Goldmine
Jazz
Album Price Guide

Tim Neely

Published by

**krause
publications**

700 E. State Street • Iola, WI 54990-0001
Telephone: 715/445-2214

Please call or write for our free catalog of music publications.
Our toll-free number to place an order or obtain a free catalog is 800-258-0929
or please use our regular business telephone 715-445-2214
for editorial comment and further information.

ISBN: 0-87341-384-9
Library of Congress: 99-68155
Printed in the United States of America

Table of Contents

Introduction: All That Jazz

I am not a jazz expert. I listen to and enjoy much of the music in the same way I listen to and enjoy classical music. But I can't discuss the relative merits of various tenor saxophonists, or whether bebop or fusion or "smooth jazz" meant the death of jazz (various people have said "yes" to all three at different times). So don't even ask, please!

What I do know is pretty clear: Six years have passed since the last major jazz price guide, and it was time for a new one. And having done eight prior record price guides, I dove in. I learned a lot in the process, and I hope you will, too.

This isn't my first experience with pricing jazz: Selected artists and listings appeared in both the *Standard Catalog Of American Records 1950-1975* and the *Goldmine Record Album Price Guide*. But for the vast scope of recorded jazz, I solicited advice. What should such a book include? What should it not include? Unfortunately, I got almost as many answers as there were people who replied. But there was consensus on a couple of things.

We asked whether a jazz price guide should include 45s. The general consensus was that it shouldn't, as most jazz collectors don't find them that interesting, and they would consume space better occupied by more album listings. In general, those few collectible jazz 45s are songs that were charted hits, such as "Take Five" or "Watermelon Man" or "Cast Your Fate to the Wind." Even then, most of the interest isn't from jazz collectors, it's from chart collectors.

Some did express an interest in seeing 7-inch extended plays listed, as sometimes these contained alternate takes of tracks that appeared on 12-inch LPs. But for now, we've decided to stick with the format that most jazz aficionados collect – the full-length album.

(That said, there is a small, active group of jazz collectors who are after 78s, especially from the 1920s and early to mid 1930s. In fact, long before anyone was collecting rock 'n' roll records, some of the rarest jazz 78s were bringing hundreds of dollars, and some still do. To learn more about some of these sought-after 78s, I suggest the *American Premium Record Guide* by Les Docks, which is available from most of the same places as the book you are now reading is found.)

The other area of consensus was to bring the listings up to date, to make it a more complete book. Jazz didn't suddenly end in 1969. Entire genres of jazz, such as fusion and the avant-garde influenced by the Chicago-based AACM (American Association for Creative Musicians), and entire important labels, such as Pablo, ECM, CTI, Strata-East, Chiaroscuro, Muse and Concord Jazz, were missing from prior jazz price guides. Also missing was the vast quantity of high-quality vinyl reissues from the 1980s, which serve as an affordable way to buy music that would otherwise be tough to find. (In the case of Blue Note, some albums that had been scheduled but canceled in the 1960s were actually issued, finally, in the 1980s, often with the originally assigned number!)

We have done just that in this book. Listings will start to taper off around 1989, as that is the last year that jazz albums came out on vinyl to the masses. (Most jazz released since 1990 on records has been geared to the audiophile market.) Even so, this book will give you a broad overview of the large numbers of jazz LPs out there, waiting to be bought, played and loved.

Market observations

The market for jazz records, in general, is much smaller and more concentrated near major metropolitan areas than for rock and pop records.

It's smaller because fewer people are exposed to jazz from a young age. People tend to collect what they grew up with, and for most record collectors, that's the popular music of the day. In the years since jazz was first recorded in 1917, the only time that jazz was also America's most popular music was during the early 1940s, the height of the swing/big band era.

It's more concentrated toward the cities because, if someone is going to be exposed to jazz at a young age, this is where it's most likely to happen. A large population base can support more kinds of clubs and more kinds of radio formats than smaller ones. And though the number of full-time jazz radio stations (even including "smooth jazz" stations) is small, you're more likely to find one near a large city. Even public radio isn't a guarantee of finding jazz on the air: In Wisconsin, which has two statewide 24-hour public radio networks, exactly six hours a week (out of a possible 336) are dedicated to jazz.

Also, some of the biggest collector base is overseas, especially on the European mainland and Japan. Jazz is one of the few great American art forms, yet international audiences have often had a far greater appreciation for it than Americans have. In the late 1990s, much of Asia went through an economic crisis, and that had a negative effect on the jazz album market. While values for many rare rock, R&B and related records were skyrocketing in the 1996-99 era, the same was not true for most jazz records. Many of the values you'll see within are similar to, or in some cases down from, where they were six years ago.

The greatest increases are coming from an area loosely defined by the words "soul jazz," "acid jazz" or "kozmigroov." Much of this music dates from the late 1960s to the middle 1970s and has never been documented in an American price guide before. It is sought after by club disc jockeys for, among other reasons, the unique "breaks" and samples that can be found on these previously ignored albums. Certain labels are loaded with this danceable, funky jazz, including the Fantasy-era Prestige label (numbers in the 10000 series), Strata-East, Black Jazz and Tribe. Many dealers in this type of music have separate sections in their advertisements for just these labels, much in the same way more "mainstream" jazz ads have sections for their Blue Note LPs.

Almost by definition, a popular jazz album sells far fewer copies than a popular rock album. Million-selling jazz records just don't happen very often. (Blue Note had only one gold record before 1994, and that was not by a jazz heavyweight, but by the group War.) Thus it may take longer to fill in the gaps in a jazz album collection than in a corresponding rock collection, as there are fewer copies out there. Conversely, there is less demand for jazz records than rock records, thus they are less expensive than an equally rare rock album in most cases. Almost every album in this book is undervalued compared to its true rarity.

Will this situation change any time soon? It's hard to say. For years, blues records were undervalued compared to their rarity. But this is no longer the case, as values have gone up faster in blues than in any other genre of music. Could jazz be next? If Americans ever gain the same appreciation for what they have given the world that Europeans and Asians have, it could happen.

What's in here, and what isn't

Trying to define jazz is like trying to define God: There is no 100 percent right answer. One person's orthodoxy is someone else's heresy. In a broad sense, though, you can define jazz by the roughly 40,000 albums included in this book.

Inside you'll find myriad styles – New Orleans and Chicago-style Dixieland, swing and big band, bebop, cool, West Coast, fusion, "soul jazz," "smooth jazz," "third stream," avant-garde, progressive, and combinations of these. There are male and female singers, vocal groups, soloists, duos, trios, quartets, quintets, all the way up to groups with 50 or more members. Every instrument you can think of is covered, from the expected (saxophone, piano, trumpet) to the unexpected (harp, bassoon, bagpipes).

Though not strictly jazz, we've included ragtime in this book. Ragtime piano, as personified by turn-of-the-20th-century pianists and composers such as Scott Joplin, was an important precursor to the jazz piano styles that came later. We could not ignore it, even if those who were playing it were not always jazz musicians.

We've also included some people (usually vocalists) who are better known as rock or pop musicians if they made records with a jazz feel. For many of these artists, we only felt comfortable including a partial discography, because the rest of their output could not be considered even remotely related to jazz. (Examples: Nat King Cole, Bing Crosby, Johnnie Ray, Dinah Shore, the band Chicago.) For others, we chose to list the entire discography, even if some of the albums can't be considered jazz, because trying to pick and choose would be more difficult than letting the listener decide. (Examples: Rosemary Clooney, Frank Sinatra and Frank Zappa.)

Another thing we've added to this book is "revival" artists, those for whom time stood still at a certain phase of jazz (usually Dixieland or swing) but didn't record until years after those forms were popular. In Britain, they call this "trad jazz," and it's best personified by people like Kenny Ball, Chris Barber, Acker Bilk, Ken Colyer and Monty Sunshine, along with former pop star Ian Whitcomb. Among the best known American artists in this realm are Pete Fountain and Al Hirt. Literally all over the world, there are "trad jazz" bands that only play Dixieland or swing music; in the United States, several record labels have cropped up to service this market (most notably GHB, Stomp Off and Timeless), not to mention almost the entire city of New Orleans.

We could not ignore the spoken-word and hip-hop artists who have discovered the wide variety and feeling of jazz, both sampled and live, and used it in their work. Some of the most important of these are included in this book.

Also in here are several vital foreign labels. Among these are ECM, from Germany; Black Saint and Soul Note, from Italy; and SteepleChase, from Japan. Unlike prior overseas labels, which tended to work out a distribution deal with an American label, most of these were only occasionally distributed by a major label in the States. (ECM had a Warner Bros. distribution deal during the height of Pat Metheny's popularity.) Instead, they contracted with an independent distributor, sometimes even only a sole sales representative, in the U.S. The same records pressed in Italy, Germany or Japan thus were available here. While most of our other *Goldmine* books omit imports, we could not ignore these important labels, even though few of them ever actually manufactured or recorded anything, or even had a tangible presence, in the States. We did not, however, include imported versions of American labels. (For example, none of the Japanese Blue Note editions are in here.)

We did draw some other lines, some of them quite precarious.

Jazz and the blues are closely related. But only those blues artists who were usually accompanied by jazz musicians are in here. Those who were usually self-accompanied are not. For example, Bessie Smith and Joe Turner are in here, but Robert Johnson is not. (In 1973, however, the Smithsonian Institution included a Robert Johnson track in its landmark set *The Smithsonian Collection of Classic Jazz.*)

I also learned how fuzzy the borders between jazz fusion and progressive rock can be. Some prog-rock musicians made jazz albums outside their groups; those are here, but the music of their parent groups are not.

We also have consciously tried to avoid "new age" music. Again, the line between jazz and new age can be pretty blurry. If they were known to have done anything truly "jazzy," for example John Klemmer or Paul Winter, they are here. If not, such as most of the Windham Hill stable of artists, they aren't.

Of course, albums not issued on vinyl are not here – no Fourplay, Kevin Mahogany or Diana Krall, to cite three well-known examples, as none of them started recording until after jazz became 99 and 44/100 percent CD only.

All that said, I'm open to suggestions for future editions. I think I've included every major artist (and many minor ones) who had at least one album of material on vinyl. I doubt I'd remove anyone who is here already, but I certainly will listen to suggestions about who belongs that isn't here.

Grading your records

When it comes to records, and how much you'll get for them, remember this above all:

Condition is (almost) everything!

Yes, it's possible to get a high price for a beat-up record, if it's exceptionally rare. But for common material, if it's not in at least Very Good condition – and preferably closer to Near Mint – you won't get many buyers. Or at least you won't the second time around. So accurately grading your discs is important, whether you're selling your records to a dealer or selling them to another collector.

Visual or play grading? In an ideal world, every record would be played before it is graded. But the time involved makes it impractical for most dealers, and anyway, it's rare that you get a chance to hear a record before you buy through the mail. Some advertisers play-grade everything and say so. But unless otherwise noted, records are visually graded.

How to grade. Look at everything about a record -- its playing surface, its label, its edges -- under a strong light. Then, based on your overall impression, give it a grade based on the following criteria:

Mint (M): Absolutely perfect in every way -- certainly never played, possibly even still sealed. (More on still sealed under "Other considerations.") Should be used sparingly as a grade, if at all.

Near Mint (NM or M-): A nearly perfect record. Many dealers won't give a grade higher than this, implying (perhaps correctly) that no record is ever truly perfect.

The record should show no obvious signs of wear. An LP jacket should have no creases, folds, seam splits or any other noticeable similar defect. No cut-out holes, either. And of course, the same should be true of any other inserts, such as posters, lyric sleeves and the like.

Basically, an LP in Near Mint condition looks as if you just got it home from a new record store and removed the shrink wrap.

Near Mint is the highest price listed in all *Goldmine* price guides. Anything that exceeds this grade, in the opinion of both buyer and seller, is worth significantly more than the highest *Goldmine* book value.

Very Good Plus (VG+): Generally worth 50 percent of the Near Mint value.

A Very Good Plus record will show some signs that it was played and otherwise handled by a previous owner who took good care of it.

Record surfaces may show some slight signs of wear and may have slight scuffs or very light scratches that don't affect one's listening experience. Slight warps that do not affect the sound are OK.

The label may have some ring wear or discoloration, but it should be barely noticeable. The center hole will not have been misshapen by repeated play.

LP inner sleeves will have some slight ring wear, lightly turned-up corners, or a slight seam split. An LP jacket may have slight signs of wear also and may be marred by a cut-out hole, indentation or corner indicating it was taken out of print and sold at a discount.

In general, if not for a couple minor things wrong with it, this would be Near Mint. All but the most mint-crazy collectors will find a Very Good Plus record highly acceptable.

A synonym used by some collectors and dealers for "Very Good Plus" is "Excellent."

Very Good (VG): Generally worth 25 percent of the Near Mint value.

Many of the defects found in a VG+ record will be more pronounced in a VG disc.

Surface noise will be evident upon playing, especially in soft passages and during a song's intro and fade, but will not overpower the music otherwise. Groove wear will start to be noticeable, as will light scratches (deep enough to feel with a fingernail) that will affect the sound.

Labels may be marred by writing, or have tape or stickers (or their residue) attached. The same will be true of picture sleeves or LP covers. However, it will not have all of these problems at the same time, only two or three of them.

This *Goldmine* price guide lists Very Good as the lowest price. This, *not* the Near Mint price, should be your guide when determining how much a record is worth, as that is the price a dealer will normally pay you for a Near Mint record.

Good (G), Good Plus (G+): Generally worth 10-15 percent of the Near Mint value.

Good does not mean Bad! A record in Good or Good Plus condition can be put onto a turntable and will play through without skipping. But it will have significant surface noise and scratches and visible groove wear (on a styrene record, the groove will be starting to turn white).

A jacket or sleeve will have seam splits, especially at the bottom or on the spine. Tape, writing, ring wear or other defects will start to over-whelm the object.

If it's a common item, you'll probably find another copy in better shape eventually. Pass it up. But if it's something you have been seeking for years, and the price is right, get it ... but keep looking to upgrade.

Poor (P), Fair (F): Generally worth 0-5 percent of the Near Mint price.

The record is cracked, badly warped, and won't play through without skipping or repeating. The LP jacket barely keeps the LP inside it. Inner sleeves are fully seam split, crinkled, and written upon.

Except for impossibly rare records otherwise unattainable, records in this condition should be bought or sold for no more than a few cents each.

Other grading considerations. Most dealers give a separate grade to the record and its cover. In an ad, a record's grade is listed first, followed by that of the jacket, unless noted otherwise.

With **Still Sealed (SS)** records, let the buyer beware, unless it's a U.S. pressing from the last 10-15 years or so. It's too easy to re-seal one. Yes, some legitimately never-opened LPs from the 1960s still exist, and some of them bring rather fancy prices. But if you're looking for a specific pressing, the only way you can know for sure is to open the record. Also, European imports are not factory-sealed, so if you see them advertised as sealed, someone other than the manufacturer sealed them.

Common collecting abbreviations

In addition to the letters used to designate a record's grade, it's not uncommon to see other abbreviations used in dealer advertisements. Knowing the more common ones helps to prevent confusion. Here are some that pertain to albums:

boot: bootleg (illegal pressing)
cc: cut corner
co: cutout
coh: cut-out hole
cov, cv, cvr: cover
dh: drill hole
dj: disc jockey (promotional) record
gf: gatefold (cover)
imp: import
ins: insert
lbl: label
m, mo: monaural (mono)
nap: (does) not affect play
noc: number on cover
nol: number on label
obi: not actually an abbreviation, "obi" is the Japanese word for "sash" and is used to describe the strip of paper usually wrapped around Japanese (and occasional US) pressings of LPs.
orig: original
pr, pro, promo: promotional record
q: quadraphonic
re: reissue
rec: record
ri: reissue

rw: ring wear
s: stereo
sl: slight
sm: saw mark
soc: sticker on cover
sol: sticker on label
ss: still sealed
s/t: self-titled
st: stereo
sw: shrink wrap
toc: tape on cover
tol: tape on label
ts: taped seam
w/: with
wlp: white label promo
wobc: writing on back cover
woc: writing on cover
wofc: writing on front cover
wol: writing on label
wr: wear
wrp: warp
xol: "x" on label

Some notes on the pricing

The prices listed in here were determined from many sources.

The more common items reflect a consensus of used record shops and collectors, plus prices in ads and online over the past few months. In some ways, these items are more difficult to get a handle on; they sell without much publicity because of their low value, thus they aren't reported as often.

The rarer items are often the matter of conjecture because they so rarely come up for public sale. A high auction price for a truly rare piece can be the only way such an item's "worth" can be gauged, no matter what someone says about the value being inflated. Records, as with all collectibles, are only worth what someone will pay for them.

Because of the inexact nature of this undertaking, we urge you to use a book such as this as a guide and not as the final word on pricing.

We, too, can always use more input on the subject. See the **How you can help** section for more information.

And by the way, the publisher of the book does not engage in the buying and selling of records. So the prices listed in here should not be construed as "offers to buy" or "offers to sell" from Krause Publications.

Some notes on promotional records

When it comes to jazz albums, almost all interest is in regular stock copies. For most promos, there is little or no premium attached to them, and in many cases, they bring *less* than the stock copies.

At first, this doesn't make sense. As fewer places sell or play jazz records, you'd think there would be even fewer promo records than normal, and thus they'd be more rare. But think of this: Because of that lack of promotional need, if someone did need a promo, it's far more likely to be a "designate" promo. These are identical to stock copies – the same label, the same number, the same everything – but are merely stamped on the front or back cover with (usually) a gold or rubber-stamped "For Promotion Only" indicator (or words to that effect). There's nothing special about these records for the most part; any time the record company wants to create a promo, it can take a stock copy and stamp it! And because the covers are defaced, they often bring less than a stock copy.

Exceptions would include artists in whom there is interest outside the jazz community, such as many of the crossover singers listed within. Even then, promos that attract the most interest are those with custom promotional labels. Most of the time, these are white versions of the regular label, thus the term "white label promo." Of course, the label isn't always white; sometimes it's yellow or blue or pink or some other color. But it will always have as part of the label typesetting, "Promotional Copy" or "Audition Copy" or "Demonstration" or some other such term. Sometimes, the label will be almost identical to the stock versions, but some sort of words alluding to the promotional nature of the record will have been added to the typeset copy.

Again, for most jazz albums, it's the stock copies that are more sought after than the promos. Strange – but true.

Making sense of the main listings

We've told you about most of the features in the book. Let's break down a listing to see what a line means.

The artist's name is in bold, all capital letters. They are mostly alphabetized the way our computer did, so blame any things that seem out of order on it. I think we caught most of the way-out things, but if not, let us know and we'll get 'em the next time.

For most of the artists in the book, we have, at the very least, identified what instrument(s) they are best known for playing. For groups that were reasonably stable, we've listed their members and sometimes their instruments, with those performers who have their own entries in ALL CAPITAL LETTERS; for those with frequent turnover, we've tried to note a couple of the founders or members of longest duration.

We haven't attempted to identify anyone with a certain kind of jazz, because many of them cannot be narrowly defined. How do you define Miles Davis, for example? Or Duke Ellington? We have, at times, added some limited non-instrumental information. For example, if someone is truly "influential" or "first," we tried to mention that. We also mentioned songs or compositions by which they are known, if they tower over the rest of the catalog. And in some cases, we mention where a rock or pop fan might have heard them in unexpected places. (For example, the saxophone player on the Doors' "Touch Me" is in here, as is a group that shared a bill with the Beatles at the Cavern Club and a guitarist who played on most of the Partridge Family's hits.) Also listed here are cross-references. Many of these are not complete, but we'll also work on that more thoroughly the next time.

Then we have grouped the discographies alphabetically by record label. With the constant flow of reissues and the frequent label hopping that even the most successful artists seemed to do, trying to put releases in chronological order would have been a logistical nightmare. (If you're that interested in a chronological discography, many of the more prominent artists in this book have fans with web sites. Some of the artists have their own "official" sites, too. Literally dozens of complete jazz artist discographies are on the Internet, and most can be found by using a good search engine.)

Under each record label are individual listings in numerical order, ignoring prefixes. This may result in some things appearing to be way out of order. For example, because they have numbers approximately 6,800 apart, mono and stereo versions of the same albums on Columbia will rarely be adjacent to each other. This is also true of other labels with separate mono and stereo numbering systems, such as Mercury, Liberty, Imperial, Blue Note and many more. However, as the RCA Victor, Capitol and Prestige label generally used the same numbers for mono and stereo, those versions are usually listed next to each other.

Each line starts with a check box, which you can use to keep track of what you have. Then comes the record number. You'll also find the title of the record as best as we can determine (you'd be surprised how often the title differs between the record and the jacket!); the year of release; and the value in Very Good, Very Good-Plus and Near Mint condition.

For many listings, you'll see a letter or two in brackets after the record number. These designate something special about the listing as follows:

B: the album is listed as stereo, but some of the tracks are in mono (the "B" means "both" stereo and mono)

DJ: some sort of promotional copy, usually for radio stations, and not meant for public sale

EP: a 12-inch extended play album, usually with only four to six tracks; it normally is no more than half the length of a regular album

M: mono record (all 12-inch albums released either in mono only or in both mono and stereo before 1968)

P: the album is listed as stereo, but only part of it is "true" two-channel stereo

PD: picture disc (graphics actually appear as part of the record; these were popular in the late 1970s to early 1980s and, for some artists, are their only valuable albums today)

Q: quadraphonic record (mostly from the years 1972-76, these were usually remixed, sometimes radically, to play on systems with four separate speakers)

R: the album is listed as stereo, but actually is all, or almost all, rechanneled stereo (called "Duophonic" by Capitol or "Enhanced for Stereo" or "Simulated Stereo" by Decca); these almost always are less sought-after than the same material in "true mono"

S: stereo record (again, when the record was pressed both in mono and stereo). If we're not sure of an album's "true" stereo content, or if we know an album is all, or almost all, true stereo, we use "S."

10: a 10-inch album, most of which are from the early years of LPs, 1948-54, and quite difficult to find in top condition

(x) where x is a number: the number of records in a set

Finally, some items have lines in italics following them. That defines something about the item listed above, such as who also is on the record, or a color of label or vinyl.

Making sense of the listings in back

Because of the nature of these items, we've used a slightly different format for the four sections that appear after the letter Z. These four sections are "Original Cast Recordings," "Soundtracks," "Television Albums" and "Various Artists Collections."

Within each category, these are arranged alphabetically by the **title** of the release, again as our computer did them, and ignoring the words "A," "An" or "The." The exception is if the title begins with a number. Computers have this nasty tendency to put these first, before things beginning with "A." We've moved them to where they would be if the number were spelled out. For example, if an album begins with the number "10," we moved it as if it were actually "Ten."

Underneath each title are the applicable releases, arranged alphabetically and numerically by label. Those lines start with a check box, then are followed by the label and number listed together; any applicable abbreviations in brackets (which are the same as in the rest of the book – M for mono, S for stereo, etc.); the year of release; and the prices in three grades of condition.

What is a "deep groove," anyway?

At times, collectors of the Blue Note record label make Elvis Presley and Beatles collectors seem, well, ordinary. Some Blue Note aficionados collect even the most apparently insignificant variations of the label, including whether the label has the registered trademark symbol ® on it or not.

This book doesn't get that picayune. Our listings for pre-1967 albums on Blue Note tend to focus on variations of the address on the record label. There are several of these, but the most valuable are what is known as the "deep groove" versions. All mono and many stereo albums on the label pressed in 1960 or earlier exist with a "deep groove," and they are always more collectible than those copies that don't have the "deep groove."

So what is this "deep groove"?

Despite the connotations of the term, "deep groove" has nothing to do with the playing surface. Instead, it has to do with the area where the label is affixed. One of the pressing plants Blue Note used to make its early LPs used a manufacturing system that left an indentation (or a "deep groove") under the label on both sides. This circular groove, which is visible to the naked eye and can be felt by a fingertip, is about the circumference of a half-dollar coin.

This indentation must be present on both sides of the album to get the "deep groove" premium. Albums with the groove on only one side do not get "deep groove" prices.

By the way, Blue Note is not the only record label to exist with the "deep groove," though it's the only one to command a premium because of it. Using a few LPs I have nearby as I write this, I discover that other labels have grooves with a narrower diameter, closer to the size of a quarter (some on RCA), and many (Decca, Columbia, et al.) have much larger circular grooves, with about a 2 3/4 inch diameter. It appears as if the closest match to the Blue Note "deep groove" appears on albums pressed by Capitol on the West Coast. That would be ironic, considering that today, EMI-Capitol Records owns the Blue Note catalog and trademarks.

Mono vs. stereo: It all depends

One of the conversations I had with a jazz collector when I was starting to prepare this book went something like this:

"Are you going to fix the stereo prices in the book?"

"What do you mean?" I replied.

"Not all the stereo albums are worth less than the mono albums," he answered.

I said I'd look into it. And I found that my inquisitor was partially right.

In my research, I've found that in the early days of stereo, say from 1960 back, mono albums generally bring more than the stereo counterparts, especially on independent labels that specialized in jazz. While such producers as Norman Granz and Rudy Van Gelder began recording jazz in stereo as far back as 1956, for the most part it was done to give them some more freedom in mixing the final result to mono. Once stereo hit the marketplace, labels such as Verve, Fantasy and Atlantic, among others, realized they had stereo tapes in their possession, but often the same care was not taken in creating a pleasing stereo mix as had been taken for the original mono mix. Thus, for original pressings of these early stereo recordings, the mono albums are more desirable.

That said, though, the major labels such as Columbia and RCA Victor had their stereo act in gear earlier than the independents. At times, early stereo by a Columbia artist such as Miles Davis brings a *lot* more than the original mono version. For example, Miles' *Kind Of Blue* is considered a landmark jazz album for a lot of reasons, not the least of which is that it sounds absolutely fabulous in stereo and has been sought by audiophiles for years, especially on the original red and black "6-eye" label. It's no accident that one of the jazz albums issued by Classic Records in its lauded audiophile vinyl series was *Kind Of Blue*.

By approximately 1961, even the jazz indies had their stereo act together. Stereo was here to stay, and much as with pop music, the stereo copies after about this time are more sought after than the mono versions. This doesn't include reissues; for example, Verve albums reissued with MGM distribution (only a "V" or "V6" prefix) that had originally come out with an "MGV" or "MGVS" prefix still go for more in mono than in stereo, unless the opposite is true with the originals.

Then the tide turns again in 1967 or so. In that case, it's not that the mono mixes are superior, it's that they are so difficult to find. By mid-1968, nearly every label had discontinued mono entirely except for some archival reissues.

Think about this, too: When the reissue boom hit with the advent of the compact disc in the 1980s, record companies had a choice of which mix to reissue, mono or stereo. Nine times out of ten, if not more often, it's the stereo mix that came out again. (The exceptions were mostly where the album was not recorded in stereo.) Remember, we're talking jazz here, which by definition has a smaller market than most other forms of music. You can market somewhat more to the "purists" in jazz than in more popular areas. So where were the mono reissues?

No matter what the preference is on mono or stereo, nobody seems to like the "electronically reprocessed" stereo, or "Duophonic" or "Enhanced for Stereo" albums, as they are sometimes called. The values for these are always lower than mono, and some collectors won't buy them at all!

Selling your records

At some point, perhaps after looking through this book, you may decide that you want to sell your collection. Good for you! And you want to take them to your local used record store with the idea that you'll get the prices you see in this book. Bad for you!

What the values in here reflect are **retail** prices – what a collector might pay for the item from a dealer, and **not** what a dealer will pay a collector for resale. Too many non-collectors (and even some collectors) don't understand that.

I know one dealer who has told me that he won't buy records from someone who tells him they consulted a price guide first. While that is extreme, it shows the distrust some dealers have for books like this and how the public uses (and abuses) them.

Just as importantly, the highest values are for records in the best condition (re-read the section on **Grading your records**). And there is a reason for that: Truly pristine records are very difficult to find! Many collectors are willing to pay handsomely for them – but for many of the records in this book, Near Mint examples aren't even known to exist!

One reason we've expanded the price listing to three grades of condition is to reflect that. There's a tendency to look at the highest price listed for something and assume that's what your record is worth. More realistically, though, such a small percentage of records are truly Near Mint – especially from the 1950s and 1960s – that your own records, if you were a typical accumulator and not a collector, are considerably less than Near Mint.

Even if you do end up trying to sell to a dealer, choose him or her carefully. Many dealers want nothing to do with jazz because they have no clientele for it. It's always best to find someone who has a customer base for your kind of LP.

There is only one way you'll be able to get anything close to the prices listed for most items, and that's to sell them direct to the collector.

The "old-fashioned" way is through record collecting magazines. The oldest and most widely read remains *Goldmine,* which was founded in 1974. Published every two weeks, the magazine is loaded with ads from people selling records of all kinds and from all eras. *Goldmine* has advertising salespeople who will help you put your ad together for maximum impact. To see what *Goldmine* is about, pick up a copy. It is available at all Tower Records stores in the U.S., most Barnes and Noble and Borders bookstores and hundreds of independent record dealers. If you still can't find a copy, call 1-800-258-0929.

Admittedly, *Goldmine*'s jazz content is somewhat limited. But there are jazz collectors who read the paper, so if you do have jazz albums for sale, you will have much less competition than you might in some other places. Also, in every other issue there is a section called "Jazz Sides," which has a short interview with a jazz musician and many CD reviews.

The "new" way to sell records and other memorabilia is over the Internet. The most popular method is through the online auction, and the most popular of these sites is eBay (www.ebay.com).

Online selling seems to draw two widely different audiences. One is very much the same audience as a stand-alone record store, except on a global scale rather than a regional one. Browsers who know next to nothing about record collecting and the relative scarcity of the listed pieces are common. These are people who can sometimes be fooled into paying too much for a common piece, especially certain million-selling compact discs, because of three magic letters: "OOP," short for "out of print." Just because something's out of print doesn't mean it has vanished off the face of the earth!

The other audience drawn to online sales are the hyper-specialists, and this is often where items can justifiably go for much larger sums than in a retail store. Thanks to search engines on most of the better sites, a fan of, say, Miles Davis can type in the words "Miles Davis" and find nothing but the Miles Davis-related material. People who specialize in one artist will usually pay more – sometimes a lot more – than someone who collects a more broad range of artists. But because they are specialists, they also know which items are common, so they don't get taken on the easy stuff.

I have bought records over the web, and have yet to have significant problems. It's faster than "snail mail" and less expensive than a long-distance telephone call. But it's not perfect. Just as in real life, it pays to be wary.

As a seller, you are reaching a larger audience than you would in a record collecting magazine, but also a much less targeted one. The Internet seems to be a good place to sell lower-priced items that might take up valuable space in an expensive print ad. But many more valuable pieces sit or fetch less than they might through more traditional means.

Also, many sellers have found that eBay overreacts if you say you are selling a promo. Promos are an accepted part of record collecting; there's even an entire book on collecting promotional records and CDs, and it's from the same publisher as this book. Despite that, eBay can, and does, remove these items, almost at random, for no good reason. (It's one thing if you're selling an advance copy of a CD that hasn't been issued to the general public yet. It's another to try to sell a 25-year-old vinyl promo.) So if you're selling promos, use synonyms or code words to keep the eBay police away.

As a buyer, you have to watch out for overgraded, under-described items. Photos of the items help. Also, buying from someone who deals in records as a primary area rather than as an obvious sideline to his/her Beanie Baby business is recommended. Look for dealers with strong feedback ratings; that is a sign of satisfied customers. Also, check for use of something resembling the *Goldmine* grading system. People who say their albums are in "good condition" don't know record collecting, because "good" is a low grade in the world of records (as it is in some other collecting areas, such as coins).

Also as a buyer, don't be afraid to e-mail the seller if you have any questions about the item. If you don't get a satisfactory answer, or get no answer at all, don't bid.

We feel the online world will continue to grow in importance over time. At some point it may become *the* biggest market for collectible records. So we'll continue to keep an eye on it. But it's still in its infancy compared to other proven selling methods.

Jazz collectors, unite!

Rock and pop music have many regional collectors organizations, but none that span a wide geographic area. Jazz collectors, however, have had a place to go for over 35 years.

The International Association of Jazz Record Collectors (IAJRC) was founded in 1964 and incorporated in 1975. Worldwide, it has over 1,200 dues-paying members who are into all kinds of jazz and formats, from Dixieland to fusion and from cylinder to CD.

Its main objectives are to promote jazz in all its forms, to preserve it and encourage collecting and researching it through publications, reissues of vintage recordings and an annual convention.

Regular membership is $25 a year. (An entire family can join for $30; students with ID can join for $20.) That fee brings you four editions of the *IAJRC Journal,* which publishes numerous reviews, historical articles and discographies; access to the association's lending library; discounts on recordings issued by the IAJRC label (records and CDs); access to the group's annual convention, which has been held in numerous locations around the world and features everything from a record sale to jam sessions with famous artists; and a complete membership directory arranged both alphabetically and by state/country.

To join the IAJRC, send dues to Dick Peters, IAJRC, 12366 Port Quinlan Ave., Port Charlotte, FL 33981 USA. Or check its web site: www.geocities.com/BourbonStreet/3910/bensum.htm

Sign up as a new member by mentioning the web site and you'll get a special bonus.

How you can help

In this book you'll find roughly 40,000 jazz and jazz-related albums. But it's far from every jazz album in existence. We can use your help in filling in some gaps.

These areas include, but are not limited to, the following:

Blue Note Records. We've already got a lot on the label, as you'll see. But there's more information we need.

For example, we'd like to know which albums saw reissue with a United Artists Records address on the label, which would cover the years from about 1970 through 1979. The original Blue Note slowly petered out during this time, but some of the older albums remained available. With a few exceptions, we don't know exactly which ones.

Also, were any mono LPs issued with Liberty Records addresses other than the ones we already list? Were any albums that originally came out with Lexington Ave. addresses on the label reissued with W. 63rd St. addresses? Basically, any variation we don't list, we're interested in hearing about.

Prestige Records. Another of the key collectible jazz labels, we again are seeking reissue information.

Prestige had several label changes in its history, and we're pretty sure that many of the Prestige albums listed within with only one version actually exist with more than one variation. But we aren't sure which ones. Not every Prestige album saw reissue after its first edition; some came out with new numbers and artwork. So we can't draw blanket conclusions.

Missing entries. Unless otherwise noted, we have not intentionally left out any albums from a listed artist's discography. With those exceptions, if it isn't listed, it's not in our database. That doesn't mean your LP is necessarily rare; it's just that we missed it along the way. If you're aware of an album we omitted, we'd like to know.

Released/unreleased entries. Some albums in this book are listed as "canceled" or "unreleased." That's because they were scheduled by the record company, but for whatever reasons, were not issued. However, as we have already found out, some supposedly "canceled" albums were actually released after all. Also, it's possible that we list an album with an appropriate value, but it really never did come out. Either way, we'd like to know.

Year of release. There are a lot of question marks in the listings, especially with 1970s and 1980s albums. At times, discerning the exact year of release can be tricky, because it doesn't necessarily correspond with the year an album was recorded. Most jazz albums are recorded quickly, and many artists recorded frequently. But because of record companies not wanting to flood the market with new material, some sessions were withheld, often for months, sometimes for years (even decades in a few instances). One thing we may do in the future is denote the year of recording in the notes under the listing for some tardily-released material.

Anything else that may be of help. For example, did we, by chance, miss someone who belongs?

I can be reached by mail:

Tim Neely
Goldmine Jazz Album Price Guide
700 E. State St.
Iola, WI 54990

Or you can call:
(715) 445-4612, extension 782

Or you can e-mail:
neelyt@krause.com

If you write, please include a daytime (Central Time) phone number where you can be reached if I have any questions.

We also have a fax number, but before sending any large contributions that way, please contact me by phone or e-mail.

Because of the volume of replies, I may not reply to you immediately, or at all. Rest assured that I read or hear (as the case may be) all messages addressed to me and take all under advisement.

Bibliography and Webography

As I noted earlier, I am not a jazz expert. I consulted many people, literally dozens of books and hundreds of web sites to compile the information you are now holding. Here are some of the sources that were consulted over and over again.

Case, Brian, and Stan Britt. *The Harmony Illustrated Encyclopedia of Jazz, Third Edition.* Harmony Books, New York, 1986.

Holtje, Steve, and Nancy Ann Lee, eds. *MusicHound Jazz: The Essential Album Guide.* Visible Ink Press, Detroit, 1998.

Popular Recordaid, October 1969.

Schwann-1 Catalog; *Schwann-2 Record and Tape Guide*; *The New Schwann*; *Schwann Spectrum.* Assorted editions, September 1971 through Winter 1999.

Umphred, Neal. *Goldmine's Price Guide to Collectible Jazz Albums 1949-1969, 2nd Edition.* Krause Publications, Iola, Wis., 1994.

www.altavista.com
Simply, AltaVista is the best search engine on the Web for finding specific pages on specific people.

www.bsnpubs.com/discog
Both Sides Now is a newsletter published by Mike Callahan that reviews (mostly) reissued CDs for their stereo content and the quality of the sound. But its best, and probably more important, work is its online album discographies. The most comprehensive site of its kind on the Internet, it lists all the known albums, in numerical order, on hundreds of labels, large and small. Mostly a rock and pop resource, it does have some jazz labels mixed in.

www.counterpoint-music.com
This is the site of Counterpoint Music, which sells jazz and blues CDs. It has a wonderful browse function, in which you can look up hundreds of artists, find out what instruments they play, and even often find out who else is on their CDs. Even if you don't buy anything from them, it's a great reference source.

www.dpo.uab.edu/~moudry/discintr.htm
Want a definitive Web discography of Sun Ra, who has one of the most complicated discographies in the history of recorded music? Here it is.

www.eclipse.net/~fitzgera/labels/homepage.htm
Similar to the Both Sides Now page, this one lists only jazz labels. Here are links to vinyl discographies of dozens of labels, from A-Records to Zim. Most of the big ones are included.

www.ecmrecords.com
The web site of Munich-based ECM Records. It lists everything in print on the label, plus gives extensive cross-references on who plays what on which albums. You also can still order vinyl from them direct from Germany, if you don't mind paying in deutsche marks.

www.jazzmart.com/jrm.home.htm
The home page for Chicago's Jazz Record Mart, one of America's best known, and most influential, jazz stores. Owner Bob Koester also has a record label called Delmark, which is linked from this site. This site has hundreds of sealed 1980s and current LPs for sale, plus many collector's items and lots of first-hand history as well.

www.mosaicrecords.com
The web site of Mosaic Records, the firm that puts out amazing limited-edition collections of the "complete" works of jazz greats. It not only lists the sets it currently has in print, it also has its out-of-print items noted. For in-print items, a complete sessionography of the material in the box is included on the site.

www.ncpr.org/tenspot/pages/nuten.html
Home page for "Jazz @ the Ten Spot," a radio show on North Country Public Radio in Canton, New York. Loaded with birthdays (and instruments played) of jazz artists, well-known and otherwise. Click on the link "The Jazz Calendar."

www.nfo.net
"The Original Big Bands Database." In addition to listing every significant (and many less significant) jazz and dance band from the 1920s through the 1950s, it has history sections, song listings, a glossary and even a section on currently working big bands.

www.redhotjazz.com
"A History of Jazz Before 1930," it contains biographies, sound samples and extensive discographies of hundreds of early jazz artists.

Acknowledgments

Putting this book together at times felt like going uphill on downhill skis. But you finally have it in your hands, and gee, where do I start?

Well, I've already mentioned many of the sources on the Web and in print whose past research was invaluable.

I received literally hundreds of suggestions for additions and corrections to prior jazz price guides put out by Krause Publications. Some were one or two entries here and there, including confirmation of the existence of Cal Tjader's album *Latin For Dancers,* Fantasy 8019, with a nearly actual-size photocopy of the LP cover and its liner notes. You all know who you are, and I thank you.

Some of the best were the annotated photocopies of record jackets and labels. Stephen Schroeder of Albuquerque, New Mexico has been sending me information like this for several years, and finally, much of his jazz data has been integrated into this book. Also, John Beznik of the Mammoth Music Mart in Skokie, Illinois, a jazz fan himself, supplied many illustrations of LPs that came through the MMM donation bins. The Mammoth Music Mart, which takes place in late September or early October annually, is a massive fund-raiser for ALS (Lou Gehrig's disease) research. It has literally hundreds of thousands of music-related items for sale (including a lot of jazz albums) over a 10-day period, all of which is donated and much of which is inexpensive. It's worth checking out at least once in your life.

I also got long lists of albums from Bruce Krohmer of Takoma Park, Maryland and Jim DeLuco of Southington, Connecticut. Many of these entries had not appeared in any price guide before. Thanks to both. And Bill Hamilton of San Diego, California, who has helped with each of the last four price guides, was there again for this one.

My own jazz collection is fairly sparse, so I relied on others for most of the illustrations. We found a stash of LP cover illustrations hiding in the *Goldmine* files just before we went to press (a big thank you to associate editor Cathy Bernardy). Many of the other illustrations came from Diane Landre of Waupaca, Wisconsin, a jazz collector almost in our own backyard, and from Greg Loescher, *Goldmine* magazine editor.

Speaking of Greg, I thank him for having the patience to see me through on this project and for suspending my regular *Goldmine* column so I could get this done. I also thank Don Gulbrandsen, Krause book division managing editor, for patience beyond the call of duty. Deb Schellin deserves a big thank you for speeding up the process by about a month with some help getting things into the database. Thanks, too, to our efficient proofreading and book production staffs, who got this turned around quickly.

Of course I want to thank the usual family members (hello Mom, Sue, Ed, Phillip, Mary, Ric, Beth, Steve, Eileen, Rick, Nancy, Terence, Stephanie, Jacquelyn, Emily) and the Creator, who keep me grounded.

Finally, I want to thank the Rev. George Wiskirchen, C.S.C. for his "Introduction to Jazz" course at the University of Notre Dame that I took so many years ago. I never could have known that it would ever come in so handy again. He probably doesn't know me from Adam, but without his course, not only would I have not known how to finish this book, but I wouldn't have known where to start.

Tim Neely
April 2000

Number	Title	Yr	VG	VG+	NM

A

ABDUL-MALIK, AHMED
Bassist and composer, a pioneer of "world music."
NEW JAZZ

Number	Title	Yr	VG	VG+	NM
❏ NJLP-8266 [M]	The Music of Ahmed Abdul-Malik	1961	10.00	20.00	40.00
-- Purple label					
❏ NJLP-8266 [M]	The Music of Ahmed Abdul-Malik	1965	6.25	12.50	25.00
-- Blue label, trident logo at right					
❏ NJLP-8282 [M]	Sounds of Africa	1962	10.00	20.00	40.00
-- Purple label					
❏ NJLP-8282 [M]	Sounds of Africa	1965	6.25	12.50	25.00
-- Blue label, trident logo at right					

PRESTIGE
❏ PRLP-16003 [M]	Eastern Moods	1963	7.50	15.00	30.00

RCA VICTOR
❏ LPM-2015 [M]	East Meets West	1959	7.50	15.00	30.00
❏ LSP-2015 [S]	East Meets West	1959	10.00	20.00	40.00

RIVERSIDE
❏ RLP 12-287 [M]	Jazz Sahara	1958	12.50	25.00	50.00
❏ RLP-1121 [S]	Jazz Sahara	1959	10.00	20.00	40.00

STATUS
❏ ST-8303 [M]	Spellbound	1965	7.50	15.00	30.00

ABERCROMBIE, JOHN
Guitarist, sometimes mandolin player. Also see RICHIE BEIRACH.
ECM
❏ 1047	Timeless	1974	2.50	5.00	10.00
❏ 1061	Gateway	1975	2.50	5.00	10.00
❏ 1105	Gateway 2	1977	2.50	5.00	10.00
❏ 1117	Characters	1978	2.50	5.00	10.00
❏ 1133	Arcade	1979	2.50	5.00	10.00
❏ 1164	John Abercrombie Quartet	1980	2.50	5.00	10.00
❏ 1191	M	1981	2.50	5.00	10.00
❏ 25009	Night	1984	2.00	4.00	8.00

JAM
❏ 5001	Straight Flight	198?	2.50	5.00	10.00

ABERCROMBIE, JOHN, AND RALPH TOWNER
Also see each artist's individual listings.
ECM
❏ 1080	Sargasso Sea	1976	2.50	5.00	10.00
❏ 1207	Five Years Later	1981	2.50	5.00	10.00

ABRAMS, MUHAL RICHARD
Piano and synthesizer player, also a composer and a co-founder of the Association for the Advancement of Creative Musicians. Also see ANTHONY BRAXTON.
ARISTA/NOVUS
❏ 3000	Lifea Blinec	1978	2.50	5.00	10.00
❏ 3007	Spiral/Live	1979	2.50	5.00	10.00

BLACK SAINT
❏ BSR 0003	Sightsong	1975	3.00	6.00	12.00
-- Featuring Malachi Favors					
❏ BSR 0017	1-OQA + 19	1978	3.00	6.00	12.00
❏ BSR 0032	Spihumonesty	1980	2.50	5.00	10.00
❏ BSR 0033	Lifelong Ambitions	1980	2.50	5.00	10.00
-- With Leroy Jenkins					
❏ BSR 0041	Mama and Daddy	1981	2.50	5.00	10.00
❏ BSR 0051	Duet	1981	2.50	5.00	10.00
-- With Amina Claudine Myers					
❏ BSR 0061	Blues Forever	1981	2.50	5.00	10.00
❏ BSR 0071	Rejoicing with the Light	1983	2.50	5.00	10.00
❏ BSR 0081	View From Within	1984	2.50	5.00	10.00
❏ BSR 0091	Colors in Thirty-Third	1987	2.50	5.00	10.00
❏ 120103	The Hearinga Suite	1989	3.00	6.00	12.00

DELMARK
❏ DS-413	Levels and Degrees of Light	1968	5.00	10.00	20.00
❏ DS-423	Young at Heart, Wise in Time	1970	5.00	10.00	20.00
❏ DS-430	Things to Come From Those Now Gone	1972	3.75	7.50	15.00

INDIA NAVIGATION
❏ IN-1058	Afrisong	1975	3.75	7.50	15.00

ACOUSTIC ALCHEMY
Group led by acoustic guitarists Nick Webb and Greg Carmichael.
MCA MASTER SERIES
❏ MCA-5816	Red Dust and Spanish Lace	1987	2.50	5.00	10.00
❏ MCA-6291	Blue Chip	1989	2.50	5.00	10.00
❏ MCA-42125	Natural Elements	1988	2.50	5.00	10.00

ADAMS, GEORGE
Tenor saxophone player.
BLUE NOTE
❏ B1-91984	Nightingale	1989	2.50	5.00	10.00

ECM
❏ 1141	Sound Suggestions	1979	3.00	6.00	12.00

TIMELESS
❏ 322	Paradise Space Shuttle	1981	3.00	6.00	12.00

ADAMS, GEORGE-DON PULLEN QUARTET
Also see each artist's individual listings.
BLUE NOTE
❏ BLJ-46907	A Song Everlasting	1987	2.50	5.00	10.00
❏ BT-85122	Breakthrough	1986	2.50	5.00	10.00

SOUL NOTE
❏ SN-1004	Don't Lose Control	198?	3.00	6.00	12.00
❏ SN-1094	Live at the Village Vanguard	1985	3.00	6.00	12.00
❏ 121144-1	Live at the Village Vanguard 2	199?	2.50	5.00	10.00

TIMELESS
❏ LPSJP-147	Earth Beams	1990	3.00	6.00	12.00

ADAMS, GEORGE- DANNIE RICHMOND QUARTET
Also see each artist's individual listings.
SOUL NOTE
❏ SN-1007	Hand to Hand	1980	3.00	6.00	12.00
❏ SN-1057	Gentleman's Agreement	1983	3.00	6.00	12.00

ADAMS, JERRI
Female singer.
COLUMBIA
❏ CL 916 [M]	It's Cool Inside	1956	10.00	20.00	40.00
❏ CL 1258 [M]	Play for Keeps	1958	10.00	20.00	40.00

ADAMS, PEPPER
Baritone saxophone player.
FANTASY
❏ OJC-031 [M]	10 to 4 at the 5 Spot	198?	2.50	5.00	10.00
-- Reissue of Riverside 12-265					

INNER CITY
❏ 3014	Julian	1976	3.00	6.00	12.00

INTERLUDE
❏ MO-502 [M]	Pepper Adams 5	1959	12.50	25.00	50.00
-- Reissue of Mode 112					
❏ ST-1002 [S]	Pepper Adams 5	1959	10.00	20.00	40.00
-- Reissue of Mode 112; remixed into stereo					

MODE
❏ LP-112 [M]	Pepper Adams 5	1957	20.00	40.00	80.00
-- With Mel Lewis					

MUSE
❏ MR-5182	Reflectory	1979	2.50	5.00	10.00
❏ MR-5213	The Master	1980	2.50	5.00	10.00

PALO ALTO
❏ 8009	Urban Dreams	1982	2.50	5.00	10.00

PRESTIGE
❏ PRST-7677	Encounter	1969	5.00	10.00	20.00
-- With Zoot Sims					

REGENT
❏ MG-6066 [M]	The Cool Sound of Pepper Adams	1958	17.50	35.00	70.00

RIVERSIDE
❏ RLP 12-265 [M]	10 to 4 at the 5 Spot	1958	12.50	25.00	50.00
❏ RLP-1104 [S]	10 to 4 at the 5 Spot	1959	10.00	20.00	40.00

SAVOY
❏ MG-12211 [M]	The Cool Sound of Pepper Adams	196?	5.00	10.00	20.00
-- Reissue of Regent 6066					

SAVOY JAZZ
❏ SJL-1142	Pure Pepper	198?	2.50	5.00	10.00
-- Reissue of Savoy 12211					

WARWICK
❏ W-2041 [M]	Out of This World	1961	10.00	20.00	40.00
-- With Donald Byrd					

WORKSHOP JAZZ
❏ WSJ-219 [M]	Pepper Adams Plays the Compositions of Charles Mingus	1964	15.00	30.00	60.00
❏ WSJS-219 [S]	Pepper Adams Plays the Compositions of Charles Mingus	1964	17.50	35.00	70.00

WORLD PACIFIC
❏ PJM-407 [M]	Critic's Choice	1957	20.00	40.00	80.00
-- With Mel Lewis					

Number	Title	Yr	VG	VG+	NM
❑ WPM-407 [M]	Critic's Choice	1958	17.50	35.00	70.00
-- With Mel Lewis; reissue with new prefix					
ZIM					
❑ 2000	Ephemera	197?	3.75	7.50	15.00

ADAMS, PEPPER, AND FRANK FOSTER
Also see each artist's individual listings.

Number	Title	Yr	VG	VG+	NM
MUSE					
❑ MR-5313	Generations	1986	2.50	5.00	10.00

ADAMS, PEPPER, AND JIMMY KNEPPER
Also see each artist's individual listings.

Number	Title	Yr	VG	VG+	NM
METROJAZZ					
❑ E-1004 [M]	The Pepper-Knepper Quartet	1958	20.00	40.00	80.00
❑ SE-1004 [S]	The Pepper-Knepper Quartet	1959	15.00	30.00	60.00

ADDERLEY, CANNONBALL
Also sax player and bandleader. Member of MILES DAVIS' group during the *Kind Of Blue* era. His band's recording of the JOE ZAWINUL composition "Mercy, Mercy, Mercy," when released as an edited 45, was one of the biggest jazz hits of the 1960s. Also see NAT ADDERLEY; RAY BROWN; ERIC DOLPHY; GIL EVANS; THE NUTTY SQUIRRELS; NANCY WILSON.

Number	Title	Yr	VG	VG+	NM
ARCHIVE OF FOLK AND JAZZ					
❑ 261	Cannonball Adderley and John Coltrane	1973	3.00	6.00	12.00
-- Abridged reissue of Limelight 86009					
BLUE NOTE					
❑ BM-LA169-F	Somethin' Else	1973	2.50	5.00	10.00
-- Reissue					
❑ LT-169	Somethin' Else	1981	2.50	5.00	10.00
-- Another reissue					
❑ BLP-1595 [M]	Somethin' Else	1958	37.50	75.00	150.00
-- "Deep groove" version (deep indentation under label on both sides)					
❑ BLP-1595 [M]	Somethin' Else	1958	25.00	50.00	100.00
-- Regular version with W. 63rd St. address on label					
❑ BLP-1595 [M]	Somethin' Else	1963	6.25	12.50	25.00
-- With New York, USA address on label					
❑ BST-1595 [S]	Somethin' Else	1959	25.00	50.00	100.00
-- "Deep groove" version (deep indentation under label on both sides)					
❑ BST-1595 [S]	Somethin' Else	1959	18.75	37.50	75.00
-- Regular version with W. 63rd St. address on label					
❑ B1-46338	Somethin' Else	1997	5.00	10.00	20.00
-- Audiophile reissue					
❑ BST-81595 [S]	Somethin' Else	1963	5.00	10.00	20.00
-- With New York, USA address on label					
❑ BST-81595 [S]	Somethin' Else	1966	3.75	7.50	15.00
-- With "A Division of Liberty Records" on label					
❑ BST-81595	Somethin' Else	1984	2.50	5.00	10.00
-- "The Finest in Jazz Since 1939" label					
❑ BST-81595	Somethin' Else	199?	6.25	12.50	25.00
-- Classic Records reissue					
CAPITOL					
❑ ST-162	Cannonball in Person	1968	3.75	7.50	15.00
❑ SKAO-404	Country Preacher	1970	3.75	7.50	15.00
❑ ST-484	Experience in E, Tensity, Dialogues	1970	3.75	7.50	15.00
❑ SWBB-636 [(2)]	The Price You Got to Pay to Be Free	1971	3.75	7.50	15.00
❑ STBB-697 [(2)]	Walk Tall/Quiet Nights	1971	3.75	7.50	15.00
❑ SWBO-812 [(2)]	Cannonball Adderley and Friends	1971	3.75	7.50	15.00
❑ SWBO-846 [(2)]	The Black Messiah	1972	3.75	7.50	15.00
❑ ST 2203 [S]	Domination	1964	5.00	10.00	20.00
❑ T 2203 [M]	Domination	1964	3.75	7.50	15.00
❑ ST 2216 [S]	Fiddler on the Roof	1965	5.00	10.00	20.00
❑ T 2216 [M]	Fiddler on the Roof	1965	3.75	7.50	15.00
❑ ST 2284 [S]	Live Session	1965	5.00	10.00	20.00
❑ T 2284 [M]	Live Session	1965	3.75	7.50	15.00
❑ SM-2399	Cannonball Adderley -- Live!	1976	2.50	5.00	10.00
❑ ST 2399 [S]	Cannonball Adderley -- Live!	1965	5.00	10.00	20.00
❑ T 2399 [M]	Cannonball Adderley -- Live!	1965	3.75	7.50	15.00
❑ ST 2531 [S]	Great Love Themes	1966	5.00	10.00	20.00
❑ T 2531 [M]	Great Love Themes	1966	3.75	7.50	15.00
❑ ST 2617 [S]	Why Am I Treated So Bad?	1966	5.00	10.00	20.00
❑ T 2617 [M]	Why Am I Treated So Bad?	1966	3.75	7.50	15.00
❑ SM-2663	Mercy, Mercy, Mercy!	1976	2.50	5.00	10.00
❑ ST 2663 [S]	Mercy, Mercy, Mercy!	1967	3.75	7.50	15.00
❑ ST-8-2663 [S]	Mercy, Mercy, Mercy!	1967	5.00	10.00	20.00
-- Capitol Record Club edition					
❑ T 2663 [M]	Mercy, Mercy, Mercy!	1967	6.25	12.50	25.00
❑ ST 2822 [S]	74 Miles Away -- Walk Tall	1967	3.75	7.50	15.00
❑ T 2822 [M]	74 Miles Away -- Walk Tall	1967	6.25	12.50	25.00
❑ SKAO 2939	The Best of Cannonball Adderley	1968	3.75	7.50	15.00
❑ ST 2987	Accent on Africa	1968	3.75	7.50	15.00
❑ ST-11008	Fiddler on the Roof	1972	3.00	6.00	12.00
-- Reissue of 2216					
❑ SABB-11120 [(2)]	The Soul of the Bible	1973	3.75	7.50	15.00

Number	Title	Yr	VG	VG+	NM
❑ ST-11121	Happy People	1973	3.00	6.00	12.00
❑ SVBB-11233 [(2)]	Cannonball Adderley and Friends	1974	3.00	6.00	12.00
-- Reissue of 812					
❑ ST-11484	Music, You All	1975	3.00	6.00	12.00
❑ SM-11817	Cannonball Adderley and Friends, Vol. 1	1978	2.50	5.00	10.00
❑ SM-11838	Cannonball Adderley and Friends, Vol. 2	1978	2.50	5.00	10.00
❑ SN-16002	The Best of Cannonball Adderley	1979	2.00	4.00	8.00
❑ SN-16153	Mercy, Mercy, Mercy!	1981	2.00	4.00	8.00
-- Budget-line reissues					
DOBRE					
❑ 1008	Cannonball, Volume 1	1977	3.00	6.00	12.00
EMARCY					
❑ EMS-2-404 [(2)]	Beginnings	1976	3.75	7.50	15.00
❑ MG-36043 [M]	Julian "Cannonball" Adderley	1955	15.00	30.00	60.00
❑ MG-36063 [M]	Julian "Cannonball" Adderley and Strings	1956	15.00	30.00	60.00
❑ MG-36077 [M]	In the Land of Hi-Fi	1956	15.00	30.00	60.00
❑ MG-36110 [M]	Sophisticated Swing	1957	15.00	30.00	60.00
❑ MG-36135 [M]	Cannonball's Sharpshooters	1958	15.00	30.00	60.00
❑ MG-36146 [M]	Jump for Joy	1958	15.00	30.00	60.00
FANTASY					
❑ FSP 2 [DJ]	Big Man Sampler	1975	5.00	10.00	20.00
❑ OJC-032	Things Are Getting Better	1982	2.50	5.00	10.00
❑ OJC-035	Cannonball Adderley Quintet in San Francisco	1982	2.50	5.00	10.00
❑ OJC-105	Know What I Mean?	1984	2.50	5.00	10.00
❑ OJC-142	Cannonball Adderley Sextet in New York	1985	2.50	5.00	10.00
❑ OJC-258	African Waltz	1987	2.50	5.00	10.00
❑ OJC-306	The Cannonball Adderley Quintet Plus	1988	2.50	5.00	10.00
❑ OJC-361	Portrait of Cannonball	1989	2.50	5.00	10.00
❑ OJC-435	Nippon Soul	1990	3.00	6.00	12.00
❑ 9435	Inside Straight	1973	3.00	6.00	12.00
❑ 9445	Love, Sex and the Zodiac	1974	3.00	6.00	12.00
❑ 9455	Pyramid	1974	3.00	6.00	12.00
❑ 9505	Lovers	1975	3.00	6.00	12.00
❑ 79004 [(2)]	Phenix	1975	3.75	7.50	15.00
❑ 79006 [(2)]	Big Man	1976	3.75	7.50	15.00
LANDMARK					
❑ LLP-1301	The Cannonball Adderley Collection Vol. 1: Them Dirty Blues	1987	2.50	5.00	10.00
❑ LLP-1302	The Cannonball Adderley Collection Vol. 2: Cannonball's Bossa Nova	1987	2.50	5.00	10.00
❑ LLP-1303	The Cannonball Adderley Collection Vol. 3: Jazz Workshop Revisited	1987	2.50	5.00	10.00
❑ LLP-1304	The Cannonball Adderley Collection Vol. 4: Cannonball and the Poll-Winners	1987	2.50	5.00	10.0
❑ LLP-1305	The Cannonball Adderley Collection Vol. 5: At the Lighthouse	1987	2.50	5.00	10.00
❑ LLP-1306	The Cannonball Adderley Collection Vol. 6: Cannonball Takes Charge	1987	2.50	5.00	10.00
❑ LLP-1307	The Cannonball Adderley Collection Vol. 7: Cannonball in Europe	1987	2.50	5.00	10.00
LIMELIGHT					
❑ LM 82009 [M]	Cannonball and Coltrane	1964	6.25	12.50	25.00
-- Reissue of Mercury 20449					
❑ LS 86009 [S]	Cannonball and Coltrane	1964	5.00	10.00	20.00
-- Reissue of Mercury 60449					
MERCURY					
❑ MG-20449 [M]	Cannonball Adderley Quintet in Chicago	1959	12.50	25.00	50.00
❑ MG-20530 [M]	Jump for Joy	1960	10.00	20.00	40.00
-- Reissue of EmArcy 36146					
❑ MG-20531 [M]	Cannonball's Sharpshooters	1960	10.00	20.00	40.00
-- Reissue of EmArcy 36135					
❑ MG-20616 [M]	Cannonball En Route	1961	10.00	20.00	40.00
❑ MG-20652 [M]	The Lush Side of Cannonball Adderley	1961	10.00	20.00	40.00
-- Reissue of EmArcy 36063					
❑ SR-60449 [S]	Cannonball Adderley Quintet in Chicago	1960	10.00	20.00	40.00
❑ SR-60530 [S]	Jump for Joy	1960	7.50	15.00	30.00
❑ SR-60531 [S]	Cannonball's Sharpshooters	1960	7.50	15.00	30.00
❑ SR-60616 [S]	Cannonball En Route	1961	7.50	15.00	30.00
❑ SR-60652 [R]	The Lush Side of Cannonball Adderley	1961	7.50	15.00	30.00
MILESTONE					
❑ 9030	Cannonball Adderley in New Orleans	197?	3.00	6.00	12.00
❑ 9106	The Sextet	198?	2.50	5.00	10.00
❑ 47001 [(2)]	Eight Giants	1973	3.75	7.50	15.00

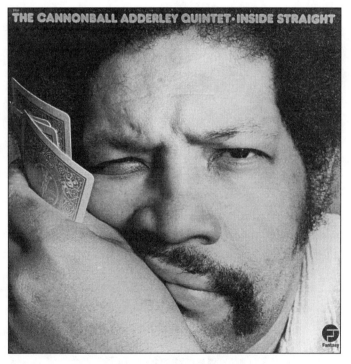

Julian "Cannonball" Adderley was one of the most influential alto saxophone players in jazz. (Top left) *Presenting Cannonball* was his first full-length album, issued on Savoy in 1955. Reissues of this album replace the band photo with a stack of cannonballs. (Top right) This album was from Adderley's short tenure with Mercury in 1960-61. (Bottom left) "Mercy, Mercy, Mercy," written by band member Joe Zawinul, became an unexpected hit in 1967. This is the album from which the single was taken. (Bottom right) Adderley moved to the Fantasy label in the early 1970s, where he stayed until his death. His first album for his new label was *Inside Straight*.

Number	Title	Yr	VG	VG+	NM
❑ 47029 [(2)]	The Japanese Concerts	1975	3.00	6.00	12.00
❑ 47039 [(2)]	Coast to Coast	1976	3.75	7.50	15.00
❑ 47053 [(2)]	What I Mean	1979	3.75	7.50	15.00
❑ 47059 [(2)]	Alabama/Africa	1982	3.00	6.00	12.00

PABLO LIVE

Number	Title	Yr	VG	VG+	NM
❑ 2308-238	What Is This Thing Called Soul	1984	2.50	5.00	10.00

RIVERSIDE

Number	Title	Yr	VG	VG+	NM
❑ RLP 12-269 [M]	Portrait of Cannonball	1958	12.50	25.00	50.00
❑ RLP 12-286 [M]	Things Are Getting Better	1959	12.50	25.00	50.00
❑ RLP 12-303 [M]	Cannonball Takes Charge	1959	12.50	25.00	50.00
❑ RLP 12-311 [M]	Cannonball Adderley Quintet in San Francisco	1959	12.50	25.00	50.00
❑ RLP 12-322 [M]	Them Dirty Blues	1960	12.50	25.00	50.00
❑ RLP 344 [M]	Cannonball Adderley Quintet at the Lighthouse	1960	10.00	20.00	40.00
❑ RLP 355 [M]	Cannonball Adderley and the Poll-Winners	1960	10.00	20.00	40.00
❑ RLP 377 [M]	African Waltz	1961	10.00	20.00	40.00
❑ RLP 388 [M]	Cannonball Adderley Quintet Plus	1961	10.00	20.00	40.00
❑ RLP 404 [M]	Cannonball Adderley Sextet In New York	1962	7.50	15.00	30.00
❑ RLP 416 [M]	Cannonball's Greatest Hits	1962	10.00	20.00	40.00
❑ RLP 433 [M]	Know What I Mean?	1962	7.50	15.00	30.00
❑ RLP 444 [M]	Jazz Workshop Revisited	1963	7.50	15.00	30.00
❑ RLP 455 [M]	Cannonball's Bossa Nova	1963	7.50	15.00	30.00
❑ RLP 477 [M]	Nippon Soul -- Recorded in Concert in Tokyo	1964	6.25	12.50	25.00
❑ RM 499 [M]	Cannonball in Europe	1967	5.00	10.00	20.00
❑ RLP 1128 [S]	Things Are Getting Better	1959	10.00	20.00	40.00
❑ RLP 1148 [S]	Cannonball Takes Charge	1959	10.00	20.00	40.00
❑ RLP 1157 [S]	Cannonball Adderley Quintet in San Francisco	1959	10.00	20.00	40.00
❑ RLP 1170 [S]	Them Dirty Blues	1960	10.00	20.00	40.00
❑ RS 3038	The Best of Cannonball Adderley	1968	3.75	7.50	15.00
❑ RS 3041	Planet Earth	1969	3.75	7.50	15.00
❑ 6051	Know What I Mean?	197?	3.00	6.00	12.00
-- Reissue of 9433					
❑ 6062	Cannonball Adderley Quintet in San Francisco	197?	3.00	6.00	12.00
-- Reissue of 1157					
❑ 6108	Cannonball Adderley Sextet in New York	197?	3.00	6.00	12.00
-- Reissue of 9404					
❑ 6122	Things Are Getting Better	197?	3.00	6.00	12.00
-- Reissue of 1128					
❑ RS 9344 [S]	Cannonball Adderley Quintet at the Lighthouse	1960	7.50	15.00	30.00
❑ RS 9355 [S]	Cannonball Adderley and the Poll-Winners	1960	7.50	15.00	30.00
❑ RS 9377 [S]	African Waltz	1961	7.50	15.00	30.00
❑ RS 9388 [S]	Cannonball Adderley Quintet Plus	1961	7.50	15.00	30.00
❑ RS 9404 [S]	Cannonball Adderley Sextet In New York	1962	7.50	15.00	30.00
❑ RS 9416 [S]	Cannonball's Greatest Hits	1962	7.50	15.00	30.00
❑ RS 9433 [S]	Know What I Mean?	1962	7.50	15.00	30.00
❑ RS 9444 [S]	Jazz Workshop Revisited	1963	7.50	15.00	30.00
❑ RS 9455 [S]	Cannonball's Bossa Nova	1963	7.50	15.00	30.00
❑ RS 9477 [S]	Nippon Soul -- Recorded in Concert in Tokyo	1964	6.25	12.50	25.00
❑ RS 9499 [S]	Cannonball in Europe	1967	3.75	7.50	15.00

SAVOY

Number	Title	Yr	VG	VG+	NM
❑ MG-12018 [M]	Presenting Cannonball	1955	20.00	40.00	80.00
-- Band pictured on cover					
❑ MG-12018 [M]	Presenting Cannonball	196?	10.00	20.00	40.00
-- Instead of picturing the band, the front cover features cannonballs					

SAVOY JAZZ

Number	Title	Yr	VG	VG+	NM
❑ SJC-401	Presenting Cannonball	1985	2.50	5.00	10.00
-- Reissue of Savoy 12018					
❑ SJL-1195	Discoveries	1989	2.50	5.00	10.00
❑ SJL-2206	Spontaneous Combustion	1976	3.00	6.00	12.00

WONDERLAND/RIVERSIDE

Number	Title	Yr	VG	VG+	NM
❑ RLP 1435 [M]	A Child's Introduction to Jazz	196?	12.50	25.00	50.00
-- Adderley narrates an album introducing the works of such artists as Armstrong, Monk, Waller, etc.					

ADDERLEY, CANNONBALL AND NAT
Also see each artist's individual listings.

LIMELIGHT

Number	Title	Yr	VG	VG+	NM
❑ LM 82032 [M]	Them Adderleys	1964	6.25	12.50	25.00
❑ LS 86032 [S]	Them Adderleys	1964	5.00	10.00	20.00

ADDERLEY, NAT
Cornet player who also played trumpet, mellophone and flugel horn. Best known as a sideman in the band of his brother, CANNONBALL ADDERLEY.

A&M

Number	Title	Yr	VG	VG+	NM
❑ LP-2005 [M]	You, Baby	1968	6.25	12.50	25.00
-- Mono is promo only					
❑ SP-3005 [S]	You, Baby	1968	3.00	6.00	12.00
❑ SP9-3005	You, Baby	198?	3.75	7.50	15.00
-- Audiophile reissue					
❑ SP-3017	Calling Out Loud	1969	3.00	6.00	12.00

ATLANTIC

Number	Title	Yr	VG	VG+	NM
❑ 1439 [M]	Autobiography	1965	3.75	7.50	15.00
❑ SD 1439 [S]	Autobiography	1965	5.00	10.00	20.00
❑ 1460 [M]	Sayin' Something	1966	3.75	7.50	15.00
❑ SD 1460 [S]	Sayin' Something	1966	5.00	10.00	20.00
❑ 1475 [M]	Live at Memory Lane	1967	5.00	10.00	20.00
❑ SD 1475 [S]	Live at Memory Lane	1967	3.75	7.50	15.00

CAPITOL

Number	Title	Yr	VG	VG+	NM
❑ SVBB-11025 [(2)]	Cannonball Adderley Presents Soul Zodiac	1972	10.00	20.00	40.00

EMARCY

Number	Title	Yr	VG	VG+	NM
❑ MG-36091 [M]	Introducing Nat Adderley	1955	20.00	40.00	80.00
❑ MG-36100 [M]	To the Ivy League from Nat	1956	20.00	40.00	80.00

FANTASY

Number	Title	Yr	VG	VG+	NM
❑ OJC-255	Branching Out	1987	2.50	5.00	10.00
-- Reissue of Riverside 12-285					
❑ OJC-363	The Work Song	198?	2.50	5.00	10.00
-- Reissue of Riverside 1167					
❑ OJC-648	In the Bag	1991	3.00	6.00	12.00
-- Reissue of Jazzland 975					

GALAXY

Number	Title	Yr	VG	VG+	NM
❑ 5120	Little New York Midtown Music	197?	2.50	5.00	10.00

JAZZLAND

Number	Title	Yr	VG	VG+	NM
❑ JLP-47 [M]	Naturally!	1961	7.50	15.00	30.00
❑ JLP-75 [M]	In the Bag	1962	7.50	15.00	30.00
❑ JLP-947 [S]	Naturally!	1961	10.00	20.00	40.00
❑ JLP-975 [S]	In the Bag	1962	10.00	20.00	40.00

LITTLE DAVID

Number	Title	Yr	VG	VG+	NM
❑ LD 1012	Hummin'	1975	3.00	6.00	12.00

MILESTONE

Number	Title	Yr	VG	VG+	NM
❑ MSP-9009	Natural Soul	1968	3.75	7.50	15.00
❑ MSP-9016	The Scavenger	1968	3.75	7.50	15.00
❑ 47047 [(2)]	Work Songs	197?	3.00	6.00	12.00

PRESTIGE

Number	Title	Yr	VG	VG+	NM
❑ 10090	Double Exposure	1974	3.00	6.00	12.00

RIVERSIDE

Number	Title	Yr	VG	VG+	NM
❑ RLP 12-285 [M]	Branching Out	1958	12.50	25.00	50.00
❑ RLP 12-301 [M]	Much Brass	1959	12.50	25.00	50.00
❑ RLP 12-318 [M]	The Work Song	1960	10.00	20.00	40.00
❑ RLP-330 [M]	That's Right!	1960	7.50	15.00	30.00
❑ RM-474 [M]	Little Big Horn!	1964	7.50	15.00	30.00
❑ RLP-1143 [S]	Much Brass	1959	12.50	25.00	50.00
❑ RLP-1167 [S]	The Work Song	1960	12.50	25.00	50.00
❑ 6041	The Work Song	197?	3.00	6.00	12.00
-- Reissue					
❑ RS-9330 [S]	That's Right!	1960	10.00	20.00	40.00
❑ RS-9474 [S]	Little Big Horn!	1964	10.00	20.00	40.00

SAVOY

Number	Title	Yr	VG	VG+	NM
❑ MG-12021 [M]	That's Nat	1955	20.00	40.00	80.00

SAVOY JAZZ

Number	Title	Yr	VG	VG+	NM
❑ SJL-1128	That's Nat	198?	2.50	5.00	10.00
-- Reissue of Savoy 12021					

STEEPLECHASE

Number	Title	Yr	VG	VG+	NM
❑ SCS-1059	Don't Look Back	198?	2.50	5.00	10.00

THERESA

Number	Title	Yr	VG	VG+	NM
❑ TR-117	On the Move	198?	2.50	5.00	10.00
❑ TR-122	Blue Autumn	1987	2.50	5.00	10.00

WING

Number	Title	Yr	VG	VG+	NM
❑ MGW-60000 [M]	Introducing Nat Adderley	1956	12.50	25.00	50.00

AIR
Trio with Henry Threadgill on saxes and horns, Fred Hopkins on bass, and Steve McCall on drums and percussion. New Air featured Threadgill and Hopkins with Pheeroan Ak Laff on percussion.

ANTILLES

Number	Title	Yr	VG	VG+	NM
❑ 1007	80 Degrees Below '82	1982	2.50	5.00	10.00

ARISTA/NOVUS

Number	Title	Yr	VG	VG+	NM
❑ 3002	Open Air Suit	1978	3.00	6.00	12.00
❑ 3008	Montreux	1979	3.00	6.00	12.00
❑ 3014	Air Lore	1980	3.00	6.00	12.00

BLACK SAINT

Number	Title	Yr	VG	VG+	NM
❑ BSR-0032	Live Air	198?	3.00	6.00	12.00

Number	Title	Yr	VG	VG+	NM
❏ BSR-0049	Air Mail	198?	3.00	6.00	12.00
❏ BSR-0084	Live at Montreal International Jazz Festival	198?	2.50	5.00	10.00

-- As "New Air"

INDIA NAVIGATION

Number	Title	Yr	VG	VG+	NM
❏ IN-1057	Air Song	1975	3.75	7.50	15.00
❏ IN-1064	Air Raid	1976	3.75	7.50	15.00

NESSA

Number	Title	Yr	VG	VG+	NM
❏ 12	Time	1978	3.75	7.50	15.00

AIRTO
Full name: Airto Moreira. Percussionist who was with MILES DAVIS' *Bitches Brew*-era band and CHICK COREA'S original Return To Forever. Also see DEODATO/AIRTO; FLORA PURIM.

ACCORD

Number	Title	Yr	VG	VG+	NM
❏ SN-7184	Brazilian Heatwave	198?	2.50	5.00	10.00

ARISTA

Number	Title	Yr	VG	VG+	NM
❏ AL 4068	Identity	1975	2.50	5.00	10.00
❏ AL 4116	Promises of the Sun	1976	2.50	5.00	10.00

BUDDAH

Number	Title	Yr	VG	VG+	NM
❏ BDS-21-SK	Natural Feelings	1970	3.75	7.50	15.00
❏ BDS-5085	Seeds on the Ground	1971	3.75	7.50	15.00
❏ BDA-5668 [(2)]	Essential Airto	197?	3.00	6.00	12.00

CTI

Number	Title	Yr	VG	VG+	NM
❏ 6020	Free	1972	3.00	6.00	12.00
❏ 6028	Fingers	1973	3.00	6.00	12.00
❏ CTSQ-6028 [Q]	Fingers	1974	5.00	10.00	20.00
❏ 8000	Free	197?	2.50	5.00	10.00

-- Reissue of 6020

SALVATION

Number	Title	Yr	VG	VG+	NM
❏ 701	Virgin Land	1974	3.00	6.00	12.00

WARNER BROS.

Number	Title	Yr	VG	VG+	NM
❏ BS 3084	I'm Fine, How Are You?	1977	2.50	5.00	10.00
❏ BSK 3279	Touching You, Touching Me	1979	2.50	5.00	10.00

AKIYOSHI, TOSHIKO
Piano player and bandleader. She also recorded as Toshiko Mariano when she was married to Charlie Mariano.

CANDID

Number	Title	Yr	VG	VG+	NM
❏ CD-8012 [M]	Toshiko Mariano Quartet	1960	10.00	20.00	40.00
❏ CD-8015 [M]	Toshiko Mariano	1960	10.00	20.00	40.00
❏ CS-9012 [S]	Toshiko Mariano Quartet	1960	12.50	25.00	50.00
❏ CS-9015 [S]	Toshiko Mariano	1960	12.50	25.00	50.00

CONCORD JAZZ

Number	Title	Yr	VG	VG+	NM
❏ CJ-69	Finesse	1980	2.50	5.00	10.00
❏ CJ-324	Interlude	1987	2.50	5.00	10.00

DAUNTLESS

Number	Title	Yr	VG	VG+	NM
❏ DM-4308 [M]	The Country and Western Sounds of Jazz	1963	10.00	20.00	40.00
❏ DS-6308 [S]	The Country and Western Sounds of Jazz	1963	12.50	25.00	50.00

INNER CITY

Number	Title	Yr	VG	VG+	NM
❏ 6046	Dedications	1977	3.00	6.00	12.00
❏ 6066	Notorious Tourist from the East	1978	3.00	6.00	12.00

METROJAZZ

Number	Title	Yr	VG	VG+	NM
❏ E-1001 [M]	United Notions	1958	12.50	25.00	50.00
❏ SE-1001 [S]	United Notions	1959	10.00	20.00	40.00

NORGRAN

Number	Title	Yr	VG	VG+	NM
❏ MGN-22 [10]	Toshiko's Piano	1954	37.50	75.00	150.00

STORYVILLE

Number	Title	Yr	VG	VG+	NM
❏ STLP-912 [M]	The Toshiko Trio	1956	15.00	30.00	60.00
❏ STLP-918 [M]	Toshiko Akiyoshi, Her Trio, Her Quartet	1957	15.00	30.00	60.00

VEE JAY

Number	Title	Yr	VG	VG+	NM
❏ LP-2505 [M]	Jazz in Japan	1964	7.50	15.00	30.00

-- As "Toshiko Mariano and Her Big Band"

VERVE

Number	Title	Yr	VG	VG+	NM
❏ MGV-8273 [M]	The Many Sides of Toshiko	1958	15.00	30.00	60.00
❏ V-8273 [M]	The Many Sides of Toshiko	1961	6.25	12.50	25.00

AKIYOSHI, TOSHIKO, AND LEON SASH
Also see each artist's individual listings.

VERVE

Number	Title	Yr	VG	VG+	NM
❏ MGV-8236 [M]	Toshiko and Leon Sash at Newport	1958	15.00	30.00	60.00
❏ V-8236 [M]	Toshiko and Leon Sash at Newport	1961	6.25	12.50	25.00

AKIYOSHI, TOSHIKO-LEW TABACKIN BIG BAND
Lew Tabackin is Akiyoshi's second husband. Also see each artist's individual listings.

JAM

Number	Title	Yr	VG	VG+	NM
❏ 003	Farewell to Mingus	1981	2.50	5.00	10.00
❏ 006	Tanuki's Night Out	1982	2.50	5.00	10.00

RCA VICTOR

Number	Title	Yr	VG	VG+	NM
❏ AFL1-0723	Tales of a Courtesan	1978	2.50	5.00	10.00

-- Reissue with new prefix

Number	Title	Yr	VG	VG+	NM
❏ JPL1-0723	Tales of a Courtesan	1976	3.75	7.50	15.00
❏ AFL1-1350	Long Yellow Road	1978	2.50	5.00	10.00

-- Reissue with new prefix

Number	Title	Yr	VG	VG+	NM
❏ JPL1-1350	Long Yellow Road	1976	3.75	7.50	15.00
❏ CPL2-2242 [(2)]	Road Time	1977	5.00	10.00	20.00
❏ AFL1-2678	Insights	1978	3.00	6.00	12.00
❏ AFL1-3019	Kogun	1979	3.00	6.00	12.00

-- Recorded in 1974

ALBAM, MANNY
Arranger and composer, also a baritone and tenor saxophone player. Also see STEVE ALLEN AND MANNY ALBAM.

ABC IMPULSE!

Number	Title	Yr	VG	VG+	NM
❏ AS-19 [S]	Jazz Goes to the Movies	196?	3.00	6.00	12.00

-- Reissue of Impulse! AS-19

CORAL

Number	Title	Yr	VG	VG+	NM
❏ CRL 57142 [M]	The Jazz Greats of Our Time	1957	10.00	20.00	40.00
❏ CRL 57173 [M]	The Jazz Greats of Our Time, Volume 2	1957	10.00	20.00	40.00
❏ CRL 57207 [M]	West Side Story	1958	10.00	20.00	40.00
❏ CRL 57231 [M]	Sophisticated Lady -- The Songs of Duke Ellington	1958	10.00	20.00	40.00
❏ CRL 59101 [M]	The Blues Is Everybody's Business	195?	10.00	20.00	40.00

DECCA

Number	Title	Yr	VG	VG+	NM
❏ DL 4517 [M]	Music from West Side Story	1964	3.75	7.50	15.00
❏ DL 74517 [S]	Music from West Side Story	1964	5.00	10.00	20.00

DOT

Number	Title	Yr	VG	VG+	NM
❏ DLP-9004 [M]	Jazz New York	1958	10.00	20.00	40.00
❏ DLP-9008 [M]	Steve's Song	1958	10.00	20.00	40.00

IMPULSE!

Number	Title	Yr	VG	VG+	NM
❏ A-19 [M]	Jazz Goes to the Movies	1962	6.25	12.50	25.00
❏ AS-19 [S]	Jazz Goes to the Movies	1962	7.50	15.00	30.00

MERCURY

Number	Title	Yr	VG	VG+	NM
❏ MG-20325 [M]	With All My Love	1958	10.00	20.00	40.00

RCA VICTOR

Number	Title	Yr	VG	VG+	NM
❏ LPM-1211 [M]	The RCA Victor Jazz Workshop	1956	12.50	25.00	50.00
❏ LPM-1279 [M]	The Drum Suite	1956	12.50	25.00	50.00
❏ LPM-2432 [M]	More Double Exposure	1961	5.00	10.00	20.00
❏ LSA-2432 [S]	More Double Exposure	1961	7.50	15.00	30.00
❏ LPM-2508 [M]	I Had the Craziest Dream	1962	5.00	10.00	20.00
❏ LSA-2508 [S]	I Had the Craziest Dream	1962	6.25	12.50	25.00

SOLID STATE

Number	Title	Yr	VG	VG+	NM
❏ SM-17000 [M]	Brass on Fire	1966	3.75	7.50	15.00
❏ SM-17009 [M]	The Soul of the City	1966	5.00	10.00	20.00
❏ SS-18000 [S]	Brass on Fire	1966	5.00	10.00	20.00
❏ SS-18009 [S]	The Soul of the City	1966	3.75	7.50	15.00

TOP RANK

Number	Title	Yr	VG	VG+	NM
❏ RM-313 [M]	Double Exposure	1960	10.00	20.00	40.00

UNITED ARTISTS

Number	Title	Yr	VG	VG+	NM
❏ UAL-3079 [M]	Drum Feast	1959	7.50	15.00	30.00
❏ UAS-6079 [S]	Drum Feast	1959	10.00	20.00	40.00

VOCALION

Number	Title	Yr	VG	VG+	NM
❏ VL 3678 [M]	West Side Story	196?	3.75	7.50	15.00

ALBANY, JOE
Pianist.

ELEKTRA MUSICIAN

Number	Title	Yr	VG	VG+	NM
❏ 60161	Portrait of an Artist	1983	2.50	5.00	10.00

INNER CITY

Number	Title	Yr	VG	VG+	NM
❏ 2003	Birdtown Birds	197?	3.75	7.50	15.00

INTERPLAY

Number	Title	Yr	VG	VG+	NM
❏ 7723	Bird Lives	1979	3.00	6.00	12.00

REVELATION

Number	Title	Yr	VG	VG+	NM
❏ 16	Proto-Bopper	197?	3.75	7.50	15.00
❏ 25	At Home Alone	197?	3.75	7.50	15.00

RIVERSIDE

Number	Title	Yr	VG	VG+	NM
❏ RS-3023	The Legendary Jazz Pianist	1968	3.75	7.50	15.00

STEEPLECHASE

Number	Title	Yr	VG	VG+	NM
❏ SCS-1003	Birdtown Birds	198?	2.50	5.00	10.00

-- Reissue of Inner City 2003

ALBANY, JOE, AND WARNE MARSH
Also see each artist's individual listings.

FANTASY

Number	Title	Yr	VG	VG+	NM
❏ OJC-1749 [M]	The Right Combination	1990	3.00	6.00	12.00

-- Reissue of Riverside 12-270

Number	Title	Yr	VG	VG+	NM
RIVERSIDE					
❏ RLP 12-270 [M]	The Right Combination	1958	20.00	40.00	80.00

ALBANY, JOE, AND NIELS-HENNING ORSTED PEDERSEN
Also see each artist's individual listings.

Number	Title	Yr	VG	VG+	NM
INNER CITY					
❏ 2019	Two's Company	197?	3.75	7.50	15.00
STEEPLECHASE					
❏ SCS-1019	Two's Company	198?	2.50	5.00	10.00
-- Reissue of Inner City 2019					

ALBRIGHT, LOLA
Female vocalist.

Number	Title	Yr	VG	VG+	NM
COLUMBIA					
❏ CL 1327 [M]	Dreamsville	1959	10.00	20.00	40.00
❏ CS 8133 [S]	Dreamsville	1959	12.50	25.00	50.00

ALBRIGHT, MAX
Drummer.

Number	Title	Yr	VG	VG+	NM
MOTIF					
❏ 502 [M]	Mood for Max	1956	15.00	30.00	60.00

ALDEN, HOWARD
Guitarist, both of the six- and seven-string varieties.

Number	Title	Yr	VG	VG+	NM
CONCORD JAZZ					
❏ CJ-378	The Howard Alden Trio	1988	2.50	5.00	10.00
FAMOUS DOOR					
❏ HL-154	Swinging Into Prominence	1988	2.50	5.00	10.00
STOMP OFF					
❏ SOS-1200	Howard Alden Plays the Music of Harry Reser	1991	3.00	6.00	12.00

ALDEN, HOWARD-DAN BARRETT QUINTET
Also see each artist's individual listings.

Number	Title	Yr	VG	VG+	NM
CONCORD JAZZ					
❏ CJ-349	Swing Street	1988	2.50	5.00	10.00

ALESS, TONY
Pianist.

Number	Title	Yr	VG	VG+	NM
ROOST					
❏ RST-2202 [M]	Tony Aless and His Long Island Suite	1955	20.00	40.00	80.00

ALEXANDER, BOB
See AL KLINK AND BOB ALEXANDER.

ALEXANDER, JOE, AND BOBBY TIMMONS
Alexander plays tenor saxophone. Also see BOBBY TIMMONS.

Number	Title	Yr	VG	VG+	NM
JAZZLAND					
❏ JLP-23 [M]	Blue Jubilee	1960	7.50	15.00	30.00
❏ JLP-923 [S]	Blue Jubilee	1960	10.00	20.00	40.00

ALEXANDER, MONTY
Pianist.

Number	Title	Yr	VG	VG+	NM
BASF					
❏ 20913	Here Comes the Sun	197?	3.00	6.00	12.00
❏ 25103	We've Only Just Begun	1972	3.00	6.00	12.00
❏ 25352	Rass!	197?	3.00	6.00	12.00
CONCORD JAZZ					
❏ CJ-108	Facets	1980	2.50	5.00	10.00
❏ CJ-231	Reunion in Europe	1982	2.50	5.00	10.00
❏ CJ-287	Full Steam Ahead	1985	2.50	5.00	10.00
CONCORD PICANTE					
❏ CJP-124	Ivory and Steel	1981	2.50	5.00	10.00
❏ CJP-359	Jamboree	1988	2.50	5.00	10.00
MGM					
❏ SE-4736	Taste of Freedom	1971	3.75	7.50	15.00
PABLO					
❏ 2310 826	Jamento	1978	3.00	6.00	12.00
❏ 2310 836	Monty Alexander in Tokyo	1979	3.00	6.00	12.00
PACIFIC JAZZ					
❏ PJ-86 [M]	Alexander the Great	1966	5.00	10.00	20.00
❏ ST-86 [S]	Alexander the Great	1966	6.25	12.50	25.00
❏ PJ-10094 [M]	Spooky	1966	5.00	10.00	20.00
❏ ST-20094 [S]	Spooky	1966	6.25	12.50	25.00
PAUSA					
❏ 7032	Now Is the Time	197?	3.00	6.00	12.00
❏ 7083	Montreux Alexander Live	197?	3.00	6.00	12.00
❏ 7129	With Love	198?	2.50	5.00	10.00

Number	Title	Yr	VG	VG+	NM
RCA VICTOR					
❏ LPM-3930 [M]	Zing	1968	6.25	12.50	25.00
❏ LSP-3930 [S]	Zing	1968	3.75	7.50	15.00
VERVE					
❏ V6-8790	This Is Monty Alexander	1970	3.75	7.50	15.00
VERVE/MPS					
❏ 821 151-1	The Duke Ellington Songbook	1984	2.50	5.00	10.00

ALEXANDER, MONTY / RAY BROWN / HERB ELLIS
Also see each artist's individual listings.

Number	Title	Yr	VG	VG+	NM
CONCORD JAZZ					
❏ CJ-136	Trio	1981	2.50	5.00	10.00
❏ CJ-193	Triple Treat	1982	2.50	5.00	10.00
❏ CJ-253	Overseas Special	1983	2.50	5.00	10.00
❏ CJ-338	Triple Treat II	1988	2.50	5.00	10.00
❏ CJ-394	Triple Treat III	1989	2.50	5.00	10.00

ALEXANDER, MONTY/NIELS-HENNING ORSTED PEDERSEN/ GRADY TATE
Also see each artist's individual listings.

Number	Title	Yr	VG	VG+	NM
SOUL NOTE					
❏ 121152-1	Threesome	198?	3.00	6.00	12.00

ALEXANDER, MONTY, AND ERNEST RANGLIN
Also see each artist's individual listings.

Number	Title	Yr	VG	VG+	NM
PAUSA					
❏ 7110	Just Friends	198?	2.50	5.00	10.00

ALEXANDER, ROLAND
Tenor saxophone player and sometimes a pianist.

Number	Title	Yr	VG	VG+	NM
NEW JAZZ					
❏ NJLP-8267 [M]	Pleasure Bent	1962	12.50	25.00	50.00
-- Purple label					
❏ NJLP-8267 [M]	Pleasure Bent	1965	6.25	12.50	25.00
-- Blue label, trident at right					

ALEXANDRIA, LOREZ
Female vocalist.

Number	Title	Yr	VG	VG+	NM
ABC IMPULSE!					
❏ AS-62	Alexandria the Great	1968	3.00	6.00	12.00
-- Reissue of Impulse! AS-62					
❏ AS-76	More of the Great Lorez Alexandria	1968	3.00	6.00	12.00
-- Reissue of Impulse! AS-76					
ARGO					
❏ LP-663 [M]	Early in the Morning	1960	10.00	20.00	40.00
❏ LPS-663 [S]	Early in the Morning	1960	12.50	25.00	50.00
-- With the Ramsey Lewis Trio					
❏ LP-682 [M]	Sing No Sad Songs for Me	1961	10.00	20.00	40.00
❏ LPS-682 [S]	Sing No Sad Songs for Me	1961	12.50	25.00	50.00
❏ LP-694 [M]	Deep Roots	1962	10.00	20.00	40.00
❏ LPS-694 [S]	Deep Roots	1962	12.50	25.00	50.00
❏ LP-720 [M]	For Swingers Only	1963	10.00	20.00	40.00
❏ LPS-720 [S]	For Swingers Only	1963	12.50	25.00	50.00
CADET					
❏ LPS-682	Sing No Sad Songs for Me	1966	5.00	10.00	20.00
-- Reissue of Argo 682					
DISCOVERY					
❏ 782	How Will I Remember You?	1978	2.50	5.00	10.00
❏ 800	A Woman Knows	1979	2.50	5.00	10.00
❏ 826	Lorez Alexandria Sings Johnny Mercer	1981	2.50	5.00	10.00
❏ 905	Harlem Butterfly (Sings the Songs of Johnny Mercer Vol. 2)	1984	2.50	5.00	10.00
IMPULSE!					
❏ A-62 [M]	Alexandria the Great	1964	6.25	12.50	25.00
❏ AS-62 [S]	Alexandria the Great	1964	7.50	15.00	30.00
❏ A-76 [M]	More of the Great Lorez Alexandria	1965	6.25	12.50	25.00
❏ AS-76 [S]	More of the Great Lorez Alexandria	1965	7.50	15.00	30.00
KING					
❏ 542 [M]	This Is Lorez	1956	25.00	50.00	100.00
-- Black label, crownless "King"					
❏ 565 [M]	Lorez Sings Prez	1956	25.00	50.00	100.00
-- Black label, crownless "King"					
❏ 657 [M]	The Band Swings, Lorez Sings	1959	25.00	50.00	100.00
-- Black label, crownless "King"					
❏ S-657 [S]	The Band Swings, Lorez Sings	1959	37.50	75.00	150.00
-- Dark blue label, crownless "King"					
❏ 676 [M]	Singing Songs Everyone Knows	1959	25.00	50.00	100.00
-- Black label, crownless "King"					
MCA					
❏ 29000	Alexandria the Great	198?	2.00	4.00	8.00
-- Reissue of ABC Impulse! AS-62					

Number	Title	Yr	VG	VG+	NM
TREND					
❑ TR-538	Tangerine (Sings the Songs of Johnny Mercer Vol. 3)	1986	2.50	5.00	10.00
❑ TR-547	Dear to My Heart	1988	2.50	5.00	10.00

ALFRED, CHUZ; OLA HANSON; CHUCK LEE
Alfred is a saxophone player; Hanson plays trombone

Number	Title	Yr	VG	VG+	NM
SAVOY					
❑ MG-12030 [M]	Jazz Young Blood	1955	15.00	30.00	60.00

ALLEN, BYRON, TRIO
The other members of his trio were Ted Robinson and Maceo Gilchrist.

Number	Title	Yr	VG	VG+	NM
ESP-DISK					
❑ 1005 [M]	The Byron Allen Trio	1965	5.00	10.00	20.00
❑ S-1005 [S]	The Byron Allen Trio	1965	6.25	12.50	25.00

ALLEN, DAVID
Male vocalist. Also includes releases as "David Allyn."

Number	Title	Yr	VG	VG+	NM
EVEREST					
❑ SD-1224 [S]	David Allen	1964	5.00	10.00	20.00
❑ LP-5224 [M]	David Allen	1964	3.75	7.50	15.00
PACIFIC JAZZ					
❑ PJM-408 [M]	A Sure Thing	1957	15.00	30.00	60.00
❑ ST-1006 [S]	A Sure Thing	1959	15.00	30.00	60.00
WORLD PACIFIC					
❑ ST-1295 [S]	David Allen Sings the Jerome Kern Songbook	1960	7.50	15.00	30.00
❑ WP-1250 [M]	Let's Face the Music and Dance	1958	10.00	20.00	40.00
❑ WP-1295 [M]	David Allen Sings the Jerome Kern Songbook	1960	7.50	15.00	30.00

ALLEN, HENRY "RED"
Highly influential trumpet player of the Dixieland and swing eras, also a singer and composer.

Number	Title	Yr	VG	VG+	NM
AMERICAN RECORDING SOCIETY					
❑ G-436 [M]	Traditional Jazz	195?	10.00	20.00	40.00
COLUMBIA					
❑ CL 2447 [M]	Feelin' Good	1966	3.75	7.50	15.00
❑ CS 9247 [S]	Feelin' Good	1966	5.00	10.00	20.00
PRESTIGE					
❑ PRST-7755	Memorial Album	1968	3.75	7.50	15.00
RCA VICTOR					
❑ LPV-556 [M]	Henry "Red" Allen	1965	5.00	10.00	20.00
❑ LPM-1509 [M]	Ride, Red, Ride in Hi-Fi	1957	12.50	25.00	50.00
SWINGVILLE					
❑ SWLP-2034 [M]	Mr. Allen	1962	10.00	20.00	40.00
-- Purple label					
❑ SWLP-2034 [M]	Mr. Allen	1965	5.00	10.00	20.00
-- Blue label, trident logo at right					
❑ SWST-2034 [S]	Mr. Allen	1962	12.50	25.00	50.00
-- Red label					
❑ SWST-2034 [S]	Mr. Allen	1965	6.25	12.50	25.00
-- Blue label, trident logo at right					
VERVE					
❑ MGV-1025 [M]	Red Allen Plays King Oliver	1959	12.50	25.00	50.00
❑ V-1025 [M]	Red Allen Plays King Oliver	1961	5.00	10.00	20.00
❑ V6-1025 [S]	Red Allen Plays King Oliver "X"	1961	6.25	12.50	25.00
❑ LVA-3033 [M]	Ridin' with Red	1955	12.50	25.00	50.00

ALLEN, HENRY "RED", AND KID ORY
Also see each artist's individual listings.

Number	Title	Yr	VG	VG+	NM
VERVE					
❑ MGV-1018 [M]	Henry "Red" Allen Meets Kid Ory	1957	12.50	25.00	50.00
❑ V-1018 [M]	Henry "Red" Allen Meets Kid Ory	1961	5.00	10.00	20.00
❑ V6-1018 [S]	Henry "Red" Allen Meets Kid Ory	1961	5.00	10.00	20.00
❑ MGV-1020 [M]	We've Got Rhythm	1958	12.50	25.00	50.00
❑ V-1020 [M]	We've Got Rhythm	1961	5.00	10.00	20.00
❑ V6-1020 [S]	We've Got Rhythm	1961	5.00	10.00	20.00
❑ MGVS-6076 [S]	Henry "Red" Allen Meets Kid Ory	1959	10.00	20.00	40.00
❑ MGVS-6121 [S]	We've Got Rhythm	1959	10.00	20.00	40.00

ALLEN, HENRY "RED", AND RED NORVO
Also see each artist's individual listings.

Number	Title	Yr	VG	VG+	NM
BRUNSWICK					
❑ BL 58044 [10]	Battle of Jazz, Vol. 6	1953	15.00	30.00	60.00

ALLEN, HENRY "RED"; JACK TEAGARDEN; KID ORY
Also see each artist's individual listings.

Number	Title	Yr	VG	VG+	NM
VERVE					
❑ UMV-2624	Verve at Newport	198?	2.50	5.00	10.00
❑ MGV-8233 [M]	Red Allen, Jack Teagarden & Kid Ory at Newport	1958	12.50	25.00	50.00
❑ V-8233 [M]	Red Allen, Jack Teagarden & Kid Ory at Newport	1961	5.00	10.00	20.00

ALLEN, STEVE
Pianist, composer and comedian in many different styles. The below list includes only his jazz-oriented work. See the *Standard Catalog of American Records* for other LPs.

Number	Title	Yr	VG	VG+	NM
CORAL					
❑ CRL 57018 [M]	Jazz for Tonight	1956	6.25	12.50	25.00
❑ CRL 57028 [M]	Let's Dance	1956	6.25	12.50	25.00
DECCA					
❑ DL 8151 [M]	Steve Allen's All Star Jazz Concert, Vol. 1	1955	7.50	15.00	30.00
❑ DL 8152 [M]	Steve Allen's All Star Jazz Concert, Vol. 2	1955	7.50	15.00	30.00
DOT					
❑ DLP 3480 [M]	Bossa Nova Jazz	1963	3.75	7.50	15.00
❑ DLP 3515 [M]	Gravy Waltz and 11 Current Hits!	1963	3.75	7.50	15.00
❑ DLP 25380 [S]	Bossa Nova Jazz	1963	5.00	10.00	20.00
❑ DLP 25515 [S]	Gravy Waltz and 11 Current Hits!	1963	5.00	10.00	20.00
FORUM					
❑ F-9014 [M]	Steve Allen at the Round Table	196?	5.00	10.00	20.00
❑ FS-9014 [S]	Steve Allen at the Round Table	196?	3.75	7.50	15.00
ROULETTE					
❑ R-25053 [M]	Steve Allen at the Round Table	1959	6.25	12.50	25.00
❑ SR-25053 [S]	Steve Allen at the Round Table	1959	5.00	10.00	20.00

ALLEN, STEVE, AND MANNY ALBAM
Also see each artist's individual listings.

Number	Title	Yr	VG	VG+	NM
DOT					
❑ DLP 3194 [M]	...And All That Jazz	1959	6.25	12.50	25.00
❑ DLP 25194 [S]	...And All That Jazz	1959	5.00	10.00	20.00

ALLISON, MOSE
Male vocalist and pianist. Also see THE MANHATTAN ALL STARS.

Number	Title	Yr	VG	VG+	NM
ATLANTIC					
❑ 1389 [M]	I Don't Worry About a Thing	1962	3.75	7.50	15.00
❑ SD 1389 [S]	I Don't Worry About a Thing	1962	5.00	10.00	20.00
❑ 1398 [M]	Swingin' Machine	1963	3.75	7.50	15.00
❑ SD 1398 [S]	Swingin' Machine	1963	5.00	10.00	20.00
❑ 1424 [M]	The Word from Mose	1964	3.00	6.00	12.00
❑ SD 1424 [S]	The Word from Mose	1964	3.75	7.50	15.00
❑ 1450 [M]	Mose Alive!	1966	3.00	6.00	12.00
❑ SD 1450 [S]	Mose Alive!	1966	3.75	7.50	15.00
❑ 1456 [M]	Wild Man on the Loose	1966	3.00	6.00	12.00
❑ SD 1456 [S]	Wild Man on the Loose	1966	3.75	7.50	15.00
❑ SD 1511	I've Been Doin' Some Thinkin'	1969	3.75	7.50	15.00
❑ SD 1542	The Best of Mose Allison	1970	3.00	6.00	12.00
❑ SD 1550	Hello There, Universe	1971	3.00	6.00	12.00
❑ SD 1584	Western Man	1972	3.00	6.00	12.00
❑ SD 1627	Mose in Your Ear	1973	3.00	6.00	12.00
❑ SD 1691	Your Mind on Vacation	197?	3.00	6.00	12.00
BLUE NOTE					
❑ B1-48015	Ever Since the World Ended	1988	2.50	5.00	10.00
❑ B1-93840	My Backyard	1990	3.00	6.00	12.00
COLUMBIA					
❑ CL 1444 [M]	The Transfiguration of Hiram Brown	1960	5.00	10.00	20.00
❑ CL 1565 [M]	I Love the Life I Live	1960	5.00	10.00	20.00
-- Red and black label with six "eye" logos					
❑ CS 8240 [S]	The Transfiguration of Hiram Brown	1960	6.25	12.50	25.00
❑ CS 8365 [S]	I Love the Life I Live	1960	6.25	12.50	25.00
-- Red and black label with six "eye" logos					
❑ C 30564	Retrospective	1971	3.00	6.00	12.00
ELEKTRA MUSICIAN					
❑ 60125	Middle Class White Boy	1983	2.50	5.00	10.00
❑ 60237	Lessons in Living	1984	2.50	5.00	10.00
EPIC					
❑ LA 16031 [M]	Take to the Hills	1962	3.75	7.50	15.00
❑ BA 17031 [S]	Take to the Hills	1962	5.00	10.00	20.00
❑ LN 24183 [M]	V-8 Ford Blues	1966	3.00	6.00	12.00
❑ BN 26183 [S]	V-8 Ford Blues	1966	3.75	7.50	15.00
FANTASY					
❑ OJC-075	Back Country Suite	198?	2.50	5.00	10.00
-- Reissue of Prestige 7091					
❑ OJC-457	Local Color	1990	3.00	6.00	12.00
-- Reissue of Prestige 7121					
❑ OJC-6004	Greatest Hits	1988	3.00	6.00	12.00

Number	Title	Yr	VG	VG+	NM
PRESTIGE					
❏ PRLP-7091 [M] Back Country Suite		1957	15.00	30.00	60.00
-- With "W. 50th St., NYC" address on label					
❏ PRLP-7121 [M] Local Color		1958	15.00	30.00	60.00
-- With "W. 50th St., NYC" address on label					
❏ PRLP-7137 [M] Young Man Blues		1958	15.00	30.00	60.00
-- With "W. 50th St., NYC" address on label					
❏ PRLP-7152 [M] Creek Bank		1959	10.00	20.00	40.00
-- Yellow label with Bergenfield, NJ address on label					
❏ PRLP-7189 [M] Autumn Song		1960	10.00	20.00	40.00
-- Yellow label with Bergenfield, NJ address on label					
❏ PRLP-7215 [M] Ramblin' with Mose		1961	10.00	20.00	40.00
-- Yellow label with Bergenfield, NJ address on label					
❏ PRLP-7279 [M] The Seventh Son -- Mose Allison Sings		1963	10.00	20.00	40.00
-- Yellow label with Bergenfield, NJ address on label					
❏ PRST-7279 [S] The Seventh Son -- Mose Allison Sings		1963	12.50	25.00	50.00
-- Silver label					
❏ PRLP-7423 [M] Down Home Piano		1966	5.00	10.00	20.00
-- Blue label, trident logo at right					
❏ PRST-7423 [S] Down Home Piano		1966	6.25	12.50	25.00
-- Blue label, trident logo at right					
❏ PRLP-7446 [M] Mose Allison Plays for Lovers		1967	6.25	12.50	25.00
❏ PRST-7446 [S] Mose Allison Plays for Lovers		1967	5.00	10.00	20.00
❏ 10052 The Seventh Son -- Mose Allison Sings		197?	3.00	6.00	12.00
-- Reissue of PRST-7279					
❏ 24002 [(2)] Mose Allison		1972	3.75	7.50	15.00
❏ 24055 [(2)] Creek Bank		197?	3.75	7.50	15.00
❏ 24089 [(2)] Ol' Devil Mose		1980	3.75	7.50	15.00

ALMEIDA, LAURINDO

Guitarist, composer, arranger, bossa nova pioneer, he also has recorded and composed in the classical vein. As it can be difficult to separate them, all his known LPs are listed below. Also see HERB ELLIS; STAN GETZ AND LAURINDO ALMEIDA; THE MODERN JAZZ QUARTET.

Number	Title	Yr	VG	VG+	NM
ANGEL					
❏ S-36050	Duets with the Spanish Guitar	197?	3.00	6.00	12.00
❏ S-36051	Duets with the Spanish Guitar, Vol. 2	197?	3.00	6.00	12.00
❏ S-36064	Clair de Lune	197?	2.50	5.00	10.00
❏ S-36076	Duets with the Spanish Guitar, Vol. 3	197?	3.00	6.00	12.00
❏ S-37322	Prelude	197?	2.50	5.00	10.00
CAPITOL					
❏ H-193 [10]	Guitar Concert	1950	20.00	40.00	80.00
❏ SM-1759	Viva Bossa Nova!	197?	2.50	5.00	10.00
❏ ST 1759 [S]	Viva Bossa Nova!	1962	5.00	10.00	20.00
❏ T 1759 [M]	Viva Bossa Nova!	1962	3.75	7.50	15.00
❏ ST 1872 [S]	Ole! Bossa Nova	1963	5.00	10.00	20.00
❏ T 1872 [M]	Ole! Bossa Nova	1963	3.75	7.50	15.00
❏ ST 1946 [S]	It's a Bossa Nova World	1963	5.00	10.00	20.00
❏ T 1946 [M]	It's a Bossa Nova World	1963	3.75	7.50	15.00
❏ ST 2063 [S]	Broadway Solo Guitar	1964	3.75	7.50	15.00
❏ T 2063 [M]	Broadway Solo Guitar	1964	3.00	6.00	12.00
❏ ST 2197 [S]	Guitar from Ipanema	1964	3.75	7.50	15.00
❏ T 2197 [M]	Guitar from Ipanema	1964	3.00	6.00	12.00
❏ T 2345 [M]	Suenos (Dreams)	1965	3.00	6.00	12.00
❏ ST 2419 [S]	New Broadway-Hollywood Hits	1965	3.75	7.50	15.00
❏ T 2419 [M]	New Broadway-Hollywood Hits	1965	3.00	6.00	12.00
❏ SM-2701	A Man and a Woman	197?	2.50	5.00	10.00
❏ ST 2701 [S]	A Man and a Woman	1967	3.75	7.50	15.00
❏ T 2701 [M]	A Man and a Woman	1967	3.00	6.00	12.00
❏ ST 2866	The Look of Love	1968	3.00	6.00	12.00
❏ P 8295 [M]	Guitar Music of Spain	196?	3.75	7.50	15.00
❏ P 8367 [M]	Vistas d'Espana	196?	3.75	7.50	15.00
❏ P 8406 [M]	Duets with the Spanish Guitar	196?	3.00	6.00	12.00
-- Regular cover					
❏ PAO 8406 [M]	Duets with the Spanish Guitar	196?	3.75	7.50	15.00
-- Gatefold cover					
❏ P 8461 [M]	For My True Love	196?	3.00	6.00	12.00
❏ SP 8461 [S]	For My True Love	196?	3.75	7.50	15.00
❏ P 8482 [M]	Songs of Enchantment	196?	3.75	7.50	15.00
❏ SP 8482 [S]	Songs of Enchantment	196?	5.00	10.00	20.00
❏ P 8497 [M]	Music of the Spanish Guitar	196?	3.00	6.00	12.00
❏ SP 8497 [S]	Music of the Spanish Guitar	196?	3.75	7.50	15.00
❏ P 8521 [M]	The Spanish Guitars of Laurindo Almeida	196?	3.00	6.00	12.00
❏ SP 8521 [S]	The Spanish Guitars of Laurindo Almeida	196?	3.75	7.50	15.00
❏ P 8532 [M]	Conversations with the Guitar	196?	3.00	6.00	12.00
❏ SP 8532 [S]	Conversations with the Guitar	196?	3.75	7.50	15.00
❏ P 8546 [M]	The Guitar Worlds of Laurindo Almeida	196?	3.00	6.00	12.00
❏ SP 8546 [S]	The Guitar Worlds of Laurindo Almeida	196?	3.75	7.50	15.00
❏ P 8571 [M]	Reverie	196?	3.00	6.00	12.00

Number	Title	Yr	VG	VG+	NM
❏ SP 8571 [S]	Reverie	196?	3.75	7.50	15.00
❏ P 8625 [M]	Concerto de Copacabana	196?	3.00	6.00	12.00
❏ SP 8625 [S]	Concerto de Copacabana	196?	3.75	7.50	15.00
❏ DP 8686 [R]	The Best of Laurindo Almeida	1969	3.00	6.00	12.00
CONCORD CONCERTO					
❏ CC-2001	First Concerto for Guitar and Orchestra	197?	2.50	5.00	10.00
❏ CC-2003	Laurindo Almeida with Bud Shank	198?	2.50	5.00	10.00
CONCORD JAZZ					
❏ CJ-84	Chamber Jazz	197?	2.50	5.00	10.00
❏ CJ-328	Artistry in Rhythm	1984	2.50	5.00	10.00
CORAL					
❏ CRL 56049 [10]	A Guitar Recital of Famous Serenades	1952	20.00	40.00	80.00
❏ CRL 56086 [10]	Latin Melodies	1952	20.00	40.00	80.00
❏ CRL 57056 [M]	A Guitar Recital of Famous Serenades	1956	12.50	25.00	50.00
CRYSTAL CLEAR					
❏ CCS-8001	Virtuoso Guitar	1978	6.25	12.50	25.00
-- Direct-to-disc recording; plays at 45 rpm					
❏ CCS-8007	New Directions	1979	6.25	12.50	25.00
-- Direct-to-disc recording					
DOBRE					
❏ 1000	Latin Guitar	1977	2.50	5.00	10.00
❏ 1024	Trio	197?	2.50	5.00	10.00
INNER CITY					
❏ 6031	Concierto de Aranjuez	1979	2.50	5.00	10.00
ORION					
❏ 7259	The Art of Laurindo Almeida	197?	2.50	5.00	10.00
PACIFIC JAZZ					
❏ PJLP-7 [10]	Laurindo Almeida Quartet	1953	30.00	60.00	120.00
❏ PJLP-13 [10]	Laurindo Almeida Quartet, Vol. 2	1954	30.00	60.00	120.00
❏ PJ-1204 [M]	Laurindo Almeida Quartet Featuring Bud Shank	1955	20.00	40.00	80.00
-- Reissue of 10-inch Pacific Jazz LPs					
PAUSA					
❏ 9009	Brazilliance	1983	2.50	5.00	10.00
-- Reissue					
PRO ARTE					
❏ PAD-235	3 Guitars 3	1985	2.50	5.00	10.00
-- With Sharon Isbin and Larry Coryell					
WORLD PACIFIC					
❏ WP-1204 [M]	Laurindo Almeida Quartet Featuring Bud Shank	1958	12.50	25.00	50.00
-- Reissue of Pacific Jazz 1204					
❏ WP-1412 [M]	Brazilliance, Vol. 1	1962	7.50	15.00	30.00
-- Reissue of World Pacific 1204					
❏ ST-1419 [S]	Brazilliance, Vol. 2	1962	6.25	12.50	25.00
❏ WP-1419 [M]	Brazilliance, Vol. 2	1962	7.50	15.00	30.00
❏ ST-1425 [S]	Brazilliance, Vol. 3	1962	6.25	12.50	25.00
❏ WP-1425 [M]	Brazilliance, Vol. 3	1962	7.50	15.00	30.00

ALMEIDA, LAURINDO, AND CHARLIE BYRD

Also see each artist's individual listings.

Number	Title	Yr	VG	VG+	NM
CONCORD PICANTE					
❏ P-150	Brazilian Soul	198?	2.50	5.00	10.00
❏ P-211	Latin Odyssey	1983	2.50	5.00	10.00
❏ CJ-290	Tango	1986	2.50	5.00	10.00

ALMERICO, TONY

New Orleans-style trumpeter and bandleader.

Number	Title	Yr	VG	VG+	NM
IMPERIAL					
❏ LP-9151 [M]	French Quarter Jazz	1961	5.00	10.00	20.00
❏ LP-12072 [S]	French Quarter Jazz	1961	6.25	12.50	25.00

ALMOND, JOHNNY

Baritone saxophone player.

Number	Title	Yr	VG	VG+	NM
DERAM					
❏ DES 18030	Music Machine	1969	3.75	7.50	15.00

ALPERT, HERB

Trumpet player. Best known for his 1960s pop material with the Tijuana Brass, his 1970s and 1980s material is more adventurous and often touches on jazz, thus it is included here.

Number	Title	Yr	VG	VG+	NM
A&M					
❏ SP-3714	Rise	1980	2.00	4.00	8.00
-- Reissue of 4790					
❏ SP-3717	Beyond	1980	2.00	4.00	8.00
❏ SP-3728	Magic Man	1981	2.00	4.00	8.00
❏ SP-3731	Fandango	1982	2.00	4.00	8.00
❏ SP-4591	Just You and Me	1976	2.50	5.00	10.00
❏ SP-4790	Rise	1979	2.50	5.00	10.00

Number	Title	Yr	VG	VG+	NM
❑ SP-4949	Blow Your Own Horn	1983	2.00	4.00	8.00
❑ SP-5082	Wild Romance	1985	2.00	4.00	8.00
❑ SP-5125	Keep Your Eye on Me	1987	2.00	4.00	8.00
❑ SP-5209	Under a Spanish Moon	1988	2.00	4.00	8.00
❑ SP-5273	My Abstract Heart	1989	2.00	4.00	8.00
❑ 75021 5345 1	North on South Street	1991	3.00	6.00	12.00

MOBILE FIDELITY

Number	Title	Yr	VG	VG+	NM
❑ 1-053	Rise	1981	6.25	12.50	25.00

-- *Audiophile vinyl*

ALPERT, HERB/HUGH MASEKELA
Also see each artist's individual listings.
A&M

Number	Title	Yr	VG	VG+	NM
❑ SP-3150	Herb Alpert/Hugh Masekela	198?	2.00	4.00	8.00

HORIZON

❑ 728	Herb Alpert/Hugh Masekela	1978	2.50	5.00	10.00

ALPERT, TRIGGER
Bass player.
RIVERSIDE

Number	Title	Yr	VG	VG+	NM
❑ RLP 12-225 [M]	Trigger Happy!	1956	20.00	40.00	80.00

-- *White label, blue print*

❑ RLP 12-225 [M]	Trigger Happy!	195?	10.00	20.00	40.00

-- *Blue label with microphone logo*

ALVIN, DANNY
Drummer and bandleader.
JAZZOLOGY

Number	Title	Yr	VG	VG+	NM
❑ 8 [M]	Danny Alvin and the Kings of Dixieland	1964	5.00	10.00	20.00
❑ S-8 [S]	Danny Alvin and the Kings of Dixieland	1964	5.00	10.00	20.00

STEPHENY

❑ MF-4002 [M]	Club Basin Street	1957	12.50	25.00	50.00

AMERICAN JAZZ ENSEMBLE, THE
EPIC

Number	Title	Yr	VG	VG+	NM
❑ LA 16040 [M]	New Dimensions	1962	5.00	10.00	20.00
❑ BA 17040 [S]	New Dimensions	1962	6.25	12.50	25.00

RCA VICTOR

❑ LPM-2557 [M]	The American Jazz Ensemble in Rome	1962	5.00	10.00	20.00
❑ LSP-2557 [S]	The American Jazz Ensemble in Rome	1962	6.25	12.50	25.00

AMMONS, ALBERT
Boogie-woogie pianist and father of GENE AMMONS.
BLUE NOTE

Number	Title	Yr	VG	VG+	NM
❑ BLP-7017 [10]	Boogie Woogie Classics	1951	75.00	150.00	300.00

COMMODORE

❑ XFL-15357 [M]	The Boogie Woogie and the Blues	198?	3.00	6.00	12.00

MERCURY

❑ MG-25012 [10]	Boogie Woogie Piano	1950	37.50	75.00	150.00

AMMONS, ALBERT/MEADE LUX LEWIS
Also see each artist's individual listings.
MOSAIC

Number	Title	Yr	VG	VG+	NM
❑ M3-103 [(3)]	The Complete Blue Note	199?	10.00	20.00	40.00

-- *Recordings of Albert Ammons and Meade Lux Lewis*

AMMONS, ALBERT, AND PETE JOHNSON
Also see each artist's individual listings.
RCA VICTOR

Number	Title	Yr	VG	VG+	NM
❑ LPT-9 [10]	8 to the Bar	1952	25.00	50.00	100.00

AMMONS, GENE
Nicknamed "Jug." Tenor saxophone player.
ARGO

Number	Title	Yr	VG	VG+	NM
❑ 697 [M]	Dig Him	1962	7.50	15.00	30.00
❑ S-697 [S]	Dig Him	1962	6.25	12.50	25.00
❑ 698 [M]	Just Jug	1962	7.50	15.00	30.00
❑ S-698 [S]	Just Jug	1962	6.25	12.50	25.00

CADET

❑ LP-783 [M]	Make It Happen	1967	6.25	12.50	25.00
❑ LPS-783 [S]	Make It Happen	1967	3.75	7.50	15.00

CHESS

❑ LP 1442 [M]	Soulful Saxophone	1959	10.00	20.00	40.00
❑ CH2-92514 [(2)]	Early Visions	198?	3.00	6.00	12.00

EMARCY

Number	Title	Yr	VG	VG+	NM
❑ EMS-2-400 [(2)]	The "Jug" Sessions	197?	3.00	6.00	12.00
❑ MG-26031 [10]	With or Without	1954	30.00	60.00	120.00

ENJA

❑ 3093	Gene Ammons in Sweden	198?	2.50	5.00	10.00

FANTASY

❑ OJC-013	The Happy Blues	198?	2.50	5.00	10.00
❑ OJC-014	All-Star Sessions	198?	2.50	5.00	10.00
❑ OJC-129	Jammin' in Hi-Fi	198?	2.50	5.00	10.00
❑ OJC-192	Blue Gene	1985	2.50	5.00	10.00
❑ OJC-211	Jammin' with Gene	1986	2.50	5.00	10.00
❑ OJC-244	Funky	1987	2.50	5.00	10.00
❑ OJC-297	Boss Tenor	1988	2.50	5.00	10.00
❑ OJC-351	Bad! Bossa Nova	198?	2.50	5.00	10.00
❑ OJC-395	Live in Chicago	198?	2.50	5.00	10.00
❑ OJC-651	The Big Sound	1991	3.00	6.00	12.00
❑ OJC-6005	Gene Ammons' Greatest Hits, Vol. 1: The Sixties	1988	3.00	6.00	12.00

MOODSVILLE

❑ MVLP-18 [M]	Nice and Cool	1961	12.50	25.00	50.00

-- *Originals have green label*

❑ MVLP-18 [M]	Nice and Cool	1965	6.25	12.50	25.00

-- *Second editions have blue label with trident at right*

❑ MVLP-28 [M]	The Soulful Moods of Gene Ammons	1963	12.50	25.00	50.00

-- *Originals have green label*

❑ MVLP-28 [M]	The Soulful Moods of Gene Ammons	1965	6.25	12.50	25.00

-- *Second editions have blue label with trident at right*

❑ MVST-28 [S]	The Soulful Moods of Gene Ammons	1963	10.00	20.00	40.00

PRESTIGE

❑ PRLP-107 [10]	Gene Ammons	1951	50.00	100.00	200.00
❑ PRLP-112 [10]	Tenor Sax Favorites, Volume 1	1951	50.00	100.00	200.00
❑ PRLP-127 [10]	Gene Ammons Favorites, Volume 2	1952	50.00	100.00	200.00
❑ PRLP-149 [10]	Gene Ammons Favorites, Volume 3	1953	50.00	100.00	200.00
❑ PRLP-211 [10]	Gene Ammons Jazz Session	1955	50.00	100.00	200.00
❑ 2514	Blue Groove	198?	2.50	5.00	10.00
❑ PRLP-7039 [M]	Hi Fidelity Jam Session	1956	25.00	50.00	100.00
❑ PRLP-7039 [M]	The Happy Blues	1960	12.50	25.00	50.00

-- *Retitled version of "Hi Fidelity Jam Session"*

❑ PRLP-7050 [M]	Gene Ammons All-Star Session	1956	25.00	50.00	100.00

-- *Compilation of Prestige 107 and 127*

❑ PRLP-7050 [M]	Woofin' and Tweetin'	1960	12.50	25.00	50.00

-- *Retitled version of "Gene Ammons All-Star Session"*

❑ PRLP-7060 [M]	Jammin' with Gene	1956	25.00	50.00	100.00
❑ PRLP-7060 [M]	Not Really the Blues	1960	12.50	25.00	50.00

-- *Retitled version of "Jammin' with Gene"*

❑ PRLP-7083 [M]	Funky	1957	25.00	50.00	100.00

-- *Originals have yellow label, "W. 50th St., NYC" address*

❑ PRLP-7110 [M]	Jammin' in Hi-Fi with Gene	1957	25.00	50.00	100.00

-- *Originals have yellow label, "W. 50th St., NYC" address*

❑ PRLP-7132 [M]	The Big Sound	1958	25.00	50.00	100.00

-- *Originals have yellow label, "W. 50th St., NYC" address*

❑ PRLP-7146 [M]	Blue Gene	1958	12.50	25.00	50.00

-- *Originals have yellow label, Bergenfield, N.J. address*

❑ PRLP-7176 [M]	The Twister	1960	12.50	25.00	50.00

-- *Originals have yellow label, Bergenfield, N.J. address; reissue of 7110*

❑ PRLP-7180 [M]	Boss Tenor	1960	12.50	25.00	50.00

-- *Originals have yellow label, Bergenfield, N.J. address*

❑ PRST-7180 [S]	Boss Tenor	1960	10.00	20.00	40.00

-- *Originals have silver label*

❑ PRLP-7192 [M]	Jug	1960	12.50	25.00	50.00

-- *Originals have yellow label, Bergenfield, N.J. address*

❑ PRST-7192 [S]	Jug	1960	10.00	20.00	40.00

-- *Originals have silver label*

❑ PRLP-7201 [M]	Groove Blues	1961	12.50	25.00	50.00

-- *Originals have yellow label, Bergenfield, N.J. address*

❑ PRLP-7208 [M]	Up Tight!	1961	12.50	25.00	50.00

-- *Originals have yellow label, Bergenfield, N.J. address*

❑ PRST-7208 [S]	Up Tight!	1961	10.00	20.00	40.00

-- *Originals have silver label*

❑ PRLP-7238 [M]	Twistin' the Jug	1962	12.50	25.00	50.00

-- *Originals have yellow label, Bergenfield, N.J. address*

❑ PRST-7238 [S]	Twistin' the Jug	1962	10.00	20.00	40.00

-- *Originals have silver label*

❑ PRLP-7257 [M]	Bad! Bossa Nova	1962	7.50	15.00	30.00

-- *Originals have yellow label, Bergenfield, N.J. address; some copies have a cover calling this "Jungle Soul! (ca' purange)"*

❑ PRST-7257 [S]	Bad! Bossa Nova	1962	10.00	20.00	40.00

-- *Originals have silver label*

❑ PRLP-7270 [M]	Preachin'	1963	7.50	15.00	30.00

-- *Originals have yellow label, Bergenfield, N.J. address*

❑ PRST-7270 [S]	Preachin'	1963	10.00	20.00	40.00

-- *Originals have silver label*

❑ PRLP-7275 [M]	Soul Summit, Volume 2	1963	7.50	15.00	30.00

-- *Originals have yellow label, Bergenfield, N.J. address*

Number	Title	Yr	VG	VG+	NM
❏ PRST-7275 [S]	Soul Summit, Volume 2	1963	10.00	20.00	40.00
-- Originals have silver label					
❏ PRLP-7287 [M]	Late Hour Special	1964	7.50	15.00	30.00
-- Originals have yellow label, Bergenfield, N.J. address					
❏ PRST-7287 [S]	Late Hour Special	1964	10.00	20.00	40.00
-- Originals have silver label					
❏ PRLP-7320 [M]	Velvet Soul	1964	7.50	15.00	30.00
-- Originals have yellow label, Bergenfield, N.J. address					
❏ PRST-7320 [S]	Velvet Soul	1964	10.00	20.00	40.00
-- Originals have silver label					
❏ PRLP-7369 [M]	Angel Eyes	1965	6.25	12.50	25.00
-- Originals have blue label with trident at right					
❏ PRST-7369 [S]	Angel Eyes	1965	7.50	15.00	30.00
-- Originals have blue label with trident at right					
❏ PRLP-7400 [M]	Sock!	1966	6.25	12.50	25.00
-- Originals have blue label with trident at right					
❏ PRST-7400 [S]	Sock!	1966	7.50	15.00	30.00
-- Originals have blue label with trident at right					
❏ PRLP-7445 [M]	Boss Soul!	1967	6.25	12.50	25.00
-- Originals have blue label with trident at right					
❏ PRST-7445 [S]	Boss Soul!	1967	7.50	15.00	30.00
-- Originals have blue label with trident at right					
❏ PRLP-7495 [M]	Gene Ammons Live in Chicago	1967	5.00	10.00	20.00
-- Originals have blue label with trident at right					
❏ PRST-7495 [S]	Gene Ammons Live in Chicago	1967	6.25	12.50	25.00
-- Originals have blue label with trident at right					
❏ PRLP-7534 [M]	Boss Tenor	1967	6.25	12.50	25.00
-- Originals have blue label with trident at right					
❏ PRST-7534 [S]	Boss Tenor	1967	5.00	10.00	20.00
-- Originals have blue label with trident at right					
❏ PRST-7552	Jungle Soul	1968	5.00	10.00	20.00
-- Reissue of 7257					
❏ PRST-7654	The Happy Blues -- Jam Session, Vol. 1	1969	3.75	7.50	15.00
-- Second reissue of 7039					
❏ PRST-7708	The Best of Gene Ammons for Beautiful People	1969	5.00	10.00	20.00
❏ PRST-7739	The Boss Is Back!	1970	5.00	10.00	20.00
❏ PRST-7771	Jammin' Jam Sessions, Vol. 2	1970	3.00	6.00	12.00
❏ PRST-7774	The Best of Gene Ammons	1970	5.00	10.00	20.00
❏ P-7862	Night Lights	1985	2.50	5.00	10.00
❏ 10006	Black Cat	197?	3.75	7.50	15.00
❏ 10010	Chase	197?	3.75	7.50	15.00
❏ 10019	You Talk That Talk!	197?	3.75	7.50	15.00
❏ 10021	Brother Jug	197?	3.75	7.50	15.00
❏ 10022	My Way	197?	3.75	7.50	15.00
❏ 10023	The Boss Is Back	197?	3.00	6.00	12.00
-- Reissue of 7739					
❏ 10040	Free Again	197?	3.00	6.00	12.00
❏ 10058	Got My Own	197?	3.00	6.00	12.00
❏ 10070	Big Bad Jug	197?	3.00	6.00	12.00
❏ 10078	Gene Ammons and Friends at Montreux	197?	3.00	6.00	12.00
❏ 10080	Brasswind	197?	3.00	6.00	12.00
❏ 10084	Greatest Hits	197?	3.00	6.00	12.00
❏ 10093	Goodbye	197?	3.00	6.00	12.00
❏ 24036 [(2)]	Juganthology	197?	3.75	7.50	15.00
❏ 24058 [(2)]	The Gene Ammons Story: The 78 Era	197?	3.75	7.50	15.00
❏ 24071 [(2)]	The Gene Ammons Story: Organ Combos	197?	3.75	7.50	15.00
❏ 24079 [(2)]	The Gene Ammons Story: Gentle Jug	197?	3.75	7.50	15.00
❏ 24098 [(2)]	The Big Sound of Gene Ammons	1981	3.00	6.00	12.00
SAVOY					
❏ SJL-1103	Red Top	197?	3.00	6.00	12.00
❏ MG-14033 [M]	Golden Saxophone	1961	7.50	15.00	30.00
STATUS					
❏ 18	Nice & Cool	197?	3.00	6.00	12.00
UPFRONT					
❏ UPF-116	Nothing But Soul	1968	3.00	6.00	12.00
-- Reissue of Vee-Jay material					
VEE JAY					
❏ LP-3024 [M]	Juggin' Around	1961	10.00	20.00	40.00
❏ LPS-3024 [S]	Juggin' Around	1961	7.50	15.00	30.00
WING					
❏ MGW-12156 [M]	Light, Bluesy and Moody	1963	3.75	7.50	15.00
-- Reissue of EmArcy 10-inch LP					
❏ SRW-16156 [R]	Light, Bluesy and Moody	1963	2.50	5.00	10.00

AMMONS, GENE, AND RICHARD "GROOVE" HOLMES
Also see each artist's individual listings.
PACIFIC JAZZ

Number	Title	Yr	VG	VG+	NM
❏ PJ-32 [M]	Groovin' with Jug	1961	10.00	20.00	40.00
❏ ST-32 [S]	Groovin' with Jug	1961	7.50	15.00	30.00

AMMONS, GENE, AND SONNY STITT
Also see each artist's individual listings.
CADET

Number	Title	Yr	VG	VG+	NM
❏ LP-785 [M]	Jug and Sonny	1967	5.00	10.00	20.00
❏ LPS-785 [S]	Jug and Sonny	1967	3.75	7.50	15.00
CHESS					
❏ LP 1455 [M]	Jug and Sonny	1960	10.00	20.00	40.00
❏ CH-91549	Jug and Sonny	198?	2.50	5.00	10.00
PRESTIGE					
❏ PRLP-7234 [M]	Soul Summit	1962	12.50	25.00	50.00
❏ PRST-7234 [S]	Soul Summit	1962	10.00	20.00	40.00
❏ PRLP-7454 [M]	Soul Summit	1967	5.00	10.00	20.00
❏ PRST-7454 [S]	Soul Summit	1967	3.75	7.50	15.00
❏ PRST-7606	We'll Be Together Again	1969	3.75	7.50	15.00
❏ PRST-7823	Blues Up	197?	3.00	6.00	12.00
❏ 10019	You Talk That Talk	197?	3.75	7.50	15.00
❏ 10100	Together Again for the Last Time	197?	3.00	6.00	12.00
VERVE					
❏ V-8426 [M]	Boss Tenors	1962	5.00	10.00	20.00
❏ V6-8426 [S]	Boss Tenors	1962	6.25	12.50	25.00
❏ V-8468 [M]	Boss Tenors in Orbit	1962	5.00	10.00	20.00
❏ V6-8468 [S]	Boss Tenors in Orbit	1962	6.25	12.50	25.00

AMRAM, DAVID
French horn player and composer; also dabbles in piano, guitar, flute and whistle. Also has written operas and classical orchestral works.
ELEKTRA MUSICIAN

Number	Title	Yr	VG	VG+	NM
❏ 60195	Latin Jazz Celebration	1983	2.50	5.00	10.00
FLYING FISH					
❏ FF-057	Havana/New York	1977	3.00	6.00	12.00
❏ FF-094	Friends, At Home/Around the World	1979	2.50	5.00	10.00
❏ FC-27752	No More Walls	198?	2.50	5.00	10.00
❏ FC-27753	Autobiography	198?	2.50	5.00	10.00

AMRAM-BARROW QUARTET, THE
Also see DAVID AMRAM.
DECCA

Number	Title	Yr	VG	VG+	NM
❏ DL 8558 [M]	Jazz Studio No. 6	1957	12.50	25.00	50.00

AMY, CURTIS
Saxophone player (soprano, alto, tenor and baritone) and occasional flutist as well. He played the sax solo on the Doors' hit single "Touch Me."
PACIFIC JAZZ

Number	Title	Yr	VG	VG+	NM
❏ PJ-62 [M]	Tippin' On Through -- Recorded "Live" at the Lighthouse	1962	6.25	12.50	25.00
❏ ST-62 [S]	Tippin' On Through -- Recorded "Live" at the Lighthouse	1962	7.50	15.00	30.00
PALOMAR					
❏ G-24003 [M]	Sounds of Hollywood and Broadway	1965	3.75	7.50	15.00
❏ GS-34003 [S]	Sounds of Hollywood and Broadway	1965	5.00	10.00	20.00
VERVE					
❏ V-8684 [M]	Mustang	1966	3.75	7.50	15.00
❏ V6-8684 [S]	Mustang	1966	5.00	10.00	20.00

AMY, CURTIS, AND DUPREE BOLTON
Bolton's instrument is the trumpet. Also see CURTIS AMY.
PACIFIC JAZZ

Number	Title	Yr	VG	VG+	NM
❏ PJ-70 [M]	Katanga!	1963	6.25	12.50	25.00
❏ ST-70 [S]	Katanga!	1963	15.00	30.00	60.00
-- Red vinyl					
❏ ST-70 [S]	Katanga!	1963	7.50	15.00	30.00
-- Black vinyl					

AMY, CURTIS, AND PAUL BRYANT
Also see each artist's individual listings.
KIMBERLY

Number	Title	Yr	VG	VG+	NM
❏ 2020 [M]	This Is the Blues	1963	5.00	10.00	20.00
❏ 11020 [S]	This Is the Blues	1963	6.25	12.50	25.00
PACIFIC JAZZ					
❏ PJ-9 [M]	The Blues Message	1960	7.50	15.00	30.00
❏ ST-9 [S]	The Blues Message	1960	10.00	20.00	40.00
❏ PJ-26 [M]	Meetin' Here	1961	7.50	15.00	30.00
❏ ST-26 [S]	Meetin' Here	1961	10.00	20.00	40.00

AMY, CURTIS, AND FRANK BUTLER
Also see each artist's individual listings.
PACIFIC JAZZ

Number	Title	Yr	VG	VG+	NM
❏ PJ-19 [M]	Groovin' Blue	1961	7.50	15.00	30.00
❏ ST-19 [S]	Groovin' Blue	1961	10.00	20.00	40.00

Number	Title	Yr	VG	VG+	NM

AMY, CURTIS, AND VICTOR FELDMAN
Also see each artist's individual listings.
PACIFIC JAZZ
| ❑ PJ-46 [M] | Way Down | 1962 | 6.25 | 12.50 | 25.00 |
| ❑ ST-46 [S] | Way Down | 1962 | 7.50 | 15.00 | 30.00 |

ANDERSEN, ARLID
Bass player.
ECM
❑ 1082	Shimri	1976	3.00	6.00	12.00
❑ 1127	Green Shading Into Blue	1978	3.00	6.00	12.00
❑ 1236	A Molde Concert	1981	3.00	6.00	12.00

ANDERSON, CAT
Trumpeter, mostly with the DUKE ELLINGTON orchestra.
CLASSIC JAZZ
| ❑ 142 | Cat Speaks | 1978 | 3.00 | 6.00 | 12.00 |
EMARCY
| ❑ MG-36142 [M] | Cat on a Hot Tin Roof | 1958 | 12.50 | 25.00 | 50.00 |
INNER CITY
| ❑ 1143 | Cat Anderson | 198? | 2.50 | 5.00 | 10.00 |
MERCURY
| ❑ MG-20522 [M] | Cat on a Hot Tin Roof | 1959 | 10.00 | 20.00 | 40.00 |
| ❑ SR-60199 [S] | Cat on a Hot Tin Roof | 1959 | 10.00 | 20.00 | 40.00 |

ANDERSON, CHRIS
Pianist.
JAZZLAND
| ❑ JLP-57 [M] | Inverted Images | 1961 | 7.50 | 15.00 | 30.00 |
| ❑ JLP-957 [S] | Inverted Images | 1961 | 10.00 | 20.00 | 40.00 |

ANDERSON, ERNESTINE
Female vocalist.
CONCORD JAZZ
❑ CJ-31	Hello Like Before	1977	3.00	6.00	12.00
❑ CJ-54	Live from Concord to London	1978	3.00	6.00	12.00
❑ CJ-109	Sunshine	1980	2.50	5.00	10.00
❑ CJ-147	Never Make Your Move Too Soon	1982	2.50	5.00	10.00
❑ CJ-214	Big City	1983	2.50	5.00	10.00
❑ CJ-263	When the Sun Goes Down	1985	2.50	5.00	10.00
❑ CJ-319	Be Mine Tonight	1987	2.50	5.00	10.00
MERCURY
❑ MG-20354 [M]	Hot Cargo	1958	10.00	20.00	40.00
❑ MG-20400 [M]	Ernestine Anderson	1959	10.00	20.00	40.00
❑ MG-20492 [M]	Fascinating Ernestine	1959	10.00	20.00	40.00
❑ MG-20496 [M]	My Kinda Swing	1959	10.00	20.00	40.00
❑ MG-20582 [M]	Moanin'	1960	10.00	20.00	40.00
❑ SR-60074 [S]	Ernestine Anderson	1959	12.50	25.00	50.00
❑ SR-60171 [S]	Fascinating Ernestine	1959	12.50	25.00	50.00
❑ SR-60175 [S]	My Kinda Swing	1959	12.50	25.00	50.00
❑ SR-60242 [S]	Moanin'	1960	12.50	25.00	50.00
SUE
| ❑ LP 1015 [M] | The New Sound of Ernestine Anderson | 1963 | 5.00 | 10.00 | 20.00 |
WING
| ❑ MGW-12281 [M] | Ernestine Anderson | 1964 | 3.00 | 6.00 | 12.00 |
| ❑ SRW-16281 [S] | Ernestine Anderson | 1964 | 3.75 | 7.50 | 15.00 |

ANDERSON, IVIE, AND LENA HORNE
Female singer. One of the first featured solo singers with a jazz band, Anderson sang on the original version of the DUKE ELLINGTON classic "It Don't Mean A Thing (If It Ain't Got That Swing)." Also see LENA HORNE.
JAZZTONE
| ❑ J-1262 [M] | Lena and Ivie | 1956 | 10.00 | 20.00 | 40.00 |

ANDERSON, RAY
Trombone player.
GRAMAVISION
| ❑ R1-79453 | What Because | 1990 | 3.00 | 6.00 | 12.00 |
MINOR MUSIC
| ❑ MM-007 | You Be | 1986 | 3.00 | 6.00 | 12.00 |
SOUL NOTE
| ❑ SN-1087 | Right Down Your Alley | 1985 | 3.00 | 6.00 | 12.00 |

ANDERZA, EARL
Alto saxophone player.
PACIFIC JAZZ
| ❑ PJ-65 [M] | Outa Sight | 1963 | 6.25 | 12.50 | 25.00 |
| ❑ ST-65 [S] | Outa Sight | 1963 | 7.50 | 15.00 | 30.00 |

ANDRE'S CUBAN ALL-STARS
CLEF
| ❑ MGC-515 [10] | Cubano | 1954 | 25.00 | 50.00 | 100.00 |
-- This was reissued on 12-inch as part of a JACK COSTANZO album.

ANDREWS, ERNIE
Male vocalist.
DISCOVERY
| ❑ 825 | From the Heart | 198? | 3.00 | 6.00 | 12.00 |
GENE NORMAN PRESENTS
❑ GNP-28 [M]	In the Dark	1957	10.00	20.00	40.00
❑ GNP-42 [M]	Ernie Andrews	1959	10.00	20.00	40.00
❑ GNP-43 [M]	Travelin' Light	1959	10.00	20.00	40.00
❑ GNPS-10008 [S]	Travelin' Light	1959	10.00	20.00	40.00
GNP CRESCENDO
| ❑ GNPS-10008 [S] | Travelin' Light | 196? | 3.75 | 7.50 | 15.00 |

ANDREWS, GAYLE
Female vocalist?
HI-LIFE
| ❑ HL-54 [M] | Love's a Snap | 195? | 7.50 | 15.00 | 30.00 |

ANDY AND THE BEY SISTERS
Vocal group. Andy Bey also is a pianist.
PRESTIGE
❑ PRLP-7346 [M]	Now! Hear!	1964	10.00	20.00	40.00
❑ PRST-7346 [S]	Now! Hear!	1964	12.50	25.00	50.00
❑ PRLP-7411 [M]	'Round About Midnight	1965	10.00	20.00	40.00
❑ PRST-7411 [S]	'Round About Midnight	1965	12.50	25.00	50.00

ANNA MARIE
Female vocalist, possibly Anna Marie Wooldridge, who later recorded as ABBEY LINCOLN.
VESTA
| ❑ LP-101 [10] | Anna Marie | 1955 | 20.00 | 40.00 | 80.00 |

ANTHONY, RAY
Trumpeter and bandleader. Member of the GLENN MILLER orchestra before starting his own band after World War II. Most of his albums are in an easy-listening vein.
AERO SPACE
| ❑ 1007 | Around the World | 197? | 2.50 | 5.00 | 10.00 |
CAPITOL
❑ L 292 [10]	Houseparty Hop	195?	10.00	20.00	40.00
❑ H 476 [10]	I Remember Glenn Miller	1954	10.00	20.00	40.00
❑ T 563 [M]	Goden Horn	1955	3.75	7.50	15.00
❑ T 723 [M]	Dream Dancing	1956	3.75	7.50	15.00
❑ T 749 [M]	Jazz Session at the Tower	1956	10.00	20.00	40.00
❑ T 831 [M]	Star Dancing	1957	3.75	7.50	15.00
❑ T 866 [M]	Young Ideas	1957	3.75	7.50	15.00
❑ T 917 [M]	Moments Together	1958	3.75	7.50	15.00
❑ T 969 [M]	The Dream Girl	1958	3.75	7.50	15.00
❑ T 1029 [M]	Dancing Over the Waves	1958	3.75	7.50	15.00
❑ T 1066 [M]	Ray Anthony Plays Steve Allen	1958	3.75	7.50	15.00
❑ T 1200 [M]	Sound Spectacular	1959	3.75	7.50	15.00
❑ ST 1252 [S]	More Dream Dancing	1959	3.75	7.50	15.00
❑ T 1252 [M]	More Dream Dancing	1959	3.00	6.00	12.00
❑ T 1371 [M]	Arthur Murray Favorites -- Fox	1960	3.00	6.00	12.00
❑ ST 1420 [S]	Dancing Alone Together	1960	3.75	7.50	15.00
❑ T 1420 [M]	Dancing Alone Together	1960	3.00	6.00	12.00
❑ ST 1421 [S]	The New Ray Anthony Show	1960	3.75	7.50	15.00
❑ T 1421 [M]	The New Ray Anthony Show	1960	3.00	6.00	12.00
❑ T 1477 [M]	The Hits of Ray Anthony	1960	3.00	6.00	12.00
❑ ST 1608 [S]	Dream Dancing Medley	1961	3.75	7.50	15.00
❑ T 1608 [M]	Dream Dancing Medley	1961	3.00	6.00	12.00
❑ ST 1668 [S]	Twist with Ray Anthony	1961	3.75	7.50	15.00
❑ T 1668 [M]	Twist with Ray Anthony	1961	3.00	6.00	12.00
❑ ST 1752 [S]	Worried Mind	1962	3.75	7.50	15.00
❑ T 1752 [M]	Worried Mind	1962	3.00	6.00	12.00
❑ ST 1783 [S]	I Almost Lost My Mind	1962	3.75	7.50	15.00
❑ T 1783 [M]	I Almost Lost My Mind	1962	3.00	6.00	12.00
❑ ST 1917 [S]	Smash Hits of '63	1963	3.75	7.50	15.00
❑ T 1917 [M]	Smash Hits of '63	1963	3.00	6.00	12.00
❑ ST 2043 [S]	Charade and Other Top Themes	1964	3.75	7.50	15.00
❑ T 2043 [M]	Charade and Other Top Themes	1964	3.00	6.00	12.00
❑ ST 2150 [S]	My Love, Forgive Me	1964	3.75	7.50	15.00
❑ T 2150 [M]	My Love, Forgive Me	1964	3.00	6.00	12.00
❑ ST 2188 [S]	Swim, Swim, C'mon, Let's Swim	1964	3.75	7.50	15.00
❑ T 2188 [M]	Swim, Swim, C'mon, Let's Swim	1964	3.00	6.00	12.00
❑ ST 2457 [S]	Dream Dancing Today	1966	3.75	7.50	15.00
❑ T 2457 [M]	Dream Dancing Today	1966	3.00	6.00	12.00
❑ ST 2530 [S]	Hit Songs to Remember	1966	3.75	7.50	15.00
❑ T 2530 [M]	Hit Songs to Remember	1966	3.00	6.00	12.00
❑ M-11978	Fox Trots	1979	2.50	5.00	10.00

Number	Title	Yr	VG	VG+	NM
CIRCLE					
❑ CLP-96	Sweet and Swingin' 1949-1953	1987	2.50	5.00	10.00
HINDSIGHT					
❑ HSR-240	Young Man with a Horn	1988	2.50	5.00	10.00
RANWOOD					
❑ 8059	Love Is for the Two of Us	197?	2.50	5.00	10.00
❑ 8082	Now	197?	2.50	5.00	10.00
❑ 8083	I Get the Blues When It Rains	197?	2.50	5.00	10.00
❑ 8153	Golden Hits	197?	2.50	5.00	10.00

APPLEYARD, PETER
Vibraphone player.

Number	Title	Yr	VG	VG+	NM
AUDIO FIDELITY					
❑ AFLP-1901 [M]	The Vibe Sound of Peter Appleyard	1958	10.00	20.00	40.00
❑ AFSD-5901 [S]	The Vibe Sound of Peter Appleyard	1958	10.00	20.00	40.00

ARGO, TONY

Number	Title	Yr	VG	VG+	NM
SAVOY					
❑ MG-12157 [M]	Jazz Argosy	1960	10.00	20.00	40.00

ARISTOCRATS OF DIXIELAND, THE
Members: Joe Perkins; George Palmer; Bob Bruce; Bob Eastman; Jim Morton; Bill Seabrook.

Number	Title	Yr	VG	VG+	NM
AUDIOPHILE					
❑ AP-129	Florida Blues	1979	2.50	5.00	10.00

ARMSTRONG, LIL HARDIN
Pianist, female vocalist, composer, arranger and bandleader. The second wife of LOUIS ARMSTRONG, she played on many Hot Five and Hot Seven sessions.

Number	Title	Yr	VG	VG+	NM
RIVERSIDE					
❑ RLP 12-120 [M]	Satchmo and Me	1956	15.00	30.00	60.00
-- White label, blue print					
❑ RLP 12-120 [M]	Satchmo and Me	195?	10.00	20.00	40.00
-- Blue label with microphone logo at top					
❑ RLP-401 [M]	Lil Armstrong and Her Orchestra	1962	7.50	15.00	30.00
❑ RLP-9401 [R]	Lil Armstrong and Her Orchestra	1962	3.75	7.50	15.00

ARMSTRONG, LOUIS
Nickname: "Satchmo." Cornet and trumpet player, male vocalist, certainly the most influential jazz musician of the first half of the 20th century, if not of all time. Also see BING CROSBY AND LOUIS ARMSTRONG; ELLA FITZGERALD AND LOUIS ARMSTRONG; KING OLIVER.

Number	Title	Yr	VG	VG+	NM
ABC					
❑ S-650	What a Wonderful World	1968	7.50	15.00	30.00
ACCORD					
❑ SN-7161	Mr. Music	1982	2.50	5.00	10.00
AMSTERDAM					
❑ AMS 12009	Louis Armstrong and His Friends	1970	3.75	7.50	15.00
ARCHIVE OF FOLK AND JAZZ					
❑ 258	Louis "Satchmo" Armstrong	197?	3.00	6.00	12.00
❑ 312	Louis Armstrong, Vol. 2	197?	2.50	5.00	10.00
AUDIO FIDELITY					
❑ AFLP-1930 [M]	Louis Armstrong Plays King Oliver	1960	7.50	15.00	30.00
❑ AFLP-2128 [M]	Ain't Gonna Give Nobody None of My Jelly Roll	1964	3.75	7.50	15.00
❑ AFLP-2132 [M]	The Best of Louis Armstrong	1964	3.75	7.50	15.00
❑ AFSD-5930 [S]	Louis Armstrong Plays King Oliver	1960	10.00	20.00	40.00
❑ AFSD-6128 [S]	Ain't Gonna Give Nobody None of My Jelly Roll	1964	5.00	10.00	20.00
❑ AFSD-6132 [S]	The Best of Louis Armstrong	1964	5.00	10.00	20.00
❑ AFSD-6241	Louis Armstrong	196?	3.75	7.50	15.00
BIOGRAPH					
❑ C-5	Great Soloists	1973	3.00	6.00	12.00
❑ C-6	Louis Armstrong Plays the Blues	1973	3.00	6.00	12.00
BLUEBIRD					
❑ AXM2-5519 [(2)]	Young Louis (1932-1933)	1984	3.00	6.00	12.00
❑ 5920-1-RB [(2)]	Pops: The 1940s Small Band Sides	1987	3.75	7.50	15.00
❑ 8310-1-RB	What a Wonderful World	1988	2.50	5.00	10.00
❑ 9759-1-RB	Louis Armstrong & His Orchestra 1932-33: Laughin' Louie	1989	3.00	6.00	12.00
BRUNSWICK					
❑ BL 58004 [10]	Armstrong Classics	1950	25.00	50.00	100.00
❑ BL 754136	I Will Wait for You	1968	3.75	7.50	15.00
BUENA VISTA					
❑ BV-4044	Disney Swings the Satchmo Way	1968	10.00	20.00	40.00
CHIAROSCURO					
❑ 2002	Snake Rag	1977	3.00	6.00	12.00

Number	Title	Yr	VG	VG+	NM
❑ 2003	Great Alternatives	1977	3.00	6.00	12.00
❑ 2006	Sweetheart	1977	3.00	6.00	12.00
COLUMBIA					
❑ CL 591 [M]	Louis Armstrong Plays W.C. Handy	1954	10.00	20.00	40.00
❑ CL 708 [M]	Satch Plays Fats	1955	10.00	20.00	40.00
❑ CL 840 [M]	Ambassador Satch	1956	10.00	20.00	40.00
❑ CL 851 [M]	The Louis Armstrong Story, Volume 1	1956	7.50	15.00	30.00
❑ CL 852 [M]	The Louis Armstrong Story, Volume 2	1956	7.50	15.00	30.00
❑ CL 853 [M]	The Louis Armstrong Story, Volume 3	1956	7.50	15.00	30.00
❑ CL 854 [M]	The Louis Armstrong Story, Volume 4	1956	7.50	15.00	30.00
❑ CL 1077 [M]	Satchmo the Great	1957	7.50	15.00	30.00
❑ CL 2638 [M]	Louis Armstrong's Greatest Hits	1967	5.00	10.00	20.00
❑ CL 6335 [10]	Louis Armstrong Plays W.C. Handy, Volume 2	1955	10.00	20.00	40.00
❑ CS 9438 [R]	Louis Armstrong's Greatest Hits	1967	3.00	6.00	12.00
❑ PC 9438 [R]	Louis Armstrong's Greatest Hits	198?	2.00	4.00	8.00
-- Budget-line reissue					
❑ CG 30416 [(2)]	The Genius of Louis Armstrong, Vol. 1	1971	3.75	7.50	15.00
COLUMBIA MASTERWORKS					
❑ ML 4383 [M]	The Louis Armstrong Story, Volume 1	1951	12.50	25.00	50.00
❑ ML 4384 [M]	The Louis Armstrong Story, Volume 2	1951	12.50	25.00	50.00
❑ ML 4385 [M]	The Louis Armstrong Story, Volume 3	1951	12.50	25.00	50.00
❑ ML 4386 [M]	The Louis Armstrong Story, Volume 4	1951	12.50	25.00	50.00
COLUMBIA MUSICAL TREASURIES					
❑ P4M 5676 [(4)]	40 Greatest Hits	197?	5.00	10.00	20.00
DECCA					
❑ DX 108 [(2) M]	Satchmo at Symphony Hall	1954	18.75	37.50	75.00
-- Black labels, silver print					
❑ DX 155 [(4) M]	Satchmo, A Musical Autobiography	1956	25.00	50.00	100.00
-- Black labels, silver print					
❑ DXM 155 [(4) M]	Satchmo, A Musical Autobiography	1960	10.00	20.00	40.00
-- Black labels with color bars					
❑ DXB 183 [(2) M]	The Best of Louis Armstrong	196?	7.50	15.00	30.00
❑ DL 4137 [M]	Satchmo's Golden Favorites	1961	5.00	10.00	20.00
❑ DL 4227 [M]	I Love Jazz	1962	5.00	10.00	20.00
❑ DL 4230 [M]	Satchmo, A Musical Autobiography,1926-1927	1962	6.25	12.50	25.00
❑ DL 4245 [M]	King Louis	1962	5.00	10.00	20.00
❑ DL 4330 [M]	Satchmo, A Musical Autobiography, 1928-1930	1962	6.25	12.50	25.00
❑ DL 4331 [M]	Satchmo, A Musical Autobiography, 1930-1934	1962	6.25	12.50	25.00
❑ DL 5225 [10]	New Orleans to New York	1950	18.75	37.50	75.00
❑ DL 5279 [10]	New Orleans Days	1950	18.75	37.50	75.00
❑ DL 5280 [10]	Jazz Concert	1950	18.75	37.50	75.00
❑ DL 5401 [10]	Satchmo Serenades	1952	18.75	37.50	75.00
❑ DL 5532 [10]	Latter-Day Louis	1954	18.75	37.50	75.00
❑ DL 5536 [10]	Louis Armstrong-Gordon Jenkins	1954	18.75	37.50	75.00
❑ DXSB 7183 [(2) R]	The Best of Louis Armstrong	196?	3.75	7.50	15.00
❑ DL 8037 [M]	Satchmo at Symphony Hall, Volume 1	1954	10.00	20.00	40.00
-- Black label, silver print					
❑ DL 8037 [M]	Satchmo at Symphony Hall, Volume 1	1960	3.75	7.50	15.00
-- Black label with color bars					
❑ DL 8038 [M]	Satchmo at Symphony Hall, Volume 2	1954	10.00	20.00	40.00
-- Black label, silver print					
❑ DL 8038 [M]	Satchmo at Symphony Hall, Volume 2	1960	3.75	7.50	15.00
-- Black label with color bars					
❑ DL 8041 [M]	Satchmo at Pasadena	1954	10.00	20.00	40.00
-- Black label, silver print					
❑ DL 8041 [M]	Satchmo at Pasadena	1960	3.75	7.50	15.00
-- Black label with color bars					
❑ DL 8126 [M]	Satchmo Sings	1955	10.00	20.00	40.00
-- Black label, silver print					
❑ DL 8126 [M]	Satchmo Sings	1960	3.75	7.50	15.00
-- Black label with color bars					
❑ DL 8168 [M]	Louis Armstrong at the Crescendo, Volume 1	1955	10.00	20.00	40.00
-- Black label, silver print					
❑ DL 8169 [M]	Louis Armstrong at the Crescendo, Volume 2	1955	10.00	20.00	40.00
-- Black label, silver print					

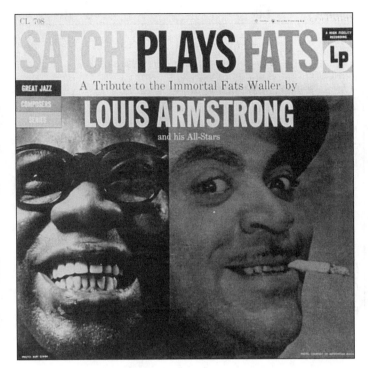

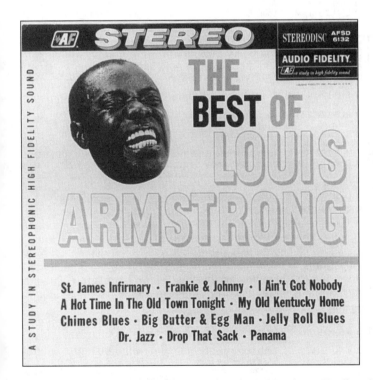

Without Louis Armstrong, you probably don't have jazz. He directly or indirectly influenced almost every musician that heard him. Only Charlie Parker looms as large in the pantheon of jazz greats. (Top left) "Satchmo" recorded for Columbia for a few years in the mid-1950s, and this tribute album to Fats Waller was one of the resulting albums. (Top right) This 1961 release on RCA Victor compiled some of his classic 1930s swing sides onto an album. (Bottom left) While the songs on this Audio Fidelity album are among Armstrong's best, they are stereo re-recordings from the early 1960s. (Bottom right) His rendition of "Hello, Dolly!" was a most unexpected chart-topping hit during the height of Beatlemania in 1964. This resulting album knocked the Beatles off the top of the album charts temporarily as well.

Number	Title	Yr	VG	VG+	NM
❏ DL 8211 [M]	Satchmo Serenades	1956	10.00	20.00	40.00
-- Black label, silver print					
❏ DL 8211 [M]	Satchmo Serenades	1960	3.75	7.50	15.00
-- Black label with color bars					
❏ DL 8283 [M]	New Orleans Jazz	1956	10.00	20.00	40.00
-- Black label, silver print					
❏ DL 8283 [M]	New Orleans Jazz	1960	3.75	7.50	15.00
-- Black label with color bars					
❏ DL 8284 [M]	Jazz Classics	1956	10.00	20.00	40.00
-- Black label, silver print					
❏ DL 8284 [M]	Jazz Classics	1960	3.75	7.50	15.00
-- Black label with color bars					
❏ DL 8327 [M]	Satchmo's Collector's Items	1957	10.00	20.00	40.00
-- Black label, silver print					
❏ DL 8327 [M]	Satchmo's Collector's Items	1960	3.75	7.50	15.00
-- Black label with color bars					
❏ DL 8329 [M]	New Orleans Nights	1957	10.00	20.00	40.00
-- Black label, silver print					
❏ DL 8329 [M]	New Orleans Nights	1960	3.75	7.50	15.00
-- Black label with color bars					
❏ DL 8329 [M]	New Orleans Nights	1960	3.75	7.50	15.00
-- Black label with color bars					
❏ DL 8330 [M]	Satchmo on Stage	1957	10.00	20.00	40.00
-- Black label, silver print					
❏ DL 8330 [M]	Satchmo on Stage	1960	3.75	7.50	15.00
-- Black label with color bars					
❏ DL 8488 [M]	Louis and the Angels	1957	10.00	20.00	40.00
-- Black label, silver print					
❏ DL 8488 [M]	Louis and the Angels	1960	3.75	7.50	15.00
-- Black label with color bars					
❏ DL 8741 [M]	Louis and the Good Book	1960	3.75	7.50	15.00
-- Black label with color bars					
❏ DL 8781 [M]	Louis and the Good Book	1958	10.00	20.00	40.00
-- Black label, silver print					
❏ DL 8840 [M]	Satchmo in Style	1958	10.00	20.00	40.00
-- Black label, silver print					
❏ DL 8840 [M]	Satchmo in Style	1960	3.75	7.50	15.00
-- Black label with color bars					
❏ DL 8963 [M]	Satchmo, A Musical Autobiography, 1923-1925	1960	6.25	12.50	25.00
❏ DL 9225 [M]	Rare Items (1935-1944)	196?	5.00	10.00	20.00
❏ DL 9233 [M]	Young Louis the Sideman (1924-1927)	196?	5.00	10.00	20.00
❏ DL 74137 [R]	Satchmo's Golden Favorites	1961	3.00	6.00	12.00
❏ DL 74227 [R]	I Love Jazz	1962	3.00	6.00	12.00
❏ DL 74245 [R]	King Louis	1962	3.00	6.00	12.00
❏ DL 74330 [R]	A Musical Autobiography, 1928-1930	1962	3.00	6.00	12.00
❏ DL 78963 [R]	Satchmo, A Musical Autobiography, 1923-1925	196?	3.00	6.00	12.00
❏ DL 79225 [R]	Rare Items (1935-1944)	196?	3.00	6.00	12.00
❏ DL 79233 [R]	Young Louis the Sideman (1924-1927)	196?	3.00	6.00	12.00
GNP CRESCENDO					
❏ 9050	Pasadena Concert, Vol. II	1987	2.50	5.00	10.00
❏ 11001 [(2)]	An Evening with Louis Armstrong	1977	3.75	7.50	15.00
HARMONY					
❏ HS 11316	Louis Armstrong	197?	3.00	6.00	12.00
❏ KH 31236	The Louis Armstrong Saga	1971	3.00	6.00	12.00
KAPP					
❏ KL-1364 [M]	Hello, Dolly!	1964	3.00	6.00	12.00
❏ KS-3364 [S]	Hello, Dolly!	1964	3.75	7.50	15.00
MCA					
❏ 538	Hello, Dolly!	197?	2.50	5.00	10.00
-- Reissue of Kapp LP					
❏ 1300	Louis and the Good Book	197?	2.50	5.00	10.00
-- Reissue of Decca 8741					
❏ 1301	Young Louis the Sideman	197?	2.50	5.00	10.00
-- Reissue of Decca 9233					
❏ 1304	Back in New York	197?	2.50	5.00	10.00
❏ 1306	Louis with Guest Stars	197?	2.50	5.00	10.00
❏ 1312	Swing That Music!	197?	2.50	5.00	10.00
❏ 1316	Satchmo Serenades	197?	2.50	5.00	10.00
-- Reissue of Decca 8211					
❏ 1322	Satchmo's Collector's Items	197?	2.50	5.00	10.00
-- Reissue of Decca 8327					
❏ 1334	Satchmo For Ever!	197?	2.50	5.00	10.00
❏ 1335	Old Favorites	197?	2.50	5.00	10.00
❏ 2-4013 [(2)]	Louis Armstrong at the Crescendo	197?	3.00	6.00	12.00
-- Reissue of Decca 8168/8169 in one sleeve					
❏ 2-4035 [(2)]	The Best of Louis Armstrong	197?	3.00	6.00	12.00
-- Reissue of Decca 7183					
❏ 2-4057 [(2)]	Satchmo at Symphony Hall	197?	3.00	6.00	12.00
-- Reissue of Decca 108					
❏ 10006 [(4)]	Satchmo, A Musical Autobiography	197?	6.25	12.50	25.00
-- Reissue of Decca 155					
❏ 25204	What a Wonderful World	1988	2.50	5.00	10.00
-- Reissue of ABC 650					
❏ 42328	Louis Armstrong of New Orleans	1990	3.00	6.00	12.00
MERCURY					
❏ MG-21081 [M]	Louis Armstrong Sings Louis Armstrong	1965	3.00	6.00	12.00
❏ SR-61081 [S]	Louis Armstrong Sings Louis Armstrong	1965	3.75	7.50	15.00
METRO					
❏ M-510 [M]	Hello, Louis	1965	3.00	6.00	12.00
❏ MS-510 [S]	Hello, Louis	1965	3.75	7.50	15.00
MILESTONE					
❏ 2010	Early Portrait	197?	2.50	5.00	10.00
❏ 47017 [(2)]	Louis Armstrong and King Oliver	197?	3.00	6.00	12.00
MOSAIC					
❏ MQ8-146 [(8)]	The Complete Decca Studio Recordings of Louis Armstrong and the All-Stars	199?	37.50	75.00	150.00
MURRAY HILL					
❏ 930633 [(2)]	Louis Armstrong Plays Dixieland Trumpet	197?	3.75	7.50	15.00
PABLO					
❏ 2310-941	Mack the Knife	1990	3.00	6.00	12.00
PAIR					
❏ PDL2-1042 [(2)]	The Jazz Legend	1986	3.00	6.00	12.00
PAUSA					
❏ 9018	The Greatest of Louis Armstrong	1983	2.50	5.00	10.00
RCA VICTOR					
❏ LPT 7 [10]	Louis Armstrong Town Hall Concert	1951	20.00	40.00	80.00
❏ LJM-1005 [M]	Louis Armstrong Sings the Blues	1954	12.50	25.00	50.00
❏ LPM-1443 [M]	Town Hall Concert Plus	1957	12.50	25.00	50.00
❏ LPM-2322 [M]	A Rare Batch of Satch	1961	6.25	12.50	25.00
❏ LPM-2971 [M]	Louis Armstrong in the '30s/in the '40s	1964	5.00	10.00	20.00
❏ LSP-2971(e) [R]	Louis Armstrong in the '30s/in the '40s	1964	3.00	6.00	12.00
❏ VPM-6044 [(2)]	July 4, 1900/July 6, 1971	1971	5.00	10.00	20.00
RIVERSIDE					
❏ RLP 12-101 [M]	The Young Louis Armstrong	195?	10.00	20.00	40.00
-- Blue label					
❏ RLP 12-101 [M]	The Young Louis Armstrong	1956	20.00	40.00	80.00
-- White label, blue print					
❏ RLP 12-122 [M]	Louis Armstrong 1923	195?	10.00	20.00	40.00
-- Blue label					
❏ RLP 12-122 [M]	Louis Armstrong 1923	1956	20.00	40.00	80.00
-- White label, blue print					
❏ RLP-1001 [10]	Louis Armstrong Plays the Blues	1953	25.00	50.00	100.00
❏ RLP-1029 [10]	Louis Armstrong with King Oliver's Creole Jazz Band 1923	1953	25.00	50.00	100.00
SEAGULL					
❏ LG-8206	Greatest Hits: Live in Concert	198?	3.00	6.00	12.00
STORYVILLE					
❏ 4012	Louis Armstrong and His All-Stars	1980	2.50	5.00	10.00
SWING					
❏ SW-8450	Louis and the Big Bands	1984	2.50	5.00	10.00
VANGUARD					
❏ VSD 91/92 [(2)]	Essential Louis Armstrong	1977	3.75	7.50	15.00
❏ VMS 73129	Essential Louis Armstrong, Vol. 1	1986	2.00	4.00	8.00
VERVE					
❏ MGV-4012 [M]	Louis Under the Stars	1957	12.50	25.00	50.00
❏ MGVS-4012	Louis Under the Stars	199?	6.25	12.50	25.00
-- Classic Records reissue					
❏ V-4012 [M]	Louis Under the Stars	1961	5.00	10.00	20.00
❏ V6-4012 [S]	Louis Under the Stars	1961	3.75	7.50	15.00
❏ MGV-4035 [M]	I've Got the World on a String	1959	12.50	25.00	50.00
❏ MGVS-4035	I've Got the World on a String	199?	6.25	12.50	25.00
-- Classic Records reissue					
❏ V-4035 [M]	I've Got the World on a String	1961	5.00	10.00	20.00
❏ V6-4035 [S]	I've Got the World on a String	1961	3.75	7.50	15.00
❏ MGVS-6044 [S]	Louis Under the Stars	1960	10.00	20.00	40.00
❏ MGVS-6101 [S]	I've Got the World on a String	1960	10.00	20.00	40.00
❏ V-8569 [M]	The Essential Louis A.	1963	3.00	6.00	12.00
❏ V6-8569 [S]	The Essential Louis A.	1963	3.75	7.50	15.00
❏ V-8595 [M]	The Best of Louis Armstrong	1964	3.00	6.00	12.00
❏ V6-8595 [S]	The Best of Louis Armstrong	1964	3.75	7.50	15.00
VOCALION					
❏ VL 3851 [M]	Here's Louis Armstrong	196?	3.75	7.50	15.00
❏ VL 73851 [R]	Here's Louis Armstrong	196?	2.50	5.00	10.00
❏ VL 73871 [R]	The One and Only Louis Armstrong	1968	2.50	5.00	10.00

Number	Title	Yr	VG	VG+	NM
WING					
❏ SR-16381	Great Louis	196?	2.50	5.00	10.00

ARMSTRONG, LOUIS, AND SIDNEY BECHET
Also see each artist's individual listings.

Number	Title	Yr	VG	VG+	NM
JOLLY ROGER					
❏ 5029 [M]	Louis Armstrong and Sidney Bechet	195?	10.00	20.00	40.00

ARMSTRONG, LOUIS, AND DUKE ELLINGTON
Also see each artist's individual listings.

Number	Title	Yr	VG	VG+	NM
MOBILE FIDELITY					
❏ 2-155 [(2)]	The Great Reunion	1984	20.00	40.00	80.00
-- Audiophile vinyl					
PICKWICK					
❏ PC-3033	Louis Armstrong and Duke Ellington	196?	2.50	5.00	10.00
ROULETTE					
❏ RE-108 [(2)]	The Duke Ellington-Louis Armstrong Era	1973	3.75	7.50	15.00
❏ R 52074 [M]	Together for the First Time	1961	6.25	12.50	25.00
❏ SR 52074 [S]	Together for the First Time	1961	5.00	10.00	20.00
❏ R 52103 [M]	The Great Reunion	1963	5.00	10.00	20.00
❏ SR 52103 [S]	The Great Reunion	1963	6.25	12.50	25.00

ARMSTRONG, LOUIS, AND THE MILLS BROTHERS
The Mills Brothers, a male vocal group, are not included in this book by themselves. Also see LOUIS ARMSTRONG; COUNT BASIE AND THE MILLS BROTHERS.

Number	Title	Yr	VG	VG+	NM
DECCA					
❏ DL 5509 [10]	Louis Armstrong and the Mills Brothers	1954	15.00	30.00	60.00

ARMSTRONG, LOUIS, AND OSCAR PETERSON
Also see each artist's individual listings.

Number	Title	Yr	VG	VG+	NM
VERVE					
❏ MGVS-6062 [S]	Louis Armstrong Meets Oscar Peterson	1960	10.00	20.00	40.00
❏ MGV-8322 [M]	Louis Armstrong Meets Oscar Peterson	1959	12.50	25.00	50.00
❏ V-8322 [M]	Louis Armstrong Meets Oscar Peterson	1961	5.00	10.00	20.00
❏ V6-8322 [S]	Louis Armstrong Meets Oscar Peterson	1961	3.75	7.50	15.00

ARNOLD, BUDDY
Tenor saxophonist. Also plays clarinet and oboe. Played in the STAN KENTON band.

Number	Title	Yr	VG	VG+	NM
ABC-PARAMOUNT					
❏ ABC-114 [M]	Wailing	1956	15.00	30.00	60.00

ARNOLD, HARRY
Alto saxophone player, clarinet player, bandleader, composer.

Number	Title	Yr	VG	VG+	NM
ATCO					
❏ 33-120 [M]	I Love Harry Arnold (And All That Jazz)	1960	10.00	20.00	40.00
EMARCY					
❏ MG-36139 [M]	Harry Arnold and His Orchestra	1958	12.50	25.00	50.00
❏ SR-80006 [S]	Harry Arnold and His Orchestra	1958	10.00	20.00	40.00
JAZZLAND					
❏ JLP-65 [M]	Harry Arnold's Great Big Band and Friends	1962	6.25	12.50	25.00
❏ JLP-965 [S]	Harry Arnold's Great Big Band and Friends	1962	7.50	15.00	30.00
JAZZTONE					
❏ J-1270 [M]	The Jazztone Mystery Band	1958	10.00	20.00	40.00
RIVERSIDE					
❏ RM-7526 [M]	Let's Dance on Broadway	196?	5.00	10.00	20.00
❏ RM-7536 [M]	Dancing on Broadway to the Music of Cole Porter	196?	5.00	10.00	20.00
❏ RS-97526 [S]	Let's Dance on Broadway	196?	6.25	12.50	25.00
❏ RS-97536 [S]	Dancing on Broadway to the Music of Cole Porter	196?	6.25	12.50	25.00

ART ENSEMBLE OF CHICAGO
Influential quintet: LESTER BOWIE (horns), Malachi Favors (bass and strings), Joseph Jarman (reeds), ROSCOE MITCHELL (reeds) and Don Moye (percussion, post-1973). Fontella Bass ("Rescue Me") was an early female vocalist.

Number	Title	Yr	VG	VG+	NM
AECO					
❏ 004	Kabalaba	1978	3.75	7.50	15.00
ARISTA/FREEDOM					
❏ AL 1903 [(2)]	The Paris Session	197?	3.75	7.50	15.00
ATLANTIC					
❏ SD 1639	Bap-Tizum	1973	3.75	7.50	15.00
❏ SD 1651	Fanfare for the Warriors	1974	3.75	7.50	15.00
❏ 90046	Fanfare for the Warriors	1983	2.50	5.00	10.00
-- Reissue of 1651					
DELMARK					
❏ DS-432/433 [(2)]	Live at Mandel Hall	1974	3.75	7.50	15.00
DIW					
❏ 8005	Live in Japan	1986	2.50	5.00	10.00
❏ 8011	Naked	1987	2.50	5.00	10.00
❏ 8014	Ancient to the Future	1987	2.50	5.00	10.00
❏ 8021/22 [(2)]	The Complete Live in Japan	198?	3.75	7.50	15.00
❏ 8033	The Alternate Express	1989	3.00	6.00	12.00
❏ 8038	Art Ensemble of Soweto	1990	3.00	6.00	12.00
ECM					
❏ 1126	Nice Guys	1979	3.00	6.00	12.00
❏ 1167	Full Force	1980	3.00	6.00	12.00
❏ 1211 [(2)]	Urban Bushmen	1982	3.75	7.50	15.00
❏ 25014	The Third Decade	1985	2.50	5.00	10.00
INNER CITY					
❏ 1004	Certain Blacks	197?	3.00	6.00	12.00
NESSA					
❏ N-3	People in Sorrow	1969	6.25	12.50	25.00
❏ N-4	Les Stances a Sophie	1970	6.25	12.50	25.00
-- With Fontella Bass					
❏ N-5	Old/Quartet	1975	5.00	10.00	20.00
PAULA					
❏ LPS-4001	Chi-Congo	197?	3.75	7.50	15.00
PRESTIGE					
❏ 10049	Art Ensemble of Chicago with Fontella Bass	1972	3.75	7.50	15.00
❏ 10064	Phase One	197?	3.75	7.50	15.00

ARTER, CARL
Pianist.

Number	Title	Yr	VG	VG+	NM
EARWIG					
❏ LPS-4905	Song from Far Away	1986	2.50	5.00	10.00

ARTHUR, BROOKS

Number	Title	Yr	VG	VG+	NM
VERVE					
❏ V-8650 [M]	Sole Forms	1966	3.75	7.50	15.00
❏ V6-8650 [S]	Sole Forms	1966	3.75	7.50	15.00
❏ V6-8779	Traces	1969	3.75	7.50	15.00

ASH, MARVIN
Pianist.

Number	Title	Yr	VG	VG+	NM
CAPITOL					
❏ H 188 [10]	Honky Tonk Piano	1950	15.00	30.00	60.00
DECCA					
❏ DL 8346 [M]	New Orleans at Midnight	1957	10.00	20.00	40.00
JAZZ MAN					
❏ LPJM-335 [10]	Marvin Ash	1954	12.50	25.00	50.00
JUMP					
❏ JL-4 [10]	Marvin Ash	1954	12.50	25.00	50.00

ASHBY, DOROTHY
Harp player.

Number	Title	Yr	VG	VG+	NM
ARGO					
❏ LP-690 [M]	Dorothy Ashby	1962	6.25	12.50	25.00
❏ LPS-690 [S]	Dorothy Ashby	1962	7.50	15.00	30.00
ATLANTIC					
❏ 1447 [M]	The Fantastic Jazz Harp of Dorothy Ashby	1966	3.75	7.50	15.00
❏ SD 1447 [S]	The Fantastic Jazz Harp of Dorothy Ashby	1966	5.00	10.00	20.00
CADET					
❏ LP-690 [M]	Dorothy Ashby	1966	3.00	6.00	12.00
-- Reissue of Argo LP-690					
❏ LPS-690 [S]	Dorothy Ashby	1966	3.75	7.50	15.00
-- Reissue of Argo LPS-690					
❏ LPS-809	Afro-Harping	1968	3.75	7.50	15.00
❏ LPS-825	Dorothy's Harp	1969	3.75	7.50	15.00
❏ LPS-841	Rubaiyat	1970	3.75	7.50	15.00
CHESS					
❏ CH-91555	Afro-Harping	198?	2.50	5.00	10.00
-- Reissue of Cadet 809					
JAZZLAND					
❏ JLP-61 [M]	Soft Winds	1961	6.25	12.50	25.00
❏ JLP-961 [S]	Soft Winds	1961	7.50	15.00	30.00
NEW JAZZ					
❏ NJLP-8209 [M]	In a Minor Groove	1958	15.00	30.00	60.00
-- Purple label					

Number	Title	Yr	VG	VG+	NM
❏ NJLP-8209 [M]	In a Minor Groove	1965	6.25	12.50	25.00
-- Blue label, trident logo at right					
PRESTIGE					
❏ PRLP-7140 [M]	Hip Harp	1958	15.00	30.00	60.00
❏ PRLP-7638	The Best of Dorothy Ashby	1969	3.75	7.50	15.00
-- Reissue of 7140					
❏ PRLP-7639	Dorothy Plays for Beautiful People	1969	3.75	7.50	15.00
-- Reissue of New Jazz 8209					
REGENT					
❏ MG-6039 [M]	Dorothy Ashby -- Jazz Harpist	1957	15.00	30.00	60.00
SAVOY					
❏ MG-12212 [M]	Dorothy Ashby -- Jazz Harpist	196?	3.75	7.50	15.00
-- Reissue of Regent 6039					

ASHBY, HAROLD
Tenor saxophone player.

Number	Title	Yr	VG	VG+	NM
GEMINI					
❏ GMLP-60-1	The Viking	1988	2.50	5.00	10.00
PROGRESSIVE					
❏ PRO-7040	Presenting Harold Ashby	1979	2.50	5.00	10.00

ASHBY, IRVING
Guitarist. Member of NAT KING COLE's trio in the late 1940s.

Number	Title	Yr	VG	VG+	NM
AUDIOPHILE					
❏ AP-133	Memoirs	1980	2.50	5.00	10.00

ASMUSSEN, SVEND
Violinist.

Number	Title	Yr	VG	VG+	NM
ANGEL					
❏ ANG.60000 [10]	Svend Asmussen and His Unmelancholy Danes	1955	15.00	30.00	60.00
❏ ANG.60010 [10]	Rhythm Is Our Business	1955	15.00	30.00	60.00
BRUNSWICK					
❏ BL 58051 [10]	Hot Fiddle	1953	20.00	40.00	80.00
DOCTOR JAZZ					
❏ FW 39150	June Night	1983	3.00	6.00	12.00
EPIC					
❏ LN 3210 [M]	Skol!	1955	12.50	25.00	50.00

ASMUSSEN, SVEND / STEPHANE GRAPPELLI
Also see each artist's individual listings.

Number	Title	Yr	VG	VG+	NM
STORYVILLE					
❏ SLP-4088	Two of a Kind	198?	3.00	6.00	12.00

ASTAIRE, FRED
Male vocalist.

Number	Title	Yr	VG	VG+	NM
CHOREO					
❏ A-1 [M]	Three Evenings with Fred Astaire	1961	10.00	20.00	40.00
CLEF					
❏ MGC-662 [M]	The Fred Astaire Story, Volume 1	1955	12.50	25.00	50.00
-- Reissue of Mercury 1001					
❏ MGC-663 [M]	The Fred Astaire Story, Volume 2	1955	12.50	25.00	50.00
-- Reissue of Mercury 1002					
❏ MGC-664 [M]	The Fred Astaire Story, Volume 3	1955	12.50	25.00	50.00
-- Reissue of Mercury 1003					
❏ MGC-665 [M]	The Fred Astaire Story, Volume 4	1955	12.50	25.00	50.00
-- Reissue of Mercury 1004					
EPIC					
❏ LN 3103 [M]	Nothing Thrilled Us Half As Much	1955	12.50	25.00	50.00
❏ LN 3137 [M]	The Best of Fred Astaire	1955	12.50	25.00	50.00
❏ FLM 13103 [M]	Nothing Thrilled Us Half As Much	196?	5.00	10.00	20.00
-- Reissue of 3103					
❏ FLS 15103 [R]	Nothing Thrilled Us Half As Much	196?	3.75	7.50	15.00
KAPP					
❏ KL-1165 [M]	Fred Astaire Now	1959	6.25	12.50	25.00
❏ KS-3165 [S]	Fred Astaire Now	1959	7.50	15.00	30.00
MERCURY					
❏ MGC-1001 [M]	The Fred Astaire Story, Volume 1	1954	25.00	50.00	100.00
❏ MGC-1001/4 [(4) M]	The Fred Astaire Story	1953	250.00	500.00	1,000.
-- Spiral-bound four-record set, pressed on blue vinyl, autographed by Fred Astaire					
❏ MGC-1002 [M]	The Fred Astaire Story, Volume 2	1954	25.00	50.00	100.00

Number	Title	Yr	VG	VG+	NM
❏ MGC-1003 [M]	The Fred Astaire Story, Volume 3	1954	25.00	50.00	100.00
❏ MGC-1004 [M]	The Fred Astaire Story, Volume 4	1954	25.00	50.00	100.00
VERVE					
❏ MGV-2010 [M]	Mr. Top Hat	1956	12.50	25.00	50.00
❏ MGV-2114 [M]	Easy to Dance With	1958	12.50	25.00	50.00
VOCALION					
❏ VL 3716 [M]	Fred Astaire	1964	3.75	7.50	15.00

AULD, GEORGIE
Tenor saxophone player, also plays alto and soprano saxes as well as clarinet.

Number	Title	Yr	VG	VG+	NM
ABC-PARAMOUNT					
❏ ABC-287 [M]	Georgie Auld Plays for Melancholy Babies	1958	10.00	20.00	40.00
❏ ABCS-287 [S]	Georgie Auld Plays for Melancholy Babies	1959	7.50	15.00	30.00
ALLEGRO					
❏ 3102 [M]	Jazz Concert	1953	10.00	20.00	40.00
APOLLO					
❏ LAP-102 [10]	Concert in Jazz	1951	20.00	40.00	80.00
CORAL					
❏ CRL 56060 [10]	Tenderly	1952	20.00	40.00	80.00
❏ CRL 56085 [10]	Manhattan	1953	20.00	40.00	80.00
❏ CRL 57029 [M]	Lullaby of Broadway	1956	10.00	20.00	40.00
❏ CRL 57032 [M]	Misty	1956	10.00	20.00	40.00
DISCOVERY					
❏ DL 3007 [10]	That's Auld	1950	20.00	40.00	80.00
EMARCY					
❏ MG-36060 [M]	In the Land of Hi-Fi	1955	10.00	20.00	40.00
❏ MG-36090 [M]	Dancing in the Land of Hi-Fi	1956	10.00	20.00	40.00
JARO					
❏ JAM-5003 [M]	Hawaii on the Rocks	1959	7.50	15.00	30.00
MUSICRAFT					
❏ 501	Georgie Auld and His Orchestra, Vol. 1	197?	2.50	5.00	10.00
❏ 509	Georgie Auld and His Orchestra, Vol. 2	197?	2.50	5.00	10.00
PHILIPS					
❏ PHM 200-096 [M]	Georgie Auld Plays to the Winners	1963	3.75	7.50	15.00
❏ PHM 200-116 [M]	Here's to the Losers	1963	3.75	7.50	15.00
❏ PHS 600-096 [S]	Georgie Auld Plays to the Winners	1963	5.00	10.00	20.00
❏ PHS 600-116 [S]	Here's to the Losers	1963	5.00	10.00	20.00
ROOST					
❏ RST-403 [10]	Georgie Auld Quintet	1951	20.00	40.00	80.00
TOP RANK					
❏ RM-306 [M]	The Melody Lingers On	1959	10.00	20.00	40.00
❏ RM-333 [M]	Good Enough to Keep	1960	10.00	20.00	40.00
UNITED ARTISTS					
❏ UAL-3068 [M]	Manhattan with Strings	1959	10.00	20.00	40.00
❏ UAS-6068 [S]	Manhattan with Strings	1959	7.50	15.00	30.00
XANADU					
❏ 190	Homage	197?	2.50	5.00	10.00

AUSTIN, CLAIRE
Female vocalist.

Number	Title	Yr	VG	VG+	NM
CONTEMPORARY					
❏ C-5002 [M]	When Your Lover Has Gone	1956	12.50	25.00	50.00
FANTASY					
❏ OJC-1711	When Your Lover Has Gone	198?	3.00	6.00	12.00
-- Reissue of Contemporary 5002					
GHB					
❏ S-22	Claire Austin and the Great Excelsior Band	197?	3.75	7.50	15.00
GOOD TIME JAZZ					
❏ L-24 [10]	Claire Austin Sings the Blues	1954	30.00	60.00	120.00
JAZZOLOGY					
❏ 52	Goin' Crazy	197?	3.75	7.50	15.00

AUSTRALIAN ALL STARS, THE

Number	Title	Yr	VG	VG+	NM
BETHLEHEM					
❏ BCP-6070 [M]	Jazz for Beach-Niks	1963	10.00	20.00	40.00
❏ BCP-6073 [M]	Jazz for Surf-Niks	1963	10.00	20.00	40.00

Number	Title	Yr	VG	VG+	NM

AUSTRALIAN JAZZ QUARTET, THE
Members were Bryce Rohde, Errol Buddle and JACK BROKENSHA – all from Down Under – with American Dick Healy.

BETHLEHEM

Number	Title	Yr	VG	VG+	NM
❏ BCP-1031 [10]	The Australian Jazz Quartet	195?	15.00	30.00	60.00
❏ BCP-6002 [M]	The Australian Jazz Quartet/ Quintet	1955	10.00	20.00	40.00
❏ BCP-6002	The Australian Jazz Quartet	197?	3.75	7.50	15.00
-- Reissue distributed by RCA Victor					
❏ BCP-6003 [M]	The Australian Jazz Quartet	1955	10.00	20.00	40.00
❏ BCP-6012 [M]	The Australian Jazz Quartet at the Varsity Drag	1956	10.00	20.00	40.00
❏ BCP-6015 [M]	The Australian Jazz Quartet Plus One	1957	10.00	20.00	40.00
❏ BCP-6022 [M]	The Australian Jazz Quartet Plays the Best of Broadway Musical Hits	1957	10.00	20.00	40.00
❏ BCP-6029 [M]	The Australian Jazz Quartet In Free Style	1959	10.00	20.00	40.00
❏ BCP-6030 [M]	Three Penny Opera	1959	10.00	20.00	40.00

AYERS, ROY
Vibraphone player. Fronted a jazz-funk (fusion) band called Roy Ayers' Ubiquity, the releases of which are included below.

ATLANTIC

Number	Title	Yr	VG	VG+	NM
❏ 1488 [M]	Virgo Vibes	1967	5.00	10.00	20.00
❏ SD 1488 [S]	Virgo Vibes	1967	3.75	7.50	15.00
❏ SD 1514	Stoned Soul Picnic	1968	5.00	10.00	20.00
❏ SD 1538	Daddy Bug	1969	5.00	10.00	20.00

COLUMBIA

Number	Title	Yr	VG	VG+	NM
❏ FC 39422	In the Dark	1984	2.50	5.00	10.00

ICHIBAN

Number	Title	Yr	VG	VG+	NM
❏ ICH-1028	Drive	198?	2.50	5.00	10.00
❏ ICH-1040	Wake Up	198?	2.50	5.00	10.00

POLYDOR

Number	Title	Yr	VG	VG+	NM
❏ PD 5022	He's Coming	1972	3.00	6.00	12.00
❏ PD 5045	Red, Black and Green	1973	3.00	6.00	12.00
❏ PD 6016	Virgo Red	1973	3.00	6.00	12.00
❏ PD 6032	Change Up the Groove	1974	2.50	5.00	10.00
❏ PD 6046	A Tear to a Smile	1975	2.50	5.00	10.00
❏ PD 6057	Mystic Voyage	1976	2.50	5.00	10.00
❏ PD-1-6070	Everybody Loves the Sunshine	1976	2.50	5.00	10.00
❏ PD-1-6078	Red, Black and Green	1976	2.50	5.00	10.00
-- Reissue of 5045					
❏ PD-1-6091	Vibrations	1977	2.50	5.00	10.00
❏ PD-1-6108	Lifeline	1977	2.50	5.00	10.00
❏ PD-1-6126	Let's Do It	1978	2.50	5.00	10.00
❏ PD-1-6159	You Send Me	1978	2.50	5.00	10.00
❏ PD-1-6204	Fever	1979	2.50	5.00	10.00
❏ PD-1-6246	No Stranger to Love	1979	2.50	5.00	10.00
❏ PD-1-6301	Love Fantasy	1980	2.50	5.00	10.00
❏ PD-1-6327	Africa, Center of the World	1981	2.50	5.00	10.00
❏ PD-1-6348	Feeling Good	1982	2.50	5.00	10.00

UNITED ARTISTS

Number	Title	Yr	VG	VG+	NM
❏ UAL-3325 [M]	West Coast Vibes	1964	5.00	10.00	20.00
❏ UAS-6325 [S]	West Coast Vibes	1964	6.25	12.50	25.00

AYERS, ROY, AND WAYNE HENDERSON
Also see each artist's individual listings.

POLYDOR

Number	Title	Yr	VG	VG+	NM
❏ PD-1-6179	Step Into Our Life	1978	2.50	5.00	10.00
❏ PD-1-6276	Prime Time	1980	2.50	5.00	10.00

AYLER, ALBERT
Tenor and alto sax player.

ABC IMPULSE!

Number	Title	Yr	VG	VG+	NM
❏ AS-9155 [S]	Live at the Village Vanguard	1968	3.00	6.00	12.00
❏ AS-9165	Love Cry	1968	5.00	10.00	20.00
❏ AS-9175	New Grass	1969	5.00	10.00	20.00
❏ AS-9191	Music Is the Healing Force of the Universe	1969	5.00	10.00	20.00
❏ AS-9208	The Last Album	1971	5.00	10.00	20.00
❏ AS-9257 [(2)]	Re-evaluations: The Impulse Years	1974	3.75	7.50	15.00
❏ IA-9336 [(2)]	Live at the Village Vanguard	1978	3.75	7.50	15.00

ARISTA/FREEDOM

Number	Title	Yr	VG	VG+	NM
❏ AL 1000	Vibrations	1976	3.75	7.50	15.00
❏ AL 1018	Witches and Devils	1977	3.75	7.50	15.00

ESP-DISK'

Number	Title	Yr	VG	VG+	NM
❏ 1002 [M]	Spiritual Unity	1965	6.25	12.50	25.00
❏ 1010 [M]	Bells	1965	6.25	12.50	25.00
-- Black vinyl					
❏ 1010 [M]	Bells	1965	12.50	25.00	50.00
-- Yellow vinyl					
❏ S-1010 [S]	Bells	1965	5.00	10.00	20.00
❏ 1016 [M]	New York Eye and Ear Control	1966	6.25	12.50	25.00
❏ S-1016 [S]	New York Eye and Ear Control	1966	5.00	10.00	20.00
❏ 1020 [M]	Spirits Rejoice	1966	6.25	12.50	25.00
❏ S-1020 [S]	Spirits Rejoice	1966	5.00	10.00	20.00

FANTASY

Number	Title	Yr	VG	VG+	NM
❏ 6016 [M]	My Name Is Albert Ayler	196?	5.00	10.00	20.00
❏ 86016 [S]	My Name Is Albert Ayler	196?	6.25	12.50	25.00

GNP CRESCENDO

Number	Title	Yr	VG	VG+	NM
❏ GNPS-9022	The First Recordings	1973	3.00	6.00	12.00

IMPULSE!

Number	Title	Yr	VG	VG+	NM
❏ A-9155 [M]	Live at the Village Vanguard	1967	7.50	15.00	30.00
❏ AS-9155 [S]	Live at the Village Vanguard	1967	6.25	12.50	25.00

MCA

Number	Title	Yr	VG	VG+	NM
❏ 4129 [(2)]	Live at the Village Vanguard	198?	3.00	6.00	12.00
-- Reissue of ABC Impulse 9336					

AZAMA, ETHEL
Female vocalist.

LIBERTY

Number	Title	Yr	VG	VG+	NM
❏ LRP-3104 [M]	Exotic Dreams	1959	5.00	10.00	20.00
❏ LRP-3142 [M]	Cool Heat	1960	10.00	20.00	40.00
❏ LST-7104 [S]	Exotic Dreams	1959	7.50	15.00	30.00
❏ LST-7142 [S]	Cool Heat	1960	12.50	25.00	50.00

AZIMUTH
John Taylor, Norma Winstone and Kenny Wheeler.

ECM

Number	Title	Yr	VG	VG+	NM
❏ 1099	Azimuth	1977	2.50	5.00	10.00
❏ 1130	The Touchstone	1978	2.50	5.00	10.00
❏ 1163	Depart	1979	2.50	5.00	10.00
❏ 1289	Azimuth '85	1985	2.50	5.00	10.00

AZYMUTH
Jose Roberto Bertrami, Alex Malheiros and Ivan Conti.

INTIMA

Number	Title	Yr	VG	VG+	NM
❏ D1-73517	Tudo Bern	1989	3.00	6.00	12.00

MILESTONE

Number	Title	Yr	VG	VG+	NM
❏ M-9089	Light as a Feather	1979	3.00	6.00	12.00
❏ M-9097	Outubro	1980	3.00	6.00	12.00
❏ M-9101	Telecommunication	1981	2.50	5.00	10.00
❏ M-9109	Cascades	1982	2.50	5.00	10.00
❏ M-9128	Flame	1984	2.50	5.00	10.00
❏ M-9134	Spectrum	1985	2.50	5.00	10.00
❏ M-9143	Tightrope Walker	1987	2.50	5.00	10.00
❏ M-9156	Crazy Rhythm	1988	2.50	5.00	10.00
❏ M-9169	Carioca	1989	3.00	6.00	12.00

Number	Title	Yr	VG	VG+	NM

B

BABASIN, HARRY
Bass player and celloist. Also see THE JAZZPICKERS.
MODE

Number	Title	Yr	VG	VG+	NM
❑ LP-119 [M]	Jazz Pickers	1957	25.00	50.00	100.00

NOCTURNE

❑ NLP-3 [10]	Harry Babasin Quartet	1954	37.50	75.00	150.00

BABASIN, HARRY/TERRY GIBBS
Also see each artist's individual listings.
PREMIER

❑ PM-2010 [M]	Pick 'n' Pat	1963	3.75	7.50	15.00
❑ PS-2010 [R]	Pick 'n' Pat	1963	2.50	5.00	10.00

BACH, STEVE
Keyboard player.
CAFÉ

❑ 59-00733	Holiday	1986	3.00	6.00	12.00
❑ 59-00736	Zero Gravity	1987	3.00	6.00	12.00

EAGLE

❑ SM-4220	Child's Play	1986	3.00	6.00	12.00

SOUNDWINGS

❑ SW-2112	More Than a Dream	1989	3.00	6.00	12.00

BAGLEY, DON
Bass player.
DOT

❑ DLP-3070 [M]	Basically Bagley	1957	12.50	25.00	50.00
❑ DLP-9007 [M]	The Soft Sell	1959	12.50	25.00	50.00
❑ DLP-25070 [S]	Basically Bagley	1959	10.00	20.00	40.00
❑ DLP-29007 [S]	The Soft Sell	1959	10.00	20.00	40.00

REGENT

❑ MG-6061 [M]	Jazz on the Rocks	1957	15.00	30.00	60.00

SAVOY

❑ MG-12210 [M]	Jazz on the Rocks	196?	5.00	10.00	20.00

BAILEY, BENNY
Trumpeter. Played in the group led by QUINCY JONES.
ARGO

❑ LP-668 [M]	The Music of Quincy Jones	1961	6.25	12.50	25.00
❑ LPS-668 [S]	The Music of Quincy Jones	1961	7.50	15.00	30.00

CANDID

❑ CD-8011 [M]	Big Brass	1960	7.50	15.00	30.00
❑ CS-9011 [S]	Big Brass	1960	10.00	20.00	40.00

GEMINI

❑ GMLP-69-1	While My Lady Sleeps	1990	3.00	6.00	12.00

BAILEY, BUSTER
Clarinet player, sometimes played saxophone.
FELSTED

❑ SJA-2003 [S]	All About Memphis	1959	10.00	20.00	40.00
❑ FAJ-7003 [M]	All About Memphis	1959	10.00	20.00	40.00

BAILEY, DAVE
Drummer.
EPIC

❑ LA 16008 [M]	One Foot in the Gutter	1960	7.50	15.00	30.00
❑ LA 16011 [M]	Gettin' Into Something	1960	7.50	15.00	30.00
❑ LA 16021 [M]	Two Feet in the Gutter	1961	7.50	15.00	30.00
❑ BA 17008 [S]	One Foot in the Gutter	1960	12.50	25.00	50.00
❑ BA 17008 [S]	One Foot in the Gutter	199?	6.25	12.50	25.00
-- Classic Records reissue					
❑ BA 17011 [S]	Gettin' Into Something	1960	10.00	20.00	40.00
❑ BA 17021 [S]	Two Feet in the Gutter	1961	10.00	20.00	40.00

JAZZ LINE

❑ 33-01 [M]	Bash!	1961	10.00	20.00	40.00

JAZZTIME

❑ JS-003 [S]	Reaching Out	1961	10.00	20.00	40.00
-- Reissued under GRANT GREEN's name					
❑ JT-003 [M]	Reaching Out	1961	7.50	15.00	30.00

BAILEY, MILDRED
Female singer. One of the very first featured vocalists with a jazz band when she filled that role for PAUL WHITEMAN.
ALLEGRO

❑ 3119 [M]	Mildred Bailey Sings	1955	15.00	30.00	60.00
❑ 4009 [10]	Mildred Bailey Songs	1952	20.00	40.00	80.00
❑ 4040 [10]	Mildred Bailey Songs	1954	20.00	40.00	80.00

ARCHIVE OF FOLK AND JAZZ

Number	Title	Yr	VG	VG+	NM
❑ 269	Mildred Bailey	197?	3.00	6.00	12.00

COLUMBIA

❑ C3L 22 [(3)]	Her Greatest Performances	1962	12.50	25.00	50.00
-- With booklet; originals have red and black labels with six "eye" logos					
❑ CL 6094 [10]	Serenade	1950	15.00	30.00	60.00

DECCA

❑ DL 5133 [10]	Mildred Bailey Memorial Album	1950	15.00	30.00	60.00
❑ DL 5387 [10]	The Rockin' Chair Lady	195?	15.00	30.00	60.00

HINDSIGHT

❑ HSR-133	Mildred Bailey 1944	198?	2.50	5.00	10.00

MONMOUTH-EVERGREEN

❑ 6814	All of Me	196?	3.75	7.50	15.00

REGENT

❑ MG-6032 [M]	Me and the Blues	1957	12.50	25.00	50.00

ROYALE

❑ VLP 6078 [10]	Mildred Bailey Sings	195?	20.00	40.00	80.00

SAVOY

❑ MG-12219 [M]	Me and the Blues	196?	5.00	10.00	20.00

SAVOY JAZZ

❑ SJL-1151	The Majestic Mildred Bailey	198?	3.00	6.00	12.00

SUNBEAM

❑ 209	Radio Show 1944-45	197?	3.00	6.00	12.00

BAILEY, PEARL
Female singer.
COLUMBIA

❑ CL 6099 [10]	Pearl Bailey Entertains	1950	12.50	25.00	50.00

CORAL

❑ CRL 56068 [10]	Say Si Si	1953	12.50	25.00	50.00
❑ CRL 56078 [10]	I'm with You	1954	12.50	25.00	50.00
❑ CRL 57037 [M]	Pearl Bailey	1957	10.00	20.00	40.00
❑ CRL 57162 [M]	Cultured Pearl	1958	10.00	20.00	40.00

MERCURY

❑ MG-20187 [M]	The One and Only Pearl Bailey Sings	1956	10.00	20.00	40.00
❑ MG-20277 [M]	The Intoxicating Pearl Bailey	1957	10.00	20.00	40.00

ROULETTE

❑ R-25012 [M]	Pearl Bailey A Broad	1957	7.50	15.00	30.00
-- Black label original					
❑ SR-25012 [R]	Pearl Bailey A Broad	196?	3.00	6.00	12.00
❑ R-25016 [M]	Pearl Bailey Sings for Adults Only	1959	5.00	10.00	20.00
-- Originals have a white label with colored spokes					
❑ SR-25016 [S]	Pearl Bailey Sings for Adults Only	1959	6.25	12.50	25.00
-- Originals have a white label with colored spokes					
❑ R-25037 [M]	St. Louis Blues	1958	7.50	15.00	30.00
-- Black label original					
❑ SR-25037 [S]	St. Louis Blues	1959	7.50	15.00	30.00
-- Originals have a white label with colored spokes					
❑ R-25063 [M]	Pearl Bailey Sings Porgy and Bess and Other Gershwin Melodies	1959	5.00	10.00	20.00
-- Originals have a white label with colored spokes					
❑ SR-25063 [S]	Pearl Bailey Sings Porgy and Bess and Other Gershwin Melodies	1959	6.25	12.50	25.00
-- Originals have a white label with colored spokes					
❑ R-25101 [M]	More Songs for Adults Only	1960	5.00	10.00	20.00
-- Originals have a white label with colored spokes					
❑ SR-25101 [S]	More Songs for Adults Only	1960	6.25	12.50	25.00
-- Originals have a white label with colored spokes					
❑ R-25116 [M]	Songs of the Bad Old Days	1960	5.00	10.00	20.00
-- Originals have a white label with colored spokes					
❑ SR-25116 [S]	Songs of the Bad Old Days	1960	6.25	12.50	25.00
-- Originals have a white label with colored spokes					
❑ R-25125 [M]	Naughty But Nice	1960	5.00	10.00	20.00
-- Originals have a white label with colored spokes					
❑ SR-25125 [S]	Naughty But Nice	1960	6.25	12.50	25.00
-- Originals have a white label with colored spokes					
❑ R-25144 [M]	The Best of Pearl Bailey	1961	5.00	10.00	20.00
-- Originals have a white label with colored spokes					
❑ SR-25144 [S]	The Best of Pearl Bailey	1961	6.25	12.50	25.00
-- Originals have a white label with colored spokes					
❑ R-25155 [M]	Pearl Bailey Sings Songs of Harold Arlen	1961	5.00	10.00	20.00
-- Originals have a white label with colored spokes					
❑ SR-25155 [S]	Pearl Bailey Sings Songs of Harold Arlen	1961	6.25	12.50	25.00
-- Originals have a white label with colored spokes					
❑ R-25167 [M]	Happy Sounds	1962	5.00	10.00	20.00
-- Originals have a white label with colored spokes					
❑ SR-25167 [S]	Happy Sounds	1962	6.25	12.50	25.00
-- Originals have a white label with colored spokes					
❑ R-25181 [M]	Come On, Let's Play with Pearlie Mae	1962	5.00	10.00	20.00
-- Originals have a white label with colored spokes					

Number	Title	Yr	VG	VG+	NM
❑ SR-25181 [S]	Come On, Let's Play with Pearlie Mae	1962	6.25	12.50	25.00
-- Originals have a white label with colored spokes					
❑ R-25195 [M]	About Good Little Girls and Bad Little Boys	1963	5.00	10.00	20.00
-- Originals have a pink and orange label					
❑ SR-25195 [S]	About Good Little Girls and Bad Little Boys	1963	6.25	12.50	25.00
-- Originals have a pink and orange label					
❑ R-25222 [M]	C'est La Vie	1963	5.00	10.00	20.00
-- Originals have a pink and orange label					
❑ SR-25222 [S]	C'est La Vie	1963	6.25	12.50	25.00
-- Originals have a pink and orange label					
❑ R-25259 [M]	The Risque World of Pearl Bailey	1964	3.75	7.50	15.00
❑ SR-25259 [S]	The Risque World of Pearl Bailey	1964	5.00	10.00	20.00
❑ R-25271 [M]	Songs by James Van Heusen	1964	3.75	7.50	15.00
❑ SR-25271 [S]	Songs by James Van Heusen	1964	5.00	10.00	20.00
❑ R-25300 [M]	For Women Only	1965	3.75	7.50	15.00
❑ SR-25300 [S]	For Women Only	1965	5.00	10.00	20.00
VOCALION					
❑ VL 3621 [M]	Gems by Pearl Bailey	1958	6.25	12.50	25.00

BAILEY, VICTOR
Bass player.
ATLANTIC

Number	Title	Yr	VG	VG+	NM
❑ 81978	Bottoms Up	1989	3.00	6.00	12.00

BAKER, BUDDY
Trombone player.
VERVE

Number	Title	Yr	VG	VG+	NM
❑ MGV-2006 [M]	Two in Love	1956	12.50	25.00	50.00
❑ V-2006 [M]	Two in Love	1961	5.00	10.00	20.00

BAKER, CHET
Trumpeter, fluegel horn player and occasional singer. Also see RUSS FREEMAN; STAN GETZ; THE MARIACHI BRASS; GERRY MULLIGAN.
ANALOGUE PRODUCTIONS

Number	Title	Yr	VG	VG+	NM
❑ AAPJ-016	Chet	199?	6.25	12.50	25.00
-- Audiophile reissue					
ARTISTS HOUSE					
❑ 9411	Once Upon a Summertime	1978	3.00	6.00	12.00
BAINBRIDGE					
❑ 1040	Albert's House	198?	2.50	5.00	10.00
BLUE NOTE					
❑ B1-92932	Let's Get Lost/The Best of Chet Baker	1989	3.00	6.00	12.00
BLUEBIRD					
❑ 2001-1-RB	The Italian Sessions	1990	3.00	6.00	12.00
BOPLICITY					
❑ BOP-13	Cool Out	198?	2.50	5.00	10.00
CADENCE JAZZ					
❑ CJ-1019	Improviser	198?	2.50	5.00	10.00
COLPIX					
❑ CP-476 [M]	Chet Baker Sings and Plays	1964	10.00	20.00	40.00
❑ SCP-476 [S]	Chet Baker Sings and Plays	1964	12.50	25.00	50.00
COLUMBIA					
❑ CL 549 [M]	Chet Baker and Strings	1954	20.00	40.00	80.00
-- Maroon label, gold print					
❑ CL 549 [M]	Chet Baker and Strings	1955	12.50	25.00	50.00
-- Red and black label with six "eye" logos					
CROWN					
❑ CST-317 [R]	Chet Baker Quintette	196?	3.75	7.50	15.00
❑ CLP-5317 [M]	Chet Baker Quintette	196?	5.00	10.00	20.00
CTI					
❑ 6050	She Was Too Good to Me	1974	3.00	6.00	12.00
ENJA					
❑ 4016	Peace	1982	2.50	5.00	10.00
❑ R1-79600	The Last Great Concert: My Favorite Songs Vol. 1	1989	3.00	6.00	12.00
❑ R1-79624	The Last Great Concert: My Favorite Songs Vol. 2	1989	3.00	6.00	12.00
FANTASY					
❑ OJC-087	Chet	198?	3.00	6.00	12.00
-- Reissue of Riverside 1135					
❑ OJC-137	Chet Baker Plays the Best of Lerner and Loewe	198?	3.00	6.00	12.00
-- Reissue of Riverside 1152					
❑ OJC-207	Chet Baker in New York	1985	3.00	6.00	12.00
-- Reissue of Riverside 1119					
❑ OJC-303	It Could Happen to You -- Chet Baker Sings	1988	2.50	5.00	10.00
-- Reissue of Riverside 1120					

Number	Title	Yr	VG	VG+	NM
❑ OJC-370	Chet Baker in Milan	198?	3.00	6.00	12.00
-- Reissue of Jazzland 18					
❑ OJC-405	Once Upon a Summertime	1989	2.50	5.00	10.00
-- Peissue of Galaxy 5150					
❑ OJC-492	Chet Baker with Fifty Italian Strings	1991	3.00	6.00	12.00
-- Reissue of Jazzland 921					
GALAXY					
❑ 5150	Once Upon a Summertime	1977	3.75	7.50	15.00
HARMONY					
❑ HL 7320 [M]	Love Walked In	1962	5.00	10.00	20.00
HORIZON					
❑ 726	You Can't Go Home Again	1977	3.00	6.00	12.00
INNER CITY					
❑ 1120	Broken Wing	198?	2.50	5.00	10.00
JAZZLAND					
❑ JLP-11 [M]	Chet Baker and Orchestra	1960	10.00	20.00	40.00
❑ JLP-18 [M]	Chet Baker in Milan	1960	10.00	20.00	40.00
❑ JLP-21 [M]	Chet Baker with Fifty Italian Strings	1960	10.00	20.00	40.00
❑ JLP-911 [S]	Chet Baker and Orchestra	1960	10.00	20.00	40.00
❑ JLP-918 [S]	Chet Baker in Milan	1960	10.00	20.00	40.00
❑ JLP-921 [S]	Chet Baker with Fifty Italian Strings	1960	10.00	20.00	40.00
LIMELIGHT					
❑ LM-82003 [M]	Baby Breeze	1964	6.25	12.50	25.00
❑ LM-82019 [M]	Baker's Holiday	1965	6.25	12.50	25.00
❑ LS-86003 [S]	Baby Breeze	1964	7.50	15.00	30.00
❑ LS-86019 [S]	Baker's Holiday	1965	7.50	15.00	30.00
MOSAIC					
❑ MR4-113 [(4)]	The Complete Pacific Jazz Live Recordings of the Chet Baker Quartet with Russ Freeman	199?	20.00	40.00	80.00
❑ MR4-122 [(4)]	The Complete Pacific Jazz Studio Recordings of the Chet Baker Quartet with Russ Freeman	199?	20.00	40.00	80.00
PACIFIC JAZZ					
❑ PJLP-3 [10]	Chet Baker Quartet	1953	50.00	100.00	200.00
❑ PJLP-6 [10]	Chet Baker Quartet Featuring Russ Freeman	1953	50.00	100.00	200.00
❑ PJLP-9 [10]	Chet Baker Ensemble	1954	50.00	100.00	200.00
❑ PJLP-11 [10]	Chet Baker Sings	1954	50.00	100.00	200.00
❑ PJLP-15 [10]	Chet Baker Sextet	1954	50.00	100.00	200.00
❑ PJ-1202 [M]	Chet Baker Sings and Plays with Bud Shank, Russ Freeman and Strings	1955	30.00	60.00	120.00
❑ PJ-1203 [M]	Jazz at Ann Arbor	1955	30.00	60.00	120.00
❑ PJ-1206 [M]	The Trumpet Artistry of Chet Baker	1955	30.00	60.00	120.00
❑ PJ-1218 [M]	Chet Baker in Europe	1956	30.00	60.00	120.00
❑ PJ-1222 [M]	Chet Baker Sings	1956	30.00	60.00	120.00
❑ PJ-1224 [M]	Chet Baker and Crew	1956	30.00	60.00	120.00
❑ PJ-1229 [M]	Chet Baker Big Band	1957	30.00	60.00	120.00
PAUSA					
❑ 9011	The Trumpet Artistry of Chet Baker	198?	2.50	5.00	10.00
PRESTIGE					
❑ PRLP-7449 [M]	Smokin' with the Chet Baker Quintet	1966	5.00	10.00	20.00
❑ PRST-7449 [S]	Smokin' with the Chet Baker Quintet	1966	6.25	12.50	25.00
❑ PRLP-7460 [M]	Groovin' with the Chet Baker Quintet	1966	5.00	10.00	20.00
❑ PRST-7460 [S]	Groovin' with the Chet Baker Quintet	1966	6.25	12.50	25.00
❑ PRLP-7478 [M]	Comin' On with the Chet Baker Quintet	1967	6.25	12.50	25.00
❑ PRST-7478 [S]	Comin' On with the Chet Baker Quintet	1967	5.00	10.00	20.00
❑ PRLP-7496 [M]	Cool Burnin' with the Chet Baker Quintet	1967	7.50	15.00	30.00
❑ PRST-7496 [S]	Cool Burnin' with the Chet Baker Quintet	1967	5.00	10.00	20.00
❑ PRLP-7512 [M]	Boppin' with the Chet Baker Quintet	1967	7.50	15.00	30.00
❑ PRST-7512 [S]	Boppin' with the Chet Baker Quintet	1967	5.00	10.00	20.00
RIVERSIDE					
❑ RLP 12-278 [M]	It Could Happen to You -- Chet Baker Sings	1958	12.50	25.00	50.00
❑ RLP 12-281 [M]	Chet Baker in New York	1958	12.50	25.00	50.00
❑ RLP 12-299 [M]	Chet	1959	12.50	25.00	50.00
❑ RLP 12-307 [M]	Chet Baker Plays Lerner and Loewe	1959	12.50	25.00	50.00
❑ RLP-1119 [S]	Chet Baker in New York	1959	10.00	20.00	40.00
❑ RLP-1120 [S]	It Could Happen to You -- Chet Baker Sings	1959	10.00	20.00	40.00

Number	Title	Yr	VG	VG+	NM
❑ RLP-1135 [S]	Chet	1959	10.00	20.00	40.00
❑ RLP-1152 [S]	Chet Baker Plays Lerner and Loewe	1959	10.00	20.00	40.00
❑ 6095	Chet Baker in New York	197?	3.00	6.00	12.00
-- Reissue					
SCEPTER					
❑ 540 [M]	Angel Eyes	1966	5.00	10.00	20.00
❑ S-540 [S]	Angel Eyes	1966	6.25	12.50	25.00
STEEPLECHASE					
❑ SCS-1122	The Touch of Your Lips	1980	3.00	6.00	12.00
❑ SCS-1131	No Problem	198?	3.00	6.00	12.00
❑ SCS-1142	Daybreak	1981	3.00	6.00	12.00
❑ SCS-1168	This Is Always	198?	2.50	5.00	10.00
❑ SCS-1180	Someday My Prince Will Come	198?	2.50	5.00	10.00
TIMELESS					
❑ LPSJP-192	Mr. B.	1990	3.00	6.00	12.00
❑ LPSJP-251	As Time Goes By	1990	3.00	6.00	12.00
❑ LPSJP-252	Cool Cat: Chet Baker Plays, Chet Baker Sings	1990	3.00	6.00	12.00
TRIP					
❑ 5569	Chet Baker Sings and Plays Billie Holiday	197?	2.50	5.00	10.00
VERVE					
❑ V6-8798	Blood, Chet and Tears	1969	3.75	7.50	15.00
WORLD PACIFIC					
❑ ST-1004 [S]	Chet Baker and Crew	1959	15.00	30.00	60.00
❑ WP-1202 [M]	Chet Baker Sings and Plays with Bud Shank, Russ Freeman and Strings	1958	20.00	40.00	80.00
-- Reissue of Pacific Jazz 1202					
❑ WP-1203 [M]	Jazz at Ann Arbor	1958	20.00	40.00	80.00
-- Reissue of Pacific Jazz 1203					
❑ WP-1206 [M]	The Trumpet Artistry of Chet Baker	1958	20.00	40.00	80.00
-- Reissue of Pacific Jazz 1206					
❑ WP-1218 [M]	Chet Baker in Europe	1958	20.00	40.00	80.00
-- Reissue of Pacific Jazz 1218					
❑ WP-1222 [M]	Chet Baker Sings	1958	20.00	40.00	80.00
-- Reissue of Pacific Jazz 1222					
❑ WP-1224 [M]	Chet Baker and Crew	1958	20.00	40.00	80.00
-- Reissue of Pacific Jazz 1224					
❑ WP-1229 [M]	Chet Baker Big Band	1958	20.00	40.00	80.00
-- Reissue of Pacific Jazz 1229					
❑ WP-1249 [M]	Pretty/Groovy	1958	25.00	50.00	100.00
❑ ST-1826 [R]	Chet Baker Sings	1964	5.00	10.00	20.00
❑ WP-1826 [M]	Chet Baker Sings	1964	7.50	15.00	30.00
-- Reissue of World Pacific 1222					
❑ WP-1842 [M]	Hat's Off	1966	5.00	10.00	20.00
❑ WP-1847 [M]	Quietly, There	1966	5.00	10.00	20.00
❑ WP-1852 [M]	Double Shot	1967	5.00	10.00	20.00
❑ WP-1858 [M]	Into My Life	1967	6.25	12.50	25.00
❑ WPS-21842 [S]	Hat's Off	1966	6.25	12.50	25.00
❑ WPS-21847 [S]	Quietly, There	1966	6.25	12.50	25.00
❑ WPS-21852 [S]	Double Shot	1967	6.25	12.50	25.00
❑ WPS-21858 [S]	Into My Life	1967	5.00	10.00	20.00
❑ WPS-21859 [S]	In the Mood	1968	5.00	10.00	20.00

BAKER, CHET, AND PAUL BLEY
Also see each artist's individual listings.
STEEPLECHASE

Number	Title	Yr	VG	VG+	NM
❑ SCS-1207	Diane	198?	2.50	5.00	10.00

BAKER, CHET; JIM HALL; HUBERT LAWS
Also see each artist's individual listings.
CTI

Number	Title	Yr	VG	VG+	NM
❑ 9007	Studio Trieste	1983	2.50	5.00	10.00

BAKER, CHET, AND LEE KONITZ
Also see each artist's individual listings.
INDIA NAVIGATION

Number	Title	Yr	VG	VG+	NM
❑ IN-1052	In Concert	198?	3.00	6.00	12.00

BAKER, CHET, AND ART PEPPER
Also see each artist's individual listings.
PACIFIC JAZZ

Number	Title	Yr	VG	VG+	NM
❑ PJ-18 [M]	Picture of Health	1961	12.50	25.00	50.00
❑ PJ-1234 [M]	Playboys	1957	37.50	75.00	150.00
-- Pacific Jazz records come in World Pacific covers					
WORLD PACIFIC					
❑ PJ-1234 [M]	Playboys	1958	30.00	60.00	120.00
❑ WP-1234 [M]	Playboys	1958	20.00	40.00	80.00

BAKER, DAVID, AND HIS 21ST CENTURY BEBOP BAND
Baker is a trombone player.
LAUREL

Number	Title	Yr	VG	VG+	NM
❑ LR-503	David Baker and His 21st Century Bebop Band	1984	3.00	6.00	12.00
❑ LR-504	RSVP	1985	3.00	6.00	12.00
❑ LR-505	Struttin'	1986	3.00	6.00	12.00

BAKER, JOSEPHINE
Female singer.
COLUMBIA

Number	Title	Yr	VG	VG+	NM
❑ FL 9532 [10]	Josephine Baker	1951	25.00	50.00	100.00
❑ FL 9533 [10]	Chansons Americaines	1951	25.00	50.00	100.00
COLUMBIA MASTERWORKS					
❑ ML 2608 [10]	Josephine Baker Sings	1952	20.00	40.00	80.00
❑ ML 2609 [10]	Chansons Americaines	1952	20.00	40.00	80.00
❑ ML 2613 [10]	Encores Americaines	1952	20.00	40.00	80.00
JOLLY ROGER					
❑ 5015 [10]	Josephine Baker	1951	12.50	25.00	50.00
MERCURY					
❑ MG-25105 [10]	The Inimitable Josephine Baker	1952	20.00	40.00	80.00
❑ MG-25151 [10]	Avec Josephine Baker	1952	20.00	40.00	80.00
RCA VICTOR RED SEAL					
❑ LM-2427 [M]	The Fabulous Josephine Baker	1960	3.75	7.50	15.00
-- Original with "shaded dog" label					
❑ LSC-2427 [S]	The Fabulous Josephine Baker	1960	10.00	20.00	40.00
-- Original with "shaded dog" label					

BAKER, LAVERN
Mostly a rhythm and blues singer – those releases are listed in the *Standard Catalog Of American Records 1950-1975*. She did do one jazz album, listed below.
ATLANTIC

Number	Title	Yr	VG	VG+	NM
❑ 1281 [M]	LaVern Baker Sings Bessie Smith	1958	30.00	60.00	120.00
-- Black label					
❑ 1281 [M]	LaVern Baker Sings Bessie Smith	1960	5.00	10.00	20.00
-- Red and purple label, "fan" logo in black					
❑ 1281 [M]	LaVern Baker Sings Bessie Smith	1960	7.50	15.00	30.00
-- Red and purple label, "fan" logo in white					
❑ SD 1281 [S]	LaVern Baker Sings Bessie Smith	1959	37.50	75.00	150.00
-- Green label					
❑ SD 1281 [S]	LaVern Baker Sings Bessie Smith	1960	10.00	20.00	40.00
-- Green and blue label, "fan" logo in white					
❑ SD 1281 [S]	LaVern Baker Sings Bessie Smith	1963	6.25	12.50	25.00
-- Green and blue label, "fan" logo in black					
❑ 90980	LaVern Baker Sings Bessie Smith	1989	3.00	6.00	12.00
-- Reissue of SD 1281					

BAKER, SHORTY
Trumpeter.
KING

Number	Title	Yr	VG	VG+	NM
❑ 608 [M]	Broadway Beat	1958	20.00	40.00	80.00

BAKER, SHORTY, AND DOC CHEATHAM
Also see each artist's individual listings.
SWINGVILLE

Number	Title	Yr	VG	VG+	NM
❑ SVLP-2021 [M]	Shorty & Doc	1961	12.50	25.00	50.00
-- Purple label					
❑ SVLP-2021 [M]	Shorty & Doc	1965	6.25	12.50	25.00
-- Blue label with trident logo at right					

BALDWIN, BOB
Keyboard player and pianist.
ATLANTIC

Number	Title	Yr	VG	VG+	NM
❑ 82098	Rejoice	1990	3.00	6.00	12.00
MALACO					
❑ MJ-1501	I've Got a Long Way to Go	1988	2.50	5.00	10.00

BALES, BURT
Pianist.
ABC-PARAMOUNT

Number	Title	Yr	VG	VG+	NM
❑ ABC-181 [M]	Jazz from the San Francisco Waterfront	1957	10.00	20.00	40.00
CAVALIER					
❑ 5007 [10]	On the Waterfront	195?	15.00	30.00	60.00
EUPHONIC					
❑ ESR-1210 [M]	New Orleans Ragtime	196?	7.50	15.00	30.00
GOOD TIME JAZZ					
❑ L-19 [10]	New Orleans Joys	1954	12.50	25.00	50.00

(Top left) Josephine Baker was a dancer, singer and actress who transcended jazz. During her lifetime, she was more celebrated in France, which she adopted as her home, than her native United States. This is one of her Mercury 10-inch albums. (Top right) Count Basie came out of Kansas City with one of the most innovative of the big bands, one that often had the flexibility of a much smaller group. Many of his early soloists became leaders in bebop. This album, on the Happy Tiger label, is also sought after by collectors of Beatles-related material. (Bottom left) Sidney Bechet helped popularize the soprano saxophone as a jazz instrument. This album was one of the many collections of vintage jazz recordings issued on the RCA subsidiary "X" in 1954-55; some of these compilations are as collectible as the original 78s! (Bottom right) Max Bennett, a bass player, recorded several albums for the Bethlehem label in the 1950s, including this one. Bennett was later the co-founder of the fusion band L.A. Express with Tom Scott.

Number	Title	Yr	VG	VG+	NM

BALES & LINGLE
BURT BALES and PAUL LINGLE, both pianists.
GOOD TIME JAZZ
| ❏ L-12025 [M] | They Tore My Playhouse Down | 1955 | 10.00 | 20.00 | 40.00 |

BALL, KENNY
Trumpeter and bandleader. His "Midnight in Moscow" was a hit single in 1962.
JAZZOLOGY
| ❏ 65 | In Concert in the USA, Volume 1 | 1979 | 2.50 | 5.00 | 10.00 |
| ❏ 66 | In Concert in the USA, Volume 2 | 1979 | 2.50 | 5.00 | 10.00 |
KAPP
❏ KL-1276 [M]	Midnight in Moscow	1962	5.00	10.00	20.00
❏ KL-1285 [M]	It's Trad	1962	5.00	10.00	20.00
❏ KL-1294 [M]	Recorded Live	1962	5.00	10.00	20.00
❏ KL-1314 [M]	More	1963	3.75	7.50	15.00
❏ KL-1340 [M]	Big Ones	1963	3.75	7.50	15.00
❏ KL-1348 [M]	Washington Square and the Best of Kenny Ball	1964	3.75	7.50	15.00
❏ KL-1392 [M]	For the Jet Set	1964	3.75	7.50	15.00
❏ KS-3276 [S]	Midnight in Moscow	1962	5.00	10.00	20.00
❏ KS-3285 [S]	It's Trad	1962	5.00	10.00	20.00
❏ KS-3294 [S]	Recorded Live	1962	5.00	10.00	20.00
❏ KS-3314 [S]	More	1963	5.00	10.00	20.00
❏ KS-3340 [S]	Big Ones	1963	5.00	10.00	20.00
❏ KS-3348 [S]	Washington Square and the Best of Kenny Ball	1964	5.00	10.00	20.00
❏ KS-3392 [S]	For the Jet Set	1964	5.00	10.00	20.00

BALL, ROCKY, AND THE RAZ'MATAZ JAZZ BAND
Banjo player.
BONFIRE
❏ 501	Hot Dixieland Jazz	198?	2.50	5.00	10.00
❏ 502	For Your Listening Pleasure	198?	2.50	5.00	10.00
❏ 503	Salute to Li'l Wally	198?	2.50	5.00	10.00

BALL, RONNIE
Pianist.
SAVOY
| ❏ MG-12075 [M] | All About Ronnie | 1956 | 10.00 | 20.00 | 40.00 |

BALLOU, MONTE, AND HIS NEW CASTLE JAZZ BAND
Banjo player and bandleader. Also see THE FAMOUS CASTLE JAZZ BAND.
GHB
| ❏ GHB-155 | They're Moving Willie's Grave to Dig a Sewer | 1986 | 2.50 | 5.00 | 10.00 |

BALMER, DAN
Guitarist. Formerly a member of TOM GRANT's band.
CMG
| ❏ CML-8013 | Becoming Became | 1989 | 3.00 | 6.00 | 12.00 |

BANG, BILLY
Violinist. Also see STRING TRIO OF NEW YORK.
CELLULOID
| ❏ CELL-5004 | Outline #12 | 198? | 3.00 | 6.00 | 12.00 |
SOUL NOTE
❏ SN-1016	Rainbow Gladiator	1981	3.00	6.00	12.00
❏ SN-1036	Invitation	1982	3.00	6.00	12.00
❏ SN-1086	The Fire from Within	1985	3.00	6.00	12.00
❏ 121136	Live at Carlos 1	1987	3.00	6.00	12.00

BANJO KINGS, THE
Banjo players Dick Roberts and Red Roundtree with a revolving cast of backing musicians.
GOOD TIME JAZZ
❏ L-15 [10]	The Banjo Kings	1953	12.50	25.00	50.00
❏ L-12015 [M]	The Banjo Kings	1955	10.00	20.00	40.00
❏ L-12015 [M]	The Banjo Kings, Vol. 1	198?	2.50	5.00	10.00
-- Reissue with revised title and thinner vinyl					
❏ L-12029 [M]	Nostalgia Revisited	1956	10.00	20.00	40.00
❏ L-12036 [M]	The Banjo Kings Go West	1957	10.00	20.00	40.00
❏ L-12047 [M]	The Banjo Kings Enjoy the Good Old Days	1958	10.00	20.00	40.00
❏ S-12047 [S]	The Banjo Kings Enjoy the Good Old Days	1959	7.50	15.00	30.00

BARBARIN, PAUL
Drummer and bandleader.
ATLANTIC
| ❏ 1215 [M] | New Orleans Jazz | 1955 | 12.50 | 25.00 | 50.00 |
| -- Black label | | | | | |

Number	Title	Yr	VG	VG+	NM
❏ 1215 [M]	New Orleans Jazz	1961	5.00	10.00	20.00
-- Multi-color label, white "fan" logo at right					
❏ 1215 [M]	New Orleans Jazz	1963	3.75	7.50	15.00
-- Multi-color label, black "fan" logo at right					
❏ SD 1215 [S]	New Orleans Jazz	1959	12.50	25.00	50.00
-- Green label					
❏ SD 1215 [S]	New Orleans Jazz	1961	5.00	10.00	20.00
-- Multi-color label, white "fan" logo at right					
❏ SD 1215 [S]	New Orleans Jazz	1963	3.75	7.50	15.00
-- Multi-color label, black "fan" logo at right					

CIRCLE
| ❏ 408 [10] | Paul Barbarin's New Orleans Band | 1951 | 20.00 | 40.00 | 80.00 |
CONCERT HALL JAZZ
| ❏ 1006 [10] | New Orleans Jamboree | 1954 | 12.50 | 25.00 | 50.00 |
GHB
❏ GHB-2 [M]	Paul Barbarin and His New Orleans Jazz Band	1962	5.00	10.00	20.00
❏ GHB-140 [M]	Bourbon St. Beat	197?	3.00	6.00	12.00
-- Reissue of Southland LP					
JAZZTONE
| ❏ J-1205 [M] | New Orleans Jamboree | 1955 | 10.00 | 20.00 | 40.00 |
NOBILITY
| ❏ 708 | Last Journey of a Jazzman | 196? | 5.00 | 10.00 | 20.00 |
SOUTHLAND
| ❏ SLP-237 [M] | Bourbon St. Beat | 195? | 10.00 | 20.00 | 40.00 |
STORYVILLE
| ❏ 4049 [M] | Jazz from New Orleans | 198? | 2.50 | 5.00 | 10.00 |

BARBARIN, PAUL / SHARKEY BONANO
Also see each artist's individual listings.
RIVERSIDE
❏ RLP 12-217 [M]	New Orleans Contrasts	1955	15.00	30.00	60.00
-- White label, blue print					
❏ RLP 12-217 [M]	New Orleans Contrasts	195?	10.00	20.00	40.00
-- Blue label with microphone logo					

BARBARIN, PAUL, AND PUNCH MILLER
Also see each artist's individual listings.
ATLANTIC
| ❏ 1410 [M] | Paul Barbarin and Punch Miller | 1963 | 5.00 | 10.00 | 20.00 |
| ❏ SD 1410 [S] | Paul Barbarin and Punch Miller | 1963 | 6.25 | 12.50 | 25.00 |

BARBARIN, PAUL / JOHNNY ST. CYR
St. Cyr played guitar and banjo. Also see PAUL BARBARIN.
SOUTHLAND
| ❏ SLP-212 [M] | Paul Barbarin and His Jazz Band/Johnny St. Cyr and His Hot Five | 1955 | 10.00 | 20.00 | 40.00 |

BARBARY, RICHARD
A&M
| ❏ SP-3010 | Soul Machine | 1969 | 5.00 | 10.00 | 20.00 |

BARBER, CHRIS
Trombonist and bandleader. His version of "Petite Fleur" was a top-five pop hit in 1959.
ATLANTIC
| ❏ 1292 [M] | Here Is Chris Barber | 1959 | 10.00 | 20.00 | 40.00 |
COLPIX
| ❏ CP-404 [M] | Petite But Great | 1959 | 7.50 | 15.00 | 30.00 |
GHB
| ❏ GHB-40 [M] | Collaboration | 1967 | 3.75 | 7.50 | 15.00 |
LAURIE
❏ 1001 [M]	Petite Fleur	1959	10.00	20.00	40.00
❏ LLP-1003 [M]	Trad Jazz Volume 1	1960	7.50	15.00	30.00
❏ LLP-1009 [M]	Chris Barber's "American" Jazz Band	1962	7.50	15.00	30.00

BARBER, PATRICIA
Pianist and female singer.
PREMONITION
❏ PREM 737-1	Café Blue	199?	7.50	15.00	30.00
-- Audiophile vinyl					
❏ PREM 747-1	Modern Cool	1998	6.25	12.50	25.00
-- Audiophile vinyl					

BARBIERI, GATO
Tenor saxophone player.
A&M
❏ SP-3029	Fire and Passion	198?	2.50	5.00	10.00
❏ SP-3188	Euphoria	198?	2.00	4.00	8.00
-- Budget-line reissue					

Number	Title	Yr	VG	VG+	NM
❏ SP-3247	Caliente!	198?	2.00	4.00	8.00
-- Budget-line reissue					
❏ SP-4597	Caliente!	1976	2.50	5.00	10.00
❏ SP-4655	Ruby, Ruby	1977	2.50	5.00	10.00
❏ SP-4710	Tropico	1978	2.50	5.00	10.00
❏ SP-4774	Euphoria	1979	2.50	5.00	10.00
ABC IMPULSE!					
❏ AS-9248	Chapter One -- Latin America	1973	3.00	6.00	12.00
❏ AS-9263	Chapter Two -- Hasta Siempre	1974	3.00	6.00	12.00
❏ AS-9279	Chapter Three -- Viva Emiliano Zapata	1974	3.00	6.00	12.00
❏ AS-9303	Chapter Four -- Alive in New York	1975	3.00	6.00	12.00
DR. JAZZ					
❏ W2X 39204 [(2)]	Gato...Para Los Amigos	1985	3.00	6.00	12.00
❏ FW 40183	Apasionado	1986	2.50	5.00	10.00
ESP-DISK'					
❏ 1049	In Search of the Mystery	1968	5.00	10.00	20.00
FLYING DUTCHMAN					
❏ BDL1-0550	Yesterdays	1974	3.00	6.00	12.00
❏ BDL1-1147	El Gato	1976	3.00	6.00	12.00
❏ BXL1-2826	3rd World	1978	2.50	5.00	10.00
-- Reissue of 10117					
❏ BXL1-2827	Fenix	1978	2.50	5.00	10.00
-- Reissue of 10144					
❏ BXL1-2828	El Pampero	1978	2.50	5.00	10.00
-- Reissue of 10151					
❏ BXL1-2829	Under Fire	1978	2.50	5.00	10.00
-- Reissue of 10156					
❏ BXL1-2830	Bolivia	1978	2.50	5.00	10.00
-- Reissue of 10158					
❏ AYL1-3815	3rd World	1980	2.00	4.00	8.00
-- Budget-line reissue					
❏ AYL1-3816	Yesterdays	1980	2.00	4.00	8.00
-- Budget-line reissue					
❏ AYL1-3817	El Gato	1980	2.00	4.00	8.00
-- Budget-line reissue					
❏ FD 10117	3rd World	1970	3.75	7.50	15.00
❏ FD 10144	Fenix	1972	3.75	7.50	15.00
❏ FD 10151	El Pampero	1973	3.75	7.50	15.00
❏ FD 10156	Under Fire	1973	3.00	6.00	12.00
❏ FD 10158	Bolivia	1973	3.00	6.00	12.00
❏ FD 10165	Legend	1974	3.00	6.00	12.00
MCA					
❏ 29002	Chapter Two -- Hasta Siempre	1981	2.00	4.00	8.00
-- Reissue of Impulse 9263					
❏ 29003	Chapter Four -- Alive in New York	1981	2.00	4.00	8.00
-- Reissue of Impulse 9303					
UNITED ARTISTS					
❏ UA-LA045-F	Last Tango in Paris	1973	3.00	6.00	12.00

BARBIERI, GATO & DOLLAR BRAND
Also see each artist's individual listings.

Number	Title	Yr	VG	VG+	NM
ARISTA FREEDOM					
❏ AL 1003	Confluence	1975	3.00	6.00	12.00

BARBOSA-LIMA, CARLOS
Acoustic guitarist who also plays classical music.

Number	Title	Yr	VG	VG+	NM
CONCORD CONCERTO					
❏ CC-2005	Carlos Barbosa-Lima Plays the Music of Jobim and Gershwin	1983	2.50	5.00	10.00
❏ CC-2006	Carlos Barbosa-Lima Plays the Music of Luiz Bonfa and Cole Porter	1984	2.50	5.00	10.00
❏ CC-2008	Carlos Barbosa-Lima Plays The Entertainer and Other Works by Scott Joplin	1985	2.50	5.00	10.00
❏ CC-2009	Impressions	1991	3.00	6.00	12.00

BARBOSA-LIMA, CARLOS, AND SHARON ISBIN
Sharon Isbin is an acoustic guitarist usually associated with classical music.

Number	Title	Yr	VG	VG+	NM
CONCORD CONCERTO					
❏ CC-2012	Rhapsody in Blue/West Side Story	1988	2.50	5.00	10.00
CONCORD PICANTE					
❏ CJP-320	Brazil, With Love	1987	2.50	5.00	10.00

BARKER, WARREN
Composer and conductor.

Number	Title	Yr	VG	VG+	NM
WARNER BROS.					
❏ W 1205 [M]	"The King and I" for Orchestra	1958	5.00	10.00	20.00
❏ WS 1205 [S]	"The King and I" for Orchestra	1958	6.25	12.50	25.00
❏ W 1290 [M]	TV Guide -- Top TV Themes	1959	7.50	15.00	30.00
❏ WS 1290 [S]	TV Guide -- Top TV Themes	1959	10.00	20.00	40.00

BARNES, CHERYL
Female singer.

Number	Title	Yr	VG	VG+	NM
OPTIMISM					
❏ OP-3105	Cheryl	198?	3.00	6.00	12.00

BARNES, EMILE
Clarinet player.

Number	Title	Yr	VG	VG+	NM
AMERICAN MUSIC					
❏ LP-641 [10]	New Orleans Trad Jazz	1952	12.50	25.00	50.00
JAZZOLOGY					
❏ JCE-23 [M]	Too Well Thou Lov'st	1967	3.00	6.00	12.00
❏ JCE-34 [M]	Emil Barnes and His New Orleans Music	197?	3.00	6.00	12.00

BARNES, GEORGE
Guitarist. Also see RUBY BRAFF AND GEORGE BARNES.

Number	Title	Yr	VG	VG+	NM
DECCA					
❏ DL 8658 [M]	Guitars -- By George	1957	10.00	20.00	40.00
-- Black label, silver print					
GRAND AWARD					
❏ GA 33-358 [M]	Guitar in Velvet	195?	6.25	12.50	25.00
MERCURY					
❏ PPS-2011 [M]	Guitar Galaxies	1961	7.50	15.00	30.00
❏ PPS-6011 [S]	Guitar Galaxies	1961	10.00	20.00	40.00
❏ MG-20956 [M]	Guitar Galaxies	1962	6.25	12.50	25.00
❏ SR-60956 [S]	Guitar Galaxies	1962	7.50	15.00	30.00

BARNES, GEORGE, AND KARL KRESS
Also see each artist's individual listings.

Number	Title	Yr	VG	VG+	NM
UNITED ARTISTS					
❏ UAL 3335 [M]	Town Hall Concert	1963	6.25	12.50	25.00
❏ UAS 6335 [S]	Town Hall Concert	1963	7.50	15.00	30.00
❏ UAL 14033 [M]	Something Tender	1961	6.25	12.50	25.00
❏ UAS 15033 [S]	Something Tender	1961	7.50	15.00	30.00

BARNES, MAE
Female singer.

Number	Title	Yr	VG	VG+	NM
ATLANTIC					
❏ ALS-404 [10]	Fun with Mae Barnes	1953	100.00	200.00	400.00
VANGUARD					
❏ VRS-9036 [M]	Meet Mae Barnes	1958	12.50	25.00	50.00

BARNET, CHARLIE
Saxophone player (alto, tenor, baritone), male singer, bandleader.

Number	Title	Yr	VG	VG+	NM
AIRCHECK					
❏ 5	Charlie Barnet and His Orchestra 1945	197?	2.50	5.00	10.00
❏ 30	Charlie Barnet On the Air Vol. 2	198?	2.50	5.00	10.00
ALAMAC					
❏ QSR 2446	Charlie Barnet & His Orchestra	198?	2.50	5.00	10.00
AVA					
❏ A-10 [M]	Charlie Barnet !?!?!?!?!?!?!	1962	6.25	12.50	25.00
❏ AS-10 [S]	Charlie Barnet !?!?!?!?!?!?!	1962	7.50	15.00	30.00
BLUEBIRD					
❏ AXM2-5526 [(2)]	The Complete Charlie Barnet Vol. 1, 1935-37	197?	3.75	7.50	15.00
❏ AXM2-5577 [(2)]	The Complete Charlie Barnet Vol. 2, 1939	197?	3.75	7.50	15.00
❏ AXM2-5581 [(2)]	The Complete Charlie Barnet Vol. 3, 1939-40	197?	3.75	7.50	15.00
❏ AXM2-5585 [(2)]	The Complete Charlie Barnet Vol. 4, 1940	197?	3.75	7.50	15.00
❏ AXM2-5587 [(2)]	The Complete Charlie Barnet Vol. 5, 1940-41	197?	3.75	7.50	15.00
❏ AXM2-5590 [(2)]	The Complete Charlie Barnet Vol. 6, 1940-41	197?	3.75	7.50	15.00
BRIGHT ORANGE					
❏ XBO-706 [S]	The Stereophonic Sound of the Charlie Barnet Orchestra	196?	3.75	7.50	15.00
CAPITOL					
❏ H 235 [10]	Big Bands	195?	15.00	30.00	60.00
❏ H 325 [10]	The Modern Idiom	195?	15.00	30.00	60.00
❏ T 624 [M]	Classics in Jazz	1955	12.50	25.00	50.00
❏ ST 1403 [S]	Jazz Oasis	1960	6.25	12.50	25.00
❏ T 1403 [M]	Jazz Oasis	1960	5.00	10.00	20.00
CHOREO					
❏ A-10 [M]	Charlie Barnet !?!?!?!?!?!?!	196?	5.00	10.00	20.00
❏ AS-10 [S]	Charlie Barnet !?!?!?!?!?!?!	196?	6.25	12.50	25.00
-- Some copies have Choreo logo on front cover, but Ava labels and back cover					

Number	Title	Yr	VG	VG+	NM
CIRCLE					
❏ CLP-65	Charlie Barnet and His Orchestra 1941	198?	2.50	5.00	10.00
CLEF					
❏ MGC-114 [10]	Charlie Barnet Plays Charlie Barnet	1953	25.00	50.00	100.00
❏ MGC-139 [10]	Dance with Charlie Barnet	1953	25.00	50.00	100.00
❏ MGC-164 [10]	Charlie Barnet Dance Session, Vol. 1	1954	25.00	50.00	100.00
❏ MGC-165 [10]	Charlie Barnet Dance Session, Vol. 2	1954	25.00	50.00	100.00
❏ MGC-638 [M]	One Night Stand	1955	20.00	40.00	80.00
COLUMBIA					
❏ CL 639 [M]	Town Hall Jazz Concert	195?	10.00	20.00	40.00
-- Black and red label with six "eye" logos					
❏ CL 639 [M]	Town Hall Jazz Concert	1955	12.50	25.00	50.00
-- Maroon label, gold print					
CREATIVE WORLD					
❏ ST 1056	Charlie Barnet Big Band 1967	197?	3.00	6.00	12.00
-- Reissue of Vault LPS-9004					
CROWN					
❏ CLP-5114 [M]	A Tribute to Harry James	195?	5.00	10.00	20.00
❏ CLP-5127 [M]	Charlie Barnet Presents a Salute to Harry James	195?	5.00	10.00	20.00
❏ CLP-5134 [M]	On Stage with Charlie Barnet	1959	5.00	10.00	20.00
DECCA					
❏ DL 8098 [M]	Hop on the Skyliner	195?	12.50	25.00	50.00
EVEREST					
❏ SDBR-1008 [S]	Cherokee	1959	5.00	10.00	20.00
❏ LPBR-5008 [M]	Cherokee	1958	6.25	12.50	25.00
❏ LPBR-5059 [M]	More Charlie Barnet	196?	5.00	10.00	20.00
❏ SDBR-5059 [S]	More Charlie Barnet	196?	6.25	12.50	25.00
HEP					
❏ 2005	Live at Basin Street East	198?	2.50	5.00	10.00
MCA					
❏ 4069 [(2)]	The Best of Charlie Barnet	197?	3.00	6.00	12.00
MERCURY					
❏ MGC-114 [10]	Charlie Barnet Plays Charlie Barnet	1952	37.50	75.00	150.00
RCA VICTOR					
❏ LPV-551 [M]	Charlie Barnet (Volume 1)	1968	5.00	10.00	20.00
❏ LPV-567 [M]	Charlie Barnet (Volume 2)	1969	5.00	10.00	20.00
❏ LPM-1091 [M]	Redskin Romp	1955	12.50	25.00	50.00
❏ LPM-2081 [M]	The Great Dance Bands	1960	5.00	10.00	20.00
❏ LPT-3062 [10]	Rockin' in Rhythm	195?	20.00	40.00	80.00
SUNSET					
❏ SUS-5150	Cherokee	1967	3.00	6.00	12.00
SWING					
❏ 103 [M]	Charlie Barnet and His Orchestra	195?	10.00	20.00	40.00
TIME-LIFE					
❏ STBB-07 [(2)]	Big Bands	198?	3.75	7.50	15.00
VAULT					
❏ LP-9004 [M]	Charlie Barnet Big Band 1967	1967	5.00	10.00	20.00
❏ LPS-9004 [S]	Charlie Barnet Big Band 1967	1967	3.75	7.50	15.00
VERVE					
❏ MGV-2007 [M]	Dance Bash	1956	12.50	25.00	50.00
❏ V-2007 [M]	Dance Bash	1961	5.00	10.00	20.00
❏ MGV-2027 [M]	Dancing Party	1956	12.50	25.00	50.00
❏ V-2027 [M]	Dancing Party	1961	5.00	10.00	20.00
❏ MGV-2031 [M]	For Dancing Lovers	1956	12.50	25.00	50.00
❏ V-2031 [M]	For Dancing Lovers	1961	5.00	10.00	20.00
❏ MGV-2040 [M]	Lonely Street	1957	12.50	25.00	50.00
❏ V-2040 [M]	Lonely Street	1961	5.00	10.00	20.00

BARR, WALT
Guitarist.

Number	Title	Yr	VG	VG+	NM
MUSE					
❏ 5172	First Visit	1978	3.75	7.50	15.00
❏ 5210	East Winds	1979	3.75	7.50	15.00
❏ 5238	Artful Dancer	1980	3.75	7.50	15.00

BARRETT, DAN
Trombone player, both slide and valve.

Number	Title	Yr	VG	VG+	NM
CONCORD JAZZ					
❏ CJ-331	Strictly Instrumental	1988	2.50	5.00	10.00

BARRETT, EMMA
Known as "Sweet Emma." Pianist and female singer.

Number	Title	Yr	VG	VG+	NM
GHB					
❏ 141 [M]	Sweet Emma Barrett and Her New Orleans Music	1969	3.00	6.00	12.00
-- Reissue of Southland 241					
❏ 142 [M]	Emma Barrett at Disneyland	1969	3.00	6.00	12.00
-- Reissue of Southland 242					
NOBILITY					
❏ 711 [M]	The Bell Gal and Her New Orleans Jazz	196?	5.00	10.00	20.00
RIVERSIDE					
❏ RLP-364 [M]	Sweet Emma	1960	10.00	20.00	40.00
❏ RS-9364 [R]	Sweet Emma	196?	5.00	10.00	20.00
SOUTHLAND					
❏ 241 [M]	Sweet Emma Barrett and Her New Orleans Music	1964	5.00	10.00	20.00
❏ 242 [M]	Emma Barrett at Disneyland	1967	5.00	10.00	20.00

BARRETTO, RAY
Percussionist (mostly congas) and bandleader. Also a legendary figure in Latin samba music. Had a hit single in 1963 with "El Watusi."

Number	Title	Yr	VG	VG+	NM
ATLANTIC					
❏ SD 2-509 [(2)]	Tomorrow: Ray Barretto Live	197?	3.75	7.50	15.00
❏ SD 19140	Eye of the Beholder	1977	3.00	6.00	12.00
❏ SD 19198	Can You	1978	3.00	6.00	12.00
CTI					
❏ 9002	La Cuna	198?	2.50	5.00	10.00
FANIA					
❏ SLP-346	Acid	196?	5.00	10.00	20.00
❏ SLP-362	Hard Hands	1970	5.00	10.00	20.00
❏ SLP-378	Together	197?	5.00	10.00	20.00
❏ SLP-388	Barretto Head Sounds	197?	5.00	10.00	20.00
❏ SLP-391	Power	197?	5.00	10.00	20.00
❏ SLP-403	The Message	197?	5.00	10.00	20.00
❏ SLP-410	From the Beginning	197?	5.00	10.00	20.00
FANTASY					
❏ 24713 [(2)]	Carnaval	197?	3.75	7.50	15.00
TICO					
❏ LP-1087 [M]	Charanga Moderna	1962	5.00	10.00	20.00
❏ SLP-1087 [S]	Charanga Moderna	1962	6.25	12.50	25.00
❏ LP-1099 [M]	The Hit Latin Style of Ray Barretto	1963	5.00	10.00	20.00
❏ SLP-1099 [S]	The Hit Latin Style of Ray Barretto	1963	6.25	12.50	25.00
❏ LP-1102 [M]	La Moderna De Siempre	1963	5.00	10.00	20.00
❏ SLP-1102 [S]	La Moderna De Siempre	1963	6.25	12.50	25.00
❏ LP-1114 [M]	Guajira y Guaguanco	1964	5.00	10.00	20.00
❏ SLP-1114 [S]	Guajira y Guaguanco	1964	6.25	12.50	25.00
❏ SLP-1205	Something to Remember	1969	3.75	7.50	15.00
❏ CLP-1314	Lo Mejor De Ray Barretto	1973	3.75	7.50	15.00

BARRON, BILL
Tenor saxophone player. Also a soprano saxophone player and flutist.

Number	Title	Yr	VG	VG+	NM
AUDIO FIDELITY					
❏ AFLP-2123 [M]	Now Hear This!	1964	5.00	10.00	20.00
❏ AFSD-6123 [S]	Now Hear This!	1964	6.25	12.50	25.00
DAUNTLESS					
❏ DM-4312 [M]	West Side Story Bossa Nova	1963	6.25	12.50	25.00
❏ DS-6312 [S]	West Side Story Bossa Nova	1963	7.50	15.00	30.00
MUSE					
❏ 5235	Jazz Caper	1978	3.00	6.00	12.00
❏ 5306	Variations in Blue	1983	3.00	6.00	12.00
SAVOY					
❏ MG-12160 [M]	The Tenor Stylings of Bill Barron	1961	10.00	20.00	40.00
❏ MG-12163 [M]	Modern Windows	1962	10.00	20.00	40.00
❏ MG-12183 [M]	Hot Line	1965	6.25	12.50	25.00
❏ MG-12303	Motivation	197?	3.75	7.50	15.00
SAVOY JAZZ					
❏ SJL-1160	The Hot Line	1986	2.50	5.00	10.00
❏ SJL-1184	Nebulae	1987	2.50	5.00	10.00

BARRON, KENNY
Pianist.

Number	Title	Yr	VG	VG+	NM
BLACK HAWK					
❏ 50601	1 + 1 + 1	1986	3.00	6.00	12.00
CRISS CROSS					
❏ 3008	Geen Chimneys	1983	3.00	6.00	12.00
EASTWIND					
❏ 709	Spiral	1982	3.00	6.00	12.00
LIMETREE					
❏ 20	Landscape	1984	3.00	6.00	12.00
MUSE					
❏ MR-5014	Sunset to Dawn	1973	3.00	6.00	12.00
❏ MR-5044	Peruvian Blue	1974	3.00	6.00	12.00
❏ MR-5080	Lucifer	1975	3.00	6.00	12.00
❏ MR-5220	Golden Lotus	1980	3.00	6.00	12.00

Number	Title	Yr	VG	VG+	NM
WHY NOT					
❏ 25032	Imo Live	1982	3.00	6.00	12.00
WOLF					
❏ 1203	Innocence	1978	3.75	7.50	15.00
XANADU					
❏ 188	Kenny Barron at the Piano	1981	3.00	6.00	12.00

BARRON, KENNY, AND TED DUNBAR
Also see each artist's individual listings.

Number	Title	Yr	VG	VG+	NM
MUSE					
❏ MR-5140	In Tandem	1975	3.00	6.00	12.00

BARTLEY, CHARLENE
Female singer.

Number	Title	Yr	VG	VG+	NM
RCA VICTOR					
❏ LPM-1478 [M]	Weekend of a Private Secretary	1957	12.50	25.00	50.00

BARTZ, GARY
Alto and soprano saxophone player and composer.

Number	Title	Yr	VG	VG+	NM
ARISTA					
❏ AL 4263	Bartz	1979	3.00	6.00	12.00
CAPITOL					
❏ ST-11647	My Sanctuary	1977	3.00	6.00	12.00
❏ SW-11789	Love Affair	1978	3.00	6.00	12.00
CATALYST					
❏ 7610	Ju Ju Man	1976	3.00	6.00	12.00
MILESTONE					
❏ 9006	Libra	1968	5.00	10.00	20.00
❏ 9018	Another Earth	1969	5.00	10.00	20.00
❏ 9027	Home!	1970	5.00	10.00	20.00
❏ 9031	Harlem Bush Music -- Taifa	1971	5.00	10.00	20.00
❏ 9032	Harlem Bush Music -- Uhuru	1972	5.00	10.00	20.00
PRESTIGE					
❏ 10057	Juju St. Songs	197?	3.75	7.50	15.00
❏ 10068	Follow the Medicine Man	197?	3.75	7.50	15.00
❏ 10083	Singerella -- A Ghetto Fairy Tale	197?	3.75	7.50	15.00
❏ 10092	The Shadow 'Do	1975	3.75	7.50	15.00
❏ 66001 [(2)]	I've Known Rivers	197?	5.00	10.00	20.00
VEE JAY					
❏ VJS-3068	Love Song	1977	3.00	6.00	12.00

BASIE, COUNT
Pianist, organist and bandleader. Also see TONY BENNETT; TERESA BREWER; EDDIE DAVIS; ELLA FITZGERALD; ARTHUR PRYSOCK; FRANK SINATRA; SARAH VAUGHAN; JACKIE WILSON.

Number	Title	Yr	VG	VG+	NM
ABC					
❏ 570 [M]	Basie's Swingin' -- Voices Singin'	1966	5.00	10.00	20.00
❏ S-570 [S]	Basie's Swingin' -- Voices Singin'	1966	6.25	12.50	25.00
❏ 4001	16 Great Performances	1974	3.00	6.00	12.00
ABC IMPULSE!					
❏ AS-15 [S]	Count Basie and the Kansas City Seven	1968	3.00	6.00	12.00
❏ IA-9351 [(2)]	Retrospective Sessions	1978	3.00	6.00	12.00
ACCORD					
❏ SN-7183	Command Performance	1981	2.50	5.00	10.00
AMERICAN RECORDING SOCIETY					
❏ G-401 [M]	Count Basie	1956	10.00	20.00	40.00
❏ G-402 [M]	The Band That Swings the Blues	1956	10.00	20.00	40.00
❏ G-422 [M]	Basie's Best	1957	10.00	20.00	40.00
❏ G-435 [M]	Mainstream Jazz Swing	1957	10.00	20.00	40.00
ARCHIVE OF FOLK AND JAZZ					
❏ 318	Savoy Ballroom 1937	197?	2.50	5.00	10.00
BASF					
❏ 25111 [(2)]	Basic Basie	1973	3.75	7.50	15.00
BRIGHT ORANGE					
❏ XBO-702	Count Basie Featuring B.B. King	196?	5.00	10.00	20.00
BRUNSWICK					
❏ BL 54012 [M]	Count Basie	1957	10.00	20.00	40.00
❏ BL 754127	Basie's in the Bag	196?	3.75	7.50	15.00
BULLDOG					
❏ BDL-2020	20 Golden Pieces of Count Basie	198?	2.50	5.00	10.00
CLEF					
❏ MCG-120 [10]	Count Basie and His Orchestra Collates	1953	50.00	100.00	200.00
❏ MCG-146 [10]	Count Basie Sextet	1954	50.00	100.00	200.00
❏ MGC-148 [10]	Count Basie Big Band	1954	50.00	100.00	200.00
❏ MGC-626 [M]	Count Basie Dance Session #1	1954	25.00	50.00	100.00
❏ MGC-633 [M]	Basie Jazz	1954	25.00	50.00	100.00

Number	Title	Yr	VG	VG+	NM
❏ MGC-647 [M]	Count Basie Jazz Session #2	1955	25.00	50.00	100.00
❏ MGC-666 [M]	Basie	1955	25.00	50.00	100.00
❏ MGC-685 [M]	The Count	1956	20.00	40.00	80.00
❏ MGC-706 [M]	The Swinging Count	1956	15.00	30.00	60.00
❏ MGC-722 [M]	The Band of Distinction	1956	15.00	30.00	60.00
❏ MGC-723 [M]	Basie Roars Again	1956	15.00	30.00	60.00
❏ MGC-724 [M]	The King of Swing	1956	15.00	30.00	60.00
❏ MGC-729 [M]	Basie Rides Again!	1956	15.00	30.00	60.00
❏ MGC-749 [M]	Basie in Europe	1956	---	---	---
-- Canceled; released as Verve 8199					
COLISEUM					
❏ 51003	The Happiest Millionaire	1968	3.75	7.50	15.00
COLUMBIA					
❏ CL 754 [M]	Classics	1955	10.00	20.00	40.00
❏ CL 901 [M]	Blues By Basie	1956	10.00	20.00	40.00
❏ CL 997 [M]	One O'Clock Jump	1956	10.00	20.00	40.00
❏ CL 2560 [10]	Basie Bash	1956	20.00	40.00	80.00
❏ CL 6079 [10]	Dance Parade	1949	25.00	50.00	100.00
❏ G 31224 [(2)]	Super Chief	1972	3.75	7.50	15.00
COLUMBIA JAZZ MASTERPIECES					
❏ CJ 40608	The Essential Count Basie, Volume 1	1987	2.50	5.00	10.00
❏ CJ 40835	The Essential Count Basie, Volume 2	1987	2.50	5.00	10.00
❏ CJ 44150	The Essential Count Basie, Volume 3	1988	2.50	5.00	10.00
COLUMBIA JAZZ ODYSSEY					
❏ PC 36824	Blues by Basie	1981	2.00	4.00	8.00
COLUMBIA SPECIAL PRODUCTS					
❏ P 14355	The Count	198?	2.00	4.00	8.00
COMMAND					
❏ 33-905 [M]	Broadway Basie's...Way	1966	3.00	6.00	12.00
❏ SD 905 [S]	Broadway Basie's...Way	1966	3.75	7.50	15.00
❏ 33-912 [M]	Hollywood Basie's Way	1967	3.75	7.50	15.00
❏ SD 912 [S]	Hollywood Basie's Way	1967	3.00	6.00	12.00
❏ CQ-40004 [Q]	Broadway Basie's...Way	1972	5.00	10.00	20.00
DAYBREAK					
❏ 2005	Have a Nice Day	1971	3.00	6.00	12.00
DECCA					
❏ DXB 170 [(2) M]	The Best of Count Basie	196?	6.25	12.50	25.00
❏ DL 5111 [10]	Count Basie at the Piano	1950	25.00	50.00	100.00
❏ DXSB 7170 [(2) R]	The Best of Count Basie	196?	3.75	7.50	15.00
❏ DL 8049 [M]	Count Basie and His Orchestra	1954	12.50	25.00	50.00
❏ DL 78049 [R]	Count Basie and His Orchestra	196?	3.00	6.00	12.00
DOCTOR JAZZ					
❏ FW 39520	Afrique	1985	2.00	4.00	8.00
DOT					
❏ DLP-25902	Straight Ahead	1969	3.75	7.50	15.00
❏ DLP-25938	Standing Ovation	1969	3.75	7.50	15.00
EMARCY					
❏ MG-26023 [10]	Jazz Royalty	1954	17.50	35.00	70.00
EPIC					
❏ LG 1021 [10]	The Old Count and the New Count -- Basie	1954	17.50	35.00	70.00
❏ LN 1117 [10]	Rock the Blues	1955	17.50	35.00	70.00
❏ LN 3107 [M]	Lester Leaps In	1955	12.50	25.00	50.00
-- With Lester Young					
❏ LN 3168 [M]	Let's Go to Prez	1955	12.50	25.00	50.00
-- With Lester Young					
❏ LN 3169 [M]	Basie's Back in Town	1955	12.50	25.00	50.00
FANTASY					
❏ OJC-379	Basie Big Band Montreux '77	1989	2.50	5.00	10.00
-- Reissue of Pablo Live 2308 209					
❏ OJC-449	Kansas City 6	1990	3.00	6.00	12.00
-- Reissue of Pablo 2310 871					
❏ OJC-600	Kansas City 3/For the Second Time	1991	3.00	6.00	12.00
-- Reissue of Pablo 2310 878					
FLYING DUTCHMAN					
❏ FD 10138	Afrique	1972	3.00	6.00	12.00
FORUM					
❏ F-9032 [M]	Kansas City Suite	196?	3.00	6.00	12.00
❏ SF-9032 [S]	Kansas City Suite	196?	3.75	7.50	15.00
-- Reissue of Roulette 52056					
❏ F-9060 [M]	One More Time	196?	3.00	6.00	12.00
❏ SF-9060 [S]	One More Time	196?	3.75	7.50	15.00
-- Reissue of Roulette 52024					
❏ F-9063 [M]	Not Now -- I'll Tell You When	196?	3.00	6.00	12.00
❏ SF-9063 [S]	Not Now -- I'll Tell You When	196?	3.75	7.50	15.00
-- Reissue of Roulette 52044					
GROOVE MERCHANT					
❏ 2001	Evergreens	1972	3.00	6.00	12.00

Number	Title	Yr	VG	VG+	NM
HAPPY TIGER					
❏ 1007	Basie on the Beatles	196?	6.25	12.50	25.00
HARMONY					
❏ HL 7229 [M]	Basie's Best	1960	3.75	7.50	15.00
❏ HS 11371	Just in Time	1970	3.00	6.00	12.00
IMPULSE!					
❏ A-15 [M]	Count Basie and the Kansas City Seven	1962	7.50	15.00	30.00
❏ AS-15 [S]	Count Basie and the Kansas City Seven	1962	10.00	20.00	40.00
INTERMEDIA					
❏ QS-5028	The Deacon	198?	2.50	5.00	10.00
❏ QS-5039	The Classic Count	198?	2.50	5.00	10.00
JAZZ ARCHIVES					
❏ JA-16	The Count at the Chatterbox, 1937	198?	2.50	5.00	10.00
❏ JA-41	At the Famous Door, 1938-1939	198?	2.50	5.00	10.00
JAZZ MAN					
❏ 5006	Ain't It the Truth	198?	2.50	5.00	10.00
JAZZ PANORAMA					
❏ 1803 [10]	Count Basie and Lester Young	1951	25.00	50.00	100.00
MCA					
❏ 718	16 Greatest Performances	198?	2.00	4.00	8.00
❏ 4050 [(2)]	The Best of Count Basie	197?	3.00	6.00	12.00
❏ 4108 [(2)]	Good Morning Blues	197?	3.00	6.00	12.00
❏ 4130 [(2)]	Retrospective Sessions	198?	2.50	5.00	10.00
❏ 4163 [(2)]	Showtime	198?	2.50	5.00	10.00
❏ 29003	Count Basie and the Kansas City Seven	198?	2.00	4.00	8.00
❏ 29004	Straight Ahead	198?	2.00	4.00	8.00
❏ 29005	Standing Ovation	198?	2.00	4.00	8.00
❏ 42324	One O'Clock Jump	1990	3.00	6.00	12.00
MCA/IMPULSE!					
❏ 5656	Count Basie and the Kansas City Seven	1986	2.00	4.00	8.00
MERCURY					
❏ MG-25105 [10]	Count Basie and His Kansas City Seven	1952	25.00	50.00	100.00
❏ MGC-120 [10]	Count Basie and His Orchestra Collates	1952	55.00	110.00	220.00
METRO					
❏ M-516 [M]	Count Basie	1965	3.75	7.50	15.00
❏ MS-516 [S]	Count Basie	1965	3.00	6.00	12.00
MGM					
❏ GAS-126	Count Basie (Golden Archive Series)	1970	3.75	7.50	15.00
MOBILE FIDELITY					
❏ 1-129	Basie Plays Hefti	1985	20.00	40.00	80.00
-- Audiophile vinyl					
❏ 1-237	April in Paris	1995	10.00	20.00	40.00
-- Audiophile vinyl					
MOSAIC					
❏ MR12-135 [(12)]	The Complete Roulette Live Recordings of Count Basie and His Orchestra	199?	50.00	100.00	200.00
❏ M15Q-149 [(15)]	The Complete Roulette Studio Recordings of Count Basie and His Orchestra	199?	50.00	100.00	200.00
PABLO					
❏ 2310 709	The Bosses	1974	3.00	6.00	12.00
❏ 2310 712	Trio	1974	3.00	6.00	12.00
❏ 2310 718	Basie Jam	1975	3.00	6.00	12.00
❏ 2310 745	Basie and Zoot	1976	3.00	6.00	12.00
❏ 2310 750	Basie Jam/Montreux '75	1976	3.00	6.00	12.00
❏ 2310 756	Basie Big Band	1975	3.00	6.00	12.00
❏ 2310 767	I Told You So	1976	3.00	6.00	12.00
❏ 2310 786	Basie Jam #2	1977	3.00	6.00	12.00
❏ 2310 797	Prime Time	1977	3.00	6.00	12.00
❏ 2310 840	Basie Jam #3	1979	2.50	5.00	10.00
❏ 2310 852	The Best of Basie	1980	2.50	5.00	10.00
❏ 2310 859	Kansas City Shout	1980	3.00	6.00	12.00
-- With Joe Turner and Eddie "Cleanhead" Vinson					
❏ 2310 871	Kansas City 6	198?	2.50	5.00	10.00
❏ 2310 874	Farmers Market Barbecue	1982	2.50	5.00	10.00
❏ 2310 891	Me & You	1983	2.50	5.00	10.00
❏ 2310 901	88 Basie Street	1987	2.50	5.00	10.00
❏ 2310 919	Mostly Blues...And Some Others	1987	2.50	5.00	10.00
❏ 2310 920	Fancy Pants	1987	2.50	5.00	10.00
❏ 2310 924	Count Basie Get Together	1987	2.50	5.00	10.00
❏ 2310 925	Basie and His Friends	1988	2.50	5.00	10.00
❏ 2405 408	The Best of the Count Basie Band	198?	2.50	5.00	10.00
PABLO LIVE					
❏ 2308 207	Basie Big Band Montreux '77	1977	3.00	6.00	12.00
❏ 2308 209	Basie Jam/Montreux '77	1977	3.00	6.00	12.00
❏ 2308 246	Live in Japan, 1978	198?	2.50	5.00	10.00
PABLO TODAY					
❏ 2312 112	On the Road	1980	2.50	5.00	10.00
❏ 2312 126	Kansas City 5	198?	2.50	5.00	10.00
❏ 2312 131	Warm Breeze	198?	2.50	5.00	10.00
PAIR					
❏ PDL2-1045 [(2)]	Basic Basie	1986	3.00	6.00	12.00
PAUSA					
❏ 7105	High Voltage	198?	2.50	5.00	10.00
PICKWICK					
❏ PC-3028 [M]	His Hits of the 60's	196?	3.75	7.50	15.00
❏ SPC-3028 [S]	His Hits of the 60's	196?	3.00	6.00	12.00
❏ SPC-3500	Everything's Coming Up Roses	197?	2.50	5.00	10.00
PRESTIGE					
❏ 24109 [(2)]	Reunions	197?	3.00	6.00	12.00
QUINTESSENCE					
❏ 25151	Everything's Coming Up Roses	197?	2.50	5.00	10.00
RCA CAMDEN					
❏ CAL-395 [M]	The Count	1958	6.25	12.50	25.00
❏ CAL-497 [M]	Basie's Basement	1959	6.25	12.50	25.00
❏ CAL-514 [M]	Count Basie in Kansas City	1959	6.25	12.50	25.00
RCA VICTOR					
❏ LPV-514 [M]	Count Basie in Kansas City	196?	3.75	7.50	15.00
❏ LPM-1112 [M]	Count Basie	1955	12.50	25.00	50.00
❏ AFM1-5180	Kansas City Style	1985	2.50	5.00	10.00
REPRISE					
❏ R-6070 [M]	This Time by Basie! Hits of the 50's and 60's	1963	5.00	10.00	20.00
❏ R9-6070 [S]	This Time by Basie! Hits of the 50's and 60's	1963	6.25	12.50	25.00
❏ R-6153 [M]	Pop Goes the Basie	1965	3.75	7.50	15.00
❏ RS-6153 [S]	Pop Goes the Basie	1965	5.00	10.00	20.00
ROULETTE					
❏ RB-1 [(2) M]	The Count Basie Story	1960	10.00	20.00	40.00
❏ SRB-1 [(2) S]	The Count Basie Story	1960	12.50	25.00	50.00
❏ RE-102 [(2)]	Echoes of an Era (The Count Basie Years)	1971	3.75	7.50	15.00
❏ RE-107 [(2)]	Echoes of an Era (The Vocal Years)	1971	3.75	7.50	15.00
❏ RE-118 [(2)]	The Best of Count Basie	1971	3.75	7.50	15.00
❏ RE-124 [(2)]	Kansas City Suite/Easin' It	1973	3.75	7.50	15.00
❏ SR 42009	Fantail	1968	3.75	7.50	15.00
❏ SR 42015	The Kid from Red Bank	1968	3.75	7.50	15.00
❏ R 52003 [M]	Basie	1958	7.50	15.00	30.00
❏ SR 52003 [S]	Basie	1958	7.50	15.00	30.00
-- Black vinyl					
❏ SR 52003 [S]	Basie	1958	25.00	50.00	100.00
-- Red vinyl					
❏ R 52011 [M]	Basie Plays Hefti	1958	7.50	15.00	30.00
❏ SR 52011 [S]	Basie Plays Hefti	1958	7.50	15.00	30.00
❏ R 52024 [M]	One More Time	1959	7.50	15.00	30.00
❏ SR 52024 [S]	One More Time	1959	7.50	15.00	30.00
❏ R 52028 [M]	Breakfast, Dance & Barbeque	1959	7.50	15.00	30.00
❏ SR 52028 [S]	Breakfast, Dance & Barbeque	1959	7.50	15.00	30.00
❏ R 52032 [M]	Chairman of the Board	1959	7.50	15.00	30.00
❏ SR 52032 [S]	Chairman of the Board	1959	7.50	15.00	30.00
❏ R 52036 [M]	Dance Along with Basie	1959	7.50	15.00	30.00
❏ SR 52036 [S]	Dance Along with Basie	1959	7.50	15.00	30.00
❏ R 52044 [M]	Not Now -- I'll Tell You When	1960	6.25	12.50	25.00
❏ SR 52044 [S]	Not Now -- I'll Tell You When	1960	7.50	15.00	30.00
❏ R 52051 [M]	String Along with Basie	1960	6.25	12.50	25.00
❏ SR 52051 [S]	String Along with Basie	1960	7.50	15.00	30.00
❏ R 52056 [M]	Benny Carter's Kansas City Suite	1960	6.25	12.50	25.00
❏ SR 52056 [S]	Benny Carter's Kansas City Suite	1960	7.50	15.00	30.00
❏ R 52065 [M]	Basie at Birdland	1961	6.25	12.50	25.00
❏ SR 52065 [S]	Basie at Birdland	1961	7.50	15.00	30.00
❏ R 52081 [M]	The Best of Basie	1962	3.75	7.50	15.00
❏ SR 52081 [S]	The Best of Basie	1962	5.00	10.00	20.00
❏ R 52086 [M]	The Legend	1962	5.00	10.00	20.00
❏ SR 52086 [S]	The Legend	1962	6.25	12.50	25.00
❏ R 52089 [M]	The Best of Basie, Volume 2	1962	3.75	7.50	15.00
❏ SR 52089 [S]	The Best of Basie, Volume 2	1962	5.00	10.00	20.00
❏ R 52099 [M]	Count Basie in Sweden	1963	5.00	10.00	20.00
❏ SR 52099 [S]	Count Basie in Sweden	1963	6.25	12.50	25.00
❏ R 52106 [M]	Easin' It	1963	5.00	10.00	20.00
❏ SR 52106 [S]	Easin' It	1963	6.25	12.50	25.00
❏ R 52111 [(2) M]	The World of Count Basie	1964	10.00	20.00	40.00
❏ SR 52111 [(2) S]	The World of Count Basie	1964	12.50	25.00	50.00
❏ R 52113 [M]	Back with Basie	1964	5.00	10.00	20.00
❏ SR 52113 [S]	Back with Basie	1964	6.25	12.50	25.00
SOLID STATE					
❏ 18032	Basie Meets Bond	1968	3.75	7.50	15.00
-- Reissue of United Artists LP					

Number	Title	Yr	VG	VG+	NM
UNITED ARTISTS					
❑ UAL-3480 [M]	Basie Meets Bond	1966	6.25	12.50	25.00
❑ UAS-6480 [S]	Basie Meets Bond	1966	7.50	15.00	30.00
UPFRONT					
❑ UPF-142	Count Basie and His Orchestra	1969	3.00	6.00	12.00
VEE JAY					
❑ VJS-3054	I Got Rhythm	198?	3.00	6.00	12.00
VERVE					
❑ VSP-12 [M]	Inside Basie, Outside	1966	3.75	7.50	15.00
❑ VSPS-12 [S]	Inside Basie, Outside	1966	5.00	10.00	20.00
❑ VE-2-2517 [(2)]	16 Men Swinging	197?	3.00	6.00	12.00
❑ VE-2-2542 [(2)]	Paradise Squat	197?	3.00	6.00	12.00
❑ UMV-1-2619	Count Basie at Newport	198?	2.50	5.00	10.00
❑ UMV-1-2641	April in Paris	198?	2.50	5.00	10.00
❑ MGVS-6024 [S]	Count Basie at Newport	1960	12.50	25.00	50.00
❑ MGV-8012 [M]	April in Paris	1957	12.50	25.00	50.00
❑ V-8012 [M]	April in Paris	1961	5.00	10.00	20.00
❑ MGV-8018 [M]	Basie Roars Again	1957	12.50	25.00	50.00
-- Reissue of Clef 723					
❑ V-8018 [M]	Basie Roars Again	1961	5.00	10.00	20.00
❑ MGV-8070 [M]	The Count	1957	12.50	25.00	50.00
-- Reissue of Clef 120					
❑ V-8070 [M]	The Count	1961	5.00	10.00	20.00
❑ MGV-8090 [M]	The Swinging Count!	1957	12.50	25.00	50.00
-- Reissue of Clef 706					
❑ V-8090 [M]	The Swinging Count!	1961	5.00	10.00	20.00
❑ MGV-8103 [M]	The Band of Distinction	1957	12.50	25.00	50.00
-- Reissue of Clef 722					
❑ V-8103 [M]	The Band of Distinction	1961	5.00	10.00	20.00
❑ MGV-8104 [M]	The King of Swing	1957	12.50	25.00	50.00
❑ V-8104 [M]	The King of Swing	1961	5.00	10.00	20.00
--Reissue of Clef 724					
❑ MGV-8108 [M]	Basie Rides Again!	1957	12.50	25.00	50.00
-- Reissue of Clef 729					
❑ V-8108 [M]	Basie Rides Again!	1961	5.00	10.00	20.00
❑ MGV-8199 [M]	Basie in London	1957	12.50	25.00	50.00
❑ V-8199 [M]	Basie in London	1961	5.00	10.00	20.00
❑ MGV-8243 [M]	Count Basie at Newport	1958	12.50	25.00	50.00
❑ V-8243 [M]	Count Basie at Newport	1961	5.00	10.00	20.00
❑ V6-8243 [S]	Count Basie at Newport	1961	5.00	10.00	20.00
❑ MGV-8291 [M]	Hall of Fame	1958	12.50	25.00	50.00
❑ V-8291 [M]	Hall of Fame	1961	5.00	10.00	20.00
❑ V-8407 [M]	The Essential Count Basie	1961	3.75	7.50	15.00
❑ V6-8407 [S]	The Essential Count Basie	1961	5.00	10.00	20.00
❑ V-8511 [M]	On My Way and Shoutin' Again!	1963	3.75	7.50	15.00
❑ V6-8511 [S]	On My Way and Shoutin' Again!	1963	5.00	10.00	20.00
❑ V-8549 [M]	Li'l Ol' Groovemaker…Basie!	1963	3.75	7.50	15.00
❑ V6-8549 [S]	Li'l Ol' Groovemaker…Basie!	1963	5.00	10.00	20.00
❑ V-8563 [M]	More Hits of the 50's and 60's	1963	3.75	7.50	15.00
❑ V6-8563 [S]	More Hits of the 50's and 60's	1963	5.00	10.00	20.00
❑ V-8596 [M]	Verve's Choice -- Best of Count Basie	1964	3.75	7.50	15.00
❑ V6-8596 [S]	Verve's Choice -- Best of Count Basie	1964	5.00	10.00	20.00
❑ V-8597 [M]	Basie Land	1964	3.75	7.50	15.00
❑ V6-8597 [S]	Basie Land	1964	5.00	10.00	20.00
❑ V-8616 [M]	Basie Picks the Winners	1965	3.75	7.50	15.00
❑ V6-8616 [S]	Basie Picks the Winners	1965	5.00	10.00	20.00
❑ V-8659 [M]	Basie's Beatle Bag	1966	7.50	15.00	30.00
❑ V6-8659 [S]	Basie's Beatle Bag	1966	10.00	20.00	40.00
❑ V-8687 [M]	Basie's Beat	1967	5.00	10.00	20.00
❑ V6-8687 [S]	Basie's Beat	1967	3.75	7.50	15.00
❑ V6-8783	Basie	1969	3.75	7.50	15.00
❑ V6-8831	The Newport Years	1973	3.00	6.00	12.00
❑ 821 291-1	Basic Basie	198?	2.50	5.00	10.00
❑ 825 194-1	High Voltage (Basic Basie Vol. 2)	198?	2.50	5.00	10.00

BASIE, COUNT, AND SAMMY DAVIS, JR.
Also see each artist's individual listings.

Number	Title	Yr	VG	VG+	NM
VERVE					
❑ V-8605 [M]	Our Shining Hour	1965	3.75	7.50	15.00
❑ V6-8605 [S]	Our Shining Hour	1965	5.00	10.00	20.00

BASIE, COUNT, AND BILLY ECKSTINE
Also see each artist's individual listings.

Number	Title	Yr	VG	VG+	NM
ROULETTE					
❑ SR 42017	Count Basie and Billy Eckstine	1968	3.75	7.50	15.00
-- Reissue					
❑ R 52029 [M]	Basie/Eckstine, Incorporated	1959	6.25	12.50	25.00
❑ SR 52029 [S]	Basie/Eckstine, Incorporated	1959	7.50	15.00	30.00

BASIE, COUNT, AND DUKE ELLINGTON
Also see each artist's individual listings.

Number	Title	Yr	VG	VG+	NM
ACCORD					
❑ SN-7200	Heads of State	1982	2.50	5.00	10.00

BASIE, COUNT, AND MAYNARD FERGUSON
Also see each artist's individual listings.

Number	Title	Yr	VG	VG+	NM
ROULETTE					
❑ R 52117 [M]	Big Band Scene '65	1965	5.00	10.00	20.00
❑ SR 52117 [S]	Big Band Scene '65	1965	6.25	12.50	25.00

BASIE, COUNT, AND DIZZY GILLESPIE
Also see each artist's individual listings.

Number	Title	Yr	VG	VG+	NM
PABLO					
❑ 2310 833	The Gifted Ones	1979	2.50	5.00	10.00
VERVE					
❑ V-8560 [M]	The Count Basie Band and the Dizzy Gillespie Band at Newport	1963	5.00	10.00	20.00
❑ V6-8560 [S]	The Count Basie Band and the Dizzy Gillespie Band at Newport	1963	6.25	12.50	25.00

BASIE, COUNT, AND THE MILLS BROTHERS
The Mills Brothers, a male vocal group, are not included in this book by themselves. Also see LOUIS ARMSTRONG AND THE MILLS BROTHERS; COUNT BASIE.

Number	Title	Yr	VG	VG+	NM
DOT					
❑ DLP-25838	The Board of Directors	1968	3.75	7.50	15.00

BASIE, COUNT, AND OSCAR PETERSON
Also see each artist's individual listings.

Number	Title	Yr	VG	VG+	NM
PABLO					
❑ 2310 722	"Satch" and "Josh"	1975	3.00	6.00	12.00
❑ 2310 802	Satch and Josh Again	1978	2.50	5.00	10.00
❑ 2310 843	Night Rider	1979	2.50	5.00	10.00
❑ 2310 896	The Timekeepers	198?	3.00	6.00	12.00
❑ 2310 923	Yessir, That's My Baby	1987	2.50	5.00	10.00

BASIE, COUNT, AND JOE WILLIAMS
Also see each artist's individual listings.

Number	Title	Yr	VG	VG+	NM
CLEF					
❑ MGC-678 [M]	Count Basie Swings/Joe Williams Sings	1955	12.50	25.00	50.00
ROULETTE					
❑ R 52021 [M]	Memories Ad Lib	1959	7.50	15.00	30.00
❑ SR 52021 [S]	Memories Ad Lib	1959	10.00	20.00	40.00
❑ R 52033 [M]	Everyday I Have the Blues	1959	7.50	15.00	30.00
❑ SR 52033 [S]	Everyday I Have the Blues	1959	10.00	20.00	40.00
❑ R 52054 [M]	Just the Blues	1960	7.50	15.00	30.00
❑ SR 52054 [S]	Just the Blues	1960	10.00	20.00	40.00
❑ R 52093 [M]	Back to Basie and Blues	1963	6.25	12.50	25.00
❑ SR 52093 [S]	Back to Basie and Blues	1963	7.50	15.00	30.00
VANGUARD					
❑ VRS-8508 [M]	A Night at Count Basie's	1955	12.50	25.00	50.00
VERVE					
❑ MGV-2016 [M]	The Greatest! Count Basie Swings/Joe Williams Sings Standards	1956	12.50	25.00	50.00
❑ UMV-1-2650	The Greatest	198?	2.50	5.00	10.00
❑ MGVS-6006 [S]	The Greatest! Count Basie Swings/Joe Williams Sings Standards	1960	10.00	20.00	40.00
❑ MGV-8063 [M]	Count Basie Swings/Joe Williams Sings	1957	10.00	20.00	40.00
-- Reissue of Clef 678					
❑ V-8488 [M]	Count Basie Swings/Joe Williams Sings	1962	6.25	12.50	25.00
-- Reissue of 8063					
❑ V6-8488 [R]	Count Basie Swings/Joe Williams Sings	1962	3.00	6.00	12.00

BASIE, COUNT; JOE WILLIAMS; LAMBERT, HENDRICKS AND ROSS
Also see each artist's individual listings.

Number	Title	Yr	VG	VG+	NM
ROULETTE					
❑ R 52018 [M]	Sing Along with Basie	1959	5.00	10.00	20.00
❑ SR 52018 [S]	Sing Along with Basie	1959	6.25	12.50	25.00

BASIN STREET SIX, THE
New Orleans Dixieland band that served to introduce PETE FOUNTAIN.

Number	Title	Yr	VG	VG+	NM
CIRCLE					
❑ L-403 [10]	Dixieland from New Orleans	1951	12.50	25.00	50.00
EMARCY					
❑ MG-26012 [10]	The Basin Street Six	1954	12.50	25.00	50.00
MERCURY					
❑ MG-20151 [M]	Strictly Dixie	195?	10.00	20.00	40.00
❑ MG-25111 [10]	The Basin Street Six	1951	12.50	25.00	50.00

Number	Title	Yr	VG	VG+	NM

BASS, MARTHA AND FONTELLA
Female singers. Fontella Bass also appeared with ART ENSEMBLE OF CHICAGO.
SOUL NOTE

Number	Title	Yr	VG	VG+	NM
❏ SN-1006	From the Root to the Source	197?	3.00	6.00	12.00

BASSO-VALDAMBRINI OCTET, THE
VERVE

Number	Title	Yr	VG	VG+	NM
❏ MGVS-6152 [S]	The New Sound from Italy	1960	10.00	20.00	40.00
❏ MGV-20009 [M]	Jazz Festival, Milan	1960	10.00	20.00	40.00
❏ V-20009 [M]	Jazz Festival, Milan	1961	5.00	10.00	20.00
❏ MGV-20011 [M]	The New Sound from Italy	1960	10.00	20.00	40.00
❏ V-20011 [M]	The New Sound from Italy	1961	5.00	10.00	20.00
❏ V6-20011 [S]	The New Sound from Italy	1961	5.00	10.00	20.00

BAUDUC, RAY, AND NAPPY LAMARE
Ray Bauduc is a drummer, male singer and bandleader; Nappy LaMare is a guitarist and male singer.
CAPITOL

Number	Title	Yr	VG	VG+	NM
❏ T 877 [M]	Riverboat Dandies	1957	10.00	20.00	40.00

MERCURY

Number	Title	Yr	VG	VG+	NM
❏ MG-205?? [M]	On a Swinging Date	1960	7.50	15.00	30.00
❏ SR-60186 [S]	On a Swinging Date	1960	6.25	12.50	25.00

BAUER, BILLY
Guitarist.
AD LIB

Number	Title	Yr	VG	VG+	NM
❏ AAL-5501 [10]	Let's Have a Session	1955	50.00	100.00	200.00

INTERPLAY

Number	Title	Yr	VG	VG+	NM
❏ IP-8603	Anthology	198?	3.00	6.00	12.00

NORGRAN

Number	Title	Yr	VG	VG+	NM
❏ MGN-1082 [M]	Billy Bauer Plectrist	1956	20.00	40.00	80.00

VERVE

Number	Title	Yr	VG	VG+	NM
❏ MGV-8172 [M]	Billy Bauer Plectrist	1957	12.50	25.00	50.00
❏ V-8172 [M]	Billy Bauer Plectrist	1961	5.00	10.00	20.00

BAY CITY JAZZ BAND, THE
San Francisco-based group. Those who appear on both albums are Sanford Newbauer, Everett Farey, Walt Yost, Roy Giomi, Don Keeler and Lloyd Byassee.
GOOD TIME JAZZ

Number	Title	Yr	VG	VG+	NM
❏ S-10053 [S]	Golden Days	196?	3.75	7.50	15.00
❏ L-12017 [M]	The Bay City Jazz Band	1955	7.50	15.00	30.00
❏ L-12053 [M]	Golden Days	1957	7.50	15.00	30.00

BAYARD, EDDIE, AND THE NEW ORLEANS CLASSIC JAZZ ORCHESTRA
Cornet player and bandleader.
STOMP OFF

Number	Title	Yr	VG	VG+	NM
❏ SOS-1145	The Owls' Hoot	1987	3.00	6.00	12.00

BAYETE
Also see TODD COCHRAN.
PRESTIGE

Number	Title	Yr	VG	VG+	NM
❏ 10045	Worlds Around the Sun	1972	7.50	15.00	30.00
❏ 10062	Seeking Other Beauty	1973	7.50	15.00	30.00

BEAL, JEFF
Trumpeter and composer.
ANTILLES

Number	Title	Yr	VG	VG+	NM
❏ 90???	Liberation	1987	2.50	5.00	10.00
❏ 91237	Perpetual Motion	1989	2.50	5.00	10.00

BEAN, BILLY
Guitarist. Also see JOHNNY PISANO AND BILLY BEAN.
RIVERSIDE

Number	Title	Yr	VG	VG+	NM
❏ RLP-380 [M]	The Trio	1961	10.00	20.00	40.00
❏ RS-9380 [S]	The Trio	1961	12.50	25.00	50.00

BECHET, SIDNEY
Soprano saxophone player and sometimes clarinetist. Also see ALBERT NICHOLAS.
ARCHIVE OF FOLK AND JAZZ

Number	Title	Yr	VG	VG+	NM
❏ 228	Sidney Bechet with Guest Artist Lionel Hampton	1969	3.00	6.00	12.00
❏ 323	Sidney Bechet Volume 2	197?	3.00	6.00	12.00

ATLANTIC

Number	Title	Yr	VG	VG+	NM
❏ ALS-118 [10]	Sidney Bechet Solos	1952	30.00	60.00	120.00
❏ 1206 [M]	Sidney Bechet Duets	1956	20.00	40.00	80.00

-- With Muggsy Spanier
BLUE NOTE

Number	Title	Yr	VG	VG+	NM
❏ BLP-1201 [M]	Jazz Classics, Volume 1	1955	37.50	75.00	150.00

-- "Deep groove" version (deep indentation under label on both sides)

Number	Title	Yr	VG	VG+	NM
❏ BLP-1201 [M]	Jazz Classics, Volume 1	1955	25.00	50.00	100.00
-- Regular edition, Lexington Ave. address on label					
❏ BLP-1202 [M]	Jazz Classics, Volume 2	1955	37.50	75.00	150.00
-- "Deep groove" version (deep indentation under label on both sides)					
❏ BLP-1202 [M]	Jazz Classics, Volume 2	1955	25.00	50.00	100.00
-- Regular edition, Lexington Ave. address on label					
❏ BLP-1203 [M]	Giant of Jazz, Volume 1	1955	37.50	75.00	150.00
-- "Deep groove" version (deep indentation under label on both sides)					
❏ BLP-1203 [M]	Giant of Jazz, Volume 1	1955	25.00	50.00	100.00
-- Regular edition, Lexington Ave. address on label					
❏ BLP-1204 [M]	Giant of Jazz, Volume 2	1955	37.50	75.00	150.00
-- "Deep groove" version (deep indentation under label on both sides)					
❏ BLP-1204 [M]	Giant of Jazz, Volume 2	1955	25.00	50.00	100.00
-- Regular edition, Lexington Ave. address on label					
❏ BLP-1207 [M]	The Fabulous Sidney Bechet	1956	30.00	60.00	120.00
-- "Deep groove" version (deep indentation under label on both sides)					
❏ BLP-1207 [M]	The Fabulous Sidney Bechet	1956	20.00	40.00	80.00
-- Regular edition, Lexington Ave. address on label					
❏ BLP-7001 [10]	Sidney Bechet's Blue Note Jazz Men	1950	100.00	200.00	400.00
❏ BLP-7002 [10]	Jazz Classics, Volume 1	1950	62.50	125.00	250.00
❏ BLP-7003 [10]	Jazz Classics, Volume 2	1950	62.50	125.00	250.00
❏ BLP-7008 [10]	Days Beyond Recall	1951	62.50	125.00	250.00
❏ BLP-7009 [10]	Sidney Bechet with the Blue Note Jazz Men	1951	62.50	125.00	250.00
❏ BLP-7014 [10]	Sidney Bechet's Blue Note Jazz Men, Volume 2	1951	62.50	125.00	250.00
❏ BLP-7020 [10]	The Fabulous Sidney Bechet and His Hot Six	1952	62.50	125.00	250.00
❏ BLP-7022 [10]	The Port of Harlem Six	1952	62.50	125.00	250.00
❏ BLP-7024 [10]	Jazz Festival Concert, Paris 1952 -- Volume 1	1953	62.50	125.00	250.00
❏ BLP-7025 [10]	Jazz Festival Concert, Paris 1952 -- Volume 2	1953	62.50	125.00	250.00
❏ BLP-7026 [10]	Dixie by the Fabulous Sidney Bechet	1953	62.50	125.00	250.00
❏ BLP-7029 [10]	Olympia Concert, Paris 1954 -- Volume 1	1954	62.50	125.00	250.00
❏ BLP-7030 [10]	Olympia Concert, Paris 1954 -- Volume 2	1954	62.50	125.00	250.00
❏ BST-81201 [R]	Jazz Classics, Volume 1	1968	3.00	6.00	12.00
-- With "A Division of Liberty Records" on label					
❏ BST-81202 [R]	Jazz Classics, Volume 2	1968	3.00	6.00	12.00
-- With "A Division of Liberty Records" on label					
❏ BST-81203 [R]	Giant of Jazz, Volume 1	1968	3.00	6.00	12.00
-- With "A Division of Liberty Records" on label					
❏ BST-81204 [R]	Giant of Jazz, Volume 2	1968	3.00	6.00	12.00
-- With "A Division of Liberty Records" on label					
❏ BST-81207 [R]	The Fabulous Sidney Bechet	1968	3.00	6.00	12.00
-- With "A Division of Liberty Records" on label					

BLUEBIRD

Number	Title	Yr	VG	VG+	NM
❏ AXM2-5516 [(2)]	Master Musician	197?	3.75	7.50	15.00

BRUNSWICK

Number	Title	Yr	VG	VG+	NM
❏ BL 54037 [M]	Sidney Bechet in Paris	1958	12.50	25.00	50.00
❏ BL 54048 [M]	The Sidney Bechet Story	1959	10.00	20.00	40.00

COLUMBIA

Number	Title	Yr	VG	VG+	NM
❏ CL 836 [M]	Grand Master of the Soprano Sax and Clarinet	1956	12.50	25.00	50.00
-- Red and black label with six "eye" logos					
❏ CL 1410 [M]	Sidney Bechet In Concert at the Brussels Fair	1960	7.50	15.00	30.00
-- Red and black label with six "eye" logos					

COMMODORE

Number	Title	Yr	VG	VG+	NM
❏ FL-20020 [10]	New Orleans Style, Old and New	1952	30.00	60.00	120.00

DIAL

Number	Title	Yr	VG	VG+	NM
❏ LP-301 [10]	Black Stick	195?	75.00	150.00	300.00
❏ LP-302 [10]	Sidney Bechet with Wally Bishop's Orchestra	195?	75.00	150.00	300.00

GNP CRESCENDO

Number	Title	Yr	VG	VG+	NM
❏ GNP-9012	Sidney Bechet	197?	3.00	6.00	12.00
❏ GNP-9037	The Legendary Sidney Bechet	197?	3.00	6.00	12.00

GOOD TIME JAZZ

Number	Title	Yr	VG	VG+	NM
❏ L-12013 [M]	King of the Soprano Saxophone	1955	12.50	25.00	50.00

JAZZ PANORAMA

Number	Title	Yr	VG	VG+	NM
❏ 1801 [10]	Sidney Bechet, Vol. 1	1951	25.00	50.00	100.00
❏ 1809 [10]	Sidney Bechet, Vol. 2	1951	25.00	50.00	100.00

JAZZOLOGY

Number	Title	Yr	VG	VG+	NM
❏ 35	The Genius	197?	3.00	6.00	12.00

JOLLY ROGER

Number	Title	Yr	VG	VG+	NM
❏ 5028 [10]	Sidney Bechet	1954	12.50	25.00	50.00

LONDON

Number	Title	Yr	VG	VG+	NM
❏ WV 91050 [10]	La Nuit Est Une Sorciere	1955	15.00	30.00	60.00

MCA

Number	Title	Yr	VG	VG+	NM
❏ 1330	Blackstick	198?	2.50	5.00	10.00

Number	Title	Yr	VG	VG+	NM
MOSAIC					
❑ MR6-110 [(6)]	The Complete Blue Note Recordings of Sidney Bechet	199?	25.00	50.00	100.00
RCA VICTOR					
❑ LPT-22 [10]	Sidney Bechet	1951	37.50	75.00	150.00
❑ LPT-31 [10]	Treasury of Immortal	1951	37.50	75.00	150.00
❑ LPV-510 [M]	Bechet of New Orleans	1965	5.00	10.00	20.00
❑ LPV-535 [M]	Blue Bechet	1966	5.00	10.00	20.00
REPRISE					
❑ R-6076 [M]	The Immortal Sidney Bechet	1963	6.25	12.50	25.00
❑ R9-6076 [R]	The Immortal Sidney Bechet	1963	5.00	10.00	20.00
RIVERSIDE					
❑ RLP-2516 [10]	Sidney Bechet and His Soprano	1955	62.50	125.00	250.00
RONDO-LETTE					
❑ A 24 [M]	Jam Session Vintage 1946	1953	7.50	15.00	30.00
SAVOY					
❑ MG-15013 [10]	Sidney Bechet	1952	50.00	100.00	200.00
STINSON					
❑ 46 [R]	Haitian Moods	196?	3.00	6.00	12.00
STORYVILLE					
❑ 4028	Sessions	198?	2.50	5.00	10.00
❑ STLP-301 [10]	Sidney Bechet at Storyville, Vol. 1	1954	50.00	100.00	200.00
❑ STLP-306 [10]	Sidney Bechet at Storyville, Vol. 2	1954	50.00	100.00	200.00
❑ STLP-902 [M]	Sidney Bechet at Storyville	1955	12.50	25.00	50.00
"X"					
❑ LVA-3024 [10]	Sidney Bechet and the New Orleans Feetwarmers	1954	25.00	50.00	100.00

BECHET, SIDNEY, AND EDDIE CONDON
Also see each artist's individual listings.

Number	Title	Yr	VG	VG+	NM
SAVOY					
❑ MG-12208 [M]	We Dig Dixieland	196?	5.00	10.00	20.00

BECHET, SIDNEY, AND BUNK JOHNSON
Also see each artist's individual listings.

Number	Title	Yr	VG	VG+	NM
JAZZ ARCHIVES					
❑ JA-48	Bechet, Bunk and Boston 1945	198?	2.50	5.00	10.00

BECHET, SIDNEY, AND WINGY MANONE
Also see each artist's individual listings.

Number	Title	Yr	VG	VG+	NM
JAZZ ARCHIVES					
❑ JA-29	Together at Town Hall, 1947	198?	2.50	5.00	10.00

BECHET, SIDNEY, AND MARTY MARSALA
Marty Marsala is a trumpeter. Also see SIDNEY BECHET.

Number	Title	Yr	VG	VG+	NM
JAZZ ARCHIVES					
❑ JA-44	Jazz from California	198?	2.50	5.00	10.00

BECHET, SIDNEY, AND MEZZ MEZZROW
Also see each artist's individual listings.

Number	Title	Yr	VG	VG+	NM
CLASSIC JAZZ					
❑ 28 [(2)]	Sidney Bechet and Mezz Mezzrow	198?	3.00	6.00	12.00
JAZZ ARCHIVES					
❑ JA-39	Really the Blues Concert	198?	2.50	5.00	10.00

BECHET, SIDNEY/OMER SIMEON
Also see each artist's individual listings.

Number	Title	Yr	VG	VG+	NM
JAZZTONE					
❑ J-1213 [M]	Jazz A La Creole	1955	10.00	20.00	40.00

BECHET, SIDNEY, AND MARTIAL SOLAL
Also see each artist's individual listings.

Number	Title	Yr	VG	VG+	NM
WORLD PACIFIC					
❑ PJ-1236 [M]	Young Ideas	1957	20.00	40.00	80.00
❑ WP-1236 [M]	Young Ideas	1957	12.50	25.00	50.00
-- Reissue with new prefix					

BECHET, SIDNEY, AND BOB WILBER
Also see each artist's individual listings.

Number	Title	Yr	VG	VG+	NM
COMMODORE					
❑ 15774	New Orleans Style Old and New	198?	2.50	5.00	10.00

BECK, JOE
Electric guitarist. DAVID SANBORN was in his band on the Kudu album, before the latter became famous; when reissued in 1979, both artists were credited equally.

Number	Title	Yr	VG	VG+	NM
CTI					
❑ 8002	Beck & Sanborn	1979	2.50	5.00	10.00
-- Reissue of Kudu 21 with new title					

Number	Title	Yr	VG	VG+	NM
CTI/CBS ASSOCIATED					
❑ FZ 40805	Beck & Sanborn	1987	2.50	5.00	10.00
KUDU					
❑ 21	Beck	1975	3.00	6.00	12.00
POLYDOR					
❑ PD-1-6092	Watch the Time	1976	2.50	5.00	10.00

BECK, PIA
Pianist and female singer.

Number	Title	Yr	VG	VG+	NM
EPIC					
❑ LN 3269 [M]	Dutch Treat	1956	10.00	20.00	40.00

BEE, DAVID
Alto saxophone player.

Number	Title	Yr	VG	VG+	NM
BALLY					
❑ BAL-12005 [M]	Belgian Jazz	1956	7.50	15.00	30.00
JUBILEE					
❑ JLP-1076 [M]	Dixieland at the World's Fair	1958	6.25	12.50	25.00

BEEBE, JIM, 'S CHICAGO JAZZ
Trombone player and bandleader.

Number	Title	Yr	VG	VG+	NM
DELMARK					
❑ DS-218	Saturday Night Function	1979	2.50	5.00	10.00
❑ DS-219	Cornet Chop Suey	1980	2.50	5.00	10.00
-- With Tommy Bridges					

BEIDERBECKE, BIX
Cornet player, bandleader and occasional pianist. Also see JEAN GOLDKETTE; PAUL WHITEMAN.

Number	Title	Yr	VG	VG+	NM
ARCHIVE OF FOLK AND JAZZ					
❑ 317	Bix Beiderbecke	197?	2.50	5.00	10.00
BLUEBIRD					
❑ 6845-1-R	Bix Lives!	1989	3.00	6.00	12.00
COLUMBIA					
❑ CL 507 [M]	The Bix Beiderbecke Story, Volume 1: Bix and His Gang	1953	10.00	20.00	40.00
-- Maroon label, gold print					
❑ GL 507 [M]	The Bix Beiderbecke Story, Volume 1: Bix and His Gang	1952	12.50	25.00	50.00
-- Black label, silver print					
❑ CL 508 [M]	The Bix Beiderbecke Story, Volume 2: Bix and Tram	1953	10.00	20.00	40.00
-- Maroon label, gold print					
❑ GL 508 [M]	The Bix Beiderbecke Story, Volume 2: Bix and Tram	1952	12.50	25.00	50.00
-- Black label, silver print					
❑ CL 509 [M]	The Bix Beiderbecke Story, Volume 3: The Whiteman Years	1953	10.00	20.00	40.00
-- Maroon label, gold print					
❑ GL 509 [M]	The Bix Beiderbecke Story, Volume 3: The Whiteman Years	1952	12.50	25.00	50.00
-- Black label, silver print					
❑ CL 844 [M]	The Bix Beiderbecke Story, Volume 1: Bix and His Gang	1956	7.50	15.00	30.00
-- Red and black label with six "eye" logos					
❑ CL 844 [M]	The Bix Beiderbecke Story, Volume 1: Bix and His Gang	1963	5.00	10.00	20.00
-- "Guaranteed High Fidelity" label					
❑ CL 844 [M]	The Bix Beiderbecke Story, Volume 1: Bix and His Gang	1966	3.75	7.50	15.00
-- "360 Sound" label					
❑ CL 845 [M]	The Bix Beiderbecke Story, Volume 2: Bix and Tram	1956	7.50	15.00	30.00
-- Red and black label with six "eye" logos					
❑ CL 845 [M]	The Bix Beiderbecke Story, Volume 2: Bix and Tram	1963	5.00	10.00	20.00
-- "Guaranteed High Fidelity" label					
❑ CL 845 [M]	The Bix Beiderbecke Story, Volume 2: Bix and Tram	1966	3.75	7.50	15.00
-- "360 Sound" label					
❑ CL 846 [M]	The Bix Beiderbecke Story, Volume 3: The Whiteman Years	1956	7.50	15.00	30.00
-- Red and black label with six "eye" logos					
❑ CL 846 [M]	The Bix Beiderbecke Story, Volume 3: The Whiteman Years	1963	5.00	10.00	20.00
-- "Guaranteed High Fidelity" label					
❑ CL 846 [M]	The Bix Beiderbecke Story, Volume 3: The Whiteman Years	1966	3.75	7.50	15.00
-- "360 Sound" label					
COLUMBIA MASTERWORKS					
❑ ML 4811 [M]	The Bix Beiderbecke Story, Volume 1	1950	17.50	35.00	70.00
❑ ML 4812 [M]	The Bix Beiderbecke Story, Volume 2	1950	17.50	35.00	70.00
❑ ML 4813 [M]	The Bix Beiderbecke Story, Volume 3	1950	17.50	35.00	70.00

Number	Title	Yr	VG	VG+	NM

JAZZ TREASURY

❑ S-1003	Bix Beiderbecke with the Wolverines	197?	3.00	6.00	12.00

JOLLY ROGER

❑ 5010 [10]	Bix Beiderbecke	1954	12.50	25.00	50.00

MILESTONE

❑ 47019 [(2)]	Bix Beiderbecke and the Chicago Cornets	197?	3.75	7.50	15.00

RCA VICTOR

❑ LPM-2323 [M]	The Bix Beiderbecke Legend	1961	6.25	12.50	25.00
-- "Long Play" on label					
❑ LPM-2323 [M]	The Bix Beiderbecke Legend	1963	3.75	7.50	15.00
-- "Mono" or "Monaural" on label					

RIVERSIDE

❑ RLP 12-123 [M]	Bix Beiderbecke and the Wolverines	195?	7.50	15.00	30.00
-- Blue label with microphone logo					
❑ RLP 12-123 [M]	Bix Beiderbecke and the Wolverines	1956	12.50	25.00	50.00
-- White label, blue print					
❑ RLP-1023 [10]	Early Bix	1954	20.00	40.00	80.00
❑ RLP-1050 [10]	Bix Beiderbecke and the Wolverines	1954	20.00	40.00	80.00

BEIRACH, RICHIE
Pianist.
ECM

❑ 1054	Eon	197?	3.75	7.50	15.00
❑ 1104	Hubris	1977	3.00	6.00	12.00
❑ 1142	Elm	1979	3.00	6.00	12.00

MAGENTA

❑ MA-0202	Breathing of Statues	1985	2.50	5.00	10.00

PATHFINDER

❑ PTF-8617	Antarctica	1987	2.50	5.00	10.00

BEIRACH, RICHIE, AND JOHN ABERCROMBIE
Also see each artist's individual listings.
PATHFINDER

❑ PTF-8701	Emerald City	1988	2.50	5.00	10.00

BELGRAVE, MARCUS
Trumpeter and flugel horn player.
TRIBE

❑ 2228	Gemini II	1975	3.75	7.50	15.00

BELL, AARON
Mostly a bass player, though also plays piano, trumpet and tuba. Also see THE MANHATTAN ALL STARS.
HERALD

❑ HLP-0100 [M]	Three Swinging Bells	1955	15.00	30.00	60.00

LION

❑ L-70111 [M]	Music from "77 Sunset Strip"	1959	6.25	12.50	25.00
❑ L-70112 [M]	Music from "Peter Gunn"	1959	6.25	12.50	25.00
❑ L-70113 [M]	Music from "Victory at Sea"	1959	6.25	12.50	25.00

RCA VICTOR

❑ LPM-1876 [M]	After the Party's Over	1958	12.50	25.00	50.00

BELL, CHARLES
Pianist.
ATLANTIC

❑ 1400 [M]	Another Dimension	1963	3.75	7.50	15.00
❑ SD 1400 [S]	Another Dimension	1963	5.00	10.00	20.00

COLUMBIA

❑ CL 1582 [M]	The Charles Bell Contemporary Jazz Quartet	1961	5.00	10.00	20.00
❑ CS 8382 [S]	The Charles Bell Contemporary Jazz Quartet	1961	6.25	12.50	25.00

GATEWAY

❑ 7012 [M]	Charles Bell in Concert	1964	3.75	7.50	15.00
❑ S-7012 [S]	Charles Bell in Concert	1964	5.00	10.00	20.00

BELL, DEE
Female singer.
CONCORD JAZZ

❑ CJ-206	Let There Be Love	1982	2.50	5.00	10.00

BELL, GRAEME
Pianist and bandleader.
ANGEL

❑ ANG.60002 [10]	Inside Jazz Down Under	1954	15.00	30.00	60.00

JAZZOLOGY

❑ J-75	Graeme Bell Jazz	197?	3.00	6.00	12.00

BELL, MARTY
Male singer. He is backed on the below album by DON ELLIOTT.
RIVERSIDE

❑ RLP 12-206 [M]	The Voice of Marty Bell	1956	15.00	30.00	60.00
-- White label, blue print					
❑ RLP 12-206 [M]	The Voice of Marty Bell	1957	10.00	20.00	40.00
-- Blue label, microphone logo					

BELLETTO, AL
Mostly an alto saxophone player, he also plays baritone sax and clarinet.
CAPITOL

❑ T 751 [M]	Half and Half	1956	12.50	25.00	50.00
❑ T 901 [M]	Whisper Not	1957	12.50	25.00	50.00
❑ T 6506 [M]	The Al Belletto Sextette	1955	15.00	30.00	60.00
❑ T 6514 [M]	Sounds and Songs	1955	15.00	30.00	60.00

KING

❑ 716 [M]	The Big Sound	1961	12.50	25.00	50.00

BELLSON, LOUIS
Drummer, bandleader, arranger and composer.
ABC IMPULSE!

❑ AS-9107 [S]	Thunderbird	1968	3.00	6.00	12.00
-- Reissue of Impulse AS-9107					

CAPITOL

❑ H 348 [10]	Just Jazz All-Stars	1952	50.00	100.00	200.00

CONCORD JAZZ

❑ CJ-20	The Louis Bellson 7 Live at the Concord Festival	1977	3.00	6.00	12.00
❑ CJ-36	Louis Bellson and His Big Band	1977	3.00	6.00	12.00
❑ CJ-64	Prime Time	1978	3.00	6.00	12.00
❑ CJ-73	Raincheck	1978	3.00	6.00	12.00
❑ CJ-105	Dynamite!	1979	3.00	6.00	12.00
❑ CJ-141	Side Track	198?	3.00	6.00	12.00
❑ CJ-157	London Scene	198?	3.00	6.00	12.00
❑ CJ-350	Live at the Jazz Showcase	1988	3.00	6.00	12.00

DISCWASHER

❑ 002	Note Smoking	1979	6.25	12.50	25.00
-- Direct-to-disc recording					

IMPULSE!

❑ A-9107 [M]	Thunderbird	1966	6.25	12.50	25.00
❑ AS-9107 [S]	Thunderbird	1966	7.50	15.00	30.00

NORGRAN

❑ MGN-7 [10]	The Amazing Artistry of Louis Bellson	1954	50.00	100.00	200.00
❑ MGN-14 [10]	The Exciting Mr. Bellson (And His Big Band)	1954	50.00	100.00	200.00
❑ MGN-1007 [M]	Journey Into Love	1954	37.50	75.00	150.00
❑ MGN-1011 [M]	Louis Bellson and His Drums	1954	37.50	75.00	150.00
❑ MGN-1020 [M]	The Driving Louis Bellson	1955	25.00	50.00	100.00
❑ MGN-1046 [M]	Skin Deep	1955	25.00	50.00	100.00
❑ MGN-1085 [M]	Concerto for Drums	1956	---	---	---
-- Canceled					
❑ MGN-1099 [M]	The Hawk Talks	1956	20.00	40.00	80.00
-- Reissue of 1020					

PABLO

❑ 2310 755	Explosion	1975	3.75	7.50	15.00
❑ 2310 813	Sunshine Rock	1978	3.00	6.00	12.00
❑ 2310 834	Matterhorn	1979	3.00	6.00	12.00
❑ 2310 838	Jam	1979	3.00	6.00	12.00
❑ 2310 880	London Gig	198?	3.00	6.00	12.00
❑ 2310 899	Cool, Cool Blue	198?	3.00	6.00	12.00
❑ 2405 407	The Best of Louis Bellson	198?	3.00	6.00	12.00

PROJECT 3

❑ PR 5029 SD	Breakthrough!	1968	3.75	7.50	15.00

ROULETTE

❑ R-52087 [M]	Big Band Jazz from the Summit	1962	5.00	10.00	20.00
❑ SR-52087 [S]	Big Band Jazz from the Summit	1962	6.25	12.50	25.00
❑ R-65002 [M]	Around the World in Percussion	1962	5.00	10.00	20.00
❑ SR-65002 [S]	Around the World in Percussion	1962	6.25	12.50	25.00

SEAGULL

❑ LG-8208	Louis Bellson and Orchestra	198?	2.50	5.00	10.00

VERVE

❑ MGV-2123 [M]	The Brilliant Bellson Sound	1960	12.50	25.00	50.00
❑ V-2123 [M]	The Brilliant Bellson Sound	1960	5.00	10.00	20.00
❑ V6-2123 [S]	The Brilliant Bellson Sound	1960	5.00	10.00	20.00
❑ MGV-2131 [M]	Louis Bellson Swings Jules Styne	1960	12.50	25.00	50.00
❑ V-2131 [M]	Louis Bellson Swings Jules Styne	1960	5.00	10.00	20.00
❑ V6-2131 [S]	Louis Bellson Swings Jules Styne	1960	5.00	10.00	20.00

Number	Title	Yr	VG	VG+	NM
❑ MGVS-6093 [S]	The Brilliant Bellson Sound	1960	10.00	20.00	40.00
❑ MGVS-6138 [S]	Louis Bellson Swings Jules Styne	1960	10.00	20.00	40.00
❑ MGV-8016 [M]	Concerto for Drums	1957	12.50	25.00	50.00
-- Reissue of Norgran 1011					
❑ V-8016 [M]	Concerto for Drums	1961	5.00	10.00	20.00
❑ MGV-8137 [M]	Skin Deep	1957	12.50	25.00	50.00
-- Reissue of Norgran 1046					
❑ V-8137 [M]	Skin Deep	1957	5.00	10.00	20.00
❑ MGV-8186 [M]	The Hawk Talks	1957	12.50	25.00	50.00
-- Reissue of Norgran 1099					
❑ V-8186 [M]	The Hawk Talks	1957	5.00	10.00	20.00
❑ MGV-8193 [M]	Drumorama!	1957	12.50	25.00	50.00
❑ V-8193 [M]	Drumorama!	1957	5.00	10.00	20.00
❑ MGV-8256 [M]	Louis Bellson at the Flamingo	1958	12.50	25.00	50.00
❑ V-8256 [M]	Louis Bellson at the Flamingo	1958	5.00	10.00	20.00
❑ MGV-8258 [M]	Let's Call It Swing	1958	12.50	25.00	50.00
❑ V-8258 [M]	Let's Call It Swing	1958	5.00	10.00	20.00
❑ MGV-8280 [M]	Music, Romance and Especially Love	1958	12.50	25.00	50.00
❑ V-8280 [M]	Music, Romance and Especially Love	1958	5.00	10.00	20.00
❑ MGV-8354 [M]	Drummer's Holiday	1959	12.50	25.00	50.00
❑ V-8354 [M]	Drummer's Holiday	1959	5.00	10.00	20.00
VOSS					
❑ VLP1-42936	Note Smoking	1988	2.50	5.00	10.00
-- Reissue of Discwasher 002					

BELLSON, LOUIS/RAY BROWN/PAUL SMITH
Also see each artist's individual listings.

PAUSA					
❑ 7167	Intensive Care	1978	3.00	6.00	12.00
VOSS					
❑ VLP1-42933	Intensive Care	1988	2.50	5.00	10.00
-- Reissue					

BELLSON, LOUIS, AND GENE KRUPA
Also see each artist's individual listings.

ROULETTE					
❑ R-52098 [M]	The Mighty Two	1962	5.00	10.00	20.00
❑ SR-52098 [S]	The Mighty Two	1962	6.25	12.50	25.00

BELLSON, LOUIS, AND WALFREDO DE LOS REYES
Reyes is a drummer and percussionist most often associated with Cuban and Puerto Rican music. Also see LOUIS BELLSON.

FANTASY					
❑ OJC-632	Ecue Ritmos Cubanos	1991	3.00	6.00	12.00
-- Reissue of Pablo 2310 807					
PABLO					
❑ 2310 807	Ecue Ritmos Cubanos	1978	3.00	6.00	12.00

BELLSON, LOUIS, AND LALO SCHIFRIN
Also see each artist's individual listings.

ROULETTE					
❑ R-52120 [M]	Explorations	1964	3.75	7.50	15.00
❑ SR-52120 [S]	Explorations	1964	5.00	10.00	20.00

BELVIN, JESSE
Primarily a rhythm and blues singer, the below album is in a jazz vein.

RCA VICTOR					
❑ LPM-2105 [M]	Mr. Easy	1960	7.50	15.00	30.00
❑ LSP-2105 [S]	Mr. Easy	1960	10.00	20.00	40.00

BENNETT, BETTY
Female singer.

ATLANTIC					
❑ 1226 [M]	Nobody Else But Me	1956	25.00	50.00	100.00
-- Black label					
❑ 1226 [M]	Nobody Else But Me	1961	10.00	20.00	40.00
-- Multicolor label, white "fan" logo					
KAPP					
❑ KL-1052 [M]	Blue Sunday	1957	10.00	20.00	40.00
TREND					
❑ TL-1006 [10]	Betty Bennett Sings Previn Arrangements	1954	30.00	60.00	120.00
UNITED ARTISTS					
❑ UAL-3070 [M]	I Love to Sing	1959	10.00	20.00	40.00
❑ UAS-6070 [S]	I Love to Sing	1959	12.50	25.00	50.00

BENNETT, MAX
Bass player. Was a member of TOM SCOTT's L.A. Express in the 1970s.

BETHLEHEM					
❑ BCP-48 [M]	Johnny Jaguar	1957	17.50	35.00	70.00
❑ BCP-50 [M]	Max Bennett Plays	1957	17.50	35.00	70.00
❑ BCP-1028 [10]	Max Bennett Quintet	1955	30.00	60.00	120.00
PALO ALTO					
❑ TBA-216	The Drifter	1986	2.50	5.00	10.00

BENNETT, RICHARD RODNEY
Pianist and composer. Also has worked in the classical realm.

AUDIOPHILE					
❑ AP-168	Harold Arlen's Songs	1982	2.50	5.00	10.00
❑ AP-206	Take Love Easy	1985	2.50	5.00	10.00
DRG					
❑ SL-5182	A Different Side of Sondheim	1978	2.50	5.00	10.00
❑ DRG-6102	Special Occasions	1979	2.50	5.00	10.00

BENNETT, TONY
Male singer. Mostly a pop singer in the 1950s and 1960s ("Because of You," "Cold, Cold Heart" and "I Left My Heart In San Francisco" are among his hits), he turned to the jazz repertoire in the 1970s and beyond. For a more complete discography, see the *Standard Catalog Of American Records 1950-1975*.

COLUMBIA					
❑ FC 40344	The Art of Excellence	1986	2.50	5.00	10.00
❑ CG 40424 [(2)]	Tony Bennett Jazz	1987	3.00	6.00	12.00
❑ FC 44029	Bennett/Berlin	1987	2.50	5.00	10.00
DRG					
❑ MRS-910	Make Magnificent Music	1985	2.50	5.00	10.00
❑ DARC-2-2102 [(2)]	The Rodgers and Hart Songbook	1986	3.75	7.50	15.00
IMPROV					
❑ 7112	Life Is Beautiful	197?	3.00	6.00	12.00
❑ 7113	Tony Bennett Sings Rodgers and Hart	197?	3.00	6.00	12.00
❑ 7120	Tony Bennett Sings More s Rodger and Hart	1978	3.00	6.00	12.00
❑ 7123	Beautiful Music	1979	3.00	6.00	12.00

BENNETT, TONY, AND COUNT BASIE
Also see each artist's individual listings.

COLUMBIA					
❑ CL 1294 [M]	Tony Bennett In Person	1959	6.25	12.50	25.00
❑ CS 8104 [S]	Tony Bennett In Person	1959	10.00	20.00	40.00
ROULETTE					
❑ R 25072 [M]	Count Basie Swings/Tony Bennett Sings	1961	6.25	12.50	25.00
❑ R 25231 [M]	Bennett and Basie Strike Up the Band	1963	5.00	10.00	20.00
❑ SR 25072 [S]	Count Basie Swings/Tony Bennett Sings	1961	7.50	15.00	30.00
❑ SR 25231 [S]	Bennett and Basie Strike Up the Band	1963	6.25	12.50	25.00

BENNETT, TONY, AND BILL EVANS
Also see each artist's individual listings.

DRG					
❑ MRS-901	Together Again	1985	2.00	4.00	8.00
FANTASY					
❑ 9489	The Tony Bennett/Bill Evans Album	197?	3.00	6.00	12.00
IMPROV					
❑ 7117	Together Again	1978	3.00	6.00	12.00
MOBILE FIDELITY					
❑ 1-117	The Tony Bennett/Bill Evans Album	1981	10.00	20.00	40.00
-- Audiophile vinyl					

BENOIT, DAVID
Pianist and composer.

AVI					
❑ AV-6025	Heavier Than Yesterday	1977	3.75	7.50	15.00
❑ AV-6074	Can You Imagine	1980	3.00	6.00	12.00
❑ AV-6138	Digits	1984	3.00	6.00	12.00
❑ AV-6214	Stages	1983	3.00	6.00	12.00
❑ AV-8620	Christmastime	1985	3.00	6.00	12.00
❑ AV-8712	Waves of Raves	1986	3.00	6.00	12.00
GRP					
❑ 1035	Freedom at Midnight	1986	3.00	6.00	12.00
❑ 1047	Every Step of the Way	1987	3.00	6.00	12.00
❑ 9587	Urban Daydreams	1989	3.00	6.00	12.00

Number	Title	Yr	VG	VG+	NM
❏ 9595	Waiting for Spring	1989	3.00	6.00	12.00
❏ 9621	Inner Motion	1990	3.00	6.00	12.00

SPINDLETOP

Number	Title	Yr	VG	VG+	NM
❏ STP-104	This Side Up	1986	3.00	6.00	12.00

BENSON, GEORGE

Guitarist and male singer who had many hit singles as a vocalist from the mid-1970s into the early 1980s.

A&M

Number	Title	Yr	VG	VG+	NM
❏ SP-3014	Shape of Things to Come	1969	5.00	10.00	20.00
-- Brown label					
❏ SP-3014	Shape of Things to Come	1976	3.00	6.00	12.00
-- Silvery label					
❏ SP-3014	Shape of Things to Come	198?	3.75	7.50	15.00
-- Audiophile reissue					
❏ SP-3020	Tell It Like It Is	1969	5.00	10.00	20.00
-- Brown label					
❏ SP-3020	Tell It Like It Is	1976	3.00	6.00	12.00
-- Silvery label					
❏ SP-3020	Tell It Like It Is	198?	3.75	7.50	15.00
-- Audiophile reissue					
❏ SP-3028	The Other Side of Abbey Road	1970	6.25	12.50	25.00
-- Brown label					
❏ SP-3028	The Other Side of Abbey Road	1976	3.00	6.00	12.00
-- Silvery label					
❏ SP-3028	The Other Side of Abbey Road	198?	3.75	7.50	15.00
-- Audiophile reissue					
❏ SP-3203	The Best of George Benson	1983	2.50	5.00	10.00

COLUMBIA

Number	Title	Yr	VG	VG+	NM
❏ CL 2525 [M]	The Most Exciting New Guitarist on the Jazz Scene Today -- It's Uptown	1966	5.00	10.00	20.00
❏ CL 2613 [M]	The George Benson Cook Book	1967	5.00	10.00	20.00
❏ CS 9325 [S]	The Most Exciting New Guitarist on the Jazz Scene Today --It's Uptown	1966	5.00	10.00	20.00
-- Red "360 Sound" label					
❏ CS 9325	The Most Exciting New Guitarist on the Jazz Scene Today -- It's Uptown	1976	2.50	5.00	10.00
-- Orange label					
❏ PC 9325	The Most Exciting New Guitarist on the Jazz Scene Today -- It's Uptown	198?	2.00	4.00	8.00
-- Reissue with new prefix					
❏ CS 9413 [S]	The George Benson Cook Book	1967	5.00	10.00	20.00
-- Red "360 Sound" label					
❏ CS 9413	The George Benson Cook Book	1976	2.50	5.00	10.00
-- Orange label					
❏ PC 9413	The George Benson Cook Book	198?	2.00	4.00	8.00
-- Reissue with new prefix					
❏ CG 33569 [(2)]	Benson Burner	1976	3.00	6.00	12.00

CTI

Number	Title	Yr	VG	VG+	NM
❏ 6009	Beyond the Blue Horizon	1971	3.00	6.00	12.00
❏ 6015	White Rabbit	1972	3.00	6.00	12.00
❏ 6033	Body Talk	1973	3.00	6.00	12.00
❏ 6045	Bad Benson	1974	3.00	6.00	12.00
❏ 6062	Good King Bad	1976	3.00	6.00	12.00
❏ 6069	Benson & Farrell	1976	3.00	6.00	12.00
❏ 6072	George Benson In Concert -- Carnegie Hall	1976	3.00	6.00	12.00
❏ 8009	White Rabbit	198?	2.50	5.00	10.00
❏ 8014	Take Five	198?	2.50	5.00	10.00
❏ 8030	Cast Your Fate to the Wind	198?	2.50	5.00	10.00
❏ 8031	Summertime: In Concert	198?	2.50	5.00	10.00

FANTASY

Number	Title	Yr	VG	VG+	NM
❏ OJC-461	New Boss Guitar	1990	3.00	6.00	12.00
-- Reissue of Prestige 7310					

MOBILE FIDELITY

Number	Title	Yr	VG	VG+	NM
❏ 1-011	Breezin'	1979	15.00	30.00	60.00
-- Audiophile vinyl					

POLYDOR

Number	Title	Yr	VG	VG+	NM
❏ PD-1-6084	Blue Benson	1976	2.50	5.00	10.00

PRESTIGE

Number	Title	Yr	VG	VG+	NM
❏ PRLP-7310 [M]	The New Boss Guitar of George Benson	1964	6.25	12.50	25.00
❏ PRST-7310 [S]	The New Boss Guitar of George Benson	1964	7.50	15.00	30.00
❏ 24072 [(2)]	George Benson & Jack McDuff	1976	3.75	7.50	15.00

VERVE

Number	Title	Yr	VG	VG+	NM
❏ V6-8749	Giblet Gravy	1968	5.00	10.00	20.00
❏ V6-8771	Goodies	1969	5.00	10.00	20.00

WARNER BROS.

Number	Title	Yr	VG	VG+	NM
❏ BS 2919	Breezin'	1976	3.75	7.50	15.00
-- With no mention of "This Masquerade" on front cover					
❏ BS 2919	Breezin'	1976	2.50	5.00	10.00
-- With "Contains This Masquerade" on front cover					
❏ BSK 2983	In Flight	1977	2.50	5.00	10.00
❏ BSK 3111	Breezin'	1977	2.00	4.00	8.00
-- Reissue of 2919					
❏ 2WS 3139 [(2)]	Weekend in L.A.	1978	3.00	6.00	12.00
❏ 2BSK 3277	Livin' Inside Your Love	1979	3.00	6.00	12.00
❏ HS 3453	Give Me the Night	1980	2.50	5.00	10.00
❏ 2HS 3577 [(2)]	The George Benson Collection	1981	3.00	6.00	12.00
❏ 23744	In Your Eyes	1983	2.50	5.00	10.00
❏ 25178	20/20	1985	2.50	5.00	10.00
❏ 25475	While the City Sleeps…	1986	2.50	5.00	10.00
❏ 25705	Twice the Love	1988	2.50	5.00	10.00
❏ 25907	Tenderly	1989	3.00	6.00	12.00
❏ 26295	Big Boss Band	1990	3.75	7.50	15.00

BENSON, GEORGE, AND EARL KLUGH

Also see each artist's individual listings.

WARNER BROS.

Number	Title	Yr	VG	VG+	NM
❏ 25580	Collaboration	1987	2.50	5.00	10.00

BENTON, WALTER

Tenor saxophone player.

JAZZLAND

Number	Title	Yr	VG	VG+	NM
❏ JLP-28 [M]	Out of This World	1960	10.00	20.00	40.00
❏ JLP-928 [S]	Out of This World	1960	10.00	20.00	40.00

BERG, BOB

Tenor saxophone player, also sometimes heard on soprano sax.

RED

Number	Title	Yr	VG	VG+	NM
❏ VPA-178	Steppin' -- Live in Europe	1985	3.00	6.00	12.00

XANADU

Number	Title	Yr	VG	VG+	NM
❏ 159	New Birth	1978	3.75	7.50	15.00

BERGAMO, JOHN

Percussionist and composer.

CMP

Number	Title	Yr	VG	VG+	NM
❏ CMP-27-ST	On the Edge	1987	2.50	5.00	10.00

BERGER, BENGT

Drummer, percussionist and bandleader.

ECM

Number	Title	Yr	VG	VG+	NM
❏ 1179	Bitter Funeral Beer	1981	3.00	6.00	12.00

BERGER, KARL

Vibraphone and pianist.

CMC

Number	Title	Yr	VG	VG+	NM
❏ 00101 [(2)]	Peace Church	197?	5.00	10.00	20.00

ENJA

Number	Title	Yr	VG	VG+	NM
❏ 2022	With Silence	1974	3.75	7.50	15.00

ESP-DISK'

Number	Title	Yr	VG	VG+	NM
❏ 1041 [M]	Karl Berger	1967	7.50	15.00	30.00
❏ S-1041 [S]	Karl Berger	1967	5.00	10.00	20.00

MILESTONE

Number	Title	Yr	VG	VG+	NM
❏ MSP-9026	Tune In	1969	3.75	7.50	15.00

BERGMAN, BORAH

Pianist.

CHIAROSCURO

Number	Title	Yr	VG	VG+	NM
❏ 118	Solo	1972	3.75	7.50	15.00
❏ 125	Discovery	1973	3.75	7.50	15.00
❏ 158	Bursts of Joy	1979	3.00	6.00	12.00

SOUL NOTE

Number	Title	Yr	VG	VG+	NM
❏ SN-1030	New Frontier	1984	3.00	6.00	12.00
❏ SN-1080	Upside Down Visions	1985	3.00	6.00	12.00

BERIGAN, BUNNY

Trumpeter and male singer.

BIOGRAPH

Number	Title	Yr	VG	VG+	NM
❏ C-10	Bunny Berigan 1932-37	197?	3.00	6.00	12.00

BLUEBIRD

Number	Title	Yr	VG	VG+	NM
❏ AXM2-5584 [(2)]	The Complete Bunny Berigan, Volume 1	197?	3.75	7.50	15.00
❏ 5657-1-RB [(2)]	The Complete Bunny Berigan, Volume 2	1987	3.75	7.50	15.00
❏ 9953-1-RB [(2)]	The Complete Bunny Berigan, Volume 3	1990	3.75	7.50	15.00

EPIC

Number	Title	Yr	VG	VG+	NM
❏ LN 3109 [M]	Take It, Bunny!	1955	12.50	25.00	50.00
❏ LA 16004 [M]	Bunny Berigan and His Boys	196?	5.00	10.00	20.00

HINDSIGHT

Number	Title	Yr	VG	VG+	NM
❏ HSR-239	Bunny Berigan 1937-38	1988	2.50	5.00	10.00

Number	Title	Yr	VG	VG+	NM
JAZZ ARCHIVES					
❏ JA-11	Down by the Old Mill Stream	198?	2.50	5.00	10.00
RCA CAMDEN					
❏ CAL-550 [M]	Bunny	195?	5.00	10.00	20.00
RCA VICTOR					
❏ LPT-10 [10]	Bunny Berigan 1937-38	1951	20.00	40.00	80.00
❏ LPV-550 [M]	Bunny	1966	5.00	10.00	20.00
❏ LPT-1003 [M]	Bunny Berigan Plays Again	1952	12.50	25.00	50.00
❏ LPM-2078 [M]	Great Dance Bands of the 30s and 40s	1959	10.00	20.00	40.00

BERIGAN, BUNNY, AND WINGY MANONE
Also see each artist's individual listings.

Number	Title	Yr	VG	VG+	NM
"X"					
❏ LVA-3034 [10]	Swing Session 1934	1954	20.00	40.00	80.00

BERIGAN, BUNNY/JACK TEAGARDEN
Also see each artist's individual listings.

Number	Title	Yr	VG	VG+	NM
FOLKWAYS					
❏ FJ-2819	The Big Band Sound of Bunny Berigan and Jack Teagarden	1982	3.00	6.00	12.00

BERK, DICK, AND THE JAZZ ADOPTION AGENCY
Drummer and bandleader.

Number	Title	Yr	VG	VG+	NM
DISCOVERY					
❏ DS-877	The Rare One	1985	2.50	5.00	10.00
❏ DS-890	Big Jake	1986	2.50	5.00	10.00
❏ DS-922	More Birds Less Feathers	1987	2.50	5.00	10.00
TREND					
❏ 550	Lover	198?	2.50	5.00	10.00

BERLINER, JAY
Acoustic guitarist.

Number	Title	Yr	VG	VG+	NM
MAINSTREAM					
❏ 384	Bananas Not Equal	1973	3.75	7.50	15.00

BERLINER, PAUL, AND KUDU
Ethnomusicologist and occasional male singer who plays a variety of traditional African instruments.

Number	Title	Yr	VG	VG+	NM
FLYING FISH					
❏ FF-092	The Sun Rises Later Here	1979	3.75	7.50	15.00

BERMAN, SONNY
Trumpeter.

Number	Title	Yr	VG	VG+	NM
ESOTERIC					
❏ ES-532 [M]	Sonny Berman 1946	1954	30.00	60.00	120.00

BERNE, TIM
Alto saxophone player.

Number	Title	Yr	VG	VG+	NM
COLUMBIA					
❏ FC 40530	Fulton Street Maul	1987	3.00	6.00	12.00
❏ FC 44073	Sanctified Dreams	1987	3.00	6.00	12.00
EMPIRE					
❏ EPC 24K	The Five Year Plan	1979	5.00	10.00	20.00
❏ EPC 36K	7X	1980	5.00	10.00	20.00
❏ EPC 48K	Spectres	1981	5.00	10.00	20.00
❏ EPC 60K-2 [(2)]	Songs and Rituals in Real Time	1982	6.25	12.50	25.00
JMT					
❏ 834 431-1	Fractured Fairy Tales	1989	3.75	7.50	15.00
SOUL NOTE					
❏ SN-1061	The Ancestors	1983	3.00	6.00	12.00
❏ SN-1091	Mutant Variations	1984	3.00	6.00	12.00

BERNE, TIM, AND BILL FRISELL
Also see each artist's individual listings.

Number	Title	Yr	VG	VG+	NM
EMPIRE					
❏ EPC 72K	...Theoretically	1984	5.00	10.00	20.00
MINOR MUSIC					
❏ 008	...Theoretically	1986	3.75	7.50	15.00

BERNHARDT, WARREN
Pianist.

Number	Title	Yr	VG	VG+	NM
ARISTA/NOVUS					
❏ AN 3001	Solo Piano	1978	3.00	6.00	12.00
❏ AN 3011	Floating	1979	3.00	6.00	12.00
❏ AN 3020	Manhattan Update	1980	3.00	6.00	12.00

BERNHART, MILT
Trombonist.

Number	Title	Yr	VG	VG+	NM
DECCA					
❏ DL 9214 [M]	The Sounds of Bernhart	1959	7.50	15.00	30.00
❏ DL 79214 [S]	The Sounds of Bernhart	1959	10.00	20.00	40.00
RCA VICTOR					
❏ LPM-1123 [M]	Modern Brass	1955	12.50	25.00	50.00

BERNSTEIN, LEONARD
Composer and conductor, mostly in the classical realm. The below album features the first Columbia recordings of MILES DAVIS.

Number	Title	Yr	VG	VG+	NM
COLUMBIA					
❏ CL 919 [M]	What Is Jazz?	1956	12.50	25.00	50.00
-- Red and black label with six "eye" logos					

BERRY, BILL
Trumpeter and flugel horn player.

Number	Title	Yr	VG	VG+	NM
CONCORD JAZZ					
❏ CJ-27	Hello Rev	1977	3.00	6.00	12.00
❏ CJ-75	Shortcake	1978	3.00	6.00	12.00
DIRECTIONAL SOUND					
❏ 5002 [M]	Jazz and Swinging Percussion	1963	5.00	10.00	20.00
❏ S-5002 [S]	Jazz and Swinging Percussion	1963	6.25	12.50	25.00
PARADE					
❏ SP-353 [M]	Broadway Escapades	196?	5.00	10.00	20.00
REAL TIME					
❏ 101	For Duke	1980	6.25	12.50	25.00
-- Direct-to-disc recording					

BERRY, CHU
Tenor saxophone player.

Number	Title	Yr	VG	VG+	NM
COMMODORE					
❏ XFL 15353	A Giant of the Tenor Sax	198?	2.50	5.00	10.00
❏ FL-20024 [10]	Chu Berry Memorial	1952	62.50	125.00	250.00
❏ DL-30017 [M]	Chu Berry	1959	20.00	40.00	80.00
ENCORE					
❏ EE 22007	Chu (1936-1940)	1968	3.75	7.50	15.00
EPIC					
❏ LG 3124 [M]	Chu	1955	20.00	40.00	80.00
MAINSTREAM					
❏ S-6038 [R]	Sittin' In	1965	3.75	7.50	15.00
❏ 56038 [M]	Sittin' In	1965	7.50	15.00	30.00

BERT, EDDIE
Trombonist.

Number	Title	Yr	VG	VG+	NM
DISCOVERY					
❏ DL-3020 [M]	Eddie Bert Quintet	1953	25.00	50.00	100.00
JAZZTONE					
❏ J-1223 [M]	Modern Moods	1956	10.00	20.00	40.00
SAVOY					
❏ MG-12015 [M]	Musician of the Year	1955	15.00	30.00	60.00
❏ MG-12019 [M]	Encore	1955	15.00	30.00	60.00
SAVOY JAZZ					
❏ SJL-1186	Kaleidoscope	198?	2.50	5.00	10.00
SOMERSET					
❏ SF-5200 [M]	Like Cool	1958	10.00	20.00	40.00
-- Reissue of Trans World LP					
TRANS WORLD					
❏ TWLP-208 [M]	Let's Dig Bert	1955	25.00	50.00	100.00

BERT, EDDIE/BILLY BYERS/JOE NEWMAN
Also see each artist's individual listings.

Number	Title	Yr	VG	VG+	NM
JAZZTONE					
❏ J-1276 [M]	East Coast Sounds	1959	10.00	20.00	40.00

BERTONCINI, GENE
Acoustic guitarist.

Number	Title	Yr	VG	VG+	NM
EVOLUTION					
❏ 3001	Evolution	1969	3.75	7.50	15.00

BERTONCINI, GENE, AND MICHAEL MOORE
Michael Moore is a bass player. Also see GENE BERTONCINI.

Number	Title	Yr	VG	VG+	NM
OMNISOUND					
❏ GJB-3333	Bridges	198?	3.00	6.00	12.00
❏ GJB-3334	Close Ties	198?	3.00	6.00	12.00
STASH					
❏ ST-258	O Grande Amor: A Bossa Nova Collection	1986	2.50	5.00	10.00
❏ ST-272	Strollin'	1987	2.50	5.00	10.00

Number	Title	Yr	VG	VG+	NM
BETTERS, HAROLD					
Trombonist.					
GATEWAY					
❑ GLP-7001 [M]	Harold Betters at the Encore	1964	5.00	10.00	20.00
❑ GS-7001 [S]	Harold Betters at the Encore	1964	3.75	7.50	15.00
❑ GLP-7004 [M]	Take Off	1964	5.00	10.00	20.00
❑ GS-7004 [S]	Take Off	1964	3.75	7.50	15.00
❑ GLP-7008 [M]	Even Better	1966	5.00	10.00	20.00
❑ GS-7008 [S]	Even Better	1966	3.75	7.50	15.00
❑ GLP-7009 [M]	Harold Betters Meets Slide	1966	5.00	10.00	20.00
❑ GLP-7009 [S]	Harold Betters Meets Slide	1966	3.75	7.50	15.00
❑ GLP-7014 [M]	Do Anything You Wanna	1966	5.00	10.00	20.00
❑ GS-7014 [S]	Do Anything You Wanna	1966	3.75	7.50	15.00
❑ GLP-7015 [M]	Swingin' on the Railroad	1966	5.00	10.00	20.00
❑ GS-7015 [S]	Swingin' on the Railroad	1966	3.75	7.50	15.00
❑ 7017	The Best of Betters	197?	3.00	6.00	12.00
❑ 7021	Jazz Showcase	197?	3.00	6.00	12.00
REPRISE					
❑ R-6195 [M]	Ram-Bunk-Shush	1965	3.75	7.50	15.00
❑ RS-6195 [S]	Ram-Bunk-Shush	1965	5.00	10.00	20.00
❑ R-6208 [M]	Out of Sight and Sound	1966	3.75	7.50	15.00
❑ RS-6208 [S]	Out of Sight and Sound	1966	5.00	10.00	20.00
❑ R-6241 [M]	Funk City Express	1966	3.75	7.50	15.00
❑ RS-6241 [S]	Funk City Express	1966	5.00	10.00	20.00
BICKERT, ED					
Guitarist.					
CONCORD JAZZ					
❑ CJ-216	Ed Bickert at Toronto's Bourbon Street	1982	2.50	5.00	10.00
❑ CJ-232	Bye Bye Baby	1983	2.50	5.00	10.00
❑ CJ-284	I Wished on the Moon	1985	2.50	5.00	10.00
❑ CJ-380	Third Floor Richard	1989	2.50	5.00	10.00
PM					
❑ PMR-010	Ed Bickert	1976	3.00	6.00	12.00
BICKERT, ED, AND DON THOMPSON					
Also see each artist's individual listings.					
SACKVILLE					
❑ 4005	Ed Bickert & Don Thompson	198?	2.50	5.00	10.00
❑ 4010	Dance to the Lady	198?	2.50	5.00	10.00
BIGARD, BARNEY					
Clarinetist and tenor saxophone player.					
LIBERTY					
❑ LRP-3072 [M]	Jazz Hall of Fame	1957	10.00	20.00	40.00
BIGARD, BARNEY, AND ART HODES					
Also see each artist's individual listings.					
DELMARK					
❑ DS-211	Bucket's Got a Hole In It	1969	3.75	7.50	15.00
BIGARD, BARNEY/ALBERT NICHOLAS					
Also see each artist's individual listings.					
RCA VICTOR					
❑ LPV-566 [M]	Barney Bigard/Albert Nicholas	1966	5.00	10.00	20.00
BILK, ACKER					
Clarinetist and bandleader. His rendition of "Stranger on the Shore" was a chart-topper in both the United States and his native Great Britain.					
ATCO					
❑ 33-129 [M]	Stranger on the Shore	1961	3.75	7.50	15.00
❑ SD 33-129 [S]	Stranger on the Shore	1961	5.00	10.00	20.00
❑ 33-144 [M]	Above the Stars	1962	3.75	7.50	15.00
❑ SD 33-144 [S]	Above the Stars	1962	5.00	10.00	20.00
❑ 33-150 [M]	Only You	1963	3.75	7.50	15.00
❑ SD 33-150 [S]	Only You	1963	5.00	10.00	20.00
❑ 33-158 [M]	Call Me Mister	1963	3.75	7.50	15.00
❑ SD 33-158 [S]	Call Me Mister	1963	5.00	10.00	20.00
❑ 33-168 [M]	A Touch of Latin	1964	3.00	6.00	12.00
❑ SD 33-168 [S]	A Touch of Latin	1964	3.75	7.50	15.00
❑ 33-170 [M]	Great Themes from Great Foreign Films	1965	3.00	6.00	12.00
❑ SD 33-170 [S]	Great Themes from Great Foreign Films	1965	3.75	7.50	15.00
❑ 33-181 [M]	Acker Bilk in Paris	1966	3.00	6.00	12.00
❑ SD 33-181 [S]	Acker Bilk in Paris	1966	3.75	7.50	15.00
GNP CRESCENDO					
❑ GNPS-2116	The Best of Acker Bilk: His Clarinet and Strings	198?	2.50	5.00	10.00
❑ GNPS-2171	The Best of Acker Bilk: His Clarinet and Strings, Volume 2	198?	2.50	5.00	10.00

Number	Title	Yr	VG	VG+	NM
❑ GNPS-2191	Acker Bilk Plays Lennon and McCartney	1988	3.00	6.00	12.00
REPRISE					
❑ R-6031 [M]	A Stranger No More	1962	5.00	10.00	20.00
❑ RS-6031 [R]	A Stranger No More	1962	3.75	7.50	15.00
BILK, ACKER, AND KEN COLYER					
Also see each artist's individual listings.					
STOMP OFF					
❑ SOS-1119	It Looks Like a Big Time Tonight	198?	2.50	5.00	10.00
BILK, ACKER, AND BENT FABRIC					
Also see each artist's individual listings.					
ATCO					
❑ 33-175 [M]	Together	1965	3.00	6.00	12.00
❑ SD 33-175 [S]	Together	1965	3.75	7.50	15.00
BISHOP, JOHN					
Guitarist.					
TANGERINE					
❑ TRCS-1508	Bishop's Whirl	1969	3.75	7.50	15.00
❑ TRCS-1513	John Bishop Plays His Guitar	1970	3.75	7.50	15.00
BISHOP, WALTER, JR.					
Pianist.					
BLACK JAZZ					
❑ 2	Coral Keys	1972	3.75	7.50	15.00
❑ QD-14 [Q]	Keeper of My Soul	1974	3.75	7.50	15.00
COTILLION					
❑ SD 236	Walter Bishop	1969	5.00	10.00	20.00
INTERPLAY					
❑ IP-8605	Just in Time	1988	2.50	5.00	10.00
JAZZTIME					
❑ JS-002 [S]	Speak Low	1961	7.50	15.00	30.00
❑ JT-002 [M]	Speak Low	1961	6.25	12.50	25.00
MUSE					
❑ 5060	Valley Land	1976	3.00	6.00	12.00
❑ 5066	Speak Low	1976	3.00	6.00	12.00
-- Reissue of Jazztime JS-002					
❑ 5142	Soul Village	1977	3.00	6.00	12.00
❑ 5151	Cubicle	1978	3.00	6.00	12.00
❑ 5183	Hot House	1979	3.00	6.00	12.00
PRESTIGE					
❑ PRST-7730	The Walter Bishop Trio 1965	1969	5.00	10.00	20.00
SEABREEZE					
❑ 1002	Soliloquy	1975	3.00	6.00	12.00
XANADU					
❑ 114	Bish Bash	1977	3.00	6.00	12.00
BIVONA, GUS					
Alto saxophone player.					
MERCURY					
❑ MG-20157 [M]	Hey, Dig That Crazy Band	195?	7.50	15.00	30.00
BLACK BOTTOM STOMPERS (ENGLAND)					
Named after one of the great early jazz bands, this group plays traditional Dixieland-style material. Many changes of personnel over the years, with John Goddard (trombone) appearing to have been a constant.					
STOMP OFF					
❑ SOS-1045	Stomp Off, Let's Go	1982	2.50	5.00	10.00
BLACK BOTTOM STOMPERS (SWITZERLAND)					
Similar to its UK namesake, this group plays traditional Dixieland-style material.					
STOMP OFF					
❑ SOS-1130	Four O'Clock Blues	1987	2.50	5.00	10.00
BLACK EAGLE JAZZ BAND					
See NEW BLACK EAGLE JAZZ BAND.					
BLACKBYRDS, THE					
Mostly vocal group founded by DONALD BYRD, though he is not a member.					
FANTASY					
❑ FPM-4004 [Q]	Flying Start	1975	6.25	12.50	25.00
❑ F-9444	The Blackbyrds	1974	3.75	7.50	15.00
❑ F-9472	Flying Start	1974	3.75	7.50	15.00
❑ F-9490	City Life	1975	3.75	7.50	15.00
❑ F-9518	Unfinished Business	1976	3.75	7.50	15.00
❑ F-9535	Action	1977	3.00	6.00	12.00
❑ F-9570	Night Grooves	1978	3.00	6.00	12.00
❑ F-9602	Better Days	1980	3.00	6.00	12.00

Number	Title	Yr	VG	VG+	NM

BLACKMAN, CINDY
Drummer.
MUSE
❏ MR-5341	Arcane	1988	3.00	6.00	12.00

BLAIR, SALLIE
Female singer.
BETHLEHEM
❏ BCP-6009 [M]	Squeeze Me	1957	20.00	40.00	80.00

MGM
❏ E-3723 [M]	Hello, Tiger!	1959	10.00	20.00	40.00
❏ SE-3723 [S]	Hello, Tiger!	1959	12.50	25.00	50.00

BLAKE, BETTY
Female singer.
BETHLEHEM
❏ BCP-6058 [M]	Betty Blake Sings in a Tender Mood	1962	10.00	20.00	40.00
❏ BCPS-6058 [S]	Betty Blake Sings in a Tender Mood	1962	12.50	25.00	50.00

BLAKE, EUBIE
Pianist and composer.
BIOGRAPH
❏ 1011	Blues & Ragtime	1972	3.00	6.00	12.00
❏ 1012	Blues & Spirituals	1972	3.00	6.00	12.00

COLUMBIA
❏ C2S 847 [(2)]	The Eighty-Six Years of Eubie Blake	1969	5.00	10.00	20.00

-- Red "360 Sound" labels

❏ C2S 847 [(2)]	The Eighty-Six Years of Eubie Blake	1970	3.75	7.50	15.00

-- Orange labels

EUBIE BLAKE MUSIC
❏ EBM-1	Eubie Blake Featuring Ivan Harold Browning	197?	3.00	6.00	12.00
❏ EBM-2	Rags to Classics: Charlestown Rag	197?	3.00	6.00	12.00
❏ EBM-3	Eubie Blake with Edith Wilson and Ivan Harold Browning	197?	3.00	6.00	12.00
❏ EBM-4	Early Rare Recordings	197?	3.00	6.00	12.00
❏ EBM-5	Live Concert	197?	3.00	6.00	12.00
❏ EBM-6	Introducing Jim Hession	197?	3.00	6.00	12.00
❏ EBM-7	Early Rare Recordings, Vol. 2	197?	3.00	6.00	12.00
❏ EBM-8	Eubie Blake and His Proteges	197?	3.00	6.00	12.00
❏ EBM-9	Song Hits	197?	3.00	6.00	12.00

QUICKSILVER
❏ QS-9003	Tricky Fingers	198?	2.50	5.00	10.00

BLAKE, RAN
Pianist. Also see JAKI BYARD.
ARISTA/NOVUS
❏ AN 3006	Rapport	1978	3.00	6.00	12.00
❏ AN 3019	Film Noir	1980	3.00	6.00	12.00

ESP-DISK'
❏ 1011 [M]	Ran Blake Plays Solo Piano	1965	5.00	10.00	20.00
❏ S-1011 [S]	Ran Blake Plays Solo Piano	1965	5.00	10.00	20.00

GC
❏ 4176	Take One	197?	3.00	6.00	12.00
❏ 4177	Take Two	197?	3.00	6.00	12.00

GM RECORDINGS
❏ GM-3007	Painted Rhythms: The Compleat Ran Blake, Vol. 1	1987	3.00	6.00	12.00
❏ GM-3008	Painted Rhythms: The Compleat Ran Blake, Vol. 2	1989	3.00	6.00	12.00

IAI
❏ 37.38.42	Breakthru	1976	3.00	6.00	12.00

MILESTONE
❏ MSP-9021	The Blue Potato	1969	3.75	7.50	15.00

OWL
❏ 012	The Realization of a Dream	1978	3.75	7.50	15.00
❏ 017	Third Stream Recompositions	1977	3.75	7.50	15.00
❏ 029	Portrait of Doktor Mabuse	1978	3.75	7.50	15.00
❏ 041	Vertigo	1986	3.75	7.50	15.00

SOUL NOTE
❏ SN-1027	Duke Dreams	198?	3.00	6.00	12.00
❏ SN-1077	Suffield Gothic	1983	3.00	6.00	12.00

BLAKEY, ART, AND THE JAZZ MESSENGERS
Blakey was a drummer and bandleader. The Jazz Messengers were a somewhat fluid organization of musicians. Some of the below albums credit only Art Blakey; others only the Jazz Messengers; others credit both.

ABC IMPULSE!
❏ AS-7 [S]	Art Blakey!!!! Jazz Messengers!!!!	1968	3.00	6.00	12.00

-- Reissue of Impulse AS-7

❏ AS-45 [S]	A Jazz Message	1968	3.00	6.00	12.00

-- Reissue of Impulse AS-45

ARCHIVE OF FOLK AND JAZZ
❏ 332	Jazz Messengers	197?	2.50	5.00	10.00

BETHLEHEM
❏ BCP-6015	The Finest of Art Blakey	197?	3.00	6.00	12.00

-- Reissue of 6027, distributed by RCA Victor

❏ BCP-6023 [M]	Hard Drive	1957	20.00	40.00	80.00
❏ BCP-6027 [M]	Art Blakey's Big Band	1958	20.00	40.00	80.00
❏ BCPS-6027 [S]	Art Blakey's Big Band	1959	12.50	25.00	50.00
❏ BCP-6037	Hard Drive	197?	3.00	6.00	12.00

-- Reissue of 6023, distributed by RCA Victor

BLUE NOTE
❏ BN-LA473-J2 [(2)]	Live Messengers	1975	3.75	7.50	15.00
❏ LT-1065	Once Upon a Groove	1980	2.50	5.00	10.00
❏ BLP-1507 [M]	At the Café Bohemia, Volume 1	1956	37.50	75.00	150.00

-- "Deep groove" version (deep indentation under label on both sides)

❏ BLP-1507 [M]	At the Café Bohemia, Volume 1	1956	25.00	50.00	100.00

-- Regular version, Lexington Ave. address on label

❏ BLP-1507 [M]	At the Café Bohemia, Volume 1	1957	12.50	25.00	50.00

-- With W. 63rd St. address on label

❏ BLP-1507 [M]	At the Café Bohemia, Volume 1	1963	6.25	12.50	25.00

-- With "New York, USA" address on label

❏ BLP-1508 [M]	At the Café Bohemia, Volume 2	1956	37.50	75.00	150.00

-- "Deep groove" version (deep indentation under label on both sides)

❏ BLP-1508 [M]	At the Café Bohemia, Volume 2	1956	25.00	50.00	100.00

-- Regular version, Lexington Ave. address on label

❏ BLP-1508 [M]	At the Café Bohemia, Volume 2	1957	12.50	25.00	50.00

-- With W. 63rd St. address on label

❏ BLP-1508 [M]	At the Café Bohemia, Volume 2	1963	6.25	12.50	25.00

-- With "New York, USA" address on label

❏ BLP-1521 [M]	A Night at Birdland, Volume 1	1956	50.00	100.00	200.00

-- "Deep groove" version (deep indentation under label on both sides)

❏ BLP-1521 [M]	A Night at Birdland, Volume 1	1956	25.00	50.00	100.00

-- Regular version, Lexington Ave. address on label

❏ BLP-1521 [M]	A Night at Birdland, Volume 1	1957	12.50	25.00	50.00

-- With W. 63rd St. address on label

❏ BLP-1521 [M]	A Night at Birdland, Volume 1	1963	6.25	12.50	25.00

-- With "New York, USA" address on label

❏ BLP-1522 [M]	A Night at Birdland, Volume 2	1956	50.00	100.00	200.00

-- "Deep groove" version (deep indentation under label on both sides)

❏ BLP-1522 [M]	A Night at Birdland, Volume 2	1956	25.00	50.00	100.00

-- Regular version, Lexington Ave. address on label

❏ BLP-1522 [M]	A Night at Birdland, Volume 2	1957	12.50	25.00	50.00

-- With W. 63rd St. address on label

❏ BLP-1522 [M]	A Night at Birdland, Volume 2	1963	6.25	12.50	25.00

-- With "New York, USA" address on label

❏ BLP-1554 [M]	Orgy in Rhythm, Volume 1	1957	37.50	75.00	150.00

-- "Deep groove" version (deep indentation under label on both sides)

❏ BLP-1554 [M]	Orgy in Rhythm, Volume 1	1957	25.00	50.00	100.00

-- Regular version, with W. 63rd St. address on label

❏ BLP-1554 [M]	Orgy in Rhythm, Volume 1	1963	6.25	12.50	25.00

-- With "New York, USA" address on label

❏ BLP-1555 [M]	Orgy in Rhythm, Volume 2	1957	37.50	75.00	150.00

-- "Deep groove" version (deep indentation under label on both sides)

❏ BLP-1555 [M]	Orgy in Rhythm, Volume 2	1957	25.00	50.00	100.00

-- Regular version, with W. 63rd St. address on label

❏ BLP-1555 [M]	Orgy in Rhythm, Volume 2	1963	6.25	12.50	25.00

-- With "New York, USA" address on label

❏ BLP-4003 [M]	Art Blakey and the Jazz Messengers	1958	37.50	75.00	150.00

-- "Deep groove" version (deep indentation under label on both sides)

❏ BLP-4003 [M]	Art Blakey and the Jazz Messengers	1958	25.00	50.00	100.00

-- Regular version, with W. 63rd St. address on label

❏ BLP-4003 [M]	Art Blakey and the Jazz Messengers	1963	6.25	12.50	25.00

-- With "New York, USA" address on label

❏ BST-4003 [S]	Art Blakey and the Jazz Messengers	1959	25.00	50.00	100.00

-- "Deep groove" version (deep indentation under label on both sides)

❏ BST-4003 [S]	Art Blakey and the Jazz Messengers	1959	20.00	40.00	80.00

-- Regular version, with W. 63rd St. address on label

❏ BST-4003 [S]	Art Blakey and the Jazz Messengers	1963	5.00	10.00	20.00

-- With "New York, USA" address on label

❏ BLP-4004 [M]	Holiday for Skins, Volume 1	1958	50.00	100.00	200.00

-- "Deep groove" version (deep indentation under label on both sides)

Number	Title	Yr	VG	VG+	NM
❑ BLP-4004 [M]	Holiday for Skins, Volume 1	1958	37.50	75.00	150.00
-- Regular version, with W. 63rd St. address on label					
❑ BLP-4004 [M]	Holiday for Skins, Volume 1	1963	6.25	12.50	25.00
-- With "New York, USA" address on label					
❑ BST-4004 [S]	Holiday for Skins, Volume 1	1959	37.50	75.00	150.00
-- "Deep groove" version (deep indentation under label on both sides)					
❑ BST-4004 [S]	Holiday for Skins, Volume 1	1959	30.00	60.00	120.00
-- Regular version, with W. 63rd St. address on label					
❑ BST-4004 [S]	Holiday for Skins, Volume 1	1963	5.00	10.00	20.00
-- With "New York, USA" address on label					
❑ BLP-4005 [M]	Holiday for Skins, Volume 2	1958	50.00	100.00	200.00
-- "Deep groove" version (deep indentation under label on both sides)					
❑ BLP-4005 [M]	Holiday for Skins, Volume 2	1958	37.50	75.00	150.00
-- Regular version, with W. 63rd St. address on label					
❑ BLP-4005 [M]	Holiday for Skins, Volume 2	1963	6.25	12.50	25.00
-- With "New York, USA" address on label					
❑ BST-4005 [S]	Holiday for Skins, Volume 2	1959	37.50	75.00	150.00
-- "Deep groove" version (deep indentation under label on both sides)					
❑ BST-4005 [S]	Holiday for Skins, Volume 2	1959	30.00	60.00	120.00
-- Regular version, with W. 63rd St. address on label					
❑ BST-4005 [S]	Holiday for Skins, Volume 2	1963	5.00	10.00	20.00
-- With "New York, USA" address on label					
❑ BLP-4015 [M]	At the Jazz Corner of the World, Volume 1	1958	30.00	60.00	120.00
-- "Deep groove" version (deep indentation under label on both sides)					
❑ BLP-4015 [M]	At the Jazz Corner of the World, Volume 1	1958	20.00	40.00	80.00
-- Regular version, with W. 63rd St. address on label					
❑ BLP-4015 [M]	At the Jazz Corner of the World, Volume 1	1963	6.25	12.50	25.00
-- With "New York, USA" address on label					
❑ BLP-4016 [M]	At the Jazz Corner of the World, Volume 2	1958	30.00	60.00	120.00
-- "Deep groove" version (deep indentation under label on both sides)					
❑ BLP-4016 [M]	At the Jazz Corner of the World, Volume 2	1958	20.00	40.00	80.00
-- Regular version, with W. 63rd St. address on label					
❑ BLP-4016 [M]	At the Jazz Corner of the World, Volume 2	1963	6.25	12.50	25.00
-- With "New York, USA" address on label					
❑ BLP-4029 [M]	The Big Beat	1960	25.00	50.00	100.00
-- "Deep groove" version (deep indentation under label on both sides)					
❑ BLP-4029 [M]	The Big Beat	1960	20.00	40.00	80.00
-- Regular version, with W. 63rd St. address on label					
❑ BLP-4029 [M]	The Big Beat	1963	6.25	12.50	25.00
-- With "New York, USA" address on label					
❑ BLP-4049 [M]	A Night in Tunisia	1960	25.00	50.00	100.00
-- "Deep groove" version (deep indentation under label on both sides)					
❑ BLP-4049 [M]	A Night in Tunisia	1960	20.00	40.00	80.00
-- Regular version, with W. 63rd St. address on label					
❑ BLP-4049 [M]	A Night in Tunisia	1963	6.25	12.50	25.00
-- With "New York, USA" address on label					
❑ BLP-4054 [M]	Meet You at the Jazz Corner of the World, Volume 1	1960	17.50	35.00	70.00
-- With W. 63rd St. address on label					
❑ BLP-4054 [M]	Meet You at the Jazz Corner of the World, Volume 1	1963	6.25	12.50	25.00
-- With "New York, USA" address on label					
❑ BLP-4055 [M]	Meet You at the Jazz Corner of the World, Volume 2	1960	17.50	35.00	70.00
-- With W. 63rd St. address on label					
❑ BLP-4055 [M]	Meet You at the Jazz Corner of the World, Volume 2	1963	6.25	12.50	25.00
-- With "New York, USA" address on label					
❑ BLP-4090 [M]	Mosaic	1961	20.00	40.00	80.00
-- With 61st St. address on label					
❑ BLP-4090 [M]	Mosaic	1963	6.25	12.50	25.00
-- With "New York, USA" address on label					
❑ BLP-4097 [M]	The African Beat	1961	20.00	40.00	80.00
-- With 61st St. address on label					
❑ BLP-4097 [M]	The African Beat	1963	6.25	12.50	25.00
-- With "New York, USA" address on label					
❑ BLP-4104 [M]	Buhaina's Delight	1962	7.50	15.00	30.00
❑ BLP-4156 [M]	The Freedom Rider	1964	7.50	15.00	30.00
❑ BLP-4170 [M]	Free for All	1965	7.50	15.00	30.00
❑ BLP-4193 [M]	Indestructible	1966	7.50	15.00	30.00
❑ BLP-4245 [M]	Like Someone in Love	1967	10.00	20.00	40.00
❑ BLP-5037 [10]	A Night at Birdland, Volume 1	1954	75.00	150.00	300.00
❑ BLP-5038 [10]	A Night at Birdland, Volume 2	1954	75.00	150.00	300.00
❑ BLP-5039 [10]	A Night at Birdland, Volume 3	1954	75.00	150.00	300.00
❑ B1-46516	Moanin'	199?	3.75	7.50	15.00
-- Audiophile reissue of 84003					
❑ B1-46523	Mosaic	199?	3.75	7.50	15.00
-- Audiophile reissue					
❑ BST-81507 [R]	At the Café Bohemia, Volume 1	1968	2.50	5.00	10.00
-- With "A Division of Liberty Records" on label					
❑ BST-81507 [M]	At the Café Bohemia, Volume 1	1985	2.50	5.00	10.00
-- "The Finest in Jazz Since 1939" reissue					
❑ BST-81508 [R]	At the Café Bohemia, Volume 2	1968	2.50	5.00	10.00
-- With "A Division of Liberty Records" on label					
❑ B1-81508	At the Café Bohemia, Volume 2	1987	2.50	5.00	10.00
-- "The Finest in Jazz Since 1939" reissue					
❑ BST-81521 [R]	A Night at Birdland, Volume 1	1968	2.50	5.00	10.00
-- With "A Division of Liberty Records" on label					
❑ BST-81522 [R]	A Night at Birdland, Volume 2	1968	2.50	5.00	10.00
-- With "A Division of Liberty Records" on label					
❑ BST-81554 [R]	Orgy in Rhythm, Volume 1	1968	2.50	5.00	10.00
-- With "A Division of Liberty Records" on label					
❑ BST-81555 [R]	Orgy in Rhythm, Volume 2	1968	2.50	5.00	10.00
-- With "A Division of Liberty Records" on label					
❑ BST-84003 [S]	Art Blakey and the Jazz Messengers	196?	3.00	6.00	12.00
-- With "A Division of Liberty Records" on label					
❑ BST-84004 [S]	Holiday for Skins, Volume 1	196?	3.00	6.00	12.00
-- With "A Division of Liberty Records" on label					
❑ BST-84005 [S]	Holiday for Skins, Volume 2	196?	3.00	6.00	12.00
-- With "A Division of Liberty Records" on label					
❑ BST-84015 [S]	At the Jazz Corner of the World, Volume 1	1959	20.00	40.00	80.00
-- "Deep groove" version (deep indentation under label on both sides)					
❑ BST-84015 [S]	At the Jazz Corner of the World, Volume 1	1959	15.00	30.00	60.00
-- Regular version, with W. 63rd St. address on label					
❑ BST-84015 [S]	At the Jazz Corner of the World, Volume 1	1963	5.00	10.00	20.00
-- With "New York, USA" address on label					
❑ BST-84015 [S]	At the Jazz Corner of the World, Volume 1	196?	3.00	6.00	12.00
-- With "A Division of Liberty Records" on label					
❑ BST-84016 [S]	At the Jazz Corner of the World, Volume 2	1959	20.00	40.00	80.00
-- "Deep groove" version (deep indentation under label on both sides)					
❑ BST-84016 [S]	At the Jazz Corner of the World, Volume 2	1959	15.00	30.00	60.00
-- Regular version, with W. 63rd St. address on label					
❑ BST-84016 [S]	At the Jazz Corner of the World, Volume 2	1963	5.00	10.00	20.00
-- With "New York, USA" address on label					
❑ BST-84016 [S]	At the Jazz Corner of the World, Volume 2	196?	3.00	6.00	12.00
-- With "A Division of Liberty Records" on label					
❑ BST-84029 [S]	The Big Beat	1960	15.00	30.00	60.00
-- With W. 63rd St. address on label					
❑ BST-84029 [S]	The Big Beat	1963	5.00	10.00	20.00
-- With "New York, USA" address on label					
❑ BST-84029 [S]	The Big Beat	196?	3.00	6.00	12.00
-- With "A Division of Liberty Records" on label					
❑ BST-84029 [S]	The Big Beat	1985	2.50	5.00	10.00
-- "The Finest in Jazz Since 1939" reissue					
❑ BST-84049 [S]	A Night in Tunisia	1960	15.00	30.00	60.00
-- With W. 63rd St. address on label					
❑ BST-84049 [S]	A Night in Tunisia	1963	5.00	10.00	20.00
-- With "New York, USA" address on label					
❑ BST-84049 [S]	A Night in Tunisia	196?	3.00	6.00	12.00
-- With "A Division of Liberty Records" on label					
❑ B1-84049	A Night in Tunisia	1989	2.50	5.00	10.00
-- "The Finest in Jazz Since 1939" reissue					
❑ BST-84054 [S]	Meet You at the Jazz Corner of the World, Volume 1	1960	15.00	30.00	60.00
-- With W. 63rd St. address on label					
❑ BST-84054 [S]	Meet You at the Jazz Corner of the World, Volume 1	1963	5.00	10.00	20.00
-- With "New York, USA" address on label					
❑ BST-84054 [S]	Meet You at the Jazz Corner of the World, Volume 1	196?	3.00	6.00	12.00
-- With "A Division of Liberty Records" on label					
❑ BST-84055 [S]	Meet You at the Jazz Corner of the World, Volume 2	1960	15.00	30.00	60.00
-- With W. 63rd St. address on label					
❑ BST-84055 [S]	Meet You at the Jazz Corner of the World, Volume 2	1963	5.00	10.00	20.00
-- With "New York, USA" address on label					
❑ BST-84055 [S]	Meet You at the Jazz Corner of the World, Volume 2	196?	3.00	6.00	12.00
-- With "A Division of Liberty Records" on label					
❑ BST-84090 [S]	Mosaic	1961	15.00	30.00	60.00
-- With 61st St. address on label					
❑ BST-84090 [S]	Mosaic	1963	5.00	10.00	20.00
-- With "New York, USA" address on label					
❑ BST-84090 [S]	Mosaic	196?	3.00	6.00	12.00
-- With "A Division of Liberty Records" on label					
❑ BST-84097 [S]	The African Beat	1961	15.00	30.00	60.00
-- With 61st St. address on label					
❑ BST-84097 [S]	The African Beat	1963	6.25	12.50	25.00
-- With "New York, USA" address on label					
❑ BST-84097 [S]	The African Beat	196?	3.00	6.00	12.00
-- With "A Division of Liberty Records" on label					
❑ BST-84104 [S]	Buhaina's Delight	1962	10.00	20.00	40.00
-- With "New York, USA" address on label					
❑ BST-84104 [S]	Buhaina's Delight	196?	3.00	6.00	12.00
-- With "A Division of Liberty Records" on label					

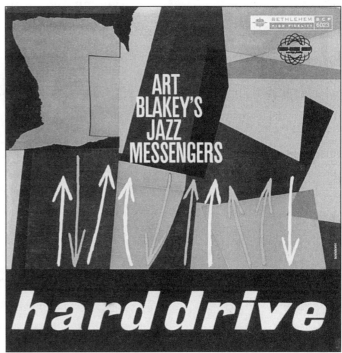

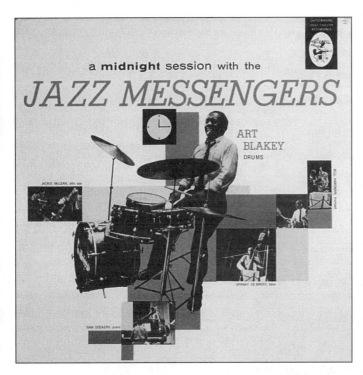

Art Blakey not only was influential as a jazz drummer, but his band, the Jazz Messengers, was the home of countless musicians who became prominent on their own. (Top left) *A Night at Birdland, Volume 1* was issued in 1956 and featured the work of legendary bebop trumpeter Clifford Brown, who had died young shortly before this recording was issued. (Top right) You might think that with a title like *Hard Drive*, this album might date from the computer era, but it was issued by the Bethlehem label in 1957. (Bottom left) New York's Elektra label was known primarily for its folk music releases in its first decade of existence, but Blakey and the Messengers had this one LP issued on the label in 1957. (Bottom right) Into the 1980s, Blakey recorded for the Concord Jazz label. This album features among its musicians the young Wynton Marsalis.

Number	Title	Yr	VG	VG+	NM
❏ BST-84156 [S]	The Freedom Rider	1964	10.00	20.00	40.00
-- With "New York, USA" address on label					
❏ BST-84156 [S]	The Freedom Rider	196?	3.00	6.00	12.00
-- With "A Division of Liberty Records" on label					
❏ BST-84170 [S]	Free for All	1965	10.00	20.00	40.00
-- With "New York, USA" address on label					
❏ BST-84170 [S]	Free for All	196?	3.00	6.00	12.00
-- With "A Division of Liberty Records" on label					
❏ BST-84193 [S]	Indestructible	1966	10.00	20.00	40.00
-- With "New York, USA" address on label					
❏ BST-84193 [S]	Indestructible	196?	3.00	6.00	12.00
-- With "A Division of Liberty Records" on label					
❏ BST-84193 [S]	Indestructible	1986	2.50	5.00	10.00
-- "The Finest in Jazz Since 1939" reissue					
❏ BST-84245 [S]	Like Someone in Love	1967	10.00	20.00	40.00
-- With "New York, USA" address on label					
❏ BST-84245 [S]	Like Someone in Love	196?	3.00	6.00	12.00
-- With "A Division of Liberty Records" on label					
❏ B1-84245	Like Someone in Love	1989	2.50	5.00	10.00
-- "The Finest in Jazz Since 1939" reissue					
❏ BST-84258 [S]	The Witch Doctor	1969	5.00	10.00	20.00
-- With "A Division of Liberty Records" on label					
❏ BST-84347	Roots and Herbs	1970	3.00	6.00	12.00
-- With "Liberty/UA" on label					
❏ B1-93205	The Best of Art Blakey and the Jazz Messengers	1989	3.00	6.00	12.00
BLUEBIRD					
❏ 6286-1-RB	Theory of Art	1987	2.50	5.00	10.00
CADET					
❏ LP-4049 [M]	Tough!	1966	6.25	12.50	25.00
❏ LPS-4049 [S]	Tough!	1966	7.50	15.00	30.00
CATALYST					
❏ 7902	Jazz Messengers '70	197?	3.00	6.00	12.00
COLUMBIA					
❏ CL 897 [M]	The Jazz Messengers	1956	20.00	40.00	80.00
-- Red and black label with six "eye" logos					
❏ CL 1002 [M]	Drum Suite	1957	12.50	25.00	50.00
-- Red and black label with six "eye" logos					
❏ CL 1040 [M]	Hard Bop	1957	15.00	30.00	60.00
-- Red and black label with six "eye" logos					
❏ FC 38036	The Original Jazz Messengers -- A Quarter Century Ago	1982	2.50	5.00	10.00
CONCORD JAZZ					
❏ CJ-68	In This Korner	1978	2.50	5.00	10.00
❏ CJ-168	Straight Ahead	1982	2.50	5.00	10.00
❏ CJ-196	Keystone Three	1983	2.50	5.00	10.00
❏ CJ-256	New York Scene	1984	2.50	5.00	10.00
❏ CJ-307	Live at Kimballs	1987	2.50	5.00	10.00
ELEKTRA					
❏ EKL-120 [M]	A Midnight Session with the Jazz Messengers	1957	20.00	40.00	80.00
EMARCY					
❏ MG-26030 [10]	Blakey	1954	62.50	125.00	250.00
EPIC					
❏ LA 16009 [M]	Paris Concert	1960	7.50	15.00	30.00
❏ LA 16017 [M]	Art Blakey in Paris	1961	7.50	15.00	30.00
❏ BA 17009 [S]	Paris Concert	1960	10.00	20.00	40.00
❏ BA 17017 [S]	Art Blakey in Paris	1961	10.00	20.00	40.00
FANTASY					
❏ OJC-038	Caravan	198?	2.50	5.00	10.00
❏ OJC-090	Ugetsu	198?	2.50	5.00	10.00
❏ OJC-145	Kyoto	198?	2.50	5.00	10.00
GNP CRESCENDO					
❏ GNPS-2182	Live at Sweet Basil	1986	2.50	5.00	10.00
IMPULSE!					
❏ A-7 [M]	Art Blakey!!!! Jazz Messengers!!!!	1961	7.50	15.00	30.00
❏ AS-7 [S]	Art Blakey!!!! Jazz Messengers!!!!	1961	10.00	20.00	40.00
❏ A-45 [M]	A Jazz Message	1963	7.50	15.00	30.00
❏ AS-45 [S]	A Jazz Message	1963	10.00	20.00	40.00
JOSIE					
❏ JOZ-3501 [M]	Cu-Bop	1962	10.00	20.00	40.00
-- Reissue of Jubilee LP					
❏ JS-3501 [S]	Cu-Bop	1962	7.50	15.00	30.00
JUBILEE					
❏ JLP-1049 [M]	Cu-Bop	1958	20.00	40.00	80.00
LIMELIGHT					
❏ LM-82001 [M]	'S Make It	1965	5.00	10.00	20.00
❏ LM-82019 [M]	Soul Finger	1965	5.00	10.00	20.00
❏ LM-82034 [M]	Buttercorn Lady	1966	5.00	10.00	20.00
❏ LM-82038 [M]	Hold On, I'm Coming	1966	5.00	10.00	20.00
❏ LS-86001 [S]	'S Make It	1965	6.25	12.50	25.00
❏ LS-86019 [S]	Soul Finger	1965	6.25	12.50	25.00
❏ LS-86034 [S]	Buttercorn Lady	1966	6.25	12.50	25.00
❏ LS-86038 [S]	Hold On, I'm Coming	1966	6.25	12.50	25.00
MCA IMPULSE!					
❏ MCA-5648	A Jazz Message	1986	2.00	4.00	8.00
-- Reissue					
MILESTONE					
❏ 47008 [(2)]	Thermo	197?	3.75	7.50	15.00
MOSAIC					
❏ MR10-141 [(10)]	The Complete Blue Note Recordings of Art Blakey's 1960 Jazz Messengers	199?	30.00	60.00	120.00
ODYSSEY					
❏ PC 36809	Hard Bop	1981	2.50	5.00	10.00
❏ PC 37021	The Jazz Messengers	1981	2.50	5.00	10.00
PACIFIC JAZZ					
❏ PJ-15 [M]	Ritual	1961	10.00	20.00	40.00
-- Reissue of 402					
❏ PJM-402 [M]	Ritual	1957	20.00	40.00	80.00
PRESTIGE					
❏ 10047	Child's Dance	197?	3.00	6.00	12.00
❏ 10067	Buhaina	197?	3.00	6.00	12.00
❏ 10076	Anthenagin	197?	3.00	6.00	12.00
RCA VICTOR					
❏ LPM-2654 [M]	A Night in Tunisia	1963	10.00	20.00	40.00
-- Reissue of Vik 1115					
❏ LSP-2654 [R]	A Night in Tunisia	1963	5.00	10.00	20.00
RIVERSIDE					
❏ RS-438 [M]	Caravan	1962	6.25	12.50	25.00
❏ RS-464 [M]	Ugetsu	1963	6.25	12.50	25.00
❏ RS-493 [M]	Kyoto	1966	5.00	10.00	20.00
❏ RS-3022	Ugetsu	1968	3.00	6.00	12.00
❏ 6074	Caravan	197?	3.00	6.00	12.00
❏ RS-9438 [S]	Caravan	1962	7.50	15.00	30.00
❏ RS-9464 [S]	Ugetsu	1963	7.50	15.00	30.00
❏ RS-9493 [S]	Kyoto	1966	6.25	12.50	25.00
ROULETTE					
❏ SR-5003	Backgammon	1976	3.00	6.00	12.00
❏ SR-5008	Gypsy Folk Tales	1977	3.00	6.00	12.00
SAVOY					
❏ MG-12171 [M]	Art Blakey and the Jazz Messengers	1960	7.50	15.00	30.00
SAVOY JAZZ					
❏ SJL-1112	Mirage	197?	2.50	5.00	10.00
SOLID STATE					
❏ 18033	Three Blind Mice	1969	3.00	6.00	12.00
SOUL NOTE					
❏ 121105-1	Not Yet	1989	3.00	6.00	12.00
❏ 121155-1	I Get a Kick Out of You	1990	3.00	6.00	12.00
TIMELESS					
❏ 301	In My Prime, Vol. 1	1979	3.00	6.00	12.00
❏ SJP-307	Feel the Wind	1990	3.00	6.00	12.00
❏ 317	Reflections in Blue	1980	3.00	6.00	12.00
TRIP					
❏ 5019	Art Blakey and the Jazz Messengers	197?	2.50	5.00	10.00
❏ 5034	Art Blakey and the Jazz Messengers Live	197?	2.50	5.00	10.00
❏ 5505	Buttercorn Lady	197?	2.50	5.00	10.00
UNITED ARTISTS					
❏ UAS-5633	Three Blind Mice	197?	2.50	5.00	10.00
❏ UAJ-14002 [M]	Three Blind Mice	1962	10.00	20.00	40.00
❏ UAJS-15002 [S]	Three Blind Mice	1962	12.50	25.00	50.00
VEE JAY					
❏ VJS-3066	Bag of Blues Featuring Buddy DeFranco	1977	3.00	6.00	12.00
VIK					
❏ LX-1103 [M]	Art Blakey and the Jazz Messengers Play Selections from Lerner and Loewe	1957	25.00	50.00	100.00
❏ LX-1115 [M]	A Night in Tunisia	1958	25.00	50.00	100.00

BLAKEY, ART, AND THE JAZZ MESSENGERS/ ELMO HOPE

PACIFIC JAZZ

Number	Title	Yr	VG	VG+	NM
❏ PJ-33 [M]	The Jazz Messengers and Elmo Hope	1962	10.00	20.00	40.00

BLAKEY, ART, AND THE JAZZ MESSENGERS WITH THELONIOUS MONK

Also see each artist's individual listings.

ATLANTIC

Number	Title	Yr	VG	VG+	NM
❏ 1278 [M]	Art Blakey's Jazz Messengers with Thelonious Monk	1958	12.50	25.00	50.00
-- Black label					
❏ 1278 [M]	Art Blakey's Jazz Messengers with Thelonious Monk	1960	5.00	10.00	20.00
-- Multicolor label, white "fan" logo					

Number	Title	Yr	VG	VG+	NM
❑ 1278 [M]	Art Blakey's Jazz Messengers with Thelonious Monk	1963	3.75	7.50	15.00
-- Multicolor label, black "fan" logo					
❑ SD 1278 [S]	Art Blakey's Jazz Messengers with Thelonious Monk	1959	10.00	20.00	40.00
-- Green label					
❑ SD 1278 [S]	Art Blakey's Jazz Messengers with Thelonious Monk	1960	3.75	7.50	15.00
-- Multicolor label, white "fan" logo					
❑ SD 1278 [S]	Art Blakey's Jazz Messengers with Thelonious Monk	1963	3.00	6.00	12.00
-- Multicolor label, black "fan" logo					
ODYSSEY					
❑ 32-16-0246	Art Blakey with the Original Jazz Messengers	1968	3.75	7.50	15.00

BLAKEY, ART, AND THE JAZZ MESSENGERS/MAX ROACH
Also see each artist's individual listings.
CHESS

❑ CH2-92511 [(2)]	Percussion Discussion	198?	3.75	7.50	15.00

BLANCHARD, PIERRE
Violinist. Also see LEE KONITZ.
SUNNYSIDE

❑ SSC-1023	Music for String Quartet, Jazz Trio, Violin and Lee Konitz	1988	2.50	5.00	10.00

BLANCHARD, TERENCE, AND DONALD HARRISON
Blanchard is a trumpeter; Harrison is an alto saxophone player. Both are alumni of ART BLAKEY AND HIS JAZZ MESSENGERS.
COLUMBIA

❑ BFC 40335	Nascence	1986	2.50	5.00	10.00
❑ FC 40830	Crystal Star	1987	2.50	5.00	10.00
❑ FC 44216	Black Pearl	1988	2.50	5.00	10.00
GEORGE WEIN COLLECTION					
❑ GW-3002	New York Second Line	1984	3.00	6.00	12.00
❑ GW-3008	Discernment	1986	3.00	6.00	12.00

BLAZING REDHEADS
Quartet consisting of Danielle Dowers, drums; Michaelle Goerlitz, timbales/congas/percussion; Klaudia Promessi, saxophone/flute; and Donna Viscuso, saxophone/flute/piccolo/harmonica.
REFERENCE RECORDINGS

| ❑ RR-26 | Blazing Redheads | 1988 | 5.00 | 10.00 | 20.00 |
| ❑ RR-41 | Crazed Women | 1991 | 5.00 | 10.00 | 20.00 |

BLEY, CARLA
Pianist, composer and conductor.
ECM

❑ 25003	Heavy Heart	1984	2.50	5.00	10.00
ECM/WATT					
❑ ECM W-11	Social Studies	1980	3.00	6.00	12.00
❑ ECM W-12	Live!	1982	3.00	6.00	12.00
❑ ECM W-12 1/2	I Hate to Sing	1982	3.00	6.00	12.00
❑ ECM W-14	Heavy Heart	1983	3.00	6.00	12.00
JCOA					
❑ 3-LP-EOTH [(3)]	Escalator Over the Hill	1971	6.25	12.50	25.00
WATT					
❑ 1	Tropic Appetites	1974	3.75	7.50	15.00
❑ 6	Dinner Music	1976	3.75	7.50	15.00
❑ 8	European Tour 1977	1978	3.75	7.50	15.00
❑ 9	Musique Mecanique	1979	3.75	7.50	15.00

BLEY, PAUL
Pianist and synthesizer player. Also see CHET BAKER AND PAUL BLEY.
ARISTA/FREEDOM

❑ AL 1901 [(2)]	Copenhagen and Haarlem	197?	3.75	7.50	15.00
DEBUT					
❑ DLP-7 [10]	Introducing Paul Bley	1954	75.00	150.00	300.00
ECM					
❑ 1010	Ballads	1973	3.75	7.50	15.00
❑ 1023	Open to Love	1974	3.00	6.00	12.00
EMARCY					
❑ MG-36092 [M]	Paul Bley	1955	25.00	50.00	100.00
ESP-DISK'					
❑ 1008 [M]	Barrage	1965	3.75	7.50	15.00
❑ S-1008 [S]	Barrage	1965	5.00	10.00	20.00
❑ 1021 [M]	Closer	1966	3.75	7.50	15.00
❑ S-1021 [S]	Closer	1966	5.00	10.00	20.00
FANTASY					
❑ OJC-201	Introducing Paul Bley	198?	2.50	5.00	10.00
-- Reissue of Debut 7					

Number	Title	Yr	VG	VG+	NM
GENE NORMAN					
❑ GNP-31 [M]	Solemn Meditation	1957	6.25	12.50	25.00
GNP CRESCENDO					
❑ GNPS-31 [R]	Solemn Meditation	197?	2.50	5.00	10.00
❑ GT-3002	Solemn Meditation	198?	2.50	5.00	10.00
IAI					
❑ 373839	Quiet Song	1975	3.00	6.00	12.00
-- With Jimmy Giuffre and Bill Connors					
❑ 373840	Alone Again	1975	3.00	6.00	12.00
❑ 373841	Turning Point	1975	3.00	6.00	12.00
-- With John Gilmore					
❑ 373853	Axis	1978	3.00	6.00	12.00
INNER CITY					
❑ 1007	Live at the Hillcrest 1958	197?	3.00	6.00	12.00
LIMELIGHT					
❑ LM-82060 [M]	Mr. Joy	1967	5.00	10.00	20.00
❑ LS-86060 [S]	Mr. Joy	1967	3.75	7.50	15.00
MILESTONE					
❑ 9033	Synthesizer Show	197?	3.75	7.50	15.00
❑ 9046	Paul Bley and Scorpio	197?	3.75	7.50	15.00
OWL					
❑ 034	Tears	198?	3.00	6.00	12.00
SAVOY					
❑ MG-12182 [M]	Footloose!	1964	6.25	12.50	25.00
SAVOY JAZZ					
❑ SJL-1148	Floater	198?	2.50	5.00	10.00
❑ SJL-1175	Syndrome	1987	2.50	5.00	10.00
❑ SJL-1192	Turns	1988	2.50	5.00	10.00
SOUL NOTE					
❑ SN-1085	Sonor	1984	3.00	6.00	12.00
❑ SN-1090	Tango Palace	1985	3.00	6.00	12.00
STEEPLECHASE					
❑ SCS-1214	My Standard	198?	2.50	5.00	10.00
WING					
❑ MGW-60001 [M]	Paul Bley	1956	12.50	25.00	50.00

BLEY, PAUL; GARY PEACOCK
Also see each artist's individual listings.
ECM

❑ 1003	Paul Bley with Gary Peacock	1973	3.75	7.50	15.00

BLEY, PAUL; GARY PEACOCK; BARRY ALTSCHUL
Barry Altschul is a drummer. Also see PAUL BLEY; GARY PEACOCK.
IAI

| ❑ 373844 | Virtuosi | 1976 | 3.00 | 6.00 | 12.00 |
| ❑ 373849 | Japan Suite | 1977 | 3.00 | 6.00 | 12.00 |

BLEY, PAUL, AND NIELS-HENNING ORSTED PEDERSEN
Also see each artist's individual listings.
INNER CITY

❑ 2005	Paul Bley and Niels-Henning Orsted Pedersen	197?	3.00	6.00	12.00
STEEPLECHASE					
❑ SCS-1005	Paul Bley and Niels-Henning Orsted Pedersen	198?	2.50	5.00	10.00

BLOOD, SWEAT AND TEARS
Jazz-rock band formed by Al Kooper, who appeared only on *Child Is Father to the Man*. He was replaced by lead singer David Clayton-Thomas. The group's jazz quotient varied from album to album.
ABC

❑ 1015	Brand New Day	1977	2.50	5.00	10.00
COLUMBIA					
❑ CS 9619	Child Is Father to the Man	1968	3.75	7.50	15.00
-- Red "360 Sound" label					
❑ CS 9619	Child Is Father to the Man	1970	2.50	5.00	10.00
-- Orange label					
❑ PC 9619	Child Is Father to the Man	1980	2.00	4.00	8.00
❑ CS 9720	Blood, Sweat and Tears	1969	3.75	7.50	15.00
-- Red "360 Sound" label					
❑ CS 9720	Blood, Sweat and Tears	1970	2.50	5.00	10.00
-- Orange label					
❑ PC 9720	Blood, Sweat and Tears	1980	2.00	4.00	8.00
❑ KC 30090	Blood, Sweat and Tears 3	1970	2.50	5.00	10.00
❑ PC 30090	Blood, Sweat and Tears 3	1986	2.00	4.00	8.00
❑ CQ 30994 [Q]	Blood, Sweat and Tears	1972	5.00	10.00	20.00
❑ KC 30590	BS&T: 4	1971	2.50	5.00	10.00
❑ CQ 31170 [Q]	Blood, Sweat and Tears' Greatest Hits	1972	5.00	10.00	20.00
❑ KC 31170	Blood, Sweat and Tears' Greatest Hits	1972	2.50	5.00	10.00
-- With the single versions of "You've Made Me So Very Happy," "Spinning Wheel," and "And When I Die" (all in mono)					

Number	Title	Yr	VG	VG+	NM
❑ PC 31170	Blood, Sweat and Tears' Greatest Hits	1980	2.00	4.00	8.00
❑ KC 31780	New Blood	1972	2.50	5.00	10.00
❑ KC 32180	No Sweat	1973	2.50	5.00	10.00
❑ CQ 32929 [Q]	Mirror Image	1974	5.00	10.00	20.00
❑ PC 32929	Mirror Image	1974	2.50	5.00	10.00
❑ PC 33484	New City	1975	2.50	5.00	10.00
❑ PC 34233	More Than Ever	1976	2.50	5.00	10.00
❑ HC 49619	Child Is Father to the Man	1981	12.50	25.00	50.00

-- Half-speed mastered edition

DIRECT DISK

Number	Title	Yr	VG	VG+	NM
❑ SD-16605	Blood, Sweat and Tears	1981	15.00	30.00	60.00

MCA

Number	Title	Yr	VG	VG+	NM
❑ L33-1865 [DJ]	Nuclear Blues	1980	3.75	7.50	15.00

-- Promo only on gold vinyl

| ❑ 3061 | Nuclear Blues | 1980 | 2.50 | 5.00 | 10.00 |
| ❑ 3227 | Blood, Sweat and Tears | 1981 | --- | --- | --- |

-- Canceled?

MOBILE FIDELITY

Number	Title	Yr	VG	VG+	NM
❑ 1-251	Blood, Sweat and Tears	1996	30.00	60.00	120.00

-- Audiophile vinyl; fewer than 2,000 pressed

BLUE BIRD SOCIETY ORCHESTRA, THE
STASH

Number	Title	Yr	VG	VG+	NM
❑ ST-268	The Blue Bird Society Orchestra	1987	2.50	5.00	10.00

BLUE STARS, THE
Vocal group from France. Their version of "Lullaby of Birdland" was a top-20 U.S. pop hit in early 1956.
EMARCY

Number	Title	Yr	VG	VG+	NM
❑ MG-36067 [M]	Lullaby of Birdland	1956	10.00	20.00	40.00

BLUIETT, HAMIET
Baritone saxophone player, sometimes a flutist. Also see WORLD SAXOPHONE QUARTET.
BLACK SAINT

Number	Title	Yr	VG	VG+	NM
❑ BSR-0014	Resolution	198?	3.00	6.00	12.00

CHIAROSCURO

| ❑ CH-182 | Orchestra, Duo and Sextet | 1978 | 3.00 | 6.00 | 12.00 |

INDIA NAVIGATION

❑ IN-1025	Endangered Species	1976	3.00	6.00	12.00
❑ IN-1030	Birthright	1977	3.00	6.00	12.00
❑ IN-1039	S.O.S.	1979	3.00	6.00	12.00

SOUL NOTE

| ❑ SN-1018 | Dangerously Suite | 198? | 3.00 | 6.00 | 12.00 |
| ❑ SN-1088 | Ebu | 1985 | 3.00 | 6.00 | 12.00 |

BLYTHE, ARTHUR
Alto saxophone player and bandleader.
ADELPHI

Number	Title	Yr	VG	VG+	NM
❑ 5008	Bush Baby	1978	3.00	6.00	12.00

COLUMBIA

❑ JC 35638	Lenox Avenue Breakdown	1979	2.50	5.00	10.00
❑ JC 36300	In the Tradition	1979	2.50	5.00	10.00
❑ JC 36583	Illusions	1980	2.50	5.00	10.00
❑ PC 36583	Illusions	198?	2.00	4.00	8.00

-- Budget-line reissue

❑ FC 37427	Blythe Spirit	1981	2.50	5.00	10.00
❑ FC 38163	Elaborations	1982	2.50	5.00	10.00
❑ FC 38661	Light Blue	1983	2.50	5.00	10.00
❑ FC 39411	Put Sunshine In It	1984	2.50	5.00	10.00
❑ FC 40237	Da-Da	1986	2.50	5.00	10.00

INDIA NAVIGATION

| ❑ IN-1029 | The Grip | 1977 | 3.00 | 6.00 | 12.00 |
| ❑ IN-1038 | Metamorphosis | 1979 | 3.00 | 6.00 | 12.00 |

BLYTHE, JIMMY
Pianist; pioneer in the "boogie-woogie" style.
EUPHORIA

Number	Title	Yr	VG	VG+	NM
❑ EES-101	Messin' Around	198?	3.00	6.00	12.00
❑ EES-102	Messin' Around, Vol. 2	198?	3.00	6.00	12.00

RIVERSIDE

| ❑ RLP-1031 [10] | Chicago Stomps and the Dixie Four | 1954 | 20.00 | 40.00 | 80.00 |
| ❑ RLP-1036 [10] | Jimmy Blythe's State Street Ramblers | 1954 | 20.00 | 40.00 | 80.00 |

BOBO, WILLIE
Percussionist (generally congas, timbales and drums) and occasional male singer.
BLUE NOTE

Number	Title	Yr	VG	VG+	NM
❑ BN-LA711-G	Tomorrow Is Here	1977	3.00	6.00	12.00

COLUMBIA

Number	Title	Yr	VG	VG+	NM
❑ JC 35734	Hell of an Act to Follow	1978	3.00	6.00	12.00

MGM

❑ 10007	Spanish Grease	197?	3.00	6.00	12.00
❑ 10011	Uno, Dos, Tres	197?	3.00	6.00	12.00
❑ 10012	Spanish Blues Band	197?	3.00	6.00	12.00

ROULETTE

| ❑ R-52097 [M] | Bobo's Beat | 1962 | 6.25 | 12.50 | 25.00 |
| ❑ SR-52097 [S] | Bobo's Beat | 1962 | 7.50 | 15.00 | 30.00 |

SUSSEX

| ❑ SUS-7003 | Do What You Want to Do | 1971 | 3.00 | 6.00 | 12.00 |

TICO

| ❑ ST-1108 [S] | Do That Thing | 1963 | 7.50 | 15.00 | 30.00 |
| ❑ T-1108 [M] | Do That Thing | 1963 | 6.25 | 12.50 | 25.00 |

TRIP

| ❑ 5013 | Latin Beat | 1974 | 2.50 | 5.00 | 10.00 |

VERVE

❑ V-8631 [M]	Spanish Grease	1965	3.75	7.50	15.00
❑ V6-8631 [S]	Spanish Grease	1965	5.00	10.00	20.00
❑ V-8648 [M]	Uno, Dos, Tres	1966	3.75	7.50	15.00
❑ V6-8648 [S]	Uno, Dos, Tres	1966	5.00	10.00	20.00
❑ V-8669 [M]	Feelin' So Good	1966	3.75	7.50	15.00
❑ V6-8669 [S]	Feelin' So Good	1966	5.00	10.00	20.00
❑ V-8685 [M]	Juicy	1967	5.00	10.00	20.00
❑ V6-8685 [S]	Juicy	1967	5.00	10.00	20.00
❑ V-8699 [M]	Bobo Motion	1967	5.00	10.00	20.00
❑ V6-8699 [S]	Bobo Motion	1967	5.00	10.00	20.00
❑ V6-8736	Spanish Blues Band	1968	5.00	10.00	20.00
❑ V6-8772	A New Dimension	1969	3.75	7.50	15.00
❑ V6-8781	Evil Ways	1969	3.75	7.50	15.00

BOCAGE, PETER
His most prominent instruments were the violin and trumpet, though he also played banjo, xylophone, mandolin, guitar, trombone and baritone horn.
JAZZOLOGY

Number	Title	Yr	VG	VG+	NM
❑ JCE-29	San Jacinto Hall	1978	2.50	5.00	10.00
❑ JCE-32	Peter Bocage with His Creole Serenaders	1979	2.50	5.00	10.00

RIVERSIDE

| ❑ RLP-379 [M] | Peter Bocage with His Creole Serenaders | 1961 | 6.25 | 12.50 | 25.00 |
| ❑ RLP-9379 [S] | Peter Bocage with His Creole Serenaders | 1961 | 7.50 | 15.00 | 30.00 |

BOCIAN, MICHAEL
Guitarist and composer.
GM RECORDINGS

Number	Title	Yr	VG	VG+	NM
❑ GM-3002	For This Gift	1982	2.50	5.00	10.00

BOFILL, ANGELA
Female singer.
ARISTA

Number	Title	Yr	VG	VG+	NM
❑ AL8-8000	Too Tough	198?	2.00	4.00	8.00

-- Reissue of 9616

| ❑ AL8-8125 | Something About You | 198? | 2.00 | 4.00 | 8.00 |

-- Reissue of 9576

❑ AL8-8198	Teaser	1983	2.50	5.00	10.00
❑ AL8-8258	Let Me Be the One	1984	2.50	5.00	10.00
❑ AL8-8396	Tell Me Tomorrow	1985	2.50	5.00	10.00
❑ AL8-8425	The Best of Angela Bofill	1986	2.50	5.00	10.00
❑ AL 9576	Something About You	1981	2.50	5.00	10.00
❑ AL 9616	Too Tough	1983	2.50	5.00	10.00

ARISTA/GRP

❑ GL 5000	Angie	1978	3.00	6.00	12.00
❑ GL 5501	Angel of the Night	1979	3.00	6.00	12.00
❑ GL8-8060	Angel of the Night	198?	2.00	4.00	8.00

-- Reissue of 5501

| ❑ GLB-8302 | Angie | 198? | 2.00 | 4.00 | 8.00 |

-- Reissue of 5000

CAPITOL

| ❑ C1-48335 | Intuition | 1988 | 2.50 | 5.00 | 10.00 |

BOHANNON, GEORGE
Trombonist. Also has played tenor sax, flute, piano and bass.
WORKSHOP JAZZ

Number	Title	Yr	VG	VG+	NM
❑ WSJ-207 [M]	Boss Bossa Nova	1963	20.00	40.00	80.00
❑ WSJ-214 [M]	Bold Bohannon	1964	---	---	---

-- Canceled?

BOLCOM, WILLIAM
Pianist and composer.
JAZZOLOGY

Number	Title	Yr	VG	VG+	NM
❑ JCE-72	William Bolcom Plays His Own Rags	198?	2.50	5.00	10.00

Number	Title	Yr	VG	VG+	NM
NONESUCH					
❑ N-71257	Heliotrope Bouquet (Piano Rags, 1900-70)	1971	3.00	6.00	12.00
❑ N-71299	Pastimes and Piano Rags	1972	3.00	6.00	12.00
BOLL WEEVIL JAZZ BAND					
GHB					
❑ 31 [M]	Volume 1	1966	3.00	6.00	12.00
❑ 32 [M]	Volume 2: Just a Little While	1966	3.00	6.00	12.00
❑ 33 [M]	Volume 3: One More Time	1966	3.00	6.00	12.00
❑ 34 [M]	Volume 4: One More Time Again	1966	3.00	6.00	12.00
❑ 48	Volume 5: A Hot Band Is Hard to Find	1968	2.50	5.00	10.00
❑ 89	Red Hot in Memphis	197?	2.50	5.00	10.00
BOLLING, CLAUDE					
Pianist and composer.					
BALLY					
❑ BAL-12003 [M]	French Jazz	1956	10.00	20.00	40.00
CBS MASTERWORKS					
❑ FM 36691	California Suite	1980	2.50	5.00	10.00
-- With Hubert Laws and Shelly Manne					
❑ FM 36731	Toot Suite for Trumpet and Jazz Piano	1980	2.50	5.00	10.00
-- With Maurice Andre					
❑ M3 36845 [(3)]	Bolling	1981	6.25	12.50	25.00
-- Combines 33233, 35128, and 35864 in one box					
❑ FM 37264	Concerto for Classic Guitar and Jazz Piano	1981	2.50	5.00	10.00
-- With Alexandre Lagoya; reissue of RCA Red Seal 0149					
❑ FM 37798	Suite for Jazz Piano and Chamber Orchestra	1982	2.50	5.00	10.00
❑ FM 39059	Suite for Cello and Jazz Piano Trio	1984	2.50	5.00	10.00
-- With Yo-Yo Ma, others					
❑ FM 39244	Jazz A La Francaise	1985	2.50	5.00	10.00
❑ FM 39245	Big Band	1985	2.50	5.00	10.00
❑ FM 42474	Bolling Plays Ellington, Vol. 1	1988	2.50	5.00	10.00
❑ FM 42476	Bolling Plays Ellington, Vol. 2	1988	2.50	5.00	10.00
COLUMBIA					
❑ PC 33277	Original Ragtime	1975	2.50	5.00	10.00
❑ FM 39009	Original Ragtime	1984	2.00	4.00	8.00
-- Reissue of 33277					
COLUMBIA MASTERWORKS					
❑ M 33233	Suite for Flute and Jazz Piano	1975	2.50	5.00	10.00
-- With Jean-Pierre Rampal					
❑ M 35128	Suite for Violin and Jazz Piano	1978	2.50	5.00	10.00
-- With Pinchas Zuckerman					
❑ M 35864	Picnic Suite for Flute, Guitar and Jazz Piano	1979	2.50	5.00	10.00
-- With Jean-Pierre Rampal and Alexandre Lagoya					
DRG					
❑ SL-5201	Nuances	1986	2.50	5.00	10.00
JAZZ MAN					
❑ 5018	Rolling with Bolling	198?	2.50	5.00	10.00
-- Reissue of Omega OSL-6					
MERCURY					
❑ 812 569-1	Bolling Blues	1983	2.50	5.00	10.00
OMEGA					
❑ OKL-6 [M]	Rolling with Bolling	1960	6.25	12.50	25.00
❑ OSL-6 [S]	Rolling with Bolling	1960	7.50	15.00	30.00
PHILIPS					
❑ PHM 200-204 [M]	Two-Beat Mozart	1966	3.75	7.50	15.00
❑ PHS 600-204 [S]	Two-Beat Mozart	1966	5.00	10.00	20.00
RCA RED SEAL					
❑ FRL1-0149	Concerto for Classic Guitar and Jazz Piano	1973	3.00	6.00	12.00
-- With Alexandre Lagoya					
BONANO, SHARKEY					
Trumpeter. Also see PAUL BARBARIN.					
CAPITOL					
❑ H 266 [10]	Sharkey's Southern Comfort	1951	12.50	25.00	50.00
❑ T 266 [M]	Kings of Dixieland	1954	10.00	20.00	40.00
CIRCLE					
❑ LP-422 [10]	Sharkey Bonano	1951	12.50	25.00	50.00
GMB					
❑ 122	Sharkey Bonano and His Kings of Dixieland	198?	2.50	5.00	10.00
ROULETTE					
❑ R-25112 [M]	Dixieland at the Roundtable	1960	6.25	12.50	25.00

Number	Title	Yr	VG	VG+	NM
SOUTHLAND					
❑ SLP-205 [10]	New Orleans Dixieland Session	1954	12.50	25.00	50.00
❑ 205 [M]	New Orleans Jam Session	1961	7.50	15.00	30.00
❑ 222 [M]	Kings of Dixieland	1959	7.50	15.00	30.00
BONANO, SHARKEY, AND LIZZIE MILES					
Also see each artist's individual listings.					
CAPITOL					
❑ H 367 [10]	Midnight on Bourbon Street	1952	12.50	25.00	50.00
❑ T 367 [M]	Midnight on Bourbon Street	1954	10.00	20.00	40.00
❑ T 792 [M]	A Night in Old New Orleans	1956	10.00	20.00	40.00
BOND, JAMES, SEXTETTE					
MIRWOOD					
❑ M-7001 [M]	The James Bond Songbook	1966	6.25	12.50	25.00
❑ S-7001 [S]	The James Bond Songbook	1966	7.50	15.00	30.00
BONFA, LUIZ					
Guitarist and composer. Also see STAN GETZ; PAUL WINTER.					
ATLANTIC					
❑ 8028 [M]	The Fabulous Guitar of Luiz Bonfa/Amor!	1959	10.00	20.00	40.00
-- Black label					
❑ 8028 [M]	The Fabulous Guitar of Luiz Bonfa/Amor!	1960	7.50	15.00	30.00
-- White "bullseye" label					
❑ 8028 [M]	The Fabulous Guitar of Luiz Bonfa/Amor!	1961	5.00	10.00	20.00
-- Multicolor label, white "fan" logo at right					
❑ 8028 [M]	The Fabulous Guitar of Luiz Bonfa/Amor!	1963	3.75	7.50	15.00
-- Multicolor label, black "fan" logo at right					
❑ SD 8028 [S]	The Fabulous Guitar of Luiz Bonfa/Amor!	1959	12.50	25.00	50.00
-- Green label					
❑ SD 8028 [S]	The Fabulous Guitar of Luiz Bonfa/Amor!	1960	10.00	20.00	40.00
-- White "bullseye" label					
❑ SD 8028 [S]	The Fabulous Guitar of Luiz Bonfa/Amor!	1961	6.25	12.50	25.00
-- Multicolor label, white "fan" logo at right					
❑ SD 8028 [S]	The Fabulous Guitar of Luiz Bonfa/Amor!	1963	5.00	10.00	20.00
-- Multicolor label, black "fan" logo at right					
CAPITOL					
❑ T 10134 [M]	Brazilian Guitar	1958	10.00	20.00	40.00
-- Turquoise label					
DOT					
❑ DLP-3804 [M]	Luiz Bonfa	1967	5.00	10.00	20.00
❑ DLP-25804 [S]	Luiz Bonfa	1967	3.75	7.50	15.00
❑ DLP-25825	Luiz Bonfa Plays Great Songs	1968	3.75	7.50	15.00
❑ DLP-25881	Bonfa	1968	3.75	7.50	15.00
EPIC					
❑ LN 24124 [M]	Softly	1964	3.75	7.50	15.00
❑ BN 26124 [S]	Softly	1964	5.00	10.00	20.00
PHILIPS					
❑ PHM 200-087 [M]	Brazil's King of the Bossa Nova and Guitar	1963	3.75	7.50	15.00
❑ PHM 200-199 [M]	Braziliana	1965	3.00	6.00	12.00
❑ PHM 200-208 [M]	The Brazilian Scene	1966	3.00	6.00	12.00
❑ PHS 600-087 [S]	Brazil's King of the Bossa Nova and Guitar	1963	5.00	10.00	20.00
❑ PHS 600-199 [S]	Braziliana	1965	3.75	7.50	15.00
❑ PHS 600-208 [S]	The Brazilian Scene	1966	3.75	7.50	15.00
VERVE					
❑ V-8522 [M]	Luiz Bonfa Plays and Sings Bossa Nova	1963	3.75	7.50	15.00
❑ V6-8522 [S]	Luiz Bonfa Plays and Sings Bossa Nova	1963	5.00	10.00	20.00
BONNEMERE, EDDIE					
Pianist.					
PRESTIGE					
❑ PRLP-7354 [M]	Jazz Oriented	1965	5.00	10.00	20.00
❑ PRST-7354 [S]	Jazz Oriented	1965	6.25	12.50	25.00
ROOST					
❑ RST-419 [10]	Piano Mambo with Bonnemere	1954	12.50	25.00	50.00
❑ RST-2236 [M]	Piano Bon Bons	1959	7.50	15.00	30.00
❑ SLP-2236 [S]	Piano Bon Bons	1959	10.00	20.00	40.00
❑ RST-2241 [M]	The Sound of Memory	1960	7.50	15.00	30.00
❑ SLP-2241 [S]	The Sound of Memory	1960	10.00	20.00	40.00

Number	Title	Yr	VG	VG+	NM

BOSTIC, EARL
Alto saxophone player and bandleader.
GRAND PRIX
Number	Title	Yr	VG	VG+	NM
❏ K-404 [M]	The Grand Prix Series	196?	3.75	7.50	15.00
❏ KS-404 [R]	The Grand Prix Series	196?	3.00	6.00	12.00
❏ K-416 [M]	Wild Man	196?	3.75	7.50	15.00
❏ KS-416 [R]	Wild Man	196?	3.00	6.00	12.00

KING
❏ 295-64 [10]	Earl Bostic and His Alto Sax	1951	100.00	200.00	400.00
-- Red vinyl					
❏ 295-64 [10]	Earl Bostic and His Alto Sax	1951	50.00	100.00	200.00
-- Black vinyl					
❏ 295-65 [10]	Earl Bostic and His Alto Sax	1951	100.00	200.00	400.00
-- Red vinyl					
❏ 295-65 [10]	Earl Bostic and His Alto Sax	1951	50.00	100.00	200.00
-- Black vinyl					
❏ 295-66 [10]	Earl Bostic and His Alto Sax	1951	100.00	200.00	400.00
-- Red vinyl					
❏ 295-66 [10]	Earl Bostic and His Alto Sax	1951	50.00	100.00	200.00
-- Black vinyl					
❏ 295-72 [10]	Earl Bostic and His Alto Sax	1952	50.00	100.00	200.00
❏ 295-76 [10]	Earl Bostic and His Alto Sax	1952	50.00	100.00	200.00
❏ 295-77 [10]	Earl Bostic and His Alto Sax	1952	50.00	100.00	200.00
❏ 295-78 [10]	Earl Bostic and His Alto Sax	1952	50.00	100.00	200.00
❏ 295-79 [10]	Earl Bostic and His Alto Sax	1952	50.00	100.00	200.00
❏ 295-95 [10]	Earl Bostic Plays the Old Standards	1954	50.00	100.00	200.00
❏ 295-103 [10]	Earl Bostic and His Alto Sax	1954	50.00	100.00	200.00
❏ 395-500 [M]	Dance to the Best of Bostic	1956	25.00	50.00	100.00
-- Original cover with Earl Bostic pictured					
❏ 395-500 [M]	Dance to the Best of Bostic	195?	20.00	40.00	80.00
-- Second cover with girl in a swimsuit pictured					
❏ 395-503 [M]	Bostic for You	1956	25.00	50.00	100.00
❏ 395-515 [M]	Alto-Tude	1956	25.00	50.00	100.00
❏ 395-525 [M]	Dance Time	1956	20.00	40.00	80.00
❏ 395-529 [M]	Let's Dance with Earl Bostic	1956	20.00	40.00	80.00
❏ 395-547 [M]	Invitation to Dance	1956	20.00	40.00	80.00
❏ 558 [M]	C'mon and Dance with Earl Bostic	1956	20.00	40.00	80.00
❏ KS-558 [S]	C'mon and Dance with Earl Bostic	1959	37.50	75.00	150.00
❏ 571 [M]	Hits of the Swing Age	1957	20.00	40.00	80.00
❏ 583 [M]	Showcase of Swinging Dance Hits	1958	20.00	40.00	80.00
❏ 597 [M]	Alto Magic in Hi-Fi	1958	20.00	40.00	80.00
❏ KS-597 [S]	Alto Magic in Hi-Fi	1959	37.50	75.00	150.00
❏ 602 [M]	Sweet Tunes of the Fantastic Fifties	1959	12.50	25.00	50.00
❏ KS-602 [S]	Sweet Tunes of the Fantastic Fifties	1959	25.00	50.00	100.00
❏ 613 [M]	Bostic Workshop	1959	12.50	25.00	50.00
❏ KS-613 [S]	Bostic Workshop	1959	25.00	50.00	100.00
❏ 620 [M]	Sweet Tunes from the Roaring Twenties	1959	12.50	25.00	50.00
❏ KS-620 [S]	Sweet Tunes from the Roaring Twenties	1959	25.00	50.00	100.00
❏ 632 [M]	Sweet Tunes of the Swinging Thirties	1959	12.50	25.00	50.00
❏ KS-632 [S]	Sweet Tunes of the Swinging Thirties	1959	25.00	50.00	100.00
❏ 640 [M]	Sweet Tunes of the Sentimental Forties	1960	12.50	25.00	50.00
❏ KS-640 [S]	Sweet Tunes of the Sentimental Forties	1960	20.00	40.00	80.00
❏ 662 [M]	Musical Pearls	1960	12.50	25.00	50.00
❏ KS-662 [S]	Musical Pearls	1960	20.00	40.00	80.00
❏ 705 [M]	Hit Tunes of Big Broadway Shows	1960	12.50	25.00	50.00
❏ KS-705 [S]	Hit Tunes of Big Broadway Shows	1960	20.00	40.00	80.00
❏ 786 [M]	By Popular Demand	1961	12.50	25.00	50.00
❏ 827 [M]	Earl Bostic Plays Bossa Nova	1963	12.50	25.00	50.00
❏ 838 [M]	Songs of the Fantastic Fifties, Volume 2	1963	12.50	25.00	50.00
❏ 846 [M]	Jazz As I Feel It	1963	12.50	25.00	50.00
❏ 881 [M]	The Best of Earl Bostic, Volume 2	1964	12.50	25.00	50.00
❏ 900 [M]	The New Sound	1964	12.50	25.00	50.00
❏ 921 [M]	The Great Hits of 1964	1964	12.50	25.00	50.00
❏ 947 [M]	24 Songs That Earl Loved the Most	1966	10.00	20.00	40.00
❏ KS-1048 [S]	Harlem Nocturne	1969	6.25	12.50	25.00
❏ K-5010X	14 Original Greatest Hits	1977	3.00	6.00	12.00

PHILIPS
| ❏ PHM 200-262 [M] | The Song Is Not Ended | 1967 | 6.25 | 12.50 | 25.00 |
| ❏ PHS 600-262 [S] | The Song Is Not Ended | 1967 | 6.25 | 12.50 | 25.00 |

BOSTIC, EARL/JIMMY LUNCEFORD
Also see each artist's individual listings.
ALLEGRO ELITE
Number	Title	Yr	VG	VG+	NM
❏ 4053 [10]	Earl Bostic/Jimmy Lunceford Orchestras	195?	10.00	20.00	40.00

BOSWELL, CONNEE
Female singer. Also a pianist, saxophone player, violinist and cellist.
DECCA
❏ DL 5390 [10]	Connee Boswell	1951	20.00	40.00	80.00
❏ DL 5445 [10]	Singing the Blues	1952	20.00	40.00	80.00
❏ DL 8356 [M]	Connee	1956	12.50	25.00	50.00

DESIGN
❏ DLP-68 [M]	Connee Boswell Sings Irving Berlin	196?	3.00	6.00	12.00
❏ DLPS-68 [R]	Connee Boswell Sings Irving Berlin	196?	2.00	4.00	8.00
❏ DLP-101 [M]	The New Sound of Connee Boswell	196?	3.00	6.00	12.00
❏ DLPS-101 [R]	The New Sound of Connee Boswell	196?	2.00	4.00	8.00

RCA VICTOR
| ❏ LPM-1426 [M] | Connee Boswell and the Original Memphis Five | 1957 | 10.00 | 20.00 | 40.00 |

BOTHWELL, JOHNNY
Alto saxophone player and bandleader.
BRUNSWICK
| ❏ BL 58033 [10] | Presenting Johnny Bothwell | 1953 | 25.00 | 50.00 | 100.00 |

BOULOU
See BOULOU FERRE.

BOURBON STREET STOMPERS, THE
TIME
| ❏ S-2118 [S] | We Like Dixieland | 196? | 5.00 | 10.00 | 20.00 |
| ❏ 52118 [M] | We Like Dixieland | 196? | 3.75 | 7.50 | 15.00 |

BOWIE, LESTER
Trumpeter and flugel horn player. Also see ART ENSEMBLE OF CHICAGO.
BLACK SAINT
| ❏ BSR-0020 | Fifth Power | 197? | 3.00 | 6.00 | 12.00 |
ECM
❏ 1209	The Great Pretender	1981	3.00	6.00	12.00
❏ 23789	All the Magic	1984	2.50	5.00	10.00
❏ 25034	I Only Have Eyes for You	1985	2.50	5.00	10.00
MUSE
❏ MR-5055	Fast Last!	1975	3.00	6.00	12.00
❏ MR-5081	Rope-a-Dope	1975	3.00	6.00	12.00
❏ MR-5337	Hello Dolly	1987	2.50	5.00	10.00
NESSA
| ❏ N-1 | Numbers 1 and 2 | 1968 | 6.25 | 12.50 | 25.00 |
VENTURE
| ❏ 90650 | Twilight Dreams | 1988 | 2.50 | 5.00 | 10.00 |

BOWIE, LESTER, AND PHILIP WILSON
Also see each artist's individual listings.
IAI
| ❏ 373854 | Duet | 1978 | 3.00 | 6.00 | 12.00 |

BOWIE, PAT
Female singer.
PRESTIGE
❏ PRLP-7385 [M]	Out of Sight	1965	7.50	15.00	30.00
❏ PRST-7385 [S]	Out of Sight	1965	7.50	15.00	30.00
❏ PRLP-7437 [M]	Feelin' Good	1967	7.50	15.00	30.00
❏ PRST-7437 [S]	Feelin' Good	1967	6.25	12.50	25.00

BOWN, PATTI
Pianist.
COLUMBIA
| ❏ CL 1379 [M] | Patti Bown Plays Big Piano | 1959 | 7.50 | 15.00 | 30.00 |

BOYD, ROCKY
Tenor saxophone player.
JAZZTIME
| ❏ JS-001 [S] | Ease It | 1961 | 7.50 | 15.00 | 30.00 |
| ❏ JT-001 [M] | Ease It | 1961 | 6.25 | 12.50 | 25.00 |

Number	Title	Yr	VG	VG+	NM
BRACE, JANET					
Female singer.					
ABC-PARAMOUNT					
❑ ABC-116 [M]	Special Delivery	1956	12.50	25.00	50.00
BRACKEEN, CHARLES					
Tenor and soprano saxophone player.					
SILKHEART					
❑ SH-105	Bannar	198?	3.00	6.00	12.00
❑ SH-110	Attainment	198?	3.00	6.00	12.00
❑ SH-111	Worshippers Come Nigh	198?	3.00	6.00	12.00
STRATA-EAST					
❑ 19736	Rhythm X	1974	3.00	6.00	12.00
BRACKEEN, JOANNE					
Pianist and composer.					
ANTILLES					
❑ 1001	Special Identity	198?	2.50	5.00	10.00
CHOICE					
❑ CRS 1009	Snooze	1976	3.00	6.00	12.00
❑ CRS 1016	Tring-a-Ling	1977	3.00	6.00	12.00
❑ CRS 1024	Prism	1978	3.00	6.00	12.00
COLUMBIA					
❑ JC 36075	Keyed In	1979	2.50	5.00	10.00
❑ JC 36593	Ancient Dynasty	1980	2.50	5.00	10.00
CONCORD JAZZ					
❑ CJ-280	Havin' Fun	1985	2.50	5.00	10.00
❑ CJ-316	Fi-Fi Goes to Heaven	1987	2.50	5.00	10.00
PAUSA					
❑ 7045	Mythical Magic	1979	3.00	6.00	12.00
TIMELESS					
❑ TI-302	Aft	1980	3.00	6.00	12.00
BRADFORD, BOBBY					
Trumpeter. Also see JOHN CARTER AND BOBBY BRADFORD.					
EMANEM					
❑ 3302	Love's Dream	1976	5.00	10.00	20.00
NESSA					
❑ N-17	Bobby Bradford with John Stevens and the Spontaneous Music Ensemble, Vol. 1	198?	2.50	5.00	10.00
❑ N-18	Bobby Bradford with John Stevens and the Spontaneous Music Ensemble, Vol. 2	198?	2.50	5.00	10.00
SOUL NOTE					
❑ 121168-1	One Night Stand	1990	3.00	6.00	12.00
BRADFORD, CLEA					
Female singer.					
CADET					
❑ LPS-810	Her Point of View	1969	3.75	7.50	15.00
MAINSTREAM					
❑ S-6042 [S]	Clea Bradford Now	1965	7.50	15.00	30.00
❑ 56042 [M]	Clea Bradford Now	1965	6.25	12.50	25.00
NEW JAZZ					
❑ NJLP-8320 [M]	Clea Bradford with Clark Terry	1963	---	---	---
-- Canceled					
STATUS					
❑ ST-8320 [M]	Clea Bradford with Clark Terry	1965	10.00	20.00	40.00
TRU-SOUND					
❑ TRU-15005 [M]	These Dues	1962	12.50	25.00	50.00
BRADFORD, PERRY					
Male singer, composer and pianist.					
CRISPUS ATTUCKS					
❑ 101 [M]	The Perry Bradford Story	1957	15.00	30.00	60.00
BRADLEY, WILL					
Trombonist and bandleader.					
EPIC					
❑ LG 1005 [10]	Boogie Woogie	1954	30.00	60.00	120.00
❑ LN 1127 [10]	The House of Bradley	1954	30.00	60.00	120.00
❑ LN 3115 [M]	Boogie Woogie	1955	12.50	25.00	50.00
❑ LN 3199 [M]	The House of Bradley	1955	12.50	25.00	50.00
RCA VICTOR					
❑ LPM-2098 [M]	Big Band Boogie	1960	10.00	20.00	40.00
❑ LSP-2098 [S]	Big Band Boogie	1960	12.50	25.00	50.00
WALDORF MUSIC HALL					
❑ MH 33-122 [10]	Jazz Encounter	195?	10.00	20.00	40.00
❑ MH 33-132 [10]	Jazz -- Dixieland and Chicago Style	195?	10.00	20.00	40.00
BRADSHAW, EVANS					
Pianist.					
RIVERSIDE					
❑ RLP 12-263 [M]	Look Out for Evans Bradshaw	1958	10.00	20.00	40.00
❑ RLP 12-296 [M]	Pieces of Eighty-Eight	1959	10.00	20.00	40.00
❑ RLP-1136 [S]	Pieces of Eighty-Eight	1959	7.50	15.00	30.00
BRAFF, RUBY					
Cornet player and trumpeter.					
ABC-PARAMOUNT					
❑ ABC-141 [M]	Ruby Braff Featuring Dave McKenna	1956	10.00	20.00	40.00
AMERICAN RECORDING SOCIETY					
❑ G-445 [M]	Hey, Ruby	1957	10.00	20.00	40.00
BETHLEHEM					
❑ BCP-5 [M]	Omnibus	1955	12.50	25.00	50.00
❑ BCP-82 [M]	Handful of Cool Jazz	1958	10.00	20.00	40.00
❑ BCP-1005 [10]	Ruby Braff Quartet	1954	30.00	60.00	120.00
❑ BCP-1032 [10]	Holiday in Braff	1955	25.00	50.00	100.00
❑ BCP-1034 [10]	Ball at Bethlehem	1955	25.00	50.00	100.00
❑ BCP-6043 [M]	The Best of Braff	1960	7.50	15.00	30.00
❑ BCP-6043	Adoration of the Melody	197?	3.75	7.50	15.00
-- Reissue material, distributed by RCA Victor					
BLACK LION					
❑ 127	Hear Me Talkin'	197?	3.00	6.00	12.00
CHIAROSCURO					
❑ 115	International Quartet Plus Three	1972	3.75	7.50	15.00
CONCERT HALL JAZZ					
❑ 1210 [M]	Little Big Horn	1955	12.50	25.00	50.00
CONCORD JAZZ					
❑ CJ-381	Me, Myself and I	1989	3.00	6.00	12.00
EPIC					
❑ LN 3377 [M]	Braff!	1957	12.50	25.00	50.00
FINESSE					
❑ FW 37988	Very Sinatra	1983	3.00	6.00	12.00
JAZZTONE					
❑ J-1210 [M]	Little Big Horn	1955	10.00	20.00	40.00
RCA VICTOR					
❑ LPM-1008 [M]	To Fred Astaire with Love	1955	12.50	25.00	50.00
❑ LPM-1332 [M]	The Magic Horn of Ruby Braff	1956	10.00	20.00	40.00
❑ LPM-1510 [M]	Salute to Bunny in Hi-Fi	1957	10.00	20.00	40.00
❑ LPM-1966 [M]	Easy Now	1959	7.50	15.00	30.00
❑ LSP-1966 [S]	Easy Now	1959	10.00	20.00	40.00
SACKVILLE					
❑ 3022	Ruby Braff with the Ed Brickert Trio	198?	2.50	5.00	10.00
STEREO-CRAFT					
❑ RTN-507 [M]	You're Getting to Be a Habit with Me	1959	7.50	15.00	30.00
❑ RTS-507 [S]	You're Getting to Be a Habit with Me	1959	10.00	20.00	40.00
STORYVILLE					
❑ STLP-320 [10]	Hustlin' and Bustlin'	1955	20.00	40.00	80.00
❑ STLP-908 [M]	Hustlin' and Bustlin'	1956	12.50	25.00	50.00
UNITED ARTISTS					
❑ UAL-3045 [M]	Blowing Around the Around	1959	7.50	15.00	30.00
❑ UAL-4093 [M]	Ruby Braff-Marshall Brown Sextet	1960	7.50	15.00	30.00
❑ UAS-5093 [S]	Ruby Braff-Marshall Brown Sextet	1960	10.00	20.00	40.00
❑ UAS-6045 [S]	Blowing Around the Around	1959	10.00	20.00	40.00
VANGUARD					
❑ VRS-8504 [M]	The Ruby Braff Special	1955	10.00	20.00	40.00
WARNER BROS.					
❑ W 1273 [M]	Ruby Braff Goes Girl Crazy	1959	7.50	15.00	30.00
❑ WS 1273 [S]	Ruby Braff Goes Girl Crazy	1959	10.00	20.00	40.00
BRAFF, RUBY, AND GEORGE BARNES					
Also see each artist's individual listings.					
CHIAROSCURO					
❑ 121	The Ruby Braff-George Barnes Quartet	1973	3.75	7.50	15.00
❑ 126	Live at the New School	1975	3.75	7.50	15.00
CONCORD JAZZ					
❑ CJ-5	The Ruby Braff-George Barnes Quartet Plays Gershwin	1975	3.00	6.00	12.00
❑ CJ-7	The Ruby Braff-George Barnes Quartet Salutes Rodgers and Hart	1976	3.00	6.00	12.00

Number	Title	Yr	VG	VG+	NM
BRAFF, RUBY, AND SCOTT HAMILTON					
Also see each artist's individual listings.					
CONCORD JAZZ					
❑ CJ-274	A First	1985	2.50	5.00	10.00
❑ CJ-296	A Sailboat in the Moonlight	1986	2.50	5.00	10.00
BRAFF, RUBY, AND DICK HYMAN					
Also see each artist's individual listings.					
CONCORD JAZZ					
❑ CJ-393	Music from My Fair Lady	1989	3.00	6.00	12.00
GEORGE WEIN COLLECTION					
❑ GW-3003	America the Beautiful	198?	2.50	5.00	10.00
BRAFF, RUBY, AND ELLIS LARKINS					
Also see each artist's individual listings.					
CHIAROSCURO					
❑ 117	The Grand Reunion	1972	3.75	7.50	15.00
VANGUARD					
❑ VRS-8019 [10]	Inventions in Jazz -- Volume 1	1955	20.00	40.00	80.00
❑ VRS-8020 [10]	Inventions in Jazz -- Volume 2	1955	20.00	40.00	80.00
❑ VRS-8507 [M]	Two By Two	1956	10.00	20.00	40.00
❑ VRS-8516 [M]	Pocketful of Dreams	1957	10.00	20.00	40.00
BRAFF, RUBY; PEE WEE RUSSELL; BOBBY HENDERSON					
Also see each artist's individual listings.					
VERVE					
❑ MGV-8241 [M]	The Ruby Braff Octet with Pee Wee Russell and Bobby Henderson at Newport	1958	12.50	25.00	50.00
❑ V-8241 [M]	The Ruby Braff Octet with Pee Wee Russell and Bobby Henderson at Newport	1961	6.25	12.50	25.00
BRAITH, GEORGE					
Tenor and soprano saxophone player.					
BLUE NOTE					
❑ BLP-4148 [M]	Two Souls in One	1963	10.00	20.00	40.00
-- With "New York, USA" on label					
❑ BLP-4161 [M]	Soul Dream	1964	10.00	20.00	40.00
-- With "New York, USA" on label					
❑ BLP-4171 [M]	Extension	1964	10.00	20.00	40.00
-- With "New York, USA" on label					
❑ BST-84148 [S]	Two Souls in One	1963	12.50	25.00	50.00
-- With "New York, USA" on label					
❑ BST-84148 [S]	Two Souls in One	1966	5.00	10.00	20.00
-- With "A Division of Liberty Records" on label					
❑ BST-84161 [S]	Soul Dream	1964	12.50	25.00	50.00
-- With "New York, USA" on label					
❑ BST-84161 [S]	Soul Dream	1966	5.00	10.00	20.00
-- With "A Division of Liberty Records" on label					
❑ BST-84171 [S]	Extension	1964	12.50	25.00	50.00
-- With "New York, USA" on label					
❑ BST-84171 [S]	Extension	1966	5.00	10.00	20.00
-- With "A Division of Liberty Records" on label					
PRESTIGE					
❑ PRLP-7474 [M]	Laughing Soul	1967	6.25	12.50	25.00
❑ PRST-7474 [S]	Laughing Soul	1967	5.00	10.00	20.00
❑ PRLP-7515 [M]	Musart	1967	6.25	12.50	25.00
❑ PRST-7515 [S]	Musart	1967	5.00	10.00	20.00
BRAND, DOLLAR					
See ABDULLAH IBRAHIM.					
BRASS COMPANY, THE					
Group led by BILL HARDMAN.					
SACKVILLE					
❑ 3006	Sangoma	198?	2.50	5.00	10.00
STRATA-EAST					
❑ 19752	Colors	1974	2.50	5.00	10.00
BRASS ENSEMBLE OF THE JAZZ AND CLASSICAL MUSIC SOCIETY, THE					
Members: MILES DAVIS; URBIE GREEN; J.J. JOHNSON; OSIE JOHNSON.					
COLUMBIA					
❑ CL 941 [M]	Music for Brass	1956	15.00	30.00	60.00
BRAUFMAN, ALAN					
Alto saxophone player, clarinetist and flutist.					
INDIA NAVIGATION					
❑ IN-1024	Valley of Search	197?	3.00	6.00	12.00

Number	Title	Yr	VG	VG+	NM
BRAXTON, ANTHONY					
Alto saxophone player and composer. Also plays other saxes, clarinet, flute, piano and percussion.					
ANTILLES					
❑ 1005	Six Compositions: Quartet	1981	3.00	6.00	12.00
ARISTA					
❑ AL 4032	New York, Fall 1974	1975	3.75	7.50	15.00
❑ AL 4064	5 Pieces 1975	1975	3.75	7.50	15.00
❑ AL 4080	Creative Orchestra Music 1976	1976	3.75	7.50	15.00
❑ AL 4181	For Trio	1978	3.75	7.50	15.00
❑ A2L 5002 [(2)]	Montreux/Berlin	197?	5.00	10.00	20.00
❑ A2L 8602 [(2)]	Alto Sax Improvisations '79	1979	3.75	7.50	15.00
ARISTA FREEDOM					
❑ AL 1902 [(2)]	The Complete Braxton 1971	1978	5.00	10.00	20.00
BLACK SAINT					
❑ BSR-0066	Four Compositions: Quartet 1983	1983	3.00	6.00	12.00
❑ BSR-0086	Four Compositions: Quartet 1984	1985	3.00	6.00	12.00
❑ 120116-1	Six Monk Compositions	1987	3.00	6.00	12.00
BLUEBIRD					
❑ 6626-1-RB	Anthony Braxton Live	1988	2.50	5.00	10.00
CONCORD JAZZ					
❑ CJ-213	A Ray Brown 3	1982	3.00	6.00	12.00
DELMARK					
❑ DS-415	Three Compositions of New Jazz	1969	5.00	10.00	20.00
❑ DS-420/421 [(2)]	For Alto	1971	6.25	12.50	25.00
❑ DS-428	Together Alone	1973	5.00	10.00	20.00
-- With Joseph Jarman					
HAT HUT					
❑ 1984 [(2)]	Composition 98	1981	3.75	7.50	15.00
❑ 1995/96 [(2)]	Open Aspects '82	1982	3.75	7.50	15.00
❑ 2019 [(2)]	Performance	1983	3.75	7.50	15.00
INNER CITY					
❑ 1008	Saxophone Improvisations -- Series F	197?	3.75	7.50	15.00
❑ 2015	In the Tradition	197?	3.75	7.50	15.00
❑ 2045	In the Tradition, Volume 2	1974	3.75	7.50	15.00
MAGENTA					
❑ MA-0203	Seven Standards 1985	1986	3.00	6.00	12.00
❑ MA-0205	Seven Standards 1985, Volume 2	1986	3.00	6.00	12.00
SACKVILLE					
❑ 3007	Trio and Duet	198?	2.50	5.00	10.00
SOUND ASPECTS					
❑ SAS-009	Anthony Braxton with the Robert Schumann Quartet	1986	3.00	6.00	12.00
STEEPLECHASE					
❑ SCS-1015	In the Tradition	198?	2.50	5.00	10.00
❑ SCS-1045	In the Tradition, Volume 2	198?	2.50	5.00	10.00
BRAXTON, ANTHONY, AND MUHAL RICHARD ABRAMS					
Also see each artist's individual listings.					
ARISTA					
❑ AL 4101	Duets	1976	3.75	7.50	15.00
BRAXTON, ANTHONY, AND DEREK BAILEY					
Derek Bailey is a guitarist. Also see ANTHONY BRAXTON.					
EMANEM					
❑ 3313	Duo 1	197?	3.75	7.50	15.00
❑ 3314	Duo 2	197?	3.75	7.50	15.00
INNER CITY					
❑ 1041	Live at Wigmore	198?	3.00	6.00	12.00
BREAKSTONE, JOSHUA					
Guitarist and composer.					
CONTEMPORARY					
❑ C-14025	Echoes	1987	2.50	5.00	10.00
❑ C-14040	Evening Star	1988	2.50	5.00	10.00
❑ C-14050	Self-Portrait in Swing	1989	2.50	5.00	10.00
BRECKER BROTHERS, THE					
Also see MICHAEL BRECKER; RANDY BRECKER.					
ARISTA					
❑ AL 4037	The Brecker Brothers	1975	2.50	5.00	10.00
❑ AL 4061	Back to Back	1976	2.50	5.00	10.00
❑ AL 4122	Don't Stop the Music	1977	2.50	5.00	10.00
❑ AL 4185	Heavy Metal Be-Bop	1978	2.50	5.00	10.00
❑ AB 4272	Détente	1979	2.50	5.00	10.00
❑ AL 9550	Straphangin'	1981	2.50	5.00	10.00

Number	Title	Yr	VG	VG+	NM

BRECKER, MICHAEL
Tenor saxophone player. Also see THE BRECKER BROTHERS; DREAMS.
GRP

Number	Title	Yr	VG	VG+	NM
❑ 9622	Now You See It (Now You Don't)	1990	3.00	6.00	12.00

BRECKER, RANDY
Trumpeter. Also see THE BRECKER BROTHERS; DREAMS.
MCA

❑ 6334	Toe to Toe	1990	3.00	6.00	12.00
SOLID STATE					
❑ 18051	Score	1969	3.75	7.50	15.00

BREGMAN, BUDDY
Pianist, composer and conductor. Also see BING CROSBY.
VERVE

❑ MGV-2042 [M]	Swingin' Kicks	1957	12.50	25.00	50.00
❑ V-2042 [M]	Swingin' Kicks	1961	5.00	10.00	20.00
❑ V6-2042 [S]	Swingin' Kicks	1961	3.75	7.50	15.00
❑ MGV-2064 [M]	Funny Face	1958	12.50	25.00	50.00
❑ V-2064 [M]	Funny Face	1961	5.00	10.00	20.00
❑ MGV-2093 [M]	The Gershwin Anniversary Album	1959	12.50	25.00	50.00
❑ V-2093 [M]	The Gershwin Anniversary Album	1961	5.00	10.00	20.00
❑ MGV-2094 [M]	Dig Buddy Bregman in Hi-Fi	1959	12.50	25.00	50.00
❑ V-2094 [M]	Dig Buddy Bregman in Hi-Fi	1961	5.00	10.00	20.00
❑ MGVS-6013 [S]	Swingin' Kicks	1960	10.00	20.00	40.00
WORLD PACIFIC					
❑ ST-1024 [S]	Swingin' Standards	1959	7.50	15.00	30.00
❑ WP-1263 [M]	Swingin' Standards	1959	7.50	15.00	30.00

BREWER, TERESA
Female singer. Her 1950s and 1960s material was pop-oriented and is not listed here. It can be found in the *Standard Catalog of American Records 1950-1975*.
DOCTOR JAZZ

❑ ASLP 804	Good News	198?	2.50	5.00	10.00
❑ FW 38534	I Dig Big Band Singers	1983	2.50	5.00	10.00
❑ W2X 39521 [(2)]	Live at Carnegie Hall and Montreux, Switzerland	1984	3.00	6.00	12.00
❑ FW 40232	Midnight Café	1986	2.50	5.00	10.00
❑ FW 40951	Good News	198?	2.00	4.00	8.00
FLYING DUTCHMAN					
❑ BSL1-0577	Good News	1974	3.00	6.00	12.00
PROJECT 3					
❑ 5108	Come Follow the Band	1982	2.50	5.00	10.00

BREWER, TERESA, AND SVEND ASMUSSEN
Also see each artist's individual listings.
DOCTOR JAZZ

❑ FW 40233	On the Good Ship Lollipop	1987	2.50	5.00	10.00

BREWER, TERESA, AND COUNT BASIE
Also see each artist's individual listings.
DOCTOR JAZZ

❑ FW 38836	Songs of Bessie Smith	1984	2.00	4.00	8.00
FLYING DUTCHMAN					
❑ FD 10161	Songs of Bessie Smith	1973	3.00	6.00	12.00

BREWER, TERESA, AND MERCER ELLINGTON
Also see each artist's individual listings.
DOCTOR JAZZ

❑ FW 40031	The Cotton Connection	1985	2.50	5.00	10.00

BREWER, TERESA, AND STEPHANE GRAPPELLI
Also see each artist's individual listings.
DOCTOR JAZZ

❑ FW 38448	On the Road Again	198?	2.50	5.00	10.00

BRIDGEWATER, DEE DEE
Female singer.
ATLANTIC

❑ SD 18188	Dee Dee Bridgewater	1976	3.00	6.00	12.00
ELEKTRA					
❑ 6E-119	Just Family	1978	2.50	5.00	10.00
❑ 6E-188	Bad for Me	1979	2.50	5.00	10.00
❑ 6E-306	Dee Dee Bridgewater	1980	2.50	5.00	10.00
MCA/IMPULSE					
❑ MCA-6331	Live in Paris	1989	3.00	6.00	12.00

BRIGGS, KAREN
Violinist.
VITAL

Number	Title	Yr	VG	VG+	NM
❑ VTL-009	Karen	1996	5.00	10.00	20.00

BRIGHT, RONNELL
Pianist, bandleader and composer.
REGENT

❑ MG-6041 [M]	Bright's Spot	1957	10.00	20.00	40.00
SAVOY					
❑ MG-12206 [M]	Bright's Spot	196?	7.50	15.00	30.00
-- *Reissue of Regent LP*					
VANGUARD					
❑ VRS-8512 [M]	Bright's Flight	1957	10.00	20.00	40.00

BRIGNOLA, NICK
Baritone saxophone player. Also has played most of the other saxes, clarinet, flute and piccolo on record.
BEE HIVE

❑ BH-7000	Baritone Madness	1977	3.00	6.00	12.00
❑ BH-7010	Burn Brigade	1979	3.00	6.00	12.00
DISCOVERY					
❑ DS-917	Northern Lights	1986	2.50	5.00	10.00
INTERPLAY					
❑ IP-7719	New York Bound	198?	3.00	6.00	12.00
SEA BREEZE					
❑ SB-2003	L.A. Bound	198?	3.00	6.00	12.00

BRISKER, GORDON
Tenor saxophone player, also an occasional flute and piano player.
DISCOVERY

❑ DS-923	About Charlie	1987	2.50	5.00	10.00
❑ DS-938	New Beginning	1987	2.50	5.00	10.00
SEA BREEZE					
❑ SB-2016	Cornerstone	1985	2.50	5.00	10.00

BRITT, PAT
Saxophone player.
CATALYST

❑ 7612	Starsong	1976	3.00	6.00	12.00
CRESTVIEW					
❑ CR-3075 [M]	Jazz from San Francisco	1967	5.00	10.00	20.00
❑ CRS-3075 [S]	Jazz from San Francisco	1967	3.75	7.50	15.00
VEE JAY					
❑ VJS-3064	Jazz from San Francisco	1975	3.00	6.00	12.00
❑ VJS-3070	Jazzman	1975	3.00	6.00	12.00

BROADBENT, ALAN
Pianist.
DISCOVERY

❑ DS-929	Everything I Love	1987	2.50	5.00	10.00
GRANITE					
❑ 7901	Palette	1979	3.00	6.00	12.00
TREND					
❑ TR-546	Another Time	1988	2.50	5.00	10.00

BROCK, HERBIE
Pianist.
SAVOY

❑ MG-12066 [M]	Herbie Brock Solo	1956	10.00	20.00	40.00
❑ MG-12069 [M]	Brock's Tops	1956	10.00	20.00	40.00

BROCK, JIM
Percussionist.
REFERENCE RECORDINGS

❑ RR-31	Tropic Affair	198?	3.75	7.50	15.00

BRODIE, HUGH, AND IMPULSE
Brodie is a tenor and soprano saxophone player.
CADENCE JAZZ

❑ CJ-1004	Live and Cooking at the Wild Oat	1981	2.00	4.00	8.00

BROKENSHA, JACK
Vibraphone player. Also see THE AUSTRALIAN JAZZ QUARTET.
SAVOY

❑ MG-12180	And Then I Said	1962	7.50	15.00	30.00

BROOKMEYER, BOB

Valve trombonist, arranger, composer and sometimes piano player. Also see THE MANHATTAN JAZZ ALL STARS; GERRY MULLIGAN; JIMMY RANEY; BUD SHANK; PHIL URSO.

Number	Title	Yr	VG	VG+	NM
ATLANTIC					
❏ 1320 [M]	Portrait of the Artist	1960	12.50	25.00	50.00
-- Black label					
❏ 1320 [M]	Portrait of the Artist	1961	6.25	12.50	25.00
-- Multicolor label, white "fan" logo at right					
❏ SD 1320 [S]	Portrait of the Artist	1960	12.50	25.00	50.00
-- Green label					
❏ SD 1320 [S]	Portrait of the Artist	1961	5.00	10.00	20.00
-- Multicolor label, white "fan" logo at right					
CLEF					
❏ MGC-644 [M]	Bob Brookmeyer Plays Bob Brookmeyer and Some Others	1955	25.00	50.00	100.00
❏ MGC-732 [M]	The Modernity of Bob Brookmeyer	1956	17.50	35.00	70.00
COLUMBIA					
❏ CL 2237 [M]	Bob Brookmeyer and Friends	1965	3.75	7.50	15.00
❏ CS 9037 [S]	Bob Brookmeyer and Friends	1965	5.00	10.00	20.00
CROWN					
❏ CLP-5318 [M]	Bob Brookmeyer	196?	3.75	7.50	15.00
FANTASY					
❏ OJC-1729	The Dual Role of Bob Brookmeyer	1990	3.00	6.00	12.00
-- Reissue of Prestige 7066					
FINESSE					
❏ FW 37488	Through a Looking Glass	198?	2.50	5.00	10.00
GRYPHON					
❏ 785 [(2)]	Bob Brookmeyer's Small Band	1978	3.75	7.50	15.00
MERCURY					
❏ MG-20600 [M]	Jazz Is a Kick	1960	6.25	12.50	25.00
❏ SR-60600 [S]	Jazz Is a Kick	1960	7.50	15.00	30.00
NEW JAZZ					
❏ NJLP-8294 [M]	Revelation	1963	12.50	25.00	50.00
-- Purple label					
❏ NJLP-8294 [M]	Revelation	1965	6.25	12.50	25.00
-- Blue label, trident logo at right					
ODYSSEY					
❏ PC 36804	Bob Brookmeyer and Friends	1980	2.50	5.00	10.00
-- Reissue of Columbia 9037					
PACIFIC JAZZ					
❏ PJLP-16 [10]	Bob Brookmeyer Quartet	1954	37.50	75.00	150.00
PRESTIGE					
❏ PRLP-214 [10]	Bob Brookmeyer with Jimmy	1955	37.50	75.00	150.00
❏ PRLP-7066 [M]	The Dual Role of Bob Brookmeyer	1956	20.00	40.00	80.00
SONET					
❏ 778	Back Again	1979	3.00	6.00	12.00
STORYVILLE					
❏ STLP-305 [10]	Bob Brookmeyer Featuring Al Cohn	1954	75.00	150.00	300.00
TODAY'S JAZZ					
❏ J-1239 [M]	Bob Brookmeyer and Zoot Sims	196?	7.50	15.00	30.00
TRIP					
❏ 5568	Jazz Is a Kick	197?	2.50	5.00	10.00
UNITED ARTISTS					
❏ UAL-4008 [M]	Kansas City Revisited	1959	12.50	25.00	50.00
❏ UAS-5008 [S]	Kansas City Revisited	1959	10.00	20.00	40.00
VERVE					
❏ MGV-8111 [M]	The Modernity of Bob Brookmeyer	1957	12.50	25.00	50.00
❏ V-8111 [M]	The Modernity of Bob Brookmeyer	1961	7.50	15.00	30.00
❏ MGV-8385 [M]	The Blues, Hot and Cold	1960	12.50	25.00	50.00
❏ V-8385 [M]	The Blues, Hot and Cold	1961	7.50	15.00	30.00
❏ V6-8385 [S]	The Blues, Hot and Cold	1961	6.25	12.50	25.00
❏ V-8413 [M]	7 X Wilder	1961	6.25	12.50	25.00
❏ V6-8413 [S]	7 X Wilder	1961	7.50	15.00	30.00
❏ V-8455 [M]	Gloomy Sunday and Other Bright Moments	1962	6.25	12.50	25.00
❏ V6-8455 [S]	Gloomy Sunday and Other Bright Moments	1962	7.50	15.00	30.00
❏ V-8498 [M]	Trombone Jazz Samba	1962	6.25	12.50	25.00
❏ V6-8498 [S]	Trombone Jazz Samba	1962	7.50	15.00	30.00
VIK					
❏ LX-1071 [M]	Brookmeyer	1957	12.50	25.00	50.00
WORLD PACIFIC					
❏ PJ-1233 [M]	Traditionalism Revisited	1958	20.00	40.00	80.00

BROOKMEYER, BOB, AND BILL EVANS

Also see each artist's individual listings.

Number	Title	Yr	VG	VG+	NM
UNITED ARTISTS					
❏ UAL-3044 [M]	The Ivory Hunters -- Double Barreled Piano	1959	12.50	25.00	50.00
❏ UAS-6044 [S]	The Ivory Hunters -- Double Barreled Piano	1959	10.00	20.00	40.00

BROOKMEYER, BOB; JIM HALL; JIMMY RANEY

Also see each artist's individual listings.

Number	Title	Yr	VG	VG+	NM
KIMBERLY					
❏ 2021 [M]	Brookmeyer and Guitars	1963	7.50	15.00	30.00
❏ 11021 [S]	Brookmeyer and Guitars	1963	5.00	10.00	20.00
WORLD PACIFIC					
❏ PJ-1239 [M]	The Street Swingers	1957	25.00	50.00	100.00
❏ WP-1239 [M]	The Street Swingers	1958	12.50	25.00	50.00
-- Reissue with new prefix					

BROOKMEYER, BOB, AND MEL LEWIS

Also see each artist's individual listings.

Number	Title	Yr	VG	VG+	NM
GRYPHON					
❏ 912	Live at the Village Vanguard	1980	3.00	6.00	12.00

BROOKMEYER, BOB, AND ZOOT SIMS

Also see each artist's individual listings.

Number	Title	Yr	VG	VG+	NM
JAZZTONE					
❏ J-1239 [M]	Bob Brookmeyer and Zoot Sims	1956	10.00	20.00	40.00
STORYVILLE					
❏ STLP-907 [M]	Tonight's Jazz Today	1956	20.00	40.00	80.00
❏ STLP-914 [M]	Whoo-eeee!	1956	20.00	40.00	80.00

BROOKS, CECIL, III

Drummer.

Number	Title	Yr	VG	VG+	NM
MUSE					
❏ MR-5377	The Collective	1989	3.00	6.00	12.00

BROOKS, DONNA

Female singer.

Number	Title	Yr	VG	VG+	NM
DAWN					
❏ DLP-1105 [M]	I'll Take Romance	1956	30.00	60.00	120.00

BROOKS, JOHN BENSON

Pianist, bandleader, arranger and composer.

Number	Title	Yr	VG	VG+	NM
DECCA					
❏ DL 75018	Avant Slant	1968	5.00	10.00	20.00
RIVERSIDE					
❏ RLP 12-276 [M]	The Alabama Concerto	1958	12.50	25.00	50.00
❏ RLP-1123 [S]	The Alabama Concerto	1959	10.00	20.00	40.00
VIK					
❏ LX-1083 [M]	Folk Jazz U.S.A.	1957	10.00	20.00	40.00

BROOKS, RANDY

Trumpeter and bandleader.

Number	Title	Yr	VG	VG+	NM
CIRCLE					
❏ CLP-035	Randy Brooks and His Orchestra 1945-47	198?	2.50	5.00	10.00
DECCA					
❏ DL 8201 [M]	Trumpet Moods	195?	7.50	15.00	30.00

BROOKS, ROY

Drummer.

Number	Title	Yr	VG	VG+	NM
IM-HOTEP					
❏ CS-030	Ethnic Expressions	197?	3.75	7.50	15.00
MUSE					
❏ MR-5003	Free Slave	197?	3.75	7.50	15.00
WORKSHOP JAZZ					
❏ WSJ-220 [M]	Roy Brooks Beat	1964	12.50	25.00	50.00
❏ WSJS-220 [S]	Roy Brooks Beat	1964	15.00	30.00	60.00

BROOKS, TINA

Real name: Harold Floyd Brooks. Tenor saxophone player.

Number	Title	Yr	VG	VG+	NM
BLUE NOTE					
❏ BLP-4041 [M]	True Blue	1960	125.00	250.00	500.00
❏ BLP-4052 [M]	Back to the Tracks	1960	---	---	---
-- Canceled					
❏ B1-28975	True Blue	1994	3.00	6.00	12.00
❏ BST-84041 [S]	True Blue	1960	---	---	---
-- Canceled					
❏ BST-84052 [S]	Back to the Tracks	1960	---	---	---
-- Canceled					

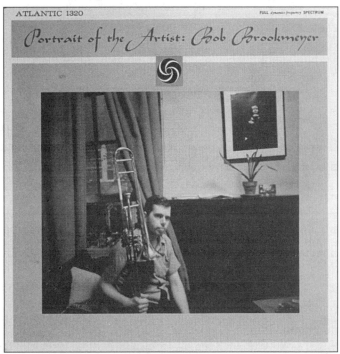

Bob Brookmeyer, jazz's foremost valve trombone player, recorded extensively in the 1950s and 1960s, then vanished into session and studio work before returning to jazz in the late 1970s. Here are some of his early works. (Top left) *The Modernity of Bob Brookmeyer* was issued on the Clef label in 1956, just before Norman Granz folded his three labels (Clef, Norgran, Down Home) into one (Verve). (Top right) *Brookmeyer* resulted from his only session for the Vik label, a subsidiary of RCA Victor and the successor to the former "X" label. (Bottom left) In its early days, United Artists Records was a player in the jazz field, and this 1959 album was one of the label's first. (Bottom right) Brookmeyer continued his label-hopping, this time to the more established Atlantic label. Once again, he stayed long enough to do exactly one album, and *Portrait of the Artist* resulted.

Number	Title	Yr	VG	VG+	NM
❏ BST-84052 [S]	Back to the Tracks	199?	7.50	15.00	30.00
-- *Classic Records reissue; first U.S. vinyl issue*					
MOSAIC					
❏ MR4-106 [(4)]	The Complete Blue Note Recordings of the Tina Brooks Quintets	199?	12.50	25.00	50.00

BROOM, BOBBY
Guitarist.
ARISTA

Number	Title	Yr	VG	VG+	NM
❏ AL8-8253	Bobby Broom	1984	2.50	5.00	10.00
ARISTA/GRP					
❏ GL 5504	Clean Sweep	1981	2.50	5.00	10.00

BROTHER MATTHEW
Alto saxophone player.
ABC-PARAMOUNT

Number	Title	Yr	VG	VG+	NM
❏ ABC-121	Brother Matthew	1956	12.50	25.00	50.00

BROUSSARD, JULES
Saxophone player and flutist.
HEADFIRST

Number	Title	Yr	VG	VG+	NM
❏ 796	Jules Broussard	198?	3.00	6.00	12.00

BROWN, BOOTS / DAN DREW
Boots Brown and His Blockbusters are Shorty Rogers, Milt Bernhart, Bud Shank, Jimmy Giuffre, Gerry Mulligan, Marty Paich, Jimmy Wyble, Howard Rumsey, Roy Harte and J. J. Johnson. Dan Drew and His Daredevils are Eddie Bert, Al Cohn, Osie Johnson, Buddy Jones, Elliott Lawrence, Charlie O'Kane and Nick Travis.
GROOVE

Number	Title	Yr	VG	VG+	NM
❏ LG-1000 [M]	Rock That Boat	1955	75.00	150.00	300.00

BROWN, CLIFFORD
Trumpeter. Considered to be among the greatest of bebop trumpet players, he died at age 26 in an auto accident. Also see TADD DAMERON; BOB GORDON; GIGI GRYCE; SONNY ROLLINS.
BLUE NOTE

Number	Title	Yr	VG	VG+	NM
❏ BN-LA267-G	Brownie Eyes	1974	3.00	6.00	12.00
❏ BLP-1526 [M]	Clifford Brown Memorial Album	1956	50.00	100.00	200.00
-- *"Deep groove" version (deep indentation under label on both sides)*					
❏ BLP-1526 [M]	Clifford Brown Memorial Album	1956	37.50	75.00	150.00
-- *Regular edition, Lexington Ave. address on label*					
❏ BLP-1526 [M]	Clifford Brown Memorial Album	196?	12.50	25.00	50.00
-- *With W. 63rd St. address on label*					
❏ BLP-1526 [M]	Clifford Brown Memorial Album	196?	6.25	12.50	25.00
-- *With "New York, USA" address on label*					
❏ BLP-5032 [10]	New Star on the Horizon	1953	125.00	250.00	500.00
❏ BLP-5047 [10]	Clifford Brown Quartet	1954	125.00	250.00	500.00
❏ BST-81526 [R]	Clifford Brown Memorial Album	1967	3.00	6.00	12.00
-- *With "A Division of Liberty Records" on label*					
❏ BST-81526	Clifford Brown Memorial Album	1985	2.50	5.00	10.00
-- *"The Finest in Jazz Since 1939" reissue*					
❏ BST-84428	Alternate Takes	198?	3.00	6.00	12.00
COLUMBIA					
❏ C 32284	The Beginning and the End	197?	3.00	6.00	12.00
-- *Reissue with new prefix*					
❏ KC 32284	The Beginning and the End	1973	3.75	7.50	15.00
EMARCY					
❏ MG-36005 [M]	Clifford Brown with Strings	1955	30.00	60.00	120.00
❏ MG-36102 [M]	Clifford Brown All Stars	1956	30.00	60.00	120.00
FANTASY					
❏ OJC-017	Clifford Brown Memorial	198?	2.50	5.00	10.00
❏ OJC-357	Clifford Brown Quartet in Paris	198?	2.50	5.00	10.00
❏ OJC-358	Clifford Brown Sextet in Paris	198?	2.50	5.00	10.00
❏ OJC-359	Clifford Brown Big Band in Paris	198?	2.50	5.00	10.00
JAZZTONE					
❏ J-1281 [M]	Jazz Messages	195?	10.00	20.00	40.00
LIMELIGHT					
❏ 2-8201 [(2) M]	The Immortal Clifford Brown	1965	10.00	20.00	40.00
❏ 2-8601 [(2) R]	The Immortal Clifford Brown	1965	6.25	12.50	25.00
MERCURY					
❏ MG-20827 [M]	Remember Clifford	1963	10.00	20.00	40.00
❏ SR-60827 [R]	Remember Clifford	1963	6.25	12.50	25.00
MOSAIC					
❏ MR5-104 [(5)]	The Complete Blue Note and Pacific Jazz Recordings of Clifford Brown	199?	20.00	40.00	80.00
NEW JAZZ					
❏ NJLP-8301 [M]	Clifford Brown	1963	---	---	---
-- *Canceled*					
PACIFIC JAZZ					
❏ PJ-3 [M]	Jazz Immortal	1956	37.50	75.00	150.00
❏ PJLP-19 [10]	The Clifford Brown Ensemble	1955	75.00	150.00	300.00

Number	Title	Yr	VG	VG+	NM
❏ LN-10126	Jazz Immortal	198?	2.50	5.00	10.00
PRESTIGE					
❏ PRLP-7055 [M]	Clifford Brown Memorial	1956	20.00	40.00	80.00
❏ PRST-7662 [R]	Clifford Brown Memorial Album	1969	3.00	6.00	12.00
❏ PRST-7761	Clifford Brown Quartet in Paris	1969	3.00	6.00	12.00
❏ PRST-7794	Clifford Brown Sextet in Paris	1970	3.00	6.00	12.00
❏ PRST-7840	Clifford Brown Big Band in Paris	1970	3.00	6.00	12.00
❏ PRLP-16008 [M]	Clifford Brown	1964	10.00	20.00	40.00
❏ 24020 [(2)]	Clifford Brown in Paris	1971	3.75	7.50	15.00
TRIP					
❏ 5502	Clifford Brown with Strings	197?	2.50	5.00	10.00

BROWN, CLIFFORD, AND ART FARMER
Also see each artist's individual listings.
PRESTIGE

Number	Title	Yr	VG	VG+	NM
❏ PRLP-167 [10]	Clifford Brown and Art Farmer with the Swedish All Stars	1953	75.00	150.00	300.00

BROWN, CLIFFORD, AND MAX ROACH
Also see each artist's individual listings.
ELEKTRA MUSICIAN

Number	Title	Yr	VG	VG+	NM
❏ 60026	Pure Genius	1982	3.00	6.00	12.00
EMARCY					
❏ MG-26043 [10]	Clifford Brown and Max Roach	1954	100.00	200.00	400.00
❏ MG-36008 [M]	Brown and Roach Incorporated	1955	30.00	60.00	120.00
❏ MG-36036 [M]	Clifford Brown and Max Roach	1955	30.00	60.00	120.00
❏ MG-36037 [M]	A Study in Brown	1955	30.00	60.00	120.00
❏ MG-36070 [M]	Clifford Brown and Max Roach at Basin Street	1956	30.00	60.00	120.00
GENE NORMAN					
❏ GNP-5 [10]	Clifford Brown and Max Roach, Vol. 1	1954	37.50	75.00	150.00
❏ GNP-7 [10]	Clifford Brown and Max Roach, Vol. 2	1954	37.50	75.00	150.00
❏ GNP-18 [M]	The Best of Max Roach and Clifford Brown In Concert	1955	30.00	60.00	120.00
MAINSTREAM					
❏ MRL-386 [M]	Daahoud	197?	3.00	6.00	12.00
TRIP					
❏ 5511	Clifford Brown and Max Roach at Basin Street	197?	2.50	5.00	10.00
❏ 5520	Brown and Roach Incorporated	197?	2.50	5.00	10.00
❏ 5530	A Study in Brown	197?	2.50	5.00	10.00
❏ 5537	Best Coast Jazz	197?	2.50	5.00	10.00
❏ 5540	Jordu	197?	2.50	5.00	10.00
❏ 5550	All Stars	197?	2.50	5.00	10.00

BROWN, DONALD
Best known as a pianist, Brown also is a bass player, trumpeter, drummer and composer.
MUSE

Number	Title	Yr	VG	VG+	NM
❏ MR-5385	Sources of Inspiration	198?	2.50	5.00	10.00
SUNNYSIDE					
❏ SSC-1025	Early Bird	1988	2.50	5.00	10.00

BROWN, LAWRENCE
Trombonist.
ABC IMPULSE!

Number	Title	Yr	VG	VG+	NM
❏ AS-89	Inspired Abandon	1968	3.00	6.00	12.00
CLEF					
❏ MGC-682 [M]	Slide Trombone	1955	30.00	60.00	120.00
IMPULSE!					
❏ A-89 [M]	Inspired Abandon	1965	6.25	12.50	25.00
❏ AS-89 [S]	Inspired Abandon	1965	7.50	15.00	30.00
VERVE					
❏ MGV-8067 [M]	Slide Trombone	1957	12.50	25.00	50.00
❏ V-8067 [M]	Slide Trombone	1961	5.00	10.00	20.00

BROWN, LES
Saxophone player and bandleader.
CAPITOL

Number	Title	Yr	VG	VG+	NM
❏ T 657 [M]	College Classics	1955	7.50	15.00	30.00
-- *Turquoise or gray label*					
❏ T 659 [M]	The Les Brown All Stars	1955	7.50	15.00	30.00
-- *Turquoise or gray label*					
❏ T 746 [M]	Les Brown's in Town	1956	7.50	15.00	30.00
-- *Turquoise or gray label*					
❏ T 886 [M]	Composer's Holiday	1957	7.50	15.00	30.00
-- *Turquoise or gray label*					
❏ T 959 [M]	Concert Modern	1958	7.50	15.00	30.00
-- *Turquoise or gray label*					

Number	Title	Yr	VG	VG+	NM
❏ SM-1174	The Les Brown Story	1976	2.00	4.00	8.00

-- *Reissue with new prefix*

Number	Title	Yr	VG	VG+	NM
❏ ST 1174 [S]	The Les Brown Story	1959	6.25	12.50	25.00

-- *Black colorband label, logo at left*

❏ T 1174 [M]	The Les Brown Story	1959	6.25	12.50	25.00

-- *Black colorband label, logo at left*

CIRCLE

❏ CLP-90	Les Brown and His Orchestra 1946	1986	2.50	5.00	10.00

COLUMBIA

❏ CL 539 [M]	Dance with Les Brown	1954	7.50	15.00	30.00

-- *Maroon label, gold print*

❏ CL 649 [M]	Sentimental Journey	1955	7.50	15.00	30.00

-- *Maroon label, gold print*

❏ CL 649 [M]	Sentimental Journey	1955	6.25	12.50	25.00

-- *Red and black label with six "eye" logos*

❏ CL 1??? [M]	The Lerner and Loewe Bandbook	1960	3.75	7.50	15.00

-- *Red and black label with six "eye" logos*

❏ CL 1497 [M]	Bandland	1960	3.75	7.50	15.00

-- *Red and black label with six "eye" logos*

❏ CL 1818 [M]	Revolution in Sound	1962	3.75	7.50	15.00

-- *Red and black label with six "eye" logos*

❏ CL 2030 [M]	Explosive Sound	1964	3.75	7.50	15.00

-- *"Guaranteed High Fidelity" on label*

❏ CL 2119 [M]	The Young Beat	1964	3.75	7.50	15.00

-- *"Guaranteed High Fidelity" on label*

❏ CL 2512 [10]	I've Got My Love to Keep Me	1955	10.00	20.00	40.00
❏ CL 2561 [10]	The Cool Classics	1955	10.00	20.00	40.00
❏ CL 6060 [10]	Dance Parade	1949	10.00	20.00	40.00
❏ CS 8??? [S]	Bandland	1960	5.00	10.00	20.00

-- *Red and black label with six "eye" logos*

❏ CS 8394 [S]	The Lerner and Loewe Bandbook	1960	5.00	10.00	20.00

-- *Red and black label with six "eye" logos*

❏ CS 8618 [S]	Revolution in Sound	1962	5.00	10.00	20.00

-- *Red and black label with six "eye" logos*

❏ CS 8830 [S]	Explosive Sound	1964	5.00	10.00	20.00

-- *"360 Sound Stereo" in black on label*

❏ CS 8919 [S]	The Young Beat	1964	5.00	10.00	20.00

-- *"360 Sound Stereo" in black on label*

COLUMBIA SPECIAL PRODUCTS

❏ P 14361	Sentimental Journey	198?	2.50	5.00	10.00

CORAL

❏ CX-1 [(2) M]	Les Brown Concert at the Palladium	1953	15.00	30.00	60.00
❏ CRL 56026 [10]	Over the Rainbow	1951	12.50	25.00	50.00
❏ CRL 56030 [10]	The Sound of Renown	1951	12.50	25.00	50.00
❏ CRL 56046 [10]	You're My Everything	1952	12.50	25.00	50.00
❏ CRL 56077 [10]	Musical Weather Vane	1953	12.50	25.00	50.00
❏ CRL 56094 [10]	Les Dance	1953	12.50	25.00	50.00
❏ CRL 56108 [10]	Invitation	1954	12.50	25.00	50.00
❏ CRL 56109 [10]	Time to Dance	1954	12.50	25.00	50.00
❏ CRL 56116 [10]	Les Dream	1954	12.50	25.00	50.00
❏ CRL 57000 [M]	Les Brown Concert at the Palladium, Part 1	1954	7.50	15.00	30.00
❏ CRL 57001 [M]	Les Brown Concert at the Palladium, Part 1	1954	7.50	15.00	30.00
❏ CRL 57030 [M]	The Sound of Renown	1955	6.25	12.50	25.00
❏ CRL 57051 [M]	Open House	1956	6.25	12.50	25.00
❏ CRL 57058 [M]	More from Les	1956	6.25	12.50	25.00
❏ CRL 57165 [M]	Love Letters in the Sand	1957	6.25	12.50	25.00
❏ CRL 57300 [M]	Swing Song Book	1959	6.25	12.50	25.00
❏ CRL 57311 [M]	Jazz Song Book	1959	6.25	12.50	25.00
❏ CRL 757300 [S]	Swing Song Book	1959	7.50	15.00	30.00
❏ CRL 757311 [S]	Jazz Song Book	1959	7.50	15.00	30.00

DAYBREAK

❏ 2007	New Horizons	1972	3.00	6.00	12.00

DECCA

❏ DL 4607 [M]	In Town	1965	3.00	6.00	12.00
❏ DL 4768 [M]	A Sign of the Times	1966	3.00	6.00	12.00
❏ DL 4965 [M]	The World of the Young	1968	5.00	10.00	20.00
❏ DL 74607 [S]	In Town	1965	3.75	7.50	15.00
❏ DL 74768 [S]	A Sign of the Times	1966	3.75	7.50	15.00
❏ DL 74965 [S]	The World of the Young	1968	3.00	6.00	12.00

FANTASY

❏ F-9650	Digital Swing	1987	3.00	6.00	12.00

GREAT AMERICAN

❏ 1010	Les Brown Goes Direct to Disc	1981	5.00	10.00	20.00

HARMONY

❏ HL 7100 [M]	Les Brown's Greatest	196?	3.00	6.00	12.00
❏ HL 7211 [M]	Sentimental Journey	196?	3.00	6.00	12.00
❏ HL 7335 [M]	Hits from The Sound of Music, My Fair Lady, Camelot and Others	1965	3.00	6.00	12.00
❏ HS 11135 [S]	Hits from The Sound of Music, My Fair Lady, Camelot and Others	1965	3.00	6.00	12.00
❏ KH 32015	The Beat of the Bands	1972	2.50	5.00	10.00

HINDSIGHT

Number	Title	Yr	VG	VG+	NM
❏ HSR-103	Les Brown and His Orchestra 1944-45	198?	2.50	5.00	10.00
❏ HSR-131	Les Brown and His Orchestra 1949	198?	2.50	5.00	10.00
❏ HSR-132	Les Brown and His Orchestra Vol. 3	198?	2.50	5.00	10.00
❏ HSR-199	Les Brown and His Orchestra 1956-57	198?	2.50	5.00	10.00

INSIGHT

❏ 213	Les Brown and His Orchestra, 1949	198?	2.50	5.00	10.00

MCA

❏ 4070 [(2)]	The Best of Les Brown	1974	3.00	6.00	12.00

VOCALION

❏ VL 3618 [M]	Les Dance	196?	3.00	6.00	12.00

BROWN, MARION

Alto saxophone player.

ABC IMPULSE!

❏ AS-9139	Three for Shepp	1968	3.00	6.00	12.00
❏ AS-9252	Geechee Recollections	1973	3.00	6.00	12.00
❏ AS-9275	Sweet Earth Flying	1974	3.00	6.00	12.00
❏ ASD-9304	Vista	1975	3.00	6.00	12.00

ARISTA FREEDOM

❏ AL 1001	Porto Novo	1975	3.00	6.00	12.00
❏ AL 1904 [(2)]	Duets	1975	3.75	7.50	15.00

ECM

❏ 1004	Afternoon of a Georgia Faun	197?	3.75	7.50	15.00

ESP-DISK'

❏ 1022 [M]	Marion Brown Quartet	1966	5.00	10.00	20.00
❏ S-1022 [S]	Marion Brown Quartet	1966	3.75	7.50	15.00
❏ 1040 [M]	Why Not?	1967	5.00	10.00	20.00
❏ S-1040 [S]	Why Not?	1967	3.75	7.50	15.00

IMPULSE!

❏ A-9139 [M]	Three for Shepp	1967	7.50	15.00	30.00
❏ AS-9139 [S]	Three for Shepp	1967	5.00	10.00	20.00

SWEET EARTH

❏ SER-1001	Solo Saxophone	1978	3.00	6.00	12.00

TIMELESS

❏ TI-314	La Placita -- Live in Willisau	197?	3.00	6.00	12.00

BROWN, MARION, AND GUNTER HAMPEL

Also see each artist's individual listings.

IAI

❏ 373855	Reeds 'n Vibes	1978	3.00	6.00	12.00

BROWN, MARION, AND ELLIOTT SCHWARTZ

Schwartz is a pianist and composer. Also see MARION BROWN.

CENTURY

❏ 41746	Soundways	1973	3.75	7.50	15.00

BROWN, MEL

Drummer.

ABC

❏ AA-1103	Actor of Music	1978	3.00	6.00	12.00

ABC IMPULSE!

❏ A-9152 [M]	Chicken Fat	1967	7.50	15.00	30.00
❏ AS-9152 [S]	Chicken Fat	1967	5.00	10.00	20.00
❏ A-9169 [M]	The Wizard	1968	10.00	20.00	40.00
❏ AS-9169 [S]	The Wizard	1968	5.00	10.00	20.00
❏ A-9180 [M]	Blues for We	1969	12.50	25.00	50.00
❏ AS-9180 [S]	Blues for We	1969	5.00	10.00	20.00
❏ AS-9186	I'd Rather Suck My Thumb	1970	5.00	10.00	20.00
❏ AS-9209	Fifth	1971	5.00	10.00	20.00
❏ AS-9249 [Q]	Big Foot Country Girl	1974	3.75	7.50	15.00

BLUESWAY

❏ 6064	18 Pounds of Uncleaned Chittlins	1973	3.75	7.50	15.00

BROWN, ODELL

Organist.

CADET

❏ LP-775 [M]	Raising the Roof	1966	3.75	7.50	15.00
❏ LPS-775 [S]	Raising the Roof	1966	5.00	10.00	20.00
❏ LP-788 [M]	Mellow Yellow	1967	5.00	10.00	20.00
❏ LPS-788 [S]	Mellow Yellow	1967	3.75	7.50	15.00
❏ LP-800 [M]	Ducky	1967	5.00	10.00	20.00
❏ LPS-800 [S]	Ducky	1967	3.75	7.50	15.00
❏ LPS-823	Odell Brown Plays Otis Redding	1969	3.75	7.50	15.00
❏ LPS-838	Free Delivery	1970	3.75	7.50	15.00

Number	Title	Yr	VG	VG+	NM
PAULA					
❑ 4005	Odell Brown	1974	3.00	6.00	12.00
BROWN, OSCAR, JR.					
Singer, poet and composer.					
ATLANTIC					
❑ SD 1629	Movin' On	1972	3.75	7.50	15.00
❑ SD 1649	Brother Where Are You	1973	3.75	7.50	15.00
❑ SD 18106	Fresh	1974	3.00	6.00	12.00
COLUMBIA					
❑ CL 1577 [M]	Sin and Soul	1960	6.25	12.50	25.00
-- *Red and black label with six "eye" logos*					
❑ CL 1774 [M]	Between Heaven and Hell	1962	6.25	12.50	25.00
-- *Red and black label with six "eye" logos*					
❑ CL 1873 [M]	In a New Mood	1963	5.00	10.00	20.00
-- *Red label, "Guaranteed High Fidelity" in black*					
❑ CL 2025 [M]	Oscar Brown Jr. Tells It Like It Is	1964	5.00	10.00	20.00
-- *Red label, "Guaranteed High Fidelity" in black*					
❑ CS 8377 [S]	Sin and Soul	1960	7.50	15.00	30.00
-- *Red and black label with six "eye" logos*					
❑ CS 8574 [S]	Between Heaven and Hell	1962	7.50	15.00	30.00
-- *Red and black label with six "eye" logos*					
❑ CS 8673 [S]	In a New Mood	1963	6.25	12.50	25.00
-- *Red label, "360 Sound Stereo" in black*					
❑ CS 8825 [S]	Oscar Brown Jr. Tells It Like It Is	1964	6.25	12.50	25.00
-- *Red label, "360 Sound Stereo" in black*					
FONTANA					
❑ MGF-27540 [M]	Mr. Oscar Brown Goes to Washington	1965	3.75	7.50	15.00
❑ MGF-27549 [M]	Finding a New Friend	1966	3.75	7.50	15.00
❑ SRF-67540 [S]	Mr. Oscar Brown Goes to Washington	1965	5.00	10.00	20.00
❑ SRF-67549 [S]	Finding a New Friend	1966	5.00	10.00	20.00
BROWN, PETE					
Alto and tenor saxophone player; also has played trumpet and violin.					
BETHLEHEM					
❑ BCP-1011 [10]	Peter the Great	1954	30.00	60.00	120.00
VERVE					
❑ MGVS-6133 [S]	From the Heart	1960	10.00	20.00	40.00
❑ MGV-8365 [M]	From the Heart	1958	12.50	25.00	50.00
❑ V-8365 [M]	From the Heart	1962	5.00	10.00	20.00
❑ V6-8365 [S]	From the Heart	1962	3.75	7.50	15.00
BROWN, PETE/JONAH JONES					
Also see each artist's individual listings.					
BETHLEHEM					
❑ BCP-4 [M]	Jazz Kaleidoscope	1957	20.00	40.00	80.00
BROWN, PUD					
Tenor saxophone player and clarinetist.					
JAZZOLOGY					
❑ J-166	Pud Brown Plays Clarinet	198?	2.50	5.00	10.00
BROWN, PUD, AND EDDIE MILLER					
Also see each artist's individual listings.					
NEW ORLEANS JAZZ					
❑ NORJC-001	Jazz for Two	198?	2.50	5.00	10.00
BROWN, RAY					
Bass player. Also see THE POLL WINNERS; ANDRE PREVIN.					
BLUESWAY					
❑ BLS-6056	Hard Times	1971	3.75	7.50	15.00
CONCORD JAZZ					
❑ CJ-19	Brown's Bag	1976	3.00	6.00	12.00
❑ CJ-102	The Ray Brown Trio Live at the Concord Jazz Festival	1979	3.00	6.00	12.00
❑ CJ-213	Ray Brown 3	1982	2.50	5.00	10.00
❑ CJ-268	Soular Energy	1985	2.50	5.00	10.00
❑ CJ-293	Don't Forget the Blues	1986	2.50	5.00	10.00
❑ CJ-315	The Red Hot Ray Brown Trio	1987	2.50	5.00	10.00
❑ CJ-375	Bam Bam Bam	1989	3.00	6.00	12.00
CONTEMPORARY					
❑ C-7641	Something for Lester	1978	2.50	5.00	10.00
FANTASY					
❑ OJC-412	Something for Lester	1990	3.00	6.00	12.00
NORGRAN					
❑ MGN-1105 [M]	Bass Hit!	1956	---	---	---
-- *Canceled; released on Verve 8022*					
VERVE					
❑ VSP-10 [M]	Two for the Blues	1966	3.00	6.00	12.00
❑ VSPS-10 [S]	Two for the Blues	1966	3.75	7.50	15.00
❑ UMV-2117	This Is Ray Brown	198?	2.50	5.00	10.00
❑ MGV-8022 [M]	Bass Hit!	1957	12.50	25.00	50.00
❑ V-8022 [M]	Bass Hit!	1961	5.00	10.00	20.00
❑ MGV-8290 [M]	This Is Ray Brown	1958	12.50	25.00	50.00
❑ V-8290 [M]	This Is Ray Brown	1961	5.00	10.00	20.00
❑ MGV-8390 [M]	Jazz Cello	1960	12.50	25.00	50.00
❑ V-8390 [M]	Jazz Cello	1961	5.00	10.00	20.00
❑ V-8444 [M]	Ray Brown with the All Star Big Band Featuring Cannonball Adderley	1962	6.25	12.50	25.00
❑ V6-8444 [S]	Ray Brown with the All Star Big Band Featuring Cannonball Adderley	1962	7.50	15.00	30.00
❑ V-8580 [M]	Much in Common	1964	6.25	12.50	25.00
❑ V6-8580 [S]	Much in Common	1964	7.50	15.00	30.00
-- *With Milt Jackson*					
❑ V-8615 [M]	Ray Brown/Milt Jackson	1965	6.25	12.50	25.00
❑ V6-8615 [S]	Ray Brown/Milt Jackson	1965	7.50	15.00	30.00
BROWN, RAY, AND JIMMIE ROWLES					
Also see each artist's individual listings.					
CONCORD JAZZ					
❑ CJ-66	As Good As Gold	1977	3.00	6.00	12.00
❑ CJ-122	Tasty	1979	3.00	6.00	12.00
BROWN, REUBEN, AND RICHIE COLE					
Brown is a pianist. Also see RICHIE COLE.					
ADELPHIA					
❑ AD-5001	Starburst	1976	3.00	6.00	12.00
BROWN, RONNIE					
Pianist.					
PHILIPS					
❑ PHM 200-130 [M]	Jazz for Everyone	1964	3.75	7.50	15.00
❑ PHS 600-130 [S]	Jazz for Everyone	1964	5.00	10.00	20.00
BROWN, RUTH					
Female singer. Most of her recordings are in the rhythm and blues field and are located in the Standard Catalog of American Records 1950-1975.					
ATLANTIC					
❑ 1308 [M]	Last Date with Ruth Brown	1959	50.00	100.00	200.00
-- *Black label*					
❑ 1308 [M]	Last Date with Ruth Brown	1961	12.50	25.00	50.00
-- *Red and purple label, "fan" logo in white*					
❑ SD 1308 [S]	Last Date with Ruth Brown	1959	75.00	150.00	300.00
-- *Green label*					
❑ SD 1308 [S]	Last Date with Ruth Brown	1961	15.00	30.00	60.00
-- *Blue and green label, "fan" logo in white*					
DOBRE					
❑ 1041	You Don't Know Me	1978	3.00	6.00	12.00
FANTASY					
❑ F-9661	Have a Good Time	1988	3.00	6.00	12.00
❑ F-9662	Blues on Broadway	1989	3.00	6.00	12.00
MAINSTREAM					
❑ 369	Softly	1972	3.00	6.00	12.00
❑ S-6034 [S]	Ruth Brown '65	1965	7.50	15.00	30.00
❑ 56034 [M]	Ruth Brown '65	1965	6.25	12.50	25.00
SDEG					
❑ 4023	Brown, Black and Beautiful	198?	3.00	6.00	12.00
SKYE					
❑ LP-13	Black Is Brown and Brown Is Beautiful	1970	3.75	7.50	15.00
BROWN, TED					
Tenor saxophone player.					
CRISS CROSS					
❑ 1031	Free Spirit	1988	3.00	6.00	12.00
VANGUARD					
❑ VRS-8515 [M]	Free Wheeling	1956	125.00	250.00	500.00
BROWN, WINI					
Female singer.					
SAVOY JAZZ					
❑ SJL-1163 [M]	Miss Brown for You	1986	2.50	5.00	10.00
BROWNE, BRIAN					
Pianist.					
JAZZIMAGE					
❑ JZ-105	Beatles	198?	3.75	7.50	15.00

Number	Title	Yr	VG	VG+	NM
BROWNE, TOM					

Trumpeter.

ARISTA

Number	Title	Yr	VG	VG+	NM
❑ AL 8107	Rockin' Radio	1983	2.00	4.00	8.00
❑ AL8-8249	Tommy Gun	1984	2.00	4.00	8.00

GRP/ARISTA

Number	Title	Yr	VG	VG+	NM
❑ GL 5003	Browne Sugar	1979	2.50	5.00	10.00
❑ GL 5008	Love Approach	1980	2.50	5.00	10.00
❑ GL 5502	Love Approach	1981	2.00	4.00	8.00
-- Reissue of 5008					
❑ GL 5503	Magic	1981	2.50	5.00	10.00
❑ GL 5507	Yours Truly	1981	2.50	5.00	10.00

MALACO

Number	Title	Yr	VG	VG+	NM
❑ MJ-1500	No Longer I	1989	3.00	6.00	12.00

BRUBECK, DAVE

Pianist, composer and bandleader. His quartet was one of the most popular and influential jazz groups of the late 1950s and early 1960s. Also see PAUL DESMOND.

ATLANTIC

Number	Title	Yr	VG	VG+	NM
❑ SD 2-317 [(2)]	The Art of Dave Brubeck: The Fantasy Years	1975	3.75	7.50	15.00
❑ SD 1606	Truth Is Fallen	1972	3.00	6.00	12.00
❑ SD 1607	The Last Set at Newport	1972	3.00	6.00	12.00
❑ SD 1641	We're All Together Again for the First Time	1973	3.00	6.00	12.00
❑ SD 1645	Two Generations of Brubeck	1974	3.00	6.00	12.00
❑ SD 1660	Brother, The Great Spirit Made Us All	1974	3.00	6.00	12.00
❑ SD 1684	All the Things We Are	1976	3.00	6.00	12.00

COLUMBIA

Number	Title	Yr	VG	VG+	NM
❑ C2L 26 [(2) M]	The Dave Brubeck Quartet at Carnegie Hall	1963	6.25	12.50	25.00
-- Red "Guaranteed High Fidelity" label					
❑ C2L 26 [(2) M]	The Dave Brubeck Quartet at Carnegie Hall	1966	3.75	7.50	15.00
-- Red "360 Sound" label					
❑ CL 566 [M]	Jazz Goes to College	1954	20.00	40.00	80.00
-- Dark red label, gold print; released at the same time as 6321 and 6322					
❑ CL 566 [M]	Jazz Goes to College	1955	12.50	25.00	50.00
-- Red/black label with six "eye" logos					
❑ CL 566 [M]	Jazz Goes to College	1962	5.00	10.00	20.00
-- Red "Guaranteed High Fidelity" label					
❑ CL 566 [M]	Jazz Goes to College	1966	3.00	6.00	12.00
-- Red "360 Sound" label					
❑ CL 590 [M]	Dave Brubeck at Storyville: 1954	1954	20.00	40.00	80.00
-- Dark red label, gold print; released at the same time as 6330 and 6331					
❑ CL 590 [M]	Dave Brubeck at Storyville: 1954	1955	12.50	25.00	50.00
-- Red/black label with six "eye" logos					
❑ CL 590 [M]	Dave Brubeck at Storyville: 1954	1962	5.00	10.00	20.00
-- Red "Guaranteed High Fidelity" label					
❑ CL 590 [M]	Dave Brubeck at Storyville: 1954	1966	3.00	6.00	12.00
-- Red "360 Sound" label					
❑ CL 622 [M]	Brubeck Time	1955	15.00	30.00	60.00
-- Red/black label with six "eye" logos					
❑ CL 622 [M]	Brubeck Time	1962	5.00	10.00	20.00
-- Red "Guaranteed High Fidelity" label					
❑ CL 622 [M]	Brubeck Time	1966	3.00	6.00	12.00
-- Red "360 Sound" label					
❑ CL 699 [M]	Jazz: Red Hot and Cool	1955	15.00	30.00	60.00
-- Red/black label with six "eye" logos					
❑ CL 699 [M]	Jazz: Red Hot and Cool	1962	5.00	10.00	20.00
-- Red "Guaranteed High Fidelity" label					
❑ CL 699 [M]	Jazz: Red Hot and Cool	1966	3.00	6.00	12.00
-- Red "360 Sound" label					
❑ C2S 826 [(2) S]	The Dave Brubeck Quartet at Carnegie Hall	1963	7.50	15.00	30.00
-- Red label, "360 Sound" in black					
❑ C2S 826 [(2) S]	The Dave Brubeck Quartet at Carnegie Hall	1966	5.00	10.00	20.00
-- Red label, "360 Sound" in white					
❑ C2S 826 [(2)]	The Dave Brubeck Quartet at Carnegie Hall	1971	3.75	7.50	15.00
-- Orange label					
❑ CL 878 [M]	Brubeck Plays Brubeck	1956	15.00	30.00	60.00
-- Red/black label with six "eye" logos					
❑ CL 878 [M]	Brubeck Plays Brubeck	1962	5.00	10.00	20.00
-- Red "Guaranteed High Fidelity" label					
❑ CL 878 [M]	Brubeck Plays Brubeck	1966	3.00	6.00	12.00
-- Red "360 Sound" label					
❑ CL 932 [M]	American Jazz Festival at Newport '56	1956	12.50	25.00	50.00
-- Red/black label with six "eye" logos					
❑ CL 932 [M]	American Jazz Festival at Newport '56	1962	5.00	10.00	20.00
-- Red "Guaranteed High Fidelity" label					
❑ CL 984 [M]	Jazz Impressions of the U.S.A.	1957	12.50	25.00	50.00
-- Red/black label with six "eye" logos					
❑ CL 984 [M]	Jazz Impressions of the U.S.A.	1962	5.00	10.00	20.00
-- Red "Guaranteed High Fidelity" label					
❑ CL 984 [M]	Jazz Impressions of the U.S.A.	1966	3.00	6.00	12.00
-- Red "360 Sound" label					
❑ CL 1034 [M]	Jazz Goes to Junior College	1957	10.00	20.00	40.00
-- Red/black label with six "eye" logos					
❑ CL 1034 [M]	Jazz Goes to Junior College	1962	5.00	10.00	20.00
-- Red "Guaranteed High Fidelity" label					
❑ CL 1034 [M]	Jazz Goes to Junior College	1966	3.00	6.00	12.00
-- Red "360 Sound" label					
❑ CL 1059 [M]	Dave Digs Disney	1957	10.00	20.00	40.00
-- Red/black label with six "eye" logos					
❑ CL 1059 [M]	Dave Digs Disney	1962	5.00	10.00	20.00
-- Red "Guaranteed High Fidelity" label					
❑ CL 1059 [M]	Dave Digs Disney	1966	3.00	6.00	12.00
-- Red "360 Sound" label					
❑ CL 1169 [M]	Dave Brubeck Quartet in Europe	1958	10.00	20.00	40.00
-- Red/black label with six "eye" logos					
❑ CL 1169 [M]	Dave Brubeck Quartet in Europe	1962	5.00	10.00	20.00
-- Red "Guaranteed High Fidelity" label					
❑ CL 1169 [M]	Dave Brubeck Quartet in Europe	1966	3.00	6.00	12.00
-- Red "360 Sound" label					
❑ CL 1249 [M]	Newport 1958	1958	10.00	20.00	40.00
-- Red/black label with six "eye" logos					
❑ CL 1249 [M]	Newport 1958	1962	5.00	10.00	20.00
-- Red "Guaranteed High Fidelity" label					
❑ CL 1249 [M]	Newport 1958	1966	3.00	6.00	12.00
-- Red "360 Sound" label					
❑ CL 1251 [M]	Jazz Impressions of Eurasia	1958	10.00	20.00	40.00
-- Red/black label with six "eye" logos					
❑ CL 1251 [M]	Jazz Impressions of Eurasia	1962	5.00	10.00	20.00
-- Red "Guaranteed High Fidelity" label					
❑ CL 1251 [M]	Jazz Impressions of Eurasia	1966	3.00	6.00	12.00
-- Red "360 Sound" label					
❑ CL 1347 [M]	Gone with the Wind	1959	10.00	20.00	40.00
-- Red/black label with six "eye" logos					
❑ CL 1347 [M]	Gone with the Wind	1962	5.00	10.00	20.00
-- Red "Guaranteed High Fidelity" label					
❑ CL 1347 [M]	Gone with the Wind	1966	3.00	6.00	12.00
-- Red "360 Sound" label					
❑ CL 1397 [M]	Time Out	1960	6.25	12.50	25.00
-- Red/black label with six "eye" logos					
❑ CL 1397 [M]	Time Out Featuring "Take Five"	1962	3.75	7.50	15.00
-- Red "Guaranteed High Fidelity" label; beginning with this issue, the cover was altered to emphasize the hit					
❑ CL 1397 [M]	Time Out Featuring "Take Five"	1966	3.00	6.00	12.00
-- Red "360 Sound" label					
❑ CL 1439 [M]	Southern Scene	1960	6.25	12.50	25.00
-- Red/black label with six "eye" logos					
❑ CL 1439 [M]	Southern Scene	1962	3.75	7.50	15.00
-- Red "Guaranteed High Fidelity" label					
❑ CL 1439 [M]	Southern Scene	1966	3.00	6.00	12.00
-- Red "360 Sound" label					
❑ CL 1454 [M]	The Riddle	1960	6.25	12.50	25.00
-- Red/black label with six "eye" logos					
❑ CL 1454 [M]	The Riddle	1962	3.75	7.50	15.00
-- Red "Guaranteed High Fidelity" label					
❑ CL 1454 [M]	The Riddle	1966	3.00	6.00	12.00
-- Red "360 Sound" label					
❑ CL 1466 [M]	Bernstein Plays Brubeck Plays Bernstein	1960	6.25	12.50	25.00
-- Red/black label with six "eye" logos					
❑ CL 1466 [M]	Bernstein Plays Brubeck Plays Bernstein	1962	3.75	7.50	15.00
-- Red "Guaranteed High Fidelity" label					
❑ CL 1466 [M]	Bernstein Plays Brubeck Plays Bernstein	1966	3.00	6.00	12.00
-- Red "360 Sound" label					
❑ CL 1553 [M]	Brubeck and Rushing	1961	6.25	12.50	25.00
-- Red/black label with six "eye" logos					
❑ CL 1553 [M]	Brubeck and Rushing	1962	3.75	7.50	15.00
-- Red "Guaranteed High Fidelity" label					
❑ CL 1553 [M]	Brubeck and Rushing	1966	3.00	6.00	12.00
-- Red "360 Sound" label					
❑ CL 1609 [M]	Tonight Only!	1961	6.25	12.50	25.00
-- Red/black label with six "eye" logos					
❑ CL 1609 [M]	Tonight Only!	1962	3.75	7.50	15.00
-- Red "Guaranteed High Fidelity" label					
❑ CL 1609 [M]	Tonight Only!	1966	3.00	6.00	12.00
-- Red "360 Sound" label					
❑ CL 1690 [M]	Time Further Out	1961	6.25	12.50	25.00
-- Red/black label with six "eye" logos					
❑ CL 1690 [M]	Time Further Out	1962	3.75	7.50	15.00
-- Red "Guaranteed High Fidelity" label					
❑ CL 1690 [M]	Time Further Out	1966	3.00	6.00	12.00
-- Red "360 Sound" label					

Number	Title	Yr	VG	VG+	NM
❑ CL 1775 [M]	Countdown -- Time in Outer Space	1962	7.50	15.00	30.00
-- Red/black label with six "eye" logos					
❑ CL 1775 [M]	Countdown -- Time in Outer Space	1962	3.75	7.50	15.00
-- Red "Guaranteed High Fidelity" label					
❑ CL 1775 [M]	Countdown -- Time in Outer Space	1966	3.00	6.00	12.00
-- Red "360 Sound" label					
❑ CL 1963 [M]	Brandenburg Gate Revisited	1963	5.00	10.00	20.00
-- Red "Guaranteed High Fidelity" label					
❑ CL 1963 [M]	Brandenburg Gate Revisited	1966	3.00	6.00	12.00
-- Red "360 Sound" label					
❑ CL 1998 [M]	Bossa Nova U.S.A.	1963	5.00	10.00	20.00
-- Red "Guaranteed High Fidelity" label					
❑ CL 1998 [M]	Bossa Nova U.S.A.	1966	3.00	6.00	12.00
-- Red "360 Sound" label					
❑ CL 2127 [M]	Time Changes	1964	5.00	10.00	20.00
-- Red "Guaranteed High Fidelity" label					
❑ CL 2127 [M]	Time Changes	1966	3.00	6.00	12.00
-- Red "360 Sound" label					
❑ CL 2212 [M]	Jazz Impressions of Japan	1964	5.00	10.00	20.00
-- Red "Guaranteed High Fidelity" label					
❑ CL 2212 [M]	Jazz Impressions of Japan	1966	3.00	6.00	12.00
-- Red "360 Sound" label					
❑ CL 2275 [M]	Jazz Impressions of New York	1965	5.00	10.00	20.00
-- Red "Guaranteed High Fidelity" label					
❑ CL 2275 [M]	Jazz Impressions of New York	1966	3.00	6.00	12.00
-- Red "360 Sound" label					
❑ CL 2316 [M]	Take Five	1965	5.00	10.00	20.00
-- Red "Guaranteed High Fidelity" label					
❑ CL 2316 [M]	Take Five	1966	3.00	6.00	12.00
-- Red "360 Sound" label					
❑ CL 2348 [M]	Angel Eyes	1965	5.00	10.00	20.00
-- Red "Guaranteed High Fidelity" label					
❑ CL 2348 [M]	Angel Eyes	1966	3.00	6.00	12.00
-- Red "360 Sound" label					
❑ CL 2437 [M]	My Favorite Things	1966	3.75	7.50	15.00
❑ CL 2484 [M]	Dave Brubeck's Greatest Hits	1966	3.75	7.50	15.00
❑ CL 2512 [M]	Time In	1966	3.75	7.50	15.00
❑ CL 2602 [M]	Anything Goes! Dave Brubeck Quartet Plays Cole Porter	1966	3.75	7.50	15.00
❑ CL 2695 [M]	Bravo Brubeck!	1967	5.00	10.00	20.00
❑ CL 2712 [M]	Jackpot	1967	5.00	10.00	20.00
❑ CL 6321 [10]	Jazz Goes to College, Volume 1	1954	25.00	50.00	100.00
❑ CL 6322 [10]	Jazz Goes to College, Volume 2	1954	25.00	50.00	100.00
❑ CL 6330 [10]	Dave Brubeck at Storyville: 1954, Volume 1	1954	20.00	40.00	80.00
❑ CL 6331 [10]	Dave Brubeck at Storyville: 1954, Volume 2	1954	20.00	40.00	80.00
❑ CS 8058 [S]	Jazz Impressions of Eurasia	1959	12.50	25.00	50.00
-- Red/black label with six "eye" logos					
❑ CS 8058 [S]	Jazz Impressions of Eurasia	1962	6.25	12.50	25.00
-- Red label, "360 Sound" in black					
❑ CS 8058 [S]	Jazz Impressions of Eurasia	1966	3.75	7.50	15.00
-- Red label, "360 Sound" in white					
❑ CS 8082 [S]	Newport 1958	1959	12.50	25.00	50.00
-- Red/black label with six "eye" logos					
❑ CS 8082 [S]	Newport 1958	1962	6.25	12.50	25.00
-- Red label, "360 Sound" in black					
❑ CS 8082 [S]	Newport 1958	1966	3.75	7.50	15.00
-- Red label, "360 Sound" in white					
❑ CS 8090 [S]	Dave Digs Disney	1959	12.50	25.00	50.00
-- Red/black label with six "eye" logos					
❑ CS 8090 [S]	Dave Digs Disney	1962	6.25	12.50	25.00
-- Red label, "360 Sound" in black					
❑ CS 8090 [S]	Dave Digs Disney	1966	3.75	7.50	15.00
-- Red label, "360 Sound" in white					
❑ CS 8156 [S]	Gone with the Wind	1959	12.50	25.00	50.00
-- Red/black label with six "eye" logos					
❑ CS 8156 [S]	Gone with the Wind	1962	6.25	12.50	25.00
-- Red label, "360 Sound" in black					
❑ CS 8156 [S]	Gone with the Wind	1966	3.75	7.50	15.00
-- Red label, "360 Sound" in white					
❑ CS 8156	Gone with the Wind	1971	3.00	6.00	12.00
-- Orange label					
❑ CS 8192 [S]	Time Out	1960	7.50	15.00	30.00
-- Red/black label with six "eye" logos					
❑ CS 8192 [S]	Time Out Featuring "Take Five"	1962	5.00	10.00	20.00
-- Red label, "360 Sound" in black; beginning with this issue, the cover was altered to emphasize the hit					
❑ CS 8192 [S]	Time Out Featuring "Take Five"	1966	3.75	7.50	15.00
-- Red label, "360 Sound" in white					
❑ CS 8192	Time Out Featuring "Take Five"	1971	3.00	6.00	12.00
-- Orange label					
❑ PC 8192	Time Out	1981	2.00	4.00	8.00
-- Reissue with new prefix					
❑ CS 8235 [S]	Southern Scene	1960	7.50	15.00	30.00
-- Red/black label with six "eye" logos					
❑ CS 8235 [S]	Southern Scene	1962	5.00	10.00	20.00
-- Red label, "360 Sound" in black					
❑ CS 8235 [S]	Southern Scene	1966	3.75	7.50	15.00
-- Red label, "360 Sound" in white					
❑ CS 8248 [S]	The Riddle	1960	7.50	15.00	30.00
-- Red/black label with six "eye" logos					
❑ CS 8248 [S]	The Riddle	1962	5.00	10.00	20.00
-- Red label, "360 Sound" in black					
❑ CS 8248 [S]	The Riddle	1966	3.75	7.50	15.00
-- Red label, "360 Sound" in white					
❑ CS 8257 [S]	Brubeck Plays Bernstein Plays Brubeck	1960	7.50	15.00	30.00
-- Red/black label with six "eye" logos					
❑ CS 8257 [S]	Brubeck Plays Bernstein Plays Brubeck	1962	5.00	10.00	20.00
-- Red label, "360 Sound" in black					
❑ CS 8257 [S]	Brubeck Plays Bernstein Plays Brubeck	1966	3.75	7.50	15.00
-- Red label, "360 Sound" in white					
❑ CS 8257	Brubeck Plays Bernstein Plays Brubeck	1971	3.00	6.00	12.00
-- Orange label					
❑ CS 8353 [S]	Brubeck and Rushing	1961	7.50	15.00	30.00
-- Red/black label with six "eye" logos					
❑ CS 8353 [S]	Brubeck and Rushing	1962	5.00	10.00	20.00
-- Red label, "360 Sound" in black					
❑ CS 8353 [S]	Brubeck and Rushing	1966	3.75	7.50	15.00
-- Red label, "360 Sound" in white					
❑ CS 8409 [S]	Tonight Only!	1961	7.50	15.00	30.00
-- Red/black label with six "eye" logos					
❑ CS 8409 [S]	Tonight Only!	1962	5.00	10.00	20.00
-- Red label, "360 Sound" in black					
❑ CS 8409 [S]	Tonight Only!	1966	3.75	7.50	15.00
-- Red label, "360 Sound" in white					
❑ CS 8490 [S]	Time Further Out	1961	7.50	15.00	30.00
-- Red/black label with six "eye" logos					
❑ CS 8490 [S]	Time Further Out	1962	5.00	10.00	20.00
-- Red label, "360 Sound" in black					
❑ CS 8490 [S]	Time Further Out	1966	3.75	7.50	15.00
-- Red label, "360 Sound" in white					
❑ CS 8490	Time Further Out	1971	3.00	6.00	12.00
-- Orange label					
❑ PC 8490	Time Further Out	1981	2.00	4.00	8.00
-- Reissue with new prefix					
❑ CS 8575 [S]	Countdown -- Time in Outer Space	1962	10.00	20.00	40.00
-- Red/black label with six "eye" logos					
❑ CS 8575 [S]	Countdown -- Time in Outer Space	1962	5.00	10.00	20.00
-- Red label, "360 Sound" in black					
❑ CS 8575 [S]	Countdown -- Time in Outer Space	1966	3.75	7.50	15.00
-- Red label, "360 Sound" in white					
❑ CS 8645 [R]	Jazz: Red Hot and Cool	1963	3.75	7.50	15.00
-- Red label, "360 Sound" in black					
❑ CS 8645 [R]	Jazz: Red Hot and Cool	1966	3.00	6.00	12.00
-- Red label, "360 Sound" in white					
❑ CS 8763 [S]	Brandenburg Gate Revisited	1963	6.25	12.50	25.00
-- Red label, "360 Sound" in black					
❑ CS 8763 [S]	Brandenburg Gate Revisited	1966	3.75	7.50	15.00
-- Red label, "360 Sound" in white					
❑ CS 8798 [S]	Bossa Nova U.S.A.	1963	6.25	12.50	25.00
-- Red label, "360 Sound" in black					
❑ CS 8798 [S]	Bossa Nova U.S.A.	1966	3.75	7.50	15.00
-- Red label, "360 Sound" in white					
❑ CS 8927 [S]	Time Changes	1964	6.25	12.50	25.00
-- Red label, "360 Sound" in black					
❑ CS 8927 [S]	Time Changes	1966	3.75	7.50	15.00
-- Red label, "360 Sound" in white					
❑ CS 9012 [S]	Jazz Impressions of Japan	1964	6.25	12.50	25.00
-- Red label, "360 Sound" in black					
❑ CS 9012 [S]	Jazz Impressions of Japan	1966	3.75	7.50	15.00
-- Red label, "360 Sound" in white					
❑ CS 9012	Jazz Impressions of Japan	1971	3.00	6.00	12.00
-- Orange label					
❑ PC 9012	Jazz Impressions of Japan	1981	2.00	4.00	8.00
-- Reissue with new prefix					
❑ CS 9075 [S]	Jazz Impressions of New York	1965	6.25	12.50	25.00
-- Red label, "360 Sound" in black					
❑ CS 9075 [S]	Jazz Impressions of New York	1966	3.75	7.50	15.00
-- Red label, "360 Sound" in white					
❑ CS 9075	Jazz Impressions of New York	1971	3.00	6.00	12.00
-- Orange label					
❑ PC 9075	Jazz Impressions of New York	1981	2.00	4.00	8.00
-- Reissue with new prefix					
❑ CS 9116 [S]	Take Five	1965	6.25	12.50	25.00
-- Red label, "360 Sound" in black					
❑ CS 9116 [S]	Take Five	1966	3.75	7.50	15.00
-- Red label, "360 Sound" in white					
❑ CS 9148 [S]	Angel Eyes	1965	6.25	12.50	25.00
-- Red label, "360 Sound" in black					
❑ CS 9148 [S]	Angel Eyes	1966	3.75	7.50	15.00
-- Red label, "360 Sound" in white					

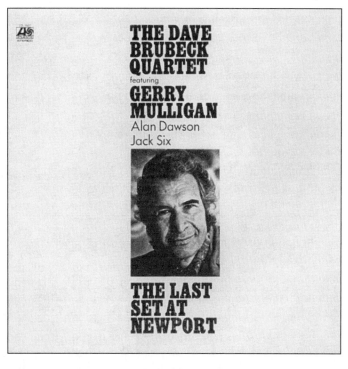

During the height of his popularity, Dave Brubeck was quite a controversial figure in jazz circles. That said, he did introduce jazz to new audiences by playing the college circuit as much as the nightclubs, and he expanded its horizons by making odd time signatures swing (such as the famous 5/4 "Take Five"). Also, one of his quartet members was esteemed alto sax man Paul Desmond. Plus he sold a lot of albums, a rarity in jazz in the 1950s and 1960s. (Top left) Before settling into the quartet format, Brubeck also made albums with trios and octets. This 10-inch LP was the first release on the brand-new Fantasy label, in 1951. (Top right) Many of his college concerts ended up as live albums. Here's a gig recorded at Oberlin College in Ohio and issued on Fantasy. (Bottom left) After the success of *Time Out*, the LP that contained "Take Five," Brubeck continued to explore odd meters, perhaps to excess. This is one of the resulting albums. (Bottom right) In the early 1970s, Brubeck signed with Atlantic's jazz division. He did this live set at the Newport Jazz Festival with Gerry Mulligan.

Number	Title	Yr	VG	VG+	NM
❑ CS 9237 [S]	My Favorite Things	1966	5.00	10.00	20.00
-- Red "360 Sound" label					
❑ CS 9284 [S]	Dave Brubeck's Greatest Hits	1966	5.00	10.00	20.00
-- Red "360 Sound" label					
❑ CS 9284	Dave Brubeck's Greatest Hits	1971	3.00	6.00	12.00
-- Orange label					
❑ PC 9284	Dave Brubeck's Greatest Hits	1981	2.00	4.00	8.00
-- Reissue with new prefix					
❑ CS 9312 [S]	Time In	1966	5.00	10.00	20.00
-- Red "360 Sound" label					
❑ CS 9312	Time In	1971	3.00	6.00	12.00
-- Orange label					
❑ PC 9312	Time In	1981	2.00	4.00	8.00
-- Reissue with new prefix					
❑ CS 9402 [S]	Anything Goes! Dave Brubeck Quartet Plays Cole Porter	1966	5.00	10.00	20.00
-- Red "360 Sound" label					
❑ CS 9402	Anything Goes! Dave Brubeck Quartet Plays Cole Porter	1971	3.00	6.00	12.00
-- Orange label					
❑ PC 9402	Anything Goes! Dave Brubeck Quartet Plays Cole Porter	1981	2.00	4.00	8.00
-- Reissue with new prefix					
❑ CS 9495 [S]	Bravo Brubeck!	1967	3.75	7.50	15.00
-- Red "360 Sound" label					
❑ CS 9495	Bravo Brubeck!	1971	3.00	6.00	12.00
-- Orange label					
❑ CS 9512 [S]	Jackpot	1967	3.75	7.50	15.00
-- Red "360 Sound" label					
❑ CS 9572	The Last Time We Saw Paris	1971	3.00	6.00	12.00
-- Orange label					
❑ CS 9672	The Last Time We Saw Paris	1968	3.75	7.50	15.00
-- Red "360 Sound" label					
❑ CS 9704	Compadres	1968	3.75	7.50	15.00
-- Red "360 Sound" label					
❑ CS 9704	Compadres	1971	3.00	6.00	12.00
-- Orange label					
❑ CS 9749	Blues Roots	1969	3.75	7.50	15.00
-- Red "360 Sound" label					
❑ CS 9749	Blues Roots	1971	3.00	6.00	12.00
-- Orange label					
❑ CS 9897	Brubeck in Amsterdam	1969	3.75	7.50	15.00
-- Red "360 Sound" label					
❑ CS 9897	Brubeck in Amsterdam	1971	3.00	6.00	12.00
-- Orange label					
❑ C 30522	The Summit Sessions	1971	3.00	6.00	12.00
❑ G 30625 [(2)]	Adventures in Time	1971	3.75	7.50	15.00
❑ KG 31298 [(2)]	Brubeck On Campus	1972	3.75	7.50	15.00
❑ KC 32143	Brubeck at the Berlin Philharmonic	1973	3.00	6.00	12.00
❑ KG 32761 [(2)]	All-Time Greatest Hits	1974	3.75	7.50	15.00
❑ CG 33666 [(2)]	Gone with the Wind/Time Out	1975	3.75	7.50	15.00
❑ PC 37022	A Place in Time	1981	2.50	5.00	10.00
-- Reissue of Odyssey LP					

COLUMBIA JAZZ MASTERPIECES

Number	Title	Yr	VG	VG+	NM
❑ CJ 40455	The Dave Brubeck Quartet Plays Music from West Side Story and Other Shows and Films	1987	2.50	5.00	10.00
❑ CJ 40585	Time Out	1987	2.50	5.00	10.00
❑ CJ 40627	Gone with the Wind	1987	2.50	5.00	10.00
❑ CJ 45149	Jazz Goes to College	1989	2.50	5.00	10.00

COLUMBIA/CLASSIC

Number	Title	Yr	VG	VG+	NM
❑ CS 8192	Time Out	1995	6.25	12.50	25.00
-- Audiophile vinyl					

CONCORD JAZZ

Number	Title	Yr	VG	VG+	NM
❑ CJ-103	Back Home	1979	2.50	5.00	10.00
❑ CJ-129	Tritonis	1980	2.50	5.00	10.00
❑ CJ-178	Paper Moon	1982	2.50	5.00	10.00
❑ CJ-198	Concord on a Summer Night	1982	2.50	5.00	10.00
❑ CJ-259	For Iola	1985	2.50	5.00	10.00
❑ CJ-299	Reflections	1986	2.50	5.00	10.00
❑ CJ-317	Blue Rondo	1987	2.50	5.00	10.00
❑ CJ-353	Moscow Night	1988	2.50	5.00	10.00

CROWN

Number	Title	Yr	VG	VG+	NM
❑ CLP-5406 [M]	The Greats	196?	3.75	7.50	15.00
❑ CLP 5470 [M]	Dave Brubeck and the George Nielson Quartet	196?	3.75	7.50	15.00

DECCA

Number	Title	Yr	VG	VG+	NM
❑ DL 710156 [(2)]	The Light in the Wilderness	1968	3.75	7.50	15.00
❑ DL 710175	The Gates of Justice	1969	3.00	6.00	12.00
❑ DL 710181	Brubeck/Mulligan/Cincinnati	1972	3.00	6.00	12.00

DIRECT DISK

Number	Title	Yr	VG	VG+	NM
❑ 106 [(2)]	A Cut Above	1979	6.25	12.50	25.00

FANTASY

Number	Title	Yr	VG	VG+	NM
❑ 3-1 [10]	Dave Brubeck Trio	1951	37.50	75.00	150.00
❑ 3-2 [10]	Dave Brubeck Trio	1951	37.50	75.00	150.00
❑ 3-3 [10]	Dave Brubeck Octet	1951	37.50	75.00	150.00
❑ 3-4 [10]	Dave Brubeck Trio	1952	37.50	75.00	150.00
❑ 3-5 [10]	Dave Brubeck Quartet with Paul Desmond	1952	37.50	75.00	150.00

Number	Title	Yr	VG	VG+	NM
❑ 3-7 [10]	Dave Brubeck Quartet with Paul Desmond	1952	37.50	75.00	150.00
❑ 3-8 [10]	Jazz at Storyville	1953	37.50	75.00	150.00
❑ 3-10 [10]	Jazz at the Blackhawk	1953	37.50	75.00	150.00
❑ 3-11 [10]	Jazz at Oberlin	1953	37.50	75.00	150.00
❑ 3-13 [10]	Jazz at the College of the Pacific	1954	37.50	75.00	150.00
❑ 3-16 [10]	Old Sounds from San Francisco	1954	37.50	75.00	150.00
❑ 3-20 [10]	Paul and Dave's Jazz Interwoven	1955	37.50	75.00	150.00
❑ OJC-046	Jazz at Oberlin	198?	2.50	5.00	10.00
-- Reissue of 3245					
❑ OJC-047	Jazz at the College of the Pacific	198?	2.50	5.00	10.00
-- Reissue of 3223					
❑ OJC-101	The Dave Brubeck Octet	198?	2.50	5.00	10.00
-- Reissue of Fantasy 3239					
❑ OJC-150	Re-Union	198?	2.50	5.00	10.00
❑ OJC-200	Brubeck A La Mode	1985	2.50	5.00	10.00
❑ OJC-236	Near Myth	1986	2.50	5.00	10.00
-- Reissue of Fantasy 3319					
❑ 3204 [M]	Dave Brubeck Trio	1956	25.00	50.00	100.00
-- Dark red vinyl; reissue of 3-1					
❑ 3204 [M]	Dave Brubeck Trio	195?	15.00	30.00	60.00
-- Black vinyl, red label, non-flexible vinyl					
❑ 3204 [M]	Dave Brubeck Trio	196?	10.00	20.00	40.00
-- Black vinyl, red label, flexible vinyl					
❑ 3205 [M]	Dave Brubeck Trio: Distinctive Rhythm Instrumentals	1956	25.00	50.00	100.00
-- Dark red vinyl; reissue of 3-2					
❑ 3205 [M]	Dave Brubeck Trio: Distinctive Rhythm Instrumentals	195?	15.00	30.00	60.00
-- Black vinyl, red label, non-flexible vinyl					
❑ 3205 [M]	Dave Brubeck Trio: Distinctive Rhythm Instrumentals	196?	10.00	20.00	40.00
-- Black vinyl, red label, flexible vinyl					
❑ 3210 [M]	Jazz at the Blackhawk	1956	25.00	50.00	100.00
-- Dark red vinyl; reissue of 3-10					
❑ 3210 [M]	Jazz at the Blackhawk	195?	15.00	30.00	60.00
-- Black vinyl, red label, non-flexible vinyl					
❑ 3210 [M]	Jazz at the Blackhawk	196?	10.00	20.00	40.00
-- Black vinyl, red label, flexible vinyl					
❑ 3223 [M]	Jazz at the College of the Pacific	1956	25.00	50.00	100.00
-- Dark red vinyl; reissue of 3-13					
❑ 3223 [M]	Jazz at the College of the Pacific	195?	15.00	30.00	60.00
-- Black vinyl, red label, non-flexible vinyl					
❑ 3223 [M]	Jazz at the College of the Pacific	196?	10.00	20.00	40.00
-- Black vinyl, red label, flexible vinyl					
❑ 3229 [M]	Brubeck-Desmond	1956	25.00	50.00	100.00
-- Dark red vinyl; reissue of 3-5					
❑ 3229 [M]	Brubeck-Desmond	195?	15.00	30.00	60.00
-- Black vinyl, red label, non-flexible vinyl					
❑ 3229 [M]	Brubeck-Desmond	196?	10.00	20.00	40.00
-- Black vinyl, red label, flexible vinyl					
❑ 3230 [M]	Dave Brubeck Quartet	1956	25.00	50.00	100.00
-- Dark red vinyl; reissue of 3-7					
❑ 3230 [M]	Dave Brubeck Quartet	195?	15.00	30.00	60.00
-- Black vinyl, red label, non-flexible vinyl					
❑ 3230 [M]	Dave Brubeck Quartet	196?	10.00	20.00	40.00
-- Black vinyl, red label, flexible vinyl					
❑ 3239 [M]	Dave Brubeck Octet	1956	25.00	50.00	100.00
-- Dark red vinyl; reissue of 3-3					
❑ 3239 [M]	Dave Brubeck Octet	195?	15.00	30.00	60.00
-- Black vinyl, red label, flexible vinyl					
❑ 3239 [M]	Dave Brubeck Octet	196?	10.00	20.00	40.00
-- Black vinyl, red label, flexible vinyl					
❑ 3240 [M]	Brubeck Desmond: Jazz at Storyville	1957	25.00	50.00	100.00
-- Dark red vinyl; reissue of 3-8					
❑ 3240 [M]	Brubeck Desmond: Jazz at Storyville	195?	15.00	30.00	60.00
-- Black vinyl, red label, non-flexible vinyl					
❑ 3240 [M]	Brubeck Desmond: Jazz at Storyville	196?	10.00	20.00	40.00
-- Black vinyl, red label, flexible vinyl					
❑ 3245 [M]	Jazz at Oberlin	1957	25.00	50.00	100.00
-- Dark red vinyl; reissue of 3-11					
❑ 3245 [M]	Jazz at Oberlin	195?	15.00	30.00	60.00
-- Black vinyl, red label, non-flexible vinyl					
❑ 3245 [M]	Jazz at Oberlin	196?	10.00	20.00	40.00
-- Black vinyl, red label, flexible vinyl					
❑ 3249 [M]	Brubeck & Desmond at Wilshire-Ebell	1957	25.00	50.00	100.00
-- Dark red vinyl					
❑ 3249 [M]	Brubeck & Desmond at Wilshire-Ebell	195?	15.00	30.00	60.00
-- Black vinyl, red label, non-flexible vinyl					
❑ 3249 [M]	Brubeck & Desmond at Wilshire-Ebell	196?	10.00	20.00	40.00
-- Black vinyl, red label, flexible vinyl					
❑ 3259 [M]	Dave Brubeck Plays and Plays and Plays and Plays and...	1958	15.00	30.00	60.00
-- Red vinyl					

Number	Title	Yr	VG	VG+	NM
❏ 3259 [M]	Dave Brubeck Plays and Plays and Plays and Plays and...	195?	10.00	20.00	40.00
-- Black vinyl, red label, non-flexible vinyl					
❏ 3259 [M]	Dave Brubeck Plays and Plays and Plays and Plays and...	196?	7.50	15.00	30.00
-- Black vinyl, red label, flexible vinyl					
❏ 3268 [M]	Re-Union	1958	15.00	30.00	60.00
-- Red vinyl					
❏ 3268 [M]	Re-Union	195?	10.00	20.00	40.00
-- Black vinyl, red label, non-flexible vinyl					
❏ 3268 [M]	Re-Union	196?	7.50	15.00	30.00
-- Black vinyl, red label, flexible vinyl					
❏ 3298 [M]	Two Knights at the Black Hawk	1959	15.00	30.00	60.00
-- Red vinyl					
❏ 3298 [M]	Two Knights at the Black Hawk	1959	10.00	20.00	40.00
-- Black vinyl, red label, non-flexible vinyl					
❏ 3298 [M]	Two Knights at the Black Hawk	196?	7.50	15.00	30.00
-- Black vinyl, red label, flexible vinyl					
❏ 3301 [M]	Brubeck A La Mode	1960	15.00	30.00	60.00
-- Red vinyl					
❏ 3301 [M]	Brubeck A La Mode	196?	7.50	15.00	30.00
-- Black vinyl, red label, flexible vinyl					
❏ 3301 [M]	Brubeck A La Mode	1960	10.00	20.00	40.00
-- Black vinyl, red label, non-flexible vinyl					
❏ 3319 [M]	Near-Myth	1961	15.00	30.00	60.00
-- Red vinyl					
❏ 3319 [M]	Near-Myth	196?	7.50	15.00	30.00
-- Black vinyl, red label, flexible vinyl					
❏ 3319 [M]	Near-Myth	1961	10.00	20.00	40.00
-- Black vinyl, red label, non-flexible vinyl					
❏ 3331 [M]	Dave Brubeck Trio Featuring Cal Tjader	1962	15.00	30.00	60.00
-- Red vinyl					
❏ 3331 [M]	Dave Brubeck Trio Featuring Cal Tjader	196?	7.50	15.00	30.00
-- Black vinyl, red label, flexible vinyl					
❏ 3331 [M]	Dave Brubeck Trio Featuring Cal Tjader	1962	10.00	20.00	40.00
-- Black vinyl, red label, non-flexible vinyl					
❏ 3332 [M]	Brubeck Tjader	1962	15.00	30.00	60.00
-- Red vinyl					
❏ 3332 [M]	Brubeck Tjader	196?	7.50	15.00	30.00
-- Black vinyl, red label, flexible vinyl					
❏ 3332 [M]	Brubeck Tjader	1962	10.00	20.00	40.00
-- Black vinyl, red label, non-flexible vinyl					
❏ MPF-4528	Greatest Hits from the Fantasy Years	198?	2.50	5.00	10.00
❏ 8007 [S]	Re-Union	1962	12.50	25.00	50.00
-- Blue vinyl					
❏ 8007 [S]	Re-Union	196?	7.50	15.00	30.00
-- Black vinyl, blue label, non-flexible vinyl					
❏ 8007 [S]	Re-Union	196?	5.00	10.00	20.00
-- Black vinyl, blue label, flexible vinyl					
❏ 8047 [S]	Brubeck A La Mode	1962	12.50	25.00	50.00
-- Blue vinyl					
❏ 8047 [S]	Brubeck A La Mode	196?	7.50	15.00	30.00
-- Black vinyl, blue label, non-flexible vinyl					
❏ 8047 [S]	Brubeck A La Mode	196?	5.00	10.00	20.00
-- Black vinyl, blue label, flexible vinyl					
❏ 8063 [S]	Near-Myth	1962	12.50	25.00	50.00
-- Blue vinyl					
❏ 8063 [S]	Near-Myth	196?	7.50	15.00	30.00
-- Black vinyl, blue label, non-flexible vinyl					
❏ 8063 [S]	Near-Myth	196?	5.00	10.00	20.00
-- Black vinyl, blue label, flexible vinyl					
❏ 8069 [R]	Jazz at Oberlin	1962	10.00	20.00	40.00
-- Blue vinyl					
❏ 8069 [R]	Jazz at Oberlin	196?	5.00	10.00	20.00
-- Black vinyl, blue label, non-flexible vinyl					
❏ 8069 [R]	Jazz at Oberlin	196?	3.75	7.50	15.00
-- Black vinyl, blue label, flexible vinyl					
❏ 8073 [R]	Dave Brubeck Trio Featuring Cal Tjader	1962	10.00	20.00	40.00
-- Blue vinyl					
❏ 8073 [R]	Dave Brubeck Trio Featuring Cal Tjader	1962	5.00	10.00	20.00
-- Black vinyl, blue label, non-flexible vinyl					
❏ 8073 [R]	Dave Brubeck Trio Featuring Cal Tjader	196?	3.75	7.50	15.00
-- Black vinyl, blue label, flexible vinyl					
❏ 8074 [R]	Brubeck Tjader	196?	3.75	7.50	15.00
-- Black vinyl, blue label, flexible vinyl					
❏ 8074 [R]	Brubeck Tjader	1962	10.00	20.00	40.00
-- Blue vinyl					
❏ 8074 [R]	Brubeck Tjader	1962	5.00	10.00	20.00
-- Black vinyl, blue label, non-flexible vinyl					
❏ 8078 [R]	Jazz at the College of the Pacific	1962	10.00	20.00	40.00
❏ 8078 [R]	Jazz at the College of the Pacific	196?	5.00	10.00	20.00
-- Black vinyl, blue label, non-flexible vinyl					
❏ 8078 [R]	Jazz at the College of the Pacific	196?	3.75	7.50	15.00
-- Black vinyl, blue label, flexible vinyl					
❏ 8080 [R]	Jazz at Storyville	1962	10.00	20.00	40.00
-- Blue vinyl					
❏ 8080 [R]	Jazz at Storyville	1962	5.00	10.00	20.00
-- Black vinyl, blue label, non-flexible vinyl					
❏ 8080 [R]	Jazz at Storyville	196?	3.75	7.50	15.00
-- Black vinyl, blue label, flexible vinyl					
❏ 8081 [R]	Two Knights at the Blackhawk	1962	10.00	20.00	40.00
-- Blue vinyl					
❏ 8081 [R]	Two Knights at the Blackhawk	1962	5.00	10.00	20.00
-- Black vinyl, blue label, non-flexible vinyl					
❏ 8081 [R]	Two Knights at the Blackhawk	196?	3.75	7.50	15.00
-- Black vinyl, blue label, flexible vinyl					
❏ 8092 [R]	Brubeck-Desmond	1962	10.00	20.00	40.00
-- Blue vinyl					
❏ 8092 [R]	Brubeck-Desmond	1962	5.00	10.00	20.00
-- Black vinyl, blue label, non-flexible vinyl					
❏ 8092 [R]	Brubeck-Desmond	196?	3.75	7.50	15.00
-- Black vinyl, blue label, flexible vinyl					
❏ 8093 [R]	Dave Brubeck Quartet	1962	10.00	2.00	40.00
-- Blue vinyl					
❏ 8093 [R]	Dave Brubeck Quartet	1962	5.00	10.00	20.00
-- Black vinyl, blue label, non-flexible vinyl					
❏ 8093 [R]	Dave Brubeck Quartet	196?	3.75	7.50	15.00
-- Black vinyl, blue label, flexible vinyl					
❏ 8094 [R]	Dave Brubeck Octet	1962	10.00	20.00	40.00
-- Blue vinyl					
❏ 8094 [R]	Dave Brubeck Octet	1962	5.00	10.00	20.00
-- Black vinyl, blue label, flexible vinyl					
❏ 8094 [R]	Dave Brubeck Octet	196?	3.75	7.50	15.00
-- Black vinyl, blue label, flexible vinyl					
❏ 8095 [S]	Brubeck and Desmond at Wilshire-Ebell	1962	12.50	25.00	50.00
-- Blue vinyl					
❏ 8095 [S]	Brubeck and Desmond at Wilshire-Ebell	1962	7.50	15.00	30.00
-- Black vinyl, blue label, non-flexible vinyl					
❏ 8095 [S]	Brubeck and Desmond at Wilshire-Ebell	196?	5.00	10.00	20.00
-- Black vinyl, blue label, flexible vinyl					
❏ 24726 [(2)]	The Dave Brubeck Trio	198?	3.75	7.50	15.00
❏ 24727 [(2)]	Brubeck-Desmond	1982	3.75	7.50	15.00
❏ 24728 [(2)]	Stardust	198?	3.75	7.50	15.00

HARMONY

Number	Title	Yr	VG	VG+	NM
❏ HS 11253	Instant Brubeck	1968	3.00	6.00	12.00
❏ HS 11336	Gone with the Wind	1969	3.00	6.00	12.00

HORIZON

Number	Title	Yr	VG	VG+	NM
❏ SP-703	1975: The Duets	1975	3.00	6.00	12.00
❏ SP-714	The Dave Brubeck Quartet 25th Anniversary	1976	3.00	6.00	12.00

JAZZTONE

Number	Title	Yr	VG	VG+	NM
❏ J-1272 [M]	Best of Brubeck	195?	10.00	20.00	40.00

MOBILE FIDELITY

Number	Title	Yr	VG	VG+	NM
❏ 1-216	We're All Together Again for the First Time	1994	15.00	30.00	60.00
-- Audiophile vinyl					

MOON

Number	Title	Yr	VG	VG+	NM
❏ 028	St. Louis Blues	1992	5.00	10.00	20.00

ODYSSEY

Number	Title	Yr	VG	VG+	NM
❏ 32-16-0248	A Place in Time	197?	3.00	6.00	12.00

TOMATO

Number	Title	Yr	VG	VG+	NM
❏ 7018	The New Brubeck Quartet at Montreux	1978	3.00	6.00	12.00

BRUCE, LENNY

Stand-up comedian who was highly influenced by 1950s jazz life.

BIZARRE

Number	Title	Yr	VG	VG+	NM
❏ 2XS 6329 [(2)]	The Berkeley Concert	1969	6.25	12.50	25.00

DOUGLAS

Number	Title	Yr	VG	VG+	NM
❏ 2	To Is a Preposition, Come Is a Verb	196?	5.00	10.00	20.00
❏ 788	The Essential Lenny Bruce Politics	1968	5.00	10.00	20.00
❏ Z 30872	What I Was Arrested For	1971	3.75	7.50	15.00
-- Reissue of 2					

FANTASY

Number	Title	Yr	VG	VG+	NM
❏ 7001 [M]	Interviews of Our Times	1959	25.00	50.00	100.00
-- Opaque, non-flexible red vinyl; tan cover with Lenny Bruce's name blacked out throughout the back					
❏ 7001 [M]	Interviews of Our Times	1959	10.00	20.00	40.00
-- Non-flexible black vinyl; cover changed to blue tint					
❏ 7001 [M]	Interviews of Our Times	1962	10.00	20.00	40.00
-- Translucent, flexible red vinyl					
❏ 7001 [M]	Interviews of Our Times	1962	5.00	10.00	20.00
-- Flexible black vinyl					
❏ 7003 [M]	The Sick Humor of Lenny Bruce	1959	25.00	50.00	100.00
-- Opaque, non-flexible red vinyl					

Number	Title	Yr	VG	VG+	NM
❏ 7003 [M]	The Sick Humor of Lenny Bruce	1959	10.00	20.00	40.00
-- Non-flexible black vinyl					
❏ 7003 [M]	The Sick Humor of Lenny Bruce	1962	10.00	20.00	40.00
-- Translucent, flexible red vinyl					
❏ 7003 [M]	The Sick Humor of Lenny Bruce	1962	5.00	10.00	20.00
-- Flexible black vinyl					
❏ 7007 [M]	I Am Not a Nut, Elect Me	1960	25.00	50.00	100.00
-- Opaque, non-flexible red vinyl					
❏ 7007 [M]	I Am Not a Nut, Elect Me	1960	10.00	20.00	40.00
-- Non-flexible black vinyl					
❏ 7007 [M]	I Am Not a Nut, Elect Me	1962	10.00	20.00	40.00
-- Translucent, flexible red vinyl					
❏ 7007 [M]	I Am Not a Nut, Elect Me	1962	5.00	10.00	20.00
-- Flexible black vinyl					
❏ 7011 [M]	Lenny Bruce, American	1961	25.00	50.00	100.00
-- Opaque, non-flexible red vinyl					
❏ 7011 [M]	Lenny Bruce, American	1961	10.00	20.00	40.00
-- Non-flexible black vinyl					
❏ 7011 [M]	Lenny Bruce, American	1962	10.00	20.00	40.00
-- Translucent, flexible red vinyl					
❏ 7011 [M]	Lenny Bruce, American	1962	5.00	10.00	20.00
-- Flexible black vinyl					
❏ 7012 [M]	The Best of Lenny Bruce	1962	12.50	25.00	50.00
-- Red vinyl					
❏ 7012 [M]	The Best of Lenny Bruce	1962	5.00	10.00	20.00
-- Black vinyl					
❏ 7017	Thank You Masked Man	1971	3.75	7.50	15.00
❏ 34201 [(3)]	Lenny Bruce at the Curran Theater	1971	10.00	20.00	40.00
❏ 79003 [(2)]	The Real Lenny Bruce	1975	5.00	10.00	20.00

LENNY BRUCE

Number	Title	Yr	VG	VG+	NM
❏ LB-3001/2 [M]	Lenny Bruce Is Out Again	196?	75.00	150.00	300.00
-- Privately pressed version with white labels and Lenny's address on cover					
❏ LB-9001/2 [10]	Warning: Sale of This Album...	1962	125.00	250.00	500.00
-- Privately pressed LP with routines used as evidence in Lenny's obscenity trial					

PHILLIES

Number	Title	Yr	VG	VG+	NM
❏ PHLP-4010 [M]	Lenny Bruce Is Out Again	1966	25.00	50.00	100.00
-- Reissue of Lenny Bruce 3001/2					

UNITED ARTISTS

Number	Title	Yr	VG	VG+	NM
❏ UAL 3580 [M]	The Midnight Concert	1967	6.25	12.50	25.00
❏ UAS 6580	The Midnight Concert	1967	5.00	10.00	20.00
❏ UAS 6794	The Midnight Concert	1972	3.75	7.50	15.00
-- Reissue of 6580					
❏ UAS 9800 [(3)]	Lenny Bruce/Carnegie Hall	1972	6.25	12.50	25.00

WARNER/SPECTOR

Number	Title	Yr	VG	VG+	NM
❏ SP 9101	The Law, the Language and Lenny Bruce	1975	3.75	7.50	15.00

BRUEL, MAX
Baritone saxophone player.
EMARCY

Number	Title	Yr	VG	VG+	NM
❏ MG-36062 [M]	Cool Bruel	1955	15.00	30.00	60.00

BRUNEL, BUNNY
Bass player.
INNER CITY

Number	Title	Yr	VG	VG+	NM
❏ 1102	Touch	198?	2.50	5.00	10.00
❏ 1162	Ivanhoe	198?	2.50	5.00	10.00

BRUNIOUS, WENDELL
Trumpeter. Member of the touring version of PRESERVATION HALL JAZZ BAND.
GHB

Number	Title	Yr	VG	VG+	NM
❏ GHB-194	Wendell Brunious and His New Orleans Jazz Band in the Tradition	198?	2.50	5.00	10.00

BRUNIS, GEORG
Trombonist. Member of NEW ORLEANS RHYTHM KINGS.
COMMODORE

Number	Title	Yr	VG	VG+	NM
❏ FL-20008 [10]	King of the Tailgate Trombone	1950	20.00	40.00	80.00
❏ DL 30015 [M]	King of the Tailgate Trombone	1959	10.00	20.00	40.00

JAZZOLOGY

Number	Title	Yr	VG	VG+	NM
❏ J-012	Georg Brunis and His Rhythm	1965	3.75	7.50	15.00

JOLLY ROGER

Number	Title	Yr	VG	VG+	NM
❏ 5024 [10]	Georg Brunis and the New Orleans Rhythm Kings	1954	12.50	25.00	50.00

RIVERSIDE

Number	Title	Yr	VG	VG+	NM
❏ RLP-1024 [10]	Georg Brunis and the Original New Orleans Rhythm Kings	1954	20.00	40.00	80.00

BRYAN, JOY
Female singer.
CONTEMPORARY

Number	Title	Yr	VG	VG+	NM
❏ M-3604 [M]	Make the Man Love Me	1961	10.00	20.00	40.00
❏ S-7604 [S]	Make the Man Love Me	1961	12.50	25.00	50.00

MODE

Number	Title	Yr	VG	VG+	NM
❏ LP-108 [M]	Joy Bryan Sings	1957	20.00	40.00	80.00

BRYANT, BOBBY
Trumpeter.
CADET

Number	Title	Yr	VG	VG+	NM
❏ LP-795 [M]	Ain't Doing Too B-A-D, Bad	1967	5.00	10.00	20.00
❏ LPS-795 [S]	Ain't Doing Too B-A-D, Bad	1967	3.75	7.50	15.00
❏ CA-50011	Swahili Strut	1972	3.00	6.00	12.00

VEE JAY

Number	Title	Yr	VG	VG+	NM
❏ VJS-3059	Big Band Blues	1974	5.00	10.00	20.00

WORLD PACIFIC

Number	Title	Yr	VG	VG+	NM
❏ ST-20159	The Jazz Excursion Into "Hair"	1969	3.75	7.50	15.00

BRYANT, CLORA
Trumpeter and female singer.
MODE

Number	Title	Yr	VG	VG+	NM
❏ LP-106 [M]	Gal with a Horn	1957	25.00	50.00	100.00

BRYANT, PAUL
Organist. Also see CURTIS AMY AND PAUL BRYANT.
FANTASY

Number	Title	Yr	VG	VG+	NM
❏ 3357 [M]	Something's Happening	1963	5.00	10.00	20.00
❏ 3363 [M]	Groove Time	1964	5.00	10.00	20.00
❏ 8357 [S]	Something's Happening	1963	6.25	12.50	25.00
❏ 8363 [S]	Groove Time	1964	6.25	12.50	25.00

PACIFIC JAZZ

Number	Title	Yr	VG	VG+	NM
❏ PJ-12 [M]	Burnin'	1961	10.00	20.00	40.00

BRYANT, RAY
Pianist and composer. Also see THE PRESTIGE BLUES SWINGERS.
ATLANTIC

Number	Title	Yr	VG	VG+	NM
❏ SD 1564	MCMLXX	1970	3.75	7.50	15.00
❏ SD 1626	Alone at Montreux	1972	3.00	6.00	12.00

CADET

Number	Title	Yr	VG	VG+	NM
❏ LP-767 [M]	Gotta Travel On	1966	3.75	7.50	15.00
❏ LPS-767 [S]	Gotta Travel On	1966	5.00	10.00	20.00
❏ LP-778 [M]	Lonesome Traveler	1966	3.75	7.50	15.00
❏ LPS-778 [S]	Lonesome Traveler	1966	5.00	10.00	20.00
❏ LP-781 [M]	Slow Freight	1967	3.75	7.50	15.00
❏ LPS-781 [S]	Slow Freight	1967	5.00	10.00	20.00
❏ LP-793 [M]	The Ray Bryant Touch	1967	5.00	10.00	20.00
❏ LPS-793 [S]	The Ray Bryant Touch	1967	3.75	7.50	15.00
❏ LP-801 [M]	Take a Bryant Step	1967	5.00	10.00	20.00
❏ LPS-801 [S]	Take a Bryant Step	1967	3.75	7.50	15.00
❏ LPS-818	Up Above the Rock	1968	3.75	7.50	15.00
❏ LPS-830	Sound Ray	1969	3.75	7.50	15.00
❏ 50038 [(2)]	It Was a Very Good Year	1973	3.75	7.50	15.00
❏ 50052	In the Cut	1974	3.00	6.00	12.00

CLASSIC JAZZ

Number	Title	Yr	VG	VG+	NM
❏ 130	Hot Turkey	198?	2.50	5.00	10.00

COLUMBIA

Number	Title	Yr	VG	VG+	NM
❏ CL 1449 [M]	Little Susie	1960	5.00	10.00	20.00
❏ CL 1476 [M]	The Madison Time	1960	6.25	12.50	25.00
❏ CL 1633 [M]	Con Alma	1961	5.00	10.00	20.00
❏ CL 1746 [M]	Dancing the Big Twist	1962	5.00	10.00	20.00
❏ CL 1867 [M]	Hollywood Jazz Beat	1962	5.00	10.00	20.00
❏ CS 8244 [S]	Little Susie	1960	6.25	12.50	25.00
❏ CS 8276 [S]	The Madison Time	1960	7.50	15.00	30.00
❏ CS 8433 [S]	Con Alma	1961	6.25	12.50	25.00
❏ CS 8546 [S]	Dancing the Big Twist	1962	6.25	12.50	25.00
❏ CS 8667 [S]	Hollywood Jazz Beat	1962	6.25	12.50	25.00

COLUMBIA JAZZ MASTERPIECES

Number	Title	Yr	VG	VG+	NM
❏ CJ 44058	Con Alma	1988	2.50	5.00	10.00

EMARCY

Number	Title	Yr	VG	VG+	NM
❏ 832 235-1	Ray Bryant Plays Basie and Ellington	1987	3.00	6.00	12.00
❏ 832 589-1	The Ray Bryant Trio Today	1988	3.00	6.00	12.00
❏ 836 368-1	Golden Earrings	1989	3.00	6.00	12.00

EPIC

Number	Title	Yr	VG	VG+	NM
❏ LN 3279 [M]	Ray Bryant Trio	1956	17.50	35.00	70.00

FANTASY

Number	Title	Yr	VG	VG+	NM
❏ OJC-213	Alone with the Blues	1987	2.50	5.00	10.00
-- Reissue					
❏ OJC-371	Montreux '77	1989	2.50	5.00	10.00
-- Reissue of Pablo Live 2308 201					

NEW JAZZ

Number	Title	Yr	VG	VG+	NM
❏ NJLP-8213 [M]	Alone with the Blues	1959	12.50	25.00	50.00
-- Purple label					

Number	Title	Yr	VG	VG+	NM
❑ NJLP-8213 [M]	Alone with the Blues	1965	6.25	12.50	25.00
-- Blue label with trident logo					
❑ NJLP-8227 [M]	Ray Bryant Trio	1959	12.50	25.00	50.00
-- Purple label; reissue of Prestige 7098					
❑ NJLP-8227 [M]	Ray Bryant Trio	1965	6.25	12.50	25.00
-- Blue label with trident logo					
PABLO					
❑ 2310 764	Here's Ray Bryant	1976	2.50	5.00	10.00
❑ 2310 798	Solo Piano	1976	2.50	5.00	10.00
❑ 2310 820	All Blues	1978	2.50	5.00	10.00
❑ 2310 860	Potpourri	1981	2.50	5.00	10.00
❑ 2405 402	The Best of Ray Bryant	198?	2.50	5.00	10.00
PABLO LIVE					
❑ 2308 201	Montreux '77	1977	2.50	5.00	10.00
PRESTIGE					
❑ PRLP-7098 [M]	Ray Bryant Trio	1957	17.50	35.00	70.00
❑ PRLP-7837	Alone with the Blues	1971	3.75	7.50	15.00
-- Reissue of New Jazz 8213					
❑ 24038 [(2)]	Me and the Blues	1973	3.75	7.50	15.00
SIGNATURE					
❑ SM-6008 [M]	Ray Bryant Plays	1960	50.00	100.00	200.00
❑ SS-6008 [S]	Ray Bryant Plays	1960	62.50	125.00	250.00
SUE					
❑ LP-1016 [M]	Groove House	1963	10.00	20.00	40.00
❑ LPS-1016 [S]	Groove House	1963	12.50	25.00	50.00
❑ LP-1019 [M]	Live at Basin Street	1964	10.00	20.00	40.00
❑ LPS-1019 [S]	Live at Basin Street	1964	12.50	25.00	50.00
❑ LP-1032 [M]	Cold Turkey	1964	10.00	20.00	40.00
❑ LPS-1032 [S]	Cold Turkey	1964	12.50	25.00	50.00
❑ LP-1036 [M]	Ray Bryant Soul	1965	10.00	20.00	40.00
❑ LPS-1036 [S]	Ray Bryant Soul	1965	12.50	25.00	50.00

BRYANT, RUSTY
Tenor and alto saxophone player.

Number	Title	Yr	VG	VG+	NM
DOT					
❑ DLP-3006 [M]	All Night Long	1956	10.00	20.00	40.00
-- Maroon label					
❑ DLP-3079 [M]	Rusty Bryant Plays Jazz	1957	10.00	20.00	40.00
❑ DLP-3353 [M]	America's Greatest Jazz	1961	3.75	7.50	15.00
❑ DLP-25353 [S]	America's Greatest Jazz	1961	5.00	10.00	20.00
FANTASY					
❑ OJC-331	Rusty Bryant Returns	1988	2.50	5.00	10.00
-- Reissue of Prestige 7626					
PRESTIGE					
❑ PRST-7626	Rusty Bryant Returns	1969	3.00	6.00	12.00
❑ PRST-7735	Night Train Now!	1970	3.00	6.00	12.00
❑ PRST-7798	Soul Liberation	1971	3.00	6.00	12.00
❑ 10013	Fire Eater	1972	3.00	6.00	12.00
❑ 10037	Wild Fire	1972	3.00	6.00	12.00
❑ 10053	Friday Night Funk	1973	3.00	6.00	12.00
❑ 10073	For the Good Times	1974	3.00	6.00	12.00
❑ 10085	Until It's Time for You to Go	1974	3.00	6.00	12.00

BUCCI, JOE
Organist.

Number	Title	Yr	VG	VG+	NM
CAPITOL					
❑ ST 1840 [S]	Wild About Basie	1963	5.00	10.00	20.00
❑ T 1840 [M]	Wild About Basie	1963	3.75	7.50	15.00

BUCKLEY, LORD
Stand-up comedian and MC popular in jazz circles in the 1950s.

Number	Title	Yr	VG	VG+	NM
CRESTVIEW					
❑ CRV-801 [M]	The Best of Lord Buckley	1963	12.50	25.00	50.00
❑ CRV7-801 [S]	The Best of Lord Buckley	1963	15.00	30.00	60.00
ELEKTRA					
❑ EKS-74047	The Best of Lord Buckley	1969	6.25	12.50	25.00
-- Reissue of Crestview 7-801					
RCA VICTOR					
❑ LPM-3246 [10]	Hipsters, Flipsters and Finger Poppin' Daddies, Knock Me Your Lobes	1955	75.00	150.00	300.00
REPRISE					
❑ RS 6389	A Most Immaculately Hip Aristocrat	1970	6.25	12.50	25.00
-- Reissue of Straight 1054					
STRAIGHT					
❑ STS-1054	A Most Immaculately Hip Aristocrat	1970	10.00	20.00	40.00
VAYA					
❑ 101/2 [M]	Euphoria, Volume 1	1955	37.50	75.00	150.00
❑ 107/8 [M]	Euphoria, Volume 2	1955	50.00	100.00	200.00
❑ 1715 [10]	Euphoria	195?	75.00	150.00	300.00
-- Red vinyl					

Number	Title	Yr	VG	VG+	NM
WORLD PACIFIC					
❑ WP-1279 [M]	The Way Out Humor of Lord Buckley	1959	30.00	60.00	120.00
-- With "Far Out Humor" on the back cover					
❑ WP-1279 [M]	The Way Out Humor of Lord Buckley	1959	25.00	50.00	100.00
-- With correct "Way Out Humor" on the back cover					
❑ WP-1815 [M]	Lord Buckley in Concert	1964	12.50	25.00	50.00
-- Reissue of 1279					
❑ WP-1849 [M]	Blowing His Mind (and Yours, Too)	1966	12.50	25.00	50.00
❑ WPS-21879	Buckley's Best	1968	10.00	20.00	40.00
❑ WPS-21889	Bad Rapping of the Marquis de Sade	1969	7.50	15.00	30.00

BUCKNER, MILT
Organist; sometimes a piano and vibraphone player.

Number	Title	Yr	VG	VG+	NM
ARGO					
❑ LP-660 [M]	Mighty High	1960	3.75	7.50	15.00
❑ LPS-660 [S]	Mighty High	1960	5.00	10.00	20.00
❑ LP-670 [M]	Please Mr. Organ Player	1960	3.75	7.50	15.00
❑ LPS-670 [S]	Please Mr. Organ Player	1960	5.00	10.00	20.00
❑ LP-702 [M]	Midnight Mood	1962	3.75	7.50	15.00
❑ LPS-702 [S]	Midnight Mood	1962	5.00	10.00	20.00
BASF					
❑ 20631	Chords	1972	3.75	7.50	15.00
BETHLEHEM					
❑ BCP-6072 [M]	The New World of Milt Buckner	1963	7.50	15.00	30.00
CAPITOL					
❑ T 642 [M]	Rockin' with Milt	1955	12.50	25.00	50.00
-- Turquoise or gray label					
❑ T 722 [M]	Rockin' Hammond	1956	12.50	25.00	50.00
-- Turquoise or gray label					
❑ T 938 [M]	Send Me Softly	1958	12.50	25.00	50.00
-- Turquoise or gray label					
CLASSIC JAZZ					
❑ 141	Green Onions	198?	2.50	5.00	10.00
JAZZ MAN					
❑ 5012	Rockin' Again	198?	3.00	6.00	12.00
PRESTIGE					
❑ PRST-7668	Milt Buckner in Europe '66	1969	3.75	7.50	15.00
REGENT					
❑ MG-6004 [M]	Organ -- Sweet 'n' Swing	195?	7.50	15.00	30.00
SAVOY					
❑ MG-15023 [10]	Milt Buckner Piano	1953	30.00	60.00	120.00

BUCKNER, TEDDY
Trumpeter, bandleader, sometimes a flugel horn player.

Number	Title	Yr	VG	VG+	NM
AIRCHECK					
❑ 10	Teddy Buckner and His Orchestra 1955	198?	2.50	5.00	10.00
DIXIELAND JUBILEE					
❑ DJ-503 [M]	In Concert at the Dixieland Jubilee	195?	5.00	10.00	20.00
❑ DJS-503 [R]	In Concert at the Dixieland Jubilee	196?	3.00	6.00	12.00
❑ DJ-504 [M]	Teddy Buckner and His Dixieland Band	195?	5.00	10.00	20.00
❑ DJS-504 [R]	Teddy Buckner and His Dixieland Band	195?	3.00	6.00	12.00
❑ DJ-505 [M]	A Salute to Louis Armstrong	1959	5.00	10.00	20.00
❑ DJS-505 [S]	A Salute to Louis Armstrong	1959	3.75	7.50	15.00
❑ DJ-507 [M]	Teddy Buckner and the All Stars	1959	5.00	10.00	20.00
❑ DJS-507 [S]	Teddy Buckner and the All Stars	1959	3.75	7.50	15.00
❑ DJ-510 [M]	Teddy Buckner on the Sunset Strip	1960	5.00	10.00	20.00
❑ DJS-510 [S]	Teddy Buckner on the Sunset Strip	1960	3.75	7.50	15.00
❑ DJS-516	Teddy Buckner at the Crescendo	196?	3.75	7.50	15.00
GENE NORMAN					
❑ GNP-?? [10]	Dixieland Jubilee	195?	12.50	25.00	50.00
-- Red vinyl					
❑ GNP-11 [M]	Teddy Buckner	1955	10.00	20.00	40.00
GNP CRESCENDO					
❑ GNP-68 [M]	Midnight in Moscow	1962	3.00	6.00	12.00
❑ GNPS-68 [S]	Midnight in Moscow	1962	3.75	7.50	15.00

BUCKSHOT LEFONQUE
Jazz/funk/hip-hop group led by BRANFORD MARSALIS.

Number	Title	Yr	VG	VG+	NM
COLUMBIA					
❑ C2 57322 [(2)]	Buckshot LeFonque	1994	3.75	7.50	15.00
❑ C 67584	Music Evolution	1997	3.00	6.00	12.00

Number	Title	Yr	VG	VG+	NM
BUDIMIR, DENNIS					

Guitarist. Also a session musician who, among other jobs, played on most of the Partridge Family's albums!

MAINSTREAM

Number	Title	Yr	VG	VG+	NM
❑ S-6059 [S]	Creeper	1966	6.25	12.50	25.00
❑ 56059 [M]	Creeper	1966	5.00	10.00	20.00

REVELATION

❑ REV-1 [S]	Alone Together	1967	5.00	10.00	20.00
❑ REV-M1 [M]	Alone Together	1967	6.25	12.50	25.00
❑ REV-4	A Second Coming	1968	5.00	10.00	20.00
❑ REV-8	Sprung Free!	1969	5.00	10.00	20.00
❑ REV-14	Session with Albert	1971	5.00	10.00	20.00

BUDWIG, MONTY
Bass player.
CONCORD JAZZ

❑ CJ-79	Dig	198?	2.50	5.00	10.00

BUG ALLEY
Canadian vocal and instrumental group featuring Karen Young.
P.M.

❑ PMR-019	Bug Alley	1980	3.75	7.50	15.00

BUNCH, JOHN
Pianist.
AUDIOPHILE

❑ AP-184	Jubilee	1982	2.50	5.00	10.00

CHIAROSCURO

❑ 144	John Bunch Plays Music of Kurt Weill	1975	3.00	6.00	12.00

CONCORD JAZZ

❑ CJ-328	The Best Thing for You	1987	2.50	5.00	10.00

FAMOUS DOOR

❑ 107	John's Bunch	1976	3.00	6.00	12.00
❑ 114	John's Other Bunch	1977	3.00	6.00	12.00
❑ 118	Slick Funk	1978	3.00	6.00	12.00

BUNKER, LARRY
Drummer, percussionist and vibraphone player.
VAULT

❑ LP-9005 [M]	Live at Shelly's Manne-Hole	1966	5.00	10.00	20.00
❑ LPS-9005 [S]	Live at Shelly's Manne-Hole	1966	3.75	7.50	15.00

BURGER, JACK
Drummer, most notably on bongos.
HIFI

❑ R-803 [M]	Let's Play Bongos!	1957	10.00	20.00	40.00
❑ R-804 [M]	The End on Bongos!	1957	10.00	20.00	40.00
❑ R-809 [M]	Let's Play Congas	1958	7.50	15.00	30.00
❑ RS-809 [S]	Let's Play Congas	1959	10.00	20.00	40.00

BURKE, CHRIS, AND HIS NEW ORLEANS MUSIC
Clarinet player.
GHB

❑ 175	True to New Orleans	1985	2.50	5.00	10.00

BURKE, RAY
Clarinet and saxophone player. Also see JOHNNY WIGGS.
NEW ORLEANS

❑ 7202	Speakeasy Boys (1937-49)	198?	2.50	5.00	10.00

SOUTHLAND

❑ SLP-209 [10]	Contemporary New Orleans Jazz	1955	12.50	25.00	50.00

BURKE, VINNIE
Bass player. Also see OSCAR PETTIFORD; BUCKY PIZZARELLI.
ABC-PARAMOUNT

❑ ABC-139 [M]	The Vinnie Burke All Stars	1956	12.50	25.00	50.00
❑ ABC-170 [M]	The Vinnie Burke String Jazz Quartet	1957	12.50	25.00	50.00

BETHLEHEM

❑ BCP-1010 [10]	East Coast Jazz 2	1954	30.00	60.00	120.00

BURNETT, CARL
Drummer.
DISCOVERY

❑ 819	Carl Burnett Plays the Music of Richard Rodgers	198?	2.50	5.00	10.00

BURNS, RALPH
Pianist, arranger and composer.
BETHLEHEM

❑ BCP-68 [M]	Bijou	1957	12.50	25.00	50.00

CLEF

❑ MGC-115 [10]	Free Forms	1953	50.00	100.00	200.00

DECCA

❑ DL 8235 [M]	Jazz Studio 5	1956	20.00	40.00	80.00
❑ DL 8555 [M]	The Masters Revisited	1957	15.00	30.00	60.00
❑ DL 9068 [M]	New York's a Song	1959	10.00	20.00	40.00
❑ DL 9207 [M]	Very Warm for Jazz	1959	10.00	20.00	40.00
❑ DL 9215 [M]	Porgy and Bess	1959	7.50	15.00	30.00
❑ DL 79068 [S]	New York's a Song	1959	12.50	25.00	50.00
❑ DL 79207 [S]	Very Warm for Jazz	1959	12.50	25.00	50.00
❑ DL 79215 [S]	Porgy and Bess	1959	10.00	20.00	40.00

EPIC

❑ LN 24015 [M]	Swingin' Down the Lane	1962	7.50	15.00	30.00
❑ BN 26015 [S]	Swingin' Down the Lane	1962	10.00	20.00	40.00

JAZZTONE

❑ J-1228 [M]	Spring Sequence	1956	12.50	25.00	50.00

MERCURY

❑ MGC-115 [10]	Free Forms	1952	62.50	125.00	250.00

MGM

❑ E-3616 [M]	The Swinging Seasons	1958	12.50	25.00	50.00
❑ SE-3616 [S]	The Swinging Seasons	1959	10.00	20.00	40.00

NORGRAN

❑ MGN-1028 [M]	Ralph Burns Among the JATP's	1955	30.00	60.00	120.00

PERIOD

❑ SPL-1105 [10]	Spring Sequence	1955	30.00	60.00	120.00
❑ SPL-1109 [10]	Bijou	1955	30.00	60.00	120.00

VERVE

❑ MGV-8121 [M]	Ralph Burns Among the JATP's	1957	12.50	25.00	50.00
❑ V-8121 [M]	Ralph Burns Among the JATP's	1961	5.00	10.00	20.00

WARWICK

❑ W-5001 [M]	Where There's Burns There's Fire	1961	10.00	20.00	40.00
❑ W-5001 ST [S]	Where There's Burns There's Fire	1961	12.50	25.00	50.00

BURNS, RALPH/BILLIE HOLIDAY
Also see each artist's individual listings.
CLEF

❑ MGC-718 [M]	The Free Forms of Ralph Burns/The Songs of Billie Holiday	1956	30.00	60.00	120.00

VERVE

❑ MGV-8098 [M]	Jazz Recital	1957	12.50	25.00	50.00
❑ V-8098 [M]	Jazz Recital	1961	5.00	10.00	20.00

BURNS, ROY
Drummer.
ROULETTE

❑ R-52095 [M]	Skin Burns	1963	5.00	10.00	20.00
❑ SR-52095 [S]	Skin Burns	1963	6.25	12.50	25.00

BURRELL, DAVE
Pianist. Also see BEAVER HARRIS 360 DEGREE MUSIC EXPERIENCE.
ARISTA FREEDOM

❑ AL 1906 [(2)]	High Won/High Two	1975	3.75	7.50	15.00

DOUGLAS

❑ SD 798	High	1969	5.00	10.00	20.00

HAT ART

❑ 2025 [(2)]	Windward Passages	1987	3.75	7.50	15.00
-- *Reissue of Hat Hut 05*					

HAT HUT

❑ 05 [(2)]	Windward Passages	1979	5.00	10.00	20.00

BURRELL, KENNY
Guitarist. Also see CHARLIE BYRD; JOHN JENKINS; FRANK WESS.
ARGO

❑ LP-655 [M]	A Night at the Vanguard	1959	7.50	15.00	30.00
❑ LPS-655 [S]	A Night at the Vanguard	1959	10.00	20.00	40.00

BLUE NOTE

❑ BLP-1523 [M]	Introducing Kenny Burrell	1956	50.00	100.00	200.00
-- *"Deep groove" version (deep indentation under label on both sides)*					
❑ BLP-1523 [M]	Introducing Kenny Burrell	1956	37.50	75.00	150.00
-- *Regular version, Lexington Ave. address on label*					
❑ BLP-1523 [M]	Introducing Kenny Burrell	1957	12.50	25.00	50.00
-- *W. 63rd St., NYC address on label*					
❑ BLP-1523 [M]	Introducing Kenny Burrell	1963	6.25	12.50	25.00
-- *New York, USA address on label*					
❑ BLP-1543 [M]	Kenny Burrell, Volume 2	1957	50.00	100.00	200.00
-- *"Deep groove" version (deep indentation under label on both sides)*					
❑ BLP-1543 [M]	Kenny Burrell, Volume 2	1957	37.50	75.00	150.00
-- *Regular version, Lexington Ave. address on label*					

Number	Title	Yr	VG	VG+	NM
❏ BLP-1543 [M]	Kenny Burrell, Volume 2	1957	12.50	25.00	50.00
-- W. 63rd St., NYC address on label					
❏ BLP-1543 [M]	Kenny Burrell, Volume 2	1963	6.25	12.50	25.00
-- New York, USA address on label					
❏ BLP-1596 [M]	Blue Lights, Volume 1	1958	25.00	50.00	100.00
-- "Deep groove" version (deep indentation under label on both sides)					
❏ BLP-1596 [M]	Blue Lights, Volume 1	1958	17.50	35.00	70.00
-- Regular version, W. 63rd St., NYC address on label					
❏ BLP-1596 [M]	Blue Lights, Volume 1	1963	6.25	12.50	25.00
-- New York, USA address on label					
❏ BST-1596 [S]	Blue Lights, Volume 1	1959	25.00	50.00	100.00
-- "Deep groove" version (deep indentation under label on both sides)					
❏ BST-1596 [S]	Blue Lights, Volume 1	1959	17.50	35.00	70.00
-- Regular version, W. 63rd St., NYC address on label					
❏ BST-1596 [S]	Blue Lights, Volume 1	1963	6.25	12.50	25.00
-- New York, USA address on label					
❏ BLP-1597 [M]	Blue Lights, Volume 2	1958	25.00	50.00	100.00
-- "Deep groove" version (deep indentation under label on both sides)					
❏ BLP-1597 [M]	Blue Lights, Volume 2	1958	17.50	35.00	70.00
-- Regular version, W. 63rd St., NYC address on label					
❏ BLP-1597 [M]	Blue Lights, Volume 2	1963	6.25	12.50	25.00
-- New York, USA address on label					
❏ BST-1597 [S]	Blue Lights, Volume 2	1959	25.00	50.00	100.00
-- "Deep groove" version (deep indentation under label on both sides)					
❏ BST-1597 [S]	Blue Lights, Volume 2	1959	17.50	35.00	70.00
-- Regular version, W. 63rd St., NYC address on label					
❏ BST-1597 [S]	Blue Lights, Volume 2	1963	6.25	12.50	25.00
-- New York, USA address on label					
❏ BLP-4021 [M]	On View at the Five Spot Café	1960	25.00	50.00	100.00
-- "Deep groove" version (deep indentation under label on both sides)					
❏ BLP-4021 [M]	On View at the Five Spot Café	1960	17.50	35.00	70.00
-- Regular version, W. 63rd St., NYC address on label					
❏ BLP-4021 [M]	On View at the Five Spot Café	1963	6.25	12.50	25.00
-- New York, USA address on label					
❏ BLP-4123 [M]	Midnight Blue	1963	7.50	15.00	30.00
-- New York, USA address on label					
❏ BST-81523 [R]	Introducing Kenny Burrell	1967	3.00	6.00	12.00
-- "A Division of Liberty Records" on label					
❏ BST-81543 [R]	Kenny Burrell, Volume 2	1967	3.00	6.00	12.00
-- "A Division of Liberty Records" on label					
❏ BST-81596 [S]	Blue Lights, Volume 1	1967	3.75	7.50	15.00
-- "A Division of Liberty Records" on label					
❏ BST-81597 [S]	Blue Lights, Volume 2	1967	3.75	7.50	15.00
-- "A Division of Liberty Records" on label					
❏ BST-84021 [S]	On View at the Five Spot Café	1960	15.00	30.00	60.00
-- W. 63rd St., NYC address on label					
❏ BST-84021 [S]	On View at the Five Spot Café	1963	6.25	12.50	25.00
-- New York, USA address on label					
❏ BST-84021 [S]	On View at the Five Spot Café	1967	3.75	7.50	15.00
-- "A Division of Liberty Records" on label					
❏ BST-84123 [S]	Midnight Blue	1963	10.00	20.00	40.00
-- New York, USA address on label					
❏ BST-84123 [S]	Midnight Blue	1967	3.75	7.50	15.00
-- "A Division of Liberty Records" on label					
❏ BST-84123	Midnight Blue	1985	2.50	5.00	10.00
-- "The Finest in Jazz Since 1939" reissue					
❏ B1-85137	Generation	1987	2.50	5.00	10.00
❏ B1-90260	Pieces of Blue and the Blues	1988	2.50	5.00	10.00
CADET					
❏ LP-769 [M]	Men at Work	1965	3.75	7.50	15.00
❏ LPS-769 [S]	Men at Work	1965	5.00	10.00	20.00
-- Reissue of Argo 655					
❏ LP-772 [M]	The Tender Gender	1966	3.75	7.50	15.00
❏ LPS-772 [S]	The Tender Gender	1966	5.00	10.00	20.00
❏ LP-779 [M]	Have Yourself a Soulful Little Christmas	1966	3.75	7.50	15.00
❏ LPS-779 [S]	Have Yourself a Soulful Little Christmas	1966	5.00	10.00	20.00
❏ LP-798 [M]	Ode to 52nd Street	1967	5.00	10.00	20.00
❏ LPS-798 [S]	Ode to 52nd Street	1967	3.75	7.50	15.00
CHESS					
❏ CH-9316	A Night at the Vanguard	1990	3.00	6.00	12.00
-- Reissue of Argo 655					
❏ CH-60019 [(2)]	Cool Cookin'	1973	3.75	7.50	15.00
❏ CH2-92509 [(2)]	Recapitulation	198?	3.00	6.00	12.00
COLUMBIA					
❏ CL 1703 [M]	Weaver of Dreams	1961	5.00	10.00	20.00
❏ CS 8503 [S]	Weaver of Dreams	1961	6.25	12.50	25.00
CONCORD JAZZ					
❏ CJ-45	Tin Tin Deo	1978	2.50	5.00	10.00
❏ CJ-83	When Lights Are Low	1978	2.50	5.00	10.00
❏ CJ-121	Moon and Sand	1980	2.50	5.00	10.00
CONTEMPORARY					
❏ C-14058	Guiding Spirit	1990	3.00	6.00	12.00
CTI					
❏ 6011	God Bless the Child	1970	3.00	6.00	12.00

Number	Title	Yr	VG	VG+	NM
DENON					
❏ 7533	Lush Life	1979	3.75	7.50	15.00
❏ 7541	'Round Midnight	1979	3.75	7.50	15.00
FANTASY					
❏ OJC-019	Kenny Burrell	198?	2.50	5.00	10.00
-- Reissue of Prestige 7088					
❏ OJC-216	Two Guitars	198?	2.50	5.00	10.00
❏ OJC-427	All Night Long	1990	3.00	6.00	12.00
❏ OJC-456	All Day Long	1990	3.00	6.00	12.00
❏ MPF-4506	For Duke	1981	2.50	5.00	10.00
❏ F-9417	'Round Midnight	1972	3.00	6.00	12.00
❏ F-9427	Both Feet on the Ground	1973	3.00	6.00	12.00
❏ F-9458	Up the Street	1974	3.00	6.00	12.00
❏ F-9514	Sky Street	1975	3.00	6.00	12.00
❏ F-9558	Stormy Monday	1977	3.00	6.00	12.00
❏ 79005 [(2)]	Ellington Is Forever	197?	3.75	7.50	15.00
❏ 79008 [(2)]	Ellington Is Forever, Vol. 2	197?	3.75	7.50	15.00
KAPP					
❏ KL-1326 [M]	Lotta Bossa Nova	1962	5.00	10.00	20.00
❏ KS-3326 [S]	Lotta Bossa Nova	1962	6.25	12.50	25.00
MOODSVILLE					
❏ MVLP-29 [M]	Bluesy Burrell	1963	10.00	20.00	40.00
-- Green label					
❏ MVLP-29 [M]	Bluesy Burrell	1965	5.00	10.00	20.00
-- Blue label with trident logo					
❏ MVST-29 [S]	Bluesy Burrell	1963	10.00	20.00	40.00
-- Green label					
❏ MVST-29 [S]	Bluesy Burrell	1965	6.25	12.50	25.00
-- Blue label with trident logo					
MUSE					
❏ 5144	Handcrafted	1979	2.50	5.00	10.00
❏ 5216	Live at the Village Vanguard	1979	2.50	5.00	10.00
❏ 5241	Kenny Burrell in New York	1982	2.50	5.00	10.00
❏ 5264	Listen to the Dawn	1982	2.50	5.00	10.00
❏ 5281	Groovin' High	1983	2.50	5.00	10.00
❏ 5317	A La Carte	1984	2.50	5.00	10.00
PAUSA					
❏ 9000	Midnight	198?	2.50	5.00	10.00
PRESTIGE					
❏ PRLP-7073 [M]	All Night Long	1957	25.00	50.00	100.00
-- Actually an all-star session; reissued as a Kenny Burrell album, thus it is listed here					
❏ PRLP-7081 [M]	All Day Long	1957	25.00	50.00	100.00
-- Actually an all-star session; reissued as a Kenny Burrell album, thus it is listed here					
❏ PRLP-7088 [M]	Kenny Burrell	1957	20.00	40.00	80.00
❏ PRLP-7277 [M]	All Day Long	1963	12.50	25.00	50.00
-- Reissue of 7081					
❏ PRST-7277 [R]	All Day Long	1963	5.00	10.00	20.00
❏ PRLP-7289 [M]	All Night Long	1964	12.50	25.00	50.00
-- Reissue of 7073					
❏ PRST-7289 [R]	All Night Long	1964	5.00	10.00	20.00
❏ PRLP-7308 [M]	Blue Moods	1964	7.50	15.00	30.00
-- Reissue of 7088					
❏ PRST-7308 [R]	Blue Moods	1964	5.00	10.00	20.00
❏ PRLP-7315 [M]	Soul Call	1964	6.25	12.50	25.00
❏ PRST-7315 [S]	Soul Call	1964	7.50	15.00	30.00
❏ PRLP-7347 [M]	Crash	1964	6.25	12.50	25.00
❏ PRST-7347 [S]	Crash	1964	7.50	15.00	30.00
❏ PRLP-7448 [M]	The Best of Kenny Burrell	1967	7.50	15.00	30.00
❏ PRST-7448 [S]	The Best of Kenny Burrell	1967	5.00	10.00	20.00
❏ PRST-7578	Out of This World	1968	3.75	7.50	15.00
-- Reissue of Moodsville 29					
❏ 24025 [(2)]	All Day Long & All Night Long	197?	3.75	7.50	15.00
-- Reissue of both albums in one package					
SAVOY JAZZ					
❏ SJL-1121	Monday Stroll	198?	2.50	5.00	10.00
-- Reissue					
VERVE					
❏ UMV-2070	Guitar Forms	198?	2.50	5.00	10.00
-- Reissue of 8612					
❏ V-8553 [M]	Blue Bash!	1963	5.00	10.00	20.00
❏ V6-8553 [S]	Blue Bash!	1963	6.25	12.50	25.00
❏ V-8612 [M]	Guitar Forms	1965	3.75	7.50	15.00
❏ V6-8612 [S]	Guitar Forms	1965	5.00	10.00	20.00
❏ V-8656 [M]	A Generation Ago Today	1966	3.75	7.50	15.00
❏ V6-8656 [S]	A Generation Ago Today	1966	5.00	10.00	20.00
❏ V-8746 [M]	Blues-- The Common Ground	1968	5.00	10.00	20.00
❏ V6-8746 [S]	Blues-- The Common Ground	1968	3.75	7.50	15.00
❏ V6-8751	Night Song	1968	3.75	7.50	15.00
❏ V6-8773	Asphalt Canyon Suite	1969	3.75	7.50	15.00
VOSS					
❏ VLP1-42930	Heritage	1988	2.50	5.00	10.00

Number	Title	Yr	VG	VG+	NM

BURRELL, KENNY, AND JOHN COLTRANE
Also see each artist's individual listings.
FANTASY

Number	Title	Yr	VG	VG+	NM
❏ OJC-079	The Cats	198?	2.50	5.00	10.00
-- Reissue of New Jazz 8217					
❏ OJC-300	Kenny Burrell and John Coltrane	1987	2.50	5.00	10.00

NEW JAZZ

Number	Title	Yr	VG	VG+	NM
❏ NJLP-8217 [M]	The Cats	1959	20.00	40.00	80.00
-- Purple label					
❏ NJLP-8217 [M]	The Cats	1965	6.25	12.50	25.00
-- Blue label with trident logo					
❏ NJLP-8276 [M]	Kenny Burrell with John Coltrane	1962	15.00	30.00	60.00
-- Purple label					
❏ NJLP-8276 [M]	Kenny Burrell with John Coltrane	1965	6.25	12.50	25.00
-- Blue label with trident logo					

PRESTIGE

Number	Title	Yr	VG	VG+	NM
❏ PRLP-7532 [M]	Kenny Burrell Quintet with John Coltrane	1967	7.50	15.00	30.00
❏ PRST-7532 [S]	Kenny Burrell Quintet with John Coltrane	1967	5.00	10.00	20.00
❏ 24059 [(2)]	Kenny Burrell & John Coltrane	197?	3.75	7.50	15.00
-- Reissue of New Jazz and Prestige LPs in one package					

BURRELL, KENNY; TINY GRIMES; BILL JENNINGS
Also see each artist's individual listings.
STATUS

Number	Title	Yr	VG	VG+	NM
❏ ST-8318 [M]	Guitar Soul	1965	10.00	20.00	40.00

BURRELL, KENNY, AND JIMMY RANEY
Also see each artist's individual listings.
PRESTIGE

Number	Title	Yr	VG	VG+	NM
❏ PRLP-7119 [M]	Two Guitars	1957	20.00	40.00	80.00

BURRELL, KENNY, AND GROVER WASHINGTON. JR.
Also see each artist's individual listings.
BLUE NOTE

Number	Title	Yr	VG	VG+	NM
❏ BT-85106	Togethering	1985	2.50	5.00	10.00

BURROUGH, ROSLYN
Female singer.
SUNNYSIDE

Number	Title	Yr	VG	VG+	NM
❏ SSC-1009	Love Is Here	1985	2.50	5.00	10.00

BURTON, ANN
Female singer.
INNER CITY

Number	Title	Yr	VG	VG+	NM
❏ 6026	By Myself Alone	1974	3.00	6.00	12.00

BURTON, GARY
Vibraphone player.
ATLANTIC

Number	Title	Yr	VG	VG+	NM
❏ SD 2-321 [(2)]	Turn of the Century	1975	3.75	7.50	15.00
❏ SD 1531	Throb	1969	3.00	6.00	12.00
❏ SD 1560	Good Vibes	1970	3.00	6.00	12.00
❏ SD 1577	Gary Burton with Keith Jarrett	1971	3.00	6.00	12.00
❏ SD 1597	Paris Encounter	1972	3.00	6.00	12.00
❏ SD 1598	Alone at Last	1971	3.00	6.00	12.00

BLUEBIRD

Number	Title	Yr	VG	VG+	NM
❏ 6280-1-RB	Artist's Choice	1987	2.50	5.00	10.00

ECM

Number	Title	Yr	VG	VG+	NM
❏ 1030	The New Quartet	1973	3.00	6.00	12.00
❏ 1040	Seven Songs for Quartet and Chamber Orchestra	1974	3.00	6.00	12.00
❏ 1051	Ring	1975	3.00	6.00	12.00
❏ 1055	Hotel Hello	1974	3.00	6.00	12.00
❏ 1072	Dreams So Real	1976	3.00	6.00	12.00
❏ 1092	Passengers	1977	3.00	6.00	12.00
❏ 1111	Times Square	1978	3.00	6.00	12.00
❏ 1184	Easy As Pie	1979	3.00	6.00	12.00
❏ 1226	Picture This	1980	3.00	6.00	12.00
❏ 25024	Real Life Hits	1985	2.50	5.00	10.00

GRP

Number	Title	Yr	VG	VG+	NM
❏ GR-9569	Times Like These	1988	2.50	5.00	10.00
❏ GR-9598	Reunion	1990	3.00	6.00	12.00

RCA CAMDEN

Number	Title	Yr	VG	VG+	NM
❏ ACL1-0200	Norwegian Wood	1973	2.50	5.00	10.00

RCA VICTOR

Number	Title	Yr	VG	VG+	NM
❏ LPM-2420 [M]	New Vibe Man in Town	1961	5.00	10.00	20.00
❏ LSP-2420 [S]	New Vibe Man in Town	1961	6.25	12.50	25.00
❏ LPM-2665 [M]	Who Is Gary Burton?	1963	5.00	10.00	20.00
❏ LSP-2665 [S]	Who Is Gary Burton?	1963	6.25	12.50	25.00
❏ LPM-2880 [M]	Something's Coming	1964	5.00	10.00	20.00
❏ LSP-2880 [S]	Something's Coming	1964	6.25	12.50	25.00
❏ LPM-3360 [M]	The Groovy Sound of Music	1965	3.75	7.50	15.00
❏ LSP-3360 [S]	The Groovy Sound of Music	1965	5.00	10.00	20.00
❏ LPM-3642 [M]	The Time Machine	1966	3.75	7.50	15.00
❏ LSP-3642 [S]	The Time Machine	1966	5.00	10.00	20.00
❏ LPM-3719 [M]	Tennessee Firebird	1966	3.75	7.50	15.00
❏ LSP-3719 [S]	Tennessee Firebird	1966	5.00	10.00	20.00
❏ LPM-3835 [M]	Duster	1967	5.00	10.00	20.00
❏ LSP-3835 [S]	Duster	1967	3.75	7.50	15.00
❏ LPM-3901 [M]	Lofty Fake Anagram	1967	5.00	10.00	20.00
❏ LSP-3901 [S]	Lofty Fake Anagram	1967	3.75	7.50	15.00
❏ LPM-3985 [M]	Gary Burton Quartet In Concert	1968	7.50	15.00	30.00
❏ LSP-3985 [S]	Gary Burton Quartet In Concert	1968	3.75	7.50	15.00
❏ LSP-3988	A Genuine Tong Funeral	1968	3.75	7.50	15.00
❏ LSP-4098	Country Roads and Other Places	1969	3.75	7.50	15.00

BURTON, GARY, AND CHICK COREA
Also see each artist's individual listings.
ECM

Number	Title	Yr	VG	VG+	NM
❏ 1024	Crystal Silence	1973	3.00	6.00	12.00
❏ 1140	Duet	1978	3.00	6.00	12.00
❏ 1182 [(2)]	Gary Burton and Chick Corea In Concert	1979	3.75	7.50	15.00
❏ 23797	Lyric Suite for Sextet	1983	2.50	5.00	10.00

BURTON, GARY; SONNY ROLLINS; CLARK TERRY
Also see each artist's individual listings.
RCA VICTOR

Number	Title	Yr	VG	VG+	NM
❏ LPM-2725 [M]	Three in Jazz	1963	3.75	7.50	15.00
❏ LSP-2725 [S]	Three in Jazz	1963	5.00	10.00	20.00

BURTON, JOE
Pianist.
ACE

Number	Title	Yr	VG	VG+	NM
❏ LP-1002 [M]	Joe Burton Plays	1959	---	---	---
-- Canceled?					

CORAL

Number	Title	Yr	VG	VG+	NM
❏ CRL 57098 [M]	Joe Burton Session	1957	10.00	20.00	40.00
❏ CRL 57175 [M]	Here I Am in Love Again	1958	10.00	20.00	40.00
❏ CRL 757175 [S]	Here I Am in Love Again	1959	7.50	15.00	30.00

JODAY

Number	Title	Yr	VG	VG+	NM
❏ J-1000 [M]	The Subtle Sound of Joe Burton	1963	3.75	7.50	15.00
❏ JS-1000 [S]	The Subtle Sound of Joe Burton	1963	5.00	10.00	20.00

REGENT

Number	Title	Yr	VG	VG+	NM
❏ MG-6036 [M]	Jazz Pretty	1957	12.50	25.00	50.00

BUSH, CHARLIE
Guitarist.
REVELATION

Number	Title	Yr	VG	VG+	NM
❏ REV-33	Local Living Legend	1979	3.00	6.00	12.00

BUSHKIN, JOE
Pianist and composer.
ATLANTIC

Number	Title	Yr	VG	VG+	NM
❏ ALR-108 [10]	I Love a Piano	1950	12.50	25.00	50.00

CAPITOL

Number	Title	Yr	VG	VG+	NM
❏ T 711 [M]	Midnight Rhapsody	1956	7.50	15.00	30.00
-- Turquoise or gray label					
❏ T 759 [M]	Skylight Rhapsody	1956	7.50	15.00	30.00
-- Turquoise or gray label					
❏ T 832 [M]	A Fellow Needs a Girl	1957	7.50	15.00	30.00
-- Turquoise or gray label					
❏ T 911 [M]	Bushkin Spotlights Berlin	1958	7.50	15.00	30.00
-- Turquoise or gray label					
❏ ST 1094 [S]	Blue Angels	1959	7.50	15.00	30.00
-- Black colorband label, logo at left					
❏ T 1094 [M]	Blue Angels	1959	5.00	10.00	20.00
-- Black colorband label, logo at left					

COLUMBIA

Number	Title	Yr	VG	VG+	NM
❏ CL 6152 [10]	Piano Moods	195?	12.50	25.00	50.00
❏ CL 6201 [10]	After Hours	195?	12.50	25.00	50.00
❏ CS 9615	Doctor Dolittle	1968	3.00	6.00	12.00

DECCA

Number	Title	Yr	VG	VG+	NM
❏ DL 4731 [M]	Night Sounds of San Francisco	1965	3.00	6.00	12.00
❏ DL 74731 [S]	Night Sounds of San Francisco	1965	3.75	7.50	15.00

Number	Title	Yr	VG	VG+	NM
EPIC					
☐ LN 3345 [M]	Piano After Midnight	1956	7.50	15.00	30.00
REPRISE					
☐ R-6119 [M]	In Concert, Town Hall	1964	3.75	7.50	15.00
☐ RS-6119 [S]	In Concert, Town Hall	1964	5.00	10.00	20.00
ROYALE					
☐ 18118 [10]	Joe Bushkin	195?	12.50	25.00	50.00

BUTLER, ARTIE
Organist, better known as an arranger, mostly for pop singers.

Number	Title	Yr	VG	VG+	NM
A&M					
☐ SP-3007	Have You Met Miss Jones?	1968	7.50	15.00	30.00

BUTLER, BILLY
Guitarist.

Number	Title	Yr	VG	VG+	NM
FANTASY					
☐ OJC-334	Guitar Soul	1988	3.00	6.00	12.00
-- Reissue of Prestige 7734					
PRESTIGE					
☐ PRST-7622	This Is Billy Butler	1968	6.25	12.50	25.00
☐ PRST-7734	Guitar Soul	1969	6.25	12.50	25.00
☐ PRST-7797	Yesterday, Today and Tomorrow	1970	6.25	12.50	25.00
☐ PRST-7854	Night Life	1971	6.25	12.50	25.00

BUTLER, FRANK
Drummer. Also see CURTIS AMY.

Number	Title	Yr	VG	VG+	NM
XANADU					
☐ 152	The Stepper	1977	2.50	5.00	10.00
☐ 169	Wheelin' and Dealin'	1978	2.50	5.00	10.00

BUTTERFIELD, BILLY
Trumpeter. Also see BOBBY HACKETT.

Number	Title	Yr	VG	VG+	NM
CAPITOL					
☐ H 201 [10]	Stardusting	1950	12.50	25.00	50.00
☐ H 424 [10]	Classics in Jazz	195?	12.50	25.00	50.00
CIRCLE					
☐ CLP-037	Billy Butterfield with Ted Easton's Jazz Band	1977	3.00	6.00	12.00
COLUMBIA					
☐ CL 1514 [M]	Billy Blows His Horn	1960	5.00	10.00	20.00
☐ CL 1673 [M]	The Golden Horn	1961	5.00	10.00	20.00
☐ CS 8??? [S]	Billy Blows His Horn	1960	6.25	12.50	25.00
☐ CS 8473 [S]	The Golden Horn	1961	6.25	12.50	25.00
EPIC					
☐ LA 16026 [M]	Billy Plays Bix	1962	7.50	15.00	30.00
☐ BA 17026 [S]	Billy Plays Bix	1962	10.00	20.00	40.00
ESSEX					
☐ ESLP-111 [10]	Far Away Places	195?	12.50	25.00	50.00
☐ 401 [M]	Billy Butterfield at Princeton	1955	10.00	20.00	40.00
☐ 402 [M]	Billy Butterfield Goes to NYU	1955	10.00	20.00	40.00
☐ 403 [M]	Billy Butterfield at Amherst	1955	10.00	20.00	40.00
☐ 404 [M]	Billy Butterfield at Rutgers	1955	10.00	20.00	40.00
HINDSIGHT					
☐ HSR-173	Billy Butterfield 1946	198?	2.50	5.00	10.00
JAZZOLOGY					
☐ J-93	Watch What Happens	198?	2.50	5.00	10.00
☐ J-117	Just Friends	1984	2.50	5.00	10.00
RCA VICTOR					
☐ LPM-1212 [M]	New York Land Dixie	1956	10.00	20.00	40.00
☐ LPM-1441 [M]	They're Playing Our Song	1957	10.00	20.00	40.00
☐ LPM-1590 [M]	Thank You for a Lovely Evening	1958	7.50	15.00	30.00
WESTMINSTER					
☐ WL-3020 [10]	Billy Butterfield	1954	12.50	25.00	50.00
☐ WL-6006 [M]	Dancing for Two in Love	1955	10.00	20.00	40.00

BUTTERFIELD, ERSKINE
Pianist , male singer and composer.

Number	Title	Yr	VG	VG+	NM
CIRCLE					
☐ CLP-062	Tuesday and Ten	198?	2.50	5.00	10.00
DAVIS					
☐ JD-104 [M]	Piano Cocktail	1951	10.00	20.00	40.00

BYARD, JAKI
Pianist.

Number	Title	Yr	VG	VG+	NM
MUSE					
☐ 5007	There'll Be Some Changes Made	1974	5.00	10.00	20.00
☐ 5173	Family Man	1978	3.75	7.50	15.00
NEW JAZZ					
☐ NJLP-8256 [M]	Here's Jaki	1961	15.00	30.00	60.00
-- Purple label					
☐ NJLP-8256 [M]	Here's Jaki	1965	7.50	15.00	30.00
-- Blue label with trident logo at right					
☐ NJLP-8273 [M]	Hi-Fly	1962	15.00	30.00	60.00
-- Purple label					
☐ NJLP-8273 [M]	Hi-Fly	1965	7.50	15.00	30.00
-- Blue label with trident logo at right					
PRESTIGE					
☐ PRLP-7397 [M]	Out Front	1965	7.50	15.00	30.00
-- Blue label with trident logo at right					
☐ PRST-7397 [S]	Out Front	1965	10.00	20.00	40.00
-- Blue label with trident logo at right					
☐ PRST-7397 [S]	Out Front	1968	6.25	12.50	25.00
-- Blue label with trident logo in circle at top					
☐ PRLP-7419 [M]	Live!	1966	7.50	15.00	30.00
-- Blue label with trident logo at right					
☐ PRST-7419 [S]	Live!	1966	10.00	20.00	40.00
-- Blue label with trident logo at right					
☐ PRST-7419 [S]	Live!	1968	6.25	12.50	25.00
-- Blue label with trident logo in circle at top					
☐ PRLP-7463 [M]	Freedom Together	1967	10.00	20.00	40.00
-- Blue label with trident logo at right					
☐ PRST-7463 [S]	Freedom Together	1967	10.00	20.00	40.00
-- Blue label with trident logo at right					
☐ PRST-7463 [S]	Freedom Together	1968	6.25	12.00	25.00
-- Blue label with trident logo in circle at top					
☐ PRLP-7477 [M]	Live! Volume 2	1967	10.00	20.00	40.00
-- Blue label with trident logo at right					
☐ PRST-7477 [S]	Live! Volume 2	1967	10.00	20.00	40.00
-- Blue label with trident logo at right					
☐ PRST-7477 [S]	Live! Volume 2	1968	6.25	12.50	25.00
-- Blue label with trident logo in circle at top					
☐ PRLP-7524 [M]	On the Spot	1967	12.50	25.00	50.00
-- Blue label with trident logo at right					
☐ PRST-7524 [S]	On the Spot	1967	10.00	20.00	40.00
-- Blue label with trident logo at right					
☐ PRST-7524 [S]	On the Spot	1968	6.25	12.50	25.00
-- Blue label with trident logo in circle at top					
☐ PRST-7550	The Sunshine of My Soul	1968	6.25	12.50	25.00
☐ PRST-7573	Jaki Byard with Strings!	1968	6.25	12.50	25.00
☐ PRST-7615	The Jaki Byard Experience	1969	6.25	12.50	25.00
☐ PRST-7686	Solo Piano	1969	6.25	12.50	25.00
☐ 24086 [(2)]	Giant Steps	197?	5.00	10.00	20.00
SOUL NOTE					
☐ SN-1031	To Them -- To Us	198?	3.00	6.00	12.00
☐ SN-1075	Phantasies	1985	3.00	6.00	12.00
☐ 121125	Foolin' Myself	199?	3.00	6.00	12.00
☐ 121175	Phantasies II	199?	3.00	6.00	12.00

BYARD, JAKI, AND RAN BLAKE
Also see each artist's individual listings.

Number	Title	Yr	VG	VG+	NM
SOUL NOTE					
☐ SN-1022	Improvisations	198?	3.00	6.00	12.00

BYAS, DON
Tenor saxophone player. Also see MARY LOU WILLIAMS.

Number	Title	Yr	VG	VG+	NM
ATLANTIC					
☐ ALR-117 [10]	Don Byas Solos	1952	62.50	125.00	250.00
BATTLE					
☐ B-6121 [M]	April in Paris	1963	7.50	15.00	30.00
☐ BS-6121 [S]	April in Paris	1963	10.00	20.00	40.00
BLACK LION					
☐ 160	Anthropology	1973	3.75	7.50	15.00
DIAL					
☐ LP-216 [10]	Tenor Saxophone Concerto	1951	75.00	150.00	300.00
DISCOVERY					
☐ 3022 [10]	Don Byas with Beryl Booker	1954	37.50	75.00	150.00
EMARCY					
☐ MG-26026 [10]	Don Byas Sax	1954	30.00	60.00	120.00
GNP CRESCENDO					
☐ GNP-9027	Don Byas	197?	3.00	6.00	12.00
NORGRAN					
☐ MGN-12 [10]	In France "Don Byas Et Ses Rhythmes"	1954	37.50	75.00	150.00
ONYX					
☐ 208	Midnight at Minton's	197?	3.75	7.50	15.00
PRESTIGE					
☐ PRST-7598	Don Byas In Paris	1969	5.00	10.00	20.00
☐ PRST-7692	Don Byas Meets Ben Webster	1969	5.00	10.00	20.00
REGENT					
☐ MG-6044 [M]	Jazz Free and Easy	1957	20.00	40.00	80.00
SAVOY					
☐ SJL-2213 [(2)]	Savoy Jam Party	197?	3.75	7.50	15.00
☐ MG-9007 [10]	Don Byas Sax	1952	37.50	75.00	150.00
☐ MG-12203	Jazz Free and Easy	196?	5.00	10.00	20.00

Number	Title	Yr	VG	VG+	NM
❏ MG-15043 [10]	Tenor Sax Solos	1955	30.00	60.00	120.00
SEECO					
❏ SLP-35 [10]	Don Byas Favorites	1955	30.00	60.00	120.00

BYAS, DON/ BERNARD PEIFFER
Also see each artist's individual listings.
CLEF

Number	Title	Yr	VG	VG+	NM
❏ MGC-748 [M]	Jazz from Saint-Germain Des Pres	1956	---	---	---
-- Canceled					
VERVE					
❏ MGV-8119 [M]	Jazz from Saint-Germain Des Pres	1957	12.50	25.00	50.00
❏ V-8119 [M]	Jazz from Saint-Germain Des Pres	1961	5.00	10.00	20.00

BYAS, DON, AND BUD POWELL
Also see each artist's individual listings.
COLUMBIA

Number	Title	Yr	VG	VG+	NM
❏ JC 35755	A Tribute to Cannonball	1979	3.00	6.00	12.00

BYAS, DON/BUDDY TATE
Also see each artist's individual listings.
ALLEGRO

Number	Title	Yr	VG	VG+	NM
❏ 1741 [M]	All Star Jazz	1956	10.00	20.00	40.00

BYERS, BILLY
Trombonist and arranger.
CONCERT HALL JAZZ

Number	Title	Yr	VG	VG+	NM
❏ 1217 [M]	Byers' Guide	1955	12.50	25.00	50.00
RCA VICTOR					
❏ LPM-1269 [M]	The Jazz Workshop	1956	15.00	30.00	60.00

BYRD, CHARLIE
Guitarist and composer. Also see STAN GETZ.
COLUMBIA

Number	Title	Yr	VG	VG+	NM
❏ CS 1053	Let It Be	1970	3.00	6.00	12.00
❏ CL 2337 [M]	Brazilian Byrd	1965	3.75	7.50	15.00
-- "Guaranteed High Fidelity" on label					
❏ CL 2337 [M]	Brazilian Byrd	1965	3.00	6.00	12.00
-- "360 Sound Mono" on label					
❏ CL 2435 [M]	Travellin' Man Recorded Live	1966	3.00	6.00	12.00
❏ CL 2504 [M]	A Touch of Gold	1966	3.00	6.00	12.00
❏ CL 2555 [M]	Christmas Carols for Solo Guitar	1966	3.75	7.50	15.00
❏ CL 2592 [M]	Byrdland	1967	5.00	10.00	20.00
❏ CL 2652 [M]	Hollywood Byrd	1967	5.00	10.00	20.00
❏ CL 2692 [M]	More Brazilian Byrd	1967	5.00	10.00	20.00
❏ CS 9137 [S]	Brazilian Byrd	1965	3.75	7.50	15.00
-- Red label, "360 Sound" in white					
❏ CS 9137 [S]	Brazilian Byrd	1965	5.00	10.00	20.00
-- Red label, "360 Sound" in black					
❏ CS 9137	Brazilian Byrd	1971	2.50	5.00	10.00
-- Orange label					
❏ PC 9137	Brazilian Byrd	198?	2.00	4.00	8.00
-- Reissue with new prefix					
❏ CS 9235 [S]	Travellin' Man Recorded Live	1966	3.75	7.50	15.00
❏ CS 9304 [S]	A Touch of Gold	1966	3.75	7.50	15.00
❏ CS 9355 [S]	Christmas Carols for Solo Guitar	1966	5.00	10.00	20.00
❏ CS 9392 [S]	Byrdland	1967	3.75	7.50	15.00
❏ CS 9452 [S]	Hollywood Byrd	1967	3.75	7.50	15.00
❏ CS 9492 [S]	More Brazilian Byrd	1967	3.75	7.50	15.00
❏ CS 9582	Sketches of Brazil (Music of Villa Lobos)	1968	3.75	7.50	15.00
❏ CS 9627 [M]	Hit Trip	1968	6.25	12.50	25.00
-- "Special Mono Radio Station Copy" with white label					
❏ CS 9627 [S]	Hit Trip	1968	3.75	7.50	15.00
❏ CS 9667	Delicately	1968	3.75	7.50	15.00
❏ CS 9747	The Great Byrd	1968	3.75	7.50	15.00
❏ CS 9841	Aquarius	1969	3.75	7.50	15.00
❏ CS 9869	Let Go	1969	3.75	7.50	15.00
❏ CS 9970	The Greatest Hits of the 60's	1970	3.00	6.00	12.00
❏ C 30380	A Stroke of Genius	1971	3.00	6.00	12.00
❏ G 30622 [(2)]	For All We Know	1971	3.75	7.50	15.00
❏ C 31025	Onda Nuevo	1972	3.00	6.00	12.00
❏ CG 31967 [(2)]	The World of Charlie Byrd	1972	3.75	7.50	15.00
CONCORD JAZZ					
❏ CJ-82	Blue Byrd	1979	2.50	5.00	10.00
❏ CJ-252	Isn't It Romantic	1984	2.50	5.00	10.00
❏ CJ-304	Byrd & Brass	1986	2.50	5.00	10.00
❏ CJ-374	It's a Wonderful World	1989	3.00	6.00	12.00
CONCORD PICANTE					
❏ P-114	Sugarloaf Suite	1980	2.50	5.00	10.00
❏ P-173	Brazilville	1981	2.50	5.00	10.00

Number	Title	Yr	VG	VG+	NM
CRYSTAL CLEAR					
❏ 8002	Charlie Byrd	1979	7.50	15.00	30.00
-- Direct-to-disc recording; plays at 45 rpm					
FANTASY					
❏ OJC-107	Bossa Nova Pelos Passaros	198?	2.50	5.00	10.00
-- Reissue of Riverside 436					
❏ OJC-262	Byrd at the Gate	1987	2.50	5.00	10.00
-- Reissue of Riverside 9467					
❏ F-9429	Crystal Silence	1973	3.00	6.00	12.00
❏ F-9466	Byrd by the Sea	1974	3.00	6.00	12.00
❏ F-9496	Top Hat	1975	3.00	6.00	12.00
IMPROV					
❏ 7116	Charlie Byrd Swings Downtown	1977	3.00	6.00	12.00
MILESTONE					
❏ 47005 [(2)]	Latin Byrd	1973	3.75	7.50	15.00
❏ 47049 [(2)]	Charlie Byrd in Greenwich Village	1978	3.75	7.50	15.00
MOBILE FIDELITY					
❏ 1-515	Byrd at the Gate	1982	10.00	20.00	40.00
-- Audiophile vinyl					
OFFBEAT					
❏ OJ-3001 [M]	Jazz at the Show Boat, Volume 1	1959	6.25	12.50	25.00
❏ OJ-3005 [M]	Jazz at the Show Boat, Volume 2	1959	6.25	12.50	25.00
❏ OJ-3006 [M]	Jazz at the Show Boat, Volume 3	1959	6.25	12.50	25.00
❏ OJ-3007 [M]	Charlie's Choice	1960	6.25	12.50	25.00
❏ OLP-3009 [M]	Blues Sonata	1960	6.25	12.50	25.00
❏ OS-93001 [S]	Jazz at the Show Boat, Volume 1	1959	7.50	15.00	30.00
❏ OS-93005 [S]	Jazz at the Show Boat, Volume 2	1959	7.50	15.00	30.00
❏ OS-93006 [S]	Jazz at the Show Boat, Volume 3	1959	7.50	15.00	30.00
❏ OS-93007 [S]	Charlie's Choice	1960	7.50	15.00	30.00
❏ OS-93009 [S]	Blues Sonata	1960	7.50	151.00	30.00
PICKWICK					
❏ SPC-3042	Byrd and the Herd	196?	3.00	6.00	12.00
RIVERSIDE					
❏ RM-427 [M]	Latin Impressions	1962	5.00	10.00	20.00
❏ RM-436 [M]	Bossa Nova Pelos Passaros	1962	5.00	10.00	20.00
❏ RM-448 [M]	Byrd's Word	1963	5.00	10.00	20.00
❏ RM-449 [M]	Byrd in the Wind	1963	5.00	10.00	20.00
❏ RM-450 [M]	Mr. Guitar	1963	5.00	10.00	20.00
❏ RM-451 [M]	The Guitar Artistry of Charlie Byrd	1963	5.00	10.00	20.00
❏ RM-452 [M]	Charlie Byrd at the Village	1963	5.00	10.00	20.00
❏ RM-453 [M]	Blues Sonata	1963	5.00	10.00	20.00
❏ RM-454 [M]	Once More! Bossa Nova	1963	5.00	10.00	20.00
❏ RM-467 [M]	Byrd at the Gate	1964	5.00	10.00	20.00
❏ RM-481 [M]	Byrd Song	1966	3.75	7.50	15.00
❏ RM-498 [M]	Solo Flight	1967	5.00	10.00	20.00
❏ RS-3005	The Guitar Artistry of Charlie Byrd	1968	3.75	7.50	15.00
❏ RS-3044	Byrd Man with Strings	1969	3.75	7.50	15.00
❏ 6054	Blues Sonata	197?	2.50	5.00	10.00
❏ RS-9427 [S]	Latin Impressions	1962	6.25	12.50	25.00
❏ RS-9436 [S]	Bossa Nova Pelos Passaros	1962	6.25	12.50	25.00
❏ RS-9448 [S]	Byrd's Word	1963	6.25	12.50	25.00
❏ RS-9449 [S]	Byrd in the Wind	1963	6.25	12.50	25.00
❏ RS-9450 [S]	Mr. Guitar	1963	6.25	12.50	25.00
❏ RS-9451 [S]	The Guitar Artistry of Charlie Byrd	1963	6.25	12.50	25.00
❏ RS-9452 [S]	Charlie Byrd at the Village	1963	6.25	12.50	25.00
❏ RS-9453 [S]	Blues Sonata	1963	6.25	12.50	25.00
❏ RS-9454 [S]	Once More! Bossa Nova	1963	6.25	12.50	25.00
❏ RS-9467 [S]	Byrd at the Gate	1964	6.25	12.50	25.00
❏ RS-9481 [S]	Byrd Song	1966	5.00	10.00	20.00
❏ RS-9498 [S]	Solo Flight	1967	3.75	7.50	15.00
SAVOY					
❏ MG-12099 [M]	Jazz Recital	1957	10.00	20.00	40.00
❏ MG-12116 [M]	Blues for Night People	1957	10.00	20.00	40.00
SAVOY JAZZ					
❏ SJL-1121	Midnight Guitar	1980	2.50	5.00	10.00
❏ SJL-1131	First Flight	1980	2.50	5.00	10.00

BYRD, CHARLIE, AND FATHER MALCOLM BOYD
Boyd, a priest popular in the Summer of Love era, reads excerpts from his works with Byrd's guitar accompaniment.
COLUMBIA

Number	Title	Yr	VG	VG+	NM
❏ CL 2548 [M]	Are You Running With Me, Jesus?	1966	3.75	7.50	15.00
❏ CL 2657 [M]	Happening Prayers for Now	1967	3.75	7.50	15.00

Number	Title	Yr	VG	VG+	NM
❑ CS 9348 [S]	Are You Running With Me, Jesus?	1966	5.00	10.00	20.00
❑ CS 9457 [S]	Happening Prayers for Now	1967	3.75	7.50	15.00

BYRD, CHARLIE, HERB ELLIS & BARNEY KESSEL
Also see each artist's individual listings.

CONCORD JAZZ

Number	Title	Yr	VG	VG+	NM
❑ C-4	The Great Guitars	197?	3.00	6.00	12.00
❑ C-23	The Great Guitars	197?	3.00	6.00	12.00
❑ CJ-131	The Great Guitars at the Winery	1981	2.50	5.00	10.00
❑ CJ-209	The Great Guitars at Charlie's Georgetown	1982	2.50	5.00	10.00
❑ CJD-1002	Straight Tracks	1986	5.00	10.00	20.00

-- *Direct-to-disc recording*

BYRD, DONALD
Trumpeter and flugel horn player. Discovered the vocal group THE BLACKBYRDS. Also see PEPPER ADAMS; KENNY DREW; ART FARMER; RED GARLAND; THE JAZZ LAB; HANK MOBLEY.

AMERICAN RECORDING SOCIETY

Number	Title	Yr	VG	VG+	NM
❑ G-437 [M]	Modern Jazz	1957	10.00	20.00	40.00

BLUE NOTE

Number	Title	Yr	VG	VG+	NM
❑ BN-LA047-F	Black Byrd	1973	3.75	7.50	15.00
❑ LO-047	Black Byrd	1981	2.00	4.00	8.00
-- *Reissue of LA047*					
❑ BN-LA140-G	Street Lady	1974	3.75	7.50	15.00
❑ BN-LA368-G	Sleeping Into Tomorrow	1975	3.75	7.50	15.00
❑ BN-LA549-G	Places and Spaces	1975	3.75	7.50	15.00
❑ LW-549	Places and Spaces	1981	2.00	4.00	8.00
-- *Reissue of LA549*					
❑ BN-LA633-G	Caricatures	1976	3.75	7.50	15.00
❑ BN-LA700-G	Donald Byrd's Best	1976	3.75	7.50	15.00
❑ LT-991	Chant	1980	3.00	6.00	12.00
❑ LT-1096	Creeper	1981	3.00	6.00	12.00
❑ BLP-4007 [M]	Off to the Races	1959	30.00	60.00	120.00
-- *"Deep groove" version (deep indentation under label on both sides)*					
❑ BLP-4007 [M]	Off to the Races	1959	20.00	40.00	80.00
-- *W. 63rd St., NYC address on label*					
❑ BLP-4007 [M]	Off to the Races	1963	6.25	12.50	25.00
-- *"New York, USA" address on label*					
❑ BST-4007 [S]	Off to the Races	1959	20.00	40.00	80.00
-- *"Deep groove" version (deep indentation under label on both sides)*					
❑ BST-4007 [S]	Off to the Races	1959	15.00	30.00	60.00
-- *W. 63rd St., NYC address on label*					
❑ BST-4007 [S]	Off to the Races	1963	6.25	12.50	25.00
-- *"New York, USA" address on label*					
❑ BLP-4019 [M]	Byrd in Hand	1959	30.00	60.00	120.00
-- *"Deep groove" version (deep indentation under label on both sides)*					
❑ BLP-4019 [M]	Byrd in Hand	1959	20.00	40.00	80.00
-- *W. 63rd St., NYC address on label*					
❑ BLP-4019 [M]	Byrd in Hand	1963	6.25	12.50	25.00
-- *"New York, USA" address on label*					
❑ BLP-4026 [M]	Fuego	1960	30.00	60.00	120.00
-- *"Deep groove" version (deep indentation under label on both sides)*					
❑ BLP-4026 [M]	Fuego	1960	20.00	40.00	80.00
-- *W. 63rd St., NYC address on label*					
❑ BLP-4026 [M]	Fuego	1963	6.25	12.50	25.00
-- *"New York, USA" address on label*					
❑ BLP-4048 [M]	Byrd in Flight	1960	30.00	60.00	120.00
-- *"Deep groove" version (deep indentation under label on both sides)*					
❑ BLP-4048 [M]	Byrd in Flight	1960	20.00	40.00	80.00
-- *W. 63rd St., NYC address on label*					
❑ BLP-4048 [M]	Byrd in Flight	1963	6.25	12.50	25.00
-- *"New York, USA" address on label*					
❑ BLP-4060 [M]	Donald Byrd at the Half Note Café, Volume 1	1961	20.00	40.00	80.00
-- *W. 63rd St., NYC address on label*					
❑ BLP-4060 [M]	Donald Byrd at the Half Note Café, Volume 1	1963	6.25	12.50	25.00
-- *"New York, USA" address on label*					
❑ BLP-4061 [M]	Donald Byrd at the Half Note Café, Volume 2	1961	20.00	40.00	80.00
-- *W. 63rd St., NYC address on label*					
❑ BLP-4061 [M]	Donald Byrd at the Half Note Café, Volume 2	1963	6.25	12.50	25.00
-- *"New York, USA" address on label*					
❑ BLP-4075 [M]	The Cat Walk	1961	20.00	40.00	80.00
-- *61st St,, New York address on label*					
❑ BLP-4075 [M]	The Cat Walk	1963	6.25	12.50	25.00
-- *"New York, USA" address on label*					
❑ BLP-4101 [M]	Royal Flush	1962	5.00	10.00	20.00
❑ BLP-4118 [M]	Free Form	1963	5.00	10.00	20.00
❑ BLP-4124 [M]	A New Perspective	1964	5.00	10.00	20.00
❑ BLP-4188 [M]	I'm Tryin' to Get Home	1965	5.00	10.00	20.00
❑ BLP-4238 [M]	Mustang!	1966	5.00	10.00	20.00
❑ BLP-4259 [M]	Blackjack	1967	6.25	12.50	25.00
❑ LN-10054	Street Lady	1981	2.00	4.00	8.00
-- *Budget-line reissue*					

Number	Title	Yr	VG	VG+	NM
❑ B1-31875	Kofi	1995	3.75	7.50	15.00
❑ B1-36195	Electric Byrd	1996	3.75	7.50	15.00
❑ BST-84007 [S]	Byrd in Hand	1967	3.00	6.00	12.00
-- *"A Division of Liberty Records" on label*					
❑ BST-84019 [S]	Byrd in Hand	1959	15.00	30.00	60.00
-- *W. 63rd St., NYC address on label*					
❑ BST-84019 [S]	Byrd in Hand	1963	6.25	12.50	25.00
-- *"New York, USA" address on label*					
❑ BST-84019 [S]	Byrd in Hand	1967	3.00	6.00	12.00
-- *"A Division of Liberty Records" on label*					
❑ BST-84019	Byrd in Hand	198?	2.50	5.00	10.00
-- *"The Finest in Jazz Since 1939" reissue*					
❑ BST-84026 [S]	Fuego	1959	15.00	30.00	60.00
-- *W. 63rd St., NYC address on label*					
❑ BST-84026 [S]	Fuego	1963	6.25	12.50	25.00
-- *"New York, USA" address on label*					
❑ BST-84026 [S]	Fuego	1967	3.00	6.00	12.00
-- *"A Division of Liberty Records" on label*					
❑ BST-84048 [S]	Byrd in Flight	1960	15.00	30.00	60.00
-- *W. 63rd St., NYC address on label*					
❑ BST-84048 [S]	Byrd in Flight	1963	6.25	12.50	25.00
-- *"New York, USA" address on label*					
❑ BST-84048 [S]	Byrd in Flight	1967	3.00	6.00	12.00
-- *"A Division of Liberty Records" on label*					
❑ BST-84060 [S]	Donald Byrd at the Half Note Café, Volume 1	1961	15.00	30.00	60.00
-- *W. 63rd St., NYC address on label*					
❑ BST-84060 [S]	Donald Byrd at the Half Note Café, Volume 1	1963	6.25	12.50	25.00
-- *"New York, USA" address on label*					
❑ BST-84060 [S]	Donald Byrd at the Half Note , Café Volume 1	1967	3.00	6.00	12.00
-- *"A Division of Liberty Records" on label*					
❑ BST-84061 [S]	Donald Byrd at the Half Note Café, Volume 2	1961	15.00	30.00	60.00
-- *W. 63rd St., NYC address on label*					
❑ BST-84061 [S]	Donald Byrd at the Half Note Café, Volume 2	1963	6.25	12.50	25.00
-- *"New York, USA" address on label*					
❑ BST-84061 [S]	Donald Byrd at the Half Note Café, Volume 2	1967	3.00	6.00	12.00
-- *"A Division of Liberty Records" on label*					
❑ BST-84075 [S]	The Cat Walk	1961	15.00	30.00	60.00
-- *61st St,, New York address on label*					
❑ BST-84075 [S]	The Cat Walk	1963	6.25	12.50	25.00
-- *"New York, USA" address on label*					
❑ BST-84075 [S]	The Cat Walk	1967	3.00	6.00	12.00
-- *"A Division of Liberty Records" on label*					
❑ BST-84101 [S]	Royal Flush	1962	6.25	12.50	25.00
-- *"New York, USA" address on label*					
❑ BST-84101 [S]	Royal Flush	1967	3.00	6.00	12.00
-- *"A Division of Liberty Records" on label*					
❑ BST-84118 [S]	Free Form	1963	6.25	12.50	25.00
-- *"New York, USA" address on label*					
❑ BST-84118 [S]	Free Form	1967	3.00	6.00	12.00
-- *"A Division of Liberty Records" on label*					
❑ BST-84118	Free Form	1986	2.50	5.00	10.00
-- *"The Finest in Jazz Since 1939" reissue*					
❑ BST-84124 [S]	A New Perspective	1964	6.25	12.50	25.00
-- *"New York, USA" address on label*					
❑ BST-84124 [S]	A New Perspective	1967	3.00	6.00	12.00
-- *"A Division of Liberty Records" on label*					
❑ BST-84124	A New Perspective	198?	2.50	5.00	10.00
-- *"The Finest in Jazz Since 1939" reissue*					
❑ BST-84188 [S]	I'm Tryin' to Get Home	1965	6.25	12.50	25.00
-- *"New York, USA" address on label*					
❑ BST-84188 [S]	I'm Tryin' to Get Home	1967	3.00	6.00	12.00
-- *"A Division of Liberty Records" on label*					
❑ BST-84188	I'm Tryin' to Get Home	1986	2.50	5.00	10.00
-- *"The Finest in Jazz Since 1939" reissue*					
❑ BST-84238 [S]	Mustang!	1966	6.25	12.50	25.00
-- *"New York, USA" address on label*					
❑ BST-84238 [S]	Mustang!	1967	3.00	6.00	12.00
-- *"A Division of Liberty Records" on label*					
❑ BST-84259 [S]	Blackjack	1967	5.00	10.00	20.00
❑ BST-84292	Slow Drag	1968	5.00	10.00	20.00
❑ BST-84319	Fancy Free	1969	5.00	10.00	20.00
❑ BST-84349	Electric	1970	5.00	10.00	20.00
❑ BST-84380	Ethiopian Nights	1972	5.00	10.00	20.00
❑ B1-89796	Fancy Free	1993	3.75	7.50	15.00

DELMARK

Number	Title	Yr	VG	VG+	NM
❑ DS-407	First Flight	1990	3.00	6.00	12.00

DISCOVERY

Number	Title	Yr	VG	VG+	NM
❑ 869	September Afternoon	198?	2.50	5.00	10.00

ELEKTRA

Number	Title	Yr	VG	VG+	NM
❑ 6E-144	Thank You for F.U.M.L. (Funking Up My Life)	1978	2.50	5.00	10.00
❑ 6E-247	Donald Byrd and 125th St., N.Y.C.	1980	2.50	5.00	10.00

Number	Title	Yr	VG	VG+	NM
❏ 5E-531	Love Byrd	1981	2.50	5.00	10.00
❏ 60188	Words, Sounds, Colors and Shapes	1982	2.50	5.00	10.00
LANDMARK					
❏ LLP-1516	Harlem Blues	1988	2.50	5.00	10.00
❏ LLP-1523	Getting Down to Business	1990	3.00	6.00	12.00
SAVOY					
❏ MG-12032 [M]	Byrd's Word	1956	25.00	50.00	100.00
❏ MG-12064 [M]	The Jazz Message of Donald Byrd	1956	30.00	60.00	120.00
SAVOY JAZZ					
❏ SJL-1101	Long Green	198?	2.50	5.00	10.00
❏ SJL-1114	Star Eyes	198?	2.50	5.00	10.00
TRANSITION					
❏ TRLP-4 [M]	Byrd's Eye View	1956	150.00	300.00	600.00
❏ TRLP-5 [M]	Byrd Jazz	1956	150.00	300.00	600.00
❏ TRLP-17 [M]	Byrd Blows on Beacon Hill	1956	150.00	300.00	600.00
TRIP					
❏ 5000 [(2)]	Two Sides of Donald Byrd	1974	3.75	7.50	15.00
VERVE					
❏ V-8609 [M]	Up with Donald Byrd	1965	5.00	10.00	20.00
❏ V6-8609 [S]	Up with Donald Byrd	1965	6.25	12.50	25.00

BYRD, DONALD; HANK MOBLEY; KENNY BURRELL
Also see each artist's individual listings.

Number	Title	Yr	VG	VG+	NM
STATUS					
❏ ST-8317 [M]	Donald Byrd, Hank Mobley & Kenny Burrell	1965	10.00	20.00	40.00

BYRNE, BOBBY
Trombonist and bandleader.

Number	Title	Yr	VG	VG+	NM
COMMAND					
❏ RS 33-894 [M]	1966 -- Magnificent Movie Themes	1966	3.00	6.00	12.00
❏ RS 894 SD [S]	1966 -- Magnificent Movie Themes	1966	3.75	7.50	15.00
❏ RS 928 SD	Sound in the 8th Dimension	1968	5.00	10.00	20.00
GRAND AWARD					
❏ GA 206 SD [S]	Great Song Hits of the Tommy and Jimmy Dorsey Orchestras	1958	10.00	20.00	40.00
❏ GA 207 SD [S]	Great Song Hits of the Glenn Miller Orchestra	1958	10.00	20.00	40.00
❏ GA 225 SD [S]	Great Themes of America's Greatest Bands	1959	10.00	20.00	40.00
❏ GA 248 SD [S]	The Jazzbone's Connected to the Trombone	1959	10.00	20.00	40.00
❏ GA 33-381 [M]	Great Song Hits of the Glenn Miller Orchestra	1958	7.50	15.00	30.00
❏ GA 33-382 [M]	Great Song Hits of the Tommy and Jimmy Dorsey Orchestras	1958	7.50	15.00	30.00
❏ GA 33-392 [M]	Great Themes of America's Greatest Bands	1958	7.50	15.00	30.00
❏ GA 33-416 [M]	The Jazzbone's Connected to the Trombone	1959	7.50	15.00	30.00
WALDORF MUSIC HALL					
❏ MH 33-121 [10]	Dixieland Jazz	195?	10.00	20.00	40.00

BYRNE, BOBBY; WILL BRADLEY; BUD FREEMAN
Also see each artist's individual listings.

Number	Title	Yr	VG	VG+	NM
GRAND AWARD					
❏ GA 33-313 [M]	Jazz, Dixieland-Chicago	1955	10.00	20.00	40.00

BYRON, GEORGE
Male singer.

Number	Title	Yr	VG	VG+	NM
ATLANTIC					
❏ 1293 [M]	Premiere Performance	1958	10.00	20.00	40.00
-- Black label					
❏ SD 1293 [S]	Premiere Performance	1958	12.50	25.00	50.00
-- Green label					

Number	Title	Yr	VG	VG+	NM

C

CABLES, GEORGE
Pianist.
CONTEMPORARY
Number	Title	Yr	VG	VG+	NM
❑ C-14001	Cables' Vision	1979	3.75	7.50	15.00
❑ C-14014	Phantom of the City	198?	3.00	6.00	12.00
❑ C-14015	Circle	198?	3.00	6.00	12.00
❑ C-14030	By George: The Music of George Gershwin	1987	2.50	5.00	10.00

CABO FRIO
Fusion band from New York.
ZEBRA
Number	Title	Yr	VG	VG+	NM
❑ ZR-5002	Just Having Fun	198?	3.00	6.00	12.00
❑ ZEB-5685	Right On the Money	1986	2.50	5.00	10.00
❑ ZEB-5990	Cabo Frio	198?	2.50	5.00	10.00

CACIA, PAUL
Trumpeter and bandleader.
HAPPY HOUR
Number	Title	Yr	VG	VG+	NM
❑ HH 5004	Quantum Leap	198?	2.50	5.00	10.00
❑ HH 6001	Paul Cacia Presents The Alumni Tribute to Stan Kenton	198?	2.50	5.00	10.00

OUTSTANDING
Number	Title	Yr	VG	VG+	NM
❑ OUTS-056	Quantum Leap	1986	3.00	6.00	12.00

CAFÉ NOIR
So-called "gypsy jazz" quartet: Randy Erwin (vocals); Gail Hess (violin); Lyle West (guitar), Jason Bucklin (guitar).
GAJO
Number	Title	Yr	VG	VG+	NM
❑ GR-1001	Café Noir	1988	2.50	5.00	10.00

CAHEN, FRANCOIS
Pianist, former member of French progressive rock band Magma.
INNER CITY
Number	Title	Yr	VG	VG+	NM
❑ 1118	Great Winds	1979	3.75	7.50	15.00

CAIN, JACKIE, AND ROY KRAL
Wife-and-husband vocal duo. Kral also is a pianist.
ABC-PARAMOUNT
Number	Title	Yr	VG	VG+	NM
❑ ABC-120 [M]	The Glory of Love	1956	12.50	25.00	50.00
❑ ABC-163 [M]	Bits and Pieces	1957	12.50	25.00	50.00
❑ ABC-207 [M]	Free and Easy	1958	12.50	25.00	50.00
❑ ABC-267 [M]	In the Spotlight	1959	10.00	20.00	40.00
❑ ABCS-267 [S]	In the Spotlight	1959	12.50	25.00	50.00

AUDIOPHILE
Number	Title	Yr	VG	VG+	NM
❑ AP-230	One More Rose (A Tribute to the Lyrics of Alan Jay Lerner)	1988	2.50	5.00	10.00

BRUNSWICK
Number	Title	Yr	VG	VG+	NM
❑ BL 54026 [M]	Jackie Cain and Roy Kral	1957	12.50	25.00	50.00

CAPITOL
Number	Title	Yr	VG	VG+	NM
❑ ST 2936	Grass	1968	3.75	7.50	15.00

COLUMBIA
Number	Title	Yr	VG	VG+	NM
❑ CL 1469 [M]	Sweet and Low Down	1960	6.25	12.50	25.00
❑ CL 1704 [M]	Double Take	1961	6.25	12.50	25.00
❑ CL 1934 [M]	Like Sing	1963	5.00	10.00	20.00
❑ CS 8260 [S]	Sweet and Low Down	1960	7.50	15.00	30.00
❑ CS 8504 [S]	Double Take	1961	7.50	15.00	30.00
❑ CS 8734 [S]	Like Sing	1963	6.25	12.50	25.00

CONCORD JAZZ
Number	Title	Yr	VG	VG+	NM
❑ CJ-115	Star Sounds	1979	3.00	6.00	12.00
❑ CJ-149	East of Suez	1981	3.00	6.00	12.00
❑ CJ-186	High Standards	198?	3.00	6.00	12.00

CONTEMPORARY
Number	Title	Yr	VG	VG+	NM
❑ C-14046	Full Circle	1989	3.00	6.00	12.00

CTI
Number	Title	Yr	VG	VG+	NM
❑ 6019	Time and Love	1972	3.75	7.50	15.00
❑ 6040	A Wilder Alias	1974	3.75	7.50	15.00

DISCOVERY
Number	Title	Yr	VG	VG+	NM
❑ 907	We've Got It: The Music of Cy Coleman	1986	2.50	5.00	10.00

FANTASY
Number	Title	Yr	VG	VG+	NM
❑ F-9643	Bogie	1986	2.50	5.00	10.00

FINESSE
Number	Title	Yr	VG	VG+	NM
❑ FW 38324	A Stephen Sondheim Collection	1983	2.50	5.00	10.00

MCA
Number	Title	Yr	VG	VG+	NM
❑ 4169 [(2)]	Jackie & Roy	198?	3.00	6.00	12.00

REGENT
Number	Title	Yr	VG	VG+	NM
❑ MG-6057 [M]	Jackie & Roy	1957	12.50	25.00	50.00

ROULETTE
Number	Title	Yr	VG	VG+	NM
❑ R-25278 [M]	By Jupiter & Girl Crazy	1964	5.00	10.00	20.00
❑ SR-25278 [S]	By Jupiter & Girl Crazy	1964	6.25	12.50	25.00

SAVOY
Number	Title	Yr	VG	VG+	NM
❑ MG-12198 [M]	Jackie and Roy	196?	5.00	10.00	20.00

STORYVILLE
Number	Title	Yr	VG	VG+	NM
❑ STLP-322 [10]	Jackie & Roy	1955	30.00	60.00	120.00
❑ STLP-904 [M]	Storyville Presents Jackie & Roy	1955	15.00	30.00	60.00
❑ STLP-915 [M]	Sing Baby, Sing!	1956	15.00	30.00	60.00

STUDIO 7
Number	Title	Yr	VG	VG+	NM
❑ 402	By the Sea	1978	3.00	6.00	12.00

VERVE
Number	Title	Yr	VG	VG+	NM
❑ V-8668 [M]	Changes	1966	5.00	10.00	20.00
❑ V6-8668 [S]	Changes	1966	6.25	12.50	25.00
❑ V-8688 [M]	Lovesick	1967	6.25	12.50	25.00
❑ V6-8688 [S]	Lovesick	1967	5.00	10.00	20.00

CAIOLA, AL
Guitarist. Most of his work is in a more pop vein; for a more complete listing, see the *Standard Catalog of American Records 1950-1975*.
CHANCELLOR
Number	Title	Yr	VG	VG+	NM
❑ CHL-5008 [M]	Great Pickin'	1960	6.25	12.50	25.00
❑ CHS-5008 [S]	Great Pickin'	1960	7.50	15.00	30.00

SAVOY
Number	Title	Yr	VG	VG+	NM
❑ MG-12033 [M]	Deep in a Dream	1955	10.00	20.00	40.00
❑ MG-12057 [M]	Serenade in Blue	1956	10.00	20.00	40.00

UNITED ARTISTS
Number	Title	Yr	VG	VG+	NM
❑ UAL-3299 [M]	Cleopatra and All That Jazz	1963	6.25	12.50	25.00
❑ UAS-6299 [S]	Cleopatra and All That Jazz	1963	7.50	15.00	30.00

CALIFORNIA RAMBLERS, THE
Early white jazz band, none of whom were from California.
BIOGRAPH
Number	Title	Yr	VG	VG+	NM
❑ 12020	Miss Annabelle Lee 1925-27	197?	2.50	5.00	10.00
❑ 12021	Hallelujah, Vol. 2 1925-29	197?	2.50	5.00	10.00

CALIMAN, HADLEY
Tenor and soprano saxophone player and sometimes flutist.
CATALYST
Number	Title	Yr	VG	VG+	NM
❑ 7604	Projecting	1976	3.00	6.00	12.00
❑ 77??	Celebration	1977	3.00	6.00	12.00

MAINSTREAM
Number	Title	Yr	VG	VG+	NM
❑ MRL-318	Hadley Caliman	1971	5.00	10.00	20.00
❑ MRL-342	Iapetus	1972	5.00	10.00	20.00

CALLENDER, RED
Bass player and sometimes tuba player.
CROWN
Number	Title	Yr	VG	VG+	NM
❑ CLP-5012 [M]	Callender Speaks Low	1957	10.00	20.00	40.00
❑ CLP-5025 [M]	Swingin' Suite	1957	10.00	20.00	40.00

LEGEND
Number	Title	Yr	VG	VG+	NM
❑ 1005	Basin Street Bass	197?	3.00	6.00	12.00

METROJAZZ
Number	Title	Yr	VG	VG+	NM
❑ E-1007 [M]	The Lowest	1958	12.50	25.00	50.00
❑ SE-1007 [S]	The Lowest	1959	10.00	20.00	40.00

MODERN
Number	Title	Yr	VG	VG+	NM
❑ MLP-1201 [M]	Swingin' Suite	1956	20.00	40.00	80.00

CALLOWAY, CAB
Male singer and bandleader. Best known for the "hi-de-ho" chorus of the song "Minnie the Moocher."
BRUNSWICK
Number	Title	Yr	VG	VG+	NM
❑ BL 58101 [10]	Cab Calloway	1954	25.00	50.00	100.00

COLUMBIA
Number	Title	Yr	VG	VG+	NM
❑ CG 32593 [(2)]	The Hi De Ho Man	1973	5.00	10.00	20.00

CORAL
Number	Title	Yr	VG	VG+	NM
❑ CRL 57408 [M]	Blues Make Me Happy	1962	6.25	12.50	25.00
❑ CRL 757408 [S]	Blues Make Me Happy	1962	7.50	15.00	30.00

EPIC
Number	Title	Yr	VG	VG+	NM
❑ LN 3265 [M]	Swing Showman	1957	12.50	25.00	50.00

GLENDALE
Number	Title	Yr	VG	VG+	NM
❑ GLS 9007	Cab Calloway	198?	2.50	5.00	10.00

GONE
Number	Title	Yr	VG	VG+	NM
❑ LP-101 [M]	Cotton Club Revue '58	1958	20.00	40.00	80.00

MCA
Number	Title	Yr	VG	VG+	NM
❑ 1344	Mr. Hi-De-Ho	198?	2.50	5.00	10.00

Number	Title	Yr	VG	VG+	NM
P.I.P.					
❏ 6801	Cab Calloway '68	1968	5.00	10.00	20.00
RCA VICTOR					
❏ LPM-2021 [M]	Hi De Hi De Ho	1958	7.50	15.00	30.00
❏ LSP-2021 [S]	Hi De Hi De Ho	1958	10.00	20.00	40.00
VOCALION					
❏ VL 73820	The Blues	196?	3.00	6.00	12.00

CAMERON, BRUCE
Cornet player.

Number	Title	Yr	VG	VG+	NM
DISCOVERY					
❏ 793	With All My Love	198?	2.50	5.00	10.00
SEA BREEZE					
❏ 9801	Jet Away	198?	2.50	5.00	10.00

CAMERON, DOUG
Violinist.

Number	Title	Yr	VG	VG+	NM
SPINDLETOP					
❏ STP-103	Freeway Mentality	1986	3.00	6.00	12.00

CAMERON, JOHN
Pianist, keyboard player, arranger and composer.

Number	Title	Yr	VG	VG+	NM
DERAM					
❏ DES 18033	Off Centre	1969	5.00	10.00	20.00

CAMILO, MICHEL
Pianist.

Number	Title	Yr	VG	VG+	NM
EPIC					
❏ OE 45295	On Fire	1989	3.00	6.00	12.00
PORTRAIT					
❏ OR 44482	Michael Camilo	1988	2.50	5.00	10.00

CAMP, RED
Pianist.

Number	Title	Yr	VG	VG+	NM
COOK					
❏ LP-1087 [10]	Camp Inventions: Bold New Design for Jazz Piano	1955	12.50	25.00	50.00
❏ LP-1089 [10]	Red Camp	1955	12.50	25.00	50.00
❏ LP-5005 [M]	Camp Has a Ball	1957	10.00	20.00	40.00

CAMPBELL, JOHN
Pianist.

Number	Title	Yr	VG	VG+	NM
CONTEMPORARY					
❏ C-14053	After Hours	1989	3.00	6.00	12.00
❏ C-14061	Turning Point	1991	3.75	7.50	15.00

CANADIAN ALL STARS, THE

Number	Title	Yr	VG	VG+	NM
DISCOVERY					
❏ DL-3025 [10]	The Canadian All Stars	1954	20.00	40.00	80.00

CANAL STREET RAGTIMERS
Members: Roy Bower, Tony Smith, Martin Rodger, Chris Brown, John Featherhouse, Derek Gracie, Colin Knight, Derek Hamer.

Number	Title	Yr	VG	VG+	NM
GHB					
❏ 4 [M]	Canal Street Ragtimers	196?	3.00	6.00	12.00

CANDIDO
Drummer, especially prominent on congas and bongos.

Number	Title	Yr	VG	VG+	NM
ABC-PARAMOUNT					
❏ ABC-125 [M]	Candido Featuring Al Cohn	1956	12.50	25.00	50.00
❏ ABC-180 [M]	The Volcanic Candido	1957	12.50	25.00	50.00
❏ ABC-236 [M]	In Indigo	1958	12.50	25.00	50.00
❏ ABCS-236 [S]	In Indigo	1959	10.00	20.00	40.00
❏ ABC-286 [M]	Latin Fire	1959	10.00	20.00	40.00
❏ ABCS-286 [S]	Latin Fire	1959	12.50	25.00	50.00
BLUE NOTE					
❏ BST-84357	Beautiful	1970	3.75	7.50	15.00
POLYDOR					
❏ PD-5063	Drum Fever	1973	3.00	6.00	12.00
RCA VICTOR					
❏ LPM-2027 [M]	Beautiful	1959	7.50	15.00	30.00
❏ LSP-2027 [S]	Beautiful	1959	10.00	20.00	40.00
ROULETTE					
❏ R-52078 [M]	Conga Soul	1962	5.00	10.00	20.00
❏ SR-52078 [S]	Conga Soul	1962	6.25	12.50	25.00
SOLID STATE					
❏ 18066	The Thousand Finger Man	1969	3.75	7.50	15.00

CANDOLI BROTHERS, THE
Also see CONTE CANDOLI; PETE CANDOLI.

Number	Title	Yr	VG	VG+	NM
DOT					
❏ DLP-3062 [M]	The Brothers Candoli	1957	12.50	25.00	50.00
❏ DLP-3168 [M]	Bell, Book and Candoli	1959	7.50	15.00	30.00
❏ DLP-25168 [S]	Bell, Book and Candoli	1959	6.25	12.50	25.00
IMPULSE!					
❏ 29064	The Brothers Candoli	198?	2.50	5.00	10.00
MERCURY					
❏ MG-20515 [M]	Two for the Money	1959	7.50	15.00	30.00
❏ SR-60191 [S]	Two for the Money	1959	6.25	12.50	25.00
WARNER BROS.					
❏ W 1462 [M]	The Brothers Candoli	1962	5.00	10.00	20.00
❏ WS 1462 [S]	The Brothers Candoli	1962	6.25	12.50	25.00

CANDOLI, CONTE
Trumpeter. Also see THE CANDOLI BROTHERS.

Number	Title	Yr	VG	VG+	NM
ANDEX					
❏ A-3002 [M]	Mucho Calor	1958	12.50	25.00	50.00
❏ AS-3002 [S]	Mucho Calor	1959	10.00	20.00	40.00
BETHLEHEM					
❏ BCP-30 [M]	Toots Sweet	1956	20.00	40.00	80.00
❏ BCP-1016 [10]	Sincerely, Conte Candoli	1954	37.50	75.00	150.00
CROWN					
❏ CST-190 [R]	Little Band, Big Jazz	196?	6.25	12.50	25.00
-- Red vinyl					
❏ CST-190 [R]	Little Band, Big Jazz	196?	3.00	6.00	12.00
-- Black vinyl					
❏ CLP-5162 [M]	Little Band, Big Jazz	1960	5.00	10.00	20.00

CANDOLI, CONTE, AND STAN LEVEY
Also see each artist's individual listings.

Number	Title	Yr	VG	VG+	NM
BETHLEHEM					
❏ BCP-9 [M]	West Coasting	1956	20.00	40.00	80.00

CANDOLI, CONTE, AND FRANK ROSOLINO
Also see each artist's individual listings.

Number	Title	Yr	VG	VG+	NM
RCA VICTOR					
❏ TPL1-1509	Conversation	197?	3.00	6.00	12.00

CANDOLI, CONTE, AND PHIL WOODS
Also see each artist's individual listings.

Number	Title	Yr	VG	VG+	NM
PAUSA					
❏ PR-7189	Old Acquaintance	1986	2.50	5.00	10.00

CANDOLI, PETE
Trumpeter. Also see THE CANDOLI BROTHERS.

Number	Title	Yr	VG	VG+	NM
DECCA					
❏ DL 4761 [M]	Moscow Mule (And Many More Kicks)	1966	3.75	7.50	15.00
❏ DL 74761 [S]	Moscow Mule (And Many More Kicks)	1966	5.00	10.00	20.00
KAPP					
❏ KL-1230 [M]	For Pete's Sake	1960	5.00	10.00	20.00
❏ KS-3230 [S]	For Pete's Sake	1960	6.25	12.50	25.00
SOMERSET					
❏ SF-17200 [M]	Blues, When Your Lover Has Gone	1963	5.00	10.00	20.00
❏ SFS-17200 [S]	Blues, When Your Lover Has Gone	1963	6.25	12.50	25.00

CAPERS, VALERIE
Pianist, arranger and composer.

Number	Title	Yr	VG	VG+	NM
ATLANTIC					
❏ SD 3003	Portrait in Soul	1970	3.75	7.50	15.00

CAPP-PIERCE JUGGERNAUT, THE
Big band: Frank Capp (drummer) and Nat Pierce (pianist), leaders.

Number	Title	Yr	VG	VG+	NM
CONCORD JAZZ					
❏ CJ-40	Juggernaut	1979	3.00	6.00	12.00
❏ CJ-72	Live at the Century Plaza	1980	3.00	6.00	12.00
❏ CJ-183	The Juggernaut Orchestra Strikes Again	1981	3.00	6.00	12.00
❏ CJ-336	Live at the Alley Cat	1988	2.50	5.00	10.00

CAPRARO, JOE
Banjo player.

Number	Title	Yr	VG	VG+	NM
SOUTHLAND					
❏ 220 [M]	Dixieland	1959	5.00	10.00	20.00

Number	Title	Yr	VG	VG+	NM
CARAM, ANA					
Female singer.					
CHESKY					
❑ JR-28	Rio After Dark	199?	6.25	12.50	25.00
-- Audiophile vinyl					
CARAMIA, TONY					
Pianist.					
STOMP OFF					
❑ SOS-1209	Hot Ivories	1991	3.75	7.50	15.00
CARBO, GLADYS					
Female singer.					
SOUL NOTE					
❑ 121197	Street Cries	1990	3.00	6.00	12.00
CAREY, DAVE					
British bandleader.					
LAURIE					
❑ LLP-1004 [M]	Bandwagon Plus 2	1959	6.25	12.50	25.00
CAREY, MUTT					
Trumpeter. Member of "Spike's Seven Pods of Pepper Orchestra," the KID ORY-led group that made the first jazz record released by black musicians (1922).					
RIVERSIDE					
❑ RLP-1042 [10]	Mutt Carey Plays the Blues	1954	25.00	50.00	100.00
CAREY, MUTT, AND PUNCH MILLER					
Punch Miller is a trumpeter and male singer. Also see MUTT CAREY.					
SAVOY					
❑ MG-12038 [M]	Jazz -- New Orleans	196?	5.00	10.00	20.00
❑ MG-12050 [M]	Jazz -- New Orleans, Vol. 2	196?	5.00	10.00	20.00
SAVOY JAZZ					
❑ SJC-415	New Orleans Jazz	1985	2.50	5.00	10.00
CARISI, JOHN					
Trumpeter.					
COLUMBIA					
❑ CL 1419 [M]	The New Jazz Sound of "Show Boat"	1960	6.25	12.50	25.00
❑ CS 8??? [S]	The New Jazz Sound of "Show Boat"	1960	7.50	15.00	30.00
CARLTON, LARRY					
Guitarist. Also see THE CRUSADERS.					
BLUE THUMB					
❑ BTS-46	Singing/Playing	1972	3.75	7.50	15.00
GRP					
❑ 9611	Collection	1990	3.00	6.00	12.00
MCA					
❑ 5689	Alone/But Never Alone	1986	2.00	4.00	8.00
❑ 6237	On Solid Ground	1988	2.00	4.00	8.00
❑ 6322	Christmas at Our House	1989	2.50	5.00	10.00
❑ 42003	Discovery	1987	2.00	4.00	8.00
UNI					
❑ 73036	With a Little Help from My Friends	1968	5.00	10.00	20.00
WARNER BROS.					
❑ BSK 3221	Larry Carlton	1978	2.50	5.00	10.00
❑ BSK 3380	Strikes Twice	1980	2.50	5.00	10.00
❑ BSK 3635	Sleepwalk	1981	2.50	5.00	10.00
❑ 23834	Friends	1983	2.00	4.00	8.00
CARMICHAEL, HOAGY					
Pianist, male singer and composer. He co-wrote "Star Dust," one of the most recorded songs in music history.					
BIOGRAPH					
❑ 37	Stardust (1927-30)	198?	2.50	5.00	10.00
BLUEBIRD					
❑ 8333-1-RB	Stardust, And Much More	1989	3.00	6.00	12.00
BOOK-OF-THE-MONTH					
❑ 61-5450 [(3)]	Hoagy Carmichael	1984	7.50	15.00	30.00
CAPITOL					
❑ ST 1819 [S]	I Can Dream, Can't I?	1963	6.25	12.50	25.00
❑ T 1819 [M]	I Can Dream, Can't I?	1963	5.00	10.00	20.00
DECCA					
❑ DL 5068 [10]	Stardust Road	1950	20.00	40.00	80.00
❑ DL 8588 [M]	Stardust Road	1958	7.50	15.00	30.00
GOLDEN					
❑ LP-198-18 [M]	Havin' a Party	1958	7.50	15.00	30.00
JAZZTONE					
❑ J-1266 [M]	Hoagy Sings Carmichael	1957	7.50	15.00	30.00
KIMBERLY					
❑ 2023 [M]	The Legend of Hoagy Carmichael	1962	6.25	12.50	25.00
❑ 11023 [R]	The Legend of Hoagy Carmichael	196?	5.00	10.00	20.00
MCA					
❑ 1507	Stardust Road	198?	2.50	5.00	10.00
❑ 20196	Hong Kong Blues	198?	2.50	5.00	10.00
PACIFIC JAZZ					
❑ PJ-1223 [M]	Hoagy Sings Carmichael	1956	15.00	30.00	60.00
PAUSA					
❑ 9006	Hoagy Sings Carmichael	198?	2.50	5.00	10.00
RCA VICTOR					
❑ LPT-3072 [10]	Old Rockin' Chair	1953	20.00	40.00	80.00
❑ CPL1-3370(e)	A Legendary Performer and Composer	1979	3.75	7.50	15.00
TOTEM					
❑ 1039	The 1944-45 V-Disc Sessions	198?	2.50	5.00	10.00
CARMICHAEL, JUDY					
Pianist.					
STATIRAS					
❑ SLP-8072	Two-Handed Stride	1985	3.00	6.00	12.00
❑ SLP-8074	Jazz Piano	1985	3.00	6.00	12.00
❑ SLP-8078	Pearls	1986	3.00	6.00	12.00
CARN, DOUG					
Keyboard player (mostly organ).					
SAVOY					
❑ MG-12195	The Doug Carn Trio	1969	5.00	10.00	20.00
TABLIGHI					
❑ 100	Ah Rahman!	1978	3.00	6.00	12.00
CARN, DOUG, AND JEAN CARN					
Jean Carn, Doug's then-wife, is a female singer. Also see DOUG CARN.					
BLACK JAZZ					
❑ 3	Infant Eyes	1971	3.75	7.50	15.00
❑ QD-8 [Q]	Spirit of the New Land	1972	3.75	7.50	15.00
❑ QT-16 [Q]	Revelation	1973	3.75	7.50	15.00
OVATION					
❑ 1702	Higher Ground	197?	3.00	6.00	12.00
CARNEY, HARRY					
Baritone saxophone player. Also played clarinet and bass clarinet.					
CLEF					
❑ MGC-640 [M]	Harry Carney with Strings	1955	20.00	40.00	80.00
VERVE					
❑ MGV-2028 [M]	Moods for Girl and Boy	1957	12.50	25.00	50.00
-- Reissue of Clef 640					
❑ V-2028 [M]	Moods for Girl and Boy	1957	5.00	10.00	20.00
CARPENTER, IKE					
Pianist.					
ALADDIN					
❑ LP-811 [M]	Lights Out	1957	---	---	---
-- Unreleased					
DISCOVERY					
❑ DL 3003 [10]	Dancers in Love	1949	75.00	150.00	300.00
INTRO					
❑ 950 [10]	Lights Out	1952	75.00	150.00	300.00
SCORE					
❑ SLP-4010 [M]	Lights Out	1957	37.50	75.00	150.00
CARR, GEORGIA					
Female singer.					
ROULETTE					
❑ R-25077 [M]	Shy	1960	6.25	12.50	25.00
❑ SR-25077 [S]	Shy	1960	7.50	15.00	30.00
TOPS					
❑ L-1617 [M]	Songs by a Moody Miss	195?	7.50	15.00	30.00
VEE JAY					
❑ LP-1105 [M]	Rocks in My Bed	1964	5.00	10.00	20.00
❑ VJS-1105 [S]	Rocks in My Bed	1964	6.25	12.50	25.00

Number	Title	Yr	VG	VG+	NM
CARR, HELEN					
Female singer.					
BETHLEHEM					
❑ BCP-1027 [10]	Down in the Depths on the 90th Floor	1955	30.00	60.00	120.00
❑ BCP-45 [M]	Why Do I Love You	1956	15.00	30.00	60.00
CARR, IAN, AND NUCLEUS					
Carr is a trumpet and fluegel horn player. On the below albums, the other members of Nucleus included Brian Smith (tenor sax, soprano sax, percussion); Geoff Castle (electric piano, synthesizer); Billy Kristian (bass) and Roger Sellers (drums).					
CAPITOL					
❑ ST-11771	In Flagrante Delicto	1978	3.00	6.00	12.00
❑ ST-11916	Out of the Long Dark	1979	3.00	6.00	12.00
CARR, JOYCE					
Female singer.					
AUDIOPHILE					
❑ AP-148	Joyce Carr	198?	3.00	6.00	12.00
CARR, LARRY					
Pianist.					
AUDIOPHILE					
❑ AP-223	Fit as a Fiddle	198?	3.00	6.00	12.00
CARR, LODI					
Female singer.					
LAURIE					
❑ LLP-1007 [M]	Lady Bird	1960	6.25	12.50	25.00
CARR, RICHARD					
Violinist.					
AUDIOPHILE					
❑ AP-194	Afternoon in New York	1984	3.00	6.00	12.00
PROGRESSIVE					
❑ P-7047	String Vibrations	1986	3.00	6.00	12.00
CARRINGTON, TERRI LYNN					
Drummer.					
VERVE					
❑ 837 697-1	Real Life Story	1989	3.75	7.50	15.00
CARROLL, BAIKIDA					
Trumpeter and composer.					
HAT HUT					
❑ M/N [(2)]	The Spoken Word	197?	5.00	10.00	20.00
SOUL NOTE					
❑ SN-1023	Shadows & Reflections	198?	3.00	6.00	12.00
CARROLL, BARBARA					
Pianist.					
ATLANTIC					
❑ ALR-132 [10]	Piano Panorama	195?	20.00	40.00	80.00
BLUE NOTE					
❑ BN-LA645-G	Barbara Carroll	1976	3.75	7.50	15.00
DISCOVERY					
❑ 847	Barbara Carrol at the Piano	1980	3.00	6.00	12.00
KAPP					
❑ KL-1113 [M]	Flower Drum Song	1958	6.25	12.50	25.00
❑ KS-3??? [S]	Flower Drum Song	1958	6.25	12.50	25.00
LIVINGSTON					
❑ 1081 [10]	Barbara Carroll Trio	1953	20.00	40.00	80.00
RCA VICTOR					
❑ LJM-1001 [M]	Barbara Carroll Trio	1954	12.50	25.00	50.00
❑ LJM-1023 [M]	Lullabies in Rhythm	1955	12.50	25.00	50.00
❑ LPM-1137 [M]	Have You Met Miss Carroll?	1956	12.50	25.00	50.00
❑ LPM-1296 [M]	We Just Couldn't Say Goodbye	1956	12.50	25.00	50.00
❑ LPM-1396 [M]	It's a Wonderful World	1957	12.50	25.00	50.00
SESAC					
❑ N-3201 [M]	Why Not?	1959	7.50	15.00	30.00
❑ SN-3201 [S]	Why Not?	1959	10.00	20.00	40.00
UNITED ARTISTS					
❑ UA-LA778-H	From the Beginning	1978	5.00	10.00	20.00
VERVE					
❑ MGV-2063 [M]	Funny Face	1957	15.00	30.00	60.00
-- Orange label					
❑ MGV-2063 [M]	Funny Face	1957	12.50	25.00	50.00
-- Black label					
❑ MGV-2092 [M]	The Best of George and Ira Gershwin	1958	10.00	20.00	40.00

Number	Title	Yr	VG	VG+	NM
❑ V-2092 [M]	The Best of George and Ira Gershwin	1961	5.00	10.00	20.00
❑ MGV-2095 [M]	Barbara	1958	10.00	20.00	40.00
❑ V-2095 [M]	Barbara	1961	5.00	10.00	20.00
WARNER BROS.					
❑ W 1543 [M]	"Hello Dolly" and "What Makes Sammy Run"	1964	3.00	6.00	12.00
❑ WS 1543 [S]	"Hello Dolly" and "What Makes Sammy Run"	1964	3.75	7.50	15.00
CARROLL, BARBARA/MARY LOU WILLIAMS					
Also see each artist's individual listings.					
ATLANTIC					
❑ 1271 [M]	Ladies in Jazz	1958	12.50	25.00	50.00
-- Black label					
❑ 1271 [M]	Ladies in Jazz	1961	5.00	10.00	20.00
-- Multi-color label, white "fan" logo					
CARROLL, JOE					
Male singer.					
CHARLIE PARKER					
❑ PLP-802 [M]	The Man with the Happy Sound	1962	7.50	15.00	30.00
❑ PLP-802S [S]	The Man with the Happy Sound	1962	7.50	15.00	30.00
EPIC					
❑ LN 3272 [M]	Joe Carroll	1956	12.50	25.00	50.00
CARSON, ERNIE					
Cornet player, pianist and bandleader.					
GHB					
❑ 95	Brother Lowdown	197?	2.50	5.00	10.00
❑ 125	Ernie Carson and the Original Cottonmouth Jazz Band at the Hookers' Ball	1980	2.50	5.00	10.00
❑ 162	Southern Comfort	198?	2.50	5.00	10.00
JAZZOLOGY					
❑ JCE-5	Eleanor Buck, A Celebration Service, Sept. 18, 1983	1984	2.50	5.00	10.00
❑ J-45	The Carson-Bornemann All Stars	198?	2.50	5.00	10.00
❑ 54	Ernie Carson and the Capitol City Jazz Band	198?	2.50	5.00	10.00
❑ J-89	Ernie Carson and Rhythm	1983	2.50	5.00	10.00
CARSON, ERNIE, AND BOB GREEN					
GHB					
❑ 56	Strutters, Volume 1	197?	2.50	5.00	10.00
❑ 57	Strutters, Volume 2	197?	2.50	5.00	10.00
CARTER, BENNY					
Alto and tenor saxophone player, clarinetist, trumpeter, pianist, arranger, composer and bandleader. (Whew!)					
ABC IMPULSE!					
❑ AS-12 [S]	Further Definitions	1968	3.00	6.00	12.00
❑ AS-9116 [S]	Additions to Further Definitions	1968	3.00	6.00	12.00
ANALOGUE PRODUCTIONS					
❑ AP-13	Jazz Giant	199?	7.50	15.00	30.00
-- Audiophile reissue					
AUDIO LAB					
❑ AL-1505 [M]	The Fabulous Benny Carter	1959	37.50	75.00	150.00
CLEF					
❑ MGC-141 [10]	Cosmopolite	1953	50.00	100.00	200.00
CONCORD JAZZ					
❑ CJ-285	A Gentleman and His Music	1985	2.50	5.00	10.00
CONTEMPORARY					
❑ C-3555 [M]	Jazz Giant	1958	12.50	25.00	50.00
❑ M-3561 [M]	Swingin' the Twenties	1959	10.00	20.00	40.00
❑ S-7028 [S]	Jazz Giant	1960	7.50	15.00	30.00
-- Reissue of Stereo Records 7028					
❑ S-7555 [S]	Jazz Giant	197?	3.00	6.00	12.00
-- Reissue of 7028					
❑ S-7561 [S]	Swingin' the Twenties	1959	10.00	20.00	40.00
FANTASY					
❑ OJC-167	Jazz Giant	198?	2.50	5.00	10.00
-- Reissue of Contemporary 7555					
❑ OJC-339	Swingin' the Twenties	198?	2.50	5.00	10.00
-- Reissue of Contemporary 7561					
❑ OJC-374	Montreux '77	1988	2.50	5.00	10.00
-- Reissue of Pablo Live 2308 204					
HINDSIGHT					
❑ HSR-218	Benny Carter and His Orchestra 1944	1985	2.50	5.00	10.00
IMPULSE!					
❑ A-12 [M]	Further Definitions	1962	6.25	12.50	25.00
❑ AS-12 [S]	Further Definitions	1962	7.50	15.00	30.00

(Top left) Benny Carter played a lot of different instruments and recorded for several decades. Here's one of his earlier releases, on the Norgran label, complete with David Stone Martin cover. (Top right) Ron Carter, a bass player, recorded four albums for Creed Taylor's CTI label in the early 1970s, of which Blues Farm was the first. (Bottom left) June Christy had been a singer with the Stan Kenton Orchestra before going solo in the mid-1950s. Her albums are popular among both jazz and female vocalist collectors. *June's Got Rhythm* was issued in 1958. (Bottom right) Al Cohn was best known as an arranger with Woody Herman and Artie Shaw, and for his band with Zoot Sims, but he also recorded with his own group for RCA Victor in the mid-1950s. This LP cover deftly illustrates Cohn's many musical skills.

Number	Title	Yr	VG	VG+	NM
❑ A-9116 [M]	Additions to Further Definitions	1966	7.50	15.00	30.00
❑ AS-9116 [S]	Additions to Further Definitions	1966	10.00	20.00	40.00
MCA					
❑ 29006	Further Definitions	198?	2.00	4.00	8.00
❑ 29066	Additions to Further Definitions	198?	2.00	4.00	8.00
MCA IMPULSE!					
❑ MCA-5651	Further Definitions	1986	2.50	5.00	10.00
MOVIETONE					
❑ 1020 [M]	Autumn Leaves	1967	5.00	10.00	20.00
❑ 72020 [S]	Autumn Leaves	1967	3.75	7.50	15.00
NORGRAN					
❑ MGN-10 [10]	The Urbane Mr. Carter	1954	37.50	75.00	150.00
❑ MGN-21 [10]	The Formidable Benny Carter	1954	37.50	75.00	150.00
❑ MGN-1015 [M]	Benny Carter Plays Pretty	1955	30.00	60.00	120.00
❑ MGN-1025 [M]	Benny Carter	1955	---	---	---
-- Canceled					
❑ MGN-1044 [M]	New Jazz Sounds	1955	20.00	40.00	80.00
-- With Dizzy Gillespie, Bill Harris					
❑ MGN-1058 [M]	Alone Together	1956	20.00	40.00	80.00
-- With Oscar Peterson					
❑ MGN-1070 [M]	Cosmopolite	1956	20.00	40.00	80.00
PABLO					
❑ 2310 768	The King	1975	3.00	6.00	12.00
❑ 2310 781	Carter, Gillespie, Inc.	1976	3.00	6.00	12.00
-- With Dizzy Gillespie					
❑ 2310 922	Wonderland	1987	2.50	5.00	10.00
❑ 2310 926	Benny Carter Meets Oscar Peterson	1987	2.50	5.00	10.00
❑ 2310 935	My Kind of Trouble	1989	3.00	6.00	12.00
❑ 2405 409	The Best of Benny Carter	198?	2.50	5.00	10.00
PABLO LIVE					
❑ 2308 204	Montreux '77	1978	3.00	6.00	12.00
❑ 2308 216	Live and Well in Japan	1979	3.00	6.00	12.00
PRESTIGE					
❑ 2513	Opening Blues	198?	2.50	5.00	10.00
❑ PR-7643	Benny Carter 1933	1969	3.75	7.50	15.00
STEREO RECORDS					
❑ S-7028 [S]	Jazz Giant	1959	10.00	20.00	40.00
STORYVILLE					
❑ 4047	Summer Serenade	1981	2.50	5.00	10.00
SWING					
❑ SW-8403	Benny Carter and His Orchestra 1938 and 1946	1985	2.50	5.00	10.00
20TH CENTURY-FOX					
❑ TFM-3134 [M]	Benny Carter in Paris	1963	5.00	10.00	20.00
❑ TFS-4134 [S]	Benny Carter in Paris	1963	6.25	12.50	25.00
UNITED ARTISTS					
❑ UAL-3055 [M]	"Can Can" and "Anything Goes"	1959	7.50	15.00	30.00
❑ UAL-4017 [M]	Aspects	1960	7.50	15.00	30.00
❑ UAL-4073 [M]	"Can Can" and "Anything Goes"	1960	5.00	10.00	20.00
❑ UAL-4080 [M]	Jazz Calendar	1960	5.00	10.00	20.00
❑ UAL-4094 [M]	Sax A La Carter	1961	5.00	10.00	20.00
❑ UAS-5017 [S]	Aspects	1960	10.00	20.00	40.00
❑ UAS-5073 [S]	"Can Can" and "Anything Goes"	1960	6.25	12.50	25.00
❑ UAS-5080 [S]	Jazz Calendar	1960	6.25	12.50	25.00
❑ UAS-5094 [S]	Sax A La Carter	1961	6.25	12.50	25.00
❑ UAS-6055 [S]	"Can Can" and "Anything Goes"	1959	10.00	20.00	40.00
VERVE					
❑ MGV-2025 [M]	Moonglow -- Love Songs by Benny Carter	1957	15.00	30.00	60.00
-- Reissue of Norgran 1015					
❑ MGV-8135 [M]	New Jazz Sounds	1957	15.00	30.00	60.00
-- Reissue of Norgran 1044					
❑ MGV-8148 [M]	Alone Together	1957	15.00	30.00	60.00
-- Reissue of Norgran 1058					
❑ MGV-8160 [M]	Cosmopolite	1957	15.00	30.00	60.00
-- Reissue of Norgran 1070					
❑ V-2025 [M]	Moonglow -- Love Songs by Benny Carter	1961	5.00	10.00	20.00
❑ V-8135 [M]	New Jazz Sounds	1961	5.00	10.00	20.00
❑ V-8148 [M]	Alone Together	1961	5.00	10.00	20.00
❑ V-8160 [M]	Cosmopolite	1961	5.00	10.00	20.00

CARTER, BENNY; COLEMAN HAWKINS; BEN WEBSTER
Also see each artist's individual listings.

BLUEBIRD

Number	Title	Yr	VG	VG+	NM
❑ 9683-1-RB	Three Great Swing Saxophonists	1989	3.00	6.00	12.00

CARTER, BENNY; BEN WEBSTER; BARNEY BIGARD
Also see each artist's individual listings.

SWINGVILLE

Number	Title	Yr	VG	VG+	NM
❑ SVLP-2032 [M]	B.B.B. & Co.	1962	10.00	20.00	40.00
-- Purple label					
❑ SVLP-2032 [M]	B.B.B. & Co.	1965	5.00	10.00	20.00
-- Blue label, trident logo at right					

Number	Title	Yr	VG	VG+	NM
❑ SVST-2032 [S]	B.B.B. & Co.	1962	12.50	25.00	50.00
-- Red label					
❑ SVST-2032 [S]	B.B.B. & Co.	1965	6.25	12.50	25.00
-- Blue label, trident logo at right					

CARTER, BETTY
Female singer. Also see RAY CHARLES AND BETTY CARTER.

ABC IMPULSE!

Number	Title	Yr	VG	VG+	NM
❑ AS-9321 [(2)]	What a Little Moonlight	197?	5.00	10.00	20.00
ABC-PARAMOUNT					
❑ ABC-363 [M]	The Modern Sound of Betty Carter	1960	15.00	30.00	60.00
❑ ABCS-363 [S]	The Modern Sound of Betty Carter	1960	20.00	40.00	80.00
ATCO					
❑ 33-152 [M]	'Round Midnight	1963	12.50	25.00	50.00
❑ SD 33-152 [S]	'Round Midnight	1963	15.00	30.00	60.00
BET-CAR					
❑ 1001	Betty Carter	1970	7.50	15.00	30.00
❑ 1002	The Betty Carter Album	197?	7.50	15.00	30.00
❑ 1003 [(2)]	The Audience with Betty Carter	198?	5.00	10.00	20.00
PEACOCK					
❑ PLP-90 [M]	Out There with Betty Carter	1958	30.00	60.00	120.00
ROULETTE					
❑ SR-5000	Finally	1969	6.25	12.50	25.00
❑ SR-5001	'Round Midnight	197?	5.00	10.00	20.00
❑ SR-5005	Now It's My Turn	1976	5.00	10.00	20.00
UNITED ARTISTS					
❑ UAL 3379 [M]	Inside Betty Carter	1964	12.50	25.00	50.00
❑ UAS-5639	Inside Betty Carter	1971	5.00	10.00	20.00
-- Reissue of 6379					
❑ UAS 6379 [S]	Inside Betty Carter	1964	15.00	30.00	60.00
VERVE					
❑ 835 661-1	Look What I Got	1988	3.00	6.00	12.00
❑ 835 682-1	The Betty Carter Album	1988	3.00	6.00	12.00
-- Reissue of Bet-Car 1002					
❑ 835 684-1 [(2)]	The Audience with Betty Carter	1988	3.75	7.50	15.00
-- Reissue of Bet-Car 1003					
❑ 843 991-1	Droppin' Things	1990	3.75	7.50	15.00

CARTER, JOHN
Clarinetist. Also an alto and tenor saxophone player and flutist. Also see CLARINET SUMMIT.

BLACK SAINT

Number	Title	Yr	VG	VG+	NM
❑ BSR-0047	Night Fire	1982	3.00	6.00	12.00
❑ BSR-0057	Dauwhe	1983	3.00	6.00	12.00
FLYING DUTCHMAN					
❑ FDS-109	John Carter	1969	5.00	10.00	20.00
GRAMAVISION					
❑ 18-8603	Castles of Ghana	1986	3.00	6.00	12.00
❑ 18-8704	Dance of the Love Ghosts	1987	3.00	6.00	12.00
❑ 18-8809	Ghosts	1988	3.00	6.00	12.00
❑ 79422	Shadows on the Wall	1989	3.00	6.00	12.00

CARTER, JOHN, AND BOBBY BRADFORD
Also see each artist's individual listings.

FLYING DUTCHMAN

Number	Title	Yr	VG	VG+	NM
❑ FDS-108	Flight for Four	1969	5.00	10.00	20.00
❑ FDS-128	Self Determination Music	1970	5.00	10.00	20.00
❑ FD-10108	Flight for Four	1971	3.75	7.50	15.00
-- Reissue of 108					
❑ FD-10128	Self Determination Music	1971	3.75	7.50	15.00
-- Reissue of 128					
REVELATION					
❑ 9	The New Art Ensemble	1977	3.75	7.50	15.00
❑ 18	Secrets	1978	3.75	7.50	15.00

CARTER, RON
Bass player.

CTI

Number	Title	Yr	VG	VG+	NM
❑ 6027	Blues Farm	1973	3.75	7.50	15.00
❑ 6036	All Blues	1974	3.75	7.50	15.00
❑ 6050	Spanish Blue	1975	3.75	7.50	15.00
❑ 6063	Yellow and Green	1976	3.75	7.50	15.00
❑ 8001	Blues Farm	1979	2.50	5.00	10.00
-- Reissue of 6027					
ELEKTRA MUSICIAN					
❑ 60214	Etudes	1984	2.50	5.00	10.00
EMARCY					
❑ 836 366-1	All Alone	1989	3.00	6.00	12.00
EMBRYO					
❑ 521	Uptown Conversation	1970	5.00	10.00	20.00

Number	Title	Yr	VG	VG+	NM
FANTASY					
❏ OJC-432	Where?	1990	3.00	6.00	12.00
KUDU					
❏ 25	Anything Goes	1976	3.75	7.50	15.00
MILESTONE					
❏ 9073	Pastels	1976	3.00	6.00	12.00
❏ 9082	Peg Leg	1977	3.00	6.00	12.00
❏ 9086	A Song for You	1978	3.00	6.00	12.00
❏ 9088	Parade	1978	3.00	6.00	12.00
❏ 9092	Pick 'Em	1979	3.00	6.00	12.00
❏ 9096	New York Slick	1979	3.00	6.00	12.00
❏ 9099	Patrao	1980	3.00	6.00	12.00
❏ 9100	Super Strings	1981	3.00	6.00	12.00
❏ 9107	Pardait	1981	3.00	6.00	12.00
❏ 55004 [(2)]	Piccolo	1977	3.75	7.50	15.00
NEW JAZZ					
❏ NJLP-8265 [M]	Where?	1961	20.00	40.00	80.00
-- With Eric Dolphy and Mal Waldron; purple label					
❏ NJLP-8265 [M]	Where?	1965	6.25	12.50	25.00
-- With Eric Dolphy and Mal Waldron;; blue label, trident logo at right					

CARTER, RON, AND JIM HALL
Also see each artist's individual listings.

Number	Title	Yr	VG	VG+	NM
CONCORD JAZZ					
❏ CJ-245	Live at Village West	1983	2.50	5.00	10.00
❏ CJ-270	Telephone	1985	2.50	5.00	10.00

CARTER, RON; HERBIE HANCOCK; TONY WILLIAMS
Also see each artist's individual listings.

Number	Title	Yr	VG	VG+	NM
MILESTONE					
❏ 9105	Third Plane	1981	3.00	6.00	12.00

CARVIN, MICHAEL
Drummer and bandleader.

Number	Title	Yr	VG	VG+	NM
INNER CITY					
❏ 2038	The Camel	1975	3.75	7.50	15.00
MUSE					
❏ MR-5352	First Time	1988	2.50	5.00	10.00
❏ MR-5370	Between You and Me	1989	3.00	6.00	12.00
STEEPLECHASE					
❏ SCS-1038	The Camel	198?	2.50	5.00	10.00

CARY, DICK
Pianist. Also a trumpeter and alto horn player.

Number	Title	Yr	VG	VG+	NM
BELL					
❏ BLP-44 [M]	Hot and Cool	1961	7.50	15.00	30.00
CIRCLE					
❏ CLP-018	The Amazing Dick Cary	198?	2.50	5.00	10.00
FAMOUS DOOR					
❏ HL-140	California Doings	1980	3.00	6.00	12.00
GOLDEN CREST					
❏ GC-3024 [M]	Dixieland Goes Progressive	1958	12.50	25.00	50.00
STEREOCRAFT					
❏ RTN-106 [S]	Hot and Cool	196?	6.25	12.50	25.00

CASEY, AL
Guitarist. Not the same Al Casey who was involved in the careers of Duane Eddy and Lee Hazlewood, among others.

Number	Title	Yr	VG	VG+	NM
MOODSVILLE					
❏ MVLP-12 [M]	The Al Casey Quartet	1960	12.50	25.00	50.00
-- Green label					
❏ MVLP-12 [M]	The Al Casey Quartet	1965	6.25	12.50	25.00
-- Blue label, trident logo at right					
SWINGVILLE					
❏ SVLP-2007 [M]	Buck Jumpin'	1960	12.50	25.00	50.00
-- Purple label					
❏ SVLP-2007 [M]	Buck Jumpin'	1965	6.25	12.50	25.00
-- Blue label, trident logo at right					

CASIMIR, JOHN
Clarinet player and bandleader.

Number	Title	Yr	VG	VG+	NM
JAZZOLOGY					
❏ JCE-5	Casimir's Paragon Jazz Band	1967	3.75	7.50	15.00
❏ JCE-21	Tomorrow Tomorrow	1967	3.75	7.50	15.00

CASIOPEA
Japanese fusion band.

Number	Title	Yr	VG	VG+	NM
ALFA					
❏ AAA 10002	Eyes of the Mind	1981	3.75	7.50	15.00

Number	Title	Yr	VG	VG+	NM
MILESTONE					
❏ M-9133	Zoom	1985	3.00	6.00	12.00

CASTLE JAZZ BAND, THE
See THE FAMOUS CASTLE JAZZ BAND.

CASTLE, LEE
Trumpeter and bandleader.

Number	Title	Yr	VG	VG+	NM
CELEBRITY					
❏ CEL-203 [M]	World Famous Dixieland Favorites	1952	10.00	20.00	40.00
DAVIS					
❏ JD-105 [M]	Dixieland Heaven	1951	15.00	30.00	60.00

CASTLE, PAULA
Female singer.

Number	Title	Yr	VG	VG+	NM
BETHLEHEM					
❏ BCP-1036 [10]	Paula Castle	1955	20.00	40.00	80.00

CASTRO, JOE
Pianist.

Number	Title	Yr	VG	VG+	NM
ATLANTIC					
❏ 1264 [M]	Mood Jazz	1957	12.50	25.00	50.00
-- Black label					
❏ 1264 [M]	Mood Jazz	1961	5.00	10.00	20.00
-- Multicolor label with white "fan" logo					
❏ SD 1264 [S]	Mood Jazz	1959	10.00	20.00	40.00
-- Green label					
❏ SD 1264 [S]	Mood Jazz	1961	3.75	7.50	15.00
-- Multicolor label with white "fan" logo					
❏ 1324 [M]	Groove Funk Soul	1960	10.00	20.00	40.00
-- Black label					
❏ SD 1324 [S]	Groove Funk Soul	1960	12.50	25.00	50.00
-- Green label					

CATALYST
Jazz-funk band: Eddie Green (keyboards), Odean Pope (tenor sax), Sherman Ferguson (drums) and Alphonso Johnson and Tyrone Brown (bass players).

Number	Title	Yr	VG	VG+	NM
COBBLESTONE					
❏ 9018	Catalyst	1972	5.00	10.00	20.00
MUSE					
❏ MR-5025	Perception	1973	3.75	7.50	15.00
❏ MR-5042	Unity	1974	3.75	7.50	15.00
❏ MR-5069	A Tear and a Smile	1975	3.75	7.50	15.00
❏ MR-5170	Catalyst	198?	3.00	6.00	12.00

CATHCART, DICK
Trumpeter and arranger.

Number	Title	Yr	VG	VG+	NM
WARNER BROS.					
❏ W 1275 [M]	Bix/MCMLIX	1959	6.25	12.50	25.00
❏ WS 1275 [S]	Bix/MCMLIX	1959	7.50	15.00	30.00

CATHERINE, PHILIP
Guitarist. Also see LARRY CORYELL.

Number	Title	Yr	VG	VG+	NM
WARNER BROS.					
❏ BS 2950	Nairam	1977	3.75	7.50	15.00

CATINGUB, MATT
Alto saxophone player, pianist, bandleader, arranger and composer.

Number	Title	Yr	VG	VG+	NM
REFERENCE RECORDINGS					
❏ RR-14	Your Friendly Neighborhood Big Band	1985	5.00	10.00	20.00
-- Plays at 45 rpm					
SEA BREEZE					
❏ SB-2013	My Mommy and Me	1983	2.50	5.00	10.00
❏ SB-2025	Hi-Tech Big Band	1985	2.50	5.00	10.00
❏ SB-3006	In the Land of the Long White Cloud	1990	3.00	6.00	12.00

CAVANAUGH, PAGE
Pianist and male singer.

Number	Title	Yr	VG	VG+	NM
CAPITOL					
❏ T 879 [M]	Fats Sent Me	1957	10.00	20.00	40.00
❏ T 1001 [M]	Swingin' Down the Road from Paris to Rome	1958	10.00	20.00	40.00
"X"					
❏ LX-3027 [10]	Page Cavanaugh Trio	1954	12.50	25.00	50.00

CELESTIN, OSCAR
Cornet player and bandleader.

Number	Title	Yr	VG	VG+	NM
FOLKLYRIC					
❏ 9030	Oscar "Papa" Celestin and His New Orleans Jazz Band	198?	2.50	5.00	10.00

Number	Title	Yr	VG	VG+	NM
IMPERIAL					
❏ LP-9125 [M]	Dixieland King	1961	5.00	10.00	20.00
❏ LP-9149 [M]	Birth of the Blues	1961	5.00	10.00	20.00
❏ LP-9199 [M]	Oscar "Papa" Celestin's New Orleans Jazz Band	1962	5.00	10.00	20.00
❏ LP-12062 [S]	Dixieland King	1961	3.75	7.50	15.00
❏ LP-12199 [S]	Oscar "Papa" Celestin's New Orleans Jazz Band	1962	3.75	7.50	15.00
JAZZOLOGY					
❏ JCE-28	Ragtime Band	1968	2.50	5.00	10.00
SOUTHLAND					
❏ SLP-206 [10]	Papa's Golden Wedding	1955	12.50	25.00	50.00

CELL BLOCK SEVEN
DIXIELAND JUBILEE

Number	Title	Yr	VG	VG+	NM
❏ DJ-506 [M]	A Dixieland Riot	195?	12.50	25.00	50.00
❏ DJS-506 [R]	A Dixieland Riot	196?	3.00	6.00	12.00

CENTIPEDE
55-piece band of British progressive rock and jazz musicians. The below album was originally issued on the Neon label in the UK in 1971.
RCA VICTOR

Number	Title	Yr	VG	VG+	NM
❏ CPL2-5042 [(2)]	Septober Energy	1974	12.50	25.00	50.00

CENTURY 22 FEATURING GEORGE SHAW
TBA

Number	Title	Yr	VG	VG+	NM
❏ TB-209	Flight 2201	198?	2.50	5.00	10.00

CHALLIS, BILL
Arranger and bandleader.
CIRCLE

Number	Title	Yr	VG	VG+	NM
❏ CLP-71	Bill Challis and His Orchestra: 1936	198?	2.50	5.00	10.00
❏ CLP-72	Bill Challis and His Orchestra: More 1936	198?	2.50	5.00	10.00

CHALOFF, SERGE
Baritone saxophone player. Also see THE FOUR BROTHERS.
CAPITOL

Number	Title	Yr	VG	VG+	NM
❏ T 742 [M]	Blue Serge	1956	25.00	50.00	100.00
-- Turquoise label					
❏ T 742 [M]	Blue Serge	1959	15.00	30.00	60.00
-- Black colorband label, logo at left					
❏ T 6510 [M]	Boston Blow-Up	1955	25.00	50.00	100.00
❏ M-11032	Blue Serge	1972	3.75	7.50	15.00
MOSAIC					
❏ MQ5-147 [(5)]	The Complete Serge Chaloff Sessions	1993	15.00	30.00	60.00
STORYVILLE					
❏ STLP-317 [10]	The Fable of Mable	1954	50.00	100.00	200.00
❏ STLP-350 [10]	Serge & Boots	1955	50.00	100.00	200.00

CHALOFF, SERGE/OSCAR PETTIFORD
Also see each artist's individual listings.
MERCER

Number	Title	Yr	VG	VG+	NM
❏ LP-1003 [10]	New Stars, New Sounds, Volume 2	1951	37.50	75.00	150.00

CHAMBERLAND, LINC
Guitarist.
MUSE

Number	Title	Yr	VG	VG+	NM
❏ MR-5064	A Place Within	1976	3.00	6.00	12.00
❏ MR-5263	Yet to Come	1981	2.50	5.00	10.00

CHAMBERS, JOE
Drummer and sometime vibraphone player.
MUSE

Number	Title	Yr	VG	VG+	NM
❏ MR-5035	The Almoravid	1973	3.00	6.00	12.00

CHAMBERS, JOE, AND LARRY YOUNG
Also see each artist's individual listings.
MUSE

Number	Title	Yr	VG	VG+	NM
❏ MR-5165	Double Exposure	1977	3.00	6.00	12.00

CHAMBERS, PAUL
Bass player. Also see KENNY DREW; ROY HAYNES; THE JAZZ MODES.
BLUE NOTE

Number	Title	Yr	VG	VG+	NM
❏ BLP-1534 [M]	Whims of Chambers	1956	37.50	75.00	150.00
-- "Deep groove" version (deep indentation under label on both sides)					
❏ BLP-1534 [M]	Whims of Chambers	1956	25.00	50.00	100.00
-- Regular version, Lexington Ave., NY address on label					

Number	Title	Yr	VG	VG+	NM
❏ BLP-1534 [M]	Whims of Chambers	1963	6.25	12.50	25.00
-- "New York, USA" address on label					
❏ BLP-1564 [M]	Paul Chambers Quintet	1957	37.50	75.00	150.00
-- "Deep groove" version (deep indentation under label on both sides)					
❏ BLP-1564 [M]	Paul Chambers Quintet	1957	20.00	40.00	80.00
-- Regular version, W. 63rd St. address on label					
❏ BLP-1564 [M]	Paul Chambers Quintet	1963	6.25	12.50	25.00
-- "New York, USA" address on label					
❏ BST-1564 [S]	Paul Chambers Quintet	1959	25.00	50.00	100.00
-- "Deep groove" version (deep indentation under label on both sides)					
❏ BST-1564 [S]	Paul Chambers Quintet	1959	15.00	30.00	60.00
-- Regular version, W. 63rd St. address on label					
❏ BST-1564 [S]	Paul Chambers Quintet	1963	5.00	10.00	20.00
-- "New York, USA" address on label					
❏ BLP-1569 [M]	Bass on Top	1957	37.50	75.00	150.00
-- "Deep groove" version (deep indentation under label on both sides)					
❏ BLP-1569 [M]	Bass on Top	1957	20.00	40.00	80.00
-- Regular version, W. 63rd St. address on label					
❏ BLP-1569 [M]	Bass on Top	1963	6.25	12.50	25.00
-- "New York, USA" address on label					
❏ BST-1569 [S]	Bass on Top	1959	25.00	50.00	100.00
-- "Deep groove" version (deep indentation under label on both sides)					
❏ BST-1569 [S]	Bass on Top	1959	15.00	30.00	60.00
-- Regular version, W. 63rd St. address on label					
❏ BST-1569 [S]	Bass on Top	1963	5.00	10.00	20.00
-- "New York, USA" address on label					
❏ BST-81534 [R]	Whims of Chambers	196?	3.00	6.00	12.00
-- "A Division of Liberty Records" on label					
❏ BST-81564 [S]	Paul Chambers Quintet	196?	3.00	6.00	12.00
-- "A Division of Liberty Records" on label					
❏ BST-81569 [S]	Bass on Top	196?	3.00	6.00	12.00
-- "A Division of Liberty Records" on label					
EPITAPH					
❏ E-4001	Paul Chambers 1935-1969	1975	3.75	7.50	15.00
IMPERIAL					
❏ LP-9182 [M]	A Jazz Delegation from the East: Chambers' Music	1961	10.00	20.00	40.00
❏ LP-12182 [S]	A Jazz Delegation from the East: Chambers' Music	1961	7.50	15.00	30.00
JAZZ WEST					
❏ JWLP-7 [M]	A Jazz Delegation from the East: Chambers' Music	1956	150.00	300.00	600.00
SCORE					
❏ SLP-4033 [M]	A Jazz Delegation from the East: Chambers' Music	1958	20.00	40.00	80.00
TRIP					
❏ 5026 [(2)]	Just Friends	197?	3.75	7.50	15.00
VEE JAY					
❏ LP-1014 [M]	Go	1959	10.00	20.00	40.00
❏ SR-1014 [S]	Go	1959	12.50	25.00	50.00
❏ VJS-1014 [S]	Go	198?	3.00	6.00	12.00
-- Reissue on thinner vinyl					
❏ LP-3012 [M]	First Bassman	1960	7.50	15.00	30.00
❏ SR-3012 [S]	First Bassman	1960	10.00	20.00	40.00
❏ VJS-3012 [S]	First Bassman	198?	3.00	6.00	12.00
-- Reissue on thinner vinyl					

CHAMBERS, PAUL, AND JOHN COLTRANE
Also see each artist's individual listings.
BLUE NOTE

Number	Title	Yr	VG	VG+	NM
❏ BN-LA451-H2 [(2)] High Step		1975	3.75	7.50	15.00
-- Reissue of Blue Note 1534 plus other material					

CHAMBLEE, EDDIE
Tenor saxophone player.
EMARCY

Number	Title	Yr	VG	VG+	NM
❏ MG-36124 [M]	Chamblee Music	1958	12.50	25.00	50.00
❏ MG-36131 [M]	Doodlin'	1958	12.50	25.00	50.00
❏ SR-80007 [S]	Doodlin'	1959	10.00	20.00	40.00
MERCURY					
❏ SR-60127 [S]	Chamblee Music	1960	6.25	12.50	25.00
PRESTIGE					
❏ PRLP-7321 [M]	The Rocking Tenor Sax of Eddie Chamblee	1964	6.25	12.50	25.00
-- Yellow label					
❏ PRST-7321 [S]	The Rocking Tenor Sax of Eddie Chamblee	1964	7.50	15.00	30.00
-- Silver label					

CHANCLER, NDUGU
Drummer.
MCA

Number	Title	Yr	VG	VG+	NM
❏ 6302	Old Friends, New Friends	1989	3.00	6.00	12.00

Number	Title	Yr	VG	VG+	NM
CHAPIN, JIM					

Drummer.

CLASSIC JAZZ

Number	Title	Yr	VG	VG+	NM
❏ 6 [M]	Jim Chapin Sextet	197?	2.50	5.00	10.00
❏ 7 [M]	Skin Tight	197?	2.50	5.00	10.00

PRESTIGE

❏ PRLP-213 [10]	Jim Chapin Sextet	1955	62.50	125.00	250.00

CHARLES, RAY

Pianist and male singer. Impossible to classify, Charles recorded all kinds of music during his long career; the below are his most jazz-oriented. For a more complete listing, see the *Standard Catalog of American Records 1950-1975*. Also see DAVID NEWMAN.

ABC IMPULSE!

❏ AS-2 [S]	Genius + Soul = Jazz	1968	3.00	6.00	12.00

ARCHIVE OF FOLK AND JAZZ

❏ 244	Ray Charles	1970	3.00	6.00	12.00
❏ 292	Ray Charles, Vol. 2	197?	2.50	5.00	10.00
❏ 358	Rockin' with Ray	1979	2.50	5.00	10.00

ATLANTIC

❏ 1259 [M]	The Great Ray Charles	1957	12.50	25.00	50.00
-- Black label					
❏ 1259 [M]	The Great Ray Charles	1960	6.25	12.50	25.00
-- Red and white label, white fan logo on right					
❏ 1259 [M]	The Great Ray Charles	1962	5.00	10.00	20.00
-- Red and white label, black fan logo on right					
❏ SD 1259 [S]	The Great Ray Charles	1959	12.50	25.00	50.00
-- Green label					
❏ SD 1259 [S]	The Great Ray Charles	1960	6.25	12.50	25.00
-- Blue and green label, white fan logo on right					
❏ SD 1259 [S]	The Great Ray Charles	1962	5.00	10.00	20.00
-- Blue and green label, black fan logo on right					
❏ 1289 [M]	Ray Charles at Newport	1958	12.50	25.00	50.00
-- Black label					
❏ 1289 [M]	Ray Charles at Newport	1960	6.25	12.50	25.00
-- Red and white label, white fan logo on right					
❏ 1289 [M]	Ray Charles at Newport	1962	5.00	10.00	20.00
-- Red and white label, black fan logo on right					
❏ SD 1289 [S]	Ray Charles at Newport	1959	12.50	25.00	50.00
-- Green label					
❏ SD 1289 [S]	Ray Charles at Newport	1960	6.25	12.50	25.00
-- Blue and green label, white fan logo on right					
❏ SD 1289 [S]	Ray Charles at Newport	1962	5.00	10.00	20.00
-- Blue and green label, black fan logo on right					
❏ 1312 [M]	The Genius of Ray Charles	1960	10.00	20.00	40.00
-- Black label					
❏ 1312 [M]	The Genius of Ray Charles	1960	10.00	20.00	40.00
-- White "bullseye" label					
❏ 1312 [M]	The Genius of Ray Charles	1960	6.25	12.50	25.00
-- Red and white label, white fan logo on right					
❏ 1312 [M]	The Genius of Ray Charles	1962	5.00	10.00	20.00
-- Red and white label, black fan logo on right					
❏ SD 1312 [S]	The Genius of Ray Charles	1960	12.50	25.00	50.00
-- Green label					
❏ SD 1312 [S]	The Genius of Ray Charles	1960	12.50	25.00	50.00
-- White "bullseye" label					
❏ SD 1312 [S]	The Genius of Ray Charles	1960	6.25	12.50	25.00
-- Blue and green label, white fan logo on right					
❏ SD 1312 [S]	The Genius of Ray Charles	1962	5.00	10.00	20.00
-- Blue and green label, black fan logo on right					
❏ SD 1312 [S]	The Genius of Ray Charles	1968	5.00	10.00	20.00
-- Brown and purple label					
❏ 1369 [M]	The Genius After Hours	1961	6.25	12.50	25.00
-- Red and white label, white fan logo on right					
❏ 1369 [M]	The Genius After Hours	1962	5.00	10.00	20.00
-- Red and white label, black fan logo on right					
❏ SD 1369 [S]	The Genius After Hours	1961	7.50	15.00	30.00
-- Blue and green label, white fan logo on right					
❏ SD 1369 [S]	The Genius After Hours	1962	6.25	12.50	25.00
-- Blue and green label, black fan logo on right					
❏ SD 1543	The Best of Ray Charles	1970	3.00	6.00	12.00
❏ 90464	The Genius After Hours	1986	2.50	5.00	10.00
-- Reissue					

BARONET

❏ B-111 [M]	The Artistry of Ray Charles	196?	3.00	6.00	12.00
❏ BS-111 [R]	The Artistry of Ray Charles	196?	2.50	5.00	10.00
❏ B-117 [M]	The Great Ray Charles	196?	3.00	6.00	12.00
❏ BS-117 [R]	The Great Ray Charles	196?	2.50	5.00	10.00

CORONET

❏ CX-173 [M]	Ray Charles	196?	3.00	6.00	12.00
❏ CXS-173 [R]	Ray Charles	196?	2.50	5.00	10.00

CROSSOVER

❏ 9007	My Kind of Jazz, Part 3	1976	3.00	6.00	12.00

DUNHILL COMPACT CLASSICS

❏ DZL-038	Genius + Soul = Jazz	1988	3.75	7.50	15.00
-- Clear vinyl reissue					

HOLLYWOOD

❏ 504 [M]	The Original Ray Charles	1959	37.50	75.00	150.00

Number	Title	Yr	VG	VG+	NM
❏ 505 [M]	The Fabuolus Ray Charles	1959	37.50	75.00	150.00

IMPULSE!

❏ A-2 [M]	Genius + Soul = Jazz	1961	6.25	12.50	25.00
❏ AS-2 [S]	Genius + Soul = Jazz	1961	7.50	15.00	30.00

PREMIER

❏ PM 2004 [M]	The Great Ray Charles	196?	3.00	6.00	12.00
❏ PS 2004 [R]	The Great Ray Charles	196?	2.50	5.00	10.00
❏ PS 6001 [R]	Fantastic Ray Charles	196?	2.50	5.00	10.00

TANGERINE

❏ 1512	My Kind of Jazz	1970	3.00	6.00	12.00
❏ 1516	My Kind of Jazz No. II	1973	3.00	6.00	12.00

CHARLES, RAY, AND BETTY CARTER

Also see each artist's individual listings.

ABC

❏ S-385 [S]	Ray Charles and Betty Carter	1967	5.00	10.00	20.00

ABC-PARAMOUNT

❏ 385 [M]	Ray Charles and Betty Carter	1961	10.00	20.00	40.00
❏ S-385 [S]	Ray Charles and Betty Carter	1961	15.00	30.00	60.00

DCC COMPACT CLASSICS

❏ LPZ-2005	Ray Charles and Betty Carter	1995	20.00	40.00	80.00
-- Audiophile vinyl					

DUNHILL COMPACT CLASSICS

❏ DZL-039	Ray Charles and Betty Carter	1988	3.75	7.50	15.00
-- Clear vinyl reissue					

CHARLES, RAY & MILT JACKSON

Also see each artist's individual listings.

ATLANTIC

❏ 1279 [M]	Soul Brothers	1958	12.50	25.00	50.00
-- Black label					
❏ 1279 [M]	Soul Brothers	1960	6.25	12.50	25.00
-- Red and white label, white fan logo on right					
❏ 1279 [M]	Soul Brothers	1962	5.00	10.00	20.00
-- Red and white label, black fan logo on right					
❏ SD 1279 [S]	Soul Brothers	1959	12.50	25.00	50.00
-- Green label					
❏ SD 1279 [S]	Soul Brothers	1960	6.25	12.50	25.00
-- Blue and green label, white fan logo on right					
❏ SD 1279 [S]	Soul Brothers	1962	5.00	10.00	20.00
-- Blue and green label, black fan logo on right					
❏ 1360 [M]	Soul Meeting	1961	6.25	12.50	25.00
-- Red and white label, white fan logo on right					
❏ 1360 [M]	Soul Meeting	1962	5.00	10.00	20.00
-- Red and white label, black fan logo on right					
❏ SD 1360 [S]	Soul Meeting	1961	7.50	15.00	30.00
-- Blue and green label, white fan logo on right					
❏ SD 1360 [S]	Soul Meeting	1962	6.25	12.50	25.00
-- Blue and green label, black fan logo on right					

CHARLES, RAY, AND CLEO LAINE

Also see each artist's individual listings.

RCA VICTOR

❏ CPL2-1831 [(2)]	Porgy & Bess	1976	3.75	7.50	15.00
❏ DJL1-2163	Porgy & Bess	1976	5.00	10.00	20.00
-- Promo-only excerpts from 2-record set					

CHARLES, TEDDY

Vibraphone player. Also see LEE KONITZ; MANHATTAN ALL STARS; PRESTIGE JAZZ QUARTET.

ATLANTIC

❏ 1229 [M]	The Teddy Charles Tentet	1956	20.00	40.00	80.00
-- Black label					
❏ 1229 [M]	The Teddy Charles Tentet	1961	7.50	15.00	30.00
-- Multicolor label with white "fan" logo					
❏ 1274 [M]	Word from Bird	1956	20.00	40.00	80.00
-- Black label					
❏ 1274 [M]	Word from Bird	1961	7.50	15.00	30.00
-- Multicolor label with white "fan" logo					

BETHLEHEM

❏ BCP-6032 [M]	Salute to Hamp	1959	12.50	25.00	50.00
❏ BCP-6044 [M]	On Campus -- Ivy League Jazz Concert	1960	12.50	25.00	50.00

ELEKTRA

❏ EKL-136 [M]	Vibe-Rant	1957	15.00	30.00	60.00

FANTASY

❏ OJC-122	Collaboration: West	198?	2.50	5.00	10.00
-- Reissue of Prestige 7028					

JOSIE

❏ JJS-3505 [S]	Teddy Charles Trio Plays Duke Ellington	1963	7.50	15.00	30.00
❏ JOZ-3505 [M]	Teddy Charles Trio Plays Duke Ellington	1963	7.50	15.00	30.00

Number	Title	Yr	VG	VG+	NM
JUBILEE					
❑ JGS-1047 [S]	Three for Duke	1959	10.00	20.00	40.00
❑ JLP-1047 [M]	Three for Duke	1957	12.50	25.00	50.00
NEW JAZZ					
❑ NJLP-1106 [10]	Teddy Charles New Directions Quartet	1955	75.00	150.00	300.00
PRESTIGE					
❑ PRLP-132 [10]	Teddy Charles and His Trio	1952	50.00	100.00	200.00
❑ PRLP-143 [10]	New Directions Vol. 1	1953	50.00	100.00	200.00
❑ PRLP-150 [10]	New Directions Vol. 2	1953	50.00	100.00	200.00
❑ PRLP-164 [10]	New Directions Vol. 3	1953	50.00	100.00	200.00
❑ PRLP-169 [10]	New Directions Vol. 4	1954	50.00	100.00	200.00
❑ PRLP-178 [10]	New Directions Vol. 5	1954	50.00	100.00	200.00
-- With Bob Brookmeyer					
❑ PRLP-206 [10]	Teddy Charles New Directions Quartet	1955	50.00	100.00	200.00
-- Reissue of New Jazz 1106					
❑ PRLP-7028 [M]	Collaboration: West	1956	25.00	50.00	100.00
-- Yellow label					
❑ PRLP-7028 [M]	Collaboration: West	196?	7.50	15.00	30.00
-- Blue label, trident logo on right					
❑ PRLP-7078 [M]	Evolution	1957	25.00	50.00	100.00
-- Yellow label					
❑ PRLP-7078 [M]	Evolution	196?	7.50	15.00	30.00
-- Blue label, trident logo on right					
SAVOY					
❑ MG-12174 [M]	The Vibe-Rant Quintet	1961	7.50	15.00	30.00
-- Reissue of Elektra LP					
SOUL NOTE					
❑ 121183	Live at the Verona Jazz Festival, 1988	1990	3.00	6.00	12.00
UNITED ARTISTS					
❑ UAL-3365 [M]	Russia Goes Jazz	1964	6.25	12.50	25.00
❑ UAS-6365 [S]	Russia Goes Jazz	1964	7.50	15.00	30.00
WARWICK					
❑ W-2033 [M]	Jazz in the Garden of the Museum of Modern Art	1960	12.50	25.00	50.00

CHARLESTON CITY ALL-STARS
Studio group composed of members of Enoch Light's Light Brigade.

Number	Title	Yr	VG	VG+	NM
GRAND AWARD					
❑ GA 201 SD [S]	The Roaring 20's	1958	5.00	10.00	20.00
❑ GA 211 SD [S]	The Roaring 20's, Volume 2	1958	5.00	10.00	20.00
❑ GA 229 SD [S]	The Roaring 20's, Volume 3	1958	5.00	10.00	20.00
❑ GA 243 SD [S]	Dixieland	1959	3.75	7.50	15.00
❑ GA 33-327 [M]	The Roaring 20's	1957	3.75	7.50	15.00
❑ GA 33-340 [M]	The Roaring 20's, Volume 2	1957	3.75	7.50	15.00
❑ GA 33-353 [M]	The Roaring 20's, Volume 3	1957	3.75	7.50	15.00
❑ GA 33-370 [M]	The Roaring 20's, Volume 4	1958	3.75	7.50	15.00
❑ GA 33-411 [M]	Dixieland	1959	3.00	6.00	12.00
WALDORF MUSIC HALL					
❑ MH 33-142 [M]	The Roaring 20's	195?	5.00	10.00	20.00

CHARQUET & CO.

Number	Title	Yr	VG	VG+	NM
STOMP OFF					
❑ SOS-1008	Crazy Quilt	197?	3.00	6.00	12.00
❑ SOS-1039	Live at Joseph Lam Club	198?	2.50	5.00	10.00
❑ SOS-1053	Everybody Stomp	198?	2.50	5.00	10.00
❑ SOS-1076	Jungle Jamboree	198?	2.50	5.00	10.00
❑ SOS-1195	You'll Long for Me	198?	2.50	5.00	10.00

CHARTERS, ANN
Pianist.

Number	Title	Yr	VG	VG+	NM
GNP CRESCENDO					
❑ GNPS-9021	A Joplin Bouquet	197?	2.50	5.00	10.00
❑ GNPS-9032	The Genius of Scott Joplin	197?	2.50	5.00	10.00
KICKING MULE					
❑ 101	Scott Joplin and His Friends	198?	2.50	5.00	10.00

CHASE
Jazz-rock nonet (four horns, four-piece rhythm section, lead vocalist). Fronted by Bill Chase (trumpet), who had played in the MAYNARD FERGUSON, WOODY HERMAN and STAN KENTON bands.

Number	Title	Yr	VG	VG+	NM
EPIC					
❑ E 30472	Chase	1971	3.00	6.00	12.00
❑ EQ 30472 [Q]	Chase	1973	5.00	10.00	20.00
❑ KE 31097	Ennea	1972	3.00	6.00	12.00
❑ EQ 32572 [Q]	Pure Music	1974	5.00	10.00	20.00
❑ KE 32572	Pure Music	1974	3.00	6.00	12.00
❑ EG 33737 [(2)]	Chase/Ennea	1976	3.75	7.50	15.00

CHEATHAM, DOC
Trumpeter and male singer.

Number	Title	Yr	VG	VG+	NM
CLASSIC JAZZ					
❑ 113	Good for What Ails Ya	1977	3.00	6.00	12.00

CHEATHAM, DOC, AND SAMMY PRICE
Also see each artist's individual listings.

Number	Title	Yr	VG	VG+	NM
SACKVILLE					
❑ 3013	Doc & Sammy	198?	3.00	6.00	12.00
❑ 3024	Sweet Substitute	198?	3.00	6.00	12.00
❑ 3029	Black Beauty	198?	3.00	6.00	12.00

CHEATHAM, JEANNIE AND JIMMY
Jeannie is a pianist and female singer. Jimmy is a trombone player.

Number	Title	Yr	VG	VG+	NM
CONCORD JAZZ					
❑ CJ-258	Sweet Baby Blues	1985	2.50	5.00	10.00
❑ CJ-297	Midnight Mama	1986	2.50	5.00	10.00
❑ CJ-321	Homeward Bound	1987	2.50	5.00	10.00
❑ CJ-373	Back to the Neighborhood	1989	3.00	6.00	12.00

CHERRY, DON
Trumpeter. Also see JOHN COLTRANE; JAZZ COMPOSERS ORCHESTRA; STEVE LACY.

Number	Title	Yr	VG	VG+	NM
ANTILLES					
❑ 7034	The Eternal Now	197?	3.00	6.00	12.00
ATLANTIC					
❑ SD 18217	Hear and Now	197?	3.00	6.00	12.00
BASF					
❑ 20980	Eternal Rhythm	1972	5.00	10.00	20.00
BLACK SAINT					
❑ BSR-0013	Old and New Dreams	198?	3.00	6.00	12.00
BLUE NOTE					
❑ BLP-4226 [M]	Complete Communion	1966	6.25	12.50	25.00
❑ BLP-4247 [M]	Symphony for Improvisers	1966	6.25	12.50	25.00
❑ BST-84226 [S]	Complete Communion	1966	7.50	15.00	30.00
-- "New York, USA" address on label					
❑ BST-84226 [S]	Complete Communion	1968	3.75	7.50	15.00
-- "A Division of Liberty Records" on label					
❑ BST-84247 [S]	Symphony for Improvisers	1966	7.50	15.00	30.00
-- "New York, USA" address on label					
❑ BST-84247 [S]	Symphony for Improvisers	1968	3.75	7.50	15.00
-- "A Division of Liberty Records" on label					
❑ BST-84311	Where Is Brooklyn?	1969	6.25	12.50	25.00
-- "A Division of Liberty Records" on label					
ECM					
❑ 1230	El Corazon	198?	3.00	6.00	12.00
-- With Ed Blackwell					
HORIZON					
❑ HP-717	Don Cherry	197?	3.00	6.00	12.00
INNER CITY					
❑ IC 1009	Togetherness	197?	5.00	10.00	20.00
JCOA					
❑ 1006	Relativity Suite	1974	5.00	10.00	20.00
MOSAIC					
❑ MQ3-145 [(3)]	The Complete Blue Note Recordings of Don Cherry	199?	10.00	20.00	40.00

CHESTER, BOB
Bandleader and arranger.

Number	Title	Yr	VG	VG+	NM
CIRCLE					
❑ 44	Bob Chester and His Orchestra: 1940-41	198?	2.50	5.00	10.00
❑ 74	Bob Chester and His Orchestra: More 1940-41	198?	2.50	5.00	10.00

CHICAGO
Mostly a rock band with some jazz elements. By 1972, most of its jazz tendencies had been superseded. For a more complete listing, see the *Standard Catalog of American Records 1950-1975*.

Number	Title	Yr	VG	VG+	NM
ACCORD					
❑ SN-7140	Toronto Rock 'n Roll Revival, Part I	1982	3.00	6.00	12.00
-- Reissue of Magnum LP					
COLUMBIA					
❑ GP 8 [(2)]	Chicago Transit Authority	1969	6.25	12.50	25.00
-- Red labels with "360 Sound" at bottom					
❑ GP 8 [(2)]	Chicago Transit Authority	1970	5.00	10.00	20.00
-- Orange labels; most copies add a Roman numeral "I" to the title on spine					
❑ KGP 24 [(2)]	Chicago	1970	10.00	20.00	40.00
-- Red labels with "360 Sound" at bottom; label and spine call the album "Chicago"					
❑ KGP 24 [(2)]	Chicago II	1970	6.25	12.50	25.00
-- Red labels with "360 Sound" at bottom; label and spine call the album "Chicago II"					
❑ KGP 24 [(2)]	Chicago II	1970	5.00	10.00	20.00
-- Orange labels					
❑ C2 30110 [(2)]	Chicago III	1971	5.00	10.00	20.00
❑ C2Q 30110 [(2) Q]	Chicago III	1974	7.50	15.00	30.00

Number	Title	Yr	VG	VG+	NM
❏ C2G 30863 [(2)]	Chicago at Carnegie Hall, Vol. 1 & 2	1971	5.00	10.00	20.00

-- First half of the 4-LP box, possibly for Columbia Record Club only

Number	Title	Yr	VG	VG+	NM
❏ C2G 30864 [(2)]	Chicago at Carnegie Hall, Vol. 3 & 4	1971	5.00	10.00	20.00

-- Second half of the 4-LP box, possibly for Columbia Record Club only

Number	Title	Yr	VG	VG+	NM
❏ C4Q 30865 [(4) Q]	Chicago at Carnegie Hall	1971	12.50	25.00	50.00
❏ C4X 30865 [(4)]	Chicago at Carnegie Hall	1971	10.00	20.00	40.00

-- With box, 4 posters and program. Deduct for missing items.

Number	Title	Yr	VG	VG+	NM
❏ GQ 33255 [(2) Q]	Chicago Transit Authority	1975	6.25	12.50	25.00
❏ GQ 33258 [(2) Q]	Chicago II	1975	6.25	12.50	25.00

MAGNUM

Number	Title	Yr	VG	VG+	NM
❏ MR 604	Chicago Transit Authority Live in Concert	1978	5.00	10.00	20.00

-- Taken from their 1969 Toronto Rock 'n Roll Revival performance

MOBILE FIDELITY

Number	Title	Yr	VG	VG+	NM
❏ 2-128 [(2)]	Chicago Transit Authority	1983	20.00	40.00	80.00

-- Audiophile vinyl

CHICAGO HOT SIX
Led by Roy Rubenstein.
GHB

Number	Title	Yr	VG	VG+	NM
❏ 176	Stompin' at the Good Time	1982	2.50	5.00	10.00

CHICAGO RHYTHM
JAZZOLOGY

Number	Title	Yr	VG	VG+	NM
❏ J-127	'Round Evening	198?	2.50	5.00	10.00
❏ J-157	Caution Blues	198?	2.50	5.00	10.00

STOMP OFF

Number	Title	Yr	VG	VG+	NM
❏ SOS-1026	Chicago Rhythm	198?	2.50	5.00	10.00
❏ SOS-1059	One in a Million	1982	2.50	5.00	10.00
❏ SOS-1164	Made in Chicago	1989	3.00	6.00	12.00

CHILDERS, BUDDY
Trumpeter.
LIBERTY

Number	Title	Yr	VG	VG+	NM
❏ LJH-6009 [M]	Sam Songs	1956	10.00	20.00	40.00
❏ LJH-6013 [M]	Buddy Childers Quartet	1957	10.00	20.00	40.00

TREND

Number	Title	Yr	VG	VG+	NM
❏ TR-539	Just Buddy's	1986	3.00	6.00	12.00

CHILDS, BILLY
Pianist.
WINDHAM HILL

Number	Title	Yr	VG	VG+	NM
❏ WH-0113	Take For Example This	1988	3.00	6.00	12.00
❏ WH-0118	Twilight Is Upon Us	1989	3.00	6.00	12.00

CHILDS, SUE
STUDIO 4

Number	Title	Yr	VG	VG+	NM
❏ 200 [M]	Sue Childs	195?	12.50	25.00	50.00

CHITTISON, HERMAN
Pianist.
AUDIOPHILE

Number	Title	Yr	VG	VG+	NM
❏ AP-39 [M]	The Melody Lingers On	1986	2.50	5.00	10.00

COLUMBIA

Number	Title	Yr	VG	VG+	NM
❏ CL 6134 [10]	Herman Chittison	1950	12.50	25.00	50.00
❏ CL 6182 [10]	Herman Chittison Trio	1951	12.50	25.00	50.00

ROYALE

Number	Title	Yr	VG	VG+	NM
❏ 1824 [10]	Cocktail Time	195?	10.00	20.00	40.00

CHRISTIAN, CHARLIE
Guitarist. Also see BENNY GOODMAN.
ARCHIVE OF FOLK AND JAZZ

Number	Title	Yr	VG	VG+	NM
❏ 219	Charlie Christian	197?	2.50	5.00	10.00

COLUMBIA

Number	Title	Yr	VG	VG+	NM
❏ G 30779 [(2)]	Solo Flight -- The Genius of Charlie Christian	1972	5.00	10.00	20.00

COLUMBIA JAZZ MASTERPIECES

Number	Title	Yr	VG	VG+	NM
❏ CJ 40846	Charlie Christian -- The Genius of the Electric Guitar	1986	3.75	7.50	15.00

COUNTERPOINT

Number	Title	Yr	VG	VG+	NM
❏ 548 [M]	The Harlem Jazz Scene 1941	195?	15.00	30.00	60.00

ESOTERIC

Number	Title	Yr	VG	VG+	NM
❏ ESJ-1 [10]	Jazz Immortal	1951	50.00	100.00	200.00

-- Red vinyl

Number	Title	Yr	VG	VG+	NM
❏ ES-548 [M]	The Harlem Jazz Scene 1941	1956	20.00	40.00	80.00

CHRISTY, JUNE
Female singer.
CAPITOL

Number	Title	Yr	VG	VG+	NM
❏ H 516 [10]	Something Cool	1954	20.00	40.00	80.00
❏ SM-516 [R]	Something Cool	197?	2.50	5.00	10.00
❏ T 516 [M]	Something Cool	1955	12.50	25.00	50.00

-- Turquoise label

Number	Title	Yr	VG	VG+	NM
❏ T 516 [M]	Something Cool	1959	6.25	12.50	25.00

-- Black label with colorband

Number	Title	Yr	VG	VG+	NM
❏ T 656 [M]	Duets	1955	10.00	20.00	40.00

-- Turquoise label

Number	Title	Yr	VG	VG+	NM
❏ T 725 [M]	The Misty Miss Christy	1956	10.00	20.00	40.00

-- Turquoise label

Number	Title	Yr	VG	VG+	NM
❏ T 833 [M]	June -- Fair and Warmer!	1957	10.00	20.00	40.00

-- Turquoise label

Number	Title	Yr	VG	VG+	NM
❏ T 902 [M]	Gone for the Day	1957	10.00	20.00	40.00

-- Turquoise label

Number	Title	Yr	VG	VG+	NM
❏ T 1006 [M]	This Is June Christy!	1958	10.00	20.00	40.00

-- Turquoise label

Number	Title	Yr	VG	VG+	NM
❏ ST 1076 [S]	June's Got Rhythm	1958	10.00	20.00	40.00

-- Black label with colorband, Capitol logo at left

Number	Title	Yr	VG	VG+	NM
❏ T 1076 [M]	June's Got Rhythm	1958	7.50	15.00	30.00

-- Black label with colorband, Capitol logo at left

Number	Title	Yr	VG	VG+	NM
❏ ST 1114 [S]	The Song Is June!	1959	10.00	20.00	40.00

-- Black label with colorband, Capitol logo at left

Number	Title	Yr	VG	VG+	NM
❏ T 1114 [M]	The Song Is June!	1959	7.50	15.00	30.00

-- Black label with colorband, Capitol logo at left

Number	Title	Yr	VG	VG+	NM
❏ ST 1202 [S]	June Christy Recalls Those Kenton Days	1959	10.00	20.00	40.00

-- Black label with colorband, Capitol logo at left

Number	Title	Yr	VG	VG+	NM
❏ T 1202 [M]	June Christy Recalls Those Kenton Days	1959	7.50	15.00	30.00

-- Black label with colorband, Capitol logo at left

Number	Title	Yr	VG	VG+	NM
❏ ST 1308 [S]	Ballads for Night People	1959	10.00	20.00	40.00

-- Black label with colorband, Capitol logo at left

Number	Title	Yr	VG	VG+	NM
❏ T 1308 [M]	Ballads for Night People	1959	7.50	15.00	30.00

-- Black label with colorband, Capitol logo at left

Number	Title	Yr	VG	VG+	NM
❏ STBO 1327 [(2) S]	Road Show	1960	10.00	20.00	40.00

-- Black label with colorband, Capitol logo at left

Number	Title	Yr	VG	VG+	NM
❏ TBO 1327 [(2) M]	Road Show	1960	7.50	15.00	30.00

-- Black label with colorband, Capitol logo at left

Number	Title	Yr	VG	VG+	NM
❏ ST 1398 [S]	The Cool School	1960	10.00	20.00	40.00

-- Black label with colorband, Capitol logo at left

Number	Title	Yr	VG	VG+	NM
❏ T 1398 [M]	The Cool School	1960	7.50	15.00	30.00

-- Black label with colorband, Capitol logo at left

Number	Title	Yr	VG	VG+	NM
❏ ST 1498 [S]	Off Beat	1961	12.50	25.00	50.00

-- Black label with colorband, Capitol logo at left

Number	Title	Yr	VG	VG+	NM
❏ T 1498 [M]	Off Beat	1961	10.00	20.00	40.00

-- Black label with colorband, Capitol logo at left

Number	Title	Yr	VG	VG+	NM
❏ ST 1586 [S]	Do-Re-Mi	1961	12.50	25.00	50.00

-- Black label with colorband, Capitol logo at left

Number	Title	Yr	VG	VG+	NM
❏ T 1586 [M]	Do-Re-Mi	1961	10.00	20.00	40.00

-- Black label with colorband, Capitol logo at left

Number	Title	Yr	VG	VG+	NM
❏ ST 1605 [S]	That Time of Year	1961	12.50	25.00	50.00

-- Black label with colorband, Capitol logo at left

Number	Title	Yr	VG	VG+	NM
❏ T 1605 [M]	That Time of Year	1961	10.00	20.00	40.00
❏ ST 1693 [S]	The Best of June Christy	1962	7.50	15.00	30.00

-- Black logo with colorband

Number	Title	Yr	VG	VG+	NM
❏ T 1693 [M]	The Best of June Christy	1962	6.25	12.50	25.00

-- Black label with colorband

Number	Title	Yr	VG	VG+	NM
❏ ST 1845 [S]	Big Band Specials	1962	6.25	12.50	25.00
❏ T 1845 [M]	Big Band Specials	1962	5.00	10.00	20.00
❏ ST 1953 [S]	The Intimate June Christy	1963	6.25	12.50	25.00
❏ T 1953 [M]	The Intimate June Christy	1963	5.00	10.00	20.00
❏ ST 2410 [S]	Something Broadway, Something Latin	1965	7.50	15.00	30.00
❏ T 2410 [M]	Something Broadway, Something Latin	1965	6.25	12.50	25.00
❏ SM-11961	The Best of June Christy	1979	2.50	5.00	10.00

DISCOVERY

Number	Title	Yr	VG	VG+	NM
❏ DS-836	Impromptu	1982	3.00	6.00	12.00
❏ DS-911	Interlude	1986	2.50	5.00	10.00
❏ DS-919	The Misty Miss Christy	1986	2.50	5.00	10.00

HINDSIGHT

Number	Title	Yr	VG	VG+	NM
❏ HSR-219	June Christy, Vol. 1	1986	2.50	5.00	10.00
❏ HSR-235	June Christy, Vol. 2	1988	2.50	5.00	10.00

PAUSA

Number	Title	Yr	VG	VG+	NM
❏ 9039	Big Band Specials	198?	2.50	5.00	10.00

CHRYSANTHEMUM RAGTIME BAND
STOMP OFF

Number	Title	Yr	VG	VG+	NM
❏ SOS-1047	Bringin' 'Em Back Alive!	1983	2.50	5.00	10.00
❏ SOS-1079	Come On and Hear	1984	2.50	5.00	10.00
❏ SOS-1123	Preserves	1987	2.50	5.00	10.00
❏ SOS-1168	Dancing on the Edge of the World	1988	2.50	5.00	10.00
❏ SOS-1196	Joy Rag	1989	2.50	5.00	10.00

Number	Title	Yr	VG	VG+	NM
CIRCLE					
Barry Altschul (drums); ANTHONY BRAXTON; CHICK COREA; DAVE HOLLAND.					
ECM					
❏ 1018/19 [(2)]	Paris Concert	197?	5.00	10.00	20.00
CIRILLO, WALLY/BOBBY SCOTT					
Cirillo is a pianist and composer. Also see BOBBY SCOTT.					
SAVOY					
❏ MG-15055 [10]	Cirillo and Scott	1955	20.00	40.00	80.00
CLARINET SUMMIT					
Alvin Batiste; JOHN CARTER; JIMMY HAMILTON; DAVID MURRAY.					
INDIA NAVIGATION					
❏ IN-1062	In Concert at the Public Theater, Vol. 1	1985	3.00	6.00	12.00
❏ IN-1067	In Concert at the Public Theater, Vol. 2	1985	3.00	6.00	12.00
CLARK, ALICE					
Female singer.					
MAINSTREAM					
❏ MRL-362	Alice Clark	1972	5.00	10.00	20.00
CLARK, DOTTIE					
Female singer.					
MAINSTREAM					
❏ S-6006 [S]	I'm Lost	1966	6.25	12.50	25.00
❏ 56006 [M]	I'm Lost	1966	5.00	10.00	20.00
CLARK, JOHN					
French horn player and occasional guitarist.					
ECM					
❏ 1176	Faces	1981	3.00	6.00	12.00
CLARK, SONNY					
Pianist and composer.					
BLUE NOTE					
❏ BLP-1570 [M]	Dial "S" for Sonny	1957	37.50	75.00	150.00
-- "Deep groove" version (deep indentation under label on both sides)					
❏ BLP-1570 [M]	Dial "S" for Sonny	1957	20.00	40.00	80.00
-- Regular version, W. 63rd St. address on label					
❏ BLP-1570 [M]	Dial "S" for Sonny	1963	6.25	12.50	25.00
-- "New York, USA" address on label					
❏ BST-1570 [S]	Dial "S" for Sonny	1959	25.00	50.00	100.00
-- "Deep groove" version (deep indentation under label on both sides)					
❏ BST-1570 [S]	Dial "S" for Sonny	1959	15.00	30.00	60.00
-- Regular version, W. 63rd St. address on label					
❏ BST-1570 [S]	Dial "S" for Sonny	1963	5.00	10.00	20.00
-- "New York, USA" address on label					
❏ BLP-1576 [M]	Sonny's Crib	1957	37.50	75.00	150.00
-- "Deep groove" version (deep indentation under label on both sides)					
❏ BLP-1576 [M]	Sonny's Crib	1957	20.00	40.00	80.00
-- Regular version, W. 63rd St. address on label					
❏ BLP-1576 [M]	Sonny's Crib	1963	6.25	12.50	25.00
-- "New York, USA" address on label					
❏ BST-1576 [S]	Sonny's Crib	1959	25.00	50.00	100.00
-- "Deep groove" version (deep indentation under label on both sides)					
❏ BST-1576 [S]	Sonny's Crib	1959	15.00	30.00	60.00
-- Regular version, W. 63rd St. address on label					
❏ BST-1576 [S]	Sonny's Crib	1963	5.00	10.00	20.00
-- "New York, USA" address on label					
❏ BLP-1579 [M]	Sonny Clark Trio	1958	37.50	75.00	150.00
-- "Deep groove" version (deep indentation under label on both sides)					
❏ BLP-1579 [M]	Sonny Clark Trio	1958	20.00	40.00	80.00
-- Regular version, W. 63rd St. address on label					
❏ BLP-1579 [M]	Sonny Clark Trio	1963	6.25	12.50	25.00
-- "New York, USA" address on label					
❏ BST-1579 [S]	Sonny Clark Trio	1959	25.00	50.00	100.0
-- "Deep groove" version (deep indentation under label on both sides)					
❏ BST-1579 [S]	Sonny Clark Trio	1959	15.00	30.00	60.00
-- Regular version, W. 63rd St. address on label					
❏ BST-1579 [S]	Sonny Clark Trio	1963	5.00	10.00	20.00
-- "New York, USA" address on label					
❏ BLP-1588 [M]	Cool Struttin'	1958	37.50	75.00	150.00
-- "Deep groove" version (deep indentation under label on both sides)					
❏ BLP-1588 [M]	Cool Struttin'	1958	20.00	40.00	80.00
-- Regular version, W. 63rd St. address on label					
❏ BLP-1588 [M]	Cool Struttin'	1963	6.25	12.50	25.00
-- "New York, USA" address on label					
❏ BST-1588 [S]	Cool Struttin'	1959	15.00	30.00	60.00
-- Regular version, W. 63rd St. address on label					
❏ BST-1588 [S]	Cool Struttin'	1959	25.00	50.00	100.00
-- "Deep groove" version (deep indentation under label on both sides)					
❏ BST-1588 [S]	Cool Struttin'	1963	5.00	10.00	20.00
-- "New York, USA" address on label					

Number	Title	Yr	VG	VG+	NM
❏ BLP-1592 [M]	Cool Struttin' -- Volume 2	1959	---	---	---
-- Canceled					
❏ BST-1592 [S]	Cool Struttin' -- Volume 2	1959	---	---	---
-- Canceled					
❏ BLP-4091 [M]	Leapin' and Lopin'	1961	15.00	30.00	60.00
-- 61st St. address on label					
❏ BLP-4091 [M]	Leapin' and Lopin'	1963	5.00	10.00	20.00
-- "New York, USA" address on label					
❏ BST-81570 [S]	Dial "S" for Sonny	1967	3.75	7.50	15.00
-- "A Division of Liberty Records" on label					
❏ BST-81576 [S]	Sonny's Crib	1967	3.75	7.50	15.00
-- "A Division of Liberty Records" on label					
❏ BST-81579 [S]	Sonny Clark Trio	1967	3.75	7.50	15.00
-- "A Division of Liberty Records" on label					
❏ BST-81588 [S]	Cool Struttin'	1967	3.75	7.50	15.00
-- "A Division of Liberty Records" on label					
❏ BST-81588 [S]	Cool Struttin'	1970	3.00	6.00	12.00
-- "Liberty/UA" on label					
❏ B1-81588	Cool Struttin'	1987	2.50	5.00	10.00
-- "The Finest in Jazz Since 1939" reissue					
❏ BST-84091 [S]	Leapin' and Lopin'	1961	20.00	40.00	80.00
-- 61st St. address on label					
❏ BST-84091 [S]	Leapin' and Lopin'	1963	6.25	12.50	25.00
-- "New York, USA" address on label					
❏ BST-84091 [S]	Leapin' and Lopin'	1967	3.75	7.50	15.00
-- "A Division of Liberty Records" on label					
TIME					
❏ S-2101 [S]	Sonny Clark Trio	1962	7.50	15.00	30.00
❏ 52101 [M]	Sonny Clark Trio	1962	6.25	12.50	25.00
❏ ST-70010 [S]	Sonny Clark Trio	1960	12.50	25.00	50.00
❏ T-70010 [M]	Sonny Clark Trio	1960	10.00	20.00	40.00
XANADU					
❏ 121	Memorial Album	197?	3.00	6.00	12.00
CLARK, SPENCER					
Bass saxophone player.					
AUDIOPHILE					
❏ 131	Spencer Clark and His Bass Sax Play Sweet & Hot	1978	3.00	6.00	12.00
CLARKE, BUCK					
Drummer, mostly on congas and bongos.					
ARGO					
❏ LP-4007 [M]	Drum Sum	1961	6.25	12.50	25.00
❏ LPS-4007 [S]	Drum Sum	1961	7.50	15.00	30.00
❏ LP-4021 [M]	The Buck Clarke Sound	1963	6.25	12.50	25.00
❏ LPS-4021 [S]	The Buck Clarke Sound	1963	7.50	15.00	30.00
OFFBEAT					
❏ OLP-3003 [M]	Cool Hands	1960	7.50	15.00	30.00
❏ OS-93003 [S]	Cool Hands	1960	10.00	20.00	40.00
CLARKE, KEN					
Pianist.					
MGM					
❏ E-205 [10]	Jazz Piano	1953	12.50	25.00	50.00
CLARKE, KENNY					
Drummer. An early member of THE MODERN JAZZ QUARTET. Also see THE CLARKE-BOLAND BIG BAND.					
EPIC					
❏ LN 3376 [M]	Kenny Clarke Plays Andre Hodeir	1957	10.00	20.00	40.00
PRESTIGE					
❏ PRST-7605	Paris Bebop Sessions	1969	3.75	7.50	15.00
SAVOY					
❏ MG-12006 [M]	Telefunken Blues	1955	15.00	30.00	60.00
❏ MG-12017 [M]	Bohemia After Dark	1955	15.00	30.00	60.00
❏ MG-12065 [M]	Klook's Clique	1956	15.00	30.00	60.00
❏ MG-15051 [10]	Kenny Clarke, Vol. 1	195?	37.50	75.00	150.00
❏ MG-15053 [10]	Kenny Clarke, Vol. 2	195?	37.50	75.00	150.00
SAVOY JAZZ					
❏ SJL-1111	Kenny Clarke Meets the Detroit Jazzmen	198?	2.50	5.00	10.00
SOUL NOTE					
❏ SN-1078	Pieces of Time	1983	3.00	6.00	12.00
SWING					
❏ SW-8411	Kenny Clarke in Paris Vol. 1	1986	2.50	5.00	10.00
CLARKE, KENNY, AND ERNIE WILKINS					
Also see each artist's individual listings.					
SAVOY					
❏ MG-12007 [M]	Plenty for Kenny	1955	15.00	30.00	60.00

Number	Title	Yr	VG	VG+	NM

CLARKE, STANLEY
Bassist. Also see RETURN TO FOREVER.
EPIC
❏ JE 36506	Rocks, Pebbles and Sand	1980	2.50	5.00	10.00
❏ PE 36973	Stanley Clarke	1981	2.00	4.00	8.00
-- Reissue of Nemperor 431					
❏ PE 36974	Journey to Love	1981	2.00	4.00	8.00
-- Reissue of Nemperor 433					
❏ PE 36975	School Days	1981	2.00	4.00	8.00
-- Reissue of Nemperor 900					
❏ FE 38386	Let Me Know You	1982	2.50	5.00	10.00
❏ FE 38688	Time Exposure	1984	2.50	5.00	10.00
❏ FE 40040	Find Out!	1985	2.50	5.00	10.00
❏ FE 40275	Hideaway	1986	2.50	5.00	10.00
NEMPEROR
❏ SD 431	Stanley Clarke	1974	3.00	6.00	12.00
❏ SD 433	Journey to Love	1975	3.00	6.00	12.00
❏ SD 439	School Days	1976	3.00	6.00	12.00
❏ SD 900	School Days	1978	2.50	5.00	10.00
-- Reissue of 439					
❏ JZ 35303	Modern Man	1978	2.50	5.00	10.00
❏ PZ 35305	Modern Man	1985	2.00	4.00	8.00
-- Reissue with new prefix					
❏ KZ2 35680 [(2)]	I Wanna Play for You	1979	3.00	6.00	12.00
POLYDOR
❏ PD-5531	Children of Forever	1973	3.00	6.00	12.00
❏ 827 559-1	Children of Forever	1985	2.00	4.00	8.00
-- Reissue					
PORTRAIT
❏ OR 40923	If This Bass Could Only Talk	1988	2.50	5.00	10.00

CLARKE, STANLEY, AND GEORGE DUKE
Also see each artist's individual listings.
EPIC
❏ FE 36918	The Clarke/Duke Project	1981	2.50	5.00	10.00
❏ PE 36918	The Clarke/Duke Project	198?	2.00	4.00	8.00
-- Budget-line reissue					
❏ FE 38934	The Clarke/Duke Project II	1983	2.50	5.00	10.00

CLARKE-BOLAND BIG BAND, THE
KENNY CLARKE and Francy Boland (pianist).
ATLANTIC
❏ 1401 [M]	Jazz Is Universal	1963	7.50	15.00	30.00
❏ SD 1401 [S]	Jazz Is Universal	1963	10.00	20.00	40.00
❏ 1404 [M]	The Clarke-Boland Big Band	1963	7.50	15.00	30.00
❏ SD 1404 [S]	The Clarke-Boland Big Band	1963	10.00	20.00	40.00
BASF
❏ 25102 [(2)]	The Big Band Sound	1971	5.00	10.00	20.00
❏ 29686	All Smiles	1972	3.75	7.50	15.00
BLACK LION
❏ 131	At Her Majesty's Pleasure	1974	3.75	7.50	15.00
BLUE NOTE
❏ BLP-4092 [M]	The Golden Eight	1961	12.50	25.00	50.00
-- 61st St. address on label					
❏ BLP-4092 [M]	The Golden Eight	1963	6.25	12.50	25.00
-- "New York, USA" address on label					
❏ BST-84092 [S]	The Golden Eight	1961	12.50	25.00	50.00
-- 61st St. address on label					
❏ BST-84092 [S]	The Golden Eight	1963	5.00	10.00	20.00
-- "New York, USA" address on label					
❏ BST-84092 [S]	The Golden Eight	1967	3.75	7.50	15.00
-- "A Division of Liberty Records" on label					
COLUMBIA
❏ CL 2314 [M]	Now Hear Our Meanin'	1965	3.75	7.50	15.00
❏ CS 9114 [S]	Now Hear Our Meanin'	1965	5.00	10.00	20.00
MUSE
❏ MR-5056	Open Door	197?	3.00	6.00	12.00
PAUSA
❏ 7097	Sax No End	198?	2.50	5.00	10.00
POLYDOR
❏ 24-4501	Volcano	1970	3.75	7.50	15.00
PRESTIGE
❏ PRST-7634	Fire, Heat, Soul and Guts	1969	3.75	7.50	15.00
❏ PRST-7699	Let's Face the Music	1969	3.75	7.50	15.00
❏ PRST-7760	Latin Kaleidoscope	1970	3.75	7.50	15.00

CLASSIC JAZZ ENSEMBLE
With Armin Von der Heydt (clarinet), Steve Jensen (trumpet, cornet) and others.
DELMARK
❏ DE-221	Classic Blues	1989	2.50	5.00	10.00

CLASSIC JAZZ QUARTET, THE
Dick Sudhalter (cornet); Joe Muranyi (clarinet and alto sax); Dick Wellstood (piano); Marty Grotz (guitar, vocals).
JAZZOLOGY
❏ J-139	The Classic Jazz Quartet	1985	2.50	5.00	10.00
STOMP OFF
❏ SOS-1125	MCMLXXXVI	1986	2.50	5.00	10.00

CLAY, JAMES
Flutist and tenor saxophone player.
RIVERSIDE
❏ RLP-349 [M]	A Double Dose of Soul	1961	7.50	15.00	30.00
-- Blue label					
❏ RS-9349 [S]	A Double Dose of Soul	1961	10.00	20.00	40.00
-- Black label					

CLAY, JAMES, AND DAVID "FATHEAD" NEWMAN
Also see each artist's individual listings.
FANTASY
❏ OJC-257	The Sound of the Wide Open Spaces!!!	1987	2.50	5.00	10.00
RIVERSIDE
❏ RLP 12-327 [M]	The Sound of the Wide Open Spaces!!!	1960	7.50	15.00	30.00
-- Blue label					
❏ RLP-1178 [S]	The Sound of the Wide Open Spaces!!!	1960	10.00	20.00	40.00
-- Black label					

CLAYTON BROTHERS, THE
Jeff Clayton (saxophone, flute) and John Clayton (bass).
CONCORD JAZZ
❏ CJ-89	The Clayton Brothers	1978	2.50	5.00	10.00
❏ CJ-138	It's All in the Family	1980	2.50	5.00	10.00

CLAYTON, BUCK
Trumpeter.
ALLEGRO ELITE
❏ 4121	Buck Clayton All Stars	195?	10.00	20.00	40.00
CHIAROSCURO
❏ 132	A Buck Clayton Jam Session	1974	3.00	6.00	12.00
❏ 143	A Buck Clayton Jam Session, Vol. II	1975	3.00	6.00	12.00
❏ 152	A Buck Clayton Jam Session, Vol. III: Jazz Party Time	1976	3.00	6.00	12.00
❏ 163	A Buck Clayton Jam Session, Vol. IV: Jay Hawk	1977	3.00	6.00	12.00
COLUMBIA
❏ CL 548 [M]	The Huckle-Buck and Robbins' Nest: A Jam Session	1954	12.50	25.00	50.00
-- Maroon label, gold print					
❏ CL 548 [M]	The Huckle-Buck and Robbins' Nest: A Jam Session	1955	7.50	15.00	30.00
-- Red and black label with six "eye" logos					
❏ CL 567 [M]	How Hi the Fi: A Jam Session	1954	12.50	25.00	50.00
-- Maroon label, gold print					
❏ CL 567 [M]	How Hi the Fi: A Jam Session	1955	7.50	15.00	30.00
-- Red and black label with six "eye" logos					
❏ CL 614 [M]	Buck Clayton Jams Benny Goodman	1955	12.50	25.00	50.00
-- Maroon label, gold print					
❏ CL 614 [M]	Buck Clayton Jams Benny Goodman	1955	7.50	15.00	30.00
-- Red and black label with six "eye" logos					
❏ CL 701 [M]	Jumpin' at the Woodside	1955	10.00	20.00	40.00
-- Red and black label with six "eye" logos					
❏ CL 808 [M]	Jazz Spectacular	1956	10.00	20.00	40.00
-- Red and black label with six "eye" logos					
❏ CL 882 [M]	All the Cats Join In	1956	10.00	20.00	40.00
-- Red and black label with six "eye" logos					
❏ CL 1320 [M]	Songs for Swingers	1959	6.25	12.50	25.00
-- Red and black label with six "eye" logos					
❏ CL 6325 [10]	Moten Swing -- Sentimental Journey	1954	15.00	30.00	60.00
❏ CL 6326 [10]	How Hi the Fi: A Jam Session	1954	15.00	30.00	60.00
❏ CS 8123 [S]	Songs for Swingers	1959	7.50	15.00	30.00
-- Red and black label with six "eye" logos					
COLUMBIA JAZZ MASTERPIECES
❏ CJ 44291	Jam Sessions from the Vaults	1988	3.00	6.00	12.00
FANTASY
❏ OJC-1709	The Classic Swing of Buck Clayton	1985	3.00	6.00	12.00
INNER CITY
❏ 7009	Passport to Paradise	1980	2.50	5.00	10.00

Number	Title	Yr	VG	VG+	NM
JAZZTONE					
❏ J-1225 [M]	Meet Buck Clayton	1956	10.00	20.00	40.00
STASH					
❏ ST-281	A Swingin' Dream	1989	3.00	6.00	12.00
STEEPLECHASE					
❏ SCC-6006/7 [(2)]	Copenhagen Concert	198?	3.75	7.50	15.00
VANGUARD					
❏ 103/104 [(2)]	Essential Buck Clayton	197?	3.75	7.50	15.00

CLAYTON, BUCK; RUBY BRAFF; MEL POWELL
Also see each artist's individual listings.

Number	Title	Yr	VG	VG+	NM
VANGUARD					
❏ VRS-8008 [10]	Buck Meets Ruby	1954	12.50	25.00	50.00
❏ VRS-8514 [M]	Buckin' the Blues	1957	10.00	20.00	40.00
❏ VRS-8517 [M]	Buck Meets Ruby and Mel	1957	10.00	20.00	40.00

CLAYTON, BUCK/WILD BILL DAVISON
Also see each artist's individual listings.

Number	Title	Yr	VG	VG+	NM
JAZZTONE					
❏ J-1267 [M]	Singing Trumpets	1957	10.00	20.00	40.00

CLAYTON, BUCK, AND BUDDY TATE
Also see each artist's individual listings.

Number	Title	Yr	VG	VG+	NM
PRESTIGE					
❏ 24040 [(2)]	Kansas City Nights	1974	3.75	7.50	15.00
SWINGVILLE					
❏ SVLP-2017 [M]	Buck and Buddy	1961	12.50	25.00	50.00
-- Purple label					
❏ SVLP-2017 [M]	Buck and Buddy	1965	6.25	12.50	25.00
-- Blue label, trident logo at right					
❏ SVLP-2030 [M]	Buck and Buddy Blow the Blues	1962	10.00	20.00	40.00
-- Purple label					
❏ SVLP-2030 [M]	Buck and Buddy Blow the Blues	1965	5.00	10.00	20.00
-- Blue label, trident logo at right					
❏ SVST-2030 [S]	Buck and Buddy Blow the Blues	1962	12.50	25.00	50.00
-- Red label					
❏ SVST-2030 [S]	Buck and Buddy Blow the Blues	1965	6.25	12.50	25.00
-- Blue label, trident logo at right					

CLAYTON, KID
Trumpeter.

Number	Title	Yr	VG	VG+	NM
FOLKWAYS					
❏ FJ-2859	The First Kid Clayton Session (1952)	1983	3.00	6.00	12.00
JAZZOLOGY					
❏ JCE-22	Exit Stares	1967	3.00	6.00	12.00

CLAYTON, STEVE

Number	Title	Yr	VG	VG+	NM
SOVEREIGN					
❏ SOV-500	Inner Spark	1985	2.50	5.00	10.00
❏ SOV-501	All Aglow Again	1986	2.50	5.00	10.00

CLEVELAND, JIMMY
Trombone player. Also see SONNY ROLLINS.

Number	Title	Yr	VG	VG+	NM
EMARCY					
❏ MG-26003 [M]	Rhythm Crazy	1964	6.25	12.50	25.00
❏ MG-36066 [M]	Introducing Jimmy Cleveland and His All Stars	1956	12.50	25.00	50.00
❏ MG-36126 [M]	Cleveland Style	1958	12.50	25.00	50.00
MERCURY					
❏ MG-20442 [M]	A Map of Jimmy Cleveland	1959	10.00	20.00	40.00
❏ MG-20553 [M]	Cleveland Style	1960	10.00	20.00	40.00
❏ SR-60117 [S]	A Map of Jimmy Cleveland	1959	7.50	15.00	30.00
❏ SR-60121 [S]	Cleveland Style	1959	7.50	15.00	30.00

CLIFTON, BILL
Pianist.

Number	Title	Yr	VG	VG+	NM
COLUMBIA					
❏ CL 6166 [10]	Piano Moods	1951	12.50	25.00	50.00

CLINTON, LARRY
Bandleader, composer and arranger.

Number	Title	Yr	VG	VG+	NM
CIRCLE					
❏ 58	Larry Clinton and His Orchestra 1941 and 1949	198?	2.50	5.00	10.00
EVEREST					
❏ SDBR-1096 [S]	My Million Sellers	196?	6.25	12.50	25.00
❏ LPBR-5096 [M]	My Million Sellers	196?	5.00	10.00	20.00
HINDSIGHT					
❏ HSR-109	Larry Clinton and His Orchestra 1937-38	198?	2.50	5.00	10.00

Number	Title	Yr	VG	VG+	NM
RCA CAMDEN					
❏ CAL-434 [M]	Dance Date	1958	5.00	10.00	20.00
SUNBEAM					
❏ 208	Larry Clinton and His Orchestra 1937-41	198?	2.50	5.00	10.00

CLOONEY, ROSEMARY
Female singer. More pop-oriented on her Columbia recordings, after a retirement she started a second successful career as a jazz singer on the Concord Jazz label.

Number	Title	Yr	VG	VG+	NM
COLUMBIA					
❏ CL 585 [M]	Hollywood's Best	1955	12.50	25.00	50.00
❏ CL 872 [M]	Blue Rose	1956	10.00	20.00	40.00
❏ CL 969 [M]	Clooney Tunes	1957	20.00	40.00	80.00
❏ CL 1006 [M]	Ring Around the Rosie	1957	10.00	20.00	40.00
-- With the Hi-Lo's					
❏ CL 1230 [M]	Rosie's Greatest Hits	1958	10.00	20.00	40.00
-- Six "eye" logos on label					
❏ CL 1230 [M]	Rosie's Greatest Hits	1962	6.25	12.50	25.00
-- "Guaranteed High Fidelity" on label					
❏ CL 1230 [M]	Rosie's Greatest Hits	1965	3.75	7.50	15.00
-- "360 Sound Mono" on label					
❏ CL 2525 [10]	Tenderly	1955	12.50	25.00	50.00
❏ CL 2569 [10]	Children's Favorites	1955	12.50	25.00	50.00
❏ CL 2572 [10]	A Date with the King	1956	12.50	25.00	50.00
❏ CL 2581 [10]	On Stage	1956	12.50	25.00	50.00
❏ CL 2597 [10]	My Fair Lady	1956	12.50	25.00	50.00
❏ CL 6224 [10]	Hollywood's Best	1952	15.00	30.00	60.00
❏ CL 6297 [10]	Rosemary Clooney (While We're Young)	1954	15.00	30.00	60.00
❏ CL 6338 [10]	White Christmas	1954	15.00	30.00	60.00
COLUMBIA SPECIAL PRODUCTS					
❏ P 13083	Hollywood's Best	197?	3.00	6.00	12.00
❏ P 13085	Blue Rose	197?	3.00	6.00	12.00
❏ P 14382	Come On-a My House	197?	3.00	6.00	12.00
CONCORD JAZZ					
❏ CJ-47	Everything's Coming Up Rosie	1978	3.00	6.00	12.00
❏ CJ-60	Rosie Sings Bing	1979	3.00	6.00	12.00
❏ CJ-81	Here's to My Lady	1979	3.00	6.00	12.00
❏ CJ-112	Rosemary Clooney Sings Ira Gershwin	1980	3.00	6.00	12.00
❏ CJ-144	With Love	1981	3.00	6.00	12.00
❏ CJ-185	Rosemary Clooney Sings Cole Porter	1982	3.00	6.00	12.00
❏ CJ-210	Rosemary Clooney Sings Harold Arlen	1983	3.00	6.00	12.00
❏ CJ-226	My Buddy	1984	3.00	6.00	12.00
-- With Woody Herman					
❏ CJ-255	Rosemary Clooney Sings the Music of Irving Berlin	1985	3.00	6.00	12.00
❏ CJ-282	Rosemary Clooney Sings Ballads	1985	3.00	6.00	12.00
❏ CJ-308	Rosemary Clooney Sings the Music of Jimmy Van Heusen	1987	3.00	6.00	12.00
❏ CJ-333	Rosemary Clooney Sings the Lyrics of Johnny Mercer	1988	3.00	6.00	12.00
❏ CJ-364	Show Tunes	1989	3.00	6.00	12.00
CORAL					
❏ CRL 57266 [M]	Swing Around Rosie	1959	7.50	15.00	30.00
❏ CRL 757266 [S]	Swing Around Rosie	1959	10.00	20.00	40.00
HARMONY					
❏ HL 7123 [M]	Rosemary Clooney in High Fidelity	195?	6.25	12.50	25.00
❏ HL 7213 [M]	Hollywood Hits	195?	6.25	12.50	25.00
❏ HL 7454 [M]	Mixed Emotions	1968	5.00	10.00	20.00
❏ HL 9501 [M]	Rosemary Clooney Sings for Children	196?	5.00	10.00	20.00
❏ HS 11254 [R]	Mixed Emotions	1968	3.00	6.00	12.00
HINDSIGHT					
❏ HSR-234	Rosemary Clooney 1951-1952	1988	2.50	5.00	10.00
HOLIDAY					
❏ 1946	Christmas with Rosemary Clooney	1981	2.50	5.00	10.00
MGM					
❏ E-3687 [M]	Oh, Captain!	1958	10.00	20.00	40.00
❏ E-3782 [M]	Hymns from the Heart	1959	7.50	15.00	30.00
❏ SE-3782 [S]	Hymns from the Heart	1959	10.00	20.00	40.00
❏ E-3834 [M]	Rosie Clooney Swings Softly	1960	7.50	15.00	30.00
❏ SE-3834 [S]	Rosie Clooney Swings Softly	1960	10.00	20.00	40.00
RCA VICTOR					
❏ LPM-2133 [M]	A Touch of Tabasco	1960	5.00	10.00	20.00
❏ LSP-2133 [S]	A Touch of Tabasco	1960	7.50	15.00	30.00
❏ LPM-2212 [M]	Clap Hands, Here Comes Rosie	1960	5.00	10.00	20.00
❏ LSP-2212 [S]	Clap Hands, Here Comes Rosie	1960	7.50	15.00	30.00
❏ LPM-2265 [M]	Rosie Solves the Swingin' Riddle	1961	5.00	10.00	20.00
❏ LSP-2265 [S]	Rosie Solves the Swingin' Riddle	1961	7.50	15.00	30.00

Number	Title	Yr	VG	VG+	NM
❏ LPM-2565 [M]	Country Hits from the Heart	1963	5.00	10.00	20.00
❏ LSP-2565 [S]	Country Hits from the Heart	1963	7.50	15.00	30.00
REPRISE					
❏ R-6088 [M]	Love	1963	7.50	15.00	30.00
❏ R9-6088 [S]	Love	1963	10.00	20.00	40.00
❏ R-6108 [M]	Thanks for Nothing	1964	7.50	15.00	30.00
❏ RS-6108 [S]	Thanks for Nothing	1964	10.00	20.00	40.00

CLOONEY, ROSEMARY, AND BING CROSBY
Also see each artist's individual listings.

CAPITOL					
❏ ST 2300 [S]	That Travelin' Two-Beat	1965	7.50	15.00	30.00
❏ T 2300 [M]	That Travelin' Two-Beat	1965	5.00	10.00	20.00
RCA CAMDEN					
❏ CAS-2330	Rendezvous	1968	3.75	7.50	15.00
RCA VICTOR					
❏ LPM-1854 [M]	Fancy Meeting You Here	1958	5.00	10.00	20.00
❏ LSP-1854 [S]	Fancy Meeting You Here	1958	7.50	15.00	30.00

COATES, JOHN, JR.
Pianist.

OMNISOUND					
❏ 1004	The Jazz Piano of John Coates, Jr.	197?	3.00	6.00	12.00
❏ 1015	Alone and Live at the Deer Head	1977	3.00	6.00	12.00
❏ 1021	After the Before	1978	3.00	6.00	12.00
❏ 1022 [(2)]	In the Open Space	1979	3.75	7.50	15.00
❏ 1024	Rainbow Road	1979	3.00	6.00	12.00
❏ 1032	Tokyo Concert	1980	3.00	6.00	12.00
❏ 1038 [(2)]	Pocono Friends	1981	3.75	7.50	15.00
❏ 1045	Pocono Friends Encore	1982	3.00	6.00	12.00
SAVOY					
❏ MG-12082 [M]	Portrait	1956	10.00	20.00	40.00

COBB, ARNETT
Tenor saxophone player.

APOLLO					
❏ LAP-105 [10]	Swingin' with Arnett Cobb	1952	62.50	125.00	250.00
BEE HIVE					
❏ BH-7017	Keep On Pushin'	1985	3.00	6.00	12.00
CLASSIC JAZZ					
❏ 102	The Wild Man from Texas	1976	3.75	7.50	15.00
FANTASY					
❏ OJC-219	Party Time	198?	2.50	5.00	10.00
❏ OJC-323	Smooth Sailing	1988	2.50	5.00	10.00
HOME COOKING					
❏ HCS-114	The Wild Man from Texas	1990	3.00	6.00	12.00
-- Reissue of Classic Jazz 102					
MOODSVILLE					
❏ MVLP-14 [M]	Ballads by Cobb	1961	12.50	25.00	50.00
-- Green label					
❏ MVLP-14 [M]	Ballads by Cobb	1965	6.25	12.50	25.00
-- Blue label, trident logo at right					
MUSE					
❏ MR-5191	Live at Sandy's	1977	3.00	6.00	12.00
❏ MR-5236	More Live at Sandy's	1979	3.00	6.00	12.00
PRESTIGE					
❏ PRLP-7151 [M]	Blow, Arnett, Blow	1959	12.50	25.00	50.00
-- Yellow label					
❏ PRLP-7151 [M]	Blow, Arnett, Blow	1963	6.25	12.50	25.00
-- Blue label, trident logo at right					
❏ PRST-7151 [R]	Blow, Arnett, Blow	196?	3.00	6.00	12.00
❏ PRLP-7165 [M]	Party Time	1959	12.50	25.00	50.00
-- Yellow label					
❏ PRLP-7165 [M]	Party Time	1963	6.25	12.50	25.00
-- Blue label, trident logo at right					
❏ PRLP-7175 [M]	More Party Time	1960	12.50	25.00	50.00
-- Yellow label					
❏ PRLP-7175 [M]	More Party Time	1963	6.25	12.50	25.00
-- Blue label, trident logo at right					
❏ PRLP-7184 [M]	Smooth Sailing	1960	12.50	25.00	50.00
-- Yellow label					
❏ PRLP-7184 [M]	Smooth Sailing	1963	6.25	12.50	25.00
-- Blue label, trident logo at right					
❏ PRLP-7216 [M]	Movin' Right Along	1961	12.50	25.00	50.00
-- Yellow label					
❏ PRLP-7216 [M]	Movin' Right Along	1963	6.25	12.50	25.00
-- Blue label, trident logo at right					
❏ PRLP-7227 [M]	Sizzlin'	1962	10.00	20.00	40.00
-- Yellow label					
❏ PRLP-7227 [M]	Sizzlin'	1963	5.00	10.00	20.00
-- Blue label, trident logo at right					
❏ PRST-7227 [S]	Sizzlin'	1962	12.50	25.00	50.00
-- Silver label					

Number	Title	Yr	VG	VG+	NM
❏ PRST-7227 [S]	Sizzlin'	1963	6.25	12.50	25.00
-- Blue label, trident logo at right					
❏ PRST-7711	The Best of Arnett Cobb	1969	3.75	7.50	15.00
❏ PRST-7835	Go Power!	1970	3.75	7.50	15.00
PROGRESSIVE					
❏ 7037	Arnett Cobb Is Back!	1978	3.00	6.00	12.00
❏ 7054	Funky Butt	1981	3.00	6.00	12.00

COBB, ARNETT; DIZZY GILLESPIE; JEWEL BROWN
Brown is a pianist and female singer. Also see ARNETT COBB; DIZZY GILLESPIE.

FANTASY					
❏ F-9659	Show Time	1987	3.00	6.00	12.00

COBB, JUNIE C.
Pianist. On other recordings, he played clarinet, alto saxophone and tenor sax.

RIVERSIDE					
❏ RLP-415 [M]	Junie C. Cobb and His New Hometown Band	1962	5.00	10.00	20.00
❏ RS-9415 [S]	Junie C. Cobb and His New Hometown Band	1962	6.25	12.50	25.00

COBHAM, BILLY
Drummer. Also see MAHAVISHNU ORCHESTRA.

ATLANTIC					
❏ SD 7268	Spectrum	1973	3.75	7.50	15.00
❏ SD 7300	Crosswinds	1974	3.00	6.00	12.00
❏ SD 18121	Total Eclipse	1974	3.00	6.00	12.00
❏ SD 18139	Shabazz (Recorded Live in Europe)	1975	3.00	6.00	12.00
❏ SD 18149	A Funky Thide of Sings	1975	2.50	5.00	10.00
❏ SD 18166	Life & Times	1976	2.50	5.00	10.00
❏ SD 19174	Inner Conflicts	1978	2.50	5.00	10.00
❏ SD 19238	The Best of Billy Cobham	1979	2.50	5.00	10.00
COLUMBIA					
❏ JC 34939	Magic	1977	2.50	5.00	10.00
❏ JC 35457	Simplicity of Expression -- Depth of Thought	1978	2.50	5.00	10.00
❏ JC 35993	B.C.	1979	2.50	5.00	10.00
❏ JC 36400	The Best of Billy Cobham	1980	2.50	5.00	10.00
ELEKTRA MUSICIAN					
❏ 60123	Observations &	1982	2.50	5.00	10.00
GRP					
❏ GR-1020	Warning	1986	2.50	5.00	10.00
❏ GR-1027	Power Play	1986	2.50	5.00	10.00
❏ GR-1040	Picture This	1987	2.50	5.00	10.00
❏ GR-9575	Billy's Best Hits	1988	2.50	5.00	10.00

COBHAM, BILLY, AND GEORGE DUKE
Also see each artist's individual listings.

ATLANTIC					
❏ SD 18194	Live On Tour in Europe	1976	2.50	5.00	10.00

COCHRAN, CHARLES
Male singer.

AUDIOPHILE					
❏ AP-177	Haunted Heart	1982	3.00	6.00	12.00

COCHRAN, TODD
Pianist and keyboard player.

VITAL					
❏ VTL-001 [(2)]	Todd	1991	5.00	10.00	20.00

COCHRANE, MICHAEL
Pianist.

SOUL NOTE					
❏ SN-1151	Elements	198?	3.00	6.00	12.00

CODONA
Trio whose name comes from the first two letters of each participant -- COLLIN WALCOTT; DON CHERRY; NANA VASCONCELOS.

ECM					
❏ 1132	Codona	1979	3.00	6.00	12.00
❏ 1177	Codona 2	1980	3.00	6.00	12.00
❏ 23785	Codona 3	1983	3.00	6.00	12.00

COE, JIMMY
Baritone, alto and tenor saxophone player and bandleader.

DELMARK					
❏ DL-443	After Hours Joint	1989	2.50	5.00	10.00

Number	Title	Yr	VG	VG+	NM

COHN, AL
Tenor saxophone player and arranger. Also see BOOTS BROWN; CANDIDO; THE FOUR BROTHERS; THE FOUR MOST; ZOOT SIMS.
BIOGRAPH
| ❏ 12063 | Be Loose | 197? | 2.50 | 5.00 | 10.00 |
CONCORD JAZZ
❏ CJ-155	Nonpareil	1981	2.50	5.00	10.00
❏ CJ-194	Overtures	1982	2.50	5.00	10.00
❏ CJ-241	Standards of Excellence	1983	2.50	5.00	10.00
CORAL
| ❏ CRL 57118 [M] | Al Cohn Quintet | 1957 | 12.50 | 25.00 | 50.00 |
DAWN
| ❏ DLP-1110 [M] | Cohn on the Saxophone | 1956 | 30.00 | 60.00 | 120.00 |
PRESTIGE
| ❏ PRST-7819 | Broadway 1954 | 1970 | 3.00 | 6.00 | 12.00 |
PROGRESSIVE
| ❏ PLP-3002 [10] | Al Cohn Quartet | 1953 | 75.00 | 150.00 | 300.00 |
| ❏ PLP-3004 [10] | Al Cohn Quintet | 1953 | 75.00 | 150.00 | 300.00 |
RCA VICTOR
❏ LJM-1024 [M]	Mr. Music	1955	20.00	40.00	80.00
❏ LPM-1116 [M]	The Natural Seven	1955	20.00	40.00	80.00
❏ LPM-1161 [M]	Four Brass, One Tenor	1956	20.00	40.00	80.00
❏ LPM-1207 [M]	That Old Feeling	1956	20.00	40.00	80.00
❏ LPM-2312 [M]	Son of Drum Suite	1960	10.00	20.00	40.00
❏ LSP-2312 [S]	Son of Drum Suite	1960	12.50	25.00	50.00
SAVOY
| ❏ MG-12048 [M] | Cohn's Tones | 1956 | 20.00 | 40.00 | 80.00 |
SAVOY JAZZ
| ❏ SJL-1126 | The Progressive | 197? | 2.50 | 5.00 | 10.00 |
TIMELESS
| ❏ LPSJP-259 | Rifftide | 1990 | 3.00 | 6.00 | 12.00 |
XANADU
❏ 110	Play It Now	1975	2.50	5.00	10.00
❏ 138	America	1976	2.50	5.00	10.00
❏ 179	No Problem	1979	2.50	5.00	10.00

COHN, AL; SCOTT HAMILTON; BUDDY TATE
Also see each artist's individual listings.
CONCORD JAZZ
| ❏ CJ-172 | Tour de Force | 198? | 2.50 | 5.00 | 10.00 |

COHN, AL; RICH KAMUCA; BILL PERKINS
Also see each artist's individual listings.
RCA VICTOR
| ❏ LPM-1162 [M] | The Brothers | 1955 | 20.00 | 40.00 | 80.00 |

COHN, AL, AND BILLY MITCHELL
Also see each artist's individual listings.
XANADU
| ❏ 180 | Xanadu in Africa | 1979 | 2.50 | 5.00 | 10.00 |
| ❏ 185 | Night Flight to Dakar | 1980 | 2.50 | 5.00 | 10.00 |

COHN, AL/SHORTY ROGERS
Also see each artist's individual listings.
RCA VICTOR
| ❏ LJM-1020 [M] | East Coast -- West Coast Scene | 1954 | 37.50 | 75.00 | 150.00 |

COHN, AL, AND JIMMY ROWLES
Also see each artist's individual listings.
XANADU
| ❏ 145 | Heavy Love | 1978 | 2.50 | 5.00 | 10.00 |

COHN, AL, AND ZOOT SIMS
Also see each artist's individual listings.
ABUNDANT SOUNDS
| ❏ 1 [M] | Either Way | 1960 | 25.00 | 50.00 | 100.00 |
CORAL
| ❏ CRL 57171 [M] | Al and Zoot | 1958 | 12.50 | 25.00 | 50.00 |
MERCURY
| ❏ MG-20606 [M] | You 'n Me | 1960 | 7.50 | 15.00 | 30.00 |
| ❏ SR-60606 [S] | You 'n Me | 1960 | 10.00 | 20.00 | 40.00 |
MUSE
❏ MR-5016	Body and Soul	1974	3.75	7.50	15.00
❏ MR-5356	Body and Soul	1988	2.50	5.00	10.00
-- Reissue of 5016					
RCA VICTOR
| ❏ LPM-1282 [M] | From A to Z | 1956 | 20.00 | 40.00 | 80.00 |
SONET
| ❏ 684 | Motoring Along | 197? | 3.00 | 6.00 | 12.00 |

TRIP
| ❏ 5548 | You 'n Me | 197? | 2.50 | 5.00 | 10.00 |
ZIM
| ❏ 2002 | Either Way | 197? | 3.00 | 6.00 | 12.00 |

COHN, STEVE
Pianist.
CADENCE JAZZ
| ❏ CJ-1020 | Shapes Sounds Theories | 198? | 2.00 | 4.00 | 8.00 |

COIL, PAT
Pianist, composer and arranger.
SHEFFIELD LABS
❏ TLP-31 [(2)]	Steps	1991	10.00	20.00	40.00
-- Audiophile vinyl					
❏ TLP-34	Just Ahead	1993	6.25	12.50	25.00
-- Audiophile vinyl					

COKER, DOLO
Pianist.
XANADU
❏ 139	Dolo!	1976	2.50	5.00	10.00
❏ 142	California Hard	1976	2.50	5.00	10.00
❏ 153	Third Down	1977	2.50	5.00	10.00
❏ 178	All Alone	1979	2.50	5.00	10.00

COKER, JERRY
Tenor saxophone player and arranger.
FANTASY
❏ 3214 [M]	Modern Music from Indiana University	1956	15.00	30.00	60.00
-- Red vinyl					
❏ 3214 [M]	Modern Music from Indiana University	1957	10.00	20.00	40.00
-- Black vinyl					
REVELATION
| ❏ 45 | A Re-Emergence | 1983 | 3.00 | 6.00 | 12.00 |
| ❏ 47 | Rebirth | 1984 | 3.00 | 6.00 | 12.00 |

COLA, GEORGE "KID SHEIK"
Trumpeter and male singer.
GHB
❏ GHB-187	Kid Sheik in England	1986	2.50	5.00	10.00
❏ GHB-47	Kid Sheik Plays Blues and Standards	197?	2.50	5.00	10.00
❏ GHB-76	Stompers	197?	2.50	5.00	10.00
JAZZOLOGY
| ❏ JCE-31 | Kid Sheik and Sheik's Swingers | 1967 | 3.00 | 6.00 | 12.00 |

COLBY, MARK
Tenor and soprano saxophone player.
COLUMBIA
| ❏ JC 35298 | Serpentine Fire | 1978 | 2.50 | 5.00 | 10.00 |
| ❏ JC 35725 | One Good Turn | 1979 | 2.50 | 5.00 | 10.00 |

COLD SWEAT
Craig Harris, David Murray, George Adams and Arthur Blythe are in this group.
JMT
| ❏ 834 426-1 | Cold Sweat Plays J.B. | 1989 | 3.75 | 7.50 | 15.00 |

COLE, COZY
Drummer. Had an unexpected pop hit in 1958 with the instrumental "Topsy II."
AUDITION
| ❏ 33-5943 [M] | Cozy Cole | 1955 | 12.50 | 25.00 | 50.00 |
BETHLEHEM
| ❏ BCP-21 [M] | Jazz at the Metropole Café | 1955 | 12.50 | 25.00 | 50.00 |
CHARLIE PARKER
| ❏ PLP-403 [M] | A Cozy Conaption of Carmen | 1962 | 5.00 | 10.00 | 20.00 |
| ❏ PLP-403S [S] | A Cozy Conaption of Carmen | 1962 | 6.25 | 12.50 | 25.00 |
COLUMBIA
| ❏ CL 2553 [M] | It's a Rockin' Thing | 1965 | 3.75 | 7.50 | 15.00 |
| ❏ CS 9353 [S] | It's a Rockin' Thing | 1965 | 5.00 | 10.00 | 20.00 |
CORAL
❏ CRL 57423 [M]	Drum Beat Dancing Feet	1962	3.75	7.50	15.00
❏ CRL 57457 [M]	It's a Cozy World	1964	3.75	7.50	15.00
❏ CRL 757423 [S]	Drum Beat Dancing Feet	1962	5.00	10.00	20.00
❏ CRL 757457 [S]	It's a Cozy World	1964	5.00	10.00	20.00
FELSTED
| ❏ 2002 [S] | Cozy's Caravan/Earl's Backroom | 1958 | 10.00 | 20.00 | 40.00 |
| ❏ 7002 [M] | Cozy's Caravan/Earl's Backroom | 1958 | 12.50 | 25.00 | 50.00 |

Number	Title	Yr	VG	VG+	NM
GRAND AWARD					
❑ GA 33-334 [M]	After Hours	1956	10.00	20.00	40.00
KING					
❑ 673 [M]	Cozy Cole	1959	15.00	30.00	60.00
LOVE					
❑ 500M [M]	Topsy	1959	25.00	50.00	100.00
❑ 500S [S]	Topsy	1959	50.00	100.00	200.00
PARIS					
❑ 122 [M]	Cozy Cole and His All-Stars	1958	12.50	25.00	50.00
PLYMOUTH					
❑ P 12-155 [M]	Cozy Cole and His All-Stars	195?	7.50	15.00	30.00
SAVOY					
❑ MG-12197 [M]	Concerto for Cozy	196?	5.00	10.00	20.00
WHO'S WHO IN JAZZ					
❑ 21003	Lionel Hampton Presents Cozy Cole & Marty Napoleon	1977	2.50	5.00	10.00

COLE, COZY/JIMMY McPARTLAND
Also see each artist's individual listings.

Number	Title	Yr	VG	VG+	NM
WALDORF MUSIC HALL					
❑ MH 33-153 [10]	After Hours	195?	12.50	25.00	50.00

COLE, IKE
Male singer, brother of Nat.

Number	Title	Yr	VG	VG+	NM
DEE GEE					
❑ 4001	Ike Cole's Tribute to His Brother	1966	10.00	20.00	40.00

COLE, NAT KING
First renowned as a piano player in The King Cole Trio, then as a male singer. The other members of the Trio were Oscar Moore (guitar) and Wesley Prince (bass). For a more complete listing, including his pop material, see the *Standard Catalog of American Records 1950-1975*.

Number	Title	Yr	VG	VG+	NM
ARCHIVE OF FOLK AND JAZZ					
❑ 290	Nature Boy	197?	2.50	5.00	10.00
CAPITOL					
❑ H 8 [10]	The King Cole Trio	1950	25.00	50.00	100.00
❑ H 29 [10]	The King Cole Trio, Volume 2	1950	25.00	50.00	100.00
❑ H 59 [10]	The King Cole Trio, Volume 3	1950	25.00	50.00	100.00
❑ H 156 [10]	Nat King Cole at the Piano	1950	25.00	50.00	100.00
❑ H 177 [10]	The King Cole Trio, Volume 4	1950	17.50	35.00	70.00
❑ H 213 [10]	Harvest of Hits	1950	17.50	35.00	70.00
❑ H 220 [10]	The Nat King Cole Trio	1950	15.00	30.00	60.00
❑ H 332 [10]	Penthouse Serenade	1951	15.00	30.00	60.00
❑ H 420 [10]	Nat King Cole Sings for Two in Love	1953	12.50	25.00	50.00
❑ H 514 [10]	Tenth Anniversary Album	1954	12.50	25.00	50.00
❑ T 592 [M]	Instrumental Classics	1955	10.00	20.00	40.00
❑ W 689 [M]	The Piano Style of Nat King Cole	1956	10.00	20.00	40.00
-- Turquoise label					
❑ W 689 [M]	The Piano Style of Nat King Cole	1958	7.50	15.00	30.00
-- Black label with colorband, "Capitol" at left					
❑ W 689 [M]	The Piano Style of Nat King Cole	1962	5.00	10.00	20.00
-- Black label with colorband, "Capitol" at top					
❑ W 782 [M]	After Midnight	1956	10.00	20.00	40.00
-- Turquoise label					
❑ W 782 [M]	After Midnight	1958	7.50	15.00	30.00
-- Black label with colorband, "Capitol" at left					
❑ W 782 [M]	After Midnight	1962	5.00	10.00	20.00
-- Black label with colorband, "Capitol" at top					
❑ SM-1675	Nat King Cole Sings/George Shearing Plays	197?	2.00	4.00	8.00
-- Reissue with new prefix					
❑ SW 1675 [S]	Nat King Cole Sings/George Shearing Plays	1962	7.50	15.00	30.00
-- Black label with colorband, "Capitol" at left					
❑ SW 1675 [S]	Nat King Cole Sings/George Shearing Plays	1963	5.00	10.00	20.00
-- Black label with colorband, "Capitol" at top					
❑ W 1675 [M]	Nat King Cole Sings/George Shearing Plays	1962	6.25	12.50	25.00
-- Black label with colorband, "Capitol" at left					
❑ W 1675 [M]	Nat King Cole Sings/George Shearing Plays	1963	3.75	7.50	15.00
-- Black label with colorband, "Capitol" at top					
❑ SW 1713 [S]	Nat King Cole Sings the Blues	1962	6.25	12.50	25.00
-- Black label with colorband, "Capitol" at left					
❑ W 1713 [M]	Nat King Cole Sings the Blues	1962	5.00	10.00	20.00
-- Black label with colorband, "Capitol" at left					
❑ SW 1929 [S]	Nat King Cole Sings the Blues, Volume 2	1963	5.00	10.00	20.00
❑ W 1929 [M]	Nat King Cole Sings the Blues, Volume 2	1963	3.75	7.50	15.00
❑ T 2311 [M]	The Nat King Cole Trio	1965	3.00	6.00	12.00
❑ M-11033 [M]	Trio Days	1972	3.75	7.50	15.00

Number	Title	Yr	VG	VG+	NM
❑ N-16260	The Best of the King Cole Trio -- Volume 1	1982	2.00	4.00	8.00
❑ N-16281	The Best of the King Cole Trio -- Volume 2	1982	2.00	4.00	8.00
DECCA					
❑ DL 8260 [M]	In the Beginning	1956	10.00	20.00	40.00
-- Black label, silver print					
❑ DL 8260 [M]	In the Beginning	1960	6.25	12.50	25.00
-- Black label with color bars					
MARK 56					
❑ 739 [(2)]	Early 1940s	197?	3.75	7.50	15.00
MCA					
❑ 4020 [(2)]	From the Very Beginning	197?	3.00	6.00	12.00
MOBILE FIDELITY					
❑ 1-081	Nat King Cole Sings/George Shearing Plays	1981	10.00	20.00	40.00
-- Audiophile vinyl					
MOSAIC					
❑ MR27-138 [(27)]	The Complete Capitol Recordings of the Nat King Cole Trio	1991	150.00	300.00	600.00
SAVOY JAZZ					
❑ SJL-1205	Nat King Cole & The King Cole Trio	1989	3.00	6.00	12.00
SCORE					
❑ SLP-4019 [M]	The King Cole Trio and Lester Young	1957	20.00	40.00	80.00
TRIP					
❑ 7	The Nat "King" Cole Trio	197?	3.00	6.00	12.00
VERVE					
❑ VSP-14 [M]	Nat Cole at JATP	1966	3.75	7.50	15.00
❑ VSPS-14 [R]	Nat Cole at JATP	1966	3.00	6.00	12.00
❑ VSP-25 [M]	Nat Cole at JATP 2	1966	3.75	7.50	15.00
❑ VSPS-25 [R]	Nat Cole at JATP 2	1966	3.00	6.00	12.00

COLE, RICHIE
Alto saxophone player.

Number	Title	Yr	VG	VG+	NM
ADELPHI					
❑ AD 5001	Starburst	1976	5.00	10.00	20.00
CONCORD JAZZ					
❑ CJ-314	Pure Imagination	1987	2.50	5.00	10.00
MILESTONE					
❑ M-9152	Popbop	1987	2.50	5.00	10.00
❑ M-9162	Signature	1988	2.50	5.00	10.00
MUSE					
❑ MR-5119	New York Afternoon	1976	2.50	5.00	10.00
❑ MR-5155	Alto Madness	1977	2.50	5.00	10.00
❑ MR-5192	Keeper of the Flame	1978	2.50	5.00	10.00
❑ MR-5207	Hollywood Madness	1979	2.50	5.00	10.00
❑ MR-5245	Cool "C"	1981	2.50	5.00	10.00
❑ MR-5270	Alive at the Village Vanguard	1981	2.50	5.00	10.00
❑ MR-5295	Some Things Speak for Themselves	1982	2.50	5.00	10.00
PALO ALTO					
❑ PA-8023	Return to Alto Acres	1982	2.50	5.00	10.00
❑ PA-8036	Alto Annie's Theme	1983	2.50	5.00	10.00
❑ PA-8070	Bossa Nova Eyes	1985	2.50	5.00	10.00

COLE, RICHIE, AND HANK CRAWFORD
Also see each artist's individual listings.

Number	Title	Yr	VG	VG+	NM
MILESTONE					
❑ M-9180	Bossa International	1990	3.00	6.00	12.00

COLE, RICHIE, AND ERIC KLOSS
Also see each artist's individual listings.

Number	Title	Yr	VG	VG+	NM
MUSE					
❑ MR-5082	Battle of the Saxes	1976	2.50	5.00	10.00

COLE, RICHIE, AND BOOTS RANDOLPH
Randolph is a pop, rock and country saxophone player whose solo recordings are outside the scope of this book. Also see RICHIE COLE.

Number	Title	Yr	VG	VG+	NM
PALO ALTO					
❑ PA-8041	Yakety Madness	1983	2.50	5.00	10.00

COLE, RICHIE, AND PHIL WOODS
Also see each artist's individual listings.

Number	Title	Yr	VG	VG+	NM
MUSE					
❑ MR-5237	Side By Side	1980	2.50	5.00	10.00

COLEMAN, BILL
Trumpeter, sometimes a fluegel horn player and male singer.

Number	Title	Yr	VG	VG+	NM
BLACK LION					
❑ 128	London!	197?	3.00	6.00	12.00

Number	Title	Yr	VG	VG+	NM
❏ 212	Mainstream at Montreux	1974	3.00	6.00	12.00

DRG

Number	Title	Yr	VG	VG+	NM
❏ SL-5200	Blowing for the Cats: The Final Big Band Sessions	198?	2.50	5.00	10.00

SWING

Number	Title	Yr	VG	VG+	NM
❏ SW-8402	Paris 1936-38	198?	2.50	5.00	10.00
❏ SW-8410	Bill Coleman with George Duvivier & Co.	198?	2.50	5.00	10.00

COLEMAN, CY
Pianist.

BENIDA

Number	Title	Yr	VG	VG+	NM
❏ LP-1023A [10]	Cy Coleman	1955	12.50	25.00	50.00

CAPITOL

Number	Title	Yr	VG	VG+	NM
❏ ST 1952 [S]	Piano Witchcraft	1963	6.25	12.50	25.00
❏ T 1952 [M]	Piano Witchcraft	1963	5.00	10.00	20.00
❏ ST 2355 [S]	The Art of Love	1965	5.00	10.00	20.00
❏ T 2355 [M]	The Art of Love	1965	3.75	7.50	15.00

COLUMBIA

Number	Title	Yr	VG	VG+	NM
❏ CL 2578 [M]	If My Friends Could See Me Now	1966	3.00	6.00	12.00
❏ CS 9378 [S]	If My Friends Could See Me Now	1966	3.75	7.50	15.00
❏ C 32804	Broadway Tunesmith	1973	2.50	5.00	10.00

DRG

Number	Title	Yr	VG	VG+	NM
❏ SL-5205	Comin' Home	1988	2.50	5.00	10.00

EVEREST

Number	Title	Yr	VG	VG+	NM
❏ SDBR-1092 [S]	Playboy's Penthouse	196?	7.50	15.00	30.00
❏ LPBR-5092 [M]	Playboy's Penthouse	196?	6.25	12.50	25.00

MGM

Number	Title	Yr	VG	VG+	NM
❏ SE-4501	Ages of Rock	1968	6.25	12.50	25.00

WESTMINSTER

Number	Title	Yr	VG	VG+	NM
❏ WLP-15001 [M]	Cool Coleman	195?	10.00	20.00	40.00

COLEMAN, EARL
Male singer.

ATLANTIC

Number	Title	Yr	VG	VG+	NM
❏ SD 8172	Love Songs	1968	3.75	7.50	15.00

FANTASY

Number	Title	Yr	VG	VG+	NM
❏ OJC-187	Earl Coleman Returns	1986	2.50	5.00	10.00

PRESTIGE

Number	Title	Yr	VG	VG+	NM
❏ PRLP-7045 [M]	Earl Coleman Returns	1956	12.50	25.00	50.00
-- Yellow label					
❏ PRLP-7045 [M]	Earl Coleman Returns	196?	6.25	12.50	25.00
-- Blue label, trident logo at right					

STASH

Number	Title	Yr	VG	VG+	NM
❏ 243	Stardust	1984	2.50	5.00	10.00

XANADU

Number	Title	Yr	VG	VG+	NM
❏ 147	A Song for You	1978	3.00	6.00	12.00
❏ 175	There's Something About an Old Love	1979	3.00	6.00	12.00

COLEMAN, ERNIE

WARNER BROS.

Number	Title	Yr	VG	VG+	NM
❏ W 1261 [M]	Be Gentle, Please	1959	6.25	12.50	25.00
❏ WS 1261 [S]	Be Gentle, Please	1959	7.50	15.00	30.00

COLEMAN, GEORGE
Alto and tenor saxophone player.

THERESA

Number	Title	Yr	VG	VG+	NM
❏ TR-120	Manhattan Panorama	1986	2.50	5.00	10.00
❏ TR-126	George Coleman at Yoshi's	1989	3.00	6.00	12.00

TIMELESS

Number	Title	Yr	VG	VG+	NM
❏ 312	Meditation	197?	3.00	6.00	12.00

COLEMAN, GLORIA
Organist.

ABC IMPULSE!

Number	Title	Yr	VG	VG+	NM
❏ AS-47	Soul Sisters	1968	3.00	6.00	12.00

IMPULSE!

Number	Title	Yr	VG	VG+	NM
❏ A-47 [M]	Soul Sisters	1963	6.25	12.50	25.00
❏ AS-47 [S]	Soul Sisters	1963	7.50	15.00	30.00

MAINSTREAM

Number	Title	Yr	VG	VG+	NM
❏ MRL-322	Gloria Coleman Sings and Swings -- Organ	1972	3.00	6.00	12.00

COLEMAN, ORNETTE
Alto saxophone player, composer, tenor saxophone player, trumpeter, violinist. Gave birth to "free jazz," named after his Atlantic album of the same name.

ABC IMPULSE!

Number	Title	Yr	VG	VG+	NM
❏ AS-9178	Ornette at 12	1968	6.25	12.50	25.00
❏ AS-9187	Crisis	1969	6.25	12.50	25.00

ANTILLES

Number	Title	Yr	VG	VG+	NM
❏ AN-2001	Of Human Feelings	198?	3.75	7.50	15.00

ARISTA FREEDOM

Number	Title	Yr	VG	VG+	NM
❏ AL 1900 [(2)]	The Great London Concert	1978	5.00	10.00	20.00

ARTISTS HOUSE

Number	Title	Yr	VG	VG+	NM
❏ 1	Body Meta	1977	5.00	10.00	20.00
❏ 6	Soapsuds	1978	5.00	10.00	20.00

ATLANTIC

Number	Title	Yr	VG	VG+	NM
❏ 1317 [M]	The Shape of Jazz to Come	1959	10.00	20.00	40.00
-- "Bullseye" label					
❏ 1317 [M]	The Shape of Jazz to Come	1960	6.25	12.50	25.00
-- Multicolor label, white "fan" logo					
❏ 1317 [M]	The Shape of Jazz to Come	1963	3.75	7.50	15.00
-- Multicolor label, black "fan" logo					
❏ SD 1317 [S]	The Shape of Jazz to Come	1959	12.50	25.00	50.00
-- "Bullseye" label					
❏ SD 1317 [S]	The Shape of Jazz to Come	1960	7.50	15.00	30.00
-- Multicolor label, white "fan" logo					
❏ SD 1317 [S]	The Shape of Jazz to Come	1963	5.00	10.00	20.00
-- Multicolor label, black "fan" logo					
❏ SD 1317 [S]	The Shape of Jazz to Come	1969	3.00	6.00	12.00
-- Red and green label					
❏ 1327 [M]	Change of the Century	1960	7.50	15.00	30.00
-- Multicolor label, white "fan" logo					
❏ 1327 [M]	Change of the Century	1963	3.75	7.50	15.00
-- Multicolor label, black "fan" logo					
❏ SD 1327 [S]	Change of the Century	1960	10.00	20.00	40.00
-- Multicolor label, white "fan" logo					
❏ SD 1327 [S]	Change of the Century	1963	5.00	10.00	20.00
-- Multicolor label, black "fan" logo					
❏ SD 1327 [S]	Change of the Century	1969	3.00	6.00	12.00
-- Red and green label					
❏ 1353 [M]	This Is Our Music	1960	7.50	15.00	30.00
-- Multicolor label, white "fan" logo					
❏ 1353 [M]	This Is Our Music	1963	3.75	7.50	15.00
-- Multicolor label, black "fan" logo					
❏ SD 1353 [S]	This Is Our Music	1960	10.00	20.00	40.00
-- Multicolor label, white "fan" logo					
❏ SD 1353 [S]	This Is Our Music	1963	5.00	10.00	20.00
-- Multicolor label, black "fan" logo					
❏ SD 1353 [S]	This Is Our Music	1969	3.00	6.00	12.00
-- Red and green label					
❏ 1364 [M]	Free Jazz	1961	10.00	20.00	40.00
-- Multicolor label, white "fan" logo					
❏ 1364 [M]	Free Jazz	1963	5.00	10.00	20.00
-- Multicolor label, black "fan" logo					
❏ SD 1364 [S]	Free Jazz	1961	12.50	25.00	50.00
-- Multicolor label, white "fan" logo					
❏ SD 1364 [S]	Free Jazz	1963	6.25	12.50	25.00
-- Multicolor label, black "fan" logo					
❏ SD 1364 [S]	Free Jazz	1969	3.00	6.00	12.00
-- Red and green label					
❏ 1378 [M]	Ornette	1961	7.50	15.00	30.00
-- Multicolor label, white "fan" logo					
❏ 1378 [M]	Ornette	1963	3.75	7.50	15.00
-- Multicolor label, black "fan" logo					
❏ SD 1378 [S]	Ornette	1961	10.00	20.00	40.00
-- Multicolor label, white "fan" logo					
❏ SD 1378 [S]	Ornette	1963	5.00	10.00	20.00
-- Multicolor label, black "fan" logo					
❏ SD 1378 [S]	Ornette	1969	3.00	6.00	12.00
-- Red and green label					
❏ 1394 [M]	Ornette on Tenor	1962	5.00	10.00	20.00
-- Multicolor label, black "fan" logo					
❏ SD 1394 [S]	Ornette on Tenor	1962	6.25	12.50	25.00
-- Multicolor label, black "fan" logo					
❏ SD 1394 [S]	Ornette on Tenor	1969	3.00	6.00	12.00
-- Red and green label					
❏ SD 1558	The Best of Ornette Coleman	1970	3.75	7.50	15.00
❏ SD 1572	The Art of Improvisors	1971	3.75	7.50	15.00
❏ SD 1588	Twins	1972	3.75	7.50	15.00
❏ SD 8810	Twins	198?	3.00	6.00	12.00

BLUE NOTE

Number	Title	Yr	VG	VG+	NM
❏ BLP-4210 [M]	Town Hall Concert, Volume 1	1965	---	---	---
-- Canceled					
❏ BLP-4211 [M]	Town Hall Concert, Volume 2	1965	---	---	---
-- Canceled					
❏ BLP-4224 [M]	Ornette Coleman at the Golden Circle, Stockholm, Volume 1	1965	7.50	15.00	30.00
❏ BLP-4225 [M]	Ornette Coleman at the Golden Circle, Stockholm, Volume 2	1965	7.50	15.00	30.00
❏ BLP-4246 [M]	The Empty Foxhole	1966	7.50	15.00	30.00
❏ B1-28982	The Empty Foxhole	1994	3.75	7.50	15.00
❏ BST-84210 [S]	Town Hall Concert, Volume 1	1965	---	---	---
-- Canceled					
❏ BST-84211 [S]	Town Hall Concert, Volume 2	1965	---	---	---
-- Canceled					

Number	Title	Yr	VG	VG+	NM
❏ BST-84224 [S]	Ornette Coleman at the Golden Circle, Stockholm, Volume 1	1965	10.00	20.00	40.00
-- "New York, USA" on label					
❏ BST-84224 [S]	Ornette Coleman at the Golden Circle, Stockholm, Volume 1	1967	3.75	7.50	15.00
-- "A Division of Liberty Records" on label					
❏ BST-84225 [S]	Ornette Coleman at the Golden Circle, Stockholm, Volume 2	1965	10.00	20.00	40.00
-- "New York, USA" on label					
❏ BST-84225 [S]	Ornette Coleman at the Golden Circle, Stockholm, Volume 2	1967	3.75	7.50	15.00
-- "A Division of Liberty Records" on label					
❏ BST-84246 [S]	The Empty Foxhole	1966	10.00	20.00	40.00
-- "New York, USA" on label					
❏ BST-84246 [S]	The Empty Foxhole	1967	7.50	15.00	30.00
-- "A Division of Liberty Records" on label					
❏ BST-84287	New York Is Now!	1968	6.25	12.50	25.00
❏ BST-84356	Love Call	1970	5.00	10.00	20.00
COLUMBIA					
❏ KC 31061	Science Fiction	1972	5.00	10.00	20.00
❏ KC 31562	Skies of America	1972	5.00	10.00	20.00
❏ CG 33669 [(2)]	Science Fiction/Skies of America	1976	5.00	10.00	20.00
❏ FC 38029	Broken Shadows	198?	3.00	6.00	12.00
CONTEMPORARY					
❏ C-3551 [M]	The Music of Ornette Coleman -- Something Else!	1958	30.00	60.00	120.00
❏ M-3569 [M]	Tomorrow Is the Question	1959	20.00	40.00	80.00
❏ S-7551 [S]	The Music of Ornette Coleman -- Something Else!	1959	20.00	40.00	80.00
❏ S-7569 [S]	Tomorrow Is the Question	1959	15.00	30.00	60.00
ESP-DISK'					
❏ 1006 [M]	Town Hall Concert, December 1962	1965	5.00	10.00	20.00
❏ S-1006 [S]	Town Hall Concert, December 1962	1965	6.25	12.50	25.00
FANTASY					
❏ OJC-163	The Music of Ornette Coleman -- Something Else!	198?	3.00	6.00	12.00
-- Reissue of Contemporary 7551					
❏ OJC-342	Tomorrow Is the Question	198?	3.00	6.00	12.00
-- Reissue of Contemporary 7569					
FLYING DUTCHMAN					
❏ 123	Friends and Neighbors	1970	5.00	10.00	20.00
❏ FD-10123	Friends and Neighbors	1972	3.75	7.50	15.00
-- Reissue of 123					
HORIZON					
❏ 722	Dancing in Your Head	1977	3.75	7.50	15.00
IAI					
❏ 373852	Classics, Volume 1	197?	5.00	10.00	20.00
INNER CITY					
❏ 1001	Live at the Hillcrest Club 1958	197?	5.00	10.00	20.00
MOON					
❏ MLP-022	Broken Shadows	1992	3.75	7.50	15.00
PORTRAIT					
❏ OR 44301	Virgin Beauty	1988	3.75	7.50	15.00
RCA VICTOR					
❏ LPM-2982 [M]	The Music of Ornette Coleman	1964	6.25	12.50	25.00
❏ LSP-2982 [S]	The Music of Ornette Coleman	1964	7.50	15.00	30.00

COLEMAN, STEVE
Alto saxophone player.

Number	Title	Yr	VG	VG+	NM
JMT					
❏ 834 425-1	Strata Institute Cipher Syntax	1988	3.00	6.00	12.00
❏ 850001	Motherland Pulse	1985	3.75	7.50	15.00
❏ 860005	On the Edge of Tomorrow	1986	3.75	7.50	15.00
❏ 870010	World Expansion	1987	3.75	7.50	15.00
NOVUS					
❏ 63180-1 [EP]	A Tale of 3 Cities The EP	1995	3.00	6.00	12.00

COLES, JOHNNY
Trumpeter.

Number	Title	Yr	VG	VG+	NM
BLUE NOTE					
❏ BLP-4144 [M]	Little Johnny C	1963	10.00	20.00	40.00
-- "New York, USA" on label					
❏ BST-84144 [S]	Little Johnny C	1963	12.50	25.00	50.00
-- "New York, USA" on label					
❏ BST-84144 [S]	Little Johnny C	1967	3.75	7.50	15.00
-- "A Division of Liberty Records" on label					
EPIC					
❏ LA 16015 [M]	The Warm Sound	1961	30.00	60.00	120.00
❏ BA 17015 [S]	The Warm Sound	1961	37.50	75.00	150.00
MAINSTREAM					
❏ MRL-346	Katumbo (Dance)	1972	5.00	10.00	20.00

COLIANNI, JOHN
Pianist.

Number	Title	Yr	VG	VG+	NM
CONCORD JAZZ					
❏ CJ-309	John Colianni	1987	2.50	5.00	10.00
❏ CJ-367	Blues-O-Matic	1989	3.00	6.00	12.00

COLINA, MICHAEL
Keyboard player, composer and producer.

Number	Title	Yr	VG	VG+	NM
PRIVATE MUSIC					
❏ 2041-1-P	The Shadow of Urbano	1988	2.50	5.00	10.00

COLLETTE, BUDDY
Saxophone player (alto, tenor), clarinet player, flutist, composer.

Number	Title	Yr	VG	VG+	NM
ABC-PARAMOUNT					
❏ ABC-179 [M]	Calm, Cool and Collette	1957	15.00	30.00	60.00
CHALLENGE					
❏ CHL-603 [M]	Everybody's Buddy	1958	12.50	25.00	50.00
CONTEMPORARY					
❏ C-3522 [M]	Man of Many Parts	1956	12.50	25.00	50.00
❏ C-3531 [M]	Nice Day with Buddy Collette	1957	12.50	25.00	50.00
❏ S-7522 [S]	Man of Many Parts	1959	10.00	20.00	40.00
❏ S-7531 [S]	Nice Day with Buddy Collette	1959	10.00	20.00	40.00
CROWN					
❏ CLP-5019 [M]	Bongo Madness	195?	6.25	12.50	25.00
DIG					
❏ LP-101 [M]	Tanganyika	1956	25.00	50.00	100.00
DOOTO					
❏ DTL-245 [M]	Buddy's Best	1957	25.00	50.00	100.00
-- Red vinyl					
❏ DTL-245 [M]	Buddy's Best	1957	15.00	30.00	60.00
-- Black vinyl					
EMARCY					
❏ MG-36133 [M]	Swingin' Shepherds	1958	12.50	25.00	50.00
❏ SR-80005 [S]	Swingin' Shepherds	1959	10.00	20.00	40.00
FANTASY					
❏ OJC-239	Man of Many Parts	198?	2.50	5.00	10.00
INTERLUDE					
❏ MO-505 [M]	Modern Interpretations of Porgy & Bess	196?	7.50	15.00	30.00
❏ ST-1005 [S]	Modern Interpretations of Porgy & Bess	196?	10.00	20.00	40.00
LEGEND					
❏ 1004	Now and Then	1974	3.00	6.00	12.00
MERCURY					
❏ MG-20447 [M]	At the Cinema	1959	10.00	20.00	40.00
❏ SR-60132 [S]	At the Cinema	1959	10.00	20.00	40.00
MUSIC & SOUND					
❏ 1001 [M]	Polynesia	196?	7.50	15.00	30.00
❏ S-1001 [S]	Polynesia	196?	10.00	20.00	40.00
RGB					
❏ 2001	Block Buster	1975	3.00	6.00	12.00
SOUL NOTE					
❏ 121165	Flute Talk	1990	3.75	7.50	15.00
SPECIALTY					
❏ SP-5002 [M]	Jazz Loves Paris	1960	12.50	25.00	50.00
SURREY					
❏ S-1009 [M]	Buddy Collette on Broadway	1965	3.75	7.50	15.00
❏ SS-1009 [S]	Buddy Collette on Broadway	1965	5.00	10.00	20.00
TAMPA					
❏ TP-34 [M]	Star Studded Cast	1959	20.00	40.00	80.00
WORLD PACIFIC					
❏ ST-1823 [S]	Warm Winds	1964	6.25	12.50	25.00
❏ WP-1823 [M]	Warm Winds	1964	5.00	10.00	20.00

COLLIE, MAX, AND HIS RHYTHM ACES
Trombonist and bandleader.

Number	Title	Yr	VG	VG+	NM
GHB					
❏ GHB-63	On Tour in the U.S.A.	198?	2.50	5.00	10.00

COLLINS, AL "JAZZBO"
Famous jazz radio announcer who lent his name to the below recordings.

Number	Title	Yr	VG	VG+	NM
ABC IMPULSE!					
❏ AS-9150 [S]	A Lovely Bunch of Al "Jazzbo" Collins	1968	3.75	7.50	15.00
CORAL					
❏ CRL 57035 [M]	East Coast Jazz Scene	1956	20.00	40.00	80.00
EVEREST					
❏ SDBR-1097 [S]	Swingin' at the Opera	1960	10.00	20.00	40.00
❏ LPBR-5097 [M]	Swingin' at the Opera	1960	7.50	15.00	30.00

Number	Title	Yr	VG	VG+	NM
IMPULSE!					
❑ A-9150 [M]	A Lovely Bunch of Al "Jazzbo" Collins	1967	10.00	20.00	40.00
❑ AS-9150 [S]	A Lovely Bunch of Al "Jazzbo" Collins	1967	7.50	15.00	30.00
OLD TOWN					
❑ LP-2001 [M]	In the Purple Grotto	1961	7.50	15.00	30.00

COLLINS, CAL
Guitarist.

Number	Title	Yr	VG	VG+	NM
CONCORD JAZZ					
❑ CJ-59	Cincinnati to L.A.	1977	2.50	5.00	10.00
❑ CJ-71	Cal Collins In San Francisco	1978	2.50	5.00	10.00
❑ CJ-95	Blues on My Mind	1979	2.50	5.00	10.00
❑ CJ-119	By Myself	1980	2.50	5.00	10.00
❑ CJ-137	Interplay	1981	2.50	5.00	10.00
❑ CJ-166	Cross Country	1981	2.50	5.00	10.00
FAMOUS DOOR					
❑ HL-123	Ohio Boss Guitar	198?	2.50	5.00	10.00
PAUSA					
❑ 7159	Milestones	198?	2.50	5.00	10.00

COLLINS, DICK
Trumpeter and composer.

Number	Title	Yr	VG	VG+	NM
RCA VICTOR					
❑ LJM-1019 [M]	Horn of Plenty	1955	15.00	30.00	60.00
❑ LJM-1027 [M]	King Richard the Swing Hearted	1955	15.00	30.00	60.00

COLLINS, JOYCE
Pianist.

Number	Title	Yr	VG	VG+	NM
DISCOVERY					
❑ 828	Moment to Moment	198?	2.50	5.00	10.00
JAZZLAND					
❑ JLP-24 [M]	The Girl Here Plays Mean Piano	1960	6.25	12.50	25.00
❑ JLP-924 [S]	The Girl Here Plays Mean Piano	1960	7.50	15.00	30.00

COLLINS, LEE
Trumpeter.

Number	Title	Yr	VG	VG+	NM
NEW ORLEANS					
❑ 7203 [M]	Night at Victory Club	198?	2.50	5.00	10.00

COLONNA, JERRY
Trombone player.

Number	Title	Yr	VG	VG+	NM
LIBERTY					
❑ SL-9004 [M]	Jerry Colonna Plays Trombone	1957	10.00	20.00	40.00

COLTRANE, ALICE
Pianist, organist and harp player.

Number	Title	Yr	VG	VG+	NM
ABC IMPULSE!					
❑ AS-9156	The Monastic Trio	1968	3.00	6.00	12.00
❑ AS-9185	Huntington Ashram Monastery	1969	3.00	6.00	12.00
❑ AS-9196	Ptah the El Daoud	1969	3.00	6.00	12.00
❑ AS-9203	Journey in Satchidananda	1970	3.00	6.00	12.00
❑ AS-9210	Universal Consciousness	1971	2.50	5.00	10.00
❑ AS-9218	World Galaxy	1972	2.50	5.00	10.00
❑ AS-9224	Lord of Lords	1972	2.50	5.00	10.00
❑ AS-9232 [(2)]	Reflection On Creation and Space	1973	3.00	6.00	12.00
GRP/IMPULSE!					
❑ IMP-228	Journey in Satchidananda	1997	3.75	7.50	15.00
WARNER BROS.					
❑ BS 2916	Eternity	1975	2.50	5.00	10.00
❑ BS 2986	Radha Krsna	1976	2.50	5.00	10.00
❑ BS 3077	Transcendence	1977	2.50	5.00	10.00
❑ 2WS 3218 [(2)]	Transfiguration	1978	3.00	6.00	12.00

COLTRANE, ALICE, AND CARLOS SANTANA
Also see each artist's individual entries.

Number	Title	Yr	VG	VG+	NM
COLUMBIA					
❑ KC 32900	Illuminations	1974	2.50	5.00	10.00

COLTRANE, JOHN
Tenor and soprano saxophone player. One of the most important and influential figures in jazz history. Also see CANNONBALL ADDERLEY; KENNY BURRELL; TADD DAMERON; MILES DAVIS; RAY DRAPER; WILBUR HARDEN; MILT JACKSON; THELONIOUS MONK; CECIL TAYLOR.

Number	Title	Yr	VG	VG+	NM
ABC IMPULSE!					
❑ AS-6 [S]	Africa/Brass	1968	3.75	7.50	15.00
❑ AS-10 [S]	Live at the Village Vanguard	1968	3.75	7.50	15.00
❑ AS-21 [S]	Coltrane	1968	3.75	7.50	15.00
❑ AS-30 [S]	Duke Ellington and John Coltrane	1968	3.75	7.50	15.00

Number	Title	Yr	VG	VG+	NM
❑ AS-32 [S]	Ballads	1968	3.75	7.50	15.00
❑ AS-40 [S]	John Coltrane + Johnny Hartman	1968	3.75	7.50	15.00
❑ AS-42 [S]	Impressions	1968	3.75	7.50	15.00
❑ AS-50 [S]	Coltrane Live at Birdland	1968	3.75	7.50	15.00
❑ AS-66 [S]	Crescent	1968	3.75	7.50	15.00
❑ AS-77 [S]	A Love Supreme	1968	3.75	7.50	15.00
❑ AS-85 [S]	The John Coltrane Quartet Plays	1968	3.75	7.50	15.00
❑ AS-94 [S]	New Thing at Newport	1968	3.75	7.50	15.00
❑ AS-95 [S]	Ascension	1968	3.75	7.50	15.00
-- With "Edition II" in dead wax					
❑ AS-9106 [S]	Kulu Se Mama	1968	3.75	7.50	15.00
❑ AS-9110 [S]	Meditations	1968	3.75	7.50	15.00
❑ AS-9120 [S]	Expression	1968	3.75	7.50	15.00
❑ AS-9124 [S]	Live at the Village Vanguard Again!	1968	3.75	7.50	15.00
❑ AS-9140 [S]	Om	1968	3.75	7.50	15.00
❑ AS-9148	Cosmic Music	1969	5.00	10.00	20.00
-- Reissue of Coltrane LP					
❑ AS-9161	Selflessness	1969	5.00	10.00	20.00
❑ AS-9165	Transition	1969	5.00	10.00	20.00
❑ AS-9200 [(2)]	Greatest Years	1971	5.00	10.00	20.00
❑ AS-9202 [(2)]	Live in Seattle	1971	5.00	10.00	20.00
❑ AS-9211	Sun Ship	1971	5.00	10.00	20.00
❑ AS-9223 [(2)]	Greatest Years, Volume 2	1973	3.75	7.50	15.00
❑ AS-9225	Infinity	1973	3.00	6.00	12.00
❑ IA-9246 [(2)]	Concert Japan	1973	3.75	7.50	15.00
❑ IA-9273	Africa/Brass, Volume 2	1974	3.00	6.00	12.00
❑ IA-9277	Interstellar Space	1974	3.00	6.00	12.00
❑ IA-9278 [(2)]	Greatest Years, Volume 3	1974	3.75	7.50	15.00
❑ IA-9306 [(2)]	The Gentle Side of John Coltrane	1976	3.75	7.50	15.00
❑ IA-9325 [(2)]	The Other Village Vanguard Tapes	1977	3.75	7.50	15.00
❑ IA-9332	First Meditations	1978	3.00	6.00	12.00
❑ IZ-9345 [(2)]	The Mastery of John Coltrane Vol.1: Feelin' Good	1978	3.00	6.00	12.00
❑ IZ-9346 [(2)]	The Mastery of John Coltrane Vol. 2: Different Drum	1978	3.00	6.00	12.00
❑ IA-9360	The Mastery of John Coltrane Vol. 3: Jupiter Variation	1978	3.00	6.00	12.00
❑ IZ-9361 [(2)]	The Mastery of John Coltrane Vol. 4: Trane's Moods	1978	3.00	6.00	12.00
ATLANTIC					
❑ SD 2-313 [(2)]	The Art of John Coltrane	1973	3.75	7.50	15.00
❑ 1311 [M]	Giant Steps	1959	12.50	25.00	50.00
-- Black label					
❑ 1311 [M]	Giant Steps	1960	6.25	12.50	25.00
-- Orange and purple label, white fan logo					
❑ 1311 [M]	Giant Steps	1962	3.75	7.50	15.00
-- Orange and purple label, black fan logo					
❑ SD 1311 [S]	Giant Steps	1959	15.00	30.00	60.00
-- Green label					
❑ SD 1311 [S]	Giant Steps	1960	6.25	12.50	25.00
-- Green and blue label, white fan logo					
❑ SD 1311 [S]	Giant Steps	1962	2.75	7.50	15.00
-- Green and blue label, black fan logo					
❑ SD 1311 [S]	Giant Steps	1969	3.00	6.00	12.00
-- Red and green label					
❑ 1354 [M]	Coltrane Jazz	1960	7.50	15.00	30.00
-- Orange and purple label, white fan logo					
❑ 1354 [M]	Coltrane Jazz	1962	3.75	7.50	15.00
-- Orange and purple label, black fan logo					
❑ SD 1354 [S]	Coltrane Jazz	1960	7.50	15.00	30.00
-- Green and blue label, white fan logo					
❑ SD 1354 [S]	Coltrane Jazz	1962	3.75	7.50	15.00
-- Green and blue label, black fan logo					
❑ SD 1354 [S]	Coltrane Jazz	1969	3.00	6.00	12.00
-- Red and green label					
❑ 1361 [M]	My Favorite Things	1961	7.50	15.00	30.00
-- Orange and purple label, white fan logo					
❑ 1361 [M]	My Favorite Things	1962	3.75	7.50	15.00
-- Orange and purple label, black fan logo					
❑ SD 1361 [S]	My Favorite Things	1961	7.50	15.00	30.00
-- Green and blue label, white fan logo					
❑ SD 1361 [S]	My Favorite Things	1962	3.75	7.50	15.00
-- Green and blue label, black fan logo					
❑ SD 1361 [S]	My Favorite Things	1969	3.00	6.00	12.00
-- Red and green label					
❑ 1373 [M]	Ole' Coltrane	1961	7.50	15.00	30.00
-- Orange and purple label, white fan logo					
❑ 1373 [M]	Ole' Coltrane	1962	3.75	7.50	15.00
-- Orange and purple label, black fan logo					
❑ SD 1373 [S]	Ole' Coltrane	1961	7.50	15.00	30.00
-- Green and blue label, white fan logo					
❑ SD 1373 [S]	Ole' Coltrane	1962	3.75	7.50	15.00
-- Green and blue label, black fan logo					
❑ SD 1373 [S]	Ole' Coltrane	1969	3.00	6.00	12.00
-- Red and green label					

Even today, listeners who discover John Coltrane for the first time can't help but be amazed at many of his solos. Some of the results may not be to everyone's tastes, but you can't help but marvel at the virtuosity. (Top left, top right and bottom left) In many ways, the time Coltrane spent on the Prestige label in the middle and late 1950s was the foundation for what was to come. In addition to recording with Miles Davis' group, he led numerous sessions, some of which resulted in the albums *Coltrane* (his first as a leader), *Soultrane* (released in 1958) and *Bahia* (not issued until 1965). (Bottom right) Trane's last recording, *Expression*, released shortly after his death in 1967, continues to show Coltrane evolving. The remnants of the group on this album, including his wife Alice and Pharoah Sanders, are today seen as the founders of the "kozmigroov" sound.

Number	Title	Yr	VG	VG+	NM
❑ 1382 [M]	Coltrane Plays the Blues	1962	7.50	15.00	30.00
❑ SD 1382 [S]	Coltrane Plays the Blues	1962	7.50	51.00	30.00
-- Green and blue label, black fan logo					
❑ SD 1382 [S]	Coltrane Plays the Blues	1969	3.00	6.00	12.00
-- Red and green label					
❑ 1419 [M]	Coltrane's Sound	1964	6.25	12.50	25.00
❑ SD 1419 [S]	Coltrane's Sound	1964	6.25	12.50	25.00
-- Green and blue label, black fan logo					
❑ SD 1419 [S]	Coltrane's Sound	1969	3.00	6.00	12.00
-- Red and green label					
❑ 1451 [M]	The Avant Garde	1966	6.25	12.50	25.00
❑ SD 1451 [S]	The Avant Garde	1966	6.25	12.50	25.00
-- Green and blue label, black fan logo					
❑ SD 1451 [S]	The Avant Garde	1969	3.00	6.00	12.00
-- Red and green label					
❑ SD 1541	The Best of John Coltrane	1969	3.00	6.00	12.00
❑ SD 1553	The Coltrane Legacy	1971	3.00	6.00	12.00
❑ 90014	The Avant Garde	1983	2.50	5.00	10.00
❑ 90462	Countdown	1986	2.50	5.00	10.00

ATLANTIC/RHINO

Number	Title	Yr	VG	VG+	NM
❑ R1-71984 [(12)]	The Heavyweight Champion: The Complete Atlantic Recordings	1995	50.00	100.00	200.00

BLUE NOTE

Number	Title	Yr	VG	VG+	NM
❑ BLP-1577 [M]	Blue Train	1957	37.50	75.00	150.00
-- "Deep groove" version (deep indentation under label on both sides)					
❑ BLP-1577 [M]	Blue Train	1957	25.00	50.00	100.00
-- Regular version, W. 63rd St., NYC address on label					
❑ BLP-1577 [M]	Blue Train	196?	7.50	15.00	30.00
-- New York, USA address on label					
❑ BST-1577 [S]	Blue Train	1959	30.00	60.00	120.00
-- "Deep groove" version (deep indentation under label on both sides)					
❑ BST-1577 [S]	Blue Train	1959	20.00	40.00	80.00
-- Regular version, W. 63rd St., NYC address on label					
❑ BST-1577 [S]	Blue Train	196?	6.25	12.50	25.00
-- New York, USA address on label					
❑ B1-46095	Blue Train	1997	3.75	7.50	15.00
❑ B1-81577	Blue Train	1988	2.50	5.00	10.00
-- Reissue with new prefix					
❑ BST-81577	Blue Train	1967	3.75	7.50	15.00
-- "A Division of Liberty Records" on label					
❑ BST-81577	Blue Train	198?	2.50	5.00	10.00
-- "The Finest in Jazz Since 1939" reissue					

COLTRANE

Number	Title	Yr	VG	VG+	NM
❑ AU-4950	Cosmic Music	1966	75.00	150.00	300.00
❑ AU-5000	Cosmic Music	1966	50.00	100.00	200.00

DCC COMPACT CLASSICS

Number	Title	Yr	VG	VG+	NM
❑ LPZ-2032	Lush Life	1997	6.25	12.50	25.00
-- Audiophile vinyl					

FANTASY

Number	Title	Yr	VG	VG+	NM
❑ OJC-020	Coltrane	198?	2.50	5.00	10.00
❑ OJC-021	Soultrane	198?	2.50	5.00	10.00
❑ OJC-078	Settin' the Pace	198?	2.50	5.00	10.00
❑ OJC-127	Tenor Conclave	1991	3.00	6.00	12.00
❑ OJC-131	Lush Life	198?	2.50	5.00	10.00
❑ OJC-189	Traneing In	1986	2.50	5.00	10.00
❑ OJC-246	Standard Coltrane	1987	2.50	5.00	10.00
❑ OJC-292	Interplay for Two Trumpets and Two Tenors	1988	2.50	5.00	10.00
❑ OJC-352	Black Pearls	1989	2.50	5.00	10.00
❑ OJC-393	Dakar	1989	2.50	5.00	10.00
❑ OJC-394	Last Trane	1989	2.50	5.00	10.00
❑ OJC-415	Bahia	1990	3.00	6.00	12.00
❑ OJC-460	Cattin' with Coltrane and Quinchette	1990	3.00	6.00	12.00

GRP/IMPULSE!

Number	Title	Yr	VG	VG+	NM
❑ GR-155	A Love Supreme	1995	3.75	7.50	15.00
❑ GR-156	Ballads	1995	3.75	7.50	15.00
❑ GR-157	John Coltrane + Johnny Hartman	1995	3.75	7.50	15.00
❑ IMP-166	Duke Ellington and John Coltrane	1997	3.75	7.50	15.00
❑ IMP-167	Sun Ship	1997	3.75	7.50	15.00
❑ IMP-169	Stellar Regions	1995	3.75	7.50	15.00
❑ IMP-198	Coltrane Live at Birdland	1997	3.75	7.50	15.00
❑ IMP-200	Crescent	1997	3.75	7.50	15.00
❑ IMP-213	Live at the Village Vanguard Again!	1997	3.75	7.50	15.00
❑ IMP-214	The John Coltrane Quartet Plays	1997	3.75	7.50	15.00
❑ IMP-215	Coltrane	1997	3.75	7.50	15.00

IMPULSE!

Number	Title	Yr	VG	VG+	NM
❑ A-6 [M]	Africa/Brass	1961	7.50	15.00	30.00
❑ AS-6 [S]	Africa/Brass	1961	10.00	20.00	40.00
❑ A-10 [M]	Live at the Village Vanguard	1962	7.50	15.00	30.00
❑ AS-10 [S]	Live at the Village Vanguard	1962	10.00	20.00	40.00
❑ A-21 [M]	Coltrane	1962	7.50	15.00	30.00
❑ AS-21 [S]	Coltrane	1962	10.00	20.00	40.00

Number	Title	Yr	VG	VG+	NM
❑ A-30 [M]	Duke Ellington and John Coltrane	1963	7.50	15.00	30.00
❑ AS-30 [S]	Duke Ellington and John Coltrane	1963	10.00	20.00	40.00
❑ A-32 [M]	Ballads	1963	7.50	15.00	30.00
❑ AS-32 [S]	Ballads	1963	10.00	20.00	40.00
❑ A-40 [M]	John Coltrane + Johnny Hartman	1963	10.00	20.00	40.00
❑ AS-40 [S]	John Coltrane + Johnny Hartman	1963	12.50	25.00	50.00
❑ A-42 [M]	Impressions	1963	6.25	12.50	25.00
❑ AS-42 [S]	Impressions	1963	7.50	15.00	30.00
❑ A-50 [M]	Coltrane Live at Birdland	1963	6.25	12.50	25.00
❑ AS-50 [S]	Coltrane Live at Birdland	1963	7.50	15.00	30.00
❑ A-66 [M]	Crescent	1964	6.25	12.50	25.00
❑ AS-66 [S]	Crescent	1964	7.50	15.00	30.00
❑ A-77 [M]	A Love Supreme	1965	7.50	15.00	30.00
❑ AS-77 [S]	A Love Supreme	1965	10.00	20.00	40.00
❑ A-85 [M]	The John Coltrane Quartet Plays	1965	6.25	12.50	25.00
❑ AS-85 [S]	The John Coltrane Quartet Plays	1965	7.50	15.00	30.00
❑ A-94 [M]	New Thing at Newport	1965	6.25	12.50	25.00
❑ AS-94 [S]	New Thing at Newport	1965	7.50	15.00	30.00
❑ A-95 [M]	Ascension	1965	20.00	40.00	80.00
-- Without "Edition II" in dead wax					
❑ A-95 [M]	Ascension	1966	6.25	12.50	25.00
-- With "Edition II" in dead wax					
❑ AS-95 [S]	Ascension	1965	25.00	50.00	100.00
-- Without "Edition II" in dead wax					
❑ AS-95 [S]	Ascension	1966	7.50	15.00	30.00
-- With "Edition II" in dead wax					
❑ A-9106 [M]	Kulu Se Mama	1966	6.25	12.50	25.00
❑ AS-9106 [S]	Kulu Se Mama	1966	7.50	15.00	30.00
❑ A-9110 [M]	Meditations	1966	6.25	12.50	25.00
❑ AS-9110 [S]	Meditations	1966	7.50	15.00	30.00
❑ A-9120 [M]	Expression	1967	7.50	15.00	30.00
❑ AS-9120 [S]	Expression	1967	6.25	12.50	25.00
❑ A-9124 [M]	Live at the Village Vanguard Again!	1967	7.50	15.00	30.00
❑ AS-9124 [S]	Live at the Village Vanguard Again!	1967	6.25	12.50	25.00
❑ A-9140 [M]	Om	1967	7.50	15.00	30.00
❑ AS-9140 [S]	Om	1967	6.25	12.50	25.00

MCA

Number	Title	Yr	VG	VG+	NM
❑ 4131 [(2)]	Greatest Years	1981	2.50	5.00	10.00
❑ 4132 [(2)]	Greatest Years, Volume 2	1981	2.50	5.00	10.00
❑ 4133 [(2)]	Greatest Years, Volume 3	1981	2.50	5.00	10.00
❑ 4134 [(2)]	Live in Seattle	1981	2.50	5.00	10.00
❑ 4135 [(2)]	Concert Japan	1981	2.50	5.00	10.00
❑ 4136 [(2)]	The Gentle Side of John Coltrane	1981	2.50	5.00	10.00
❑ 4137 [(2)]	The Other Village Vanguard Tapes	1981	2.50	5.00	10.00
❑ 4138 [(2)]	The Mastery of John Coltrane Vol. 1: Feelin' Good	1981	2.50	5.00	10.00
❑ 4139 [(2)]	The Mastery of John Coltrane Vol. 2: Different Drum	1981	2.50	5.00	10.00
❑ 4140 [(2)]	The Mastery of John Coltrane Vol. 4: Trane's Moods	1981	2.50	5.00	10.00
❑ 29007	Africa/Brass	1981	2.00	4.00	8.00
❑ 29008	Africa/Brass, Volume 2	1981	2.00	4.00	8.00
❑ 29009	Live at the Village Vanguard	1981	2.00	4.00	8.00
❑ 29010	Live at the Village Vanguard Again!	1981	2.00	4.00	8.00
❑ 29011	Coltrane	1981	2.00	4.00	8.00
❑ 29012	Ballads	1981	2.00	4.00	8.00
❑ 29013	John Coltrane + Johnny Hartman	1981	2.00	4.00	8.00
❑ 29014	Impressions	1981	2.00	4.00	8.00
❑ 29015	Coltrane Live at Birdland	1981	2.00	4.00	8.00
❑ 29016	Crescent	1981	2.00	4.00	8.00
❑ 29017	A Love Supreme	1981	2.00	4.00	8.00
❑ 29018	The John Coltrane Quartet Plays	1981	2.00	4.00	8.00
❑ 29019	New Thing at Newport	1981	2.00	4.00	8.00
❑ 29020	Ascension	1981	2.00	4.00	8.00
❑ 29021	Kulu Se Mama	1981	2.00	4.00	8.00
❑ 29022	Meditations	1981	2.00	4.00	8.00
❑ 29023	Expression	1981	2.00	4.00	8.00
❑ 29024	Om	1981	2.00	4.00	8.00
❑ 29025	Cosmic Music	1981	2.00	4.00	8.00
❑ 29026	Selflessness	1981	2.00	4.00	8.00
❑ 29027	Transition	1981	2.00	4.00	8.00
❑ 29028	Sun Ship	1981	2.00	4.00	8.00
❑ 29029	Interstellar Space	1981	2.00	4.00	8.00
❑ 29030	First Meditations	1981	2.00	4.00	8.00
❑ 29031	The Mastery of John Coltrane Vol. 3: Jupiter Variation	1981	2.00	4.00	8.00
❑ 29032	Duke Ellington and John Coltrane	1981	2.00	4.00	8.00

Number	Title	Yr	VG	VG+	NM
MCA/IMPULSE!					
❑ 5660	A Love Supreme	1986	2.50	5.00	10.00
❑ 5661	John Coltrane + Johnny Hartman	1986	2.50	5.00	10.00
❑ 5883	Coltrane	1987	2.50	5.00	10.00
❑ 5885	Ballads	1987	2.50	5.00	10.00
❑ 5887	Impressions	1987	2.50	5.00	10.00
❑ 5889	Crescent	1987	2.50	5.00	10.00
❑ 33109	Coltrane Live at Birdland	198?	2.50	5.00	10.00
❑ 33110	The John Coltrane Quartet Plays	198?	2.50	5.00	10.00
❑ 39103	Duke Ellington and John Coltrane	1988	2.50	5.00	10.00
❑ 39118	Om	1988	2.50	5.00	10.00
❑ 39136	Live at the Village Vanguard	1988	2.50	5.00	10.00
❑ 42231	Africa/Brass	1988	2.50	5.00	10.00
❑ 42232	Africa/Brass, Volume 2	1988	2.50	5.00	10.00
PABLO					
❑ 2405 417	The Best of John Coltrane	198?	2.50	5.00	10.00
PABLO LIVE					
❑ 2308 217	The Paris Concert	1980	3.00	6.00	12.00
❑ 2308 222	European Tour	1981	3.00	6.00	12.00
❑ 2308 227	Bye Bye Blackbird	1981	3.00	6.00	12.00
❑ 2620 101 [(2)]	Afro Blue Impressions	198?	3.00	6.00	12.00
PRESTIGE					
❑ PRLP-7105 [M]	Coltrane	1957	25.00	50.00	100.00
-- Yellow label					
❑ PRLP-7105 [M]	Coltrane	1964	7.50	15.00	30.00
-- Blue label with trident logo					
❑ PRLP-7123 [M]	John Coltrane and the Red Garland Trio	1957	25.00	50.00	100.00
-- Yellow label					
❑ PRLP-7123 [M]	Traneing In	1964	7.50	15.00	30.00
-- Blue label with trident logo; reissue with new title					
❑ PRLP-7142 [M]	Soultrane	1958	20.00	40.00	80.00
-- Yellow label					
❑ PRLP-7142 [M]	Soultrane	1964	6.25	12.50	25.00
-- Blue label with trident logo					
❑ PRLP-7158 [M]	Cattin' with Coltrane and Quinchette	1959	20.00	40.00	80.00
-- Yellow label					
❑ PRLP-7158 [M]	Cattin' with Coltrane and Quinchette	1964	6.25	12.50	25.00
-- Blue label with trident logo					
❑ PRLP-7188 [M]	Lush Life	1960	20.00	40.00	80.00
-- Yellow label					
❑ PRLP-7188 [M]	Lush Life	1964	6.25	12.50	25.00
-- Blue label with trident logo					
❑ PRLP-7213 [M]	Settin' the Pace	1961	20.00	40.00	80.00
-- Yellow label					
❑ PRLP-7213 [M]	Settin' the Pace	1964	6.25	12.50	25.00
-- Blue label with trident logo					
❑ PRLP-7243 [M]	Standard Coltrane	1962	10.00	20.00	40.00
-- Yellow label					
❑ PRLP-7243 [M]	Standard Coltrane	1964	6.25	12.50	25.00
-- Blue label with trident logo					
❑ PRST-7243 [S]	Standard Coltrane	1962	12.50	25.00	50.00
-- Silver label					
❑ PRST-7243 [S]	Standard Coltrane	1964	6.25	12.50	25.00
-- Blue label with trident logo					
❑ PRLP-7247 [M]	Mating Call	1962	10.00	20.00	40.00
-- Yellow label					
❑ PRLP-7247 [M]	Mating Call	1964	6.25	12.50	25.00
-- Blue label with trident logo					
❑ PRST-7247 [R]	Mating Call	196?	6.25	12.50	25.00
-- Silver label					
❑ PRST-7247 [R]	Mating Call	1964	5.00	10.00	20.00
-- Blue label with trident logo					
❑ PRLP-7249 [M]	Tenor Conclave	1962	10.00	20.00	40.00
-- Yellow label					
❑ PRLP-7249 [M]	Tenor Conclave	1964	6.25	12.50	25.00
-- Blue label with trident logo					
❑ PRST-7249 [R]	Tenor Conclave	196?	6.25	12.50	25.00
-- Silver label					
❑ PRST-7249 [R]	Tenor Conclave	1964	5.00	10.00	20.00
-- Blue label with trident logo					
❑ PRLP-7268 [M]	Stardust	1963	10.00	20.00	40.00
-- Yellow label					
❑ PRLP-7268 [M]	Stardust	1964	6.25	12.50	25.00
-- Blue label with trident logo					
❑ PRST-7268 [S]	Stardust	1963	10.00	20.00	40.00
-- Silver label					
❑ PRST-7268 [S]	Stardust	1964	6.25	12.50	25.00
-- Blue label with trident logo					
❑ PRLP-7280 [M]	Dakar	1963	10.00	20.00	40.00
-- Yellow label					
❑ PRLP-7280 [M]	Dakar	1964	6.25	12.50	25.00
-- Blue label with trident logo					
❑ PRST-7280 [S]	Dakar	1963	10.00	20.00	40.00
-- Silver label					

Number	Title	Yr	VG	VG+	NM
❑ PRST-7280 [S]	Dakar	1964	6.25	12.50	25.00
-- Blue label with trident logo					
❑ PRLP-7292 [M]	The Believer	1964	6.25	12.50	25.00
-- Blue label with trident logo					
❑ PRLP-7292 [M]	The Believer	1964	10.00	20.00	40.00
-- Yellow label					
❑ PRST-7292 [S]	The Believer	1964	10.00	20.00	40.00
-- Silver label					
❑ PRST-7292 [S]	The Believer	1964	6.25	12.50	25.00
-- Blue label with trident logo					
❑ PRLP-7316 [M]	Black Pearls	1964	10.00	20.00	40.00
-- Yellow label					
❑ PRLP-7316 [M]	Black Pearls	1964	6.25	12.50	25.00
-- Blue label with trident logo					
❑ PRST-7316 [S]	Black Pearls	1964	10.00	20.00	40.00
-- Silver label					
❑ PRST-7316 [S]	Black Pearls	1964	6.25	12.50	25.00
-- Blue label with trident logo					
❑ PRLP-7353 [M]	Bahia	1965	6.25	12.50	25.00
❑ PRST-7353 [S]	Bahia	1965	6.25	12.50	25.00
❑ PRLP-7378 [M]	The Last Trane	1965	6.25	12.50	25.00
❑ PRST-7378 [S]	The Last Trane	1965	6.25	12.50	25.00
❑ PRLP-7426 [M]	John Coltrane Plays for Lovers	1966	6.25	12.50	25.00
❑ PRST-7426 [S]	John Coltrane Plays for Lovers	1966	6.25	12.50	25.00
❑ PRLP-7531 [M]	Soultrane	1967	6.25	12.50	25.00
❑ PRST-7531 [R]	Soultrane	1967	3.00	6.00	12.00
❑ PRST-7581 [R]	Lush Life	1968	3.00	6.00	12.00
❑ PRST-7609 [R]	The First Trane	1969	3.00	6.00	12.00
❑ PRST-7651 [R]	Traneing In	1969	3.00	6.00	12.00
❑ PRST-7670 [R]	Two Tenors	1969	3.00	6.00	12.00
❑ PRST-7725	Mating Call	1970	3.00	6.00	12.00
❑ PRST-7746	Trane's Reign	1970	3.00	6.00	12.00
❑ PRST-7825	The Master	1971	3.00	6.00	12.00
❑ 24003 [(2)]	John Coltrane	1972	3.75	7.50	15.00
❑ 24014 [(2)]	More Lasting Than Bronze	1973	3.75	7.50	15.00
❑ 24037 [(2)]	Black Pearls	1974	3.75	7.50	15.00
❑ 24056 [(2)]	The Stardust Session	197?	3.75	7.50	15.00
❑ 24069 [(2)]	Wheelin'	197?	3.00	6.00	12.00
❑ 24084 [(2)]	On a Misty Night	198?	3.00	6.00	12.00
❑ 24094 [(2)]	Rain or Shine	198?	3.00	6.00	12.00
❑ 24104 [(2)]	Dakar	198?	3.00	6.00	12.00
❑ 24110 [(2)]	Bahia	198?	3.00	6.00	12.00
SOLID STATE					
❑ SM-17025 [M]	Coltrane Time	1968	6.25	12.50	25.00
❑ SS-18025 [S]	Coltrane Time	1968	3.75	7.50	15.00
TRIP					
❑ 5001 [(2)]	Trane Tracks	1974	3.75	7.50	15.00
UNITED ARTISTS					
❑ UAS-5638	Coltrane Time	1972	3.00	6.00	12.00
-- Reissue of 15001					
❑ UAJ-14001 [M]	Coltrane Time	1962	10.00	20.00	40.00
❑ UAJS-15001 [S]	Coltrane Time	1962	12.50	25.00	50.00

COLUMBO, CHRIS
Drummer.

Number	Title	Yr	VG	VG+	NM
STRAND					
❑ SL-1044 [M]	Jazz Rediscovered	1962	7.50	15.00	30.00
❑ SLS-1044 [S]	Jazz Rediscovered	1962	10.00	20.00	40.00
❑ SL-1095 [M]	Summertime	1963	7.50	15.00	30.00
❑ SLS-1095 [S]	Summertime	1963	10.00	20.00	40.00

COLYER, KEN
British trumpeter, cornet player, guitarist, male singer and bandleader.

Number	Title	Yr	VG	VG+	NM
GHB					
❑ 161	Live at the 100 Club	198?	2.50	5.00	10.00
LONDON					
❑ PB 904 [10]	New Orleans to London	1954	12.50	25.00	50.00
❑ LL 1340 [M]	Back to the Delta	1956	10.00	20.00	40.00
❑ LL 1618 [M]	Club Session with Colyer	1957	10.00	20.00	40.00
STORYVILLE					
❑ SLP-144	Ken's Early Days	197?	3.00	6.00	12.00

COMMANDERS, THE
Led by Eddie Grady.

Number	Title	Yr	VG	VG+	NM
DECCA					
❑ DL 8117 [M]	Dance Party	1955	10.00	20.00	40.00

COMPOSER'S WORKSHOP ENSEMBLE, THE
Led by WARREN SMITH.

Number	Title	Yr	VG	VG+	NM
STRATA-EAST					
❑ 1972-3	The Composer's Workshop Ensemble	197?	7.50	15.00	30.00
❑ 7422	(We've Been) Around	1974	7.50	15.00	30.00

Number	Title	Yr	VG	VG+	NM
CON BRIO					
PLUG					
❑ PLUG-4	Con Brio	1986	3.00	6.00	12.00
CONCORD ALL STARS, THE					
Collection of artists, all of whom are or were signed to the Concord Jazz label.					
CONCORD JAZZ					
❑ CJ-347	Take 8	1988	2.50	5.00	10.00
❑ CJ-348	Ow!	1988	2.50	5.00	10.00
CONCORD FESTIVAL ALL STARS, THE					
Collection of artists, all of whom are or were signed to the Concord Jazz label.					
CONCORD JAZZ					
❑ CJ-366	20th Anniversary	1989	3.00	6.00	12.00
CONCORD JAZZ ALL STARS, THE					
Collection of artists, all of whom are or were signed to the Concord Jazz label.					
CONCORD JAZZ					
❑ CJ-182	The Concord Jazz All Stars at Northsea Jazz Festival	1982	3.00	6.00	12.00
❑ CJ-205	The Concord Jazz All Stars at Northsea Jazz Festival, Vol. 2	1982	3.00	6.00	12.00
CONCORD SUPER BAND, THE					
Collection of artists, all of whom are or were signed to the Concord Jazz label.					
CONCORD JAZZ					
❑ CJ-80 [(2)]	The Concord Super Band in Tokyo	1979	3.75	7.50	15.00
❑ CJ-120 [(2)]	CSB II	1980	3.75	7.50	15.00
CONDON, EDDIE					
Guitarist, banjo player, vocalist and bandleader. Also see SIDNEY BECHET.					
ATLANTIC					
❑ 90461	That Toddlin' Town: Chicago Jazz Revisited	1986	2.50	5.00	10.00
CHIAROSCURO					
❑ 108	Town Hall Concerts, Volume 1	197?	3.00	6.00	12.00
❑ 113	Town Hall Concerts, Volume 2	197?	3.00	6.00	12.00
❑ 154	Eddie Condon in Japan	1978	3.00	6.00	12.00
COLUMBIA					
❑ CL 616 [M]	Jammin' at Condon's	1955	12.50	25.00	50.00
-- Maroon label, gold print					
❑ CL 616 [M]	Jammin' at Condon's	1955	10.00	20.00	40.00
-- Red and black label with six "eye" logos					
❑ CL 632 [M]	Chicago Style Jazz	1955	10.00	20.00	40.00
-- Red and black label with six "eye" logos					
❑ CL 719 [M]	Bixieland	1955	10.00	20.00	40.00
-- Red and black label with six "eye" logos					
❑ CL 881 [M]	Eddie Condon's Treasury of Jazz	1956	10.00	20.00	40.00
-- Red and black label with six "eye" logos					
❑ CL 1089 [M]	The Roaring Twenties	1958	10.00	20.00	40.00
-- Red and black label with six "eye" logos					
❑ KG 31564 [(2)]	The World of Eddie Condon	1972	4.50	9.00	18.00
❑ PG 31564 [(2)]	The World of Eddie Condon	197?	3.75	7.50	15.00
-- Reissue with new prefix					
COMMODORE					
❑ XFL-14427	Windy City Seven/Jam Sessions at Commodore	198?	2.50	5.00	10.00
❑ XFL-15355	The Liederkranz Sessions	198?	2.50	5.00	10.00
❑ XFL-16568	A Good Band Is Hard to Find	198?	2.50	5.00	10.00
❑ FL 20,022 [M]	Ballin' the Jack	195?	12.50	25.00	50.00
DECCA					
❑ DL 5137 [10]	George Gershwin Jazz Concert	1950	12.50	25.00	50.00
❑ DL 5203 [10]	Jazz Concert at Eddie Condon's	1950	12.50	25.00	50.00
❑ DL 5218 [10]	Jazz Concert at Eddie Condon's	1950	12.50	25.00	50.00
❑ DL 5246 [10]	We Call It Music	1951	12.50	25.00	50.00
❑ DL 8282 [M]	Ivy League Jazz	195?	10.00	20.00	40.00
❑ DL 9234 [M]	Gershwin Program (1941-1945)	1968	6.25	12.50	25.00
❑ DL 79234 [R]	Gershwin Program (1941-1945)	1968	3.00	6.00	12.00
DESIGN					
❑ DLP-47 [M]	Confidentially...It's Condon	196?	3.00	6.00	12.00
DOT					
❑ DLP-3141 [M]	Dixieland Dance Party	1958	10.00	20.00	40.00
EPIC					
❑ LA 16024 [M]	Midnight in Moscow	1962	3.75	7.50	15.00
❑ BA 17024 [S]	Midnight in Moscow	1962	5.00	10.00	20.00
JAZZ PANORAMA					
❑ 1805 [10]	Eddie Condon	1951	10.00	20.00	40.00
JAZZOLOGY					
❑ JCE-10	Eddie Condon Concert	196?	3.75	7.50	15.00
❑ J-50	Eddie Condon Jazz	197?	3.75	7.50	15.00
❑ J-73	The Spirit of Condon	1979	3.00	6.00	12.00
❑ J-101/2 [(2)]	1944 Jam Sessions	198?	3.75	7.50	15.00
❑ JCE-1001/2 [(2)]	Town Hall Concerts, Volume 1	1988	3.75	7.50	15.00
❑ JCE-1003/4 [(2)]	Town Hall Concerts, Volume 2	1988	3.75	7.50	15.00
❑ JCE-1005/6 [(2)]	Town Hall Concerts, Volume 3	1988	3.75	7.50	15.00
❑ JCE-1007/8 [(2)]	Town Hall Concerts, Volume 4	1990	3.75	7.50	15.00
❑ JCE-1009/10 [(2)]	Town Hall Concerts, Volume 5	1990	3.75	7.50	15.00
❑ JCE-1011/12 [(2)]	Town Hall Concerts, Volume 6	1990	3.75	7.50	15.00
❑ JCE-1013/14 [(2)]	Town Hall Concerts, Volume 7	1992	3.75	7.50	15.00
JOLLY ROGER					
❑ 5018 [10]	Eddie Condon and His Orchestra Featuring Pee Wee Russell	1954	10.00	20.00	40.00
❑ 5025 [10]	Eddie Condon	1954	10.00	20.00	40.00
MAINSTREAM					
❑ S-6024 [R]	Eddie Condon: A Legend	1965	3.75	7.50	15.00
❑ 56024 [M]	Eddie Condon: A Legend	1965	6.25	12.50	25.00
MCA					
❑ 4071 [(2)]	The Best of Eddie Condon	197?	3.75	7.50	15.00
-- Black rainbow labels					
MCA CORAL					
❑ 20013	Sunny Day	198?	2.50	5.00	10.00
MGM					
❑ E-3651 [M]	Eddie Condon Is Uptown Now	1960	6.25	12.50	25.00
❑ SE-3651 [S]	Eddie Condon Is Uptown Now	1960	7.50	15.00	30.00
MOSAIC					
❑ MQ7-152 [(7)]	The Complete CBS Recordings of Eddie Condon and His All-Stars	199?	30.00	60.00	120.00
SAVOY					
❑ MG-12055 [M]	Ringside at Condon's	1956	10.00	20.00	40.00
TRIP					
❑ 5800 [(2)]	Eddie Condon and His Jazz Concert Orchestra	197?	3.75	7.50	15.00
"X"					
❑ LX-3005 [M]	Eddie Condon's Hot Shots	1954	12.50	25.00	50.00
CONNELLY, PEGGY					
Female singer.					
BETHLEHEM					
❑ BCP-53 [M]	That Old Black Magic	1957	30.00	60.00	120.00
CONNICK, HARRY, JR.					
Pianist, male singer and guitarist.					
COLUMBIA					
❑ BFC 40702	Harry Connick, Jr.	1987	3.00	6.00	12.00
❑ FC 44369	20	1988	3.00	6.00	12.00
❑ SC 45319	When Harry Met Sally... (soundtrack)	1989	3.00	6.00	12.00
❑ C 46146	We Are in Love	1990	3.75	7.50	15.00
❑ C 46223	Lofty's Roach Souffle	1990	3.75	7.50	15.00
CONNOR, CHRIS					
Female singer.					
ABC					
❑ ABC-585 [M]	Chris Connor Now	1966	5.00	10.00	20.00
❑ ABCS-585 [S]	Chris Connor Now	1966	6.25	12.50	25.00
ABC-PARAMOUNT					
❑ ABC-529 [M]	Gentle Bossa Nova	1965	5.00	10.00	20.00
❑ ABCS-529 [S]	Gentle Bossa Nova	1965	6.25	12.50	25.00
ATLANTIC					
❑ 2-601 [(2) M]	Chris Connor Sings the George Gershwin Almanac of Song	1957	25.00	50.00	100.00
-- Black label					
❑ 2-601 [(2) M]	Chris Connor Sings the George Gershwin Almanac of Song	196?	5.00	10.00	20.00
-- Multi-color label, black "fan" logo					
❑ 2-601 [(2) M]	Chris Connor Sings the George Gershwin Almanac of Song	196?	10.00	20.00	40.00
-- Multi-color label, white "fan" logo					
❑ 1228 [M]	Chris Connor	1956	12.50	25.00	50.00
-- Black label					
❑ 1228 [M]	Chris Connor	196?	5.00	10.00	20.00
-- Multi-color label, white "fan" logo					
❑ 1228 [M]	Chris Connor	196?	3.00	6.00	12.00
-- Multi-color label, black "fan" logo					
❑ SD 1228 [S]	Chris Connor	1958	15.00	30.00	60.00
-- Green label					
❑ SD 1228 [S]	Chris Connor	196?	6.25	12.50	25.00
-- Multi-color label, white "fan" logo					
❑ SD 1228 [S]	Chris Connor	196?	3.75	7.50	15.00
-- Multi-color label, black "fan" logo					
❑ 1240 [M]	He Loves Me, He Loves Me Not	1956	12.50	25.00	50.00
-- Black label					

(Top left) Eddie Condon was a pioneer in so-called "Chicago jazz" before World War II. He continued to record traditionally-styled material long after that; the above album on Columbia, one of his best, was issued in 1955. (Top right) Chris Connor, another former Stan Kenton singer, helped keep Bethlehem Records in business in the 1950s with her big-selling (for the time) albums, including this one. (Bottom left) Curtis Counce, a bass player, led some sessions on the Contemporary label in the late 1950s. This one, *Carl's Blues*, featured pianist Carl Perkins, who died shortly after it was recorded. (Bottom right) Hank Crawford first made a name for himself as Ray Charles' musical director. On his own, he's the epitome of "soul jazz," as shown on this 1983 album for Milestone, *Indigo Blue*.

Number	Title	Yr	VG	VG+	NM
❑ 1240 [M]	He Loves Me, He Loves Me Not	1960	10.00	20.00	40.00
-- White "bullseye" label					
❑ 1240 [M]	He Loves Me, He Loves Me Not	196?	3.00	6.00	12.00
-- Multi-color label, black "fan" logo					
❑ 1240 [M]	He Loves Me, He Loves Me Not	196?	5.00	10.00	20.00
-- Multi-color label, white "fan" logo					
❑ SD 1240 [S]	He Loves Me, He Loves Me Not	1958	15.00	30.00	60.00
-- Green label					
❑ SD 1240 [S]	He Loves Me, He Loves Me Not	1960	12.50	25.00	50.00
-- White "bullseye" label					
❑ SD 1240 [S]	He Loves Me, He Loves Me Not	196?	3.75	7.50	15.00
-- Multi-color label, black "fan" logo					
❑ SD 1240 [S]	He Loves Me, He Loves Me Not	196?	6.25	12.50	25.00
-- Multi-color label, white "fan" logo					
❑ 1286 [M]	A Jazz Date with Chris Connor	1958	12.50	25.00	50.00
-- Black label					
❑ 1286 [M]	A Jazz Date with Chris Connor	196?	3.00	6.00	12.00
-- Multi-color label, black "fan" logo					
❑ 1286 [M]	A Jazz Date with Chris Connor	196?	5.00	10.00	20.00
-- Multi-color label, white "fan" logo					
❑ 1290 [M]	Chris Craft	1958	12.50	25.00	50.00
-- Black label					
❑ 1290 [M]	Chris Craft	196?	5.00	10.00	20.00
-- Multi-color label, white "fan" logo					
❑ 1290 [M]	Chris Craft	196?	3.00	6.00	12.00
-- Multi-color label, black "fan" logo					
❑ 1307 [M]	Ballads of the Sad Café	1959	12.50	25.00	50.00
-- Black label					
❑ 1307 [M]	Ballads of the Sad Café	196?	5.00	10.00	20.00
-- Multi-color label, white "fan" logo					
❑ 1307 [M]	Ballads of the Sad Café	196?	3.00	6.00	12.00
-- Multi-color label, black "fan" logo					
❑ SD 1307 [S]	Ballads of the Sad Café	1959	15.00	30.00	60.00
-- Green label					
❑ SD 1307 [S]	Ballads of the Sad Café	196?	6.25	12.50	25.00
-- Multi-color label, white "fan" logo					
❑ SD 1307 [S]	Ballads of the Sad Café	196?	3.75	7.50	15.00
-- Multi-color label, black "fan" logo					
❑ 1309 [M]	Chris Connor Sings the George Gershwin Almanac of Song, Vol. 1	1959	10.00	20.00	40.00
-- Black label					
❑ 1309 [M]	Chris Connor Sings the George Gershwin Almanac of Song, Vol. 1	196?	5.00	10.00	20.00
-- Multi-color label, white "fan" logo					
❑ 1309 [M]	Chris Connor Sings the George Gershwin Almanac of Song, Vol. 1	196?	3.00	6.00	12.00
-- Multi-color label, black "fan" logo					
❑ 1310 [M]	Chris Connor Sings the George Gershwin Almanac of Song, Vol. 2	1959	10.00	20.00	40.00
-- Black label					
❑ 1310 [M]	Chris Connor Sings the George Gershwin Almanac of Song, Vol. 2	196?	5.00	10.00	20.00
-- Multi-color label, white "fan" logo					
❑ 1310 [M]	Chris Connor Sings the George Gershwin Almanac of Song, Vol. 2	196?	3.00	6.00	12.00
-- Multi-color label, black "fan" logo					
❑ 8014 [M]	I Miss You So	1957	12.50	25.00	50.00
-- Black label					
❑ 8014 [M]	I Miss You So	196?	3.00	6.00	12.00
-- Multi-color label, black "fan" logo					
❑ 8014 [M]	I Miss You So	196?	5.00	10.00	20.00
-- Multi-color label, white "fan" logo					
❑ 8014 [M]	I Miss You So	1960	10.00	20.00	40.00
-- White "bullseye" label					
❑ 8032 [M]	Witchcraft	1959	12.50	25.00	50.00
-- Black label					
❑ 8032 [M]	Witchcraft	196?	5.00	10.00	20.00
-- Multi-color label, white "fan" logo					
❑ 8032 [M]	Witchcraft	196?	3.00	6.00	12.00
-- Multi-color label, black "fan" logo					
❑ SD 8032 [S]	Witchcraft	1959	15.00	30.00	60.00
-- Green label					
❑ SD 8032 [S]	Witchcraft	196?	3.75	7.50	15.00
-- Multi-color label, black "fan" logo					
❑ SD 8032 [S]	Witchcraft	196?	6.25	12.50	25.00
-- Multi-color label, white "fan" logo					
❑ 8040 [M]	Chris In Person	1959	12.50	25.00	50.00
-- Black labe					
❑ 8040 [M]	Chris In Person	196?	3.00	6.00	12.00
-- Multi-color label, black "fan" logo					
❑ 8040 [M]	Chris In Person	196?	5.00	10.00	20.00
-- Multi-color label, white "fan" logo					
❑ SD 8040 [S]	Chris In Person	1959	15.00	30.00	60.00
-- Green label					
❑ SD 8040 [S]	Chris In Person	196?	3.75	7.50	15.00
-- Multi-color label, black "fan" logo					
❑ SD 8040 [S]	Chris In Person	196?	6.25	12.50	25.00
-- Multi-color label, white "fan" logo					
❑ 8046 [M]	A Portrait of Chris	196?	3.00	6.00	12.00
-- Multi-color label, black "fan" logo					

Number	Title	Yr	VG	VG+	NM
❑ 8046 [M]	A Portrait of Chris	1960	10.00	20.00	40.00
-- Multi-color label, white "fan" logo					
❑ SD 8046 [S]	A Portrait of Chris	196?	3.75	7.50	15.00
-- Multi-color label, black "fan" logo					
❑ SD 8046 [S]	A Portrait of Chris	1960	12.50	25.00	50.00
-- Multi-color label, white "fan" logo					
❑ 8061 [M]	Free Spirits	1962	7.50	15.00	30.00
-- Multi-color label, black "fan" logo					
❑ SD 8061 [S]	Free Spirits	1962	10.00	20.00	40.00
-- Multi-color label, black "fan" logo					
AUDIOPHILE					
❑ AP-208	Sweet and Swinging	199?	3.75	7.50	15.00
BAINBRIDGE					
❑ 6230	Sketches	198?	2.50	5.00	10.00
-- Reissue of Stanyan 10029					
BETHLEHEM					
❑ BCP-20 [M]	This Is Chris	1955	15.00	30.00	60.00
❑ BCP-56 [M]	Chris	1957	15.00	30.00	60.00
❑ 2BP-1001 [(2)]	The Finest	197?	3.75	7.50	15.00
❑ BCP-1001 [10]	Chris Connor Sings Lullabys of Birdland	1954	20.00	40.00	80.00
❑ BCP-1002 [10]	Chris Connor Sings Lullabys for Lovers	1954	20.00	40.00	80.00
❑ BCP-6004 [M]	Chris Connor Sings Lullabys of Birdland	1955	12.50	25.00	50.00
❑ BCP-6010	Cocktails and Dusk	197?	3.00	6.00	12.00
CONTEMPORARY					
❑ C-14023	Classic	1987	3.00	6.00	12.00
❑ C-14038	New Again	1988	3.00	6.00	12.00
FM					
❑ 300 [M]	Chris Connor at the Village Gate	1963	12.50	25.00	50.00
❑ S-300 [S]	Chris Connor at the Village Gate	1963	15.00	30.00	60.00
❑ 312 [M]	A Weekend in Paris	1964	12.50	25.00	50.00
❑ S-312 [S]	A Weekend in Paris	1964	15.00	30.00	60.00
PROGRESSIVE					
❑ 7028	Sweet and Singing	1979	3.00	6.00	12.00
STANYAN					
❑ 10029	Sketches	1972	3.75	7.50	15.00
STASH					
❑ 232	Love Being Here with You	1984	3.00	6.00	12.00

CONNOR, CHRIS, AND MAYNARD FERGUSON
Also see each artist's individual listings.

Number	Title	Yr	VG	VG+	NM
ATLANTIC					
❑ 8049 [M]	Double Exposure	196?	3.00	6.00	12.00
-- Multi-color label, black "fan" logo					
❑ 8049 [M]	Double Exposure	1961	7.50	15.00	30.00
-- Multi-color label, white "fan" logo					
❑ SD 8049 [S]	Double Exposure	196?	3.75	7.50	15.00
-- Multi-color label, black "fan" logo					
❑ SD 8049 [S]	Double Exposure	1961	10.00	20.00	40.00
-- Multi-color label, white "fan" logo					
❑ 90143	Double Exposure	198?	2.50	5.00	10.00
-- Reissue					
ROULETTE					
❑ R 52068 [M]	Two's Company	1961	7.50	15.00	30.00
-- White label with colored spokes					
❑ SR 52068 [S]	Two's Company	1961	10.00	20.00	40.00
-- White label with colored spokes					

CONNORS, BILL
Guitarist.

Number	Title	Yr	VG	VG+	NM
ECM					
❑ 1057	Theme to the Gaurdian	197?	3.75	7.50	15.00
❑ 1120	Of Mist and Melting	1977	3.75	7.50	15.00
❑ 1158	Swimming with a Hole in My Body	1979	3.00	6.00	12.00
PATHFINDER					
❑ PTF-8503	Step It	1985	2.50	5.00	10.00
❑ PTF-8620	Double Up	1986	2.50	5.00	10.00
❑ PTF-8707	Assembler	1987	2.50	5.00	10.00

CONNORS, NORMAN
Drummer and bandleader.

Number	Title	Yr	VG	VG+	NM
ACCORD					
❑ SN-7210	Just Imagine	1982	2.00	4.00	8.00
ARISTA					
❑ AB 4177	This Is Your Life	1978	2.50	5.00	10.00
❑ AB 4216	Invitation	1979	2.50	5.00	10.00
❑ AL 9534	Take It to the Limit	1980	2.50	5.00	10.00
❑ AL 9575	Mr. C.	1981	2.50	5.00	10.00
BUDDAH					
❑ BDS-5142	Love from the Sun	1973	3.00	6.00	12.00

Number	Title	Yr	VG	VG+	NM
❑ BDS-5611	Slewfoot	1974	3.00	6.00	12.00
❑ BDS-5643	Saturday Night Special	1975	2.50	5.00	10.00
❑ BDS-5655	You Are My Starship	1976	2.50	5.00	10.00
❑ BDS-5674	Dance of Magic	1977	2.50	5.00	10.00
-- Reissue of Cobblestone 9024					
❑ BDS-5675	Dark of Light	1977	2.50	5.00	10.00
-- Reissue of Cobblestone 9035					
❑ BDS-5682	Romantic Journey	1977	2.50	5.00	10.00
❑ BDS-5716	The Best of Norman Connors & Friends	1978	2.50	5.00	10.00
CAPITOL					
❑ C1-48515	Passion	1988	2.50	5.00	10.00
COBBLESTONE					
❑ 9024	Dance of Magic	1972	3.75	7.50	15.00
❑ 9035	Dark of Light	1973	3.75	7.50	15.00

CONTEMPORARY JAZZ ENSEMBLE, THE
PRESTIGE

Number	Title	Yr	VG	VG+	NM
❑ PRLP-163 [10]	New Sounds from Rochester	1953	25.00	50.00	100.00

CONTI, ROBERT
Guitarist. Also see JOE PASS.
DISCOVERY

Number	Title	Yr	VG	VG+	NM
❑ 834	Robert Conti Jazz Quintet	1981	3.00	6.00	12.00
TREND					
❑ TR-519	Solo Guitar	198?	5.00	10.00	20.00
-- Direct-to-disc recording					
❑ TR-540	Laura	1986	3.00	6.00	12.00

CONTINENTAL OCTETTE, THE
CROWN

Number	Title	Yr	VG	VG+	NM
❑ CLP-5220	Modern Jazz Greats	196?	5.00	10.00	20.00

COOK, JUNIOR
Tenor saxophone player.
JAZZLAND

Number	Title	Yr	VG	VG+	NM
❑ JLP-58 [M]	Junior's Cookin'	1961	10.00	20.00	40.00
❑ JLP-958 [S]	Junior's Cookin'	1961	12.50	25.00	50.00
MUSE					
❑ MR-5159	Good Cookin'	1979	3.00	6.00	12.00
❑ MR-5218	Something's Cookin'	1981	3.00	6.00	12.00

COOL BRITONS, THE
Also see THE SWINGING SWEDES.
BLUE NOTE

Number	Title	Yr	VG	VG+	NM
❑ BLP-5052 [10]	New Sounds from Olde England	1954	75.00	150.00	300.00

COON, JACKIE
Cornet and fluegel horn player.
SEA BREEZE

Number	Title	Yr	VG	VG+	NM
❑ SB-1009	Jazzin' Around	1987	2.50	5.00	10.00

COOPER, BOB
Tenor saxophone player and composer. Also played oboe.
CAPITOL

Number	Title	Yr	VG	VG+	NM
❑ ST 1586 [S]	Do Re Mi	1961	7.50	15.00	30.00
❑ T 1586 [M]	Do Re Mi	1961	6.25	12.50	25.00
❑ H 6501 [10]	Bob Cooper	1954	20.00	40.00	80.00
❑ T 6501 [M]	Bob Cooper	1955	12.50	25.00	50.00
❑ H 6513 [10]	Shifting Winds	1955	15.00	30.00	60.00
❑ T 6513 [M]	Shifting Winds	1955	12.50	25.00	50.00
CONTEMPORARY					
❑ C-3544 [M]	Coop!	1958	12.50	25.00	50.00
❑ S-7012 [S]	Coop!	1959	10.00	20.00	40.00
-- Reissue of Stereo Records 7012					
❑ C-14017	In a Mellotone	1986	2.50	5.00	10.00
DISCOVERY					
❑ 822	Bob Cooper Plays the Music of Michel Legrand	1981	3.00	6.00	12.00
FANTASY					
❑ OJC-161	Coop!	198?	2.50	5.00	10.00
STEREO RECORDS					
❑ S-7012 [S]	Coop!	1958	12.50	25.00	50.00
TREND					
❑ TR-518	Tenor Sax Impressions	198?	5.00	10.00	20.00
-- Direct-to-disc recording					
WORLD PACIFIC					
❑ WPM-411 [M]	Bob Cooper Swings TV	1958	12.50	25.00	50.00

COOPER, JEROME
Drummer.
ABOUT TIME

Number	Title	Yr	VG	VG+	NM
❑ 1002	The Unpredictability of Predictability	1979	2.50	5.00	10.00
❑ 1008	Outer and Interactions	1988	2.50	5.00	10.00
HAT HUT					
❑ 07	For the People	1980	3.00	6.00	12.00

CORBIN, HAROLD
ROULETTE

Number	Title	Yr	VG	VG+	NM
❑ R-52079 [M]	Soul Brother	1961	6.25	12.50	25.00
❑ SR-52079 [S]	Soul Brother	1961	7.50	15.00	30.00

CORCORAN, CORKY
Tenor saxophone player.
CELESTIAL

Number	Title	Yr	VG	VG+	NM
❑ Vol. 1 [M]	Sounds of Jazz	1958	62.50	125.00	250.00
-- Red vinyl					
❑ Vol. 1 [M]	Sounds of Jazz	1958	30.00	60.00	120.00
-- Black vinyl					
EPIC					
❑ LN 3319 [M]	The Sound of Love	1956	20.00	40.00	80.00

COREA, CHICK
Pianist, keyboard and synthesizer player, composer and bandleader. Also see CIRCLE; RETURN TO FOREVER.
ATLANTIC

Number	Title	Yr	VG	VG+	NM
❑ SD 2-305 [(2)]	Inner Space	1973	3.75	7.50	15.00
BLUE NOTE					
❑ BN-LA395-H2 [(2)]	Chick Corea	1975	3.75	7.50	15.00
❑ LWB-395 [(2)]	Chick Corea	1981	2.50	5.00	10.00
-- Reissue with new prefix					
❑ BN-LA472-H2 [(2)]	Circling In	1976	3.75	7.50	15.00
❑ BN-LA882-J2 [(2)]	Circulus	1978	3.75	7.50	15.00
❑ BST-84353	Song of Singing	1970	5.00	10.00	20.00
❑ B1-90055	Now He Sings, Now He Sobs	1988	3.00	6.00	12.00
-- Reissue					
ECM					
❑ 1009	A.R.C.	197?	3.00	6.00	12.00
❑ 1014	Piano Improvisations, Vol. 1	1974	3.00	6.00	12.00
❑ 1020	Piano Improvisations, Vol. 2	197?	3.00	6.00	12.00
❑ 1232 [(2)]	Trio Music	198?	3.00	6.00	12.00
❑ 23797	Lyric Suite for Sextet	1984	2.50	5.00	10.00
❑ 25005	Children's Songs	1985	2.50	5.00	10.00
❑ 25013	Voyage	1985	2.50	5.00	10.00
ELEKTRA/MUSICIAN					
❑ 60167	Again & Again	1984	2.50	5.00	10.00
GROOVE MERCHANT					
❑ 530	Sundance	1974	3.00	6.00	12.00
-- Reissue of 2202					
❑ 2202	Sundance	1972	5.00	10.00	20.00
❑ 4406 [(2)]	Piano Giants	197?	3.75	7.50	15.00
GRP					
❑ GR-1026	The Chick Corea Electric Band	1987	2.50	5.00	10.00
❑ GR-1036	Light Years	1987	2.50	5.00	10.00
❑ GR-1053	Eye of the Beholder	1988	2.50	5.00	10.00
❑ GR-9582	The Chick Corea Akoustic Band	1989	3.00	6.00	12.00
❑ GR-9601	Inside Out	1991	3.75	7.50	15.00
MUSE					
❑ 5011	Bliss!	1973	3.75	7.50	15.00
PACIFIC JAZZ					
❑ LN-10057	Now He Sings, Now He Sobs	1981	2.50	5.00	10.00
-- Reissue of Solid State 18039					
POLYDOR					
❑ PD-6062	The Leprechaun	1976	2.50	5.00	10.00
❑ PD-1-6130	The Mad Hatter	1978	2.50	5.00	10.00
❑ PD-1-6160	Friends	1978	2.50	5.00	10.00
❑ PD-1-6176	Secret Agent	1979	2.50	5.00	10.00
❑ PD-1-6208	Delphi I	1979	2.50	5.00	10.00
❑ PD-2-6334 [(2)]	Delphi II & III	1982	3.00	6.00	12.00
❑ PD-2-9003 [(2)]	My Spanish Heart	1976	3.00	6.00	12.00
QUINTESSENCE					
❑ 25011	Before Forever	1978	3.00	6.00	12.00
SOLID STATE					
❑ SS-18039	Now He Sings, Now He Sobs	1969	5.00	10.00	20.00
❑ SS-18055	Chick Corea "Is"	1969	5.00	10.00	20.00
VORTEX					
❑ 2004	Tones	1971	5.00	10.00	20.00
WARNER BROS.					
❑ BSK 3425	Tap Step	1980	2.50	5.00	10.00

Number	Title	Yr	VG	VG+	NM
❏ BSK 3552	Three Quartets	1981	2.50	5.00	10.00
❏ 23699	Touchstone	1983	2.50	5.00	10.00

CORWIN, BOB
Pianist.
RIVERSIDE
❏ RLP 12-220 [M]	Bob Corwin Quartet with Don Elliott	1956	20.00	40.00	80.00
-- White label, blue print					
❏ RLP 12-220 [M]	Bob Corwin Quartet with Don Elliott	1957	10.00	20.00	40.00
-- Blue label with microphone logo					

CORYELL, LARRY
Guitarist. Also see JAZZ COMPOSERS ORCHESTRA.
ARISTA
❏ AL 4052	Level One	1975	3.75	7.50	15.00
❏ AL 4077	Aspects	1976	3.75	7.50	15.00
❏ AL 4108	The Lion and the Ram	1977	3.75	7.50	15.00
ARISTA/NOVUS
❏ AN 3005	European Imperssions	1978	3.00	6.00	12.00
❏ AN 3017	Tributaries	1979	3.00	6.00	12.00
CONCORD JAZZ
❏ CJ-289	Together	1986	2.50	5.00	10.00
FLYING DUTCHMAN
❏ 51-1000	Fairyland	1971	5.00	10.00	20.00
❏ FD-10139	Barefoot Boy	1971	3.75	7.50	15.00
MEGA
❏ 607	Fairyland	197?	3.75	7.50	15.00
-- Reissue of Flying Dutchman 51-1000					
MUSE
❏ MR-5303	Comin' Home	1985	2.50	5.00	10.00
❏ MR-5319	Equipoise	1986	2.50	5.00	10.00
❏ MR-5350	Toku Do	1988	3.00	6.00	12.00
RCA VICTOR
❏ AYL1-3961	Barefoot Boy	198?	2.00	4.00	8.00
-- Reissue of Flying Dutchman 10139					
SHANACHIE
❏ 97005	The Dragon Gate	1990	3.75	7.50	15.00
STEEPLECHASE
❏ SCS-1187	A Quiet Day in Spring	1983	2.50	5.00	10.00
VANGUARD
❏ VSD-75/76 [(2)]	The Essential Larry Coryell	1975	3.75	7.50	15.00
❏ VSD-6509	Lady Coryell	1969	3.75	7.50	15.00
❏ VSD-6547	Coryell	1969	3.75	7.50	15.00
❏ VSD-6558	Spaces	1970	3.75	7.50	15.00
❏ VSD-6573	Larry Coryell at the Village Gate	1971	3.75	7.50	15.00
❏ VSQ-40006 [Q]	Larry Coryell at the Village Gate	197?	5.00	10.00	20.00
❏ VSQ-40013 [Q]	Offering	197?	5.00	10.00	20.00
❏ VSQ-40023 [Q]	The Real Great Escape	197?	5.00	10.00	20.00
❏ VSQ-40036 [Q]	Introducing the Eleventh House	1974	5.00	10.00	20.00
❏ VSD-79319	Offering	1972	3.75	7.50	15.00
❏ VSD-79329	The Real Great Escape	1973	3.75	7.50	15.00
❏ VSD-79342	Introducing the Eleventh House	1974	3.75	7.50	15.00
❏ VSD-79345	Spaces	1974	3.00	6.00	12.00
-- Reissue of 6558 with new cover					
❏ VSD-79353	The Restful Mind	1975	3.00	6.00	12.00
❏ VSD-79360	Another Side of Larry Coryell	1975	3.75	7.50	15.00
❏ VSD-79367	Planet End	1975	3.00	6.00	12.00
❏ VSD-79375	Basics	1976	3.00	6.00	12.00
❏ VSD-79410	Larry Coryell and the Eleventh House at Montreux	1978	3.00	6.00	12.00
❏ VSD-79426	Return	1979	3.00	6.00	12.00

CORYELL, LARRY, AND PHILIP CATHERINE
Also see each artist's individual listings.
ELEKTRA
❏ 6E-123	Twin House	1977	3.00	6.00	12.00
❏ 6E-153	Splendid	1978	3.00	6.00	12.00

CORYELL, LARRY, AND BRIAN KEANE
Keane is a guitarist in the new-age genre. Also see LARRY CORYELL.
FLYING FISH
❏ FF-337	Just Like Being Born	1985	3.00	6.00	12.00

CORYELL, LARRY, AND STEVE KHAN
Also see each artist's individual listings.
ARISTA
❏ AB 4156	Two for the Road	1978	3.00	6.00	12.00

CORYELL, LARRY, AND ALPHONSE MOUZON
Also see each artist's individual listings.
ATLANTIC
❏ SD 18220	Back Together Again	1977	3.00	6.00	12.00

COSMIC TWINS, THE
Ron Burton and John Lewis.
STRATA-EAST
❏ SES-7410	The Waterbearers	1974	7.50	15.00	30.00

COSTA, EDDIE
Vibraphone player and pianist. Also see THE MANHATTAN JAZZ SEPTETTE; JOHN MEHEGAN.
CORAL
❏ CRL 57230 [M]	Guys and Dolls Like Vibes	1958	12.50	25.00	50.00
DOT
❏ DLP-3206 [M]	The House of Blue Lights	1959	10.00	20.00	40.00
❏ DLP-25206 [S]	The House of Blue Lights	1959	12.50	25.00	50.00
INTERLUDE
❏ MO-508 [M]	Eddie Costa Quintet	1959	10.00	20.00	40.00
-- Reissue of Mode 118					
❏ ST-1008 [S]	Eddie Costa Quintet	1959	7.50	15.00	30.00
JOSIE
❏ JOZ-3509 [M]	Eddie Costa with the Burke Trio	1963	5.00	10.00	20.00
❏ JSS-2509 [S]	Eddie Costa with the Burke Trio	1963	6.25	12.50	25.00
MODE
❏ LP-118 [M]	Eddie Costa Quintet	1957	25.00	50.00	100.00

COSTA, EDDIE, AND ART FARMER
Also see each artist's individual listings.
PREMIER
❏ PM-2002 [M]	In Their Own Sweet Way	1962	3.75	7.50	15.00
❏ PMS-2002 [R]	In Their Own Sweet Way	196?	2.00	4.00	8.00

COSTA, EDDIE/MAT MATTHEWS AND DON ELLIOTT
Also see each artist's individual listings.
VERVE
❏ MGV-8237 [M]	Eddie Costa with Rolf Kuhn and Dick Johnson/Mat Matthews and Don Elliott at Newport	1958	10.00	20.00	40.00
❏ V-8237 [M]	Eddie Costa with Rolf Kuhn and Dick Johnson/Mat Matthews and Don Elliott at Newport	1961	5.00	10.00	20.00

COSTA, JOHNNY
Pianist and composer.
CORAL
❏ CRL 57117 [M]	The Most Beautiful Girl in the World	1957	7.50	15.00	30.00
SAVOY
❏ MG-12052 [M]	The Amazing Johnny Costa	1956	12.50	25.00	50.00
❏ MG-15056 [10]	Johnny Costa	1955	20.00	40.00	80.00
SAVOY JAZZ
❏ SJL-1190	Neighborhood	198?	2.50	5.00	10.00

COSTANZO, JACK
Bongo player.
GENE NORMAN
❏ GNP-19 [M]	Mr. Bongo	1955	12.50	25.00	50.00
LIBERTY
❏ LRP-3093 [M]	Latin Fever	1958	6.25	12.50	25.00
❏ LRP-3109 [M]	Bongo Fever	1959	6.25	12.50	25.00
❏ LRP-3137 [M]	Afro Can-Can	1960	6.25	12.50	25.00
❏ LRP-3177 [M]	Learn-Play Bongos	1960	6.25	12.50	25.00
❏ LRP-3195 [M]	Naked City	1961	6.25	12.50	25.00
❏ LST-7020 [S]	Latin Fever	1958	7.50	15.00	30.00
❏ LST-7109 [S]	Bongo Fever	1959	7.50	15.00	30.00
❏ LST-7137 [S]	Afro Can-Can	1960	7.50	15.00	30.00
❏ LST-7195 [S]	Naked City	1961	7.50	15.00	30.00
NORGRAN
❏ MGN-32 [10]	Afro-Cubano	1954	37.50	75.00	150.00
SUNSET
❏ SUM-1134 [M]	Bongo Fever	196?	3.00	6.00	12.00
❏ SUS-5134 [S]	Bongo Fever	196?	3.00	6.00	12.00

COSTANZO, JACK/ANDRE'S CUBAN ALL STARS
Also see each artist's individual listings.
NORGRAN
❏ MGN-1067 [M]	Afro-Cubano	1956	25.00	50.00	100.00
-- Combined reissue of Norgran 32 (by the former) and Clef 515 (by the latter)					

Number	Title	Yr	VG	VG+	NM
VERVE					
❏ MGV-8157 [M]	Afro-Cubano	1957	12.50	25.00	50.00
❏ V-8157 [M]	Afro-Cubano	1961	6.25	12.50	25.00
COTTRELL, LOUIS					
Clarinetist and saxophone player.					
NOBILITY					
❏ LP-703	Dixieland Hall Presents Louis Cottrell and His New Orleans Jazz	197?	3.75	7.50	15.00
RIVERSIDE					
❏ RLP-385 [M]	Bourbon Street	1961	5.00	10.00	20.00
❏ RS-9385 [S]	Bourbon Street	1961	6.25	12.50	25.00
COTTRELL, LOUIS/HERB HALL					
Hall played clarinet and saxophone. Also see LOUIS COTTRELL.					
GHB					
❏ 156	Clarinet Legends	198?	2.50	5.00	10.00
COULTER, CLIFF					
Pianist (mostly electric).					
ABC IMPULSE!					
❏ AS-9197	Eastside San Jose	1971	5.00	10.00	20.00
❏ AS-9216	Do It Now!	1972	5.00	10.00	20.00
COUNCE, CURTIS					
Bass player.					
ANALOGUE PRODUCTIONS					
❏ AP-3006	You Get More Bounce with Curtis Counce	199?	3.75	7.50	15.00
BOPLICITY					
❏ BOP-7	Exploring the Future	198?	3.00	6.00	12.00
-- Reissue of Dooto LP					
CONTEMPORARY					
❏ C-3526 [M]	Curtis Counce Group	1957	20.00	40.00	80.00
❏ M-3539 [M]	You Get More Bounce with Curtis Counce	1957	20.00	40.00	80.00
❏ M-3574 [M]	Carl's Blues	1960	10.00	20.00	40.00
❏ S-7526 [S]	Curtis Counce Group	1959	15.00	30.00	60.00
❏ S-7526 [S]	Landslide	196?	7.50	15.00	30.00
-- Retitled version of "Curtis Counce Group"					
❏ C-7539	Counceltation	197?	5.00	10.00	20.00
-- Retitled version of "You Get More Bounce with Curtis Counce"					
❏ S-7539 [S]	You Get More Bounce with Curtis Counce	1959	15.00	30.00	60.00
❏ S-7574 [S]	Carl's Blues	1960	12.50	25.00	50.00
❏ C-7655	Sonority	198?	5.00	10.00	20.00
DOOTO					
❏ DTL-247 [M]	Exploring the Future	1958	12.50	25.00	50.00
FANTASY					
❏ OJC-159	You Get More Bounce with Curtis Counce	198?	2.50	5.00	10.00
-- Reissue of Contemporary 7539					
❏ OJC-423	Carl's Blues	1990	3.00	6.00	12.00
-- Reissue of Contemporary 7574					
COWELL, STANLEY					
Pianist.					
ARISTA FREEDOM					
❏ AL 1009	Beautiful Circles	197?	3.00	6.00	12.00
❏ AL 1032	Blues for the Viet Cong	197?	3.00	6.00	12.00
ECM					
❏ 1026	Illusion Suite	1973	6.25	12.50	25.00
GALAXY					
❏ 5104	Waiting for ...	1977	3.00	6.00	12.00
❏ 5111	Talkin' Bout Love	1978	3.00	6.00	12.00
❏ 5125	Equipoise	1979	3.00	6.00	12.00
❏ 5131	New World	1979	3.00	6.00	12.00
STRATA-EAST					
❏ SES-19743	Musa-Ancestral Streams	1974	5.00	10.00	20.00
❏ SES-19765	Regeneration	1976	5.00	10.00	20.00
COX, IDA					
Female singer.					
FANTASY					
❏ OJC-1758	Blues for Rampart Street	198?	3.75	7.50	15.00
-- Reissue of Riverside 9374					
RIVERSIDE					
❏ RLP-374 [M]	Blues for Rampart Street	1961	7.50	15.00	30.00
❏ RS-9374 [S]	Blues for Rampart Street	1961	10.00	20.00	40.00
COX, KENNY, CONTEMPORARY JAZZ QUINTET					
Cox is a pianist.					
BLUE NOTE					
❏ BST-84302	Introducing Kenny Cox	1969	5.00	10.00	20.00
❏ BST-84339	Multidirection	1970	5.00	10.00	20.00
COX, SONNY					
CADET					
❏ LP-765 [M]	The Wailer	1966	3.75	7.50	15.00
❏ LPS-765 [S]	The Wailer	1966	5.00	10.00	20.00
CRAM, PAUL					
Tenor saxophone player, composer and arranger.					
ONARI/A&M					
❏ 006	Blue Tales in Time	1982	3.00	6.00	12.00
CRAWFORD, HANK					
Saxophone player (tenor, alto and baritone), pianist and composer.					
ATLANTIC					
❏ SD 2-315 [(2)]	The Art of Hank Crawford	1973	3.75	7.50	15.00
❏ 1356 [M]	More Soul	1960	5.00	10.00	20.00
-- Purple and red label, white fan logo					
❏ 1356 [M]	More Soul	1962	3.00	6.00	12.00
-- Purple and red label, black fan logo					
❏ SD 1356 [S]	More Soul	1960	6.25	12.50	25.00
-- Green and blue label, white fan logo					
❏ SD 1356 [S]	More Soul	1962	3.75	7.50	15.00
-- Green and blue label, black fan logo					
❏ 1372 [M]	The Soul Clinic	1961	5.00	10.00	20.00
-- Purple and red label, white fan logo					
❏ 1372 [M]	The Soul Clinic	1962	3.00	6.00	12.00
-- Purple and red label, black fan logo					
❏ SD 1372 [S]	The Soul Clinic	1961	6.25	12.50	25.00
-- Green and blue label, white fan logo					
❏ SD 1372 [S]	The Soul Clinic	1962	3.75	7.50	15.00
-- Green and blue label, black fan logo					
❏ 1387 [M]	From the Heart	1962	3.75	7.50	15.00
❏ SD 1387 [S]	From the Heart	1962	5.00	10.00	20.00
❏ 1405 [M]	Soul of the Ballad	1963	3.75	7.50	15.00
❏ SD 1405 [S]	Soul of the Ballad	1963	5.00	10.00	20.00
❏ 1423 [M]	True Blue	1964	3.75	7.50	15.00
❏ SD 1423 [S]	True Blue	1964	5.00	10.00	20.00
❏ 1436 [M]	Dig These Blues	1965	3.75	7.50	15.00
❏ SD 1436 [S]	Dig These Blues	1965	5.00	10.00	20.00
❏ 1455 [M]	After Hours	1966	3.75	7.50	15.00
❏ SD 1455 [S]	After Hours	1966	5.00	10.00	20.00
❏ 1470 [M]	Mr. Blues	1967	5.00	10.00	20.00
❏ SD 1470 [S]	Mr. Blues	1967	3.75	7.50	15.00
❏ SD 1503	Double Cross	1968	3.75	7.50	15.00
❏ SD 1523	Mr. Blues Plays Lady Soul	1969	3.75	7.50	15.00
❏ SD 1557	The Best of Hank Crawford	1970	3.75	7.50	15.00
COTILLION					
❏ SD 18003	It's a Funny Thing to Do	1971	3.00	6.00	12.00
KUDU					
❏ 06	Help Me Make It	1972	3.00	6.00	12.00
❏ 08	We've Got a Good Thing	1973	3.00	6.00	12.00
❏ 15	Wildflower	1974	3.00	6.00	12.00
❏ 19	Don't You Worry 'Bout a Thing	1975	3.00	6.00	12.00
❏ 26	I Hear a Symphony	1976	3.00	6.00	12.00
❏ 33	Hank Crawford's Back	1977	3.00	6.00	12.00
❏ 35	Tico Rico	1977	3.00	6.00	12.00
❏ 39	Cajun Sunrise	1979	3.00	6.00	12.00
MILESTONE					
❏ 9112	Midnight Ramble	1983	2.50	5.00	10.00
❏ 9119	Indigo Blue	1984	2.50	5.00	10.00
❏ 9129	Down on the Deuce	1985	2.50	5.00	10.00
❏ 9140	Roadhouse Symphony	1986	2.50	5.00	10.00
❏ 9149	Mr. Chips	1987	2.50	5.00	10.00
❏ 9168	Night Beat	1988	2.50	5.00	10.00
❏ 9182	Groove Master	1990	3.00	6.00	12.00
MOBILE FIDELITY					
❏ 1-224	Soul of the Ballad	1995	6.25	12.50	25.00
-- Audiophile vinyl					
CRAWFORD, HANK, AND JIMMY MCGRIFF					
Also see each artist's individual listings.					
MILESTONE					
❏ 9142	Soul Survivors	1986	2.50	5.00	10.00
❏ 9153	Steppin' Up	1988	2.50	5.00	10.00
❏ 9177	On the Blue Side	1990	3.00	6.00	12.00
CRAWFORD, RAY					
Guitarist.					
CANDID					
❏ CJM-8028 [M]	Smooth Groove	1963	6.25	12.50	25.00

CREATIVE CONSTRUCTION COMPANY   104

Number	Title	Yr	VG	VG+	NM
❑ CJS-9028 [S]	Smooth Groove	1963	7.50	15.00	30.00
DOBRE					
❑ 1021	One Step at a Time	1978	3.00	6.00	12.00

CREATIVE CONSTRUCTION COMPANY
ANTHONY BRAXTON, LEO SMITH, LEROY JENKINS and Steve McCall.

Number	Title	Yr	VG	VG+	NM
MUSE					
❑ MR-5071	Volume 1	1975	3.75	7.50	15.00
❑ MR-5097	Volume 2	1976	3.75	7.50	15.00

CREEKMORE, TOM
Number	Title	Yr	VG	VG+	NM
DISCOVERY					
❑ DS-791	She Is It	198?	2.50	5.00	10.00

CREQUE, NEAL
Keyboard player (electric piano and organ).

Number	Title	Yr	VG	VG+	NM
COBBLESTONE					
❑ 9005	Creque	1971	3.75	7.50	15.00
❑ 9023	Contrast!	1972	3.00	6.00	12.00
MUSE					
❑ MR-5029	Neal Creque and the Hands of Time	1973	3.00	6.00	12.00
❑ MR-5226	Black Velvet Rose	1980	2.50	5.00	10.00

CREVELING, CAROLE
Number	Title	Yr	VG	VG+	NM
EUTERPE					
❑ ETP-101 [M]	Carole Creveling	1955	12.50	25.00	50.00

CRINER, CLYDE
Pianist and synthesizer player.

Number	Title	Yr	VG	VG+	NM
NOVUS					
❑ 3029-1-N	Behind the Sun	1988	2.50	5.00	10.00
❑ 3066-1-N	The Color of Dark	1989	3.00	6.00	12.00
TERRA					
❑ T-4	New England	1985	3.00	6.00	12.00

CRISPELL, MARILYN
Pianist.

Number	Title	Yr	VG	VG+	NM
BLACK SAINT					
❑ BSR-0069	Live in Berlin	1984	3.00	6.00	12.00
❑ 120069	Live in Berlin	198?	2.50	5.00	10.00
-- Reissue of 0069					
CADENCE JAZZ					
❑ CJR-1015	Spirit Music	1983	2.50	5.00	10.00

CRISS, SONNY
Alto saxophone player.

Number	Title	Yr	VG	VG+	NM
ABC IMPULSE!					
❑ AS-9312	Warm and Sonny	197?	3.75	7.50	15.00
❑ AS-9326	The Joy of Sax	197?	3.75	7.50	15.00
CLEF					
❑ MGC-122 [10]	Sonny Criss Collates	1953	62.50	125.00	250.00
FANTASY					
❑ OJC-430	This Is Sonny Criss!	1990	3.00	6.00	12.00
-- Reissue of Prestige 7511					
❑ OJC-655	Portrait of Sonny Criss	1991	3.00	6.00	12.00
-- Reissue of Prestige 7526					
IMPERIAL					
❑ LP-9006 [M]	Jazz U.S.A.	1956	50.00	100.00	200.00
❑ LP-9020 [M]	Go Man: It's Sonny Criss & Modern Jazz	1956	50.00	100.00	200.00
❑ LP-9024 [M]	Sonny Criss Plays Cole Porter	1956	50.00	100.00	200.00
❑ LP-9205 [M]	Criss Cross	1963	20.00	40.00	80.00
❑ LP-12205 [R]	Criss Cross	1963	5.00	10.00	20.00
MERCURY					
❑ MGC-122 [10]	Sonny Criss Collates	1953	---	---	---
-- Cover exists, but all known copies contain Clef labels					
MUSE					
❑ MR-5068	Crisscraft	1975	3.75	7.50	15.00
❑ MR-5089	Out of Nowhere	1976	3.75	7.50	15.00
PABLO					
❑ 2310 929	Intermission Riff	1988	2.50	5.00	10.00
PEACOCK					
❑ PLP-91 [M]	At the Crossroads	1959	37.50	75.00	150.00
PRESTIGE					
❑ PRLP-7511 [M]	This Is Sonny Criss!	1966	6.25	12.50	25.00
❑ PRST-7511 [S]	This Is Sonny Criss!	1966	7.50	15.00	30.00
❑ PRLP-7526 [M]	Portrait of Sonny Criss	1967	7.50	15.00	30.00
❑ PRST-7526 [S]	Portrait of Sonny Criss	1967	6.25	12.50	25.00

Number	Title	Yr	VG	VG+	NM
❑ PRLP-7530 [M]	Up, Up and Away	1967	10.00	20.00	40.00
❑ PRST-7530 [S]	Up, Up and Away	1967	6.25	12.50	25.00
❑ PRST-7558	The Beat Goes On	1968	5.00	10.00	20.00
❑ PRST-7576	Sonny's Dream	1968	5.00	10.00	20.00
❑ PRST-7610	Rockin' in Rhythm	1969	5.00	10.00	20.00
❑ PRST-7628	I'll Catch the Sun	1969	5.00	10.00	20.00
❑ PRST-7742	Hits of the 60s	1970	3.75	7.50	15.00
XANADU					
❑ 105	Saturday Morning	197?	3.75	7.50	15.00
❑ 200	Memorial Album	198?	2.50	5.00	10.00

CRISS, SONNY, AND KENNY DORHAM
Also see each artist's individual listings.

Number	Title	Yr	VG	VG+	NM
ABC IMPULSE!					
❑ IA-9337 [(2)]	Bopmasters	197?	5.00	10.00	20.00
MCA					
❑ 4141 [(2)]	Bopmasters	198?	3.00	6.00	12.00
-- Reissue of ABC Impulse! 9337					

CROOK, HAL
Trombone player.

Number	Title	Yr	VG	VG+	NM
OMNISOUND					
❑ 1039	Hello Heaven	198?	2.50	5.00	10.00

CROSBY, BING
Male singer. Not only was he the most popular singer of the first half of the 20th century, he was one of the most influential. While most of his vocals were influenced by jazz, the below covers only his "jazziest," mostly his pre-Decca material. For a more complete listing of Bing's hundreds of albums, see the *Standard Catalog of American Records 1950-1975.*

Number	Title	Yr	VG	VG+	NM
BIOGRAPH					
❑ M-1	When the Blue of the Night Meets the Gold of the Day	197?	2.50	5.00	10.00
❑ C-13	Bing Crosby 1929-33	1973	3.00	6.00	12.00
BRUNSWICK					
❑ BL 54005 [M]	The Voice of Bing in the 1930s	1957	6.25	12.50	25.00
❑ BL 58000 [10]	Bing Crosby, Volume 1	1950	12.50	25.00	50.00
❑ BL 58001 [10]	Bing Crosby, Volume 2	1950	12.50	25.00	50.00
COLUMBIA					
❑ C2L 43 [(2)]	Bing in Hollywood 1930-1934	196?	3.75	7.50	15.00
-- Red "360 Sound" labels					
❑ C2L 43 [(2)]	Bing in Hollywood 1930-1934	1971	3.00	6.00	12.00
-- Orange labels					
❑ CL 2502 [10]	Der Bingle	1955	10.00	20.00	40.00
❑ CL 6027 [10]	Crosby Classics	1949	12.50	25.00	50.00
❑ CL 6105 [10]	Crosby Classics, Volume 2	1950	12.50	25.00	50.00
❑ C 35093	Bing Crosby Collection, Vol. 1	1977	2.50	5.00	10.00
❑ C 35094	Bing Crosby Collection, Vol. 2	1977	2.50	5.00	10.00
❑ C4X 44229 [(4)]	The Crooner: The Columbia Years	1988	10.00	20.00	40.00
COLUMBIA SPECIAL PRODUCTS					
❑ P 14369	Bing	197?	2.50	5.00	10.00
DAYBREAK					
❑ 2014	Bing and Basie	1972	3.00	6.00	12.00
DECCA					
❑ DL 5064 [10]	Cole Porter Songs	1950	12.50	25.00	50.00
❑ DL 5126 [10]	Stardust	1950	12.50	25.00	50.00
❑ DL 5323 [10]	Bing and the Dixieland Bands	1951	12.50	25.00	50.00
❑ DL 5390 [10]	Bing and Connee	1953	12.50	25.00	50.00
-- With Connee Boswell					
HARMONY					
❑ HL 7094 [M]	Crosby Classics	1958	3.75	7.50	15.00
❑ HS 11313 [R]	Crosby Classics	196?	2.50	5.00	10.00
MCA					
❑ 1502	Rare 1930-31 Brunswick Recordings	198?	2.50	5.00	10.00
MOBILE FIDELITY					
❑ 1-260	Bing Sings Whilst Bregman Swings	1996	5.00	10.00	20.00
-- Audiophile vinyl					
RCA VICTOR					
❑ LPM-1473 [M]	Bing with a Beat	1957	6.25	12.50	25.00
VERVE					
❑ MGV 2020 [M]	Bing Sings Whilst Bregman Swings	1956	12.50	25.00	50.00
❑ V-2020 [M]	Bing Sings Whilst Bregman Swings	1961	6.25	12.50	25.00
"X"					
❑ XLVA-4250 [M]	Young Bing Crosby	1955	12.50	25.00	50.00

CROSBY, BING, AND LOUIS ARMSTRONG
Also see each artist's individual listings.

Number	Title	Yr	VG	VG+	NM
CAPITOL					
❑ SM-11735	Bing Crosby and Louis Armstrong	1977	2.50	5.00	10.00

Number	Title	Yr	VG	VG+	NM
MGM					
❏ E-3882 [M]	Bing and Satchmo	1960	3.75	7.50	15.00
❏ SE-3882 [S]	Bing and Satchmo	1960	5.00	10.00	20.00

CROSBY, BOB
Male singer and bandleader.

AIRCHECK

Number	Title	Yr	VG	VG+	NM
❏ 17	Bob Crosby and His Orchestra	197?	2.50	5.00	10.00
CAPITOL					
❏ H 293 [10]	Bob Crosby and His Bobcats	1952	12.50	25.00	50.00
❏ T 293 [M]	Bob Crosby and His Bobcats	1955	10.00	20.00	40.00
❏ T 1556 [M]	The Hits of Bob Crosby's Bobcats	1961	5.00	10.00	20.00
CIRCLE					
❏ 1	Bob Crosby and His Orchestra	198?	2.50	5.00	10.00
❏ 34	Bob Crosby and His Orchestra 1938-39	198?	2.50	5.00	10.00
COLUMBIA					
❏ CL 766 [M]	The Bob Crosby Show	1956	7.50	15.00	30.00
CORAL					
❏ CRL 56000 [10]	Swinging at the Sugar Bowl	1950	12.50	25.00	50.00
❏ CRL 56003 [10]	Dixieland Jazz 1	1950	12.50	25.00	50.00
❏ CRL 56018 [10]	Marches in Dixieland Style	1950	12.50	25.00	50.00
❏ CRL 56039 [10]	St. Louis Blues	1950	12.50	25.00	50.00
❏ CRL 57005 [M]	The Bobcats' Ball	1955	10.00	20.00	40.00
❏ CRL 57060 [M]	Bobcats' Blues	1956	10.00	20.00	40.00
❏ CRL 57061 [M]	Bobcats On Parade	1956	10.00	20.00	40.00
❏ CRL 57062 [M]	Bob Crosby in Hi-Fi	1956	10.00	20.00	40.00
❏ CRL 57089 [M]	Bob Crosby 1936-1956	1957	10.00	20.00	40.00
❏ CRL 57170 [M]	The Bobcats in Hi-Fi	1958	10.00	20.00	40.00
DECCA					
❏ DL 4856 [M]	Bob Crosby's Bobcats -- Their Greatest Hits	1967	5.00	10.00	20.00
❏ DL 8042 [M]	Five Feet of Swing	1954	10.00	20.00	40.00
❏ DL 8061 [M]	Bob Crosby's Bobcats	1954	10.00	20.00	40.00
❏ DL 74856 [R]	Bob Crosby's Bobcats -- Their Greatest Hits	1967	3.00	6.00	12.00
DOT					
❏ DLP-3136 [M]	South Pacific Blows Warm	1958	5.00	10.00	20.00
❏ DLP-3170 [M]	Petite Fleur	1959	5.00	10.00	20.00
❏ DLP-3278 [M]	Bob Crosby's Great Hits	196?	5.00	10.00	20.00
❏ DLP-3382 [M]	C'est Si Bon	196?	5.00	10.00	20.00
❏ DLP-25170 [S]	Petite Fleur	1959	6.25	12.50	25.00
❏ DLP-25278 [S]	Bob Crosby's Great Hits	196?	6.25	12.50	25.00
❏ DLP-25382 [S]	C'est Si Bon	196?	6.25	12.50	25.00
HINDSIGHT					
❏ HSR-192	Bob Crosby and His Orchestra 1941-42	198?	2.00	4.00	8.00
❏ HSR-209	Bob Crosby and His Orchestra 1952-53	1985	2.00	4.00	8.00
MCA					
❏ 253	Bob Crosby's Bobcats -- Their Greatest Hits	1974	2.50	5.00	10.00
❏ 4083 [(2)]	The Best of Bob Crosby	1974	3.00	6.00	12.00
MONMOUTH-EVERGREEN					
❏ 6815	The Bob Crosby Orchestra Live	1968	3.75	7.50	15.00
❏ 7026	Mardi Gras Parade	1970	3.75	7.50	15.00
PAUSA					
❏ 9034	This Hits of Bob Crosby's Bobcats	198?	2.50	5.00	10.00
-- Reissue of Capitol 1556					
SUNBEAM					
❏ 216	The Bob Crosby Orchestra 1938-39	197?	2.50	5.00	10.00

CROSSE, JON
Tenor saxophone player.

JAZZ CAT

Number	Title	Yr	VG	VG+	NM
❏ JCR-101	Lullabies Go Jazz	1986	2.50	5.00	10.00

CROSSFIRE
Australian fusion band.

HEADFIRST

Number	Title	Yr	VG	VG+	NM
❏ HF 9704	East of Where	198?	2.50	5.00	10.00

CROSSING POINT

CLAY PIGEON

Number	Title	Yr	VG	VG+	NM
❏ CP-1027	Listener Friendly	1986	3.75	7.50	15.00
OPTIMISM					
❏ OP-5001	Listener Friendly	1988	2.50	5.00	10.00
❏ OP-5002	Point of No Return	1988	2.50	5.00	10.00

CROSSINGS
Dan Carillo (guitar) and Marc Irwin with guests.

IRIS

Number	Title	Yr	VG	VG+	NM
❏ IL-1000	Crossings of the Spirit	198?	2.50	5.00	10.00
❏ IL-1001	Child's Play	198?	2.50	5.00	10.00

CROTHERS, CONNIE
Pianist.

INNER CITY

Number	Title	Yr	VG	VG+	NM
❏ IC-2022	Perception	1974	3.75	7.50	15.00
JAZZ					
❏ JR-4 [(2)]	Solo	1980	3.75	7.50	15.00
NEW ARTISTS					
❏ NA-1002	Concert at Cooper Union	198?	2.50	5.00	10.00
STEEPLECHASE					
❏ SCS-1022	Perception	1986	3.00	6.00	12.00

CROTHERS, CONNIE/LENNY POPKIN QUARTET
Also see each artist's individual listings.

NEW ARTISTS

Number	Title	Yr	VG	VG+	NM
❏ NA-1005	Love Energy	1989	3.00	6.00	12.00

CROTHERS, CONNIE, AND RICHARD TABNICK
Tabnick is an alto saxophone player. Also see CONNIE CROTHERS.

NEW ARTISTS

Number	Title	Yr	VG	VG+	NM
❏ NA-1003	Duo Dimension	1987	2.50	5.00	10.00

CRUSADERS, THE
Originally known as the Jazz Crusaders, whose records are included below. Members included Wilton Felder (tenor saxophone), Wayne Henderson (trombone), JOE SAMPLE (piano) and Nesbit "Stix" Hooper (drums).

ABC BLUE THUMB

Number	Title	Yr	VG	VG+	NM
❏ 6022	Chain Reaction	1975	2.50	5.00	10.00
❏ 6024	Those Southern Knights	1976	2.50	5.00	10.00
❏ 6027 [(2)]	The Best of the Crusaders	1976	3.00	6.00	12.00
❏ 6029	Free As the Wind	1977	2.50	5.00	10.00
❏ 6030	Images	1978	2.50	5.00	10.00
❏ 9002 [(2)]	Southern Comfort	1974	3.00	6.00	12.00
BLUE NOTE					
❏ BN-LA170-G [(2)]	Tough Talk	1974	3.00	6.00	12.00
❏ BN-LA530-H2 [(2)]	Young Rabbits	1977	3.00	6.00	12.00
❏ LWB-530 [(2)]	Young Rabbits	1981	2.50	5.00	10.00
-- Reissue of BN-LA530-H2					
❏ LT-1046	Live Sides	1980	2.50	5.00	10.00
BLUE THUMB					
❏ BT-6001 [(2)]	Crusaders 1	1972	3.75	7.50	15.00
❏ BT-6007	Unsung Heroes	1973	3.00	6.00	12.00
❏ BT-6010	Scratch	1974	3.00	6.00	12.00
❏ BT-7000 [(2)]	The 2nd Crusade	1973	3.75	7.50	15.00
CHISA					
❏ 804	Old Socks, New Shoes...New Socks, Old Shoes	1970	3.00	6.00	12.00
-- As "Jazz Crusaders"					
❏ 807	Pass the Plate	1971	3.00	6.00	12.00
CRUSADERS					
❏ 16000	Street Life	1982	6.25	12.50	25.00
-- Audiophile vinyl					
❏ 16002	Ongaku-Kai: Live in Japan	1982	6.25	12.50	25.00
-- Audiophile vinyl					
LIBERTY					
❏ LST-11005	Give Peace a Chance	1970	3.75	7.50	15.00
-- As "Jazz Crusaders"					
MCA					
❏ 3094	Street Life	1979	2.50	5.00	10.00
❏ 5124	Rhapsody and Blues	1980	2.50	5.00	10.00
❏ 5254	Standing Tall	1981	2.50	5.00	10.00
❏ 5429	Ghetto Blaster	1984	2.50	5.00	10.00
❏ 5781	The Good and Bad Times	1987	2.50	5.00	10.00
❏ 6006 [(2)]	The Best of the Crusaders	1980	2.50	5.00	10.00
-- Reissue of Blue Thumb 6027					
❏ 6014 [(2)]	Crusaders 1	198?	2.50	5.00	10.00
-- Reissue of Blue Thumb 6001					
❏ 6015 [(2)]	2nd Crusade	198?	2.50	5.00	10.00
-- Reissue of Blue Thumb 7000					
❏ 6016 [(2)]	Southern Comfort	198?	2.50	5.00	10.00
-- Reissue of Blue Thumb 9002					
❏ 8017 [(2)]	Royal Jam	1982	3.00	6.00	12.00
❏ 37072	Scratch	198?	2.00	4.00	8.00
-- Reissue of Blue Thumb 6010					
❏ 37073	Free As the Wind	198?	2.00	4.00	8.00
-- Reissue of Blue Thumb 6029					
❏ 37074	Images	198?	2.00	4.00	8.00
-- Reissue of Blue Thumb 6030					

Number	Title	Yr	VG	VG+	NM
❑ 37146	Chain Reaction	198?	2.00	4.00	8.00
-- Reissue of Blue Thumb 6022					
❑ 37147	Those Southern Knights	198?	2.00	4.00	8.00
-- Reissue of Blue Thumb 6024					
❑ 37174	Rhapsody and Blues	198?	2.00	4.00	8.00
-- Reissue of 5124					
❑ 37240	Standing Tall	1985	2.00	4.00	8.00
-- Reissue of 5254					
❑ 42087	The Vocal Album	1988	2.50	5.00	10.00
❑ 42168	Life in the Modern World	1988	2.50	5.00	10.00
MOBILE FIDELITY					
❑ 1-010	Chain Reaction	1979	5.00	10.00	20.00
-- Audiophile vinyl					
MOTOWN					
❑ M5-195V1	The Crusaders At Their Best	1981	2.50	5.00	10.00
❑ M 796	The Crusaders At Their Best	1973	3.00	6.00	12.00
MOWEST					
❑ 118	Hollywood	1972	3.00	6.00	12.00
PACIFIC JAZZ					
❑ PJ-27 [M]	Freedom Sound	1961	6.25	12.50	25.00
❑ ST-27 [S]	Freedom Sound	1961	7.50	15.00	30.00
❑ PJ-43 [M]	Lookin' Ahead	1962	6.25	12.50	25.00
❑ ST-43 [S]	Lookin' Ahead	1962	7.50	15.00	30.00
-- Black vinyl					
❑ ST-43 [S]	Lookin' Ahead	1962	15.00	30.00	60.00
-- Yellow vinyl					
❑ PJ-57 [M]	The Jazz Crusaders at the Lighthouse	1962	6.25	12.50	25.00
❑ ST-57 [S]	The Jazz Crusaders at the Lighthouse	1962	7.50	15.00	30.00
❑ PJ-68 [M]	Tough Talk	1963	6.25	12.50	25.00
❑ ST-68 [S]	Tough Talk	1963	7.50	15.00	30.00
❑ PJ-76 [M]	Heat Wave	1963	6.25	12.50	25.00
❑ ST-76 [S]	Heat Wave	1963	7.50	15.00	30.00
❑ PJ-83 [M]	Stretchin' Out	1964	6.25	12.50	25.00
❑ ST-83 [S]	Stretchin' Out	1964	7.50	15.00	30.00
❑ PJ-87 [M]	The Thing	1964	6.25	12.50	25.00
❑ ST-87 [S]	The Thing	1964	7.50	15.00	30.00
❑ PJ-10092 [M]	Chili Con Soul	1965	5.00	10.00	20.00
❑ PJ-10098 [M]	The Jazz Crusaders at the Lighthouse '66	1966	5.00	10.00	20.00
❑ PJ-10106 [M]	Talk That Talk	1966	5.00	10.00	20.00
❑ PJ-10115 [M]	The Festival Album	1967	6.25	12.50	25.00
❑ PJ-10124 [M]	Uh Huh	1967	6.25	12.50	25.00
❑ ST-20092 [S]	Chili Con Soul	1965	6.25	12.50	25.00
❑ ST-20098 [S]	The Jazz Crusaders at the Lighthouse '66	1966	6.25	12.50	25.00
❑ ST-20106 [S]	Talk That Talk	1966	6.25	12.50	25.00
❑ ST-20115 [S]	The Festival Album	1967	5.00	10.00	20.00
❑ ST-20124 [S]	Uh Huh	1967	5.00	10.00	20.00
❑ ST-20131	The Jazz Crusaders at the Lighthouse '68	1968	5.00	10.00	20.00
❑ ST-20136	Powerhouse	1968	5.00	10.00	20.00
❑ ST-20165	The Jazz Crusaders at the Lighthouse '69	1969	5.00	10.00	20.00
❑ ST-20175	The Best of the Jazz Crusaders	1969	5.00	10.00	20.00
PAUSA					
❑ 9005	The Best of the Jazz Crusaders	1979	2.50	5.00	10.00
-- As "Jazz Crusaders"					

CRYSTAL
Among the members were Charlie Camorata (keyboards), Jim Lucas (bass) and Peter Cardarelli (saxophone).

Number	Title	Yr	VG	VG+	NM
BLACKHAWK					
❑ BKH-51501	Clear	1986	2.50	5.00	10.00

CUBER, RONNIE
Baritone saxophone player.

Number	Title	Yr	VG	VG+	NM
XANADU					
❑ 135	Cuber Libre	1976	3.75	7.50	15.00
❑ 156	The Eleventh Day of Aquarius	1978	3.75	7.50	15.00

CULLUM, JIM (SR.)
Clarinet player and bandleader.

Number	Title	Yr	VG	VG+	NM
AUDIOPHILE					
❑ 107	Eloquent Clarinet	1972	3.00	6.00	12.00

CULLUM, JIM (JR.)
Cornet player and bandleader. Son of the above Jim Cullum.

Number	Title	Yr	VG	VG+	NM
JAZZOLOGY					
❑ 132	Life in Memphis	198?	2.50	5.00	10.00
STOMP OFF					
❑ SOS-1148	Super Satch	1987	2.50	5.00	10.00

CUNIMONDO, FRANK
Pianist, keyboard player and occasional vocalist.

Number	Title	Yr	VG	VG+	NM
MONDO					
❑ M-101	Communication	197?	2.50	5.00	10.00
❑ M-102	The Lamp Is Low	197?	2.50	5.00	10.00
❑ M-103	Introducing Lynn Marino	197?	2.50	5.00	10.00
❑ M-104	Echoes	197?	2.50	5.00	10.00
❑ M-105	Sagittarius	197?	2.50	5.00	10.00
❑ S1-90175	The Top Shelf Collection	197?	2.50	5.00	10.00

CUOZZO, MIKE
Tenor saxophone player.

Number	Title	Yr	VG	VG+	NM
JUBILEE					
❑ JLP-1027 [M]	Mike Cuozzo	1957	10.00	20.00	40.00
SAVOY					
❑ MG-12051 [M]	Mighty Mike	1956	10.00	20.00	40.00

CURRAN, ED

Number	Title	Yr	VG	VG+	NM
SAVOY					
❑ MG-12191 [M]	Elysa	1967	5.00	10.00	20.00

CURRENT EVENTS
Among the members was pianist Darrell Grant.

Number	Title	Yr	VG	VG+	NM
VERVE FORECAST					
❑ 839 388-1	Current Events	1989	3.75	7.50	15.00

CURSON, TED
Trumpeter, fluegel horn player and piccolo trumpet player.

Number	Title	Yr	VG	VG+	NM
ARISTA FREEDOM					
❑ AL 1021	Tears	197?	3.75	7.50	15.00
❑ AL 1030	Flip Top	197?	3.75	7.50	15.00
ATLAN.TIC					
❑ 1441 [M]	The New Thing and the Blue Thing	1965	5.00	10.00	20.00
❑ SD 1441 [S]	The New Thing and the Blue Thing	1965	6.25	12.50	25.00
AUDIO FIDELITY					
❑ AFLP-2123 [M]	Now Hear This	1964	5.00	10.00	20.00
❑ AFSD-6123 [S]	Now Hear This	1964	6.25	12.50	25.00
FANTASY					
❑ OJC-1744	Fire Down Below	1990	3.00	6.00	12.00
INDIA NAVIGATION					
❑ IN-1054	Blue Piccolo	1976	3.75	7.50	15.00
INNER CITY					
❑ IC 1017	Jubilant Power	1976	3.00	6.00	12.00
INTERPLAY					
❑ 7716	Blowin' Away	1978	3.00	6.00	12.00
❑ 7722	The Trio	1979	3.00	6.00	12.00
❑ 7726	I Heard Mingus	1980	3.00	6.00	12.00
OLD TOWN					
❑ LP-2003 [M]	Plenty of Horn	1961	50.00	100.00	200.00
PRESTIGE					
❑ PRLP-7263 [M]	Fire Down Below	1963	7.50	15.00	30.00
-- Yellow label, Bergenfield, N.J. address					
❑ PRLP-7263 [M]	Fire Down Below	1965	5.00	10.00	20.00
-- Blue label with trident logo at right					
❑ PRST-7263 [S]	Fire Down Below	1963	10.00	20.00	40.00
-- Silver label, Bergenfield, N.J. address					
❑ PRST-7263 [S]	Fire Down Below	1965	6.25	12.50	25.00
-- Blue label with trident logo at right					

CYRILLE, ANDREW
Drummer and percussionist.

Number	Title	Yr	VG	VG+	NM
BLACK SAINT					
❑ BSR-0025	Metamusician's Stomp	1979	3.00	6.00	12.00
ICTUS					
❑ 0009	The Loop	197?	3.75	7.50	15.00
IPS					
❑ 002	Celebration	1977	3.75	7.50	15.00
❑ 003	Junction	1978	3.75	7.50	15.00
SOUL. NOTE					
❑ SN-1012	Special People	1981	3.00	6.00	12.00
❑ SN-1062	The Navigator	1982	3.00	6.00	12.00
❑ SN-1078	Pieces of Time	198?	3.00	6.00	12.00

CYRILLE, ANDREW, AND MILFORD GRAVES
Also see each artist's individual listings.

Number	Title	Yr	VG	VG+	NM
IPS					
❑ 001	Dialogue of the Drums	1974	5.00	10.00	20.00

CYRILLE, ANDREW; JEANNE LEE; JIMMY LYONS
Also see each artist's individual listings.

Number	Title	Yr	VG	VG+	NM
BLACK SAINT					
❑ BSR-0030	Nuba	198?	3.00	6.00	12.00

Number	Title	Yr	VG	VG+	NM

D

D'AMBROSIO, MEREDITH
Pianist and female singer.
PALO ALTO
❑ 8019	Little Jazz Bird	1982	3.00	6.00	12.00

SHIAH
❑ SR-109	Another Time	198?	3.75	7.50	15.00

SPRING INC.
❑ SPR	Lost in His Arms	1978	3.75	7.50	15.00

SUNNYSIDE
❑ SSC-1011	It's Your Dance	1985	2.50	5.00	10.00
❑ SSC-1017	Another Time	1987	2.50	5.00	10.00
❑ SSC-1018	Lost in His Arms	1987	2.50	5.00	10.00
❑ SSC-1028	The Cove	1988	2.50	5.00	10.00
❑ SSC-1039	South to a Warmer Place	1989	3.00	6.00	12.00

D'AMICO, HANK
Clarinet and saxophone player. Also see AARON SACHS.
BETHLEHEM
❑ BCP-1006 [10]	Hank's Holiday	1954	30.00	60.00	120.00

D'ANDREA, FRANCO
Pianist.
RED
❑ NS-201	My One and Only Love	198?	3.00	6.00	12.00
❑ NS-202	No Idea of Time	1985	3.00	6.00	12.00

D'RIVERA, PAQUITO
Saxophone player and clarinetist, originally from Cuba. Also see IRAKERE.
COLUMBIA
❑ FC 37374	Paquito Blowin'	1981	2.50	5.00	10.00
❑ FC 38177	Mariel	1982	2.50	5.00	10.00
❑ FC 38899	Live at the Keystone Korner	1983	2.50	5.00	10.00
❑ FC 39584	Why Not!	1984	2.50	5.00	10.00
❑ FC 40156	Explosion	1985	2.50	5.00	10.00
❑ FC 40583	Manhattan Burn	1987	2.50	5.00	10.00
❑ FC 44077	Celebration	1988	2.50	5.00	10.00

DA COSTA, PAULINHO
Percussionist. Regularly used as a session musician by other jazz and rock artists.
FANTASY
❑ OJC-630	Agora	1991	3.00	6.00	12.00

PABLO
❑ 2310 785	Agora	1976	3.75	7.50	15.00

PABLO TODAY
❑ 2312 102	Happy People	1979	3.00	6.00	12.00

DAGRADI, TONY
Saxophone player, primarily tenor sax.
GRAMAVISION
❑ 8001	Oasis	1981	3.00	6.00	12.00
❑ 8103	Lunar Eclipse	1982	3.00	6.00	12.00

ROUNDER
❑ 2071	Dreams of Love	1988	2.50	5.00	10.00

DAHLANDER, NILS-BERTIL "BERT"
Drummer.
VERVE
❑ MGV-8253 [M]	Skol	1958	12.50	25.00	50.00
❑ V-8253 [M]	Skol	1961	5.00	10.00	20.00

DAILEY, ALBERT
Pianist. Also see STAN GETZ.
COLUMBIA
❑ KC 31278	Day After the Dawn	1973	3.75	7.50	15.00

MUSE
❑ MR-5256	Textures	198?	2.50	5.00	10.00

STEEPLECHASE
❑ SCS-1107	That Old Feeling	198?	2.50	5.00	10.00

DAILY, PETE
Cornet player and bandleader.
CAPITOL
❑ H 183 [10]	Dixieland Band	1950	12.50	25.00	50.00
❑ T 183 [M]	Dixieland Band	1954	10.00	20.00	40.00
❑ H 385 [10]	Dixie by Daily	1953	12.50	25.00	50.00
❑ T 385 [M]	Dixie by Daily	1954	10.00	20.00	40.00

Number	Title	Yr	VG	VG+	NM

DAILY, PETE/PHIL NAPOLEON
Also see each artist's individual listings.
DECCA
❑ DL 5261 [10]	Pete Daily/Phil Napoleon	195?	12.50	25.00	50.00

DALEY, JOE
Tenor saxophone player. Also a clarinet player, flutist and composer.
RCA VICTOR
❑ LPM-2763 [M]	Joe Daley at Newport '63	1963	5.00	10.00	20.00
❑ LSP-2763 [S]	Joe Daley at Newport '63	1963	6.25	12.50	25.00

DALINE
See DALINE JONES.

DALLWITZ, DAVE
Australian trombonist, pianist, composer and bandleader.
STOMP OFF
❑ SOS-1098	Nostalgia	1985	2.50	5.00	10.00
❑ SOS-1112	Elephant Stomp	1987	2.50	5.00	10.00

DALTO, JORGE
Pianist and keyboard player.
CONCORD PICANTE
❑ CJP-275	Urban Oasis	1985	2.50	5.00	10.00

DAMERON, TADD
Pianist, arranger, composer and bandleader.
FANTASY
❑ OJC-055	Fontainebleu	198?	2.50	5.00	10.00
-- Reissue of Prestige 7037					
❑ OJC-143	The Magic Touch of Tadd Dameron	198?	2.50	5.00	10.00
-- Reissue of Riverside 9419					
❑ OJC-212	Mating Call	198?	2.50	5.00	10.00
-- Reissue of Prestige 7070					

JAZZLAND
❑ JLP-50 [M]	Fats Navarro Featured with the Tadd Dameron Quintet	1962	12.50	25.00	50.00
❑ JLP-68 [M]	The Tadd Dameron Band	1962	12.50	25.00	50.00

NEW JAZZ
❑ NJLP-8300 [M]	Dameronia	1963	---	---	---
-- Canceled; reassigned to Prestige 16007					

PRESTIGE
❑ PRLP-159 [10]	A Study in Dameronia	1953	50.00	100.00	200.00
❑ PRLP-7037 [M]	Fontainebleu	1956	25.00	50.00	100.00
❑ PRLP-7070 [M]	Mating Call	1956	25.00	50.00	100.00
-- Reissued as 7247 and 7725 as a John Coltrane LP; see his listings					
❑ PRST-7842	Memorial Album	1970	3.75	7.50	15.00
❑ PRLP-16007 [M]	Dameronia	1964	10.00	20.00	40.00

RIVERSIDE
❑ RLP-419 [M]	The Magic Touch of Tadd Dameron	1962	10.00	20.00	40.00
❑ RS-3019	Good Bait	1968	5.00	10.00	20.00
❑ RS-9419 [S]	The Magic Touch of Tadd Dameron	1962	12.50	25.00	50.00

DANCY, MEL
MAINSTREAM
❑ MRL-378	A Little Lovin'	1972	3.00	6.00	12.00

DANE, BARBARA
Female singer and guitarist.
BARBARY COAST
❑ 33014 [M]	Trouble in Mind	1959	10.00	20.00	40.00
-- Reissue of San Francisco LP					

CAPITOL
❑ ST 1758 [S]	On My Way	1962	10.00	20.00	40.00
❑ T 1758 [M]	On My Way	1962	7.50	15.00	30.00

DOT
❑ DLP-3177 [M]	Living with the Blues	1959	7.50	15.00	30.00
❑ DLP-25177 [S]	Living with the Blues	1959	10.00	20.00	40.00

FOLKWAYS
❑ FA-2468	Barbara Dane and the Chambers Brothers	1966	12.50	25.00	50.00
❑ FA-2471	Folk Songs	1966	7.50	15.00	30.00

HORIZON
❑ WP-1602 [M]	When I Was a Young Girl	1962	7.50	15.00	30.00
❑ WPS-1602 [S]	When I Was a Young Girl	1962	10.00	20.00	40.00
-- Black vinyl					
❑ WPS-1602 [S]	When I Was a Young Girl	1962	15.00	30.00	60.00
-- Gold vinyl					

Number	Title	Yr	VG	VG+	NM
PAREDON					
❏ 1003	FTA! Songs of the GI Resistance	1970	3.75	7.50	15.00
❏ 1014	I Hate the Capitalist System	1973	3.75	7.50	15.00
❏ 1046	When We Make It Through	1982	3.75	7.50	15.00
SAN FRANCISCO					
❏ 33014 [M]	Trouble in Mind	1957	15.00	30.00	60.00

DANIEL, TED
Trumpeter.

Number	Title	Yr	VG	VG+	NM
UJAMAA					
❏ 1001	Ted Daniel	197?	3.00	6.00	12.00

DANIELS, EDDIE
Clarinet and tenor saxophone player; also a composer.

Number	Title	Yr	VG	VG+	NM
CHOICE					
❏ 1002	A Flower for All Seasons	1974	3.00	6.00	12.00
COLUMBIA					
❏ JC 36290	Morning Thunder	1980	2.50	5.00	10.00
GRP					
❏ GR-1024	Breakthrough	198?	2.50	5.00	10.00
❏ GR-1034	To Bird with Love	1987	2.50	5.00	10.00
❏ GR-1050	Memos from Paradise: The Music of Roger Kellaway	1988	2.50	5.00	10.00
❏ GR-9584	Blackwood	1989	3.00	6.00	12.00
MUSE					
❏ MR-5154	Brief Encounter	1978	3.00	6.00	12.00
PRESTIGE					
❏ PRLP-7506 [M]	First Prize	1967	10.00	20.00	40.00
❏ PRST-7506 [S]	First Prize	1967	6.25	12.50	25.00

DANIELS, HALL

Number	Title	Yr	VG	VG+	NM
JUMP					
❏ JL-9 [10]	Hall Daniels Septet	1955	20.00	40.00	80.00
-- Issued on blue vinyl					

DANIELS, MIKE, AND HIS DELTA JAZZMEN
Daniels is a trumpeter and bandleader.

Number	Title	Yr	VG	VG+	NM
STOMP OFF					
❏ SOS-1203	Together Again -- Thirty Years On!	1991	3.00	6.00	12.00

DANKO, HAROLD
Pianist.

Number	Title	Yr	VG	VG+	NM
DREAMSTREET					
❏ 104	Coincidence	1980	3.00	6.00	12.00
INNER CITY					
❏ IC-1029	Harold Danko Quartet Featuring Gregory Herbert	1978	3.00	6.00	12.00
❏ IC-1069	Chasin' Bad Guys	1979	3.00	6.00	12.00
SUNNYSIDE					
❏ SSC-1008	Ink and Water	1985	2.50	5.00	10.00
❏ SSC-1033	Alone But Not Forgotten	1989	3.00	6.00	12.00

DANKO, HAROLD, AND KIRK LIGHTSEY
Also see each artist's individual listings.

Number	Title	Yr	VG	VG+	NM
SUNNYSIDE					
❏ SSC-1004	Shorter by Two	1985	2.50	5.00	10.00

DANKO, HAROLD, AND RUFUS REID
Also see each artist's individual listings.

Number	Title	Yr	VG	VG+	NM
SUNNYSIDE					
❏ SSC-1001	Mirth Song	1985	2.50	5.00	10.00

DANKWORTH, JOHN
British saxophone and clarinet player, bandleader and composer.

Number	Title	Yr	VG	VG+	NM
DRG					
❏ MRS-507	Movies 'N' Me	198?	2.50	5.00	10.00
FONTANA					
❏ MGF-27543 [M]	Zodiac Variations	1966	3.75	7.50	15.00
❏ SRF-67543 [S]	Zodiac Variations	1966	5.00	10.00	20.00
❏ SRF-67603	The Sophisticated Johnnie Dankworth	1969	5.00	10.00	20.00
IAJRC					
❏ LP 39	Johnny Dankworth's Big Band In the Fifties	198?	2.50	5.00	10.00
MCA CLASSICS					
❏ 25932	Crossing Over the Bridge	1987	2.50	5.00	10.00
ROULETTE					
❏ R-52040 [M]	England's Ambassador of Jazz	1960	5.00	10.00	20.00
❏ SR-52040 [S]	England's Ambassador of Jazz	1960	6.25	12.50	25.00
❏ R-52059 [M]	Collaboration	1961	5.00	10.00	20.00
❏ SR-52059 [S]	Collaboration	1961	6.25	12.50	25.00
❏ R-52096 [M]	Jazz from Abroad	1963	5.00	10.00	20.00
❏ SR-52096 [S]	Jazz from Abroad	1963	6.25	12.50	25.00

DANKWORTH, JOHN/BILLY STRAYHORN
Also see each artist's individual listings.

Number	Title	Yr	VG	VG+	NM
ROULETTE					
❏ RE-121 [(2)]	Echoes of an Era	1973	3.75	7.50	15.00

DAPOGNY, JIM
Pianist and bandleader.

Number	Title	Yr	VG	VG+	NM
JAZZOLOGY					
❏ J-120	Jim Dapogny's Chicago Jazz Band	1983	2.50	5.00	10.00
❏ J-140	Back Home in Illinois	1984	2.50	5.00	10.00

DAPOGNY, JIM, AND BUTCH THOMPSON
Also see each artist's individual listings.

Number	Title	Yr	VG	VG+	NM
STOMP OFF					
❏ SOS-1183	How Could We Be So Blue?	1988	2.50	5.00	10.00

DARCH, BOB
Pianist.

Number	Title	Yr	VG	VG+	NM
UNITED ARTISTS					
❏ UAL-3120 [M]	Ragtime Piano	1960	5.00	10.00	20.00
❏ UAS-6120 [S]	Ragtime Piano	1960	6.25	12.50	25.00

DARDANELLE
Female singer.

Number	Title	Yr	VG	VG+	NM
AUDIOPHILE					
❏ AP-32	Gold Braid	1983	2.50	5.00	10.00
❏ AP-145	Echoes Singing Ladies	1982	2.50	5.00	10.00
❏ AP-191	A Woman's Intuition	198?	2.50	5.00	10.00
❏ AP-214	Down Home	1985	2.50	5.00	10.00
STASH					
❏ ST-202	Songs for New Lovers	1978	2.50	5.00	10.00
❏ ST-217	The Colors of My Life	198?	2.50	5.00	10.00

DARDANELLE AND VIVIAN LORD
Also see each artist's individual listings.

Number	Title	Yr	VG	VG+	NM
STASH					
❏ ST-231	The Two of Us	1983	2.50	5.00	10.00

DARENSBOURG, JOE
Clarinet player.

Number	Title	Yr	VG	VG+	NM
GHB					
❏ 90	Barrelhousin' with Joe	197?	2.50	5.00	10.00
GNP CRESCENDO					
❏ GNP-514	Yellow Dog Blues	197?	2.50	5.00	10.00
❏ GNP-515	Petite Fleur	197?	2.50	5.00	10.00

DARK
Jazz/fusion/world music band: Mark Nauseef (drums, percussion), Leonice Shinneman (percussion), Mark London Sims (bass), Miroslav Tadic (guitar).

Number	Title	Yr	VG	VG+	NM
CMP					
❏ 28	Dark	1987	3.00	6.00	12.00

DARLING, DAVID
Cellist.

Number	Title	Yr	VG	VG+	NM
ECM					
❏ 1161	Journal October	1980	3.00	6.00	12.00
❏ 1219	Cycles	198?	2.50	5.00	10.00

DARR, ALICE
Female singer.

Number	Title	Yr	VG	VG+	NM
CHARLIE PARKER					
❏ PLP-611 [M]	I Only Know How to Cry	1962	7.50	15.00	30.00
❏ PLP-611S [S]	I Only Know How to Cry	1962	10.00	20.00	40.00

DARTMOUTH INDIAN CHIEFS

Number	Title	Yr	VG	VG+	NM
TRANSITION					
❏ TRLP-23 [M]	Chiefly Jazz	1956	30.00	60.00	120.00

DASH, JULIAN
Tenor saxophone player and composer. Co-writer of "Tuxedo Junction."

Number	Title	Yr	VG	VG+	NM
MASTER JAZZ					
❏ 8106	Portrait	1970	5.00	10.00	20.00

Number	Title	Yr	VG	VG+	NM

DAUGHERTY, JACK
Trumpeter, conductor, composer and arranger. Best known as the producer of the early hits by the Carpenters!
A&M
| ❏ SP-3038 | Jack Daugherty and the Class of '71 | 1971 | 5.00 | 10.00 | 20.00 |
MONTEREY
| ❏ 100 | Carmel by the Sea | 1976 | 3.75 | 7.50 | 15.00 |

DAVENPORT, WALLACE
Trumpeter.
GHB
| ❏ 146 | Darkness on the Delta | 198? | 2.50 | 5.00 | 10.00 |

DAVIDSON, LOWELL
Pianist and composer.
ESP-DISK'
| ❏ 1012 [M] | Lowell Davidson Trio | 1965 | 3.75 | 7.50 | 15.00 |
| ❏ S-1012 [S] | Lowell Davidson Trio | 1965 | 5.00 | 10.00 | 20.00 |

DAVIS, ANTHONY
Pianist and composer.
GRAMAVISION
❏ 8101	Episteme	1981	3.00	6.00	12.00
❏ 8201	I've Known Rivers	1982	3.00	6.00	12.00
❏ 8303	Hemispheres	1983	3.00	6.00	12.00
❏ 8401	Middle Passage	1984	3.00	6.00	12.00
❏ 8612	Undine	1986	3.00	6.00	12.00
❏ R1-79441	Trio Squared	1989	3.00	6.00	12.00
INDIA NAVIGATION
❏ IN-1036	Songs for the Old World	1978	3.75	7.50	15.00
❏ IN-1041	Hidden Voices	1979	3.75	7.50	15.00
❏ IN-1047	Lady in the Mirror	1980	3.75	7.50	15.00
❏ IN-1056	Variations in Dream-Time	1981	3.75	7.50	15.00
PAUSA
| ❏ 7120 | Under the Double Moon | 198? | 2.50 | 5.00 | 10.00 |
SACKVILLE
| ❏ 3020 | Of Blues and Dreams | 198? | 2.50 | 5.00 | 10.00 |

DAVIS, ART
Bass player.
INTERPLAY
| ❏ 7728 | Reemergence | 197? | 3.00 | 6.00 | 12.00 |
SOUL NOTE
| ❏ 121143 | Life | 1985 | 3.00 | 6.00 | 12.00 |

DAVIS, BOB
Pianist.
STEPHENY
| ❏ MF-4000 [M] | Jazz in Orbit | 1958 | 15.00 | 30.00 | 60.00 |
| ❏ MFS-8003 [S] | Jazz in Orbit | 1960 | 12.50 | 25.00 | 50.00 |
ZEPHYR
| ❏ 12001 [M] | Jazz from the North Coast | 1959 | 12.50 | 25.00 | 50.00 |

DAVIS, CHARLES
Baritone saxophone player. Also has played tenor and alto saxes.
STRATA-EAST
| ❏ 7425 | Ingia! | 1974 | 3.75 | 7.50 | 15.00 |
WEST 54
| ❏ 8006 | Dedicated to Tadd | 1979 | 3.00 | 6.00 | 12.00 |

DAVIS, EDDIE "LOCKJAW"
Tenor saxophone player.
BETHLEHEM
| ❏ BCP-6035 [M] | Eddie's Function | 197? | 3.75 | 7.50 | 15.00 |

-- *Reissue material, distributed by RCA Victor*

| ❏ BCP-6069 [M] | The Best of Eddie "Lockjaw" Davis | 1963 | 10.00 | 20.00 | 40.00 |
| ❏ BCPS-6069 [R] | The Best of Eddie "Lockjaw" Davis | 196? | 5.00 | 10.00 | 20.00 |
CLASSIC JAZZ
| ❏ 116 | Sweet and Lovely | 197? | 3.00 | 6.00 | 12.00 |
ENJA
| ❏ 3097 | Jaws' Blues | 1981 | 3.00 | 6.00 | 12.00 |
FANTASY
❏ OJC-384	Montreux '77	1989	3.00	6.00	12.00
❏ OJC-403	Afro-Jaws	1989	3.00	6.00	12.00
❏ OJC-429	Trane Whistle	1990	3.00	6.00	12.00
❏ OJC-629	Straight Ahead	1991	3.00	6.00	12.00
❏ OJC-652	The Eddie "Lockjaw" Davis Cookbook, Vol. 1	1991	3.00	6.00	12.00
❏ OJC-653	The Eddie "Lockjaw" Davis Cookbook, Vol. 2	1991	3.00	6.00	12.00

INNER CITY
| ❏ IC-2058 | Swingin' Till the Girls Come Home | 1976 | 3.75 | 7.50 | 15.00 |
JAZZLAND
| ❏ JLP-97 [M] | Alma Alegre | 1962 | 6.25 | 12.50 | 25.00 |
| ❏ JLP-997 [S] | Alma Alegre | 1962 | 7.50 | 15.00 | 30.00 |
KING
❏ 395-506 [M]	Modern Jazz Expression	1956	25.00	50.00	100.00
❏ 395-526 [M]	Jazz with a Horn	1957	25.00	50.00	100.00
❏ 566 [M]	Jazz with a Beat	1957	25.00	50.00	100.00
❏ 599 [M]	Big Beat Jazz	1958	25.00	50.00	100.00
❏ 606 [M]	Uptown	1958	25.00	50.00	100.00
❏ 637 [M]	This and That	1959	25.00	50.00	100.00
MUSE
| ❏ MR-5202 | Heavy Hitter | 1979 | 3.00 | 6.00 | 12.00 |
PABLO
| ❏ 2310 778 | Straight Ahead | 197? | 3.75 | 7.50 | 15.00 |
| ❏ 2405 414 | The Best of Eddie "Lockjaw" Davis | 198? | 2.50 | 5.00 | 10.00 |
PABLO LIVE
| ❏ 2308 214 | Montreux '77 | 1978 | 3.00 | 6.00 | 12.00 |
PRESTIGE
| ❏ PRLP-7141 [M] | The Eddie "Lockjaw" Davis Cookbook | 1958 | 20.00 | 40.00 | 80.00 |

-- *Cover photo features Davis with no hat*

| ❏ PRLP-7141 [M] | The Eddie "Lockjaw" Davis Cookbook | 1959 | 12.50 | 25.00 | 50.00 |

-- *Cover photo features Davis with hat*

❏ PRLP-7161 [M]	The Eddie "Lockjaw" Davis Cookbook, Vol. 2	1959	12.50	25.00	50.00
❏ PRLP-7206 [M]	Trane Whistle	1961	12.50	25.00	50.00
❏ PRLP-7219 [M]	The Eddie "Lockjaw" Davis Cookbook, Vol. 3	1961	12.50	25.00	50.00
❏ PRST-7219 [S]	The Eddie "Lockjaw" Davis Cookbook, Vol. 3	1961	10.00	20.00	40.00
❏ PRLP-7242 [M]	Goin' to the Meeting	1962	10.00	20.00	40.00
❏ PRST-7242 [S]	Goin' to the Meeting	1962	12.50	25.00	50.00
❏ PRLP-7261 [M]	I Only Have Eyes for You	1963	10.00	20.00	40.00
❏ PRST-7261 [S]	I Only Have Eyes for You	1963	12.50	25.00	50.00
❏ PRLP-7271 [M]	Trackin'	1963	10.00	20.00	40.00
❏ PRST-7271 [S]	Trackin'	1963	12.50	25.00	50.00
❏ PRST-7660	In the Kitchen	1969	3.75	7.50	15.00

-- *Reissue of 7141 in (rechanneled?) stereo*

| ❏ PRST-7782 | The Rev. | 197? | 3.75 | 7.50 | 15.00 |

-- *Reissue of 7161 in (rechanneled?) stereo*

| ❏ PRST-7834 | Stolen Moments | 197? | 3.75 | 7.50 | 15.00 |

-- *Reissue of 7206 in (rechanneled?) stereo*

| ❏ 24039 [(2)] | The Eddie "Lockjaw" Davis Cookbook | 197? | 5.00 | 10.00 | 20.00 |

RCA VICTOR
❏ LPM-3652 [M]	Lock the Fox	1966	5.00	10.00	20.00
❏ LSP-3652 [S]	Lock the Fox	1966	6.25	12.50	25.00
❏ LPM-3741 [M]	The Fox and the Hounds	1967	6.25	12.50	25.00
❏ LSP-3741 [S]	The Fox and the Hounds	1967	5.00	10.00	20.00
❏ LPM-3882 [M]	Love Calls	1967	6.25	12.50	25.00
❏ LSP-3882 [S]	Love Calls	1967	5.00	10.00	20.00
RIVERSIDE
❏ RLP-373 [M]	Afro-Jaws	1961	7.50	15.00	30.00
❏ RLP-430 [M]	Jawbreakers	1962	7.50	15.00	30.00
❏ RS-9373 [S]	Afro-Jaws	1961	10.00	20.00	40.00
❏ RS-9430 [S]	Jawbreakers	1962	10.00	20.00	40.00
ROOST
| ❏ LP-422 [10] | Goodies | 1954 | 37.50 | 75.00 | 150.00 |
| ❏ RST-2227 [M] | Eddie Davis Trio | 1957 | 25.00 | 50.00 | 100.00 |
ROULETTE
| ❏ R-52007 [M] | Count Basie Presents Eddie Davis | 1958 | 15.00 | 30.00 | 60.00 |

-- *White label with color spokes*

| ❏ R-52007 [M] | Count Basie Presents Eddie Davis | 1963 | 6.25 | 12.50 | 25.00 |

-- *Orange and yellow "roulette wheel" label*

| ❏ SR-52007 [S] | Count Basie Presents Eddie Davis | 1959 | 12.50 | 25.00 | 50.00 |

-- *White label with color spokes*

| ❏ SR-52007 [S] | Count Basie Presents Eddie Davis | 1963 | 5.00 | 10.00 | 20.00 |

-- *Orange and yellow "roulette wheel" label*

| ❏ R-52019 [M] | Eddie Davis Trio | 1959 | 15.00 | 30.00 | 60.00 |

-- *White label with color spokes*

| ❏ R-52019 [M] | Eddie Davis Trio | 1963 | 6.25 | 12.50 | 25.00 |

-- *Orange and yellow "roulette wheel" label*

| ❏ SR-52019 [S] | Eddie Davis Trio | 1959 | 12.50 | 25.00 | 50.00 |

-- *White label with color spokes*

| ❏ SR-52019 [S] | Eddie Davis Trio | 1963 | 5.00 | 10.00 | 20.00 |

-- *Orange and yellow "roulette wheel" label*

Number	Title	Yr	VG	VG+	NM
STEEPLECHASE					
❑ SCS-1058	Swingin' Till the Girls Come Home	198?	2.50	5.00	10.00
❑ SCS-1181	All of Me	198?	2.50	5.00	10.00

DAVIS, EDDIE "LOCKJAW", AND HARRY "SWEETS" EDISON
Also see each artist's individual listings.

Number	Title	Yr	VG	VG+	NM
PABLO					
❑ 2310 882	Jazz at the Philharmonic 1983	1983	3.00	6.00	12.00
STORYVILLE					
❑ 4004	Eddie "Lockjaw" Davis and Harry "Sweets" Edison	197?	3.00	6.00	12.00

DAVIS, EDDIE "LOCKJAW", AND JOHNNY GRIFFIN
Also see each artist's individual listings.

Number	Title	Yr	VG	VG+	NM
FANTASY					
❑ OJC-264	Griff & Lock	1987	2.50	5.00	10.00
JAZZLAND					
❑ JLP-31 [M]	Tough Tenors	1960	10.00	20.00	40.00
❑ JLP-39 [M]	Lookin' at Monk	1961	10.00	20.00	40.00
❑ JLP-42 [M]	Griff & Lock	1961	10.00	20.00	40.00
❑ JLP-60 [M]	Blues Up and Down	1961	10.00	20.00	40.00
❑ JLP-76 [M]	Tough Tenor Favorites	1962	10.00	20.00	40.00
❑ JLP-931 [S]	Tough Tenors	1960	12.50	25.00	50.00
❑ JLP-939 [S]	Lookin' at Monk	1961	12.50	25.00	50.00
❑ JLP-942 [S]	Griff & Lock	1961	12.50	25.00	50.00
❑ JLP-960 [S]	Blues Up and Down	1961	12.50	25.00	50.00
❑ JLP-976 [S]	Tough Tenor Favorites	1962	12.50	25.00	50.00
MILESTONE					
❑ 47035 [(2)]	The Toughest Tenors	198?	3.75	7.50	15.00
PAUSA					
❑ 7062	The Tough Tenors Again 'n' Again	197?	2.50	5.00	10.00
PRESTIGE					
❑ PRLP-7191 [M]	The Tenor Scene	1961	12.50	25.00	50.00
❑ PRLP-7282 [M]	Battle Stations	1963	7.50	15.00	30.00
❑ PRST-7282 [S]	Battle Stations	1963	10.00	20.00	40.00
❑ PRLP-7309 [M]	The First Set -- Recorded Live at Minton's	1964	7.50	15.00	30.00
❑ PRST-7309 [S]	The First Set -- Recorded Live at Minton's	1964	10.00	20.00	40.00
❑ PRLP-7330 [M]	The Midnight Show at Minton's Playhouse	1964	6.25	12.50	25.00
❑ PRST-7330 [S]	The Midnight Show at Minton's Playhouse	1964	7.50	15.00	30.00
❑ PRLP-7357 [M]	The Late Show -- Recorded Live!	1965	6.25	12.50	25.00
❑ PRST-7357 [S]	The Late Show -- Recorded Live!	1965	7.50	15.00	30.00
❑ PRLP-7407 [M]	The Breakfast Show	1965	7.50	15.00	30.00
-- Reissue of 7191					
❑ PRST-7407 [S]	The Breakfast Show	1965	6.25	12.50	25.00
❑ 24099 [(2)]	Live at Minton's	197?	3.75	7.50	15.00

DAVIS, EDDIE "LOCKJAW", AND SHIRLEY SCOTT
Also see each artist's individual listings.

Number	Title	Yr	VG	VG+	NM
FANTASY					
❑ OJC-216	Jaws	198?	2.50	5.00	10.00
❑ OJC-322	Jaws in Orbit	1988	2.50	5.00	10.00
MOODSVILLE					
❑ MVLP-4 [M]	Eddie "Lockjaw" Davis with Shirley Scott	1960	12.50	25.00	50.00
-- Green label					
❑ MVLP-4 [M]	Eddie "Lockjaw" Davis with Shirley Scott	1965	6.25	12.50	25.00
-- Blue label, trident logo on right					
❑ MVLP-30 [M]	Misty	1963	12.50	25.00	50.00
-- Green label					
❑ MVLP-30 [M]	Misty	1965	6.25	12.50	25.00
-- Blue label, trident logo on right					
❑ MVST-30 [S]	Misty	1963	12.50	25.00	50.00
-- Green label					
❑ MVST-30 [S]	Misty	1965	6.25	12.50	25.00
-- Blue label, trident logo on right					
PRESTIGE					
❑ PRLP-7154 [M]	Jaws	1959	12.50	25.00	50.00
❑ PRLP-7171 [M]	Jaws in Orbit	1959	12.50	25.00	50.00
❑ PRLP-7178 [M]	Bacalao	1960	12.50	25.00	50.00
❑ PRLP-7301 [M]	Smokin'	1964	10.00	20.00	40.00
❑ PRST-7301 [S]	Smokin'	1964	7.50	15.00	30.00
❑ PRST-7710	The Best of Eddie "Lockjaw" Davis with Shirley Scott	1970	3.75	7.50	15.00

DAVIS, EDDY
Banjo player and bandleader.

Number	Title	Yr	VG	VG+	NM
JAZZOLOGY					
❑ J-67	Eddy Davis and His Hot Jazz Orchestra	1979	2.50	5.00	10.00
❑ J-88	Eddy Davis and His Hot Jazz Orchestra	1982	2.50	5.00	10.00

DAVIS, JACKIE
Organist.

Number	Title	Yr	VG	VG+	NM
CAPITOL					
❑ T 815 [M]	Chasing Shadows	1957	10.00	20.00	40.00
-- Turquoise or gray label					
❑ T 1180 [M]	Jackie Davis Meets the Trombones	1959	7.50	15.00	30.00
-- Black colorband label, logo at left					

DAVIS, JOHNNY "SCAT"
Male singer.

Number	Title	Yr	VG	VG+	NM
KING					
❑ 626 [M]	Here's Lookin' Atcha	1959	20.00	40.00	80.00

DAVIS, MEL
Trumpeter.

Number	Title	Yr	VG	VG+	NM
EPIC					
❑ LN 3268 [M]	Trumpet with a Soul	1956	10.00	20.00	40.00
RCA CAMDEN					
❑ CAL-2127 [M]	The Big Ones of '66	1966	3.00	6.00	12.00
❑ CAS-2127 [S]	The Big Ones of '66	1966	3.75	7.50	15.00
TIME					
❑ S-2087 [S]	Shoot the Trumpet Player	1962	6.25	12.50	25.00
❑ S-2117 [S]	We Like Broadway	1963	6.25	12.50	25.00
❑ 52087 [M]	Shoot the Trumpet Player	1962	5.00	10.00	20.00
❑ 52117 [M]	We Like Broadway	1963	5.00	10.00	20.00

DAVIS, MILES
Trumpeter, bandleader and composer. The most significant post-World War II jazz musician, he experimented in everything from bebop to hip-hop, alternately enthralling and/or infuriating his fans. The number of prominent soloists and bandleaders who passed through his groups is enormous. Also see LEONARD BERNSTEIN; THE BRASS ENSEMBLE; LEE KONITZ.

Number	Title	Yr	VG	VG+	NM
ARCHIVE OF FOLK AND JAZZ					
❑ 283	Miles Davis	197?	2.50	5.00	10.00
BLUE NOTE					
❑ BLP-1501 [M]	Miles Davis, Volume 1	1955	50.00	100.00	200.00
-- "Deep groove" version (deep indentation under label on both sides)					
❑ BLP-1501 [M]	Miles Davis, Volume 1	1955	37.50	75.00	150.00
-- Regular version with Lexington Ave. address on label					
❑ BLP-1501 [M]	Miles Davis, Volume 1	1958	12.50	25.00	50.00
-- Regular version with W. 63rd St. address on label					
❑ BLP-1501 [M]	Miles Davis, Volume 1	1963	6.25	12.50	25.00
-- With New York, USA address on label					
❑ BLP-1501 [M]	Miles Davis, Volume 1	1966	3.75	7.50	15.00
-- With "A Division of Liberty Records" on label					
❑ BLP-1502 [M]	Miles Davis, Volume 2	1955	50.00	100.00	200.00
-- "Deep groove" version (deep indentation under label on both sides)					
❑ BLP-1502 [M]	Miles Davis, Volume 2	1955	37.50	75.00	150.00
-- Regular version with Lexington Ave. address on label					
❑ BLP-1502 [M]	Miles Davis, Volume 2	1958	12.50	25.00	50.00
-- Regular version with W. 63rd St. address on label					
❑ BLP-1502 [M]	Miles Davis, Volume 2	1963	6.25	12.50	25.00
-- With New York, USA address on label					
❑ BLP-1502 [M]	Miles Davis, Volume 2	1966	3.75	7.50	15.00
-- With "A Division of Liberty Records" on label					
❑ BLP-5013 [10]	Miles Davis (Young Man with a Horn)	1952	75.00	150.00	300.00
❑ BLP-5022 [10]	Miles Davis, Vol. 2	1953	75.00	150.00	300.00
❑ BLP-5040 [10]	Miles Davis, Vol. 3	1954	75.00	150.00	300.00
❑ BLP-81501	Miles Davis, Volume 1	1968	3.00	6.00	12.00
-- Rechanneled stereo version of 1501					
❑ BST-81501	Miles Davis, Volume 1	1985	2.50	5.00	10.00
-- "The Finest in Jazz Since 1939" reissue label					
❑ BLP-81502	Miles Davis, Volume 2	1968	3.00	6.00	12.00
-- Rechanneled stereo version of 1502					
❑ BST-81502	Miles Davis, Volume 2	1985	2.50	5.00	10.00
-- "The Finest in Jazz Since 1939" reissue label					
CAPITOL					
❑ H 459 [10]	Jeru	1954	62.50	125.00	250.00
-- First 33 1/3 rpm issue of some of the "Birth of the Cool" sessions					
❑ T 762 [M]	Birth of the Cool	1956	37.50	75.00	150.00
❑ T 1974 [M]	Birth of the Cool	1963	7.50	15.00	30.00
-- Reissue of 762					
❑ DT 1974 [R]	Birth of the Cool	196?	3.00	6.00	12.00
❑ M-11026 [M]	The Complete Birth of the Cool	1972	3.00	6.00	12.00
❑ N-16168 [M]	Birth of the Cool	198?	2.00	4.00	8.00
-- Budget-line reissue					
COLUMBIA					
❑ J 1	Facets	1973	3.00	6.00	12.00
❑ J 17	Miles Davis at Newport	1973	3.00	6.00	12.00
❑ C2L 20 [(2) M]	Miles Davis in Person (Friday & Saturday Nights at the Blackhawk, San Francisco)	1961	12.50	25.00	50.00
-- Six "eye" logos on label					

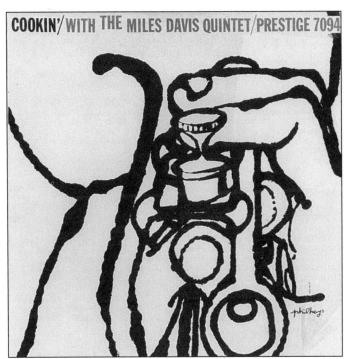
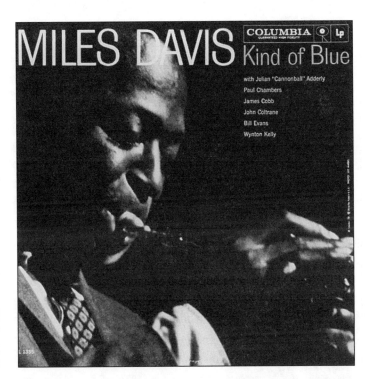
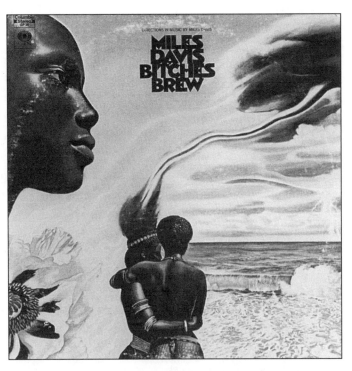

Four phases of Miles Davis' long and varied career are illustrated here. (Top left) *Birth of the Cool*, a collection of 78 rpm sides Miles recorded in 1949 and 1950, are considered exactly what the album title calls it – the beginning of the "cool" jazz epitomized by the so-called "West Coast" sound of the 1950s. (Top right) One of Miles' legendary Prestige albums, recorded in the mid-1950s and among some of the greatest quintet music ever recorded. (Bottom left) *Kind of Blue,* which has been named by more than one critic as the greatest jazz LP ever. (Bottom right) *Bitches Brew*, the two-album set that marked Miles' entry into full-fledged jazz-rock fusion, was his first gold album.

Number	Title	Yr	VG	VG+	NM
C2L 20 [(2) M]	Miles Davis in Person (Friday & Saturday Nights at the Blackhawk, San Francisco)	1963	7.50	15.00	30.00
-- "Guaranteed High Fidelity" on label					
C2L 20 [(2) M]	Miles Davis in Person (Friday & Saturday Nights at the Blackhawk, San Francisco)	1965	6.25	12.50	25.00
-- "Mono" on label					
GP 26 [(2)]	Bitches Brew	1970	10.00	20.00	40.00
-- "360 Sound Stereo" on red labels					
GP 26 [(2)]	Bitches Brew	1970	3.75	7.50	15.00
-- Orange labels					
PG 26 [(2)]	Bitches Brew	1977	3.00	6.00	12.00
-- Orange labels, new prefix					
C2S 820 [(2) S]	Miles Davis in Person (Friday & Saturday Nights at the Blackhawk, San Francisco)	1961	12.50	25.00	50.00
-- Six "eye" logos on label					
C2S 820 [(2) S]	Miles Davis in Person (Friday & Saturday Nights at the Blackhawk, San Francisco)	1963	7.50	15.00	30.00
-- "360 Sound Stereo" in black on label					
C2S 820 [(2) S]	Miles Davis in Person (Friday & Saturday Nights at the Blackhawk, San Francisco)	1965	6.25	12.50	25.00
-- "360 Sound Stereo" in white on label					
C2S 820 [(2)]	Miles Davis in Person (Friday & Saturday Nights at the Blackhawk, San Francisco)	1971	3.75	7.50	15.00
-- Orange labels					
CL 949 [M]	'Round About Midnight	1957	12.50	25.00	50.00
-- Six "eye" logos on label					
CL 949 [M]	'Round About Midnight	1963	6.25	12.50	25.00
-- "Guaranteed High Fidelity" on label					
CL 949 [M]	'Round About Midnight	1965	5.00	10.00	20.00
-- "Mono" on label					
CL 1041 [M]	Miles Ahead	1957	20.00	40.00	80.00
-- Six "eye" logos on label; cover has a white woman and her child on a sailboat					
CL 1041 [M]	Miles Ahead	1957	12.50	25.00	50.00
-- Six "eye" logos on label; cover has Miles Davis blowing his trumpet					
CL 1041 [M]	Miles Ahead	1963	6.25	12.50	25.00
-- "Guaranteed High Fidelity" on label					
CL 1041 [M]	Miles Ahead	1965	5.00	10.00	20.00
-- "Mono" on label					
CL 1193 [M]	Milestones	1958	12.50	25.00	50.00
-- Six "eye" logos on label					
CL 1193 [M]	Milestones	1963	6.25	12.50	25.00
-- "Guaranteed High Fidelity" on label					
CL 1193 [M]	Milestones	1965	5.00	10.00	20.00
-- "Mono" on label					
CL 1268 [M]	Jazz Track	1958	12.50	25.00	50.00
-- Six "eye" logos on label; with Miles and a woman on cover					
CL 1268 [M]	Jazz Track	1958	20.00	40.00	80.00
-- Six "eye" logos on label; with abstract drawing on cover					
CL 1274 [M]	Porgy and Bess	1958	12.50	25.00	50.00
-- Six "eye" logos on label					
CL 1274 [M]	Porgy and Bess	1963	6.25	12.50	25.00
-- "Guaranteed High Fidelity" on label					
CL 1274 [M]	Porgy and Bess	1965	5.00	10.00	20.00
-- "Mono" on label					
CL 1355 [M]	Kind of Blue	1959	15.00	30.00	60.00
-- Six "eye" logos on label					
CL 1355 [M]	Kind of Blue	1963	6.25	12.50	25.00
-- "Guaranteed High Fidelity" on label					
CL 1355 [M]	Kind of Blue	1965	5.00	10.00	20.00
-- "Mono" on label					
CL 1480 [M]	Sketches of Spain	1960	12.50	25.00	50.00
-- Six "eye" logos on label					
CL 1480 [M]	Sketches of Spain	1963	6.25	12.50	25.00
-- "Guaranteed High Fidelity" on label					
CL 1480 [M]	Sketches of Spain	1965	5.00	10.00	20.00
-- "Mono" on label					
CL 1656 [M]	Someday My Prince Will Come	1961	10.00	20.00	40.00
-- Six "eye" logos on label					
CL 1656 [M]	Someday My Prince Will Come	1963	6.25	12.50	25.00
-- "Guaranteed High Fidelity" on label					
CL 1656 [M]	Someday My Prince Will Come	1965	5.00	10.00	20.00
-- "Mono" on label					
CL 1669 [M]	Miles Davis in Person, Vol. 1 (Friday Nights at the Blackhawk, San Francisco)	1961	7.50	15.00	30.00
-- Six "eye" logos on label; later pressings may exist					
CL 1670 [M]	Miles Davis in Person, Vol. 2 (Saturday Nights at the Blackhawk, San Francisco)	1961	7.50	15.00	30.00
-- Six "eye" logos on label; later pressings may exist					
CL 1812 [M]	Miles Davis at Carnegie Hall	1962	12.50	25.00	50.00
-- Six "eye" logos on label					
CL 1812 [M]	Miles Davis at Carnegie Hall	1963	6.25	12.50	25.00
-- "Guaranteed High Fidelity" on label					
CL 1812 [M]	Miles Davis at Carnegie Hall	1965	5.00	10.00	20.00
-- "Mono" on label					
CL 2051 [M]	Seven Steps to Heaven	1963	6.25	12.50	25.00
-- "Guaranteed High Fidelity" on label					
CL 2051 [M]	Seven Steps to Heaven	1965	5.00	10.00	20.00
-- "Mono" on label					
CL 2106 [M]	Quiet Nights	1964	6.25	12.50	25.00
-- "Guaranteed High Fidelity" on label					
CL 2106 [M]	Quiet Nights	1965	5.00	10.00	20.00
-- "Mono" on label					
CL 2183 [M]	Miles Davis in Europe	1964	6.25	12.50	25.00
-- "Guaranteed High Fidelity" on label					
CL 2183 [M]	Miles Davis in Europe	1965	5.00	10.00	20.00
-- "Mono" on label					
CL 2306 [M]	My Funny Valentine	1965	6.25	12.50	25.00
-- "Guaranteed High Fidelity" on label					
CL 2306 [M]	My Funny Valentine	1965	5.00	10.00	20.00
-- "Mono" on label					
CL 2350 [M]	E.S.P.	1965	6.25	12.50	25.00
-- "Guaranteed High Fidelity" on label					
CL 2350 [M]	E.S.P.	1965	5.00	10.00	20.00
-- "Mono" on label					
CL 2453 [M]	"Four" & More -- Recorded Live in Concert	1966	5.00	10.00	20.00
CL 2601 [M]	Miles Smiles	1966	5.00	10.00	20.00
CL 2628 [M]	Milestones	1967	7.50	15.00	30.00
-- Reissue of 1193?					
CL 2732 [M]	Sorcerer	1967	7.50	15.00	30.00
CL 2794 [M]	Nefertiti	1968	12.50	25.00	50.00
CL 2828 [M]	Miles in the Sky	1968	20.00	40.00	80.00
CS 8021 [S]	Milestones	1959	12.50	25.00	50.00
-- Six "eye" logos on label					
CS 8021 [S]	Milestones	1963	6.25	12.50	25.00
-- "360 Sound Stereo" in black on label					
CS 8021 [S]	Milestones	1965	5.00	10.00	20.00
-- "360 Sound Stereo" in white on label					
CS 8085 [S]	Porgy and Bess	1959	12.50	25.00	50.00
-- Six "eye" logos on label					
CS 8085 [S]	Porgy and Bess	1963	6.25	12.50	25.00
-- "360 Sound Stereo" in black on label					
CS 8085 [S]	Porgy and Bess	1965	5.00	10.00	20.00
-- "360 Sound Stereo" in white on label					
CS 8085	Porgy and Bess	1971	3.00	6.00	12.00
-- Orange label					
KCS 8085	Porgy and Bess	1974	2.50	5.00	10.00
-- Orange label, new prefix					
PC 8085	Porgy and Bess	1977	2.00	4.00	8.00
-- Orange label, new prefix					
CS 8163 [S]	Kind of Blue	1959	30.00	60.00	120.00
-- Six "eye" logos on label					
CS 8163 [S]	Kind of Blue	1963	6.25	12.50	25.00
-- "360 Sound Stereo" in black on label					
CS 8163 [S]	Kind of Blue	1965	5.00	10.00	20.00
-- "360 Sound Stereo" in white on label					
CS 8163	Kind of Blue	1971	3.00	6.00	12.00
-- Orange label					
KCS 8163	Kind of Blue	1974	2.50	5.00	10.00
-- Orange label, new prefix					
PC 8163	Kind of Blue	1977	2.00	4.00	8.00
-- Orange label, new prefix					
CS 8271 [S]	Sketches of Spain	1960	20.00	40.00	80.00
-- Six "eye" logos on label					
CS 8271 [S]	Sketches of Spain	1963	6.25	12.50	25.00
-- "360 Sound Stereo" in black on label					
CS 8271 [S]	Sketches of Spain	1965	5.00	10.00	20.00
-- "360 Sound Stereo" in white on label					
CS 8271	Sketches of Spain	1971	3.00	6.00	12.00
-- Orange label					
KCS 8271	Sketches of Spain	1974	2.50	5.00	10.00
-- Orange label, new prefix					
PC 8271	Sketches of Spain	1977	2.00	4.00	8.00
-- Orange label, new prefix					
CS 8456 [S]	Someday My Prince Will Come	1961	10.00	20.00	40.00
-- Six "eye" logos on label					
CS 8456 [S]	Someday My Prince Will Come	1963	6.25	12.50	25.00
-- "360 Sound Stereo" in black on label					
CS 8456 [S]	Someday My Prince Will Come	1965	5.00	10.00	20.00
-- "360 Sound Stereo" in white on label					
CS 8456	Someday My Prince Will Come	1971	3.00	6.00	12.00
-- Orange label					
KCS 8456	Someday My Prince Will Come	1974	2.50	5.00	10.00
-- Orange label, new prefix					
PC 8456	Someday My Prince Will Come	1977	2.00	4.00	8.00
-- Orange label, new prefix					
CS 8469 [S]	Miles Davis in Person, Vol. 1 (Friday Nights at the Blackhawk, San Francisco)	1961	7.50	15.00	30.00
-- Six "eye" logos on label; later pressings may exist					
CS 8470 [S]	Miles Davis in Person, Vol. 2 (Saturday Nights at the Blackhawk, San Francisco)	1961	7.50	15.00	30.00
-- Six "eye" logos on label; later pressings may exist					
CS 8612 [S]	Miles Davis at Carnegie Hall	1962	12.50	25.00	50.00
-- Six "eye" logos on label					
CS 8612 [S]	Miles Davis at Carnegie Hall	1962	6.25	12.50	25.00
-- "360 Sound Stereo" in black on label					
CS 8612 [S]	Miles Davis at Carnegie Hall	1965	5.00	10.00	20.00
-- "360 Sound Stereo" in white on label					
CS 8612	Miles Davis at Carnegie Hall	1971	3.00	6.00	12.00
-- Orange label					

Number	Title	Yr	VG	VG+	NM
❏ KCS 8612	Miles Davis at Carnegie Hall	1974	2.50	5.00	10.00
-- Orange label, new prefix					
❏ PC 8612	Miles Davis at Carnegie Hall	1977	2.00	4.00	8.00
-- Orange label, new prefix					
❏ CS 8633 [R]	Miles Ahead	1963	3.00	6.00	12.00
-- Rechanneled stereo version of 1041					
❏ CS 8633	Miles Ahead	1971	3.00	6.00	12.00
-- Orange label					
❏ KCS 8633	Miles Ahead	1974	2.50	5.00	10.00
-- Orange label, new prefix					
❏ PC 8633	Miles Ahead	1977	2.00	4.00	8.00
-- Orange label, new prefix					
❏ CS 8649 [R]	'Round About Midnight	1963	3.00	6.00	12.00
-- Rechanneled stereo version of 949					
❏ CS 8649	'Round About Midnight	1971	3.00	6.00	12.00
-- Orange label					
❏ KCS 8649	'Round About Midnight	1974	2.50	5.00	10.00
-- Orange label, new prefix					
❏ PC 8649	'Round About Midnight	1977	2.00	4.00	8.00
-- Orange label, new prefix					
❏ CS 8851 [S]	Seven Steps to Heaven	1963	6.25	12.50	25.00
-- "360 Sound Stereo" in black on label					
❏ CS 8851 [S]	Seven Steps to Heaven	1965	5.00	10.00	20.00
-- "360 Sound Stereo" in white on label					
❏ CS 8851	Seven Steps to Heaven	1971	3.00	6.00	12.00
-- Orange label					
❏ KCS 8851	Seven Steps to Heaven	1974	2.50	5.00	10.00
-- Orange label, new prefix					
❏ PC 8851	Seven Steps to Heaven	1977	2.00	4.00	8.00
-- Orange label, new prefix					
❏ CS 8906 [S]	Quiet Nights	1964	6.25	12.50	25.00
-- "360 Sound Stereo" in black on label					
❏ CS 8906 [S]	Quiet Nights	1965	5.00	10.00	20.00
-- "360 Sound Stereo" in white on label					
❏ CS 8906	Quiet Nights	1971	3.00	6.00	12.00
-- Orange label					
❏ KCS 8906	Quiet Nights	1974	2.50	5.00	10.00
-- Orange label, new prefix					
❏ PC 8906	Quiet Nights	1977	2.00	4.00	8.00
-- Orange label, new prefix					
❏ CS 8983 [S]	Miles Davis in Europe	1964	6.25	12.50	25.00
-- "360 Sound Stereo" in black on label					
❏ CS 8983 [S]	Miles Davis in Europe	1965	5.00	10.00	20.00
-- "360 Sound Stereo" in white on label					
❏ CS 8983	Miles Davis in Europe	1971	3.00	6.00	12.00
-- Orange label					
❏ KCS 8983	Miles Davis in Europe	1974	2.50	5.00	10.00
-- Orange label, new prefix					
❏ PC 8983	Miles Davis in Europe	1977	2.00	4.00	8.00
-- Orange label, new prefix					
❏ CS 9106 [S]	My Funny Valentine	1965	6.25	12.50	25.00
-- "360 Sound Stereo" in black on label					
❏ CS 9106 [S]	My Funny Valentine	1965	5.00	10.00	20.00
-- "360 Sound Stereo" in white on label					
❏ CS 9106	My Funny Valentine	1971	3.00	6.00	12.00
-- Orange label					
❏ KCS 9106	My Funny Valentine	1974	2.50	5.00	10.00
-- Orange label, new prefix					
❏ PC 9106	My Funny Valentine	1977	2.00	4.00	8.00
-- Orange label, new prefix					
❏ CS 9150 [S]	E.S.P.	1965	6.25	12.50	25.0
-- "360 Sound Stereo" in black on label					
❏ CS 9150 [S]	E.S.P.	1965	5.00	10.00	20.00
-- "360 Sound Stereo" in white on label					
❏ CS 9150	E.S.P.	1971	3.00	6.00	12.00
-- Orange label					
❏ KCS 9150	E.S.P.	1974	2.50	5.00	10.00
-- Orange label, new prefix					
❏ PC 9150	E.S.P.	1977	2.00	4.00	8.00
-- Orange label, new prefix					
❏ CS 9253 [S]	"Four" and More -- Recorded Live in Concert	1966	5.00	10.00	20.00
-- "360 Sound Stereo" on red label					
❏ CS 9253	"Four" and More -- Recorded Live in Concert	1971	3.00	6.00	12.00
-- Orange label					
❏ KCS 9253	"Four" and More -- Recorded Live in Concert	1974	2.50	5.00	10.00
-- Orange label, new prefix					
❏ PC 9253	"Four" and More -- Recorded Live in Concert	1977	2.00	4.00	8.00
-- Orange label, new prefix					
❏ CS 9401 [S]	Miles Smiles	1966	5.00	10.00	20.00
-- "360 Sound Stereo" on red label					
❏ CS 9401	Miles Smiles	1971	3.00	6.00	12.00
-- Orange label					
❏ KCS 9401	Miles Smiles	1974	2.50	5.00	10.00
-- Orange label, new prefix					
❏ PC 9401	Miles Smiles	1977	2.00	4.00	8.00
-- Orange label, new prefix					
❏ CS 9428 [S]	Milestones	1967	5.00	10.00	20.00
-- "360 Sound Stereo" on red label; reissue of 8021?					

Number	Title	Yr	VG	VG+	NM
❏ KCS 9428	Milestones	1974	2.50	5.00	10.00
-- Orange label, new prefix					
❏ PC 9428	Milestones	1977	2.00	4.00	8.00
-- Orange label, new prefix					
❏ CS 9532 [S]	Sorcerer	1967	5.00	10.00	20.00
-- "360 Sound Stereo" on red label					
❏ CS 9532	Sorcerer	1971	3.00	6.00	12.00
-- Orange label					
❏ KCS 9532	Sorcerer	1974	2.50	5.00	10.00
-- Orange label, new prefix					
❏ PC 9532	Sorcerer	1977	2.00	4.00	8.00
-- Orange label, new prefix					
❏ CS 9594 [S]	Nefertiti	1968	5.00	10.00	20.00
-- "360 Sound Stereo" on red label					
❏ CS 9594	Nefertiti	1971	3.00	6.00	12.00
-- Orange label					
❏ KCS 9594	Nefertiti	1974	2.50	5.00	10.00
-- Orange label, new prefix					
❏ PC 9594	Nefertiti	1977	2.00	4.00	8.00
-- Orange label, new prefix					
❏ CS 9628 [S]	Miles in the Sky	1968	5.00	10.00	20.00
-- "360 Sound Stereo" on red label					
❏ CS 9628	Miles in the Sky	1971	3.00	6.00	12.00
-- Orange label					
❏ KCS 9628	Miles in the Sky	1974	2.50	5.00	10.00
-- Orange label, new prefix					
❏ PC 9628	Miles in the Sky	1977	2.00	4.00	8.00
-- Orange label, new prefix					
❏ CS 9750	Filles de Kilimanjaro	1969	5.00	10.00	20.00
-- "360 Sound Stereo" on red label					
❏ CS 9750	Filles de Kilimanjaro	1971	3.00	6.00	12.00
-- Orange label					
❏ KCS 9750	Filles de Kilimanjaro	1974	2.50	5.00	10.00
-- Orange label, new prefix					
❏ PC 9750	Filles de Kilimanjaro	1977	2.00	4.00	8.00
-- Orange label, new prefix					
❏ CS 9808	Miles Davis' Greatest Hits	1969	5.00	10.00	20.00
-- "360 Sound Stereo" on red label					
❏ CS 9808	Miles Davis' Greatest Hits	1971	3.00	6.00	12.00
-- Orange label					
❏ KCS 9808	Miles Davis' Greatest Hits	1974	2.50	5.00	10.00
-- Orange label, new prefix					
❏ PC 9808	Miles Davis' Greatest Hits	1977	2.00	4.00	8.00
-- Orange label, new prefix					
❏ CS 9875	In a Silent Way	1969	5.00	10.00	20.00
-- "360 Sound Stereo" on red label					
❏ CS 9875	In a Silent Way	1971	3.00	6.00	12.00
-- Orange label					
❏ KCS 9875	In a Silent Way	1974	2.50	5.00	10.00
-- Orange label, new prefix					
❏ PC 9875	In a Silent Way	1977	2.00	4.00	8.00
-- Orange label, new prefix					
❏ CG 30038 [(2)]	Miles Davis at Fillmore	1970	3.75	7.50	15.00
❏ KC 30455	A Tribute to Jack Johnson	1971	3.00	6.00	12.00
❏ PC 30455	A Tribute to Jack Johnson	1977	2.00	4.00	8.00
-- Orange label, new prefix					
❏ CG 30954 [(2)]	Live-Evil	1971	3.75	7.50	15.00
❏ GQ 30954 [(2) Q]	Live-Evil	1973	7.50	15.00	30.00
❏ GQ 30997 [(2) Q]	Bitches Brew	1972	10.00	20.00	40.00
❏ KC 31906	On the Corner	1972	3.00	6.00	12.00
❏ PC 31906	On the Corner	1977	2.00	4.00	8.00
-- Orange label, new prefix					
❏ KC 32025	Basic Miles -- The Classic Performances of Miles Davis	1973	3.00	6.00	12.00
❏ PC 32025	Basic Miles -- The Classic Performances of Miles Davis	198?	2.00	4.00	8.00
-- Budget-line reissue					
❏ KG 32092 [(2)]	In Concert	1973	3.75	7.50	15.00
❏ PG 32092 [(2)]	In Concert	1977	2.50	5.00	10.00
-- Orange labels, new prefix					
❏ C 32470	Jazz at the Plaza, Vol. 1	1973	3.00	6.00	12.00
❏ CG 32866 [(2)]	Big Fun	1974	3.75	7.50	15.00
❏ PG 32866 [(2)]	Big Fun	1977	3.00	6.00	12.00
-- Orange labels, new prefix					
❏ KG 33236 [(2)]	Get Up With It	1974	3.75	7.50	15.00
❏ PG 33236 [(2)]	Get Up With It	1977	2.50	5.00	10.00
-- Orange labels, new prefix					
❏ PG 33967 [(2)]	Agharta	1976	3.75	7.50	15.00
❏ PC 34396	Water Babies	1977	3.00	6.00	12.00
-- Original has no bar code					
❏ PC 34396	Water Babies	198?	2.00	4.00	8.00
-- Reissue with bar code					
❏ KC2 36278 [(2)]	Circle in the Round	1980	3.75	7.50	15.00
❏ KC2 36472 [(2)]	Directions	1981	3.75	7.50	15.00
❏ FC 36790	The Man with the Horn	1981	2.50	5.00	10.00
❏ PC 36790	The Man with the Horn	198?	2.00	4.00	8.00
-- Budget-line reissue					
❏ C6X 36976 [(6)]	The Miles Davis Collection Vol. 1: 12 Sides of Miles	1980	12.50	25.00	50.00
❏ C2 38005 [(2)]	We Want Miles	1982	3.00	6.00	12.00

Number	Title	Yr	VG	VG+	NM
❏ C2 38266 [(2)]	Live at the Plugged Nickel	1982	3.00	6.00	12.00
❏ C2 38506 [(2)]	Heard 'Round the World	1983	3.00	6.00	12.00
❏ FC 38657	Star People	1983	2.50	5.00	10.00
❏ FC 38991	Decoy	1984	2.50	5.00	10.00
❏ FC 40023	You're Under Arrest	1985	2.50	5.00	10.00
❏ HC 46790	The Man with the Horn	1982	10.00	20.00	40.00
-- Half-speed mastered edition					

COLUMBIA JAZZ MASTERPIECES

Number	Title	Yr	VG	VG+	NM
❏ CJ2 40577 [(2)]	Bitches Brew	1987	3.00	6.00	12.00
❏ CJ 40578	Sketches of Spain	1987	2.50	5.00	10.00
❏ CJ 40579	Kind of Blue	1987	2.50	5.00	10.00
❏ CJ 40580	In a Silent Way	1987	2.50	5.00	10.00
❏ CJ 40609	Live Miles: More Music from the	1987	2.50	5.00	10.00
	Legendary Carnegie Hall Concert				
❏ CJ 40610	'Round About Midnight	1987	2.50	5.00	10.00
❏ CJ 40645	Cookin' at the Plugged Nickel	1987	2.50	5.00	10.00
❏ CJ 40647	Porgy and Bess	1987	2.50	5.00	10.00
❏ CJ 40784	Miles Ahead	1987	2.50	5.00	10.00
❏ CJ 40837	Milestones	1987	2.50	5.00	10.00
❏ CJ 40947	Someday My Prince Will Come	1987	2.50	5.00	10.00
❏ CJ 44052	Miles and Coltrane	1988	2.50	5.00	10.00
❏ CJ 44151	Ballads	1988	2.50	5.00	10.00
❏ CJ 44257	Miles Davis in Person, Vol. 1	1988	2.50	5.00	10.00
	(Friday Nights at the Blackhawk, San Francisco)				
❏ CJ 44425	Miles Davis in Person, Vol. 2	1989	2.50	5.00	10.00
	(Saturday Nights at the Blackhawk, San Francisco)				

COLUMBIA SPECIAL PRODUCTS

Number	Title	Yr	VG	VG+	NM
❏ P 13811	Facets	1977	2.50	5.00	10.00

COLUMBIA/CLASSIC

Number	Title	Yr	VG	VG+	NM
❏ CS 8163 [(2)]	Kind of Blue	1997	10.00	20.00	40.00
-- Reissue; contains both the original Side 1, which was mastered slightly fast, and the "correct" Side 1 (as Side 3)					
❏ CS 8271 [S]	Sketckes of Spain	1999	6.25	12.50	25.00
-- Audiophile reissue					

CONTEMPORARY

Number	Title	Yr	VG	VG+	NM
❏ 7645	Miles Davis and the Lighthouse All-Stars At Last!	1985	3.00	6.00	12.00

DEBUT

Number	Title	Yr	VG	VG+	NM
❏ DEB 120 [M]	Blue Moods	1955	62.50	125.00	250.00

FANTASY

Number	Title	Yr	VG	VG+	NM
❏ OJC-004	The Musings of Miles	198?	2.50	5.00	10.00
-- Reissue of Prestige 7007					
❏ OJC-005	Dig Miles Davis/Sonny Rollins	198?	2.50	5.00	10.00
-- Reissue of Prestige 7012					
❏ OJC-006	Miles -- The New Miles Davis Quintet	198?	2.50	5.00	10.00
-- Reissue of Prestige 7014					
❏ OJC-012	Miles Davis and the Milt Jackson Quintet/Sextet	198?	2.50	5.00	10.00
-- Reissue of Prestige 7034					
❏ OJC-043	Blue Moods	198?	2.50	5.00	10.00
-- Reissue of Fantasy 6001					
❏ OJC-053	Miles Davis and Horns	198?	2.50	5.00	10.00
-- Reissue of Prestige 7025					
❏ OJC-071	Collector's Item	198?	2.50	5.00	10.00
-- Reissue of Prestige 7044					
❏ OJC-093	Blue Haze	198?	2.50	5.00	10.00
-- Reissue of Prestige 7054					
❏ OJC-128	Cookin' with the Miles Davis Quintet	198?	2.50	5.00	10.00
-- Reissue of Prestige 7094					
❏ OJC-190	Relaxin' with the Miles Davis Quintet	1985	2.50	5.00	10.00
-- Reissue of Prestige 7129					
❏ OJC-213	Walkin'	1987	2.50	5.00	10.00
-- Reissue of Prestige 7076					
❏ OJC-245	Bags Groove	1987	2.50	5.00	10.00
-- Reissue of Prestige 7109					
❏ OJC-296	Workin' with the Miles Davis Quintet	1987	2.50	5.00	10.00
-- Reissue of Prestige 7166					
❏ OJC-347	Miles Davis and the Modern Jazz Giants	198?	2.50	5.00	10.00
-- Reissue of Prestige 7150					
❏ OJC-391	Steamin' with the Miles Davis Quintet	1989	2.50	5.00	10.00
-- Reissue of Prestige 7200					
❏ OJC-480	Miles Davis and the Lighthouse All-Stars At Last!	1991	2.50	5.00	10.00
-- Reissue of Contemporary 7645					
❏ 6001 [M]	Blue Moods	1962	12.50	25.00	50.00
-- Reissue of Debut album; red vinyl					
❏ 6001 [M]	Blue Moods	1963	7.50	15.00	30.00
-- Black vinyl, red label					
❏ 86001 [R]	Blue Moods	1962	7.50	15.00	30.00
-- Blue vinyl					

Number	Title	Yr	VG	VG+	NM
❏ 86001 [R]	Blue Moods	1963	3.75	7.50	15.00
-- Black vinyl, blue label					

MOBILE FIDELITY

Number	Title	Yr	VG	VG+	NM
❏ 1-177	Someday My Prince Will Come	1985	20.00	40.00	80.00
-- Audiophile vinyl					

MOSAIC

Number	Title	Yr	VG	VG+	NM
❏ MQ10-158 [(10)]	The Complete Plugged Nickel Sessions	199?	37.50	75.00	150.00
❏ MQ11-164 [(11)]	Miles Davis & Gil Evans: The Complete Columbia Studio Recordings	199?	50.00	100.00	200.00
❏ MQ10-177 [(10)]	The Complete Studio Recordings of the Miles Davis Quintet 1965-June 1968	1998	37.50	75.00	150.00
❏ MQ6-183 [(6)]	The Complete Bitches Brew Sessions	1999	25.00	50.00	100.00

PAIR

Number	Title	Yr	VG	VG+	NM
❏ PDL2-1095 [(2)]	Best of Miles Davis	1986	3.00	6.00	12.00

PHILIPS

Number	Title	Yr	VG	VG+	NM
❏ 836 305-1	Elevator to the Scaffold (L'Ancenseur Pour L'Echafaud)	198?	3.00	6.00	12.00
-- Reissue of Columbia 1268					

PRESTIGE

Number	Title	Yr	VG	VG+	NM
❏ P-12 [(12)]	Chronicle: The Complete Prestige Recordings	198?	25.00	50.00	100.00
❏ PRLP-124 [10]	The New Sounds of Miles Davis	1952	62.50	125.00	250.00
❏ PRLP-140 [10]	Blue Period	1953	62.50	125.00	250.00
❏ PRLP-154 [10]	Miles Davis Plays Al Cohn Compositions	1953	62.50	125.00	250.00
❏ PRLP-161 [10]	Miles Davis Featuring Sonny	1953	62.50	125.00	250.00
❏ PRLP-182 [10]	Miles Davis Sextet	1954	62.50	125.00	250.00
❏ PRLP-185 [10]	Miles Davis Quintet	1954	62.50	125.00	250.00
❏ PRLP-187 [10]	Miles Davis Quintet Featuring Sonny Rollins	1954	62.50	125.00	250.00
❏ PRLP-196 [10]	Miles Davis All Stars, Volume 1	1955	62.50	125.00	250.00
❏ PRLP-200 [10]	Miles Davis All Stars, Volume 2	1955	62.50	125.00	250.00
❏ PRLP-7007 [M]	The Musings of Miles	1955	37.50	75.00	150.00
❏ PRLP-7012 [M]	Dig Miles Davis/Sonny Rollins	1956	37.50	75.00	150.00
-- Gray cover					
❏ PRLP-7012 [M]	Dig Miles Davis/Sonny Rollins	1957	30.00	60.00	120.00
-- Color cover					
❏ PRLP-7014 [M]	Miles -- The New Miles Davis Quintet	1956	37.50	75.00	150.00
❏ PRLP-7025 [M]	Miles Davis and Horns	1956	37.50	75.00	150.00
❏ PRLP-7034 [M]	Miles Davis and the Milt Jackson Quintet/Sextet	1956	37.50	75.00	150.00
-- With W. 50th St. address on yellow label					
❏ PRLP-7034 [M]	Miles Davis and the Milt Jackson Quintet/Sextet	196?	7.50	15.00	30.00
-- With trident on blue label					
❏ PRLP-7044 [M]	Collectors' Item	1956	30.00	60.00	120.00
-- With W. 50th St. address on yellow label					
❏ PRLP-7044 [M]	Collectors' Item	196?	7.50	15.00	30.00
-- With trident on blue label					
❏ PRLP-7054 [M]	Blue Haze	1956	30.00	60.00	120.00
-- With W. 50th St. address on yellow label					
❏ PRLP-7054 [M]	Blue Haze	196?	7.50	15.00	30.00
-- With trident on blue label					
❏ PRLP-7076 [M]	Walkin'	1957	25.00	50.00	100.00
-- With W. 50th St. address on yellow label					
❏ PRLP-7076 [M]	Walkin'	196?	7.50	15.00	30.00
-- With trident on blue label					
❏ PRLP-7094 [M]	Cookin' with the Miles Davis Quintet	1957	25.00	50.00	100.00
-- With W. 50th St. address on yellow label					
❏ PRLP-7094 [M]	Cookin' with the Miles Davis Quintet	196?	7.50	15.00	30.00
-- With trident on blue label					
❏ PRLP-7109 [M]	Bags Groove	1957	25.00	50.00	100.00
-- With W. 50th St. address on yellow label					
❏ PRLP-7109 [M]	Bags Groove	196?	7.50	15.00	30.00
-- With trident on blue label					
❏ PRLP-7129 [M]	Relaxin' with the Miles Davis Quintet	1957	25.00	50.00	100.00
-- With W. 50th St. address on yellow label					
❏ PRLP-7129 [M]	Relaxin' with the Miles Davis Quintet	1957	15.00	30.00	60.00
-- With Bergenfield, NJ address on yellow label					
❏ PRLP-7129 [M]	Relaxin' with the Miles Davis Quintet	196?	7.50	15.00	30.00
-- With trident on blue label					
❏ PRLP-7150 [M]	Miles Davis and the Modern Jazz Giants	1958	20.00	40.00	80.00
-- With Bergenfield, NJ address on yellow label					
❏ PRLP-7150 [M]	Miles Davis and the Modern Jazz Giants	196?	7.50	15.00	30.00
-- With trident on blue label					
❏ PRLP-7166 [M]	Workin' with the Miles Davis Quintet	1959	20.00	40.00	80.00
-- With Bergenfield, NJ address on yellow label					

Number	Title	Yr	VG	VG+	NM
❑ PRLP-7166 [M]	Workin' with the Miles Davis Quintet	196?	7.50	15.00	30.00
-- With trident on blue label					
❑ PRLP-7168 [M]	Early Miles	1959	20.00	40.00	80.00
-- Reissue of 7025; with Bergenfield, NJ address on yellow label					
❑ PRLP-7168 [M]	Early Miles	196?	7.50	15.00	30.00
-- With trident on blue label					
❑ PRLP-7200 [M]	Steamin' with the Miles Davis Quintet	1961	20.00	40.00	80.00
-- With Bergenfield, NJ address on yellow label					
❑ PRLP-7200 [M]	Steamin' with the Miles Davis Quintet	196?	7.50	15.00	30.00
-- With trident on blue label					
❑ PRLP-7221 [M]	The Beginning	1962	12.50	25.00	50.00
-- Reissue of 7007; with Bergenfield, NJ address on yellow label					
❑ PRLP-7221 [M]	The Beginning	196?	7.50	15.00	30.00
-- With trident on blue label					
❑ PRLP-7254 [M]	The Original Quintet	1963	12.50	25.00	50.00
-- Reissue of 7014; with Bergenfield, NJ address on yellow label					
❑ PRLP-7254 [M]	The Original Quintet	196?	7.50	15.00	30.00
-- With trident on blue label					
❑ PRST-7254 [R]	The Original Quintet	1963	5.00	10.00	20.00
❑ PRLP-7281 [M]	Diggin'	196?	7.50	15.00	30.00
-- With trident on blue label					
❑ PRLP-7281 [M]	Diggin'	1963	12.50	25.00	50.00
-- Reissue of 7012; with Bergenfield, NJ address on yellow label					
❑ PRST-7281 [R]	Diggin'	1963	5.00	10.00	20.00
❑ PRLP-7322 [M]	Miles Davis Plays Richard Rodgers	1964	7.50	15.00	30.00
❑ PRST-7322 [R]	Miles Davis Plays Richard Rodgers	1964	5.00	10.00	20.00
❑ PRLP-7352 [M]	Miles Davis Plays for Lovers	1965	7.50	15.00	30.00
❑ PRST-7352 [R]	Miles Davis Plays for Lovers	1965	5.00	10.00	20.00
❑ PRLP-7373 [M]	Jazz Classics	1965	7.50	15.00	30.00
❑ PRST-7373 [R]	Jazz Classics	1965	5.00	10.00	20.00
❑ PRLP-7457 [M]	Miles Davis' Greatest Hits	1967	5.00	10.00	20.00
❑ PRST-7457 [R]	Miles Davis' Greatest Hits	1967	3.00	6.00	12.00
❑ PRST-7540 [R]	Odyssey	1968	3.00	6.00	12.00
-- Reissue of 7034					
❑ PRST-7580 [R]	Steamin'	1968	3.00	6.00	12.00
-- Reissue of 7200					
❑ PRST-7608 [R]	Walkin'	1969	3.00	6.00	12.00
-- Reissue of 7076					
❑ PRST-7650 [R]	Miles Davis and the Modern Jazz Giants	1969	3.00	6.00	12.00
-- Reissue of 7150					
❑ PRST-7674 [R]	Early Miles	1969	3.00	6.00	12.00
-- Reissue of 7168					
❑ PRST-7744 [R]	Conception	1970	3.00	6.00	12.00
❑ PRST-7822 [R]	Miles Ahead!	1971	3.00	6.00	12.00
❑ PRST-7847	Oleo	1972	3.00	6.00	12.00
❑ 24001 [(2)]	Miles Davis	1972	3.75	7.50	15.00
❑ 24012 [(2)]	The Tallest Trees	1972	3.75	7.50	15.00
❑ 24022 [(2)]	Collector's Items	1973	3.75	7.50	15.00
❑ 24034 [(2)]	Workin' and Steamin'	1973	3.75	7.50	15.00
❑ 24054 [(2)]	Dig	197?	3.00	6.00	12.00
❑ 24064 [(2)]	Green Haze	197?	3.00	6.00	12.00
❑ 24077 [(2)]	Tune Up	197?	3.00	6.00	12.00
SAVOY JAZZ					
❑ SJL-1196	First Miles	1989	2.50	5.00	10.00
TRIP					
❑ 5015	Miles of Jazz	1974	2.50	5.00	10.00
UNITED ARTISTS					
❑ UAS-9952 [(2)]	Miles Davis	1972	3.75	7.50	15.00
-- Reissue of Blue Note material					
WARNER BROS.					
❑ 25490	Tutu	1986	2.50	5.00	10.00
❑ 25873	Amandla	1989	3.00	6.00	12.00
❑ 26938	Doo-Bop	1992	3.75	7.50	15.00

DAVIS, MILES, AND JOHN COLTRANE
Also see each artist's individual listings.
MOODSVILLE

❑ MVLP-32 [M]	Miles Davis and John Coltrane Play Richard Rodgers	1963	12.50	25.00	50.00
-- Green label					
❑ MVLP-32 [M]	Miles Davis and John Coltrane Play Richard Rodgers	1965	6.25	12.50	25.00
-- Blue label, trident logo at right					
PRESTIGE					
❑ PRLP-7322 [M]	Miles Davis and John Coltrane Play Rodgers and Hart	1964	10.00	20.00	40.00
❑ PRST-7322 [R]	Miles Davis and John Coltrane Play Rodgers and Hart	1964	5.00	10.00	20.00

DAVIS, MILES, AND TADD DAMERON
Also see each artist's individual listings.
COLUMBIA

❑ JC 34804	Paris Festival International, May 1949	1978	2.50	5.00	10.00

DAVIS, MILES, AND THELONIOUS MONK
Also see each artist's individual listings.
COLUMBIA

❑ CL 2178 [M]	Miles and Monk at Newport	1964	6.25	12.50	25.00
-- "Guaranteed High Fidelity" on label					
❑ CL 2178 [M]	Miles and Monk at Newport	1965	5.00	10.00	20.00
-- "Mono" on label					
❑ CS 8978 [S]	Miles and Monk at Newport	1964	6.25	12.50	25.00
-- "360 Sound Stereo" in black on label					
❑ CS 8978 [S]	Miles and Monk at Newport	1965	5.00	10.00	20.00
-- "360 Sound Stereo" in white on label					
❑ KCS 8978	Miles and Monk at Newport	1974	2.50	5.00	10.00
-- Orange label, new prefix					
❑ PC 8978	Miles and Monk at Newport	1977	2.00	4.00	8.00
-- Orange label, new prefix					

DAVIS, RICHARD
Bass player.
BASF

❑ 20725	Muses for Richard Davis	1973	3.75	7.50	15.00
COBBLESTONE					
❑ 9003	Philosophy of the Spiritual	1972	3.75	7.50	15.00
GALAXY					
❑ 5102	Fancy Free	1978	2.50	5.00	10.00
MUSE					
❑ MR-5002	Epistrophy & Now's the Time	1973	3.00	6.00	12.00
❑ MR-5027	Dealin'	1974	3.00	6.00	12.00
❑ MR-5083	With Understanding	1976	3.00	6.00	12.00
❑ MR-5093	As One	1977	3.00	6.00	12.00
❑ MR-5115	Harvest	1978	3.00	6.00	12.00
❑ MR-5180	Way Out West	198?	2.50	5.00	10.00
PAUSA					
❑ 7022	Jazz Wave	197?	2.50	5.00	10.00

DAVIS, SAMMY, JR.
Mostly a pop singer, he dabbled in jazz occasionally. For a more complete listing of his releases, see the *Standard Catalog of American Records 1950-1975*.
DECCA

❑ DL 8676 [M]	Mood to Be Wooed	1958	6.25	12.50	25.00
❑ DL 8981 [M]	I Got a Right to Swing	1960	5.00	10.00	20.00
❑ DL 78981 [S]	I Got a Right to Swing	1960	6.25	12.50	25.00
REPRISE					
❑ R-6236 [M]	Sammy Davis. Jr., Sings/Laurindo Almeida Plays	1966	3.00	6.00	12.00
❑ RS-6236 [S]	Sammy Davis. Jr., Sings/Laurindo Almeida Plays	1966	3.75	7.50	15.00

DAVIS, SAMMY, JR., AND COUNT BASIE
Also see each artist's individual listings.
MGM

❑ SE-4825	Sammy Davis Jr. and Count Basie	1972	2.50	5.00	10.00
-- Reissue of Verve LP?					
VERVE					
❑ V-8605 [M]	Our Shining Hour	1965	3.00	6.00	12.00
❑ V6-8605 [S]	Our Shining Hour	1965	3.75	7.50	15.00

DAVIS, SAMMY, JR. AND CARMEN McRAE
Also see each artist's individual listings.
DECCA

❑ DL 8490 [M]	Boy Meets Girl	1957	7.50	15.00	30.00

DAVIS, STANTON
Trumpeter and flugel horn player.
OUTRAGEOUS

❑ 2	Better Days	1977	3.75	7.50	15.00

DAVIS, WALTER, JR.
Pianist.
BLUE NOTE

❑ BLP-4018 [M]	Davis Cup	1959	20.00	40.00	80.00
-- Regular version with W. 63rd St. address on label					
❑ BLP-4018 [M]	Davis Cup	1959	37.50	75.00	150.00
-- "Deep groove" version (deep indentation under label on both sides)					
❑ BLP-4018 [M]	Davis Cup	1964	6.25	12.50	25.00
-- With New York, USA address on label					
❑ B1-32098	Davis Cup	1995	3.75	7.50	15.00
❑ BST-84018 [S]	Davis Cup	1959	15.00	30.00	60.00
-- Regular version with W. 63rd St. address on label					
❑ BST-84018 [S]	Davis Cup	1964	5.00	10.00	20.00
-- With New York, USA address on label					
❑ BST-84018 [S]	Davis Cup	1967	3.75	7.50	15.00
-- With "A Division of Liberty Records" on label					

Number	Title	Yr	VG	VG+	NM
RED					
❑ VPA-150	A Being Such As You	198?	3.00	6.00	12.00
❑ VPA-153	Blues Walk	198?	3.00	6.00	12.00

DAVIS, WILD BILL
Organist. Also see JOHNNY HODGES AND WILD BILL DAVIS.

Number	Title	Yr	VG	VG+	NM
CORAL					
❑ CRL 57417 [M]	One More Time	1962	5.00	10.00	20.00
❑ CRL 57427 [M]	Lover	1962	5.00	10.00	20.00
❑ CRL 757417 [S]	One More Time	1962	6.25	12.50	25.00
❑ CRL 757427 [S]	Lover	1962	6.25	12.50	25.00
EPIC					
❑ LN 1004 [10]	Here's Wild Bill Davis	1954	25.00	50.00	100.00
❑ LN 1121 [M]	On the Loose	1955	15.00	30.00	60.00
❑ LN 3118 [M]	Wild Bill Davis at Birdland	1955	15.00	30.00	60.00
❑ LN 3308 [M]	Evening Concerto	1956	15.00	30.00	60.00
EVEREST					
❑ SDBR-1014 [S]	My Fair Lady	1959	6.25	12.50	25.00
❑ SDBR-1052 [S]	Flying High	1959	7.50	15.00	30.00
❑ SDBR-1094 [S]	Dance the Madison	1960	7.50	15.00	30.00
❑ SDBR-1116 [S]	Organ Grinder's Swing	1960	7.50	15.00	30.00
❑ SDBR-1125 [S]	Dis Heah	1961	7.50	15.00	30.00
❑ SDBR-1133 [S]	The Music from "Milk and Honey"	1961	7.50	15.00	30.00
❑ LPBR-5014 [M]	My Fair Lady	1958	7.50	15.00	30.00
❑ LPBR-5052 [M]	Flying High	1959	6.25	12.50	25.00
❑ LPBR-5094 [M]	Dance the Madison	1960	6.25	12.50	25.00
❑ LPBR-5116 [M]	Organ Grinder's Swing	1960	6.25	12.50	25.00
❑ LPBR-5125 [M]	Dis Heah	1961	6.25	12.50	25.00
❑ LPBR-5133 [M]	The Music from "Milk and Honey"	1961	6.25	12.50	25.00
IMPERIAL					
❑ LP-9010 [M]	Wild Bill Davis on Broadway	1956	12.50	25.00	50.00
❑ LP-9015 [M]	Wild Bill Davis in Hollywood	1956	12.50	25.00	50.00
❑ LP-9201 [M]	Wild Wild Wild Wild Wild Wild Wild Wild Wild	1963	10.00	20.00	40.00
❑ LP-12201 [R]	Wild Wild Wild Wild Wild Wild Wild Wild Wild	1963	5.00	10.00	20.00
RCA VICTOR					
❑ LPM-3314 [M]	Free, Frantic and Funky	1965	3.75	7.50	15.00
❑ LSP-3314 [S]	Free, Frantic and Funky	1965	5.00	10.00	20.00
❑ LPM-3578 [M]	Live at Count Basie's	1966	3.75	7.50	15.00
❑ LSP-3578 [S]	Live at Count Basie's	1966	5.00	10.00	20.00
❑ LPM-3799 [M]	Midnight to Dawn	1967	5.00	10.00	20.00
❑ LSP-3799 [S]	Midnight to Dawn	1967	3.75	7.50	15.00
❑ LSP-4139	Doin' His Thing	1969	3.75	7.50	15.00
SUNSET					
❑ SUS-5191	Flying Home	196?	3.75	7.50	15.00
TANGERINE					
❑ 1509	Wonderful World	197?	3.75	7.50	15.00

DAVISON, WILD BILL
Trumpeter, cornet player and bandleader.

Number	Title	Yr	VG	VG+	NM
AIRCHECK					
❑ 31	Wild Bill Davison	198?	2.50	5.00	10.00
AUDIOPHILE					
❑ AP-149	Beautifully Wild	197?	3.00	6.00	12.00
CHIAROSCURO					
❑ 124	Live at the Rainbow Room	197?	3.75	7.50	15.00
CIRCLE					
❑ LP-405 [10]	Showcase	1951	20.00	40.00	80.00
COLUMBIA					
❑ CL 871 [M]	Pretty Wild: Wild Bill Davison with Strings	1956	10.00	20.00	40.00
❑ CL 983 [M]	Wild Bill Davison with Strings Attached	1957	10.00	20.00	40.00
COMMODORE					
❑ XFL-14939	That's a-Plenty	198?	2.50	5.00	10.00
❑ FL-20,000 [10]	Dixieland Jazz Jamboree	1950	25.00	50.00	100.00
❑ FL-30009 [M]	Mild and Wild	1959	15.00	30.00	60.00
DIXIELAND JUBILEE					
❑ DJ-508 [M]	Greatest of the Greats	1958	6.25	12.50	25.00
❑ DJS-508 [S]	Greatest of the Greats	1958	5.00	10.00	20.00
JAZZOLOGY					
❑ J-2 [M]	Wild Bill Davison's Jazzologists	1962	5.00	10.00	20.00
❑ JCE-2 [S]	Wild Bill Davison's Jazzologists	1962	3.00	6.00	12.00
❑ J-14 [M]	Rompin' and Stompin'	196?	5.00	10.00	20.00
❑ JCE-14 [S]	Rompin' and Stompin'	196?	3.00	6.00	12.00
❑ J-18	Blowin' Wild	1966	3.75	7.50	15.00
❑ J-22	After Hours	196?	3.75	7.50	15.00
❑ J-25	Surfside Jazz	196?	3.75	7.50	15.00
❑ J-30	Wild Bill Davison at Bull Run	1968	3.75	7.50	15.00
❑ J-37	Jazz on a Saturday Afternoon, Vol. 1	197?	3.00	6.00	12.00
❑ J-38	Jazz on a Saturday Afternoon, Vol. 2	197?	3.00	6.00	12.00

Number	Title	Yr	VG	VG+	NM
❑ J-39	Jazz on a Saturday Afternoon, Vol. 3	197?	3.00	6.00	12.00
❑ J-70	Wild Bill Davison and the Classic Jazz Collegium	197?	3.00	6.00	12.00
❑ J-103	Wild Bill Davison and His Jazz	198?	2.50	5.00	10.00
❑ J-121	Wild Bill Davison In London	1987	2.50	5.00	10.00
❑ J-128	Lady of the Evening	1986	2.50	5.00	10.00
❑ J-133	Live in Memphis	1986	2.50	5.00	10.00
❑ J-151	Wild Bill Davison and His 75th Anniversary Jazz Band	1986	2.50	5.00	10.00
❑ J-160	Wild Bill Davison with Freddy Randall and His Band	198?	2.50	5.00	10.00
REGENT					
❑ MG-6026 [M]	When the Saints Go Marching In	196?	5.00	10.00	20.00
RIVERSIDE					
❑ RLP 12-211 [M]	Sweet and Hot	195?	7.50	15.00	30.00
-- Blue label, microphone logo at top					
❑ RLP 12-211 [M]	Sweet and Hot	1956	15.00	30.00	60.00
-- White label, blue print					
SACKVILLE					
❑ 3002	The Jazz Giants	198?	2.50	5.00	10.00
SAVOY					
❑ MG-12035 [M]	Jazz at Storyville	1955	15.00	30.00	60.00
❑ MG-12055 [M]	Ringside at Condon's	1955	15.00	30.00	60.00
-- Reissue of two 10-inch LPs (15029 and 15030) that are listed in the Various Artists Collection area					
❑ MG-12214 [M]	Dixieland	1969	3.75	7.50	15.00
SAVOY JAZZ					
❑ SJC-403	Ringside at Condon's	198?	2.50	5.00	10.00
❑ SJL-2229 [(2)]	Individualism	198?	3.75	7.50	15.00
STORYVILLE					
❑ 4005	Wild Bill Davison with Eddie Condon's All Stars	197?	2.50	5.00	10.00
❑ 4029	Papa Bue's Viking Jazz Band	197?	2.50	5.00	10.00
❑ 4048	But Beautiful	197?	2.50	5.00	10.00

DAVISON, WILD BILL, AND EDDIE MILLER
Also see each artist's individual listings.

Number	Title	Yr	VG	VG+	NM
REALTIME					
❑ 306	Wild Bill Davison and Eddie Miller Play Hoagy Carmichael	198?	2.50	5.00	10.00

DAVISON, WILD BILL, AND RALPH SUTTON
Also see each artist's individual listings.

Number	Title	Yr	VG	VG+	NM
STORYVILLE					
❑ 4027	Together Again	197?	2.50	5.00	10.00

DAWSON, SID
Trombonist and bandleader.

Number	Title	Yr	VG	VG+	NM
DELMAR					
❑ DL-109 [10]	Sid Dawson's Riverboat Gamblers	195?	15.00	30.00	60.00

DAY, CORA LEE
Female singer.

Number	Title	Yr	VG	VG+	NM
ROULETTE					
❑ R-52048 [M]	My Crying Hour	1960	7.50	15.00	30.00
❑ SR-52048 [S]	My Crying Hour	1960	10.00	20.00	40.00

DEAN, PETER

Number	Title	Yr	VG	VG+	NM
AUDIO FIDELITY					
❑ AFSD-6280	Peter Dean in Fun City	197?	3.75	7.50	15.00
BUDDAH					
❑ BDS-5613	Four or Five Times	1974	3.75	7.50	15.00
INNER CITY					
❑ IC-4002	Only Time Will Tell	1979	3.00	6.00	12.00
MONMOUTH-EVERGREEN					
❑ 7092	Where Did the Magic Go	198?	3.00	6.00	12.00
PROJECT 3					
❑ PR 5075 SD	Ding Dong Daddy!	196?	3.75	7.50	15.00

DEAN, SUZANNE
Female singer.

Number	Title	Yr	VG	VG+	NM
NOVA					
❑ 8808-1	Dreams Come True	198?	2.50	5.00	10.00
❑ 9028-1	I Wonder	1988	2.50	5.00	10.00

DeANGELIS, JIM, AND TONY SIGNA
DeAngelis is a guitarist; Signa is a flutist.

Number	Title	Yr	VG	VG+	NM
STATIRAS					
❑ SLP-8075	Gridlock	1985	2.50	5.00	10.00

DeARANGO, BILL
Guitarist.

Number	Title	Yr	VG	VG+	NM
EMARCY					
❑ MG-26020 [10]	Bill DeArango	1954	12.50	25.00	50.00

Number	Title	Yr	VG	VG+	NM

DEARIE, BLOSSOM
Female singer and pianist. Known to some as one of the singers on the "Schoolhouse Rock" ABC cartoon series ("Figure Eight" and "Unpack Your Adjectives").
CAPITOL
| ❑ SM-2086 | May I Come In | 1976 | 2.50 | 5.00 | 10.00 |
-- Reissue with new prefix
| ❑ ST 2086 [S] | May I Come In | 1964 | 5.00 | 10.00 | 20.00 |
| ❑ T 2086 [M] | May I Come In | 1964 | 3.75 | 7.50 | 15.00 |
DAFFODIL
❑ BMD-101	Blossom Dearie Sings	197?	3.75	7.50	15.00
❑ BMD-102	1975	1975	3.75	7.50	15.00
❑ BMD-103 [(2)]	My New Celebrity Is You	197?	5.00	10.00	20.00
❑ BMD-104 [(2)]	Winchester in Apple Blossom Time	197?	5.00	10.00	20.00
❑ BMD-105	Needlepoint Magic	198?	3.00	6.00	12.00
❑ BMD-106	Simply Volume VI	1983	2.50	5.00	10.00
❑ BMD-107	Positively Volume VII	198?	2.50	5.00	10.00
❑ BMD-108	Et Tu Bruce (Volume VIII)	198?	2.50	5.00	10.00
❑ BMD-109	Chez Wahlberg, Part I	198?	3.00	6.00	12.00
❑ BMD-110	Songs of Chelsea	1987	2.50	5.00	10.00
DRG
| ❑ DARC-1105 [(2)] | Blossom Dearie On Broadway | 1980 | 3.75 | 7.50 | 15.00 |
FONTANA
| ❑ MGF-27562 [M] | Blossom Time | 1966 | 3.75 | 7.50 | 15.00 |
| ❑ SRF-67562 [S] | Blossom Time | 1966 | 5.00 | 10.00 | 20.00 |
VERVE
❑ MGV-2037 [M]	Blossom Dearie	1957	15.00	30.00	60.00
❑ V-2037 [M]	Blossom Dearie	1961	5.00	10.00	20.00
❑ MGV-2081 [M]	Give Him the Ooh-La-La	1958	15.00	30.00	60.00
❑ V-2081 [M]	Give Him the Ooh-La-La	1961	5.00	10.00	20.00
❑ MGV-2109 [M]	Blossom Dearie Sings Comden & Green	1959	15.00	30.00	60.00
❑ V-2109 [M]	Blossom Dearie Sings Comden & Green	1961	5.00	10.00	20.00
❑ V6-2109 [S]	Blossom Dearie Sings Comden & Green	1961	6.25	12.50	25.00
❑ MGV-2111 [M]	Once Upon a Summertime	1958	15.00	30.00	60.00
❑ V-2111 [M]	Once Upon a Summertime	1961	5.00	10.00	20.00
❑ V6-2111 [S]	Once Upon a Summertime	1961	6.25	12.50	25.00
❑ MGV-2125 [M]	My Gentleman Friend	1959	15.00	30.00	60.00
❑ V-2125 [M]	My Gentleman Friend	1961	5.00	10.00	20.00
❑ V6-2125 [S]	My Gentleman Friend	1961	6.25	12.50	25.00
❑ MGV-2133 [M]	Broadway Song Hits	1960	12.50	25.00	50.00
❑ V-2133 [M]	Broadway Song Hits	1961	5.00	10.00	20.00
❑ V6-2133 [S]	Broadway Song Hits	1961	6.25	12.50	25.00
❑ UMV-2639	Blossom Dearie	198?	2.50	5.00	10.00
❑ MGVS-6020 [S]	Once Upon a Summertime	1960	12.50	25.00	50.00
❑ MGVS-6050 [S]	Blossom Dearie Sings Comden & Green	1960	12.50	25.00	50.00
❑ MGVS-6112 [S]	My Gentleman Friend	1960	12.50	25.00	50.00
❑ MGVS-6139 [S]	Broadway Song Hits	1960	15.00	30.00	60.00
❑ 827 757-1	Once Upon a Summertime	1986	2.50	5.00	10.00

DeCAUTER, KOEN, AND ORANGE KELLIN
DeCauter is a reed player (often on soprano saxophone). Kellin plays clarinet.
GHB
| ❑ GHB-242 | New Orleans Swing with Koen DeCauter and Orange Kellin: A Little Piece of Paradise | 1990 | 3.00 | 6.00 | 12.00 |

DECEMBER BAND, THE
GHB
| ❑ GHB-197 | The December Band, Volume 1 | 1986 | 2.50 | 5.00 | 10.00 |
| ❑ GHB-198 | The December Band, Volume 2 | 1986 | 2.50 | 5.00 | 10.00 |

DEDRICK, RUSTY
Trumpeter, arranger and composer.
COUNTERPOINT
| ❑ 552 [M] | Salute to Bunny | 1957 | 12.50 | 25.00 | 50.00 |
ESOTERIC
| ❑ ESJ-9 [10] | Rhythm and Winds | 1955 | 25.00 | 50.00 | 100.00 |
4 CORNERS OF THE WORLD
| ❑ FC-4207 [M] | The Big Band Sound | 1964 | 3.75 | 7.50 | 15.00 |
| ❑ FCS-4207 [S] | The Big Band Sound | 1964 | 5.00 | 10.00 | 20.00 |
KEYNOTE
| ❑ 1103 [M] | Rusty Dedrick | 1955 | 15.00 | 30.00 | 60.00 |
MONMOUTH-EVERGREEN
| ❑ 6918 | Harold Arlen in Hollywood | 1969 | 3.75 | 7.50 | 15.00 |
| ❑ 7035 | Many Facets, Many Friends | 1970 | 3.75 | 7.50 | 15.00 |
MONUMENT
| ❑ MLP-6502 [M] | A Jazz Journey | 1965 | 3.75 | 7.50 | 15.00 |
| ❑ SLP-16502 [S] | A Jazz Journey | 1965 | 5.00 | 10.00 | 20.00 |

DeFRANCESCO, JOEY
Organist.
COLUMBIA
| ❑ FC 44463 | All of Me | 1989 | 3.75 | 7.50 | 15.00 |

DeFRANCO, BUDDY
Clarinet player. Also see TERRY GIBBS; GERRY MULLIGAN.
CHOICE
| ❑ 1008 | Free Sail | 1974 | 3.75 | 7.50 | 15.00 |
| ❑ 1017 | Waterbed | 1977 | 3.00 | 6.00 | 12.00 |
CLASSIC JAZZ
| ❑ 33 | Buddy DeFranco and Jim Gillis | 1978 | 3.00 | 6.00 | 12.00 |
CLEF
| ❑ MGC-149 [10] | The Buddy DeFranco Quartet | 1954 | --- | --- | --- |
-- Canceled; reassigned to Norgran 3
DECCA
| ❑ DL 4031 [M] | Pacific Standard Swingin' Time | 1961 | 5.00 | 10.00 | 20.00 |
| ❑ DL 74031 [S] | Pacific Standard Swingin' Time | 1961 | 6.25 | 12.50 | 25.00 |
DOT
| ❑ DLP-9006 [M] | Cross-Country Suite | 1958 | 10.00 | 20.00 | 40.00 |
GENE NORMAN
| ❑ GNP-2 [10] | Buddy DeFranco Takes You to the Stars | 1954 | 30.00 | 60.00 | 120.00 |
HAMILTON
| ❑ HL-133 [M] | Cross-Country Suite | 1964 | 5.00 | 10.00 | 20.00 |
| ❑ HS-12133 [R] | Cross-Country Suite | 1964 | 3.00 | 6.00 | 12.00 |
MGM
❑ E-177 [10]	King of the Clarinet	1952	30.00	60.00	120.00
❑ E-253 [10]	Buddy DeFranco with Strings	1954	25.00	50.00	100.00
❑ E-3396 [M]	Buddy DeFranco	1956	20.00	40.00	80.00
MOSAIC
| ❑ M5-117 [(5)] | The Complete Recordings of the Buddy DeFranco Quartet/Quintet with Sonny Clark | 199? | 15.00 | 30.00 | 60.00 |
NORGRAN
❑ MGN-3 [10]	The Buddy DeFranco Quartet	1954	37.50	75.00	150.00
❑ MGN-16 [10]	Pretty Moods by Buddy DeFranco	1954	37.50	75.00	150.00
❑ MGN-1006 [M]	The Progressive Mr. DeFranco	1954	30.00	60.00	120.00
❑ MGN-1012 [M]	Buddy DeFranco and His Clarinet	1954	25.00	50.00	100.00
❑ MGN-1016 [M]	Buddy DeFranco and Oscar Peterson Play George Gershwin	1955	25.00	50.00	100.00
❑ MGN-1026 [M]	Buddy DeFranco Quartet	1955	25.00	50.00	100.00
❑ MGN-1068 [M]	Jazz Tones	1956	20.00	40.00	80.00
❑ MGN-1069 [M]	Mr. Clarinet	1956	20.00	40.00	80.00
❑ MGN-1079 [M]	In a Mellow Mood	1956	20.00	40.00	80.00
❑ MGN-1085 [M]	The Buddy DeFranco Wailers	1956	20.00	40.00	80.00
❑ MGN-1094 [M]	Odalisque	1956	20.00	40.00	80.00
❑ MGN-1096 [M]	Autumn Leaves	1956	20.00	40.00	80.00
❑ MGN-1105 [M]	Broadway Showcase	1956	---	---	---
-- Canceled; reassigned to Verve 2033
PABLO
| ❑ 2310 906 | Mr. Lucky | 198? | 3.00 | 6.00 | 12.00 |
PROGRESSIVE
| ❑ 7014 | Like Someone in Love | 1979 | 3.00 | 6.00 | 12.00 |
SONET
| ❑ 724 | Boronquin | 197? | 3.00 | 6.00 | 12.00 |
VERVE
| ❑ MGV-2022 [M] | The George Gershwin Songbook | 1956 | 12.50 | 25.00 | 50.00 |
-- Reissue of Norgran 1016
❑ MGV-2033 [M]	Broadway Showcase	1957	12.50	25.00	50.00
❑ V-2033 [M]	Broadway Showcase	1961	5.00	10.00	20.00
❑ MGV-2089 [M]	Buddy DeFranco Plays Benny Goodman	1958	12.50	25.00	50.00
❑ V-2089 [M]	Buddy DeFranco Plays Benny Goodman	1961	5.00	10.00	20.00
❑ MGV-2090 [M]	Buddy DeFranco Plays Artie Shaw	1958	12.50	25.00	50.00
❑ V-2090 [M]	Buddy DeFranco Plays Artie Shaw	1961	5.00	10.00	20.00
❑ MGV-2108 [M]	I Hear Benny Goodman and Artie Shaw	1958	12.50	25.00	50.00
❑ V-2108 [M]	I Hear Benny Goodman and Artie Shaw	1961	5.00	10.00	20.00
❑ V6-2108 [S]	I Hear Benny Goodman and Artie Shaw	1961	5.00	10.00	20.00
❑ UMV-2632	Closed Session	198?	2.50	5.00	10.00
❑ MGVS-6032 [S]	I Hear Benny Goodman and Artie Shaw	1960	10.00	20.00	40.00
❑ MGVS-6051 [S]	Bravura	1960	10.00	20.00	40.00
❑ MGVS-6132 [S]	Generalissimo	1960	10.00	20.00	40.00
❑ MGVS-6150 [S]	Wholly Cats	1960	10.00	20.00	40.00
❑ MGVS-6165 [S]	Closed Session	1960	10.00	20.00	40.00
❑ MGVS-6166 [S]	Live Date!	1960	10.00	20.00	40.00
❑ MGVS-6167 [S]	Buddy DeFranco	1960	---	---	---
-- Canceled
| ❑ MGV-8158 [M] | Jazz Tones | 1957 | 12.50 | 25.00 | 50.00 |
-- Reissue of Norgran 1068
| ❑ V-8158 [M] | Jazz Tones | 1961 | 5.00 | 10.00 | 20.00 |
| ❑ MGV-8159 [M] | Mr. Clarinet | 1957 | 12.50 | 25.00 | 50.00 |
-- Reissue of Norgran 1069
| ❑ V-8159 [M] | Mr. Clarinet | 1961 | 5.00 | 10.00 | 20.00 |

Number	Title	Yr	VG	VG+	NM
❑ MGV-8169 [M]	In a Mellow Mood	1957	12.50	25.00	50.00
-- Reissue of Norgran 1079					
❑ V-8169 [M]	In a Mellow Mood	1961	5.00	10.00	20.00
❑ MGV-8175 [M]	The Buddy DeFranco Wailers	1957	12.50	25.00	50.00
-- Reissue of Norgran 1085					
❑ V-8175 [M]	The Buddy DeFranco Wailers	1961	5.00	10.00	20.00
❑ MGV-8182 [M]	Odalisque	1957	12.50	25.00	50.00
-- Reissue of Norgran 1094					
❑ V-8182 [M]	Odalisque	1961	5.00	10.00	20.00
❑ MGV-8183 [M]	Autumn Leaves	1957	12.50	25.00	50.00
-- Reissue of Norgran 1096					
❑ V-8183 [M]	Autumn Leaves	1961	5.00	10.00	20.00
❑ MGV-8210 [M]	Buddy DeFranco and the Oscar Peterson Quartet	1958	12.50	25.00	50.00
❑ V-8210 [M]	Buddy DeFranco and the Oscar Peterson Quartet	1961	5.00	10.00	20.00
❑ MGV-8221 [M]	Cooking the Blues	1958	20.00	40.00	80.00
❑ V-8221 [M]	Cooking the Blues	1961	5.00	10.00	20.00
❑ MGV-8224 [M]	Sweet and Lovely	1958	12.50	25.00	50.00
❑ V-8224 [M]	Sweet and Lovely	1961	5.00	10.00	20.00
❑ MGV-8279 [M]	I Hear Benny Goodman and Artie Shaw	1958	---	---	---
-- Canceled; issued as 2108					
❑ MGV-8315 [M]	Bravura	1959	12.50	25.00	50.00
❑ V-8315 [M]	Bravura	1961	5.00	10.00	20.00
❑ V6-8315 [S]	Bravura	1961	5.00	10.00	20.00
❑ MGV-8363 [M]	Generalissimo	1960	12.50	25.00	50.00
❑ V-8363 [M]	Generalissimo	1961	5.00	10.00	20.00
❑ V6-8363 [S]	Generalissimo	1961	5.00	10.00	20.00
❑ MGV-8375 [M]	Wholly Cats	1960	10.00	20.00	40.00
❑ V-8375 [M]	Wholly Cats	1961	5.00	10.00	20.00
❑ V6-8375 [S]	Wholly Cats	1961	5.00	10.00	20.00
❑ MGV-8382 [M]	Closed Session	1960	10.00	20.00	40.00
❑ V-8382 [M]	Closed Session	1961	5.00	10.00	20.00
❑ V6-8382 [S]	Closed Session	1961	5.00	10.00	20.00
❑ MGV-8383 [M]	Live Date!	1960	10.00	20.00	40.00
❑ V-8383 [M]	Live Date!	1961	5.00	10.00	20.00
❑ V6-8383 [S]	Live Date!	1961	5.00	10.00	20.00
❑ MGV-8384 [M]	Buddy DeFranco	1960	---	---	---
-- Canceled					

DeFRANCO, BUDDY, AND TOMMY GUMINA
Also see each artist's individual listings.
MERCURY

Number	Title	Yr	VG	VG+	NM
❑ MG-20685 [M]	Presenting the Buddy DeFranco-Tommy Gumina Quintet	1962	5.00	10.00	20.00
❑ MG-20743 [M]	Kaleidoscope	1962	5.00	10.00	20.00
❑ MG-20833 [M]	Polytones	1963	5.00	10.00	20.00
❑ MG-20900 [M]	The Girl from Ipanema	1964	5.00	10.00	20.00
❑ SR-60685 [S]	Presenting the Buddy DeFranco-Tommy Gumina Quintet	1962	6.25	12.50	25.00
❑ SR-60743 [S]	Kaleidoscope	1962	6.25	12.50	25.00
❑ SR-60833 [S]	Polytones	1963	6.25	12.50	25.00
❑ SR-60900 [S]	The Girl from Ipanema	1964	6.25	12.50	25.00

DEGEN, BOB
Pianist.
ENJA

Number	Title	Yr	VG	VG+	NM
❑ 3015	Chartreuse	198?	2.50	5.00	10.00

INNER CITY

Number	Title	Yr	VG	VG+	NM
❑ IC-3027	Children of the Night	1978	3.00	6.00	12.00

DeHAVEN, DOC
Trumpeter and bandleader.
CUCA

Number	Title	Yr	VG	VG+	NM
❑ K-3000 [M]	Dixieland Treasure	1962	5.00	10.00	20.00
❑ K-3100 [M]	Doc DeHaven On Location	1963	5.00	10.00	20.00
❑ K-3200 [M]	Doc Swings a Little	1964	5.00	10.00	20.00
❑ K-3300 [M]	Just Off State Street	1966	5.00	10.00	20.00
❑ KS-3300 [S]	Just Off State Street	1966	6.25	12.50	25.00
❑ K-3400 [M]	Erle of Madison	1967	5.00	10.00	20.00

DeJOHNETTE, JACK
Drummer and percussionist. Also a pianist and keyboard player.
COLUMBIA

Number	Title	Yr	VG	VG+	NM
❑ C 31176	Compost (Take Off Your Body)	1971	5.00	10.00	20.00

ECM

Number	Title	Yr	VG	VG+	NM
❑ 1074	Untitled	1976	3.00	6.00	12.00
❑ 1079	Pictures	1976	3.00	6.00	12.00
❑ 1103	New Rags	1977	3.00	6.00	12.00
❑ 1128	New Directions	1978	3.00	6.00	12.00
❑ 1152	Special Edition	1980	3.00	6.00	12.00
❑ 1157	New Directions in Europe	1980	3.00	6.00	12.00
❑ 1189	Tin Can Alley	1981	3.00	6.00	12.00
❑ 23790	Inflation Blues	1983	2.50	5.00	10.00
❑ 25010	Album Album	1984	2.50	5.00	10.00

IMPULSE!/MCA

Number	Title	Yr	VG	VG+	NM
❑ 5992	Irresistible Force	1987	2.50	5.00	10.00

LANDMARK

Number	Title	Yr	VG	VG+	NM
❑ LLP-1504	The Piano Album	1985	2.50	5.00	10.00

MCA

Number	Title	Yr	VG	VG+	NM
❑ 42160	Zebra	1986	2.50	5.00	10.00
❑ 42313	Parallel Realities	1990	3.75	7.50	15.00

MILESTONE

Number	Title	Yr	VG	VG+	NM
❑ MSP-9022	The DeJohnette Complex	1969	5.00	10.00	20.00
❑ MSP-9029	Have You Heard?	1970	3.75	7.50	15.00

PRESTIGE

Number	Title	Yr	VG	VG+	NM
❑ 10081	Sorcery	1974	3.75	7.50	15.00
❑ 10094	Cosmic Chicken	1975	3.75	7.50	15.00

DELANEY, JACK
Trombone player and bandleader.
SOUTHLAND

Number	Title	Yr	VG	VG+	NM
❑ LP-201 [10]	Jack Delaney and George Girard in New Orleans	1954	12.50	25.00	50.00
❑ LP-214 [10]	Jack Delaney with Lee Collins	1954	12.50	25.00	50.00
❑ LP-214 [M]	Jack Delaney and the New Orleans Jazz Babies	195?	10.00	20.00	40.00

DELEGATES, THE
Group led by BILLY LARKIN.
AURA

Number	Title	Yr	VG	VG+	NM
❑ 23002 [M]	Pigmy	1964	5.00	10.00	20.00
❑ 23003 [M]	Blue Lights	1965	5.00	10.00	20.00
❑ 83002 [S]	Pigmy	1964	6.25	12.50	25.00
❑ 83003 [S]	Blue Lights	1965	6.25	12.50	25.00

DELIRIUM TREMOLO
Members: Tom Stuip (plectrum banjo, tenor banjo); Ronald Jansen Heijtmajer (bass saxophone, alto saxophone, C-melody saxophone); Guido Nielsen (violin, piano).
STOMP OFF

Number	Title	Yr	VG	VG+	NM
❑ SOS-1177	Banjophobia	1987	2.50	5.00	10.00

DeMANO, HANK
Trumpeter.
FREEWAY

Number	Title	Yr	VG	VG+	NM
❑ FLJP-1 [M]	Hank DeMano Quartet	1955	12.50	25.00	50.00

DeMERLE, LES
Drummer.
DOBRE

Number	Title	Yr	VG	VG+	NM
❑ 1020	Transfusion	1978	3.00	6.00	12.00

PALO ALTO

Number	Title	Yr	VG	VG+	NM
❑ 8008	On Fire	1981	3.00	6.00	12.00

DENNIS, JOHN
Pianist.
DEBUT

Number	Title	Yr	VG	VG+	NM
❑ DEB-121 [M]	New Piano Expressions	1955	30.00	60.00	120.00

DENNY, DOTTY
A440

Number	Title	Yr	VG	VG+	NM
❑ AJ-505 [M]	Tribute to Edgar Sampson	1954	17.50	35.00	70.00
❑ AJ-506 [M]	Dotty Digs Duke	1954	17.50	35.00	70.00

DEODATO
Full name: Eumir Deodato. Keyboard player, pianist and arranger. His version of "Also Sprach Zarathustra (2001)" was a left-field pop hit in 1973.
ATLANTIC

Number	Title	Yr	VG	VG+	NM
❑ 82048	Somewhere Out There	1989	2.50	5.00	10.00

CTI

Number	Title	Yr	VG	VG+	NM
❑ CTS-6021	Prelude	1972	3.00	6.00	12.00
❑ CTSQ-6021 [Q]	Prelude	1973	4.50	9.00	18.00
❑ CTS-6029	Deodato 2	1973	3.00	6.00	12.00
❑ CTSQ-6029 [Q]	Deodato 2	1973	4.50	9.00	18.00
❑ 7081	2001	1977	2.50	5.00	10.00
❑ 8021	Prelude	198?	2.00	4.00	8.00
-- Reissue of 6021					

MCA

Number	Title	Yr	VG	VG+	NM
❑ 410	Whirlwinds	1974	2.50	5.00	10.00
❑ 457	Artistry	1974	2.50	5.00	10.00
❑ 491	First Cuckoo	1975	2.50	5.00	10.00
❑ 697	Very Together	198?	2.00	4.00	8.00
-- Reissue of 2219					
❑ 2219	Very Together	1976	2.50	5.00	10.00

WARNER BROS.

Number	Title	Yr	VG	VG+	NM
❑ BSK 3132	Love Island	1978	2.50	5.00	10.00

Number	Title	Yr	VG	VG+	NM
❏ BSK 3321	Knights of Fantasy	1979	2.50	5.00	10.00
❏ BSK 3467	Night Cruiser	1980	2.50	5.00	10.00
❏ BSK 3649	Happy Hour	1981	2.50	5.00	10.00
❏ 25175	Motion	1984	2.00	4.00	8.00

DEODATO/AIRTO
Also see each artist's individual listings.
CTI

Number	Title	Yr	VG	VG+	NM
❏ CTS-6041	In Concert	1974	3.00	6.00	12.00

DePARIS, SIDNEY
Trumpeter and bandleader. Also a tuba player and male singer. WILBUR DePARIS is his brother.
BLUE NOTE

Number	Title	Yr	VG	VG+	NM
❏ B-6501	DeParis Dixie	1969	5.00	10.00	20.00
❏ BLP-7016 [10]	Sidney DeParis' Blue Note Stompers	1951	75.00	150.00	300.00

DePARIS, SIDNEY/JAMES P. JOHNSON
Also see each artist's individual listings.
BLUE NOTE

Number	Title	Yr	VG	VG+	NM
❏ B-6506	Original Blue Note Jazz, Volume 3	1969	5.00	10.00	20.00

DePARIS, WILBUR
Trombone player and bandleader. Brother of SIDNEY DePARIS.
A440

Number	Title	Yr	VG	VG+	NM
❏ AJ-503 [10]	New New Orleans Jazz	1954	15.00	30.00	60.00
ATLANTIC					
❏ ALS-141 [10]	Wilbur DeParis and His Rampart Street Ramblers	1952	25.00	50.00	100.00
❏ ALS-143 [10]	Wilbur DeParis, Volume 2	1953	25.00	50.00	100.00
❏ 1219 [M]	New New Orleans Jazz	1956	12.50	25.00	50.00
-- Black label					
❏ 1219 [M]	New New Orleans Jazz	1961	5.00	10.00	20.00
-- Multicolor label, white "fan" logo					
❏ 1219 [M]	New New Orleans Jazz	1964	3.75	7.50	15.00
-- Multicolor label, black "fan" logo					
❏ SD 1219 [S]	New New Orleans Jazz	1958	10.00	20.00	40.00
-- Green label					
❏ SD 1219 [S]	New New Orleans Jazz	1961	5.00	10.00	20.00
-- Multicolor label, white "fan" logo					
❏ SD 1219 [S]	New New Orleans Jazz	1964	3.75	7.50	15.00
-- Multicolor label, black "fan" logo					
❏ 1233 [M]	Marchin' and Swingin'	1956	12.50	25.00	50.00
-- Black label					
❏ 1233 [M]	Marchin' and Swingin'	1961	5.00	10.00	20.00
-- Multicolor label, white "fan" logo					
❏ 1233 [M]	Marchin' and Swingin'	1964	3.75	7.50	15.00
-- Multicolor label, black "fan" logo					
❏ SD 1233 [S]	Marchin' and Swingin'	1958	10.00	20.00	40.00
-- Green label					
❏ SD 1233 [S]	Marchin' and Swingin'	1961	5.00	10.00	20.00
-- Multicolor label, white "fan" logo					
❏ SD 1233 [S]	Marchin' and Swingin'	1964	3.75	7.50	15.00
-- Multicolor label, black "fan" logo					
❏ 1253 [M]	Wilbur DeParis at Symphony Hall	1957	12.50	25.00	50.00
-- Black label					
❏ 1253 [M]	Wilbur DeParis at Symphony Hall	1961	5.00	10.00	20.00
-- Multicolor label, white "fan" logo					
❏ 1253 [M]	Wilbur DeParis at Symphony Hall	1964	3.75	7.50	15.00
-- Multicolor label, black "fan" logo					
❏ SD 1253 [S]	Wilbur DeParis at Symphony Hall	1958	10.00	20.00	40.00
-- Green label					
❏ SD 1253 [S]	Wilbur DeParis at Symphony Hall	1961	5.00	10.00	20.00
-- Multicolor label, white "fan" logo					
❏ SD 1253 [S]	Wilbur DeParis at Symphony Hall	1964	3.75	7.50	15.00
-- Multicolor label, black "fan" logo					
❏ 1288 [M]	Wilbur DeParis Plays Cole Porter	1958	12.50	25.00	50.00
-- Black label					
❏ 1288 [M]	Wilbur DeParis Plays Cole Porter	1961	5.00	10.00	20.00
-- Multicolor label, white "fan" logo					
❏ 1288 [M]	Wilbur DeParis Plays Cole Porter	1964	3.75	7.50	15.00
-- Multicolor label, black "fan" logo					
❏ 1300 [M]	Something Old, New, Gay, Blue	1958	12.50	25.00	50.00
-- Black label					
❏ 1300 [M]	Something Old, New, Gay, Blue	1961	5.00	10.00	20.00
-- Multicolor label, white "fan" logo					
❏ 1300 [M]	Something Old, New, Gay, Blue	1964	3.75	7.50	15.00
-- Multicolor label, black "fan" logo					
❏ SD 1300 [S]	Something Old, New, Gay, Blue	1958	10.00	20.00	40.00
-- Green label					
❏ SD 1300 [S]	Something Old, New, Gay, Blue	1961	5.00	10.00	20.00
-- Multicolor label, white "fan" logo					
❏ SD 1300 [S]	Something Old, New, Gay, Blue	1964	3.75	7.50	15.00
-- Multicolor label, black "fan" logo					
❏ 1318 [M]	That's a-Plenty	1959	12.50	25.00	50.00
-- Black label					

Number	Title	Yr	VG	VG+	NM
❏ 1318 [M]	That's a-Plenty	1961	5.00	10.00	20.00
-- Multicolor label, white "fan" logo					
❏ 1318 [M]	That's a-Plenty	1964	3.75	7.50	15.00
-- Multicolor label, black "fan" logo					
❏ SD 1318 [S]	That's a-Plenty	1959	10.00	20.00	40.00
-- Green label					
❏ SD 1318 [S]	That's a-Plenty	1961	5.00	10.00	20.00
-- Multicolor label, white "fan" logo					
❏ SD 1318 [S]	That's a-Plenty	1964	3.75	7.50	15.00
-- Multicolor label, black "fan" logo					
❏ 1336 [M]	The Wild Jazz Age	1960	6.25	12.50	25.00
-- Multicolor label, white "fan" logo					
❏ 1336 [M]	The Wild Jazz Age	1964	3.75	7.50	15.00
-- Multicolor label, black "fan" logo					
❏ SD 1336 [S]	The Wild Jazz Age	1960	7.50	15.00	30.00
-- Multicolor label, white "fan" logo					
❏ SD 1336 [S]	The Wild Jazz Age	1964	5.00	10.00	20.00
-- Multicolor label, black "fan" logo					
❏ 1363 [M]	Wilbur DeParis on the Riviera	1961	6.25	12.50	25.00
-- Multicolor label, white "fan" logo					
❏ 1363 [M]	Wilbur DeParis on the Riviera	1964	3.75	7.50	15.00
-- Multicolor label, black "fan" logo					
❏ SD 1363 [S]	Wilbur DeParis on the Riviera	1961	7.50	15.00	30.00
-- Multicolor label, white "fan" logo					
❏ SD 1363 [S]	Wilbur DeParis on the Riviera	1964	5.00	10.00	20.00
-- Multicolor label, black "fan" logo					
❏ SD 1552	Over and Over Again	1970	3.75	7.50	15.00
HERITAGE					
❏ SS-1207 [M]	Wilbur DeParis	1956	12.50	25.00	50.00

DePARIS, WILBUR, AND JIMMY WITHERSPOON
Also see each artist's individual listings.
ATLANTIC

Number	Title	Yr	VG	VG+	NM
❏ 1266 [M]	New Orleans Blues	1957	17.50	35.00	70.00
-- Black label					
❏ 1266 [M]	New Orleans Blues	1961	7.50	15.00	30.00
-- Multicolor label, white "fan" logo					
❏ 1266 [M]	New Orleans Blues	1964	6.25	12.50	25.00
-- Multicolor label, black "fan" logo					

DeRISE, JOE
Pianist and male singer.
AUDIOPHILE

Number	Title	Yr	VG	VG+	NM
❏ AP-153	House of Flowers	1981	3.00	6.00	12.00
❏ AP-174	The Blues Are Out of Town	1982	3.00	6.00	12.00
❏ AP-215	The Joe DeRise Tentette Is About You Mad	1986	2.50	5.00	10.00
❏ AP-231	Joe DeRise Sings and Plays the Jimmy Van Heusen Anthology, Vol. 1	1989	2.50	5.00	10.00
❏ AP-232	Joe DeRise Sings and Plays the Jimmy Van Heusen Anthology, Vol. 2	1989	2.50	5.00	10.00
❏ AP-233	Joe DeRise Sings and Plays the Jimmy Van Heusen Anthology, Vol. 3	1989	2.50	5.00	10.00
BETHLEHEM					
❏ BCP-51 [M]	Joe DeRise with the Australian Jazz Quintet	1956	12.50	25.00	50.00
❏ BCP-1039 [10]	Joe DeRise Sings	1955	25.00	50.00	100.00
INNER CITY					
❏ IC-4003	I'll Remember Suzanne	1979	3.00	6.00	12.00

DES PLANTES, TED
Pianist and bandleader.
JAZZOLOGY

Number	Title	Yr	VG	VG+	NM
❏ J-125	Ted Des Plantes and His Buddies	1983	2.50	5.00	10.00
STOMP OFF					
❏ SOS-1136	Swedish-American Hot Jazz Collaboration	1987	2.50	5.00	10.00

DESCENDANTS OF MIKE & PHOEBE, THE
STRATA-EAST

Number	Title	Yr	VG	VG+	NM
❏ SES-19744	A Spirit Speaks	1973	15.00	30.00	60.00

DESMARAIS, LORRAINE
Pianist.
JAZZIMAGE

Number	Title	Yr	VG	VG+	NM
❏ JZ-100	Lorraine Desmarais Trio	1984	3.00	6.00	12.00
❏ JZ-106	Andiamo	1985	3.00	6.00	12.00

DESMOND, PAUL
Alto saxophone player. Long-time member of DAVE BRUBECK's classic quartet. Wrote the hit "Take Five." Also see GERRY MULLIGAN.
A&M

Number	Title	Yr	VG	VG+	NM
❏ SP-3015	Summertime	1969	3.00	6.00	12.00
❏ SP-3024	From the Hot Afternoon	1969	3.00	6.00	12.00
❏ SP-3032	Bridge Over Troubled Water	1970	3.00	6.00	12.00

Number	Title	Yr	VG	VG+	NM
ARTISTS HOUSE					
❏ 2	Paul Desmond	1979	2.50	5.00	10.00
CTI					
❏ CTS-6039	Skylark	1974	2.50	5.00	10.00
❏ CTS-6059	Pure Desmond	1975	2.50	5.00	10.00
CTI/CBS ASSOCIATED					
❏ FZ 40806	Pure Desmond	1987	2.50	5.00	10.00
-- *Reissue of CTI 6059*					
❏ FZ 44170	Skylark	1988	2.50	5.00	10.00
-- *Reissue of CTI 6039*					
DISCOVERY					
❏ 840	East of the Sun	198?	2.50	5.00	10.00
FANTASY					
❏ 3-21 [10]	Paul Desmond	1955	25.00	50.00	100.00
❏ OJC-119	Paul Desmond Quartet Featuring Don Elliott	198?	2.50	5.00	10.00
-- *Reissue of Fantasy 3235*					
❏ 3235 [M]	Paul Desmond Quartet Featuring Don Elliott	1956	20.00	40.00	80.00
-- *Red vinyl*					
❏ 3235 [M]	Paul Desmond Quartet Featuring Don Elliott	1957	10.00	20.00	40.00
-- *Black vinyl, red label, non-flexible vinyl*					
❏ 3235 [M]	Paul Desmond Quartet Featuring Don Elliott	1962	5.00	10.00	20.00
-- *Black vinyl, red label, flexible vinyl*					
FINESSE					
❏ FW 37487	Paul Desmond and the Modern Jazz Quartet	1981	2.50	5.00	10.00
HORIZON					
❏ 850 [(2)]	Paul Desmond Live	1976	3.75	7.50	15.00
MOSAIC					
❏ M6-120 [(6)]	The Complete Recordings of the Paul Desmond Quartet with Jim Hall	199?	17.50	35.00	70.00
RCA CAMDEN					
❏ ACL1-0201	Samba de Orfeo	1973	2.50	5.00	10.00
RCA VICTOR					
❏ LPM-2438 [M]	Desmond Blue	1961	7.50	15.00	30.00
❏ LSP-2438 [S]	Desmond Blue	1961	7.50	15.00	30.00
❏ LPM-2569 [M]	Take Ten	1962	6.25	12.50	25.00
❏ LSP-2569 [S]	Take Ten	1962	7.50	15.00	30.00
❏ LPM-2654 [M]	Two of a Mind	1963	6.25	12.50	25.00
❏ LSP-2654 [S]	Two of a Mind	1963	7.50	15.00	30.00
❏ ANL1-2807	Pure Gold	1978	2.50	5.00	10.00
❏ LPM-3320 [M]	Boss Antigua	1965	5.00	10.00	20.00
❏ LSP-3320 [S]	Boss Antigua	1965	6.25	12.50	25.00
❏ LPM-3407 [M]	Glad to Be Unhappy	1965	5.00	10.00	20.00
❏ LSP-3407 [S]	Glad to Be Unhappy	1965	6.25	12.50	25.00
❏ LPM-3480 [M]	Easy Living	1965	5.00	10.00	20.00
❏ LSP-3480 [S]	Easy Living	1965	6.25	12.50	25.00
WARNER BROS.					
❏ W 1356 [M]	First Place Again	1960	7.50	15.00	30.00
❏ WS 1356 [S]	First Place Again	1960	7.50	15.00	30.00

DeSOUZA, RAUL
Trombonist.

Number	Title	Yr	VG	VG+	NM
CAPITOL					
❏ ST-11648	Sweet Lucy	1977	3.00	6.00	12.00
❏ SW-11774	Don't Ask My Neighbors	1978	3.00	6.00	12.00
❏ ST-11918	'Til Tomorrow Comes	1979	3.00	6.00	12.00
MILESTONE					
❏ 9061	Colors	1975	3.75	7.50	15.00

DEUCE
Jean Fineberg (saxophone, flute) and Ellen Seeling (trumpet).

Number	Title	Yr	VG	VG+	NM
REDWOOD					
❏ R-8602	Deuce	1986	3.00	6.00	12.00

DEUCHAR, JIMMY
Trumpeter and mellophone player.

Number	Title	Yr	VG	VG+	NM
CONTEMPORARY					
❏ C-3529 [M]	Pub Crawling	1957	12.50	25.00	50.00
DISCOVERY					
❏ DL-2004 [10]	New Sounds from England	1953	20.00	40.00	80.00

DIAZ MENA, ANTONIO
Conga player.

Number	Title	Yr	VG	VG+	NM
AUDIO FIDELITY					
❏ AFLP-2117 [M]	Eso Es En Latin Jazz Man	1963	3.75	7.50	15.00
❏ AFSD-6117 [S]	Eso Es En Latin Jazz Man	1963	5.00	10.00	20.00

DICKENSON, VIC
Trombone player and occasional male singer.

Number	Title	Yr	VG	VG+	NM
JAZZTONE					
❏ J-1259 [M]	Slidin' Swing	1956	10.00	20.00	40.00
SACKVILLE					
❏ 2015	Just Friends	198?	3.00	6.00	12.00
SONET					
❏ 720	Trombone Cholly	197?	2.50	5.00	10.00
STORYVILLE					
❏ STLP-920 [M]	Vic's Boston Story	1957	10.00	20.00	40.00
VANGUARD					
❏ VRS-99/100 [(2)]	The Essential Vic Dickenson	197?	3.75	7.50	15.00
❏ VRS-8001 [10]	Vic Dickenson Septet, Volume 1	1953	12.50	25.00	50.00
❏ VRS-8002 [10]	Vic Dickenson Septet, Volume 2	1953	12.50	25.00	50.00
❏ VRS-8012 [10]	Vic Dickenson Septet, Volume 3	1954	12.50	25.00	50.00
❏ VRS-8013 [10]	Vic Dickenson Septet, Volume 4	1954	12.50	25.00	50.00
❏ VRS-8520 [M]	Vic Dickenson Showcase, Volume 1	1958	10.00	20.00	40.00
❏ VRS-8521 [M]	Vic Dickenson Showcase, Volume 2	1958	10.00	20.00	40.00

DICKENSON, VIC, AND JOE THOMAS
Thomas played trumpet. Also see VIC DICKENSON.

Number	Title	Yr	VG	VG+	NM
ATLANTIC					
❏ 1303 [M]	Mainstream	1958	12.50	25.00	50.00
-- *Black label*					
❏ 1303 [M]	Mainstream	1961	5.00	10.00	20.00
-- *Multicolor label, white "fan" logo*					
❏ SD 1303 [S]	Mainstream	1958	10.00	20.00	40.00
-- *Green label*					
❏ SD 1303 [S]	Mainstream	1961	5.00	10.00	20.00
-- *Multicolor label, white "fan" logo*					

DICKERSON, DWIGHT
Pianist.

Number	Title	Yr	VG	VG+	NM
DISCOVERY					
❏ DS-792	Sooner or Later	1978	3.00	6.00	12.00

DICKERSON, WALT
Vibraphone player, composer and arranger. Also see PIERRE DORGE.

Number	Title	Yr	VG	VG+	NM
AUDIO FIDELITY					
❏ AFLP-2131 [M]	Unity	1963	5.00	10.00	20.00
❏ AFLP-2217 [M]	Vibes in Motion	1968	6.25	12.50	25.00
-- *Reissue of Dauntless 4313*					
❏ AFSD-6131 [S]	Unity	1963	6.25	12.50	25.00
❏ AFSD-6217 [S]	Vibes in Motion	1968	3.75	7.50	15.00
-- *Reissue of Dauntless 6313*					
DAUNTLESS					
❏ DM-4313 [M]	Jazz Impressions of "Lawrence of Arabia"	1963	6.25	12.50	25.00
❏ DS-6313 [S]	Jazz Impressions of "Lawrence of Arabia"	1963	7.50	15.00	30.00
INNER CITY					
❏ IC-2042	Peace	1976	3.75	7.50	15.00
MGM					
❏ E-4358 [M]	Impressions of "A Patch of Blue"	1965	5.00	10.00	20.00
❏ SE-4358 [S]	Impressions of "A Patch of Blue"	1965	6.25	12.50	25.00
NEW JAZZ					
❏ NJLP-8254 [M]	This Is Walt Dickerson	1961	12.50	25.00	50.00
-- *Purple label*					
❏ NJLP-8254 [M]	This Is Walt Dickerson	1965	6.25	12.50	25.00
-- *Blue label, trident logo at right*					
❏ NJLP-8268 [M]	A Sense of Direction	1962	12.50	25.00	50.00
-- *Purple label*					
❏ NJLP-8268 [M]	A Sense of Direction	1965	6.25	12.50	25.00
-- *Blue label, trident logo at right*					
❏ NJLP-8275 [M]	Relativity	1962	12.50	25.00	50.00
-- *Purple label*					
❏ NJLP-8275 [M]	Relativity	1965	6.25	12.50	25.00
-- *Blue label, trident logo at right*					
❏ NJLP-8283 [M]	To My Queen	1962	12.50	25.00	50.00
-- *Purple label*					
❏ NJLP-8283 [M]	To My Queen	1965	6.25	12.50	25.00
-- *Blue label, trident logo at right*					
SOUL NOTE					
❏ SN-1028	Life Rays	1982	3.00	6.00	12.00
STEEPLECHASE					
❏ SCS-1042	Peace	197?	2.50	5.00	10.00
-- *Reissue of Inner City 2042*					
❏ SCS-1070	Serendipity	197?	3.00	6.00	12.00
❏ SCS-1089	Divine Gemini	197?	3.00	6.00	12.00
❏ SCS-1112	To My Queen Revisited	1978	3.00	6.00	12.00
❏ SCS-1115	Landscape with Open Door	1978	3.00	6.00	12.00
❏ SCS-1126	Visions	1979	3.00	6.00	12.00

Number	Title	Yr	VG	VG+	NM
❑ SCS-1130	To My Son	1979	3.00	6.00	12.00
❑ SCS-1146	I Hear You John	198?	3.00	6.00	12.00
❑ SCS-1213	Tenderness	198?	3.00	6.00	12.00
❑ SCD-17002	Shades of Love	198?	6.25	12.50	25.00
-- Direct-to-disc recording					

DICKIE, NEVILLE
Pianist.
STOMP OFF
❑ SOS-1052	Eye Openers	1982	2.50	5.00	10.00
❑ SOS-1096	Taken in Stride	1986	2.50	5.00	10.00
❑ SOS-1176	Neville Dickie Meets Fats, the Lion and the Lamb	1988	2.50	5.00	10.00

DIGABLE PLANETS
Hip-hop group; most of its samples and influences came from jazz. Its biggest hit single, "Rebirth of Slick (Cool Like Dat)," samples Art Blakey.
PENDULUM
❑ E1-30654	Blowout Comb	1994	3.00	6.00	12.00
❑ 61414	Reachin' (A New Refutation of Time and Space)	1993	3.00	6.00	12.00

DIGGS, DAVID
Keyboard player, composer, arranger and producer.
INSTANT JOY
❑ 1002	Supercook!	198?	2.50	5.00	10.00
PALO ALTO
| ❑ 8037 | Realworld | 198? | 2.50 | 5.00 | 10.00 |
PBR
| ❑ 9 | Out on a Limb | 197? | 3.00 | 6.00 | 12.00 |
| ❑ 12 | Elusion | 1979 | 3.00 | 6.00 | 12.00 |
TBA
| ❑ TB-207 | Streetshadows | 1985 | 2.50 | 5.00 | 10.00 |
| ❑ TB-213 | Right Before Your Eyes | 1986 | 2.50 | 5.00 | 10.00 |

DiMEOLA, AL
Guitarist. Sometimes a keyboard player and percussionist. Also see RETURN TO FOREVER.
COLUMBIA
❑ PC 34074	Land of the Midnight Sun	1976	2.50	5.00	10.00
-- Original issue with no bar code					
❑ PC 34074	Land of the Midnight Sun	1980	2.00	4.00	8.00
-- Budget-line reissue with bar code					
❑ JC 34461	Elegant Gypsy	197?	2.00	4.00	8.00
-- Reissue with new prefix					
❑ PC 34461	Elegant Gypsy	1976	2.50	5.00	10.00
-- Original issue with no bar code					
❑ PC 35561	Elegant Gypsy	198?	2.00	4.00	8.00
-- Budget-line reissue with bar code					
❑ JC 35277	Casino	1978	2.50	5.00	10.00
❑ PC 35277	Casino	1980	2.00	4.00	8.00
-- Budget-line reissue					
❑ C2X 36270 [(2)]	Splendido Hotel	1980	3.00	6.00	12.00
❑ FC 37654	Electric Rendezvous	1982	2.50	5.00	10.00
❑ PC 37654	Electric Rendezvous	198?	2.00	4.00	8.00
-- Budget-line reissue					
❑ FC 38373	Tour de Force -- "Live"	1982	2.50	5.00	10.00
❑ FC 38944	Scenario	1983	2.50	5.00	10.00
❑ HC 44461	Elegant Gypsy	198?	10.00	20.00	40.00
-- Half-speed mastered edition					
❑ HC 46454	Electric Rendezvous	198?	12.50	25.00	50.00
-- Half-speed mastered edition					
❑ HC 47152	Friday Night in San Francisco	198?	12.50	25.00	50.00
-- Half-speed mastered edition					
EMI-MANHATTAN
| ❑ MLT-46995 | Tirami Su | 1987 | 2.50 | 5.00 | 10.00 |
MANHATTAN
| ❑ ST-53002 | Cielo E Terra | 1985 | 2.50 | 5.00 | 10.00 |
| ❑ ST-53011 | Soaring Through a Dream | 1987 | 2.50 | 5.00 | 10.00 |

DIRECT FLIGHT
DIRECT DISC
| ❑ DD-104 | Spectrum | 1980 | 6.25 | 12.50 | 25.00 |
| -- Direct-to-disc recording | | | | | |

DIRTY DOZEN JAZZ BAND, THE
COLUMBIA
| ❑ FC 45042 | Voodoo | 1989 | 3.75 | 7.50 | 15.00 |
GEORGE WEIN COLLECTION
| ❑ GW-3005 | My Feet Can't Fail Me Now | 1984 | 3.00 | 6.00 | 12.00 |
ROUNDER
| ❑ 2052 | Live: Mardi Gras in Montreux | 1986 | 3.00 | 6.00 | 12.00 |

DITMAS, BRUCE
Drummer.
CHIAROSCURO
| ❑ 195 | Aeray Dust | 1977 | 3.75 | 7.50 | 15.00 |

DIXIE SMALL FRY, THE
The five members were all between the ages of 11 and 13 when this was recorded.
LIBERTY
| ❑ LRP-3057 [M] | The Dixie Small Fry in Hi-Fi | 1957 | 10.00 | 20.00 | 40.00 |
| ❑ LST-7010 [S] | The Dixie Small Fry in Hi-Fi | 1958 | 10.00 | 20.00 | 40.00 |

DIXIE STOMPERS, THE
DELMAR
❑ DL-112 [10]	The Dixie Stompers Play New Orleans Jazz	195?	20.00	40.00	80.00
❑ DL-113 [10]	Wake the Levee	195?	20.00	40.00	80.00
❑ DL-204 [M]	Jazz at Westminster College	195?	15.00	30.00	60.00
-- Blue vinyl; label says "DL-201" though cover says "204"					
RCA VICTOR
| ❑ LPM-1212 [M] | New York Land Dixie | 1956 | 20.00 | 40.00 | 80.00 |

DIXIELAND RHYTHM KINGS, THE
Also see TONY PARENTI.
BLACKBIRD
| ❑ 12006 | A Trip to Waukesha | 197? | 3.75 | 7.50 | 15.00 |
EMPIRICAL
| ❑ LP-102 [10] | The Dixieland Rhythm Kings | 1954 | 20.00 | 40.00 | 80.00 |
GHB
| ❑ GHB-7 | The Dixieland Rhythm Kings | 1963 | 3.75 | 7.50 | 15.00 |
RIVERSIDE
❑ RLP 12-210 [M]	Dixieland in Hi-Fi	1956	15.00	30.00	60.00
-- White label, blue print					
❑ RLP 12-210 [M]	Dixieland in Hi-Fi	1957	12.50	25.00	50.00
-- Blue label, microphone logo					
❑ RLP 12-259 [M]	The Dixieland Rhythm Kings at the Hi-Fi Jazz Band Ball	1958	10.00	20.00	40.00
❑ RLP 12-289 [M]	Jazz in Retrospect	1959	10.00	20.00	40.00
❑ RLP-2505 [10]	New Orleans Jazz Party	1954	20.00	40.00	80.00

DIXON, BILL
Trumpeter, flugel horn player, pianist and composer. Also see ARCHIE SHEPP.
CADENCE JAZZ
| ❑ CJ-1024/25 [(2)] | Collection | 1985 | 5.00 | 10.00 | 20.00 |
RCA VICTOR
| ❑ LPM-3844 [M] | Intents and Purposes | 1967 | 7.50 | 15.00 | 30.00 |
| ❑ LSP-3844 [S] | Intents and Purposes | 1967 | 5.00 | 10.00 | 20.00 |
SAVOY
| ❑ MG-12184 | The Bill Dixon 7-Tette | 1964 | 5.00 | 10.00 | 20.00 |
SOUL NOTE
❑ SN-1008	Bill Dixon in Italy, Volume 1	1980	3.00	6.00	12.00
❑ SN-1011	Bill Dixon in Italy, Volume 2	1981	3.00	6.00	12.00
❑ SN-1037/38 [(2)]	November 1981	1982	3.75	7.50	15.00
❑ 121111	Thoughts	1987	3.00	6.00	12.00
❑ 121138	Son of Sisyphus	1990	3.75	7.50	15.00

DIXON, ERIC
Tenor saxophone player and flutist.
MASTER JAZZ
| ❑ 8124 | Eric's Edge | 197? | 3.75 | 7.50 | 15.00 |

DIZRHYTHMIA
Members: Jakko Jakszyck (guitar, sitar, piano, synthesizers, vocals); Gavin Harrison (drums, percussion); Danny Thompson (bass); Pandit Dinesh (tabla, percussion); Sultan Khan (sarangi).
ANTILLES
| ❑ 91026 | Disrhythmia | 1988 | 2.50 | 5.00 | 10.00 |

DJAVAN
Male singer and composer.
COLUMBIA
| ❑ FC 44276 | Bird of Paradise | 1988 | 2.50 | 5.00 | 10.00 |

DOBBINS, BILL
Pianist, composer and arranger.
ADVENT
| ❑ 5003 | Textures | 1974 | 3.75 | 7.50 | 15.00 |
OMNISOUND
| ❑ 1036 | Dedications | 1980 | 2.50 | 5.00 | 10.00 |
| ❑ 1041 | Where One Relaxes | 1981 | 2.50 | 5.00 | 10.00 |
TELARC
| ❑ 5003 | Textures | 198? | 2.50 | 5.00 | 10.00 |
| -- Reissue of Advent LP | | | | | |

Number	Title	Yr	VG	VG+	NM

DODD, BILLY
JAZZOLOGY
❑ J-130	Doctor Billy Dodd and Friends	1985	2.50	5.00	10.00
❑ J-161	Billy Dodd's Swing All-Stars, Volume One	198?	2.50	5.00	10.00
❑ J-162	Billy Dodd's Swing All-Stars, Volume Two	198?	2.50	5.00	10.00

DODDS, BABY
Drummer. Brother of JOHNNY DODDS.
AMERICAN MUSIC
❑ 1 [M]	Baby Dodds No. 1	1951	12.50	25.00	50.00
❑ 2 [M]	Baby Dodds No. 2	1951	12.50	25.00	50.00
❑ 3 [M]	Baby Dodds No. 3	1951	12.50	25.00	50.00
FOLKWAYS
❑ FP-30 [10]	Footnotes to Jazz, Vol. 1 -- Baby Dodds' Drum Solos	1951	15.00	30.00	60.00
GHB
❑ GHB-50	Jazz A La Creole	1969	3.75	7.50	15.00

DODDS, JOHNNY
Clarinetist and sometimes saxophone player.
BIOGRAPH
❑ 12024	Johnny Dodds and Tommy Ladner, 1923-28	198?	2.50	5.00	10.00
BRUNSWICK
❑ BL 58016 [10]	The King of New Orleans Clarinets	1951	25.00	50.00	100.00
HERWIN
❑ 115	Paramount Recordings Vol. 1: 1926-1929	198?	3.00	6.00	12.00
JOLLY ROGER
❑ 5012 [10]	Johnny Dodds	1954	12.50	25.00	50.00
MCA
❑ 1328	Spirit of New Orleans	198?	2.50	5.00	10.00
❑ 42326	South Side Chicago Jazz	1990	3.75	7.50	15.00
MILESTONE
❑ M-2002 [M]	The Immortal Johnny Dodds	1967	5.00	10.00	20.00
❑ M-2011	Chicago Mess Around	1968	5.00	10.00	20.00
RCA VICTOR
❑ LPV-558 [M]	Sixteen Rare Recordings	1965	6.25	12.50	25.00
RIVERSIDE
❑ RLP 12-104 [M]	Johnny Dodds' New Orleans Clarinet	1956	15.00	30.00	60.00
-- White label, blue print					
❑ RLP 12-104 [M]	Johnny Dodds' New Orleans Clarinet	195?	10.00	20.00	40.00
-- Blue label with microphone logo					
❑ RLP 12-135 [M]	In the Alley: Johnny Dodds, Volume 2	1961	10.00	20.00	40.00
❑ RLP-1002 [10]	Johnny Dodds, Volume 1	1953	20.00	40.00	80.00
❑ RLP-1015 [10]	Johnny Dodds, Volume 2	1953	20.00	40.00	80.00
"X"
❑ LX-3006 [10]	Johnny Dodds' Washboard Band	1954	15.00	30.00	60.00

DODDS, JOHNNY/JIMMY NOONE
Also see each artist's individual listings.
BRUNSWICK
❑ BL 58046 [10]	Battle of Jazz, Volume 8	1953	20.00	40.00	80.00

DODDS, JOHNNY, AND KID ORY
Also see each artist's individual listings.
EPIC
❑ LN 3207 [M]	Johnny Dodds and Kid Ory	1956	12.50	25.00	50.00
❑ LA 16004 [M]	Johnny Dodds and Kid Ory	1960	6.25	12.50	25.00

DODSON, MARGE
Female singer.
COLUMBIA
❑ CL 1309 [M]	In the Still of the Night	1959	7.50	15.00	30.00
❑ CL 1458 [M]	New Voice in Town	1960	7.50	15.00	30.00
❑ CS 8258 [S]	New Voice in Town	1960	10.00	20.00	40.00

DOGGETT, BILL
Pianist, organist and arranger. As much rhythm & blues as he was jazz, he's best known for his 1956 hit record "Honky Tonk."
ABC-PARAMOUNT
❑ 507 [M]	Wow!	1965	5.00	10.00	20.00
❑ S-507 [S]	Wow!	1965	6.25	12.50	25.00
AFTER HOURS
❑ AFT-4112	The Right Choice	1991	3.75	7.50	15.00

COLUMBIA
Number	Title	Yr	VG	VG+	NM
❑ CL 1814 [M]	Oops!	1962	5.00	10.00	20.00
❑ CL 1942 [M]	Prelude to the Blues	1963	5.00	10.00	20.00
❑ CL 2082 [M]	Fingertips	1963	5.00	10.00	20.00
❑ CS 8614 [S]	Oops!	1962	6.25	12.50	25.00
❑ CS 8742 [S]	Prelude to the Blues	1963	6.25	12.50	25.00
❑ CS 8882 [S]	Fingertips	1963	6.25	12.50	25.00
KING
❑ 295-82 [10]	Bill Doggett -- His Organ and Combo	1955	37.50	75.00	150.00
❑ 295-83 [10]	Bill Doggett -- His Organ and Combo, Volume 2	1955	37.50	75.00	150.00
❑ 295-89 [10]	All-Time Christmas Favorites	1955	50.00	100.00	200.00
❑ 295-102 [10]	Sentimentally Yours	1956	37.50	75.00	150.00
❑ 395-502 [M]	Moondust	1957	15.00	30.00	60.00
❑ 395-514 [M]	Hot Doggett	1957	15.00	30.00	60.00
❑ 395-523 [M]	As You Desire	1957	15.00	30.00	60.00
❑ KLP-523 [M]	As You Desire	1987	2.50	5.00	10.00
-- Reissue with "Highland Records" on label					
❑ 395-531 [M]	Everybody Dance to the Honky Tonk	1958	15.00	30.00	60.00
❑ 395-532 [M]	Dame Dreaming	1958	15.00	30.00	60.00
❑ KLP-532 [M]	Dame Dreaming	1987	2.50	5.00	10.00
-- Reissue with "Highland Records" on label					
❑ 395-533 [M]	A Salute to Ellington	1958	15.00	30.00	60.00
❑ 395-557 [M]	The Doggett Beat for Dancing Feet	1958	15.00	30.00	60.00
❑ KLP-557 [M]	The Doggett Beat for Dancing Feet	1987	2.50	5.00	10.00
-- Reissue with "Highland Records" on label					
❑ 395-563 [M]	Candle Glow	1958	15.00	30.00	60.00
❑ 395-582 [M]	Swingin' Easy	1959	15.00	30.00	60.00
❑ 395-585 [M]	Dance Awhile	1959	15.00	30.00	60.00
❑ KLP-585 [M]	Dance Awhile	1987	2.50	5.00	10.00
-- Reissue with "Highland Records" on label					
❑ 395-600 [M]	A Bill Doggett Christmas	1959	10.00	20.00	40.00
❑ 395-609 [M]	Hold It	1959	15.00	30.00	60.00
❑ 633 [M]	High and Wide	1959	12.50	25.00	50.00
❑ 641 [M]	Big City Dance Party	1959	12.50	25.00	50.00
❑ 667 [M]	Bill Doggett On Tour	1959	12.50	25.00	50.00
❑ 706 [M]	For Reminiscent Lovers, Romantic Songs	1960	12.50	25.00	50.00
❑ 723 [M]	Back Again with More	1960	12.50	25.00	50.00
❑ 759 [M]	Bonanza of 24 Songs	1960	12.50	25.00	50.00
❑ 778 [M]	The Many Moods of Bill Doggett	1960	12.50	25.00	50.00
❑ KLP-778 [M]	The Many Moods of Bill Doggett	1987	2.50	5.00	10.00
-- Reissue with "Highland Records" on label					
❑ 830 [M]	American Songs in the Bossa Nova Style	1963	10.00	20.00	40.00
❑ 868 [M]	Impressions	1964	10.00	20.00	40.00
❑ 908 [M]	The Best of Bill Doggett	1964	10.00	20.00	40.00
❑ 959 [M]	Bonanza of 24 Hit Songs	1966	7.50	15.00	30.00
❑ KS-1078	Honky Tonk Popcorn	1969	12.50	25.00	50.00
❑ KS-1097	The Nearness of You	1970	6.25	12.50	25.00
❑ KS-1101	Ram-Bunk-Shush	1970	6.25	12.50	25.00
❑ KS-1104	Sentimental Journey	1970	6.25	12.50	25.00
❑ KS-1108	Soft	1970	6.25	12.50	25.00
❑ K-5009	14 Original Greatest Hits	1977	2.50	5.00	10.00
POWER PAK
❑ 269	Hold It!	197?	2.50	5.00	10.00
ROULETTE
❑ R 25330 [M]	Honky Tonk A La Mod	1966	5.00	10.00	20.00
❑ SR 25330 [S]	Honky Tonk A La Mod	1966	6.25	12.50	25.00
STARDAY
❑ 3023	16 Bandstand Favorites	197?	2.50	5.00	10.00
WARNER BROS.
❑ W 1404 [M]	3,046 People Danced 'Til 4 AM	1960	5.00	10.00	20.00
❑ WS 1404 [S]	3,046 People Danced 'Til 4 AM	1960	6.25	12.50	25.00
❑ W 1421 [M]	The Band with the Beat	1961	5.00	10.00	20.00
❑ WS 1421 [S]	The Band with the Beat	1961	6.25	12.50	25.00
❑ W 1452 [M]	Bill Doggett Swings	1962	5.00	10.00	20.00
❑ WS 1452 [S]	Bill Doggett Swings	1962	6.25	12.50	25.00
WHO'S WHO IN JAZZ
❑ 21002	Lionel Hampton Presents Bill Doggett	1977	3.00	6.00	12.00

DOKY, NIELS LAN
Pianist.
MILESTONE
❑ M-9178	Dreams	1990	3.75	7.50	15.00
STORYVILLE
❑ SLP-4117	Here or There	1986	2.50	5.00	10.00
❑ SLP-4140	The Target	1987	2.50	5.00	10.00
❑ SLP-4144	The Truth	1988	2.50	5.00	10.00
❑ SLP-4160	Daybreak	1989	3.00	6.00	12.00

Number	Title	Yr	VG	VG+	NM

DOLDINGER, KLAUS
Tenor saxophone player, clarinetist, soprano saxophone player and composer.
PHILIPS
Number	Title	Yr	VG	VG+	NM
❑ PHM 200-125 [M]Dig Doldinger		1966	5.00	10.00	20.00
❑ PHS 600-125 [S] Dig Doldinger		1966	6.25	12.50	25.00

WORLD PACIFIC
| ❑ WPS-20176 | Blues Happening | 1969 | 5.00 | 10.00 | 20.00 |

DOLPHY, ERIC
Alto saxophone player, flutist, clarinetist and bass clarinetist. Also see THE JAZZ ARTISTS GUILD; THE LATIN JAZZ QUINTET; ORCHESTRA USA.
ARCHIVE OF FOLK AND JAZZ
| ❑ 227 | Eric Dolphy and Cannonball Adderley | 1968 | 3.00 | 6.00 | 12.00 |

BLUE NOTE
❑ BLP-4163 [M]	Out to Lunch!	1964	12.50	25.00	50.00
❑ B1-46524	Out to Lunch!	199?	3.75	7.50	15.00
-- Reissue of 84163					
❑ BST-84163 [S]	Out to Lunch!	1964	20.00	40.00	80.00
-- "New York, USA" on label					
❑ BST-84163 [S]	Out to Lunch!	1966	3.75	7.50	15.00
-- "A Division of Liberty Records" on label					
❑ BST-84163 [S]	Out to Lunch!	1970	3.75	7.50	15.00
-- "Liberty/UA" on label					
❑ BST-84163 [S]	Out to Lunch!	1972	3.00	6.00	12.00
-- "United Artists" on label					
❑ BST-84163 [S]	Out to Lunch!	1985	3.00	6.00	12.00
-- "The Finest in Jazz Since 1939" reissue					
❑ BT-85131	Other Aspects	1987	5.00	10.00	20.00

CELLULOID
| ❑ CELL-5014 | Conversations | 198? | 2.50 | 5.00 | 10.00 |
| ❑ CELL-5015 | Iron Man | 198? | 2.50 | 5.00 | 10.00 |

DOUGLAS
❑ SD 785	Iron Man	1969	6.25	12.50	25.00
❑ 6002 [(2)]	Jitterbug Waltz	197?	3.75	7.50	15.00
❑ Z 30873	Iron Man	1971	5.00	10.00	20.00

EPITAPH
| ❑ E-4010 | Eric Dolphy 1928-1964 | 1975 | 3.75 | 7.50 | 15.00 |

EXODUS
❑ EX-6005 [M]	The Memorial Album	1966	5.00	10.00	20.00
-- Reissue of Vee Jay LP-2503					
❑ EXS-6005 [S]	The Memorial Album	1966	5.00	10.00	20.00
-- Reissue of Vee Jay LPS-2503					

FANTASY
❑ OJC-022	Outward Bound	198?	2.50	5.00	10.00
-- Reissue of New Jazz 8236					
❑ OJC-023	Out There	198?	2.50	5.00	10.00
-- Reissue of New Jazz 8252					
❑ OJC-133	Eric Dolphy at the Five Spot	198?	2.50	5.00	10.00
-- Reissue of New Jazz 8260					
❑ OJC-247	Eric Dolphy at the Five Spot, Volume 2	198?	2.50	5.00	10.00
-- Reissue of Prestige 7294					
❑ OJC-353	Eric Dolphy Memorial Album	198?	2.50	5.00	10.00
-- Reissue of Prestige 7334					
❑ OJC-400	Far Cry	1989	3.00	6.00	12.00
-- Reissue of New Jazz 8270					
❑ OJC-413	Eric Dolphy in Europe, Volume 1	1990	3.00	6.00	12.00
-- Reissue of Prestige 7304					
❑ OJC-414	Eric Dolphy in Europe, Volume 2	1990	3.00	6.00	12.00
-- Reissue of Prestige 7350					
❑ OJC-415	Eric Dolphy in Europe, Volume 3	1990	3.00	6.00	12.00
-- Reissue of Prestige 7366					

FM
| ❑ 308 [M] | Conversations | 1963 | 10.00 | 20.00 | 40.00 |
| ❑ S-308 [S] | Conversations | 1963 | 12.50 | 25.00 | 50.00 |

FONTANA
| ❑ 822 226-1 | Last Date | 1986 | 2.50 | 5.00 | 10.00 |

GM
| ❑ GM-3005 | Vintage Dolphy | 1986 | 3.75 | 7.50 | 15.00 |

INNER CITY
| ❑ IC-3017 [(2)] | The Berlin Concerts | 1978 | 3.75 | 7.50 | 15.00 |

LIMELIGHT
| ❑ LM-82013 [M] | Last Date | 1964 | 7.50 | 15.00 | 30.00 |
| ❑ LS-86013 [S] | Last Date | 1964 | 10.00 | 20.00 | 40.00 |

NEW JAZZ
❑ NJLP-8236 [M]	Outward Bound	1960	30.00	60.00	120.00
❑ NJLP-8252 [M]	Out There	1960	30.00	60.00	120.00
-- Purple label					
❑ NJLP-8252 [M]	Out There	1965	7.50	15.00	30.00
-- Blue label, trident logo at right					
❑ NJLP-8260 [M]	Eric Dolphy at the Five Spot	1961	25.00	50.00	100.00
-- Purple label					
❑ NJLP-8260 [M]	Eric Dolphy at the Five Spot	1965	7.50	15.00	30.00
-- Blue label, trident logo at right					
❑ NJLP-8270 [M]	Far Cry	1962	25.00	50.00	100.00
-- Purple label					
❑ NJLP-8270 [M]	Far Cry	1965	7.50	15.00	30.00
-- Blue label, trident logo at right					

PRESTIGE
❑ MPP-2503	Caribe	198?	2.50	5.00	10.00
❑ MPP-2517	Dash One	198?	2.50	5.00	10.00
❑ PRLP-7294 [M]	Eric Dolphy at the Five Spot, Volume 2	1964	10.00	20.00	40.00
-- Yellow label					
❑ PRLP-7294 [M]	Eric Dolphy at the Five Spot, Volume 2	1965	5.00	10.00	20.00
-- Blue label, trident logo at right					
❑ PRST-7294 [S]	Eric Dolphy at the Five Spot, Volume 2	1964	12.50	25.00	50.00
-- Silver label					
❑ PRST-7294 [S]	Eric Dolphy at the Five Spot, Volume 2	1965	6.25	12.50	25.00
-- Blue label, trident logo at right					
❑ PRLP-7304 [M]	Eric Dolphy in Europe, Volume 1	1964	10.00	20.00	40.00
-- Yellow label					
❑ PRLP-7304 [M]	Eric Dolphy in Europe, Volume 1	1965	5.00	10.00	20.00
-- Blue label, trident logo at right					
❑ PRST-7304 [S]	Eric Dolphy in Europe, Volume 1	1964	12.50	25.00	50.00
-- Silver label					
❑ PRST-7304 [S]	Eric Dolphy in Europe, Volume 1	1965	6.25	12.50	25.00
-- Blue label, trident logo at right					
❑ PRLP-7311 [M]	Outward Bound	1964	12.50	25.00	50.00
-- Yellow label					
❑ PRLP-7311 [M]	Outward Bound	1965	6.25	12.50	25.00
-- Blue label, trident logo at right					
❑ PRST-7311 [S]	Outward Bound	1964	10.00	20.00	40.00
-- Silver label					
❑ PRST-7311 [S]	Outward Bound	1965	5.00	10.00	20.00
-- Blue label, trident logo at right					
❑ PRLP-7334 [M]	Eric Dolphy Memorial Album	1964	5.00	10.00	20.00
❑ PRST-7334 [S]	Eric Dolphy Memorial Album	1964	6.25	12.50	25.00
❑ PRLP-7350 [M]	Eric Dolphy in Europe, Volume 2	1965	5.00	10.00	20.00
❑ PRST-7350 [S]	Eric Dolphy in Europe, Volume 2	1965	6.25	12.50	25.00
❑ PRLP-7366 [M]	Eric Dolphy in Europe, Volume 3	1965	5.00	10.00	20.00
❑ PRST-7366 [S]	Eric Dolphy in Europe, Volume 3	1965	6.25	12.50	25.00
❑ PRLP-7382 [M]	Here and There	1965	5.00	10.00	20.00
❑ PRST-7382 [S]	Here and There	1965	6.25	12.50	25.00
❑ PRST-7611	Live at the Five Spot, Volume 1	1969	3.75	7.50	15.00
❑ PRST-7652	Out There	1969	3.75	7.50	15.00
❑ PRST-7747	Far Cry	1970	3.75	7.50	15.00
❑ PRST-7826	Live at the Five Spot, Volume 2	1971	3.75	7.50	15.00
❑ PRST-7843	Where?	1971	3.75	7.50	15.00
❑ 24008 [(2)]	Eric Dolphy	197?	5.00	10.00	20.00
❑ 24027 [(2)]	Copenhagen Concert	197?	5.00	10.00	20.00
❑ 24053 [(2)]	Magic	197?	3.75	7.50	15.00
❑ 24070 [(2)]	Status	197?	3.75	7.50	15.00
❑ 34002 [(3)]	Great Concert	1974	6.25	12.50	25.00

TRIP
| ❑ 5012 | The Greatness of Eric Dolphy | 197? | 3.00 | 6.00 | 12.00 |
| ❑ 5506 | Last Date | 197? | 3.00 | 6.00 | 12.00 |

VEE JAY
| ❑ LP-2503 [M] | The Memorial Album | 1964 | 7.50 | 15.00 | 30.00 |
| ❑ LPS-2503 [S] | The Memorial Album | 1964 | 10.00 | 20.00 | 40.00 |

DOMNERUS, ARNE
Alto saxophone player and clarinetist. Also see BENGT HALLBERG.
PRESTIGE
| ❑ PRLP-134 [10] | New Sounds from Sweden, Volume 4 | 1952 | 62.50 | 125.00 | 250.00 |

RCA CAMDEN
| ❑ CAL-417 [M] | Swedish Modern Jazz | 1958 | 7.50 | 15.00 | 30.00 |

RCA VICTOR
| ❑ LPT-3032 [10] | Around the World in Jazz | 1953 | 62.50 | 125.00 | 250.00 |

DOMNERUS, ARNE/LARS GULLIN
Also see each artist's individual listings.
PRESTIGE
| ❑ PRLP-133 [10] | New Sounds from Sweden, Volume 3 | 1952 | 62.50 | 125.00 | 250.00 |

DONAHUE, SAM
Tenor saxophone player and trumpeter.
CAPITOL
❑ H 613 [10]	For Young Moderns in Love	1955	15.00	30.00	60.00
❑ T 613 [M]	For Young Moderns in Love	1956	10.00	20.00	40.00
❑ H 626 [10]	Classics in Jazz	1955	12.50	25.00	50.00

Number	Title	Yr	VG	VG+	NM
DONALD, BARBARA					

Trumpeter.

CADENCE JAZZ

Number	Title	Yr	VG	VG+	NM
❑ CJ-1011	Olympia Live	198?	2.50	5.00	10.00
❑ CJ-1017	Past & Tomorrows	198?	2.50	5.00	10.00

DONALDSON, BOBBY

Drummer and bandleader.

GOLDEN CREST

Number	Title	Yr	VG	VG+	NM
❑ GC-1003	Unlimited	196?	5.00	10.00	20.00

SAVOY

Number	Title	Yr	VG	VG+	NM
❑ MG-12128 [M]	Dixieland Jazz Party	1958	10.00	20.00	40.00
❑ SST-13003 [S]	Dixieland Jazz Party	1959	7.50	15.00	30.00

WORLD WIDE

Number	Title	Yr	VG	VG+	NM
❑ 20005	Bobby Donaldson and the 7th Avenue Stompers	196?	5.00	10.00	20.00

DONALDSON, LOU

Alto saxophone player.

ARGO

Number	Title	Yr	VG	VG+	NM
❑ LP-724 [M]	Signifyin'	1963	6.25	12.50	25.00
❑ LPS-724 [S]	Signifyin'	1963	6.25	12.50	25.00
❑ LP-734 [M]	Possum Head	1964	6.25	12.50	25.00
❑ LPS-734 [S]	Possum Head	1964	6.25	12.50	25.00
❑ LP-747 [M]	Cole Slaw	1965	6.25	12.50	25.00
❑ LPS-747 [S]	Cole Slaw	1965	6.25	12.50	25.00

BLUE NOTE

Number	Title	Yr	VG	VG+	NM
❑ BN-LA024-F	Sophisticated Lou	1972	3.75	7.50	15.00
❑ BN-LA109-F	Sassy Soul Strut	1973	3.75	7.50	15.00
❑ BN-LA259-G	Sweet Lou	1974	3.75	7.50	15.00
❑ LT-1028	Midnight Sun	1980	2.50	5.00	10.00
❑ BLP-1537 [M]	Lou Donaldson Quartet/Quintet/Sextet	1957	50.00	100.00	200.00
-- "Deep groove" version (deep indentation under label on both sides)					
❑ BLP-1537 [M]	Lou Donaldson Quartet/Quintet/Sextet	1957	37.50	75.00	150.00
-- Regular version with Lexington Ave. address on label					
❑ BLP-1537 [M]	Lou Donaldson Quartet/Quintet/Sextet	1957	10.00	20.00	40.00
-- Regular version with W. 63rd St. address on label					
❑ BLP-1537 [M]	Lou Donaldson Quartet/Quintet/Sextet	1963	6.25	12.50	25.00
-- With New York, USA address on label					
❑ BLP-1545 [M]	Wailing with Lou	1957	30.00	60.00	120.00
-- "Deep groove" version (deep indentation under label on both sides)					
❑ BLP-1545 [M]	Wailing with Lou	1957	20.00	40.00	80.00
-- Regular version with W. 63rd St. address on label					
❑ BLP-1545 [M]	Wailing with Lou	1963	6.25	12.50	25.00
-- With New York, USA address on label					
❑ BLP-1566 [M]	Swing and Soul	1957	30.00	60.00	120.00
-- "Deep groove" version (deep indentation under label on both sides)					
❑ BLP-1566 [M]	Swing and Soul	1957	20.00	40.00	80.00
-- Regular version with W. 63rd St. address on label					
❑ BLP-1566 [M]	Swing and Soul	1963	6.25	12.50	25.00
-- With New York, USA address on label					
❑ BST-1566 [S]	Swing and Soul	1959	20.00	40.00	80.00
-- "Deep groove" version (deep indentation under label on both sides)					
❑ BST-1566 [S]	Swing and Soul	1959	12.50	25.00	50.00
-- Regular version with W. 63rd St. address on label					
❑ BST-1566 [S]	Swing and Soul	1963	5.00	10.00	20.00
-- With New York, USA address on label					
❑ BLP-1591 [M]	Lou Takes Off	1958	30.00	60.00	120.00
-- "Deep groove" version (deep indentation under label on both sides)					
❑ BLP-1591 [M]	Lou Takes Off	1958	20.00	40.00	80.00
-- Regular version with W. 63rd St. address on label					
❑ BLP-1591 [M]	Lou Takes Off	1963	6.25	12.50	25.00
-- With New York, USA address on label					
❑ BST-1591 [S]	Lou Takes Off	1959	20.00	40.00	80.00
-- "Deep groove" version (deep indentation under label on both sides)					
❑ BST-1591 [S]	Lou Takes Off	1959	12.50	25.00	50.00
-- Regular version with W. 63rd St. address on label					
❑ BST-1591 [S]	Lou Takes Off	1963	5.00	10.00	20.00
-- With New York, USA address on label					
❑ BLP-1593 [M]	Blues Walk	1958	30.00	60.00	120.00
-- "Deep groove" version (deep indentation under label on both sides)					
❑ BLP-1593 [M]	Blues Walk	1958	20.00	40.00	80.00
-- Regular version with W. 63rd St. address on label					
❑ BLP-1593 [M]	Blues Walk	1963	6.25	12.50	25.00
-- With New York, USA address on label					
❑ BST-1593 [S]	Blues Walk	1959	20.00	40.00	80.00
-- "Deep groove" version (deep indentation under label on both sides)					
❑ BST-1593 [S]	Blues Walk	1959	12.50	25.00	50.00
-- Regular version with W. 63rd St. address on label					
❑ BST-1593 [S]	Blues Walk	1963	5.00	10.00	20.00
-- With New York, USA address on label					
❑ BLP-4012 [M]	LD + 3	1959	30.00	60.00	120.00
-- "Deep groove" version (deep indentation under label on both sides)					
❑ BLP-4012 [M]	LD + 3	1959	20.00	40.00	80.00
-- Regular version with W. 63rd St. address on label					
❑ BLP-4012 [M]	LD + 3	1963	6.25	12.50	25.00
-- With New York, USA address on label					
❑ BST-4012 [S]	LD + 3	1960	20.00	40.00	80.00
-- "Deep groove" version (deep indentation under label on both sides)					
❑ BST-4012 [S]	LD + 3	1960	12.50	25.00	50.00
-- Regular version with W. 63rd St. address on label					
❑ BST-4012 [S]	LD + 3	1963	5.00	10.00	20.00
-- With New York, USA address on label					
❑ BLP-4025 [M]	The Time Is Right	1960	30.00	60.00	120.00
-- "Deep groove" version (deep indentation under label on both sides)					
❑ BLP-4025 [M]	The Time Is Right	1960	20.00	40.00	80.00
-- Regular version with W. 63rd St. address on label					
❑ BLP-4025 [M]	The Time Is Right	1963	6.25	12.50	25.00
-- With New York, USA address on label					
❑ BLP-4036 [M]	Sunny Side Up	1960	30.00	60.00	120.00
-- "Deep groove" version (deep indentation under label on both sides)					
❑ BLP-4036 [M]	Sunny Side Up	1960	20.00	40.00	80.00
-- Regular version with W. 63rd St. address on label					
❑ BLP-4036 [M]	Sunny Side Up	1963	6.25	12.50	25.00
-- With New York, USA address on label					
❑ BLP-4053 [M]	Light Foot	1960	20.00	40.00	80.00
-- With W. 63rd St. address on label					
❑ BLP-4053 [M]	Light Foot	1963	6.25	12.50	25.00
-- With New York, USA address on label					
❑ BLP-4066 [M]	Here 'Tis	1961	20.00	40.00	80.00
-- With W. 63rd St. address on label					
❑ BLP-4066 [M]	Here 'Tis	1963	6.25	12.50	25.00
-- With New York, USA address on label					
❑ BLP-4079 [M]	Gravy Train	1962	20.00	40.00	80.00
-- With 61st St. address on label					
❑ BLP-4079 [M]	Gravy Train	1963	6.25	12.50	25.00
-- With New York, USA address on label					
❑ BLP-4108 [M]	The Natural Soul	1963	6.25	12.50	25.00
❑ BLP-4125 [M]	Good Gracious	1963	6.25	12.50	25.00
❑ 4254/84254	Sweet Slumber	1967	---	---	---
-- Canceled					
❑ BLP-4263 [M]	Alligator Boogaloo	1967	7.50	15.00	30.00
❑ BLP-4271 [M]	Mr. Shing-a-Ling	1968	7.50	15.00	30.00
❑ BLP-5021 [10]	Lou Donaldson Quintet/Quartet	1953	50.00	100.00	200.00
❑ BLP-5030 [10]	Lou Donaldson-Clifford Brown	1954	50.00	100.00	200.00
❑ BLP-5055 [10]	Lou Donaldson Sextet, Volume 2	1955	50.00	100.00	200.00
❑ B1-28267	Hot Dog	1994	3.75	7.50	15.00
-- Reissue of 84318					
❑ B1-31248	Everything I Play Is Funky	1995	3.75	7.50	15.00
-- Reissue of 84337					
❑ B1-31876	The Scorpion: Live at the Cadillac Club	1995	3.75	7.50	15.00
❑ B1-32095	Sunny Side Up	1995	3.75	7.50	15.00
-- Reissue of 84036					
❑ B1-81537	Lou Donaldson Quartet/Quintet/Sextet	1989	2.50	5.00	10.00
-- Reissue of 1537					
❑ BST-81591 [S]	Lou Takes Off	1966	3.00	6.00	12.00
-- With "A Division of Liberty Records" on label					
❑ BST-81593 [S]	Blues Walk	1967	3.00	6.00	12.00
-- With "A Division of Liberty Records" on label					
❑ BST-81593	Blues Walk	1985	2.50	5.00	10.00
-- "The Finest in Jazz Since 1939" reissue					
❑ BST-84025 [S]	The Time Is Right	1960	12.50	25.00	50.00
-- With W. 63rd St. address on label					
❑ BST-84025 [S]	The Time Is Right	1963	5.00	10.00	20.00
-- With New York, USA address on label					
❑ BST-84036 [S]	Sunny Side Up	1960	12.50	25.00	50.00
-- With W. 63rd St. address on label					
❑ BST-84036 [S]	Sunny Side Up	1963	5.00	10.00	20.00
-- With New York, USA address on label					
❑ BST-84053 [S]	Light Foot	1960	12.50	25.00	50.00
-- With W. 63rd St. address on label					
❑ BST-84053 [S]	Light Foot	1963	5.00	10.00	20.00
-- With New York, USA address on label					
❑ BST-84066 [S]	Here 'Tis	1961	12.50	25.00	50.00
-- With W. 63rd St. address on label					
❑ BST-84066 [S]	Here 'Tis	1963	5.00	10.00	20.00
-- With New York, USA address on label					
❑ BST-84066 [S]	Here 'Tis	1967	3.00	6.00	12.00
-- With "A Division of Liberty Records" on label					
❑ BST-84079 [S]	Gravy Train	1962	12.50	25.00	50.00
-- With 61st St. address on label					
❑ BST-84079 [S]	Gravy Train	1963	5.00	10.00	20.00
-- With New York, USA address on label					
❑ BST-84079 [S]	Gravy Train	1967	3.00	6.00	12.00
-- With "A Division of Liberty Records" on label					
❑ BST-84108 [S]	The Natural Soul	1963	6.25	12.50	25.00
❑ BST-84108 [S]	The Natural Soul	1967	3.00	6.00	12.00
-- With "A Division of Liberty Records" on label					
❑ BST-84108	The Natural Soul	1987	2.50	5.00	10.00
-- "The Finest in Jazz Since 1939" reissue					
❑ BST-84125 [S]	Good Gracious	1963	6.25	12.50	25.00

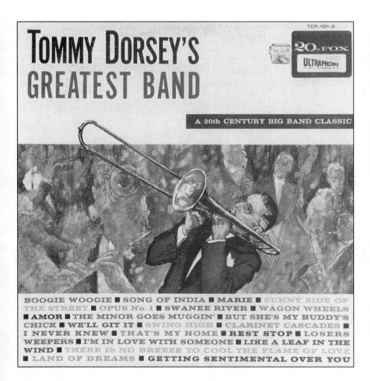

(Top left) Proof that some collectible jazz can come from outside the United States comes in this hard-to-find RCA Victor 10-inch LP by Swede Arne Domnerus. (Top right) Lou Donaldson's recording career spans 40 years; he's considered a "soul jazz" pioneer. Here's one of the LPs from his earliest period, on the Blue Note label. (Bottom left) Tommy Dorsey was one of the great swing trombonists, plus he had a great band, too. He helped make Frank Sinatra a star, among others. This is one of the scarcer of the many posthumous Dorsey compilations. (Bottom right) Pianist Kenny Drew's trio goes through *Pal Joey* on this album for Riverside, which is among his best.

Number	Title	Yr	VG	VG+	NM
❏ BST-84125 [S]	Good Gracious	1967	3.00	6.00	12.00
-- With "A Division of Liberty Records" on label					
❏ BST-84254	Lush Life	1986	2.50	5.00	10.00
-- "The Finest in Jazz Since 1939" label; first issue of this LP					
❏ BST-84263 [S]	Alligator Boogaloo	1967	5.00	10.00	20.00
❏ BST-84271 [S]	Mr. Shing-a-Ling	1968	5.00	10.00	20.00
❏ BST-84280	Midnight Creeper	1968	5.00	10.00	20.00
❏ BST-84299	Say It Loud!	1969	5.00	10.00	20.00
❏ BST-84318	Hot Dog	1969	5.00	10.00	20.00
❏ BST-84337	Everything I Play Is Funky	1970	3.75	7.50	15.00
❏ BST-84359	Pretty Things	1970	3.75	7.50	15.00
❏ BST-84370	Cosmos	1971	3.75	7.50	15.00
❏ B1-89794	Pretty Things	1993	3.75	7.50	15.00
-- Reissue of 84359					
CADET					
❏ LP-724 [M]	Signifyin'	1966	5.00	10.00	20.00
-- Reissue of Argo 724					
❏ LPS-724 [S]	Signifyin'	1966	3.75	7.50	15.00
-- Reissue of Argo 724					
❏ LP-734 [M]	Possum Head	1966	5.00	10.00	20.00
-- Reissue of Argo 734					
❏ LPS-734 [S]	Possum Head	1966	3.75	7.50	15.00
-- Reissue of Argo 734					
❏ LP-747 [M]	Cole Slaw	1966	5.00	10.00	20.00
-- Reissue of Argo 747					
❏ LPS-747 [S]	Cole Slaw	1966	3.75	7.50	15.00
-- Reissue of Argo 747					
❏ LP-759 [M]	Musty Rusty	1966	6.25	12.50	25.00
❏ LPS-759 [S]	Musty Rusty	1966	6.25	12.50	25.00
❏ LP-768 [M]	Rough House Blues	1966	6.25	12.50	25.00
❏ LPS-768 [S]	Rough House Blues	1966	6.25	12.50	25.00
❏ LP-789 [M]	Blowin' in the Wind	1967	6.25	12.50	25.00
❏ LPS-789 [S]	Blowin' in the Wind	1967	5.00	10.00	20.00
❏ LPS-815	Lou Donaldson At His Best	1969	5.00	10.00	20.00
❏ LPS-842	Fried Buzzard -- Lou Donaldson Live	1970	5.00	10.00	20.00
CHESS					
❏ 2CA 60007	Ha' Mercy	1972	3.00	6.00	12.00
COTILLION					
❏ SD 9905	A Different Scene	1976	3.00	6.00	12.00
❏ SD 9915	Color As a Way of Life	1977	3.00	6.00	12.00
MUSE					
❏ 5247	Sweet Poppa Lou	1982	3.00	6.00	12.00
❏ 5292	Back Street	1983	3.00	6.00	12.00
SUNSET					
❏ SUS-5258	Down Home	1969	3.00	6.00	12.00
❏ SUS-5318	I Won't Cry Anymore	1970	3.00	6.00	12.00
TIMELESS					
❏ SJP-153	Forgotten Man	198?	2.50	5.00	10.00

DONALDSON, WALTER
Composer ("Makin' Whoopee," "Carolina in the Morning" and dozens of others).

Number	Title	Yr	VG	VG+	NM
MONMOUTH-EVERGREEN					
❏ 7059	The Greatest Song Hits	197?	3.00	6.00	12.00

DONATO, JOAO
Pianist, organist and sometimes trombone player.

Number	Title	Yr	VG	VG+	NM
BLUE THUMB					
❏ BT-21	A Bad Donato	1972	3.75	7.50	15.00
-- Distributed by Famous Music					
❏ BT-8821	A Bad Donato	1970	5.00	10.00	20.00
-- Distributed by Capitol					
MUSE					
❏ MR-5017	Joao Donato	197?	3.00	6.00	12.00
RCA VICTOR					
❏ LPM-3473 [M]	The New Sound of Brazil	1966	3.75	7.50	15.00
❏ LSP-3473 [S]	The New Sound of Brazil	1966	5.00	10.00	20.00

DONEGAN, DOROTHY
Pianist.

Number	Title	Yr	VG	VG+	NM
AUDIOPHILE					
❏ AP-209	The Explosive Dorothy Donegan	198?	2.50	5.00	10.00
CAPITOL					
❏ ST 1135 [S]	Dorothy Donegan Live!	1959	10.00	20.00	40.00
❏ T 1135 [M]	Dorothy Donegan Live!	1959	7.50	15.00	30.00
❏ ST 1226 [S]	Donnybrook with Dorothy	1960	10.00	20.00	40.00
❏ T 1226 [M]	Donnybrook with Dorothy	1960	7.50	15.00	30.00
FORUM					
❏ F-9003 [M]	Dorothy Donegan at the Embers	196?	3.75	7.50	15.00
-- Reissue of Roulette R-25010					
❏ SF-9003 [R]	Dorothy Donegan at the Embers	196?	3.00	6.00	12.00
JUBILEE					
❏ LP-11 [10]	Dorothy Donegan Trio	1955	20.00	40.00	80.00

Number	Title	Yr	VG	VG+	NM
❏ JLP-1013 [M]	September Song	1956	15.00	30.00	60.00
MGM					
❏ E-278 [10]	Dorothy Donegan Piano	1954	20.00	40.00	80.00
PROGRESSIVE					
❏ PRO-7056	The Explosive Dorothy Donegan	198?	3.00	6.00	12.00
ROULETTE					
❏ R-25010 [M]	Dorothy Donegan at the Embers	1957	12.50	25.00	50.00
❏ R-25154 [M]	It Happened One Night	1961	7.50	15.00	30.00
❏ SR-25154 [S]	It Happened One Night	1961	10.00	20.00	40.00

DONELIAN, ARMEN
Pianist.

Number	Title	Yr	VG	VG+	NM
SUNNYSIDE					
❏ SSC-1019	A Reverie	1987	2.50	5.00	10.00
❏ SSC-1031	Secrets	1988	2.50	5.00	10.00

DORGE, PIERRE
Danish guitarist, bandleader, composer and arranger.

Number	Title	Yr	VG	VG+	NM
STEEPLECHASE					
❏ SCS-1132	Ballad Round Left Corner	1979	3.00	6.00	12.00
❏ SCS-1162	Pierre Dorge and the New Jungle Orchestra	1982	3.00	6.00	12.00
❏ SCS-1188	Brikama	198?	2.50	5.00	10.00
❏ SCS-1208	Even the Moon Is Dancing	198?	2.50	5.00	10.00
❏ SCS-1228	Johnny Lives	198?	2.50	5.00	10.00

DORGE, PIERRE, AND WALT DICKERSON
Also see each artist's individual entries.

Number	Title	Yr	VG	VG+	NM
STEEPLECHASE					
❏ SCS-1115	Landscape with Open Door	1978	3.00	6.00	12.00

DORHAM, KENNY
Trumpeter, composer and arranger. Also see THE JAZZ ARTISTS GUILD.

Number	Title	Yr	VG	VG+	NM
ABC-PARAMOUNT					
❏ ABC-122 [M]	Kenny Dorham and the Jazz Prophets	1956	20.00	40.00	80.00
BAINBRIDGE					
❏ 1043	Show Boat	198?	2.50	5.00	10.00
❏ 1048	Kenny Dorham	198?	2.50	5.00	10.00
BLUE NOTE					
❏ BLP-1524 [M]	'Round About Midnight at the Café Bohemia	1956	50.00	100.00	200.00
-- "Deep groove" version (deep indentation under label on both sides)					
❏ BLP-1524 [M]	'Round About Midnight at the Café Bohemia	1956	37.50	75.00	150.00
-- Regular version with Lexington Ave. address on label					
❏ BLP-1524 [M]	'Round About Midnight at the Café Bohemia	1963	7.50	15.00	30.00
-- "New York, USA" address on label					
❏ BLP-1535 [M]	Kenny Dorham Octet/Sextet	1956	50.00	100.00	200.00
-- "Deep groove" version (deep indentation under label on both sides)					
❏ BLP-1535 [M]	Kenny Dorham Octet/Sextet	1956	37.50	75.00	150.00
-- Regular version with Lexington Ave. address on label					
❏ BLP-1535 [M]	Kenny Dorham Octet/Sextet	1963	7.50	15.00	30.00
-- "New York, USA" address on label					
❏ BLP-4063 [M]	Whistle Stop	1961	20.00	40.00	80.00
-- W. 63rd St. address on label					
❏ BLP-4063 [M]	Whistle Stop	1963	7.50	15.00	30.00
-- "New York, USA" address on label					
❏ BLP-4127 [M]	Una Mas	1963	7.50	15.00	30.00
-- "New York, USA" address on label					
❏ BLP-4181 [M]	Trompeta Toccata	1964	7.50	15.00	30.00
-- "New York, USA" address on label					
❏ BLP-5055 [10]	Afro-Cuban Holiday	1955	75.00	150.00	300.00
❏ B1-28978	Whistle Stop	1994	3.75	7.50	15.00
❏ BST-84063 [S]	Whistle Stop	1961	15.00	30.00	60.00
-- W. 63rd St. address on label					
❏ BST-84063 [S]	Whistle Stop	1963	6.25	12.50	25.00
-- "New York, USA" address on label					
❏ BST-84063 [S]	Whistle Stop	1966	3.75	7.50	15.00
-- "A Division of Liberty Records" on label					
❏ BST-84063 [S]	Whistle Stop	197?	3.00	6.00	12.00
-- "United Artists" on label					
❏ BST-84127 [S]	Una Mas	1963	10.00	20.00	40.00
-- "New York, USA" address on label					
❏ BST-84127 [S]	Una Mas	1966	3.75	7.50	15.00
-- "A Division of Liberty Records" on label					
❏ BST-84127 [S]	Una Mas	197?	3.00	6.00	12.00
-- "United Artists" on label					
❏ BST-84181 [S]	Trompeta Toccata	1964	10.00	20.00	40.00
-- "New York, USA" address on label					
❏ BST-84181 [S]	Trompeta Toccata	1966	3.75	7.50	15.00
-- "A Division of Liberty Records" on label					
❏ BST-84181	Trompeta Toccata	1985	2.50	5.00	10.00
-- "The Finest in Jazz Since 1939" reissue					

Number	Title	Yr	VG	VG+	NM
DEBUT					
❑ DLP-9 [10]	Kenny Dorham Quintet	1954	75.00	150.00	300.00
FANTASY					
❑ OJC-028	Jazz Contrasts	198?	2.50	5.00	10.00
❑ OJC-113	Kenny Dorham Quintet	198?	2.50	5.00	10.00
-- Reissue of Debut 9					
❑ OJC-134	Blue Spring	198?	2.50	5.00	10.00
❑ OJC-250	Quiet Kenny	1987	2.50	5.00	10.00
-- Reissue of New Jazz 8225					
❑ OJC-463	2 Horns 2 Rhythm	1990	3.00	6.00	12.00
-- Reissue of Riverside 255					
JARO					
❑ JAM-5007 [M]	The Arrival of Kenny Dorham	1960	100.00	200.00	400.00
❑ JAS-8007 [S]	The Arrival of Kenny Dorham	1960	100.00	200.00	400.00
JAZZLAND					
❑ JLP-3 [M]	The Swingers	1960	10.00	20.00	40.00
❑ JLP-14 [M]	Kenny Dorham and Friends	1960	10.00	20.00	40.00
❑ JLP-82 [M]	Kenny Dorham and Friends	1962	5.00	10.00	20.00
❑ JLP-903 [S]	The Swingers	1960	12.50	25.00	50.00
❑ JLP-914 [S]	Kenny Dorham and Friends	1960	12.50	25.00	50.00
❑ JLP-982 [S]	Kenny Dorham and Friends	1962	6.25	12.50	25.00
MILESTONE					
❑ 47036 [(2)]	But Beautiful	197?	3.75	7.50	15.00
MUSE					
❑ MR-5053	Ease It	1974	3.75	7.50	15.00
NEW JAZZ					
❑ NJLP-8225 [M]	Quiet Kenny	1959	20.00	40.00	80.00
-- Purple label					
❑ NJLP-8225 [M]	Quiet Kenny	1965	6.25	12.50	25.00
-- Blue label, trident logo at right					
PACIFIC JAZZ					
❑ PJ-41 [M]	Inta Somethin' -- Recorded Live at the Jazz Workshop	1962	7.50	15.00	30.00
❑ ST-41 [S]	Inta Somethin' -- Recorded Live at the Jazz Workshop	1962	10.00	20.00	40.00
PRESTIGE					
❑ PRST-7754	Kenny Dorham 1959	1970	5.00	10.00	20.00
RIVERSIDE					
❑ 6075	Jazz Contrasts	197?	3.75	7.50	15.00
❑ RLP 12-239 [M]	Jazz Contrasts	1957	20.00	40.00	80.00
-- White label, blue print					
❑ RLP 12-239 [M]	Jazz Contrasts	1959	10.00	20.00	40.00
-- Blue label, microphone logo					
❑ RLP 12-255 [M]	2 Horns 2 Rhythm	1957	12.50	25.00	50.00
❑ RLP 12-275 [M]	This Is the Moment!	1958	12.50	25.00	50.00
❑ RLP 12-297 [M]	Blue Spring	1959	12.50	25.00	50.00
❑ RLP-1105 [S]	Jazz Contrasts	1959	7.50	15.00	30.00
-- Black label, microphone logo					
❑ RLP-1139 [S]	Blue Spring	1959	10.00	20.00	40.00
STEEPLECHASE					
❑ SCC-6010	Short Story	198?	3.00	6.00	12.00
❑ SCC-6011	Scandia Skies	198?	3.00	6.00	12.00
TIME					
❑ S-2004 [S]	Jazz Contemporary	1960	12.50	25.00	50.00
❑ S-2024 [S]	Show Boat	1960	12.50	25.00	50.00
❑ 52004 [M]	Jazz Contemporary	1960	10.00	20.00	40.00
❑ 52024 [M]	Show Boat	1960	10.00	20.00	40.00
UNITED ARTISTS					
❑ UAS-5631	Matador	1971	5.00	10.00	20.00
-- Reissue of 15007					
❑ UAJ-14007 [M]	Matador	1962	7.50	15.00	30.00
❑ UAJS-15007 [S]	Matador	1962	10.00	20.00	40.00
XANADU					
❑ 125	Memorial Album	197?	3.75	7.50	15.00

DORHAM, KENNY/CLARK TERRY

Also see each artist's individual listings.

Number	Title	Yr	VG	VG+	NM
JAZZLAND					
❑ JLP-10 [M]	Top Trumpets	1960	10.00	20.00	40.00
❑ JLP-910 [S]	Top Trumpets	1960	12.50	25.00	50.00

DOROUGH, BOB

Pianist and male singer. Best known as the musical director of the ABC cartoon series "Schoolhouse Rock."

Number	Title	Yr	VG	VG+	NM
BETHLEHEM					
❑ BCP-11 [M]	Devil May Care	1955	30.00	60.00	120.00
❑ BCP-6023	Yardbird Suite	197?	5.00	10.00	20.00
-- Reissue of 11, distributed by RCA Victor					
CLASSIC JAZZ					
❑ 18	An Excursion Through Oliver	197?	3.75	7.50	15.00
❑ 19	The Medieval Jazz Quartet Plus 3	197?	3.75	7.50	15.00

Number	Title	Yr	VG	VG+	NM
FOCUS					
❑ FL-336 [M]	Better Than Anything	1967	6.25	12.50	25.00
❑ FS-336 [S]	Better Than Anything	1967	5.00	10.00	20.00
INNER CITY					
❑ IC-1023	Just About Everything	197?	3.75	7.50	15.00
LAISSEZ-FAIRE					
❑ 02	Beginning to See the Light	1976	5.00	10.00	20.00
MUSIC MINUS ONE					
❑ 225 [M]	Oliver	1963	6.25	12.50	25.00

DORSEY BROTHERS, THE

Big bands in which both JIMMY DORSEY and TOMMY DORSEY appeared.

Number	Title	Yr	VG	VG+	NM
CIRCLE					
❑ 20	The Dorsey Brothers Orchestra 1935	198?	2.50	5.00	10.00
COLUMBIA					
❑ C2L 8 [(2)]	The Fabulous Dorseys in Hi-Fi	1958	10.00	20.00	40.00
-- Red and black labels with six "eye" logos					
❑ CL 1240 [M]	Sentimental and Swinging	1958	6.25	12.50	25.00
-- Red and black label with six "eye" logos					
DECCA					
❑ DL 8631 [M]	Dixieland Jazz	1958	6.25	12.50	25.00
-- Black label, silver print					
❑ DL 8631 [M]	Dixieland Jazz	1961	3.75	7.50	15.00
-- Black label with color bars					
❑ DL 8654 [M]	The Swinging Dorseys	1958	6.25	12.50	25.00
-- Black label, silver print					
❑ DL 8654 [M]	The Swinging Dorseys	1961	3.75	7.50	15.00
-- Black label with color bars					
DESIGN					
❑ DLP-20 [M]	Their Shining Hour	196?	3.00	6.00	12.00
❑ DLPS-20 [R]	Their Shining Hour	196?	2.50	5.00	10.00
MCA					
❑ 1505	The 1934-35 Decca Sessions	198?	2.50	5.00	10.00
RIVERSIDE					
❑ RLP 12-811 [M]	A Backward Glance	1958	15.00	30.00	60.00
❑ RLP-1008 [10]	Jazz of the Roaring Twenties	1953	20.00	40.00	80.00
❑ RLP-1051 [10]	The Dorsey Brothers with the California Ramblers	1955	20.00	40.00	80.00
SUNBEAM					
❑ 210	The Fabulous Dorsey Brothers	197?	2.50	5.00	10.00
❑ 224	The Fabulous Dorsey Brothers, Volume 2	197?	2.50	5.00	10.00
❑ 301	The Dorsey Brothers 1934	197?	2.50	5.00	10.00

DORSEY, JIMMY

Clarinetist, alto saxophone player, trumpeter, cornet player and bandleader. Also see THE DORSEY BROTHERS.

Number	Title	Yr	VG	VG+	NM
ATLANTIC					
❑ 81801	Dorsey, Then and Now	1988	2.50	5.00	10.00
CIRCLE					
❑ 30	Jimmy Dorsey and His Orchestra 1939-40	198?	2.50	5.00	10.00
❑ 46	Jimmy Dorsey and His Orchestra Mostly 1940	198?	2.50	5.00	10.00
COLUMBIA					
❑ CL 608 [M]	Dixie by Dorsey	1955	7.50	15.00	30.00
-- Red and black label with six "eye" logos					
❑ CL 608 [M]	Dixie by Dorsey	1955	10.00	20.00	40.00
-- Maroon label with gold print					
❑ CL 6095 [10]	Dixie by Dorsey	1950	12.50	25.00	50.00
❑ CL 6114 [10]	Dorseyland Band	1950	12.50	25.00	50.00
CORAL					
❑ CRL 56004 [10]	Contrasting Music, Volume 1	1950	12.50	25.00	50.00
❑ CRL 56008 [10]	Contrasting Music, Volume 2	1950	12.50	25.00	50.00
❑ CRL 56033 [10]	Gershwin Music	1950	12.50	25.00	50.00
DECCA					
❑ DL 4853 [M]	Jimmy Dorsey's Greatest Hits	1967	5.00	10.00	20.00
❑ DL 5091 [10]	Latin American Favorites	1950	12.50	25.00	50.00
❑ DL 8153 [M]	Latin American Favorites	1955	7.50	15.00	30.00
-- Black label, silver print					
❑ DL 8609 [M]	The Great Jimmy Dorsey	1957	6.25	12.50	25.00
-- Black label, silver print					
❑ DL 74853 [R]	Jimmy Dorsey's Greatest Hits	1967	3.00	6.00	12.00
DOT					
❑ DLP-3437 [M]	So Rare	1962	5.00	10.00	20.00
-- Reissue of Fraternity LP					
❑ DLP-25437 [R]	So Rare	196?	3.00	6.00	12.00
FRATERNITY					
❑ F-1008 [M]	Fabulous Jimmy Dorsey	1957	7.50	15.00	30.00
HINDSIGHT					
❑ HSR-101	Jimmy Dorsey and His Orchestra 1939-40	198?	2.50	5.00	10.00

Number	Title	Yr	VG	VG+	NM
❑ HSR-153	Jimmy Dorsey and His Orchestra 1942-44	198?	2.50	5.00	10.00
❑ HSR-165	Jimmy Dorsey and His Orchestra 1949, 1951	198?	2.50	5.00	10.00
❑ HSR-178	Jimmy Dorsey and His Orchestra 1950	198?	2.50	5.00	10.00
❑ HSR-203	Jimmy Dorsey and His Orchestra 1948	198?	2.50	5.00	10.00

INSIGHT

Number	Title	Yr	VG	VG+	NM
❑ 210	Jimmy Dorsey and His Orchestra 1939-42	198?	2.50	5.00	10.00

MCA

Number	Title	Yr	VG	VG+	NM
❑ 232	Jimmy Dorsey's Greatest Hits	197?	2.50	5.00	10.00
-- Reissue of Decca 74853					
❑ 4073 [(2)]	The Best of Jimmy Dorsey	197?	3.00	6.00	12.00

POWER PAK

Number	Title	Yr	VG	VG+	NM
❑ 244	Jimmy Dorsey Plays His Biggest Hits	197?	2.50	5.00	10.00

TIME-LIFE

Number	Title	Yr	VG	VG+	NM
❑ STBB-10 [(2)]	Jimmy Dorsey	1984	3.75	7.50	15.00

TRIP

Number	Title	Yr	VG	VG+	NM
❑ 5815	So Rare!	197?	2.50	5.00	10.00

DORSEY, TOMMY

Trombonist, trumpet player and bandleader. Starred items (*) include one or more tracks with FRANK SINATRA as vocalist. Also see THE DORSEY BROTHERS.

BLUEBIRD

Number	Title	Yr	VG	VG+	NM
❑ AXM2-5521 [(2)]	The Complete Tommy Dorsey, Volume 1	197?	3.75	7.50	15.00
❑ AXM2-5549 [(2)]	The Complete Tommy Dorsey, Volume 2	197?	3.75	7.50	15.00
❑ AXM2-5560 [(2)]	The Complete Tommy Dorsey, Volume 3	197?	3.75	7.50	15.00
❑ AXM2-5564 [(2)]	The Complete Tommy Dorsey, Volume 4	197?	3.75	7.50	15.00
❑ AXM2-5573 [(2)]	The Complete Tommy Dorsey, Volume 5	197?	3.75	7.50	15.00
❑ AXM2-5578 [(2)]	The Complete Tommy Dorsey, Volume 6	197?	3.75	7.50	15.00
❑ AXM2-5582 [(2)]	The Complete Tommy Dorsey, Volume 7	197?	3.75	7.50	15.00
❑ AXM2-5586 [(2)]	The Complete Tommy Dorsey, Volume 8	197?	3.75	7.50	15.00
❑ 9987-1-RB	Yes, Indeed!	1990	3.75	7.50	15.00

DECCA

Number	Title	Yr	VG	VG+	NM
❑ DL 5317 [10]	Tommy Dorsey Plays Howard	1951	12.50	25.00	50.00
❑ DL 5448 [10]	In a Sentimental Mood	1952	12.50	25.00	50.00
❑ DL 5449 [10]	Tenderly	1952	12.50	25.00	50.00
❑ DL 5452 [10]	Your Invitation to Dance	1952	12.50	25.00	50.00

HARMONY

Number	Title	Yr	VG	VG+	NM
❑ HL 7324 [M]	On the Sentimental Side	196?	3.75	7.50	15.00
❑ KH 32014	The Beat of the Big Bands	1972	2.50	5.00	10.00

MCA

Number	Title	Yr	VG	VG+	NM
❑ 732	Sentimental	198?	2.00	4.00	8.00
❑ 4074 [(2)]	The Best of Tommy Dorsey	197?	3.00	6.00	12.00

MOVIETONE

Number	Title	Yr	VG	VG+	NM
❑ MTM-1004 [M]	Tommy Dorsey's Hullaballoo	196?	3.75	7.50	15.00
❑ MTM-1019 [M]	The Tommy Dorsey Years	1967	3.75	7.50	15.00
❑ MTS-72004 [R]	Tommy Dorsey's Hullaballoo	196?	3.00	6.00	12.00
❑ MTS-72019 [R]	The Tommy Dorsey Years	1967	3.00	6.00	12.00

PICKWICK

Number	Title	Yr	VG	VG+	NM
❑ PTP-2035 [(2)]	I'm Getting Sentimental*	197?	3.00	6.00	12.00

RCA CAMDEN

Number	Title	Yr	VG	VG+	NM
❑ ADL2-0178 [(2)]	I'll See You in My Dreams*	1973	3.75	7.50	15.00
❑ CAL-650 [M]	The One and Only Tommy Dorsey*	1961	3.75	7.50	15.00
❑ CAS-650(e) [R]	The One and Only Tommy Dorsey*	196?	2.50	5.00	10.00
❑ CAL-800 [M]	Dedicated to You*	1964	3.75	7.50	15.00
❑ CAS-800(e) [R]	Dedicated to You*	1964	2.50	5.00	10.00
❑ CXS-9027 [(2)]	I'm Getting Sentimental*	1972	3.75	7.50	15.00

RCA VICTOR

Number	Title	Yr	VG	VG+	NM
❑ LPT-10 [M]	Getting Sentimental with Tommy Dorsey*	1951	20.00	40.00	80.00
❑ ALPT-15 [M]	All Time Hits*	1951	20.00	40.00	80.00
❑ LPM-22 [10]	Tommy Dorsey Plays Cole Porter for Dancing	1951	12.50	25.00	50.00
❑ ANL1-1087	The Best of Tommy Dorsey	1976	2.50	5.00	10.00
❑ ANL1-1586	Pure Gold*	1976	2.50	5.00	10.00
❑ LPM-1229 [M]	Yes Indeed*	1956	12.50	25.00	50.00
❑ LPM-1425 [M]	Tommy Dorsey Plays Cole Porter and Jerome Kern	1956	6.25	12.50	25.00
❑ LPM-1432 [M]	Tribute to Dorsey, Volume 1*	1956	10.00	20.00	40.00
❑ LPM-1433 [M]	Tribute to Dorsey, Volume 2*	1956	10.00	20.00	40.00
❑ LPM-1643 [M]	Having a Wonderful Time*	1958	10.00	20.00	40.00
❑ ANL1-2162(e)	On the Sunny Side of the Street	1977	2.50	5.00	10.00
❑ LPT-3005 [M]	This Is Tommy Dorsey*	1952	20.00	40.00	80.00
❑ LPT-3018 [10]	This Is Tommy Dorsey	1952	12.50	25.00	50.00
❑ LPM-3674 [M]	The Best of Tommy Dorsey*	1966	5.00	10.00	20.00
❑ LSP-3674 [R]	The Best of Tommy Dorsey*	1966	3.00	6.00	12.00
❑ LPM-6003 [(2) M]	That Sentimental Gentleman*	1957	20.00	40.00	80.00
-- Box set					
❑ VPM-6038 [(2)]	This Is Tommy Dorsey*	197?	6.25	12.50	25.00
❑ VPM-6064 [(2)]	This Is Tommy Dorsey, Volume 2*	197?	6.25	12.50	25.00
❑ VPM-6087 [(2)]	Tommy Dorsey with the Clambake Seven	197?	5.00	10.00	20.00

SUNBEAM

Number	Title	Yr	VG	VG+	NM
❑ 201	Tommy Dorsey and His Orchestra 1935-39	197?	2.50	5.00	10.00
❑ 220	Tommy Dorsey and His Orchestra 1944-46	197?	2.50	5.00	10.00

TIME-LIFE

Number	Title	Yr	VG	VG+	NM
❑ STBB-02 [(2)]	Tommy Dorsey*	1983	5.00	10.00	20.00

20TH CENTURY FOX

Number	Title	Yr	VG	VG+	NM
❑ TCF 101/2 [(2) M]	Tommy Dorsey's Greatest Band	1959	7.50	15.00	30.00
❑ TFM-3157 [M]	This Is Tommy Dorsey and His Greatest Band, Vol. 1	196?	5.00	10.00	20.00
❑ TFM-3158 [M]	This Is Tommy Dorsey and His Greatest Band, Vol. 2	196?	5.00	10.00	20.00
❑ TFS-4157 [R]	This Is Tommy Dorsey and His Greatest Band, Vol. 1	196?	3.00	6.00	12.00
❑ TFS-4158 [R]	This Is Tommy Dorsey and His Greatest Band, Vol. 2	196?	3.00	6.00	12.00

VOCALION

Number	Title	Yr	VG	VG+	NM
❑ VL 3613 [M]	Dance Party	196?	3.75	7.50	15.00
❑ VL 73613 [R]	Dance Party	196?	2.50	5.00	10.00

DORSEY, TOMMY, ORCHESTRA (WARREN COVINGTON, DIRECTOR)

Covington, a trombonist, became leader of the Dorsey band after Tommy's death. This version of the band had a hit single in 1958 with "Tea for Two Cha Cha."

DECCA

Number	Title	Yr	VG	VG+	NM
❑ DL 4120 [M]	Dance to the Songs Everybody Knows	1960	3.75	7.50	15.00
❑ DL 4130 [M]	Tricky Trombones	1961	3.75	7.50	15.00
❑ DL 8802 [M]	The Fabulous Arrangements of Tommy Dorsey	1958	3.75	7.50	15.00
❑ DL 8842 [M]	Tea for Two Cha Chas	1958	3.75	7.50	15.00
❑ DL 8904 [M]	Dance and Romance	1959	3.75	7.50	15.00
❑ DL 8943 [M]	More Tea for Two Cha Chas	1959	3.75	7.50	15.00
❑ DL 8980 [M]	It Takes Two to Cha-Cha...	1959	3.75	7.50	15.00
❑ DL 8996 [M]	It Takes Two to Bunny Hop..	1960	3.75	7.50	15.00
❑ DL 74120 [S]	Dance to the Songs Everybody Knows	1960	5.00	10.00	20.00
❑ DL 74130 [S]	Tricky Trombones	1961	5.00	10.00	20.00
❑ DL 78802 [S]	The Fabulous Arrangements of Tommy Dorsey	1958	5.00	10.00	20.00
❑ DL 78842 [S]	Tea for Two Cha Chas	1958	5.00	10.00	20.00
❑ DL 78904 [S]	Dance and Romance	1959	5.00	10.00	20.00
❑ DL 78943 [S]	More Tea for Two Cha Chas	1959	5.00	10.00	20.00
❑ DL 78980 [S]	It Takes Two to Cha-Cha...	1959	5.00	10.00	20.00
❑ DL 78996 [S]	It Takes Two to Bunny Hop..	1960	5.00	10.00	20.00

MCA

Number	Title	Yr	VG	VG+	NM
❑ 178	Tea for Two Cha Chas	197?	2.50	5.00	10.00
-- Reissue of Decca 78842					
❑ 180	More Tea for Two Cha Chas	197?	2.50	5.00	10.00
-- Reissue of Decca 78943					
❑ 185	It Takes Two to Bunny Hop..	197?	2.50	5.00	10.00
-- Reissue of Decca 78996					
❑ 534	It Takes Two to Cha-Cha...	197?	2.50	5.00	10.00
-- Reissue of Decca 78996					

DOUBLE IMAGE

DAVE SAMUELS and DAVID FRIEDMAN form the core of this group.

CELESTIAL HARMONIES

Number	Title	Yr	VG	VG+	NM
❑ CEL-015	In Lands I Never Saw	1986	2.50	5.00	10.00

ECM

Number	Title	Yr	VG	VG+	NM
❑ 1146	Dawn	1978	3.00	6.00	12.00

ENJA

Number	Title	Yr	VG	VG+	NM
❑ 2096	Double Image	198?	3.00	6.00	12.00

INNER CITY

Number	Title	Yr	VG	VG+	NM
❑ IC-3013	Double Image	1978	3.75	7.50	15.00

DOUBLE SIX OF PARIS, THE

Vocal group formed in France, also known as "Les Double Six": Jacques Danjean, Jeannine "Mimi" Perrin, Claude Germain, Ward Swingle, Christine Legrand, Jean-Claude Briodin. Also see DIZZY GILLESPIE; THE SWINGLE SINGERS.

CAPITOL

Number	Title	Yr	VG	VG+	NM
❑ ST 10259 [S]	The Double Six of Paris	1961	6.25	12.50	25.00

Number	Title	Yr	VG	VG+	NM
❏ T 10259 [M]	The Double Six of Paris	1961	5.00	10.00	20.00
PHILIPS					
❏ PHM 200-026 [M]	Swingin' Singin'	1962	5.00	10.00	20.00
❏ PHM 200-141 [M]	The Double Six of Paris Sings Ray Charles	1964	5.00	10.00	20.00
❏ PHS 600-026 [S]	Swingin' Singin'	1962	6.25	12.50	25.00
❏ PHS 600-141 [S]	The Double Six of Paris Sings Ray Charles	1964	6.25	12.50	25.00

DOWN HOME JAZZ BAND, THE
STOMP OFF

Number	Title	Yr	VG	VG+	NM
❏ SOS-1171	Hambone Kelly's Favorites	1987	2.50	5.00	10.00
❏ SOS-1190	Yerba Buena Style	1988	2.50	5.00	10.00
❏ SOS-1199	The San Francisco Jazz Tradition	1989	2.50	5.00	10.00
❏ SOS-1217	The Down Home Jazz Band in New Orleans	1990	2.50	5.00	10.00

DOYLE, ARTHUR
Tenor saxophone player.
AUDIBLE HISS

Number	Title	Yr	VG	VG+	NM
❏ AHS-004	Arthur Doyle Plays and Sings from the Songbook, Volume One	1995	3.00	6.00	12.00
ECSTATIC PEACE					
❏ 29	Arthur Doyle Plays More Alabama Feeling	1990	3.00	6.00	12.00

DRAKE, DONNA
Female singer.
LUXOR

Number	Title	Yr	VG	VG+	NM
❏ LP-1 [M]	The Wynton Kelly Trio Introduces Donna Drake -- Donna Sings Dinah	1968	7.50	15.00	30.00
❏ LPS-1 [S]	The Wynton Kelly Trio Introduces Donna Drake -- Donna Sings Dinah	1968	5.00	10.00	20.00

DRAPER, RAY
Tuba player and composer.
JOSIE

Number	Title	Yr	VG	VG+	NM
❏ JLPS-3004 [S]	Tuba Jazz	1963	5.00	10.00	20.00
❏ JOZ-3004 [M]	Tuba Jazz	1963	6.25	12.50	25.00
JUBILEE					
❏ JLP-1090 [M]	Tuba Jazz	1959	12.50	25.00	50.00
NEW JAZZ					
❏ NJLP-8228 [M]	Ray Draper Quintet Featuring John Coltrane	1958	15.00	30.00	60.00
-- Purple label					
❏ NJLP-8228 [M]	Ray Draper Quintet Featuring John Coltrane	1965	6.25	12.50	25.00
-- Blue label, trident logo at right					
PRESTIGE					
❏ PRLP-7096 [M]	Tuba Sounds	1957	20.00	40.00	80.00

DREAMS
Jazz-rock group. Among its members were MICHAEL BRECKER, RANDY BRECKER and BILLY COBHAM.
COLUMBIA

Number	Title	Yr	VG	VG+	NM
❏ C 30225	Dreams	1970	3.75	7.50	15.00
❏ C 30960	Imagine My Surprise	1971	3.75	7.50	15.00

DREW, DAN
See BOOTS BROWN.

DREW, KENNY
Pianist.
BLUE NOTE

Number	Title	Yr	VG	VG+	NM
❏ BLP-4059 [M]	Undercurrent	1961	20.00	40.00	80.00
-- "W. 63rd St." address on label					
❏ BLP-4059 [M]	Undercurrent	1964	6.25	12.50	25.00
-- "New York, USA" address on label					
❏ BLP-5023 [10]	Introducing the Kenny Drew Trio	1953	100.00	200.00	400.00
❏ BST-84059 [S]	Undercurrent	1961	20.00	40.00	80.00
-- "W. 63rd St." address on label					
❏ BST-84059 [S]	Undercurrent	1964	6.25	12.50	25.00
-- "New York, USA" address on label					
❏ BST-84059 [S]	Undercurrent	1966	3.75	7.50	15.00
-- "A Division of Liberty Records" on label					
FANTASY					
❏ OJC-065	Kenny Drew Trio	198?	2.50	5.00	10.00
❏ OJC-483	This Is New	1991	3.00	6.00	12.00
❏ OJC-6007	Kenny Drew Trio/Quartet/Quintet	198?	3.00	6.00	12.00
INNER CITY					
❏ IC-2007	Everything I Love	1973	3.75	7.50	15.00
❏ IC-2034	If You Could See Me Now	1974	3.75	7.50	15.00

Number	Title	Yr	VG	VG+	NM
❏ IC-2048	Morning	1975	3.75	7.50	15.00
JAZZ WEST					
❏ JWLP-4 [M]	Walkin' and Talkin' with the Kenny Drew Quartet	1955	75.00	150.00	300.00
JUDSON					
❏ L-3004 [M]	Harry Warren Showcase	1957	12.50	25.00	50.00
❏ L-3005 [M]	Harold Arlen Showcase	1957	12.50	25.00	50.00
NORGRAN					
❏ MGN-29 [10]	The Ideation of Kenny Drew	1954	62.50	125.00	250.00
❏ MGN-1002 [M]	Progressive Piano	1954	50.00	100.00	200.00
❏ MGN-1066 [M]	The Modernity of Kenny Drew	1956	37.50	75.00	150.00
RIVERSIDE					
❏ RLP 12-224 [M]	Kenny Drew Trio	195?	12.50	25.00	50.00
-- Blue label, microphone logo at top					
❏ RLP 12-224 [M]	Kenny Drew Trio	1956	37.50	75.00	150.00
-- White label, blue print					
❏ RLP 12-236 [M]	This Is New	195?	12.50	25.00	50.00
-- Blue label, microphone logo at top					
❏ RLP 12-236 [M]	This Is New	1957	37.50	75.00	150.00
-- White label, blue print					
❏ RLP 12-249 [M]	Pal Joey	1957	12.50	25.00	50.00
❏ RLP 12-811 [M]	I Love Jerome Kern	1956	37.50	75.00	150.00
❏ RLP-1112 [S]	Pal Joey	1959	10.00	20.00	40.00
❏ 6037	Kenny Drew Trio	197?	3.00	6.00	12.00
❏ 6066	This Is New	197?	3.00	6.00	12.00
❏ 6106	Pal Joey	197?	3.00	6.00	12.00
SOUL NOTE					
❏ SN-1031	Your Soft Eyes	1980	3.00	6.00	12.00
❏ SN-1040	It Might As Well Be Spring	1981	3.00	6.00	12.00
❏ SN-1081	Kenny Drew and Far Away	1983	3.00	6.00	12.00
❏ 121031	Your Soft Eyes	198?	2.50	5.00	10.00
-- Reissue of 1031					
❏ 121081	Kenny Drew and Far Away	198?	2.50	5.00	10.00
-- Reissue of 1081					
STEEPLECHASE					
❏ SCS-1007	Everything I Love	198?	3.00	6.00	12.00
-- Reissue of Inner City 2007					
❏ SCS-1016	Dark Beauty	198?	3.00	6.00	12.00
❏ SCS-1034	If You Could See Me Now	198?	3.00	6.00	12.00
-- Reissue of Inner City 2034					
❏ SCS-1048	Morning	198?	3.00	6.00	12.00
❏ SCS-1077	Lite Flite	198?	3.00	6.00	12.00
❏ SCS-1106	In Concert	198?	3.00	6.00	12.00
❏ SCS-1129	Ruby, My Dear	1977	3.00	6.00	12.00
VERVE					
❏ MGV-8156 [M]	The Modernity of Kenny Drew	1957	---	---	---
-- Canceled?					
XANADU					
❏ 166	Home Is Where the Soul Is	197?	3.00	6.00	12.00
❏ 167	For Sure	197?	3.00	6.00	12.00

DREW, KENNY; DONALD BYRD; HANK MOBLEY
Also see each artist's individual listings.
JAZZLAND

Number	Title	Yr	VG	VG+	NM
❏ JLP-6 [M]	Hard Bop	1960	12.50	25.00	50.00
-- Reissue of Riverside 236					
❏ JLP-906 [S]	Hard Bop	1960	10.00	20.00	40.00

DREW, KENNY; PAUL CHAMBERS; PHILLY JOE JONES
Also see each artist's individual listings.
JAZZLAND

Number	Title	Yr	VG	VG+	NM
❏ JLP-9 [M]	The Tough Piano Trio	1960	12.50	25.00	50.00
-- Reissue of Riverside 224					
❏ JLP-909 [S]	The Tough Piano Trio	1960	10.00	20.00	40.00

DREW, KENNY, AND NIELS-HENNING ORSTED PEDERSEN
Also see each artist's individual listings.
INNER CITY

Number	Title	Yr	VG	VG+	NM
❏ IC-2002	Duo	1973	3.75	7.50	15.00
❏ IC-2010	Duo 2	1974	3.75	7.50	15.00
❏ IC-2031	Duo Live in Concert	1974	3.75	7.50	15.00
STEEPLECHASE					
❏ SCS-1002	Duo	198?	3.00	6.00	12.00
-- Reissue of Inner City 2002					
❏ SCS-1010	Duo 2	198?	3.00	6.00	12.00
-- Reissue of Inner City 2010					
❏ SCS-1031	Duo Live in Concert	198?	3.00	6.00	12.00
-- Reissue of Inner City 2031					

DRY JACK
Fusion band formed by Chuck Lamb (keyboards) and Rich Lamb (bass).
INNER CITY

Number	Title	Yr	VG	VG+	NM
❏ IC-1063	Magical Elements	1978	3.75	7.50	15.00
❏ IC-1075	Whale City	1979	3.75	7.50	15.00

Number	Title	Yr	VG	VG+	NM	Number	Title	Yr	VG	VG+	NM

DRY THROAT FIVE, THE
Members: Bertrand Neyroud (clarinet, melodica); René Hagmann (alto saxophone, clarinet, trombone, cornet, trumpet, tuba); Raymond Graisier (washboard, drums, metallophone); Pierre-Alain Maret (banjo); Michel Rudaz (tuba)

STOMP OFF
Number	Title	Yr	VG	VG+	NM
❏ SOS-1114	Who's Blue?	1986	2.50	5.00	10.00
❏ SOS-1151	My Melancholy Baby	1989	2.50	5.00	10.00

DUDZIAK, URSZULA
Female singer.
ARISTA
| ❏ AL 4065 | Urszula | 1975 | 3.75 | 7.50 | 15.00 |
| ❏ AL 4132 | Midnight Rain | 1976 | 3.75 | 7.50 | 15.00 |
COLUMBIA
| ❏ KC 32902 | Newborn Light | 1972 | 5.00 | 10.00 | 20.00 |
INNER CITY
| ❏ IC-1066 | Future Talk | 1979 | 3.75 | 7.50 | 15.00 |

DUGGAN, LAR
Pianist.
PHILO
| ❏ PH-9002 | From the Lake Studies | 198? | 3.00 | 6.00 | 12.00 |

DUKE'S MEN, THE
Small groups from DUKE ELLINGTON's orchestra, many of which contain The Duke.
EPIC
| ❏ LG 3108 [M] | The Duke's Men | 1955 | 12.50 | 25.00 | 50.00 |
| ❏ LN 3237 [M] | Ellington's Sidekicks | 1956 | 12.50 | 25.00 | 50.00 |

DUKE, DOUGLAS
Organist.
HERALD
| ❏ HLP-0102 [M] | Sounds Impossible | 1956 | 12.50 | 25.00 | 50.00 |
REGENT
| ❏ MG-6013 [M] | Jazz Organist | 196? | 7.50 | 15.00 | 30.00 |

DUKE, GEORGE
Pianist, keyboard player and male singer. Also see STANLEY CLARKE.
ELEKTRA
| ❏ 60398 | Thief in the Night | 1985 | 2.50 | 5.00 | 10.00 |
| ❏ 60778 | Night After Night | 1989 | 2.50 | 5.00 | 10.00 |
EPIC
| ❏ PE 34469 | From Me to You | 1977 | 2.50 | 5.00 | 10.00 |

-- Originals have no bar code

| ❏ PE 34469 | From Me to You | 198? | 2.00 | 4.00 | 8.00 |

-- Budget-line reissue with bar code

| ❏ JE 34883 | Reach For It | 1977 | 2.50 | 5.00 | 10.00 |
| ❏ PE 34883 | Reach For It | 198? | 2.00 | 4.00 | 8.00 |

-- Budget-line reissue

| ❏ JE 35366 | Don't Let Go | 1978 | 2.50 | 5.00 | 10.00 |
| ❏ PE 35366 | Don't Let Go | 198? | 2.00 | 4.00 | 8.00 |

-- Budget-line reissue

❏ JE 35701	Follow the Rainbow	1979	2.50	5.00	10.00
❏ JE 36263	Master of the Game	1979	2.50	5.00	10.00
❏ PE 36263	Master of the Game	198?	2.00	4.00	8.00

-- Budget-line reissue

❏ FE 36483	A Brazilian Love Affair	1980	2.50	5.00	10.00
❏ FE 37532	Dream On	1982	2.50	5.00	10.00
❏ FE 38208	1976 Solo Album	1983	2.50	5.00	10.00
❏ FE 39262	Rendezvous	1984	2.50	5.00	10.00
MPS/BASF
❏ 22018	Faces in Reflection	1974	3.00	6.00	12.00
❏ 22835	Liberated Fantasies	1976	2.50	5.00	10.00
❏ 25355	Feel	1974	2.50	5.00	10.00
❏ 25613	The Aura Will Prevail	1975	2.50	5.00	10.00
❏ 25671	I Love the Blues, She Heard My Cry	1975	2.50	5.00	10.00
PACIFIC JAZZ
| ❏ PJ-LA891-H | George Duke | 1978 | 2.50 | 5.00 | 10.00 |
| ❏ LN-10127 | Save the Country | 198? | 2.00 | 4.00 | 8.00 |
PAUSA
| ❏ 7042 | The Aura Will Prevail | 198? | 2.00 | 4.00 | 8.00 |

-- Reissue of MPS/BASF 25613

| ❏ 7070 | I Love the Blues | 1980 | 2.00 | 4.00 | 8.00 |
PICKWICK
| ❏ SPC-3588 | Save the Country | 1978 | 2.00 | 4.00 | 8.00 |
VERVE/MPS
| ❏ 821 665-1 | Feel | 1984 | 2.00 | 4.00 | 8.00 |

-- Reissue of MPS/BASF 25355

| ❏ 821 837-1 | The Aura Will Prevail | 1984 | 2.00 | 4.00 | 8.00 |

-- Reissue of Pausa 7042

DUKE, KENO
Drummer.
STRATA-EAST
| ❏ SES-7416 | Sense of Values | 1974 | 6.25 | 12.50 | 25.00 |
TRIDENT
| ❏ 501 | Crest of the Wave | 197? | 5.00 | 10.00 | 20.00 |

DUKES OF DIXIELAND, THE
Founded by Frank Assunto (trumpet) and Fred Assunto (trombone) in the late 1940s.
AUDIO FIDELITY
❏ AFLP-1823 [M]	You Have to Hear It to Believe It -- The Dukes of Dixieland, Vol. 1	1956	3.75	7.50	15.00
❏ AFLP-1840 [M]	You Have to Hear It to Believe It -- The Dukes of Dixieland, Vol. 2	1957	3.75	7.50	15.00
❏ AFLP-1851 [M]	Marching Along with the Dukes of Dixieland, Vol. 3	1957	3.75	7.50	15.00
❏ AFLP-1860 [M]	The Dukes of Dixieland On Bourbon Street, Vol. 4	1958	3.75	7.50	15.00
❏ AFLP-1862 [M]	Mardi Gras Time	1958	3.75	7.50	15.00
❏ AFLP-1891 [M]	The Dukes of Dixieland On Campus	1959	3.75	7.50	15.00
❏ AFLP-1892 [M]	Up the Mississippi	1959	3.75	7.50	15.00
❏ AFLP-1918 [M]	Carnegie Hall Concert	1959	3.75	7.50	15.00
❏ AFLP-1924 [M]	Louie and the Dukes	196?	3.75	7.50	15.00
❏ AFLP-1928 [M]	Piano Ragtime (Vol. 11)	196?	3.75	7.50	15.00
❏ AFLP-1956 [M]	The Best of the Dukes of Dixieland	1961	3.75	7.50	15.00
❏ AFLP-1976 [M]	More of the Best of the Dukes of Dixieland	1962	3.75	7.50	15.00
❏ AFSD-5823 [S]	You Have to Hear It to Believe It -- The Dukes of Dixieland, Vol. 1	196?	5.00	10.00	20.00
❏ AFSD-5840 [S]	You Have to Hear It to Believe It -- The Dukes of Dixieland, Vol. 2	196?	5.00	10.00	20.00
❏ AFSD-5851 [S]	Marching Along with the Dukes of Dixieland, Vol. 3	1958	5.00	10.00	20.00
❏ AFSD-5860 [S]	The Dukes of Dixieland On Bourbon Street, Vol. 4	1958	5.00	10.00	20.00
❏ AFSD-5862 [S]	Mardi Gras Time	1958	5.00	10.00	20.00
❏ AFSD-5891 [S]	The Dukes of Dixieland On Campus	1959	5.00	10.00	20.00
❏ AFSD-5892 [S]	Up the Mississippi	1959	5.00	10.00	20.00
❏ AFSD-5918 [S]	Carnegie Hall Concert	1959	3.75	7.50	15.00
❏ AFSD-5924 [S]	Louie and the Dukes	196?	3.75	7.50	15.00
❏ AFSD-5928 [S]	Piano Ragtime (Vol. 11)	196?	3.75	7.50	15.00
❏ AFSD-5956 [S]	The Best of the Dukes of Dixieland	1961	3.75	7.50	15.00
❏ AFSD-5976 [S]	More of the Best of the Dukes of Dixieland	1962	3.75	7.50	15.00
❏ AFSD-6172	Tailgating	1967	3.00	6.00	12.00
❏ AFSD-6174	The Dukes of Dixieland On Parade	1967	3.00	6.00	12.00
COLUMBIA
❏ CL 1728 [M]	Breakin' It Up on Broadway	1962	3.00	6.00	12.00
❏ CL 2194 [M]	Struttin' at the World's Fair	1964	3.00	6.00	12.00
❏ CS 8528 [S]	Breakin' It Up on Broadway	1962	3.75	7.50	15.00
❏ CS 8994 [S]	Struttin' at the World's Fair	1964	3.75	7.50	15.00
DECCA
❏ DL 4653 [M]	"Live" At Bourbon Street, Chicago	1965	3.00	6.00	12.00
❏ DL 4708 [M]	Come On and Hear	1966	3.00	6.00	12.00
❏ DL 4807 [M]	Sunrise, Sunset	1966	3.00	6.00	12.00
❏ DL 4863 [M]	Come to the Cabaret	1967	3.75	7.50	15.00
❏ DL 4864 [M]	Thoroughly Modern Millie	1967	3.75	7.50	15.00
❏ DL 74653 [S]	"Live" At Bourbon Street, Chicago	1965	3.75	7.50	15.00
❏ DL 74708 [S]	Come On and Hear	1966	3.75	7.50	15.00
❏ DL 74807 [S]	Sunrise, Sunset	1966	3.75	7.50	15.00
❏ DL 74863 [S]	Come to the Cabaret	1967	3.00	6.00	12.00
❏ DL 74864 [S]	Thoroughly Modern Millie	1967	3.00	6.00	12.00
❏ DL 74975	Dixieland's Greatest Hits	1968	3.00	6.00	12.00
HARMONY
| ❏ HL 7349 [M] | Best of the Dukes of Dixieland | 1965 | 3.00 | 6.00 | 12.00 |
| ❏ HS 11149 [S] | Best of the Dukes of Dixieland | 1965 | 3.00 | 6.00 | 12.00 |
MCA
| ❏ 268 | Dixieland's Greatest Hits | 1973 | 2.50 | 5.00 | 10.00 |

-- Reissue of Decca 74975

RCA VICTOR
| ❏ LPM-2097 [M] | The Dukes of Dixieland at the Jazz Band Ball | 1960 | 3.00 | 6.00 | 12.00 |
| ❏ LSP-2097(e) [R] | The Dukes of Dixieland at the Jazz Band Ball | 1960 | 3.75 | 7.50 | 15.00 |
VIK
| ❏ LX-1025 [M] | The Dukes of Dixieland at the Jazz Band Ball | 1956 | 7.50 | 15.00 | 30.00 |
VOCALION
| ❏ VL 73846 | Hello, Dolly! | 1968 | 2.50 | 5.00 | 10.00 |

Number	Title	Yr	VG	VG+	NM

DUKES, JOE, AND JACK McDUFF
Drummer. Also see JACK McDUFF.
PRESTIGE
| ❏ PRLP-7324 [M] | Soulful Drums | 1964 | 6.25 | 12.50 | 25.00 |
| ❏ PRST-7324 [S] | Soulful Drums | 1964 | 7.50 | 15.00 | 30.00 |

DUNBAR, TED
Guitarist and composer. Also see KENNY BARRON.
XANADU
❏ 155	Opening Remarks	1978	3.75	7.50	15.00
❏ 181	Secundum Artem	1980	3.00	6.00	12.00
❏ 196	Jazz Guitarist	1982	3.00	6.00	12.00

DUNCAN, DANNY
"X"
| ❏ LVA-3040 [10] | Ragtime Jamboree | 1955 | 12.50 | 25.00 | 50.00 |

DUNCAN, SAMMY
JAZZOLOGY
❏ J-64	Sammy Duncan and His Underground All Stars	197?	2.50	5.00	10.00
❏ J-77	Jazz and Blues	1979	2.50	5.00	10.00
❏ J-84	Swingin' Jazz	1980	2.50	5.00	10.00
❏ J-118	When the Saints Go Marching In	1987	2.50	5.00	10.00
❏ J-119	When You're Swingin'	1987	2.50	5.00	10.00
NATIONAL RECORDING CO.
❏ NRC-LPA 1	Cool Dixieland Jazz from Out of the South	197?	3.00	6.00	12.00

DUNN, DOROTHY
See ANNIE ROSS.

DUPREE, CORNELL
Guitarist.
ANTILLES
| ❏ 90984 | Coast to Coast | 1988 | 2.50 | 5.00 | 10.00 |
ATLANTIC
| ❏ SD 7311 | Teasin' | 1975 | 3.00 | 6.00 | 12.00 |

DURAN, EDDIE
Guitarist.
CONCORD JAZZ
| ❏ CJ-94 | Ginza | 1979 | 3.00 | 6.00 | 12.00 |
| ❏ CJ-271 | One by One | 1985 | 2.50 | 5.00 | 10.00 |
FANTASY
❏ 3247 [M]	Jazz Guitarist	195?	10.00	20.00	40.00
-- Black vinyl					
❏ 3247 [M]	Jazz Guitarist	1957	20.00	40.00	80.00
-- Red vinyl					
❏ OJC-120	Jazz Guitarist	198?	2.50	5.00	10.00

DuSHON, JEAN
Female singer. Early in her career (1961), she had a one-off 45 rpm single on Atco produced by Phil Spector. Also see RAMSEY LEWIS.
ARGO
| ❏ LP-4039 [M] | Make Way for Jean DuShon | 1964 | 6.25 | 12.50 | 25.00 |
| ❏ LPS-4039 [S] | Make Way for Jean DuShon | 1964 | 7.50 | 15.00 | 30.00 |

DUTCH SWING COLLEGE BAND, THE
Founded by Peter Schilperoort, Frans Vink and Joost van Os on May 5, 1945 (Liberation Day, the end of the German occupation of the Netherlands).
ARCHIVE OF FOLK AND JAZZ
| ❏ 341 | The Dutch Swing College Band | 1979 | 2.50 | 5.00 | 10.00 |
EPIC
| ❏ LN 3211 [M] | Dixieland Goes Dutch | 1955 | 10.00 | 20.00 | 40.00 |
PHILIPS
| ❏ PHM 200-010 [M] | Dixie Goes Dutch | 1962 | 3.75 | 7.50 | 15.00 |
| ❏ PHS 600-010 [S] | Dixie Goes Dutch | 1962 | 5.00 | 10.00 | 20.00 |
TIMELESS
| ❏ 516 | The Dutch Swing College Band At Its Best | 198? | 2.50 | 5.00 | 10.00 |
| ❏ 525 | The Dutch Swing College Band | 198? | 2.50 | 5.00 | 10.00 |

DYANI, JOHNNY
Bass player, pianist and male singer. Also see THREE.
STEEPLECHASE
❏ SCS-1098	Witchdoctor's Son	197?	3.00	6.00	12.00
❏ SCS-1109	Song for Biko	1978	3.00	6.00	12.00
❏ SCS-1163	Mbizo	1982	3.00	6.00	12.00
❏ SCS-1186	Afrika	198?	3.00	6.00	12.00
❏ SCS-1209	Angolan City	198?	3.00	6.00	12.00

DYANI, JOHNNY; OKAY TEMIZ; MONGEZI FEZA
Temiz is a percussionist; Feza played trumpet. Also see JOHNNY DYANI.
ANTILLES
| ❏ AN-7035 | Music for Xaba | 197? | 7.50 | 15.00 | 30.00 |

Number	Title	Yr	VG	VG+	NM

E

EAGER, ALLAN
Alto and tenor saxophone player.
SAVOY
Number	Title	Yr	VG	VG+	NM
❑ MG-9015 [10]	New Trends in Modern Music, Volume 2	1952	62.50	125.00	250.00
❑ MG-15044 [10]	Tenor Sax	1954	50.00	100.00	200.00

EAGLE BRASS BAND, THE
Members: John Ewing, Alex Less (trombones); Benny Booker (tuba); Joe Darensbourg (clarinet); Floyd Turnham (alto sax); Sam Lee (tenor sax); Teddy Edwards (snare drum); Barry Martyn (bass drum); Wendell Eugene, Mike Owen (trombones); Chris Burke (clarinet).
GHB
| ❑ GHB-60 | The Eagle Brass Band | 1978 | 2.50 | 5.00 | 10.00 |
| ❑ GHB-170 | The Last of the Line | 1986 | 2.50 | 5.00 | 10.00 |

EARDLEY, JON
Trumpeter.
FANTASY
| ❑ OJC-123 | Jon Eardley Seven | 198? | 2.50 | 5.00 | 10.00 |
| ❑ OJC-1746 | From Hollywood to New York | 1988 | 2.50 | 5.00 | 10.00 |
NEW JAZZ
| ❑ NJLP-1105 [10] | Jon Eardley in Hollywood | 1954 | 50.00 | 100.00 | 200.00 |
PRESTIGE
❑ PRLP-205 [10]	Jon Eardley in Hollywood	1955	37.50	75.00	150.00
❑ PRLP-207 [10]	Hey There	1955	37.50	75.00	150.00
❑ PRLP-7033 [M]	Jon Eardley Seven	1956	25.00	50.00	100.00

EARLAND, CHARLES
Organist.
COLUMBIA
❑ FC 37573	Earland's Jam	1982	2.50	5.00	10.00
❑ FC 38547	Earland's Street Themes	1983	2.50	5.00	10.00
❑ JC 36449	Coming to You Live	1980	2.50	5.00	10.00
FANTASY
| ❑ OJC-335 | Black Talk! | 1988 | 2.50 | 5.00 | 10.00 |
| -- Reissue of Prestige 7758 | | | | | |
MERCURY
❑ SRM-1-1049	Odyssey	1976	2.50	5.00	10.00
❑ SRM-1-1139	The Great Pyramid	1976	2.50	5.00	10.00
❑ SRM-1-1149	Revelation	1977	2.50	5.00	10.00
❑ SRM-1-3720	Perception	1978	2.50	5.00	10.00
MILESTONE
| ❑ M-9165 | Front Burner | 1988 | 2.50 | 5.00 | 10.00 |
| ❑ M-9175 | Third Degree Burn | 1989 | 2.50 | 5.00 | 10.00 |
MUSE
❑ MR-5126	Smokin'	1978	2.50	5.00	10.00
❑ MR-5156	Mama Roots	1979	2.50	5.00	10.00
❑ MR-5181	Infant Eyes	1980	2.50	5.00	10.00
❑ MR-5201	Pleasant Afternoon	1981	2.50	5.00	10.00
❑ MR-5240	In the Pocket	1984	2.50	5.00	10.00
PRESTIGE
❑ 2501	Burners	1982	2.50	5.00	10.00
❑ PRST-7758	Black Talk!	1970	5.00	10.00	20.00
❑ PRST-7815	Black Drops	1970	3.75	7.50	15.00
❑ 10009	Living Black!	1971	3.00	6.00	12.00
❑ 10018	Soul Story	1971	3.00	6.00	12.00
❑ 10024	Black Talk!	1971	2.50	5.00	10.00
-- Reissue of 7758					
❑ 10029	Black Drops	1971	2.50	5.00	10.00
-- Reissue of 7815					
❑ 10041	Intensity	1972	3.00	6.00	12.00
❑ 10051	Live at the Lighthouse	1972	3.00	6.00	12.00
❑ 10061	Charles III	1973	3.00	6.00	12.00
❑ 10095	Kharma	· 1975	3.00	6.00	12.00
❑ 66002 [(2)]	Leaving This Planet	1974	3.75	7.50	15.00
TRIP
| ❑ 5004 | Charles Earland | 1974 | 2.50 | 5.00 | 10.00 |

EASLEY, BILL
Tenor saxophone player and clarinetist.
SUNNYSIDE
| ❑ SSC-1022 | Wind Inventions | 1988 | 2.50 | 5.00 | 10.00 |

EAST NEW YORK ENSEMBLE DE PARIS, THE
FOLKWAYS
| ❑ F-33867 | At the Helm | 1974 | 3.75 | 7.50 | 15.00 |

EASTERN REBELLION
The core of the group on these recordings was Cedar Walton (piano), Sam Jones (bass) and Billy Higgins (drums).
TIMELESS
Number	Title	Yr	VG	VG+	NM
❑ 306	Eastern Rebellion	1976	3.75	7.50	15.00
❑ 318	Eastern Rebellion II	1977	3.75	7.50	15.00

EASTON, TED
Drummer and bandleader.
CIRCLE
| ❑ 12 | A Salute to Satchmo | 198? | 2.50 | 5.00 | 10.00 |

EASY RIDERS JAZZ BAND, THE
Led by Big Bill Bissonette.
JAZZ CRUSADE
| ❑ 1002 | My Life Will Be Sweeter Someday | 1963 | 10.00 | 20.00 | 40.00 |

EATON, CLEVELAND
Bass player. Formerly in the RAMSEY LEWIS Trio.
OVATION
| ❑ OV-1703 | Instant Hip | 1974 | 5.00 | 10.00 | 20.00 |
| ❑ OV-1742 | Keep Love Alive | 197? | 3.75 | 7.50 | 15.00 |

EATON, JOHN
Pianist. May or may not be the same person as below.
CHIAROSCURO
| ❑ CH-137 | Solo Piano | 1975 | 3.00 | 6.00 | 12.00 |
| ❑ CH-174 | Like Old Times | 1977 | 3.00 | 6.00 | 12.00 |

EATON, JOHNNY
Pianist. May or may not be the same person as above.
COLUMBIA
| ❑ CL 737 [M] | College Jazz: Modern | 1956 | 10.00 | 20.00 | 40.00 |
| ❑ CL 996 [M] | Far Out, Far In | 1957 | 10.00 | 20.00 | 40.00 |

EAVES, HUBERT
Keyboard player.
INNER CITY
| ❑ IC-6012 | Esoteric Funk | 1976 | 5.00 | 10.00 | 20.00 |

ECHOES OF HARLEM
This is the title of this jazz album – no artist is listed, but it's all by the same band.
ROYALE
| ❑ LP-18128 [10] | Echoes of Harlem | 195? | 20.00 | 40.00 | 80.00 |

ECKSTINE, BILLY
Male singer and bandleader. Also an occasional trumpeter and valve trombone player. Also see COUNT BASIE; EARL "FATHA" HINES.
AUDIO LAB
| ❑ AL-1549 [M] | Mr. B | 1960 | 30.00 | 60.00 | 120.00 |
DELUXE
| ❑ FA-2010 [M] | Billy Eckstine and His Orchestra | 195? | 20.00 | 40.00 | 80.00 |
EMARCY
❑ MG-26025 [10]	Blues for Sale	1954	30.00	60.00	120.00
❑ MG-26027 [10]	The Love Songs of Mr. B	1954	30.00	60.00	120.00
❑ MG-36010 [M]	I Surrender, Dear	1955	20.00	40.00	80.00
❑ MG-36029 [M]	Blues for Sale	1955	20.00	40.00	80.00
❑ MG-36030 [M]	The Love Songs of Mr. B	1955	20.00	40.00	80.00
❑ MG-36129 [M]	Billy Eckstine's Imagination	1958	15.00	30.00	60.00
ENTERPRISE
❑ ENS-1013	Stormy	1971	3.75	7.50	15.00
❑ ENS-1017	Feel the Warm	1971	3.75	7.50	15.00
❑ ENS-5004	Senior Soul	1972	3.75	7.50	15.00
FORUM
| ❑ F-9027 [M] | Once More with Feeling | 196? | 3.75 | 7.50 | 15.00 |
| ❑ SF-9027 [S] | Once More with Feeling | 196? | 3.75 | 7.50 | 15.00 |
KING
| ❑ 295-12 [10] | The Great Mr. B | 1953 | 75.00 | 150.00 | 300.00 |
LION
| ❑ L-70057 [M] | The Best of Billy Eckstine | 1958 | 6.25 | 12.50 | 25.00 |
MERCURY
❑ MG-20333 [M]	Billy's Best	1958	10.00	20.00	40.00
❑ MG-20637 [M]	Broadway, Bongos and Mr. B	1961	6.25	12.50	25.00
❑ MG-20674 [M]	Billy Eckstine and Quincy Jones at Basin St. East	1962	6.25	12.50	25.00
❑ MG-20736 [M]	Don't Worry 'Bout Me	1962	6.25	12.50	25.00
❑ MG-20796 [M]	The Golden Hits of Billy Eckstine	1963	3.75	7.50	15.00
❑ SR-60086 [S]	Billy's Best	1958	12.50	25.00	50.00
❑ SR-60637 [S]	Broadway, Bongos and Mr. B	1961	7.50	15.00	30.00

Number	Title	Yr	VG	VG+	NM
❑ SR-60674 [S]	Billy Eckstine and Quincy Jones at Basin St. East	1962	7.50	15.00	30.00
❑ SR-60736 [S]	Don't Worry 'Bout Me	1962	7.50	15.00	30.00
❑ SR-60796 [S]	The Golden Hits of Billy Eckstine	1963	5.00	10.00	20.00

METRO

Number	Title	Yr	VG	VG+	NM
❑ M-537 [M]	Everything I Have Is Yours	1965	3.75	7.50	15.00
❑ MS-537 [R]	Everything I Have Is Yours	1965	3.00	6.00	12.00

MGM

Number	Title	Yr	VG	VG+	NM
❑ E-153 [10]	Billy Eckstine Sings Rodgers & Hammerstein	1952	37.50	75.00	150.00
❑ E-219 [10]	Tenderly	1953	37.50	75.00	150.00
❑ E-257 [10]	I Let a Song Go Out of My Heart	1954	37.50	75.00	150.00
❑ E-523 [10]	Songs by Billy Eckstine	1951	40.00	80.00	160.00
❑ E-548 [10]	Favorites	1951	40.00	80.00	160.00
❑ E-3176 [M]	Mr. B with a Beat	1955	12.50	25.00	50.00
❑ E-3209 [M]	Rendezvous	1955	12.50	25.00	50.00
❑ E-3275 [M]	That Old Feeling	1956	12.50	25.00	50.00

MOTOWN

Number	Title	Yr	VG	VG+	NM
❑ M 632 [M]	Prime of My Life	1965	5.00	10.00	20.00
❑ MS 632 [S]	Prime of My Life	1965	6.25	12.50	25.00
❑ M 646 [M]	My Way	1966	5.00	10.00	20.00
❑ MS 646 [S]	My Way	1966	6.25	12.50	25.00
❑ MS 677	For Love of Ivy	1969	6.25	12.50	25.00

NATIONAL

Number	Title	Yr	VG	VG+	NM
❑ NLP-2001 [10]	Billy Eckstine Sings	1949	50.00	100.00	200.00

REGENT

Number	Title	Yr	VG	VG+	NM
❑ MG-6052 [M]	Prisoner of Love	1957	12.50	25.00	50.00
❑ MG-6053 [M]	The Duke, the Blues and Me	1957	12.50	25.00	50.00
❑ MG-6054 [M]	My Deep Blue Dream	1957	12.50	25.00	50.00
❑ MG-6058 [M]	You Call It Madness	1957	12.50	25.00	50.00

ROULETTE

Number	Title	Yr	VG	VG+	NM
❑ R-25052 [M]	No Cover, No Minimum	1961	6.25	12.50	25.00
❑ SR-25052 [S]	No Cover, No Minimum	1961	7.50	15.00	30.00
❑ R-25104 [M]	Once More with Feeling	1962	6.25	12.50	25.00
❑ SR-25104 [S]	Once More with Feeling	1962	7.50	15.00	30.00

SAVOY

Number	Title	Yr	VG	VG+	NM
❑ 1127	Billy Eckstine Sings	1979	3.00	6.00	12.00
❑ SJL-2214 [(2)]	Mr. B and the Band/The Savoy Sessions	1976	3.75	7.50	15.00

TRIP

Number	Title	Yr	VG	VG+	NM
❑ 5567	The Modern Sound of Mr. B	197?	2.50	5.00	10.00

VERVE

Number	Title	Yr	VG	VG+	NM
❑ 819 442-1 [(2)]	Everything I Have Is Yours: The MGM Years	1986	3.75	7.50	15.00

XANADU

Number	Title	Yr	VG	VG+	NM
❑ 207	I Want to Talk About You	1987	2.50	5.00	10.00

EDISON, HARRY "SWEETS"
Trumpeter. Also see EDDIE "LOCKJAW" DAVIS; ROY ELDREDGE; BUDDY RICH; BEN WEBSTER; LESTER YOUNG.

AMERICAN RECORDING SOCIETY

Number	Title	Yr	VG	VG+	NM
❑ G-430 [M]	Sweets	1957	10.00	20.00	40.00

CLEF

Number	Title	Yr	VG	VG+	NM
❑ MGC-717 [M]	Sweets	1956	20.00	40.00	80.00

LIBERTY

Number	Title	Yr	VG	VG+	NM
❑ LRP-3484 [M]	When Lights Are Low	1966	5.00	10.00	20.00
❑ LST-7484 [S]	When Lights Are Low	1966	6.25	12.50	25.00

PABLO

Number	Title	Yr	VG	VG+	NM
❑ 2310 780	Lights	1976	3.75	7.50	15.00
❑ 2310 806	Simply Sweets	1977	3.75	7.50	15.00
❑ 2310 934	For My Pals	198?	3.00	6.00	12.00

PABLO LIVE

Number	Title	Yr	VG	VG+	NM
❑ 2308 237	'S Wonderful	198?	3.00	6.00	12.00

PACIFIC JAZZ

Number	Title	Yr	VG	VG+	NM
❑ PJLP-4 [10]	Harry Edison Quartet	1953	37.50	75.00	150.00
❑ PJ-11 [M]	The Inventive Harry Edison	1960	12.50	25.00	50.00

ROULETTE

Number	Title	Yr	VG	VG+	NM
❑ R-52023 [M]	Sweetenings	1960	10.00	20.00	40.00
❑ SR-52023 [S]	Sweetenings	1960	10.00	20.00	40.00
❑ R-52041 [M]	Patented by Edison	1960	7.50	15.00	30.00
❑ SR-52041 [S]	Patented by Edison	1960	10.00	20.00	40.00

SUE

Number	Title	Yr	VG	VG+	NM
❑ LP-1030 [M]	Sweets for the Sweet	1964	10.00	20.00	40.00
❑ STLP-1030 [S]	Sweets for the Sweet	1964	12.50	25.00	50.00

VEE JAY

Number	Title	Yr	VG	VG+	NM
❑ LP-1104 [M]	For the Sweet Taste of Love	1964	7.50	15.00	30.00
❑ LPS-1104 [S]	For the Sweet Taste of Love	1964	10.00	20.00	40.00
❑ VJS-3065	Home with Sweets	1975	5.00	10.00	20.00

VERVE

Number	Title	Yr	VG	VG+	NM
❑ MGVS-6016 [S]	Harry Edison Swings Buck Clayton, And Vice Versa	1959	10.00	20.00	40.00
❑ MGVS-6037 [S]	The Swinger	1960	10.00	20.00	40.00
❑ MGVS-6118 [S]	Mr. Swing	1960	10.00	20.00	40.00
❑ MGV-8097 [M]	Sweets	1957	12.50	25.00	50.00
❑ V-8097 [M]	Sweets	1961	5.00	10.00	20.00
❑ MGV-8211 [M]	Gee Baby, Ain't I Good to You?	1958	12.50	25.00	50.00
❑ V-8211 [M]	Gee Baby, Ain't I Good to You?	1961	5.00	10.00	20.00
❑ MGV-8293 [M]	Harry Edison Swings Buck Clayton, And Vice Versa	1958	12.50	25.00	50.00
❑ V-8293 [M]	Harry Edison Swings Buck Clayton, And Vice Versa	1961	5.00	10.00	20.00
❑ V6-8293 [S]	Harry Edison Swings Buck Clayton, And Vice Versa	1961	5.00	10.00	20.00
❑ MGV-8295 [M]	The Swinger	1959	12.50	25.00	50.00
❑ V-8295 [M]	The Swinger	1961	5.00	10.00	20.00
❑ V6-8295 [S]	The Swinger	1961	5.00	10.00	20.00
❑ MGV-8353 [M]	Mr. Swing	1959	12.50	25.00	50.00
❑ V-8353 [M]	Mr. Swing	1961	5.00	10.00	20.00
❑ V6-8358 [S]	Mr. Swing	1961	5.00	10.00	20.00

EDWARDS, EDDIE
Trombone player and violinist.

COMMODORE

Number	Title	Yr	VG	VG+	NM
❑ FL-20,003 [10]	Eddie Edwards' Original Dixieland Jazz Band	1950	15.00	30.00	60.00

EDWARDS, TEDDY
Tenor saxophone player.

CONTEMPORARY

Number	Title	Yr	VG	VG+	NM
❑ M-3583 [M]	Teddy's Ready	1960	6.25	12.50	25.00
❑ M-3588 [M]	Together Again	1961	7.50	15.00	30.00
❑ M-3592 [M]	Good Gravy	1961	6.25	12.50	25.00
❑ M-3606 [M]	Heart and Soul	1962	6.25	12.50	25.00
❑ S-7583 [S]	Teddy's Ready	1960	7.50	15.00	30.00
❑ S-7588 [S]	Together Again	1961	10.00	20.00	40.00
❑ S-7592 [S]	Good Gravy	1961	7.50	15.00	30.00
❑ S-7606 [S]	Heart and Soul	1962	7.50	15.00	30.00

FANTASY

Number	Title	Yr	VG	VG+	NM
❑ OJC-177	Heart and Soul	198?	2.50	5.00	10.00
❑ OJC-424	Together Again	1990	3.00	6.00	12.00

MUSE

Number	Title	Yr	VG	VG+	NM
❑ MR-5045	Feelin's	1974	3.00	6.00	12.00

PACIFIC JAZZ

Number	Title	Yr	VG	VG+	NM
❑ PJ-6 [M]	It's About Time	1960	10.00	20.00	40.00
❑ ST-6 [S]	It's About Time	1960	10.00	20.00	40.00
❑ PJ-14 [M]	Sunset Eyes	1961	10.00	20.00	40.00

PRESTIGE

Number	Title	Yr	VG	VG+	NM
❑ PRLP-7518 [M]	Nothin' But the Truth	1967	7.50	15.00	30.00
❑ PRST-7518 [S]	Nothin' But the Truth	1967	6.25	12.50	25.00
❑ PRLP-7522 [M]	It's Alright	1967	7.50	15.00	30.00
❑ PRST-7522 [S]	It's Alright	1967	6.25	12.50	25.00

STEEPLECHASE

Number	Title	Yr	VG	VG+	NM
❑ SCS-1147	Out of This World	1980	3.00	6.00	12.00

XANADU

Number	Title	Yr	VG	VG+	NM
❑ 134	Inimitable	1976	3.00	6.00	12.00

EGAN, MARK
Bass player. Also see ELEMENTS.

GRP

Number	Title	Yr	VG	VG+	NM
❑ GR-9572	A Touch of Light	1988	2.50	5.00	10.00

HIP POCKET

Number	Title	Yr	VG	VG+	NM
❑ HP-104	Mosaic	1985	2.50	5.00	10.00

EGILSSON, ARNI
Bass player.

INNER CITY

Number	Title	Yr	VG	VG+	NM
❑ IC-1103	Bassus Erectus	1981	3.00	6.00	12.00

EITHER/ORCHESTRA, THE
Ten-piece band led by saxophone player and composer Russ Gershon.

ACCURATE

Number	Title	Yr	VG	VG+	NM
❑ AC-2222	Dial "E" for Either/Orchestra	1987	3.00	6.00	12.00
❑ AC-3232	Radium	1989	3.00	6.00	12.00

ELDRIDGE, ROY
Best known as a trumpeter, he also played fluegel horn and piano. Also see COLEMAN HAWKINS; EARL "FATHA" HINES; THE JAZZ ARTISTS GUILD; OSCAR PETERSON; ART TATUM; LESTER YOUNG.

AMERICAN RECORDING SOCIETY

Number	Title	Yr	VG	VG+	NM
❑ G-420 [M]	Swing Goes Dixie	1956	10.00	20.00	40.00

CLEF

Number	Title	Yr	VG	VG+	NM
❑ MGC-113 [10]	Roy Eldridge Collates	1953	37.50	75.00	150.00

Number	Title	Yr	VG	VG+	NM
❏ MGC-150 [10]	The Roy Eldridge Quintet	1954	37.50	75.00	150.00
❏ MGC-162 [10]	The Strolling Mr. Eldridge	1954	37.50	75.00	150.00
❏ MGC-683 [M]	Little Jazz	1956	25.00	50.00	100.00
❏ MGC-704 [M]	Rockin' Chair	1956	25.00	50.00	100.00
❏ MGC-705 [M]	Dale's Wail	1956	25.00	50.00	100.00
❏ MGC-716 [M]	Mr. Jazz	1956	---	---	---
-- Canceled					
COLUMBIA					
❏ C2 38033 [(2)]	Early Years	1983	3.00	6.00	12.00
DIAL					
❏ LP-304 [10]	Little Jazz Four: Trumpet Fantasy	1953	100.00	200.00	400.00
DISCOVERY					
❏ DL-2009 [10]	Roy Eldridge with Zoot Sims	1954	30.00	60.00	120.00
EMARCY					
❏ MG-36084 [M]	Roy's Got Rhythm	1956	20.00	40.00	80.00
FANTASY					
❏ OJC-373	Montreux '77	1989	3.00	6.00	12.00
❏ OJC-628	Happy Time	1991	3.00	6.00	12.00
GNP CRESCENDO					
❏ GNP-9009	Roy Eldridge	197?	3.00	6.00	12.00
JAZZ ARCHIVES					
❏ JA-14	Arcadia Shuffle	198?	2.50	5.00	10.00
LONDON					
❏ PB 375 [10]	Roy Eldridge Quartet	1954	30.00	60.00	120.00
MASTER JAZZ					
❏ 8110	The Nifty Cat	1970	5.00	10.00	20.00
❏ 8121	The Nifty Cat Strikes West	197?	5.00	10.00	20.00
MCA					
❏ 1355	All the Cats Join In	198?	2.50	5.00	10.00
MERCURY					
❏ MGC-113 [10]	Roy Eldridge Collates	1952	50.00	100.00	200.00
METRO					
❏ M-513 [M]	Roy Eldridge	1965	3.00	6.00	12.00
❏ MS-513 [R]	Roy Eldridge	1965	2.50	5.00	10.00
PABLO					
❏ 2310 746	Happy Time	1975	3.75	7.50	15.00
❏ 2310 766	What It's All About	1976	3.75	7.50	15.00
❏ 2310 869	Little Jazz	198?	3.00	6.00	12.00
❏ 2310 928	Loose Walk	198?	2.50	5.00	10.00
❏ 2405 413	The Best of Roy Eldridge	198?	2.50	5.00	10.00
PABLO LIVE					
❏ 2308 203	Montreux '77	1978	3.00	6.00	12.00
PRESTIGE					
❏ PRLP-114 [10]	Roy Eldridge in Sweden	1951	62.50	125.00	250.00
VERVE					
❏ MGV-1010 [M]	Swing Goes Dixie	1957	12.50	25.00	50.00
❏ V-1010 [M]	Swing Goes Dixie	1961	5.00	10.00	20.00
❏ VE-2-2531 [(2)]	Dale's Wail	198?	3.75	7.50	15.00
❏ UMV-2686	Rockin' Chair	198?	2.50	5.00	10.00
❏ MGV-8068 [M]	Little Jazz	1957	12.50	25.00	50.00
-- Reissue of Clef 683					
❏ V-8068 [M]	Little Jazz	1961	5.00	10.00	20.00
❏ MGV-8088 [M]	Rockin' Chair	1957	12.50	25.00	50.00
-- Reissue of Clef 704					
❏ V-8088 [M]	Rockin' Chair	1961	5.00	10.00	20.00
❏ MGV-8089 [M]	Dale's Wail	1957	12.50	25.00	50.00
-- Reissue of Clef 705					
❏ V-8089 [M]	Dale's Wail	1961	5.00	10.00	20.00
❏ MGV-8389 [M]	Swingin' on the Town	1960	12.50	25.00	50.00
❏ V-8389 [M]	Swingin' on the Town	1961	5.00	10.00	20.00
XANADU					
❏ 140	Roy Eldridge at Jerry Newman's	198?	2.50	5.00	10.00

ELDRIDGE, ROY, AND BENNY CARTER
Also see each artist's individual listings.

Number	Title	Yr	VG	VG+	NM
AMERICAN RECORDING SOCIETY					
❏ G-413 [M]	The Urbane Jazz of Roy Eldridge and Benny Carter	1957	10.00	20.00	40.00
VERVE					
❏ MGV-8202 [M]	The Urbane Jazz of Roy Eldridge and Benny Carter	1957	12.50	25.00	50.00
❏ V-8202 [M]	The Urbane Jazz of Roy Eldridge and Benny Carter	1961	5.00	10.00	20.00

ELDRIDGE, ROY, AND DIZZY GILLESPIE
Also see each artist's individual listings.

Number	Title	Yr	VG	VG+	NM
CLEF					
❏ MGC-641 [M]	Roy and Diz	1955	37.50	75.00	150.00
❏ MGC-671 [M]	Roy and Diz, Volume 2	1955	37.50	75.00	150.00
❏ MGC-730 [M]	Trumpet Battle	1956	25.00	50.00	100.00

Number	Title	Yr	VG	VG+	NM
❏ MGC-731 [M]	The Trumpet Kings	1956	25.00	50.00	100.00
PABLO					
❏ 2310 816	Jazz Maturity	1977	3.75	7.50	15.00
VERVE					
❏ VSP-28 [M]	Soul Mates	1966	3.75	7.50	15.00
❏ VSPS-28 [R]	Soul Mates	1966	3.00	6.00	12.00
❏ MGV-8109 [M]	Trumpet Battle	1957	12.50	25.00	50.00
❏ V-8109 [M]	Trumpet Battle	1961	5.00	10.00	20.00
❏ MGV-8110 [M]	The Trumpet Kings	1957	12.50	25.00	50.00
❏ V-8110 [M]	The Trumpet Kings	1961	5.00	10.00	20.00

ELDRIDGE, ROY; DIZZY GILLESPIE; HARRY "SWEETS" EDISON
Also see each artist's individual listings.

Number	Title	Yr	VG	VG+	NM
VERVE					
❏ MGV-8212 [M]	Tour de Force	1958	12.50	25.00	50.00
❏ V-8212 [M]	Tour de Force	1961	5.00	10.00	20.00

ELDRIDGE, ROY/SAMMY PRICE
Also see each artist's individual listings.

Number	Title	Yr	VG	VG+	NM
BRUNSWICK					
❏ BL 58045 [10]	Battle of Jazz, Volume 7	1953	15.00	30.00	60.00

ELEMENTS
Fusion band led by MARK EGAN and drummer Danny Gottlieb.

Number	Title	Yr	VG	VG+	NM
ANTILLES					
❏ AN-1017	The Elements	198?	2.50	5.00	10.00
-- Reissue of Philo album					
❏ AN-1021	Forward Motion	198?	2.50	5.00	10.00
NOVUS					
❏ 3031-1-N	Illumination	1988	2.50	5.00	10.00
❏ 3058-1-N	Liberal Arts	1989	3.00	6.00	12.00
PHILO					
❏ 9011	The Elements	198?	3.75	7.50	15.00

ELEVENTH HOUSE, THE
See LARRY CORYELL.

ELGART, BILL
Drummer.

Number	Title	Yr	VG	VG+	NM
MARK LEVINSON					
❏ 3	A Life	1980	6.25	12.50	25.00

ELGART, CHARLIE

Number	Title	Yr	VG	VG+	NM
NOVUS					
❏ 3045-1-N	Signs of Life	1988	2.50	5.00	10.00
❏ 3068-1-N	Balance	1989	3.00	6.00	12.00

ELGART, LARRY
Alto saxophone player and bandleader. Also see LES AND LARRY ELGART.

Number	Title	Yr	VG	VG+	NM
BRUNSWICK					
❏ BL 58054 [10]	Impressions of Outer Space	1954	15.00	30.00	60.00
DECCA					
❏ DL 5526 [10]	The Larry Elgart Band with Strings	1954	25.00	50.00	100.00
❏ DL 8034 [M]	Music for Barefoot Ballerinas	1955	10.00	20.00	40.00
MGM					
❏ E-3891 [M]	Sophisticated Sixties	1960	3.75	7.50	15.00
❏ SE-3891 [S]	Sophisticated Sixties	1960	5.00	10.00	20.00
❏ E-3896 [M]	The Shape of Sounds to Come	1961	3.75	7.50	15.00
❏ SE-3896 [S]	The Shape of Sounds to Come	1961	5.00	10.00	20.00
❏ E-3961 [M]	Visions	1961	3.75	7.50	15.00
❏ SE-3961 [S]	Visions	1961	5.00	10.00	20.00
❏ E-4007 [M]	The City	1961	3.75	7.50	15.00
❏ SE-4007 [S]	The City	1961	5.00	10.00	20.00
❏ E-4028 [M]	Music in Motion!	1962	3.75	7.50	15.00
❏ SE-4028 [S]	Music in Motion!	1962	5.00	10.00	20.00
❏ E-4080 [M]	More Music in Motion!	1962	3.75	7.50	15.00
❏ SE-4080 [S]	More Music in Motion!	1962	5.00	10.00	20.00
PROJECT 3					
❏ PR 5102	The Larry Elgart Dance Band	1979	2.50	5.00	10.00
RCA CAMDEN					
❏ CAL-575 [M]	Easy Goin' Swing	1960	3.00	6.00	12.00
❏ CAS-575 [S]	Easy Goin' Swing	1960	3.75	7.50	15.00
❏ CXS-9036 [(2)]	That Old Feeling	1972	3.00	6.00	12.00
RCA VICTOR					
❏ LPM-1961 [M]	Larry Elgart and His Orchestra	1959	3.75	7.50	15.00
❏ LSP-1961 [S]	Larry Elgart and His Orchestra	1959	5.00	10.00	20.00
❏ LPM-2045 [M]	New Sounds at the Roosevelt	1959	3.75	7.50	15.00
❏ LSP-2045 [S]	New Sounds at the Roosevelt	1959	5.00	10.00	20.00
❏ LPM-2166 [M]	Saratoga	1960	3.75	7.50	15.00
❏ LSP-2166 [S]	Saratoga	1960	5.00	10.00	20.00

Number	Title	Yr	VG	VG+	NM
❑ AFL1-4095	Flight of the Condor	1981	2.50	5.00	10.00
❑ AFL1-4343	Hooked on Swing	1982	2.50	5.00	10.00
❑ AFL1-4589	Hooked on Swing, Volume 2	1983	2.50	5.00	10.00
❑ AFL1-4850	Larry Elgart and His Manhattan Swing Orchestra	1984	2.50	5.00	10.00
❑ AYL1-5025	Hooked on Swing	1984	2.00	4.00	8.00
-- Budget-line reissue					
❑ AYL1-5026	Hooked on Swing, Volume 2	1984	2.00	4.00	8.00
-- Budget-line reissue					
❑ AYL1-7178	(The Theme from) La Cage Aux Folles	1986	2.00	4.00	8.00

ELGART, LES
Trumpeter and bandleader. Also see LES AND LARRY ELGART.
CIRCLE
| ❑ CLP-126 | Les Elgart and His Orchestra | 198? | 2.50 | 5.00 | 10.00 |
COLUMBIA
❑ CL 536 [M]	Sophisticated Swing	1953	7.50	15.00	30.00
-- Maroon label, gold print					
❑ CL 594 [M]	Just One More Dance	1954	7.50	15.00	30.00
-- Maroon label, gold print					
❑ CL 619 [M]	The Band of the Year	1955	10.00	20.00	40.00
-- Maroon label, gold print; first LP appearance of "Bandstand Boogie"					
❑ CL 684 [M]	The Dancing Sound	1955	7.50	15.00	30.00
❑ CL 803 [M]	For Dancers Only	1956	7.50	15.00	30.00
❑ CL 873 [M]	The Elgart Touch	1956	7.50	15.00	30.00
-- Red and black label, six "eye" logos					
❑ CL 1008 [M]	For Dancers Also	1957	6.25	12.50	25.00
❑ CL 1052 [M]	Les and Larry Elgart and Their Orchestra	1957	5.00	10.00	20.00
❑ CL 1123 [M]	Sound Ideas	1958	5.00	10.00	20.00
❑ CL 1291 [M]	Les Elgart On Tour	1959	5.00	10.00	20.00
❑ CL 1350 [M]	The Great Sound of Les Elgart	1959	5.00	10.00	20.00
❑ CL 1450 [M]	The Band with That Sound	1960	5.00	10.00	20.00
❑ CL 1500 [M]	Designs for Dancing	1960	5.00	10.00	20.00
❑ CL 1567 [M]	Half Satin - Half Latin	1961	5.00	10.00	20.00
❑ CL 1659 [M]	It's De-Lovely	1961	5.00	10.00	20.00
❑ CL 1785 [M]	The Twist Goes to College	1962	5.00	10.00	20.00
❑ CL 1890 [M]	Best Band on Campus	1963	5.00	10.00	20.00
❑ CL 2503 [10]	Prom Date	1954	10.00	20.00	40.00
❑ CL 2578 [10]	Campus Hop	1955	10.00	20.00	40.00
❑ CL 2590 [10]	More of Les	1955	10.00	20.00	40.00
❑ CL 6287 [10]	Just One More Dance	195?	10.00	20.00	40.00
❑ CS 8002 [S]	Sound Ideas	1958	6.25	12.50	25.00
❑ CS 8092 [S]	Les and Larry Elgart and Their Orchestra	1959	6.25	12.50	25.00
❑ CS 8103 [S]	Les Elgart On Tour	1959	6.25	12.50	25.00
❑ CS 8159 [S]	The Great Sound of Les Elgart	1959	6.25	12.50	25.00
❑ CS 8245 [S]	The Band with That Sound	1960	6.25	12.50	25.00
❑ CS 8291 [S]	Designs for Dancing	1960	6.25	12.50	25.00
❑ CS 8367 [S]	Half Satin - Half Latin	1961	6.25	12.50	25.00
❑ CS 8459 [S]	It's De-Lovely	1961	6.25	12.50	25.00
❑ CS 8585 [S]	The Twist Goes to College	1962	6.25	12.50	25.00
❑ CS 8690 [S]	Best Band on Campus	1963	6.25	12.50	25.00
COLUMBIA SPECIAL PRODUCTS
| ❑ P 13168 | The Greatest Dance Band in the Land | 197? | 2.50 | 5.00 | 10.00 |
HARMONY
| ❑ HL 7374 [M] | The Greatest Dance Band in the Land | 196? | 3.00 | 6.00 | 12.00 |
| ❑ HS 11174 [R] | The Greatest Dance Band in the Land | 196? | 2.50 | 5.00 | 10.00 |

ELGART, LES AND LARRY
Twice the Elgart brothers joined in a big band. The first time, from 1953-59, is included in the LES ELGART listings. The second time, from 1963-70, is listed below. Also see LARRY ELGART.
COLUMBIA
❑ CL 2112 [M]	Big Band Hootenanny	1963	3.75	7.50	15.00
❑ CL 2221 [M]	Command Performance! Les & Larry Elgart Play the Great Dance Hits	1964	3.75	7.50	15.00
❑ CL 2301 [M]	The New Elgart Touch	1965	3.75	7.50	15.00
❑ CL 2355 [M]	Elgart Au-Go-Go	1965	3.75	7.50	15.00
❑ CL 2511 [M]	Sound of the Times	1966	3.75	7.50	15.00
❑ CL 2591 [M]	Warm and Sensuous	1966	3.75	7.50	15.00
❑ CL 2633 [M]	Girl Watchers	1967	5.00	10.00	20.00
❑ CL 2780 [M]	The Wonderful World of Today's Hits	1968	6.25	12.50	25.00
❑ CS 8912 [S]	Big Band Hootenanny	1963	5.00	10.00	20.00
❑ CS 9021 [S]	Command Performance! Les & Larry Elgart Play the Great Dance Hits	1964	5.00	10.00	20.00
❑ CS 9101 [S]	The New Elgart Touch	1965	5.00	10.00	20.00
❑ CS 9155 [S]	Elgart Au-Go-Go	1965	5.00	10.00	20.00
❑ CS 9311 [S]	Sound of the Times	1966	5.00	10.00	20.00
❑ CS 9391 [S]	Warm and Sensuous	1966	5.00	10.00	20.00
❑ CS 9433 [S]	Girl Watchers	1967	3.75	7.50	15.00

Number	Title	Yr	VG	VG+	NM
❑ CS 9580 [S]	The Wonderful World of Today's Hits	1968	3.75	7.50	15.00
❑ CS 9722	Les & Larry Elgart's Greatest Hits	1968	3.75	7.50	15.00
❑ PC 38341	Swingtime	1982	2.50	5.00	10.00
HARMONY					
❑ KH 32053	Wonderful World	1972	2.50	5.00	10.00
SWAMPFIRE					
❑ 201	Nashville Country Piano	196?	3.00	6.00	12.00
❑ 202	Nashville Country Brass	196?	3.00	6.00	12.00
❑ 203	Nashville Country Guitars	196?	3.00	6.00	12.00
❑ 207	Bridge Over Troubled Water	1971	3.00	6.00	12.00

ELIAS, ELIANE
Pianist and female singer.
BLUE NOTE
❑ BST-46994	Illusions	1987	2.50	5.00	10.00
❑ B1-48785	Cross Currents	1988	2.50	5.00	10.00
❑ B1-91411	So Far So Close	1989	3.00	6.00	12.00

ELIOVSON, STEVE
Guitarist.
ECM
| ❑ 1198 | Dawn Dance | 198? | 2.50 | 5.00 | 10.00 |

ELLIAS, RODDY
Guitarist and composer.
INNER CITY
| ❑ IC-1081 | A Night for Stars | 1980 | 2.50 | 5.00 | 10.00 |

ELLINGSON, PAUL
Pianist.
IVY JAZZ
| ❑ IJ1-E1-2 [(2)] | Solo Piano Jazz | 198? | 3.75 | 7.50 | 15.00 |

ELLINGTON, DUKE
Pianist, composer, arranger and bandleader – simply, one of America's greatest musical figures. Also see LOUIS ARMSTRONG; JOHN COLTRANE; THE DUKE'S MEN; THE ELLINGTONIANS; ELLA FITZGERALD; COLEMAN HAWKINS; JOHNNY HODGES; FRANK SINATRA.
AAMCO
❑ ALP-301 [M]	The Royal Concert of Duke Ellington, Vol. 1	196?	7.50	15.00	30.00
-- Reissue of Bethlehem material					
❑ ALP-313 [M]	The Royal Concert of Duke Ellington, Vol. 2	196?	7.50	15.00	30.00
-- Reissue of Bethlehem material					
ABC IMPULSE!
❑ 9256 [(2)]	Ellingtonia: Reevaluations, The Impulse Years	1973	3.75	7.50	15.00
❑ 9285 [(2)]	Ellingtonia, Volume 2	1974	3.75	7.50	15.00
❑ IA-9350 [(2)]	Great Tenor Encounters	1978	3.75	7.50	15.00
AIRCHECK
| ❑ 4 | Duke on the Air | 197? | 2.50 | 5.00 | 10.00 |
| ❑ 29 | Duke on the Air, Vol. 2 | 198? | 2.50 | 5.00 | 10.00 |
ALLEGRO
❑ 1591 [M]	Duke Ellington and His Orchestra Play	1955	12.50	25.00	50.00
❑ 3082 [M]	Duke Ellington	1953	12.50	25.00	50.00
❑ 4014 [10]	Duke Ellington and His Orchestra Play	1954	25.00	50.00	100.00
❑ 4038 [10]	Duke Ellington and His Orchestra Play	1954	25.00	50.00	100.00
ARCHIVE OF FOLK AND JAZZ
❑ 221	Early Duke Ellington	1968	3.00	6.00	12.00
❑ 249	Early Duke Ellington Vol. 2	1970	3.00	6.00	12.00
❑ 266	Early Duke Ellington Vol. 3	1972	3.00	6.00	12.00
❑ 327	Duke Ellington at Carnegie Hall	197?	3.00	6.00	12.00
ATLANTIC
❑ SD 2-304 [(2)]	The Great Paris Concert	1972	3.75	7.50	15.00
❑ QD 1580 [Q]	New Orleans Suite	1974	6.25	12.50	25.00
❑ SD 1580	New Orleans Suite	1971	3.00	6.00	12.00
❑ SD 1665	Recollections of the Big Band Era	1974	3.00	6.00	12.00
❑ SD 1688	Jazz Violin Session	1976	3.00	6.00	12.00
❑ 90043	Recollections of the Big Band Era	1982	2.50	5.00	10.00
BASF
| ❑ 21704 | Collages | 1973 | 3.00 | 6.00 | 12.00 |
BETHLEHEM
| ❑ BCP-60 [M] | Historically Speaking, The Duke | 1956 | 15.00 | 30.00 | 60.00 |
| ❑ BCP-6005 [M] | Duke Ellington Presents | 1956 | 15.00 | 30.00 | 60.00 |

Number	Title	Yr	VG	VG+	NM
❏ BCP-6013	The Bethlehem Years, Vol. 1	197?	2.50	5.00	10.00
BIOGRAPH					
❏ M-2	Band Shorts (1929-1935)	1978	2.50	5.00	10.00
BLUE NOTE					
❏ BT-85129	Money Jungle	1986	2.50	5.00	10.00
-- Reissue of United Artists 15017					
BLUEBIRD					
❏ 5659-1-RB [(4)]	Duke Ellington: The Blanton-Webster Band	1986	6.25	12.50	25.00
❏ 6287-1-RB	And His Mother Called Him Bill	1987	2.00	4.00	8.00
-- Reissue of RCA Victor 3906					
❏ 6641-1-RB [(4)]	Black, Brown and Beige	1988	6.25	12.50	25.00
❏ 6852-1-RB	Early Ellington	1989	2.50	5.00	10.00
BRIGHT ORANGE					
❏ 709	The Stereophonic Sound of Duke Ellington	1973	3.00	6.00	12.00
BRUNSWICK					
❏ BL 54007 [M]	Early Ellington	1954	12.50	25.00	50.00
❏ BL 58002 [10]	Ellingtonia, Volume 1	1950	25.00	50.00	100.00
❏ BL 58012 [10]	Ellingtonia, Volume 2	1950	25.00	50.00	100.00
BULLDOG					
❏ BDL-2021	20 Golden Pieces of Duke Ellington	198?	2.50	5.00	10.00
CAPITOL					
❏ H 440 [10]	Premiered by Ellington	1953	25.00	50.00	100.00
❏ H 477 [10]	The Duke Plays Ellington	1954	25.00	50.00	100.00
❏ T 477 [M]	The Duke Plays Ellington	1954	10.00	20.00	40.00
-- Turquoise label					
❏ T 477 [M]	The Duke Plays Ellington	1958	5.00	10.00	20.00
-- Black label with colorband, logo at left					
❏ T 521 [M]	Ellington '55	1955	10.00	20.00	40.00
-- Turquoise label					
❏ T 521 [M]	Ellington '55	1958	5.00	10.00	20.00
-- Black label with colorband, logo at left					
❏ T 637 [M]	Dance to the Duke	1955	10.00	20.00	40.00
-- Turquoise label					
❏ T 637 [M]	Dance to the Duke	1958	5.00	10.00	20.00
-- Black label with colorband, logo at left					
❏ T 679 [M]	Ellington Showcase	1956	10.00	20.00	40.00
-- Turquoise label					
❏ T 679 [M]	Ellington Showcase	1958	5.00	10.00	20.00
-- Black label with colorband, logo at left					
❏ DT 1602 [R]	The Best of Duke Ellington	1961	3.00	6.00	12.00
❏ SM-1602	The Best of Duke Ellington	197?	2.50	5.00	10.00
-- Reissue with new prefix					
❏ T 1602 [M]	The Best of Duke Ellington	1961	5.00	10.00	20.00
❏ M-11058	Piano Reflections	1972	3.00	6.00	12.00
❏ M-11674	Ellington '55	1977	2.50	5.00	10.00
❏ N-16172	The Best of Duke Ellington	198?	2.00	4.00	8.00
-- Budget-line reissue					
CIRCLE					
❏ CLP-101	Duke Ellington World Broadcasting Series, Vol. 1	1986	2.50	5.00	10.00
❏ CLP-102	Duke Ellington World Broadcasting Series, Vol. 2	1986	2.50	5.00	10.00
❏ CLP-103	Duke Ellington World Broadcasting Series, Vol. 3	1986	2.50	5.00	10.00
❏ CLP-104	Duke Ellington World Broadcasting Series, Vol. 4	199?	2.50	5.00	10.00
❏ CLP-105	Duke Ellington World Broadcasting Series, Vol. 5 (1943)	199?	2.50	5.00	10.00
❏ CLP-106	Duke Ellington World Broadcasting Series, Vol. 6 (1945)	1988	2.50	5.00	10.00
❏ CLP-108	Duke Ellington World Broadcasting Series, Vol. 8 (1945)	1988	2.50	5.00	10.00
❏ CLP-109	Duke Ellington World Broadcasting Series, Vol. 9 (1945)	1988	2.50	5.00	10.00
COLUMBIA					
❏ C3L 27 [M (3)]	The Ellington Era, Vol. 1	1963	10.00	20.00	40.00
❏ C3L 39 [M (3)]	The Ellington Era, Vol. 2	1964	10.00	20.00	40.00
❏ CL 558 [M]	The Music of Duke Ellington	1954	12.50	25.00	50.00
-- Maroon label with gold print					
❏ CL 558 [M]	The Music of Duke Ellington	1956	10.00	20.00	40.00
-- Red and black label with six "eye" logos					
❏ CL 558 [M]	The Music of Duke Ellington	1963	3.75	7.50	15.00
-- Red label with "Guaranteed High Fidelity" or "360 Sound Mono"					
❏ CL 663 [M]	Blue Light	1955	10.00	20.00	40.00
❏ CL 825 [M]	Masterpieces by Ellington	1956	10.00	20.00	40.00
-- Reissue of Columbia Masterworks 4418					
❏ CL 825 [M]	Masterpieces by Ellington	1963	3.75	7.50	15.00
-- Red label with "Guaranteed High Fidelity" or "360 Sound Mono"					
❏ CL 830 [M]	Hi-Fi Ellington Uptown	1956	10.00	20.00	40.00
❏ CL 830 [M]	Hi-Fi Ellington Uptown	1963	3.75	7.50	15.00
-- Red label with "Guaranteed High Fidelity" or "360 Sound Mono"					
❏ CL 848 [M]	Liberian Suite	1956	10.00	20.00	40.00
-- Reissue of Columbia 6073					

Number	Title	Yr	VG	VG+	NM
❏ CL 934 [M]	Ellington at Newport '56	1957	10.00	20.00	40.00
-- Red and black label with six "eye" logos					
❏ CL 934 [M]	Ellington at Newport '56	1963	3.75	7.50	15.00
-- Red label with "Guaranteed High Fidelity" or "360 Sound Mono"					
❏ CL 951 [M]	A Drum Is a Woman	1957	10.00	20.00	40.00
❏ CL 1033 [M]	Such Sweet Thunder	1957	10.00	20.00	40.00
❏ CL 1085 [M]	Ellington Indigos	1958	6.25	12.50	25.00
❏ CL 1085 [M]	Ellington Indigos	1963	3.75	7.50	15.00
-- Red label with "Guaranteed High Fidelity" or "360 Sound Mono"					
❏ CL 1162 [M]	Brown, Black and Beige	1958	6.25	12.50	25.00
❏ CL 1198 [M]	The Cosmic Scene	1959	20.00	40.00	80.00
❏ CL 1245 [M]	Newport 1958	1959	6.25	12.50	25.00
❏ CL 1282 [M]	Duke Ellington at the Bal Masque	1959	6.25	12.50	25.00
❏ CL 1323 [M]	Duke Ellington Jazz Party	1959	6.25	12.50	25.00
❏ CL 1400 [M]	Festival Session	1960	6.25	12.50	25.00
❏ CL 1445 [M]	Blues in Orbit	1960	6.25	12.50	25.00
❏ CL 1541 [M]	The Nutcracker Suite	1960	7.50	15.00	30.00
❏ CL 1546 [M]	Piano in the Background	1960	7.50	15.00	30.00
❏ CL 1546 [M]	Piano in the Background	1963	3.75	7.50	15.00
-- Red label with "Guaranteed High Fidelity" or "360 Sound Mono"					
❏ CL 1597 [M]	Peer Gynt Suite/Suite Thursday	1961	6.25	12.50	25.00
❏ CL 1715 [M]	First Time	1962	6.25	12.50	25.00
❏ CL 1790 [M]	All American	1962	5.00	10.00	20.00
❏ CL 1907 [M]	Midnight in Paris	1963	5.00	10.00	20.00
❏ CL 2522 [10]	Duke's Mixture	1955	20.00	40.00	80.00
❏ CL 2562 [10]	Here's the Duke	1955	20.00	40.00	80.00
❏ CL 2593 [10]	Al Hibbler with the Duke	1956	20.00	40.00	80.00
❏ CL 6024 [10]	Mood Ellington	1949	25.00	50.00	100.00
❏ CL 6073 [10]	Liberian Suite	1949	25.00	50.00	100.00
❏ CS 8015 [S]	Brown, Black and Beige	1958	7.50	15.00	30.00
❏ CS 8053 [S]	Ellington Indigos	1958	7.50	15.00	30.00
❏ CS 8053 [S]	Ellington Indigos	1963	3.75	7.50	15.00
-- Red label with "360 Sound Stereo"					
❏ PC 8053	Ellington Indigos	198?	2.00	4.00	8.00
-- Budget-line reissue					
❏ CS 8072 [S]	Newport 1958	1959	7.50	15.00	30.00
❏ CS 8098 [S]	Duke Ellington at the Bal Masque	1959	7.50	15.00	30.00
❏ CS 8127 [S]	Duke Ellington Jazz Party	1959	7.50	15.00	30.00
❏ CS 8241 [S]	Blues in Orbit	1960	7.50	15.00	30.00
❏ CS 8341 [S]	The Nutcracker Suite	1960	10.00	20.00	40.00
❏ CS 8346 [S]	Piano in the Background	1960	10.00	20.00	40.00
❏ CS 8346 [S]	Piano in the Background	1963	3.75	7.50	15.00
-- Red label with "360 Sound Stereo"					
❏ CS 8397 [S]	Peer Gynt Suite/Suite Thursday	1961	7.50	15.00	30.00
❏ CS 8515 [S]	First Time	1962	7.50	15.00	30.00
❏ CS 8590 [S]	All American	1962	6.25	12.50	25.00
❏ CS 8648 [R]	Ellington at Newport	1963	3.00	6.00	12.00
❏ PC 8648	Ellington at Newport	198?	2.00	4.00	8.00
-- Budget-line reissue					
❏ CS 8829 [S]	Midnight in Paris	1963	6.25	12.50	25.00
❏ CS 9629	Duke Ellington's Greatest Hits	1969	3.75	7.50	15.00
❏ KG 32064 [(2)]	Duke Ellington Presents Ivie Anderson	1973	3.75	7.50	15.00
❏ C 32471	Jazz at the Plaza -- Vol. II	1973	3.00	6.00	12.00
❏ G 32564 [(2)]	The World of Duke Ellington	1974	3.75	7.50	15.00
❏ KG 33341 [(2)]	The World of Duke Ellington, Volume 2	1975	3.75	7.50	15.00
❏ CG 33961 [(2)]	The World of Duke Ellington, Volume 3	1975	3.75	7.50	15.00
❏ PC 37340	It Don't Mean a Thing	1981	2.00	4.00	8.00
-- Reissue					
❏ FC 38028	The Girl's Suite & Perfume Suite	1982	2.50	5.00	10.00
COLUMBIA JAZZ MASTERPIECES					
❏ CJ 40586	First Time	1987	2.50	5.00	10.00
-- Reissue of Columbia 8515					
❏ CJ 40587	Ellington at Newport	1987	2.50	5.00	10.00
-- Reissue of Columbia 934					
❏ CJ 40712	Duke Ellington Jazz Party	1987	2.50	5.00	10.00
-- Reissue of Columbia 8127					
❏ CJ 40836	Uptown	1987	2.50	5.00	10.00
❏ CJ 44051	Blues in Orbit	1988	2.50	5.00	10.00
-- Reissue of Columbia 8241					
❏ CJ 44444	Ellington Indigos	1989	2.50	5.00	10.00
-- Reissue of Columbia 8053					
COLUMBIA JAZZ ODYSSEY					
❏ PC 36979	The Festival Session	1981	2.50	5.00	10.00
COLUMBIA MASTERWORKS					
❏ ML 4418 [M]	Masterpieces by Ellington	1951	25.00	50.00	100.00
❏ ML 4639 [M]	Ellington Uptown	1951	25.00	50.00	100.00
-- Blue or green label, gold print					
❏ ML 4639 [M]	Ellington Uptown	195?	12.50	25.00	50.00
-- Oddly, this exists as a reissue on the red and black "6 eye" label					
COLUMBIA SPECIAL PRODUCTS					
❏ P 14359	Suite Thursday/Controversial Suite/Harlem Suite	198?	2.50	5.00	10.00

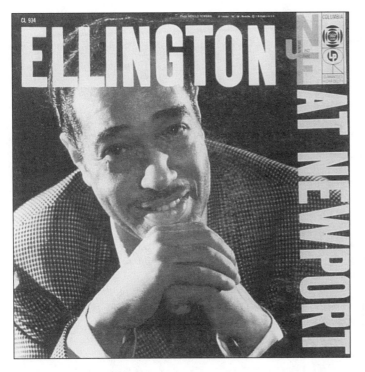

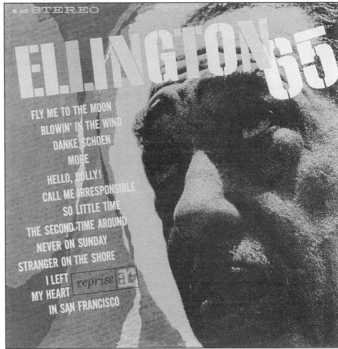

Not only is Duke Ellington among the giants of jazz, he's among the giants of American popular music, period. He truly is, as a prominent biography notes, "beyond category." (Top left) An early 10-inch LP that was a compilation of sides recorded for Victor in the early 1940s, it's a tough find today. (Top right) *Ellington Uptown* was issued in 1951, originally as part of the Columbia "Masterworks" numbering series, a rarity for a jazz artist. (Bottom left) *Ellington at Newport*, recorded in 1956, was a steady seller for Columbia, so much so that, even converted to rechanneled stereo, it remained in print into the 1980s on vinyl. (Bottom right) Ellington's time at the Reprise label in the mid-1960s is among his most underappreciated. He still could put his unique spin on hits of the day, as *Ellington '65* showed.

Number	Title	Yr	VG	VG+	NM
DAYBREAK					
❑ DR 2017	The Symphonic Ellington	1973	3.00	6.00	12.00
DECCA					
❑ DL 75069	Duke Ellington in Canada	1969	3.75	7.50	15.00
❑ DL 79224 [R]	Duke Ellington, Volume 1 -- In the Beginning	1958	6.25	12.50	25.00
-- Black label, silver print					
❑ DL 79224 [R]	Duke Ellington, Volume 1 -- In the Beginning	1961	3.75	7.50	15.00
-- Black label with color bars					
❑ DL 79241 [R]	Duke Ellington, Volume 2 -- Hot in Harlem	1959	6.25	12.50	25.00
-- Black label, silver print					
❑ DL 79241 [R]	Duke Ellington, Volume 2 -- Hot in Harlem	1961	3.75	7.50	15.00
-- Black label with color bars					
❑ DL 79247 [R]	Duke Ellington, Volume 3 -- Rockin' in Rhythm	1959	6.25	12.50	25.00
-- Black label, silver print					
❑ DL 79247 [R]	Duke Ellington, Volume 3 -- Rockin' in Rhythm	1961	3.75	7.50	15.00
-- Black label with color bars					
❑ DL 9224 [M]	Duke Ellington, Volume 1 -- In the Beginning	1958	10.00	20.00	40.00
-- Black label, silver print					
❑ DL 9224 [M]	Duke Ellington, Volume 1 -- In the Beginning	1961	6.25	12.50	25.00
-- Black label with color bars					
❑ DL 9241 [M]	Duke Ellington, Volume 2 -- Hot in Harlem	1959	10.00	20.00	40.00
-- Black label, silver print					
❑ DL 9241 [M]	Duke Ellington, Volume 2 -- Hot in Harlem	1961	6.25	12.50	25.00
-- Black label with color bars					
❑ DL 9247 [M]	Duke Ellington, Volume 3 -- Rockin' in Rhythm	1959	10.00	20.00	40.00
-- Black label, silver print					
❑ DL 9247 [M]	Duke Ellington, Volume 3 -- Rockin' in Rhythm	1961	6.25	12.50	25.00
-- Black label with color bars					
DISCOVERY					
❑ 841	Concert in the Virgin Islands	198?	2.50	5.00	10.00
-- Reissue of Reprise 6185					
❑ 871	Afro Bossa	198?	2.50	5.00	10.00
-- Reissue of Reprise 6069					
DO YOU LIKE JAZZ					
❑ P 13293	Monologue	1973	3.00	6.00	12.00
DOCTOR JAZZ					
❑ W2X 39137 [(2)]	All-Star Road Band	1984	3.00	6.00	12.00
❑ W2X 40012 [(2)]	All-Star Road Band, Vol. 2	1985	3.00	6.00	12.00
❑ FW 40030	Happy Reunion	1985	2.50	5.00	10.00
❑ FW 40359	New Mood Indigo	1986	2.50	5.00	10.00
FANTASY					
❑ OJC-108	Great Times!	198?	2.50	5.00	10.00
-- Reissue of Riverside 9475					
❑ OJC-446	The Ellington Suites	1990	2.50	5.00	10.00
-- Reissue of Pablo 2310 762					
❑ OJC-469	Latin American Suite	1990	2.50	5.00	10.00
-- Reissue of 8419					
❑ OJC-623	Duke Ellington Featuring Paul Gonsalves	1991	3.00	6.00	12.00
-- Reissue of 9636					
❑ OJC-624	The Intimacy of the Blues	1991	3.00	6.00	12.00
-- Reissue of 9640					
❑ OJC-633	Up in Duke's Workshop	1991	3.00	6.00	12.00
-- Reissue of Pablo 2310 815					
❑ OJC-645	The Afro-Eurasian Eclipse	1991	3.00	6.00	12.00
-- Reissue of 9498					
❑ F-8407/8 [(2)]	Duke Ellington's Second Sacred Concert	1971	3.75	7.50	15.00
❑ F-8419	Latin American Suite	1971	3.00	6.00	12.00
❑ F-9433	Yale Concert	1974	3.00	6.00	12.00
❑ F-9462	The Pianist	1974	3.00	6.00	12.00
❑ F-9498	Afro-American Eclipse	1976	3.00	6.00	12.00
❑ F-9636	Duke Ellington Featuring Paul Gonsalves	198?	2.50	5.00	10.00
❑ F-9640	The Intimacy of the Blues	1986	2.50	5.00	10.00
FLYING DUTCHMAN					
❑ BXL1-2832	It Don't Mean a Thing	1978	2.50	5.00	10.00
-- Reissue					
❑ 10112	My People	1969	3.75	7.50	15.00
❑ 10166	It Don't Mean a Thing	1973	3.00	6.00	12.00
FOLKWAYS					
❑ FJ-2968	First Annual Tour of the Pacific Northwest, Spring, 1952	198?	2.50	5.00	10.00
GALAXY					
❑ 4807	Duke Ellington and His Famous Orchestra and Soloists	197?	3.75	7.50	15.00
GNP CRESCENDO					
❑ GNP-9045	The 1953 Pasadena Concert	1986	2.50	5.00	10.00
❑ GNP-9049	The 1954 Los Angeles Concert	1987	2.50	5.00	10.00
HALL OF FAME					
❑ 625/6/7 [(3)]	The Immortal Duke Ellington	197?	5.00	10.00	20.00
HARMONY					
❑ HL 7436 [M]	Fantasies	1967	3.75	7.50	15.00
❑ HS 11236 [R]	Fantasies	1967	3.00	6.00	12.00
❑ HS 11323	In My Solitude	1969	3.00	6.00	12.00
❑ H 30566	Duke Ellington's Greatest Hits Live	1971	3.00	6.00	12.00
HINDSIGHT					
❑ HSR-125	Duke Ellington 1946	198?	2.50	5.00	10.00
❑ HSR-126	Duke Ellington 1946, Volume 2	198?	2.50	5.00	10.00
❑ HSR-127	Duke Ellington 1946, Volume 3	198?	2.50	5.00	10.00
❑ HSR-128	Duke Ellington 1947	198?	2.50	5.00	10.00
❑ HSR-129	Duke Ellington 1947, Volume 2	198?	2.50	5.00	10.00
IAJRC					
❑ LP-45	Fairfield, Connecticut Jazz Fest 1956	198?	2.00	4.00	8.00
INTERMEDIA					
❑ QS-5002	Sophisticated Duke	198?	2.50	5.00	10.00
❑ QS-5020	Lullaby of Birdland	198?	2.50	5.00	10.00
❑ QS-5021	Do Nothin' Till You Hear from Me	198?	2.50	5.00	10.00
❑ QS-5063	Satin Doll	198?	2.50	5.00	10.00
JAZZ ODYSSEY					
❑ 32-16-0252	Nutcracker and Peer Gynt Suites	196?	3.00	6.00	12.00
JAZZ PANORAMA					
❑ 1802 [10]	Duke Ellington -- Vol. 1	1951	25.00	50.00	100.00
❑ 1811 [10]	Duke Ellington -- Vol. 2	1951	25.00	50.00	100.00
❑ 1816 [10]	Duke Ellington -- Vol. 3	1951	25.00	50.00	100.00
JAZZBIRD					
❑ 2009	Meadowbrook to Manhattan	1980	2.50	5.00	10.00
LONDON					
❑ AL-3551 [10]	The Duke -- 1926	195?	25.00	50.00	100.00
MCA					
❑ 1358	Duke Ellington, Volume 1 -- In the Beginning	198?	2.00	4.00	8.00
-- Reissue of 2075					
❑ 1359	Duke Ellington, Volume 2 -- Hot in Harlem	198?	2.00	4.00	8.00
-- Reissue of 2076					
❑ 1360	Duke Ellington, Volume 3 -- Rockin' in Rhythm	198?	2.00	4.00	8.00
-- Reissue of 2077					
❑ 2075	Duke Ellington, Volume 1 -- In the Beginning	197?	2.50	5.00	10.00
-- Reissue of Decca 79224					
❑ 2076	Duke Ellington, Volume 2 -- Hot in Harlem	197?	2.50	5.00	10.00
-- Reissue of Decca 79241					
❑ 2077	Duke Ellington, Volume 3 -- Rockin' in Rhythm	197?	2.50	5.00	10.00
-- Reissue of Decca 79247					
❑ 4142 [(2)]	Great Tenor Encounters	198?	3.00	6.00	12.00
-- Reissue of Impulse! 9350					
❑ 42325	The Brunswick Era, Vol. 1	1990	3.00	6.00	12.00
MOBILE FIDELITY					
❑ 1-214	Anatomy of a Murder	1995	10.00	20.00	40.00
-- Audiophile vinyl					
MOSAIC					
❑ MQ8-160 [(8)]	The Complete Capitol Recordings of Duke Ellington	199?	37.50	75.00	150.00
MUSICRAFT					
❑ 2002	Carnegie Hall Concert	1986	2.50	5.00	10.00
PABLO					
❑ 2310 703	Duke's Big 4	1974	3.00	6.00	12.00
❑ 2310 721	This One's for Blanton	197?	3.00	6.00	12.00
❑ 2310 762	The Ellington Suites	197?	3.00	6.00	12.00
❑ 2310 787	Intimate	197?	3.00	6.00	12.00
❑ 2310 815	Up in Duke's Workshop	1980	2.50	5.00	10.00
❑ 2405 401	The Best of Duke Ellington	198?	2.50	5.00	10.00
PABLO LIVE					
❑ 2308 245	Harlem	198?	2.50	5.00	10.00
❑ 2308 247	In the Uncommon Market	198?	2.50	5.00	10.00
PAIR					
❑ PDL2-1011 [(2)]	Original Recordings by Duke Ellington	1986	3.00	6.00	12.00
PICCADILLY					
❑ 3524	Classic Ellington	198?	2.50	5.00	10.00

Number	Title	Yr	VG	VG+	NM
PICKWICK					
❑ SPC-3390	We Love You Madly	197?	2.50	5.00	10.00
PRESTIGE					
❑ 24029 [(2)]	The Golden Duke	1973	3.75	7.50	15.00
❑ 24045 [(2)]	Duke Ellington's Second Sacred Concert	1974	3.00	6.00	12.00
-- Reissue of Fantasy 8407/8					
❑ 24073 [(2)]	The Carnegie Hall Concerts: December 1944	197?	3.75	7.50	15.00
❑ 24074 [(2)]	The Carnegie Hall Concerts: January 1946	197?	3.75	7.50	15.00
❑ 24075 [(2)]	The Carnegie Hall Concerts: December 1947	197?	3.75	7.50	15.00
❑ 34003 [(3)]	The Carnegie Hall Concerts: January 1943	197?	5.00	10.00	20.00
RCA CAMDEN					
❑ ACL2-0152 [(2)]	Mood Indigo	1973	3.75	7.50	15.00
❑ CAL-394 [M]	Duke Ellington at Tanglewood	1958	5.00	10.00	20.00
❑ CAL-459 [M]	Duke Ellington at the Cotton Club	1959	5.00	10.00	20.00
❑ ACL-7052	The Duke at Tanglewood	197?	2.50	5.00	10.00
-- Reissue of RCA Red Seal LSC-2857					
RCA VICTOR					
❑ WPT-11 [10]	Duke Ellington	1951	25.00	50.00	100.00
❑ LPV-506 [M]	Daybreak Express	1964	5.00	10.00	20.00
❑ LPV-517 [M]	Jumpin' Punkins	1965	5.00	10.00	20.00
❑ LPV-541 [M]	Johnny Come Lately	1967	5.00	10.00	20.00
❑ LPV-553 [M]	Pretty Woman	1968	5.00	10.00	20.00
❑ LPV-568 [M]	Flaming Youth	1969	5.00	10.00	20.00
❑ LJM-1002 [M]	Seattle Concert	1954	12.50	25.00	50.00
❑ LPT-1004 [M]	Ellington's Greatest	1954	10.00	20.00	40.00
❑ APL1-1023	Eastbourne Performance	1974	3.00	6.00	12.00
❑ LPM-1092 [M]	Duke and His Men	1955	10.00	20.00	40.00
❑ LPM-1364 [M]	In a Mellotone	1957	10.00	20.00	40.00
❑ LPM-1715 [M]	Duke Ellington at His Very Best	1958	10.00	20.00	40.00
❑ ANL1-2811	Pure Gold	1978	2.50	5.00	10.00
❑ LPT-3017 [10]	This Is Duke Ellington and His Orchestra	1952	25.00	50.00	100.00
❑ LPT-3067 [10]	Duke Ellington Plays the Blues	1952	25.00	50.00	100.00
❑ LPM-3576 [M]	The Popular Duke Ellington	1966	3.75	7.50	15.00
❑ LPM-3582 [M]	Concert of Sacred Music	1966	3.75	7.50	15.00
❑ LPM-3782 [M]	Far East Suite	1967	6.25	12.50	25.00
❑ LPM-3906 [M]	And His Mother Called Him Bill	1968	12.50	25.00	50.00
❑ CPL2-4098 [(2)]	Sophisticated Ellington	1983	3.00	6.00	12.00
❑ LPM-6009 [(2) M]	The Indispensible Duke Ellington	1961	12.50	25.00	50.00
❑ LSP-3576 [S]	The Popular Duke Ellington	1966	5.00	10.00	20.00
❑ LSP-3582 [S]	Concert of Sacred Music	1966	5.00	10.00	20.00
❑ LSP-3782 [S]	Far East Suite	1967	3.75	7.50	15.00
❑ LSP-3906 [S]	And His Mother Called Him Bill	1968	3.75	7.50	15.00
❑ VPM-6042 [(2)]	This Is Duke Ellington	1972	3.75	7.50	15.00
RCA VICTOR RED SEAL					
❑ LM-2857 [M]	The Duke at Tanglewood	1966	3.75	7.50	15.00
❑ LSC-2857 [S]	The Duke at Tanglewood	1966	5.00	10.00	20.00
REPRISE					
❑ R-6069 [M]	Afro-Bossa	1962	5.00	10.00	20.00
❑ R9-6069 [S]	Afro-Bossa	1962	5.00	10.00	20.00
❑ R-6097 [M]	The Symphonic Ellington	1963	5.00	10.00	20.00
❑ R9-6097 [S]	The Symphonic Ellington	1963	5.00	10.00	20.00
❑ R-6122 [M]	Ellington '65: Hits of the '60s/ This Time by Ellington	1964	5.00	10.00	20.00
❑ RS-6122 [S]	Ellington '65: Hits of the '60s/ This Time by Ellington	1964	5.00	10.00	20.00
❑ R-6141 [M]	Mary Poppins	1964	5.00	10.00	20.00
❑ RS-6141 [S]	Mary Poppins	1964	5.00	10.00	20.00
❑ R-6154 [M]	Ellington '66	1965	5.00	10.00	20.00
❑ RS-6154 [S]	Ellington '66	1965	3.75	7.50	15.00
❑ R-6168 [M]	Will Big Bands Ever Come Back?	1965	5.00	10.00	20.00
❑ RS-6168 [S]	Will Big Bands Ever Come Back?	1965	3.75	7.50	15.00
❑ R-6185 [M]	Concert in the Virgin Islands	1965	5.00	10.00	20.00
❑ RS-6185 [S]	Concert in the Virgin Islands	1965	3.75	7.50	15.00
❑ R-6234 [M]	Duke Ellington's Greatest Hits	1967	5.00	10.00	20.00
❑ RS-6234 [S]	Duke Ellington's Greatest Hits	1967	3.75	7.50	15.00
RIVERSIDE					
❑ RLP-12-129 [M]	Birth of Big Band Jazz	195?	7.50	15.00	30.00
-- Blue label with mike logo					
❑ RLP-12-129 [M]	Birth of Big Band Jazz	1956	15.00	30.00	60.00
-- White label, blue print					
❑ RLP-475 [M]	Great Times!	1963	6.25	12.50	25.00
❑ RS-9475 [S]	Great Times!	1963	6.25	12.50	25.00
RONDO-LETTE					
❑ A-7 [M]	Duke Ellington and Orchestra	1958	7.50	15.00	30.00
ROULETTE					
❑ 108 [(2)]	Echoes of An Era	1971	3.75	7.50	15.00
ROYALE					
❑ 18143 [10]	Duke Ellington and His Orchestra	195?	12.50	25.00	50.00
❑ 18152 [10]	Duke Ellington Plays Ellington	195?	12.50	25.00	50.00
SOLID STATE					
❑ SM-18022	Money Jungle	1968	3.75	7.50	15.00
-- Reissue of United Artists 15017					
❑ SS-19000 [(2)]	75th Birthday	1970	5.00	10.00	20.00
STANYAN					
❑ 10105	For Always	197?	3.00	6.00	12.00
STORYVILLE					
❑ SLP-4003	Duke Ellington and His Orchestra	198?	2.50	5.00	10.00
SUPER MAJESTIC					
❑ 2000	Duke Ellington	197?	3.00	6.00	12.00
SUTTON					
❑ SU-276 [M]	Duke Meets Leonard Feather	196?	3.00	6.00	12.00
TREND					
❑ 2004	Carnegie Hall Concert	198?	2.50	5.00	10.00
❑ 529	The Symphonic Ellington	1982	5.00	10.00	20.00
UNITED ARTISTS					
❑ UXS-92 [(2)]	Togo Bravo Suite	1972	3.75	7.50	15.00
❑ UAS-5632	Money Jungle	1972	3.00	6.00	12.00
-- Reissue					
❑ UAJ-14017 [M]	Money Jungle	1962	10.00	20.00	40.00
❑ UAJS-15017 [S]	Money Jungle	1962	10.00	20.00	40.00
VEE JAY					
❑ VJS-3061	Love You Madly	198?	2.50	5.00	10.00
VERVE					
❑ V-8701 [M]	Soul Call	1967	3.75	7.50	15.00
❑ V6-8701 [S]	Soul Call	1967	3.00	6.00	12.00
"X"					
❑ LVA-3037 [10]	Duke Ellington Plays	1955	25.00	50.00	100.00

ELLINGTON, DUKE, ORCHESTRA (MERCER ELLINGTON, DIRECTOR)

Recordings made after Duke's son Mercer took over the orchestra in 1974.

Number	Title	Yr	VG	VG+	NM
DOCTOR JAZZ					
❑ FW 40029	Hot and Bothered: A Re-Creation	1986	2.50	5.00	10.00
❑ FW 40359	New Mood Indigo	1987	2.50	5.00	10.00
FANTASY					
❑ F-9481	Continuum	1975	3.00	6.00	12.00
GRP					
❑ GR-1038	Digital Duke	1987	2.50	5.00	10.00
HOLIDAY					
❑ HDY 1916	Take the Holiday Train	1980	2.00	4.00	8.00

ELLINGTON, MERCER

Trumpet player, bandleader and composer; took over the DUKE ELLINGTON ORCHESTRA after his father's death.

Number	Title	Yr	VG	VG+	NM
CORAL					
❑ CRL 572?? [M]	Black and Tan Fantasy	1958	7.50	15.00	30.00
❑ CRL 57225 [M]	Stepping Into Swing Society	1958	7.50	15.00	30.00
❑ CRL 57293 [M]	Colors in Rhythm	1959	7.50	15.00	30.00
❑ CRL 7572?? [S]	Black and Tan Fantasy	1958	10.00	20.00	40.00
❑ CRL 757225 [S]	Stepping Into Swing Society	1958	10.00	20.00	40.00
❑ CRL 757293 [S]	Colors in Rhythm	1959	10.00	20.00	40.00
MCA					
❑ 349	Black and Tan Fantasy	197?	3.00	6.00	12.00

ELLINGTONIANS, THE

Assorted members of DUKE ELLINGTON's orchestra. Also see THE DUKE'S MEN.

Number	Title	Yr	VG	VG+	NM
MERCER					
❑ LP-1004 [10]	The Ellingtonians with Al Hibbler	1951	30.00	60.00	120.00

ELLIOT, MIKE

Guitarist.

Number	Title	Yr	VG	VG+	NM
ASI					
❑ 5001	Natural Life	197?	2.50	5.00	10.00
❑ 5003	Atrio	197?	2.50	5.00	10.00
❑ 5007	City Traffic	197?	2.50	5.00	10.00
PAUSA					
❑ 7139	Diffusion	1981	2.50	5.00	10.00

ELLIOT, RICHARD

Tenor saxophone player.

Number	Title	Yr	VG	VG+	NM
INTIMA					
❑ SJ-73233	Trolltown	1987	3.00	6.00	12.00
❑ SJE-73283	Initial Approach	1987	2.50	5.00	10.00
-- Reissue of ITI album					
❑ D1-73321	The Power of Suggestion	1988	3.00	6.00	12.00

Number	Title	Yr	VG	VG+	NM
❑ D1-73348	Take to the Skies	1989	3.00	6.00	12.00
ITI					
❑ JL-030	Initial Approach	198?	3.75	7.50	15.00

ELLIOTT, DON
Mellophone player, male singer, and occasional trumpeter and vibraphone player. Also see BOB CORWIN; PAUL DESMOND; THE NUTTY SQUIRRELS; CAL TJADER.

Number	Title	Yr	VG	VG+	NM
ABC-PARAMOUNT					
❑ ABC-106 [M]	Musical Offering	1956	10.00	20.00	40.00
❑ ABC-142 [M]	Don Elliott at the Modern Jazz Room	1956	10.00	20.00	40.00
❑ ABC-190 [M]	The Voices of Don Elliott	1957	12.50	25.00	50.00
❑ ABC-228 [M]	Jamaica Jazz	1958	10.00	20.00	40.00
❑ ABCS-228 [S]	Jamaica Jazz	1959	7.50	15.00	30.00
BETHLEHEM					
❑ BCP-12 [M]	Mellophone	1955	12.50	25.00	50.00
❑ BCP-15 [M]	Don Elliott Sings	1955	12.50	25.00	50.00
COLUMBIA					
❑ PC 33799	Rejuvenation	1975	3.00	6.00	12.00
DECCA					
❑ DL 9208 [M]	The Mello Sound	1958	10.00	20.00	40.00
❑ DL 79208 [S]	The Mello Sound	1958	12.50	25.00	50.00
DESIGN					
❑ DLP-69 [M]	Music for the Sensational 60's	196?	3.75	7.50	15.00
❑ DLPS-69 [S]	Music for the Sensational 60's	196?	3.00	6.00	12.00
HALLMARK					
❑ 317 [M]	Pal Joey	1957	12.50	25.00	50.00
JAZZLAND					
❑ JLP-15 [M]	Double Trumpet Doings	1960	10.00	20.00	40.00
❑ JLP-915 [S]	Double Trumpet Doings	1960	7.50	15.00	30.00
RCA VICTOR					
❑ LJM-1007 [M]	Don Elliott Quintet	1954	15.00	30.00	60.00
RIVERSIDE					
❑ RLP 12-218 [M]	Counterpoint for Six Valves	195?	10.00	20.00	40.00
-- Blue label, microphone logo					
❑ RLP 12-218 [M]	Counterpoint for Six Valves	1956	25.00	50.00	100.00
-- White label, blue print					
❑ RLP-2517 [10]	Six Valves	1955	30.00	60.00	120.00
SAVOY					
❑ MG-9033 [10]	The Versatile Don Elliott	1953	30.00	60.00	120.00
VANGUARD					
❑ VRS-8016 [10]	Doubles in Brass	1954	25.00	50.00	100.00

ELLIOTT, DON/SAM MOST
Also see each artist's individual listings.

Number	Title	Yr	VG	VG+	NM
JAZZTONE					
❑ J-1256 [M]	Doubles in Jazz	1957	10.00	20.00	40.00
VANGUARD					
❑ VRS-8522 [M]	Doubles in Jazz	1957	15.00	30.00	60.00
-- Partial reissue of 8016 and 8014					

ELLIS, ANITA
Female singer.

Number	Title	Yr	VG	VG+	NM
ELEKTRA					
❑ EKL-179 [M]	The World in My Arms	1959	10.00	20.00	40.00
EPIC					
❑ LN 3280 [M]	I Wonder What Became of Me	1956	10.00	20.00	40.00
❑ LN 3419 [M]	Him	1958	10.00	20.00	40.00

ELLIS, DON
Trumpeter, composer and bandleader.

Number	Title	Yr	VG	VG+	NM
ATLANTIC					
❑ SD 18227	Survival/Music from Other Galaxies and Planets	1977	3.00	6.00	12.00
❑ SD 19178	Live at Montreux	1977	3.00	6.00	12.00
BARNABY					
❑ BR-5020	How Time Passes	197?	3.00	6.00	12.00
-- Reissue of Candid LP					
BASF					
❑ 25123	Soaring	1973	3.75	7.50	15.00
❑ 25341	Haiku	1974	3.75	7.50	15.00
CANDID					
❑ CJM-8004 [M]	How Time Passes	1961	12.50	25.00	50.00
❑ CJS-9004 [S]	How Time Passes	1961	15.00	30.00	60.00
COLUMBIA					
❑ CL 2785 [M]	Electric Bath	1968	7.50	15.00	30.00
❑ CS 9585 [S]	Electric Bath	1968	3.75	7.50	15.00
❑ CS 9668	Shock Treatment	1968	3.75	7.50	15.00
❑ CS 9721	Autumn	1969	3.75	7.50	15.00
❑ CS 9889	The New Don Ellis Band Goes Underground	1969	5.00	10.00	20.00

Number	Title	Yr	VG	VG+	NM
❑ CG 30243 [(2)]	Don Ellis at the Fillmore	197?	3.75	7.50	15.00
-- Reissue with new prefix					
❑ G 30243 [(2)]	Don Ellis at the Fillmore	1970	5.00	10.00	20.00
❑ CG 30927 [(2)]	Tears of Joy	197?	3.75	7.50	15.00
-- Reissue with new prefix					
❑ G 30927 [(2)]	Tears of Joy	1971	5.00	10.00	20.00
❑ KC 31766	Connection	1972	3.75	7.50	15.00
FANTASY					
❑ OJC-431	New Ideas	1990	3.00	6.00	12.00
NEW JAZZ					
❑ NJLP-8257 [M]	New Ideas	1961	12.50	25.00	50.00
-- Purple label					
❑ NJLP-8257 [M]	New Ideas	1965	6.25	12.50	25.00
-- Blue label, trident logo at right					
PACIFIC JAZZ					
❑ PJ-55 [M]	Essence	1962	7.50	15.00	30.00
❑ ST-55 [S]	Essence	1962	10.00	20.00	40.00
❑ PJ-10112 [M]	Don Ellis "Live" At Monterey	1967	5.00	10.00	20.00
❑ PJ-10123 [M]	Live in 3/2 3/4 Time	1967	5.00	10.00	20.00
❑ ST-20112 [S]	Don Ellis "Live" At Monterey	1967	3.75	7.50	15.00
❑ ST-20123 [S]	Live in 3/2 3/4 Time	1967	3.75	7.50	15.00
PAUSA					
❑ 7028	Soaring	1979	2.50	5.00	10.00
-- Reissue of BASF 25123					
PRESTIGE					
❑ PRST-7607	New Ideas	1969	3.75	7.50	15.00

ELLIS, HERB
Guitarist.

Number	Title	Yr	VG	VG+	NM
COLUMBIA					
❑ CL 2330 [M]	Herb Ellis Guitar	1965	3.75	7.50	15.00
❑ CS 9130 [S]	Herb Ellis Guitar	1965	5.00	10.00	20.00
CONCORD JAZZ					
❑ CJ-77	Soft and Mellow	1979	2.50	5.00	10.00
❑ CJ-116	Herb Ellis at Montreux, Summer 1979	1980	2.50	5.00	10.00
❑ CJ-181	Herb Mix	1982	2.50	5.00	10.00
DOT					
❑ DLP-3678 [M]	The Man with the Guitar	1965	3.75	7.50	15.00
❑ DLP-25678 [S]	The Man with the Guitar	1965	5.00	10.00	20.00
EPIC					
❑ LA 16034 [M]	The Midnight Roll	1962	6.25	12.50	25.00
❑ LA 16036 [M]	Three Guitars in Bossa Nova Time	1963	5.00	10.00	20.00
❑ LA 16039 [M]	Herb Ellis and "Stuff" Smith Together	1963	5.00	10.00	20.00
❑ BA 17034 [S]	The Midnight Roll	1962	7.50	15.00	30.00
❑ BA 17036 [S]	Three Guitars in Bossa Nova Time	1963	6.25	12.50	25.00
❑ BA 17039 [S]	Herb Ellis and "Stuff" Smith Together	1963	6.25	12.50	25.00
NORGRAN					
❑ MGN-1081 [M]	Ellis in Wonderland	1956	25.00	50.00	100.00
VERVE					
❑ MGVS-6045 [S]	Herb Ellis Meets Jimmy Giuffre	1960	10.00	20.00	40.00
❑ MGVS-6164 [S]	Thank You, Charlie Christian	1960	10.00	20.00	40.00
❑ MGV-8171 [M]	Ellis in Wonderland	1957	12.50	25.00	50.00
-- Reissue of Norgran 1081					
❑ V-8171 [M]	Ellis in Wonderland	1961	5.00	10.00	20.00
❑ MGV-8252 [M]	Nothing But the Blues	1958	12.50	25.00	50.00
❑ V-8252 [M]	Nothing But the Blues	1961	5.00	10.00	20.00
❑ MGV-8278 [M]	Herb Ellis	1958	---	---	---
-- Canceled					
❑ MGV-8311 [M]	Herb Ellis Meets Jimmy Giuffre	1959	12.50	25.00	50.00
❑ V-8311 [M]	Herb Ellis Meets Jimmy Giuffre	1961	5.00	10.00	20.00
❑ V6-8311 [S]	Herb Ellis Meets Jimmy Giuffre	1961	5.00	10.00	20.00
❑ MGV-8381 [M]	Thank You, Charlie Christian	1960	12.50	25.00	50.00
❑ V-8381 [M]	Thank You, Charlie Christian	1961	5.00	10.00	20.00
❑ V6-8381 [S]	Thank You, Charlie Christian	1961	5.00	10.00	20.00
❑ V-8448 [M]	Softly...But With That Feeling	1962	5.00	10.00	20.00
❑ V6-8448 [S]	Softly...But With That Feeling	1962	6.25	12.50	25.00

ELLIS, HERB, AND RAY BROWN
Also see each artist's individual listings.

Number	Title	Yr	VG	VG+	NM
CONCORD JAZZ					
❑ CJ-3	Soft Shoe	197?	3.00	6.00	12.00
❑ CJ-6	After You've Gone	197?	3.00	6.00	12.00
❑ CJ-10	Rhythm Willie	197?	3.00	6.00	12.00
❑ CJ-12	Hot Tracks	1977	3.00	6.00	12.00

ELLIS, HERB, AND RED MITCHELL
Also see each artist's individual listings.

Number	Title	Yr	VG	VG+	NM
CONCORD JAZZ					
❑ CJ-372	Doggin' Around	1989	3.00	6.00	12.00

Number	Title	Yr	VG	VG+	NM

ELLIS, HERB, AND REMO PALMIER
Also see each artist's individual listings.
CONCORD JAZZ
| ❑ CJ-56 | Windflower | 1978 | 3.00 | 6.00 | 12.00 |

ELLIS, HERB, AND JOE PASS
Also see each artist's individual listings.
CONCORD JAZZ
| ❑ CJ-1 | Jazz/Concord | 197? | 3.75 | 7.50 | 15.00 |
| ❑ CJ-2 | Seven Come Eleven | 197? | 3.75 | 7.50 | 15.00 |
PABLO
| ❑ 2310 714 | Two for the Road | 1974 | 3.75 | 7.50 | 15.00 |

ELLIS, HERB, AND ROSS TOMPKINS
Also see each artist's individual listings.
CONCORD JAZZ
| ❑ CJ-17 | A Pair to Draw On | 1977 | 3.00 | 6.00 | 12.00 |

ELLIS, LLOYD
Guitarist.
CARLTON
| ❑ LP 12/104 [M] | Fastest Guitar in the World | 1958 | 12.50 | 25.00 | 50.00 |
FAMOUS DOOR
| ❑ HL-100 | Las Vegas 3 AM | 197? | 3.00 | 6.00 | 12.00 |
TREY
| ❑ T-902 [M] | So Tall, So Cool | 1960 | 7.50 | 15.00 | 30.00 |

ELLIS, PEE WEE
Tenor saxophone player.
SAVOY
| ❑ SJL-3301 | Home in the Country | 1976 | 5.00 | 10.00 | 20.00 |

ELMAN, ZIGGY
Trumpeter and bandleader.
CIRCLE
| ❑ 70 | Ziggy Elman and His Orchestra 1947 | 198? | 2.50 | 5.00 | 10.00 |
MGM
❑ E-163 [10]	Dancing with Zig	1952	12.50	25.00	50.00
❑ E-535 [10]	Ziggy Elman and His Orchestra	195?	12.50	25.00	50.00
❑ E-3389 [M]	Sentimental Trumpet	1956	10.00	20.00	40.00
SUNBEAM
| ❑ 202 | Angels Sing 1938-39 | 198? | 2.50 | 5.00 | 10.00 |

ELSTAK, NEDLEY
Trumpeter.
ESP-DISK'
| ❑ 1076 | The Machine | 1969 | 5.00 | 10.00 | 20.00 |

ELY, CHET
GHB
| ❑ 67 | Til Times Get Better | 197? | 2.50 | 5.00 | 10.00 |

EMMONS, BUDDY
Steel guitar player, better known in the country-western realm.
MERCURY
| ❑ MG-20843 [M] | Steel Guitar Jazz | 1963 | 20.00 | 40.00 | 80.00 |
| ❑ SR-60843 [S] | Steel Guitar Jazz | 1963 | 25.00 | 50.00 | 100.00 |

ENEVOLDSEN, BOB
Trombone player (both slide and valve), bass clarinet player, and tenor saxophone player.
LIBERTY
| ❑ LJH-6008 [M] | Smorgasboard | 1956 | 12.50 | 25.00 | 50.00 |
NOCTURNE
| ❑ NLP-6 [M] | Bob Enevoldsen Quintet | 1954 | 37.50 | 75.00 | 150.00 |
TAMPA
❑ TP-14 [M]	Reflections in Jazz	1957	25.00	50.00	100.00
-- Colored vinyl					
❑ TP-14 [M]	Reflections in Jazz	1958	12.50	25.00	50.00
-- Black vinyl					

ENNIS, ETHEL
Female singer.
BASF
| ❑ 25121 | 10 Sides of Ethel Ennis | 1973 | 3.75 | 7.50 | 15.00 |
CAPITOL
| ❑ T 941 | Change of Scenery | 1957 | 10.00 | 20.00 | 40.00 |

JUBILEE
❑ JLP-1021 [M]	Lullabies for Losers	1956	12.50	25.00	50.00
❑ JLP-5024 [M]	Ethel Ennis Sings	1963	5.00	10.00	20.00
❑ SJLP-5024 [S]	Ethel Ennis Sings	1963	6.25	12.50	25.00
RCA CAMDEN
| ❑ ACL1-0157 | God Bless the Child | 1973 | 2.50 | 5.00 | 10.00 |
RCA VICTOR
❑ LPM-2786 [M]	This Is Ethel Ennis	1964	5.00	10.00	20.00
❑ LSP-2786 [S]	This Is Ethel Ennis	1964	6.25	12.50	25.00
❑ LPM-2984 [M]	Eyes for You	1964	5.00	10.00	20.00
❑ LSP-2984 [S]	Eyes for You	1964	6.25	12.50	25.00

ENNIS, SKINNAY
Male singer.
HINDSIGHT
| ❑ HSR-164 | Skinnay Ennis 1947-48 | 198? | 2.50 | 5.00 | 10.00 |

ENRIQUEZ, BOBBY
Pianist.
GNP CRESCENDO
❑ GNPS-2144	The Wildman	198?	2.00	4.00	8.00
❑ GNPS-2148	The Wildman Meets the Madman	198?	2.00	4.00	8.00
❑ GNPS-2151	Prodigious Piano	198?	2.00	4.00	8.00
❑ GNPS-2155	Espana	198?	2.50	5.00	10.00
❑ GNPS-2161	Live in Tokyo	198?	2.00	4.00	8.00
❑ GNPS-2168	Live in Tokyo, Volume II	198?	2.00	4.00	8.00
❑ GNPS-2179	Live at Concerts by the Sea	1985	2.00	4.00	8.00
❑ GNPS-2183	Live at Concerts by the Sea, Volume II	1986	2.00	4.00	8.00
PORTRAIT
| ❑ FR 44160 | Wild Piano | 1988 | 3.00 | 6.00 | 12.00 |

ENSEMBLE AL-SALAAM, THE
STRATA-EAST
| ❑ SES-7418 | The Sojourner | 1974 | 10.00 | 20.00 | 40.00 |

ENYARD, RON, AND PAULA OWEN
Enyard is a drummer. Owen is a female singer.
CADENCE JAZZ
| ❑ CJR-1031 | Red, Green and Blues (In Living Black and White) | 1987 | 2.50 | 5.00 | 10.00 |

ERICSON, ROLF
Trumpeter.
EMARCY
| ❑ MG-36106 [M] | Rolf Ericson and His All American Stars | 1957 | 12.50 | 25.00 | 50.00 |

ERNEY, DEWEY
Male vocalist.
DISCOVERY
| ❑ DS-881 | A Beautiful Friendship | 1982 | 2.50 | 5.00 | 10.00 |

ERSKINE, PETER
Drummer.
CONTEMPORARY
| ❑ C-14010 | Peter Erskine | 1983 | 3.00 | 6.00 | 12.00 |
FANTASY
| ❑ OJC-610 | Peter Erskine | 1991 | 3.00 | 6.00 | 12.00 |
PASSPORT
| ❑ 88032 | Transition | 198? | 2.50 | 5.00 | 10.00 |

ERVIN, BOOKER
Tenor saxophone player. Also see BOOKER LITTLE.
BARNABY
| ❑ Z 30560 | That's It! | 1971 | 3.75 | 7.50 | 15.00 |
| -- Reissue of Candid 9014 | | | | | |
BETHLEHEM
❑ BCP-6025	The Book Cooks	197?	3.75	7.50	15.00
-- Reissue with RCA Victor distrbution					
❑ BCP-6048 [M]	The Book Cooks	1961	10.00	20.00	40.00
BLUE NOTE
❑ BN-LA488-H2 [(2)]	Back from the Gig	1975	5.00	10.00	20.00
❑ 4134/84134	Back from the Gig	1963	---	---	---
-- Canceled					
❑ BST-84283	The In Between	1969	7.50	15.00	30.00
❑ BST-84314	Booker Ervin	1969	---	---	---
-- Canceled					

Number	Title	Yr	VG	VG+	NM
CANDID					
❏ CJM-8014 [M]	That's It!	1961	10.00	20.00	40.00
❏ CJS-9014 [S]	That's It!	1961	12.50	25.00	50.00
PACIFIC JAZZ					
❏ PJ-10199 [M]	Structurally Sound	1968	10.00	20.00	40.00
❏ ST-20199 [S]	Structurally Sound	1968	5.00	10.00	20.00
PRESTIGE					
❏ PRLP-7293 [M]	Exultation!	1964	6.25	12.50	25.00
❏ PRST-7293 [S]	Exultation!	1964	7.50	15.00	30.00
❏ PRLP-7295 [M]	The Freedom Book	1964	6.25	12.50	25.00
❏ PRST-7295 [S]	The Freedom Book	1964	7.50	15.00	30.00
❏ PRLP-7318 [M]	The Song Book	1964	6.25	12.50	25.00
❏ PRST-7318 [S]	The Song Book	1964	7.50	15.00	30.00
❏ PRLP-7340 [M]	The Blues Book	1965	6.25	12.50	25.00
❏ PRST-7340 [S]	The Blues Book	1965	7.50	15.00	30.00
❏ PRLP-7386 [M]	The Space Book	1965	6.25	12.50	25.00
❏ PRST-7386 [S]	The Space Book	1965	7.50	15.00	30.00
❏ PRLP-7417 [M]	Groovin' High	1966	5.00	10.00	20.00
❏ PRST-7417 [S]	Groovin' High	1966	6.25	12.50	25.00
❏ PRLP-7435 [M]	Settin' the Pace	1967	6.25	12.50	25.00
❏ PRST-7435 [S]	Settin' the Pace	1967	5.00	10.00	20.00
❏ PRLP-7462 [M]	The Trance	1967	6.25	12.50	25.00
❏ PRST-7462 [S]	The Trance	1967	5.00	10.00	20.00
❏ PRLP-7499 [M]	Heavy!	1968	7.50	15.00	30.00
❏ PRST-7499 [S]	Heavy!	1968	5.00	10.00	20.00
❏ PRST-7844	Exultation!	197?	3.75	7.50	15.00
-- Reissue of 7293					
❏ 24091 [(2)]	Freedom and the Space Sessions	1979	3.75	7.50	15.00
SAVOY					
❏ MG-12154 [M]	Cookin'	1960	12.50	25.00	50.00
SAVOY JAZZ					
❏ SJL-1119	Down in the Dumps	198?	2.50	5.00	10.00

ERVIN, BOOKER/HORACE PARLAN
Also see each artist's individual listings.

Number	Title	Yr	VG	VG+	NM
INNER CITY					
❏ IC-3006	Lament	1977	3.75	7.50	15.00

ERWIN, PEE WEE
Trumpeter.

Number	Title	Yr	VG	VG+	NM
BRUNSWICK					
❏ BL 54011 [M]	The Land of Dixie	1956	10.00	20.00	40.00
CADENCE					
❏ CLP-1011 [M]	Dixieland at Grandview Inn	1956	10.00	20.00	40.00
JAZZOLOGY					
❏ J-80	Swingin' That Music	1981	2.50	5.00	10.00
STRAND					
❏ SL-1001 [M]	Peter Meets the Wolf in Dixieland	1959	12.50	25.00	50.00
❏ SLS-1001 [S]	Peter Meets the Wolf in Dixieland	1959	15.00	30.00	60.00
URANIA					
❏ UJLP-1202 [M]	Accent on Dixieland	1955	10.00	20.00	40.00

ESCHETE, RON
Seven-string guitarist.

Number	Title	Yr	VG	VG+	NM
BAINBRIDGE					
❏ BT-6264	Stump Jumper	1986	2.50	5.00	10.00
❏ BT-6267	Christmas Impressions	1986	2.50	5.00	10.00
MUSE					
❏ MR-5186	To Let You Know I Care	1979	3.00	6.00	12.00
❏ MR-5246	Line-Up	1980	3.00	6.00	12.00
MUSIC IS MEDICINE					
❏ 9055	Christmas Impressions	1982	3.75	7.50	15.00

ESCOVEDO, PETE
Percussionist, male vocalist and bandleader.

Number	Title	Yr	VG	VG+	NM
CROSSOVER					
❏ CR-5002	Yesterday's Memories, Tomorrow's Dreams	1987	3.00	6.00	12.00
❏ CR-5005	Mister E.	1988	3.00	6.00	12.00

ESCOVEDO, PETE AND SHEILA
Sheila Escovedo, Pete's daughter, is a drummer, percussionist and female vocalist. She is better known to pop and R&B fans as Prince protégé "Sheila E."

Number	Title	Yr	VG	VG+	NM
FANTASY					
❏ F-9524	Solo Two	1976	3.75	7.50	15.00
❏ F-9545	Happy Together	1977	3.75	7.50	15.00

ESHELMAN, DAVE, JAZZ GARDEN BIG BAND
Eshelman is a trombonist, bandleader, arranger and composer.

Number	Title	Yr	VG	VG+	NM
SEA BREEZE					
❏ SB-2039	Deep Voices	1989	3.00	6.00	12.00

ETHNIC HERITAGE ENSEMBLE, THE
Led by drummer and percussionist Kahil El'Zabar, other members include Joe Bowie (trombone), Harold Atu Murray (flute, thumb piano and various percussion instruments) and Ed Wilkerson (tenor sax).

Number	Title	Yr	VG	VG+	NM
RED					
❏ VPA-156	Impressions	198?	3.75	7.50	15.00
SILKHEART					
❏ SH-108	Ancestral Song	198?	3.00	6.00	12.00

ETHRIDGE, KELLIS

Number	Title	Yr	VG	VG+	NM
INNER CITY					
❏ IC-1109	Tomorrow Sky	1980	2.50	5.00	10.00

EUBANKS, KEVIN
Guitarist.

Number	Title	Yr	VG	VG+	NM
ELEKTRA MUSICIAN					
❏ 60213	Guitarist	1983	3.75	7.50	15.00
GRP					
❏ GR-1008	Sundance	1984	2.50	5.00	10.00
❏ GR-1029	Face to Face	1985	2.50	5.00	10.00
❏ GR-1031	Opening Night	1985	2.50	5.00	10.00
❏ GR-1041	Heat of Heat	1986	2.50	5.00	10.00
❏ GR-1054	Shadow Prophets	1988	2.50	5.00	10.00
❏ GR-9580	The Searcher	1989	3.00	6.00	12.00

EUBANKS, ROBIN
Trombone player. KEVIN EUBANKS is his brother.

Number	Title	Yr	VG	VG+	NM
JMT					
❏ 834 424-1	Different Perspectives	1988	2.50	5.00	10.00
❏ 834 433-1	Dedication	1989	3.00	6.00	12.00

EUREKA BRASS BAND, THE
The leader was trumpeter Percy Humphrey.

Number	Title	Yr	VG	VG+	NM
ATLANTIC					
❏ 1408 [M]	The Eureka Brass Band	1963	3.75	7.50	15.00
❏ SD 1408 [S]	The Eureka Brass Band	1963	5.00	10.00	20.00
-- Multicolor label with black "fan" logo at right					
❏ SD 1408 [S]	The Eureka Brass Band	1969	2.50	5.00	10.00
-- Red and green label					
FOLKWAYS					
❏ FA-2642 [M]	Music of New Orleans	195?	12.50	25.00	50.00
PAX					
❏ LP-9001 [10]	New Orleans Parade	1954	15.00	30.00	60.00

EUROPEAN CLASSIC JAZZ BAND, THE

Number	Title	Yr	VG	VG+	NM
STOMP OFF					
❏ SOS-1070	Whip Me with Plenty of Love	1984	2.50	5.00	10.00

EUROPEAN CLASSIC JAZZ TRIO, THE

Number	Title	Yr	VG	VG+	NM
STOMP OFF					
❏ SOS-1142	That's Like It Ought to Be	1988	2.50	5.00	10.00

EUROPEAN JAZZ QUARTET, THE

Number	Title	Yr	VG	VG+	NM
PULSE					
❏ 3001 [M]	New Jazz from the Old World	1957	12.50	25.00	50.00

EVANS, BILL (1)
Pianist. Also see BOB BROOKMEYER; GARY McFARLAND.

Number	Title	Yr	VG	VG+	NM
COLUMBIA					
❏ C 30855	The Bill Evans Album	1971	3.75	7.50	15.00
❏ PC 30855	The Bill Evans Album	198?	2.00	4.00	8.00
-- Budget-line reissue					
❏ KC 31490	Living Time: Events I-VIII	1972	3.75	7.50	15.00
❏ CG 33672 [(2)]	The Bill Evans Album/Living Time	1976	3.75	7.50	15.00
CTI					
❏ 6004	Montreux II	1971	3.75	7.50	15.00
ELEKTRA MUSICIAN					
❏ 60164	The Paris Concert, Volume 1	1984	3.00	6.00	12.00
❏ 60311	The Paris Concert, Volume 2	1986	3.00	6.00	12.00
FANTASY					
❏ OJC-025	New Jazz Conceptions	1982	2.50	5.00	10.00
❏ OJC-037	Explorations	198?	2.50	5.00	10.00
❏ OJC-068	Everybody Digs Bill Evans	198?	2.50	5.00	10.00

Number	Title	Yr	VG	VG+	NM
❏ OJC-088	Portrait in Jazz	198?	2.50	5.00	10.00
❏ OJC-140	Sunday at the Village Vanguard	198?	2.50	5.00	10.00
❏ OJC-210	Waltz for Debby	198?	2.50	5.00	10.00
❏ OJC-263	Bill Evans at Shelly's Manne-Hole	1987	2.50	5.00	10.00
❏ OJC-308	Interplay	198?	2.50	5.00	10.00
❏ OJC-345	The Tokyo Concert	1990	3.00	6.00	12.00
❏ OJC-369	How My Heart Sings	198?	2.50	5.00	10.00
❏ OJC-434	Moonbeams	1990	3.00	6.00	12.00
❏ OJC-470	Intuition	1990	3.00	6.00	12.00
❏ OJC-622	Since We Met	1991	3.00	6.00	12.00
❏ F-9457	The Tokyo Concert	1974	3.00	6.00	12.00
❏ F-9475	Intuition	1975	3.00	6.00	12.00
❏ F-9501	Since We Met	1975	3.00	6.00	12.00
❏ F-9510	Montreux III	1976	3.00	6.00	12.00
❏ F-9529	Quintessence	1976	3.00	6.00	12.00
❏ F-9542	Alone (Again)	1977	3.00	6.00	12.00
❏ F-9568	Crosscurrents	1978	3.00	6.00	12.00
❏ F-9593	I Will Say Goodbye	1980	3.00	6.00	12.00
❏ F-9608	Re: The Person I Knew	198?	2.50	5.00	10.00
❏ F-9618	Eloquence	198?	2.50	5.00	10.00
❏ F-9630	From the 70s	198?	2.50	5.00	10.00

MGM

❏ SE-4723	From Left to Right	1970	3.75	7.50	15.00

MILESTONE

❏ 9125	More from the Vanguard	198?	2.50	5.00	10.00
❏ 9151	Jazzhouse	1988	2.50	5.00	10.00
❏ 9164	You're Gonna Hear from Me	198?	2.50	5.00	10.00
❏ 9170	The Solo Sessions, Volume 1	1989	3.00	6.00	12.00
❏ 47002 [(2)]	The Village Vanguard Sessions	197?	3.75	7.50	15.00
❏ 47024 [(2)]	Peace Piece & Others	197?	3.75	7.50	15.00
❏ 47034 [(2)]	Spring Leaves	197?	3.75	7.50	15.00
❏ 47046 [(2)]	The Second Trio	197?	3.75	7.50	15.00
❏ 47063 [(2)]	Conception	198?	3.75	7.50	15.00
❏ 47066 [(2)]	The Interplay Sessions	198?	3.00	6.00	12.00
❏ 47068 [(2)]	Time Remembered	198?	3.00	6.00	12.00

MOSAIC

❏ MQ10-171 [(10)]	The Final Village Vanguard Sessions -- June 1980	1996	45.00	90.00	180.00

PAUSA

❏ 7050	Symbiosis	1979	2.50	5.00	10.00

RIVERSIDE

❏ R-018 [(18)]	The Complete Riverside Recordings	1985	50.00	100.00	200.00
❏ RLP 12-223 [M]	New Jazz Conceptions	1956	125.00	250.00	500.00

-- Photo on cover, label is white with blue print

❏ RLP 12-223 [M]	New Jazz Conceptions	1958	7.50	15.00	30.00

-- New label, label is blue with microphone logo at top

❏ RLP 12-291 [M]	Everybody Digs Bill Evans	1958	10.00	20.00	40.00
❏ RLP 12-315 [M]	Portrait in Jazz	1959	10.00	20.00	40.00
❏ RLP 1129 [S]	Everybody Digs Bill Evans	1959	7.50	15.00	30.00
❏ RLP 1162 [S]	Portrait in Jazz	1959	7.50	15.00	30.00
❏ RLP-351 [M]	Explorations	1960	7.50	15.00	30.00
❏ RLP-376 [M]	Sunday at the Village Vanguard	1961	6.25	12.50	25.00
❏ RLP-399 [M]	Waltz for Debby	1961	6.25	12.50	25.00
❏ RLP-428 [M]	Moonbeams	1962	6.25	12.50	25.00
❏ RLP-445 [M]	Interplay	1963	6.25	12.50	25.00
❏ RLP-473 [M]	How My Heart Sings!	1964	6.25	12.50	25.00
❏ RLP-487 [M]	Bill Evans at Shelly's Manne-Hole, Hollywood, California	1965	5.00	10.00	20.00
❏ RM-3001 [M]	Polka Dots and Moonbeams	1967	3.75	7.50	15.00
❏ RS-3001 [S]	Polka Dots and Moonbeams	1967	3.00	6.00	12.00
❏ RM-3006 [M]	Live at the Village Vanguard	1967	3.75	7.50	15.00
❏ RS-3006 [S]	Live at the Village Vanguard	1967	3.00	6.00	12.00
❏ RS-3013	Live at Shelly's Manne-Hole	1968	3.00	6.00	12.00
❏ RS-3042	Peace Pieces	1969	3.00	6.00	12.00
❏ 6038	Explorations	197?	3.00	6.00	12.00
❏ 6090	Everybody Digs Bill Evans	197?	3.00	6.00	12.00
❏ 6118	Waltz for Debby	197?	3.00	6.00	12.00
❏ 6175	Moonbeams	198?	2.50	5.00	10.00
❏ 6197	Bill Evans at Shelly's Manne-Hole	198?	2.50	5.00	10.00
❏ RS-9351 [S]	Explorations	1960	7.50	15.00	30.00
❏ RS-9376 [S]	Sunday at the Village Vanguard	1961	7.50	15.00	30.00
❏ RS-9399 [S]	Waltz for Debby	1961	7.50	15.00	30.00
❏ RS-9428 [S]	Moonbeams	1962	7.50	15.00	30.00
❏ RS-9445 [S]	Interplay	1963	7.50	15.00	30.00
❏ RS-9473 [S]	How My Heart Sings!	1964	7.50	15.00	30.00
❏ RS-9487 [S]	Bill Evans at Shelly's Manne-Hole, Hollywood, California	1965	6.25	12.50	25.00

TIMELESS

❏ LPSJP-331	Consecration I	1990	3.75	7.50	15.00
❏ LPSJP-332	Consecration II	1990	3.75	7.50	15.00

VERVE

❏ UMV-2053	The Bill Evans Trio at Town Hall	198?	2.50	5.00	10.00

Number	Title	Yr	VG	VG+	NM
❏ UMV-2106	Intermodulation	198?	2.50	5.00	10.00
❏ UMV-2107	A Simple Matter of Conviction	198?	2.50	5.00	10.00
❏ VE-2-2509 [(2)]	Trios and Duos	197?	3.75	7.50	15.00
❏ VE-2-2545 [(2)]	California Here I Come	198?	3.00	6.00	12.00
❏ V-8497 [M]	Empathy	1962	6.25	12.50	25.00
❏ V6-8497 [S]	Empathy	1962	7.50	15.00	30.00
❏ V-8526 [M]	Conversations with Myself	1963	5.00	10.00	20.00
❏ V6-8526 [S]	Conversations with Myself	1963	6.25	12.50	25.00
❏ V-8578 [M]	Bill Evans Trio '64	1964	3.75	7.50	15.00
❏ V6-8578 [S]	Bill Evans Trio '64	1964	5.00	10.00	20.00
❏ V-8613 [M]	Bill Evans Trio '65	1965	3.75	7.50	15.00
❏ V6-8613 [S]	Bill Evans Trio '65	1965	5.00	10.00	20.00
❏ V-8640 [M]	Bill Evans Trio with Symphony Orchestra	1965	3.75	7.50	15.00
❏ V6-8640 [S]	Bill Evans Trio with Symphony Orchestra	1965	5.00	10.00	20.00
❏ V-8655 [M]	Intermodulation	1966	3.75	7.50	15.00
❏ V6-8655 [S]	Intermodulation	1966	5.00	10.00	20.00
❏ V-8675 [M]	A Simple Matter of Conviction	1966	3.75	7.50	15.00
❏ V6-8675 [S]	A Simple Matter of Conviction	1966	5.00	10.00	20.00
❏ V-8683 [M]	Bill Evans at Town Hall	1966	3.75	7.50	15.00
❏ V6-8683 [S]	Bill Evans at Town Hall	1966	5.00	10.00	20.00
❏ V-8727 [M]	Further Conversations with Myself	1967	5.00	10.00	20.00
❏ V6-8727 [S]	Further Conversations with Myself	1967	3.75	7.50	15.00
❏ V-8747 [M]	The Best of Bill Evans	1967	5.00	10.00	20.00
❏ V6-8747 [S]	The Best of Bill Evans	1967	3.75	7.50	15.00
❏ V6-8762	Bill Evans at the Montreux Jazz Festival	1968	3.75	7.50	15.00
❏ V6-8777	What's New	1968	3.75	7.50	15.00
❏ V6-8792	Bill Evans Alone	1969	3.75	7.50	15.00
❏ V3HB-8841 [(3)]	Return Engagement	1973	5.00	10.00	20.00
❏ 827 844-1	Bill Evans at the Montreux Jazz Festival	1986	2.50	5.00	10.00

VERVE/CLASSIC

❏ V6-8762	Bill Evans at the Montreux Jazz Festival	199?	6.25	12.50	25.00

-- Reissue on audiophile vinyl

WARNER BROS.

❏ BSK 3177	New Conversations	1977	3.00	6.00	12.00
❏ BSK 3293	Affinity	1978	3.00	6.00	12.00
❏ HS 3411	We Will Meet Again	1979	3.00	6.00	12.00
❏ HS 3504	You Must Believe in Spring	1980	3.00	6.00	12.00

EVANS, BILL (1), AND JIM HALL

Also see each artist's individual listings.

BLUE NOTE

❏ B1-90583	Undercurrent	1988	2.50	5.00	10.00

SOLID STATE

❏ SS-18018	Undercurrent	1968	5.00	10.00	20.00

UNITED ARTISTS

❏ UAJ-14003 [M]	Undercurrent	1962	10.00	20.00	40.00
❏ UAJS-15003 [S]	Undercurrent	1962	12.50	25.00	50.00
❏ UAS-5640	Undercurrent	197?	3.75	7.50	15.00

EVANS, BILL (2)

No relation to the more prominent man above, he is a saxophone player; he also plays flute and keyboards and is a composer.

BLUE NOTE

❏ BT-85111	The Alternative Man	1985	2.50	5.00	10.00

ELEKTRA MUSICIAN

❏ 60349	Living in the Crest of a Wave	1986	2.50	5.00	10.00

EVANS, DOC

Cornet player and bandleader.

AUDIOPHILE

❏ AP-4	Down in Jungle Town	1987	2.50	5.00	10.00
❏ AP-11 [M]	Doc Evans and His Band, Volume 1	195?	10.00	20.00	40.00
❏ AP-12 [M]	Doc Evans and His Band, Volume 2	195?	10.00	20.00	40.00
❏ AP-29 [M]	Dixieland Session	195?	10.00	20.00	40.00
❏ AP-31 [M]	The Cornet Artistry of Doc Evans	195?	10.00	20.00	40.00
❏ AP-33 [M]	Traditional Jazz	195?	10.00	20.00	40.00

-- Red vinyl

❏ AP-34 [M]	Traditional Jazz	195?	10.00	20.00	40.00

-- Red vinyl

❏ AP-44 [M]	Traditional Jazz	195?	10.00	20.00	40.00

-- Red vinyl

❏ AP-45 [M]	Traditional Jazz	195?	10.00	20.00	40.00
❏ AP-50 [M]	Classics of the 20's	195?	10.00	20.00	40.00

-- Red vinyl

❏ AP-95 [M]	Doc Evans at the Gas Light	196?	5.00	10.00	20.00

Number	Title	Yr	VG	VG+	NM
❏ AP-95	Doc Evans at the Gas Light	1989	2.50	5.00	10.00
-- Reissue with same number					
❏ AS-95 [S]	Doc Evans at the Gas Light	196?	6.25	12.50	25.00
❏ XL-328 [M]	Traditional Jazz	195?	10.00	20.00	40.00
❏ XL-329 [M]	Traditional Jazz	195?	10.00	20.00	40.00
❏ APS-5968	Reminiscing in Dixieland	196?	6.25	12.50	25.00
-- Red vinyl					

CONCERT DISC

Number	Title	Yr	VG	VG+	NM
❏ CS-48	Muskrat Ramble	196?	6.25	12.50	25.00

FOLKWAYS

Number	Title	Yr	VG	VG+	NM
❏ FA-2855	Doc Evans and His Dixieland Jazz Band	195?	5.00	10.00	20.00

JAZZOLOGY

Number	Title	Yr	VG	VG+	NM
❏ J-85	Jazz Heritage, Volume 1	197?	2.50	5.00	10.00
❏ J-86	Blues in Dixieland	197?	2.50	5.00	10.00
❏ J-87	Command Performance	197?	2.50	5.00	10.00

SOMA

Number	Title	Yr	VG	VG+	NM
❏ MG-100 [M]	Dixieland Concert	1953	12.50	25.00	50.00
❏ MG-101 [10]	Dixieland Concert	1953	12.50	25.00	50.00
❏ MG-1201 [M]	Classic Jazz at Carleton	1954	10.00	20.00	40.00

EVANS, GIL
Pianist, keyboard player, arranger and composer.

ABC IMPULSE!

Number	Title	Yr	VG	VG+	NM
❏ AS-4 [S]	Out of the Cool	1968	3.75	7.50	15.00
❏ AS-9 [S]	Into the Hot	1968	3.75	7.50	15.00
❏ IA-9340 [(2)]	The Great Arrangers	1978	3.75	7.50	15.00

AMPEX

Number	Title	Yr	VG	VG+	NM
❏ A-10102	Gil Evans	1971	3.75	7.50	15.00

ANTILLES

Number	Title	Yr	VG	VG+	NM
❏ AN-1010	Priestess	198?	2.50	5.00	10.00

ARTISTS HOUSE

Number	Title	Yr	VG	VG+	NM
❏ 14	Where Flamingoes Fly	198?	2.50	5.00	10.00

ATLANTIC

Number	Title	Yr	VG	VG+	NM
❏ QD 1643 [Q]	Svengali	1973	5.00	10.00	20.00
❏ SD 1643	Svengali	1973	3.00	6.00	12.00
❏ 90048	Svengali	1983	2.00	4.00	8.00

BLUE NOTE

Number	Title	Yr	VG	VG+	NM
❏ BN-LA461-H2 [(2)]	Pacific Standard Time	1975	3.75	7.50	15.00

EMARCY

Number	Title	Yr	VG	VG+	NM
❏ 836 401-1	Rhythm-A-Ning	1989	3.00	6.00	12.00

FANTASY

Number	Title	Yr	VG	VG+	NM
❏ OJC-346	Gil Evans Plus Ten	198?	2.50	5.00	10.00

IMPULSE!

Number	Title	Yr	VG	VG+	NM
❏ A-4 [M]	Out of the Cool	1961	6.25	12.50	25.00
❏ AS-4 [S]	Out of the Cool	1961	7.50	15.00	30.00
❏ A-9 [M]	Into the Hot	1962	6.25	12.50	25.00
❏ AS-9 [S]	Into the Hot	1962	7.50	15.00	30.00

INNER CITY

Number	Title	Yr	VG	VG+	NM
❏ IC-1110	Little Wing	198?	3.00	6.00	12.00

MCA

Number	Title	Yr	VG	VG+	NM
❏ 4143 [(2)]	The Great Arrangers	198?	2.50	5.00	10.00
❏ 29033	Out of the Cool	198?	2.00	4.00	8.00
❏ 29034	Into the Hot	198?	2.00	4.00	8.00

MCA IMPULSE!

Number	Title	Yr	VG	VG+	NM
❏ 5653	Out of the Cool	1986	2.50	5.00	10.00

NEW JAZZ

Number	Title	Yr	VG	VG+	NM
❏ NJLP-8215 [M]	Big Stuff	1959	12.50	25.00	50.00
-- Purple label					
❏ NJLP-8215 [M]	Big Stuff	1965	6.25	12.50	25.00
-- Blue label, trident logo at right					

PACIFIC JAZZ

Number	Title	Yr	VG	VG+	NM
❏ PJ-28 [M]	America's #1 Arranger	1961	7.50	15.00	30.00
❏ PJ-40 [M]	Cannonball Adderley/Gil Evans	1962	6.25	12.50	25.00
❏ ST-40 [S]	Cannonball Adderley/Gil Evans	1962	7.50	15.00	30.00

PRESTIGE

Number	Title	Yr	VG	VG+	NM
❏ PRLP-7120 [M]	Gil Evans Plus Ten	1957	20.00	40.00	80.00
❏ PRST-7756	Big Stuff	1970	3.75	7.50	15.00
❏ 24049 [(2)]	An Arranger's Touch	197?	3.75	7.50	15.00

RCA VICTOR

Number	Title	Yr	VG	VG+	NM
❏ CPL1-0667	Gil Evans Plays Jimi Hendrix	1974	5.00	10.00	20.00
❏ APL1-1057	There Comes a Time	1976	3.00	6.00	12.00
❏ LPM-1057 [M]	There Comes a Time	1955	20.00	40.00	80.00

VERVE

Number	Title	Yr	VG	VG+	NM
❏ V-8555 [M]	The Individualism of Gil Evans	1963	5.00	10.00	20.00
❏ V6-8555 [S]	The Individualism of Gil Evans	1963	6.25	12.50	25.00
❏ V6-8838	Previously Unreleased Recordings	1974	3.00	6.00	12.00

WORLD PACIFIC

Number	Title	Yr	VG	VG+	NM
❏ ST-1011 [S]	New Bottle, Old Wine	1959	10.00	20.00	40.00
❏ ST-1027 [S]	Great Jazz Standards	1959	10.00	20.00	40.00

Number	Title	Yr	VG	VG+	NM
❏ WP-1246 [M]	New Bottle, Old Wine	1958	12.50	25.00	50.00
❏ WP-1270 [M]	Great Jazz Standards	1959	12.50	25.00	50.00

EVANS, JOHN
Pianist.

OMEGA

Number	Title	Yr	VG	VG+	NM
❏ OL-49 [M]	Mainstream Jazz Piano	1960	5.00	10.00	20.00
❏ OSL-49 [S]	Mainstream Jazz Piano	1960	5.00	10.00	20.00

EVANS, LEE
Pianist.

CAPITOL

Number	Title	Yr	VG	VG+	NM
❏ ST 1625 [S]	Big Piano/Big Band/Big Sound	1962	5.00	10.00	20.00
❏ T 1625 [M]	Big Piano/Big Band/Big Sound	1962	3.75	7.50	15.00
❏ ST 1847 [S]	The Lee Evans Trio	1963	5.00	10.00	20.00
❏ T 1847 [M]	The Lee Evans Trio	1963	3.75	7.50	15.00

EVANS, RICHARD
Bass player.

ARGO

Number	Title	Yr	VG	VG+	NM
❏ LP-658 [M]	Richard's Almanac	1960	7.50	15.00	30.00
❏ LPS-658 [S]	Richard's Almanac	1960	10.00	20.00	40.00
❏ LP-675 [M]	Home Cookin'	1961	6.25	12.50	25.00
❏ LPS-675 [S]	Home Cookin'	1961	7.50	15.00	30.00

EVERGREEN CLASSIC JAZZ BAND

STOMP OFF

Number	Title	Yr	VG	VG+	NM
❏ SOS-1202	Trust Me... I'm a Musician	1991	2.50	5.00	10.00

EVERYMAN BAND
Members: Michael Suchorsky (drums); DAVID TORN (guitar); Bruce Yaw (bass); MARTY FOGEL (saxophones).

ECM

Number	Title	Yr	VG	VG+	NM
❏ 1234	Everyman Band	1983	3.00	6.00	12.00
❏ 1290	Without Warning	1985	2.50	5.00	10.00

EWELL, DON
Pianist.

ANALOGUE PRODUCTIONS

Number	Title	Yr	VG	VG+	NM
❏ APJ-19	Yellow Dog Blues	199?	6.25	12.50	25.00
-- Audiophile reissue on red vinyl					

AUDIOPHILE

Number	Title	Yr	VG	VG+	NM
❏ APS-5966	Yellow Dog Blues	196?	5.00	10.00	20.00

CHIAROSCURO

Number	Title	Yr	VG	VG+	NM
❏ 106	Jazz Portrait of the Artist	1972	3.75	7.50	15.00
❏ 127	Take It in Stride	1973	3.75	7.50	15.00
❏ 130	Don Ewell	1974	3.75	7.50	15.00

GHB

Number	Title	Yr	VG	VG+	NM
❏ 30	Don Ewell in New Orleans	196?	5.00	10.00	20.00

GOOD TIME JAZZ

Number	Title	Yr	VG	VG+	NM
❏ S-10043 [S]	The Man Here Plays Fine Piano	1960	6.25	12.50	25.00
❏ S-10046 [S]	Free 'N Easy	1960	6.25	12.50	25.00
❏ L-12021 [M]	Music to Listen to Don Ewell By	1955	10.00	20.00	40.00
❏ L-12043 [M]	The Man Here Plays Fine Piano	1956	10.00	20.00	40.00
❏ L-12046 [M]	Free 'N Easy	1956	10.00	20.00	40.00

JAZZOLOGY

Number	Title	Yr	VG	VG+	NM
❏ J-29	Don Ewell and the All-Stars	197?	2.50	5.00	10.00
❏ J-69	Don Ewell Quintet	198?	2.50	5.00	10.00
❏ JCE-84	Don Ewell and Bob Greene Together!	198?	2.50	5.00	10.00

NEW ORLEANS

Number	Title	Yr	VG	VG+	NM
❏ NOR-7209	Don Ewell and Herb Hall in New Orleans	198?	2.50	5.00	10.00

STOMP OFF

Number	Title	Yr	VG	VG+	NM
❏ SOS-1077	Chicago '57	198?	2.50	5.00	10.00

WINDIN' BALL

Number	Title	Yr	VG	VG+	NM
❏ LP-101 [10]	Don Ewell	1953	12.50	25.00	50.00
❏ LP-102 [10]	Don Ewell and Mama Yancey	1953	12.50	25.00	50.00
❏ LP-103 [M]	Don Ewell Plays Tunes Played by the King Oliver Band	195?	7.50	15.00	30.00
❏ LP-103 [10]	Don Ewell Plays Tunes Played by the King Oliver Band	1953	12.50	25.00	50.00

EX-HERMANITES, THE
See TERRY GIBBS AND BILL HARRIS.

EYEBALL
Fusion band led by Dutch pianist and composer Jasper van't Hof.

CMP

Number	Title	Yr	VG	VG+	NM
❏ CMP-11-ST	Eyeball	198?	3.00	6.00	12.00

Number	Title	Yr	VG	VG+	NM	Number	Title	Yr	VG	VG+	NM

EYERMANN, TIM, AND EAST COAST OFFERING
Eyermann is a soprano, alto and tenor saxophone player and clarinetist.
BLUEMOON

Number	Title	Yr	VG	VG+	NM
❏ R1-79151	Jazz on L	1989	3.00	6.00	12.00
❏ R1-79163	Outside/Inside	1990	3.00	6.00	12.00

INNER CITY

Number	Title	Yr	VG	VG+	NM
❏ IC-1095	Aloha	198?	3.00	6.00	12.00

MCA

Number	Title	Yr	VG	VG+	NM
❏ 5494	East Coast Offering	1985	2.50	5.00	10.00
❏ 5589	Walkin' With You	1986	2.50	5.00	10.00

EYGES, DAVID
Cello player.
MUSIC UNLIMITED

Number	Title	Yr	VG	VG+	NM
❏ 7431	The Arrow	1981	3.00	6.00	12.00
❏ 7432	Crossroads	1982	3.00	6.00	12.00

EZELL, WILLIAM
RIVERSIDE

Number	Title	Yr	VG	VG+	NM
❏ RLP-1043 [10]	Gin Mill Jazz	1954	20.00	40.00	80.00

Number	Title	Yr	VG	VG+	NM

F

FABRIC, BENT
Danish pianist. Also see ACKER BILK.
ATCO
❑ 33-148 [M]	Alley Cat	1962	3.75	7.50	15.00
❑ SD 33-148 [S]	Alley Cat	1962	5.00	10.00	20.00
❑ 33-155 [M]	The Happy Puppy	1963	3.00	6.00	12.00
❑ SD 33-155 [S]	The Happy Puppy	1963	3.75	7.50	15.00
❑ 33-164 [M]	Organ Grinder's Swing	1964	3.00	6.00	12.00
❑ SD 33-164 [S]	Organ Grinder's Swing	1964	3.75	7.50	15.00
❑ 33-173 [M]	The Drunken Penguin	1965	3.00	6.00	12.00
❑ SD 33-173 [S]	The Drunken Penguin	1965	3.75	7.50	15.00
❑ 33-185 [M]	Never Tease Tigers	1966	3.00	6.00	12.00
❑ SD 33-185 [S]	Never Tease Tigers	1966	3.75	7.50	15.00
❑ 33-202 [M]	Operation Lovebirds	1967	3.00	6.00	12.00
❑ SD 33-202 [S]	Operation Lovebirds	1967	3.75	7.50	15.00
❑ 33-221 [M]	Relax	1967	3.75	7.50	15.00
❑ SD 33-221 [S]	Relax	1967	3.00	6.00	12.00

FADDIS, JON
Trumpeter.
BUDDAH
❑ BDS-5727	Good and Plenty	1979	3.00	6.00	12.00
CONCORD JAZZ
| ❑ CJ-291 | Legacy | 1986 | 2.50 | 5.00 | 10.00 |
EPIC
| ❑ OE 45266 | Into the FaddisPhere | 1989 | 3.75 | 7.50 | 15.00 |
PABLO
| ❑ 2310 765 | Youngblood | 1977 | 3.75 | 7.50 | 15.00 |

FAGERQUIST, DON
Trumpeter.
MODE
❑ LP-124 [M]	Music to Fill a Void	1957	25.00	50.00	100.00

FAME, GEORGIE
British organist, keyboard player and male vocalist.
EPIC
❑ BN 26368	The Ballad of Bonnie and Clyde	1968	6.25	12.50	25.00
IMPERIAL
❑ LP-9282 [M]	Yeh, Yeh	1965	6.25	12.50	25.00
❑ LP-9331 [M]	Get Away	1966	6.25	12.50	25.00
❑ LP-12282 [P]	Yeh, Yeh	1965	7.50	15.00	30.00
❑ LP-12331 [R]	Get Away	1966	5.00	10.00	20.00
ISLAND
| ❑ ILPS 9293 | Georgie Fame | 1975 | 2.50 | 5.00 | 10.00 |

FAME, GEORGIE, AND ANNIE ROSS
Also see each artist's individual listings.
DRG
❑ 5197	Georgie Fame and Annie Ross in Hoagland	198?	3.00	6.00	12.00

FAMOUS CASTLE JAZZ BAND, THE
GOOD TIME JAZZ
❑ S-7021 [S]	The Famous Castle Jazz Band in Stereo	1959	7.50	15.00	30.00
❑ S-10030 [S]	The Famous Castle Jazz Band in Stereo	197?	2.50	5.00	10.00
❑ S-10037 [S]	The Famous Castle Jazz Band Plays the Five Pennies	1959	7.50	15.00	30.00
❑ L-12030 [M]	The Famous Castle Jazz Band in Hi-Fi	1957	10.00	20.00	40.00
❑ L-12037 [M]	The Famous Castle Jazz Band Plays the Five Pennies	1959	10.00	20.00	40.00
STEREO RECORDS
| ❑ S-7021 [S] | The Famous Castle Jazz Band in Stereo | 1958 | 10.00 | 20.00 | 40.00 |

FARLOW, TAL
Guitarist.
AMERICAN RECORDING SOCIETY
❑ G-418 [M]	The Swinging Guitar of Tal Farlow	1957	10.00	20.00	40.00
BLUE NOTE
| ❑ BLP-5042 [10] | Tal Farlow Quartet | 1954 | 75.00 | 150.00 | 300.00 |
CONCORD JAZZ
| ❑ CJ-26 | Sign of the Times | 1976 | 3.00 | 6.00 | 12.00 |
| ❑ CJ-57 | Tal Farlow '78 | 1978 | 3.00 | 6.00 | 12.00 |

Number	Title	Yr	VG	VG+	NM
❑ CJ-154	Chromatic Palette	1981	3.00	6.00	12.00
❑ CJ-204	Cookin' on All Burners	1982	3.00	6.00	12.00
❑ CJ-266	The Legendary Tal Farlow	1986	2.50	5.00	10.00

FANTASY
❑ OJC-356	The Return of Tal Farlow/1969	198?	2.50	5.00	10.00
INNER CITY
| ❑ IC-1099 | Trilogy | 197? | 3.00 | 6.00 | 12.00 |
NORGRAN
❑ MGN-19 [10]	The Tal Farlow Album	1954	37.50	75.00	150.00
❑ MGN-1014 [M]	The Artistry of Tal Farlow	1955	30.00	60.00	120.00
❑ MGN-1027 [M]	The Interpretations of Tal Farlow	1955	30.00	60.00	120.00
❑ MGN-1030 [M]	A Recital by Tal Farlow	1955	25.00	50.00	100.00
❑ MGN-1047 [M]	The Tal Farlow Album	1955	25.00	50.00	100.00
❑ MGN-1097 [M]	Autumn in New York	1956	25.00	50.00	100.00
❑ MGN-1101 [M]	Fascinating Rhythm	1956	25.00	50.00	100.00
❑ MGN-1102 [M]	Tal	1956	25.00	50.00	100.00
PRESTIGE
| ❑ 24042 [(2)] | Guitar Player | 197? | 5.00 | 10.00 | 20.00 |
| ❑ PRST-7732 | The Return of Tal Farlow/1969 | 1969 | 5.00 | 10.00 | 20.00 |
VERVE
❑ UMV-2565	Tal	198?	2.50	5.00	10.00
❑ UMV-2584	The Tal Farlow Album	198?	2.50	5.00	10.00
❑ MGVS-6143 [S]	The Guitar Artistry of Tal Farlow	1960	10.00	20.00	40.00
❑ MGVS-6144 [S]	Tal Farlow Plays the Music of Harold Arlen	1960	---	---	---
-- Canceled					
❑ MGV-8011 [M]	The Interpretations of Tal Farlow	1957	12.50	25.00	50.00
-- Reissue of Norgran 1027					
❑ V-8011 [M]	The Interpretations of Tal Farlow	1961	5.00	10.00	20.00
❑ MGV-8021 [M]	Tal	1957	12.50	25.00	50.00
-- Reissue of Norgran 1102					
❑ V-8021 [M]	Tal	1961	5.00	10.00	20.00
❑ MGV-8123 [M]	A Recital by Tal Farlow	1957	12.50	25.00	50.00
-- Reissue of Norgran 1030					
❑ V-8123 [M]	A Recital by Tal Farlow	1961	5.00	10.00	20.00
❑ MGV-8138 [M]	The Tal Farlow Album	1957	12.50	25.00	50.00
-- Reissue of Norgran 1047					
❑ V-8138 [M]	The Tal Farlow Album	1961	5.00	10.00	20.00
❑ MGV-8184 [M]	Autumn in New York	1957	12.50	25.00	50.00
-- Reissue of Norgran 1097					
❑ V-8184 [M]	Autumn in New York	1961	5.00	10.00	20.00
❑ MGV-8201 [M]	The Swinging Guitar of Tal Farlow	1957	12.50	25.00	50.00
❑ V-8201 [M]	The Swinging Guitar of Tal Farlow	1961	5.00	10.00	20.00
❑ MGV-8289 [M]	This Is Tal Farlow	1958	12.50	25.00	50.00
❑ V-8289 [M]	This Is Tal Farlow	1961	5.00	10.00	20.00
❑ MGV-8370 [M]	The Guitar Artistry of Tal Farlow	1960	12.50	25.00	50.00
❑ V-8370 [M]	The Guitar Artistry of Tal Farlow	1961	5.00	10.00	20.00
❑ V6-8370 [S]	The Guitar Artistry of Tal Farlow	1961	3.75	7.50	15.00
❑ MGV-8371 [M]	Tal Farlow Plays the Music of Harold Arlen	1960	12.50	25.00	50.00
❑ V-8371 [M]	Tal Farlow Plays the Music of Harold Arlen	1961	5.00	10.00	20.00
❑ 815 236-1 [(2)]	Poppin' and Burnin'	198?	3.00	6.00	12.00
XANADU
| ❑ 109 | The Fuerst Set | 197? | 3.00 | 6.00 | 12.00 |
| ❑ 119 | The Second Set | 197? | 3.00 | 6.00 | 12.00 |

FARMER, ART
Trumpeter and fluegel horn player. Also played something called the "flumpet," a hybrid of the two instruments, starting in 1989. Also see CLIFFORD BROWN; EDDIE COSTA; BENNIE GREEN; THE JAZZTET; THE PRESTIGE BLUES SWINGERS.
ABC-PARAMOUNT
❑ ABC-200 [M]	Last Night When We Were Young	1958	15.00	30.00	60.00
ARGO
❑ LP-678 [M]	Art	1961	6.25	12.50	25.00
❑ LPS-678 [S]	Art	1961	7.50	15.00	30.00
❑ LP-738 [M]	Perception	1964	6.25	12.50	25.00
❑ LPS-738 [S]	Perception	1964	7.50	15.00	30.00
ATLANTIC
❑ 1412 [M]	Interaction	1963	6.25	12.50	25.00
❑ SD 1412 [S]	Interaction	1963	7.50	15.00	30.00
❑ 1421 [M]	Live at the Half Note	1964	6.25	12.50	25.00
❑ SD 1421 [S]	Live at the Half Note	1964	7.50	15.00	30.00
❑ 1430 [M]	To Sweden with Love	1964	5.00	10.00	20.00
❑ SD 1430 [S]	To Sweden with Love	1964	6.25	12.50	25.00
❑ 1442 [M]	Sing Me Softly of the Blues	1965	5.00	10.00	20.00
❑ SD 1442 [S]	Sing Me Softly of the Blues	1965	6.25	12.50	25.00
COLUMBIA
❑ CL 2588 [M]	Baroque Sketches	1966	5.00	10.00	20.00
❑ CL 2649 [M]	The Time and the Place	1967	6.25	12.50	25.00
❑ CL 2746 [M]	Art Farmer Plays the Great Jazz Hits	1967	7.50	15.00	30.00
❑ CS 9388 [S]	Baroque Sketches	1966	5.00	10.00	20.00

Number	Title	Yr	VG	VG+	NM
❏ CS 9449 [S]	The Time and the Place	1967	5.00	10.00	20.00
❏ CS 9546 [S]	Art Farmer Plays the Great Jazz Hits	1967	5.00	10.00	20.00
❏ C2 38232 [(2)]	Time and Place	198?	3.00	6.00	12.00
COLUMBIA JAZZ ODYSSEY					
❏ PC 36826	Art Farmer Plays the Great Jazz Hits	1980	2.50	5.00	10.00
CONCORD JAZZ					
❏ CJ-179	Work of Art	198?	3.00	6.00	12.00
❏ CJ-212	Warm Valley	1982	3.00	6.00	12.00
CONTEMPORARY					
❏ C-3554 [M]	Portrait of Art Farmer	1958	12.50	25.00	50.00
❏ S-7027 [S]	Portrait of Art Farmer	1959	7.50	15.00	30.00
❏ S-7554	Portrait of Art Farmer	197?	3.75	7.50	15.00
❏ S-7636	On the Road	197?	3.75	7.50	15.00
❏ C-14029	Something to Live For: The Music of Billy Strayhorn	1987	2.50	5.00	10.00
❏ C-14042	Blame It on My Youth	198?	2.50	5.00	10.00
❏ C-14055	Ph. D.	1989	3.00	6.00	12.00
CTI					
❏ 7073	Crawl	1977	3.75	7.50	15.00
❏ 7080	Something You Got	1977	3.75	7.50	15.00
❏ 7083	Big Blues	1978	3.75	7.50	15.00
❏ 9000	Yama	198?	3.00	6.00	12.00
FANTASY					
❏ OJC-018	Two Trumpets	198?	2.50	5.00	10.00
❏ OJC-054	The Art Farmer Septet	198?	2.50	5.00	10.00
❏ OJC-072	When Farmer Met Gryce	198?	2.50	5.00	10.00
❏ OJC-166	Portrait of Art	198?	2.50	5.00	10.00
❏ OJC-241	Art Farmer Quintet	1987	2.50	5.00	10.00
❏ OJC-398	Farmer's Market	1989	3.00	6.00	12.00
❏ OJC-478	On the Road	1990	3.00	6.00	12.00
INNER CITY					
❏ IC-6004	The Summer Knows	197?	3.75	7.50	15.00
❏ IC-6014	To Duke with Love	197?	3.75	7.50	15.00
❏ IC-6024	Live at Boomer's	197?	3.75	7.50	15.00
MAINSTREAM					
❏ MRL-332	Homecoming	1971	5.00	10.00	20.00
❏ MRL-371	Gentle Eyes	1972	5.00	10.00	20.00
MERCURY					
❏ MG-20786 [M]	Listen to Art Farmer and the Orchestra	1963	5.00	10.00	20.00
❏ SR-60786 [S]	Listen to Art Farmer and the Orchestra	1963	6.25	12.50	25.00
MOON					
❏ MLP-014	Art Worker	199?	3.75	7.50	15.00
NEW JAZZ					
❏ NJLP-8203 [M]	Farmer's Market	1958	25.00	50.00	100.00
-- Yellow label					
❏ NJLP-8203 [M]	Farmer's Market	1958	12.50	25.00	50.00
-- Purple label					
❏ NJLP-8203 [M]	Farmer's Market	1965	6.25	12.50	25.00
-- Blue label, trident logo at right					
❏ NJLP-8258 [M]	Early Art	1961	10.00	20.00	40.00
-- Purple label					
❏ NJLP-8258 [M]	Early Art	1965	6.25	12.50	25.00
-- Blue label, trident logo at right					
❏ NJLP-8278 [M]	Work of Art	1962	10.00	20.00	40.00
-- Purple label					
❏ NJLP-8278 [M]	Work of Art	1965	6.25	12.50	25.00
-- Blue label, trident logo at right					
❏ NJLP-8289 [M]	Evening in Casablanca	1962	10.00	20.00	40.00
-- Purple label					
❏ NJLP-8289 [M]	Evening in Casablanca	1965	6.25	12.50	25.00
-- Blue label, trident logo at right					
PAUSA					
❏ 7133	From Vienna with Art	198?	3.00	6.00	12.00
❏ 9025	Modern Art	198?	2.50	5.00	10.00
PRESTIGE					
❏ PRLP-162 [10]	Art Farmer Septet	1953	50.00	100.00	200.00
❏ PRLP-177 [10]	Art Farmer Quintet Featuring Sonny Rollins	1954	50.00	100.00	200.00
❏ PRLP-181 [10]	Art Farmer Quintet	1954	50.00	100.00	200.00
❏ PRLP-193 [10]	Art Farmer Quartet	1954	50.00	100.00	200.00
❏ PRLP-209 [10]	Art Farmer Quintet	1955	50.00	100.00	200.00
❏ PRLP-7017 [M]	Art Farmer Quintet Featuring Gigi Gryce	1956	25.00	50.00	100.00
❏ PRLP-7031 [M]	Art Farmer Septet	1956	25.00	50.00	100.00
❏ PRLP-7062 [M]	Two Trumpets	1956	25.00	50.00	100.00
❏ PRLP-7085 [M]	When Farmer Met Gryce	1957	25.00	50.00	100.00
❏ PRLP-7092 [M]	Three Trumpets	1957	25.00	50.00	100.00
❏ PRLP-7344 [(2) M]	Trumpets All Out	1964	12.50	25.00	50.00
❏ PRST-7344 [(2) R]	Trumpets All Out	1964	7.50	15.00	30.00
❏ PRST-7665	Early Art	1969	3.75	7.50	15.00

Number	Title	Yr	VG	VG+	NM
❏ 24032 [(2)]	Farmer's Market	197?	3.75	7.50	15.00
SCEPTER					
❏ S-521 [M]	The Many Faces of Art Farmer	1964	5.00	10.00	20.00
❏ SS-521 [S]	The Many Faces of Art Farmer	1964	6.25	12.50	25.00
SOUL NOTE					
❏ SN-1026	I'll Take Manhattan	198?	3.00	6.00	12.00
❏ SN-1046	Mirage	1983	3.00	6.00	12.00
❏ SN-1076	You Make Me Smile	1985	3.00	6.00	12.00
STEREO RECORDS					
❏ S-7027 [S]	Portrait of Art Farmer	1958	10.00	20.00	40.00
UNITED ARTISTS					
❏ UAL-4007 [M]	Modern Art	1958	12.50	25.00	50.00
❏ UAL-4047 [M]	Brass Shout	1959	12.50	25.00	50.00
❏ UAL-4062 [M]	Aztec Suite	1959	12.50	25.00	50.00
❏ UAS-5007 [S]	Modern Art	1959	10.00	20.00	40.00
❏ UAS-5047 [S]	Brass Shout	1959	10.00	20.00	40.00
❏ UAS-5062 [S]	Aztec Suite	1959	10.00	20.00	40.00

FARMER, ART/ART TAYLOR
Also see each artist's individual listings.

PRESTIGE					
❏ PRLP-7342 [(2) M]	Hard Cookin'	1964	12.50	25.00	50.00
❏ PRST-7342 [(2) R]	Hard Cookin'	1964	7.50	15.00	30.00

FARR, JIMMY

CIRCLE					
❏ CLP-26	Best by Farr	197?	2.50	5.00	10.00

FARRAH, SHAMEK
Alto saxophone player.

STRATA-EAST					
❏ SES-7412	First Impressions	1974	10.00	20.00	40.00

FARRELL, JOE
Tenor and soprano saxophone player, flutist and clarinetist. Also see FUSE ONE.

CONTEMPORARY					
❏ C-14002	Sonic Text	1980	3.00	6.00	12.00
CTI					
❏ 6003	Joe Farrell Quartet	1970	5.00	10.00	20.00
❏ 6014	Outback	1971	5.00	10.00	20.00
❏ 6023	Moon Germs	1972	5.00	10.00	20.00
❏ 6034	Penny Arcade	1973	3.75	7.50	15.00
❏ 6042	Upon This Rock	1974	3.75	7.50	15.00
❏ 6053	Canned Funk	1975	3.75	7.50	15.00
❏ 6065	Song of the Wind	1976	3.75	7.50	15.00
❏ 8003	Moon Germs	197?	2.50	5.00	10.00
-- Reissue of 6023					
❏ 8005	Outback	197?	2.50	5.00	10.00
-- Reissue of 6014					
JAZZ A LA CARTE					
❏ 4	Farrell's Inferno	1979	3.75	7.50	15.00
WARNER BROS.					
❏ BS 3121	La Cathedral y El Toro	1977	3.00	6.00	12.00
❏ BSK 3225	Night Dancing	1978	3.00	6.00	12.00
XANADU					
❏ 174	Skateboard Park	1979	3.75	7.50	15.00

FARRELL, JOE; FLORA PURIM; AIRTO MOREIRA
Also see each artist's individual listings (for Moreira, see AIRTO).

REFERENCE RECORDINGS					
❏ RR-24	Three-Way Mirror	1989	5.00	10.00	20.00

FASCIANI, GUY

INNER CITY					
❏ IC-1161	The Stairway Caper	198?	3.75	7.50	15.00

FASOLI, CLAUDIO
Tenor and soprano saxophone player.

SOUL NOTE					
❏ SN-1071	Lido	1983	3.75	7.50	15.00

FATOOL, NICK
Drummer and bandleader.

JAZZOLOGY					
❏ J-158	Nick Fatool's Jazz Band -- Spring of '87	1987	2.50	5.00	10.00

FATTBURGER
Members in the 1980s: Tom Aros (percussion); Carl Evans Jr. (keyboards); Mark Hunter (bass); Kevin Koch (drums); Steve Laury (guitar).

INTIMA					
❏ SJ-73287	Good News	1987	2.50	5.00	10.00

Number	Title	Yr	VG	VG+	NM
❏ D1-73334	Living in Paradise	1988	2.50	5.00	10.00
❏ D1-73503	Time Will Tell	1989	3.00	6.00	12.00

OPTIMISM

Number	Title	Yr	VG	VG+	NM
❏ OP-2001	One of a Kind	198?	3.00	6.00	12.00

FAVERO, ALBERTO
Argentinean saxophone player, composer and conductor.
CATALYST

Number	Title	Yr	VG	VG+	NM
❏ 7914	Suite Trane	197?	3.00	6.00	12.00

FAVRE, PIERRE
Drummer and percussionist.
ECM

Number	Title	Yr	VG	VG+	NM
❏ 1274	Singing Drums	1985	3.00	6.00	12.00

FAWKES, WALLY
Clarinetist and bandleader.
STOMP OFF

Number	Title	Yr	VG	VG+	NM
❏ SOS-1060	That's the Blues, Old Man	198?	2.50	5.00	10.00
❏ SOS-1144	Whatever Next!	1988	2.50	5.00	10.00

FAYE, FRANCES
Pianist and female singer.
BETHLEHEM

Number	Title	Yr	VG	VG+	NM
❏ BCP-23 [M]	I'm Wild Again	1955	12.50	25.00	50.00
❏ BCP-62 [M]	Relaxin' with Frances Faye	1957	10.00	20.00	40.00
❏ BCP-6006	Bad, Bad, Frances Faye	1976	3.75	7.50	15.00
-- Reissue of 23, distributed by RCA Victor					
❏ BCP-6017 [M]	Frances Faye Sings Folk Songs	1957	10.00	20.00	40.00

CAPITOL

Number	Title	Yr	VG	VG+	NM
❏ H 512 [10]	No Reservations	1954	20.00	40.00	80.00
❏ T 512 [M]	No Reservations	1955	12.50	25.00	50.00
-- Turquoise or gray label					
❏ T 512 [M]	No Reservations	1958	7.50	15.00	30.00
-- Black label with colorband, logo at left					

GENE NORMAN

Number	Title	Yr	VG	VG+	NM
❏ GNP-41 [M]	Caught in the Act	1958	10.00	20.00	40.00
❏ GNP-92 [M]	Caught in the Act, Volume 2	1959	10.00	20.00	40.00

GNP CRESCENDO

Number	Title	Yr	VG	VG+	NM
❏ GNP-41 [M]	Caught in the Act	196?	3.75	7.50	15.00
❏ GNPS-41 [S]	Caught in the Act	196?	3.00	6.00	12.00
❏ GNP-92 [M]	Caught in the Act, Volume 2	196?	3.75	7.50	15.00
❏ GNPS-92 [S]	Caught in the Act, Volume 2	196?	3.00	6.00	12.00

IMPERIAL

Number	Title	Yr	VG	VG+	NM
❏ LP-9059 [M]	Frances Faye Swings Fats Domino	1958	10.00	20.00	40.00
❏ LP-9063 [M]	Frances Faye	1959	---	---	---
-- Canceled					
❏ LP-9158 [M]	Frances Faye Sings the Blues	1961	10.00	20.00	40.00
❏ LP-12007 [S]	Frances Faye Swings Fats Domino	1959	12.50	25.00	50.00

REGINA

Number	Title	Yr	VG	VG+	NM
❏ R-315 [M]	You Gotta Go! Go! Go!	1964	6.25	12.50	25.00
❏ RS-315 [S]	You Gotta Go! Go! Go!	1964	7.50	15.00	30.00

VERVE

Number	Title	Yr	VG	VG+	NM
❏ MGV-2147 [M]	Frances Faye in Frenzy	1961	10.00	20.00	40.00
❏ V-2147 [M]	Frances Faye in Frenzy	1961	5.00	10.00	20.00
❏ V-8434 [M]	Swinging All the Way with Frances Faye	1962	5.00	10.00	20.00
❏ V6-8434 [S]	Swinging All the Way with Frances Faye	1962	6.25	12.50	25.00

FAZOLA, IRVING
Clarinetist and saxophone player.
MERCURY

Number	Title	Yr	VG	VG+	NM
❏ MG-25016 [10]	Irving Fazola and His Dixielanders	1950	12.50	25.00	50.00

FAZOLA, IRVING/GEORGE HARTMAN
Also see IRVING FAZOLA.
EMARCY

Number	Title	Yr	VG	VG+	NM
❏ MG-36022 [M]	New Orleans Express	1954	10.00	20.00	40.00

FEATHER
Vocal group.
DISCOVERY

Number	Title	Yr	VG	VG+	NM
❏ DS-821	Goin' Through Changes	198?	2.50	5.00	10.00
❏ DS-867	Chen Yu Lips	198?	2.50	5.00	10.00
❏ DS-903	Zanzibar	1986	2.50	5.00	10.00

FEATHER, LEONARD
Best known as a jazz critic and author, Feather didn't merely write on the subject; he also was a pianist, arranger and composer.
ABC-PARAMOUNT

Number	Title	Yr	VG	VG+	NM
❏ ABC-110 [M]	Swingin' on the Vibories	1956	15.00	30.00	60.00

INTERLUDE

Number	Title	Yr	VG	VG+	NM
❏ MO-511 [M]	Leonard Feather Presents 52nd Street	1959	10.00	20.00	40.00
❏ ST-1011 [S]	Leonard Feather Presents 52nd Street	1959	7.50	15.00	30.00

MAINSTREAM

Number	Title	Yr	VG	VG+	NM
❏ MRL-348	Night Blooming Jazzmen	1972	5.00	10.00	20.00
❏ MRL-388	Freedom Jazz Dance	1974	5.00	10.00	20.00

MGM

Number	Title	Yr	VG	VG+	NM
❏ E-270 [10]	Winter Sequence	1954	30.00	60.00	120.00
❏ E-3494 [M]	Hi-Fi Suite	1957	12.50	25.00	50.00
❏ E-3650 [M]	Oh, Captain!	1958	12.50	25.00	50.00

MODE

Number	Title	Yr	VG	VG+	NM
❏ LP-127 [M]	Leonard Feather Presents Bop	1957	15.00	30.00	60.00

FEATHER, LORRAINE
Female singer and composer. Also see FULL SWING.
CONCORD JAZZ

Number	Title	Yr	VG	VG+	NM
❏ CJ-78	Sweet Lorraine	1979	3.00	6.00	12.00

FELDER, WILTON
Bass player and composer. Also see THE CRUSADERS.
ABC

Number	Title	Yr	VG	VG+	NM
❏ AA-1109	We All Have a Star	1978	3.75	7.50	15.00

MCA

Number	Title	Yr	VG	VG+	NM
❏ AA-1109	We All Have a Star	1979	2.50	5.00	10.00
-- Reissue of ABC 1109					
❏ 5144	Inherit the Wind	1980	2.50	5.00	10.00
❏ 5406	Gentle Fire	1983	2.50	5.00	10.00
❏ 5510	Secrets	1985	2.50	5.00	10.00
❏ 27031	Inherit the Wind	198?	2.00	4.00	8.00
-- Reissue					
❏ 42096	Love Is a Rush	1987	2.50	5.00	10.00

FELDMAN, VICTOR
Vibraphone player and pianist. Also see CURTIS AMY.
AVA

Number	Title	Yr	VG	VG+	NM
❏ A-19 [M]	Soviet Jazz Themes	1963	6.25	12.00	25.00
❏ AS-19 [S]	Soviet Jazz Themes	1963	6.25	12.00	25.00

CHOICE

Number	Title	Yr	VG	VG+	NM
❏ 1005	Your Smile	1974	3.75	7.50	15.00

CONCORD JAZZ

Number	Title	Yr	VG	VG+	NM
❏ CJ-38	Artful Dodger	197?	3.00	6.00	12.00

CONTEMPORARY

Number	Title	Yr	VG	VG+	NM
❏ C-3541 [M]	Suite Sixteen	1957	10.00	20.00	40.00
❏ C-3549 [M]	The Arrival of Victor Feldman	1958	10.00	20.00	40.00
❏ C-5005 [M]	Latinsville	1960	10.00	20.00	40.00
❏ S-7541 [S]	Suite Sixteen	1959	7.50	15.00	30.00
❏ S-7549 [S]	The Arrival of Victor Feldman	1959	7.50	15.00	30.00
❏ S-9005 [S]	Latinsville	1960	7.50	15.00	30.00

FANTASY

Number	Title	Yr	VG	VG+	NM
❏ OJC-268	The Arrival of Victor Feldman	1987	2.50	5.00	10.00
❏ OJC-402	Merry Olde Soul	1989	3.00	6.00	12.00

INTERLUDE

Number	Title	Yr	VG	VG+	NM
❏ MO-510 [M]	With Mallets Aforethought	1959	10.00	20.00	40.00
-- Reissue of Mode LP					

MODE

Number	Title	Yr	VG	VG+	NM
❏ LP-120 [M]	Victor Feldman on Vibes	1957	15.00	30.00	60.00

NAUTILUS

Number	Title	Yr	VG	VG+	NM
❏ NR-50	The Secret of the Andes	1982	5.00	10.00	20.00
-- Audiophile vinyl					

PALO ALTO

Number	Title	Yr	VG	VG+	NM
❏ PA-8053	The Secret of the Andes	1982	2.50	5.00	10.00
❏ PA-8056	To Chopin with Love	1983	2.50	5.00	10.00
❏ PA-8066	Fiesta	1984	2.50	5.00	10.00

RIVERSIDE

Number	Title	Yr	VG	VG+	NM
❏ RLP-366 [M]	Merry Ole Soul	1961	6.25	12.00	25.00
❏ RS-9366 [S]	Merry Ole Soul	1961	6.25	12.00	25.00

VEE JAY

Number	Title	Yr	VG	VG+	NM
❏ LP-1096 [M]	Love Me with All Your Heart	1964	7.50	15.00	30.00
❏ LP-2507 [S]	It's a Wonderful World	1965	5.00	10.00	20.00

WORLD PACIFIC

Number	Title	Yr	VG	VG+	NM
❏ ST-1807 [S]	Stop the World, I Want to Get Off	1962	5.00	10.00	20.00
-- Black vinyl					

Number	Title	Yr	VG	VG+	NM
❏ ST-1807 [S]	Stop the World, I Want to Get Off	1962	12.50	25.00	50.00
-- Yellow vinyl					
❏ WP-1807 [M]	Stop the World, I Want to Get Off	1962	7.50	15.00	30.00

FELICE, DEE, TRIO
Produced by James Brown.
BETHLEHEM

Number	Title	Yr	VG	VG+	NM
❏ B-10000	In Heat	1969	12.50	25.00	50.00

FELICE, ERNICE
Accordion player.
CAPITOL

Number	Title	Yr	VG	VG+	NM
❏ H 192 [10]	Ernice Felice Quartet	1950	15.00	30.00	60.00

FENIX JAZZ BAND OF ARGENTINA, THE
STOMP OFF

Number	Title	Yr	VG	VG+	NM
❏ SOS-1129	Grandpa's Spells	1987	2.50	5.00	10.00

FERGUSON, ALLYN
Composer and arranger.
AVA

Number	Title	Yr	VG	VG+	NM
❏ A-32 [M]	Pictures at an Exhibition Framed in Jazz	1963	6.25	12.50	25.00
❏ AS-32 [S]	Pictures at an Exhibition Framed in Jazz	1963	7.50	15.00	30.00

DISCOVERY

Number	Title	Yr	VG	VG+	NM
❏ DS-810	Pictures at an Exhibition Framed in Jazz	1980	3.00	6.00	12.00
-- Reissue of AS-32					

FERGUSON, MAYNARD
Trumpeter and bandleader. Also see CHRIS CONNOR.
BASF

Number	Title	Yr	VG	VG+	NM
❏ 20662	Trumpet Rhapsody	1973	3.00	6.00	12.00

BLACK HAWK

Number	Title	Yr	VG	VG+	NM
❏ BKH-50101	Body and Soul	1986	2.50	5.00	10.00

BLUEBIRD

Number	Title	Yr	VG	VG+	NM
❏ 6455-1-RB	The Bluebird Dreamband	1987	2.50	5.00	10.00

CAMEO

Number	Title	Yr	VG	VG+	NM
❏ C-1046 [M]	The New Sounds of Maynard Ferguson	1963	5.00	10.00	20.00
❏ SC-1046 [S]	The New Sounds of Maynard Ferguson	1963	6.25	12.50	25.00
❏ C-1066 [M]	Come Blow Your Horn	1964	5.00	10.00	20.00
❏ SC-1066 [S]	Come Blow Your Horn	1964	6.25	12.50	25.00

COLUMBIA

Number	Title	Yr	VG	VG+	NM
❏ C 30466	M.F. Horn	1971	3.00	6.00	12.00
❏ PC 30466	M.F. Horn	198?	2.00	4.00	8.00
-- Budget-line reissue					
❏ C 31117	Alive and Well in London	1972	3.00	6.00	12.00
❏ PC 31117	Alive and Well in London	198?	2.00	4.00	8.00
-- Budget-line reissue					
❏ KC 31709	M.F. Horn Two	1972	3.00	6.00	12.00
❏ PC 31709	M.F. Horn Two	198?	2.00	4.00	8.00
-- Budget-line reissue					
❏ KC 32403	M.F. Horn/3	1973	3.00	6.00	12.00
❏ PC 32403	M.F. Horn/3	198?	2.00	4.00	8.00
-- Budget-line reissue					
❏ KG 32732 [(2)]	M.F. Horn 4 & 5/Live at Jimmy's	1973	3.75	7.50	15.00
❏ PG 32732 [(2)]	M.F. Horn 4 & 5/Live at Jimmy's	198?	2.50	5.00	10.00
-- Budget-line reissue					
❏ KC 33007	Chameleon	1974	3.00	6.00	12.00
❏ PC 33007	Chameleon	1975	2.50	5.00	10.00
-- Early reissue of KC 33007; no bar code					
❏ PC 33007	Chameleon	1980	2.00	4.00	8.00
-- Budget-line reissue with bar code					
❏ CG 33660 [(2)]	M.F. Horn/M.F. Horn Two	1975	3.75	7.50	15.00
❏ PC 33953	Primal Scream	1976	2.50	5.00	10.00
-- No bar code					
❏ PC 34457	Conquistador	1977	2.50	5.00	10.00
-- No bar code					
❏ PC 34457	Conquistador	1980	2.00	4.00	8.00
-- Budget-line reissue with bar code					
❏ PCQ 34457 [Q]	Conquistador	1977	5.00	10.00	20.00
❏ JC 34971	New Vintage	1977	2.50	5.00	10.00
❏ JC 35480	Carnival	1978	2.50	5.00	10.00
❏ PC 35480	Carnival	1980	2.00	4.00	8.00
-- Budget-line reissue					
❏ JC 36124	Hot	1979	2.50	5.00	10.00
❏ JC 36361	The Best of Maynard Ferguson	1980	2.50	5.00	10.00
❏ PC 36361	The Best of Maynard Ferguson	1986	2.00	4.00	8.00
-- Budget-line reissue					

Number	Title	Yr	VG	VG+	NM
❏ JC 36766	It's My Time	1980	2.50	5.00	10.00
❏ PC 36978	Maynard Ferguson	1981	2.50	5.00	10.00
❏ FC 37713	Hollywood	1982	2.50	5.00	10.00
❏ HC 44457	Conquistador	1982	12.50	25.00	50.00
-- Half-speed mastered edition					

EMARCY

Number	Title	Yr	VG	VG+	NM
❏ EMS-2-406 [(2)]	Stratospheric	1976	3.00	6.00	12.00
❏ MG-26017 [10]	Maynard Ferguson's Hollywood Party	1954	25.00	50.00	100.00
❏ MG-26024 [10]	Dimensions	1954	25.00	50.00	100.00
❏ MG-36009 [M]	Jam Session Featuring Maynard Ferguson	1955	12.50	25.00	50.00
❏ MG-36021 [M]	Maynard Ferguson Octet	1955	15.00	30.00	60.00
❏ MG-36044 [M]	Dimensions	1956	12.50	25.00	50.00
❏ MG-36046 [M]	Maynard Ferguson's Hollywood Party	1956	12.50	25.00	50.00
❏ MG-36076 [M]	Around the Horn with Maynard Ferguson	1956	12.50	25.00	50.00
❏ MG-36114 [M]	Boy with Lots of Brass	1957	12.50	25.00	50.00

ENTERPRISE

Number	Title	Yr	VG	VG+	NM
❏ S-13-101	Ridin' High	1968	3.75	7.50	15.00

FORUM

Number	Title	Yr	VG	VG+	NM
❏ F-9035 [M]	Jazz for Dancing	196?	3.00	6.00	12.00
❏ SF-9035 [S]	Jazz for Dancing	196?	3.75	7.50	15.00

INTIMA

Number	Title	Yr	VG	VG+	NM
❏ SJ-73279	High Voltage	1987	3.00	6.00	12.00
❏ D1-73390	Big Bop Nouveau	1990	3.00	6.00	12.00

MAINSTREAM

Number	Title	Yr	VG	VG+	NM
❏ MRL-316	Screamin' Blue	1971	3.00	6.00	12.00
❏ MRL-359	Dues	1972	3.00	6.00	12.00
❏ MRL-372	6 By 6	1973	3.00	6.00	12.00
❏ 805 [(2)]	Big "F"	1974	3.75	7.50	15.00
❏ S-6031 [S]	Color Him Wild	1965	5.00	10.00	20.00
❏ S-6045 [S]	The Blues Roar	1965	5.00	10.00	20.00
❏ S-6060 [S]	Maynard Ferguson Sextet	1966	5.00	10.00	20.00
❏ 56031 [M]	Color Him Wild	1965	3.75	7.50	15.00
❏ 56045 [M]	The Blues Roar	1965	3.75	7.50	15.00
❏ 56060 [M]	Maynard Ferguson Sextet	1966	3.75	7.50	15.00

MERCURY

Number	Title	Yr	VG	VG+	NM
❏ MG-20556 [M]	Boy with Lots of Brass	1960	7.50	15.00	30.00
❏ SR-60124 [S]	Boy with Lots of Brass	1960	7.50	15.00	30.00

MOSAIC

Number	Title	Yr	VG	VG+	NM
❏ MQ14-156 [(14)]	The Complete Roulette Recordings of the Maynard Ferguson Orchestra	199?	62.50	125.00	250.00

NAUTILUS

Number	Title	Yr	VG	VG+	NM
❏ NR-57	Storm	1983	10.00	20.00	40.00
-- Audiophile vinyl					

PALO ALTO

Number	Title	Yr	VG	VG+	NM
❏ PA-8052	Storm	1983	2.50	5.00	10.00
❏ PA-8077	Live from San Francisco	1985	2.50	5.00	10.00

PAUSA

Number	Title	Yr	VG	VG+	NM
❏ 7037	Trumpet Rhapsody	1980	2.50	5.00	10.00
-- Reissue of BASF LP					

PRESTIGE

Number	Title	Yr	VG	VG+	NM
❏ PRLP-7636	Maynard Ferguson 1969	1969	3.75	7.50	15.00

ROULETTE

Number	Title	Yr	VG	VG+	NM
❏ SK-101 [(2)]	The Ferguson Years	197?	3.75	7.50	15.00
❏ RE-116 [(2)]	A Message from Newport/ Newport Suite	1972	3.75	7.50	15.00
-- Reissue of 52012 and 52047 in one package					
❏ RE-122 [(2)]	Maynard '61/Si! Si! M.F.	1973	3.75	7.50	15.00
-- Reissue of 52064 and 52084 in one package					
❏ R 52012 [M]	A Message from Newport	1958	6.25	12.50	25.00
❏ SR 52012 [S]	A Message from Newport	1958	6.25	12.50	25.00
❏ R 52027 [M]	A Message from Birdland	1959	6.25	12.50	25.00
❏ SR 52027 [S]	A Message from Birdland	1959	6.25	12.50	25.00
❏ R 52038 [M]	Maynard Ferguson Plays Jazz for Dancing	1959	6.25	12.50	25.00
❏ SR 52038 [S]	Maynard Ferguson Plays Jazz for Dancing	1959	6.25	12.50	25.00
❏ R 52047 [M]	Newport Suite	1960	6.25	12.50	25.00
❏ SR 52047 [S]	Newport Suite	1960	6.25	12.50	25.00
❏ R 52055 [M]	Let's Face the Music and Dance	1960	6.25	12.50	25.00
❏ SR 52055 [S]	Let's Face the Music and Dance	1960	6.25	12.50	25.00
❏ R 52058 [M]	Swingin' My Way Through College	1960	6.25	12.50	25.00
❏ SR 52058 [S]	Swingin' My Way Through College	1960	6.25	12.50	25.00
❏ R 52064 [M]	Maynard '61	1961	6.25	12.50	25.00
❏ SR 52064 [S]	Maynard '61	1961	6.25	12.50	25.00
❏ R 52083 [M]	Maynard '62	1962	3.75	7.50	15.00
❏ SR 52083 [S]	Maynard '62	1962	5.00	10.00	20.00
❏ R 52084 [M]	Si! Si! M.F.	1962	3.75	7.50	15.00

Number	Title	Yr	VG	VG+	NM
❑ SR 52084 [S]	Si! Si! M.F.	1962	5.00	10.00	20.00
❑ R 52097 [M]	Maynard '63	1963	3.75	7.50	15.00
❑ SR 52097 [S]	Maynard '63	1963	5.00	10.00	20.00
❑ R 52107 [M]	Maynard '64	1964	3.75	7.50	15.00
❑ SR 52107 [S]	Maynard '64	1964	5.00	10.00	20.00
❑ R 52110 [M]	The World of Maynard Ferguson	1964	3.75	7.50	15.00
❑ SR 52110 [S]	The World of Maynard Ferguson	1964	5.00	10.00	20.00

TRIP

Number	Title	Yr	VG	VG+	NM
❑ 5507	Dimensions	197?	2.00	4.00	8.00
❑ 5525	Jam Session Featuring Maynard Ferguson	197?	2.00	4.00	8.00
❑ 5558	Around the Horn with Maynard Ferguson	197?	2.00	4.00	8.00

FERLINGHETTI, LAWRENCE
Jazz-influenced beat poet.
FANTASY

Number	Title	Yr	VG	VG+	NM
❑ 7004 [M] -- Red vinyl	The Impeachment of Eisenhower	1958	50.00	100.00	200.00
❑ 7004 [M] -- Black vinyl	The Impeachment of Eisenhower	1958	25.00	50.00	100.00

FERRE, BOULOU
Guitarist.
4 CORNERS OF THE WORLD

Number	Title	Yr	VG	VG+	NM
❑ FCL-4211 [M]	Boulou with the Paris All Stars	1966	5.00	10.00	20.00
❑ FCS-4211 [S]	Boulou with the Paris All Stars	1966	6.25	12.50	25.00
❑ FCL-4234 [M]	Jazz/Left Bank	1967	6.25	12.50	25.00
❑ FCS-4234 [S]	Jazz/Left Bank	1967	5.00	10.00	20.00
-- As "Boulou with the Paris All Stars"					

STEEPLECHASE

Number	Title	Yr	VG	VG+	NM
❑ SCS-1210	Relax and Enjoy	198?	3.00	6.00	12.00
❑ SCS-1222	Nuages	198?	3.00	6.00	12.00

FERRE, BOULOU AND ELOIS
Elois Ferre is a guitarist. Also see BOULOU FERRE.
STEEPLECHASE

Number	Title	Yr	VG	VG+	NM
❑ SCS-1120	Pour Django	198?	3.00	6.00	12.00
❑ SCS-1140	Gypsy Dreams	198?	3.00	6.00	12.00

FERRE, BOULOU/NIELS-HENNING ORSTED PEDERSEN/ ELOIS FERRE
Also see BOULOU AND ELOIS FERRE; NIELS-HENNING ORSTED PEDERSEN.
STEEPLECHASE

Number	Title	Yr	VG	VG+	NM
❑ SCS-1171	Trinity	1982	3.00	6.00	12.00

FETTIG, MARY
Alto and soprano saxophone player and flutist.
CONCORD JAZZ

Number	Title	Yr	VG	VG+	NM
❑ CJ-273	In Good Company	1985	2.50	5.00	10.00

FIELDING, JANE
Female singer.
JAZZ WEST

Number	Title	Yr	VG	VG+	NM
❑ LP-3 [M]	Jazz Trio for Voice, Piano and Bass	1955	75.00	150.00	300.00
❑ LP-5 [M]	Embers Glow	1956	75.00	150.00	300.00

FIELDING, JERRY
Bandleader, arranger and composer. Also see THE HI-LO'S.
ABC-PARAMOUNT

Number	Title	Yr	VG	VG+	NM
❑ ABC-542 [M]	Hollywood Brass	1966	3.75	7.50	15.00
❑ ABCS-542 [S]	Hollywood Brass	1966	5.00	10.00	20.00

COMMAND

Number	Title	Yr	VG	VG+	NM
❑ RS 33-921 [M]	Near East Brass	1967	7.50	15.00	30.00
❑ RS 921 SD [S]	Near East Brass	1967	3.75	7.50	15.00

DECCA

Number	Title	Yr	VG	VG+	NM
❑ DL 8100 [M]	Sweet with a Beat	1955	7.50	15.00	30.00
❑ DL 8371 [M]	Swingin' in Hi-Fi	1956	7.50	15.00	30.00
❑ DL 8450 [M]	Fielding's Formula	1957	7.50	15.00	30.00
❑ DL 8669 [M]	Hollywood Wind Jazztet	1958	7.50	15.00	30.00

KAPP

Number	Title	Yr	VG	VG+	NM
❑ KL-1026 [M]	Dance Concert	1956	12.50	25.00	50.00

SIGNATURE

Number	Title	Yr	VG	VG+	NM
❑ SM-1028 [M]	Favorite Christmas Music	1960	5.00	10.00	20.00
❑ SS-1028 [S]	Favorite Christmas Music	1960	6.25	12.50	25.00

TIME

Number	Title	Yr	VG	VG+	NM
❑ S-2042 [S]	Magnificence in Brass	196?	5.00	10.00	20.00
❑ S-2059 [S]	A Bit of Ireland	196?	5.00	10.00	20.00
❑ S-2119 [S]	We Like Brass	196?	5.00	10.00	20.00
❑ 52042 [M]	Magnificence in Brass	196?	3.75	7.50	15.00

Number	Title	Yr	VG	VG+	NM
❑ 52059 [M]	A Bit of Ireland	196?	3.75	7.50	15.00
❑ 52119 [M]	We Like Brass	196?	3.75	7.50	15.00

TREND

Number	Title	Yr	VG	VG+	NM
❑ TL-1000 [10]	Jerry Fielding and His Great New Orchestra	1953	30.00	60.00	120.00
❑ TL-1004 [10]	Jerry Fielding Plays a Dance Concert	1954	25.00	50.00	100.00

FIELDS, BRANDON
Tenor saxophone player.
NOVA

Number	Title	Yr	VG	VG+	NM
❑ 8602	The Other Side of the Story	1986	2.50	5.00	10.00
❑ 8811	The Traveler	1988	2.50	5.00	10.00

FIELDS, HERBIE
Tenor saxophone player and clarinetist.
DECCA

Number	Title	Yr	VG	VG+	NM
❑ DL 8130 [M]	Blow Hot -- Blow Cool	1956	10.00	20.00	40.00

FRATERNITY

Number	Title	Yr	VG	VG+	NM
❑ F-1011 [M]	Fields in Clover	1959	15.00	30.00	60.00

RKO UNIQUE

Number	Title	Yr	VG	VG+	NM
❑ ULP-146 [M]	A Night at Kitty's	1957	12.50	25.00	50.00

FIELDS, SHEP
Bandleader and arranger.
CIRCLE

Number	Title	Yr	VG	VG+	NM
❑ 38	Shep Fields and His Rippling Rhythm Orchestra 1947-50	198?	2.50	5.00	10.00
❑ 133	Shep Fields and His Orchestra 1947-51	199?	2.50	5.00	10.00

DOT

Number	Title	Yr	VG	VG+	NM
❑ DLP-3348 [M]	The Rippling Rhythm of Shep Fields	1960	3.75	7.50	15.00
❑ DLP-25348 [S]	The Rippling Rhythm of Shep Fields	1960	5.00	10.00	20.00

GOLDEN CREST

Number	Title	Yr	VG	VG+	NM
❑ 3037 [M]	Rippling Rhythms	196?	5.00	10.00	20.00
❑ S-3037 [R]	Rippling Rhythms	196?	3.00	6.00	12.00
❑ 3061 [M]	Shep Fields at the Shamrock Hilton	196?	5.00	10.00	20.00
❑ S-3061 [R]	Shep Fields at the Shamrock Hilton	196?	3.00	6.00	12.00

HINDSIGHT

Number	Title	Yr	VG	VG+	NM
❑ HSR-160	Shep Fields' New Music, 1942-44	198?	2.50	5.00	10.00
❑ HSR-179	Shep Fields and His Orchestra	198?	2.50	5.00	10.00

JUBILEE

Number	Title	Yr	VG	VG+	NM
❑ JLP-1056 [M]	Cocktails, Dinner and Dancing	1958	5.00	10.00	20.00

SUNBEAM

Number	Title	Yr	VG	VG+	NM
❑ 316	Shep Fields and His Rippling Rhythm Orchestra 1936-38	198?	2.50	5.00	10.00

FINE, MILO
Percussionist and bandleader.
FUSETRON

Number	Title	Yr	VG	VG+	NM
❑ 010	Another Outbreak of Iconoclasm (Two Eggs, Slightly Beaten)	1995	3.75	7.50	15.00

HAT ART

Number	Title	Yr	VG	VG+	NM
❑ 2033	Old Eyes	1983	3.00	6.00	12.00

HAT HUT

Number	Title	Yr	VG	VG+	NM
❑ 1R01	Old Eyes	1980	3.75	7.50	15.00
❑ E	Hah!	1977	3.75	7.50	15.00
❑ H	The Constant Extension of Inescapable Tradition	1978	3.75	7.50	15.00
❑ S/T [(2)]	MFG in Minnesota	1978	5.00	10.00	20.00

SHIH SHIH WU AI

Number	Title	Yr	VG	VG+	NM
❑ 2	Improvisations (Being Free)	1975	2.50	5.00	10.00
❑ 3	Against the Betrayers	1980	2.50	5.00	10.00
❑ 4	Lucid Anarchists (Meat with Two Potatoes)	1981	2.50	5.00	10.00
❑ 5	Get Down! Shove It! It's Tango Time!	1986	2.50	5.00	10.00
❑ 6	April/October 1991	1992	3.75	7.50	15.00

FIREHOUSE FIVE PLUS TWO, THE
Jazz band comprising employees of the Walt Disney Company, led by trombonist Ward Kimball. The personnel changed frequently over the years.
GOOD TIME JAZZ

Number	Title	Yr	VG	VG+	NM
❑ L-1 [10]	The Firehouse Five Plus Two, Volume 1	1953	12.50	25.00	50.00
❑ L-2 [10]	The Firehouse Five Plus Two, Volume 2	1953	12.50	25.00	50.00

Number	Title	Yr	VG	VG+	NM
❑ L-6 [10]	The Firehouse Five Plus Two, Volume 3	1953	12.50	25.00	50.00
❑ L-16 [10]	The Firehouse Five Plus Two, Volume 4	1953	12.50	25.00	50.00
❑ L-23 [10]	The Firehouse Five Plus Two Goes South!, Volume 5	1954	15.00	30.00	60.00
❑ S-10028 [S]	The Firehouse Five Plus Two Goes to Sea	1960	6.25	12.50	25.00
❑ S-10038 [S]	The Firehouse Five Plus Two Crashes a Party	1960	6.25	12.50	25.00
❑ S-10040 [S]	Dixieland Favorites	1960	6.25	12.50	25.00
❑ S-10044 [S]	Around the World	1960	6.25	12.50	25.00
❑ S-10049 [S]	The Firehouse Five Plus Two at Disneyland	1960	6.25	12.50	25.00
❑ S-10052 [S]	The Firehouse Five Plus Two Goes to a Fire	1960	6.25	12.50	25.00
❑ S-10054 [S]	Twenty Years Later	1960	6.25	12.50	25.00
❑ L-12010 [M]	The Firehouse Five Story, Volume 1	1955	7.50	15.00	30.00
❑ L-12011 [M]	The Firehouse Five Story, Volume 2	1955	7.50	15.00	30.00
❑ L-12012 [M]	The Firehouse Five Story, Volume 3	1955	7.50	15.00	30.00
❑ L-12014 [M]	The Firehouse Five Plus Two Plays for Lovers	1955	7.50	15.00	30.00
❑ L-12018 [M]	The Firehouse Five Plus Two Goes South!	1955	7.50	15.00	30.00
❑ L-12028 [M]	The Firehouse Five Plus Two Goes to Sea	1956	7.50	15.00	30.00
❑ L-12038 [M]	The Firehouse Five Plus Two Crashes a Party	1957	7.50	15.00	30.00
❑ L-12040 [M]	Dixieland Favorites	1957	7.50	15.00	30.00
❑ L-12044 [M]	Around the World	1958	7.50	15.00	30.00
❑ L-12049 [M]	The Firehouse Five Plus Two at Disneyland	1958	7.50	15.00	30.00
❑ L-12052 [M]	The Firehouse Five Plus Two Goes to a Fire	1959	6.25	12.50	25.00
❑ L-12054 [M]	Twenty Years Later	1959	6.25	12.50	25.00

STEREO RECORDS

Number	Title	Yr	VG	VG+	NM
❑ S-7005 [S]	The Firehouse Five Plus Two Goes to Sea	1959	10.00	20.00	40.00

FIRST HOUSE
Members: Ken Stubbs (alto saxophone); Django Bates (piano, tenor horn); Mick Hutton (bass); Martin France (drums).
ECM

Number	Title	Yr	VG	VG+	NM
❑ 1307	Erendira	1987	2.50	5.00	10.00
❑ 1393	Cantilena	1990	3.00	6.00	12.00

FIRST JAZZ PIANO QUARTET, THE
Members: Irving Joseph; Bernie Leighton; Morris Nanton; Moe Weschler.
WARNER BROS.

Number	Title	Yr	VG	VG+	NM
❑ W 1274 [M]	The First Jazz Piano Quartet	1959	6.25	12.50	25.00
❑ WS 1274 [S]	The First Jazz Piano Quartet	1959	7.50	15.00	30.00

FISCHER, CLARE
Pianist, organist, keyboard player and composer.
ATLANTIC

Number	Title	Yr	VG	VG+	NM
❑ SD 1520	Thesaurus	1969	3.75	7.50	15.00

COLUMBIA

Number	Title	Yr	VG	VG+	NM
❑ CL 2691 [M]	Songs for Rainy Day Lovers	1967	6.25	12.50	25.00
❑ CS 9491 [S]	Songs for Rainy Day Lovers	1967	3.75	7.50	15.00

DISCOVERY

Number	Title	Yr	VG	VG+	NM
❑ DS-786	America	1978	3.00	6.00	12.00
❑ DS-798	'Twas Only Yesterday	1978	3.00	6.00	12.00
❑ DS-807	Duality	1979	3.00	6.00	12.00
❑ DS-817	Salsa Picante	1979	3.00	6.00	12.00
❑ DS-820	Alone Together	198?	2.50	5.00	10.00
❑ DS-835	Machacha	198?	2.50	5.00	10.00
❑ DS-852	Clare Fischer and the Sometimes Voices	1982	2.50	5.00	10.00
❑ DS-914	Crazy Bird	1984	2.50	5.00	10.00
❑ DS-921	Free Fall	1986	2.50	5.00	10.00
❑ DS-934	By and With Himself	1987	2.50	5.00	10.00

LIGHT

Number	Title	Yr	VG	VG+	NM
❑ 5544	Love Is Surrender	197?	3.00	6.00	12.00

PACIFIC JAZZ

Number	Title	Yr	VG	VG+	NM
❑ PJ-52 [M]	First Time Out	1962	6.25	12.50	25.00
❑ ST-52 [S]	First Time Out	1962	7.50	15.00	30.00
❑ PJ-67 [M]	Surging Ahead	1963	6.25	12.50	25.00
❑ ST-67 [S]	Surging Ahead	1963	7.50	15.00	30.00
❑ PJ-77 [M]	Extension	1963	6.25	12.50	25.00
❑ ST-77 [S]	Extension	1963	7.50	15.00	30.00
❑ PJ-10096 [M]	Manteca	1966	3.75	7.50	15.00
❑ ST-20096 [S]	Manteca	1966	5.00	10.00	20.00

PAUSA

Number	Title	Yr	VG	VG+	NM
❑ 7086	2 Plus 2	198?	2.50	5.00	10.00

REVELATION

Number	Title	Yr	VG	VG+	NM
❑ REV-2	Easy Living	1968	3.75	7.50	15.00
❑ REV-6	One to Get Ready, Four to Go	1968	3.75	7.50	15.00
❑ REV-13	The Great White Hope	1969	3.75	7.50	15.00
❑ REV-15	Reclamation Act of 1972	1972	3.75	7.50	15.00
❑ REV-23	T'Da-a-a!	1976	3.75	7.50	15.00
❑ REV-26	The State of His Art	1976	3.00	6.00	12.00
❑ REV-31	Jazz Song	1979	3.00	6.00	12.00
❑ REV-37	Head, Heart and Hands	198?	2.50	5.00	10.00

WORLD PACIFIC

Number	Title	Yr	VG	VG+	NM
❑ WP-1830 [M]	So Danco Samba	1964	5.00	10.00	20.00
❑ ST-21830 [S]	So Danco Samba	1964	6.25	12.50	25.00

FISCHER, LOU
Bassist. Also see THE CRUSADERS.
SEA BREEZE

Number	Title	Yr	VG	VG+	NM
❑ SB-2012	Royal St.	198?	2.50	5.00	10.00

FISCHER, WILLIAM S.
Moog synthesizer player, composer and arranger.
EMBRYO

Number	Title	Yr	VG	VG+	NM
❑ 529	Circles	1970	3.75	7.50	15.00

FISELE, JERRY
DELMAR

Number	Title	Yr	VG	VG+	NM
❑ DL-101 [10]	Jerry Fisele and the Fabulous Windy City Six	1954	12.50	25.00	50.00

FISHER, EDDIE
Guitarist and occasional male singer, this is not the pop singer of the 1950s.
CADET

Number	Title	Yr	VG	VG+	NM
❑ LPS-828	The Third Cup	1969	3.75	7.50	15.00
❑ CA-848	The Next Hundred Years	1971	3.75	7.50	15.00

STANG

Number	Title	Yr	VG	VG+	NM
❑ 1032	Hot Lunch	1977	3.75	7.50	15.00

FISHER, ELLIOT
Violinist (regular and electronic).
DOBRE

Number	Title	Yr	VG	VG+	NM
❑ 1003	In the Land of Make Believe	1976	5.00	10.00	20.00

FISHER, KING
Trumpeter and bandleader.
JAZZOLOGY

Number	Title	Yr	VG	VG+	NM
❑ J-13	King Fisher and His All Stars	196?	3.00	6.00	12.00

FITCH, MAL
Male singer, pianist and composer.
EMARCY

Number	Title	Yr	VG	VG+	NM
❑ MG-36041 [M]	Mal Fitch	1956	12.50	25.00	50.00

FITE, BUDDY
Guitarist.
BELL

Number	Title	Yr	VG	VG+	NM
❑ 6058	Buddy Fite and Friend	1970	3.75	7.50	15.00

CYCLONE

Number	Title	Yr	VG	VG+	NM
❑ CY 4100	Buddy Fite	1971	3.00	6.00	12.00
❑ CY 4110	Changes	1972	3.00	6.00	12.00

DIFFERENT DRUMMER

Number	Title	Yr	VG	VG+	NM
❑ 1001	Buddy Fite Plays for Satin Dolls	197?	3.75	7.50	15.00

FITZGERALD, ELLA
Female singer, one of the giants of jazz.
ARCHIVE OF FOLK AND JAZZ

Number	Title	Yr	VG	VG+	NM
❑ 276	Ella Fitzgerald	1973	3.00	6.00	12.00

ATLANTIC

Number	Title	Yr	VG	VG+	NM
❑ SD 1631	Ella Loves Cole	1972	3.00	6.00	12.00

BAINBRIDGE

Number	Title	Yr	VG	VG+	NM
❑ 6223	Things Ain't What They Used to Be	1982	2.50	5.00	10.00

-- Reissue of Reprise 6432

BASF

Number	Title	Yr	VG	VG+	NM
❑ 20712	Watch What Happens	1972	3.00	6.00	12.00

CAPITOL

Number	Title	Yr	VG	VG+	NM
❑ ST 2685 [S]	Brighten the Corner	1967	3.75	7.50	15.00
❑ T 2685 [M]	Brighten the Corner	1967	5.00	10.00	20.00
❑ ST 2805 [S]	Ella Fitzgerald's Christmas	1967	3.00	6.00	12.00

Number	Title	Yr	VG	VG+	NM
❏ T 2805 [M]	Ella Fitzgerald's Christmas	1967	5.00	10.00	20.00
❏ ST 2888	Misty Blue	1968	3.75	7.50	15.00
❏ ST 2960	Thirty by Ella	1968	3.75	7.50	15.00
❏ SM-11793	Brighten the Corner	1978	2.50	5.00	10.00
❏ SN-16276	Thirty by Ella	1983	2.50	5.00	10.00
-- Budget-line reissue					
COLUMBIA					
❏ KG 32557 [(2)]	Carnegie Hall & Newport Jazz Festival 1973	1973	3.75	7.50	15.00
DECCA					
❏ DXB 156 [(2) M]	The Best of Ella	1959	10.00	20.00	40.00
-- Black labels, silver print					
❏ DXB 156 [(2) M]	The Best of Ella	1961	6.25	12.50	25.00
-- Black labels with color bars					
❏ DL 4129 [M]	Golden Favorites	1961	5.00	10.00	20.00
❏ DL 4446 [M]	Stairway to the Stars	1964	3.75	7.50	15.00
❏ DL 4447 [M]	Early Ella	1964	3.75	7.50	15.00
❏ DL 4451 [M]	Ella Sings Gershwin	1964	3.75	7.50	15.00
❏ DL 4887 [M]	Smooth Sailing	1967	3.75	7.50	15.00
❏ DL 5084 [10]	Souvenir Album	1950	30.00	60.00	120.00
❏ DL 5300 [10]	Ella Fitzgerald Sings Gershwin Songs	1951	30.00	60.00	120.00
❏ DXSB 7156 [(2) R]	The Best of Ella	196?	5.00	10.00	20.00
❏ DL 8068 [M]	Songs in a Mellow Mood	1954	12.50	25.00	50.00
❏ DL 8149 [M]	Lullabies of Birdland	1955	12.50	25.00	50.00
❏ DL 8155 [M]	Sweet and Hot	1955	12.50	25.00	50.00
❏ DL 8378 [M]	Ella Sings Gershwin	1957	10.00	20.00	40.00
❏ DL 8477 [M]	Ella and Her Fellas	1957	10.00	20.00	40.00
❏ DL 8695 [M]	The First Lady of Song	1958	10.00	20.00	40.00
❏ DL 8696 [M]	Miss Ella Fitzgerald and Mr. Nelson Riddle Invite You to Listen and Relax	1958	10.00	20.00	40.00
❏ DL 8832 [M]	For Sentimental Reasons	1958	10.00	20.00	40.00
❏ DL 74129 [R]	Golden Favorites	1961	3.00	6.00	12.00
❏ DL 74446 [R]	Stairway to the Stars	1964	3.00	6.00	12.00
❏ DL 74447 [R]	Early Ella	1964	3.00	6.00	12.00
❏ DL 74451 [R]	Ella Sings Gershwin	1964	3.00	6.00	12.00
❏ DL 74887 [R]	Smooth Sailing	1967	3.00	6.00	12.00
FANTASY					
❏ OJC-376	Montreux '77	1989	3.00	6.00	12.00
-- Reissue of Pablo Live 2308 206					
❏ OJC-442	Ella & Nice	1990	3.00	6.00	12.00
-- Reissue of Pablo Live 2308 234					
INTERMEDIA					
❏ QS-5049	Ella by Starlight	198?	2.50	5.00	10.00
MCA					
❏ 215	Ella Sings Gershwin	1973	2.50	5.00	10.00
❏ 734	Memories	198?	2.50	5.00	10.00
❏ 4016 [(2)]	The Best of Ella, Vol. 2	1973	3.75	7.50	15.00
❏ 4047 [(2)]	The Best of Ella	197?	3.75	7.50	15.00
METRO					
❏ M-500 [M]	Ella Fitzgerald	1965	3.00	6.00	12.00
❏ MS-500 [S]	Ella Fitzgerald	1965	3.00	6.00	12.00
❏ M-567 [M]	The World of Ella Fitzgerald	1966	3.00	6.00	12.00
❏ MS-567 [S]	The World of Ella Fitzgerald	1966	3.00	6.00	12.00
MGM					
❏ GAS-130	Ella Fitzgerald (Golden Archive Series)	1970	3.75	7.50	15.00
PABLO					
❏ 2310 702	Take Love Easy	1974	3.00	6.00	12.00
❏ 2310 711	Ella in London	1974	3.00	6.00	12.00
❏ 2310 751	Montreux '75	1976	3.00	6.00	12.00
❏ 2310 759	Ella and Oscar	1976	3.00	6.00	12.00
❏ 2310 772	Again	1977	3.00	6.00	12.00
❏ 2310 814	Dream Dancing	1978	3.00	6.00	12.00
❏ 2310 825	Lady Time	1978	3.00	6.00	12.00
❏ 2310 829	Fine and Mellow	1979	3.00	6.00	12.00
❏ 2310 888	Speak Love	1983	2.50	5.00	10.00
❏ 2310 921	Easy Living	1987	2.50	5.00	10.00
❏ 2310 938	All That Jazz	1990	3.00	6.00	12.00
❏ 2405 421	The Best of Ella Fitzgerald	198?	2.50	5.00	10.00
❏ 2630 201 [(2)]	Ella Embraces Jobim	1981	3.75	7.50	15.00
PABLO LIVE					
❏ 2308 206	Montreux '77	1978	3.00	6.00	12.00
❏ 2308 234	Ella & Nice	197?	3.75	7.50	15.00
❏ 2308 242	Stockholm Concert 1966	198?	2.50	5.00	10.00
PABLO TODAY					
❏ 2312 110	A Perfect Match	1980	3.00	6.00	12.00
❏ 2312 132	A Classy Pair	1983	2.50	5.00	10.00
❏ 2312 138	The Best Is Yet to Come	1982	2.50	5.00	10.00
❏ 2312 140	Nice Work If You Can Get It	198?	2.50	5.00	10.00
PAUSA					
❏ 7130	Love You Madly	198?	2.50	5.00	10.00
PICKWICK					
❏ SPC-3259	Misty Blues	1974	2.50	5.00	10.00

Number	Title	Yr	VG	VG+	NM
PRESTIGE					
❏ PRLP-7685	Sunshine of Your Love	1970	3.75	7.50	15.00
REPRISE					
❏ RS-6354	Ella	1969	3.75	7.50	15.00
❏ RS-6432	Things Ain't What They Used to Be	1971	3.00	6.00	12.00
SUNBEAM					
❏ 205	Ella Fitzgerald and Her Orchestra, 1940	197?	2.50	5.00	10.00
VERVE					
❏ V-10-4 [(4) M]	Ella Fitzgerald Sings the Duke Ellington Song Book	196?	12.50	25.00	50.00
❏ V-29-5 [(5) M]	Ella Fitzgerald Sings the George and Ira Gershwin Song Book	196?	25.00	50.00	100.00
-- Reissue of MGV-4029					
❏ V6-29-5 [(5) S]	Ella Fitzgerald Sings the George and Ira Gershwin Song Book	196?	25.00	50.00	100.00
-- Reissue of MGVS-6082					
❏ VE-2-2511 [(2)]	The Cole Porter Song Book	197?	3.75	7.50	15.00
❏ VE-2-2519 [(2)]	The Rodgers and Hart Song Book	197?	3.75	7.50	15.00
❏ VE-2-2525 [(2)]	The George Gershwin Song Book	1978	3.75	7.50	15.00
❏ VE-2-2535 [(2)]	The Duke Ellington Song Book	1979	3.75	7.50	15.00
❏ VE-1-2539	Ella Wishes You a Swinging Christmas	198?	3.00	6.00	12.00
❏ VE-2-2540 [(2)]	The Duke Ellington Song Book, Vol. 2	1982	3.75	7.50	15.00
❏ MGV-4001-2 [(2) M]	Ella Fitzgerald Sings the Cole Porter Song Book	1956	20.00	40.00	80.00
❏ V-4001-2 [(2) M]	Ella Fitzgerald Sings the Cole Porter Song Book	1961	6.25	12.50	25.00
❏ MGV-4002-2 [(2) M]	Ella Fitzgerald Sings the Rodgers & Hart Song Book	1956	20.00	40.00	80.00
❏ V-4002-2 [(2) M]	Ella Fitzgerald Sings the Rodgers and Hart Song Book	1961	6.25	12.50	25.00
❏ MGV-4004 [M]	Like Someone in Love	1957	12.50	25.00	50.00
❏ V-4004 [M]	Like Someone in Love	1961	5.00	10.00	20.00
❏ V6-4004 [S]	Like Someone in Love	1961	5.00	10.00	20.00
❏ MGV-4008-2 [(2) M]	Ella Fitzgerald Sings the Duke Ellington Song Book, Vol. 1	1957	20.00	40.00	80.00
❏ V-4008-2 [(2) M]	Ella Fitzgerald Sings the Duke Ellington Song Book, Vol. 1	1961	6.25	12.50	25.00
❏ MGV-4009-2 [(2) M]	Ella Fitzgerald Sings the Duke Ellington Song Book, Vol. 2	1957	20.00	40.00	80.00
❏ V-4009-2 [(2) M]	Ella Fitzgerald Sings the Duke Ellington Song Book, Vol. 2	1961	6.25	12.50	25.00
❏ MGV-4010-4 [(4) M]	Ella Fitzgerald Sings the Duke Ellington Song Book	1957	37.50	75.00	150.00
-- Combines 4008 and 4009 into one package					
❏ MGV-4013 [M]	Ella Fitzgerald Sings the Gershwin Song Book	1957	12.50	25.00	50.00
❏ MGV-4019-2 [(2) M]	Ella Fitzgerald Sings the Irving Berlin Song Book	1958	20.00	40.00	80.00
❏ V-4019-2 [(2) M]	Ella Fitzgerald Sings the Irving Berlin Song Book	1961	6.25	12.50	25.00
❏ V6-4019-2 [(2) S]	Ella Fitzgerald Sings the Irving Berlin Song Book	1961	6.25	12.50	25.00
❏ MGV-4021 [M]	Ella Swings Lightly	1958	12.50	25.00	50.00
❏ V-4021 [M]	Ella Swings Lightly	1961	5.00	10.00	20.00
❏ V6-4021 [S]	Ella Swings Lightly	1961	5.00	10.00	20.00
❏ MGV-4022 [M]	Ella Fitzgerald Sings the Rodgers & Hart Song Book, Vol. 1	1959	12.50	25.00	50.00
❏ V-4022 [M]	Ella Fitzgerald Sings the Rodgers & Hart Song Book, Vol. 1	1961	5.00	10.00	20.00
❏ V6-4022 [S]	Ella Fitzgerald Sings the Rodgers & Hart Song Book, Vol. 1	1961	5.00	10.00	20.00
❏ MGV-4023 [M]	Ella Fitzgerald Sings the Rodgers & Hart Song Book, Vol. 2	1959	12.50	25.00	50.00
❏ V-4023 [M]	Ella Fitzgerald Sings the Rodgers & Hart Song Book, Vol. 2	1961	5.00	10.00	20.00
❏ V6-4023 [S]	Ella Fitzgerald Sings the Rodgers & Hart Song Book, Vol. 2	1961	5.00	10.00	20.00
❏ MGV-4024 [M]	Ella Fitzgerald Sings the George and Ira Gershwin Song Book, Vol. 1	1959	12.50	25.00	50.00
❏ V-4024 [M]	Ella Fitzgerald Sings the George and Ira Gershwin Song Book, Vol. 1	1961	5.00	10.00	20.00
❏ V6-4024 [S]	Ella Fitzgerald Sings the George and Ira Gershwin Song Book, Vol. 1	1961	5.00	10.00	20.00
❏ MGV-4025 [M]	Ella Fitzgerald Sings the George and Ira Gershwin Song Book, Vol. 2	1959	12.50	25.00	50.00
❏ V-4025 [M]	Ella Fitzgerald Sings the George and Ira Gershwin Song Book, Vol. 2	1961	5.00	10.00	20.00
❏ V6-4025 [S]	Ella Fitzgerald Sings the George and Ira Gershwin Song Book, Vol. 2	1961	5.00	10.00	20.00
❏ MGV-4026 [M]	Ella Fitzgerald Sings the George and Ira Gershwin Song Book, Vol. 3	1959	12.50	25.00	50.00

Known to one generation as the singer who shatters glass in the original "Is it live or is it Memorex?" cassette tape commercial, Ella Fitzgerald will forever be known to all generations as among the foremost interpreters of American popular song. (Top left) Her most celebrated albums were her "songbook" series, in which she took on the works of one composer per album and made them her own. One of these is the pictured take on the Cole Porter songbook. (Top right) Jazz musicians have been recording Christmas songs almost as long as there has been recorded jazz, but Ella's Verve Christmas album remains essential. (Bottom left) Ella stole some of Bobby Darin's thunder when her own version of "Mack the Knife" became a hit single. This is the album from which her hit version came. (Bottom right) In the late 1960s, Ella recorded for Capitol in, to be honest, the least satisfying phase of her career. One of the resulting albums, before her artistic renaissance on Norman Granz's new Pablo label, was *Misty Blue*.

Number	Title	Yr	VG	VG+	NM
❏ V-4026 [M]	Ella Fitzgerald Sings the George and Ira Gershwin Song Book, Vol. 3	1961	5.00	10.00	20.00
❏ V6-4026 [S]	Ella Fitzgerald Sings the George and Ira Gershwin Song Book, Vol. 3	1961	5.00	10.00	20.00
❏ MGV-4027 [M]	Ella Fitzgerald Sings the George and Ira Gershwin Song Book, Vol. 4	1959	12.50	25.00	50.00
❏ V-4027 [M]	Ella Fitzgerald Sings the George and Ira Gershwin Song Book, Vol. 4	1961	5.00	10.00	20.00
❏ V6-4027 [S]	Ella Fitzgerald Sings the George and Ira Gershwin Song Book, Vol. 4	1961	5.00	10.00	20.00
❏ MGV-4028 [M]	Ella Fitzgerald Sings the George and Ira Gershwin Song Book, Vol. 5	1959	12.50	25.00	50.00
❏ V-4028 [M]	Ella Fitzgerald Sings the George and Ira Gershwin Song Book, Vol. 5	1961	5.00	10.00	20.00
❏ V6-4028 [S]	Ella Fitzgerald Sings the George and Ira Gershwin Song Book, Vol. 5	1961	5.00	10.00	20.00
❏ MGV-4029-5 [(5) M]	Ella Fitzgerald Sings the George and Ira Gershwin Song Book	1959	62.50	125.00	250.00
-- Box set with 4024 through 4028 plus bonus 10-inch LP
❏ MGV-4029-5 [(5) M]	Ella Fitzgerald Sings the George and Ira Gershwin Song Book	1959	125.00	250.00	500.00
-- Box set with 4024 through 4028 plus bonus 10-inch LP, all in walnut box with leather pockets
❏ MGV-4030 [M]	Ella Fitzgerald Sings the Irving Berlin Song Book, Vol. 1	1959	12.50	25.00	50.00
❏ V-4030 [M]	Ella Fitzgerald Sings the Irving Berlin Song Book, Vol. 1	1961	5.00	10.00	20.00
❏ V6-4030 [S]	Ella Fitzgerald Sings the Irving Berlin Song Book, Vol. 1	1961	5.00	10.00	20.00
❏ MGV-4031 [M]	Ella Fitzgerald Sings the Irving Berlin Song Book, Vol. 2	1959	12.50	25.00	50.00
❏ V-4031 [M]	Ella Fitzgerald Sings the Irving Berlin Song Book, Vol. 2	1961	5.00	10.00	20.00
❏ V6-4031 [S]	Ella Fitzgerald Sings the Irving Berlin Song Book, Vol. 2	1961	5.00	10.00	20.00
❏ MGV-4032 [M]	Sweet Songs for Swingers	1959	12.50	25.00	50.00
❏ V-4032 [M]	Sweet Songs for Swingers	1961	5.00	10.00	20.00
❏ V6-4032 [S]	Sweet Songs for Swingers	1961	5.00	10.00	20.00
❏ MGV-4034 [M]	Hello, Love	1959	12.50	25.00	50.00
❏ V-4034 [M]	Hello, Love	1961	5.00	10.00	20.00
❏ V6-4034 [S]	Hello, Love	1961	5.00	10.00	20.00
❏ MGV-4036 [M]	Get Happy!	1960	10.00	20.00	40.00
❏ V-4036 [M]	Get Happy!	1961	5.00	10.00	20.00
❏ V6-4036 [S]	Get Happy!	1961	5.00	10.00	20.00
❏ MGV-4041 [M]	Mack the Knife -- Ella in Berlin	1960	10.00	20.00	40.00
❏ V-4041 [M]	Mack the Knife -- Ella in Berlin	1961	5.00	10.00	20.00
❏ V6-4041 [S]	Mack the Knife -- Ella in Berlin	1961	5.00	10.00	20.00
❏ MGV-4042 [M]	Ella Wishes You a Swinging Christmas	1960	12.50	25.00	50.00
❏ V-4042 [M]	Ella Wishes You a Swinging Christmas	1961	10.00	20.00	40.00
❏ V6-4042 [S]	Ella Wishes You a Swinging Christmas	1961	12.50	25.00	50.00
❏ MGV-4043 [M]	Let No Man Write My Epitaph	1961	10.00	20.00	40.00
❏ V-4043 [M]	Let No Man Write My Epitaph	1961	5.00	10.00	20.00
❏ V6-4043 [S]	Let No Man Write My Epitaph	1961	5.00	10.00	20.00
❏ MGV-4046-2 [(2) M]	Ella Fitzgerald Sings the Harold Arlen Song Book	1961	15.00	30.00	60.00
❏ MGV-4049 [M]	Ella Fitzgerald Sings Cole Porter	1961	10.00	20.00	40.00
❏ V-4049 [M]	Ella Fitzgerald Sings Cole Porter	1961	5.00	10.00	20.00
❏ MGV-4050 [M]	Ella Fitzgerald Sings More Cole Porter	1961	10.00	20.00	40.00
❏ V-4050 [M]	Ella Fitzgerald Sings More Cole Porter	1961	5.00	10.00	20.00
❏ MGV-4052 [M]	Ella in Hollywood	1961	10.00	20.00	40.00
❏ V-4052 [M]	Ella in Hollywood	1961	5.00	10.00	20.00
❏ V-4053 [M]	Clap Hands, Here Comes Charley	1962	10.00	20.00	40.00
❏ V6-4053 [S]	Clap Hands, Here Comes Charley	1962	37.50	75.00	150.00
❏ V-4054 [M]	Ella Swings Brightly with Nelson	1962	7.50	15.00	30.00
❏ V6-4054 [S]	Ella Swings Brightly with Nelson	1962	7.50	15.00	30.00
❏ V-4055 [M]	Ella Swings Gently with Nelson	1962	7.50	15.00	30.00
❏ V6-4055 [S]	Ella Swings Gently with Nelson	1962	7.50	15.00	30.00
❏ V-4056 [M]	Rhythm Is My Business	1962	7.50	15.00	30.00
❏ V6-4056 [S]	Rhythm Is My Business	1962	7.50	15.00	30.00
❏ V-4057 [M]	Ella Fitzgerald Sings the Harold Arlen Song Book, Vol. 1	1962	7.50	15.00	30.00
❏ V6-4057 [S]	Ella Fitzgerald Sings the Harold Arlen Song Book, Vol. 1	1962	7.50	15.00	30.00
❏ V-4058 [M]	Ella Fitzgerald Sings the Harold Arlen Song Book, Vol. 2	1962	7.50	15.00	30.00
❏ V6-4058 [S]	Ella Fitzgerald Sings the Harold Arlen Song Book, Vol. 2	1962	7.50	15.00	30.00
❏ V-4059 [M]	Ella Sings Broadway	1963	6.25	12.50	25.00
❏ V6-4059 [S]	Ella Sings Broadway	1963	6.25	12.50	25.00
❏ V-4060 [M]	Ella Fitzgerald Sings the Jerome Kern Song Book	1963	6.25	12.50	25.00
❏ V6-4060 [S]	Ella Fitzgerald Sings the Jerome Kern Song Book	1963	6.25	12.50	25.00
❏ V-4061 [M]	Ella and Basie!	1963	6.25	12.50	25.00
❏ V6-4061 [S]	Ella and Basie!	1963	6.25	12.50	25.00
❏ V-4062 [M]	These Are the Blues	1963	6.25	12.50	25.00
❏ V6-4062 [S]	These Are the Blues	1963	6.25	12.50	25.00
❏ V-4063 [M]	The Best of Ella Fitzgerald	1964	3.75	7.50	15.00
❏ V6-4063 [S]	The Best of Ella Fitzgerald	1964	3.75	7.50	15.00
❏ V-4064 [M]	Hello, Dolly!	1964	6.25	12.50	25.00
❏ V6-4064 [S]	Hello, Dolly!	1964	6.25	12.50	25.00
❏ V-4065 [M]	Ella at Juan Les Pins	1964	6.25	12.50	25.00
❏ V6-4065 [S]	Ella at Juan Les Pins	1964	6.25	12.50	25.00
❏ V-4066 [M]	A Tribute to Cole Porter	1964	6.25	12.50	25.00
❏ V6-4066 [S]	A Tribute to Cole Porter	1964	6.25	12.50	25.00
❏ V-4067 [M]	Ella Fitzgerald Sings the Johnny Mercer Song Book	1965	5.00	10.00	20.00
❏ V6-4067 [S]	Ella Fitzgerald Sings the Johnny Mercer Song Book	1965	5.00	10.00	20.00
❏ V-4068 [M]	Porgy & Bess	1965	5.00	10.00	20.00
❏ V6-4068 [S]	Porgy & Bess	1965	5.00	10.00	20.00
❏ V-4069 [M]	Ella in Hamburg	1966	5.00	10.00	20.00
❏ V6-4069 [S]	Ella in Hamburg	1966	5.00	10.00	20.00
❏ V-4070 [M]	Ella at Duke's Place	1966	5.00	10.00	20.00
❏ V6-4070 [S]	Ella at Duke's Place	1966	5.00	10.00	20.00
❏ V-4071 [M]	Whisper Not	1966	5.00	10.00	20.00
❏ V6-4071 [S]	Whisper Not	1966	5.00	10.00	20.00
❏ V-4072 [M]	Ella & Duke at Cote d'Azur	1967	6.25	12.50	25.00
❏ V6-4072 [S]	Ella & Duke at Cote d'Azur	1967	3.75	7.50	15.00
❏ MGVS-6000 [S]	Like Someone in Love	1960	10.00	20.00	40.00
❏ MGVS-6005-2 [(2) S]	Ella Fitzgerald Sings the Irving Berlin Song Book	1960	15.00	30.00	60.00
❏ MGVS-6009 [S]	Ella Fitzgerald Sings the Rodgers & Hart Song Book, Vol. 1	1960	10.00	20.00	40.00
❏ MGVS-6010 [S]	Ella Fitzgerald Sings the Rodgers & Hart Song Book, Vol. 2	1960	10.00	20.00	40.00
❏ MGVS-6019 [S]	Ella Swings Lightly	1960	10.00	20.00	40.00
❏ MGVS-6026 [S]	Ella Fitzgerald at the Opera House	1960	10.00	20.00	40.00
❏ MGVS-6052 [S]	Ella Fitzgerald Sings the Irving Berlin Song Book, Vol. 1	1960	10.00	20.00	40.00
❏ MGVS-6053 [S]	Ella Fitzgerald Sings the Irving Berlin Song Book, Vol. 2	1960	10.00	20.00	40.00
❏ MGVS-6072 [S]	Sweet Songs for Swingers	1960	10.00	20.00	40.00
❏ MGVS-6077 [S]	Ella Fitzgerald Sings the George and Ira Gershwin Song Book, Vol. 1	1960	10.00	20.00	40.00
❏ MGVS-6078 [S]	Ella Fitzgerald Sings the George and Ira Gershwin Song Book, Vol. 2	1960	10.00	20.00	40.00
❏ MGVS-6079 [S]	Ella Fitzgerald Sings the George and Ira Gershwin Song Book, Vol. 3	1960	10.00	20.00	40.00
❏ MGVS-6080 [S]	Ella Fitzgerald Sings the George and Ira Gershwin Song Book, Vol. 4	1960	10.00	20.00	40.00
❏ MGVS-6081 [S]	Ella Fitzgerald Sings the George and Ira Gershwin Song Book, Vol. 5	1960	10.00	20.00	40.00
❏ MGVS-6082-5 [(5) S]	Ella Fitzgerald Sings the George and Ira Gershwin Song Book	1960	50.00	100.00	200.00
-- Box set with 6077 through 6081 plus bonus 10-inch LP
❏ MGVS-6100 [S]	Hello, Love	1960	10.00	20.00	40.00
❏ MGVS-6102 [S]	Get Happy!	1960	10.00	20.00	40.00
❏ MGVS-6163 [S]	Mack the Knife -- Ella in Berlin	1960	10.00	20.00	40.00
❏ MGVS-7000 [S]	Ella Fitzgerald Sings the Gershwin Song Book	1959	12.50	25.00	50.00
❏ MGV-8264 [M]	Ella Fitzgerald at the Opera House	1958	12.50	25.00	50.00
❏ V-8264 [M]	Ella Fitzgerald at the Opera House	1961	5.00	10.00	20.00
❏ V6-8264 [S]	Ella Fitzgerald at the Opera House	1961	5.00	10.00	20.00
❏ MGV-8288 [M]	One O'Clock Jump	1958	12.50	25.00	50.00
❏ V-8288 [M]	One O'Clock Jump	1961	5.00	10.00	20.00
❏ V-8670 [M]	Ella Fitzgerald Sings the Jerome Kern Song Book	1967	---	---	---
-- Canceled reissue
❏ V-8720 [M]	The Best of Ella Fitzgerald	1967	3.75	7.50	15.00
❏ V6-8720 [S]	The Best of Ella Fitzgerald	1967	3.00	6.00	12.00
❏ V-8745 [M]	Ella "Live"	1968	7.50	15.00	30.00
❏ V6-8745 [S]	Ella "Live"	1968	3.75	7.50	15.00
❏ V6-8795 [S]	The Best of Ella Fitzgerald, Vol. 2	1969	3.00	6.00	12.00
❏ V6-8817 [(2)]	History	1973	3.75	7.50	15.00
❏ MGVS-64042 [S]	Ella Wishes You a Swinging Christmas	1960	15.00	30.00	60.00
❏ 817 526-1 [(2)]	The Harold Arlen Song Book	1984	3.75	7.50	15.00
❏ 821 693-1 [(2)]	The Rodgers and Hart Song Book	198?	3.00	6.00	12.00
❏ 823 247-1	The Johnny Mercer Song Book	1985	2.50	5.00	10.00
❏ 823 278-1 [(2)]	The Cole Porter Song Book	198?	3.00	6.00	12.00
❏ 823 279-1 [(2)]	The George and Ira Gershwin Songbook (Highlights)	198?	3.00	6.00	12.00

Number	Title	Yr	VG	VG+	NM
❏ 825 024-1 [(5)]	The George and Ira Gershwin Songbook (Complete)	198?	6.25	12.50	25.00
❏ 825 098-1	Lady Be Good	1985	2.50	5.00	10.00
❏ 825 669-1	The Jerome Kern Song Book	1985	2.50	5.00	10.00
❏ 825 670-1	Mack the Knife -- Ella in Berlin	1985	2.50	5.00	10.00
❏ 827 150-1	Ella Wishes You a Swinging Christmas	198?	2.50	5.00	10.00
❏ 827 163-1 [(2)]	The Duke Ellington Song Book, Vol. 1	198?	3.00	6.00	12.00
❏ 827 169-1 [(2)]	The Duke Ellington Song Book, Vol. 2	198?	3.00	6.00	12.00
❏ 829 533-1 [(2)]	The Irving Berlin Song Book	1988	3.00	6.00	12.00
❏ 835 454-1	Ella in Rome: The Birthday Concert	1988	2.50	5.00	10.00

VOCALION

Number	Title	Yr	VG	VG+	NM
❏ VL 3797 [M]	Ella Fitzgerald	1967	3.00	6.00	12.00
❏ VL 73797 [R]	Ella Fitzgerald	1967	3.00	6.00	12.00

FITZGERALD, ELLA, AND BILLIE HOLIDAY
Also see each artist's individual listings.
AMERICAN RECORDING SOCIETY

Number	Title	Yr	VG	VG+	NM
❏ G-433 [M]	Ella Fitzgerald and Billie Holiday at Newport	1957	10.00	20.00	40.00

VERVE

Number	Title	Yr	VG	VG+	NM
❏ MGVS-6022 [S]	Ella Fitzgerald and Billie Holiday at Newport	1960	10.00	20.00	40.00
❏ MGV-8234 [M]	Ella Fitzgerald and Billie Holiday at Newport	1958	12.50	25.00	50.00
❏ V-8234 [M]	Ella Fitzgerald and Billie Holiday at Newport	1961	5.00	10.00	20.00
❏ V6-8234 [S]	Ella Fitzgerald and Billie Holiday at Newport	1961	5.00	10.00	20.00
❏ V-8826	Newport Years	1973	3.00	6.00	12.00

FITZGERALD, ELLA, AND LOUIS ARMSTRONG
Also see each artist's individual listings.
METRO

Number	Title	Yr	VG	VG+	NM
❏ M-601 [M]	Louis and Ella	1967	3.00	6.00	12.00
❏ MS-601 [S]	Louis and Ella	1967	3.00	6.00	12.00

MOBILE FIDELITY

Number	Title	Yr	VG	VG+	NM
❏ 2-248 [(2)]	Ella and Louis Again	1996	37.50	75.00	150.00
-- Audiophile vinyl					

VERVE

Number	Title	Yr	VG	VG+	NM
❏ VE-1-2507	Porgy and Bess	197?	2.50	5.00	10.00
❏ MGV-4003 [M]	Ella and Louis	1956	12.50	25.00	50.00
❏ V-4003 [M]	Ella and Louis	1961	5.00	10.00	20.00
❏ MGV-4006-2 [(2) M]	Ella and Louis Again	1956	20.00	40.00	80.00
❏ V-4006-2 [(2) M]	Ella and Louis Again	1961	6.25	12.50	25.00
❏ MGV-4011-2 [(2) M]	Porgy and Bess	1957	20.00	40.00	80.00
❏ V-4011-2 [(2) M]	Porgy and Bess	1961	6.25	12.50	25.00
❏ V6-4011-2 [(2) S]	Porgy and Bess	1961	6.25	12.50	25.00
❏ MGV-4017 [M]	Ella and Louis Again, Vol. 1	1958	12.50	25.00	50.00
❏ V-4017 [M]	Ella and Louis Again, Vol. 1	1961	5.00	10.00	20.00
❏ MGV-4018 [M]	Ella and Louis Again, Vol. 2	1958	12.50	25.00	50.00
❏ V-4018 [M]	Ella and Louis Again, Vol. 2	1961	5.00	10.00	20.00
❏ MGVS-6040-2 [(2) S]	Porgy and Bess	1960	15.00	30.00	60.00
❏ V6-8811 [(2)]	Ella and Louis	1972	3.75	7.50	15.00
❏ 827 475-1 [(2)]	Porgy and Bess	198?	3.00	6.00	12.00

FIVE BROTHERS
Members: Frank Capp; BOB ENEVOLDSEN; HERBIE HARPER; RED MITCHELL; Don Overburg.
TAMPA

Number	Title	Yr	VG	VG+	NM
❏ TP-25 [M]	Five Brothers	1957	37.50	75.00	150.00
-- Colored vinyl					
❏ TP-25 [M]	Five Brothers	1958	20.00	40.00	80.00
-- Black vinyl					

FIVE, THE
Members: CONTE CANDOLI; BUDDY CLARK; PETE JOLLY; MEL LEWIS; BILL PERKINS.
RCA VICTOR

Number	Title	Yr	VG	VG+	NM
❏ LPM-1121 [M]	The Five	1955	20.00	40.00	80.00

FIVE-A-SLIDE
AUDIOPHILE

Number	Title	Yr	VG	VG+	NM
❏ AP-180	Five-a-Slide	198?	3.00	6.00	12.00

FLAHIVE, LARRY
Pianist.
SEA BREEZE

Number	Title	Yr	VG	VG+	NM
❏ SB-2020	Standard Flay	1983	2.50	5.00	10.00

FLANAGAN, TOMMY
Pianist. Also see THE NEW YORK JAZZ SEPTET.
ENJA

Number	Title	Yr	VG	VG+	NM
❏ 4014	Confirmation	1982	3.00	6.00	12.00
❏ 4022	Giant Steps	1983	3.00	6.00	12.00

FANTASY

Number	Title	Yr	VG	VG+	NM
❏ OJC-182	The Tommy Flanagan Trio	198?	2.50	5.00	10.00
❏ OJC-372	Montreux '77	1989	3.00	6.00	12.00
❏ OJC-473	Something Borrowed, Something Blue	1990	3.00	6.00	12.00

GALAXY

Number	Title	Yr	VG	VG+	NM
❏ 5110	Something Borrowed, Something Blue	1978	3.00	6.00	12.00

INNER CITY

Number	Title	Yr	VG	VG+	NM
❏ IC-1071	Tommy Flanagan Plays the Music of Harold Arlen	1980	3.00	6.00	12.00
❏ IC-1084	Trinity	198?	2.50	5.00	10.00
❏ IC-3009	Eclypso	1977	3.75	7.50	15.00
❏ IC-3029	Ballads and Blues	1979	3.75	7.50	15.00

MOODSVILLE

Number	Title	Yr	VG	VG+	NM
❏ MVLP-9 [M]	The Tommy Flanagan Trio	1960	12.50	25.00	50.00
-- Green label					
❏ MVLP-9 [M]	The Tommy Flanagan Trio	1965	6.25	12.50	25.00
-- Blue label, trident logo at right					

ONYX

Number	Title	Yr	VG	VG+	NM
❏ 206	The Tommy Flanagan Trio and Sextet	197?	3.75	7.50	15.00

PABLO

Number	Title	Yr	VG	VG+	NM
❏ 2310 724	Tokyo Recital	1975	3.75	7.50	15.00
❏ 2405 410	The Best of Tommy Flanagan	198?	2.50	5.00	10.00

PABLO LIVE

Number	Title	Yr	VG	VG+	NM
❏ 2308 202	Montreux '77	1978	3.75	7.50	15.00

PRESTIGE

Number	Title	Yr	VG	VG+	NM
❏ PRLP-7134 [M]	Overseas	1958	37.50	75.00	150.00
❏ PRST-7632	Overseas	1969	3.75	7.50	15.00

REGENT

Number	Title	Yr	VG	VG+	NM
❏ MG-6055 [M]	Jazz...It's Magic	1958	20.00	40.00	80.00

SAVOY JAZZ

Number	Title	Yr	VG	VG+	NM
❏ SJL-1158	Jazz... It's Magic	1986	2.50	5.00	10.00

STATIRAS

Number	Title	Yr	VG	VG+	NM
❏ SLP-8073	The Magnificent	1985	2.50	5.00	10.00

TIMELESS

Number	Title	Yr	VG	VG+	NM
❏ SJP-301	Jazz Poet	1990	3.00	6.00	12.00

FLANAGAN, TOMMY, AND HANK JONES
Also see each artist's individual listings.
GALAXY

Number	Title	Yr	VG	VG+	NM
❏ 5113	Our Delights	1978	3.00	6.00	12.00
❏ 5152	More Delights	1985	2.50	5.00	10.00

FLEMING, KING
Pianist and composer.
ARGO

Number	Title	Yr	VG	VG+	NM
❏ LP-4004 [M]	Misty Night	1961	6.25	12.50	25.00
❏ LPS-4004 [S]	Misty Night	1961	7.50	15.00	30.00
❏ LP-4019 [M]	Stand By!	1962	6.25	12.50	25.00
❏ LPS-4019 [S]	Stand By!	1962	7.50	15.00	30.00

CADET

Number	Title	Yr	VG	VG+	NM
❏ LP-4053 [M]	Weary Traveler	1966	3.75	7.50	15.00
❏ LPS-4053 [S]	Weary Traveler	1966	5.00	10.00	20.00

FLINT, SHELBY
Female singer. Best known as a pop-folk singer in the early 1960s ("Angel on My Shoulder" was her hit), years later she returned as a jazz vocalist.
MAD SATYR

Number	Title	Yr	VG	VG+	NM
❏ MSR-101	You've Been On My Mind	1982	6.25	12.50	25.00

FLORENCE, BOB
Pianist, male singer and composer.
CARLTON

Number	Title	Yr	VG	VG+	NM
❏ LP 12/115 [M]	Name Band: 1959	1959	10.00	20.00	40.00
❏ STLP 12/115 [S]	Name Band: 1959	1959	15.00	30.00	60.00

DISCOVERY

Number	Title	Yr	VG	VG+	NM
❏ DS-832	Westlake	1982	2.50	5.00	10.00

ERA

Number	Title	Yr	VG	VG+	NM
❏ EL-20003 [M]	Bob Florence and Trio	1956	25.00	50.00	100.00

TREND

Number	Title	Yr	VG	VG+	NM
❏ TR-523	Live at Concerts by the Sea	1980	2.50	5.00	10.00
❏ TR-536	Magic Time	1984	2.50	5.00	10.00
❏ TR-545	Trash Can City	1987	2.50	5.00	10.00

Number	Title	Yr	VG	VG+	NM

WORLD PACIFIC

❑ WP-1860 [M]	Pet Project: The Bob Florence	196?	5.00	10.00	20.00
	Big Band Plays Petula Clark Hits				
❑ WPS-21860 [S]	Pet Project: The Bob Florence	196?	6.25	12.50	25.00
	Big Band Plays Petula Clark Hits				

FLORES, CHUCK
Drummer.
CONCORD JAZZ

❑ CJ-49	Drum Flower	1978	3.00	6.00	12.00

DOBRE

❑ 1001	Flores Azules	1976	3.00	6.00	12.00

FLORY, MED
Alto, tenor and baritone saxophone player. Also an arranger and composer.
JOSIE

❑ JJS-3506 [S]	Med Flory Big Band	1963	5.00	10.00	20.00
❑ JOZ-3506 [M]	Med Flory Big Band	1963	6.25	12.50	25.00

JUBILEE

❑ JLP-1066 [M]	Jazzwave	1958	12.50	25.00	50.00
❑ SDJLP-1066 [S]	Jazzwave	1959	10.00	20.00	40.00

FLYING ISLAND
Members: Bill Baron (drums, percussion); Jeff Bova (keyboards, trumpet); Faith Fraioli (violin); Thom Preli (bass); Ray Smith (guitar).
VANGUARD

❑ VSD-79359	Flying Island	197?	3.75	7.50	15.00
❑ VSD-79368	Another Kind of Space	197?	3.75	7.50	15.00

FOGEL, MARTY
Tenor saxophone player. Also see EVERYMAN BAND.
CMP

❑ CMP-37-ST	Many Bobbing Heads, At Last	1990	3.00	6.00	12.00

FOL, RAYMOND
Pianist.
PHILIPS

❑ PHM 200-198 [M]	Vivaldi's Four Seasons in Jazz	1966	3.00	6.00	12.00
❑ PHS 600-198 [S]	Vivaldi's Four Seasons in Jazz	1966	3.75	7.50	15.00

FOLEY, GEORGE
Pianist.
STOMP OFF

❑ SOS-1085	I Like It	1985	2.50	5.00	10.00
❑ SOS-1187	Smiles and Kisses	1991	3.00	6.00	12.00

FORD, RICKY
Tenor saxophone player.
MUSE

❑ MR-5188	Manhattan Plaza	1979	3.00	6.00	12.00
❑ MR-5227	Flying Colors	1981	2.50	5.00	10.00
❑ MR-5250	Tenor for the Times	1982	2.50	5.00	10.00
❑ MR-5275	Interpretations	198?	2.50	5.00	10.00
❑ MR-5296	Future's Gold	198?	2.50	5.00	10.00
❑ MR-5314	Shorter Ideas	1985	2.50	5.00	10.00
❑ MR-5322	Looking Ahead	1987	2.50	5.00	10.00
❑ MR-5349	Saxotic Stomp	1988	2.50	5.00	10.00

NEW WORLD

❑ 204	Loxodonta Africana	1977	3.75	7.50	15.00

FOREFRONT, THE
Group of four trumpets, bass and drums founded by Bobby Lewis.
AFI

❑ 21557	Incantation	197?	5.00	10.00	20.00

FORETICH, HERMAN
Clarinetist.
AUDIOPHILE

❑ AP-124	Herman Foretich and His Atlanta	196?	3.75	7.50	15.00
	Swing Quartet				

JAZZOLOGY

❑ J-144	The Foretich Four	1987	2.50	5.00	10.00

FORMAN, BRUCE
Guitarist.
CHOICE

❑ 1026	Coast to Coast	1980	3.00	6.00	12.00

CONCORD JAZZ

❑ CJ-251	Full Circle	1984	2.50	5.00	10.00
❑ CJ-332	There Are Times	1988	2.50	5.00	10.00

Number	Title	Yr	VG	VG+	NM
❑ CJ-368	Pardon Me!	1989	3.00	6.00	12.00

MUSE

❑ MR-5251	River Journey	1981	2.50	5.00	10.00
❑ MR-5273	20/20	1982	2.50	5.00	10.00
❑ MR-5299	In Transit	1982	2.50	5.00	10.00
❑ MR-5315	The Bash	1985	2.50	5.00	10.00

FORMAN, BRUCE, AND GEORGE CABLES
Also see each artist's individual listings.
CONCORD JAZZ

❑ CJ-279	Dynamics	1985	2.50	5.00	10.00

FORMAN, MITCHELL
Keyboard player.
MAGENTA

❑ MA-0201	Train of Thought	198?	3.00	6.00	12.00

SOUL NOTE

❑ SN-1050	Childhood Dreams	198?	3.00	6.00	12.00
❑ SN-1070	Only a Memory	198?	3.00	6.00	12.00

FORREST, EUGENE "FLIP"
SAVOY

❑ MG-14392	I Heard It on the Radio	197?	5.00	10.00	20.00

FORREST, HELEN
Female singer.
AUDIOPHILE

❑ AP-47	On the Sunny Side of the Street	1958	10.00	20.00	40.00

CAPITOL

❑ T 704 [M]	Voice of the Name Bands	1956	12.50	25.00	50.00

STASH

❑ ST-225	Now and Forever	198?	3.00	6.00	12.00

FORREST, JIMMY
Tenor saxophone player. Also see OLIVER NELSON.
DELMARK

❑ DS-404	All the Gin Is Gone	196?	3.00	6.00	12.00
❑ DS-427	Black Forrest	196?	3.00	6.00	12.00
❑ DS-435	Night Train	197?	3.00	6.00	12.00

FANTASY

❑ OJC-097	Out of the Forrest	198?	2.50	5.00	10.00
❑ OJC-199	Forrest Fire	1985	2.50	5.00	10.00
❑ OJC-350	Most Much!	198?	2.50	5.00	10.00

NEW JAZZ

❑ NJLP-8250 [M]	Forrest Fire	1960	15.00	30.00	60.00
-- Purple label					
❑ NJLP-8250 [M]	Forrest Fire	1965	7.50	15.00	30.00
-- Blue label with trident logo at right					
❑ NJLP-8293 [M]	Soul Street	1962	15.00	30.00	60.00
-- Purple label					
❑ NJLP-8293 [M]	Soul Street	1965	7.50	15.00	30.00
-- Blue label with trident logo at right					

PALO ALTO

❑ 8021	Heart of the Forrest	198?	3.00	6.00	12.00

PRESTIGE

❑ PRLP-7202 [M]	Out of the Forrest	1961	10.00	20.00	40.00
-- Yellow label					
❑ PRLP-7202 [M]	Out of the Forrest	1965	5.00	10.00	20.00
-- Blue label with trident logo at right					
❑ PRLP-7218 [M]	Most Much!	1961	10.00	20.00	40.00
-- Yellow label					
❑ PRLP-7218 [M]	Most Much!	1965	5.00	10.00	20.00
-- Blue label with trident logo at right					
❑ PRLP-7235 [M]	Sit Down and Relax with Jimmy	1962	10.00	20.00	40.00
	Forrest				
-- Yellow label					
❑ PRLP-7235 [M]	Sit Down and Relax with Jimmy	1965	5.00	10.00	20.00
	Forrest				
-- Blue label with trident logo at right					
❑ PRST-7235 [S]	Sit Down and Relax with Jimmy	1962	15.00	30.00	60.00
	Forrest				
-- Silver label					
❑ PRST-7235 [S]	Sit Down and Relax with Jimmy	1965	6.25	12.50	25.00
	Forrest				
-- Blue label with trident logo at right					

UNITED

❑ 002 [10]	Night Train	1955	30.00	60.00	120.00

Number	Title	Yr	VG	VG+	NM

FORREST, JIMMY, AND MILES DAVIS
Also see each artist's individual listings.
PRESTIGE
Number	Title	Yr	VG	VG+	NM
❏ PRST-7858	Live at the Barrel	197?	3.00	6.00	12.00
❏ PRST-7860	Live at the Barrel, Volume 2	197?	3.00	6.00	12.00

FORRESTER, BOBBY
Organist.
DOBRE
❏ 1012	Organist	197?	3.00	6.00	12.00

FORTUNE, SONNY
Alto and tenor saxophone player, clarinetist and flutist. Also see STAN HUNTER.
ATLANTIC
❏ SD 18225	Serengeti Minstrel	1977	3.00	6.00	12.00
❏ SD 19187	Infinity Is	1978	3.00	6.00	12.00
❏ SD 19239	With Sound Reason	1979	3.00	6.00	12.00
HORIZON
| ❏ 704 | Awakening | 1975 | 3.75 | 7.50 | 15.00 |
| ❏ 711 | Waves | 1976 | 3.75 | 7.50 | 15.00 |
STRATA-EAST
| ❏ SES-7423 | Long Before Our Mothers Cried | 1974 | 5.00 | 10.00 | 20.00 |

FOSTER, CHUCK
Bandleader, reeds player and male singer.
CIRCLE
❏ 68	Chuck Foster and His Orchestra 1945-46	198?	2.50	5.00	10.00
HINDSIGHT
| ❏ HSR-115 | Chuck Foster and His Orchestra 1940 | 198? | 2.50 | 5.00 | 10.00 |
| ❏ HSR-171 | Chuck Foster and His Orchestra 1938-39 | 198? | 2.50 | 5.00 | 10.00 |
SEA BREEZE
| ❏ SB-2023 | Long Overdue | 1985 | 2.50 | 5.00 | 10.00 |

FOSTER, FRANK
Tenor saxophone player and composer. Also see ELMO HOPE; PAUL QUINICHETTE.
ARGO
❏ LP-717 [M]	Basie Is Our Boss	1963	6.25	12.50	25.00
❏ LPS-717 [S]	Basie Is Our Boss	1963	7.50	15.00	30.00
BLUE NOTE
❏ BLP-5043 [10]	Frank Foster Quintet	1954	100.00	200.00	400.00
❏ BST-84278	Manhattan Fever	1968	6.25	12.50	25.00
❏ BST-84316	Frank Foster	1969	---	---	---
-- Canceled
MAINSTREAM
| ❏ MRL-349 | The Loud Minority | 1972 | 5.00 | 10.00 | 20.00 |
PRESTIGE
❏ PRLP-7461 [M]	Fearless	1966	6.25	12.50	25.00
❏ PRST-7461 [S]	Fearless	1966	7.50	15.00	30.00
❏ PRLP-7479 [M]	Soul Outing!	1967	7.50	15.00	30.00
❏ PRST-7479 [S]	Soul Outing!	1967	6.25	12.50	25.00
STEEPLECHASE
| ❏ SCS-1170 | A House That Love Built | 1982 | 3.00 | 6.00 | 12.00 |

FOSTER, FRANK, AND FRANK WESS
Also see each artist's individual listings.
CONCORD JAZZ
❏ CJ-276	Frankly Speaking	1986	2.50	5.00	10.00
PABLO
| ❏ 2310 905 | Two for the Blues | 198? | 3.00 | 6.00 | 12.00 |
SAVOY JAZZ
| ❏ SJL-2249 [(2)] | Two Franks Please! | 198? | 3.00 | 6.00 | 12.00 |

FOSTER, GARY
Saxophone player, clarinetist and flutist.
REVELATION
❏ REV-5	Subconsciously	1968	5.00	10.00	20.00
❏ REV-19	Grand Clu Classe	197?	5.00	10.00	20.00

FOSTER, HERMAN
Pianist.
ARGO
❏ LP-727 [M]	Ready and Willing	1964	5.00	10.00	20.00
❏ LPS-727 [S]	Ready and Willing	1964	6.25	12.50	25.00
EPIC
❏ LA 16010 [M]	Have You Heard?	1960	5.00	10.00	20.00
❏ LA 16016 [M]	The Explosive Piano of Herman Foster	1961	5.00	10.00	20.00
❏ BA 17010 [S]	Have You Heard?	1960	6.25	12.50	25.00
❏ BA 17016 [S]	The Explosive Piano of Herman Foster	1961	6.25	12.50	25.00

FOSTER, RONNIE
Organist and keyboard player. Also see FUSE ONE.
BLUE NOTE
❏ BN-LA098-G	Sweet Revival	1973	3.75	7.50	15.00
❏ BN-LA261-G	On the Avenue	1974	3.75	7.50	15.00
❏ BN-LA425-G	Cheshire Cat	1975	3.75	7.50	15.00
❏ B1-32082	Two Headed Freap	1995	3.75	7.50	15.00
-- Reissue of 84382
| ❏ BST-84382 | Two Headed Freap | 1972 | 5.00 | 10.00 | 20.00 |
COLUMBIA
| ❏ JC 35373 | Love Satellite | 1978 | 3.00 | 6.00 | 12.00 |
| ❏ JC 36019 | Delight | 1979 | 3.00 | 6.00 | 12.00 |

FOUGERAT, TONY
GHB
❏ GHB-89	Every Man a King	197?	2.50	5.00	10.00
❏ GHB-147	Live at the Maple Leaf Bar	198?	2.50	5.00	10.00

FOUNTAIN, PETE
Clarinetist.
ARCHIVE OF FOLK AND JAZZ
❏ 257	New Orleans All-Stars	197?	2.50	5.00	10.00
CAPITOL
| ❏ SN-16224 | Pete Fountain and Friends | 1982 | 2.00 | 4.00 | 8.00 |
| ❏ SN-16225 | Way Down Yonder in New Orleans | 1982 | 2.00 | 4.00 | 8.00 |
CORAL
❏ CXS-710 [(2)]	The Best of Pete Fountain	1969	3.75	7.50	15.00
❏ CRL 57200 [M]	Lawrence Welk Presents Pete Fountain	1958	5.00	10.00	20.00
❏ CRL 57282 [M]	Pete Fountain's New Orleans	1959	3.75	7.50	15.00
❏ CRL 57284 [M]	The Blues	1959	3.75	7.50	15.00
❏ CRL 57313 [M]	Pete Fountain Day	1960	3.75	7.50	15.00
❏ CRL 57314 [M]	Pete Fountain at the Bateau Lounge	1960	3.75	7.50	15.00
❏ CRL 57333 [M]	Pete Fountain Salutes the Great Clarinetists	1960	3.75	7.50	15.00
❏ CRL 57357 [M]	Pete Fountain On Tour	1961	3.75	7.50	15.00
❏ CRL 57359 [M]	Pete Fountain's French Quarter	1961	3.75	7.50	15.00
❏ CRL 57378 [M]	I Love Paris	1961	3.75	7.50	15.00
❏ CRL 57394 [M]	Swing Low Sweet Chariot	1962	3.75	7.50	15.00
❏ CRL 57401 [M]	Pete Fountain's Music from Dixie	1962	3.75	7.50	15.00
❏ CRL 57419 [M]	New Orleans Scene	1963	3.75	7.50	15.00
❏ CRL 57424 [M]	Plenty of Pete	1963	3.00	6.00	12.00
❏ CRL 57429 [M]	New Orleans at Midnight	1964	3.00	6.00	12.00
❏ CRL 57440 [M]	South Rampart Street Parade	1963	3.00	6.00	12.00
❏ CRL 57453 [M]	Pete's Place	1964	3.00	6.00	12.00
❏ CRL 57460 [M]	Licorice Stick	1964	3.00	6.00	12.00
❏ CRL 57473 [M]	Mr. Stick Man	1965	3.00	6.00	12.00
❏ CRL 57474 [M]	Standing Room Only	1965	3.00	6.00	12.00
❏ CRL 57484 [M]	Mood Indigo	1966	3.00	6.00	12.00
❏ CRL 57486 [M]	A Taste of Honey	1966	3.00	6.00	12.00
❏ CRL 57487 [M]	Candy Clarinet -- Merry Christmas from Pete Fountain	1966	3.00	6.00	12.00
❏ CRL 57488 [M]	I've Got You Under My Skin	1967	3.00	6.00	12.00
❏ CRL 57496 [M]	Music to Turn You On	1967	3.75	7.50	15.00
❏ CRL 57499 [M]	Pete Fountain Plays Bert	1968	3.75	7.50	15.00
❏ CRL 757282 [S]	Pete Fountain's New Orleans	1959	5.00	10.00	20.00
❏ CRL 757284 [S]	The Blues	1959	5.00	10.00	20.00
❏ CRL 757313 [S]	Pete Fountain Day	1960	5.00	10.00	20.00
❏ CRL 757314 [S]	Pete Fountain at the Bateau Lounge	1960	5.00	10.00	20.00
❏ CRL 757333 [S]	Pete Fountain Salutes the Great Clarinetists	1960	5.00	10.00	20.00
❏ CRL 757357 [S]	Pete Fountain On Tour	1961	5.00	10.00	20.00
❏ CRL 757359 [S]	Pete Fountain's French Quarter	1961	5.00	10.00	20.00
❏ CRL 757378 [S]	I Love Paris	1961	5.00	10.00	20.00
❏ CRL 757394 [S]	Swing Low Sweet Chariot	1962	5.00	10.00	20.00
❏ CRL 757401 [S]	Pete Fountain's Music from Dixie	1962	5.00	10.00	20.00
❏ CRL 757419 [S]	New Orleans Scene	1963	5.00	10.00	20.00
❏ CRL 757424 [S]	Plenty of Pete	1963	3.75	7.50	15.00
❏ CRL 757429 [S]	New Orleans at Midnight	1964	3.75	7.50	15.00
❏ CRL 757440 [S]	South Rampart Street Parade	1963	3.75	7.50	15.00
❏ CRL 757453 [S]	Pete's Place	1964	3.75	7.50	15.00
❏ CRL 757460 [S]	Licorice Stick	1964	3.75	7.50	15.00
❏ CRL 757473 [S]	Mr. Stick Man	1965	3.75	7.50	15.00
❏ CRL 757474 [S]	Standing Room Only	1965	3.75	7.50	15.00
❏ CRL 757484 [S]	Mood Indigo	1966	3.75	7.50	15.00
❏ CRL 757486 [S]	A Taste of Honey	1966	3.75	7.50	15.00
❏ CRL 757487 [S]	Candy Clarinet -- Merry Christmas from Pete Fountain	1966	3.75	7.50	15.00
❏ CRL 757488 [S]	I've Got You Under My Skin	1967	3.75	7.50	15.00

Number	Title	Yr	VG	VG+	NM
❏ CRL 757496 [S]	Music to Turn You On	1967	3.00	6.00	12.00
❏ CRL 757499 [S]	Pete Fountain Plays Bert	1968	3.00	6.00	12.00
❏ CRL 757503	Walking Through New Orleans	1968	3.00	6.00	12.00
❏ CRL 757505	Those Were the Days	1969	3.00	6.00	12.00
❏ CRL 757507	Both Sides Now	1969	3.00	6.00	12.00
❏ CRL 757510	Make Your Own Kind of Music	1970	3.00	6.00	12.00
❏ CRL 757511	Golden Favorites	1970	3.00	6.00	12.00
❏ CRL 757513	Dr. Fountain's Magical Licorice	1971	3.00	6.00	12.00
❏ CRL 757516	Something/Misty	1971	3.00	6.00	12.00
❏ CRL 757517	New Orleans Tennessee	1971	3.00	6.00	12.00
DECCA					
❏ DL 75374	Pete Fountain's New Orleans	1972	3.00	6.00	12.00
-- Reissue of Coral 757282					
❏ DL 75375	The Blues	1972	3.00	6.00	12.00
-- Reissue of Coral 757284					
❏ DL 75377	Mr. New Orleans	1972	3.00	6.00	12.00
❏ DL 75378	Dr. Fountain's Magical Licorice	1972	2.50	5.00	10.00
-- Reissue of Coral 757513					
❏ DL 75379	Something/Misty	1972	2.50	5.00	10.00
-- Reissue of Coral 757516					
❏ DL 75380	New Orleans Tennessee	1972	3.00	6.00	12.00
-- Reissue of Coral 757517					
FIRST AMERICAN					
❏ 7706	New Orleans Jazz	1978	2.50	5.00	10.00
INTERMEDIA					
❏ QS-5038	Down on Rampart Street	198?	2.00	4.00	8.00
MCA					
❏ 165	Mr. New Orleans	1973	2.50	5.00	10.00
-- Reissue of Decca 75377					
❏ 176	Something/Misty	1973	2.50	5.00	10.00
-- Reissue of Decca 75379					
❏ 336	Crescent City	1974	2.50	5.00	10.00
❏ 505	Pete Fountain's New Orleans	1974	2.50	5.00	10.00
-- Reissue of Decca 75374					
❏ 506	The Blues	1974	2.50	5.00	10.00
-- Reissue of Decca 75375					
❏ 507	Dr. Fountain's Magical Licorice	1974	2.50	5.00	10.00
-- Reissue of Decca 75378					
❏ 508	New Orleans Tennessee	1974	2.50	5.00	10.00
-- Reissue of Decca 75380					
❏ 4032 [(2)]	The Best of Pete Fountain	197?	3.00	6.00	12.00
-- Reissue of Coral 710					
❏ 4095 [(2)]	The Best of Pete Fountain, Vol. 2	197?	3.00	6.00	12.00
PICKWICK					
❏ SPC-3024	Pete Fountain	196?	3.00	6.00	12.00
❏ SPC-3201	High Society	1971	2.50	5.00	10.00
RCA CAMDEN					
❏ CAL-727 [M]	Dixieland	1962	3.00	6.00	12.00
❏ CAS-727 [S]	Dixieland	1962	3.00	6.00	12.00
RCA VICTOR					
❏ LPM-2097 [M]	Pete Fountain at the Jazz Band Ball	1960	3.75	7.50	15.00
❏ LSP-2097 [S]	Pete Fountain at the Jazz Band Ball	1960	5.00	10.00	20.00
VOCALION					
❏ VL 3803 [M]	And the Angels Sing	1967	3.00	6.00	12.00
❏ VL 73803 [S]	And the Angels Sing	1967	3.00	6.00	12.00

FOUNTAIN, PETE, AND "BIG" TINY LITTLE
CORAL

Number	Title	Yr	VG	VG+	NM
❏ CRL 57334 [M]	Mr. New Orleans Meets Mr. Honky Tonk	1961	3.75	7.50	15.00
❏ CRL 757334 [S]	Mr. New Orleans Meets Mr. Honky Tonk	1961	5.00	10.00	20.00

FOUNTAIN, PETE, AND AL HIRT
Also see each artist's individual listings.
CORAL

Number	Title	Yr	VG	VG+	NM
❏ CRL 57389 [M]	Bourbon Street	1962	3.75	7.50	15.00
❏ CRL 757389 [S]	Bourbon Street	1962	5.00	10.00	20.00
MONUMENT					
❏ 8602 [(2)]	Super I	1975	2.50	5.00	10.00

FOUR BROTHERS, THE
Members: SERGE CHALOFF; AL COHN; ZOOT SIMS; HERBIE STEWARD.
VIK

Number	Title	Yr	VG	VG+	NM
❏ LX-1096 [M]	The Four Brothers -- Together Again	1957	20.00	40.00	80.00

FOUR MOST, THE
Members: AL COHN; HANK JONES; MUNDELL LOWE; MAT MATHEWS; OSCAR PETTIFORD; JOE PUMA; GENE QUILL.
DAWN

Number	Title	Yr	VG	VG+	NM
❏ DLP-1111 [M]	The Four Most	1956	20.00	40.00	80.00

FOURTH WAY, THE
Early electric jazz group: MIKE NOCK (keyboards); RON McCLURE (bass), Michael White (violin); Eddie Marshall (drums).
CAPITOL

Number	Title	Yr	VG	VG+	NM
❏ ST-317	The Fourth Way	1969	6.25	12.50	25.00
HARVEST					
❏ SKAO-423	The Sun and Moon Have Come Together	1970	5.00	10.00	20.00
❏ ST-666	Werewolf	1971	5.00	10.00	20.00

FRANCIS, PANAMA
Drummer and bandleader.
CLASSIC JAZZ

Number	Title	Yr	VG	VG+	NM
❏ 149	Panama Francis and His Savoy Sultans, Volume 1	197?	2.50	5.00	10.00
❏ 150	Panama Francis and His Savoy Sultans, Volume 2	197?	2.50	5.00	10.00
EPIC					
❏ BN 629 [S]	Exploding Drums	1959	7.50	15.00	30.00
❏ LN 3839 [M]	Exploding Drums	1959	7.50	15.00	30.00
STASH					
❏ ST-218	Grooving	198?	2.50	5.00	10.00
❏ ST-223	Everything Swings	198?	2.50	5.00	10.00
20TH CENTURY FOX					
❏ TFM-6101 [M]	Tough Talk	196?	6.25	12.50	25.00
❏ TFS-6101 [S]	Tough Talk	196?	7.50	15.00	30.00

FRANKLIN, ARETHA
Female singer and pianist. In her pre-Atlantic days, "The Queen of Soul" was anything but. Much of her Columbia output was jazzy or pop-oriented. For a more complete listing, see the *Standard Catalog of American Records 1950-1975*.
COLUMBIA

Number	Title	Yr	VG	VG+	NM
❏ CL 1612 [M]	Aretha	1961	12.50	25.00	50.00
-- Red and black label with six "eye" logos					
❏ CL 1612 [M]	Aretha	1963	5.00	10.00	20.00
-- "Guaranteed High Fidelity" on label					
❏ CL 1612 [M]	Aretha	1965	3.75	7.50	15.00
-- "360 Sound Mono" on label					
❏ CL 1761 [M]	The Electrifying Aretha Franklin	1962	10.00	20.00	40.00
-- Red and black label with six "eye" logos					
❏ CL 1761 [M]	The Electrifying Aretha Franklin	1963	5.00	10.00	20.00
-- "Guaranteed High Fidelity" on label					
❏ CL 1761 [M]	The Electrifying Aretha Franklin	1965	3.75	7.50	15.00
-- "360 Sound Mono" on label					
❏ CL 1876 [M]	The Tender, The Moving, The Swinging Aretha Franklin	1962	10.00	20.00	40.00
-- Red and black label with six "eye" logos					
❏ CL 1876 [M]	The Tender, The Moving, The Swinging Aretha Franklin	1963	5.00	10.00	20.00
-- "Guaranteed High Fidelity" on label					
❏ CL 1876 [M]	The Tender, The Moving, The Swinging Aretha Franklin	1965	3.75	7.50	15.00
-- "360 Sound Mono" on label					
❏ CL 2079 [M]	Laughing on the Outside	1963	5.00	10.00	20.00
-- "Guaranteed High Fidelity" on label					
❏ CL 2079 [M]	Laughing on the Outside	1965	3.75	7.50	15.00
-- "360 Sound Mono" on label					
❏ CL 2163 [M]	Unforgettable	1964	5.00	10.00	20.00
-- "Guaranteed High Fidelity" on label					
❏ CL 2163 [M]	Unforgettable	1965	3.75	7.50	15.00
-- "360 Sound Mono" on label					
❏ CL 2281 [M]	Runnin' Out of Fools	1964	5.00	10.00	20.00
-- "Guaranteed High Fidelity" on label					
❏ CL 2281 [M]	Runnin' Out of Fools	1965	3.75	7.50	15.00
-- "360 Sound Mono" on label					
❏ CL 2351 [M]	Yeah!!!	1965	5.00	10.00	20.00
-- "Guaranteed High Fidelity" on label					
❏ CL 2351 [M]	Yeah!!!	1966	3.75	7.50	15.00
-- "360 Sound Mono" on label					
❏ CL 2521 [M]	Soul Sister	1966	5.00	10.00	20.00
❏ CL 2629 [M]	Take It Like You Give It	1967	6.25	12.50	25.00
❏ CL 2673 [M]	Aretha Franklin's Greatest Hits	1967	6.25	12.50	25.00
❏ CL 2754 [M]	Take a Look	1967	7.50	15.00	30.00
❏ CS 8412 [S]	Aretha	1961	20.00	40.00	80.00
-- Red and black label with six "eye" logos					
❏ CS 8412 [S]	Aretha	1963	6.25	12.50	25.00
-- "360 Sound Stereo" on label					
❏ CS 8561 [S]	The Electrifying Aretha Franklin	1962	12.50	25.00	50.00
-- Red and black label with six "eye" logos					
❏ CS 8561 [S]	The Electrifying Aretha Franklin	1963	6.25	12.50	25.00
-- "360 Sound Stereo" on label					
❏ CS 8676 [S]	The Tender, The Moving, The Swinging Aretha Franklin	1962	12.50	25.00	50.00
-- Red and black label with six "eye" logos					
❏ CS 8676 [S]	The Tender, The Moving, The Swinging Aretha Franklin	1963	6.25	12.50	25.00
-- "360 Sound Stereo" on label					

Number	Title	Yr	VG	VG+	NM
❏ CS 8879 [S]	Laughing on the utside	1963	6.25	12.50	25.00
-- "360 Sound Stereo" on label					
❏ CS 8963 [S]	Unforgettable	1964	6.25	12.50	25.00
-- "360 Sound Stereo" on label					
❏ CS 9081 [S]	Runnin' Out of Fools	1964	6.25	12.50	25.00
-- "360 Sound Stereo" on label					
❏ CS 9151 [S]	Yeah!!!	1965	6.25	12.50	25.00
-- "360 Sound Stereo" on label					
❏ CS 9321 [S]	Soul Sister	1966	6.25	12.50	25.00
-- "360 Sound Stereo" on label					
❏ CS 9429 [S]	Take It Like You Give It	1967	5.00	10.00	20.00
-- "360 Sound Stereo" on label					
❏ CS 9473 [S]	Aretha Franklin's Greatest Hits	1967	5.00	10.00	20.00
-- "360 Sound Stereo" on label					
❏ CS 9554 [S]	Take a Look	1967	5.00	10.00	20.00
-- "360 Sound Stereo" on label					
❏ CS 9601	Aretha Franklin's Greatest Hits, Volume 2	1968	5.00	10.00	20.00
-- "360 Sound Stereo" on label					
❏ CS 9776	Soft and Beautiful	1969	5.00	10.00	20.00
-- "360 Sound Stereo" on label					
❏ CS 9956	Today I Sing the Blues	1970	3.75	7.50	15.00
-- "360 Sound Stereo" on label					
❏ KC 31953	The First 12 Sides	1973	3.00	6.00	12.00
❏ KG 31355 [(2)]	In the Beginning/The World of Aretha Franklin 1960-1967	1972	5.00	10.00	20.00
❏ C2 37377 [(2)]	The Legendary Queen of Soul	1981	3.00	6.00	12.00
❏ PC 38042	Sweet Bitter Love	1982	2.50	5.00	10.00
❏ FC 40105	Aretha Franklin Sings the Blues	1985	2.50	5.00	10.00
❏ FC 40708	Aretha After Hours	1987	2.50	5.00	10.00
COLUMBIA SPECIAL PRODUCTS					
❏ C 10589	Take a Look	1971	3.00	6.00	12.00
HARMONY					
❏ HS 11349	Once in a Lifetime	1969	3.00	6.00	12.00
❏ HS 11418	Two Sides of Love	1970	3.00	6.00	12.00
❏ KH 30606	Greatest Hits 1960-1965	1971	3.00	6.00	12.00

FRANKLIN, HENRY
Bass player.
BLACK JAZZ

Number	Title	Yr	VG	VG+	NM
❏ QD-7	The Skipper	1972	5.00	10.00	20.00
❏ QD-17	The Skipper At Home	1974	5.00	10.00	20.00
CATALYST					
❏ 7618	Tribal Dance	1976	3.00	6.00	12.00
OVATION					
❏ OV-1801	Blue Lights	197?	3.75	7.50	15.00

FRANKLIN, RODNEY
Keyboard player.
COLUMBIA

Number	Title	Yr	VG	VG+	NM
❏ JC 35558	In the Center	1978	2.50	5.00	10.00
❏ JC 36122	You'll Never Know	1979	2.50	5.00	10.00
❏ JC 36747	Rodney Franklin	1980	2.50	5.00	10.00
❏ FC 37154	Endless Flight	1982	2.50	5.00	10.00
❏ FC 38198	Learning to Love	1983	2.50	5.00	10.00
❏ FC 38953	Marathon	1984	2.50	5.00	10.00
❏ FC 39962	Sky Dance	1985	2.50	5.00	10.00
❏ FC 40307	It Takes Two	1986	2.50	5.00	10.00
NOVUS					
❏ 3038-1-N	King of Diamonds	1988	2.50	5.00	10.00

FRANKS, MICHAEL
Male singer.
BRUT

Number	Title	Yr	VG	VG+	NM
❏ 6005	Michael Franks	1973	5.00	10.00	20.00
DIRECT DISK					
❏ SD-16611	Tiger in the Rain	1980	7.50	15.00	30.00
-- Audiophile vinyl					
DRG					
❏ SL-5210	Previously Unavailable	1989	3.00	6.00	12.00
-- Reissue of John Hammond LP					
JOHN HAMMOND					
❏ BFW 38664	Previously Unavailable	1983	3.75	7.50	15.00
REPRISE					
❏ MS 2230	The Art of Tea	1975	2.50	5.00	10.00
WARNER BROS.					
❏ BS 3004	Sleeping Gypsy	1977	2.50	5.00	10.00
❏ BSK 3167	Burchfield Nines	1978	2.50	5.00	10.00
❏ BSK 3294	Tiger in the Rain	1979	2.50	5.00	10.00
❏ BSK 3427	One Bad Habit	1980	2.50	5.00	10.00
❏ BSK 3648	Objects of Desire	1981	2.50	5.00	10.00
❏ 23962	Passionfruit	1983	2.00	4.00	8.00
❏ 25275	Skin Dive	1985	2.00	4.00	8.00

Number	Title	Yr	VG	VG+	NM
❏ 25570	The Camera Never Lies	1987	2.00	4.00	8.00
❏ 26183	Blue Pacific	1990	3.00	6.00	12.00

FRANZETTI, CARLOS
Pianist, composer and arranger.
INNER CITY

Number	Title	Yr	VG	VG+	NM
❏ IC-1113	Galaxy Dust	1980	3.00	6.00	12.00
PROGRESSIVE					
❏ PRO-7030	Prometheus	198?	3.00	6.00	12.00

FRASER, HUGH
Trombonist and pianist.
JAZZIMAGE

Number	Title	Yr	VG	VG+	NM
❏ JZ-115	Looking Up	1988	2.50	5.00	10.00

FRAZIER, CAESAR
Organist and male singer.
EASTBOUND

Number	Title	Yr	VG	VG+	NM
❏ 900?	Hail Caesar!	1973	12.50	25.00	50.00
❏ 9009	Caesar Frazier '74	1974	10.00	20.00	40.00
WESTBOUND					
❏ 206	Caesar Frazier '75	1975	7.50	15.00	30.00
❏ WT 6103	Another Life	1978	7.50	15.00	30.00

FREE FLIGHT
Founded by flutist Jim Walker; MIKE GARSON has been a near-permanent member also. The rest of the group varies from year to year.
ARABESQUE

Number	Title	Yr	VG	VG+	NM
❏ 8130	Free Flight	1981	3.00	6.00	12.00
CBS					
❏ BFM 42143	Illumination	1986	2.50	5.00	10.00
PALO ALTO					
❏ PA-8024	The Jazz/Classical Union	1982	2.50	5.00	10.00
❏ PA-8050	Soaring	1983	2.50	5.00	10.00
❏ PA-8075	Beyond the Clouds	1984	2.50	5.00	10.00
VOSS					
❏ VLP1-42932	Free Flight	1988	2.50	5.00	10.00
-- Reissue of Arabesque LP					

FREE MUSIC QUARTET, THE
ESP-DISK'

Number	Title	Yr	VG	VG+	NM
❏ 1083	Free Music One and Two	1969	5.00	10.00	20.00

FREEDMAN, BOB
Pianist. Also a saxophone player and composer.
COBBLESTONE

Number	Title	Yr	VG	VG+	NM
❏ 9009	Journeys of Odysseus	1972	5.00	10.00	20.00
SAVOY					
❏ MG-15040 [10]	Piano Moods	1954	12.50	25.00	50.00

FREEMAN, BUD
Tenor saxophone player, clarinetist and composer. Also see BOBBY BYRNE; JOE MARSALA.
BETHLEHEM

Number	Title	Yr	VG	VG+	NM
❏ BCP-29 [M]	Newport News	1955	20.00	40.00	80.00
❏ BCP-6033	Test of Time	197?	3.00	6.00	12.00
-- Reissue, distributed by RCA Victor					
CAPITOL					
❏ H 625 [10]	Classics in Jazz	1955	20.00	40.00	80.00
❏ T 625 [M]	Classics in Jazz	1955	12.50	25.00	50.00
CHIAROSCURO					
❏ 135	The Joy of Sax	1975	3.75	7.50	15.00
CIRCLE					
❏ 10	Bud Freeman and Jimmy McPartland Meet the Ted Easton Jazz Band	198?	2.50	5.00	10.00
COLUMBIA					
❏ CL 2558 [10]	Jazz -- Chicago Style	1955	20.00	40.00	80.00
❏ CL 6107 [10]	Comes Jazz	1950	25.00	50.00	100.00
COMMODORE					
❏ XFL-14941	Three's No Crowd	198?	3.00	6.00	12.00
DECCA					
❏ DL 5213 [10]	Wolverine Jazz	1950	25.00	50.00	100.00
DOT					
❏ DLP-3166 [M]	Bud Freeman and His Summa Cum Laude Trio	1959	10.00	20.00	40.00
❏ DLP-3254 [M]	Midnight Session	1960	7.50	15.00	30.00
❏ DLP-25166 [S]	Bud Freeman and His Summa Cum Laude Trio	1959	7.50	15.00	30.00
❏ DLP-25254 [S]	Midnight Session	1960	10.00	20.00	40.00

Number	Title	Yr	VG	VG+	NM
EMARCY					
❏ MG-36013 [M]	Midnight at Eddie Condon's	1955	15.00	30.00	60.00
FANTASY					
❏ OJC-183	Bud Freeman All Stars	198?	2.50	5.00	10.00
-- Reissue of Swingville 2012					
HALO					
❏ 50275 [M]	Bud Freeman	195?	3.75	7.50	15.00
HARMONY					
❏ HL 7046 [M]	Bud Freeman and His All-Star Jazz	1957	6.25	12.50	25.00
JAZZ ARCHIVES					
❏ JA-38	Summer Concert 1960	198?	2.50	5.00	10.00
JAZZOLOGY					
❏ J-165	The Compleat Bud Freeman	198?	2.50	5.00	10.00
MONMOUTH-EVERGREEN					
❏ 7022	The Compleat Bud Freeman	1970	5.00	10.00	20.00
PARAMOUNT					
❏ CJS-105 [10]	Bud Freeman and the Chicagoans	195?	20.00	40.00	80.00
PROMENADE					
❏ 2134 [M]	Dixieland U.S.A.	196?	3.00	6.00	12.00
RCA VICTOR					
❏ LPM-1508 [M]	Chicago Austin High School Jazz in Hi-Fi	1957	12.50	25.00	50.00
SWINGVILLE					
❏ SVLP-2012 [M]	Bud Freeman All Stars	1960	12.50	25.00	50.00
-- Purple label					
❏ SVLP-2012 [M]	Bud Freeman All Stars	1965	6.25	12.50	25.00
-- Blue label with trident logo at right					
TRIP					
❏ 5529	Midnight at Eddie Condon's	197?	2.50	5.00	10.00
UNITED ARTISTS					
❏ UAJ-14033 [M]	Something Tender -- Bud Freeman and Two Guitars	1963	10.00	20.00	40.00
❏ UAJS-15033 [S]	Something Tender -- Bud Freeman and Two Guitars	1963	12.50	25.00	50.00

FREEMAN, BUD, AND BUDDY TATE
Also see each artist's individual listings.

Number	Title	Yr	VG	VG+	NM
CIRCLE					
❏ 69	Two Beautiful	198?	2.50	5.00	10.00

FREEMAN, CHICO
Tenor saxophone player. Also a trumpeter, keyboard player and composer. Also see THE YOUNG LIONS.

Number	Title	Yr	VG	VG+	NM
BLACK SAINT					
❏ BSR-0036	No Time Left	1977	3.00	6.00	12.00
BLACKHAWK					
❏ BKH-50801	The Pied Piper	1986	2.50	5.00	10.00
CONTEMPORARY					
❏ C-7640	Beyond the Rain	1978	3.00	6.00	12.00
❏ C-14005	Peaceful Heart, Gentle Spirit	1980	3.00	6.00	12.00
❏ C-14008	Destiny's Dance	1981	3.00	6.00	12.00
ELEKTRA/MUSICIAN					
❏ 60163	Tradition in Transition	1983	2.50	5.00	10.00
❏ 60361	Tangents	1984	2.50	5.00	10.00
FANTASY					
❏ OJC-479	Beyond the Rain	1991	2.50	5.00	10.00
INDIA NAVIGATION					
❏ IN-1031	Chico	1977	3.75	7.50	15.00
❏ IN-1035	Kings of Mali	1978	3.75	7.50	15.00
❏ IN-1042	The Outside Within	1981	3.00	6.00	12.00
❏ IN-1045	Spirit Sensitive	1979	3.75	7.50	15.00
❏ IN-1059	The Search	1981	3.00	6.00	12.00
❏ IN-1063	Morning Prayer	198?	3.00	6.00	12.00

FREEMAN, GEORGE
Guitarist.

Number	Title	Yr	VG	VG+	NM
DELMARK					
❏ DS-424	Birth Sign	197?	3.00	6.00	12.00
GROOVE MERCHANT					
❏ 519	New Improved Funk	1973	3.75	7.50	15.00
❏ 3305	Man and Woman	1975	3.75	7.50	15.00

FREEMAN, RUSS
Pianist. Not the same Russ Freeman who is with THE RIPPINGTONS.

Number	Title	Yr	VG	VG+	NM
PACIFIC JAZZ					
❏ PJLP-8 [10]	The Russ Freeman Trio	1953	30.00	60.00	120.00
❏ PJ-1212 [M]	Trio: Russ Freeman/Richard Twardzik	1956	25.00	50.00	100.00
❏ PJ-1232 [M]	Quartet: Russ Freeman/Chet Baker	1957	25.00	50.00	100.00
-- Label says Pacific Jazz, but cover is on World Pacific					
WORLD PACIFIC					
❏ WP-1212 [M]	Trio: Russ Freeman/Richard Twardzik	1958	12.50	25.00	50.00
❏ WP-1232 [M]	Quartet: Russ Freeman/Chet Baker	1958	12.50	25.00	50.00
-- Both label and cover are on World Pacific					

FREEMAN, STAN
Pianist, harpsichordist and composer. Best known for his harpsichord work on the ROSEMARY CLOONEY hit "Come On-a My House."

Number	Title	Yr	VG	VG+	NM
AUDIOPHILE					
❏ AP-202	Not a Care in the World	1986	2.50	5.00	10.00
COLUMBIA					
❏ CL 1120 [M]	Stan Freeman Swings "The Music Man"	1958	7.50	15.00	30.00
❏ CL 6158 [10]	Piano Moods	1951	12.50	25.00	50.00
❏ CL 6193 [10]	Come On-a Stan's House	1951	15.00	30.00	60.00
HARMONY					
❏ HL 7067 [M]	Stan Freeman Plays 30 All-Time Hits	195?	5.00	10.00	20.00

FREEMAN, VON
Tenor saxophone player.

Number	Title	Yr	VG	VG+	NM
ATLANTIC					
❏ SD 1628	Doin' It Right Now	1972	3.00	6.00	12.00
NESSA					
❏ 6	Have No Fear	1975	3.75	7.50	15.00
❏ 11	Serenade and Blues	197?	3.75	7.50	15.00

FRENCH MARKET JAZZ BAND, THE

Number	Title	Yr	VG	VG+	NM
FLYING DUTCHMAN					
❏ BDL1-1239	The French Market Jazz Band	1976	2.50	5.00	10.00

FRENCH, ALBERT "PAPA"
Banjo player and bandleader.

Number	Title	Yr	VG	VG+	NM
NOBILITY					
❏ LP-702 [M]	A Night at Dixieland Hall	195?	10.00	20.00	40.00

FRIEDMAN, DAVID
Vibraphone player.

Number	Title	Yr	VG	VG+	NM
ENJA					
❏ 3089	Of the Wind's Eye	1982	3.00	6.00	12.00
INNER CITY					
❏ IC-3004	Futures Passed	1976	3.00	6.00	12.00
❏ IC-6005	Winter Love April Joy	1979	3.00	6.00	12.00

FRIEDMAN, DON
Pianist.

Number	Title	Yr	VG	VG+	NM
PRESTIGE					
❏ PRLP-7488 [M]	Metamorphosis	1966	6.25	12.50	25.00
❏ PRST-7488 [S]	Metamorphosis	1966	7.50	15.00	30.00
PROGRESSIVE					
❏ PRO-7036	Hot Knepper and Pepper	198?	3.00	6.00	12.00
RIVERSIDE					
❏ RLP-384 [M]	A Day in the City	1961	10.00	20.00	40.00
❏ RLP-431 [M]	Circle Waltz	1962	7.50	15.00	30.00
❏ RLP-463 [M]	Flashback	1963	7.50	15.00	30.00
❏ RLP-485 [M]	Dreams and Explorations	1965	5.00	10.00	20.00
❏ 6082	Circle Waltz	197?	3.75	7.50	15.00
-- Reissue of 9431					
❏ 6094	Flashback	197?	3.75	7.50	15.00
-- Reissue of 9463					
❏ RS-9384 [S]	A Day in the City	1961	12.50	25.00	50.00
❏ RS-9431 [S]	Circle Waltz	1962	10.00	20.00	40.00
❏ RS-9463 [S]	Flashback	1963	10.00	20.00	40.00
❏ RS-9485 [S]	Dreams and Explorations	1965	6.25	12.50	25.00

FRIENDS
Jazz-rock band featuring JOHN ABERCROMBIE and Marc Cohen.

Number	Title	Yr	VG	VG+	NM
OBLIVION					
❏ OD-3	Friends	1974	5.00	10.00	20.00

FRIESEN, DAVID
Bass player.

Number	Title	Yr	VG	VG+	NM
INNER CITY					
❏ IC-1019	Star Dance	1977	3.00	6.00	12.00
❏ IC-1027	Waterfall Rainbow	1978	3.00	6.00	12.00
❏ IC-1086	Other Mansions	1980	3.00	6.00	12.00

Number	Title	Yr	VG	VG+	NM
MUSE					
❑ MR-5109	Color Pool	197?	3.00	6.00	12.00
❑ MR-5255	Storyteller	1981	2.50	5.00	10.00
STEEPLECHASE					
❑ SCS-1138	Paths Beyond Tracing	1980	3.00	6.00	12.00

FRIESEN, DAVID, AND JOHN STOWELL
Stowell is a guitarist. Also see DAVID FRIESEN.

Number	Title	Yr	VG	VG+	NM
INNER CITY					
❑ IC-1061	Through the Listening Glass	1979	3.00	6.00	12.00

FRIESEN, EUGENE
Cellist. Member of the PAUL WINTER Consort.

LIVING MUSIC					
❑ LM-0007	New Friend	1986	2.50	5.00	10.00

FRIGO, JOHNNY
Violinist.

MERCURY					
❑ MG-20285 [M]	I Love Johnny Frigo, He Swings	1957	7.50	15.00	30.00

FRISELL, BILL
Guitarist.

ECM					
❑ 1241	In Line	198?	2.50	5.00	10.00
❑ 25026	Rambler	1985	2.50	5.00	10.00
ELEKTRA/MUSICIAN					
❑ 60843	Before We Were Born	1988	2.50	5.00	10.00

FRISELL, BILL, AND VERNON REID
Reid, a guitarist, was later with the rock band Living Colour. Also see BILL FRISELL.

MINOR MUSIC					
❑ MM-005	Smash and Scatteration	1984	3.75	7.50	15.00

FRISHBERG, DAVE
Pianist, male singer and composer.

CONCORD JAZZ					
❑ CJ-37	Getting Some Fun Out	197?	3.00	6.00	12.00
❑ CJ-74	You're a Lucky Guy	1978	3.00	6.00	12.00
FANTASY					
❑ F-9638	Live at Vine Street	1985	2.50	5.00	10.00
❑ F-9651	Can't Take You Nowhere	1987	2.50	5.00	10.00
OMNISOUND					
❑ 1040	Songbook	198?	2.50	5.00	10.00
❑ 1051	Songbook, Volume 2	198?	2.50	5.00	10.00

FROEBA, FRANK
Pianist.

DECCA					
❑ DL 5043 [10]	Back Room Piano	1950	12.50	25.00	50.00
❑ DL 5048 [10]	Old Time Piano	1950	12.50	25.00	50.00
ROYALE					
❑ 1818 [10]	Old Time Piano	1954	10.00	20.00	40.00
VARSITY					
❑ 6031 [10]	Boys in the Backroom	1950	12.50	25.00	50.00

FROM THE OTHER SIDE JAZZ BAND
Among the members: Mike Greenblatt.

SOUL NOTE					
❑ 121106	From the Other Side	1990	3.00	6.00	12.00

FRONTIERE, DOMINIC
Accordion player, bandleader and composer.

COLUMBIA					
❑ CL 1273 [M]	Pagan Festival	1958	10.00	20.00	40.00
❑ CL 1427 [M]	Love Eyes: The Moods of Romance	1960	7.50	15.00	30.00
❑ CS 8224 [S]	Love Eyes: The Moods of Romance	1960	10.00	20.00	40.00
LIBERTY					
❑ LRP-3015 [M]	Fabulous!	1956	10.00	20.00	40.00
❑ LRP-3032 [M]	Dom Frontiere Plays the Classics	1957	10.00	20.00	40.00
❑ LJH-6002 [M]	The Dom Frontiere Sextet	1956	12.50	25.00	50.00
❑ LST-7008 [S]	Mr. Accordion	1958	10.00	20.00	40.00
-- *Evidently not issued in mono*					

FRUSCELLA, TONY
Trumpeter.

ATLANTIC					
❑ 1220 [M]	Tony Fruscella	1955	20.00	40.00	80.00

FUKUMURA, HIROSHI
Trombone player.

Number	Title	Yr	VG	VG+	NM
INNER CITY					
❑ IC-6067	Hunt Up Wind	198?	3.00	6.00	12.00

FULL CIRCLE
Among this fusion band's members are Karl Lundberg (keyboards, vocals); Anders Bostrom (flute, piccolo) and Philip Hamilton (vocals, percussion).

COLUMBIA					
❑ FC 40966	Full Circle	1988	2.50	5.00	10.00
❑ FC 44474	Myth America	1989	3.00	6.00	12.00

FULL FAITH AND CREDIT BIG BAND, THE

PALO ALTO					
❑ PA-8001	Debut	198?	2.50	5.00	10.00
❑ PA-8003	JazzFaire	198?	2.50	5.00	10.00

FULL MOON

DOUGLAS					
❑ KZ 31904	Full Moon	1972	3.75	7.50	15.00

FULL SWING
Female vocal trio. Also see LORRAINE FEATHER.

CYPRESS					
❑ YL 0109	In Full Swing	1988	2.50	5.00	10.00
❑ YL 0128	The End of the Sky	1989	3.00	6.00	12.00
PLANET					
❑ BXL1-4426	Good Times Are Back!	1982	2.50	5.00	10.00

FULLER, CURTIS
Trombone player.

ABC IMPULSE!					
❑ AS-22 [S]	Cabin in the Sky	1968	3.00	6.00	12.00
BEE HIVE					
❑ BH-7007	Fire and Filigree	197?	3.00	6.00	12.00
BLUE NOTE					
❑ BLP-1567 [M]	The Opener	1957	30.00	60.00	120.00
-- *"Deep groove" version (deep indentation under label on both sides)*					
❑ BLP-1567 [M]	The Opener	1957	20.00	40.00	80.00
-- *Regular version with W. 63rd St. address on label*					
❑ BLP-1567 [M]	The Opener	1963	6.25	12.50	25.00
-- *"New York, USA" address on label*					
❑ BST-1567 [S]	The Opener	1959	20.00	40.00	80.00
-- *"Deep groove" version (deep indentation under label on both sides)*					
❑ BST-1567 [S]	The Opener	1959	12.50	25.00	50.00
-- *Regular version with W. 63rd St. address on label*					
❑ BST-1567 [S]	The Opener	1963	5.00	10.00	20.00
-- *"New York, USA" address on label*					
❑ BLP-1572 [M]	Bone and Bari	1957	30.00	60.00	120.00
-- *"Deep groove" version (deep indentation under label on both sides)*					
❑ BLP-1572 [M]	Bone and Bari	1957	20.00	40.00	80.00
-- *Regular version with W. 63rd St. address on label*					
❑ BLP-1572 [M]	Bone and Bari	1963	6.25	12.50	25.00
-- *"New York, USA" address on label*					
❑ BST-1572 [S]	Bone and Bari	1959	20.00	40.00	80.00
-- *"Deep groove" version (deep indentation under label on both sides)*					
❑ BST-1572 [S]	Bone and Bari	1959	12.50	25.00	50.00
-- *Regular version with W. 63rd St. address on label*					
❑ BST-1572 [S]	Bone and Bari	1963	5.00	10.00	20.00
-- *"New York, USA" address on label*					
❑ BLP-1583 [M]	Curtis Fuller, Volume 3	1958	30.00	60.00	120.00
-- *"Deep groove" version (deep indentation under label on both sides)*					
❑ BLP-1583 [M]	Curtis Fuller, Volume 3	1958	20.00	40.00	80.00
-- *Regular version with W. 63rd St. address on label*					
❑ BLP-1583 [M]	Curtis Fuller, Volume 3	1963	6.25	12.50	25.00
-- *"New York, USA" address on label*					
❑ BST-1583 [S]	Curtis Fuller, Volume 3	1959	20.00	40.00	80.00
-- *"Deep groove" version (deep indentation under label on both sides)*					
❑ BST-1583 [S]	Curtis Fuller, Volume 3	1959	12.50	25.00	50.00
-- *Regular version with W. 63rd St. address on label*					
❑ BST-1583 [S]	Curtis Fuller, Volume 3	1963	5.00	10.00	20.00
-- *"New York, USA" address on label*					
❑ BST-81567 [S]	The Opener	1967	3.75	7.50	15.00
-- *"A Division of Liberty Records" on label*					
❑ BST-81572 [S]	Bone and Bari	1967	3.75	7.50	15.00
-- *"A Division of Liberty Records" on label*					
❑ BST-81583 [S]	Curtis Fuller, Volume 3	1967	3.75	7.50	15.00
-- *"A Division of Liberty Records" on label*					
EPIC					
❑ LA 16013 [M]	The Magnificent Trombone	1961	7.50	15.00	30.00
❑ LA 16020 [M]	South American Cookin'	1961	10.00	20.00	40.00
❑ BA 17013 [S]	The Magnificent Trombone	1961	10.00	20.00	40.00
❑ BA 17020 [S]	South American Cookin'	1961	12.50	25.00	50.00
FANTASY					
❑ OJC-077	New Trombone	198?	2.50	5.00	10.00

Number	Title	Yr	VG	VG+	NM
IMPULSE!					
❏ A-13 [M]	Soul Trombone	1962	6.25	12.50	25.00
❏ AS-13 [S]	Soul Trombone	1962	7.50	15.00	30.00
❏ A-22 [M]	Cabin in the Sky	1962	6.25	12.50	25.00
❏ AS-22 [S]	Cabin in the Sky	1962	7.50	15.00	30.00
MAINSTREAM					
❏ MRL-333	Crankin'	1971	5.00	10.00	20.00
❏ MRL-370	Smokin'	1972	5.00	10.00	20.00
NEW JAZZ					
❏ NJLP-8277 [M]	Curtis Fuller with Red Garland	1962	12.50	25.00	50.00
-- Purple label					
❏ NJLP-8277 [M]	Curtis Fuller with Red Garland	1965	6.25	12.50	25.00
-- Blue label, trident logo at right					
❏ NJLP-8305 [M]	Curtis Fuller and Hampton Hawes with French Horns	1963	---	---	--
-- Canceled; re-assigned to Status label					
PRESTIGE					
❏ PRLP-7107 [M]	New Trombone	1957	25.00	50.00	100.00
REGENT					
❏ MG-6055 [M]	Jazz...It's Magic	1957	20.00	40.00	80.00
SAVOY					
❏ MG-12141 [M]	Blues-Ette	1959	12.50	25.00	50.00
❏ MG-12143 [M]	The Curtis Fuller Jazztet with Benny Golson	1959	10.00	20.00	40.00
❏ MG-12144 [M]	Imagination	1959	10.00	20.00	40.00
❏ MG-12151 [M]	Curtis Fuller	1960	10.00	20.00	40.00
❏ MG-12164 [M]	Images of Curtis Fuller	1960	10.00	20.00	40.00
❏ MG-12209 [M]	Jazz...It's Magic	196?	5.00	10.00	20.00
❏ ST-13006 [S]	Blues-Ette	1959	10.00	20.00	40.00
SAVOY JAZZ					
❏ SJL-1135	Blues-Ette	198?	2.50	5.00	10.00
❏ SJL-2239 [(2)]	All-Star Sextets	197?	3.00	6.00	12.00
SMASH					
❏ MGS-27034 [M]	Jazz Conference Abroad	1962	6.25	12.50	25.00
❏ SRS-67034 [S]	Jazz Conference Abroad	1962	7.50	15.00	30.00
STATUS					
❏ ST-8305 [M]	Curtis Fuller and Hampton Hawes with French Horns	1965	10.00	20.00	40.00
UNITED ARTISTS					
❏ UAL-4051 [M]	Sliding Easy	1959	12.50	25.00	50.00
❏ UAS-5051 [S]	Sliding Easy	1959	10.00	20.00	40.00
WARWICK					
❏ W-2038 [M]	Boss of the Soul Stream Trombone	1961	7.50	15.00	30.00
❏ W-2038ST [S]	Boss of the Soul Stream Trombone	1961	12.50	25.00	50.00

FULLER, GIL
Bandleader and composer.

Number	Title	Yr	VG	VG+	NM
PACIFIC JAZZ					
❏ PJ-93 [M]	Gil Fuller and the Monterey Jazz Orchestra with Dizzy Gillespie	1965	6.25	12.50	25.00
❏ ST-93 [S]	Gil Fuller and the Monterey Jazz Orchestra with Dizzy Gillespie	1965	7.50	15.00	30.00
❏ LN-10060	Gil Fuller and the Monterey Jazz Orchestra with Dizzy Gillespie	198?	2.00	4.00	8.00
-- Budget-line reissue					
❏ PJ-10101 [M]	Night Flight	1966	5.00	10.00	20.00
❏ LN-10128	Night Flight	198?	2.00	4.00	8.00
-- Budget-line reissue					
❏ ST-20101 [S]	Night Flight	1966	6.25	12.50	25.00

FULLER, JERRY
Clarinetist.

Number	Title	Yr	VG	VG+	NM
ANDEX					
❏ A-3008 [M]	Clarinet Portrait	1958	10.00	20.00	40.00
❏ AS-3008 [S]	Clarinet Portrait	1959	7.50	15.00	30.00

FUNK INC.
Members in the 1970s: Eugene Barr (tenor saxophone); Bobby Watley (organ); Steve Weakley; Jimmy Munford; Cecil Hunt (percussion).

Number	Title	Yr	VG	VG+	NM
PRESTIGE					
❏ 10031	Funk Inc.	1971	3.75	7.50	15.00
❏ 10043	Chicken Lickin'	1972	3.75	7.50	15.00
❏ 10059	Hangin' Out	1973	3.75	7.50	15.00
❏ 10071	Superfunk	1973	3.75	7.50	15.00
❏ 10087	Priced to Sell	1974	3.75	7.50	15.00

FUSE ONE
All-star group: JOE FARRELL; JOHN McLAUGHLIN; RONNIE FOSTER; STANLEY CLARKE; Ndugu (drums); PAULINHO DA COSTA,; Lenny White (drums); Marcus Miller (bass); WYNTON MARSALIS; DAVE VALENTIN; GEORGE BENSON.

Number	Title	Yr	VG	VG+	NM
CTI					
❏ 9003	Fuse One	1980	3.00	6.00	12.00
❏ 9006	Silk	1981	3.00	6.00	12.00

FUTTERMAN, JOEL
Pianist, curved soprano saxophone player and Indian flutist.

Number	Title	Yr	VG	VG+	NM
SILKHEART					
❏ SH-125	Vision in Time	1991	3.00	6.00	12.00

FUTURE PROSPECT

Number	Title	Yr	VG	VG+	NM
OPTIMISM					
❏ OP-7001	Future Prospect	198?	2.50	5.00	10.00

Number	Title	Yr	VG	VG+	NM

G

GADD GANG, THE
Drummer and percussionist Steve Gadd with CORNELL DUPREE, EDDIE GOMEZ, Richard Tee (keyboards) and guests.
COLUMBIA

Number	Title	Yr	VG	VG+	NM
❏ FC 40864	The Gadd Gang	1987	2.50	5.00	10.00
❏ FC 44327	Here and Now	1988	3.00	6.00	12.00

GAFA, AL
Guitarist.
PABLO

❏ 2310 782	Leblon Beach	1976	3.00	6.00	12.00

GAILLARD, SLIM
Best known as a guitarist and male singer. Also a pianist, vibraphone player, tenor saxophone player and composer; he co-wrote "Flat Foot Floogie" and "Cement Mixer (Put-ti Put-ti)," among others.
ALLEGRO ELITE

❏ 4050 [10]	Slim Gaillard Plays	195?	7.50	15.00	30.00

CLEF

❏ MGC-126 [10]	Mish Mash	1953	25.00	50.00	100.00
❏ MGC-138 [10]	Slim Cavorts	1953	25.00	50.00	100.00

DISC

❏ DLP-505 [10]	Opera in Vout	195?	50.00	100.00	200.00

DOT

❏ DLP-25190 [S]	Slim Gaillard Rides Again	1959	10.00	20.00	40.00
❏ DLP-3190 [M]	Slim Gaillard Rides Again	1959	7.50	15.00	30.00

KING

❏ 295-80 [10]	Slim Gaillard/Boogie	195?	25.00	50.00	100.00

MCA

❏ 1508	The Dot Sessions	198?	2.50	5.00	10.00

MERCURY

❏ MGC-126 [10]	Mish Mash	1953	---	---	---

-- Canceled; reassigned to Clef 126
NORGRAN

❏ MGN-13 [10]	Slim Gaillard and His Musical Aggregation Wherever They May Be	1954	25.00	50.00	100.00

VERVE

❏ MGV-2013 [M]	Smorgasbord, Help Yourself	1956	12.50	25.00	50.00
❏ V-2013 [M]	Smorgasbord, Help Yourself	1961	5.00	10.00	20.00

GAILLARD, SLIM/DIZZY GILLESPIE
Also see each artist's individual listings.
ULTRAPHONIC

❏ ULP-50273 [M]	Gaillard and Gillespie	1958	10.00	20.00	40.00

GAILLARD, SLIM/MEADE LUX LEWIS
Also see each artist's individual listings.
CLEF

❏ MGC-506 [10]	Boogie Woogie at the Philharmonic	1954	25.00	50.00	100.00

MERCURY

❏ MGC-506 [10]	Boogie Woogie at the Philharmonic	1951	37.50	75.00	150.00

GAINEN, MAURY
DISCOVERY

❏ DS-855	Jazz Sunrise	198?	2.50	5.00	10.00

GALASSO, MICHAEL
Violinist.
ECM

❏ 1245	Scenes	198?	3.00	6.00	12.00

GALAXY ALL-STARS, THE
GALAXY

❏ GXY-95001 [(2)]	Live Under the Sky	1979	3.75	7.50	15.00

GALBRAITH, BARRY
Guitarist. Also see THE MANHATTAN JAZZ SEPTETTE.
DECCA

❏ DL 9200 [M]	Guitar and the Wind	1958	12.50	25.00	50.00
❏ DL 79200 [S]	Guitar and the Wind	1959	10.00	20.00	40.00

GALE, EDDIE
Trumpeter.
BLUE NOTE

Number	Title	Yr	VG	VG+	NM
❏ BST-84294	Eddie Gale's Ghetto Music	1968	6.25	12.50	25.00
❏ BST-84320	Black Rhythm Happening	1969	6.25	12.50	25.00

GALE, ERIC
Guitarist.
COLUMBIA

❏ PC 34421	Ginseng	1977	2.50	5.00	10.00

-- Original edition with no bar code

❏ JC 34938	Multiplication	1978	2.50	5.00	10.00
❏ JC 35715	Part of You	1979	2.50	5.00	10.00
❏ JC 36363	The Best of Eric Gale	1980	2.50	5.00	10.00
❏ JC 36570	Touch of Silk	1981	2.50	5.00	10.00

ELEKTRA/MUSICIAN

❏ 60022	Blue Horizon	1982	2.50	5.00	10.00
❏ 60198	Island Breeze	1984	2.50	5.00	10.00

EMARCY

❏ 836 369-1	In a Jazz Tradition	1989	3.00	6.00	12.00

KUDU

❏ 11	Forecast	1973	3.75	7.50	15.00

GALLAGHER, BRIAN
Saxophone player, flutist and vocalist.
CYPRESS

❏ 0126	Coming Home	1989	3.00	6.00	12.00

GALLERY
Members: David Samuels (vibraharp, marimba); Michael DiPasqua (drums, percussion); Paul McCandless (soprano saxophone, oboe, English horn); David Darling (cello); Ratzo Harris (bass).
ECM

❏ 1206	Gallery	1982	3.00	6.00	12.00

GALLODORO, AL
Clarinetist and saxophone player. Also see FREDDIE GARDNER.
ARCO

❏ AL-3 [10]	Al Gallodoro Concert	1950	12.50	25.00	50.00

COLUMBIA

❏ CL 6188 [10]	Al Gallodoro	1951	12.50	25.00	50.00

GALLOWAY, JIM
Soprano, baritone and tenor saxophone player and clarinetist.
SACKVILLE

❏ 2007	Three Is Company	198?	2.50	5.00	10.00
❏ 4002	The Metro Stompers	198?	2.50	5.00	10.00
❏ 4011	Thou Swell	198?	2.50	5.00	10.00

GALPER, HAL
Pianist.
BLACKHAWK

❏ BKH 529	Naturally	1987	3.75	7.50	15.00

CENTURY

❏ 1120	Speak with a Single Voice	1978	3.75	7.50	15.00

CONCORD JAZZ

❏ CJ-383	Portrait	1988	2.50	5.00	10.00

ENJA

❏ 4006	Speak with a Single Voice	198?	3.00	6.00	12.00

INNER CITY

❏ IC-2067	Reach Out	1978	3.75	7.50	15.00
❏ IC-3012	Now Hear This	1977	3.75	7.50	15.00

MAINSTREAM

❏ MRL-337	The Guerrilla Band	1971	5.00	10.00	20.00
❏ MRL-354	Wild Bird	1972	5.00	10.00	20.00
❏ MRL-398	Inner Journey	1974	5.00	10.00	20.00

STEEPLECHASE

❏ SCS-1067	Reach Out	198?	3.00	6.00	12.00

-- Reissue of Inner City 2067

GAMALON
Fusion band led by guitarists Bruce Brucato and George Puleo.
AMHERST

❏ AMH-3318	Gamalon	1988	3.75	7.50	15.00

GAMBRELL, FREDDIE
Pianist. Also see CHICO HAMILTON.
WORLD PACIFIC

❏ WP-1256 [M]	Freddie Gambrell	1959	12.50	25.00	50.00

Number	Title	Yr	VG	VG+	NM

GAMBRELL, FREDDIE, AND PAUL HORN
Also see each artist's individual lstings.
WORLD PACIFIC

Number	Title	Yr	VG	VG+	NM
❏ ST-1023 [S]	Mikado	1959	7.50	15.00	30.00
❏ WP-1262 [M]	Mikado	1959	10.00	20.00	40.00

GANDELMAN, LEO
Tenor saxophone player.
VERVE FORECAST

❏ 836 424-1	Western World	1989	3.00	6.00	12.00

GANELIN TRIO, THE
From the former Soviet Union: Vyacheslav Ganelin (piano, guitar, percussion); Vladimir Tarasov (drums, percussion); Vladimir Chekasin (reeds).
HAT ART

❏ 2027 [(2)]	Non Troppo	1986	3.75	7.50	15.00

GANG STARR
Hip-hop duo influenced by jazz. Also see GURU.
CHRYSALIS

❏ F1-21798	Step In the Arena	1991	3.75	7.50	15.00
❏ F1-21910	Daily Operation	1992	3.75	7.50	15.00
❏ F1-28435	Hard to Earn	1994	3.75	7.50	15.00

VIRGIN

❏ 45585 [(3)]	Moment of Truth	1998	3.75	7.50	15.00
❏ 47279 [(4)]	Full Clip -- A Decade of Gang Starr	1999	5.00	10.00	20.00

WILD PITCH

❏ 2001	No More Mr. Nice Guy	1989	3.75	7.50	15.00
❏ E1-98709	No More Mr. Nice Guy	1992	3.00	6.00	12.00

GANNON, JIM
Guitarist.
CATALYST

❏ 7605	Gannon's Back in Town	1976	3.75	7.50	15.00

GARBAREK, JAN
Saxophone (soprano, tenor, bass) player. Also a clarinetist, flutist and percussionist.
ECM

❏ 1093	Dis	1977	3.00	6.00	12.00
❏ 1118	Places	1978	2.50	5.00	10.00
❏ 1135	Photo With…	1978	2.50	5.00	10.00
❏ 1151	Magico	1979	2.50	5.00	10.00
❏ 1200	Eventyr	1981	2.50	5.00	10.00
❏ 1223	Paths, Prints	1982	2.50	5.00	10.00
❏ 23798	Wayfarer	1984	2.50	5.00	10.00
❏ 25033	It's OK to Listen to the Gray Voice	1985	2.50	5.00	10.00

FLYING DUTCHMAN

❏ FD-10125	The Esoteric Circle	1971	5.00	10.00	20.00

GARBAREK, JAN, AND KJELL JOHNSEN
Johnsen is a pipe organ player. Also see JAN GARBAREK.
ECM

❏ 1169	Aftenland	1980	2.50	5.00	10.00

GARBAREK, JAN, AND TERJE RYPDAL
Also see each artist's individual listings.
ARISTA FREEDOM

❏ AL 1031	Esoteric	197?	3.00	6.00	12.00

GARBAREK, JAN, AND BOBO STENSON
Stenson is a pianist. Also see JAN GARBAREK.
ECM

❏ 1041	Witchi-Tai-To	1973	3.00	6.00	12.00
❏ 1075	Dansere	1976	3.00	6.00	12.00

GARCIA, DICK
Guitarist.
DAWN

❏ DLP-1106 [M]	A Message from Dick Garcia	1956	12.50	25.00	50.00

SEECO

❏ SLP-428 [M]	A Message from Dick Garcia	1958	10.00	20.00	40.00

GARCIA, RUSS
Guitarist, arranger and composer.
ABC-PARAMOUNT

❏ ABC-147 [M]	The Johnny Evergreens	1956	12.50	25.00	50.00

BETHLEHEM

❏ BCP-46 [M]	Four Horns and a Lush Life	1956	12.50	25.00	50.00
❏ BCP-1040 [10]	Wigville	1955	50.00	100.00	200.00
❏ BCP-6044	I'll Never Forget What's Her Name	1978	3.00	6.00	12.00

-- Reissue, distributed by RCA Victor
DISCOVERY

❏ DS-814	I Lead a Charmed Life	1980	3.00	6.00	12.00

KAPP

❏ KL-1050 [M]	Listen to the Music of Russell Garcia	1957	12.50	25.00	50.00

LIBERTY

❏ LRP-3062 [M]	Enchantment (The Music of Joe Greene)	1958	6.25	12.50	25.00
❏ LRP-3084 [M]	Fantastica	1958	7.50	15.00	30.00
❏ LST-7005 [S]	Fantastica	1958	10.00	20.00	40.00

VERVE

❏ MGV-2088 [M]	The Warm Feeling	1957	12.50	25.00	50.00
❏ V-2088 [M]	The Warm Feeling	1961	5.00	10.00	20.00

GARCIA, RUSS, AND MARTY PAICH
Also see each artist's individual listings.
BETHLEHEM

❏ BCP-6039 [M]	Jazz Music for Birds and Hep Cats	1960	12.50	25.00	50.00
❏ SBCP-6039 [S]	Jazz Music for Birds and Hep Cats	1960	12.50	25.00	50.00

GARDNER, FREDDY, AND AL GALLODORO
Gardner played clarinet and tenor, alto and baritone saxophones. Also see AL GALLODORO.
COLUMBIA

❏ CL 623 [M]	The Immortal Freddy Gardner and Al Gallodoro	1954	10.00	20.00	40.00

-- Maroon label, gold print
GARDONY, LASZLO
Pianist.
ANTILLES

❏ 90694	The Secret	1988	3.00	6.00	12.00
❏ 91250	The Legend of Tsumi	1989	3.00	6.00	12.00

GARI, RALPH
Clarinetist. Also played alto saxophone, flute, piccolo and English horn.
EMARCY

❏ MG-36019 [M]	Ralph Gari	1955	12.50	25.00	50.00

GARLAND, HANK
Guitarist. Also known as a session musician for country artists.
COLUMBIA

❏ CL 1572 [M]	Jazz Winds from a New Direction	1961	7.50	15.00	30.00
❏ CL 1913 [M]	The Unforgettable Guitar of Hank Garland	1962	7.50	15.00	30.00
❏ CS 8372 [S]	Jazz Winds from a New Direction	1961	10.00	20.00	40.00
❏ CS 8713 [S]	The Unforgettable Guitar of Hank Garland	1962	10.00	20.00	40.00

HARMONY

❏ HL 7231 [M]	Velvet Guitar	196?	5.00	10.00	20.00
❏ HS 11028 [S]	Velvet Guitar	196?	6.25	12.50	25.00

SESAC

❏ SN-2301/2 [M]	Subtle Swing	196?	25.00	50.00	100.00

GARLAND, RED
Pianist. Also see JOHN COLTRANE; CURTIS FULLER; COLEMAN HAWKINS.
FANTASY

❏ OJC-061	Groovy	198?	2.50	5.00	10.00

-- Reissue of Prestige 7113

❏ OJC-073	Red Garland's Piano	198?	2.50	5.00	10.00

-- Reissue of Prestige 7086

❏ OJC-126	A Garland of Red	198?	2.50	5.00	10.00

-- Reissue of Prestige 7064

❏ OJC-193	All Kinds of Weather	1985	2.50	5.00	10.00

-- Reissue of Prestige 7148

❏ OJC-224	The Red Garland Trio	198?	2.50	5.00	10.00

-- Reissue of Moodsville 6

❏ OJC-265	Bright and Breezy	1987	2.50	5.00	10.00

-- Reissue of Jazzland 948

❏ OJC-293	All Morning Long	1988	2.50	5.00	10.00

-- Reissue of Prestige 7130

❏ OJC-295	Red in Bluesville	198?	2.50	5.00	10.00

-- Reissue of Prestige 7157

❏ OJC-349	High Pressure	198?	2.50	5.00	10.00

-- Reissue of Prestige 7209

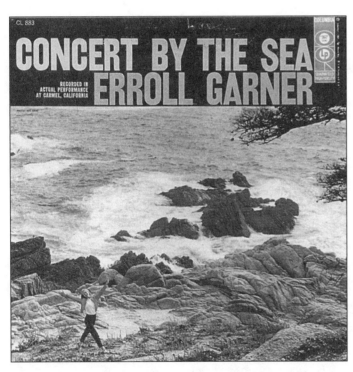

(Top left) Russ Garcia was a jazz guitarist before it was cool to be a jazz guitarist. His early 10-inch album, *Wigville,* not only is sought after for its music but for its interesting cover. (Top right) Red Garland, who had been a boxer before taking up the piano, played on some of the great Miles Davis Prestige sessions. On his own, he recorded some stellar albums for the label, including *Soul Junction* with guest John Coltrane. (Bottom left) Early in his career, pianist Erroll Garner recorded with Charlie Parker. But he's better known for his solo work, including the original version of the romantic ballad "Misty." Here's one of his albums from his association with Columbia. (Bottom right) Saxophone player Herb Geller sometimes recorded with his wife Lorraine, whose own solo album is among the most sought-after original jazz LPs. This album on Jubilee is probably most noteworthy for its cheesy cover.

Number	Title	Yr	VG	VG+	NM
❑ OJC-360	Red Garland & Eddie "Lockjaw" Davis	198?	2.50	5.00	10.00
-- Reissue of Moodsville 1					
❑ OJC-392	Dig It!	1989	3.00	6.00	12.00
-- Reissue of Prestige 7229					
❑ OJC-428	Manteca	1990	3.00	6.00	12.00
-- Reissue of Prestige 7139					
❑ OJC-472	Crossings	1990	3.00	6.00	12.00
-- Reissue of Galaxy 5106					
❑ OJC-481	Soul Junction	1991	3.00	6.00	12.00
-- Reissue of Prestige 7181					
❑ OJC-647	Red Alert	1991	3.00	6.00	12.00
-- Reissue of Galaxy 5109					
GALAXY					
❑ 5106	Crossings	1978	3.00	6.00	12.00
❑ 5109	Red Alert	1978	3.00	6.00	12.00
❑ 5115	Equinox	1979	3.00	6.00	12.00
❑ 5129	Stepping Out	198?	2.50	5.00	10.00
❑ 5135	Strike Up the Band	198?	2.50	5.00	10.00
JAZZLAND					
❑ JLP-48 [M]	Bright and Breezy	1961	7.50	15.00	30.00
❑ JLP-62 [M]	The Nearness of You -- Ballads Played by Red Garland	1962	7.50	15.00	30.00
❑ JLP-73 [M]	Solar	1962	7.50	15.00	30.00
❑ JLP-87 [M]	Red's Good Groove!	1963	7.50	15.00	30.00
❑ JLP-948 [S]	Bright and Breezy	1961	10.00	20.00	40.00
❑ JLP-962 [S]	The Nearness of You -- Ballads Played by Red Garland	1962	10.00	20.00	40.00
❑ JLP-973 [S]	Solar	1962	10.00	20.00	40.00
❑ JLP-987 [S]	Red's Good Groove!	1963	10.00	20.00	40.00
MOODSVILLE					
❑ MVLP-1 [M]	Red Garland & Eddie "Lockjaw" Davis	1960	12.50	25.00	50.00
-- Green label					
❑ MVLP-1 [M]	Red Garland & Eddie "Lockjaw" Davis	1965	6.25	12.50	25.00
-- Blue label, trident logo at right					
❑ MVLP-3 [M]	Red Alone -- Vol. 3	1960	12.50	25.00	50.00
-- Green label					
❑ MVLP-3 [M]	Red Alone -- Vol. 3	1965	6.25	12.50	25.00
-- Blue label, trident logo at right					
❑ MVLP-6 [M]	The Red Garland Trio	1960	12.50	25.00	50.00
-- Green label					
❑ MVLP-6 [M]	The Red Garland Trio	1965	6.25	12.50	25.00
-- Blue label, trident logo at right					
❑ MVLP-10 [M]	Alone with the Blues	1960	12.50	25.00	50.00
-- Green label					
❑ MVLP-10 [M]	Alone with the Blues	1965	6.25	12.50	25.00
-- Blue label, trident logo at right					
MUSE					
❑ MR-5130	Feelin' Red	1980	3.00	6.00	12.00
❑ MR-5311	I Left My Heart	1985	2.50	5.00	10.00
NEW JAZZ					
❑ NJLP-8314 [M]	Li'l Darlin'	1963	---	---	---
-- Canceled; reassigned to Status					
❑ NJLP-8325 [M]	High Pressure	1963	---	---	---
-- Canceled; reassigned to Status					
❑ NJLP-8326 [M]	Red Garland Live!	1963	---	---	---
-- Canceled; reassigned to Status					
PRESTIGE					
❑ PRLP-7064 [M]	A Garland of Red	1956	20.00	40.00	80.00
-- W. 50th St., New York address on label					
❑ PRLP-7064 [M]	A Garland of Red	1958	15.00	30.00	60.00
-- Yellow label with Bergenfield, N.J. address					
❑ PRLP-7086 [M]	Red Garland's Piano	1957	20.00	40.00	80.00
-- W. 50th St., New York address on label					
❑ PRLP-7086 [M]	Red Garland's Piano	1958	15.00	30.00	60.00
-- Yellow label with Bergenfield, N.J. address					
❑ PRLP-7113 [M]	Groovy	1957	20.00	40.00	80.00
-- W. 50th St., New York address on label					
❑ PRLP-7113 [M]	Groovy	1958	15.00	30.00	60.00
-- Yellow label with Bergenfield, N.J. address					
❑ PRLP-7130 [M]	All Morning Long	1958	20.00	40.00	80.00
-- W. 50th St., New York address on label					
❑ PRLP-7130 [M]	All Morning Long	1958	15.00	30.00	60.00
-- Yellow label with Bergenfield, N.J. address					
❑ PRLP-7139 [M]	Manteca	1958	12.50	25.00	50.00
-- Yellow label with Bergenfield, N.J. address					
❑ PRLP-7148 [M]	All Kinds of Weather	1958	12.50	25.00	50.00
-- Yellow label with Bergenfield, N.J. address					
❑ PRLP-7157 [M]	Red in Bluesville	1959	12.50	25.00	50.00
-- Yellow label with Bergenfield, N.J. address					
❑ PRLP-7170 [M]	Red Garland at the Prelude	1959	12.50	25.00	50.00
-- Yellow label with Bergenfield, N.J. address					
❑ PRLP-7181 [M]	Soul Junction	1960	12.50	25.00	50.00
-- Yellow label with Bergenfield, N.J. address					
❑ PRLP-7193 [M]	Rojo	1961	10.00	20.00	40.00
-- Yellow label with Bergenfield, N.J. address					

Number	Title	Yr	VG	VG+	NM
❑ PRLP-7209 [M]	High Pressure	1961	12.50	25.00	50.00
-- Yellow label with Bergenfield, N.J. address					
❑ PRLP-7229 [M]	Dig It!	1962	10.00	20.00	40.00
❑ PRST-7258 [S]	When There Are Grey Skies	1963	10.00	20.00	40.00
❑ PRLP-7258 [M]	When There Are Grey Skies	1963	7.50	15.00	30.00
❑ PRST-7229 [S]	Dig It!	1962	12.50	25.00	50.00
❑ PRLP-7276 [M]	Can't See for Lookin'	1963	7.50	15.00	30.00
❑ PRST-7276 [S]	Can't See for Lookin'	1963	10.00	20.00	40.00
❑ PRLP-7288 [M]	Halleloo-Y'all	1964	7.50	15.00	30.00
❑ PRST-7288 [S]	Halleloo-Y'all	1964	10.00	20.00	40.00
❑ PRLP-7307 [M]	Soul Burnin'	1964	6.25	12.50	25.00
❑ PRST-7307 [S]	Soul Burnin'	1964	7.50	15.00	30.00
❑ PRST-7658	Red Garland Revisited!	1969	3.75	7.50	15.00
❑ PRST-7752	P.C. Blues	1970	3.75	7.50	15.00
❑ PRST-7838	It's a Blue World	1971	3.75	7.50	15.00
❑ 24023 [(2)]	Jazz Junction	1972	3.75	7.50	15.00
❑ 24078 [(2)]	Rediscovered Masters	1979	3.75	7.50	15.00
❑ 24090 [(2)]	Saying Something	1980	3.75	7.50	15.00
RIVERSIDE					
❑ 6099	Bright and Breezy	197?	3.75	7.50	15.00
STATUS					
❑ ST-8314 [M]	Li'l Darlin'	1965	7.50	15.00	30.00
❑ ST-8325 [M]	High Pressure	1965	7.50	15.00	30.00
❑ ST-8326 [M]	Red Garland Live!	1965	7.50	15.00	30.00

GARNER, ERROLL

Pianist and composer; wrote the standard "Misty." Also see DODO MARMAROSA; KAY STARR; ART TATUM.

Number	Title	Yr	VG	VG+	NM
ABC-PARAMOUNT					
❑ 365 [M]	Dreamstreet	1961	5.00	10.00	20.00
❑ S-365 [S]	Dreamstreet	1961	6.25	12.50	25.00
❑ 395 [M]	Closeup in Swing	1961	5.00	10.00	20.00
❑ S-395 [S]	Closeup in Swing	1961	6.25	12.50	25.00
ARCHIVE OF FOLK AND JAZZ					
❑ 245	Erroll Garner	1970	2.50	5.00	10.00
ATLANTIC					
❑ ALR-109 [10]	Rhapsody	1950	20.00	40.00	80.00
❑ ALR-112 [10]	Erroll Garner at the Piano	1951	20.00	40.00	80.00
❑ ALR-128 [10]	Passport to Fame	1952	25.00	50.00	100.00
❑ ALR-135 [10]	Piano Solos, Volume 2	1952	20.00	40.00	80.00
❑ 1227 [M]	The Greatest Garner	1956	10.00	20.00	40.00
-- Black label					
❑ 1227 [M]	The Greatest Garner	1961	3.75	7.50	15.00
-- Multi-color label with white "fan" logo					
❑ 1227 [M]	The Greatest Garner	196?	3.00	6.00	12.00
-- Multi-color label with black "fan" logo					
❑ 1315 [M]	Perpetual Motion	1959	10.00	20.00	40.00
-- Black label					
BARONET					
❑ B-109 [M]	Informal Piano Improvisations	1962	3.00	6.00	12.00
❑ BS-109 [R]	Informal Piano Improvisations	1962	2.50	5.00	10.00
BLUE NOTE					
❑ BLP-5007 [10]	Overture to Dawn, Volume 1	1952	50.00	100.00	200.00
❑ BLP-5008 [10]	Overture to Dawn, Volume 2	1952	50.00	100.00	200.00
❑ BLP-5014 [10]	Overture to Dawn, Volume 3	1953	50.00	100.00	200.00
❑ BLP-5015 [10]	Overture to Dawn, Volume 4	1953	50.00	100.00	200.00
❑ BLP-5016 [10]	Overture to Dawn, Volume 5	1953	50.00	100.00	200.00
CLARION					
❑ 610 [M]	Serenade in Blue	1966	3.00	6.00	12.00
❑ SD 610 [S]	Serenade in Blue	1966	3.00	6.00	12.00
COLUMBIA					
❑ C2L 9 [(2) M]	Paris Impressions	1958	10.00	20.00	40.00
❑ CL 535 [M]	Erroll Garner	1953	15.00	30.00	60.00
-- Red label with gold print					
❑ CL 535 [M]	Erroll Garner	1956	7.50	15.00	30.00
-- Red and black label with six "eye" logos					
❑ CL 583 [M]	Gems	1954	15.00	30.00	60.00
-- Red label with gold print					
❑ CL 583 [M]	Gems	1956	7.50	15.00	30.00
-- Red and black label with six "eye" logos					
❑ CL 617 [M]	Gone Garner Gonest	1955	15.00	30.00	60.00
-- Red label with gold print					
❑ CL 617 [M]	Gone Garner Gonest	1956	7.50	15.00	30.00
-- Red and black label with six "eye" logos					
❑ CL 667 [M]	Erroll Garner Plays for Dancing	1956	7.50	15.00	30.00
❑ CL 883 [M]	Concert by the Sea	1956	7.50	15.00	30.00
❑ CL 939 [M]	The Most Happy Piano	1957	7.50	15.00	30.00
❑ CL 1014 [M]	Other Voices	1957	7.50	15.00	30.00
❑ CL 1060 [M]	Soliloquy	1957	7.50	15.00	30.00
❑ CL 1141 [M]	Encores in Hi-Fi	1958	7.50	15.00	30.00
❑ CL 1216 [M]	Paris Impressions, Volume 1	1958	5.00	10.00	20.00
❑ CL 1217 [M]	Paris Impressions, Volume 2	1958	5.00	10.00	20.00
❑ CL 1452 [M]	The One and Only Erroll Garner	1960	5.00	10.00	20.00
❑ CL 1512 [M]	Swinging Solos	1960	5.00	10.00	20.00
❑ CL 1587 [M]	The Provocative Erroll Garner	1961	5.00	10.00	20.00

Number	Title	Yr	VG	VG+	NM
❏ CL 2540 [10]	Garnerland	1955	15.00	30.00	60.00
❏ CL 2606 [10]	He's Here! He's Gone! He's	1956	15.00	30.00	60.00
❏ CL 6139 [10]	Piano Moods	1950	20.00	40.00	80.00
❏ CL 6173 [10]	Gems	1951	20.00	40.00	80.00
❏ CL 6209 [10]	Solo Flight	1952	20.00	40.00	80.00
❏ CL 6259 [10]	Erroll Garner Plays for Dancing	1953	20.00	40.00	80.00
❏ CS 8252 [S]	The One and Only Erroll Garner	1960	6.25	12.50	25.00
❏ CS 8312 [S]	Swinging Solos	1960	6.25	12.50	25.00
❏ CS 8387 [S]	The Provocative Erroll Garner	1961	6.25	12.50	25.00
❏ CS 9820 [R]	Other Voices	1970	3.00	6.00	12.00
❏ CS 9821 [R]	Concert by the Sea	1970	3.00	6.00	12.00
❏ PG 33424 [(2)]	Play It Again, Erroll!	1975	3.00	6.00	12.00
COLUMBIA JAZZ MASTERPIECES					
❏ CJ 40863	Long Ago and Far Away	1987	3.00	6.00	12.00
COLUMBIA SPECIAL PRODUCTS					
❏ P 14386	Dreamy	1978	2.50	5.00	10.00
DIAL					
❏ LP-205 [10]	Erroll Garner, Volume 1	1950	50.00	100.00	200.00
❏ LP-902 [M]	Free Piano Improvisations Recorded by Baron Timme Rosenkranz at One of His Famous Gaslight Jazz Sessions	1949	75.00	150.00	300.00
EMARCY					
❏ MG-26016 [10]	Garnering	1954	20.00	40.00	80.00
❏ MG-26042 [10]	Gone with Garner	1954	20.00	40.00	80.00
❏ MG-36001 [M]	Contrasts	1955	7.50	15.00	30.00
❏ MG-36026 [M]	Garnering	1955	7.50	15.00	30.00
❏ MG-36069 [M]	Erroll!	1956	7.50	15.00	30.00
❏ 826 224-1	Erroll Garner Plays Gershwin and Kern	1986	2.50	5.00	10.00
❏ 832 994-1	The Erroll Garner Collection Vol. 1: Easy to Love	1988	2.50	5.00	10.00
❏ 834 935-1	The Erroll Garner Collection Vol. 2: Dancing on the Ceiling	1989	2.50	5.00	10.00
HALL OF FAME					
❏ 610	Early Erroll	198?	2.50	5.00	10.00
HARMONY					
❏ HS 11268	One More Time	1968	3.00	6.00	12.00
JAZZTONE					
❏ J-1269 [M]	Early Erroll	1957	10.00	20.00	40.00
KING					
❏ 295-17 [10]	Piano Stylist	1952	20.00	40.00	80.00
❏ 395-540 [M]	Piano Variations	1958	12.50	25.00	50.00
LONDON					
❏ APS 640	Magician	1973	3.00	6.00	12.00
❏ XPS 617	Gemini	1972	3.00	6.00	12.00
MERCURY					
❏ MG-20009 [M]	Erroll Garner at the Piano	1953	12.50	25.00	50.00
❏ MG-20055 [M]	Mambo Moves Garner	1954	12.50	25.00	50.00
❏ MG-20063 [M]	Solitaire	1954	12.50	25.00	50.00
❏ MG-20090 [M]	Afternoon of an Elf	1955	12.50	25.00	50.00
❏ MG-20662 [M]	Erroll Garner Plays Misty	1962	3.75	7.50	15.00
❏ MG-20803 [M]	The Best of Erroll Garner	1963	3.75	7.50	15.00
❏ MG-20859 [M]	New Kind of Love	1963	3.75	7.50	15.00
❏ MG-21308 [M]	Feeling Is Believing	1964	3.75	7.50	15.00
❏ MG-25117 [10]	Erroll Garner at the Piano	1951	20.00	40.00	80.00
❏ MG-25157 [10]	Gone with Garner	1951	20.00	40.00	80.00
❏ SR-60662 [S]	Erroll Garner Plays Misty	1962	5.00	10.00	20.00
❏ SR-60803 [S]	The Best of Erroll Garner	1963	5.00	10.00	20.00
❏ SR-60859 [S]	New Kind of Love	1963	5.00	10.00	20.00
❏ SR-61308 [S]	Feeling Is Believing	1964	5.00	10.00	20.00
❏ 826 457-1	Afternoon of an Elf	1986	2.50	5.00	10.00
-- Reissue					
MGM					
❏ E-4335 [M]	Now Playing: Erroll Garner	1966	3.00	6.00	12.00
❏ SE-4335 [S]	Now Playing: Erroll Garner	1966	3.75	7.50	15.00
❏ E-4361 [M]	Campus Concert	1966	3.00	6.00	12.00
❏ SE-4361 [S]	Campus Concert	1966	3.75	7.50	15.00
❏ E-4463 [M]	That's My Kick	1967	3.75	7.50	15.00
❏ SE-4463 [S]	That's My Kick	1967	3.00	6.00	12.00
❏ E-4520 [M]	Up in Erroll's Room	1967	3.75	7.50	15.00
❏ SE-4520 [S]	Up in Erroll's Room	1967	3.00	6.00	12.00
PICKWICK					
❏ SPC-3254	Deep Purple	197?	2.50	5.00	10.00
REPRISE					
❏ R 6080 [DJ]	One World Concert	1963	10.00	20.00	40.00
-- Six-song sampler -- three on each side -- on a 12-inch record that plays at 45 rpm. This comes in a different cover than the stock copy that is clearly marked "Special 45 RPM Preview Record" on the top front.					
❏ R 6080 [M]	One World Concert	1963	5.00	10.00	20.00
❏ RS 6080 [S]	One World Concert	1963	6.25	12.50	25.00
RONDO-LETTE					
❏ A-15 [M]	Erroll Garner	1958	6.25	12.50	25.00
SAVOY					
❏ MG-12002 [M]	Penthouse Serenade	1955	7.50	15.00	30.00

Number	Title	Yr	VG	VG+	NM
❏ MG-12003 [M]	Serenade to "Laura"	1955	7.50	15.00	30.00
❏ MG-15000 [10]	Erroll Garner Plays Piano Solos	1950	20.00	40.00	80.00
❏ MG-15001 [10]	Erroll Garner Plays Piano Solos, Volume 2	1950	20.00	40.00	80.00
❏ MG-15002 [10]	Erroll Garner Plays Piano Solos, Volume 3	1950	20.00	40.00	80.00
❏ MG-15003 [10]	Erroll Garner Plays Piano Solos, Volume 4	1950	20.00	40.00	80.00
❏ MG-15026 [10]	Erroll Garner at the Piano	1953	20.00	40.00	80.00
SAVOY JAZZ					
❏ SJC-411	Penthouse Serenade	1985	2.50	5.00	10.00
❏ SJL-1118	Yesterdays	198?	2.50	5.00	10.00
❏ SJL-2207 [(2)]	Elf	198?	3.00	6.00	12.00
TRIP					
❏ 5519	Garnering	197?	2.50	5.00	10.00
WING					
❏ MGW 12134	Erroll Garner Moods	196?	3.00	6.00	12.00

GARNER, ERROLL/PETE JOHNSON
Also see each artist's individual listings.

GRAND AWARD					
❏ GA 33-321 [M]	Jazz Piano	1956	20.00	40.00	80.00
-- With removable David Stone Martin cover still attached					
❏ GA 33-321 [M]	Jazz Piano	1956	6.25	12.50	25.00
-- Without removable cover					

GARNER, ERROLL/OSCAR PETERSON/ART TATUM
Also see each artist's individual listings.

RCA CAMDEN					
❏ CAL-882 [M]	Great Jazz Pianists of Our Time	196?	3.75	7.50	15.00
❏ CAS-882 [R]	Great Jazz Pianists of Our Time	196?	3.00	6.00	12.00

GARNER, ERROLL/BILLY TAYLOR
Also see each artist's individual listings.

SAVOY					
❏ MG-12008 [M]	Erroll Garner/Billy Taylor	1955	12.50	25.00	50.00

GARNER, MORRIS

THUNDERBIRD					
❏ TH-1958 [M]	The Worst of Morris Garner	196?	6.25	12.50	25.00

GARNETT, CARLOS
Saxophone player and male singer.

MUSE					
❏ MR-5040	Black Love	1973	3.75	7.50	15.00
❏ MR-5057	Journey to Enlightenment	1974	5.00	10.00	20.00
❏ MR-5079	Let the Melody Ring On	1975	7.50	15.00	30.00
❏ MR-5104	Cosmos Nucleus	1976	10.00	20.00	40.00
❏ MR-5133	New Love	1977	10.00	20.00	40.00

GARRETT, KENNY
Alto saxophone player.

ATLANTIC					
❏ 82046	Prisoner of Love	1989	3.00	6.00	12.00

GARSON, MIKE
Pianist and composer.

CONTEMPORARY					
❏ C-14003	Avant Garson	1979	3.00	6.00	12.00
JAZZ HOUNDS					
❏ 0005	Jazzical	1982	3.00	6.00	12.00
REFERENCE RECORDINGS					
❏ RR-20	Serendipity	1987	3.75	7.50	15.00
❏ RR-37	The Oxnard Sessions	1991	5.00	10.00	20.00
❏ RR-53 [(2)]	The Oxnard Sessions, Volume 2	1993	6.25	12.50	25.00

GARSON, MIKE, AND JIM WALKER
Walker is a flutist. Also see MIKE GARSON.

REFERENCE RECORDINGS					
❏ RR-18	Reflections	1987	3.75	7.50	15.00

GASCA, LUIS
Trumpeter. Also a session musician for rock artists such as Van Morrison.

ATLANTIC					
❏ SD 1527	Little Giant	1970	3.75	7.50	15.00
BLUE THUMB					
❏ BTS-37	Luis Gasca	1972	3.75	7.50	15.00
FANTASY					
❏ F-9461	Born to Love You	1974	3.75	7.50	15.00
❏ F-9504	Collage	1975	3.75	7.50	15.00

Number	Title	Yr	VG	VG+	NM

GASKIN, LEONARD
Bass player.
SWINGVILLE
❑ SVLP-2031 [M]	At the Jazz Band Ball	1962	10.00	20.00	40.00
-- Purple label					
❑ SVLP-2031 [M]	At the Jazz Band Ball	1965	5.00	10.00	20.00
-- Blue label, trident logo at right					
❑ SVST-2031 [S]	At the Jazz Band Ball	1962	12.50	25.00	50.00
-- Red label					
❑ SVST-2031 [S]	At the Jazz Band Ball	1965	6.25	12.50	25.00
-- Blue label, trident logo at right					
❑ SVLP-2033 [M]	At the Darktown Strutters' Ball	1962	10.00	20.00	40.00
-- Purple label					
❑ SVLP-2033 [M]	At the Darktown Strutters' Ball	1965	5.00	10.00	20.00
-- Blue label, trident logo at right					
❑ SVST-2033 [S]	At the Darktown Strutters' Ball	1962	12.50	25.00	50.00
-- Red label					
❑ SVST-2033 [S]	At the Darktown Strutters' Ball	1965	6.25	12.50	25.00
-- Blue label, trident logo at right					

GASLINI, GIORGIO
Pianist, composer and conductor.
SOUL NOTE
❑ SN-1020	Gaslini Plays Monk	1981	3.00	6.00	12.00
❑ SN-1120	Schumann Reflections	1984	3.00	6.00	12.00
❑ 121020	Gaslini Plays Monk	199?	2.50	5.00	10.00
-- Reissue of 1020					
❑ 121120	Schumann Reflections	199?	2.50	5.00	10.00
-- Reissue of 1120					
❑ 121220	Multipli	199?	3.00	6.00	12.00
❑ 121270	Ayler's Wings	1991	3.00	6.00	12.00

GATEWAY
See JOHN ABERCROMBIE.

GAULT, BILLY
Pianist.
INNER CITY
❑ IC-2027	When Destiny Calls	197?	3.75	7.50	15.00
STEEPLECHASE
❑ SCS-1027	When Destiny Calls	198?	2.50	5.00	10.00

GAUTHE, JACQUES
Clarinetist and soprano saxophone player.
GHB
❑ GHB-179	Riz A La Creole	1987	2.50	5.00	10.00
STOMP OFF
❑ SOS-1170	Cassoulet Stomp	1989	2.50	5.00	10.00

GAVIN, KEVIN
Male singer.
CHARLIE PARKER
❑ PLP-810 [M]	Hey! This Is Kevin Gavin	1962	7.50	15.00	30.00
❑ PLP-810S [S]	Hey! This Is Kevin Gavin	1962	10.00	20.00	40.00

GAYLE, CHARLES
Tenor saxophone player, bass clarinetist, keyboard player, pianist and violist.
SILKHEART
❑ SH-115	Always Born	1988	2.50	5.00	10.00
❑ SH-116	Homeless	1988	2.50	5.00	10.00
❑ SH-117	Spirits Before	1988	2.50	5.00	10.00

GAYLE, ROZELLE
MERCURY
❑ MG-20374 [M]	Like, Be My Guest	1958	10.00	20.00	40.00

GEE, MATTHEW
Trombonist. Also see JOHNNY GRIFFIN.
RIVERSIDE
❑ RLP 12-221 [M]	Jazz by Gee!	1956	20.00	40.00	80.00
-- White label, blue print					
❑ RLP 12-221 [M]	Jazz by Gee!	1958	10.00	20.00	40.00
-- Blue label, microphone logo at top					

GEISSMAN, GRANT
Guitarist and composer.
BLUEMOON
❑ R1-79152	Take Another Look	1990	3.00	6.00	12.00
CONCORD JAZZ
❑ CJ-62	Good Stuff	1978	3.00	6.00	12.00
PAUSA
❑ 7150	Put Away Childish Toys	198?	3.00	6.00	12.00

TBA
❑ TB-217	Drinkin' from the Money River	198?	3.00	6.00	12.00
❑ TB-224	Snapshots	198?	3.00	6.00	12.00
❑ TB-241	All My Tomorrows	1989	3.00	6.00	12.00

GELB, LARRY
Pianist.
CADENCE JAZZ
❑ 1012	The Language of Blue	198?	2.50	5.00	10.00

GELLER, HERB
Alto saxophone player. Also a soprano sax player, flutist and male singer.
ATCO
❑ 33-109 [M]	Gypsy	1959	10.00	20.00	40.00
ATLANTIC
❑ SD 1681	Rhyme and Reason	1975	3.00	6.00	12.00
EMARCY
❑ MG-26045 [10]	Herb Geller Plays	1954	30.00	60.00	120.00
❑ MG-36024 [M]	The Gellers	1955	25.00	50.00	100.00
❑ MG-36040 [M]	The Herb Geller Sextette	1955	20.00	40.00	80.00
❑ MG-36045 [M]	Herb Geller Plays	1955	20.00	40.00	80.00
JOSIE
❑ JLPS-3502 [S]	Alto Saxophone	1962	5.00	10.00	20.00
❑ JOZ-3502 [M]	Alto Saxophone	1962	6.25	12.50	25.00
JUBILEE
❑ JLP-1044 [M]	Fire in the West	1957	12.50	25.00	50.00
❑ SDJLP-1044 [S]	Fire in the West	1959	10.00	20.00	40.00
❑ JG-1094 [M]	Stax of Sax	1959	12.50	25.00	50.00

GELLER, LORRAINE
Pianist.
DOT
❑ DLP-3174 [M]	Lorraine Geller at the Piano	1959	125.00	250.00	500.00

GENERATION BAND, THE
All-star group led by VICTOR FELDMAN. Other members have included LEE RITENOUR and TOM SCOTT.
NAUTILUS
❑ NR-62	Soft Shoulder	198?	10.00	20.00	40.00
-- Audiophile vinyl					
PALO ALTO
❑ PA-8054	Soft Shoulder	198?	3.00	6.00	12.00
TBA
❑ TB-202	Call of the Wild	198?	2.50	5.00	10.00
❑ TB-208	High Visibility	1985	2.50	5.00	10.00

GEORGIA GRINDERS, THE
STOMP OFF
❑ SOS-1068	A Tribute to Roy Palmer	1984	2.50	5.00	10.00

GETZ, EDDIE
Alto saxophone player.
MGM
❑ E-3462 [M]	The Eddie Getz Quintette	1957	12.50	25.00	50.00

GETZ, STAN
Influential and popular tenor saxophone player and bandleader. Also see DIZZY GILLESPIE; LIONEL HAMPTON; BILLIE HOLIDAY; MODERN JAZZ SOCIETY; GERRY MULLIGAN; CAL TJADER.
A&M
❑ SP-5297	Apasionado	1990	3.75	7.50	15.00
AMERICAN RECORDING SOCIETY
❑ G-407 [M]	Cool Jazz of Stan Getz	1956	10.00	20.00	40.00
❑ G-428 [M]	Intimate Portrait	1957	10.00	20.00	40.00
❑ G-443 [M]	Stan Getz '57	1957	10.00	20.00	40.00
BLACKHAWK
❑ BKH-51101	Voyage	1986	2.50	5.00	10.00
BLUE RIBBON
❑ BR-8012 [M]	Rhythms	1961	5.00	10.00	20.00
❑ BS-8012 [R]	Rhythms	1961	2.50	5.00	10.00
CLEF
❑ MGC-137 [10]	Stan Getz Plays	1953	50.00	100.00	200.00
❑ MGC-143 [10]	The Artistry of Stan Getz	1953	50.00	100.00	200.00
COLUMBIA
❑ PC 32706	Captain Marvel	1974	3.75	7.50	15.00
❑ PC 33703	Best of Two Worlds	1975	3.75	7.50	15.00
❑ JC 34873	The Peacocks	1977	3.00	6.00	12.00
❑ JC 35992	Children of the World	1979	3.00	6.00	12.00
❑ JC 36403	The Best of Stan Getz	1980	3.00	6.00	12.00
❑ FC 38272	The Master	1983	2.50	5.00	10.00

Even before he helped to popularize Brazilian music in the 1960s, Stan Getz was a respected tenor sax player and had a long legacy of recordings. (Top left) One of his first sessions as a leader resulted in *New Sounds in Modern Music*, an early Savoy-label 10-inch LP that is quite rare today. (Top right) *Stan Getz '57* was actually the third issue of the recordings contained within. It originally was on two 10-inch LPs on the Clef label, then was reissued as a single 12-inch disc on Norgran before this reissue on the early Verve label. (Bottom left) This compilation of early material appeared on the budget Crown label. Look closely and you can see what the LP cost when it came out! (Bottom right) After the massive success of his collaboration with Charlie Byrd, *Jazz Samba*, Getz followed immediately with this album, which only cemented the hold the bossa nova had on America in the 1962-63 era.

Number	Title	Yr	VG	VG+	NM
❑ CJ 44047	The Lyrical Stan Getz	1988	3.00	6.00	12.00
CONCORD JAZZ					
❑ CJ-158	The Dolphin	198?	3.00	6.00	12.00
❑ CJ-188	Pure Getz	1983	3.00	6.00	12.00
CROWN					
❑ CLP-5002 [M]	Groovin' High	1957	10.00	20.00	40.00
-- Reissue of Modern 1202					
❑ CLP-5284 [M]	Groovin' High	196?	5.00	10.00	20.00
-- Reissue of 5002					
DALE					
❑ 21 [10]	In Retrospect	1951	75.00	150.00	300.00
EMARCY					
❑ 838 771-1	Billy Highstreet Samba	1990	3.00	6.00	12.00
FANTASY					
❑ OJC-121	Stan Getz Quartets	198?	2.50	5.00	10.00
-- Reissue of Prestige 7002					
HALL OF FAME					
❑ 606	Stan Getz and His Tenor Sax	197?	3.00	6.00	12.00
INNER CITY					
❑ 1040 [(2)]	Gold	1977	3.00	6.00	12.00
INTERMEDIA					
❑ QS-5057	Stella by Starlight	198?	2.50	5.00	10.00
JAZZ MAN					
❑ 5014	Forrest Eyes	1982	3.00	6.00	12.00
JAZZTONE					
❑ J-1230 [M]	Stan Getz	1956	10.00	20.00	40.00
❑ J-1240 [M]	Stan Getz '57	1957	10.00	20.00	40.00
METRO					
❑ M-501 [M]	The Melodic Stan Getz	1965	3.00	6.00	12.00
❑ MS-501 [S]	The Melodic Stan Getz	1965	3.75	7.50	15.00
METRONOME					
❑ BLP-6 [M]	The Sound	1956	12.50	25.00	50.00
MGM					
❑ SE-4696	Marrakesh Express	1970	3.75	7.50	15.00
MODERN					
❑ MLP-1202 [M]	Groovin' High	1956	37.50	75.00	150.00
MOSAIC					
❑ M4-131 [(4)]	The Complete Recordings of the Stan Getz Quintet with Jimmy Raney	199?	12.50	25.00	50.00
NEW JAZZ					
❑ NJLP-8214 [M]	Long Island Sound	1959	15.00	30.00	60.00
-- Reissue of Prestige 7002; purple label					
❑ NJLP-8214 [M]	Long Island Sound	1965	6.25	12.50	25.00
-- Blue label with trident logo on right					
NORGRAN					
❑ MGN-1000 [M]	Interpretations by the Stan Getz Quintet	1954	30.00	60.00	120.00
❑ MGN-1008 [M]	Interpretations by the Stan Getz Quintet #2	1954	30.00	60.00	120.00
❑ MGN-1029 [M]	Interpretations by the Stan Getz Quintet #3	1955	37.50	75.00	150.00
❑ MGN-1032 [M]	West Coast Jazz	1955	37.50	75.00	150.00
❑ MGN-1042 [M]	Stan Getz Plays	1955	25.00	50.00	100.00
-- Reissue of Clef 137 and 143 on one 12-inch LP					
❑ MGN-1087 [M]	Stan Getz '56	1956	25.00	50.00	100.00
❑ MGN-1088 [M]	More West Coast Jazz with Stan Getz	1956	25.00	50.00	100.00
❑ MGN-2000-2 [(2) M]	Stan Getz at the Shrine	1955	50.00	100.00	200.00
-- Boxed set with booklet					
PICKWICK					
❑ SPC-3031	Stan Getz In Concert	197?	2.50	5.00	10.00
PRESTIGE					
❑ PRLP-102 [10]	Stan Getz and the Tenor Sax Stars	1951	50.00	100.00	200.00
❑ PRLP-104 [10]	Stan Getz, Volume 2	1951	50.00	100.00	200.00
❑ PRLP-108 [10]	Stan Getz-Lee Konitz	1951	50.00	100.00	200.00
❑ PRLP-7002 [M]	Stan Getz Quartets	1955	25.00	50.00	100.00
❑ PRLP-7255 [M]	Early Stan	1963	10.00	20.00	40.00
❑ PRST-7255 [R]	Early Stan	1963	5.00	10.00	20.00
❑ PRLP-7256 [M]	Stan Getz' Greatest Hits	1963	10.00	20.00	40.00
❑ PRST-7256 [R]	Stan Getz' Greatest Hits	1963	5.00	10.00	20.00
❑ PRLP-7337 [M]	Stan Getz' Greatest Hits	1967	6.25	12.50	25.00
-- Reissue of PRLP 7256					
❑ PRST-7337 [R]	Stan Getz' Greatest Hits	1967	3.75	7.50	15.00
-- Reissue of PRST 7256					
❑ PRLP-7434 [M]	Getz Plays Jazz Classics	1967	6.25	12.50	25.00
-- Reissue of PRLP 7255					
❑ PRST-7434 [R]	Getz Plays Jazz Classics	1967	3.75	7.50	15.00
-- Reissue of PRST 7255					
❑ PRLP-7516 [M]	Preservation	1967	6.25	12.50	25.00
❑ PRST-7516 [R]	Preservation	1967	3.75	7.50	15.00
❑ 24019 [(2)]	Stan Getz	197?	3.75	7.50	15.00

Number	Title	Yr	VG	VG+	NM
❑ 24088 [(2)]	Early Getz	197?	3.00	6.00	12.00
ROOST					
❑ RK-103 [(2) M]	The Stan Getz Years	1964	10.00	20.00	40.00
❑ RKS-103 [(2) R]	The Stan Getz Years	1964	6.25	12.50	25.00
❑ R-402 [10]	Stan Getz	1950	50.00	100.00	200.00
❑ R-404 [10]	Stan Getz and the Swedish All Stars	1951	50.00	100.00	200.00
❑ R-407 [10]	Jazz at Storyville	1952	37.50	75.00	150.00
❑ R-411 [10]	Jazz at Storyville, Volume 2	1952	37.50	75.00	150.00
❑ R-417 [10]	Chamber Music	1953	37.50	75.00	150.00
❑ R-420 [10]	Jazz at Storyville, Volume 3	1954	37.50	75.00	150.00
❑ R-423 [10]	Split Kick	1954	37.50	75.00	150.00
❑ LP-2207 [M]	The Sounds of Stan Getz	1956	20.00	40.00	80.00
-- Reissue of R-402					
❑ LP-2209 [M]	Storyville	1956	20.00	40.00	80.00
-- Reissue of R-407 and half of R-411					
❑ LP-2225 [M]	Storyville, Volume 2	1957	20.00	40.00	80.00
-- Reissue of R-423 and the other half of R-411					
❑ LP-2249 [M]	The Greatest of Stan Getz	1963	7.50	15.00	30.00
❑ SLP-2249 [R]	The Greatest of Stan Getz	1963	3.75	7.50	15.00
❑ LP-2251 [M]	Moonlight in Vermont	1963	7.50	15.00	30.00
❑ SLP-2251 [R]	Moonlight in Vermont	1963	3.75	7.50	15.00
❑ LP-2255 [M]	Modern World	1963	7.50	15.00	30.00
❑ SLP-2255 [R]	Modern World	1963	3.75	7.50	15.00
❑ LP-2258 [M]	Getz Age	1963	7.50	15.00	30.00
❑ SLP-2258 [R]	Getz Age	1963	3.75	7.50	15.00
ROULETTE					
❑ RE-119 [(2)]	The Best of Stan Getz	1972	3.75	7.50	15.00
❑ RE-123 [(2)]	Stan Getz/Sonny Stitt	1973	3.75	7.50	15.00
SAVOY					
❑ MG-9004 [10]	New Sounds in Modern Music	1951	75.00	150.00	300.00
SAVOY JAZZ					
❑ SJL-1105	Opus de Bop	197?	3.00	6.00	12.00
STEEPLECHASE					
❑ SCS-1073/4 [(2)]	Live at Montmartre	1986	3.00	6.00	12.00
VERVE					
❑ VSP-2 [M]	Eloquence	1966	3.75	7.50	15.00
❑ VSPS-2 [R]	Eloquence	1966	2.50	5.00	10.00
❑ VSP-22 [M]	Another Time, Another Place	1966	3.75	7.50	15.00
❑ VSPS-22 [R]	Another Time, Another Place	1966	2.50	5.00	10.00
❑ VSP-31 [M]	Stan Getz Plays Blues	1966	3.75	7.50	15.00
❑ VSPS-31 [R]	Stan Getz Plays Blues	1966	2.50	5.00	10.00
❑ UMV-2071	Focus	198?	2.50	5.00	10.00
-- Reissue					
❑ UMV-2075	Getz Au Go Go	198?	2.50	5.00	10.00
-- Reissue					
❑ UMV-2100	Jazz Samba Encore	198?	2.50	5.00	10.00
-- Reissue					
❑ VE-2-2510 [(2)]	The Corea/Evans Sessions	1976	3.75	7.50	15.00
❑ VR-1-2528	Focus	1977	2.50	5.00	10.00
-- Reissue of 8412					
❑ UMV-2614	Stan Getz in Stockholm	198?	2.50	5.00	10.00
-- Reissue					
❑ MGVS-6160 [S]	Cool Velvet -- Stan Getz and Strings	1960	---	---	---
-- Unreleased					
❑ MGV-8028 [M]	West Coast Jazz	1957	12.50	25.00	50.00
-- Reissue of Norgran 1032					
❑ V-8028 [M]	West Coast Jazz	1961	5.00	10.00	20.00
-- Reissue of MGV-8028					
❑ V6-8028 [R]	West Coast Jazz	196?	3.00	6.00	12.00
❑ MGV-8029 [M]	Stan Getz '57	1957	12.50	25.00	50.00
-- Reissue of Norgran 1087 with revised title					
❑ V-8029 [M]	Stan Getz '57	1961	5.00	10.00	20.00
-- Reissue of MGV-8029					
❑ MGV-8122 [M]	Interpretations by the Stan Getz Quintet #3	1957	12.50	25.00	50.00
-- Reissue of Norgran 1029					
❑ V-8122 [M]	Interpretations by the Stan Getz Quintet #3	1961	5.00	10.00	20.00
-- Reissue of MGV-8122					
❑ MGV-8133 [M]	Stan Getz Plays	1957	12.50	25.00	50.00
-- Reissue of Norgran 1042					
❑ V-8133 [M]	Stan Getz Plays	1961	5.00	10.00	20.00
-- Reissue of MGV-8133					
❑ V6-8133 [R]	Stan Getz Plays	196?	3.00	6.00	12.00
❑ MGV-8177 [M]	More West Coast Jazz with Stan Getz	1957	12.50	25.00	50.00
-- Reissue of Norgran 1088					
❑ V-8177 [M]	More West Coast Jazz with Stan Getz	1961	5.00	10.00	20.00
-- Reissue of MGV-8177					
❑ V6-8177 [R]	More West Coast Jazz with Stan Getz	196?	3.00	6.00	12.00
❑ MGV-8188-2 [M]	Stan Getz at the Shrine	1957	25.00	50.00	100.00
-- Reissue of Norgran 2000-2					
❑ V-8188-2 [(2) M]	Stan Getz at the Shrine	1961	6.25	12.50	25.00
-- Reissue of MGV-8188-2					

Number	Title	Yr	VG	VG+	NM
❏ V6-8188-2 [(2) R]Stan Getz at the Shrine		196?	3.75	7.50	15.00
❏ MGV-8200 [M]	Stan Getz and the Cool Sounds	1957	12.50	25.00	50.00
-- Reissue of American Recording Society 407 with new name					
❏ V-8200 [M]	Stan Getz and the Cool Sounds	1961	5.00	10.00	20.00
-- Reissue of MGV-8200					
❏ V6-8200 [R]	Stan Getz and the Cool Sounds	196?	3.00	6.00	12.00
❏ MGV-8213 [M]	Stan Getz in Stockholm	1958	12.50	25.00	50.00
-- Reissue of American Recording Society 428 with new name					
❏ V-8213 [M]	Stan Getz in Stockholm	1961	5.00	10.00	20.00
-- Reissue of MGV-8213					
❏ V6-8213 [R]	Stan Getz in Stockholm	196?	3.00	6.00	12.00
❏ MGV-8263 [M]	Stan Meets Chet	1958	15.00	30.00	60.00
-- With Chet Baker					
❏ V-8263 [M]	Stan Meets Chet	1961	5.00	10.00	20.00
-- Reissue of MGV-8263					
❏ V6-8263 [R]	Stan Meets Chet	196?	3.00	6.00	12.00
❏ MGV-8294 [M]	The Steamer	1959	12.50	25.00	50.00
❏ V-8294 [M]	The Steamer	1961	5.00	10.00	20.00
-- Reissue of MGV-8294					
❏ V6-8294 [R]	The Steamer	196?	3.00	6.00	12.00
❏ MGV-8296 [M]	Award Winner	1959	12.50	25.00	50.00
❏ V-8296 [M]	Award Winner	1961	5.00	10.00	20.00
-- Reissue of MGV-8296					
❏ V6-8296 [R]	Award Winner	196?	3.00	6.00	12.00
❏ MGV-8321 [M]	The Soft Swing	1959	12.50	25.00	50.00
❏ V-8321 [M]	The Soft Swing	1961	5.00	10.00	20.00
-- Reissue of MGV-8321					
❏ V6-8321 [R]	The Soft Swing	196?	3.00	6.00	12.00
❏ MGV-8331 [M]	Imported from Europe	1959	12.50	25.00	50.00
❏ V-8331 [M]	Imported from Europe	1961	5.00	10.00	20.00
-- Reissue of MGV-8331					
❏ V6-8331 [R]	Imported from Europe	196?	3.00	6.00	12.00
❏ MGV-8356 [M]	Stan Getz Quintet	1960	---	---	---
-- Unreleased					
❏ MGV-8379 [M]	Cool Velvet -- Stan Getz and Strings	1960	12.50	25.00	50.00
❏ V-8379 [M]	Cool Velvet -- Stan Getz and Strings	1961	5.00	10.00	20.00
-- Reissue of MGV-8379					
❏ V6-8379 [S]	Cool Velvet -- Stan Getz and Strings	1961	5.00	10.00	20.00
❏ MGV-8393-2 [(2) M]	Stan Getz At Large	1960	15.00	30.00	60.00
❏ V-8393-2 [(2) M] Stan Getz At Large		1961	6.25	12.50	25.00
-- Reissue of MGV-8393-2					
❏ V6-8393-2 [(2) R]Stan Getz At Large		1961	3.75	7.50	15.00
❏ MGV-8401 [M]	Stan Getz At Large, Volume 1	1960	---	---	---
-- Unreleased					
❏ MGV-8402 [M]	Stan Getz At Large, Volume 2	1960	---	---	---
-- Unreleased					
❏ V-8412 [M]	Focus	1961	6.25	12.50	25.00
❏ V6-8412 [S]	Focus	1961	5.00	10.00	20.00
❏ V-8494 [M]	Big Band Bossa Nova	1962	5.00	10.00	20.00
❏ V6-8494 [S]	Big Band Bossa Nova	1962	6.25	12.50	25.00
❏ V-8523 [M]	Jazz Samba Encore!	1963	5.00	10.00	20.00
-- With Luiz Bonfa					
❏ V6-8523 [S]	Jazz Samba Encore!	1963	6.25	12.50	25.00
-- With Luiz Bonfa					
❏ V-8554 [M]	Reflections	1964	3.75	7.50	15.00
❏ V6-8554 [S]	Reflections	1964	5.00	10.00	20.00
❏ V-8600 [M]	Getz Au Go Go	1964	3.75	7.50	15.00
❏ V6-8600 [S]	Getz Au Go Go	1964	5.00	10.00	20.00
❏ V-8693 [M]	Sweet Rain	1967	6.25	12.50	25.00
❏ V6-8693 [S]	Sweet Rain	1967	3.75	7.50	15.00
❏ V-8707 [M]	Voices	1967	6.25	12.50	25.00
❏ V6-8707 [S]	Voices	1967	3.75	7.50	15.00
❏ V-8719 [M]	The Best of Stan Getz	1967	6.25	12.50	25.00
❏ V6-8719 [S]	The Best of Stan Getz	1967	3.75	7.50	15.00
❏ V-8752 [M]	What the World Needs Now -- Stan Getz Plays Bacharach and David	1968	7.50	15.00	30.00
❏ V6-8752 [S]	What the World Needs Now -- Stan Getz Plays Bacharach and David	1968	3.75	7.50	15.00
❏ V6-8780	Didn't We	1969	3.75	7.50	15.00
❏ V6-8802-2 [(2)]	Dynasty	1971	5.00	10.00	20.00
❏ V6-8807	Communications '72	1972	3.75	7.50	15.00
❏ V6-8815-2 [(2)]	History of Stan Getz	1973	3.75	7.50	15.00
❏ V3HB-8844 [(2)]	Return Engagement	1974	3.75	7.50	15.00
❏ 815 239-1	Stan the Man	1983	2.50	5.00	10.00
❏ 821 725-1	Getz Au Go Go	198?	2.50	5.00	10.00
-- Reissue					
❏ 823 242-1 [(2)]	The Corea/Evans Sessions	198?	3.00	6.00	12.00
-- Reissue					
❏ 823 611-1 [(5)]	The Girl from Ipanema: The Bossa Nova Years	1984	12.50	25.00	50.00
❏ 823 613-1	Jazz Samba Encore	198?	2.50	5.00	10.00
-- Reissue					

GETZ, STAN, AND LAURINDO ALMEIDA
Also see each artist's individual listings.
VERVE

Number	Title	Yr	VG	VG+	NM
❏ V-8665 [M]	Stan Getz with Guest Artist Laurindo Almeida	1965	3.75	7.50	15.00
❏ V6-8665 [S]	Stan Getz with Guest Artist Laurindo Almeida	1965	5.00	10.00	20.00

GETZ, STAN, AND CHET BAKER
Also see each artist's individual listings.
STORYVILLE

❏ 4090	Line for Lyons	1984	2.50	5.00	10.00

GETZ, STAN, AND BOB BROOKMEYER
Also see each artist's individual listings.
VERVE

❏ V-8418 [M]	Stan Getz and Bob Brookmeyer (Recorded Fall 1961)	1961	5.00	10.00	20.00
❏ V6-8418 [S]	Stan Getz and Bob Brookmeyer (Recorded Fall 1961)	1961	5.00	10.00	20.00

GETZ, STAN, AND CHARLIE BYRD
Also see each artist's individual listings.
DCC COMPACT CLASSICS

❏ LPZ-2011	Jazz Samba	1995	6.25	12.50	25.00
-- Audiophile vinyl					

VERVE

❏ UMJ-3158	Jazz Samba	198?	2.50	5.00	10.00
❏ V-8432 [M]	Jazz Samba	1962	5.00	10.00	20.00
❏ V6-8432 [S]	Jazz Samba	1962	6.25	12.50	25.00
❏ 810 061-1	Jazz Samba	198?	2.50	5.00	10.00
-- Reissue					

GETZ, STAN, AND ALBERT DAILEY
Also see each artist's individual listings.
ELEKTRA/MUSICIAN

❏ 60370	Poetry	1985	2.50	5.00	10.00

GETZ, STAN, AND BILL EVANS
Also see each artist's individual listings.
VERVE

❏ V3G-8833	Previously Unreleased Recordings	1974	3.00	6.00	12.00

GETZ, STAN, AND JOAO GILBERTO
Also see each artist's individual listings.
MOBILE FIDELITY

❏ 1-208	Getz/Gilberto	1994	12.50	25.00	50.00
-- Audiophile vinyl					

VERVE

❏ UMV-2099	Getz/Gilberto	198?	2.50	5.00	10.00
-- Reissue					
❏ V-8545 [M]	Getz/Gilberto	1964	3.75	7.50	15.00
❏ V6-8545 [S]	Getz/Gilberto	1964	5.00	10.00	20.00
❏ V-8623 [M]	Getz/Gilberto #2	1965	3.75	7.50	15.00
❏ V6-8623 [S]	Getz/Gilberto #2	1965	5.00	10.00	20.00
❏ 810 048-1	Getz/Gilberto	198?	2.50	5.00	10.00
-- Reissue					

GETZ, STAN; DIZZY GILLESPIE; SONNY STITT
Also see each artist's individual listings.
VERVE

❏ MGV-8198 [M]	For Musicians Only	1958	20.00	40.00	80.00
❏ V-8198 [M]	For Musicians Only	1961	6.25	12.50	25.00

GETZ, STAN, AND WARDELL GRAY
Also see each artist's individual listings.
DAWN

❏ DLP-1126 [M]	Tenors Anyone?	1958	20.00	40.00	80.00

SEECO

❏ SLP-7 [10]	Highlights in Modern Jazz	1954	50.00	100.00	200.00

GETZ, STAN, AND J.J. JOHNSON
Also see each artist's individual listings.
VERVE

❏ MGVS-6027 [S]	Stan Getz and J.J. Johnson at the Opera House	1960	10.00	20.00	40.00
❏ MGV-8265 [M]	Stan Getz and J.J. Johnson at the Opera House	1958	12.50	25.00	50.00
❏ V-8265 [M]	Stan Getz and J.J. Johnson at the Opera House	1961	5.00	10.00	20.00

Number	Title	Yr	VG	VG+	NM
❏ V6-8265 [S]	Stan Getz and J.J. Johnson at the Opera House	1961	3.75	7.50	15.00
❏ MGV-8405 [M]	Stan Getz and J.J. Johnson	1961	---	---	---
-- Unreleased					

GETZ, STAN, AND GERRY MULLIGAN
Also see each artist's individual listings.
MAINSTREAM

Number	Title	Yr	VG	VG+	NM
❏ MRL 364	Yesterday	1972	3.75	7.50	15.00

GETZ, STAN, AND OSCAR PETERSON
Also see each artist's individual listings.
VERVE

Number	Title	Yr	VG	VG+	NM
❏ UMV-2665	Stan Getz and the Oscar Peterson Trio	198?	2.50	5.00	10.00
-- Reissue					
❏ MGV-8251 [M]	Stan Getz and the Oscar Peterson Trio	1958	12.50	25.00	50.00
❏ V-8251 [M]	Stan Getz and the Oscar Peterson Trio	1961	5.00	10.00	20.00
-- Reissue of MGV-8251					
❏ V6-8251 [R]	Stan Getz and the Oscar Peterson Trio	196?	3.00	6.00	12.00
❏ MGV-8348 [M]	Stan Getz with Gerry Mulligan and the Oscar Peterson Trio	1959	12.50	25.00	50.00
❏ V-8348 [M]	Stan Getz with Gerry Mulligan and the Oscar Peterson Trio	1961	5.00	10.00	20.00
-- Reissue of MGV-8348					
❏ V6-8348 [R]	Stan Getz with Gerry Mulligan and the Oscar Peterson Trio	1961	3.00	6.00	12.00

GETZ, STAN, AND HORACE SILVER
Also see each artist's individual listings.
BARONET

Number	Title	Yr	VG	VG+	NM
❏ B-102 [M]	A Pair of Kings	1962	3.75	7.50	15.00
❏ BS-102 [R]	A Pair of Kings	196?	2.50	5.00	10.00

GETZ, STAN, AND ZOOT SIMS
Also see each artist's individual listings.
FANTASY

Number	Title	Yr	VG	VG+	NM
❏ OJC-008	The Brothers	1982	2.50	5.00	10.00
PRESTIGE					
❏ PRLP-7022 [M]	The Brothers	1956	37.50	75.00	150.00
❏ PRLP-7252 [M]	The Brothers	1963	12.50	25.00	50.00

GHIGLIONI, TIZIANA
Female singer.
SOUL NOTE

Number	Title	Yr	VG	VG+	NM
❏ SN-1056	Sounds of Love	1984	3.00	6.00	12.00
❏ 121056	Sounds of Love	198?	2.50	5.00	10.00
❏ 121156	Somebody Special	198?	3.00	6.00	12.00

GIBBONS, SHANNON
Female singer.
SOUL NOTE

Number	Title	Yr	VG	VG+	NM
❏ 121163	Shannon Gibbons	1987	3.00	6.00	12.00

GIBBS, MICHAEL
Trombonist, pianist, arranger, bandleader and composer.
DERAM

Number	Title	Yr	VG	VG+	NM
❏ DES 18048	Michael Gibbs	1970	5.00	10.00	20.00

GIBBS, MICHAEL, AND GARY BURTON
Also see each artist's individual listings.
POLYDOR

Number	Title	Yr	VG	VG+	NM
❏ PD-6503	In the Public Interest	197?	3.75	7.50	15.00

GIBBS, TERRY
Vibraphone player and percussionist. Also see HARRY BABASIN.
ABC IMPULSE!

Number	Title	Yr	VG	VG+	NM
❏ AS-58 [S]	Take It from Me	1968	3.75	7.50	15.00
BRUNSWICK					
❏ BL 54009 [M]	Terry	1955	12.50	25.00	50.00
❏ BL 56055 [10]	Terry Gibbs Quartet	1954	25.00	50.00	100.00
CONTEMPORARY					
❏ C-7647	Dream Band	1986	2.50	5.00	10.00
❏ C-7652	Volume 2: The Sundown Sessions	1987	2.50	5.00	10.00
❏ C-7654	Volume 3: Flying Home	1988	2.50	5.00	10.00
❏ C-7656	Volume 4: Main Stem	1990	3.00	6.00	12.00
❏ C-14022	The Latin Connection	1986	2.50	5.00	10.00

Number	Title	Yr	VG	VG+	NM
DOT					
❏ DLP-3726 [M]	Reza	1966	3.75	7.50	15.00
❏ DLP-25726 [S]	Reza	1966	5.00	10.00	20.00
EMARCY					
❏ MG-36047 [M]	Terry Gibbs	1956	12.50	25.00	50.00
❏ MG-36064 [M]	Vibes on Velvet	1956	12.50	25.00	50.00
❏ MG-36075 [M]	Mallets A-Plenty	1956	12.50	25.00	50.00
❏ MG-36103 [M]	Swingin' Terry Gibbs	1957	12.50	25.00	50.00
❏ MG-36128 [M]	Terry Plays the Duke	1958	12.50	25.00	50.00
❏ MG-36138 [M]	Steve Allen's All Stars	1958	12.50	25.00	50.00
❏ MG-36148 [M]	More Vibes on Velvet	1958	12.50	25.00	50.00
❏ SR-80004 [S]	Steve Allen's All Stars	1959	10.00	20.00	40.00
IMPULSE!					
❏ A-58 [M]	Take It from Me	1964	6.25	12.50	25.00
❏ AS-58 [S]	Take It from Me	1964	7.50	15.00	30.00
INTERLUDE					
❏ MO-506 [M]	Vibrations	1959	10.00	20.00	40.00
❏ ST-1006 [S]	Vibrations	1959	7.50	15.00	30.00
JAZZ A LA CARTE					
❏ 1 [(2)]	Live at the Lord	1978	3.75	7.50	15.00
❏ 2	Smoke 'Em Up	1978	3.00	6.00	12.00
LIMELIGHT					
❏ LM-82005 [M]	El Nutto	1964	5.00	10.00	20.00
❏ LS-86005 [S]	El Nutto	1964	6.25	12.50	25.00
MAINSTREAM					
❏ S-6048 [S]	It's Time We Met	1965	5.00	10.00	20.00
❏ 56048 [M]	It's Time We Met	1965	3.75	7.50	15.00
MCA					
❏ 29035	Take It from Me	198?	2.00	4.00	8.00
MERCURY					
❏ MG-20440 [M]	Launching a New Sound in Music	1959	10.00	20.00	40.00
❏ MG-20518 [M]	Steve Allen's All Stars	1960	7.50	15.00	30.00
❏ MG-20704 [M]	Explosion!	1962	3.75	7.50	15.00
❏ MG-20812 [M]	Jewish Melodies in Jazztime	1963	3.75	7.50	15.00
❏ SR-60112 [S]	Launching a New Sound in Music	1959	7.50	15.00	30.00
❏ SR-60195 [S]	Steve Allen's All Stars	1960	6.25	12.50	25.00
❏ SR-60704 [S]	Explosion!	1962	5.00	10.00	20.00
❏ SR-60812 [S]	Jewish Melodies in Jazztime	1963	5.00	10.00	20.00
MODE					
❏ LP-123 [M]	A Jazz Band Ball	1957	20.00	40.00	80.00
ROOST					
❏ LP-2260 [M]	El Latino	1965	3.75	7.50	15.00
❏ RS-2260 [S]	Latino	1965	5.00	10.00	20.00
TIME					
❏ S-2105 [S]	Hootenanny My Way	1963	7.50	15.00	30.00
❏ S-2120 [S]	Terry Gibbs with Sal Nistico	196?	6.25	12.50	25.00
❏ 52105 [M]	Hootenanny My Way	1963	6.25	12.50	25.00
❏ 52120 [M]	Terry Gibbs with Sal Nistico	196?	5.00	10.00	20.00
TRIP					
❏ 5545	Launching a New Band	197?	2.50	5.00	10.00
VERVE					
❏ MGV-2134 [M]	Swing Is Here!	1960	10.00	20.00	40.00
❏ V-2134 [M]	Swing Is Here!	1961	5.00	10.00	20.00
❏ V6-2134 [S]	Swing Is Here!	1961	5.00	10.00	20.00
❏ MGV-2136 [M]	Music from Cole Porter's "Can-Can"	1960	10.00	20.00	40.00
❏ V-2136 [M]	Music from Cole Porter's "Can-Can"	1961	5.00	10.00	20.00
❏ V6-2136 [S]	Music from Cole Porter's "Can-Can"	1961	5.00	10.00	20.00
❏ MGV-2151 [M]	The Exciting Terry Gibbs Big Band	1960	10.00	20.00	40.00
❏ V-2151 [M]	The Exciting Terry Gibbs Big Band	1961	5.00	10.00	20.00
❏ V6-2151 [S]	The Exciting Terry Gibbs Big Band	1961	6.25	12.50	25.00
❏ MGVS-6140 [S]	Swing Is Here!	1960	10.00	20.00	40.00
❏ MGVS-6145 [S]	Music from Cole Porter's "Can-Can"	1960	10.00	20.00	40.00
❏ V-8447 [M]	That Swing Thing	1962	5.00	10.00	20.00
❏ V6-8447 [S]	That Swing Thing	1962	6.25	12.50	25.00
❏ V-8496 [M]	Straight Ahead	1962	5.00	10.00	20.00
❏ V6-8496 [S]	Straight Ahead	1962	6.25	12.50	25.00
WING					
❏ MGW-12255 [M]	Terry Plays the Duke	196?	3.75	7.50	15.00
❏ SRW-16255 [R]	Terry Plays the Duke	196?	2.50	5.00	10.00
XANADU					
❏ 210	Bopstacle Course	198?	2.50	5.00	10.00

Number	Title	Yr	VG	VG+	NM

GIBBS, TERRY, AND BILL HARRIS
Also see each artist's individual listings.
MODE
| ❏ LP-129 [M] | The Ex-Hermanites | 1957 | 20.00 | 40.00 | 80.00 |
PREMIER
| ❏ PM-2006 [M] | Woodchoppers' Ball | 1963 | 3.75 | 7.50 | 15.00 |
| ❏ PS-2006 [R] | Woodchoppers' Ball | 1963 | 2.50 | 5.00 | 10.00 |

GIBBS, TERRY, AND BUDDY DeFRANCO
Also see each artist's individual listings.
CONTEMPORARY
| ❏ C-14036 | Chicago Fire | 1987 | 2.50 | 5.00 | 10.00 |
| ❏ C-14056 | Air Mail Special | 1990 | 3.00 | 6.00 | 12.00 |
PALO ALTO
| ❏ PA-8011 | Jazz Party -- First Time Together | 1982 | 2.50 | 5.00 | 10.00 |

GIBSON, DON
Pianist. Not to be confused with the country singer of the same name.
JAZZOLOGY
| ❏ J-40 | The Al Capone Memorial Jazz Band | 197? | 3.00 | 6.00 | 12.00 |

GIFFORD, WALT
DELMARK
| ❏ DS-204 [M] | Walt Gifford's New Yorkers | 1959 | 3.00 | 6.00 | 12.00 |

GIL, GILBERTO
Guitarist and male singer.
BRAZILOID
| ❏ BR-4000 | Soy Loco Por Ti America | 1988 | 3.00 | 6.00 | 12.00 |
| ❏ BR-4009 | Ao Vivo Em Toquio | 1989 | 3.00 | 6.00 | 12.00 |
ELEKTRA
| ❏ 6E-167 | Nightingale | 1979 | 3.00 | 6.00 | 12.00 |
PHILIPS
| ❏ 832 216-1 | Gilberto Gil | 1988 | 2.50 | 5.00 | 10.00 |

GILBERT & SULLIVAN JAZZ WORKSHOP, THE
Members: MEL LEWIS (gong, drums); Bobby Gibbons (guitar); Milt Bernhart (trombone) JOHN GRAAS (French horn) Frank Flynn (vibes); Red Mandel (flute, clarinet); Cappy Lewis (trumpet); Morty Cobb (bass); John Rotella (baritone and alto saxophones).
ANDEX
| ❏ A-27101 [M] | The Coolest Mikado | 1961 | 5.00 | 10.00 | 20.00 |
| ❏ AS-27101 [S] | The Coolest Mikado | 1961 | 6.25 | 12.50 | 25.00 |

GILBERT, ANN
Female singer.
GROOVE
| ❏ LG-1004 [M] | The Many Moods of Ann | 1956 | 12.50 | 25.00 | 50.00 |

GILBERT, RONNIE
Female singer. Best known as a member of the folk group The Weavers, the below LP has a backing band of jazz musicians.
RCA VICTOR
| ❏ LPM-1591 [M] | In Hi-Fi, The Legend of Bessie Smith | 1958 | 10.00 | 20.00 | 40.00 |

GILBERTO, ASTRUD
Female singer.
CTI
| ❏ CTS-6008 | Astrud Gilberto with Stanley Turrentine | 1970 | 3.00 | 6.00 | 12.00 |
ELEKTRA/MUSICIAN
| ❏ 60760 | Live in Montreux | 1988 | 2.50 | 5.00 | 10.00 |
PERCEPTION
| ❏ 29 | Now | 1973 | 2.50 | 5.00 | 10.00 |
VERVE
❏ V-8608 [M]	The Astrud Gilberto Album	1965	3.00	6.00	12.00
❏ V6-8608 [S]	The Astrud Gilberto Album	1965	3.75	7.50	15.00
❏ V-8629 [M]	The Shadow of Your Smile	1965	3.00	6.00	12.00
❏ V6-8629 [S]	The Shadow of Your Smile	1965	3.75	7.50	15.00
❏ V-8643 [M]	Look to the Rainbow	1966	3.00	6.00	12.00
❏ V6-8643 [S]	Look to the Rainbow	1966	3.75	7.50	15.00
❏ V-8673 [M]	A Certain Smile, A Certain Sadness	1966	3.00	6.00	12.00
❏ V6-8673 [S]	A Certain Smile, A Certain Sadness	1966	3.75	7.50	15.00
❏ V-8708 [M]	Beach Samba	1967	3.00	6.00	12.00
❏ V6-8708 [S]	Beach Samba	1967	3.75	7.50	15.00
❏ V6-8754	Windy	1968	3.00	6.00	12.00
❏ V6-8776	I Haven't Got Anything Better to	1969	3.00	6.00	12.00
❏ V6-8793	September 17, 1969	1969	3.00	6.00	12.00
❏ 821 566-1	Look to the Rainbow	1986	2.50	5.00	10.00
-- Reissue of V6-8643					

GILBERTO, JOAO
Guitarist and male singer. Also see STAN GETZ.
ATLANTIC
❏ 8070 [M]	The Boss of the Bossa Nova	1963	3.75	7.50	15.00
❏ SD 8070 [S]	The Boss of the Bossa Nova	1963	5.00	10.00	20.00
❏ 8076 [M]	The Warm World of Joao Gilberto	1964	3.75	7.50	15.00
❏ SD 8076 [S]	The Warm World of Joao Gilberto	1964	5.00	10.00	20.00
CAPITOL
❏ ST 2160 [S]	Joao Gilberto and Antonio Carlos Jobim	1964	5.00	10.00	20.00
❏ T 2160 [M]	Joao Gilberto and Antonio Carlos Jobim	1964	3.75	7.50	15.00
❏ ST 10280 [S]	Pops in Portuguese	196?	6.25	12.50	25.00
❏ T 10280 [M]	Pops in Portuguese	196?	5.00	10.00	20.00
WARNER BROS.
| ❏ BS 3053 | Amoroso | 1978 | 2.50 | 5.00 | 10.00 |
| ❏ BSK 3613 | Brasel | 1981 | 2.50 | 5.00 | 10.00 |

GILL, JOHN
Pianist.
STOMP OFF
❏ SOS-1066	Finger Buster	1984	2.50	5.00	10.00
❏ SOS-1094	I Lost My Heart in Dixie Land	1986	2.50	5.00	10.00
❏ SOS-1126	Down Home Blues	1987	2.50	5.00	10.00
❏ SOS-1156	Some Sweet Day	1988	2.50	5.00	10.00
❏ SOS-1157	Big City Blues	1988	2.50	5.00	10.00

GILLESPIE, DIZZY
Trumpeter, male singer and composer; one of the most important figures in jazz history. His visual trademarks were the upturned bell on his instrument and his puffed-out cheeks as he played. Also see COUNT BASIE; ROY ELDRIDGE; GIL FULLER; SLIM GAILLARD; STAN GETZ; THE MODERN JAZZ SEXTET; CHARLIE PARKER; THE QUINTET.
ALLEGRO
❏ 3017 [M]	Dizzy Gillespie Plays	195?	30.00	60.00	120.00
❏ 3083 [M]	Dizzy Gillespie	195?	30.00	60.00	120.00
❏ 4023 [10]	Dizzy Gillespie	195?	50.00	100.00	200.00
❏ 4108 [10]	Dizzy Gillespie Plays	195?	50.00	100.00	200.00
AMERICAN RECORDING SOCIETY
| ❏ G-405 [M] | Jazz Creations/Dizzy Gillespie | 1955 | 25.00 | 50.00 | 100.00 |
| ❏ G-423 [M] | Big Band Jazz | 1955 | 25.00 | 50.00 | 100.00 |
ARCHIVE OF FOLK AND JAZZ
❏ 237	Dizzy Gillespie	1970	2.50	5.00	10.00
❏ 272	Dizzy Gillespie, Volume 2	197?	2.50	5.00	10.00
❏ 346	The King of Bop	198?	2.50	5.00	10.00
ATLANTIC
❏ ALR-138 [10]	Dizzy Gillespie	1952	100.00	200.00	400.00
❏ ALR-142 [10]	Dizzy Gillespie, Vol. 2	1952	100.00	200.00	400.00
❏ 1257 [M]	Dizzy at Home and Abroad	1957	25.00	50.00	100.00
-- Black label					
❏ 1257 [M]	Dizzy at Home and Abroad	1961	7.50	15.00	30.00
-- Multi-color label with white "fan" logo					
❏ 81646	Closer to the Source	1986	2.50	5.00	10.00
BANDSTAND
| ❏ BDLP-1513 | Groovin' High | 1992 | 3.75 | 7.50 | 15.00 |
BARONET
| ❏ 105 [M] | A Handful of Modern Jazz | 1961 | 10.00 | 20.00 | 40.00 |
BLUE NOTE
| ❏ BLP-5017 [10] | Horn of Plenty | 1953 | 75.00 | 150.00 | 300.00 |
BLUEBIRD
| ❏ 5785-1-RB [(2)] | Dizziest | 1987 | 3.75 | 7.50 | 15.00 |
BULLDOG
| ❏ BDL-2006 | 20 Golden Pieces of Dizzy Gillespie | 198? | 2.50 | 5.00 | 10.00 |
CLEF
| ❏ MGC-136 [10] | Dizzy Gillespie with Strings | 1953 | 50.00 | 100.00 | 200.00 |
CONTEMPORARY
| ❏ C-2504 [10] | Dizzy in Paris | 1953 | 50.00 | 100.00 | 200.00 |
COUNTERPOINT
| ❏ C-5548 | Dizzy Gillespie, 1941 | 197? | 3.00 | 6.00 | 12.00 |
DEE GEE
| ❏ LP-1000 [10] | Dizzy Gillespie | 1950 | 75.00 | 150.00 | 300.00 |
DIAL
| ❏ 212 [10] | Modern Trumpets | 1952 | 100.00 | 200.00 | 400.00 |

Number	Title	Yr	VG	VG+	NM
DISCOVERY					
❑ DL-3013 [10]	Dizzy Gillespie Plays, Johnny Richards Conducts	1950	75.00	150.00	300.00
ELEKTRA/MUSICIAN					
❑ 60300	One Night in Washington	1984	2.50	5.00	10.00
EMARCY					
❑ EMS-2-410 [(2)]	Composer's Concepts	197?	3.75	7.50	15.00
FANTASY					
❑ OJC-381	Dizzy Gillespie Jam: Montreux '77	1989	2.50	5.00	10.00
❑ OJC-443	Dizzy's Big Four	1990	2.50	5.00	10.00
❑ OJC-447	Afro-Cuban Jazz Moods	1990	3.00	6.00	12.00
GATEWAY					
❑ 7025	Sweet Soul	198?	3.00	6.00	12.00
GENE NORMAN					
❑ GNP-4 [10]	Dizzy Gillespie with His Original Big Band	195?	50.00	100.00	200.00
❑ GNP-23 [M]	Dizzy Gillespie and His Big Band	1957	20.00	40.00	80.00
GNP CRESCENDO					
❑ GNP-23 [M]	Dizzy Gillespie and His Big Band	196?	5.00	10.00	20.00
❑ GNPS-23 [R]	Dizzy Gillespie and His Big Band	196?	3.00	6.00	12.00
❑ GNP-9006	Paris Concert	197?	2.50	5.00	10.00
❑ GNP-9028	Dizzy!	197?	2.50	5.00	10.00
GRP					
❑ GR-1012	New Faces	198?	2.50	5.00	10.00
GWP					
❑ 2023	Souled Out	197?	3.75	7.50	15.00
IMPULSE!					
❑ AS-9149	Swing Low, Sweet Cadillac!	1967	5.00	10.00	20.00
INTERMEDIA					
❑ QS-5033	Body & Soul Featuring Sarah Vaughan	198?	2.50	5.00	10.00
JAZZ MAN					
❑ 5017	The Giant	198?	3.00	6.00	12.00
❑ 5021	The Source	198?	3.00	6.00	12.00
LIMELIGHT					
❑ LM-82007 [M]	Jambo Caribe	1964	5.00	10.00	20.00
❑ LM-82022 [M]	The New Continent	1965	5.00	10.00	20.00
❑ LM-82042 [M]	The Melody Lingers On	1967	5.00	10.00	20.00
❑ LS-86007 [S]	Jambo Caribe	1964	6.25	12.50	25.00
❑ LS-86022 [S]	The New Continent	1965	6.25	12.50	25.00
❑ LS-86042 [S]	The Melody Lingers On	1967	6.25	12.50	25.00
MAINSTREAM					
❑ MRL-325	Dizzy Gillespie with the Mitchell-Ruff Duo	1972	3.75	7.50	15.00
MCA					
❑ 29036	Swing Low, Sweet Cadillac	198?	2.00	4.00	8.00
MOON					
❑ MLP-035	Angel City	1992	3.75	7.50	15.00
MUSICRAFT					
❑ MVS-2009	Groovin' High	1986	2.50	5.00	10.00
❑ MVS-2010	One Bass Hit	1986	2.50	5.00	10.00
NORGRAN					
❑ MGN-1003 [M]	Afro Dizzy	1954	30.00	60.00	120.00
❑ MGN-1023 [M]	Dizzy and Strings	1955	30.00	60.00	120.00
❑ MGN-1083 [M]	Jazz Recital	1956	30.00	60.00	120.00
❑ MGN-1084 [M]	World Statesman	1956	30.00	60.00	120.00
❑ MGN-1090 [M]	Diz Big Band	1956	30.00	60.00	120.00
PABLO					
❑ 2310 719	Dizzy's Big Four	1975	3.00	6.00	12.00
❑ 2310 749	Dizzy's Big Seven: Montreux '75	1976	3.00	6.00	12.00
❑ 2310 771	Afro-Cuban Jazz Moods	1976	3.00	6.00	12.00
❑ 2310 784	Party	1977	3.00	6.00	12.00
❑ 2310 794	Free Ride	1977	3.00	6.00	12.00
❑ 2310 885	The Best of Dizzy Gillespie	198?	2.50	5.00	10.00
❑ 2310 889	In Helsinki: To a Finland Station	198?	2.50	5.00	10.00
❑ 2312 136	The Alternate Blues	198?	2.50	5.00	10.00
❑ 2405 411	The Best of Dizzy Gillespie	198?	2.50	5.00	10.00
❑ 2625 708 [(2)]	Bahiana	1976	3.75	7.50	15.00
PABLO LIVE					
❑ 2308 211	Dizzy Gillespie Jam: Montreux '77	1977	3.00	6.00	12.00
❑ 2308 226	Digital Dizzy at Montreux 1980	1980	3.00	6.00	12.00
❑ 2308 229	Summertime	1980	3.00	6.00	12.00
PERCEPTION					
❑ 2	The Real Thing	197?	3.75	7.50	15.00
❑ 13	Portrait of Jenny	1971	3.75	7.50	15.00
PHILIPS					
❑ PHM 200-048 [M]	Dizzy at the French Riviera	1962	5.00	10.00	20.00
❑ PHM 200-070 [M]	New Wave!	1962	5.00	10.00	20.00
❑ PHM 200-091 [M]	Something Old, Something New	1963	5.00	10.00	20.00
❑ PHM 200-106 [M]	Dizzy Gillespie and the Double Six of Paris	1963	5.00	10.00	20.00
❑ PHM 200-123 [M]	Dizzy Gillespie Goes Hollywood	1964	5.00	10.00	20.00
❑ PHS 600-048 [S]	Dizzy at the French Riviera	1962	6.25	12.50	25.00
❑ PHS 600-070 [S]	New Wave!	1962	6.25	12.50	25.00
❑ PHS 600-091 [S]	Something Old, Something New	1963	6.25	12.50	25.00
❑ PHS 600-106 [S]	Dizzy Gillespie and the Double Six of Paris	1963	6.25	12.50	25.00
❑ PHS 600-123 [S]	Dizzy Gillespie Goes Hollywood	1964	6.25	12.50	25.00
❑ 822 897-1	Dizzy Gillespie on the Frence Riviera	1986	2.50	5.00	10.00
PHOENIX					
❑ 2	The Small Groups	197?	2.50	5.00	10.00
❑ 4	The Big Bands	197?	2.50	5.00	10.00
PRESTIGE					
❑ PRST-7818	Dizzy Gillespie at Salle Plevel '48	1970	3.00	6.00	12.00
❑ 24030 [(2)]	In the Beginning	197?	3.75	7.50	15.00
❑ 24047 [(2)]	The Giant	197?	3.75	7.50	15.00
RCA VICTOR					
❑ LPV-530 [M]	Dizzy Gillespie	1966	6.25	12.50	25.00
❑ LJM-1009 [M]	Dizzier and Dizzier	1954	30.00	60.00	120.00
❑ LPM-2398 [M]	The Greatest of Dizzy Gillespie	1961	12.50	25.00	50.00
-- "Long Play" on label					
REGENT					
❑ MG-6043 [M]	School Days	1957	25.00	50.00	100.00
REPRISE					
❑ R-6072 [M]	Dateline: Europe	1963	5.00	10.00	20.00
❑ R9-6072 [S]	Dateline: Europe	1963	6.25	12.50	25.00
RONDO-LETTE					
❑ A-11 [M]	Dizzy Gillespie	195?	7.50	15.00	30.00
ROOST					
❑ R-414 [10]	Dizzy Over Paris	1953	62.50	125.00	250.00
❑ LP-2214 [M]	Concert in Paris	1957	30.00	60.00	120.00
SAVOY					
❑ MG-12020 [M]	Groovin' High	1955	15.00	30.00	60.00
❑ MG-12047 [M]	The Champ	1956	15.00	30.00	60.00
❑ MG-12110 [M]	The Dizzy Gillespie Story	1957	15.00	30.00	60.00
SAVOY JAZZ					
❑ SJC-402	The Dizzy Gillespie Story	1985	2.50	5.00	10.00
❑ SJL-2209 [(2)]	Dee Gee Days	197?	3.75	7.50	15.00
SOLID STATE					
❑ SS-18034	Live at the Village Vanguard	1968	5.00	10.00	20.00
❑ SS-18054	My Way	1969	5.00	10.00	20.00
❑ SS-18061	Cornucopia	1969	5.00	10.00	20.00
TIMELESS					
❑ LPSJP-250	Dizzy Gillespie Meets the Phil Woods Quintet	1990	3.00	6.00	12.00
TRIP					
❑ 5566	Something Old, Something New	197?	2.50	5.00	10.00
VERVE					
❑ VSP-7 [M]	Night in Tunisia	1966	3.75	7.50	15.00
❑ VSPS-7 [S]	Night in Tunisia	1966	3.75	7.50	15.00
❑ VE-2-2505 [(2)]	Dizzy, Rollins & Stitt	197?	3.75	7.50	15.00
❑ VE-2-2524 [(2)]	Diz and Roy	197?	3.75	7.50	15.00
❑ UMV-2605	An Electrifying Evening with the Dizzy Gillespie Quintet	198?	2.50	5.00	10.00
❑ UMV-2692	Have Trumpet, Will Excite	198?	2.50	5.00	10.00
❑ MGVS-6023 [S]	Dizzy Gillespie at Newport	1960	15.00	30.00	60.00
❑ MGVS-6047 [S]	Have Trumpet, Will Excite	1960	15.00	30.00	60.00
❑ MGVS-6068 [S]	The Ebullient Mr. Gillespie	1960	15.00	30.00	60.00
❑ MGVS-6117 [S]	Greatest Trumpet of Them All	1960	15.00	30.00	60.00
❑ MGV-8017 [M]	Dizzy in Greece	1957	15.00	30.00	60.00
❑ V-8017 [M]	Dizzy in Greece	1961	6.25	12.50	25.00
❑ MGV-8173 [M]	Jazz Recital	1957	15.00	30.00	60.00
❑ V-8173 [M]	Jazz Recital	1961	6.25	12.50	25.00
❑ MGV-8174 [M]	World Statesman	1957	15.00	30.00	60.00
❑ V-8174 [M]	World Statesman	1961	6.25	12.50	25.00
❑ MGV-8178 [M]	Diz Big Band	1957	17.50	35.00	70.00
❑ V-8178 [M]	Diz Big Band	1961	6.25	12.50	25.00
❑ MGV-8191 [M]	Afro Dizzy	1957	15.00	30.00	60.00
❑ MGV-8208 [M]	Manteca	1958	15.00	30.00	60.00
❑ V-8208 [M]	Manteca	1961	6.25	12.50	25.00
❑ MGV-8214 [M]	Dizzy Gillespie and Stuff Smith	1958	15.00	30.00	60.00
❑ V-8214 [M]	Dizzy Gillespie and Stuff Smith	1961	6.25	12.50	25.00
❑ MGV-8242 [M]	Dizzy Gillespie at Newport	1958	15.00	30.00	60.00
❑ V-8242 [M]	Dizzy Gillespie at Newport	1961	6.25	12.50	25.00
❑ V6-8242 [S]	Dizzy Gillespie at Newport	1961	6.25	12.50	25.00
❑ MGV-8260 [M]	Duets	1958	15.00	30.00	60.00
-- With Sonny Rollins and Sonny Stitt					
❑ MGV-8313 [M]	Have Trumpet, Will Excite	1959	15.00	30.00	60.00
❑ V-8313 [M]	Have Trumpet, Will Excite	1961	6.25	12.50	25.00
❑ V6-8313 [S]	Have Trumpet, Will Excite	1961	6.25	12.50	25.00
❑ MGV-8328 [M]	The Ebullient Mr. Gillespie	1959	15.00	30.00	60.00

Among popular and influential jazz musicians, few were as instantly recognizable as Dizzy Gillespie, thanks to his trumpet with the upturned bell and the way his cheeks puffed out when he played. But oh, could he play! (Top left) A very early solo album from Gillespie was this 1950 10-incher on the Discovery label. Before this he was best known for his time with Charlie Parker. (Top right) Speaking of those two legends' time together, here's one of many albums released after Parker's death. This one was on the respected Roost label. (Bottom left) Gillespie spent some time in the late 1950s and early 1960s with Norman Granz' Verve label. This album was one of the early stereo releases on Verve. (Bottom right) The only album Gillespie recorded for the Impulse! label was this one from 1967.

Number	Title	Yr	VG	VG+	NM
❏ V-8328 [M]	The Ebullient Mr. Gillespie	1961	6.25	12.50	25.00
❏ V6-8328 [S]	The Ebullient Mr. Gillespie	1961	6.25	12.50	25.00
❏ MGV-8352 [M]	Greatest Trumpet of Them All	1959	15.00	30.00	60.00
❏ V-8352 [M]	Greatest Trumpet of Them All	1961	6.25	12.50	25.00
❏ V6-8352 [S]	Greatest Trumpet of Them All	1961	6.25	12.50	25.00
❏ MGV-8386 [M]	Portrait of Duke	1960	15.00	30.00	60.00
❏ V-8386 [M]	Portrait of Duke	1961	6.25	12.50	25.00
❏ MGV-8394 [M]	Gillespiana	1960	15.00	30.00	60.00
❏ V-8394 [M]	Gillespiana	1961	6.25	12.50	25.00
❏ V6-8394 [S]	Gillespiana	1961	6.25	12.50	25.00
❏ V-8401 [M]	An Electrifying Evening with the Dizzy Gillespie Quintet	1961	5.00	10.00	20.00
❏ V6-8401 [S]	An Electrifying Evening with the Dizzy Gillespie Quintet	1961	6.25	12.50	25.00
❏ V-8411 [M]	Perceptions	1961	5.00	10.00	20.00
❏ V6-8411 [S]	Perceptions	1961	6.25	12.50	25.00
❏ V-8423 [M]	Carnegie Hall Concert	1962	5.00	10.00	20.00
❏ V6-8423 [S]	Carnegie Hall Concert	1962	6.25	12.50	25.00
❏ V-8477 [M]	Dizzy, Rollins & Stitt	1962	5.00	10.00	20.00
-- Reissue of MGV-8260					
❏ V6-8477 [S]	Dizzy, Rollins & Stitt	1962	6.25	12.50	25.00
❏ V-8560 [M]	Dizzy at Newport	1964	5.00	10.00	20.00
❏ V6-8560 [S]	Dizzy at Newport	1964	6.25	12.50	25.00
❏ V-8566 [M]	The Essential Dizzy Gillespie	1964	5.00	10.00	20.00
❏ V6-8566 [S]	The Essential Dizzy Gillespie	1964	6.25	12.50	25.00
❏ V6-8830	The Newport Years	197?	3.00	6.00	12.00
❏ 821 662-1	The Reunion Big Band	198?	2.50	5.00	10.00
WING					
❏ MGW-12318 [M]	The New Wave!	1966	3.00	6.00	12.00
❏ SRW-16318 [S]	The New Wave!	1966	3.00	6.00	12.00

GILLESPIE, DIZZY, AND STAN GETZ
Also see each artist's individual listings.

NORGRAN

Number	Title	Yr	VG	VG+	NM
❏ MGN-2 [10]	The Dizzy Gillespie-Stan Getz Sextet #1	1954	75.00	150.00	300.00
❏ MGN-18 [10]	The Dizzy Gillespie-Stan Getz Sextet #2	1954	75.00	150.00	300.00
❏ MGN-1050 [M]	Diz and Getz	1956	30.00	60.00	120.00
VERVE					
❏ MGV-8141 [M]	Diz and Getz	1957	20.00	40.00	80.00
-- Reissue of Norgran 1050					
❏ V-8141 [M]	Diz and Getz	1961	6.25	12.50	25.00
❏ VE-2-2521 [(2)]	Diz and Getz	197?	3.75	7.50	15.00

GILLESPIE, DIZZY/JIMMY McPARTLAND
Also see each artist's individual listings.

MGM

Number	Title	Yr	VG	VG+	NM
❏ E-3286 [M]	Hot vs. Cool	1955	20.00	40.00	80.00

GILLESPIE, DIZZY, AND CHARLIE PARKER
Also see each artist's individual listings.

ROOST

Number	Title	Yr	VG	VG+	NM
❏ SK-106 [(2) M]	The Beginning: Diz and Bird	1960	25.00	50.00	100.00
❏ LP-2234 [M]	Diz 'n' Bird In Concert	1959	20.00	40.00	80.00

GILLESPIE, DIZZY, AND DJANGO REINHARDT
Also see each artist's individual listings.

CLEF

Number	Title	Yr	VG	VG+	NM
❏ MGC-747 [M]	Jazz from Paris	1956	---	---	---
-- Canceled; reassigned to Verve					
VERVE					
❏ MGV-8015 [M]	Jazz from Paris	1957	15.00	30.00	60.00
❏ V-8015 [M]	Jazz from Paris	1961	6.25	12.50	25.00

GINSBERG, ALLEN
Jazz-influenced beat poet.

ATLANTIC

Number	Title	Yr	VG	VG+	NM
❏ 4001 [M]	Allen Ginsburg Reads Kaddish	1966	7.50	15.00	30.00
FANTASY					
❏ F-7006 [M]	Howl and Other Poems	1959	100.00	200.00	400.00
-- Red vinyl					
❏ F-7006 [M]	Howl and Other Poems	1959	50.00	100.00	200.00
-- Black non-flexible vinyl					

GIRARD, GEORGE
Trumpeter and bandleader.

VIK

Number	Title	Yr	VG	VG+	NM
❏ LX-1058 [M]	Jam Session on Bourbon Street	1957	10.00	20.00	40.00
❏ LX-1063 [M]	Stompin' at the Famous Door	1957	10.00	20.00	40.00

GISMONTI, EGBERTO
Pianist, guitarist, flutist and male singer.

ECM

Number	Title	Yr	VG	VG+	NM
❏ 1089	Danca Das Cabecas	1976	3.00	6.00	12.00
❏ 1116	Sol Do Meio Dia	1978	3.00	6.00	12.00
❏ 1136	Solo	1979	2.50	5.00	10.00
❏ 1203 [(2)]	Sanfona	1981	3.75	7.50	15.00

GISMONTI, EGBERTO, AND NANA VASCONCELOS
Also see each artist's individual listings.

ECM

Number	Title	Yr	VG	VG+	NM
❏ 25015	Duas Vozes	1985	2.50	5.00	10.00

GIUFFRE, JIMMY
Clarinetist, saxophone player (tenor and baritone) and flutist. Also see HERB ELLIS; LEE KONITZ.

ATLANTIC

Number	Title	Yr	VG	VG+	NM
❏ 1238 [M]	The Jimmy Giuffre Clarinet	1956	12.50	25.00	50.00
-- Black label					
❏ 1238 [M]	The Jimmy Giuffre Clarinet	1960	5.00	10.00	20.00
-- Multicolor label, white "fan" logo at right					
❏ 1238 [M]	The Jimmy Giuffre Clarinet	1963	3.75	7.50	15.00
-- Multicolor label, black "fan" logo at right					
❏ 1254 [M]	The Jimmy Giuffre Three	1957	12.50	25.00	50.00
-- Black label					
❏ 1254 [M]	The Jimmy Giuffre Three	1960	5.00	10.00	20.00
-- Multicolor label, white "fan" logo at right					
❏ 1254 [M]	The Jimmy Giuffre Three	1963	3.75	7.50	15.00
-- Multicolor label, black "fan" logo at right					
❏ 1276 [M]	Music Man	1958	12.50	25.00	50.00
-- Black label					
❏ 1276 [M]	Music Man	1960	5.00	10.00	20.00
-- Multicolor label, white "fan" logo at right					
❏ 1276 [M]	Music Man	1963	3.75	7.50	15.00
-- Multicolor label, black "fan" logo at right					
❏ SD 1276 [S]	Music Man	1959	12.50	25.00	50.00
-- Green label					
❏ SD 1276 [S]	Music Man	1960	5.00	10.00	20.00
-- Multicolor label, white "fan" logo at right					
❏ SD 1276 [S]	Music Man	1963	3.75	7.50	15.00
-- Multicolor label, black "fan" logo at right					
❏ 1282 [M]	Trav'lin' Light	1958	12.50	25.00	50.00
-- Black label					
❏ 1282 [M]	Trav'lin' Light	1960	5.00	10.00	20.00
-- Multicolor label, white "fan" logo at right					
❏ 1282 [M]	Trav'lin' Light	1963	3.75	7.50	15.00
-- Multicolor label, black "fan" logo at right					
❏ SD 1282 [S]	Trav'lin' Light	1959	12.50	25.00	50.00
-- Green label					
❏ SD 1282 [S]	Trav'lin' Light	1960	5.00	10.00	20.00
-- Multicolor label, white "fan" logo at right					
❏ SD 1282 [S]	Trav'lin' Light	1963	3.75	7.50	15.00
-- Multicolor label, black "fan" logo at right					
❏ 1295 [M]	Four Brothers Sound	1959	12.50	25.00	50.00
-- Black label					
❏ 1295 [M]	Four Brothers Sound	1960	5.00	10.00	20.00
-- Multicolor label, white "fan" logo at right					
❏ SD 1295 [S]	Four Brothers Sound	1959	12.50	25.00	50.00
-- Green label					
❏ SD 1295 [S]	Four Brothers Sound	1960	5.00	10.00	20.00
-- Multicolor label, white "fan" logo at right					
❏ 1330 [M]	Western Suite	1960	6.25	12.50	25.00
-- Multicolor label, white "fan" logo at right					
❏ 1330 [M]	Western Suite	1963	3.75	7.50	15.00
-- Multicolor label, black "fan" logo at right					
❏ SD 1330 [S]	Western Suite	1960	7.50	15.00	30.00
-- Multicolor label, white "fan" logo at right					
❏ SD 1330 [S]	Western Suite	1963	3.75	7.50	15.00
-- Multicolor label, black "fan" logo at right					
❏ 90144	Jimmy Giuffre Clarinet	198?	2.50	5.00	10.00
CAPITOL					
❏ H 549 [10]	Jimmy Giuffre	1954	37.50	75.00	150.00
❏ T 549 [M]	Jimmy Giuffre	1955	20.00	40.00	80.00
❏ T 634 [M]	Tangents in Jazz	1955	20.00	40.00	80.00
CHOICE					
❏ 1001	Music for People, Birds, Butterflies and Mosquitos	1974	3.75	7.50	15.00
❏ 1011	River Chant	1975	3.75	7.50	15.00
COLUMBIA					
❏ CL 1964 [M]	Free Fall	1963	3.75	7.50	15.00
❏ CS 8764 [S]	Free Fall	1963	5.00	10.00	20.00
IAI					
❏ 373859	Jimmy Giuffre at the IAI Festival	1978	3.00	6.00	12.00
SOUL NOTE					
❏ SN-1058	Dragonfly	1983	3.00	6.00	12.00
❏ SN-1108	Quasar	1986	3.00	6.00	12.00

Number	Title	Yr	VG	VG+	NM
❏ 121058	Dragonfly	199?	2.50	5.00	10.00
❏ 121108	Quasar	199?	2.50	5.00	10.00
❏ 121158	Liquid Dancers	1991	3.75	7.50	15.00
VERVE					
❏ MGVS-6039 [S]	Seven Pieces	1960	7.50	15.00	30.00
❏ MGVS-6095 [S]	The Easy Way	1960	7.50	15.00	30.00
❏ MGVS-6130 [S]	Ad Lib	1960	7.50	15.00	30.00
❏ MGV-8307 [M]	Seven Pieces	1959	10.00	20.00	40.00
❏ V-8307 [M]	Seven Pieces	1961	5.00	10.00	20.00
❏ V6-8307 [S]	Seven Pieces	1961	3.75	7.50	15.00
❏ MGV-8337 [M]	The Easy Way	1960	10.00	20.00	40.00
❏ V-8337 [M]	The Easy Way	1961	5.00	10.00	20.00
❏ V6-8337 [S]	The Easy Way	1961	3.75	7.50	15.00
❏ MGV-8361 [M]	Ad Lib	1960	10.00	20.00	40.00
❏ V-8361 [M]	Ad Lib	1961	5.00	10.00	20.00
❏ V6-8361 [S]	Ad Lib	1961	3.75	7.50	15.00
❏ MGV-8387 [M]	The Jimmy Giuffre Quartet In Person	1961	10.00	20.00	40.00
❏ V-8387 [M]	The Jimmy Giuffre Quartet In Person	1961	5.00	10.00	20.00
❏ V6-8387 [S]	The Jimmy Giuffre Quartet In Person	1961	6.25	12.50	25.00
❏ MGV-8395 [M]	Piece for Clarinet and String Orchestra	1961	10.00	20.00	40.00
❏ V-8395 [M]	Piece for Clarinet and String Orchestra	1961	5.00	10.00	20.00
❏ V6-8395 [S]	Piece for Clarinet and String Orchestra	1961	6.25	12.50	25.00
❏ MGV-8397 [M]	Fusion	1961	10.00	20.00	40.00
❏ V-8397 [M]	Fusion	1961	5.00	10.00	20.00
❏ V6-8397 [S]	Fusion	1961	6.25	12.50	25.00
❏ MGV-8402 [M]	Thesis	1961	10.00	20.00	40.00
❏ V-8402 [M]	Thesis	1961	5.00	10.00	20.00
❏ V6-8402 [S]	Thesis	1961	6.25	12.50	25.00

GIUFFRE, JIMMY, AND MARTY PAICH
Also see each artist's individual listings.
GNP CRESCENDO

Number	Title	Yr	VG	VG+	NM
❏ GNPS-9040	Tenors West	197?	2.50	5.00	10.00

GLASEL, JOHN
Trumpeter.
ABC-PARAMOUNT

Number	Title	Yr	VG	VG+	NM
❏ ABC-165 [M]	Jazz Session	1957	12.50	25.00	50.00
GOLDEN CREST					
❏ 1002 [M]	Jazz Unlimited	1960	7.50	15.00	30.00

GLENN, ROGER
Flutist, vibraphone player and percussionist.
FANTASY

Number	Title	Yr	VG	VG+	NM
❏ F-9516	Reachin'	1976	3.00	6.00	12.00

GLENN, TYREE
Trombonist and vibraphone player.
ROULETTE

Number	Title	Yr	VG	VG+	NM
❏ R-25009 [M]	Tyree Glenn at the Embers	1957	10.00	20.00	40.00
❏ R-25050 [M]	Tyree Glenn at the Roundtable	1959	10.00	20.00	40.00
❏ SR-25050 [S]	Tyree Glenn at the Roundtable	1959	7.50	15.00	30.00
❏ R-25075 [M]	Try a Little Tenderness	1959	10.00	20.00	40.00
❏ SR-25075 [S]	Try a Little Tenderness	1959	7.50	15.00	30.00
❏ R-25115 [M]	Let's Have a Ball	1960	6.25	12.50	25.00
❏ SR-25115 [S]	Let's Have a Ball	1960	7.50	15.00	30.00
❏ R-25138 [M]	Tyree Glenn at London House in Chicago	1961	5.00	10.00	20.00
❏ SR-25138 [S]	Tyree Glenn at London House in Chicago	1961	6.25	12.50	25.00
❏ R-25184 [M]	The Trombone Artistry of Tyree Glenn	1962	5.00	10.00	20.00
❏ SR-25184 [S]	The Trombone Artistry of Tyree Glenn	1962	6.25	12.50	25.00

GOLD, SANFORD
Pianist.
PRESTIGE

Number	Title	Yr	VG	VG+	NM
❏ PRLP-7019 [M]	Piano d'Or	1956	15.00	30.00	60.00

GOLDBERG, STU
Pianist.
PAUSA

Number	Title	Yr	VG	VG+	NM
❏ 7036	Solos, Duos, Trio	1978	2.50	5.00	10.00
❏ 7095	Variations by Goldberg	1980	2.50	5.00	10.00
❏ 7123	Eye of the Beholder	1981	2.50	5.00	10.00

GOLDEN AGE JAZZ BAND
Led by banjo player Dick Oxtot.
ARHOOLIE

Number	Title	Yr	VG	VG+	NM
❏ 4007	Golden Age Jazz Band	197?	3.75	7.50	15.00

GOLDEN EAGLE JAZZ BAND
STOMP OFF

Number	Title	Yr	VG	VG+	NM
❏ SOS-1080	Oh My Babe	1985	2.50	5.00	10.00
❏ SOS-1100	Young Woman's Blues	1986	2.50	5.00	10.00

GOLDEN STATE JAZZ BAND
STOMP OFF

Number	Title	Yr	VG	VG+	NM
❏ SOS-1006	Alive and At Bay	1983	2.50	5.00	10.00

GOLDIE, DON
Trumpeter.
ARGO

Number	Title	Yr	VG	VG+	NM
❏ LP-708 [M]	Trumpet Caliente	1963	6.25	12.50	25.00
❏ LPS-708 [S]	Trumpet Caliente	1963	7.50	15.00	30.00
❏ LP-4010 [M]	Brilliant!	1961	6.25	12.50	25.00
❏ LPS-4010 [S]	Brilliant!	1961	7.50	15.00	30.00
JAZZOLOGY					
❏ J-135	Don Goldie's Jazz Express	1986	2.50	5.00	10.00
VERVE					
❏ V-8475 [M]	Trumpet Exodus	1962	6.25	12.50	25.00
❏ V6-8475 [S]	Trumpet Exodus	1962	7.50	15.00	30.00

GOLDKETTE, JEAN
Pianist and bandleader.
"X"

Number	Title	Yr	VG	VG+	NM
❏ LVA-3017 [10]	Jean Goldkette and His Orchestra Featuring Bix Beiderbecke	1954	15.00	30.00	60.00

GOLDSBURY, MACK
Saxophone player.
MUSE

Number	Title	Yr	VG	VG+	NM
❏ MR-5194	Anthropo-logic	1979	2.50	5.00	10.00

GOLDSTEIN, GIL
Pianist, accordion player and arranger.
CHIAROSCURO

Number	Title	Yr	VG	VG+	NM
❏ 201	Pure As Rain	1978	3.00	6.00	12.00
MUSE					
❏ MR-5229	Wrapped in a Cloud	1980	2.50	5.00	10.00

GOLIA, VINNY
Multi-instrumentalist credited with playing 19 different woodwind instruments.
NINE WINDS

Number	Title	Yr	VG	VG+	NM
❏ NW 0101	Spirits in Fellowship	1977	3.00	6.00	12.00
❏ NW 0102	Openhearted	1978	3.00	6.00	12.00
❏ NW 0103 [(2)]	... In the Right Order ...	1979	3.75	7.50	15.00
❏ NW 0104	Solo	1980	3.00	6.00	12.00
❏ NW 0108	Slice of Life	1981	3.00	6.00	12.00
❏ NW 0109	The Gift of Fury	1982	3.00	6.00	12.00
❏ NW 0110 [(3)]	Compositions for Large Ensemble	1984	5.00	10.00	20.00
❏ NW 0117	Goin' Ahead	1985	3.00	6.00	12.00
❏ NW 0120 [(2)]	Facts of Their Own Lives	1986	3.75	7.50	15.00
❏ NW 0127	Out for Blood	1989	3.00	6.00	12.00

GOLSON, BENNY
Tenor saxophone player and composer. Also see CURTIS FULLER; THE JAZZTET; RAHSAAN ROLAND KIRK.
ARGO

Number	Title	Yr	VG	VG+	NM
❏ LP-681 [M]	Take a Number from 1 to 10	1961	7.50	15.00	30.00
❏ LPS-681 [S]	Take a Number from 1 to 10	1961	10.00	20.00	40.00
❏ LP-716 [M]	Free	1963	7.50	15.00	30.00
❏ LPS-716 [S]	Free	1963	10.00	20.00	40.00
AUDIO FIDELITY					
❏ AFLP-1978 [M]	Pop + Jazz = Swing	1962	3.75	7.50	15.00
❏ AFLP-2150 [M]	Just Jazz	1966	3.75	7.50	15.00
❏ AFSD-5978 [S]	Pop + Jazz = Swing	1962	5.00	10.00	20.00
❏ AFSD-6150 [S]	Just Jazz	1966	5.00	10.00	20.00
COLUMBIA					
❏ JC 35359	I'm Always Dancin' to the Music	1978	2.50	5.00	10.00
❏ PC 34678	Killer Joe	1977	2.50	5.00	10.00
CONTEMPORARY					
❏ C-3552 [M]	Benny Golson's New York Scene	1958	12.50	25.00	50.00

Number	Title	Yr	VG	VG+	NM
FANTASY					
❑ OJC-164	New York Scene	198?	2.50	5.00	10.00
-- Reissue of Contemporary 3552					
❑ OJC-226	Groovin' with Golson	198?	2.50	5.00	10.00
-- Reissue of New Jazz 8220					
❑ OJC-1750	The Other Side of Benny Golson	1990	3.00	6.00	12.00
-- Reissue of Riverside 290					
JAZZLAND					
❑ JLP-85 [M]	Reunion	1962	10.00	20.00	40.00
❑ JLP-985 [S]	Reunion	1962	7.50	15.00	30.00
MERCURY					
❑ MG-20801 [M]	Turning Point	1963	3.75	7.50	15.00
❑ SR-60801 [S]	Turning Point	1963	5.00	10.00	20.00
MILESTONE					
❑ 47048 [(2)]	Blues On Down	198?	3.75	7.50	15.00
NEW JAZZ					
❑ NJLP-8220 [M]	Groovin' with Golson	1959	12.50	25.00	50.00
-- Purple label					
❑ NJLP-8220 [M]	Groovin' with Golson	1965	6.25	12.50	25.00
-- Blue label, trident logo at right					
❑ NJLP-8235 [M]	Gone with Golson	1960	12.50	25.00	50.00
-- Purple label					
❑ NJLP-8235 [M]	Gone with Golson	1965	6.25	12.50	25.00
-- Blue label, trident logo at right					
❑ NJLP-8248 [M]	Gettin' With It	1960	12.50	25.00	50.00
-- Purple label					
❑ NJLP-8248 [M]	Gettin' With It	1965	6.25	12.50	25.00
-- Blue label, trident logo at right					
PRESTIGE					
❑ PRLP-7361 [M]	Stockholm Sojourn	1965	5.00	10.00	20.00
❑ PRST-7361 [S]	Stockholm Sojourn	1965	6.25	12.50	25.00
RIVERSIDE					
❑ RLP 12-256 [M]	The Modern Touch of Benny Golson	1957	15.00	30.00	60.00
❑ RLP 12-290 [M]	The Other Side of Benny Golson	1958	15.00	30.00	60.00
❑ 6070	The Modern Touch	197?	3.00	6.00	12.00
SWING					
❑ SW-8418	Benny Golson in Paris	1987	2.50	5.00	10.00
TIMELESS					
❑ LPSJP-177	California Message	1990	3.00	6.00	12.00
UNITED ARTISTS					
❑ UAL-4020 [M]	Benny Golson and the Philadelphians	1959	12.50	25.00	50.00
❑ UAS-5020 [S]	Benny Golson and the Philadelphians	1959	10.00	20.00	40.00
VERVE					
❑ V-8710 [M]	Turn In, Turn On	1967	5.00	10.00	20.00
❑ V6-8710 [S]	Turn In, Turn On	1967	3.75	7.50	15.00

GOMEZ, EDDIE
Bass player.

Number	Title	Yr	VG	VG+	NM
COLUMBIA					
❑ FC 44214	Power Play	1988	2.50	5.00	10.00

GONSALVES, PAUL
Tenor saxophone player.

Number	Title	Yr	VG	VG+	NM
ABC IMPULSE!					
❑ AS-41 [S]	Cleopatra Feelin' Jazzy	1967	3.75	7.50	15.00
❑ AS-52 [S]	Salt and Pepper	1967	3.75	7.50	15.00
❑ AS-55 [S]	Tell It the Way It Is	1967	3.75	7.50	15.00
ARGO					
❑ LP-626 [M]	Cookin'	1958	12.50	25.00	50.00
❑ LPS-626 [S]	Cookin'	1959	10.00	20.00	40.00
BLACK LION					
❑ 191	Just a Sittin' and a Rockin'	197?	3.75	7.50	15.00
CATALYST					
❑ 7913	Buenos Aires	197?	3.75	7.50	15.00
FANTASY					
❑ OJC-203	Gettin' Together	198?	2.50	5.00	10.00
IMPULSE!					
❑ A-41 [M]	Cleopatra Feelin' Jazzy	1963	6.25	12.50	25.00
❑ AS-41 [S]	Cleopatra Feelin' Jazzy	1963	7.50	15.00	30.00
❑ A-52 [M]	Salt and Pepper	1963	6.25	12.50	25.00
❑ AS-52 [S]	Salt and Pepper	1963	7.50	15.00	30.00
❑ A-55 [M]	Tell It the Way It Is	1963	6.25	12.50	25.00
❑ AS-55 [S]	Tell It the Way It Is	1963	7.50	15.00	30.00
JAZZLAND					
❑ JLP-36 [M]	Gettin' Together	1961	7.50	15.00	30.00
❑ JLP-936 [S]	Gettin' Together	1961	10.00	20.00	40.00

GONSALVES, PAUL, AND ROY ELDREDGE
Also see each artist's individual listings.

Number	Title	Yr	VG	VG+	NM
FANTASY					
❑ F-9646	Mexican Bandit Meets Pittsburgh Pirate	1986	2.50	5.00	10.00

GONSALVES, VIRGIL
Baritone saxophone player, clarinetist and male singer.

Number	Title	Yr	VG	VG+	NM
LIBERTY					
❑ LJH-6010 [M]	Jazz San Francisco Style	1956	12.50	25.00	50.00
NOCTURNE					
❑ NLP-8 [10]	Virgil Gonsalves	1954	20.00	40.00	80.00
OMEGA					
❑ OML-1047 [M]	Jazz at Monterey	1959	10.00	20.00	40.00

GONZALES, BABS
Female singer.

Number	Title	Yr	VG	VG+	NM
CHIAROSCURO					
❑ 2025	Live at Small's Paradise	197?	3.75	7.50	15.00
DAUNTLESS					
❑ DM-4311 [M]	Sunday Afternoon at Small's Paradise	1963	10.00	20.00	40.00
❑ DS-6311 [S]	Sunday Afternoon at Small's Paradise	1963	12.50	25.00	50.00
HOPE					
❑ 001 [M]	Voila!	1958	37.50	75.00	150.00
JARO					
❑ JAM-5000 [M]	Cool Philosophy	1959	20.00	40.00	80.00
❑ JAS-8000 [S]	Cool Philosophy	1959	25.00	50.00	100.00

GONZALES, JERRY
Trumpeter and fluegel horn player.

Number	Title	Yr	VG	VG+	NM
AMERICAN CLAVE					
❑ 1001	Ya Yo Me Cure	198?	3.00	6.00	12.00
ENJA					
❑ 4040	The River Is Deep	1982	3.00	6.00	12.00
❑ R1-79609	Obatala	1990	3.00	6.00	12.00

GOODE, BRAD
Trumpeter.

Number	Title	Yr	VG	VG+	NM
DELMARK					
❑ DS-440	Shock of the New	1989	3.00	6.00	12.00

GOODMAN, BENNY
Clarinet player and bandleader known as "The King of Swing." Also see BEN POLLACK.

Number	Title	Yr	VG	VG+	NM
AIRCHECK					
❑ 16	Benny Goodman and His Orchestra	197?	3.00	6.00	12.00
❑ 16	Benny Goodman and His Orchestra On the Air, Vol. 1	1986	2.50	5.00	10.00
-- Reissue of above with revised title					
❑ 32	Benny Goodman and His Orchestra On the Air, Vol. 2	1986	2.50	5.00	10.00
❑ 34	Benny Goodman and His Orchestra On the Air, Vol. 3	1986	2.50	5.00	10.00
ARCHIVE OF FOLK AND JAZZ					
❑ 277	Benny Goodman	1973	3.00	6.00	12.00
BIOGRAPH					
❑ C-1	Great Soloist 1929-33	197?	2.50	5.00	10.00
BLUEBIRD					
❑ AXM2-5505 [(2)]	The Complete Benny Goodman, Vol. 1 (1935)	197?	3.00	6.00	12.00
❑ AXM2-5515 [(2)]	The Complete Benny Goodman, Vol. 2 (1935-36)	197?	3.00	6.00	12.00
❑ AXM2-5532 [(2)]	The Complete Benny Goodman, Vol. 3 (1936)	197?	3.00	6.00	12.00
❑ AXM2-5537 [(2)]	The Complete Benny Goodman, Vol. 4 (1936-37)	197?	3.00	6.00	12.00
❑ AXM2-5557 [(2)]	The Complete Benny Goodman, Vol. 5 (1937-38)	197?	3.00	6.00	12.00
❑ AXM2-5566 [(2)]	The Complete Benny Goodman, Vol. 6 (1938)	197?	3.00	6.00	12.00
❑ AXM2-5567 [(2)]	The Complete Benny Goodman, Vol. 7 (1938-39)	197?	3.00	6.00	12.00
❑ AXM2-5568 [(2)]	The Complete Benny Goodman, Vol. 8 (1936-39)	197?	3.00	6.00	12.00
BRUNSWICK					
❑ BL 54010 [M]	Benny Goodman 1927-34	1954	7.50	15.00	30.00
❑ BL 58015 [10]	Chicago Jazz Classics	1950	12.50	25.00	50.00

It's never been seriously disputed that Benny Goodman was "The King of Swing," but he also continued to keep up with the times, as his later groups often had serious bebop musicians. In fact, his small groups of the 1930s can be seen as a breeding ground for what became known as bebop. (Top left) The most famous and important jazz concert in history was Goodman's 1938 concert at staid Carnegie Hall. Even today, more than 60 years later, fascination with this gig remains high; another CD reissue mastered from the original acetates came out in late 1999. (Top right) One of the Columbia albums in "The King of Swing" series. (Bottom left) *Swing Into Spring* was an album compiled for the Texaco service station chain and sold there. (Bottom right) *Seven Come Eleven*, released in 1983, consisted of small-group recordings made in 1975.

Number	Title	Yr	VG	VG+	NM
CAPITOL					
❑ H 202 [10]	Session for Six	1950	12.50	25.00	50.00
❑ H 295 [10]	Easy Does It	1952	12.50	25.00	50.00
❑ H 343 [10]	The Benny Goodman Trio	1952	12.50	25.00	50.00
❑ T 395 [M]	Session for Six	1953	10.00	20.00	40.00
-- Turquoise label					
❑ T 395 [M]	Session for Six	1958	5.00	10.00	20.00
-- Black label with colorband, Capitol logo on left					
❑ H 409 [10]	The Benny Goodman Band	1953	12.50	25.00	50.00
❑ T 409 [M]	The Benny Goodman Band	1953	10.00	20.00	40.00
-- Turquoise label					
❑ T 409 [M]	The Benny Goodman Band	1958	5.00	10.00	20.00
-- Black label with colorband, Capitol logo on left					
❑ H 441 [10]	The Goodman Touch	1953	12.50	25.00	50.00
❑ T 441 [M]	The Goodman Touch	1953	10.00	20.00	40.00
-- Turquoise label					
❑ T 441 [M]	The Goodman Touch	1958	5.00	10.00	20.00
-- Black label with colorband, Capitol logo on left					
❑ H 479 [10]	Small Combo 1947	1954	12.50	25.00	50.00
❑ H1-565 [10]	B.G. in Hi-Fi (Volume 1)	1955	7.50	15.00	30.00
❑ H2-565 [10]	B.G. in Hi-Fi (Volume 2)	1955	7.50	15.00	30.00
❑ W 565 [M]	B.G. in Hi-Fi	1955	10.00	20.00	40.00
-- Turquoise label					
❑ W 565 [M]	B.G. in Hi-Fi	1958	5.00	10.00	20.00
-- Black label with colorband, Capitol logo on left					
❑ T 668 [M]	Mostly Sextets	1956	7.50	15.00	30.00
-- Turquoise label					
❑ T 668 [M]	Mostly Sextets	1958	5.00	10.00	20.00
-- Black label with colorband, Capitol logo on left					
❑ T 669 [M]	Benny Goodman Combos	1956	7.50	15.00	30.00
-- Turquoise label					
❑ T 669 [M]	Benny Goodman Combos	1958	5.00	10.00	20.00
-- Black label with colorband, Capitol logo on left					
❑ S 706 [M]	Selections Featured in "The Benny Goodman Story"	1956	7.50	15.00	30.00
-- Turquoise label					
❑ S 706 [M]	Selections Featured in "The Benny Goodman Story"	1958	5.00	10.00	20.00
-- Black label with colorband, Capitol logo on left					
❑ SM-706	Selections Featured in "The Benny Goodman Story"	197?	2.50	5.00	10.00
-- Reissue of S 706					
❑ DT 1514 [R]	The Hits of Benny Goodman	1961	3.00	6.00	12.00
❑ SM-1514	The Hits of Benny Goodman	197?	2.50	5.00	10.00
-- Reissue of DT 1514					
❑ T 1514 [M]	The Hits of Benny Goodman	1961	5.00	10.00	20.00
-- Black label with colorband, Capitol logo on left					
❑ T 1514 [M]	The Hits of Benny Goodman	1963	3.75	7.50	15.00
-- Black label with colorband, Capitol logo on top					
❑ ST 2157 [S]	Hello Benny!	1964	3.75	7.50	15.00
❑ T 2157 [M]	Hello Benny!	1964	3.00	6.00	12.00
❑ ST 2282 [S]	Made in Japan	1965	3.75	7.50	15.00
❑ T 2282 [M]	Made in Japan	1965	3.00	6.00	12.00
CENTURY					
❑ 1150	The King of Swing Direct to Disc	1979	7.50	15.00	30.00
-- Direct-to-disc audiophile recording					
CHESS					
❑ LP-1440 [DJ]	Benny Rides Again	1960	25.00	50.00	100.00
-- Multi-color swirl vinyl					
❑ LP-1440 [M]	Benny Rides Again	1960	12.50	25.00	50.00
❑ LPS-1440 [S]	Benny Rides Again	1960	7.50	15.00	30.00
CLASSICS RECORD LIBRARY					
❑ RL-7673 [(3) M]	An Album of Swing Classics	1967	12.50	25.00	50.00
❑ RLS-7673 [(3) S]	An Album of Swing Classics	1967	10.00	20.00	40.00
-- Above two were compiled for Book-of-the-Month Club					
COLUMBIA					
❑ GL 102 [10]	Let's Hear the Melody	1950	15.00	30.00	60.00
❑ CL 500 [M]	Combos	1952	10.00	20.00	40.00
-- Maroon label with gold print					
❑ CL 500 [M]	Combos	1955	7.50	15.00	30.00
-- Red and black label with six "eye" logos					
❑ GL 500 [M]	Combos	1951	12.50	25.00	50.00
-- Black label, silver print					
❑ CL 501 [M]	Bands	1952	10.00	20.00	40.00
-- Maroon label with gold print					
❑ CL 501 [M]	Bands	1955	7.50	15.00	30.00
-- Red and black label with six "eye" logos					
❑ GL 501 [M]	Bands	1951	12.50	25.00	50.00
-- Black label, silver print					
❑ CL 516 [M]	The Benny Goodman Trio Plays for the Fletcher Henderson Fund	1953	10.00	20.00	40.00
-- Maroon label with gold print					
❑ CL 516 [M]	The Benny Goodman Trio Plays for the Fletcher Henderson Fund	1955	7.50	15.00	30.00
-- Red and black label with six "eye" logos					
❑ GL 516 [M]	The Benny Goodman Trio Plays for the Fletcher Henderson Fund	1952	12.50	25.00	50.00
-- Reissue of Martin Block 1000; black label, silver print					
❑ CL 523 [M]	Benny Goodman Presents Eddie Sauter Arrangements	1953	10.00	20.00	40.00
-- Maroon label with gold print					
❑ CL 523 [M]	Benny Goodman Presents Eddie Sauter Arrangements	1955	7.50	15.00	30.00
-- Red and black label with six "eye" logos					
❑ GL 523 [M]	Benny Goodman Presents Eddie Sauter Arrangements	1953	12.50	25.00	50.00
-- Black label, silver print					
❑ CL 524 [M]	Benny Goodman Presents Fletcher Henderson Arrangements	1953	10.00	20.00	40.00
-- Maroon label with gold print					
❑ CL 524 [M]	Benny Goodman Presents Fletcher Henderson Arrangements	1955	7.50	15.00	30.00
-- Red and black label with six "eye" logos					
❑ GL 524 [M]	Benny Goodman Presents Fletcher Henderson Arrangements	1953	12.50	25.00	50.00
-- Black label, silver print					
❑ CL 534 [M]	Benny Goodman and His Orchestra	1953	10.00	20.00	40.00
-- Maroon label with gold print					
❑ CL 534 [M]	Benny Goodman and His Orchestra	1955	7.50	15.00	30.00
-- Red and black label with six "eye" logos					
❑ CL 552 [M]	The New Benny Goodman Sextet	1954	10.00	20.00	40.00
-- Maroon label with gold print					
❑ CL 552 [M]	The New Benny Goodman Sextet	1955	7.50	15.00	30.00
-- Red and black label with six "eye" logos					
❑ CL 652 [M]	The Benny Goodman Sextet and Orchestra with Charlie Christian	1955	7.50	15.00	30.00
-- Red and black label with six "eye" logos					
❑ CL 652 [M]	The Benny Goodman Sextet and Orchestra with Charlie Christian	1963	5.00	10.00	20.00
-- Red label with "Guaranteed High Fidelity" or "Mono" at bottom					
❑ CL 814 [M]	Carnegie Hall Jazz Concert, Volume 1	1956	7.50	15.00	30.00
-- Red and black label with six "eye" logos					
❑ CL 814 [M]	Carnegie Hall Jazz Concert, Volume 1	1963	5.00	10.00	20.00
-- Red label with "Guaranteed High Fidelity" or "Mono" at bottom					
❑ CL 815 [M]	Carnegie Hall Jazz Concert, Volume 2	1956	7.50	15.00	30.00
-- Red and black label with six "eye" logos					
❑ CL 815 [M]	Carnegie Hall Jazz Concert, Volume 2	1963	5.00	10.00	20.00
-- Red label with "Guaranteed High Fidelity" or "Mono" at bottom					
❑ CL 816 [M]	Carnegie Hall Jazz Concert, Volume 3	1956	7.50	15.00	30.00
-- Red and black label with six "eye" logos					
❑ CL 816 [M]	Carnegie Hall Jazz Concert, Volume 3	1963	5.00	10.00	20.00
-- Red label with "Guaranteed High Fidelity" or "Mono" at bottom					
❑ CL 817 [M]	The King of Swing, Volume 1	1956	7.50	15.00	30.00
❑ CL 818 [M]	The King of Swing, Volume 2	1956	7.50	15.00	30.00
❑ CL 819 [M]	The King of Swing, Volume 3	1956	7.50	15.00	30.00
❑ CL 820 [M]	The Great Benny Goodman	1956	7.50	15.00	30.00
-- Red and black label with six "eye" logos					
❑ CL 820 [M]	The Great Benny Goodman	1963	5.00	10.00	20.00
-- Red label with "Guaranteed High Fidelity" or "Mono" at bottom					
❑ CL 821 [M]	Vintage Goodman	1956	7.50	15.00	30.00
❑ CL 1247 [M]	Benny Goodman in Brussels, Volume 1	1958	7.50	15.00	30.00
❑ CL 1248 [M]	Benny Goodman in Brussels, Volume 2	1958	7.50	15.00	30.00
❑ CL 1324 [M]	The Happy Session	1959	7.50	15.00	30.00
❑ CL 1579 [M]	Benny Goodman Swings Again	1960	7.50	15.00	30.00
❑ CL 2483 [M]	Benny Goodman's Greatest Hits	1966	3.75	7.50	15.00
❑ CL 2533 [10]	Benny at the Ballroom	1955	10.00	20.00	40.00
-- Retitled reissue of 6100					
❑ CL 2564 [10]	The B.G. Six	1955	10.00	20.00	40.00
-- Retitled reissue of 6052					
❑ CL 6033 [10]	Benny Goodman and Peggy Lee	1949	20.00	40.00	80.00
❑ CL 6048 [10]	Dance Parade	1949	12.50	25.00	50.00
❑ CL 6052 [10]	Goodman Sextet Session	1949	12.50	25.00	50.00
❑ CL 6100 [10]	Dance Parade, Volume 2	1950	12.50	25.00	50.00
❑ CL 6302 [10]	Let's Hear the Melody	1951	12.50	25.00	50.00
-- Reissue of GL 102					
❑ CS 8075 [S]	Benny Goodman in Brussels, Volume 1	1959	10.00	20.00	40.00
❑ CS 8129 [S]	The Happy Session	1959	6.25	12.50	25.00
❑ CS 8379 [S]	Benny Goodman Swings Again	1960	6.25	12.50	25.00
❑ CS 8643 [R]	The Great Benny Goodman	1962	3.00	6.00	12.00
❑ PC 8643	The Great Benny Goodman	198?	2.00	4.00	8.00
-- Reissue					
❑ CS 9283 [S]	Benny Goodman's Greatest Hits	1966	3.00	6.00	12.00
-- "360 Sound Stereo" on label					
❑ PC 9283	Benny Goodman's Greatest Hits	198?	2.00	4.00	8.00
-- Reissue					

Number	Title	Yr	VG	VG+	NM
❑ XTV 28995/6 [M]	Swing Into Spring	1959	5.00	10.00	20.00
-- Special item made for Texaco service stations					
❑ KG 31547 [(2)]	The All-Time Greatest Hits of Benny Goodman	1972	3.75	7.50	15.00
❑ PG 31547 [(2)]	The All-Time Greatest Hits of Benny Goodman	197?	3.00	6.00	12.00
-- Reissue					
❑ PG 33405 [(2)]	Solid Gold Instrumentals	1975	3.00	6.00	12.00
❑ FC 38265	Seven Come Eleven	1983	2.50	5.00	10.00

COLUMBIA MASTERWORKS

Number	Title	Yr	VG	VG+	NM
❑ OSL 160 [(2) M]	Carnegie Hall Jazz Concert	1956	18.75	37.50	75.00
-- Gray and black labels with six "eye" logos					
❑ OSL 160 [(2) M]	Carnegie Hall Jazz Concert	1963	10.00	20.00	40.00
-- Gray labels with "Columbia" at top					
❑ OSL 180 [(2) M]	The King of Swing	1956	18.75	37.50	75.00
-- Gray and black labels with six "eye" logos					
❑ OSL 180 [(2) M]	The King of Swing	1963	10.00	20.00	40.00
-- Gray labels with "Columbia" at top					
❑ SL 160 [(2) M]	Carnegie Hall Jazz Concert	1950	25.00	50.00	100.00
-- Green labels					
❑ SL 176 [(6) M]	King of Swing	1950	37.50	75.00	150.00
❑ SL 180 [(2) M]	1937-38 Jazz Concert No. 2	1950	18.75	37.50	75.00
❑ ML 4358 [M]	Carnegie Hall Jazz Concert, Volume 1	1950	10.00	20.00	40.00
❑ ML 4359 [M]	Carnegie Hall Jazz Concert, Volume 2	1950	10.00	20.00	40.00
❑ ML 4590 [M]	1937-38 Jazz Concert No. 2, Volume 1	1950	10.00	20.00	40.00
❑ ML 4591 [M]	1937-38 Jazz Concert No. 2, Volume 2	1950	10.00	20.00	40.00
❑ ML 4613 [M]	King of Swing, Volume 1	1950	10.00	20.00	40.00
❑ ML 4614 [M]	King of Swing, Volume 2	1950	10.00	20.00	40.00
❑ ML 6205 [M]	Meeting at the Summit	1961	3.75	7.50	15.00
-- With the Columbia Jazz Combo and the Columbia Orchestra					
❑ MS 6805 [S]	Meeting at the Summit	1961	5.00	10.00	20.00
-- With the Columbia Jazz Combo and the Columbia Orchestra					

COLUMBIA MUSICAL TREASURY

Number	Title	Yr	VG	VG+	NM
❑ P4M 5678 [(4)]	The Best of Benny Goodman	197?	7.50	15.00	30.00
-- Issued by Columbia House					

COMMAND

Number	Title	Yr	VG	VG+	NM
❑ RS-921	Benny Goodman & Paris: Listen to the Magic	1967	3.75	7.50	15.00

DECCA

Number	Title	Yr	VG	VG+	NM
❑ DXB 188 [(2) M]	The Benny Goodman Story	1956	15.00	30.00	60.00
-- Black label, silver print					
❑ DXB 188 [(2) M]	The Benny Goodman Story	1961	10.00	20.00	40.00
-- Black label with color bars					
❑ DXSB 7188 [(2) R]	The Benny Goodman Story	196?	3.75	7.50	15.00
❑ DL 8252 [M]	The Benny Goodman Story, Volume 1	1956	7.50	15.00	30.00
-- Black label, silver print					
❑ DL 8252 [M]	The Benny Goodman Story, Volume 1	1961	5.00	10.00	20.00
-- Black label with color bars					
❑ DL 8253 [M]	The Benny Goodman Story, Volume 2	1956	7.50	15.00	30.00
-- Black label, silver print					
❑ DL 8253 [M]	The Benny Goodman Story, Volume 2	1961	5.00	10.00	20.00
-- Black label with color bars					
❑ DL 78252 [R]	The Benny Goodman Story, Volume 1	1961	2.50	5.00	10.00
❑ DL 78253 [R]	The Benny Goodman Story, Volume 2	1961	2.50	5.00	10.00

DOCTOR JAZZ

Number	Title	Yr	VG	VG+	NM
❑ W2X 40350 [(2)]	Airplay	1986	3.00	6.00	12.00

GIANTS OF JAZZ

Number	Title	Yr	VG	VG+	NM
❑ 1030	The Benny Goodman Caravans -- Big Band Broadcasts Vol. 1: Ciribiribin	1985	2.50	5.00	10.00
❑ 1033	The Benny Goodman Caravans -- Big Band Broadcasts Vol. 2: Swingin' Down the Lane	1985	2.50	5.00	10.00
❑ 1034	The Benny Goodman Caravans -- The Small Groups, Vol. 1	1985	2.50	5.00	10.00
❑ 1036	The Benny Goodman Caravans -- Big Band Broadcasts Vol. 3: One O'Clock Jump	1985	2.50	5.00	10.00
❑ 1039	The Benny Goodman Caravans -- Big Band Broadcasts Vol. 4: Sing, Sing, Sing	1985	2.50	5.00	10.00

HARMONY

Number	Title	Yr	VG	VG+	NM
❑ HL 7005 [M]	Peggy Lee Sings with Benny Goodman	1957	5.00	10.00	20.00
❑ HL 7190 [M]	Swing with Benny Goodman in High Fidelity	196?	3.75	7.50	15.00
❑ HL 7225 [M]	Swing Time	196?	3.75	7.50	15.00
❑ HL 7278 [M]	Swingin' Benny Goodman Sextet	196?	3.75	7.50	15.00
❑ HS 11090 [R]	Swing with Benny Goodman in High Fidelity	196?	2.50	5.00	10.00

Number	Title	Yr	VG	VG+	NM
❑ HS 11271 [R]	Sing, Sing, Sing	1968	2.50	5.00	10.00

INTERMEDIA

Number	Title	Yr	VG	VG+	NM
❑ QS-5046	All the Cats Join In	198?	2.50	5.00	10.00

LONDON

Number	Title	Yr	VG	VG+	NM
❑ PS 918/9 [(2)]	Live at Carnegie Hall 1978	1979	3.75	7.50	15.00

LONDON PHASE 4

Number	Title	Yr	VG	VG+	NM
❑ SPB-21 [(2)]	Benny Goodman Today	1971	3.75	7.50	15.00
❑ SP-44182/3 [(2)]	Benny Goodman On Stage	1972	3.75	7.50	15.00

MARTIN BLOCK

Number	Title	Yr	VG	VG+	NM
❑ MB-1000 [M]	The Benny Goodman Trio Plays for the Fletcher Henderson Fund	1951	15.00	30.00	60.00

MCA

Number	Title	Yr	VG	VG+	NM
❑ 4018 [(2)]	Jazz Holiday	197?	3.00	6.00	12.00

MEGA

Number	Title	Yr	VG	VG+	NM
❑ 606	Let's Dance Again	1974	2.50	5.00	10.00
❑ 51-5002	Let's Dance Again	1971	3.00	6.00	12.00
-- Reissue of 51-5002					

MGM

Number	Title	Yr	VG	VG+	NM
❑ 3E-9 [(3) M]	The Benny Goodman Treasure Chest	1959	37.50	75.00	150.00
❑ E-3788 [M]	Performance Recordings, Volume 1	1959	6.25	12.50	25.00
❑ E-3788 [M]	The Benny Goodman Treasure Chest, Volume 1	198?	2.00	4.00	8.00
-- Reissue on blue and gold label					
❑ E-3789 [M]	Performance Recordings, Volume 2	1959	6.25	12.50	25.00
❑ E-3789 [M]	The Benny Goodman Treasure Chest, Volume 2	198?	2.00	4.00	8.00
-- Reissue on blue and gold label					
❑ E-3790 [M]	Performance Recordings, Volume 3	1959	6.25	12.50	25.00
❑ E-3790 [M]	The Benny Goodman Treasure Chest, Volume 3	198?	2.00	4.00	8.00
-- Reissue on blue and gold label					
❑ E-3810 [M]	The Sound of Music	1960	5.00	10.00	20.00
❑ SE-3810 [S]	The Sound of Music	1960	6.25	12.50	25.00

MOSAIC

Number	Title	Yr	VG	VG+	NM
❑ MQ6-148 [(6)]	The Complete Capitol Small Group Recordings of Benny Goodman 1944-1955	199?	25.00	50.00	100.00

MUSICMASTERS

Number	Title	Yr	VG	VG+	NM
❑ MM-20112 Z	Let's Dance	1986	2.50	5.00	10.00
-- From the PBS TV special of 1985					

PAIR

Number	Title	Yr	VG	VG+	NM
❑ PDL2-1014 [(2)]	Original Recordings by Benny Goodman	1986	3.00	6.00	12.00
❑ PDL2-1054 [(2)]	Original Recordings by Benny Goodman, Volume 2	1986	3.00	6.00	12.00
❑ PDL2-1093 [(2)]	Original Recordings by Benny Goodman, Volume 3	1986	3.00	6.00	12.00

PAUSA

Number	Title	Yr	VG	VG+	NM
❑ 9031	The Benny Goodman Trios (and One Duet)	198?	2.50	5.00	10.00

PICKWICK

Number	Title	Yr	VG	VG+	NM
❑ SPC-3270	Let's Dance	197?	2.50	5.00	10.00
❑ SPC-3529	Francaise	197?	2.50	5.00	10.00

PRESTIGE

Number	Title	Yr	VG	VG+	NM
❑ PRST-7644	Benny Goodman and the Giants of Swing	1969	3.75	7.50	15.00

RCA CAMDEN

Number	Title	Yr	VG	VG+	NM
❑ CAL-624 [M]	Swing, Swing, Swing	1960	3.75	7.50	15.00
❑ CAS-624(e) [R]	Swing, Swing, Swing	1960	2.50	5.00	10.00
❑ CAL-872 [M]	Benny Goodman and His Orchestra Featuring Great Vocalists of Our Times	1965	3.75	7.50	15.00
❑ CAS-872 [S]	Benny Goodman and His Orchestra Featuring Great Vocalists of Our Times	1965	3.00	6.00	12.00

RCA VICTOR

Number	Title	Yr	VG	VG+	NM
❑ WPT 12 [10]	Benny Goodman	1951	12.50	25.00	50.00
❑ LPT-17 [10]	A Treasury of Immortal Performances	1951	12.50	25.00	50.00
❑ WPT 26 [10]	Immortal Performances	1952	12.50	25.00	50.00
❑ LPV-521 [M]	B.G. The Small Groups	1965	3.75	7.50	15.00
❑ ANL1-0973	Pure Gold	1974	2.50	5.00	10.00
❑ LPT-1005 [M]	Benny Goodman	1954	10.00	20.00	40.00
❑ LPM-1099 [M]	The Golden Age of Benny	1955	10.00	20.00	40.00
❑ LPM-1226 [M]	The Benny Goodman Trio/Quartet/Quintet	1956	10.00	20.00	40.00
❑ LPM-1239 [M]	This Is Benny Goodman	1956	10.00	20.00	40.00
❑ LPM-2247 [M]	The Kingdom of Swing	1960	5.00	10.00	20.00
❑ LSP-2247 [S]	The Kingdom of Swing	1960	6.25	12.50	25.00
❑ CPL1-2470	A Legendary Performer	1977	2.50	5.00	10.00
❑ LPM-2968 [M]	Together Again	1964	3.75	7.50	15.00
❑ LSP-2968 [S]	Together Again	1964	5.00	10.00	20.00
❑ LPT-3004 [10]	Benny Goodman Quartet	1952	12.50	25.00	50.00

Number	Title	Yr	VG	VG+	NM
❏ LPT-3056 [10]	This Is Benny Goodman and His Orchestra	1954	12.50	25.00	50.00
❏ AFL1-4005(e)	The Best of Benny Goodman	1977	2.50	5.00	10.00
-- Reissue of LSP-4005					
❏ LSP-4005	The Best of Benny Goodman	1968	3.75	7.50	15.00
❏ LOC-6008 [(2) M]	Benny Goodman in Moscow	1962	5.00	10.00	20.00
❏ LSO-6008 [(2) S]	Benny Goodman in Moscow	1962	6.25	12.50	25.00
❏ VPM-6040 [(2)]	This Is Benny Goodman	1972	3.75	7.50	15.00
❏ VPM-6063 [(2)]	This Is Benny Goodman, Vol. 2	1973	3.75	7.50	15.00
❏ LPT-6703 [(5) M]	The Golden Age of Swing	1956	150.00	300.00	600.00
-- Five-record set in white vinyl binder with bound-in booklet					
SUNBEAM					
❏ 100	The Let's Dance Broadcasts 1934-35, Volume 1	197?	2.50	5.00	10.00
❏ 104	The Let's Dance Broadcasts 1934-35, Volume 2	197?	2.50	5.00	10.00
❏ 105	Benny Goodman On the Air 1935-36, Volume 1	197?	2.50	5.00	10.00
❏ 106	Benny Goodman In a Mellotone Manner 1930-31	197?	2.50	5.00	10.00
❏ 107	Benny Goodman On the Side 1929-31	197?	2.50	5.00	10.00
❏ 111	Benny Goodman Accompanies Girls 1931-33	197?	2.50	5.00	10.00
❏ 112	Rare Benny Goodman 1927-29	197?	2.50	5.00	10.00
❏ 113	The Hotsy Totsy Gang 1928-29	197?	2.50	5.00	10.00
❏ 114	Whoopee Makers 1928-29	197?	2.50	5.00	10.00
❏ 116/27 [(12)]	Manhattan Room 1937	197?	15.00	30.00	60.00
❏ 128/32 [(5)]	From the Congress Hotel, Chicago, 1935-36	197?	6.25	12.50	25.00
❏ 133	Benny Goodman 1933	197?	2.50	5.00	10.00
❏ 135	Benny Goodman and the Modernists 1934-35	197?	2.50	5.00	10.00
❏ 138	Benny Goodman and His Orchestra 1931-33, Volume 1	197?	2.50	5.00	10.00
❏ 139	Benny Goodman and His Orchestra 1931-33, Volume 2	197?	2.50	5.00	10.00
❏ 140	Benny Goodman and His Orchestra 1931-33, Volume 3	197?	2.50	5.00	10.00
❏ 141	The Benny Goodman Boys 1928-29	197?	2.50	5.00	10.00
❏ 142	Benny Goodman On V-Disc 1939-48, Volume 1	197?	2.50	5.00	10.00
❏ 143	Benny Goodman On V-Disc 1939-48, Volume 2	197?	2.50	5.00	10.00
❏ 144	Benny Goodman On V-Disc 1939-48, Volume 3	197?	2.50	5.00	10.00
❏ 145	Fitch Bandwagon 1945	197?	2.50	5.00	10.00
❏ 146	Camel Caravan 1937, Volume 1	197?	2.50	5.00	10.00
❏ 147	Camel Caravan 1937, Volume 2	197?	2.50	5.00	10.00
❏ 148	Benny Goodman 1934	197?	2.50	5.00	10.00
❏ 149	Jam Session 1935-37	197?	2.50	5.00	10.00
❏ 150	The Let's Dance Broadcasts 1934-35, Volume 3	197?	2.50	5.00	10.00
❏ 151	The Benny Goodman Show 1946	197?	2.50	5.00	10.00
❏ 152 [(2)]	Benny Goodman and His Orchestra 1937-38	197?	3.00	6.00	12.00
❏ 153	Benny Goodman On the Air 1935-36, Volume 2	197?	2.50	5.00	10.00
❏ 154	Benny Goodman 1946	197?	2.50	5.00	10.00
❏ 156	Broadcasts from Hollywood	197?	2.50	5.00	10.00
VERVE					
❏ MGV-4013 [M]	The Superlative Goodman, Volume 1	1958	---	---	--
-- Canceled					
❏ MGV-4014 [M]	The Superlative Goodman, Volume 2	1958	---	---	---
-- Canceled					
❏ MGV-4015-2 [(2) M]	The Superlative Goodman	1958	---	---	---
-- Canceled					
❏ V-8582 [M]	The Essential Benny Goodman	1964	3.75	7.50	15.00
❏ V6-8582 [S]	The Essential Benny Goodman	1964	3.75	7.50	15.00
WESTINGHOUSE					
❏ (no #) [(5) M]	Benny in Brussels	1958	25.00	50.00	100.00
❏ (no #) [M]	Benny Goodman Plays World Favorites in High Fidelity	1958	7.50	15.00	30.00

GOODMAN, BENNY/CHARLIE BARNET
Also see each artist's individual listings.
CAPITOL

Number	Title	Yr	VG	VG+	NM
❏ M-11061	BeBop Spoken Here	197?	3.00	6.00	12.00

GOODMAN, JERRY, AND JAN HAMMER
Goodman, a violinist, was a member of the first MAHAVISHNU ORCHESTRA, as was Hammer. Also see JAN HAMMER.
NEMPEROR

Number	Title	Yr	VG	VG+	NM
❏ SD 430	Like Children	197?	2.50	5.00	10.00

GOODRICK, MICK
Guitarist.
ECM

| ❏ 1139 | In Pas(s)ing | 1979 | 3.00 | 6.00 | 12.00 |

GOODWIN, BILL
Drummer.
OMNISOUND

| ❏ 1029 | Bill Goodwin's Solar Energy | 1981 | 2.50 | 5.00 | 10.00 |
| ❏ 1050 | Network | 1983 | 2.50 | 5.00 | 10.00 |

GORDON, BOB
Baritone saxophone player. Also see JACK MONTROSE.
PACIFIC JAZZ

❏ PJLP-12 [10]	Meet Mr. Gordon	1954	30.00	60.00	120.00
TAMPA					
❏ TP-26 [M]	Jazz Impressions	1957	25.00	50.00	100.00
-- Colored vinyl					
❏ TP-26 [M]	Jazz Impressions	1958	12.50	25.00	50.00
-- Black vinyl					

GORDON, BOB/CLIFFORD BROWN
Also see each artist's individual listings.
PACIFIC JAZZ

| ❏ PJ-3 [M] | Jazz Immortal | 1960 | 12.50 | 25.00 | 50.00 |
| ❏ PJ-1214 [M] | The Bob Gordon Quintet/The Clifford Brown Ensemble | 1956 | 25.00 | 50.00 | 100.00 |

GORDON, BOBBY
Clarinetist.
DECCA

❏ DL 4394 [M]	Warm and Sentimental	1963	3.00	6.00	12.00
❏ DL 4507 [M]	Young Man's Fancy	1964	3.00	6.00	12.00
❏ DL 4726 [M]	The Lamp Is Low	1966	3.00	6.00	12.00
❏ DL 74394 [S]	Warm and Sentimental	1963	3.75	7.50	15.00
❏ DL 74507 [S]	Young Man's Fancy	1964	3.75	7.50	15.00
❏ DL 74726 [S]	The Lamp Is Low	1966	3.75	7.50	15.00

GORDON, DEXTER
Tenor saxophone player. Also see WARDELL GRAY.
BASF

❏ 20698	A Day in Copenhagen	197?	3.75	7.50	15.00
BETHLEHEM					
❏ BCP-36 [M]	Daddy Plays the Horn	1956	30.00	60.00	120.00
❏ BCP-6008	The Bethlehem Years	197?	3.00	6.00	12.00
-- Reissue, distributed by RCA Victor					
BLACK LION					
❏ 108	The Montmartre Collection	197?	3.75	7.50	15.00
BLUE NOTE					
❏ BN-LA393-H2 [(2)]	Dexter Gordon	1975	3.75	7.50	15.00
❏ LT-989	Clubhouse	1980	3.00	6.00	12.00
❏ LT-1051	Landslide	1980	3.00	6.00	12.00
❏ BLP-4077 [M]	Doin' Allright	1961	37.50	75.00	150.00
-- With W. 63rd St. address on label					
❏ BLP-4077 [M]	Doin' Allright	1963	6.25	12.50	25.00
-- With "New York, USA" address on label					
❏ BLP-4083 [M]	Dexter Calling	1961	15.00	30.00	60.00
-- With 61st. St. address on label					
❏ BLP-4083 [M]	Dexter Calling	1963	6.25	12.50	25.00
-- With "New York, USA" address on label					
❏ BLP-4112 [M]	Go	1962	7.50	15.00	30.00
-- With "New York, USA" address on label					
❏ BLP-4133 [M]	A Swingin' Affair	1963	7.50	15.00	30.00
-- With "New York, USA" address on label					
❏ BLP-4146 [M]	Our Man in Paris	1963	7.50	15.00	30.00
-- With "New York, USA" address on label					
❏ BLP-4176 [M]	One Flight Up	1964	7.50	15.00	30.00
-- With "New York, USA" address on label					
❏ BLP-4204 [M]	Gettin' Around	1965	7.50	15.00	30.00
-- With "New York, USA" address on label					
❏ BST-84077 [S]	Doin' Allright	1961	50.00	100.00	200.00
-- With W. 63rd St. address on label					
❏ BST-84077 [S]	Doin' Allright	1963	7.50	15.00	30.00
-- With "New York, USA" address on label					
❏ BST-84077 [S]	Doin' Allright	1967	3.75	7.50	15.00
-- With "A Division of Liberty Records" on label					

Number	Title	Yr	VG	VG+	NM
❏ BST-84077	Doin' Allright	1985	2.50	5.00	10.00
-- "The Finest in Jazz Since 1939" reissue					
❏ BST-84083 [S]	Dexter Calling	1961	20.00	40.00	80.00
-- With 61st. St. address on label					
❏ BST-84083 [S]	Dexter Calling	1963	7.50	15.00	30.00
-- With "New York, USA" address on label					
❏ BST-84083 [S]	Dexter Calling	1967	3.75	7.50	15.00
-- With "A Division of Liberty Records" on label					
❏ BST-84112 [S]	Go	1962	10.00	20.00	40.00
-- With "New York, USA" address on label					
❏ BST-84112 [S]	Go	1967	3.75	7.50	15.00
-- With "A Division of Liberty Records" on label					
❏ BST-84112	Go	1985	2.50	5.00	10.00
-- "The Finest in Jazz Since 1939" reissue					
❏ BST-84133 [S]	A Swingin' Affair	1963	10.00	20.00	40.00
-- With "New York, USA" address on label					
❏ BST-84133 [S]	A Swingin' Affair	1967	3.75	7.50	15.00
-- With "A Division of Liberty Records" on label					
❏ BST-84133	A Swingin' Affair	199?	7.50	15.00	30.00
-- Classic Records 180-gram audiophile reissue					
❏ BST-84146 [S]	Our Man in Paris	1963	10.00	20.00	40.00
-- With "New York, USA" address on label					
❏ BST-84146 [S]	Our Man in Paris	1967	3.75	7.50	15.00
-- With "A Division of Liberty Records" on label					
❏ BST-84148	Our Man in Paris	1987	2.50	5.00	10.00
-- "The Finest in Jazz Since 1939" reissue					
❏ BST-84176 [S]	One Flight Up	1964	10.00	20.00	40.00
-- With "New York, USA" address on label					
❏ BST-84176 [S]	One Flight Up	1967	3.75	7.50	15.00
-- With "A Division of Liberty Records" on label					
❏ BST-84176	One Flight Up	1986	2.50	5.00	10.00
-- "The Finest in Jazz Since 1939" reissue					
❏ BST-84204 [S]	Gettin' Around	1965	10.00	20.00	40.00
-- With "New York, USA" address on label					
❏ BST-84204 [S]	Gettin' Around	1967	3.75	7.50	15.00
-- With "A Division of Liberty Records" on label					
❏ BABB-85112	Nights at the Keystone	198?	3.00	6.00	12.00
❏ BT-85135	The Other Side of 'Round Midnight	1987	3.00	6.00	12.00
❏ B1-91139	The Best of Dexter Gordon	1988	3.00	6.00	12.00
BOPLICITY					
❏ BOP-6	Dexter Blows Hot and Cool	198?	2.50	5.00	10.00
COLUMBIA					
❏ PG 34650 [(2)]	Homecoming	1977	3.75	7.50	15.00
❏ JC 34989	Sophisticated Giant	1977	3.00	6.00	12.00
❏ JC 35608	Manhattan Symphonie	1978	3.00	6.00	12.00
❏ PC 35608	Manhattan Symphonie	198?	2.00	4.00	8.00
-- Budget-line reissue					
❏ JC 35987	Great Encounters	1979	2.50	5.00	10.00
❏ JC 36356	The Best of Dexter Gordon	1979	2.50	5.00	10.00
❏ JC 36853	Gotham City	1980	2.50	5.00	10.00
DIAL					
❏ LP-204 [10]	Dexter Gordon Quintet	1950	100.00	200.00	400.00
DISCOVERY					
❏ 79005	American Classic	1995	3.75	7.50	15.00
DOOTO					
❏ DL-207 [M]	Dexter Blows Hot and Cool	196?	12.50	25.00	50.00
DOOTONE					
❏ DL-207 [M]	Dexter Blows Hot and Cool	1956	62.50	125.00	250.00
-- Red vinyl					
❏ DL-207 [M]	Dexter Blows Hot and Cool	1957	30.00	60.00	120.00
-- Black vinyl					
ELEKTRA/MUSICIAN					
❏ 60126	American Classic	1983	2.50	5.00	10.00
FANTASY					
❏ OJC-299	Tower of Power	198?	2.50	5.00	10.00
INNER CITY					
❏ IC-2006	The Meeting	1973	3.75	7.50	15.00
❏ IC-2020	The Source	1973	3.75	7.50	15.00
❏ IC-2025	The Apartment	197?	3.75	7.50	15.00
❏ IC-2030	More Than You Know	197?	3.75	7.50	15.00
❏ IC-2040	Stable Mable	1975	3.75	7.50	15.00
❏ IC-2050	Swiss Nights	1975	3.75	7.50	15.00
❏ IC-2060	Bouncin'	197?	3.75	7.50	15.00
❏ IC-2080	Biting the Apple	1977	3.00	6.00	12.00
JAZZ MAN					
❏ 5023	Dexter Gordon at Montmartre	198?	2.50	5.00	10.00
JAZZLAND					
❏ JLP-29 [M]	The Resurgence of Dexter Gordon	1960	12.50	25.00	50.00
❏ JLP-929 [S]	The Resurgence of Dexter Gordon	1960	15.00	30.00	60.00
PAUSA					
❏ 7058	A Day in Copenhagen	1980	2.50	5.00	10.00
PRESTIGE					
❏ 2502	The Ballad Album	198?	2.50	5.00	10.00

Number	Title	Yr	VG	VG+	NM
❏ 2511	Resurgence	198?	2.50	5.00	10.00
❏ PRST-7623	The Tower of Power	1969	5.00	10.00	20.00
❏ PRST-7680	More Power	1969	5.00	10.00	20.00
❏ PRST-7763	A Day in Copenhagen	1970	5.00	10.00	20.00
❏ PRST-7829	Panther!	1971	5.00	10.00	20.00
❏ 10020	Jumpin' Blues	197?	3.75	7.50	15.00
❏ 10051	Ca' Purange	197?	3.75	7.50	15.00
❏ 10069	Generation	197?	3.75	7.50	15.00
❏ 10079	Blues A La Suisse	197?	3.75	7.50	15.00
❏ 10091	Tangerine	197?	3.75	7.50	15.00
SAVOY					
❏ MG-9003 [10]	All Star Series -- Dexter Gordon	1951	62.50	125.00	250.00
❏ MG-9016 [10]	New Trends in Modern Jazz, Volume 3	1952	62.50	125.00	250.00
❏ MG-12130 [M]	Dexter Rides Again	1958	25.00	50.00	100.00
SAVOY JAZZ					
❏ SJC-407	Jazz Concert, West Coast	1985	2.50	5.00	10.00
❏ SJL-1154	Master Takes: The Savoy Recordings	198?	2.50	5.00	10.00
❏ SJL-2211 [(2)]	Long Tall Dexter	197?	3.75	7.50	15.00
❏ SJL-2222 [(2)]	The Hunt	197?	3.75	7.50	15.00
STEEPLECHASE					
❏ SCC-1080	Biting the Apple	198?	2.50	5.00	10.00
❏ SCS-1025	The Apartment	198?	2.50	5.00	10.00
❏ SCS-1030	More Than You Know	198?	2.50	5.00	10.00
❏ SCS-1040	Stable Mable	198?	2.50	5.00	10.00
❏ SCS-1050	Swiss Nights, Volume 1	198?	2.50	5.00	10.00
❏ SCS-1060	Bouncin'	198?	2.50	5.00	10.00
❏ SCS-1090	Swiss Nights, Volume 2	198?	2.50	5.00	10.00
❏ SCS-1110	Swiss Nights, Volume 3	198?	2.50	5.00	10.00
❏ SCS-1136	Something Different	1980	3.00	6.00	12.00
❏ SCS-1145	Strings & Things	198?	3.00	6.00	12.00
❏ SCS-1156	Lullaby for a Monster	198?	2.50	5.00	10.00
❏ SCS-1206	The Shadow of Your Smile	198?	3.00	6.00	12.00
❏ SCC-6004	Cry Me a River	198?	3.00	6.00	12.00
❏ SCC-6008	Cheese Cake	198?	3.00	6.00	12.00
❏ SCC-6015	I Want More	198?	3.00	6.00	12.00
❏ SCC-6022	It's You or No One	198?	3.00	6.00	12.00
❏ SCC-6028	Billie's Bounce	198?	3.00	6.00	12.00
WHO'S WHO IN JAZZ					
❏ 21011	Who's Who Presents Dexter Gordon and Lionel Hampton	1977	3.00	6.00	12.00

GORDON, DEXTER/HOWARD McGHEE

Also see each artist's individual listings.

Number	Title	Yr	VG	VG+	NM
JAZZTONE					
❏ J-1235 [M]	The Chase	1956	10.00	20.00	40.00

GORDON, FRANK

Trumpeter.

Number	Title	Yr	VG	VG+	NM
SOUL NOTE					
❏ SN-1096	Clarion Echoes	1986	2.50	5.00	10.00

GORDON, GRAY

Saxophone player and bandleader.

Number	Title	Yr	VG	VG+	NM
HINDSIGHT					
❏ HSR-206	Gray Gordon and His Tic Toc Rhythm 1939	198?	2.50	5.00	10.00

GORDON, HONI

Female singer.

Number	Title	Yr	VG	VG+	NM
PRESTIGE					
❏ PRLP-7230 [M]	Honi Gordon Sings	1962	10.00	20.00	40.00
❏ PRST-7230 [S]	Honi Gordon Sings	1962	12.50	25.00	50.00

GORDON, JOE

Trumpeter.

Number	Title	Yr	VG	VG+	NM
CONTEMPORARY					
❏ M-3597 [M]	Lookin' Good	1961	7.50	15.00	30.00
❏ S-7597 [S]	Lookin' Good	1961	10.00	20.00	40.00
EMARCY					
❏ MG-26046 [10]	Introducing Joe Gordon	1954	37.50	75.00	150.00
❏ MG-36025 [M]	Introducing Joe Gordon	1955	25.00	50.00	100.00
FANTASY					
❏ OJC-174	Lookin' Good	198?	2.50	5.00	10.00
TRIP					
❏ 5535	Introducing Joe Gordon	197?	2.50	5.00	10.00

GORDON, JOHN

Number	Title	Yr	VG	VG+	NM
STRATA-EAST					
❏ SES-19760	Step by Step	197?	5.00	10.00	20.00

Number	Title	Yr	VG	VG+	NM
GORDON, JON					
Trombone player.					
GEMINI TAURUS					
❏ TRLP-827	Beginning and Endings	1989	3.00	6.00	12.00
GORRILL, LIZ					
Pianist and female singer.					
JAZZ RECORDS					
❏ JR-2 [(2)]	I Feel Like I'm Home	198?	3.75	7.50	15.00
❏ JR-7	True Fun	198?	3.00	6.00	12.00
GORRILL, LIZ, AND ANDY FITE					
Fite is a guitarist. Also see LIZ GORRILL.					
NEW ARTISTS					
❏ NA-1004	Phantasmagoria	1988	2.50	5.00	10.00
GOSSEZ, PIERRE					
Clarinetist and saxophone player.					
VANGUARD CARDINAL					
❏ C-10061	Bach Takes a Trip	1969	5.00	10.00	20.00
GOTTLIEB, DANNY					
Drummer. Also see ELEMENTS.					
ATLANTIC					
❏ 81806	Aquamarine	1988	2.50	5.00	10.00
❏ 81958	Whirlwind	1989	3.00	6.00	12.00
GOULD, CHUCK					
Bandleader and male singer.					
VIK					
❏ LX-1123 [M]	Chuck Gould Plays A La Fletcher Henderson	1957	12.50	25.00	50.00
GOWANS, BRAD					
Trombone player, arranger and bandleader.					
RCA VICTOR					
❏ LJM-3000 [10]	Brad Gowans' New York Nine	1954	12.50	25.00	50.00
GOYKOVICH, DUSKO					
Trumpeter and fluegel horn player.					
ENJA					
❏ 2020	After Hours	197?	3.00	6.00	12.00
GOZZO, CONRAD					
Trumpeter.					
RCA VICTOR					
❏ LPM-1124 [M]	Goz the Great	1955	12.50	25.00	50.00
GRAAS, JOHN					
French horn player. Also see THE GILBERT & SULLIVAN JAZZ WORKSHOP.					
ANDEX					
❏ A-3003 [M]	Premiere in Jazz	1958	12.50	25.00	50.00
❏ AS-3003 [S]	Premiere in Jazz	1959	10.00	20.00	40.00
DECCA					
❏ DL 8079 [M]	Jazz Studio 2	1954	12.50	25.00	50.00
❏ DL 8104 [M]	Jazz Studio 3	1955	12.50	25.00	50.00
❏ DL 8343 [M]	Jazz Lab 1	1956	12.50	25.00	50.00
❏ DL 8478 [M]	Jazz Lab 2	1957	12.50	25.00	50.00
❏ DL 8677 [M]	Jazzmantics	1958	12.50	25.00	50.00
EMARCY					
❏ MG-36117 [M]	Coup de Graas	1958	12.50	25.00	50.00
KAPP					
❏ KL-1046 [M]	French Horn Jazz	1957	12.50	25.00	50.00
MERCURY					
❏ SR-80020 [S]	Coup de Graas	1959	10.00	20.00	40.00
TREND					
❏ TL-1005 [10]	French Horn Jazz	1954	30.00	60.00	120.00
GRACEN, THELMA					
Female singer.					
EMARCY					
❏ MG-36096 [M]	Thelma Gracen	1956	50.00	100.00	200.00
WING					
❏ MGW-60005 [M]	Thelma Gracen	1956	37.50	75.00	150.00

Number	Title	Yr	VG	VG+	NM
GRAHAM, ED					
Drummer.					
M&K REALTIME					
❏ 106	Hot Stix	1980	10.00	20.00	40.00
-- Direct-to-disc recording; plays at 45 rpm					
GRAMERCY SIX, THE					
No relation to the ARTIE SHAW Gramercy Five. Among the members: Nick Fatool, Al Henderson, Jud DeNaut, Shorty Sherrock, Eddie Rosa.					
EDISON INTERNATIONAL					
❏ P-502 [M]	Great Swinging Sounds Vol. 1	1959	7.50	15.00	30.00
GRAND DOMINION JAZZ BAND					
Organized by Michael Cox (banjo). Other members: Bob Pelland (piano); Bob Jackson (trumpet); Jim Armstrong (trombone); Greey Green (clarinet, alto saxophone); Mike Duffy (bass); Stephen Joseph (drums).					
GHB					
❏ GHB-174	Grand Dominion Jazz Band	1984	2.50	5.00	10.00
STOMP OFF					
❏ SOS-1139	Don't Give Up the Ship	1987	2.50	5.00	10.00
❏ SOS-1189	Ain't Nobody Got the Blues Like Me	1988	2.50	5.00	10.00
GRANT, TOM					
Pianist, keyboard player and male singer.					
CMG					
❏ CML-8007	Heart of the City	198?	2.00	4.00	8.00
❏ CML-8008	Tom Grant	198?	2.00	4.00	8.00
❏ CML-8009	Just the Right Moment	198?	2.00	4.00	8.00
❏ CML-8010	Take Me to Your Dream	198?	2.00	4.00	8.00
PAUSA					
❏ 7145	Tom Grant	198?	2.50	5.00	10.00
❏ 7174	Just the Right Moment	1985	2.50	5.00	10.00
❏ 7199	Take Me to Your Dream	1986	2.50	5.00	10.00
GRAPPELLI, STEPHANE					
Violinist.					
ANGEL					
❏ DS-37790	Brandenberg Boogie (Music of Bach)	1980	3.00	6.00	12.00
❏ DS-37886	We've Got the World on a String	198?	3.00	6.00	12.00
❏ DS-38063	Just One of Those Things	198?	3.00	6.00	12.00
ARCHIVE OF FOLK AND JAZZ					
❏ 311	Stephane Grappelli	197?	3.00	6.00	12.00
ARSITA FREEDOM					
❏ AL 1033	The Parisian	197?	3.00	6.00	12.00
ATLANTIC					
❏ 1391 [M]	Feeling + Finesse = Jazz	1962	3.75	7.50	15.00
❏ SD 1391 [S]	Feeling + Finesse = Jazz	1962	5.00	10.00	20.00
❏ 82095	Olympia '88	1990	3.00	6.00	12.00
❏ 90140	Feeling + Finesse = Jazz	198?	2.50	5.00	10.00
BARCLAY					
❏ 820007	Music to Pass the Time	196?	5.00	10.00	20.00
BASF					
❏ 20876	Afternoon in Paris	1972	3.75	7.50	15.00
BLACK LION					
❏ 047 [(2)]	I Got Rhythm	1974	5.00	10.00	20.00
❏ 211	Just One of the Things	1974	3.75	7.50	15.00
❏ 313	Talk of the Town	1975	3.00	6.00	12.00
CLASSIC JAZZ					
❏ 23 [(2)]	Homage to Django	197?	5.00	10.00	20.00
❏ 24	Stephane Grappelli and Bill Coleman	197?	3.75	7.50	15.00
COLUMBIA					
❏ JC 35415	Uptown Dance	1978	2.50	5.00	10.00
CONCORD JAZZ					
❏ CJ-139	Stephane Grappelli at the Winery	1980	2.50	5.00	10.00
❏ CJ-169	Vintage 1981	1981	2.50	5.00	10.00
❏ CJ-225	Stephanova	1983	2.50	5.00	10.00
DOCTOR JAZZ					
❏ FW 38727	Live at Carnegie Hall	1983	2.50	5.00	10.00
EMARCY					
❏ MG-36120 [M]	Improvisations	1957	15.00	30.00	60.00
FANTASY					
❏ OJC-441	Tivoli Gardens	1990	2.50	5.00	10.00
GRP					
❏ GR-1032	Stephane Grappelli Plays Jerome Kern	1987	2.50	5.00	10.00

Number	Title	Yr	VG	VG+	NM
PABLO LIVE					
❑ 2308 220	Tivoli Gardens	1979	3.00	6.00	12.00
PAUSA					
❑ 7041	Young Django	1979	2.50	5.00	10.00
❑ 7071	Afternoon in Paris	1979	2.50	5.00	10.00
❑ 7098	Violinspiration	198?	2.50	5.00	10.00
VANGUARD					
❑ VMS-73130	Satin Doll, Volume 1	198?	2.50	5.00	10.00
❑ VSD-81/82 [(2)]	Satin Doll	197?	3.75	7.50	15.00
VERVE					
❑ 815 672-1	Young Django	198?	2.50	5.00	10.00

GRAPPELLI, STEPHANE, AND TERESA BREWER
Also see each artist's individual listings.

Number	Title	Yr	VG	VG+	NM
DOCTOR JAZZ					
❑ FW 38448	On the Road Again	1983	2.50	5.00	10.00

GRAPPELLI, STEPHANE, AND VASSAR CLEMENTS
Clements is a fiddler/violinist best known for his bluegrass music; he does not have an entry in this book. Also see STEPHANE GRAPPELLI.

Number	Title	Yr	VG	VG+	NM
FLYING FISH					
❑ FF-421	Together at Last	1987	2.50	5.00	10.00

GRAPPELLI, STEPHANE, AND DAVID GRISMAN
Also see each artist's individual listings.

Number	Title	Yr	VG	VG+	NM
WARNER BROS.					
❑ BSK 3550	Live	1981	2.50	5.00	10.00

GRAPPELLI, STEPHANE, AND HANK JONES
Also see each artist's individual listings.

Number	Title	Yr	VG	VG+	NM
MUSE					
❑ MR-5287	A Two-fer	198?	2.50	5.00	10.00

GRAPPELLI, STEPHANE, AND BARNEY KESSEL
Also see each artist's individual listings.

Number	Title	Yr	VG	VG+	NM
BLACK LION					
❑ 105	I Remember Django	197?	3.75	7.50	15.00
JAZZ MAN					
❑ 5008	I Remember Django	198?	2.50	5.00	10.00
MOBILE FIDELITY					
❑ 1-111	I Remember Django	1984	12.50	25.00	50.00
-- Audiophile vinyl					

GRAPPELLI, STEPHANE, AND YO-YO MA
Ma is a cellist best known in the classical realm; he does not have an entry in this book. Also see STEPHANE GRAPPELLI.

Number	Title	Yr	VG	VG+	NM
CBS					
❑ FM 45574	Anything Goes: The Music of Cole Porter	1989	3.00	6.00	12.00

GRAPPELLI, STEPHANE, AND JEAN-LUC PONTY
Also see each artist's individual listings.

Number	Title	Yr	VG	VG+	NM
ARCHIVE OF FOLK AND JAZZ					
❑ 355	Violin Summit	1980	2.50	5.00	10.00
PAUSA					
❑ 7074	Giants	1979	2.50	5.00	10.00

GRAPPELLI, STEPHANE, AND GEORGE SHEARING
Also see each artist's individual listings.

Number	Title	Yr	VG	VG+	NM
VERVE					
❑ 821 868-1	The Reunion	1985	2.50	5.00	10.00

GRAPPELLI, STEPHANE, AND McCOY TYNER
Also see each artist's individual listings.

Number	Title	Yr	VG	VG+	NM
MILESTONE					
❑ M-9181	One on One	1990	3.00	6.00	12.00

GRAVES, CONLEY
Pianist.

Number	Title	Yr	VG	VG+	NM
DECCA					
❑ DL 8220 [M]	Genius at Work	1956	10.00	20.00	40.00
❑ DL 8412 [M]	Piano Dynamics	1957	10.00	20.00	40.00
❑ DL 8475 [M]	Rendezvous in Paris	1957	10.00	20.00	40.00
LIBERTY					
❑ LPR-3007 [M]	V.I.P. (Very Important Pianist)	1956	10.00	20.00	40.00
NOCTURNE					
❑ NLP-4 [10]	Piano Artistry	1954	25.00	50.00	100.00

GRAVES, JOE
Trumpeter.

Number	Title	Yr	VG	VG+	NM
CAPITOL					
❑ ST 1977 [S]	The Great New Swingers	1963	7.50	15.00	30.00
❑ T 1977 [M]	The Great New Swingers	1963	6.25	12.50	25.00

GRAVES, MILFORD
Drummer. Also see THE NEW YORK ART QUARTET.

Number	Title	Yr	VG	VG+	NM
ESP-DISK'					
❑ 1015 [M]	Milford Graves Percussion Ensemble	1966	5.00	10.00	20.00
❑ S-1015 [S]	Milford Graves Percussion Ensemble	1966	6.25	12.50	25.00
IPS					
❑ 004	Babi	197?	3.75	7.50	15.00
❑ 290	Nommo	197?	3.75	7.50	15.00

GRAVINE, ANITA
Female singer.

Number	Title	Yr	VG	VG+	NM
STASH					
❑ ST-256	I Always Knew	1985	2.50	5.00	10.00

GRAY, GLEN
Saxophone player and bandleader. Also see JONAH JONES.

Number	Title	Yr	VG	VG+	NM
CAPITOL					
❑ W 747 [M]	Casa Loma in Hi-Fi!	1956	6.25	12.50	25.00
❑ SM-1022	Sounds of the Great Bands!	197?	2.50	5.00	10.00
-- Reissue					
❑ SW 1022 [S]	Sounds of the Great Bands!	1959	3.75	7.50	15.00
❑ W 1022 [S]	Sounds of the Great Bands!	1959	3.00	6.00	12.00
❑ SM-1067	Sounds of the Great Bands Volume 2	197?	2.50	5.00	10.00
-- Reissue					
❑ ST 1067 [S]	Sounds of the Great Bands Volume 2	1959	3.75	7.50	15.00
❑ T 1067 [M]	Sounds of the Great Bands Volume 2	1959	3.00	6.00	12.00
❑ ST 1234 [S]	Solo Spotlight	1960	3.75	7.50	15.00
❑ T 1234 [M]	Solo Spotlight	1960	3.00	6.00	12.00
❑ ST 1289 [S]	Swingin' Decade	1960	3.75	7.50	15.00
❑ T 1289 [M]	Swingin' Decade	1960	3.00	6.00	12.00
❑ ST 1400 [S]	Swingin' Southern Style	1961	3.75	7.50	15.00
❑ T 1400 [M]	Swingin' Southern Style	1961	3.00	6.00	12.00
❑ ST 1506 [S]	Please Mr. Gray…More Sounds of the Great Bands	1961	3.75	7.50	15.00
❑ T 1506 [M]	Please Mr. Gray…More Sounds of the Great Bands	1961	3.00	6.00	12.00
❑ DT 1588 [R]	Sounds of the Great Casa Loma Band	1961	3.00	6.00	12.00
❑ SM-1588	Sounds of the Great Casa Loma Band	197?	2.50	5.00	10.00
-- Reissue					
❑ T 1588 [M]	Sounds of the Great Casa Loma Band	1961	3.75	7.50	15.00
❑ ST 1615 [S]	Shall We Swing?	1961	3.75	7.50	15.00
❑ T 1615 [M]	Shall We Swing?	1961	3.00	6.00	12.00
❑ ST 1739 [S]	Sounds of the Great Bands Volume 5: They All Swung the Blues	1962	3.75	7.50	15.00
❑ T 1739 [M]	Sounds of the Great Bands Volume 5: They All Swung the Blues	1962	3.00	6.00	12.00
❑ SM-1812	Themes of the Great Bands	197?	2.50	5.00	10.00
-- Reissue					
❑ ST 1812 [S]	Themes of the Great Bands	1963	3.75	7.50	15.00
❑ T 1812 [M]	Themes of the Great Bands	1963	3.00	6.00	12.00
❑ ST 1938 [S]	Sounds of the Great Bands Volume 7: Today's Best	1963	3.00	6.00	12.00
❑ T 1938 [M]	Sounds of the Great Bands Volume 7: Today's Best	1963	2.50	5.00	10.00
❑ ST 2014 [S]	Sounds of the Great Bands Volume 8: More of Today's Best	1964	3.00	6.00	12.00
❑ T 2014 [M]	Sounds of the Great Bands Volume 8: More of Today's Best	1964	2.50	5.00	10.00
❑ ST 2131 [S]	Sounds of the Great Bands in Latin	1964	3.00	6.00	12.00
❑ T 2131 [M]	Sounds of the Great Bands in Latin	1964	2.50	5.00	10.00
CIRCLE					
❑ 16	Glen Gray and the Casa Loma Orchestra	198?	2.50	5.00	10.00
CORAL					
❑ CRL 56006 [10]	Hoagy Carmichael Songs	1950	12.50	25.00	50.00
❑ CRL 56009 [10]	Glen Gray Souvenirs	1950	12.50	25.00	50.00
CREATIVE WORLD					
❑ ST-1055	Shall We Swing?	197?	2.50	5.00	10.00

Number	Title	Yr	VG	VG+	NM
DECCA					
❑ DL 5089 [10]	Musical Smoke Rings	1950	12.50	25.00	50.00
❑ DL 5397 [10]	No-Name Jive	1953	12.50	25.00	50.00
❑ DL 8570 [M]	Smoke Rings	1957	5.00	10.00	20.00
❑ DL 75016 [R]	Greatest Hits	1968	3.00	6.00	12.00
HARMONY					
❑ HL 7045 [M]	The Great Recordings of Glen Gray	1957	5.00	10.00	20.00
HINDSIGHT					
❑ HSR-104	Glen Gray and the Casa Loma Orchestra, 1939-1940	198?	2.50	5.00	10.00
❑ HSR-120	Glen Gray and the Casa Loma Orchestra, 1943-1946	198?	2.50	5.00	10.00
INSIGHT					
❑ 214	Glen Gray and the Casa Loma Orchestra, 1939-1946	198?	2.50	5.00	10.00
MCA					
❑ 122	Greatest Hits	1973	2.50	5.00	10.00
-- Reissue of Decca 75016					
❑ 4076 [(2)]	The Best of Glen Gray	197?	3.00	6.00	12.00
❑ 20199	Smoke Rings	198?	2.00	4.00	8.00

GRAY, JERRY
Arranger and composer best known for his work with the GLENN MILLER band; he, in fact, took over its reins following Miller's death.

Number	Title	Yr	VG	VG+	NM
CRAFTSMAN					
❑ 8035 [M]	More Miller Hits	195?	5.00	10.00	20.00
DECCA					
❑ DL 5266 [10]	Dance to the Music of Gray	1950	12.50	25.00	50.00
❑ DL 5375 [10]	A Tribute to Glenn Miller	1951	12.50	25.00	50.00
❑ DL 5478 [10]	Dance Time	1952	12.50	25.00	50.00
❑ DL 8101 [M]	Jerry Gray and His Orchestra	1955	10.00	20.00	40.00
DOT					
❑ DLP-3741 [M]	This Is Jerry Gray	1966	3.00	6.00	12.00
❑ DLP-25741 [S]	This Is Jerry Gray	1966	3.75	7.50	15.00
GOLDEN TONE					
❑ C-4005 [M]	Glenn Miller Favorites	196?	3.00	6.00	12.00
HINDSIGHT					
❑ HSR-212	Jerry Gray and His Orchestra 1952	198?	2.50	5.00	10.00
LIBERTY					
❑ LRP-3038 [M]	Hi-Fi Shades of Gray	1956	10.00	20.00	40.00
❑ LRP-3089 [M]	Jerry Gray at the Hollywood Palladium	1958	10.00	20.00	40.00
❑ LST-7002 [S]	Hi-Fi Shades of Gray	1958	10.00	20.00	40.00
❑ LST-7013 [S]	Jerry Gray at the Hollywood Palladium	1958	10.00	20.00	40.00
TOPS					
❑ L-1627 [M]	A Salute to Glenn Miller	1958	5.00	10.00	20.00
❑ L-1640 [M]	Glenn Miller Greats	1958	5.00	10.00	20.00
VOCALION					
❑ VL 3602 [M]	A Tribute to Glenn Miller	196?	5.00	10.00	20.00
WARNER BROS.					
❑ W 1446 [M]	Singin' and Swingin'	1962	5.00	10.00	20.00
❑ WS 1446 [S]	Singin' and Swingin'	1962	6.25	12.50	25.00

GRAY, WARDELL
Tenor saxophone player. Also see LOUIS BELLSON; STAN GETZ.

Number	Title	Yr	VG	VG+	NM
CROWN					
❑ CLP-5004 [M]	Way Out Wardell	1957	10.00	20.00	40.00
-- Original have black label with the word "crown" in small letters at top					
❑ CLP-5293 [M]	Wardell Gray	196?	3.75	7.50	15.00
-- Gray label					
FANTASY					
❑ OJC-050	Wardell Gray Memorial, Volume 1	1982	2.50	5.00	10.00
-- Reissue of Prestige 7008					
❑ OJC-051	Wardell Gray Memorial, Volume 2	1982	2.50	5.00	10.00
-- Reissue of Prestige 7009					
MODERN					
❑ MLP-1204 [M]	Way Out Wardell	1956	37.50	75.00	150.00
PHILOLOGY/SPHERE					
❑ W-14	Light Gray, Vol. 1	198?	2.50	5.00	10.00
❑ W-36	Light Gray, Vol. 2	198?	2.50	5.00	10.00
PRESTIGE					
❑ PRLP-115 [10]	Wardell Gray Tenor Sax	1951	62.50	125.00	250.00
❑ PRLP-128 [10]	Jazz Concert	1952	62.50	125.00	250.00

Number	Title	Yr	VG	VG+	NM
❑ PRLP-147 [10]	Wardell Gray's Los Angeles Stars	1953	62.50	125.00	250.00
❑ PRLP-7008 [M]	Wardell Gray Memorial, Volume 1	1955	25.00	50.00	100.00
❑ PRLP-7009 [M]	Wardell Gray Memorial, Volume 2	1955	25.00	50.00	100.00
❑ PRLP-7343 [(2) M]	Wardell Gray Memorial Album	1964	10.00	20.00	40.00
❑ PRST-7343 [(2) R]	Wardell Gray Memorial Album	1964	5.00	10.00	20.00
❑ 24062 [(2)]	Central Ave.	197?	3.75	7.50	15.00
XANADU					
❑ 146	Live in Hollywood	197?	3.00	6.00	12.00

GRAY, WARDELL, AND DEXTER GORDON
Also see each artist's individual listings.

Number	Title	Yr	VG	VG+	NM
DECCA					
❑ DL 7025 [10]	The Chase and the Steeple Chase	1952	62.50	125.00	250.00
JAZZTONE					
❑ J-1235 [M]	The Chase and the Steeple Chase	1956	12.50	25.00	50.00
MCA					
❑ 1336	The Chase and the Steeple Chase	198?	2.50	5.00	10.00

GRAYE, TONY

Number	Title	Yr	VG	VG+	NM
FUTURA					
❑ 55514	Let's Swing Away	197?	3.75	7.50	15.00
❑ 55515	The Blue Horn of Tony Graye	197?	3.75	7.50	15.00
ZIM					
❑ ZMS-2001	Oh Gee!	1975	3.75	7.50	15.00

GREAT EXCELSIOR JAZZ BAND
Led by pianist Ray Skjelbred.

Number	Title	Yr	VG	VG+	NM
VOYAGER					
❑ VRLP-202	Hot Jazz from the Territory	198?	2.50	5.00	10.00
❑ VRLP-203	Roast Chestnuts	198?	2.50	5.00	10.00
❑ VRLP-204	Remembering Joe	198?	2.50	5.00	10.00

GREAT GUITARS, THE
See CHARLIE BYRD, HERB ELLIS & BARNEY KESSEL.

GREAT JAZZ TRIO, THE
Members: RON CARTER; HANK JONES; TONY WILLIAMS.

Number	Title	Yr	VG	VG+	NM
EAST WIND					
❑ 10005	Direct from L.A.	1978	6.25	12.50	25.00
-- Direct-to-disc recording					
INNER CITY					
❑ IC-6003	Love for Sale	1976	3.00	6.00	12.00
❑ IC-6013	The Great Jazz Trio at the Village Vanguard	1977	3.00	6.00	12.00
❑ IC-6023	Kindness, Joy, Love and Happiness	1978	3.00	6.00	12.00
❑ IC-6030	Milestones	1979	3.00	6.00	12.00

GREEN, BENNIE
Trombonist. Also see J.J. JOHNSON.

Number	Title	Yr	VG	VG+	NM
BAINBRIDGE					
❑ 1048	Bennie Green	198?	2.50	5.00	10.00
BARBARY					
❑ M 33015 [M]	Play More Than You Can Stand	196?	6.25	12.50	25.00
BETHLEHEM					
❑ BCP-4019 [M]	Hornful of Soul	196?	5.00	10.00	20.00
-- Reissue of 6054					
❑ BCP-6018	Cat Walk	197?	3.75	7.50	15.00
-- Reissue of 6054, distributed by RCA Victor					
❑ BCP-6054 [M]	Hornful of Soul	1961	7.50	15.00	30.00
BLUE NOTE					
❑ BLP-1587 [M]	Back on the Scene	1958	30.00	60.00	120.00
-- "Deep groove" version (deep indentation under label on both sides)					
❑ BLP-1587 [M]	Back on the Scene	1958	20.00	40.00	80.00
-- Regular version with W. 63rd St. address on label					
❑ BLP-1587 [M]	Back on the Scene	1963	6.25	12.50	25.00
-- With "New York, USA" address on label					
❑ BST-1587 [S]	Back on the Scene	1959	20.00	40.00	80.00
-- "Deep groove" version (deep indentation under label on both sides)					
❑ BST-1587 [S]	Back on the Scene	1959	15.00	30.00	60.00
-- Regular version with W. 63rd St. address on label					
❑ BLP-1599 [M]	Soul Stirrin'	1958	30.00	60.00	120.00
-- "Deep groove" version (deep indentation under label on both sides)					

Number	Title	Yr	VG	VG+	NM
❑ BLP-1599 [M]	Soul Stirrin'	1958	20.00	40.00	80.00
-- Regular version with W. 63rd St. address on label					
❑ BLP-1599 [M]	Soul Stirrin'	1963	6.25	12.50	25.00
-- With "New York, USA" address on label					
❑ BST-1599 [S]	Soul Stirrin'	1959	20.00	40.00	80.00
-- "Deep groove" version (deep indentation under label on both sides)					
❑ BST-1599 [S]	Soul Stirrin'	1959	15.00	30.00	60.00
-- Regular version with W. 63rd St. address on label					
❑ BLP-4010 [M]	Walkin' and Talkin'	1959	30.00	60.00	120.00
-- "Deep groove" version (deep indentation under label on both sides)					
❑ BLP-4010 [M]	Walkin' and Talkin'	1959	20.00	40.00	80.00
-- Regular version with W. 63rd St. address on label					
❑ BLP-4010 [M]	Walkin' and Talkin'	1963	6.25	12.50	25.00
-- With "New York, USA" address on label					
❑ BST-4010 [S]	Walkin' and Talkin'	1959	20.00	40.00	80.00
-- "Deep groove" version (deep indentation under label on both sides)					
❑ BST-4010 [S]	Walkin' and Talkin'	1959	15.00	30.00	60.00
-- Regular version with W. 63rd St. address on label					
❑ BST-81587 [S]	Back on the Scene	1963	5.00	10.00	20.00
-- With "New York, USA" address on label					
❑ BST-81587 [S]	Back on the Scene	1967	3.75	7.50	15.00
-- With "A Division of Liberty Records" on label					
❑ BST-81599 [S]	Soul Stirrin'	1963	5.00	10.00	20.00
-- With "New York, USA" address on label					
❑ BST-81599 [S]	Soul Stirrin'	1967	3.75	7.50	15.00
-- With "A Division of Liberty Records" on label					
❑ BST-84010 [S]	Walkin' and Talkin'	1963	5.00	10.00	20.00
-- With "New York, USA" address on label					
❑ BST-84010 [S]	Walkin' and Talkin'	1967	3.75	7.50	15.00
-- With "A Division of Liberty Records" on label					
ENRICA					
❑ 2002 [M]	Bennie Green Swings the Blues	1960	7.50	15.00	30.00
❑ S-2002 [S]	Bennie Green Swings the Blues	1960	10.00	20.00	40.00
FANTASY					
❑ OJC-1728	Bennie Green Blows His Horn	198?	2.50	5.00	10.00
❑ OJC-1752	Walkin' Down	198?	2.50	5.00	10.00
JAZZLAND					
❑ JLP-43 [M]	Glidin' Along	1961	6.25	12.50	25.00
❑ JLP-943 [S]	Glidin' Along	1961	7.50	15.00	30.00
PRESTIGE					
❑ PRLP-210 [10]	Bennie Blows His Horn	1955	37.50	75.00	150.00
❑ PRLP-7041 [M]	Bennie Green and Art Farmer	1956	25.00	50.00	100.00
❑ PRLP-7049 [M]	Walking Down	1956	25.00	50.00	100.00
❑ PRLP-7052 [M]	Bennie Green Blows His Horn	1956	25.00	50.00	100.00
❑ PRLP-7160 [M]	Bennie Green Blows His Horn	1959	20.00	40.00	80.00
❑ PRST-7776	The Best of Bennie Green	1970	3.75	7.50	15.00
RCA VICTOR					
❑ LPM-2376 [M]	Futura	1961	6.25	12.50	25.00
❑ LSP-2376 [S]	Futura	1961	7.50	15.00	30.00
TIME					
❑ S-2021 [S]	Bennie Green	1960	12.50	25.00	50.00
❑ 52021 [M]	Bennie Green	1960	10.00	20.00	40.00
VEE JAY					
❑ LP-1005 [M]	The Swingin'est	1959	12.50	25.00	50.00
❑ SR-1005 [S]	The Swingin'est	1959	12.50	25.00	50.00
-- This LP was reissued as "Juggin' Around" by GENE AMMONS on Vee Jay 3024					
❑ VJS-1005 [S]	The Swingin'est	198?	2.50	5.00	10.00
-- Reissue on thinner vinyl					

GREEN, BENNIE/PAUL QUINICHETTE
Also see each artist's individual listings.
DECCA
Number	Title	Yr	VG	VG+	NM
❑ DL 8176 [M]	Blow Your Horn	1955	12.50	25.00	50.00

GREEN, BUNKY
Alto saxophone player (sometimes tenor) and bandleader.
ARGO
Number	Title	Yr	VG	VG+	NM
❑ LP-753 [M]	Testifyin' Time	1965	6.25	12.50	25.00
❑ LPS-753 [S]	Testifyin' Time	1965	7.50	15.00	30.00
CADET					
❑ LP-753 [M]	Testifyin' Time	1966	3.75	7.50	15.00
❑ LPS-753 [S]	Testifyin' Time	1966	5.00	10.00	20.00
❑ LP-766 [M]	Playin' for Keeps	1966	6.25	12.50	25.00
❑ LPS-766 [S]	Playin' for Keeps	1966	7.50	15.00	30.00
❑ LP-780 [M]	The Latinization of Bunky Green	1967	7.50	15.00	30.00
❑ LPS-780 [S]	The Latinization of Bunky Green	1967	6.25	12.50	25.00
VANGUARD					
❑ VSD-79387	Transformations	197?	3.00	6.00	12.00
❑ VSD-79413	Visions	1978	3.00	6.00	12.00
❑ VSD-79425	Places We've Never Been	1979	3.00	6.00	12.00

GREEN, BYRDIE
Female singer.
PRESTIGE
Number	Title	Yr	VG	VG+	NM
❑ PRLP-7503 [M]	The Golden Thrush Speaks	1967	5.00	10.00	20.00
❑ PRST-7503 [S]	The Golden Thrush Speaks	1967	3.75	7.50	15.00
❑ PRLP-7509 [M]	I Got It Bad	1967	5.00	10.00	20.00
❑ PRST-7509 [S]	I Got It Bad	1967	3.75	7.50	15.00
❑ PRST-7574	Sister Byrdie	1968	3.75	7.50	15.00

GREEN, FREDDIE
Guitarist.
RCA VICTOR
Number	Title	Yr	VG	VG+	NM
❑ LPM-1210 [M]	Mr. Rhythm	1956	12.50	25.00	50.00

GREEN, GRANT
Guitarist.
BLUE NOTE
Number	Title	Yr	VG	VG+	NM
❑ BN-LA037-G [(2)]	Live at the Lighthouse	1973	5.00	10.00	20.00
❑ LT-990	Solid	1980	3.00	6.00	12.00
❑ LT-1032	Nigeria	1980	3.00	6.00	12.00
❑ BLP-4064 [M]	Grant's First Stand	1961	20.00	40.00	80.00
-- With W. 63rd St. address on label					
❑ BLP-4064 [M]	Grant's First Stand	1963	6.25	12.50	25.00
-- With New York, USA address on label					
❑ BLP-4071 [M]	Green Street	1961	15.00	30.00	60.00
-- With W. 63rd St. address on label					
❑ BLP-4071 [M]	Green Street	1963	6.25	12.50	25.00
-- With New York, USA address on label					
❑ BLP-4086 [M]	Grant Stand	1962	15.00	30.00	60.00
-- With 61st St. address on label					
❑ BLP-4086 [M]	Grant Stand	1963	6.25	12.50	25.00
-- With New York, USA address on label					
❑ BLP-4099 [M]	Sunday Mornin'	1962	15.00	30.00	60.00
-- With 61st St. address on label					
❑ BLP-4099 [M]	Sunday Mornin'	1963	6.25	12.50	25.00
-- With New York, USA address on label					
❑ BLP-4111 [M]	The Latin Bit	1962	10.00	20.00	40.00
❑ BLP-4132 [M]	Feelin' the Spirit	1963	10.00	20.00	40.00
❑ BLP-4139 [M]	Am I Blue	1963	10.00	20.00	40.00
❑ BLP-4154 [M]	Idle Moments	1964	10.00	20.00	40.00
❑ BLP-4183 [M]	Talkin' About!	1964	10.00	20.00	40.00
❑ BLP-4202 [M]	I Want to Hold Your Hand	1964	10.00	20.00	40.00
❑ BLP-4253 [M]	Street of Dreams	1967	12.50	25.00	50.00
❑ BLP-84064 [S]	Grant's First Stand	1961	15.00	30.00	60.00
-- With W. 63rd St. address on label					
❑ BLP-84064 [S]	Grant's First Stand	1963	5.00	10.00	20.00
-- With New York, USA address on label					
❑ BLP-84064 [S]	Grant's First Stand	1968	3.00	6.00	12.00
-- With "A Division of Liberty Records" on label					
❑ BLP-84071 [S]	Green Street	1961	12.50	25.00	50.00
-- With W. 63rd St. address on label					
❑ BLP-84071 [S]	Green Street	1963	5.00	10.00	20.00
-- With New York, USA address on label					
❑ BLP-84071 [S]	Green Street	1968	3.00	6.00	12.00
-- With "A Division of Liberty Records" on label					
❑ BLP-84086 [S]	Grant Stand	1962	12.50	25.00	50.00
-- With 61st St. address on label					
❑ BLP-84086 [S]	Grant Stand	1963	5.00	10.00	20.00
-- With New York, USA address on label					
❑ BLP-84086 [S]	Grant Stand	1968	3.00	6.00	12.00
-- With "A Division of Liberty Records" on label					
❑ BLP-84099 [S]	Sunday Mornin'	1962	12.50	25.00	50.00
-- With 61st St. address on label					
❑ BLP-84099 [S]	Sunday Mornin'	1963	5.00	10.00	20.00
-- With New York, USA address on label					
❑ BLP-84099 [S]	Sunday Mornin'	1968	3.00	6.00	12.00
-- With "A Division of Liberty Records" on label					
❑ BLP-84111 [S]	The Latin Bit	1962	10.00	20.00	40.00
-- With New York, USA address on label					
❑ BLP-84111 [S]	The Latin Bit	1968	3.00	6.00	12.00
-- With "A Division of Liberty Records" on label					
❑ BLP-84132 [S]	Feelin' the Spirit	1963	10.00	20.00	40.00
-- With New York, USA address on label					
❑ BLP-84132 [S]	Feelin' the Spirit	1968	3.00	6.00	12.00
-- With "A Division of Liberty Records" on label					
❑ BLP-84139 [S]	Am I Blue	1963	10.00	20.00	40.00
-- With New York, USA address on label					
❑ BLP-84139 [S]	Am I Blue	1968	3.00	6.00	12.00
-- With "A Division of Liberty Records" on label					
❑ BLP-84154 [S]	Idle Moments	1964	10.00	20.00	40.00
-- With New York, USA address on label					
❑ BLP-84154 [S]	Idle Moments	1968	3.00	6.00	12.00
-- With "A Division of Liberty Records" on label					
❑ BLP-84183 [S]	Talkin' About!	1964	10.00	20.00	40.00
-- With New York, USA address on label					
❑ BLP-84183 [S]	Talkin' About!	1968	3.00	6.00	12.00
-- With "A Division of Liberty Records" on label					
❑ BLP-84202 [S]	I Want to Hold Your Hand	1964	10.00	20.00	40.00
-- With New York, USA address on label					
❑ BLP-84202 [S]	I Want to Hold Your Hand	1968	3.00	6.00	12.00
-- With "A Division of Liberty Records" on label					
❑ BLP-84253 [S]	Street of Dreams	1967	10.00	20.00	40.00
❑ BLP-84310	Goin' West	1969	10.00	20.00	40.00
❑ BLP-84327	Carryin' On	1969	10.00	20.00	40.00

Number	Title	Yr	VG	VG+	NM
❑ BLP-84340	Green Is Beautiful	1970	6.25	12.50	25.00
❑ BLP-84360	Alive!	1970	6.25	12.50	25.00
❑ BLP-84373	Visions	1971	5.00	10.00	20.00
❑ BLP-84413	Shades of Green	1972	5.00	10.00	20.00
❑ BLP-84432	Born to Be Blue	1985	3.00	6.00	12.00
COBBLESTONE					
❑ 9001	Iron City	1972	3.75	7.50	15.00
DELMARK					
❑ DL-404 [M]	All the Gin Is Gone	1966	6.25	12.50	25.00
❑ DS-404 [S]	All the Gin Is Gone	1966	6.25	12.50	25.00
❑ DL-427 [M]	Black Forrest	1966	6.25	12.50	25.00
❑ DS-427 [S]	Black Forrest	1966	6.25	12.50	25.00
MOSAIC					
❑ M5-133 [(5)]	The Complete Blue Note Recordings of Grant Green with Sonny Clark	199?	15.00	30.00	60.00
MUSE					
❑ MR-5014	Green Blues	1973	3.75	7.50	15.00
❑ MR-5120	Iron City	197?	3.00	6.00	12.00
VERVE					
❑ V-8627 [M]	His Majesty, King Funk	1965	7.50	15.00	30.00
❑ V6-8627 [S]	His Majesty, King Funk	1965	7.50	15.00	30.00

GREEN, PHIL
LONDON

Number	Title	Yr	VG	VG+	NM
❑ LPB-17 [10]	Rhythm on Reeds	1950	12.50	25.00	50.00

GREEN, URBIE
Trombonist. Also see THE BRASS ENSEMBLE OF THE JAZZ & CLASSICAL MUSIC SOCIETY; THE MANHATTAN JAZZ SEPTETTE.
ABC-PARAMOUNT

Number	Title	Yr	VG	VG+	NM
❑ ABC-101 [M]	Blues and Other Shades of Green	1955	15.00	30.00	60.00
❑ ABC-137 [M]	All About Urbie Green	1956	12.50	25.00	50.00
BETHLEHEM					
❑ BCP-14 [M]	East Coast Jazz, Volume 6	1955	20.00	40.00	80.00
❑ BCP-6041	The Lyrical Language of Urbie Green	197?	3.00	6.00	12.00
-- Reissue of 14, distributed by RCA Victor					
BLUE NOTE					
❑ BLP-5036 [10]	Urbie Green Septet	1954	62.50	125.00	250.00
COMMAND					
❑ RS 33-815 [M]	The Persuasive Trombone of Urbie Green	1960	3.00	6.00	12.00
❑ RS 815 SD [S]	The Persuasive Trombone of Urbie Green	1960	3.75	7.50	15.00
❑ RS 33-838 [M]	The Persuasive Trombone of Urbie Green, Volume 2	1962	3.00	6.00	12.00
❑ RS 838 SD [S]	The Persuasive Trombone of Urbie Green, Volume 2	1962	3.75	7.50	15.00
❑ RS 33-857 [M]	Urbie Green and His 6-Tet	1963	3.00	6.00	12.00
❑ RS 857 SD [S]	Urbie Green and His 6-Tet	1963	3.75	7.50	15.00
CTI					
❑ 7070	The Fox	1976	3.00	6.00	12.00
❑ 7079	Senor Blues	1977	3.00	6.00	12.00
PROJECT 3					
❑ PR 5014 SD	21 Trombones	1967	3.00	6.00	12.00
❑ PR 5024 SD	21 Trombones, Volume 2	1968	3.00	6.00	12.00
❑ PR 5052 SD	Green Power	1970	3.00	6.00	12.00
❑ PR 5066 SD	Bein' Green	1972	3.00	6.00	12.00
❑ PR 5087 SD	Big Beautiful Band	1974	2.50	5.00	10.00
RCA VICTOR					
❑ LPM-1667 [M]	Let's Face the Music and Dance	1958	10.00	20.00	40.00
❑ LSP-1667 [S]	Let's Face the Music and Dance	1958	10.00	20.00	40.00
❑ LPM-1969 [M]	Best of the New Broadway Show Hits	1959	10.00	20.00	40.00
❑ LSP-1969 [S]	Best of the New Broadway Show Hits	1959	10.00	20.00	40.00
VANGUARD					
❑ VRS-8010 [10]	Urbie Green and His Band	1954	30.00	60.00	120.00
"X"					
❑ LXA-3026 [10]	A Cool Yuletide	1954	30.00	60.00	120.00

GREEN, URBIE/VIC DICKENSON
Also see each artist's individual listings.
JAZZTONE

Number	Title	Yr	VG	VG+	NM
❑ J-1259 [M]	Urbie Green Octet/Slidin' Swing	1957	10.00	20.00	40.00

GREEN, WILLIAM
Saxophone player and flutist.
EVEREST

Number	Title	Yr	VG	VG+	NM
❑ SDBR-1213 [S]	Shades of Green	1963	5.00	10.00	20.00
❑ LPBR-5213 [M]	Shades of Green	1963	3.75	7.50	15.00

GREENE, BOB
Pianist and bandleader.
RCA VICTOR

Number	Title	Yr	VG	VG+	NM
❑ ARL1-0504	The World of Jelly Roll Morton	1974	3.00	6.00	12.00

GREENE, BURTON
Pianist.
COLUMBIA

Number	Title	Yr	VG	VG+	NM
❑ CS 9784	Presenting Burton Greene	1969	3.75	7.50	15.00
ESP-DISK'					
❑ 1024 [M]	Burton Greene	1966	6.25	12.50	25.00
❑ S-1024 [S]	Burton Greene	1966	5.00	10.00	20.00
❑ S-1074	Burton Greene Concert Tour	1968	6.25	12.50	25.00

GREENE, BURTON, AND ALAN SILVA
Silva is a pianist. Also see BURTON GREENE.
HAT HUT

Number	Title	Yr	VG	VG+	NM
❑ 15 [(2)]	Ongoing Strings	198?	3.75	7.50	15.00

GREENE, DODO
Female singer.
BLUE NOTE

Number	Title	Yr	VG	VG+	NM
❑ BLP-9001 [M]	My Hour of Need	1962	12.50	25.00	50.00
-- With W. 63rd St. address on label					
❑ BLP-9001 [M]	My Hour of Need	1963	6.25	12.50	25.00
-- With "New York, USA" address on label					
❑ BST-89001 [S]	My Hour of Need	1967	5.00	10.00	20.00
-- With "A Division of Liberty Records" on label					

GREENIDGE, ROBERT, AND MICHAEL UTLEY
Greenidge plays steel drums; Utley is a keyboard player, composer and producer. Both are also members of Jimmy Buffett's Coral Reefer Band.
MCA MASTER SERIES

Number	Title	Yr	VG	VG+	NM
❑ 5695	Mad Music	1985	2.50	5.00	10.00
❑ 6258	Heat	1989	3.00	6.00	12.00
❑ 42045	Jubilee	1987	2.50	5.00	10.00

GREENWICH, SONNY
Guitarist.
PM

Number	Title	Yr	VG	VG+	NM
❑ PMR-016	Evol-ution: Love's Opposite	1978	3.75	7.50	15.00

GREY, AL
Trombonist.
ARGO

Number	Title	Yr	VG	VG+	NM
❑ LP-653 [M]	The Last of the Big Plungers	1960	6.25	12.50	25.00
❑ LPS-653 [S]	The Last of the Big Plungers	1960	6.25	12.50	25.00
❑ LP-677 [M]	The Thinking Man's Trombone	1961	5.00	10.00	20.00
❑ LPS-677 [S]	The Thinking Man's Trombone	1961	6.25	12.50	25.00
❑ LP-689 [M]	Al Grey and the Billy Mitchell	1962	5.00	10.00	20.00
❑ LPS-689 [S]	Al Grey and the Billy Mitchell	1962	6.25	12.50	25.00
❑ LP-700 [M]	Snap Your Fingers	1962	5.00	10.00	20.00
❑ LPS-700 [S]	Snap Your Fingers	1962	6.25	12.50	25.00
❑ LP-711 [M]	Night Song	1963	5.00	10.00	20.00
❑ LPS-711 [S]	Night Song	1963	6.25	12.50	25.00
❑ LP-718 [M]	Having a Ball	1963	5.00	10.00	20.00
❑ LPS-718 [S]	Having a Ball	1963	6.25	12.50	25.00
❑ LP-731 [M]	Boss Bones	1964	5.00	10.00	20.00
❑ LPS-731 [S]	Boss Bones	1964	6.25	12.50	25.00
CLASSIC JAZZ					
❑ 118	Grey's Mood	197?	3.75	7.50	15.00
COLUMBIA					
❑ FC 38505	Struttin' and Shoutin'	1983	2.50	5.00	10.00
TANGERINE					
❑ TRC-1504 [M]	Shades of Grey	1965	3.75	7.50	15.00
❑ TRCS-1504 [S]	Shades of Grey	1965	5.00	10.00	20.00

GREY, AL, AND WILD BILL DAVIS
Also see each artist's individual listings.
CLASSIC JAZZ

Number	Title	Yr	VG	VG+	NM
❑ 103	Keybone	197?	3.75	7.50	15.00

GRICE, JANET
Bassoonist. Also has played the recorder.
OPTIMISM

Number	Title	Yr	VG	VG+	NM
❑ OP-3203	Song for Andy	1988	2.50	5.00	10.00

GRIER, JIMMY
Clarinetist, saxophone player and bandleader.
HINDSIGHT

Number	Title	Yr	VG	VG+	NM
❑ HSR-177	Jimmy Grier and His Orchestra 1935-36	198?	2.50	5.00	10.00

Number	Title	Yr	VG	VG+	NM
GRIFFIN, DELLA					
Female singer.					
DOBRE					
❑ 1009	Della Griffin Sings	1978	3.00	6.00	12.00
GRIFFIN, DICK					
Trombonist.					
STRATA-EAST					
❑ SES-19747	The Eighth Wonder	1975	5.00	10.00	20.00
GRIFFIN, JOHNNY					
Tenor saxophone player. Also see THELONIOUS MONK; WILBUR WARE.					
ARGO					
❑ LP-624 [M]	Johnny Griffin Quartet	1958	12.50	25.00	50.00
BLACK LION					
❑ 304	You Leave Me Breathless	197?	3.75	7.50	15.00
BLUE NOTE					
❑ BLP-1533 [M]	Introducing Johnny Griffin	1956	50.00	100.00	200.00
-- "Deep groove" version (deep indentation under label on both sides)					
❑ BLP-1533 [M]	Introducing Johnny Griffin	1956	37.50	75.00	150.00
-- Regular version, Lexington Ave. address on label					
❑ BLP-1533 [M]	Introducing Johnny Griffin	1957	15.00	30.00	60.00
-- With "W. 63rd St." address on label					
❑ BLP-1533 [M]	Introducing Johnny Griffin	1963	6.25	12.50	25.00
-- With "New York, USA" address on label					
❑ BLP-1559 [M]	A Blowing Session	1957	37.50	75.00	150.00
-- "Deep groove" version (deep indentation under label on both sides)					
❑ BLP-1559 [M]	A Blowing Session	1957	25.00	50.00	100.00
-- Regular version, "W. 63rd St." address on label					
❑ BLP-1559 [M]	A Blowing Session	1963	6.25	12.50	25.00
-- With "New York, USA" address on label					
❑ BLP-1580 [M]	The Congregation	1958	30.00	60.00	120.00
-- "Deep groove" version (deep indentation under label on both sides)					
❑ BLP-1580 [M]	The Congregation	1958	20.00	40.00	80.00
-- Regular version, "W. 63rd St." address on label					
❑ BLP-1580 [M]	The Congregation	1963	6.25	12.50	25.00
-- With "New York, USA" address on label					
❑ BST-1580 [S]	The Congregation	1959	20.00	40.00	80.00
-- "Deep groove" version (deep indentation under label on both sides)					
❑ BST-1580 [S]	The Congregation	1959	15.00	30.00	60.00
-- Regular version, "W. 63rd St." address on label					
❑ BST-1580 [S]	The Congregation	1963	5.00	10.00	20.00
-- With "New York, USA" address on label					
❑ BT-46536	Introducing Johnny Griffin	198?	2.50	5.00	10.00
-- Another "The Finest in Jazz Since 1939" reissue					
❑ BST-81580 [S]	The Congregation	1967	3.75	7.50	15.00
-- With "A Division of Liberty Records" on label					
❑ BST-85133	Introducing Johnny Griffin	1985	2.50	5.00	10.00
-- "The Finest in Jazz Since 1939" reissue					
❑ B1-89383	The Congregation	1994	3.75	7.50	15.00
-- "The Finest in Jazz Since 1939" reissue					
EMARCY					
❑ MG-26001 [M]	Night Lady	1967	10.00	20.00	40.00
❑ SR-66001 [S]	Night Lady	1967	6.25	12.50	25.00
FANTASY					
❑ OJC-136	The Little Giant	198?	2.50	5.00	10.00
❑ OJC-485	The Big Soul-Band	1990	3.00	6.00	12.00
GALAXY					
❑ 5117	Return of the Griffin	1979	3.00	6.00	12.00
❑ 5126	Bush Dance	1979	3.00	6.00	12.00
❑ 5132	NYC Underground	1980	3.00	6.00	12.00
❑ 5139	To the Ladies	1981	3.00	6.00	12.00
❑ 5146	Call It Whatchawaana	1984	3.00	6.00	12.00
INNER CITY					
❑ IC-2004	Blues for Harvey	1973	3.75	7.50	15.00
❑ IC-6042 [(2)]	Live Tokyo	197?	5.00	10.00	20.00
JAZZLAND					
❑ JLP-93 [M]	The Little Giant	1961	10.00	20.00	40.00
❑ JLP-993 [S]	The Little Giant	1961	7.50	15.00	30.00
MILESTONE					
❑ 47014 [(2)]	Big Soul	197?	5.00	10.00	20.00
❑ 47054 [(2)]	Little Giant	197?	3.75	7.50	15.00
MOON					
❑ MLP-004	Body and Soul	1992	3.75	7.50	15.00
RIVERSIDE					
❑ RLP 12-264 [M]	Johnny Griffin Sextet	1958	12.50	25.00	50.00
❑ RLP 12-274 [M]	Way Out!	1958	12.50	25.00	50.00
❑ RLP 12-304 [M]	The Little Giant	1959	12.50	25.00	50.00
❑ RLP 12-331 [M]	The Big Soul-Band	1960	10.00	20.00	40.00
❑ RLP-338 [M]	Studio Jazz Party	1960	10.00	20.00	40.00
❑ RLP-368 [M]	Change of Pace	1961	7.50	15.00	30.00
❑ RLP-387 [M]	White Gardenia	1961	7.50	15.00	30.00
❑ RLP-420 [M]	The Kerry Dancers	1962	6.25	12.50	25.00
❑ RLP-437 [M]	Grab This!	1962	6.25	12.50	25.00
❑ RLP-462 [M]	Do Nothing 'Til You Hear from Me	1963	6.25	12.50	25.00
❑ RLP-479 [M]	Wade in the Water	1964	5.00	10.00	20.00
❑ RLP-1149 [S]	The Little Giant	1959	10.00	20.00	40.00
❑ RLP-1171 [S]	The Big Soul-Band	1960	7.50	15.00	30.00
❑ 6145	Studio Jazz Party	198?	3.00	6.00	12.00
❑ RS-9338 [S]	Studio Jazz Party	1960	7.50	15.00	30.00
❑ RS-9368 [S]	Change of Pace	1961	7.50	15.00	30.00
❑ RS-9387 [S]	White Gardenia	1961	7.50	15.00	30.00
❑ RS-9420 [S]	The Kerry Dancers	1962	7.50	15.00	30.00
❑ RS-9437 [S]	Grab This!	1962	7.50	15.00	30.00
❑ RS-9462 [S]	Do Nothing 'Til You Hear from Me	1963	7.50	15.00	30.00
❑ RS-9479 [S]	Wade in the Water	1964	6.25	12.50	25.00
STEEPLECHASE					
❑ SCS-1004	Blues for Harvey	198?	3.00	6.00	12.00
TIMELESS					
❑ LPSJP-121	The Jamfs Are Coming	1990	2.50	5.00	10.00
-- Reissue of 311					
❑ 311	The Jamfs Are Coming	198?	3.00	6.00	12.00
GRIFFIN, JOHNNY, AND MATTHEW GEE					
Also see each artist's individual listings.					
ATLANTIC					
❑ 1431 [M]	Soul Groove	1965	5.00	10.00	20.00
❑ SD 1431 [S]	Soul Groove	1965	6.25	12.50	25.00
GRIFFITH, JOHNNY					
Keyboard player; a member of the Motown studio band.					
WORKSHOP JAZZ					
❑ WSJ 205 [M]	Jazz	1963	50.00	100.00	200.00
GRIMES, HENRY					
Bass player.					
ESP-DISK'					
❑ 1027 [M]	Henry Grimes Trio	1966	5.00	10.00	20.00
❑ S-1027 [S]	Henry Grimes Trio	1966	6.25	12.50	25.00
GRIMES, TINY					
Guitarist (four- and six-string) and male singer. Also see KENNY BURRELL; THE PRESTIGE BLUES SWINGERS.					
CLASSIC JAZZ					
❑ 114	Some Groovy Fours	197?	3.00	6.00	12.00
COLLECTABLES					
❑ COL-5304	Tiny Grimes Featuring Screamin' Jay Hawkins	198?	2.50	5.00	10.00
❑ COL-5317	Tiny Grimes and His Rocking Highlanders, Volume 2	198?	2.50	5.00	10.00
❑ COL-5321	Tiny Grimes and Friends	198?	2.50	5.00	10.00
FANTASY					
❑ OJC-191	Callin' the Blues	1985	2.50	5.00	10.00
MUSE					
❑ MR-5012	Profoundly Blue	1974	3.00	6.00	12.00
PRESTIGE					
❑ PRLP-7138 [M]	Blues Grooves	1958	25.00	50.00	100.00
❑ PRLP-7144 [M]	Callin' the Blues	1958	25.00	50.00	100.00
SWINGVILLE					
❑ SVLP-2002 [M]	Tiny in Swingville	1960	12.50	25.00	50.00
-- Purple label					
❑ SVLP-2002 [M]	Tiny in Swingville	1965	6.25	12.50	25.00
-- Blue label, trident logo at right					
❑ SVLP-2004 [M]	Callin' the Blues	1960	12.50	25.00	50.00
-- Purple label					
❑ SVLP-2004 [M]	Callin' the Blues	1965	6.25	12.50	25.00
-- Blue label, trident logo at right					
UNITED ARTISTS					
❑ UAL-3232 [M]	Big Time Guitar	1962	6.25	12.50	25.00
❑ UAS-6232 [S]	Big Time Guitar	1962	7.50	15.00	30.00
GRISMAN, DAVID					
Mandolin player. Also see STEPHANE GRAPPELLI.					
HORIZON					
❑ SP-731	Hot Dawg	1979	3.00	6.00	12.00
KALEIDOSCOPE					
❑ 5	David Grisman Quintet	1977	5.00	10.00	20.00
ROUNDER					
❑ 0069	The Rounder Album	1976	3.00	6.00	12.00
❑ 0169	Here Today	198?	2.50	5.00	10.00
❑ 0190	Acoustic Christmas	1983	3.00	6.00	12.00
❑ 0251/2 [(2)]	Home Is Where the Heart Is	1988	3.00	6.00	12.00

Number	Title	Yr	VG	VG+	NM

SUGAR HILL
| ❏ SH-3713 | Early Dawg | 198? | 2.50 | 5.00 | 10.00 |

WARNER BROS.
❏ BSK 3469	David Grisman Quintet '80	1980	2.50	5.00	10.00
❏ BSK 3618	Mondo Mando	1982	2.50	5.00	10.00
❏ 23804	Dawg Jazz	1983	2.50	5.00	10.00

ZEBRA/ACOUSTIC
| ❏ ZEA-6153 | Acousticity | 1986 | 2.50 | 5.00 | 10.00 |

GRISSOM, JIMMY
Male singer.

ARGO
| ❏ LP-729 [M] | World of Trouble | 1963 | 6.25 | 12.50 | 25.00 |
| ❏ LPS-729 [S] | World of Trouble | 1963 | 7.50 | 15.00 | 30.00 |

GROLNICK, DON, AND MICHAEL BRECKER
Grolnick was a pianist, producer and composer. Also see MICHAEL BRECKER.

HIP POCKET
| ❏ HP-0106 | Hearts and Numbers | 1985 | 2.50 | 5.00 | 10.00 |

GROOVE COLLECTIVE
Members: Gordon Clay aka Nappy G (timbales, vocals); Jay Rodriguez (saxophone, flute, vocals); Genji Siriasi (drums); Richard Worth (flute, vocals); Christopher Theberge (percussion); Jonathan Maron (guitar); William Ware III (vibes); David Jenson (tenor sax); Josh Roseman (trombone); Fabio Morgera (trumpet).

REPRISE
| ❏ 45541 [(2)] | Groove Collective | 1994 | 5.00 | 10.00 | 20.00 |

GROOVE, MAX
Pianist and keyboard player.

OPTIMISM
| ❏ OP-3108 | Center of Gravity | 198? | 2.50 | 5.00 | 10.00 |

GROSSMAN, STEVE
Soprano and tenor saxophone player.

ATLANTIC
| ❏ SD 19230 | Perspective | 1979 | 2.50 | 5.00 | 10.00 |

PM
| ❏ PMR-002 | Some Shapes to Come | 1974 | 3.00 | 6.00 | 12.00 |
| ❏ PMR-012 | Terra Firma | 1977 | 3.00 | 6.00 | 12.00 |

RED
| ❏ VPA 176 | Way Out East | 1985 | 3.00 | 6.00 | 12.00 |
| ❏ VPA 189 | Love Is the Thing | 1986 | 3.00 | 6.00 | 12.00 |

GROSZ, MARTY
Guitarist.

RIVERSIDE
| ❏ RLP 12-268 [M] | Hurrah for Bix | 1958 | 10.00 | 20.00 | 40.00 |
| ❏ RLP-1109 [S] | Hurrah for Bix | 1959 | 7.50 | 15.00 | 30.00 |

STOMP OFF
| ❏ SOS-1158 | Marty Grosz and the Keepers of the Flame | 1988 | 2.50 | 5.00 | 10.00 |
| ❏ SOS-1214 | Unsaturated Fats | 1991 | 2.50 | 5.00 | 10.00 |

GROUP, THE
Vocal group: Larry Benson, Anne Gable, Tom Kampman.

RCA VICTOR
| ❏ LPM-2663 [M] | The Group | 1963 | 5.00 | 10.00 | 20.00 |
| ❏ LSP-2663 [S] | The Group | 1963 | 6.25 | 12.50 | 25.00 |

GROVE, DICK
Pianist, arranger and composer.

PACIFIC JAZZ
| ❏ PJ-74 [M] | Little Bird Suite | 1963 | 5.00 | 10.00 | 20.00 |
| ❏ ST-74 [S] | Little Bird Suite | 1963 | 6.25 | 12.50 | 25.00 |

GRUNING, TOM

INNER CITY
| ❏ IC-1119 | Midnight Lullaby | 198? | 3.00 | 6.00 | 12.00 |

GRUNTZ, GEORGE
Pianist, composer and bandleader.

PHILIPS
| ❏ PHM 200-162 [M] | Bach Humbug | 1964 | 3.75 | 7.50 | 15.00 |
| ❏ PHS 600-162 [S] | Bach Humbug | 1964 | 5.00 | 10.00 | 20.00 |

GRUSIN, DAVE
Pianist, composer and arranger also known for his many film and television scores, not included below.

COLUMBIA
| ❏ CL 2344 [M] | Kaleidoscope | 1965 | 5.00 | 10.00 | 20.00 |
| ❏ CS 9144 [S] | Kaleidoscope | 1965 | 6.25 | 12.50 | 25.00 |

EPIC
❏ BN 622 [S]	Subways Are for Sleeping	1962	6.25	12.50	25.00
❏ LN 3829 [M]	Subways Are for Sleeping	1962	5.00	10.00	20.00
❏ LN 24023 [M]	Piano Strings and Moonlight	1962	6.25	12.50	25.00
❏ BN 26023 [S]	Piano Strings and Moonlight	1962	7.50	15.00	30.00

GRP
❏ GR-1001	Dave Grusin and the NY/LA Dream Band	198?	2.50	5.00	10.00
❏ GR-1006	Night-Lines	198?	2.50	5.00	10.00
❏ GR-1011	One of a Kind	198?	2.50	5.00	10.00
❏ GR-1018	Mountain Dance	198?	2.00	4.00	8.00
-- Another reissue of GRP/Arista 5010					
❏ GR-1037	Cinemagic	1987	2.50	5.00	10.00
❏ GR-1051	Sticks and Stones	1988	2.50	5.00	10.00
❏ GR-9579	The Dave Grusin Collection	1989	3.00	6.00	12.00
❏ GR-9592	Migration	1989	3.00	6.00	12.00

GRP/ARISTA
❏ GL 5010	Mountain Dance	1980	2.50	5.00	10.00
❏ GL 5506	Live in Japan	1981	2.50	5.00	10.00
❏ GL 5510	Out of the Shadows	1982	2.50	5.00	10.00
❏ GL8-8058	Mountain Dance	198?	2.00	4.00	8.00
-- Budget-line reissue					
❏ GL8-8139	Out of the Shadows	198?	2.00	4.00	8.00
-- Budget-line reissue					

POLYDOR
| ❏ PD-1-6118 | One of a Kind | 1977 | 3.75 | 7.50 | 15.00 |

SHEFFIELD LABS
| ❏ 5 | Discovered Again! | 1976 | 6.25 | 12.50 | 25.00 |
| -- Direct-to-disc recording | | | | | |

SHEFFIELD TREASURY
| ❏ ST-500 | Discovered Again! | 198? | 5.00 | 10.00 | 20.00 |
| -- Reissue of Sheffield Labs 5 | | | | | |

GRUSIN, DAVE, AND LEE RITENOUR
Also see each artist's individual listings.

GRP
| ❏ GRPA-1015 | Harlequin | 1985 | 2.50 | 5.00 | 10.00 |

GRYCE, GIGI
Alto saxophone player and flutist. Also see ART FARMER.

BLUE NOTE
❏ BLP-5049 [10]	Gigi Gryce's Jazztime Paris	1954	75.00	150.00	300.00
❏ BLP-5050 [10]	Gigi Gryce and His Little Band, Volume 2	1954	75.00	150.00	300.00
❏ BLP-5051 [10]	Gigi Gryce Quintet/Sextet, Volume	1954	75.00	150.00	300.00

FANTASY
| ❏ OJC-081 | The Rat Race Blues | 198? | 2.50 | 5.00 | 10.00 |

MERCURY
| ❏ MG-20628 [M] | Reminiscin' | 1961 | 7.50 | 15.00 | 30.00 |
| ❏ SR-60628 [S] | Reminiscin' | 1961 | 10.00 | 20.00 | 40.00 |

METROJAZZ
| ❏ E-1006 [M] | Gigi Gryce | 1958 | 20.00 | 40.00 | 80.00 |
| ❏ SE-1006 [S] | Gigi Gryce | 1959 | 15.00 | 30.00 | 60.00 |

NEW JAZZ
❏ NJLP-8230 [M]	Sayin' Somethin'!	1959	12.50	25.00	50.00
-- Purple label					
❏ NJLP-8230 [M]	Sayin' Somethin'!	1965	6.25	12.50	25.00
-- Blue label, trident logo at right					
❏ NJLP-8246 [M]	The Hap'nin's	1960	12.50	25.00	50.00
-- Purple label					
❏ NJLP-8246 [M]	The Hap'nin's	1965	6.25	12.50	25.00
-- Blue label, trident logo at right					
❏ NJLP-8262 [M]	The Rat Race Blues	1961	12.50	25.00	50.00
-- Purple label					
❏ NJLP-8262 [M]	The Rat Race Blues	1965	6.25	12.50	25.00
-- Blue label, trident logo at right					

SAVOY
| ❏ MG-12137 [M] | Nica's Tempo | 1958 | 20.00 | 40.00 | 80.00 |

SIGNAL
| ❏ S-1201 [M] | Gigi Gryce Quartet | 1955 | 75.00 | 150.00 | 300.00 |

GRYCE, GIGI, AND CLIFFORD BROWN
Also see each artist's individual listings.

BLUE NOTE
| ❏ BLP-5048 [10] | Gigi Gryce-Clifford Brown Sextet | 1954 | 100.00 | 200.00 | 400.00 |

Number	Title	Yr	VG	VG+	NM

GRYCE, GIGI, AND DONALD BYRD
See THE JAZZ LAB.

GUARALDI, VINCE
Pianist and composer. Best known for his music for the early "Peanuts" TV specials and for the hit tune "Cast Your Fate to the Wind."
FANTASY

Number	Title	Yr	VG	VG+	NM
❑ OJC-149	Vince Guaraldi Trio	198?	2.50	5.00	10.00
-- Reissue of 3225					
❑ OJC-235	A Flower Is a Lovesome Thing	198?	2.50	5.00	10.00
-- Reissue of 3257					
❑ OJC-272	Modern Music from San Francisco	1987	2.50	5.00	10.00
-- Reissue of 3213					
❑ OJC-287	Jazz Impressions	1987	2.50	5.00	10.00
-- Reissue of 8359					
❑ OJC-289	Live at the El Matador	1987	2.50	5.00	10.00
-- Reissue of 8371					
❑ OJC-437	Jazz Impressions of Black Orpheus (Cast Your Fate to the Wind)	198?	2.50	5.00	10.00
-- Reissue of 8089					
❑ 3213 [M]	Modern Music from San Francisco	1956	12.50	25.00	50.00
-- Red vinyl					
❑ 3213 [M]	Modern Music from San Francisco	195?	6.25	12.50	25.00
-- Black vinyl, red label, non-flexible vinyl					
❑ 3225 [M]	Vince Guaraldi Trio	1956	12.50	25.00	50.00
-- Red vinyl					
❑ 3225 [M]	Vince Guaraldi Trio	195?	6.25	12.50	25.00
-- Black vinyl, red label, non-flexible vinyl					
❑ 3225 [M]	Vince Guaraldi Trio	196?	3.75	7.50	15.00
-- Black vinyl, red label, flexible vinyl					
❑ 3257 [M]	A Flower Is a Lovesome Thing	1958	10.00	20.00	40.00
-- Red vinyl					
❑ 3257 [M]	A Flower Is a Lovesome Thing	195?	6.25	12.50	25.00
-- Black vinyl, red label, non-flexible vinyl					
❑ 3257 [M]	A Flower Is a Lovesome Thing	196?	3.75	7.50	15.00
-- Black vinyl, red label, flexible vinyl					
❑ 3337 [M]	Jazz Impressions of Black Orpheus (Cast Your Fate to the Wind)	1962	10.00	20.00	40.00
-- Red vinyl					
❑ 3337 [M]	Jazz Impressions of Black Orpheus (Cast Your Fate to the Wind)	1962	3.75	7.50	15.00
-- Black vinyl, red label, flexible vinyl					
❑ 3337 [M]	Jazz Impressions of Black Orpheus (Cast Your Fate to the Wind)	1962	6.25	12.50	25.00
-- Black vinyl, red label, non-flexible vinyl					
❑ 3352 [M]	Vince Guaraldi in Person	1963	6.25	12.50	25.00
❑ 3356 [M]	Vince Guaraldi and Bola Sete and Friends	1964	6.25	12.50	25.00
❑ 3358 [M]	Tour de Force	1964	6.25	12.50	25.00
❑ 3359 [M]	Jazz Impressions	1965	6.25	12.50	25.00
❑ 3360 [M]	The Latin Side of Vince Guaraldi	1965	6.25	12.50	25.00
❑ 3362 [M]	From All Sides	1966	5.00	10.00	20.00
❑ 3367 [M]	Vince Guaraldi at Grace Cathedral	1967	5.00	10.00	20.00
❑ 3371 [M]	Live at the El Matador	1967	5.00	10.00	20.00
❑ MPF-4505	Vince Guaraldi's Greatest Hits	1981	3.00	6.00	12.00
❑ 5019	A Charlie Brown Christmas	1964	7.50	15.00	30.00
❑ 8089 [S]	Jazz Impressions of Black Orpheus (Cast Your Fate to the Wind)	1962	10.00	20.00	40.00
-- Blue vinyl					
❑ 8089 [S]	Jazz Impressions of Black Orpheus (Cast Your Fate to the Wind)	1962	6.25	12.50	25.00
-- Black vinyl, blue label, non-flexible vinyl					
❑ 8089 [S]	Jazz Impressions of Black Orpheus (Cast Your Fate to the Wind)	1962	3.75	7.50	15.00
-- Black vinyl, blue label, flexible vinyl					
❑ 8352 [S]	Vince Guaraldi in Person	1963	6.25	12.50	25.00
❑ 8356 [S]	Vince Guaraldi and Bola Sete and Friends	1964	6.25	12.50	25.00
❑ 8358 [S]	Tour de Force	1964	6.25	12.50	25.00
❑ 8359 [S]	Jazz Impressions	1965	6.25	12.50	25.00
❑ 8360 [S]	The Latin Side of Vince Guaraldi	1965	6.25	12.50	25.00
❑ 8362 [S]	From All Sides	1966	5.00	10.00	20.00
❑ 8367 [S]	Vince Guaraldi at Grace Cathedral	1967	5.00	10.00	20.00
❑ 8371 [S]	Live at the El Matador	1967	5.00	10.00	20.00
❑ 8377	Live-Live-Live	1968	5.00	10.00	20.00
❑ 8430	A Boy Named Charlie Brown -- Jazz Impressions	1971	5.00	10.00	20.00
-- Reissue of 85017					
❑ 8431	A Charlie Brown Christmas	1971	6.25	12.50	25.00
-- Reissue of 85019; dark blue label					
❑ 8431	A Charlie Brown Christmas	1988	3.75	7.50	15.00
-- Remastered version with "1988" on back cover. Lighter blue label. Also has a bonus track.					
❑ 85017	A Boy Named Charlie Brown -- Jazz Impressions	196?	6.25	12.50	25.00
❑ 85019 [S]	A Charlie Brown Christmas	1964	10.00	20.00	40.00

MOBILE FIDELITY
Number	Title	Yr	VG	VG+	NM
❑ 1-112	Jazz Impressions of Black Orpheus (Cast Your Fate to the Wind)	1983	12.50	25.00	50.00
-- Audiophile vinyl					

WARNER BROS.
Number	Title	Yr	VG	VG+	NM
❑ WS 1747	Oh Good Grief!	1968	5.00	10.00	20.00
❑ WS 1775	Eclectic	1969	3.75	7.50	15.00
❑ WS 1828	Alma-Ville	1970	3.75	7.50	15.00

GUARALDI, VINCE/CONTE CANDOLI
Also see each artist's individual listings.
CROWN
Number	Title	Yr	VG	VG+	NM
❑ CLP-5417 [M]	Vince Guaraldi and the Conte Candoli All Stars	1963	3.00	6.00	12.00
❑ CST-417 [R]	Vince Guaraldi and the Conte Candoli All Stars	1963	2.50	5.00	10.00

PREMIER
Number	Title	Yr	VG	VG+	NM
❑ PM-2009 [M]	Vince Guaraldi-Conte Candoli Quartet	1963	3.00	6.00	12.00
❑ PS-2009 [R]	Vince Guaraldi-Conte Candoli Quartet	1963	2.50	5.00	10.00

GUARALDI, VINCE/FRANK ROSOLINO
Also see each artist's individual listings.
PREMIER
Number	Title	Yr	VG	VG+	NM
❑ PM-2014 [M]	Vince Guaraldi-Frank Rosolino Quintet	1963	3.00	6.00	12.00
❑ PS-2014 [R]	Vince Guaraldi-Frank Rosolino Quintet	1963	2.50	5.00	10.00

GUARNIERI, JOHNNY
Pianist and composer. Also see BERNIE LEIGHTON.
CLASSIC JAZZ
Number	Title	Yr	VG	VG+	NM
❑ 105	Gliss Me Again	197?	3.00	6.00	12.00

CORAL
Number	Title	Yr	VG	VG+	NM
❑ CRL 57085 [M]	Songs of Hudson and DeLange	1957	10.00	20.00	40.00
❑ CRL 57086 [M]	The Duke Again	1957	10.00	20.00	40.00

DOBRE
Number	Title	Yr	VG	VG+	NM
❑ 1017	Johnny Guarnieri Plays Walter Donaldson	197?	3.00	6.00	12.00

DOT
Number	Title	Yr	VG	VG+	NM
❑ DLP-3647 [M]	Piano Dimensions	1965	3.00	6.00	12.00
❑ DLP-25647 [S]	Piano Dimensions	1965	3.75	7.50	15.00

GOLDEN CREST
Number	Title	Yr	VG	VG+	NM
❑ GC-3020 [M]	Johnny Guarnieri Plays Johnny Guarnieri	1958	10.00	20.00	40.00

JIM TAYLOR PRESENTS
Number	Title	Yr	VG	VG+	NM
❑ 102	Johnny Guarnieri Plays Harry Warren	197?	3.00	6.00	12.00

RCA CAMDEN
Number	Title	Yr	VG	VG+	NM
❑ CAL-345 [M]	Cheerful Little Earful	1958	3.75	7.50	15.00
❑ CAL-391 [M]	Side by Side	1958	3.75	7.50	15.00

ROYALE
Number	Title	Yr	VG	VG+	NM
❑ 1296 [M]	An Hour of Modern Music	1952	10.00	20.00	40.00
❑ VLP 6047 [10]	Johnny Guarnieri/Tony Mottola/Bob Haggart/Cozy Cole	195?	12.50	25.00	50.00

SAVOY
Number	Title	Yr	VG	VG+	NM
❑ MG-15007 [10]	Hot Piano	1951	20.00	40.00	80.00

SOUNDS GREAT
Number	Title	Yr	VG	VG+	NM
❑ SG-5001	Echoes of Ellington	198?	2.50	5.00	10.00

TAZ-JAZ
Number	Title	Yr	VG	VG+	NM
❑ 1001	Superstride	1976	3.00	6.00	12.00
❑ 1002	Stealin' Apples	1977	3.00	6.00	12.00

GUESNON, GEORGE
Guitarist, banjo player and male singer.
JAZZ CRUSADE
Number	Title	Yr	VG	VG+	NM
❑ 2011	Echoes from New Orleans	196?	3.75	7.50	15.00

JAZZOLOGY
Number	Title	Yr	VG	VG+	NM
❑ JCE-11	Creole Blues	1967	3.75	7.50	15.00

GULDA, FRIEDRICH
Pianist also known for his straight classical work.
COLUMBIA
Number	Title	Yr	VG	VG+	NM
❑ CL 2251 [M]	From Vienna with Jazz	1964	3.00	6.00	12.00
❑ CL 2346 [M]	The Ineffable Friedrich Gulda	1965	3.00	6.00	12.00
❑ CS 9051 [S]	From Vienna with Jazz	1964	3.75	7.50	15.00
❑ CS 9146 [S]	The Ineffable Friedrich Gulda	1965	3.75	7.50	15.00

Number	Title	Yr	VG	VG+	NM

RCA VICTOR

❏ LPM-1355 [M]	Friedrich Gulda at Birdland	1957	12.50	25.00	50.00

GULLIN, LARS
Baritone saxophone player. Also see ARNE DOMNERUS; BENGT HALLBERG.
ATLANTIC

❏ 1246 [M]	Baritone Sax	1956	30.00	60.00	120.00
-- Black label					
❏ 1246 [M]	Baritone Sax	1960	12.50	25.00	50.00
-- Multicolor label, white "fan" logo at right					

CONTEMPORARY

❏ C-2505 [10]	Modern Sounds	1953	62.50	125.00	250.00

EASTWEST

❏ 4003 [M]	Lars Gullin Swings	196?	10.00	20.00	40.00

EMARCY

❏ MG-26041 [10]	Lars Gullin Quartet	1954	50.00	100.00	200.00
❏ MG-26044 [10]	Gullin's Garden	1954	50.00	100.00	200.00
❏ MG-36012 [M]	Lars Gullin	1955	30.00	60.00	120.00
❏ MG-36059 [M]	Lars Gullin with the Moretone Singers	1955	30.00	60.00	120.00

PRESTIGE

❏ PRLP-144 [10]	New Sounds from Sweden, Volume 5	1953	50.00	100.00	200.00
❏ PRLP-151 [10]	New Sounds from Sweden, Volume 7	1953	50.00	100.00	200.00

GULLY LOW JAZZ BAND
Led by David Ostwald.
GHB

❏ GHB-163	In Dreamland	1984	2.50	5.00	10.00

GUMBS, ONAJE ALLAN
Pianist.
STEEPLECHASE

❏ SCS-1069	Onaje	198?	3.00	6.00	12.00

ZEBRA/MCA

❏ ZEB-42120	That Special Part of Me	1988	2.50	5.00	10.00

GURU
Jazz-influenced rapper, one-half of GANG STARR.
CHRYSALIS

❏ F1-21998	Jazzmatazz Vol. 1	1993	5.00	10.00	20.00
❏ F1-34290 [(2)]	Jazzmatazz Vol. 2: The New Reality	1995	3.75	7.50	15.00

GUSTAFSSON, RUNE
Guitarist.
ATLANTIC

❏ SD 8234	Rune at the Top	1969	3.00	6.00	12.00

GNP CRESCENDO

❏ GNPS-2118	Move	1976	2.50	5.00	10.00

PABLO TODAY

❏ 2312 106	The Sweetest Sounds	1979	3.00	6.00	12.00

GWALTNEY, TOMMY
Clarinetist and alto saxophone player.
RIVERSIDE

❏ RLP-353 [M]	Goin' to Kansas City	1960	7.50	15.00	30.00
❏ RS-9353 [S]	Goin' to Kansas City	1960	10.00	20.00	40.00

Number	Title	Yr	VG	VG+	NM

H

HACKETT, BOBBY
Cornet player, trumpeter and guitarist. Also see JACK TEAGARDEN.

BRUNSWICK
Number	Title	Yr	VG	VG+	NM
❏ BL 56014 [10]	Trumpet Solos	1950	12.50	25.00	50.00

CAPITOL
Number	Title	Yr	VG	VG+	NM
❏ H 458 [10]	Soft Lights	1954	12.50	25.00	50.00
❏ T 458 [M]	Soft Lights	1955	10.00	20.00	40.00
-- Turquoise or gray label					
❏ T 458 [M]	Soft Lights	1958	6.25	12.50	25.00
-- Black colorband label, logo at left					
❏ T 575 [M]	In a Mellow Mood	1955	10.00	20.00	40.00
-- Turquoise or gray label					
❏ T 575 [M]	In a Mellow Mood	1958	6.25	12.50	25.00
-- Black colorband label, logo at left					
❏ T 692 [M]	Coast Concert	1956	10.00	20.00	40.00
-- Turquoise or gray label					
❏ T 692 [M]	Coast Concert	1958	6.25	12.50	25.00
-- Black colorband label, logo at left					
❏ T 719 [M]	Rendezvous	1956	10.00	20.00	40.00
-- Turquoise or gray label					
❏ T 719 [M]	Rendezvous	1958	6.25	12.50	25.00
-- Black colorband label, logo at left					
❏ T 857 [M]	Gotham Jazz Scene	1957	10.00	20.00	40.00
-- Turquoise or gray label					
❏ T 857 [M]	Gotham Jazz Scene	1958	6.25	12.50	25.00
-- Black colorband label, logo at left					
❏ SM-933	Jazz Ultimate	1976	2.50	5.00	10.00
-- Reissue with new prefix					
❏ ST 933 [S]	Jazz Ultimate	1959	7.50	15.00	30.00
-- Black colorband label, logo at left					
❏ T 933 [M]	Jazz Ultimate	1958	10.00	20.00	40.00
-- Turquoise or gray label					
❏ T 933 [M]	Jazz Ultimate	1958	6.25	12.50	25.00
-- Black colorband label, logo at left					
❏ T 1002 [M]	Don't Take Your Love from Me	1958	10.00	20.00	40.00
-- Turquoise or gray label					
❏ T 1002 [M]	Don't Take Your Love from Me	1958	6.25	12.50	25.00
-- Black colorband label, logo at left					
❏ ST 1077 [S]	Bobby Hackett at the Embers	1958	7.50	15.00	30.00
❏ T 1077 [M]	Bobby Hackett at the Embers	1958	6.25	12.50	25.00
❏ ST 1172 [S]	Blues with a Kick	1959	7.50	15.00	30.00
❏ T 1172 [M]	Blues with a Kick	1959	6.25	12.50	25.00
❏ ST 1235 [S]	Bobby Hackett Quartet	1959	7.50	15.00	30.00
❏ T 1235 [M]	Bobby Hackett Quartet	1959	6.25	12.50	25.00
❏ ST 1413 [S]	Easy Beat	1960	6.25	12.50	25.00
❏ T 1413 [M]	Easy Beat	1960	5.00	10.00	20.00

CHIAROSCURO
Number	Title	Yr	VG	VG+	NM
❏ 105	Live at Roosevelt Grill	1972	3.00	6.00	12.00
❏ 138	Live at Roosevelt Grill, Volume 2	197?	3.00	6.00	12.00
❏ 161	Live at Roosevelt Grill, Volume 3	197?	3.00	6.00	12.00

COLUMBIA
Number	Title	Yr	VG	VG+	NM
❏ CL 1602 [M]	Dream Awhile	1961	5.00	10.00	20.00
❏ CL 1729 [M]	The Most Beautiful Horn in the World	1962	5.00	10.00	20.00
❏ CL 1895 [M]	Night Love	1962	3.75	7.50	15.00
❏ CL 2566 [10]	The Bobby Hackett Horn	1955	12.50	25.00	50.00
❏ CL 6156 [10]	Jazz Session	1951	12.50	25.00	50.00
❏ CS 8402 [S]	Dream Awhile	1961	6.25	12.50	25.00
❏ CS 8529 [S]	The Most Beautiful Horn in the World	1962	6.25	12.50	25.00
❏ CS 8695 [S]	Night Love	1962	5.00	10.00	20.00

COMMODORE
Number	Title	Yr	VG	VG+	NM
❏ FL-20016 [10]	Horn A Plenty	1951	12.50	25.00	50.00

DOBRE
Number	Title	Yr	VG	VG+	NM
❏ 1004	Thanks Bobby	197?	2.50	5.00	10.00

ENCORE
Number	Title	Yr	VG	VG+	NM
❏ EE 22003 [M]	The Bobby Hackett Horn	1968	3.00	6.00	12.00

EPIC
Number	Title	Yr	VG	VG+	NM
❏ LN 3106 [M]	The Hackett Horn	1956	10.00	20.00	40.00
❏ FLM 13107 [M]	The Swingin'est Gals in Town	196?	3.75	7.50	15.00
❏ FLS 15107 [S]	The Swingin'est Gals in Town	196?	5.00	10.00	20.00
❏ LA 16037 [M]	Oliver!	1963	3.00	6.00	12.00
❏ BA 17037 [S]	Oliver!	1963	3.75	7.50	15.00
❏ LN 24061 [M]	The Music of Mancini	1963	3.00	6.00	12.00
❏ LN 24080 [M]	The Music of Bert Kaempfert	1964	3.00	6.00	12.00
❏ LN 24099 [M]	Hello, Louis!	1964	3.00	6.00	12.00
❏ LN 24155 [M]	The Trumpet's Greatest Hits	1965	3.00	6.00	12.00
❏ LN 24174 [M]	A String of Pearls	1966	3.00	6.00	12.00
❏ LN 24220 [M]	Tony Bennett's Greatest Hits	1966	3.00	6.00	12.00
❏ BN 26061 [S]	The Music of Mancini	1963	3.75	7.50	15.00
❏ BN 26080 [S]	The Music of Bert Kaempfert	1964	3.75	7.50	15.00
❏ BN 26099 [S]	Hello, Louis!	1964	3.75	7.50	15.00
❏ BN 26155 [S]	The Trumpet's Greatest Hits	1965	3.75	7.50	15.00
❏ BN 26174 [S]	A String of Pearls	1966	3.75	7.50	15.00
❏ BN 26220 [S]	Tony Bennett's Greatest Hits	1966	3.75	7.50	15.00

FLYING DUTCHMAN
Number	Title	Yr	VG	VG+	NM
❏ BDL1-0829	Strike Up the Band	1975	3.00	6.00	12.00
❏ FD-10159	What a Wonderful World	1973	3.00	6.00	12.00

JAZZOLOGY
Number	Title	Yr	VG	VG+	NM
❏ JCE-76	Live from Manassas	1979	2.50	5.00	10.00
❏ J-111	Bobby Hackett and His Orchestra, 1943	198?	2.50	5.00	10.00

PAUSA
Number	Title	Yr	VG	VG+	NM
❏ 9038	Coast Concert	198?	2.50	5.00	10.00

PICKWICK
Number	Title	Yr	VG	VG+	NM
❏ PC-3012 [M]	Bobby Hackett with Strings	1966	3.00	6.00	12.00
❏ SPC-3012 [S]	Bobby Hackett with Strings	1966	2.50	5.00	10.00

PROJECT 3
Number	Title	Yr	VG	VG+	NM
❏ PR 5006 SD	That Midnight Touch	1967	3.00	6.00	12.00
❏ PR 5016 SD	A Time for Love	1968	3.00	6.00	12.00
❏ PR 5034 SD	This Is My Bag	1969	3.00	6.00	12.00
❏ PR 6033 [(2)]	Memorable and Mellow	198?	3.00	6.00	12.00

SEAGULL
Number	Title	Yr	VG	VG+	NM
❏ LG-8201	Goodnight My Love	198?	2.50	5.00	10.00

SESAC
Number	Title	Yr	VG	VG+	NM
❏ N-4101 [M]	The Spirit Swings Me	1960	6.25	12.50	25.00
❏ SN-4101 [S]	The Spirit Swings Me	1960	7.50	15.00	30.00
❏ N-4105 [M]	Candlelight and Romance	1960	6.25	12.50	25.00
❏ SN-4105 [S]	Candlelight and Romance	1960	7.50	15.00	30.00

STORYVILLE
Number	Title	Yr	VG	VG+	NM
❏ 4059	Sextet Recordings	198?	2.50	5.00	10.00

VERVE
Number	Title	Yr	VG	VG+	NM
❏ V-8698 [M]	Creole Cookin'	1967	3.75	7.50	15.00
❏ V6-8698 [S]	Creole Cookin'	1967	3.00	6.00	12.00

HACKETT, BOBBY, AND BILLY BUTTERFIELD
Also see each artist's individual listings.

VERVE
Number	Title	Yr	VG	VG+	NM
❏ V-8723 [M]	Bobby/Billy/Brazil	1967	3.75	7.50	15.00
❏ V6-8723 [S]	Bobby/Billy/Brazil	1967	3.00	6.00	12.00

HACKETT, BOBBY/MAX KAMINSKY
Also see each artist's individual listings.

BRUNSWICK
Number	Title	Yr	VG	VG+	NM
❏ BL 58043 [10]	Battle of Jazz, Vol. 5	1953	12.50	25.00	50.00

HADEN, CHARLIE
Bass player and occasional male singer.

ABC IMPULSE!
Number	Title	Yr	VG	VG+	NM
❏ AS-9183	Liberation Music Orchestra	1969	10.00	20.00	40.00

ECM
Number	Title	Yr	VG	VG+	NM
❏ 23794	Ballad of the Fallen	1982	2.50	5.00	10.00

HORIZON
Number	Title	Yr	VG	VG+	NM
❏ SP-710	Closeness	197?	3.75	7.50	15.00
❏ SP-727	The Golden Number	1978	3.75	7.50	15.00

SOUL NOTE
Number	Title	Yr	VG	VG+	NM
❏ 121172	Silence	1990	3.00	6.00	12.00

VERVE
Number	Title	Yr	VG	VG+	NM
❏ 831 673-1	Quartet West	1987	2.50	5.00	10.00
❏ 837 031-1	Quartet West in Angel City	1988	2.50	5.00	10.00

HADEN, CHARLIE, AND HAMPTON HAWES
Also see each artist's individual listings.

ARTISTS HOUSE
Number	Title	Yr	VG	VG+	NM
❏ 4	As Long As There's Music	1979	3.00	6.00	12.00

HADEN, CHARLIE; JAN GARBAREK; EGBERTO GISMONTI
Also see each artist's individual listings.

ECM
Number	Title	Yr	VG	VG+	NM
❏ 1170	Folk Songs	1979	3.00	6.00	12.00

HAGGART, BOB
Bass player, composer and bandleader. Also see YANK LAWSON.

COMMAND
Number	Title	Yr	VG	VG+	NM
❏ RS 33-849 [M]	Big Noise from Winnetka	1963	3.00	6.00	12.00
❏ RS 849 SD [S]	Big Noise from Winnetka	1963	3.75	7.50	15.00

JAZZOLOGY
Number	Title	Yr	VG	VG+	NM
❏ J-74	Sentimental Journey	1980	2.50	5.00	10.00
❏ J-94	Bob Haggart Enjoys Carolina in the Morning	1982	2.50	5.00	10.00
❏ J-149	A Portrait of Bix	1986	2.50	5.00	10.00

Number	Title	Yr	VG	VG+	NM

HAHN, JERRY
Guitarist.
ARHOOLIE

| 8006 | Jerry Hahn Quintet | 197? | 3.75 | 7.50 | 15.00 |

CHANGES

| LP-7001 | Arabein | 1968 | 5.00 | 10.00 | 20.00 |

FANTASY

| F-9426 | Moses | 1974 | 3.75 | 7.50 | 15.00 |

HAIG, AL
Pianist.
ARCHIVE OF FOLK AND JAZZ

| 293 | Jazz Will o' the Wisp | 197? | 2.50 | 5.00 | 10.00 |

COUNTERPOINT

| C-551 [M] | Jazz Will o' the Wisp | 1957 | 25.00 | 50.00 | 100.00 |

ESOTERIC

| ESJ-7 [10] | Al Haig Trio | 1954 | 50.00 | 100.00 | 200.00 |

INNER CITY

| IC-1073 | Al Haig Plays Music of Jerome Kern | 197? | 3.00 | 6.00 | 12.00 |

INTERPLAY

| 7707 | Portrait of Bud Powell | 1978 | 3.00 | 6.00 | 12.00 |
| 7713 | Serendipity | 1978 | 3.00 | 6.00 | 12.00 |

MINT

| AL-711 [M] | Al Haig Today | 1964 | 37.50 | 75.00 | 150.00 |

PACIFIC JAZZ

| PJLP-18 [10] | Al Haig Trio | 1955 | 37.50 | 75.00 | 150.00 |

PERIOD

| SPL-1104 [10] | Al Haig Quartet | 1954 | 37.50 | 75.00 | 150.00 |

PRESTIGE

| PRST-7841 | Al Haig Trio and Quartet | 1970 | 3.75 | 7.50 | 15.00 |

SEABREEZE

1001	Piano Interpretation	1976	3.00	6.00	12.00
1005	Interplay	1977	3.00	6.00	12.00
1006	Piano Time	1977	3.00	6.00	12.00
1008	Manhattan Memories	1978	3.00	6.00	12.00

SEECO

| SLP-7 [10] | Highlights in Modern Jazz | 195? | 30.00 | 60.00 | 120.00 |

XANADU

| 206 | Live in Hollywood | 198? | 2.50 | 5.00 | 10.00 |

HAIG, AL, AND JIMMY RANEY
Also see each artist's individual listings.
CHOICE

| 1010 | Strings Attached | 197? | 3.00 | 6.00 | 12.00 |

HAIG, AL/MARY LOU WILLIAMS
Also see each artist's individual listings.
PRESTIGE

| PRLP-175 [10] | Piano Moderns | 1953 | 50.00 | 100.00 | 200.00 |

HAKIM, OMAR
Drummer. Also an occasional guitarist and male singer.
GRP

| GR-9585 | Rhythm Deep | 1989 | 3.00 | 6.00 | 12.00 |

HAKIM, SADIK
Pianist.
STEEPLECHASE

| SCS-1091 | Witches, Goblins | 198? | 3.00 | 6.00 | 12.00 |

HALE, CORKY
Pianist, harpist and female singer.
GENE NORMAN

| GNP-17 [M] | Corky Hale | 1956 | 12.50 | 25.00 | 50.00 |

GNP CRESCENDO

| GNP-17 [M] | Corky Hale | 196? | 3.75 | 7.50 | 15.00 |
| GNP-9035 | Corky Hale Plays Gershwin and Duke | 197? | 3.00 | 6.00 | 12.00 |

STASH

| ST-245 | Harp Beat | 198? | 3.00 | 6.00 | 12.00 |

HALEN, CARL
Cornet player and trumpeter.
EMPIRICAL

| LP-101 [10] | Gin Bottle Seven | 1957 | 12.50 | 25.00 | 50.00 |

RIVERSIDE

| RLP 12-231 [M] | Gin Bottle Jazz | 1958 | 15.00 | 30.00 | 60.00 |
| -- White label, blue print | | | | | |

RLP 12-231 [M]	Gin Bottle Jazz	1959	7.50	15.00	30.00
-- Blue label, microphone logo at top					
RLP 12-261 [M]	Whoopee Makers' Jazz	1958	10.00	20.00	40.00
RLP-1103 [S]	Whoopee Makers' Jazz	1958	7.50	15.00	30.00

HALL BROTHERS JAZZ BAND, THE
Led by pianist Mike Polad. Also see KID THOMAS.
GHB

GHB-11 [M]	Hall Brothers Jazz Band	1964	3.00	6.00	12.00
GHBS-11 [S]	Hall Brothers Jazz Band	1964	3.75	7.50	15.00
GHB-46 [M]	Sweet Like This	196?	3.00	6.00	12.00
GHBS-46 [S]	Sweet Like This	196?	3.75	7.50	15.00

STOMP OFF

| SOS-1013 | Waiting at the End of the Road | 198? | 2.50 | 5.00 | 10.00 |
| SOS-1062 | Fizz Water | 198? | 2.50 | 5.00 | 10.00 |

HALL, ADELAIDE
Female singer.
MONMOUTH-EVERGREEN

| 7080 | That Wonderful... | 1970 | 5.00 | 10.00 | 20.00 |

HALL, BECKY
Female singer.
AAMCO

| ALP-324 [M] | A Tribute to Bessie Smith | 1958 | 7.50 | 15.00 | 30.00 |

HALL, EDMOND
Clarinetist. Also a baritone saxophone player. Also see MIFF MOLE.
BLUE NOTE

| B-6505 [M] | Celestial Express | 1969 | 5.00 | 10.00 | 20.00 |

CIRCLE

| C-52 | Rompin' in '44 | 198? | 2.50 | 5.00 | 10.00 |

MOSAIC

| M6-109 [(6)] | The Complete Edmond Hall/ | 199? | 25.00 | 50.00 | 100.00 |
| | James P. Johnson/Sidney De Paris/ Vic Dickenson Blue Note Sessions | | | | |

MOUNT VERNON

| MVM-124 | Rumpus on Rampart St. | 197? | 3.00 | 6.00 | 12.00 |

STORYVILLE

| 4009 | Live at Club Hangover, Volume 4 | 198? | 2.50 | 5.00 | 10.00 |

UNITED ARTISTS

| UAL-4028 [M] | Petite Fleur | 1959 | 10.00 | 20.00 | 40.00 |
| UAS-5028 [S] | Petite Fleur | 1959 | 7.50 | 15.00 | 30.00 |

HALL, EDMOND/SIDNEY DePARIS
Also see each artist's individual listings.
BLUE NOTE

| BLP-7007 [10] | Jamming in Jazz Hall | 1951 | 50.00 | 100.00 | 200.00 |

HALL, EDMOND/ART HODES
Also see each artist's individual listings.
BLUE NOTE

| B-6504 [M] | Original Blue Note Jazz, Volume 1 | 1969 | 5.00 | 10.00 | 20.00 |

HALL, GEORGE
Violinist and bandleader.
HINDSIGHT

| HSR-144 | George Hall and His Orchestra 1937 | 198? | 2.50 | 5.00 | 10.00 |

HALL, HERB
Alto and baritone saxophone player.
BIOGRAPH

| 3003 | Herb Hall Quartet | 196? | 3.75 | 7.50 | 15.00 |

HALL, JIM
Guitarist. Also see BOB BROOKMEYER; BILL EVANS; ZOOT SIMS.
BASF

| 20708 | It's Nice to Be with You | 1972 | 3.75 | 7.50 | 15.00 |

CONCORD JAZZ

CJ-161	Circles	1982	2.50	5.00	10.00
CJ-298	Jim Hall's Three	1986	2.50	5.00	10.00
CJ-384	All Across the City	1989	3.00	6.00	12.00

CTI

| 6060 | Concierto | 1977 | 3.00 | 6.00 | 12.00 |

FANTASY

| OJC-649 | Where Would I Be | 1991 | 3.00 | 6.00 | 12.00 |

HORIZON

| SP-705 | Live | 1975 | 3.00 | 6.00 | 12.00 |

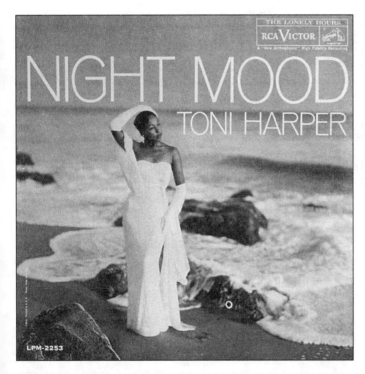

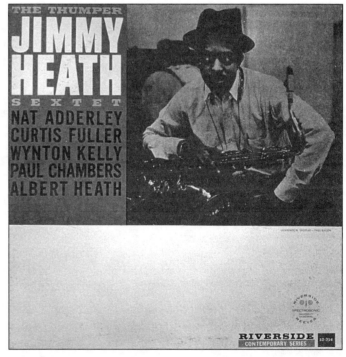

(Top left) Jim Hall's first album, on its original Pacific Jazz edition, is pretty self-explanatory. After a long absence from recording as a leader, he returned with albums on five different labels in the 1970s and 1980s, most recently on vinyl from Concord Jazz. (Top right) Bengt Hallberg was part of the 1950s "Swedish Invasion" of jazz artists. His self-titled album on Epic is a tough one to find. (Bottom left) Toni Harper is another all-but-forgotten female jazz singer. She did albums on Verve and RCA Victor, including this one, with a very attractive cover. (Bottom right) Jimmy Heath played tenor and alto sax and had lots of well-known friends, as this album, *The Thumper*, illustrates.

Number	Title	Yr	VG	VG+	NM
❑ SP-715	Commitment	1976	3.00	6.00	12.00
MILESTONE					
❑ 9037	Where Would I Be	1973	3.75	7.50	15.00
PACIFIC JAZZ					
❑ PJ-10 [M]	Good Friday Blues	1960	10.00	20.00	40.00
❑ PJ-79 [M]	Jazz Guitar	1963	7.50	15.00	30.00
❑ ST-79 [S]	Jazz Guitar	1963	6.25	12.50	25.00
❑ PJ-1227 [M]	Jazz Guitar	1957	20.00	40.00	80.00
PAUSA					
❑ 7112	In a Sentimental Mood	198?	2.50	5.00	10.00
WORLD PACIFIC					
❑ WP-1227 [M]	Jazz Guitar	1958	12.50	25.00	50.00

HALL, JIM, AND RON CARTER
Also see each artist's individual listings.

Number	Title	Yr	VG	VG+	NM
FANTASY					
❑ OJC-467	Alone Together	1990	3.00	6.00	12.00
MILESTONE					
❑ 9045	Alone Together	1974	3.75	7.50	15.00

HALL, JIM, AND RED MITCHELL
Also see each artist's individual listings.

Number	Title	Yr	VG	VG+	NM
ARTISTS HOUSE					
❑ 5	Jim Hall and Red Mitchell	1979	3.00	6.00	12.00

HALLBERG, BENGT
Pianist. Also see REINHOLD SVENSSON.

Number	Title	Yr	VG	VG+	NM
EPIC					
❑ LN 3375 [M]	Bengt Hallberg	1957	25.00	50.00	100.00
PRESTIGE					
❑ PRLP-176 [10]	Bengt Hallberg's Swedish All-Stars	1953	45.00	90.00	180.00

HALLBERG, BENGT/ARNE DOMNERUS
Also see each artist's individual listings.

Number	Title	Yr	VG	VG+	NM
PRESTIGE					
❑ PRLP-145 [10]	New Sounds from Sweden, Volume 6	1953	50.00	100.00	200.00

HALLBERG, BENGT/LARS GULLIN
Also see each artist's individual listings.

Number	Title	Yr	VG	VG+	NM
PRESTIGE					
❑ PRLP-121 [10]	New Sounds from Sweden, Volume 2	1952	50.00	100.00	200.00

HALLEY, PAUL
Pianist, organist and composer.

Number	Title	Yr	VG	VG+	NM
GRAMAVISION					
❑ 7704	Nightwatch	198?	2.50	5.00	10.00
LIVING MUSIC					
❑ LM-0009	Pianosong	1986	2.50	5.00	10.00

HAMBRO, LENNY
Alto saxophone player.

Number	Title	Yr	VG	VG+	NM
COLUMBIA					
❑ CL 757 [M]	Message from Hambro	1956	10.00	20.00	40.00
EPIC					
❑ LN 3361 [M]	The Nature of Things	1956	10.00	20.00	40.00
SAVOY					
❑ MG-15031 [10]	Mambo Hambro	1954	12.50	25.00	50.00

HAMILTON, CHICO
Drummer and bandleader. Also see LAURINDO ALMEIDA

Number	Title	Yr	VG	VG+	NM
ABC IMPULSE!					
❑ AS-29 [S]	Passin' Thru	1968	3.75	7.50	15.00
❑ AS-59 [S]	Man from Two Worlds	1968	3.75	7.50	15.00
❑ AS-82 [S]	Chi Chi Chico	1968	3.75	7.50	15.00
❑ AS-9102 [S]	El Chico	1968	3.75	7.50	15.00
❑ AS-9114 [S]	The Further Adventures of El Chico	1968	3.75	7.50	15.00
❑ AS-9130 [S]	The Dealer	1968	3.75	7.50	15.00
❑ AS-9174	The Best of Chico Hamilton	1969	3.75	7.50	15.00
❑ AS-9213 [(2)]	His Great Hits	1971	5.00	10.00	20.00
BLUE NOTE					
❑ BN-LA520-G	Peregrinations	1975	3.00	6.00	12.00
❑ BN-LA622-G	Chico Hamilton & Players	1976	3.00	6.00	12.00
COLUMBIA					
❑ CL 1590 [M]	Selections from "Bye Bye Birdie"	1961	5.00	10.00	20.00
❑ CL 1619 [M]	Chico Hamilton Special	1961	5.00	10.00	20.00

Number	Title	Yr	VG	VG+	NM
❑ CL 1807 [M]	Drumfusion	1962	5.00	10.00	20.00
❑ CS 8390 [S]	Selections from "Bye Bye Birdie"	1961	6.25	12.50	25.00
❑ CS 8419 [S]	Chico Hamilton Special	1961	6.25	12.50	25.00
❑ CS 8607 [S]	Drumfusion	1962	6.25	12.50	25.00
DECCA					
❑ DL 8614 [M]	Jazz from the Sweet Smell of Success	1957	12.50	25.00	50.00
DISCOVERY					
❑ 831	Gongs East	1981	2.50	5.00	10.00
-- *Reissue of Warner Bros. 1271*					
ELEKTRA					
❑ 6E-257	Nomad	1980	2.50	5.00	10.00
ENTERPRISE					
❑ SD 7501	The Master	1974	3.00	6.00	12.00
FLYING DUTCHMAN					
❑ 10135	Exigente	1971	3.75	7.50	15.00
IMPULSE!					
❑ A-29 [M]	Passin' Thru	1963	6.25	12.50	25.00
❑ AS-29 [S]	Passin' Thru	1963	7.50	15.00	30.00
❑ A-59 [M]	Man from Two Worlds	1964	6.25	12.50	25.00
❑ AS-59 [S]	Man from Two Worlds	1964	7.50	15.00	30.00
❑ A-82 [M]	Chi Chi Chico	1965	5.00	10.00	20.00
❑ AS-82 [S]	Chi Chi Chico	1965	6.25	12.50	25.00
❑ A-9102 [M]	El Chico	1965	5.00	10.00	20.00
❑ AS-9102 [S]	El Chico	1965	6.25	12.50	25.00
❑ A-9114 [M]	The Further Adventures of El Chico	1966	5.00	10.00	20.00
❑ AS-9114 [S]	The Further Adventures of El Chico	1966	6.25	12.50	25.00
❑ A-9130 [M]	The Dealer	1966	5.00	10.00	20.00
❑ AS-9130 [S]	The Dealer	1966	6.25	12.50	25.00
JAZZTONE					
❑ J-1264 [M]	Delightfully Modern	1957	10.00	20.00	40.00
MCA					
❑ 637	Man from Two Worlds	198?	2.00	4.00	8.00
-- *Reissue of Impulse! 59*					
❑ 638	El Chico	198?	2.00	4.00	8.00
-- *Reissue of Impulse! 9102*					
❑ 29037	Passin' Thru	198?	2.50	5.00	10.00
-- *Reissue of Impulse! 29*					
❑ 29038	The Best of Chico Hamilton	198?	2.50	5.00	10.00
-- *Reissue of Impulse! 9174*					
MERCURY					
❑ SRM-1-1163	Catwalk	1977	3.00	6.00	12.00
NAUTILUS					
❑ NR-13	Reaching for the Top	1981	7.50	15.00	30.00
-- *Audiophile vinyl*					
PACIFIC JAZZ					
❑ PJLP-17 [10]	Chico Hamilton Trio	1955	25.00	50.00	100.00
❑ PJ-39 [M]	Spectacular	1962	6.25	12.50	25.00
-- *Reissue of 1209*					
❑ PJ-1209 [M]	Chico Hamilton Quintet	1955	18.75	37.50	75.00
❑ PJ-1216 [M]	Chico Hamilton Quintet In Hi-Fi	1956	18.75	37.50	75.00
❑ PJ-1220 [M]	Chico Hamilton Trio	1956	18.75	37.50	75.00
❑ PJ-1225 [M]	Chico Hamilton Quintet	1957	18.75	37.50	75.00
❑ PJ-1231 [M]	Chico Hamilton Plays the Music of Fred Katz	1957	18.75	37.50	75.00
REPRISE					
❑ R-6078 [M]	A Different Journey	1963	7.50	15.00	30.00
❑ R9-6078 [S]	A Different Journey	1963	10.00	20.00	40.00
SOLID STATE					
❑ 18043	The Gamut	1969	3.75	7.50	15.00
❑ 18050	Headhunters	1969	3.75	7.50	15.00
SOUL NOTE					
❑ 121 191-1	Reunion	1989	3.00	6.00	12.00
SUNSET					
❑ SUS-5215	Easy Livin'	196?	3.00	6.00	12.00
WARNER BROS.					
❑ W 1245 [M]	Chico Hamilton Quintet with Strings Attached	1958	12.50	25.00	50.00
❑ WS 1245 [S]	Chico Hamilton Quintet with Strings Attached	1958	15.00	30.00	60.00
❑ W 1271 [M]	Gongs East	1958	12.50	25.00	50.00
❑ WS 1271 [S]	Gongs East	1958	15.00	30.00	60.00
❑ W 1344 [M]	The Three Faces of Chico	1959	12.50	25.00	50.00
❑ WS 1344 [S]	The Three Faces of Chico	1959	15.00	30.00	60.00
WORLD PACIFIC					
❑ ST-1003 [S]	South Pacific in Hi-Fi	1958	10.00	20.00	40.00
❑ ST-1005 [S]	Chico Hamilton Quintet	1958	10.00	20.00	40.00
❑ ST-1008 [S]	The Chico Hamilton Trio Featuring Freddie Gambrell	1958	10.00	20.00	40.00
❑ ST-1016 [S]	Ellington Suite	1959	10.00	20.00	40.00
❑ WP-1216 [M]	Chico Hamilton Quintet In Hi-Fi	1958	12.50	25.00	50.00

Number	Title	Yr	VG	VG+	NM
❏ WP-1225 [M]	Chico Hamilton Quintet	1958	12.50	25.00	50.00
❏ WP-1231 [M]	Chico Hamilton Plays the Music of Fred Katz	1958	12.50	25.00	50.00
❏ PJ-1238 [M]	South Pacific in Hi-Fi	1957	12.50	25.00	50.00
❏ WP-1238 [M]	South Pacific in Hi-Fi	1958	10.00	20.00	40.00
❏ PJ-1242 [M]	The Chico Hamilton Trio Featuring Freddie Gambrell	1957	12.50	25.00	50.00
❏ WP-1242 [M]	The Chico Hamilton Trio Featuring Freddie Gambrell	1958	10.00	20.00	40.00
❏ WP-1258 [M]	Ellington Suite	1959	12.50	25.00	50.00
❏ WP-1287 [M]	The Original Hamilton Quintet	1960	12.50	25.00	50.00

HAMILTON, DAVE
Vibraphone player.
WORKSHOP JAZZ

Number	Title	Yr	VG	VG+	NM
❏ WSJ-206 [M]	Blue Vibrations	1963	20.00	40.00	80.00

HAMILTON, JEFF
Drummer.
CONCORD JAZZ

Number	Title	Yr	VG	VG+	NM
❏ CJ-187	Indiana	1982	2.50	5.00	10.00

HAMILTON, JIMMY
Clarinetist and tenor saxophone player.
EVEREST

Number	Title	Yr	VG	VG+	NM
❏ SDBR-1100 [S]	Swing Low, Sweet Chariot	1960	7.50	15.00	30.00
❏ LPBR-5100 [M]	Swing Low, Sweet Chariot	1960	6.25	12.50	25.00

SWINGVILLE

Number	Title	Yr	VG	VG+	NM
❏ SVLP-2022 [M]	It's About Time	1961	12.50	25.00	50.00
-- Purple label					
❏ SVLP-2022 [M]	It's About Time	1965	6.25	12.50	25.00
-- Blue label, trident logo at right					
❏ SVLP-2028 [M]	Can't Help Swingin'	1961	12.50	25.00	50.00
-- Purple label					
❏ SVLP-2028 [M]	Can't Help Swingin'	1965	6.25	12.50	25.00
-- Blue label, trident logo at right					

URANIA

Number	Title	Yr	VG	VG+	NM
❏ UJLP-1003 [10]	Clarinet in Hi-Fi	1954	30.00	60.00	120.00
❏ UJLP-1204 [M]	Accent on Clarinet	1955	12.50	25.00	50.00
❏ UJLP-1208 [M]	Clarinet in Hi-Fi	1955	12.50	25.00	50.00

HAMILTON, SCOTT
Tenor saxophone player.
CONCORD JAZZ

Number	Title	Yr	VG	VG+	NM
❏ CJ-42	Scott Hamilton Is a Good Wind Who Is Blowing Us No Ill	1977	3.00	6.00	12.00
❏ CJ-61	Scott Hamilton 2	1978	3.00	6.00	12.00
❏ CJ-127	Tenorshoes	1980	2.50	5.00	10.00
❏ CJ-165	Apples and Oranges	1981	2.50	5.00	10.00
❏ CJ-197	Close Up	1982	2.50	5.00	10.00
❏ CJ-233	In Concert	1984	2.50	5.00	10.00
❏ CJ-254	The Second Set	1984	2.50	5.00	10.00
❏ CJ-311	The Right Time	1987	2.50	5.00	10.00

FAMOUS DOOR

Number	Title	Yr	VG	VG+	NM
❏ 119	The Swinging Young Scott	197?	5.00	10.00	20.00

PROGRESSIVE

Number	Title	Yr	VG	VG+	NM
❏ 7026	Grand Appearance	1979	2.50	5.00	10.00

HAMILTON, SCOTT; JAKE HANNA; DAVE McKENNA
Also see each artist's individual listings.
CONCORD JAZZ

Number	Title	Yr	VG	VG+	NM
❏ CJ-305	Major League	1986	2.50	5.00	10.00

HAMILTON, SCOTT, AND BUDDY TATE
Also see each artist's individual listings.
CONCORD JAZZ

Number	Title	Yr	VG	VG+	NM
❏ CJ-85	Back to Back	1979	3.00	6.00	12.00
❏ CJ-148	Scott's Buddy	1981	2.50	5.00	10.00

HAMILTON, SCOTT, AND WARREN VACHE
Also see each artist's individual listings.
CONCORD JAZZ

Number	Title	Yr	VG	VG+	NM
❏ CJ-70	With Scott's Band in New York	1978	3.00	6.00	12.00
❏ CJ-111	Skyscrapers	1980	2.50	5.00	10.00

HAMLIN, JOHNNY
Accordion player.
ARGO

Number	Title	Yr	VG	VG+	NM
❏ LP-4001 [M]	Johnny Hamlin Quintet	1961	6.25	12.50	25.00
❏ LPS-4001 [S]	Johnny Hamlin Quintet	1961	7.50	15.00	30.00

HAMMACK, BOBBY
Pianist.
LIBERTY

Number	Title	Yr	VG	VG+	NM
❏ LRP-3016 [M]	Power House	1956	10.00	20.00	40.00

HAMMER, ATLE
Trombonist.
GEMINI TAURUS

Number	Title	Yr	VG	VG+	NM
❏ GMLP-65	Arizona Blue	1991	3.75	7.50	15.00

HAMMER, BOB
Pianist, composer and arranger.
ABC-PARAMOUNT

Number	Title	Yr	VG	VG+	NM
❏ ABC-497 [M]	Beatle Jazz	1964	7.50	15.00	30.00
❏ ABCS-497 [S]	Beatle Jazz	1964	10.00	20.00	40.00

HAMMER, JAN
Keyboard player, composer and bandleader. A onetime member of MAHAVISHNU ORCHESTRA, he is best known for his television theme from Miami Vice.
ELEKTRA

Number	Title	Yr	VG	VG+	NM
❏ 6E-173	Black Sheep	1979	2.50	5.00	10.00
❏ 6E-232	Hammer	1979	2.50	5.00	10.00

MCA

Number	Title	Yr	VG	VG+	NM
❏ 42103	Escape from Television	1988	2.50	5.00	10.00

NEMPEROR

Number	Title	Yr	VG	VG+	NM
❏ SD 432	The First Seven Days	1975	3.00	6.00	12.00
❏ SD 437	Oh, Yeah?	1976	3.00	6.00	12.00
❏ JZ 35003	Melodies	1977	2.50	5.00	10.00
❏ PZ 35003	Melodies	198?	2.00	4.00	8.00
-- Budget-line reissue					
❏ BZ 40382	The Early Years (1974-1977)	1986	2.50	5.00	10.00

HAMMOND, JOHNNY
Organist and occasional pianist. He also recorded as Johnny "Hammond" Smith; the below listings include those albums as well as the Johnny Hammond ones.
KUDU

Number	Title	Yr	VG	VG+	NM
❏ 01	Breakout	1971	3.00	6.00	12.00
❏ 04	Wild Horses/Rock Steady	1972	3.00	6.00	12.00
❏ 10	The Prophet	1973	3.00	6.00	12.00
❏ 16	Higher Ground	1974	3.00	6.00	12.00

MILESTONE

Number	Title	Yr	VG	VG+	NM
❏ 9062	Gears	1975	3.75	7.50	15.00
❏ 9068	Forever Taurus	1976	3.75	7.50	15.00
❏ 9076	Storm Warning	1977	3.75	7.50	15.00
❏ 9083	Don't Let the System Get You	1978	3.75	7.50	15.00

NEW JAZZ

Number	Title	Yr	VG	VG+	NM
❏ NJLP-8221 [M]	All Soul	1959	12.50	25.00	50.00
-- Purple label					
❏ NJLP-8221 [M]	All Soul	1965	6.25	12.50	25.00
-- Blue label with trident logo					
❏ NJLP-8229 [M]	That Good Feelin'	1959	12.50	25.00	50.00
-- Purple label					
❏ NJLP-8229 [M]	That Good Feelin'	1965	6.25	12.50	25.00
-- Blue label with trident logo					
❏ NJLP-8241 [M]	Talk That Talk	1960	12.50	25.00	50.00
-- Purple label					
❏ NJLP-8241 [M]	Talk That Talk	1965	6.25	12.50	25.00
-- Blue label with trident logo					
❏ NJLP-8288 [M]	Look Out!	1962	12.50	25.00	50.00
-- Purple label					
❏ NJLP-8288 [M]	Look Out!	1965	6.25	12.50	25.00
-- Blue label with trident logo					

PRESTIGE

Number	Title	Yr	VG	VG+	NM
❏ PRLP-7203 [M]	Stimulation	1961	10.00	20.00	40.00
-- Yellow label					
❏ PRLP-7203 [M]	Stimulation	1965	6.25	12.50	25.00
-- Blue label with trident logo					
❏ PRLP-7217 [M]	Gettin' the Message	1961	10.00	20.00	40.00
-- Yellow label					
❏ PRLP-7217 [M]	Gettin' the Message	1965	6.25	12.50	25.00
-- Blue label with trident logo					
❏ PRLP-7408 [M]	The Stinger	1965	5.00	10.00	20.00
❏ PRST-7408 [S]	The Stinger	1965	6.25	12.50	25.00
❏ PRLP-7420 [M]	Opus de Funk	1966	5.00	10.00	20.00
❏ PRST-7420 [S]	Opus de Funk	1966	6.25	12.50	25.00
❏ PRLP-7464 [M]	The Stinger Meets the Golden Thrush	1966	5.00	10.00	20.00
❏ PRST-7464 [S]	The Stinger Meets the Golden Thrush	1966	6.25	12.50	25.00
❏ PRLP-7482 [M]	Love Potion #9	1967	6.25	12.50	25.00
❏ PRST-7482 [S]	Love Potion #9	1967	5.00	10.00	20.00
❏ PRLP-7494 [M]	Ebb Tide	1967	6.25	12.50	25.00
❏ PRST-7494 [S]	Ebb Tide	1967	5.00	10.00	20.00
❏ PRST-7549	Soul Flowers	1968	5.00	10.00	20.00

Number	Title	Yr	VG	VG+	NM
❏ PRST-7564	Dirty Grape	1968	5.00	10.00	20.00
❏ PRST-7588	Nasty	1968	5.00	10.00	20.00
❏ PRST-7681	Soul Talk	1969	5.00	10.00	20.00
❏ PRST-7705	The Best of Johnny "Hammond" Smith	1969	3.75	7.50	15.00
❏ PRST-7736	Black Feeling	1969	3.75	7.50	15.00
❏ PRST-7777	Best for Lovers	1970	3.75	7.50	15.00
❏ PRST-7786	Stimulation	1970	3.75	7.50	15.00
❏ PRST-7846	Good 'Nuff	1970	3.75	7.50	15.00
❏ 10002	Here It 'Tis	1971	3.75	7.50	15.00
❏ 10015	What's Going On	1971	3.75	7.50	15.00

RIVERSIDE

Number	Title	Yr	VG	VG+	NM
❏ RLP-442 [M]	Black Coffee	1963	6.25	12.50	25.00
❏ RLP-466 [M]	Mr. Wonderful	1963	6.25	12.50	25.00
❏ RLP-482 [M]	Open House!	1965	5.00	10.00	20.00
❏ RLP-496 [M]	A Little Taste	1965	5.00	10.00	20.00
❏ RS-9442 [S]	Black Coffee	1963	7.50	15.00	30.00
❏ RS-9466 [S]	Mr. Wonderful	1963	7.50	15.00	30.00
❏ RS-9482 [S]	Open House!	1965	6.25	12.50	25.00
❏ RS-9496 [S]	A Little Taste	1965	6.25	12.50	25.00

SALVATION

Number	Title	Yr	VG	VG+	NM
❏ 702	A Gambler's Life	1974	3.00	6.00	12.00

HAMPEL, GUNTER

Vibraphone player, flutist, bass clarinetist, baritone saxophone player and occasional male singer, percussionist and pianist.

BIRTH

Number	Title	Yr	VG	VG+	NM
❏ 001	The 8th of July, 1969	1969	10.00	20.00	40.00
❏ 002	Dances	1970	7.50	15.00	30.00
❏ 003	Symphony No. 5 and 6	1970	7.50	15.00	30.00
❏ 005	People Symphony	1970	7.50	15.00	30.00
❏ 007	Spirits	1971	5.00	10.00	20.00
❏ 008	Familie	1972	5.00	10.00	20.00
❏ 009	Angel	1972	5.00	10.00	20.00
❏ 0010	Waltz for 3 Universes in a Corridor	1972	5.00	10.00	20.00
❏ 0011	Broadway/Folksong	1972	5.00	10.00	20.00
❏ 0012	I Love Being with You	1972	5.00	10.00	20.00
❏ 0013	Unity Dance	1973	5.00	10.00	20.00
❏ 0016	Out from Under	1974	5.00	10.00	20.00
❏ 0017	Journey to the Song Within	1974	5.00	10.00	20.00
❏ 0021/0022 [(2)]	Celebrations	1974	7.50	15.00	30.00
❏ 0023	Ruomi	1975	5.00	10.00	20.00
❏ 0024	Cosmic Dancer	1975	5.00	10.00	20.00
❏ 0025	Enfant Terrible	1976	5.00	10.00	20.00
❏ 0026	Transformation	1976	5.00	10.00	20.00
❏ 0027	That Came Down on Me	1978	5.00	10.00	20.00
❏ 0028	All Is Real	1978	5.00	10.00	20.00
❏ 0029	Vogelfrei	1978	5.00	10.00	20.00
❏ 0030	Freedom of the Universe	1978	5.00	10.00	20.00
❏ 0031	All the Things You Could Be If Charles Mingus Was Your Daddy	1980	5.00	10.00	20.00
❏ 0032	A Place to Be with Us	1981	5.00	10.00	20.00
❏ 0033	Life on This Planet 1981	1981	5.00	10.00	20.00
❏ 0034	Cavana	1982	5.00	10.00	20.00
❏ 0035	Generator	1982	5.00	10.00	20.00
❏ 0036	Companion	1983	5.00	10.00	20.00
❏ 0038	Jubilation	1984	5.00	10.00	20.00
❏ 0039	Fresh Heat	1985	5.00	10.00	20.00

ESP-DISK'

Number	Title	Yr	VG	VG+	NM
❏ 1042 [M]	Music from Europe	1967	6.25	12.50	25.00
❏ S-1042 [S]	Music from Europe	1967	5.00	10.00	20.00

FLYING DUTCHMAN

Number	Title	Yr	VG	VG+	NM
❏ 126	The 8th of July, 1969	1970	10.00	20.00	40.00
❏ FD-10126	The 8th of July, 1969	1971	5.00	10.00	20.00

FMP

Number	Title	Yr	VG	VG+	NM
❏ 0770	Wellen/Waves	1980	3.75	7.50	15.00

HORO

Number	Title	Yr	VG	VG+	NM
❏ 33/34 [(2)]	Oasis	1978	7.50	15.00	30.00

KHARMA

Number	Title	Yr	VG	VG+	NM
❏ PK 8	Flying Carpet	1978	3.00	6.00	12.00

HAMPEL, GUNTER, AND BOULOU FERRE

Also see each artist's individual listings.

BIRTH

Number	Title	Yr	VG	VG+	NM
❏ 006	Espace	1970	6.25	12.50	25.00

HAMPTON, LIONEL

Vibraphone player (essentially the father of jazz vibes), he also was a drummer, pianist, male singer and bandleader. Also see BENNY GOODMAN.

ABC IMPULSE!

Number	Title	Yr	VG	VG+	NM
❏ AS-78 [S]	You Better Know It	1968	3.75	7.50	15.00

AMERICAN RECORDING SOCIETY

Number	Title	Yr	VG	VG+	NM
❏ G-403 [M]	The Swinging Jazz of Lionel Hampton	1956	10.00	20.00	40.00

ARCHIVE OF FOLK AND JAZZ

Number	Title	Yr	VG	VG+	NM
❏ 348	Hamp in Paris	197?	2.50	5.00	10.00

ATLANTIC

Number	Title	Yr	VG	VG+	NM
❏ 81644	Sentimental Journey	1986	2.50	5.00	10.00

AUDIO FIDELITY

Number	Title	Yr	VG	VG+	NM
❏ AFLP-1849 [M]	Lionel	1957	7.50	15.00	30.00
❏ AFLP-1913 [M]	Hamp's Big Band	1958	7.50	15.00	30.00
❏ AFSD-5849 [S]	Lionel	1958	10.00	20.00	40.00
❏ AFSD-5913 [S]	Hamp's Big Band	1958	10.00	20.00	40.00

BLUE NOTE

Number	Title	Yr	VG	VG+	NM
❏ BLP-5046 [10]	Rockin' and Groovin'	1954	75.00	150.00	300.00

BLUEBIRD

Number	Title	Yr	VG	VG+	NM
❏ AXM6-5536 [(6)]	The Complete Lionel Hampton	197?	12.50	25.00	50.00
❏ 6458-1-RB	Hot Mallets	1987	2.50	5.00	10.00

BRUNSWICK

Number	Title	Yr	VG	VG+	NM
❏ BL 754182	Them Changes	1972	3.75	7.50	15.00
❏ BL 754190	Please Sunrise	1973	3.75	7.50	15.00
❏ BL 754198	There It Is!	1974	3.75	7.50	15.00
❏ BL 754203	Stop! I Don't Need No Sympathy	1974	3.75	7.50	15.00
❏ BL 754213	Off Into a Black Thing	1977	3.00	6.00	12.00

CLASSIC JAZZ

Number	Title	Yr	VG	VG+	NM
❏ 136	Jazz Giants '77	198?	2.50	5.00	10.00

CLEF

Number	Title	Yr	VG	VG+	NM
❏ MGC-142 [10]	The Lionel Hampton Quartet	1953	30.00	60.00	120.00
❏ MGC-611 [M]	The Lionel Hampton Quartet	1954	20.00	40.00	80.00
❏ MGC-628 [M]	The Lionel Hampton Quintet	1954	20.00	40.00	80.00
❏ MGC-642 [M]	The Lionel Hampton Quintet, Volume 2	1955	25.00	50.00	100.00
❏ MGC-667 [M]	The Lionel Hampton Quartet and Quintet	1955	25.00	50.00	100.00
❏ MGC-670 [M]	Lionel Hampton Big Band	1955	25.00	50.00	100.00
❏ MGC-673 [M]	The Lionel Hampton Quartet	1955	20.00	40.00	80.00
❏ MGC-714 [M]	Lionel Hampton Plays Love Songs	1956	17.50	35.00	70.00
❏ MGC-726 [M]	King of the Vibes	1956	17.50	35.00	70.00
❏ MGC-727 [M]	Air Mail Special	1956	17.50	35.00	70.00
❏ MGC-735 [M]	Flying Home	1956	17.50	35.00	70.00
❏ MGC-736 [M]	Swingin' with Hamp	1956	17.50	35.00	70.00
❏ MGC-737 [M]	Hamp Roars Again	1956	---	---	---
-- Canceled					
❏ MGC-738 [M]	Hamp!	1956	17.50	35.00	70.00
❏ MGC-744 [M]	Hamp's Big Four	1956	17.50	35.00	70.00

COLUMBIA

Number	Title	Yr	VG	VG+	NM
❏ CL 711 [M]	Wailin' at the Trianon	1956	10.00	20.00	40.00
❏ CL 1304 [M]	Golden Vibes	1959	6.25	12.50	25.00
❏ CL 1486 [M]	Silver Vibes	1960	6.25	12.50	25.00
❏ CL 1661 [M]	Soft Vibes	1961	5.00	10.00	20.00
❏ CS 8110 [S]	Golden Vibes	1959	5.00	10.00	20.00
❏ CS 8277 [S]	Silver Vibes	1960	5.00	10.00	20.00
❏ CS 8461 [S]	Soft Vibes	1961	5.00	10.00	20.00

CONTEMPORARY

Number	Title	Yr	VG	VG+	NM
❏ C-3502 [M]	Hampton in Paris	1955	12.50	25.00	50.00

DECCA

Number	Title	Yr	VG	VG+	NM
❏ DL 4194 [M]	The Original Star Dust	1962	3.75	7.50	15.00
❏ DL 4296 [M]	Hamp's Golden Favorites	1962	3.75	7.50	15.00
❏ DL 5230 [10]	Boogie Woogie	1950	20.00	40.00	80.00
❏ DL 5297 [10]	Moonglow	1951	20.00	40.00	80.00
❏ DL 7013 [10]	Just Jazz	1962	20.00	40.00	80.00
❏ DL 8088 [M]	All American Award Concert at Carnegie Hall	1955	12.50	25.00	50.00
-- Black label, silver print					
❏ DL 8088 [M]	All American Award Concert at Carnegie Hall	196?	5.00	10.00	20.00
-- Black label with color bars					
❏ DL 8230 [M]	Moonglow	1956	12.50	25.00	50.00
-- Black label, silver print					
❏ DL 8230 [M]	Moonglow	196?	5.00	10.00	20.00
-- Black label with color bars					
❏ DL 9055 [M]	Just Jazz	1958	12.50	25.00	50.00
❏ DL 74194 [S]	The Original Star Dust	1962	5.00	10.00	20.00
❏ DL 74296 [S]	Hamp's Golden Favorites	1962	5.00	10.00	20.00

EMARCY

Number	Title	Yr	VG	VG+	NM
❏ MG-27537 [10]	Hamp in Paris	1954	25.00	50.00	100.00
❏ MG-27538 [10]	Crazy Hamp	1954	25.00	50.00	100.00
❏ MG-36032 [M]	Hamp in Paris	1955	12.50	25.00	50.00
❏ MG-36034 [M]	Crazy Rhythm	1955	12.50	25.00	50.00
❏ MG-36035 [M]	Jam Session in Paris	1955	12.50	25.00	50.00

EPIC

Number	Title	Yr	VG	VG+	NM
❏ LN 3190 [M]	Apollo Hall Concert 1954	1955	12.50	25.00	50.00
❏ LA 16027 [M]	Many Splendored Vibes	1962	5.00	10.00	20.00
❏ BA 17027 [S]	Many Splendored Vibes	1962	6.25	12.50	25.00

Number	Title	Yr	VG	VG+	NM
FOLKWAYS					
❑ FJ-2871	A Jazz Man for All Seasons	196?	3.75	7.50	15.00
GATEWAY					
❑ 7020	Jazz Showcase	197?	3.00	6.00	12.00
GENE NORMAN					
❑ GNP-15 [M]	Lionel Hampton with the Just Jazz All-Stars	1956	12.50	25.00	50.00
GLAD HAMP					
❑ GH-1001 [M]	The Many Sides of Lionel Hampton	1961	6.25	12.50	25.00
❑ GHS-1001 [S]	The Many Sides of Lionel Hampton	1961	7.50	15.00	30.00
❑ GH-1003 [M]	The Exciting Hamp in Europe	1962	6.25	12.50	25.00
❑ GHS-1003 [S]	The Exciting Hamp in Europe	1962	7.50	15.00	30.00
❑ GH-1004 [M]	Bossa Nova Jazz	1963	6.25	12.50	25.00
❑ GHS-1004 [S]	Bossa Nova Jazz	1963	7.50	15.00	30.00
❑ GH-1005 [M]	Lionel Hampton on Tour	1963	6.25	12.50	25.00
❑ GHS-1005 [S]	Lionel Hampton on Tour	1963	7.50	15.00	30.00
❑ GH-1006 [M]	Hamp in Japan	1964	6.25	12.50	25.00
❑ GHS-1006 [S]	Hamp in Japan	1964	7.50	15.00	30.00
❑ GH-1007 [M]	East Meets West	1965	6.25	12.50	25.00
❑ GHS-1007 [S]	East Meets West	1965	7.50	15.00	30.00
❑ GH-1009 [M]	A Taste of Hamp	1965	6.25	12.50	25.00
❑ GHS-1009 [S]	A Taste of Hamp	1965	7.50	15.00	30.00
❑ GHS-1011	Hamp Stamps	1967	3.75	7.50	15.00
❑ GH-1020	Lionel Hampton's Big Band Live	198?	2.50	5.00	10.00
❑ GH-1021	Chameleon	198?	2.50	5.00	10.00
❑ GH-1022	Outrageous	198?	2.50	5.00	10.00
❑ GH-1023	Made in Japan	198?	2.50	5.00	10.00
❑ GH-1024	Ambassador at Large	198?	2.50	5.00	10.00
❑ GH-1026	One of a Kind	1988	2.50	5.00	10.00
❑ GH-3050 [M]	All That Twistin' Jazz	1962	6.25	12.50	25.00
❑ GHS-3050 [S]	All That Twistin' Jazz	1962	7.50	15.00	30.00
GNP CRESCENDO					
❑ GNP-15 [M]	Lionel Hampton with the Just Jazz All-Stars	196?	5.00	10.00	20.00
❑ GNPS-15 [R]	Lionel Hampton with the Just Jazz All-Stars	196?	3.00	6.00	12.00
GROOVE MERCHANT					
❑ 4400 [(2)]	The Works!	197?	3.75	7.50	15.00
HARMONY					
❑ HL 7115 [M]	Hamp in Hi-Fi	1958	5.00	10.00	20.00
❑ HL 7281 [M]	The One and Only Lionel Hampton	1961	5.00	10.00	20.00
❑ KH 32165	Good Vibes	1972	2.50	5.00	10.00
HINDSIGHT					
❑ HSR-237	Lionel Hampton Septet 1962	1988	2.50	5.00	10.00
IMPULSE!					
❑ A-78 [M]	You Better Know It	1965	6.25	12.50	25.00
❑ AS-78 [S]	You Better Know It	1965	7.50	15.00	30.00
JAZZ MAN					
❑ 5011	Lionel Hampton and His Giants	198?	2.50	5.00	10.00
JAZZTONE					
❑ J-1040 [10]	Visit on a Skyscraper	195?	12.50	25.00	50.00
❑ J-1238 [M]	The Fabulous Lionel Hampton and His All-Stars	1957	10.00	20.00	40.00
❑ J-1246 [M]	Lionel Hampton's All Star Groups	1957	10.00	20.00	40.00
LION					
❑ L-70064 [M]	Lionel Hampton and His Orchestra	1958	5.00	10.00	20.00
MCA					
❑ 204	Golden Favorites	197?	2.50	5.00	10.00
❑ 1315	Steppin' Out	198?	2.50	5.00	10.00
❑ 1331	Sweatin' with Hamp	198?	2.50	5.00	10.00
❑ 1351	Rarities	198?	2.50	5.00	10.00
❑ 4057 [(2)]	The Best of Lionel Hampton	197?	3.00	6.00	12.00
❑ 42329	Gene Norman Presents Just Jazz	1990	3.00	6.00	12.00
MGM					
❑ E-285 [10]	Oh, Rock	1954	30.00	60.00	120.00
❑ E-3386 [M]	Oh, Rock	1956	12.50	25.00	50.00
NORGRAN					
❑ MGN-1080 [M]	Lionel Hampton and His Giants	1956	25.00	50.00	100.00
PERFECT					
❑ 12002 [M]	Lionel Hampton Swings	1959	7.50	15.00	30.00
❑ 14002 [S]	Lionel Hampton Swings	1959	10.00	20.00	40.00
QUINTESSENCE					
❑ 25031	Flyin'	197?	3.00	6.00	12.00
RCA CAMDEN					
❑ CAL-317 [M]	Open House	1957	5.00	10.00	20.00
❑ CAL-402 [M]	Jivin' the Vibes	1958	5.00	10.00	20.00
RCA VICTOR					
❑ LPT-18 [10]	A Treasury of Immortal Performances	1951	25.00	50.00	100.00

Number	Title	Yr	VG	VG+	NM
❑ LJM-1000 [M]	Hot Mallets	1954	12.50	25.00	50.00
❑ LPM-1422 [M]	Jazz Flamenco	1957	12.50	25.00	50.00
❑ LPM-2318 [M]	Swing Classics	1961	6.25	12.50	25.00
❑ LSP-2318 [R]	Swing Classics	196?	3.75	7.50	15.00
❑ LPM-3917 [M]	Lionel Hampton Plays Bert Kaempfert	1968	6.25	12.50	25.00
❑ LSP-3917 [S]	Lionel Hampton Plays Bert Kaempfert	1968	3.75	7.50	15.00
SWING					
❑ SW-8415	Lionel Hampton in Paris	1987	2.50	5.00	10.00
TIMELESS					
❑ LPSJP-142	Lionel Hampton's All Star Band at Newport '78	1990	3.00	6.00	12.00
❑ 303	Live in Emmen, Holland	197?	3.00	6.00	12.00
UPFRONT					
❑ UPF-153	Jammin'	197?	3.00	6.00	12.00
VERVE					
❑ MGV-2018 [M]	Lionel Hampton Plays Love Songs	1957	12.50	25.00	50.00
❑ V-2018 [M]	Lionel Hampton Plays Love Songs	1961	5.00	10.00	20.00
❑ VE-2-2543 [(2)]	Blues Ain't News to Me	198?	3.75	7.50	15.00
❑ MGV-8019 [M]	Travelin' Band	1957	12.50	25.00	50.00
❑ V-8019 [M]	Travelin' Band	1961	5.00	10.00	20.00
❑ MGV-8105 [M]	King of the Vibes	1957	12.50	25.00	50.00
❑ V-8105 [M]	King of the Vibes	1961	5.00	10.00	20.00
❑ MGV-8106 [M]	Air Mail Special	1957	12.50	25.00	50.00
❑ V-8106 [M]	Air Mail Special	1961	5.00	10.00	20.00
❑ MGV-8112 [M]	Flying Home	1957	12.50	25.00	50.00
❑ V-8112 [M]	Flying Home	1961	5.00	10.00	20.00
❑ MGV-8113 [M]	Swingin' with Hamp	1957	12.50	25.00	50.00
❑ V-8113 [M]	Swingin' with Hamp	1961	5.00	10.00	20.00
❑ MGV-8114 [M]	Hamp!	1957	12.50	25.00	50.00
❑ V-8114 [M]	Hamp!	1961	5.00	10.00	20.00
❑ MGV-8117 [M]	Hamp's Big Four	1957	12.50	25.00	50.00
❑ V-8117 [M]	Hamp's Big Four	1961	5.00	10.00	20.00
❑ MGV-8170 [M]	Lionel Hampton and His Giants	1957	12.50	25.00	50.00
❑ V-8170 [M]	Lionel Hampton and His Giants	1961	5.00	10.00	20.00
❑ MGV-8215 [M]	The Genius of Lionel Hampton	1958	12.50	25.00	50.00
❑ V-8215 [M]	The Genius of Lionel Hampton	1961	5.00	10.00	20.00
❑ MGV-8223 [M]	Lionel Hampton '58	1958	12.50	25.00	50.00
❑ V-8223 [M]	Lionel Hampton '58	1961	5.00	10.00	20.00
❑ MGV-8226 [M]	Hallelujah Hamp	1958	12.50	25.00	50.00
❑ V-8226 [M]	Hallelujah Hamp	1961	5.00	10.00	20.00
❑ MGV-8228 [M]	The High and the Mighty	1958	12.50	25.00	50.00
❑ V-8228 [M]	The High and the Mighty	1961	5.00	10.00	20.00
❑ MGV-8275 [M]	Lionel Hampton	1958	---	---	---
-- Canceled					
WHO'S WHO IN JAZZ					
❑ 21008	Who's Who Presents Lionel Hampton	1977	3.00	6.00	12.00
❑ 21017	Blackout	1978	3.00	6.00	12.00

HAMPTON, LIONEL, AND SVEND ASMUSSEN
Also see each artist's individual listings.

Number	Title	Yr	VG	VG+	NM
SONET					
❑ 779	As Time Goes By	1979	3.00	6.00	12.00

HAMPTON, LIONEL, AND STAN GETZ
Also see each artist's individual listings.

Number	Title	Yr	VG	VG+	NM
NORGRAN					
❑ MGN-1037 [M]	Hamp and Getz	1955	25.00	50.00	100.00
VERVE					
❑ MGV-8128 [M]	Hamp and Getz	1957	12.50	25.00	50.00
❑ V-8128 [M]	Hamp and Getz	1961	5.00	10.00	20.00

HAMPTON, LIONEL; ART TATUM; BUDDY RICH
Also see each artist's individual listings.

Number	Title	Yr	VG	VG+	NM
CLEF					
❑ MGC-709 [M]	The Hampton-Tatum-Rich Trio	1956	20.00	40.00	80.00
VERVE					
❑ MGV-8093 [M]	The Hampton-Tatum-Rich Trio	1957	12.50	25.00	50.00
❑ V-8093 [M]	The Hampton-Tatum-Rich Trio	1961	5.00	10.00	20.00

HAMPTON, LIONEL, AND CHARLIE TEAGARDEN
Also see each artist's individual listings.

Number	Title	Yr	VG	VG+	NM
CORAL					
❑ CRL 57438 [M]	The Great Hamp and Little T.	1963	5.00	10.00	20.00
❑ CRL 757438 [S]	The Great Hamp and Little T.	1963	6.25	12.50	25.00

HAMPTON, SLIDE
Trombonist, thus the nickname "Slide." Also has played tuba. Also see HAROLD BETTERS.

Number	Title	Yr	VG	VG+	NM
ATLANTIC					
❑ 1339 [M]	Sister Salvation	1960	7.50	15.00	30.00
-- Multicolor label, white "fan" logo at right					

Number	Title	Yr	VG	VG+	NM
❏ 1339 [M]	Sister Salvation	1962	3.75	7.50	15.00
-- Multicolor label, black "fan" logo at right					
❏ SD 1339 [S]	Sister Salvation	1960	10.00	20.00	40.00
-- Multicolor label, white "fan" logo at right					
❏ SD 1339 [S]	Sister Salvation	1962	5.00	10.00	20.00
-- Multicolor label, black "fan" logo at right					
❏ 1362 [M]	Somethin' Sanctified	1961	7.50	15.00	30.00
-- Multicolor label, white "fan" logo at right					
❏ 1362 [M]	Somethin' Sanctified	1962	3.75	7.50	15.00
-- Multicolor label, black "fan" logo at right					
❏ SD 1362 [S]	Somethin' Sanctified	1961	10.00	20.00	40.00
-- Multicolor label, white "fan" logo at right					
❏ SD 1362 [S]	Somethin' Sanctified	1962	5.00	10.00	20.00
-- Multicolor label, black "fan" logo at right					
❏ 1379 [M]	Jazz with a Twist	1962	6.25	12.50	25.00
❏ SD 1379 [S]	Jazz with a Twist	1962	7.50	15.00	30.00
❏ 1396 [M]	Explosion!	1962	5.00	10.00	20.00
❏ SD 1396 [S]	Explosion!	1962	6.25	12.50	25.00

CHARLIE PARKER

Number	Title	Yr	VG	VG+	NM
❏ PLP-803 [M]	Two Sides of Slide	1962	6.25	12.50	25.00
❏ PLP-803S [S]	Two Sides of Slide	1962	6.25	12.50	25.00

EPIC

Number	Title	Yr	VG	VG+	NM
❏ LA 16030 [M]	Drum Suite	1963	5.00	10.00	20.00
❏ BA 17030 [S]	Drum Suite	1963	6.25	12.50	25.00

STRAND

Number	Title	Yr	VG	VG+	NM
❏ SL-1006 [M]	Slide Hampton and His Horn of Plenty	1959	10.00	20.00	40.00
❏ SLS-1006 [S]	Slide Hampton and His Horn of Plenty	1959	10.00	20.00	40.00

HANCOCK, HERBIE
Pianist, keyboard player and composer. Also see HEADHUNTERS.

BLUE NOTE

Number	Title	Yr	VG	VG+	NM
❏ BN-LA152-F	Succotash	1974	3.00	6.00	12.00
❏ BN-LA399-H2 [(2)]	Herbie Hancock	1975	3.75	7.50	15.00
❏ BLP-4109 [M]	Takin' Off	1962	12.50	25.00	50.00
❏ BLP-4126 [M]	My Point of View	1963	8.75	17.50	35.00
❏ BLP-4147 [M]	Inventions and Dimensions	1963	8.75	17.50	35.00
❏ BLP-4175 [M]	Empyrean Isles	1964	8.75	17.50	35.00
❏ BLP-4195 [M]	Maiden Voyage	1965	8.75	17.50	35.00
❏ B1-46339	Maiden Voyage	1997	5.00	10.00	20.00
-- Audiophile reissue					
❏ BST-84109 [S]	Takin' Off	1962	10.00	20.00	40.00
-- With New York, USA address on label					
❏ BST-84109 [S]	Takin' Off	1967	3.75	7.50	15.00
-- With "A Division of Liberty Records" on label					
❏ BST-84109	Takin' Off	1987	2.50	5.00	10.00
-- "The Finest in Jazz Since 1939" reissue					
❏ BST-84126 [S]	My Point of View	1963	8.75	17.50	35.00
-- With New York, USA address on label					
❏ BST-84126 [S]	My Point of View	1967	3.75	7.50	15.00
-- With "A Division of Liberty Records" on label					
❏ BST-84126	My Point of View	1987	2.50	5.00	10.00
-- "The Finest in Jazz Since 1939" reissue					
❏ BST-84147 [S]	Inventions and Dimensions	1963	8.75	17.50	35.00
-- With New York, USA address on label					
❏ BST-84147 [S]	Inventions and Dimensions	1967	3.75	7.50	15.00
-- With "A Division of Liberty Records" on label					
❏ BST-84147	Inventions and Dimensions	1987	2.50	5.00	10.00
-- "The Finest in Jazz Since 1939" reissue					
❏ BST-84175 [S]	Empyrean Isles	1964	8.75	17.50	35.00
-- With New York, USA address on label					
❏ BST-84175 [S]	Empyrean Isles	1967	3.75	7.50	15.00
-- With "A Division of Liberty Records" on label					
❏ BST-84175	Empyrean Isles	1985	2.50	5.00	10.00
-- "The Finest in Jazz Since 1939" reissue					
❏ BST-84195 [S]	Maiden Voyage	1965	8.75	17.50	35.00
-- With New York, USA address on label					
❏ BST-84195 [S]	Maiden Voyage	1967	3.75	7.50	15.00
-- With "A Division of Liberty Records" on label					
❏ BST-84195 [S]	Maiden Voyage	1985	2.50	5.00	10.00
-- "The Finest in Jazz Since 1939" reissue					
❏ BST-84279	Speak Like a Child	1968	3.75	7.50	15.00
❏ BST-84279	Speak Like a Child	1986	2.50	5.00	10.00
-- "The Finest in Jazz Since 1939" reissue					
❏ BST-84321	The Prisoner	1969	3.75	7.50	15.00
❏ BST-84321	The Prisoner	1987	2.50	5.00	10.00
-- "The Finest in Jazz Since 1939" reissue					
❏ BST-84407	The Best of Herbie Hancock	1971	3.75	7.50	15.00
❏ B1-91142	The Best of Herbie Hancock	1988	2.50	5.00	10.00

COLUMBIA

Number	Title	Yr	VG	VG+	NM
❏ KC 32212	Sextant	1973	3.00	6.00	12.00
❏ PC 32212	Sextant	198?	2.00	4.00	8.00
-- Budget-line reissue					
❏ CQ 32371 [Q]	Head Hunters	1973	6.25	12.50	25.00
❏ KC 32371	Head Hunters	1973	3.00	6.00	12.00
❏ PC 32371	Head Hunters	197?	2.00	4.00	8.00
-- Reissue (with or without bar code)					

Number	Title	Yr	VG	VG+	NM
❏ PC 32965	Thrust	1974	3.00	6.00	12.00
-- No bar code on cover					
❏ PC 32965	Thrust	198?	2.00	4.00	8.00
-- Budget-line reissue with bar code					
❏ PCQ 32965 [Q]	Thrust	1974	6.25	12.50	25.00
❏ PC 33812	Man-Child	1975	3.00	6.00	12.00
-- No bar code on cover					
❏ PC 33812	Man-Child	198?	2.00	4.00	8.00
-- Budget-line reissue with bar code					
❏ PC 34280	Secrets	1976	3.00	6.00	12.00
-- No bar code on cover					
❏ PC 34280	Secrets	198?	2.00	4.00	8.00
-- Budget-line reissue with bar code					
❏ PCQ 34280 [Q]	Secrets	1976	6.25	12.50	25.00
❏ PG 34688 [(2)]	V.S.O.P.	1977	3.75	7.50	15.00
❏ JC 34907	Sunlight	1978	3.00	6.00	12.00
❏ C2 34976 [(2)]	V.S.O.P. Quintet	1978	3.75	7.50	15.00
❏ JC 35764	Feets Don't Fail Me Now	1979	3.00	6.00	12.00
❏ PC 35764	Feets Don't Fail Me Now	198?	2.00	4.00	8.00
-- Budget-line reissue					
❏ JC 36309	The Best of Herbie Hancock	1979	3.00	6.00	12.00
❏ JC 36415	Monster	1980	2.50	5.00	10.00
❏ PC 36415	Monster	198?	2.00	4.00	8.00
-- Budget-line reissue					
❏ JC 36578	Mr. Hands	1980	2.50	5.00	10.00
❏ PC 36578	Mr. Hands	198?	2.00	4.00	8.00
-- Budget-line reissue					
❏ FC 37387	Magic Windows	1981	2.50	5.00	10.00
❏ PC 37387	Magic Windows	198?	2.00	4.00	8.00
-- Budget-line reissue					
❏ FC 37928	Lite Me Up	1982	2.50	5.00	10.00
❏ PC 37928	Lite Me Up	198?	2.00	4.00	8.00
-- Budget-line reissue					
❏ FC 38814	Future Shock	1983	2.50	5.00	10.00
❏ FC 39478	Sound-System	1984	2.50	5.00	10.00
❏ PC 39478	Sound-System	1985	2.00	4.00	8.00
-- Budget-line reissue					
❏ FC 39870	Village Life	1985	2.50	5.00	10.00
❏ 8C8 39913 [EP]	Hardrock	1984	3.00	6.00	12.00
-- Picture disc					
❏ FC 40025	Perfect Machine	1988	2.50	5.00	10.00
❏ SC 40464	'Round Midnight	1986	2.50	5.00	10.00

MGM

Number	Title	Yr	VG	VG+	NM
❏ E-4447 [M]	Blow-Up	1967	8.75	17.50	35.00
❏ SE-4447 [S]	Blow-Up	1967	10.00	20.00	40.00
-- Also includes one track by the Yardbirds					

PAUSA

Number	Title	Yr	VG	VG+	NM
❏ 9002	Succotash	198?	2.50	5.00	10.00

TRIP

Number	Title	Yr	VG	VG+	NM
❏ UPF-194	Traces	197?	3.00	6.00	12.00

WARNER BROS.

Number	Title	Yr	VG	VG+	NM
❏ WS 1834	Fat Albert Rotunda	1970	3.75	7.50	15.00
❏ WS 1898	Mwandishi	1971	3.75	7.50	15.00
❏ BS 2617	Crossings	1972	3.75	7.50	15.00
❏ 2WS 2807 [(2)]	Treasure Chest	1974	3.75	7.50	15.00

HANCOCK, HERBIE, AND CHICK COREA
Also see each artist's individual listings.

COLUMBIA

Number	Title	Yr	VG	VG+	NM
❏ PC2 35663 [(2)]	An Evening with Herbie Hancock and Chick Corea	1979	3.00	6.00	12.00

POLYDOR

Number	Title	Yr	VG	VG+	NM
❏ PD-2-6238 [(2)]	An Evening with Chick Corea and Herbie Hancock	1979	3.00	6.00	12.00

HANDY, CAP'N JOHN
Alto saxophone player. Not the same person as the JOHN HANDY below.

GHB

Number	Title	Yr	VG	VG+	NM
❏ GHB-38	Everybody's Talking	1967	3.00	6.00	12.00
❏ GHBS-41	All Aboard, Volume 1	1967	3.00	6.00	12.00
❏ GHBS-42	All Aboard, Volume 2	1967	3.00	6.00	12.00
❏ GHBS-43	All Aboard, Volume 3	1967	3.00	6.00	12.00
❏ GHB-166	Cap'n John Handy with Geoff Bull and Bary Martyn's Band	1986	2.50	5.00	10.00

RCA VICTOR

Number	Title	Yr	VG	VG+	NM
❏ LPM-3762 [M]	Introducing Cap'n John Handy	1967	6.25	12.50	25.00
❏ LSP-3762 [S]	Introducing Cap'n John Handy	1967	3.75	7.50	15.00
❏ LSP-3929	New Orleans and the Blues	1968	3.00	6.00	12.00

HANDY, GEORGE
Pianist.

"X"

Number	Title	Yr	VG	VG+	NM
❏ LXA-1004 [M]	Handyland, U.S.A.	1954	15.00	30.00	60.00
❏ LXA-1032 [M]	By George! Handy, Of Course	1954	15.00	30.00	60.00

Number	Title	Yr	VG	VG+	NM

HANDY, JOHN
Saxophone (soprano, alto, tenor, baritone) player and bandleader. Best known in pop and R&B circles for his 1976 hit single "Hard Work," he is not the same person as the CAP'N JOHN HANDY above.
ABC IMPULSE!
| AS-9314 | Hard Work | 1976 | 2.50 | 5.00 | 10.00 |
| AS-9324 | Carnival | 1977 | 2.50 | 5.00 | 10.00 |
COLUMBIA
CL 2462 [M]	Recorded Live at the Monterey Jazz Festival	1966	3.75	7.50	15.00
CL 2567 [M]	The Second John Handy Album	1966	3.75	7.50	15.00
CL 2697 [M]	New View	1967	3.75	7.50	15.00
CS 9262 [S]	Recorded Live at the Monterey Jazz Festival	1966	3.75	7.50	15.00
CS 9367 [S]	The Second John Handy Album	1966	3.75	7.50	15.00
CS 9497 [S]	New View	1967	3.00	6.00	12.00
CS 9689	Projections	1968	3.00	6.00	12.00
MILESTONE
| M-9173 | Centerpiece, With Class | 1989 | 3.00 | 6.00 | 12.00 |
ROULETTE
R 52042 [M]	In the Ver-nac'-u-lar	1960	5.00	10.00	20.00
SR 52042 [S]	In the Ver-nac'-u-lar	1960	6.25	12.50	25.00
R 52088 [M]	No Coast Jazz	1962	5.00	10.00	20.00
SR 52088 [S]	No Coast Jazz	1962	6.25	12.50	25.00
R 52121 [M]	John Handy Jazz	1964	3.75	7.50	15.00
SR 52121 [S]	John Handy Jazz	1964	5.00	10.00	20.00
R 52124 [M]	Quote, Unquote	1964	3.75	7.50	15.00
SR 52124 [S]	Quote, Unquote	1964	5.00	10.00	20.00
WARNER BROS.
| BSK 3170 | Where Go the Boats | 1978 | 2.50 | 5.00 | 10.00 |
| BSK 3242 | Handy Dandy Man | 1978 | 2.50 | 5.00 | 10.00 |

HANDY, W.C.
Cornet player and bandleader, but far more influential as a composer ("St. Louis Blues" is a jazz standard, and "Beale Street Blues" and "Memphis Blues" helped spread the music).
DRG
| SL-5192 | Father of the Blues | 1980 | 2.50 | 5.00 | 10.00 |
HERITAGE
| 0052 [10] | Blues Revisited | 195? | 30.00 | 60.00 | 120.00 |

HANNA, JAKE
Drummer.
CONCORD JAZZ
CJ-11	Jake Hanna and Carl Fontana Live	1975	3.00	6.00	12.00
CJ-22	Kansas City Express	1976	3.00	6.00	12.00
CJ-35	Jake Hanna Takes Manhattan	1977	3.00	6.00	12.00

HANNA, KEN
Trumpeter, composer, arranger and conductor.
CAPITOL
| T 6512 [M] | Jazz for Dancers | 1955 | 10.00 | 20.00 | 40.00 |

HANNA, ROLAND
Pianist.
ARISTA FREEDOM
| AL 1010 | Perugia | 1975 | 3.00 | 6.00 | 12.00 |
ATCO
33-108 [M]	Destry Rides Again	1959	10.00	20.00	40.00
SD 33-108 [S]	Destry Rides Again	1959	10.00	20.00	40.00
33-121 [M]	Easy to Love	1960	7.50	15.00	30.00
SD 33-121 [S]	Easy to Love	1960	10.00	20.00	40.00
AUDIOPHILE
| AP-157 | This Must Be Love | 198? | 2.50 | 5.00 | 10.00 |
BASF
| 20875 | Child of Gemini | 1972 | 6.25 | 12.50 | 25.00 |
BEE HIVE
| BH-7013 | Roland Hanna and the New York Jazz Quartet in Chicago | 198? | 2.50 | 5.00 | 10.00 |
CHOICE
| 1003 | Sir Elf | 1974 | 3.75 | 7.50 | 15.00 |
INNER CITY
| IC-1072 | Roland Hanna Plays Music of Alec Wilder | 197? | 3.00 | 6.00 | 12.00 |
PROGRESSIVE
| 7012 | Time for the Dancers | 1978 | 3.00 | 6.00 | 12.00 |
STORYVILLE
| 4018 | Swing Me No Waltzes | 198? | 2.50 | 5.00 | 10.00 |
WEST 54TH
| 8003 | A Gift from the Magi | 1979 | 3.00 | 6.00 | 12.00 |

HANNA, ROLAND, AND GEORGE MRAZ
Also see each artist's individual listings.
CHOICE
| 1018 | Sir Elf Plus One | 1978 | 3.75 | 7.50 | 15.00 |

HANNIBAL
Full name: Hannibal Marvin Peterson. Trumpeter and percussionist.
ATLANTIC
| 81973 | Visions of a New World | 1989 | 3.00 | 6.00 | 12.00 |

HANRAHAN, KIP
Percussionist, composer and arranger.
AMERICAN CLAVE
1007	Coup De Tete	198?	3.00	6.00	12.00
1008/9 [(2)]	Desire Develops an Edge	1984	3.75	7.50	15.00
1010	Vertical's Currency	1985	3.00	6.00	12.00
1011 [EP]	A Few Short Notes from the End of the Run	198?	3.00	6.00	12.00
PANGAEA
| 42137 | Days & Nights of Blue Luck Inverted | 1987 | 5.00 | 10.00 | 20.00 |

HANSON, OLA
See CHUZ ALFRED.

HAPPY JAZZ BAND, THE
Members: Cliff Brewton, piano; Benny Valfre, banjo; Harvey Kindervater, drums; Willson Davis, sousaphone; Gene McKinney, trombone; Jim Cullum Jr.., cornet; Jim Cullum Sr., clarinet.
AUDIOPHILE
AP-86 [M]	Jazz from the San Antonio River	196?	3.00	6.00	12.00
APS-86 [S]	Jazz from the San Antonio River	196?	3.75	7.50	15.00
AP-87 [M]	Real Stuff	196?	3.00	6.00	12.00
APS-87 [S]	Real Stuff	196?	3.75	7.50	15.00
AP-93 [M]	Jim Cullum's Happy Jazz Band	196?	3.00	6.00	12.00
APS-93 [S]	Jim Cullum's Happy Jazz Band	196?	3.75	7.50	15.00
AP-96 [M]	Goose Pimples	196?	3.00	6.00	12.00
APS-96 [S]	Goose Pimples	196?	3.75	7.50	15.00
AP-114	College Street Caper	196?	3.00	6.00	12.00
AP-200	High Society	196?	3.00	6.00	12.00
HAPPY JAZZ
| HJ-201 | Zacatecas | 1969 | 3.00 | 6.00 | 12.00 |
| HJ-202 | We've Had Mighty Good Weather | 1970 | 3.00 | 6.00 | 12.00 |

HAQUE, FAREED
Guitarist.
PANGAEA
| 42156 | Voices Rising | 1988 | 2.50 | 5.00 | 10.00 |
| 82012 | Manresa | 1989 | 3.00 | 6.00 | 12.00 |

HARDAWAY, BOB
Tenor saxophone player. Also see EDDIE SHU.
BETHLEHEM
| BCP-1028 [10] | Bob Hardaway | 1955 | 30.00 | 60.00 | 120.00 |

HARDEN, WILBUR
Fluegel horn player and trumpeter.
SAVOY
MG-12127 [M]	Mainstream 1958/The East Coast Jazz Scene Featuring John Coltrane	1958	15.00	30.00	60.00
MG-12131 [M]	Jazz Way Out	1958	12.50	25.00	50.00
MG-12134 [M]	The King and I	1958	12.50	25.00	50.00
MG-12136 [M]	Tanganyika Suite	1958	12.50	25.00	50.00
SST-13002 [S]	The King and I	1959	10.00	20.00	40.00
SST-13004 [S]	Jazz Way Out	1959	10.00	20.00	40.00
SST-13005 [S]	Tanganyika Suite	1959	10.00	20.00	40.00

HARDIMAN, DAVID
Trumpeter and bandleader.
THERESA
| 104 | It'll Be Alright | 197? | 2.50 | 5.00 | 10.00 |

HARDING, ELLERINE
Female singer.
MAINSTREAM
| MRL-377 | Ellerine Harding | 1972 | 2.50 | 5.00 | 10.00 |

Number	Title	Yr	VG	VG+	NM

HARDMAN, BILL
Trumpeter. Also see JACKIE McLEAN.
MUSE
❑ MR-5152	Home	1978	3.00	6.00	12.00
❑ MR-5184	Politely	1981	3.00	6.00	12.00
❑ MR-5259	Focus	198?	2.50	5.00	10.00
SAVOY
| ❑ MG-12170 [M] | Bill Hardman Quintet | 1961 | 15.00 | 30.00 | 60.00 |
SAVOY JAZZ
| ❑ SJL-1164 | Saying Something | 1986 | 2.50 | 5.00 | 10.00 |

HARDY, HAGOOD
Vibraphone player and composer.
CAPITOL
❑ ST-11488	The Homecoming	1975	2.50	5.00	10.00
❑ ST-11552	Maybe Tomorrow	1976	2.50	5.00	10.00
❑ SN-16300	The Homecoming	198?	2.00	4.00	8.00
-- Budget-line reissue					

HARGROVE, ROY
Trumpeter.
NOVUS
| ❑ 3082-1-N | Diamond in the Rough | 1990 | 3.00 | 6.00 | 12.00 |

HARIAN, KENT
Bandleader.
CARAVAN
| ❑ LP-15611 [M] | Echoes of Joy | 1956 | 62.50 | 125.00 | 250.00 |

HARLEY, RUFUS
Perhaps the world's only jazz bagpipes player.
ATLANTIC
❑ SD 1504	Tribute to Courage	1969	3.75	7.50	15.00
❑ SD 1539	King/Queens	1970	3.75	7.50	15.00
❑ 3001 [M]	Bagpipe Blues	1967	6.25	12.50	25.00
❑ SD 3001 [S]	Bagpipe Blues	1967	3.75	7.50	15.00
❑ SD 3006	Scotch & Soul	1968	3.75	7.50	15.00

HARNELL, JOE
Pianist, most of whose recordings are more in a pop vein.
JUBILEE
❑ JLP-1015 [M]	Piano Inventions of Jo Harnell	1956	12.50	25.00	50.00
❑ JGM-5020 [M]	Joe Harnell and His Trio	1963	3.75	7.50	15.00
-- Reissue of 1015					

HARPER BROTHERS, THE
Led by Winard Harper (drums) and Phillip Harper (trumpet).
VERVE
| ❑ 837 033-1 | The Harper Brothers | 1988 | 2.50 | 5.00 | 10.00 |

HARPER, BILLY
Tenor saxophone player.
BLACK SAINT
| ❑ BSR-0001 | Black Saint | 198? | 3.75 | 7.50 | 15.00 |
SOUL NOTE
| ❑ SN-1001 | Billy Harper In Europe | 198? | 3.75 | 7.50 | 15.00 |
STRATA-EAST
| ❑ SES-19739 | Capra Black | 1973 | 10.00 | 20.00 | 40.00 |

HARPER, HERBIE
Trombonist.
BETHLEHEM
| ❑ BCP-1025 [10] | Herbie Harper | 1955 | 30.00 | 60.00 | 120.00 |
LIBERTY
| ❑ LRP-6003 [M] | Herbie Harper | 1956 | 20.00 | 40.00 | 80.00 |
MODE
| ❑ LP-100 [M] | Herbie Harper Sextet | 1957 | 25.00 | 50.00 | 100.00 |
NOCTURNE
| ❑ NLP-1 [10] | Herbie Harper Quintet | 1954 | 37.50 | 75.00 | 150.00 |
| ❑ NLP-7 [10] | Herbie Harper | 1954 | 37.50 | 75.00 | 150.00 |
SEABREEZE
| ❑ SBD-101 | Herbie Harper Revisited | 1981 | 3.00 | 6.00 | 12.00 |
TAMPA
❑ TP-11 [M]	Herbie Harper Quintet	1957	25.00	50.00	100.00
-- Red vinyl					
❑ TP-11 [M]	Herbie Harper Quintet	1958	12.50	25.00	50.00
-- Black vinyl					

HARPER, TONI
Female singer.
RCA VICTOR
❑ LPM-2092 [M]	Lady Lonely	1960	6.25	12.50	25.00
❑ LSP-2092 [S]	Lady Lonely	1960	7.50	15.00	30.00
❑ LPM-2253 [M]	Night Mood	1960	6.25	12.50	25.00
❑ LSP-2253 [S]	Night Mood	1960	7.50	15.00	30.00
VERVE
| ❑ MGV-2001 [M] | Toni Harper Sings | 1956 | 20.00 | 40.00 | 80.00 |
| ❑ V-2001 [M] | Toni Harper Sings | 1961 | 7.50 | 15.00 | 30.00 |

HARPER, WALT
Pianist.
GATEWAY
❑ 7005 [M]	Harper's Ferry	1964	3.75	7.50	15.00
❑ 7016 [M]	On the Road	1966	5.00	10.00	20.00
❑ S-7016 [S]	On the Road	1966	3.75	7.50	15.00

HARRELL, TOM
Trumpeter, fluegel horn player and composer.
BLACKHAWK
| ❑ BKH-50901 | The Play of Light | 1986 | 2.50 | 5.00 | 10.00 |
CONTEMPORARY
❑ C-14043	Stories	1988	2.50	5.00	10.00
❑ C-14054	Sail Away	1989	3.00	6.00	12.00
❑ C-14059	Form	1990	3.00	6.00	12.00

HARRIOTT, JOE
Alto saxophone player, also played baritone and tenor saxes.
ATLANTIC
❑ 1465 [M]	Indo-Jazz Suite	1966	3.00	6.00	12.00
❑ SD 1465 [S]	Indo-Jazz Suite	1966	3.75	7.50	15.00
❑ 1482 [M]	Indo-Jazz Fusions	1967	3.75	7.50	15.00
❑ SD 1482 [S]	Indo-Jazz Fusions	1967	3.00	6.00	12.00
CAPITOL
| ❑ DT 10351 [R] | Abstract | 1962 | 3.00 | 6.00 | 12.00 |
| ❑ T 10351 [M] | Abstract | 1962 | 5.00 | 10.00 | 20.00 |
JAZZLAND
❑ JLP-37 [M]	Southern Horizons	1961	6.25	12.50	25.00
❑ JLP-49 [M]	Free Form	1961	6.25	12.50	25.00
❑ JLP-937 [S]	Southern Horizons	1961	7.50	15.00	30.00
❑ JLP-949 [S]	Free Form	1961	7.50	15.00	30.00

HARRIS, ART
Pianist and composer.
KAPP
| ❑ KL-1015 [M] | Jazz Goes to Post-Graduate School | 1956 | 10.00 | 20.00 | 40.00 |

HARRIS, ART, AND MITCH LEIGH
Leigh is a bassoonist and composer (co-writer of "The Impossible Dream"). Also see ART HARRIS.
EPIC
| ❑ LG 1010 [10] | Modern Woodwind Expressions | 1954 | 12.50 | 25.00 | 50.00 |
| ❑ LN 3200 [M] | New Jazz in Hi-Fi | 1956 | 10.00 | 20.00 | 40.00 |
KAPP
| ❑ KL-1011 [M] | Baroque Band and Brass Choir -- Jazz 1775 | 1956 | 10.00 | 20.00 | 40.00 |

HARRIS, BARRY
Pianist.
ARGO
| ❑ LP-644 [M] | Breakin' It Up | 1959 | 10.00 | 20.00 | 40.00 |
| ❑ LPS-644 [S] | Breakin' It Up | 1959 | 7.50 | 15.00 | 30.00 |
CADET
| ❑ LP-644 [M] | Breakin' It Up | 1966 | 5.00 | 10.00 | 20.00 |
| ❑ LPS-644 [S] | Breakin' It Up | 1966 | 3.75 | 7.50 | 15.00 |
FANTASY
| ❑ OJC-208 | Barry Harris at the Jazz Workshop | 1986 | 2.50 | 5.00 | 10.00 |
| ❑ OJC-486 | Preminado | 1991 | 3.00 | 6.00 | 12.00 |
MILESTONE
| ❑ 47050 [(2)] | Stay Right With It | 197? | 3.75 | 7.50 | 15.00 |
PRESTIGE
❑ PRLP-7498 [M]	Luminescence	1967	7.50	15.00	30.00
❑ PRST-7498 [S]	Luminescence	1967	5.00	10.00	20.00
❑ PRST-7600	Bull's Eye	1969	5.00	10.00	20.00
❑ PRST-7733	Magnificent!	1970	5.00	10.00	20.00
RIVERSIDE
| ❑ RLP 12-326 [M] | Barry Harris at the Jazz Workshop | 1960 | 7.50 | 15.00 | 30.00 |

Number	Title	Yr	VG	VG+	NM
❏ RLP-354 [M]	Preminado	1961	7.50	15.00	30.00
❏ RLP-392 [M]	Listen to Barry Harris	1961	7.50	15.00	30.00
❏ RLP-413 [M]	Newer Than New	1962	6.25	12.50	25.00
❏ RLP-435 [M]	Chasin' the Bird	1962	6.25	12.50	25.00
❏ RLP-1177 [S]	Barry Harris at the Jazz Workshop	1960	10.00	20.00	40.00
❏ 6047	Preminado	197?	3.00	6.00	12.00
❏ 6123	Barry Harris at the Jazz Workshop	197?	3.00	6.00	12.00
❏ RS-9354 [S]	Preminado	1961	10.00	20.00	40.00
❏ RS-9392 [S]	Listen to Barry Harris	1961	10.00	20.00	40.00
❏ RS-9413 [S]	Newer Than New	1962	7.50	15.00	30.00
❏ RS-9435 [S]	Chasin' the Bird	1962	7.50	15.00	30.00
XANADU					
❏ 113	Barry Harris Plays Tadd Dameron	1975	3.00	6.00	12.00
❏ 130	Live in Tokyo	1976	3.00	6.00	12.00
❏ 154	Barry Harris Plays Barry Harris	1978	3.00	6.00	12.00
❏ 177	Tokyo: 1976	1980	3.00	6.00	12.00
❏ 213	The Bird of Red and Gold	1990	3.75	7.50	15.00

HARRIS, BEAVER
Drummer.

Number	Title	Yr	VG	VG+	NM
BLACK SAINT					
❏ BSR-0006/7 [(2)]	In-Sanity	198?	4.50	9.00	18.00
CADENCE JAZZ					
❏ 1002	Live at Nyon	198?	3.00	6.00	12.00
❏ 1003	Negcaumongus	198?	2.50	5.00	10.00
RED					
❏ VPA-146	360 Degree Aeutopia	198?	3.00	6.00	12.00
❏ VPA-151	Safe	198?	3.00	6.00	12.00
SOUL NOTE					
❏ SN-1002	Beautiful Africa	198?	3.75	7.50	15.00

HARRIS, BEAVER, AND DON PULLEN
Also see each artist's individual listings.

Number	Title	Yr	VG	VG+	NM
HANNIBAL					
❏ HNBL-2701	A Well Kept Secret	198?	2.50	5.00	10.00

HARRIS, BILL (1)
This Bill Harris is a trombonist. Also see TERRY GIBBS; CHUBBY JACKSON.

Number	Title	Yr	VG	VG+	NM
CLEF					
❏ MGC-125 [10]	Bill Harris Collates	1953	37.50	75.00	150.00
FANTASY					
❏ 3263 [M]	Bill Harris and Friends	1958	10.00	20.00	40.00
-- Red vinyl					
❏ 3263 [M]	Bill Harris and Friends	1959	6.25	12.50	25.00
-- Black vinyl					
❏ OJC-083	Bill Harris and Friends	198?	2.50	5.00	10.00
MERCURY					
❏ MGC-125 [10]	Bill Harris Collates	1953	---	---	---
-- Canceled					
NORGRAN					
❏ MGN-1062 [M]	The Bill Harris Herd	1956	30.00	60.00	120.00
VERVE					
❏ MGV-8152 [M]	The Bill Harris Herd	1957	---	---	---
-- Canceled?					
XANADU					
❏ 191	Memorial Album	198?	3.00	6.00	12.00

HARRIS, BILL (1), AND CHARLIE VENTURA
Also see each artist's individual listings.

Number	Title	Yr	VG	VG+	NM
PHOENIX					
❏ 11	Live at the Three Deuces	197?	2.50	5.00	10.00
❏ 14	Aces	197?	2.50	5.00	10.00

HARRIS, BILL (2)
This Bill Harris is a guitarist.

Number	Title	Yr	VG	VG+	NM
EMARCY					
❏ MG-36097 [M]	Bill Harris	1956	10.00	20.00	40.00
❏ MG-36113 [M]	The Harris Touch	1957	10.00	20.00	40.00
MERCURY					
❏ MG-20552 [M]	The Harris Touch	1960	7.50	15.00	30.00
❏ SR-60552 [S]	The Harris Touch	1960	6.25	12.50	25.00
WING					
❏ MGW-12220 [M]	Great Guitar Sounds	1963	5.00	10.00	20.00
❏ SRW-16220 [S]	Great Guitar Sounds	1963	3.75	7.50	15.00

HARRIS, CRAIG
Trombonist.

Number	Title	Yr	VG	VG+	NM
INDIA NAVIGATION					
❏ IN-1060	Aboriginal Affairs	198?	3.00	6.00	12.00
JMT					
❏ 834 408-1	Shelter	1987	3.00	6.00	12.00
❏ 834 415-1	Blackout in the Square Root of Soul	1988	3.00	6.00	12.00
SOUL NOTE					
❏ SN-1055	Black Bone	198?	3.00	6.00	12.00

HARRIS, DON "SUGARCANE"
Violinist, male singer and composer who also worked in R&B (The Squires, Don & Dewey) and rock (Frank Zappa, Pure Food & Drug Act).

Number	Title	Yr	VG	VG+	NM
BASF					
❏ 20878	Fiddler on the Rock	1972	3.75	7.50	15.00
❏ 21293	Sugarcane's Got the Blues	1972	3.75	7.50	15.00
❏ 21792	Cup Full of Dreams	1973	3.75	7.50	15.00
❏ 21912	I'm On Your Case	1974	3.75	7.50	15.00
EPIC					
❏ E 30027	Sugarcane	1971	3.75	7.50	15.00

HARRIS, EDDIE
Tenor saxophone player and composer.

Number	Title	Yr	VG	VG+	NM
ANGELACO					
❏ AN 3002	Sounds Incredible	1980	3.00	6.00	12.00
ATLANTIC					
❏ SD 2-311 [(2)]	Excursions	1973	3.75	7.50	15.00
❏ 1448 [M]	The In Sound	1966	3.00	6.00	12.00
❏ SD 1448 [S]	The In Sound	1966	3.75	7.50	15.00
❏ 1453 [M]	Mean Greens	1966	3.00	6.00	12.00
❏ SD 1453 [S]	Mean Greens	1966	3.75	7.50	15.00
❏ 1478 [M]	The Tender Storm	1967	3.75	7.50	15.00
❏ SD 1478 [S]	The Tender Storm	1967	3.75	7.50	15.00
❏ SD 1495	The Electrifying Eddie Harris	1968	3.75	7.50	15.00
❏ SD 1506	Plug Me In	1968	3.75	7.50	15.00
❏ SD 1517	Silver Cycles	1969	3.75	7.50	15.00
❏ SD 1529	High Voltage	1969	3.75	7.50	15.00
❏ 1545 [M-DJ]	The Best of Eddie Harris	1970	6.25	12.50	25.00
-- Promo-only white label mono pressing					
❏ SD 1545	The Best of Eddie Harris	1970	3.75	7.50	15.00
❏ SD 1554	Come On Down!	1970	3.75	7.50	15.00
❏ SD 1573	Free Speech	1971	3.75	7.50	15.00
❏ SD 1595	Eddie Harris Live at Newport	1971	3.00	6.00	12.00
❏ SD 1611	Instant Death	1972	3.00	6.00	12.00
❏ SD 1625	Eddie Harris Sings the Blues	1973	3.00	6.00	12.00
❏ SD 1647	E.H. in the U.K.	1974	3.00	6.00	12.00
❏ SD 1659	Is It In	1974	3.00	6.00	12.00
❏ SD 1669	I Need Some Money	1975	3.00	6.00	12.00
❏ SD 1675	Bad Luck Is All I Have	1975	3.00	6.00	12.00
❏ SD 1683	Why You're Overweight	1976	3.00	6.00	12.00
❏ SD 1698	How Can You Live Like That	1977	3.00	6.00	12.00
❏ SD 8807	The Versatile Eddie Harris	1982	2.50	5.00	10.00
❏ SW-94771	Instant Death	1972	3.75	7.50	15.00
-- Capitol Record Club edition					
BUDDAH					
❏ BDS 4004	Sculpture	1969	3.00	6.00	12.00
COLUMBIA					
❏ CL 2168 [M]	Cool Sax, Warm Heart	1964	3.75	7.50	15.00
❏ CL 2295 [M]	Cool Sax from Hollywood to Broadway	1965	3.75	7.50	15.00
❏ CS 8968 [S]	Cool Sax, Warm Heart	1964	5.00	10.00	20.00
❏ CS 9095 [S]	Cool Sax from Hollywood to Broadway	1965	5.00	10.00	20.00
❏ CS 9681 [M]	Here Comes the Judge	1968	6.25	12.50	25.00
-- Mono copies are promo only					
❏ CS 9681 [S]	Here Comes the Judge	1968	3.75	7.50	15.00
EXODUS					
❏ EX-6002 [M]	For Bird and Bags	1966	3.75	7.50	15.00
GNP CRESCENDO					
❏ GNPS-2073 [(2)]	Black Sax	1973	3.75	7.50	15.00
JANUS					
❏ 3020	Smokin'	1970	3.00	6.00	12.00
MUTT & JEFF					
❏ 5018	The Real Electrifying Eddie Harris	1982	3.00	6.00	12.00
RCA VICTOR					
❏ AFL1-3402	Playin' With Myself	1980	2.50	5.00	10.00
❏ APL1-2942	I'm Tired	1978	2.50	5.00	10.00
STEEPLECHASE					
❏ 1151	Eddie Harris Steps Up	1981	2.50	5.00	10.00
SUNSET					
❏ SUS-5234	The Explosive Eddie Harris	1969	3.00	6.00	12.00

Number	Title	Yr	VG	VG+	NM
TRADITION					
❏ 2067	Genius	1969	3.00	6.00	12.00
TRIP					
❏ 5005 [(2)]	Shades of Eddie Harris	1974	3.00	6.00	12.00
VEE JAY					
❏ VJLP 1081 [M]	The Theme from Exodus and Other Film Spectaculars	1964	3.75	7.50	15.00
❏ VJLPS 1081 [S]	The Theme from Exodus and Other Film Spectaculars	1964	5.00	10.00	20.00
❏ LP 3016 [M]	Exodus to Jazz	1961	7.50	15.00	30.00
❏ SR 3016 [S]	Exodus to Jazz	1961	10.00	20.00	40.00
❏ VJS-3016	Exodus to Jazz	198?	2.50	5.00	10.00
-- Reissue with thinner vinyl					
❏ LP 3025 [M]	Mighty Like a Rose	1961	7.50	15.00	30.00
❏ SR 3025 [S]	Mighty Like a Rose	1961	10.00	20.00	40.00
❏ LP 3027 [M]	Jazz for "Breakfast at Tiffany's"	1961	7.50	15.00	30.00
❏ SR 3027 [S]	Jazz for "Breakfast at Tiffany's"	1961	10.00	20.00	40.00
❏ LP 3028 [M]	A Study in Jazz	1962	5.00	10.00	20.00
❏ SR 3028 [S]	A Study in Jazz	1962	7.50	15.00	30.00
❏ LP 3031 [M]	Eddie Harris Goes to the Movies	1962	5.00	10.00	20.00
❏ SR 3031 [S]	Eddie Harris Goes to the Movies	1962	7.50	15.00	30.00
❏ LP 3034 [M]	Bossa Nova	1963	5.00	10.00	20.00
❏ SR 3034 [S]	Bossa Nova	1963	7.50	15.00	30.00
❏ LP 3037 [M]	Half and Half	1963	6.25	12.50	25.00
❏ SR 3037 [S]	Half and Half	1963	7.50	15.00	30.00
❏ VJS-3058	For Bird and Bags	198?	2.50	5.00	10.00

HARRIS, GENE
Pianist. Also see THE THREE SOUNDS.

Number	Title	Yr	VG	VG+	NM
BLUE NOTE					
❏ BN-LA141-G [(2)]	Yesterday, Today and Tomorrow	1973	6.25	12.50	25.00
❏ BN-LA313-G	Astral Signal	1974	5.00	10.00	20.00
❏ BN-LA519-G	Nexus	1975	3.75	7.50	15.00
❏ BN-LA634-G	Special Way	1976	3.75	7.50	15.00
❏ BN-LA760-H	Tone Tantrum	1977	3.75	7.50	15.00
❏ BST-84378	The Three Sounds	1971	5.00	10.00	20.00
❏ BST-84423	Gene Harris of the Three Sounds	1972	5.00	10.00	20.00
CONCORD JAZZ					
❏ CJ-303	The Gene Harris Trio Plus One	1986	2.50	5.00	10.00
JAM					
❏ 008	Hot Lips	198?	3.00	6.00	12.00
JUBILEE					
❏ JLP-1005 [M]	Our Love Is Here to Stay	1955	12.50	25.00	50.00
❏ JGM-1115 [M]	Genie in My Soul	1959	10.00	20.00	40.00

HARRIS, HAROLD
Pianist.

Number	Title	Yr	VG	VG+	NM
VEE JAY					
❏ LP-3018 [M]	Here's Harold	1962	6.25	12.50	25.00
❏ SR-3018 [S]	Here's Harold	1962	7.50	15.00	30.00
❏ LP-3036 [M]	Harold Harris at the Playboy Club	1963	6.25	12.50	25.00
❏ SR-3036 [S] ,	Harold Harris at the Playboy Club	1963	7.50	15.00	30.00

HARRISON, CASS

Number	Title	Yr	VG	VG+	NM
MGM					
❏ E-3388 [M]	The Duke and I	1956	10.00	20.00	40.00
❏ E-3495 [M]	Wrappin' It Up	1957	10.00	20.00	40.00

HARRISON, WENDELL
Clarinetist and tenor saxophone player.

Number	Title	Yr	VG	VG+	NM
REBIRTH					
❏ WHR-015	Dreams of a Love Supreme	1985	2.50	5.00	10.00
❏ WHR-016	Organic Dream	1985	2.50	5.00	10.00
❏ WHR-040	Reawakening	1985	2.50	5.00	10.00
❏ WHR-140	Birth of a Fossil	1986	2.50	5.00	10.00
❏ WHR-150	"Wait" Broke the Wagon Down	1987	2.50	5.00	10.00
❏ WHR-160	Carnivorous Lady	1988	3.00	6.00	12.00
TRIBE					
❏ PRSD-2212	Evening with the Devil	197?	25.00	50.00	100.00
❏ PRSD-4002	Message from the Tribe, Vol. 3	197?	25.00	50.00	100.00
WENHA					
❏ 015	Dreams of a Love Supreme	198?	12.50	25.00	50.00
❏ 016	Organic Dream	198?	10.00	20.00	40.00
❏ 2212	Evening with the Devil	198?	5.00	10.00	20.00
-- Reissue of Tribe 2212					
❏ 4002	Message from the Tribe	198?	5.00	10.00	20.00
-- Reissue of Tribe 4002					

HARROW, NANCY
Female singer.

Number	Title	Yr	VG	VG+	NM
ATLANTIC					
❏ 8075 [M]	You Never Know	1963	6.25	12.50	25.00

Number	Title	Yr	VG	VG+	NM
❏ SD 8075 [S]	You Never Know	1963	7.50	15.00	30.00
AUDIOPHILE					
❏ AP-142	Anything Goes	1979	3.00	6.00	12.00
CANDID					
❏ CD-8008 [M]	Wild Women Don't Have the Blues	1962	7.50	15.00	30.00
❏ CD-9008 [S]	Wild Women Don't Have the Blues	1962	10.00	20.00	40.00

HART, BILLY
Drummer.

Number	Title	Yr	VG	VG+	NM
GRAMAVISION					
❏ 18-8502	Oshumare	1986	3.00	6.00	12.00
HORIZON					
❏ SP-725	Enchance	1978	3.00	6.00	12.00

HART, JOHN
Guitarist.

Number	Title	Yr	VG	VG+	NM
BLUE NOTE					
❏ B1-93476	One Down	1990	3.75	7.50	15.00

HARTH, ALFRED
Multi-instrumentalist (tenor sax; alto sax; baritone sax; trumpet; trombone; clarinet; bass clarinet; cello; male singer).

Number	Title	Yr	VG	VG+	NM
ECM					
❏ 1264	This Earth	198?	2.50	5.00	10.00

HARTMAN, GEORGE
See IRVING FAZOLA.

HARTMAN, JOHNNY
Male vocalist.

Number	Title	Yr	VG	VG+	NM
ABC IMPULSE!					
❏ AS-57 [S]	I Just Dropped By to Say Hello	1968	3.00	6.00	12.00
❏ AS-74 [S]	The Voice That Is	1968	3.00	6.00	12.00
ABC-PARAMOUNT					
❏ ABC-574 [M]	The Unforgettable Johnny Hartman	1966	7.50	15.00	30.00
❏ ABCS-574 [S]	The Unforgettable Johnny Hartman	1966	10.00	20.00	40.00
AUDIOPHILE					
❏ AP-181	This One's for Tedi	1981	3.00	6.00	12.00
BEE HIVE					
❏ BH-7012	Once in Every Life	198?	2.50	5.00	10.00
BETHLEHEM					
❏ BCP-43 [M]	Songs from the Heart	1956	20.00	40.00	80.00
❏ BCP-6014 [M]	All of Me: The Debonair Mr. Hartman	1957	20.00	40.00	80.00
❏ BCP-6045	All of Me	197?	3.00	6.00	12.00
-- Reissue, distributed by RCA Victor					
IMPULSE!					
❏ A-57 [M]	I Just Dropped By to Say Hello	1964	7.50	15.00	30.00
❏ AS-57 [S]	I Just Dropped By to Say Hello	1964	10.00	20.00	40.00
❏ A-74 [M]	The Voice That Is	1965	7.50	15.00	30.00
❏ AS-74 [S]	The Voice That Is	1965	10.00	20.00	40.00
MCA					
❏ 29039	I Just Dropped By to Say Hello	1980	2.50	5.00	10.00
❏ 29040	The Voice That Is	1980	2.50	5.00	10.00
MUSICOR					
❏ 2502	Johnny Hartman, Johnny Hartman	1976	3.00	6.00	12.00
REGENT					
❏ MG-6014 [M]	Just You, Just Me	1956	20.00	40.00	80.00
SAVOY JAZZ					
❏ SJL-1134	First, Lasting and Always	198?	2.50	5.00	10.00

HARVEY, LAURENCE
The below are spoken-word recordings with a jazz background. Harvey is much better known as an actor (The Manchurian Candidate, among others).

Number	Title	Yr	VG	VG+	NM
ATLANTIC					
❏ 1367 [M]	This Is My Beloved	1962	10.00	20.00	40.00
❏ SD 1367 [S]	This Is My Beloved	1962	12.50	25.00	50.00

HASHIM, MICHAEL
Alto and soprano saxophone player.

Number	Title	Yr	VG	VG+	NM
STASH					
❏ 227	Peacocks	1983	2.50	5.00	10.00

Number	Title	Yr	VG	VG+	NM
HASSELBACH, MARK					

Best known as a trumpeter, but also plays fluegel horn, flute, trombone and keyboards, with an occasional turn as drummer or bass player.

JAZZIMAGE

Number	Title	Yr	VG	VG+	NM
❏ JZ-104	Hasselblast	198?	3.00	6.00	12.00

HASSELL, JON

Trumpeter. A pioneer in ambient music, he has collaborated with Brian Eno.

ECM

❏ 1327	Power Spot	1987	3.00	6.00	12.00

INTUITION

❏ C1-46880	The Surgeon of the Nightsky Restores Dead Things by the Power of Sound	1988	3.00	6.00	12.00
❏ C1-91186	Flash of the Spirit	1989	3.00	6.00	12.00

LOVELY

❏ 1021	Vernal Equinox	1978	3.75	7.50	15.00

OPAL/WARNER BROS.

❏ 26153	City: Works of Fiction	1990	3.75	7.50	15.00

TOMATO

❏ TOM-7019	Earthquake Island	1979	3.75	7.50	15.00

HATZA, GREG

Organist.

CORAL

❏ CRL 57493 [M]	The Wizardry of Greg Hatza	1962	3.00	6.00	12.00
❏ CRL 57495 [M]	Organized Jazz	1963	3.75	7.50	15.00
❏ CRL 757493 [S]	The Wizardry of Greg Hatza	1962	3.75	7.50	15.00
❏ CRL 757495 [S]	Organized Jazz	1963	5.00	10.00	20.00

HAUSER, FRITZ

Drummer.

HAT ART

❏ 2023 [(2)]	Solodrumming	1986	3.75	7.50	15.00

HAVENS, BOB

Trombonist and bandleader.

GHB

❏ GHB-143 [M]	Bob Havens' New Orleans All-Stars	1969	3.00	6.00	12.00

SOUTHLAND

❏ 226 [M]	Bob Havens in New Orleans	1961	3.75	7.50	15.00
❏ 243 [M]	Bob Havens' New Orleans All-Stars	1966	3.00	6.00	12.00

HAWES, HAMPTON

Pianist. Also see CURTIS FULLER; FREDDIE REDD.

ARISTA FREEDOM

❏ AL 1020	Live at the Montmartre	1976	3.00	6.00	12.00
❏ AL 1043	Copenhagen Night Music	1977	3.00	6.00	12.00

BLACK LION

❏ 122	Spanish Steps	197?	3.75	7.50	15.00

CONCORD JAZZ

❏ CJ-222	Recorded Live at the Great American Music Hall	198?	2.50	5.00	10.00

CONTEMPORARY

❏ C-3505 [M]	Hampton Hawes	1955	12.50	25.00	50.00
❏ C-3515 [M]	This Is Hampton Hawes	1956	12.50	25.00	50.00
❏ C-3523 [M]	Everybody Likes Hampton Hawes	1956	12.50	25.00	50.00
❏ C-3545 [M]	All Night Session! Volume 1	1958	12.50	25.00	50.00
❏ C-3546 [M]	All Night Session! Volume 2	1958	12.50	25.00	50.00
❏ C-3547 [M]	All Night Session! Volume 3	1958	12.50	25.00	50.00
❏ C-3553 [M]	Four! Hampton Hawes!!!	1958	12.50	25.00	50.00
❏ M-3589 [M]	For Real!	1959	10.00	20.00	40.00
❏ M-3614 [M]	The Green Leaves of Summer	1964	7.50	15.00	30.00
❏ M-3616 [M]	Here and Now	1965	5.00	10.00	20.00
❏ M-3621 [M]	The Seance	1966	5.00	10.00	20.00
❏ M-3631 [M]	I'm All Smiles	1967	6.25	12.50	25.00
❏ S-7545 [S]	All Night Session! Volume 1	1960	10.00	20.00	40.00
❏ S-7546 [S]	All Night Session! Volume 2	1960	10.00	20.00	40.00
❏ S-7547 [S]	All Night Session! Volume 3	1960	10.00	20.00	40.00
❏ S-7553 [S]	Four! Hampton Hawes!!!	1960	10.00	20.00	40.00
❏ S-7589 [S]	For Real!	1959	7.50	15.00	30.00
❏ S-7614 [S]	The Green Leaves of Summer	1964	10.00	20.00	40.00
❏ S-7616 [S]	Here and Now	1965	6.25	12.50	25.00
❏ S-7621 [S]	The Seance	1966	6.25	12.50	25.00
❏ S-7631 [S]	I'm All Smiles	1967	5.00	10.00	20.00

ENJA

❏ 3099	Live at Jazz Showcase in Chicago, Vol. 1	198?	3.00	6.00	12.00

FANTASY

❏ OJC-165	Four! Hampton Hawes!!!	198?	2.50	5.00	10.00
❏ OJC-178	I'm All Smiles	198?	2.50	5.00	10.00
❏ OJC-316	Hampton Hawes	198?	2.50	5.00	10.00
❏ OJC-318	This Is Hampton Hawes	198?	2.50	5.00	10.00
❏ OJC-421	Everybody Likes Hampton Hawes	1990	3.00	6.00	12.00
❏ OJC-455	Seance	1990	3.00	6.00	12.00
❏ OJC-476	The Green Leaves of Summer	1991	3.00	6.00	12.00
❏ OJC-638	All Night Session! Volume 1	1991	3.00	6.00	12.00
❏ OJC-639	All Night Session! Volume 2	1991	3.00	6.00	12.00
❏ OJC-640	All Night Session! Volume 3	1991	3.00	6.00	12.00

JAZZ MAN

❏ 5022	Spanish Steps	198?	2.50	5.00	10.00

MOON

❏ MLP-005	Autumn Leaves in Paris	199?	3.75	7.50	15.00

PRESTIGE

❏ PRLP-212 [10]	Hampton Hawes Quartet	1955	25.00	50.00	100.00
❏ PRST-7695	Hampton Hawes in Europe	1969	3.75	7.50	15.00
❏ 10046	The Universe	1972	3.75	7.50	15.00
❏ 10060	Blues for Walls	1973	3.75	7.50	15.00
❏ 10077	Playin' in the Yard	1974	3.75	7.50	15.00
❏ 10088	Northern Windows	1974	3.75	7.50	15.00

RCA VICTOR

❏ JPL1-1508	Challenge	1976	3.00	6.00	12.00

STEREO RECORDS

❏ S-7026 [S]	Four! Hampton Hawes!!!	1959	12.50	25.00	50.00

VANTAGE

❏ VLP-1 [10]	Hamp Hawes	1954	37.50	75.00	150.00

VAULT

❏ LPS-9009	Hampton Hawes Plays Movie Musicals	1969	5.00	10.00	20.00
❏ LPS-9010	High in the Sky	1970	5.00	10.00	20.00

XANADU

❏ 161	Memorial Album	198?	3.00	6.00	12.00

HAWES, HAMPTON/PAUL CHAMBERS

Also see each artist's individual listings.

XANADU

❏ 104	The East/West Conspiracy	197?	3.00	6.00	12.00

HAWKINS, COLEMAN

Tenor saxophone player. A favorite among audiophiles, his "Body and Soul" is a standard. Also see EARL "FATHA" HINES; SONNY ROLLINS; CLARK TERRY.

ABC IMPULSE!

❏ AS-26 [S]	Duke Ellington Meets Coleman Hawkins	1968	3.75	7.50	15.00
❏ AS-28 [S]	Desafinado	1968	3.75	7.50	15.00
❏ AS-34 [S]	Today and Now	1968	3.75	7.50	15.00
❏ AS-87 [S]	Wrapped Tight	1968	3.75	7.50	15.00
❏ AS-9258 [(2)]	Reevaluations: The Impulse Years	197?	3.75	7.50	15.00

ADVANCE

❏ LSP-9 [10]	Coleman Hawkins Favorites	1951	75.00	150.00	300.00

AMERICAN RECORDING SOCIETY

❏ G-316 [M]	Coleman Hawkins and His Orchestra	1956	12.50	25.00	50.00

APOLLO

❏ LAP-101 [10]	Coleman Hawkins All Stars	1951	75.00	150.00	300.00

ARCHIVE OF FOLK AND JAZZ

❏ 252	Coleman Hawkins	197?	2.50	5.00	10.00

BLUEBIRD

❏ 5658-1-RB [(2)]	Body and Soul	1986	3.75	7.50	15.00

BRUNSWICK

❏ BL 58030 [10]	Tenor Sax	1952	50.00	100.00	200.00

CAPITOL

❏ H 327 [10]	Classics in Jazz	1952	62.50	125.00	250.00
❏ T 819 [M]	Gilded Hawk	1957	20.00	40.00	80.00
❏ M-11030	Hollywood Stampede	1973	3.75	7.50	15.00

COMMODORE

❏ XFL-14936	Coleman Hawkins	198?	2.50	5.00	10.00
❏ FL-20,025 [10]	King of the Tenor Sax	1952	75.00	150.00	300.00

CONCERT HALL JAZZ

❏ J-1201 [M]	Improvisations Unlimited	1955	15.00	30.00	60.00

CONTINENTAL

❏ 16006 [M]	On the Bean	1962	6.25	12.50	25.00
❏ S-16006 [S]	On the Bean	1962	7.50	15.00	30.00

CROWN

❏ CST-206 [R]	Coleman Hawkins and His Orchestra	196?	2.50	5.00	10.00
❏ CST-224 [R]	The Hawk Swing	196?	2.50	5.00	10.00
❏ CLP-5181 [M]	Coleman Hawkins and His Orchestra	1960	5.00	10.00	20.00

Number	Title	Yr	VG	VG+	NM
❏ CLP-5207 [M]	The Hawk Swing	1961	5.00	10.00	20.00
DECCA					
❏ DL 4081 [M]	The Hawk Blows at Midnight	1961	7.50	15.00	30.00
❏ DL 8127 [M]	The Hawk Talks	1955	20.00	40.00	80.00
❏ DL 74081 [S]	The Hawk Blows at Midnight	1961	10.00	20.00	40.00
EMARCY					
❏ MG-26013 [10]	The Bean	1954	50.00	100.00	200.00
FANTASY					
❏ OJC-027	The Hawk Flies High	1982	2.50	5.00	10.00
❏ OJC-096	Soul	198?	2.50	5.00	10.00
❏ OJC-181	At Ease with Coleman Hawkins	1985	2.50	5.00	10.00
❏ OJC-225	The Coleman Hawkins All Stars	198?	2.50	5.00	10.00
❏ OJC-294	Hawk Eyes	1988	2.50	5.00	10.00
❏ OJC-418	Coleman Hawkins Plus the Red Garland Trio	1990	3.00	6.00	12.00
❏ OJC-420	Night Hawk	1990	3.00	6.00	12.00
❏ OJC-6001	In a Mellow Tone	1988	2.50	5.00	10.00
FELSTED					
❏ SJA-2005 [S]	The High and Mighty Hawk	1959	20.00	40.00	80.00
❏ FAJ-7005 [M]	The High and Mighty Hawk	1959	15.00	30.00	60.00
GNP CRESCENDO					
❏ GNP-9003	Coleman Hawkins in Holland	197?	2.50	5.00	10.00
GRP IMPULSE!					
❏ 227 [S]	Desafinado	199?	3.75	7.50	15.00
-- Reissue on audiophile vinyl					
IMPULSE!					
❏ A-26 [M]	Duke Ellington Meets Coleman Hawkins	1962	6.25	12.00	25.00
❏ AS-26 [S]	Duke Ellington Meets Coleman Hawkins	1962	7.50	15.00	30.00
❏ A-28 [M]	Desafinado	1963	6.25	12.50	25.00
❏ AS-28 [S]	Desafinado	1963	7.50	15.00	30.00
❏ A-34 [M]	Today and Now	1963	6.25	12.50	25.00
❏ AS-34 [S]	Today and Now	1963	7.50	15.00	30.00
❏ A-87 [M]	Wrapped Tight	1965	6.25	12.50	25.00
❏ AS-87 [S]	Wrapped Tight	1965	7.50	15.00	30.00
JAZZ MAN					
❏ 5042	Jazz Reunion	198?	2.50	5.00	10.00
JAZZTONE					
❏ J-1201 [M]	Timeless Jazz	1955	12.50	25.00	50.00
-- Reissue of Concert Hall Jazz 1201					
MAINSTREAM					
❏ S-6037 [R]	Meditations	1965	3.75	7.50	15.00
❏ 56037 [M]	Meditations	1965	6.25	12.50	25.00
MASTER JAZZ					
❏ 8115	The High and Mighty Hawk	197?	3.00	6.00	12.00
MILESTONE					
❏ 47015 [(2)]	The Hawk Flies	197?	`3.75	7.50	15.00
MOODSVILLE					
❏ MVLP-7 [M]	At Ease with Coleman Hawkins	1960	12.50	25.00	50.00
-- Green label					
❏ MVLP-7 [M]	At Ease with Coleman Hawkins	1965	6.25	12.50	25.00
-- Blue label, trident logo at right					
❏ MVLP-15 [M]	The Hawk Relaxes	1961	12.50	25.00	50.00
-- Green label					
❏ MVLP-15 [M]	The Hawk Relaxes	1965	6.25	12.50	25.00
-- Blue label, trident logo at right					
❏ MVLP-23 [M]	Good Old Broadway	1962	10.00	20.00	40.00
-- Green label					
❏ MVST-23 [S]	Good Old Broadway	1962	12.50	25.00	50.00
-- Green label					
❏ MVST-23 [S]	Good Old Broadway	1965	6.25	12.50	25.00
-- Blue label, trident logo at right					
❏ MVLP-23 [M]	Good Old Broadway	1965	5.00	10.00	20.00
-- Blue label, trident logo at right					
❏ MVLP-25 [M]	The Jazz Version of No Strings	1962	10.00	20.00	40.00
-- Green label					
❏ MVLP-25 [M]	The Jazz Version of No Strings	1965	5.00	10.00	20.00
-- Blue label, trident logo at right					
❏ MVST-25 [S]	The Jazz Version of No Strings	1962	12.50	25.00	50.00
-- Green label					
❏ MVST-25 [S]	The Jazz Version of No Strings	1965	6.25	12.50	25.00
-- Blue label, trident logo at right					
❏ MVLP-31 [M]	Make Someone Happy	1963	10.00	20.00	40.00
-- Green label					
❏ MVLP-31 [M]	Make Someone Happy	1965	5.00	10.00	20.00
-- Blue label, trident logo at right					
❏ MVST-31 [S]	Make Someone Happy	1963	12.50	25.00	50.00
-- Green label					
❏ MVST-31 [S]	Make Someone Happy	1965	6.25	12.50	25.00
-- Blue label, trident logo at right					
MOON					
❏ MLP-018	Coleman Hawkins Vs. Oscar Peterson	199?	3.75	7.50	15.00

Number	Title	Yr	VG	VG+	NM
PABLO					
❏ 2310 707	Sirius	197?	3.75	7.50	15.00
❏ 2310 933	Bean Stalkin'	198?	3.00	6.00	12.00
PHILIPS					
❏ PHM 200-022 [M]	Jazz at the Metropole	1962	5.00	10.00	20.00
❏ PHS 600-022 [S]	Jazz at the Metropole	1962	6.25	12.50	25.00
PHOENIX					
❏ 8	In Concert	197?	2.50	5.00	10.00
❏ 13	Centerpiece	197?	2.50	5.00	10.00
PRESTIGE					
❏ PRLP-7149 [M]	Soul	1958	20.00	40.00	80.00
❏ PRLP-7156 [M]	Hawk Eyes	1958	20.00	40.00	80.00
❏ PRST-7647	Pioneers	1969	3.75	7.50	15.00
❏ PRST-7671	Night Hawk	1969	3.75	7.50	15.00
❏ PRST-7753	Blues Groove	1970	3.75	7.50	15.00
❏ PRST-7824	Bean and the Boys	1970	3.75	7.50	15.00
❏ PRST-7824	Coleman Hawkins and the Boys	1971	3.00	6.00	12.00
❏ PRST-7857	Hawk Eyes!	1971	3.75	7.50	15.00
❏ 24051 [(2)]	Jam Session in Swingville	198?	3.00	6.00	12.00
❏ 24083 [(2)]	The Real Thing	198?	3.00	6.00	12.00
❏ 24106 [(2)]	Moonglow	198?	3.00	6.00	12.00
QUINTESSENCE					
❏ 25371	Golden Hawk	1979	2.50	5.00	10.00
RCA VICTOR					
❏ LJM-1017 [M]	Hawk In Flight	1955	20.00	40.00	80.00
❏ LPM-1281 [M]	Hawk in Hi-Fi	1956	20.00	40.00	80.00
❏ LPV-501 [M]	Body and Soul	1965	5.00	10.00	20.00
RIVERSIDE					
❏ RLP 12-117/8 [(2) M]	Coleman Hawkins: A Documentary	1956	50.00	100.00	200.00
❏ RLP 12-233 [M]	The Hawk Flies High	1957	25.00	50.00	100.00
-- White label, blue print					
❏ RLP 12-233 [M]	The Hawk Flies High	1959	12.50	25.00	50.00
-- Blue label, microphone logo at top					
❏ 3049	Think Deep	1970	3.75	7.50	15.00
SAVOY					
❏ MG-12013 [M]	The Hawk Returns	1955	30.00	60.00	120.00
❏ MG-15039 [10]	The Hawk Talks	1954	50.00	100.00	200.00
SAVOY JAZZ					
❏ SJL-1123	Coleman Hawkins Meets the Big Sax Section	1979	2.50	5.00	10.00
STINSON					
❏ SLP-22 [10]	Originals with Hawkins	1950	75.00	150.00	300.00
❏ SLP-22 [M]	Originals with Hawkins	195?	10.00	20.00	40.00
SUNBEAM					
❏ 204	Coleman Hawkins at the Savoy 1940	197?	2.50	5.00	10.00
SWINGVILLE					
❏ SVLP-2001 [M]	Coleman Hawkins Plus the Red Garland Trio	1960	12.50	25.00	50.00
-- Purple label					
❏ SVLP-2001 [M]	Coleman Hawkins Plus the Red Garland Trio	1965	6.25	12.50	25.00
-- Blue label, trident logo at right					
❏ SVLP-2005 [M]	The Coleman Hawkins All Stars	1960	12.50	25.00	50.00
-- Purple label					
❏ SVLP-2005 [M]	The Coleman Hawkins All Stars	1965	6.25	12.50	25.00
-- Blue label, trident logo at right					
❏ SVLP-2016 [M]	Night Hawk	1961	12.50	25.00	50.00
-- Purple label					
❏ SVLP-2016 [M]	Night Hawk	1965	6.25	12.50	25.00
-- Blue label, trident logo at right					
❏ SVLP-2024 [M]	Things Ain't What They Used to Be	1961	10.00	20.00	40.00
-- Purple label					
❏ SVLP-2024 [M]	Things Ain't What They Used to Be	1965	5.00	10.00	20.00
-- Blue label, trident logo at right					
❏ SVST-2024 [S]	Things Ain't What They Used to Be	1961	12.50	25.00	50.00
-- Red label					
❏ SVST-2024 [S]	Things Ain't What They Used to Be	1965	6.25	12.50	25.00
-- Blue label, trident logo at right					
❏ SVLP-2025 [M]	Years Ago	1961	10.00	20.00	40.00
-- Purple label					
❏ SVLP-2025 [M]	Years Ago	1965	5.00	10.00	20.00
-- Blue label, trident logo at right					
❏ SVST-2025 [S]	Years Ago	1961	12.50	25.00	50.00
-- Red label					
❏ SVST-2025 [S]	Years Ago	1965	6.25	12.50	25.00
-- Blue label, trident logo at right					
❏ SVLP-2035 [M]	Blues Groove	1962	12.50	25.00	50.00
-- Purple label					

Number	Title	Yr	VG	VG+	NM
❏ SVLP-2035 [M]	Blues Groove	1965	6.25	12.50	25.00
-- Blue label, trident logo at right					
❏ SVST-2035 [S]	Blues Groove	1962	10.00	20.00	40.00
-- Red label					
❏ SVST-2035 [S]	Blues Groove	1965	5.00	10.00	20.00
-- Blue label, trident logo at right					
❏ SVLP-2038 [M]	Soul	1962	12.50	25.00	50.00
-- Purple label					
❏ SVLP-2038 [M]	Soul	1965	6.25	12.50	25.00
-- Blue label, trident logo at right					
❏ SVST-2038 [S]	Soul	1962	10.00	20.00	40.00
-- Red label					
❏ SVST-2038 [S]	Soul	1965	5.00	10.00	20.00
-- Blue label, trident logo at right					
❏ SVLP-2039 [M]	Hawk Eyes	1962	12.50	25.00	50.00
-- Purple label					
❏ SVLP-2039 [M]	Hawk Eyes	1965	6.25	12.50	25.00
-- Blue label, trident logo at right					
❏ SVST-2039 [S]	Hawk Eyes	1962	10.00	20.00	40.00
-- Red label					
❏ SVST-2039 [S]	Hawk Eyes	1965	5.00	10.00	20.00
-- Blue label, trident logo at right					
TRIP					
❏ 5515	Coleman Hawkins and the Trumpet Kings	197?	2.50	5.00	10.00
URANIA					
❏ UJLP-1201 [M]	Accent on Tenor Sax	1955	25.00	50.00	100.00
❏ UJLP-41201 [R]	Accent on Tenor Sax	196?	5.00	10.00	20.00
VERVE					
❏ UMV-2532	Coleman Hawkins Encounters Ben Webster	198?	2.50	5.00	10.00
❏ UMV-2623	Coleman Hawkins at Newport	198?	2.50	5.00	10.00
❏ MGVS-6033 [S]	The Genius of Coleman Hawkins	1960	10.00	20.00	40.00
❏ MGVS-6066 [S]	Coleman Hawkins Encounters Ben Webster	1960	10.00	20.00	40.00
❏ MGVS-6066 [S]	Coleman Hawkins Encounters Ben Webster	199?	6.25	12.50	25.00
-- Classic Records reissue on audiophile vinyl					
❏ MGVS-6110 [S]	Coleman Hawkins and His Confreres with the Oscar Peterson Trio	1960	10.00	20.00	40.00
❏ MGV-8261 [M]	The Genius of Coleman Hawkins	1958	12.50	25.00	50.00
❏ V-8261 [M]	The Genius of Coleman Hawkins	1961	6.25	12.50	25.00
❏ V6-8261 [S]	The Genius of Coleman Hawkins	1961	5.00	10.00	20.00
❏ MGV-8327 [M]	Coleman Hawkins Encounters Ben Webster	1959	12.50	25.00	50.00
❏ V-8327 [M]	Coleman Hawkins Encounters Ben Webster	1961	6.25	12.50	25.00
❏ V6-8327 [S]	Coleman Hawkins Encounters Ben Webster	1961	5.00	10.00	20.00
❏ MGV-8346 [M]	Coleman Hawkins and His Confreres with the Oscar Peterson Trio	1959	12.50	25.00	50.00
❏ V-8346 [M]	Coleman Hawkins and His Confreres with the Oscar Peterson Trio	1961	6.25	12.50	25.00
❏ V6-8346 [S]	Coleman Hawkins and His Confreres with the Oscar Peterson Trio	1961	5.00	10.00	20.00
❏ V-8509 [M]	Hawkins! Alive! At the Village Gate	1963	6.25	12.50	25.00
❏ V6-8509 [S]	Hawkins! Alive! At the Village Gate	1963	7.50	15.00	30.00
❏ V-8568 [M]	The Essential Coleman Hawkins	1964	5.00	10.00	20.00
❏ V6-8568 [S]	The Essential Coleman Hawkins	1964	6.25	12.50	25.00
❏ V6-8829	The Newport Years	197?	3.75	7.50	15.00
❏ 825 673-1	The Genius of Coleman Hawkins	1986	2.50	5.00	10.00
VIK					
❏ LX-1059 [M]	The Hawk in Paris	1957	20.00	40.00	80.00
WORLD WIDE					
❏ MGS-20001 [S]	Coleman Hawkins with the Basie Saxophone Section	1958	12.50	25.00	50.00
XANADU					
❏ 111	Thanks for the Memory	198?	2.50	5.00	10.00
❏ 189	Dutch Treat	198?	2.50	5.00	10.00
❏ 195	Jazz Tones	198?	2.50	5.00	10.00

HAWKINS, COLEMAN/GEORGIE AULD
Also see each artist's individual listings.

Number	Title	Yr	VG	VG+	NM
GRAND AWARD					
❏ GA 33-316 [M]	Jazz Concert	1955	25.00	50.00	100.00
-- With wrap-around cover intact					
❏ GA 33-316 [M]	Jazz Concert	1955	12.50	25.00	50.00
-- Without wrap-around cover					

HAWKINS, COLEMAN, AND BENNY CARTER
Also see each artist's individual listings.

Number	Title	Yr	VG	VG+	NM
MOON					
❏ MLP-001	Jammin' the Blues	199?	3.75	7.50	15.00

Number	Title	Yr	VG	VG+	NM
SWING					
❏ 8403	Coleman Hawkins and Benny	1985	2.50	5.00	10.00

HAWKINS, COLEMAN, AND ROY ELDRIDGE
Also see each artist's individual listings.

Number	Title	Yr	VG	VG+	NM
PHOENIX					
❏ 3	Coleman Hawkins and Roy Eldredge 1939	197?	2.50	5.00	10.00
VERVE					
❏ MGVS-6028 [S]	At the Opera House	1960	10.00	20.00	40.00
❏ MGV-8266 [M]	At the Opera House	1958	12.50	25.00	50.00
❏ V-8266 [M]	At the Opera House	1961	6.25	12.50	25.00
❏ V6-8266 [S]	At the Opera House	1961	5.00	10.00	20.00

HAWKINS, COLEMAN; ROY ELDRIDGE; PETE BROWN; JO JONES
Also see each artist's individual listings.

Number	Title	Yr	VG	VG+	NM
VERVE					
❏ MGV-8240 [M]	All Stars at Newport	1958	12.50	25.00	50.00
❏ V-8240 [M]	All Stars at Newport	1961	5.00	10.00	20.00

HAWKINS, COLEMAN; ROY ELDRIDGE; JOHNNY HODGES
Also see each artist's individual listings.

Number	Title	Yr	VG	VG+	NM
VERVE					
❏ V-8509 [M]	Alive at the Village Gate	1963	5.00	10.00	20.00
❏ V6-8509 [S]	Alive at the Village Gate	1963	6.25	12.50	25.00
❏ V6-8509 [S]	Alive at the Village Gate	199?	6.25	12.50	25.00
-- Classic Records reissue on audiophile vinyl					

HAWKINS, COLEMAN, AND FRANK HUNTER
Also see each artist's individual listings.

Number	Title	Yr	VG	VG+	NM
MIRA					
❏ M-3003 [M]	The Hawk and the Hunter	1965	5.00	10.00	20.00
❏ MS-3003 [S]	The Hawk and the Hunter	1965	6.25	12.50	25.00

HAWKINS, COLEMAN, AND BUD POWELL
Also see each artist's individual listings.

Number	Title	Yr	VG	VG+	NM
BLACK LION					
❏ 159	Hawk in Germany	197?	3.00	6.00	12.00

HAWKINS, COLEMAN, AND PEE WEE RUSSELL
Also see each artist's individual listings.

Number	Title	Yr	VG	VG+	NM
CANDID					
❏ CD-8020 [M]	Jazz Reunion	1960	10.00	20.00	40.00
❏ CS-9020 [S]	Jazz Reunion	1960	10.00	20.00	40.00

HAWKINS, COLEMAN, AND CLARK TERRY
Also see each artist's individual listings.

Number	Title	Yr	VG	VG+	NM
COLUMBIA					
❏ CL 1991 [M]	Back in Bean's Bag	1963	3.75	7.50	15.00
❏ CS 8791 [S]	Back in Bean's Bag	1963	5.00	10.00	20.00
❏ CS 8791 [S]	Back in Bean's Bag	1999	6.25	12.50	25.00
-- Classic Records reissue on audiophile vinyl					

HAWKINS, COLEMAN/BEN WEBSTER
Also see each artist's individual listings.

Number	Title	Yr	VG	VG+	NM
BRUNSWICK					
❏ BL 54016 [M]	The Big Sounds of Coleman Hawkins and Ben Webster	1956	20.00	40.00	80.00

HAWKINS, COLEMAN, AND LESTER YOUNG
Also see each artist's individual listings.

Number	Title	Yr	VG	VG+	NM
DOCTOR JAZZ					
❏ FW 38446	Classic Tenors	1983	2.50	5.00	10.00
FLYING DUTCHMAN					
❏ BXM1-2823	Classic Tenors	1978	3.00	6.00	12.00
ZIM					
❏ 1000	Coleman Hawkins and Lester	197?	2.50	5.00	10.00

HAWKINS, ERSKINE
Trumpeter, bandleader and composer. Wrote "Tuxedo Junction."

Number	Title	Yr	VG	VG+	NM
CORAL					
❏ CRL 56051 [10]	After Hours	1954	30.00	60.00	120.00
DECCA					
❏ DL 4081 [M]	The Hawk Blows at Midnight	1960	7.50	15.00	30.00
❏ DL 74081 [S]	The Hawk Blows at Midnight	1960	10.00	20.00	40.00
IMPERIAL					
❏ LP-9191 [M]	25 Golden Years of Jazz, Volume 1	1962	6.25	12.50	25.00

Number	Title	Yr	VG	VG+	NM
❑ LP-9197 [M]	25 Golden Years of Jazz, Volume 2	1962	6.25	12.50	25.00
❑ LP-12191 [S]	25 Golden Years of Jazz, Volume 1	1962	7.50	15.00	30.00
❑ LP-12197 [S]	25 Golden Years of Jazz, Volume 2	1962	7.50	15.00	30.00

RCA VICTOR

Number	Title	Yr	VG	VG+	NM
❑ LPM-2227 [M]	After Hours	1960	10.00	20.00	40.00

HAWKS, BILLY
Organist and male singer.
PRESTIGE

Number	Title	Yr	VG	VG+	NM
❑ PRLP-7501 [M]	New Genius of the Blues	1967	6.25	12.50	25.00
❑ PRST-7501 [S]	New Genius of the Blues	1967	5.00	10.00	20.00
❑ PRST-7556	More Heavy Soul	1968	5.00	10.00	20.00

HAYES, ALVIN
Trombone player.
PALO ALTO/TBA

Number	Title	Yr	VG	VG+	NM
❑ TBA-221	Star Gaze	1987	2.50	5.00	10.00

HAYES, CLANCY
Banjo player and male singer.
DELMARK

Number	Title	Yr	VG	VG+	NM
❑ DE-210 [M]	Oh By Jingo	1965	5.00	10.00	20.00
❑ DS-9210 [S]	Oh By Jingo	1965	6.25	12.50	25.00

DOWN HOME

Number	Title	Yr	VG	VG+	NM
❑ MGD-3 [M]	Clancy Hayes Sings	1956	15.00	30.00	60.00

GOOD TIME JAZZ

Number	Title	Yr	VG	VG+	NM
❑ S-10050 [S]	Swingin' Minstrel	1963	6.25	12.50	25.00
❑ L-12050 [M]	Swingin' Minstrel	1963	5.00	10.00	20.00

VERVE

Number	Title	Yr	VG	VG+	NM
❑ MGV-1003 [M]	Clancy Hayes Sings	1957	10.00	20.00	40.00

HAYES, LOUIS
Drummer and bandleader.
GRYPHON

Number	Title	Yr	VG	VG+	NM
❑ 787	Variety Is the Spice of Life	1979	3.00	6.00	12.00

MUSE

Number	Title	Yr	VG	VG+	NM
❑ MR-5052	Breath of Life	197?	3.00	6.00	12.00
❑ MR-5125	Real Thing	1977	3.00	6.00	12.00

VEE JAY

Number	Title	Yr	VG	VG+	NM
❑ LP-3010 [M]	Louis Hayes	1960	10.00	20.00	40.00
❑ SR-3010 [S]	Louis Hayes	1960	12.50	25.00	50.00

HAYES, LOUIS, AND JUNIOR COOK
Also see each artist's individual listings.
TIMELESS

Number	Title	Yr	VG	VG+	NM
❑ 307	Ichi-Ban	197?	3.00	6.00	12.00

HAYES, MARTHA
Female singer.
JUBILEE

Number	Title	Yr	VG	VG+	NM
❑ JLP-1023 [M]	A Hayes Named Martha	1956	12.50	25.00	50.00

HAYES, TUBBY
Tenor and soprano saxophone player, flutist and vibraphone player. Also see THE JAZZ COURIERS; DIZZY REECE.
EPIC

Number	Title	Yr	VG	VG+	NM
❑ LA 16019 [M]	Introducing Tubby	1961	10.00	20.00	40.00
❑ LA 16023 [M]	Tubby the Tenor	1962	10.00	20.00	40.00
❑ BA 17019 [S]	Introducing Tubby	1961	12.50	25.00	50.00
❑ BA 17023 [S]	Tubby the Tenor	1962	12.50	25.00	50.00
❑ BA 17023 [S]	Tubby the Tenor	199?	6.25	12.50	25.00
-- Classic Records reissue on audiophile vinyl					

IMPERIAL

Number	Title	Yr	VG	VG+	NM
❑ LP-9046 [M]	Little Giant of Jazz	1957	20.00	40.00	80.00

SMASH

Number	Title	Yr	VG	VG+	NM
❑ MGS-27026 [M]	Tubby's Back in Town	1963	10.00	20.00	40.00
❑ SRS-67026 [S]	Tubby's Back in Town	1963	12.50	25.00	50.00

HAYNES, GRAHAM
Cornet player.
MUSE

Number	Title	Yr	VG	VG+	NM
❑ MR-5402	What Time It Be!	1991	3.00	6.00	12.00

HAYNES, ROY
Drummer.
ABC IMPULSE!

Number	Title	Yr	VG	VG+	NM
❑ AS-23	Out of the Afternoon	1968	3.75	7.50	15.00

EMARCY

Number	Title	Yr	VG	VG+	NM
❑ MG-26048 [10]	Bushman's Holiday	1954	37.50	75.00	150.00

GALAXY

Number	Title	Yr	VG	VG+	NM
❑ 5103	Thank You	1978	3.00	6.00	12.00
❑ 5116	Vistalite	1979	3.00	6.00	12.00

IMPULSE!

Number	Title	Yr	VG	VG+	NM
❑ A-23 [M]	Out of the Afternoon	1962	7.50	15.00	30.00
❑ AS-23 [S]	Out of the Afternoon	1962	10.00	20.00	40.00

MAINSTREAM

Number	Title	Yr	VG	VG+	NM
❑ MRL-313	Hip Ensemble	1971	5.00	10.00	20.00
❑ MRL-351	Senyah	1972	5.00	10.00	20.00

MCA

Number	Title	Yr	VG	VG+	NM
❑ 639	Out of the Afternoon	1980	2.50	5.00	10.00

NEW JAZZ

Number	Title	Yr	VG	VG+	NM
❑ NJLP-8245 [M]	Just Us	1960	20.00	40.00	80.00
-- Purple label					
❑ NJLP-8245 [M]	Just Us	1965	6.25	12.50	25.00
-- Blue label, trident logo at right					
❑ NJLP-8286 [M]	Cracklin'	1962	20.00	40.00	80.00
-- Purple label					
❑ NJLP-8286 [M]	Cracklin'	1965	6.25	12.50	25.00
-- Blue label, trident logo at right					
❑ NJLP-8287 [M]	Cymbalism	1962	20.00	40.00	80.00
-- Purple label					
❑ NJLP-8287 [M]	Cymbalism	1965	6.25	12.50	25.00
-- Blue label, trident logo at right					

PACIFIC JAZZ

Number	Title	Yr	VG	VG+	NM
❑ PJ-82 [M]	People	1964	7.50	15.00	30.00
❑ ST-82 [S]	People	1964	10.00	20.00	40.00

PRESTIGE

Number	Title	Yr	VG	VG+	NM
❑ 2504	Bad News	198?	3.00	6.00	12.00

HAYNES, ROY/QUINCY JONES
Also see each artist's individual listings.
EMARCY

Number	Title	Yr	VG	VG+	NM
❑ MG-36083 [M]	Jazz Abroad	1956	20.00	40.00	80.00

HAYNES, ROY; PHINEAS NEWBORN; PAUL CHAMBERS
Also see each artist's individual listings.
FANTASY

Number	Title	Yr	VG	VG+	NM
❑ OJC-196	We Three	1986	2.50	5.00	10.00

NEW JAZZ

Number	Title	Yr	VG	VG+	NM
❑ NJLP-8210 [M]	We Three	1958	25.00	50.00	100.00

HAZEL, MONK
Drummer and occasional cornet and mellophone player.
SOUTHLAND

Number	Title	Yr	VG	VG+	NM
❑ SLP-217 [M]	Monk Hazel	1956	10.00	20.00	40.00

HAZELL, EDDIE
Guitarist and male singer.
AUDIOPHILE

Number	Title	Yr	VG	VG+	NM
❑ AP-137	Sugar, Don't You Know	1979	3.00	6.00	12.00
❑ AP-179	Live at Gulliver's -- I Go for That!	1984	2.50	5.00	10.00

MONMOUTH-EVERGREEN

Number	Title	Yr	VG	VG+	NM
❑ 7075	Take Your Shoes Off, Baby	197?	3.00	6.00	12.00

HAZILLA, JON
Drummer.
CADENCE JAZZ

Number	Title	Yr	VG	VG+	NM
❑ CJR-1035	Chicplacity	1988	2.50	5.00	10.00

HEADHUNTERS
HERBIE HANCOCK's backing band on his classic album of the same name: Blackbird McKnight (guitar); Bennie Maupin (saxophones, clarinet); Paul Jackson (bass); Bill Summers (percussion); Mike Clark (bass).
ARISTA

Number	Title	Yr	VG	VG+	NM
❑ AL 4038	Survival of the Fittest	1975	2.50	5.00	10.00
❑ AB 4146	Straight	1978	2.50	5.00	10.00

HEALY, PAT
Female singer.
WORLD PACIFIC

Number	Title	Yr	VG	VG+	NM
❑ WP-409 [M]	Just Before Dawn	1958	20.00	40.00	80.00

HEARD, J.C.
Drummer and male singer.
ARGO

Number	Title	Yr	VG	VG+	NM
❑ LP-633 [M]	This Is Me, J.C.	1958	10.00	20.00	40.00
❑ LPS-633 [S]	This Is Me, J.C.	1959	7.50	15.00	30.00

Number	Title	Yr	VG	VG+	NM
HEATH BROTHERS, THE					
Led by ALBERT HEATH and Percy Heath (bass).					
ANTILLES					
❑ AN-1003	Brotherly Love	1982	3.00	6.00	12.00
❑ AN-1016	Brothers and Others	198?	3.00	6.00	12.00
COLUMBIA					
❑ FC 36374	Live at the Public Theatre	1980	3.00	6.00	12.00
❑ FC 37126	Expressions of Life	1981	3.00	6.00	12.00
❑ JC 35573	Passin' Thru	1978	3.00	6.00	12.00
❑ JC 35816	In Motion: The Heath Brothers and Brass Choir	1979	3.00	6.00	12.00
STRATA-EAST					
❑ SES-19766	Marchin' On	1975	6.25	12.50	25.00
HEATH, ALBERT					
Drummer. Also see THE HEATH BROTHERS.					
MUSE					
❑ MR-5031	Kwanza (The First)	1974	5.00	10.00	20.00
O'BE					
❑ LP-301	Kawaida	1969	10.00	20.00	40.00
TRIP					
❑ 5032	Kawaida	1974	6.25	12.50	25.00
-- As "Kuumba Toudie Heath"					
HEATH, JIMMY					
Tenor and alto saxophone player and composer. Also see THE RIVERSIDE JAZZ STARS.					
COBBLESTONE					
❑ CST-9012	The Gap Sealer	197?	3.75	7.50	15.00
FANTASY					
❑ OJC-6006	Nice People	198?	2.50	5.00	10.00
LANDMARK					
❑ LLP-1506	New Picture	1986	2.50	5.00	10.00
❑ LLP-1514	Peer Pleasure	1987	2.50	5.00	10.00
MILESTONE					
❑ 47025 [(2)]	Fast Company	197?	3.75	7.50	15.00
MUSE					
❑ MR-5028	Love and Understanding	1974	3.75	7.50	15.00
❑ MR-5138	Jimmy	197?	3.75	7.50	15.00
RIVERSIDE					
❑ RLP 12-314 [M]	The Thumper	1960	10.00	20.00	40.00
❑ RLP 12-333 [M]	Really Big	1960	7.50	15.00	30.00
❑ RLP-372 [M]	The Quota	1961	7.50	15.00	30.00
❑ RLP-400 [M]	Triple Threat	1962	7.50	15.00	30.00
❑ RLP-465 [M]	Swamp Soul	1963	7.50	15.00	30.00
❑ RLP-486 [M]	On the Trail	1965	5.00	10.00	20.00
❑ RLP-1160 [S]	The Thumper	1960	10.00	20.00	40.00
❑ RLP-1188 [S]	Really Big	1960	10.00	20.00	40.00
❑ 6060	Swamp Seed	197?	3.00	6.00	12.00
❑ RS-9372 [S]	The Quota	1961	10.00	20.00	40.00
❑ RS-9400 [S]	Triple Threat	1962	10.00	20.00	40.00
❑ RS-9465 [S]	Swamp Soul	1963	10.00	20.00	40.00
❑ RS-9486 [S]	On the Trail	1965	6.25	12.50	25.00
XANADU					
❑ 118	Picture of Heath	1976	3.00	6.00	12.00
HEATH, TED					
British trombone player and bandleader.					
ARCHIVE OF FOLK AND JAZZ					
❑ 215	Ted Heath's Big Band	1970	2.50	5.00	10.00
LONDON					
❑ PS 116 [S]	Hits I Missed	1958	6.25	12.50	25.00
❑ PS 117 [S]	All Time Top Twelve	1958	6.25	12.50	25.00
❑ PS 138 [S]	Swing Session	1958	6.25	12.50	25.00
❑ PS 140 [S]	Ted Heath Swings in High Stereo	1958	6.25	12.50	25.00
-- Stereo version of LL 1475					
❑ PS 148 [S]	Shall We Dance	1959	6.25	12.50	25.00
❑ PS 159 [S]	Great Film Hits	1959	6.25	12.50	25.00
❑ PS 171 [S]	Pop Hits from the Classics	1959	6.25	12.50	25.00
❑ PS 172 [S]	Big Band Blues	1959	6.25	12.50	25.00
❑ PS 174 [S]	My Very Good Friends The Bandleaders	1959	6.25	12.50	25.00
❑ PS 175 [S]	The Hits of the Twenties	1960	5.00	10.00	20.00
❑ PS 184 [S]	The Big Band Dixie Sound	1960	5.00	10.00	20.00
❑ PS 187 [S]	Ted Heath in Concert	1960	5.00	10.00	20.00
❑ PS 190 [S]	Songs for the Young at Heart	1960	5.00	10.00	20.00
❑ PS 216 [S]	The Hits of the Thirties	1961	5.00	10.00	20.00
❑ PS 219 [S]	Latin Swingers	1961	5.00	10.00	20.00
❑ LPB-340 [10]	Tempo for Dancing	195?	10.00	20.00	40.00
❑ LPB-374 [10]	Ted Heath and His Orchestra	195?	10.00	20.00	40.00
❑ LB-511 [10]	Listen to My Music	195?	10.00	20.00	40.00
❑ PS 535	21st Anniversary Album	1968	3.00	6.00	12.00
❑ LB-732 [10]	Black and White Magic	195?	10.00	20.00	40.00
❑ LL 750 [M]	Ted Heath Strikes Up the Band	1953	5.00	10.00	20.00
❑ LL 802 [M]	Ted Heath at the London Palladium	1953	5.00	10.00	20.00
❑ LL 978 [M]	Ted Heath Plays the Music of Fats Waller	1954	5.00	10.00	20.00
❑ LL 1000 [M]	The 100th London Palladium Concert	1955	5.00	10.00	20.00
❑ LL 1211 [M]	Jazz Concert at the London Palladium, Vol. 3	1955	5.00	10.00	20.00
❑ LL 1217 [M]	Gershwin for Moderns	1956	5.00	10.00	20.00
❑ LL 1279 [M]	Kern for Moderns	1956	5.00	10.00	20.00
❑ LL 1379 [M]	Jazz Concert at the London Palladium, Vol. 4	1956	5.00	10.00	20.00
❑ LL 1475 [M]	Ted Heath Swings in Hi-Fi	1956	5.00	10.00	20.00
❑ LL 1500 [M]	Rodgers for Moderns	1956	5.00	10.00	20.00
❑ LL 1564 [M]	Ted Heath's First American Tour	1956	5.00	10.00	20.00
❑ LL 1566 [M]	Ted Heath at Carnegie Hall	1956	5.00	10.00	20.00
❑ LL 1676 [M]	A Yank in Europe	1956	5.00	10.00	20.00
❑ LL 1716 [M]	All Time Top Twelve	1957	5.00	10.00	20.00
❑ LL 1721 [M]	Spotlight on Sidemen	1957	5.00	10.00	20.00
❑ LL 1737 [M]	Showcase	1957	5.00	10.00	20.00
❑ LL 1743 [M]	Tribute to the Fabulous Dorseys	1957	5.00	10.00	20.00
❑ LL 1749 [M]	Rhapsody in Blue	1957	5.00	10.00	20.00
❑ LL 3047 [M]	Things to Come	1958	5.00	10.00	20.00
❑ LL 3057 [M]	Hits I Missed	1958	5.00	10.00	20.00
❑ LL 3058 [M]	Old English	1958	5.00	10.00	20.00
❑ LL 3062 [M]	Shall We Dance	1959	5.00	10.00	20.00
❑ LL 3106 [M]	Great Film Hits	1959	5.00	10.00	20.00
❑ LL 3124 [M]	Pop Hits from the Classics	1959	5.00	10.00	20.00
❑ LL 3125 [M]	Big Band Blues	1959	5.00	10.00	20.00
❑ LL 3127 [M]	My Very Good Friends The Bandleaders	1959	5.00	10.00	20.00
❑ LL 3128 [M]	The Hits of the Twenties	1960	3.75	7.50	15.00
❑ LL 3138 [M]	The Big Band Dixie Sound	1960	3.75	7.50	15.00
❑ LL 3143 [M]	Ted Heath in Concert	1960	3.75	7.50	15.00
❑ LL 3146 [M]	Songs for the Young at Heart	1960	3.75	7.50	15.00
❑ LL 3192 [M]	The Hits of the Thirties	1961	3.75	7.50	15.00
❑ LL 3195 [M]	Latin Swingers	1961	3.75	7.50	15.00
❑ LL 3325 [M]	Big Band Spirituals	1963	3.00	6.00	12.00
❑ LL 3367 [M]	New Palladium Performances	1964	3.00	6.00	12.00
LONDON PHASE 4					
❑ SP 44002 [S]	Big Band Percussion	1961	3.75	7.50	15.00
❑ SP 44017	Big Band Bash	1962	3.75	7.50	15.00
❑ SP 44023	Satin Strings and Bouncing Brass	1963	3.75	7.50	15.00
❑ SP 44036 [S]	Big Band Spirituals	1963	3.75	7.50	15.00
❑ SP 44038	Swing vs. Latin	1964	3.75	7.50	15.00
❑ SP 44046 [S]	New Palladium Performances	1964	3.00	6.00	12.00
❑ SP 44063	The Sound of Music	1965	3.00	6.00	12.00
❑ SP 44074	Chartbusters	1966	3.00	6.00	12.00
❑ SP 44079	Pow!	1966	3.00	6.00	12.00
❑ P 54074 [M]	Big Band Percussion	1961	3.00	6.00	12.00
RICHMOND					
❑ B 20034 [M]	Big Band Beat	196?	3.00	6.00	12.00
❑ B 20037 [M]	Ted Heath Plays Gershwin	196?	3.00	6.00	12.00
❑ B 20082 [M]	Ted Heath Plays the Music of Fats Waller	196?	3.00	6.00	12.00
❑ B 20096 [M]	Big Band Gershwin	196?	3.00	6.00	12.00
❑ B 20097 [M]	Big Band Kern	196?	3.00	6.00	12.00
❑ B 20098 [M]	Big Band Rodgers	196?	3.00	6.00	12.00
HEATH, TED, BAND					
Recorded after Heath's retirement, the group was led by trombonist Don Lusher.					
LONDON PHASE 4					
❑ SP 44104	Swing Is King	1968	3.00	6.00	12.00
❑ SP 44113	Swing Is King, Volume 2	1969	3.00	6.00	12.00
❑ SP 44140	Big Ones	1970	3.00	6.00	12.00
❑ SP 44148	Beatles, Bach and Bacharach	1971	3.75	7.50	15.00
❑ SP 44164	Those Were the Days	1971	3.00	6.00	12.00
❑ SP 44177	Big Band Themes Revisited	197?	2.50	5.00	10.00
❑ SP 44178	Big Band Themes Revisited, Volume 2	197?	2.50	5.00	10.00
❑ SP 44186	Salute to Glenn Miller	1972	2.50	5.00	10.00
❑ SP 44220	The Ted Heath Band Salutes the Duke	197?	2.50	5.00	10.00
❑ SP 44228	The Ted Heath Band Salutes Tommy Dorsey	197?	2.50	5.00	10.00
❑ SP 44284	Coast to Coast	1977	2.50	5.00	10.00
HECKMAN, DON					
Clarinetist and bandleader.					
ICTUS					
❑ 101	Summerlin Improvisational Jazz Workshop	1967	15.00	30.00	60.00

Number	Title	Yr	VG	VG+	NM

HEFTI, NEAL
Trumpeter, pianist, composer and arranger best known for his soundtrack work, with his "Batman Theme" the most popular.
COLUMBIA
| ❏ CL 1516 [M] | Light and Right | 1960 | 5.00 | 10.00 | 20.00 |
| ❏ CS 8316 [S] | Light and Right | 1960 | 6.25 | 12.50 | 25.00 |
CORAL
❏ CX 2 [(2) M]	Hollywood Song Book	1959	10.00	20.00	40.00
❏ 7CX 2 [(2) S]	Hollywood Song Book	1959	15.00	30.00	60.00
❏ CRL 56083 [10]	Swingin' on a Coral Reef	1953	12.50	25.00	50.00
❏ CRL 57241 [M]	Hollywood Song Book, Volume 1	1958	5.00	10.00	20.00
❏ CRL 57242 [M]	Hollywood Song Book, Volume 2	1958	5.00	10.00	20.00
❏ CRL 57256 [M]	Music U.S.A.	1959	5.00	10.00	20.00
❏ CRL 757241 [S]	Hollywood Song Book, Volume 1	1959	7.50	15.00	30.00
❏ CRL 757242 [S]	Hollywood Song Book, Volume 2	1959	7.50	15.00	30.00
❏ CRL 757256 [S]	Music U.S.A.	1959	7.50	15.00	30.00
EPIC
❏ LN 3113 [M]	Singing Instrumentals	1956	12.50	25.00	50.00
❏ LN 3440 [M]	Singing Instrumentals	1958	7.50	15.00	30.00
❏ LN 3481 [M]	Pardon My Do-Wah	1958	7.50	15.00	30.00
RCA VICTOR
❏ LPM-3573 [M]	Batman Theme (and 11 Other Bat-Songs)	1966	12.50	25.00	50.00
❏ LSP-3573 [S]	Batman Theme (and 11 Other Bat-Songs)	1966	15.00	30.00	60.00
❏ LPM-3621 [M]	Hefti in Gotham City	1966	12.50	25.00	50.00
❏ LSP-3621 [S]	Hefti in Gotham City	1966	15.00	30.00	60.00
REPRISE
❏ R-6018 [M]	Themes from TV's Top 12	1962	6.25	12.50	25.00
❏ R9-6018 [S]	Themes from TV's Top 12	1962	7.50	15.00	30.00
❏ R-6039 [M]	Jazz Pops	1962	5.00	10.00	20.00
❏ R9-6039 [S]	Jazz Pops	1962	6.25	12.50	25.00
"X"
| ❏ LXA-3021 [10] | Music of Rudolf Frimi | 1954 | 12.50 | 25.00 | 50.00 |

HEIDT, HORACE
Bandleader.
HINDSIGHT
| ❏ HSR-194 | Horace Heidt and His Musical Knights 1939 | 198? | 2.50 | 5.00 | 10.00 |
| ❏ HSR-202 | Horace Heidt and His Musical Knights 1943-45 | 198? | 2.50 | 5.00 | 10.00 |
SUNBEAM
| ❏ 4 | Horace Heidt and His Orchestra 1927-29 | 198? | 2.50 | 5.00 | 10.00 |

HELIOCENTRIC
Members: Norn Scutti; Al von Seggern; Jeff Pressing; John Leftwich.
DISCOVERY
| ❏ 806 | Heliocentric | 1979 | 3.00 | 6.00 | 12.00 |

HELLBORG, JONAS
Bass player.
DAY EIGHT
❏ DEM 001	The Bassic Thing	1982	5.00	10.00	20.00
❏ DEM 002	All Our Steps	1983	3.75	7.50	15.00
❏ DEM 004	Elegant Punk	1984	3.00	6.00	12.00
❏ DEM 006	Axis	1986	3.00	6.00	12.00
❏ DEM 009	Bass	1988	3.00	6.00	12.00
❏ DEM 01?	Jonas Hellborg Group	1988	3.00	6.00	12.00

HELM, BOB
Clarinetist.
RIVERSIDE
| ❏ RLP-2510 [10] | Bob Helm | 1954 | 20.00 | 40.00 | 80.00 |

HELM, BOB/LU WATTERS
Also see each artist's individual listings.
RIVERSIDE
| ❏ RLP 12-213 [M] | San Francisco Style | 1956 | 15.00 | 30.00 | 60.00 |

HEMPHILL, JULIUS
Alto and tenor saxophone player, flutist and male singer.
ARISTA FREEDOM
| ❏ AL 1012 | 'Coon Bid'ness | 1975 | 5.00 | 10.00 | 20.00 |
| ❏ AL 1028 | Dogon A.D. | 1976 | 6.25 | 12.50 | 25.00 |
BLACK SAINT
| ❏ BSR-0015 | Raw Material and Residuals | 197? | 3.75 | 7.50 | 15.00 |
| ❏ BSR-0040 | Flat-Out Jump Suite | 198? | 3.75 | 7.50 | 15.00 |

ELEKTRA/MUSICIAN
| ❏ 60831 | Julius Hemphill's Big Band | 1988 | 2.50 | 5.00 | 10.00 |
MBARI
❏ 5001	Dogon A.D.	1972	12.50	25.00	50.00
❏ (# unknown)	'Coon Bid'ness	1974	10.00	20.00	40.00
❏ (# unknown) [(2)]	Blue Boye	1977	15.00	30.00	60.00
MINOR MUSIC
| ❏ MM-003 | Georgia Blue | 1985 | 3.00 | 6.00 | 12.00 |
RED
| ❏ VPA-138 | Live in New York | 1976 | 3.75 | 7.50 | 15.00 |
SACKVILLE
| ❏ 3018 | Buster Bee | 198? | 3.00 | 6.00 | 12.00 |

HENDERSON, BILL
Male singer.
DISCOVERY
❏ 779	Live at the Times	1978	3.00	6.00	12.00
❏ 802	Street of Dreams	1979	3.00	6.00	12.00
❏ 846	Tribute to Johnny Mercer	1982	3.00	6.00	12.00
MGM
| ❏ E-4128 [M] | Bill Henderson with the Oscar Peterson Trio | 1963 | 6.25 | 12.50 | 25.00 |
| ❏ SE-4128 [S] | Bill Henderson with the Oscar Peterson Trio | 1963 | 7.50 | 15.00 | 30.00 |
VEE JAY
❏ LP-1015 [M]	Bill Henderson Sings	1959	6.25	12.50	25.00
❏ SR-1015 [S]	Bill Henderson Sings	1959	10.00	20.00	40.00
❏ LP-1031 [M]	Bill Henderson	1961	6.25	12.50	25.00
❏ SR-1031 [S]	Bill Henderson	1961	10.00	20.00	40.00
VERVE
| ❏ V-8619 [M] | When My Dreamboat Comes Home | 1965 | 5.00 | 10.00 | 20.00 |
| ❏ V6-8619 [S] | When My Dreamboat Comes Home | 1965 | 6.25 | 12.50 | 25.00 |

HENDERSON, BOBBY
Pianist. Also a trumpeter and male singer. Also see RUBY BRAFF.
CHIAROSCURO
| ❏ 102 | Home in the Clouds | 1971 | 3.75 | 7.50 | 15.00 |
-- Reissue of Halcyon 102
| ❏ 122 | Last Recordings | 1973 | 3.75 | 7.50 | 15.00 |
HALCYON
| ❏ 102 | Home in the Clouds | 1970 | 5.00 | 10.00 | 20.00 |
VANGUARD
| ❏ VRS-8511 [M] | Handful of Keys | 1955 | 10.00 | 20.00 | 40.00 |

HENDERSON, EDDIE
Trumpeter.
BLUE NOTE
| ❏ BN-LA464-G | Sunburst | 1975 | 5.00 | 10.00 | 20.00 |
| ❏ BN-LA636-G | Heritage | 1976 | 5.00 | 10.00 | 20.00 |
CAPITOL
❏ ST-11761	Comin' Through	1977	3.75	7.50	15.00
❏ SW-11846	Mahal	1978	3.00	6.00	12.00
❏ ST-11984	Runnin' To Your Love	1979	3.00	6.00	12.00
CAPRICORN
| ❏ CP 0118 | Realization | 1973 | 3.75 | 7.50 | 15.00 |
| ❏ CP 0122 | Inside Out | 1974 | 3.75 | 7.50 | 15.00 |

HENDERSON, FLETCHER
Pianist, bandleader, arranger. His band was a precursor to, and a heavy influence on, the Swing Era.
BIOGRAPH
| ❏ C-12 | Fletcher Henderson 1924-41 | 197? | 3.00 | 6.00 | 12.00 |
| ❏ 12039 | Fletcher Henderson 1923-27 | 197? | 3.00 | 6.00 | 12.00 |
BLUEBIRD
| ❏ AXM2-5507 [(2)] | The Complete Fletcher Henderson | 197? | 3.75 | 7.50 | 15.00 |
COLUMBIA
| ❏ C4L 19 [(4) M] | The Fletcher Henderson Story | 1961 | 25.00 | 50.00 | 100.00 |
-- Box set with booklet; red and black labels with six "eye" logos
| ❏ C4L 19 [(4) M] | The Fletcher Henderson Story | 1963 | 12.50 | 25.00 | 50.00 |
-- Red "Guaranteed High Fidelity" labels
| ❏ C4L 19 [(4) M] | The Fletcher Henderson Story | 1966 | 7.50 | 15.00 | 30.00 |
-- Red "360 Sound Mono" labels
DECCA
| ❏ DL 6025 [10] | Fletcher Henderson Memorial | 1952 | 37.50 | 75.00 | 150.00 |
| ❏ DL 9227 [M] | Fletcher Henderson: First Impression (Vol. 1 1924-1931) | 1958 | 12.50 | 25.00 | 50.00 |
-- Black label, silver print

Number	Title	Yr	VG	VG+	NM
❑ DL 9227 [M]	Fletcher Henderson: First Impression (Vol. 1 1924-1931)	1961	7.50	15.00	30.00
-- Black label with color bars					
❑ DL 9228 [M]	Fletcher Henderson: The Swing's the Thing (Vol. 2 1931-1934)	1958	12.50	25.00	50.00
-- Black label, silver print					
❑ DL 9228 [M]	Fletcher Henderson: The Swing's the Thing (Vol. 2 1931-1934)	1961	7.50	15.00	30.00
-- Black label with color bars					
❑ DL 79227 [R]	Fletcher Henderson: First Impression (Vol. 1 1924-1931)	196?	3.75	7.50	15.00
❑ DL 79228 [R]	Fletcher Henderson: The Swing's the Thing (Vol. 2 1931-1934)	196?	3.75	7.50	15.00

HISTORICAL

Number	Title	Yr	VG	VG+	NM
❑ 13	Fletcher Henderson 1923-24	1967	5.00	10.00	20.00
❑ 18	Fletcher Henderson Volume 2: 1923-25	1967	5.00	10.00	20.00

JAZZTONE

❑ J-1285 [M]	The Big Reunion	1958	7.50	15.00	30.00

MCA

❑ 1310	First Impressions	198?	2.50	5.00	10.00
❑ 1318	The Swing's the Thing	198?	2.50	5.00	10.00
❑ 1346	The Rarest Fletcher	198?	2.50	5.00	10.00

MILESTONE

❑ M-2005	The Immortal Fletcher Henderson	196?	6.25	12.50	25.00

RIVERSIDE

❑ RLP-1055 [10]	Fletcher Henderson	1954	37.50	75.00	150.00

SAVOY JAZZ

❑ SJL-1152	The Crown King of Swing	198?	2.50	5.00	10.00

SUTTON

❑ SSL-286 [M]	Fletcher Henderson with Slam Stewart	195?	6.25	12.50	25.00

SWING

❑ SW-8445/6 [(2)]	Fletcher Henderson and His Dixie Stompers 1925-1928	198?	3.75	7.50	15.00

"X"

❑ LVA-3013 [10]	Fletcher Henderson and His Connie's Inn Orchestra	1954	37.50	75.00	150.00

HENDERSON, JOE

Primarily a tenor saxophone player, he also has played soprano sax and flute.

BLUE NOTE

Number	Title	Yr	VG	VG+	NM
❑ BLP-4140 [M]	Page One	1963	6.25	12.50	25.00
❑ BLP-4152 [M]	Our Thing	1963	6.25	12.50	25.00
❑ BLP-4166 [M]	In 'n Out	1964	6.25	12.50	25.00
❑ BLP-4189 [M]	Inner Urge	1965	6.25	12.50	25.00
❑ BLP-4227 [M]	Mode for Joe	1966	6.25	12.50	25.00
❑ BST-84140 [S]	Page One	1963	7.50	15.00	30.00
-- "New York, USA" address on label					
❑ BST-84140 [S]	Page One	1967	3.75	7.50	15.00
-- "A Division of Liberty Records" on label					
❑ BST-84152 [S]	Our Thing	1963	7.50	15.00	30.00
-- "New York, USA" address on label					
❑ BST-84152 [S]	Our Thing	1967	3.75	7.50	15.00
-- "A Division of Liberty Records" on label					
❑ BST-84166 [S]	In 'n Out	1964	7.50	15.00	30.00
-- "New York, USA" address on label					
❑ BST-84166 [S]	In 'n Out	1967	3.75	7.50	15.00
-- "A Division of Liberty Records" on label					
❑ BST-84189 [S]	Inner Urge	1965	7.50	15.00	30.00
-- "New York, USA" address on label					
❑ BST-84189 [S]	Inner Urge	1967	3.75	7.50	15.00
-- "A Division of Liberty Records" on label					
❑ BST-84227 [S]	Mode for Joe	1966	7.50	15.00	30.00
-- "New York, USA" address on label					
❑ BST-84227 [S]	Mode for Joe	1967	3.75	7.50	15.00
-- "A Division of Liberty Records" on label					
❑ BT-85123	State of the Tenor	1987	2.50	5.00	10.00
❑ BT-85126	State of the Tenor Vol. 2: Live at the Village Vanguard	1987	2.50	5.00	10.00

CONTEMPORARY

❑ C-14006	Relaxin' at Camarillo	198?	3.00	6.00	12.00

FANTASY

❑ OJC-465	The Kicker	1990	3.00	6.00	12.00

MILESTONE

❑ M-9008	The Kicker	1968	5.00	10.00	20.00
❑ M-9017	Tetragon	1969	5.00	10.00	20.00
❑ M-9024	Power to the People	1970	5.00	10.00	20.00
❑ M-9028	If You're Not Part	1970	5.00	10.00	20.00
❑ M-9034	In Pursuit of Blackness	1971	5.00	10.00	20.00
❑ M-9040	Black Is the Color	1972	5.00	10.00	20.00
❑ M-9047	Joe Henderson In Japan	1972	5.00	10.00	20.00
❑ M-9050	Multiple	1973	3.75	7.50	15.00
❑ M-9053	Elements	1974	3.75	7.50	15.00
❑ M-9057	Canyon Lady	1974	3.75	7.50	15.00
❑ M-9066	Black Miracle	1975	3.75	7.50	15.00
❑ M-9071	Black Narcissus	1975	3.75	7.50	15.00
❑ 47058 [(2)]	Foresight	198?	3.75	7.50	15.00

PAUSA

❑ 7075	Mirror, Mirror	1980	2.50	5.00	10.00

HENDERSON, WAYNE

Trombonist. Also see THE CRUSADERS.

ABC

❑ AB-1020	Big Daddy's Place	1977	2.50	5.00	10.00

POLYDOR

❑ PD-1-6145	Living on a Dream	1978	2.50	5.00	10.00
❑ PD-1-6227	Emphasized	1980	2.50	5.00	10.00

HENDRICKS, JON

Male singer. Also see LAMBERT, HENDRICKS & BAVAN; LAMBERT, HENDRICKS & ROSS.

COLUMBIA

Number	Title	Yr	VG	VG+	NM
❑ CL 1583 [M]	Evolution of the Blues	1961	7.50	15.00	30.00
❑ CL 1805 [M]	Fast Livin' Blues	1962	7.50	15.00	30.00
❑ CS 8383 [S]	Evolution of the Blues	1961	10.00	20.00	40.00
❑ CS 8605 [S]	Fast Livin' Blues	1962	10.00	20.00	40.00

ENJA

❑ 4032	Cloudburst	198?	3.00	6.00	12.00

MUSE

❑ MR-5258	Love	1982	2.50	5.00	10.00

REPRISE

❑ R-6089 [M]	Salud!	1964	6.25	12.50	25.00
❑ R9-6089 [S]	Salud!	1964	7.50	15.00	30.00

SMASH

❑ MGS-27069 [M]	Recorded In Person at the Trident	1963	6.25	12.50	25.00
❑ SRS-67069 [S]	Recorded In Person at the Trident	1963	7.50	15.00	30.00

STANYAN

❑ 10132	September Songs	197?	3.00	6.00	12.00

WORLD PACIFIC

❑ WP-1283 [M]	A Good Git-Together	1959	20.00	40.00	80.00

HENDRICKS, MICHELE

Female singer.

MUSE

❑ MR-5336	Carryin' On	1988	2.50	5.00	10.00
❑ MR-5363	Keepin' Me Satisfied	1989	3.00	6.00	12.00

HENKE, MEL

Pianist and composer.

CONTEMPORARY

❑ C-5001 [M]	Dig Mel Henke	1955	12.50	25.00	50.00
❑ C-5003 [M]	Now Spin This	1956	12.50	25.00	50.00

DOBRE

❑ 1031	Love Touch	197?	3.00	6.00	12.00

WARNER BROS.

❑ W 1472 [M]	La Dolce Henke	1962	10.00	20.00	40.00
❑ WS 1472 [S]	La Dolce Henke	1962	12.50	25.00	50.00

HENRIQUE, LUIZ

Male singer.

FONTANA

❑ MGF-27553 [M]	Listen to Me	1966	5.00	10.00	20.00
❑ SRF-67553 [S]	Listen to Me	1966	6.25	12.50	25.00

VERVE

❑ V-8697 [M]	Barra Limpa	1967	7.50	15.00	30.00
❑ V6-8697 [S]	Barra Limpa	1967	5.00	10.00	20.00

HENRY'S BOOTBLACKS

STOMP OFF

❑ SOS-1149	Hullabaloo	1988	2.50	5.00	10.00

HENRY, ERNIE

Alto saxophone player.

FANTASY

❑ OJC-086	Last Chorus	198?	2.50	5.00	10.00
❑ OJC-102	Presenting Ernie Henry	198?	2.50	5.00	10.00
❑ OJC-1722	Seven Standards and a Blues	198?	2.50	5.00	10.00

RIVERSIDE

❑ RLP 12-222 [M]	Presenting Ernie Henry	1956	30.00	60.00	120.00

Number	Title	Yr	VG	VG+	NM
❏ RLP 12-248 [M]	Seven Standards and a Blues	1957	25.00	50.00	100.00
❏ RLP 12-266 [M]	Last Chorus	1958	20.00	40.00	80.00
❏ 6040	Presenting Ernie Henry	197?	3.75	7.50	15.00

HENSON-CONANT, DEBORAH
Harpist and female singer.
GRP
Number	Title	Yr	VG	VG+	NM
❏ GR-9578	On the Rise	1989	3.75	7.50	15.00

HERBECK, RAY
Saxophone player, clarinetist and bandleader.
CIRCLE
Number	Title	Yr	VG	VG+	NM
❏ CLP-78	Modern Music with Romance	198?	2.50	5.00	10.00

GLENDALE
Number	Title	Yr	VG	VG+	NM
❏ 6025	Live and Romantic	1985	2.50	5.00	10.00

HERBERT, MORT
Bass player and composer.
SAVOY
Number	Title	Yr	VG	VG+	NM
❏ MG-12073 [M]	Night People	1956	10.00	20.00	40.00

HERBIG, GARY
Saxophone, bass clarinet and flute player.
HEADFIRST
Number	Title	Yr	VG	VG+	NM
❏ A-723	Gary Herbig	198?	2.50	5.00	10.00

HERDSMEN, THE
Various members of WOODY HERMAN's band: Ralph Burns; Jerry Coker; Dick Collins; Chuck Flores; Dick Haffner; Red Kelly; Bill Perkins; Cy Touff.
FANTASY
Number	Title	Yr	VG	VG+	NM
❏ 3201 [M]	The Herdsmen Play Paris	1955	20.00	40.00	80.00
-- Green vinyl					
❏ 3201 [M]	The Herdsmen Play Paris	1955	10.00	20.00	40.00
-- Black vinyl					

HERMAN, WOODY
Bandleader, saxophone player and clarinetist. Also see THE EX-HERMANITES; THE FOUR BROTHERS; THE HERDSMEN; THE SMALL HERD.
ACCORD
Number	Title	Yr	VG	VG+	NM
❏ SN-7185	All Star Session	1981	2.50	5.00	10.00

AMERICAN RECORDING SOCIETY
Number	Title	Yr	VG	VG+	NM
❏ G-410 [M]	The Progressive Big Band Sound	1956	10.00	20.00	40.00

ARCHIVE OF FOLK AND JAZZ
Number	Title	Yr	VG	VG+	NM
❏ 316	Woody Herman, Vol. 2	197?	2.50	5.00	10.00
❏ 338	Woody Herman, Vol. 2	197?	2.50	5.00	10.00

ATLANTIC
Number	Title	Yr	VG	VG+	NM
❏ 1328 [M]	Woody Herman at the Monterey Jazz Festival	1960	10.00	20.00	40.00
❏ SD 1328 [S]	Woody Herman at the Monterey Jazz Festival	1960	7.50	15.00	30.00
❏ 90044	Woody Herman at the Monterey Jazz Festival	1982	2.50	5.00	10.00
-- Reissue of 1328					

BRUNSWICK
Number	Title	Yr	VG	VG+	NM
❏ BL 54024 [M]	The Swinging Herman Herd	1957	10.00	20.00	40.00

BULLDOG
Number	Title	Yr	VG	VG+	NM
❏ 2005	20 Golden Pieces of Woody	198?	2.50	5.00	10.00

CADET
Number	Title	Yr	VG	VG+	NM
❏ LPS-819	Light My Fire	1969	3.00	6.00	12.00
❏ LPS-835	Heavy Exposure	1969	3.00	6.00	12.00
❏ LPS-845	Woody	1970	3.00	6.00	12.00

CAPITOL
Number	Title	Yr	VG	VG+	NM
❏ H 324 [10]	Classics in Jazz	1952	17.50	35.00	70.00
❏ T 324 [M]	Classics in Jazz	1955	10.00	20.00	40.00
❏ T 560 [M]	The Woody Herman Band	1955	10.00	20.00	40.00
❏ T 658 [M]	Road Band	1955	10.00	20.00	40.00
❏ T 748 [M]	Jackpot!	1956	10.00	20.00	40.00
❏ T 784 [M]	Blues Groove	1956	10.00	20.00	40.00
❏ DT 1554 [R]	The Hits of Woody Herman	1961	3.00	6.00	12.00
❏ SM-1554	The Hits of Woody Herman	197?	2.00	4.00	8.00
❏ T 1554 [M]	The Hits of Woody Herman	1961	5.00	10.00	20.00
❏ M-11034	Early Autumn	1972	2.50	5.00	10.00

CENTURY
Number	Title	Yr	VG	VG+	NM
❏ CRDD-1080	Road Father	1979	6.25	12.50	25.00
-- Direct-to-disc recording					
❏ CR-1110	Chick, Donald, Walter and	1978	3.00	6.00	12.00

CHESS
Number	Title	Yr	VG	VG+	NM
❏ 402 [(2)]	Double Exposure	197?	3.75	7.50	15.00

CLEF
Number	Title	Yr	VG	VG+	NM
❏ MGC-745 [M]	Jazz, the Utmost!	1956	20.00	40.00	80.00

COLUMBIA
Number	Title	Yr	VG	VG+	NM
❏ C3L 25 [(3) M]	The Thundering Herds	1963	12.50	25.00	50.00
❏ CL 592 [M]	The Three Herds	1955	12.50	25.00	50.00
-- Maroon label with gold print					
❏ CL 592 [M]	The Three Herds	1956	7.50	15.00	30.00
-- Red and black label with six "eye" logos					
❏ CL 651 [M]	Music for Tired Lovers	1955	10.00	20.00	40.00
❏ CL 2357 [M]	My Kind of Broadway	1965	3.00	6.00	12.00
❏ CL 2436 [M]	Woody's Winners	1965	3.00	6.00	12.00
❏ CL 2491 [M]	Woody Herman's Greatest Hits	1966	3.00	6.00	12.00
❏ CL 2509 [10]	Ridin' Herd	1955	15.00	30.00	60.00
❏ CL 2552 [M]	The Jazz S(w)inger	1966	3.00	6.00	12.00
❏ CL 2563 [10]	Woody!	1955	15.00	30.00	60.00
❏ CL 2693 [M]	Woody Live -- East & West	1967	3.75	7.50	15.00
❏ CL 6026 [10]	Sequence in Jazz	1949	17.50	35.00	70.00
❏ CL 6049 [10]	Dance Parade	1949	17.50	35.00	70.00
❏ CL 6092 [10]	Woody Herman and His Woodchoppers	1950	17.50	35.00	70.00
❏ CS 9157 [S]	My Kind of Broadway	1965	3.75	7.50	15.00
❏ CS 9236 [S]	Woody's Winners	1965	3.75	7.50	15.00
❏ CS 9291 [S]	Woody Herman's Greatest Hits	1966	3.75	7.50	15.00
❏ CS 9352 [S]	The Jazz S(w)inger	1966	3.75	7.50	15.00
❏ CS 9493 [S]	Woody Live -- East & West	1967	3.00	6.00	12.00
❏ PC 9291	Woody Herman's Greatest Hits	198?	2.00	4.00	8.00
-- Reissue with new prefix					
❏ C 32530	Jazz Hoot	1974	3.00	6.00	12.00

CONCORD JAZZ
Number	Title	Yr	VG	VG+	NM
❏ CJ-170	Woody Herman and Friends at the Monterey Jazz Festival 1979	198?	3.00	6.00	12.00
❏ CJ-191	Live at the Concord Jazz Festival	1982	3.00	6.00	12.00
❏ CJ-240	World Class	1983	3.00	6.00	12.00
❏ CJ-302	50th Anniversary Tour	1986	3.00	6.00	12.00
❏ CJ-330	Woody's Gold Star	1987	3.00	6.00	12.00

CORAL
Number	Title	Yr	VG	VG+	NM
❏ CRL 56005 [10]	Blue Prelude	1950	17.50	35.00	70.00
❏ CRL 56010 [10]	Woody Herman Souvenirs	1950	17.50	35.00	70.00
❏ CRL 56090 [10]	Woody's Best	1953	17.50	35.00	70.00

CROWN
Number	Title	Yr	VG	VG+	NM
❏ CLP 5180 [M]	The New Swingin' Herman Band	1960	5.00	10.00	20.00

DECCA
Number	Title	Yr	VG	VG+	NM
❏ DL 4484 [M]	Woody Herman's Golden Hits	1964	3.75	7.50	15.00
❏ DL 8133 [M]	Woodchopper's Ball	1955	10.00	20.00	40.00
❏ DL 9229 [M]	The Turning Point -- 1943-44	1967	3.75	7.50	15.00
❏ DL 74484 [R]	Woody Herman's Golden Hits	1964	2.50	5.00	10.00
❏ DL 79229 [R]	The Turning Point -- 1943-44	1967	2.50	5.00	10.00

DIAL
Number	Title	Yr	VG	VG+	NM
❏ LP-210 [10]	Swinging with the Woodchoppers	1950	37.50	75.00	150.00

DISCOVERY
Number	Title	Yr	VG	VG+	NM
❏ 815	The Third Herd	198?	2.50	5.00	10.00
❏ 845	The Third Herd, Volume 2	198?	2.50	5.00	10.00

EVEREST
Number	Title	Yr	VG	VG+	NM
❏ SDBR-1003 [S]	The Herd Rides Again…In Stereo	1958	10.00	20.00	40.00
❏ SDBR-1032 [S]	Moody Woody	1958	10.00	20.00	40.00
❏ EV-1222 [S]	The Best of Woody Herman	1963	5.00	10.00	20.00
❏ LPBR-5003 [M]	The Herd Rides Again	1958	7.50	15.00	30.00
❏ LPBR-5032 [M]	Moody Woody	1958	7.50	15.00	30.00
❏ EV-5222 [M]	The Best of Woody Herman	1963	3.75	7.50	15.00

FANTASY
Number	Title	Yr	VG	VG+	NM
❏ OJC-344	Giant Steps	198?	2.50	5.00	10.00
-- Reissue of 9432					
❏ FPM-4003 [Q]	Children of Lima	1975	5.00	10.00	20.00
❏ 8414	Brand New	1971	3.00	6.00	12.00
❏ 9416	The Raven Speaks	1972	3.00	6.00	12.00
❏ F-9432	Giant Steps	1973	3.00	6.00	12.00
❏ F-9452	The Thundering Herd	1973	3.00	6.00	12.00
❏ F-9470	The Herd at Montreux	1974	3.00	6.00	12.00
❏ F-9477	Children of Lima	1975	3.00	6.00	12.00
❏ F-9499	King Cobra	1976	3.00	6.00	12.00
❏ F-9609	Feelin' So Blue	1982	2.50	5.00	10.00

FORUM
Number	Title	Yr	VG	VG+	NM
❏ F-9016 [M]	Woody Herman Sextet at the Round Table	196?	5.00	10.00	20.00
❏ FS-9016 [S]	Woody Herman Sextet at the Round Table	196?	6.25	12.50	25.00

HARMONY
Number	Title	Yr	VG	VG+	NM
❏ HL 7013 [M]	Bijou	1957	5.00	10.00	20.00
❏ HL 7093 [M]	Summer Sequence	1957	5.00	10.00	20.00

HINDSIGHT
Number	Title	Yr	VG	VG+	NM
❏ HSR-116	Woody Herman and His Orchestra 1937	198?	2.50	5.00	10.00
❏ HSR-134	Woody Herman and His Orchestra 1944	198?	2.50	5.00	10.00

INSIGHT
Number	Title	Yr	VG	VG+	NM
❏ 208	Woody Herman and His Orchestra 1937-44	198?	2.50	5.00	10.00

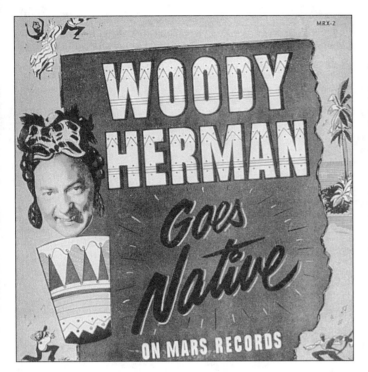

Woody Herman led numerous big bands and "Herds," as he dubbed them, for almost 50 years, helping to launch numerous careers in the process. (Top left) One of his earliest full-length LPs was *Woody Herman Goes Native*, issued on the forgotten Mars label. (Top right) His fame as a bandleader obscured the fact that Herman was a pretty good clarinet player. Here's an early reissue of an album that originally came out on the Clef label. (Bottom left) Woody Herman as a solo artist, with Frank DeVol's orchestra backing him up, appears on this 1958 Verve album. (Bottom right) By 1960, Herman was on his "Fourth Herd," as this album for Jazzland amply illustrates.

Number	Title	Yr	VG	VG+	NM
JAZZLAND					
❏ JLP-17 [M]	The Fourth Herd	1960	6.25	12.50	25.00
❏ JLP-917 [S]	The Fourth Herd	1960	6.25	12.50	25.00
LION					
❏ L-70059 [M]	The Herman Herd at Carnegie Hall	1958	6.25	12.50	25.00
MARS					
❏ MRX-1 [10]	Dance Date on Mars	1952	37.50	75.00	150.00
❏ MRX-2 [10]	Woody Herman Goes Native	1953	37.50	75.00	150.00
MCA					
❏ 219	Golden Favorites	1973	2.50	5.00	10.00
❏ 4077 [(2)]	The Best of Woody Herman	197?	3.75	7.50	15.00
METRO					
❏ M-514 [M]	Woody Herman	1966	3.75	7.50	15.00
❏ MS-514 [R]	Woody Herman	1966	2.50	5.00	10.00
MGM					
❏ E-158 [10]	Woody Herman at Carnegie Hall, 1946, Vol. 1	1952	17.50	35.00	70.00
❏ E-159 [10]	Woody Herman at Carnegie Hall, 1946, Vol. 2	1952	17.50	35.00	70.00
❏ E-192 [10]	The Third Herd	1953	17.50	35.00	70.00
❏ E-284 [10]	Blue Flame	1955	17.50	35.00	70.00
❏ E-3043 [M]	Carnegie Hall 1946	1953	12.50	25.00	50.00
-- Compiles 158 and 159 on one 12-inch LP					
❏ E-3385 [M]	Hi-Fi-ing Herd	1956	10.00	20.00	40.00
MOBILE FIDELITY					
❏ 1-219	The Fourth Herd	1994	7.50	15.00	30.00
-- Audiophile vinyl					
PHILIPS					
❏ PHM 200-004 [M]	Swing Low, Sweet Chariot	1962	3.75	7.50	15.00
❏ PHM 200-065 [M]	Woody Herman 1963	1963	3.75	7.50	15.00
❏ PHM 200-092 [M]	Encore: Woody Herman 1963	1963	3.75	7.50	15.00
❏ PHM 200-118 [M]	Woody Herman: 1964	1964	3.75	7.50	15.00
❏ PHM 200-131 [M]	The Swinging Herman Herd Recorded Live	1964	3.75	7.50	15.00
❏ PHM 200-171 [M]	Woody's Big Band Goodies	1965	3.75	7.50	15.00
❏ PHS 600-004 [S]	Swing Low, Sweet Chariot	1962	5.00	10.00	20.00
❏ PHS 600-065 [S]	Woody Herman 1963	1963	5.00	10.00	20.00
❏ PHS 600-092 [S]	Encore: Woody Herman 1963	1963	5.00	10.00	20.00
❏ PHS 600-118 [S]	Woody Herman: 1964	1964	5.00	10.00	20.00
❏ PHS 600-131 [S]	The Swinging Herman Herd Recorded Live	1964	5.00	10.00	20.00
❏ PHS 600-171 [S]	Woody's Big Band Goodies	1965	5.00	10.00	20.00
PICCADILY					
❏ 3333	It's Coolin' Time	198?	2.50	5.00	10.00
PICKWICK					
❏ SPC-3591	Blowin' Up a Storm	1978	2.50	5.00	10.00
RCA VICTOR					
❏ BGL2-2203 [(2)]	40th Anniversary Carnegie Hall Concert	1977	3.75	7.50	15.00
ROULETTE					
❏ R 25067 [M]	Woody Herman Sextet at the Round Table	1959	7.50	15.00	30.00
❏ SR 25067 [S]	Woody Herman Sextet at the Round Table	1959	10.00	20.00	40.00
SUNBEAM					
❏ 206	Woody Herman and His Orchestra 1936	198?	2.50	5.00	10.00
SUNSET					
❏ SUM-1139 [M]	Blowin' Up a Storm	1966	2.50	5.00	10.00
❏ SUS-5139 [S]	Blowin' Up a Storm	1966	3.00	6.00	12.00
TRIP					
❏ 5547	Woody 1963	1974	2.50	5.00	10.00
VERVE					
❏ VSP-1 [M]	The First Herd at Carnegie Hall	1966	3.75	7.50	15.00
❏ VSPS-1 [R]	The First Herd at Carnegie Hall	1966	2.50	5.00	10.00
❏ VSP-26 [M]	Woody Herman's Woodchoppers & The First Herd Live at Carnegie Hall	1966	3.75	7.50	15.00
❏ VSPS-26 [R]	Woody Herman's Woodchoppers & The First Herd Live at Carnegie Hall	1966	2.50	5.00	10.00
❏ MGV-2030 [M]	Early Autumn	1957	10.00	20.00	40.00
❏ V-2030 [M]	Early Autumn	1963	3.75	7.50	15.00
❏ MGV-2069 [M]	Songs for Hip Lovers	1957	10.00	20.00	40.00
❏ V-2069 [M]	Songs for Hip Lovers	1963	3.75	7.50	15.00
❏ MGV-2096 [M]	Love Is the Sweetest Thing -- Sometimes	1958	10.00	20.00	40.00
❏ V-2096 [M]	Love Is the Sweetest Thing -- Sometimes	1963	3.75	7.50	15.00
❏ MGV-8014 [M]	Jazz, the Utmost!	1957	10.00	20.00	40.00
-- Reissue of Clef LP					
❏ V-8014 [M]	Jazz, the Utmost!	1963	3.75	7.50	15.00
❏ MGV-8216 [M]	Men from Mars	1958	10.00	20.00	40.00
❏ MGV-8255 [M]	Woody Herman '58	1958	10.00	20.00	40.00
❏ V-8255 [M]	Woody Herman '58	1963	3.75	7.50	15.00
❏ V-8558 [M]	Hey! Heard the Herd?	1963	5.00	10.00	20.00
-- Reissue of Verve 8216					
❏ V6-8558 [S]	Hey! Heard the Herd?	1963	3.75	7.50	15.00
❏ V6-8764	Concerto for Herd	1968	5.00	10.00	20.00
WHO'S WHO IN JAZZ					
❏ 21013	Lionel Hampton Presents Woody Herman	1979	3.00	6.00	12.00
WING					
❏ MGW-12329 [M]	Woody's Big Band Goodies	1966	2.50	5.00	10.00
❏ SRW-16329 [S]	Woody's Big Band Goodies	1966	3.00	6.00	12.00

HERMAN, WOODY/TITO PUENTE

Also see each artist's individual listings.

Number	Title	Yr	VG	VG+	NM
EVEREST					
❏ SDBR-1010 [S]	Herman's Heat and Puente's Beat	1958	10.00	20.00	40.00
❏ LPBR-5010 [M]	Herman's Heat and Puente's Beat	1958	10.00	20.00	40.00

HERMETO

Brazilian multi-instrumentalist.

Number	Title	Yr	VG	VG+	NM
MUSE					
❏ MR-5086	Hermeto	197?	3.00	6.00	12.00
WARNER BROS.					
❏ BS 2980	Slaves Mass	1976	3.75	7.50	15.00

HERSCH, FRED

Pianist.

Number	Title	Yr	VG	VG+	NM
CHESKY					
❏ 90	Dancing in the Dark	1993	5.00	10.00	20.00
CONCORD JAZZ					
❏ CJ-267	Horizons	1985	2.50	5.00	10.00

HERSEY, BAIRD

Number	Title	Yr	VG	VG+	NM
ARISTA NOVUS					
❏ AN 3004	Lookin' for That Groove	1977	3.00	6.00	12.00
❏ AN 3016	Have You Heard	1979	3.00	6.00	12.00

HERWIG, CONRAD

Trombonist.

Number	Title	Yr	VG	VG+	NM
SEA BREEZE					
❏ SB-2034	With Every Breath	1987	2.50	5.00	10.00

HEYWOOD, EDDIE

Pianist, composer, bandleader and arranger. Best known for his piano solo on the hit version of "Canadian Sunset" with Hugo Winterhalter's orchestra.

Number	Title	Yr	VG	VG+	NM
BRUNSWICK					
❏ BL 58036 [10]	Eddie Heywood '45	1953	12.50	25.00	50.00
CAPITOL					
❏ ST-163	Soft Summer Breeze	1969	3.00	6.00	12.00
❏ ST 2833	With Love and Strings	1968	3.00	6.00	12.00
COLUMBIA					
❏ CL 6157 [10]	Piano Moods	1951	12.50	25.00	50.00
COMMODORE					
❏ XFL-15876	The Biggest Little Band of the Forties	198?	3.00	6.00	12.00
❏ FL-20007 [10]	Eight Selections	1950	18.75	37.50	75.00
CORAL					
❏ CRL 57095 [M]	Featuring Eddie Heywood	1957	10.00	20.00	40.00
DECCA					
❏ DL 8202 [M]	Lightly and Politely	1956	7.50	15.00	30.00
❏ DL 8270 [M]	Swing Low Sweet Heywood	1956	7.50	15.00	30.00
EMARCY					
❏ MG-36042 [M]	Eddie Heywood	1955	10.00	20.00	40.00
EPIC					
❏ LN 3327 [M]	Eddie Heywood at Twilight	1956	7.50	15.00	30.00
LIBERTY					
❏ LRP-3250 [M]	Eddie Heywood's Golden Encores	1962	3.00	6.00	12.00
❏ LRP-3313 [M]	Canadian Sunset Bossa Nova	1963	3.00	6.00	12.00
❏ LST-7250 [S]	Eddie Heywood's Golden Encores	1962	3.75	7.50	15.00
❏ LST-7313 [S]	Canadian Sunset Bossa Nova	1963	3.75	7.50	15.00
MAINSTREAM					
❏ S-6001 [S]	Begin the Beguine	1964	3.75	7.50	15.00
❏ 96001 [M]	Begin the Beguine	1964	3.00	6.00	12.00
MERCURY					
❏ MG-20445 [M]	Breezin' Along with the Breeze	1959	5.00	10.00	20.00
❏ MG-20590 [M]	Eddie Heywood at the Piano	1960	5.00	10.00	20.00

Number	Title	Yr	VG	VG+	NM
❏ MG-20632 [M]	One for My Baby	1960	5.00	10.00	20.00
❏ SR-60115 [S]	Breezin' Along with the Breeze	1959	6.25	12.50	25.00
❏ SR-60248 [S]	Eddie Heywood at the Piano	1960	6.25	12.50	25.00
❏ SR-60632 [S]	One for My Baby	1960	6.25	12.50	25.00

MGM

Number	Title	Yr	VG	VG+	NM
❏ E-135 [10]	It's Easy to Remember	1952	12.50	25.00	50.00
❏ E-3093 [M]	Pianorama	1955	10.00	20.00	40.00
❏ E-3260 [M]	Eddie Heywood	1956	10.00	20.00	40.00

RCA VICTOR

Number	Title	Yr	VG	VG+	NM
❏ LPM-1466 [M]	The Touch of Eddie Heywood	1957	7.50	15.00	30.00
❏ LPM-1529 [M]	Canadian Sunset	1957	7.50	15.00	30.00
❏ LSP-1529 [S]	Canadian Sunset	1958	10.00	20.00	40.00
❏ LPM-1900 [M]	The Keys and I	1958	7.50	15.00	30.00

SUNSET

Number	Title	Yr	VG	VG+	NM
❏ SUM-1121 [M]	An Affair to Remember	196?	3.00	6.00	12.00
❏ SUS-5121 [S]	An Affair to Remember	196?	3.00	6.00	12.00

VOCALION

Number	Title	Yr	VG	VG+	NM
❏ VL 3748 [M]	The Piano Stylings of Eddie Heywood	1966	3.75	7.50	15.00
❏ VL 73748 [R]	The Piano Stylings of Eddie Heywood	1966	3.00	6.00	12.00

WING

Number	Title	Yr	VG	VG+	NM
❏ MGW-12137 [M]	Eddie Heywood	196?	3.75	7.50	15.00
❏ MGW-12287 [M]	Breezin' Along	196?	3.75	7.50	15.00
❏ SRW-16137 [S]	Eddie Heywood	196?	3.00	6.00	12.00
❏ SRW-16287 [S]	Breezin' Along	196?	3.00	6.00	12.00

HI-LO'S, THE
Vocal group: Gene Puerling; Bob Strassen (replaced by Don Shelton in 1959); Clark Burroughs; Bob Morse.

COLUMBIA

Number	Title	Yr	VG	VG+	NM
❏ CL 952 [M]	Suddenly It's the Hi-Lo's	1957	7.50	15.00	30.00
❏ CL 1023 [M]	Now Hear This	1957	7.50	15.00	30.00
❏ CL 1259 [M]	The Hi-Lo's and All That Jazz	1958	7.50	15.00	30.00
❏ CL 1416 [M]	Broadway Playbill	1959	7.50	15.00	30.00
❏ CL 1509 [M]	All Over the Place	1960	6.25	12.50	25.00
❏ CL 1723 [M]	This Time It's Love	1962	6.25	12.50	25.00
❏ CS 8057 [S]	Love Nest	1958	10.00	20.00	40.00
❏ CS 8077 [S]	The Hi-Lo's and All That Jazz	1958	10.00	20.00	40.00
❏ CS 8213 [S]	Broadway Playbill	1959	10.00	20.00	40.00
❏ CS 8300 [S]	All Over the Place	1960	7.50	15.00	30.00
❏ CS 8523 [S]	This Time It's Love	1962	7.50	15.00	30.00

COLUMBIA SPECIAL PRODUCTS

Number	Title	Yr	VG	VG+	NM
❏ P 14387	Harmony in Jazz	1978	3.00	6.00	12.00

DRG

Number	Title	Yr	VG	VG+	NM
❏ SL 5184	Clap Yo' Hands	198?	3.00	6.00	12.00

KAPP

Number	Title	Yr	VG	VG+	NM
❏ KL 1027 [M]	The Hi-Lo's and the Jerry Fielding Band	1956	7.50	15.00	30.00
❏ KL 1184 [M]	Under Glass	1959	6.25	12.50	25.00
-- Reissue of Starlite 7005					
❏ KL 1194 [M]	On Hand	1960	6.25	12.50	25.00
-- Reissue of Starlite 7008					

MCA

Number	Title	Yr	VG	VG+	NM
❏ 4171 [(2)]	The Hi-Lo's Collection	197?	3.75	7.50	15.00

OMEGA

Number	Title	Yr	VG	VG+	NM
❏ OSL-11 [S]	The Hi-Lo's in Stereo	195?	7.50	15.00	30.00

PAUSA

Number	Title	Yr	VG	VG+	NM
❏ 7040	Back Again	198?	3.00	6.00	12.00
❏ 7093	Now	198?	3.00	6.00	12.00

REPRISE

Number	Title	Yr	VG	VG+	NM
❏ R-6066 [M]	The Hi-Lo's Happen to Bossa Nova	1963	5.00	10.00	20.00
❏ R9-6066 [S]	The Hi-Lo's Happen to Bossa Nova	1963	6.25	12.50	25.00

STARLITE

Number	Title	Yr	VG	VG+	NM
❏ 6004 [10]	Listen!	1955	15.00	30.00	60.00
❏ 6005 [10]	The Hi-Lo's, I Presume	1955	15.00	30.00	60.00
❏ 7005 [M]	Under Glass	1956	10.00	20.00	40.00
❏ 7006 [M]	Listen!	1956	10.00	20.00	40.00
-- Reissue of 6004					
❏ 7007 [M]	The Hi-Lo's. I Presume	1956	10.00	20.00	40.00
-- Reissue of 6005					
❏ 7008 [M]	On Hand	1956	10.00	20.00	40.00

HIBBLER, AL
Male singer, best known for his 1955 hit version of "Unchained Melody."

ARGO

Number	Title	Yr	VG	VG+	NM
❏ LP-601 [M]	Melodies by Al Hibbler	1956	10.00	20.00	40.00
-- Reissue of Marterry LP					

ATLANTIC

Number	Title	Yr	VG	VG+	NM
❏ 1251 [M]	After the Lights Go Down Low	1957	12.50	25.00	50.00
-- Black label					

Number	Title	Yr	VG	VG+	NM
❏ 1251 [M]	After the Lights Go Down Low	1961	6.25	12.50	25.00
-- Mostly red label, white fan logo					
❏ 1251 [M]	After the Lights Go Down Low	1963	5.00	10.00	20.00
-- Mostly red label, black fan logo					

BRUNSWICK

Number	Title	Yr	VG	VG+	NM
❏ BL 54036 [M]	Al Hibbler with the Ellingtonians	1957	12.50	25.00	50.00

DECCA

Number	Title	Yr	VG	VG+	NM
❏ DL 8328 [M]	Starring Al Hibbler	1956	7.50	15.00	30.00
❏ DL 8420 [M]	Here's Hibbler	1957	7.50	15.00	30.00
❏ DL 8697 [M]	Torchy and Blue	1958	7.50	15.00	30.00
❏ DL 8757 [M]	Hits by Hibbler	1958	7.50	15.00	30.00
❏ DL 8862 [M]	Al Hibbler Remembers the Big Songs of the Big Bands	1959	7.50	15.00	30.00
❏ DL 78862 [S]	Al Hibbler Remembers the Big Songs of the Big Bands	1959	10.00	20.00	40.00

DISCOVERY

Number	Title	Yr	VG	VG+	NM
❏ 842	It's Monday Every Day	198?	3.00	6.00	12.00
-- Reissue of Reprise LP					

LMI

Number	Title	Yr	VG	VG+	NM
❏ 10001 [M]	Early One Morning	1964	7.50	15.00	30.00

MARTERRY

Number	Title	Yr	VG	VG+	NM
❏ LP-601 [M]	Melodies by Al Hibbler	1956	20.00	40.00	80.00

MCA

Number	Title	Yr	VG	VG+	NM
❏ 4098 [(2)]	The Best of Al Hibbler	197?	3.75	7.50	15.00

NORGRAN

Number	Title	Yr	VG	VG+	NM
❏ MGN-4 [10]	Al Hibbler Favorites	1954	37.50	75.00	150.00
❏ MGN-15 [10]	Al Hibbler Sings Duke Ellington	1954	37.50	75.00	150.00

OPEN SKY

Number	Title	Yr	VG	VG+	NM
❏ OSR-3126	For Sentimental Reasons	1986	3.00	6.00	12.00

REPRISE

Number	Title	Yr	VG	VG+	NM
❏ R-2005 [M]	It's Monday Every Day	1961	7.50	15.00	30.00
❏ R9-2005 [S]	It's Monday Every Day	1961	10.00	20.00	40.00

SCORE

Number	Title	Yr	VG	VG+	NM
❏ SLP-4013 [M]	I Surrender, Dear	1957	25.00	50.00	100.00

VERVE

Number	Title	Yr	VG	VG+	NM
❏ MGV-4000 [M]	Al Hibbler Sings Love Songs	1956	15.00	30.00	60.00
❏ V-4000 [M]	Al Hibbler Sings Love Songs	1961	5.00	10.00	20.00

HICKS, JOHN
Pianist.

STRATA-EAST

Number	Title	Yr	VG	VG+	NM
❏ SES-8002	Hells Bells	1979	3.75	7.50	15.00

THERESA

Number	Title	Yr	VG	VG+	NM
❏ TR-115	Some Other Time	1983	3.00	6.00	12.00
❏ TR-119	John Hicks	1986	3.00	6.00	12.00
❏ TR-123	John Hicks In Concert	1987	3.00	6.00	12.00

WEST 54TH

Number	Title	Yr	VG	VG+	NM
❏ 8004	After the Morning	1980	3.00	6.00	12.00

HIGGINBOTHAM, J.C.
Trombonist.

JAZZOLOGY

Number	Title	Yr	VG	VG+	NM
❏ J-28	J.C. Higginbotham Comes Home!	1968	3.00	6.00	12.00

HIGGINS, BILLY
Drummer and composer.

CONTEMPORARY

Number	Title	Yr	VG	VG+	NM
❏ C-14024	Bridgework	1987	2.50	5.00	10.00

RED

Number	Title	Yr	VG	VG+	NM
❏ VPA-141	Soweto	1979	3.00	6.00	12.00
❏ VPA-164	Once More	198?	3.00	6.00	12.00

HIGGINS, EDDIE
Pianist, clarinetist and bass player.

ATLANTIC

Number	Title	Yr	VG	VG+	NM
❏ 1446 [M]	Soulero	1966	3.75	7.50	15.00
❏ SD 1446 [S]	Soulero	1966	5.00	10.00	20.00

VEE JAY

Number	Title	Yr	VG	VG+	NM
❏ LP-3017 [M]	Eddie Higgins	1961	7.50	15.00	30.00
❏ SR-3017 [S]	Eddie Higgins	1961	10.00	20.00	40.00

HIGH SOCIETY JAZZ BAND, THE

STOMP OFF

Number	Title	Yr	VG	VG+	NM
❏ SOS-1010	Shake It and Break It	1981	3.00	6.00	12.00
❏ SOS-1166	'Lasses Candy	1989	2.50	5.00	10.00

HIGHER PRIMATES
Members: Glenn Davis, Peter LeMaitre, Ron Glick (percussion); Ed Schuller, Roy Cumming, Ratso Harris (bass); Mark Reboul (saxophone); Herb Robertson (trumpet).

GM

Number	Title	Yr	VG	VG+	NM
❏ 3003	Environmental Impressions	1985	2.50	5.00	10.00

Number	Title	Yr	VG	VG+	NM
HIGHTOWER, DONNA					
Female singer.					
CAPITOL					
❏ ST 1133 [S]	Take One	1959	12.50	25.00	50.00
❏ T 1133 [M]	Take One	1959	10.00	20.00	40.00
❏ ST 1273 [S]	Gee Baby...Ain't I Good to You	1959	12.50	25.00	50.00
❏ T 1273 [M]	Gee Baby...Ain't I Good to You	1959	10.00	20.00	40.00
HILDINGER, DAVE					
Pianist and vibraphone player.					
BATON					
❏ 1204 [M]	The Young Moderns	1957	10.00	20.00	40.00
HILL, ANDREW					
Pianist.					
ARISTA FREEDOM					
❏ AL 1007	Spiral	1975	3.75	7.50	15.00
❏ AL 1023	Montreux	1976	3.75	7.50	15.00
ARTISTS HOUSE					
❏ 9	From California with Love	1979	3.00	6.00	12.00
BLUE NOTE					
❏ BN-LA459-H2 [(2)]	One for One	1975	5.00	10.00	20.00
❏ LN-1030	Dance with Andrew Hill	1980	3.00	6.00	12.00
❏ BLP-4151 [M]	Black Fire	1963	7.50	15.00	30.00
❏ BLP-4159 [M]	Judgment!	1964	7.50	15.00	30.00
❏ BLP-4160 [M]	Smoke Stack	1964	7.50	15.00	30.00
❏ BLP-4167 [M]	Point of Departure	1964	7.50	15.00	30.00
❏ BLP-4203 [M]	Andrew!!! -- The Music of Andrew Hill	1965	---	---	---
-- Not known to exist					
❏ BLP-4217 [M]	Compulsion	1965	6.25	12.50	25.00
❏ BLP-4233 [M]	One for One	1966	---	---	---
-- Canceled					
❏ B1-28981	Judgment!	1994	3.75	7.50	15.00
❏ B1-32097	Smokestack	1995	3.75	7.50	15.00
❏ BST-84151 [S]	Black Fire	1963	10.00	20.00	40.00
-- With "New York, USA" address on label					
❏ BST-84151 [S]	Black Fire	1967	3.75	7.50	15.00
-- With "A Division of Liberty Records" on label					
❏ BST-84159 [S]	Judgment!	1964	10.00	20.00	40.00
-- With "New York, USA" address on label					
❏ BST-84159 [S]	Judgment!	1967	3.75	7.50	15.00
-- With "A Division of Liberty Records" on label					
❏ BST-84160 [S]	Smoke Stack	1964	10.00	20.00	40.00
-- With "New York, USA" address on label					
❏ BST-84160 [S]	Smoke Stack	1967	3.75	7.50	15.00
-- With "A Division of Liberty Records" on label					
❏ BST-84167 [S]	Point of Departure	1964	10.00	20.00	40.00
-- With "New York, USA" address on label					
❏ BST-84167 [S]	Point of Departure	1967	3.75	7.50	15.00
-- With "A Division of Liberty Records" on label					
❏ BST-84203 [S]	Andrew!!! -- The Music of Andrew Hill	1967	6.25	12.50	25.00
-- With "A Division of Liberty Records" on label; version with "New York, USA" on label not known to exist					
❏ BST-84217 [S]	Compulsion	1965	7.50	15.00	30.00
-- With "New York, USA" address on label					
❏ BST-84217 [S]	Compulsion	1967	3.75	7.50	15.00
-- With "A Division of Liberty Records" on label					
❏ BST-84233 [S]	One for One	1966	---	---	---
-- Canceled					
❏ BST-84303	Grass Roots	1968	5.00	10.00	20.00
❏ BST-84330	Lift Every Voice	1969	5.00	10.00	20.00
❏ B1-92051	Internal Spirit	198?	2.50	5.00	10.00
INNER CITY					
❏ IC-2026	Invitation	1975	3.75	7.50	15.00
❏ IC-2044	Divine Revelation	1976	3.75	7.50	15.00
❏ IC-6022	Nefertiti	1977	3.75	7.50	15.00
MOSAIC					
❏ MQ10-161 [(10)]	The Complete Andrew Hill Blue Note Sessions	199?	45.00	90.00	180.00
SOUL NOTE					
❏ SN-1010	Faces of Hope	198?	3.00	6.00	12.00
❏ SN-1013	Strange Serenade	198?	3.00	6.00	12.00
❏ 121110	Verona Rag	199?	3.00	6.00	12.00
❏ 121113	Shades	199?	3.00	6.00	12.00
STEEPLECHASE					
❏ SCS-1026	Invitation	198?	3.00	6.00	12.00
❏ SCS-1044	Divine Revelation	198?	3.00	6.00	12.00
WARWICK					
❏ W-2002 [M]	So in Love	1960	15.00	30.00	60.00
❏ W-2002ST [S]	So in Love	1960	20.00	40.00	80.00

Number	Title	Yr	VG	VG+	NM
HILL, BUCK					
Tenor saxophone player.					
MUSE					
❏ MR-5384	Capital Hill	198?	2.50	5.00	10.00
STEEPLECHASE					
❏ SCS-1095	This Is Buck Hill	1979	3.75	7.50	15.00
❏ SCS-1123	Scope	1980	3.75	7.50	15.00
❏ SCS-1160	Easy to Love	198?	3.75	7.50	15.00
❏ SCS-1173	Impressions	198?	3.75	7.50	15.00
HILL, VINSON					
Pianist.					
SAVOY					
❏ MG-12187 [M]	The Vinson Hill Trio	1966	7.50	15.00	30.00
HIMBER, RICHARD					
Bandleader.					
CIRCLE					
❏ 7	Richard Himber and His Orchestra: 1939-1940	198?	2.50	5.00	10.00
HINES, EARL "FATHA"					
Pianist, male singer and composer. Also see COZY COLE; JOHNNY HODGES.					
ABC IMPULSE!					
❏ AS-9108 [S]	Once Upon a Time	1968	3.75	7.50	15.00
ADVANCE					
❏ 4 [10]	Fats Waller Memorial Set	1951	37.50	75.00	150.00
ARCHIVE OF FOLK AND JAZZ					
❏ 246	Earl "Fatha" Hines	1970	3.00	6.00	12.00
❏ 322	Earl "Fatha" Hines, Volume 2	197?	2.50	5.00	10.00
ATLANTIC					
❏ ALS-120 [10]	Earl Hines: QRS Solos	1952	50.00	100.00	200.00
AUDIOPHILE					
❏ APS-111	My Tribute to Louis	1971	3.75	7.50	15.00
❏ APS-112	Earl Hines Comes In Handy	197?	3.75	7.50	15.00
❏ APS-113	Hines Does Hoagy	197?	3.75	7.50	15.00
BASF					
❏ 20749	Fatha and His Flock On Tour	1972	3.75	7.50	15.00
BIOGRAPH					
❏ 12055	Solo Walk in Tokyo	197?	2.50	5.00	10.00
❏ 12056	Earl Hines in New Orleans	197?	2.50	5.00	10.00
BLACK LION					
❏ 112	Tea for Two	1973	3.00	6.00	12.00
❏ 200	Tour De Force	1974	3.00	6.00	12.00
BLUEBIRD					
❏ AXM2-5508 [(2)]	Fatha Jumps	197?	3.75	7.50	15.00
BRUNSWICK					
❏ BL 58035 [10]	Earl Hines Plays Fats Waller	1953	30.00	60.00	120.00
CAPITOL					
❏ ST 1971 [S]	Earl "Fatha" Hines	1963	7.50	15.00	30.00
❏ T 1971 [M]	Earl "Fatha" Hines	1963	6.25	12.50	25.00
CHIAROSCURO					
❏ 101	Quintessential Recording Session	1971	3.75	7.50	15.00
-- Reissue of Halcyon 101					
❏ 116 [(2)]	An Evening with Hines	1972	5.00	10.00	20.00
❏ 120	Quintessential Continued	1973	3.75	7.50	15.00
❏ 131	Quintessential 1974	1974	3.75	7.50	15.00
❏ 157	Live at the New School	1974	3.00	6.00	12.00
❏ 180	Live at the New School, Volume 2	1977	3.00	6.00	12.00
❏ 200	Earl Hines in New Orleans	1978	3.00	6.00	12.00
CLASSIC JAZZ					
❏ 31 [(2)]	Earl Hines Plays Gershwin	1974	3.75	7.50	15.00
❏ 144	Earl Hines at Sundown	198?	3.00	6.00	12.00
COLUMBIA					
❏ CL 2320 [M]	The New Earl Hines Trio	1965	5.00	10.00	20.00
❏ CL 6171 [10]	Piano Moods	1951	30.00	60.00	120.00
❏ CS 9120 [S]	The New Earl Hines Trio	1965	6.25	12.50	25.00
COLUMBIA JAZZ MASTERPIECES					
❏ CJ 44197	Live at the Village Vanguard	1988	2.50	5.00	10.00
CONTACT					
❏ 2 [M]	Spontaneous Explorations	1964	6.25	12.50	25.00
❏ S-2 [S]	Spontaneous Explorations	1964	7.50	15.00	30.00
CRAFTSMEN					
❏ 8041 [M]	Swingin' and Singin'	1960	6.25	12.50	25.00
DECCA					
❏ DL 9221 [M]	Southside Swing (1934-35)	1967	6.25	12.50	25.00
❏ DL 9235 [M]	Earl Hines at the Apex Club	1968	6.25	12.50	25.00
❏ DL 75048	Fatha Blows Best	1969	3.75	7.50	15.00
❏ DL 79221 [R]	Southside Swing (1934-35)	1967	3.00	6.00	12.00

Number	Title	Yr	VG	VG+	NM
❏ DL 79235 [R]	Earl Hines at the Apex Club	1968	3.00	6.00	12.00
DELMARK					
❏ DS-212	Earl Hines At Home	1969	3.00	6.00	12.00
DIAL					
❏ LP-303 [10]	Earl Hines Trio	1952	62.50	125.00	250.00
❏ LP-306 [10]	Earl Hines All Stars	1953	62.50	125.00	250.00
ENSIGN					
❏ 22021	Earl Hines Rhythm	1969	5.00	10.00	20.00
EPIC					
❏ LN 3223 [M]	Oh, Fatha!	1956	12.50	25.00	50.00
❏ LN 3501 [M]	Earl "Fatha" Hines	1958	12.50	25.00	50.00
FANTASY					
❏ OJC-1740	A Monday Date	198?	2.50	5.00	10.00
❏ 3217 [M]	"Fatha" Plays "Fats"	1956	25.00	50.00	100.00
-- Red vinyl					
❏ 3217 [M]	"Fatha" Plays "Fats"	195?	12.50	25.00	50.00
-- Black vinyl					
❏ 3238 [M]	Earl "Fatha" Hines Solo	1956	25.00	50.00	100.00
-- Red vinyl					
❏ 3238 [M]	Earl "Fatha" Hines Solo	195?	12.50	25.00	50.00
-- Black vinyl					
❏ 8381	Incomparable	1968	3.00	6.00	12.00
FLYING DUTCHMAN					
❏ FD-10147 [(2)]	The Mighty Fatha	1973	3.75	7.50	15.00
FOCUS					
❏ FM-335 [M]	The Real Earl Hines In Concert	1965	6.25	12.50	25.00
❏ FS-335 [S]	The Real Earl Hines In Concert	1965	7.50	15.00	30.00
GNP CRESCENDO					
❏ GNP-9010	Earl "Fatha" Hines in Paris	197?	2.50	5.00	10.00
❏ GNP-9042	Earl "Fatha" Hines All-Stars	197?	2.50	5.00	10.00
❏ GNP-9043	Earl "Fatha" Hines All-Stars, Vol. 2	197?	2.50	5.00	10.00
❏ GNPS-9054	Live at the Crescendo	1992	3.00	6.00	12.00
HALCYON					
❏ 101	The Quintessential Recording Session	196?	5.00	10.00	20.00
HALL OF FAME					
❏ 609	Earl "Fatha" Hines All-Stars	197?	2.50	5.00	10.00
IMPROV					
❏ 7114	Live at the Downtown Club	1976	3.00	6.00	12.00
IMPULSE!					
❏ A-9108 [M]	Once Upon a Time	1966	6.25	12.50	25.00
❏ AS-9108 [S]	Once Upon a Time	1966	7.50	15.00	30.00
INNER CITY					
❏ IC-1142	Paris Session	198?	3.00	6.00	12.00
JAZZ PANORAMA					
❏ 7 [M]	All Stars	1961	10.00	20.00	40.00
M&K					
❏ 105	"Fatha"	1979	6.25	12.50	25.00
-- Direct-to-disc recording					
MASTER JAZZ					
❏ 8101	Blues and Things	1970	3.75	7.50	15.00
❏ 8109	Hines '65	1971	3.75	7.50	15.00
❏ 8114	Earl Hines Plays Duke Ellington	1971	3.75	7.50	15.00
❏ 8126 [(2)]	Earl Hines Plays Duke Ellington, Volumes 2 and 3	1973	5.00	10.00	20.00
❏ 8132	Earl Hines Plays Duke Ellington, Volume 4	1975	3.00	6.00	12.00
MCA					
❏ 1311	South Side Swing	198?	2.50	5.00	10.00
❏ 29070	Once Upon a Time	198?	2.50	5.00	10.00
MERCURY					
❏ MG-25018 [10]	Earl Hines and the All Stars	1950	62.50	125.00	250.00
MGM					
❏ E-3832 [M]	Earl's Pearls	1960	6.25	12.50	25.00
❏ SE-3832 [S]	Earl's Pearls	1960	7.50	15.00	30.00
MILESTONE					
❏ 2012	Monday Date 1928	197?	3.00	6.00	12.00
MUSE					
❏ DE-602	The Legendary Little Theatre Concert of 1964, Volume 1	198?	2.50	5.00	10.00
❏ MR-2001/2 [(2)]	The Legendary Little Theatre Concert of 1964	198?	3.75	7.50	15.00
NOCTURNE					
❏ NLP-5 [10]	Earl "Fatha" Hines	1954	37.50	75.00	150.00
PRESTIGE					
❏ 2515	Boogie Woogie on St. Louis Blues	198?	3.00	6.00	12.00
❏ 24043 [(2)]	Another Monday Date	197?	3.75	7.50	15.00

Number	Title	Yr	VG	VG+	NM
QUICKSILVER					
❏ QS-9000	Live and in Living Jazz	198?	2.50	5.00	10.00
❏ QS-9001	Fatha	198?	2.50	5.00	10.00
RCA VICTOR					
❏ LPT-20 [10]	Earl Hines with Billy Eckstine	1953	30.00	60.00	120.00
❏ LPV-512 [M]	The Grand Terrace Band	1965	6.25	12.50	25.00
❏ LPM-3380 [M]	Up to Date	1965	5.00	10.00	20.00
❏ LSP-3380 [S]	Up to Date	1965	6.25	12.50	25.00
RIVERSIDE					
❏ RLP-398 [M]	A Monday Date	1961	7.50	15.00	30.00
❏ RS-9398 [R]	A Monday Date	196?	5.00	10.00	20.00
ROYALE					
❏ 18166 [10]	Eal "Fatha" Hines -- Great Piano Solos	195?	30.00	60.00	120.00
STORYVILLE					
❏ 4063	Earl Hines at the Club Hangover	198?	2.50	5.00	10.00
TIARA					
❏ TMT-7524 [M]	Earl "Fatha" Hines with Buck Clayton	195?	5.00	10.00	20.00
TOPS					
❏ L-1599 [M]	"Fatha"	195?	7.50	15.00	30.00
TRIP					
❏ J-3	All-Star Session	1970	3.00	6.00	12.00
VERVE					
❏ VSP-35 [M]	Life with Fatha	1966	5.00	10.00	20.00
❏ VSPS-35 [R]	Life with Fatha	1966	3.00	6.00	12.00
WHO'S WHO IN JAZZ					
❏ 21004	Lionel Hampton Presents Earl	1978	3.00	6.00	12.00
"X"					
❏ LVA-3023 [10]	Piano Solos	1954	30.00	60.00	120.00
XANADU					
❏ 203	Varieties!	1985	2.50	5.00	10.00

HINES, EARL "FATHA," AND TERESA BREWER

Also see each artist's individual listings.

Number	Title	Yr	VG	VG+	NM
DOCTOR JAZZ					
❏ FW 38810	We Love You Fats	1983	2.50	5.00	10.00

HINES, EARL "FATHA," AND JAKI BYARD

Also see each artist's individual listings.

Number	Title	Yr	VG	VG+	NM
VERVE/MPS					
❏ 825 195-1	Duet	1985	2.50	5.00	10.00

HINES, EARL "FATHA," AND ROY ELDRIDGE

Also see each artist's individual listings.

Number	Title	Yr	VG	VG+	NM
LIMELIGHT					
❏ LM-82028 [M]	The Grand Reunion, Volume 2	1965	5.00	10.00	20.00
❏ LS-86028 [S]	The Grand Reunion, Volume 2	1965	6.25	12.50	25.00
XANADU					
❏ 106	At the Village Vanguard	197?	3.00	6.00	12.00

HINES, EARL "FATHA," AND PAUL GONSALVES

Also see each artist's individual listings.

Number	Title	Yr	VG	VG+	NM
BLACK LION					
❏ 306	It Don't Mean a Thing	197?	3.00	6.00	12.00

HINES, EARL "FATHA," AND COLEMAN HAWKINS

Also see each artist's individual listings.

Number	Title	Yr	VG	VG+	NM
LIMELIGHT					
❏ LM-82020 [M]	The Grand Reunion	1965	5.00	10.00	20.00
❏ LS-86020 [S]	The Grand Reunion	1965	6.25	12.50	25.00
TRIP					
❏ 5557	The Grand Reunion	197?	2.50	5.00	10.00

HINES, EARL "FATHA," AND BUDD JOHNSON

Also see each artist's individual listings.

Number	Title	Yr	VG	VG+	NM
CLASSIC JAZZ					
❏ 129	Linger Awhile	197?	3.00	6.00	12.00

HINES, EARL "FATHA," AND MARVA JOSIE

Josie is a female singer. Also see EARL "FATHA" HINES.

Number	Title	Yr	VG	VG+	NM
CATALYST					
❏ 7622	His Old Lady and Me	197?	3.00	6.00	12.00

HINES, EARL "FATHA," AND MAXINE SULLIVAN

Also see each artist's individual listings.

Number	Title	Yr	VG	VG+	NM
CHIAROSCURO					
❏ 107	Live at the Overseas Press Club	1971	3.75	7.50	15.00

Number	Title	Yr	VG	VG+	NM
HINO, TERUMASA					
Trumpeter.					
CATALYST					
❑ 7901	Fuji	197?	3.00	6.00	12.00
❑ 7910	At the Berlin Jazz Festival '71	197?	3.00	6.00	12.00
ENJA					
❑ 2028	Taro's Mood	197?	3.75	7.50	15.00
INNER CITY					
❑ IC-6027	Speak to Loneliness	197?	3.00	6.00	12.00
❑ IC-6065	May Dance	197?	3.00	6.00	12.00
❑ IC-6068	City Connection	198?	3.00	6.00	12.00
❑ IC-6069	Daydream	198?	3.00	6.00	12.00
HINTON, MILT					
Bass player.					
BETHLEHEM					
❑ BCP-10 [M]	East Coast Jazz Series #5	1957	12.50	25.00	50.00
❑ BCP-1020 [10]	Milt Hinton Quartet	1955	20.00	40.00	80.00
CHIAROSCURO					
❑ 188	Trio	1978	3.00	6.00	12.00
EPIC					
❑ LN 3271 [M]	The Rhythm Section	1956	12.50	25.00	50.00
FAMOUS DOOR					
❑ 104	Here Swings The Judge	197?	3.75	7.50	15.00
HINTON, MILT; WENDELL MARSHALL; BULL RUTHER					
All of the above are bass players. Also see MILT HINTON.					
RCA VICTOR					
❑ LPM-1107 [M]	Basses Loaded!	1955	20.00	40.00	80.00
HINZE, CHRIS					
Flutist and composer.					
ATLANTIC					
❑ SD 19185	Bamboo	1978	3.00	6.00	12.00
COLUMBIA					
❑ KC 33363	Sister Slick	1975	3.00	6.00	12.00
HIPP, JUTTA					
Pianist.					
BLUE NOTE					
❑ BLP-1515 [M]	Jutta Hipp at the Hickory House, Volume 1	1956	62.50	125.00	250.00
-- "Deep groove" version (deep indentation under label on both sides)					
❑ BLP-1515 [M]	Jutta Hipp at the Hickory House, Volume 1	1956	50.00	100.00	200.00
-- Regular version, Lexington Ave. address on label					
❑ BLP-1515 [M]	Jutta Hipp at the Hickory House, Volume 1	1963	7.50	15.00	30.00
-- With "New York, USA" address on label					
❑ BLP-1516 [M]	Jutta Hipp at the Hickory House, Volume 2	1956	62.50	125.00	250.00
-- "Deep groove" version (deep indentation under label on both sides)					
❑ BLP-1516 [M]	Jutta Hipp at the Hickory House, Volume 2	1956	50.00	100.00	200.00
-- Regular version, Lexington Ave. address on label					
❑ BLP-1516 [M]	Jutta Hipp at the Hickory House, Volume 2	1963	7.50	15.00	30.00
-- With "New York, USA" address on label					
❑ BLP-1530 [M]	Jutta Hipp with Zoot Sims	1956	62.50	125.00	250.00
-- "Deep groove" version (deep indentation under label on both sides)					
❑ BLP-1530 [M]	Jutta Hipp with Zoot Sims	1956	50.00	100.00	200.00
-- Regular version, Lexington Ave. address on label					
❑ BLP-1530 [M]	Jutta Hipp with Zoot Sims	1963	7.50	15.00	30.00
-- With "New York, USA" address on label					
❑ BLP-5056 [10]	New Faces-New Sounds from Germany	1955	75.00	150.00	300.00
MGM					
❑ E-3157 [M]	Cool Europe	1955	37.50	75.00	150.00
HIROTA, JOJI					
Percussionist and singer.					
INNER CITY					
❑ IC-1127	Wheel of Fortune	198?	3.00	6.00	12.00
HIRT, AL					
Trumpeter and occasional male singer. One of the most popular musicians of the 1960s Dixieland revival.					
ACCORD					
❑ SN-7187	Java	1981	2.00	4.00	8.00
ALLEGIANCE					
❑ AV-5018	Showtime	1985	2.00	4.00	8.00
❑ AV-5032	Blues Line	1986	2.00	4.00	8.00

Number	Title	Yr	VG	VG+	NM
AUDIO FIDELITY					
❑ AFLP-1877 [M]	Swingin' Dixie (At Dan's Pier 600 in New Orleans)	1959	3.75	7.50	15.00
❑ AFLP-1878 [M]	Swingin' Dixie	1959	3.75	7.50	15.00
❑ AFLP-1926 [M]	Swingin' Dixie (Vol. 3)	1961	3.75	7.50	15.00
❑ AFLP-1927 [M]	Swingin' Dixie (Vol. 4)	1961	3.75	7.50	15.00
❑ AFSD-5877 [S]	Swingin' Dixie (At Dan's Pier 600 in New Orleans)	1959	5.00	10.00	20.00
❑ AFSD-5878 [S]	Swingin' Dixie	1959	5.00	10.00	20.00
❑ AFSD-5926 [S]	Swingin' Dixie (Vol. 3)	1961	5.00	10.00	20.00
❑ AFSD-5927 [S]	Swingin' Dixie (Vol. 4)	1961	5.00	10.00	20.00
❑ AF-6282	Hirt...So Good!	1978	2.50	5.00	10.00
CORAL					
❑ CRL 57402 [M]	Al Hirt in New Orleans	1962	3.00	6.00	12.00
❑ CRL 757402 [S]	Al Hirt in New Orleans	1962	3.75	7.50	15.00
CROWN					
❑ CST-457 [S]	The Dawn Busters	196?	3.00	6.00	12.00
❑ CLP-5457 [M]	The Dawn Busters	196?	3.00	6.00	12.00
GHB					
❑ 107	Mardi Gras Parade Music	197?	2.50	5.00	10.00
GWP					
❑ 2002	Paint Your Wagon	1970	2.50	5.00	10.00
❑ 2004	Al Hirt Gold	1971	2.50	5.00	10.00
❑ 2005	Al Hirt Country	1971	2.50	5.00	10.00
METRO					
❑ M-517 [M]	Al Hirt	1965	2.50	5.00	10.00
❑ MS-517 [S]	Al Hirt	1965	3.00	6.00	12.00
MONUMENT					
❑ 6642	Raw Sugar/Sweet Sauce/Banana Puddin'	1976	2.00	4.00	8.00
-- Reissue of 32913					
❑ 7603	Jumbo's Gumbo	1977	2.00	4.00	8.00
-- Reissue of 33885					
❑ KZ 32913	Raw Sugar/Sweet Sauce/Banana Puddin'	1974	2.50	5.00	10.00
❑ PZ 33885	Jumbo's Gumbo	1975	2.50	5.00	10.00
PAIR					
❑ PDL2-1048 [(2)]	New Orleans By Night	1986	3.00	6.00	12.00
RCA CAMDEN					
❑ CAL-2138 [M]	Struttin' Down Royal Street	1967	3.00	6.00	12.00
❑ CAS-2138 [S]	Struttin' Down Royal Street	1967	2.50	5.00	10.00
❑ CAS-2316	Al's Place	1970	2.50	5.00	10.00
❑ CAS-2573	Have a Merry Little	1971	2.50	5.00	10.00
❑ CXS-9015 [(2)]	Al Hirt Blows His Own Horn	1972	3.00	6.00	12.00
RCA VICTOR					
❑ ANL1-1034	The Best of Al Hirt	1975	2.50	5.00	10.00
❑ LPM-2354 [M]	Al (He's the King) Hirt and His Band	1961	3.00	6.00	12.00
❑ LSP-2354 [S]	Al (He's the King) Hirt and His Band	1961	3.75	7.50	15.00
❑ LPM-2366 [M]	The Greatest Horn in the World	1961	3.00	6.00	12.00
❑ LSP-2366 [S]	The Greatest Horn in the World	1961	3.75	7.50	15.00
❑ LPM-2446 [M]	Horn A-Plenty	1962	3.00	6.00	12.00
❑ LSP-2446 [S]	Horn A-Plenty	1962	3.75	7.50	15.00
❑ LPM-2497 [M]	Al Hirt at the Mardi Gras	1962	3.00	6.00	12.00
❑ LSP-2497 [S]	Al Hirt at the Mardi Gras	1962	3.75	7.50	15.00
❑ LPM-2584 [M]	Trumpet and Strings	1962	3.00	6.00	12.00
❑ LSP-2584 [S]	Trumpet and Strings	1962	3.75	7.50	15.00
❑ LPM-2607 [M]	Our Man in New Orleans	1963	3.00	6.00	12.00
❑ LSP-2607 [S]	Our Man in New Orleans	1963	3.75	7.50	15.00
❑ LM-2729 [M]	"Pops" Goes the Trumpet	1964	3.75	7.50	15.00
❑ LSC-2729 [S]	"Pops" Goes the Trumpet	1964	5.00	10.00	20.00
-- With the Boston Pops Orchestra conducted by Arthur Fiedler					
❑ LPM-2733 [M]	Honey in the Horn	1963	3.00	6.00	12.00
❑ LSP-2733 [S]	Honey in the Horn	1963	3.75	7.50	15.00
❑ LPM-2917 [M]	Cotton Candy	1964	3.00	6.00	12.00
❑ LSP-2917 [S]	Cotton Candy	1964	3.75	7.50	15.00
❑ LPM-2965 [M]	Sugar Lips	1964	3.00	6.00	12.00
❑ LSP-2965 [S]	Sugar Lips	1964	3.75	7.50	15.00
❑ LPM-3309 [M]	The Best of Al Hirt	1965	3.00	6.00	12.00
❑ LSP-3309 [S]	The Best of Al Hirt	1965	3.75	7.50	15.00
❑ LPM-3337 [M]	That Honey Horn Sound	1965	3.00	6.00	12.00
❑ LSP-3337 [S]	That Honey Horn Sound	1965	3.75	7.50	15.00
❑ LPM-3416 [M]	Live at Carnegie Hall	1965	3.00	6.00	12.00
❑ LSP-3416 [S]	Live at Carnegie Hall	1965	3.75	7.50	15.00
❑ LPM-3417 [M]	The Sound of Christmas	1965	2.50	5.00	10.00
❑ LSP-3417 [S]	The Sound of Christmas	1965	3.00	6.00	12.00
❑ LPM-3492 [M]	They're Playing Our Song	1966	3.00	6.00	12.00
❑ LSP-3492 [S]	They're Playing Our Song	1966	3.75	7.50	15.00
❑ LPM-3556 [M]	The Best of Al Hirt, Volume 2	1966	3.00	6.00	12.00
❑ LSP-3556 [S]	The Best of Al Hirt, Volume 2	1966	3.75	7.50	15.00
❑ LPM-3579 [M]	The Happy Trumpet	1966	3.00	6.00	12.00
❑ LSP-3579 [S]	The Happy Trumpet	1966	3.75	7.50	15.00
❑ LPM-3653 [M]	Latin in the Horn	1966	3.00	6.00	12.00
❑ LSP-3653 [S]	Latin in the Horn	1966	3.75	7.50	15.00

Number	Title	Yr	VG	VG+	NM
❏ LPM-3716 [M]	The Horn Meets the Hornet	1967	3.00	6.00	12.00
❏ LSP-3716 [S]	The Horn Meets the Hornet	1967	3.75	7.50	15.00
❏ LPM-3773 [M]	Music to Watch Girls By	1967	3.75	7.50	15.00
❏ LSP-3773 [S]	Music to Watch Girls By	1967	3.75	7.50	15.00
❏ LPM-3878 [M]	Soul in the Horn	1967	3.75	7.50	15.00
❏ LSP-3878 [S]	Soul in the Horn	1967	3.75	7.50	15.00
❏ LPM-3917 [M]	Al Hirt Plays Bert Kaempfert	1968	5.00	10.00	20.00
❏ LSP-3917 [S]	Al Hirt Plays Bert Kaempfert	1968	3.75	7.50	15.00
❏ LPM-3979 [M]	Unforgettable	1968	6.25	12.50	25.00
❏ LSP-3979 [S]	Unforgettable	1968	3.00	6.00	12.00
❏ LSP-4020	In Love with You	1968	3.00	6.00	12.00
❏ LSP-4101	Al Hirt Now	1969	3.00	6.00	12.00
❏ LSP-4161	Here in My Heart	1969	3.00	6.00	12.00
❏ LSP-4247	Al Hirt	1970	3.00	6.00	12.00
❏ VPS-6025 [(2)]	This Is Al Hirt	1970	3.75	7.50	15.00
❏ VPS-6057 [(2)]	This Is Al Hirt, Volume 2	1972	3.75	7.50	15.00

VERVE

Number	Title	Yr	VG	VG+	NM
❏ MGV-1012 [M]	Swinging Dixie from Dan's Pier 600	1957	12.50	25.00	50.00
❏ MGV-1027 [M]	Blockbustin' Dixie!	195?	10.00	20.00	40.00
❏ V-1027 [M]	Blockbustin' Dixie!	1961	5.00	10.00	20.00

VOCALION

Number	Title	Yr	VG	VG+	NM
❏ VL 73907	Floatin' Down to Cotton Town	1970	2.50	5.00	10.00

WYNCOTE

Number	Title	Yr	VG	VG+	NM
❏ 9089	The Dawn Busters	196?	2.50	5.00	10.00

HIRT, AL, AND ANN-MARGRET
Ann-Margret is a female singer whose solo recordings are outside the jazz realm. Also see AL HIRT.
RCA VICTOR

Number	Title	Yr	VG	VG+	NM
❏ LPM-2690 [M]	Beauty and the Beard	1964	6.25	12.50	25.00
❏ LSP-2690 [S]	Beauty and the Beard	1964	7.50	15.00	30.00

HITTMAN, JEFF, AND YOSHITAKA UEMATSU
Hittman plays tenor saxophone; Uematsu is a drummer.
SOUL NOTE

Number	Title	Yr	VG	VG+	NM
❏ 121137	Mosaic	1990	3.75	7.50	15.00

HODEIR, ANDRE
Composer and conductor.
EMARCY

Number	Title	Yr	VG	VG+	NM
❏ SR-66005	Plain Old Blues	1967	3.75	7.50	15.00

JAZZOLOGY

Number	Title	Yr	VG	VG+	NM
❏ J-7	Summit Meeting	1965	3.75	7.50	15.00

PHILIPS

Number	Title	Yr	VG	VG+	NM
❏ PHM 200-073 [M]	Jazz Et Al	1963	6.25	12.50	25.00
❏ PHS 600-073 [S]	Jazz Et Al	1963	7.50	15.00	30.00

SAVOY

Number	Title	Yr	VG	VG+	NM
❏ MG-12104 [M]	American Jazzmen Play Andre Hodeir	1957	10.00	20.00	40.00
❏ MG-12113 [M]	Andre Hodeir Presents the Paris Scene	1957	10.00	20.00	40.00

SAVOY JAZZ

Number	Title	Yr	VG	VG+	NM
❏ SJL-1194	Essais	198?	2.50	5.00	10.00

HODES, ART
Pianist. Also see EDMOND HALL.
AUDIOPHILE

Number	Title	Yr	VG	VG+	NM
❏ AP-54	Mostly Blues	196?	3.75	7.50	15.00
❏ AP-54	Some Legendary Art	1986	2.50	5.00	10.00
-- Retitled reissue					

BLUE NOTE

Number	Title	Yr	VG	VG+	NM
❏ B-6502 [M]	The Funky Side of Art Hodes	1969	5.00	10.00	20.00
❏ B-6508 [M]	Sittin' In	1969	5.00	10.00	20.00
❏ BLP-7004 [10]	The Best in Two-Beat	1950	62.50	125.00	250.00
❏ BLP-7005 [10]	Art Hodes' Hot Five	1950	62.50	125.00	250.00
❏ BLP-7006 [10]	Dixieland Jubilee	1950	62.50	125.00	250.00
❏ BLP-7015 [10]	Dixieland Clambake	1951	62.50	125.00	250.00
❏ BLP-7021 [10]	Out of the Backroom	1952	62.50	125.00	250.00

CAPITOL

Number	Title	Yr	VG	VG+	NM
❏ M-11030	Hollywood Stampede	1973	3.00	6.00	12.00

DELMARK

Number	Title	Yr	VG	VG+	NM
❏ DS-211	My Bucket's Got a Hole In It	1969	3.75	7.50	15.00
❏ DS-213	Hodes' Art	197?	3.00	6.00	12.00
❏ DS-215	Friar's Inn Revisited	197?	3.00	6.00	12.00

DOTTED EIGHTH

Number	Title	Yr	VG	VG+	NM
❏ 1000 [M]	Art for Art's Sake	195?	12.50	25.00	50.00

EMARCY

Number	Title	Yr	VG	VG+	NM
❏ MG-26104 [10]	Jazz Chicago Style	1954	20.00	40.00	80.00

EUPHONIC

Number	Title	Yr	VG	VG+	NM
❏ 1207	The Art of Hodes	198?	2.50	5.00	10.00
❏ 1213	I Remember Bessie	198?	2.50	5.00	10.00
❏ 1218	When Music Was Music	198?	2.50	5.00	10.00

GHB

Number	Title	Yr	VG	VG+	NM
❏ 171	Art Hodes and the Magolia Jazz Band, Vol. 1	1984	2.50	5.00	10.00
❏ 172	Art Hodes and the Magolia Jazz Band, Vol. 2	1984	2.50	5.00	10.00

JAZZOLOGY

Number	Title	Yr	VG	VG+	NM
❏ J-20	Andre Hodeir with the All-Star Stompers	1966	3.75	7.50	15.00
❏ J-46 [M]	For Art's Sake	196?	5.00	10.00	20.00
❏ J-58	Home Cookin'	1974	3.00	6.00	12.00
❏ J-74	Down Home Blues	197?	3.00	6.00	12.00
❏ J-79	Echoes of Chicago	1979	3.00	6.00	12.00
❏ J-83	The Jazz Record Story, Vol. 2	1979	2.50	5.00	10.00
❏ J-104	Apex Blues	198?	2.50	5.00	10.00
❏ J-113	The Trios	198?	2.50	5.00	10.00
❏ J-155	Art Hodes and His Blues Six-Blues Groove	198?	2.50	5.00	10.00

MERCURY

Number	Title	Yr	VG	VG+	NM
❏ MG-20185 [M]	Chicago Style Jazz	1957	12.50	25.00	50.00

MOSAIC

Number	Title	Yr	VG	VG+	NM
❏ M5-114 [(5)]	The Complete Art Hodes Blue Note Sessions	199?	20.00	40.00	80.00

MUSE

Number	Title	Yr	VG	VG+	NM
❏ MR-5252	Someone to Watch Over Me	1981	2.50	5.00	10.00
❏ MR-5279	Just the Two of Us	1982	2.50	5.00	10.00

PARAMOUNT

Number	Title	Yr	VG	VG+	NM
❏ LP-113 [M]	The Trios	1955	20.00	40.00	80.00

PRESTIGE

Number	Title	Yr	VG	VG+	NM
❏ 24083 [(2)]	The Real Thing	198?	3.75	7.50	15.00

RIVERSIDE

Number	Title	Yr	VG	VG+	NM
❏ RLP-1012 [10]	Chicago Rhythm Kings	1953	20.00	40.00	80.00

SACKVILLE

Number	Title	Yr	VG	VG+	NM
❏ 3039	Blues in the Night	198?	2.50	5.00	10.00

STOMP OFF

Number	Title	Yr	VG	VG+	NM
❏ SOS-1184	The Music of Lovie Austin	1988	2.50	5.00	10.00

STORYVILLE

Number	Title	Yr	VG	VG+	NM
❏ 4057	Selections from the Gutter	198?	2.50	5.00	10.00

HODGES, JOHNNY
Alto saxophone, and occasional soprano saxophone, player. Also see GERRY MULLIGAN.
ABC IMPULSE!

Number	Title	Yr	VG	VG+	NM
❏ AS-61 [S]	Everybody Knows	1968	3.75	7.50	15.00

AMERICAN RECORDING SOCIETY

Number	Title	Yr	VG	VG+	NM
❏ G-421 [M]	Johnny Hodges and the Ellington All-Stars	195?	10.00	20.00	40.00

BLUEBIRD

Number	Title	Yr	VG	VG+	NM
❏ 5903-1-RB	Triple Play	1987	2.50	5.00	10.00

CLEF

Number	Title	Yr	VG	VG+	NM
❏ MGC-111 [10]	Johnny Hodges Collates	1953	37.50	75.00	150.00
❏ MGC-128 [10]	Johnny Hodges Collates #2	1953	50.00	100.00	200.00
❏ MGC-151 [10]	Swing with Johnny Hodges	1954	---	---	---
-- Canceled; reassigned to Norgran					

DOT

Number	Title	Yr	VG	VG+	NM
❏ DLP-3682 [M]	Johnny Hodges with Lawrence Welk's Orchestra	1966	3.75	7.50	15.00
❏ DLP-25682 [S]	Johnny Hodges with Lawrence Welk's Orchestra	1966	5.00	10.00	20.00

ENCORE

Number	Title	Yr	VG	VG+	NM
❏ EE-22001 [M]	Hodge Podge	1968	3.75	7.50	15.00

EPIC

Number	Title	Yr	VG	VG+	NM
❏ LN 3105 [M]	Hodge Podge	1955	15.00	30.00	60.00

FLYING DUTCHMAN

Number	Title	Yr	VG	VG+	NM
❏ 120	Three Shades of Blue	1971	5.00	10.00	20.00
❏ FD-10120	Three Shades of Blue	1972	3.75	7.50	15.00

IMPULSE!

Number	Title	Yr	VG	VG+	NM
❏ A-61 [M]	Everybody Knows	1964	6.25	12.50	25.00
❏ AS-61 [S]	Everybody Knows	1964	7.50	15.00	30.00

JAZZ PANORAMA

Number	Title	Yr	VG	VG+	NM
❏ 1806 [10]	Johnny Hodges	1951	37.50	75.00	150.00

MASTER JAZZ

Number	Title	Yr	VG	VG+	NM
❏ 8107	Memory	1970	3.75	7.50	15.00

MCA

Number	Title	Yr	VG	VG+	NM
❏ 29071	Everybody Knows	198?	2.50	5.00	10.00

MERCER

Number	Title	Yr	VG	VG+	NM
❏ LP-1000 [10]	Johnny Hodges, Vol. 1	1951	37.50	75.00	150.00
❏ LP-1006 [10]	Johnny Hodges, Vol. 2	1951	37.50	75.00	150.00

Number	Title	Yr	VG	VG+	NM
MERCURY					
❏ MGC-111 [10]	Johnny Hodges Collates	1952	62.50	125.00	250.00
❏ MGC-128 [10]	Johnny Hodges Collates #2	1953	---	---	---
-- Canceled; reassigned to Clef					
MGM					
❏ SE-4715	Tribute	1970	3.75	7.50	15.00
MOSAIC					
❏ M6-126 [(6)]	The Complete Johnny Hodges Recordings 1951-1956	199?	25.00	50.00	100.00
NORGRAN					
❏ MGN-1 [10]	Swing with Johnny Hodges	1954	50.00	100.00	200.00
❏ MGN-1004 [M]	Memories of Ellington	1954	37.50	75.00	150.00
❏ MGN-1009 [M]	More of Johnny Hodges	1954	37.50	75.00	150.00
❏ MGN-1024 [M]	Johnny Hodges Dance Bash	1955	37.50	75.00	150.00
❏ MGN-1045 [M]	Creamy	1955	37.50	75.00	150.00
❏ MGN-1048 [M]	Castle Rock	1955	30.00	60.00	120.00
❏ MGN-1055 [M]	Ellingtonia '56	1956	25.00	50.00	100.00
❏ MGN-1059 [M]	In a Tender Mood	1956	25.00	50.00	100.00
❏ MGN-1060 [M]	Used to Be Duke	1956	25.00	50.00	100.00
❏ MGN-1061 [M]	The Blues	1956	25.00	50.00	100.00
❏ MGN-1091 [M]	Perdido	1956	25.00	50.00	100.00
❏ MGN-1092 [M]	In a Mellow Tone	1956	25.00	50.00	100.00
ONYX					
❏ 216	Ellingtonia	197?	3.00	6.00	12.00
PABLO LIVE					
❏ 2620 102 [(2)]	Sportpalast, Berlin	1978	3.75	7.50	15.00
PRESTIGE					
❏ 24103 [(2)]	Caravan	198?	3.75	7.50	15.00
RCA VICTOR					
❏ LPV-533 [M]	Things Ain't What They Used to Be	1966	5.00	10.00	20.00
❏ LPT-3000 [10]	Alto Sax	1952	37.50	75.00	150.00
❏ LPM-3867 [M]	Triple Play	1967	7.50	15.00	30.00
❏ LSP-3867 [S]	Triple Play	1967	5.00	10.00	20.00
STORYVILLE					
❏ 4073	A Man and His Music	198?	3.00	6.00	12.00
VERVE					
❏ VSP-3 [M]	Johnny Hodges and All the Duke's Men	1966	3.00	6.00	12.00
❏ VSPS-3 [R]	Johnny Hodges and All the Duke's Men	1966	2.50	5.00	10.00
❏ VSP-20 [M]	Alto Blues	1966	3.00	6.00	12.00
❏ VSPS-20 [R]	Alto Blues	1966	2.50	5.00	10.00
❏ UMV-2525	The Big Sound	198?	2.50	5.00	10.00
❏ VE2-2532 [(2)]	The Smooth One	1979	3.75	7.50	15.00
❏ MGVS-6017 [S]	Creamy	1960	10.00	20.00	40.00
❏ MGVS-6048 [S]	The Prettiest Gershwin	1960	10.00	20.00	40.00
❏ MGVS-6055 [S]	Back to Back -- Duke Ellington and Johnny Hodges Play the Blues	1960	10.00	20.00	40.00
❏ MGVS-6109 [S]	Side by Side	1960	10.00	20.00	40.00
❏ MGVS-6109 [S]	Side by Side	199?	6.25	12.50	25.00
-- Classic Records reissue on audiophile vinyl					
❏ MGVS-6115 [S]	The Smooth One	1960	---	---	---
-- Canceled					
❏ MGVS-6120 [S]	Not So Dukish	1960			
-- Canceled					
❏ MGVS-6123 [S]	Blues-a-Plenty	1960			
-- Unreleased					
❏ MGV-8136 [M]	Creamy	1957	12.50	25.00	50.00
-- Reissue of Norgran 1045					
❏ V-8136 [M]	Creamy	1961	5.00	10.00	20.00
❏ MGV-8139 [M]	Castle Rock	1957	12.50	25.00	50.00
-- Reissue of Norgran 1048					
❏ V-8139 [M]	Castle Rock	1961	5.00	10.00	20.00
❏ MGV-8145 [M]	Ellingtonia '56	1957	12.50	25.00	50.00
-- Reissue of Norgran 1055					
❏ V-8145 [M]	Ellingtonia '56	1961	5.00	10.00	20.00
❏ MGV-8149 [M]	In a Tender Mood	1957	12.50	25.00	50.00
-- Reissue of Norgran 1059					
❏ V-8149 [M]	In a Tender Mood	1961	5.00	10.00	20.00
❏ MGV-8150 [M]	Used to Be Duke	1957	12.50	25.00	50.00
-- Reissue of Norgran 1060					
❏ V-8150 [M]	Used to Be Duke	1961	5.00	10.00	20.00
❏ MGV-8151 [M]	The Blues	1957	12.50	25.00	50.00
-- Reissue of Norgran 1061					
❏ V-8151 [M]	The Blues	1961	5.00	10.00	20.00
❏ MGV-8179 [M]	Perdido	1957	12.50	25.00	50.00
-- Reissue of Norgran 1091					
❏ V-8179 [M]	Perdido	1961	5.00	10.00	20.00
❏ MGV-8180 [M]	In a Mellow Tone	1957	12.50	25.00	50.00
-- Reissue of Norgran 1092					
❏ V-8180 [M]	In a Mellow Tone	1961	5.00	10.00	20.00
❏ MGV-8203 [M]	Duke's in Bed	1957	12.50	25.00	50.00
❏ V-8203 [M]	Duke's in Bed	1961	5.00	10.00	20.00
❏ MGV-8271 [M]	The Big Sound	1958	12.50	25.00	50.00
❏ V-8271 [M]	The Big Sound	1961	5.00	10.00	20.00

Number	Title	Yr	VG	VG+	NM
❏ V6-8271 [S]	The Big Sound	1961	5.00	10.00	20.00
❏ MGV-8314 [M]	The Prettiest Gershwin	1959	12.50	25.00	50.00
❏ V-8314 [M]	The Prettiest Gershwin	1961	5.00	10.00	20.00
❏ V6-8314 [S]	The Prettiest Gershwin	1961	5.00	10.00	20.00
❏ MGV-8317 [M]	Back to Back -- Duke Ellington and Johnny Hodges Play the Blues	1959	12.50	25.00	50.00
❏ V-8317 [M]	Back to Back -- Duke Ellington and Johnny Hodges Play the Blues	1961	5.00	10.00	20.00
❏ V6-8317 [S]	Back to Back -- Duke Ellington and Johnny Hodges Play the Blues	1961	5.00	10.00	20.00
❏ MGV-8345 [M]	Side by Side	1959	12.50	25.00	50.00
❏ V-8345 [M]	Side by Side	1961	5.00	10.00	20.00
❏ V6-8345 [S]	Side by Side	1961	5.00	10.00	20.00
❏ MGV-8350 [M]	The Smooth One	1960	---	---	---
-- Canceled					
❏ MGV-8355 [M]	Not So Dukish	1960	12.50	25.00	50.00
❏ V-8355 [M]	Not So Dukish	1961	5.00	10.00	20.00
❏ MGV-8358 [M]	Blues-a-Plenty	1960	12.50	25.00	50.00
❏ V-8358 [M]	Blues-a-Plenty	1961	5.00	10.00	20.00
❏ V6-8358 [S]	Blues-a-Plenty	1961	5.00	10.00	20.00
❏ V6-8358 [S]	Blues-a-Plenty	199?	6.25	12.50	25.00
-- Classic Records reissue on audiophile vinyl					
❏ MGV-8391 [M]	Johnny Hodges	1961	---	---	---
-- Canceled					
❏ V-8452 [M]	Johnny Hodges with Billy Strayhorn	1962	6.25	12.50	25.00
❏ V6-8452 [S]	Johnny Hodges with Billy Strayhorn	1962	7.50	15.00	30.00
❏ V-8492 [M]	The Eleventh Hour	1962	6.25	12.50	25.00
❏ V6-8492 [S]	The Eleventh Hour	1962	7.50	15.00	30.00
❏ V/V6-8546	Johnny Hodges	1963	---	---	---
-- Canceled					
❏ V-8561 [M]	Sandy's Gone	1963	6.25	12.50	25.00
❏ V6-8561 [S]	Sandy's Gone	1963	7.50	15.00	30.00
❏ V-8680 [M]	Blue Notes	1966	3.75	7.50	15.00
❏ V6-8680 [S]	Blue Notes	1966	5.00	10.00	20.00
❏ V-8726 [M]	Don't Sleep in the Subway	1967	5.00	10.00	20.00
❏ V6-8726 [S]	Don't Sleep in the Subway	1967	3.75	7.50	15.00
❏ V6-8753	Rippin' and Runnin'	1968	3.75	7.50	15.00
❏ V6-8834	Previously Unreleased Recordings	1973	3.75	7.50	15.00
❏ 827 758-1	Castle Rock	1986	2.50	5.00	10.00

HODGES, JOHNNY, AND WILD BILL DAVIS
Also see each artist's individual listings.

Number	Title	Yr	VG	VG+	NM
RCA VICTOR					
❏ LPM-3393 [M]	Con-Soul and Sax	1965	5.00	10.00	20.00
❏ LSP-3393 [S]	Con-Soul and Sax	1965	6.25	12.50	25.00
❏ LPM-3706 [M]	Eddie Hodges and Wild Bill Davis In Atlantic City	1966	3.75	7.50	15.00
❏ LSP-3706 [S]	Eddie Hodges and Wild Bill Davis In Atlantic City	1966	5.00	10.00	20.00
VERVE					
❏ V-8406 [M]	Blue Hodges	1961	5.00	10.00	20.00
❏ V6-8406 [S]	Blue Hodges	1961	6.25	12.50	25.00
❏ V-8570 [M]	A Mess of Blues	1964	5.00	10.00	20.00
❏ V6-8570 [S]	A Mess of Blues	1964	6.25	12.50	25.00
❏ V-8599 [M]	Blue Rabbit	1964	5.00	10.00	20.00
❏ V6-8599 [S]	Blue Rabbit	1964	6.25	12.50	25.00
❏ V-8617 [M]	Joe's Blues	1965	5.00	10.00	20.00
❏ V6-8617 [S]	Joe's Blues	1965	6.25	12.50	25.00
❏ V-8630 [M]	Wings and Things	1965	5.00	10.00	20.00
❏ V6-8630 [S]	Wings and Things	1965	6.25	12.50	25.00
❏ V-8635 [M]	Blue Pyramid	1965	5.00	10.00	20.00
❏ V6-8635 [S]	Blue Pyramid	1965	6.25	12.50	25.00

HODGES, JOHNNY, AND EARL "FATHA" HINES
Also see each artist's individual listings.

Number	Title	Yr	VG	VG+	NM
VERVE					
❏ V-8647 [M]	Stride Right	1966	5.00	10.00	20.00
❏ V6-8647 [S]	Stride Right	1966	6.25	12.50	25.00
❏ V-8732 [M]	Swing's Our Thing	1967	6.25	12.50	25.00
❏ V6-8732 [S]	Swing's Our Thing	1967	3.75	7.50	15.00

HOFMANN, HOLLY
Flutist.

Number	Title	Yr	VG	VG+	NM
CAPRI					
❏ 74011	Take Note	1989	3.00	6.00	12.00

HOGGARD, JAY
Vibraphone player.

Number	Title	Yr	VG	VG+	NM
CONTEMPORARY					
❏ C-14007	Rain Forest	1980	3.00	6.00	12.00
GRAMAVISION					
❏ GR-8204	Love Survives	1983	2.50	5.00	10.00

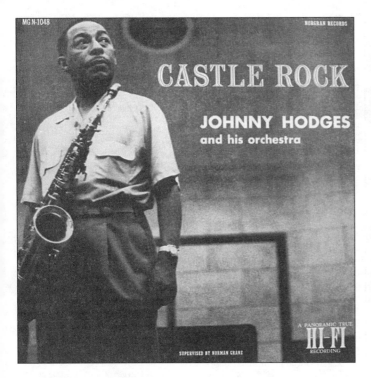

(Top left) Johnny Hodges is best known as an alto saxophone player, though he sometimes played soprano. A key member of Duke Ellington's orchestra, he had ample chance to record on his own. Here is one of his approximately one dozen albums that was released on the Norgran label. (Top right) Billie Holiday's *Lady in Satin*, recorded in 1958 when she was about a year away from dying, is considered a classic among audiophiles, though most of her best material was recorded in the 78 rpm era. (Bottom left) Bill Holman, though a tenor sax player, was best known in jazz circles as one of the arrangers for the early Stan Kenton Orchestra. He did get to record on his own, though, with this album as one of the results. (Bottom right) Helen Humes, who replaced Billie Holiday in the Count Basie Orchestra, was a fine singer as well. She did three excellent albums for the Contemporary label in the late 1950s, of which *Songs I Like to Sing* was the first.

Number	Title	Yr	VG	VG+	NM
GRP/ARISTA					
❏ GL 5004	Days Like These	1979	3.00	6.00	12.00
INDIA NAVIGATION					
❏ IN-1040	Solo Vibes Concert	1979	3.75	7.50	15.00
❏ IN-1049	Mystic Winds, Tropic Breezes	1981	3.00	6.00	12.00
❏ IN-1068	Riverside Dance	1985	3.00	6.00	12.00
MUSE					
❏ MR-5383	Overview	1989	3.00	6.00	12.00
❏ MR-5410	The Little Tiger	1991	3.75	7.50	15.00

HOLDSWORTH, ALLAN
Guitarist.
CTI
Number	Title	Yr	VG	VG+	NM
❏ 6068	Velvet	197?	3.75	7.50	15.00

HOLIDAY, BILLIE
Female singer, one of the greatest jazz vocalists ever. Also see RALPH BURNS; ELLA FITZGERALD; TEDDY WILSON.

Number	Title	Yr	VG	VG+	NM
AMERICAN RECORDING SOCIETY					
❏ G-409 [M]	Billie Holiday Sings	1956	15.00	30.00	60.00
-- Reissue of Clef 713					
❏ G-431 [M]	Lady Sings the Blues	1957	15.00	30.00	60.00
-- Reissue of Clef 721					
ARCHIVE OF FOLK AND JAZZ					
❏ 265	Billie Holiday	197?	3.00	6.00	12.00
❏ 310	Billie Holiday, Vol. 2	197?	3.00	6.00	12.00
ATLANTIC					
❏ 1614	Strange Fruit	1972	3.75	7.50	15.00
BLACKHAWK					
❏ BKH-50701	Billie Holiday at Monterey	1986	2.50	5.00	10.00
BULLDOG					
❏ 1007	Billie's Blues	198?	2.50	5.00	10.00
CLEF					
❏ MGC-118 [10]	Billie Holiday Sings	1953	45.00	90.00	180.00
❏ MGC-144 [10]	An Evening with Billie Holiday	1954	45.00	90.00	180.00
❏ MGC-161 [10]	Billie Holiday Favorites	1954	45.00	90.00	180.00
❏ MGC-169 [10]	Billie Holiday at Jazz at the Philharmonic	1955	45.00	90.00	180.00
❏ MGC-669 [M]	Music for Torching	1955	25.00	50.00	100.00
❏ MGC-686 [M]	A Recital by Billie Holiday	1956	30.00	60.00	120.00
-- Reissue of 144 and 161 as one 12-inch LP					
❏ MGC-690 [M]	Solitude -- Songs by Billie Holiday	1956	30.00	60.00	120.00
-- Reissue of 118					
❏ MGC-713 [M]	Velvet Moods	1956	30.00	60.00	120.00
❏ MGC-721 [M]	Lady Sings the Blues	1956	30.00	60.00	120.00
COLLECTABLES					
❏ COL-5142	Fine and Mellow	198?	3.00	6.00	12.00
COLUMBIA					
❏ C3L 21 [(3) M]	The Golden Years	1962	12.50	25.00	50.00
-- Red and black label with six "eye" logos					
❏ C3L 21 [(3) M]	The Golden Years	1963	6.25	12.50	25.00
-- Red "Guaranteed High Fidelity" or "360 Sound" label					
❏ C3L 40 [(3) M]	The Golden Years, Volume 2	1966	7.50	15.00	30.00
❏ CL 637 [M]	Lady Day	1954	17.50	35.00	70.00
-- Maroon label, gold print					
❏ CL 637 [M]	Lady Day	1956	10.00	20.00	40.00
-- Red and black label with six "eye" logos					
❏ CL 637 [M]	Lady Day	1962	3.75	7.50	15.00
-- Red "Guaranteed High Fidelity" or "360 Sound" label					
❏ CL 1157 [M]	Lady in Satin	1958	10.00	20.00	40.00
-- Red and black label with six "eye" logos					
❏ CL 1157 [M]	Lady in Satin	1962	3.75	7.50	15.00
-- Red "Guaranteed High Fidelity" or "360 Sound" label					
❏ CL 2666 [M]	Billie Holiday's Greatest Hits	1967	3.75	7.50	15.00
❏ CL 6129 [10]	Billie Holiday Sings	1950	50.00	100.00	200.00
❏ CL 6163 [10]	Billie Holiday Favorites	1951	50.00	100.00	200.00
❏ CS 8048 [S]	Lady in Satin	1958	10.00	20.00	40.00
-- Red and black label with six "eye" logos					
❏ CS 8048 [S]	Lady in Satin	1962	3.75	7.50	15.00
-- Red "Guaranteed High Fidelity" or "360 Sound" label					
❏ CS 8048 [S]	Lady in Satin	1999	6.25	12.50	25.00
-- Classic Records reissue on audiophile vinyl					
❏ G 30782 [(2)]	God Bless the Child	1972	5.00	10.00	20.00
❏ C 32060	The Original Recordings	1973	3.75	7.50	15.00
❏ PC 32080	Billie's Blues	198?	2.00	4.00	8.00
-- Reissue of Harmony LP					
❏ CG 32121 [(2)]	The Billie Holiday Story, Volume 1	1973	3.75	7.50	15.00
❏ CG 32124 [(2)]	The Billie Holiday Story, Volume 2	1973	3.75	7.50	15.00
❏ CG 32127 [(2)]	The Billie Holiday Story, Volume 3	1973	3.75	7.50	15.00
COLUMBIA JAZZ MASTERPIECES					
❏ CJ 40247	Lady in Satin	1987	2.50	5.00	10.00
❏ CJ 40646	The Quintessential Billie Holiday, Vol. 1	1987	2.50	5.00	10.00
❏ CJ 40790	The Quintessential Billie Holiday, Vol. 2	1987	2.50	5.00	10.00
❏ CJ 44048	The Quintessential Billie Holiday, Vol. 3	1988	2.50	5.00	10.00
❏ CJ 44252	The Quintessential Billie Holiday, Vol. 4	1988	2.50	5.00	10.00
❏ CJ 44423	The Quintessential Billie Holiday, Vol. 5	1989	2.50	5.00	10.00
❏ C 45449	The Quintessential Billie Holiday, Vol. 6	1990	2.50	5.00	10.00
❏ C 46180	The Quintessential Billie Holiday, Vol. 7	1990	2.50	5.00	10.00
COLUMBIA MUSICAL TREASURY					
❏ P3M 5869 [(3)]	The Golden Years	197?	5.00	10.00	20.00
COLUMBIA SPECIAL PRODUCTS					
❏ P 14338	Swing, Brother, Swing	198?	2.50	5.00	10.00
COMMODORE					
❏ FL-20005 [10]	Billie Holiday, Volume 1	1950	62.50	125.00	250.00
❏ FL-20006 [10]	Billie Holiday, Volume 2	1950	62.50	125.00	250.00
❏ DL-30008 [M]	Billie Holiday	1959	12.50	25.00	50.00
-- Reissue of 20006					
❏ DL-30011 [M]	Billie Holiday with Eddie Heywood and His Orchestra	1959	12.50	25.00	50.00
-- Reissue of 20005					
CROWN					
❏ CST-380 [R]	Billie Holiday & Vivian Fears	196?	3.00	6.00	12.00
❏ CLP-5380 [M]	Billie Holiday & Vivian Fears	196?	5.00	10.00	20.00
DECCA					
❏ DXB-161 [(2) M]	The Billie Holiday Story	1959	5.00	10.00	20.00
❏ DL 5345 [10]	Lover Man	1951	50.00	100.00	200.00
❏ DXSB-7161 [(2) R]	The Billie Holiday Story	1959	3.75	7.50	15.00
❏ DL 8215 [M]	The Lady Sings	1956	15.00	30.00	60.00
❏ DL 8701 [M]	The Blues Are Brewin'	1958	15.00	30.00	60.00
❏ DL 8702 [M]	Lover Man	1958	15.00	30.00	60.00
❏ DL 75040	Billie Holiday's Greatest Hits	1968	3.00	6.00	12.00
ESP-DISK'					
❏ 3002	The Lady Lives, Vol. 1	1973	3.00	6.00	12.00
❏ 3003	The Lady Lives, Vol. 2	1973	3.00	6.00	12.00
HALL					
❏ 622	I've Gotta Right to Sing	197?	3.00	6.00	12.00
HARMONY					
❏ KH 32080	Billie's Blues	1973	2.50	5.00	10.00
INTERMEDIA					
❏ QS-5076	Billie Holiday Talks and Sings	198?	2.50	5.00	10.00
JAZZ MAN					
❏ 5005	Billie Holiday at Storyville	198?	2.50	5.00	10.00
JAZZTONE					
❏ J-1209 [M]	Billie Holiday Sings	1955	12.50	25.00	50.00
-- Reissue of Commodore 20005					
JOLLY ROGER					
❏ 5020 [10]	Billie Holiday, Volume 1	1954	25.00	50.00	100.00
❏ 5021 [10]	Billie Holiday, Volume 2	1954	25.00	50.00	100.00
❏ 5022 [10]	Billie Holiday, Volume 3	1954	25.00	50.00	100.00
MAINSTREAM					
❏ S-6000 [R]	The Commodore Recordings	1965	3.00	6.00	12.00
❏ S-6022 [R]	Once Upon a Time	1965	3.00	6.00	12.00
❏ 56000 [M]	The Commodore Recordings	1965	6.25	12.50	25.00
❏ 56022 [M]	Once Upon a Time	1965	6.25	12.50	25.00
MCA					
❏ 275	Billie Holiday's Greatest Hits	1973	2.50	5.00	10.00
-- Reissue of Decca 75040					
❏ 4006 [(2)]	The Billie Holiday Story	1973	3.00	6.00	12.00
-- Reissue of Decca 7161					
METRO					
❏ M-515 [M]	Billie Holiday	1965	3.75	7.50	15.00
❏ MS-515 [R]	Billie Holiday	1965	3.00	6.00	12.00
MGM					
❏ GAS-122	Billie Holiday (Golden Archive Series)	1970	3.00	6.00	12.00
❏ E-3764 [M]	Billie Holiday	1959	10.00	20.00	40.00
❏ SE-3764 [S]	Billie Holiday	1959	12.50	25.00	50.00
❏ M3G-4948	Archetypes	1974	3.00	6.00	12.00
MOBILE FIDELITY					
❏ 1-247	Body and Soul	1996	30.00	60.00	120.00
-- Audiophile vinyl					
MONMOUTH/EVERGREEN					
❏ 7046	Gallant Lady	1973	3.00	6.00	12.00
PARAMOUNT					
❏ PA-6059	Songs and Conversations	1973	3.00	6.00	12.00

Number	Title	Yr	VG	VG+	NM
PICKWICK					
❏ PC-3335	Billie Holiday Sings the Blues	197?	2.50	5.00	10.00
RIC					
❏ R-2001 [M]	Rare Live Recordings	1964	6.25	12.50	25.00
SCORE					
❏ SLP-4014 [M]	Billie Holiday Sings the Blues	1957	30.00	60.00	120.00
SOLID STATE					
❏ 18040	Lady Love	1969	3.00	6.00	12.00
SUNSET					
❏ SUM-1147 [M]	Shades of Blue	1967	3.00	6.00	12.00
❏ SUS-5147 [R]	Shades of Blue	1967	2.50	5.00	10.00
TOTEM					
❏ 1037	Billie Holiday On the Air	198?	2.50	5.00	10.00
TRIP					
❏ 5024	Billie Holiday Live	1974	2.50	5.00	10.00
UNITED ARTISTS					
❏ UAS-5625	Lady Love	1972	2.50	5.00	10.00
-- Reissue of 15014					
❏ UAJ-14014 [M]	Lady Love	1962	10.00	20.00	40.00
❏ UASJ-15014 [S]	Lady Love	1962	12.50	25.00	50.00
VERVE					
❏ VSP-5 [M]	Lady	1966	3.75	7.50	15.00
❏ VSPS-5 [R]	Lady	1966	3.00	6.00	12.00
❏ VE-2-2503 [(2)]	The First Verve Sessions	1976	3.75	7.50	15.00
❏ VE-2-2515 [(2)]	Stormy Blues	1976	3.75	7.50	15.00
❏ VE-2-2529 [(2)]	All or Nothing at All	198?	3.75	7.50	15.00
❏ MGVS-6021 [S]	Songs for Distingue Lovers	1960	15.00	30.00	60.00
❏ MGVS-6021 [S]	Songs for Distingue Lovers	199?	6.25	12.50	25.00
-- Classic Records reissue on audiophile vinyl					
❏ MGVS-6021-45 [(2) S]	Songs for Distingue Lovers	1999	5.00	10.00	20.00
-- Classic Records reissue on two 12-inch 45-rpm records					
❏ MGV-8026 [M]	Music for Torching	1957	10.00	20.00	40.00
-- Reissue of Clef 669					
❏ V-8026 [M]	Music for Torching	1961	5.00	10.00	20.00
❏ MGV-8027 [M]	A Recital by Billie Holiday	1957	10.00	20.00	40.00
❏ -- Reissue of Clef 686					
❏ V-8027 [M]	A Recital by Billie Holiday	1961	5.00	10.00	20.00
❏ MGV-8074 [M]	Solitude -- Songs by Billie Holiday	1957	10.00	20.00	40.00
-- Reissue of Clef 690					
❏ V-8074 [M]	Solitude -- Songs by Billie Holiday	1961	5.00	10.00	20.00
❏ V6-8074 [R]	Solitude -- Songs by Billie Holiday	196?	3.00	6.00	12.00
❏ MGV-8096 [M]	Velvet Moods	1957	10.00	20.00	40.00
-- Reissue of Clef 713					
❏ V-8096 [M]	Velvet Moods	1961	5.00	10.00	20.00
❏ MGV-8099 [M]	Lady Sings the Blues	1957	10.00	20.00	40.00
-- Reissue of Clef 721					
❏ V-8099 [M]	Lady Sings the Blues	1957	5.00	10.00	20.00
❏ MGV-8197 [M]	Body and Soul	1957	15.00	30.00	60.00
❏ V-8197 [M]	Body and Soul	1961	5.00	10.00	20.00
❏ MGV-8257 [M]	Songs for Distingue Lovers	1958	15.00	30.00	60.00
❏ V-8257 [M]	Songs for Distingue Lovers	1961	5.00	10.00	20.00
❏ V6-8257 [S]	Songs for Distingue Lovers	1961	6.25	12.50	25.00
❏ MGV-8302 [M]	Stay with Me	1959	12.50	25.00	50.00
❏ V-8302 [M]	Stay with Me	1961	5.00	10.00	20.00
❏ MGV-8329 [M]	All or Nothing at All	1959	12.50	25.00	50.00
❏ V-8329 [M]	All or Nothing at All	1959	5.00	10.00	20.00
❏ V6-8329 [R]	All or Nothing at All	196?	3.00	6.00	12.00
❏ MGV-8338-2 [(2) M]	The Unforgettable Lady Day	1959	20.00	40.00	80.00
❏ V-8338-2 [(2) M]	The Unforgettable Lady Day	1961	6.25	12.50	25.00
❏ V-8410 [M]	The Essential Billie Holiday	1961	5.00	10.00	20.00
❏ V6-8410 [R]	The Essential Billie Holiday	1961	3.00	6.00	12.00
❏ V-8505 [M]	The Essential Jazz Vocals	1963	5.00	10.00	20.00
❏ V6-8505 [R]	The Essential Jazz Vocals	1963	3.00	6.00	12.00
❏ V6-8808 [R]	The Best of Billie Holiday	1973	2.50	5.00	10.00
❏ 2-V6S-8816 [(2)]	History of the Real Billie Holiday	1973	3.75	7.50	15.00
❏ 817 359-1 [(2)]	Embraceable You	198?	3.00	6.00	12.00
❏ 823 230-1 [(2)]	Stormy Blues	198?	3.00	6.00	12.00
❏ 823 233-1 [(2)]	History of the Real Billie Holiday	198?	3.00	6.00	12.00
❏ 823 246-1	The Billie Holiday Songbook	198?	2.50	5.00	10.00
❏ 827 160-1	All or Nothing at All	1987	2.50	5.00	10.00

HOLIDAY, BILLIE, AND STAN GETZ

Number	Title	Yr	VG	VG+	NM
DALE					
❏ 25 [10]	Billie and Stan	1951	100.00	200.00	400.00

HOLIDAY, BILLIE/AL HIBBLER
Also see each artist's individual listings.

Number	Title	Yr	VG	VG+	NM
IMPERIAL					
❏ LP-9185 [M]	Billie Holiday, Al Hibbler and the Blues	1962	12.50	25.00	50.00
❏ LP-12185 [R]	Billie Holiday, Al Hibbler and the Blues	196?	7.50	15.00	30.00

HOLIDAY, JOE
Tenor saxophone player.

Number	Title	Yr	VG	VG+	NM
DECCA					
❏ DL 8487 [M]	Holiday for Jazz	1957	15.00	30.00	60.00
PRESTIGE					
❏ PRLP-131 [10]	Joe Holiday	1952	50.00	100.00	200.00

HOLIDAY, JOE/BILLY TAYLOR
Also see each artist's individual listings.

Number	Title	Yr	VG	VG+	NM
PRESTIGE					
❏ PRLP-171 [10]	Mambo Jazz	1953	37.50	75.00	150.00

HOLLAND, DAVE
Bass player. The first album below was as "David Holland." Also see CIRCLE.

Number	Title	Yr	VG	VG+	NM
ECM					
❏ 1027	Conference of the Birds	1974	3.75	7.50	15.00
❏ 1109	Emerald Tears	1978	3.00	6.00	12.00
❏ 23787	Life Cycle	1983	2.50	5.00	10.00
❏ 25001	Jumpin' In	1984	2.50	5.00	10.00
❏ 25032	Seeds of Time	1985	2.50	5.00	10.00

HOLLIDAY, JUDY
Female singer. Best known as an actress, she won an Oscar for her performance in Born Yesterday.

Number	Title	Yr	VG	VG+	NM
COLUMBIA					
❏ CL 1153 [M]	Trouble Is a Man	1958	7.50	15.00	30.00
❏ CS 8041 [S]	Trouble Is a Man	1959	10.00	20.00	40.00
DRG					
❏ MRS-602	Trouble Is a Man	198?	2.50	5.00	10.00

HOLLIDAY, JUDY, AND GERRY MULLIGAN
Also see each artist's individual listings.

Number	Title	Yr	VG	VG+	NM
DRG					
❏ SL-5191	Holliday with Mulligan	1979	3.00	6.00	12.00

HOLLOWAY, RED
Tenor saxophone player.

Number	Title	Yr	VG	VG+	NM
CONCORD JAZZ					
❏ CJ-322	Red Holloway & Company	1987	2.50	5.00	10.00
FANTASY					
❏ OJC-327	Cookin' Together	1988	2.50	5.00	10.00
JAM					
❏ 014	Hittin' the Road Again	198?	3.00	6.00	12.00
PRESTIGE					
❏ PRLP-7299 [M]	Burner	1964	12.50	25.00	50.00
-- Yellow label, Bergenfield, N.J. address					
❏ PRLP-7299 [M]	Burner	1965	6.25	12.50	25.00
-- Blue label, trident logo at right					
❏ PRST-7299 [S]	Burner	1964	12.50	25.00	50.00
-- Yellow label, Bergenfield, N.J. address					
❏ PRST-7299 [S]	Burner	1965	6.25	12.50	25.00
-- Blue label, trident logo at right					
❏ PRLP-7325 [M]	Cookin' Together	1964	7.50	15.00	30.00
❏ PRST-7325 [S]	Cookin' Together	1964	10.00	20.00	40.00
❏ PRLP-7390 [M]	Sax, Strings and Soul	1965	5.00	10.00	20.00
❏ PRST-7390 [S]	Sax, Strings and Soul	1965	6.25	12.50	25.00
❏ PRLP-7473 [M]	Red Soul	1966	5.00	10.00	20.00
❏ PRST-7473 [S]	Red Soul	1966	6.25	12.50	25.00
❏ PRST-7778	Best of the Soul Organ Giants	1970	3.75	7.50	15.00
STEEPLECHASE					
❏ SCS-1192	Nica's Dream	198?	3.00	6.00	12.00

HOLLOWAY, RED, AND CLARK TERRY
Also see each artist's individual listings.

Number	Title	Yr	VG	VG+	NM
CONCORD JAZZ					
❏ CJ-390	Locksmith Blues	1989	3.00	6.00	12.00

HOLLYDAY, CHRISTOPHER
Alto saxophone player.

Number	Title	Yr	VG	VG+	NM
JAZZ BEAT					
❏ 102	Oh Brother!	198?	3.75	7.50	15.00

Number	Title	Yr	VG	VG+	NM
NOVUS					
❏ 3055-1-N	Christopher Hollyday	1989	3.00	6.00	12.00
❏ 3087-1-N	On Course	1990	3.75	7.50	15.00
RBI					
❏ 402	Reverence	1988	3.75	7.50	15.00

HOLLYWOOD JAZZ QUINTET, THE
GATEWAY

Number	Title	Yr	VG	VG+	NM
❏ 7018	Neon	1979	3.00	6.00	12.00
❏ 7019	Nuances	1980	3.00	6.00	12.00

HOLLYWOOD SAXOPHONE QUARTET, THE
LIBERTY

Number	Title	Yr	VG	VG+	NM
❏ LRP-3047 [M]	Gold Rush Suite	1957	10.00	20.00	40.00
❏ LRP-3080 [M]	Sax Appeal	1958	7.50	15.00	30.00
❏ LRP-6005 [M]	The Hollywood Saxophone Quartet	1955	10.00	20.00	40.00

HOLMAN, BILL
Tenor saxophone player, arranger and composer.
ANDEX

Number	Title	Yr	VG	VG+	NM
❏ A-3004 [M]	In a Jazz Orbit	1958	10.00	20.00	40.00
❏ AS-3004 [S]	In a Jazz Orbit	1959	7.50	15.00	30.00
❏ A-3005 [M]	Jive for Five	1958	10.00	20.00	40.00
❏ AS-3005 [S]	Jive for Five	1959	7.50	15.00	30.00
CAPITOL					
❏ ST 1464 [S]	Great Big Band	1960	7.50	15.00	30.00
❏ T 1464 [M]	Great Big Band	1960	6.25	12.50	25.00
❏ H 6500 [10]	The Bill Holman Octet	1954	30.00	60.00	120.00
CORAL					
❏ CRL 57188 [M]	The Fabulous Bill Holman	1958	20.00	40.00	80.00
CREATIVE WORLD					
❏ ST-1053	Great Big Band	197?	3.75	7.50	15.00

HOLMES, RICHARD "GROOVE"
Organist. Also see JIMMY WITHERSPOON.
BLUE NOTE

Number	Title	Yr	VG	VG+	NM
❏ BST-84372	Comin' On Home	1971	3.00	6.00	12.00
FANTASY					
❏ OJC-329	Soul Message	1988	2.50	5.00	10.00
-- Reissue of Prestige 7435					
FLYING DUTCHMAN					
❏ BDL1-1537	I'm in the Mood for Love	1976	3.00	6.00	12.00
GROOVE MERCHANT					
❏ 505	American Pie	1972	3.00	6.00	12.00
❏ 512	Night Glider	1972	3.00	6.00	12.00
❏ 527	New Groove	1973	3.00	6.00	12.00
❏ 4402 [(2)]	Hunk-A-Funk	1975	3.75	7.50	15.00
MUSE					
❏ 5134	Shippin' Out	1978	2.50	5.00	10.00
❏ 5167	Good Vibrations	1979	2.50	5.00	10.00
❏ 5239	Broadway	1981	2.50	5.00	10.00
❏ 5358	Blues All Day Long	1989	2.50	5.00	10.00
PACIFIC JAZZ					
❏ PJ-23 [M]	Richard "Groove" Holmes	1961	6.25	12.50	25.00
❏ ST-23 [S]	Richard "Groove" Holmes	1961	7.50	15.00	30.00
❏ PJ-32 [M]	Groovin' with Jug	1961	7.50	15.00	30.00
❏ ST-32 [S]	Groovin' with Jug	1961	10.00	20.00	40.00
❏ PJ-51 [M]	Somethin' Special	1962	5.00	10.00	20.00
❏ ST-51 [S]	Somethin' Special	1962	6.25	12.50	25.00
❏ PJ-59 [M]	After Hours	1962	5.00	10.00	20.00
❏ ST-59 [S]	After Hours	1962	6.25	12.50	25.00
❏ PJ-10105 [M]	Tell It Like It Tis	1966	3.75	7.50	15.00
❏ LN-10130	Groovin' with Jug	198?	2.00	4.00	8.00
-- Budget-line reissue					
❏ ST-20105 [S]	Tell It Like It Tis	1966	5.00	10.00	20.00
❏ ST-20153	Workin' on a Groovy Thing	1969	3.75	7.50	15.00
❏ ST-20163	X-77	1969	3.75	7.50	15.00
❏ ST-20171	Come Together	1970	3.75	7.50	15.00
PRESTIGE					
❏ PRLP-7435 [M]	Soul Message	1966	3.75	7.50	15.00
❏ PRST-7435 [S]	Soul Message	1966	5.00	10.00	20.00
❏ PRLP-7468 [M]	Living Soul	1966	3.75	7.50	15.00
❏ PRST-7468 [S]	Living Soul	1966	5.00	10.00	20.00
❏ PRLP-7485 [M]	Misty	1966	3.75	7.50	15.00
❏ PRST-7485 [S]	Misty	1966	5.00	10.00	20.00
❏ PRLP-7493 [M]	Spicy	1967	5.00	10.00	20.00
❏ PRST-7493 [S]	Spicy	1967	3.75	7.50	15.00
❏ PRLP-7497 [M]	Super Cool	1967	5.00	10.00	20.00
❏ PRST-7497 [S]	Super Cool	1967	3.75	7.50	15.00
❏ PRLP-7514 [M]	Get Up and Get It	1967	5.00	10.00	20.00
❏ PRST-7514 [S]	Get Up and Get It	1967	3.75	7.50	15.00

Number	Title	Yr	VG	VG+	NM
❏ PRST-7543	Soul Power	1968	3.75	7.50	15.00
❏ PRST-7570	The Groover	1968	3.75	7.50	15.00
❏ PRST-7601	That Healin' Feelin'	1969	3.75	7.50	15.00
❏ PRST-7700	The Best of Richard "Groove" Holmes	1969	3.75	7.50	15.00
❏ PRST-7741	Soul Mist	1970	3.75	7.50	15.00
❏ PRST-7768	The Best for Beautiful People	1971	3.75	7.50	15.00
❏ PRST-7778	The Best of Soul Organ Giants	1972	3.00	6.00	12.00
VERSATILE					
❏ MSG 6003	Dancing in the Sun	1977	3.75	7.50	15.00
WARNER BROS.					
❏ W 1553 [M]	Book of the Blues	1964	5.00	10.00	20.00
❏ WS 1553 [S]	Book of the Blues	1964	6.25	12.50	25.00
WORLD PACIFIC					
❏ ST-20147	Welcome Home	1968	5.00	10.00	20.00

HOLT, RED
Drummer, formerly with the RAMSEY LEWIS Trio. Also see YOUNG-HOLT UNLIMITED.
ARGO

Number	Title	Yr	VG	VG+	NM
❏ LP-696 [M]	Look Out! Look Out!	1962	5.00	10.00	20.00
❏ LPS-696 [S]	Look Out! Look Out!	1962	6.25	12.50	25.00
PAULA					
❏ 4006	Isaac, Isaac, Isaac	197?	3.75	7.50	15.00
❏ 4007	The Other Side of the Moon	197?	3.75	7.50	15.00

HOMI & JARVIS
Also see JOHN JARVIS.
GRP

Number	Title	Yr	VG	VG+	NM
❏ GR-1005	Friend of a Friend	1984	2.50	5.00	10.00

HONEY DREAMERS, THE
Vocal group.
FANTASY

Number	Title	Yr	VG	VG+	NM
❏ 3207 [M]	The Honey Dreamers Sing Gershwin	1956	20.00	40.00	80.00
-- Red vinyl					
❏ 3207 [M]	The Honey Dreamers Sing Gershwin	195?	10.00	20.00	40.00
-- Black vinyl					

HOOPER, LES
Composer, arranger and conductor. Also a male singer and keyboard player.
CHURCHILL

Number	Title	Yr	VG	VG+	NM
❏ 67234	Dorian Blue	1977	3.00	6.00	12.00
❏ 67235	Hoopla	1978	3.00	6.00	12.00
CREATIVE WORLD					
❏ ST-3002	Look What They've Done	197?	3.75	7.50	15.00
JAZZ HOUNDS					
❏ 0004	Raisin' the Roof	1982	3.00	6.00	12.00
PAUSA					
❏ 7185	Hoopla	1986	2.50	5.00	10.00

HOOPER, STIX
Drummer. Also see THE CRUSADERS.
MCA

Number	Title	Yr	VG	VG+	NM
❏ 3180	The World Within	1980	2.50	5.00	10.00

HOOPES, RONNIE
Pianist.
REVELATION

Number	Title	Yr	VG	VG+	NM
❏ 21	Respect for a Great Tradition	1973	3.75	7.50	15.00

HOPE, ELMO
Pianist and composer. Also see ART BLAKEY.
AUDIO FIDELITY

Number	Title	Yr	VG	VG+	NM
❏ AFLP-2119 [M]	Sounds from Riker's Island	1963	7.50	15.00	30.00
❏ AFSD-6119 [S]	Sounds from Riker's Island	1963	10.00	20.00	40.00
BEACON					
❏ B-401 [M]	High Hopes	1961	7.50	15.00	30.00
❏ BS-401 [S]	High Hopes	1961	10.00	20.00	40.00
BLUE NOTE					
❏ BLP-5029 [10]	Elmo Hope Trio	1953	75.00	150.00	300.00
❏ BLP-5044 [10]	Elmo Hope Quintet	1954	75.00	150.00	300.00
CELEBRITY					
❏ 209 [M]	Elmo Hope Trio	1962	6.25	12.50	25.00
❏ S-209 [S]	Elmo Hope Trio	1962	7.50	15.00	30.00
CONTEMPORARY					
❏ M-3620 [M]	The Elmo Hope Trio	1966	6.25	12.50	25.00
❏ S-7620 [S]	The Elmo Hope Trio	1966	7.50	15.00	30.00

Number	Title	Yr	VG	VG+	NM
FANTASY					
❏ OJC-1703	Hope Meets Foster	1985	2.50	5.00	10.00
❏ OJC-1751	Meditations	198?	2.50	5.00	10.00
❏ OJC-477	Elmo Hope Trio	1991	3.00	6.00	12.00
HIFI					
❏ J-616 [M]	Elmo Hope	1960	10.00	20.00	40.00
❏ JS-616 [S]	Elmo Hope	1960	12.50	25.00	50.00
INNER CITY					
❏ IC-1018	Last Sessions	197?	3.75	7.50	15.00
❏ IC-1037	Last Sessions, Volume 2	1978	3.75	7.50	15.00
MILESTONE					
❏ 47037 [(2)]	All Star Sessions	197?	3.75	7.50	15.00
PRESTIGE					
❏ PRLP-7010 [M]	Meditations	1956	30.00	60.00	120.00
❏ PRLP-7021 [M]	Hope Meets Foster	1956	30.00	60.00	120.00
❏ PRLP-7021 [M]	Wail, Frank, Wail	1957	20.00	40.00	80.00
-- Retitled reissue of above album					
❏ PRLP-7043 [M]	Informal Jazz	1956	30.00	60.00	120.00
❏ PRST-7675	Elmo Hope Memorial Album	1969	3.75	7.50	15.00
RIVERSIDE					
❏ RLP-381 [M]	Homecoming!	1961	10.00	20.00	40.00
❏ RLP-408 [M]	Hope-Full	1962	6.25	12.50	25.00
❏ 6161	Homecoming!	198?	3.00	6.00	12.00
❏ RS-9381 [S]	Homecoming!	1961	12.50	25.00	50.00
❏ RS-9408 [S]	Hope-Full	1962	7.50	15.00	30.00

HOPE, STAN
Pianist.

Number	Title	Yr	VG	VG+	NM
MAINSTREAM					
❏ MRL-327	Stan Hope	1972	3.75	7.50	15.00

HOPKINS, CLAUDE
Pianist, composer and bandleader.

Number	Title	Yr	VG	VG+	NM
CHIAROSCURO					
❏ 114	Crazy Fingers	1972	3.75	7.50	15.00
DESIGN					
❏ DLP-30 [M]	Golden Era of Dixieland Jazz 1887-1937	1957	6.25	12.50	25.00
JAZZ ARCHIVES					
❏ JA-27	Singin' in the Rain	198?	2.50	5.00	10.00
SWINGVILLE					
❏ SVLP-2009 [M]	Yes Indeed	1960	12.50	25.00	50.00
-- Purple label					
❏ SVLP-2009 [M]	Yes Indeed	1965	6.25	12.50	25.00
-- Blue label, trident logo at right					
❏ SVLP-2020 [M]	Let's Jam	1961	12.50	25.00	50.00
-- Purple label					
❏ SVLP-2020 [M]	Let's Jam	1965	6.25	12.50	25.00
-- Blue label, trident logo at right					
❏ SVLP-2041 [M]	Swing Time	1962	12.50	25.00	50.00
-- Purple label					
❏ SVLP-2041 [M]	Swing Time	1965	6.25	12.50	25.00
-- Blue label, trident logo at right					

HOPKINS, KENYON
Composer.

Number	Title	Yr	VG	VG+	NM
VERVE					
❏ V-8694 [M]	Dream Songs	1967	5.00	10.00	20.00
❏ V6-8694 [S]	Dream Songs	1967	3.00	6.00	12.00

HOPKINS, LINDA
Female singer.

Number	Title	Yr	VG	VG+	NM
PALO ALTO					
❏ PA-8034	How Blue Can You Get	1982	2.50	5.00	10.00

HORENSTEIN, STEPHEN
Baritone and tenor saxophone player and composer.

Number	Title	Yr	VG	VG+	NM
SOUL NOTE					
❏ SN-1099	Collages: Jerusalem '85	1986	3.00	6.00	12.00

HORN, PAUL
Flutist, also has played clarinet and alto saxophone. His 1968 Epic album Inside is considered one of the first "New Age" recordings.

Number	Title	Yr	VG	VG+	NM
ABC IMPULSE!					
❏ IA-9356 [(2)]	Plenty of Horn	1978	3.75	7.50	15.00
ARCHIVE OF FOLK AND JAZZ					
❏ 308	Paul Horn	197?	2.50	5.00	10.00
BLUE NOTE					
❏ BN-LA529-H2 [(2)]	Paul Horn in India	1975	3.75	7.50	15.00

Number	Title	Yr	VG	VG+	NM
COLUMBIA					
❏ CL 1677 [M]	The Sound of Paul Horn	1961	6.25	12.50	25.00
❏ CL 1922 [M]	Profile of a Jazz Musician	1962	3.75	7.50	15.00
❏ CL 2050 [M]	Impressions of "Cleopatra"	1963	3.75	7.50	15.00
❏ CS 8477 [S]	The Sound of Paul Horn	1961	7.50	15.00	30.00
❏ CS 8722 [S]	Profile of a Jazz Musician	1962	5.00	10.00	20.00
❏ CS 8850 [S]	Impressions of "Cleopatra"	1963	5.00	10.00	20.00
DOT					
❏ DLP-3091 [M]	House of Horn	1957	12.50	25.00	50.00
❏ DLP-9002 [M]	Plenty of Horn	1958	12.50	25.00	50.00
❏ DLP-29002 [S]	Plenty of Horn	1959	10.00	20.00	40.00
EPIC					
❏ BXN 26466	Inside	1969	3.75	7.50	15.00
❏ PE 26466	Inside	198?	2.00	4.00	8.00
-- Budget-line reissue with new prefix					
❏ KE 31600	Inside II	1971	3.75	7.50	15.00
❏ KE 32837	Visions	1973	3.00	6.00	12.00
❏ KE 33561	Paul Horn + Nexus	1975	3.00	6.00	12.00
❏ PE 34231	Altura do Sol	1976	3.00	6.00	12.00
HIFI					
❏ J-615 [M]	Something Blue	1960	7.50	15.00	30.00
❏ JS-615 [S]	Something Blue	1960	10.00	20.00	40.00
ISLAND					
❏ ILSD 6 [(2)]	Special Edition	197?	5.00	10.00	20.00
KUCKUCK					
❏ KU-060/061 [(2)]	Inside the Great Pyramid	198?	5.00	10.00	20.00
❏ 11062	Inside the Taj Mahal	198?	3.00	6.00	12.00
❏ 11075	Inside the Cathedral	198?	3.00	6.00	12.00
❏ 11083	The Peace Album	1988	3.00	6.00	12.00
❏ 12060 [(2)]	Inside the Great Pyramid	198?	3.75	7.50	15.00
-- Reissue with new number					
LOST LAKE					
❏ LL-0091	Sketches: A Collection	1986	3.00	6.00	12.00
MCA					
❏ 4144 [(2)]	Plenty of Horn	198?	3.00	6.00	12.00
OVATION					
❏ OV-1405	Concert Ensemble	1970	3.75	7.50	15.00
RCA VICTOR					
❏ LPM-3386 [M]	Cycle	1965	3.75	7.50	15.00
❏ LSP-3386 [S]	Cycle	1965	5.00	10.00	20.00
❏ LPM-3414 [M]	Jazz Suite on the Mass Texts	1965	3.75	7.50	15.00
❏ LSP-3414 [S]	Jazz Suite on the Mass Texts	1965	5.00	10.00	20.00
❏ LPM-3519 [M]	Here's That Rainy Day	1966	3.75	7.50	15.00
❏ LSP-3519 [S]	Here's That Rainy Day	1966	5.00	10.00	20.00
❏ LPM-3613 [M]	Monday, Monday	1966	3.75	7.50	15.00
❏ LSP-3613 [S]	Monday, Monday	1966	5.00	10.00	20.00
WORLD PACIFIC					
❏ WP-1266 [M]	Impressions	1959	12.50	25.00	50.00

HORN, SHIRLEY
Pianist and female singer.

Number	Title	Yr	VG	VG+	NM
ABC-PARAMOUNT					
❏ ABC-538 [M]	Travelin' Light	1965	10.00	20.00	40.00
❏ ABCS-538 [S]	Travelin' Light	1965	12.50	25.00	50.00
MERCURY					
❏ MG-20761 [M]	Loads of Love	1963	12.50	25.00	50.00
❏ MG-20835 [M]	Shirley Horn with Horns	1963	12.50	25.00	50.00
❏ SR-60761 [S]	Loads of Love	1963	15.00	30.00	60.00
❏ SR-60835 [S]	Shirley Horn with Horns	1963	15.00	30.00	60.00
❏ SR-60835 [S]	Shirley Horn with Horns	199?	6.25	12.50	25.00
-- Classic Records reissue on audiophile vinyl					
STEEPLECHASE					
❏ SCS-1023	Garden of the Blues	198?	3.00	6.00	12.00
❏ SCS-1111	A Lazy Afternoon	1979	3.00	6.00	12.00
❏ SCS-1157	All Night Long	1981	3.00	6.00	12.00
❏ SCS-1164	Violets for Your Furs	1982	3.00	6.00	12.00
STEREO-CRAFT					
❏ RTN-16 [M]	Embers and Ashes	1961	15.00	30.00	60.00
❏ RTS-16 [S]	Embers and Ashes	1961	20.00	40.00	80.00
VERVE					
❏ 832 235-1	I Thought About You	1987	2.50	5.00	10.00
❏ 837 933-1	Close Enough for Love	1989	3.00	6.00	12.00

HORNE, LENA
Female singer.

Number	Title	Yr	VG	VG+	NM
ACCORD					
❏ SN-7190	Standing Room Only	198?	2.50	5.00	10.00
BLUEBIRD					
❏ 9985-1-RB	Stormy Weather: The Legendary Lena	1990	3.00	6.00	12.00

Number	Title	Yr	VG	VG+	NM
BUDDAH					
❏ BDS-5084	Nature's Baby	1971	3.00	6.00	12.00
❏ BDS-5669 [(2)]	The Essential Lena Horne	197?	3.00	6.00	12.00
BULLDOG					
❏ BDL-2000	20 Golden Pieces of Lena Horne	198?	2.50	5.00	10.00
CHARTER					
❏ CLP-101 [M]	Lena Sings Your Requests	1963	3.75	7.50	15.00
❏ CLS-101 [S]	Lena Sings Your Requests	1963	5.00	10.00	20.00
❏ CLP-106 [M]	Like Latin	1964	3.75	7.50	15.00
❏ CLS-106 [S]	Like Latin	1964	5.00	10.00	20.00
DRG					
❏ MRS-501	Lena Horne With Lennie Hayton & the Marty Paich Orchestra	1985	2.50	5.00	10.00
❏ MRS-510	Lena Goes Latin	1986	2.50	5.00	10.00
JAZZTONE					
❏ J-1262 [M]	Lena and Ivie	1957	12.50	25.00	50.00
LIBERTY					
❏ LN-10194	Lena in Hollywood	198?	2.00	4.00	8.00
LION					
❏ L-70050 [M]	I Feel So Smoochie	1959	5.00	10.00	20.00
MGM					
❏ E-545 [10]	Lena Horne Sings	1952	12.50	25.00	50.00
❏ M3G-5409	The One and Only	197?	2.50	5.00	10.00
MOBILE FIDELITY					
❏ 2-094 [(2)]	Lena Horne: The Lady and Her Music	1982	10.00	20.00	40.00
-- Audiophile vinyl					
MOVIETONE					
❏ MTM 71005 [M]	Once in a Lifetime	196?	3.75	7.50	15.00
❏ MTS 72005 [S]	Once in a Lifetime	196?	5.00	10.00	20.00
PAIR					
❏ PDL2-1055 [(2)]	Lena	1986	3.00	6.00	12.00
QWEST					
❏ 2QW 3597 [(2)]	Lena Horne: The Lady and Her Music	1981	3.00	6.00	12.00
RCA VICTOR					
❏ BGL1-1026	Lena and Michel	1975	3.00	6.00	12.00
-- With Michel Legrand					
❏ LOC-1028 [M]	Lena Horne at the Waldorf Astoria	1957	7.50	15.00	30.00
❏ LSO-1028 [S]	Lena Horne at the Waldorf Astoria	1957	10.00	20.00	40.00
❏ LPM-1148 [M]	It's Love	1955	12.50	25.00	50.00
❏ LPM-1375 [M]	Stormy Weather	1956	12.50	25.00	50.00
❏ BGL1-1799	Lena	1976	3.00	6.00	12.00
❏ LPM-1879 [M]	Give the Lady What She Wants	1958	7.50	15.00	30.00
❏ LSP-1879 [S]	Give the Lady What She Wants	1958	10.00	20.00	40.00
❏ LPM-1895 [M]	Songs of Burke and Van Heusen	1959	7.50	15.00	30.00
❏ LSP-1895 [S]	Songs of Burke and Van Heusen	1959	10.00	20.00	40.00
❏ LPM-2364 [M]	Lena Horne at the Sands	1961	6.25	12.50	25.00
❏ LSP-2364 [S]	Lena Horne at the Sands	1961	7.50	15.00	30.00
❏ LPM-2465 [M]	Lena on the Blue Side	1962	6.25	12.50	25.00
❏ LSP-2465 [S]	Lena on the Blue Side	1962	7.50	15.00	30.00
❏ LPM-2587 [M]	Lena...Lovely and Alive	1963	6.25	12.50	25.00
❏ LSP-2587 [S]	Lena...Lovely and Alive	1963	7.50	15.00	30.00
❏ LPT-3061 [10]	This Is Lena Horne	1952	12.50	25.00	50.00
❏ AYL1-4389	Lena, A New Album	1983	2.00	4.00	8.00
-- "Best Buy Series" reissue					
SKYE					
❏ 15	Lena & Gabor	1970	3.75	7.50	15.00
-- With Gabor Szabo					
STANYAN					
❏ POW-3006	Stormy Weather	198?	2.50	5.00	10.00
-- Reissue of 10126					
❏ 10126	Stormy Weather	197?	3.00	6.00	12.00
SUNBEAM					
❏ 212	A Date with Lena Horne	198?	2.50	5.00	10.00
-- With Fletcher Henderson and His Orchestra					
THREE CHERRIES					
❏ TC-44411	The Men in My Life	1989	2.50	5.00	10.00
TOPS					
❏ L-910 [10]	Moanin' Low	195?	10.00	20.00	40.00
❏ L-931 [10]	Lena Horne Sings	195?	10.00	20.00	40.00
❏ L-1502 [M]	Lena Horne	1958	5.00	10.00	20.00
20TH CENTURY FOX					
❏ TF-4115 [M]	Here's Lena Now	1964	3.75	7.50	15.00
❏ TFS-4115 [S]	Here's Lena Now	1964	5.00	10.00	20.00
UNITED ARTISTS					
❏ UAL 3433 [M]	Feelin' Good	1965	3.75	7.50	15.00
❏ UAL 3470 [M]	Lena in Hollywood	1966	3.75	7.50	15.00
❏ UAL 3496 [M]	Soul	1966	3.75	7.50	15.00
❏ UAS 6433 [S]	Feelin' Good	1965	5.00	10.00	20.00
❏ UAS 6470 [S]	Lena in Hollywood	1966	5.00	10.00	20.00
❏ UAS 6496 [S]	Soul	1966	5.00	10.00	20.00

HORNE, LENA, AND HARRY BELAFONTE

Belafonte is a male singer not otherwise listed in this book. Also see LENA HORNE.

Number	Title	Yr	VG	VG+	NM
RCA VICTOR					
❏ LOC-1507 [M]	Porgy and Bess	1959	6.25	12.50	25.00
❏ LSO-1507 [S]	Porgy and Bess	1959	10.00	20.00	40.00

HORTA, TONINHO

Guitarist, pianist and male singer.

Number	Title	Yr	VG	VG+	NM
VERVE FORECAST					
❏ 835 183-1	Diamond Land	1988	2.50	5.00	10.00
❏ 839 734-1	Moonstone	1989	3.00	6.00	12.00

HORVITZ, WAYNE

Pianist, organist, keyboard player and composer.

Number	Title	Yr	VG	VG+	NM
BLACK SAINT					
❏ BSR-0059	Some Order, Long Understood	1982	3.00	6.00	12.00
ELEKTRA/MUSICIAN					
❏ 60759	This New Generation	1988	2.50	5.00	10.00

HOT ANTIC JAZZ BAND, THE

Members include: Michel Bastide (cornet, trombone, vocals); Jean-François Bonnel (clarinet, cornet, saxophones, vocals); Bernard Antherieu (clarinet, alto saxophone, banjo, vocals); Philippe Raspail (tenor sax, clarinet, alto sax, vocals); Martin Seck (piano, vocals); Jean-Pierre Dubois (banjo, clarinet, kazoo, vocals); Christian Lefevre (tuba, trombone, vocals).

Number	Title	Yr	VG	VG+	NM
STOMP OFF					
❏ SOS-1044	I Got the Stinger	1982	2.50	5.00	10.00
❏ SOS-1058	We Love You Jabbo	1983	2.50	5.00	10.00
❏ SOS-1099	Jazz Battle	1985	2.50	5.00	10.00
❏ SOS-1154	Puttin' On the Ritz	1988	2.50	5.00	10.00

HOT COTTON JAZZ BAND, THE

Members include Gene Rush (piano) and Bob Baker (clarinet).

Number	Title	Yr	VG	VG+	NM
GHB					
❏ 168	Stompin' Room Only, Vol. 1	1984	2.50	5.00	10.00
❏ 169	Stompin' Room Only, Vol. 2	1984	2.50	5.00	10.00
❏ 188	Take Your Tomorrow	1986	2.50	5.00	10.00

HOT JAZZ ORCHESTRA

Number	Title	Yr	VG	VG+	NM
REVELATION					
❏ 28	Hot Jazz Orchestra	1979	2.50	5.00	10.00

HOTEL EDISON ROOF ORCHESTRA, THE

Number	Title	Yr	VG	VG+	NM
STOMP OFF					
❏ SOS-1169	Breakaway	1988	2.50	5.00	10.00

HOUGHTON, STEVE

Drummer and percussionist.

Number	Title	Yr	VG	VG+	NM
SEABREEZE					
❏ SB-2018	The Steve Houghton Album	198?	2.50	5.00	10.00

HOUN, FRED, AND THE AFRO-ASIAN MUSIC ENSEMBLE

Houn is a baritone saxophone player and bandleader.

Number	Title	Yr	VG	VG+	NM
SOUL NOTE					
❏ SN-1117	Tomorrow Is Now!	1986	3.00	6.00	12.00
❏ 121117	Tomorrow Is Now!	198?	3.00	6.00	12.00
-- Reissue of 1117					
❏ 121167	We Refuse to Be Used and Abused	1990	3.75	7.50	15.00

HOWARD, DAVE

Male singer.

Number	Title	Yr	VG	VG+	NM
CHOREO					
❏ C-5 [M]	I Love Everybody	1961	6.25	12.50	25.00
❏ CS-5 [S]	I Love Everybody	1961	7.50	15.00	30.00

HOWARD, EDDY

Male singer, guitarist, trombonist and bandleader. His biggest hit was "(It's No) Sin" in 1951.

Number	Title	Yr	VG	VG+	NM
CIRCLE					
❏ 29	Eddy Howard 1949-1952	198?	2.50	5.00	10.00
❏ 79	Eddy Howard 1949-1953	1985	2.50	5.00	10.00
HINDSIGHT					
❏ HSR-119	Eddy Howard 1946-1951	198?	2.50	5.00	10.00
❏ HSR-156	Eddy Howard 1945-1948	198?	2.50	5.00	10.00
❏ HSR-405 [(2)]	Eddy Howard and His Orchestra Play 22 Original Big Band Favorites	198?	3.00	6.00	12.00

Number	Title	Yr	VG	VG+	NM
INSIGHT					
❏ 205	Eddy Howard and His Orchestra 1945-1951	198?	2.50	5.00	10.00
MERCURY					
❏ MG-20112 [M]	Singing in the Rain	195?	6.25	12.50	25.00
❏ MG-20312 [M]	Paradise Isle	195?	6.25	12.50	25.00
❏ MG-20432 [M]	Great for Dancing	1958	5.00	10.00	20.00
❏ MG-20562 [M]	Eddy Howard's Golden Hits	1961	3.75	7.50	15.00
❏ MG-20593 [M]	More Eddy Howard's Golden Hits	1962	3.75	7.50	15.00
❏ MG-20665 [M]	Eddy Howard Sings and Plays the Great Old Waltzes	1962	3.75	7.50	15.00
❏ MG-20817 [M]	Eddy Howard Sings and Plays the Great Band Hits	196?	3.75	7.50	15.00
❏ MG-20910 [M]	Intimately Yours	1965	3.75	7.50	15.00
❏ MG-21014 [M]	Softly and Sincerely	196?	3.75	7.50	15.00
❏ SR-60104 [S]	Great for Dancing	1959	6.25	12.50	25.00
❏ SR-60562 [S]	Eddy Howard's Golden Hits	1961	5.00	10.00	20.00
❏ SR-60593 [S]	More Eddy Howard's Golden Hits	1962	5.00	10.00	20.00
❏ SR-60665 [S]	Eddy Howard Sings and Plays the Great Old Waltzes	1962	5.00	10.00	20.00
❏ SR-60817 [S]	Eddy Howard Sings and Plays the Great Band Hits	196?	5.00	10.00	20.00
❏ SR-60910 [S]	Intimately Yours	1965	5.00	10.00	20.00
❏ SR-61014 [S]	Softly and Sincerely	196?	5.00	10.00	20.00
WING					
❏ MGW-12104 [M]	Saturday Night Dance Date	196?	3.00	6.00	12.00
❏ MGW-12171 [M]	Words of Love	196?	3.00	6.00	12.00
❏ MGW-12171 [M]	Eddy Howard Sings Words of Love	196?	3.00	6.00	12.00
❏ MGW-12194 [M]	Sleepy Serenade	196?	3.00	6.00	12.00
❏ MGW-12249 [M]	The Velvet Voice	196?	3.00	6.00	12.00
❏ SRW-16104 [S]	Saturday Night Dance Date	196?	3.00	6.00	12.00
❏ SRW-16171 [S]	Words of Love	196?	3.00	6.00	12.00
❏ SRW-16171 [S]	Eddy Howard Sings Words of Love	196?	3.00	6.00	12.00
❏ SRW-16194 [S]	Sleepy Serenade	196?	3.00	6.00	12.00
❏ SRW-16249 [S]	The Velvet Voice	196?	3.00	6.00	12.00
HOWARD, GEORGE					
Soprano and alto saxophone player.					
GRP					
❏ GR-9629	Love and Understanding	1991	3.75	7.50	15.00
MCA					
❏ 5855	A Nice Place to Be	1987	2.50	5.00	10.00
❏ 6335	Personal	1990	3.00	6.00	12.00
❏ 42145	Reflections	1988	2.50	5.00	10.00
PALO ALTO					
❏ TB-201	Steppin' Out	198?	2.50	5.00	10.00
❏ TB-205	Dancing in the Sun	198?	2.50	5.00	10.00
❏ TB-210	Love Will Follow	1987	2.50	5.00	10.00
❏ PA-8035	Asphalt Garden	1982	3.00	6.00	12.00
HOWARD, JIM					
Guitarist.					
SEABREEZE					
❏ SB-2005	No Compromise	1983	2.50	5.00	10.00
HOWARD, JOE					
Trombonist.					
KING					
❏ 661 [M]	The Golden Sound	1959	12.50	25.00	50.00
SUNSET					
❏ SU-3001 [M]	Patterns for Trombone	1955	10.00	20.00	40.00
HOWARD, KID					
Trumpeter and bandleader.					
GHB					
❏ 23	Kid Howard at San Jacinto Hall	1966	3.00	6.00	12.00
JAZZOLOGY					
❏ JCE-14	Kid Howard and the Vida Jazz Band	1967	3.00	6.00	12.00
❏ JCE-18	Kid Howard's Olympia Band	1967	3.00	6.00	12.00
HOWARD, NOAH					
Alto saxophone player.					
ALTOSAX					
❏ 1001	Patterns	197?	3.75	7.50	15.00
❏ 25055	Quartetto	197?	3.75	7.50	15.00
CHIAROSCURO					
❏ 2016	Oie	1979	3.00	6.00	12.00

Number	Title	Yr	VG	VG+	NM
ESP-DISK'					
❏ 1031 [M]	Noah Howard Quartet	1966	5.00	10.00	20.00
❏ S-1031 [S]	Noah Howard Quartet	1966	6.25	12.50	25.00
❏ S-1064 [S]	Live at Judson Hall	1969	5.00	10.00	20.00
❏ 1073	Noah Howard	1968	---	---	---
-- Canceled					
HOWELL, MICHAEL					
Guitarist.					
CATALYST					
❏ 7615	Alone	1976	3.00	6.00	12.00
MILESTONE					
❏ M-9048	Looking Glass	1973	3.00	6.00	12.00
❏ M-9054	In the Silence	1974	3.00	6.00	12.00
HUBBARD, DAVE					
Tenor saxophone player.					
MAINSTREAM					
❏ MRL-317	Dave Hubbard	1971	3.75	7.50	15.00
HUBBARD, FREDDIE					
Trumpeter, fluegel horn player and composer.					
ABC IMPULSE!					
❏ AS-27 [S]	The Artistry of Freddie Hubbard	1968	3.00	6.00	12.00
❏ AS-38 [S]	The Body and Soul of Freddie Hubbard	1968	3.00	6.00	12.00
❏ AS-9237 [(2)]	Re-Evaluation: The Impulse Years	1973	3.75	7.50	15.00
ATLANTIC					
❏ SD 2-314 [(2)]	The Art of Freddie Hubbard	1974	3.75	7.50	15.00
❏ 1477 [M]	Backlash	1967	6.25	12.50	25.00
❏ SD 1477 [S]	Backlash	1967	3.75	7.50	15.00
❏ SD 1501	High Pressure Blues	1969	3.75	7.50	15.00
❏ SD 1526	Soul Experiment	1970	3.00	6.00	12.00
❏ SD 1549	Black Angel	1971	3.00	6.00	12.00
❏ 80108	Sweet Return	1983	2.50	5.00	10.00
❏ 90466	Backlash	1986	2.00	4.00	8.00
-- Reissue of SD 1477					
BASF					
❏ 10726	The Hub of Hubbard	1972	3.00	6.00	12.00
BLUE NOTE					
❏ BN-LA356-H [(2)]	Freddie Hubbard	1975	3.75	7.50	15.00
❏ BLP-4040 [M]	Open Sesame	1960	30.00	60.00	120.00
-- "Deep groove" version (deep indentation under label on both sides)					
❏ BLP-4040 [M]	Open Sesame	1960	20.00	40.00	80.00
-- Regular version with W. 63rd St. address on label					
❏ BLP-4040 [M]	Open Sesame	1963	5.00	10.00	20.00
-- With New York, USA address on label					
❏ BLP-4056 [M]	Goin' Up	1960	20.00	40.00	80.00
-- With W. 63rd St. address on label					
❏ BLP-4056 [M]	Goin' Up	1963	5.00	10.00	20.00
-- With New York, USA address on label					
❏ BLP-4073 [M]	Hub Cap	1961	20.00	40.00	80.00
-- With W. 63rd St. address on label					
❏ BLP-4073 [M]	Hub Cap	1963	5.00	10.00	20.00
-- With New York, USA address on label					
❏ BLP-4085 [M]	Ready for Freddie	1961	20.00	40.00	80.00
-- With 61st St. address on label					
❏ BLP-4085 [M]	Ready for Freddie	1963	5.00	10.00	20.00
-- With New York, USA address on label					
❏ BLP-4115 [M]	Hub Tones	1962	6.25	12.50	25.00
❏ 4135/84135	Here to Stay	1963	---	---	---
-- Scheduled, but unreleased until 1985					
❏ BLP-4172 [M]	Breaking Point	1964	6.25	12.50	25.00
❏ BLP-4196 [M]	Blue Spirits	1965	6.25	12.50	25.00
❏ BLP-4207 [M]	The Night of the Cookers -- Live at Club Le Marchal, Vol. 1	1965	6.25	12.50	25.00
❏ BLP-4208 [M]	The Night of the Cookers -- Live at Club Le Marchal, Vol. 2	1965	6.25	12.50	25.00
❏ B1-32094	Ready for Freddie	1995	3.00	6.00	12.00
-- "The Finest in Jazz Since 1939" reissue					
❏ BJT-48017	The Eternal Triangle	1988	3.00	6.00	12.00
❏ BST-84040 [S]	Open Sesame	1960	15.00	30.00	60.00
-- With W. 63rd St. addresss on label					
❏ BST-84040 [S]	Open Sesame	1963	6.25	12.50	25.00
-- With New York, USA address on label					
❏ BST-84040 [S]	Open Sesame	1967	3.75	7.50	15.00
-- With "A Division of Liberty Records" on label					
❏ BST-84040	Open Sesame	1989	2.50	5.00	10.00
-- "The Finest in Jazz Since 1939" reissue					
❏ BST-84040 [S]	Open Sesame	199?	6.25	12.50	25.00
-- Classic Records reissue on audiophile vinyl					
❏ BST-84056 [S]	Goin' Up	1960	15.00	30.00	60.00
-- With W. 63rd St. address on label					
❏ BST-84056 [S]	Goin' Up	1963	6.25	12.50	25.00
-- With New York, USA address on label					

Number	Title	Yr	VG	VG+	NM
❑ BST-84056 [S] Goin' Up		1967	3.75	7.50	15.00
-- With "A Division of Liberty Records" on label					
❑ BST-84073 [S] Hub Cap		1961	15.00	30.00	60.00
-- With W. 63rd St. addresss on label					
❑ BST-84073 [S] Hub Cap		1963	6.25	12.50	25.00
-- With New York, USA address on label					
❑ BST-84073 [S] Hub Cap		1967	3.75	7.50	15.00
-- With "A Division of Liberty Records" on label					
❑ BST-84073 Hub Cap		198?	2.50	5.00	10.00
-- "The Finest in Jazz Since 1939" reissue					
❑ BST-84085 [S] Ready for Freddie		1961	15.00	30.00	60.00
-- With 61st St. addresss on label					
❑ BST-84085 [S] Ready for Freddie		1963	6.25	12.50	25.00
-- With New York, USA address on label					
❑ BST-84085 [S] Ready for Freddie		1967	3.75	7.50	15.00
-- With "A Division of Liberty Records" on label					
❑ BST-84115 [S] Hub-Tones		1962	7.50	15.00	30.00
-- With New York, USA address on label					
❑ BST-84115 [S] Hub-Tones		1967	3.75	7.50	15.00
-- With "A Division of Liberty Records" on label					
❑ BST-84115 Hub-Tones		1985	2.50	5.00	10.00
-- "The Finest in Jazz Since 1939" reissue					
❑ BST-84135 Here to Stay		1985	3.00	6.00	12.00
❑ BST-84172 [S] Breaking Point		1964	7.50	15.00	30.00
-- With New York, USA address on label					
❑ BST-84172 [S] Breaking Point		1967	3.75	7.50	15.00
-- With "A Division of Liberty Records" on label					
❑ BST-84196 [S] Blue Spirits		1965	7.50	15.00	30.00
-- With New York, USA address on label					
❑ BST-84196 [S] Blue Spirits		1967	3.75	7.50	15.00
-- With "A Division of Liberty Records" on label					
❑ BST-84196 Blue Spirits		1987	2.50	5.00	10.00
-- "The Finest in Jazz Since 1939" reissue					
❑ BST-84207 [S] The Night of the Cookers -- Live at Club Le Marchal, Vol. 1		1965	7.50	15.00	30.00
-- With New York, USA address on label					
❑ BST-84207 [S] The Night of the Cookers -- Live at Club Le Marchal, Vol. 1		1967	3.75	7.50	15.00
-- With "A Division of Liberty Records" on label					
❑ BST-84208 [S] The Night of the Cookers -- Live at Club Le Marchal, Vol. 2		1965	7.50	15.00	30.00
-- With New York, USA address on label					
❑ BST-84208 [S] The Night of the Cookers -- Live at Club Le Marchal, Vol. 2		1967	3.75	7.50	15.00
-- With "A Division of Liberty Records" on label					
❑ B1-85121 Doubletake		1987	2.50	5.00	10.00
❑ B1-85139 Life-Flight		1987	2.50	5.00	10.00
❑ B1-90905 Times 'R Changin'		1989	3.00	6.00	12.00
❑ B1-93202 The Best of Freddie Hubbard		1989	3.00	6.00	12.00
COLUMBIA					
❑ KC 33048 High Energy		1974	2.50	5.00	10.00
❑ PC 33556 Liquid Love		1975	2.50	5.00	10.00
❑ PC 34166 Windjammer		1976	2.50	5.00	10.00
❑ PC 34902 Bundle of Joy		1977	2.50	5.00	10.00
❑ JC 35386 Super Blue		1978	2.50	5.00	10.00
❑ JC 36015 Love Connection		1979	2.50	5.00	10.00
❑ JC 36358 The Best of Freddie Hubbard		1979	2.50	5.00	10.00
❑ FC 36418 Skagly		1980	2.50	5.00	10.00
CTI					
❑ CTS-6001 Red Clay		1970	3.00	6.00	12.00
❑ CTS-6007 The Straight Life		1971	3.00	6.00	12.00
❑ CTS-6013 First Light		1972	3.00	6.00	12.00
❑ CTS-6018 Sky Dive		1973	2.50	5.00	10.00
❑ CTS-6036 Keep Your Soul Together		1974	2.50	5.00	10.00
❑ CTS-6044 Freddie Hubbard In Concert		1974	2.50	5.00	10.00
❑ CTS-6047 The Baddest Hubbard		1974	2.50	5.00	10.00
❑ CTS-6056 Polar AC		1975	2.50	5.00	10.00
❑ 8016 Red Clay		198?	2.00	4.00	8.00
-- Reissue of 6001					
❑ 8017 First Light		198?	2.00	4.00	8.00
-- Reissue of 6013					
❑ 8022 The Straight Life		198?	2.00	4.00	8.00
-- Reissue of 6007					
CTI/CBS ASSOCIATED					
❑ FZ 40687 First Light		1987	2.50	5.00	10.00
ELEKTRA MUSICIAN					
❑ 60029 Ride Like the Wind		1982	2.50	5.00	10.00
ENJA					
❑ 3095 Outpost		1981	2.50	5.00	10.00
FANTASY					
❑ 9610 Splash		1981	2.50	5.00	10.00
❑ 9615 Keystone Bop		1982	2.50	5.00	10.00
❑ 9626 A Little Night Music		1983	2.50	5.00	10.00
❑ 9635 Classics		1984	2.50	5.00	10.00
IMPULSE!					
❑ A-27 [M] The Artistry of Freddie Hubbard		1962	6.25	12.50	25.00
❑ AS-27 [S] The Artistry of Freddie Hubbard		1962	7.50	15.00	30.00
❑ A-38 [M] The Body and Soul of Freddie Hubbard		1963	6.25	12.50	25.00
❑ AS-38 [S] The Body and Soul of Freddie Hubbard		1963	7.50	15.00	30.00
LIBERTY					
❑ LT-1110 Mistral		1981	2.50	5.00	10.00
PABLO					
❑ 2310-884 The Best of Freddie Hubbard		1983	2.50	5.00	10.00
❑ 2312-134 Born to Be Blue		1982	2.50	5.00	10.00
PABLO LIVE					
❑ 2620-113 [(2)] Live at the Northsea Jazz Festival, The Hague, 1980		1983	3.00	6.00	12.00
PABLO TODAY					
❑ 2312-134 Born to Be Blue		198?	2.50	5.00	10.00
PAUSA					
❑ 7122 Rollin'		1982	2.50	5.00	10.00
PHOENIX 10					
❑ PHX 318 Extended		1981	2.00	4.00	8.00
PICCADILLY					
❑ 3467 Intrepid Fox		198?	2.50	5.00	10.00
QUINTESSENCE					
❑ 25161 Skylark		1978	2.50	5.00	10.00
REAL TIME					
❑ 305 Back to Birdland		198?	2.50	5.00	10.00

HUBBARD, FREDDIE, AND OSCAR PETERSON
Also see each artist's individual listings.
PABLO

Number	Title	Yr	VG	VG+	NM
❑ 2310-876 Face to Face		198?	2.50	5.00	10.00

HUBBARD, FREDDIE, AND STANLEY TURRENTINE
Also see each artist's individual listings.
CTI

| ❑ CTS-6044 In Concert, Volume 1 | | 1974 | 2.50 | 5.00 | 10.00 |
| ❑ CTS-6049 In Concert, Volume 2 | | 1975 | 2.50 | 5.00 | 10.00 |

HUBBELL, FRANK
PHILIPS

| ❑ PHS 600-293 Frank Hubbell and the Stompers | | 1969 | 3.75 | 7.50 | 15.00 |

HUBNER, ABBI, AND HIS LOW DOWN WIZARDS
STOMP OFF

| ❑ SOS-1093 Twenty Years, Live in Concert | | 1986 | 2.50 | 5.00 | 10.00 |

HUCKO, PEANUTS
Clarinetist and tenor saxophone player.
CIRCLE

❑ C-21 Peanuts		198?	2.50	5.00	10.00
GRAND AWARD					
❑ GA 33-331 [M] Tribute to Benny Goodman		1956	10.00	20.00	40.00
JAZZTONE					
❑ J-1250 [M] In the Style of Benny Goodman		1957	7.50	15.00	30.00
WALDORF MUSIC HALL					
❑ MH 33-153 [10] A Tribute to Benny Goodman		1956	7.50	15.00	30.00

HUCKO, PEANUTS/RAY McKINLEY
Also see each artist's individual listings.
GRAND AWARD

| ❑ GA 33-333 [M] The Swingin' 30s | | 1956 | 10.00 | 20.00 | 40.00 |

HUCKO, PEANUTS, AND RALPH SUTTON
Also see each artist's individual listings.
CHIAROSCURO

| ❑ 167 Live at Condon's | | 1978 | 3.00 | 6.00 | 12.00 |

HUDSON, DEAN
There was no Dean Hudson; it was a fictitious name used by various groups of University of Florida big-band musicians to imply continuity.
CIRCLE

❑ C-13 Dean Hudson and His Orchestra 1942-1948		198?	2.50	5.00	10.00
❑ C-40 Dean Hudson and His Orchestra -- Now!		1982	2.50	5.00	10.00
❑ C-86 More Dean Hudson and His Orchestra 1941 and 1948		198?	2.50	5.00	10.00
❑ CLP-136 Dean Hudson and His Orchestra 1943-1944		198?	2.50	5.00	10.00

Number	Title	Yr	VG	VG+	NM
HUG, ARMAND					
Pianist.					
CIRCLE					
❑ L-411 [10]	New Orleans 88	1951	12.50	25.00	50.00
GHB					
❑ 144	Armand Hug	1988	2.50	5.00	10.00
GOLDEN CREST					
❑ GC-3045 [M]	New Orleans Piano	196?	3.75	7.50	15.00
❑ GC-3064	Rags and Blues	196?	3.75	7.50	15.00
JAZZOLOGY					
❑ J-83	Armand Hug Plays Bix	197?	3.00	6.00	12.00
LAND O' JAZZ					
❑ 3475	Autobiography in Jazz	197?	3.00	6.00	12.00
PARAMOUNT					
❑ LP-114 [10]	Armand Hug Plays Armand Piron	1954	12.50	25.00	50.00
SOUTHLAND					
❑ 228 [M]	Dixieland	1961	3.75	7.50	15.00
❑ 244 [M]	Piano in New Orleans	196?	3.75	7.50	15.00
HUG, ARMAND/EDDIE MILLER					
Also see each artist's individual listings.					
GHB					
❑ 121	Armand Hug and His New Orleans Dixielanders/Eddie Miller and His New Orleans Rhythm Pals	198?	2.50	5.00	10.00
LAND O' JAZZ					
❑ 5876	Just Friends	198?	2.50	5.00	10.00
HUGHES, LANGSTON					
The below are spoken-word recordings.					
FOLKWAYS					
❑ FA-7312 [10]	The Story of Jazz for Children	1954	12.50	25.00	50.00
-- With booklet					
MGM					
❑ E-3697 [M]	The Weary Blues	1958	12.50	25.00	50.00
-- Yellow label					
VERVE					
❑ VSP-36 [M]	The Weary Blues	1966	5.00	10.00	20.00
❑ VSPS-36 [R]	The Weary Blues	1966	3.00	6.00	12.00
HUGHES, RHETA					
Female singer.					
COLUMBIA					
❑ CL 2385 [M]	Introducing An Electrifying New Star	1965	7.50	15.00	30.00
❑ CS 9185 [S]	Introducing An Electrifying New Star	1965	10.00	20.00	40.00
HUMAN ARTS ENSEMBLE					
Membership included Charles "Bobo" Shaw (drums, bugle); Joseph Bowie (trombone); Luther Thomas (alto saxophone); James Emery (guitar); John Lindberg (bass).					
ARISTA FREEDOM					
❑ AF 1022	Under the Sun	1975	3.00	6.00	12.00
❑ AF 1039	Whisper of Dharma	1977	3.00	6.00	12.00
HUMES, HELEN					
Female singer.					
AUDIOPHILE					
❑ AP-107	Helen Humes	197?	3.00	6.00	12.00
CLASSIC JAZZ					
❑ 110	Sneakin' Around	197?	3.00	6.00	12.00
❑ 120	Let the Good Times Roll	197?	3.00	6.00	12.00
COLUMBIA					
❑ KC 33488	The Talk of the Town	1975	2.50	5.00	10.00
CONTEMPORARY					
❑ M-3571 [M]	'Tain't Nobody's Biz-Ness If I Do	1960	10.00	20.00	40.00
❑ M-3582 [M]	Songs I Like to Sing	1960	10.00	20.00	40.00
❑ M-3598 [M]	Swingin' with Humes	1961	7.50	15.00	30.00
❑ S-7571 [S]	'Tain't Nobody's Biz-Ness If I Do	1960	10.00	20.00	40.00
❑ S-7582 [S]	Songs I Like to Sing	1960	10.00	20.00	40.00
❑ S-7598 [S]	Swingin' with Humes	1961	10.00	20.00	40.00
FANTASY					
❑ OJC-171	Songs I Like to Sing	198?	2.50	5.00	10.00
❑ OJC-453	'Tain't Nobody's Biz-Ness If I Do	1990	3.00	6.00	12.00
❑ OJC-608	Swingin' with Humes	1991	3.75	7.50	15.00
JAZZ MAN					
❑ 5003	On the Sunny Side of the Street	198?	2.50	5.00	10.00
JAZZOLOGY					
❑ J-55	Incomparable	197?	3.00	6.00	12.00
MUSE					
❑ MR-5217	Helen Humes with the Muse All Stars	197?	2.50	5.00	10.00
❑ MR-5233	Helen	1980	2.50	5.00	10.00
SAVOY JAZZ					
❑ SJL-1159	"E-Baba-Le-Ba": The Rhythm & Blues Years	1986	2.50	5.00	10.00
HUMPHREY, BOBBI					
Flutist and female singer.					
BLUE NOTE					
❑ BN-LA142-G	Blacks and Blues	1974	2.50	5.00	10.00
❑ BN-LA344-G	Satin Doll	1974	2.50	5.00	10.00
❑ BN-LA550-G	Fancy Dancer	1975	2.50	5.00	10.00
❑ BN-LA699-G	The Best of Bobbi Humphrey	1976	2.50	5.00	10.00
❑ BST-84379	Flute-In	1971	3.00	6.00	12.00
❑ BST-84421	Dig This	1972	3.00	6.00	12.00
EPIC					
❑ PE 34704	Tailor Made	1977	2.50	5.00	10.00
❑ JE 35338	Freestyle	1978	2.50	5.00	10.00
❑ JE 35607	The Good Life	1979	2.50	5.00	10.00
❑ JE 36368	The Best of Bobbi Humphrey	1980	2.50	5.00	10.00
HUMPHREY, EARL					
Trombonist and bandleader. Percy and Willie were his brothers.					
BIOGRAPH					
❑ CEN-11	Earl Humphrey and His Footwarmers	197?	3.00	6.00	12.00
HUMPHREY, PAUL					
Drummer. Had a pop and R&B hit with "Cool Aid" in 1971.					
BLUE THUMB					
❑ BTS 47	Supermellow	1973	3.00	6.00	12.00
❑ BTS 66	America, Wake Up!	1974	3.00	6.00	12.00
DISCOVERY					
❑ DS-850	Paul Humphrey Sextet	1981	2.50	5.00	10.00
LIZARD					
❑ 20106	Paul Humphrey & the Cool Aid Chemists	1971	3.75	7.50	15.00
HUMPHREY, PERCY					
Trumpeter. He, Earl and Willie were brothers.					
BIOGRAPH					
❑ CEN-13	Percy Humphrey at Manny's	197?	3.00	6.00	12.00
GHB					
❑ 85	Percy Humphrey and the Crescent City Joymakers	197?	2.50	5.00	10.00
JAZZOLOGY					
❑ JCE-26	Percy Humphrey and the Crescent City Joymakers	197?	3.00	6.00	12.00
PEARL					
❑ PS-3	Climax Rag	197?	3.75	7.50	15.00
RIVERSIDE					
❑ RLP-378 [M]	Percy Humphrey's Crescent City Joymakers	1961	7.50	15.00	30.00
❑ RS-9378 [R]	Percy Humphrey's Crescent City Joymakers	196?	3.75	7.50	15.00
HUMPHREY, WILLIE					
Clarinetist, brother of Earl and Percy.					
GHB					
❑ 248	New Orleans Jazz from Willie Humphrey	198?	2.50	5.00	10.00
HUNDLEY, CRAIG					
Keyboard player.					
WORLD PACIFIC					
❑ WPS-21896	The Craig Hundley Trio Plays with the Big Boys	1969	3.75	7.50	15.00
❑ WPS-21900	Rhapsody in Blue	1970	3.75	7.50	15.00
HUNT, PEE WEE					
Trombonist, male singer and bandleader.					
ALLEGRO					
❑ 1633 [M]	Dixieland	1956	6.25	12.50	25.00
CAPITOL					
❑ H 203 [10]	Straight from Dixie	1950	10.00	20.00	40.00
❑ H 312 [10]	Dixieland Detour	1952	10.00	20.00	40.00
❑ H 492 [10]	Swingin' Around	1954	10.00	20.00	40.00
❑ T 573 [M]	Dixieland Classics	1955	7.50	15.00	30.00

Number	Title	Yr	VG	VG+	NM
❑ T 783 [M]	Pee Wee and Fingers	1956	7.50	15.00	30.00
❑ ST 1362 [S]	Pee Wee Hunt's Dance Party	1960	5.00	10.00	20.00
❑ T 1362 [M]	Pee Wee Hunt's Dance Party	1960	3.75	7.50	15.00
❑ DT 1853 [R]	The Best of Pee Wee Hunt	1962	3.00	6.00	12.00
❑ T 1853 [M]	The Best of Pee Wee Hunt	1962	3.75	7.50	15.00

ROYALE

Number	Title	Yr	VG	VG+	NM
❑ 18153 [10]	Pee Wee Hunt and His Dixieland Band	195?	10.00	20.00	40.00

SOLITAIRE

Number	Title	Yr	VG	VG+	NM
❑ 507 [10]	Dixieland Capers	195?	7.50	15.00	30.00

HUNT, PEE WEE/PEE WEE RUSSELL
Also see each artist's individual listings.

RONDO-LETTE

Number	Title	Yr	VG	VG+	NM
❑ A 2 [M]	Dixieland: Pee Wee Hunt and Pee Wee Russell	195?	6.25	12.50	25.00

HUNTER, ALBERTA
Female singer.

COLUMBIA

Number	Title	Yr	VG	VG+	NM
❑ JC 36430	Amtrak Blues	1980	2.50	5.00	10.00
❑ FC 37691	The Glory of Alberta Hunter	1982	3.00	6.00	12.00
❑ PC 37691	The Glory of Alberta Hunter	1985	2.00	4.00	8.00
-- Budget-line reissue					
❑ FC 38970	Look for the Silver Lining	1984	2.50	5.00	10.00

DRG

Number	Title	Yr	VG	VG+	NM
❑ SL-5195	Legendary Alberta Hunter	198?	2.50	5.00	10.00

FANTASY

Number	Title	Yr	VG	VG+	NM
❑ OBC-510	Alberta Hunter with Lovie Austin's Blues Serenaders	198?	2.50	5.00	10.00

RIVERSIDE

Number	Title	Yr	VG	VG+	NM
❑ RLP-418 [M]	Alberta Hunter with Lovie Austin's Blues Serenaders	1962	7.50	15.00	30.00
❑ RS-9418 [R]	Alberta Hunter with Lovie Austin's Blues Serenaders	196?	3.75	7.50	15.00

STASH

Number	Title	Yr	VG	VG+	NM
❑ ST-115	Classic Alberta Hunter: The Thirties	198?	2.50	5.00	10.00

HUNTER, FRANK
Arranger and composer.

JUBILEE

Number	Title	Yr	VG	VG+	NM
❑ JLP-1020 [M]	Sounds of Hunter	1956	12.50	25.00	50.00

HUNTER, LURLEAN
Female singer.

ATLANTIC

Number	Title	Yr	VG	VG+	NM
❑ 1344 [M]	Blue and Sentimental	1960	12.50	25.00	50.00
❑ SD 1344 [S]	Blue and Sentimental	1960	15.00	30.00	60.00

RCA VICTOR

Number	Title	Yr	VG	VG+	NM
❑ LPM-1151 [M]	Lonesome Gal	1955	25.00	50.00	100.00

VIK

Number	Title	Yr	VG	VG+	NM
❑ LX-1061 [M]	Night Life	1956	20.00	40.00	80.00
❑ LX-1116 [M]	Stepping Out	1957	20.00	40.00	80.00

HUNTER, STAN, AND SONNY FORTUNE
Hunter is a keyboard player, Also see SONNY FORTUNE.

PRESTIGE

Number	Title	Yr	VG	VG+	NM
❑ PRLP-7458 [M]	Trip on the Strip	1967	7.50	15.00	30.00
❑ PRST-7458 [S]	Trip on the Strip	1967	5.00	10.00	20.00

HUSSAIN, ZAKIR
Tabla (Indian drum) player.

ECM

Number	Title	Yr	VG	VG+	NM
❑ 1349	Making Music	1987	2.50	5.00	10.00

HUTCHERSON, BOBBY
Vibraphone and marimba player.

BLUE NOTE

Number	Title	Yr	VG	VG+	NM
❑ BN-LA257-G	Cirrus	1973	3.00	6.00	12.00
❑ BN-LA396-G	Linger Lane	1974	3.00	6.00	12.00
❑ BN-LA551-G	Montara	1975	3.00	6.00	12.00
❑ BN-LA615-G	Waiting	1976	3.00	6.00	12.00
❑ BN-LA710-G	View from Inside	1977	3.00	6.00	12.00
❑ BN-LA789-H	Knucklebean	1977	3.00	6.00	12.00
❑ LT-996	Spiral	1979	2.50	5.00	10.00
❑ LT-1044	Patterns	1980	2.50	5.00	10.00
❑ LT-1086	Medina	1980	2.50	5.00	10.00
❑ BLP-4198 [M]	Dialogue	1965	6.25	12.50	25.00
❑ BLP-4213 [M]	Components	1966	6.25	12.50	25.00
❑ BLP-4231 [M]	Happenings	1967	7.50	15.00	30.00

Number	Title	Yr	VG	VG+	NM
❑ BLP-4244 [M]	Stick-Up!	1968	---	---	---
-- Scheduled for release in mono, but evidently never came out					
❑ B1-28268	San Francisco	1994	3.75	7.50	15.00
-- Reissue					
❑ B1-29027	Components	1994	3.75	7.50	15.00
-- Reissue					
❑ B1-33583	Patterns	1995	3.75	7.50	15.00
-- Reissue					
❑ BST-84198 [S]	Dialogue	1965	7.50	15.00	30.00
-- With "New York, USA" address on label					
❑ BST-84198 [S]	Dialogue	1967	3.75	7.50	15.00
-- With "A Division of Liberty Records" on label					
❑ BST-84198	Dialogue	198?	2.50	5.00	10.00
-- "The Finest in Jazz Since 1939" reissue					
❑ BST-84213 [S]	Components	1966	7.50	15.00	30.00
-- With "New York, USA" address on label					
❑ BST-84213 [S]	Components	1967	3.75	7.50	15.00
-- With "A Division of Liberty Records" on label					
❑ BST-84231 [S]	Happenings	1967	3.75	7.50	15.00
-- With "A Division of Liberty Records" on label					
❑ BST-84231 [S]	Happenings	1967	6.25	12.50	25.00
-- With "New York, USA" address on label					
❑ BST-84244 [S]	Stick-Up!	1968	5.00	10.00	20.00
-- With "A Division of Liberty Records" on label					
❑ BST-84291	Total Eclipse	1969	5.00	10.00	20.00
-- With "A Division of Liberty Records" on label					
❑ BST-84291	Total Eclipse	1985	2.50	5.00	10.00
-- "The Finest in Jazz Since 1939" reissue					
❑ BST-84333	Bobby Hutcherson Now	1969	5.00	10.00	20.00
-- With "A Division of Liberty Records" on label					
❑ BST-84362	San Francisco	1970	5.00	10.00	20.00
❑ BST-84376	Head On	1971	3.75	7.50	15.00
❑ BST-84416	Natural Illusions	1972	3.75	7.50	15.00

COLUMBIA

Number	Title	Yr	VG	VG+	NM
❑ JC 35550	Highway 1	1978	2.50	5.00	10.00
❑ JC 35814	Conception: The Gift of Love	1979	2.50	5.00	10.00
❑ FC 36402	Un Poco Loco	1980	2.50	5.00	10.00

CONTEMPORARY

Number	Title	Yr	VG	VG+	NM
❑ C-14009	Solo/Quartet	1982	3.00	6.00	12.00

FANTASY

Number	Title	Yr	VG	VG+	NM
❑ OJC-425	Solo/Quartet	1990	3.00	6.00	12.00

LANDMARK

Number	Title	Yr	VG	VG+	NM
❑ LLP-501	Good Bait	1985	3.00	6.00	12.00
❑ LLP-1508	Color Schemes	1986	3.00	6.00	12.00
❑ LLP-1513	In the Vanguard	1987	3.00	6.00	12.00
❑ LLP-1517	Cruisin' the 'Bird	1988	3.00	6.00	12.00
❑ LLP-1522	Ambos Mundos	1989	3.75	7.50	15.00

THERESA

Number	Title	Yr	VG	VG+	NM
❑ TR-124	Farewell Keystone	1989	3.00	6.00	12.00

HYLTON, JACK
British pianist, organist, male singer and bandleader.

FLAPPER

Number	Title	Yr	VG	VG+	NM
❑ 702	Jack Hylton and His Orchestra 1925-28: Light Music from the Variety Stage	198?	2.50	5.00	10.00

HYMAN, DICK
Pianist, harpsichord player, organist, Moog synthesizer pioneer, bandleader, arranger and composer. His version of "Moritat (Mack the Knife)" was second only to Bobby Darin's in sales.

CHIAROSCURO

Number	Title	Yr	VG	VG+	NM
❑ 198	Themes and Variations on "A Child Is Born"	1978	2.50	5.00	10.00

COLUMBIA MASTERWORKS

Number	Title	Yr	VG	VG+	NM
❑ M 32587	Ferdinand "Jelly Roll" Morton -- Transcriptions for Orchestra	1974	3.00	6.00	12.00

COMMAND

Number	Title	Yr	VG	VG+	NM
❑ RS 33-811 [M]	Provocative Piano	1960	3.75	7.50	15.00
❑ RS 811 SD [S]	Provocative Piano	1960	5.00	10.00	20.00
❑ RS 33-824 [M]	Provocative Piano Volume 2	1961	3.75	7.50	15.00
❑ RS 824 SD [S]	Provocative Piano Volume 2	1961	5.00	10.00	20.00
❑ RS 33-832 [M]	The Dick Hyman Trio	1961	3.75	7.50	15.00
❑ RS 832 SD [S]	The Dick Hyman Trio	1961	5.00	10.00	20.00
❑ RS 33-856 [M]	Electrodynamics	1963	3.75	7.50	15.00
❑ RS 856 SD [S]	Electrodynamics	1963	5.00	10.00	20.00
❑ RS 33-862 [M]	Fabulous	1963	3.75	7.50	15.00
❑ RS 862 SD [S]	Fabulous	1963	5.00	10.00	20.00
❑ RS 33-875 [M]	Keyboard Kaleidoscope	1964	3.75	7.50	15.00
❑ RS 875 SD [S]	Keyboard Kaleidoscope	1964	5.00	10.00	20.00
❑ RS 33-891 [M]	The Man from O.R.G.A.N.	1965	5.00	10.00	20.00
❑ RS 891 SD [S]	The Man from O.R.G.A.N.	1965	6.25	12.50	25.00
❑ RS 33-899 [M]	Happening!	1966	3.75	7.50	15.00
❑ RS 899 SD [S]	Happening!	1966	5.00	10.00	20.00
❑ RS 33-911 [M]	Brazilian Impressions	1966	3.75	7.50	15.00
❑ RS 911 SD [S]	Brazilian Impressions	1966	5.00	10.00	20.00
❑ RS 924 SD	Mirrors	1967	5.00	10.00	20.00

Number	Title	Yr	VG	VG+	NM
❏ RS 938 SD	Moog -- The Electric Eclectics of Dick Hyman	1968	7.50	15.00	30.00
❏ RS 946 SD	The Age of Electronicus	1969	7.50	15.00	30.00
❏ RS 951 SD	Concerto Electro	1970	7.50	15.00	30.00
GRAPEVINE					
❏ 3309	Waltz Dressed in Blue	1978	3.00	6.00	12.00
MGM					
❏ E-3280 [M]	The Dick Hyman Trio Swings	1954	6.25	12.50	25.00
-- Yellow label					
❏ E-3329 [M]	The "Unforgettable" Sound of the Dick Hyman Trio	1955	6.25	12.50	25.00
-- Yellow label					
❏ E-3379 [M]	Behind a Shady Nook	1956	6.25	12.50	25.00
-- Yellow label					
❏ E-3483 [M]	Red Sails in the Sunset	1957	6.25	12.50	25.00
-- Yellow label					
❏ E-3494 [M]	Hi-Fi Suite	1957	6.25	12.50	25.00
-- Yellow label					
❏ E-3535 [M]	60 Great All-Time Songs, Vol. 1	1957	5.00	10.00	20.00
-- Yellow label					
❏ E-3536 [M]	60 Great All-Time Songs, Vol. 2	1957	5.00	10.00	20.00
-- Yellow label					
❏ E-3537 [M]	60 Great All-Time Songs, Vol. 3	1957	5.00	10.00	20.00
-- Yellow label					
❏ E-3553 [M]	Rockin' Sax and Rollin' Organ	1958	6.25	12.50	25.00
-- Yellow label					
❏ E-3586 [M]	60 Great All-Time Songs, Vol. 4	1958	5.00	10.00	20.00
-- Yellow label					
❏ E-3587 [M]	60 Great All-Time Songs, Vol. 5	1958	5.00	10.00	20.00
-- Yellow label					
❏ E-3588 [M]	60 Great All-Time Songs, Vol. 6	1958	5.00	10.00	20.00
-- Yellow label					
❏ E-3606 [M]	Dick Hyman and Harpsichord in Hi-Fi	1958	5.00	10.00	20.00
-- Yellow label					
❏ E-3642 [M]	Gigi	1958	5.00	10.00	20.00
-- Yellow label					
❏ E-3724 [M]	60 Great Songs That Say "I Love You"	1959	5.00	10.00	20.00
-- Yellow label					
❏ E-3725 [M]	60 Great Songs from Broadway Musicals	1959	5.00	10.00	20.00
-- Yellow label					
❏ E-3747 [M]	Whoop-Up!	1959	5.00	10.00	20.00
-- Yellow label					
❏ E-3808 [M]	Strictly Organic	1960	5.00	10.00	20.00
❏ E-4119 [M]	Moon Gas	1963	5.00	10.00	20.00
❏ SE-4119 [S]	Moon Gas	1963	7.50	15.00	30.00
❏ SE-4649	Space Reflex	1969	3.75	7.50	15.00
MONMOUTH-EVERGREEN					
❏ 7065	Genius at Play	197?	3.75	7.50	15.00
PROJECT 3					
❏ PR 5054 SD	The Sensuous Piano of "D"	1970	3.75	7.50	15.00
❏ PR 5057 SD	Fantomfingers	1971	3.75	7.50	15.00
❏ PR 5070 SD	Piano Solos	1972	3.75	7.50	15.00
❏ PR 5080 SD	Traditional Jazz Piano	1973	3.75	7.50	15.00
REFERENCE RECORDINGS					
❏ RR-33	Dick Hyman Plays Fats Waller	1991	6.25	12.50	25.00
SEAGULL					
❏ LG-8209	Love Story	198?	2.50	5.00	10.00
STOMP OFF					
❏ SOS-1141	Gulf Coast Blues: The Music of Clarence Williams	1987	2.50	5.00	10.00

Number	Title	Yr	VG	VG+	NM

I

IBRAHIM, ABDULLAH
Pianist, male singer, cellist, flutist and soprano saxophone player. Originally recorded under the name "Dollar Brand"; those albums are also listed below.
BLACK LION
| ❏ 192 | This Is Dollar Brand | 197? | 3.00 | 6.00 | 12.00 |
BLACKHAWK
| ❏ BKH-50207 | Water from an Ancient Well | 1986 | 2.50 | 5.00 | 10.00 |
CHIAROSCURO
❏ 187	Journey	1978	3.00	6.00	12.00
❏ 2004	Cape Town Fringe	197?	3.00	6.00	12.00
❏ 2012	Soweto	197?	3.00	6.00	12.00
DENON
| ❏ 7537 | Anthems for the New Nations | 1978 | 3.00 | 6.00 | 12.00 |
ELEKTRA
| ❏ 6E-252 | African Marketplace | 1980 | 2.50 | 5.00 | 10.00 |
ENJA
❏ 2026	African Sketchbook	197?	3.75	7.50	15.00
❏ 2032	African Space Program	197?	3.75	7.50	15.00
❏ 2048	Good News from Africa	1976	3.75	7.50	15.00
❏ R1-79601	Mindif (Original Soundtrack Recording for the Film "Chocolat")	1989	3.75	7.50	15.00
❏ R1-79617	African River	1990	3.75	7.50	15.00
INNER CITY
❏ IC-3003	Children of Africa	197?	3.00	6.00	12.00
❏ IC-3031	Tears and Laughter	1979	3.00	6.00	12.00
❏ IC-6049	Ode to Duke Ellington	198?	2.50	5.00	10.00
REPRISE
| ❏ R-6111 [M] | Duke Ellington Presents the Dollar Brand Trio | 1965 | 5.00 | 10.00 | 20.00 |
| ❏ RS-6111 [S] | Duke Ellington Presents the Dollar Brand Trio | 1965 | 6.25 | 12.50 | 25.00 |
SACKVILLE
| ❏ 3009 | African Portraits | 198? | 2.50 | 5.00 | 10.00 |
WEST 54
| ❏ 8011 | Memories | 1979 | 3.00 | 6.00 | 12.00 |

ILORI, SOLOMON
Guitarist, percussionist and male singer.
BLUE NOTE
❏ BLP-4136 [M]	African High Life	1963	15.00	30.00	60.00
❏ BST-84136 [S]	African High Life	1963	20.00	40.00	80.00
-- With "New York, USA" address on label					
❏ BST-84136 [S]	African High Life	1967	6.25	12.50	25.00
-- With "A Division of Liberty Records" on label					

IND, PETER
Bass player.
WAVE
| ❏ W-1 [M] | Looking Out | 1961 | 6.25 | 12.50 | 25.00 |
| ❏ WS-1 [S] | Looking Out | 1961 | 7.50 | 15.00 | 30.00 |

INSTANT COMPOSERS POOL (ICP ORCHESTRA)
A fluid organization with MISHA MENGELBERG as the constant.
ICP
❏ 020	Tetterettet	1977	6.25	12.50	25.00
❏ 022	Live Soncino	1980	6.25	12.50	25.00
❏ 026	The ICP Orchestra Performs Nichols-Monk	1987	3.75	7.50	15.00

INTERNATIONAL JAZZ BAND
Members: Kid Thomas Valentine, BILL BISSONETTE, Sammy Rimington, Emanuel Paul, Bill Sinclair, Dick Griffith, Dick McCarthy, Barry Martyn.
GHB
| ❏ 20 | International Jazz Band Volume 1 | 1966 | 3.75 | 7.50 | 15.00 |
| ❏ 21 | International Jazz Band Volume 2 | 1966 | 3.75 | 7.50 | 15.00 |

INTERNATIONAL JAZZ GROUP
Led by Andre Persiany.
SWING
| ❏ SW-8407 | International Jazz Group, Volume 1 | 198? | 2.50 | 5.00 | 10.00 |
| ❏ SW-8416 | International Jazz Group, Volume 2 | 1987 | 2.50 | 5.00 | 10.00 |

IRAKERE
Cuban jazz band founded by Chucho Valdes (piano), ARTURO SANDOVAL, PAQUITO D'RIVERA and Oscar Valdes. Many membership changes in its history.
COLUMBIA
| ❏ JC 35655 | Irakere | 1979 | 3.00 | 6.00 | 12.00 |
| ❏ JC 36107 | Irakere II | 1980 | 3.00 | 6.00 | 12.00 |
MILESTONE
| ❏ M-9103 | Chekere Son | 198? | 3.00 | 6.00 | 12.00 |
| ❏ M-9111 | El Coco | 198? | 3.00 | 6.00 | 12.00 |

IRVIN, BOOKER
See BOOKER ERVIN.

IRVIN, TINY
Female singer.
EARWIG
| ❏ LPS-4903 | You Don't Know What Love Is | 1986 | 3.00 | 6.00 | 12.00 |

IRVINE, WELDON
Organist, pianist and keyboard player.
NODLEW
| ❏ 1001 | Liberated Brother | 1972 | 25.00 | 50.00 | 100.00 |
| ❏ 1002 | Time Capsule | 1973 | 25.00 | 50.00 | 100.00 |
RCA VICTOR
❏ APL1-0703	Cosmic Vortex	1974	20.00	40.00	80.00
❏ APL1-0909	Spirit Man	1975	20.00	40.00	80.00
❏ APL1-1363	Sinbad	1976	20.00	40.00	80.00
STRATA-EAST
| ❏ SES-19479 | In Harmony | 1974 | 10.00 | 20.00 | 40.00 |

ISAACS, IKE
Guitarist.
RGB
| ❏ 2000 | Ike Isaccs at the Pied Piper | 197? | 3.00 | 6.00 | 12.00 |

ISHAM, MARK
Trumpeter, keyboard player and composer.
VIRGIN
| ❏ 90900 | Castalia | 1988 | 2.50 | 5.00 | 10.00 |
WINDHAM HILL
❏ WH-1027	Vapor Drawings	1983	2.50	5.00	10.00
❏ WH-1041	Film Music of Mark Isham	1985	2.50	5.00	10.00
❏ WH-1080	Tibet	1989	3.00	6.00	12.00

ITOH, KIMIKO
Female singer.
COLUMBIA
| ❏ FC 44203 | For Lovers Only | 1988 | 2.50 | 5.00 | 10.00 |
| ❏ FC 45214 | Follow Me | 1989 | 3.00 | 6.00 | 12.00 |

Number	Title	Yr	VG	VG+	NM

J

J.F.K. QUINTET, THE
Among the members of this group were Andrew White on alto saxophone and Walter Booker on bass.
RIVERSIDE
❏ RLP-396 [M]	New Frontiers from Washington	1961	7.50	15.00	30.00
❏ RLP-424 [M]	Young Ideas	1962	7.50	15.00	30.00
❏ RS-9396 [S]	New Frontiers from Washington	1961	10.00	20.00	40.00
❏ RS-9424 [S]	Young Ideas	1962	10.00	20.00	40.00

J.J. & KAI
See J.J. JOHNSON AND KAI WINDING.

JACINTHA
Female singer.
GROOVE NOTE
❏ 2001	Here's to Ben	1999	6.25	12.50	25.00
-- Audiophile vinyl					

JACK PINE SAVAGES, THE
JIM TAYLOR PRESENTS
❏ 104	The Beiderbecke Legend Is Alive and Well	197?	3.75	7.50	15.00

JACKIE AND ROY
See JACKIE CAIN AND ROY KRAL.

JACKSON, CALVIN
Pianist and composer.
COLUMBIA
❏ CL 756 [M]	Calvin JacksonAlive and the All Stars Quartet	1956	12.50	25.00	50.00
❏ CL 824 [M]	Rave Notice	1956	12.50	25.00	50.00
LIBERTY
❏ LRP-3071 [M]	Jazz Variations	1957	10.00	20.00	40.00
"X"
❏ LXA-1005 [M]	Calvin Jackson at the Plaza	1954	12.50	25.00	50.00

JACKSON, CHUBBY
Bass player.
ARGO
❏ LP-614 [M]	Chubby's Back	1957	12.50	25.00	50.00
❏ LPS-614 [S]	Chubby's Back	1959	10.00	20.00	40.00
❏ LP-625 [M]	I'm Entitled to You	1958	12.50	25.00	50.00
EVEREST
❏ SDBR-1009 [S]	Chubby Takes Over	1959	10.00	20.00	40.00
❏ SDBR-1029 [S]	The Big Three	1959	10.00	20.00	40.00
❏ SDBR-1041 [S]	Jazz Then Till Now	1960	10.00	20.00	40.00
❏ LPBR-5009 [M]	Chubby Takes Over	1959	7.50	15.00	30.00
❏ LPBR-5029 [M]	The Big Three	1959	7.50	15.00	30.00
❏ LPBR-5041 [M]	Jazz Then Till Now	1960	7.50	15.00	30.00
LAURIE
❏ LLP-2011 [M]	Twist Calling	1962	6.25	12.50	25.00
NEW JAZZ
❏ NJLP-105 [10]	Chubby Jackson and His All Star Band	1950	100.00	200.00	400.00
-- Either an original or erroneous pressing of Prestige 105					
PRESTIGE
❏ PRLP-105 [10]	Chubby Jackson and His All Star Band	1951	75.00	150.00	300.00
❏ PRST-7641	Chubby Jackson Sextet and Big Band	1969	5.00	10.00	20.00
RAINBOW
❏ 708 [10]	Chubby Jackson	1951	50.00	100.00	200.00
STEREO-CRAFT
❏ RTN-108 [M]	The Big Three	195?	12.50	25.00	50.00
❏ RTS-108 [S]	The Big Three	195?	12.50	25.00	50.00

JACKSON, CHUBBY, AND BILL HARRIS (2)
Also see each artist's individual listings.
EMARCY
❏ MG-26003 [10]	The Small Herd	1954	25.00	50.00	100.00
❏ MG-26012 [M]	Out of the Herd	1965	5.00	10.00	20.00
❏ SR-66012 [R]	Out of the Herd	1965	3.00	6.00	12.00
MERCURY
❏ MG-25076 [10]	Jazz Journey	1950	75.00	150.00	300.00

JACKSON, FRANZ
Tenor saxophone player, clarinetist, male singer and arranger.
PINNACLE
❏ 102 [M]	No Saints	1961	5.00	10.00	20.00
❏ 104 [M]	Night at Red Arrow	196?	3.75	7.50	15.00
❏ S-104 [S]	Night at Red Arrow	196?	5.00	10.00	20.00
❏ 109 [M]	Franz Jackson	1966	5.00	10.00	20.00
RIVERSIDE
❏ RLP-406 [M]	Franz Jackson and the Original Jass All-Stars	1962	7.50	15.00	30.00
❏ RS-9406 [R]	Franz Jackson and the Original Jass All-Stars	196?	3.75	7.50	15.00

JACKSON, FRED
Tenor saxophone player.
BLUE NOTE
❏ BLP-4094 [M]	Hootin' 'N Tootin'	1962	15.00	30.00	60.00
-- With 61st St. address on label					
❏ BLP-4094 [M]	Hootin' 'N Tootin'	1963	6.25	12.50	25.00
-- With "New York, USA" address on label					
❏ BST-84094 [S]	Hootin' 'N Tootin'	1962	20.00	40.00	80.00
-- With 61st St. address on label					
❏ BST-84094 [S]	Hootin' 'N Tootin'	1963	7.50	15.00	30.00
-- With "New York, USA" address on label					
❏ BST-84094 [S]	Hootin' 'N Tootin'	1967	5.00	10.00	20.00
-- With "A Division of Liberty Records" on label					

JACKSON, MARY ANNE
Pianist; actually STEVE ALLEN in disguise. (The woman on the cover is Allen's maid.)
HANOVER
❏ HM-8009 [M]	The Wild Piano of Mary Anne Jackson	1959	20.00	40.00	80.00

JACKSON, MICHAEL GREGORY
Guitarist.
ARISTA/NOVUS
❏ AN 3015	Heart & Center	1979	3.75	7.50	15.00
BIJA
❏ 1000	Clarity	1976	6.25	12.50	25.00
ENJA
❏ 4026	Cowboys, Cartoons and Assorted Candy	1982	3.75	7.50	15.00
IAI
❏ 373857	Karmonic Suite	1978	5.00	10.00	20.00

JACKSON, MILT
Vibraphone player, occasional pianist and male singer. He was the co-founder of THE MODERN JAZZ QUARTET. Also see RAY BROWN; MILES DAVIS; HOWARD McGHEE.
ABC IMPULSE!
❏ AS-14 [S]	Statements	1968	3.75	7.50	15.00
❏ AS-70 [S]	Jazz n' Samba	1968	3.75	7.50	15.00
❏ AS-9189	That's the Way It Is	1969	5.00	10.00	20.00
❏ AS-9193	Memphis Jackson	1969	5.00	10.00	20.00
❏ AS-9230	Milt Jackson Quartet	1973	3.00	6.00	12.00
❏ AS-9282 [(2)]	The Impulse Years	1974	3.75	7.50	15.00
ATLANTIC
❏ SD 2-319 [(2)]	The Art of Milt Jackson	197?	3.75	7.50	15.00
❏ 1242 [M]	Ballads and Blues	1956	10.00	20.00	40.00
-- Black label					
❏ 1242 [M]	Ballads and Blues	1961	5.00	10.00	20.00
-- Multicolor label, white "fan" logo at right					
❏ 1242 [M]	Ballads and Blues	1963	3.75	7.50	15.00
-- Multicolor label, black "fan" logo at right					
❏ 1269 [M]	Plenty, Plenty Soul	1957	10.00	20.00	40.00
-- Black label					
❏ 1269 [M]	Plenty, Plenty Soul	1961	5.00	10.00	20.00
-- Multicolor label, white "fan" logo at right					
❏ 1269 [M]	Plenty, Plenty Soul	1963	3.75	7.50	15.00
-- Multicolor label, black "fan" logo at right					
❏ SD 1269 [S]	Plenty, Plenty Soul	1959	10.00	20.00	40.00
-- Green label					
❏ SD 1269 [S]	Plenty, Plenty Soul	1961	5.00	10.00	20.00
-- Multicolor label, white "fan" logo at right					
❏ SD 1269 [S]	Plenty, Plenty Soul	1963	3.75	7.50	15.00
-- Multicolor label, black "fan" logo at right					
❏ 1294 [M]	Bags & Flutes	1958	10.00	20.00	40.00
-- Black label					
❏ 1294 [M]	Bags & Flutes	1961	5.00	10.00	20.00
-- Multicolor label, white "fan" logo at right					
❏ 1294 [M]	Bags & Flutes	1963	3.75	7.50	15.00
-- Multicolor label, black "fan" logo at right					
❏ SD 1294 [S]	Bags & Flutes	1959	10.00	20.00	40.00
-- Green label					
❏ SD 1294 [S]	Bags & Flutes	1961	5.00	10.00	20.00
-- Multicolor label, white "fan" logo at right					

Number	Title	Yr	VG	VG+	NM
❏ SD 1294 [S]	Bags & Flutes	1963	3.75	7.50	15.00
-- Multicolor label, black "fan" logo at right					
❏ 1316 [M]	Bean Bags	1959	10.00	20.00	40.00
-- Black label					
❏ 1316 [M]	Bean Bags	1961	5.00	10.00	20.00
-- Multicolor label, white "fan" logo at right					
❏ 1316 [M]	Bean Bags	1963	3.75	7.50	15.00
-- Multicolor label, black "fan" logo at right					
❏ SD 1316 [S]	Bean Bags	1959	10.00	20.00	40.00
-- Green label					
❏ SD 1316 [S]	Bean Bags	1961	5.00	10.00	20.00
-- Multicolor label, white "fan" logo at right					
❏ SD 1316 [S]	Bean Bags	1963	3.75	7.50	15.00
-- Multicolor label, black "fan" logo at right					
❏ 1342 [M]	Ballad Artistry	1960	5.00	10.00	20.00
-- Multicolor label, white "fan" logo at right					
❏ 1342 [M]	Ballad Artistry	1963	3.75	7.50	15.00
-- Multicolor label, black "fan" logo at right					
❏ SD 1342 [S]	Ballad Artistry	1960	6.25	12.50	25.00
-- Multicolor label, white "fan" logo at right					
❏ SD 1342 [S]	Ballad Artistry	1963	5.00	10.00	20.00
-- Multicolor label, black "fan" logo at right					
❏ 1417 [M]	Vibrations	1964	3.75	7.50	15.00
❏ SD 1417 [S]	Vibrations	1964	5.00	10.00	20.00
❏ SD 8811	Plenty, Plenty Soul	198?	2.50	5.00	10.00
❏ 90465	Bean Bags	1986	2.50	5.00	10.00
BLUE NOTE					
❏ BN-LA590-H2 [(2)]	All Star Bags	1976	3.75	7.50	15.00
❏ BLP-1509 [M]	Milt Jackson	1956	25.00	50.00	100.00
-- Regular version with Lexington Ave. address on label					
❏ BLP-1509 [M]	Milt Jackson	1956	37.50	75.00	150.00
-- "Deep groove" version (deep indentation under label on both sides)					
❏ BLP-1509 [M]	Milt Jackson	1963	6.25	12.50	25.00
-- With "New York, USA" address on label					
❏ BLP-5011 [10]	Wizard of the Vibes	1952	75.00	150.00	300.00
❏ B1-81509	Milt Jackson	1987	2.50	5.00	10.00
-- "The Finest in Jazz Since 1939" reissue					
❏ BST-81509 [R]	Milt Jackson	196?	3.75	7.50	15.00
-- With "A Division of Liberty Records" on label					
CTI					
❏ 6024	Sunflower	1973	3.75	7.50	15.00
❏ 6038	Goodbye	1974	3.75	7.50	15.00
❏ 6046	Olinga	1974	3.75	7.50	15.00
❏ 8004	Sunflower	197?	2.50	5.00	10.00
-- Reissue of 6024					
DEE GEE					
❏ 1002 [10]	Milt Jackson	1952	75.00	150.00	300.00
EASTWEST					
❏ 90991	Bebop	1988	3.00	6.00	12.00
FANTASY					
❏ OJC-001	Milt Jackson Quartet	1982	3.75	7.50	15.00
❏ OJC-260	Invitation	1987	2.50	5.00	10.00
❏ OJC-309	"Live" at the Village Gate	1988	2.50	5.00	10.00
❏ OJC-366	Big Bags	198?	2.50	5.00	10.00
❏ OJC-375	Montreux '77	198?	2.50	5.00	10.00
❏ OJC-404	For Someone I Love	1989	3.00	6.00	12.00
❏ OJC-448	Feelings	1990	2.50	5.00	10.00
❏ OJC-601	It Don't Mean a Thing If You Can't Tap Your Foot To It	1991	3.75	7.50	15.00
GNP CRESCENDO					
❏ GNP-9007	Milt Jackson	197?	2.50	5.00	10.00
IMPULSE!					
❏ A-14 [M]	Statements	1962	6.25	12.50	25.00
❏ AS-14 [S]	Statements	1962	7.50	15.00	30.00
❏ A-70 [M]	Jazz n' Samba	1964	6.25	12.50	25.00
❏ AS-70 [S]	Jazz n' Samba	1964	7.50	15.00	30.00
LIMELIGHT					
❏ LM-82006 [M]	In a New Setting	1964	5.00	10.00	20.00
❏ LM-82024 [M]	At the Museum of Modern Art	1965	5.00	10.00	20.00
❏ LM-82045 [M]	Born Free	1966	5.00	10.00	20.00
❏ LS-86006 [S]	In a New Setting	1964	6.25	12.50	25.00
❏ LS-86024 [S]	At the Museum of Modern Art	1965	6.25	12.50	25.00
❏ LS-86045 [S]	Born Free	1966	6.25	12.50	25.00
MILESTONE					
❏ 47006 [(2)]	Big Band Bags	1972	3.75	7.50	15.00
PABLO					
❏ 2310 753	The Big 4 at Montreux '75	1976	3.00	6.00	12.00
❏ 2310 757	The Big 3	1976	3.00	6.00	12.00
❏ 2310 774	Feelings	1976	3.00	6.00	12.00
❏ 2310 822	Milt Jackson with Count Basie and the Big Band, Volume 1	1978	3.00	6.00	12.00
❏ 2310 823	Milt Jackson with Count Basie and the Big Band, Volume 2	1978	3.00	6.00	12.00
❏ 2310 832	Soul Believer	1979	3.00	6.00	12.00
❏ 2310 842	Bag's Bag	1979	3.00	6.00	12.00

Number	Title	Yr	VG	VG+	NM
❏ 2310 867	Big Mouth	198?	3.00	6.00	12.00
❏ 2310 873	Ain't But a Few of Us Left	198?	3.00	6.00	12.00
❏ 2310 897	Milt Jackson & Co.	198?	3.00	6.00	12.00
❏ 2310 909	It Don't Mean a Thing If You Can't Tap Your Foot To It	1986	3.75	7.50	15.00
❏ 2310 916	Brother Jim	1987	2.50	5.00	10.00
❏ 2310 932	A London Bridge	1988	3.00	6.00	12.00
❏ 2405 405	The Best of Milt Jackson	198?	2.50	5.00	10.00
PABLO LIVE					
❏ 2308 205	Montreux '77	1977	3.00	6.00	12.00
❏ 2308 235	Live in London: Memories of Thelonious Monk	198?	3.00	6.00	12.00
❏ 2620 103 [(2)]	Kosei Nenkin	197?	3.75	7.50	15.00
PABLO TODAY					
❏ 2312 124	Nightmist	198?	3.00	6.00	12.00
PRESTIGE					
❏ PRLP-183 [10]	Milt Jackson Quintet	1954	50.00	100.00	200.00
❏ PRLP-7003 [M]	Milt Jackson	1955	30.00	60.00	120.00
❏ PRLP-7224 [M]	Soul Pioneers	1962	10.00	20.00	40.00
❏ PRST-7655	The Complete Milt Jackson	1969	3.75	7.50	15.00
❏ 24048 [(2)]	Opus de Funk	197?	3.75	7.50	15.00
QUINTESSENCE					
❏ 25391	Milt Jackson (1961-69)	1980	2.50	5.00	10.00
RIVERSIDE					
❏ RLP-429 [M]	Big Bags	1962	5.00	10.00	20.00
❏ RLP-446 [M]	Invitation	1963	5.00	10.00	20.00
❏ RLP-478 [M]	For Someone I Love	1966	5.00	10.00	20.00
❏ RLP-495 [M]	"Live" at the Village Gate	1967	6.25	12.50	25.00
❏ 3021	Bags and Brass	1968	3.75	7.50	15.00
❏ RS-9429 [S]	Big Bags	1962	6.25	12.50	25.00
❏ RS-9446 [S]	Invitation	1963	6.25	12.50	25.00
❏ RS-9478 [S]	For Someone I Love	1966	6.25	12.50	25.00
❏ RS-9495 [S]	"Live" at the Village Gate	1967	5.00	10.00	20.00
SAVOY					
❏ MG-12042 [M]	Roll 'Em Bags	1955	12.50	25.00	50.00
❏ MG-12046 [M]	Milt Jackson Quartette	1955	12.50	25.00	50.00
❏ MG-12061 [M]	Meet Milt	1956	12.50	25.00	50.00
❏ MG-12070 [M]	Jazz Skyline	1956	12.50	25.00	50.00
❏ MG-12080 [M]	Jackson's Ville	1956	12.50	25.00	50.00
❏ MG-15058 [10]	Milt Jackson	1954	37.50	75.00	150.00
SAVOY JAZZ					
❏ SJC-410	The Jazz Skyline	1985	2.50	5.00	10.00
❏ SJL-1106	The First Q	197?	2.50	5.00	10.00
❏ SJL-1130	Bluesology	198?	2.50	5.00	10.00
❏ SJL-2204 [(2)]	Second Nature	197?	3.00	6.00	12.00
TRIP					
❏ 5553	At the Museum of Modern Art	197?	2.50	5.00	10.00
UNITED ARTISTS					
❏ UAL-4022 [M]	Bags' Opus	1959	10.00	20.00	40.00
❏ UAS-5022 [S]	Bags' Opus	1959	7.50	15.00	30.00
VERVE					
❏ V6-8761	Milt Jackson and the Hip String Quartet	1969	3.75	7.50	15.00

JACKSON, MILT, AND MONTY ALEXANDER
Also see each artist's individual listings.
PABLO

❏ 2310 804	Soul Fusion	1978	3.00	6.00	12.00

JACKSON, MILT, AND JOHN COLTRANE
Also see each artist's individual listings.
ATLANTIC

❏ 1368 [M]	Bags and Trane	1961	7.50	15.00	30.00
-- Multicolor label, white "fan" logo at right					
❏ 1368 [M]	Bags and Trane	1963	5.00	10.00	20.00
-- Multicolor label, black "fan" logo at right					
❏ SD 1368 [S]	Bags and Trane	1961	10.00	20.00	40.00
-- Multicolor label, white "fan" logo at right					
❏ SD 1368 [S]	Bags and Trane	1963	6.25	12.50	25.00
-- Multicolor label, black "fan" logo at right					

JACKSON, MILT, AND WES MONTGOMERY
Also see each artist's individual listings.
FANTASY

❏ OJC-234	Bags Meets Wes	198?	2.50	5.00	10.00
RIVERSIDE					
❏ RLP-407 [M]	Bags Meets Wes	1962	5.00	10.00	20.00
❏ 6058	Bags Meets Wes	197?	3.00	6.00	12.00
❏ RS-9407 [S]	Bags Meets Wes	1962	6.25	12.50	25.00

JACKSON, MUNYUNGO
Percussionist.
VITAL MUSIC

❏ VTL-002	Munyungo	199?	3.75	7.50	15.00

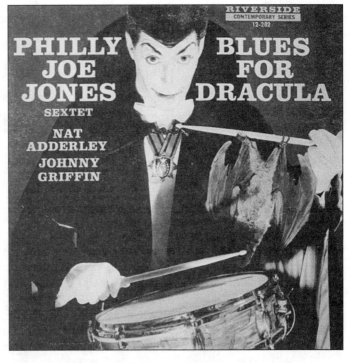

(Top left) Milt Jackson, vibraphone player extraordinaire and co-founder of the Modern Jazz Quartet, made plenty of albums as a leader. His only one on the early United Artists label is pictured above. (Top right) Many years before Chuck Mangione became a major star with "Feels So Good" and other similar material, he was in a band with his brother Gap called The Jazz Brothers. They did three albums for Riverside before splitting up. During the height of Mangione's popularity, the originals skyrocketed in price, but are much more reasonable now. (Bottom left) Elvin Jones was the drummer with John Coltrane from 1960-65, during which time Coltrane made some of his most important albums. After leaving, his first new release was *Dear John C.* in 1966. (Bottom right) Philly Joe Jones, an in-demand drummer in the 1950s, made his first album as a leader with *Blues for Dracula*, which he starts with a dead-on impersonation of Bela Lugosi as Dracula before he gets into the really good stuff.

Number	Title	Yr	VG	VG+	NM
JACKSON, PAUL, JR.					
Guitarist.					
ATLANTIC					
❑ 81841	I Came to Play	1988	2.50	5.00	10.00
❑ 82065	Out of the Shadows	1990	3.00	6.00	12.00
JACKSON, RONALD SHANNON					
Drummer and percussionist; has also played flute on record.					
ABOUT TIME					
❑ AT-1003	Eye on You	1980	5.00	10.00	20.00
ANTILLES					
❑ AN-1008	Man Dance	1982	3.75	7.50	15.00
❑ AN-1015	Barbeque Dog	1983	3.75	7.50	15.00
CARAVAN OF DREAMS					
❑ 009	When Colors Play	1987	3.75	7.50	15.00
❑ 012	Texas	1988	3.75	7.50	15.00
❑ 85005	Live at the Caravan of Dreams	1986	3.75	7.50	15.00
ISLAND					
❑ 90247	Decode Yourself	1985	2.50	5.00	10.00
MOERS					
❑ 01081	Street Priest	1981	5.00	10.00	20.00
❑ 01086	Nasty	1981	5.00	10.00	20.00
OAO/CELLULOID					
❑ 5011	Pulse	1984	3.75	7.50	15.00
JACKSON, WILLIS					
Tenor saxophone player.					
ATLANTIC					
❑ SD 18145	The Way We Were	1975	3.00	6.00	12.00
CADET					
❑ LP-763 [M]	Smoking with Willis	1966	3.75	7.50	15.00
❑ LPS-763 [S]	Smoking with Willis	1966	5.00	10.00	20.00
COTILLION					
❑ SD 9908	Willis Jackson Plays with Feeling	1977	3.75	7.50	15.00
CTI					
❑ 6024	Sunflower	1972	3.75	7.50	15.00
FANTASY					
❑ OJC-220	Cool Gator	198?	2.50	5.00	10.00
❑ OJC-321	Please, Mr. Jackson	1988	2.50	5.00	10.00
MOODSVILLE					
❑ MVLP-17 [M]	In My Solitude	1961	12.50	25.00	50.00
-- Green label					
❑ MVLP-17 [M]	In My Solitude	1965	6.25	12.50	25.00
-- Blue label, trident logo at right					
MUSE					
❑ MR-5036	West Africa	1974	3.00	6.00	12.00
❑ MR-5048	Headed and Gutted	1975	3.00	6.00	12.00
❑ MR-5100	In the Valley	1976	3.00	6.00	12.00
❑ MR-5146	The Gator Horn	1978	3.00	6.00	12.00
❑ MR-5162	Bar Wars	1978	3.00	6.00	12.00
❑ MR-5200	Lockin' Horns	1979	3.00	6.00	12.00
❑ MR-5294	Nothing Butt	198?	2.50	5.00	10.00
❑ MR-5316	Ya Understand Me?	198?	2.50	5.00	10.00
PRESTIGE					
❑ 2516	Gatorade	198?	3.00	6.00	12.00
❑ PRLP-7162 [M]	Please, Mr. Jackson	1959	12.50	25.00	50.00
❑ PRLP-7172 [M]	Cool Gator	1959	12.50	25.00	50.00
❑ PRLP-7183 [M]	Blue Gator	1960	12.50	25.00	50.00
❑ PRLP-7196 [M]	Really Groovin'	1961	12.50	25.00	50.00
❑ PRLP-7211 [M]	Cookin' Sherry	1961	7.50	15.00	30.00
❑ PRST-7211 [S]	Cookin' Sherry	1961	10.00	20.00	40.00
❑ PRLP-7232 [M]	Thunderbird	1962	7.50	15.00	30.00
❑ PRST-7232 [S]	Thunderbird	1962	10.00	20.00	40.00
❑ PRLP-7260 [M]	Bossa Nova Plus	1962	7.50	15.00	30.00
❑ PRST-7260 [S]	Bossa Nova Plus	1962	10.00	20.00	40.00
❑ PRLP-7264 [M]	Neapolitan Nights	1963	7.50	15.00	30.00
❑ PRST-7264 [S]	Neapolitan Nights	1963	10.00	20.00	40.00
❑ PRLP-7273 [M]	Loose...	1963	7.50	15.00	30.00
❑ PRST-7273 [S]	Loose...	1963	10.00	20.00	40.00
❑ PRLP-7285 [M]	Grease 'n' Gravy	1963	7.50	15.00	30.00
❑ PRST-7285 [S]	Grease 'n' Gravy	1963	10.00	20.00	40.00
❑ PRLP-7296 [M]	The Good Life	1964	7.50	15.00	30.00
❑ PRST-7296 [S]	The Good Life	1964	10.00	20.00	40.00
❑ PRLP-7317 [M]	More Gravy	1964	7.50	15.00	30.00
❑ PRST-7317 [S]	More Gravy	1964	10.00	20.00	40.00
❑ PRLP-7329 [M]	Boss Shoutin'	1964	6.25	12.50	25.00
❑ PRST-7329 [S]	Boss Shoutin'	1964	7.50	15.00	30.00
❑ PRLP-7348 [M]	Live! Jackson's Action	1965	6.25	12.50	25.00
❑ PRST-7348 [S]	Live! Jackson's Action	1965	7.50	15.00	30.00
❑ PRLP-7364 [M]	Together Again	1965	6.25	12.50	25.00
❑ PRST-7364 [S]	Together Again	1965	7.50	15.00	30.00
❑ PRLP-7380 [M]	Live! Action	1965	6.25	12.50	25.00
❑ PRST-7380 [S]	Live! Action	1965	7.50	15.00	30.00
❑ PRLP-7396 [M]	Soul Night -- Live!	1965	6.25	12.50	25.00
❑ PRST-7396 [S]	Soul Night -- Live!	1965	7.50	15.00	30.00
❑ PRLP-7412 [M]	Tell It...	1966	5.00	10.00	20.00
❑ PRST-7412 [S]	Tell It...	1966	6.25	12.50	25.00
❑ PRLP-7428 [M]	Together Again...Again	1966	5.00	10.00	20.00
❑ PRST-7428 [S]	Together Again...Again	1966	6.25	12.50	25.00
❑ PRST-7551	Soul Grabber	1968	5.00	10.00	20.00
❑ PRST-7571	Star Bag	1968	5.00	10.00	20.00
❑ PRST-7602	Swivel Hips	1969	5.00	10.00	20.00
❑ PRST-7648	Gator's Groove	1969	5.00	10.00	20.00
❑ PRST-7702	The Best of Willis Jackson with Brother Jack McDuff	1969	3.75	7.50	15.00
❑ PRST-7770	The Best -- Soul Stompin'	1971	3.75	7.50	15.00
❑ PRST-7783	Please Mr. Jackson	1970	5.00	10.00	20.00
❑ PRST-7830	Keep On a-Blowing	1971	5.00	10.00	20.00
❑ PRST-7850	Blue Gator	197?	3.75	7.50	15.00
TRIP					
❑ 5007 [(2)]	Mellow Blues	197?	3.00	6.00	12.00
❑ 5028	Funky Reggae	197?	2.50	5.00	10.00
❑ 5030	Willis Jackson Plays Around with the Hits	197?	2.50	5.00	10.00
VERVE					
❑ V-8589 [M]	'Gator Tails	1964	3.75	7.50	15.00
❑ V6-8589 [S]	'Gator Tails	1964	5.00	10.00	20.00
❑ V6-8782	Willis Jackson	1969	3.75	7.50	15.00
JACOBY, DON					
Trumpeter.					
DECCA					
❑ DL 4241 [M]	The Swinging Big Sound	1963	3.75	7.50	15.00
❑ DL 74241 [S]	The Swinging Big Sound	1963	5.00	10.00	20.00
JACQUET, ILLINOIS					
Tenor saxophone player. Also see REX STEWART; LESTER YOUNG.					
ALADDIN					
❑ LP-708 [10]	Illinois Jacquet and His Tenor Sax	1954	62.50	125.00	250.00
❑ LP-803 [M]	Illinois Jacquet and His Tenor Sax	1956	20.00	40.00	80.00
APOLLO					
❑ LP-104 [10]	Illinois Jacquet Jam Session	1951	75.00	150.00	300.00
ARGO					
❑ LP-722 [M]	Message	1963	6.25	12.50	25.00
❑ LPS-722 [S]	Message	1963	7.50	15.00	30.00
❑ LP-735 [M]	Desert Winds	1964	6.25	12.50	25.00
❑ LPS-735 [S]	Desert Winds	1964	7.50	15.00	30.00
❑ LP-746 [M]	Illinois Jacquet Plays Cole Porter	1964	6.25	12.50	25.00
❑ LPS-746 [S]	Illinois Jacquet Plays Cole Porter	1964	7.50	15.00	30.00
ATLANTIC					
❑ 81816	Jacquet's Got It!	1988	2.50	5.00	10.00
BLACK LION					
❑ 146	Genius at Work	197?	3.75	7.50	15.00
CADET					
❑ LP-722 [M]	Message	1966	3.75	7.50	15.00
❑ LPS-722 [S]	Message	1966	5.00	10.00	20.00
❑ LP-735 [M]	Desert Winds	1966	3.75	7.50	15.00
❑ LPS-735 [S]	Desert Winds	1966	5.00	10.00	20.00
❑ LP-746 [M]	Bosses of the Ballad	1966	3.75	7.50	15.00
❑ LPS-746 [S]	Bosses of the Ballad	1966	5.00	10.00	20.00
❑ LP-754 [M]	Spectrum	1965	5.00	10.00	20.00
❑ LPS-754 [S]	Spectrum	1965	6.25	12.50	25.00
❑ LP-773 [M]	Go Power!	1966	5.00	10.00	20.00
❑ LPS-773 [S]	Go Power!	1966	6.25	12.50	25.00
CHESS					
❑ CH-91554	The Message	198?	2.50	5.00	10.00
CLASSIC JAZZ					
❑ 112	Illinois Jacquet with Wild Bill Davis	1978	3.00	6.00	12.00
❑ 146	Jacquet's Street	198?	3.00	6.00	12.00
CLEF					
❑ MGC-112 [10]	Illinois Jacquet Collates	1953	37.50	75.00	150.00
❑ MGC-129 [10]	Illinois Jacquet Collates #2	1953	37.50	75.00	150.00
❑ MGC-167 [10]	Jazz by Jacquet	1954	37.50	75.00	150.00
❑ MGC-622 [M]	Jazz Moods	1955	30.00	60.00	120.00
❑ MGC-676 [M]	Illinois Jacquet Septet	1955	30.00	60.00	120.00
❑ MGC-700 [M]	Jazz Moods by Illinois Jacquet	1956	25.00	50.00	100.00
❑ MGC-701 [M]	Port of Rico	1956	25.00	50.00	100.00
❑ MGC-702 [M]	Groovin' with Jacquet	1956	30.00	60.00	120.00
❑ MGC-750 [M]	Swing's the Thing	1956	25.00	50.00	100.00
EPIC					
❑ LA 16033 [M]	Illinois Jacquet	1963	7.50	15.00	30.00

Number	Title	Yr	VG	VG+	NM
❑ BA 17033 [S]	Illinois Jacquet	1963	10.00	20.00	40.00
❑ BA 17033 [S]	Illinois Jacquet	199?	6.25	12.50	25.00
-- Classic Records reissue on audiophile vinyl					
FANTASY					
❑ OJC-417	Bottoms Up!	1990	3.00	6.00	12.00
❑ OJC-614	The Blues -- That's Me	1991	3.75	7.50	15.00
GROOVE NOTE					
❑ 2003 [(2)]	Birthday Party	1999	7.50	15.00	30.00
-- Audiophile vinyl; one record has the entire album, the other has two tracks at 45 rpm					
IMPERIAL					
❑ LP-9184 [M]	Flying Home	1962	7.50	15.00	30.00
❑ LP-12184 [S]	Flying Home	1962	10.00	20.00	40.00
JAZZ MAN					
❑ 5034	Genius at Work	198?	3.00	6.00	12.00
JRC					
❑ 11434	Birthday Party	197?	3.75	7.50	15.00
MERCURY					
❑ MGC-112 [10]	Illinois Jacquet Collates	1952	62.50	125.00	250.00
❑ MGC-129 [10]	Illinois Jacquet Collates #2	1953	---	---	---
-- Canceled; issued on Clef					
MOSAIC					
❑ MQ6-165 [(6)]	The Complete Illinois Jacquet Sessions 1945-50	199?	25.00	50.00	100.00
PRESTIGE					
❑ PRST-7575	Bottoms Up!	1968	6.25	12.50	25.00
❑ PRST-7597	The King!	1968	6.25	12.50	25.00
❑ PRST-7629	The Soul Explosion	1969	6.25	12.50	25.00
❑ PRST-7731	The Blues -- That's Me	1969	6.25	12.50	25.00
❑ 24057 [(2)]	How High the Moon	197?	3.75	7.50	15.00
RCA VICTOR					
❑ LPM-3236 [10]	Black Velvet	1954	62.50	125.00	250.00
ROULETTE					
❑ R-52035 [M]	Illinois Jacquet Flies Again	1959	12.50	25.00	50.00
❑ SR-52035 [S]	Illinois Jacquet Flies Again	1959	10.00	20.00	40.00
SAVOY					
❑ MG-15024 [10]	Tenor Sax	1953	50.00	100.00	200.00
VERVE					
❑ VE-2-2544 [(2)]	The Cool Rage	198?	3.75	7.50	15.00
❑ MGV-8023 [M]	Swing's the Thing	1957	12.50	25.00	50.00
-- Reissue of Clef 750					
❑ V-8023 [M]	Swing's the Thing	1961	6.25	12.50	25.00
❑ MGV-8061 [M]	Illinois Jacquet and His Orchestra	1957	12.50	25.00	50.00
-- Reissue of Clef 676					
❑ V-8061 [M]	Illinois Jacquet and His Orchestra	1961	6.25	12.50	25.00
❑ MGV-8084 [M]	Jazz Moods by Illinois Jacquet	1957	12.50	25.00	50.00
-- Reissue of Clef 700					
❑ V-8084 [M]	Jazz Moods by Illinois Jacquet	1961	6.25	12.50	25.00
❑ MGV-8085 [M]	Port of Rico	1957	12.50	25.00	50.00
-- Reissue of Clef 701					
❑ V-8085 [M]	Port of Rico	1961	6.25	12.50	25.00
❑ MGV-8086 [M]	Groovin' with Jacquet	1957	12.50	25.00	50.00
-- Reissue of Clef 702					
❑ V-8086 [M]	Groovin' with Jacquet	1961	6.25	12.50	25.00

JACQUET, ILLINOIS, AND BEN WEBSTER
Also see each artist's individual listings.

Number	Title	Yr	VG	VG+	NM
CLEF					
❑ MGC-680 [M]	"The Kid" and "The Brute"	1955	30.00	60.00	120.00
VERVE					
❑ MGV-8065 [M]	"The Kid" and "The Brute"	1957	12.50	25.00	50.00
-- Reissue of Clef 680					
❑ V-8065 [M]	"The Kid" and "The Brute"	1961	5.00	10.00	20.00

JACQUET, RUSSELL
Trumpeter and occasional male singer.

Number	Title	Yr	VG	VG+	NM
KING					
❑ 295-81 [10]	Russell Jacquet and His All Stars	1954	62.50	125.00	250.00

JAFFE, ANDY
Pianist.

Number	Title	Yr	VG	VG+	NM
STASH					
❑ ST-247	Manhattan Projections	1985	2.50	5.00	10.00

JAMAL, AHMAD
Pianist. His most popular recordings were on Argo/Cadet and featured a trio with Israel Crosby (bass) and Vernell Fournier (drums).

Number	Title	Yr	VG	VG+	NM
ABC					
❑ S-660	Tranquility	1968	3.00	6.00	12.00

Number	Title	Yr	VG	VG+	NM
ABC IMPULSE!					
❑ AS-9176	At the Top -- Poinciana Revisited	1969	3.75	7.50	15.00
❑ AS-9194	Awakening	1970	3.75	7.50	15.00
❑ AS-9217	Freelight	1971	3.00	6.00	12.00
❑ AS-9226	Outertimeinnerspace	1972	3.00	6.00	12.00
❑ AS-9260 [(2)]	Re-Evaluations: The Impulse Years	1975	3.00	6.00	12.00
ARGO					
❑ LP-602 [M]	Chamber Music of New Jazz	1956	7.50	15.00	30.00
-- Reissue of Creative 602					
❑ LP-610 [M]	Count 'Em 88	1957	7.50	15.00	30.00
❑ LP-628 [M]	But Not for Me/Ahmad Jamal at the Pershing	1958	7.50	15.00	30.00
❑ LPS-628 [S]	But Not for Me/Ahmad Jamal at the Pershing	1958	10.00	20.00	40.00
❑ LP-636 [M]	Ahmad Jamal, Volume IV	1958	7.50	15.00	30.00
❑ LPS-636 [S]	Ahmad Jamal, Volume IV	1958	10.00	20.00	40.00
❑ LP-638 [(2) M]	Portfolio of Ahmad Jamal	1959	10.00	20.00	40.00
❑ LPS-638 [(2) S]	Portfolio of Ahmad Jamal	1959	12.50	25.00	50.00
❑ LP-646 [M]	Jamal at the Penthouse	1959	7.50	15.00	30.00
❑ LPS-646 [S]	Jamal at the Penthouse	1959	10.00	20.00	40.00
❑ LP-662 [M]	Happy Moods	1960	5.00	10.00	20.00
❑ LPS-662 [S]	Happy Moods	1960	6.25	12.50	25.00
❑ LP-667 [M]	Ahmad Jamal at the Pershing Volume 2	1961	5.00	10.00	20.00
❑ LPS-667 [S]	Ahmad Jamal at the Pershing Volume 2	1961	6.25	12.50	25.00
❑ LP-673 [M]	Listen to Ahmad Jamal	1961	5.00	10.00	20.00
❑ LPS-673 [S]	Listen to Ahmad Jamal	1961	6.25	12.50	25.00
❑ LP-685 [M]	Alhambra	1961	5.00	10.00	20.00
❑ LPS-685 [S]	Alhambra	1961	6.25	12.50	25.00
❑ LP-691 [M]	All of You	1962	5.00	10.00	20.00
❑ LPS-691 [S]	All of You	1962	6.25	12.50	25.00
❑ LP-703 [M]	Ahmad Jamal at the Blackhawk	1962	5.00	10.00	20.00
❑ LPS-703 [S]	Ahmad Jamal at the Blackhawk	1962	6.25	12.50	25.00
❑ LP-712 [M]	Macanudo	1963	5.00	10.00	20.00
❑ LPS-712 [S]	Macanudo	1963	6.25	12.50	25.00
❑ LP-719 [M]	Poin'-ci-an'a	1963	5.00	10.00	20.00
❑ LPS-719 [S]	Poin'-ci-an'a	1963	6.25	12.50	25.00
❑ LP-733 [M]	"Naked City" Theme	1964	5.00	10.00	20.00
❑ LPS-733 [S]	"Naked City" Theme	1964	6.25	12.50	25.00
❑ LP-751 [M]	The Roar of the Greasepaint	1965	5.00	10.00	20.00
❑ LPS-751 [S]	The Roar of the Greasepaint	1965	6.25	12.50	25.00
❑ LP-758 [M]	Extensions	1965	5.00	10.00	20.00
❑ LPS-758 [S]	Extensions	1965	6.25	12.50	25.00
ATLANTIC					
❑ 81258 [(2)]	Digital Works	1985	3.00	6.00	12.00
❑ 81645	Rossiter Road	1986	2.50	5.00	10.00
❑ 81699 [(2)]	Live at the Montreal Jazz Festival 1985	1986	3.00	6.00	12.00
❑ 81793	Crystal	1987	2.50	5.00	10.00
CADET					
❑ LP-628 [M]	But Not for Me/Ahmad Jamal at the Pershing	1966	3.00	6.00	12.00
❑ LPS-628 [S]	But Not for Me/Ahmad Jamal at the Pershing	1966	3.75	7.50	15.00
❑ LP-636 [M]	Ahmad Jamal, Volume IV	1966	3.00	6.00	12.00
❑ LPS-636 [S]	Ahmad Jamal, Volume IV	1966	3.75	7.50	15.00
❑ LP-638 [(2) M]	Portfolio of Ahmad Jamal	1966	3.75	7.50	15.00
❑ LPS-638 [(2) S]	Portfolio of Ahmad Jamal	1966	5.00	10.00	20.00
❑ LP-646 [M]	Jamal at the Penthouse	1966	3.00	6.00	12.00
❑ LPS-646 [S]	Jamal at the Penthouse	1966	3.75	7.50	15.00
❑ LP-662 [M]	Happy Moods	1966	3.00	6.00	12.00
❑ LPS-662 [S]	Happy Moods	1966	3.75	7.50	15.00
❑ LP-667 [M]	Ahmad Jamal at the Pershing Volume 2	1966	3.00	6.00	12.00
❑ LPS-667 [S]	Ahmad Jamal at the Pershing Volume 2	1966	3.75	7.50	15.00
❑ LP-673 [M]	Listen to Ahmad Jamal	1966	3.00	6.00	12.00
❑ LPS-673 [S]	Listen to Ahmad Jamal	1966	3.75	7.50	15.00
❑ LP-685 [M]	Alhambra	1966	3.00	6.00	12.00
❑ LPS-685 [S]	Alhambra	1966	3.75	7.50	15.00
❑ LP-691 [M]	All of You	1966	3.00	6.00	12.00
❑ LPS-691 [S]	All of You	1966	3.75	7.50	15.00
❑ LP-703 [M]	Ahmad Jamal at the Blackhawk	1966	3.00	6.00	12.00
❑ LPS-703 [S]	Ahmad Jamal at the Blackhawk	1966	3.75	7.50	15.00
❑ LP-712 [M]	Macanudo	1966	3.00	6.00	12.00
❑ LPS-712 [S]	Macanudo	1966	3.75	7.50	15.00
❑ LP-719 [M]	Poin'-ci-an'a	1966	3.00	6.00	12.00
❑ LPS-719 [S]	Poin'-ci-an'a	1966	3.75	7.50	15.00
❑ LP-733 [M]	"Naked City" Theme	1966	3.00	6.00	12.00
❑ LPS-733 [S]	"Naked City" Theme	1966	3.75	7.50	15.00
❑ LP-751 [M]	The Roar of the Greasepaint	1966	3.00	6.00	12.00
❑ LPS-751 [S]	The Roar of the Greasepaint	1966	3.75	7.50	15.00
❑ LP-758 [M]	Extensions	1966	3.00	6.00	12.00

Number	Title	Yr	VG	VG+	NM
❏ LPS-758 [S]	Extensions	1965	3.75	7.50	15.00
❏ LP-764 [M]	Rhapsody	1966	3.75	7.50	15.00
❏ LPS-764 [S]	Rhapsody	1966	5.00	10.00	20.00
❏ LP-777 [M]	Heat Wave	1966	3.75	7.50	15.00
❏ LPS-777 [S]	Heat Wave	1966	5.00	10.00	20.00
❏ LP-786 [M]	Standard Eyes	1967	3.75	7.50	15.00
❏ LPS-786 [S]	Standard Eyes	1967	5.00	10.00	20.00
❏ LP-792 [M]	Cry Young	1967	5.00	10.00	20.00
❏ LPS-792 [S]	Cry Young	1967	3.75	7.50	15.00
❏ LPS-807	The Bright, the Blue and the Beautiful	1968	3.75	7.50	15.00
❏ 50035 [(2)]	Inspiration	1974	3.75	7.50	15.00

CATALYST

Number	Title	Yr	VG	VG+	NM
❏ 7606	Live at Oil Can Harry's	1978	3.00	6.00	12.00

CHESS

❏ CH-91553	Poinciana	198?	2.50	5.00	10.00

CREATIVE

❏ LP-602 [M]	Chamber Music of New Jazz	1956	12.50	25.00	50.00

EPIC

❏ BN 627 [R]	Ahmad Jamal Trio	196?	5.00	10.00	20.00
❏ BN 634 [S]	The Piano Scene of Ahmad Jamal	1959	5.00	10.00	20.00
❏ LN 3212 [M]	Ahmad Jamal Trio	1956	12.50	25.00	50.00
-- Yellow label with lines around rim					
❏ LN 3212 [M]	Ahmad Jamal Trio	1963	6.25	12.50	25.00
-- Yellow label, no lines around rim					
❏ LN 3631 [M]	The Piano Scene of Ahmad Jamal	1959	7.50	15.00	30.00

GRP/IMPULSE!

❏ 226	The Awakening	199?	3.75	7.50	15.00
-- Reissue on audiophile vinyl					

MCA

❏ 29041	At the Top -- Poinciana Revisited	198?	2.00	4.00	8.00
-- Reissue of Impulse! 9178					
❏ 29042	Awakening	198?	2.00	4.00	8.00
-- Reissue of Impulse! 9194					
❏ 29043	Freelight	198?	2.00	4.00	8.00
-- Reissue of Impulse! 9217					

MCA/IMPULSE!

❏ 5644	Awakening	1986	2.50	5.00	10.00
-- Another reissue of Impulse! 9194					

MOTOWN

❏ M8-945	Night Song	1981	2.50	5.00	10.00

20TH CENTURY

❏ T-417	Ahmad Jamal '73	1973	2.50	5.00	10.00
❏ T-432	Jamaica	1974	2.50	5.00	10.00
❏ T-459	Jamal Plays Jamal	1975	2.50	5.00	10.00
❏ T-515	Steppin' Out with a Dream	1977	2.50	5.00	10.00
❏ T-600	Genetic Walk	1980	2.50	5.00	10.00
❏ T-622	Intervals	1980	2.50	5.00	10.00
❏ T-631	Greatest Hits	1981	2.50	5.00	10.00

JAMAL, KHAN
Vibraphone and marimbas player.

STASH

❏ ST-278	Infinity	1988	2.50	5.00	10.00

STEEPLECHASE

❏ SCS-1196	Dark Warrior	198?	3.00	6.00	12.00

JAMES, BOB
Pianist, keyboard player, composer and arranger.

CBS MASTERWORKS

❏ IM 39540	Rameau	1985	2.50	5.00	10.00

COLUMBIA

❏ FC 38678	The Genie (Themes & Variations from the TV Series "Taxi")	1983	2.50	5.00	10.00

CTI

❏ CTS-6043	One	1974	3.00	6.00	12.00
❏ CTS-6057	Two	1975	3.00	6.00	12.00
❏ CTS-6063	Three	1976	3.00	6.00	12.00
❏ 7074	BJ4	1977	3.00	6.00	12.00

ESP-DISK'

❏ 1009 [M]	Explosions	1965	5.00	10.00	20.00
❏ S-1009 [S]	Explosions	1965	6.25	12.50	25.00

MERCURY

❏ MG-20768 [M]	Bold Conceptions	1963	5.00	10.00	20.00
❏ SR-60768 [S]	Bold Conceptions	1963	6.25	12.50	25.00

TAPPAN ZEE

❏ JC 34896	Heads	1977	2.50	5.00	10.00
❏ PC 34896	Heads	1985	---	3.00	6.00
-- Budget-line reissue					
❏ JC 35594	Touchdown	1978	2.50	5.00	10.00

Number	Title	Yr	VG	VG+	NM
❏ PC 35594	Touchdown	1985	---	3.00	6.00
-- Budget-line reissue					
❏ JC 36056	Lucky Seven	1979	2.50	5.00	10.00
❏ PC 36056	Lucky Seven	1985	---	3.00	6.00
-- Budget-line reissue					
❏ JC 36422	"H"	1980	2.50	5.00	10.00
❏ C2X 36786 [(2)]	All Around the Town	1981	3.00	6.00	12.00
❏ FC 36835	One	1981	2.50	5.00	10.00
-- Reissue of CTI 6043					
❏ PC 36835	One	1985	---	3.00	6.00
-- Budget-line reissue					
❏ FC 36836	Two	1981	2.50	5.00	10.00
-- Reissue of CTI 6057					
❏ PC 36836	Two	1985	---	3.00	6.00
-- Budget-line reissue					
❏ FC 36837	Three	1981	2.50	5.00	10.00
-- Reissue of CTI 6063					
❏ PC 36837	Three	1985	---	3.00	6.00
-- Budget-line reissue					
❏ FC 36838	BJ4	1981	2.50	5.00	10.00
-- Reissue of CTI 7074					
❏ PC 36838	BJ4	1985	---	3.00	6.00
-- Budget-line reissue					
❏ FC 37495	Sign of the Times	1981	2.50	5.00	10.00
❏ FC 38067	Hands Down	1982	2.50	5.00	10.00
❏ FC 38801	Foxie	1983	2.50	5.00	10.00
❏ FC 39580	12	1985	2.50	5.00	10.00
❏ HC 45594	Touchdown	1982	7.50	15.00	30.00
-- Half-speed mastered edition					
❏ HC 47495	Sign of the Times	1982	7.50	15.00	30.00
-- Half-speed mastered edition					

WARNER BROS.

❏ 25495	Obsession	1986	2.50	5.00	10.00
❏ 25757	Ivory Coast	1988	2.50	5.00	10.00
❏ 26256	Grand Piano Canyon	1990	3.00	6.00	12.00

JAMES, BOB, AND EARL KLUGH
Also see each artist's individual listings.

CAPITOL

❏ SMAS-12244	Two of a Kind	1982	2.50	5.00	10.00

MOBILE FIDELITY

❏ 1-124	Two of a Kind	1984	10.00	20.00	40.00
-- Audiophile vinyl					

TAPPAN ZEE

❏ FC 36241	One on One	1979	2.50	5.00	10.00
❏ HC 46241	One on One	198?	7.50	15.00	30.00
-- Half-speed mastered edition					

JAMES, BOB, AND DAVID SANBORN
Also see each artist's individual listings.

WARNER BROS.

❏ 25393	Double Vision	1986	2.50	5.00	10.00

JAMES, DWIGHT

CADENCE JAZZ

❏ CJ-1014	Inner Heat	198?	2.50	5.00	10.00

JAMES, GREGORY
Guitarist.

INNER CITY

❏ IC-1050	Alicia	1978	3.75	7.50	15.00

JAMES, HARRY
Trumpeter and bandleader. Items with an asterisk (*) feature at least one track with FRANK SINATRA on vocals.

AIRCHECK

❏ 18	Harry James On the Air	197?	2.50	5.00	10.00
❏ 33	Harry James On the Air, Vol. 2	1986	2.50	5.00	10.00

BAINBRIDGE

❏ BT-6252	Ciribiribin	1982	2.50	5.00	10.00

CAPITOL

❏ W 654 [M]	Harry James in Hi-Fi	1955	7.50	15.00	30.00
❏ W 712 [M]	More Harry James in Hi-Fi	1956	7.50	15.00	30.00
❏ T 874 [M]	Wild About Harry	1957	7.50	15.00	30.00
❏ T 1093 [M]	Harry's Choice	1958	7.50	15.00	30.00
❏ DT 1515 [R]	The Hits of Harry James	1961	3.00	6.00	12.00
❏ M-1515	The Hits of Harry James	197?	3.00	6.00	12.00
-- Mono reissue					
❏ T 1515 [M]	The Hits of Harry James	1961	5.00	10.00	20.00
-- Black colorband label, logo at left					
❏ T 1515 [M]	The Hits of Harry James	1962	3.75	7.50	15.00
-- Black colorband label, logo at top					

CIRCLE

❏ 5	Harry James and His Orchestra with Dick Haymes	198?	2.50	5.00	10.00

Number	Title	Yr	VG	VG+	NM
❑ 39	Harry James and His Orchestra 1954	198?	2.50	5.00	10.00
COLUMBIA					
❑ CL 522 [M]	One Night Stand	1953	10.00	20.00	40.00
-- Maroon label, gold print					
❑ GL 522 [M]	One Night Stand	1953	12.50	25.00	50.00
-- Black label, silver print					
❑ CL 553 [M]	Trumpet After Midnight	1954	10.00	20.00	40.00
-- Maroon label, gold print					
❑ CL 562 [M]	Dancing in Person with Harry James at the Hollywood Palladium	1954	10.00	20.00	40.00
-- Maroon label, gold print					
❑ CL 581 [M]	Soft Lights, Sweet Trumpet	1954	10.00	20.00	40.00
-- Maroon label, gold print					
❑ CL 615 [M]	Juke Box Jamboree	1955	10.00	20.00	40.00
-- Maroon label, gold print					
❑ CL 655 [M]	*All Time Favorites	1955	10.00	20.00	40.00
-- Maroon label, gold print					
❑ CL 669 [M]	Jazz Session	1955	10.00	20.00	40.00
❑ CL 2527 [10]	The Man with the Horn	1955	12.50	25.00	50.00
❑ CL 2630 [M]	*Harry James' Greatest Hits	1967	5.00	10.00	20.00
❑ CL 6009 [10]	*All Time Favorites	1949	12.50	25.00	50.00
❑ CL 6044 [10]	Trumpet Time	1950	12.50	25.00	50.00
❑ CL 6088 [10]	Dance Parade	1950	12.50	25.00	50.00
❑ CL 6138 [10]	Your Dance Date	1951	12.50	25.00	50.00
❑ CL 6207 [10]	Soft Lights, Sweet Trumpet	1952	12.50	25.00	50.00
❑ CS 9430 [R]	*Harry James' Greatest Hits	1967	3.00	6.00	12.00
-- Red "360 Sound" label					
❑ CS 9430 [R]	*Harry James' Greatest Hits	1970	2.50	5.00	10.00
-- Orange label					
❑ PC 9430	*Harry James' Greatest Hits	198?	2.00	4.00	8.00
-- Budget-line reissue					
DOT					
❑ DLP-3728 [M]	Live at the Riverboat	1966	3.00	6.00	12.00
❑ DLP-3735 [M]	Harry James and His Western Friends	1966	3.00	6.00	12.00
❑ DLP-3801 [M]	Our Leader	1967	3.75	7.50	15.00
❑ DLP-25728 [S]	Live at the Riverboat	1966	3.75	7.50	15.00
❑ DLP-25735 [S]	Harry James and His Western Friends	1966	3.75	7.50	15.00
❑ DLP-25801 [S]	Our Leader	1967	3.00	6.00	12.00
HARMONY					
❑ HL 7159 [M]	Harry James and His Great Vocalists	196?	3.75	7.50	15.00
❑ HL 7162 [M]	Harry James Plays Trumpet Rhapsody	196?	3.75	7.50	15.00
❑ HL 7191 [M]	Harry James Plays the Songs That Sold a Million	196?	3.75	7.50	15.00
❑ HL 7269 [M]	Strictly Instrumental	196?	3.75	7.50	15.00
❑ HS 11245 [R]	Harry James Plays the Songs That Sold a Million	196?	2.50	5.00	10.00
❑ HS 11326	Laura	1969	2.50	5.00	10.00
❑ KH 32018	Best of the Big Bands	1972	2.50	5.00	10.00
HINDSIGHT					
❑ HSR-102	Harry James and His Orchestra 1943-46	198?	2.50	5.00	10.00
❑ HSR-123	Harry James and His Orchestra 1943-46	198?	2.50	5.00	10.00
❑ HSR-135	Harry James and His Orchestra 1948-49	198?	2.50	5.00	10.00
❑ HSR-141	Harry James and His Orchestra 1943-46, Vol. 4	198?	2.50	5.00	10.00
❑ HSR-142	Harry James and His Orchestra 1943-53	198?	2.50	5.00	10.00
❑ HSR-150	Harry James and His Orchestra 1947-49	198?	2.50	5.00	10.00
❑ HSR-406 [(2)]	Harry James and His Orchestra Play 22 Original Big Band Recordings	198?	3.00	6.00	12.00
INSIGHT					
❑ 203	Harry James and His Orchestra 1943-53	198?	2.50	5.00	10.00
JAZZ ARCHIVES					
❑ JA-31	Young Harry James	198?	2.50	5.00	10.00
LONDON PHASE 4					
❑ SP-44109	Golden Trumpet	1968	3.75	7.50	15.00
LONGINES SYMPHONETTE					
❑ LS-217 [(5)]	Harry James Dance Band Spectacular	196?	7.50	15.00	30.00
METRO					
❑ M-536 [M]	Harry Not Jesse	1966	3.00	6.00	12.00
❑ MS-536 [S]	Harry Not Jesse	1966	3.00	6.00	12.00
MGM					
❑ E-3778 [M]	Harry James and His New Swingin' Band	1959	5.00	10.00	20.00
❑ SE-3778 [S]	Harry James and His New ' Swingin Band	1959	6.25	12.50	25.00

Number	Title	Yr	VG	VG+	NM
❑ E-3848 [M]	Harry James Today	1960	5.00	10.00	20.00
❑ SE-3848 [S]	Harry James Today	1960	6.25	12.50	25.00
❑ E-4003 [M]	Requests on the Road	1961	5.00	10.00	20.00
❑ SE-4003 [S]	Requests on the Road	1961	6.25	12.50	25.00
❑ E-4058 [M]	The Solid Gold Trumpet	1962	3.75	7.50	15.00
❑ SE-4058 [S]	The Solid Gold Trumpet	1962	5.00	10.00	20.00
❑ E-4137 [M]	Double Dixie	1963	3.75	7.50	15.00
❑ SE-4137 [S]	Double Dixie	1963	5.00	10.00	20.00
❑ E-4214 [M]	25th Anniversary Album	1964	3.00	6.00	12.00
❑ SE-4214 [S]	25th Anniversary Album	1964	3.75	7.50	15.00
❑ E-4265 [M]	New Versions of Down Beat Favorites	1965	3.00	6.00	12.00
❑ SE-4265 [S]	New Versions of Down Beat Favorites	1965	3.75	7.50	15.00
❑ E-4274 [M]	In a Relaxed Mood	1965	3.00	6.00	12.00
❑ SE-4274 [S]	In a Relaxed Mood	1965	3.75	7.50	15.00
PAIR					
❑ PDL2-1158 [(2)]	Big Band Favorites	1986	3.00	6.00	12.00
PAUSA					
❑ 9037	More Harry James in Hi-Fi	198?	2.50	5.00	10.00
PICKWICK					
❑ PC-3006 [M]	Mr. Trumpet	196?	3.75	7.50	15.00
❑ SPC-3006 [R]	Mr. Trumpet	196?	2.50	5.00	10.00
❑ PC-3044 [M]	You Made Me Love You	196?	3.75	7.50	15.00
❑ SPC-3044 [R]	You Made Me Love You	196?	2.50	5.00	10.00
❑ SPC-3126	The Shadow of Your Smile	196?	2.50	5.00	10.00
SAVOY JAZZ					
❑ SJL-2262 [(2)]	First Team Player on the Jazz Varsity	198?	3.00	6.00	12.00
SHEFFIELD LABS					
❑ 3	The King James Version	1976	3.75	7.50	15.00
-- Direct-to-disc recording					
❑ 6	Comin' From a Good Place	1978	3.75	7.50	15.00
-- Direct-to-disc recording					
❑ 11	Still Harry After All These Years	1979	3.75	7.50	15.00
-- Direct-to-disc recording					
SUNBEAM					
❑ 203	Harry James and His Orchestra 1940	197?	2.50	5.00	10.00
❑ 217	Harry James and His Orchestra 1954	197?	2.50	5.00	10.00

JAMES, WOODY
PAUSA					
❑ 7020	Crystallizations	198?	2.50	5.00	10.00
SEA BREEZE					
❑ SB-2011	Hardcore Jazz	198?	2.50	5.00	10.00
❑ SB-2015	Zinger	1985	2.50	5.00	10.00

JANIS, CONRAD
Trombonist and bandleader.

CIRCLE					
❑ L-404 [10]	Conrad Janis' Tailgate Jazz Band	1951	12.50	25.00	50.00
JUBILEE					
❑ JLP-7 [10]	Conrad Janis and His Tailgaters	1954	12.50	25.00	50.00
❑ JLP-1010 [M]	Conrad Janis and His Tailgate Five	1955	10.00	20.00	40.00
RIVERSIDE					
❑ RLP 12-215 [M]	Dixieland Jam Session	1956	12.50	25.00	50.00
-- White label, blue print					
❑ RLP 12-215 [M]	Dixieland Jam Session	1959	7.50	15.00	30.00
-- Blue label, microphone label at top					

JARMAN, JOSEPH
Tenor saxophone player and a founder of ART ENSEMBLE OF CHICAGO.

AECO					
❑ 002	Sunbound	1979	3.75	7.50	15.00
DELMARK					
❑ DS-410	Song for	1968	5.00	10.00	20.00
❑ DS-417	As If It Were the Seasons	1969	5.00	10.00	20.00

JARMAN, JOSEPH, AND DON MOYE
Moye is a drummer and percussionist. Also see ART ENSEMBLE OF CHICAGO; JOSEPH JARMAN.

BLACK SAINT					
❑ BSR-0042	Black Paladins	198?	3.00	6.00	12.00
❑ BSR-0052	Earth Passage	198?	3.00	6.00	12.00
INDIA NAVIGATION					
❑ IN-1033 [(2)]	Egwu-Anwu	1978	5.00	10.00	20.00

JAROSLAV
Keyboard player and male vocalist.

COLUMBIA					
❑ JC 35537	Checkin' In	1978	3.00	6.00	12.00

Number	Title	Yr	VG	VG+	NM

JARRE, JEAN-MICHEL
Synthesizer and keyboard player, a pioneer in what has become known as "electronica."
DREYFUS/POLYDOR
811 551-1 [(2)]	The Concerts in China	1983	3.00	6.00	12.00
823 763-1	Zoolook	1984	2.00	4.00	8.00
827 885-1	Oxygene	1987	2.00	4.00	8.00
829 125-1	Rendez-Vous	1986	2.00	4.00	8.00
829 456-1	Equinoxe	1987	2.00	4.00	8.00
829 457-1	Magnetic Fields	1987	2.00	4.00	8.00
833 170-1	Concerts Houston/Lyon	1987	2.50	5.00	10.00
MOBILE FIDELITY
| 1-212 | Oxygene | 1995 | 5.00 | 10.00 | 20.00 |
-- Audiophile vinyl
| 1-227 | Equinoxe | 1995 | 5.00 | 10.00 | 20.00 |
-- Audiophile vinyl
POLYDOR
PD-1-6112	Oxygene	1977	2.50	5.00	10.00
PD-1-6175	Equinoxe	1979	2.50	5.00	10.00
PD-1-6225	Magnetic Fields	1981	2.50	5.00	10.00

JARREAU, AL
Male singer.
BAINBRIDGE
| BT-6237 | Al Jarreau 1965 | 1982 | 2.00 | 4.00 | 8.00 |
MOBILE FIDELITY
| 1-019 | All Fly Home | 1980 | 5.00 | 10.00 | 20.00 |
-- Audiophile vinyl
REPRISE
MS 2224	We Got By	1975	2.50	5.00	10.00
MS 2248	Glow	1976	2.50	5.00	10.00
25778	Heart's Horizon	1988	2.50	5.00	10.00
WARNER BROS.
2WS 3052 [(2)]	Look to the Rainbow/Live in Europe	1977	3.00	6.00	12.00
BSK 3229	All Fly Home	1978	2.50	5.00	10.00
BSK 3434	This Time	1980	2.00	4.00	8.00
BSK 3576	Breakin' Away	1981	2.00	4.00	8.00
23801	Jarreau	1983	2.00	4.00	8.00
25106	High Crime	1984	2.00	4.00	8.00
25331	Al Jarreau in London	1985	2.00	4.00	8.00
25477	L Is for Lover	1986	2.00	4.00	8.00

JARRETT, KEITH
Pianist, organist and keyboard player. Also an occasional flutist and soprano saxophone player.
ABC IMPULSE!
AS-9240	Fort Yawuh	1973	3.00	6.00	12.00
AS-9274	Treasure Island	1974	3.00	6.00	12.00
AS-9301	Death and the Flower	1974	3.00	6.00	12.00
AS-9305	Backhand	1975	2.50	5.00	10.00
AS-9315	Mysteries	1976	2.50	5.00	10.00
AS-9322	Shades	1976	2.50	5.00	10.00
AS-9331	Byablue	1977	2.50	5.00	10.00
IA-9334	Bop-Be	1977	2.50	5.00	10.00
IA-9348	The Best of Keith Jarrett	1978	2.50	5.00	10.00
ATLANTIC
SD 1596	Mourning of a Star	1971	3.00	6.00	12.00
SD 1612	Birth	1972	3.00	6.00	12.00
SD 1673	El Juicio (The Judgment)	1975	2.50	5.00	10.00
SD 8808	Somewhere Before	198?	2.00	4.00	8.00
-- Reissue of Vortex 2012
COLUMBIA
| KG 31580 [(2)] | Expectations | 1972 | 3.75 | 7.50 | 15.00 |
ECM
1017	Facing You	1973	2.50	5.00	10.00
1033/4 [(2)]	In the Light	1976	3.00	6.00	12.00
1035/6/7 [(3)]	Solo Concerts	1974	5.00	10.00	20.00
1049	Luminessence	1974	2.50	5.00	10.00
1050	Belonging	1974	2.50	5.00	10.00
1064/5 [(2)]	The Koln Concert	1976	3.00	6.00	12.00
1070	Arbour Zena	1976	2.50	5.00	10.00
1085	Survivors' Suite	1977	2.50	5.00	10.00
1086/7 [(2)]	Hymns/Spheres	1977	3.00	6.00	12.00
1090	Staircase/Hourglass/Sundial/Sand	1977	3.00	6.00	12.00
1100 [(10)]	The Sun Bear Concerts	1977	20.00	40.00	80.00
1115	My Song	1978	2.50	5.00	10.00
1150	Eyes of the Heart	1979	2.50	5.00	10.00
1171 [(2)]	Nude Ants	1979	3.00	6.00	12.00
1174	Sacred Hymns	1981	2.50	5.00	10.00
1201 [(2)]	Invocations/The Moth and the Flame	1981	3.00	6.00	12.00
1227 [(3)]	Concerts	1982	5.00	10.00	20.00
1228	Concerts	1982	2.50	5.00	10.00
-- Abridged version of 1227

23793	Standards, Volume 1	1983	2.50	5.00	10.00
25007	Changes	1984	2.50	5.00	10.00
25023	Standards, Volume 2	1985	2.50	5.00	10.00
25041	Standards Live	1986	2.50	5.00	10.00
MCA
| 29044 | Fort Yawuh | 1980 | 2.00 | 4.00 | 8.00 |
-- Reissue of Impulse 9240
| 29045 | Treasure Island | 1980 | 2.00 | 4.00 | 8.00 |
-- Reissue of Impulse 9274
| 29046 | Death and the Flower | 1980 | 2.00 | 4.00 | 8.00 |
-- Reissue of Impulse 9301
| 29047 | Byablue | 1980 | 2.00 | 4.00 | 8.00 |
-- Reissue of Impulse 9331
| 29048 | Bop-Be | 1980 | 2.00 | 4.00 | 8.00 |
-- Reissue of Impulse 9334
| 39106 | Treasure Island | 198? | 2.50 | 5.00 | 10.00 |
-- Another reissue of Impulse 9274
VORTEX
2006	Life Between the Exit Signs	1969	5.00	10.00	20.00
2008	Restoration Ruin	1969	5.00	10.00	20.00
2012	Somewhere Before	1970	5.00	10.00	20.00

JARRETT, KEITH, AND JACK DeJOHNETTE
Also see each artist's individual listings.
ECM
| 1021 | Ruta & Daitya | 1973 | 2.50 | 5.00 | 10.00 |

JARRETT, SCOTT
Pianist and male singer.
GRP/ARISTA
| GL 5007 | Without Rhyme or Reason | 1979 | 2.50 | 5.00 | 10.00 |

JARVIS, JOHN
Pianist and composer.
CRYSTAL CLEAR
| 8004 | Evolutions | 1980 | 5.00 | 10.00 | 20.00 |
-- Direct-to-disc recording
MCA
5690	So Far So Good	1986	2.50	5.00	10.00
5963	Something Constructive	1987	2.50	5.00	10.00
6263	Whatever Works	1988	2.50	5.00	10.00

JASEN, DAVE
Pianist.
BLUE GOOSE
| 3001 | Fingerbustin' Ragtime | 197? | 3.00 | 6.00 | 12.00 |
| 3002 | Rompin', Stompin' Ragtime | 197? | 3.00 | 6.00 | 12.00 |
EUPHONIC
| 1206 | Creative Ragtime | 196? | 3.00 | 6.00 | 12.00 |
FOLKWAYS
| FC-3561 | Rip-Roarin' Ragtime | 1977 | 2.50 | 5.00 | 10.00 |

JASMINE
Members: Roger Rosenberg; Bill O'Connell; Carmen Lundy.
WEST 54
| 8007 | Jasmine | 1980 | 3.00 | 6.00 | 12.00 |

JASPAR, BOBBY
Tenor saxophone player and flutist. Also see THE NUTTY SQUIRRELS.
EMARCY
| MG-36105 [M] | Bobby Jaspar and His All Stars | 1957 | 20.00 | 40.00 | 80.00 |
RIVERSIDE
| RLP 12-240 [M] | Bobby Jaspar | 1957 | 20.00 | 40.00 | 80.00 |
-- White label, blue print
| RLP 12-240 [M] | Bobby Jaspar | 1959 | 10.00 | 20.00 | 40.00 |
-- Blue label, microphone label at top
| 6156 | Tenor and Flute | 198? | 3.00 | 6.00 | 12.00 |
SWING
| SW-8413 | Bobby Jaspar In Paris | 1986 | 2.50 | 5.00 | 10.00 |

JAUME, ANDRE
Reeds player.
HAT ART
| 2003 [(2)] | Musique Pour 3 & 8: Errance | 1986 | 3.75 | 7.50 | 15.00 |
HAT HUT
| R | Saxanimalier | 1979 | 3.00 | 6.00 | 12.00 |
| 1989/90 [(2)] | Musique Pour 8: L'oc | 1981 | 5.00 | 10.00 | 20.00 |

JAUME, ANDRE, AND JOE McPHEE
Also see each artist's individual listings.
HAT HUT
| 12 [(2)] | Tales and Prophecies | 1980 | 5.00 | 10.00 | 20.00 |

Number	Title	Yr	VG	VG+	NM

JAZZ ARTISTS GUILD, THE
Members: ERIC DOLPHY; KENNT DORHAM; ROY ELDRIDGE; JO JONES; ABBEY LINCLON; CHARLES MINGUS; MAX ROACH.
CANDID

❑ CD-8022 [M]	Newport Rebels	1960	10.00	20.00	40.00
❑ CS-9022 [S]	Newport Rebels	1960	12.50	25.00	50.00

JAZZ BROTHERS, THE
Led by CHUCK MANGIONE and his brother GAP MANGIONE.
RIVERSIDE

❑ RLP-335 [M]	Jazz Brothers	1960	6.25	12.50	25.00
❑ RLP-371 [M]	Hey, Baby!	1961	6.25	12.50	25.00
❑ RLP-405 [M]	Spring Fever	1962	6.25	12.50	25.00
❑ RS-9335 [S]	Jazz Brothers	1960	7.50	15.00	30.00
❑ RS-9371 [S]	Hey, Baby!	1961	7.50	15.00	30.00
❑ RS-9405 [S]	Spring Fever	1962	7.50	15.00	30.00

JAZZ CITY
Members include Pete Christlieb (tenor sax) and Harry Kevis Jr. (drums).
RAHMP

❑ 2	Jazz City	197?	5.00	10.00	20.00

JAZZ CITY ALL-STARS, THE
BETHLEHEM

❑ BCP-79 [M]	Jazz City Presents	1957	12.50	25.00	50.00

JAZZ COMPOSERS ORCHESTRA
JCOA

❑ LP-1001/2 [(2)]	Jazz Composers Orchestra	1968	15.00	30.00	60.00

JAZZ CONTEMPORARIES
STRATA-EAST

❑ SES 1972-2	Reasons in Tonality	1972	3.75	7.50	15.00

JAZZ CORPS, THE
Members: Tommy Peltier (cornet, fluegel horn); [RAHSAAN] ROLAND KIRK (tenor sax, flute, baritone sax); Fred Rodriguez (tenor and alto saxes, flute); Lynn Blessing (vibes); Bill Plummer (bass); Maurice Miller (drums).
PACIFIC JAZZ

❑ PJ-10116 [M]	The Jazz Corps Under the Direction of Tommy Peltier	1967	6.25	12.50	25.00
❑ LN-10131	The Jazz Corps Under the Direction of Tommy Peltier	198?	2.50	5.00	10.00
-- Budget-line reissue					
❑ ST-20116 [S]	The Jazz Corps Under the Direction of Tommy Peltier	1967	3.75	7.50	15.00

JAZZ COURIERS, THE
British group whose members included TUBBY HAYES; Kenny Nepper; Ronnie Scott; Phil Seamen; Terry Shannon.
CARLTON

❑ LP 12-116 [M]	The Couriers of Jazz	1959	12.50	25.00	50.00
❑ ST 12-116 [S]	The Couriers of Jazz	1959	10.00	20.00	40.00

JAZZLAND

❑ JLP-34 [M]	Message from Britain	1961	6.25	12.50	25.00
❑ JLP-934 [S]	Message from Britain	1961	7.50	15.00	30.00

WHIPPET

❑ WLP-700 [M]	The Jazz Couriers	1956	30.00	60.00	120.00

JAZZ CRUSADERS, THE
See THE CRUSADERS.

JAZZ EXPONENTS, THE
Members: Norm Diamond; Bill Elliott; Jack Gridley; Dick Rionda.
ARGO

❑ LP-622 [M]	The Jazz Exponents	1958	10.00	20.00	40.00

JAZZ FIVE, THE
Members: Vic Arch; Malcolm Cecil; Brian Dee; Bill Eyden; Barry Klein.
RIVERSIDE

❑ RLP-361 [M]	The Hooter	1961	6.25	12.50	25.00
❑ RS-9361 [S]	The Hooter	1961	7.50	15.00	30.00

JAZZ INTERACTIONS ORCHESTRA, THE
Members: Joe Newman (trumpet, conductor); Ernie Royal, Ray Copeland, Burt Collins, Marvin Stamm (trumpets); Benny Powell, Paul Faulise, Wayne Andre, Jimmy Cleveland (trombones); Jimmy Buffington, Ray Alonge (French horns); Don Butterfield (tubs); Phil Woods, George Marge (alto sax, flute); Jerry Dodgion, Zoot Sims (tenor sax); Danny Bank (bass, bass clarinet, flute); Patti Bown (piano); Ron Carter, George Duvivier (bass); Ed Shaughnessy (drums); Bobby Rosengarden (percussion); Oliver Nelson (composer, arranger, conductor).
VERVE

❑ V-8731 [M]	Jazzhattan Suite	1967	5.00	10.00	20.00
❑ V6-8731 [S]	Jazzhattan Suite	1967	3.00	6.00	12.00

JAZZ LAB, THE
Led by CHARLIE BYRD and GIGI GRYCE.
COLUMBIA

❑ CL 998 [M]	Jazz Lab	1957	20.00	40.00	80.00
❑ CL 1058 [M]	Modern Jazz Perspective/Jazz Lab, Volume 2	1957	20.00	40.00	80.00

JAZZLAND

❑ JLP-1 [M]	Jazz Lab	1960	7.50	15.00	30.00
❑ JLP-901 [S]	Jazz Lab	1960	10.00	20.00	40.00

JOSIE

❑ JOZ-3500 [M]	Gigi Gryce and Donald Byrd	1962	10.00	20.00	40.00
-- Reissue of Jubilee album					
❑ JS-3500 [R]	Gigi Gryce and Donald Byrd	196?	5.00	10.00	20.00

JUBILEE

❑ JLP-1059 [M]	Jazz Lab	1958	25.00	50.00	100.00

RIVERSIDE

❑ RLP 12-229 [M]	Gigi Gryce and the Jazz Lab	1957	25.00	50.00	100.00
-- White label, blue print					
❑ RLP 12-229 [M]	Gigi Gryce and the Jazz Lab	1959	12.50	25.00	50.00
-- Blue label, microphone logo at top					
❑ RLP-1110 [S]	Gigi Gryce and the Jazz Lab	1959	12.50	25.00	50.00

JAZZ MEMBERS BIG BAND
SEA BREEZE

❑ SB-2014	May Day	1985	2.50	5.00	10.00
❑ SB-2028	Live at Fitzgerald	1986	2.50	5.00	10.00

JAZZ MESSENGERS, THE
See ART BLAKEY.

JAZZ MODES, THE
See LES JAZZ MODES.

JAZZ O'MANIACS, THE
STOMP OFF

❑ SOS-1046	Have You Ever Felt This Way	198?	2.50	5.00	10.00
❑ SOS-1071	Sweet Mumtaz	1984	2.50	5.00	10.00

JAZZ PIANO QUARTET, THE
Members: ROLAND HANNA; DICK HYMAN; HANK JONES; MARIAN McPARTLAND.
RCA VICTOR

❑ CPL1-0680	Let It Happen	1974	3.75	7.50	15.00

JAZZ SYMPHONICS
RENFRO

❑ LP-12369	The Beginning	1968	15.00	30.00	60.00

JAZZ WARRIORS
Led by COURTNEY PINE with a constantly changing membership.
ANTILLES

❑ 90681	Out of Many, One People	1987	2.50	5.00	10.00

JAZZ WAVE, LTD., THE
See THAD JONES-MEL LEWIS ORCHESTRA.

JAZZMOBILE ALL-STARS, THE
Led by BILLY TAYLOR. Other members: Jimmy Owens (trumpet, fluegel horn); FRANK WESS; TED DUNBAR; Victor Gaskin (bass); Bobby Thomas (drums).
TAYLOR-MADE

❑ TL-1003	The Jazzmobile All Stars	1989	3.00	6.00	12.00

JAZZPICKERS, THE
Led by HARRY BABASIN. Other members at different times included BUDDY COLLETTE; TERRY GIBBS; and RED NORVO.
EMARCY

❑ MG-36111 [M]	The Jazzpickers	1957	12.50	25.00	50.00
❑ MG-36123 [M]	Command Performance	1958	12.50	25.00	50.00

MERCURY

❑ SR-80013 [S]	For Moderns Only	1959	10.00	20.00	40.00

JAZZTET, THE
Featuring ART FARMER and BENNY GOLSON.
ARGO

❑ LP-664 [M]	Meet the Jazztet	1960	7.50	15.00	30.00
❑ LPS-664 [S]	Meet the Jazztet	1960	10.00	20.00	40.00
❑ LP-672 [M]	Big City Sounds	1961	6.25	12.50	25.00
❑ LPS-672 [S]	Big City Sounds	1961	7.50	15.00	30.00
❑ LP-684 [M]	The Jazztet and John Lewis	1961	6.25	12.50	25.00

Number	Title	Yr	VG	VG+	NM
❑ LPS-684 [S]	The Jazztet and John Lewis	1961	7.50	15.00	30.00
❑ LP-688 [M]	The Jazztet at Birdhouse	1961	6.25	12.50	25.00
❑ LPS-688 [S]	The Jazztet at Birdhouse	1961	7.50	15.00	30.00
CADET					
❑ LP-664 [M]	Meet the Jazztet	1966	3.75	7.50	15.00
❑ LPS-664 [S]	Meet the Jazztet	1966	5.00	10.00	20.00
CONTEMPORARY					
❑ C-14034	Real Time	1988	2.50	5.00	10.00
MERCURY					
❑ MG-20698 [M]	Here and Now	1962	6.25	12.50	25.00
❑ MG-20737 [M]	Another Git-Together	1962	6.25	12.50	25.00
❑ SR-60698 [S]	Here and Now	1962	7.50	15.00	30.00
❑ SR-60737 [S]	Another Git-Together	1962	7.50	15.00	30.00
SOUL NOTE					
❑ SN-1066	Moment to Moment	1984	3.00	6.00	12.00

JEANNEAU, FRANCOIS
Saxophone player, arranger and composer.
INNER CITY

Number	Title	Yr	VG	VG+	NM
❑ IC-1022	Techniques Douces	197?	3.75	7.50	15.00

JEFFERSON, CARTER
Saxophone player.
TIMELESS

Number	Title	Yr	VG	VG+	NM
❑ 309	The Rise of Atlantis	1979	3.00	6.00	12.00

JEFFERSON, EDDIE
Male singer; popularized "vocalese," the art of putting lyrics to jazz solos.
FANTASY

Number	Title	Yr	VG	VG+	NM
❑ OJC-307	Letter from Home	1988	2.50	5.00	10.00
❑ OJC-396	Body and Soul	1989	3.00	6.00	12.00
❑ OJC-613	Come Along with Me	1991	3.00	6.00	12.00
INNER CITY					
❑ IC-1016	Jazz Singer	197?	3.75	7.50	15.00
❑ IC-1033	Main Man	1978	3.75	7.50	15.00
MUSE					
❑ MR-5043	Things Are Getting Better	1974	3.00	6.00	12.00
❑ MR-5063	Still On the Planet	1976	3.00	6.00	12.00
❑ MR-5127	The Live-Liest	197?	3.00	6.00	12.00
PRESTIGE					
❑ PRST-7619	Body and Soul	1969	5.00	10.00	20.00
❑ PRST-7698	Come Along with Me	1969	5.00	10.00	20.00
❑ 24095 [(2)]	There I Go Again	198?	3.75	7.50	15.00
RIVERSIDE					
❑ RLP-411 [M]	Letter from Home	1962	7.50	15.00	30.00
❑ RS-9411 [S]	Letter from Home	1962	10.00	20.00	40.00

JEFFERSON, RON
Drummer. Also see LES JAZZ MODES.
CATALYST

Number	Title	Yr	VG	VG+	NM
❑ 7601	Vous Etes Swing	1976	3.00	6.00	12.00
PACIFIC JAZZ					
❑ PJ-36 [M]	Love Lifted Me	1962	7.50	15.00	30.00
❑ ST-36 [S]	Love Lifted Me	1962	10.00	20.00	40.00

JEFFREY, PAUL
Tenor saxophone player.
MAINSTREAM

Number	Title	Yr	VG	VG+	NM
❑ MRL-376	Family	1972	3.75	7.50	15.00
❑ MRL-390	Watershed	1973	3.75	7.50	15.00
❑ MRL-406	Paul Jeffrey	1973	3.75	7.50	15.00
SAVOY					
❑ MG-12192 [M]	Electrifying Sounds	1968	5.00	10.00	20.00

JEFFRIES, FRAN
Female singer.
WARWICK

Number	Title	Yr	VG	VG+	NM
❑ W-2020 [M]	Fran Can Really Hang You Up the Most	1960	5.00	10.00	20.00

JEFFRIES, HERB
Male singer.
BETHLEHEM

Number	Title	Yr	VG	VG+	NM
❑ BCP-72 [M]	Say It Isn't So	1957	15.00	30.00	60.00
CORAL					
❑ CRL 56044 [10]	Time on My Hands	1951	25.00	50.00	100.00
MERCURY					
❑ MG-25089 [10]	Magenta Moods	1950	25.00	50.00	100.00
❑ MG-25091 [10]	Just Jeffries	1950	25.00	50.00	100.00

JENKINS, JOHN
Alto saxophone player. Also see PHIL WOODS.
BLUE NOTE

Number	Title	Yr	VG	VG+	NM
❑ BLP-1573 [M]	John Jenkins with Kenny Burrell	1958	30.00	60.00	120.00
-- "Deep groove" version (deep indentation under label on both sides)					
❑ BLP-1573 [M]	John Jenkins with Kenny Burrell	1958	20.00	40.00	80.00
-- Regular version with W. 63rd St., New York address on label					
❑ BLP-1573 [M]	John Jenkins with Kenny Burrell	1963	6.25	12.50	25.00
-- With "New York, USA" address on label					
❑ BST-1573 [S]	John Jenkins with Kenny Burrell	1959	20.00	40.00	80.00
-- "Deep groove" version (deep indentation under label on both sides)					
❑ BST-1573 [S]	John Jenkins with Kenny Burrell	1959	12.50	25.00	50.00
-- Regular version with W. 63rd St., New York address on label					
❑ BST-1573 [S]	John Jenkins with Kenny Burrell	1963	5.00	10.00	20.00
-- With "New York, USA" address on label					
❑ BST-81573 [S]	John Jenkins with Kenny Burrell	1967	3.75	7.50	15.00
-- With "A Division of Liberty Records" on label					
REGENT					
❑ MG-6056 [M]	Jazz Eyes	1957	25.00	50.00	100.00
SAVOY					
❑ MG-12201 [M]	Jazz Eyes	196?	5.00	10.00	20.00

JENKINS, JOHN; CLIFF JORDAN; BOBBY TIMMONS
Also see each artist's individual listings.
FANTASY

Number	Title	Yr	VG	VG+	NM
❑ OJC-251	Jenkins, Jordan & Timmons	1987	2.50	5.00	10.00
NEW JAZZ					
❑ NJLP-8232 [M]	Jenkins, Jordan & Timmons	1960	15.00	30.00	60.00
❑ NJLP-8232 [M]	Jenkins, Jordan & Timmons	1965	6.25	12.50	25.00

JENKINS, LEROY
Violinist.
BLACK SAINT

Number	Title	Yr	VG	VG+	NM
❑ BSR-0022	The Legend of Ai Glatson	198?	3.00	6.00	12.00
❑ BSR-0060	Mixed Quartet	198?	3.00	6.00	12.00
❑ BSR-0083	Urban Blues	1985	3.00	6.00	12.00
INDIA NAVIGATION					
❑ IN-1028	Solo Concert	1977	3.00	6.00	12.00
JCOA					
❑ LP-1010	For Players Only	1975	3.75	7.50	15.00
TOMATO					
❑ TOM-8001	Space Minds, New Worlds	1979	3.75	7.50	15.00

JENKINS, LEROY, AND MUHAL RICHARD ABRAMS
Also see each artist's individual listings.
BLACK SAINT

Number	Title	Yr	VG	VG+	NM
❑ BSR-0033	Duo	198?	3.00	6.00	12.00

JENKINS, MARV
OROVOX

Number	Title	Yr	VG	VG+	NM
❑ 1001 [M]	Marv Jenkins Arrives	196?	10.00	20.00	40.00
❑ S-1001 [S]	Marv Jenkins Arrives	196?	10.00	20.00	40.00
REPRISE					
❑ R-6077 [M]	Good Little Man at the Rubaiyat Room	1963	5.00	10.00	20.00
❑ R9-6077 [S]	Good Little Man at the Rubaiyat Room	1963	6.25	12.50	25.00

JENKS, GLENN
Pianist.
STOMP OFF

Number	Title	Yr	VG	VG+	NM
❑ SOS-1179	Ragtime Alchemy	1989	2.50	5.00	10.00

JENNEY, JACK
Trombonist.
COLUMBIA

Number	Title	Yr	VG	VG+	NM
❑ GL 100 [10]	The Golden Era	1949	12.50	25.00	50.00
COLUMBIA MASTERWORKS					
❑ ML 4803 [M]	Jack Jenney	195?	20.00	40.00	80.00

JENNINGS, BILL
Guitarist. Also see KENNY BURRELL.
AUDIO LAB

Number	Title	Yr	VG	VG+	NM
❑ AL-1514 [M]	Guitar/Vibes	1959	25.00	50.00	100.00
KING					
❑ 295-105 [10]	Jazz Interlude	195?	62.50	125.00	250.00
❑ 295-106 [10]	The Fabulous Guitar of Bill	195?	62.50	125.00	250.00
❑ 398-508 [M]	Mood Indigo	1955	25.00	50.00	100.00
❑ 398-527 [M]	Billy in the Lion's Den	1956	25.00	50.00	100.00

Number	Title	Yr	VG	VG+	NM
PRESTIGE					
❏ PRLP-7164 [M]	Enough Said!	1959	12.50	25.00	50.00
❏ PRLP-7177 [M]	Glide On	1960	12.50	25.00	50.00
❏ PRST-7788	Enough Said!	1970	3.00	6.00	12.00
❏ PRST-7836	Glide On	1971	3.00	6.00	12.00

JERNIGAN, DOUG, AND BUCKY PIZZARELLI
Jernigan is a pedal steel guitar player. Also see BUCKY PIZZARELLI.

Number	Title	Yr	VG	VG+	NM
FLYING FISH					
❏ 043	Doug and Bucky	1977	3.00	6.00	12.00

JETSTREAM
Also see GEORGE SHAW.

Number	Title	Yr	VG	VG+	NM
PALO ALTO					
❏ TB-211	Around the World	198?	2.50	5.00	10.00

JEWKES, NOEL
Saxophone player and flutist.

Number	Title	Yr	VG	VG+	NM
REVELATION					
❏ 30	Just Passin' Thru	1980	3.00	6.00	12.00

JOBIM, ANTONIO CARLOS
Guitarist, pianist, composer and arranger. Also see STAN GETZ; HERBIE MANN; FRANK SINATRA.

Number	Title	Yr	VG	VG+	NM
A&M					
❏ SP-3002	Wave	1968	3.00	6.00	12.00
❏ SP-3031	Tide	1970	3.00	6.00	12.00
CTI					
❏ 6002	Stone Flower	1973	3.00	6.00	12.00
DISCOVERY					
❏ DS-848	A Certain Mr. Jobim	198?	2.50	5.00	10.00
PHILIPS					
❏ 832 766-1	Personalidade Series	1988	2.50	5.00	10.00
VERVE					
❏ V-8547 [M]	The Composer of "Desafinado" Plays	1963	3.00	6.00	12.00
❏ V6-8547 [S]	The Composer of "Desafinado" Plays	1963	3.75	7.50	15.00
❏ 833 234-1	Passaim	1988	2.50	5.00	10.00
WARNER BROS.					
❏ W 1611 [M]	The Wonderful World of Antonio Carlos Jobim	1966	3.75	7.50	15.00
❏ WS 1611 [S]	The Wonderful World of Antonio Carlos Jobim	1966	5.00	10.00	20.00
❏ W 1636 [M]	Love, Strings	1966	3.75	7.50	15.00
❏ WS 1636 [S]	Love, Strings	1966	5.00	10.00	20.00
-- Gold label					
❏ BS 2928	Urubu	1976	2.50	5.00	10.00
❏ 2BS 3409 [(2)]	Terra Brasilis	1981	3.00	6.00	12.00

JOHANSSON, JAN
Pianist.

Number	Title	Yr	VG	VG+	NM
DOT					
❏ DLP-3416 [M]	Sweden Non-Stop	1962	5.00	10.00	20.00
❏ DLP-25416 [S]	Sweden Non-Stop	1962	6.25	12.50	25.00

JOHANSSON, LASSE
Guitarist.

Number	Title	Yr	VG	VG+	NM
KICKING MULE					
❏ KM-170	King Porter Stomp -- The Music of Jelly Roll Morton	198?	3.00	6.00	12.00

JOHNSON, ALPHONSO
Bass player.

Number	Title	Yr	VG	VG+	NM
EPIC					
❏ PE 34118	Moonshadows	1975	2.50	5.00	10.00
❏ PE 34364	Yesterday's Dreams	1976	2.50	5.00	10.00
❏ JE 34869	Spellbound	1977	2.50	5.00	10.00
❏ JE 36521	The Best of Alphonso Johnson	1979	2.50	5.00	10.00

JOHNSON, ARNOLD
Bandleader.

Number	Title	Yr	VG	VG+	NM
CIRCLE					
❏ 32	Swinging the Classics	198?	2.50	5.00	10.00

JOHNSON, BUDD
Saxophone player (mostly tenor), occasional male singer, composer and arranger. Also see THE JPJ QUARTET.

Number	Title	Yr	VG	VG+	NM
ARGO					
❏ LP-721 [M]	French Cookin'	1963	6.25	12.50	25.00
❏ LPS-721 [S]	French Cookin'	1963	7.50	15.00	30.00

Number	Title	Yr	VG	VG+	NM
❏ LP-736 [M]	Ya! Ya!	1964	6.25	12.50	25.00
❏ LPS-736 [S]	Ya! Ya!	1964	7.50	15.00	30.00
❏ LP-748 [M]	Off the Wall	1965	6.25	12.50	25.00
❏ LPS-748 [S]	Off the Wall	1965	7.50	15.00	30.00
FANTASY					
❏ OJC-209	Budd Johnson and the Four Brass Giants	1985	2.50	5.00	10.00
❏ OJC-1720	Let's Swing	198?	2.50	5.00	10.00
FELSTED					
❏ SJA-2007 [S]	Blues A La Mode	1959	20.00	40.00	80.00
❏ FAJ-7007 [M]	Blues A La Mode	1959	15.00	30.00	60.00
MASTER JAZZ					
❏ 8119	Blues A La Mode	197?	3.00	6.00	12.00
RIVERSIDE					
❏ RLP-343 [M]	Budd Johnson and the Four Brass Giants	1960	10.00	20.00	40.00
❏ RS-9343 [S]	Budd Johnson and the Four Brass Giants	1960	12.50	25.00	50.00
SWINGVILLE					
❏ SVLP-2015 [M]	Let's Swing	1961	12.50	25.00	50.00
-- Purple label					
❏ SVLP-2015 [M]	Let's Swing	1965	6.25	12.50	25.00
-- Blue label, trident logo at right					

JOHNSON, BUDDY
Pianist, male singer, arranger, composer and bandleader.

Number	Title	Yr	VG	VG+	NM
MCA					
❏ 1356	Fine Brown Frame	198?	2.50	5.00	10.00
MERCURY					
❏ MG-20209 [M]	Rock 'n' Roll	195?	20.00	40.00	80.00
❏ MG-20322 [M]	Walkin'	195?	20.00	40.00	80.00
❏ MG-20330 [M]	Buddy Johnson Wails	195?	20.00	40.00	80.00
❏ MG-20347 [M]	Swing Me	195?	20.00	40.00	80.00
❏ SR-60072 [S]	Buddy Johnson Wails	195?	25.00	50.00	100.00
WING					
❏ MGW-12005 [M]	Rock 'n' Roll	1956	37.50	75.00	150.00
❏ MGW-12111 [M]	Rock 'n' Roll Stage Show	1963	10.00	20.00	40.00

JOHNSON, BUDDY & ELLA
Ella is a female singer. Also see BUDDY JOHNSON.

Number	Title	Yr	VG	VG+	NM
MERCURY					
❏ MG-20347 [M]	Swing Me	195?	20.00	40.00	80.00
ROULETTE					
❏ R 25085 [M]	Go Ahead and Rock and Roll	1959	20.00	40.00	80.00
❏ SR 25085 [S]	Go Ahead and Rock and Roll	1959	30.00	60.00	120.00

JOHNSON, BUNK
Trumpeter. One of the earliest known jazz musicians, he had a second go-round after being rediscovered in the 1940s. Also see ERNESTINE WASHINGTON.

Number	Title	Yr	VG	VG+	NM
AMERICAN MUSIC					
❏ 638 [10]	Bunk Plays the Blues -- The Spirituals	1951	15.00	30.00	60.00
❏ 644 [10]	Bunk Johnson Talking	1952	15.00	30.00	60.00
COLUMBIA					
❏ CL 520 [M]	Bunk Johnson and His Band	1953	12.50	25.00	50.00
-- Maroon label, gold print					
❏ CL 520 [M]	Bunk Johnson and His Band	1955	10.00	20.00	40.00
-- Red and black label with six "eye" logos					
❏ GL 520 [M]	Bunk Johnson and His Band	1952	15.00	30.00	60.00
-- Black label, silver print					
❏ CL 829 [M]	Bunk Johnson	1955	10.00	20.00	40.00
-- Red and black label with six "eye" logos					
COLUMBIA MASTERWORKS					
❏ ML 4802 [M]	The Last Testament of a Great New Orleans Jazzman	1950	20.00	40.00	80.00
COMMODORE					
❏ DL-30007 [M]	The Bunk Johnson Band	1952	12.50	25.00	50.00
FOLKLYRIC					
❏ 9047	Bunk Johnson and His New Orleans Jazz Band	1986	2.50	5.00	10.00
GHB					
❏ 101	Spicy Advice	198?	2.50	5.00	10.00
GOOD TIME JAZZ					
❏ L-17 [10]	Bunk Johnson and the Yerba Buena Jazz Band	1953	12.50	25.00	50.00
❏ L-12048 [M]	Bunk Johnson and His Superior Jazz Band	1962	7.50	15.00	30.00
MAINSTREAM					
❏ S-6039 [R]	Bunk Johnson -- A Legend	1965	3.00	6.00	12.00
❏ 56039 [M]	Bunk Johnson -- A Legend	1965	5.00	10.00	20.00
TRIP					
❏ J-2	Bunk Johnson	1970	3.00	6.00	12.00

Number	Title	Yr	VG	VG+	NM
JOHNSON, BUNK, AND LU WATTERS					

Also see each artist's individual listings.

GOOD TIME JAZZ

Number	Title	Yr	VG	VG+	NM
❑ L-12024 [M]	Bunk and Lu	195?	10.00	20.00	40.00

JOHNSON, CHARLIE

Pianist and bandleader.

"X"

Number	Title	Yr	VG	VG+	NM
❑ LVA-3026 [10]	Harlem in the Twenties, Vol. 2	1954	15.00	30.00	60.00

JOHNSON, DAVID EARLE

Drummer, percussionist and male singer.

CMP

Number	Title	Yr	VG	VG+	NM
❑ CMP-14-ST	Hip Address	1980	3.00	6.00	12.00
❑ CMP-20-ST	Skin Deep -- Yeah!	1981	3.00	6.00	12.00

VANGUARD

Number	Title	Yr	VG	VG+	NM
❑ VSD-79401	Time Free	197?	2.50	5.00	10.00

JOHNSON, DAVID EARLE; JAN HAMMER; JOHN ABERCROMBIE

Also see each artist's individual listings.

PLUG

Number	Title	Yr	VG	VG+	NM
❑ 1	The Midweek Blues	1986	3.00	6.00	12.00

JOHNSON, DICK

Clarinetist, saxophone player (soprano, alto and tenor) and flutist. Also see EDDIE COSTA.

CONCORD JAZZ

Number	Title	Yr	VG	VG+	NM
❑ CJ-107	Dick Johnson Plays Alto Sax & Flute & Soprano Sax & Clarinet	1979	2.50	5.00	10.00
❑ CJ-135	Spider's Blues	1980	2.50	5.00	10.00
❑ CJ-146	Piano Mover	1980	2.50	5.00	10.00
❑ CJ-167	Swing Shift	1981	2.50	5.00	10.00

EMARCY

Number	Title	Yr	VG	VG+	NM
❑ MG-36081 [M]	Music for Swinging Moderns	1956	20.00	40.00	80.00

RIVERSIDE

Number	Title	Yr	VG	VG+	NM
❑ RLP 12-253 [M]	Most Likely...	1957	12.50	25.00	50.00

JOHNSON, EDDIE

Tenor saxophone player.

NESSA

Number	Title	Yr	VG	VG+	NM
❑ N-22	Indian Summer	1981	3.00	6.00	12.00

JOHNSON, HENRY

Guitarist.

MCA

Number	Title	Yr	VG	VG+	NM
❑ 6329	Never Too Much	1990	3.00	6.00	12.00

JOHNSON, J.J.

Trombonist, arranger and composer. Also see THE BRASS ENSEMBLE OF THE JAZZ & CLASSICAL MUSIC SOCIETY; STAN GETZ; SONNY STITT.

ABC IMPULSE!

Number	Title	Yr	VG	VG+	NM
❑ AS-68 [S]	Proof Positive	1968	3.75	7.50	15.00

BLUE NOTE

Number	Title	Yr	VG	VG+	NM
❑ BLP-1505 [M]	The Eminent Jay Jay Johnson, Volume 1	1955	37.50	75.00	150.00
-- "Deep groove" version (deep indentation under label on both sides)					
❑ BLP-1505 [M]	The Eminent Jay Jay Johnson, Volume 1	1955	25.00	50.00	100.00
-- Regular version, Lexington Ave. address on label					
❑ BLP-1505 [M]	The Eminent Jay Jay Johnson, Volume 1	1963	6.25	12.50	25.00
-- "New York, USA" address on label					
❑ BLP-1506 [M]	The Eminent Jay Jay Johnson, Volume 2	1955	37.50	75.00	150.00
-- "Deep groove" version (deep indentation under label on both sides)					
❑ BLP-1506 [M]	The Eminent Jay Jay Johnson, Volume 2	1955	25.00	50.00	100.00
-- Regular version, Lexington Ave. address on label					
❑ BLP-1506 [M]	The Eminent Jay Jay Johnson, Volume 2	1963	6.25	12.50	25.00
-- "New York, USA" address on label					
❑ BLP-5028 [10]	Jay Jay Johnson All Stars	1953	75.00	150.00	300.00
❑ BLP-5057 [10]	Jay Jay Johnson, Volume 2	1955	75.00	150.00	300.00
❑ BLP-5070 [10]	Jay Jay Johnson, Volume 3	1955	75.00	150.00	300.00
❑ BST-81505 [R]	The Eminent Jay Jay Johnson, Volume 1	1967	3.00	6.00	12.00
❑ B1-81505	The Eminent J.J. Johnson, Volume 1	1989	3.00	6.00	12.00
-- "The Finest in Jazz Since 1939" reissue					
❑ BST-81506 [R]	The Eminent Jay Jay Johnson, Volume 2	1967	3.00	6.00	12.00
❑ B1-81506	The Eminent J.J. Johnson, Volume 2	1989	3.75	7.50	15.00
-- "The Finest in Jazz Since 1939" reissue					

COLUMBIA

Number	Title	Yr	VG	VG+	NM
❑ CL 935 [M]	"J" Is for Jazz	1956	12.50	25.00	50.00
-- Red and black label with six "eye" logos					
❑ CL 935 [M]	"J" Is for Jazz	1963	3.75	7.50	15.00
-- Red label with "Guaranteed High Fidelity" or "360 Sound Mono" at bottom					
❑ CL 1030 [M]	First Place	1957	12.50	25.00	50.00
-- Red and black label with six "eye" logos					
❑ CL 1030 [M]	First Place	1963	3.75	7.50	15.00
-- Red label with "Guaranteed High Fidelity" or "360 Sound Mono" at bottom					
❑ CL 1084 [M]	Dial J.J. 5	1957	12.50	25.00	50.00
-- Red and black label with six "eye" logos					
❑ CL 1084 [M]	Dial J.J. 5	1963	3.75	7.50	15.00
-- Red label with "Guaranteed High Fidelity" or "360 Sound Mono" at bottom					
❑ CL 1161 [M]	J.J. In Person	1958	12.50	25.00	50.00
-- Red and black label with six "eye" logos					
❑ CL 1161 [M]	J.J. In Person	1963	3.75	7.50	15.00
-- Red label with "Guaranteed High Fidelity" or "360 Sound Mono" at bottom					
❑ CL 1303 [M]	Blue Trombone	1959	10.00	20.00	40.00
-- Red and black label with six "eye" logos					
❑ CL 1303 [M]	Blue Trombone	1963	3.00	6.00	12.00
-- Red label with "Guaranteed High Fidelity" or "360 Sound Mono" at bottom					
❑ CL 1383 [M]	Really Livin'	1959	10.00	20.00	40.00
-- Red and black label with six "eye" logos					
❑ CL 1383 [M]	Really Livin'	1963	3.00	6.00	12.00
-- Red label with "Guaranteed High Fidelity" or "360 Sound Mono" at bottom					
❑ CL 1547 [M]	Trombones and Voices	1960	7.50	15.00	30.00
-- Red and black label with six "eye" logos					
❑ CL 1547 [M]	Trombones and Voices	1963	3.00	6.00	12.00
-- Red label with "Guaranteed High Fidelity" or "360 Sound Mono" at bottom					
❑ CL 1606 [M]	J.J. Inc	1961	7.50	15.00	30.00
-- Red and black label with six "eye" logos					
❑ CL 1606 [M]	J.J. Inc	1963	3.00	6.00	12.00
-- Red label with "Guaranteed High Fidelity" or "360 Sound Mono" at bottom					
❑ CL 1737 [M]	A Touch of Satin	1962	10.00	20.00	40.00
-- Red and black label with six "eye" logos					
❑ CL 1737 [M]	A Touch of Satin	1963	3.75	7.50	15.00
-- Red label with "Guaranteed High Fidelity" or "360 Sound Mono" at bottom					
❑ CS 8009 [S]	J.J. In Person	1959	10.00	20.00	40.00
-- Red and black label with six "eye" logos					
❑ CS 8009 [S]	J.J. In Person	1963	3.00	6.00	12.00
-- Red label with "360 Sound Stereo" in black or white at bottom					
❑ CS 8109 [S]	Blue Trombone	1959	12.50	25.00	50.00
-- Red and black label with six "eye" logos					
❑ CS 8109 [S]	Blue Trombone	1963	3.75	7.50	15.00
-- Red label with "360 Sound Stereo" in black or white at bottom					
❑ CS 8178 [S]	Really Livin'	1959	12.50	25.00	50.00
-- Red and black label with six "eye" logos					
❑ CS 8178 [S]	Really Livin'	1963	3.75	7.50	15.00
-- Red label with "360 Sound Stereo" in black or white at bottom					
❑ CS 8347 [S]	Trombones and Voices	1960	10.00	20.00	40.00
-- Red and black label with six "eye" logos					
❑ CS 8347 [S]	Trombones and Voices	1963	3.75	7.50	15.00
-- Red label with "360 Sound Stereo" in black or white at bottom					
❑ CS 8406 [S]	J.J. Inc	1961	10.00	20.00	40.00
-- Red and black label with six "eye" logos					
❑ CS 8406 [S]	J.J. Inc	1963	3.75	7.50	15.00
-- Red label with "360 Sound Stereo" in black or white at bottom					
❑ CS 8537 [S]	A Touch of Satin	1962	12.50	25.00	50.00
-- Red and black label with six "eye" logos					
❑ CS 8537 [S]	A Touch of Satin	1963	5.00	10.00	20.00
-- Red label with "360 Sound Stereo" in black or white at bottom					

COLUMBIA JAZZ ODYSSEY

Number	Title	Yr	VG	VG+	NM
❑ PC 36808	J.J. Inc.	1979	2.50	5.00	10.00

IMPULSE!

Number	Title	Yr	VG	VG+	NM
❑ A-68 [M]	Proof Positive	1965	6.25	12.50	25.00
❑ AS-68 [S]	Proof Positive	1965	7.50	15.00	30.00

MCA

Number	Title	Yr	VG	VG+	NM
❑ 29072	Proof Positive	1980	2.50	5.00	10.00

MILESTONE

Number	Title	Yr	VG	VG+	NM
❑ M-9093	Pinnacles	1979	3.00	6.00	12.00

MOSAIC

Number	Title	Yr	VG	VG+	NM
❑ MQ11-169 [(11)]	The Complete Columbia J.J. Johnson Small Group Sessions	199?	50.00	100.00	200.00

PABLO TODAY

Number	Title	Yr	VG	VG+	NM
❑ 2312 123	Concepts in Blue	1980	3.00	6.00	12.00

PRESTIGE

Number	Title	Yr	VG	VG+	NM
❑ 24067 [(2)]	Early Bones	198?	3.00	6.00	12.00

RCA VICTOR

Number	Title	Yr	VG	VG+	NM
❑ LPM-3350 [M]	J.J.!	1965	5.00	10.00	20.00
❑ LSP-3350 [S]	J.J.!	1965	6.25	12.50	25.00
❑ LPM-3458 [M]	Goodies	1965	5.00	10.00	20.00
❑ LSP-3458 [S]	Goodies	1965	6.25	12.50	25.00
❑ LPM-3544 [M]	Broadway Express	1966	5.00	10.00	20.00
❑ LSP-3544 [S]	Broadway Express	1966	6.25	12.50	25.00
❑ LPM-3833 [M]	The Total J.J. Johnson	1967	7.50	15.00	30.00
❑ LSP-3833 [S]	The Total J.J. Johnson	1967	5.00	10.00	20.00

Number	Title	Yr	VG	VG+	NM
REGENT					
❑ MG-6001 [M]	Jazz South Pacific	1956	12.50	25.00	50.00
SAVOY JAZZ					
❑ SJL-2232 [(2)]	Mad Bebop	198?	3.00	6.00	12.00
VERVE					
❑ V-8530 [M]	J.J.'s Broadway	1963	5.00	10.00	20.00
❑ V6-8530 [S]	J.J.'s Broadway	1963	6.25	12.50	25.00

JOHNSON, J.J., AND NAT ADDERLEY
Also see each artist's individual listings.

Number	Title	Yr	VG	VG+	NM
PABLO LIVE					
❑ 2620 109 [(2)]	Yokohama Concert	1977	3.75	7.50	15.00

JOHNSON, J.J./BENNIE GREEN
Also see each artist's individual listings.

Number	Title	Yr	VG	VG+	NM
PRESTIGE					
❑ PRLP-123 [10]	Modern Jazz Trombones, Volume 2	1952	50.00	100.00	200.00

JOHNSON, J.J., AND JOE PASS
Also see each artist's individual listings.

Number	Title	Yr	VG	VG+	NM
PABLO					
❑ 2310 911	We'll Be Together Again	198?	2.50	5.00	10.00

JOHNSON, J.J., AND KAI WINDING
Also see each artist's individual listings.

Number	Title	Yr	VG	VG+	NM
A&M					
❑ SP-3008	Israel	1968	5.00	10.00	20.00
❑ SP-3016	Betwixt and Between	1969	5.00	10.00	20.00
❑ SP-3027	Stonebone	1970	---	---	---
-- Canceled					
ABC IMPULSE!					
❑ AS-1 [S]	The Great Kai & J.J.	1968	3.00	6.00	12.00
BETHLEHEM					
❑ BCP-6001 [M]	Kai + J.J.	1955	12.50	25.00	50.00
❑ BCP-6001 [M]	The Finest Kai Winding and J.J. Johnson	197?	3.00	6.00	12.00
-- Reissue with new title, distributed by RCA Victor					
COLUMBIA					
❑ CL 742 [M]	Trombone for Two	1956	12.50	25.00	50.00
-- Red label with "360 Sound Stereo" in black or white at bottom					
❑ CL 742 [M]	Trombone for Two	1963	5.00	10.00	20.00
-- Red label with "Guaranteed High Fidelity" or "360 Sound Mono" at bottom					
❑ CL 892 [M]	J.J. Johnson, Kai Winding + 6	1956	12.50	25.00	50.00
-- Red label with "360 Sound Stereo" in black or white at bottom					
❑ CL 892 [M]	J.J. Johnson, Kai Winding + 6	1963	5.00	10.00	20.00
-- Red label with "Guaranteed High Fidelity" or "360 Sound Mono" at bottom					
❑ CL 973 [M]	Jay and Kai	1957	12.50	25.00	50.00
-- Red label with "360 Sound Stereo" in black or white at bottom					
❑ CL 973 [M]	Jay and Kai	1963	5.00	10.00	20.00
-- Red label with "Guaranteed High Fidelity" or "360 Sound Mono" at bottom					
❑ CL 2573 [10]	Kai + J.J.	1955	20.00	40.00	80.00
COLUMBIA JAZZ ODYSSEY					
❑ PC 37001 [M]	J.J. Johnson, Kai Winding + 6	198?	2.50	5.00	10.00
IMPULSE!					
❑ A-1 [M]	The Great Kai & J.J.	1961	7.50	15.00	30.00
❑ AS-1 [S]	The Great Kai & J.J.	1961	10.00	20.00	40.00
MCA					
❑ 29061	The Great Kai & J.J.	1980	2.50	5.00	10.00
PRESTIGE					
❑ PRLP-109 [10]	Modern Jazz Trombones	1951	50.00	100.00	200.00
❑ PRLP-195 [10]	Jay and Kai	1954	50.00	100.00	200.00
❑ PRLP-7253 [M]	Looking Back	1963	12.50	25.00	50.00
❑ PRST-7253 [R]	Looking Back	1963	7.50	15.00	30.00
SAVOY					
❑ MG-12010 [M]	Jay and Kai	1955	20.00	40.00	80.00
❑ MG-12106 [M]	J.J. Johnson's Jazz Quintets	1957	20.00	40.00	80.00
❑ MG-15038 [10]	Jay and Kai	1954	30.00	60.00	120.00
❑ MG-15048 [10]	Jay and Kai, Volume 2	1955	25.00	50.00	100.00
❑ MG-15049 [10]	Jay and Kai, Volume 3	1955	25.00	50.00	100.00
VIK					
❑ LXA-1040 [M]	An Afternoon at Birdland	1956	20.00	40.00	80.00

JOHNSON, J.J.; KAI WINDING; BENNIE GREEN
Also see each artist's individual listings.

Number	Title	Yr	VG	VG+	NM
DEBUT					
❑ DLP-5 [10]	Jazz Workshop, Volume 1	1953	50.00	100.00	200.00
❑ DLP-14 [10]	Jazz Workshop, Volume 2	1955	50.00	100.00	200.00
❑ DEB-126 [M]	Four Trombones	1958	25.00	50.00	100.00
FANTASY					
❑ OJC-091	Trombones by Three	198?	2.50	5.00	10.00

Number	Title	Yr	VG	VG+	NM
❑ 6005 [M]	Four Trombones	1963	12.50	25.00	50.00
-- Red vinyl					
❑ 6005 [M]	Four Trombones	1963	7.50	15.00	30.00
-- Black vinyl					
❑ 86005 [R]	Four Trombones	1963	5.00	10.00	20.00
-- Black vinyl					
❑ 86005 [R]	Four Trombones	1963	10.00	20.00	40.00
-- Blue vinyl					
PRESTIGE					
❑ PRLP-7023 [M]	Trombones by Three	1956	20.00	40.00	80.00
❑ PRLP-7030 [M]	J.J. Johnson, Kai Winding, Bennie Green	1956	20.00	40.00	80.00

JOHNSON, JAMES P.
Pianist, composer and arranger, he was a pioneer in what became known as "stride piano." Also see SIDNEY DePARIS; OMER SIMEON.

Number	Title	Yr	VG	VG+	NM
BIOGRAPH					
❑ 1003	Rare Piano Rolls	1972	3.00	6.00	12.00
❑ 1009	Rare Piano Rolls, Volume 2	1972	3.00	6.00	12.00
BLUE NOTE					
❑ BLP-7011 [10]	Stomps, Rags and Blues	1951	75.00	150.00	300.00
❑ BLP-7012 [10]	Jazz Band Ball	1951	75.00	150.00	300.00
COLUMBIA					
❑ CL 1780 [M]	Father of the Stride Piano	1961	6.25	12.50	25.00
-- Red and black label with six "eye" logos					
❑ CL 1780 [M]	Father of the Stride Piano	1963	3.75	7.50	15.00
-- All-red label, "Guaranteed High Fidelity" or "360 Sound Mono" at bottom					
DECCA					
❑ DL 5190 [10]	The Daddy of the Piano	1950	25.00	50.00	100.00
❑ DL 5228 [10]	James P. Johnson Plays Fats Waller Favorites	1951	25.00	50.00	100.00
FOLKWAYS					
❑ FJ-2816	Striding in Dixieland	196?	5.00	10.00	20.00
❑ FJ-2842 [M]	Yamekraw	1962	5.00	10.00	20.00
❑ FJ-2850	The Original James P. Johnson	196?	5.00	10.00	20.00
RIVERSIDE					
❑ RLP 12-105 [M]	Rediscovered Early Solos	1955	15.00	30.00	60.00
-- White label, blue print					
❑ RLP 12-105 [M]	Rediscovered Early Solos	1959	10.00	20.00	40.00
-- Blue label, microphone logo at top					
❑ RLP 12-151 [M]	Backwater Blues	1955	15.00	30.00	60.00
-- White label, blue print					
❑ RLP 12-151 [M]	Backwater Blues	1959	10.00	20.00	40.00
-- Blue label, microphone logo at top					
❑ RLP-1011 [10]	Rent Party	1953	30.00	60.00	120.00
❑ RLP-1046 [10]	Early Harlem Piano, Vol. 2	1954	30.00	60.00	120.00
❑ RLP-1056 [10]	Harlem Rent Party	1955	25.00	50.00	100.00
SOUNDS					
❑ 1204	Father of the Stride Piano	196?	3.75	7.50	15.00
STINSON					
❑ SLP-21 [10]	New York Jazz	1950	30.00	60.00	120.00
❑ SLP-21 [M]	New York Jazz	195?	12.50	25.00	50.00

JOHNSON, LAMONT
Pianist, composer and arranger.

Number	Title	Yr	VG	VG+	NM
MAINSTREAM					
❑ MRL-328	Sun, Moon and Stars	1972	3.75	7.50	15.00

JOHNSON, MARC
Bass player.

Number	Title	Yr	VG	VG+	NM
ECM					
❑ 25040	Bass Desires	1986	2.50	5.00	10.00

JOHNSON, OSIE
Drummer, male singer and arranger. Also see THE BRASS ENSEMBLE OF THE JAZZ & CLASSICAL MUSIC SOCIETY; THE MANHATTAN JAZZ SEPTETTE.

Number	Title	Yr	VG	VG+	NM
BETHLEHEM					
❑ BCP-66 [M]	The Happy Jazz of Osie Johnson	1957	12.50	25.00	50.00
PERIOD					
❑ SPL-1108 [10]	Osie's Oasis	1955	20.00	40.00	80.00
❑ SPL-1112 [10]	Johnson's Whacks	1955	20.00	40.00	80.00
RCA VICTOR					
❑ LPM-1369 [M]	A Bit of the Blues	1957	10.00	20.00	40.00

JOHNSON, PETE
Pianist. Also see ALBERT AMMONS; ERROLL GARNER; JOE TURNER.

Number	Title	Yr	VG	VG+	NM
BLUE NOTE					
❑ BLP-7019 [10]	Boogie Woogie Blues and Skiffle	1952	75.00	150.00	300.00
BRUNSWICK					
❑ BL 58041 [10]	Boogie Woogie Mood	1953	20.00	40.00	80.00
MCA					
❑ 1333	Boogie Woogie Mood	198?	2.50	5.00	10.00

Number	Title	Yr	VG	VG+	NM
MOSAIC					
❏ M-119	The Pete Johnson/Earl Hines/ Teddy Bunn Blue Note Sessions	199?	5.00	10.00	20.00
RIVERSIDE					
❏ RLP-1056 [10]	Jumpin' with Pete Johnson	1955	20.00	40.00	80.00
SAVOY					
❏ MG-14018 [M]	Pete's Blues	1958	30.00	60.00	120.00
SAVOY JAZZ					
❏ SJL-414	Pete's Blues	1985	2.50	5.00	10.00

JOHNSON, PETE/HADDA BROOKS
Also see each artist's individual listings.

Number	Title	Yr	VG	VG+	NM
CROWN					
❏ CLP-5058 [M]	Boogie	195?	5.00	10.00	20.00

JOHNSON, PLAS
Tenor saxophone player. He is the soloist on the original soundtrack version of the theme from The Pink Panther.

Number	Title	Yr	VG	VG+	NM
CAPITOL					
❏ ST 1281 [S]	This Must Be the Plas!	1960	7.50	15.00	30.00
❏ T 1281 [M]	This Must Be the Plas!	1960	6.25	12.50	25.00
❏ ST 1503 [S]	Mood for the Blues	1961	7.50	15.00	30.00
❏ T 1503 [M]	Mood for the Blues	1961	6.25	12.50	25.00
CONCORD JAZZ					
❏ CJ-15	Blues	1975	2.50	5.00	10.00
❏ CJ-24	Positively	1976	2.50	5.00	10.00
TAMPA					
❏ TP-24 [M]	Bop Me, Daddy	1957	25.00	50.00	100.00
-- Colored vinyl					
❏ TP-24 [M]	Bop Me, Daddy	1958	12.50	25.00	50.00
-- Black vinyl					

JOHNSON, RUDOLPH
Saxophone player.

Number	Title	Yr	VG	VG+	NM
BLACK JAZZ					
❏ 4	Spring Rain	1971	6.25	12.50	25.00
❏ 11	Second Coming	1972	6.25	12.50	25.00
OVATION					
❏ OV-1805	Time and Space	1977	3.75	7.50	15.00

JOHNSON, WAYNE
Guitarist.

Number	Title	Yr	VG	VG+	NM
INNER CITY					
❏ IC-1098	Arrowhead	198?	3.00	6.00	12.00
ZEBRA					
❏ ZR-5003	Everybody's Painting Pictures	1984	3.00	6.00	12.00
ZEBRA/MCA					
❏ 42228	Spirit of the Dancer	1988	2.50	5.00	10.00

JOLLY, PETE
Pianist. Also see THE FIVE.

Number	Title	Yr	VG	VG+	NM
A&M					
❏ SP-3033	Seasons	1969	3.00	6.00	12.00
❏ SP-4145	Herb Alpert Presents Pete Jolly	1968	3.00	6.00	12.00
❏ SP-4184	Give a Damn	1970	3.00	6.00	12.00
AVA					
❏ A-22 [M]	Little Bird	1963	5.00	10.00	20.00
❏ AS-22 [S]	Little Bird	1963	6.25	12.50	25.00
❏ A-39 [M]	Sweet September	1963	5.00	10.00	20.00
❏ AS-39 [S]	Sweet September	1963	6.25	12.50	25.00
❏ A-51 [M]	Hello Jolly	1964	5.00	10.00	20.00
❏ AS-51 [S]	Hello Jolly	1964	6.25	12.50	25.00
CHARLIE PARKER					
❏ PLP-825 [M]	Pete Jolly Gasses Everybody	1962	5.00	10.00	20.00
❏ PLP-825S [S]	Pete Jolly Gasses Everybody	1962	6.25	12.50	25.00
COLUMBIA					
❏ CL 2397 [M]	Too Much, Baby	1965	5.00	10.00	20.00
❏ CS 9197 [S]	Too Much, Baby	1965	6.25	12.50	25.00
MAINSTREAM					
❏ S-6114	The Best of Pete Jolly	196?	3.75	7.50	15.00
METROJAZZ					
❏ E-1014 [M]	Impossible	1958	8.75	17.50	35.00
❏ SE-1014 [S]	Impossible	1958	8.75	17.50	35.00
MGM					
❏ E-4127 [M]	5 O'Clock Shadows	1963	5.00	10.00	20.00
❏ SE-4127 [S]	5 O'Clock Shadows	1963	6.25	12.50	25.00
RCA VICTOR					
❏ LPM-1105 [M]	Jolly Jumps In	1955	12.50	25.00	50.00
❏ LPM-1125 [M]	Duo, Trio, Quartet	1955	12.50	25.00	50.00
❏ LPM-1367 [M]	When Lights Are Low	1957	12.50	25.00	50.00

Number	Title	Yr	VG	VG+	NM
STEREO FIDELITY					
❏ SFS-11000 [S]	Continental Jazz	1960	6.25	12.50	25.00
TRIP					
❏ TLP-5817	A Touch of Jazz	197?	2.50	5.00	10.00

JONES BOYS, THE
A collaboration of unrelated musicians, all with the last name of Jones: Eddie, Jimmy, Jo, Quincy, Renauld and Thad.

Number	Title	Yr	VG	VG+	NM
PERIOD					
❏ SPL-1210 [M]	The Jones Boys	1954	20.00	40.00	80.00

JONES BROTHERS, THE
A collaboration of Joneses who really were brothers: Elvin, Hank and Thad.

Number	Title	Yr	VG	VG+	NM
METROJAZZ					
❏ E-1003 [M]	Keepin' Up with the Joneses	1958	20.00	40.00	80.00
❏ SE-1003 [S]	Keepin' Up with the Joneses	1958	15.00	30.00	60.00

JONES, BOBBY
Clarinetist and tenor saxophone player.

Number	Title	Yr	VG	VG+	NM
ENJA					
❏ 2046	Hill Country Suite	1975	3.75	7.50	15.00

JONES, BOOGALOO JOE
Guitarist.

Number	Title	Yr	VG	VG+	NM
PRESTIGE					
❏ PRST-7557	Mind Bender	1968	5.00	10.00	20.00
❏ PRST-7617	My Fire! More of the Psychedelic Soul Jazz Guitar of Joe Jones	1968	5.00	10.00	20.00
❏ PRST-7697	Boogaloo Joe	1969	5.00	10.00	20.00
❏ PRST-7766	Right On Brother!	1970	5.00	10.00	20.00
❏ 10004	No Way!	1971	6.25	12.50	25.00
❏ 10035	What It Is	1971	7.50	15.00	30.00
❏ 10056	Snake Rhythm Rock	1972	7.50	15.00	30.00
❏ 10072	Black Whip	1973	7.50	15.00	30.00

JONES, CARMELL
Trumpeter, composer and arranger. Also see TRICKY LOFTON.

Number	Title	Yr	VG	VG+	NM
PACIFIC JAZZ					
❏ PJ-29 [M]	The Remarkable Carmell Jones	1961	10.00	20.00	40.00
❏ ST-29 [S]	The Remarkable Carmell Jones	1961	12.50	25.00	50.00
❏ PJ-53 [M]	Business Meetin'	1962	10.00	20.00	40.00
❏ ST-53 [S]	Business Meetin'	1962	12.50	25.00	50.00
-- Black vinyl					
❏ ST-53 [S]	Business Meetin'	1962	20.00	40.00	80.00
-- Colored vinyl					
PRESTIGE					
❏ PRLP-7401 [M]	Jay Hawk Talk	1965	7.50	15.00	30.00
❏ PRST-7401 [S]	Jay Hawk Talk	1965	10.00	20.00	40.00
❏ PRST-7669	Carmell Jones in Europe	1969	5.00	10.00	20.00

JONES, CONNIE
Trumpeter.

Number	Title	Yr	VG	VG+	NM
JAZZOLOGY					
❏ J-49	Connie Jones with the Crescent City Jazz Band	197?	2.50	5.00	10.00

JONES, DALINE
Female singer.

Number	Title	Yr	VG	VG+	NM
TBA					
❏ TBA-220	Secret Fantasy	1986	3.00	6.00	12.00
❏ TBA-231	Share the Love	1987	3.00	6.00	12.00

JONES, DILL
Pianist.

Number	Title	Yr	VG	VG+	NM
CHIAROSCURO					
❏ 112	The Music of Bix Beiderbecke	197?	3.75	7.50	15.00
PALO ALTO					
❏ PA-8016	Earth Jones	1982	3.00	6.00	12.00

JONES, ELVIN
Drummer. Also see THE JONES BROTHERS; PHILLY JOE JONES.

Number	Title	Yr	VG	VG+	NM
ABC IMPULSE!					
❏ AS-88 [S]	Dear John C.	1968	3.75	7.50	15.00
❏ AS-9160	Heavy Sounds	1968	5.00	10.00	20.00
❏ AS-9283	The Impulse Years	197?	3.75	7.50	15.00
ATLANTIC					
❏ 1443 [M]	And Then Again	1965	5.00	10.00	20.00
❏ SD 1443 [S]	And Then Again	1965	6.25	12.50	25.00
❏ 1485 [M]	Midnight Walk	1967	5.00	10.00	20.00
❏ SD 1485 [S]	Midnight Walk	1967	6.25	12.50	25.00

BLUE NOTE

Number	Title	Yr	VG	VG+	NM
BN-LA015-G [(2)]	Live at the Lighthouse	1973	5.00	10.00	20.00
BN-LA110-F	Mr. Jones	1973	3.75	7.50	15.00
BN-LA506-H2 [(2)]	Prime Element	1976	5.00	10.00	20.00
BST-84282	Puttin' It Together	1968	6.25	12.50	25.00
BST-84305	The Ultimate Elvin Jones	1969	6.25	12.50	25.00
BST-84331	Poly-Currents	1969	6.25	12.50	25.00
BST-84331	Poly-Currents	1986	2.50	5.00	10.00
-- "The Finest in Jazz Since 1939" reissue					
BST-84361	Coalition	1970	6.25	12.50	25.00
BST-84369	Genesis	1971	5.00	10.00	20.00
BST-84414	Elvin Jones	1972	5.00	10.00	20.00

ENJA

Number	Title	Yr	VG	VG+	NM
2036	Live at the Vanguard	1974	3.75	7.50	15.00

FANTASY

Number	Title	Yr	VG	VG+	NM
OJC-259	Elvin!	1987	2.50	5.00	10.00

IMPULSE!

Number	Title	Yr	VG	VG+	NM
A-88 [M]	Dear John C.	1965	6.25	12.50	25.00
AS-88 [S]	Dear John C.	1965	7.50	15.00	30.00

MCA

Number	Title	Yr	VG	VG+	NM
29068	Dear John C.	1980	2.50	5.00	10.00

PAUSA

Number	Title	Yr	VG	VG+	NM
7052	Rememberance	1979	2.50	5.00	10.00

PM

Number	Title	Yr	VG	VG+	NM
004	Live at Town Hall	197?	3.75	7.50	15.00
005	On the Mountain	197?	3.75	7.50	15.00

QUICKSILVER

Number	Title	Yr	VG	VG+	NM
QS-4001	Brother John	198?	2.50	5.00	10.00

RIVERSIDE

Number	Title	Yr	VG	VG+	NM
RLP-409 [M]	Elvin!	1962	6.25	12.50	25.00
6192	Elvin!	198?	3.00	6.00	12.00
RS-9409 [S]	Elvin!	1962	7.50	15.00	30.00

VANGUARD

Number	Title	Yr	VG	VG+	NM
VSD-79362	New Agenda	1975	3.75	7.50	15.00
VSD-79372	Main Force	1976	3.75	7.50	15.00
VSD-79389	Time Capsule	1977	3.75	7.50	15.00

JONES, ELVIN, AND THE JIMMY GARRISON SEXTETTE

Garrison is a bass player. Also see ELVIN JONES.

IMPULSE!

Number	Title	Yr	VG	VG+	NM
A-49 [M]	Illumination	1963	6.25	12.50	25.00
AS-49 [S]	Illumination	1963	7.50	15.00	30.00

JONES, ETTA

Female singer.

FANTASY

Number	Title	Yr	VG	VG+	NM
OJC-221	Something Nice	198?	2.50	5.00	10.00
OJC-298	Don't Go to Strangers	198?	2.50	5.00	10.00

KING

Number	Title	Yr	VG	VG+	NM
544 [M]	The Jones Girl...Etta	1956	25.00	50.00	100.00
707 [M]	Etta Jones Sings	1960	12.50	25.00	50.00

MUSE

Number	Title	Yr	VG	VG+	NM
MR-5099	Ms. Jones to You	197?	3.00	6.00	12.00
MR-5145	Mother's Eyes	1977	3.00	6.00	12.00
MR-5175	If You Could See Me Now	1979	3.00	6.00	12.00
MR-5214	Save Your Love for Me	1981	2.50	5.00	10.00
MR-5262	Love Me with All of Your Heart	198?	2.50	5.00	10.00
MR-5333	Fine and Mellow	1987	2.50	5.00	10.00
MR-5351	I'll Be Seeing You	1989	3.00	6.00	12.00
MR-5379	Sugar	1989	3.00	6.00	12.00
MR-5411	Christmas with Etta Jones	1989	3.00	6.00	12.00

PRESTIGE

Number	Title	Yr	VG	VG+	NM
PRLP-7186 [M]	Don't Go to Strangers	1960	10.00	20.00	40.00
-- Yellow label					
PRLP-7186 [M]	Don't Go to Strangers	1964	5.00	10.00	20.00
-- Blue label, trident logo at right					
PRST-7186 [S]	Don't Go to Strangers	1960	12.50	25.00	50.00
-- Silver label					
PRST-7186 [S]	Don't Go to Strangers	1964	6.25	12.50	25.00
-- Blue label, trident logo at right					
PRLP-7194 [M]	Something Nice	1961	12.50	25.00	50.00
-- Yellow label					
PRLP-7194 [M]	Something Nice	1964	6.25	12.50	25.00
-- Blue label, trident logo at right					
PRLP-7204 [M]	So Warm -- Etta Jones and Strings	1961	10.00	20.00	40.00
-- Yellow label					
PRLP-7204 [M]	So Warm -- Etta Jones and Strings	1964	5.00	10.00	20.00
-- Blue label, trident logo at right					
PRST-7204 [S]	So Warm -- Etta Jones and Strings	1961	12.50	25.00	50.00
-- Silver label					
PRST-7204 [S]	So Warm -- Etta Jones and Strings	1964	6.25	12.50	25.00
-- Blue label, trident logo at right					
PRLP-7214 [M]	From the Heart	1961	10.00	20.00	40.00
-- Yellow label					
PRLP-7214 [M]	From the Heart	1964	5.00	10.00	20.00
-- Blue label, trident logo at right					
PRST-7214 [S]	From the Heart	1961	12.50	25.00	50.00
-- Silver label					
PRST-7214 [S]	From the Heart	1964	6.25	12.50	25.00
-- Blue label, trident logo at right					
PRLP-7241 [M]	Lonely and Blue	1962	10.00	20.00	40.00
-- Yellow label					
PRLP-7241 [M]	Lonely and Blue	1964	5.00	10.00	20.00
-- Blue label, trident logo at right					
PRST-7241 [S]	Lonely and Blue	1962	12.50	25.00	50.00
-- Silver label					
PRST-7241 [S]	Lonely and Blue	1964	6.25	12.50	25.00
-- Blue label, trident logo at right					
PRLP-7272 [M]	Love Shout	1963	10.00	20.00	40.00
-- Yellow label					
PRLP-7272 [M]	Love Shout	1964	5.00	10.00	20.00
-- Blue label, trident logo at right					
PRST-7272 [S]	Love Shout	1963	12.50	25.00	50.00
-- Silver label					
PRST-7272 [S]	Love Shout	1964	6.25	12.50	25.00
-- Blue label, trident logo at right					
PRLP-7284 [M]	Holler!	1963	10.00	20.00	40.00
-- Yellow label					
PRLP-7284 [M]	Holler!	1964	5.00	10.00	20.00
-- Blue label, trident logo at right					
PRST-7284 [S]	Holler!	1963	12.50	25.00	50.00
-- Silver label					
PRST-7284 [S]	Holler!	1964	6.25	12.50	25.00
-- Blue label, trident logo at right					
PRLP-7443 [M]	Etta Jones' Greatest Hits	1967	6.25	12.50	25.00
PRST-7443 [S]	Etta Jones' Greatest Hits	1967	5.00	10.00	20.00

ROULETTE

Number	Title	Yr	VG	VG+	NM
R-25329 [M]	Etta Jones Sings	1965	5.00	10.00	20.00
SR-25329 [S]	Etta Jones Sings	1965	6.25	12.50	25.00

WESTBOUND

Number	Title	Yr	VG	VG+	NM
203	Etta Jones '75	1975	5.00	10.00	20.00

JONES, HANK

Pianist. Also see THE FOUR MOST; THE JONES BROTHERS; THE TRIO.

ABC-PARAMOUNT

Number	Title	Yr	VG	VG+	NM
ABC-496 [M]	This Is Ragtime Now	1964	5.00	10.00	20.00
ABCS-496 [S]	This Is Ragtime Now	1964	6.25	12.50	25.00

ARGO

Number	Title	Yr	VG	VG+	NM
LP-728 [M]	Here's Love	1963	5.00	10.00	20.00
LPS-728 [S]	Here's Love	1963	6.25	12.50	25.00

CAPITOL

Number	Title	Yr	VG	VG+	NM
ST 1044 [S]	The Talented Touch of Hank Jones	1958	7.50	15.00	30.00
T 1044 [M]	The Talented Touch of Hank Jones	1958	10.00	20.00	40.00
ST 1175 [S]	Porgy and Bess	1959	7.50	15.00	30.00
T 1175 [M]	Porgy and Bess	1959	10.00	20.00	40.00

CLEF

Number	Title	Yr	VG	VG+	NM
MGC-100 [10]	Hank Jones Piano	1953	30.00	60.00	120.00
MGC-707 [M]	Urbanity -- Piano Solos by Hank Jones	1956	25.00	50.00	100.00

CONCORD JAZZ

Number	Title	Yr	VG	VG+	NM
CJ-391	Lazy Afternoon	1989	3.00	6.00	12.00

FANTASY

Number	Title	Yr	VG	VG+	NM
OJC-471	Just for Fun	1990	3.00	6.00	12.00

GALAXY

Number	Title	Yr	VG	VG+	NM
5105	Just for	1977	3.00	6.00	12.00
5108	Tiptoe Tapdance	1978	3.00	6.00	12.00
5123	Ain't Misbehavin'	1979	3.00	6.00	12.00

GOLDEN CREST

Number	Title	Yr	VG	VG+	NM
GC-3042 [M]	Hank Jones Swings "Gigi"	1958	12.50	25.00	50.00
GCS-3042 [S]	Hank Jones Swings "Gigi"	196?	5.00	10.00	20.00
GC-5002 [S]	Hank Jones Swings "Gigi"	1959	10.00	20.00	40.00

INNER CITY

Number	Title	Yr	VG	VG+	NM
IC-6020	Hanky Panky	197?	3.00	6.00	12.00

MERCURY

Number	Title	Yr	VG	VG+	NM
MGC-100 [10]	Hank Jones Piano	195?	37.50	75.00	150.00
MG-25022 [10]	Hank Jones Piano	1950	50.00	100.00	200.00
MG-35014 [10]	Hank Jones Piano	1950	50.00	100.00	200.00

MUSE

Number	Title	Yr	VG	VG+	NM
MR-5123	Bop Redux	1977	3.00	6.00	12.00
MR-5169	Grovin' High	1979	3.00	6.00	12.00

PAUSA

Number	Title	Yr	VG	VG+	NM
7051	Have You Met This Jones?	1979	2.50	5.00	10.00

Number	Title	Yr	VG	VG+	NM
PROGRESSIVE					
❑ 7004	Arigato	1976	3.00	6.00	12.00
RCA VICTOR					
❑ LPM-2570 [M]	Arrival Time	1962	6.25	12.50	25.00
❑ LSP-2570 [S]	Arrival Time	1962	7.50	15.00	30.00
SAVOY					
❑ MG-12037 [M]	Hank Jones Quartet-Quintet	1955	20.00	40.00	80.00
❑ MG-12053 [M]	The Trio	1956	20.00	40.00	80.00
❑ MG-12084 [M]	Have You Met Hank Jones	1956	20.00	40.00	80.00
❑ MG-12087 [M]	Hank Jones Trio	1956	20.00	40.00	80.00
SAVOY JAZZ					
❑ SJL-1124	Hank Jones	198?	2.50	5.00	10.00
❑ SJL-1138	Relaxin' at Camarillo	198?	2.50	5.00	10.00
❑ SJL-1193	Bluebird	198?	2.50	5.00	10.00
VERVE					
❑ MGV-8091 [M]	Urbanity -- Piano Solos by Hank Jones	1957	20.00	40.00	80.00
❑ V-8091 [M]	Urbanity -- Piano Solos by Hank Jones	1961	6.25	12.50	25.00

JONES, HANK; RAY BROWN; JIMMIE SMITH
Also see each artist's individual listings.

Number	Title	Yr	VG	VG+	NM
CONCORD JAZZ					
❑ CJ-32	Hank Jones/Ray Brown/Jimmie Smith	197?	3.00	6.00	12.00

JONES, HANK, AND JOHN LEWIS
Also see each artist's individual listings.

Number	Title	Yr	VG	VG+	NM
LITTLE DAVID					
❑ LD 1079	An Evening with Two Grand Pianos	1980	3.00	6.00	12.00

JONES, HANK, AND RED MITCHELL
Also see each artist's individual listings.

Number	Title	Yr	VG	VG+	NM
TIMELESS					
❑ SJP-283	Duo	1990	3.75	7.50	15.00

JONES, ISHAM
Bandleader and composer.

Number	Title	Yr	VG	VG+	NM
RCA VICTOR					
❑ LPV-504 [M]	The Great Isham Jones and His Orchestra	1966	5.00	10.00	20.00

JONES, JO
Drummer. Also see COLEMAN HAWKINS; JAZZ ARTISTS GUILD; THE JONES BOYS.

Number	Title	Yr	VG	VG+	NM
ARCHIVE OF FOLK AND JAZZ					
❑ 329	Jo Jones	197?	2.50	5.00	10.00
EVEREST					
❑ SDBR-1023 [S]	Jo Jones Trio	1959	7.50	15.00	30.00
❑ SDBR-1099 [S]	Vamp Till Ready	1960	7.50	15.00	30.00
❑ SDBR-1110 [S]	Percussion and Bass	1960	7.50	15.00	30.00
❑ LPBR-5023 [M]	Jo Jones Trio	1959	6.25	12.50	25.00
❑ LPBR-5099 [M]	Vamp Till Ready	1960	6.25	12.50	25.00
❑ LPBR-5110 [M]	Percussion and Bass	1960	6.25	12.50	25.00
JAZZTONE					
❑ J-1242 [M]	Jo Jones Special	1956	12.50	25.00	50.00
PABLO					
❑ 2310 799	Main Man	1976	3.75	7.50	15.00
VANGUARD					
❑ VSD-2031 [S]	Jo Jones Plus Two	1959	7.50	15.00	30.00
❑ VRS-8503 [M]	Jo Jones Special	1955	15.00	30.00	60.00
❑ VRS-8525 [M]	Jo Jones Plus Two	1959	10.00	20.00	40.00

JONES, JONAH
Trumpeter and male singer. Also see PETE BROWN; JACK TEAGARDEN.

Number	Title	Yr	VG	VG+	NM
ANGEL					
❑ ANG.60005 [10]	Jonah Wails -- 1st Blast	1954	18.75	37.50	75.00
❑ ANG.60006 [10]	Jonah Wails -- 2nd Blast	1954	18.75	37.50	75.00
BETHLEHEM					
❑ BCP-1014 [10]	Jonah Jones Sextet	1954	20.00	40.00	80.00
CAPITOL					
❑ T 839 [M]	Muted Jazz	1957	10.00	20.00	40.00
❑ T 963 [M]	Swingin' On Broadway	1958	10.00	20.00	40.00
❑ ST 1039 [S]	Jumpin' with Jonah	1958	7.50	15.00	30.00
❑ T 1039 [M]	Jumpin' with Jonah	1958	6.25	12.50	25.00
❑ ST 1083 [S]	Swingin' at the Cinema	1958	7.50	15.00	30.00
❑ T 1083 [M]	Swingin' at the Cinema	1958	6.25	12.50	25.00
❑ ST 1115 [S]	Jonah Jumps Again	1959	7.50	15.00	30.00
❑ T 1115 [M]	Jonah Jumps Again	1959	6.25	12.50	25.00
❑ ST 1193 [S]	I Dig Chicks	1959	6.25	12.50	25.00
❑ T 1193 [M]	I Dig Chicks	1959	5.00	10.00	20.00

Number	Title	Yr	VG	VG+	NM
❑ ST 1237 [S]	Swingin' 'Round the World	1959	6.25	12.50	25.00
❑ T 1237 [M]	Swingin' 'Round the World	1959	5.00	10.00	20.00
❑ ST 1375 [S]	Hit Me Again!	1960	6.25	12.50	25.00
❑ T 1375 [M]	Hit Me Again!	1960	5.00	10.00	20.00
❑ ST 1405 [S]	A Touch of Blue	1960	6.25	12.50	25.00
❑ T 1405 [M]	A Touch of Blue	1960	5.00	10.00	20.00
❑ ST 1532 [S]	The Unsinkable Molly Brown	1961	6.25	12.50	25.00
❑ T 1532 [M]	The Unsinkable Molly Brown	1961	5.00	10.00	20.00
❑ ST 1557 [S]	Great Instrumental Hits Styled by Jonah Jones	1961	6.25	12.50	25.00
❑ T 1557 [M]	Great Instrumental Hits Styled by Jonah Jones	1961	5.00	10.00	20.00
❑ ST 1641 [S]	Broadway Swings Again	1961	6.25	12.50	25.00
❑ T 1641 [M]	Broadway Swings Again	1961	5.00	10.00	20.00
❑ SM-1660	Jonah Jones/Glenn Gray	197?	2.50	5.00	10.00
❑ ST 1660 [S]	Jonah Jones/Glenn Gray	1961	6.25	12.50	25.00
❑ T 1660 [M]	Jonah Jones/Glenn Gray	1961	5.00	10.00	20.00
❑ ST 1773 [S]	Jazz Bonus	1962	5.00	10.00	20.00
❑ T 1773 [M]	Jazz Bonus	1962	3.75	7.50	15.00
❑ ST 1948 [S]	And Now, In Person -- Jonah Jones	1963	5.00	10.00	20.00
❑ T 1948 [M]	And Now, In Person -- Jonah Jones	1963	3.75	7.50	15.00
❑ ST 2087 [S]	Blowin' Up a Storm	1964	5.00	10.00	20.00
❑ T 2087 [M]	Blowin' Up a Storm	1964	3.75	7.50	15.00
❑ ST 2594 [S]	The Best of Jonah Jones	1966	3.00	6.00	12.00
❑ T 2594 [M]	The Best of Jonah Jones	1966	3.75	7.50	15.00
CIRCLE					
❑ CLP-83	1944: Butterflies in the Rain	198?	2.50	5.00	10.00
DECCA					
❑ DL 4638 [M]	Hello Broadway	1965	3.00	6.00	12.00
❑ DL 4688 [M]	On the Sunny Side of the Street	1966	3.00	6.00	12.00
❑ DL 4765 [M]	Tijuana Taxi	1966	3.00	6.00	12.00
❑ DL 4800 [M]	Sweet with a Beat	1967	3.75	7.50	15.00
❑ DL 74638 [S]	Hello Broadway	1965	3.75	7.50	15.00
❑ DL 74688 [S]	On the Sunny Side of the Street	1966	3.75	7.50	15.00
❑ DL 74765 [S]	Tijuana Taxi	1966	3.75	7.50	15.00
❑ DL 74800 [S]	Sweet with a Beat	1967	3.00	6.00	12.00
GROOVE					
❑ LG-1001 [M]	Jonah Jones at the Embers	1956	12.50	25.00	50.00
HALL OF FAME					
❑ 613	After Hours Jazz	198?	2.50	5.00	10.00
JAZZ MAN					
❑ 5009	Confessin'	1981	2.50	5.00	10.00
MOTOWN					
❑ M-683	Along Came Jonah	1969	10.00	20.00	40.00
❑ M-690	Little Dis, Little Dat	1970	10.00	20.00	40.00
PICKWICK					
❑ SPC-3008	Swing Along	196?	3.00	6.00	12.00
RCA CAMDEN					
❑ CAS-2328	Jonah Jones Quartet	1969	3.00	6.00	12.00
RCA VICTOR					
❑ LPM-2004 [M]	Jonah Jones at the Embers	1959	10.00	20.00	40.00
-- Reissue of Groove and Vik LP					
SWING					
❑ 8408	Paris 1954	198?	2.50	5.00	10.00
VIK					
❑ LXA-1135 [M]	Jonah Jones at the Embers	1958	10.00	20.00	40.00
-- Reissue of Groove LP					

JONES, JONAH, AND EARL "FATHA" HINES
Also see each artist's individual listings.

Number	Title	Yr	VG	VG+	NM
CHIAROSCURO					
❑ 118	Back on the Street	1973	3.00	6.00	12.00

JONES, JONAH/CHARLIE SHAVERS
Also see each artist's individual listings.

Number	Title	Yr	VG	VG+	NM
BETHLEHEM					
❑ BCP-6034 [M]	Sounds of the Trumpets	1959	10.00	20.00	40.00

JONES, PHILLY JOE
Drummer. Also see KENNY DREW.

Number	Title	Yr	VG	VG+	NM
ATLANTIC					
❑ 1340 [M]	Philly Joe's Beat	1960	6.25	12.50	25.00
-- Multicolor label, white "fan" logo on right					
❑ 1340 [M]	Philly Joe's Beat	1963	3.75	7.50	15.00
-- Multicolor label, black "fan" logo on right					
❑ SD 1340 [S]	Philly Joe's Beat	1960	7.50	15.00	30.00
-- Multicolor label, white "fan" logo on right					
❑ SD 1340 [S]	Philly Joe's Beat	1963	3.75	7.50	15.00
-- Multicolor label, black "fan" logo on right					
BLACK LION					
❑ 142	Trailways Express	197?	3.00	6.00	12.00

Number	Title	Yr	VG	VG+	NM
FANTASY					
❑ OJC-230	Blues for Dracula	198?	2.50	5.00	10.00
❑ OJC-484	Showcase	1991	3.00	6.00	12.00
GALAXY					
❑ 5112	Philly Mignon	1978	3.00	6.00	12.00
❑ 5122	Advance!	1980	3.00	6.00	12.00
❑ 5153	Drum Song	1985	2.50	5.00	10.00
RIVERSIDE					
❑ 6055	Blues for Dracula	197?	3.75	7.50	15.00
❑ 6193	Showcase	198?	3.00	6.00	12.00
❑ RLP 12-282 [M]	Blues for Dracula	1958	12.50	25.00	50.00
❑ RLP 12-302 [M]	Drums Around the World	1959	12.50	25.00	50.00
❑ RLP 12-313 [M]	Showcase	1959	12.50	25.00	50.00
❑ RLP-1147 [S]	Drums Around the World	1959	10.00	20.00	40.00
❑ RLP-1159 [S]	Showcase	1959	10.00	20.00	40.00
UPTOWN					
❑ 27.11	To Tadd with Love	198?	3.00	6.00	12.00
❑ 27.15	Look, Stop, Listen	198?	3.00	6.00	12.00

JONES, PHILLY JOE, AND ELVIN JONES
Also see each artist's individual listings.

Number	Title	Yr	VG	VG+	NM
ATLANTIC					
❑ 1428 [M]	Together	1964	6.25	12.50	25.00
❑ SD 1428 [S]	Together	1964	7.50	15.00	30.00

JONES, QUINCY
Bandleader, producer, composer, arranger, record company executive, and a trumpeter, too. The below list includes some of his soundtrack work. Also see BILLY ECKSTINE; ROY HAYNES; THE JONES BOYS.

Number	Title	Yr	VG	VG+	NM
A&M					
❑ SP-3023	Walking in Space	1969	3.00	6.00	12.00
❑ SP-3030	Gula Matari	1970	3.00	6.00	12.00
❑ SP-3037	Smackwater Jack	1971	3.00	6.00	12.00
❑ SP-3041	You've Got It Bad Girl	1973	3.00	6.00	12.00
❑ SP-3191	Body Heat	1982	2.00	4.00	8.00
-- Budget-line reissue					
❑ SP-3200	The Best	1982	2.00	4.00	8.00
❑ SP-3248	The Dude	198?	2.00	4.00	8.00
-- Budget-line reissue					
❑ SP-3249	Sounds…And Stuff Like That!	198?	2.00	4.00	8.00
-- Budget-line reissue					
❑ SP-3278	The Best, Vol. 2	1985	2.00	4.00	8.00
❑ SP-3617	Body Heat	1974	2.50	5.00	10.00
❑ SP-3705 [(2)]	I Heard That!!	1976	3.00	6.00	12.00
❑ SP-3721	The Dude	1981	2.50	5.00	10.00
❑ SP-4526	Mellow Madness	1975	2.50	5.00	10.00
❑ SP-4626	Roots	1977	2.50	5.00	10.00
❑ SP-4685	Sounds…And Stuff Like That!	1978	2.50	5.00	10.00
❑ SP-6507 [(2)]	I Heard That!!	198?	2.50	5.00	10.00
-- Budget-line reissue					
❑ QU-53041 [Q]	You've Got It Bad Girl	1974	5.00	10.00	20.00
❑ QU-53617 [Q]	Body Heat	1974	5.00	10.00	20.00
❑ QU-54526 [Q]	Mellow Madness	1975	5.00	10.00	20.00
ABC					
❑ D-782 [(2)]	Mode	1973	3.00	6.00	12.00
ABC IMPULSE!					
❑ AS-11 [S]	The Quintessence	1968	3.75	7.50	15.00
❑ IA-9342 [(2)]	Quintessential Charts	1978	3.00	6.00	12.00
ABC-PARAMOUNT					
❑ 149 [M]	This Is How I Feel About Jazz	1956	25.00	50.00	100.00
❑ 186 [M]	Go West, Man!	1957	25.00	50.00	100.00
CHESS					
❑ CH-91562	The Music of Quincy Jones	198?	2.50	5.00	10.00
COLGEMS					
❑ COM-107 [M]	In Cold Blood	1967	5.00	10.00	20.00
❑ COS-107 [S]	In Cold Blood	1967	6.25	12.50	25.00
EMARCY					
❑ MG-36083 [M]	Jazz Abroad	1956	25.00	50.00	100.00
❑ 818 177-1 [(2)]	The Birth of a Band	1984	3.00	6.00	12.00
GRP/IMPULSE!					
❑ 222	The Quintessence	199?	3.75	7.50	15.00
-- Reissue on audiophile vinyl					
IMPULSE!					
❑ A-11 [M]	The Quintessence	1962	7.50	15.00	30.00
❑ AS-11 [S]	The Quintessence	1962	10.00	20.00	40.00
LIBERTY					
❑ LOM-16004 [M]	Enter Laughing	1967	6.25	12.50	25.00
❑ LOS-17004 [S]	Enter Laughing	1967	7.50	15.00	30.00
MCA					
❑ 4145 [(2)]	Quintessential Charts	198?	2.50	5.00	10.00
-- Reissue of ABC Impulse 9342					
❑ 5578	The Slugger's Wife	1985	3.00	6.00	12.00

Number	Title	Yr	VG	VG+	NM
MCA/IMPULSE!					
❑ 5728	The Quintessence	1986	2.00	4.00	8.00
MERCURY					
❑ SRM-2-623 [(2)]	Ndeda	1972	3.75	7.50	15.00
❑ PPS-2014 [M]	Around the World	1961	7.50	15.00	30.00
❑ PPS-6014 [S]	Around the World	1961	10.00	20.00	40.00
❑ MG-20444 [M]	Birth of a Band	1959	12.50	25.00	50.00
❑ MG-20561 [M]	The Great, Wide World of Quincy Jones	1960	12.50	25.00	50.00
❑ MG-20612 [M]	I Dig Dancers	1960	10.00	20.00	40.00
❑ MG-20653 [M]	Quincy Jones at Newport '61	1961	7.50	15.00	30.00
❑ MG-20751 [M]	Big Band Bossa Nova	1962	7.50	15.00	30.00
❑ MG-20799 [M]	Quincy Jones Plays Hip Hits	1963	7.50	15.00	30.00
❑ MG-20863 [M]	Quincy Jones Explores the Music of Henry Mancini	1964	5.00	10.00	20.00
❑ MG-20938 [M]	Golden Boy	1964	5.00	10.00	20.00
❑ MG-21011 [M]	The Pawnbroker	1964	5.00	10.00	20.00
❑ MG-21025 [M]	Mirage	1965	5.00	10.00	20.00
❑ MG-21050 [M]	Quincy Jones Plays for Pussycats	1965	5.00	10.00	20.00
❑ MG-21063 [M]	Quincy's Got a Brand New Bag	1965	5.00	10.00	20.00
❑ MG-21070 [M]	Slender Thread	1966	5.00	10.00	20.00
❑ SR-60129 [S]	Birth of a Band	1959	15.00	30.00	60.00
❑ SR-60221 [S]	The Great, Wide World of Quincy Jones	1960	15.00	30.00	60.00
❑ SR-60612 [S]	I Dig Dancers	1960	12.50	25.00	50.00
❑ SR-60653 [S]	Quincy Jones at Newport '61	1961	10.00	20.00	40.00
❑ SR-60751 [S]	Big Band Bossa Nova	1962	10.00	20.00	40.00
❑ SR-60799 [S]	Quincy Jones Plays Hip Hits	1963	10.00	20.00	40.00
❑ SR-60863 [S]	Quincy Jones Explores the Music of Henry Mancini	1964	6.25	12.50	25.00
❑ SR-60938 [S]	Golden Boy	1964	6.25	12.50	25.00
❑ SR-61011 [S]	The Pawnbroker	1964	6.25	12.50	25.00
❑ SR-61025 [S]	Mirage	1965	6.25	12.50	25.00
❑ SR-61050 [S]	Quincy Jones Plays for Pussycats	1965	6.25	12.50	25.00
❑ SR-61063 [S]	Quincy's Got a Brand New Bag	1965	6.25	12.50	25.00
❑ SR-61070 [S]	Slender Thread	1966	6.25	12.50	25.00
MOBILE FIDELITY					
❑ 1-078	You've Got It Bad Girl	1981	6.25	12.50	25.00
-- Audiophile vinyl					
NAUTILUS					
❑ NR-52	The Dude	198?	10.00	20.00	40.00
-- Audiophile vinyl					
PRESTIGE					
❑ PRLP-172 [10]	Quincy Jones with the Swedish-American All Stars	1953	50.00	100.00	200.00
QWEST					
❑ 25356 [(2)]	The Color Purple	1985	5.00	10.00	20.00
-- Boxed set on purple vinyl					
❑ 25389 [(2)]	The Color Purple	1985	3.75	7.50	15.00
-- Gatefold package on purple vinyl					
❑ 26020	Back on the Block	1989	3.00	6.00	12.00
TRIP					
❑ 5514	The Great Wide World of Quincy Jones	1974	2.00	4.00	8.00
❑ 5554	Live at Newport '61	197?	2.00	4.00	8.00
UNITED ARTISTS					
❑ UAS-5214	They Call Me Mister Tibbs	1970	6.25	12.50	25.00
WING					
❑ SRW-16398	Around the World	1969	3.00	6.00	12.00

JONES, RICHARD M.
Pianist.

Number	Title	Yr	VG	VG+	NM
FOLKWAYS					
❑ FJ-2817	Chicago Dixieland in the Forties	198?	3.00	6.00	12.00
PAX					
❑ 6010 [10]	New Orleans Style	1954	20.00	40.00	80.00
RIVERSIDE					
❑ RLP-1017 [10]	Richard M. Jones and Clarence Williams	1953	20.00	40.00	80.00

JONES, RODNEY
Guitarist.

Number	Title	Yr	VG	VG+	NM
TIMELESS					
❑ 323	Articulation	1979	3.00	6.00	12.00

JONES, RUFUS
Drummer.

Number	Title	Yr	VG	VG+	NM
CAMEO					
❑ C-1076 [M]	Five on Eight	1964	6.25	12.50	25.00
❑ SC-1076 [S]	Five on Eight	1964	7.50	15.00	30.00

JONES, SAM
Bass player.

Number	Title	Yr	VG	VG+	NM
FANTASY					
❏ OJC-6008	Right Down in Front	198?	2.50	5.00	10.00
INTERPLAY					
❏ 7720	The Bassist	1979	3.00	6.00	12.00
MUSE					
❏ MR-5149	Something in Common	1977	3.75	7.50	15.00
RIVERSIDE					
❏ RLP 12-324 [M]	The Soul Society	1960	10.00	20.00	40.00
❏ RLP-358 [M]	The Chant!	1961	7.50	15.00	30.00
❏ RLP-432 [M]	Down Home	1962	7.50	15.00	30.00
❏ RLP-1172 [S]	The Soul Society	1960	10.00	20.00	40.00
❏ 6079	Soul Society	197?	3.75	7.50	15.00
❏ RS-9358 [S]	The Chant!	1961	10.00	20.00	40.00
❏ RS-9432 [S]	Down Home	1962	10.00	20.00	40.00
SEA BREEZE					
❏ 2004	Something New	1979	3.00	6.00	12.00
STEEPLECHASE					
❏ SCS-1097	Visitation	198?	3.00	6.00	12.00
XANADU					
❏ 129	Cello Again	197?	3.00	6.00	12.00
❏ 150	Changes and Things	1978	3.00	6.00	12.00

JONES, SPIKE, AND THE CITY SLICKERS
Drummer and bandleader, best known as a master parodist of both classical and popular music of his day.

Number	Title	Yr	VG	VG+	NM
CORNOGRAPHIC					
❏ 1001	King of Corn	197?	2.50	5.00	10.00
HINDSIGHT					
❏ HSR-185	The Uncollected Spike Jones 1946	198?	2.50	5.00	10.00
LIBERTY					
❏ LRP-3140 [M]	Omnibust	1959	12.50	25.00	50.00
❏ LRP-3154 [M]	60 Years of Music America Hates Best	1960	12.50	25.00	50.00
❏ LRP-3338 [M]	Washington Square	1963	5.00	10.00	20.00
❏ LRP-3349 [M]	Spike Jones' New Band	1964	7.50	15.00	30.00
❏ LRP-3370 [M]	My Man	1964	5.00	10.00	20.00
❏ LRP-3401 [M]	Spike Jones Plays Hank Williams Hits	1965	5.00	10.00	20.00
❏ LST-7140 [S]	Omnibust	1959	37.50	75.00	150.00
-- Red vinyl					
❏ LST-7140 [S]	Omnibust	1959	18.75	37.50	75.00
-- Black vinyl					
❏ LST-7154 [S]	60 Years of Music America Hates Best	1960	18.75	37.50	75.00
❏ LST-7338 [S]	Washington Square	1963	6.25	12.50	25.00
❏ LST-7349 [S]	Spike Jones' New Band	1964	10.00	20.00	40.00
❏ LST-7370 [S]	My Man	1964	6.25	12.50	25.00
❏ LST-7401 [S]	Spike Jones Plays Hank Williams Hits	1965	6.25	12.50	25.00
RCA GOLD SEAL					
❏ AGL1-4142	Spike Jones Is Murdering the Classics!	1982	2.00	4.00	8.00
-- Reissue					
RCA RED SEAL					
❏ LSC-3235 [R]	Spike Jones Is Murdering the Classics!	1971	5.00	10.00	20.00
RCA VICTOR					
❏ LPT-18 [10]	Spike Jones Plays the Charleston	1952	50.00	100.00	200.00
❏ ANL1-1035	The Best of Spike Jones	1975	2.50	5.00	10.00
-- Reissue					
❏ LPM-2224 [M]	Thank You Music Lovers	1960	12.50	25.00	50.00
❏ ANL1-2312	The Best of Spike Jones, Volume 2	1977	2.50	5.00	10.00
-- Reissue					
❏ LPM-3054 [10]	Bottoms Up	1952	50.00	100.00	200.00
❏ LPM-3128 [10]	Spike Jones Murders Carmen and Kids the Classics	1953	50.00	100.00	200.00
❏ AYL1-3748	The Best of Spike Jones, Volume 1	1980	2.00	4.00	8.00
-- "Best Buy Series" reissue					
❏ LPM-3849 [M]	The Best of Spike Jones	1967	6.25	12.50	25.00
❏ LSP-3849 [R]	The Best of Spike Jones	1967	5.00	10.00	20.00
❏ AYL1-3870	The Best of Spike Jones, Volume 2	1981	2.00	4.00	8.00
-- "Best Buy Series" reissue					
RHINO					
❏ R1 70196	It's a Spike Jones Christmas	1988	3.00	6.00	12.00
❏ R1 70261	Dinner Music...For People Who Aren't Very Hungry	1988	3.00	6.00	12.00
UNITED ARTISTS					
❏ UA-LA439-E	The Very Best of Spike Jones	1975	3.00	6.00	12.00
VERVE					
❏ MGV-2021 [M]	Let's Sing a Song for Christmas	1956	12.50	25.00	50.00
❏ V-2021 [M]	Let's Sing a Song for Christmas	1961	7.50	15.00	30.00
❏ MGV-4005 [M]	Dinner Music...For People Who Aren't Very Hungry	1957	12.50	25.00	50.00
❏ V-4005 [M]	Dinner Music...For People Who Aren't Very Hungry	1961	6.25	12.50	25.00
WARNER BROS.					
❏ W 1332 [M]	Spike Jones in Hi-Fi	1959	10.00	20.00	40.00
❏ WS 1332 [S]	Spike Jones in Stereo	1959	12.50	25.00	50.00

JONES, TAMIKO
Female singer. Also see HERBIE MANN.

Number	Title	Yr	VG	VG+	NM
A&M					
❏ SP-3011	I'll Be Anything for You	1969	5.00	10.00	20.00
DECEMBER					
❏ 8500	Tamiko	1970	5.00	10.00	20.00

JONES, THAD
Trumpeter, cornet player, arranger and composer. Also see THE JONES BOYS; THE JONES BROTHERS; SONNY ROLLINS; FRANK WESS.

Number	Title	Yr	VG	VG+	NM
BIOGRAPH					
❏ 12059	Greetings and Salutations	197?	3.00	6.00	12.00
BLUE NOTE					
❏ BLP-1513 [M]	Detroit-New York Junction	1956	50.00	100.00	200.00
-- "Deep groove" version (deep indentation under label on both sides)					
❏ BLP-1513 [M]	Detroit-New York Junction	1956	37.50	75.00	150.00
-- Regular version, Lexington Ave. address on label					
❏ BLP-1513 [M]	Detroit-New York Junction	1963	6.25	12.50	25.00
-- With "New York, USA" address on label					
❏ BLP-1527 [M]	The Magnificent Thad Jones	1956	50.00	100.00	200.00
-- "Deep groove" version (deep indentation under label on both sides)					
❏ BLP-1527 [M]	The Magnificent Thad Jones	1956	37.50	75.00	150.00
-- Regular version, Lexington Ave. address on label					
❏ BLP-1527 [M]	The Magnificent Thad Jones	1963	6.25	12.50	25.00
-- With "New York, USA" address on label					
❏ BLP-1546 [M]	The Magnificent Thad Jones, Volume 3	1957	37.50	75.00	150.00
-- "Deep groove" version (deep indentation under label on both sides)					
❏ BLP-1546 [M]	The Magnificent Thad Jones, Volume 3	1957	30.00	60.00	120.00
-- Regular version, W. 63rd St., NY address on label					
❏ BLP-1546 [M]	The Magnificent Thad Jones, Volume 3	1963	6.25	12.50	25.00
-- With "New York, USA" address on label					
❏ BST-81513 [R]	Detroit-New York Junction	1967	3.00	6.00	12.00
-- With "A Division of Liberty Records" on label					
❏ BST-81527 [R]	The Magnificent Thad Jones	1967	3.00	6.00	12.00
-- With "A Division of Liberty Records" on label					
❏ BST-81546 [R]	The Magnificent Thad Jones, Volume 3	1967	3.00	6.00	12.00
-- With "A Division of Liberty Records" on label					
DEBUT					
❏ DLP-12 [10]	The Fabulous Thad Jones	1954	75.00	150.00	300.00
❏ DLP-17 [10]	Jazz Collaborations	1954	75.00	150.00	300.00
❏ DEB-127 [M]	Thad Jones	1958	50.00	100.00	200.00
FANTASY					
❏ 6004 [M]	The Fabulous Thad Jones	1962	12.50	25.00	50.00
-- Red vinyl					
❏ 6004 [M]	The Fabulous Thad Jones	1962	6.25	12.50	25.00
-- Black vinyl					
❏ 86004 [R]	The Fabulous Thad Jones	1962	7.50	15.00	30.00
-- Blue vinyl					
❏ 86004 [R]	The Fabulous Thad Jones	1962	3.75	7.50	15.00
-- Black vinyl					
❏ OJC-625	The Fabulous Thad Jones	1991	3.75	7.50	15.00
MOSAIC					
❏ MQ5-172 [(5)]	The Complete Blue Note/UA/Roulette Recordings of Thad Jones	199?	25.00	50.00	100.00
PERIOD					
❏ SPL-1208 [M]	Mad Thad	1956	37.50	75.00	150.00
PRESTIGE					
❏ 2506	Thad Jones and Charles Mingus	198?	3.00	6.00	12.00
❏ PRLP-7118 [M]	After Hours	1957	20.00	40.00	80.00
STEEPLECHASE					
❏ SCS-1197	Three and One	198?	3.00	6.00	12.00
UNITED ARTISTS					
❏ UAL-4025 [M]	Motor City Scene	1959	20.00	40.00	80.00
❏ UAS-5025 [S]	Motor City Scene	1959	15.00	30.00	60.00

JONES, THAD, AND PEPPER ADAMS
Also see each artist's individual listings.

Number	Title	Yr	VG	VG+	NM
MILESTONE					
❏ MLP-1001 [M]	Mean What You Say	1966	5.00	10.00	20.00
❏ MSP-9001 [S]	Mean What You Say	1966	6.25	12.50	25.00

Number	Title	Yr	VG	VG+	NM

JONES, THAD-MEL LEWIS ORCHESTRA
Also see each artist's individual listings.
ARTISTS HOUSE

Number	Title	Yr	VG	VG+	NM
❏ 3	Quartet	1980	3.00	6.00	12.00

BLUE NOTE
❏ BN-LA392-H [(2)]	Thad Jones/Mel Lewis	1975	3.75	7.50	15.00
❏ BST-84346	Consummation	1970	5.00	10.00	20.00
❏ BST-89905 [(2)]	The Jazz Wave Ltd. On Tour (Volume 1)	1970	6.25	12.50	25.00

HORIZON
❏ SP-701	Suite for Pops	1975	3.00	6.00	12.00
❏ SP-707	New Life	1976	3.00	6.00	12.00
❏ SP-724	Live in Munich	1978	3.00	6.00	12.00

MOSAIC
❏ MQ7-151 [(7)]	The Complete Solid State Recordings of the Thad Jones-Mel Lewis Orchestra	199?	37.50	75.00	150.00

PAUSA
❏ 7012	Thad Jones-Mel Lewis Orchestra and Manuel De Sica	198?	2.50	5.00	10.00

PHILADELPHIA INT'L.
❏ KZ 33152	Potpourri	1974	3.75	7.50	15.00

RCA VICTOR
❏ AFL1-3423	Thad Jones/Mel Lewis and Umo	1980	3.75	7.50	15.00

SOLID STATE
❏ SM-17003 [M]	Presenting Thad Jones, Mel Lewis and the Jazz Orchestra	1966	5.00	10.00	20.00
❏ SM-17016 [M]	Live at the Village Vanguard	1967	6.25	12.50	25.00
❏ SS-18003 [S]	Presenting Thad Jones, Mel Lewis and the Jazz Orchestra	1966	5.00	10.00	20.00
❏ SS-18016 [S]	Live at the Village Vanguard	1967	3.75	7.50	15.00
❏ SS-18041	Thad Jones and Mel Lewis Featuring Miss Ruth Brown	1968	3.75	7.50	15.00
❏ SS-18048	Monday Night	1969	3.75	7.50	15.00
❏ SS-18058	Central Park North	1969	3.75	7.50	15.00

JOPLIN, SCOTT
Pianist and composer. He was a pioneer in ragtime music, a precursor to jazz piano.
BIOGRAPH
❏ 1006	Scott Joplin 1916: Classic Solos	197?	2.50	5.00	10.00
❏ 1008	Ragtime, Vol. 2	197?	2.50	5.00	10.00
❏ 1010	Ragtime, Vol. 3	197?	2.50	5.00	10.00

JORDAN, CLIFFORD
Tenor saxophone player. Also see JOHN JENKINS.
ATLANTIC
❏ 1444 [M]	These Are My Roots	1965	6.25	12.50	25.00
❏ SD 1444 [S]	These Are My Roots	1965	7.50	15.00	30.00

BEE HIVE
❏ BH-7018	Dr. Chicago	1986	2.50	5.00	10.00

BLUE NOTE
❏ BLP-1549 [M]	Blowing In from Chicago	1957	30.00	60.00	120.00
-- "Deep groove" version (deep indentation under label on both sides)					
❏ BLP-1549 [M]	Blowing In from Chicago	1957	20.00	40.00	80.00
-- Regular version, W. 63rd St., NY address on label					
❏ BLP-1549 [M]	Blowing In from Chicago	1963	6.25	12.50	25.00
-- With "New York, USA" address on label					
❏ BLP-1565 [M]	Clifford Jordan	1957	30.00	60.00	120.00
-- "Deep groove" version (deep indentation under label on both sides)					
❏ BLP-1565 [M]	Clifford Jordan	1957	20.00	40.00	80.00
-- Regular version, W. 63rd St., NY address on label					
❏ BLP-1565 [M]	Clifford Jordan	1963	6.25	12.50	25.00
-- With "New York, USA" address on label					
❏ BST-1565 [S]	Clifford Jordan	1959	20.00	40.00	80.00
-- "Deep groove" version (deep indentation under label on both sides)					
❏ BST-1565 [S]	Clifford Jordan	1959	15.00	30.00	60.00
-- Regular version, W. 63rd St., NY address on label					
❏ BST-1565 [S]	Clifford Jordan	1963	5.00	10.00	20.00
-- With "New York, USA" address on label					
❏ BLP-1582 [M]	Cliff Craft	1958	30.00	60.00	120.00
-- "Deep groove" version (deep indentation under label on both sides)					
❏ BLP-1582 [M]	Cliff Craft	1958	20.00	40.00	80.00
-- Regular version, W. 63rd St., NY address on label					
❏ BLP-1582 [M]	Cliff Craft	1963	6.25	12.50	25.00
-- With "New York, USA" address on label					
❏ BST-1582 [S]	Cliff Craft	1959	20.00	40.00	80.00
-- "Deep groove" version (deep indentation under label on both sides)					
❏ BST-1582 [S]	Cliff Craft	1959	15.00	30.00	60.00
-- Regular version, W. 63rd St., NY address on label					
❏ BST-1582 [S]	Cliff Craft	1963	5.00	10.00	20.00
-- With "New York, USA" address on label					
❏ BST-81549 [R]	Blowing In from Chicago	1967	3.00	6.00	12.00
-- With "A Division of Liberty Records" on label					
❏ BST-81565 [S]	Clifford Jordan	1967	3.75	7.50	15.00
-- With "A Division of Liberty Records" on label					

Number	Title	Yr	VG	VG+	NM
❏ BST-81582 [S]	Cliff Craft	1967	3.75	7.50	15.00
-- With "A Division of Liberty Records" on label					
❏ BST-81582 [S]	Cliff Craft	199?	6.25	12.50	25.00
-- Classic Records reissue on audiophile vinyl					

FANTASY
❏ OJC-147	Starting Time	198?	2.50	5.00	10.00
❏ OJC-494	Bearcat	1991	3.75	7.50	15.00

INNER CITY
❏ IC-2033	Firm Roots	197?	3.75	7.50	15.00
❏ IC-2047	The Highest Mountain	197?	3.75	7.50	15.00

JAZZLAND
❏ JLP-40 [M]	A Story Tale	1961	7.50	15.00	30.00
❏ JLP-52 [M]	Starting Time	1961	7.50	15.00	30.00
❏ JLP-69 [M]	Bearcat	1962	7.50	15.00	30.00
❏ JLP-940 [S]	A Story Tale	1961	10.00	20.00	40.00
❏ JLP-952 [S]	Starting Time	1961	10.00	20.00	40.00
❏ JLP-969 [S]	Bearcat	1962	10.00	20.00	40.00

MUSE
❏ MR-5076	Night of the Mark VII	197?	3.00	6.00	12.00
❏ MR-5105	Remembering Me-Me	197?	3.00	6.00	12.00
❏ MR-5128	Inward Fire	197?	3.00	6.00	12.00
❏ MR-5163	The Adventurer	197?	3.00	6.00	12.00

RIVERSIDE
❏ RLP-340 [M]	Spellbound	1960	10.00	20.00	40.00
❏ RS-9340 [S]	Spellbound	1960	7.50	15.00	30.00

SOUL NOTE
❏ SN-1084	Repetition	1984	3.00	6.00	12.00

STEEPLECHASE
❏ SCS-1033	Film Roots	198?	3.00	6.00	12.00
❏ SCS-1047	The Highest Mountain	198?	3.00	6.00	12.00
❏ SCS-1071	On Stage, Volume 1	197?	3.00	6.00	12.00
❏ SCS-1092	On Stage, Volume 2	198?	3.00	6.00	12.00
❏ SCS-1104	On Stage, Volume 3	198?	3.00	6.00	12.00
❏ SCS-1198	Half Note	198?	3.00	6.00	12.00

STRATA-EAST
❏ SES 1972-1	In the World	1972	5.00	10.00	20.00
❏ SES 19737/8 [(2)]	Glass Bead Games	1974	6.25	12.50	25.00

VORTEX
❏ 2010	Soul Fountain	1970	5.00	10.00	20.00

JORDAN, DUKE
Pianist.
BLUE NOTE
❏ BLP-4046 [M]	Flight to Jordan	1960	20.00	40.00	80.00
-- With W. 63rd St., NY address on label					
❏ BLP-4046 [M]	Flight to Jordan	1963	6.25	12.50	25.00
-- With "New York, USA" address on label					
❏ BST-84046 [S]	Flight to Jordan	1960	15.00	30.00	60.00
-- With W. 63rd St., NY address on label					
❏ BST-84046 [S]	Flight to Jordan	1963	5.00	10.00	20.00
-- With "New York, USA" address on label					
❏ BST-84046 [S]	Flight to Jordan	1967	3.75	7.50	15.00
-- With "A Division of Liberty Records" on label					

CHARLIE PARKER
❏ PLP-805 [M]	East and West of Jazz	1962	6.25	12.50	25.00
❏ PLP-805S [S]	East and West of Jazz	1962	7.50	15.00	30.00

INNER CITY
❏ IC-2011	Flight to Denmark	197?	3.75	7.50	15.00
❏ IC-2024	Two Loves	197?	3.75	7.50	15.00
❏ IC-2046	Duke's Delight	197?	3.75	7.50	15.00

NEW JAZZ
❏ NJ-810 [10]	Jordu	195?	50.00	100.00	200.00

PRESTIGE
❏ PRST-7849	Jordu	1970	3.00	6.00	12.00

SAVOY
❏ MG-12149 [M]	Duke Jordan	1959	20.00	40.00	80.00

SAVOY JAZZ
❏ SJL-1169	Flight to Jordan	1986	2.50	5.00	10.00

SIGNAL
❏ S-1202 [M]	Duke Jordan	1955	62.50	125.00	250.00

STEEPLECHASE
❏ SCS-1011	Flight to Denmark	198?	3.00	6.00	12.00
❏ SCS-1024	Two Loves	198?	3.00	6.00	12.00
❏ SCS-1046	Duke's Delight	198?	3.00	6.00	12.00
❏ SCS-1053	Misty Thursday	198?	3.00	6.00	12.00
❏ SCS-1063/4 [(2)]	Live in Japan	198?	3.75	7.50	15.00
❏ SCS-1088	Flight to Japan	198?	3.00	6.00	12.00
❏ SCS-1103	Duke's Artistry	1978	3.00	6.00	12.00
❏ SCS-1127	Lover Man	198?	3.00	6.00	12.00
❏ SCS-1135	Change of Pace	1979	3.00	6.00	12.00
❏ SCS-1143	Midnight Moonlight	198?	3.00	6.00	12.00
❏ SCS-1150	Great Session	198?	3.00	6.00	12.00

Number	Title	Yr	VG	VG+	NM
❏ SCS-1165	Thinking of You	198?	3.00	6.00	12.00
❏ SCS-1175	Truth	198?	3.00	6.00	12.00
❏ SCS-1189	Tivol One	198?	3.00	6.00	12.00
❏ SCS-1193	Tivol Two	198?	3.00	6.00	12.00
❏ SCS-1211	Wait and See	198?	3.00	6.00	12.00

JORDAN, DUKE/HALL OVERTON
Overton is a pianist. Also see DUKE JORDAN.
SAVOY

Number	Title	Yr	VG	VG+	NM
❏ MG-12145 [M]	Do It Yourself Jazz	1959	25.00	50.00	100.00
❏ MG-12146 [M]	Jazz Laboratory Series	1959	25.00	50.00	100.00

SIGNAL

Number	Title	Yr	VG	VG+	NM
❏ S-101/2 [M]	Jazz Laboratory Series	1955	62.50	125.00	250.00

-- Deduct 20 percent if book is missing

JORDAN, KENT
Flutist.
COLUMBIA

Number	Title	Yr	VG	VG+	NM
❏ FC 39325	No Question About It	1984	2.50	5.00	10.00

JORDAN, LOUIS
Alto saxophone player, male singer, bandleader and composer. Considered to be a major influence on rhythm 'n' blues and rock 'n' roll.
CIRCLE

Number	Title	Yr	VG	VG+	NM
❏ 53	Louis Jordan and the Tympany Five: 1944-45	198?	2.50	5.00	10.00
❏ 97	More Louis Jordan and His Tympany Five	198?	2.50	5.00	10.00

CLASSIC JAZZ

Number	Title	Yr	VG	VG+	NM
❏ 148	I Believe in Music	198?	3.00	6.00	12.00

DECCA

Number	Title	Yr	VG	VG+	NM
❏ DL 5035 [M]	Greatest Hits	1968	7.50	15.00	30.00
❏ DL 8551 [M]	Let the Good Times Roll	1958	25.00	50.00	100.00

-- Black label, silver print

Number	Title	Yr	VG	VG+	NM
❏ DL 75035 [R]	Greatest Hits	1968	3.75	7.50	15.00

MCA

Number	Title	Yr	VG	VG+	NM
❏ 274	Greatest Hits	197?	2.50	5.00	10.00
❏ 1337	Greatest Hits, Vol. 2	198?	2.50	5.00	10.00
❏ 4079 [(2)]	The Best of Louis Jordan	197?	3.00	6.00	12.00

MERCURY

Number	Title	Yr	VG	VG+	NM
❏ MG-20242 [M]	Somebody Up There Digs Me	1957	30.00	60.00	120.00
❏ MG-20331 [M]	Man, We're Wailin'	1958	30.00	60.00	120.00

SCORE

Number	Title	Yr	VG	VG+	NM
❏ SLP-4007 [M]	Go Blow Your Horn	1957	50.00	100.00	200.00

TANGERINE

Number	Title	Yr	VG	VG+	NM
❏ 1503 [M]	Hallelujah	1964	5.00	10.00	20.00
❏ S-1503 [S]	Hallelujah	1964	6.25	12.50	25.00

WING

Number	Title	Yr	VG	VG+	NM
❏ MGW-12126 [M]	Somebody Up There Digs Me	1962	6.25	12.50	25.00

JORDAN, SHEILA
Female singer.
BLACKHAWK

Number	Title	Yr	VG	VG+	NM
❏ BKH-50501	The Crossing	1986	2.50	5.00	10.00

BLUE NOTE

Number	Title	Yr	VG	VG+	NM
❏ BLP-9002 [M]	Portrait of Sheila Jordan	1962	37.50	75.00	150.00

-- With W. 63rd St., NY address on label

Number	Title	Yr	VG	VG+	NM
❏ BLP-9002 [M]	Portrait of Sheila Jordan	1963	6.25	12.50	25.00

-- With "New York, USA" address on label

Number	Title	Yr	VG	VG+	NM
❏ BST-89002 [R]	Portrait of Sheila Jordan	1967	3.00	6.00	12.00

-- With "A Division of Liberty Records" on label

MUSE

Number	Title	Yr	VG	VG+	NM
❏ MR-5366	Old Time Feeling	1989	3.00	6.00	12.00
❏ MR-5390	Lost and Found	1990	3.75	7.50	15.00

PALO ALTO

Number	Title	Yr	VG	VG+	NM
❏ PA-8038	Old Time Feeling	1982	3.00	6.00	12.00

STEEPLECHASE

Number	Title	Yr	VG	VG+	NM
❏ SCS-1081	Sheila	1978	3.00	6.00	12.00

WAVE

Number	Title	Yr	VG	VG+	NM
❏ W-1 [M]	Looking Out	1961	15.00	30.00	60.00
❏ WS-1 [S]	Looking Out	1961	20.00	40.00	80.00

JORDAN, STANLEY
Guitarist.
BLUE NOTE

Number	Title	Yr	VG	VG+	NM
❏ BT-85101	Magic Touch	1985	2.50	5.00	10.00
❏ BT-85130	Standards Volume 1	1985	2.50	5.00	10.00
❏ B1-92356	Cornucopia	1990	3.75	7.50	15.00

EMI MANHATTAN

Number	Title	Yr	VG	VG+	NM
❏ E1-48682	Flying Home	1988	2.50	5.00	10.00

JORDAN, TAFT
Trumpeter and male singer.
MERCURY

Number	Title	Yr	VG	VG+	NM
❏ MG-20429 [M]	The Moods of Taft Jordan	1959	10.00	20.00	40.00
❏ SR-60101 [S]	The Moods of Taft Jordan	1959	10.00	20.00	40.00

MOODSVILLE

Number	Title	Yr	VG	VG+	NM
❏ MVLP-21 [M]	Mood Indigo -- Taft Jordan Plays Duke Ellington	1961	12.50	25.00	50.00

-- Green label

Number	Title	Yr	VG	VG+	NM
❏ MVLP-21 [M]	Mood Indigo -- Taft Jordan Plays Duke Ellington	1965	6.25	12.50	25.00

-- Blue label, trident logo at right

JORGENSMANN, THEO
Clarinetist.
CMP

Number	Title	Yr	VG	VG+	NM
❏ CMP-4-ST	Go Ahead Clarinet	198?	2.50	5.00	10.00
❏ CMP-6-ST	Song of BoWaGe	198?	2.50	5.00	10.00
❏ CMP-15-ST	Next Adventure	198?	2.50	5.00	10.00
❏ CMP-19-ST	Laterna Magica	198?	2.50	5.00	10.00

JOYRIDE
Ten-member all-star band.
NOVA

Number	Title	Yr	VG	VG+	NM
❏ 8705	Joyride	1987	2.50	5.00	10.00

JPJ QUARTET, THE
Members: BUDD JOHNSON; DILL JONES; Bill Pemberton (bass); Oliver Jackson (drums).
MASTER JAZZ

Number	Title	Yr	VG	VG+	NM
❏ 8111	Montreux '71	1972	3.75	7.50	15.00

JUJU
See ONENESS OF JUJU.

JUNGLE CRAWLERS, THE
STOMP OFF

Number	Title	Yr	VG	VG+	NM
❏ SOS-1084	Stompin' On Down	1985	2.50	5.00	10.00

JURGENS, DICK
Trumpeter and bandleader.
HINDSIGHT

Number	Title	Yr	VG	VG+	NM
❏ HSR-111	Dick Jurgens and His Orchestra 1937-39	198?	2.50	5.00	10.00
❏ HSR-138	Dick Jurgens and His Orchestra 1937-38	198?	2.50	5.00	10.00
❏ HSR-191	Dick Jurgens and His Orchestra 1938	198?	2.50	5.00	10.00

JURIS, VIC
Guitarist.
MUSE

Number	Title	Yr	VG	VG+	NM
❏ MR-5150	Road Song	1978	3.75	7.50	15.00
❏ MR-5206	Horizon Drive	1979	3.75	7.50	15.00
❏ MR-5265	Bleecker Street	1982	3.00	6.00	12.00

Number	Title	Yr	VG	VG+	NM

K

KALAPARUSHA
See KALAPARUSHA MAURICE McINTYRE.

KALLAO, ALEX
Pianist.
BATON
| ❏ BL-1205 [M] | Alex Kallao in Concert, University of Ottawa | 1954 | 15.00 | 30.00 | 60.00 |

RCA VICTOR
| ❏ LJM-1011 [M] | Evening at the Embers | 1954 | 12.50 | 25.00 | 50.00 |

KAMINSKY, MAX
Trumpeter. Also see BOBBY HACKETT.
CHIAROSCURO
| ❏ 176 | When Summer Is Gone | 1977 | 3.00 | 6.00 | 12.00 |
COMMODORE
| ❏ FL-20019 [10] | Max Kaminsky | 1952 | 12.50 | 25.00 | 50.00 |
CONCERT HALL JAZZ
| ❏ 1009 [10] | Windy City Jazz | 1955 | 12.50 | 25.00 | 50.00 |
JAZZTONE
| ❏ J-1208 [M] | Windy City Six | 1955 | 10.00 | 20.00 | 40.00 |
MGM
| ❏ E-261 [10] | When the Saints Go Marching In | 1954 | 12.50 | 25.00 | 50.00 |
RCA VICTOR
| ❏ LJM-3003 [10] | Jazz on the Campus, Ltd. | 1954 | 12.50 | 25.00 | 50.00 |
UNITED ARTISTS
| ❏ UAL-3174 [M] | Max Goes East | 1961 | 5.00 | 10.00 | 20.00 |
| ❏ UAS-6174 [S] | Max Goes East | 1961 | 6.25 | 12.50 | 25.00 |

KAMUCA, RICHIE
Tenor saxophone player. Also see AL COHN; BILL PERKINS.
CONCORD JAZZ
❏ CJ-38	Drop Me Off in Harlem	197?	3.00	6.00	12.00
❏ CJ-41	Richie	1977	3.00	6.00	12.00
❏ CJ-96	Charlie	1979	3.00	6.00	12.00
FANTASY
| ❏ OJC-1760 | West Coast Jazz in Hi-Fi | 198? | 2.50 | 5.00 | 10.00 |
HIFI
❏ R-604 [M]	Jazz Erotica	1957	15.00	30.00	60.00
❏ J-609 [M]	West Coast Jazz in Hi-Fi	1959	7.50	15.00	30.00
❏ JS-609 [S]	West Coast Jazz in Hi-Fi	1959	10.00	20.00	40.00
JAZZZ
| ❏ 104 | Richie Kamuca 1976 | 1976 | 3.00 | 6.00 | 12.00 |
MODE
| ❏ LP-102 [M] | Richie Kamuka Quartet | 1957 | 20.00 | 40.00 | 80.00 |

KAPLAN, ARTIE
Baritone saxophone player, producer and arranger.
HOPI
| ❏ VHS 901 | Confessions of a Male Chauvinist Pig | 1971 | 6.25 | 12.50 | 25.00 |

KAPLAN, LEIGH
Pianist.
CAMBRIA
| ❏ C-1016 | Shades of Dring | 198? | 2.50 | 5.00 | 10.00 |
| ❏ C-1019 | Dizzy Fingers | 1987 | 2.50 | 5.00 | 10.00 |

KARMA
HORIZON
| ❏ SP-713 | Celebration | 1976 | 3.75 | 7.50 | 15.00 |
| ❏ SP-723 | For Everybody | 1977 | 3.75 | 7.50 | 15.00 |

KARUKAS
Full name: Gregg Karukas. Keyboard player and pianist.
OPTIMISM
| ❏ OP-3101 | The Nightowl | 1988 | 2.50 | 5.00 | 10.00 |

KASAI, KIMIKO
Female singer.
CATALYST
| ❏ 7900 | One for the Lady | 1977 | 3.00 | 6.00 | 12.00 |

KASSEL, ART
Bandleader.
HINDSIGHT
| ❏ HSR-162 | Kassels In The Air Orchestra 1944 | 198? | 2.50 | 5.00 | 10.00 |

| ❏ HSR-170 | Kassels In The Air Orchestra 1945 | 198? | 2.50 | 5.00 | 10.00 |
KAPP
| ❏ KL-1248 [M] | Dance to the Music of Art Kassel | 1962 | 5.00 | 10.00 | 20.00 |
| ❏ KS-3248 [S] | Dance to the Music of Art Kassel | 1962 | 5.00 | 10.00 | 20.00 |

KATINDIG, BOY
Keyboard player and composer.
PAUSA
| ❏ 7137 | Midnight Lady | 198? | 2.50 | 5.00 | 10.00 |

KATZ, BRUCE
Keyboard player and pianist.
AUDIOQUEST
| ❏ AQ-1012 | Crescent Crawl | 1992 | 3.00 | 6.00 | 12.00 |
| ❏ AQ-1026 | Transformation | 1994 | 3.00 | 6.00 | 12.00 |

KATZ, DICK
Pianist and composer.
ATLANTIC
❏ 1314 [M]	Piano and Pin	1959	10.00	20.00	40.00
-- Black label					
❏ 1314 [M]	Piano and Pin	1961	6.25	12.50	25.00
-- Multicolor label, white "fan" logo at right					
❏ SD 1314 [S]	Piano and Pin	1959	10.00	20.00	40.00
-- Green label					
❏ SD 1314 [S]	Piano and Pin	1961	5.00	10.00	20.00
-- Multicolor label, white "fan" logo at right					

KATZ, DICK; DEREK SMITH; RENE URTREGER
All three are pianists. Also see DICK KATZ; DEREK SMITH.
ATLANTIC
❏ 1287 [M]	John Lewis Presents Jazz Piano International	1958	10.00	20.00	40.00
-- Black label					
❏ 1287 [M]	John Lewis Presents Jazz Piano International	1961	6.25	12.50	25.00
-- Multicolor label, white "fan" logo at right					

KATZ, FRED
Pianist and cellist.
DECCA
❏ DL 9202 [M]	Soulo Cello	1958	10.00	20.00	40.00
❏ DL 9213 [M]	4-5-6 Trio	1958	10.00	20.00	40.00
❏ DL 9217 [M]	Fred Katz and Jammers	1958	10.00	20.00	40.00
❏ DL 79202 [S]	Soulo Cello	1958	7.50	15.00	30.00
❏ DL 79213 [S]	4-5-6 Trio	1958	7.50	15.00	30.00
❏ DL 79217 [S]	Fred Katz and Jammers	1958	7.50	15.00	30.00
WARNER BROS.
| ❏ W 1277 [M] | Folk Songs for Far Out Folks | 1959 | 6.25 | 12.50 | 25.00 |
| ❏ WS 1277 [S] | Folk Songs for Far Out Folks | 1959 | 7.50 | 15.00 | 30.00 |

KAWAGUCHI, GEORGE, AND ART BLAKEY
Kawaguchi is a drummer. Also see ART BLAKEY.
STORYVILLE
| ❏ 4100 | Killer Joe | 1982 | 3.00 | 6.00 | 12.00 |

KAWASAKI, RYO
Guitarist.
INNER CITY
| ❏ IC-6006 | Eight Mile Road | 197? | 3.75 | 7.50 | 15.00 |
| ❏ IC-6016 | Prism | 197? | 3.75 | 7.50 | 15.00 |
RCA VICTOR
| ❏ APL1-1855 | Juice | 1977 | 3.75 | 7.50 | 15.00 |

KAYE, MILTON
Pianist.
GOLDEN CREST
| ❏ GC-31032 [(2)] | Ragtime at the Rosebud | 197? | 3.00 | 6.00 | 12.00 |

KAYE, SAMMY
Clarinet player, more famous as a bandleader.
COLUMBIA
❏ CL 561 [M]	Swing and Sway with Sammy Kaye	195?	7.50	15.00	30.00
❏ CL 668 [M]	Music, Maestro, Please!	195?	7.50	15.00	30.00
❏ CL 885 [M]	My Fair Lady (For Dancing)	1956	5.00	10.00	20.00
❏ CL 891 [M]	What Makes Sammy Swing and Sway	1956	5.00	10.00	20.00

Number	Title	Yr	VG	VG+	NM
❏ CL 964 [M]	Sunday Serenade	1957	5.00	10.00	20.00
❏ CL 1018 [M]	Popular American Waltzes	1957	5.00	10.00	20.00
❏ CL 1236 [M]	Strauss Waltzes for Dancing	1959	3.75	7.50	15.00
❏ CL 2541 [10]	Christmas Serenade	1955	10.00	20.00	40.00
-- "House Party Series" issue					
❏ CL 6155 [10]	Sunday Serenade	1953	10.00	20.00	40.00
DECCA					
❏ DL 4070 [M]	Christmas Day with Sammy Kaye	1960	3.00	6.00	12.00
❏ DL 4071 [M]	Sing and Sway with Sammy Kaye	1960	3.00	6.00	12.00
❏ DL 4121 [M]	Dance to My Golden Favorites	1961	3.00	6.00	12.00
❏ DL 4154 [M]	Songs I Wish I Had Played...The First Time Around	1961	3.00	6.00	12.00
❏ DL 4215 [M]	Sexy Strings and Subtle Saxes	1962	3.00	6.00	12.00
❏ DL 4247 [M]	New Twists on Old Favorites	1962	3.00	6.00	12.00
❏ DL 4306 [M]	For Your Dancing Pleasure	1962	3.00	6.00	12.00
❏ DL 4357 [M]	Come Dance with Me	1963	3.00	6.00	12.00
❏ DL 4424 [M]	Dreamy Serenades	1963	3.00	6.00	12.00
❏ DL 4502 [M]	Come Dance to the Hits	1964	3.00	6.00	12.00
❏ DL 4590 [M]	Come Dance with Me (Vol. 2)	1965	3.00	6.00	12.00
❏ DL 4655 [M]	Dancetime	1965	3.00	6.00	12.00
❏ DL 4687 [M]	Swing and Sway Au-Go-Go	1965	3.00	6.00	12.00
❏ DL 4754 [M]	Shall We Dance	1966	3.00	6.00	12.00
❏ DL 4823 [M]	Let's Face the Music	1967	3.00	6.00	12.00
❏ DL 4862 [M]	Swing & Sway in Hawaii	1967	3.75	7.50	15.00
❏ DL 4924 [M]	Dance and Be Happy	1967	3.75	7.50	15.00
❏ DL 4970 [M]	Glory of Love	1967	3.75	7.50	15.00
❏ DL 74070 [S]	Christmas Day with Sammy Kaye	1960	3.75	7.50	15.00
❏ DL 74071 [S]	Sing and Sway with Sammy Kaye	1960	3.75	7.50	15.00
❏ DL 74121 [S]	Dance to My Golden Favorites	1961	3.75	7.50	15.00
❏ DL 74154 [S]	Songs I Wish I Had Played...The First Time Around	1961	3.75	7.50	15.00
❏ DL 74215 [S]	Sexy Strings and Subtle Saxes	1962	3.75	7.50	15.00
❏ DL 74247 [S]	New Twists on Old Favorites	1962	3.75	7.50	15.00
❏ DL 74306 [S]	For Your Dancing Pleasure	1962	3.75	7.50	15.00
❏ DL 74357 [S]	Come Dance with Me	1963	3.75	7.50	15.00
❏ DL 74424 [S]	Dreamy Serenades	1963	3.75	7.50	15.00
❏ DL 74502 [S]	Come Dance to the Hits	1964	3.75	7.50	15.00
❏ DL 74590 [S]	Come Dance with Me (Vol. 2)	1965	3.75	7.50	15.00
❏ DL 74655 [S]	Dancetime	1965	3.75	7.50	15.00
❏ DL 74687 [S]	Swing and Sway Au-Go-Go	1965	3.75	7.50	15.00
❏ DL 74754 [S]	Shall We Dance	1966	3.75	7.50	15.00
❏ DL 74823 [S]	Let's Face the Music	1967	3.75	7.50	15.00
❏ DL 74862 [S]	Swing & Sway in Hawaii	1967	3.00	6.00	12.00
❏ DL 74924 [S]	Dance and Be Happy	1967	3.00	6.00	12.00
❏ DL 74970 [S]	Glory of Love	1967	3.00	6.00	12.00
❏ DL 75106	The 30's Are Here to Stay	1968	3.00	6.00	12.00
HARMONY					
❏ HL 7187 [M]	Dancing with Sammy Kaye in Hi-Fi	196?	3.75	7.50	15.00
❏ HL 7230 [M]	In a Dancing Mood	196?	3.75	7.50	15.00
❏ HL 7321 [M]	My Fair Lady	1964	3.75	7.50	15.00
❏ HL 7357 [M]	Beautiful Waltzes for Dancing	196?	3.75	7.50	15.00
❏ HS 11087 [R]	Dancing with Sammy Kaye in Hi-Fi	196?	3.00	6.00	12.00
❏ HS 11121 [R]	My Fair Lady	1964	3.00	6.00	12.00
❏ HS 11157 [R]	Beautiful Waltzes for Dancing	196?	3.00	6.00	12.00
❏ HS 11261	All-Time Waltz Favorites	1968	3.00	6.00	12.00
❏ HS 11377	Harbor Lights	1970	2.50	5.00	10.00
❏ KH 32013	Best of the Big Bands	1971	2.50	5.00	10.00
HINDSIGHT					
❏ HSR-158	1940-41	198?	2.50	5.00	10.00
❏ HSR-163	1942-43	198?	2.50	5.00	10.00
❏ HSR-207	1944-46	198?	2.50	5.00	10.00
❏ HSR-402 [(2)]	22 Original Big Band Recordings	198?	3.00	6.00	12.00
MCA					
❏ 191	Dance to My Golden Favorites	1973	2.50	5.00	10.00
-- Reissue of Decca 74121					
❏ 205	Plays Swing & Sway	1973	2.50	5.00	10.00
-- Reissue of Decca 74306					
❏ 278	The 30's Are Here to Stay	197?	2.50	5.00	10.00
-- Reissue of Decca material					
❏ 4027 [(2)]	The Best of Sammy Kaye	197?	3.00	6.00	12.00
PROJECT 3					
❏ 5065	Brand New Recordings	1972	3.00	6.00	12.00
RCA CAMDEN					
❏ CAL-355 [M]	Swing and Sway with Sammy Kaye	1957	5.00	10.00	20.00
RCA VICTOR					
❏ LPM-3966 [M]	The Best of Sammy Kaye	1967	5.00	10.00	20.00
❏ LSP-3966 [R]	The Best of Sammy Kaye	1967	3.00	6.00	12.00
❏ VPM-6070 [(2)]	This Is Sammy Kaye	1972	3.00	6.00	12.00
VOCALION					
❏ VL 73919	Theme from "Love Story"	1971	2.50	5.00	10.00

KAZ, FRED
Pianist.
ATLANTIC

Number	Title	Yr	VG	VG+	NM
❏ 1335 [M]	Eastern Exposure	1960	6.25	12.50	25.00
-- Multicolor label, white "fan" logo at right					
❏ SD 1335 [S]	Eastern Exposure	1960	7.50	15.00	30.00
-- Multicolor label, white "fan" logo at right					

KEATING, JOHNNY
Trombonist, pianist, arranger and composer.
BALLY
| ❏ BAL-12001 [M] | English Jazz | 1956 | 12.50 | 25.00 | 50.00 |
DOT
| ❏ DLP-3066 [M] | Swinging Scots | 1957 | 10.00 | 20.00 | 40.00 |

KEENE, BOB
Clarinet player and bandleader, best known as the founder of the Del-Fi record label.
ANDEX
| ❏ S-4001 [M] | Solo for 7 | 1958 | 12.50 | 25.00 | 50.00 |
DEL-FI
| ❏ DFLP-1202 [M] | Unforgettable Love Songs of the 50's | 1959 | 10.00 | 20.00 | 40.00 |
| ❏ DFLP-1222 [M] | Twist to Radio KRLA | 1962 | 7.50 | 15.00 | 30.00 |
GENE NORMAN
| ❏ GNP-149 [10] | Bob Keene | 1954 | 12.50 | 25.00 | 50.00 |

KEISER TWINS, THE
Peter Keiser (bass) and Walter Keiser (drums).
CBS
| ❏ FM 44737 | The Keiser Twins | 1988 | 2.50 | 5.00 | 10.00 |

KELLAWAY, ROGER
Pianist, bass player, arranger and composer.
A&M
| ❏ SP-3034 | Cello Quartet | 1970 | 3.00 | 6.00 | 12.00 |
| ❏ SP-3618 | Come to the Meadow | 1974 | 2.50 | 5.00 | 10.00 |
CHOICE
| ❏ CRS-6833 | Ain't Misbehavin' | 1989 | 2.50 | 5.00 | 10.00 |
DISCWASHER
| ❏ 003 | Nostalgia Suite | 1979 | 5.00 | 10.00 | 20.00 |
DOBRE
| ❏ 1045 | Say That Again | 1978 | 2.50 | 5.00 | 10.00 |
PACIFIC JAZZ
❏ LN-10070	Spirit Feel	198?	2.00	4.00	8.00
-- Budget-line reissue					
❏ PJ-10122 [M]	Spirit Feel	196?	5.00	10.00	20.00
❏ ST-20122 [S]	Spirit Feel	196?	3.75	7.50	15.00
PRESTIGE
| ❏ PRLP-7399 [M] | The Roger Kellaway Trio | 1965 | 6.25 | 12.50 | 25.00 |
| ❏ PRST-7399 [S] | The Roger Kellaway Trio | 1965 | 7.50 | 15.00 | 30.00 |
REGINA
| ❏ R-298 [M] | Portraits | 1964 | 5.00 | 10.00 | 20.00 |
| ❏ RS-298 [S] | Portraits | 1964 | 6.25 | 12.50 | 25.00 |
VOSS
| ❏ VLP1-42935 | Nostalgia Suite | 1988 | 2.50 | 5.00 | 10.00 |
WORLD PACIFIC
| ❏ WP-21861 [M] | Stride | 1967 | 5.00 | 10.00 | 20.00 |
| ❏ WPS-21861 [S] | Stride | 1967 | 3.75 | 7.50 | 15.00 |

KELLAWAY, ROGER, AND RED MITCHELL
Also see each artist's individual listings.
STASH
| ❏ ST-271 | Fifty/Fifty | 1988 | 2.50 | 5.00 | 10.00 |

KELLER, ALLEN
Male singer.
CHARLIE PARKER
| ❏ PLP-817 [M] | A New Look at the World | 1962 | 6.25 | 12.50 | 25.00 |
| ❏ PLP-817S [S] | A New Look at the World | 1962 | 7.50 | 15.00 | 30.00 |

KELLER, HAL
Pianist.
SAND
| ❏ 7 [M] | Hal Keller Debut | 1957 | 12.50 | 25.00 | 50.00 |
SOUND
| ❏ 602 [M] | Hal Keller Debut | 1959 | 10.00 | 20.00 | 40.00 |

Number	Title	Yr	VG	VG+	NM
KELLEY, PAT					
Guitarist.					
NOVA					
❏ 8704-1	Views of the Future	1988	2.50	5.00	10.00
KELLEY, PECK					
Pianist and bandleader.					
COMMODORE					
❏ XF2-17017 [(2)]	Peck Kelley Jam	198?	3.00	6.00	12.00
KELLIN, ORANGE					
Clarinetist.					
BIOGRAPH					
❏ CEN-7	Orange Kellin in New Orleans	197?	2.50	5.00	10.00
KELLY, BEVERLY					
Female singer.					
AUDIO FIDELITY					
❏ AFLP-1874 [M]	Beverly Kelly Sings	1958	7.50	15.00	30.00
❏ AFSD-5874 [S]	Beverly Kelly Sings	1958	10.00	20.00	40.00
RIVERSIDE					
❏ RLP-328 [M]	Love Locked Out	1960	6.25	12.50	25.00
❏ RLP-345 [M]	Bev Kelly In Person	1960	6.25	12.50	25.00
❏ 6042	Bev Kelly In Person	197?	3.00	6.00	12.00
❏ 6052	Love Locked Out	197?	3.00	6.00	12.00
❏ RS-9328 [S]	Love Locked Out	1960	7.50	15.00	30.00
❏ RS-9345 [S]	Bev Kelly In Person	1960	7.50	15.00	30.00
KELLY, ED					
Pianist, organist, arranger and composer.					
THERESA					
❏ 103	Music from the Black Museum	197?	3.00	6.00	12.00
❏ 106	Ed Kelly and Friend	197?	3.75	7.50	15.00
KELLY, GEORGE					
Tenor saxophone player.					
STASH					
❏ 240	George Kelly Plays Music of Don Redman	198?	2.50	5.00	10.00
KELLY, JACK					
JUBILEE					
❏ JLP-21 [10]	Jack Kelly's Badinage	1955	12.50	25.00	50.00
KELLY, JOE					
BLACKBIRD					
❏ 4001	Blackbird Presents Joe Kelly	197?	3.00	6.00	12.00
KELLY, JULIE					
Female singer.					
PAUSA					
❏ 7154	We're On Our Way	198?	2.50	5.00	10.00
❏ 7186	Never Let Me Go	1986	2.50	5.00	10.00
KELLY, JULIE, AND TOM GARVIN					
Garvin is a pianist. Also see JULIE KELLY.					
CMG					
❏ CML-8017	Some Other Time	1989	3.00	6.00	12.00
KELLY, NANCY					
Female singer and arranger.					
AMHERST					
❏ AMH-3317	Live Jazz	1988	2.50	5.00	10.00
KELLY, WYNTON					
Pianist and composer. Also see DONNA DRAKE; STEVE LACY.					
BLUE NOTE					
❏ BLP-5025 [10]	Piano Interpretations by Wynton Kelly	1953	75.00	150.00	300.00
DELMARK					
❏ DS-441	The Last Trio Session	1989	3.00	6.00	12.00
EPITAPH					
❏ E-4007	Wynton Kelly 1931-1971	1975	3.75	7.50	15.00
FANTASY					
❏ OJC-033	Kelly Blue	198?	2.50	5.00	10.00
❏ OJC-401	Wynton Kelly Piano	1989	3.00	6.00	12.00
JAZZLAND					
❏ JLP-83 [M]	Whisper Not	1962	7.50	15.00	30.00
❏ JLP-983 [S]	Whisper Not	1962	6.25	12.50	25.00

Number	Title	Yr	VG	VG+	NM
MILESTONE					
❏ 9004	Full View	1968	3.75	7.50	15.00
❏ 47026 [(2)]	Keep It Moving	197?	3.75	7.50	15.00
RIVERSIDE					
❏ RLP 12-254 [M]	Wynton Kelly Piano	1957	12.50	25.00	50.00
❏ RLP 12-298 [M]	Kelly Blue	1959	12.50	25.00	50.00
❏ RLP-1142 [S]	Kelly Blue	1959	10.00	20.00	40.00
❏ 6043	Whisper Not	197?	3.00	6.00	12.00
❏ 6114	Kelly Blue	197?	3.00	6.00	12.00
TRIP					
❏ 5010 [(2)]	Smokin'	197?	3.00	6.00	12.00
VEE JAY					
❏ LP-1016 [M]	Kelly Great	1960	7.50	15.00	30.00
❏ SR-1016 [S]	Kelly Great	1960	10.00	20.00	40.00
❏ VJ-1086 [M]	Best of Wynton Kelly	1964	5.00	10.00	20.00
❏ VJS-1086 [S]	Best of Wynton Kelly	1964	6.25	12.50	25.00
❏ LP-3004 [M]	Kelly Great	1960	6.25	12.50	25.00
-- Reissue of LP-1016					
❏ SR-3004 [S]	Kelly Great	1960	7.50	15.00	30.00
-- Reissue of SR-1016					
❏ LP-3011 [M]	Kelly at Midnight	1960	6.25	12.50	25.00
❏ SR-3011 [S]	Kelly at Midnight	1960	7.50	15.00	30.00
❏ LP-3022 [M]	Wynton Kelly	1961	6.25	12.50	25.00
❏ SR-3022 [S]	Wynton Kelly	1961	7.50	15.00	30.00
❏ VJS-3038	Someday My Prince Will Come	1977	3.75	7.50	15.00
❏ VJS-3071	Wynton Kelly In Concert	1977	3.75	7.50	15.00
❏ VJS-3072-2 [(2)]	Final Notes	1977	5.00	10.00	20.00
VERVE					
❏ V-8576 [M]	Comin' In the Back Door	1964	3.75	7.50	15.00
❏ V6-8576 [S]	Comin' In the Back Door	1964	5.00	10.00	20.00
❏ V-8588 [M]	It's All Right	1964	3.75	7.50	15.00
❏ V6-8588 [S]	It's All Right	1964	5.00	10.00	20.00
❏ V-8622 [M]	Undiluted	1965	3.75	7.50	15.00
❏ V6-8622 [S]	Undiluted	1965	5.00	10.00	20.00
❏ V-8633 [M]	Smokin' at the Half Note	1965	3.75	7.50	15.00
❏ V6-8633 [S]	Smokin' at the Half Note	1965	5.00	10.00	20.00
XANADU					
❏ 198	Blues On Purpose	198?	2.50	5.00	10.00
KEMP, HAL					
Bandleader.					
CIRCLE					
❏ C-25	Hal Kemp and His Orchestra 1934	198?	2.50	5.00	10.00
HINDSIGHT					
❏ HSR-143	Hal Kemp and His Orchestra 1934	198?	2.50	5.00	10.00
❏ HSR-161	Hal Kemp and His Orchestra 1934, 198? Volume 2		2.50	5.00	10.00
❏ HSR-222	Hal Kemp and His Orchestra 1936	198?	2.50	5.00	10.00
KENIA					
Female singer.					
ZEBRA					
❏ ZEB-5967	Initial Thrill	1987	3.00	6.00	12.00
❏ ZEB-42149	Distant Horizon: Rio/New York	1988	3.00	6.00	12.00
KENNEDY, CHARLIE					
See CHARLIE VENTURA.					
KENNEY, BEVERLY					
Female singer.					
DECCA					
❏ DL 8743 [M]	Beverly Kenney Sings for Playboys	1958	50.00	100.00	200.00
❏ DL 8850 [M]	Born to Be Blue	1959	50.00	100.00	200.00
❏ DL 8948 [M]	Like Yesterday	1960	37.50	75.00	150.00
❏ DL 78948 [S]	Like Yesterday	1960	50.00	100.00	200.00
ROOST					
❏ RST-2206 [M]	Beverly Kenney Sings for Johnny Smith	1956	37.50	75.00	150.00
❏ RST-2212 [M]	Come Swing with Me	1956	37.50	75.00	150.00
❏ RST-2218 [M]	Beverly Kenney with Jimmy Jones and the Basie-ites	1957	37.50	75.00	150.00
KENNY G					
Saxophone player, mostly soprano and alto.					
ARISTA					
❏ AL8-8192	G Force	1984	2.00	4.00	8.00
❏ AL8-8282	Gravity	1985	2.00	4.00	8.00

Number	Title	Yr	VG	VG+	NM
❏ ALB6-8299	Kenny G	1985	2.00	4.00	8.00
-- Reissue of 9608					
❏ AL8-8427	Duotones	1986	2.00	4.00	8.00
❏ AL-8457	Silhouette	1988	2.00	4.00	8.00
❏ A2L-8613 [(2)]	Kenny G Live	1989	3.00	6.00	12.00
❏ AL 9608	Kenny G	1983	2.50	5.00	10.00

KENT, MARSHALL
HERWIN

Number	Title	Yr	VG	VG+	NM
❏ 301	Pallet on the Floor	197?	3.75	7.50	15.00

KENTON, STAN

Pianist, bandleader, composer and arranger. He pioneered what became known as "progressive jazz."

CAPITOL

Number	Title	Yr	VG	VG+	NM
❏ H 155 [10]	Encores	1950	15.00	30.00	60.00
❏ T 155 [M]	Encores	195?	10.00	20.00	40.00
-- Turquoise label					
❏ DT 167 [R]	Artistry in Rhythm	1969	2.50	5.00	10.00
❏ H 167 [10]	Artistry in Rhythm	1950	15.00	30.00	60.00
❏ SM-167 [R]	Artistry in Rhythm	1975	2.00	4.00	8.00
-- Reissue with new prefix					
❏ T 167 [M]	Artistry in Rhythm	195?	10.00	20.00	40.00
-- Turquoise label					
❏ T 167 [M]	Artistry in Rhythm	1959	3.75	7.50	15.00
-- Black label with colorband, Capitol logo at left					
❏ T 167 [M]	Artistry in Rhythm	1962	3.00	6.00	12.00
-- Black label with colorband, Capitol logo at top					
❏ H 172 [10]	A Presentation of Progressive Jazz	1950	15.00	30.00	60.00
❏ T 172 [M]	A Presentation of Progressive Jazz	195?	10.00	20.00	40.00
❏ P 189 [10]	Innovations in Modern Music	1950	15.00	30.00	60.00
❏ H 190 [10]	Milestones	1950	15.00	30.00	60.00
❏ T 190 [M]	Milestones	195?	10.00	20.00	40.00
-- Turquoise label					
❏ L 248 [10]	Stan Kenton Presents	1951	15.00	30.00	60.00
❏ T 248 [M]	Stan Kenton Presents	195?	10.00	20.00	40.00
-- Turquoise label					
❏ ST-305	Music from "Hair"	1969	3.75	7.50	15.00
❏ H 353 [10]	City of Glass	1952	15.00	30.00	60.00
❏ H 358 [10]	Classics	1952	15.00	30.00	60.00
❏ T 358 [M]	Classics	195?	10.00	20.00	40.00
-- Turquoise label					
❏ H 383 [10]	New Concepts of Artistry in Rhythm	1953	15.00	30.00	60.00
❏ T 383 [M]	New Concepts of Artistry in Rhythm	195?	10.00	20.00	40.00
-- Turquoise label					
❏ H 386 [10]	Prologue: This Is an Orchestra	1953	15.00	30.00	60.00
❏ H 421 [10]	Popular Favorites	1953	15.00	30.00	60.00
❏ T 421 [M]	Popular Favorites	195?	10.00	20.00	40.00
-- Turquoise label					
❏ H 426 [10]	Sketches on Standards	1953	15.00	30.00	60.00
❏ T 426 [M]	Sketches on Standards	195?	10.00	20.00	40.00
-- Turquoise label					
❏ H 460 [10]	This Modern World	1953	15.00	30.00	60.00
❏ H 462 [10]	Portraits on Standards	1953	15.00	30.00	60.00
❏ T 462 [M]	Portraits on Standards	195?	10.00	20.00	40.00
-- Turquoise label					
❏ W 524 [M]	Kenton Showcase	1954	10.00	20.00	40.00
❏ H 525 [10]	Kenton Showcase -- The Music of Bill Russo	1954	15.00	30.00	60.00
❏ H 526 [10]	Kenton Showcase -- The Music of Bill Holman	1954	15.00	30.00	60.00
❏ TDB 569 [(4) M]	The Kenton Era	1955	25.00	50.00	100.00
-- Box set with 44-page book					
❏ STCL-575 [(3)]	Stan Kenton	1970	5.00	10.00	20.00
❏ T 656 [M]	Duet	1955	10.00	20.00	40.00
-- With June Christy; turquoise label					
❏ T 666 [M]	Contemporary Concepts	1955	10.00	20.00	40.00
-- Turquoise label					
❏ W 724 [M]	Kenton in Hi-Fi	1956	10.00	20.00	40.00
-- Turquoise label					
❏ T 731 [M]	Cuban Fire!	1956	10.00	20.00	40.00
-- Turquoise label					
❏ T 731 [M]	Cuban Fire!	1959	5.00	10.00	20.00
-- Black label with colorband, Capitol logo at left					
❏ T 731 [M]	Cuban Fire!	1962	3.75	7.50	15.00
-- Black label with colorband, Capitol logo at top					
❏ T 736 [M]	City of Glass/This Modern World	1956	10.00	20.00	40.00
-- Combination of 353 and 460 onto one 12-inch LP, turquoise label					
❏ T 810 [M]	Kenton with Voices	1957	10.00	20.00	40.00
-- Turquoise label					
❏ T 932 [M]	Rendezvous with Kenton	1957	10.00	20.00	40.00
-- Turquoise label					
❏ T 995 [M]	Back to Balboa	1958	10.00	20.00	40.00
-- Turquoise label					

Number	Title	Yr	VG	VG+	NM
❏ ST 1068 [S]	The Ballad Style of Stan Kenton	1959	5.00	10.00	20.00
-- Black label with colorband, Capitol logo at left					
❏ ST 1068 [S]	The Ballad Style of Stan Kenton	1962	3.00	6.00	12.00
-- Black label with colorband, Capitol logo at top					
❏ T 1068 [M]	The Ballad Style of Stan Kenton	1959	6.25	12.50	25.00
-- Black label with colorband, Capitol logo at left					
❏ T 1068 [M]	The Ballad Style of Stan Kenton	1962	3.75	7.50	15.00
-- Black label with colorband, Capitol logo at top					
❏ ST 1130 [S]	Lush Interlude	1959	5.00	10.00	20.00
-- Black label with colorband, Capitol logo at left					
❏ T 1130 [M]	Lush Interlude	1959	6.25	12.50	25.00
-- Black label with colorband, Capitol logo at left					
❏ ST 1166 [S]	The Stage Door Swings	1959	5.00	10.00	20.00
-- Black label with colorband, Capitol logo at left					
❏ T 1166 [M]	The Stage Door Swings	1959	6.25	12.50	25.00
-- Black label with colorband, Capitol logo at left					
❏ ST 1276 [S]	The Kenton Touch	1960	5.00	10.00	20.00
-- Black label with colorband, Capitol logo at left					
❏ T 1276 [M]	The Kenton Touch	1960	6.25	12.50	25.00
-- Black label with colorband, Capitol logo at left					
❏ SW 1305 [S]	Viva Kenton!	1960	5.00	10.00	20.00
-- Black label with colorband, Capitol logo at left					
❏ W 1305 [M]	Viva Kenton!	1960	6.25	12.50	25.00
-- Black label with colorband, Capitol logo at left					
❏ STBO 1327 [(2) S]	Road Show	1960	7.50	15.00	30.00
-- Black label with colorband, Capitol logo at left					
❏ STBO 1327 [(2) S]	Road Show	1962	3.75	7.50	15.00
-- Black label with colorband, Capitol logo at top					
❏ TBO 1327 [(2) M]	Road Show	1960	10.00	20.00	40.00
-- Black label with colorband, Capitol logo at left					
❏ TBO 1327 [(2) M]	Road Show	1962	5.00	10.00	20.00
-- Black label with colorband, Capitol logo at top					
❏ ST 1394 [S]	Standards in Silhouette	1960	5.00	10.00	20.00
-- Black label with colorband, Capitol logo at left					
❏ ST 1394 [S]	Standards in Silhouette	1962	3.00	6.00	12.00
-- Black label with colorband, Capitol logo at top					
❏ T 1394 [M]	Standards in Silhouette	1960	6.25	12.50	25.00
-- Black label with colorband, Capitol logo at left					
❏ T 1394 [M]	Standards in Silhouette	1962	3.75	7.50	15.00
-- Black label with colorband, Capitol logo at top					
❏ ST 1460 [S]	Kenton at the Las Vegas Tropicana	1961	5.00	10.00	20.00
-- Black label with colorband, Capitol logo at left					
❏ T 1460 [M]	Kenton at the Las Vegas Tropicana	1961	6.25	12.50	25.00
-- Black label with colorband, Capitol logo at left					
❏ ST 1533 [S]	The Romantic Approach	1961	5.00	10.00	20.00
-- Black label with colorband, Capitol logo at left					
❏ ST 1533 [S]	The Romantic Approach	1961	3.00	6.00	12.00
-- Black label with colorband, Capitol logo at top					
❏ T 1533 [M]	The Romantic Approach	1961	6.25	12.50	25.00
-- Black label with colorband, Capitol logo at left					
❏ T 1533 [M]	The Romantic Approach	1961	3.75	7.50	15.00
-- Black label with colorband, Capitol logo at top					
❏ ST 1609 [S]	Kenton's West Side Story	1961	5.00	10.00	20.00
-- Black label with colorband, Capitol logo at left					
❏ ST 1609 [S]	Kenton's West Side Story	1961	3.00	6.00	12.00
-- Black label with colorband, Capitol logo at top					
❏ T 1609 [M]	Kenton's West Side Story	1961	3.75	7.50	15.00
-- Black label with colorband, Capitol logo at top					
❏ T 1609 [M]	Kenton's West Side Story	1961	6.25	12.50	25.00
-- Black label with colorband, Capitol logo at left					
❏ ST 1621 [S]	A Merry Christmas	1961	5.00	10.00	20.00
❏ T 1621 [M]	A Merry Christmas	1961	3.75	7.50	15.00
❏ ST 1674 [S]	The Sophisticated Approach	1962	3.75	7.50	15.00
-- Black label with colorband, Capitol logo at top					
❏ T 1674 [M]	The Sophisticated Approach	1962	3.00	6.00	12.00
-- Black label with colorband, Capitol logo at top					
❏ ST 1796 [S]	Adventures in Jazz	1962	3.75	7.50	15.00
-- Black label with colorband, Capitol logo at top					
❏ T 1796 [M]	Adventures in Jazz	1962	3.00	6.00	12.00
-- Black label with colorband, Capitol logo at top					
❏ ST 1844 [S]	Adventures in Time	1963	3.75	7.50	15.00
-- Black label with colorband, Capitol logo at top					
❏ T 1844 [M]	Adventures in Time	1963	3.00	6.00	12.00
-- Black label with colorband, Capitol logo at top					
❏ ST 1931 [S]	Artistry in Bossa Nova	1963	3.75	7.50	15.00
❏ T 1931 [M]	Artistry in Bossa Nova	1963	3.00	6.00	12.00
❏ ST 1985 [S]	Adventures in Blues	1963	3.75	7.50	15.00
-- Black label with colorband, Capitol logo at top					
❏ T 1985 [M]	Adventures in Blues	1963	3.00	6.00	12.00
-- Black label with colorband, Capitol logo at top					
❏ ST 2132 [S]	Artistry in Voices and Brass	1964	3.75	7.50	15.00
-- Black label with colorband, Capitol logo at top					
❏ T 2132 [M]	Artistry in Voices and Brass	1964	3.00	6.00	12.00
-- Black label with colorband, Capitol logo at top					
❏ STAO 2217 [S]	Kenton Plays Wagner	1964	3.75	7.50	15.00
-- Black label with colorband, Capitol logo at top					

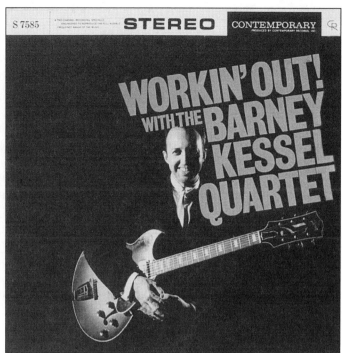

(Top left) The most fertile times for Stan Kenton's "progressive jazz" music were the early to mid 1950s. This 10-inch album for Capitol spotlighted one of his top arrangers, Bill Holman. There was a simultaneous 10-inch album that focused on another Kenton arranger, Bill Russo. (Top right) Guitarist Barney Kessel played on countless pop and rock sessions, including some with Elvis Presley and the Beach Boys, but his first love was jazz. He made some very good examples for the Contemporary label, of which this album is one. (Bottom left) Rahsaan Roland Kirk, blind from a young age, joined with another blind musician, Al Hibbler, for this 1973 release on Atlantic. (Bottom right) Gene Krupa was responsible for one of the most famous drum solos in jazz history, that in Benny Goodman's "Sing, Sing, Sing," and he went on from there to a long career. This is an album from the very earliest days of Verve Records, from 1956.

Number	Title	Yr	VG	VG+	NM
❏ TAO 2217 [M]	Kenton Plays Wagner	1964	3.00	6.00	12.00
-- *Black label with colorband, Capitol logo at top*					
❏ DT 2327 [R]	Stan Kenton's Greatest Hits	1965	2.50	5.00	10.00
-- *Black label with colorband, Capitol logo at top*					
❏ SM-2327	Stan Kenton's Greatest Hits	197?	2.00	4.00	8.00
-- *Reissue with new prefix*					
❏ T 2327 [M]	Stan Kenton's Greatest Hits	1965	3.00	6.00	12.00
-- *Black label with colorband, Capitol logo at top*					
❏ MAS 2424 [M]	Stan Kenton Conducts the Los Angeles Neophonic Orchestra	1966	3.00	6.00	12.00
-- *Black label with colorband, Capitol logo at top*					
❏ SMAS 2424 [S]	Stan Kenton Conducts the Los Angeles Neophonic Orchestra	1966	3.75	7.50	15.00
-- *Black label with colorband, Capitol logo at top*					
❏ ST 2655 [S]	Kenton Plays for Today	1966	3.75	7.50	15.00
-- *Black label with colorband, Capitol logo at top*					
❏ T 2655 [M]	Kenton Plays for Today	1966	3.00	6.00	12.00
-- *Black label with colorband, Capitol logo at top*					
❏ ST 2810	The World We Know	1968	3.00	6.00	12.00
❏ ST 2932	Jazz Compositions of Dee Barton	1968	3.00	6.00	12.00
❏ ST 2974	Finian's Rainbow	1968	3.00	6.00	12.00
❏ STCL 2989 [(3)]	The Stan Kenton Deluxe Set	1968	5.00	10.00	20.00
❏ M-11027	Artistry in Jazz	1972	2.50	5.00	10.00
❏ SM-11794 [M]	Cuban Fire!	1978	2.50	5.00	10.00
-- *Reissue of Capitol T 731*					
❏ STBB-12016 [(2)]	The Comprehensive Kenton	1979	3.75	7.50	15.00
❏ SM-12037	Kenton's West Side Story	1979	2.50	5.00	10.00
-- *Reissue of Capitol ST 1609*					
❏ N-16182	Stan Kenton's Greatest Hits	1984	2.00	4.00	8.00
-- *Budget-line reissue*					

CREATIVE WORLD

❏ ST 1001	Kenton's Christmas	1970	3.00	6.00	12.00
❏ ST 1002 [R]	New Concepts of Artistry in	197?	2.50	5.00	10.00
-- *Reissue of Capitol T 383*					
❏ ST 1003 [R]	Contemporary Concepts	197?	2.00	4.00	8.00
-- *Reissue of Capitol T 666*					
❏ ST 1004 [R]	Kenton in Stereo	197?	2.50	5.00	10.00
-- *Reissue of Capitol W 724*					
❏ ST 1005	Lush Interlude	197?	2.50	5.00	10.00
-- *Reissue of Capitol ST 1130*					
❏ ST 1006 [R]	City of Glass/This Modern World	197?	2.00	4.00	8.00
-- *Reissue of Capitol T 736*					
❏ ST 1007	Kenton's West Side Story	197?	2.50	5.00	10.00
-- *Reissue of Capitol ST 1609*					
❏ ST 1008 [R]	Cuban Fire!	197?	2.00	4.00	8.00
-- *Reissue of Capitol T 731*					
❏ ST 1009 [R]	Innovations in Modern Music	197?	2.00	4.00	8.00
-- *Reissue of Capitol P 189*					
❏ ST 1010	Adventures in Jazz	197?	2.50	5.00	10.00
-- *Reissue of Capitol ST 1796*					
❏ ST 1011	Adventures in Time	197?	2.50	5.00	10.00
-- *Reissue of Capitol ST 1844*					
❏ ST 1012	Adventures in Blues	197?	2.50	5.00	10.00
-- *Reissue of Capitol ST 1985*					
❏ ST 1013	Stan Kenton Conducts the Los Angeles Neophonic Orchestra	197?	2.50	5.00	10.00
-- *Reissue of Capitol SMAS 2424*					
❏ ST 1015 [(2)]	Live at Redlands University	1971	2.50	5.00	10.00
❏ ST 1017	The Romantic Approach	197?	2.00	4.00	8.00
-- *Reissue of Capitol ST 1533*					
❏ ST 1018	The Sophisticated Approach	197?	2.50	5.00	10.00
-- *Reissue of Capitol ST 1674*					
❏ ST 1019	Road Show, Volume 1	197?	2.50	5.00	10.00
-- *Partial reissue of Capitol STBO 1327*					
❏ ST 1020	Road Show, Volume 2	197?	2.50	5.00	10.00
-- *Partial reissue of Capitol STBO 1327*					
❏ ST 1022	Jazz Compositions of Dee Barton	197?	2.50	5.00	10.00
-- *Reissue of Capitol ST 2932*					
❏ ST 1023 [R]	Stan Kenton Presents	197?	2.00	4.00	8.00
-- *Reissue of Capitol T 248*					
❏ ST 1024	Kenton Plays Wagner	197?	2.50	5.00	10.00
-- *Reissue of Capitol STAO 2217*					
❏ ST 1025	Adventures in Standards	197?	2.50	5.00	10.00
❏ ST 1026 [R]	Kenton Showcase	197?	2.00	4.00	8.00
-- *Reissue of Capitol W 524*					
❏ ST 1027 [R]	Collector's Choice	197?	2.00	4.00	8.00
❏ ST 1028 [R]	The Fabulous Alumni of Stan Kenton	197?	2.00	4.00	8.00
❏ STCL 1029 [R]	Some Women I've Known	197?	2.00	4.00	8.00
❏ ST 1030 [(4) R]	The Kenton Era	197?	5.00	10.00	20.00
-- *Reissue of Capitol TDB 569*					
❏ ST 1031	Back to Balboa	197?	2.50	5.00	10.00
-- *Reissue of Capitol T 995*					
❏ ST 1032	Kenton at the Las Vegas Tropicana	197?	2.50	5.00	10.00
-- *Reissue of Capitol ST 1460*					
❏ ST 1033	The Kenton Touch	197?	2.50	5.00	10.00
-- *Reissue of Capitol ST 1276*					

Number	Title	Yr	VG	VG+	NM
❏ ST 1034 [R]	Encores	197?	2.00	4.00	8.00
-- *Reissue of Capitol T 155*					
❏ ST 1035 [R]	The Christy Years	197?	2.00	4.00	8.00
❏ ST 1036 [R]	Kenton By Request, Vol. I	197?	2.00	4.00	8.00
❏ ST 1037 [R]	A Concert in Progessive Jazz	197?	2.00	4.00	8.00
-- *Reissue of Capitol T 172*					
❏ ST 1038	Artistry in Voices and Brass	197?	2.50	5.00	10.00
-- *Reissue of Capitol ST 2132*					
❏ ST 1039 [Q]	Live at Brigham Young	1971	3.75	7.50	15.00
❏ ST 1040	Kenton By Request, Vol. II	197?	2.00	4.00	8.00
❏ ST 1041 [R]	Sketches on Standards	197?	2.00	4.00	8.00
-- *Reissue of Capitol T 426*					
❏ ST 1042 [R]	Portraits on Standards	197?	2.00	4.00	8.00
-- *Reissue of Capitol T 462*					
❏ ST 1043 [R]	Artistry in Rhythm	197?	2.00	4.00	8.00
-- *Reissue of Capitol DT 167*					
❏ ST 1044	The Stage Door Swings	197?	2.50	5.00	10.00
-- *Reissue of Capitol ST 1166*					
❏ ST 1045	Artistry in Bossa Nova	197?	2.50	5.00	10.00
❏ ST 1046	Stan Kenton with Jean Turner	197?	2.50	5.00	10.00
❏ ST 1047 [R]	Milestones	197?	2.00	4.00	8.00
-- *Reissue of Capitol T 190*					
❏ ST 1048 [R]	Duet	197?	2.00	4.00	8.00
-- *Reissue of Capitol T 656*					
❏ ST 1049	Standards in Silhouette	197?	2.50	5.00	10.00
-- *Reissue of Capitol ST 1394*					
❏ ST 1050 [R]	The Lighter Side of Stan Kenton	197?	2.00	4.00	8.00
❏ ST 1057	Rendezvous with Kenton	197?	2.50	5.00	10.00
-- *Reissue of Capitol T 932*					
❏ ST 1058 [(2) Q]	Live at Butler University	1972	5.00	10.00	20.00
❏ ST 1059 [(2) Q]	Stan Kenton with the Four Freshmen at Butler University	1972	5.00	10.00	20.00
❏ ST 1060 [(2) Q]	National Anthems of the World	1972	5.00	10.00	20.00
❏ ST 1061 [R]	Stan Kenton -- Formative Years	197?	2.00	4.00	8.00
-- *Reissue of Decca DL 8259*					
❏ ST 1062 [R]	Kenton By Request, Vol. III	197?	2.00	4.00	8.00
❏ ST 1063	Viva Kenton!	197?	2.50	5.00	10.00
-- *Reissue of Capitol SW 1305*					
❏ ST 1064 [R]	Kenton By Request, Vol. IV	197?	2.00	4.00	8.00
❏ ST 1065	Birthday in Britain	1973	2.50	5.00	10.00
❏ ST 1066 [R]	Kenton By Request, Vol. V	197?	2.00	4.00	8.00
❏ ST 1067	Too Much	197?	2.50	5.00	10.00
❏ ST 1068	The Ballad Style of Stan Kenton	197?	2.00	4.00	8.00
-- *Reissue of Capitol ST 1068*					
❏ ST 1069	Kenton By Request, Vol. VI	197?	2.50	5.00	10.00
❏ ST 1070	7.5 on the Richter Scale	197?	2.50	5.00	10.00
❏ ST 1071	Solo	1973	2.50	5.00	10.00
❏ ST 1072	Kenton Plays Chicago	1974	2.50	5.00	10.00
❏ ST 1073	Fire, Fury and Fun	1974	2.50	5.00	10.00
❏ ST 1074	Hits in Concert	197?	2.50	5.00	10.00
❏ ST 1076	Kenton '76	1976	2.50	5.00	10.00
❏ ST 1077	Journey Into Capricorn	1977	2.50	5.00	10.00
❏ ST 1078 [R]	The Jazz Compositions of Stan Kenton	197?	2.00	4.00	8.00
❏ ST 1079	Street of Dreams	197?	2.50	5.00	10.00
❏ ST 1080	The Exciting Stan Kenton	197?	2.50	5.00	10.00
❏ CW-3005	Stan Kenton Presents Gabe Baltazar	1979	2.50	5.00	10.00

DECCA

❏ DL 8259 [M]	Stan Kenton -- Formative Years	195?	6.25	12.50	25.00
-- *All-black label with silver print*					
❏ DL 8259 [M]	Stan Kenton -- Formative Years	1960	3.75	7.50	15.00
-- *Black label with color bars*					

HINDSIGHT

❏ HSR-118	Stan Kenton 1941	1984	2.00	4.00	8.00
❏ HSR-124	Stan Kenton 1941, Volume 2	1984	2.00	4.00	8.00
❏ HSR-136	Stan Kenton 1943-44	1984	2.00	4.00	8.00
❏ HSR-147	Stan Kenton 1944-45	1984	2.00	4.00	8.00
❏ HSR-157	Stan Kenton 1945-47	1984	2.00	4.00	8.00
❏ HSR-195	Stan Kenton 1962	1984	2.00	4.00	8.00

INSIGHT

❏ 206	Stan Kenton and His Orchestra, Volume 1	197?	2.50	5.00	10.00
❏ 217	Stan Kenton and His Orchestra, Volume 2	197?	2.50	5.00	10.00

LONDON PHASE 4

❏ BP 44179/80 [(2)]	Stan Kenton Today	1972	10.00	20.00	40.00
❏ ST-44276	Live in Europe	1976	2.50	5.00	10.00

MOBILE FIDELITY

❏ 1-091	Kenton Plays Wagner	1982	6.25	12.50	25.00
-- *Audiophile vinyl*					

MOSAIC

❏ M6-136 [(6)]	The Complete Capitol Recordings of the Holman and Russo Charts	199?	30.00	60.00	120.00
❏ MQ10-163 [(10)]	The Complete Capitol Studio Recordings of Stan Kenton 1943-47	199?	50.00	100.00	200.00

Number	Title	Yr	VG	VG+	NM
SUNBEAM					
❑ 213	Artistry in Rhythm, 1944-45	197?	2.50	5.00	10.00
KENTON, STAN, AND TEX RITTER					
Ritter is a male country-western singer not otherwise listed in this book. Also see STAN KENTON.					
CAPITOL					
❑ ST 1757 [S]	Stan Kenton/Tex Ritter	1962	20.00	40.00	80.00
❑ T 1757 [M]	Stan Kenton/Tex Ritter	1962	15.00	30.00	60.00
KENYATTA, ROBIN					
Alto saxophone player and flutist.					
ATLANTIC					
❑ SD 1633	Gypsy Man	1972	5.00	10.00	20.00
❑ SD 1644	Terra Nova	1973	3.75	7.50	15.00
❑ SD 1656	Stompin' at the Savoy	1974	3.75	7.50	15.00
ECM					
❑ 1008	The Girl from Martinique	197?	5.00	10.00	20.00
MUSE					
❑ MR-5062	Nomusa	1975	3.00	6.00	12.00
❑ MR-5095	Beggars	1979	3.00	6.00	12.00
VORTEX					
❑ 2005	Until	1969	5.00	10.00	20.00
KEPPARD, FREDDIE					
Cornet player and bandleader.					
HERWIN					
❑ 101	Freddie Keppard 1926	197?	3.00	6.00	12.00
MILESTONE					
❑ 2014	Freddie Keppard and Tommy Ladnier	197?	3.00	6.00	12.00
KEROUAC, JACK					
Jazz-influenced beat poet and author.					
DOT					
❑ DLP-3154 [M]	Poetry for the Beat Generation	1959	250.00	500.00	1,000.
-- Acknowledged to be extremely rare; the same performance is on Hanover 5000					
HANOVER					
❑ HML-5000 [M]	Poetry for the Beat Generation	1959	62.50	125.00	250.00
❑ HML-5006 [M]	Blues and Haikus	1959	62.50	125.00	250.00
-- STEVE ALLEN plays piano behind Kerouac on this album					
RHINO					
❑ R1-70939 [(4)]	The Jack Kerouac Collection	1990	15.00	30.00	60.00
-- Box set compiling the Hanover and Verve LPs plus an LP of unreleased material					
VERVE					
❑ MGV-15005 [M]	Readings on the Beat Generation	1960	62.50	125.00	250.00
KERR, BROOKS					
Pianist.					
CHIAROSCURO					
❑ 2001	Soda Fountain Rag	197?	3.00	6.00	12.00
KERR, BROOKS, AND PAUL QUINICHETTE					
Also see each artist's individual listings.					
FAMOUS DOOR					
❑ 106	Preview	197?	3.75	7.50	15.00
KESL, LENNIE					
Male singer.					
REVELATION					
❑ 29	Walkin' On Air	1978	3.00	6.00	12.00
KESSEL, BARNEY					
Guitarist. Also see THE POLL WINNERS.					
BLACK LION					
❑ 130	Swinging Easy	197?	3.00	6.00	12.00
❑ 210	Summertime in Montreux	197?	3.00	6.00	12.00
❑ 310	Blue Soul	197?	3.75	7.50	15.00
CONCORD JAZZ					
❑ CJ-9	Barney Plays Kessel	197?	3.00	6.00	12.00
❑ CJ-33	Soaring	1976	3.00	6.00	12.00
❑ CJ-164	Jellybeans	1981	2.50	5.00	10.00
❑ CJ-221	Solo	1982	2.50	5.00	10.00
CONTEMPORARY					
❑ C-2508 [10]	Barney Kessel, Volume 1	1953	30.00	60.00	120.00
❑ C-2514 [10]	Barney Kessel, Volume 2	1954	30.00	60.00	120.00
❑ C-3511 [M]	Easy Like	1956	20.00	40.00	80.00
❑ C-3512 [M]	Kessel Plays Standards	1956	20.00	40.00	80.00
❑ C-3513 [M]	To Swing or Not to Swing	1956	20.00	40.00	80.00

Number	Title	Yr	VG	VG+	NM
❑ C-3521 [M]	Music to Listen to Barney Kessel By	1956	15.00	30.00	60.00
❑ M-3563 [M]	Barney Kessel Plays "Carmen"	1959	10.00	20.00	40.00
❑ M-3565 [M]	Some Like It Hot	1959	10.00	20.00	40.00
❑ M-3585 [M]	Workin' Out!	1960	10.00	20.00	40.00
❑ M-3603 [M]	Let's Cook!	1962	6.25	12.50	25.00
❑ M-3613 [M]	Swingin' Party	1963	5.00	10.00	20.00
❑ M-3618 [M]	Feeling Free	1965	5.00	10.00	20.00
❑ S-7521 [S]	Music to Listen to Barney Kessel By	1959	10.00	20.00	40.00
❑ S-7563 [S]	Barney Kessel Plays "Carmen"	1959	7.50	15.00	30.00
❑ S-7565 [S]	Some Like It Hot	1959	7.50	15.00	30.00
❑ S-7585 [S]	Workin' Out!	1960	7.50	15.00	30.00
❑ S-7603 [S]	Let's Cook!	1962	6.25	12.50	25.00
❑ S-7613 [S]	Swingin' Party	1963	6.25	12.50	25.00
❑ S-7618 [S]	Feeling Free	1965	6.25	12.50	25.00
❑ C-14033	Spontaneous Combustion	1987	2.50	5.00	10.00
❑ C-14044	Red Hot and Blues	198?	2.50	5.00	10.00
EMERALD					
❑ 1401 [M]	On Fire	1965	3.75	7.50	15.00
❑ 2401 [S]	On Fire	1965	5.00	10.00	20.00
FANTASY					
❑ OJC-153	Easy Like	198?	2.50	5.00	10.00
❑ OJC-168	Some Like It Hot	198?	2.50	5.00	10.00
❑ OJC-179	Feeling Free	198?	2.50	5.00	10.00
❑ OJC-238	Kessel Plays Standards	198?	2.50	5.00	10.00
❑ OJC-269	Barney Kessel Plays "Carmen"	198?	2.50	5.00	10.00
❑ OJC-317	To Swing or Not to Swing	1987	2.50	5.00	10.00
RCA CAMDEN					
❑ CAS-2404	Guitarra	1970	2.50	5.00	10.00
REPRISE					
❑ R-6019 [M]	Breakfast at Tiffany's	1961	3.75	7.50	15.00
❑ R9-6019 [S]	Breakfast at Tiffany's	1961	5.00	10.00	20.00
❑ R-6049 [M]	Bossa Nova	1962	3.75	7.50	15.00
❑ R9-6049 [S]	Bossa Nova	1962	5.00	10.00	20.00
❑ R-6073 [M]	Kessel/Jazz	1963	3.75	7.50	15.00
❑ R9-6073 [S]	Kessel/Jazz	1963	5.00	10.00	20.00
STEREO RECORDS					
❑ S-7001 [S]	Music to Listen to Barney Kessel By	1958	12.50	25.00	50.00
KESSEL, BARNEY, AND HERB ELLIS					
Also see each artist's individual listings.					
CONCORD JAZZ					
❑ CJ-34	Butterfly	1976	3.00	6.00	12.00
KESSEL, BARNEY, AND STEPHANE GRAPPELLI					
Also see each artist's individual listings.					
BLACK LION					
❑ 173	Limehouse Blues	197?	3.75	7.50	15.00
KESSEL, BARNEY, AND RED MITCHELL					
JAZZ MAN					
❑ 5025	Two Way Conversation	198?	2.50	5.00	10.00
KESSLER, SIEGFRIED, AND DAUNIK LAZRO					
Kessler is a pianist. Also see DAUNIK LAZRO.					
HAT HUT					
❑ 3502	Aeros	1982	3.00	6.00	12.00
KEYS, CALVIN					
Guitarist.					
BLACK JAZZ					
❑ 5	Shawn-neeq	1972	5.00	10.00	20.00
OVATION					
❑ OV-1804	Criss Cross	1978	3.00	6.00	12.00
KHAN, STEVE					
Guitarist.					
ANTILLES					
❑ AN-1018	Eyewitness	1981	2.50	5.00	10.00
❑ AN-1020	Casa Loco	1983	2.50	5.00	10.00
ARISTA/NOVUS					
❑ AN 3023	Evidence	1980	3.00	6.00	12.00
COLUMBIA					
❑ JC 34857	Tightrope	1977	2.50	5.00	10.00
❑ JC 35539	The Blue Man	1978	2.50	5.00	10.00
❑ JC 36129	Arrows	1979	2.50	5.00	10.00
❑ JC 36406	The Best of Steve Khan	1980	2.50	5.00	10.00

Number	Title	Yr	VG	VG+	NM

KICKLIGHTER, RICHY
Guitarist.
ICHIBAN

Number	Title	Yr	VG	VG+	NM
❏ ICH-1019	Just for Kicks	198?	2.50	5.00	10.00
❏ ICH-1051	In the Night	198?	2.50	5.00	10.00

KID SHEIK
See GEORGE "KID SHEIK" COLA.

KID THOMAS
Real name: Thomas Valentine. Trumpeter and bandleader.
AMERICAN MUSIC

Number	Title	Yr	VG	VG+	NM
❏ 642 [10]	Kid Thomas	1952	12.50	25.00	50.00

ARHOOLIE

❏ 1016	New Orleans Jazz	1967	3.00	6.00	12.00

GHB

❏ GHB-24 [M]	Kid Thomas + The Hall Brothers Jazz Band	196?	5.00	10.00	20.00
❏ GHB-80	Kid Thomas and His Algiers Stompers	197?	3.00	6.00	12.00
❏ GHB-291	Kid Thomas in England	198?	2.50	5.00	10.00

JAZZOLOGY

❏ JCE-13	Sonnets from Algiers	1967	3.00	6.00	12.00

RIVERSIDE

❏ RLP-365 [M]	Kid Thomas and His Algiers Stompers	1961	7.50	15.00	30.00
❏ RLP-386 [M]	Kid Thomas and His Algiers Stompers	1961	7.50	15.00	30.00
❏ RS-9365 [R]	Kid Thomas and His Algiers Stompers	1961	5.00	10.00	20.00
❏ RS-9386 [R]	Kid Thomas and His Algiers Stompers	1961	5.00	10.00	20.00

KIKUCHI, MASABUMI
Pianist.
CATALYST

❏ 7916	Matrix	197?	3.00	6.00	12.00

INNER CITY

❏ IC-6021	Wishes/Kochi	1979	3.75	7.50	15.00

KILIMANJARO
Members: Paul Asbell (various guitars); Bill Kinzie (drums, percussion); Tony Markellis (basses); Chas Eller (keyboards, pianos); Rafael Cruz (congas, percussion).
PHILO

❏ 9001	Kilimanjaro	1979	3.00	6.00	12.00
❏ 9005	Kilimanjaro 2	1981	3.00	6.00	12.00

KIMBALL, JEANETTE
Pianist.
NEW ORLEANS

❏ 7208	Sophisticated Lady	198?	2.50	5.00	10.00

KIMURA, YOSHIKO
INNER CITY

❏ IC-6043	Memories	1978	3.75	7.50	15.00

KINCAIDE, DEAN
Saxophone player, bandleader, arranger and composer.
WEATHERS

❏ 5610 [M]	Arranged for You	1954	12.50	25.00	50.00

KINESIS
HEADFIRST

❏ 9705	New Life	198?	2.50	5.00	10.00

KING CURTIS
Tenor saxophone player, best known for his session work with legendary early R&B and rock 'n' roll artists.
ATCO

❏ 33-113 [M]	Have Tenor Sax, Will Blow	1959	10.00	20.00	40.00
❏ SD 33-113 [S]	Have Tenor Sax, Will Blow	1959	15.00	30.00	60.00
❏ 33-189 [M]	That Lovin' Feeling	1966	5.00	10.00	20.00
❏ SD 33-189 [S]	That Lovin' Feeling	1966	6.25	12.50	25.00
❏ 33-198 [M]	Live at Small's Paradise	1966	5.00	10.00	20.00
❏ SD 33-198 [S]	Live at Small's Paradise	1966	6.25	12.50	25.00
❏ 33-211 [M]	The Great Memphis Hits	1967	5.00	10.00	20.00
❏ SD 33-211 [S]	The Great Memphis Hits	1967	6.25	12.50	25.00
❏ 33-231 [M]	King Size Soul	1967	6.25	12.50	25.00
❏ SD 33-231 [S]	King Size Soul	1967	5.00	10.00	20.00
❏ 33-247 [M]	Sweet Soul	1968	7.50	15.00	30.00
❏ SD 33-247 [S]	Sweet Soul	1968	5.00	10.00	20.00
❏ SD 33-266	The Best of King Curtis	1968	5.00	10.00	20.00
❏ SD 33-293	Instant Groove	1969	5.00	10.00	20.00
❏ SD 33-338	Get Ready	1970	5.00	10.00	20.00
❏ SD 33-359	Live at Fillmore West	1971	5.00	10.00	20.00
❏ SD 33-385	Everybody's Talkin'	1972	5.00	10.00	20.00

ATLANTIC

❏ SD 1637	Blues Montreux	1973	3.00	6.00	12.00

CAPITOL

❏ ST 1756 [S]	Country Soul	1963	10.00	20.00	40.00
❏ T 1756 [M]	Country Soul	1963	7.50	15.00	30.00
❏ ST 2095 [S]	Soul Serenade	1964	7.50	15.00	30.00
❏ T 2095 [M]	Soul Serenade	1964	6.25	12.50	25.00
❏ ST 2341 [S]	King Curtis Plays the Hits Made Famous by Sam Cooke	1965	7.50	15.00	30.00
❏ T 2341 [M]	King Curtis Plays the Hits Made Famous by Sam Cooke	1965	6.25	12.50	25.00
❏ ST 2858	The Best of King Curtis	1968	6.25	12.50	25.00
❏ SM-11798	Soul Serenade	1978	2.50	5.00	10.00
-- Reissue					
❏ SM-11963	The Best of King Curtis	1979	2.50	5.00	10.00
-- Reissue					

CLARION

❏ 615 [M]	The Great "K" Curtis	1966	5.00	10.00	20.00
❏ SD 615 [S]	The Great "K" Curtis	1966	6.25	12.50	25.00

COLLECTABLES

❏ COL-5119	Soul Twist	198?	2.50	5.00	10.00
❏ COL-5156	Golden Classics: Enjoy...The Best of King Curtis	198?	2.50	5.00	10.00

ENJOY

❏ ENLP-2001 [M]	Soul Twist	1962	12.50	25.00	50.00

EVEREST

❏ SDBR-1121 [S]	Azure	1961	18.75	37.50	75.00
❏ LPBR-5121 [M]	Azure	1961	12.50	25.00	50.00

FANTASY

❏ OJC-198	The New Scene of King Curtis	1985	2.50	5.00	10.00
-- Reissue of New Jazz 8237					
❏ OBC-512	Trouble in Mind	1988	2.50	5.00	10.00
-- Reissue of Tru-Sound 15001					

NEW JAZZ

❏ NJLP-8237 [M]	The New Scene of King Curtis	1960	15.00	30.00	60.00
-- Purple label					
❏ NJLP-8237 [M]	The New Scene of King Curtis	1965	7.50	15.00	30.00
-- Blue label with trident logo on right					

PRESTIGE

❏ PRLP-7222 [M]	Soul Meeting	1962	12.50	25.00	50.00
❏ PRST-7222 [S]	Soul Meeting	1962	18.75	37.50	75.00
❏ PRST-7709	The Best of King Curtis	1969	3.75	7.50	15.00
❏ PRST-7775	The Best of King Curtis -- One More Time	1970	3.75	7.50	15.00
❏ PRST-7789	King Soul	1970	3.75	7.50	15.00
❏ PRST-7833	Soul Meeting	1971	3.75	7.50	15.00
-- Reissue of 7222					
❏ 24033 [(2)]	Jazz Groove	198?	3.75	7.50	15.00

RCA CAMDEN

❏ CAS-2242	Sax in Motion	1968	3.75	7.50	15.00

RCA VICTOR

❏ LPM-2492 [M]	Arthur Murray's Music for Dancing: The Twist!	1962	6.25	12.50	25.00
❏ LSP-2492 [S]	Arthur Murray's Music for Dancing: The Twist!	1962	7.50	15.00	30.00

TRU-SOUND

❏ TS-15001 [M]	Trouble in Mind	1961	12.50	25.00	50.00
❏ TS-15008 [M]	It's Party Time	1962	12.50	25.00	50.00
❏ TS-15009 [M]	Doin' the Dixie Twist	1962	12.50	25.00	50.00

KING PLEASURE
Male singer; the acknowledged inventor of "vocalese" (basically, putting words to jazz solos).
HIFI

❏ R-425 [M]	Golden Days	1960	10.00	20.00	40.00
❏ RS-425 [S]	Golden Days	1960	12.50	25.00	50.00

PRESTIGE

❏ PRLP-208 [10]	King Pleasure Sings	1955	50.00	100.00	200.00

UNITED ARTISTS

❏ UAJ-14031 [M]	Mr. Jazz	1962	10.00	20.00	40.00
❏ UAJS-15031 [S]	Mr. Jazz	1962	12.50	25.00	50.00

KING PLEASURE/ANNIE ROSS
Also see each artist's individual listings.
PRESTIGE

❏ PRLP-7128 [M]	King Pleasure Sings/Annie Ross Sings	1957	25.00	50.00	100.00

Number	Title	Yr	VG	VG+	NM
KING'S MEN FIVE, THE					
CUCA					
❑ 1130 [M]	The King's Men Five	1965	5.00	10.00	20.00
KING, MORGANA					
Female singer.					
ASCOT					
❑ AM 13014 [M]	The Winter of My Discontent	1964	6.25	12.50	25.00
❑ AM 13019 [M]	The End of a Love Affair	1965	6.25	12.50	25.00
-- Reissue of United Artists 30020					
❑ AM 13020 [M]	Everybody Loves Saturday Night	1965	6.25	12.50	25.00
❑ AM 13025 [M]	More Morgana	1965	6.25	12.50	25.00
❑ AS 16014 [S]	The Winter of My Discontent	1964	7.50	15.00	30.00
❑ AS 16019 [S]	The End of a Love Affair	1965	7.50	15.00	30.00
-- Reissue of United Artists 40020					
❑ AS 16020 [S]	Everybody Loves Saturday Night	1965	7.50	15.00	30.00
❑ AS 16025 [S]	More Morgana	1965	7.50	15.00	30.00
EMARCY					
❑ MG-36079 [M]	For You, For Me, Forever More	1956	20.00	40.00	80.00
MAINSTREAM					
❑ MRL-321	Taste of Honey	1972	3.75	7.50	15.00
❑ MRL-355	Cuore di Mama	1974	3.75	7.50	15.00
❑ S-6015 [S]	With a Taste of Honey	1964	6.25	12.50	25.00
❑ S-6052 [S]	Miss Morgana King	1965	6.25	12.50	25.00
❑ 56015 [M]	With a Taste of Honey	1964	5.00	10.00	20.00
❑ 56052 [M]	Miss Morgana King	1965	5.00	10.00	20.00
MERCURY					
❑ MG-20231 [M]	Morgana King Sings the Blues	1958	20.00	40.00	80.00
MUSE					
❑ MR-5166	Stretchin' Out	1977	2.50	5.00	10.00
❑ MR-5190	Everything Must Change	1978	2.50	5.00	10.00
❑ MR-5224	Higher Ground	1979	2.50	5.00	10.00
❑ MR-5257	Looking Through the Eyes of Love	1981	2.50	5.00	10.00
❑ MR-5301	Portraits	1983	2.50	5.00	10.00
❑ MR-5326	Simply Eloquent	1986	2.50	5.00	10.00
❑ MR-5339	Another Time, Another Space	1988	2.50	5.00	10.00
PARAMOUNT					
❑ PAS-6067	New Beginnings	1973	3.00	6.00	12.00
RCA CAMDEN					
❑ CAL-543 [M]	The Greatest Songs Ever Swung	1959	5.00	10.00	20.00
❑ CAS-543 [S]	The Greatest Songs Ever Swung	1959	7.50	15.00	30.00
REPRISE					
❑ R 6192 [M]	It's a Quiet Thing	1966	5.00	10.00	20.00
❑ RS 6192 [S]	It's a Quiet Thing	1966	6.25	12.50	25.00
❑ R 6205 [M]	Wild Is Love	1966	5.00	10.00	20.00
❑ RS 6205 [S]	Wild Is Love	1966	6.25	12.50	25.00
❑ R 6257 [M]	Gemini Changes	1967	5.00	10.00	20.00
❑ RS 6257 [S]	Gemini Changes	1967	6.25	12.50	25.00
TRIP					
❑ 5533	Morgana King Sings	197?	2.50	5.00	10.00
UNITED ARTISTS					
❑ UAL 3028 [M]	Folk Songs A La King	1960	10.00	20.00	40.00
❑ UAS 6028 [S]	Folk Songs A La King	1960	12.50	25.00	50.00
❑ UAL 30020 [M]	Let Me Love You	1960	12.50	25.00	50.00
❑ UAS 40020 [S]	Let Me Love You	1960	15.00	30.00	60.00
VERVE					
❑ V-5061 [M]	I Know How It Feels	1968	6.25	12.50	25.00
❑ V6-5061 [S]	I Know How It Feels	1968	6.25	12.50	25.00
WING					
❑ MGW-12307 [M]	More Morgana King	1965	3.75	7.50	15.00
❑ SRW-16307 [S]	More Morgana King	1965	5.00	10.00	20.00
KING, SANDRA					
Female singer and pianist.					
AUDIOPHILE					
❑ AP-197	Songs by Vernon Duke	1984	3.00	6.00	12.00
KING, TEDDI					
Female singer.					
AUDIOPHILE					
❑ AP-117	Lovers and Losers	1976	3.00	6.00	12.00
❑ AP-150	Someone to Light Up Your Life	1979	3.00	6.00	12.00
CORAL					
❑ CRL 57278 [M]	All the King's Songs	1959	15.00	30.00	60.00
❑ CRL 757278 [S]	All the King's Songs	1959	20.00	40.00	80.00
RCA VICTOR					
❑ LPM-1147 [M]	Bidin' My Time	1956	20.00	40.00	80.00
❑ LPM-1313 [M]	To You from Teddi King	1957	20.00	40.00	80.00
❑ LPM-1454 [M]	A Girl and Her Songs	1957	20.00	40.00	80.00
STORYVILLE					
❑ STLP-302 [10]	'Round Midnight	1954	50.00	100.00	200.00
❑ STLP-314 [10]	Storyville Presents Teddi King	1954	50.00	100.00	200.00
❑ STLP-903 [M]	Now In Vogue	1956	30.00	60.00	120.00
KING, TEDDI, AND DAVE McKENNA					
Also see each artist's individual listings.					
INNER CITY					
❑ IC-1044	This Is New	1977	3.00	6.00	12.00
KINSEY, TONY					
Drummer and occasional pianist.					
LONDON					
❑ LL 1672 [M]	Kinsey Come On	1957	12.50	25.00	50.00
KIRBY, JOHN					
Bass player, bandleader and arranger. Also see SARAH VAUGHAN.					
CIRCLE					
❑ 14	John Kirby and His Orchestra 1941	198?	2.50	5.00	10.00
❑ 64	John Kirby and His Orchestra 1941-42	198?	2.50	5.00	10.00
CLASSIC JAZZ					
❑ 22	The Biggest Little Band in the Land	197?	2.50	5.00	10.00
COLUMBIA					
❑ CL 502 [M]	John Kirby and His Orchestra	1953	10.00	20.00	40.00
-- Maroon label, gold print					
❑ GL 502 [M]	John Kirby and His Orchestra	1951	12.50	25.00	50.00
-- Black label, silver print					
❑ CG 33557 [(2)]	Boss of the Bass	1975	3.75	7.50	15.00
COLUMBIA MASTERWORKS					
❑ ML 4801 [10]	John Kirby and His Orchestra	195?	15.00	30.00	60.00
EPITAPH					
❑ E-4004	John Kirby 1908-1952	1975	3.00	6.00	12.00
HARMONY					
❑ HL 7124 [M]	Intimate Swing	1958	5.00	10.00	20.00
TRIP					
❑ 5802	The Biggest Little Band	197?	2.50	5.00	10.00
KIRCHNER, BILL					
Saxophone player, arranger, composer and jazz historian. (He won a Grammy for his liner notes for a Miles Davis boxed set.)					
SEA BREEZE					
❑ SB-2010	What It Is to Be Frank	1982	2.50	5.00	10.00
❑ SB-2017	Infant Eyes	1983	2.50	5.00	10.00
KIRK, ANDY					
Bass saxophone and tuba player, also a bandleader.					
CORAL					
❑ CRL 56019 [10]	Andy Kirk Souvenir Album -- Vol. 1	1951	25.00	50.00	100.00
DECCA					
❑ DL 79232	Instrumentally	1968	3.75	7.50	15.00
MAINSTREAM					
❑ MRL-399	March 1936	1975	3.00	6.00	12.00
MCA					
❑ 1308	Instrumentally Speaking	198?	2.50	5.00	10.00
❑ 1343	The Lady Who Swings the Band	198?	2.50	5.00	10.00
❑ 4105 [(2)]	The Best of Andy Kirk and the Clouds of Joy	197?	3.00	6.00	12.00
RCA VICTOR					
❑ LPM-1302 [M]	A Mellow Bit of Rhythm	1956	10.00	20.00	40.00
KIRK, RAHSAAN ROLAND					
Versatile musician who played tenor, baritone and bass saxophones, stritch, manzello, clarinet, flute, piccolo, trumpet, English horn, pipes, harmonica, whistle, harmonium, percussion, et al. – sometimes more than one at a time – and even sang once in a while. Also see THE JAZZ CORDS.					
ABC					
❑ AA-1106	Cry	1978	3.00	6.00	12.00
ARGO					
❑ LP-669 [M]	Introducing Roland Kirk	1960	7.50	15.00	30.00
❑ LPS-669 [S]	Introducing Roland Kirk	1960	10.00	20.00	40.00
ATLANTIC					
❑ SD 2-303 [(2)]	The Art of Rahsaan Roland Kirk	1973	5.00	10.00	20.00
❑ SD 2-907 [(2)]	Bright Moments	1974	5.00	10.00	20.00
❑ SD 2-1003 [(2)]	Vibration	1978	3.75	7.50	15.00
❑ 1502 [M]	The Inflated Tear	1968	6.25	12.50	25.00
❑ SD 1502 [S]	The Inflated Tear	1968	3.75	7.50	15.00

Number	Title	Yr	VG	VG+	NM
❑ SD 1518	Left and Right	1969	3.75	7.50	15.00
❑ SD 1534	Volunteered Slavery	1969	3.75	7.50	15.00
❑ SD 1575	Rahsaan Rahsaan	1970	3.75	7.50	15.00
❑ SD 1578	Natural Black Inventions	1971	3.75	7.50	15.00
❑ SD 1592	The Best of Rahsaan Roland Kirk	1972	3.75	7.50	15.00
❑ SD 1601	Blacknuss	1972	3.75	7.50	15.00
❑ SD 1630	Meeting of the Times	1973	3.75	7.50	15.00
❑ SD 1640	Prepare Thyself to Deal with a Miracle	1974	3.75	7.50	15.00
❑ SD 1674	The Case of the 3-Sided Dream in Audio Color	1975	3.75	7.50	15.00
❑ SD 1686	Other Folks' Music	1976	3.00	6.00	12.00
❑ 3007 [M]	Here Comes the Whistle Man	1967	6.25	12.50	25.00
❑ SD 3007 [S]	Here Comes the Whistle Man	1967	3.75	7.50	15.00
❑ 90045	The Inflated Tear	1983	2.50	5.00	10.00
BETHLEHEM					
❑ BCP-6016	Early Roots	197?	3.00	6.00	12.00
-- Reissue of 6064, distributed by RCA Victor					
❑ BCP-6064 [M]	Third Dimension	1962	37.50	75.00	150.00
EMARCY					
❑ EMS-2-411 [(2)]	Kirk's Works	1975	3.75	7.50	15.00
FANTASY					
❑ OJC-459	Kirk's Work	1990	3.00	6.00	12.00
KING					
❑ 539 [M]	Triple Threat	1956	62.50	125.00	250.00
LIMELIGHT					
❑ LM-82008 [M]	I Talk with Spirits	1964	5.00	10.00	20.00
❑ LM-82027 [M]	Rip, Rig and Panic	1965	5.00	10.00	20.00
❑ LM-82033 [M]	Slightly Latin	1966	5.00	10.00	20.00
❑ LS-86008 [S]	I Talk with Spirits	1964	6.25	12.50	25.00
❑ LS-86027 [S]	Rip, Rig and Panic	1965	6.25	12.50	25.00
❑ LS-86033 [S]	Slightly Latin	1966	6.25	12.50	25.00
MERCURY					
❑ MG-20679 [M]	We Free Kings	1962	6.25	12.50	25.00
❑ MG-20748 [M]	Domino	1962	6.25	12.50	25.00
❑ MG-20800 [M]	Reeds and Deeds	1963	6.25	12.50	25.00
❑ MG-20844 [M]	Roland Kirk Meets the Benny Golson Orchestra	1963	6.25	12.50	25.00
❑ MG-20894 [M]	Kirk in Copenhagen	1963	6.25	12.50	25.00
❑ MG-20939 [M]	Gifts and Messages	1964	6.25	12.50	25.00
❑ SR-60679 [S]	We Free Kings	1962	7.50	15.00	30.00
❑ SR-60748 [S]	Domino	1962	7.50	15.00	30.00
❑ SR-60800 [S]	Reeds and Deeds	1963	7.50	15.00	30.00
❑ SR-60844 [S]	Roland Kirk Meets the Benny Golson Orchestra	1963	7.50	15.00	30.00
❑ SR-60894 [S]	Kirk in Copenhagen	1963	7.50	15.00	30.00
❑ SR-60939 [S]	Gifs and Messages	1964	7.50	15.00	30.00
❑ 826 455-1	We Free Kings	1986	2.50	5.00	10.00
PRESTIGE					
❑ PRLP-7210 [M]	Kirk's Work	1961	10.00	20.00	40.00
❑ PRLP-7450 [M]	Funk Underneath	1967	6.25	12.50	25.00
❑ PRST-7450 [R]	Funk Underneath	1967	3.75	7.50	15.00
❑ 24080 [(2)]	Pre-Rahsaan	1978	3.75	7.50	15.00
TRIP					
❑ 5503	Domino	197?	2.50	5.00	10.00
❑ 5512	Kirk in Copenhagen	197?	2.50	5.00	10.00
❑ 5541	We Free Kings	197?	2.50	5.00	10.00
VERVE					
❑ V-8709 [M]	Now Please Don't You Cry, Beautiful Edith	1967	6.25	12.50	25.00
❑ V6-8709 [S]	Now Please Don't You Cry, Beautiful Edith	1967	5.00	10.00	20.00
WARNER BROS.					
❑ BS 2918	The Return of the 5,000 Pound Man	1976	2.50	5.00	10.00
❑ BS 2982	Kirkatron	1977	2.50	5.00	10.00
❑ BSK 3035	Boogie-Woogie String Along for Real	1977	2.50	5.00	10.00

KIRKLAND, LEROY
Guitarist.
IMPERIAL

Number	Title	Yr	VG	VG+	NM
❑ LP-9198 [M]	Twistin', Mashin' and All That Jazz	1962	3.75	7.50	15.00
❑ LP-12198 [S]	Twistin', Mashin' and All That Jazz	1962	5.00	10.00	20.00

KITAEV, ANDREI, AND BILL DOUGLASS
Kitaev is a pianist, Douglass plays bass.
REFERENCE RECORDINGS

Number	Title	Yr	VG	VG+	NM
❑ RR-6	First Takes	198?	5.00	10.00	20.00

KITAJIMA, OSAMU
Keyboard and synthesizer player. Also plays koto, guitar and percussion.
ARISTA

Number	Title	Yr	VG	VG+	NM
❑ AL 9570	Dragon King	1982	2.50	5.00	10.00
HEADFIRST					
❑ 9706	Masterless Samurai	198?	2.50	5.00	10.00

KITAMURA, EIJI
Clarinetist.
CONCORD JAZZ

Number	Title	Yr	VG	VG+	NM
❑ CJ-152	Swing Eiji	198?	2.50	5.00	10.00
❑ CJ-217	Seven Stars	198?	2.50	5.00	10.00

KITTRELL, JEAN
Female singer and bandleader.
GHB

Number	Title	Yr	VG	VG+	NM
❑ 51	'Tain't Nobody's Bizness	197?	3.00	6.00	12.00

KITTYHAWK
Featuring Paul Edwards, Dan Bortz (on the first EMI America LP) and Randy Strom (on the other two LPs), who play the Chapman Stick, a 10- or 12-stringed instrument that combines guitar and bass but is tapped like a piano (rather than strummed or plucked) to make sounds.
EMI AMERICA

Number	Title	Yr	VG	VG+	NM
❑ SW-17029	Kittyhawk	1980	3.00	6.00	12.00
❑ ST-17053	Race for the Oasis	1981	3.00	6.00	12.00
ZEBRA					
❑ ZR-5001	Fanfare	1984	3.00	6.00	12.00

KLEMMER, JOHN
Tenor and soprano saxophone player.
ABC

Number	Title	Yr	VG	VG+	NM
❑ D-836	Fresh Feathers	1974	3.75	7.50	15.00
❑ D-922	Touch	1975	3.75	7.50	15.00
❑ D-950	Barefoot Ballet	1976	3.00	6.00	12.00
❑ AA-1068	Arabesque	1978	3.00	6.00	12.00
❑ AA-1106	Cry	1978	3.00	6.00	12.00
❑ AA-1116	Brazilia	1979	3.00	6.00	12.00
❑ AB-1007	LifeStyle (Living & Loving)	1977	3.00	6.00	12.00
ABC IMPULSE!					
❑ AS-9214	Constant Throb	1973	3.75	7.50	15.00
❑ AS-9220	Waterfalls	1973	3.75	7.50	15.00
❑ AS-9244	Intensity	1974	3.75	7.50	15.00
❑ AS-9269	Magic and Movement	1974	3.75	7.50	15.00
ARISTA/NOVUS					
❑ 3500	Nexus	1979	3.00	6.00	12.00
BLUEBIRD					
❑ 6577-1-RB	Nexus One	1987	2.50	5.00	10.00
CADET					
❑ LP 797 [M]	Involvement	1967	7.50	15.00	30.00
❑ LPS 797 [S]	Involvement	1967	5.00	10.00	20.00
❑ LPS 808	And We Were Lovers	1968	5.00	10.00	20.00
CADET CONCEPT					
❑ LPS 321	Blowin' Gold	1969	5.00	10.00	20.00
❑ LPS 326	All the Children Cried	1970	5.00	10.00	20.00
❑ LPS 330	Eruptions	1971	5.00	10.00	20.00
CHESS					
❑ 2ACMJ-401 [(2)]	Magic Moments	1976	3.75	7.50	15.00
❑ CH2-92501 [(2)]	Blowin' Gold	198?	3.00	6.00	12.00
ELEKTRA					
❑ 6E-284	Magnificent Madness	1980	2.50	5.00	10.00
❑ 5E-527	Hush	1981	2.50	5.00	10.00
❑ 5E-566	Solo Saxophone II: Life	1982	2.50	5.00	10.00
ELEKTRA/MUSICIAN					
❑ 60197	Finesse	1983	2.50	5.00	10.00
MCA					
❑ AA-1116	Brazilia	1979	2.50	5.00	10.00
-- Reissue of ABC 1116					
❑ 6007 [(2)]	The Best of John Klemmer, Volume One/Mosaic	198?	2.50	5.00	10.00
-- Reissue of MCA 8014					
❑ 6017 [(2)]	The Best of John Klemmer, Volume Two/The Impulse Years	1982	3.00	6.00	12.00
❑ 6246	Music	1989	2.50	5.00	10.00
❑ 8014 [(2)]	The Best of John Klemmer, Volume One/Mosaic	1979	3.75	7.50	15.00
❑ 37012	Fresh Feathers	1980	2.00	4.00	8.00
-- Reissue of ABC 836					
❑ 37013	Barefoot Ballet	1980	2.00	4.00	8.00
-- Reissue of ABC 950					

Number	Title	Yr	VG	VG+	NM
❏ 37014	LifeStyle (Living & Loving)	1980	2.00	4.00	8.00
-- Reissue of ABC 1007					
❏ 37015	Arabesque	1980	2.00	4.00	8.00
-- Reissue of ABC 1068					
❏ 37016	Cry	1980	2.00	4.00	8.00
-- Reissue of ABC 1106					
❏ 37017	Constant Throb	1980	2.00	4.00	8.00
-- Reissue					
❏ 37018	Waterfalls	1980	2.00	4.00	8.00
-- Reissue					
❏ 37019	Intensity	1980	2.00	4.00	8.00
-- Reissue					
❏ 37020	Magic and Movement	1980	2.00	4.00	8.00
-- Reissue					
❏ 37115	Brazilia	1980	2.00	4.00	8.00
-- Reissue of MCA 1116					
❏ 37152	Touch	198?	2.00	4.00	8.00
-- Reissue of ABC 922					

MOBILE FIDELITY
| ❏ 1-006 | Touch | 1979 | 7.50 | 15.00 | 30.00 |
| -- Audiophile vinyl | | | | | |

NAUTILUS
❏ NR-4	Straight from the Heart	1980	20.00	40.00	80.00
-- Audiophile vinyl					
❏ NR-22	Finesse	1981	20.00	40.00	80.00
-- Audiophile vinyl					

KLEMMER, JOHN, AND EDDIE HARRIS
Also see each artist's individual listings.
CRUSADERS
| ❏ 16015 | Two Tone | 1982 | 6.25 | 12.50 | 25.00 |
| -- Part of MCA's "Audiophile Series" | | | | | |

KLINK, AL/BOB ALEXANDER
Klink is an alto and tenor saxophone player. Alexander is a trombonist.
GRAND AWARD
❏ GA 33-525 [M]	Progressive Jazz	1956	20.00	40.00	80.00
-- With removable outer cover					
❏ GA 33-525 [M]	Progressive Jazz	1956	7.50	15.00	30.00
-- Without removable outer cover					

KLOSS, ERIC
Alto and tenor saxophone player.
COBBLESTONE
| ❏ 9006 | Doors | 1972 | 5.00 | 10.00 | 20.00 |

MUSE
❏ MR-5019	One, Two, Free	1973	3.75	7.50	15.00
❏ MR-5038	Essence	1974	3.75	7.50	15.00
❏ MR-5077	Bodies' Warmth	1975	3.75	7.50	15.00
❏ MR-5147	Now	1978	3.00	6.00	12.00
❏ MR-5196	Celebration	1979	3.00	6.00	12.00
❏ MR-5291	Doors	198?	3.00	6.00	12.00
-- Reissue of Cobblestone 9006					

PRESTIGE
❏ PRLP-7442 [M]	Introducing Eric Kloss	1966	5.00	10.00	20.00
❏ PRST-7442 [S]	Introducing Eric Kloss	1966	6.25	12.50	25.00
❏ PRLP-7469 [M]	Love and All That Jazz	1966	5.00	10.00	20.00
❏ PRST-7469 [S]	Love and All That Jazz	1966	6.25	12.50	25.00
❏ PRLP-7486 [M]	Grits & Gravy	1967	6.25	12.50	25.00
❏ PRST-7486 [S]	Grits & Gravy	1967	5.00	10.00	20.00
❏ PRLP-7520 [M]	First Class Kloss	1967	7.50	15.00	30.00
❏ PRST-7520 [S]	First Class Kloss	1967	5.00	10.00	20.00
❏ PRST-7535	Life Force	1968	5.00	10.00	20.00
❏ PRST-7565	We're Goin' Up	1968	3.75	7.50	15.00
❏ PRST-7594	Sky Shadows	1969	3.75	7.50	15.00
❏ PRST-7627	In the Land of the Giants	1969	3.75	7.50	15.00
❏ PRST-7689	To Hear Is to See!	1970	3.75	7.50	15.00
❏ PRST-7793	Consciousness!	1970	3.75	7.50	15.00

KLOSS, ERIC, AND GIL GOLDSTEIN
Also see each artist's individual listings.
OMNISOUND
| ❏ 1044 | Sharing | 1981 | 3.00 | 6.00 | 12.00 |

KLOSS, ERIC, AND BARRY MILES
Also see each artist's individual listings.
MUSE
| ❏ MR-5112 | Together | 1976 | 3.75 | 7.50 | 15.00 |

KLUGH, EARL
Guitarist and keyboard player. Also see GEORGE BENSON; BOB JAMES.
BLUE NOTE
| ❏ BN-LA596-G | Earl Klugh | 1976 | 2.50 | 5.00 | 10.00 |

Number	Title	Yr	VG	VG+	NM
❏ BN-LA667-G	Living Inside Your Love	1976	2.50	5.00	10.00
❏ LO-667	Living Inside Your Love	198?	2.00	4.00	8.00
-- Reissue with new prefix					
❏ BN-LA737-H	Finger Paintings	1977	2.50	5.00	10.00
❏ LO-737	Finger Paintings	198?	2.00	4.00	8.00
-- Reissue with new prefix					
❏ LN-10163	Earl Klugh	198?	2.00	4.00	8.00
-- Budget-line reissue					

CAPITOL
❏ ST-12253	Low Ride	1983	2.50	5.00	10.00
❏ ST-12323	Wishful Thinking	1984	2.50	5.00	10.00
❏ ST-12372	Nightsongs	1984	2.50	5.00	10.00
❏ ST-12405	Key Notes (Greatest Hits)	1985	2.50	5.00	10.00

LIBERTY
❏ LMAS-877	Magic in Your Eyes	198?	2.00	4.00	8.00
-- Reissue of United Artists 877					
❏ LO-942	Heart String	198?	2.00	4.00	8.00
-- Reissue of United Artists 942					
❏ LT-1079	Late Night Guitar	1980	2.50	5.00	10.00
❏ LN-10231	Heart String	198?	2.00	4.00	8.00
-- Budget-line reissue					
❏ LN-10233	Living Inside Your Love	198?	2.00	4.00	8.00
-- Budget-line reissue					
❏ LN-10257	Finger Paintings	198?	2.00	4.00	8.00
-- Budget-line reissue					
❏ LN-10308	Crazy for You	1986	2.00	4.00	8.00
-- Budget-line reissue					
❏ LT-51113	Crazy for You	1981	2.50	5.00	10.00

MOBILE FIDELITY
❏ 1-025	Finger Paintings	1979	7.50	15.00	30.00
-- Audiophile vinyl					
❏ UHQR 1-025	Finger Paintings	1982	30.00	60.00	120.00
-- "Ultra High Quality" audiophile vinyl in box					
❏ 1-076	Late Night Guitar	1981	12.50	25.00	50.00
-- Audiophile vinyl					

NAUTILUS
| ❏ NR-46 | Crazy for You | 198? | 10.00 | 20.00 | 40.00 |
| -- Audiophile vinyl | | | | | |

UNITED ARTISTS
❏ UA-LA877-H	Magic in Your Eyes	1978	2.50	5.00	10.00
❏ UA-LA942-H	Heart String	1979	2.50	5.00	10.00
❏ LT-1026	Dream Come True	1980	2.50	5.00	10.00

WARNER BROS.
❏ 25262	Soda Fountain Shuffle	1985	2.50	5.00	10.00
❏ 25478	Life Stories	1986	2.50	5.00	10.00
❏ 25902	Whispers and Promises	1989	3.00	6.00	12.00
❏ 26018	Solo Guitar	1989	3.00	6.00	12.00

KNAPP, JAMES
Trumpeter and composer.
ECM
| ❏ 1194 | First Avenue | 198? | 3.00 | 6.00 | 12.00 |

KNEE, BERNIE
Male singer, best known for his work in advertising jingles.
AUDIOPHILE
| ❏ AP-144 | Bernie Knee | 198? | 3.00 | 6.00 | 12.00 |

KNEPPER, JIMMY
Trombonist. Also see PEPPER ADAMS; TONY SCOTT.
BETHLEHEM
❏ BCP-77 [M]	A Swinging Introduction to Jimmy Knepper	1957	15.00	30.00	60.00
❏ BCP-6031	Idol of the Flies	197?	3.00	6.00	12.00
-- Reissue, distributed by RCA Victor					

DEBUT
| ❏ DEB-129 [M] | New Faces | 1956 | --- | --- | --- |
| -- Canceled | | | | | |

INNER CITY
| ❏ IC-6047 | Knepper in L.A. | 197? | 3.00 | 6.00 | 12.00 |

SOUL NOTE
| ❏ SN-1092 | I Dream Too Much | 1984 | 3.00 | 6.00 | 12.00 |

STEEPLECHASE
| ❏ SCS-1061 | Cunningbird | 1977 | 3.00 | 6.00 | 12.00 |

KNIGHT, BOBBY, 'S GREAT AMERICAN TROMBONE CO.
Knight, a bass and tenor trombonist and arranger, is joined by Carl Fontana, Charles Loper, Lew McCreary and Frank Rosolino on trombones and Phil Teele on bass trombone, with additional backing musicians.
SEA BREEZE
| ❏ SB-2009 | Cream of the Crop | 198? | 2.50 | 5.00 | 10.00 |

Number	Title	Yr	VG	VG+	NM
KNIGHTS OF DIXIELAND, THE					
JAZZOLOGY					
❏ J-4 [M]	A Night with the Knights of Dixieland	1964	3.75	7.50	15.00
KNOPF, PAUL					
Pianist.					
PLAYBACK					
❏ PLP-500 [M]	The Outcat	1959	10.00	20.00	40.00
❏ PLP-500ST [S]	The Outcat	1959	12.50	25.00	50.00
❏ PLP-501 [M]	Enigma of a Day	1959	10.00	20.00	40.00
❏ PLP-501ST [S]	Enigma of a Day	1959	12.50	25.00	50.00
❏ PLP-502 [M]	And the Walls Came Tumbling Down	1960	10.00	20.00	40.00
❏ PLP-502ST [S]	And the Walls Came Tumbling Down	1960	12.50	25.00	50.00
❏ PLP-503 [M]	Paul Knoft Trio	1960	10.00	20.00	40.00
❏ PLP-503ST [S]	Paul Knoft Trio	1960	12.50	25.00	50.00
❏ PLP-600 [M]	Music from the Morgue	1961	10.00	20.00	40.00
❏ PLP-600ST [S]	Music from the Morgue	1961	12.50	25.00	50.00
KOCH, MERLE					
Pianist.					
AUDIOPHILE					
❏ AP-126	The Polite Jazz Quartet	1978	2.50	5.00	10.00
❏ AP-135	Merle Koch and Eddie Miller at Michele's	1979	2.50	5.00	10.00
JAZZOLOGY					
❏ J-80	Jazz Piano	197?	2.50	5.00	10.00
KOFFMAN, MOE					
Flutist, saxophone player and composer, best known for "The Swingin' Shepherd Blues."					
ASCOT					
❏ AM 13001 [M]	Moe Koffman Plays for the Teens	1962	5.00	10.00	20.00
❏ AS 16001 [S]	Moe Koffman Plays for the Teens	1962	6.25	12.50	25.00
JUBILEE					
❏ JLP-1037 [M]	Cool and Hot Sax	1957	10.00	20.00	40.00
❏ JLP-1074 [M]	The Shepherd Swings Again	1958	10.00	20.00	40.00
KAMA SUTRA					
❏ KSBS-2018	Moe's Curried Soul	1970	5.00	10.00	20.00
SOUNDWINGS/DUKE STREET					
❏ SW 2108	Oop-Pop-A-Da	1988	3.00	6.00	12.00
-- With Dizzy Gillespie					
UNITED ARTISTS					
❏ UAJ-14029 [M]	Tales of Koffman	1963	6.25	12.50	25.00
❏ UAJS-15029 [S]	Tales of Koffman	1963	7.50	15.00	30.00
KOHANNA, DEE					
ROCK CREEK					
❏ 001	Eclipse	1979	3.75	7.50	15.00
KOHLMAN, FREDDIE					
Drummer.					
MGM					
❏ E-297 [10]	New Orleans Now -- New Orleans Then	1955	20.00	40.00	80.00
KOINONIA					
Members: Abraham Laboriel (bass, acoustic guitar); Justo Almario (saxophone); Bill Maxwell (drums); Lou Pardini (keyboards, vocals); Harlan Rogers (keyboards).					
BREAKER					
❏ 9946	More Than a Feeling	1983	2.50	5.00	10.00
❏ 9970	Celebration	1984	2.50	5.00	10.00
KOLLER, HANS					
Tenor and baritone saxophone player.					
DISCOVERY					
❏ DL-2005 [10]	Hans Koller	1954	20.00	40.00	80.00
VANGUARD					
❏ VRS-8509 [M]	Hans Across the Sea	1956	12.50	25.00	50.00
KONITZ, LEE					
Alto saxophone player. Also see STAN GETZ; GERRY MULLIGAN; LENNY TRISTANO.					
ATLANTIC					
❏ 1217 [M]	Lee Konitz with Warne Marsh	1955	20.00	40.00	80.00
-- Black label					
❏ 1217 [M]	Lee Konitz with Warne Marsh	1961	6.25	12.50	25.00
-- Multicolor label, white "fan" logo at right					
❏ 1258 [M]	Inside Hi-Fi	1957	15.00	30.00	60.00
-- Black label					
❏ 1258 [M]	Inside Hi-Fi	1961	6.25	12.50	25.00
-- Multicolor label, white "fan" logo at right					
❏ SD 1258 [S]	Inside Hi-Fi	1958	15.00	30.00	60.00
-- Green label					
❏ SD 1258 [S]	Inside Hi-Fi	1961	5.00	10.00	20.00
-- Multicolor label, white "fan" logo at right					
❏ 1273 [M]	The Real Lee Konitz	1958	12.50	25.00	50.00
-- Black label					
❏ 1273 [M]	The Real Lee Konitz	1961	6.25	12.50	25.00
-- Multicolor label, white "fan" logo at right					
❏ SD 8235	Duets	1969	3.75	7.50	15.00
❏ 90050	Lee Konitz with Warne Marsh	198?	2.50	5.00	10.00
CHIAROSCURO					
❏ 166	The Quartet	1976	3.00	6.00	12.00
❏ 186	The Nonet	1977	3.00	6.00	12.00
CHOICE					
❏ 1019	Tenorlee	1977	3.00	6.00	12.00
FANTASY					
❏ OJC-186	Subconscious-Lee	198?	2.50	5.00	10.00
❏ OJC-466	Duets	1990	3.00	6.00	12.00
GROOVE MERCHANT					
❏ 3306	Chicago and All That Jazz	197?	5.00	10.00	20.00
IAI					
❏ 37.38.45	Pyramid	1977	3.75	7.50	15.00
INNER CITY					
❏ IC-2035	Lone-Lee	1975	3.75	7.50	15.00
JAZZTONE					
❏ J-1275 [M]	Jazz at Storyville	1957	10.00	20.00	40.00
MIESTONE					
❏ 9060	Satori	197?	5.00	10.00	20.00
MILESTONE					
❏ 9013	Duets	1968	5.00	10.00	20.0
❏ 9025	Peacemeal	1968	5.00	10.00	20.00
❏ 9038	Spirits	1969	5.00	10.00	20.00
PAUSA					
❏ 7019	Lee Konitz Meets Warne Marsh Again	198?	2.50	5.00	10.00
PRESTIGE					
❏ PRLP-116 [10]	Lee Konitz -- The New Sounds	1951	75.00	150.00	300.00
❏ PRLP-7004 [M]	Lee Konitz Groups	1955	37.50	75.00	150.00
❏ PRLP-7250 [M]	Subconscious-Lee	1962	12.50	25.00	50.00
❏ 24081 [(2)]	First Sessions 1949-50	198?	3.00	6.00	12.00
PROGRESSIVE					
❏ 7003	Figure and Spirit	1977	3.75	7.50	15.00
ROOST					
❏ LP-416 [10]	Originalee	1953	50.00	100.00	200.00
ROULETTE					
❏ SR-5006	The Nonet	1976	3.75	7.50	15.00
SOUL NOTE					
❏ SN-1069	Live at Laren	198?	3.00	6.00	12.00
❏ 121119	Ideal Scene	198?	3.00	6.00	12.00
❏ 121169	The New York Album	1990	3.00	6.00	12.00
STEEPLECHASE					
❏ SCS-1035	Lone-Lee	198?	3.00	6.00	12.00
❏ SCS-1072	Jazz & Juan	198?	3.00	6.00	12.00
❏ SCS-1119	Yes, Yes Nonet	1979	3.00	6.00	12.00
STORYVILLE					
❏ STLP-304 [10]	Lee Konitz at Storyville	1954	50.00	100.00	200.00
❏ STLP-313 [10]	Konitz	1954	50.00	100.00	200.00
❏ STLP-323 [10]	Lee Konitz in Harvard Square	1955	37.50	75.00	150.00
❏ STLP-901 [M]	Lee Konitz at Storyville	1956	30.00	60.00	120.00
SUNNYSIDE					
❏ SSC-1003	Dovetail	1985	2.50	5.00	10.00
VERVE					
❏ UMV-2563	Motion	198?	2.50	5.00	10.00
❏ MGVS-6035 [S]	An Image -- Lee Konitz with Strings	1959	7.50	15.00	30.00
❏ MGVS-6073 [S]	Lee Konitz Meets Jimmy Giuffre	1959	7.50	15.00	30.00
❏ MGVS-6131 [S]	You and Lee	1960	7.50	15.00	30.00
❏ MGV-8209 [M]	Very Cool	1958	12.50	25.00	50.00
❏ V-8209 [M]	Very Cool	1961	6.25	12.50	25.00
❏ MGV-8281 [M]	Tranquility	1958	12.50	25.00	50.00
❏ V-8281 [M]	Tranquility	1961	6.25	12.50	25.00
❏ MGV-8286 [M]	An Image -- Lee Konitz with Strings	1958	10.00	20.00	40.00
❏ V-8286 [M]	An Image -- Lee Konitz with Strings	1961	6.25	12.50	25.00
❏ V6-8286 [S]	An Image -- Lee Konitz with Strings	1961	5.00	10.00	20.00
❏ MGV-8335 [M]	Lee Konitz Meets Jimmy Giuffre	1959	10.00	20.00	40.00

Number	Title	Yr	VG	VG+	NM
❑ V-8335 [M]	Lee Konitz Meets Jimmy Giuffre	1961	5.00	10.00	20.00
❑ V6-8335 [S]	Lee Konitz Meets Jimmy Giuffre	1961	3.75	7.50	15.00
❑ MGV-8362 [M]	You and Lee	1960	10.00	20.00	40.00
❑ V-8362 [M]	You and Lee	1961	5.00	10.00	20.00
❑ V6-8362 [S]	You and Lee	1961	3.75	7.50	15.00
❑ V-8399 [M]	Motion	1961	5.00	10.00	20.00
❑ V6-8399 [S]	Motion	1961	6.25	12.50	25.00

KONITZ, LEE/MILES DAVIS/TEDDY CHARLES
Also see each artist's individual listings.
NEW JAZZ

❑ NJLP-8295 [M]	Ezz-Thetic	1962	12.50	25.00	50.00
-- Purple label					
❑ NJLP-8295 [M]	Ezz-Thetic	1965	6.25	12.50	25.00
-- Blue label, trident logo at right					
PRESTIGE					
❑ PRST-7827	Ezz-Thetic	1970	3.00	6.00	12.00

KONITZ, LEE, AND HAL GALPER
Also see each artist's individual listings.
INNER CITY

❑ IC-2057	Windows	1976	3.75	7.50	15.00
STEEPLECHASE					
❑ SCS-1057	Windows	198?	3.00	6.00	12.00

KONITZ, LEE, AND RED MITCHELL
Also see each artist's individual listings.
INNER CITY

❑ IC-2018	I Concentrate on You	1975	3.75	7.50	15.00
STEEPLECHASE					
❑ SCS-1018	I Concentrate on You	198?	3.00	6.00	12.00

KONITZ, LEE, AND MARTIAL SOLAI
Also see each artist's individual listings.
PAUSA

❑ 7138	Duo: Live at Berlin Jazz Days 1980	198?	2.50	5.00	10.00

KONRAD, BERND
Soprano, alto, tenor, baritone and bass saxophone player and bass clarinetist.
HAT HUT

❑ 3509	Traumtanzer	198?	3.00	6.00	12.00

KOONSE, DAVE AND LARRY
Both are guitarists.
DOBRE

❑ 1035	Father and Son	197?	3.00	6.00	12.00

KRAL, IRENE
Female singer.
AVA

❑ A-33 [M]	Better Than Anything	1963	10.00	20.00	40.00
❑ AS-33 [S]	Better Than Anything	1963	12.50	25.00	50.00
CATALYST					
❑ 7625	Kral Space	1977	3.00	6.00	12.00
CHOICE					
❑ CRS 1012	Where Is Love?	197?	3.00	6.00	12.00
❑ CRS 1020	Gentle Rain	197?	3.00	6.00	12.00
DRG					
❑ MRS-505	Irene Kral and the Junior Mance Trio	198?	2.50	5.00	10.00
MAINSTREAM					
❑ S-6058 [S]	Wonderful Life	1965	10.00	20.00	40.00
❑ 56058 [M]	Wonderful Life	1965	7.50	15.00	30.00
UNITED ARTISTS					
❑ UAL-3052 [M]	Steve Irene O!	1959	30.00	60.00	120.00
❑ UAL-4016 [M]	The Band and I	1959	30.00	60.00	120.00
❑ UAS-5016 [S]	The Band and I	1959	37.50	75.00	150.00
❑ UAS-6052 [S]	Steve Irene O!	1959	37.50	75.00	150.00

KRESS, CARL
Guitarist; one of the first jazz guitarists.
CAPITOL

❑ H 368 [10]	Classics in Jazz	1953	12.50	25.00	50.00

KRESS, CARL, AND GEORGE BARNES
See GEORGE BARNES.

KRESTON, JUDY, AND DAVID LAHM
Kreston is a female singer; Lahm is a pianist.
PLUG

Number	Title	Yr	VG	VG+	NM
❑ PLUG-6	Here In Love Lies the Answer	1986	3.00	6.00	12.00

KRIVDA, ERNIE
Tenor saxophone player.
CADENCE JAZZ

❑ CJR-1028	Tough Tenor Red Hot	1987	2.50	5.00	10.00
INNER CITY					
❑ IC-1031	Satanic	1977	3.75	7.50	15.00
❑ IC-1043	Alchemist	1978	3.75	7.50	15.00
❑ IC-1083	Glory Strut	198?	3.00	6.00	12.00

KROG, KARIN, AND DEXTER GORDON
Krog is a female singer and sometimes percussionist. Also see DEXTER GORDON.
STORYVILLE

❑ 4045	Some Other Spring	198?	3.00	6.00	12.00

KRONOS QUARTET
Jazz and classical string quartet: David Hurrington (violin); John Sherba (violin); Hank Dutt (viola); Joan Jeanrenaud (cello).
LANDMARK

❑ LLP-1505	Monk Suite (Music of Monk & Ellington)	1985	3.00	6.00	12.00
❑ LLP-1510	Music of Bill Evans	1986	3.00	6.00	12.00
REFERENCE RECORDINGS					
❑ RR-9	In Formation	198?	6.25	12.50	25.00
-- Audiophile vinyl					

KRUPA, GENE
Drummer and bandleader.
AIRCHECK

❑ 35	Gene Krupa on the Air, 1944-46	198?	2.50	5.00	10.00
AMERICAN RECORDING SOCIETY					
❑ L-411 [M]	Gene Krupa Quartet	1956	10.00	20.00	40.00
❑ L-427 [M]	Drummer Man	1957	10.00	20.00	40.00
CLEF					
❑ MGC-121 [10]	The Gene Krupa Trio Collates	1953	20.00	40.00	80.00
-- With either Clef or Mercury cover					
❑ MGC-147 [10]	The Gene Krupa Sextet #1	1954	20.00	40.00	80.00
❑ MGC-152 [10]	The Gene Krupa Sextet #2	1954	20.00	40.00	80.00
❑ MGC-500 [M]	The Gene Krupa Trio at Jazz at the Philharmonic	1953	15.00	30.00	60.00
❑ MGC-514 [10]	Gene Krupa Trio	1953	20.00	40.00	80.00
❑ MGC-607 [M]	Gene Krupa	1954	---	---	---
-- Canceled					
❑ MGC-627 [M]	Sing, Sing, Sing -- The Rocking Mr. Krupa and His Orchestra	1954	15.00	30.00	60.00
❑ MGC-631 [M]	The Gene Krupa Sextet #3	1954	15.00	30.00	60.00
❑ MGC-668 [M]	The Gene Krupa Quartet	1955	15.00	30.00	60.00
❑ MGC-684 [M]	Krupa and Rich	1955	15.00	30.00	60.00
❑ MGC-687 [M]	The Exciting Gene Krupa and His Quartet	1956	15.00	30.00	60.00
❑ MGC-703 [M]	Drum Boogie	1956	15.00	30.00	60.00
❑ MGC-710 [M]	Krupa's Wail	1956	---	---	---
-- Canceled					
❑ MGC-728 [M]	The Driving Gene Krupa Plays with His Sextet	1956	15.00	30.00	60.00
COLUMBIA					
❑ C2L 29 [(2) M]	Drummin' Man	1962	12.50	25.00	50.00
-- Red and black labels with six "eye" logos; box set with booklet; deduct 20 percent if book is missing					
❑ C2L 29 [(2) M]	Drummin' Man	1963	5.00	10.00	20.00
-- Red labels, "Guaranteed High Fidelity" or "360 Sound Mono" on label					
❑ CL 641 [M]	Gene Krupa's Sidekicks	1955	7.50	15.00	30.00
-- Red and black label with six "eye" logos					
❑ CL 641 [M]	Gene Krupa's Sidekicks	1955	10.00	20.00	40.00
-- Maroon label, gold print					
❑ CL 735 [M]	Gene Krupa	1956	7.50	15.00	30.00
-- Red and black label with six "eye" logos					
❑ CL 735 [M]	Gene Krupa	1963	3.75	7.50	15.00
-- Red label, "Guaranteed High Fidelity" or "360 Sound Mono" on label					
❑ CL 2515 [10]	Drummin' Man	1955	12.50	25.00	50.00
❑ CL 6017 [10]	Gene Krupa	1949	25.00	50.00	100.00
❑ CL 6066 [10]	Dance Parade	1949	25.00	50.00	100.00
❑ KG 32663 [(2)]	Gene Krupa, His Orchestra and Anita O'Day	1974	3.75	7.50	15.00
COLUMBIA SPECIAL PRODUCTS					
❑ P 14379	Krupa Swings	197?	2.50	5.00	10.00
ENCORE					
❑ EE 22027	That Drummer's Band	196?	3.75	7.50	15.00

Number	Title	Yr	VG	VG+	NM
HARMONY					
❏ HL 7252 [M]	The Gene Krupa Story in Music	1960	3.75	7.50	15.00
INTERMEDIA					
❏ QS-5050	Hot Drums	198?	2.50	5.00	10.00
MERCURY					
❏ MGC-121 [10]	The Gene Krupa Trio Collates	1953	---	---	---
-- Covers exist, but all contain Clef labels (see Clef section)					
❏ MGC-500 [M]	The Gene Krupa Trio at Jazz at the Philharmonic	1953	20.00	40.00	80.00
❏ MGC-514 [10]	Gene Krupa Trio	1953	30.00	60.00	120.00
METRO					
❏ M-518 [M]	Gene Krupa	1965	3.75	7.50	15.00
❏ MS-518 [R]	Gene Krupa	1965	3.00	6.00	12.00
MGM					
❏ GAS-132	Gene Krupa (Golden Archive Series)	1970	3.00	6.00	12.00
RCA CAMDEN					
❏ CAL-340 [M]	Mutiny in the Parlor	1958	5.00	10.00	20.00
SUNBEAM					
❏ 225	The World's Greatest Drummer	197?	2.50	5.00	10.00
VERVE					
❏ VSP-4 [M]	That Drummer's Band	1966	3.75	7.50	15.00
❏ VSPS-4 [R]	That Drummer's Band	1966	3.00	6.00	12.00
❏ MGV-2008 [M]	Drummer Man -- Gene Krupa in Highest-Fi	1956	15.00	30.00	60.00
-- Orange label					
❏ MGV-2008 [M]	Drummer Man -- Gene Krupa in Highest-Fi	1957	12.50	25.00	50.00
-- Black label					
❏ V-2008 [M]	Drummer Man -- Gene Krupa in Highest-Fi	1961	6.25	12.50	25.00
❏ UMV-2594	The Exciting Gene Krupa	198?	2.50	5.00	10.00
❏ MGV-4016 [M]	Gene Krupa Plays the Classics	1958	---	---	---
-- Canceled					
❏ MGVS-6008 [S]	Gene Krupa Plays Gerry Mulligan Arrangements	1959	10.00	20.00	40.00
❏ MGVS-6042 [S]	Big Noise from Winnetka -- Gene Krupa at the London House	1960	10.00	20.00	40.00
❏ MGVS-6148 [S]	Gene Krupa	1960	---	---	---
-- Canceled					
❏ MGV-8031 [M]	The Gene Krupa Trio	1957	12.50	25.00	50.00
❏ V-8031 [M]	The Gene Krupa Trio	1961	6.25	12.50	25.00
❏ MGV-8069 [M]	Krupa and Rich	1957	12.50	25.00	50.00
❏ V-8069 [M]	Krupa and Rich	1961	6.25	12.50	25.00
❏ MGV-8071 [M]	The Exciting Gene Krupa and His Quartet	1957	12.50	25.00	50.00
❏ V-8071 [M]	The Exciting Gene Krupa and His Quartet	1961	6.25	12.50	25.00
❏ MGV-8087 [M]	Drum Boogie	1957	12.50	25.00	50.00
❏ V-8087 [M]	Drum Boogie	1961	6.25	12.50	25.00
❏ MGV-8107 [M]	The Driving Gene Krupa	1957	12.50	25.00	50.00
❏ V-8107 [M]	The Driving Gene Krupa	1961	6.25	12.50	25.00
❏ MGV-8190 [M]	Sing, Sing, Sing	1957	12.50	25.00	50.00
❏ V-8190 [M]	Sing, Sing, Sing	1961	6.25	12.50	25.00
❏ MGV-8204 [M]	The Jazz Rhythms of Gene Krupa	1957	12.50	25.00	50.00
❏ V-8204 [M]	The Jazz Rhythms of Gene Krupa	1961	6.25	12.50	25.00
❏ MGV-8276 [M]	Krupa Rocks	1958	12.50	25.00	50.00
❏ V-8276 [M]	Krupa Rocks	1961	6.25	12.50	25.00
❏ MGV-8292 [M]	Gene Krupa Plays Gerry Mulligan Arrangements	1958	12.50	25.00	50.00
❏ V-8292 [M]	Gene Krupa Plays Gerry Mulligan Arrangements	1961	6.25	12.50	25.00
❏ V6-8292 [S]	Gene Krupa Plays Gerry Mulligan Arrangements	1961	5.00	10.00	20.00
❏ MGV-8300 [M]	Hey! Here's Gene Krupa	1959	12.50	25.00	50.00
❏ V-8300 [M]	Hey! Here's Gene Krupa	1961	6.25	12.50	25.00
❏ MGV-8310 [M]	Big Noise from Winnetka -- Gene Krupa at the London House	1959	12.50	25.00	50.00
❏ V-8310 [M]	Big Noise from Winnetka -- Gene Krupa at the London House	1961	6.25	12.50	25.00
❏ V6-8310 [S]	Big Noise from Winnetka -- Gene Krupa at the London House	1961	5.00	10.00	20.00
❏ MGV-8369 [M]	The Drum Battle	1960	12.50	25.00	50.00
❏ MGV-8373 [M]	Gene Krupa	1960	---	---	---
-- Canceled					
❏ V-8400 [M]	Krupa and Rich	1961	6.25	12.50	25.00
❏ V6-8400 [S]	Krupa and Rich	1961	5.00	10.00	20.00
❏ V-8414 [M]	Percussion King	1961	3.75	7.50	15.00
❏ V6-8414 [S]	Percussion King	1961	5.00	10.00	20.00
❏ V-8450 [M]	Classics in Percussion	1962	3.75	7.50	15.00
❏ V6-8450 [S]	Classics in Percussion	1962	5.00	10.00	20.00
❏ V-8484 [M]	The Original Drum Battle	1962	3.75	7.50	15.00
❏ V6-8484 [R]	The Original Drum Battle	196?	3.00	6.00	12.00
❏ V-8571 [M]	Let Me Off Uptown -- The Essential Gene Krupa	1964	3.75	7.50	15.00
❏ V6-8571 [S]	Let Me Off Uptown -- The Essential Gene Krupa	1964	5.00	10.00	20.00
❏ V-8584 [M]	The Great New Gene Krupa Quartet Featuring Charlie Ventura	1964	3.75	7.50	15.00
❏ V6-8584 [S]	The Great New Gene Krupa Quartet Featuring Charlie Ventura	1964	5.00	10.00	20.00
❏ V-8594 [M]	Verve's Choice -- The Best of Gene Krupa	1964	3.75	7.50	15.00
❏ V6-8594 [S]	Verve's Choice -- The Best of Gene Krupa	1964	3.00	6.00	12.00
❏ 827 843-1	Drummer Man	1986	2.50	5.00	10.00

KRUPA, GENE; LIONEL HAMPTON; TEDDY WILSON

Also see each artist's individual listings.

Number	Title	Yr	VG	VG+	NM
CLEF					
❏ MGC-681 [M]	Selections from "The Benny Goodman Story"	1956	20.00	40.00	80.00
VERVE					
❏ MGV-8066 [M]	Gene Krupa-Lionel Hampton-Teddy Wilson with Red Callender	1957	12.50	25.00	50.00
-- Reissue of Clef 681 with new title					
❏ V-8066 [M]	Gene Krupa-Lionel Hampton-Teddy Wilson with Red Callender	1961	6.25	12.50	25.00

KRUPA, GENE, AND CHARLIE VENTURA

Also see each artist's individual listings.

Number	Title	Yr	VG	VG+	NM
COMMODORE					
❏ FL-20028 [10]	The Krupa-Ventura Trio	1950	25.00	50.00	100.00

KUHN, JOACHIM

Pianist. Also see ROLF KUHN.

Number	Title	Yr	VG	VG+	NM
ATLANTIC					
❏ SD 1695	Springfever	1976	3.00	6.00	12.00
❏ SD 19193	Sunshower	1978	2.50	5.00	10.00
CMP					
❏ CMP-22-ST	I'm Not Dreaming	1986	2.50	5.00	10.00
❏ CMP-26-ST	Distance	1987	2.50	5.00	10.00
❏ CMP-29-ST	Wandlungen/Transformations	1987	2.50	5.00	10.00

KUHN, PETER

Clarinetist and bass clarinetist.

Number	Title	Yr	VG	VG+	NM
HAT HUT					
❏ 09	Ghost of a Trance	1980	3.75	7.50	15.00
SOUL NOTE					
❏ SN-1043	The Kill	1981	3.00	6.00	12.00

KUHN, ROLF

Clarinetist.

Number	Title	Yr	VG	VG+	NM
URANIA					
❏ US-1220 [M]	Sound of Jazz	1962	6.25	12.50	25.00
❏ US-41220 [S]	Sound of Jazz	1962	7.50	15.00	30.00
VANGUARD					
❏ VRS-8510 [M]	Streamline	1955	10.00	20.00	40.00

KUHN, ROLF AND JOACHIM

Also see each artist's individual listings.

Number	Title	Yr	VG	VG+	NM
ABC IMPULSE!					
❏ AS-9150	Impressions of New York	1968	5.00	10.00	20.00

KUHN, STEVE

Pianist.

Number	Title	Yr	VG	VG+	NM
ABC IMPULSE!					
❏ AS-9136 [S]	The October Suite	1968	3.00	6.00	12.00
BUDDAH					
❏ BDS-5098	Steve Kuhn	1972	3.75	7.50	15.00
CONTACT					
❏ CM-5 [M]	Steve Kuhn Trio Featuring Steve Swallow and Pete LaRoca	1965	5.00	10.00	20.00
❏ CS-5 [S]	Steve Kuhn Trio Featuring Steve Swallow and Pete LaRoca	1965	6.25	12.50	25.00
ECM					
❏ 1052	Trance	197?	3.00	6.00	12.00
❏ 1058	Ecstasy	197?	3.00	6.00	12.00
❏ 1094	Motility	1977	3.00	6.00	12.00
❏ 1124	Non-Fiction	1978	3.00	6.00	12.00
❏ 1213	Last Year's Waltz	1982	2.50	5.00	10.00
IMPULSE!					
❏ A-9136 [M]	The October Suite	1967	6.25	12.50	25.00

Number	Title	Yr	VG	VG+	NM
❏ AS-9136 [S]	The October Suite	1967	5.00	10.00	20.00

MUSE

❏ MR-5106	Raindrops/Live in New York	1978	3.00	6.00	12.00

PRESTIGE

❏ PRST-7694	Steve Kuhn in Europe	1969	3.75	7.50	15.00

KUHN, STEVE, AND TOSHIKO AKIYOSHI
Also see each artist's individual listings.

DAUNTLESS

❏ DM-4308 [M]	The Country & Western Sound for Jazz Pianos	1963	5.00	10.00	20.00
❏ DS-6308 [S]	The Country & Western Sound for Jazz Pianos	1963	6.25	12.50	25.00

KUHN, STEVE, AND SHEILA JORDAN
Also see each artist's individual listings.

ECM

❏ 1159	Playground	1979	3.00	6.00	12.00

KUSTBANDET
New Orleans-style Dixieland music from a band based in Stockholm, Sweden.

STOMP OFF

❏ SOS-1178	The New Call of the Freaks	1989	3.00	6.00	12.00

KYNARD, CHARLES
Organist, pianist and composer.

FANTASY

❏ OJC-333	Reelin' with the Feelin'	1988	2.50	5.00	10.00

MAINSTREAM

❏ MRL-331	Charles Kynard	1972	5.00	10.00	20.00
❏ MRL-368	Woga	1973	5.00	10.00	20.00
❏ MRL-389	Your Mama Don't Dance	1973	5.00	10.00	20.00

PACIFIC JAZZ

❏ PJ-72 [M]	Where It's At!	1963	7.50	15.00	30.00
❏ ST-72 [S]	Where It's At!	1963	10.00	20.00	40.00

PRESTIGE

❏ PRST-7599	Professor Soul	1968	5.00	10.00	20.00
❏ PRST-7630	The Soul Brotherhood	1969	5.00	10.00	20.00
❏ PRST-7688	Reelin' with the Feelin'	1969	5.00	10.00	20.00
❏ PRST-7796	Afro-disiac	1970	5.00	10.00	20.00
❏ 10008	Wa-tu-wa-zui	1971	5.00	10.00	20.00

WORLD PACIFIC

❏ ST-1823 [S]	Warm Winds	1964	7.50	15.00	30.00
❏ WP-1823 [M]	Warm Winds	1964	6.25	12.50	25.00

Number	Title	Yr	VG	VG+	NM

L

L.A. 4
Members: LAURINDO ALMEIDA; RAY BROWN; SHELLY MANNE; BUD SHANK.
CONCORD JAZZ
Number	Title	Yr	VG	VG+	NM
❏ CJ-8	Scores	197?	3.75	7.50	15.00
❏ CJ-18	The L.A. 4	197?	3.00	6.00	12.00
❏ CJ-63	Watch What Happens	1978	3.00	6.00	12.00
❏ CJ-100	Live at Montreux, 1979	1980	2.50	5.00	10.00
❏ CJ-130	Zaca	1980	2.50	5.00	10.00
❏ CJ-156	Montage	1981	2.50	5.00	10.00
❏ CJ-199	Just Friends	1981	2.50	5.00	10.00
-- Regular version					
❏ CJ-215	Executive Suite	1982	2.50	5.00	10.00
❏ CJ-1001	Just Friends	1980	5.00	10.00	20.00
-- Direct-to-disc recording					

EAST WIND
Number	Title	Yr	VG	VG+	NM
❏ 10003	Pavanne Pour Une Infante Defunte	197?	7.50	15.00	30.00
-- Audiophile issue					
❏ 10004	Going Home	197?	7.50	15.00	30.00
-- Audiophile issue					

L.A. JAZZ CHOIR, THE
Founded and directed by Gerald Eskelin.
MOBILE FIDELITY
Number	Title	Yr	VG	VG+	NM
❏ 1-096	Listen	1982	20.00	40.00	80.00
-- Audiophile vinyl					

PAUSA
Number	Title	Yr	VG	VG+	NM
❏ 7184	From All Sides	1986	3.00	6.00	12.00

L.A. JAZZ ENSEMBLE, THE
Led by ROLAND VAZQUEZ.
PBR
Number	Title	Yr	VG	VG+	NM
❏ 8	Urantia	197?	3.00	6.00	12.00

L.A. JAZZ WORKSHOP, THE
AM-PM
Number	Title	Yr	VG	VG+	NM
❏ 16	The Shopwork Shuffle	1986	2.50	5.00	10.00

SEA BREEZE
Number	Title	Yr	VG	VG+	NM
❏ SB-2021	Stan's Donuts	198?	2.50	5.00	10.00

LaBARBERA, PAT
Saxophone player.
PM
Number	Title	Yr	VG	VG+	NM
❏ 009	Pass It On	197?	3.00	6.00	12.00

LACY, STEVE
Soprano saxophone player.
ADELPHI
Number	Title	Yr	VG	VG+	NM
❏ 5004	Raps	1977	3.00	6.00	12.00

BARNABY
Number	Title	Yr	VG	VG+	NM
❏ BR-5013	Straight Horn	1977	3.75	7.50	15.00

BLACK SAINT
Number	Title	Yr	VG	VG+	NM
❏ BSR-0008	Trickles	198?	3.00	6.00	12.00
❏ BSR-0035	Troubles	198?	3.00	6.00	12.00

CANDID
Number	Title	Yr	VG	VG+	NM
❏ CD-8007 [M]	The Straight Horn of Steve Lacy	1960	10.00	20.00	40.00
❏ CS-9007 [S]	The Straight Horn of Steve Lacy	1960	12.50	25.00	50.00

EMANEM
Number	Title	Yr	VG	VG+	NM
❏ 301	Steve Lacy Solo	1973	3.75	7.50	15.00
❏ 304	The Crust	1974	3.75	7.50	15.00
❏ 3310	Saxophone Special	1975	3.75	7.50	15.00
❏ 3316	School Days	1975	3.75	7.50	15.00

ESP-DISK'
Number	Title	Yr	VG	VG+	NM
❏ 1060 [M]	The Forest and the Zoo	1967	7.50	15.00	30.00
❏ S-1060 [S]	The Forest and the Zoo	1967	5.00	10.00	20.00

FANTASY
Number	Title	Yr	VG	VG+	NM
❏ OJC-063	Reflections: Steve Lacy Plays Thelonious Monk	198?	2.50	5.00	10.00
❏ OJC-130	Steve Lacy Soprano Sax	198?	2.50	5.00	10.00
❏ OJC-1755	Evidence	198?	2.50	5.00	10.00

HAT ART
Number	Title	Yr	VG	VG+	NM
❏ 2006 [(2)]	Blinks	1986	3.75	7.50	15.00
❏ 2014 [(2)]	N.Y. Capers	1986	3.75	7.50	15.00
❏ 2022 [(2)]	Futurities	1986	3.75	7.50	15.00
❏ 2029 [(2)]	The Way	1987	3.75	7.50	15.00

HAT HUT
Number	Title	Yr	VG	VG+	NM
❏ 03 [(2)]	The Way	1979	5.00	10.00	20.00
❏ 14 [(2)]	Capers	1980	3.75	7.50	15.00
❏ 1982/3 [(2)]	Ballets	1982	3.75	7.50	15.00
❏ 1985/86 [(2)]	Songs	1982	3.75	7.50	15.00
❏ 20	Tips	1980	3.00	6.00	12.00
❏ 2001 [(2)]	Prospectus	198?	3.75	7.50	15.00
❏ F	Clinkers	1977	3.75	7.50	15.00
❏ K/L [(2)]	Stamps	1978	5.00	10.00	20.00

NEW JAZZ
Number	Title	Yr	VG	VG+	NM
❏ NJLP-8206 [M]	Reflections: Steve Lacy Plays Thelonious Monk	1958	25.00	50.00	100.00
-- Purple label					
❏ NJLP-8206 [M]	Reflections: Steve Lacy Plays Thelonious Monk	1965	6.25	12.50	25.00
-- Blue label, trident logo at right					
❏ NJLP-8271 [M]	Evidence	1962	20.00	40.00	80.00
-- Purple label					
❏ NJLP-8271 [M]	Evidence	1965	6.25	12.50	25.00
-- Blue label, trident logo at right					
❏ NJLP-8308 [M]	Wynton Kelly with Steve Lacy	1963	---	---	---
-- Canceled; issued on Status					

NOVUS
Number	Title	Yr	VG	VG+	NM
❏ 3021-1-N	Momentum	1988	2.50	5.00	10.00
❏ 3049-1-N	The Door	1989	3.00	6.00	12.00
❏ 3079-1-N	Anthem	1990	3.00	6.00	12.00

PRESTIGE
Number	Title	Yr	VG	VG+	NM
❏ 2505	Evidence	198?	3.00	6.00	12.00
❏ PRLP-7125 [M]	Steve Lacy Soprano Sax	1956	25.00	50.00	100.00

QED
Number	Title	Yr	VG	VG+	NM
❏ 997	School Days	197?	3.00	6.00	12.00

RED
Number	Title	Yr	VG	VG+	NM
❏ VPA-120	Axieme Vol. 1	198?	3.00	6.00	12.00
❏ VPA-121	Axieme Vol. 2	198?	3.00	6.00	12.00

SILKHEART
Number	Title	Yr	VG	VG+	NM
❏ SH-102	The Gleam	198?	2.50	5.00	10.00
❏ SH-103	One Fell Swoop	198?	2.50	5.00	10.00

SOUL NOTE
Number	Title	Yr	VG	VG+	NM
❏ SN-1035	The Flame	198?	3.00	6.00	12.00
❏ 121135	The Condor	1990	3.75	7.50	15.00
❏ 121160	Only Monk	199?	3.75	7.50	15.00
❏ 121185	The Window	199?	3.75	7.50	15.00
❏ 121210	More Monk	199?	3.75	7.50	15.00

STATUS
Number	Title	Yr	VG	VG+	NM
❏ ST-8308 [M]	Wynton Kelly with Steve Lacy	1965	10.00	20.00	40.00

LACY, STEVE, AND MICHAEL SMITH
Also see each artist's individual listings.
IAI
Number	Title	Yr	VG	VG+	NM
❏ 37.38.47	Sidelines	197?	3.75	7.50	15.00

LACY, STEVE, AND MAL WALDRON
Also see each artist's individual listings.
HAT ART
Number	Title	Yr	VG	VG+	NM
❏ 2015 [(2)]	Herbe de L'Oubli & Snake-Out	1986	3.75	7.50	15.00

HAT HUT
Number	Title	Yr	VG	VG+	NM
❏ 3501	Snake-Out	198?	3.00	6.00	12.00

LADNIER, TOMMY
Trumpeter.
RIVERSIDE
Number	Title	Yr	VG	VG+	NM
❏ RLP-1019 [10]	Ida Cox with Tommy Ladnier	1953	25.00	50.00	100.00
❏ RLP-1026 [10]	Early Ladnier	1954	25.00	50.00	100.00
❏ RLP-1044 [10]	Tommy Ladnier Plays the Blues	1954	25.00	50.00	100.00

"X"
Number	Title	Yr	VG	VG+	NM
❏ LVA-3027 [M]	Tommy Ladnier	1954	15.00	30.00	60.00

LaFORGE, JACK
Male singer.
AUDIO FIDELITY
Number	Title	Yr	VG	VG+	NM
❏ AFLP-2161 [M]	Hit the Road Jack	196?	3.75	7.50	15.00
❏ AFSD-6161 [S]	Hit the Road Jack	196?	5.00	10.00	20.00

REGINA
Number	Title	Yr	VG	VG+	NM
❏ R-282 [M]	I Remember You	196?	5.00	10.00	20.00
❏ RS-282 [S]	I Remember You	196?	6.25	12.50	25.00
❏ R-288 [M]	Unchain My Heart	196?	5.00	10.00	20.00
❏ RS-288 [S]	Unchain My Heart	196?	6.25	12.50	25.00
❏ R-301 [M]	You Fascinate Me So	196?	5.00	10.00	20.00
❏ RS-301 [S]	You Fascinate Me So	196?	6.25	12.50	25.00
❏ R-309 [M]	Comin' Home Baby	196?	5.00	10.00	20.00
❏ RS-309 [S]	Comin' Home Baby	196?	6.25	12.50	25.00
❏ R-313 [M]	Promise Her Anything	196?	5.00	10.00	20.00
❏ RS-313 [S]	Promise Her Anything	196?	6.25	12.50	25.00
❏ R-314 [M]	Jazz Portrait of Jack LaForge	196?	5.00	10.00	20.00

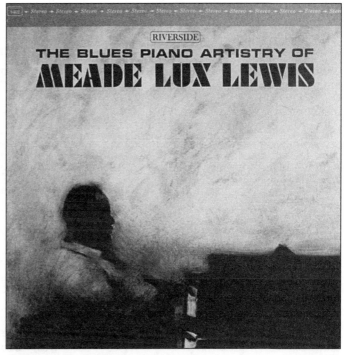

(Top left) Steve Lacy's first album as a leader, *Soprano Sax* in 1956, was the start of a productive career that led in many musical directions, and eventually to Paris and some of his best work for the Hat Hut label. (Top right) Prolific as both a singer and songwriter – she wrote the last three verses of her famous version of Little Willie John's "Fever" – Peggy Lee had hits in the 1940s, 1950s and 1960s. *Dream Street* was a collection issued by Decca in 1957 after she left for a second stint at the Capitol label. (Bottom left) One of the rarest of the early Blue Note 10-inch LPs is this trio album recorded by Wade Legge; it's his only known recording as a leader. (Bottom right) *The Blues Piano Artistry of Meade Lux Lewis* is just that – it's only him, one of the great boogie-woogie pianists, without any other instruments. These were new recordings, some of the last he would make before his death in 1964.

Number	Title	Yr	VG	VG+	NM
❏ RS-314 [S]	Jazz Portrait of Jack LaForge	196?	6.25	12.50	25.00
❏ R-319 [M]	Goldfinger	1965	5.00	10.00	20.00
❏ RS-319 [S]	Goldfinger	1965	6.25	12.50	25.00
❏ R-327 [M]	Our Crazy Affair	196?	5.00	10.00	20.00
❏ RS-327 [S]	Our Crazy Affair	196?	6.25	12.50	25.00
❏ R-716 [M]	Hawaii and I	196?	5.00	10.00	20.00
❏ RS-716 [S]	Hawaii and I	196?	6.25	12.50	25.00

LAGGERS, MAX, AND THE STOMPERS
GHB

Number	Title	Yr	VG	VG+	NM
❏ GHB-157	In the New Orleans Tradition	198?	2.50	5.00	10.00

LAGRENE, BIRELI
Guitarist.
ANTILLES

Number	Title	Yr	VG	VG+	NM
❏ AN-1002	Routes to Django	1981	3.00	6.00	12.00
❏ AN-1009	15	198?	2.50	5.00	10.00

BLUE NOTE

Number	Title	Yr	VG	VG+	NM
❏ BT-48016	Inferno	1987	2.50	5.00	10.00
❏ B1-90967	Foreign Affairs	1988	2.50	5.00	10.00

LAHM, DAVID
Pianist.
PALO ALTO

Number	Title	Yr	VG	VG+	NM
❏ PA-8027	Real Jazz for Folks Who Feel Jazz	198?	3.00	6.00	12.00

PLUG

Number	Title	Yr	VG	VG+	NM
❏ PLUG-7	The Highest Standards	1986	2.50	5.00	10.00

LAINE, CLEO
Female singer.
BUDDAH

Number	Title	Yr	VG	VG+	NM
❏ BDS-5607	Day by Day	1972	3.75	7.50	15.00

CBS

Number	Title	Yr	VG	VG+	NM
❏ FM 39211	Let the Music Take You	1984	2.50	5.00	10.00
❏ FM 39736	That Old Feeling	1985	2.50	5.00	10.00

DRG

Number	Title	Yr	VG	VG+	NM
❏ MRS-502	Cleo Lane with John Dankworth's Orchestra	198?	2.50	5.00	10.00
❏ MR2S-608 [(2)]	An Evening with Cleo Lane and the John Dankworth Quartet	198?	3.00	6.00	12.00
❏ DARC2-2101	Cleo at Carnegie: The 10th Anniversary Concert	198?	3.00	6.00	12.00
❏ SL-5198	One More Day	198?	2.50	5.00	10.00

FONTANA

Number	Title	Yr	VG	VG+	NM
❏ MGF-27531 [M]	Shakespeare and All That Jazz	1966	3.75	7.50	15.00
❏ MGF-27552 [M]	Woman to Woman	1967	5.00	10.00	20.00
❏ SRF-67531 [S]	Shakespeare and All That Jazz	1966	5.00	10.00	20.00
❏ SRF-67552 [S]	Woman to Woman	1967	3.75	7.50	15.00

GNP CRESCENDO

Number	Title	Yr	VG	VG+	NM
❏ GNPS-9024	Cleo's Choice	197?	2.50	5.00	10.00

JAZZ MAN

Number	Title	Yr	VG	VG+	NM
❏ 5033	Live at Wavendon Festival	198?	2.50	5.00	10.00

RCA

Number	Title	Yr	VG	VG+	NM
❏ 7702-1-R	Cleo Sings Sondheim	1988	2.50	5.00	10.00

RCA VICTOR

Number	Title	Yr	VG	VG+	NM
❏ AFL1-1937	Best Friends	1978	2.50	5.00	10.00
-- Reissue with new prefix					
❏ APL1-1937	Best Friends	1976	3.00	6.00	12.00
❏ AFL1-2407	Return to Carnegie Hall	1978	2.50	5.00	10.00
-- Reissue with new prefix					
❏ APL1-2407	Return to Carnegie Hall	1977	3.00	6.00	12.00
❏ AFL1-2926	Gonna Get Through	1978	2.50	5.00	10.00
❏ AYL1-3751	Live at Carnegie Hall	1980	2.00	4.00	8.00
-- Budget-line reissue					
❏ AYL1-3805	A Beautiful Thing	1980	2.00	4.00	8.00
-- Budget-line reissue					
❏ AFL1-5000	I Am a Song	1978	2.50	5.00	10.00
-- Reissue with new prefix					
❏ LPL1-5000	I Am a Song	1973	3.75	7.50	15.00
❏ AFL1-5015	Live at Carnegie Hall	1978	2.50	5.00	10.00
-- Reissue with new prefix					
❏ LPL1-5015	Live at Carnegie Hall	1973	3.75	7.50	15.00
❏ AFL1-5059	A Beautiful Thing	1978	2.50	5.00	10.00
-- Reissue with new prefix					
❏ CPL1-5059	A Beautiful Thing	1974	3.75	7.50	15.00
❏ AFL1-5113	Born Friday	1978	2.50	5.00	10.00
-- Reissue with new prefix					
❏ LPL1-5113	Born Friday	197?	3.00	6.00	12.00

STANYAN

Number	Title	Yr	VG	VG+	NM
❏ 10067	Day by Day	197?	3.00	6.00	12.00
❏ 10122	Easy Livin'	197?	3.00	6.00	12.00

LAINE, CLEO, AND JAMES GALWAY
Galway is a mostly classical flutist whose solo work is outside the scope of this book.
RCA RED SEAL

Number	Title	Yr	VG	VG+	NM
❏ ARL1-3628	Sometimes When We Touch	198?	2.50	5.00	10.00

LAINE, CLEO, AND DUDLEY MOORE
Also see each artist's individual listings.
FINESSE

Number	Title	Yr	VG	VG+	NM
❏ FW 38091	Smilin' Through	1983	3.00	6.00	12.00

LAINE, FRANKIE
Mostly a male pop singer, Laine made some forays into jazzy music as listed below.
COLUMBIA

Number	Title	Yr	VG	VG+	NM
❏ CL 808 [M]	Jazz Spectacular	1956	7.50	15.00	30.00
❏ CL 12?? [M]	Reunion in Rhythm	1959	5.00	10.00	20.00
❏ CS 8087 [S]	Reunion in Rhythm	1959	7.50	15.00	30.00

HINDSIGHT

Number	Title	Yr	VG	VG+	NM
❏ HSR-216	Frankie Laine with Carl Fischer and His Orchestra, 1947	1985	2.50	5.00	10.00

LAIRD, RICK
Bass player.
TIMELESS

Number	Title	Yr	VG	VG+	NM
❏ 308	Soft Focus	197?	3.00	6.00	12.00

LAKE, OLIVER
Saxophone player. Also see WORLD SAXOPHONE QUARTET.
ARISTA/FREEDOM

Number	Title	Yr	VG	VG+	NM
❏ AF 1008	Heavy Spirits	1975	3.75	7.50	15.00
❏ AF 1024	Ntu	1976	3.75	7.50	15.00

ARISTA/NOVUS

Number	Title	Yr	VG	VG+	NM
❏ AN 3003	Life Dance Of Is	1978	3.00	6.00	12.00
❏ AN 3010	Focus	1977	3.00	6.00	12.00

BLACK SAINT

Number	Title	Yr	VG	VG+	NM
❏ BSR-0044	Prophet	198?	3.00	6.00	12.00
❏ BSR-0054	Clevont Fitzhubert	198?	3.00	6.00	12.00

GRAMAVISION

Number	Title	Yr	VG	VG+	NM
❏ 8106	Oliver Lake & Jump Up	198?	2.50	5.00	10.00
❏ 8206	Plug It	198?	2.50	5.00	10.00

LALA, MIKE
GHB

Number	Title	Yr	VG	VG+	NM
❏ GHB-120	Mike Lala and His Dixie Six	198?	2.50	5.00	10.00

LAMARCH, SUSAN
STOMP OFF

Number	Title	Yr	VG	VG+	NM
❏ SOS-1032	Vamp 'Til Ready	198?	2.50	5.00	10.00

LAMB, JOSEPH
Pianist.
FOLKWAYS

Number	Title	Yr	VG	VG+	NM
❏ FJ-3562 [M]	Classic Ragtime	1960	5.00	10.00	20.00

LAMB, NATALIE, AND SAMMY PRICE
Lamb is a female singer. Also see SAMMY PRICE.
GHB

Number	Title	Yr	VG	VG+	NM
❏ GHB-84	Natalie Lamb and Sammy Price and the Blues	198?	2.50	5.00	10.00

LAMBERT, DAVE
Male singer. Also see LAMBERT, HENDRICKS AND BAVAN; LAMBERT, HENDRICKS AND ROSS.
UNITED ARTISTS

Number	Title	Yr	VG	VG+	NM
❏ UAL-3084 [M]	Dave Lambert Sings and Swings Alone	1959	10.00	20.00	40.00
❏ UAS-6084 [S]	Dave Lambert Sings and Swings Alone	1959	12.50	25.00	50.00

LAMBERT, DONALD
Pianist.
JAZZOLOGY

Number	Title	Yr	VG	VG+	NM
❏ JCE-59	Giant Stride	197?	2.50	5.00	10.00

LAMBERT, HENDRICKS AND BAVAN
Successor vocal trio to LAMBERT, HENDRICKS AND ROSS consisting of DAVE LAMBERT; JON HENDRICKS; Yolanda Bavan.
BLUEBIRD

Number	Title	Yr	VG	VG+	NM
❏ 6282-1-RB	Swingin' Til the Girls Come Home	1987	2.50	5.00	10.00

Number	Title	Yr	VG	VG+	NM
RCA VICTOR					
❏ LPM-2635 [M]	Live at Basin Street East	1963	7.50	15.00	30.00
❏ LSP-2635 [S]	Live at Basin Street East	1963	10.00	20.00	40.00
❏ LPM-2747 [M]	Lambert, Hendricks and Bavan at Newport	1963	7.50	15.00	30.00
❏ LSP-2747 [S]	Lambert, Hendricks and Bavan at Newport	1963	10.00	20.00	40.00
❏ LPM-2861 [M]	Lambert, Hendricks and Bavan at the Village Gate	1964	7.50	15.00	30.00
❏ LSP-2861 [S]	Lambert, Hendricks and Bavan at the Village Gate	1964	10.00	20.00	40.00

LAMBERT, HENDRICKS AND ROSS
Vocal trio: DAVE LAMBERT; JON HENDRICKS; ANNIE ROSS.

Number	Title	Yr	VG	VG+	NM
ABC IMPULSE!					
❏ AS-83 [S]	Sing a Song of Basie	1968	3.75	7.50	15.00
ABC-PARAMOUNT					
❏ ABC-223 [M]	Sing a Song of Basie	1958	12.50	25.00	50.00
❏ ABCS-223 [S]	Sing a Song of Basie	1958	12.50	25.00	50.00
COLUMBIA					
❏ CL 1403 [M]	The Hottest New Group in Jazz	1959	7.50	15.00	30.00
-- Black and red label with six "eye" logos					
❏ CL 1403 [M]	The Hottest New Group in Jazz	1963	3.75	7.50	15.00
-- Red label with "Guaranteed High Fidelity" or "360 Sound Mono" at bottom					
❏ CL 1510 [M]	Lambert, Hendricks and Ross Sing Ellington	1960	7.50	15.00	30.00
-- Black and red label with six "eye" logos					
❏ CL 1510 [M]	Lambert, Hendricks and Ross Sing Ellington	1963	3.75	7.50	15.00
-- Red label with "Guaranteed High Fidelity" or "360 Sound Mono" at bottom					
❏ CL 1675 [M]	High Flying	1961	7.50	15.00	30.00
-- Black and red label with six "eye" logos					
❏ CL 1675 [M]	High Flying	1963	3.75	7.50	15.00
-- Red label with "Guaranteed High Fidelity" or "360 Sound Mono" at bottom					
❏ CS 8198 [S]	The Hottest New Group in Jazz	1959	10.00	20.00	40.00
-- Black and red label with six "eye" logos					
❏ CS 8198 [S]	The Hottest New Group in Jazz	1963	5.00	10.00	20.00
-- Red label with "360 Sound Stereo" at bottom					
❏ CS 8310 [S]	Lambert, Hendricks and Ross Sing Ellington	1960	10.00	20.00	40.00
-- Black and red label with six "eye" logos					
❏ CS 8310 [S]	Lambert, Hendricks and Ross Sing Ellington	1963	5.00	10.00	20.00
-- Red label with "360 Sound Stereo" at bottom					
❏ CS 8475 [S]	High Flying	1961	10.00	20.00	40.00
-- Black and red label with six "eye" logos					
❏ CS 8475 [S]	High Flying	1963	5.00	10.00	20.00
-- Red label with "360 Sound Stereo" at bottom					
❏ C 32911	The Best of Lambert, Hendricks and Ross	197?	2.50	5.00	10.00
-- First reissue with new prefix					
❏ KC 32911	The Best of Lambert, Hendricks and Ross	1973	3.75	7.50	15.00
-- Original edition					
❏ PC 32911	The Best of Lambert, Hendricks and Ross	198?	2.00	4.00	8.00
-- Second reissue with new prefix and bar code					
COLUMBIA JAZZ ODYSSEY					
❏ PC 37020	Lambert, Hendricks and Ross with the Ike Isaacs Trio	1983	2.50	5.00	10.00
IMPULSE!					
❏ A-83 [M]	Sing a Song of Basie	1965	6.25	12.50	25.00
-- Reissue of ABC-Paramount ABC-223					
❏ AS-83 [S]	Sing a Song of Basie	1965	7.50	15.00	30.00
-- Reissue of ABC-Paramount ABCS-223					
MCA					
❏ 29049	Sing a Song of Basie	1980	2.00	4.00	8.00
ODYSSEY					
❏ 32-16-0292	Way-Out Voices	1968	3.75	7.50	15.00
ROULETTE					
❏ R-52018 [M]	Sing Along with Basie	1959	10.00	20.00	40.00
❏ SR-52018 [S]	Sing Along with Basie	1959	12.50	25.00	50.00
WORLD PACIFIC					
❏ ST-1025 [S]	The Swingers!	1959	12.50	25.00	50.00
❏ WP-1264 [M]	The Swingers!	1959	10.00	20.00	40.00

LAMBSON, ROGER
Saxophone player.

Number	Title	Yr	VG	VG+	NM
SEA BREEZE					
❏ SB-2035	Dreams of Mexico	198?	2.50	5.00	10.00

LAMOND, DON
Drummer.

Number	Title	Yr	VG	VG+	NM
COMMAND					
❏ RS 33-842	Off Beat Percussion	1962	3.75	7.50	15.00
❏ RS 842 SD	Off Beat Percussion	1962	5.00	10.00	20.00
PROGRESSIVE					
❏ PRO-7067	Extraordinary	198?	2.50	5.00	10.00

LANCASTER, BYARD
Alto and soprano saxophone player, flutist and bass clarinetist.

Number	Title	Yr	VG	VG+	NM
VORTEX					
❏ 2003	It's Not Up to Us	1968	7.50	15.00	30.00

LAND, HAROLD
Tenor saxophone player. Also see RED MITCHELL.

Number	Title	Yr	VG	VG+	NM
BLUE NOTE					
❏ LT-1057	Take Aim	1980	2.50	5.00	10.00
CADET					
❏ LPS-813	The Peace-Maker	1968	3.75	7.50	15.00
CONTEMPORARY					
❏ C-3550 [M]	Harold in the Land of Hi-Fi	1958	20.00	40.00	80.00
❏ M-3550 [M]	Grooveyard	1959	15.00	30.00	60.00
-- Reissue with new title					
❏ M-3619 [M]	The Fox	1965	5.00	10.00	20.00
❏ S-7550 [S]	Grooveyard	1959	12.50	25.00	50.00
❏ S-7619 [S]	The Fox	1965	6.25	12.50	25.00
FANTASY					
❏ OJC-146	West Coast Blues!	198?	2.50	5.00	10.00
❏ OJC-162	In the Land of Jazz	198?	2.50	5.00	10.00
❏ OJC-343	The Fox	198?	2.50	5.00	10.00
❏ OJC-493	Eastward Ho! Harold Land in New York	1991	3.00	6.00	12.00
HIFI					
❏ J-612 [M]	The Fox	1960	15.00	30.00	60.00
❏ SJ-612 [S]	The Fox	1960	20.00	40.00	80.00
IMPERIAL					
❏ LP-12247 [S]	Jazz Impressions of Folk Music	1963	7.50	15.00	30.00
❏ LP-9247 [M]	Jazz Impressions of Folk Music	1963	6.25	12.50	25.00
JAZZLAND					
❏ JLP-20 [M]	West Coast Blues!	1960	10.00	20.00	40.00
❏ JLP-33 [M]	Eastward Ho! Harold Land in New York	1961	10.00	20.00	40.00
❏ JLP-920 [S]	West Coast Blues!	1960	12.50	25.00	50.00
❏ JLP-933 [S]	Eastward Ho! Harold Land in New York	1961	12.50	25.00	50.00
MAINSTREAM					
❏ MRL-314	New Shade of Blue	1971	3.75	7.50	15.00
❏ MRL-344	Choma (Burn)	1972	3.75	7.50	15.00
❏ MRL-367	Damisi	1973	3.75	7.50	15.00
MUSE					
❏ MR-5272	Xocia's Dance	198?	2.50	5.00	10.00

LAND, HAROLD, AND BLUE MITCHELL
Also see each artist's individual listings.

Number	Title	Yr	VG	VG+	NM
CONCORD JAZZ					
❏ CJ-44	Mapenzi	1977	3.00	6.00	12.00

LANDE, ART
Pianist.

Number	Title	Yr	VG	VG+	NM
ECM					
❏ 1081	Rubisa Patrol	197?	3.75	7.50	15.00
❏ 1106	Desert	197?	3.75	7.50	15.00
1750 ARCH					
❏ 1769	The Eccentricities of Earl Dant	1978	3.75	7.50	15.00
❏ 1778	The Story of Ba-Ku	1979	3.75	7.50	15.00

LANDE, ART, AND JAN GARBAREK
Also see each artist's individual listings.

Number	Title	Yr	VG	VG+	NM
ECM					
❏ 1038	Red Lanta	197?	3.75	7.50	15.00

LANDE, ART; DAVE SAMUELS; PAUL McCANDLESS
Also see each artist's individual listings.

Number	Title	Yr	VG	VG+	NM
ECM					
❏ 1208	Skylight	1982	3.00	6.00	12.00

LANE, STEVE, AND THE SOUTHERN STOMPERS
Lane is a cornet player and bandleader.

Number	Title	Yr	VG	VG+	NM
STOMP OFF					
❏ SOS-1040	Snake Rag	198?	2.50	5.00	10.00

LANG, EDDIE
Guitarist, considered the first jazz guitar virtuoso.

Number	Title	Yr	VG	VG+	NM
YAZOO					
❏ 1059	Virtuoso	198?	2.50	5.00	10.00

Number	Title	Yr	VG	VG+	NM

LANG, RONNIE
Alto saxophone player.
TOPS
| ❑ L-1521 [M] | Modern Jazz | 1958 | 6.25 | 12.50 | 25.00 |

LANGDON, JIM
CUCA
| ❑ 1100 [M] | Jim Langdon Trio | 1965 | 5.00 | 10.00 | 20.00 |

LANGFORD, BILL
Organist.
FANTASY
| ❑ 8396 | Gangbusters and Lollipops | 197? | 2.50 | 5.00 | 10.00 |

LaPORTA, JOHN
Clarinetist.
DEBUT
| ❑ DLP-10 [10] | The John LaPorta Quintet | 1954 | 50.00 | 100.00 | 200.00 |
| ❑ DEB-122 [M] | Three Moods | 1955 | 37.50 | 75.00 | 150.00 |
EVEREST
| ❑ SDBR-1037 [S] | The Most Minor | 1959 | 10.00 | 20.00 | 40.00 |
| ❑ LPBR-5037 [M] | The Most Minor | 1959 | 7.50 | 15.00 | 30.00 |
FANTASY
❑ 3228 [M]	Conceptions	1956	15.00	30.00	60.00
-- Red vinyl					
❑ 3228 [M]	Conceptions	1956	7.50	15.00	30.00
-- Black vinyl					
❑ 3237 [M]	South American Brothers	1956	15.00	30.00	60.00
-- Red vinyl					
❑ 3237 [M]	South American Brothers	1956	7.50	15.00	30.00
-- Black vinyl					
❑ 3248 [M]	The Clarinet Artistry of John LaPorta	1957	15.00	30.00	60.00
-- Red vinyl					
❑ 3248 [M]	The Clarinet Artistry of John LaPorta	1957	7.50	15.00	30.00
-- Black vinyl					
MUSIC MINUS ONE
| ❑ 4003 [M] | Eight Men In Search of a Drummer | 1961 | 6.25 | 12.50 | 25.00 |

LARKIN, BILLY
Pianist. Also see THE DELEGATES.
WORLD PACIFIC
❑ WP-1837 [M]	Hole in the Wall	1966	5.00	10.00	20.00
❑ WP-1843 [M]	Ain't That a Groove	1966	5.00	10.00	20.00
❑ WP-1850 [M]	Hold On	1967	5.00	10.00	20.00
❑ WPS-21837 [S]	Hole in the Wall	1966	6.25	12.50	25.00
❑ WPS-21843 [S]	Ain't That a Groove	1966	6.25	12.50	25.00
❑ WPS-21850 [S]	Hold On	1967	6.25	12.50	25.00

LARKINS, ELLIS
Pianist. Also see RUBY BRAFF.
ANTILLES
| ❑ DGTL-101 | Ellis Larkins | 198? | 3.75 | 7.50 | 15.00 |
CLASSIC JAZZ
| ❑ 145 | Smooth One | 1977 | 3.00 | 6.00 | 12.00 |
DECCA
❑ DL 5391 [10]	Blues in the Night	1952	12.50	25.00	50.00
❑ DL 8303 [M]	Manhattan at Midnight	1956	10.00	20.00	40.00
❑ DL 9205 [M]	The Soft Touch	1958	7.50	15.00	30.00
❑ DL 9211 [M]	Blue and Sentimental	1958	7.50	15.00	30.00
❑ DL 79205 [S]	The Soft Touch	1958	6.25	12.50	25.00
❑ DL 79211 [S]	Blue and Sentimental	1958	6.25	12.50	25.00
STANYAN
❑ 10011	Hair	1969	3.00	6.00	12.00
❑ 10024	Lost in the Wood	197?	3.00	6.00	12.00
❑ 10074 [(2)]	Ellis Larkins Plays Bacharach and McKuen	197?	3.75	7.50	15.00
STORYVILLE
| ❑ STLP-316 [10] | Perfume and Rain | 1955 | 20.00 | 40.00 | 80.00 |
| ❑ STLP-913 [M] | Do Nothin' Till You Hear from Me | 1956 | 12.50 | 25.00 | 50.00 |

LARKINS, ELLIS, AND TONY MIDDLETON
Middleton is a male singer. Also see ELLIS LARKINS.
CONCORD JAZZ
| ❑ CJ-134 | Swingin' for Hamp | 1979 | 2.50 | 5.00 | 10.00 |

LARKINS, ELLIS/LEE WILEY
Also see each artist's individual listings.
STORYVILLE
| ❑ STLP-911 [M] | Duologue | 1956 | 15.00 | 30.00 | 60.00 |

LaROCA, PETE
Drummer and composer.
BLUE NOTE
❑ BLP-4205 [M]	Basra	1965	7.50	15.00	30.00
❑ B1-32091	Basra	1995	3.75	7.50	15.00
-- "The Finest in Jazz Since 1939" reissue					
❑ BST-84205 [S]	Basra	1965	10.00	20.00	40.00
-- With "New York, USA" address on label					
❑ BST-84205 [S]	Basra	1967	3.75	7.50	15.00
-- With "A Division of Liberty Records" on label					
DOUGLAS
| ❑ SD 782 | Turkish Woman at the Bath | 1969 | 3.75 | 7.50 | 15.00 |
MUSE
| ❑ MR-5011 | Bliss | 197? | 3.00 | 6.00 | 12.00 |

LaROCCA, NICK
Cornet player. Also see ORIGINAL DIXIELAND JASS (JAZZ) BAND.
SOUTHLAND
| ❑ 230 [M] | Nick LaRocca and His Dixieland Band | 196? | 5.00 | 10.00 | 20.00 |

LARSEN, MORTON G.
Pianist.
STOMP OFF
| ❑ SOS-1009 | Morton G. Larsen Plays Robert Clemente | 198? | 2.50 | 5.00 | 10.00 |

LARSEN, NEIL
Keyboard player.
A&M
❑ SP-3116	Jungle Fever	1980	2.50	5.00	10.00
-- Reissue of Horizon 733					
❑ SP-3117	High Gear	1980	2.50	5.00	10.00
HORIZON
| ❑ SP-733 | Jungle Fever | 1978 | 3.75 | 7.50 | 15.00 |

LASHA, PRINCE
Flutist and composer.
CONTEMPORARY
❑ M-3610 [M]	The Cry	1963	6.25	12.50	25.00
❑ S-7610 [S]	The Cry	1963	7.50	15.00	30.00
❑ S-7617	Firebirds	1968	6.25	12.50	25.00

LASHLEY, BARBARA, AND RAY SKJELBRED
Lashley is a female singer. Also see RAY SKJELBRED.
STOMP OFF
| ❑ SOS-1152 | Sweet and Lowdown | 1988 | 2.50 | 5.00 | 10.00 |

LASK, ULRICH
Saxophone player.
ECM
| ❑ 1217 | Lask | 198? | 3.00 | 6.00 | 12.00 |
| ❑ 1268 | Sucht und Ordnung | 1985 | 3.00 | 6.00 | 12.00 |

LAST EXIT
Members: Peter Brotzmann (reeds); Sonny Sharrock (guitar); BILL LASWELL (bass); RONALD SHANNON JACKSON (drums, vocals).
CELLULOID
| ❑ CELL-8140 | Cassette Recordings '87 | 1988 | 3.00 | 6.00 | 12.00 |
ENEMY
| ❑ 88561-8176-1 | Last Exit | 1986 | 5.00 | 10.00 | 20.00 |
| ❑ 88561-8178-1 | The Noise of Trouble | 1987 | 3.75 | 7.50 | 15.00 |
VENTURE
| ❑ 91015 | Iron Path | 1988 | 3.00 | 6.00 | 12.00 |

LAST POETS, THE
Proto-rap group highly influenced by jazz.
BLUE THUMB
| ❑ BT-39 | Chastisement | 1972 | 7.50 | 15.00 | 30.00 |
| ❑ BT-52 | At Last | 1973 | 7.50 | 15.00 | 30.00 |
CASABLANCA
| ❑ NBLP 7051 | Delights of the Garden | 1977 | 6.25 | 12.50 | 25.00 |
CELLULOID
| ❑ 6101 | The Last Poets | 198? | 2.50 | 5.00 | 10.00 |
| ❑ 6105 | This Is Madness | 198? | 2.50 | 5.00 | 10.00 |

Number	Title	Yr	VG	VG+	NM	Number	Title	Yr	VG	VG+	NM
❑ 6108	Oh My People	198?	2.50	5.00	10.00	❑ A-69 [M]	Live at Pep's	1964	6.25	12.50	25.00
❑ 6136	Delights of the Garden	198?	2.50	5.00	10.00	❑ AS-69 [S]	Live at Pep's	1964	7.50	15.00	30.00
COLLECTABLES						❑ A-84 [M]	1984	1965	6.25	12.50	25.00
❑ COL-6500	Right On!	198?	2.50	5.00	10.00	❑ AS-84 [S]	1984	1965	7.50	15.00	30.00
DOUGLAS						❑ A-92 [M]	Psychicemotus	1966	6.25	12.50	25.00
❑ 3	The Last Poets	1970	12.50	25.00	50.00	❑ AS-92 [S]	Psychicemotus	1966	7.50	15.00	30.00
❑ Z 30583	This Is Madness	1971	12.50	25.00	50.00	❑ A-9117 [M]	A Flat, G Flat and C	1966	6.25	12.50	25.00
❑ Z 30811	The Last Poets	1971	10.00	20.00	40.00	❑ AS-9117 [S]	A Flat, G Flat and C	1966	7.50	15.00	30.00
JUGGERNAUT						❑ A-9125 [M]	The Golden Flute	1966	6.25	12.50	25.00
❑ 8802	Right On!	1971	12.50	25.00	50.00	❑ AS-9125 [S]	The Golden Flute	1966	7.50	15.00	30.00
-- As "The Original Last Poets"						**LANDMARK**					
						❑ LLP-502	Yusef Lateef in Nigeria	1985	2.50	5.00	10.00
LASWELL, BILL						**MCA**					
Bass player. Also see LAST EXIT.						❑ 4146 [(2)]	Live Session	198?	3.00	6.00	12.00
ELEKTRA/MUSICIAN						**MILESTONE**					
❑ 60221	Basslines	1984	2.50	5.00	10.00	❑ 47009 [(2)]	The Many Faces of Yusef Lateef	1973	3.75	7.50	15.00
VENTURE						**MOODSVILLE**					
❑ 90888	Hear No Evil	1988	2.50	5.00	10.00	❑ MVLP-22 [M]	Eastern Sounds	1961	10.00	20.00	40.00
						-- Green label, silver print					
LASWELL, BILL, AND PETER BROTZMANN						❑ MVST-22 [S]	Eastern Sounds	1961	12.50	25.00	50.00
One-half of LAST EXIT. Also see BILL LASWELL.						-- Green label, silver print					
CELLULOID						**NEW JAZZ**					
❑ CELL-5016	Low Life	198?	3.00	6.00	12.00	❑ NJLP-8218 [M]	Other Sounds	1959	12.50	25.00	50.00
						-- Purple label					
LATARSKI, DON						❑ NJLP-8218 [M]	Other Sounds	1965	6.25	12.50	25.00
Guitarist.						-- Blue label, trident logo at right					
INNER CITY						❑ NJLP-8234 [M]	Cry! Tender	1960	12.50	25.00	50.00
❑ IC-1114	Haven	198?	3.00	6.00	12.00	-- Purple label					
PAUSA						❑ NJLP-8234 [M]	Cry! Tender	1965	6.25	12.50	25.00
❑ 7146	Lifeline	1983	2.50	5.00	10.00	-- Blue label, trident logo at right					
						❑ NJLP-8261 [M]	The Sounds of Yusef	1961	12.50	25.00	50.00
LATEEF, YUSEF						-- Reissue of Prestige 7122; purple label					
Flutist, tenor saxophone player, oboist, occasional bassoonist and player of more exotic reed instruments as well.						❑ NJLP-8261 [M]	The Sounds of Yusef	1965	6.25	12.50	25.00
ABC IMPULSE!						-- Blue label, trident logo at right					
❑ AS-56 [S]	Jazz Around the World	1968	3.00	6.00	12.00	❑ NJLP-8272 [M]	Into Something	1962	12.50	25.00	50.00
❑ AS-69 [S]	Live at Pep's	1968	3.00	6.00	12.00	-- Purple label					
❑ AS-84 [S]	1984	1968	3.00	6.00	12.00	❑ NJLP-8272 [M]	Into Something	1965	6.25	12.50	25.00
❑ AS-92 [S]	Psychicemotus	1968	3.00	6.00	12.00	-- Blue label, trident logo at right					
❑ AS-9117 [S]	A Flat, G Flat and C	1968	3.00	6.00	12.00	**PRESTIGE**					
❑ AS-9125 [S]	The Golden Flute	1968	3.00	6.00	12.00	❑ PRLP-7122 [M]	The Sounds of Yusef	1957	25.00	50.00	100.00
❑ AS-9259 [(2)]	Re-evaluations: The Impulse Years	1974	3.75	7.50	15.00	-- Yellow label					
❑ AS-9310	Club Date	197?	3.00	6.00	12.00	❑ PRLP-7319 [M]	Eastern Sounds	1964	6.25	12.50	25.00
❑ IA-9353 [(2)]	Yusef Lateef Live!	1978	3.75	7.50	15.00	❑ PRLP-7398 [M]	The Sounds of Yusef Lateef	1966	5.00	10.00	20.00
ARCHIVE OF FOLK AND JAZZ						❑ PRLP-7447 [M]	Yusef Lateef Plays for Lovers	1967	6.25	12.50	25.00
❑ 285	Yusef Lateef	197?	2.50	5.00	10.00	❑ PRST-7319 [S]	Eastern Sounds	1964	6.25	12.50	25.00
ARGO						-- Reissue of Moodsville 22					
❑ LP-634 [M]	Live at Cranbrook	1959	7.50	15.00	30.00	❑ PRST-7398 [S]	The Sounds of Yusef Lateef	1966	6.25	12.50	25.00
ATLANTIC						❑ PRST-7447 [S]	Yusef Lateef Plays for Lovers	1967	5.00	10.00	20.00
❑ SD 2-1000 [(2)]	10 Years	1977	3.75	7.50	15.00	❑ PRST-7637	Into Something	1966	3.75	7.50	15.00
❑ SD 1499	The Complete Lateef	1968	3.75	7.50	15.00	❑ PRST-7653	Expressions	1969	3.75	7.50	15.00
❑ SD 1508	The Blue Lateef	1969	3.75	7.50	15.00	❑ PRST-7748	Cry! Tender	1970	3.75	7.50	15.00
❑ SD 1525	Yusef Lateef's Detroit	1969	3.75	7.50	15.00	❑ PRST-7832	Imagination	1971	3.75	7.50	15.00
❑ SD 1548	The Diverse Lateef	1971	3.75	7.50	15.00	❑ 24007 [(2)]	Yusef Lateef	1972	3.75	7.50	15.00
❑ SD 1563	Suite 16	1970	3.75	7.50	15.00	❑ 24035 [(2)]	Blues for the Orient	1974	3.75	7.50	15.00
❑ SD 1591	The Best of Yusef Lateef	1971	3.75	7.50	15.00	❑ 24105 [(2)]	Yusef's Bag	197?	3.75	7.50	15.00
❑ SD 1602	Gentle Giant	1972	3.00	6.00	12.00	**RIVERSIDE**					
❑ SD 1635	Hush 'n' Thunder	1973	3.00	6.00	12.00	❑ RLP-12-325 [M]	Three Faces of Yusef Lateef	1960	10.00	20.00	40.00
❑ SD 1650	Part of the Search	1974	3.00	6.00	12.00	❑ RLP-337 [M]	The Centaur and the Phoenix	1960	10.00	20.00	40.00
❑ SD 1685	The Doctor Is In... And Out	1976	3.00	6.00	12.00	❑ RLP-1176 [S]	Three Faces of Yusef Lateef	1960	10.00	20.00	40.00
❑ 81663	Concerto for Yusef Lateef	1988	2.50	5.00	10.00	❑ RS-3011	This Is Yusef Lateef	1968	3.75	7.50	15.00
CADET						❑ RLP-9337 [S]	The Centaur and the Phoenix	1960	10.00	20.00	40.00
❑ LP-634 [M]	Live at Cranbrook	1966	3.75	7.50	15.00	**SAVOY**					
❑ LPS-816	Live at Cranbrook	1969	3.00	6.00	12.00	❑ MG-12103 [M]	Jazz Mood	1957	12.50	25.00	50.00
CHARLIE PARKER						❑ MG-12109 [M]	Jazz for the Thinker	1957	12.50	25.00	50.00
❑ PLP-814 [M]	Lost in Sound	1962	6.25	12.50	25.00	❑ MG-12117 [M]	Prayer to the East	1957	12.50	25.00	50.00
❑ PLP-814S [S]	Lost in Sound	1962	7.50	15.00	30.00	❑ MG-12120 [M]	Jazz and the Sounds of Nature	1958	12.50	25.00	50.00
CTI						❑ MG-12139 [M]	The Dreamer	1958	12.50	25.00	50.00
❑ 7082	Autophysiopsychic	1978	3.00	6.00	12.00	❑ MG-12140 [M]	The Fabric of Jazz	1958	12.50	25.00	50.00
❑ 7088	In a Temple Garden	1979	3.00	6.00	12.00	❑ SR-13007 [S]	The Dreamer	1959	12.50	25.00	50.00
DELMARK						❑ SR-13008 [S]	The Fabric of Jazz	1959	12.50	25.00	50.00
❑ DL-407 [M]	Yusef!	1965	5.00	10.00	20.00	**SAVOY JAZZ**					
❑ DS-407 [S]	Yusef!	1965	6.25	12.50	25.00	❑ SJL-2205	Morning	1976	3.00	6.00	12.00
FANTASY						❑ SJL-2226	Gong!	197?	3.00	6.00	12.00
❑ OJC-399	Other Sounds	1989	2.50	5.00	10.00	❑ SJL-2238 [(2)]	Angel Eyes	1979	3.75	7.50	15.00
❑ OJC-482	Cry! Tender	1991	3.00	6.00	12.00	**TRIP**					
❑ OJC-612	Eastern Sounds	1991	3.00	6.00	12.00	❑ 5018	Outside Blues	1973	2.50	5.00	10.00
IMPULSE!						**VERVE**					
❑ A-56 [M]	Jazz Around the World	1963	6.25	12.50	25.00	❑ MGV-8217 [M]	Before Dawn	1958	25.00	50.00	100.00
❑ AS-56 [S]	Jazz Around the World	1963	7.50	15.00	30.00	❑ V-8217 [M]	Before Dawn	1961	6.25	12.50	25.00
						LATIN ALL-STARS, THE					
						CROWN					
						❑ CLP 5159 [M]	Jazz Heat-Bongo Beat	1959	6.25	12.50	25.00

Number	Title	Yr	VG	VG+	NM

LATIN JAZZ QUINTET, THE
Members: Charles Simons (vibraphone); Gene Casey (piano); Bill Ellington (bass); Manuel Ramos (drums, timbales); Juan Amalbert (congas).

NEW JAZZ
Number	Title	Yr	VG	VG+	NM
❏ NJLP-8251 [M]	Caribe	1960	12.50	25.00	50.00
-- Purple label					
❏ NJLP-8251 [M]	Caribe	1965	6.25	12.50	25.00
-- Blue label, trident logo at right					
❏ NJLP-8321 [M]	Latin Soul	1963	---	---	---
-- Reassigned to Status					

STATUS
| ❏ ST-8321 [M] | Latin Soul | 1965 | 10.00 | 20.00 | 40.00 |

TRIP
| ❏ 8008 | Oh! Pharaoh Speak | 197? | 3.00 | 6.00 | 12.00 |

TRU-SOUND
| ❏ TRU-15003 [M] | Hot Sauce | 1962 | 10.00 | 20.00 | 40.00 |
| ❏ TRU-15012 [M] | The Latin Jazz Quintet | 1962 | 10.00 | 20.00 | 40.00 |

UNITED ARTISTS
| ❏ UAL-4071 [M] | The Latin Jazz Quintet | 1960 | 7.50 | 15.00 | 30.00 |
| ❏ UAS-5071 [S] | The Latin Jazz Quintet | 1960 | 10.00 | 20.00 | 40.00 |

LAUER, CHRISTOF
Tenor saxophone player.
CMP
| ❏ CMP-39-ST | Christof Lauer | 1990 | 3.00 | 6.00 | 12.00 |

LAURENCE, BABY
Tap dancer. Laurence dances to the music of a jazz band on the below LP.
CLASSIC JAZZ
| ❏ 30 | Dancemaster | 197? | 2.50 | 5.00 | 10.00 |

LAVERNE, ANDY
Pianist.
STEEPLECHASE
| ❏ SCS-1086 | Another World | 198? | 3.00 | 6.00 | 12.00 |

LAVITZ, T.
Piano and keyboard player. Member of The Dixie Dregs (not included in this book).
INTIMA
| ❏ D1-73512 | T. Lavitz and the Bad Habits | 1989 | 3.00 | 6.00 | 12.00 |

LAWRENCE, ARNIE
Alto saxophone (and other reed instruments) player.
DOCTOR JAZZ
| ❏ FW 38445 | Arnie Lawrence and Treasure Island | 1983 | 2.50 | 5.00 | 10.00 |

EMBRYO
| ❏ SD 525 | Inside an Hour Glass | 1970 | 5.00 | 10.00 | 20.00 |

PROJECT 3
| ❏ PR-5011 | You're Gonna Hear from Me | 1967 | 5.00 | 10.00 | 20.00 |
| ❏ PR-5028 | Look Toward a Dream | 1968 | 5.00 | 10.00 | 20.00 |

LAWRENCE, AZAR
Alto saxophone player.
PRESTIGE
❏ 10086	Bridge Into a New Age	1973	3.75	7.50	15.00
❏ 10097	Summer Solstice	1975	3.75	7.50	15.00
❏ 10099	People Moving	1976	3.75	7.50	15.00

LAWRENCE, ELLIOT
Pianist, bandleader and composer.
DECCA
| ❏ DL 5274 [10] | College Prom | 1950 | 12.50 | 25.00 | 50.00 |
| ❏ DL 5353 [10] | Moonlight on the Campus | 1951 | 12.50 | 25.00 | 50.00 |

FANTASY
❏ OJC-117	Elliot Lawrence Plays Gerry Mulligan Arrangements	198?	2.50	5.00	10.00
❏ 3206 [M]	Elliot Lawrence Plays Gerry Mulligan Arrangements	1956	12.50	25.00	50.00
-- Red vinyl					
❏ 3206 [M]	Elliot Lawrence Plays Gerry Mulligan Arrangements	1956	7.50	15.00	30.00
-- Black vinyl, red label, non-flexible vinyl					
❏ 3206 [M]	Elliot Lawrence Plays Gerry Mulligan Arrangements	196?	5.00	10.00	20.00
-- Black vinyl, red label, flexible vinyl					
❏ 3219 [M]	Elliot Lawrence Plays Tiny Kahn and Johnny Mandel Arrangements	1956	12.50	25.00	50.00
-- Red vinyl					
❏ 3219 [M]	Elliot Lawrence Plays Tiny Kahn and Johnny Mandel Arrangements	1956	7.50	15.00	30.00
-- Black vinyl, red label, non-flexible vinyl					

Number	Title	Yr	VG	VG+	NM
❏ 3219 [M]	Elliot Lawrence Plays Tiny Kahn and Johnny Mandel Arrangements	196?	5.00	10.00	20.00
-- Black vinyl, red label, flexible vinyl					
❏ 3226 [M]	Dream	1956	12.50	25.00	50.00
-- Red vinyl					
❏ 3226 [M]	Dream	1956	7.50	15.00	30.00
-- Black vinyl, red label, non-flexible vinyl					
❏ 3226 [M]	Dream	196?	5.00	10.00	20.00
-- Black vinyl, red label, flexible vinyl					
❏ 3236 [M]	Swinging at the Steel Pier	1956	12.50	25.00	50.00
-- Red vinyl					
❏ 3236 [M]	Swinging at the Steel Pier	1956	7.50	15.00	30.00
-- Black vinyl, red label, non-flexible vinyl					
❏ 3236 [M]	Swinging at the Steel Pier	196?	5.00	10.00	20.00
-- Black vinyl, red label, flexible vinyl					
❏ 3246 [M]	Elliot Lawrence Plays for Swinging Dancers	1957	10.00	20.00	40.00
-- Red vinyl					
❏ 3246 [M]	Elliot Lawrence Plays for Swinging Dancers	1957	6.25	12.50	25.00
-- Black vinyl, red label, non-flexible vinyl					
❏ 3246 [M]	Elliot Lawrence Plays for Swinging Dancers	196?	3.75	7.50	15.00
-- Black vinyl, red label, flexible vinyl					
❏ 3261 [M]	Dream On -- Dance On	1958	10.00	20.00	40.00
-- Red vinyl					
❏ 3261 [M]	Dream On -- Dance On	1958	6.25	12.50	25.00
-- Black vinyl, red label, non-flexible vinyl					
❏ 3261 [M]	Dream On -- Dance On	196?	3.75	7.50	15.00
-- Black vinyl, red label, flexible vinyl					
❏ 3290 [M]	Big Band Sound	1959	10.00	20.00	40.00
-- Red vinyl					
❏ 3290 [M]	Big Band Sound	1959	6.25	12.50	25.00
-- Black vinyl, red label, non-flexible vinyl					
❏ 3290 [M]	Big Band Sound	196?	3.75	7.50	15.00
-- Black vinyl, red label, flexible vinyl					
❏ 8002 [S]	Dream On -- Dance On	196?	7.50	15.00	30.00
-- Blue vinyl					
❏ 8002 [S]	Dream On -- Dance On	196?	5.00	10.00	20.00
-- Black vinyl, blue label, non-flexible vinyl					
❏ 8002 [S]	Dream On -- Dance On	196?	3.00	6.00	12.00
-- Black vinyl, blue label, flexible vinyl					
❏ 8021 [S]	Elliot Lawrence Plays for Swinging Dancers	196?	7.50	15.00	30.00
-- Blue vinyl					
❏ 8021 [S]	Elliot Lawrence Plays for Swinging Dancers	196?	5.00	10.00	20.00
-- Black vinyl, blue label, non-flexible vinyl					
❏ 8021 [S]	Elliot Lawrence Plays for Swinging Dancers	196?	3.00	6.00	12.00
-- Black vinyl, blue label, flexible vinyl					
❏ 8031 [S]	Big Band Sound	196?	7.50	15.00	30.00
-- Blue vinyl					
❏ 8031 [S]	Big Band Sound	196?	5.00	10.00	20.00
-- Black vinyl, blue label, non-flexible vinyl					
❏ 8031 [S]	Big Band Sound	196?	3.00	6.00	12.00
-- Black vinyl, blue label, flexible vinyl					

HINDSIGHT
| ❏ HSR-182 | Elliot Lawrence and His Orchestra 1946 | 198? | 2.50 | 5.00 | 10.00 |

JAZZTONE
| ❏ J-1279 [M] | Big Band Modern | 1958 | 10.00 | 20.00 | 40.00 |

MOBILE FIDELITY
| ❏ 2-229 [(2)] | The Music of Elliot Lawrence | 1995 | 7.50 | 15.00 | 30.00 |
| -- Audiophile vinyl | | | | | |

SESAC
| ❏ N-1153 [M] | Jump Steady | 1960 | 7.50 | 15.00 | 30.00 |
| ❏ SN-1153 [S] | Jump Steady | 1960 | 10.00 | 20.00 | 40.00 |

TOP RANK
| ❏ RM-304 [M] | Music for Trapping (Tender, That Is) | 1959 | 10.00 | 20.00 | 40.00 |

VIK
| ❏ LX-1113 [M] | Jazz Goes Broadway | 1958 | 10.00 | 20.00 | 40.00 |

LAWRENCE, GARY
Pianist and bandleader.
BLUE GOOSE
| ❏ 2020 | Gary Lawrence and His Sizzling Syncopators | 1979 | 2.50 | 5.00 | 10.00 |

LAWRENCE, MIKE
Flugel horn player, trumpeter, bass player and synthesizer player.
OPTIMISM
| ❏ OP-3104 | Nightwind | 198? | 2.50 | 5.00 | 10.00 |

Number	Title	Yr	VG	VG+	NM

LAWRENCE, T.J.
EAGLE
| ❏ SM-4194 | Illuminations | 1985 | 2.50 | 5.00 | 10.00 |

LAWS, HUBERT
Flutist, pianist, saxophone player and composer.
ATLANTIC
❏ 1432 [M]	The Laws of Jazz	1965	3.00	6.00	12.00
❏ SD 1432 [S]	The Laws of Jazz	1965	3.75	7.50	15.00
❏ 1452 [M]	Flute By-Laws	1966	3.00	6.00	12.00
❏ SD 1452 [S]	Flute By-Laws	1966	3.75	7.50	15.00
❏ SD 1509	Laws Cause	1970	3.00	6.00	12.00
❏ SD 1624	Wild Flower	1973	2.50	5.00	10.00
❏ SD 8813	The Laws of Jazz	198?	2.00	4.00	8.00
-- Reissue of 1432					
CBS
| ❏ M 39858 | Blanchard: New Earth | 1985 | 3.00 | 6.00 | 12.00 |
| | Symphony; Telemann: Suite in A; Amazing Grace | | | | |
COLUMBIA
❏ PC 34330	Romeo and Juliet	1976	3.00	6.00	12.00
❏ JC 35022	Say It with Silence	1978	2.50	5.00	10.00
❏ JC 35708	Land of Passion	1979	2.50	5.00	10.00
❏ FC 36365	The Best of Hubert Laws	198?	2.50	5.00	10.00
❏ JC 36396	Family	1980	2.50	5.00	10.00
❏ FC 38850	Make It Last	1983	2.50	5.00	10.00
CTI
❏ CTX-3 + 3 [(2)]	In the Beginning	1974	3.75	7.50	15.00
❏ 1002	Crying Song	1970	5.00	10.00	20.00
❏ 6000	Crying Song	1970	3.00	6.00	12.00
-- Reissue of 1002					
❏ 6006	Afro-Classic	1971	3.00	6.00	12.00
❏ 6012	Rite of Spring	1972	3.00	6.00	12.00
❏ 6022	Morning Star	1972	3.00	6.00	12.00
❏ 6025	Carnegie Hall	1973	3.00	6.00	12.00
❏ 6058	The Chicago Theme	1975	3.00	6.00	12.00
❏ 6065	Then There Was Light, Vol. 1	1976	3.00	6.00	12.00
❏ 6066	Then There Was Light, Vol. 2	1976	3.00	6.00	12.00
❏ 7075	San Francisco	1976	3.00	6.00	12.00
❏ 8015	The Chicago Theme	198?	2.00	4.00	8.00
-- Reissue of 6058					
❏ 8019	Afro-Classic	198?	2.00	4.00	8.00
-- Reissue of 6006					
❏ 8020	Rite of Spring	198?	2.00	4.00	8.00
-- Reissue of 6012					

LAWS, RONNIE
Soprano saxophone player.
BLUE NOTE
❏ BN-LA452-G	Pressure Sensitive	1975	3.00	6.00	12.00
❏ BN-LA628-G	Fever	1976	3.00	6.00	12.00
❏ BN-LA730-H	Friends and Strangers	1977	2.50	5.00	10.00
CAPITOL
| ❏ ST-12261 | Mr. Nice Guy | 1983 | 2.50 | 5.00 | 10.00 |
| ❏ ST-12375 | Classic Masters | 1984 | 2.50 | 5.00 | 10.00 |
COLUMBIA
| ❏ BFC 40089 | Mirror Town | 1986 | 2.50 | 5.00 | 10.00 |
| ❏ FC 40902 | All Day Rhythm | 1987 | 2.50 | 5.00 | 10.00 |
LIBERTY
❏ LO-628	Fever	198?	2.00	4.00	8.00
-- Reissue of Blue Note 628					
❏ LW-730	Friends and Strangers	198?	2.00	4.00	8.00
-- Reissue of Blue Note 730					
❏ LO-881	Flame	198?	2.00	4.00	8.00
-- Reissue of United Artists 881					
❏ LT-1001	Every Generation	1981	2.00	4.00	8.00
-- Reissue of United Artists 1001					
❏ LN-10164	Pressure Sensitive	198?	2.00	4.00	8.00
-- Reissue of Blue Note 452					
❏ LN-10232	Flame	198?	2.00	4.00	8.00
-- Budget-line reissue					
❏ LN-10255	Fever	198?	2.00	4.00	8.00
-- Budget-line reissue					
❏ LN-10307	Solid Ground	1986	2.00	4.00	8.00
-- Budget-line reissue					
❏ LO-51087	Solid Ground	1981	2.50	5.00	10.00
UNITED ARTISTS
| ❏ UA-LA881-H | Flame | 1978 | 2.50 | 5.00 | 10.00 |
| ❏ LT-1001 | Every Generation | 1980 | 2.50 | 5.00 | 10.00 |

LAWSON, DEE
ROULETTE
| ❏ R-52017 [M] | 'Round Midnight | 1958 | 7.50 | 15.00 | 30.00 |
| ❏ SR-52017 [S] | 'Round Midnight | 1958 | 10.00 | 20.00 | 40.00 |

LAWSON, HUGH
Pianist.
SOUL NOTE
| ❏ SN-1052 | Colour | 1983 | 3.00 | 6.00 | 12.00 |
STORYVILLE
| ❏ 4078 | Prime Time | 198? | 2.50 | 5.00 | 10.00 |

LAWSON, JANET
Female singer.
INNER CITY
| ❏ IC-1118 | Janet Lawson Quintet | 1981 | 3.00 | 6.00 | 12.00 |
OMNISOUND
| ❏ 1052 | Dreams Can Be | 1983 | 3.00 | 6.00 | 12.00 |

LAWSON, STELLA
STASH
| ❏ 235 | Goin' For It | 198? | 2.50 | 5.00 | 10.00 |

LAWSON, YANK
Trumpeter and bandleader.
ABC-PARAMOUNT
❏ ABC-518 [M]	Big Yank Is Here	1965	3.75	7.50	15.00
❏ ABCS-518 [S]	Big Yank Is Here	1965	5.00	10.00	20.00
❏ ABC-567 [M]	Ole Dixie	1965	3.75	7.50	15.00
❏ ABCS-567 [S]	Ole Dixie	1965	5.00	10.00	20.00
AUDIOPHILE
| ❏ AP-221 | Yank Lawson Plays Mostly Blues | 1986 | 2.50 | 5.00 | 10.00 |
BRUNSWICK
| ❏ BL 58035 [10] | Yank Lawson | 1953 | 15.00 | 30.00 | 60.00 |
DOCTOR JAZZ
| ❏ FW 40064 | That's a Plenty | 1985 | 2.50 | 5.00 | 10.00 |
RIVERSIDE
| ❏ RLP-2509 [10] | Yank Lawson's Dixieland Jazz | 1954 | 20.00 | 40.00 | 80.00 |

LAWSON, YANK, AND BOB HAGGART
Also known as the Lawson-Haggart Jazz Band and the World's Greatest Jazz Band, both of which are covered below. Also see each artist's individual listings.
ATLANTIC
| ❏ SD 1570 | Live at the Roosevelt Grill | 1970 | 3.75 | 7.50 | 15.00 |
| ❏ SD 1582 | What's New? | 1971 | 3.75 | 7.50 | 15.00 |
DECCA
❏ DL 5368 [10]	Lawson-Haggart Band Play Jelly Roll's Jazz	1952	15.00	30.00	60.00
❏ DL 5427 [10]	College Fight Songs	1952	15.00	30.00	60.00
❏ DL 5437 [10]	Lawson-Haggart Band Play King Oliver's Jazz	1952	15.00	30.00	60.00
❏ DL 5439 [10]	Lawson-Haggart Band	1952	15.00	30.00	60.00
❏ DL 5456 [10]	Blues on the River	1952	15.00	30.00	60.00
❏ DL 5502 [10]	Windy City Jazz	1953	15.00	30.00	60.00
❏ DL 5529 [10]	South of the Mason-Dixon Line	1954	15.00	30.00	60.00
❏ DL 5533 [10]	Louis' Hot Fives and Sevens	1954	15.00	30.00	60.00
❏ DL 8182 [M]	Lawson-Haggart Band Play Jelly Roll's Jazz	1955	10.00	20.00	40.00
❏ DL 8195 [M]	Lawson-Haggart Band Play King Oliver's Jazz	1955	10.00	20.00	40.00
❏ DL 8196 [M]	Blues on the River	1955	10.00	20.00	40.00
❏ DL 8197 [M]	South of the Mason-Dixon Line	1955	10.00	20.00	40.00
❏ DL 8198 [M]	Windy City Jazz	1955	10.00	20.00	40.00
❏ DL 8200 [M]	Louis' Hot Fives and Sevens	1955	10.00	20.00	40.00
❏ DL 8453 [M]	Hold That Tiger	1956	7.50	15.00	30.00
❏ DL 8801 [M]	Boppin' at the Hop	1959	7.50	15.00	30.00
❏ DL 78801 [S]	Boppin' at the Hop	1959	10.00	20.00	40.00
EVEREST
❏ SDBR-1040 [S]	Junior Prom	1959	5.00	10.00	20.00
❏ SDBR-1084 [S]	Dixieland Goes West	1960	6.25	12.50	25.00
❏ LPBR-5040 [M]	Junior Prom	1959	6.25	12.50	25.00
❏ LPBR-5084 [M]	Dixieland Goes West	1960	5.00	10.00	20.00
PROJECT 3
| ❏ PR-5033 | The World's Greatest Jazz Band | 1968 | 5.00 | 10.00 | 20.00 |
| ❏ PR-5039 | Extra | 1969 | 5.00 | 10.00 | 20.00 |
STINSON
| ❏ SLP-59 [10] | Lawson-Haggart with Jerry Jerome and His Orchestra | 1957 | 6.25 | 12.50 | 25.00 |

LAZAR, SAM
Organist.
ARGO
❏ LP-714 [M]	Soul Merchant	1963	6.25	12.50	25.00
❏ LPS-714 [S]	Soul Merchant	1963	7.50	15.00	30.00
❏ LP-4002 [M]	Space Flight	1961	7.50	15.00	30.00

Number	Title	Yr	VG	VG+	NM
❑ LPS-4002 [S]	Space Flight	1961	10.00	20.00	40.00
❑ LP-4015 [M]	Playback	1962	7.50	15.00	30.00
❑ LPS-4015 [S]	Playback	1962	10.00	20.00	40.00

LAZRO, DAUNIK
Baritone and alto saxophone player.
HAT ART

❑ 2010 [(2)]	Sweet Zee	1986	3.75	7.50	15.00

HAT HUT

❑ 11	Entrance Gates Tshee Park	198?	3.75	7.50	15.00

LEA, BARBARA
Female singer.
AUDIOPHILE

❑ AP-86	A Woman in Love	197?	3.00	6.00	12.00
❑ AP-119	The Devil Is Afraid of Music	197?	3.00	6.00	12.00
❑ AP-125	Remembering Lee Wiley	197?	3.00	6.00	12.00
❑ AP-175	Do It Again	1984	2.50	5.00	10.00

FANTASY

❑ OJC-1713	Barbara Lea	198?	2.50	5.00	10.00
❑ OJC-1742	Lea in Love	1990	3.00	6.00	12.00

PRESTIGE

❑ PRLP-7065 [M]	Barbara Lea	1956	37.50	75.00	150.00
❑ PRLP-7100 [M]	Lea in Love	1957	37.50	75.00	150.00

RIVERSIDE

❑ RLP-2518 [10]	A Woman in Love	1955	50.00	100.00	200.00

LEA, BARBARA, AND BOB DOROUGH
Also see each artist's individual listings.
AUDIOPHILE

❑ AP-165	Hoagy's Children	1981	3.00	6.00	12.00

LEADBELLY
One of America's greatest folk singers, the below is "jazz" in name only.
CAPITOL

❑ H 369 [10]	Classics in Jazz	1953	62.50	125.00	250.00

LEADERS, THE
Collaboration of bandleaders and composers: CHICO FREEMAN; CECIL McBEE; KIRK LIGHTSEY; LESTER BOWIE; ARTHUR BLYTHE; and Famadou Don Moye.
BLACK SAINT

❑ 120119	Out Here Like This	1989	3.75	7.50	15.00
❑ 120129	Unforeseen Blessings	1990	3.75	7.50	15.00

LEAHEY, HARRY
Guitarist.
OMNISOUND

❑ 1031	Still Waters	198?	2.50	5.00	10.00
❑ 1042	Silver Threads	198?	2.50	5.00	10.00

LEARY, JAMES
Bass player.
VITAL MUSIC

❑ VTL-003	James	199?	3.75	7.50	15.00
❑ VTL-005	James II	199?	3.75	7.50	15.00

LEE, CHUCK
See CHUZ ALFRED.

LEE, EDDIE
Pianist and vibraphone player.
GEORGIAN

❑ GR 2001 [M]	Windy City Profile	1958	10.00	20.00	40.00

LEE, JEANNE, AND RAN BLAKE
Lee is a female singer. Also see RAN BLAKE.
BLUEBIRD

❑ 6461-1-RB	The Legendary Duets	1987	3.00	6.00	12.00

RCA VICTOR

❑ LPM-2500 [M]	The Newest Sound Around	1962	7.50	15.00	30.00
❑ LSP-2500 [S]	The Newest Sound Around	1962	10.00	20.00	40.00

LEE, JOHN, AND GERRY BROWN
Lee plays bass and synthesizers; Brown is a drummer and percussionist.
BLUE NOTE

❑ BN-LA541-G	Mango Sunrise	1976	3.00	6.00	12.00
❑ BN-LA701-G	Still Can't Say Enough	1977	3.00	6.00	12.00

LEE, JULIA
Female singer, pianist and composer.
CAPITOL

Number	Title	Yr	VG	VG+	NM
❑ H 228 [10]	Party Time	1950	30.00	60.00	120.00
❑ T 228 [M]	Party Time	195?	20.00	40.00	80.00

LEE, JULIE
PAUSA

❑ 9020	Julie Lee and Her Boyfriends	198?	2.50	5.00	10.00

LEE, PEGGY
Female singer.
A&M

❑ SP-4547	Mirrors	1975	3.00	6.00	12.00

ARCHIVE OF FOLK AND JAZZ

❑ 294	Peggy Lee	197?	2.50	5.00	10.00

ATLANTIC

❑ SD 18108	Let's Love	1974	3.00	6.00	12.00

CAPITOL

❑ ST-105	Two Shows Nightly	1969	50.00	100.00	200.00
-- Withdrawn immediately after release					
❑ H 151 [10]	Rendezvous with Peggy Lee	1952	25.00	50.00	100.00
❑ T 151 [M]	Rendezvous with Peggy Lee	1954	12.50	25.00	50.00
-- Turquoise or gray label					
❑ T 151 [M]	Rendezvous with Peggy Lee	1959	6.25	12.50	25.00
-- Black label with colorband, Capitol logo at left					
❑ H 204 [10]	My Best to You	1952	25.00	50.00	100.00
❑ T 204 [M]	My Best to You	1954	12.50	25.00	50.00
-- Turquoise or gray label					
❑ T 204 [M]	My Best to You	1959	6.25	12.50	25.00
-- Black label with colorband, Capitol logo at left					
❑ ST-382	Is That All There Is?	1969	3.00	6.00	12.00
❑ SM-386	Is That All There Is?	197?	2.50	5.00	10.00
-- Reissue with new prefix					
❑ DKAO-377	Peggy Lee's Greatest	1969	3.00	6.00	12.00
❑ ST-463	Bridge Over Troubled Water	1970	3.00	6.00	12.00
❑ STBB-517 [(2)]	Folks Who Live on the Hill/Broadway Ala Lee	1970	3.75	7.50	15.00
❑ STCL-576 [(3)]	Peggy Lee	1970	6.25	12.50	25.00
❑ ST-622	Make It with You	1970	3.00	6.00	12.00
❑ ST-810	Where Did They Go	1971	3.00	6.00	12.00
❑ ST 864 [S]	The Man I Love	1959	7.50	15.00	30.00
❑ T 864 [M]	The Man I Love	1957	12.50	25.00	50.00
-- Turquoise label					
❑ T 864 [M]	The Man I Love	1959	6.25	12.50	25.00
-- Black label with colorband, Capitol logo at left					
❑ ST 975 [S]	Jump for Joy	1959	7.50	15.00	30.00
❑ T 975 [M]	Jump for Joy	1958	10.00	20.00	40.00
-- Turquoise or gray label					
❑ T 975 [M]	Jump for Joy	1959	6.25	12.50	25.00
-- Black label with colorband, Capitol logo at left					
❑ ST 1049 [S]	Things Are Swingin'	1959	7.50	15.00	30.00
❑ T 1049 [M]	Things Are Swingin'	1958	6.25	12.50	25.00
❑ ST 1131 [S]	I Like Men	1959	7.50	15.00	30.00
❑ T 1131 [M]	I Like Men	1959	6.25	12.50	25.00
❑ ST 1213 [S]	Alright, Okay, You Win	1959	7.50	15.00	30.00
❑ T 1213 [M]	Alright, Okay, You Win	1959	6.25	12.50	25.00
❑ ST 1219 [S]	Beauty and the Beast	1959	7.50	15.00	30.00
-- With George Shearing; black label with colorband, Capitol logo at left					
❑ ST 1219 [S]	Beauty and the Beast	1962	5.00	10.00	20.00
-- With George Shearing; black label with colorband, Capitol logo at top					
❑ T 1219 [M]	Beauty and the Beast	1959	6.25	12.50	25.00
-- With George Shearing; black label with colorband, Capitol logo at left					
❑ T 1219 [M]	Beauty and the Beast	1962	3.75	7.50	15.00
-- With George Shearing; black label with colorband, Capitol logo at top					
❑ SM-1290	Latin Ala Lee!	1977	2.50	5.00	10.00
-- Reissue with new prefix					
❑ ST 1290 [S]	Latin Ala Lee!	1960	6.25	12.50	25.00
-- Black label with colorband, Capitol logo at left					
❑ ST 1290 [S]	Latin Ala Lee!	1962	3.75	7.50	15.00
-- Black label with colorband, Capitol logo at top					
❑ T 1290 [M]	Latin Ala Lee!	1960	5.00	10.00	20.00
-- Black label with colorband, Capitol logo at left					
❑ T 1290 [M]	Latin Ala Lee!	1962	3.00	6.00	12.00
-- Black label with colorband, Capitol logo at top					
❑ ST 1366 [S]	All Aglow Again	1960	6.25	12.50	25.00
-- Black label with colorband, Capitol logo at left					
❑ ST 1366 [S]	All Aglow Again	1962	3.75	7.50	15.00
-- Black label with colorband, Capitol logo at top					
❑ T 1366 [M]	All Aglow Again	1960	5.00	10.00	20.00
-- Black label with colorband, Capitol logo at left					
❑ T 1366 [M]	All Aglow Again	1962	3.00	6.00	12.00
-- Black label with colorband, Capitol logo at top					
❑ ST 1401 [S]	Pretty Eyes	1960	6.25	12.50	25.00
❑ ST 1401 [S]	Pretty Eyes	1962	3.75	7.50	15.00
-- Black label with colorband, Capitol logo at top					

Number	Title	Yr	VG	VG+	NM
❑ T 1401 [M]	Pretty Eyes	1960	5.00	10.00	20.00
-- Black label with colorband, Capitol logo at left					
❑ T 1401 [M]	Pretty Eyes	1962	3.00	6.00	12.00
-- Black label with colorband, Capitol logo at top					
❑ ST 1423 [S]	Christmas Carousel	1960	6.25	12.50	25.00
❑ T 1423 [M]	Christmas Carousel	1960	5.00	10.00	20.00
❑ ST 1475 [S]	Ole Ala Lee!	1961	6.25	12.50	25.00
❑ T 1475 [M]	Ole Ala Lee!	1961	5.00	10.00	20.00
❑ SM-1520	Basin Street East	1977	2.50	5.00	10.00
-- Reissue with new prefix					
❑ ST 1520 [S]	Basin Street East	1961	6.25	12.50	25.00
-- Black label with colorband, Capitol logo at left					
❑ ST 1520 [S]	Basin Street East	1962	3.75	7.50	15.00
-- Black label with colorband, Capitol logo at top					
❑ T 1520 [M]	Basin Street East	1961	5.00	10.00	20.00
-- Black label with colorband, Capitol logo at left					
❑ T 1520 [M]	Basin Street East	1962	3.00	6.00	12.00
-- Black label with colorband, Capitol logo at top					
❑ ST 1630 [S]	If You Go	1962	6.25	12.50	25.00
❑ T 1630 [M]	If You Go	1962	5.00	10.00	20.00
❑ ST 1671 [S]	Blue Cross Country	1962	6.25	12.50	25.00
❑ T 1671 [M]	Blue Cross Country	1962	5.00	10.00	20.00
❑ DT 1743 [R]	Bewitching-Lee!	1962	3.75	7.50	15.00
❑ T 1743 [M]	Bewitching-Lee!	1962	6.25	12.50	25.00
-- Black "The Star Line" label					
❑ ST 1772 [S]	Sugar 'n' Spice	1962	6.25	12.50	25.00
❑ T 1772 [M]	Sugar 'n' Spice	1962	5.00	10.00	20.00
❑ ST 1850 [S]	Mink Jazz	1963	6.25	12.50	25.00
❑ T 1850 [M]	Mink Jazz	1963	5.00	10.00	20.00
❑ SM-1857	I'm a Woman	1977	2.50	5.00	10.00
-- Reissue with new prefix					
❑ ST 1857 [S]	I'm a Woman	1963	6.25	12.50	25.00
❑ T 1857 [M]	I'm a Woman	1963	5.00	10.00	20.00
❑ ST 1969 [S]	In Love Again	1963	6.25	12.50	25.00
❑ T 1969 [M]	In Love Again	1963	5.00	10.00	20.00
❑ ST 2096 [S]	In the Name of Love	1964	5.00	10.00	20.00
❑ T 2096 [M]	In the Name of Love	1964	3.75	7.50	15.00
❑ ST 2320 [S]	Pass Me By	1965	5.00	10.00	20.00
❑ T 2320 [M]	Pass Me By	1965	3.75	7.50	15.00
❑ ST 2388 [S]	That Was Then, Now Is Now	1965	5.00	10.00	20.00
❑ T 2388 [M]	That Was Then, Now Is Now	1965	3.75	7.50	15.00
❑ ST 2390 [S]	Happy Holiday	1965	3.75	7.50	15.00
❑ T 2390 [M]	Happy Holiday	1965	3.00	6.00	12.00
❑ ST 2469 [S]	Guitars Ala Lee	1966	5.00	10.00	20.00
❑ T 2469 [M]	Guitars Ala Lee	1966	3.75	7.50	15.00
❑ ST 2475 [S]	Big $pender	1966	5.00	10.00	20.00
❑ T 2475 [M]	Big $pender	1966	3.75	7.50	15.00
❑ ST 2732 [S]	Extra Special	1967	3.75	7.50	15.00
❑ T 2732 [M]	Extra Special	1967	5.00	10.00	20.00
❑ ST 2781	Somethin' Groovy	1968	3.75	7.50	15.00
❑ ST 2887	The Hits of Peggy Lee	1968	3.75	7.50	15.00
❑ ST-11077	Norma Deloris Egstrom from Jamestown, North Dakota	1972	3.00	6.00	12.00
❑ SN-16140	Peggy Lee Sings Songs of Cy Coleman	198?	2.00	4.00	8.00
COLUMBIA					
❑ CL 6033 [10]	Benny Goodman and Peggy Lee	1949	15.00	30.00	60.00
DECCA					
❑ DXB 164 [(2) M]	The Best of Peggy Lee	1964	7.50	15.00	30.00
❑ DL 4458 [M]	Lover	1964	6.25	12.50	25.00
❑ DL 4461 [M]	The Fabulous Peggy Lee	1964	6.25	12.50	25.00
❑ DL 5482 [10]	Black Coffee	1953	25.00	50.00	100.00
❑ DL 5539 [10]	Songs in an Intimate Style	1953	20.00	40.00	80.00
❑ DXSB 7164 [(2) R]	The Best of Peggy Lee	1964	5.00	10.00	20.00
❑ DL 8358 [M]	Black Coffee	1956	15.00	30.00	60.00
❑ DL 8411 [M]	Dream Street	1957	15.00	30.00	60.00
❑ DL 8591 [M]	Sea Shells	1958	15.00	30.00	60.00
❑ DL 8816 [M]	Miss Wonderful	1959	15.00	30.00	60.00
❑ DL 74458 [R]	Lover	1964	3.75	7.50	15.00
❑ DL 74461 [R]	The Fabulous Peggy Lee	1964	3.75	7.50	15.00
DRG					
❑ SL-5190	Close Enough for Love	1979	3.00	6.00	12.00
GLENDALE					
❑ 6023	You Can Depend on Me	1982	2.50	5.00	10.00
HARMONY					
❑ HL 7005 [M]	Peggy Lee Sings with Benny Goodman	195?	6.25	12.50	25.00
❑ H 30024	Miss Peggy Lee	1970	2.50	5.00	10.00
HINDSIGHT					
❑ HSR-220	Peggy Lee with the David Barbour and Billy May Bands, 1948	1985	2.50	5.00	10.00
MCA					
❑ 4049 [(2)]	The Best of Peggy Lee	197?	3.00	6.00	12.00
MERCURY					
❑ SRM-1-1172	Live in London	1977	3.00	6.00	12.00

Number	Title	Yr	VG	VG+	NM
MUSICMASTERS					
❑ 5005	Peggy Sings the Blues	1988	3.00	6.00	12.00
PAUSA					
❑ PR-9043	Sugar 'n' Spice	1985	2.50	5.00	10.00
PICKWICK					
❑ SPC-3090	Once More with Feeling	196?	2.50	5.00	10.00
❑ SPC-3192	I've Got the World	1971	2.50	5.00	10.00
VOCALION					
❑ VL 3776 [M]	So Blue	1966	3.75	7.50	15.00
❑ VL 73776 [R]	So Blue	1966	2.50	5.00	10.00
❑ VL 73903	Crazy in the Heart	1969	2.50	5.00	10.00

LEE, PERRY
Organist.
ROULETTE					
❑ R-52080 [M]	A Night at Count Basie's	1962	3.75	7.50	15.00
❑ SR-52080 [S]	A Night at Count Basie's	1962	5.00	10.00	20.00

LEE, THOMAS OBOE
Flutist (despite his name) and composer of both jazz and classical works.
GM RECORDINGS					
❑ GM-3004	Departed Feathers	1986	2.50	5.00	10.00

LEEDS, ERIC
Flutist and saxophone player; also a member of Prince's live backing group.
PAISLEY PARK					
❑ 27499	Times Square	1991	3.75	7.50	15.00

LEES, GENE
Male singer. Better known as a composer, lyricist and author.
STASH					
❑ ST-269	Gene Lees Sings the Gene Lees Songbook	1987	2.50	5.00	10.00

LEES, GENE, AND ROGER KELLAWAY
Also see each artist's individual listings.
CHOICE					
❑ CRS-6832	Leaves on the Water	1986	2.50	5.00	10.00

LEESE, TIM
MUSIC IS MEDICINE					
❑ 9036	After Hours	198?	3.00	6.00	12.00

LEFEBVRE, DAVE
Woodwinds player.
JAZZ HOUNDS					
❑ 0001	Marble Dust	198?	3.00	6.00	12.00

LEFEBVRE, GARY
Tenor and alto saxophone player.
DISCOVERY					
❑ DS-849	Gary LeFebvre Quartet	1981	3.00	6.00	12.00

LEGGE, WADE
Pianist.
BLUE NOTE					
❑ BLP-5031 [10]	Wade Legge Trio	1953	150.00	300.00	600.00

LEGGIO, CARMEN
Tenor saxophone player.
DREAMSTREET					
❑ 103	Aerial View	1979	3.00	6.00	12.00
FAMOUS DOOR					
❑ 125	Tarytown Tenor	1978	3.00	6.00	12.00
GOLDEN CREST					
❑ GCS-1000	Jazz	196?	5.00	10.00	20.00
PROGRESSIVE					
❑ PRO-7010	Smile	1980	2.50	5.00	10.00

LEGRAND, MICHEL
Pianist and composer; best known for his film scores.
BELL					
❑ 4200 [(2)]	Twenty Songs of the Century	1974	3.00	6.00	12.00
❑ 6071	Brian's Song Themes & Variations	1972	2.50	5.00	10.00
COLUMBIA					
❑ CL 555 [M]	I Love Paris	1954	10.00	20.00	40.00
❑ CL 647 [M]	Holiday in Rome	1955	6.25	12.50	25.00

Number	Title	Yr	VG	VG+	NM
❏ CL 706 [M]	Vienna Holiday	1955	6.25	12.50	25.00
❏ CL 888 [M]	Castles in Spain	1956	6.25	12.50	25.00
❏ CL 1115 [M]	Michel Legrand Plays Cole Porter	1957	6.25	12.50	25.00
❏ CL 1139 [M]	Legrand in Rio	1957	6.25	12.50	25.00
❏ CL 1250 [M]	Legrand Jazz	1958	10.00	20.00	40.00
-- Miles Davis appears on this record					
❏ CL 1437 [M]	I Love Paris	1960	6.25	12.50	25.00
❏ CS 8079 [S]	Legrand Jazz	1959	10.00	20.00	40.00
-- Miles Davis appears on this record					
❏ CS 8237 [S]	I Love Paris	1960	5.00	10.00	20.00
❏ PC 8237	I Love Paris	1987	2.00	4.00	8.00
-- Reissue with new prefix					
GRYPHON					
❏ 786	Jazz Grand	1978	2.50	5.00	10.00
HARMONY					
❏ HL 7331 [M]	I Love Paris	196?	3.00	6.00	12.00
❏ HS 11131 [S]	I Love Paris	196?	3.00	6.00	12.00
❏ KH 31540	Cole Porter, Volume II	1972	2.50	5.00	10.00
❏ KH 31549	Cole Porter, Volume I	1972	2.50	5.00	10.00
MGM					
❏ SE-4491	Cinema La Grand	1967	3.75	7.50	15.00
MOBILE FIDELITY					
❏ 1-504	Jazz Grand	198?	12.50	25.00	50.00
-- Audiophile vinyl					
PABLO TODAY					
❏ 2312-139	After the Rain	198?	2.50	5.00	10.00
PHILIPS					
❏ PHM 200-074 [M]	The Michel Legrand Big Band Plays Richard Rogers	1963	5.00	10.00	20.00
❏ PHM 200-143 [M]	Michel Legrand Sings	1964	6.25	12.50	25.00
❏ PHS 600-074 [S]	The Michel Legrand Big Band Plays Richard Rogers	1963	6.25	12.50	25.00
❏ PHS 600-143 [S]	Michel Legrand Sings	1964	7.50	15.00	30.00
RCA VICTOR					
❏ BGL1-0850	Jimmy's	1975	2.50	5.00	10.00
❏ BXL1-0850	Jimmy's	1978	2.00	4.00	8.00
-- Reissue with new prefix					
❏ BGL1-1028	Concert	1976	2.50	5.00	10.00
❏ BXL1-1028	Concert	1978	2.00	4.00	8.00
-- Reissue with new prefix					
❏ BGL1-1392	Michel Legrand and Friends	1976	2.50	5.00	10.00
❏ BXL1-1392	Michel Legrand and Friends	1978	2.00	4.00	8.00
-- Reissue with new prefix					
VERVE					
❏ V6-8760	Michel Legrand at Shelly's Mann-Hole	1969	3.00	6.00	12.00

LEIGH, CAROL
Female singer.
GHB

Number	Title	Yr	VG	VG+	NM
❏ GHB-88	Wild Women Don't Have the Blues	197?	3.00	6.00	12.00
❏ 136	You've Got to Give Me Some	1980	3.00	6.00	12.00
❏ 152	Blame It on the Blues	198?	3.00	6.00	12.00
❏ 167	Go Back Where You Stayed Last Night	198?	3.00	6.00	12.00
STOMP OFF					
❏ SOS-1064	If You Don't Know, I Know Who Will	1983	2.50	5.00	10.00
❏ SOS-1087	I'm Busy and You Can't Come In	1985	2.50	5.00	10.00

LEIGHTON, BERNIE
Pianist.
CAMEO

Number	Title	Yr	VG	VG+	NM
❏ C-1005 [M]	Dizzy Fingers	1959	7.50	15.00	30.00
COLUMBIA					
❏ CL 6112 [10]	East Side Rendezvous	1950	20.00	40.00	80.00
MONMOUTH-EVERGREEN					
❏ 7068	Bernie Leighton Plays Duke Ellington Live at Jimmy Weston's	197?	3.00	6.00	12.00

LEIGHTON, BERNIE/JOHNNY GUARNIERI
Also see each artist's individual listings.
EMARCY

Number	Title	Yr	VG	VG+	NM
❏ MG-26018 [10]	Piano Stylings	1954	20.00	40.00	80.00

LEITCH, PETER
Guitarist.
PAUSA

Number	Title	Yr	VG	VG+	NM
❏ 7132	Jump Street	1981	2.50	5.00	10.00

LELLIS, TOM
Male singer.
INNER CITY

Number	Title	Yr	VG	VG+	NM
❏ IC-1090	And In This Corner	198?	3.75	7.50	15.00

LEMER, PETER
Pianist.
ESP-DISK'

Number	Title	Yr	VG	VG+	NM
❏ 1057	Local Colour	1968	6.25	12.50	25.00

LEONARD, HARLAN
Alto saxophone player and bandleader.
RCA VICTOR

Number	Title	Yr	VG	VG+	NM
❏ LPV-531 [M]	Harlan Leonard and His Rockets	1965	6.25	12.50	25.00

LEONARD, HARVEY
Pianist.
KEYNOTE

Number	Title	Yr	VG	VG+	NM
❏ 1102 [M]	Jazz Ecstasy	1955	12.50	25.00	50.00

LEONHART, JAY
Bass player, male singer and composer.
SUNNYSIDE

Number	Title	Yr	VG	VG+	NM
❏ SSC-1006	There's Gonna Be Trouble	1985	2.50	5.00	10.00
❏ SSC-1032	The Double Cross	1989	3.00	6.00	12.00

LES JAZZ MODES
Members: JULIUS WATKINS (French horn), CHARLIE ROUSE (tenor sax), GILDO MAHONES (piano), Martin Rivera (bass) and RON JEFFERSON (drums).
ATLANTIC

Number	Title	Yr	VG	VG+	NM
❏ 1280 [M]	The Most Happy Fella	1958	20.00	40.00	80.00
-- Black label					
❏ 1280 [M]	The Most Happy Fella	1961	7.50	15.00	30.00
-- Multicolor label, white "fan" logo at right					
❏ 1306 [M]	Les Jazz Modes	1959	15.00	30.00	60.00
-- Black label					
❏ 1306 [M]	Les Jazz Modes	1961	7.50	15.00	30.00
-- Multicolor label, white "fan" logo at right					
❏ SD 1306 [S]	Les Jazz Modes	1959	15.00	30.00	60.00
-- Green label					
❏ SD 1306 [S]	Les Jazz Modes	1961	7.50	15.00	30.00
-- Multicolor label, white "fan" logo at right					
DAWN					
❏ DLP-1101 [M]	Jazzville	1956	25.00	50.00	100.00
❏ DLP-1108 [M]	Les Jazz Modes	1956	25.00	50.00	100.00
❏ DLP-1117 [M]	Mood in Scarlet	1957	25.00	50.00	100.00
SEECO					
❏ CELP-466 [M]	Smart Jazz for the Smart Set	1960	7.50	15.00	30.00

LESBERG, JACK
Bass player.
FAMOUS DOOR

Number	Title	Yr	VG	VG+	NM
❏ 120	Hollywood	1977	3.00	6.00	12.00

LESLIE, BILL
Tenor saxophone player.
ARGO

Number	Title	Yr	VG	VG+	NM
❏ LP-710 [M]	Diggin' the Chicks	1962	6.25	12.50	25.00
❏ LPS-710 [S]	Diggin' the Chicks	1962	7.50	15.00	30.00

LESMANA, INDRA
Pianist.
ZEBRA

Number	Title	Yr	VG	VG+	NM
❏ ZR-5005	Indra Lesmana and Nebula	1984	3.00	6.00	12.00
❏ ZEB-5709	For Earth and Heaven	1986	2.50	5.00	10.00

LETMAN, JOHN
Trumpeter.
BETHLEHEM

Number	Title	Yr	VG	VG+	NM
❏ BCP-6053 [M]	The Many Angles of John Letman	1961	7.50	15.00	30.00
❏ SBCP-6053 [S]	The Many Angles of John Letman	1961	10.00	20.00	40.00

LEVEY, STAN
Drummer. Also see CONTE CANDOLI; MAX ROACH.
BETHLEHEM

Number	Title	Yr	VG	VG+	NM
❏ BCP-37 [M]	This Time the Dream's On Me	1956	12.50	25.00	50.00
❏ BCP-71 [M]	Grand Stan	1957	12.50	25.00	50.00
❏ BCP-1017 [10]	Stan Levey Plays	1954	30.00	60.00	120.00

Number	Title	Yr	VG	VG+	NM
❑ BCP-6030 [M]	Stanley the Steamer	197?	3.75	7.50	15.00

-- Reissue of 37, distributed by RCA Victor

MODE

❑ LP-101 [M]	Stan Levey Quartet	1957	20.00	40.00	80.00

LEVIEV, MILCHO
Pianist.
DOBRE

❑ 1025	Piano Lesson	197?	3.00	6.00	12.00

OPTIMISM

❑ OP-2004	Destination	198?	2.50	5.00	10.00

TREND

❑ 530	Music for Big Band and Symphony Orchestra	1982	2.50	5.00	10.00

LEVIN, MARC
Cornet player.
SAVOY

❑ MG-12190 [M]	The Dragon Suite	1967	6.25	12.50	25.00

SWEET DRAGON

❑ 1	Songs, Dances and Prayers	197?	5.00	10.00	20.00

LEVIN, PETE
Pianist, organist, keyboard player, banjo player and composer.
GRAMAVISION

❑ R1-79456	Party in the Basement	1990	3.75	7.50	15.00

LEVINE, HENRY
Trumpeter.
RCA CAMDEN

❑ CAL-321 [M]	Lower Basin Street	1958	6.25	12.50	25.00

RCA VICTOR

❑ LPM-1283 [M]	Dixieland Jazz Band	1956	12.50	25.00	50.00

LEVINE, MARK
Pianist.
CATALYST

❑ 7614	Up 'Til Now	1976	3.00	6.00	12.00

CONCORD JAZZ

❑ CJ-234	Concepts	1984	2.50	5.00	10.00
❑ CJ-352	Smiley and Me	1988	2.50	5.00	10.00

LEVINSON, MARK
Bass player.
MARK LEVINSON

❑ 7	Jazz at Long Wharf	1979	7.50	15.00	30.00

-- Audiophile edition pressed at 45 rpm

LEVISTER, ALONZO
Pianist, composer and arranger.
DEBUT

❑ DEB-125 [M]	Manhattan Moondrama	1956	37.50	75.00	150.00

LEVITT, ROD
Trombonist, composer and bandleader.
RCA VICTOR

❑ LPM-3372 [M]	Insight	1965	3.75	7.50	15.00
❑ LSP-3372 [S]	Insight	1965	5.00	10.00	20.00
❑ LPM-3448 [M]	Solid Ground	1965	3.75	7.50	15.00
❑ LSP-3448 [S]	Solid Ground	1965	5.00	10.00	20.00
❑ LPM-3615 [M]	42nd Street	1966	3.75	7.50	15.00
❑ LSP-3615 [S]	42nd Street	1966	5.00	10.00	20.00

RIVERSIDE

❑ RLP-471 [M]	The Dynamic Sound Patterns of the Rod Levitt Orchestra	1964	3.75	7.50	15.00
❑ RS-9471 [S]	The Dynamic Sound Patterns of the Rod Levitt Orchestra	1964	5.00	10.00	20.00

LEVITTS, THE
Family group: Al Levitt (drums); Sean Levitt (guitar); Stella Levitt, Michele Levitt, Miron Levitt, Teresa Levitt (vocals). One of the backing musicians is CHICK COREA.
ESP-DISK'

❑ S-1095	We Are the Levitts	1970	6.25	12.50	25.00

LEVY, LOU
Pianist.
DOBRE

❑ 1042	A Touch of Class	1978	3.00	6.00	12.00

INTERPLAY

❑ 7711	Tempus Fugue It	197?	2.50	5.00	10.00

JUBILEE

Number	Title	Yr	VG	VG+	NM
❑ JLP-1101 [M]	Lou Levy Plays Baby Grand Jazz	1959	10.00	20.00	40.00
❑ SDJLP-1101 [S]	Lou Levy Plays Baby Grand Jazz	1959	10.00	20.00	40.00

NOCTURNE

❑ NLP-10 [10]	Lou Levy Trio	1954	25.00	50.00	100.00

PHILIPS

❑ PHM 200-056 [M]	The Hymn	1962	3.75	7.50	15.00
❑ PHS 600-056 [S]	The Hymn	1962	5.00	10.00	20.00

RCA VICTOR

❑ LPM-1267 [M]	Solo Scene	1956	12.50	25.00	50.00
❑ LPM-1319 [M]	Jazz in Four Colors	1956	12.50	25.00	50.00
❑ LPM-1491 [M]	A Most Musical Fella	1957	12.50	25.00	50.00

LEVY, LOU/CONTE CANDOLI
Also see each artist's individual listings.
ATLANTIC

❑ 1268 [M]	West Coast Wailers	1957	12.50	25.00	50.00

-- Black label

❑ 1268 [M]	West Coast Wailers	1961	6.25	12.50	25.00

-- Multicolor label, white "fan" logo at right

LEVY, O'DONEL
Guitarist and male singer.
GROOVE MERCHANT

❑ 501	Black Velvet	1971	6.25	12.50	25.00
❑ 507	Breeding of Mind	1972	6.25	12.50	25.00
❑ 518	Dawn of a New Day	1973	6.25	12.50	25.00
❑ 526	Simba	1974	7.50	15.00	30.00
❑ 535	Everything I Do Gonna Be Funky	1975	7.50	15.00	30.00
❑ 3313	Windows	197?	5.00	10.00	20.00
❑ 4408 [(2)]	Hands of Fire	197?	6.25	12.50	25.00

LEWES, WILSON
DIPLOMAT

❑ D-2369 [M]	The "In" Crowd	1965	2.50	5.00	10.00
❑ DS-2369 [S]	The "In" Crowd	1965	3.00	6.00	12.00
❑ D-2378 [M]	The Shadow of Your Smile	1966	2.50	5.00	10.00
❑ DS-2378 [S]	The Shadow of Your Smile	1966	3.00	6.00	12.00

LEWIS, GEORGE (1)
Clarinetist and occasional alto saxophone player.
AMERICAN MUSIC

❑ 639 [10]	The George Lewis Band in the French Quarter	1951	20.00	40.00	80.00
❑ 645 [10]	George Lewis with Kid Shots Madison	1952	20.00	40.00	80.00

ARCHIVE OF FOLK AND JAZZ

❑ 240	George Lewis	197?	2.50	5.00	10.00

ATLANTIC

❑ 1411 [M]	The George Lewis Band	1963	3.75	7.50	15.00
❑ SD 1411 [S]	The George Lewis Band	1963	5.00	10.00	20.00

BIOGRAPH

❑ CEN-1	George Lewis and His Mustache Stompers	197?	2.50	5.00	10.00

BLUE NOTE

❑ BLP-1205 [M]	George Lewis and His New Orleans Stompers, Volume 1	1955	37.50	75.00	150.00

-- "Deep groove" version (deep indentation under label on both sides)

❑ BLP-1205 [M]	George Lewis and His New Orleans Stompers, Volume 1	1955	25.00	50.00	100.00

-- Regular version, Lexington Ave. address on label

❑ BLP-1205 [M]	George Lewis and His New Orleans Stompers, Volume 1	1963	6.25	12.50	25.00

-- With "New York, USA" address on label

❑ BLP-1206 [M]	George Lewis and His New Orleans Stompers, Volume 2	1955	37.50	75.00	150.00

-- "Deep groove" version (deep indentation under label on both sides)

❑ BLP-1206 [M]	George Lewis and His New Orleans Stompers, Volume 2	1955	25.00	50.00	100.00

-- Regular version, Lexington Ave. address on label

❑ BLP-1206 [M]	George Lewis and His New Orleans Stompers, Volume 2	1963	6.25	12.50	25.00

-- With "New York, USA" address on label

❑ BLP-1208 [M]	George Lewis Concert!	1955	37.50	75.00	150.00

-- "Deep groove" version (deep indentation under label on both sides)

❑ BLP-1208 [M]	George Lewis Concert!	1955	25.00	50.00	100.00

-- Regular version, Lexington Ave. address on label

❑ BLP-1208 [M]	George Lewis Concert!	1963	6.25	12.50	25.00

-- With "New York, USA" address on label

❑ BLP-7010 [10]	George Lewis' New Orleans Stompers, Volume 1	1951	62.50	125.00	250.00

Number	Title	Yr	VG	VG+	NM
❏ BLP-7013 [10]	George Lewis' New Orleans Stompers, Volume 2	1951	62.50	125.00	250.00
❏ BLP-7027 [10]	George Lewis' New Orleans Stompers, Volume 3	1954	62.50	125.00	250.00
❏ BLP-7028 [10]	George Lewis' New Orleans Stompers, Volume 4	1954	62.50	125.00	250.00
❏ BST-81205 [R]	George Lewis and His New Orleans Stompers, Volume 1	1967	3.00	6.00	12.00
-- With "A Division of Liberty Records" on label					
❏ BST-81206 [R]	George Lewis and His New Orleans Stompers, Volume 2	1967	3.00	6.00	12.00
-- With "A Division of Liberty Records" on label					
❏ BST-81208 [R]	George Lewis Concert!	1967	3.00	6.00	12.00
-- With "A Division of Liberty Records" on label					
CAVALIER					
❏ CVLP-6004 [M]	George Lewis in Hi-Fi	1956	15.00	30.00	60.00
CIRCLE					
❏ L-421 [10]	George Lewis and His New Orleans All-Stars	1951	20.00	40.00	80.00
DELMAR					
❏ DL-201 [M]	Doctor Jazz	195?	12.50	25.00	50.00
❏ DL-202 [M]	On Parade	195?	12.50	25.00	50.00
DELMARK					
❏ DL-202	George Lewis' New Orleans Stompers	196?	6.25	12.50	25.00
❏ DL-203	George Lewis Memorial Album	196?	5.00	10.00	20.00
DISC JOCKEY					
❏ DDL-100 [(2) M]	Jazz at Ohio Union	195?	300.00	600.00	1,200.
-- Box set with booklet					
EMPIRICAL					
❏ EM-107 [10]	Spirituals in Ragtime	1956	20.00	40.00	80.00
FANTASY					
❏ OJC-1736	Jazz at Vespers	198?	2.50	5.00	10.00
❏ OJC-1739	George Lewis of New Orleans	198?	2.50	5.00	10.00
FOLKLYRIC					
❏ 9030	George Lewis and His New Orleans Ragtime Jazz Band	198?	2.50	5.00	10.00
GHB					
❏ GHB-5	George Lewis and His Ragtime Stompers	196?	3.00	6.00	12.00
❏ GHB-10	City of a Million Dreams	1964	3.00	6.00	12.00
❏ GHB-14	George Lewis in Japan, Volume 1	1965	3.00	6.00	12.00
❏ GHB-15	George Lewis in Japan, Volume 2	1965	3.00	6.00	12.00
❏ GHB-16	George Lewis in Japan, Volume 3	1965	3.00	6.00	12.00
❏ GHB-29	Easy Riders Jazz Band	1965	3.00	6.00	12.00
❏ GHB-37	For Dancers Only	1968	3.00	6.00	12.00
❏ GHB-39	Easy Riders Jazz Band	1968	3.00	6.00	12.00
❏ GHB-68	The Big Four	1970	3.00	6.00	12.00
JAZZ CRUSADE					
❏ 2004	Jazzology Poll	1965	3.00	6.00	12.00
JAZZ MAN					
❏ LP-1 [10]	George Lewis' Ragtime Band	1953	20.00	40.00	80.00
-- "Limited First Pressing Dec. 25, 1953" on label at left					
❏ LJ-331 [10]	New Orleans Music	1954	20.00	40.00	80.00
JAZZOLOGY					
❏ JCE-3 [M]	George Lewis and His Ragtime Stompers	196?	3.75	7.50	15.00
❏ SJCE-3 [S]	George Lewis and His Ragtime Stompers	196?	3.00	6.00	12.00
❏ JCE-19	Endless the Trek	1967	3.00	6.00	12.00
❏ JCE-27	George Lewis at Congo Square	196?	3.00	6.00	12.00
MOSAIC					
❏ M5-132 [(5)]	The Complete Blue Note Recordings of George Lewis	199?	25.00	50.00	100.00
PARADOX					
❏ LP-6001 [10]	George Lewis	1951	20.00	40.00	80.00
RIVERSIDE					
❏ RLP 12-207 [M]	Jazz in the Classic New Orleans Tradition	1956	12.50	25.00	50.00
-- White label, blue print					
❏ RLP 12-207 [M]	Jazz in the Classic New Orleans Tradition	1959	7.50	15.00	30.00
-- Blue label, microphone logo at top					
❏ RLP 12-230 [M]	Jazz at Vespers	1957	12.50	25.00	50.00
-- White label, blue print					
❏ RLP 12-230 [M]	Jazz at Vespers	1959	7.50	15.00	30.00
-- Blue label, microphone logo at top					
❏ RLP 12-283 [M]	George Lewis of New Orleans	1958	10.00	20.00	40.00
❏ RLP-2507 [10]	George Lewis	1954	25.00	50.00	100.00
❏ RLP-2512 [10]	George Lewis with Guest Artist Red Allen	1955	25.00	50.00	100.00

Number	Title	Yr	VG	VG+	NM
SOUTHLAND					
❏ SLP-208 [10]	George Lewis	1955	20.00	40.00	80.00
STORYVILLE					
❏ 4022	George Lewis and His Ragtime Band In Concert	197?	3.00	6.00	12.00
❏ 4049	Jazz from New Orleans	198?	2.50	5.00	10.00
❏ 4055	George Lewis at Club Hangover, Volume 1	198?	2.50	5.00	10.00
❏ 4061	George Lewis at Club Hangover, Volume 3	198?	2.50	5.00	10.00
VERVE					
❏ MGV-1019 [M]	Blues from the Bayou	1957	12.50	25.00	50.00
❏ V-1019 [M]	Blues from the Bayou	1961	5.00	10.00	20.00
❏ V6-1019 [S]	Blues from the Bayou	1961	3.75	7.50	15.00
❏ MGV-1021 [M]	Doctor Jazz	1957	12.50	25.00	50.00
❏ V-1021 [M]	Doctor Jazz	1961	5.00	10.00	20.00
❏ V6-1021 [S]	Doctor Jazz	1961	3.75	7.50	15.00
❏ MGV-1024 [M]	Hot Time in the Old Town Tonight	1957	12.50	25.00	50.00
❏ V-1024 [M]	Hot Time in the Old Town Tonight	1961	5.00	10.00	20.00
❏ V6-1024 [S]	Hot Time in the Old Town Tonight	1961	5.00	10.00	20.00
❏ MGV-1027 [M]	George Lewis' Dixieland Band	1957	12.50	25.00	50.00
❏ V-1027 [M]	George Lewis' Dixieland Band	1961	5.00	10.00	20.00
❏ UMV-2621	Verve at Newport	198?	3.00	6.00	12.00
❏ MGVS-6064 [S]	Oh, Didn't He Ramble	1960	10.00	20.00	40.00
❏ MGVS-6113 [S]	Blues from the Bayou	1960	10.00	20.00	40.00
❏ MGVS-6122 [S]	Doctor Jazz	1960	10.00	20.00	40.00
❏ MGV-8232 [M]	George Lewis and Turk Murphy at Newport	1958	12.50	25.00	50.00
❏ V-8232 [M]	George Lewis and Turk Murphy at Newport	1961	5.00	10.00	20.00
❏ MGV-8277 [M]	The Perennial George Lewis	1958	12.50	25.00	50.00
❏ V-8277 [M]	The Perennial George Lewis	1961	5.00	10.00	20.00
❏ MGV-8303 [M]	On Stage: George Lewis Concert, Volume 1	1959	12.50	25.00	50.00
❏ V-8303 [M]	On Stage: George Lewis Concert, Volume 1	1961	5.00	10.00	20.00
❏ MGV-8304 [M]	On Stage: George Lewis Concert, Volume 2	1959	12.50	25.00	50.00
❏ V-8304 [M]	On Stage: George Lewis Concert, Volume 2	1961	5.00	10.00	20.00
❏ MGV-8325 [M]	Oh, Didn't He Ramble	1959	12.50	25.00	50.00
❏ V-8325 [M]	Oh, Didn't He Ramble	1961	5.00	10.00	20.00
❏ V6-8325 [S]	Oh, Didn't He Ramble	1961	3.75	7.50	15.00

LEWIS, GEORGE (2)

Trombonist and composer.

Number	Title	Yr	VG	VG+	NM
BLACK SAINT					
❏ BSR-0016	Monads	198?	3.00	6.00	12.00
❏ BSR-0029	Homage to Charles Parker	198?	3.00	6.00	12.00
LOVELY					
❏ VR-1101	Chicago Slow Dance	198?	3.75	7.50	15.00

LEWIS, GEORGE (2), AND DOUGLAS EWART

Ewart plays many different reed instruments. Also see GEORGE LEWIS (2).

Number	Title	Yr	VG	VG+	NM
BLACK SAINT					
❏ BSR-0026	The Imaginary Suite	198?	3.00	6.00	12.00

LEWIS, JOHN

Pianist and composer. Also see THE MODERN JAZZ QUARTET; THE MODERN JAZZ SEXTET; ORCHESTRA U.S.A.

Number	Title	Yr	VG	VG+	NM
ATLANTIC					
❏ 1272 [M]	The John Lewis Piano	1958	10.00	20.00	40.00
-- Black label					
❏ 1272 [M]	The John Lewis Piano	1961	5.00	10.00	20.00
-- Multicolor label, white "fan" logo at right					
❏ 1272 [M]	The John Lewis Piano	1964	3.75	7.50	15.00
-- Multicolor label, black "fan" logo at right					
❏ 1313 [M]	Improvised Meditations and Excursions	1959	10.00	20.00	40.00
-- Black label					
❏ 1313 [M]	Improvised Meditations and Excursions	1961	5.00	10.00	20.00
-- Multicolor label, white "fan" logo at right					
❏ 1313 [M]	Improvised Meditations and Excursions	1964	3.75	7.50	15.00
-- Multicolor label, black "fan" logo at right					
❏ SD 1313 [S]	Improvised Meditations and Excursions	1959	12.50	25.00	50.00
-- Green label					
❏ SD 1313 [S]	Improvised Meditations and Excursions	1961	5.00	10.00	20.00
-- Multicolor label, white "fan" logo at right					

Number	Title	Yr	VG	VG+	NM
❑ SD 1313 [S]	Improvised Meditations and Excursions	1964	3.75	7.50	15.00
-- Multicolor label, black "fan" logo at right
❑ 1334 [M]	The Golden Striker	1960	6.25	12.50	25.00
-- Multicolor label, white "fan" logo at right
❑ 1334 [M]	The Golden Striker	1964	3.75	7.50	15.00
-- Multicolor label, black "fan" logo at right
❑ SD 1334 [S]	The Golden Striker	1960	7.50	15.00	30.00
-- Multicolor label, white "fan" logo at right
❑ SD 1334 [S]	The Golden Striker	1964	5.00	10.00	20.00
-- Multicolor label, black "fan" logo at right
❑ 1365 [M]	John Lewis Presents Jazz Abstractions	1961	6.25	12.50	25.00
-- Multicolor label, white "fan" logo at right
❑ 1365 [M]	John Lewis Presents Jazz Abstractions	1964	3.75	7.50	15.00
-- Multicolor label, black "fan" logo at right
❑ SD 1365 [S]	John Lewis Presents Jazz Abstractions	1961	7.50	15.00	30.00
-- Multicolor label, white "fan" logo at right
❑ SD 1365 [S]	John Lewis Presents Jazz Abstractions	1964	5.00	10.00	20.00
-- Multicolor label, black "fan" logo at right
❑ 1370 [M]	Original Sin	1961	6.25	12.50	25.00
-- Multicolor label, white "fan" logo at right
❑ 1370 [M]	Original Sin	1964	3.75	7.50	15.00
-- Multicolor label, black "fan" logo at right
❑ SD 1370 [S]	Original Sin	1961	7.50	15.00	30.00
-- Multicolor label, white "fan" logo at right
❑ SD 1370 [S]	Original Sin	1964	5.00	10.00	20.00
-- Multicolor label, black "fan" logo at right
❑ 1375 [M]	The Wonderful World of Jazz	1961	6.25	12.50	25.00
-- Multicolor label, white "fan" logo at right
❑ 1375 [M]	The Wonderful World of Jazz	1964	3.75	7.50	15.00
-- Multicolor label, black "fan" logo at right
❑ SD 1375 [S]	The Wonderful World of Jazz	1961	7.50	15.00	30.00
-- Multicolor label, white "fan" logo at right
❑ SD 1375 [S]	The Wonderful World of Jazz	1964	5.00	10.00	20.00
-- Multicolor label, black "fan" logo at right
❑ 1392 [M]	European Encounter	1963	3.75	7.50	15.00
❑ SD 1392 [S]	European Encounter	1963	5.00	10.00	20.00
❑ 1402 [M]	Animal Dance	1963	3.75	7.50	15.00
❑ SD 1402 [S]	Animal Dance	1963	5.00	10.00	20.00
❑ 1425 [M]	Essence	1964	3.75	7.50	15.00
❑ SD 1425 [S]	Essence	1964	5.00	10.00	20.00
❑ 90533	European Encounter	1986	2.50	5.00	10.00
❑ 90979	The Wonderful World of Jazz	1989	3.00	6.00	12.00
COLUMBIA
❑ PC 33534	P.O.V.	1976	2.50	5.00	10.00
EMARCY
❑ 834 478-1	The Garden of Delight: Delaunay's Dilemma	1989	3.00	6.00	12.00
❑ 838 036-1	Midnight in Paris	1990	3.00	6.00	12.00
FINESSE
❑ FW 37681	Album for Nancy Harrow	1982	2.50	5.00	10.00
❑ FW 38187	Kansas City Breaks	1983	2.50	5.00	10.00
PHILIPS
❑ 824 381-1	John Lewis Plays Bach's "Well-Tempered Clavier"	1985	2.50	5.00	10.00
❑ 826 698-1	The Bridge Game	1986	2.50	5.00	10.00
❑ 832 015-1	The Chess Game	1987	3.00	6.00	12.00
❑ 832 588-1	The Chess Game, Volume 2	1988	3.00	6.00	12.00
❑ 836 821-1	Bach: Preludes and Fugues, Vol. 3	1989	3.00	6.00	12.00
RCA VICTOR
❑ LPM-1742 [M]	European Windows	1958	12.50	25.00	50.00

LEWIS, JOHN, AND SACHA DISTEL
Distel is a male singer and guitarist not otherwise listed in this book. Also see JOHN LEWIS.
ATLANTIC

Number	Title	Yr	VG	VG+	NM
❑ 1267 [M]	Afternoon in Paris	1957	10.00	20.00	40.00
-- Black label
❑ 1267 [M]	Afternoon in Paris	1961	5.00	10.00	20.00
-- Multicolor label, white "fan" logo at right
❑ 1267 [M]	Afternoon in Paris	1964	3.75	7.50	15.00
-- Multicolor label, black "fan" logo at right

LEWIS, JOHN, AND BILL PERKINS
Also see each artist's individual listings.
PACIFIC JAZZ

Number	Title	Yr	VG	VG+	NM
❑ PJ-44 [M]	Grand Encounter: 2' East, 3' West	1962	10.00	20.00	40.00
-- Reissue with new number
❑ PJ-1217 [M]	Grand Encounter: 2' East, 3' West	1956	37.50	75.00	150.00

Number	Title	Yr	VG	VG+	NM
PAUSA
❑ 9019	Grand Encounter: 2' East, 3' West	198?	2.50	5.00	10.00
WORLD PACIFIC
❑ WP-1217 [M]	Grand Encounter: 2' East, 3' West	1959	25.00	50.00	100.00

LEWIS, KATHARINE HANDY
Female singer, daughter of W.C. HANDY.
FOLKWAYS

Number	Title	Yr	VG	VG+	NM
❑ FJ-3540 [M]	W.C. Handy Blues	1958	7.50	15.00	30.00

LEWIS, MEADE LUX
Pianist; one of the most popular boogie-woogie style pianists. Also see ALBERT AMMONS; SLIM GAILLARD.
ABC-PARAMOUNT

Number	Title	Yr	VG	VG+	NM
❑ ABC-164 [M]	Out of the Roaring 20's	1956	10.00	20.00	40.00
ATLANTIC
❑ ALS-133 [10]	Boogie-Woogie Interpretations	1952	25.00	50.00	100.00
BLUE NOTE
❑ BLP-7018 [10]	Boogie-Woogie Classics	1952	62.50	125.00	250.00
DISC
❑ DLP-352 [10]	Meade Lux Lewis at the Philharmonic	195?	50.00	100.00	200.00
DOWN HOME
❑ MGD-6 [M]	Cat House Piano	1955	---	---	---
-- Canceled
❑ MGD-7 [M]	Yancey's Last Ride	1956	12.50	25.00	50.00
FANTASY
❑ OJC-1759	The Blues Piano Artistry of Meade Lux Lewis	198?	2.50	5.00	10.00
MERCURY
❑ MG-25158 [10]	Meade Lux Lewis	1951	37.50	75.00	150.00
RIVERSIDE
❑ RLP-402 [M]	The Blues Piano Artistry of Meade Lux Lewis	1962	6.25	12.50	25.00
❑ RS-9402 [S]	The Blues Piano Artistry of Meade Lux Lewis	1962	7.50	15.00	30.00
STINSON
❑ 25 [M]	Meade Lux Lewis	196?	5.00	10.00	20.00
TOPS
❑ L-1533 [M]	Barrelhouse Piano	195?	7.50	15.00	30.00
VERVE
❑ MGV-1006 [M]	Cat House Piano	1957	12.50	25.00	50.00
❑ MGV-1007 [M]	Meade Lux Lewis	1957	12.50	25.00	50.00
❑ V-1006 [M]	Cat House Piano	1961	6.25	12.50	25.00
❑ V-1007 [M]	Meade Lux Lewis	1961	6.25	12.50	25.00

LEWIS, MEADE LUX, AND LOUIS BELLSON
Also see each artist's individual listings.
CLEF

Number	Title	Yr	VG	VG+	NM
❑ MGC-632 [M]	Boogie Woogie Piano and Drums	1954	15.00	30.00	60.00

LEWIS, MEL
Drummer. Also see THE FIVE; THAD JONES-MEL LEWIS ORCHESTRA.
ATLANTIC

Number	Title	Yr	VG	VG+	NM
❑ 81655	20th Anniversary	1986	2.50	5.00	10.00
FINESSE
❑ FW 37987	Make Me Smile	1984	2.50	5.00	10.00
HORIZON
❑ SP-716	Mel Lewis and Friends	1976	3.00	6.00	12.00
MODE
❑ LP-103 [M]	Mel Lewis Sextet	1957	20.00	40.00	80.00
PAUSA
❑ 7115	Live in Montreux	1981	2.50	5.00	10.00
SAN FRANCISCO
❑ 2 [M]	Got 'Cha	1957	25.00	50.00	100.00
TELARC
❑ DG-10044	Naturally	1980	3.00	6.00	12.00
VEE JAY
❑ VJS-3062	Gettin' Together	1974	5.00	10.00	20.00

LEWIS, RAMSEY
Pianist and keyboard player. Most of his Argo and Chess albums were released under the moniker "Ramsey Lewis Trio." The other two members of the classic trio were ELDEE YOUNG (bass) and RED HOLT (drums), who later formed their own groups.
ARGO

Number	Title	Yr	VG	VG+	NM
❑ 611 [M]	Gentleman of Swing	1958	12.50	25.00	50.00

Number	Title	Yr	VG	VG+	NM
❏ 611S [S]	Gentleman of Swing	1959	15.00	30.00	60.00
❏ 627 [M]	Gentleman of Jazz	1958	12.50	25.00	50.00
❏ 627S [S]	Gentleman of Jazz	1959	15.00	30.00	60.00
❏ 642 [M]	The Ramsey Lewis Trio with Lee Winchester	1959	10.00	20.00	40.00
❏ 642S [S]	The Ramsey Lewis Trio with Lee Winchester	1959	12.50	25.00	50.00
❏ 645 [M]	An Hour with the Ramsey Lewis	1959	10.00	20.00	40.00
❏ 645S [S]	An Hour with the Ramsey Lewis	1959	12.50	25.00	50.00
❏ 665 [M]	Stretching Out	1960	10.00	20.00	40.00
❏ 665S [S]	Stretching Out	1960	12.50	25.00	50.00
❏ 671 [M]	The Ramsey Lewis Trio in Chicago	1961	10.00	20.00	40.00
❏ 671S [S]	The Ramsey Lewis Trio in Chicago	1961	12.50	25.00	50.00
❏ 680 [M]	More Music from the Soil	1961	10.00	20.00	40.00
❏ 680S [S]	More Music from the Soil	1961	12.50	25.00	50.00
❏ 687 [M]	Sound of Christmas	1961	10.00	20.00	40.00
❏ 687-S [S]	Sound of Christmas	1961	12.50	25.00	50.00
❏ 693 [M]	The Sound of Spring	1962	6.25	12.50	25.00
❏ 693S [S]	The Sound of Spring	1962	7.50	15.00	30.00
❏ 701 [M]	Country Meets the Blues	1962	6.25	12.50	25.00
❏ 701S [S]	Country Meets the Blues	1962	7.50	15.00	30.00
❏ 705 [M]	Bossa Nova	1962	6.25	12.50	25.00
❏ 705S [S]	Bossa Nova	1962	7.50	15.00	30.00
❏ 715 [M]	Pot Luck	1963	6.25	12.50	25.00
❏ 715S [S]	Pot Luck	1963	7.50	15.00	30.00
❏ 723 [M]	Barefoot Sunday Blues	1963	6.25	12.50	25.00
❏ 723S [S]	Barefoot Sunday Blues	1963	7.50	15.00	30.00
❏ 732 [M]	Bach to the Blues	1964	6.25	12.50	25.00
❏ 732S [S]	Bach to the Blues	1964	7.50	15.00	30.00
❏ 741 [M]	The Ramsey Lewis Trio at the Bohemian Caverns	1964	6.25	12.50	25.00
❏ 741S [S]	The Ramsey Lewis Trio at the Bohemian Caverns	1964	7.50	15.00	30.00
❏ 745 [M]	More Sounds of Christmas	1964	6.25	12.50	25.00
❏ 745-S [S]	More Sounds of Christmas	1964	7.50	15.00	30.00
❏ LP-755 [M]	Choice! The Best of the Ramsey Lewis Trio	1965	7.50	15.00	30.00
❏ LPS-755 [S]	Choice! The Best of the Ramsey Lewis Trio	1965	10.00	20.00	40.00
❏ 757 [M]	The In Crowd	1965	6.25	12.50	25.00
❏ 757S [S]	The In Crowd	1965	7.50	15.00	30.00
CADET					
❏ 611 [M]	Gentleman of Swing	1966	3.00	6.00	12.00
❏ 611S [S]	Gentleman of Swing	1966	3.75	7.50	15.00
❏ 627 [M]	Gentleman of Jazz	1966	3.00	6.00	12.00
❏ 627S [S]	Gentleman of Jazz	1966	3.75	7.50	15.00
❏ 645 [M]	An Hour with the Ramsey Lewis	1966	3.00	6.00	12.00
❏ 645S [S]	An Hour with the Ramsey Lewis	1966	3.75	7.50	15.00
❏ 665 [M]	Stretching Out	1966	3.00	6.00	12.00
❏ 665S [S]	Stretching Out	1966	3.75	7.50	15.00
❏ 671 [M]	The Ramsey Lewis Trio in Chicago	1966	3.00	6.00	12.00
❏ 671S [S]	The Ramsey Lewis Trio in Chicago	1966	3.75	7.50	15.00
❏ 680 [M]	More Music from the Soil	1966	3.00	6.00	12.00
❏ 680S [S]	More Music from the Soil	1966	3.75	7.50	15.00
❏ 687X [M]	Sound of Christmas	1966	5.00	10.00	20.00
❏ 687X-S [S]	Sound of Christmas	1966	5.00	10.00	20.00
❏ 693 [M]	The Sound of Spring	1966	3.00	6.00	12.00
❏ 693S [S]	The Sound of Spring	1966	3.75	7.50	15.00
❏ 701 [M]	Country Meets the Blues	1966	3.00	6.00	12.00
❏ 701S [S]	Country Meets the Blues	1966	3.75	7.50	15.00
❏ 705 [M]	Bossa Nova	1966	3.00	6.00	12.00
❏ 705S [S]	Bossa Nova	1966	3.75	7.50	15.00
❏ 723 [M]	Barefoot Sunday Blues	1966	3.00	6.00	12.00
❏ 723S [S]	Barefoot Sunday Blues	1966	3.75	7.50	15.00
❏ 732 [M]	Bach to the Blues	1966	3.00	6.00	12.00
❏ 732S [S]	Bach to the Blues	1966	3.75	7.50	15.00
❏ 741 [M]	The Ramsey Lewis Trio at the Bohemian Caverns	1964	3.00	6.00	12.00
❏ 741S [S]	The Ramsey Lewis Trio at the Bohemian Caverns	1964	3.75	7.50	15.00
❏ 745 [M]	More Sounds of Christmas	1964	3.75	7.50	15.00
❏ 745-S [S]	More Sounds of Christmas	1964	5.00	10.00	20.00
❏ 750 [M]	You Better Believe It	1966	3.00	6.00	12.00
❏ 750S [S]	You Better Believe It	1966	3.75	7.50	15.00
❏ 757 [M]	The In Crowd	1965	3.00	6.00	12.00
❏ 757S [S]	The In Crowd	1965	3.75	7.50	15.00
❏ LP-715 [M]	Pot Luck	1966	3.00	6.00	12.00
❏ LPS-715 [S]	Pot Luck	1966	3.75	7.50	15.00
❏ LP-755 [M]	Choice! The Best of the Ramsey Lewis Trio	1965	3.75	7.50	15.00
❏ LPS-755 [S]	Choice! The Best of the Ramsey Lewis Trio	1965	5.00	10.00	20.00
❏ LP-761 [M]	Hang On Ramsey!	1966	3.75	7.50	15.00
❏ LPS-761 [S]	Hang On Ramsey!	1966	5.00	10.00	20.00
❏ LP-771 [M]	Swingin'	1966	3.75	7.50	15.00
❏ LPS-771 [S]	Swingin'	1966	5.00	10.00	20.00
❏ LP-774 [M]	Wade in the Water	1966	3.75	7.50	15.00
❏ LPS-774 [S]	Wade in the Water	1966	5.00	10.00	20.00
❏ LP-782 [M]	The Movie Album	1967	5.00	10.00	20.00
❏ LPS-782 [S]	The Movie Album	1967	3.75	7.50	15.00
❏ LP-790 [M]	Goin' Latin	1967	5.00	10.00	20.00
❏ LPS-790 [S]	Goin' Latin	1967	3.75	7.50	15.00
❏ LP-794 [M]	Dancing in the Street	1967	5.00	10.00	20.00
❏ LPS-794 [S]	Dancing in the Street	1967	3.75	7.50	15.00
❏ LPS-799	Up Pops Ramsey Lewis	1968	3.75	7.50	15.00
❏ LPS-811	Maiden Voyage	1968	3.75	7.50	15.00
❏ LPS-821	Mother Nature's Son	1969	3.75	7.50	15.00
❏ LPS-827	Another Voyage	1969	3.75	7.50	15.00
❏ LPS-836	Ramsey Lewis, The Piano Player	1970	3.75	7.50	15.00
❏ LPS-839	The Best of Ramsey Lewis	1970	3.75	7.50	15.00
❏ LPS-844	Them Changes	1970	3.75	7.50	15.00
❏ 50020	Groover	1973	3.00	6.00	12.00
❏ 50058 [(2)]	Solid Ivory	1974	3.75	7.50	15.00
❏ 60001	Back to the Roots	1971	3.00	6.00	12.00
❏ 60018 [(2)]	Inside Ramsey Lewis	1972	3.75	7.50	15.00
CBS					
❏ FM 42661	A Classic Encounter	1988	2.50	5.00	10.00
CHESS					
❏ 9001 [(2)]	Solid Ivory	197?	3.00	6.00	12.00
-- Reissue of Cadet 50058					
❏ CH 9716	Sound of Christmas	1984	2.50	5.00	10.00
-- Reissue of Argo 687-S					
COLUMBIA					
❏ CQ 31096 [Q]	Upendo Ni Pamoja	1972	4.50	9.00	18.00
❏ KC 31096	Upendo Ni Pamoja	1972	3.00	6.00	12.00
❏ KC 32030	Funky Serenity	1973	3.00	6.00	12.00
❏ KC 32490	Ramsey Lewis' Newly Recorded All-Time, Non-Stop Golden Hits	1973	3.00	6.00	12.00
❏ PC 32490	Ramsey Lewis' Newly Recorded All-Time, Non-Stop Golden Hits	197?	2.00	4.00	8.00
-- Reissue with new prefix					
❏ KC 32897	Solar Wind	1974	3.00	6.00	12.00
❏ KC 33194	Sun Goddess	1974	2.50	5.00	10.00
❏ PC 33194	Sun Goddess	197?	2.00	4.00	8.00
-- Reissue with new prefix					
❏ CG 33663 [(2)]	Upendo Ni Pamoja/Funky Serenity	1975	3.00	6.00	12.00
❏ PC 33800	Don't It Feel Good	1975	2.50	5.00	10.00
-- Originals have no bar code					
❏ PC 33800	Don't It Feel Good	198?	2.00	4.00	8.00
-- Budget-line reissue with bar code					
❏ PC 34173	Salongo	1976	2.50	5.00	10.00
-- Originals have no bar code					
❏ PC 34173	Salongo	198?	2.00	4.00	8.00
-- Budget-line reissue with bar code					
❏ PC 34696	Love Notes	1977	2.50	5.00	10.00
❏ JC 35018	Tequila Mockingbird	1977	2.50	5.00	10.00
❏ JC 35483	Legacy	1978	2.50	5.00	10.00
❏ PC 35483	Legacy	198?	2.00	4.00	8.00
-- Budget-line reissue					
❏ FC 36364	The Best of Ramsey Lewis	1980	2.50	5.00	10.00
❏ JC 36423	Routes	1980	2.50	5.00	10.00
❏ PC 36423	Routes	198?	2.00	4.00	8.00
-- Budget-line reissue					
❏ JC 35815	Ramsey	1979	2.50	5.00	10.00
❏ FC 37153	Three Piece Suite	1981	2.50	5.00	10.00
❏ FC 37687	Live at the Savoy	1982	2.50	5.00	10.00
❏ PC 37687	Live at the Savoy	198?	2.00	4.00	8.00
-- Budget-line reissue					
❏ FC 38294	Chance Encounter	1983	2.50	5.00	10.00
❏ FC 38787	Les Fleurs	1983	2.50	5.00	10.00
❏ FC 39158	Reunion	1983	2.50	5.00	10.00
❏ FC 40108	Fantasy	1985	2.50	5.00	10.00
❏ FC 40677	Keys to the City	1987	2.50	5.00	10.00
❏ HC 43194	Sun Goddess	1982	12.50	25.00	50.00
-- Half-speed mastered edition					
❏ FC 44190	Urban Renewal	1989	3.75	7.50	15.00
❏ HC 47687	Live at the Savoy	1982	20.00	40.00	80.00
-- Half-speed mastered edition					
COLUMBIA JAZZ ODYSSEY					
❏ PC 37019	Blues for the Night Owl	1981	2.50	5.00	10.00
EMARCY					
❏ MG-36150 [M]	Down to Earth	1958	10.00	20.00	40.00
❏ SR-80029 [S]	Down to Earth	1958	12.50	25.00	50.00
MERCURY					
❏ MG-20536 [M]	Down to Earth	1965	5.00	10.00	20.00
❏ SR-60536 [S]	Down to Earth	1965	6.25	12.50	25.00

Number	Title	Yr	VG	VG+	NM
LEWIS, RAMSEY, AND JEAN DuSHON					
Also see each artist's individual listings.					
ARGO					
❏ 750 [M]	You Better Believe It	1965	6.25	12.50	25.00
❏ 750S [S]	You Better Believe It	1965	7.50	15.00	30.00
LEWIS, RAMSEY, AND NANCY WILSON					
Also see each artist's individual listings.					
COLUMBIA					
❏ FC 39326	The Two of Us	1984	2.50	5.00	10.00
LEWIS, TED					
Clarinetist, male singer and bandleader.					
BIOGRAPH					
❏ C-7	Ted Lewis' Orchestra, Volume 1	198?	2.50	5.00	10.00
❏ C-8	Ted Lewis' Orchestra, Volume 2	198?	2.50	5.00	10.00
COLUMBIA					
❏ CL 6127 [10]	Classic Jazz	1950	12.50	25.00	50.00
DECCA					
❏ DL 4905 [M]	Ted Lewis' Greatest Hits	1967	6.25	12.50	25.00
❏ DL 8321 [M]	Is Everybody Happy?	1956	10.00	20.00	40.00
❏ DL 8322 [M]	The Medicine Man for the Blues	1956	10.00	20.00	40.00
❏ DL 74905 [R]	Ted Lewis' Greatest Hits	1967	3.75	7.50	15.00
EPIC					
❏ LN 3170 [M]	Everybody's Happy!	1955	10.00	20.00	40.00
LEWIS, WILLIE					
Alto saxophone player and bandleader.					
SWING					
❏ 8400/1 [(2)]	Willie Lewis and His Entertainers	198?	3.00	6.00	12.00
LIBBY, JERRY					
SABRINA					
❏ SA-100 [M]	Live? At Wilkins	1964	5.00	10.00	20.00
LIDSTROM, JACK					
Trumpeter.					
WORLD PACIFIC					
❏ PJ-1235 [M]	Look, Dad! They're Comin' Down the Street in Hi-Fi	1957	10.00	20.00	40.00
LIEBMAN, DAVE					
Soprano and tenor saxophone player.					
ARTISTS HOUSE					
❏ 8	Pendulum	1978	3.00	6.00	12.00
CMP					
❏ CMP-9-ST	Dedications	198?	3.00	6.00	12.00
❏ CMP-24-ST	The Loneliness of a Long-Distance Runner	1987	3.00	6.00	12.00
❏ CMP-40-ST	Chant	1990	3.75	7.50	15.00
ECM					
❏ 1039	Lookout Farm	197?	3.75	7.50	15.00
❏ 1046	Drum Ode	1975	3.75	7.50	15.00
HEADS UP					
❏ HUP-3005	The Energy of the Chance	1989	3.75	7.50	15.00
HORIZON					
❏ SP-702	Sweet Hands	1976	3.00	6.00	12.00
❏ SP-709	Fantasies	1976	3.00	6.00	12.00
❏ SP-721	Light'n Up, Please!	1977	3.00	6.00	12.00
PM					
❏ PMR-022	Memories, Dreams and Reflections	1986	3.00	6.00	12.00
❏ PMR-023	Picture Show	1986	3.00	6.00	12.00
WEST 54					
❏ 8012	First Visit	1979	3.00	6.00	12.00
LIGHTHOUSE ALL-STARS, THE					
See HOWARD RUMSEY.					
LIGHTSEY, KIRK					
Pianist.					
SUNNYSIDE					
❏ SSC-1002	Lightsey 1	1985	3.00	6.00	12.00
❏ SSC-1005	Lightsey 2	1985	3.00	6.00	12.00
❏ SSC-1014	Lightsey Live	1987	3.00	6.00	12.00
❏ SSC-1020	Everything Is Changed	198?	3.00	6.00	12.00
LIGON, BERT					
Pianist, bandleader, arranger and composer.					
INNER CITY					
❏ IC-1107	The Condor	198?	3.00	6.00	12.00
SEA BREEZE					
❏ SB-3002	Dancing Bare	198?	3.00	6.00	12.00
LIMEHOUSE JAZZ BAND, THE					
STOMP OFF					
❏ SOS-1014	Rhythm Is Our Business	1981	2.50	5.00	10.00
LINCOLN, ABBEY					
Female singer.					
BARMABY					
❏ KZ 31037	Straight Ahead	1972	3.75	7.50	15.00
CANDID					
❏ CD-8015 [M]	Straight Ahead	1960	10.00	20.00	40.00
❏ CS-9015 [S]	Straight Ahead	1960	12.50	25.00	50.00
COLUMBIA					
❏ JC 36581	What It Is	1979	2.50	5.00	10.00
FANTASY					
❏ OJC-069	Abbey Is Blue	1982	2.50	5.00	10.00
❏ OJC-085	That's Him!	198?	2.50	5.00	10.00
❏ OJC-205	It's Magic	1985	2.50	5.00	10.00
INNER CITY					
❏ IC-1117	Golden Lady	198?	3.00	6.00	12.00
❏ IC-6040	The People in Me	197?	3.75	7.50	15.00
JAZZ MAN					
❏ 5043	Straight Ahead	198?	2.50	5.00	10.00
LIBERTY					
❏ LRP-3025 [M]	Abbey Lincoln's Affair	1957	12.50	25.00	50.00
RIVERSIDE					
❏ RLP 12-251 [M]	That's Him!	1957	12.50	25.00	50.00
❏ RLP 12-277 [M]	It's Magic	1958	10.00	20.00	40.00
❏ RLP 12-308 [M]	Abbey Is Blue	1959	10.00	20.00	40.00
❏ RLP-1107 [S]	That's Him!	1958	10.00	20.00	40.00
❏ RLP-1153 [S]	Abbey Is Blue	1959	12.50	25.00	50.00
❏ 6088	Abbey Is Blue	197?	3.00	6.00	12.00
LINDBERG, JOHN					
Bass player and composer.					
BLACK SAINT					
❏ BSR-0062	Dimension 5	1982	3.00	6.00	12.00
❏ BSR-0072	Give and Take	1983	3.00	6.00	12.00
❏ BSR-0082	Trilogy of Works for Eleven Instrumentalists	1985	3.00	6.00	12.00
SOUND ASPECTS					
❏ SAS-001	The East Side Suite	1985	3.00	6.00	12.00
LINDBERG, NILS					
Pianist and composer.					
CAPITOL					
❏ ST 10367 [S]	Trisection	196?	6.25	12.50	25.00
❏ T 10367 [M]	Trisection	196?	5.00	10.00	20.00
LINDH, JAYSON					
Flutist. Also recorded under the name "Bjorn J-Son Lindh"; these are included below.					
JAS					
❏ JAS-4000	Second Carneval	1975	5.00	10.00	20.00
METRONOME					
❏ DIX-3000	Ramadan	1972	6.25	12.50	25.00
❏ DIX-3001	Cous-Cous	1973	6.25	12.50	25.00
❏ DIX-3002	Sissel	1974	6.25	12.50	25.00
STORYVILLE					
❏ 4132	Atlantis	1983	3.00	6.00	12.00
-- As "Bjorn J-Son Lindh"					
VANGUARD					
❏ VSD-79434	A Day at the Surface	1979	3.00	6.00	12.00
-- As "Bjorn J-Son Lindh"					
LINGLE, PAUL					
Pianist.					
EUPHONIC					
❏ 1217	Dance of the Witch Hazels	198?	2.50	5.00	10.00
❏ 1220	The Legend of Lingle	198?	2.50	5.00	10.00
LINN, RAY					
Trumpeter.					
DISCOVERY					
❏ DS-823	Empty Suit Blues	1981	2.50	5.00	10.00

Number	Title	Yr	VG	VG+	NM

TREND
| ❏ 515 | Chicago Jazz | 1980 | 5.00 | 10.00 | 20.00 |

-- *Direct-to-disc recording*

LINS, IVAN
Male singer and composer.
PHILIPS
| ❏ 822 672-1 | Juntos (Together) | 1986 | 2.50 | 5.00 | 10.00 |

LINSKY, JEFF
Guitarist.
CONCORD PICANTE
| ❏ CJP-363 | Up Late | 1988 | 2.50 | 5.00 | 10.00 |

LIPSKIN, MIKE
Pianist, arranger and composer.
FLYING DUTCHMAN
| ❏ FD-10140 | California | 1972 | 3.75 | 7.50 | 15.00 |

LIPSKY, HELMUT
Violinist.
JAZZIMAGE
| ❏ JZ-101 | Melosphere | 198? | 3.00 | 6.00 | 12.00 |

LIST, GARRETT
Trombonist and composer.
LOVELY
| ❏ VR-1201 | Fire and Ice | 198? | 3.00 | 6.00 | 12.00 |

LISTEN
Group led by saxophone player Mel Martin.
INNER CITY
| ❏ IC-1025 | Listen | 1977 | 3.75 | 7.50 | 15.00 |
| ❏ IC-1055 | Growing | 1978 | 3.75 | 7.50 | 15.00 |

LISTON, MELBA
Trombonist, composer and arranger.
METROJAZZ
| ❏ E-1013 [M] | Melba Liston and Her Bones | 1958 | 20.00 | 40.00 | 80.00 |
| ❏ SE-1013 [S] | Melba Liston and Her Bones | 1958 | 15.00 | 30.00 | 60.00 |

LITTLE, BOOKER
Trumpeter. Also see YOUNG MEN FROM MEMPHIS.
BAINBRIDGE
| ❏ 1041 | Booker Little | 198? | 2.50 | 5.00 | 10.00 |
BARNABY
| ❏ BR-5019 | Out Front | 1977 | 3.00 | 6.00 | 12.00 |
BETHLEHEM
| ❏ BCP-6034 | Victory and Sorrow | 197? | 3.75 | 7.50 | 15.00 |

-- *Reissue of 6061, distributed by RCA Victor*
| ❏ BCP-6061 [M] | Booker Little and Friends | 1962 | 12.50 | 25.00 | 50.00 |
CANDID
| ❏ CD-8027 [M] | Out Front | 1961 | 10.00 | 20.00 | 40.00 |
| ❏ CS-9027 [S] | Out Front | 1961 | 12.50 | 25.00 | 50.00 |
TIME
| ❏ S-2011 [S] | Booker Little | 1960 | 20.00 | 40.00 | 80.00 |
| ❏ 52011 [M] | Booker Little | 1960 | 15.00 | 30.00 | 60.00 |
UNITED ARTISTS
| ❏ UAL-4034 [M] | The Booker Little Four | 1959 | 20.00 | 40.00 | 80.00 |
| ❏ UAS-5034 [S] | The Booker Little Four | 1959 | 15.00 | 30.00 | 60.00 |

LITTLE, BOOKER, AND BOOKER ERVIN
Also see each artist's individual listings.
TCB
| ❏ 1003 | Sounds of Inner City | 197? | 10.00 | 20.00 | 40.00 |

LIVING JAZZ
Studio group featuring woodwinds player Phil Bodner.
RCA CAMDEN
❏ ACL1-0202	Manha de Carnival	1973	2.50	5.00	10.00
❏ CAL-848 [M]	The Girl from Ipanema and Other Hits	1964	2.50	5.00	10.00
❏ CAS-848 [S]	The Girl from Ipanema and Other Hits	1964	3.00	6.00	12.00
❏ CAL-878 [M]	Dear Heart and Other Favorites	1965	2.50	5.00	10.00
❏ CAS-878 [S]	Dear Heart and Other Favorites	1965	3.00	6.00	12.00
❏ CAL-914 [M]	Quiet Nights	1965	2.50	5.00	10.00
❏ CAS-914 [S]	Quiet Nights	1965	3.00	6.00	12.00
❏ CAL-985 [M]	A Lover's Concerto	1966	2.50	5.00	10.00

Number	Title	Yr	VG	VG+	NM
❏ CAS-985 [S]	A Lover's Concerto	1966	3.00	6.00	12.00
❏ CAL-2135 [M]	The Soul of Brazil	1967	3.00	6.00	12.00
❏ CAL-2196 [M]	Ode to Young Lovers	1968	3.00	6.00	12.00
❏ CAS-2135 [S]	The Soul of Brazil	1967	2.50	5.00	10.00
❏ CAS-2196 [S]	Ode to Young Lovers	1968	2.50	5.00	10.00
❏ CAS-2298	Fool on the Hill	1969	2.50	5.00	10.00
❏ CAS-2436	Hot Butter and Soul	1970	2.50	5.00	10.00

RCA VICTOR
| ❏ APL1-2386 | Hello Young Lovers | 1977 | 2.50 | 5.00 | 10.00 |

LLOYD, CHARLES
Tenor saxophone player and flutist.
A&M
| ❏ SP-3044 | Waves | 1973 | 3.00 | 6.00 | 12.00 |
| ❏ SP-3046 | Geeta | 1973 | 3.00 | 6.00 | 12.00 |
ATLANTIC
❏ 1459 [M]	Dream Weaver	1966	3.75	7.50	15.00
❏ SD 1459 [S]	Dream Weaver	1966	5.00	10.00	20.00
❏ 1473 [M]	Forest Flower	1967	3.75	7.50	15.00
❏ SD 1473 [S]	Forest Flower	1967	5.00	10.00	20.00
❏ 1481 [M]	Love-In	1967	5.00	10.00	20.00
❏ SD 1481 [S]	Love-In	1967	3.75	7.50	15.00
❏ SD 1493	Journey Within	1968	3.75	7.50	15.00
❏ SD 1500	Charles Lloyd in Europe	1969	3.75	7.50	15.00
❏ SD 1519	Soundtrack	1970	3.75	7.50	15.00
❏ SD 1556	The Best of Charles Lloyd	1970	3.75	7.50	15.00
❏ SD 1571	Charles Lloyd in the Soviet Union	1971	3.75	7.50	15.00
❏ SD 1586	Flowering of the Original	1972	3.00	6.00	12.00
BLUE NOTE
| ❏ BT-85104 | A Night in Copenhagen | 198? | 2.50 | 5.00 | 10.00 |
COLUMBIA
❏ CL 2267 [M]	Discovery!	1965	6.25	12.50	25.00
❏ CL 2412 [M]	Of Course, Of Course	1966	6.25	12.50	25.00
❏ CS 9067 [S]	Discovery!	1965	7.50	15.00	30.00
❏ CS 9212 [S]	Of Course, Of Course	1966	7.50	15.00	30.00
❏ CS 9609	Nirvana	1968	6.25	12.50	25.00
ELEKTRA MUSICIAN
| ❏ 60220 | Montreux '82 | 1983 | 2.50 | 5.00 | 10.00 |
KAPP
| ❏ KS-3634 | Moon Man | 1971 | 3.00 | 6.00 | 12.00 |
| ❏ KS-3647 | Warm Waters | 1971 | 3.00 | 6.00 | 12.00 |
PACIFIC ARTS
| ❏ 7-123 | Weavings | 1978 | 3.00 | 6.00 | 12.00 |
| ❏ 7-139 | Big Sur Tapestry | 1979 | 3.00 | 6.00 | 12.00 |

LOBO
Full name: Edu Lobo. Guitarist, male singer and composer – and unrelated to the pop singer of the early 70s who called himself "Lobo."
A&M
| ❏ SP-3035 | Sergio Mendes Presents Lobo | 1970 | 6.25 | 12.50 | 25.00 |

LoCASCIO, JOE
Pianist.
CMG
| ❏ CML-8002 | Gliders | 1988 | 2.50 | 5.00 | 10.00 |
| ❏ CML-8015 | Marionette | 1989 | 3.00 | 6.00 | 12.00 |

LOCKE, JOE
Vibraphone player.
CADENCE JAZZ
| ❏ CJR-1034 | Scenario | 1988 | 2.50 | 5.00 | 10.00 |

LOCKWOOD, DIDIER
Violinist.
GRAMAVISION
| ❏ 18-8412 | Didier Lockwood Group | 1984 | 2.50 | 5.00 | 10.00 |
| ❏ 18-8504 | Out of the Blue | 1985 | 2.50 | 5.00 | 10.00 |
INNER CITY
| ❏ IC-1092 | Surya | 1982 | 3.00 | 6.00 | 12.00 |
PAUSA
❏ 7046	New World	1979	2.50	5.00	10.00
❏ 7094	Live in Montreux	1981	2.50	5.00	10.00
❏ 7125	Fasten Seat Belts	1981	2.50	5.00	10.00

LOFSKY, LORNE
Guitarist.
PABLO TODAY
| ❏ 2312 122 | It Could Happen to You | 1979 | 3.00 | 6.00 | 12.00 |

Number	Title	Yr	VG	VG+	NM

LOFTON, CLARENCE
Pianist. Nicknamed "Cripple."
RIVERSIDE

Number	Title	Yr	VG	VG+	NM
❏ RLP-1037 [10]	Honky-Tonk and Boogie-Woogie Piano	1954	20.00	40.00	80.00

LOFTON, TRICKY, AND CARMELL JONES
Lofton plays trombone. Also see CARMELL JONES.
PACIFIC JAZZ

❏ PJ-49 [M]	Brass Bag	1962	10.00	20.00	40.00
❏ ST-49 [S]	Brass Bag	1962	12.50	25.00	50.00

LOGAN, GIUSEPPI
Alto and tenor saxophone player.
ESP-DISK'

❏ 1007 [M]	Giuseppi Logan Quartet	1965	3.75	7.50	15.00
❏ S-1007 [S]	Giuseppi Logan Quartet	1965	5.00	10.00	20.00
❏ 1013 [M]	More Giuseppi Logan	1965	3.75	7.50	15.00
❏ S-1013 [S]	More Giuseppi Logan	1965	5.00	10.00	20.00

LOMBARDO, GUY
Bandleader and violinist; his Royal Canadians were the most popular of the "sweet" big bands, and he helped make "Auld Lang Syne" a New Year's Eve staple.
CAPITOL

❏ ST-128	The New Songs -- The New Sounds	1969	2.50	5.00	10.00
❏ SM-340	Is That All There Is?	1976	2.00	4.00	8.00
-- Reissue with new prefix					
❏ ST-340	Is That All There Is?	1969	2.50	5.00	10.00
❏ STCL-578 [(3)]	Guy Lombardo	1970	6.25	12.50	25.00
❏ W 738 [M]	Lombardo in Hi-Fi	1956	5.00	10.00	20.00
-- Turquoise or gray label					
❏ W 738 [M]	Lombardo in Hi-Fi	1958	3.75	7.50	15.00
-- Black colorband label, logo at left					
❏ W 738 [M]	Lombardo in Hi-Fi	1962	3.00	6.00	12.00
-- Black colorband label, logo at top					
❏ DT 739 [R]	Your Guy Lombardo Medley	196?	2.50	5.00	10.00
❏ SM-739	Your Guy Lombardo Medley	1976	2.00	4.00	8.00
-- Reissue with new prefix					
❏ T 739 [M]	Your Guy Lombardo Medley	1956	5.00	10.00	20.00
-- Turquoise or gray label					
❏ T 739 [M]	Your Guy Lombardo Medley	1958	3.75	7.50	15.00
-- Black colorband label, logo at left					
❏ T 739 [M]	Your Guy Lombardo Medley	1962	3.00	6.00	12.00
-- Black colorband label, logo at top					
❏ DT 788 [R]	A Decade on Broadway 1946-56	196?	2.50	5.00	10.00
-- Black colorband label, logo at left					
❏ T 788 [M]	A Decade on Broadway 1946-56	1956	5.00	10.00	20.00
-- Turquoise or gray label					
❏ T 788 [M]	A Decade on Broadway 1946-56	1958	3.75	7.50	15.00
-- Black colorband label, logo at left					
❏ T 788 [M]	A Decade on Broadway 1946-56	1962	3.00	6.00	12.00
-- Black colorband label, logo at top					
❏ DT 892 [R]	Lively Guy	196?	2.50	5.00	10.00
❏ T 892 [M]	Lively Guy	1957	5.00	10.00	20.00
-- Turquoise or gray label					
❏ T 892 [M]	Lively Guy	1958	3.75	7.50	15.00
-- Black colorband label, logo at left					
❏ T 892 [M]	Lively Guy	1962	3.00	6.00	12.00
-- Black colorband label, logo at top					
❏ DT 916 [R]	A Decade on Broadway 1935-45	196?	2.50	5.00	10.00
-- Black colorband label, logo at left					
❏ T 916 [M]	A Decade on Broadway 1935-45	1958	5.00	10.00	20.00
-- Turquoise or gray label					
❏ T 916 [M]	A Decade on Broadway 1935-45	1958	3.75	7.50	15.00
-- Black colorband label, logo at left					
❏ T 916 [M]	A Decade on Broadway 1935-45	1962	3.00	6.00	12.00
-- Black colorband label, logo at top					
❏ ST 1019 [S]	Berlin by Lombardo	1959	6.25	12.50	25.00
-- Black colorband label, logo at left					
❏ ST 1019 [S]	Berlin by Lombardo	1962	3.00	6.00	12.00
-- Black colorband label, logo at top					
❏ T 1019 [M]	Berlin by Lombardo	1958	5.00	10.00	20.00
-- Turquoise or gray label					
❏ T 1019 [M]	Berlin by Lombardo	1959	3.75	7.50	15.00
-- Black colorband label, logo at left					
❏ T 1019 [M]	Berlin by Lombardo	1962	2.50	5.00	10.00
-- Black colorband label, logo at top					

Number	Title	Yr	VG	VG+	NM
❏ ST 1121 [S]	Dancing Room Only	1959	5.00	10.00	20.00
-- Black colorband label, logo at left					
❏ ST 1121 [S]	Dancing Room Only	1962	3.00	6.00	12.00
-- Black colorband label, logo at top					
❏ T 1121 [M]	Dancing Room Only	1959	3.75	7.50	15.00
-- Black colorband label, logo at left					
❏ T 1121 [M]	Dancing Room Only	1962	2.50	5.00	10.00
-- Black colorband label, logo at top					
❏ ST 1244 [S]	Your Guy Lombardo Medley, Vol. 2	1960	5.00	10.00	20.00
-- Black colorband label, logo at left					
❏ ST 1244 [S]	Your Guy Lombardo Medley, Vol. 2	1962	3.00	6.00	12.00
-- Black colorband label, logo at top					
❏ T 1244 [M]	Your Guy Lombardo Medley, Vol. 2	1960	3.75	7.50	15.00
-- Black colorband label, logo at left					
❏ T 1244 [M]	Your Guy Lombardo Medley, Vol. 2	1962	2.50	5.00	10.00
-- Black colorband label, logo at top					
❏ ST 1306 [S]	The Sweetest Waltzes This Side of Heaven	1960	5.00	10.00	20.00
-- Black colorband label, logo at top					
❏ ST 1306 [S]	The Sweetest Waltzes This Side of Heaven	1962	3.00	6.00	12.00
-- Black colorband label, logo at top					
❏ T 1306 [M]	The Sweetest Waltzes This Side of Heaven	1960	3.75	7.50	15.00
-- Black colorband label, logo at top					
❏ T 1306 [M]	The Sweetest Waltzes This Side of Heaven	1962	2.50	5.00	10.00
-- Black colorband label, logo at top					
❏ KAO 1443 [M]	Sing the Songs of Christmas	1960	3.75	7.50	15.00
❏ SKAO 1443 [S]	Sing the Songs of Christmas	1960	5.00	10.00	20.00
-- Black colorband label, logo at left					
❏ STAO 1443 [S]	Sing the Songs of Christmas	1962	3.75	7.50	15.00
-- Black colorband label, logo at top					
❏ TAO 1443 [M]	Sing the Songs of Christmas	1962	3.00	6.00	12.00
-- Black colorband label, logo at top					
❏ DT 1461 [R]	The Best of Guy Lombardo	1961	2.50	5.00	10.00
-- Black colorband label, logo at left					
❏ T 1461 [M]	The Best of Guy Lombardo	1961	5.00	10.00	20.00
-- Black colorband label, logo at left					
❏ T 1461 [M]	The Best of Guy Lombardo	1962	3.00	6.00	12.00
-- Black colorband label, logo at top					
❏ SM-1593	Drifting and Dreaming	1976	2.00	4.00	8.00
-- Reissue with new prefix					
❏ ST 1593 [S]	Drifting and Dreaming	1961	5.00	10.00	20.00
-- Black colorband label, logo at left					
❏ ST 1593 [S]	Drifting and Dreaming	1962	3.00	6.00	12.00
-- Black colorband label, logo at top					
❏ T 1593 [M]	Drifting and Dreaming	1961	3.75	7.50	15.00
-- Black colorband label, logo at top					
❏ T 1593 [M]	Drifting and Dreaming	1962	2.50	5.00	10.00
-- Black colorband label, logo at top					
❏ ST 1598 [S]	Your Guy Lombardo Medley, Vol. 3	1961	5.00	10.00	20.00
-- Black colorband label, logo at left					
❏ ST 1598 [S]	Your Guy Lombardo Medley, Vol. 3	1962	3.00	6.00	12.00
-- Black colorband label, logo at top					
❏ T 1598 [M]	Your Guy Lombardo Medley, Vol. 3	1961	3.75	7.50	15.00
-- Black colorband label, logo at top					
❏ T 1598 [M]	Your Guy Lombardo Medley, Vol. 3	1962	2.50	5.00	10.00
-- Black colorband label, logo at top					
❏ ST 1738 [S]	Waltzing with Guy Lombardo	1962	3.75	7.50	15.00
❏ T 1738 [M]	Waltzing with Guy Lombardo	1962	3.00	6.00	12.00
❏ DT 1947 [R]	The Sweetest Medleys This Side of Heaven	1963	2.50	5.00	10.00
❏ T 1947 [M]	The Sweetest Medleys This Side of Heaven	1963	3.00	6.00	12.00
❏ ST 2052 [S]	The Lombardo Touch	1964	3.75	7.50	15.00
❏ T 2052 [M]	The Lombardo Touch	1964	3.00	6.00	12.00
❏ STDL 2181 [(4) S]	The Lombardo Years	1964	7.50	15.00	30.00
❏ TDL 2181 [(4) M]	The Lombardo Years	1964	6.25	12.50	25.00
❏ ST 2298 [S]	Guy Lombardo Presents Kenny Gardner	1965	3.75	7.50	15.00
❏ T 2298 [M]	Guy Lombardo Presents Kenny Gardner	1965	3.00	6.00	12.00
❏ DT 2350 [R]	Guy Lombardo and His Royal Canadians Play Songs of Carmen Lombardo	1965	2.50	5.00	10.00
❏ T 2350 [M]	Guy Lombardo and His Royal Canadians Play Songs of Carmen Lombardo	1965	3.00	6.00	12.00
❏ ST 2481 [S]	A Wonderful Year	1966	3.75	7.50	15.00
❏ T 2481 [M]	A Wonderful Year	1966	3.00	6.00	12.00
❏ ST 2559 [S]	Guy Lombardo's Broadway	1966	3.75	7.50	15.00
❏ T 2559 [M]	Guy Lombardo's Broadway	1966	3.00	6.00	12.00

Number	Title	Yr	VG	VG+	NM
❏ ST 2639 [S]	The Sweetest Sounds Today	1967	3.00	6.00	12.00
❏ T 2639 [M]	The Sweetest Sounds Today	1967	3.75	7.50	15.00
❏ ST 2777 [S]	Lombardo Country	1967	3.00	6.00	12.00
❏ T 2777 [M]	Lombardo Country	1967	3.75	7.50	15.00
❏ ST 2825	Medleys on Parade	1968	2.50	5.00	10.00
❏ ST 2829	They're Playing Our Songs	1968	2.50	5.00	10.00
❏ SKAO 2940	The Best of Guy Lombardo, Vol. 2	1968	2.50	5.00	10.00
❏ SN-16192	Dancing Room Only	198?	2.00	4.00	8.00
-- Budget-line reissue					
❏ SN-16193	The Sweetest Waltzes This Side of Heaven	198?	2.00	4.00	8.00
-- Budget-line reissue					

DECCA

Number	Title	Yr	VG	VG+	NM
❏ DXB 185 [(2) M]	The Best of Guy Lombardo	1964	5.00	10.00	20.00
❏ DL 4123 [M]	The Sweetest Pianos This Side of Heaven	1961	3.00	6.00	12.00
❏ DL 4149 [M]	Far Away Places	1961	3.00	6.00	12.00
❏ DL 4177 [M]	New Year's Eve with Guy	1961	3.00	6.00	12.00
❏ DL 4180 [M]	Dance to the Songs Everybody Knows	1961	3.00	6.00	12.00
❏ DL 4229 [M]	The Sweetest Music This Side of Heaven (A Musical Biography 1932-1939)	1962	3.00	6.00	12.00
❏ DL 4268 [M]	The Best Songs Are the Old Songs	1962	3.75	7.50	15.00
❏ DL 4280 [M]	By Special Request	1962	3.00	6.00	12.00
❏ DL 4288 [M]	Dancing Piano	1962	3.00	6.00	12.00
❏ DL 4328 [M]	The Sweetest Music This Side of Heaven (A Musical Biography 1944-1948)	1962	3.00	6.00	12.00
❏ DL 4329 [M]	The Sweetest Music This Side of Heaven (A Musical Biography 1949-1954)	1962	3.00	6.00	12.00
❏ DL 4371 [M]	Play a Happy Song	1963	3.00	6.00	12.00
❏ DL 4380 [M]	Golden Minstrel Songs for Dancing	1963	3.00	6.00	12.00
❏ DL 4430 [M]	Golden Folk Songs	1964	2.50	5.00	10.00
❏ DL 4516 [M]	Italian Songs Everybody Knows	1964	2.50	5.00	10.00
❏ DL 4567 [M]	Snuggled on Your Shoulder	1965	2.50	5.00	10.00
❏ DL 4593 [M]	Golden Medleys	1965	2.50	5.00	10.00
❏ DL 4735 [M]	Dance Medley Time	1966	2.50	5.00	10.00
❏ DL 4812 [M]	Guy Lombardo's Greatest Hits	1966	2.50	5.00	10.00
❏ DL 5002 [10]	The Twin Pianos -- Vol. 1	195?	7.50	15.00	30.00
-- Record has "DL" prefix; sleeve may or may not have "DL"					
❏ DLP 5002 [10]	The Twin Pianos -- Vol. 1	1949	10.00	20.00	40.00
-- Both record and sleeve have "DLP" prefix					
❏ DL 5003 [10]	The Twin Pianos -- Vol. 2	195?	7.50	15.00	30.00
-- Record has "DL" prefix; sleeve may or may not have "DL"					
❏ DLP 5003 [10]	The Twin Pianos -- Vol. 2	1949	10.00	20.00	40.00
-- Both record and sleeve have "DLP" prefix					
❏ DL 5024 [10]	Sidewalks of New York	1949	10.00	20.00	40.00
❏ DL 5041 [10]	Lombardoland	1949	10.00	20.00	40.00
❏ DL 5097 [10]	Song Hits from Broadway Shows	1949	10.00	20.00	40.00
❏ DL 5127 [10]	Latin Rhythms	195?	7.50	15.00	30.00
❏ DL 5156 [10]	Hawaiian Songs for Dancing	195?	7.50	15.00	30.00
❏ DL 5193 [10]	Waltzes	195?	7.50	15.00	30.00
❏ DL 5235 [10]	Silver Jubilee -- 1925-1950	1950	7.50	15.00	30.00
❏ DL 5277 [10]	Square Dances (Without Calls)	195?	7.50	15.00	30.00
❏ DL 5322 [10]	Souvenirs	195?	7.50	15.00	30.00
❏ DL 5325 [10]	Waltzland	195?	7.50	15.00	30.00
❏ DL 5328 [10]	Lombardoland, Vol. 2	195?	7.50	15.00	30.00
❏ DL 5329 [10]	Enjoy Yourself	195?	7.50	15.00	30.00
❏ DL 5330 [10]	The Sweetest Music This Side of Heaven	195?	7.50	15.00	30.00
❏ DL 5430 [10]	Jingle Bells	195?	7.50	15.00	30.00
❏ DL 5434 [10]	Everybody Dance to the Music of Guy Lombardo	195?	7.50	15.00	30.00
❏ DXSB 7185 [(2) R]	The Best of Guy Lombardo	1964	3.75	7.50	15.00
❏ DL 8070 [M]	A Night at the Roosevelt	195?	5.00	10.00	20.00
-- Black label, silver print					
❏ DL 8070 [M]	A Night at the Roosevelt	1961	3.00	6.00	12.00
-- Black label with color bars					
❏ DL 8097 [M]	Lombardoland, U.S.A.	195?	5.00	10.00	20.00
-- Black label, silver print					
❏ DL 8097 [M]	Lombardoland, U.S.A.	1961	3.00	6.00	12.00
-- Black label with color bars					
❏ DL 8119 [M]	Twin Pianos	195?	5.00	10.00	20.00
-- Black label, silver print					
❏ DL 8119 [M]	Twin Pianos	1961	3.00	6.00	12.00
-- Black label with color bars					
❏ DL 8135 [M]	Soft and Sweet	1955	5.00	10.00	20.00
-- Black label, silver print					
❏ DL 8135 [M]	Soft and Sweet	1961	3.00	6.00	12.00
-- Black label with color bars					
❏ DL 8136 [M]	Enjoy Yourself	1955	5.00	10.00	20.00
-- Black label, silver print					
❏ DL 8136 [M]	Enjoy Yourself	1961	3.00	6.00	12.00
-- Black label with color bars					
❏ DL 8205 [M]	Waltz Time	1955	5.00	10.00	20.00
-- Black label, silver print					

Number	Title	Yr	VG	VG+	NM
❏ DL 8205 [M]	Waltz Time	1961	3.00	6.00	12.00
-- Black label with color bars					
❏ DL 8208 [M]	The Band Played On	1955	5.00	10.00	20.00
-- Black label, silver print					
❏ DL 8208 [M]	The Band Played On	1961	3.00	6.00	12.00
-- Black label with color bars					
❏ DL 8249 [M]	Lombardoland	1956	5.00	10.00	20.00
-- Black label, silver print					
❏ DL 8249 [M]	Lombardoland	1961	3.00	6.00	12.00
-- Black label with color bars					
❏ DL 8251 [M]	Twin Piano Magic	1956	5.00	10.00	20.00
-- Black label, silver print					
❏ DL 8251 [M]	Twin Piano Magic	1961	3.00	6.00	12.00
-- Black label with color bars					
❏ DL 8254 [M]	Everybody Dance	1956	5.00	10.00	20.00
-- Black label, silver print					
❏ DL 8254 [M]	Everybody Dance	1961	3.00	6.00	12.00
-- Black label with color bars					
❏ DL 8255 [M]	Oh! How We Danced	1956	5.00	10.00	20.00
-- Black label, silver print					
❏ DL 8255 [M]	Oh! How We Danced	1961	3.00	6.00	12.00
-- Black label with color bars					
❏ DL 8256 [M]	Waltzland	1956	5.00	10.00	20.00
-- Black label, silver print					
❏ DL 8256 [M]	Waltzland	1961	3.00	6.00	12.00
-- Black label with color bars					
❏ DL 8333 [M]	Silver Jubilee	1956	5.00	10.00	20.00
-- Black label, silver print					
❏ DL 8333 [M]	Silver Jubilee	1961	3.00	6.00	12.00
-- Black label with color bars					
❏ DL 8354 [M]	Jingle Bells	1956	5.00	10.00	20.00
-- Black label, silver print					
❏ DL 8354 [M]	Jingle Bells	1961	3.00	6.00	12.00
-- Black label with color bars					
❏ DL 8843 [M]	Instrumentally Yours	1959	5.00	10.00	20.00
-- Black label, silver print					
❏ DL 8843 [M]	Instrumentally Yours	1961	3.00	6.00	12.00
-- Black label with color bars					
❏ DL 8894 [M]	The Sidewalks of New York	1959	5.00	10.00	20.00
-- Black label, silver print					
❏ DL 8894 [M]	The Sidewalks of New York	1961	3.00	6.00	12.00
-- Black label with color bars					
❏ DL 8962 [M]	The Sweetest Music This Side of Heaven (A Musical Biography 1926-1932)	1960	3.75	7.50	15.00
-- Black label, silver print					
❏ DL 8962 [M]	The Sweetest Music This Side of Heaven (A Musical Biography 1926-1932)	1960	2.50	5.00	10.00
-- Black label with color bars					
❏ DL 74123 [S]	The Sweetest Pianos This Side of Heaven	1961	3.75	7.50	15.00

MCA

Number	Title	Yr	VG	VG+	NM
❏ DL 74149 [S]	Far Away Places	1961	3.75	7.50	15.00
❏ DL 74177 [S]	New Year's Eve with Guy	1961	3.75	7.50	15.00
❏ DL 74180 [S]	Dance to the Songs Everybody Knows	1961	3.75	7.50	15.00
❏ DL 74229 [S]	The Sweetest Music This Side of Heaven (A Musical Biography 1932-1939)	1962	3.75	7.50	15.00
❏ DL 74268 [R]	The Best Songs Are the Old Songs	196?	3.00	6.00	12.00
❏ DL 74280 [S]	By Special Request	1962	3.75	7.50	15.00
❏ DL 74288 [S]	Dancing Piano	1962	3.75	7.50	15.00
❏ DL 74328 [S]	The Sweetest Music This Side of Heaven (A Musical Biography 1944-1948)	1962	3.75	7.50	15.00
❏ DL 74329 [S]	The Sweetest Music This Side of Heaven (A Musical Biography 1949-1954)	1962	3.75	7.50	15.00
❏ DL 74371 [S]	Play a Happy Song	1963	3.75	7.50	15.00
❏ DL 74380 [S]	Golden Minstrel Songs for Dancing	1963	3.75	7.50	15.00
❏ DL 74430 [S]	Golden Folk Songs	1964	3.00	6.00	12.00
❏ DL 74516 [S]	Italian Songs Everybody Knows	1964	3.00	6.00	12.00
❏ DL 74567 [S]	Snuggled on Your Shoulder	1965	3.00	6.00	12.00
❏ DL 74593 [S]	Golden Medleys	1965	3.00	6.00	12.00
❏ DL 74735 [S]	Dance Medley Time	1966	3.00	6.00	12.00
❏ DL 74812 [S]	Guy Lombardo's Greatest Hits	1966	3.00	6.00	12.00
❏ DL 78354 [R]	Jingle Bells	196?	2.50	5.00	10.00
❏ DL 78962 [S]	The Sweetest Music This Side of Heaven (A Musical Biography 1926-1932)	1960	5.00	10.00	20.00
-- Black label, silver print					
❏ DL 78962 [S]	The Sweetest Music This Side of Heaven (A Musical Biography 1926-1932)	1960	3.00	6.00	12.00
-- Black label with color bars					

HINDSIGHT

Number	Title	Yr	VG	VG+	NM
❏ HSR-187	Guy Lombardo and His Royal Canadians 1950	198?	2.50	5.00	10.00

LONDON

Number	Title	Yr	VG	VG+	NM
❏ XPS 904	Every Night Is New Year's Eve	1973	2.50	5.00	10.00

MCA

Number	Title	Yr	VG	VG+	NM
❏ 89	The Best Songs Are the Old Songs	1973	2.00	4.00	8.00
-- Reissue of Decca 74268					

Number	Title	Yr	VG	VG+	NM
❏ 103	Golden Medleys	1973	2.00	4.00	8.00
-- Reissue of Decca 74593					
❏ 195	New Year's Eve with Guy Lombardo	1973	3.00	6.00	12.00
-- Reissue of Decca 74177					
❏ 197	Dance to the Songs Everybody Knows	1973	2.00	4.00	8.00
-- Reissue of Decca 74180					
❏ 201	The Sweetest Music This Side of Heaven	1973	2.00	4.00	8.00
-- Reissue of Decca 78962?					
❏ 242	Dance Medley Time	197?	2.00	4.00	8.00
-- Reissue of Decca 74735					
❏ 245	Guy Lombardo's Greatest Hits	197?	2.00	4.00	8.00
-- Reissue of Decca 74812					
❏ 4041 [(2)]	The Best of Guy Lombardo	197?	3.00	6.00	12.00
-- Black rainbow labels					
❏ 4041 [(2)]	The Best of Guy Lombardo	1977	2.50	5.00	10.00
-- Tan labels					
❏ 4041 [(2)]	The Best of Guy Lombardo	1980	2.50	5.00	10.00
-- Blue rainbow labels					
❏ 4082 [(2)]	The Best of Guy Lombardo, Vol. 2	197?	3.00	6.00	12.00
-- Black rainbow labels					
❏ 4082 [(2)]	The Best of Guy Lombardo, Vol. 2	1977	2.50	5.00	10.00
-- Tan labels					
❏ 4082 [(2)]	The Best of Guy Lombardo, Vol. 2	1980	2.50	5.00	10.00
-- Blue rainbow labels					
❏ 15000	New Year's Eve with Guy Lombardo	1974	2.50	5.00	10.00
-- Reissue of MCA 195; black rainbow label					
❏ 15000	New Year's Eve with Guy Lombardo	1977	2.00	4.00	8.00
-- Tan label					
❏ 15000	New Year's Eve with Guy Lombardo	1980	2.00	4.00	8.00
-- Blue rainbow label					
❏ 15012	Jingle Bells	197?	2.50	5.00	10.00
-- Reissue of Decca 78354; black rainbow label					
❏ 15012	Jingle Bells	1977	2.00	4.00	8.00
-- Tan label					
❏ 15012	Jingle Bells	1980	2.00	4.00	8.00
-- Blue rainbow label					
❏ 15031	Auld Lang Syne	198?	2.50	5.00	10.00
❏ 15035	I Saw Mommy Kissing Santa Claus	198?	2.50	5.00	10.00

MCA CORAL

Number	Title	Yr	VG	VG+	NM
❏ CR 20105	Here's Guy Lombardo	197?	2.50	5.00	10.00

PAIR

Number	Title	Yr	VG	VG+	NM
❏ PDL2-1046 [(2)]	Guy Lombardo	1986	3.00	6.00	12.00

PICKWICK

Number	Title	Yr	VG	VG+	NM
❏ SPC 1011	Deck the Halls	196?	2.50	5.00	10.00
-- Silver label					
❏ SPC 1011	Deck the Halls	197?	2.00	4.00	8.00
-- Reissue on black label					
❏ PTP-2009 [(2)]	The Sweet Sounds	197?	2.50	5.00	10.00
❏ SPC-3073	Sweet and Heavenly	196?	2.50	5.00	10.00
❏ SPC-3193	Enjoy Yourself	196?	2.50	5.00	10.00
❏ SPC-3257	Red Roses for a Blue Lady	197?	2.00	4.00	8.00
❏ SPC-3312	The Impossible Dream	197?	2.00	4.00	8.00
❏ SPC-3358	Alley Cat	197?	2.00	4.00	8.00
❏ SPC-3530	Seems Like Old Times	197?	2.00	4.00	8.00
❏ SPC-3530	Seems Like Old Times	197?	2.00	4.00	8.00

RCA CAMDEN

Number	Title	Yr	VG	VG+	NM
❏ CAL-255 [M]	Guy Lombardo Plays	195?	3.75	7.50	15.00
❏ CAS-255 [R]	Guy Lombardo Plays	196?	2.50	5.00	10.00
❏ CAL-445 [M]	An Evening with Guy Lombardo	195?	3.75	7.50	15.00
❏ CAS-445 [R]	An Evening with Guy Lombardo	196?	2.50	5.00	10.00
❏ CAL-578 [M]	He's My Guy	195?	3.75	7.50	15.00

RCA VICTOR

Number	Title	Yr	VG	VG+	NM
❏ CPL1-2047(e)	A Legendary Performer	1977	2.50	5.00	10.00
❏ VPM-6071 [(2)]	This Is Guy Lombardo	197?	3.00	6.00	12.00

SUNBEAM

Number	Title	Yr	VG	VG+	NM
❏ 308	On the Air 1935	197?	2.50	5.00	10.00

VOCALION

Number	Title	Yr	VG	VG+	NM
❏ VL 3605 [M]	Dance in the Moonlight	1958	3.75	7.50	15.00
❏ VL 73605 [R]	Dance in the Moonlight	196?	2.50	5.00	10.00
❏ VL 73833	Here's Guy Lombardo	1968	2.50	5.00	10.00

LONDON RAGTIME ORCHESTRA, THE

STOMP OFF

Number	Title	Yr	VG	VG+	NM
❏ SOS-1081	Bouncing Around	1985	2.50	5.00	10.00

LONDON, JULIE
Female singer.

LIBERTY

Number	Title	Yr	VG	VG+	NM
❏ MCR-1 [M]	By Myself	196?	6.25	12.50	25.00
-- Columbia Record Club exclusive					
❏ SCR-1 [S]	By Myself	196?	7.50	15.00	30.00
-- Columbia Record Club exclusive					
❏ LRP-3006 [M]	Julie Is Her Name	1956	12.50	25.00	50.00
-- Green label					
❏ LRP-3006 [M]	Julie Is Her Name	1960	5.00	10.00	20.00
-- Black label, colorband and logo at left					
❏ LRP-3012 [M]	Lonely Girl	1956	12.50	25.00	50.00
-- Green label					
❏ LRP-3012 [M]	Lonely Girl	1960	5.00	10.00	20.00
-- Black label, colorband and logo at left					
❏ LRP-3043 [M]	About the Blues	1957	10.00	20.00	40.00
-- Green label					
❏ LRP-3043 [M]	About the Blues	1960	5.00	10.00	20.00
-- Black label, colorband and logo at left					
❏ LRP-3060 [M]	Make Love to Me	1957	10.00	20.00	40.00
-- Green label					
❏ LRP-3060 [M]	Make Love to Me	1960	5.00	10.00	20.00
-- Black label, colorband and logo at left					
❏ LRP-3096 [M]	Julie	1957	10.00	20.00	40.00
-- Green label					
❏ LRP-3100 [M]	Julie Is Her Name, Volume 2	1958	10.00	20.00	40.00
-- Green label					
❏ LRP-3100 [M]	Julie Is Her Name, Volume 2	1960	5.00	10.00	20.00
-- Black label, colorband and logo at left					
❏ LRP-3105 [M]	London By Night	1958	7.50	15.00	30.00
-- Green label					
❏ LRP-3119 [M]	Swing Me an Old Song	1959	7.50	15.00	30.00
-- Green label					
❏ LRP-3130 [M]	Your Number Please	1959	7.50	15.00	30.00
-- Green label					
❏ LRP-3130 [M]	Your Number Please	1960	5.00	10.00	20.00
-- Black label, colorband and logo at left					
❏ LRP-3152 [M]	Julie...At Home	1960	7.50	15.00	30.00
❏ LRP-3164 [M]	Around Midnight	1960	7.50	15.00	30.00
❏ LRP-3171 [M]	Send for Me	1961	7.50	15.00	30.00
❏ LRP-3192 [M]	Whatever Julie Wants	1961	7.50	15.00	30.00
❏ LRP-3203 [M]	Sophisticated Lady	1962	6.25	12.50	25.00
❏ LRP-3231 [M]	Love Letters	1962	6.25	12.50	25.00
❏ LRP-3249 [M]	Love on the Rocks	1963	6.25	12.50	25.00
❏ LRP-3278 [M]	Latin in a Satin Mood	1963	6.25	12.50	25.00
❏ LRP-3291 [M]	Julie's Golden Hits	1963	6.25	12.50	25.00
-- Black cover					
❏ LRP-3291 [M]	Julie's Golden Hits	1963	6.25	12.50	25.00
-- White cover					
❏ LRP-3300 [M]	The End of the World	1963	6.25	12.50	25.00
❏ LRP-3324 [M]	The Wonderful World of Julie London	1963	6.25	12.50	25.00
❏ LRP-3342 [M]	Julie London	1964	6.25	12.50	25.00
❏ LRP-3375 [M]	Julie London In Person at the Americana	1964	6.25	12.50	25.00
❏ LRP-3392 [M]	Our Fair Lady	1965	6.25	12.50	25.00
❏ LRP-3416 [M]	Feeling Good	1965	6.25	12.50	25.00
❏ LRP-3434 [M]	All Through the Night	1965	6.25	12.50	25.00
❏ LRP-3478 [M]	For the Night People	1966	6.25	12.50	25.00
❏ LRP-3493 [M]	Nice Girls Don't Stay for Breakfast	1967	6.25	12.50	25.00
❏ LRP-3514 [M]	With Body and Soul	1967	7.50	15.00	30.00
❏ L-5501 [M]	The Best of Julie London	1962	7.50	15.00	30.00
❏ S-6601 [S]	The Best of Julie London	1962	10.00	20.00	40.00
❏ LST-7004 [S]	Julie	1958	17.50	35.00	70.00
-- Black label, silver print					
❏ LST-7012 [S]	About the Blues	1958	17.50	35.00	70.00
-- Black label, silver print					
❏ LST-7012 [S]	About the Blues	1960	6.25	12.50	25.00
-- Black label, colorband and logo at left					
❏ LST-7027 [S]	Julie Is Her Name	1958	10.00	20.00	40.00
-- Black label, silver print					
❏ LST-7027 [S]	Julie Is Her Name	1958	25.00	50.00	100.00
-- Red vinyl					
❏ LST-7027 [S]	Julie Is Her Name	1958	25.00	50.00	100.00
-- Blue vinyl					
❏ LST-7027 [S]	Julie Is Her Name	1960	6.25	12.50	25.00
-- Black label, colorband and logo at left					
❏ LST-7029 [S]	Lonely Girl	1958	10.00	20.00	40.00
-- Black label, silver print					
❏ LST-7029 [S]	Lonely Girl	1960	6.25	12.50	25.00
-- Black label, colorband and logo at left					
❏ LST-7060 [S]	Make Love to Me	1958	10.00	20.00	40.00
-- Black label, silver print					
❏ LST-7060 [S]	Make Love to Me	1960	6.25	12.50	25.00
-- Black label, colorband and logo at left					
❏ LST-7100 [S]	Julie Is Her Name, Volume 2	1958	10.00	20.00	40.00
-- Black label, silver print					
❏ LST-7100 [S]	Julie Is Her Name, Volume 2	1960	6.25	12.50	25.00
-- Black label, colorband and logo at left					

Number	Title	Yr	VG	VG+	NM
LST-7105 [S]	London By Night	1958	10.00	20.00	40.00
-- Black label, silver print					
LST-7119 [S]	Swing Me an Old Song	1959	10.00	20.00	40.00
-- Black label, silver print					
LST-7130 [S]	Your Number Please	1959	10.00	20.00	40.00
-- Black label, silver print					
LST-7130 [S]	Your Number Please	1960	6.25	12.50	25.00
-- Black label, colorband and logo at left					
LST-7152 [S]	Julie...At Home	1960	25.00	50.00	100.00
-- Blue vinyl					
LST-7152 [S]	Julie...At Home	1960	10.00	20.00	40.00
-- Black vinyl					
LST-7164 [S]	Around Midnight	1960	10.00	20.00	40.00
LST-7171 [S]	Send for Me	1961	10.00	20.00	40.00
LST-7192 [S]	Whatever Julie Wants	1961	10.00	20.00	40.00
LST-7203 [S]	Sophisticated Lady	1962	7.50	15.00	30.00
LST-7231 [S]	Love Letters	1962	7.50	15.00	30.00
LST-7249 [S]	Love on the Rocks	1963	7.50	15.00	30.00
LST-7278 [S]	Latin in a Satin Mood	1963	7.50	15.00	30.00
LST-7291 [S]	Julie's Golden Hits	1963	7.50	15.00	30.00
-- Black cover					
LST-7291 [S]	Julie's Golden Hits	1963	7.50	15.00	30.00
-- White cover					
LST-7300 [S]	The End of the World	1963	7.50	15.00	30.00
LST-7324 [S]	The Wonderful World of Julie London	1963	7.50	15.00	30.00
LST-7342 [S]	Julie London	1964	7.50	15.00	30.00
LST-7375 [S]	Julie London In Person at the Americana	1964	7.50	15.00	30.00
LST-7392 [S]	Our Fair Lady	1965	7.50	15.00	30.00
LST-7416 [S]	Feeling Good	1965	7.50	15.00	30.00
LST-7434 [S]	All Through the Night	1965	7.50	15.00	30.00
LST-7478 [S]	For the Night People	1966	7.50	15.00	30.00
LST-7493 [S]	Nice Girls Don't Stay for Breakfast	1967	6.25	12.50	25.00
LST-7514 [S]	With Body and Soul	1967	6.25	12.50	25.00
LST-7546	Easy Does It	1968	5.00	10.00	20.00
LST-7609	Yummy, Yummy, Yummy	1969	5.00	10.00	20.00
SL-9002 [M]	Calendar Girl	1956	25.00	50.00	100.00
SUNSET					
SUM-1104 [M]	Julie London	196?	3.00	6.00	12.00
SUM-1161 [M]	Soft and Sweet	196?	3.00	6.00	12.00
SUS-5104 [S]	Julie London	196?	3.75	7.50	15.00
SUS-5161 [S]	Soft and Sweet	196?	3.75	7.50	15.00
SUS-5207	Gone with the Wind	196?	3.00	6.00	12.00
UNITED ARTISTS					
UA-LA437-E	The Very Best of Julie London	1975	3.00	6.00	12.00

LONG, BARBARA
Female singer.
SAVOY

Number	Title	Yr	VG	VG+	NM
MG-12161 [M]	Soul	1961	7.50	15.00	30.00

LONG, DANNY
Pianist.
CAPITOL

| ST 1988 [S] | Jazz Furlough | 1963 | 5.00 | 10.00 | 20.00 |
| T 1988 [M] | Jazz Furlough | 1963 | 3.75 | 7.50 | 15.00 |

LONG, JOHNNY
Violinist and bandleader.
CIRCLE

| 56 | Johnny Long and His Orchestra 1941-1942 | 198? | 2.50 | 5.00 | 10.00 |

LONGMIRE, WILBERT
Guitarist.
COLUMBIA

JC 35365	Sunny Side Up	1978	2.50	5.00	10.00
JC 35754	Champagne	1979	2.50	5.00	10.00
PACIFIC JAZZ					
ST-20161	Revolution	1969	5.00	10.00	20.00

LONGNON, JEAN-LOUP
Trumpeter, composer and bandleader.
ATLANTIC

| 81829 | Jean-Loup Longnon and His New York Orchestra | 1988 | 2.50 | 5.00 | 10.00 |

LONGO, MIKE
Pianist.
GROOVE MERCHANT

| 525 | Funkia | 1974 | 5.00 | 10.00 | 20.00 |

MAINSTREAM

Number	Title	Yr	VG	VG+	NM
MRL-334	Matrix	1972	3.75	7.50	15.00
MRL-357	The Awakening	1972	3.75	7.50	15.00
PABLO					
2310 769	Talk with Spirits	197?	3.75	7.50	15.00

LONGO, PAT
Alto saxophone player and bandleader.
TOWN HALL

25	Chain Reaction	1980	2.50	5.00	10.00
30	Crocodile Tears	1981	2.50	5.00	10.00
33	Billy May for President	198?	2.50	5.00	10.00

LOOKOFSKY, HARRY
Violinist and violist. Played the string parts on the Left Banke's hit single "Walk Away Renee." (His son, Mike Brown, wrote the song and was part of the group.)
ATLANTIC

1319 [M]	Stringville	1959	10.00	20.00	40.00
-- Black label					
1319 [M]	Stringville	1961	5.00	10.00	20.00
-- Multicolor label, white "fan" logo at right					
1319 [M]	Stringville	1964	3.75	7.50	15.00
-- Multicolor label, black "fan" logo at right					
SD 1319 [S]	Stringville	1959	10.00	20.00	40.00
-- Green label					
SD 1319 [S]	Stringville	1961	3.75	7.50	15.00
-- Multicolor label, white "fan" logo at right					
SD 1319 [S]	Stringville	1964	3.00	6.00	12.00
-- Multicolor label, black "fan" logo at right					

LORBER, JEFF
Keyboard player, arranger and composer.
ARISTA

AB 4234	Water Sign	1979	2.50	5.00	10.00
AL8-8025	In the Heat of the Night	1984	2.50	5.00	10.00
AL 8119	Galaxian	198?	2.00	4.00	8.00
-- Reissue of 9545					
AL 8218	It's a Fact	198?	2.00	4.00	8.00
-- Reissue of 9583					
AL8-8269	Step by Step	1985	2.50	5.00	10.00
AL 8340	Wizard Island	198?	2.00	4.00	8.00
-- Reissue of 9516					
AL 8360	Water Sign	198?	2.00	4.00	8.00
-- Reissue of 4234					
AL 8393	Lift Off	1986	2.50	5.00	10.00
AL 9516	Wizard Island	1980	2.50	5.00	10.00
AL 9545	Galaxian	1981	2.50	5.00	10.00
AL 9583	It's a Fact	1982	2.50	5.00	10.00
INNER CITY					
IC-1026	Jeff Lorber Fusion	1977	3.75	7.50	15.00
IC-1056	Soft Space	1978	3.75	7.50	15.00
WARNER BROS.					
25492	Private Passion	1986	2.50	5.00	10.00

LORD, VIVIAN
Pianist and female singer.
STASH

| ST-241 | Love Dance | 198? | 2.50 | 5.00 | 10.00 |

LORIMER, MICHAEL
Guitarist.
DANCING CAT

| DC-3002 | Remembranza | 198? | 3.00 | 6.00 | 12.00 |

LOTTRIDGE, RICHARD, AND JOAN WILDMAN
Lottridge plays bassoon; Wildman plays piano and keyboards.
UNIVERSITY OF WISCONSIN

| UW-102 | Something New: The Unique Sounds of Jazz Bassoon | 1986 | 3.75 | 7.50 | 15.00 |

LOUISIANA REPERTORY JAZZ BAND
STOMP OFF

SOS-1029	New Orleans	198?	2.50	5.00	10.00
SOS-1055	Uptown Jazz	198?	2.50	5.00	10.00
SOS-1140	Hot and Sweet Sounds of Lost New Orleans	1987	2.50	5.00	10.00

LOUNGE LIZARDS, THE
Founded by JOHN LURIE. Revolving membership over the years.
EDITIONS EG

EGS-108	The Lounge Lizards	1981	3.00	6.00	12.00
EUROPA					
JP-2012	Live from the Drunken Boat	1983	3.75	7.50	15.00

Number	Title	Yr	VG	VG+	NM

ISLAND
| ❏ 90529 | Live in Tokyo -- Big Heart | 1986 | 2.50 | 5.00 | 10.00 |
| ❏ 90592 | No Pain for Cakes | 1987 | 2.50 | 5.00 | 10.00 |

LOUSSIER, JACQUES
Pianist.
LONDON
❏ PS 287 [S]	Bach Jazz, Vol. 1	1964	3.75	7.50	15.00
❏ PS 288 [S]	Bach Jazz, Vol. 2	1964	3.75	7.50	15.00
❏ PS 289 [S]	Bach Jazz, Vol. 3	1964	3.75	7.50	15.00
❏ PS 365 [S]	Play Bach, Vol. 4	1964	3.75	7.50	15.00
❏ PS 454/5 [(2) S]	Bach Jazz	1965	5.00	10.00	20.00
❏ PS 524	Bach Jazz, Vol. 5	1968	3.00	6.00	12.00
❏ LL 3144 [M]	Play Bach	196?	3.75	7.50	15.00
❏ LL 3287 [M]	Bach Jazz, Vol. 1	1964	3.00	6.00	12.00
❏ LL 3288 [M]	Bach Jazz, Vol. 2	1964	3.00	6.00	12.00
❏ LL 3289 [M]	Bach Jazz, Vol. 3	1964	3.00	6.00	12.00
❏ LL 3365 [M]	Play Bach, Vol. 4	1964	3.00	6.00	12.00
❏ LL 3454/5 [(2) M]	Bach Jazz	1965	3.75	7.50	15.00
❏ 820 245-1 [S]	Bach Jazz, Vol. 1	1985	2.50	5.00	10.00
❏ 820 246-1 [S]	Bach Jazz, Vol. 2	1985	2.50	5.00	10.00

LOVANO, JOE
Alto saxophone player and composer.
SOUL NOTE
| ❏ 121132 | Tones, Shapes and Colors | 1985 | 3.00 | 6.00 | 12.00 |
| ❏ 121182 | Village Rhythm | 1988 | 3.00 | 6.00 | 12.00 |

LOVETT, LEE
Pianist.
STRAND
❏ SL-1055 [M]	Jazz Dance Party	1962	5.00	10.00	20.00
❏ SLS-1055 [S]	Jazz Dance Party	1962	6.25	12.50	25.00
❏ SL-1059 [M]	Misty	1962	5.00	10.00	20.00
❏ SLS-1059 [S]	Misty	1962	6.25	12.50	25.00
WYNNE
| ❏ WLP-108 [M] | Jazz Dance Party | 195? | 7.50 | 15.00 | 30.00 |

LOWE, FRANK
Tenor saxophone player.
ARISTA/FREEDOM
| ❏ AF 1015 | Fresh | 1976 | 3.00 | 6.00 | 12.00 |
BLACK SAINT
| ❏ BSR-0005 | The Flam | 198? | 3.00 | 6.00 | 12.00 |
CADENCE JAZZ
| ❏ CJR-1007 | Skizoke | 198? | 2.50 | 5.00 | 10.00 |
ESP-DISK'
| ❏ 3013 | Black Beings | 197? | 6.25 | 12.50 | 25.00 |
SOUL NOTE
| ❏ SN-1032 | Erotic Heartbreak | 198? | 3.00 | 6.00 | 12.00 |
| ❏ SN-1082 | Decision in Paradise | 1985 | 3.00 | 6.00 | 12.00 |

LOWE, FRANK, AND EUGENE CHADBOURNE
Chadbourne is a guitarist. Also see FRANK LOWE.
QED
| ❏ 995 | Don't Punk Out | 1977 | 3.00 | 6.00 | 12.00 |

LOWE, MUNDELL
Guitarist. Also see THE FOUR MOST.
CHARLIE PARKER
| ❏ PLP-822 [M] | Blues for a Stripper | 1962 | 6.25 | 12.50 | 25.00 |
| ❏ PLP-822S [S] | Blues for a Stripper | 1962 | 7.50 | 15.00 | 30.00 |
DOBRE
| ❏ 1018 | Incomparable | 1978 | 3.00 | 6.00 | 12.00 |
FAMOUS DOOR
| ❏ HL-102 | California Guitar | 197? | 5.00 | 10.00 | 20.00 |
JAZZLAND
| ❏ JLP-8 [M] | Low-Down Guitar | 1960 | 7.50 | 15.00 | 30.00 |
OFFBEAT
| ❏ OLP-3010 [M] | Tacet for Neurotics | 1960 | 7.50 | 15.00 | 30.00 |
| ❏ OS-93010 [S] | Tacet for Neurotics | 1960 | 10.00 | 20.00 | 40.00 |
PAUSA
| ❏ 7152 | Mundell Lowe and Transit West | 1983 | 2.50 | 5.00 | 10.00 |
RCA CAMDEN
❏ CAL-490 [M]	Porgy and Bess	1959	5.00	10.00	20.00
❏ CAS-490 [S]	Porgy and Bess	1959	6.25	12.50	25.00
❏ CAL-522 [M]	TV Action Jazz!	1959	6.25	12.50	25.00
❏ CAS-522 [S]	TV Action Jazz!	1959	7.50	15.00	30.00
❏ CAL-627 [M]	TV Action Jazz! -- Volume 2	1960	6.25	12.50	25.00
❏ CAS-627 [S]	TV Action Jazz! -- Volume 2	1960	7.50	15.00	30.00

RCA VICTOR
| ❏ LJM-3002 [10] | The Mundell Lowe Quintet | 1954 | 25.00 | 50.00 | 100.00 |
RIVERSIDE
❏ RLP 12-204 [M]	The Mundell Lowe Quartet	1956	15.00	30.00	60.00
-- White label, blue print					
❏ RLP 12-204 [M]	The Mundell Lowe Quartet	1959	10.00	20.00	40.00
-- Blue label, microphone logo at top					
❏ RLP 12-208 [M]	Guitar Moods	1956	15.00	30.00	60.00
-- White label, blue print					
❏ RLP 12-208 [M]	Guitar Moods	1959	10.00	20.00	40.00
-- Blue label, microphone logo at top					
❏ RLP 12-219 [M]	New Music of Alec Wilder	1956	15.00	30.00	60.00
-- White label, blue print					
❏ RLP 12-219 [M]	New Music of Alec Wilder	1959	10.00	20.00	40.00
-- Blue label, microphone logo at top					
❏ RLP 12-238 [M]	A Grand Night for Swinging	1957	15.00	30.00	60.00
-- White label, blue print					
❏ RLP 12-238 [M]	A Grand Night for Swinging	1959	10.00	20.00	40.00
-- Blue label, microphone logo at top					
❏ 6089	Mundell Lowe Quintet	197?	3.00	6.00	12.00

LUCAS, DOUG
SHADYBROOK
| ❏ 33004 | Niara | 1975 | 3.00 | 6.00 | 12.00 |

LUCAS, REGGIE
Guitarist and composer. Wrote several of Madonna's early hit singles.
INNER CITY
| ❏ IC-6010 | Survival Themes | 197? | 3.75 | 7.50 | 15.00 |

LUCIE, LAWRENCE
Guitarist.
TOY
❏ 1001	Cool and Warm Guitar	197?	3.75	7.50	15.00
❏ 1003	Sophisticated Lady/After Sundown	1978	3.00	6.00	12.00
❏ 1005	This Is It	1979	3.00	6.00	12.00
❏ 1006	Mixed Emotions	1980	3.00	6.00	12.00

LUCRAFT, HOWARD
Guitarist and composer.
DECCA
| ❏ DL 8679 [M] | Showcase for Modern Jazz | 1958 | 7.50 | 15.00 | 30.00 |

LUDI, WERNER
Saxophone player.
HAT ART
| ❏ 2018 [(2)] | Lunatico | 1986 | 3.75 | 7.50 | 15.00 |

LUDWIG, GENE
Organist.
MUSE
| ❏ MR-5164 | Now's the Time | 1979 | 3.00 | 6.00 | 12.00 |

LUNA
ARHOOLIE
| ❏ ST-8001 | Space Swell | 1968 | 5.00 | 10.00 | 20.00 |

LUNCEFORD, JIMMIE
Multi-instrumentalist., bandleader and composer.
AIRCHECK
| ❏ 8 | Victory | 197? | 2.50 | 5.00 | 10.00 |
ALLEGRO ELITE
| ❏ 40?? [10] | Jimmie Lunceford Plays | 195? | 10.00 | 20.00 | 40.00 |
CAPITOL
| ❏ TAO 924 [M] | Jimmie Lunceford | 195? | 7.50 | 15.00 | 30.00 |
CIRCLE
| ❏ 11 | Jimmie Lunceford and His Orchestra 1940 | 198? | 2.50 | 5.00 | 10.00 |
| ❏ CLP-92 | Jimmie Lunceford and His Orchestra 1944 | 198? | 2.50 | 5.00 | 10.00 |
COLUMBIA
❏ GL 104 [10]	Lunceford Special	1950	20.00	40.00	80.00
❏ CL 634 [M]	Lunceford Special	1955	12.50	25.00	50.00
-- Maroon label, gold print					
❏ CL 634 [M]	Lunceford Special	1956	10.00	20.00	40.00
-- Red and black label with six "eye" logos					
❏ CL 2715 [M]	Lunceford Special	1967	7.50	15.00	30.00
❏ CS 9515 [R]	Lunceford Special	1967	3.75	7.50	15.00
-- Red "360 Sound" label					
COLUMBIA MASTERWORKS
| ❏ ML 4804 [M] | Lunceford Special | 195? | 15.00 | 30.00 | 60.00 |

Number	Title	Yr	VG	VG+	NM
DECCA					
❑ DL 5393 [10]	For Dancers Only	1952	15.00	30.00	60.00
❑ DL 8050 [M]	Jimmie Lunceford and His Orchestra	1954	10.00	20.00	40.00
❑ DL 9237 [M]	Rhythm Is Our Business	1968	10.00	20.00	40.00
❑ DL 9238 [M]	Harlem Shout	1968	10.00	20.00	40.00
❑ DL 79237 [R]	Rhythm Is Our Business	1968	5.00	10.00	20.00
❑ DL 79238 [R]	Harlem Shout	1968	5.00	10.00	20.00
MCA					
❑ 1302	Rhythm Is Our Business	198?	2.50	5.00	10.00
❑ 1305	Harlem Shout	198?	2.50	5.00	10.00
❑ 1307	For Dancers Only	198?	2.50	5.00	10.00
❑ 1314	Blues in the Night	198?	2.50	5.00	10.00
❑ 1320	Jimmie's Legacy	198?	2.50	5.00	10.00
❑ 1321	Last Sparks	198?	2.50	5.00	10.00
PICKWICK					
❑ SPC-3531	Blues in the Night	197?	2.50	5.00	10.00
SUNBEAM					
❑ 221	Jimmie Lunceford and Band 1939-42	197?	2.50	5.00	10.00
"X"					
❑ LX-3002 [M]	Jimmie Lunceford and His Chickasaw Syncopators	1954	15.00	30.00	60.00

LURIE, JOHN
Soprano and alto saxophone player and male singer. Also see THE LOUNGE LIZARDS.

Number	Title	Yr	VG	VG+	NM
ENIGMA					
❑ SJ-73213	Stranger Than Paradise	1986	2.50	5.00	10.00

LYLE, BOBBY
Pianist.

Number	Title	Yr	VG	VG+	NM
ATLANTIC					
❑ 81938	Ivory Dreams	1989	3.00	6.00	12.00
CAPITOL					
❑ ST-11627	Genie	1976	2.50	5.00	10.00
❑ SW-11809	New Warrior	1978	2.50	5.00	10.00

LYMAN, ABE
Bandleader and drummer.

Number	Title	Yr	VG	VG+	NM
HINDSIGHT					
❑ HSR-184	Abe Lyman and His Orchestra 1941	198?	2.50	5.00	10.00

LYMAN, ARTHUR
Vibraphone and marimba player. Best known for his long line of exotica LPs, the below is his only jazz offering.

Number	Title	Yr	VG	VG+	NM
HIFI					
❑ R-607 [M]	Leis of Jazz	1958	5.00	10.00	20.00
❑ SR-607 [S]	Leis of Jazz	1958	7.50	15.00	30.00

LYNNE, GLORIA
Female singer.

Number	Title	Yr	VG	VG+	NM
ABC IMPULSE!					
❑ AS-9311	Don't Know	1976	3.00	6.00	12.00
CANYON					
❑ 7709	Happy and In Love	1970	3.75	7.50	15.00
COLLECTABLES					
❑ COL-5138	Golden Classics	198?	2.50	5.00	10.00
DESIGN					
❑ D-177 [M]	My Funny Valentine	196?	2.50	5.00	10.00
❑ DS-177 [S]	My Funny Valentine	196?	3.00	6.00	12.00
EVEREST					
❑ ES-1001 [S]	Gloria Lynne Live! Take 1	1959	10.00	20.00	40.00
❑ SDBR-1022 [S]	Miss Gloria Lynne	1959	7.50	15.00	30.00
❑ SDBR-1063 [S]	Lonely and Sentimental	1960	7.50	15.00	30.00
❑ SDBR-1090 [S]	Try a Little Tenderness	1960	7.50	15.00	30.00
❑ SDBR-1101 [S]	Day In, Day Out	1961	7.50	15.00	30.00
❑ SDBR-1126 [S]	I'm Glad There Is You	1961	7.50	15.00	30.00
❑ SDBR-1128 [S]	He Needs Me	1961	7.50	15.00	30.00
❑ SDBR-1131 [S]	This Little Boy of Mine	1961	7.50	15.00	30.00
❑ SDBR-1132 [S]	Gloria Lynne at Basin Street East	1962	7.50	15.00	30.00
❑ SDBR-1203 [S]	Gloria Blue	1962	7.50	15.00	30.00
❑ SDBR-1208 [S]	Gloria Lynne at the Las Vegas Thunderbird	1963	7.50	15.00	30.00
❑ EV-1220 [S]	Gloria, Marty & Strings	1963	7.50	15.00	30.00
❑ EV-1226 [S]	I Wish You Love	1964	6.25	12.50	25.00
❑ EV-1228 [S]	Glorious Gloria Lynne	1964	6.25	12.50	25.00
❑ EV-1230 [S]	After Hours	1965	6.25	12.50	25.00
❑ EV-1231 [S]	The Best of Gloria Lynne	1965	5.00	10.00	20.00
❑ EV-1237 [S]	Go, Go, Go	1965	5.00	10.00	20.00
❑ EV-1238 [S]	Gloria Lynne '66	1966	5.00	10.00	20.00
❑ E-5001 [M]	Gloria Lynne Live! Take 1	1959	7.50	15.00	30.00

Number	Title	Yr	VG	VG+	NM
❑ LPBR-5022 [M]	Miss Gloria Lynne	1959	5.00	10.00	20.00
❑ LPBR-5063 [M]	Lonely and Sentimental	1960	5.00	10.00	20.00
❑ LPBR-5090 [M]	Try a Little Tenderness	1960	5.00	10.00	20.00
❑ LPBR-5101 [M]	Day In, Day Out	1961	5.00	10.00	20.00
❑ LPBR-5126 [M]	I'm Glad There Is You	1961	5.00	10.00	20.00
❑ LPBR-5128 [M]	He Needs Me	1961	5.00	10.00	20.00
❑ LPBR-5131 [M]	This Little Boy of Mine	1961	5.00	10.00	20.00
❑ LPBR-5132 [M]	Gloria Lynne at Basin Street East	1962	5.00	10.00	20.00
❑ LPBR-5203 [M]	Gloria Blue	1962	5.00	10.00	20.00
❑ LPBR-5208 [M]	Gloria Lynne at the Las Vegas Thunderbird	1963	5.00	10.00	20.00
❑ EV-5220 [M]	Gloria, Marty & Strings	1963	5.00	10.00	20.00
❑ EV-5226 [M]	I Wish You Love	1964	5.00	10.00	20.00
❑ EV-5228 [M]	Glorious Gloria Lynne	1964	5.00	10.00	20.00
❑ EV-5230 [M]	After Hours	1965	5.00	10.00	20.00
❑ EV-5231 [M]	The Best of Gloria Lynne	1965	3.75	7.50	15.00
❑ EV-5237 [M]	Go, Go, Go	1965	3.75	7.50	15.00
❑ EV-5238 [M]	Gloria Lynne '66	1966	3.75	7.50	15.00
FONTANA					
❑ MGF-27528 [M]	Intimate Moments	1964	3.75	7.50	15.00
❑ MGF-27541 [M]	Soul Serenade	1965	3.75	7.50	15.00
❑ MGF-27546 [M]	Love and a Woman	1965	3.75	7.50	15.00
❑ MGF-27555 [M]	Where It's At	1966	3.75	7.50	15.00
❑ MGF-27561 [M]	Gloria	1966	3.75	7.50	15.00
❑ MGF-27571 [M]	The Other Side of Gloria Lynne	1967	5.00	10.00	20.00
❑ SRF-67528 [S]	Intimate Moments	1964	5.00	10.00	20.00
❑ SRF-67541 [S]	Soul Serenade	1965	5.00	10.00	20.00
❑ SRF-67546 [S]	Love and a Woman	1965	5.00	10.00	20.00
❑ SRF-67555 [S]	Where It's At	1966	5.00	10.00	20.00
❑ SRF-67561 [S]	Gloria	1966	5.00	10.00	20.00
❑ SRF-67571 [S]	The Other Side of Gloria Lynne	1967	3.75	7.50	15.00
❑ SRF-67577	Here, There and Everywhere	1968	3.75	7.50	15.00
HIFI					
❑ R-440 [M]	Gloria Lynne	1966	3.75	7.50	15.00
❑ SR-440 [S]	Gloria Lynne	1966	5.00	10.00	20.00
❑ SR-441	Greatest Hits	1969	3.75	7.50	15.00
INTERMEDIA					
❑ QS-5069	Classics	198?	2.50	5.00	10.00
MERCURY					
❑ SRM-1-633	A Very Gentle Sound	1972	3.75	7.50	15.00
MUSE					
❑ MR-5381	A Time for Love	198?	2.50	5.00	10.00
SUNSET					
❑ SUM-1145 [M]	Gloria Lynne	1966	3.00	6.00	12.00
❑ SUM-1171 [M]	I Wish You Love	1967	3.00	6.00	12.00
❑ SUS-5145 [S]	Gloria Lynne	1966	3.00	6.00	12.00
❑ SUS-5171 [S]	I Wish You Love	1967	3.00	6.00	12.00
❑ SUS-5221	Golden Greats	1968	3.00	6.00	12.00
UPFRONT					
❑ 146	Gloria Lynne	197?	3.00	6.00	12.00

LYON, JIMMY
Pianist.

Number	Title	Yr	VG	VG+	NM
FINNADAR					
❑ 9034	Johnny Lyon Plays Cole Porter's Steinway and Music	198?	3.75	7.50	15.00

LYONS, JIMMY
Tenor saxophone player.

Number	Title	Yr	VG	VG+	NM
BLACK SAINT					
❑ BSR-0087	Give It Up	1986	3.00	6.00	12.00
❑ 120125	Something in Return	1990	3.75	7.50	15.00
HAT ART					
❑ 2028 [(2)]	Jump Up/What to Do About	1986	3.75	7.50	15.00
-- Reissue of Hat Hut 21					
HAT HUT					
❑ 21 [(2)]	Jump Up/What to Do About	198?	5.00	10.00	20.00
❑ 3503	Riffs	198?	3.00	6.00	12.00
❑ Y/Z/Z [(3)]	Push	1979	6.25	12.50	25.00

LYTLE, JOHNNY
Vibraphone player.

Number	Title	Yr	VG	VG+	NM
FANTASY					
❑ OJC-110	The Village Caller	198?	2.50	5.00	10.00
JAZZLAND					
❑ JLP-22 [M]	Blue Vibes	1960	6.25	12.50	25.00
❑ JLP-44 [M]	Happy Ground	1961	6.25	12.50	25.00
❑ JLP-67 [M]	Nice and Easy	1962	6.25	12.50	25.00
❑ JLP-81 [M]	Moon Child	1962	6.25	12.50	25.00
❑ JLP-922 [S]	Blue Vibes	1960	7.50	15.00	30.00
❑ JLP-944 [S]	Happy Ground	1961	7.50	15.00	30.00
❑ JLP-967 [S]	Nice and Easy	1962	7.50	15.00	30.00
❑ JLP-981 [S]	Moon Child	1962	7.50	15.00	30.00

Number	Title	Yr	VG	VG+	NM	Number	Title	Yr	VG	VG+	NM

MILESTONE

❑ 9036	Soulful Rebel	197?	3.75	7.50	15.00						
❑ 9043	People and Love	197?	3.75	7.50	15.00						

MUSE

❑ MR-5158	Everything Must Change	1978	3.00	6.00	12.00
❑ MR-5185	Fast Hands	1981	2.50	5.00	10.00
❑ MR-5271	Good Vibes	1982	2.50	5.00	10.00
❑ MR-5387	Happy Ground	1991	3.75	7.50	15.00

RIVERSIDE

❑ RLP-456 [M]	Got That Feeling	1963	5.00	10.00	20.00
❑ RLP-470 [M]	Happy Ground	1964	5.00	10.00	20.00
❑ RLP-480 [M]	The Village Caller	1965	5.00	10.00	20.00
❑ RM-3003 [M]	A Groove	1967	7.50	15.00	30.00
❑ RS-3003 [S]	A Groove	1967	5.00	10.00	20.00
❑ RS-3017	Moon Child	1968	3.75	7.50	15.00
❑ RS-9456 [S]	Got That Feeling	1963	6.25	12.50	25.00
❑ RS-9470 [S]	Happy Ground	1964	6.25	12.50	25.00
❑ RS-9480 [S]	The Village Caller	1965	6.25	12.50	25.00

SOLID STATE

❑ SS-18014	A Man and a Woman	1967	5.00	10.00	20.00
❑ SS-18044	Be Proud	1969	5.00	10.00	20.00
❑ SS-18056	Close Enough	1969	5.00	10.00	20.00

LYTTELTON, HUMPHREY

Trumpeter and bandleader.

ANGEL

❑ ANG.60008 [10]	Some Like It Hot	1955	15.00	30.00	60.00

BETHLEHEM

❑ BCP-6063 [M]	Humph Plays Standards	1961	7.50	15.00	30.00

LONDON

❑ PS 178 [S]	Humph Dedicates	1959	6.25	12.50	25.00
❑ LL 3101 [M]	I Play As I Please	195?	7.50	15.00	30.00
❑ LL 3132 [M]	Humph Dedicates	195?	7.50	15.00	30.00

SACKVILLE

❑ 3033	Humphrey Lyttelton in Canada	198?	3.00	6.00	12.00

STOMP OFF

❑ SOS-1111	Scatterbrains	1986	2.50	5.00	10.00
❑ SOS-1160	Delving Back and Forth with Humph	1989	2.50	5.00	10.00

Number	Title	Yr	VG	VG+	NM

M

M'BOOM
Percussion group led by MAX ROACH.
COLUMBIA
☐ JC 37066	M'Boom	1981	3.00	6.00	12.00
SOUL NOTE
| ☐ SN-1059 | Collage | 198? | 3.00 | 6.00 | 12.00 |

MABERN, HAROLD
Pianist. Also see THE MODERN JAZZ TRIO.
FANTASY
| ☐ OJC-330 | Rakin' and Scrapin' | 1988 | 2.50 | 5.00 | 10.00 |
PRESTIGE
☐ PRST-7568	A Few Miles from Memphis	1968	5.00	10.00	20.00
☐ PRST-7624	Rakin' and Scrapin'	1969	5.00	10.00	20.00
☐ PRST-7687	Workin' and Wailin'	1969	5.00	10.00	20.00
☐ PRST-7764	Greasy Kid Stuff	1970	5.00	10.00	20.00
SACKVILLE
| ☐ 2016 | Live at Café Des Copains | 198? | 3.00 | 6.00 | 12.00 |

MacDONALD, KEITH
LANDMARK
| ☐ LLP-1503 | This Is Keith MacDonald | 1985 | 2.50 | 5.00 | 10.00 |
| ☐ LLP-1509 | Waiting | 1986 | 2.50 | 5.00 | 10.00 |

MacDOWELL, AL
Bass player.
GRAMAVISION
| ☐ R1-79450 | Time Peace | 1990 | 3.00 | 6.00 | 12.00 |

MACERO, TEO
Tenor saxophone player and composer. Also see THE MANHATTAN JAZZ ALL-STARS.
AMERICAN CLAVE
| ☐ 1002 | Teo | 198? | 3.00 | 6.00 | 12.00 |
COLUMBIA
| ☐ CL 842 [M] | What's New? | 1956 | 12.50 | 25.00 | 50.00 |
DEBUT
| ☐ DLP-6 [10] | Explorations by Teo Macero | 1954 | 62.50 | 125.00 | 250.00 |
DOCTOR JAZZ
| ☐ FW 40111 | Acoustical Suspension | 1986 | 2.50 | 5.00 | 10.00 |
FANTASY
| ☐ OJC-1715 | Teo Macero with the Prestige Jazz Quartet | 198? | 2.50 | 5.00 | 10.00 |
FINNADAR
| ☐ 9024 | Time Plus 7 | 1979 | 3.00 | 6.00 | 12.00 |
PRESTIGE
| ☐ PRLP-7104 [M] | Teo Macero with the Prestige JazzQuartet | 1957 | 20.00 | 40.00 | 80.00 |

MACHITO
Bandleader, male singer and percussionist.
CLEF
☐ MGC-505 [10]	Afro-Cuban Jazz Suite	1953	30.00	60.00	120.00
☐ MGC-511 [10]	Machito Jazz with Flip and Bird	1953	30.00	60.00	120.00
☐ MGC-689 [M]	Afro-Cuban Jazz	1956	25.00	50.00	100.00
CORAL
| ☐ CRL 57258 [M] | Vacation at the Concord | 1959 | 10.00 | 20.00 | 40.00 |
| ☐ CRL 757258 [S] | Vacation at the Concord | 1959 | 7.50 | 15.00 | 30.00 |
DECCA
| ☐ DL 5157 [10] | Machito's Afro-Cuban | 1950 | 37.50 | 75.00 | 150.00 |
FORUM
☐ F-9038 [M]	Mi Amigo, Machito	196?	3.00	6.00	12.00
-- Reissue of Tico 1053					
☐ SF-9038 [S]	Mi Amigo, Machito	196?	3.00	6.00	12.00
☐ F-9043 [M]	Asia Minor	196?	3.00	6.00	12.00
-- Reissue of Tico 1033					
☐ SF-9043 [S]	Asia Minor	196?	3.00	6.00	12.00
GNP CRESCENDO
| ☐ GNPS-58 [R] | Machito at the Crescendo | 198? | 2.00 | 4.00 | 8.00 |
| ☐ GNPS-72 [R] | The World's Greatest Latin Band | 198? | 2.00 | 4.00 | 8.00 |
MERCURY
☐ MGC-505 [10]	Afro-Cuban Jazz Suite	1951	37.50	75.00	150.00
☐ MGC-511 [10]	Machito Jazz with Flip and Bird	1952	37.50	75.00	150.00
☐ MG-25009 [10]	Jungle Drums	1950	37.50	75.00	150.00
☐ MG-25020 [10]	Rhumbas	1950	37.50	75.00	150.00
RCA VICTOR
| ☐ LPM-3944 [M] | Machito Goes Memphis | 1968 | 10.00 | 20.00 | 40.00 |
| ☐ LSP-3944 [S] | Machito Goes Memphis | 1968 | 5.00 | 10.00 | 20.00 |
ROULETTE
☐ R-52006 [M]	Kenya	1958	10.00	20.00	40.00
☐ SR-52006 [S]	Kenya	1958	7.50	15.00	30.00
☐ R-52026 [M]	With Flute to Boot	1959	10.00	20.00	40.00
☐ SR-52026 [S]	With Flute to Boot	1959	7.50	15.00	30.00
TICO
☐ LP-138 [10]	El Niche	1956	30.00	60.00	120.00
☐ LP-1002 [M]	Cha Cha Cha at the Palladium	1955	20.00	40.00	80.00
☐ LP-1029 [M]	Asia Minor Cha Cha Cha	1956	20.00	40.00	80.00
☐ LP-1033 [M]	Si Si, No No	1957	20.00	40.00	80.00
☐ LP-1045 [M]	Inspired by "The Sun Also Rises"	1957	20.00	40.00	80.00
☐ LP-1053 [M]	Mi Amigo, Machito	1959	15.00	30.00	60.00
☐ LP-1062 [M]	Irving Berlin in Latin America	1959	15.00	30.00	60.00
☐ LP-1074 [M]	A Night with Machito	1960	12.50	25.00	50.00
☐ LPS-1074 [S]	A Night with Machito	1960	15.00	30.00	60.00
☐ LP-1084 [M]	The New Sound of Machito (El Sonido Nuevo de Machito)	1962	10.00	20.00	40.00
☐ LPS-1084 [S]	The New Sound of Machito (El Sonido Nuevo de Machito)	1962	12.50	25.00	50.00
☐ LP-1090 [M]	Variedades	1963	10.00	20.00	40.00
☐ LPS-1090 [S]	Variedades	1963	12.50	25.00	50.00
☐ LP-1094 [M]	Tremendo Cumban!	1963	10.00	20.00	40.00
☐ LPS-1094 [S]	Tremendo Cumban!	1963	12.50	25.00	50.00
☐ CLP-1314	Latin Soul Plus Jazz	1973	5.00	10.00	20.00
☐ CLP-1328	Lo Mejor De Machito Y Sus AfroCubans Con Graciela	1974	5.00	10.00	20.00
TIMELESS
| ☐ LPSJP-183 | Machito and His Salsa Big Band | 1990 | 3.00 | 6.00 | 12.00 |
VERVE
☐ VSP-19 [M]	Soul Source	1966	5.00	10.00	20.00
☐ VSPS-19 [R]	Soul Source	1966	3.00	6.00	12.00
☐ MGV-8073 [M]	Afro-Cuban Jazz	1957	12.50	25.00	50.00
☐ V-8073 [M]	Afro-Cuban Jazz	1961	5.00	10.00	20.00

MACK, DAVID
SERENUS
| ☐ SRE-1009 [M] | New Directions | 1965 | 5.00 | 10.00 | 20.00 |
| ☐ SRS-12009 [S] | New Directions | 1965 | 6.25 | 12.50 | 25.00 |

MACKAY, BRUCE
ORO
| ☐ 1 | Bruce Mackay | 196? | 5.00 | 10.00 | 20.00 |

MacKAY, DAVID, AND VICKI HAMILTON
MacKay is a pianist; Hamilton is a female singer.
ABC IMPULSE!
| ☐ AS-9184 | David MacKay and Vicki Hamilton | 1969 | 5.00 | 10.00 | 20.00 |
DISCOVERY
| ☐ 868 | Hands | 1982 | 2.50 | 5.00 | 10.00 |

MacPHERSON, FRASER
Tenor saxophone player.
CONCORD JAZZ
☐ CJ-92	Live at the Planetarium	1976	2.50	5.00	10.00
☐ CJ-224	Indian Summer	1983	2.50	5.00	10.00
☐ CJ-269	Jazz Prose	1985	2.50	5.00	10.00

MADIGAN, BETTY
Female singer.
MGM
| ☐ E-3448 [M] | Am I Blue? | 1956 | 10.00 | 20.00 | 40.00 |

MADISON, AL
GOLDEN CREST
| ☐ GC-3048 [M] | Meet Al Madison | 196? | 6.25 | 12.50 | 25.00 |

MADISON, JIMMY
Drummer.
ADELPHI
| ☐ 5007 | Bumps | 1978 | 3.00 | 6.00 | 12.00 |

MAGNOLIA JAZZ BAND
Core members: Robbie Schlosser, cornet and string bass; Bill Napier, clarinet; Paul Mehling, guitar and banjo.
STOMP OFF
| ☐ SOS-1016 | Red Onion Blues | 198? | 2.50 | 5.00 | 10.00 |
| ☐ SOS-1137 | Shake That Thing | 1987 | 2.50 | 5.00 | 10.00 |

Number	Title	Yr	VG	VG+	NM

MAGNUSSON, BOB
Bass player.
DISCOVERY
❑ 804	Revelation	1979	3.00	6.00	12.00
❑ 824	Road Work Ahead	1980	3.00	6.00	12.00
❑ 912	Song for Janet Lee	1984	2.50	5.00	10.00

TREND
❑ 528	Two Generations of Music	1981	3.75	7.50	15.00

-- Direct-to-disc recording

MAGNUSSON, JAKOB
Bass player.
OPTIMISM
❑ OP-2002	Time Zone	198?	2.50	5.00	10.00

MAHAVISHNU ORCHESTRA
Highly influential fusion group: BILLY COBHAM; JERRY GOODMAN; JAN HAMMER; RICK LAIRD; JOHN McLAUGHLIN.
COLUMBIA
❑ KC 31067	The Inner Mounting Flame	1972	3.00	6.00	12.00

-- As "Mahavishnu Orchestra with John McLaughlin"
❑ PC 31067	The Inner Mounting Flame	197?	2.00	4.00	8.00

-- Reissue with new prefix
❑ CQ 31996 [Q]	Birds of Fire	1973	5.00	10.00	20.00
❑ KC 31996	Birds of Fire	1973	2.50	5.00	10.00
❑ PC 31996	Birds of Fire	197?	2.00	4.00	8.00

-- Reissue with new prefix
❑ CQ 32766 [Q]	Between Nothingness and Eternity	1973	5.00	10.00	20.00
❑ KC 32766	Between Nothingness and Eternity	1973	2.50	5.00	10.00
❑ PC 32766	Between Nothingness and Eternity	197?	2.00	4.00	8.00

-- Reissue with new prefix
❑ KC 32957	Apocalypse	1974	2.50	5.00	10.00
❑ PC 32957	Apocalypse	197?	2.00	4.00	8.00

-- Reissue with new prefix
❑ PC 33411	Visions of the Emerald Beyond	1975	2.50	5.00	10.00

-- Original with no bar code
❑ PC 33411	Visions of the Emerald Beyond	198?	2.00	4.00	8.00

-- Reissue with bar code
❑ PC 33908	Inner Worlds	1976	2.50	5.00	10.00

-- Original with no bar code
❑ PC 33908	Inner Worlds	198?	2.00	4.00	8.00

-- Reissue with bar code
❑ JC 36394	The Best of Mahavishnu Orchestra	1980	2.50	5.00	10.00

MAHONES, GILDO
Pianist. Also see LES JAZZ MODES.
NEW JAZZ
❑ NJLP-8299 [M]	Shooting High	1963	---	---	---

-- Canceled
PRESTIGE
❑ PRLP-7339 [(2) M]	The Soulful Piano of Gildo Mahones	1964	7.50	15.00	30.00
❑ PRST-7339 [(2) S]	The Soulful Piano of Gildo Mahones	1964	10.00	20.00	40.00
❑ PRLP-16004 [M]	Shooting High	1964	10.00	20.00	40.00

MAINIERI, MIKE
Vibraphone player, producer and composer. Also see STEPS AHEAD.
ARGO
❑ LP-706 [M]	Blues on the Other Side	1963	6.25	12.50	25.00
❑ LPS-706 [S]	Blues on the Other Side	1963	7.50	15.00	30.00

ARISTA
❑ AL 4133	Love	1976	2.50	5.00	10.00

SOLID STATE
❑ SS-18029	Insight	1968	5.00	10.00	20.00
❑ SS-18049	Journey Thru an Electric Tube	1969	5.00	10.00	20.00

WARNER BROS.
❑ BSK 3586	Wanderlust	1982	2.50	5.00	10.00

MAINIERI, MIKE, AND WARREN BERNHARDT
Also see each artist's individual listings.
ARISTA/NOVUS
❑ AN 3009	Free	1978	3.00	6.00	12.00

MAKOWICZ, ADAM
Pianist.
CHOICE
❑ 1028	From My Window	198?	3.00	6.00	12.00

COLUMBIA
❑ JC 35320	Adam	1978	2.50	5.00	10.00

NOVUS
❑ 3003-1-N	Moonray	1986	2.50	5.00	10.00
❑ 3022-1-N	Naughty Baby	1988	2.50	5.00	10.00

SHEFFIELD LABS
❑ 21	The Name Is Makowicz (ma-KO-vitch)	1984	5.00	10.00	20.00

-- Audiophile vinyl

MAKOWICZ, ADAM, AND GEORGE MRAZ
Mraz is a bass player. Also see ADAM MAKOWICZ.
STASH
❑ ST-216	Classic Jazz Duets	198?	2.50	5.00	10.00

MALHEIROS, ALEX
Bass player, occasional guitarist and male singer. Also see AZYMUTH.
MILESTONE
❑ M-9131	Atlantic Forest	1985	2.50	5.00	10.00

MALINVERNI, PETE
Pianist, bandleader and composer.
SEA BREEZE
❑ SB-2037	Don't Be Shy	198?	2.50	5.00	10.00

MALLET BUSTERS
Arnold Faber and Allan Molnar.
JAZZIMAGE
❑ JZ-103	Mallet Busters	198?	2.50	5.00	10.00

MANCE, JUNIOR
Pianist. Also see WILBUR WARE.
ATLANTIC
❑ 1479 [M]	Harlem Lullaby	1967	5.00	10.00	20.00
❑ SD 1479 [S]	Harlem Lullaby	1967	3.75	7.50	15.00
❑ 1496 [M]	I Believe to My Soul	1968	6.25	12.50	25.00
❑ SD 1496 [S]	I Believe to My Soul	1968	3.75	7.50	15.00
❑ SD 1521	At the Top	1969	3.75	7.50	15.00
❑ SD 1562	With a Lotta Help from My Friends	1970	3.75	7.50	15.00

BEE HIVE
❑ BH-7015	Truckin' and Trakin'	198?	3.00	6.00	12.00

CAPITOL
❑ ST 2092 [S]	Get Ready, Set, Jump!	1964	6.25	12.50	25.00
❑ T 2092 [M]	Get Ready, Set, Jump!	1964	5.00	10.00	20.00
❑ ST 2218 [S]	Straight Ahead	1965	5.00	10.00	20.00
❑ T 2218 [M]	Straight Ahead	1965	3.75	7.50	15.00
❑ ST 2393 [S]	That's Where It Is	1965	5.00	10.00	20.00
❑ T 2393 [M]	That's Where It Is	1965	3.75	7.50	15.00

FANTASY
❑ OJC-204	Junior Mance Trio at the Village Vanguard	198?	2.50	5.00	10.00

INNER CITY
❑ IC-6018	Holy Mama	197?	3.75	7.50	15.00

JAZZLAND
❑ JLP-30 [M]	The Soulful Piano of Junior Mance	1960	6.25	12.50	25.00
❑ JLP-41 [M]	Junior Mance Trio at the Village Vanguard	1961	6.25	12.50	25.00
❑ JLP-53 [M]	Big Chief!	1961	6.25	12.50	25.00
❑ JLP-63 [M]	The Jazz Soul of Hollywood	1961	6.25	12.50	25.00
❑ JLP-77 [M]	Happy Time	1962	6.25	12.50	25.00
❑ JLP-930 [S]	The Soulful Piano of Junior Mance	1960	7.50	15.00	30.00
❑ JLP-941 [S]	Junior Mance Trio at the Village Vanguard	1961	7.50	15.00	30.00
❑ JLP-953 [S]	Big Chief!	1961	7.50	15.00	30.00
❑ JLP-963 [S]	The Jazz Soul of Hollywood	1961	7.50	15.00	30.00
❑ JLP-977 [S]	Happy Time	1962	7.50	15.00	30.00

MILESTONE
❑ M-9041	That Lovin' Feelin'	197?	3.75	7.50	15.00

POLYDOR
❑ PD-5051	Touch	1974	3.75	7.50	15.00

RIVERSIDE
❑ RLP-447 [M]	Junior's Blues	1963	6.25	12.50	25.00
❑ 6059	Soulful Piano	197?	3.00	6.00	12.00
❑ RS-9447 [S]	Junior's Blues	1963	7.50	15.00	30.00

SACKVILLE
❑ 3031	For Dancers Only	198?	2.50	5.00	10.00

VERVE
❑ MGVS-6057 [S]	Junior	1960	7.50	15.00	30.00

Number	Title	Yr	VG	VG+	NM
❏ MGV-8319 [M]	Junior	1959	10.00	20.00	40.00
❏ V-8319 [M]	Junior	1961	5.00	10.00	20.00
❏ V6-8319 [S]	Junior	1961	3.75	7.50	15.00

MANCINI, HENRY
Pianist, bandleader and composer. Most of his music is in the pop or easy-listening vein, but the below albums – including several soundtracks – are definitely jazz. For a more complete listing, see the Standard Catalog of American Records 1950-1975.
RCA VICTOR

Number	Title	Yr	VG	VG+	NM
❏ LPM-1956 [M]	The Music from Peter Gunn	1959	10.00	20.00	40.00
-- Original cover is a "block" design with "Peter Gunn" at top					
❏ LPM-1956 [M]	The Music from Peter Gunn	1959	5.00	10.00	20.00
-- Reissue cover is green/blue with huge "Peter Gunn" in center					
❏ LSP-1956 [S]	The Music from Peter Gunn	1959	12.50	25.00	50.00
-- Original cover is a "block" design with "Peter Gunn" at top					
❏ LSP-1956 [S]	The Music from Peter Gunn	1959	6.25	12.50	25.00
-- Reissue cover is green/blue with huge "Peter Gunn" in center					
❏ LPM-2040 [M]	More Music from Peter Gunn	1959	5.00	10.00	20.00
❏ LSP-2040 [S]	More Music from Peter Gunn	1959	6.25	12.50	25.00
❏ LPM-2147 [M]	The Blues and the Beat	1960	6.25	12.50	25.00
❏ LSP-2147 [S]	The Blues and the Beat	1960	7.50	15.00	30.00
❏ LPM-2198 [M]	Music from Mr. Lucky	1960	5.00	10.00	20.00
❏ LSP-2198 [S]	Music from Mr. Lucky	1960	6.25	12.50	25.00
❏ LPM-2360 [M]	Mr. Lucky Goes Latin	1961	5.00	10.00	20.00
❏ LSP-2360 [S]	Mr. Lucky Goes Latin	1961	6.25	12.50	25.00
❏ LPM-2795 [M]	The Pink Panther	1964	3.75	7.50	15.00
❏ LSP-2795 [S]	The Pink Panther	1964	5.00	10.00	20.00
❏ LPM-3694 [M]	Mancini '67	1967	3.75	7.50	15.00
❏ LSP-3694 [S]	Mancini '67	1967	3.75	7.50	15.00

MANCUSO, GUS
Baritone horn player and trombonist.
FANTASY

Number	Title	Yr	VG	VG+	NM
❏ 3223 [M]	Introducing Gus Mancuso	1956	15.00	30.00	60.00
-- Red vinyl					
❏ 3223 [M]	Introducing Gus Mancuso	1956	10.00	20.00	40.00
-- Black vinyl					
❏ 3282 [M]	Music from New Faces	1958	10.00	20.00	40.00
-- Red vinyl					
❏ 3282 [M]	Music from New Faces	1958	5.00	10.00	20.00
-- Black vinyl					
❏ 8025 [S]	Music from New Faces	1960	7.50	15.00	30.00
-- Blue vinyl					
❏ 8025 [S]	Music from New Faces	1960	3.75	7.50	15.00
-- Black vinyl					

MANDEL, MIKE
Keyboard player.
VANGUARD

Number	Title	Yr	VG	VG+	NM
❏ VSD-79409	Sky Music	1978	3.00	6.00	12.00
❏ VSD-79437	Utopia Parkway	1979	3.00	6.00	12.00

MANETTA, FESS
Pianist.
JAZZOLOGY

Number	Title	Yr	VG	VG+	NM
❏ JCE-6	Whorehouse Piano	198?	2.50	5.00	10.00

MANGELSDORF, ALBERT
Trombonist and composer.
ENJA

Number	Title	Yr	VG	VG+	NM
❏ 2006	Live in Tokyo	197?	3.75	7.50	15.00

PACIFIC JAZZ

Number	Title	Yr	VG	VG+	NM
❏ PJ-10095 [M]	Now, Jazz Ramwong	1966	3.00	6.00	12.00
❏ ST-20095 [S]	Now, Jazz Ramwong	1966	3.75	7.50	15.00

PAUSA

Number	Title	Yr	VG	VG+	NM
❏ 7055	Triologue	197?	2.50	5.00	10.00
❏ 7091	Hamburger Idylle	198?	2.50	5.00	10.00

MANGIONE, CHUCK
Fluegel horn and trumpet player; had pop success in the late 1970s with the single "Feels So Good" and several followups. Also see THE JAZZ BROTHERS.
A&M

Number	Title	Yr	VG	VG+	NM
❏ SP-3115	Chase the Clouds Away	198?	---	3.00	6.00
-- Budget-line reissue					
❏ SP-3172	Bellavia	198?	---	3.00	6.00
-- Budget-line reissue					
❏ SP-3193	Fun and Games	1983	---	3.00	6.00
-- Budget-line reissue					
❏ SP-3219	Feels So Good	198?	---	3.00	6.00
-- Budget-line reissue					
❏ SP-3220	Main Squeeze	198?	---	3.00	6.00
-- Budget-line reissue					
❏ SP-3237	70 Miles Young	198?	---	3.00	6.00
-- Budget-line reissue					
❏ SP-3282	The Best of Chuck Mangione	1985	2.50	5.00	10.00

Number	Title	Yr	VG	VG+	NM
❏ SP-3715	Fun and Games	1980	2.50	5.00	10.00
❏ SP-4518	Chase the Clouds Away	1975	2.50	5.00	10.00
❏ SP-4557	Bellavia	1975	2.50	5.00	10.00
❏ SP-4612	Main Squeeze	1976	2.50	5.00	10.00
❏ SP-4658	Feels So Good	1977	2.50	5.00	10.00
❏ SP-4911	70 Miles Young	1982	2.50	5.00	10.00
❏ SP-6513 [(2)]	Tarantella	1981	3.00	6.00	12.00
❏ SP-6700 [(2)]	Children of Sanchez	1978	3.00	6.00	12.00
❏ SP-6701 [(2)]	An Evening of Magic -- Chuck Mangione Live at the Hollywood Bowl	1979	3.00	6.00	12.00
❏ QU-54518 [Q]	Chase the Clouds Away	1975	4.50	9.00	18.00
❏ QU-54557 [Q]	Bellavia	1975	4.50	9.00	18.00

COLUMBIA

Number	Title	Yr	VG	VG+	NM
❏ FC 38101	Love Notes	1982	2.50	5.00	10.00
❏ PC 38101	Love Notes	198?	---	3.00	6.00
-- Budget-line reissue					
❏ FC 38686	Journey to a Rainbow	1983	2.50	5.00	10.00
❏ PC 38686	Journey to a Rainbow	1986	---	3.00	6.00
-- Budget-line reissue					
❏ FC 39479	Disguise	1984	2.50	5.00	10.00
❏ FC 40254	Save Tonight for Me	1986	2.50	5.00	10.00
❏ FC 40984	Eyes of the Veiled Temptress	1988	2.50	5.00	10.00

FANTASY

Number	Title	Yr	VG	VG+	NM
❏ OJC-495	Recuerdo	1991	3.00	6.00	12.00
-- Reissue of Jazzland 984					

JAZZLAND

Number	Title	Yr	VG	VG+	NM
❏ JLP-84 [M]	Recuerdo	1962	10.00	20.00	40.00
❏ JLP-984 [S]	Recuerdo	1962	12.50	25.00	50.00

MERCURY

Number	Title	Yr	VG	VG+	NM
❏ SRM-1-631	The Chuck Mangione Quartet	1972	3.00	6.00	12.00
❏ SRM-1-650	Alive!	1973	3.00	6.00	12.00
❏ SRM-1-681	Friends & Love/Highlights	1973	3.00	6.00	12.00
❏ SRM-1-684	Land of Make Believe	1973	3.00	6.00	12.00
❏ SRM-2-800 [(2)]	Friends & Love -- A Chuck Mangione Concert	1971	3.75	7.50	15.00
❏ SRM-1-1050	Encore/The Chuck Mangione Concerts	1975	2.50	5.00	10.00
❏ SRM-2-7501 [(2)]	Together: A New Chuck Mangione Concert	1971	3.75	7.50	15.00
❏ SRM-2-8601 [(2)]	The Best of Chuck Mangione	1978	3.00	6.00	12.00
❏ 824 301-1	Alive!	198?	2.00	4.00	8.00
-- Reissue of 650					

MILESTONE

Number	Title	Yr	VG	VG+	NM
❏ 47042 [(2)]	Jazz Brother	1977	3.00	6.00	12.00
-- Reissue of material issued by The Jazz Brothers					

MOBILE FIDELITY

Number	Title	Yr	VG	VG+	NM
❏ 1-068	Feels So Good	1981	6.25	12.50	25.00
-- Audiophile vinyl					

MANGIONE, GAP
Pianist, organist and keyboard player. Also see THE JAZZ BROTHERS.
A&M

Number	Title	Yr	VG	VG+	NM
❏ SP-3407	She and I	1974	2.50	5.00	10.00
❏ SP-4621	Gap Mangione!	197?	2.50	5.00	10.00
❏ SP-4694	Suite Lady	1978	2.50	5.00	10.00
❏ SP-4762	Dancin' Is Makin' Love	1979	2.50	5.00	10.00

FEELS SO GOOD

Number	Title	Yr	VG	VG+	NM
❏ FSG 9002	The Boys from Rochester	1987	3.00	6.00	12.00

GRC

Number	Title	Yr	VG	VG+	NM
❏ 9001	Diana in the Autumn Wind	1968	6.25	12.50	25.00

MERCURY

Number	Title	Yr	VG	VG+	NM
❏ SRM-1-647	Sing Along Junk	1972	3.00	6.00	12.00

MANHATTAN JAZZ ALL-STARS, THE
Members: MOSE ALLISON; AARON BELL; BOB BROOKMEYER; TEDDY CHARLES; Addison Farmer (bass); TEO MACERO; DAVE McKENNA; JIMMY RANEY; Ed Shaughnessy (drums); ZOOT SIMS; SIR CHARLES THOMPSON; NICK TRAVIS; JULIUS WATKINS; PHIL WOODS.
COLUMBIA

Number	Title	Yr	VG	VG+	NM
❏ CL 1426 [M]	Swinging Guys and Dolls	1960	6.25	12.50	25.00
❏ CS 8223 [S]	Swinging Guys and Dolls	1960	7.50	15.00	30.00

MANHATTAN JAZZ SEPTETTE, THE
Members: EDDIE COSTA, BARRY GALBRAITH, URBIE GREEN, OSIE JOHNSON, HERBIE MANN, HAL McKUSICK, OSCAR PETTIFORD.
CORAL

Number	Title	Yr	VG	VG+	NM
❏ CRL 57090 [M]	The Manhattan Jazz Septette	1956	20.00	40.00	80.00

MANHATTAN RHYTHM KINGS
Vocal and instrumental trio: Tripp Hanson; Brian Nalepka; Hal Shane.
INNER CITY

Number	Title	Yr	VG	VG+	NM
❏ IC-1124	Manhattan Rhythm Kings	198?	3.00	6.00	12.00

(Top left) Henry Mancini, in general, wasn't very jazz-oriented. But his music for the television series *Peter Gunn* sure was. Here's a copy of the scarce original jacket for the first album of *Peter Gunn* music. (Top right) Drummer Shelly Manne recorded often with the best of the West Coast's jazz musicians. This was the first of these sessions to be released, as a 10-inch album on the Contemporary label in 1953. (Bottom left) Warne Marsh, best known for his work on the tenor sax, made records over a four-decade span. This was one of his first, on the long-gone Mode label. (Bottom right) Early in Charles Mingus' career, it wasn't always easy to tell whether an album was his or not. *Jaccical Moods Vol. 2*, a 10-inch album from the Period label, has him first among the six musicians listed on the left.

Number	Title	Yr	VG	VG+	NM

MANHATTAN TRANSFER

Vocal quartet: Laurel Masse (soprano, replaced by Cheryl Bentine in 1979); Janis Siegel (alto); Alan Paul (tenor); Tim Hauser (bass).

ATLANTIC

Number	Title	Yr	VG	VG+	NM
❏ SD 16036	Mecca for Moderns	1981	2.50	5.00	10.00
❏ SD 18133	The Manhattan Transfer	1975	2.50	5.00	10.00
❏ SD 18183	Coming Out	1976	2.50	5.00	10.00
❏ SD 19163	Pastiche	1978	2.50	5.00	10.00
❏ SD 19258	Extensions	1979	2.50	5.00	10.00
❏ SD 19319	The Best of the Manhattan Transfer	1981	2.50	5.00	10.00
❏ 80104	Bodies and Souls	1983	2.50	5.00	10.00
❏ 81233	Bop Doo-Wopp	1984	3.00	6.00	12.00
❏ 81266	Vocalese	1985	2.50	5.00	10.00
❏ 81723	Live	1987	2.50	5.00	10.00
❏ 81803	Brasil	1987	2.50	5.00	10.00

CAPITOL

Number	Title	Yr	VG	VG+	NM
❏ ST-778	Jukin'	1971	3.75	7.50	15.00
-- With Gene Pistilli					
❏ ST-11405	Jukin'	1975	2.50	5.00	10.00
-- With Gene Pistilli; reissue of 778					
❏ SN-16223	Jukin'	198?	2.00	4.00	8.00
-- With Gene Pistilli; budget-line reissue					

COLUMBIA

Number	Title	Yr	VG	VG+	NM
❏ C 47079	The Offbeat of Avenues	1991	3.75	7.50	15.00

MOBILE FIDELITY

Number	Title	Yr	VG	VG+	NM
❏ 1-022	Manhattan Transfer Live	1979	5.00	10.00	20.00
-- Audiophile vinyl					
❏ 1-199	Extensions	1994	6.25	12.50	25.00
-- Audiophile vinyl					

MANN, DAVID

Tenor saxophone player.

ANTILLES

Number	Title	Yr	VG	VG+	NM
❏ 90628	Games	1988	2.50	5.00	10.00
❏ 91050	Insight	1989	3.00	6.00	12.00

MANN, ED

Percussionist.

CMP

Number	Title	Yr	VG	VG+	NM
❏ CMP-38-ST	Get Up	1988	2.50	5.00	10.00

MANN, HERBIE

Best known as a flutist, he also plays tenor saxophone. Also see LaVERN BAKER; THE MANHATTAN JAZZ SEPTETTE; NEW YORK JAZZ QUARTET; SAHIB SHIBAB.

A&M

Number	Title	Yr	VG	VG+	NM
❏ 2003 [M]	Glory of Love	1967	5.00	10.00	20.00
❏ SP-3003 [S]	Glory of Love	1967	3.00	6.00	12.00
❏ SP-3003	Glory of Love	198?	3.75	7.50	15.00
-- Audiophile reissue (labeled as such)					
❏ SP-3008	Trust in Me/Soul Flutes	1969	3.00	6.00	12.00

ATLANTIC

Number	Title	Yr	VG	VG+	NM
❏ SD 2-300 [(2)]	The Evolution of Mann	1972	3.75	7.50	15.00
❏ 1343 [M]	The Common Ground	1960	3.75	7.50	15.00
❏ SD 1343 [S]	The Common Ground	1960	5.00	10.00	20.00
❏ 1371 [M]	The Family of Mann	1961	3.75	7.50	15.00
❏ SD 1371 [S]	The Family of Mann	1961	5.00	10.00	20.00
❏ 1380 [M]	Herbie Mann at the Village Gate	1962	3.75	7.50	15.00
❏ SD 1380 [S]	Herbie Mann at the Village Gate	1962	5.00	10.00	20.00
❏ 1384 [M]	Right Now	1962	3.75	7.50	15.00
❏ SD 1384 [S]	Right Now	1962	5.00	10.00	20.00
❏ 1397 [M]	Do the Bossa Nova with Herbie Mann	1962	3.75	7.50	15.00
❏ SD 1397 [S]	Do the Bossa Nova with Herbie Mann	1962	5.00	10.00	20.00
❏ 1407 [M]	Herbie Mann Returns to the Village Gate	1963	3.75	7.50	15.00
❏ SD 1407 [S]	Herbie Mann Returns to the Village Gate	1963	5.00	10.00	20.00
❏ 1413 [M]	Herbie Mann Live at Newport	1963	3.75	7.50	15.00
❏ SD 1413 [S]	Herbie Mann Live at Newport	1963	5.00	10.00	20.00
❏ 1422 [M]	Latin Fever	1964	3.75	7.50	15.00
❏ SD 1422 [S]	Latin Fever	1964	5.00	10.00	20.00
❏ 1426 [M]	Nirvana	1964	3.75	7.50	15.00
❏ SD 1426 [S]	Nirvana	1964	5.00	10.00	20.00
❏ 1433 [M]	My Kinda Groove	1965	3.75	7.50	15.00
❏ SD 1433 [S]	My Kinda Groove	1965	5.00	10.00	20.00
❏ 1437 [M]	The Roar of the Greasepaint, The Smell of the Crowd	1965	3.75	7.50	15.00
❏ SD 1437 [S]	The Roar of the Greasepaint, The Smell of the Crowd	1965	5.00	10.00	20.00
❏ 1445 [M]	Standing Ovation at Newport	1965	3.75	7.50	15.00
❏ SD 1445 [S]	Standing Ovation at Newport	1965	5.00	10.00	20.00
❏ 1454 [M]	Herbie Mann Today	1966	3.75	7.50	15.00
❏ SD 1454 [S]	Herbie Mann Today	1966	5.00	10.00	20.00
❏ 1462 [M]	Monday Night at the Village Gate	1966	3.75	7.50	15.00
❏ SD 1462 [S]	Monday Night at the Village Gate	1966	5.00	10.00	20.00
❏ 1464 [M]	Our Mann Flute	1966	3.75	7.50	15.00
❏ SD 1464 [S]	Our Mann Flute	1966	5.00	10.00	20.00
❏ 1471 [M]	New Mann at Newport	1967	5.00	10.00	20.00
❏ SD 1471 [S]	New Mann at Newport	1967	3.75	7.50	15.00
❏ 1475 [M]	Impressions of the Middle East	1967	5.00	10.00	20.00
❏ SD 1475 [S]	Impressions of the Middle East	1967	3.75	7.50	15.00
❏ 1483 [M]	The Beat Goes On	1967	5.00	10.00	20.00
❏ SD 1483 [S]	The Beat Goes On	1967	3.75	7.50	15.00
❏ 1490 [M]	The Herbie Mann String Album	1968	6.25	12.50	25.00
❏ SD 1490 [S]	The Herbie Mann String Album	1968	3.75	7.50	15.00
❏ SD 1497	Wailing Dervishes	1968	3.75	7.50	15.00
❏ SD 1507	Windows Open	1969	3.00	6.00	12.00
❏ SD 1513	The Inspiration I Feel	1969	3.75	7.50	15.00
❏ SD 1522	Memphis Underground	1969	3.00	6.00	12.00
❏ SD 1536	Live at the Whisky A-Go-Go	1969	3.00	6.00	12.00
❏ SD 1540	Concerto Grosso in D Blues	1969	3.00	6.00	12.00
❏ SD 1544	The Best of Herbie Mann	1970	3.00	6.00	12.00
❏ SD 1610	Mississippi Gambler	1972	3.00	6.00	12.00
❏ QD 1632 [Q]	Hold On, I'm Comin'	1973	5.00	10.00	20.00
❏ SD 1632	Hold On, I'm Comin'	1973	3.00	6.00	12.00
❏ SD 1642	Turtle Bay	1973	3.00	6.00	12.00
❏ SD 1648	London Underground	1974	3.00	6.00	12.00
❏ SD 1655	Reggae	1974	3.00	6.00	12.00
❏ SD 1658	First Light	1974	3.00	6.00	12.00
❏ SD 1670	Discotheque	1975	3.00	6.00	12.00
❏ SD 1676	Waterbed	1975	3.00	6.00	12.00
❏ SD 1682	Surprises	1976	3.00	6.00	12.00
❏ 8141 [M]	Mann and a Woman	1967	5.00	10.00	20.00
❏ SD 8141 [S]	Mann and a Woman	1967	3.75	7.50	15.00
❏ SD 16046	Mellow	1981	2.50	5.00	10.00
❏ SD 18209	Bird in a Silver Cage	1977	2.50	5.00	10.00
❏ SD 19112	Herbie Mann & Fire Island	1977	2.50	5.00	10.00
❏ SD 19169	Brazil -- Once Again	1978	2.50	5.00	10.00
❏ SD 19221	Super Mann	1979	2.50	5.00	10.00
❏ SD 19252	Yellow Fever	1980	2.50	5.00	10.00
❏ 80077	Astral Island	1983	2.50	5.00	10.00
❏ 81285	See Through Spirits	1986	2.50	5.00	10.00
❏ 90141	Nirvana	1984	2.50	5.00	10.00

BETHLEHEM

Number	Title	Yr	VG	VG+	NM
❏ BCP-24 [M]	Flamingo, My Goodness -- Four Flutes, Vol. 2	1955	12.50	25.00	50.00
❏ BCP-40 [M]	The Herbie Mann-Sam Most Quintet	1956	12.50	25.00	50.00
❏ BCP-58 [M]	Herbie Mann Plays	1956	12.50	25.00	50.00
❏ BCP-63 [M]	Love and the Weather	1956	12.50	25.00	50.00
❏ BCP-1018 [10]	East Coast Jazz 4	1954	25.00	50.00	100.00
❏ BCP-6020 [M]	The Mann with the Most	1960	10.00	20.00	40.00
❏ BCP-6067 [M]	The Epitome of Jazz	1963	7.50	15.00	30.00

COLUMBIA

Number	Title	Yr	VG	VG+	NM
❏ CS 1068	Big Boss	1970	3.00	6.00	12.00
❏ CL 2388 [M]	Latin Mann	1965	3.75	7.50	15.00
❏ CS 9188 [S]	Latin Mann	1965	5.00	10.00	20.00

EMBRYO

Number	Title	Yr	VG	VG+	NM
❏ 520	Stone Flute	1970	3.00	6.00	12.00
❏ 526	Muscle Shoals Nitty Gritty	1970	3.00	6.00	12.00
❏ 531	Memphis Two-Step	1971	3.00	6.00	12.00
❏ 532	Push Push	1971	3.00	6.00	12.00

EPIC

Number	Title	Yr	VG	VG+	NM
❏ LN 3395 [M]	Salute to the Flute	1957	15.00	30.00	60.00
❏ LN 3499 [M]	Herbie Mann with the Ilcken Trio	1958	15.00	30.00	60.00

FINNADAR

Number	Title	Yr	VG	VG+	NM
❏ 9014	Gagaku and Beyond	197?	2.50	5.00	10.00

JAZZLAND

Number	Title	Yr	VG	VG+	NM
❏ JLP-5 [M]	Herbie Mann Quintet	1960	7.50	15.00	30.00
-- Reissue of Riverside 245					

MILESTONE

Number	Title	Yr	VG	VG+	NM
❏ 47010	Let Me Tell You	1973	3.00	6.00	12.00

NEW JAZZ

Number	Title	Yr	VG	VG+	NM
❏ NJLP-8211 [M]	Just Walkin'	1958	12.50	25.00	50.00
-- Purple label					
❏ NJLP-8211 [M]	Just Walkin'	1964	6.25	12.50	25.00
-- Blue label with trident logo					

PRESTIGE

Number	Title	Yr	VG	VG+	NM
❏ PRLP-7101 [M]	Flute Souffle	1957	20.00	40.00	80.00
❏ PRLP-7124 [M]	Flute Flight	1957	20.00	40.00	80.00
❏ PRLP-7136 [M]	Mann in the Morning	1958	20.00	40.00	80.00
❏ PRLP-7432 [M]	The Best of Herbie Mann	1965	3.75	7.50	15.00
❏ PRST-7432 [R]	The Best of Herbie Mann	1965	3.00	6.00	12.00
❏ PRST-7659	Herbie Mann in Sweden	1969	3.00	6.00	12.00

RIVERSIDE

Number	Title	Yr	VG	VG+	NM
❏ RLP-12-234 [M]	Sultry Serenade	1957	15.00	30.00	60.00
-- Blue on white label					

Number	Title	Yr	VG	VG+	NM
❏ RLP-12-234 [M]	Sultry Serenade	1958	10.00	20.00	40.00
-- Blue label with reel and microphone logo					
❏ RLP-12-245 [M]	Great Ideas of Western Mann	1957	10.00	20.00	40.00
❏ S-3029	Moody Mann	1969	3.00	6.00	12.00
❏ 6084	Great Ideas of Western Mann	197?	2.50	5.00	10.00
SAVOY					
❏ MG-12102 [M]	Flute Suite	1957	12.50	25.00	50.00
❏ MG-12107 [M]	Mann Alone	1957	12.50	25.00	50.00
❏ MG-12108 [M]	Yardbird Suite	1957	12.50	25.00	50.00
SAVOY JAZZ					
❏ SJL-1102	Be Bop Synthesis	197?	2.50	5.00	10.00
SOLID STATE					
❏ SS-18020	Jazz Impressions of Brazil	1968	3.00	6.00	12.00
❏ SS-18023	St. Thomas	1968	3.00	6.00	12.00
SURREY					
❏ S-1015 [M]	Big Band	1965	3.75	7.50	15.00
❏ SS-1015 [S]	Big Band	1965	5.00	10.00	20.00
TRIP					
❏ 5031	Super Mann	1974	2.50	5.00	10.00
UNITED ARTISTS					
❏ UAL-4042 [M]	African Suite	1959	7.50	15.00	30.00
❏ UAS-5042 [S]	African Suite	1959	10.00	20.00	40.00
❏ UAS-5638	Brazil Blues	1972	3.00	6.00	12.00
❏ UAJ-14009 [M]	Brasil, Bossa Nova and Blue	1962	7.50	15.00	30.00
❏ UAJ-14022 [M]	St. Thomas	1962	7.50	15.00	30.00
❏ UAJS-15009 [S]	Brasil, Bossa Nova and Blue	1962	10.00	20.00	40.00
❏ UAJS-15022 [S]	St. Thomas	1962	10.00	20.00	40.00
VERVE					
❏ VSP-8 [M]	Bongo, Conga and Flute	1966	3.75	7.50	15.00
❏ VSPS-8 [R]	Bongo, Conga and Flute	1966	3.00	6.00	12.00
❏ VSP-19 [M]	Big Band Mann	1966	3.75	7.50	15.00
❏ VSPS-19 [R]	Big Band Mann	1966	3.00	6.00	12.00
❏ MGVS-6074 [S]	Flautista! -- Herbie Mann Plays Afro-Cuban Jazz	1960	7.50	15.00	30.00
❏ MGV-8247 [M]	The Magic Flute of Herbie Mann	1958	10.00	20.00	40.00
❏ V-8247 [M]	The Magic Flute of Herbie Mann	1961	5.00	10.00	20.00
❏ MGV-8336 [M]	Flautista! -- Herbie Mann Plays Afro-Cuban Jazz	1959	10.00	20.00	40.00
❏ V-8336 [M]	Flautista! -- Herbie Mann Plays Afro-Cuban Jazz	1961	5.00	10.00	20.00
❏ V6-8336 [S]	Flautista! -- Herbie Mann Plays Afro-Cuban Jazz	1961	3.75	7.50	15.00
❏ MGV-8392 [M]	Flute, Brass, Vibes and Percussion	1960	7.50	15.00	30.00
❏ V-8392 [M]	Flute, Brass, Vibes and Percussion	1961	5.00	10.00	20.00
❏ V-8527 [M]	The Sound of Mann	1963	5.00	10.00	20.00
❏ V6-8527 [S]	The Sound of Mann	1963	3.75	7.50	15.00
❏ V6-8821 [(2)]	Et Tu Flute	1973	3.75	7.50	15.00

MANN, HERBIE, AND BUDDY COLLETTE

Also see each artist's individual listings.

Number	Title	Yr	VG	VG+	NM
INTERLUDE					
❏ MO-503 [M]	Flute Fraternity	1959	10.00	20.00	40.00
-- Reissue of Mode 114					
❏ ST-1103 [S]	Flute Fraternity	1959	7.50	15.00	30.00
MODE					
❏ LP-114 [M]	Flute Fraternity	1957	17.50	35.00	70.00

MANN, HERBIE, AND JOAO GILBERTO

Also see each artist's individual listings.

Number	Title	Yr	VG	VG+	NM
ATLANTIC					
❏ 8105 [M]	Herbie Mann and Joao Gilberto with Antonio Carlos Jobim	1965	3.75	7.50	15.00
❏ SD 8105 [S]	Herbie Mann and Joao Gilberto with Antonio Carlos Jobim	1965	5.00	10.00	20.00

MANN, HERBIE, AND MACHITO

Also see each artist's individual listings.

Number	Title	Yr	VG	VG+	NM
ROULETTE					
❏ R-52122 [M]	Afro-Jazziac	1963	3.75	7.50	15.00
❏ SR-52122 [S]	Afro-Jazziac	1963	5.00	10.00	20.00

MANNE, SHELLY

Drummer and male singer. Also see BOOTS BROWN; ART PEPPER; THE POLL WINNERS; ANDRE PREVIN; RUTH PRICE.

Number	Title	Yr	VG	VG+	NM
ABC IMPULSE!					
❏ AS-20 [S]	2 3 4	1968	3.75	7.50	15.00
ATLANTIC					
❏ 1469 [M]	Boss Sounds!	1967	3.75	7.50	15.00
❏ SD 1469 [S]	Boss Sounds!	1967	3.00	6.00	12.00
❏ 1487 [M]	Jazz Gunn	1967	5.00	10.00	20.00
❏ SD 1487 [S]	Jazz Gunn	1967	3.00	6.00	12.00

Number	Title	Yr	VG	VG+	NM
❏ 8157 [M]	Daktari	1968	6.25	12.50	25.00
❏ SD 8157 [S]	Daktari	1968	3.00	6.00	12.00
CAPITOL					
❏ SM-2173	"My Fair Lady" with Un-Original Cast	1976	2.50	5.00	10.00
-- Reissue with new prefix					
❏ ST 2173 [S]	"My Fair Lady" with Un-Original Cast	1964	5.00	10.00	20.00
❏ T 2173 [M]	"My Fair Lady" with Un-Original Cast	1964	3.75	7.50	15.00
❏ ST 2313 [S]	Manne, That's Gershwin	1965	5.00	10.00	20.00
❏ T 2313 [M]	Manne, That's Gershwin	1965	3.75	7.50	15.00
❏ ST 2610 [S]	Shelly Manne Sounds	1966	3.75	7.50	15.00
❏ T 2610 [M]	Shelly Manne Sounds	1966	3.00	6.00	12.00
CONCORD JAZZ					
❏ CJ-21	Perk Up	1976	3.00	6.00	12.00
CONTEMPORARY					
❏ C-2503 [10]	Shelly Manne and His Men	1953	37.50	75.00	150.00
❏ C-2511 [10]	Shelly Manne and His Men, Volume 2	1954	37.50	75.00	150.00
❏ C-2516 [10]	The Three	1954	37.50	75.00	150.00
❏ C-2518 [10]	The Two	1954	37.50	75.00	150.00
❏ C-3507 [M]	The West Coast Sound	1955	15.00	30.00	60.00
❏ C-3516 [M]	Swinging Sounds, Vol. 4	1956	15.00	30.00	60.00
❏ C-3519 [M]	More Swinging Sounds, Vol. 5	1957	15.00	30.00	60.00
❏ C-3525 [M]	Shelly Manne and His Friends	1957	12.50	25.00	50.00
❏ C-3527 [M]	Modern Jazz Performance of Songs from "My Fair Lady"	1957	12.50	25.00	50.00
❏ C-3533 [M]	Li'l Abner	1957	12.50	25.00	50.00
❏ C-3536 [M]	Concerto for Clarinet and Combo	1957	12.50	25.00	50.00
❏ C-3557 [M]	The Gambit	1958	12.50	25.00	50.00
❏ C-3559 [M]	Bells Are Ringing	1958	10.00	20.00	40.00
❏ C-3560 [M]	Shelly Manne Plays "Peter Gunn"	1958	12.50	25.00	50.00
❏ M-3566 [M]	Son of Gunn	1959	10.00	20.00	40.00
❏ M-3577 [M]	Shelly Manne and His Men at the Black Hawk, Vol. 1	1960	10.00	20.00	40.00
❏ M-3578 [M]	Shelly Manne and His Men at the Black Hawk, Vol. 2	1960	10.00	20.00	40.00
❏ M-3579 [M]	Shelly Manne and His Men at the Black Hawk, Vol. 3	1960	10.00	20.00	40.00
❏ M-3580 [M]	Shelly Manne and His Men at the Black Hawk, Vol. 4	1960	10.00	20.00	40.00
❏ M-3584 [M]	The Three and The Two	1960	7.50	15.00	30.00
❏ M-3593/4 [(2) M]	Live! Shelly Manne and His Men at the Manne-Hole	1961	10.00	20.00	40.00
❏ M-3599 [M]	Checkmate	1961	6.25	12.50	25.00
❏ M-3609 [M]	My Son, the Jazz Drummer!	1962	6.25	12.50	25.00
❏ M-3624 [M]	Outside	1966	6.25	12.50	25.00
❏ M-5006 [M]	Sounds Unheard Of	1962	7.50	15.00	30.00
❏ S-7025 [S]	Shelly Manne Plays "Peter Gunn"	1959	10.00	20.00	40.00
❏ S-7519 [S]	Swinging Sounds in Stereo	1959	12.50	25.00	50.00
❏ S-7527 [S]	Modern Jazz Performance of Songs from "My Fair Lady"	1959	10.00	20.00	40.00
❏ S-7533 [S]	Li'l Abner	1959	10.00	20.00	40.00
❏ S-7557 [S]	The Gambit	1959	10.00	20.00	40.00
❏ S-7559 [S]	Bells Are Ringing	1959	7.50	15.00	30.00
❏ S-7566 [S]	Son of Gunn	1959	7.50	15.00	30.00
❏ S-7577 [S]	Shelly Manne and His Men at the Black Hawk, Vol. 1	1960	7.50	15.00	30.00
❏ S-7578 [S]	Shelly Manne and His Men at the Black Hawk, Vol. 2	1960	7.50	15.00	30.00
❏ S-7579 [S]	Shelly Manne and His Men at the Black Hawk, Vol. 3	1960	7.50	15.00	30.00
❏ S-7580 [S]	Shelly Manne and His Men at the Black Hawk, Vol. 4	1960	7.50	15.00	30.00
❏ S-7593/4 [(2) S]	Live! Shelly Manne and His Men at the Manne-Hole	1961	12.50	25.00	50.00
❏ S-7599 [S]	Checkmate	1961	7.50	15.00	30.00
❏ S-7609 [S]	My Son, the Jazz Drummer!	1962	7.50	15.00	30.00
❏ S-7624 [S]	Outside	1966	7.50	15.00	30.00
❏ S-9006 [S]	Sounds Unheard Of	1962	10.00	20.00	40.00
❏ C-14018	Shelly Manne in Zurich	1986	2.50	5.00	10.00
DEE GEE					
❏ 1003 [10]	Here's That Manne	1952	75.00	150.00	300.00
DISCOVERY					
❏ 783	Rex	1976	3.00	6.00	12.00
❏ 909	Manne, That's Gershwin!	1986	2.50	5.00	10.00
-- Reissue of Capitol ST 2313					
DOCTOR JAZZ					
❏ FW 38728	Shelly Manne and His Friends	1983	2.50	5.00	10.00
FANTASY					
❏ OJC-152	The West Coast Sound	198?	2.50	5.00	10.00
❏ OJC-176	The Three and The Two	198?	2.50	5.00	10.00
❏ OJC-240	Shelly Manne and His Men at the Black Hawk, Vol. 1	198?	2.50	5.00	10.00
❏ OJC-267	Swinging Sounds, Vol. 4	1987	2.50	5.00	10.00

Number	Title	Yr	VG	VG+	NM
❑ OJC-320	More Swinging Sounds, Vol. 5	198?	2.50	5.00	10.00
❑ OJC-336	Modern Jazz Performance of Songs from "My Fair Lady"	198?	2.50	5.00	10.00
GALAXY					
❑ 5101	Essence	1978	3.00	6.00	12.00
❑ 5124	French Concert	1979	3.00	6.00	12.00
IMPULSE!					
❑ A-20 [M]	2 3 4	1962	6.25	12.50	25.00
❑ AS-20 [S]	2 3 4	1962	7.50	15.00	30.00
MAINSTREAM					
❑ MRL-375	Mannekind	1972	3.75	7.50	15.00
MCA					
❑ 29073	2 3 4	1980	2.00	4.00	8.00
STEREO RECORDS					
❑ S-7002 [S]	Modern Jazz Performance of Songs from "My Fair Lady"	1958	12.50	25.00	50.00
❑ S-7007 [S]	Swinging Sounds in Stereo	1958	15.00	30.00	60.00
❑ S-7019 [S]	Li'l Abner	1958	12.50	25.00	50.00
❑ S-7025 [S]	Shelly Manne Plays "Peter Gunn"	1958	12.50	25.00	50.00
❑ S-7030 [S]	The Gambit	1958	12.50	25.00	50.00
TREND					
❑ 525	Interpretations of Bach and Mozart	1980	3.00	6.00	12.00
❑ 526	Double Piano Jazz Quartet	1980	3.00	6.00	12.00
❑ 527	Double Piano Jazz Quartet, Volume 2	1980	3.00	6.00	12.00

MANNE, SHELLY/BILL RUSSO
Also see each artist's individual listings.
SAVOY

Number	Title	Yr	VG	VG+	NM
❑ MG-12045 [M]	Deep Purple	1955	12.50	25.00	50.00

MANONE, WINGY
Trumpeter, bandleader, male singer and composer. Also see BUNNY BERIGAN.
DECCA

Number	Title	Yr	VG	VG+	NM
❑ DL 8473 [M]	Trumpet on the Wing	1957	10.00	20.00	40.00
IMPERIAL					
❑ LP-9190 [M]	Wingy Manone on the Jazzband Bus	1962	3.75	7.50	15.00
❑ LP-12190 [S]	Wingy Manone on the Jazzband Bus	1962	5.00	10.00	20.00
RCA VICTOR					
❑ LPV-563 [M]	Wingy Manone, Volume 1	1969	5.00	10.00	20.00
STORYVILLE					
❑ 4066	Wingy Manone with Papa Bue's Viking Jazzband	198?	2.50	5.00	10.00
"X"					
❑ LVA-3014 [10]	Wingy Manone, Vol. 1	1954	12.50	25.00	50.00

MANTECA
Canadian fusion group led by Aaron Davis (keyboards) and Matt Zimbel (percussion).
SOUNDWINGS/DUKE STREET

Number	Title	Yr	VG	VG+	NM
❑ SW 2111	No Heroes	1986	2.50	5.00	10.00

MANTILLA, RAY
Percussionist.
INNER CITY

Number	Title	Yr	VG	VG+	NM
❑ IC-1052	Mantilla	1978	3.75	7.50	15.00
RED RECORD					
❑ VPA-174	Hands of Fire	198?	3.00	6.00	12.00

MANTLER, MICHAEL
Trumpeter.
ECM

Number	Title	Yr	VG	VG+	NM
❑ 23786	Something There	1984	2.50	5.00	10.00
WATT					
❑ 2	No Answer	197?	5.00	10.00	20.00
❑ 3	13 & 3/4	197?	5.00	10.00	20.00
❑ 4	Hapless Child	197?	5.00	10.00	20.00
❑ 5	Silence	197?	5.00	10.00	20.00
❑ 7	Movies	1978	3.75	7.50	15.00

MARABLE, LAWRENCE
Drummer.
JAZZ WEST

Number	Title	Yr	VG	VG+	NM
❑ LP-8 [M]	Tenor Man	1956	75.00	150.00	300.00

MARCUS, LEW
Pianist.
SAVOY

Number	Title	Yr	VG	VG+	NM
❑ MG-15006 [10]	Back Room Piano	1951	12.50	25.00	50.00

MARCUS, STEVE
Tenor saxophone player.
FLYING DUTCHMAN

Number	Title	Yr	VG	VG+	NM
❑ BDL1-1461	Sometime Other Than Now	1976	3.00	6.00	12.00
VORTEX					
❑ 2001	Tomorrow Never Knows	1968	6.25	12.50	25.00
❑ 2009	The Count's Rock Band	1969	6.25	12.50	25.00
❑ 2013	The Lord's Prayer	1969	6.25	12.50	25.00

MARCUS, WADE
Arranger and composer.
ABC IMPULSE!

Number	Title	Yr	VG	VG+	NM
❑ AS-9318	Metamorphosis	197?	3.00	6.00	12.00

MARDIN, ARIF
Composer, arranger and producer.
ATLANTIC

Number	Title	Yr	VG	VG+	NM
❑ SD 1661	Journey	1974	3.00	6.00	12.00

MARGITZA, RICK
Tenor saxophone player and composer.
BLUE NOTE

Number	Title	Yr	VG	VG+	NM
❑ B1-92279	Color	1989	3.00	6.00	12.00

MARIA, TANIA
Pianist and female singer.
CAPITOL

Number	Title	Yr	VG	VG+	NM
❑ C1-90966	Forbidden Colors	1988	2.50	5.00	10.00
CONCORD PICANTE					
❑ CJP-151	Piquant	1981	2.50	5.00	10.00
❑ CJP-175	Taurus	1982	2.50	5.00	10.00
❑ CJP-200	Come with Me	1982	2.50	5.00	10.00
❑ CJP-230	Love Explosion	1984	2.50	5.00	10.00
❑ CJP-264	The Real Tania Maria: Wild!	1985	2.50	5.00	10.00
MANHATTAN					
❑ ST-53000	Made in New York	1985	2.50	5.00	10.00
❑ ST-53045	Lady from Brazil	1986	2.50	5.00	10.00

MARIACHI BRASS, THE
Studio group modeled after the Tijuana Brass and featuring CHET BAKER. This group also did the original version of the theme from "The Dating Game."
WORLD PACIFIC

Number	Title	Yr	VG	VG+	NM
❑ WP-1839 [M]	A Taste of Tequila	1966	3.00	6.00	12.00
❑ WP-1842 [M]	Hats Off!!!	1966	3.00	6.00	12.00
❑ WP-1852 [M]	Double Shot	1966	3.00	6.00	12.00
❑ WP-1859 [M]	In the Mood	1967	3.00	6.00	12.00
❑ WPS-21839 [S]	A Taste of Tequila	1966	3.75	7.50	15.00
❑ WPS-21842 [S]	Hats Off!!!	1966	3.75	7.50	15.00
❑ WPS-21852 [S]	Double Shot	1966	3.75	7.50	15.00
❑ WPS-21859 [S]	In the Mood	1967	3.75	7.50	15.00

MARIANO, CHARLIE
Alto saxophone player. Also has played soprano sax and flute. Also see TOSHIKO AKIYOSHI; NAT PIERCE.
ATLANTIC

Number	Title	Yr	VG	VG+	NM
❑ SD 1608	The Mirror	197?	3.75	7.50	15.00
BETHLEHEM					
❑ BCP-25 [M]	Alto Sax for Young Moderns	1956	25.00	50.00	100.00
❑ BCP-49 [M]	Charlie Mariano Plays Chloe	1957	25.00	50.00	100.00
❑ BCP-1022 [10]	Charlie Mariano Sextet	1955	37.50	75.00	150.00
CATALYST					
❑ 7915	Reflections	197?	3.75	7.50	15.00
CMP					
❑ CMP-2-ST	October	198?	2.50	5.00	10.00
❑ CMP-10-ST	Crystal Balls	198?	2.50	5.00	10.00
ECM					
❑ 1256	Charlie Mariano with the Kamataka College of Percussion	1985	3.00	6.00	12.00
FANTASY					
❑ 3-10 [10]	Charlie Mariano Sextet	1953	45.00	90.00	180.00
❑ OJC-1745	Charlie Mariano Boston All Stars	1990	3.00	6.00	12.00
IMPERIAL					
❑ IMP-3006 [10]	Charlie Mariano Quintet Volume 1	1955	37.50	75.00	150.00
❑ IMP-3007 [10]	Charlie Mariano Quintet Volume 2	1955	37.50	75.00	150.00
INNER CITY					
❑ IC-1024	October	1977	3.75	7.50	15.00
INTUITION					
❑ C1-90787	Mariano	1988	2.50	5.00	10.00

Number	Title	Yr	VG	VG+	NM
PRESTIGE					
❑ PRLP-130 [10]	Charlie Mariano	1952	50.00	100.00	200.00
❑ PRLP-153 [10]	Charlie Mariano Boston All Stars	1953	50.00	100.00	200.00
REGINA					
❑ R-286 [M]	A Jazz Portrait of Charlie Mariano	1963	6.25	12.50	25.00
❑ RS-286 [S]	A Jazz Portrait of Charlie Mariano	1963	7.50	15.00	30.00

MARIANO, CHARLIE, AND JERRY DODGION
Dodgion is a flute and alto saxophone player. Also see CHARLIE MARIANO.

Number	Title	Yr	VG	VG+	NM
WORLD PACIFIC					
❑ WP-1245 [M]	Beauties of 1918	1958	12.50	25.00	50.00

MARIANO, TOSHIKO
See TOSHIKO AKIYOSHI.

MARIENTHAL, ERIC
Saxophone player (alto, tenor and soprano).

Number	Title	Yr	VG	VG+	NM
GRP					
❑ GR-1052	Voices of the Heart	1988	2.50	5.00	10.00
❑ GR-9586	Round Trip	1989	3.00	6.00	12.00

MARK-ALMOND
The constants in this British band were Jon Mark (guitar, bass, percussion, vocals) and Johnny Almond (saxophones, vibes, vocals, percussion, flute).

Number	Title	Yr	VG	VG+	NM
ABC					
❑ D-945	To the Heart	1976	2.50	5.00	10.00
BLUE THUMB					
❑ BTS 27	Mark-Almond	1971	3.00	6.00	12.00
-- Reissue of 8827					
❑ BTS 32	Mark-Almond II	1971	3.00	6.00	12.00
❑ BTS 50	The Best of Mark-Almond	1973	3.00	6.00	12.00
❑ BTS-8827	Mark-Almond	1971	3.75	7.50	15.00
COLUMBIA					
❑ KC 31917	Rising	1972	3.00	6.00	12.00
❑ PC 31917	Rising	198?	2.00	4.00	8.00
-- Budget-line reissue					
❑ KC 32486	Mark-Almond 73	1973	3.00	6.00	12.00
❑ CG 33648 [(2)]	Rising/Mark-Almond 73	1976	3.75	7.50	15.00
HORIZON					
❑ SP-730	Other People's Rooms	1978	2.50	5.00	10.00
MCA					
❑ 711	Mark-Almond II	198?	2.00	4.00	8.00
-- Reissue of Blue Thumb 32					
❑ 792	The Best of Mark-Almond	198?	2.00	4.00	8.00
-- Reissue of Blue Thumb 50					
❑ 793	To the Heart	198?	2.00	4.00	8.00
-- Reissue of ABC 945					
PACIFIC ARTS					
❑ 7-142	The Best of the Mark-Almond Band...Live	1980	2.50	5.00	10.00

MARKEWICH, REESE

Number	Title	Yr	VG	VG+	NM
MODERN AGE					
❑ MA-134 [M]	New Designs in Jazz	1958	12.50	25.00	50.00

MARKHAM, JOHN
Drummer.

Number	Title	Yr	VG	VG+	NM
FAMOUS DOOR					
❑ 121	San Francisco Jazz	1977	3.00	6.00	12.00

MARKOWITZ, MARKIE
Trumpeter.

Number	Title	Yr	VG	VG+	NM
FAMOUS DOOR					
❑ 111	Marky's Vibes	197?	3.75	7.50	15.00

MARLENE
See MARLENE VER PLANCK.

MARLOW, JANET
10-string guitarist, female singer and composer.

Number	Title	Yr	VG	VG+	NM
CMG					
❑ CML-8003	Outside the City	198?	2.50	5.00	10.00

MARMAROSA, DODO
Pianist.

Number	Title	Yr	VG	VG+	NM
ARGO					
❑ LP-4012 [M]	Dodo's Back	1961	6.25	12.50	25.00
❑ LPS-4012 [S]	Dodo's Back	1961	7.50	15.00	30.00

Number	Title	Yr	VG	VG+	NM
PHOENIX					
❑ 20	Piano Man	197?	3.00	6.00	12.00
SPOTLITE					
❑ 108	Dodo Marmarosa Trio	197?	2.50	5.00	10.00

MARMAROSA, DODO/ERROLL GARNER
Also see each artist's individual listings.

Number	Title	Yr	VG	VG+	NM
CONCERT HALL JAZZ					
❑ 1001 [10]	Piano Contrasts	1955	12.50	25.00	50.00
DIAL					
❑ LP-208 [10]	Piano Contrasts	1950	62.50	125.00	250.00

MAROCCO, FRANK
Accordion player.

Number	Title	Yr	VG	VG+	NM
DISCOVERY					
❑ 797	Jazz Accordion	1979	3.00	6.00	12.00
❑ 838	The Trio	198?	2.50	5.00	10.00
❑ 854	Road to Marocco	198?	2.50	5.00	10.00
TREND					
❑ 516	New Colors	1980	3.75	7.50	15.00
-- Direct-to-disc recording					

MAROHNIC, CHUCK
Pianist.

Number	Title	Yr	VG	VG+	NM
STEEPLECHASE					
❑ SCS-1155	Permutations	198?	3.00	6.00	12.00
❑ SCS-4002	Copenhagen Suite	198?	3.00	6.00	12.00

MARR, HANK
Pianist and organist.

Number	Title	Yr	VG	VG+	NM
KING					
❑ 829 [M]	Teentime Dance Steps	1963	7.50	15.00	30.00
❑ 899 [M]	Live at Club 502	1964	10.00	20.00	40.00
❑ 933 [M]	On and Off Stage	1965	7.50	15.00	30.00
❑ 1011 [M]	Hank Marr Plays 24 Originals	1966	5.00	10.00	20.00
❑ 1025 [M]	Sounds from the Marr-Ket Place	1968	5.00	10.00	20.00
❑ KSD-1061	Greasy Spoon	1969	5.00	10.00	20.00

MARROW, ESTHER
Female singer better known in the gospel realm.

Number	Title	Yr	VG	VG+	NM
FANTASY					
❑ 9414	Sister Woman	1972	3.75	7.50	15.00

MARSALA, JOE
Clarinetist, saxophone player, bandleader and composer. Also see RAY McKINLEY.

Number	Title	Yr	VG	VG+	NM
JAZZOLOGY					
❑ J-106	Joe Marsala and His Jazz Band, 1944	198?	2.50	5.00	10.00

MARSALA, JOE/BUD FREEMAN
Also see each artist's individual listings.

Number	Title	Yr	VG	VG+	NM
BRUNSWICK					
❑ BL 58037 [10]	Battle of Jazz, Vol. 1	1953	12.50	25.00	50.00

MARSALIS, BRANFORD
Tenor and soprano saxophone player and male singer. Also see BUCKSHOT LEFONQUE.

Number	Title	Yr	VG	VG+	NM
CBS MASTERWORKS					
❑ M 42122	Romances for Saxophone	1986	3.00	6.00	12.00
COLUMBIA					
❑ CAS 1628 [DJ]	Trio Jeepy Interchords Special	1989	3.75	7.50	15.00
❑ FC 38951	Scenes in the City	1984	2.50	5.00	10.00
❑ FC 40363	Royal Garden Blues	1986	2.50	5.00	10.00
❑ FC 40711	Renaissance	1987	2.50	5.00	10.00
❑ OC 44055	Random Abstract	1988	2.50	5.00	10.00
❑ CX2 44199 [(2)]	Trio Jeepy	1989	3.75	7.50	15.00
JAZZ PLANET					
❑ JP-5004 [(2)]	The Dark Keys	1996	7.50	15.00	30.00

MARSALIS, ELLIS
Pianist and male singer; father of Branford and Wynton.

Number	Title	Yr	VG	VG+	NM
SPINDLETOP					
❑ ST-105	Homecoming	1986	2.50	5.00	10.00

MARSALIS, WYNTON
Trumpeter and composer.

Number	Title	Yr	VG	VG+	NM
CBS					
❑ IM 42137	Carnaval	1987	2.50	5.00	10.00
COLUMBIA					
❑ FC 37574	Wynton Marsalis	1982	2.50	5.00	10.00

Number	Title	Yr	VG	VG+	NM
❏ FC 38641	Think of One	1983	2.50	5.00	10.00
❏ FC 39530	Hot House Flowers	1984	2.50	5.00	10.00
❏ FC 40009	Black Codes (From the Underground)	1985	2.50	5.00	10.00
❏ FC 40308	J Mood	1986	2.50	5.00	10.00
❏ FC 40461	Marsalis Standard Time	1987	2.50	5.00	10.00
❏ OC 45091	The Majesty of the Blues	1989	3.00	6.00	12.00
❏ FC 45287	Crescent City Christmas Card	1989	2.50	5.00	10.00
❏ C 46143	Standard Time Vol. 3 -- The Resolution of Romance	1990	3.00	6.00	12.00
❏ C 47346	Standard Time Vol. 2 -- Intimacy Calling	1991	3.75	7.50	15.00
❏ HC 47574	Wynton Marsalis	198?	7.50	15.00	30.00

-- Half-speed mastered edition

WHO'S WHO IN JAZZ

Number	Title	Yr	VG	VG+	NM
❏ 21024	Wynton Marsalis with Art Blakey and His Jazz Messengers	1981	3.75	7.50	15.00

MARSH, GEORGE
Drummer.
1750 ARCH

| ❏ 1791 | Marshland | 1982 | 3.00 | 6.00 | 12.00 |

MARSH, GEORGE, AND JOHN ABERCROMBIE
Also see each artist's individual listings.
1750 ARCH

| ❏ 1804 | Drum Strum | 198? | 3.00 | 6.00 | 12.00 |

MARSH, HUGH
Violinist.
SOUNDWINGS/DUKE STREET

| ❏ SW-210 | Shaking the Pumpkin | 1988 | 3.00 | 6.00 | 12.00 |

MARSH, MILTON
Composer, conductor and male vocalist.
STRATA-EAST

| ❏ SES-19758 | Monism | 1975 | 5.00 | 10.00 | 20.00 |

MARSH, WARNE
Tenor saxophone player. Also see LEE KONITZ.
ATLANTIC

| ❏ 1291 [M] | Warne Marsh | 1958 | 12.50 | 25.00 | 50.00 |

-- Black label

| ❏ 1291 [M] | Warne Marsh | 1961 | 6.25 | 12.50 | 25.00 |

-- Multicolor label, white "fan" logo at right

| ❏ SD 1291 [S] | Warne Marsh | 1958 | 12.50 | 25.00 | 50.00 |

-- Green label

| ❏ SD 1291 [S] | Warne Marsh | 1961 | 5.00 | 10.00 | 20.00 |

-- Multicolor label, white "fan" logo at right

DISCOVERY

| ❏ 863 | How Deep/How High | 198? | 2.50 | 5.00 | 10.00 |

IMPERIAL

| ❏ LP-9027 [M] | Jazz of Two Cities | 1957 | 20.00 | 40.00 | 80.00 |
| ❏ LP-12013 [S] | The Winds of Warne Marsh | 1959 | 15.00 | 30.00 | 60.00 |

-- Retitled version of 9027 in stereo?

INTERPLAY

❏ 7709	Warne Out	197?	3.00	6.00	12.00
❏ 8602	Two Days in the Life of Warne Marsh	1986	3.00	6.00	12.00
❏ 8604	Posthumous	1986	3.00	6.00	12.00

MODE

| ❏ LP-125 [M] | Music for Prancing | 1957 | 20.00 | 40.00 | 80.00 |

NESSA

| ❏ N-7 | All Music | 1977 | 3.00 | 6.00 | 12.00 |

REVELATION

❏ R-12	Ne Plus Ultra	1970	5.00	10.00	20.00
❏ 22	The Art of Improvising	197?	3.00	6.00	12.00
❏ 27	The Art of Improvising, Vol. 3	197?	3.00	6.00	12.00

STORYVILLE

| ❏ 4001 | Jazz Exchange, Vol. 1 | 197? | 3.00 | 6.00 | 12.00 |
| ❏ 4026 | Jazz Exchange, Vol. 2: Live at the Montmartre Club | 198? | 3.00 | 6.00 | 12.00 |

XANADU

| ❏ 151 | Live in Hollywood | 197? | 3.00 | 6.00 | 12.00 |

MARSH, WARNE; CLARE FISCHER; GARY FOSTER
Also see each artist's individual listings.
REVELATION

| ❏ 17 | First Symposium on Relaxed Improvisation | 197? | 3.75 | 7.50 | 15.00 |

MARSH, WARNE, AND SAL MOSCA
Also see each artist's individual listings.
INTERPLAY

Number	Title	Yr	VG	VG+	NM
❏ 7725	How Deep/How High	1980	3.00	6.00	12.00

MARSHALL, EDDIE
Drummer and recorder player.
TIMELESS

| ❏ 315 | Dance of the Sun | 1977 | 3.00 | 6.00 | 12.00 |

MARSHALL, JACK
Guitarist, composer and arranger. Wrote the theme to the TV show The Munsters.
CAPITOL

❏ ST 1108 [S]	18th Century Jazz	1959	6.25	12.50	25.00
❏ T 1108 [M]	18th Century Jazz	1959	5.00	10.00	20.00
❏ ST 1194 [S]	Soundsville!	1959	6.25	12.50	25.00
❏ T 1194 [M]	Soundsville!	1959	5.00	10.00	20.00
❏ ST 1351 [S]	The Marshall Swings	1960	6.25	12.50	25.00
❏ T 1351 [M]	The Marshall Swings	1960	5.00	10.00	20.00
❏ ST 1601 [S]	Songs Without Words	1961	6.25	12.50	25.00
❏ T 1601 [M]	Songs Without Words	1961	5.00	10.00	20.00
❏ ST 1727 [S]	The Twangy, Shoutin', Fantastic Big-Band Sounds of Tuff Jack	1962	10.00	20.00	40.00
❏ T 1727 [M]	The Twangy, Shoutin', Fantastic Big-Band Sounds of Tuff Jack	1962	7.50	15.00	30.00
❏ ST 1939 [S]	My Son the Surf Nut	1963	10.00	20.00	40.00
❏ T 1939 [M]	My Son the Surf Nut	1963	7.50	15.00	30.00

MARSHALL, WENDELL
See MILT HINTON.

MARTIN, ARCH
Trombonist.
ZEPHYR

| ❏ 12009 [M] | Arch Martin Quintet | 1959 | 7.50 | 15.00 | 30.00 |

MARTIN, FREDDY
Saxophone player and bandleader.
CAPITOL

| ❏ ST 1269 [S] | C'mon, Let's Dance | 1960 | 3.75 | 7.50 | 15.00 |

-- Black colorband label, logo at left

| ❏ ST 1269 [S] | C'mon, Let's Dance | 1962 | 3.00 | 6.00 | 12.00 |

-- Black colorband label, logo at top

| ❏ T 1269 [M] | C'mon, Let's Dance | 1960 | 3.00 | 6.00 | 12.00 |

-- Black colorband label, logo at left

| ❏ T 1269 [M] | C'mon, Let's Dance | 1962 | 2.50 | 5.00 | 10.00 |

-- Black colorband label, logo at top

| ❏ ST 1486 [S] | Seems Like Old Times | 1961 | 3.75 | 7.50 | 15.00 |

-- Black colorband label, logo at left

| ❏ ST 1486 [S] | Seems Like Old Times | 1962 | 3.00 | 6.00 | 12.00 |

-- Black colorband label, logo at top

| ❏ T 1486 [M] | Seems Like Old Times | 1961 | 3.00 | 6.00 | 12.00 |

-- Black colorband label, logo at left

| ❏ T 1486 [M] | Seems Like Old Times | 1962 | 2.50 | 5.00 | 10.00 |

-- Black colorband label, logo at top

❏ ST 1582 [S]	The Hits of Freddie Martin	1962	3.00	6.00	12.00
❏ T 1582 [M]	The Hits of Freddie Martin	1962	2.50	5.00	10.00
❏ ST 1889 [S]	In a Sentimental Mood	1963	3.00	6.00	12.00
❏ T 1889 [M]	In a Sentimental Mood	1963	2.50	5.00	10.00
❏ ST 2018 [S]	Tonight We Love	1964	3.00	6.00	12.00
❏ T 2018 [M]	Tonight We Love	1964	2.50	5.00	10.00
❏ ST 2028 [S]	Freddy Martin Plays the Hits	1964	3.00	6.00	12.00
❏ T 2028 [M]	Freddy Martin Plays the Hits	1964	2.50	5.00	10.00
❏ ST 2098 [S]	Best of the New Favorites	1964	3.00	6.00	12.00
❏ T 2098 [M]	Best of the New Favorites	1964	2.50	5.00	10.00
❏ ST 2163 [S]	Freddy Martin Plays the Hits, Vol. 2	1964	3.00	6.00	12.00
❏ T 2163 [M]	Freddy Martin Plays the Hits, Vol. 2	1964	2.50	5.00	10.00
❏ ST 2347 [S]	As Time Goes By	1965	3.00	6.00	12.00
❏ T 2347 [M]	As Time Goes By	1965	2.50	5.00	10.00

DECCA

❏ DL 4839 [M]	The Most Requested	1967	3.75	7.50	15.00
❏ DL 4908 [M]	Freddy Martin's Greatest Hits	1967	3.75	7.50	15.00
❏ DL 74839 [R]	The Most Requested	1967	2.50	5.00	10.00
❏ DL 74908 [R]	Freddy Martin's Greatest Hits	1967	2.50	5.00	10.00

HINDSIGHT

❏ HSR-151	Freddy Martin and His Orchestra 1940	198?	2.50	5.00	10.00
❏ HSR-169	Freddy Martin and His Orchestra 1944-46	198?	2.50	5.00	10.00
❏ HSR-190	Freddy Martin and His Orchestra 1952	198?	2.50	5.00	10.00
❏ HSR-205	Freddy Martin and His Orchestra 1948, 1952	198?	2.50	5.00	10.00

Number	Title	Yr	VG	VG+	NM
KAPP					
❏ KL-1261 [M]	Great Waltzes of the World	1962	3.00	6.00	12.00
❏ KL-1271 [M]	Great Waltzes of the World, Volume 2	1962	3.00	6.00	12.00
❏ KL-1286 [M]	Dancing Tonight	1963	3.00	6.00	12.00
❏ KL-1490 [M]	The Most Beautiful Girl in the World	1966	2.50	5.00	10.00
❏ KS-3261 [S]	Great Waltzes of the World	1962	3.75	7.50	15.00
❏ KS-3271 [S]	Great Waltzes of the World, Volume 2	1962	3.75	7.50	15.00
❏ KS-3286 [S]	Dancing Tonight	1963	3.75	7.50	15.00
❏ KS-3490 [S]	The Most Beautiful Girl in the World	1966	3.00	6.00	12.00
MCA					
❏ 258	Freddy Martin's Greatest Hits	197?	2.00	4.00	8.00
❏ 4021 [(2)]	54 Great Waltzes	197?	3.00	6.00	12.00
❏ 4080 [(2)]	The Best of Freddy Martin	197?	3.00	6.00	12.00
RCA VICTOR					
❏ LPM-1??? [M]	Freddy Martin at the Cocoanut Grove	1957	5.00	10.00	20.00
❏ LSP-4044 [R]	The Best of Freddy Martin	1969	2.50	5.00	10.00
❏ VPM-6072 [(2)]	This Is Freddy Martin	197?	3.75	7.50	15.00
SUNBEAM					
❏ 313	Music in the Martin Manner 1933-39	197?	2.50	5.00	10.00
MARTIN, JUAN					
Guitarist.					
NOVUS					
❏ 3005-1-N	Painter in Sound	1986	2.50	5.00	10.00
❏ 3036-1-N	Through the Moving Window	1988	2.50	5.00	10.00
MARTIN, RONEE					
Female singer.					
SOUNDWINGS					
❏ SW-2105	Sensation	1987	2.50	5.00	10.00
MARTIN, SPIDER					
Saxophone player.					
IMPROV					
❏ 7118	Absolutely	197?	3.00	6.00	12.00
MARTINO, PAT					
Guitarist.					
COBBLESTONE					
❏ 9015	The Visit	1972	5.00	10.00	20.00
FANTASY					
❏ OJC-195	El Hombre	198?	2.50	5.00	10.00
❏ OJC-223	Strings!	198?	2.50	5.00	10.00
❏ OJC-248	East!	198?	2.50	5.00	10.00
❏ OJC-355	Baiyina (The Clear Evidence)	198?	2.50	5.00	10.00
❏ OJC-397	Desperado	1989	3.00	6.00	12.00
MUSE					
❏ MR-5026	Live!	1974	3.00	6.00	12.00
❏ MR-5039	Consciousness	1975	3.00	6.00	12.00
❏ MR-5075	Exit	1976	3.00	6.00	12.00
❏ MR-5090	We'll Be Together Again	1977	3.00	6.00	12.00
❏ MR-5096	Footprints	1977	3.00	6.00	12.00
❏ MR-5328	The Return	198?	2.50	5.00	10.00
PRESTIGE					
❏ PRLP-7513 [M]	El Hombre	1967	6.25	12.50	25.00
❏ PRST-7513 [S]	El Hombre	1967	3.75	7.50	15.00
❏ PRLP-7547 [M]	Strings!	1967	6.25	12.50	25.00
❏ PRST-7547 [S]	Strings!	1967	3.75	7.50	15.00
❏ PRST-7562	East!	1968	3.75	7.50	15.00
❏ PRST-7589	Baiyina (The Clear Evidence)	1968	3.75	7.50	15.00
❏ PRST-7795	Desperado	1970	3.75	7.50	15.00
WARNER BROS.					
❏ BS 2921	Starbright	1976	2.50	5.00	10.00
❏ BS 2977	Joyous Lake	1977	2.50	5.00	10.00
MARX, BILL					
Pianist.					
VEE JAY					
❏ LP-3032 [M]	Jazz Kaleidoscope	1962	5.00	10.00	20.00
❏ SR-3032 [S]	Jazz Kaleidoscope	1962	6.25	12.50	25.00
❏ LP-3035 [M]	My Son, the Folk Swinger	1963	5.00	10.00	20.00
❏ SR-3035 [S]	My Son, the Folk Swinger	1963	6.25	12.50	25.00

Number	Title	Yr	VG	VG+	NM
MARX, DICK					
Pianist.					
OMEGA					
❏ OSL-2 [S]	Marx Makes Broadway	1959	7.50	15.00	30.00
-- The front cover of the above LP spells his last name "Marks," though it is spelled correctly on the label and back cover					
❏ OML-1002 [M]	Marx Makes Broadway	1958	10.00	20.00	40.00
MARX, DICK, AND JOHNNY FRIGO					
Also see each artist's individual listings.					
BRUNSWICK					
❏ BL 54006 [M]	Two Much Piano	1955	10.00	20.00	40.00
MARYLAND JAZZ BAND					
GHB					
❏ GHB-178	25 Years of Jazz with the Maryland Jazz Band	1987	2.50	5.00	10.00
MAS, JEAN-PIERRE, AND CESARIUS ALVIM					
Mas is a pianist; Alvim is a bass player.					
INNER CITY					
❏ IC-1014	Lourmel	197?	3.75	7.50	15.00
MASEKELA, HUGH					
Cornet player, flugel horn player, trumpeter, occasional percussionist and male singer, best known for his hit song "Grazing in the Grass." Also see HERB ALPERT.					
ABC IMPULSE!					
❏ IA-9343 [(2)]	African Connection	1978	3.00	6.00	12.00
BLUE THUMB					
❏ BT-62	Introducing Hedzoleh Sounds	1972	2.50	5.00	10.00
❏ BT-6003	Home Is Where the Music Is	1973	2.50	5.00	10.00
❏ BT-6015	I Am Not Afraid	1974	2.50	5.00	10.00
CASABLANCA					
❏ NBLP 7017	The Boy's Doin' It	1975	2.50	5.00	10.00
❏ NBLP 7023	Colonial Man	1976	2.50	5.00	10.00
❏ NBLP 7036	Melody Maker	1977	2.50	5.00	10.00
❏ NBLP 7079	You Told Your Mama	1978	2.50	5.00	10.00
CHISA					
❏ CS-803	Reconstruction	1970	3.00	6.00	12.00
❏ CS-808	Union of South Africa	1971	3.00	6.00	12.00
JIVE					
❏ JL-8210	Techno Bush	1984	2.50	5.00	10.00
❏ JL-8382	Waiting for the Rain	1985	2.50	5.00	10.00
MERCURY					
❏ MG-20797 [M]	The Trumpet of Hugh Masekela	1963	3.75	7.50	15.00
❏ SR-60797 [S]	The Trumpet of Hugh Masekela	1963	5.00	10.00	20.00
❏ SR-61109	Grr	1969	3.00	6.00	12.00
MGM					
❏ GAS-116	Hugh Masekela (Golden Archive Series)	1970	3.00	6.00	12.00
❏ E-4372 [M]	The Americanization of Ooga Booga	1966	3.00	6.00	12.00
❏ SE-4372 [S]	The Americanization of Ooga Booga	1966	3.75	7.50	15.00
❏ E-4415 [M]	Hugh Masekela's Next Album	1966	3.00	6.00	12.00
❏ SE-4415 [S]	Hugh Masekela's Next Album	1966	3.75	7.50	15.00
NOVUS					
❏ 3070-1-R	Uptownship	1990	3.00	6.00	12.00
UNI					
❏ 3010 [M]	Hugh Masekela's Latest	1967	3.75	7.50	15.00
❏ 3015 [M]	Hugh Masekela Is Alive and Well at the Whisky	1967	5.00	10.00	20.00
❏ 73010 [S]	Hugh Masekela's Latest	1967	3.00	6.00	12.00
❏ 73015 [S]	Hugh Masekela Is Alive and Well at the Whisky	1967	3.00	6.00	12.00
❏ 73028	The Promise of a Future	1968	3.00	6.00	12.00
❏ 73041	Masekela	1969	3.00	6.00	12.00
❏ 73051	Masekela -- Vol. 2	1970	3.00	6.00	12.00
VERVE					
❏ V6-8651 [(2)]	24 Karat Hits	1968	3.75	7.50	15.00
WARNER BROS.					
❏ 25566	Tomorrow	1987	2.50	5.00	10.00
MASLAK, KESHAVAN					
Saxophone player, clarinetist, occasional guitarist and drummer.					
BLACK SAINT					
❏ BSR-0079	Blaster Master	198?	3.00	6.00	12.00
MASON, CHRISTOPHER					
Alto saxophone player.					
OPTIMISM					
❏ OP-3218	Something Beautiful	198?	2.50	5.00	10.00

Number	Title	Yr	VG	VG+	NM

MASON, HARVEY
Drummer. Also see HEADHUNTERS.
ARISTA
❏ AL 4054	Marching in the Street	1975	3.00	6.00	12.00
❏ AL 4096	Earthmover	1976	3.00	6.00	12.00
❏ AL 4157	Funk in a Mason Jar	1978	3.00	6.00	12.00

MASON, JAMES
Guitarist.
CHIAROSCURO
❏ 189	Rhythm of Life	1978	3.00	6.00	12.00

MASSO, GEORGE
Trombonist, pianist and vibraphone player.
DREAMSTREET
❏ DR-108	Pieces of Eight	1986	2.50	5.00	10.00
FAMOUS DOOR
❏ 129	Choice N.Y.C.	197?	3.00	6.00	12.00
❏ 138	Swinging Case of Masso-ism	1981	3.00	6.00	12.00
❏ 148	No Frills, Just Music	198?	2.50	5.00	10.00

MASTER CYLINDER
Texas-based fusion band.
INNER CITY
❏ IC-1112	Elsewhere	198?	7.50	15.00	30.00

MASTERS, FRANKIE
Bandleader and male singer.
CIRCLE
❏ 62	Frankie Masters and His Orchestra 1945-46	198?	2.50	5.00	10.00

MASTERS, JOE
Pianist and composer.
COLUMBIA
❏ CL 2598	Jazz Mass	1967	6.25	12.50	25.00
❏ CS 9398	Jazz Mass	1967	5.00	10.00	20.00
DISCOVERY
❏ 785	Jazz Mass	197?	3.75	7.50	15.00

MASTERS, MARK
Composer and arranger.
SEA BREEZE
❏ SB-2022	Early Start	198?	3.00	6.00	12.00
❏ SB-2033	Silver Threads Among the Blues	1987	3.00	6.00	12.00

MASTERSOUNDS, THE
Members: Benny Barth (drums); Richie Crabtree (piano); BUDDY MONTGOMERY; MONK MONTGOMERY. Also see THE MONTGOMERY BROTHERS.
FANTASY
❏ OJC-280	Swinging with the Mastersounds	1987	2.50	5.00	10.00
❏ OJC-282	A Date with the Mastersounds	1987	2.50	5.00	10.00
❏ 3305 [M]	Swingin' with the Mastersounds	1960	10.00	20.00	40.00
-- Red vinyl					
❏ 3305 [M]	Swingin' with the Mastersounds	1962	6.25	12.50	25.00
-- Black vinyl					
❏ 3316 [M]	A Date with the Mastersounds	1961	10.00	20.00	40.00
-- Red vinyl					
❏ 3316 [M]	A Date with the Mastersounds	1962	6.25	12.50	25.00
-- Black vinyl					
❏ 3327 [M]	The Mastersounds on Tour	1961	10.00	20.00	40.00
-- Red vinyl					
❏ 3327 [M]	The Mastersounds on Tour	1962	6.25	12.50	25.00
-- Black vinyl					
❏ 8050 [S]	Swingin' with the Mastersounds	1961	7.50	15.00	30.00
-- Blue vinyl					
❏ 8050 [S]	Swingin' with the Mastersounds	1962	5.00	10.00	20.00
-- Black vinyl					
❏ 8062 [S]	A Date with the Mastersounds	1961	7.50	15.00	30.00
-- Blue vinyl					
❏ 8062 [S]	A Date with the Mastersounds	1962	5.00	10.00	20.00
-- Black vinyl					
❏ 8066 [S]	The Mastersounds on Tour	1961	7.50	15.00	30.00
-- Blue vinyl					
❏ 8066 [S]	The Mastersounds on Tour	1962	5.00	10.00	20.00
-- Black vinyl					
PACIFIC JAZZ
❏ PJM-403 [M]	Introducing the Mastersounds	1957	12.50	25.00	50.00
❏ PJM-405 [M]	The King and I	1958	12.50	25.00	50.00
WORLD PACIFIC
❏ ST-1010 [S]	Kismet	1958	7.50	15.00	30.00
❏ ST-1012 [S]	Flower Drum Song	1958	7.50	15.00	30.00
❏ ST-1017 [S]	The King and I	1959	7.50	15.00	30.00

Number	Title	Yr	VG	VG+	NM
❏ ST-1019 [S]	Ballads and Blues	1959	7.50	15.00	30.00
❏ ST-1026 [S]	The Mastersounds in Concert	1959	7.50	15.00	30.00
❏ ST-1030 [S]	Happy Holidays from Many Lands	1959	7.50	15.00	30.00
❏ WP-1243 [M]	Kismet	1958	10.00	20.00	40.00
❏ WP-1252 [M]	Flower Drum Song	1958	10.00	20.00	40.00
❏ WP-1260 [M]	Ballads and Blues	1959	10.00	20.00	40.00
❏ WP-1269 [M]	The Mastersounds in Concert	1959	10.00	20.00	40.00
❏ WP-1271 [M]	Jazz Showcase	1959	7.50	15.00	30.00
-- Reissue of Pacific Jazz 403					
❏ WP-1272 [M]	The King and I	1959	7.50	15.00	30.00
-- Reissue of Pacific Jazz 405					
❏ WP-1280 [M]	Happy Holidays from Many Lands	1959	10.00	20.00	40.00
❏ ST-1284 [S]	The Mastersounds Play Horace Silver	1960	7.50	15.00	30.00
❏ WP-1284 [M]	The Mastersounds Play Horace Silver	1960	10.00	20.00	40.00

MATERIAL
Group led by BILL LASWELL and Michael Beinhorn (synthesizers) with a flexible supporting cast.
ELEKTRA MUSICIAN
❏ 60042	Memory Serves	1982	2.50	5.00	10.00
❏ 60206	One Down	1984	2.50	5.00	10.00

MATHEWS, MAT
Accordion player. Also see EDDIE COSTA; THE FOUR MOST; THE NEW YORK JAZZ QUARTET.
AUDIOPHILE
❏ AP-219	Mat Mathews and Friends	1987	2.50	5.00	10.00
BRUNSWICK
❏ BL 54013 [M]	Bag's Groove	1956	12.50	25.00	50.00
DAWN
❏ DLP-1104 [M]	The Modern Art of Jazz	1956	20.00	40.00	80.00

MATHEWS, RONNIE
Pianist.
BEE HIVE
❏ 7008	Roots, Branches and Dances	197?	3.00	6.00	12.00
❏ 7011	Legacy	197?	3.00	6.00	12.00
PRESTIGE
❏ PRLP-7303 [M]	Doin' the Thang	1964	7.50	15.00	30.00
❏ PRST-7303 [S]	Doin' the Thang	1964	10.00	20.00	40.00
TIMELESS
❏ LPSJP-304	Selena's Dance	1990	3.00	6.00	12.00

MATHIS, JOHNNY
Male singer. Known for his pop and easy listening hits, he is backed by a jazz combo on this, his debut album. For the rest of his discography, see the *Standard Catalog of American Records 1950-1975*.
COLUMBIA
❏ CL 887 [M]	Johnny Mathis	1957	12.50	25.00	50.00
- Red and black label with six "eye" logos					

MATLOCK, MATTY
Clarinetist and arranger.
RCA VICTOR
❏ LPM-1413 [M]	Pete Kelly at Home	1957	10.00	20.00	40.00
WARNER BROS.
❏ W 1280 [M]	Four Button Dixie	1958	7.50	15.00	30.00
❏ WS 1280 [S]	Four Button Dixie	1958	10.00	20.00	40.00
"X"
❏ LXA-3035 [10]	Sports Parade	1955	12.50	25.00	50.00

MATRIX
Nonet co-founded by pianist-composer John Harmon in Appleton, Wisconsin. Among the other musicians were Mike Hale (trumpet).
PABLO TODAY
❏ 2312 121	Harvest	1980	3.00	6.00	12.00

MATTHEWS, DAVID
Pianist.
CTI
❏ 5005	Dune	1977	3.00	6.00	12.00
GNP CRESCENDO
❏ GNP-2153	Delta Lady	198?	2.50	5.00	10.00
❏ GNP-2157	Grand Cross	198?	2.50	5.00	10.00
❏ GNP-2162	Grand Connection	198?	2.50	5.00	10.00
❏ GNP-2169	Super Funky Sax	198?	2.50	5.00	10.00
❏ GNP-2174	Ice Fuse One	198?	2.50	5.00	10.00
❏ GNP-2185	Speed Demon	1986	2.50	5.00	10.00

Number	Title	Yr	VG	VG+	NM
KUDU					
❑ 30	Shoogie Wanna Boogie	1976	3.75	7.50	15.00
MUSE					
❑ MR-5073	David Matthews' Big Band at the 5 Spot	1976	2.50	5.00	10.00
❑ MR-5096	Flight	1977	2.50	5.00	10.00
MATTHEWS, ONZY					
Bandleader, composer and arranger.					
CAPITOL					
❑ ST 2099 [S]	Blues with a Touch of Elegance	1964	5.00	10.00	20.00
❑ T 2099 [M]	Blues with a Touch of Elegance	1964	3.75	7.50	15.00
MATTHEWS, WALT					
FRETLESS					
❑ 158	The Dance in Your Eye	198?	3.00	6.00	12.00
MATTSON, PHIL					
Male singer.					
DOCTOR JAZZ					
❑ FW 40349	Setting Standards	1986	2.50	5.00	10.00
MATZ, PETER					
Composer, arranger and bandleader.					
PROJECT 3					
❑ PR 5007 SD	Peter Matz Brings 'Em Back	1967	3.75	7.50	15.00
MAULAWI					
STRATA-EAST					
❑ SES 104-74	Maulawi	1974	5.00	10.00	20.00
MAUPIN, BENNIE					
Tenor and soprano saxophone player and bass clarinetist.					
ECM					
❑ 1043	The Jewel in the Lotus	197?	3.75	7.50	15.00
MERCURY					
❑ SRM-1-1148	Slow Traffic	1976	2.50	5.00	10.00
❑ SRM-1-3717	Moonscapes	1978	2.50	5.00	10.00
MAURO, TURK					
Tenor saxophone player.					
STORYVILLE					
❑ 4076	The Underdog	198?	2.50	5.00	10.00
MAXTED, BILLY					
Pianist and composer.					
BRUNSWICK					
❑ BL 58052 [10]	Honky Tonk Piano	1953	15.00	30.00	60.00
CADENCE					
❑ CLP-1005 [M]	Billy Maxted Plays Hi-Fi Keyboard	1955	10.00	20.00	40.00
❑ CLP-1012 [M]	Jazz at Nick's	1955	10.00	20.00	40.00
❑ CLP-1013 [M]	Dixieland Manhattan Style	1955	10.00	20.00	40.00
❑ CLP-3013 [M]	Dixieland Manhattan Style	1958	7.50	15.00	30.00
LIBERTY					
❑ LRP-3474 [M]	Maxted Makes It	1966	3.00	6.00	12.00
❑ LRP-3492 [M]	Satin Doll	1967	3.75	7.50	15.00
❑ LST-7474 [S]	Maxted Makes It	1966	3.75	7.50	15.00
❑ LST-7492 [S]	Satin Doll	1967	3.00	6.00	12.00
SEECO					
❑ CELP-438 [M]	Bourbon St. Billy and the Blues	1960	5.00	10.00	20.00
❑ CELP-458 [M]	Art of Jazz	1960	5.00	10.00	20.00
❑ CELP-4380 [S]	Bourbon St. Billy and the Blues	1960	6.25	12.50	25.00
❑ CELP-4580 [S]	Art of Jazz	1960	6.25	12.50	25.00
MAXWELL, JIMMIE					
Trumpeter and fluegel horn player.					
CIRCLE					
❑ 50	Let's Fall in Love	198?	2.50	5.00	10.00
MAYERL, BILLY					
Pianist, bandleader and composer.					
FLAPPER					
❑ 704/5 [(2)]	The Versatility of Billy Mayerl	198?	3.75	7.50	15.00
MAYL, GENE					
Bass player and bandleader.					
BLACKBIRD					
❑ 12006	A Trip to Waukesha	1969	3.75	7.50	15.00

Number	Title	Yr	VG	VG+	NM
JAZZOLOGY					
❑ J-6 [M]	Gene Mayl's Dixieland Rhythm Kings	1964	3.75	7.50	15.00
MAYS, BILL					
Pianist and composer.					
TREND					
❑ TR-532	Tha's Delights	1984	3.00	6.00	12.00
MAYS, LYLE					
Pianist.					
GEFFEN					
❑ GHS 24097	Lyle Mays	1986	2.50	5.00	10.00
❑ GHS 24204	Street Dreams	1988	2.50	5.00	10.00
McBEE, CECIL					
Bass player.					
ENJA					
❑ 3041	Compassion	198?	3.00	6.00	12.00
INDIA NAVIGATION					
❑ IN-1043	Alternate Spaces	197?	3.75	7.50	15.00
❑ IN-1053	Flying Out	198?	3.75	7.50	15.00
INNER CITY					
❑ IC-3023	Music from the Source	197?	3.75	7.50	15.00
STRATA-EAST					
❑ SES-7417	Mutima	1975	6.25	12.50	25.00
McBROWNE, LENNY					
Drummer.					
PACIFIC JAZZ					
❑ PJ-1 [M]	The Four Souls	1960	7.50	15.00	30.00
❑ ST-1 [S]	The Four Souls	1960	10.00	20.00	40.00
RIVERSIDE					
❑ RLP-346 [M]	Eastern Lights	1960	7.50	15.00	30.00
❑ RS-9346 [S]	Eastern Lights	1960	10.00	20.00	40.00
McCALL, MARY ANN					
Female singer. Also see CHARLIE VENTURA.					
CORAL					
❑ CRL 57276 [M]	Melancholy Baby	1959	10.00	20.00	40.00
❑ CRL 757276 [S]	Melancholy Baby	1959	12.50	25.00	50.00
DISCOVERY					
❑ 3011 [10]	Mary Ann McCall Sings	1950	50.00	100.00	200.00
JUBILEE					
❑ JLP-1078 [M]	Detour to the Moon	1958	12.50	25.00	50.00
REGENT					
❑ MG-6040 [M]	Easy Living	1957	10.00	20.00	40.00
SAVOY JAZZ					
❑ SJL-1178	Easy Living	198?	2.50	5.00	10.00
McCANN, HOOPS					
Not a real person, but a character from the Steely Dan song "Glamour Profession." All the band members had played on Steely Dan records.					
MCA					
❑ 42202	The Hoops McCann Band Plays the Music of Steely Dan	1988	2.50	5.00	10.00
McCANN, LES					
Pianist, male singer and composer. Also see CLIFFORD SCOTT.					
A&M					
❑ SP-4718	The Man	1978	2.50	5.00	10.00
❑ SP-4780	Tall, Dark and Handsome	1979	2.50	5.00	10.00
ABC IMPULSE!					
❑ AS-9329	The Music Lets Me Be	1977	2.50	5.00	10.00
❑ AS-9333	Live at the Roxy	1978	2.50	5.00	10.00
ATLANTIC					
❑ SD 2-312 [(2)]	Live at Montreux	1974	3.75	7.50	15.00
❑ SD 1516	Much Les	1969	3.75	7.50	15.00
❑ SD 1547	Comment	1970	3.75	7.50	15.00
❑ SD 1603	Invitation to Openness	1972	3.00	6.00	12.00
❑ SD 1619	Talk to the People	1972	3.00	6.00	12.00
❑ SD 1646	Layers	1973	3.00	6.00	12.00
❑ SD 1666	Another Beginning	1974	3.00	6.00	12.00
❑ SD 1679	Hustle to Survive	1975	3.00	6.00	12.00
❑ SD 1690	River High, River Low	1976	3.00	6.00	12.00
JAM					
❑ 012	The Longer You Wait	1984	2.50	5.00	10.00
LIMELIGHT					
❑ LM-82016 [M]	But Not Really	1965	3.75	7.50	15.00

Number	Title	Yr	VG	VG+	NM
❑ LM-82025 [M]	Poo Boo	1965	3.75	7.50	15.00
❑ LM-82031 [M]	Beaux J. Pooboo	1966	3.75	7.50	15.00
❑ LM-82036 [M]	Live at Shelly's Manne-Hole	1966	3.75	7.50	15.00
❑ LM-82041 [M]	Les McCann Plays the Hits	1966	3.75	7.50	15.00
❑ LM-82043 [M]	Bucket O' Grease	1967	5.00	10.00	20.00
❑ LM-82046 [M]	Live at the Bohemian Caverns, Washington, D.C.	1967	5.00	10.00	20.00
❑ LS-86016 [S]	But Not Really	1965	5.00	10.00	20.00
❑ LS-86025 [S]	Poo Boo	1965	5.00	10.00	20.00
❑ LS-86031 [S]	Beaux J. Pooboo	1966	5.00	10.00	20.00
❑ LS-86036 [S]	Live at Shelly's Manne-Hole	1966	5.00	10.00	20.00
❑ LS-86041 [S]	Les McCann Plays the Hits	1966	5.00	10.00	20.00
❑ LS-86043 [S]	Bucket O' Grease	1967	3.75	7.50	15.00
❑ LS-86046 [S]	Live at the Bohemian Caverns, Washington, D.C.	1967	3.75	7.50	15.00

PACIFIC JAZZ

Number	Title	Yr	VG	VG+	NM
❑ PJ-2 [M]	The Truth	1960	6.25	12.50	25.00
❑ ST-2 [S]	The Truth	1960	7.50	15.00	30.00
❑ PJ-7 [M]	The Shout	1960	6.25	12.50	25.00
❑ ST-7 [S]	The Shout	1960	7.50	15.00	30.00
❑ PJ-16 [M]	Les McCann in San Francisco	1961	6.25	12.50	25.00
❑ ST-16 [S]	Les McCann in San Francisco	1961	7.50	15.00	30.00
❑ PJ-25 [M]	Pretty Lady	1961	5.00	10.00	20.00
❑ ST-25 [S]	Pretty Lady	1961	6.25	12.50	25.00
❑ PJ-31 [M]	Les McCann Sings	1961	5.00	10.00	20.00
❑ ST-31 [S]	Les McCann Sings	1961	6.25	12.50	25.00
❑ PJ-45 [M]	Les McCann in New York	1962	5.00	10.00	20.00
❑ ST-45 [S]	Les McCann in New York	1962	6.25	12.50	25.00
❑ PJ-56 [M]	On Time	1962	10.00	20.00	40.00
-- Yellow vinyl					
❑ PJ-56 [M]	On Time	1962	5.00	10.00	20.00
-- Black vinyl					
❑ ST-56 [S]	On Time	1962	12.50	25.00	50.00
-- Yellow vinyl					
❑ ST-56 [S]	On Time	1962	6.25	12.50	25.00
-- Black vinyl					
❑ PJ-63 [M]	Shampoo	1962	3.75	7.50	15.00
❑ ST-63 [S]	Shampoo	1962	5.00	10.00	20.00
❑ PJ-69 [M]	The Gospel Truth	1963	3.75	7.50	15.00
❑ ST-69 [S]	The Gospel Truth	1963	5.00	10.00	20.00
❑ PJ-78 [M]	Soul Hits	1963	3.75	7.50	15.00
❑ ST-78 [S]	Soul Hits	1963	5.00	10.00	20.00
❑ PJ-81 [M]	Jazz Waltz	1964	3.75	7.50	15.00
❑ ST-81 [S]	Jazz Waltz	1964	5.00	10.00	20.00
❑ PJ-84 [M]	McCanna	1964	3.75	7.50	15.00
❑ ST-84 [S]	McCanna	1964	5.00	10.00	20.00
❑ PJ-91 [M]	McCann/Wilson	1965	3.75	7.50	15.00
-- With Gerald Wilson					
❑ ST-91 [S]	McCann/Wilson	1965	5.00	10.00	20.00
-- With Gerald Wilson					
❑ LN-10077	Les McCann In San Francisco	1980	2.00	4.00	8.00
-- Budget-line reissue					
❑ LN-10078	Les McCann In New York	1980	2.00	4.00	8.00
-- Budget-line reissue					
❑ LN-10079	Soul Hits	1980	2.00	4.00	8.00
-- Budget-line reissue					
❑ LN-10083	The Shout	1980	2.00	4.00	8.00
-- Budget-line reissue					
❑ PJ-10097 [M]	Spanish Onions	1966	3.75	7.50	15.00
❑ PJ-10107 [M]	A Bag of Gold	1966	3.75	7.50	15.00
❑ ST-20097 [S]	Spanish Onions	1966	5.00	10.00	20.00
❑ ST-20107 [S]	A Bag of Gold	1966	5.00	10.00	20.00

STONE

Number	Title	Yr	VG	VG+	NM
❑ 1906	Butterfly	1988	2.50	5.00	10.00

SUNSET

Number	Title	Yr	VG	VG+	NM
❑ SUS-5214	Django	1969	2.50	5.00	10.00
❑ SUS-5296	Unlimited	1970	2.50	5.00	10.00

WORLD PACIFIC

Number	Title	Yr	VG	VG+	NM
❑ ST-20166	More Or Les McCann	1969	3.75	7.50	15.00
❑ ST-20173	New from the Big City	1970	3.75	7.50	15.00

McCANN, LES, AND EDDIE HARRIS

Also see each artist's individual listings.

ATLANTIC

Number	Title	Yr	VG	VG+	NM
❑ SD 1537	Swiss Movement	1969	3.75	7.50	15.00
❑ SD 1583	Second Movement	1971	3.75	7.50	15.00

McCLURE, RON

Bass player, composer and arranger.

ODE/NEW ZEALAND

Number	Title	Yr	VG	VG+	NM
❑ SODE-160	Home Base	1985	3.00	6.00	12.00

McCONNELL, ROB

Trombonist (both slide and valve) and composer.

PAUSA

Number	Title		Yr	VG	VG+	NM
❑ 7031	The Rob McConnell and Boss Brass Jazz Album		1979	2.50	5.00	10.00
❑ 7067	Present Perfect		1980	2.50	5.00	10.00
❑ 7106	Trubute		198?	2.50	5.00	10.00
❑ 7140	Big Band Jazz Vol. 1		198?	2.50	5.00	10.00
❑ 7141	Big Band Jazz Vol. 2		198?	2.50	5.00	10.00
❑ 7148	Again, Vol. 1		1983	2.50	5.00	10.00

McCORKLE, SUSANNAH

Female singer.

CONCORD JAZZ

Number	Title	Yr	VG	VG+	NM
❑ CJ-370	No More Blues	1989	3.00	6.00	12.00

INNER CITY

Number	Title	Yr	VG	VG+	NM
❑ IC-1101	Songs of Johnny Mercer	198?	3.00	6.00	12.00
❑ IC-1131	Songs of Yip Harburg	198?	3.00	6.00	12.00
❑ IC-1141	Music of Harry Warren	198?	3.00	6.00	12.00
❑ IC-1151	People You Never Get to Love	1984	3.00	6.00	12.00

PAUSA

Number	Title	Yr	VG	VG+	NM
❑ 7175	Thanks for the Memory	1985	2.50	5.00	10.00
❑ 7195	How Do You Keep the Music Playing?	1986	2.50	5.00	10.00

McCOY, CLYDE

Trumpeter and bandleader.

CAPITOL

Number	Title	Yr	VG	VG+	NM
❑ DT 311 [R]	Sugar Blues	196?	3.00	6.00	12.00
❑ H 311 [10]	Sugar Blues	195?	25.00	50.00	100.00
❑ T 311 [M]	Sugar Blues	1955	12.50	25.00	50.00
-- Turquoise or gray label					
❑ T 311 [M]	Sugar Blues	1959	10.00	20.00	40.00
-- Black colorband label, logo at left					
❑ T 311 [M]	Sugar Blues	1963	6.25	12.50	25.00
-- Black colorband label, logo at top					

CIRCLE

Number	Title	Yr	VG	VG+	NM
❑ CLP-82	Sugar Blues, 1951	198?	2.50	5.00	10.00

DESIGN

Number	Title	Yr	VG	VG+	NM
❑ DLP-28 [M]	The Golden Era of the Sugar Blues	196?	3.00	6.00	12.00

HINDSIGHT

Number	Title	Yr	VG	VG+	NM
❑ HSR-180	Clyde McCoy and His Orchestra 1936	198?	2.50	5.00	10.00

MERCURY

Number	Title	Yr	VG	VG+	NM
❑ MG-20110 [M]	The Blues	195?	10.00	20.00	40.00
❑ MG-20677 [M]	Really McCoy	1961	3.75	7.50	15.00
❑ MG-20730 [M]	Blue Prelude	1962	3.75	7.50	15.00
❑ SR-60677 [S]	Really McCoy	1961	5.00	10.00	20.00
❑ SR-60730 [S]	Blue Prelude	1962	5.00	10.00	20.00

TOP RANK

Number	Title	Yr	VG	VG+	NM
❑ RM-350 [M]	Dixieland's Best Friend	1961	7.50	15.00	30.00
❑ RS-650 [S]	Dixieland's Best Friend	1961	10.00	20.00	40.00

WING

Number	Title	Yr	VG	VG+	NM
❑ MGW-12260 [M]	Dancing to the Blues	196?	3.00	6.00	12.00
❑ SRW-16260 [S]	Dancing to the Blues	196?	3.00	6.00	12.00

McCOY, FREDDIE

Vibraphone player.

COBBLESTONE

Number	Title	Yr	VG	VG+	NM
❑ 9004	Gimme Some	1972	5.00	10.00	20.00

PRESTIGE

Number	Title	Yr	VG	VG+	NM
❑ PRLP-7395 [M]	Lonely Avenue	1965	5.00	10.00	20.00
❑ PRST-7395 [S]	Lonely Avenue	1965	6.25	12.50	25.00
❑ PRLP-7444 [M]	Spider Man	1966	5.00	10.00	20.00
❑ PRST-7444 [S]	Spider Man	1966	6.25	12.50	25.00
❑ PRLP-7470 [M]	Funk Drops	1967	6.25	12.50	25.00
❑ PRST-7470 [S]	Funk Drops	1967	6.25	12.50	25.00
❑ PRLP-7487 [M]	Peas 'N' Rice	1967	7.50	15.00	30.00
❑ PRST-7487 [S]	Peas 'N' Rice	1967	6.25	12.50	25.00
❑ PRST-7542	Beans and Greens	1968	6.25	12.50	25.00
❑ PRST-7561	Soul Yogi	1968	6.25	12.50	25.00
❑ PRST-7582	Listen Here	1968	6.25	12.50	25.00
❑ PRST-7706	The Best of Freddie McCoy	1969	5.00	10.00	20.00

McCROBY, RON

Jazz whistler.

CONCORD JAZZ

Number	Title	Yr	VG	VG+	NM
❑ CJ-208	Ron McCroby Plays Puccolo	1982	2.50	5.00	10.00
❑ CJ-257	The Other Whistler	1984	2.50	5.00	10.00

PRO ARTE

Number	Title	Yr	VG	VG+	NM
❑ PAD-258	Breezin' the Classics	1985	2.50	5.00	10.00

Number	Title	Yr	VG	VG+	NM

McDERMOT, TOM
STOMP OFF

Number	Title	Yr	VG	VG+	NM
❏ SOS-1024	New Rags	198?	2.50	5.00	10.00

McDONOUGH, DICK, AND CARL KRESS
McDonough was one of the first jazz guitarists. Also see CARL KRESS.
JAZZ ARCHIVES

❏ JA-32	The Guitar Genius of Dick McDonough and Carl Kress	198?	2.50	5.00	10.00

McDUFF, JACK
Organist and composer; also known as "Brother Jack McDuff." Also see JOE DUKES.
ATLANTIC

❏ 1463 [M]	A Change Is Gonna Come	1966	3.75	7.50	15.00
❏ SD 1463 [S]	A Change Is Gonna Come	1966	5.00	10.00	20.00
❏ 1472 [M]	Tobacco Road	1967	5.00	10.00	20.00
❏ SD 1472 [S]	Tobacco Road	1967	3.75	7.50	15.00
❏ SD 1498	Double Barreled Soul	1968	3.75	7.50	15.00

BLUE NOTE

❏ BST-84322	Down Home Style	1969	3.75	7.50	15.00
❏ BST-84334	Moon Rappin'	1970	3.75	7.50	15.00
❏ BST-84348	To Seek a New Home	1970	3.75	7.50	15.00
❏ BST-84358	Who Knows	1971	3.75	7.50	15.00

CADET

❏ LPS-812	Natural Thing	1968	3.75	7.50	15.00
❏ LPS-817	Getting Our Thing Together	1969	3.75	7.50	15.00
❏ LPS-831	Gin and Orange	1970	3.75	7.50	15.00
❏ CH-50024	Check This Out	1973	3.00	6.00	12.00
❏ CH-50051	Fourth Dimension	1974	3.00	6.00	12.00
❏ CH-60017	The Healin' System	1972	3.00	6.00	12.00
❏ CH-60031	Magnetic Feel	1975	3.00	6.00	12.00

CHESS

❏ 19004	Sophisticated Funk	1976	3.00	6.00	12.00

FANTASY

❏ OJC-222	The Honeydripper	198?	2.50	5.00	10.00

-- Reissue of Prestige 7199

❏ OJC-324	Tough 'Duff	1988	2.50	5.00	10.00

-- Reissue of Prestige 7185

❏ OJC-326	Brother Jack Meets the Boss	1988	2.50	5.00	10.00

-- Reissue of Prestige 7228

MUSE

❏ MR-5361	The Re-Entry	1989	3.00	6.00	12.00

PRESTIGE

❏ PRLP-7174 [M]	Brother Jack	1960	12.50	25.00	50.00
❏ PRLP-7185 [M]	Tough 'Duff	1960	12.50	25.00	50.00
❏ PRLP-7199 [M]	The Honeydripper	1961	12.50	25.00	50.00
❏ PRLP-7220 [M]	Goodnight, It's Time to Go	1961	10.00	20.00	40.00
❏ PRST-7220 [M]	Goodnight, It's Time to Go	1961	10.00	20.00	40.00
❏ PRLP-7228 [M]	Mellow Gravy -- Brother Jack Meets the Boss	1962	10.00	20.00	40.00
❏ PRST-7228 [S]	Mellow Gravy -- Brother Jack Meets the Boss	1962	10.00	20.00	40.00
❏ PRLP-7259 [M]	Screamin'	1963	10.00	20.00	40.00
❏ PRST-7259 [S]	Screamin'	1963	10.00	20.00	40.00
❏ PRLP-7265 [M]	Somethin' Slick!	1963	10.00	20.00	40.00
❏ PRST-7265 [S]	Somethin' Slick!	1963	10.00	20.00	40.00
❏ PRLP-7274 [M]	Live!	1963	10.00	20.00	40.00
❏ PRST-7274 [S]	Live!	1963	10.00	20.00	40.00
❏ PRLP-7286 [M]	Live! At the Jazz Workshop	1964	10.00	20.00	40.00
❏ PRST-7286 [S]	Live! At the Jazz Workshop	1964	10.00	20.00	40.00
❏ PRLP-7323 [M]	The Dynamic Jack McDuff	1964	10.00	20.00	40.00
❏ PRST-7323 [S]	The Dynamic Jack McDuff	1964	10.00	20.00	40.00
❏ PRLP-7333 [M]	Prelude	1964	6.25	12.50	25.00
❏ PRST-7333 [S]	Prelude	1964	7.50	15.00	30.00
❏ PRLP-7362 [M]	The Concert McDuff Recorded Live!	1965	6.25	12.50	25.00
❏ PRST-7362 [S]	The Concert McDuff Recorded Live!	1965	7.50	15.00	30.00
❏ PRLP-7404 [M]	Silk and Soul	1965	6.25	12.50	25.00
❏ PRST-7404 [S]	Silk and Soul	1965	7.50	15.00	30.00
❏ PRLP-7422 [M]	Hot Barbeque	1966	5.00	10.00	20.00
❏ PRST-7422 [S]	Hot Barbeque	1966	6.25	12.50	25.00
❏ PRLP-7476 [M]	Walk On By	1967	6.25	12.50	25.00
❏ PRST-7476 [S]	Walk On By	1967	5.00	10.00	20.00
❏ PRLP-7481 [M]	Brother Jack McDuff's Greatest Hits	1967	6.25	12.50	25.00
❏ PRST-7481 [S]	Brother Jack McDuff's Greatest Hits	1967	5.00	10.00	20.00
❏ PRLP-7492 [M]	Hallelujah Time!	1967	6.25	12.50	25.00
❏ PRST-7492 [S]	Hallelujah Time!	1967	5.00	10.00	20.00
❏ PRST-7529	The Midnight Sun	1968	5.00	10.00	20.00
❏ PRST-7567	Soul Circle	1968	5.00	10.00	20.00
❏ PRST-7596	Jack McDuff Plays for Beautiful People	1969	5.00	10.00	20.00
❏ PRST-7642	I Got a Woman	1969	5.00	10.00	20.00
❏ PRST-7666	Steppin' Out	1969	5.00	10.00	20.00
❏ PRST-7703	Live! The Best of Brother Jack McDuff	1969	5.00	10.00	20.00
❏ PRST-7771	Best of the Big Soul Band	1970	3.75	7.50	15.00
❏ PRST-7785	Brother Jack	1970	3.75	7.50	15.00
❏ PRST-7814	Tough Duff	1971	3.75	7.50	15.00
❏ PRST-7851	On With It	1973	3.00	6.00	12.00
❏ 24013 [(2)]	Rock Candy	1972	3.75	7.50	15.00

McFARLAND, GARY
Vibraphone player, percussionist, composer, bandleader and arranger. Also see ORCHESTRA USA.
ABC IMPULSE!

❏ AS-46 [S]	Points of Departure	1968	3.00	6.00	12.00
❏ AS-9104 [S]	Tijuana Jazz	1968	3.00	6.00	12.00
❏ AS-9112 [S]	Profiles	1968	3.00	6.00	12.00
❏ AS-9122 [S]	Simpatico	1968	3.00	6.00	12.00

BUDDAH

❏ BDS 95001	Butterscotch Rum	1967	3.75	7.50	15.00

COBBLESTONE

❏ CST 9019	Requiem	1972	3.75	7.50	15.00

IMPULSE!

❏ A-46 [M]	Points of Departure	1963	5.00	10.00	20.00
❏ AS-46 [S]	Points of Departure	1963	6.25	12.50	25.00
❏ A-9104 [M]	Tijuana Jazz	1966	5.00	10.00	20.00
❏ AS-9104 [S]	Tijuana Jazz	1966	6.25	12.50	25.00
❏ A-9112 [M]	Profiles	1966	5.00	10.00	20.00
❏ AS-9112 [S]	Profiles	1966	6.25	12.50	25.00
❏ A-9122 [M]	Simpatico	1966	5.00	10.00	20.00
❏ AS-9122 [S]	Simpatico	1966	6.25	12.50	25.00

SKYE

❏ SK-2	Does the Sun Really Shine	1968	3.75	7.50	15.00
❏ SK-8	America the Beautiful	1969	3.75	7.50	15.00
❏ SK-11	Slaves	1970	3.75	7.50	15.00
❏ SK-14	Today	1970	3.75	7.50	15.00

VERVE

❏ V-8443 [M]	How to Succeed in Business Without Really Trying	1962	3.75	7.50	15.00
❏ V6-8443 [S]	How to Succeed in Business Without Really Trying	1962	5.00	10.00	20.00
❏ V-8518 [M]	The Gary McFarland Orchestra with Special Guest Soloist Bill Evans	1963	3.75	7.50	15.00
❏ V6-8518 [S]	The Gary McFarland Orchestra with Special Guest Soloist Bill Evans	1963	5.00	10.00	20.00
❏ V-8603 [M]	Soft Samba	1964	3.75	7.50	15.00
❏ V6-8603 [S]	Soft Samba	1964	5.00	10.00	20.00
❏ V-8632 [M]	The "In" Sound	1965	3.75	7.50	15.00
❏ V6-8632 [S]	The "In" Sound	1965	5.00	10.00	20.00
❏ V/V6-8674	Gary McFarland	1965	---	---	---

-- Canceled

❏ V-8682 [M]	Soft Samba Strings	1966	3.75	7.50	15.00
❏ V6-8682 [S]	Soft Samba Strings	1966	5.00	10.00	20.00
❏ V-8738 [M]	Scorpio and Other Signs	1967	5.00	10.00	20.00
❏ V6-8738 [S]	Scorpio and Other Signs	1967	3.75	7.50	15.00
❏ V6-8786	Sympathetic Vibrations	1969	3.75	7.50	15.00

McFERRIN, BOBBY
Male singer. Best known for the 1988 hit "Don't Worry Be Happy."
BLUE NOTE

❏ BT-85110	Spontaneous Inventions	1986	3.00	6.00	12.00

ELEKTRA/MUSICIAN

❏ 60023	Bobby McFerrin	1982	2.50	5.00	10.00
❏ 60366	The Voice	1985	2.50	5.00	10.00

EMI MANHATTAN

❏ E1-48059	Simple Pleasures	1988	2.00	4.00	8.00

McGARITY, LOU
Trombonist and male singer.
ARGO

❏ LP-654 [M]	Blue Lou	1960	7.50	15.00	30.00
❏ LPS-654 [S]	Blue Lou	1960	10.00	20.00	40.00

JUBILEE

❏ JGM-1108 [M]	Some Like It Hot	1959	12.50	25.00	50.00

McGHEE, HOWARD
Trumpeter and composer. Also see DEXTER GORDON; COLEMAN HAWKINS.
ARGO

❏ LP-4020 [M]	House Warmin'	1963	6.25	12.50	25.00
❏ LPS-4020 [S]	House Warmin'	1963	7.50	15.00	30.00

BETHLEHEM

❏ BCP-42 [M]	The Return of Howard McGhee	1956	20.00	40.00	80.00

Number	Title	Yr	VG	VG+	NM
❑ BCP-61 [M]	Life Is Just a Bowl of Cherries	1957	20.00	40.00	80.00
❑ BCP-6039	That Bop Thing	197?	3.00	6.00	12.00
-- Reissue of 42, distributed by RCA Victor					
❑ BCP-6055 [M]	Dusty Blue	1961	12.50	25.00	50.00
❑ BCPS-6055 [S]	Dusty Blue	1961	15.00	30.00	60.00
BLACK LION					
❑ 305	Shades of Blue	197?	3.00	6.00	12.00
BLUE NOTE					
❑ BLP-5012 [10]	Howard McGhee's All Stars/ Howard McGhee-Fats Navarro Sextet	1952	75.00	150.00	300.00
❑ BLP-5024 [10]	Howard McGhee, Volume 2	1953	75.00	150.00	300.00
CADET					
❑ LP-4020 [M]	House Warmin'	1966	3.00	6.00	12.00
❑ LPS-4020 [S]	House Warmin'	1966	3.75	7.50	15.00
CONTEMPORARY					
❑ M-3596 [M]	Maggie's Back in Town	1961	10.00	20.00	40.00
❑ S-7596 [S]	Maggie's Back in Town	1961	12.50	25.00	50.00
DIAL					
❑ LP-217 [10]	Night Music	1951	75.00	150.00	300.00
HI-LO					
❑ HL-6001 [10]	Jazz Goes to the Battlefront, Vol. 1	1952	62.50	125.00	250.00
❑ HL-6002 [10]	Jazz Goes to the Battlefront, Vol. 2	1952	62.50	125.00	250.00
SAVOY					
❑ MG-12026 [M]	Howard McGhee and Milt Jackson	1955	20.00	40.00	80.00
SAVOY JAZZ					
❑ SJL-2219 [(2)]	Maggie	197?	3.75	7.50	15.00
STEEPLECHASE					
❑ SCS-1024	Just Be There	198?	3.00	6.00	12.00
STORYVILLE					
❑ 4077	Jazzbrothers	198?	3.00	6.00	12.00
❑ 4080	Young at Heart	198?	3.00	6.00	12.00
UNITED ARTISTS					
❑ UAJ-14028 [M]	Nobody Knows You When You're Down and Out	1963	7.50	15.00	30.00
❑ UAJS-15028 [S]	Nobody Knows You When You're Down and Out	1963	10.00	20.00	40.00
ZIM					
❑ 2004	Cookin' Time	197?	3.00	6.00	12.00
❑ 2006	Live at Emerson's	197?	3.00	6.00	12.00

McGLOHON, LOONIS
Pianist and composer.
AUDIOPHILE

❑ AP-166	Loonis in London	1982	2.50	5.00	10.00

McGOVERN, PATTY, AND THOMAS TALBERT
McGovern is a female singer. Also see THOMAS TALBERT.
ATLANTIC

❑ 1245 [M]	Wednesday's Child	1956	12.50	25.00	50.00
-- Black label					
❑ 1245 [M]	Wednesday's Child	1961	6.25	12.50	25.00
-- Multicolor label, white "fan" logo at right					

McGREGOR, CHRIS, BROTHERHOOD OF BREATH
McGregor is a pianist, composer and bandleader.
VENTURE

❑ 90988	Country Cooking	1988	2.50	5.00	10.00

McGRIFF, JIMMY
Organist.
BLUE NOTE

❑ BST-84350	Electric Funk	1970	3.75	7.50	15.00
❑ BST-84364	Something to Listen To	1971	3.75	7.50	15.00
❑ BST-84374	Black Pearl	1971	3.75	7.50	15.00
CAPITOL					
❑ ST-569	Dudes Doin' Business	1970	3.75	7.50	15.00
❑ ST-616	Soul Sugar	1970	3.75	7.50	15.00
COLLECTABLES					
❑ COL-5147	Blues for Mr. Jimmy	198?	2.50	5.00	10.00
GROOVE MERCHANT					
❑ 503	Groove Grease	1972	3.75	7.50	15.00
❑ 506	Let's Stay Together	1972	3.75	7.50	15.00
❑ 509	Fly Dude	1973	3.75	7.50	15.00
❑ 520	Come Together	1973	3.00	6.00	12.00
❑ 529	If You're Ready Come Go with Me	1974	3.00	6.00	12.00
❑ 534	Main Squeeze	1975	3.00	6.00	12.00
❑ 2203	Black and Blues	1971	3.75	7.50	15.00

Number	Title	Yr	VG	VG+	NM
❑ 2205	Good Things Don't Happen Every Day	1971	3.75	7.50	15.00
❑ 3300 [(2)]	Giants of the Organ In Concert	1974	3.75	7.50	15.00
❑ 3309	Stump Juice	1976	3.00	6.00	12.00
❑ 3311	Mean Machine	1976	3.00	6.00	12.00
❑ 4403 [(2)]	Flyin' Time	197?	3.75	7.50	15.00
JAM					
❑ 002	City Lights	1982	3.00	6.00	12.00
❑ 005	Movin' Upside the Blues	1983	3.00	6.00	12.00
LRC					
❑ 9316	Tailgunner	1977	3.75	7.50	15.00
❑ 9320	Outside Looking In	1978	3.75	7.50	15.00
MILESTONE					
❑ M-9116	Countdown	1984	2.50	5.00	10.00
❑ M-9126	Skywalk	1985	2.50	5.00	10.00
❑ M-9135	State of the Art	1986	2.50	5.00	10.00
❑ M-9148	The Starting Five	1987	2.50	5.00	10.00
❑ M-9163	Blue to the 'Bone	1988	2.50	5.00	10.00
QUINTESSENCE					
❑ 25061	Soul	1978	3.00	6.00	12.00
SOLID STATE					
❑ SM-17001 [M]	The Big Band of Jimmy McGriff	1966	3.75	7.50	15.00
❑ SM-17002 [M]	A Bag Full of Soul	1966	3.75	7.50	15.00
❑ SM-17006 [M]	Cherry	1967	5.00	10.00	20.00
❑ SS-18001 [S]	The Big Band of Jimmy McGriff	1966	5.00	10.00	20.00
❑ SS-18002 [S]	A Bag Full of Soul	1966	5.00	10.00	20.00
❑ SS-18006 [S]	Cherry	1967	5.00	10.00	20.00
❑ SS-18017	A Bag Full of Blues	1968	5.00	10.00	20.00
❑ SS-18030	I've Got a New Woman	1968	5.00	10.00	20.00
❑ SS-18036	Honey	1968	5.00	10.00	20.00
❑ SS-18045	The Worm	1968	5.00	10.00	20.00
❑ SS-18053	Step I	1969	5.00	10.00	20.00
❑ SS-18060	A Thing to Come By	1969	5.00	10.00	20.00
❑ SS-18063	The Way You Look Tonight	1970	5.00	10.00	20.00
SUE					
❑ LP-1012 [M]	I've Got a Woman	1962	7.50	15.00	30.00
❑ STLP-1012 [S]	I've Got a Woman	1962	10.00	20.00	40.00
❑ LP-1013 [M]	One of Mine	1963	7.50	15.00	30.00
❑ STLP-1013 [S]	One of Mine	1963	10.00	20.00	40.00
❑ LP-1017 [M]	Jimmy McGriff at the Apollo	1963	7.50	15.00	30.00
❑ STLP-1017 [S]	Jimmy McGriff at the Apollo	1963	10.00	20.00	40.00
❑ LP-1018 [M]	Christmas with McGriff	1963	7.50	15.00	30.00
❑ STLP-1018 [S]	Christmas with McGriff	1963	10.00	20.00	40.00
❑ LP-1020 [M]	Jimmy McGriff at the Organ	1963	7.50	15.00	30.00
❑ STLP-1020 [S]	Jimmy McGriff at the Organ	1963	10.00	20.00	40.00
❑ LP-1033 [M]	Topkapi	1964	7.50	15.00	30.00
❑ STLP-1033 [S]	Topkapi	1964	10.00	20.00	40.00
❑ LP-1039 [M]	Blues for Mister Jimmy	1965	7.50	15.00	30.00
❑ STLP-1039 [S]	Blues for Mister Jimmy	1965	10.00	20.00	40.00
❑ LP-1043 [M]	Toast to Greatest Hits	1966	5.00	10.00	20.00
❑ STLP-1043 [S]	Toast to Greatest Hits	1966	6.25	12.50	25.00
SUNSET					
❑ SUS-5264	The Great Jimmy McGriff	1969	2.50	5.00	10.00
UNITED ARTISTS					
❑ UAS-5597	Jimmy McGriff and Junior Parker	1972	3.75	7.50	15.00
VEEP					
❑ VP-13515 [M]	Live Where the Action Is	1966	5.00	10.00	20.00
❑ VP-13522 [M]	Greatest Organ Hits	1967	6.25	12.50	25.00
❑ VPS-16515 [S]	Live Where the Action Is	1966	6.25	12.50	25.00
❑ VPS-16522 [S]	Greatest Organ Hits	1967	5.00	10.00	20.00

McHARGUE, ROSY
Clarinetist, saxophone player, male singer and composer.
JUMP

❑ JL-8 [10]	Dixie Combo	1955	12.50	25.00	50.00

McINTOSH, LADD
Bandleader and composer.
SEA BREEZE

❑ 2007	Energy	198?	2.50	5.00	10.00

McINTYRE, HAL
Alto saxophone player and bandleader.
COLUMBIA

❑ CL 6124 [10]	Dance Date	1950	12.50	25.00	50.00
FORUM					
❑ F-9018 [M]	It Seems Like Only Yesterday	196?	3.00	6.00	12.00
❑ SF-9018 [S]	It Seems Like Only Yesterday	196?	3.75	7.50	15.00
HINDSIGHT					
❑ HSR-172	Hal McIntyre and His Orchestra 1943-45	198?	2.50	5.00	10.00

Number	Title	Yr	VG	VG+	NM
ROULETTE					
❑ R-25079 [M]	It Seems Like Only Yesterday	1959	5.00	10.00	20.00
❑ SR-25079 [S]	It Seems Like Only Yesterday	1959	6.25	12.50	25.00

McINTYRE, KALAPARUSHA MAURICE
Tenor saxophone player, clarinetist, flutist and percussionist.

Number	Title	Yr	VG	VG+	NM
BLACK SAINT					
❑ BSR-0037	Peace and Blessings	198?	3.00	6.00	12.00
DELMARK					
❑ DS-419	Humility	1969	5.00	10.00	20.00
❑ DS-425	Forces and Feelings	197?	5.00	10.00	20.00

McINTYRE, KEN
Alto saxophone player, bass clarinetist, oboist, bassoonist, flutist.

Number	Title	Yr	VG	VG+	NM
FANTASY					
❑ OJC-252	Looking Ahead	1987	2.50	5.00	10.00
INNER CITY					
❑ IC-2014	Hindsight	197?	3.75	7.50	15.00
❑ IC-2039	Home	197?	3.75	7.50	15.00
❑ IC-2049	Open Horizon	197?	3.75	7.50	15.00
❑ IC-2065	Introducing the Vibrations	197?	3.75	7.50	15.00
NEW JAZZ					
❑ NJLP-8247 [M]	Looking Ahead	1960	12.50	25.00	50.00
-- Purple label					
❑ NJLP-8247 [M]	Looking Ahead	1965	6.25	12.50	25.00
-- Blue label, trident logo at right					
❑ NJLP-8259 [M]	Stone Blues	1961	12.50	25.00	50.00
-- Purple label					
❑ NJLP-8259 [M]	Stone Blues	1965	6.25	12.50	25.00
-- Blue label, trident logo at right					
STEEPLECHASE					
❑ SCS-1014	Hindsight	198?	3.00	6.00	12.00
❑ SCS-1039	Home	198?	3.00	6.00	12.00
❑ SCS-1049	Open Horizon	198?	3.00	6.00	12.00
❑ SCS-1065	Introducing the Vibrations	198?	3.00	6.00	12.00
❑ SCS-1114	Chasing the Sun	198?	3.00	6.00	12.00
UNITED ARTISTS					
❑ UAL-3336 [M]	Way Way Out	1964	6.25	12.50	25.00
❑ UAS-6336 [S]	Way Way Out	1964	7.50	15.00	30.00
❑ UAJ-14015 [M]	Year of the Iron Sheep	1962	7.50	15.00	30.00
❑ UAJS-15015 [S]	Year of the Iron Sheep	1962	10.00	20.00	40.00

McKAY, STUART

Number	Title	Yr	VG	VG+	NM
RCA VICTOR					
❑ LJM-1021 [M]	Stuart McKay and His Woods	1955	10.00	20.00	40.00

McKENNA, DAVE
Pianist. Also see THE MANHATTAN JAZZ ALL-STARS.

Number	Title	Yr	VG	VG+	NM
ABC-PARAMOUNT					
❑ ABC-104 [M]	Solo Piano	1956	10.00	20.00	40.00
CHIAROSCURO					
❑ 119	Piano Solos	197?	3.75	7.50	15.00
❑ 136	Dave McKenna Quartet Featuring Zoot Sims	197?	3.75	7.50	15.00
❑ 175	Dave "Fingers" McKenna	197?	3.00	6.00	12.00
❑ 202	McKenna	1978	3.00	6.00	12.00
CONCORD JAZZ					
❑ CJ-99	Giant Strides	1979	3.00	6.00	12.00
❑ CJ-123	Left Handed Complement	1980	3.00	6.00	12.00
❑ CJ-174	Dave McKenna Plays Music of Harry Warren	198?	2.50	5.00	10.00
❑ CJ-227	Celebration of Hoagy Carmichael	1984	2.50	5.00	10.00
❑ CJ-261	The Key Man	1985	2.50	5.00	10.00
❑ CJ-292	Dancing in the Dark	1986	2.50	5.00	10.00
❑ CJ-313	My Friend the Piano	1987	2.50	5.00	10.00
❑ CJ-365	No More Ouzo for Puzo	1989	3.00	6.00	12.00
EPIC					
❑ BN 527 [S]	Dave McKenna	1959	6.25	12.50	25.00
❑ LN 3558 [M]	Dave McKenna	1959	7.50	15.00	30.00
FAMOUS DOOR					
❑ 122	No Holds Barred	1978	3.00	6.00	12.00
HALCYON					
❑ 108	Cookin' at Michael's Pub	197?	3.75	7.50	15.00
SHIAH					
❑ MK-1	By Myself	198?	3.00	6.00	12.00

McKENNA, DAVE; SCOTT HAMILTON; JAKE HANNA
Also see each artist's individual listings.

Number	Title	Yr	VG	VG+	NM
CONCORD JAZZ					
❑ CJ-97	No Bass Hit	1979	3.00	6.00	12.00

McKENNA, DAVE, AND HALL OVERTON
Overton is an arrangers and composer. Also see DAVE McKENNA.

Number	Title	Yr	VG	VG+	NM
BETHLEHEM					
❑ BCP-6049 [M]	Dual Piano Jazz	1960	7.50	15.00	30.00
❑ BCPS-6049 [S]	Dual Piano Jazz	1960	7.50	15.00	30.00

McKENZIE, RED, AND EDDIE CONDON
McKenzie was a male singer, comb and kazoo player, and bandleader. Also see EDDIE CONDON.

Number	Title	Yr	VG	VG+	NM
JAZZOLOGY					
❑ J-110	Chicagoans (1944)	198?	2.50	5.00	10.00

McKINLEY, RAY
Drummer, male singer and bandleader. Also see PEANUTS HUCKO; GLENN MILLER ORCHESTRA.

Number	Title	Yr	VG	VG+	NM
ALLEGRO ELITE					
❑ 4015 [10]	Ray McKinley Plays Sauter and Others	195?	12.50	25.00	50.00
❑ 4129 [10]	Ray McKinley and His Famous Orchestra	195?	25.00	50.00	100.00
SAVOY JAZZ					
❑ SJK-2261 [(2)]	The Most Versatile Band in the World	198?	3.00	6.00	12.00

McKINLEY, RAY/JOE MARSALA
Also see each artist's individual listings.

Number	Title	Yr	VG	VG+	NM
DECCA					
❑ DL 5262 [10]	Dixieland Jazz Battle, Vol. 2	1950	12.50	25.00	50.00

McKINLEY, RAY, AND EDDIE SAUTER
Eddie Sauter was half of SAUTER-FINEGAN. Also see RAY McKINLEY.

Number	Title	Yr	VG	VG+	NM
SAVOY					
❑ MG-12024 [M]	Borderline	1955	12.50	25.00	50.00

McKINLEY, TOM, AND ED SCHULLER
McKinley is a pianist; Schuller is a bass player.

Number	Title	Yr	VG	VG+	NM
GM					
❑ 3001	Life Cycle	1982	2.50	5.00	10.00

McKINNEY'S COTTON PICKERS
Led by drummer Bill McKinney, they were an important early big band.

Number	Title	Yr	VG	VG+	NM
RCA VICTOR					
❑ LPT-24 [10]	McKinney's Cotton Pickers	1952	15.00	30.00	60.00
"X"					
❑ LVA-3031 [10]	McKinney's Cotton Pickers	1954	12.50	25.00	50.00

McKINNEY, HAROLD
Pianist.

Number	Title	Yr	VG	VG+	NM
TRIBE					
❑ 2233	Voices and Rhythms	197?	10.00	20.00	40.00

McKUSICK, HAL
Alto saxophone player, clarinetist, bass clarinetist and flutist. Also see THE MANHATTAN JAZZ SEPTETTE; THE NUTTY SQUIRRELS; BETTY ST. CLAIRE; PHIL WOODS.

Number	Title	Yr	VG	VG+	NM
BETHLEHEM					
❑ BCP-16 [M]	East Coast Jazz 6	1955	30.00	60.00	120.00
CORAL					
❑ CRL 57116 [M]	Jazz at the Academy	1957	20.00	40.00	80.00
❑ CRL 57131 [M]	Hal McKusick Quintet	1957	20.00	40.00	80.00
DECCA					
❑ DL 9209 [M]	Cross Section Saxes	1958	12.50	25.00	50.00
❑ DL 79209 [S]	Cross Section Saxes	1958	10.00	20.00	40.00
PRESTIGE					
❑ PRLP-7135 [M]	Triple Exposure	1957	20.00	40.00	80.00
RCA VICTOR					
❑ LPM-1164 [M]	Hal McKusick in the 20th Century Drawing Room	1956	17.50	35.00	70.00
❑ LPM-1366 [M]	The Jazz Workshop	1957	20.00	40.00	80.00

McLAUGHLIN, JOHN
Guitarist. Also see MAHAVISHNU ORCHESTRA; CARLOS SANTANA.

Number	Title	Yr	VG	VG+	NM
CELLULOID					
❑ CEL-5010	Devotion	198?	2.00	4.00	8.00
-- Reissue of Douglas 31568					
COLUMBIA					
❑ PC 34162	Shakti with John McLaughlin	1976	2.50	5.00	10.00
❑ PC 34372	A Handful of Secrets	1977	2.50	5.00	10.00
❑ JC 34980	Natural Elements	1977	2.50	5.00	10.00
❑ JC 35326	Electric Guitarist	1978	2.50	5.00	10.00
❑ JC 35785	Electric Dreams	1979	2.50	5.00	10.00

Number	Title	Yr	VG	VG+	NM
JC 36355	The Best of John McLaughlin	1980	2.50	5.00	10.00
FC 37152	Friday Night in San Francisco	1981	2.50	5.00	10.00
-- With Al DiMeola and Paco De Lucia					
FC 38645	Passion, Grace & Fire	1983	2.50	5.00	10.00
-- With Al DiMeola and Paco De Lucia					

DOUGLAS

Number	Title	Yr	VG	VG+	NM
4	Devotion	1970	3.75	7.50	15.00
KZ 30766	My Goals Beyond	1971	3.00	6.00	12.00
KZ 31568	Devotion	1972	3.00	6.00	12.00
-- Reissue of 4					

DOUGLAS CASABLANCA

Number	Title	Yr	VG	VG+	NM
6003	My Goals Beyond	1976	2.50	5.00	10.00
-- Reissue of Douglas 30766					

ELEKTRA/MUSICIAN

Number	Title	Yr	VG	VG+	NM
60031	My Goals Beyond	1982	2.50	5.00	10.00
-- Reissue of Douglas 30766					

POLYDOR

Number	Title	Yr	VG	VG+	NM
5510	Extrapolation	1969	3.75	7.50	15.00
PD-6074	Extrapolation	1972	3.00	6.00	12.00
-- Reissue of 5510					

RYKO ANALOGUE

Number	Title	Yr	VG	VG+	NM
RALP-0051	My Goals Beyond	1987	5.00	10.00	20.00
-- Clear vinyl reissue					

WARNER BROS.

Number	Title	Yr	VG	VG+	NM
BSK 3619	Belo Horizonte	1981	2.50	5.00	10.00
23723	Music Spoken Here	1982	2.50	5.00	10.00
25190	Mahavishnu	1985	2.50	5.00	10.00

McLEAN, JACKIE

Alto saxophone player. Also see PHIL WOODS.

ADLIB

Number	Title	Yr	VG	VG+	NM
ADL-6601 [M]	The Jackie McLean Quintet	1955	250.00	500.00	1,000.

BLUE NOTE

Number	Title	Yr	VG	VG+	NM
BN-LA457-H2 [(2)]	Jackknife	1975	5.00	10.00	20.00
-- First issue of unreleased material from 1960s					
BN-LA483-J2 [(2)]	Hipnosis	1975	5.00	10.00	20.00
LT-994	Consequences	1979	2.50	5.00	10.00
LT-1085	Vertigo	1980	2.50	5.00	10.00
BLP-4013 [M]	New Soil	1959	50.00	100.00	200.00
-- "Deep groove" version (deep indentation under label on both sides)					
BLP-4013 [M]	New Soil	1959	37.50	75.00	150.00
-- Regular version, W. 63rd St. address on label					
BLP-4013 [M]	New Soil	1963	6.25	12.50	25.00
-- With "New York, USA" address on label					
BST-4013 [S]	New Soil	1959	37.50	75.00	150.00
-- "Deep groove" version (deep indentation under label on both sides)					
BST-4013 [S]	New Soil	1959	30.00	60.00	120.00
-- Regular version, W. 63rd St. address on label					
BST-4013 [S]	New Soil	1963	5.00	10.00	20.00
-- With "New York, USA" address on label					
BLP-4024 [M]	Swing, Swang, Swingin'	1959	100.00	200.00	400.00
-- "Deep groove" version (deep indentation under label on both sides)					
BLP-4024 [M]	Swing, Swang, Swingin'	1959	75.00	150.00	300.00
-- Regular version, W. 63rd St. address on label					
BLP-4024 [M]	Swing, Swang, Swingin'	1963	6.25	12.50	25.00
-- With "New York, USA" address on label					
BLP-4038 [M]	Capuchin Swing	1960	50.00	100.00	200.00
-- "Deep groove" version (deep indentation under label on both sides)					
BLP-4038 [M]	Capuchin Swing	1960	37.50	75.00	150.00
-- Regular version, W. 63rd St. address on label					
BLP-4038 [M]	Capuchin Swing	1963	6.25	12.50	25.00
-- With "New York, USA" address on label					
BLP-4051 [M]	Jackie's Bag	1960	25.00	50.00	100.00
-- With W. 63rd St. address on label					
BLP-4051 [M]	Jackie's Bag	1963	6.25	12.50	25.00
-- With "New York, USA" address on label					
BLP-4067 [M]	Bluesnik	1961	25.00	50.00	100.00
-- With W. 63rd St. address on label					
BLP-4067 [M]	Bluesnik	1963	6.25	12.50	25.00
-- With "New York, USA" address on label					
BLP-4089 [M]	A Fickle Sonance	1961	20.00	40.00	80.00
-- With 61st St. address on label					
BLP-4089 [M]	A Fickle Sonance	1963	6.25	12.50	25.00
-- With "New York, USA" address on label					
BLP-4106 [M]	Let Freedom Ring	1962	7.50	15.00	30.00
-- With "New York, USA" address on label					
BLP-4116 [M]	Jackie McLean Quintet	1962	---	---	---
-- Canceled					
BLP-4137 [M]	One Step Beyond	1963	7.50	15.00	30.00
-- With "New York, USA" address on label					
BLP-4165 [M]	Destination... Out!	1964	7.50	15.00	30.00
-- With "New York, USA" address on label					
BLP-4179 [M]	It's Time!	1964	7.50	15.00	30.00
-- With "New York, USA" address on label					
BLP-4215 [M]	Right Now!	1965	7.50	15.00	30.00
-- With "New York, USA" address on label					
BLP-4218 [M]	Action Action Action	1965	7.50	15.00	30.00
-- With "New York, USA" address on label					
BLP-4223 [M]	Jackknife	1965	---	---	---
-- Canceled					
BLP-4236 [M]	New Frequency	1966	---	---	---
-- Canceled					
BLP-4262 [M]	New and Old Gospel	1967	7.50	15.00	30.00
B1-84013 [S]	New Soil	1989	3.00	6.00	12.00
-- "The Finest in Jazz Since 1939" reissue					
BST-84013 [S]	New Soil	1967	3.75	7.50	15.00
-- With "A Division of Liberty Records" on label					
BST-84024 [S]	Swing, Swang, Swingin'	1959	50.00	100.00	200.00
-- With W. 63rd St. address on label					
BST-84024 [S]	Swing, Swang, Swingin'	1963	5.00	10.00	20.00
-- With "New York, USA" address on label					
BST-84024 [S]	Swing, Swang, Swingin'	1967	3.75	7.50	15.00
-- With "A Division of Liberty Records" on label					
BST-84038 [S]	Capuchin Swing	1960	25.00	50.00	100.00
-- With W. 63rd St. address on label					
BST-84038 [S]	Capuchin Swing	1963	5.00	10.00	20.00
-- With "New York, USA" address on label					
BST-84038 [S]	Capuchin Swing	1967	3.75	7.50	15.00
-- With "A Division of Liberty Records" on label					
BST-84051 [S]	Jackie's Bag	1960	20.00	40.00	80.00
-- With W. 63rd St. address on label					
BST-84051 [S]	Jackie's Bag	1963	5.00	10.00	20.00
-- With "New York, USA" address on label					
BST-84051 [S]	Jackie's Bag	1967	3.75	7.50	15.00
-- With "A Division of Liberty Records" on label					
BST-84051 [S]	Jackie's Bag	1985	2.50	5.00	10.00
-- "The Finest in Jazz Since 1939" reissue					
B1-84067 [S]	Bluesnik	1989	3.00	6.00	12.00
-- "The Finest in Jazz Since 1939" reissue					
BST-84067 [S]	Bluesnik	1961	20.00	40.00	80.00
-- With W. 63rd St. address on label					
BST-84067 [S]	Bluesnik	1963	5.00	10.00	20.00
-- With "New York, USA" address on label					
BST-84067 [S]	Bluesnik	1967	3.75	7.50	15.00
-- With "A Division of Liberty Records" on label					
BST-84089 [S]	A Fickle Sonance	1961	15.00	30.00	60.00
-- With 61st St. address on label					
BST-84089 [S]	A Fickle Sonance	1963	5.00	10.00	20.00
-- With "New York, USA" address on label					
BST-84089 [S]	A Fickle Sonance	1967	3.75	7.50	15.00
-- With "A Division of Liberty Records" on label					
BST-84106 [S]	Let Freedom Ring	1962	10.00	20.00	40.00
-- With "New York, USA" address on label					
BST-84106 [S]	Let Freedom Ring	1967	5.00	10.00	20.00
-- With "A Division of Liberty Records" on label					
BST-84106 [S]	Let Freedom Ring	198?	2.50	5.00	10.00
-- "The Finest in Jazz Since 1939" reissue					
BST-84116 [S]	Jackie McLean Quintet	1962	---	---	---
-- Canceled					
BST-84137 [S]	One Step Beyond	1963	10.00	20.00	40.00
-- With "New York, USA" address on label					
BST-84137 [S]	One Step Beyond	1967	5.00	10.00	20.00
-- With "A Division of Liberty Records" on label					
BST-84137 [S]	One Step Beyond	198?	2.50	5.00	10.00
-- "The Finest in Jazz Since 1939" reissue					
BST-84165 [S]	Destination... Out!	1964	10.00	20.00	40.00
-- With "New York, USA" address on label					
BST-84165 [S]	Destination... Out!	1967	5.00	10.00	20.00
-- With "A Division of Liberty Records" on label					
BST-84179 [S]	It's Time!	1964	10.00	20.00	40.00
-- With "New York, USA" address on label					
BST-84179 [S]	It's Time!	1967	5.00	10.00	20.00
-- With "A Division of Liberty Records" on label					
BST-84215 [S]	Right Now!	1965	10.00	20.00	40.00
-- With "New York, USA" address on label					
BST-84215 [S]	Right Now!	1967	5.00	10.00	20.00
-- With "A Division of Liberty Records" on label					
BST-84218 [S]	Action Action Action	1965	10.00	20.00	40.00
-- With "New York, USA" address on label					
BST-84218 [S]	Action Action Action	1967	5.00	10.00	20.00
-- With "A Division of Liberty Records" on label					
BST-84223 [S]	Jackknife	1965	---	---	---
-- Canceled					
BST-84236 [S]	New Frequency	1966	---	---	---
-- Canceled					
BST-84262 [S]	New and Old Gospel	1967	5.00	10.00	20.00
-- With "A Division of Liberty Records" on label					
BST-84284	'Bout Soul	1968	5.00	10.00	20.00
-- With "A Division of Liberty Records" on label					
BST-84345	Demon's Dance	1969	5.00	10.00	20.00
-- With "A Division of Liberty Records" on label					
BST-84345	Demon's Dance	198?	2.50	5.00	10.00
-- "The Finest in Jazz Since 1939" reissue					
BST-84427	Tippin' the Scales	198?	3.00	6.00	12.00

BOPLICITY

Number	Title	Yr	VG	VG+	NM
BOP-2	Swing, Swang, Swingin'	198?	2.50	5.00	10.00

Number	Title	Yr	VG	VG+	NM
FANTASY					
❑ OJC-056	4, 5 and 6	198?	2.50	5.00	10.00
❑ OJC-074	Jackie McLean & Co.	198?	2.50	5.00	10.00
❑ OJC-098	McLean's Scene	198?	2.50	5.00	10.00
❑ OJC-197	Makin' the Changes	1985	2.50	5.00	10.00
❑ OJC-253	A Long Drink of the Blues	1987	2.50	5.00	10.00
❑ OJC-354	Strange Blues	198?	2.50	5.00	10.00
❑ OJC-426	Lights Out!	1990	3.00	6.00	12.00
❑ OJC-1717	Jackie's Pal -- Introducing Bill Hardman	198?	2.50	5.00	10.00
INNER CITY					
❑ IC-2001	Live at Montmartre	197?	3.75	7.50	15.00
❑ IC-2009	Ode to Super	197?	3.75	7.50	15.00
❑ IC-2013	Ghetto Lullaby	197?	3.75	7.50	15.00
❑ IC-2023	New York Calling	197?	3.75	7.50	15.00
❑ IC-6029	New Wine	1978	3.75	7.50	15.00
JOSIE					
❑ JLPS-3503 [S]	Jackie McLean Sextet	1963	5.00	10.00	20.00
❑ JOZ-3503 [M]	Jackie McLean Sextet	1963	7.50	15.00	30.00
❑ JLPS-3507 [S]	Jackie McLean Sextet	1963	5.00	10.00	20.00
❑ JOZ-3507 [M]	Jackie McLean Sextet	1963	7.50	15.00	30.00
JUBILEE					
❑ JLP-1064 [M]	The Jackie McLean Quintet	1958	20.00	40.00	80.00
❑ JLP-1093 [M]	Jackie McLean Plays Fat Jazz	1959	20.00	40.00	80.00
MOSAIC					
❑ MQ6-150 [(6)]	The Complete Blue Note 1964-66 Jackie McLean Sessions	199?	25.00	50.00	100.00
NEW JAZZ					
❑ NJLP-8212 [M]	McLean's Scene	1958	25.00	50.00	100.00
-- Purple label					
❑ NJLP-8212 [M]	McLean's Scene	1965	6.25	12.50	25.00
-- Blue label, trident logo at right					
❑ NJLP-8231 [M]	Makin' the Changes	1960	25.00	50.00	100.00
-- Purple label					
❑ NJLP-8231 [M]	Makin' the Changes	1965	6.25	12.50	25.00
-- Blue label, trident logo at right					
❑ NJLP-8253 [M]	A Long Drink of the Blues	1961	20.00	40.00	80.00
-- Purple label					
❑ NJLP-8253 [M]	A Long Drink of the Blues	1965	6.25	12.50	25.00
-- Blue label, trident logo at right					
❑ NJLP-8263 [M]	Lights Out!	1961	12.50	25.00	50.00
-- Purple label					
❑ NJLP-8263 [M]	Lights Out!	1965	6.25	12.50	25.00
-- Blue label, trident logo at right					
❑ NJLP-8279 [M]	4, 5 and 6	1962	12.50	25.00	50.00
-- Purple label					
❑ NJLP-8279 [M]	4, 5 and 6	1965	6.25	12.50	25.00
-- Blue label, trident logo at right					
❑ NJLP-8290 [M]	Steeplechase	1962	12.50	25.00	50.00
-- Purple label					
❑ NJLP-8290 [M]	Steeplechase	1965	6.25	12.50	25.00
-- Blue label, trident logo at right					
❑ NJLP-8312 [M]	Alto Madness	1963	---	---	---
-- Canceled; reassigned to Status					
❑ NJLP-8323 [M]	Jackie McLean & Co.	1963	---	---	---
-- Canceled; reassigned to Status					
PRESTIGE					
❑ 2512	Alto Madness	198?	3.00	6.00	12.00
❑ PRLP-7035 [M]	Lights Out!	1956	37.50	75.00	150.00
❑ PRLP-7048 [M]	4, 5 and 6	1956	37.50	75.00	150.00
❑ PRLP-7068 [M]	Jackie's Pal -- Introducing Bill Hardman	1956	37.50	75.00	150.00
❑ PRLP-7087 [M]	Jackie McLean & Co.	1957	30.00	60.00	120.00
❑ PRLP-7114 [M]	Alto Madness	1957	30.00	60.00	120.00
❑ PRLP-7500 [M]	Strange Blues	1967	6.25	12.50	25.00
❑ PRST-7500 [R]	Strange Blues	1967	3.75	7.50	15.00
❑ PRST-7757	Lights Out!	1970	3.75	7.50	15.00
❑ 24076 [(2)]	Contour	197?	3.75	7.50	15.00
RCA VICTOR					
❑ LPM-3230 [M]	Alto Madness	1965	5.00	10.00	20.00
❑ LSP-3230 [S]	Alto Madness	1965	6.25	12.50	25.00
STATUS					
❑ ST-8312 [M]	Alto Madness	1965	10.00	20.00	40.00
❑ ST-8323 [M]	Jackie McLean & Co.	1965	10.00	20.00	40.00
STEEPLECHASE					
❑ SCS-1001	Live at Montmartre	198?	3.00	6.00	12.00
❑ SCS-1006	The Meeting	198?	3.00	6.00	12.00
❑ SCS-1009	Ode to Super	198?	3.00	6.00	12.00
❑ SCS-1013	A Ghetto Lullaby	198?	3.00	6.00	12.00
❑ SCS-1020	The Source	198?	3.00	6.00	12.00
❑ SCS-1023	New York Calling	198?	3.00	6.00	12.00
❑ SCC-6005	Dr. Jackie	198?	3.00	6.00	12.00
TRIP					
❑ 5027 [(2)]	Two Sides of Jackie McLean	197?	3.75	7.50	15.00

Number	Title	Yr	VG	VG+	NM
McLEAN, JACKIE, AND MICHAEL CARVIN					
Also see each artist's individual listings.					
INNER CITY					
❑ IC-2028	Antiquity	197?	3.75	7.50	15.00
STEEPLECHASE					
❑ SCS-1028	Antiquity	198?	3.00	6.00	12.00
McLEAN, RENE					
Tenor and soprano saxophone player.					
INNER CITY					
❑ IC-2037	Watch Out	197?	3.75	7.50	15.00
STEEPLECHASE					
❑ SCS-1037	Watch Out!	198?	3.00	6.00	12.00
McMANUS, JILL					
CONCORD JAZZ					
❑ CJ-242	Symbols of Hopi	1984	2.50	5.00	10.00
McNABB, TED					
Bandleader.					
EPIC					
❑ BN 558 [S]	Ted McNabb and Company	1959	10.00	20.00	40.00
❑ LN 3663 [M]	Ted McNabb and Company	1959	12.50	25.00	50.00
McNEELY, JIM					
Pianist, keyboard player, bandleader and composer.					
GATEMOUTH					
❑ 1001	The Plot Thickens	1980	3.00	6.00	12.00
MUSE					
❑ MR-5378	The Plot Thickens	198?	2.50	5.00	10.00
STEEPLECHASE					
❑ SCS-4001	Rain's Dance	198?	3.00	6.00	12.00
McNEIL, JOHN					
Trumpeter.					
STEEPLECHASE					
❑ SCS-1099	Embarkation	1978	3.00	6.00	12.00
❑ SCS-1117	Faun	198?	3.00	6.00	12.00
❑ SCS-1128	Look to the Sky	198?	3.00	6.00	12.00
❑ SCS-1133	The Glass Room	1979	3.00	6.00	12.00
❑ SCS-1154	Clean Sweep	198?	3.00	6.00	12.00
❑ SCS-1183	I've Got the World on a String	198?	3.00	6.00	12.00
McNEILL, LLOYD					
Flutist.					
ASHA					
❑ 3	Washington Suite	1976	3.75	7.50	15.00
McPARTLAND, JIMMY					
Cornet player and trumpeter. Also see DIZZY GILLESPIE.					
BRUNSWICK					
❑ BL 54018 [M]	Dixieland Band	1955	12.50	25.00	50.00
❑ BL 58049 [10]	Shades of Bix	1953	20.00	40.00	80.00
EPIC					
❑ BN 506 [S]	"The Music Man" Goes Dixieland	1958	7.50	15.00	30.00
❑ LN 3371 [M]	Jimmy McPartland's Dixieland	1956	10.00	20.00	40.00
❑ LN 3463 [M]	"The Music Man" Goes Dixieland	1958	10.00	20.00	40.00
HARMONY					
❑ HS 11264	Dixieland	1968	3.00	6.00	12.00
JAZZOLOGY					
❑ J-16 [M]	Jimmy McPartland On Stage	196?	3.75	7.50	15.00
❑ J-137	One Night Stand	1986	2.50	5.00	10.00
JAZZTONE					
❑ J-1227 [M]	The Middle Road	1956	10.00	20.00	40.00
MCA					
❑ 4110 [(2)]	Shades of Bix	197?	3.00	6.00	12.00
MERCURY					
❑ MG-20??? [M]	Meet Me in Chicago	1959	6.25	12.50	25.00
❑ SR-60143 [S]	Meet Me in Chicago	1959	7.50	15.00	30.00
PALACE					
❑ M-708 [M]	Dixieland Vol. 1	196?	3.75	7.50	15.00
RCA VICTOR					
❑ LPV-549 [M]	That Happy Dixieland Jazz	1966	5.00	10.00	20.00
McPARTLAND, JIMMY/PAUL BARBARIN					
Also see each artist's individual listings.					
JAZZTONE					
❑ J-1241 [M]	Dixieland Now and Then	195?	7.50	15.00	30.00

Number	Title	Yr	VG	VG+	NM

McPARTLAND, MARIAN
Pianist.
ARGO
| ❏ LP-640 [M] | Marion McPartland at the London House | 1959 | 10.00 | 20.00 | 40.00 |
| ❏ LPS-640 [S] | Marion McPartland at the London House | 1959 | 7.50 | 15.00 | 30.00 |

BAINBRIDGE
| ❏ 1045 | Marian McPartland with Ben Tucker | 198? | 2.50 | 5.00 | 10.00 |

CAPITOL
❏ T 574 [M]	Marion McPartland at the Hickory House	1955	10.00	20.00	40.00
❏ T 699 [M]	After Dark	1956	10.00	20.00	40.00
❏ T 785 [M]	Marion McPartland Trio	1957	10.00	20.00	40.00

CONCORD JAZZ
❏ CJ-86	From This Moment On	1979	2.50	5.00	10.00
❏ CJ-101	Portrait of Marian McPartland	1980	2.50	5.00	10.00
❏ CJ-118	Marian McPartland at the Festival	1981	2.50	5.00	10.00
❏ CJ-202	Personal Choice	1982	2.50	5.00	10.00
❏ CJ-272	Willow Creek and Other Ballads	1985	2.50	5.00	10.00
❏ CJ-326	Marian McPartland Plays the Music of Billy Strayhorn	1987	2.50	5.00	10.00

DOT
| ❏ DLP-25907 | My Old Flame | 1969 | 3.75 | 7.50 | 15.00 |

HALCYON
❏ 100	Interplay	1970	3.75	7.50	15.00
❏ 103	Ambience	1971	3.75	7.50	15.00
❏ 105	Delicate Balance	1972	3.75	7.50	15.00
❏ 109	Marian McPartland Plays Alec Wilder	197?	3.75	7.50	15.00
❏ 111	Solo Concert at Haverford	197?	3.00	6.00	12.00
❏ 115	Now's the Time	1978	3.00	6.00	12.00
❏ 117	Live at the Carlyle	1979	3.00	6.00	12.00

IMPROV
| ❏ 7115 | A Fine Romance | 1976 | 3.00 | 6.00 | 12.00 |

SAVOY
❏ MG-12004 [M]	Marion McPartland in Concert	1955	12.50	25.00	50.00
❏ MG-12005 [M]	Lullaby of Birdland	1955	12.50	25.00	50.00
❏ MG-15019 [10]	Jazz at Storyville, Volume 3	1952	20.00	40.00	80.00
❏ MG-15021 [10]	Piano Moods	1952	20.00	40.00	80.00
❏ MG-15027 [10]	Marion McPartland	1953	20.00	40.00	80.00
❏ MG-15032 [10]	Jazz at the Hickory House	1953	20.00	40.00	80.00

SAVOY JAZZ
| ❏ SJL-2248 [(2)] | Marian McPartland at the Hickory House | 198? | 3.75 | 7.50 | 15.00 |

TIME
❏ S-2073 [S]	Bossa Nova Plus Soul	1963	7.50	15.00	30.00
❏ S-2189 [S]	West Side Story	196?	7.50	15.00	30.00
❏ 52073 [M]	Bossa Nova Plus Soul	1963	6.25	12.50	25.00
❏ 52189 [M]	West Side Story	196?	6.25	12.50	25.00

McPARTLAND, MARIAN AND JIMMY
Also see each artist's individual listings.
HALCYON
❏ 107	Live at the Monticello	197?	3.75	7.50	15.00
❏ 114	Swingin'	197?	3.00	6.00	12.00
❏ 116	Goin' Back a Ways	198?	3.00	6.00	12.00

IMPROV
| ❏ 7122 | Wanted! | 1977 | 3.00 | 6.00 | 12.00 |

McPARTLAND, MARIAN, AND GEORGE SHEARING
Also see each artist's individual listings.
SAVOY
| ❏ MG-12016 [M] | Great Britain's Marion McPartland and George Shearing | 1955 | 10.00 | 20.00 | 40.00 |

McPHEE, JOE
Tenor saxophone player, trumpeter, valve trombonist, clarinetist, pianist and keyboard player.
CJR
❏ 2	Nation Time	197?	6.25	12.50	25.00
❏ 3	Trinity	197?	6.25	12.50	25.00
❏ 4	Pieces of Light	197?	6.25	12.50	25.00

HAT ART
| ❏ 2033 [(2)] | Po Music: A Future Retrospective | 1987 | 3.75 | 7.50 | 15.00 |

HAT HUT
❏ A	Black Magic Man	1974	6.25	12.50	25.00
❏ C	Tenor	1976	5.00	10.00	20.00
❏ D	Rotation	1977	5.00	10.00	20.00

Number	Title	Yr	VG	VG+	NM
❏ I/J [(2)]	Graphics	1977	7.50	15.00	30.00
❏ O	Variations on a Blue Line/'Round Midnight	1978	5.00	10.00	20.00
❏ P	Glasses	1978	5.00	10.00	20.00
❏ 01	Old Eyes	1979	5.00	10.00	20.00
❏ 1987/8 [(2)]	Topology	1981	6.25	12.50	25.00

McPHERSON, CHARLES
Alto saxophone player.
MAINSTREAM
❏ MRL-329	Charles McPherson	1972	3.75	7.50	15.00
❏ MRL-365	Siku Ya Bibi	1973	3.75	7.50	15.00
❏ MRL-395	Today's Man	1974	3.75	7.50	15.00

PRESTIGE
❏ PRLP-7359 [M]	Bebop Revisited	1965	7.50	15.00	30.00
❏ PRST-7359 [S]	Bebop Revisited	1965	10.00	20.00	40.00
❏ PRLP-7427 [M]	Con Alma!	1966	7.50	15.00	30.00
❏ PRST-7427 [S]	Con Alma!	1966	10.00	20.00	40.00
❏ PRLP-7480 [M]	The Charles McPherson Quintet Live!	1967	10.00	20.00	40.00
❏ PRST-7480 [S]	The Charles McPherson Quintet Live!	1967	7.50	15.00	30.00
❏ PRST-7559	From This Moment On	1968	7.50	15.00	30.00
❏ PRST-7603	Horizons	1969	7.50	15.00	30.00
❏ PRST-7743	McPherson's Mood	1970	5.00	10.00	20.00

XANADU
❏ 115	Beautiful	1976	3.00	6.00	12.00
❏ 131	Live in Tokyo	1977	3.00	6.00	12.00
❏ 149	New Horizons	1978	3.00	6.00	12.00
❏ 170	Free Bop	1979	3.00	6.00	12.00

McRAE, CARMEN
Female singer and pianist.
ACCORD
| ❏ SN-7152 | Love Songs | 1981 | 2.50 | 5.00 | 10.00 |

ATLANTIC
❏ SD 2-904 [(2)]	The Great American Songbook	1971	5.00	10.00	20.00
❏ SD 1568	Just a Little Lovin'	1971	3.00	6.00	12.00
❏ 8143 [M]	For Once in My Life	1967	5.00	10.00	20.00
❏ SD 8143 [S]	For Once in My Life	1967	3.75	7.50	15.00
❏ SD 8165	Portrait	1968	3.75	7.50	15.00
❏ SD 8200	The Sound of Silence	1968	3.75	7.50	15.00

BAINBRIDGE
| ❏ 6221 | The Sound of Silence | 198? | 2.50 | 5.00 | 10.00 |

BETHLEHEM
| ❏ BCP-1023 [10] | Carmen McRae | 1955 | 25.00 | 50.00 | 100.00 |

BLUE NOTE
❏ BN-LA462-G	I Am Music	1975	3.00	6.00	12.00
❏ BN-LA635-G	Can't Hide Love	1976	3.00	6.00	12.00
❏ BN-LA709-H2 [(2)]	The Great Music Hall	1977	3.75	7.50	15.00
❏ LWB-709 [(2)]	The Great Music Hall	1981	3.00	6.00	12.00
-- Reissue of BN-LA709-H2					

BUDDAH
| ❏ B2D-6501 [(2)] | I'm Coming Home Again | 1979 | 3.75 | 7.50 | 15.00 |

CATALYST
| ❏ 7904 | As Time Goes By | 197? | 3.00 | 6.00 | 12.00 |

COLUMBIA
❏ CL 1730 [M]	Lover Man	1962	5.00	10.00	20.00
❏ CL 1943 [M]	Something Wonderful	1962	5.00	10.00	20.00
❏ CS 8530 [S]	Lover Man	1962	6.25	12.50	25.00
❏ CS 8743 [S]	Something Wonderful	1962	6.25	12.50	25.00

CONCORD JAZZ
❏ CJ-128	Two for the Road	1980	2.50	5.00	10.00
❏ CJ-235	You're Looking at Me: A Collection of Nat King Cole Songs	1984	2.50	5.00	10.00
❏ CJ-342	Fine and Mellow	1988	2.50	5.00	10.00

DECCA
❏ DL 8173 [M]	By Special Request	1955	12.50	25.00	50.00
-- Black label, silver print					
❏ DL 8173 [M]	By Special Request	1960	5.00	10.00	20.00
-- Black label with color bars					
❏ DL 8267 [M]	Torchy!	1956	12.50	25.00	50.00
-- Black label, silver print					
❏ DL 8267 [M]	Torchy!	1960	5.00	10.00	20.00
-- Black label with color bars					
❏ DL 8347 [M]	Blue Moon	1957	12.50	25.00	50.00
-- Black label, silver print					
❏ DL 8347 [M]	Blue Moon	1960	5.00	10.00	20.00
-- Black label with color bars					
❏ DL 8583 [M]	After Glow	1957	12.50	25.00	50.00
-- Black label, silver print					

Number	Title	Yr	VG	VG+	NM
❑ DL 8583 [M]	After Glow	1960	5.00	10.00	20.00
-- Black label with color bars					
❑ DL 8662 [M]	Mad About the Man	1958	12.50	25.00	50.00
-- Black label, silver print					
❑ DL 8662 [M]	Mad About the Man	1960	5.00	10.00	20.00
-- Black label with color bars					
❑ DL 8738 [M]	Carmen for Cool Ones	1958	12.50	25.00	50.00
-- Black label, silver print					
❑ DL 8738 [M]	Carmen for Cool Ones	1960	5.00	10.00	20.00
-- Black label with color bars					
❑ DL 8815 [M]	Birds of a Feather	1959	12.50	25.00	50.00
-- Black label, silver print					
❑ DL 8815 [M]	Birds of a Feather	1960	5.00	10.00	20.00
-- Black label with color bars					

FOCUS

Number	Title	Yr	VG	VG+	NM
❑ FL-334 [M]	Bittersweet	1964	3.75	7.50	15.00
❑ FS-334 [S]	Bittersweet	1964	5.00	10.00	20.00

GROOVE MERCHANT

❑ 522	A Whole Lot of Human Feeling	1973	3.00	6.00	12.00
❑ 531	Ms. Jazz	1974	3.00	6.00	12.00
❑ 4401 [(2)]	Velvet Soul	197?	3.75	7.50	15.00

HARMONY

❑ HL 7452 [M]	Yesterdays	1968	5.00	10.00	20.00
❑ HS 11252 [S]	Yesterdays	1968	3.00	6.00	12.00
❑ KH 32177	Carmen McRae Sings Billie Holiday	1972	2.50	5.00	10.00

JAZZ MAN

❑ 5004	Carmen McRae and the Kenny Clarke/Francy Boland Big Band	198?	2.50	5.00	10.00

KAPP

❑ KL-1117 [M]	Book of Ballads	1958	6.25	12.50	25.00
❑ KL-1135 [M]	When You're Away	1959	6.25	12.50	25.00
❑ KL-1169 [M]	Something to Swing About	1960	6.25	12.50	25.00
❑ KL-1541 [M]	This Is Carmen McRae	1967	5.00	10.00	20.00
❑ KS-3000 [S]	Book of Ballads	1958	7.50	15.00	30.00
❑ KS-3018 [S]	When You're Away	1959	7.50	15.00	30.00
❑ KS-3053 [S]	Something to Swing About	1960	7.50	15.00	30.00
❑ KS-3541 [S]	This Is Carmen McRae	1967	3.75	7.50	15.00

MAINSTREAM

❑ 309	Carmen McRae	1971	3.00	6.00	12.00
❑ 338	Carmen's Gold	1972	3.00	6.00	12.00
❑ 352	Carmen McRae In Person	1972	3.00	6.00	12.00
❑ 387	I Want You	1972	3.00	6.00	12.00
❑ 403	Live and Doin' It	1974	3.00	6.00	12.00
❑ 800 [(2)]	Alive!	1974	3.75	7.50	15.00
❑ S-6028 [S]	Second to None	1965	5.00	10.00	20.00
❑ S-6044 [S]	Haven't We Met?	1965	5.00	10.00	20.00
❑ S-6065 [S]	Woman Talk	1966	5.00	10.00	20.00
❑ S-6084 [S]	Alfie	1966	5.00	10.00	20.00
❑ S-6091 [S]	In Person/San Francisco	1967	3.75	7.50	15.00
❑ S-6110	Live & Wailin'	1968	3.75	7.50	15.00
❑ 56028 [M]	Second to None	1965	3.75	7.50	15.00
❑ 56044 [M]	Haven't We Met?	1965	3.75	7.50	15.00
❑ 56065 [M]	Woman Talk	1966	3.75	7.50	15.00
❑ 56084 [M]	Alfie	1966	3.75	7.50	15.00
❑ 56091 [M]	In Person/San Francisco	1967	5.00	10.00	20.00

MCA

❑ 4111 [(2)]	The Greatest of Carmen McRae	197?	3.00	6.00	12.00

NOVUS

❑ 3086-1-N	Carmen Sings Monk	1990	3.00	6.00	12.00

PAUSA

❑ 9003	Can't Hide Love	198?	2.50	5.00	10.00

QUINTESSENCE

❑ 25021	Ms. Jazz	1978	2.50	5.00	10.00
-- Reissue of Groove Merchant 531					

STANYAN

❑ 10115	Mad About the Man	197?	3.00	6.00	12.00

TEMPONIC

❑ 29562	Carmen	1972	3.00	6.00	12.00

TIME

❑ S-2104 [S]	Live at Sugar Hill	1960	6.25	12.50	25.00
❑ 52104 [M]	Live at Sugar Hill	1960	5.00	10.00	20.00

VOCALION

❑ VL 3697 [M]	Carmen McRae	1963	3.75	7.50	15.00
❑ VL 73828	My Foolish Heart	1969	3.00	6.00	12.00

McRITCHIE, GREIG
Arranger and composer.
CADET

❑ LP-4058 [M]	Fighting Back	1967	6.25	12.50	25.00
❑ LPS-4058 [S]	Fighting Back	1967	3.75	7.50	15.00

ZEPHYR

❑ 12005 [M]	Easy Jazz on a Fish Beat Bass	1959	12.50	25.00	250.00

McSHANN, JAY
Pianist, male singer and bandleader.
ATLANTIC

Number	Title	Yr	VG	VG+	NM
❑ SD 8800	The Last of Jay McShann	197?	3.00	6.00	12.00
❑ 90047	The Big Apple Bash	198?	2.50	5.00	10.00

CAPITOL

❑ ST 2645 [S]	McShann's Piano	1967	5.00	10.00	20.00
❑ T 2645 [M]	McShann's Piano	1967	5.00	10.00	20.00

CLASSIC JAZZ

❑ 128	Confessin' the Blues	197?	3.00	6.00	12.00

DECCA

❑ DL 5503 [10]	Kansas City Memories	1954	125.00	250.00	500.00
-- CHARLIE PARKER appears on this LP					
❑ DL 9236 [M]	Kansas City Memories	1958	50.00	100.00	200.00
❑ DL 79236 [R]	Kansas City Memories	196?	3.75	7.50	15.00

MASTER JAZZ

❑ 8113	Going to Kansas City	197?	3.75	7.50	15.00

MCA

❑ 1338	The Early Bird	198?	2.50	5.00	10.00

SACKVILLE

❑ 3006	The Man from Muskogee	198?	2.50	5.00	10.00
❑ 3011	Crazy Legs and Friday Soul	198?	2.50	5.00	10.00
❑ 3019	A Tribute to Fats Waller	198?	2.50	5.00	10.00
❑ 3021	Kansas City Hustle	198?	2.50	5.00	10.00
❑ 3025	Tuxedo Junction	198?	2.50	5.00	10.00
❑ 3035	Just a Little So and So	198?	2.50	5.00	10.00
❑ 3040	Airmail Special	198?	2.50	5.00	10.00

MECCA, LOU
Guitarist.
BLUE NOTE

❑ BLP-5067 [10]	Lou Mecca Quartet	1955	75.00	150.00	300.00

MEHEGAN, JOHN
Pianist and composer.
EPIC

❑ LA 16007 [M]	Act of Jazz	1960	5.00	10.00	20.00
❑ BA 17007 [S]	Act of Jazz	1960	6.25	12.50	25.00

PERSPECTIVE

❑ PR-1 [M]	From Barrelhouse to Bop	195?	12.50	25.00	50.00

SAVOY

❑ MG-12028 [M]	Reflections	1956	10.00	20.00	40.00
❑ MG-15054 [10]	The Last Mehegan	1955	15.00	30.00	60.00

TJ

❑ LP-1 [M]	Casual Affair	1959	10.00	20.00	40.00

MEHEGAN, JOHN, AND EDDIE COSTA
Also see each artist's individual listings.
SAVOY

❑ MG-12049 [M]	A Pair of Pianos	1956	10.00	20.00	40.00

MELDONIAN, DICK
Alto and tenor saxophone player.
PROGRESSIVE

❑ 7033	Some of These Days	1979	3.00	6.00	12.00
❑ 7058	The Jersey Swing Concerts	198?	2.50	5.00	10.00
❑ 7062	Plays Gene Roland Music	198?	2.50	5.00	10.00

STATINAS

❑ SLP-8076	It's a Wonderful World	1985	2.50	5.00	10.00

MELILLO, MIKE
Pianist.
RED RECORD

❑ VPA-170	Piano Solo	198?	3.00	6.00	12.00
❑ VPA-188	'Live and Well	1986	3.00	6.00	12.00

MELIS, MARCELLO
Bass player.
BLACK SAINT

❑ BSR-0012	New Village on the Left	198?	3.00	6.00	12.00
❑ BSR-0023	Free to Dance	198?	3.00	6.00	12.00
❑ BSR-0073	Angedras	1983	3.00	6.00	12.00

MELLE, GIL
Saxophone player and composer who later created many electronic instruments.
BLUE NOTE

❑ BLP-1517 [M]	Patterns in Jazz	1956	50.00	100.00	200.00
-- "Deep groove" version (deep indentation under label on both sides)					
❑ BLP-1517 [M]	Patterns in Jazz	1956	37.50	75.00	150.00
-- Regular version, Lexington Ave. address on label					

Number	Title	Yr	VG	VG+	NM
❏ BLP-5020 [10]	Gil Melle Quintet/Sextet	1953	75.00	150.00	300.00
❏ BLP-5033 [10]	Gil Melle Quintet, Volume 2	1953	75.00	150.00	300.00
❏ BLP-5054 [10]	Gil Melle Quintet, Volume 3	1954	75.00	150.00	300.00
❏ BLP-5063 [10]	Gil Melle Quintet, Volume 4 -- Five Impressions of Color	1954	75.00	150.00	300.00
❏ B1-92168	Mindscape	1989	3.00	6.00	12.00
FANTASY					
❏ OJC-1712	Melle Plays Primitive Modern	198?	2.50	5.00	10.00
❏ OJC-1753	Gil's Guests	198?	2.50	5.00	10.00
PRESTIGE					
❏ PRLP-7040 [M]	Melle Plays Primitive Modern	1956	20.00	40.00	80.00
❏ PRLP-7063 [M]	Gil's Guests	1956	20.00	40.00	80.00
❏ PRLP-7097 [M]	Quadrama	1957	20.00	40.00	80.00
VERVE					
❏ V6-8744	Tome VI	1968	5.00	10.00	20.00

MELLO-LARKS, THE
Vocal group: Adele Castle; Joseph Eich; Thomas Hamm; Robert Wolter.
RCA CAMDEN

Number	Title	Yr	VG	VG+	NM
❏ CAL-530 [M]	Just for a Lark	1959	10.00	20.00	40.00

MELROSE, FRANK
Pianist and composer.
ABC-PARAMOUNT

Number	Title	Yr	VG	VG+	NM
❏ (# unknown) [M]	Kansas City Frank Melrose	1956	12.50	25.00	50.00

MEMBERS ONLY
Group led by NELSON RANGELL.
MUSE

Number	Title	Yr	VG	VG+	NM
❏ MR-5332	Members Only	1987	2.50	5.00	10.00
❏ MR-5348	Members Only...Too: The Way You Make Me Feel	1989	3.00	6.00	12.00

MEMPHIS NIGHTHAWKS, THE
DELMARK

Number	Title	Yr	VG	VG+	NM
❏ DS-216	Jazz Lips	197?	3.75	7.50	15.00
GOLDEN CREST					
❏ GC-4162	Stabilizer	1977	3.00	6.00	12.00

MENDELSON, STAN
Pianist.
LAND O' JAZZ

Number	Title	Yr	VG	VG+	NM
❏ 2674	Storyville Piano	1978	2.50	5.00	10.00

MENDES, SERGIO
Pianist and bandleader best known for the jazzy pop sounds of Brasil '66.
A&M

Number	Title	Yr	VG	VG+	NM
❏ LP-116 [M]	Sergio Mendes and Brasil '66	1966	3.00	6.00	12.00
❏ LP-122 [M]	Equinox	1967	3.75	7.50	15.00
❏ SP-3108	Fool on the Hill	198?	2.00	4.00	8.00
-- Budget-line reissue					
❏ SP-3258	Greatest Hits	198?	2.00	4.00	8.00
-- Budget-line reissue					
❏ SP-3522 [(2)]	The Sergio Mendes Foursider	1973	3.75	7.50	15.00
❏ SP-4116 [S]	Sergio Mendes and Brasil '66	1966	3.75	7.50	15.00
❏ SP-4122 [S]	Equinox	1967	3.75	7.50	15.00
❏ SP-4137	Look Around	1968	3.75	7.50	15.00
❏ SP-4160	Fool on the Hill	1968	3.75	7.50	15.00
❏ SP-4197	Crystal Illusions	1969	3.75	7.50	15.00
❏ SP-4236	Ye-Me-Le	1969	3.75	7.50	15.00
❏ SP-4252	Greatest Hits	1970	3.75	7.50	15.00
❏ SP-4284	Stillness	1970	3.75	7.50	15.00
❏ SP-4315	Pais Tropical	1971	3.00	6.00	12.00
❏ SP-4353	Primal Roots	1972	3.00	6.00	12.00
❏ SP-4937	Sergio Mendes	1983	2.50	5.00	10.00
❏ SP-4984	Confetti	1984	2.50	5.00	10.00
❏ SP-5135	Sergio Mendes and Brasil '86	1986	2.50	5.00	10.00
❏ SP-5250	Arara	1989	3.00	6.00	12.00
❏ SP-6012 [(2)]	The Sergio Mendes Foursider	198?	2.50	5.00	10.00
-- Budget-line reissue					
ATLANTIC					
❏ 1434 [M]	The Swinger from Rio	1965	3.75	7.50	15.00
❏ SD 1434 [S]	The Swinger from Rio	1965	5.00	10.00	20.00
❏ 1466 [M]	Great Arrival	1966	3.75	7.50	15.00
❏ SD 1466 [S]	Great Arrival	1966	5.00	10.00	20.00
❏ 1480 [M]	The Beat of Brazil	1967	5.00	10.00	20.00
❏ SD 1480 [S]	The Beat of Brazil	1967	3.75	7.50	15.00
❏ 8112 [M]	Sergio Mendes In Person at the El Matador	1967	5.00	10.00	20.00
❏ SD 8112 [S]	Sergio Mendes In Person at the El Matador	1967	3.75	7.50	15.00
❏ SD 8177	Sergio Mendes' Favorite Things	1968	5.00	10.00	20.00

Number	Title	Yr	VG	VG+	NM
BELL					
❏ 1119	Love Music	1973	2.50	5.00	10.00
❏ 1305	Vintage 74	1974	2.50	5.00	10.00
CAPITOL					
❏ ST 2294 [S]	In a Brazilian Bag	1965	15.00	30.00	60.00
❏ T 2294 [M]	In a Brazilian Bag	1965	12.50	25.00	50.00
ELEKTRA					
❏ 6E-134	Sergio Mendes and Brasil '88	1978	2.50	5.00	10.00
❏ 6E-214	Magic Lady	1980	2.50	5.00	10.00
❏ 7E-1027	Sergio Mendes	1975	2.50	5.00	10.00
❏ EQ-1027 [Q]	Sergio Mendes	1975	3.75	7.50	15.00
❏ 7E-1055	Homecooking	1976	2.50	5.00	10.00
❏ 7E-1102	Sergio Mendes and the New Brasil '77	1977	2.50	5.00	10.00
MOBILE FIDELITY					
❏ 1-118	Sergio Mendes and Brasil '66	1984	12.50	25.00	50.00
-- Audiophile vinyl					
PHILIPS					
❏ PHM 200-263 [M]	Quiet Nights	1968	5.00	10.00	20.00
❏ PHS 600-263 [S]	Quiet Nights	1968	3.75	7.50	15.00
PICKWICK					
❏ SPC-3149	So Nice	1972	2.50	5.00	10.00
TOWER					
❏ ST 5052 [S]	In a Brazilian Bag	1966	12.50	25.00	50.00
-- Reissue of Capitol 2294					
❏ T 5052 [M]	In a Brazilian Bag	1966	10.00	20.00	40.00
-- Reissue of Capitol 2294					

MENGELBERG, MISHA
Pianist.
SOUL NOTE

Number	Title	Yr	VG	VG+	NM
❏ SN-1104	Change of Season	1985	3.00	6.00	12.00

MENZA, DON
Tenor and alto saxophone player, clarinetist and flutist.
CATALYST

Number	Title	Yr	VG	VG+	NM
❏ 7617	First Flight	1976	3.75	7.50	15.00
PALO ALTO					
❏ PA-8010	Flip Pocket	1981	3.00	6.00	12.00
PAUSA					
❏ 7170	Horn of Plenty	1985	2.50	5.00	10.00
REAL TIME					
❏ RT-301	Burnin'	198?	3.75	7.50	15.00
VOSS					
❏ VLP1-42931	Horn of Plenty	1988	2.50	5.00	10.00

MENZLES, HAMISH
MUSIC IS MEDICINE

Number	Title	Yr	VG	VG+	NM
❏ 9028	Jazz Tracks	1979	3.00	6.00	12.00

MERCER, JOHNNY
Male singer; far better known as a composer.
CAPITOL

Number	Title	Yr	VG	VG+	NM
❏ H 210 [10]	Music of Jerome Kern	1950	20.00	40.00	80.00
❏ H 214 [10]	Johnny Mercer Sings	1950	20.00	40.00	80.00
❏ T 907 [M]	Ac-Cent-Tchu-Ate the Positive	1957	12.50	25.00	50.00
JUPITER					
❏ JLP-1001 [M]	Johnny Mercer Sings Just for Fun	1956	12.50	25.00	50.00

MERCER, MABEL
Female singer.
ATLANTIC

Number	Title	Yr	VG	VG+	NM
❏ ALS-402 [10]	Songs by Mabel Mercer, Volume 1	1954	20.00	40.00	80.00
❏ ALS-403 [10]	Songs by Mabel Mercer, Volume 2	1954	20.00	40.00	80.00
❏ 2-602 [(2) M]	The Art of Mabel Mercer	1959	15.00	30.00	60.00
-- Black labels					
❏ 2-602 [(2) M]	The Art of Mabel Mercer	1961	7.50	15.00	30.00
-- Multicolor labels, white "fan" logo at right					
❏ 2-602 [(2) M]	The Art of Mabel Mercer	1963	5.00	10.00	20.00
-- Multicolor labels, black "fan" logo at right					
❏ SD 2-605 [(2)]	The Second Town Hall Concert	1969	5.00	10.00	20.00
❏ 1213 [M]	Mabel Mercer Sings Cole Porter	1955	10.00	20.00	40.00
-- Black label					
❏ 1213 [M]	Mabel Mercer Sings Cole Porter	1961	5.00	10.00	20.00
-- Multicolor label, white "fan" logo at right					
❏ 1213 [M]	Mabel Mercer Sings Cole Porter	1963	3.75	7.50	15.00
-- Multicolor label, black "fan" logo at right					
❏ 1244 [M]	Midnight at Mabel Mercer's	1956	10.00	20.00	40.00
-- Black label					

Number	Title	Yr	VG	VG+	NM
❏ 1244 [M]	Midnight at Mabel Mercer's	1961	5.00	10.00	20.00
-- Multicolor label, white "fan" logo at right					
❏ 1244 [M]	Midnight at Mabel Mercer's	1963	3.75	7.50	15.00
-- Multicolor label, black "fan" logo at right					
❏ 1301 [M]	Once in a Blue Moon	1959	10.00	20.00	40.00
-- Black label					
❏ 1301 [M]	Once in a Blue Moon	1961	5.00	10.00	20.00
-- Multicolor label, white "fan" logo at right					
❏ 1301 [M]	Once in a Blue Moon	1963	3.75	7.50	15.00
-- Multicolor label, black "fan" logo at right					
❏ SD 1301 [S]	Once in a Blue Moon	1959	12.50	25.00	50.00
-- Green label					
❏ SD 1301 [S]	Once in a Blue Moon	1961	6.25	12.50	25.00
-- Multicolor labels, white "fan" logo at right					
❏ SD 1301 [S]	Once in a Blue Moon	1963	5.00	10.00	20.00
-- Multicolor labels, black "fan" logo at right					
❏ 1322 [M]	Merely Marvelous Mabel Mercer	1960	10.00	20.00	40.00
-- Black label					
❏ 1322 [M]	Merely Marvelous Mabel Mercer	1961	5.00	10.00	20.00
-- Multicolor label, white "fan" logo at right					
❏ 1322 [M]	Merely Marvelous Mabel Mercer	1963	3.75	7.50	15.00
-- Multicolor label, black "fan" logo at right					
❏ SD 1322 [S]	Merely Marvelous Mabel Mercer	1960	12.50	25.00	50.00
-- Green label					
❏ SD 1322 [S]	Merely Marvelous Mabel Mercer	1961	6.25	12.50	25.00
-- Multicolor labels, white "fan" logo at right					
❏ SD 1322 [S]	Merely Marvelous Mabel Mercer	1963	5.00	10.00	20.00
-- Multicolor labels, black "fan" logo at right					
❏ 81264	Mabel Mercer Sings Cole Porter	1985	2.50	5.00	10.00
AUDIOPHILE					
❏ AP-161/2 [(2)]	Echoes of My Life	197?	3.75	7.50	15.00
DECCA					
❏ DL 4472 [M]	Mabel Mercer Sings	1964	3.75	7.50	15.00
❏ DL 74472 [S]	Mabel Mercer Sings	1964	5.00	10.00	20.00
STANYAN					
❏ 10108	For Always	197?	3.00	6.00	12.00

MERCER, MABEL, AND BOBBY SHORT
Also see each artist's individual listings.

Number	Title	Yr	VG	VG+	NM
ATLANTIC					
❏ SD 2-604 [(2)]	Mabel Mercer and Bobby Short at Town Hall	1968	5.00	10.00	20.00

MERIAN, LEON
Trumpeter.

Number	Title	Yr	VG	VG+	NM
SEECO					
❏ CELP-447 [M]	This Time the Swing's On Me	1960	3.75	7.50	15.00
❏ CELP-459 [M]	Fiorello!	1960	3.75	7.50	15.00
❏ CELP-4470 [S]	This Time the Swing's On Me	1960	5.00	10.00	20.00
❏ CELP-4590 [S]	Fiorello!	1960	5.00	10.00	20.00

MERIWETHER, ROY
Pianist and composer.

Number	Title	Yr	VG	VG+	NM
CAPITOL					
❏ ST-102	Soul Knight	1969	7.50	15.00	30.00
COLUMBIA					
❏ CL 2433 [M]	Soup and Onions (Soul Cookin')	1966	3.75	7.50	15.00
❏ CL 2498 [M]	Popcorn and Soul Groovin' at the Movies	1966	3.75	7.50	15.00
❏ CL 2584 [M]	Stone Truth	1967	5.00	10.00	20.00
❏ CL 2744 [M]	Soul Invader	1968	7.50	15.00	30.00
❏ CS 9233 [S]	Soup and Onions (Soul Cookin')	1966	5.00	10.00	20.00
❏ CS 9298 [S]	Popcorn and Soul Groovin' at the Movies	1966	5.00	10.00	20.00
❏ CS 9384 [S]	Stone Truth	1967	3.75	7.50	15.00
❏ CS 9544 [S]	Soul Invader	1968	3.75	7.50	15.00

MERRILL, HELEN
Female singer.

Number	Title	Yr	VG	VG+	NM
ATCO					
❏ 33-112 [M]	American Country Songs	1959	10.00	20.00	40.00
CATALYST					
❏ 7903	Helen Merrill Sings and Swings	197?	3.00	6.00	12.00
❏ 7912	Autumn Love	197?	3.00	6.00	12.00
DRG					
❏ SL-5204	The Rodgers & Hammerstein Album	1987	2.50	5.00	10.00
EMARCY					
❏ MG-36006 [M]	Helen Merrill	1955	20.00	40.00	80.00
❏ MG-36057 [M]	Helen Merrill with Strings	1955	20.00	40.00	80.00

Number	Title	Yr	VG	VG+	NM
❏ MG-36078 [M]	Dream of You	1956	15.00	30.00	60.00
❏ MG-36107 [M]	Merrill at Midnight	1957	15.00	30.00	60.00
❏ MG-36134 [M]	The Nearness of You	1958	12.50	25.00	50.00
INNER CITY					
❏ IC-1060	Something Special	1978	3.75	7.50	15.00
❏ IC-1080	Chasin' the Bird	198?	3.75	7.50	15.00
❏ IC-1125	Casa Forte	198?	3.75	7.50	15.00
LANDMARK					
❏ LLP-1308	A Shade of Difference	1986	2.50	5.00	10.00
MAINSTREAM					
❏ S-6014 [S]	The Artistry of Helen Merrill	1965	6.25	12.50	25.00
❏ 56014 [M]	The Artistry of Helen Merrill	1965	6.25	12.50	25.00
MERCURY					
❏ 826 340-1 [(4)]	The Complete Helen Merrill on Mercury	1985	10.00	20.00	40.00
METROJAZZ					
❏ E-1010 [M]	You've Got a Date with the Blues	1958	10.00	20.00	40.00
❏ SE-1010 [S]	You've Got a Date with the Blues	1958	12.50	25.00	50.00
MILESTONE					
❏ MLP-1003 [M]	The Feeling Is Mutual	1967	6.25	12.50	25.00
❏ MLS-9003 [S]	The Feeling Is Mutual	1967	5.00	10.00	20.00
❏ M-9019	Shade of Difference	1969	5.00	10.00	20.00
TRIP					
❏ 5526	Helen Merrill Sings	197?	2.50	5.00	10.00
❏ 5552	Helen Merrill with Strings	197?	2.50	5.00	10.00

MERRILL, HELEN, AND JOHN LEWIS
Also see each artist's individual listings.

Number	Title	Yr	VG	VG+	NM
MERCURY					
❏ SRM-1-1150	Helen Merrill and John Lewis	197?	2.50	5.00	10.00

MESSNER, JOHNNY
Saxophone player, clarinetist and bandleader.

Number	Title	Yr	VG	VG+	NM
HINDSIGHT					
❏ HSR-186	Johnny Messner and His Hotel McAlpin Orchestra 1939-40	198?	2.50	5.00	10.00

METHENY, MIKE
Trumpeter.

Number	Title	Yr	VG	VG+	NM
HEADFIRST					
❏ 9712	Blue Jay Sessions	198?	5.00	10.00	20.00
MCA/IMPULSE!					
❏ 5755	Day In, Night Out	1986	2.50	5.00	10.00

METHENY, PAT
Guitarist (electric, acoustic and hybrids thereof).

Number	Title	Yr	VG	VG+	NM
ECM					
❏ 1073	Bright Size Life	1976	3.00	6.00	12.00
❏ 1097	Watercolors	1977	3.00	6.00	12.00
❏ 1114	Pat Metheny Group	1978	2.50	5.00	10.00
❏ 1131	New Chautauqua	1979	2.50	5.00	10.00
❏ 1155	American Garage	1979	2.50	5.00	10.00
❏ 1180 [(2)]	80/81	1980	3.00	6.00	12.00
❏ 1216	Offramp	1982	2.50	5.00	10.00
❏ 23791 [(2)]	Travels	1983	3.00	6.00	12.00
❏ 25006	Rejoicing	1984	2.50	5.00	10.00
❏ 25008	First Circle	1984	2.50	5.00	10.00
GEFFEN					
❏ GHS 24145	Still Life (Talking)	1987	2.50	5.00	10.00
❏ GHS 24245	Letter from Home	1989	3.00	6.00	12.00
❏ GHS 24293	Question and Answer	1990	3.75	7.50	15.00

METHENY, PAT, AND ORNETTE COLEMAN
Also see each artist's individual listings.

Number	Title	Yr	VG	VG+	NM
GEFFEN					
❏ GHS 24096	Song X	1986	2.50	5.00	10.00

METHENY, PAT, AND LYLE MAYS
Also see each artist's individual listings.

Number	Title	Yr	VG	VG+	NM
ECM					
❏ 1190	As Falls Wichita, So Falls Wichita Falls	1981	2.50	5.00	10.00

METROPOLITAN JAZZ OCTET

Number	Title	Yr	VG	VG+	NM
ARGO					
❏ LP-659 [M]	The Legend of Bix	1960	7.50	15.00	30.00

Number	Title	Yr	VG	VG+	NM

MEZZROW, MEZZ
Clarinetist and bandleader.
BLUE NOTE
| ❑ BLP-7023 [10] | Mezz Mezzrow and His Band | 1952 | 75.00 | 150.00 | 300.00 |
LONDON
| ❑ TKL-93092 [10] | A La Schola Cantorum | 195? | 15.00 | 30.00 | 60.00 |
RCA VICTOR
| ❑ LJM-1006 [M] | Mezzin' Around | 1954 | 12.50 | 25.00 | 50.00 |
SWING
| ❑ SW-8409 | Paris 1955, Volume 1 | 1986 | 2.50 | 5.00 | 10.00 |
"X"
| ❑ LVA-3015 [10] | Mezz Mezzrow's Swing Session | 1954 | 25.00 | 50.00 | 100.00 |
| ❑ LVA-3027 [10] | Mezz Mezzrow | 1954 | 25.00 | 50.00 | 100.00 |

MFG
From the initials of its members: JOE McPHEE; MILO FINE; Steve Gnitka (guitar).
HAT HUT
| ❑ S/T [(2)] | MFG in Minnesota | 1978 | 7.50 | 15.00 | 30.00 |

MICROSCOPIC SEPTET, THE
Led by Phillip Johnston (soprano saxophone). Other members: Joel Forrester (piano); Paul Shapiro (tenor sax); Don Davis (alto sax); Dave Sewelson (baritone sax); David Hofstra (bass and tuba); Richard Dworkin (drums).
OSMOSIS
| ❑ (# unknown) | Off Beat Glory | 198? | 3.00 | 6.00 | 12.00 |
STASH
| ❑ ST-276 | Beauty Based on Science | 1988 | 2.50 | 5.00 | 10.00 |

MIGLIORI, JAY
Tenor and baritone saxophone player; also has played alto sax and flute.
DISCOVERY
| ❑ DS-859 | The Courage | 198? | 2.50 | 5.00 | 10.00 |
PBR
| ❑ 5 | Count the Nights and Times | 197? | 3.75 | 7.50 | 15.00 |
TRANSITION
| ❑ TRLP-18 [M] | Jay Migliori Quintet | 1956 | --- | --- | --- |
-- Canceled

MIL-COMBO, THE
Among the members are Don Mamblow, Connie Milano and Ziggi Milonzi.
CAPITOL
| ❑ T 579 [M] | The Mil-Combo | 1955 | 12.50 | 25.00 | 50.00 |

MILES, BARRY
Keyboard player and drummer.
CENTURY
| ❑ 1070 | Fusion Is... | 1979 | 5.00 | 10.00 | 20.00 |
-- Audiophile edition
CHARLIE PARKER
| ❑ PLP-804 [M] | Miles of Genius | 1962 | 6.25 | 12.50 | 25.00 |
| ❑ PLP-804S [S] | Miles of Genius | 1962 | 7.50 | 15.00 | 30.00 |
GRYPHON
| ❑ 783 | Fusion Is... | 1978 | 3.00 | 6.00 | 12.00 |
LONDON
| ❑ XPS 651 | Silverlight | 1975 | 3.00 | 6.00 | 12.00 |
| ❑ XPS 661 | Magic Theatre | 1975 | 3.00 | 6.00 | 12.00 |
MAINSTREAM
| ❑ MRL-353 | White Heat | 1973 | 3.75 | 7.50 | 15.00 |
| ❑ MRL-382 | Scatbird | 1974 | 3.75 | 7.50 | 15.00 |
POPPY
| ❑ PY-40009 | Barry Miles | 1970 | 5.00 | 10.00 | 20.00 |
RCA VICTOR
| ❑ BGL1-2200 | Sky Train | 1977 | 3.00 | 6.00 | 12.00 |

MILES, BOB
OPTIMISM
| ❑ OP-2003 | Windstorm | 198? | 2.50 | 5.00 | 10.00 |

MILES, BUTCH
Drummer.
DREAMSTREET
| ❑ 102 | Lady Be Good | 1980 | 3.00 | 6.00 | 12.00 |
FAMOUS DOOR
❑ 117	Miles of Swing	1977	3.00	6.00	12.00
❑ 124	Encore	1978	3.00	6.00	12.00
❑ 132	Butch Miles Salutes Chick Webb	1979	3.00	6.00	12.00
❑ 135	Butch Miles Swings Some Standards	1981	2.50	5.00	10.00
❑ 142	Butch Miles Salutes Gene Krupa	1982	2.50	5.00	10.00
❑ 145	Hail to the Chief	1982	2.50	5.00	10.00
❑ 150	More Miles... More Standards	1985	2.50	5.00	10.00

MILES, LIZZIE
Female singer.
COOK
❑ 1181 [10]	Queen Mother of the Rue Royale	1955	15.00	30.00	60.00
❑ 1182 [M]	Moans and Blues	195?	12.50	25.00	50.00
❑ 1183 [M]	Hot Songs My Mother Taught Me	195?	12.50	25.00	50.00
❑ 1184 [M]	Torchy Lullabies My Mother Taught Me	195?	12.50	25.00	50.00

MILESTONE JAZZSTARS, THE
Members: RON CARTER; SONNY ROLLINS; McCOY TYNER.
MILESTONE
| ❑ 55006 [(2)] | Milestone Jazzstars In Concert | 1978 | 3.75 | 7.50 | 15.00 |

MILL CITY SEVEN, THE
JAZZOLOGY
| ❑ J-19 | The Mill City Seven | 1974 | 2.50 | 5.00 | 10.00 |

MILLER, CLARENCE "BIG"
Male singer.
COLUMBIA
❑ CL 1611 [M]	Revelation and the Blues	1961	6.25	12.50	25.00
❑ CL 1808 [M]	Big Miller Sings, Twists, Shouts and Preaches	1962	6.25	12.50	25.00
❑ CS 8411 [S]	Revelation and the Blues	1961	7.50	15.00	30.00
❑ CS 8608 [S]	Big Miller Sings, Twists, Shouts and Preaches	1962	7.50	15.00	30.00
UNITED ARTISTS
| ❑ UAL-3047 [M] | Did You Ever Hear the Blues? | 1959 | 10.00 | 20.00 | 40.00 |
| ❑ UAS-6047 [S] | Did You Ever Hear the Blues? | 1959 | 15.00 | 30.00 | 60.00 |

MILLER, DON
Guitarist.
KING
| ❑ 712 [M] | The Don Miller Quartet | 1960 | 15.00 | 30.00 | 60.00 |

MILLER, EDDIE
Tenor saxophone player, clarinetist and male singer.
CAPITOL
| ❑ T 614 [M] | Classics in Jazz | 1955 | 12.50 | 25.00 | 50.00 |
FAMOUS DOOR
| ❑ 131 | It's Miller Time | 1979 | 3.00 | 6.00 | 12.00 |

MILLER, EDDIE, AND ARMAND HUG
Also see each artist's individual listings.
LAND O' JAZZ
| ❑ 5876 | Just Friends | 1979 | 3.00 | 6.00 | 12.00 |

MILLER, EDDIE/GEORGE VAN EPS
Also see each artist's individual listings.
JUMP
| ❑ JL-5 [10] | Eddie Miller/George Van Eps | 1953 | 12.50 | 25.00 | 50.00 |

MILLER, GARY
CIRCLE
| ❑ 2 | Gary Miller and the Celebration Road Show Live On Stage | 197? | 2.50 | 5.00 | 10.00 |

MILLER, GLENN
Trombonist, bandleader, arranger and composer. Led the most popular of all the big bands; it was so popular that more than five decades after his death, there is still a GLENN MILLER ORCHESTRA that tours regularly.
BLUEBIRD
❑ AXM2-5512 [(2)]	The Complete Glenn Miller Volume 1, 1938-39	1975	3.00	6.00	12.00
❑ AXM2-5514 [(2)]	The Complete Glenn Miller Volume 2, 1939	1975	3.00	6.00	12.00
❑ AXM2-5534 [(2)]	The Complete Glenn Miller Volume 3, 1939-40	197?	3.00	6.00	12.00
❑ AXM2-5558 [(2)]	The Complete Glenn Miller Volume 4, 1940	197?	3.00	6.00	12.00
❑ AXM2-5565 [(2)]	The Complete Glenn Miller Volume 5, 1940	197?	3.00	6.00	12.00
❑ AXM2-5569 [(2)]	The Complete Glenn Miller Volume 6, 1940-41	197?	3.00	6.00	12.00
❑ AXM2-5570 [(2)]	The Complete Glenn Miller Volume 7, 1941	197?	3.00	6.00	12.00

Glenn Miller was the most popular of the big-band leaders. Because of that popularity, though, the original 78s of most of his hits are common by 78 rpm standards and are not valuable. Instead, it's the reissued mono albums, especially from the 1950s, that collectors seek. (Top left) One of the earliest compilations of Miller material into an LP was this 10-incher from the early 1950s. (Top right) Until the early 1950s, recordings by Miller's Army Air Force Band, which he led in Europe in the 1943-44 era, had not been legitimately released. But radio airchecks and rehearsals were found, leading to, among others, this album with the suitably cheesy album cover. (Bottom left) Not as well-known or as important as Benny Goodman's concert there, Miller, nonetheless, played Carnegie Hall, too. (Bottom right) From the "This Is" series that RCA did in the early 1970s, here's a two-record set of Army Air Force Band material.

Number	Title	Yr	VG	VG+	NM
❑ AXM2-5571 [(2)]	The Complete Glenn Miller Volume 8, 1941-42	197?	3.00	6.00	12.00
❑ AXM2-5574 [(2)]	The Complete Glenn Miller Volume 9, 1939-42	197?	3.00	6.00	12.00
❑ 6360-1-RB	Maj. Glenn Miller and the Army Air Force Band	1987	2.50	5.00	10.00
❑ 9785-1-RB [(4)]	The Popular Recordings 1938-1942	1989	6.25	12.50	25.00

EPIC

Number	Title	Yr	VG	VG+	NM
❑ LA 16002 [M]	Glenn Miller	1960	5.00	10.00	20.00

HARMONY

Number	Title	Yr	VG	VG+	NM
❑ HS 11393 [R]	Collector's Choice	1970	3.00	6.00	12.00

INTERMEDIA

Number	Title	Yr	VG	VG+	NM
❑ QS-5045	A String of Pearls	198?	2.00	4.00	8.00

KOALA

Number	Title	Yr	VG	VG+	NM
❑ AW 14186	Chattanooga Choo Choo	1979	3.00	6.00	12.00

MERCURY

Number	Title	Yr	VG	VG+	NM
❑ 826 635-1 [(2)]	Glenn Miller In Hollywood	1986	3.00	6.00	12.00

-- Reissue of material formerly on 20th Century

MOVIETONE

Number	Title	Yr	VG	VG+	NM
❑ MTM-1003 [M]	Glenn Miller's Shindig	1965	3.75	7.50	15.00
❑ MTS-2003 [R]	Glenn Miller's Shindig	1965	2.50	5.00	10.00
❑ MTS-72018 [R]	The Glenn Miller Years	1967	3.00	6.00	12.00

PAIR

Number	Title	Yr	VG	VG+	NM
❑ PDL2-1003 [(2)]	Original Recordings, Volume 1	1986	3.00	6.00	12.00
❑ PDL2-1036 [(2)]	Original Recordings, Volume 2	1986	3.00	6.00	12.00

RCA

Number	Title	Yr	VG	VG+	NM
❑ 7648-1-R	Pure Gold	1988	---	3.00	6.00
❑ 7652-1-R	The Best of Glenn Miller	1988	---	3.00	6.00

RCA CAMDEN

Number	Title	Yr	VG	VG+	NM
❑ ACL2-0168 [(2)]	A String of Pearls	1973	3.00	6.00	12.00
❑ ACL-0503	This Time the Dream's On Me	1974	2.00	4.00	8.00
❑ CAL-751 [M]	The Great Glenn Miller	1963	3.75	7.50	15.00
❑ CAS-751(e) [R]	The Great Glenn Miller	1963	3.00	6.00	12.00
❑ CAL-829 [M]	The Original Recordings	1964	3.75	7.50	15.00
❑ CAS-829(e) [R]	The Original Recordings	1964	3.00	6.00	12.00
❑ CAL-2128 [M]	The Nearness of You and Others	1967	3.75	7.50	15.00
❑ CAS-2128 [R]	The Nearness of You and Others	1967	3.00	6.00	12.00
❑ CAS-2267	The One and Only Glenn Miller	1968	2.50	5.00	10.00
❑ CXS-9004 [(2)]	Sunrise Serenade	197?	3.00	6.00	12.00

RCA VICTOR

Number	Title	Yr	VG	VG+	NM
❑ LPT-16 [10]	Glenn Miller Concert -- Volume 1	1951	15.00	30.00	60.00
❑ LPT-30 [10]	Glenn Miller Concert -- Volume 2	1951	15.00	30.00	60.00
❑ LPT-31 [10]	Glenn Miller	1951	15.00	30.00	60.00
❑ PR-114 [M]	Glenn Miller Originals	1962	5.00	10.00	20.00

-- Promotional item for Salada Foods Inc.

Number	Title	Yr	VG	VG+	NM
❑ CPM2-0693 [(2)]	A Legendary Performer	1974	3.00	6.00	12.00
❑ ANL1-0974	Pure Gold	1975	2.00	4.00	8.00
❑ LOP-1005 [M]	The Marvelous Miller Medleys	1955	10.00	20.00	40.00
❑ LPT-1016 [M]	Juke Box Saturday Night	1955	10.00	20.00	40.00
❑ LPT-1031 [M]	The Nearness of You	1955	10.00	20.00	40.00
❑ ANL1-1139	The Chesterfield Broadcasts, Volume 1	1975	2.00	4.00	8.00
❑ LPM-1189 [M]	The Sound of Glenn Miller	1956	10.00	20.00	40.00
❑ LPM-1190 [M]	This Is Glenn Miller	1956	10.00	20.00	40.00
❑ AFL1-1192	Selections from "The Glenn Miller Story" and Other Hits	1977	2.00	4.00	8.00
❑ LPM-1192 [M]	Selections from "The Glenn Miller Story" and Other Hits	1956	10.00	20.00	40.00
❑ LSP-1192 [R]	Selections from "The Glenn Miller Story" and Other Hits	196?	3.75	7.50	15.00
❑ LPM-1193 [M]	Glenn Miller Concert	1956	10.00	20.00	40.00
❑ LPM-1494 [M]	Marvelous Miller Moods	1957	10.00	20.00	40.00
❑ LPM-1506 [M]	The Glenn Miller Carnegie Hall Concert	1957	10.00	20.00	40.00
❑ LPM-1973 [M]	The Marvelous Miller Medleys	1959	7.50	15.00	30.00
❑ LSP-1973 [R]	The Marvelous Miller Medleys	196?	3.75	7.50	15.00
❑ CPL1-2080	A Legendary Performer, Volume 2	1976	2.50	5.00	10.00
❑ CPL1-2495	A Legendary Performer, Volume 3	1977	2.50	5.00	10.00
❑ LPM-2767 [M]	Glenn Miller On the Air Volume 1	1963	3.75	7.50	15.00
❑ LSP-2767 [R]	Glenn Miller On the Air Volume 1	1963	2.50	5.00	10.00
❑ LPM-2768 [M]	Glenn Miller On the Air Volume 2	1963	3.75	7.50	15.00
❑ LSP-2768 [R]	Glenn Miller On the Air Volume 2	1963	2.50	5.00	10.00
❑ LPM-2769 [M]	Glenn Miller On the Air Volume 3	1963	3.75	7.50	15.00
❑ LSP-2769 [R]	Glenn Miller On the Air Volume 3	1963	2.50	5.00	10.00

Number	Title	Yr	VG	VG+	NM
❑ AFL1-2825	The Best of Glenn Miller Volume 3	1978	2.00	4.00	8.00
❑ LPT-3001 [10]	Glenn Miller Concert -- Volume 3	195?	15.00	30.00	60.00
❑ LPT-3002 [10]	This Is Glenn Miller	195?	15.00	30.00	60.00
❑ LPT-3036 [10]	This Is Glenn Miller -- Volume 2	195?	15.00	30.00	60.00
❑ LPT-3057 [10]	Selections from the Film "The Glenn Miller Story"	1954	15.00	30.00	60.00
❑ LPT-3067 [10]	Sunrise Serenade	1954	15.00	30.00	60.00
❑ LPM-3377 [M]	The Best of Glenn Miller	1965	3.75	7.50	15.00
❑ LSP-3377 [R]	The Best of Glenn Miller	1965	2.50	5.00	10.00
❑ LPM-3564 [M]	The Best of Glenn Miller Volume 2	1966	3.75	7.50	15.00
❑ LSP-3564 [R]	The Best of Glenn Miller Volume 2	1966	2.50	5.00	10.00
❑ LPM-3657 [M]	Blue Moonlight	1966	3.75	7.50	15.00
❑ LSP-3657 [R]	Blue Moonlight	1966	2.50	5.00	10.00
❑ AYL1-3666	Pure Gold	1980	---	3.00	6.00
❑ AYL1-3759	Selections from "The Glenn Miller Story" and Other Hits	1981	---	3.00	6.00
❑ AYL1-3809	The Best of Glenn Miller Volume 2	1981	---	3.00	6.00
❑ AYL1-3810	The Best of Glenn Miller Volume 3	1981	---	3.00	6.00
❑ AYL1-3871	The Best of Glenn Miller	1981	---	3.00	6.00
❑ LPM-3873 [M]	The Chesterfield Broadcasts, Volume 1	1967	3.75	7.50	15.00
❑ LSP-3873 [R]	The Chesterfield Broadcasts, Volume 1	1967	2.50	5.00	10.00
❑ LSP-3981 [R]	The Chesterfield Broadcasts, Volume 2	1968	3.00	6.00	12.00
❑ LSP-4125 [R]	The Best of Glenn Miller Volume 3	1969	3.00	6.00	12.00
❑ VPM-6019 [(2)]	Glenn Miller: A Memorial 1944-1969	1969	3.75	7.50	15.00
❑ VPM-6080 [(2)]	This Is Glenn Miller's Army Air Force Band	1972	3.75	7.50	15.00
❑ LPM-6100 [(3) M]	For the Very First Time...	195?	12.50	25.00	50.00

-- Black "Long Play" labels in leatherette spiral-bound binder

Number	Title	Yr	VG	VG+	NM
❑ LPM-6101 [(3) M]	Glenn Miller On the Air	1963	10.00	20.00	40.00
❑ LSP-6101 [(3) R]	Glenn Miller On the Air	1963	6.25	12.50	25.00
❑ LPT-6700 [(5) M]	Glenn Miller and His Orchestra Limited Edition	1953	37.50	75.00	150.00

-- Silver labels with red print in leatherette spiral-bound binder

Number	Title	Yr	VG	VG+	NM
❑ LPT-6700 [(5) M]	Glenn Miller and His Orchestra Limited Edition -- Second Pressing	195?	15.00	30.00	60.00

-- Black "Long Play" labels in leatherette spiral-bound binder

Number	Title	Yr	VG	VG+	NM
❑ LPT-6701 [(5) M]	Glenn Miller and His Orchestra Limited Edition Volume Two	1954	30.00	60.00	120.00

-- Black "Long Play" labels in leatherette spiral-bound binder

Number	Title	Yr	VG	VG+	NM
❑ LPT-6701 [(5) M]	Glenn Miller and His Orchestra Limited Edition Volume Two -- Second Pressing	195?	15.00	30.00	60.00

-- Black "Long Play" labels in leatherette spiral-bound binder; identified as "Second Pressing" throughout

Number	Title	Yr	VG	VG+	NM
❑ LPT-6702 [(4) M]	Glenn Miller Army Air Force Band	1955	30.00	60.00	120.00

-- Black "Long Play" labels in leatherette spiral-bound binder

Number	Title	Yr	VG	VG+	NM
❑ LPT-6702 [(4) M]	Glenn Miller Army Air Force Band	195?	15.00	30.00	60.00

-- Same as above, but in box rather than in binder

20TH CENTURY

Number	Title	Yr	VG	VG+	NM
❑ T2-904 [(2)]	Remember Glenn	197?	3.75	7.50	15.00

20TH CENTURY FOX

Number	Title	Yr	VG	VG+	NM
❑ TFM-3159 [M]	This Is Glenn Miller and His Greatest Orchestra, Volume 1	1964	3.75	7.50	15.00
❑ TFM-3160 [M]	This Is Glenn Miller and His Greatest Orchestra, Volume 2	1964	3.75	7.50	15.00
❑ TFS-4159 [R]	This Is Glenn Miller and His Greatest Orchestra, Volume 1	1964	2.50	5.00	10.00
❑ TFS-4160 [R]	This Is Glenn Miller and His Greatest Orchestra, Volume 2	1964	2.50	5.00	10.00

20TH FOX

Number	Title	Yr	VG	VG+	NM
❑ TCF-100-2 [(2) M]	Glenn Miller and His Orchestra Original Film Sound Tracks	1958	7.50	15.00	30.00
❑ TCF-100-2S [(2) R]	Glenn Miller and His Orchestra Original Film Sound Tracks	1961	5.00	10.00	20.00

MILLER, GLENN, ORCHESTRA (BUDDY DeFRANCO, DIRECTOR)

Also see BUDDY DeFRANCO.

EPIC

Number	Title	Yr	VG	VG+	NM
❑ LN 24206 [M]	Something New	1966	3.00	6.00	12.00
❑ BN 26206 [S]	Something New	1966	3.75	7.50	15.00

PARAMOUNT

Number	Title	Yr	VG	VG+	NM
❑ PAS-5034	The Glenn Miller Orchestra	1970	3.00	6.00	12.00

RCA VICTOR

Number	Title	Yr	VG	VG+	NM
❑ LPM-3819 [M]	In the Mod	1967	3.75	7.50	15.00

Number	Title	Yr	VG	VG+	NM
❑ LSP-3819 [S]	In the Mod	1967	3.00	6.00	12.00
❑ LPM-3880 [M]	The Glenn Miller Orchestra Returns to the Glen Island Casino	1968	5.00	10.00	20.00
❑ LSP-3880 [S]	The Glenn Miller Orchestra Returns to the Glen Island Casino	1968	3.00	6.00	12.00
❑ LPM-3971 [M]	The Glenn Miller Orchestra Makes the Goin' Great	1968	10.00	20.00	40.00
❑ LSP-3971 [S]	The Glenn Miller Orchestra Makes the Goin' Great	1968	3.00	6.00	12.00

MILLER, GLENN, ORCHESTRA (RAY McKINLEY, DIRECTOR)
Also see RAY McKINLEY.
EPIC

Number	Title	Yr	VG	VG+	NM
❑ LN 24133 [M]	Glenn Miller Time -- 1965	1965	3.75	7.50	15.00
❑ LN 24157 [M]	Great Songs of the 60's	1965	3.75	7.50	15.00
❑ BN 26133 [S]	Glenn Miller Time -- 1965	1965	5.00	10.00	20.00
❑ BN 26157 [S]	Great Songs of the 60's	1965	5.00	10.00	20.00

RCA VICTOR

Number	Title	Yr	VG	VG+	NM
❑ LPM-1522 [M]	The New Glenn Miller Orchestra in Hi-Fi	1957	7.50	15.00	30.00
❑ LSP-1522 [S]	The New Glenn Miller Orchestra in Hi-Fi	1958	10.00	20.00	40.00
❑ LPM-1678 [M]	Something Old, New, Borrowed and Blue	1958	7.50	15.00	30.00
❑ LSP-1678 [S]	Something Old, New, Borrowed and Blue	1958	10.00	20.00	40.00
❑ LPM-1852 [M]	The Miller Sound	1959	7.50	15.00	30.00
❑ LSP-1852 [S]	The Miller Sound	1959	10.00	20.00	40.00
❑ LPM-1948 [M]	On Tour with the New Glenn Miller Orchestra	1959	7.50	15.00	30.00
❑ LSP-1948 [S]	On Tour with the New Glenn Miller Orchestra	1959	10.00	20.00	40.00
❑ LPM-2080 [M]	The Great Dance Bands of the 30's and 40's	1960	6.25	12.50	25.00
❑ LSP-2080 [S]	The Great Dance Bands of the 30's and 40's	1960	7.50	15.00	30.00
❑ LPM-2193 [M]	Dance, Anyone?	1960	6.25	12.50	25.00
❑ LSP-2193 [S]	Dance, Anyone?	1960	7.50	15.00	30.00
❑ LPM-2270 [M]	The Authentic Sound of the New Glenn Miller Orchestra -- Today	1961	6.25	12.50	25.00
❑ LSP-2270 [S]	The Authentic Sound of the New Glenn Miller Orchestra -- Today	1961	7.50	15.00	30.00
❑ LPM-2436 [M]	Glenn Miller Time	1961	6.25	12.50	25.00
❑ LSP-2436 [S]	Glenn Miller Time	1961	7.50	15.00	30.00
❑ LPM-2519 [M]	Echoes of Glenn Miller	1962	6.25	12.50	25.00
❑ LSP-2519 [S]	Echoes of Glenn Miller	1962	7.50	15.00	30.00

MILLER, MULGREW
Pianist.
LANDMARK

Number	Title	Yr	VG	VG+	NM
❑ LLP-1507	Keys to the City	198?	2.50	5.00	10.00
❑ LLP-1511	Work!	1986	2.50	5.00	10.00
❑ LLP-1515	Wingspan	1988	2.50	5.00	10.00
❑ LLP-1519	The Countdown	1989	3.00	6.00	12.00
❑ LLP-1525	From Day to Day	1990	3.00	6.00	12.00

MILLER, PUNCH
Trumpeter and male singer. Also see PAUL BARBARIN.
HERWIN

Number	Title	Yr	VG	VG+	NM
❑ 108	Jazz Rarities 1929-30	197?	2.50	5.00	10.00

IMPERIAL

Number	Title	Yr	VG	VG+	NM
❑ LP-9160 [M]	Hongo Fongo	1962	6.25	12.50	25.00

JAZZ CRUSADE

Number	Title	Yr	VG	VG+	NM
❑ 2016	Oh Lady Be Good	196?	3.75	7.50	15.00

JAZZOLOGY

Number	Title	Yr	VG	VG+	NM
❑ JCE-12	Kid Punch	1967	3.75	7.50	15.00
❑ J-17	River's in Mourning	197?	2.50	5.00	10.00

SAVOY

Number	Title	Yr	VG	VG+	NM
❑ MG-12038 [M]	Jazz: New Orleans, Volume 1	1955	12.50	25.00	50.00
❑ MG-12050 [M]	Jazz: New Orleans, Volume 2	1955	12.50	25.00	50.00

MILLMAN, JACK
Trumpet and fluegel horn player.
DECCA

Number	Title	Yr	VG	VG+	NM
❑ DL 8156 [M]	Jazz Studio 4	1955	12.50	25.00	50.00

ERA

Number	Title	Yr	VG	VG+	NM
❑ EL-20005 [M]	Blowing Up a Storm	1956	15.00	30.00	60.00
-- Red vinyl					
❑ EL-20005 [M]	Blowing Up a Storm	1956	10.00	20.00	40.00
-- Black vinyl					

LIBERTY

Number	Title	Yr	VG	VG+	NM
❑ LJH-6007 [M]	Shades of Things to Come	1956	12.50	25.00	50.00

MINASI, DOM
Guitarist.
BLUE NOTE

Number	Title	Yr	VG	VG+	NM
❑ BN-LA258-G	When Joanna Loved Me	1974	3.75	7.50	15.00
❑ BN-LA426-G	I Have the Feeling I've Been Here	1975	3.75	7.50	15.00

MINCE, JOHNNY
Saxophone player and clarinetist.
JAZZOLOGY

Number	Title	Yr	VG	VG+	NM
❑ J-126	The Master Comes Home	1985	2.50	5.00	10.00
❑ J-163	Summer of '79	1989	2.50	5.00	10.00

MONMOUTH-EVERGREEN

Number	Title	Yr	VG	VG+	NM
❑ 7090	Summer of '79	1979	3.00	6.00	12.00

MINERVA JAZZ BAND
STOMP OFF

Number	Title	Yr	VG	VG+	NM
❑ SOS-1117	A Pile of Logs and Stone Called Home	1986	2.50	5.00	10.00

MINGUS DYNASTY
Loose aggregation of musicians, most of whom had played in various CHARLES MINGUS bands, formed after Mingus' death.
ELEKTRA

Number	Title	Yr	VG	VG+	NM
❑ 6E-248	Chair in the Sky	1980	2.50	5.00	10.00

SOUL NOTE

Number	Title	Yr	VG	VG+	NM
❑ SN-1042	Reincarnation	1982	3.00	6.00	12.00
❑ SN-1142	Mingus' Sound of Love	1988	3.00	6.00	12.00

MINGUS, CHARLES
Bass player, composer, bandleader and arranger. Also see DUKE ELLINGTON; JAZZ ARTISTS GUILD; JONI MITCHELL; THE QUINTET.
ABC IMPULSE!

Number	Title	Yr	VG	VG+	NM
❑ AS-35 [S]	Black Saint and Sinner Lady	1968	5.00	10.00	20.00
❑ AS-54 [S]	Mingus, Mingus, Mingus, Mingus, Mingus	1968	5.00	10.00	20.00
❑ AS-60 [S]	Charlie Mingus Plays Piano	1968	5.00	10.00	20.00
❑ AS-9234 [(2)]	Reevaluation -- The Impulse Years	1973	3.75	7.50	15.00

ARCHIVE OF FOLK AND JAZZ

Number	Title	Yr	VG	VG+	NM
❑ 235	Charlie Mingus	1969	3.00	6.00	12.00

ATLANTIC

Number	Title	Yr	VG	VG+	NM
❑ SD 2-302 [(2)]	The Art of Charles Mingus	1973	3.75	7.50	15.00
❑ SD 3-600 [(3)]	Passions of a Man: The Charles Mingus Anthology	1980	5.00	10.00	20.00
❑ 1237 [M]	Pithecanthropus Erectus	1956	20.00	40.00	80.00
-- Black label					
❑ 1237 [M]	Pithecanthropus Erectus	1961	6.25	12.50	25.00
-- Multicolor label, white "fan" logo at right					
❑ 1237 [M]	Pithecanthropus Erectus	1964	5.00	10.00	20.00
-- Multicolor label, black "fan" logo at right					
❑ 1260 [M]	The Clown	1957	20.00	40.00	80.00
-- Black label					
❑ 1260 [M]	The Clown	1961	6.25	12.50	25.00
-- Multicolor label, white "fan" logo at right					
❑ 1260 [M]	The Clown	1964	5.00	10.00	20.00
-- Multicolor label, black "fan" logo at right					
❑ 1305 [M]	Blues & Roots	1959	15.00	30.00	60.00
-- White "bullseye" label					
❑ 1305 [M]	Blues & Roots	1961	6.25	12.50	25.00
-- Multicolor label, white "fan" logo at right					
❑ 1305 [M]	Blues & Roots	1964	5.00	10.00	20.00
-- Multicolor label, black "fan" logo at right					
❑ SD 1305 [S]	Blues & Roots	1959	15.00	30.00	60.00
-- White "bullseye" label					
❑ SD 1305 [S]	Blues & Roots	1961	5.00	10.00	20.00
-- Multicolor label, white "fan" logo at right					
❑ SD 1305 [S]	Blues & Roots	1964	3.75	7.50	15.00
-- Multicolor label, black "fan" logo at right					
❑ 1377 [M]	Oh, Yeah	1961	6.25	12.50	25.00
-- Multicolor label, white "fan" logo at right					
❑ 1377 [M]	Oh, Yeah	1964	3.75	7.50	15.00
-- Multicolor label, black "fan" logo at right					
❑ SD 1377 [S]	Oh, Yeah	1961	7.50	15.00	30.00
-- Multicolor label, white "fan" logo at right					
❑ SD 1377 [S]	Oh, Yeah	1964	5.00	10.00	20.00
-- Multicolor label, black "fan" logo at right					
❑ 1417 [M]	Tonight at Noon	1964	6.25	12.50	25.00
❑ SD 1417 [S]	Tonight at Noon	1964	7.50	15.00	30.00
❑ SD 1555	The Best of Charles Mingus	1970	3.75	7.50	15.00
❑ SD 1653	Mingus Moves	1974	3.00	6.00	12.00
❑ SD 1667	Mingus at Carnegie Hall	1974	3.00	6.00	12.00
❑ SD 1677	Changes 1	1975	3.00	6.00	12.00
❑ SD 1678	Changes 2	1975	3.00	6.00	12.00
❑ SD 1700	3 or 4 Shades	1977	3.00	6.00	12.00

Number	Title	Yr	VG	VG+	NM
❏ SD 3001 [(2)]	Charles Mingus at Antibes	1979	3.75	7.50	15.00
❏ SD 8801	Cumbia & Jazz Fusion	197?	3.00	6.00	12.00
❏ SD 8803	Me, Myself An Eye	1979	3.00	6.00	12.00
❏ SD 8805	Something Like a Bird	1979	3.00	6.00	12.00
❏ SD 8809	Pithecanthropus Erectus	198?	2.50	5.00	10.00
❏ 90142	The Clown	198?	2.50	5.00	10.00
BARNABY					
❏ BR-5012	Charles Mingus Presents	1978	3.00	6.00	12.00
❏ BR-6015	Stormy Weather	1976	3.00	6.00	12.00
❏ Z 30561	Charles Mingus Presents the Quartet	1971	3.75	7.50	15.00
❏ KZ 31034	The Candid Recordings	1972	3.75	7.50	15.00
BETHLEHEM					
❏ BCP-65 [M]	The Jazz Experiment of Charlie Mingus	1956	25.00	50.00	100.00
❏ BCP-6019 [M]	East Coasting	1957	25.00	50.00	100.00
❏ BCP-6019	East Coasting	197?	3.75	7.50	15.00
-- Reissue, distributed by RCA Victor					
❏ BCP-6026 [M]	A Modern Jazz Symposium of Jazz and Poetry	1958	25.00	50.00	100.00
BLUEBIRD					
❏ 5644-1-RB [(2)]	New Tijuana Moods	1986	3.75	7.50	15.00
CANDID					
❏ CD-8005 [M]	Charles Mingus Presents Charles Mingus	1960	10.00	20.00	40.00
❏ CD-8021 [M]	Mingus	1960	10.00	20.00	40.00
❏ CS-9005 [S]	Charles Mingus Presents Charles Mingus	1960	12.50	25.00	50.00
❏ CS-9021 [S]	Mingus	1960	12.50	25.00	50.00
CHARLES MINGUS					
❏ JWS-001/2 [(2)]	Mingus at Monterey	1966	175.00	350.00	700.00
-- Single-pocket jacket with sepia-tone photo on front					
❏ JWS-001/2 [(2)]	Mingus at Monterey	1966	75.00	150.00	300.00
-- Gatefold jacket with color photo on front; "This album can be purchased only by mail" on back cover					
❏ JWS-001/2 [(2)]	Mingus at Monterey	1968	15.00	30.00	60.00
-- Gatefold jacket with color photo on front; distributed by Fantasy					
❏ JWS-005	My Favorite Quintet	1966	75.00	150.00	300.00
-- "This album can be purchased only by mail" on back cover					
❏ JWS-009	Town Hall Concert 1964, Vol. 1	1966	75.00	150.00	300.00
-- "This album can be purchased only by mail" on back cover					
❏ JWS-013/14 [(2)]	Special Music Written For (But Not Heard At) Monterey	1966	250.00	500.00	1,000.
-- Single-pocket jacket; "This album can be purchased only by mail" on back cover					
COLUMBIA					
❏ CL 1370 [M]	Mingus Ah Um	1959	10.00	20.00	40.00
-- Red and black label with six "eye" logos					
❏ CL 1370 [M]	Mingus Ah Um	1963	6.25	12.50	25.00
-- Red label with "Guaranteed High Fidelity" at bottom					
❏ CL 1370 [M]	Mingus Ah Um	1966	5.00	10.00	20.00
-- Red label with "360 Sound Mono" at bottom					
❏ CL 1440 [M]	Mingus Dynasty	1960	7.50	15.00	30.00
-- Red and black label with six "eye" logos					
❏ CL 1440 [M]	Mingus Dynasty	1963	5.00	10.00	20.00
-- Red label with "Guaranteed High Fidelity" at bottom					
❏ CL 1440 [M]	Mingus Dynasty	1966	3.75	7.50	15.00
-- Red label with "360 Sound Mono" at bottom					
❏ CS 8171 [S]	Mingus Ah Um	1959	15.00	30.00	60.00
-- Red and black label with six "eye" logos					
❏ CS 8171 [S]	Mingus Ah Um	1963	7.50	15.00	30.00
-- Red label with "360 Sound Stereo" in black at bottom					
❏ CS 8171 [S]	Mingus Ah Um	1966	6.25	12.50	25.00
-- Red label with "360 Sound Stereo" in white at bottom					
❏ CS 8171 [S]	Mingus Ah Um	1971	3.00	6.00	12.00
-- Orange label, "Columbia" repeated along edge					
❏ CS 8171 [S]	Mingus Ah Um	199?	6.25	12.50	25.00
-- Classic Records reissue on audiophile vinyl					
❏ PC 8171	Mingus Ah Um	198?	2.00	4.00	8.00
-- Budget-line reissue with new prefix					
❏ CS 8236 [S]	Mingus Dynasty	1960	10.00	20.00	40.00
-- Red and black label with six "eye" logos					
❏ CS 8236 [S]	Mingus Dynasty	1963	6.25	12.50	25.00
-- Red label with "360 Sound Stereo" in black at bottom					
❏ CS 8236 [S]	Mingus Dynasty	1966	5.00	10.00	20.00
-- Red label with "360 Sound Stereo" in white at bottom					
❏ CS 8236 [S]	Mingus Dynasty	1971	3.00	6.00	12.00
-- Orange label, "Columbia" repeated along edge					
❏ G 30628 [(2)]	Better Git It in Your Soul	1971	5.00	10.00	20.00
❏ CG 30628 [(2)]	Better Git It in Your Soul	197?	3.00	6.00	12.00
-- Reissue with new prefix					
❏ KC 31039	Let My Children Hear Music	1972	3.75	7.50	15.00
❏ PC 31039	Let My Children Hear Music	198?	2.00	4.00	8.00
-- Reissue with new prefix					
❏ KG 31814 [(2)]	Charles Mingus and Friends	1973	5.00	10.00	20.00
❏ JG 35717 [(2)]	Nostalgia in Times Square	1979	3.75	7.50	15.00
COLUMBIA JAZZ MASTERPIECES					
❏ CJ 40648	Mingus Ah Um	1987	2.50	5.00	10.00
❏ CJ 44050	Shoes of the Fisherman's Wife	1988	2.50	5.00	10.00

Number	Title	Yr	VG	VG+	NM
DEBUT					
❏ DLP-1 [10]	Strings and Keys	1953	125.00	250.00	500.00
❏ DEB-123 [M]	Mingus at the Bohemia	1956	50.00	100.00	200.00
❏ DEB-139 [M]	The Charlie Mingus Quintet + Max Roach	1956	---	---	---
-- Canceled					
ENJA					
❏ 3077	Mingus in Europe	198?	3.00	6.00	12.00
FANTASY					
❏ JWS-001/2 [(2)]	Mingus at Monterey	1969	5.00	10.00	20.00
-- Reissue of Charles Mingus 001/2					
❏ JWS-005	My Favorite Quintet	1969	3.75	7.50	15.00
-- Reissue of Charles Mingus 005					
❏ JWS-009	Town Hall Concert 1964, Vol. 1	1969	3.75	7.50	15.00
-- Reissue of Charles Mingus 009					
❏ OJC-042	Town Hall Concert 1964	198?	2.50	5.00	10.00
❏ OJC-045	Mingus at the Bohemia	198?	2.50	5.00	10.00
❏ OJC-237	Right Now -- Live at the Jazz Workshop	198?	2.50	5.00	10.00
❏ OJC-440	The Charlie Mingus Quartet + Max Roach	1990	3.00	6.00	12.00
❏ 6002 [M]	Chazz!	1962	12.50	25.00	50.00
-- Red vinyl					
❏ 6002 [M]	Chazz!	1962	7.50	15.00	30.00
-- Black vinyl					
❏ 6009 [M]	The Charlie Mingus Quartet + Max Roach	1963	7.50	15.00	30.00
❏ 6017 [M]	Right Now -- Live at the Jazz Workshop	1966	6.25	12.50	25.00
❏ 86002 [R]	Chazz!	196?	6.25	12.50	25.00
-- Blue vinyl					
❏ 86002 [R]	Chazz!	196?	3.75	7.50	15.00
-- Black vinyl					
❏ 86009 [R]	The Charlie Mingus Quartet + Max Roach	196?	3.75	7.50	15.00
❏ 86017 [S]	Right Now -- Live at the Jazz Workshop	1966	7.50	15.00	30.00
GATEWAY					
❏ 7026	His Final Work	1979	3.00	6.00	12.00
GRP/IMPULSE!					
❏ 217	Charlie Mingus Plays Piano	1997	5.00	10.00	20.00
-- Reissue on audiophile vinyl					
IMPULSE!					
❏ A-35 [M]	Black Saint and Sinner Lady	1963	7.50	15.00	30.00
❏ AS-35 [S]	Black Saint and Sinner Lady	1963	10.00	20.00	40.00
❏ A-54 [M]	Mingus, Mingus, Mingus, Mingus, Mingus	1963	7.50	15.00	30.00
❏ AS-54 [S]	Mingus, Mingus, Mingus, Mingus, Mingus	1963	10.00	20.00	40.00
❏ A-60 [M]	Charlie Mingus Plays Piano	1964	7.50	15.00	30.00
❏ AS-60 [S]	Charlie Mingus Plays Piano	1964	10.00	20.00	40.00
JAZZ MAN					
❏ 5002	Mingus	198?	3.00	6.00	12.00
❏ 5048	Mingus Presents	198?	3.00	6.00	12.00
JAZZTONE					
❏ J-1226 [M]	Jazz Experiment	1956	15.00	30.00	60.00
❏ J-1271 [M]	The Jazz Experiments of Charlie Mingus	1957	12.50	25.00	50.00
JOSIE					
❏ JLPS-3508 [R]	Mingus Three	1963	5.00	10.00	20.00
❏ JOZ-3508 [M]	Mingus Three	1963	7.50	15.00	30.00
JUBILEE					
❏ JLP-1054 [M]	Mingus Trio	1958	20.00	40.00	80.00
LIMELIGHT					
❏ LM-82015 [M]	Mingus Revisited	1965	6.25	12.50	25.00
❏ LS-86105 [S]	Mingus Revisited	1965	7.50	15.00	30.00
MCA IMPULSE!					
❏ MCA-5649	The Black Saint and the Sinner	1986	2.50	5.00	10.00
❏ MCA-39119	Mingus, Mingus, Mingus, Mingus, Mingus	198?	2.50	5.00	10.00
MERCURY					
❏ MG-20627 [M]	Pre-Bird	1961	7.50	15.00	30.00
❏ SR-60627 [S]	Pre-Bird	1961	10.00	20.00	40.00
MOSAIC					
❏ M4-111 [(4)]	The Complete Candid Recordings of Charles Mingus	199?	25.00	50.00	100.00
❏ MQ4-143 [(4)]	The Complete 1959 CBS Charles Mingus Sessions	199?	25.00	50.00	100.00
PERIOD					
❏ SLP-1111 [10]	Jazzical Moods, Volume 2	1955	50.00	100.00	200.00
❏ SPL-1107 [10]	Jazzical Moods, Volume 1	1955	50.00	100.00	200.00
PRESTIGE					
❏ 24010 [(2)]	Charles Mingus	197?	3.75	7.50	15.00
❏ 24028 [(2)]	Reincarnation of a Lovebird	197?	3.75	7.50	15.00

Number	Title	Yr	VG	VG+	NM
❑ 24092 [(2)]	Portrait	1980	3.75	7.50	15.00
❑ 24100 [(2)]	Mingus at Monterey	198?	3.75	7.50	15.00
❑ 34001 [(3)]	The Great Concert	197?	5.00	10.00	20.00

QUINTESSENCE

❑ 25171	Soul Fusion	197?	3.00	6.00	12.00

RCA VICTOR

❑ APL1-0939	Tijuana Moods	1974	3.00	6.00	12.00
-- Reissue of 2533					
❑ LPM-2533 [M]	Tijuana Moods	1962	10.00	20.00	40.00
❑ LSP-2533 [S]	Tijuana Moods	1962	12.50	25.00	50.00
❑ LSP-2533 [S]	Tijuana Moods	199?	6.25	12.50	25.00
-- Classic Records reissue on audiophile vinyl					

SAVOY

❑ MG-12059 [M]	Jazz Composers Workshop	1956	25.00	50.00	100.00
❑ MG-15050 [10]	Charlie Mingus	1955	50.00	100.00	200.00

SAVOY JAZZ

❑ SJL-1113	Jazz Workshop	197?	2.50	5.00	10.00

SOLID STATE

❑ SS-18019	Wonderland	1968	5.00	10.00	20.00
❑ SS-18024	Town Hall Concert	1968	5.00	10.00	20.00

TRIP

❑ 5017	Mingus Moods	197?	2.50	5.00	10.00
❑ 5040	Charles Mingus Trio and Sextet	197?	2.50	5.00	10.00
❑ 5513	Mingus Revisited	197?	2.50	5.00	10.00

UNITED ARTISTS

❑ UAL-4036 [M]	Jazz Portraits	1959	10.00	20.00	40.00
❑ UAS-5036 [S]	Jazz Portraits	1959	12.50	25.00	50.00
❑ UAS-5637	Wonderland	1972	3.00	6.00	12.00
❑ UAJ-14005 [M]	Wonderland	1962	10.00	20.00	40.00
❑ UAJ-14024 [M]	Town Hall Concert	1963	10.00	20.00	40.00
❑ UAJS-15005 [S]	Wonderland	1962	12.50	25.00	50.00
❑ UAJS-15024 [S]	Town Hall Concert	1963	12.50	25.00	50.00

WHO'S WHO IN JAZZ

❑ 21005	Lionel Hampton Presents Charles Mingus	1978	3.75	7.50	15.00

MINIMAL KIDDS
German group featuring Gebhard Ullmann (reeds) and Andreas Willers (guitar).
INTUITION

❑ C1-46879	No Age	1989	3.00	6.00	12.00

MINION, FRANK
BETHLEHEM

❑ BCP-6033 [M]	Forward Sound	1959	10.00	20.00	40.00
❑ BCP-6052 [M]	The Soft Land of Make Believe	1961	10.00	20.00	40.00
❑ BCPS-6052 [S]	The Soft Land of Make Believe	1961	12.50	25.00	50.00

MISSOURIANS, THE
Members: William Blue (clarinet, alto saxophone); Andrew Brown (clarinet, tenor saxophone); R.Q. Dickerson (trumpet); Lockwood Lewis (vocals, leader); Leroy Maxey (drums); Earres Prince (piano); George Scott (clarinet, alto saxophone); Jimmy Smith (tuba); De Priest Wheeler (trumpet); Morris White (violin).
"X"

❑ LVA-3020 [10]	Harlem in the Twenties, Volume 1	1954	12.50	25.00	50.00

MISTER SPATS
Members included Richard Shulman (piano) and Steve Evans.
PAUSA

❑ 7194	Love Speaks	1986	2.50	5.00	10.00

MIT
HAT HUT

❑ 18	MIT	198?	3.75	7.50	15.00

MITCHELL, BILLY
Tenor saxophone player. Also see AL GREY.
CATALYST

❑ 7611	Now's the Time	1976	3.00	6.00	12.00

OPTIMISM

❑ OP-2501	Faces	1987	2.50	5.00	10.00
❑ OP-2502	In Focus	1988	2.50	5.00	10.00

PAUSA

❑ 7158	Blue City Jam	198?	2.50	5.00	10.00
❑ 7192	Night Theme	1986	2.50	5.00	10.00

SMASH

❑ MGS-27027 [M]	This Is Billy Mitchell	1962	6.25	12.50	25.00
❑ MGS-27042 [M]	A Little Juicy	1962	6.25	12.50	25.00
❑ SRS-67027 [S]	This Is Billy Mitchell	1962	7.50	15.00	30.00
❑ SRS-67042 [S]	A Little Juicy	1962	7.50	15.00	30.00

TRIP

❑ 5534	Billy Mitchell with Bobby	197?	2.50	5.00	10.00

XANADU

Number	Title	Yr	VG	VG+	NM
❑ 158	Colossus of Detroit	1978	3.00	6.00	12.00
❑ 182	De Lawd's Blues	198?	2.50	5.00	10.00

MITCHELL, BLUE
Trumpeter. Also see THE MITCHELLS; THE RIVERSIDE JAZZ STARS.
ABC IMPULSE!

❑ AS-9328	African Violet	1977	3.00	6.00	12.00
❑ IA-9347	Summer Soft	1978	3.00	6.00	12.00

BLUE NOTE

❑ LT-1082	Step Lightly	1980	2.50	5.00	10.00
❑ BLP-4142 [M]	Step Lightly	1963	---	---	---
-- Canceled					
❑ BLP-4178 [M]	The Thing to Do	1964	6.25	12.50	25.00
❑ BLP-4214 [M]	Down With It	1965	6.25	12.50	25.00
❑ BLP-4228 [M]	Bring It Home to Me	1966	7.50	15.00	30.00
❑ BLP-4257 [M]	Boss Horn	1967	7.50	15.00	30.00
❑ BST-84142 [S]	Step Lightly	1963	---	---	---
-- Canceled					
❑ BST-84178 [S]	The Thing to Do	1964	7.50	15.00	30.00
-- With "New York, USA" address on label					
❑ BST-84178 [S]	The Thing to Do	1967	3.75	7.50	15.00
-- With "A Division of Liberty Records" on label					
❑ BST-84178 [S]	The Thing to Do	1985	2.50	5.00	10.00
-- "The Finest in Jazz Since 1939" reissue					
❑ BST-84214 [S]	Down With It	1965	7.50	15.00	30.00
-- With "New York, USA" address on label					
❑ BST-84214 [S]	Down With It	1967	3.75	7.50	15.00
-- With "A Division of Liberty Records" on label					
❑ BST-84228 [S]	Bring It Home to Me	1966	10.00	20.00	40.00
-- With "New York, USA" address on label					
❑ BST-84228 [S]	Bring It Home to Me	1967	3.75	7.50	15.00
-- With "A Division of Liberty Records" on label					
❑ BST-84257 [S]	Boss Horn	1967	5.00	10.00	20.00
-- With "A Division of Liberty Records" on label					
❑ BST-84272	Heads Up!	1968	5.00	10.00	20.00
❑ BST-84300	Collision in Black	1968	5.00	10.00	20.00
❑ BST-84324	Bantu Village	1969	5.00	10.00	20.00

FANTASY

❑ OJC-615	The Big Six	1991	3.75	7.50	15.00
❑ OJC-6009	Blues on My Mind	198?	2.50	5.00	10.00

JAM

❑ 5002	Last Dance	198?	2.50	5.00	10.00

MAINSTREAM

❑ MRL-315	Blue Mitchell	1971	3.75	7.50	15.00
❑ MRL-343	Vital	1972	3.75	7.50	15.00
❑ MRL-374	Blue's Blues	1973	3.75	7.50	15.00
❑ MRL-400	Graffiti Blues	1974	3.75	7.50	15.00
❑ MRL-402	Many Shades of Blue Mitchell	1974	3.75	7.50	15.00

MCA

❑ 29050	African Violet	1980	2.50	5.00	10.00
❑ 29051	Summer Soft	1980	2.50	5.00	10.00

MILESTONE

❑ 47055 [(2)]	A Blue Time	1979	3.75	7.50	15.00

MOSAIC

❑ MQ6-178 [(6)]	The Complete Blue Note Sessions	199?	25.00	50.00	100.00

RCA VICTOR

❑ APL1-1109	Stratosonic	1975	3.75	7.50	15.00
❑ APL1-1493	Funktion	1976	3.75	7.50	15.00

RIVERSIDE

❑ RLP 12-273 [M]	The Big Six	1958	12.50	25.00	50.00
❑ RLP 12-293 [M]	Out of the Blue	1958	12.50	25.00	50.00
❑ RLP 12-309 [M]	Blue Soul	1959	12.50	25.00	50.00
❑ RLP-336 [M]	Blue's Moods	1960	10.00	20.00	40.00
❑ RLP-367 [M]	Smooth as the Wind	1961	7.50	15.00	30.00
❑ RLP-414 [M]	A Sure Thing	1962	7.50	15.00	30.00
❑ RLP-439 [M]	The Cup Bearers	1963	7.50	15.00	30.00
❑ RLP-1131 [S]	Out of the Blue	1959	10.00	20.00	40.00
❑ RLP-1155 [S]	Blue Soul	1959	10.00	20.00	40.00
❑ 6045	Blue's Moods	197?	3.00	6.00	12.00
❑ RS-9336 [S]	Blue's Moods	1960	10.00	20.00	40.00
❑ RS-9367 [S]	Smooth as the Wind	1961	10.00	20.00	40.00
❑ RS-9414 [S]	A Sure Thing	1962	10.00	20.00	40.00
❑ RS-9439 [S]	The Cup Bearers	1963	10.00	20.00	40.00

MITCHELL, GROVER
Trombonist.
STASH

❑ ST-277	Truckin' with Grover Mitchell and His Orchestra	1988	2.50	5.00	10.00

Number	Title	Yr	VG	VG+	NM

MITCHELL, JONI
Female singer. Best known in the folk, pop and rock realms, the below LPs feature backing and inspiration by jazz musicians.
ASYLUM
❑ AB-202	Miles of Aisles	1974	2.50	5.00	10.00
❑ 5E-504	Mingus	1979	2.50	5.00	10.00
❑ BB-704 [(2)]	Shadows and Light	1980	3.00	6.00	12.00

MITCHELL, OLLIE
Trumpeter.
PAUSA
| ❑ 7128 | Blast Off | 198? | 2.50 | 5.00 | 10.00 |

MITCHELL, PAUL
Pianist.
VERVE
| ❑ V-8713 [M] | Live at the Atlanta Playboy Club | 1967 | 5.00 | 10.00 | 20.00 |
| ❑ V6-8713 [S] | Live at the Atlanta Playboy Club | 1967 | 3.00 | 6.00 | 12.00 |

MITCHELL, RED
Bass player. Also see THE MITCHELLS; OSCAR PETTIFORD; THE VIDEO ALL-STARS.
BETHLEHEM
| ❑ BCP-38 [M] | Jam for Your Bread | 1956 | 20.00 | 40.00 | 80.00 |
| ❑ BCP-1033 [10] | Happy Minors | 1955 | 100.00 | 200.00 | 400.00 |
CONTEMPORARY
| ❑ C-3538 [M] | Presenting Red Mitchell | 1957 | 20.00 | 40.00 | 80.00 |
FANTASY
| ❑ OJC-158 | Presenting Red Mitchell | 198? | 2.50 | 5.00 | 10.00 |
PACIFIC JAZZ
| ❑ PJ-22 [M] | Rejoice | 1961 | 7.50 | 15.00 | 30.00 |
| ❑ ST-22 [S] | Rejoice | 1961 | 10.00 | 20.00 | 40.00 |
PAUSA
| ❑ 7018 | Red Mitchell Meets Manusardi | 198? | 2.50 | 5.00 | 10.00 |
STEEPLECHASE
| ❑ SCS-1161 | Chocolate Cadillac | 198? | 3.00 | 6.00 | 12.00 |

MITCHELL, RED, AND HAROLD LAND
Also see each artist's individual listings.
ATLANTIC
| ❑ 1376 [M] | Hear Ye! | 1961 | 7.50 | 15.00 | 30.00 |
| -- Multicolor label, white "fan" logo at right |
| ❑ 1376 [M] | Hear Ye! | 1964 | 5.00 | 10.00 | 20.00 |
| -- Multicolor label, black "fan" logo at right |
| ❑ SD 1376 [S] | Hear Ye! | 1961 | 10.00 | 20.00 | 40.00 |
| -- Multicolor label, white "fan" logo at right |
| ❑ SD 1376 [S] | Hear Ye! | 1964 | 6.25 | 12.50 | 25.00 |
| -- Multicolor label, black "fan" logo at right |

MITCHELL, ROSCOE
Reeds player. Also see ART ENSEMBLE OF CHICAGO.
BLACK SAINT
| ❑ BSR-0050 | 3 X 4 Eye | 198? | 3.00 | 6.00 | 12.00 |
| ❑ BSR-0070 | Roscoe Mitchell and Sound and Space Ensembles | 198? | 3.00 | 6.00 | 12.00 |
DELMARK
| ❑ D-408 [M] | Roscoe Mitchell Sextet | 1966 | 6.25 | 12.50 | 25.00 |
| ❑ DS-408 [S] | Roscoe Mitchell Sextet | 1966 | 5.00 | 10.00 | 20.00 |
NESSA
❑ N-2	Congliptious	1968	6.25	12.50	25.00
❑ N-5	Old/Quartet	197?	3.75	7.50	15.00
❑ N-9/10 [(2)]	Nonaah	1977	6.25	12.50	25.00
❑ N-14/15 [(2)]	L-R-G/The Maze/S II Examples	1980	5.00	10.00	20.00
❑ N-20	Snurdy McGurdy and Her Dancin' Shoes	1981	3.75	7.50	15.00

MITCHELL, WHITEY
Bass player. Also see THE MITCHELLS; THE NEW YORK JAZZ QUARTET.
ABC-PARAMOUNT
| ❑ ABC-126 [M] | Whitey Mitchell Sextette | 1956 | 12.50 | 25.00 | 50.00 |

MITCHELL-RUFF DUO, THE
Featuring Dwike Mitchell (piano) and Willie Ruff (bass, French horn).
ATLANTIC
| ❑ 1374 [M] | The Catbird Seat | 1961 | 5.00 | 10.00 | 20.00 |
| -- Multicolor label, white "fan" logo at right |
| ❑ 1374 [M] | The Catbird Seat | 1964 | 3.75 | 7.50 | 15.00 |
| -- Multicolor label, black "fan" logo at right |
| ❑ SD 1374 [S] | The Catbird Seat | 1961 | 6.25 | 12.50 | 25.00 |
| -- Multicolor label, white "fan" logo at right |
| ❑ SD 1374 [S] | The Catbird Seat | 1964 | 5.00 | 10.00 | 20.00 |
| -- Multicolor label, black "fan" logo at right |

Number	Title	Yr	VG	VG+	NM

| ❑ 1458 [M] | After This Message | 1966 | 5.00 | 10.00 | 20.00 |
| ❑ SD 1458 [S] | After This Message | 1966 | 6.25 | 12.50 | 25.00 |
EPIC
| ❑ LN 3221 [M] | The Mitchell-Ruff Duo | 1956 | 10.00 | 20.00 | 40.00 |
| ❑ LN 3318 [M] | Campus Concert | 1956 | 10.00 | 20.00 | 40.00 |
FORUM
| ❑ F-9031 [M] | Jazz Mission to Moscow | 196? | 3.00 | 6.00 | 12.00 |
| -- Reissue of Roulette R-52034 |
| ❑ SF-9031 [S] | Jazz Mission to Moscow | 196? | 3.75 | 7.50 | 15.00 |
| -- Reissue of Roulette SR-52034 |
MAINSTREAM
| ❑ MRL-335 | Strayhorn | 1972 | 3.75 | 7.50 | 15.00 |
ROULETTE
❑ R-52002 [M]	Appearing Nightly	1958	10.00	20.00	40.00
❑ SR-52002 [S]	Appearing Nightly	1959	7.50	15.00	30.00
❑ R-52013 [M]	The Mitchell-Ruff Duo Plus Strings and Brass	1958	10.00	20.00	40.00
❑ SR-52013 [S]	The Mitchell-Ruff Duo Plus Strings and Brass	1959	7.50	15.00	30.00
❑ R-52025 [M]	Jazz for Juniors	1959	7.50	15.00	30.00
❑ SR-52025 [S]	Jazz for Juniors	1959	6.25	12.50	25.00
❑ R-52034 [M]	Jazz Mission to Moscow	1959	7.50	15.00	30.00
❑ SR-52034 [S]	Jazz Mission to Moscow	1959	6.25	12.50	25.00
❑ R-52037 [M]	The Sound of Music	1960	6.25	12.50	25.00
❑ SR-52037 [S]	The Sound of Music	1960	7.50	15.00	30.00

MITCHELLS, THE
Members: BLUE MITCHELL; RED MITCHELL; WHITEY MITCHELL.
METROJAZZ
| ❑ E-1012 [M] | Get Those Elephants Out'a Here | 1958 | 20.00 | 40.00 | 80.00 |
| ❑ SE-1012 [S] | Get Those Elephants Out'a Here | 1958 | 15.00 | 30.00 | 60.00 |

MJT + 3
Members: Bob Cranshaw (bass); HAROLD MABERN (piano); Walter Perkins (drums); FRANK STROZIER (alto sax); Willie Thomas (trumpet).
ARGO
| ❑ LP-621 [M] | Daddy-O Presents MJT + 3 | 1957 | 10.00 | 20.00 | 40.00 |
TRIP
| ❑ 5025 [(2)] | Branching Out | 197? | 3.00 | 6.00 | 12.00 |
VEE JAY
❑ LP-1013 [M]	Walter Perkins' MJT + 3	1959	7.50	15.00	30.00
❑ SR-1013 [S]	Walter Perkins' MJT + 3	1959	10.00	20.00	40.00
❑ LP-3008 [M]	Make Everybody Happy	1960	6.25	12.50	25.00
❑ SR-3008 [S]	Make Everybody Happy	1960	7.50	15.00	30.00
❑ LP-3014 [M]	MJT + 3	1961	6.25	12.50	25.00
❑ SR-3014 [S]	MJT + 3	1961	7.50	15.00	30.00

MOBLEY, HANK
Tenor saxophone player. Also see DONALD BYRD; KENNY DREW.
BLUE NOTE
❑ LT-995	Slice Off the Top	1979	2.50	5.00	10.00
❑ LT-1045	Thinking of Home	1980	2.50	5.00	10.00
❑ LT-1081	Third Season	1981	2.50	5.00	10.00
❑ BLP-1540 [M]	Hank Mobley with Donald Byrd and Lee Morgan	1957	75.00	150.00	300.00
-- "Deep groove" version (deep indentation under label on both sides)
❑ BLP-1540 [M]	Hank Mobley with Donald Byrd and Lee Morgan	1957	50.00	100.00	200.00
-- Regular version, Lexington Ave. address on label
❑ BLP-1540 [M]	Hank Mobley with Donald Byrd and Lee Morgan	1963	6.25	12.50	25.00
-- With "New York, USA" address on label
❑ BLP-1544 [M]	Hank Mobley and His All Stars	1957	50.00	100.00	200.00
-- "Deep groove" version (deep indentation under label on both sides)
❑ BLP-1544 [M]	Hank Mobley and His All Stars	1957	37.50	75.00	150.00
-- Regular version, W. 63rd St. address on label
❑ BLP-1544 [M]	Hank Mobley and His All Stars	1963	6.25	12.50	25.00
-- With "New York, USA" address on label
❑ BLP-1550 [M]	Hank Mobley	1957	50.00	100.00	200.00
-- "Deep groove" version (deep indentation under label on both sides)
❑ BLP-1550 [M]	Hank Mobley	1957	37.50	75.00	150.00
-- Regular version, W. 63rd St. address on label
❑ BLP-1550 [M]	Hank Mobley	1963	6.25	12.50	25.00
-- With "New York, USA" address on label
❑ BLP-1560 [M]	Hank	1957	50.00	100.00	200.00
-- "Deep groove" version (deep indentation under label on both sides)
❑ BLP-1560 [M]	Hank	1957	37.50	75.00	150.00
-- Regular version, W. 63rd St. address on label
❑ BLP-1560 [M]	Hank	1963	6.25	12.50	25.00
-- With "New York, USA" address on label
❑ BLP-1568 [M]	Hank Mobley	1957	50.00	100.00	200.00
-- "Deep groove" version (deep indentation under label on both sides)
❑ BLP-1568 [M]	Hank Mobley	1957	37.50	75.00	150.00
-- Regular version, W. 63rd St. address on label
❑ BLP-1568 [M]	Hank Mobley	1963	6.25	12.50	25.00
-- With "New York, USA" address on label

Number	Title	Yr	VG	VG+	NM
❏ BST-1568 [S]	Hank Mobley	1959	37.50	75.00	150.00
-- "Deep groove" version (deep indentation under label on both sides)					
❏ BST-1568 [S]	Hank Mobley	1959	25.00	50.00	100.00
-- Regular version, W. 63rd St. address on label					
❏ BST-1568 [S]	Hank Mobley	1963	5.00	10.00	20.00
-- With "New York, USA" address on label					
❏ BLP-1574 [M]	Peckin' Time	1958	50.00	100.00	200.00
-- "Deep groove" version (deep indentation under label on both sides)					
❏ BLP-1574 [M]	Peckin' Time	1958	37.50	75.00	150.00
-- Regular version, W. 63rd St. address on label					
❏ BLP-1574 [M]	Peckin' Time	1963	6.25	12.50	25.00
-- With "New York, USA" address on label					
❏ BLP-4031 [M]	Soul Station	1960	30.00	60.00	120.00
-- "Deep groove" version (deep indentation under label on both sides)					
❏ BLP-4031 [M]	Soul Station	1960	20.00	40.00	80.00
-- Regular version, W. 63rd St. address on label					
❏ BLP-4031 [M]	Soul Station	1963	6.25	12.50	25.00
-- With "New York, USA" address on label					
❏ BLP-4058 [M]	Roll Call	1961	20.00	40.00	80.00
-- With W. 63rd St. address on label					
❏ BLP-4058 [M]	Roll Call	1963	6.25	12.50	25.00
-- With "New York, USA" address on label					
❏ BLP-4080 [M]	Workout	1961	15.00	30.00	60.00
-- With 61st St. address on label					
❏ BLP-4080 [M]	Workout	1963	6.25	12.50	25.00
-- With "New York, USA" address on label					
❏ BLP-4149 [M]	No Room for Squares	1963	7.50	15.00	30.00
❏ BLP-4186 [M]	The Turnaround!	1964	7.50	15.00	30.00
❏ BLP-4209 [M]	Dippin'	1965	7.50	15.00	30.00
❏ BLP-4230 [M]	A Caddy for Daddy	1966	7.50	15.00	30.00
❏ BLP-4241 [M]	Hank Mobley	1966	---	---	---
-- Canceled					
❏ BLP-4273 [M]	Hi Voltage	1968	30.00	60.00	120.00
❏ BLP-5066 [10]	Hank Mobley Quartet	1955	100.00	200.00	400.00
❏ B1-33582	A Slice Off the Top	1995	3.75	7.50	15.00
-- "The Finest in Jazz Since 1939" reissue					
❏ BST-81540 [R]	Hank Mobley with Donald Byrd and Lee Morgan	1967	3.00	6.00	12.00
-- With "A Division of Liberty Records" on label					
❏ BST-81544 [R]	Hank Mobley and His All Stars	1967	3.00	6.00	12.00
-- With "A Division of Liberty Records" on label					
❏ BST-81550 [R]	Hank Mobley	1967	3.00	6.00	12.00
-- With "A Division of Liberty Records" on label					
❏ BST-81560 [R]	Hank	1967	3.00	6.00	12.00
-- With "A Division of Liberty Records" on label					
❏ BST-81568 [S]	Hank Mobley	1967	3.75	7.50	15.00
-- With "A Division of Liberty Records" on label					
❏ B1-81574	Peckin' Time	1988	2.50	5.00	10.00
-- "The Finest in Jazz Since 1939" reissue					
❏ BST-81574 [R]	Peckin' Time	1967	3.00	6.00	12.00
-- With "A Division of Liberty Records" on label					
❏ BST-84031 [S]	Soul Station	1960	15.00	30.00	60.00
-- With W. 63rd St. address on label					
❏ BST-84031 [S]	Soul Station	1963	5.00	10.00	20.00
-- With "New York, USA" address on label					
❏ BST-84031 [S]	Soul Station	1967	3.75	7.50	15.00
-- With "A Division of Liberty Records" on label					
❏ BST-84031	Soul Station	1987	2.50	5.00	10.00
-- "The Finest in Jazz Since 1939" reissue					
❏ BST-84058 [S]	Roll Call	1961	15.00	30.00	60.00
-- With W. 63rd St. address on label					
❏ BST-84058 [S]	Roll Call	1963	5.00	10.00	20.00
-- With "New York, USA" address on label					
❏ BST-84058 [S]	Roll Call	1967	3.75	7.50	15.00
-- With "A Division of Liberty Records" on label					
❏ BST-84058	Roll Call	199?	6.25	12.50	25.00
-- Classic Records reissue on audiophile vinyl					
❏ B1-84080	Workout	1988	2.50	5.00	10.00
-- "The Finest in Jazz Since 1939" reissue					
❏ BST-84080 [S]	Workout	1961	12.50	25.00	50.00
-- With 61st St. address on label					
❏ BST-84080 [S]	Workout	1963	5.00	10.00	20.00
-- With "New York, USA" address on label					
❏ BST-84080 [S]	Workout	1967	3.75	7.50	15.00
-- With "A Division of Liberty Records" on label					
❏ B1-84149	No Room for Squares	1989	3.00	6.00	12.00
-- "The Finest in Jazz Since 1939" reissue					
❏ BST-84149 [S]	No Room for Squares	1963	10.00	20.00	40.00
-- With "New York, USA" address on label					
❏ BST-84149 [S]	No Room for Squares	1967	5.00	10.00	20.00
-- With "A Division of Liberty Records" on label					
❏ B1-84186	The Turnaround!	1989	3.00	6.00	12.00
-- "The Finest in Jazz Since 1939" reissue					
❏ BST-84186 [S]	The Turnaround!	1964	10.00	20.00	40.00
-- With "New York, USA" address on label					
❏ BST-84186 [S]	The Turnaround!	1967	5.00	10.00	20.00
-- With "A Division of Liberty Records" on label					
❏ BST-84209 [S]	Dippin'	1965	10.00	20.00	40.00
-- With "New York, USA" address on label					
❏ BST-84209 [S]	Dippin'	1967	5.00	10.00	20.00
-- With "A Division of Liberty Records" on label					

Number	Title	Yr	VG	VG+	NM
❏ BST-84230 [S]	A Caddy for Daddy	1966	10.00	20.00	40.00
-- With "New York, USA" address on label					
❏ BST-84230 [S]	A Caddy for Daddy	1967	5.00	10.00	20.00
-- With "A Division of Liberty Records" on label					
❏ BST-84241 [S]	Hank Mobley	1966	---	---	---
-- Canceled					
❏ BST-84273 [S]	Hi Voltage	1968	6.25	12.50	25.00
-- With "A Division of Liberty Records" on label					
❏ BST-84273	High Voltage	1986	2.50	5.00	10.00
-- "The Finest in Jazz Since 1939" reissue					
❏ BST-84288	Reach Out!	1968	6.25	12.50	25.00
-- With "A Division of Liberty Records" on label					
❏ BST-84329	The Flip	1969	6.25	12.50	25.00
-- With "A Division of Liberty Records" on label					
❏ BST-84425	Far Away Lands	1985	2.50	5.00	10.00
❏ BST-84431	Another Workout	1986	2.50	5.00	10.00
❏ BST-84435	Straight No Filter	1986	2.50	5.00	10.00
NEW JAZZ					
❏ NJLP-8311 [M]	52nd Street Theme	1963	---	---	---
-- Canceled; reassigned to Status					
PRESTIGE					
❏ PRLP-7061 [M]	Mobley's Message	1956	37.50	75.00	150.00
❏ PRLP-7082 [M]	Mobley's Second Message	1957	37.50	75.00	150.00
❏ PRST-7661	Hank Mobley's Message	1969	3.75	7.50	15.00
❏ PRST-7667	Mobley's Second Message	1969	3.75	7.50	15.00
❏ 24063 [(2)]	Messages	197?	3.75	7.50	15.00
SAVOY					
❏ MG-12092 [M]	Jazz Message #2	1956	37.50	75.00	150.00
STATUS					
❏ ST-8311 [M]	52nd Street Theme	1965	6.25	12.50	25.00

MODERN JAZZ DISCIPLES, THE
Members: Bill Brown; Wilbur Jackson; Mike Kelly; Roy McCurdy; Curtis Peagler; Lee Tucker.

Number	Title	Yr	VG	VG+	NM
NEW JAZZ					
❏ NJLP-8222 [M]	Modern Jazz Disciples	1959	12.50	25.00	50.00
-- Purple label					
❏ NJLP-8222 [M]	Modern Jazz Disciples	1965	6.25	12.50	25.00
-- Blue label, trident logo at right					
❏ NJLP-8240 [M]	Right Down Front	1960	12.50	25.00	50.00
-- Purple label					
❏ NJLP-8240 [M]	Right Down Front	1965	6.25	12.50	25.00
-- Blue label, trident logo at right					

MODERN JAZZ ENSEMBLE, THE
See THE MODERN JAZZ SOCIETY.

MODERN JAZZ QUARTET, THE
The classic lineup was Percy Heath (bass); MILT JACKSON (vibes); Connie Kay (drums and percussion); JOHN LEWIS (piano). KENNY CLARKE was the original drummer. Also see OSCAR PETERSON; SONNY ROLLINS.

Number	Title	Yr	VG	VG+	NM
APPLE					
❏ ST-3353	Under the Jasmine Tree	1969	6.25	12.50	25.00
❏ ST-5-3353	Under the Jasmine Tree	1969	10.00	20.00	40.00
-- Capitol Record Club edition					
❏ STAO-3360	Space	1970	6.25	12.50	25.00
❏ STAO-5-3360	Space	1970	10.00	20.00	40.00
-- Capitol Record Club edition					
ATLANTIC					
❏ SD 2-301 [(2)]	The Art of the Modern Jazz Quartet	1973	3.75	7.50	15.00
❏ 2-603 [(2) M]	The European Concert	1961	7.50	15.00	30.00
-- Multicolor labels, white "fan" logo at right					
❏ 2-603 [(2) M]	The European Concert	1963	5.00	10.00	20.00
-- Multicolor labels, black "fan" logo at right					
❏ SD 2-603 [(2) S]	The European Concert	1961	10.00	20.00	40.00
-- Multicolor labels, white "fan" logo at right					
❏ SD 2-603 [(2) S]	The European Concert	1963	6.25	12.50	25.00
-- Multicolor labels, black "fan" logo at right					
❏ SD 2-603 [(2) S]	The European Concert	1969	3.75	7.50	15.00
-- Red and green labels					
❏ SD 2-909 [(2)]	The Last Concert	1975	3.75	7.50	15.00
❏ SQ 2-909 [(2) Q]	The Last Concert	1975	6.25	12.50	25.00
❏ 1231 [M]	Fontessa	1956	10.00	20.00	40.00
-- Black label					
❏ 1231 [M]	Fontessa	1960	5.00	10.00	20.00
-- Multicolor label, white "fan" logo at right					
❏ 1231 [M]	Fontessa	1963	3.75	7.50	15.00
-- Multicolor label, black "fan" logo at right					
❏ SD 1231 [S]	Fontessa	1958	7.50	15.00	30.00
-- Green label					
❏ SD 1231 [S]	Fontessa	1960	3.75	7.50	15.00
-- Multicolor label, white "fan" logo at right					
❏ SD 1231 [S]	Fontessa	1963	3.00	6.00	12.00
-- Multicolor label, black "fan" logo at right					
❏ SD 1231 [S]	Fontessa	1969	2.50	5.00	10.00
-- Red and green label					

Number	Title	Yr	VG	VG+	NM
❏ 1247 [M]	The Modern Jazz Quartet at the Music Inn	1956	10.00	20.00	40.00
-- Black label					
❏ 1247 [M]	The Modern Jazz Quartet at the Music Inn	1960	5.00	10.00	20.00
-- Multicolor label, white "fan" logo at right					
❏ 1247 [M]	The Modern Jazz Quartet at the Music Inn	1963	3.75	7.50	15.00
-- Multicolor label, black "fan" logo at right					
❏ 1265 [M]	The Modern Jazz Quartet	1957	10.00	20.00	40.00
-- Black label					
❏ 1265 [M]	The Modern Jazz Quartet	1960	5.00	10.00	20.00
-- Multicolor label, white "fan" logo at right					
❏ 1265 [M]	The Modern Jazz Quartet	1963	3.75	7.50	15.00
-- Multicolor label, black "fan" logo at right					
❏ 1284 [M]	No Sun in Venice	1958	10.00	20.00	40.00
-- Black label					
❏ 1284 [M]	No Sun in Venice	1960	5.00	10.00	20.00
-- Multicolor label, white "fan" logo at right					
❏ 1284 [M]	No Sun in Venice	1963	3.75	7.50	15.00
-- Multicolor label, black "fan" logo at right					
❏ SD 1284 [S]	No Sun in Venice	1958	7.50	15.00	30.00
-- Green label					
❏ SD 1284 [S]	No Sun in Venice	1960	3.75	7.50	15.00
-- Multicolor label, white "fan" logo at right					
❏ SD 1284 [S]	No Sun in Venice	1963	3.00	6.00	12.00
-- Multicolor label, black "fan" logo at right					
❏ SD 1284 [S]	No Sun in Venice	1969	2.50	5.00	10.00
-- Red and green label					
❏ 1299 [M]	The Modern Jazz Quartet at the Music Inn, Volume 2	1958	10.00	20.00	40.00
-- Black label					
❏ 1299 [M]	The Modern Jazz Quartet at the Music Inn, Volume 2	1960	5.00	10.00	20.00
-- Multicolor label, white "fan" logo at right					
❏ 1299 [M]	The Modern Jazz Quartet at the Music Inn, Volume 2	1963	3.75	7.50	15.00
-- Multicolor label, black "fan" logo at right					
❏ SD 1299 [S]	The Modern Jazz Quartet at the Music Inn, Volume 2	1958	7.50	15.00	30.00
-- Green label					
❏ SD 1299 [S]	The Modern Jazz Quartet at the Music Inn, Volume 2	1960	3.75	7.50	15.00
-- Multicolor label, white "fan" logo at right					
❏ SD 1299 [S]	The Modern Jazz Quartet at the Music Inn, Volume 2	1963	3.00	6.00	12.00
-- Multicolor label, black "fan" logo at right					
❏ SD 1299 [S]	The Modern Jazz Quartet at the Music Inn, Volume 2	1969	2.50	5.00	10.00
-- Red and green label					
❏ 1325 [M]	Pyramid	1960	10.00	20.00	40.00
-- Black label					
❏ 1325 [M]	Pyramid	1961	5.00	10.00	20.00
-- Multicolor label, white "fan" logo at right					
❏ 1325 [M]	Pyramid	1963	3.75	7.50	15.00
-- Multicolor label, black "fan" logo at right					
❏ SD 1325 [S]	Pyramid	1960	7.50	15.00	30.00
-- Green label					
❏ SD 1325 [S]	Pyramid	1961	3.75	7.50	15.00
-- Multicolor label, white "fan" logo at right					
❏ SD 1325 [S]	Pyramid	1963	3.00	6.00	12.00
-- Multicolor label, black "fan" logo at right					
❏ SD 1325 [S]	Pyramid	1969	2.50	5.00	10.00
-- Red and green label					
❏ 1345 [M]	Third Stream Music	1960	5.00	10.00	20.00
-- Multicolor label, white "fan" logo at right					
❏ 1345 [M]	Third Stream Music	1963	3.00	6.00	12.00
-- Multicolor label, black "fan" logo at right					
❏ SD 1345 [S]	Third Stream Music	1960	6.25	12.50	25.00
-- Multicolor label, white "fan" logo at right					
❏ SD 1345 [S]	Third Stream Music	1963	3.75	7.50	15.00
-- Multicolor label, black "fan" logo at right					
❏ SD 1345 [S]	Third Stream Music	1969	2.50	5.00	10.00
-- Red and green label					
❏ 1359 [M]	The Modern Jazz Quartet and Orchestra	1961	5.00	10.00	20.00
-- Multicolor label, white "fan" logo at right					
❏ 1359 [M]	The Modern Jazz Quartet and Orchestra	1963	3.00	6.00	12.00
-- Multicolor label, black "fan" logo at right					
❏ SD 1359 [S]	The Modern Jazz Quartet and Orchestra	1961	6.25	12.50	25.00
-- Multicolor label, white "fan" logo at right					
❏ SD 1359 [S]	The Modern Jazz Quartet and Orchestra	1963	3.75	7.50	15.00
-- Multicolor label, black "fan" logo at right					
❏ SD 1359 [S]	The Modern Jazz Quartet and Orchestra	1969	2.50	5.00	10.00
-- Red and green label					
❏ 1381 [M]	Lonely Woman	1962	3.75	7.50	15.00
❏ SD 1381 [S]	Lonely Woman	1962	5.00	10.00	20.00
-- Multicolor label, black "fan" logo at right					
❏ SD 1381 [S]	Lonely Woman	1969	2.50	5.00	10.00
-- Red and green label					
❏ 1385 [M]	The European Concert, Volume 1	1962	3.75	7.50	15.00
❏ SD 1385 [S]	The European Concert, Volume 1	1962	5.00	10.00	20.00
-- Multicolor label, black "fan" logo at right					
❏ SD 1385 [S]	The European Concert, Volume 1	1969	2.50	5.00	10.00
-- Red and green label					
❏ 1386 [M]	The European Concert, Volume 2	1962	3.75	7.50	15.00
❏ SD 1386 [S]	The European Concert, Volume 2	1962	5.00	10.00	20.00
-- Multicolor label, black "fan" logo at right					
❏ SD 1386 [S]	The European Concert, Volume 2	1969	2.50	5.00	10.00
-- Red and green label					
❏ 1390 [M]	The Comedy	1963	3.75	7.50	15.00
❏ SD 1390 [S]	The Comedy	1963	5.00	10.00	20.00
-- Multicolor label, black "fan" logo at right					
❏ SD 1390 [S]	The Comedy	1969	2.50	5.00	10.00
-- Red and green label					
❏ 1414 [M]	The Sheriff	1964	3.75	7.50	15.00
❏ SD 1414 [S]	The Sheriff	1964	5.00	10.00	20.00
-- Multicolor label, black "fan" logo at right					
❏ SD 1414 [S]	The Sheriff	1969	2.50	5.00	10.00
-- Red and green label					
❏ 1420 [M]	A Quartet Is a Quartet Is a Quartet	1964	3.75	7.50	15.00
❏ SD 1420 [S]	A Quartet Is a Quartet Is a Quartet	1964	5.00	10.00	20.00
-- Multicolor label, black "fan" logo at right					
❏ SD 1420 [S]	A Quartet Is a Quartet Is a Quartet	1969	2.50	5.00	10.00
-- Red and green label					
❏ 1429 [M]	Collaboration -- The Modern Jazz Quartet with Laurindo Almeida	1964	3.00	6.00	12.00
❏ SD 1429 [S]	Collaboration -- The Modern Jazz Quartet with Laurindo Almeida	1964	3.75	7.50	15.00
-- Multicolor label, black "fan" logo at right					
❏ SD 1429 [S]	Collaboration -- The Modern Jazz Quartet with Laurindo Almeida	1969	2.50	5.00	10.00
-- Red and green label					
❏ 1440 [M]	The Modern Jazz Quartet Plays Gershwin's "Porgy and Bess"	1965	3.00	6.00	12.00
❏ SD 1440 [S]	The Modern Jazz Quartet Plays Gershwin's "Porgy and Bess"	1965	3.75	7.50	15.00
-- Multicolor label, black "fan" logo at right					
❏ SD 1440 [S]	The Modern Jazz Quartet Plays Gershwin's "Porgy and Bess"	1969	2.50	5.00	10.00
-- Red and green label					
❏ 1449 [M]	Jazz Dialogue	1966	3.00	6.00	12.00
❏ SD 1449 [S]	Jazz Dialogue	1966	3.75	7.50	15.00
-- Multicolor label, black "fan" logo at right					
❏ SD 1449 [S]	Jazz Dialogue	1969	2.50	5.00	10.00
-- Red and green label					
❏ 1468 [M]	Blues at Carnegie Hall	1967	3.75	7.50	15.00
❏ SD 1468 [S]	Blues at Carnegie Hall	1967	3.00	6.00	12.00
-- Multicolor label, black "fan" logo at right					
❏ SD 1468 [S]	Blues at Carnegie Hall	1969	2.50	5.00	10.00
-- Red and green label					
❏ 1486 [M]	Live at the Lighthouse	1967	5.00	10.00	20.00
❏ SD 1486 [S]	Live at the Lighthouse	1967	3.00	6.00	12.00
-- Multicolor label, black "fan" logo at right					
❏ SD 1486 [S]	Live at the Lighthouse	1969	2.50	5.00	10.00
-- Red and green label					
❏ SD 1546	The Best of the Modern Jazz Quartet	1970	3.00	6.00	12.00
❏ SD 1589	Plastic Dreams	1972	3.00	6.00	12.00
❏ SD 1623	Legendary Profile	1973	3.00	6.00	12.00
❏ SD 1652	Blues on Bach	1974	3.00	6.00	12.00
❏ SQ 1652 [Q]	Blues on Bach	1974	5.00	10.00	20.00
❏ SD 8806	More from the Last Concert	198?	2.50	5.00	10.00
❏ 81761	Three Windows	1987	2.50	5.00	10.00
❏ 90049	The Modern Jazz Quartet at the Music Inn	1983	2.50	5.00	10.00
EASTWEST					
❏ 90826	For Ellington	1988	2.50	5.00	10.00
FANTASY					
❏ OJC-002	Concorde	1982	2.50	5.00	10.00
❏ OJC-057	Django	198?	2.50	5.00	10.00
❏ OJC-125	Modern Jazz Quartet/Milt Jackson Quintet	198?	2.50	5.00	10.00
LITTLE DAVID					
❏ LD 3001	In Memoriam	1975	3.00	6.00	12.00

Number	Title	Yr	VG	VG+	NM
❑ 90130	In Memoriam	198?	2.50	5.00	10.00
MOBILE FIDELITY					
❑ 1-090	Live at the Lighthouse	1982	12.50	25.00	50.00
-- Audiophile vinyl					
❑ 1-205	The Modern Jazz Quartet	1994	7.50	15.00	30.00
-- Audiophile vinyl					
❑ 1-206	Blues at Carnegie Hall	1994	7.50	15.00	30.00
-- Audiophile vinyl					
❑ 1-228	The Modern Jazz Quartet at the Music Inn, Volume 2	1995	15.00	30.00	60.00
-- Audiophile vinyl					
PABLO					
❑ 2310 917	Topsy: This One's for Basie	198?	2.50	5.00	10.00
❑ 2405 423	The Best of the Modern Jazz Quartet	198?	2.50	5.00	10.00
PABLO LIVE					
❑ 2308 243	Reunion at Budokan	198?	2.50	5.00	10.00
❑ 2308 244	Together Again... At Montreux Jazz Festival	198?	2.50	5.00	10.00
PABLO TODAY					
❑ 2312 142	Together Again	198?	2.50	5.00	10.00
PRESTIGE					
❑ PRLP-160 [10]	The Modern Jazz Quartet with Milt Jackson	1953	30.00	60.00	120.00
❑ PRLP-170 [10]	The Modern Jazz Quartet, Volume 2	1953	30.00	60.00	120.00
❑ PRLP-7005 [M]	Concorde	1955	17.50	35.00	70.00
-- Yellow label originals					
❑ PRLP-7057 [M]	Django	1956	17.50	35.00	70.00
-- Yellow label originals					
❑ PRLP-7059 [M]	Modern Jazz Quartet/Milt Jackson Quintet	1956	17.50	35.00	70.00
-- Yellow label originals					
❑ PRLP-7421 [M]	The Modern Jazz Quartet Play for Lovers	1966	5.00	10.00	20.00
❑ PRST-7421 [R]	The Modern Jazz Quartet Play for Lovers	1966	3.00	6.00	12.00
❑ PRLP-7425 [M]	The Modern Jazz Quartet Plays Jazz Classics	1966	5.00	10.00	20.00
❑ PRST-7425 [R]	The Modern Jazz Quartet Plays Jazz Classics	1966	3.00	6.00	12.00
❑ PRST-7749	First Recordings	1970	3.00	6.00	12.00
❑ 24005 [(2)]	The Modern Jazz Quartet	197?	3.75	7.50	15.00
SAVOY					
❑ MG-12046 [M]	Modern Jazz Quartet	1955	12.50	25.00	50.00
SOLID STATE					
❑ SS-18035	The Modern Jazz Quartet on Tour	1968	3.00	6.00	12.00
UNITED ARTISTS					
❑ UAL-4072 [M]	Patterns	1960	6.25	12.50	25.00
❑ UAS-5072 [S]	Patterns	1960	7.50	15.00	30.00

MODERN JAZZ QUINTET, THE
SURREY

Number	Title	Yr	VG	VG+	NM
❑ S-1030 [M]	Q.T. Hush	1966	6.25	12.50	25.00
❑ SS-1030 [S]	Q.T. Hush	1966	7.50	15.00	30.00

MODERN JAZZ SEXTET, THE
Members: Skeeter Best (guitar); DIZZY GILLESPIE (trumpet); Percy Heath (bass); JOHN LEWIS (piano); CHARLIE PERSIP (drums); SONNY STITT (alto & tenor sax).
AMERICAN RECORDING SOCIETY

Number	Title	Yr	VG	VG+	NM
❑ G-429 [M]	The Modern Jazz Sextet	1957	10.00	20.00	40.00
NORGRAN					
❑ MGN-1076 [M]	The Modern Jazz Sextet	1956	25.00	50.00	100.00
VERVE					
❑ VE-1-2533	Dizzy Meets Sonny	197?	3.00	6.00	12.00
❑ MGV-8166 [M]	The Modern Jazz Sextet	1957	15.00	30.00	60.00
❑ V-8166 [M]	The Modern Jazz Sextet	1961	6.25	12.50	25.00

MODERN JAZZ SOCIETY, THE
Members: STAN GETZ; Percy Heath; J.J. JOHNSON; Connie Kay; James Politis; Jim Poole; Janet Putnam; AARON SACHS; Gunther Schuller; TONY SCOTT; LUCKY THOMPSON; Manny Ziegler.
AMERICAN RECORDING SOCIETY

Number	Title	Yr	VG	VG+	NM
❑ G-432 [M]	A Concert of Contemporary Music	1957	10.00	20.00	40.00
NORGRAN					
❑ MGN-1040 [M]	A Concert of Contemporary Music	1955	25.00	50.00	100.00
VERVE					
❑ VSP-18 [M]	Little David's Fugue	1966	5.00	10.00	20.00
-- As "The Modern Jazz Ensemble"					
❑ VSPS-18 [R]	Little David's Fugue	1966	3.00	6.00	12.00
-- As "The Modern Jazz Ensemble"					

Number	Title	Yr	VG	VG+	NM
❑ MGV-8131 [M]	A Concert of Contemporary Music	1957	15.00	30.00	60.00
❑ V-8131 [M]	A Concert of Contemporary Music	1961	6.25	12.50	25.00

MODERN JAZZ TRIO, THE
See MJT + 3.

MODERN MANDOLIN QUARTET, THE
Members: Paul Binkley; John Imholtz; David Peters; Dana Rath.
LOST LAKE ARTS

Number	Title	Yr	VG	VG+	NM
❑ LL-0095	Modern Mandolin Quartet	1988	3.00	6.00	12.00

MOER, PAUL
Pianist.
DEL-FI

Number	Title	Yr	VG	VG+	NM
❑ DFLP-1212 [M]	Contemporary Jazz Classics	1961	5.00	10.00	20.00
❑ DFST-1212 [S]	Contemporary Jazz Classics	1961	6.25	12.50	25.00

MOFFETT, CHARLES
Drummer.
SAVOY

Number	Title	Yr	VG	VG+	NM
❑ MG-12194	The Gift	1969	5.00	10.00	20.00

MOFFETT, CHARNETT
Bass player.
BLUE NOTE

Number	Title	Yr	VG	VG+	NM
❑ BT-46993	Nett Man	1987	2.50	5.00	10.00
❑ B1-91650	Beauty Within	1989	3.75	7.50	15.00

MOFFITT, PETER
Cello player and flutist.
NOVUS

Number	Title	Yr	VG	VG+	NM
❑ 3020-1-N	Zoe's Song	1987	2.50	5.00	10.00
❑ 3059-1-N	Riverdance	1989	3.00	6.00	12.00

MOJO JAZZIN' FIVE
STOMP OFF

Number	Title	Yr	VG	VG+	NM
❑ SOS-1086	South Side Chicago Style	1985	2.50	5.00	10.00

MOLE, MIFF
Trombonist.
JAZZOLOGY

Number	Title	Yr	VG	VG+	NM
❑ JCE-5 [M]	The Immortal Miff Mole	1964	3.75	7.50	15.00
❑ J-105	Milt Mole and His World Jam Session Band, 1944	198?	2.50	5.00	10.00

MOLE, MIFF/EDMOND HALL
Also see each artist's individual listings.
BRUNSWICK

Number	Title	Yr	VG	VG+	NM
❑ BL 58042 [10]	Battle of Jazz, Volume 4	1953	15.00	30.00	60.00

MOLENAT, CLAUDE
VANGUARD

Number	Title	Yr	VG	VG+	NM
❑ VSD-319	Trumpet/Organ/Rhythm	197?	3.00	6.00	12.00

MONCUR, GRACHAN, III
Trombonist.
BLUE NOTE

Number	Title	Yr	VG	VG+	NM
❑ BLP-4153 [M]	Evolution	1963	6.25	12.50	25.00
❑ BLP-4177 [M]	Some Other Stuff	1964	6.25	12.50	25.00
❑ BST-84153 [S]	Evolution	1963	7.50	15.00	30.00
-- With "New York, USA" address on label					
❑ BST-84153 [S]	Evolution	1967	3.75	7.50	15.00
-- With "A Division of Liberty Records" on label					
❑ BST-84153 [S]	Evolution	1986	2.50	5.00	10.00
-- "The Finest in Jazz Since 1939" reissue					
❑ BST-84177 [S]	Some Other Stuff	1964	7.50	15.00	30.00
-- With "New York, USA" address on label					
❑ BST-84177 [S]	Some Other Stuff	1967	3.75	7.50	15.00
-- With "A Division of Liberty Records" on label					
JCOA					
❑ 1009	Echoes of Prayer	197?	3.75	7.50	15.00
PICCADILLY					
❑ 3520	African Concepts	198?	2.50	5.00	10.00

MONK, MEREDITH
Female singer and composer.
ECM

Number	Title	Yr	VG	VG+	NM
❑ 1197	Dolmen Music	198?	2.50	5.00	10.00

Number	Title	Yr	VG	VG+	NM
❑ 23792	Turtle Dreams	1983	2.50	5.00	10.00
LOVELY					
❑ 1051	Key	198?	2.50	5.00	10.00

MONK, THELONIOUS
Pianist and composer; one of the most influential and important post-World War II jazz figures. Also see ART BLAKEY; MILES DAVIS.

Number	Title	Yr	VG	VG+	NM
ANALOGUE PRODUCTIONS					
❑ AP-37 [(7)]	The Riverside Tenor Sessions	1999	62.50	125.00	250.00
ARCHIVE OF FOLK AND JAZZ					
❑ 336	Piano Solos	198?	2.50	5.00	10.00
BANDSTAND					
❑ BDLP-1505	Blue Monk	1992	3.00	6.00	12.00
❑ BDLP-1516	April in Paris	1992	3.00	6.00	12.00
BLACK LION					
❑ 152	Something in Blue	1972	3.00	6.00	12.00
❑ 197	The Man I Love	1973	3.00	6.00	12.00
BLUE NOTE					
❑ BN-LA579-H2 [(2)]	The Complete Genius	1976	3.75	7.50	15.00
❑ LWB-579 [(2)]	The Complete Genius	1981	3.00	6.00	12.00
-- Reissue of BN-LA579-H2					
❑ BLP-1510 [M]	Genius of Modern Music, Vol. 1	1956	50.00	100.00	200.00
-- "Deep groove" version (deep indentation under label on both sides)					
❑ BLP-1510 [M]	Genius of Modern Music, Vol. 1	1956	37.50	75.00	150.00
-- Regular edition, Lexington Ave. address on label					
❑ BLP-1510 [M]	Genius of Modern Music, Vol. 1	1963	6.25	12.50	25.00
-- "New York, USA" address on label					
❑ BLP-1511 [M]	Genius of Modern Music, Vol. 2	1956	50.00	100.00	200.00
-- "Deep groove" version (deep indentation under label on both sides)					
❑ BLP-1511 [M]	Genius of Modern Music, Vol. 2	1956	37.50	75.00	150.00
-- Regular edition, Lexington Ave. address on label					
❑ BLP-1511 [M]	Genius of Modern Music, Vol. 2	1963	6.25	12.50	25.00
-- "New York, USA" address on label					
❑ BLP-5002 [10]	Genius of Modern Music, Vol. 1	1952	100.00	200.00	400.00
❑ BLP-5009 [10]	Genius of Modern Music, Vol. 2	1952	100.00	200.00	400.00
❑ BLP-81510 [R]	Genius of Modern Music, Vol. 1	1968	2.50	5.00	10.00
❑ BLP-81511 [R]	Genius of Modern Music, Vol. 2	1968	2.50	5.00	10.00
❑ BST-81510	Genius of Modern Music, Vol. 1	1985	2.50	5.00	10.00
-- "The Finest in Jazz Since 1939" reissue					
❑ BST-81511	Genius of Modern Music, Vol. 2	1985	2.50	5.00	10.00
-- "The Finest in Jazz Since 1939" reissue					
COLUMBIA					
❑ CL 1965 [M]	Monk's Dream	1963	5.00	10.00	20.00
❑ CL 2038 [M]	Criss-Cross	1963	5.00	10.00	20.00
❑ CL 2164 [M]	Monk Big Band and Quartet In Concert	1964	5.00	10.00	20.00
❑ CL 2184 [M]	It's Monk's Time	1964	5.00	10.00	20.00
❑ CL 2291 [M]	Monk	1965	5.00	10.00	20.00
❑ CL 2349 [M]	Solo Monk	1965	5.00	10.00	20.00
❑ CL 2416 [M]	Misterioso	1966	5.00	10.00	20.00
❑ CL 2651 [M]	Straight No Chaser	1967	7.50	15.00	50.00
❑ CS 8765 [S]	Monk's Dream	1963	6.25	12.50	25.00
❑ CS 8838 [S]	Criss-Cross	1963	6.25	12.50	25.00
❑ CS 8964 [S]	Monk Big Band and Quartet In Concert	1964	6.25	12.50	25.00
❑ CS 8984 [S]	It's Monk's Time	1964	6.25	12.50	25.00
❑ CS 9091 [S]	Monk	1965	6.25	12.50	25.00
❑ CS 9149 [S]	Solo Monk	1965	6.25	12.50	25.00
❑ CS 9149	Solo Monk	1971	3.00	6.00	12.00
-- Orange label					
❑ CS 9216 [S]	Misterioso	1966	6.25	12.50	25.00
❑ CS 9451 [S]	Straight No Chaser	1967	5.00	10.00	20.00
-- Red "360 Sound" label					
❑ CS 9451	Straight No Chaser	1971	3.00	6.00	12.00
-- Orange label					
❑ CS 9632	Underground	1968	5.00	10.00	20.00
-- Red "360 Sound" label					
❑ CS 9632	Underground	1971	3.00	6.00	12.00
-- Orange label					
❑ CS 9775	Greatest Hits	1969	3.75	7.50	15.00
-- Red "360 Sound" label					
❑ CS 9775	Greatest Hits	1971	3.00	6.00	12.00
-- Orange label					
❑ CS 9806	Monk's Blues	1969	5.00	10.00	20.00
-- Red "360 Sound" label					
❑ CS 9806	Monk's Blues	1971	3.00	6.00	12.00
-- Orange label					
❑ PC 9149	Solo Monk	198?	2.00	4.00	8.00
-- Reissue with new prefix					
❑ PC 9451	Straight No Chaser	198?	2.00	4.00	8.00
-- Reissue with new prefix					
❑ PC 9632	Underground	198?	2.00	4.00	8.00
-- Reissue with new prefix					
❑ PC 9775	Greatest Hits	198?	2.00	4.00	8.00
-- Reissue with new prefix					

Number	Title	Yr	VG	VG+	NM
❑ PC 9806	Monk's Blues	198?	2.00	4.00	8.00
-- Reissue with new prefix					
❑ KG 32892 [(2)]	Who's Afraid of the Big Band Monk	1974	3.75	7.50	15.00
❑ JG 35720 [(2)]	Always Know	1979	3.75	7.50	15.00
❑ C2 38030 [(2)]	Live at the It Club	1983	3.00	6.00	12.00
❑ C2 38269 [(2)]	Live at the Jazz Workshop	1983	3.00	6.00	12.00
❑ C2 38510 [(2)]	The Tokyo Concerts	1984	3.00	6.00	12.00
COLUMBIA JAZZ MASTERPIECES					
❑ CJ 40785	Underground	1987	2.50	5.00	10.00
❑ CJ 40786	Monk's Dream	1987	2.50	5.00	10.00
❑ CJ 44297	The Composer	1988	2.50	5.00	10.00
COLUMBIA MUSICAL TREASURY					
❑ DS 338	Monk's Miracles	1967	6.25	12.50	25.00
-- Columbia Record Club exclusive					
FANTASY					
❑ OJC-010	Thelonious Monk Trio	198?	2.50	5.00	10.00
❑ OJC-016	Monk	198?	2.50	5.00	10.00
❑ OJC-024	Thelonious Monk Plays Duke Ellington	198?	2.50	5.00	10.00
❑ OJC-026	Brilliant Corners	198?	2.50	5.00	10.00
❑ OJC-059	Thelonious Monk/Sonny Rollins	198?	2.50	5.00	10.00
❑ OJC-064	The Unique Thelonious Monk	198?	2.50	5.00	10.00
❑ OJC-084	Monk's Music	198?	2.50	5.00	10.00
❑ OJC-103	Thelonious in Action	198?	2.50	5.00	10.00
❑ OJC-135	Thelonious Monk at Town Hall	198?	2.50	5.00	10.00
❑ OJC-206	Misterioso	1985	2.50	5.00	10.00
❑ OJC-231	Alone in San Francisco	1987	2.50	5.00	10.00
❑ OJC-254	Thelonious Himself	1987	2.50	5.00	10.00
❑ OJC-301	Mulligan Meets Monk	1988	2.50	5.00	10.00
❑ OJC-305	Thelonious Monk at the Blackhawk	1988	2.50	5.00	10.00
❑ OJC-362	5 By Monk By 5	1988	2.50	5.00	10.00
❑ OJC-488	Monk in Italy	1991	2.50	5.00	10.00
GATEWAY					
❑ 7023	Monk's Music	197?	3.00	6.00	12.00
GNP CRESCENDO					
❑ 9008 [(2)]	Thelonious Monk	197?	3.75	7.50	15.00
JAZZ MAN					
❑ 5017	Something in Blue	198?	2.50	5.00	10.00
MILESTONE					
❑ 9115	Evidence	198?	2.50	5.00	10.00
❑ 9124	Blues Five Spot	198?	2.50	5.00	10.00
❑ 47004 [(2)]	Pure Monk	1972	3.75	7.50	15.00
❑ 47023 [(2)]	Brilliance	197?	3.75	7.50	15.00
❑ 47033 [(2)]	Thelonious Monk In Person	197?	3.75	7.50	15.00
❑ 47043 [(2)]	Thelonious Monk at the Five Spot	1978	3.75	7.50	15.00
❑ 47052 [(2)]	The Riverside Trios	1980	3.75	7.50	15.00
❑ 47060 [(2)]	April in Paris/Live	198?	3.75	7.50	15.00
❑ 47064 [(2)]	Memorial Album	1982	3.00	6.00	12.00
❑ 47067 [(2)]	'Round Midnight	198?	3.00	6.00	12.00
MOSAIC					
❑ M4-101 [(4)]	The Complete Blue Note Recordings of Thelonious Monk	198?	25.00	50.00	100.00
❑ MR4-112 [(4)]	The Complete Black Lion and Vogue Recordings	199?	20.00	40.00	80.00
PICCADILLY					
❑ 3521	Monkisms	198?	2.50	5.00	10.00
PRESTIGE					
❑ PRLP-142 [10]	Thelonious Monk Trio	1953	50.00	100.00	200.00
❑ PRLP-166 [10]	Thelonious Monk Quintet with Sonny Rollins and Julius Watkins	1953	50.00	100.00	200.00
❑ PRLP-180 [10]	Thelonious Monk Quintet	1954	50.00	100.00	200.00
❑ PRLP-189 [10]	Thelonious Monk Trio	1954	50.00	100.00	200.00
❑ PRLP-7027 [M]	Thelonious Monk	1956	25.00	50.00	100.00
-- Reissue of 142 and 189 on one 12-inch record					
❑ PRLP-7053 [M]	Monk	1956	25.00	50.00	100.00
-- Reissue of 150					
❑ PRLP-7075 [M]	Thelonious Monk/Sonny Rollins	1957	25.00	50.00	100.00
-- Reissue of 166					
❑ PRLP-7159 [M]	Monk's Moods	1959	18.75	37.50	75.00
-- Reissue of 7027					
❑ PRLP-7169 [M]	Work	1959	18.75	37.50	75.00
-- Reissue of 7075					
❑ PRLP-7245 [M]	We See	1962	18.75	37.50	75.00
-- Reissue of 7053					
❑ PRLP-7363 [M]	The Golden Monk	1965	7.50	15.00	30.00
-- Reissue of 7245					
❑ PRST-7363 [R]	The Golden Monk	1965	3.75	7.50	15.00
❑ PRLP-7508 [M]	The High Priest	1967	7.50	15.00	30.00
-- Reissue of 7159					
❑ PRST-7508 [R]	The High Priest	1967	3.75	7.50	15.00
❑ PRST-7656	The Genius	1969	3.00	6.00	12.00
❑ PRST-7751	Reflections, Volume 1	1970	3.00	6.00	12.00
❑ PRST-7848	Blue Monk, Volume 2	197?	3.00	6.00	12.00

Number	Title	Yr	VG	VG+	NM
❑ 24006 [(2)]	Thelonious Monk	1971	3.75	7.50	15.00
RIVERSIDE					
❑ R-022 [(22)]	The Complete Riverside Recordings	1987	100.00	200.00	400.00
❑ RLP 12-201 [M]	Thelonious Monk Plays Duke Ellington	1955	100.00	200.00	400.00
-- White label with blue print					
❑ RLP 12-201 [M]	Thelonious Monk Plays Duke Ellington	1958	10.00	20.00	40.00
-- Blue label with reel and microphone logo					
❑ RLP 12-209 [M]	The Unique Thelonious Monk	1956	25.00	50.00	100.00
-- White label with blue print					
❑ RLP 12-209 [M]	The Unique Thelonious Monk	1958	10.00	20.00	40.00
-- Blue label with reel and microphone logo					
❑ RLP 12-226 [M]	Brilliant Corners	1957	25.00	50.00	100.00
-- White label with blue print					
❑ RLP 12-226 [M]	Brilliant Corners	1958	10.00	20.00	40.00
-- Blue label with reel and microphone logo					
❑ RLP 12-235 [M]	Thelonious Himself	1957	25.00	50.00	100.00
-- White label with blue print					
❑ RLP 12-235 [M]	Thelonious Himself	1958	10.00	20.00	40.00
-- Blue label with reel and microphone logo					
❑ RLP 12-242 [M]	Monk's Music	1957	25.00	50.00	100.00
-- White label with blue print					
❑ RLP 12-242 [M]	Monk's Music	1958	10.00	20.00	40.00
-- Blue label with reel and microphone logo					
❑ RLP 12-247 [M]	Mulligan Meets Monk	1957	25.00	50.00	100.00
-- White label with blue print					
❑ RLP 12-247 [M]	Mulligan Meets Monk	1958	10.00	20.00	40.00
-- Blue label with reel and microphone logo					
❑ RLP 12-262 [M]	Thelonious in Action Recorded at the Five Spot Café, New York, With Johnny Griffin	1958	10.00	20.00	40.00
❑ RLP 12-279 [M]	Misterioso	1958	10.00	20.00	40.00
❑ RLP 12-300 [M]	The Thelonious Monk Orchestra at Town Hall	1959	10.00	20.00	40.00
❑ RLP 12-305 [M]	5 By Monk By 5	1959	10.00	20.00	40.00
❑ RLP 12-312 [M]	Thelonious Alone in San Francisco	1959	10.00	20.00	40.00
❑ RLP 12-323 [M]	Thelonious Monk Quartet Plus Two at the Blackhawk	1960	10.00	20.00	40.00
❑ RLP-421 [M]	Thelonious Monk's Greatest Hits	1962	5.00	10.00	20.00
❑ RLP-443 [M]	Thelonious Monk in Italy	1963	5.00	10.00	20.00
❑ RLP-460/1 [(2) M]	April in Paris	1963	10.00	20.00	40.00
❑ RLP-483 [M]	The Thelonious Monk Story, Volume 1	1965	5.00	10.00	20.00
❑ RLP-484 [M]	The Thelonious Monk Story, Volume 2	1965	5.00	10.00	20.00
❑ RLP-491 [M]	Monk in France	1965	5.00	10.00	20.00
❑ RLP 1101 [S]	Monk's Music	1959	10.00	20.00	40.00
-- Black label with reel and microphone logo					
❑ RLP 1106 [S]	Mulligan Meets Monk	1959	10.00	20.00	40.00
-- Black label with reel and microphone logo					
❑ RLP 1133 [S]	Misterioso	1958	12.50	25.00	50.00
❑ RLP 1138 [S]	The Thelonious Monk Orchestra at Town Hall	1959	12.50	25.00	50.00
❑ RLP 1150 [S]	5 By Monk By 5	1959	12.50	25.00	50.00
❑ RLP 1158 [S]	Thelonious Alone in San Francisco	1959	12.50	25.00	50.00
❑ RLP 1171 [S]	Thelonious Monk Quartet Plus Two at the Blackhawk	1960	12.50	25.00	50.00
❑ RLP 1190 [S]	Thelonious in Action Recorded at the Five Spot Café, New York, With Johnny Griffin	1960	12.50	25.00	50.00
❑ RM-3000 [M]	Mighty Monk	1967	5.00	10.00	20.00
❑ RS-3000 [S]	Mighty Monk	1967	3.75	7.50	15.00
❑ RM-3004 [M]	Monk's Music	1967	5.00	10.00	20.00
❑ RS-3004 [S]	Monk's Music	1967	3.75	7.50	15.00
❑ RS-3009 [R]	CT Meets Monk	1968	3.00	6.00	12.00
❑ RS-3015 [R]	Monk Plays Duke	1968	3.00	6.00	12.00
❑ RS-3020X [(2) R]	Two Hours with Thelonious Monk	1969	3.75	7.50	15.00
❑ RS-3037	Best of Thelonious Monk	1969	3.00	6.00	12.00
❑ RS-3047	Panorama!	1970	3.00	6.00	12.00
❑ 6039 [M]	Thelonious Monk Plays Duke Ellington	197?	3.00	6.00	12.00
❑ 6053 [M]	Thelonious Himself	197?	3.00	6.00	12.00
❑ 6068 [M]	The Unique Thelonious Monk	197?	3.00	6.00	12.00
❑ 6086	5 By Monk By 5	197?	3.00	6.00	12.00
❑ 6102	Thelonious in Action	197?	3.00	6.00	12.00
❑ 6107	Meet Thelonious Monk and Gerry Mulligan	197?	3.00	6.00	12.00
❑ 6119	Misterioso	197?	3.00	6.00	12.00
❑ 6163	Alone in San Francisco	198?	3.00	6.00	12.00
❑ 6183	Thelonious Monk at Town Hall	198?	3.00	6.00	12.00
❑ 6198	Thelonious Monk at the Blackhawk	198?	3.00	6.00	12.00
❑ 6207	Monk's Music	1983	2.50	5.00	10.00
❑ RS-9421 [S]	Thelonious Monk's Greatest Hits	1962	6.25	12.50	25.00
❑ RS-9443 [S]	Monk in Italy	1963	6.25	12.50	25.00
❑ RS-9460/1 [(2) S]	April in Paris	1963	12.50	25.00	50.00
❑ RS-9483 [S]	The Thelonious Monk Story, Volume 1	1965	6.25	12.50	25.00
❑ RS-9484 [S]	The Thelonious Monk Story, Volume 2	1965	6.25	12.50	25.00
❑ RS-9491 [S]	Monk in France	1965	6.25	12.50	25.00
TRIP					
❑ 5022	Pure Monk	1974	2.50	5.00	10.00
XANADU					
❑ 202	Live at the Village Gate	1985	2.50	5.00	10.00

MONK, THELONIOUS, AND JOHN COLTRANE
Also see each artist's individual listings.

Number	Title	Yr	VG	VG+	NM
FANTASY					
❑ OJC-039	Thelonious Monk with John Coltrane	198?	2.50	5.00	10.00
JAZZLAND					
❑ JLP-46 [M]	Thelonious Monk with John Coltrane	1961	10.00	20.00	40.00
❑ JLP-946 [S]	Thelonious Monk with John Coltrane	1961	12.50	25.00	50.00
MILESTONE					
❑ 47011 [(2)]	Monk/Trane	1973	3.75	7.50	15.00
RIVERSIDE					
❑ RLP-490 [M]	Thelonious Monk with John Coltrane	1965	6.25	12.50	25.00
-- Reissue of Jazzland 46					
❑ RS-9490 [S]	Thelonious Monk with John Coltrane	1965	7.50	15.00	30.00
-- Reissue of Jazzland 946					

MONNIER, ALAIN

Number	Title	Yr	VG	VG+	NM
HAT HUT					
❑ 3505	Tribulat	198?	3.75	7.50	15.00

MONTANA

Number	Title	Yr	VG	VG+	NM
LABOR					
❑ 5	Montana	198?	3.00	6.00	12.00

MONTARROYOS, MARCIO
Trumpeter.

Number	Title	Yr	VG	VG+	NM
BLACK SUN					
❑ 15001	Samba Solstice	1987	3.00	6.00	12.00
COLUMBIA					
❑ FC 38952	Carioca	1983	2.50	5.00	10.00
LORIMAR					
❑ FC 37929	Magic Moment	1982	2.50	5.00	10.00
PM					
❑ 014	Marcio Montarroyos and Stone Alliance	1977	3.75	7.50	15.00

MONTEGO JOE
Percussionist.

Number	Title	Yr	VG	VG+	NM
ESP-DISK'					
❑ S-1067	Montego Joe's HARYOU Percussion Ensemble	1968	6.25	12.50	25.00
PRESTIGE					
❑ PRLP-7336 [M]	Arriba Con Montego Joe	1964	6.25	12.50	25.00
❑ PRST-7336 [S]	Arriba Con Montego Joe	1964	7.50	15.00	30.00
❑ PRLP-7413 [M]	Wild and Warm	1966	6.25	12.50	25.00
❑ PRST-7413 [S]	Wild and Warm	1966	7.50	15.00	30.00

MONTEROSE, J.R.
Tenor saxophone player.

Number	Title	Yr	VG	VG+	NM
BLUE NOTE					
❑ BLP-1536 [M]	J.R. Monterose	1956	50.00	100.00	200.00
-- "Deep groove" version (deep indentation under label on both sides)					
❑ BLP-1536 [M]	J.R. Monterose	1956	37.50	75.00	150.00
-- Regular version, Lexington Ave. address on label					
❑ BLP-1536 [M]	J.R. Monterose	1963	6.25	12.50	25.00
-- With "New York, USA" address on label					
❑ BST-81536 [R]	J.R. Monterose	1967	3.00	6.00	12.00
-- With "A Division of Liberty Records" on label					
CADENCE JAZZ					
❑ CJ-1013	Bebop Loose and Live	198?	2.50	5.00	10.00
JARO					
❑ JAM-5004 [M]	The Message	1959	100.00	200.00	400.00
❑ JAS-8004 [S]	The Message	1959	125.00	250.00	500.00
STUDIO 4					
❑ 100 [M]	J.R. Monterose in Action	195?	150.00	300.00	600.00

Number	Title	Yr	VG	VG+	NM
UPTOWN					
❏ 27.02	J.R. Monterose in Albany	198?	3.00	6.00	12.00
❏ 27.06	J.R. Monterose in Duo with Tommy Flanagan....And a Little Pleasure	198?	3.00	6.00	12.00
XANADU					
❏ 126	Straight Ahead	197?	3.00	6.00	12.00

MONTGOMERY BROTHERS, THE

BUDDY MONTGOMERY, MONK MONTGOMERY and WES MONTGOMERY. Also see THE MASTERSOUNDS; GEORGE SHEARING.

Number	Title	Yr	VG	VG+	NM
FANTASY					
❏ OJC-138	Groove Yard	198?	2.50	5.00	10.00
❏ OJC-283	The Montgomery Brothers in Canada	1987	2.50	5.00	10.00
❏ 3308 [M]	The Montgomery Brothers	1960	12.50	25.00	50.00
-- Red vinyl					
❏ 3308 [M]	The Montgomery Brothers	1960	7.50	15.00	30.00
-- Black vinyl					
❏ 3323 [M]	The Montgomery Brothers in Canada	1961	12.50	25.00	50.00
-- Red vinyl					
❏ 3323 [M]	The Montgomery Brothers in Canada	1961	7.50	15.00	30.00
-- Black vinyl					
❏ 3376 [M]	Wes' Best	1967	5.00	10.00	20.00
❏ 8052 [S]	The Montgomery Brothers	1960	10.00	20.00	40.00
-- Blue vinyl					
❏ 8052 [S]	The Montgomery Brothers	1960	6.25	12.50	25.00
-- Black vinyl					
❏ 8066 [S]	The Montgomery Brothers in Canada	1961	10.00	20.00	40.00
-- Blue vinyl					
❏ 8066 [S]	The Montgomery Brothers in Canada	1961	6.25	12.50	25.00
-- Black vinyl					
❏ 8376 [S]	Wes' Best	1967	3.75	7.50	15.00
PACIFIC JAZZ					
❏ PJ-17 [M]	Wes, Buddy and Monk Montgomery	1961	7.50	15.00	30.00
RIVERSIDE					
❏ RLP-362 [M]	Groove Yard	1961	6.25	12.50	25.00
❏ 6141	Groove Yard	198?	3.00	6.00	12.00
❏ RS-9362 [S]	Groove Yard	1961	7.50	15.00	30.00
WORLD PACIFIC					
❏ PJ-1240 [M]	The Montgomery Brothers and Five Others	1957	20.00	40.00	80.00
❏ WP-1240 [M]	The Montgomery Brothers and Five Others	1958	15.00	30.00	60.00
-- Reissue with new prefix					

MONTGOMERY, BUDDY

Vibraphone player, pianist and composer. Also see THE MASTERSOUNDS; THE MONTGOMERY BROTHERS.

Number	Title	Yr	VG	VG+	NM
ABC IMPULSE!					
❏ AS-9192	This Rather Than That	1970	5.00	10.00	20.00
BEAN					
❏ 102	Ties	197?	3.75	7.50	15.00
LANDMARK					
❏ LLP-1512	Ties of Love	1987	2.50	5.00	10.00
❏ LLP-1518	So Why Not?	1989	3.00	6.00	12.00
MILESTONE					
❏ M-9015	Two-Sided Album	1969	5.00	10.00	20.00

MONTGOMERY, DAVID, AND CECIL LYTLE

Both are pianists.

Number	Title	Yr	VG	VG+	NM
KLAVIER					
❏ 533	Rags and Blues	197?	3.00	6.00	12.00
SONIC ARTS					
❏ 6	Ragtime Piano for Four Hands	197?	5.00	10.00	20.00
-- Direct-to-disc recording					

MONTGOMERY, MARIAN

Female singer.

Number	Title	Yr	VG	VG+	NM
CAPITOL					
❏ ST 1884 [S]	Marian Montgomery Swings for Winners and Losers	1963	7.50	15.00	30.00
❏ T 1884 [M]	Marian Montgomery Swings for Winners and Losers	1963	6.25	12.50	25.00
❏ ST 1962 [S]	Let There Be Love, Let There Be Swing, Let There Be Marian Montgomery	1963	7.50	15.00	30.00
❏ T 1962 [M]	Let There Be Love, Let There Be Swing, Let There Be Marian Montgomery	1963	6.25	12.50	25.00
❏ ST 2185 [S]	Lovin' Is Livin' and Livin' Is Lovin'	1964	7.50	15.00	30.00
❏ T 2185 [M]	Lovin' Is Livin' and Livin' Is Lovin'	1964	6.25	12.50	25.00
DECCA					
❏ DL 4773 [M]	What's New?	1965	5.00	10.00	20.00
❏ DL 74773 [S]	What's New?	1965	6.25	12.50	25.00

MONTGOMERY, MONK

Bass player. Also see THE MASTERSOUNDS; THE MONTGOMERY BROTHERS.

Number	Title	Yr	VG	VG+	NM
CHISA					
❏ CS-801	It's Never Too Late	1970	5.00	10.00	20.00
❏ CS-806	Bass Odyssey	1971	5.00	10.00	20.00
PHILADELPHIA INT'L.					
❏ KZ 33153	Reality	1974	3.75	7.50	15.00

MONTGOMERY, WES

Guitarist. Also see MILT JACKSON; THE MONTGOMERY BROTHERS; JIMMY SMITH.

Number	Title	Yr	VG	VG+	NM
A&M					
❏ LP-2001 [M]	A Day in the Life	1967	5.00	10.00	20.00
❏ SP-3001 [S]	A Day in the Life	1967	3.75	7.50	15.00
❏ SP9-3001	A Day in the Life	1985	3.75	7.50	15.00
-- Audiophile reissue					
❏ SP-3006	Down Here on the Ground	1968	3.75	7.50	15.00
❏ SP9-3006	Down Here on the Ground	1985	3.75	7.50	15.00
-- Audiophile reissue					
❏ SP-3012	Road Song	1968	3.75	7.50	15.00
❏ SP9-3012	Road Song	198?	3.75	7.50	15.00
-- Audiophile reissue					
❏ SP-4247	Greatest Hits	1970	3.75	7.50	15.00
ACCORD					
❏ SN-7170	The Classic Sound of Wes Montgomery	1981	2.50	5.00	10.00
BLUE NOTE					
❏ BN-LA531-H2 [(2)]	Beginnings	1976	3.75	7.50	15.00
❏ LWB-531 [(2)]	Beginnings	1981	3.00	6.00	12.00
-- Reissue of BN-LA531-H2					
DCC COMPACT CLASSICS					
❏ LPZ-2014	Goin' Out of My Head	1996	6.25	12.50	25.00
-- Audiophile vinyl					
FANTASY					
❏ OJC-034	New Concepts in Jazz Guitar	198?	2.50	5.00	10.00
❏ OJC-036	The Incredible Jazz Guitar of Wes Montgomery	198?	2.50	5.00	10.00
❏ OJC-089	Movin' Along	198?	2.50	5.00	10.00
❏ OJC-106	Full House	198?	2.50	5.00	10.00
❏ OJC-144	Portrait of Wes	198?	2.50	5.00	10.00
❏ OJC-233	So Much Guitar!	198?	2.50	5.00	10.00
❏ OJC-261	Boss Guitar	1987	2.50	5.00	10.00
❏ OJC-368	Fusion! Wes Montgomery with Strings	198?	2.50	5.00	10.00
❏ OJC-489	Guitar on the Go	1991	3.00	6.00	12.00
MGM					
❏ GAS-120	Wes Montgomery (Golden Archive Series)	1970	3.75	7.50	15.00
MILESTONE					
❏ 9110	Encores	1983	2.50	5.00	10.00
❏ 47003 [(2)]	While We're Young	1972	3.75	7.50	15.00
❏ 47013 [(2)]	Wes Montgomery and Friends	1973	3.75	7.50	15.00
❏ 47030 [(2)]	Pretty Blue	197?	3.00	6.00	12.00
❏ 47040 [(2)]	Movin'	197?	3.00	6.00	12.00
❏ 47051 [(2)]	Groove Brothers	1979	3.00	6.00	12.00
❏ 47057 [(2)]	Yesterdays	198?	3.00	6.00	12.00
❏ 47065 [(2)]	The Alternative	198?	3.00	6.00	12.00
MOBILE FIDELITY					
❏ MFSL-508	Bumpin'	198?	7.50	15.00	30.00
-- Audiophile vinyl					
PACIFIC JAZZ					
❏ PJ-5 [M]	Montgomeryland	1960	7.50	15.00	30.00
❏ ST-5 [S]	Montgomeryland	1960	10.00	20.00	40.00
❏ PJ-10104 [M]	Easy Groove	1966	3.75	7.50	15.00
❏ PJ-10130 [M]	Kismet	1967	5.00	10.00	20.00
❏ ST-20104 [S]	Easy Groove	1966	5.00	10.00	20.00
❏ ST-20130 [S]	Kismet	1967	3.75	7.50	15.00
❏ ST-20137	Portrait of Wes Montgomery	1968	3.75	7.50	15.00
PICCADILLY					
❏ 3584	Jazz Guitar	198?	2.50	5.00	10.00
RIVERSIDE					
❏ RLP 12-310 [M]	New Concepts in Jazz Guitar	1959	7.50	15.00	30.00
❏ RLP 12-320 [M]	The Incredible Jazz Guitar of Wes Montgomery	1960	7.50	15.00	30.00
❏ RLP-342 [M]	Movin' Along	1960	6.25	12.50	25.00
❏ RLP-382 [M]	So Much Guitar!	1961	6.25	12.50	25.00
❏ RLP-434 [M]	Full House	1962	7.50	15.00	30.00

Number	Title	Yr	VG	VG+	NM
❏ RLP-459 [M]	Boss Guitar	1963	5.00	10.00	20.00
❏ RLP-472 [M]	Fusion! Wes Montgomery with Strings	1964	5.00	10.00	20.00
❏ RLP-492 [M]	Portrait of Wes	1965	3.75	7.50	15.00
❏ RLP-494 [M]	Guitar on the Go	1965	3.75	7.50	15.00
❏ RLP 1156 [S]	New Concepts in Jazz Guitar	1959	7.50	15.00	30.00
❏ RLP 1169 [S]	The Incredible Jazz Guitar of Wes Montgomery	1960	7.50	15.00	30.00
❏ RM-3002 [M]	In the Wee Small Hours	1967	3.75	7.50	15.00
-- Reissue of 472					
❏ RS-3002 [S]	In the Wee Small Hours	1967	3.00	6.00	12.00
-- Reissue of 9472					
❏ RS-3012	This Is Wes Montgomery	1968	3.00	6.00	12.00
-- Reissue of 9459					
❏ RS-3014	'Round Midnight	1968	3.00	6.00	12.00
-- Reissue of 1156					
❏ RS-3036	March 6, 1925-June 15, 1968	1968	3.00	6.00	12.00
❏ RS-3039	The Best of Wes Montgomery	1968	3.00	6.00	12.00
❏ RS-3046	Panorama	1969	3.00	6.00	12.00
❏ 6046	The Incredible Jazz Guitar of Wes Montgomery	197?	2.50	5.00	10.00
❏ 6069	Full House	197?	2.50	5.00	10.00
❏ 6080	The Dynamic New Jazz Sound of Wes Montgomery	197?	2.50	5.00	10.00
❏ 6100	So Much Guitar!	197?	2.50	5.00	10.00
❏ 6111	Boss Guitar	197?	2.50	5.00	10.00
❏ 6168	Guitar on the Go	198?	2.50	5.00	10.00
❏ 6199	Movin' Along	198?	2.50	5.00	10.00
❏ 6202	Portrait of Wes	198?	2.50	5.00	10.00
❏ 6210	Fusion! Wes Montgomery with Strings	198?	2.50	5.00	10.00
❏ RS-9342 [S]	Movin' Along	1960	6.25	12.50	25.00
❏ RS-9382 [S]	So Much Guitar!	1961	6.25	12.50	25.00
❏ RS-9434 [S]	Full House	1962	7.50	15.00	30.00
❏ RS-9459 [S]	Boss Guitar	1963	6.25	12.50	25.00
❏ RS-9472 [S]	Fusion! Wes Montgomery with Strings	1964	6.25	12.50	25.00
❏ RS-9492 [S]	Portrait of Wes	1965	5.00	10.00	20.00
❏ RS-9494 [S]	Guitar on the Go	1965	5.00	10.00	20.00

VERVE

Number	Title	Yr	VG	VG+	NM
❏ VE-2-2513 [(2)]	Small Group Recording	197?	3.75	7.50	15.00
❏ V-8610 [M]	Movin' Wes	1965	3.75	7.50	15.00
❏ V6-8610 [S]	Movin' Wes	1965	5.00	10.00	20.00
❏ V-8625 [M]	Bumpin'	1965	3.75	7.50	15.00
❏ V6-8625 [S]	Bumpin'	1965	5.00	10.00	20.00
❏ V-8642 [M]	Goin' Out of My Head	1966	3.75	7.50	15.00
❏ V6-8642 [S]	Goin' Out of My Head	1966	5.00	10.00	20.00
❏ V-8653 [M]	Tequila	1966	3.75	7.50	15.00
❏ V6-8653 [S]	Tequila	1966	5.00	10.00	20.00
❏ V-8672 [M]	California Dreaming	1967	5.00	10.00	20.00
❏ V6-8672 [S]	California Dreaming	1967	3.75	7.50	15.00
❏ V-8714 [M]	The Best of Wes Montgomery	1967	5.00	10.00	20.00
❏ V6-8714 [S]	The Best of Wes Montgomery	1967	3.75	7.50	15.00
❏ V6-8757	The Best of Wes Montgomery, Vol. 2	1968	3.75	7.50	15.00
❏ V6-8765	Willow Weep for Me	1969	3.75	7.50	15.00
❏ V6-8796	Eulogy	1970	3.75	7.50	15.00
❏ V6-8804	Just Walkin'	1971	3.00	6.00	12.00
❏ V6-8813 [(2)]	The History of Wes Montgomery	1972	3.75	7.50	15.00
❏ V3HB-8839 [(2)]	Return Engagement	1974	3.75	7.50	15.00

MONTOLIU, TETE
Pianist.
CONTEMPORARY

Number	Title	Yr	VG	VG+	NM
❏ C-14004	Lunch in L.A.	1980	3.00	6.00	12.00

ENJA

| ❏ 2040 | Songs for Love | 197? | 3.75 | 7.50 | 15.00 |

INNER CITY

❏ IC-2017	Catalonian Fire	197?	3.75	7.50	15.00
❏ IC-2021	Music for Perla	197?	3.75	7.50	15.00
❏ IC-2029	Tete!	197?	3.75	7.50	15.00

PAUSA

| ❏ 7057 | Piano for Nuria | 1979 | 2.50 | 5.00 | 10.00 |

STEEPLECHASE

❏ SCS-1054	Tete-a-Tete	197?	3.00	6.00	12.00
❏ SCS-1108	Tootie's Tempo	198?	3.00	6.00	12.00
❏ SCS-1137	I Wanna Talk About You	1980	3.00	6.00	12.00
❏ SCS-1148	Catalonian Nights Vol. 1	1980	3.00	6.00	12.00
❏ SCS-1152/3 [(2)]	Boston Concert	1981	4.50	9.00	18.00
❏ SCS-1185	Face to Face	198?	3.00	6.00	12.00
❏ SCS-1199	That's All	198?	3.00	6.00	12.00

TIMELESS

| ❏ 304 | Catalonian Folksongs | 1979 | 3.00 | 6.00 | 12.00 |

Number	Title	Yr	VG	VG+	NM

MONTROSE, JACK
Tenor saxophone player, arranger and composer.
ATLANTIC

❏ 1223 [M]	Arranged, Played, Composed by Jack Montrose with Bob Gordon	1956	20.00	40.00	80.00
-- Black label					
❏ 1223 [M]	Arranged, Played, Composed by Jack Montrose with Bob Gordon	1961	6.25	12.50	25.00
-- Multicolor label, white "fan" logo at right					
❏ 1223 [M]	Arranged, Played, Composed by Jack Montrose with Bob Gordon	1964	3.75	7.50	15.00
-- Multicolor label, black "fan" logo at right					

PACIFIC JAZZ

❏ PJ-1208 [M]	Jack Montrose Sextet	1955	20.00	40.00	80.00
-- Black vinyl					
❏ PJ-1208 [M]	Jack Montrose Sextet	1955	37.50	75.00	150.00
-- Red vinyl					

RCA VICTOR

| ❏ LPM-1451 [M] | Blues and Vanilla | 1957 | 12.50 | 25.00 | 50.00 |
| ❏ LPM-1572 [M] | The Horns Full | 1957 | 12.50 | 25.00 | 50.00 |

WORLD PACIFIC

| ❏ WP-1208 [M] | Jack Montrose Sextet | 1958 | 12.50 | 25.00 | 50.00 |

MOODY, JAMES
Tenor and alto saxophone player and flutist. Also see ART BLAKEY; THE NEW YORK JAZZ SEXTET.
ARGO

❏ LP-603 [M]	Flute 'n the Blues	1956	10.00	20.00	40.00
-- Reissue of Creative 603					
❏ LP-613 [M]	Moody's Mood for Love	1957	10.00	20.00	40.00
❏ LP-637 [M]	Last Train from Overbrook	1959	10.00	20.00	40.00
❏ LPS-637 [S]	Last Train from Overbrook	1959	7.50	15.00	30.00
❏ LP-648 [M]	James Moody	1959	10.00	20.00	40.00
❏ LPS-648 [S]	James Moody	1959	7.50	15.00	30.00
❏ LP-666 [M]	Hey! It's James Moody	1960	7.50	15.00	30.00
❏ LPS-666 [S]	Hey! It's James Moody	1960	10.00	20.00	40.00
❏ LP-679 [M]	Moody with Strings	1961	7.50	15.00	30.00
❏ LPS-679 [S]	Moody with Strings	1961	10.00	20.00	40.00
❏ LP-695 [M]	Another Bag	1962	7.50	15.00	30.00
❏ LPS-695 [S]	Another Bag	1962	10.00	20.00	40.00
❏ LP-725 [M]	Great Day	1963	6.25	12.50	25.00
❏ LPS-725 [S]	Great Day	1963	7.50	15.00	30.00
❏ LP-740 [M]	Comin' On Strong	1964	6.25	12.50	25.00
❏ LPS-740 [S]	Comin' On Strong	1964	7.50	15.00	30.00

BLUE NOTE

| ❏ BLP-5005 [10] | James Moody with Strings | 1952 | 75.00 | 150.00 | 300.00 |
| ❏ BLP-5006 [10] | James Moody and His Modernists | 1952 | 75.00 | 150.00 | 300.00 |

CADET

❏ LP-603 [M]	Flute 'n the Blues	1966	3.75	7.50	15.00
❏ LP-613 [M]	Moody's Mood for Love	1966	3.75	7.50	15.00
❏ LP-637 [M]	Last Train from Overbrook	1966	3.00	6.00	12.00
❏ LPS-637 [S]	Last Train from Overbrook	1966	3.75	7.50	15.00
❏ LP-648 [M]	James Moody	1966	3.00	6.00	12.00
❏ LPS-648 [S]	James Moody	1966	3.75	7.50	15.00
❏ LP-666 [M]	Hey! It's James Moody	1966	3.00	6.00	12.00
❏ LPS-666 [S]	Hey! It's James Moody	1966	3.75	7.50	15.00
❏ LP-679 [M]	Moody with Strings	1966	3.00	6.00	12.00
❏ LPS-679 [S]	Moody with Strings	1966	3.75	7.50	15.00
❏ LP-695 [M]	Another Bag	1966	3.00	6.00	12.00
❏ LPS-695 [S]	Another Bag	1966	3.75	7.50	15.00
❏ LP-725 [M]	Great Day	1966	3.00	6.00	12.00
❏ LPS-725 [S]	Great Day	1966	3.75	7.50	15.00
❏ LP-740 [M]	Comin' On Strong	1966	3.00	6.00	12.00
❏ LPS-740 [S]	Comin' On Strong	1966	3.75	7.50	15.00
❏ LP-756 [M]	Cookin' the Blues	1965	5.00	10.00	20.00
❏ LPS-756 [S]	Cookin' the Blues	1965	6.25	12.50	25.00
❏ 2CA-60010 [(2)]	Everything About Sax and Flute	1972	5.00	10.00	20.00

CHESS

❏ 2ACMJ-403 [(2)]	Moody's Mood	1976	3.75	7.50	15.00
❏ CH-91522	The Great Day	198?	2.50	5.00	10.00
❏ CH-91548	Flute 'n' the Blues	198?	2.50	5.00	10.00

CREATIVE

| ❏ LP-603 [M] | Flute 'n Blues | 1956 | 37.50 | 75.00 | 150.00 |

DIAL

| ❏ LP-209 [10] | James Moody, His Saxophone and His Band | 1950 | 100.00 | 200.00 | 400.00 |

EMARCY

❏ MG-26004 [10]	The Moody Story	1954	37.50	75.00	150.00
❏ MG-26040 [10]	Moodsville	1954	37.50	75.00	150.00
❏ MG-36031 [M]	The Moody Story	1955	25.00	50.00	100.00

FANTASY

| ❏ OJC-188 | James Moody's Moods | 1985 | 2.50 | 5.00 | 10.00 |

Number	Title	Yr	VG	VG+	NM
MILESTONE					
❏ M-9005	Brass Figures	1968	5.00	10.00	20.00
❏ M-9023	Blues and Other Colors	1970	5.00	10.00	20.00
MUSE					
❏ MR-5001	Never Again!	1973	3.00	6.00	12.00
❏ MR-5020	Feelin' It Together	1974	3.00	6.00	12.00
NOVUS					
❏ 3004-1-N	Something Special	1986	2.50	5.00	10.00
❏ 3026-1-N	Moving Forward	1988	2.50	5.00	10.00
❏ 3063-1-N	Sweet and Lovely	1989	3.00	6.00	12.00
PAULA					
❏ LPS-4003	Sax and Flute Man	197?	3.00	6.00	12.00
PAUSA					
❏ 7029	Too Heavy for Words	1979	2.50	5.00	10.00
PRESTIGE					
❏ PRLP-110 [10]	James Moody Favorites, No. 1	1951	50.00	100.00	200.00
❏ PRLP-125 [10]	James Moody Favorites, No. 2	1952	50.00	100.00	200.00
❏ PRLP-146 [10]	James Moody Favorites, No. 3	1953	50.00	100.00	200.00
❏ PRLP-157 [10]	Moody in France	1953	37.50	75.00	150.00
❏ PRLP-192 [10]	Moody's Mood	1954	37.50	75.00	150.00
❏ PRLP-198 [10]	James Moody and His Band	1954	37.50	75.00	150.00
❏ PRLP-7011 [M]	Hi-Fi Party	1955	25.00	50.00	100.00
❏ PRLP-7036 [M]	Wail, Moody, Wail	1956	25.00	50.00	100.00
❏ PRLP-7056 [M]	James Moody's Moods	1956	25.00	50.00	100.00
❏ PRLP-7072 [M]	Moody	1956	25.00	50.00	100.00
❏ PRLP-7179 [M]	Moody's Workshop	1960	12.50	25.00	50.00
❏ PRLP-7431 [M]	James Moody's Greatest Hits	1967	6.25	12.50	25.00
❏ PRST-7431 [R]	James Moody's Greatest Hits	1967	3.75	7.50	15.00
❏ PRLP-7441 [M]	James Moody's Greatest Hits, Volume 2	1967	6.25	12.50	25.00
❏ PRST-7441 [R]	James Moody's Greatest Hits, Volume 2	1967	3.75	7.50	15.00
❏ PRST-7554	Moody's Moods	1968	3.75	7.50	15.00
❏ PRST-7625	Don't Look Away Now!	1969	3.75	7.50	15.00
❏ PRST-7663	Moody's Workshop	1969	3.75	7.50	15.00
❏ PRST-7740	Hi-Fi Party, Volume 2	1970	3.75	7.50	15.00
❏ PRST-7853	Wail Moody Wail, Volume 3	1971	3.75	7.50	15.00
❏ 24015 [(2)]	James Moody	197?	3.75	7.50	15.00
ROOST					
❏ RST-405 [10]	James Moody in France	1951	62.50	125.00	250.00
SCEPTER					
❏ SPS-525 [S]	Running the Gamut	1965	6.25	12.50	25.00
❏ SRM-525 [M]	Running the Gamut	1965	5.00	10.00	20.00
TRIP					
❏ 5521	The Moody Story (1951-52)	197?	2.50	5.00	10.00
VANGUARD					
❏ VSD-79366	Timeless	1975	3.00	6.00	12.00
❏ VSD-79381	Sun Journey	1976	3.00	6.00	12.00
❏ VSD-79404	Beyond	1978	3.00	6.00	12.00

MOODY, JAMES/GEORGE WALLINGTON
Also see each artist's individual listings.

Number	Title	Yr	VG	VG+	NM
BLUE NOTE					
❏ B-6503 [M]	The Beginning and End of Bop	1969	7.50	15.00	30.00

MOODY, PHIL
Pianist.

Number	Title	Yr	VG	VG+	NM
SOMERSET					
❏ SF-10400 [M]	Intimate Jazz	1959	7.50	15.00	30.00

MOONDOC, JEMEEL
Alto saxophone player.

Number	Title	Yr	VG	VG+	NM
CADENCE JAZZ					
❏ CJ-1006	New York Live	198?	2.50	5.00	10.00
SOUL NOTE					
❏ SN-1041	Konstanze's Delight	1981	3.00	6.00	12.00
❏ SN-1051	Judy's Bounce	1981	3.00	6.00	12.00

MOONDOG
Percussionist, male singer and composer.

Number	Title	Yr	VG	VG+	NM
COLUMBIA					
❏ KC 30897	Moondog II	1971	6.25	12.50	25.00
COLUMBIA MASTERWORKS					
❏ MS 7335	Moondog	1969	6.25	12.50	25.00
EPIC					
❏ LG 1002 [10]	Moondog and His Friends	1954	50.00	100.00	200.00
FANTASY					
❏ OJC-1741	Moondog	1990	3.00	6.00	12.00
MUSICAL HERITAGE SOCIETY					
❏ 3803	Moondog	198?	7.50	15.00	30.00

Number	Title	Yr	VG	VG+	NM
PRESTIGE					
❏ PRLP-7042 [M]	Moondog	1956	25.00	50.00	100.00
❏ PRLP-7069 [M]	More Moondog	1957	25.00	50.00	100.00
❏ PRLP-7099 [M]	The Story of Moondog	1957	25.00	50.00	100.00

MOONEY, JOE
Accordion player, pianist, organist and male singer.

Number	Title	Yr	VG	VG+	NM
ATLANTIC					
❏ 1255 [M]	Lush Life	1958	10.00	20.00	40.00
-- Black label					
❏ 1255 [M]	Lush Life	1961	5.00	10.00	20.00
-- Multicolor label, white "fan" logo at right					
COLUMBIA					
❏ CL 2186 [M]	The Greatness of Joe Mooney	1964	3.75	7.50	15.00
❏ CL 2345 [M]	The Happiness of Joe Mooney	1965	3.00	6.00	12.00
❏ CS 8986 [S]	The Greatness of Joe Mooney	1964	5.00	10.00	20.00
❏ CS 9145 [S]	The Happiness of Joe Mooney	1965	3.75	7.50	15.00
DECCA					
❏ DL 5555 [10]	You Go to My Head	1955	12.50	25.00	50.00
❏ DL 8468 [M]	On the Rocks	1957	10.00	20.00	40.00

MOONLIGHT BROADCASTERS, THE

Number	Title	Yr	VG	VG+	NM
STOMP OFF					
❏ SOS-1193	Radio Nights	1991	2.50	5.00	10.00

MOORE, ADA
Female singer.

Number	Title	Yr	VG	VG+	NM
DEBUT					
❏ DLP-15 [10]	Jazz Workshop	1955	50.00	100.00	200.00
FANTASY					
❏ OJC-1701	Ada Moore	1985	2.50	5.00	10.00

MOORE, BREW
Tenor saxophone player. Also see FATS NAVARRO.

Number	Title	Yr	VG	VG+	NM
FANTASY					
❏ OJC-049	Brew Moore	198?	2.50	5.00	10.00
❏ OJC-100	The Brew Moore Quintet	198?	2.50	5.00	10.00
❏ 3222 [M]	The Brew Moore Quintet	1956	20.00	40.00	80.00
-- Red vinyl					
❏ 3222 [M]	The Brew Moore Quintet	1956	10.00	20.00	40.00
-- Black vinyl					
❏ 3264 [M]	Brew Moore	1958	12.50	25.00	50.00
-- Red vinyl					
❏ 3264 [M]	Brew Moore	1958	7.50	15.00	30.00
-- Black vinyl					
❏ 6013 [M]	Brew Moore in Europe	1962	10.00	20.00	40.00
-- Red vinyl					
❏ 6013 [M]	Brew Moore in Europe	1962	6.25	12.50	25.00
-- Black vinyl					
❏ 86013 [S]	Brew Moore in Europe	1962	7.50	15.00	30.00
-- Blue vinyl					
❏ 86013 [S]	Brew Moore in Europe	1962	5.00	10.00	20.00
-- Black vinyl					
SAVOY					
❏ MG-9028 [10]	Tenor Sax	1953	37.50	75.00	150.00
STEEPLECHASE					
❏ SCS-6016	If I Had You	198?	3.00	6.00	12.00
❏ SCS-6019	I Should Care	198?	3.00	6.00	12.00
STORYVILLE					
❏ 4019	No More Brew	198?	2.50	5.00	10.00

MOORE, DEBBY
Guitarist and female singer.

Number	Title	Yr	VG	VG+	NM
TOP RANK					
❏ RM-12-301 [M]	My Kind of Blues	1959	10.00	20.00	40.00

MOORE, DUDLEY
Pianist; best known as an actor.

Number	Title	Yr	VG	VG+	NM
ATLANTIC					
❏ 1403 [M]	Beyond the Fringe and All That Jazz	1963	6.25	12.50	25.00
❏ SD 1403 [S]	Beyond the Fringe and All That Jazz	1963	7.50	15.00	30.00
LONDON					
❏ PS 558	Dudley Moore Trio	1969	6.25	12.50	25.00

MOORE, GLEN, AND DAVID FRIESEN
Moore is a bass player. Also see DAVID FRIESEN.

Number	Title	Yr	VG	VG+	NM
VANGUARD					
❏ VSD-79383	Glen Moore and David Friesen In Concert	1976	3.00	6.00	12.00

MOORE, JERRY
Male singer.
ESP-DISK'

Number	Title	Yr	VG	VG+	NM
❏ 1061	Life Is a Constant Journey Home	1968	5.00	10.00	20.00

MOORE, MARILYN
Female singer.
BETHLEHEM

Number	Title	Yr	VG	VG+	NM
❏ BCP-73 [M]	Moody	1957	20.00	40.00	80.00

MOORE, OSCAR
Guitarist; member of the King Cole Trio.
CHARLIE PARKER

Number	Title	Yr	VG	VG+	NM
❏ PLP-830 [M]	The Fabulous Oscar Moore Guitar	1962	6.25	12.50	25.00
❏ PLP-830S [S]	The Fabulous Oscar Moore Guitar	1962	7.50	15.00	30.00

SKYLARK

Number	Title	Yr	VG	VG+	NM
❏ SKLP-19 [M]	Oscar Moore Trio	1954	25.00	50.00	100.00

TAMPA

Number	Title	Yr	VG	VG+	NM
❏ TP-16 [M]	Oscar Moore Trio	1957	20.00	40.00	80.00
-- Colored vinyl					
❏ TP-16 [M]	Oscar Moore Trio	1958	12.50	25.00	50.00
-- Black vinyl					
❏ TP-22 [M]	Galivantin' Guitar	1957	20.00	40.00	80.00
-- Colored vinyl					
❏ TP-22 [M]	Galivantin' Guitar	1958	12.50	25.00	50.00
-- Black vinyl					

MOORE, PHIL
Pianist, male singer and composer.
CLEF

Number	Title	Yr	VG	VG+	NM
❏ MGC-635 [M]	Music for Moderns	1954	25.00	50.00	100.00

STRAND

Number	Title	Yr	VG	VG+	NM
❏ SL-1004 [M]	Polynesian Paradise	1959	10.00	20.00	40.00
❏ SLS-1004 [S]	Polynesian Paradise	1959	12.50	25.00	50.00

MOORE, PHIL, JR.
Pianist.
ATLANTIC

Number	Title	Yr	VG	VG+	NM
❏ SD 1530	Right On	1969	3.75	7.50	15.00

MOORE, RALPH
Tenor and soprano saxophone player.
LANDMARK

Number	Title	Yr	VG	VG+	NM
❏ LLP-1520	Images	1988	2.50	5.00	10.00
❏ LLP-1526	Furthermore	1990	3.00	6.00	12.00

MOORE, REGGIE
Pianist and keyboard player.
MAINSTREAM

Number	Title	Yr	VG	VG+	NM
❏ MRL-341	Wishbone	1971	5.00	10.00	20.00
❏ MRL-380	Furioso	1972	5.00	10.00	20.00

MOORE, SHELLEY
Female singer.
ARGO

Number	Title	Yr	VG	VG+	NM
❏ LP-4016 [M]	For the First Time	1962	7.50	15.00	30.00
❏ LPS-4016 [S]	For the First Time	1962	10.00	20.00	40.00

MOORE, WILD BILL
Tenor saxophone player.
JAZZLAND

Number	Title	Yr	VG	VG+	NM
❏ JLP-38 [M]	Wild Bill's Beat	1961	7.50	15.00	30.00
❏ JLP-54 [M]	Bottom Groove	1961	7.50	15.00	30.00
❏ JLP-938 [S]	Wild Bill's Beat	1961	10.00	20.00	40.00
❏ JLP-954 [S]	Bottom Groove	1961	10.00	20.00	40.00

MOORMAN, DENNIS
Pianist.
INDIA NAVIGATION

Number	Title	Yr	VG	VG+	NM
❏ IN-1055	Circles of Destiny	198?	3.00	6.00	12.00

MORAN, GAYLE
Female singer.
WARNER BROS.

Number	Title	Yr	VG	VG+	NM
❏ BSK 3339	I Loved You Then, I Love You Now	1980	2.50	5.00	10.00

MORAN, PAT
Female singer.
AUDIO FIDELITY

Number	Title	Yr	VG	VG+	NM
❏ AFLP-1875 [M]	This Is Pat Moran	1958	10.00	20.00	40.00
❏ AFSD-5875 [S]	This Is Pat Moran	1958	12.50	25.00	50.00

BETHLEHEM

Number	Title	Yr	VG	VG+	NM
❏ BCP-6007 [M]	Pat Moran Quartet	1956	12.50	25.00	50.00
❏ BCP-6018 [M]	While at Birdland	1957	12.50	25.00	50.00

MORATH, MAX
Pianist and male vocalist.
EPIC

Number	Title	Yr	VG	VG+	NM
❏ LN 24066 [M]	Celebrated Maestro	1963	3.75	7.50	15.00
❏ BN 26066 [S]	Celebrated Maestro	1963	5.00	10.00	20.00

JAZZOLOGY

Number	Title	Yr	VG	VG+	NM
❏ JCE-52 [M]	All Play Together	1969	3.00	6.00	12.00

RCA VICTOR

Number	Title	Yr	VG	VG+	NM
❏ LSO-1159	Max Morath at the Turn of the Century	1969	6.25	12.50	25.00

SAVOY

Number	Title	Yr	VG	VG+	NM
❏ MG-12091 [M]	Introducing Max Morath	196?	5.00	10.00	20.00

VANGUARD

Number	Title	Yr	VG	VG+	NM
❏ VRS-39/40 [(2)]	The Best of Scott Joplin and Other Rag Classics	1972	3.75	7.50	15.00
❏ VSD-83/84 [(2)]	Max Morath Plays Ragtime	197?	3.75	7.50	15.00
❏ VSD-310	The World of Scott Joplin	197?	3.00	6.00	12.00
❏ VSD-351	The World of Scott Joplin, Vol. 2	197?	3.00	6.00	12.00
❏ VSD-73106 [(2)]	The Best of Scott Joplin and Other Rag Classics	198?	3.00	6.00	12.00
❏ VSD-79378	Jonah Man and Others of the Bert Williams Era	1976	2.50	5.00	10.00
❏ VSD-79391	Living a Ragtime Life: A One-Man Show	1977	3.00	6.00	12.00
❏ VSD-79402	Ragtime Women	1977	2.50	5.00	10.00
❏ VSD-79418	Max Morath in Jazz Country	1979	2.50	5.00	10.00
❏ VSD-79429	The Great American Piano Bench	1980	2.50	5.00	10.00

MOREIRA, AIRTO
See AIRTO.

MOREL, TERRY
Female singer.
BETHLEHEM

Number	Title	Yr	VG	VG+	NM
❏ BCP-47 [M]	Songs of a Woman in Love	1956	37.50	75.00	150.00

MORELLO, JOE
Drummer.
INTRO

Number	Title	Yr	VG	VG+	NM
❏ 608 [M]	Joe Morello Sextet	1957	37.50	75.00	150.00

OVATION

Number	Title	Yr	VG	VG+	NM
❏ OV-1197	Joe Morello	197?	3.75	7.50	15.00

RCA VICTOR

Number	Title	Yr	VG	VG+	NM
❏ LPM-2486 [M]	It's About Time	1961	6.25	12.50	25.00
❏ LSP-2486 [S]	It's About Time	1961	7.50	15.00	30.00

MORELLO, JOE, AND GARY BURTON
Also see each artist's individual listing.
OVATION

Number	Title	Yr	VG	VG+	NM
❏ OV-1714	Percussive Jazz	197?	3.00	6.00	12.00

MORGAN, DICK
Pianist.
RIVERSIDE

Number	Title	Yr	VG	VG+	NM
❏ RLP 12-329 [M]	Dick Morgan at the Showboat	1960	10.00	20.00	40.00
❏ RLP-347 [M]	See What I Mean?	1960	7.50	15.00	30.00
❏ RLP-383 [M]	Settin' In	1961	7.50	15.00	30.00
❏ RLP-1183 [S]	Dick Morgan at the Showboat	1960	10.00	20.00	40.00
❏ RS-9347 [S]	See What I Mean?	1960	10.00	20.00	40.00
❏ RS-9383 [S]	Settin' In	1961	10.00	20.00	40.00

MORGAN, FRANK
Alto saxophone player.
ANTILLES

Number	Title	Yr	VG	VG+	NM
❏ 91320	Mood Indigo	1989	3.00	6.00	12.00

CONTEMPORARY

Number	Title	Yr	VG	VG+	NM
❏ C-14013	Easy Living	198?	2.50	5.00	10.00
❏ C-14021	Lament	1986	2.50	5.00	10.00
❏ C-14026	Bebop Lives!	1987	2.50	5.00	10.00
❏ C-14039	Major Changes	1988	2.50	5.00	10.00
❏ C-14045	Double Image	1988	2.50	5.00	10.00
❏ C-14045	Yardbird Suite	1988	2.50	5.00	10.00

Number	Title	Yr	VG	VG+	NM
❑ C-14052	Reflections	1989	3.00	6.00	12.00

GENE NORMAN

Number	Title	Yr	VG	VG+	NM
❑ GNP-12 [M]	Frank Morgan	1955	30.00	60.00	120.00
-- Red vinyl					

GNP CRESCENDO

Number	Title	Yr	VG	VG+	NM
❑ GNPS-9014	Frank Morgan with Conte Candoli	197?	2.50	5.00	10.00

SAVOY JAZZ

Number	Title	Yr	VG	VG+	NM
❑ SJL-1201	Bird Calls	198?	2.50	5.00	10.00

WHIPPET

Number	Title	Yr	VG	VG+	NM
❑ WLP-704 [M]	Frank Morgan	1956	25.00	50.00	100.00

MORGAN, LEE
Trumpeter. Also see JOHN COLTRANE; THE YOUNG LIONS.

BLUE NOTE

Number	Title	Yr	VG	VG+	NM
❑ BN-LA224-G	Memorial Album	1974	3.75	7.50	15.00
❑ BN-LA582-J2 [(2)]	Procrastinator	1977	3.75	7.50	15.00
❑ LT-987	Sonic Boom	1979	3.00	6.00	12.00
❑ LT-1031	Taru	1980	3.00	6.00	12.00
❑ LT-1058	Tom Cat	1980	3.00	6.00	12.00
❑ LT-1091	Infinity	1981	3.00	6.00	12.00
❑ BLP-1538 [M]	Lee Morgan Indeed!	1957	62.50	125.00	250.00
-- "Deep groove" version (deep indentation under label on both sides)					
❑ BLP-1538 [M]	Lee Morgan Indeed!	1957	50.00	100.00	200.00
-- Regular edition, Lexington Ave. address on label					
❑ BLP-1538 [M]	Lee Morgan Indeed!	1963	6.25	12.50	25.00
-- "New York, USA" address on label					
❑ BLP-1541 [M]	Lee Morgan, Volume 2	1957	62.50	125.00	250.00
-- "Deep groove" version (deep indentation under label on both sides)					
❑ BLP-1541 [M]	Lee Morgan, Volume 2	1957	50.00	100.00	200.00
-- Regular edition, Lexington Ave. address on label					
❑ BLP-1541 [M]	Lee Morgan, Volume 2	1963	6.25	12.50	25.00
-- "New York, USA" address on label					
❑ BLP-1557 [M]	Lee Morgan, Volume 3	1957	37.50	75.00	150.00
-- "Deep groove" version (deep indentation under label on both sides)					
❑ BLP-1557 [M]	Lee Morgan, Volume 3	1957	25.00	50.00	100.00
-- Regular edition, W. 63rd St. address on label					
❑ BLP-1557 [M]	Lee Morgan, Volume 3	1963	6.25	12.50	25.00
-- "New York, USA" address on label					
❑ BLP-1575 [M]	City Lights	1958	37.50	75.00	150.00
-- "Deep groove" version (deep indentation under label on both sides)					
❑ BLP-1575 [M]	City Lights	1958	25.00	50.00	100.00
-- Regular edition, W. 63rd St. address on label					
❑ BLP-1575 [M]	City Lights	1963	6.25	12.50	25.00
-- "New York, USA" address on label					
❑ BST-1575 [S]	City Lights	1959	25.00	50.00	100.00
-- "Deep groove" version (deep indentation under label on both sides)					
❑ BST-1575 [S]	City Lights	1959	20.00	40.00	80.00
-- Regular edition, W. 63rd St. address on label					
❑ BST-1575 [S]	City Lights	1963	5.00	10.00	20.00
-- "New York, USA" address on label					
❑ BLP-1578 [M]	The Cooker	1958	37.50	75.00	150.00
-- "Deep groove" version (deep indentation under label on both sides)					
❑ BLP-1578 [M]	The Cooker	1958	25.00	50.00	100.00
-- Regular edition, W. 63rd St. address on label					
❑ BLP-1578 [M]	The Cooker	1963	6.25	12.50	25.00
-- "New York, USA" address on label					
❑ BST-1578 [S]	The Cooker	1959	25.00	50.00	100.00
-- "Deep groove" version (deep indentation under label on both sides)					
❑ BST-1578 [S]	The Cooker	1959	20.00	40.00	80.00
-- Regular edition, W. 63rd St. address on label					
❑ BST-1578 [S]	The Cooker	1963	5.00	10.00	20.00
-- "New York, USA" address on label					
❑ BLP-1590 [M]	Candy	1958	37.50	75.00	150.00
-- "Deep groove" version (deep indentation under label on both sides)					
❑ BLP-1590 [M]	Candy	1958	25.00	50.00	100.00
-- Regular edition, W. 63rd St. address on label					
❑ BLP-1590 [M]	Candy	1963	6.25	12.50	25.00
-- "New York, USA" address on label					
❑ BST-1590 [S]	Candy	1959	25.00	50.00	100.00
-- "Deep groove" version (deep indentation under label on both sides)					
❑ BST-1590 [S]	Candy	1959	20.00	40.00	80.00
-- Regular edition, W. 63rd St. address on label					
❑ BST-1590 [S]	Candy	1963	5.00	10.00	20.00
-- "New York, USA" address on label					
❑ BLP-4034 [M]	Lee-Way	1960	30.00	60.00	120.00
-- "Deep groove" version (deep indentation under label on both sides)					
❑ BLP-4034 [M]	Lee-Way	1960	20.00	40.00	80.00
-- Regular edition, W. 63rd St. address on label					
❑ BLP-4034 [M]	Lee-Way	1963	6.25	12.50	25.00
-- "New York, USA" address on label					
❑ BLP-4157 [M]	The Sidewinder	1964	7.50	15.00	30.00
❑ BLP-4169 [M]	Search for the New Land	1965	7.50	15.00	30.00
❑ BLP-4199 [M]	The Rumroller	1966	7.50	15.00	30.00
❑ BLP-4212 [M]	The Gigolo	1966	7.50	15.00	30.00
❑ BLP-4222 [M]	Cornbread	1967	7.50	15.00	30.00
❑ BLP-4243 [M]	Delightfulee Morgan	1967	10.00	20.00	40.00

Number	Title	Yr	VG	VG+	NM
❑ LN-10075	The Sidewinder	1981	2.50	5.00	10.00
-- Budget-line reissue					
❑ B1-32089	Lee-Way	1995	3.75	7.50	15.00
❑ B1-33579	The Procrastinator	1995	3.75	7.50	15.00
❑ B1-46137	The Sidewinder	1997	3.75	7.50	15.00
❑ BST-81578 [S]	The Cooker	1968	3.00	6.00	12.00
-- "A Division of Liberty Records" on label					
❑ BST-84034 [S]	Lee-Way	1960	12.50	25.00	50.00
-- Regular edition, W. 63rd St. address on label					
❑ BST-84034 [S]	Lee-Way	1963	5.00	10.00	20.00
-- "New York, USA" address on label					
❑ BST-84034 [S]	Lee-Way	1968	3.00	6.00	12.00
-- "A Division of Liberty Records" on label					
❑ BST-84157 [S]	The Sidewinder	1964	10.00	20.00	40.00
-- "New York, USA" address on label					
❑ BST-84157 [S]	The Sidewinder	1968	3.00	6.00	12.00
-- "A Division of Liberty Records" on label					
❑ BST-84157	The Sidewinder	1985	2.50	5.00	10.00
-- "The Finest in Jazz Since 1939" reissue					
❑ BST-84169 [S]	Search for the New Land	1965	10.00	20.00	40.00
-- "New York, USA" address on label					
❑ BST-84169 [S]	Search for the New Land	1968	3.00	6.00	12.00
-- "A Division of Liberty Records" on label					
❑ BST-84199 [S]	The Rumroller	1966	10.00	20.00	40.00
-- "New York, USA" address on label					
❑ BST-84199 [S]	The Rumroller	1968	3.00	6.00	12.00
-- "A Division of Liberty Records" on label					
❑ BST-84212 [S]	The Gigolo	1966	10.00	20.00	40.00
-- "New York, USA" address on label					
❑ BST-84212 [S]	The Gigolo	1968	3.00	6.00	12.00
-- "A Division of Liberty Records" on label					
❑ BST-84212	The Gigolo	1986	2.50	5.00	10.00
-- "The Finest in Jazz Since 1939" reissue					
❑ BST-84222 [S]	Cornbread	1967	10.00	20.00	40.00
-- "New York, USA" address on label					
❑ BST-84222 [S]	Cornbread	1968	3.00	6.00	12.00
-- "A Division of Liberty Records" on label					
❑ BST-84243 [S]	Delightfulee Morgan	1967	7.50	15.00	30.00
-- "New York, USA" address on label					
❑ BST-84243 [S]	Delightfulee Morgan	1968	3.00	6.00	12.00
-- "A Division of Liberty Records" on label					
❑ BST-84243	Delightfulee Morgan	198?	2.50	5.00	10.00
-- "The Finest in Jazz Since 1939" reissue					
❑ BST-84289	Caramba!	1969	6.25	12.50	25.00
❑ BST-84312	Charisma	1969	6.25	12.50	25.00
❑ BST-84335	The Sixth Sense	1969	6.25	12.50	25.00
❑ BST-84426	The Rajah	1984	2.50	5.00	10.00
❑ BST-84901 [(2)]	Lee Morgan	1972	5.00	10.00	20.00
❑ BST-89906 [(2)]	Lee Morgan at the Lighthouse	1970	6.25	12.50	25.00
❑ B1-91138	The Best of Lee Morgan	1988	3.00	6.00	12.00

FANTASY

Number	Title	Yr	VG	VG+	NM
❑ OJC-310	Take Twelve	198?	2.50	5.00	10.00

GNP CRESCENDO

Number	Title	Yr	VG	VG+	NM
❑ GNP-2079 [(2)]	Lee Morgan	1973	5.00	10.00	20.00

JAZZLAND

Number	Title	Yr	VG	VG+	NM
❑ JLP-80 [M]	Take Twelve	1962	7.50	15.00	30.00
❑ JLP-980 [S]	Take Twelve	1962	10.00	20.00	40.00

MOSAIC

Number	Title	Yr	VG	VG+	NM
❑ MQ6-162 [(6)]	The Complete Blue Note Lee Morgan Fifties Sessions	199?	25.00	50.00	100.00

PRESTIGE

Number	Title	Yr	VG	VG+	NM
❑ 2510	Take Twelve	198?	2.50	5.00	10.00

SAVOY

Number	Title	Yr	VG	VG+	NM
❑ MG-12091 [M]	Introducing Lee Morgan	1956	50.00	100.00	200.00

SUNSET

Number	Title	Yr	VG	VG+	NM
❑ SUS-5269	All the Way	1969	3.00	6.00	12.00

TRADITION

Number	Title	Yr	VG	VG+	NM
❑ 2079	Genius	1969	3.00	6.00	12.00

TRIP

Number	Title	Yr	VG	VG+	NM
❑ 5003 [(2)]	Two Sides of Lee Morgan	1974	3.75	7.50	15.00
❑ 5020	Speedball	1974	3.00	6.00	12.00
❑ 5029	One of a Kind	1974	3.00	6.00	12.00
❑ 5037	A Date with Lee	1974	3.00	6.00	12.00
❑ 5041 [(2)]	Live Sessions	1975	3.75	7.50	15.00

VEE JAY

Number	Title	Yr	VG	VG+	NM
❑ VJ-2508 [M]	Lee Morgan Quintet	1965	7.50	15.00	30.00
❑ VJS-2508 [S]	Lee Morgan Quintet	1965	10.00	20.00	40.00
❑ LP-3007 [M]	Here's Lee Morgan	1960	7.50	15.00	30.00
❑ SR-3007 [S]	Here's Lee Morgan	1960	10.00	20.00	40.00
❑ VJS-3007	Here's Lee Morgan	1986	3.00	6.00	12.00
-- Reissue on reactivated label					
❑ LP-3015 [M]	Expoobident	1960	7.50	15.00	30.00
❑ SR-3015 [S]	Expoobident	1960	10.00	20.00	40.00
❑ E-4000	Lee Morgan 1938-1972	198?	3.00	6.00	12.00

Number	Title	Yr	VG	VG+	NM
MORGAN, LENNY					
PALO ALTO					
❑ PA-8007	It's About Time	1981	3.00	6.00	12.00
MORGAN, RUSS					
Pianist, trombonist, bandleader and composer.					
CAPITOL					
❑ ST 1703 [S]	Medleys in the Morgan Manner	1962	3.75	7.50	15.00
❑ T 1703 [M]	Medleys in the Morgan Manner	1962	3.00	6.00	12.00
❑ ST 2158 [S]	Music in the Country Manner	1964	3.75	7.50	15.00
❑ T 2158 [M]	Music in the Country Manner	1964	3.00	6.00	12.00
CIRCLE					
❑ C-9	Russ Morgan and His Orchestra 1936	198?	2.50	5.00	10.00
❑ CLP-87	Music in the Morgan Manner (1938)	198?	2.50	5.00	10.00
DECCA					
❑ DXB 196 [(2) M]	The Best of Russ Morgan	1965	5.00	10.00	20.00
❑ DL 4503 [M]	Does Your Heart Beat for Me	1964	3.00	6.00	12.00
❑ DL 5098 [10]	Music in the Morgan Manner	1950	7.50	15.00	30.00
❑ DL 5278 [10]	College Marching Songs	195?	7.50	15.00	30.00
❑ DL 5406 [10]	Everybody Dance to the Music of Russ Morgan	195?	7.50	15.00	30.00
❑ DXSB 7196 [(2) R]	The Best of Russ Morgan	1965	3.75	7.50	15.00
❑ DL 8332 [M]	Does Your Heart Beat for Me	1956	5.00	10.00	20.00
-- Black label, silver print					
❑ DL 8332 [M]	Does Your Heart Beat for Me	196?	3.00	6.00	12.00
-- Black label with color bars					
❑ DL 8336 [M]	Tap Dancing for Pleasure	1956	5.00	10.00	20.00
-- Black label, silver print					
❑ DL 8336 [M]	Tap Dancing for Pleasure	196?	3.00	6.00	12.00
-- Black label with color bars					
❑ DL 8337 [M]	Everybody Dance	1956	5.00	10.00	20.00
-- Black label, silver print					
❑ DL 8337 [M]	Everybody Dance	196?	3.00	6.00	12.00
-- Black label with color bars					
❑ DL 8423 [M]	A Lovely Way to Spend an Evening (Songs of Jimmy McHugh)	1957	5.00	10.00	20.00
-- Black label, silver print					
❑ DL 8423 [M]	A Lovely Way to Spend an Evening (Songs of Jimmy McHugh)	196?	3.00	6.00	12.00
-- Black label with color bars					
❑ DL 8581 [M]	Cheerful Little Earful (Songs of Harry Warren)	195?	5.00	10.00	20.00
-- Black label, silver print					
❑ DL 8581 [M]	Cheerful Little Earful (Songs of Harry Warren)	196?	3.00	6.00	12.00
-- Black label with color bars					
❑ DL 8642 [M]	Velvet Violins	1957	5.00	10.00	20.00
-- Black label, silver print					
❑ DL 8642 [M]	Velvet Violins	196?	3.00	6.00	12.00
-- Black label with color bars					
❑ DL 8746 [M]	Kitten on the Keys	195?	5.00	10.00	20.00
-- Black label, silver print					
❑ DL 8746 [M]	Kitten on the Keys	196?	3.00	6.00	12.00
-- Black label with color bars					
❑ DL 8828 [M]	Songs Everybody Knows	1958	5.00	10.00	20.00
-- Black label, silver print					
❑ DL 8828 [M]	Songs Everybody Knows	196?	3.00	6.00	12.00
-- Black label with color bars					
❑ DL 74503 [S]	Does Your Heart Beat for Me	1964	3.75	7.50	15.00
❑ DL 78828 [S]	Songs Everybody Knows	1958	6.25	12.50	25.00
-- Black label, silver print					
❑ DL 78828 [S]	Songs Everybody Knows	196?	3.75	7.50	15.00
-- Black label with color bars					
EVEREST					
❑ SDBR-1054 [S]	Music in the Morgan Manner	1959	3.75	7.50	15.00
❑ SDBR-1055 [S]	Let's All Sing with Russ Morgan and Eddie Wilser	1959	3.75	7.50	15.00
❑ SDBR-1083 [S]	Dance Along	1960	3.75	7.50	15.00
❑ SDBR-1095 [S]	Russ Morgan and His Wolverine Band	1960	3.75	7.50	15.00
❑ SDBR-1129 [S]	Morgan Time	1961	3.75	7.50	15.00
❑ SDBR-1130 [S]	Russ Morgan at Catalina	1961	3.75	7.50	15.00
❑ LPBR-5054 [M]	Music in the Morgan Manner	1959	3.00	6.00	12.00
❑ LPBR-5055 [M]	Let's All Sing with Russ Morgan and Eddie Wilser	1959	3.00	6.00	12.00
❑ LPBR-5083 [M]	Dance Along	1960	3.00	6.00	12.00
❑ LPBR-5095 [M]	Russ Morgan and His Wolverine Band	1960	3.00	6.00	12.00
❑ LPBR-5129 [M]	Morgan Time	1961	3.00	6.00	12.00
❑ LPBR-5130 [M]	Russ Morgan at Catalina	1961	3.00	6.00	12.00
GNP CRESCENDO					
❑ GNPS-9015	The Best of Russ Morgan	197?	2.50	5.00	10.00
HINDSIGHT					
❑ HSR-145	Russ Morgan and His Orchestra 1937-38	198?	2.50	5.00	10.00

Number	Title	Yr	VG	VG+	NM
❑ HSR-404 [(2)]	Russ Morgan and His Orchestra Play 22 Original Big Band Recordings	198?	3.00	6.00	12.00
MCA					
❑ 92	Golden Favorites	1973	2.50	5.00	10.00
❑ 4036 [(2)]	The Best of Russ Morgan	197?	3.00	6.00	12.00
PICKWICK					
❑ PC-3016 [M]	There Goes That Song	196?	2.50	5.00	10.00
❑ SPC-3016 [S]	There Goes That Song	196?	3.00	6.00	12.00
❑ PC-3030 [M]	Dance Along	196?	2.50	5.00	10.00
❑ SPC-3030 [S]	Dance Along	196?	3.00	6.00	12.00
SUNSET					
❑ SUM-1142 [M]	Does Your Heart Beat for Me	1967	3.00	6.00	12.00
❑ SUS-5142 [S]	Does Your Heart Beat for Me	1967	2.50	5.00	10.00
VEE JAY					
❑ VJ-1125 [M]	His Greatest Hits	1964	3.75	7.50	15.00
❑ VJS-1125 [S]	His Greatest Hits	1964	5.00	10.00	20.00
❑ VJ-1139 [M]	Red Roses for a Blue Lady	1965	3.75	7.50	15.00
❑ VJS-1139 [S]	Red Roses for a Blue Lady	1965	5.00	10.00	20.00
❑ E-4009 [M]	Russ Morgan 1904-1969	1975	3.75	7.50	15.00
VOCALION					
❑ VL 3601 [M]	Let's Dance	195?	3.00	6.00	12.00
❑ VL 3695 [M]	Hoop-De-Doo Polkas and Waltzes	196?	3.00	6.00	12.00
❑ VL 3792 [M]	Music in the Morgan Manner	196?	3.00	6.00	12.00
❑ VL 73792 [R]	Music in the Morgan Manner	196?	2.50	5.00	10.00
MORRIS, AUDREY					
Female singer.					
BETHLEHEM					
❑ BCP-6010 [M]	The Voice of Audrey Morris	1956	30.00	60.00	120.00
MORRIS, MARLOWE					
Pianist and organist.					
COLUMBIA					
❑ CL 1819 [M]	Play the Thing	1962	5.00	10.00	20.00
❑ CS 8619 [S]	Play the Thing	1962	6.25	12.50	25.00
MORRISON, SAM					
Alto and soprano saxophone player.					
CHIAROSCURO					
❑ 184	Natural Layers	197?	3.00	6.00	12.00
INNER CITY					
❑ IC-6017	Dune	197?	3.75	7.50	15.00
MORRISSEY, PAT					
MERCURY					
❑ MG-20197 [M]	I'm Pat Morrissey, I Sing	1957	25.00	50.00	100.00
MORROW, BUDDY					
Trombone player and bandleader.					
EPIC					
❑ LN 24095 [M]	Big Band Beatlemania	1964	6.25	12.50	25.00
❑ LN 24171 [M]	Campus After Dark	1965	3.00	6.00	12.00
❑ BN 26095 [S]	Big Band Beatlemania	1964	7.50	15.00	30.00
❑ BN 26171 [S]	Campus After Dark	1965	3.75	7.50	15.00
HINDSIGHT					
❑ HSR-154	Buddy Morrow 1963-64	198?	2.50	5.00	10.00
MERCURY					
❑ MG-20062 [M]	Shall We Dance?	195?	7.50	15.00	30.00
❑ MG-20204 [M]	A Salute to the Fabulous Dorseys	1957	7.50	15.00	30.00
❑ MG-20221 [M]	Golden Trombone	1956	7.50	15.00	30.00
❑ MG-20290 [M]	Tribute to Tommy Dorsey	1957	7.50	15.00	30.00
❑ MG-20372 [M]	Just We Two	195?	7.50	15.00	30.00
❑ MG-20396 [M]	Night Train	195?	7.50	15.00	30.00
❑ MG-20702 [M]	Night Train Goes to Hollywood	1962	6.25	12.50	25.00
❑ MG-20764 [M]	A Collection of 33 All-Time Dance Favorites	1963	3.75	7.50	15.00
❑ SR-60009 [S]	Night Train	1958	10.00	20.00	40.00
❑ SR-60018 [S]	Just We Two	1958	10.00	20.00	40.00
❑ SR-60702 [S]	Night Train Goes to Hollywood	1962	7.50	15.00	30.00
❑ SR-60764 [S]	A Collection of 33 All-Time Dance Favorites	1963	5.00	10.00	20.00
RCA VICTOR					
❑ LPM-1427 [M]	Night Train	1956	10.00	20.00	40.00
❑ LPM-1925 [M]	Dancing Tonight To Morrow	1958	7.50	15.00	30.00
❑ LSP-1925 [S]	Dancing Tonight To Morrow	1958	10.00	20.00	40.00
❑ LPM-2018 [M]	Big Band Guitar	1959	7.50	15.00	30.00
❑ LSP-2018 [S]	Big Band Guitar	1959	10.00	20.00	40.00
❑ LPM-2042 [M]	Impact	1959	7.50	15.00	30.00
❑ LSP-2042 [S]	Impact	1959	10.00	20.00	40.00

Number	Title	Yr	VG	VG+	NM
❏ LPM-2180 [M]	Double Impact	1960	7.50	15.00	30.00
❏ LSP-2180 [S]	Double Impact	1960	10.00	20.00	40.00
❏ LPM-2208 [M]	Poe for Moderns	1960	7.50	15.00	30.00
❏ LSP-2208 [S]	Poe for Moderns	1960	10.00	20.00	40.00
WING					
❏ MGW-12102 [M]	Dance Date	196?	3.00	6.00	12.00
❏ MGW-12105 [M]	Tribute to a Sentimental Gentleman	196?	3.00	6.00	12.00
❏ SRW-16102 [R]	Dance Date	196?	3.00	6.00	12.00

MORTIMER, AZIE
BETHLEHEM

Number	Title	Yr	VG	VG+	NM
❏ BLP-10006	The Feeling of Jazz	197?	3.75	7.50	15.00

MORTON, JELLY ROLL
Pianist, male singer, arranger and composer.
ARCHIVE OF FOLK AND JAZZ

Number	Title	Yr	VG	VG+	NM
❏ 267	Jelly Roll Morton	197?	2.50	5.00	10.00
BIOGRAPH					
❏ 1004	Rare Piano Rolls 1924-1926	197?	2.50	5.00	10.00
BLUEBIRD					
❏ 6588-1-RB	Jelly Roll Morton & His Red Hot Peppers	1988	3.00	6.00	12.00
CIRCLE					
❏ L-14001 [M]	The Saga of Mr. Jelly Lord Volume 1: Jazz Started in New Orelans	1951	30.00	60.00	120.00
❏ L-14002 [M]	The Saga of Mr. Jelly Lord Volume 2: Way Down Yonder	1951	30.00	60.00	120.00
❏ L-14003 [M]	The Saga of Mr. Jelly Lord Volume 3: Jazz Is Strictly Music	1951	30.00	60.00	120.00
❏ L-14004 [M]	The Saga of Mr. Jelly Lord Volume 4: The Spanish Tinge	1951	30.00	60.00	120.00
❏ L-14005 [M]	The Saga of Mr. Jelly Lord Volume 5: Bad Man Ballads	1951	30.00	60.00	120.00
❏ L-14006 [M]	The Saga of Mr. Jelly Lord Volume 6: Jazz Piano Soloist #1	1951	30.00	60.00	120.00
❏ L-14007 [M]	The Saga of Mr. Jelly Lord Volume 7: Everyone Had His Style	1951	30.00	60.00	120.00
❏ L-14008 [M]	The Saga of Mr. Jelly Lord Volume 8: Jelly and the Blues	1951	30.00	60.00	120.00
❏ L-14009 [M]	The Saga of Mr. Jelly Lord Volume 9: Alabama Bound	1951	30.00	60.00	120.00
❏ L-14010 [M]	The Saga of Mr. Jelly Lord Volume 10: Jazz Piano Soloist #2	1951	30.00	60.00	120.00
❏ L-14011 [M]	The Saga of Mr. Jelly Lord Volume 11: In New Orleans	1951	30.00	60.00	120.00
❏ L-14012 [M]	The Saga of Mr. Jelly Lord Volume 12: I'm the Winin' Boy	1951	30.00	60.00	120.00
COMMODORE					
❏ XFL-14942	New Orleans Memories	198?	3.00	6.00	12.00
❏ DL-30000 [M]	New Orleans Memories	1950	25.00	50.00	100.00
JAZZ PANORAMA					
❏ 1804 [10]	Peppers	1951	25.00	50.00	100.00
❏ 1810 [10]	Peppers	1951	25.00	50.00	100.00
MAINSTREAM					
❏ S-6020 [R]	Jelly Roll Morton	1965	3.00	6.00	12.00
❏ 56020 [M]	Jelly Roll Morton	1965	6.25	12.50	25.00
MILESTONE					
❏ M-2003 [M]	Immortal Jelly Roll Morton	1970	3.00	6.00	12.00
❏ 47018 [(2)]	Jelly Roll Morton 1923-24	197?	3.75	7.50	15.00
RCA VICTOR					
❏ LPT-32 [10]	A Treasury of Immortal Performances	1952	25.00	50.00	100.00
❏ LPV-508 [M]	Stomps and Joys	1965	5.00	10.00	20.00
❏ LPV-524 [M]	Hot Jazz, Pop Jazz, Hokum and Hilarity	1965	5.00	10.00	20.00
❏ LPV-546 [M]	Mr. Jelly Lord	1966	5.00	10.00	20.00
❏ LPV-559 [M]	I Thought I Heard Buddy Bolden Say	1966	5.00	10.00	20.00
❏ LPM-1649 [M]	The King of New Orleans Jazz	1957	12.50	25.00	50.00
RIVERSIDE					
❏ RLP 12-102 [M]	The New Orleans Rhythm Kings with Jelly Roll Morton	1955	12.50	25.00	50.00
❏ RLP 12-111 [M]	Classic Piano Solos	1955	12.50	25.00	50.00
❏ RLP 12-128 [M]	The Incomparable Jelly Roll Morton	1956	12.50	25.00	50.00
❏ RLP 12-132 [M]	Mr. Jelly Lord	1956	12.50	25.00	50.00
❏ RLP 12-133 [M]	Jelly Roll Morton Plays and Sings	1956	12.50	25.00	50.00
❏ RLP 12-140 [M]	Rags and Blues	1956	12.50	25.00	50.00
❏ RLP-1018 [10]	Rediscovered Solos	1953	25.00	50.00	100.00
❏ RLP-1027 [10]	Jelly Roll Morton's Kings of Jazz: His Rarest Recordings	1954	25.00	50.00	100.00
❏ RLP-1038 [10]	Classic Jazz Piano, Volume 1	1954	25.00	50.00	100.00
❏ RLP-1041 [10]	Classic Jazz Piano, Volume 2	1954	25.00	50.00	100.00

Number	Title	Yr	VG	VG+	NM
❏ RLP-9001 [M]	Library of Congress Recordings Volume 1	1955	12.50	25.00	50.00
❏ RLP-9002 [M]	Library of Congress Recordings Volume 2	1955	12.50	25.00	50.00
❏ RLP-9003 [M]	Library of Congress Recordings Volume 3	1955	12.50	25.00	50.00
❏ RLP-9004 [M]	Library of Congress Recordings Volume 4	1955	12.50	25.00	50.00
❏ RLP-9005 [M]	Library of Congress Recordings Volume 5	1955	12.50	25.00	50.00
❏ RLP-9006 [M]	Library of Congress Recordings Volume 6	1955	12.50	25.00	50.00
❏ RLP-9007 [M]	Library of Congress Recordings Volume 7	1955	12.50	25.00	50.00
❏ RLP-9008 [M]	Library of Congress Recordings Volume 8	1955	12.50	25.00	50.00
❏ RLP-9009 [M]	Library of Congress Recordings Volume 9	1955	12.50	25.00	50.00
❏ RLP-9010 [M]	Library of Congress Recordings Volume 10	1955	12.50	25.00	50.00
❏ RLP-9011 [M]	Library of Congress Recordings Volume 11	1955	12.50	25.00	50.00
❏ RLP-9012 [M]	Library of Congress Recordings Volume 12	1955	12.50	25.00	50.00
TRIP					
❏ J-1	Piano Roll Solos	197?	2.50	5.00	10.00
"X"					
❏ LX-3008 [10]	Red Hot Peppers, Volume 1	1954	25.00	50.00	100.00
❏ LVA-3028 [10]	Red Hot Peppers, Volume 2	1954	25.00	50.00	100.00

MOSCA, SAL
Pianist.
CHOICE

Number	Title	Yr	VG	VG+	NM
❏ 1022	For You	1979	3.00	6.00	12.00
INTERPLAY					
❏ 7712	Sal Mosca Music	197?	3.00	6.00	12.00

MOSCHNER, PINGUIN
Tuba player.
SOUND ASPECTS

Number	Title	Yr	VG	VG+	NM
❏ 005	Tuba Love Story	1986	3.00	6.00	12.00

MOSES, BOB
Drummer and percusssionist.
GRAMAVISION

Number	Title	Yr	VG	VG+	NM
❏ 8203	When Elephants Dream of Music	198?	2.50	5.00	10.00
❏ 8307	Visit with the Great Spirit	1983	2.50	5.00	10.00

MOSES, KATHRYN
Flutist.
PM

Number	Title	Yr	VG	VG+	NM
❏ 017	Music in My Heart	1979	3.00	6.00	12.00

MOSHER, JIMMY
Saxophone player and flutist.
DISCOVERY

Number	Title	Yr	VG	VG+	NM
❏ 860	A Chick from Chelsea	1981	2.50	5.00	10.00

MOSS, ANNE MARIE
Female singer.
STASH

Number	Title	Yr	VG	VG+	NM
❏ ST-211	Don't You Know Me	198?	2.50	5.00	10.00

MOSSE, SANDY
Tenor and alto saxophone player.
ARGO

Number	Title	Yr	VG	VG+	NM
❏ LP-609 [M]	Chicago Scene	1957	10.00	20.00	40.00
❏ LP-639 [M]	Relaxin' with Sandy Mosse	1959	7.50	15.00	30.00
❏ LPS-639 [S]	Relaxin' with Sandy Mosse	1959	10.00	20.00	40.00

MOST, ABE
Clarinetist.
LIBERTY

Number	Title	Yr	VG	VG+	NM
❏ LJH-6004 [M]	Mister Clarinet	1955	12.50	25.00	50.00

MOST, SAM
Flutist, clarinetist and alto saxophone player. Also see DON ELLIOTT; HERBIE MANN; THE NUTTY SQUIRRELS.
BETHLEHEM

Number	Title	Yr	VG	VG+	NM
❏ BCP-18 [M]	I'm Nuts About the Most: East Coast Jazz, Volume 7	1955	12.50	25.00	50.00

Number	Title	Yr	VG	VG+	NM
❏ BCP-75 [M]	Sam Most Plays Bird, Bud, Monk and Miles	1957	12.50	25.00	50.00
❏ BCP-78 [M]	The Amazing Sam Most with Strings	1958	12.50	25.00	50.00
❏ BCP-6008 [M]	Musically Yours	1956	12.50	25.00	50.00

CATALYST

❏ 7609	But Beautiful	1976	3.00	6.00	12.00

DEBUT

❏ DLP-11 [10]	Sam Most Sextet	1954	75.00	150.00	300.00

VANGUARD

❏ VRS-8014 [10]	Sam Most Sextet	1954	20.00	40.00	80.00

XANADU

❏ 133	Mostly Flute	1976	3.00	6.00	12.00
❏ 141	Flute Flight	1977	3.00	6.00	12.00
❏ 160	From the Attic of My Mind	198?	2.50	5.00	10.00
❏ 173	Flute Talk	1980	3.00	6.00	12.00
❏ X-3001	Flute Talk	1980	6.25	12.50	25.00
-- Audiophile edition					

MOTEN, BENNIE
Pianist , composer and bandleader.
BLUEBIRD

❏ 9768-1-RB	Bennie Moten's Kansas City Orchestra	1989	3.00	6.00	12.00

HISTORICAL

❏ 9	Bennie Moten's Kansas City Orchestra	1966	5.00	10.00	20.00

RCA VICTOR

❏ LPV-514 [M]	Bennie Moten's Great Band of 1930-32	1965	5.00	10.00	20.00

"X"

❏ LX-3004 [10]	Kansas City Jazz, Volume 1	1954	15.00	30.00	60.00
❏ LVA-3025 [10]	Kansas City Jazz, Volume 2	1954	15.00	30.00	60.00
❏ LVA-3038 [10]	Kansas City Jazz, Volume 3	1954	15.00	30.00	60.00

MOTHER'S BOYS
AUDIOPHILE

❏ AP-100	Stompin' Hot! Singin' Sweet!	1970	3.00	6.00	12.00

MOTIAN, PAUL
Drummer.
ECM

❏ 1028	Conception Vessel	197?	3.75	7.50	15.00
❏ 1048	Tribute	197?	3.00	6.00	12.00
❏ 1108	Dance	1977	2.50	5.00	10.00
❏ 1138	Le Voyage	1979	2.50	5.00	10.00
❏ 1222	Psalm	198?	2.50	5.00	10.00
❏ 1283	It Should Have Happened a Long Time Ago	1985	3.00	6.00	12.00

SOUL NOTE

❏ SN-1074	The Story of Maryam	1983	3.00	6.00	12.00
❏ SN-1124	Jack of Clubs	1986	3.00	6.00	12.00
❏ 121224	One Time Out	1990	3.75	7.50	15.00

MOULE, KEN
Pianist, composer and arranger.
LONDON

❏ LL 1673 [M]	Ken Moule Arranges for...	1957	12.50	25.00	50.00
-- Label calls this "Cool Moule"					

MOUZON, ALPHONSE
Drummer, percussionist, keyboard player, bass player and composer.
BLUE NOTE

❏ BN-LA058-G	Essence of Mystery	1973	3.75	7.50	15.00
❏ BN-LA222-G	Funky Snakefoot	1974	5.00	10.00	20.00
❏ BN-LA398-G	Mind Transplant	1975	3.75	7.50	15.00
❏ BN-LA584-G	Man Incognito	1976	3.75	7.50	15.00

OPTIMISM

❏ OP-6001	Love, Fantasy	198?	2.50	5.00	10.00
❏ OP-6002	Early Spring	198?	2.50	5.00	10.00
❏ OP-6003	Back to Jazz	198?	2.50	5.00	10.00
❏ OP-6004	Morning Sun	198?	2.50	5.00	10.00

PAUSA

❏ 7054	Virtue	197?	2.50	5.00	10.00
❏ 7087	By All Means	198?	2.50	5.00	10.00
❏ 7107	Morning Sun	198?	2.50	5.00	10.00
❏ 7173	The Sky Is the Limit	1985	2.50	5.00	10.00
❏ 7182	The 11th House	1985	2.50	5.00	10.00
❏ 7196	Back to Jazz	1986	2.50	5.00	10.00

MOVER, BOB
Alto saxophone player.
CHOICE

❏ 1015	On the Move	1977	3.00	6.00	12.00

VANGUARD

❏ VSD-79408	Bob Mover	1978	2.50	5.00	10.00

XANADU

❏ 187	In the True Tradition	198?	2.50	5.00	10.00
❏ 194	Things Unseen	198?	2.50	5.00	10.00

MOYE, DON
Drummer and percussionist. Also see ART ENSEMBLE OF CHICAGO.
AECO

❏ 001	Sun Percussion, Vol. 1	1980	3.75	7.50	15.00

MOZIAN, ROGER KING
Trumpeter, arranger and bandleader.
CLEF

❏ MGC-166 [10]	The Colorful Music of Roger King Mozian	1954	25.00	50.00	100.00

MOZZ, THE
MESA

❏ R1-79018	Mystique and Identity	1989	3.75	7.50	15.00

MRUBATA, McCOY
Saxophone player.
JIVE

❏ 1254-1-J	Firebird	1989	3.00	6.00	12.00

MTUME UMOJA ENSEMBLE
Led by Mtume (drums, percussion, piano), who went on from this album to do some soul and funk albums, including the hit "Juicy Fruit."
STRATA-EAST

❏ SES-1972-4 [(2)]	Alkebu-Lan, Land of the Blacks	1972	12.50	25.00	50.00

MUHAMMAD, IDRIS
Drummer and percussionist.
FANTASY

❏ F-9566	You Ain't No Friend of Mine	1978	3.75	7.50	15.00
❏ F-9581	Foxhuntin'	1979	3.75	7.50	15.00
❏ F-9598	Make It Count	1980	3.75	7.50	15.00

KUDU

❏ 17	Power of Soul	1974	6.25	12.50	25.00
❏ 27	House of the Rising Sun	1976	6.25	12.50	25.00
❏ 34	Turn This Mutha Out	1977	5.00	10.00	20.00
❏ 38	Boogie to the Top	1978	5.00	10.00	20.00

PRESTIGE

❏ 10005	Black Rhythm Revolution	1971	10.00	20.00	40.00
❏ 10036	Peace and Rhythm	1971	7.50	15.00	30.00

THERESA

❏ 110	Kabsha	198?	3.75	7.50	15.00

MULLIGAN, GERRY
Baritone saxophone player, pianist, soprano saxophone player, and occasional clarinetist and male singer. Also see CHET BAKER; BOOTS BROWN; STAN GETZ; THELONIOUS MONK; OSCAR PETERSON; SHORTY ROGERS; ANNIE ROSS; PHIL SUNKEL; TEDDY WILSON.
A&M

❏ SP-3036	The Age of Steam	1971	3.75	7.50	15.00

CAPITOL

❏ H 439 [10]	Gerry Mulligan and His Ten-Tette	1953	62.50	125.00	250.00

CHIAROSCURO

❏ 155	Idol Gossip	1977	3.00	6.00	12.00

COLUMBIA

❏ CL 1307 [M]	What Is There to Say?	1959	10.00	20.00	40.00
-- Red and black label with six "eye" logos					
❏ CL 1307 [M]	What Is There to Say?	1963	3.00	6.00	12.00
-- Red label, "Guaranteed High Fidelity" or "360 Sound Mono" at bottom					
❏ CL 1932 [M]	Jeru	1963	12.50	25.00	50.00
-- Red and black label with six "eye" logos					
❏ CL 1932 [M]	Jeru	1963	7.50	15.00	30.00
-- Red label, "Guaranteed High Fidelity" at bottom					
❏ CL 1932 [M]	Jeru	1965	3.00	6.00	12.00
-- Red label, "360 Sound Mono" at bottom					
❏ CS 8116 [S]	What Is There to Say?	1959	10.00	20.00	40.00
-- Red and black label with six "eye" logos					
❏ CS 8116 [S]	What Is There to Say?	1963	3.75	7.50	15.00
-- Red label, "360 Sound Stereo" at bottom					
❏ CS 8732 [S]	Jeru	1963	7.50	15.00	30.00
-- Red label, "360 Sound Stereo" in black at bottom					

Number	Title	Yr	VG	VG+	NM
❑ CS 8732 [S]	Jeru	1965	3.75	7.50	15.00
-- Red label, "360 Sound Stereo" in white at bottom					
❑ JC 34803	The Arranger (1946-57)	1977	3.00	6.00	12.00
CONCORD JAZZ					
❑ CJ-300	Soft Lights and Sweet Music	1986	2.50	5.00	10.00
CROWN					
❑ CST-363 [R]	The Great Gerry Mulligan	196?	3.00	6.00	12.00
❑ CLP-5363 [M]	The Great Gerry Mulligan	196?	3.75	7.50	15.00
DRG					
❑ MRS-506	Gerry Mulligan and Dave Grusin	198?	2.50	5.00	10.00
❑ SL-5194	Walk on the Water	1980	2.50	5.00	10.00
EMARCY					
❑ MG-36056 [M]	Presenting the Gerry Mulligan Sextet	1955	37.50	75.00	150.00
❑ MG-36101 [M]	Mainstream of Jazz	1956	37.50	75.00	150.00
FANTASY					
❑ OJC-003	Mulligan Plays Mulligan	1982	2.50	5.00	10.00
❑ 3-6 [10]	Gerry Mulligan Quartet	1953	50.00	100.00	200.00
GENE NORMAN					
❑ GNP-3 [10]	Gerry Mulligan Quartet	1952	62.50	125.00	250.00
GRP					
❑ GR-1003	Little Big Horn	198?	2.50	5.00	10.00
JAZZTONE					
❑ J-1253 [M]	Gerry Mulligan and Chet Baker	195?	10.00	20.00	40.00
LIMELIGHT					
❑ LM-82004 [M]	Butterfly with Hiccups	1964	6.25	12.50	25.00
❑ LM-82021 [M]	If You Can't Beat 'Em, Join 'Em	1965	6.25	12.50	25.00
❑ LM-82030 [M]	Feelin' Good	1965	6.25	12.50	25.00
❑ LM-82040 [M]	Something Borrowed, Something Blue	1966	5.00	10.00	20.00
❑ LS-86004 [S]	Butterfly with Hiccups	1964	7.50	15.00	30.00
❑ LS-86021 [S]	If You Can't Beat 'Em, Join 'Em	1965	7.50	15.00	30.00
❑ LS-86030 [S]	Feelin' Good	1965	7.50	15.00	30.00
❑ LS-86040 [S]	Something Borrowed, Something Blue	1966	6.25	12.50	25.00
MERCURY					
❑ MG-20453 [M]	A Profile of Gerry Mulligan	1959	15.00	30.00	60.00
MOBILE FIDELITY					
❑ 1-179	At the Village Vanguard	1985	10.00	20.00	40.00
-- Audiophile vinyl					
❑ 1-234	Gerry Mulligan Meets Ben Webster	1995	10.00	20.00	40.00
-- Audiophile vinyl					
❑ 1-241	Blues in Time	1996	7.50	15.00	30.00
-- Audiophile vinyl					
MOSAIC					
❑ M5-102 [(5)]	The Complete Pacific Jazz and Capitol Recordings of the Original Gerry Mulligan Quartet and Tentette	198?	25.00	50.00	100.00
ODYSSEY					
❑ 32160258	What Is There to Say?	1968	3.00	6.00	12.00
❑ 32160290	Jeru	1968	3.00	6.00	12.00
PACIFIC JAZZ					
❑ PJLP-1 [10]	Gerry Mulligan Quartet	1953	75.00	150.00	300.00
❑ PJLP-2 [10]	Lee Konitz Plays with the Gerry Mulligan Quartet	1953	75.00	150.00	300.00
❑ PJLP-5 [10]	Gerry Mulligan Quartet	1953	75.00	150.00	300.00
❑ PJ-8 [M]	The Genius of Gerry Mulligan	1960	10.00	20.00	40.00
❑ PJLP-10 [10]	Lee Konitz and the Gerry Mulligan Quartet	1954	62.50	125.00	250.00
❑ PJ-38 [M]	Konitz Meets Mulligan	1962	7.50	15.00	30.00
❑ PJ-47 [M]	Reunion with Chet Baker	1962	7.50	15.00	30.00
❑ ST-47 [S]	Reunion with Chet Baker	1962	7.50	15.00	30.00
❑ PJ-50 [M]	California Concerts	1962	7.50	15.00	30.00
❑ PJ-75 [M]	Timeless	1963	7.50	15.00	30.00
❑ PJM-406 [M]	Lee Konitz with the Gerry Mulligan Quartet	1956	37.50	75.00	150.00
❑ PJ-1201 [M]	Gerry Mulligan Sextet	1955	37.50	75.00	150.00
❑ PJ-1207 [M]	The Original Mulligan Quartet	1955	37.50	75.00	150.00
❑ PJ-1210 [M]	Paris Concert	1956	37.50	75.00	150.00
❑ PJ-1228 [M]	Gerry Mulligan at Storyville	1957	37.50	75.00	150.00
❑ PJ-10102 [M]	Paris Concert	1966	5.00	10.00	20.00
❑ ST-20102 [S]	Paris Concert	1966	5.00	10.00	20.00
❑ ST-20140 [R]	The Genius of Gerry Mulligan	1968	3.75	7.50	15.00
PAR					
❑ PAD-703	Symphonic Dreams	1987	2.50	5.00	10.00
PAUSA					
❑ 9010	The Genius of Gerry Mulligan	198?	2.50	5.00	10.00
PHILIPS					
❑ PHM 200-077 [M]	Spring Is Sprung	1963	5.00	10.00	20.00
❑ PHM 200-108 [M]	Night Lights	1963	5.00	10.00	20.00
❑ PHS 600-077 [S]	Spring Is	1963	6.25	12.50	25.00

Number	Title	Yr	VG	VG+	NM
PRESTIGE					
❑ PRLP-120 [10]	Gerry Mulligan Blows	1952	75.00	150.00	300.00
❑ PRLP-141 [10]	Mulligan Too Blows	1953	75.00	150.00	300.00
❑ PRLP-7006 [M]	Mulligan Plays Mulligan	1956	25.00	50.00	100.00
-- Yellow label					
❑ PRLP-7251 [M]	Historically Speaking	1963	10.00	20.00	40.00
-- Yellow label					
❑ 24016 [(2)]	Mulligan/Baker	1972	3.75	7.50	15.00
SUNSET					
❑ SUM-1117 [M]	Concert Days	1966	3.75	7.50	15.00
❑ SUS-5117 [S]	Concert Days	1966	3.00	6.00	12.00
TRIP					
❑ 5531	Profile (1955-56)	197?	2.50	5.00	10.00
❑ 5561	Gerry Mulligan Sextet	197?	2.50	5.00	10.00
UNITED ARTISTS					
❑ UAL-4085 [M]	Nightwatch	1960	10.00	20.00	40.00
❑ UAS-5085 [S]	Nightwatch	1960	12.50	25.00	50.00
VERVE					
❑ VSP-6 [M]	Gerry's Time	1966	3.75	7.50	15.00
❑ VSPS-6 [R]	Gerry's Time	1966	3.00	6.00	12.00
❑ UMV-2057	Gerry Mulligan and the Concert Jazz Band at the Village Vanguard	198?	3.00	6.00	12.00
❑ VE-2-2537 [(2)]	Mulligan & Getz & Desmond	1980	3.75	7.50	15.00
❑ UMV-2652	Gerry Mulligan Presents a Concert in Jazz	198?	3.00	6.00	12.00
❑ UMJ-3093	Gerry Mulligan Meets Ben Webster	198?	3.00	6.00	12.00
❑ MGVS-6003 [S]	Getz Meets Mulligan in Hi-Fi	1960	10.00	20.00	40.00
❑ MGVS-6104 [S]	Gerry Mulligan Meets Ben Webster	1960	10.00	20.00	40.00
❑ MGVS-6137 [S]	Gerry Mulligan Meets Johnny Hodges	1960	---	---	---
-- Canceled					
❑ MGV-8246 [M]	The Gerry Mulligan-Paul Desmond Quartet	1958	12.50	25.00	50.00
❑ V-8246 [M]	The Gerry Mulligan-Paul Desmond Quartet	1961	5.00	10.00	20.00
❑ MGV-8249 [M]	Getz Meets Mulligan in Hi-Fi	1958	10.00	20.00	40.00
❑ V-8249 [M]	Getz Meets Mulligan in Hi-Fi	1961	5.00	10.00	20.00
❑ V6-8249 [S]	Getz Meets Mulligan in Hi-Fi	1961	6.25	12.50	25.00
❑ MGV-8343 [M]	Gerry Mulligan Meets Ben Webster	1959	10.00	20.00	40.00
❑ V-8343 [M]	Gerry Mulligan Meets Ben Webster	1961	5.00	10.00	20.00
❑ MGV-8367 [M]	Gerry Mulligan Meets Johnny Hodges	1960	10.00	20.00	40.00
❑ V-8367 [M]	Gerry Mulligan Meets Johnny Hodges	1961	5.00	10.00	20.00
❑ V6-8367 [S]	Gerry Mulligan Meets Johnny Hodges	1961	6.25	12.50	25.00
❑ MGV-8388 [M]	Gerry Mulligan and the Concert Jazz Band	1960	10.00	20.00	40.00
❑ V-8388 [M]	Gerry Mulligan and the Concert Jazz Band	1961	5.00	10.00	20.00
❑ V6-8388 [S]	Gerry Mulligan and the Concert Jazz Band	1961	6.25	12.50	25.00
❑ MGV-8396 [M]	Gerry Mulligan and the Concert Jazz Band at the Village Vanguard	1960	10.00	20.00	40.00
❑ V-8396 [M]	Gerry Mulligan and the Concert Jazz Band at the Village Vanguard	1961	5.00	10.00	20.00
❑ V6-8396 [S]	Gerry Mulligan and the Concert Jazz Band at the Village Vanguard	1961	6.25	12.50	25.00
❑ V-8415 [M]	Gerry Mulligan and the Concert Jazz Band Presents a Concert in Jazz	1961	6.25	12.50	25.00
❑ V6-8415 [S]	Gerry Mulligan and the Concert Jazz Band Presents a Concert in Jazz	1961	7.50	15.00	30.00
❑ V-8438 [M]	The Gerry Mulligan Concert Jazz Band On Tour with Guest Soloist Zoot Sims	1962	6.25	12.50	25.00
❑ V6-8438 [S]	The Gerry Mulligan Concert Jazz Band On Tour with Guest Soloist Zoot Sims	1962	7.50	15.00	30.00
❑ V-8466 [M]	The Gerry Mulligan Quartet	1962	6.25	12.50	25.00
❑ V6-8466 [S]	The Gerry Mulligan Quartet	1962	7.50	15.00	30.00
❑ V-8478 [M]	Blues in Time	1962	5.00	10.00	20.00
❑ V6-8478 [S]	Blues in Time	1962	6.25	12.50	25.00
❑ V-8515 [M]	Gerry Mulligan '63 -- The Concert Jazz Band	1963	5.00	10.00	20.00
❑ V6-8515 [S]	Gerry Mulligan '63 -- The Concert Jazz Band	1963	6.25	12.50	25.00
❑ V-8534 [M]	Gerry Mulligan Meets Ben Webster	1963	3.75	7.50	15.00
❑ V6-8534 [S]	Gerry Mulligan Meets Ben Webster	1963	5.00	10.00	20.00
❑ V-8535 [M]	Gerry Mulligan Meets Stan Getz	1963	3.75	7.50	15.00
❑ V6-8535 [S]	Gerry Mulligan Meets Stan Getz	1963	5.00	10.00	20.00
❑ V-8536 [M]	Gerry Mulligan Meets Johnny Hodges	1963	3.75	7.50	15.00
❑ V6-8536 [S]	Gerry Mulligan Meets Johnny Hodges	1963	5.00	10.00	20.00

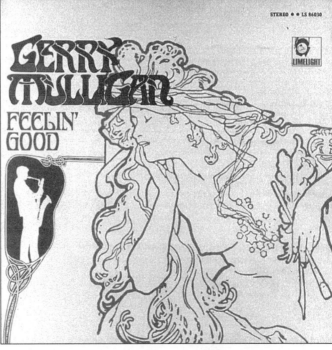

Gerry Mulligan, the most famous baritone sax player of his era, was on some of the Miles Davis *Birth of the Cool* sessions – the first 10-inch LP of those sessions was even called *Jeru*, Mulligan's nickname. He recorded frequently as a leader, as is illustrated in the listings and above. (Top left) One of his earliest sessions as a leader, and a tough one to find today, is this 10-inch LP on Capitol. (Top right) Mulligan recorded briefly for Mercury's EmArcy label in the mid-1950s, and this album was one of the two that resulted. (Bottom left) He also had a brief stopover at Columbia in 1959. Two albums resulted; this one, *Jeru*, was not issued until 1963, by which time Mulligan was with the Philips label. (Bottom right) *Feelin' Good* was one of four albums that were released during Mulligan's time with the new Limelight label from 1964 through 1966.

Number	Title	Yr	VG	VG+	NM
❏ V-8567 [M]	The Essential Gerry Mulligan	1964	3.00	6.00	12.00
❏ V6-8567 [S]	The Essential Gerry Mulligan	1964	3.75	7.50	15.00
WHO'S WHO IN JAZZ					
❏ 21007	Lionel Hampton Presents Gerry Mulligan	1978	3.00	6.00	12.00
WING					
❏ MGW-12335 [M]	Night Lights	1964	3.00	6.00	12.00
❏ SRW-16335 [S]	Night Lights	1964	3.75	7.50	15.00
WORLD PACIFIC					
❏ PJM-406 [M]	Lee Konitz with the Gerry Mulligan Quartet	1958	20.00	40.00	80.00
❏ ST-1001 [S]	The Gerry Mulligan Songbook	1958	25.00	50.00	100.00
❏ ST-1006 [S]	Gerry Mulligan at Storyville	1958	25.00	50.00	100.00
❏ ST-1007 [S]	Reunion with Chet Baker	1958	20.00	40.00	80.00
❏ WP-1201 [M]	California Concerts	1958	20.00	40.00	80.00
❏ WP-1207 [M]	The Original Mulligan Quartet	1958	20.00	40.00	80.00
❏ WP-1210 [M]	Paris Concert	1958	20.00	40.00	80.00
❏ WP-1228 [M]	Gerry Mulligan at Storyville	1958	20.00	40.00	80.00
❏ PJ-1237 [M]	The Gerry Mulligan Songbook	1957	30.00	60.00	120.00
❏ WP-1237 [M]	The Gerry Mulligan Songbook	1958	20.00	40.00	80.00
❏ PJ-1241 [M]	Reunion with Chet Baker	1957	30.00	60.00	120.00
❏ WP-1241 [M]	Reunion with Chet Baker	1958	20.00	40.00	80.00
❏ WP-1273 [M]	Lee Konitz Plays with the Gerry Mulligan Quartet	1959	20.00	40.00	80.00
-- Reissue of 406					

MULLIGAN, GERRY, AND CHET BAKER
Also see each artist's individual listings.

Number	Title	Yr	VG	VG+	NM
CTI					
❏ 6054	The Carnegie Hall Concert, Volume 1	1976	3.00	6.00	12.00
❏ 6055	The Carnegie Hall Concert, Volume 2	1976	3.00	6.00	12.00

MULLIGAN, GERRY/BUDDY DeFRANCO
Also see each artist's individual listings.

Number	Title	Yr	VG	VG+	NM
GENE NORMAN					
❏ GNP-26 [M]	The Gerry Mulligan Quartet with Chet Baker/Buddy DeFranco Quartet	1957	20.00	40.00	80.00
-- Combined reissue of two 10-inch LPs					
❏ GNP-56 [M]	The Gerry Mulligan Quartet with Chet Baker/Buddy DeFranco Quartet	196?	10.00	20.00	40.00
-- Reissue of 26					
GNP CRESCENDO					
❏ GNPS-56 [R]	The Gerry Mulligan Quartet with Chet Baker/Buddy DeFranco Quartet	196?	2.50	5.00	10.00

MULLIGAN, GERRY/PAUL DESMOND
Also see each artist's individual listings.

Number	Title	Yr	VG	VG+	NM
FANTASY					
❏ 3220 [M]	Gerry Mulligan Quartet/Paul Desmond Quintet	1956	20.00	40.00	80.00
-- Red vinyl; combined reissue of two 10-inch LPs					
❏ 3220 [M]	Gerry Mulligan Quartet/Paul Desmond Quintet	1956	10.00	20.00	40.00
-- Black vinyl					

MULLIGAN, GERRY/KAI WINDING/RED RODNEY
Also see each artist's individual listings.

Number	Title	Yr	VG	VG+	NM
NEW JAZZ					
❏ NJLP-8306 [M]	Broadway	1963	---	---	---
-- Canceled; reassigned to Status					
STATUS					
❏ ST-8306 [M]	Broadway	1965	10.00	20.00	40.00

MULLINS, ROB
Pianist, saxophone player, guitarist, bass player and drummer/percussionist.

Number	Title	Yr	VG	VG+	NM
NOVA					
❏ 8810	5th Gear	1988	2.50	5.00	10.00

MULTIPLICATION ROCK (SOUNDTRACK)
More jazz than rock, it features the vocal and composing talents of BOB DOROUGH, with BLOSSOM DEARIE also involved.

Number	Title	Yr	VG	VG+	NM
CAPITOL					
❏ SJA-11174	Multiplication Rock	1973	10.00	20.00	40.00

MUNOZ
Full name: Tisziji Munoz. Drummer and percussionist.

Number	Title	Yr	VG	VG+	NM
INDIA NAVIGATION					
❏ IN-1034	Rendezvous with Now	1978	3.75	7.50	15.00

Number	Title	Yr	VG	VG+	NM
MURIBUS, GEORGE					
CATALYST					
❏ 7602	Brazilian Tapestry	1976	3.00	6.00	12.00
❏ 7619	Trio '77	1977	3.00	6.00	12.00

MURPHY, JAC

Number	Title	Yr	VG	VG+	NM
MUSIC IS MEDICINE					
❏ 9003	Child's Gift	1978	3.00	6.00	12.00
❏ 9016	Erin Eileen	198?	3.00	6.00	12.00

MURPHY, LYLE
Saxophone, clarinet player and bandleader, but best-known as a composer and arranger.

Number	Title	Yr	VG	VG+	NM
CONTEMPORARY					
❏ C-3506 [M]	Gone with the Woodwinds	1955	15.00	30.00	60.00
GENE NORMAN					
❏ GNP-9 [10]	Four Saxophones in Twelve Tones	1954	30.00	60.00	120.00
❏ GNP-33 [M]	New Orbits in Sound	1957	12.50	25.00	50.00
❏ GNP-152 [M]	Four Saxophones in Twelve Tones	195?	12.50	25.00	50.00
INNER CITY					
❏ IC-1133	Ultimate Odyssey	198?	3.75	7.50	15.00

MURPHY, MARK
Male singer.

Number	Title	Yr	VG	VG+	NM
AUDIOPHILE					
❏ AP-132	Mark Murphy Sings Dorothy Fields and Cy Coleman	197?	2.50	5.00	10.00
CAPITOL					
❏ ST 1177 [S]	This Could Be the Start of Something	1959	7.50	15.00	30.00
❏ T 1177 [M]	This Could Be the Start of Something	1959	6.25	12.50	25.00
❏ ST 1299 [S]	Hip Parade	1960	7.50	15.00	30.00
❏ T 1299 [M]	Hip Parade	1960	6.25	12.50	25.00
❏ ST 1458 [S]	Playing the Field	1960	7.50	15.00	30.00
❏ T 1458 [M]	Playing the Field	1960	6.25	12.50	25.00
DECCA					
❏ DL 8390 [M]	Meet Mark Murphy	1957	12.50	25.00	50.00
❏ DL 8632 [M]	Let Yourself Go	1958	10.00	20.00	40.00
FANTASY					
❏ OJC-141	Rah	198?	2.50	5.00	10.00
❏ OJC-367	That's How I Love the Blues	198?	2.50	5.00	10.00
FONTANA					
❏ MGF-27537 [M]	A Swingin' Singin' Affair	1965	5.00	10.00	20.00
❏ SRF-67537 [S]	A Swingin' Singin' Affair	1965	6.25	12.50	25.00
MILESTONE					
❏ M-9145	Night Mood	1987	2.50	5.00	10.00
❏ M-9154	September Ballads	1988	2.50	5.00	10.00
MUSE					
❏ MR-5009	Bridging a Gap	197?	3.00	6.00	12.00
❏ MR-5041	Mark II	197?	3.00	6.00	12.00
❏ MR-5078	Mark Murphy Sings	1975	3.00	6.00	12.00
❏ MR-5102	Stolen Moments	1978	3.00	6.00	12.00
❏ MR-5213	Satisfaction Guaranteed	1980	2.50	5.00	10.00
❏ MR-5253	Bop for Kerouac	1981	3.00	6.00	12.00
❏ MR-5286	The Artistry of Mark Murphy	1982	2.50	5.00	10.00
❏ MR-5297	Brazil Song (Cancoes do Brasil)	1983	2.50	5.00	10.00
❏ MR-5308	Mark Murphy Sings Nat's Choice	1985	2.50	5.00	10.00
❏ MR-5320	Mark Murphy Sings Nat's Choice, Vol. 2	1986	2.50	5.00	10.00
❏ MR-5345	Living Room	1986	2.50	5.00	10.00
❏ MR-5355	Beauty and the Beast	198?	2.50	5.00	10.00
❏ MR-5359	Kerouac, Then and Now	198?	3.00	6.00	12.00
PAUSA					
❏ 7023	Midnight Mood	1979	2.50	5.00	10.00
❏ 9042	This Could Be the Start of Something	1985	2.50	5.00	10.00
RIVERSIDE					
❏ RLP-395 [M]	Rah	1961	6.25	12.50	25.00
❏ RLP-441 [M]	That's How I Love the Blues!	1962	6.25	12.50	25.00
❏ 6064	Rah	197?	3.00	6.00	12.00
❏ 6091	That's How I Love the Blues	197?	3.00	6.00	12.00
❏ RS-9395 [S]	Rah	1961	7.50	15.00	30.00
❏ RS-9441 [S]	That's How I Love the Blues!	1962	7.50	15.00	30.00

MURPHY, ROSE
Female singer.

Number	Title	Yr	VG	VG+	NM
AUDIOPHILE					
❏ 70	Rose Murphy	198?	3.00	6.00	12.00
UNITED ARTISTS					
❏ UAJ-14025 [M]	Jazz, Joy and Happiness	1962	10.00	20.00	40.00

Number	Title	Yr	VG	VG+	NM
❏ UAJS-15025 [S]	Jazz, Joy and Happiness	1962	12.50	25.00	50.00
VERVE					
❏ MGV-2070 [M]	Not Cha-Cha But Chi-Chi	1957	10.00	20.00	40.00
❏ V-2070 [M]	Not Cha-Cha But Chi-Chi	1961	5.00	10.00	20.00

MURPHY, TURK
Trombonist and bandleader. Also see GEORGE LEWIS.

Number	Title	Yr	VG	VG+	NM
ATLANTIC					
❏ SD 1613	The Many Faces of Ragtime	1972	3.00	6.00	12.00
COLUMBIA					
❏ CL 546 [M]	When the Saints Go Marching In	1953	10.00	20.00	40.00
-- Maroon label, gold print					
❏ CL 546 [M]	When the Saints Go Marching In	1955	7.50	15.00	30.00
-- Red and black label with six "eye" logos					
❏ CL 559 [M]	The Music of Jelly Roll Morton	1954	10.00	20.00	40.00
-- Maroon label, gold print					
❏ CL 559 [M]	The Music of Jelly Roll Morton	1955	7.50	15.00	30.00
-- Red and black label with six "eye" logos					
❏ CL 595 [M]	Barrelhouse Jazz	1954	10.00	20.00	40.00
-- Maroon label, gold print					
❏ CL 595 [M]	Barrelhouse Jazz	1955	7.50	15.00	30.00
-- Red and black label with six "eye" logos					
❏ CL 650 [M]	Dancing Jazz	1955	10.00	20.00	40.00
-- Maroon label, gold print					
❏ CL 650 [M]	Dancing Jazz	1955	7.50	15.00	30.00
-- Red and black label with six "eye" logos					
❏ CL 6257 [10]	Barrelhouse Jazz	1953	12.50	25.00	50.00
FORUM					
❏ F-9017 [M]	Turk Murphy and His Jazz Band at the Roundtable	196?	3.00	6.00	12.00
-- Reissue of Roulette R-25076					
❏ SF-9017 [S]	Turk Murphy and His Jazz Band at the Roundtable	196?	3.75	7.50	15.00
-- Reissue of Roulette SR-25076					
GHB					
❏ 91	Turk Murphy, Volume 1	198?	2.50	5.00	10.00
❏ 92	Turk Murphy, Volume 2	198?	2.50	5.00	10.00
❏ 93	Turk Murphy, Volume 3	198?	2.50	5.00	10.00
GOOD TIME JAZZ					
❏ L-7 [10]	Turk Murphy with Claire Austin	1952	12.50	25.00	50.00
❏ L-12026 [M]	San Francisco Jazz, Volume 1	1955	10.00	20.00	40.00
❏ L-12027 [M]	San Francisco Jazz, Volume 2	1955	10.00	20.00	40.00
MERRY MAKERS					
❏ S-105	Turk Murphy San Francisco Jazz Band	197?	3.75	7.50	15.00
❏ S-106	Turk Murphy's Jazz Band	197?	3.75	7.50	15.00
MOTHERLODE					
❏ 0103	Turk Murphy's Jazz Band, Vol. 1	1973	3.00	6.00	12.00
❏ 0104	Turk Murphy's Jazz Band, Vol. 2	1973	3.00	6.00	12.00
MPS					
❏ MC-22097	Live!	197?	3.75	7.50	15.00
RCA VICTOR					
❏ LPM-2501 [M]	Let the Good Times Roll	1962	5.00	10.00	20.00
❏ LSP-2501 [S]	Let the Good Times Roll	1962	6.25	12.50	25.00
ROULETTE					
❏ R-25076 [M]	Turk Murphy and His Jazz Band at the Roundtable	1959	5.00	10.00	20.00
❏ SR-25076 [S]	Turk Murphy and His Jazz Band at the Roundtable	1959	6.25	12.50	25.00
❏ R-25088 [M]	Music for Wise Guys	1960	5.00	10.00	20.00
❏ SR-25088 [S]	Music for Wise Guys	1960	6.25	12.50	25.00
SONIC ARTS					
❏ 14	Natural High	1979	3.75	7.50	15.00
STOMP OFF					
❏ SOS-1155	Turk at Carnegie	1988	2.50	5.00	10.00
❏ SOS-1161	Southern Stomps	1989	2.50	5.00	10.00
VERVE					
❏ MGV-1013 [M]	Music for Losers	1957	10.00	20.00	40.00
❏ V-1013 [M]	Music for Losers	1961	5.00	10.00	20.00
❏ MGV-1015 [M]	Turk Murphy on Easy Street	1957	10.00	20.00	40.00
❏ V-1015 [M]	Turk Murphy on Easy Street	1961	5.00	10.00	20.00

MURRAY, DAVID
Tenor saxophone player and bass clarinetist.

Number	Title	Yr	VG	VG+	NM
ADELPHI					
❏ 5002	Low Class Conspiracy	1976	3.75	7.50	15.00
BLACK SAINT					
❏ BSR-0018	Interboogieology	198?	3.75	7.50	15.00

Number	Title	Yr	VG	VG+	NM
❏ BSR-0039	Sweet Lovely	198?	3.00	6.00	12.00
❏ BSR-0045	Ming	198?	3.00	6.00	12.00
❏ BSR-0055	Home	198?	3.00	6.00	12.00
❏ BSR-0065	Murray's Steps	1983	3.00	6.00	12.00
❏ BSR-0075	Morning Song	1984	3.00	6.00	12.00
❏ BSR-0085	Live at Sweet Basil, Vol. 1	1985	3.00	6.00	12.00
❏ BSR-0089	Children	1986	3.00	6.00	12.00
❏ 120095	Live at Sweet Basil, Vol. 2	1986	3.00	6.00	12.00
❏ 120105	I Want to Talk About You	1990	3.75	7.50	15.00
❏ 120110	The Hill	1990	3.75	7.50	15.00
HAT ART					
❏ 2016 [(2)]	3D Family	1986	3.75	7.50	15.00
HAT HUT					
❏ U/V [(2)]	The Third Family	1979	5.00	10.00	20.00
INDIA NAVIGATION					
❏ IN-1026	Flowers for Albert	197?	3.75	7.50	15.00
❏ IN-1032	Live at the Ocean Club	1978	3.75	7.50	15.00
❏ IN-1044	Live, Volume 2	1979	3.75	7.50	15.00
PORTRAIT					
❏ OR 44432	Ming's Samba	1989	3.00	6.00	12.00
RED RECORD					
❏ VPA-129	Last of the Hipman	198?	3.00	6.00	12.00

MURRAY, SUNNY
Drummer.

Number	Title	Yr	VG	VG+	NM
ESP-DISK'					
❏ 1032 [M]	Sunny Murray	1966	5.00	10.00	20.00
❏ S-1032 [S]	Sunny Murray	1966	6.25	12.50	25.00
JIHAD					
❏ 663 [M]	Sunny's Time Now	1967	50.00	100.00	200.00

MUSIC COMPANY, THE
Studio group led by pianist DON RANDI.

Number	Title	Yr	VG	VG+	NM
MIRWOOD					
❏ M-7002 [M]	Rubber Soul Jazz	1966	5.00	10.00	20.00
❏ MS-7002 [S]	Rubber Soul Jazz	1966	6.25	12.50	25.00

MUSIC IMPROVISATION COMPANY, THE
Members: Evan Parker (soprano sax); Derek Bailey (guitar); Hugh Davies (live electronics); Jamie Muir (percussion); Christine Jeffrey (vocals).

Number	Title	Yr	VG	VG+	NM
ECM					
❏ 1005	The Music Improvisation Company	197?	3.75	7.50	15.00

MUSSO, VIDO
Tenor saxophone player and occasional clarinetist.

Number	Title	Yr	VG	VG+	NM
CROWN					
❏ CLP-5007 [M]	The Swingin'st	1957	12.50	25.00	50.00
-- Reissue of Modern LP					
❏ CLP-5029 [M]	Teenage Dance Party	1957	12.50	25.00	50.00
MODERN					
❏ MLP-1207 [M]	The Swingin'st	1956	25.00	50.00	100.00

MUSSULLI, BOOTS
Alto saxophone player.

Number	Title	Yr	VG	VG+	NM
CAPITOL					
❏ H 6506 [10]	Boots Mussulli	1955	30.00	60.00	120.00
❏ T 6506 [M]	Boots Mussulli	1955	12.50	25.00	50.00

MYERS, AMINA CLAUDINE
Female singer, keyboard player and composer.

Number	Title	Yr	VG	VG+	NM
BLACK SAINT					
❏ BSR-0078	Circle of Time	1984	3.00	6.00	12.00
MINOR MUSIC					
❏ MM-002	Jumping in the Sugar Bowl	198?	3.00	6.00	12.00
❏ MM-012	Country Girl	1987	2.50	5.00	10.00
NOVUS					
❏ 3030-1-N	Amina	1988	2.50	5.00	10.00
❏ 3064-1-N	In Touch	1989	3.00	6.00	12.00

MYRICK, BERL

Number	Title	Yr	VG	VG+	NM
STRATA-EAST					
❏ SES-102-74	Live 'n Well	1974	7.50	15.00	30.00

MYSTERIOUS FLYING ORCHESTRA, THE

Number	Title	Yr	VG	VG+	NM
RCA VICTOR					
❏ APL1-2137	The Mysterious Flying Orchestra	1977	5.00	10.00	20.00

Number	Title	Yr	VG	VG+	NM

N

NAJEE
Saxophone player, also an occasional flutist and keyboard player.
EMI
❏ E1-92248	Tokyo Blue	1990	2.50	5.00	10.00

EMI AMERICA
❏ ST-17241	Najee's Theme	1986	2.50	5.00	10.00

EMI MANHATTAN
❏ E1-90096	Day by Day	1988	2.50	5.00	10.00

NAKAMURA, TERUO
Bass player.
POLYDOR
❏ PD-1-6097	Rising Sun	1977	2.50	5.00	10.00
❏ PD-1-6119	Manhattan Special	1977	2.50	5.00	10.00

NAMYSLOVSKI, ZBIGNIEW
Alto saxophone player and arranger.
INNER CITY
❏ IC-1048	Namyslovski	197?	3.75	7.50	15.00
❏ IC-1130	Air Condition	198?	3.00	6.00	12.00

NANCE, RAY
Violinist.
SOLID STATE
❏ SS-18062	Body And Soul	1969	5.00	10.00	20.00

NANTON, MORRIS
Pianist. Also see THE FIRST JAZZ PIANO QUARTET.
PRESTIGE
❏ PRLP-7345 [M]	Preface	1964	5.00	10.00	20.00
❏ PRST-7345 [S]	Preface	1964	6.25	12.50	25.00
❏ PRLP-7409 [M]	Something We've Got	1965	5.00	10.00	20.00
❏ PRST-7409 [S]	Something We've Got	1965	6.25	12.50	25.00
❏ PRLP-7467 [M]	Soul Fingers	1966	5.00	10.00	20.00
❏ PRST-7467 [S]	Soul Fingers	1966	6.25	12.50	25.00
WARNER BROS.
❏ W-1256 [M]	Flower Drum Song	1958	6.25	12.50	25.00
❏ WS-1256 [S]	Flower Drum Song	1958	7.50	15.00	30.00
❏ W-1279 [M]	The Original Jazz Performance of "Roberta"	1959	6.25	12.50	25.00
❏ WS-1279 [S]	The Original Jazz Performance of "Roberta"	1959	7.50	15.00	30.00

NAPOLEON, PHIL
Trumpeter. Also see PETE DAILY.
CAPITOL
❏ ST 1344 [S]	Phil Napoleon and the Memphis Five	1960	5.00	10.00	20.00
❏ T 1344 [M]	Phil Napoleon and the Memphis Five	1960	6.25	12.50	25.00
COLUMBIA
❏ CL 2505 [10]	Two-Beat	1955	12.50	25.00	50.00
EMARCY
❏ MG-26008 [10]	Dixieland Classics #1	1954	15.00	30.00	60.00
❏ MG-26009 [10]	Dixieland Classics #2	1954	15.00	30.00	60.00
❏ MG-36033 [M]	Dixieland Classics	1955	12.50	25.00	50.00
JOLLY ROGER
❏ 5006 [10]	Dixieland By Phil Napoleon	1954	12.50	25.00	50.00
MERCURY
❏ MG-25079 [10]	Dixieland Classics	1953	15.00	30.00	60.00

NARAHARA, STEVE
PAUSA
❏ 7153	Sierra	1982	2.50	5.00	10.00
❏ 7177	Odyssey	1985	2.50	5.00	10.00

NARELL, ANDY
Steel pan player.
HIPPOCKET
❏ HP-0103	Light in Your Eyes	198?	2.50	5.00	10.00
❏ HP-0105	Slow Motion	1985	2.50	5.00	10.00
❏ HP-1010	Stickman	198?	3.00	6.00	12.00
INNER CITY
❏ IC-1053	Hidden Treasure	1979	3.75	7.50	15.00
WINDHAM HILL
❏ WH-0107	The Hammer	1987	2.50	5.00	10.00
❏ WH-0120	Little Secrets	1989	3.00	6.00	12.00

NARK, VAUGHN
Trumpeter, fluegel horn player and valve trombonist.
STATIRAS
❏ SLP-8070	El Tigre	1985	2.50	5.00	10.00

NASCIMENTO, MILTON
Guitarist, male singer and composer.
A&M
❏ LP-1?? [M]	Milton Nascimento	1967	7.50	15.00	30.00
❏ SP-3019	Courage	1969	5.00	10.00	20.00
❏ SP9-3019	Courage	198?	3.75	7.50	15.00
-- Audiophile reissue (clearly marked as such)					
❏ SP-41?? [S]	Milton Nascimento	1967	5.00	10.00	20.00
❏ SP-4611	Milton	1976	2.50	5.00	10.00
❏ SP-4719	Journey to Dawn	1979	3.75	7.50	15.00
COLUMBIA
❏ FC 44277	Yauarate	1987	2.50	5.00	10.00
❏ FC 45239	Miltons	1989	3.00	6.00	12.00
INTUITION
❏ B1-90790	Milagre Dos Peixes	1988	3.00	6.00	12.00
-- Originally issued in Brazil in 1973					
POLYDOR
❏ 827 638-1	Encontros E Despedidas	1986	3.00	6.00	12.00
VERVE
❏ 831 349-1	A Barca Dos Amantes	1986	3.00	6.00	12.00

NASH, PAUL
Guitarist and composer.
REVELATION
❏ 32	A Jazz Composer's Ensemble	1980	3.75	7.50	15.00
SOUL NOTE
❏ SN-1107	Second Impression	1986	3.00	6.00	12.00

NASH, TED
Clarinetist, bass clarinetist, and tenor and alto saxophone player.
COLUMBIA
❏ CL 989 [M]	Star Eyes	1957	10.00	20.00	40.00
CONCORD JAZZ
❏ CJ-106	Conception	1980	2.50	5.00	10.00
STARLITE
❏ LP-6001 [10]	Ted Nash	1954	12.50	25.00	50.00

NASH, TED & DICK
Dick Nash plays trombone. Also see TED NASH.
LIBERTY
❏ LJH-6011 [M]	The Brothers Nash	1956	12.50	25.00	50.00

NASHVILLE JAZZ MACHINE, THE
AM-PM
❏ 14	Where's Eli?	1986	2.50	5.00	10.00

NATAL, NANETTE
Female singer, composer and arranger.
BENYO
❏ BY-3334	Wild in Reverie	198?	3.00	6.00	12.00
❏ BY-3335	Hi-Fi Baby	198?	3.00	6.00	12.00

NATIONAL JAZZ ENSEMBLE
Led by bass player, arranger and composer Chuck Israels, Members included Jimmy Maxwell, Tom Harrell, Don Hayes, Dave Berger (trumpets); Jimmy Knepper, Rod Levitt, Joe Randazzo (trombones); Greg Herbert, Lawrence Feldman (alto sax); Sal Nistico, Dennis Anderson (tenor sax); Kenny Berger (baritone sax); Ben Aranov (piano); Steve Brown (guitar); Lyle Atkinson (bass); Bill Goodwin (drums); with guest soloists Lee Konitz (alto sax) and Bill Evans (piano).
CHIAROSCURO
❏ 140	National Jazz Ensemble	197?	3.00	6.00	12.00
❏ 151 [(2)]	National Jazz Ensemble, Volume 2	197?	5.00	10.00	20.00

NATIONAL YOUTH JAZZ ORCHESTRA
British band.
RCA VICTOR
❏ LPL1-5116	11 Plus	197?	3.75	7.50	15.00

NATURAL ESSENCE
Fusion group led by drummer T.S. Monk (son of Thelonious).
FANTASY
❏ F-9440	In Search of Happiness	1974	3.00	6.00	12.00

Number	Title	Yr	VG	VG+	NM

NATURAL LIFE
Also see MIKE ELLIOT.
ASI
| ❏ 5005 | Unnamed Land | 1977 | 3.00 | 6.00 | 12.00 |
| ❏ 5006 | All Music | 1977 | 3.00 | 6.00 | 12.00 |
CELEBRATION
| ❏ 5001 | Natural Life | 197? | 3.75 | 7.50 | 15.00 |
| ❏ 5005 | Unnamed Land | 1975 | 3.75 | 7.50 | 15.00 |

NATURAL PROGRESSIONS
PALO ALTO/TBA
| ❏ TBA-248 | Rumor Has It | 1989 | 3.00 | 6.00 | 12.00 |

NAUGHTON, BOBBY
Vibraphone player.
OTIC
❏ 1003	Understanding	197?	3.75	7.50	15.00
❏ 1005	The Haunt	1976	3.75	7.50	15.00
❏ 1009	Nauxtagram	1979	3.00	6.00	12.00

NAUSEEF, MARK
Drummer.
CMP
❏ CMP-16-ST	Personal Note	198?	2.50	5.00	10.00
❏ CMP-21-ST	Sura	198?	2.50	5.00	10.00
❏ CMP-25-ST	Wun Wun	1987	2.50	5.00	10.00

NAVARRO, FATS
Trumpeter. Also see TADD DAMERON; MILES DAVIS; STAN GETZ; HOWARD McGHEE.
BLUE NOTE
| ❏ BN-LA507-H2 [(2)] | Prime Source | 1976 | 3.75 | 7.50 | 15.00 |
| ❏ BLP-1531 [M] | The Fabulous Fats Navarro, Vol. 1 | 1956 | 62.50 | 125.00 | 250.00 |
| -- "Deep groove" version (deep indentation under label on both sides) |
| ❏ BLP-1531 [M] | The Fabulous Fats Navarro, Vol. 1 | 1956 | 50.00 | 10.00 | 20.00 |
| -- Regular version, Lexington Ave. address on label |
| ❏ BLP-1531 [M] | The Fabulous Fats Navarro, Vol. 1 | 1963 | 6.25 | 12.50 | 25.00 |
| -- With "New York, USA" address on label |
| ❏ BLP-1532 [M] | The Fabulous Fats Navarro, Vol. 2 | 1956 | 62.50 | 125.00 | 250.00 |
| -- "Deep groove" version (deep indentation under label on both sides) |
| ❏ BLP-1532 [M] | The Fabulous Fats Navarro, Vol. 2 | 1956 | 50.00 | 100.00 | 200.00 |
| -- Regular version, Lexington Ave. address on label |
| ❏ BLP-1532 [M] | The Fabulous Fats Navarro, Vol. 2 | 1963 | 6.25 | 12.50 | 25.00 |
| -- With "New York, USA" address on label |
| ❏ BLP-5004 [10] | Fats Navarro Memorial Album | 1952 | 125.00 | 250.00 | 500.00 |
| ❏ BST-81531 [R] | The Fabulous Fats Navarro, Vol. 1 | 196? | 3.00 | 6.00 | 12.00 |
| -- With "A Divison of Liberty Records" on label |
| ❏ BST-81531 | The Fabulous Fats Navarro, Vol. 1 | 1985 | 3.00 | 6.00 | 12.00 |
| -- "The Finest in Jazz Since 1939" reissue |
| ❏ BST-81532 [R] | The Fabulous Fats Navarro, Vol. 2 | 196? | 3.00 | 6.00 | 12.00 |
| -- With "A Divison of Liberty Records" on label |
| ❏ BST-81532 | The Fabulous Fats Navarro, Vol. 2 | 1985 | 3.00 | 6.00 | 12.00 |
| -- "The Finest in Jazz Since 1939" reissue |
MILESTONE
| ❏ 47041 [(2)] | Fats Navarro Featured with the Tadd Dameron Band | 197? | 3.75 | 7.50 | 15.00 |
RIVERSIDE
| ❏ 3019 | Good Bait | 1968 | 5.00 | 10.00 | 20.00 |
SAVOY
❏ MG-9005 [10]	New Sounds Of Modern Music	1952	75.00	150.00	300.00
❏ MG-9019 [10]	New Trends Of Jazz	1952	75.00	150.00	300.00
❏ MG-12011 [M]	Fats Navarro Memorial	1955	37.50	75.00	150.00
❏ MG-12133 [M]	Nostalgia	1958	25.00	50.00	100.00
SAVOY JAZZ
| ❏ SJC-416 | Memorial Album | 1985 | 2.50 | 5.00 | 10.00 |
| ❏ SJL-2216 [(2)] | Fat Girl | 197? | 3.00 | 6.00 | 12.00 |

NAVARRO, FATS/KAI WINDING/BREW MOORE
Also see each artist's individual listings.
SAVOY
| ❏ MG-12119 [M] | In the Beginning...Bebop | 1957 | 15.00 | 30.00 | 60.00 |

NAVARRO, JOEY
Keyboard player.
ANTILLES
| ❏ 90985 | On the Rocks | 1988 | 2.50 | 5.00 | 10.00 |

NEELY, DON
Saxophone player, clarinetist, male singer and bandleader.
MERRY MAKERS
| ❏ 108 | Don Neely's Royal Society Jazz Orchestra | 197? | 2.50 | 5.00 | 10.00 |
STOMP OFF
| ❏ SOS-1208 | Ain't That a Grand and Glorious Feeling? | 1991 | 3.00 | 6.00 | 12.00 |

NEELY, JIMMY
Pianist.
TRU-SOUND
| ❏ TRU-15002 [M] | Misirlou | 1962 | 10.00 | 20.00 | 40.00 |

NEIDLINGER, BUELL
Bass player.
ANTILLES
| ❏ AN-1014 | Swingrass '83 | 1983 | 2.50 | 5.00 | 10.00 |

NELL, BOB
Pianist.
CADENCE JAZZ
| ❏ CJR-1022 | Chasin' a Classic | 198? | 2.50 | 5.00 | 10.00 |

NELOMS, BOB
Pianist.
INDIA NAVIGATION
| ❏ IN-1050 | Pretty Music | 198? | 3.00 | 6.00 | 12.00 |

NELSON, LOUIS
Trombonist.
GHB
❏ GHB-25	The Big Four, Vol. 1	196?	3.75	7.50	15.00
❏ GHB-26	The Big Four, Vol. 2	196?	3.75	7.50	15.00
❏ 158	Everybody's Talkin' 'Bout the Piron Band	198?	2.50	5.00	10.00

NELSON, OLIVER
Alto (occasional tenor) saxophone player and composer.
ABC IMPULSE!
❏ AS-5 [S]	The Blues and the Abstract Truth	1968	3.75	7.50	15.00
❏ AS-75 [S]	More Blues and the Abstract Truth	1968	3.75	7.50	15.00
❏ AS-9113 [S]	Michelle	1968	3.75	7.50	15.00
❏ AS-9129 [S]	Sound Pieces	1968	3.75	7.50	15.00
❏ AS-9132 [S]	Happenings	1968	3.75	7.50	15.00
❏ AS-9144 [S]	The Kennedy Dream	1968	3.75	7.50	15.00
❏ AS-9147 [S]	The Spirit of '67	1968	3.75	7.50	15.00
❏ AS-9153 [S]	Live From Los Angeles	1968	3.75	7.50	15.00
❏ AS-9168 [S]	Soulful Brass	1968	5.00	10.00	20.00
❏ IA-9335 [(2)]	Three Dimensions	1978	3.75	7.50	15.00
ARGO
| ❏ LP-737 [M] | Fantabulous | 1964 | 5.00 | 10.00 | 20.00 |
| ❏ LPS-737 [S] | Fantabulous | 1964 | 6.25 | 12.50 | 25.00 |
CADET
| ❏ LP-737 [M] | Fantabulous | 1966 | 3.00 | 6.00 | 12.00 |
| ❏ LPS-737 [S] | Fantabulous | 1966 | 3.75 | 7.50 | 15.00 |
FANTASY
❏ OJC-089	Screamin' the Blues	198?	2.50	5.00	10.00
❏ OJC-099	Straight Ahead	198?	2.50	5.00	10.00
❏ OJC-227	Meet Oliver Nelson	198?	2.50	5.00	10.00
❏ OJC-325	Soul Battle	1988	2.50	5.00	10.00
FLYING DUTCHMAN
❏ 116	Black, Brown and Beautiful	1970	5.00	10.00	20.00
❏ BDL1-0592	Oliver Nelson in London	1974	3.00	6.00	12.00
❏ BDL1-0825	Skull Session	1975	3.00	6.00	12.00
❏ CYL2-1449 [(2)]	Dream Deferred	1976	3.75	7.50	15.00
❏ FD-10116	Black, Brown and Beautiful	1971	3.75	7.50	15.00
❏ -- Reissue of 116
❏ FD-10134	Berlin Dialogue	1972	3.75	7.50	15.00
❏ FD-10149	Swiss Suite	1973	3.75	7.50	15.00
GRP IMPULSE!
| ❏ IMP-154 | The Blues and the Abstract Truth | 1995 | 3.75 | 7.50 | 15.00 |
| -- Reissue on audiophile vinyl |
| ❏ IMP-212 | More Blues and the Abstract Truth | 1997 | 5.00 | 10.00 | 20.00 |
| -- Reissue on audiophile vinyl |

Number	Title	Yr	VG	VG+	NM
IMPULSE!					
❑ A-5 [M]	The Blues and the Abstract Truth	1961	12.50	25.00	50.00
-- Art cover					
❑ A-5 [M]	The Blues and the Abstract Truth	196?	5.00	10.00	20.00
-- Photo cover					
❑ AS-5 [S]	The Blues and the Abstract Truth	1961	25.00	50.00	100.00
-- Art cover					
❑ AS-5 [S]	The Blues and the Abstract Truth	196?	7.50	15.00	30.00
-- Photo cover					
❑ A-75 [M]	More Blues and the Abstract Truth	1964	6.25	12.50	25.00
❑ AS-75 [S]	More Blues and the Abstract Truth	1964	7.50	15.00	30.00
❑ A-9113 [M]	Michelle	1966	5.00	10.00	20.00
❑ AS-9113 [S]	Michelle	1966	6.25	12.50	25.00
❑ A-9129 [M]	Sound Pieces	1966	5.00	10.00	20.00
❑ AS-9129 [S]	Sound Pieces	1966	6.25	12.50	25.00
❑ A-9132 [M]	Happenings	1967	6.25	12.50	25.00
❑ AS-9132 [S]	Happenings	1967	5.00	10.00	20.00
❑ A-9144 [M]	The Kennedy Dream	1967	6.25	12.50	25.00
❑ AS-9144 [S]	The Kennedy Dream	1967	5.00	10.00	20.00
❑ A-9147 [M]	The Spirit of '67	1967	7.50	15.00	30.00
❑ AS-9147 [S]	The Spirit of '67	1967	5.00	10.00	20.00
❑ A-9153 [M]	Live From Los Angeles	1967	10.00	20.00	40.00
❑ AS-9153 [S]	Live From Los Angeles	1967	5.00	10.00	20.00
INNER CITY					
❑ IC-6008	Stolen Moments	197?	3.75	7.50	15.00
MCA					
❑ 4148 [(2)]	Three Dimensions	1980	3.00	6.00	12.00
❑ 29052	More Blues and the Abstract Truth	1980	2.50	5.00	10.00
❑ 29063	The Blues and the Abstract Truth	1980	2.50	5.00	10.00
MCA IMPULSE!					
❑ MCA-5659	The Blues and the Abstract Truth	1985	3.00	6.00	12.00"
❑ MCA-5888	More Blues and the Abstract Truth	1987	2.50	5.00	10.00
MOODSVILLE					
❑ MVLP-13 [M]	Nocturne	1960	12.50	25.00	50.00
-- Green label					
❑ MVLP-13 [M]	Nocturne	1965	6.25	12.50	25.00
-- Blue label, trident logo at right					
NEW JAZZ					
❑ NJLP-8224 [M]	Meet Oliver Nelson	1959	12.50	25.00	50.00
-- Purple label					
❑ NJLP-8224 [M]	Meet Oliver Nelson	1965	6.25	12.50	25.00
-- Blue label, trident logo at right					
❑ NJLP-8233 [M]	Takin' Care of Business	1960	12.50	25.00	50.00
-- Purple label					
❑ NJLP-8233 [M]	Takin' Care of Business	1965	6.25	12.50	25.00
-- Blue label, trident logo at right					
❑ NJLP-8243 [M]	Screamin' the Blues	1960	12.50	25.00	50.00
-- Purple label					
❑ NJLP-8243 [M]	Screamin' the Blues	1965	6.25	12.50	25.00
-- Blue label, trident logo at right					
❑ NJLP-8255 [M]	Straight Ahead	1961	12.50	25.00	50.00
-- Purple label					
❑ NJLP-8255 [M]	Straight Ahead	1965	6.25	12.50	25.00
-- Blue label, trident logo at right					
❑ NJLP-8324 [M]	Screamin' the Blues	1963	---	---	---
-- Canceled					
PRESTIGE					
❑ PRLP-7225 [M]	Afro/American Sketches	1962	10.00	20.00	40.00
❑ PRST-7225 [S]	Afro/American Sketches	1962	12.50	25.00	50.00
❑ PRLP-7236 [M]	Main Stem	1962	10.00	20.00	40.00
❑ PRST-7236 [S]	Main Stem	1962	12.50	25.00	50.00
❑ 24060 [(2)]	Images	197?	3.75	7.50	15.00
STATUS					
❑ ST-8324 [M]	Screamin' the Blues	1965	10.00	20.00	40.00
UNITED ARTISTS					
❑ UAJ-14019 [M]	Impressions of Phaedra	1962	7.50	15.00	30.00
❑ UAJS-15019 [S]	Impressions of Phaedra	1962	10.00	20.00	40.00
VERVE					
❑ V-8508 [M]	Full Nelson	1963	6.25	12.50	25.00
❑ V6-8508 [S]	Full Nelson	1963	7.50	15.00	30.00
❑ V6-8743 [S]	Leonard Feather Presents the Sound of Feeling and the Sound of Oliver Nelson	1968	5.00	10.00	20.00

NELSON, OLIVER; KING CURTIS; JIMMY FORREST

Also see each artist's individual listings.

Number	Title	Yr	VG	VG+	NM
PRESTIGE					
❑ PRLP-7223 [M]	Soul Battle	1962	10.00	20.00	40.00
❑ PRST-7223 [S]	Soul Battle	1962	12.50	25.00	50.00

NELSON, OLIVER, AND LOU DONALDSON

Also see each artist's individual listings.

Number	Title	Yr	VG	VG+	NM
CHESS					
❑ 2ACMJ-404 [(2)]	Back Talk	1976	3.75	7.50	15.00
❑ CH2-92515 [(2)]	Back Talk	198?	3.00	6.00	12.00

NELSON, OZZIE

Bandleader. Best known for his 1950s TV sitcom with wife Harriet.

Number	Title	Yr	VG	VG+	NM
AIRCHECK					
❑ 19	Ozzie Nelson and His Orchestra On the Air	198?	2.50	5.00	10.00
HINDSIGHT					
❑ HSR-107	Ozzie Nelson and His Orchestra 1940-42	198?	2.50	5.00	10.00
❑ HSR-189	Ozzie Nelson and His Orchestra 1937	198?	2.50	5.00	10.00
❑ HSR-208	Ozzie Nelson and His Orchestra 1938	198?	2.50	5.00	10.00

NELSON, RICK "COUGAR"

Trombonist.

Number	Title	Yr	VG	VG+	NM
JAZZOLOGY					
❑ J-123	Steppin' Out	198?	2.50	5.00	10.00

NEPTUNE, JOHN KAIZAN

Shakuhachi (type of Japanese flute) player.

Number	Title	Yr	VG	VG+	NM
FORTUNA					
❑ 17030	Dance for the One in Six	198?	2.50	5.00	10.00
INNER CITY					
❑ IC-6077	Bamboo	198?	3.00	6.00	12.00
❑ IC-6078	Shogun	198?	3.00	6.00	12.00
MILESTONE					
❑ M-9113	West of Somewhere	1981	3.00	6.00	12.00

NERO, PAUL

Violinist and composer.

Number	Title	Yr	VG	VG+	NM
SUNSET					
❑ LP-303 [M]	Play the Music of Paul Nero and His Hi-Fiddles	1956	15.00	30.00	60.00

NERO, PETER

Pianist. Best known for his pop and classical work, the below are jazz-oriented. The Mode LP was recorded under his real name, Bernie Nerow.

Number	Title	Yr	VG	VG+	NM
CONCORD JAZZ					
❑ CJ-48	Now	1978	2.50	5.00	10.00
MODE					
❑ LP-117 [M]	Bernie Nerow Trio	1957	20.00	40.00	80.00
PREMIER					
❑ PM-2011 [M]	Just For You	1963	5.00	10.00	20.00
❑ PS-2011 [R]	Just For You	1963	3.00	6.00	12.00

NEROW, BERNIE

See PETER NERO.

NESTICO, SAMMY

Arranger and bandleader.

Number	Title	Yr	VG	VG+	NM
MARK					
❑ 32244	Swingaphonic	1969	5.00	10.00	20.00
SEA BREEZE					
❑ SBD-103	Night Flight	1986	2.50	5.00	10.00

NEUMANN, ROGER

Saxophone player, bandleader, composer and arranger.

Number	Title	Yr	VG	VG+	NM
SEA BREEZE					
❑ SBD-102	Introducing Roger Neumann's Rather Large Band	1983	2.50	5.00	10.00

Number	Title	Yr	VG	VG+	NM

NEW AIR
See AIR.

NEW ART JAZZ ENSEMBLE, THE
See JOHN CARTER AND BOBBY BRADFORD.

NEW BLACK EAGLE JAZZ BAND
Members: Tony Pringle (trumpet); Pam Pameijer (drums); Peter Bullis (banjo); Eli Newberger (tuba); Stan Vincent (trombone); Stan MacDonald (clarinet, soprano sax); Norm Stowell (string bass); Bob Pilsbury (piano). Brian Ogilvie replaced MacDonald in 1980; Hugh Blackwell replaced Ogilvie in 1981; Billy Novick replaced Blackwell in 1986.

DIRTY SHAME

Number	Title	Yr	VG	VG+	NM
❑ 2002	On the River	197?	5.00	10.00	20.00

GHB

Number	Title	Yr	VG	VG+	NM
❑ GHB-59	New Black Eagle Jazz Band	1973	3.00	6.00	12.00

PHILO

Number	Title	Yr	VG	VG+	NM
❑ 1086	New Black Eagle Jazz Band at Symphony Hall: 10th Anniversary	198?	3.00	6.00	12.00

STOMP OFF

Number	Title	Yr	VG	VG+	NM
❑ SOS-1048	Live at the World Music Concourse	198?	2.50	5.00	10.00
❑ SOS-1054	Live at the World Music Concourse, Volume 2	198?	2.50	5.00	10.00
❑ SOS-1065	Dreaming the Hours Away	1984	2.50	5.00	10.00
❑ SOS-1091	Mt. Gretna Week-End, Vol. 1	1985	2.50	5.00	10.00
❑ SOS-1092	Mt. Gretna Week-End, Vol. 2	1985	2.50	5.00	10.00
❑ SOS-1147	Don't Monkey With It	1988	2.50	5.00	10.00

NEW GLENN MILLER ORCHESTRA
See GLENN MILLER ORCHESTRA (in the M's).

NEW HERITAGE KEYBOARD QUARTET
BLUE NOTE

Number	Title	Yr	VG	VG+	NM
❑ BN-LA099-F	New Heritage Keyboard Quartet	1973	3.00	6.00	12.00

NEW McKINNEY'S COTTON PICKERS, THE
Fronted by banjo player and male singer Dave Wilborn, who was one of the original McKINNEY'S COTTON PICKERS.

BOUNTIFUL

Number	Title	Yr	VG	VG+	NM
❑ 38000	The New McKinney's Cotton Pickers	1972	3.75	7.50	15.00
❑ 38001	You're Driving Me Crazy	1974	3.75	7.50	15.00

NEW ORLEANS ALL STARS, THE
Among the members: Raymond Burke; Jack Delaney; George Gerard; Johnny St. Cyr,.

DIXIELAND JUBILEE

Number	Title	Yr	VG	VG+	NM
❑ DJ-502	In Concert	196?	3.75	7.50	15.00

NEW ORLEANS CREOLE ORCHESTRA
SOUTHLAND

Number	Title	Yr	VG	VG+	NM
❑ 234 [M]	New Orleans Creole Jazz Band	1962	3.75	7.50	15.00

NEW ORLEANS HERITAGE HALL JAZZ BAND
Among the members: Alvin Alcorn; Louis Barbarin; Louis Cuttrell; "Frog" Joseph; Walter Lewis; Blanche Thomas.

DIXIELAND JUBILEE

Number	Title	Yr	VG	VG+	NM
❑ DJ-512	New Orleans Heritage Hall Jazz Band	197?	3.00	6.00	12.00

NEW ORLEANS NIGHTHAWKS, THE
GHB

Number	Title	Yr	VG	VG+	NM
❑ 98	The New Orleans Nighthawks	1979	2.50	5.00	10.00

NEW ORLEANS RAGTIME ORCHESTRA
Revival band led by Lars Edegran.

ARHOOLIE

Number	Title	Yr	VG	VG+	NM
❑ 1058	New Orleans Ragtime Orchestra	197?	3.00	6.00	12.00

DELMARK

Number	Title	Yr	VG	VG+	NM
❑ DS-214	Grace and Beauty	197?	3.00	6.00	12.00

VANGUARD

Number	Title	Yr	VG	VG+	NM
❑ VSD-69/70 [(2)]	New Orleans Ragtime Orchestra	197?	3.75	7.50	15.00

NEW ORLEANS RASCALS, THE
Based in Osaka, Japan.

STOMP OFF

Number	Title	Yr	VG	VG+	NM
❑ SOS-1074	Love Song of the Nile	1984	2.50	5.00	10.00
❑ SOS-1113	The New Orleans Rascals at Preservation Hall	1986	2.50	5.00	10.00

NEW ORLEANS RHYTHM KINGS
Important early white jazz band; the first to make a racially mixed jazz record when JELLY ROLL MORTON joined on piano in 1923. Original members: Louis Black (banjo); GEORG BRUNIS (trombone); Alfred Loyacano (bass); Paul Mares (cornet); Leon Roppolo (clarinet); Elmer Schobel (piano); Frank Snyder (drums).

BRUNSWICK

Number	Title	Yr	VG	VG+	NM
❑ BL 58011 [10]	Dixieland Jazz	1950	30.00	60.00	120.00

KINGS OF JAZZ

Number	Title	Yr	VG	VG+	NM
❑ NLJ-18009/10 [(2)]	New Orleans Rhythm Kings Heritage	198?	3.75	7.50	15.00

MILESTONE

Number	Title	Yr	VG	VG+	NM
❑ 47020 [(2)]	New Orleans Rhythm Kings	197?	3.75	7.50	15.00

NEW ORLEANS SHUFFLERS, THE
KINGSWAY

Number	Title	Yr	VG	VG+	NM
❑ KL-700 [M]	The New Orleans Shufflers	1955	10.00	20.00	40.00

NEW PAUL WHITEMAN ORCHESTRA
See PAUL WHITEMAN ORCHESTRA (in the W's)

NEW SUNSHINE JAZZ BAND
BIOGRAPH

Number	Title	Yr	VG	VG+	NM
❑ 12058	Too Much Mustard	197?	3.00	6.00	12.00

FLYING DUTCHMAN

Number	Title	Yr	VG	VG+	NM
❑ BDL1-0549	Old Rags	1974	3.00	6.00	12.00

NEW YANKEE RHYTHM KINGS, THE
Led by trombonist Bob Connors.

STOMP OFF

Number	Title	Yr	VG	VG+	NM
❑ SOS-1015	Jazz Band	198?	2.50	5.00	10.00
❑ SOS-1050	Live at the Strata-Capitol	1982	2.50	5.00	10.00
❑ SOS-1067	Together at Last	1984	2.50	5.00	10.00

NEW YORK ART QUARTET, THE
Members: MILFORD GRAVES; ROSWELL RUDD; JOHN TCHICAI; Lewis Worrell (bass).

ESP-DISK'

Number	Title	Yr	VG	VG+	NM
❑ 1004 [M]	The New York Art Quartet	1965	5.00	10.00	20.00
❑ S-1004 [S]	The New York Art Quartet	1965	6.25	12.50	25.00

NEW YORK BASS VIOLIN CHOIR
Founded by Bill Lee. Other members: Lisle Atkinson, RON CARTER, RICHARD DAVIS, Michael Fleming, MILT HINTON, SAM JONES.

STRATA-EAST

Number	Title	Yr	VG	VG+	NM
❑ SES-8003	New York Bass Violin Choir	1980	3.75	7.50	15.00

NEW YORK JAZZ GUITAR ENSEMBLE, THE
Among the members: PETER LEITCH; Paul Meyers.

CHOICE

Number	Title	Yr	VG	VG+	NM
❑ CRS-6831	4 On 6 x 5	1986	3.00	6.00	12.00

NEW YORK JAZZ QUARTET, THE (1)
Members: HERBIE MANN; MAT MATTHEWS; WHITEY MITCHELL; JOE PUMA.

CORAL

Number	Title	Yr	VG	VG+	NM
❑ CRL 57136 [M]	Music For Suburban Living	1958	10.00	20.00	40.00
❑ CRL 757136 [S]	Music For Suburban Living	1958	7.50	15.00	30.00

ELEKTRA

Number	Title	Yr	VG	VG+	NM
❑ EKL-115 [M]	The New York Jazz Quartet	1957	12.50	25.00	50.00
❑ EKL-118 [M]	Gone Native	1957	12.50	25.00	50.00

SAVOY

Number	Title	Yr	VG	VG+	NM
❑ MG-12172 [M]	Adam's Theme	1960	7.50	15.00	30.00
❑ MG-12175 [M]	Gone Native	1961	7.50	15.00	30.00

NEW YORK JAZZ QUARTET, THE (2)
Members: ROLAND HANNA; George Mraz (bass); revolving drummers including Richard Pratt, MARVIN "SMITTY" SMITH and GRADY TATE; FRANK WESS.

ENJA

Number	Title	Yr	VG	VG+	NM
❑ 3083	Oasis	1981	3.00	6.00	12.00

INNER CITY

Number	Title	Yr	VG	VG+	NM
❑ IC-3011	Surge	197?	3.75	7.50	15.00
❑ IC-3024	Blues for Sarka	1978	3.75	7.50	15.00

SALVATION

Number	Title	Yr	VG	VG+	NM
❑ 703	In Concert in Japan	1975	3.00	6.00	12.00

Number	Title	Yr	VG	VG+	NM

NEW YORK JAZZ REPERTORY COMPANY, THE
Directed by DICK HYMAN. Many jazz greats appeared in this band, which toured the world playing a tribute to Louis Armstrong.
ATLANTIC

❏ SD 1671	The Music of Louis Armstrong	1975	2.50	5.00	10.00

NEW YORK JAZZ SEXTET, THE
Members: RICHARD DAVIS; ART FARMER; TOMMY FLANAGAN; ALBERT HEATH; Tom McIntosh (trombone); JAMES MOODY.
SCEPTER

❏ S-526 [M]	New York Jazz Sextet	1964	5.00	10.00	20.00
❏ SS-526 [S]	New York Jazz Sextet	1964	6.25	12.50	25.00

NEW YORK MARY
Members: Joe Corsello (drums); Bruce Johnstone (baritone sax); Rick Petrone (bass).
ARISTA/FREEDOM

❏ AF 1019	New York Mary	1975	3.75	7.50	15.00
❏ AF 1035	Piece of the Apple	1976	3.75	7.50	15.00

NEW YORK ORIGINATORS, THE
PARAMOUNT

❏ RS-201 [10]	The New York Style	1952	15.00	30.00	60.00

NEW YORK SAXOPHONE QUARTET, THE
MARK

❏ 32322	The New York Saxophone Quartet	1969	5.00	10.00	20.00

STASH

❏ ST-210	New York Saxophone Quartet	198?	2.50	5.00	10.00
❏ ST-220	An American Experience	198?	2.50	5.00	10.00

20TH CENTURY FOX

❏ TFM-3150 [M]	The New York Saxophone Quartet	1964	5.00	10.00	20.00
❏ TFS-3150 [S]	The New York Saxophone Quartet	1964	6.25	12.50	25.00

NEW YORK VOICES
Vocal group: Peter Eldridge; Caprice Fox; Sara Krieger; Darmon Meader; Kim Nazarian. Lauren Kinhan replaced Krieger in 1992; Fox left in 1994.
GRP

❏ GR-9589	New York Voices	1989	3.00	6.00	12.00

NEWBERGER, ELI, AND JIMMY MAZZY
Newberger plays tuba; Mazzy is a banjo player.
STOMP OFF

❏ SOS-1109	Shake It Down	1986	2.50	5.00	10.00

NEWBORN, PHINEAS
Pianist. Also see ROY HAYNES; YOUNG MEN FROM MEMPHIS.
ATLANTIC

❏ 1235 [M]	Here Is Phineas	1956	12.50	25.00	50.00
-- Black label					
❏ 1235 [M]	Here Is Phineas	1961	5.00	10.00	20.00
-- Multicolor label, white "fan" logo at right					
❏ 1235 [M]	Here Is Phineas	1964	3.75	7.50	15.00
-- Multicolor label, black "fan" logo at right					
❏ SD 1235 [S]	Here Is Phineas	1958	12.50	25.00	50.00
-- Green label					
❏ SD 1235 [S]	Here Is Phineas	1961	3.75	7.50	15.00
-- Multicolor label, white "fan" logo at right					
❏ SD 1235 [S]	Here Is Phineas	1964	3.00	6.00	12.00
-- Multicolor label, black "fan" logo at right					
❏ SD 1672	Solo Piano	1975	3.00	6.00	12.00
❏ 90534	The Piano Artistry of Phineas Newborn	1986	2.50	5.00	10.00

CONTEMPORARY

❏ M-3600 [M]	The World of Piano!	1961	5.00	10.00	20.00
❏ M-3611 [M]	Great Jazz Piano	1962	5.00	10.00	20.00
❏ M-3615 [M]	The Newborn Touch	1964	5.00	10.00	20.00
❏ S-7600 [S]	The World of Piano!	1961	6.25	12.50	25.00
❏ S-7611 [S]	Great Jazz Piano	1962	6.25	12.50	25.00
❏ S-7615 [S]	The Newborn Touch	1964	6.25	12.50	25.00
❏ S-7622 [S]	Please Send Me Someone to Love	1969	5.00	10.00	20.00
❏ C-7648	Back Home	198?	3.00	6.00	12.00

FANTASY

❏ OJC-175	The World of Piano!	198?	2.50	5.00	10.00
❏ OJC-175	A World of Piano	198?	2.50	5.00	10.00
❏ OJC-270	The Newborn Touch	1988	2.50	5.00	10.00
❏ OJC-388	Great Jazz Piano	1989	3.00	6.00	12.00

PABLO

❏ 2310 801	Look Out, Phineas Is Back	197?	3.00	6.00	12.00

RCA VICTOR

❏ LPM-1421 [M]	Phineas' Rainbow	1957	12.50	25.00	50.00
❏ LPM-1474 [M]	While the Lady Sleeps	1957	12.50	25.00	50.00
❏ LPM-1589 [M]	Phineas Newborn Plays Jamaica	1957	12.50	25.00	50.00
❏ LPM-1873 [M]	Fabulous Phineas	1958	12.50	25.00	50.00
❏ LSP-1873 [S]	Fabulous Phineas	1958	10.00	20.00	40.00

ROULETTE

❏ R-52031 [M]	Piano Portraits	1959	6.25	12.50	25.00
❏ SR-52031 [S]	Piano Portraits	1959	7.50	15.00	30.00
❏ R-52043 [M]	I Love a Piano	1960	6.25	12.50	25.00
❏ SR-52043 [S]	I Love a Piano	1960	7.50	15.00	30.00

NEWMAN, DAVID "FATHEAD"
Tenor saxophone player; also plays alto sax and flute. Also see JAMES CLAY.
ATLANTIC

❏ 1304 [M]	Ray Charles Presents David "Fathead" Newman	1959	10.00	20.00	40.00
-- Black label					
❏ 1304 [M]	Ray Charles Presents David "Fathead" Newman	1961	3.75	7.50	15.00
-- Multicolor label with white "fan" logo					
❏ 1304 [M]	Ray Charles Presents David "Fathead" Newman	1964	3.00	6.00	12.00
-- Multicolor label with black "fan" logo					
❏ SD 1304 [S]	Ray Charles Presents David "Fathead" Newman	1959	12.50	25.00	50.00
-- Green label					
❏ SD 1304 [S]	Ray Charles Presents David "Fathead" Newman	1961	5.00	10.00	20.00
-- Multicolor label with white "fan" logo					
❏ SD 1304 [S]	Ray Charles Presents David "Fathead" Newman	1964	3.75	7.50	15.00
-- Multicolor label with black "fan" logo					
❏ 1366 [M]	Straight Ahead	1961	7.50	15.00	30.00
-- Multicolor label with white "fan" logo					
❏ 1366 [M]	Straight Ahead	1964	3.00	6.00	12.00
-- Multicolor label with black "fan" logo					
❏ SD 1366 [S]	Straight Ahead	1961	10.00	20.00	40.00
-- Multicolor label with white "fan" logo					
❏ SD 1366 [S]	Straight Ahead	1964	3.75	7.50	15.00
-- Multicolor label with black "fan" logo					
❏ 1399 [M]	Fathead Comes On	1962	7.50	15.00	30.00
❏ SD 1399 [S]	Fathead Comes On	1962	10.00	20.00	40.00
❏ SD 1489	House of David	1968	5.00	10.00	20.00
❏ SD 1505	Bigger and Better	1968	5.00	10.00	20.00
❏ SD 1524	Many Facets	1969	3.75	7.50	15.00
❏ SD 1590	The Best of David "Fathead" Newman	1972	3.75	7.50	15.00
❏ SD 1600	Lonely Avenue	1972	3.75	7.50	15.00
❏ SD 1638	The Weapon	1973	3.75	7.50	15.00
❏ SD 1662	Newmanism	1974	3.00	6.00	12.00
❏ 81725	Heads Up	1987	2.50	5.00	10.00
❏ 81965	Fire! Live at the Village Vanguard	1989	3.00	6.00	12.00

COTILLION

❏ SD 18002	Captain Buckles	1970	5.00	10.00	20.00

MUSE

❏ MR-5234	Resurgence	1981	2.50	5.00	10.00
❏ MR-5283	Still Hard Times	1982	2.50	5.00	10.00

PRESTIGE

❏ 10104	Concrete Jungle	1978	3.75	7.50	15.00
❏ 10106	Keep the Dream Alive	1978	3.75	7.50	15.00
❏ 10108	Scratch My Back	1979	3.75	7.50	15.00

WARNER BROS.

❏ BS 2917	Mr. Fathead	1976	2.50	5.00	10.00
❏ BS 2984	Front Money	1977	2.50	5.00	10.00

NEWMAN, JOE
Trumpeter. Also see EDDIE BERT.
AMERICAN RECORDING SOCIETY

❏ G-447 [M]	Basically Swing	1958	10.00	20.00	40.00
❏ G-451 [M]	New Sounds In Swing	1958	10.00	20.00	40.00

CORAL

❏ CRL 57121 [M]	The Happy Cats	1957	12.50	25.00	50.00
❏ CRL 57208 [M]	Soft Swingin' Jazz	1958	12.50	25.00	50.00

FANTASY

❏ OJC-185	Good 'N Groovy	1985	2.50	5.00	10.00
❏ OJC-419	Jive at Five	1990	3.00	6.00	12.00

JAZZTONE

❏ J-1217 [M]	New Sounds In Swing	1956	10.00	20.00	40.00
❏ J-1220 [M]	The Count's Men	1956	10.00	20.00	40.00
❏ J-1265 [M]	Swing Lightly	1957	10.00	20.00	40.00

Number	Title	Yr	VG	VG+	NM
MERCURY					
❑ MG-20696 [M]	Joe Newman At Count Basie's	1962	6.25	12.50	25.00
❑ SR-60696 [S]	Joe Newman At Count Basie's	1962	7.50	15.00	30.00
PRESTIGE					
❑ 2509	Jive at Five	198?	3.00	6.00	12.00
RAMA					
❑ LP-1003 [M]	Locking Horns	1957	30.00	60.00	120.00
RCA VICTOR					
❑ LPM-1118 [M]	All I Want To Do Is Swing	1955	25.00	50.00	100.00
❑ LPM-1198 [M]	I'm Still Swinging	1956	25.00	50.00	100.00
❑ LPM-1324 [M]	Salute To Satch	1956	20.00	40.00	80.00
ROULETTE					
❑ R-52009 [M]	Locking Horns	1958	10.00	20.00	40.00
❑ SR-52009 [S]	Locking Horns	1958	7.50	15.00	30.00
❑ R-52014 [M]	Joe Newman With Woodwinds	1958	10.00	20.00	40.00
❑ SR-52014 [S]	Joe Newman With Woodwinds	1958	7.50	15.00	30.00
STASH					
❑ ST-219	In a Mellow Mood	198?	2.50	5.00	10.00
STORYVILLE					
❑ STLP-318 [10]	Joe Newman and the Boys In the Band	1955	37.50	75.00	150.00
❑ STLP-905 [M]	I Feel Like a Newman	1956	25.00	50.00	100.00
SWINGVILLE					
❑ SVLP-2011 [M]	Jive At Five	1961	12.50	25.00	50.00
-- Purple label					
❑ SVLP-2011 [M]	Jive At Five	1965	6.25	12.50	25.00
-- Blue label, trident logo at right					
❑ SVLP-2019 [M]	Good 'N Groovy	1961	12.50	25.00	50.00
-- Purple label					
❑ SVLP-2019 [M]	Good 'N Groovy	1965	6.25	12.50	25.00
-- Blue label, trident logo at right					
❑ SVLP-2027 [M]	Joe's Hap'nin's	1961	12.50	25.00	50.00
-- Purple label					
❑ SVLP-2027 [M]	Joe's Hap'nin's	1965	6.25	12.50	25.00
-- Blue label, trident logo at right					
❑ SVST-2027 [S]	Joe's Hap'nin's	1961	12.50	25.00	50.00
-- Red label					
❑ SVST-2027 [S]	Joe's Hap'nin's	1965	6.25	12.50	25.00
-- Blue label, trident logo at right					
TRIP					
❑ 5548	Live at Basie's	197?	2.50	5.00	10.00
VANGUARD					
❑ VRS-8007 [10]	Joe Newman and His Band	1954	50.00	100.00	200.00
VIK					
❑ LX-1060 [M]	Midgets	1957	20.00	40.00	80.00
WORLD PACIFIC					
❑ ST-1288 [S]	Countin'	1960	10.00	20.00	40.00
❑ WP-1288 [M]	Countin'	1960	10.00	20.00	40.00

NEWMAN, JOE/RUBY BRAFF
Also see each artist's individual listings.

Number	Title	Yr	VG	VG+	NM
HALL OF FAME					
❑ 601	Swing Lightly	197?	2.50	5.00	10.00

NEWMAN, JOE, AND JOE WILDER
Also see each artist's individual listings.

Number	Title	Yr	VG	VG+	NM
CONCORD JAZZ					
❑ CJ-262	Joe Newman and Joe Wilder	1985	2.50	5.00	10.00

NEWPORT ALL STARS, THE
Organized by pianist GEORGE WEIN.

Number	Title	Yr	VG	VG+	NM
BASF					
❑ 20717	A Tribute to Duke	1972	3.75	7.50	15.00
BLACK LION					
❑ 303	Newport All Stars	197?	3.00	6.00	12.00
CONCORD JAZZ					
❑ CJ-343	European Tour	1988	2.50	5.00	10.00

NEWTON, CAM
Guitarist.

Number	Title	Yr	VG	VG+	NM
INNER CITY					
❑ IC-1059	The Motive Behind the Smile	1979	3.75	7.50	15.00
❑ IC-1079	Welcome Aliens	1980	3.75	7.50	15.00

NEWTON, JAMES
Flutist.

Number	Title	Yr	VG	VG+	NM
BLUE NOTE					
❑ BT-85109	The African Flower	1986	3.00	6.00	12.00
CELESTIAL HARMONIES					
❑ CEL-012	Echo Canyon	1984	3.00	6.00	12.00

Number	Title	Yr	VG	VG+	NM
❑ 13012	Echo Canyon	198?	2.50	5.00	10.00
-- Reissue with new number					
❑ 14030 [(2)]	James Newton in Venice	1988	3.00	6.00	12.00
ECM					
❑ 1214	Axum	1981	2.50	5.00	10.00
GRAMAVISION					
❑ 8205	James Newton	1982	2.50	5.00	10.00
❑ GR-8304	Luella	1983	2.50	5.00	10.00
INDIA NAVIGATION					
❑ IN-1037	Paseo Del Mar	197?	3.75	7.50	15.00
❑ IN-1046	Mystery School	1980	3.00	6.00	12.00
❑ IN-1051	Portraits	198?	3.00	6.00	12.00

NEWTON, LAUREN
Female singer.

Number	Title	Yr	VG	VG+	NM
HAT HUT					
❑ 3511	Timbre	1982	3.75	7.50	15.00

NGCUKANA, EZRA
Saxophone player and multi-instrumentalist from South Africa.

Number	Title	Yr	VG	VG+	NM
JIVE					
❑ 1250-1-J	You Think You Know Me	1989	3.00	6.00	12.00

NHOP
See NIELS-HENNING ORSTED PEDERSEN.

NICHOLAS, ALBERT
Clarinetist and saxophone player.

Number	Title	Yr	VG	VG+	NM
DELMARK					
❑ DS-209	Albert Nicholas with Art Hodes' All-Star Stompers	1964	5.00	10.00	20.00
GHB					
❑ 64	The Albert Nicholas/John Defferary Jazztet	197?	3.00	6.00	12.00

NICHOLAS, ALBERT/SIDNEY BECHET
Also see each artist's individual listings.

Number	Title	Yr	VG	VG+	NM
RIVERSIDE					
❑ RLP-12-216 [M]	Creole Reeds	1956	20.00	40.00	80.00
-- White label, blue print					
❑ RLP-12-216 [M]	Creole Reeds	1959	10.00	20.00	40.00
-- Blue label, microphone logo at top					

NICHOLAS, GEORGE "BIG NICK"
Tenor saxophone player and male singer.

Number	Title	Yr	VG	VG+	NM
INDIA NAVIGATION					
❑ IN-1061	Big and Warm	1985	3.00	6.00	12.00
❑ IN-1066	"Big Nick"	1986	3.00	6.00	12.00

NICHOLAS, JOSEPH "WOODEN JOE"
Cornet player.

Number	Title	Yr	VG	VG+	NM
AMERICA MUSIC					
❑ 640 [10]	A Nite at Artesian Hall With Wooden Joe	1951	15.00	30.00	60.00

NICHOLS, HERBIE
Pianist and composer.

Number	Title	Yr	VG	VG+	NM
BETHLEHEM					
❑ BCP-81 [M]	Love Gloom Cash and Love	1957	25.00	50.00	100.00
❑ BCP-6028	The Bethlehem Years	197?	3.00	6.00	12.00
-- Distributed by RCA Victor					
BLUE NOTE					
❑ BN-LA485-H2 [(2)]	Third World	197?	3.75	7.50	15.00
❑ BLP-1519 [M]	Herbie Nichols Trio	1956	37.50	75.00	150.00
-- "Deep groove" version (deep indentation under label on both sides)					
❑ BLP-1519 [M]	Herbie Nichols Trio	1956	25.00	50.00	100.00
-- Regular edition, Lexington Ave. address on label					
❑ BLP-1519 [M]	Herbie Nichols Trio	1963	6.25	12.50	25.00
-- With "New York, USA" address on label					
❑ BLP-5068 [10]	The Prophetic Herbie Nichols, Volume 1	1955	100.00	200.00	400.00
❑ BLP-5069 [10]	The Prophetic Herbie Nichols, Volume 2	1955	100.00	200.00	400.00
❑ BST-81519 [R]	Herbie Nichols Trio	1967	3.00	6.00	12.00
-- With "A Division of Liberty Records" on label					

NICHOLS, KEITH
Pianist.

Number	Title	Yr	VG	VG+	NM
STOMP OFF					
❑ SOS-1135	Doctors Jazz	1987	2.50	5.00	10.00

Number	Title	Yr	VG	VG+	NM
❑ SOS-1159	Chitterlin' Strut	1988	2.50	5.00	10.00

NICHOLS, NAT
Pianist.
NAJO

Number	Title	Yr	VG	VG+	NM
❑ LPS-001	Nat Nichols Trio	1967	6.25	12.50	25.00
❑ LPS-002	Spring Play	1967	6.25	12.50	25.00

NICHOLS, RED, AND THE FIVE PENNIES
Nichols played cornet. The Five Pennies were often more than five, and the membership changed often.
AUDIOPHILE

Number	Title	Yr	VG	VG+	NM
❑ AP-1 [M]	Red Nichols and Band	195?	12.50	25.00	50.00
❑ AP-7 [M]	Syncopated Chamber Music, Volume 1	195?	12.50	25.00	50.00
❑ AP-8 [M]	Syncopated Chamber Music, Volume 2	195?	12.50	25.00	50.00

BRUNSWICK

Number	Title	Yr	VG	VG+	NM
❑ BL 54008 [M]	For Collectors Only	1954	12.50	25.00	50.00
❑ BL 54047 [M]	The Red Nichols Story	1959	12.50	25.00	50.00
❑ BL 58008 [10]	Classics, Volume 1	1950	20.00	40.00	80.00
❑ BL 58009 [10]	Classics, Volume 2	1950	20.00	40.00	80.00
❑ BL 58027 [10]	Volume 3	1951	20.00	40.00	80.00

CAPITOL

Number	Title	Yr	VG	VG+	NM
❑ H 215 [10]	Jazz Time	1950	20.00	40.00	80.00
❑ T 775 [M]	Hot Pennies	1956	12.50	25.00	50.00
❑ ST 1051 [S]	Parade of the Pennies	1958	7.50	15.00	30.00
❑ T 1051 [M]	Parade of the Pennies	1958	5.00	10.00	20.00
❑ ST 1297 [S]	Dixieland Dinner Dance	1960	5.00	10.00	20.00
❑ T 1297 [M]	Dixieland Dinner Dance	1960	3.75	7.50	15.00
❑ ST 1803 [S]	The All-Time Hits of Red Nichols	1962	5.00	10.00	20.00
❑ T 1803 [M]	The All-Time Hits of Red Nichols	1962	3.75	7.50	15.00
❑ ST 2065 [S]	Blues and Old-Time Rags	1963	5.00	10.00	20.00
❑ T 2065 [M]	Blues and Old-Time Rags	1963	3.75	7.50	15.00

CIRCLE

Number	Title	Yr	VG	VG+	NM
❑ CLP-110	Red Nichols and His Orchestra	1987	2.50	5.00	10.00

HALL OF FAME

Number	Title	Yr	VG	VG+	NM
❑ 619	Red Nichols and His Five Pennies	197?	2.50	5.00	10.00

JAZZOLOGY

Number	Title	Yr	VG	VG+	NM
❑ J-90	Red Nichols and His Five Pennies	198?	2.50	5.00	10.00

MARK 56

Number	Title	Yr	VG	VG+	NM
❑ 612	Red Nichols and His Five Pennies	197?	3.00	6.00	12.00

MCA

Number	Title	Yr	VG	VG+	NM
❑ 1518	The Rarest Brunswick Masters	198?	2.50	5.00	10.00

MOBILE FIDELITY

Number	Title	Yr	VG	VG+	NM
❑ 1-093	Red Nichols and the Five Pennies at Marineland	1982	5.00	10.00	20.00

-- Audiophile vinyl
PAUSA

Number	Title	Yr	VG	VG+	NM
❑ 9022	All Time Hits	198?	2.50	5.00	10.00

PICCADILLY

Number	Title	Yr	VG	VG+	NM
❑ 3570	Big Band Series/Original Recordings	198?	2.50	5.00	10.00

SUNBEAM

Number	Title	Yr	VG	VG+	NM
❑ 12 [(2)]	Popular Concert 1928-32	197?	3.00	6.00	12.00
❑ 137	Red Nichols and His Five Pennies 1929-31	197?	2.50	5.00	10.00

NICHOLS-JACOBY DREAMLAND SYNCOPATORS
STOMP OFF

Number	Title	Yr	VG	VG+	NM
❑ SOS-1150	Territory Jazz	1988	2.50	5.00	10.00

NIEBLA, EDUARDO, AND ANTONIO FORCIONE
Niebla and Forcione are guitarists.
VENTURE

Number	Title	Yr	VG	VG+	NM
❑ 90655	Celebration	1988	2.50	5.00	10.00

NIEHAUS, LENNIE
Alto saxophone player and arranger.
CONTEMPORARY

Number	Title	Yr	VG	VG+	NM
❑ C-2513 [10]	Lennie Niehaus, Vol. 1: The Quintet	1954	30.00	60.00	120.00
❑ C-2517 [10]	Lennie Niehaus, Vol. 2: The Octet	1954	30.00	60.00	120.00
❑ C-3503 [M]	Lennie Niehaus, Vol. 3: The Octet No. 2	1955	20.00	40.00	80.00
❑ C-3510 [M]	Lennie Niehaus, Vol. 4: The Quintets & Strings	1956	20.00	40.00	80.00
❑ C-3518 [M]	The Lennie Niehaus Quintet	1956	20.00	40.00	80.00
❑ C-3524 [M]	Lennie Niehaus, Vol. 5: The Sextet	1956	20.00	40.00	80.00
❑ C-3540 [M]	Zounds! Lennie Niehaus, Vol. 2: The Octet	1957	20.00	40.00	80.00

EMARCY

Number	Title	Yr	VG	VG+	NM
❑ MG-36118 [M]	I Swing for You	1957	12.50	25.00	50.00

FANTASY

Number	Title	Yr	VG	VG+	NM
❑ OJC-319	The Lennie Niehaus Quintet	198?	2.50	5.00	10.00

MERCURY

Number	Title	Yr	VG	VG+	NM
❑ MG-20555 [M]	I Swing for You	1960	7.50	15.00	30.00
❑ SR-60123 [S]	I Swing for You	1960	6.25	12.50	25.00

NIEMACK, JUDY, AND SIMON WETTENHALL
Niemack is a female singer; Wettenhall plays trumpet.
INNER CITY

Number	Title	Yr	VG	VG+	NM
❑ IC-1115	Night Sprite	198?	3.00	6.00	12.00

SEA BREEZE

Number	Title	Yr	VG	VG+	NM
❑ 2001	By Heart	1980	3.00	6.00	12.00

NIEWOOD, GERRY
Flutist.
A&M

Number	Title	Yr	VG	VG+	NM
❑ SP-3409	Slow, Hot Wind	1977	2.50	5.00	10.00

HORIZON

Number	Title	Yr	VG	VG+	NM
❑ SP-719	Gerry Niewood and Timepiece	1976	3.00	6.00	12.00

NIGHTWIND
PAUSA

Number	Title	Yr	VG	VG+	NM
❑ 7127	A Casual Romance	198?	2.50	5.00	10.00

NIMMONS, PHIL
Clarinetist, alto saxophone player and composer.
CLEF

Number	Title	Yr	VG	VG+	NM
❑ MGC-753 [M]	The Canadian Scene Via Phil Nimmons	1955	---	---	---

-- Canceled; issued on Verve 8025
VERVE

Number	Title	Yr	VG	VG+	NM
❑ MGVS-6153 [S]	Nimmons 'n' Nine	1960	---	---	---

-- Canceled

Number	Title	Yr	VG	VG+	NM
❑ MGV-8025 [M]	The Canadian Scene Via Phil Nimmons	1957	6.25	12.50	25.00
❑ V-8025 [M]	The Canadian Scene Via Phil Nimmons	1961	5.00	10.00	20.00
❑ MGV-8376 [M]	Nimmons 'n' Nine	1960	6.25	12.50	25.00
❑ V-8376 [M]	Nimmons 'n' Nine	1961	5.00	10.00	20.00

NISTICO, SAL
Tenor saxophone player.
BEE HIVE

Number	Title	Yr	VG	VG+	NM
❑ BH-7006	Neo/Nistico	1980	3.00	6.00	12.00

JAZZLAND

Number	Title	Yr	VG	VG+	NM
❑ JLP-66 [M]	Heavyweights	1962	7.50	15.00	30.00
❑ JLP-966 [S]	Heavyweights	1962	10.00	20.00	40.00

RIVERSIDE

Number	Title	Yr	VG	VG+	NM
❑ RLP-457 [M]	Comin' On Up	1963	7.50	15.00	30.00
❑ RS-9457 [S]	Comin' On Up	1963	10.00	20.00	40.00

NO/GAP JAZZ BAND, THE
NO/GAP

Number	Title	Yr	VG	VG+	NM
❑ 7444001	Live	197?	3.75	7.50	15.00
❑ 7444002	No/Gap Jazz Band	197?	3.75	7.50	15.00

NOCK, MIKE
Pianist.
ECM

Number	Title	Yr	VG	VG+	NM
❑ 1220	Ondas	1981	2.50	5.00	10.00

IAI

Number	Title	Yr	VG	VG+	NM
❑ 373851	Almanac	197?	3.75	7.50	15.00

TIMELESS

Number	Title	Yr	VG	VG+	NM
❑ 313	In Out and Around	1978	3.00	6.00	12.00

TOMATO

Number	Title	Yr	VG	VG+	NM
❑ TOM-8009	Climbing	1979	3.75	7.50	15.00

NOONE, JIMMIE
Clarinetist and soprano and alto saxophone player. Also see JOHNNY DODDS.
BRUNSWICK

Number	Title	Yr	VG	VG+	NM
❑ BL 58006 [10]	The Apex Club Orchestra	1950	12.50	25.00	50.00

Number	Title	Yr	VG	VG+	NM

MCA
❏ 1313 — Jimmie Noone and Earl Hines at the Apex Club — 198? — 2.50 — 5.00 — 10.00

NOONE, JIMMY, JR.
STOMP OFF
❏ SOS-1121 — Jimmy Remembers Jimmie — 1986 — 2.50 — 5.00 — 10.00

NORDINE, KEN
Spoken-word performer known for his so-called "word jazz."
BLUE THUMB
❏ BTS-33 [(2)] — How Are Things in Your Town? — 1971 — 6.25 — 12.50 — 25.00
❏ BTS-35 [(2)] — Ken Nordine — 1972 — 6.25 — 12.50 — 25.00
DECCA
❏ DL 8550 [M] — Concert in the Sky — 1957 — 15.00 — 30.00 — 60.00
DOT
❏ DLP-3075 [M] — Word Jazz — 1958 — 10.00 — 20.00 — 40.00
❏ DLP-3096 [M] — Son of Word Jazz — 1958 — 10.00 — 20.00 — 40.00
❏ DLP-3115 [M] — Love Words — 1958 — 10.00 — 20.00 — 40.00
❏ DLP-3142 [M] — My Baby — 1959 — 10.00 — 20.00 — 40.00
❏ DLP-3196 [M] — Next! — 1959 — 10.00 — 20.00 — 40.00
❏ DLP-3301 [M] — Word Jazz, Vol. 2 — 1960 — 10.00 — 20.00 — 40.00
❏ DLP-25075 [S] — Word Jazz — 1959 — 12.50 — 25.00 — 50.00
❏ DLP-25096 [S] — Son of Word Jazz — 1959 — 12.50 — 25.00 — 50.00
❏ DLP-25115 [S] — Love Words — 1959 — 12.50 — 25.00 — 50.00
❏ DLP-25142 [S] — My Baby — 1959 — 12.50 — 25.00 — 50.00
❏ DLP-25196 [S] — Next! — 1959 — 12.50 — 25.00 — 50.00
❏ DLP-25301 [S] — Word Jazz, Vol. 2 — 1960 — 12.50 — 25.00 — 50.00
❏ DLP-25880 — The Best of Word Jazz — 1968 — 5.00 — 10.00 — 20.00
FM
❏ 304 [M] — Passion In the Desert — 1963 — 7.50 — 15.00 — 30.00
❏ S-304 [S] — Passion In the Desert — 1963 — 10.00 — 20.00 — 40.00
HAMILTON
❏ HL-102 [M] — The Voice of Love — 1964 — 5.00 — 10.00 — 20.00
❏ HL-12102 [S] — The Voice of Love — 1964 — 6.25 — 12.50 — 25.00
PHILIPS
❏ PHM 200-224 [M] Colors — 1966 — 5.00 — 10.00 — 20.00
❏ PHM 200-258 [M] Ken Nordine Does Robert Shure's "Twink" — 1967 — 5.00 — 10.00 — 20.00
❏ PHS 600-224 [S] Colors — 1966 — 6.25 — 12.50 — 25.00
❏ PHS 600-258 [S] Ken Nordine Does Robert Shure's "Twink" — 1967 — 6.25 — 12.50 — 25.00
SNAIL
❏ SR-1003 — Grandson of Word Jazz — 1987 — 5.00 — 10.00 — 20.00

NORMAN, GENE, GROUP
Studio band formed by record company owner Norman.
GNP CRESCENDO
❏ GNP-2015 [M] — Dylan Jazz — 1965 — 5.00 — 10.00 — 20.00
❏ GNPS-2015 [S] — Dylan Jazz — 1965 — 6.25 — 12.50 — 25.00

NORRIS, WALTER
Pianist.
ENJA
❏ 2044 — Drifting — 198? — 3.00 — 6.00 — 12.00
PROGRESSIVE
❏ PRO-7039 — Stepping on Cracks — 198? — 3.00 — 6.00 — 12.00

NORRIS, WALTER, AND GEORGE MRAZ
Mraz is a bass player. Also see WALTER NORRIS.
ENJA
❏ 2044 — Drifting — 197? — 3.75 — 7.50 — 15.00

NORRIS, WALTER, AND ALADAR PAGE
Page is a bass player. Also see WALTER NORRIS.
INNER CITY
❏ IC-3028 — Synchronicity — 1979 — 3.75 — 7.50 — 15.00

NORVO, RED
Vibraphone, xylophone and marimba player. Also an occasional pianist. Also see RED ALLEN; THE JAZZ PICKERS; CHARLIE PARKER; ART PEPPER; DINAH SHORE.
ALLEGRO
❏ 1739 [M] — Red Norvo Jazz Trio — 195? — 10.00 — 20.00 — 40.00
BLUEBIRD
❏ 6278-1-RB — Just a Mood — 1987 — 2.50 — 5.00 — 10.00
CAPITOL
❏ T 616 [M] — Classics In Jazz — 1955 — 20.00 — 40.00 — 80.00

CHARLIE PARKER
❏ PLP-833 [M] — Pretty Is the Only Way To Fly — 1962 — 6.25 — 12.50 — 25.00
❏ PLP-833S [S] — Pretty Is the Only Way To Fly — 1962 — 6.25 — 12.50 — 25.00
CIRCLE
❏ 3 — Red Norvo and His Orchestra 1938 — 198? — 2.50 — 5.00 — 10.00
COMMODORE
❏ FL-20023 [10] — Town Hall Concert, Volume 1 — 1952 — 37.50 — 75.00 — 150.00
❏ FL-20027 [10] — Town Hall Concert, Volume 2 — 1952 — 37.50 — 75.00 — 150.00
CONTEMPORARY
❏ C-3534 [M] — Music To Listen to Red Norvo By — 1957 — 12.50 — 25.00 — 50.00
❏ S-7009 [S] — Music To Listen to Red Norvo By — 1959 — 10.00 — 20.00 — 40.00
CONTINENTAL
❏ C-16005 [M] — Mainstream Jazz — 1962 — 3.75 — 7.50 — 15.00
❏ CS-16005 [S] — Mainstream Jazz — 1962 — 5.00 — 10.00 — 20.00
DECCA
❏ DL 5501 [10] — Dancing on the Ceiling — 1953 — 30.00 — 60.00 — 120.00
DIAL
❏ LP-903 [M] — Fabulous Jazz Session — 1951 — 50.00 — 100.00 — 200.00
DISCOVERY
❏ DL-3012 [10] — Red Norvo Trio — 1950 — 37.50 — 75.00 — 150.00
❏ DL-3018 [10] — Red Norvo Trio — 1952 — 37.50 — 75.00 — 150.00
❏ DL-4005 [M] — Red Norvo Trio, Volume 1 — 1951 — 30.00 — 60.00 — 120.00
DOT
❏ DLP-3126 [M] — Windjammer City Style — 1958 — 7.50 — 15.00 — 30.00
❏ DLP-25126 [S] — Windjammer City Style — 1958 — 10.00 — 20.00 — 40.00
EMARCY
❏ MG-26002 [10] — Improvisation — 1954 — 37.50 — 75.00 — 150.00
ENCORE
❏ EE-22009 — Original 1933-38 Recordings — 1968 — 3.75 — 7.50 — 15.00
EPIC
❏ LN 3128 [M] — Red Norvo and His All Stars — 1955 — 12.50 — 25.00 — 50.00
FAMOUS DOOR
❏ 105 — Vibes A La Red — 197? — 3.00 — 6.00 — 12.00
❏ 108 — Second Time Around — 197? — 3.00 — 6.00 — 12.00
❏ 116 — Red Norvo in New York — 197? — 3.00 — 6.00 — 12.00
FANTASY
❏ 3-12 [10] — Red Norvo Trio — 1953 — 37.50 — 75.00 — 150.00
-- Colored vinyl
❏ 3-12 [10] — Red Norvo Trio — 1953 — 25.00 — 50.00 — 100.00
-- Black vinyl
❏ 3-19 [M] — Red Norvo Trio — 1955 — 20.00 — 40.00 — 80.00
-- Red vinyl
❏ 3-19 [M] — Red Norvo Trio — 195? — 10.00 — 20.00 — 40.00
-- Black vinyl
❏ OJC-155 — Music to Listen to Red Norvo By — 198? — 2.50 — 5.00 — 10.00
❏ OJC-641 — Red Norvo Trio — 1991 — 3.00 — 6.00 — 12.00
❏ 3218 [M] — Red Norvo With Strings — 195? — 10.00 — 20.00 — 40.00
-- Black vinyl
❏ 3218 [M] — Red Norvo With Strings — 1956 — 20.00 — 40.00 — 80.00
-- Red vinyl
❏ 3244 [M] — The Red Norvo Trios — 195? — 10.00 — 20.00 — 40.00
-- Black vinyl
❏ 3244 [M] — The Red Norvo Trios — 1957 — 20.00 — 40.00 — 80.00
-- Red vinyl
JAZZTONE
❏ J-1277 [M] — Delightfully Light — 195? — 10.00 — 20.00 — 40.00
LIBERTY
❏ LRP-3035 [M] — Ad Lib — 1957 — 10.00 — 20.00 — 40.00
❏ LJH-6012 [M] — Vibe-rations In Hi-Fi — 1956 — 12.50 — 25.00 — 50.00
MERCURY
❏ 830 966-1 — Improvisations — 1987 — 2.50 — 5.00 — 10.00
PAUSA
❏ 9015 — All Star Sessions — 198? — 2.50 — 5.00 — 10.00
PRESTIGE
❏ 24108 [(2)] — The Trios — 198? — 3.75 — 7.50 — 15.00
RAVE
❏ 101 [M] — Red Norvo Quintet — 1956 — 20.00 — 40.00 — 80.00
RCA VICTOR
❏ LPM-1420 [M] — Hi Five — 1957 — 10.00 — 20.00 — 40.00
❏ LPM-1449 [M] — Some Of My Favorites — 1957 — 10.00 — 20.00 — 40.00
❏ LSP-1711 [S] — Red Norvo In Stereo — 1958 — 12.50 — 25.00 — 50.00
❏ LPM-1729 [M] — Red Plays the Blues — 1958 — 10.00 — 20.00 — 40.00
❏ LSP-1729 [S] — Red Plays the Blues — 1958 — 12.50 — 25.00 — 50.00
REFERENCE RECORDINGS
❏ RR-8 — The Forward Look — 1983 — 5.00 — 10.00 — 20.00
❏ RR-8-UHGR — The Forward Look — 1983 — 10.00 — 20.00 — 40.00

Number	Title	Yr	VG	VG+	NM
RONDO-LETTE					
❑ A-28 [M]	Red Norvo Trio	1958	6.25	12.50	25.00
SAVOY					
❑ MG-12088 [M]	Move!	1956	20.00	40.00	80.00
❑ MG-12093 [M]	Midnight On Cloud 69	1956	20.00	40.00	80.00
SAVOY JAZZ					
❑ SJL-2212 [(2)]	Red Norvo Trio	197?	3.00	6.00	12.00
SPOTLITE					
❑ 107	Fabulous Jam	197?	2.50	5.00	10.00
STASH					
❑ ST-230	Just Friends	1984	2.50	5.00	10.00
STEREO RECORDS					
❑ S-7009 [S]	Music To Listen To Red Norvo By	1958	12.50	25.00	50.00
TAMPA					
❑ TP-35 [M]	Norvo Naturally	1957	25.00	50.00	100.00
-- Colored vinyl					
❑ TP-35 [M]	Norvo Naturally	1958	12.50	25.00	50.00
-- Black vinyl					
"X"					
❑ LXA-3034 [M]	Red's Blue Room	1955	37.50	75.00	150.00
XANADU					
❑ 199	Time in His Hands	198?	2.50	5.00	10.00

NORVO, RED/GEORGIE AULD
Also see each artist's individual listings.

Number	Title	Yr	VG	VG+	NM
GOLDEN ERA					
❑ 15016 [M]	The Great Dance Bands, Vol. 2	195?	10.00	20.00	40.00

NORVO, RED, AND ROSS TOMPKINS
Also see each artist's individual listings.

Number	Title	Yr	VG	VG+	NM
CONCORD JAZZ					
❑ CJ-90	Red Norvo and Ross Tompkins	1979	2.50	5.00	10.00

NOTHING, CHARLIE
Imagine if The Legendary Stardust Cowboy played sax...

Number	Title	Yr	VG	VG+	NM
TAKOMA					
❑ C-1015	The Psychedelic Saxophone Of Charlie Nothing	1967	12.50	25.00	50.00

NOTO, SAM
Trumpeter.

Number	Title	Yr	VG	VG+	NM
XANADU					
❑ 103	Entrance!	1975	3.00	6.00	12.00
❑ 127	Act One	1976	3.00	6.00	12.00
❑ 144	Notes to You	1977	3.00	6.00	12.00
❑ 168	Noto-Riety	198?	2.50	5.00	10.00

NOVAC, JERRY

Number	Title	Yr	VG	VG+	NM
EMBRYO					
❑ 527	The 5th Word	1970	6.25	12.50	25.00

NOW CREATIVE ARTS JAZZ ENSEMBLE, THE

Number	Title	Yr	VG	VG+	NM
ARHOOLIE					
❑ 8002	Now	1969	5.00	10.00	20.00

NOZERO, LARRY
Alto saxophone player.

Number	Title	Yr	VG	VG+	NM
STRATA					
❑ 109-75	Time	1975	5.00	10.00	20.00

NRG ENSEMBLE
See HAL RUSSELL.

NUBIN, KATI BELL
Female singer.

Number	Title	Yr	VG	VG+	NM
VERVE					
❑ MGV-3004 [M]	Soul, Soul Searchin'	1960	20.00	40.00	80.00
❑ V-3004 [M]	Soul, Soul Searchin'	1961	10.00	20.00	40.00
❑ V6-3004 [S]	Soul, Soul Searchin'	1961	12.50	25.00	50.00
❑ MGVS-6147 [S]	Soul, Soul Searchin'	1960	---	---	---
-- Canceled					
❑ MGV-8372 [M]	Soul, Soul Searchin'	1960	---	---	---
-- Canceled					

NUNEZ, FLIP
Pianist.

Number	Title	Yr	VG	VG+	NM
CATALYST					
❑ 7603	My Own Time and Space	1976	3.00	6.00	12.00

NUROCK, KIRK
Pianist and composer.

Number	Title	Yr	VG	VG+	NM
LABOR					
❑ 13	Natural Sound	1981	3.00	6.00	12.00

NUTTY SQUIRRELS, THE
Jazz counterpart to the Chpmunks, created by DON ELLIOTT with Sascha Burland (vocals) and a band of jazz all-stars: CANNONBALL ADDERLEY; BOBBY JASPAR; HAL McKUSICK; SAM MOST; Romeo Penque (flute); Sol Schlinger (baritone sax).

Number	Title	Yr	VG	VG+	NM
COLUMBIA					
❑ CL 1589 [M]	Bird Watching	1961	7.50	15.00	30.00
❑ CS 8389 [S]	Bird Watching	1961	10.00	20.00	40.00
HANOVER					
❑ HML-8014 [M]	The Nutty Squirrels	1960	12.50	25.00	50.00
MGM					
❑ E-4272 [M]	A Hard Day's Night	1964	6.25	12.50	25.00
❑ SE-4272 [S]	A Hard Day's Night	1964	7.50	15.00	30.00

Number	Title	Yr	VG	VG+	NM

O

O'BRIEN, HOD
Pianist.
UPTOWN
| 27.08 | Bits and Pieces | 198? | 2.50 | 5.00 | 10.00 |

O'BRYANT, JIMMY
Clarinet player and bandleader.
BIOGRAPH
| 12002 [M] | Jimmy O'Bryant's Washboard Wonders 1924-26 | 1968 | 3.00 | 6.00 | 12.00 |

O'CONNELL, BILL
Pianist.
INNER CITY
| IC-1035 | Searching | 197? | 3.75 | 7.50 | 15.00 |

O'DAY, ANITA
Female singer.
ADVANCE
| LSP-8 [10] | Anita O'Day Specials | 1951 | 62.50 | 125.00 | 250.00 |
AMERICAN RECORDING SOCIETY
| G-426 [M] | For Oscar | 1957 | 10.00 | 20.00 | 40.00 |
BASF
| 20750 | Berlin Jazz Fest 1970 | 197? | 5.00 | 10.00 | 20.00 |
CLEF
| MGC-130 [10] | Anita O'Day Collates | 1953 | 37.50 | 75.00 | 150.00 |
CORAL
| CRL-56073 [10] | Singin' and Swingin' | 1953 | 37.50 | 75.00 | 150.00 |
DOCTOR JAZZ
| FW 39418 | Hi Ho Trailus Boot Whip | 198? | 2.50 | 5.00 | 10.00 |
EMILY
9579	Live at Tokyo	1979	3.75	7.50	15.00
11279	My Ship	1979	3.75	7.50	15.00
11579	Live at Mingos	1979	3.75	7.50	15.00
13081	Angel Eyes	1981	3.00	6.00	12.00
32383	The Night Has a Thousand Eyes	1983	3.00	6.00	12.00
42181	Live at the City: The Second Set	1981	3.00	6.00	12.00
83084	A Song for You	1984	3.00	6.00	12.00
92685	Big Band Concert 1985	1985	3.00	6.00	12.00
102479	Live at the City	1979	3.75	7.50	15.00
GLENDALE
| 6000 | Once Upon a Summertime | 197? | 3.00 | 6.00 | 12.00 |
| 6001 | Anita O'Day | 197? | 3.00 | 6.00 | 12.00 |
GNP CRESCENDO
| GNPS-2126 | Mello' Day | 197? | 2.50 | 5.00 | 10.00 |
NORGRAN
MGN-30 [10]	Songs By Anita O'Day	1954	37.50	75.00	150.00
MGN-1049 [M]	Anita O'Day	1955	30.00	60.00	120.00
MGN-1057 [M]	An Evening With Anita O'Day	1956	25.00	50.00	100.00
PAUSA
| 7092 | Anita O'Day in Berlin | 198? | 2.50 | 5.00 | 10.00 |
VERVE
MGV-2000 [M]	Anita	1956	20.00	40.00	80.00
V-2000 [M]	Anita	1961	5.00	10.00	20.00
MGV-2043 [M]	Pick Yourself Up with Anita O'Day	1957	20.00	40.00	80.00
V-2043 [M]	Pick Yourself Up with Anita O'Day	1961	5.00	10.00	20.00
MGV-2049 [M]	The Lady Is a Tramp	1957	15.00	30.00	60.00
V-2049 [M]	The Lady Is a Tramp	1961	5.00	10.00	20.00
MGV-2050 [M]	An Evening with Anita O'Day	1957	15.00	30.00	60.00
V-2050 [M]	An Evening with Anita O'Day	1961	5.00	10.00	20.00
MGV-2086 [M]	'S Wonderful	1957	---	---	---
-- Canceled					
MGV-2113 [M]	Anita O'Day at Mr. Kelly's	1958	12.50	25.00	50.00
V-2113 [M]	Anita O'Day at Mr. Kelly's	1961	5.00	10.00	20.00
V6-2113 [S]	Anita O'Day at Mr. Kelly's	1961	6.25	12.50	25.00
MGV-2118 [M]	Anita O'Day Swings Cole Porter	1959	12.50	25.00	50.00
V-2118 [M]	Anita O'Day Swings Cole Porter	1961	5.00	10.00	20.00
V6-2118 [S]	Anita O'Day Swings Cole Porter	1961	6.25	12.50	25.00
MGV-2141 [M]	Anita O'Day and Billy May Swing Rodgers and Hart	1960	15.00	30.00	60.00
V-2141 [M]	Anita O'Day and Billy May Swing Rodgers and Hart	1961	5.00	10.00	20.00
V6-2141 [S]	Anita O'Day and Billy May Swing Rodgers and Hart	1961	6.25	12.50	25.00
MGV-2145 [M]	Waiter, Make Mine Blues	1960	15.00	30.00	60.00
V-2145 [M]	Waiter, Make Mine Blues	1961	5.00	10.00	20.00
V6-2145 [S]	Waiter, Make Mine Blues	1961	6.25	12.50	25.00
MGV-2154 [M]	I Remember Billie Holiday	1960	---	---	---
-- Canceled					
MGV-2157 [M]	Trav'lin' Light	1960	12.50	25.00	50.00
V-2157 [M]	Trav'lin' Light	1961	5.00	10.00	20.00
V6-2157 [S]	Trav'lin' Light	1961	6.25	12.50	25.00
VE-1-2534	Big Band	197?	3.75	7.50	15.00
UMV-2536	Anita O'Day Sings the Winners	198?	3.00	6.00	12.00
UMV-2550	Anita O'Day at Mr. Kelly's	198?	3.00	6.00	12.00
UMV-2679	Cool Heat -- Anita O'Day Sings Jimmy Giuffre Arrangements	198?	3.00	6.00	12.00
UMJ-3287	Time For Two	198?	3.00	6.00	12.00
MGVS-6002 [S]	Anita O'Day Sings the Winners	1960	15.00	30.00	60.00
MGVS-6043 [S]	Anita O'Day at Mr. Kelly's	1960	15.00	30.00	60.00
MGVS-6046 [S]	Cool Heat -- Anita O'Day Sings Jimmy Giuffre Arrangements	1960	15.00	30.00	60.00
MGVS-6059 [S]	Anita O'Day Swings Cole Porter	1960	15.00	30.00	60.00
MGV-8140 [M]	The Lady Is a Tramp	1957	---	---	---
-- Canceled					
MGV-8147 [M]	An Evening with Anita O'Day	1957	---	---	---
-- Canceled					
MGV-8259 [M]	Anita Sings the Most	1958	12.50	25.00	50.00
V-8259 [M]	Anita Sings the Most	1961	5.00	10.00	20.00
MGV-8283 [M]	Anita O'Day Sings the Winners	1958	12.50	25.00	50.00
V-8283 [M]	Anita O'Day Sings the Winners	1961	5.00	10.00	20.00
V6-8283 [S]	Anita O'Day Sings the Winners	1961	6.25	12.50	25.00
MGV-8312 [M]	Cool Heat -- Anita O'Day Sings Jimmy Giuffre Arrangements	1959	12.50	25.00	50.00
V-8312 [M]	Cool Heat -- Anita O'Day Sings Jimmy Giuffre Arrangements	1961	5.00	10.00	20.00
V6-8312 [S]	Cool Heat -- Anita O'Day Sings Jimmy Giuffre Arrangements	1961	6.25	12.50	25.00
V-8442 [M]	All the Sad Young Men	1962	7.50	15.00	30.00
V6-8442 [S]	All the Sad Young Men	1962	10.00	20.00	40.00
V-8472 [M]	Time for Two	1962	7.50	15.00	30.00
V6-8472 [S]	Time for Two	1962	10.00	20.00	40.00
V-8483 [M]	This Is Anita	1962	7.50	15.00	30.00
V-8483 [R]	This Is Anita	1962	3.75	7.50	15.00
V-8485 [M]	Anita O'Day Sings the Winners	1962	5.00	10.00	20.00
V6-8485 [S]	Anita O'Day Sings the Winners	1962	6.25	12.50	25.00
V-8514 [M]	Anita O'Day and the Three Sounds	1963	6.25	12.50	25.00
V6-8514 [S]	Anita O'Day and the Three Sounds	1963	7.50	15.00	30.00
V-8572 [M]	Incomparable! Anita O'Day	1964	6.25	12.50	25.00
V6-8572 [S]	Incomparable! Anita O'Day	1964	7.50	15.00	30.00
829 261-1	Anita	1986	2.50	5.00	10.00

O'FARRILL, CHICO
Trumpeter, arranger, composer and bandleader.
ABC IMPULSE!
| AS-9135 [S] | Nine Flags | 1968 | 3.75 | 7.50 | 15.00 |
CLEF
MGC-131 [10]	Afro-Cuban	1953	50.00	100.00	200.00
MGC-132 [10]	Chico O'Farrill Jazz	1953	50.00	100.00	200.00
MGC-699 [M]	Chico O'Farrill Jazz	1956	20.00	40.00	80.00
IMPULSE!
| A-9135 [M] | Nine Flags | 1967 | 6.25 | 12.50 | 25.00 |
| AS-9135 [S] | Nine Flags | 1967 | 5.00 | 10.00 | 20.00 |
NORGRAN
MGN-9 [10]	The Second Afro-Cuban Jazz Suite	1954	37.50	75.00	150.00
MGN-27 [10]	Mambo Dance Sessions	1954	20.00	40.00	80.00
MGN-28 [10]	Latino Dance Sessions	1954	20.00	40.00	80.00
MGN-31 [10]	Chico O'Farrill	1954	20.00	40.00	80.00
VERVE
MGV-2003 [M]	Mambo/Latino Dances	1956	12.50	25.00	50.00
V-2003 [M]	Mambo/Latino Dances	1961	6.25	12.50	25.00
MGV-2024 [M]	Music From South America	1956	12.50	25.00	50.00
V-2024 [M]	Music From South America	1961	6.25	12.50	25.00
MGV-8083 [M]	Jazz North of the Border and South of the Border	1957	12.50	25.00	50.00
V-8083 [M]	Jazz North of the Border and South of the Border	1961	6.25	12.50	25.00

O'LENO, LARRY
Pianist and male singer.
PAINTED SMILES
| 1348 | Larry O'Leno Sings Billy Strayhorn | 198? | 3.00 | 6.00 | 12.00 |

O'NEAL, JOHNNY
Male singer and pianist.
CONCORD JAZZ
| CJ-228 | Coming Out | 198? | 2.50 | 5.00 | 10.00 |

Number	Title	Yr	VG	VG+	NM
OAKLEY, LEON					
Cornet player and bandleader.					
GHB					
❑ GHB-153	Leon Oakley and the Flying Duces	198?	2.50	5.00	10.00
STOMP OFF					
❑ SOS-1013	New Orleans Joys	198?	2.50	5.00	10.00
OBEIDO, RAY					
Guitarist.					
WINDHAM HILL					
❑ WH-0115	Perfect Crime	1989	3.00	6.00	12.00
ODETTA					
Female singer better known in the folk realm. For a more complete listing, see the *Standard Catalog of American Records 1950-1975*.					
RIVERSIDE					
❑ RLP-417 [M]	Odetta and the Blues	1962	6.25	12.50	25.00
❑ RS-9417 [S]	Odetta and the Blues	1962	7.50	15.00	30.00
ODRICH, RON					
Bass clarinet player.					
CLASSIC JAZZ					
❑ 35	Blackstick	1978	3.00	6.00	12.00
OGERMAN, CLAUS					
Pianist, composer and arranger.					
JAZZ MAN					
❑ 5015	Aranjuez	198?	3.00	6.00	12.00
RCA VICTOR					
❑ LPM-3366 [M]	Soul Searchin'	1965	5.00	10.00	20.00
❑ LSP-3366 [S]	Soul Searchin'	1965	6.25	12.50	25.00
❑ LPM-3455 [M]	Watusi Trumpets	1965	5.00	10.00	20.00
❑ LSP-3455 [S]	Watusi Trumpets	1965	6.25	12.50	25.00
❑ LPM-3640 [M]	Saxes Mexicano	1966	5.00	10.00	20.00
❑ LSP-3640 [S]	Saxes Mexicano	1966	6.25	12.50	25.00
UNITED ARTISTS					
❑ UAL-3206 [M]	Sing Along in German	1962	5.00	10.00	20.00
❑ UAS-6206 [S]	Sing Along in German	1962	6.25	12.50	25.00
WARNER BROS.					
❑ BS 3006	Gate of Dreams	1977	2.50	5.00	10.00
OGERMAN, CLAUS, AND MICHAEL BRECKER					
Also see each artist's individual listings.					
ECM					
❑ 23698	Cityscape	1982	2.50	5.00	10.00
OHLSON, CURTIS					
Bass player.					
INTIMA					
❑ SJE-73274	So Fast	1987	2.50	5.00	10.00
❑ D1-73358	Better Than Ever	1989	3.00	6.00	12.00
OHNO, SHUNZO					
Trumpeter.					
INNER CITY					
❑ IC-1108	Quarter Moon	198?	3.00	6.00	12.00
OLAY, RUTH					
Female singer.					
ABC					
❑ ABC-573 [M]	Soul In the Night	1966	5.00	10.00	20.00
❑ ABCS-573 [S]	Soul In the Night	1966	6.25	12.50	25.00
EMARCY					
❑ MG-36125 [M]	Olay! The New Sound Of Ruth	1958	12.50	25.00	50.00
EVEREST					
❑ SDBR-1218 [S]	Olay! OK	1963	7.50	15.00	30.00
❑ LPBR-5218 [M]	Olay! OK	1963	6.25	12.50	25.00
LAUREL					
❑ 501	Ruth Olay Sings Jazz Today	198?	3.00	6.00	12.00
MERCURY					
❑ MG-20390 [M]	Easy Living	1959	10.00	20.00	40.00
❑ SR-60069 [S]	Easy Living	1959	12.50	25.00	50.00
UNITED ARTISTS					
❑ UAL-3115 [M]	Ruth Olay In Person	1960	7.50	15.00	30.00
❑ UAS-4115 [S]	Ruth Olay In Person	1960	10.00	20.00	40.00
OLD AND NEW DREAMS					
Members: Ed Blackwell (drums); DON CHERRY; CHARLIE HADEN; DEWEY REDMAN.					
BLACK SAINT					
❑ BSR-0013	Old and New Dreams	198?	3.00	6.00	12.00
❑ 120113	A Tribute to Blackwell	1990	3.75	7.50	15.00
ECM					
❑ 1154	Old and New Dreams	1979	3.00	6.00	12.00
❑ 1205	Playing	1981	3.00	6.00	12.00
OLIPHANT, GRASELLA					
ATLANTIC					
❑ 1438 [M]	The Grass Roots	1965	3.75	7.50	15.00
❑ SD-1438 [S]	The Grass Roots	1965	5.00	10.00	20.00
OLIVER, KING					
Cornet player, bandleader and composer, an important jazz pioneer. Also see LOUIS ARMSTRONG.					
BRUNSWICK					
❑ BL 58020 [10]	King Oliver	1950	30.00	60.00	120.00
DECCA					
❑ DL 79246	Papa Joe	1969	3.75	7.50	15.00
EPIC					
❑ LN 3208 [M]	King Oliver Featuring Louis Armstrong	1956	12.50	25.00	50.00
❑ LA 16003 [M]	King Oliver and His Orchestra	1960	7.50	15.00	30.00
❑ BA 17003 [R]	King Oliver and His Orchestra	1960	5.00	10.00	20.00
HERWIN					
❑ 106	Zulus Ball/Working Man Blues	197?	3.00	6.00	12.00
LONDON					
❑ AL 3510 [10]	King Oliver Plays the Blues	195?	20.00	40.00	80.00
MCA					
❑ 1309	Papa Joe	198?	2.50	5.00	10.00
MILESTONE					
❑ M-2006	The Immortal King Oliver	197?	3.75	7.50	15.00
RCA VICTOR					
❑ LPV-529 [M]	King Oliver In New York	1965	6.25	12.50	25.00
RIVERSIDE					
❑ RLP-1007 [10]	King Oliver Plays the Blues	1953	20.00	40.00	80.00
"X"					
❑ LVA-3018 [10]	King Oliver's Uptown Jazz	1954	25.00	50.00	100.00
OLSEN, GEORGE					
Violinist and bandleader.					
RCA VICTOR					
❑ LPV-549 [M]	George Olsen and His Music	1968	5.00	10.00	20.00
OLSHER, LESLEY					
Female singer.					
VITAL					
❑ VTL-011 [(2)]	Lesley	1993	5.00	10.00	20.00
OLYMPIA BRASS BAND OF NEW ORLEANS					
AUDIOPHILE					
❑ AP-108	Olympia Brass Band of New Orleans	197?	3.00	6.00	12.00
BASF					
❑ 20678	New Orleans Street Parade	197?	3.00	6.00	12.00
BIOGRAPH					
❑ VPS-4	Here Come Da Great Olympia Jazz Band	197?	3.00	6.00	12.00
ONENESS OF JUJU					
Led by saxophone player J. Plunky Branch. Other members on the Juju LPs: Ken Shabala (bass); Lon Moshe (vibraphone); Michael Babatunde Lea (percussion); Al-Hammel Rasul (piano); Jalongo Ngoma (percussion). Personnel changes included Ronnie Toler (drums), replacing Ngoma; Muzi Branch (bass), replacing Shabala; and a female singer, Lady Eka-Ete.					
BLACK FIRE					
❑ (# unknown)	African Rhythms	1975	15.00	30.00	60.00
❑ (# unknown)	Space Jungle Luv	1976	15.00	30.00	60.00
STRATA-EAST					
❑ SES-7420	Chapter 2: Nia	1974	25.00	50.00	100.00
-- As "Juju"					
❑ SES-19735	A Message from Mozambique	1973	25.00	50.00	100.00
-- As "Juju"					
OPA					
Members: Hugo Fattoruso (keyboards, vocal, percussion); George Fattoruso (drums, vocal, percussion); Ringo Thielmann (electric bass, vocal).					
MILESTONE					
❑ M-9069	Goldenwings	1976	3.00	6.00	12.00
❑ M-9078	Magic Time	1977	3.00	6.00	12.00

Number	Title	Yr	VG	VG+	NM

OPAFIRE
Led by Norman Engeleitner (keyboards, guitar, percussion, composer). Other members include Christopher Hedge (keyboards, guitar, percussion, hammer dulcimer, mandolin, kalimba); Robert Powell (various guitars, banjo, mandolin); Michael Manning (bass); JEFF NARELL (steel pans).
NOVUS
| ❏ 3084-1-N | Opafire Featuring Norman Engeleitner | 1990 | 3.00 | 6.00 | 12.00 |

OPEN SKY
Members: David Liebman (soprano and tenor saxophone, flute, piano, percussion); Bob Moses (vibes, drums); Frank Tusa (bass).
PM
| ❏ PMR-001 | Open Sky | 1974 | 3.75 | 7.50 | 15.00 |
| ❏ PMR-003 | Spirit in the Sky | 1975 | 3.75 | 7.50 | 15.00 |

OPHELIA RAGTIME ORCHESTRA
Founded by Morten Gunnar Larsen in Oslo, Norway.
STOMP OFF
| ❏ SOS-1108 | Echoes from the Snowball Club | 1986 | 2.50 | 5.00 | 10.00 |

ORANGE THEN BLUE
Big band from Boston.
GM RECORDINGS
| ❏ GM-3006 | Music for Jazz Orchestra | 1987 | 2.50 | 5.00 | 10.00 |

ORCHESTRA OF THE EIGHTH DAY
Polish jazz/classical group led by Jan A.P. Kaczmarek.
FLYING FISH
| ❏ FF-292 | Music for the End | 198? | 3.75 | 7.50 | 15.00 |

ORCHESTRA U.S.A.
Group of more than two dozen musicians led by JOHN LEWIS. Among the names listed elsewhere who appeared on one or more of the LPs are ERIC DOLPHY; GARY McFARLAND; ZOOT SIMS; and PHIL WOODS.
COLPIX
| ❏ CP-448 [M] | Orchestra U.S.A. Debut | 1964 | 10.00 | 20.00 | 40.00 |
| ❏ SCP-448 [S] | Orchestra U.S.A. Debut | 1964 | 12.50 | 25.00 | 50.00 |
COLUMBIA
| ❏ CL 2247 [M] | Jazz Journey | 1963 | 6.25 | 12.50 | 25.00 |
| ❏ CS 9047 [S] | Jazz Journey | 1963 | 7.50 | 15.00 | 30.00 |
RCA VICTOR
| ❏ LPM-3498 [M] | The Sextet Of Orchestra U.S.A. | 1965 | 5.00 | 10.00 | 20.00 |
| ❏ LSP-3498 [S] | The Sextet Of Orchestra U.S.A. | 1965 | 6.25 | 12.50 | 25.00 |

OREGON
Members include Paul McCandless (oboe, English horn, soprano saxophone); Glen Moore (bass); and Ralph Towner (guitar, piano, synthesizers).
ECM
| ❏ 23796 | Oregon | 1983 | 2.50 | 5.00 | 10.00 |
| ❏ 25025 | Crossing | 1985 | 2.50 | 5.00 | 10.00 |
ELEKTRA
❏ 6E-154	Out of the Woods	1978	2.50	5.00	10.00
❏ 6E-224	Roots in the Sky	1979	2.50	5.00	10.00
❏ AB-304 [(2)]	In Performance	1979	3.75	7.50	15.00
MOBILE FIDELITY
| ❏ 1-514 | Distant Hills | 198? | 17.50 | 35.00 | 70.00 |
-- Audiophile vinyl
PORTRAIT
| ❏ OR 44465 | 45th Parallel | 1989 | 3.00 | 6.00 | 12.00 |
TERRA
| ❏ T-1 | Music of Another Present Era | 1985 | 2.50 | 5.00 | 10.00 |
VANGUARD
❏ VSD-109/10 [(2)]	The Essential Oregon	198?	3.75	7.50	15.00
❏ VSQ-40031 [Q]	Distant Hills	1974	6.25	12.50	25.00
❏ VSD-79326	Music of Another Present Era	197?	3.00	6.00	12.00
❏ VSD-79341	Distant Hills	1973	3.00	6.00	12.00
❏ VSD-79350	Winter Light	1974	3.00	6.00	12.00
❏ VSD-79358	In Concert	1975	3.00	6.00	12.00
❏ VSD-79370	Friends	1976	3.00	6.00	12.00
❏ VSD-79397	Violin	1978	3.00	6.00	12.00
❏ VSD-79419	Moon and Mind	1979	3.00	6.00	12.00
❏ VSD-79432	Our First Record	1980	3.00	6.00	12.00

OREGON AND ELVIN JONES
Also see each artist's individual listings.
VANGUARD
| ❏ VSD-79377 | Together | 1977 | 3.00 | 6.00 | 12.00 |

ORGAN-IZERS, THE
See ODELL BROWN.

ORIGINAL CAMELLIA JAZZ BAND
Led by Clive Wilson (trumpet).
NEW ORLEANS
| ❏ 7207 | Original Camellia Jazz Band | 198? | 2.50 | 5.00 | 10.00 |

ORIGINAL DIXIELAND JAZZ BAND, THE
Artists on the first jazz record ever released, "Livery Stable Blues" backed with "Dixie Jass (sic) Band One Step," on the Victor label in 1917. The original members of the all-white group were Eddie Edwards (trombone); NICK LaROCCA (cornet); Yellow Nunez (clarinet); Henry Ragas (piano); Tony Sbarbaro (drums).
GHB
| ❏ GHB-100 | Original Dixieland Jazz Band 1943 | 198? | 2.50 | 5.00 | 10.00 |
RCA VICTOR
| ❏ LPV-547 [M] | The Original Dixieland Jazz Band | 1968 | 5.00 | 10.00 | 20.00 |
"X"
| ❏ LX-3007 [M] | The Original Dixieland Jazz Band | 1954 | 12.50 | 25.00 | 50.00 |

ORIGINAL MEMPHIS FIVE, THE
Founded in 1917 by PHIL NAPOLEON and pianist Frank Signorelli. None of its revolving-door membership was from Memphis!
FOLKWAYS
| ❏ RBF-26 | The Original Memphis Five | 197? | 3.75 | 7.50 | 15.00 |

ORIGINAL SALTY DOGS, THE
Among the members: Lew Green Jr. (cornet); Tom Bartlett (trombone); Kim Cusack (clarinet); John Cooper (piano); Jack Kuncl (banjo); Mike Waldbridge (tuba).
BLACKBIRD
| ❏ 12003 | Traditional Classics | 1967 | 3.75 | 7.50 | 15.00 |
GHB
❏ 44	The Original Salty Dogs	1967	3.75	7.50	15.00
❏ 58	Free Wheeling	1968	3.75	7.50	15.00
❏ 62	The Right Track	197?	3.00	6.00	12.00
STOMP OFF
| ❏ SOS-1115 | Honky Tonk Town | 1987 | 2.50 | 5.00 | 10.00 |

ORLANDO, JAY
DOBRE
| ❏ 1040 | Jay Orlando Loves Earl Bostic | 197? | 3.00 | 6.00 | 12.00 |

ORNBERG, THOMAS
Soprano saxophone player, clarinetist and bandleader.
STOMP OFF
| ❏ SOS-1043 | Come Back, Sweet Papa | 198? | 2.50 | 5.00 | 10.00 |

ORPHEON CELESTA
From France.
STOMP OFF
| ❏ SOS-1083 | Gare de Lyon | 1985 | 2.50 | 5.00 | 10.00 |
| ❏ SOS-1095 | Shim-Me-Sha-Wabble | 1985 | 2.50 | 5.00 | 10.00 |

ORSTED PEDERSEN, NIELS-HENNING
Bass player. Also see JOE ALBANY; MONTY ALEXANDER; PAUL BLEY; KENNY DREW; BOULOU FERRE.
INNER CITY
| ❏ IC-2041 | Jaywalkin' | 197? | 3.75 | 7.50 | 15.00 |
STEEPLECHASE
❏ SCS-1041	Jaywalkin'	198?	3.00	6.00	12.00
❏ SCS-1083	Trio 1	198?	3.00	6.00	12.00
❏ SCS-1093	Trio 2	198?	3.00	6.00	12.00
❏ SCS-1125	Dancing on the Tables	1979	3.00	6.00	12.00

ORSTED PEDERSEN, NIELS-HENNING, AND SAM JONES
Also see each artist's individual listings.
INNER CITY
| ❏ IC-2055 | Double Bass | 197? | 3.75 | 7.50 | 15.00 |
STEEPLECHASE
| ❏ SCS-1055 | Double Bass | 198? | 3.00 | 6.00 | 12.00 |

ORSTED PEDERSEN, NIELS-HENNING, AND KENNETH KNUDSEN
Knudsen plays keyboards. Also see NIELS-HENNING ORSTED PEDERSEN.
STEEPLECHASE
| ❏ SCS-1068 | Pictures | 198? | 3.00 | 6.00 | 12.00 |

ORTEGA, ANTHONY
Alto saxophone and clarinet player.
BETHLEHEM
| ❏ BCP-79 [M] | Jazz For Young Moderns | 1957 | 12.50 | 25.00 | 50.00 |

Number	Title	Yr	VG	VG+	NM
DISCOVERY					
❏ 788	Rain Dance	1978	3.00	6.00	12.00
HERALD					
❏ HLP-0101 [M]	A Man and His Horn	1956	15.00	30.00	60.00
REVELATION					
❏ REV-3 [S]	New Dance	1968	5.00	10.00	20.00
❏ REV-M3 [M]	New Dance	1968	10.00	20.00	40.00
VANTAGE					
❏ VLP-2 [10]	Anthony Ortega	1954	30.00	60.00	120.00

ORTEGA, FRANKIE
Pianist.

Number	Title	Yr	VG	VG+	NM
DOBRE					
❏ 1043	Smokin'	197?	3.00	6.00	12.00
IMPERIAL					
❏ LP-9025 [M]	Piano Stylings	1956	6.25	12.50	25.00
❏ LP-12011 [S]	Piano Stylings	1959	5.00	10.00	20.00
JUBILEE					
❏ JLP-1051 [M]	Twinkling Pinkies	1958	6.25	12.50	25.00
❏ JLP-1080 [M]	Swingin' Abroad	1958	5.00	10.00	20.00
❏ SDJLP-1080 [S]	Swingin' Abroad	1958	6.25	12.50	25.00
❏ JGS-1106 [S]	77 Sunset Strip	1959	10.00	20.00	40.00
❏ JLP-1106 [M]	77 Sunset Strip	1959	6.25	12.50	25.00
❏ JGM-1112 [M]	Frankie Ortega at the Embers	1960	5.00	10.00	20.00
❏ JGS-1112 [S]	Frankie Ortega at the Embers	1960	6.25	12.50	25.00

ORTEGA/DOMANICO/WEST/GOODWIN
ANTHONY ORTEGA; Chuck Domanico (bass); Bob West (bass); BILL GOODWIN.

Number	Title	Yr	VG	VG+	NM
REVELATION					
❏ REV-7 [S]	Permutations	1969	6.25	12.50	25.00

ORY, KID
Trombone player and bandleader. Under the name "Spike's Seven Pods of Pepper Orchestra," his group was the first black jazz band to make recordings.

Number	Title	Yr	VG	VG+	NM
COLUMBIA					
❏ CL 835 [M]	Kid Ory	1955	12.50	25.00	50.00
❏ CL 6145 [10]	Kid Ory & His Creole Dixieland	1950	25.00	50.00	100.00
DIXIELAND JUBILEE					
❏ DJ-519	Kid Ory at the Dixieland Jubilee	198?	2.50	5.00	10.00
FOLKLYRIC					
❏ 9008	Kid Ory's Creole Jazz Band	197?	2.50	5.00	10.00
GOOD TIME JAZZ					
❏ L-21 [10]	Kid Ory's Creole Jazz Band, 1953	1954	12.50	25.00	50.00
❏ S-10041/2 [(2) S]	Kid Ory's Favorites!	1961	15.00	30.00	60.00
❏ LTJ-12004 [M]	Kid Ory's Creole Jazz Band, 1954	1954	10.00	20.00	40.00
❏ L-12008 [M]	Kid Ory's Creole Jazz Band, 1955	1955	10.00	20.00	40.00
❏ L-12016 [M]	Kid Ory's Creole Jazz Band, 1956	1955	10.00	20.00	40.00
❏ L-12022 [M]	Kid Ory's Creole Jazz Band, 1944-45	1955	10.00	20.00	40.00
❏ L-12041/2 [(2) M]	Kid Ory's Favorites!	1961	12.50	25.00	50.00
❏ M-12045 [M]	This Kid's the Greatest!	1962	7.50	15.00	30.00
STORYVILLE					
❏ 4064	Kid Ory Plays the Blues	198?	2.50	5.00	10.00
VAULT					
❏ 9006	Kid Ory Live!	196?	3.75	7.50	15.00
VERVE					
❏ MGV-1014 [M]	Song of the Wanderer	1957	12.50	25.00	50.00
❏ V-1014 [M]	Song of the Wanderer	1961	5.00	10.00	20.00
❏ V6-1014 [S]	Song of the Wanderer	1961	3.75	7.50	15.00
❏ MGV-1016 [M]	The Kid from New Orleans	1957	12.50	25.00	50.00
❏ V-1016 [M]	The Kid from New Orleans	1961	5.00	10.00	20.00
❏ MGV-1017 [M]	Kid Ory Plays W.C. Handy	1957	12.50	25.00	50.00
❏ V-1017 [M]	Kid Ory Plays W.C. Handy	1961	5.00	10.00	20.00
❏ V6-1017 [S]	Kid Ory Plays W.C. Handy	1961	3.75	7.50	15.00
❏ MGV-1022 [M]	Dance with Kid Ory or Just Listen	1957	12.50	25.00	50.00
❏ V-1022 [M]	Dance with Kid Ory or Just Listen	1961	5.00	10.00	20.00
❏ V6-1022 [S]	Dance with Kid Ory or Just Listen	1961	3.75	7.50	15.00
❏ MGV-1023 [M]	The Original Jazz	1957	12.50	25.00	50.00
❏ V-1023 [M]	The Original Jazz	1961	5.00	10.00	20.00
❏ V6-1023 [S]	The Original Jazz	1961	3.75	7.50	15.00
❏ MGV-1026 [M]	Dixieland Marching Songs	1957	12.50	25.00	50.00
❏ V-1026 [M]	Dixieland Marching Songs	1961	5.00	10.00	20.00
❏ V6-1026 [S]	Dixieland Marching Songs	1961	3.75	7.50	15.00
❏ MGV-1030 [M]	Kid Ory Sings French Traditional Songs	1957	---	---	---

-- Canceled

Number	Title	Yr	VG	VG+	NM
❏ MGVS-6011 [S]	Song of the Wanderer	1960	10.00	20.00	40.00
❏ MGVS-6061 [S]	Kid Ory Plays W.C. Handy	1960	10.00	20.00	40.00
❏ MGVS-6125 [S]	Dance with Kid Ory or Just Listen	1960	10.00	20.00	40.00
❏ MGVS-6126 [S]	The Original Jazz	1960	---	---	---
-- Canceled					
❏ MGV-8254 [M]	Kid Ory In Europe	1958	12.50	25.00	50.00
❏ V-8254 [M]	Kid Ory In Europe	1961	5.00	10.00	20.00
❏ V-8456 [M]	Storyville Nights	1962	6.25	12.50	25.00
❏ V6-8456 [S]	Storyville Nights	1962	5.00	10.00	20.00

ORY, KID/JOHNNY WITTWER
Also see KID ORY.

Number	Title	Yr	VG	VG+	NM
JAZZ MAN					
❏ LP-2 [10]	Kid Ory's Creole Band/Johnny Wittwer Trio	1954	12.50	25.00	50.00

OSBORNE, MARY
Guitarist and female singer.

Number	Title	Yr	VG	VG+	NM
STASH					
❏ ST-215	Now and Then	198?	2.50	5.00	10.00
WARWICK					
❏ W-2004 [M]	A Girl and Her Guitar	1960	25.00	50.00	100.00
❏ W-2004ST [S]	A Girl and Her Guitar	1960	30.00	60.00	120.00

OSBORNE, WILL
Drummer, male singer and bandleader. He was one of the pioneers of the singing style known as "crooning."

Number	Title	Yr	VG	VG+	NM
AIRCHECK					
❏ 37	Will Osborne and His Orchestra On the Air	198?	2.50	5.00	10.00
HINDSIGHT					
❏ HSR-197	Will Osborne and His Orchestra 1936	198?	2.50	5.00	10.00

OSTERWALD, HAZY
Vibraphone player and trumpeter.

Number	Title	Yr	VG	VG+	NM
BALLY					
❏ BAL-12004 [M]	Swiss Jazz	1956	10.00	20.00	40.00

OTB
Also known as "Out of the Blue." Original members: Ralph Bowen (tenor sax); KENNY GARRETT (alto sax); Robert Hurst (bass); Michael Philip Mossman (trumpet); Ralph Peterson (drums); Harry Pickens (piano). Personnel changes: Kenny Davis (bass) for Hurst; Billy Drummond (drums) for Peterson; Renee Rosnes (piano) for Pickens; Steve Wilson (alto sax) for Garrett.

Number	Title	Yr	VG	VG+	NM
BLUE NOTE					
❏ BT-85118	Out of the Blue	1985	3.00	6.00	12.00
❏ BT-85128	Inside Track	1986	3.00	6.00	12.00
❏ B1-85141	Live at Mt. Fuji	1987	3.00	6.00	12.00
❏ B1-93006	Spiral Staircase	1989	3.75	7.50	15.00

OTTE, HANS
Pianist and composer.

Number	Title	Yr	VG	VG+	NM
KUCKUCK					
❏ KU-069/70 [(2)]	Das Buch der Klange	1984	3.75	7.50	15.00

OUSLEY, HAROLD
Tenor saxophone player.

Number	Title	Yr	VG	VG+	NM
BETHLEHEM					
❏ BCP-6059 [M]	Tenor Sax	1961	7.50	15.00	30.00
❏ SBCP-6059 [S]	Tenor Sax	1961	10.00	20.00	40.00
COBBLESTONE					
❏ 9017	The Kid!	1971	6.25	12.50	25.00
MUSE					
❏ MR-5107	The People's Groove	197?	3.75	7.50	15.00
❏ MR-5141	Sweet Double Hipness	1979	3.00	6.00	12.00

OVERTON, HALL
See DUKE JORDAN; DAVE McKENNA.

OWENS, CHARLES
Tenor saxophone player.

Number	Title	Yr	VG	VG+	NM
DISCOVERY					
❏ 787	Two Quartets	1978	3.00	6.00	12.00
❏ 811	Music of Harry Warren, Volume 1	1980	3.00	6.00	12.00
VAULT					
❏ LP-90??	I Stand Alone	196?	12.50	25.00	50.00

Number	Title	Yr	VG	VG+	NM	Number	Title	Yr	VG	VG+	NM

OWENS, JIMMY
Trumpeter and fluegel horn player.
ATLANTIC

❏ SD 1491	Jimmy Owens-Kenny Barron Quintet	1968	5.00	10.00	20.00

-- Multicolor label, black "fan" logo at right

❏ SD 1491	Jimmy Owens-Kenny Barron Quintet	1969	3.75	7.50	15.00

-- Red and green label
HORIZON

❏ SP-712	Jimmy Owens	197?	3.00	6.00	12.00
❏ SP-729	Headin' Home	1978	3.00	6.00	12.00

OZONE, MAKOTO
Pianist.
COLUMBIA

❏ BFC 39624	Makoto Ozone	1985	2.50	5.00	10.00
❏ FC 40240	After	1986	2.50	5.00	10.00

Number	Title	Yr	VG	VG+	NM

P

PACE, JOHNNY
Male singer.
RIVERSIDE

Number	Title	Yr	VG	VG+	NM
❑ RLP 12-292 [M]	Chet Baker Introduces Johnny Pace	1958	12.50	25.00	50.00
❑ RLP-1130 [S]	Chet Baker Introduces Johnny Pace	1959	12.50	25.00	50.00

PACHECO, MIKE
Bongo drummer.
INTERLUDE

Number	Title	Yr	VG	VG+	NM
❑ MO-513 [M]	Hot Skins	1959	10.00	20.00	40.00
❑ ST-1013 [S]	Hot Skins	1959	7.50	15.00	30.00

TAMPA

Number	Title	Yr	VG	VG+	NM
❑ TP-10 [M]	Bongo Skins	1957	25.00	50.00	100.00
-- Colored vinyl					
❑ TP-10 [M]	Bongo Skins	1958	12.50	25.00	50.00
-- Black vinyl					
❑ TP-21 [M]	Bongo Session	1957	25.00	50.00	100.00
-- Colored vinyl					
❑ TP-21 [M]	Bongo Session	1958	12.50	25.00	50.00
-- Black vinyl					
❑ TP-30 [M]	Bongo Date	1957	25.00	50.00	100.00
-- Colored vinyl					
❑ TP-30 [M]	Bongo Date	1958	12.50	25.00	50.00
-- Black vinyl					

PACIFIC COAST RAGTIMERS, THE
CIRCLE

Number	Title	Yr	VG	VG+	NM
❑ CLP-1376	The Pacific Coast Ragtimers	199?	3.00	6.00	12.00

PACKHAM, GREG
Guitarist.
STASH

Number	Title	Yr	VG	VG+	NM
❑ ST-242	Action Reaction	198?	2.50	5.00	10.00

PADDOCK JAZZ BAND
Members: James Davis (trumpet, trombone); Bill Kelsey (clarinet, saxophones); Art Langston (bass); Walter Lewis (piano); Stan Williams (drums).
BIOGRAPH

Number	Title	Yr	VG	VG+	NM
❑ CEN-10	Paddock Jazz Band	197?	2.50	5.00	10.00

PAGE, HOT LIPS
Trumpeter, occasional mellophone player and male singer.
CONTINENTAL

Number	Title	Yr	VG	VG+	NM
❑ 16007 [M]	Hot and Cozy	1962	7.50	15.00	30.00

ONYX

Number	Title	Yr	VG	VG+	NM
❑ 207	After Hours	197?	3.00	6.00	12.00

XANADU

Number	Title	Yr	VG	VG+	NM
❑ 107	Trumpet at Minton's	197?	3.00	6.00	12.00

PAGE, PATTI
Female singer. Most of her material was in the pop or country-western field, but the following were released on Mercury's jazz label. For a more complete listing of her releases, see the Standard Catalog of American Records 1950-1975.
EMARCY

Number	Title	Yr	VG	VG+	NM
❑ MG-36074 [M]	In the Land of Hi-Fi	1956	12.50	25.00	50.00
❑ MG-36116 [M]	The East Side	1957	12.50	25.00	50.00
❑ MG-36136 [M]	The West Side	1957	12.50	25.00	50.00
❑ SR-60013 [S]	The West Side	1959	12.50	25.00	50.00
❑ SR-60014 [S]	The East Side	1959	12.50	25.00	50.00
❑ SR-80000 [S]	In the Land of Hi-Fi	1959	12.50	25.00	50.00

PAGE, SID, AND DAVID SHELANDER
Page is a violinist; Shelander is a pianist.
BAINBRIDGE

Number	Title	Yr	VG	VG+	NM
❑ 6257	Odyssey	198?	2.50	5.00	10.00

PAICH, MARTY
Pianist, arranger and bandleader. Also see RUSS GARCIA.
BETHLEHEM

Number	Title	Yr	VG	VG+	NM
❑ BCP-44 [M]	Jazz City Workshop	1956	20.00	40.00	80.00

CADENCE

Number	Title	Yr	VG	VG+	NM
❑ CLP-3010 [M]	Marty Paich Big Band	1958	12.50	25.00	50.00

DISCOVERY

Number	Title	Yr	VG	VG+	NM
❑ 829	I Get a Boot Out of You	198?	2.50	5.00	10.00
❑ 844	New York Scene	198?	2.50	5.00	10.00
❑ 857	What's New	198?	2.50	5.00	10.00

GENE NORMAN

Number	Title	Yr	VG	VG+	NM
❑ GNP-10 [10]	Marty Paich Octet	1955	30.00	60.00	120.00
-- Red vinyl					
❑ GNP-21 [M]	Marty Paich Octet	1956	20.00	40.00	80.00

INTERLUDE

Number	Title	Yr	VG	VG+	NM
❑ MO-509 [M]	Revel Without Pause	1959	7.50	15.00	30.00
❑ MO-514 [M]	Like Wow -- Jazz 1960	1960	7.50	15.00	30.00
❑ ST-1009 [S]	Revel Without Pause	1959	6.25	12.50	25.00
❑ ST-1014 [S]	Like Wow -- Jazz 1960	1960	6.25	12.50	25.00

MODE

Number	Title	Yr	VG	VG+	NM
❑ LP-105 [M]	Marty Paich Trio	1957	20.00	40.00	80.00
❑ LP-110 [M]	Jazz Band Ball	1957	20.00	40.00	80.00

RCA VICTOR

Number	Title	Yr	VG	VG+	NM
❑ LPM-2164 [M]	Piano Quartet	1960	5.00	10.00	20.00
❑ LSP-2164 [S]	Piano Quartet	1960	6.25	12.50	25.00
❑ LPM-2259 [M]	Piano Quartet	1960	5.00	10.00	20.00
❑ LSP-2259 [S]	Piano Quartet	1960	6.25	12.50	25.00

REPRISE

Number	Title	Yr	VG	VG+	NM
❑ R-6206 [M]	The Rock-Jazz Incident	1966	3.00	6.00	12.00
❑ RS-6206 [S]	The Rock-Jazz Incident	1966	3.75	7.50	15.00

TAMPA

Number	Title	Yr	VG	VG+	NM
❑ TP-23 [M]	Jazz for Relaxation	1957	50.00	100.00	200.00
-- Colored vinyl					
❑ TP-23 [M]	Jazz for Relaxation	1958	25.00	50.00	100.00
❑ TP-28 [M]	Marty Paich Quintet Featuring Art Pepper	1957	150.00	300.00	600.00
-- Colored vinyl					
❑ TP-28 [M]	Marty Paich Quintet Featuring Art Pepper	1958	75.00	150.00	300.00

WARNER BROS.

Number	Title	Yr	VG	VG+	NM
❑ W 1296 [M]	The Broadway Bit	1959	6.25	12.50	25.00
❑ WS 1296 [S]	The Broadway Bit	1959	7.50	15.00	30.00
❑ W 1349 [M]	I Get A Boot Out of You	1959	6.25	12.50	25.00
❑ WS 1349 [S]	I Get A Boot Out of You	1959	7.50	15.00	30.00

PALMER, JEFF
Organist.
AUDIOQUEST

Number	Title	Yr	VG	VG+	NM
❑ AQ-LP-1014	Ease On	1993	3.75	7.50	15.00

STATIRAS

Number	Title	Yr	VG	VG+	NM
❑ SLP-8081	Laser Wizzard	1987	3.00	6.00	12.00

PALMER, ROY
Trombonist.
RIVERSIDE

Number	Title	Yr	VG	VG+	NM
❑ RLP-1020 [10]	Roy Palmer's State Street Ramblers	1953	20.00	40.00	80.00

PALMER, SINGLETON
Bass and tuba player.
DIXIELAND JUBILEE

Number	Title	Yr	VG	VG+	NM
❑ DJ-511	Dixie by Gaslight	197?	2.50	5.00	10.00
❑ DJ-513	At the Opera House	197?	2.50	5.00	10.00

NORMAN

Number	Title	Yr	VG	VG+	NM
❑ NL-101 [M]	Dixie by Gaslight	1962	3.00	6.00	12.00
❑ NL-106 [M]	At the Opera House	1963	3.00	6.00	12.00
❑ NL-110 [M]	The Best Dixieland Band	1965	3.00	6.00	12.00
❑ NS-201 [S]	Dixie by Gaslight	1962	3.75	7.50	15.00
❑ NS-206 [S]	At the Opera House	1963	3.75	7.50	15.00
❑ NS-210 [S]	The Best Dixieland Band	1965	3.75	7.50	15.00

PALMIER, REMO
Guitarist.
CONCORD JAZZ

Number	Title	Yr	VG	VG+	NM
❑ CJ-76	Remo Palmier	1979	2.50	5.00	10.00

PALMIERI, EDDIE
Pianist.
EPIC

Number	Title	Yr	VG	VG+	NM
❑ JE 35523	Lucumi Macumba Voodoo	1978	2.50	5.00	10.00

INTUITION

Number	Title	Yr	VG	VG+	NM
❑ C1-91353	Sueno	1989	3.00	6.00	12.00

PAMEIJER, PAM
Drummer and percussionist.
STOMP OFF

Number	Title	Yr	VG	VG+	NM
❑ SOS-1134	Jelly Roll Morton: 100 Years	1987	2.50	5.00	10.00
❑ SOS-1172	London Blues	1988	2.50	5.00	10.00
❑ SOS-1194	Little Bits	1989	2.50	5.00	10.00

Number	Title	Yr	VG	VG+	NM

PARAMOUNT JAZZ BAND OF BOSTON
Members: Jeff Hughes (cornet, trumpet, fluegel horn); Gary Rodberg (clarinet, soprano and alto sax); Jim Mazzy (banjo, vocals); Ray Smith (drums, leader); Robin Verdier (piano); Steve Wright (saxes, clarinets, cornet).
STOMP OFF

Number	Title	Yr	VG	VG+	NM
❑ SOS-1205	Ain't Cha Glad	1991	2.50	5.00	10.00

PARAMOUNT THEATRE ORCHESTRA, THE
STOMP OFF
| ❑ SOS-1089 | Lolly Pops | 1985 | 2.50 | 5.00 | 10.00 |

PARANOISE
Members: Lloyd Fonoroff (drums); Jim Matus (guitar); Miguel Ortiz (bass). Many jazz musicians were guests on the below LP.
ANTILLES
| ❑ 90986 | Constant Fear | 1988 | 3.75 | 7.50 | 15.00 |

PARENTI, TONY
Clarinetist and baritone and alto saxophone player.
JAZZOLOGY
❑ JCE-1 [10]	Tony Parenti and His New Orleanians	1962	5.00	10.00	20.00
❑ J-1 [M]	Tony Parenti	1962	3.75	7.50	15.00
❑ J-11 [M]	Downtown Boys	1965	3.75	7.50	15.00
❑ J-15	Ragtime	196?	3.75	7.50	15.00
❑ J-21 [M]	Ragtime Jubilee	1967	3.75	7.50	15.00
❑ J-26	Jean Kittrell with Tony Parenti and His Blues Blowers	196?	3.75	7.50	15.00
❑ J-31 [M]	Night at Jimmy Ryan's	196?	3.75	7.50	15.00
❑ J-41	Jazz Goes Underground	197?	2.50	5.00	10.00
❑ J-71	The Final Bar	197?	2.50	5.00	10.00
RIVERSIDE
❑ RLP 12-205 [M]	Ragtime	195?	7.50	15.00	30.00
-- Blue label, microphone logo at top					
❑ RLP 12-205 [M]	Ragtime	1956	15.00	30.00	60.00
-- White label, blue print					

PARENTI, TONY/THE DIXIELAND RHYTHM KINGS
Also see each artist's individual listings.
JAZZTONE
| ❑ J-1273 [M] | Two Beat Bash | 195? | 10.00 | 20.00 | 40.00 |

PARHAM, TINY
Pianist, organist, celeste player, bandleader, arranger and composer.
FOLKLYRIC
| ❑ 9028 | Hot Chicago Jazz | 198? | 2.50 | 5.00 | 10.00 |
"X"
| ❑ LVA-3039 [10] | Tiny Parham's South Side Jazz | 1955 | 15.00 | 30.00 | 60.00 |

PARIS WASHBOARD
Four-piece band from France.
STOMP OFF
| ❑ SOS-1182 | When We're Smiling | 1988 | 2.50 | 5.00 | 10.00 |

PARIS, JACKIE
Male singer.
ABC IMPULSE!
| ❑ AS-17 [S] | The Song Is Paris | 1968 | 5.00 | 10.00 | 20.00 |
AUDIOPHILE
| ❑ 158 | Jackie Paris | 198? | 2.50 | 5.00 | 10.00 |
BRUNSWICK
| ❑ BL-54019 [M] | Skylark | 1957 | 25.00 | 50.00 | 100.00 |
CORAL
| ❑ CRL-56118 [10] | That Paris Mood | 195? | 20.00 | 40.00 | 80.00 |
EASTWEST
| ❑ 4002 [M] | The Jackie Paris Sound | 1958 | 20.00 | 40.00 | 80.00 |
EMARCY
| ❑ MG-36095 [M] | Songs by Jackie Paris | 1956 | 25.00 | 50.00 | 100.00 |
IMPULSE!
| ❑ A-17 [M] | The Song Is Paris | 1962 | 7.50 | 15.00 | 30.00 |
| ❑ AS-17 [S] | The Song Is Paris | 1962 | 10.00 | 20.00 | 40.00 |
TIME
| ❑ ST-70009 [S] | Jackie Paris Sings the Lyrics of Ira Gershwin | 1959 | 12.50 | 25.00 | 50.00 |
| ❑ T-70009 [M] | Jackie Paris Sings the Lyrics of Ira Gershwin | 1959 | 10.00 | 20.00 | 40.00 |
WING
| ❑ MGW-60004 [M] | Songs by Jackie Paris | 1956 | 20.00 | 40.00 | 80.00 |

PARIS, JACKIE, AND ANNE MARIE MOSS
Also see each artist's individual listings.
DIFFERENT DRUMMER
Number	Title	Yr	VG	VG+	NM
❑ 1004	Maisonette	197?	3.75	7.50	15.00

PARKER, BILLY
Percussionist.
STRATA-EAST
| ❑ SES-19754 | Freedom of Speech | 1975 | 6.25 | 12.50 | 25.00 |

PARKER, CHARLIE
Alto saxophone player and composer. He was every bit as important to jazz in the second half of the 20th century as LOUIS ARMSTRONG was in the first half. Also see DIZZY GILLESPIE; THE QUINTET.
AMERICAN RECORDING SOCIETY
| ❑ G-441 [M] | Now's the Time | 1957 | 12.50 | 25.00 | 50.00 |
ARCHIVE OF FOLK AND JAZZ
❑ 214	Charlie Parker	1969	3.00	6.00	12.00
❑ 232	Charlie Parker, Volume 2	1970	2.50	5.00	10.00
❑ 254	Charlie Parker, Vol. 3	197?	2.50	5.00	10.00
❑ 295	Charlie Parker, Vol. 4	197?	2.50	5.00	10.00
❑ 315	Charlie Parker, Vol. 5	197?	2.50	5.00	10.00
BARONET
❑ B-105 [M]	A Handful of Modern Jazz	1962	5.00	10.00	20.00
❑ BS-105 [R]	A Handful of Modern Jazz	1962	3.00	6.00	12.00
❑ B-107 [M]	The Early Bird	1962	5.00	10.00	20.00
❑ BS-107 [R]	The Early Bird	1962	3.00	6.00	12.00
BIRDLAND
| ❑ 425 [M] | A Night at Carnegie Hall | 1956 | 75.00 | 150.00 | 300.00 |
BLUE NOTE
| ❑ BT-85108 | Charlie Parker at Storyville | 198? | 3.00 | 6.00 | 12.00 |
BLUE RIBBON
| ❑ 8011 [M] | The Early Bird | 1962 | 5.00 | 10.00 | 20.00 |
| ❑ S-8011 [R] | The Early Bird | 1962 | 3.00 | 6.00 | 12.00 |
CHARLIE PARKER
❑ PLP-401 [M]	Bird Is Free	1961	10.00	20.00	40.00
❑ PLP-404 [M]	The Happy Bird	1961	10.00	20.00	40.00
❑ PLP-406 [M]	Charlie Parker	1961	10.00	20.00	40.00
❑ PLP-407 [M]	Bird Symbols	1961	10.00	20.00	40.00
❑ PLP-408 [M]	Once There Was Bird	1961	10.00	20.00	40.00
❑ CP-2-502 [(2) M]	Live at Rockland Palace, September 26, 1952	1961	12.50	25.00	50.00
❑ CP-513 [M]	Charlie Parker Plus Strings	196?	10.00	20.00	40.00
❑ PLP-701 [(3)]	Historical Masterpieces	196?	15.00	30.00	60.00
CLEF
❑ MGC-101 [10]	Charlie Parker with Strings	1958	---	---	---
-- Canceled					
❑ MGC-157 [10]	Charlie Parker	1954	100.00	200.00	400.00
❑ MGC-501 [10]	Charlie Parker with Strings	1954	100.00	200.00	400.00
-- Reissue of Mercury 501					
❑ MGC-509 [10]	Charlie Parker with Strings, No. 2	1954	100.00	200.00	400.00
-- Reissue of Mercury 509					
❑ MGC-512 [10]	Bird and Diz	1954	100.00	200.00	400.00
-- Reissue of Mercury 512					
❑ MGC-513 [10]	South of the Border	1954	100.00	200.00	400.00
-- Reissue of Mercury 513					
❑ MGC-609 [M]	Charlie Parker Big Band	1954	100.00	200.00	400.00
❑ MGC-646 [M]	The Magnificent Charlie Parker	1955	100.00	200.00	400.00
❑ MGC-675 [M]	Charlie Parker with Strings	1955	100.00	200.00	400.00
❑ MGC-725 [M]	Night and Day	1956	30.00	60.00	120.00
COLUMBIA
❑ C2 34808 [(2)]	One Night in Birdland	198?	3.00	6.00	12.00
-- Reissue with new prefix					
❑ JG 34808 [(2)]	One Night in Birdland	1977	3.75	7.50	15.00
❑ JC 34831	Summit Meeting	1977	3.00	6.00	12.00
❑ JC 34832	Bird with Strings Live	1977	3.00	6.00	12.00
CONCERT HALL JAZZ
| ❑ 1004 [10] | The Fabulous Bird | 1955 | 15.00 | 30.00 | 60.00 |
| ❑ 1017 [10] | The Art of Charlie Parker, Vol. 2 | 1955 | 15.00 | 30.00 | 60.00 |
CONTINENTAL
| ❑ 16004 [M] | Bird Lives | 1962 | 10.00 | 20.00 | 40.00 |
DEBUT
| ❑ DEB-611 [M] | Bird on 52nd Street | 196? | 12.50 | 25.00 | 50.00 |
DIAL
❑ LP-1 [M]	The Bird Blows the Blues	1949	1,000.	2,000.	4,000.
-- Mail-order offer					
❑ LP-201 [10]	Charlie Parker Quintet	1949	200.00	400.00	800.00
❑ LP-202 [10]	Charlie Parker Quintet	1949	200.00	400.00	800.00
❑ LP-203 [10]	Charlie Parker	1949	200.00	400.00	800.00
❑ LP-207 [10]	Charlie Parker Sextet	1949	200.00	400.00	800.00
❑ LP-901 [M]	The Bird Blows the Blues	1950	150.00	300.00	600.00

Number	Title	Yr	VG	VG+	NM
❏ LP-904 [M]	Alternate Masters	1951	150.00	300.00	600.00
❏ LP-905 [M]	Alternate Masters	1951	150.00	300.00	600.00
ELEKTRA/MUSICIAN					
❏ 60019	One Night in Washington	1982	2.50	5.00	10.00
FANTASY					
❏ OJC-041	Bird at St. Nick's	198?	2.50	5.00	10.00
❏ OJC-044	Jazz at Massey Hall	198?	2.50	5.00	10.00
❏ OJC-114	Bird on 52nd St.	198?	2.50	5.00	10.00
❏ 6011 [M]	Bird on 52nd St.	1964	7.50	15.00	30.00
❏ 6012 [M]	Bird at St. Nick's	1964	7.50	15.00	30.00
❏ 86011 [R]	Bird on 52nd St.	1964	3.75	7.50	15.00
❏ 86012 [R]	Bird at St. Nick's	1964	3.75	7.50	15.00
HALL OF FAME					
❏ 617	Giants of Jazz	197?	2.50	5.00	10.00
❏ 620	Takin' Off	197?	2.50	5.00	10.00
JAZZ WORKSHOP					
❏ JWS-500 [M]	Bird at St. Nick's	1958	30.00	60.00	120.00
❏ JWS-501 [M]	Bird on 52nd Street	1958	30.00	60.00	120.00
JAZZTONE					
❏ J-12?? [M]	The Art of Charlie Parker, Vol. 2	1955	12.50	25.00	50.00
❏ J-1204 [M]	Giants of Modern Jazz	1955	12.50	25.00	50.00
❏ J-1214 [M]	The Fabulous Bird	1955	12.50	25.00	50.00
❏ J-1240 [M]	The Saxes of Stan Getz and Charlie Parker	1957	12.50	25.00	50.00
LES JAZZ COOL					
❏ 101 [M]	Les Jazz Cool, Volume 1	1960	12.50	25.00	50.00
❏ 102 [M]	Les Jazz Cool, Volume 2	1960	12.50	25.00	50.00
❏ 103 [M]	Les Jazz Cool, Volume 3	1960	12.50	25.00	50.00
MERCURY					
❏ MGC-101 [10]	Charlie Parker with Strings	1950	125.00	250.00	500.00
-- Reissue of 35010					
❏ MGC-109 [10]	Charlie Parker with Strings, Volume 2	1950	125.00	250.00	500.00
❏ MGC-501 [10]	Charlie Parker with Strings	1951	125.00	250.00	500.00
-- Reissue of 101 with new number					
❏ MGC-509 [10]	Charlie Parker with Strings, Volume 2	1952	125.00	250.00	500.00
-- Reissue of 109 with new number					
❏ MGC-512 [10]	Bird and Diz	1952	125.00	250.00	500.00
❏ MGC-513 [10]	South of the Border	1952	125.00	250.00	500.00
❏ MG-35010 [10]	Charlie Parker with Strings	1950	150.00	300.00	600.00
MGM					
❏ M3G-4949	Archetypes	1974	3.00	6.00	12.00
MOSAIC					
❏ 129 [(10)]	The Complete Dean Benedetti Recordings of Charlie Parker	199?	25.00	50.00	100.00
ONYX					
❏ 221	First Recordings with Jay McShann	197?	3.00	6.00	12.00
PHOENIX					
❏ 10	New Bird	197?	2.50	5.00	10.00
❏ 12	New Bird, Vol. 2	197?	2.50	5.00	10.00
❏ 17	Yardbird in Lotusland	197?	2.50	5.00	10.00
PICKWICK					
❏ PC-3054 [M]	Yardbird	196?	3.00	6.00	12.00
❏ SPC-3054 [R]	Yardbird	196?	2.50	5.00	10.00
PRESTIGE					
❏ 24009 [(2)]	Charlie Parker	197?	3.75	7.50	15.00
❏ 24024 [(2)]	Parker/Powell/Mingus/Roach	197?	3.75	7.50	15.00
ROOST					
❏ LP-2210 [M]	All Star Sextet	1958	30.00	60.00	120.00
❏ LP-2257 [M]	The World of Charlie Parker	1963	10.00	20.00	40.00
SAVOY					
❏ MG-9000 [10]	Charlie Parker	1950	125.00	250.00	500.00
❏ MG-9001 [10]	Charlie Parker, Volume 2	1951	125.00	250.00	500.00
❏ MG-9010 [10]	Charlie Parker, Volume 3	1952	125.00	250.00	500.00
❏ MG-9011 [10]	Charlie Parker, Volume 4	1952	125.00	250.00	500.00
❏ MG-12000 [M]	Charlie Parker Memorial	1955	25.00	50.00	100.00
❏ MG-12001 [M]	The Immortal Charlie Parker	1955	25.00	50.00	100.00
❏ MG-12009 [M]	Charlie Parker Memorial, Volume 2	1955	25.00	50.00	100.00
❏ MG-12014 [M]	The Genius of Charlie Parker	1955	25.00	50.00	100.00
❏ MG-12079 [M]	The Charlie Parker Story	1956	25.00	50.00	100.00
❏ MG-12138 [M]	Bird's Night	1960	10.00	20.00	40.00
❏ MG-12152 [M]	An Evening at Home with the Bird	196?	10.00	20.00	40.00
❏ MG-12179 [M]	The "Bird" Returns	196?	7.50	15.00	30.00
❏ MG-12186 [M]	Newly Discovered Sides by the Immortal Charlie Parker	1966	7.50	15.00	30.00
SAVOY JAZZ					
❏ SJL-1107	Encores	197?	3.00	6.00	12.00
❏ SJL-1108	Bird at the Roost	197?	3.00	6.00	12.00
❏ SJL-1129	Encores, Vol. 2	198?	2.50	5.00	10.00

Number	Title	Yr	VG	VG+	NM
❏ SJL-1132	One Night in Chicago	198?	2.50	5.00	10.00
❏ SJL-1173	Bird at the Roost, Vol. 3	1987	2.50	5.00	10.00
❏ SJL-1208	Original Bird: The Beston Savoy	198?	2.50	5.00	10.00
❏ SJL-2201 [(2)]	Bird: The Savoy Recordings	197?	3.75	7.50	15.00
❏ SJL-2259 [(2)]	Bird at the Roost: The Complete Royal Roost Performances, Vol. 1	198?	3.75	7.50	15.00
❏ SJL-2260 [(2)]	Bird at the Roost: The Complete Royal Roost Performances, Vol. 2	1986	3.75	7.50	15.00
❏ SJL-5500 [(5)]	The Complete Savoy Studio Sessions	197?	7.50	15.00	30.00
SPOTLITE					
❏ 101	Charlie Parker on Dial, Vol. 1	197?	2.50	5.00	10.00
❏ 102	Charlie Parker on Dial, Vol. 2	197?	2.50	5.00	10.00
❏ 103	Charlie Parker on Dial, Vol. 3	197?	2.50	5.00	10.00
❏ 104	Charlie Parker on Dial, Vol. 4	197?	2.50	5.00	10.00
❏ 105	Charlie Parker on Dial, Vol. 5	197?	2.50	5.00	10.00
❏ 106	Charlie Parker on Dial, Vol. 6	197?	2.50	5.00	10.00
STASH					
❏ ST-260	Birth of the Bebop	1986	2.50	5.00	10.00
❏ ST-280	The Bird You Never Heard	1988	2.50	5.00	10.00
TRIP					
❏ 5035 [(2)]	The Master	197?	3.00	6.00	12.00
❏ 5039 [(2)]	Birdology	197?	3.75	7.50	15.00
VERVE					
❏ VSP-23 [M]	Bird Wings	1966	5.00	10.00	20.00
❏ VSPS-23 [R]	Bird Wings	1966	3.00	6.00	12.00
❏ UMV-2029	Now's the Time	198?	2.50	5.00	10.00
❏ UMV-2030	Swedish Schnapps	198?	2.50	5.00	10.00
❏ VE-2-2501 [(2)]	The Verve Years 1948-50	197?	3.75	7.50	15.00
❏ VE-2-2508 [(2)]	Charlie Parker Sides	197?	3.75	7.50	15.00
❏ VE-2-2512 [(2)]	The Verve Years 1950-51	197?	3.75	7.50	15.00
❏ VE-2-2523 [(2)]	The Verve Years 1952-54	197?	3.75	7.50	15.00
❏ UMV-2562	Charlie Parker with Strings	198?	2.50	5.00	10.00
❏ UMV-2617	Jazz Perennial	198?	2.50	5.00	10.00
❏ MGV-8000 [M]	The Charlie Parker Story, Volume 1	1957	20.00	40.00	80.00
❏ V-8000 [M]	The Charlie Parker Story, Volume 1	1961	6.25	12.50	25.00
❏ V6-8000 [R]	The Charlie Parker Story, Volume 1	196?	3.00	6.00	12.00
❏ MGV-8001 [M]	The Charlie Parker Story, Volume 2	1957	20.00	40.00	80.00
❏ V-8001 [M]	The Charlie Parker Story, Volume 2	1961	6.25	12.50	25.00
❏ V6-8001 [R]	The Charlie Parker Story, Volume 2	196?	3.00	6.00	12.00
❏ MGV-8002 [M]	The Charlie Parker Story, Volume 3	1957	20.00	40.00	80.00
❏ V-8002 [M]	The Charlie Parker Story, Volume 3	1961	6.25	12.50	25.00
❏ V6-8002 [R]	The Charlie Parker Story, Volume 3	196?	3.00	6.00	12.00
❏ MGV-8003 [M]	Night and Day (The Genius of Charlie Parker #1)	1957	20.00	40.00	80.00
❏ V-8003 [M]	Night and Day (The Genius of Charlie Parker #1)	1961	6.25	12.50	25.00
❏ V6-8003 [R]	Night and Day (The Genius of Charlie Parker #1)	196?	3.00	6.00	12.00
❏ MGV-8004 [M]	April in Paris (The Genius of Charlie Parker #2)	1957	20.00	40.00	80.00
❏ V-8004 [M]	April in Paris (The Genius of Charlie Parker #2)	1961	6.25	12.50	25.00
❏ V6-8004 [R]	April in Paris (The Genius of Charlie Parker #2)	196?	3.00	6.00	12.00
❏ MGV-8005 [M]	Now's the Time (The Genius of Charlie Parker #3)	1957	20.00	40.00	80.00
❏ V-8005 [M]	Now's the Time (The Genius of Charlie Parker #3)	1961	6.25	12.50	25.00
❏ V6-8005 [R]	Now's the Time (The Genius of Charlie Parker #3)	196?	3.00	6.00	12.00
❏ MGV-8006 [M]	Bird and Diz (The Genius of Charlie Parker #4)	1957	20.00	40.00	80.00
❏ V-8006 [M]	Bird and Diz (The Genius of Charlie Parker #4)	1961	6.25	12.50	25.00
❏ V6-8006 [R]	Bird and Diz (The Genius of Charlie Parker #4)	196?	3.00	6.00	12.00
❏ MGV-8007 [M]	Charlie Parker Plays Cole Porter (The Genius of Charlie Parker #5)	1957	20.00	40.00	80.00
❏ V-8007 [M]	Charlie Parker Plays Cole Porter (The Genius of Charlie Parker #5)	1961	6.25	12.50	25.00
❏ V6-8007 [R]	Charlie Parker Plays Cole Porter (The Genius of Charlie Parker #5)	196?	3.00	6.00	12.00
❏ MGV-8008 [M]	Fiesta (The Genius of Charlie Parker #6)	1957	20.00	40.00	80.00
❏ V-8008 [M]	Fiesta (The Genius of Charlie Parker #6)	1961	6.25	12.50	25.00
❏ V6-8008 [R]	Fiesta (The Genius of Charlie Parker #6)	196?	3.00	6.00	12.00

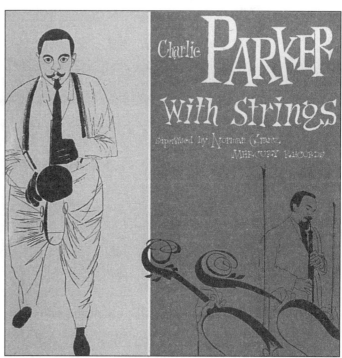

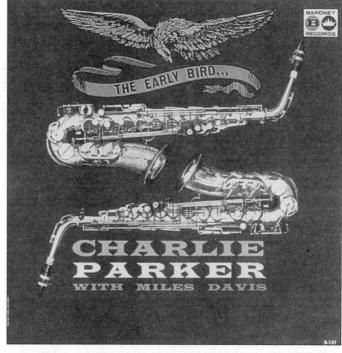

Charlie Parker is the Elvis of jazz collecting: His records, especially the originals, are more collectible and more sought-after than those of any other jazz artist, and all of the original editions of LPs issued while he was alive bring hundreds of dollars in top-notch condition. (Top left) Parker recorded for the small Los Angeles label Dial – not to be confused with the 1960s label of the same name that was home for Joe Tex – in 1946 and 1947. The original 78s are difficult to find, but even tougher are the compiled 10-inch LPs that were released by Dial during the dawn of the LP age. *Charlie Parker* is one of these. (Top right) Bird began recording for Norman Granz in the late 1940s. In fact, the first 11 albums issued on the Verve label, which united all of Granz' labels under one name, were reissues of Parker material. One of the most justifiably acclaimed of the original Granz sessions is *Charlie Parker with Strings*, here illustrated by a 10-inch cover on Mercury from the early 1950s. (Bottom left) After Parker's death in 1955, "new" albums began to hit the market with alarming speed. One of these was the live gig documented on this album on the Jazz Workshop label in 1958. This has since been reissued on Fantasy. (Bottom right) The budget labels got into the act, too. This early 1960s collection of 1940s recordings came out on the Baronet label.

Number	Title	Yr	VG	VG+	NM
❑ MGV-8009 [M]	Jazz Perennial (The Genius of Charlie Parker #7)	1957	20.00	40.00	80.00
❑ V-8009 [M]	Jazz Perennial (The Genius of Charlie Parker #7)	1961	6.25	12.50	25.00
❑ V6-8009 [R]	Jazz Perennial (The Genius of Charlie Parker #7)	196?	3.00	6.00	12.00
❑ MGV-8010 [M]	Swedish Schnapps (The Genius of Charlie Parker #8)	1957	20.00	40.00	80.00
❑ V-8010 [M]	Swedish Schnapps (The Genius of Charlie Parker #8)	1961	6.25	12.50	25.00
❑ V6-8010 [R]	Swedish Schnapps (The Genius of Charlie Parker #8)	196?	3.00	6.00	12.00
❑ MGV-8100-3 [(3) M]	The Charlie Parker Story	1957	37.50	75.00	150.00
-- Combines 8000, 8001 and 8002 in a box set					
❑ V-8100-3 [(3) M]	The Charlie Parker Story	1961	15.00	30.00	60.00
-- Combines 8000, 8001 and 8002 in a box set					
❑ V-8409 [M]	The Essential Charlie Parker	1961	6.25	12.50	25.00
❑ V6-8409 [R]	The Essential Charlie Parker	196?	3.00	6.00	12.00
❑ V6-8787 [R]	Bird Set	1969	3.75	7.50	15.00
❑ V3HB-8840 [(2)]	Return Engagement	197?	3.75	7.50	15.00
❑ 817 442-1	Bird on Verve, Vol. 1: Charlie Parker with Strings	1985	2.50	5.00	10.00
❑ 817 443-1	Bird on Verve, Vol. 2: Bird and Diz	1985	2.50	5.00	10.00
❑ 817 444-1	Bird on Verve, Vol. 3: More Charlie Parker with Strings	1985	2.50	5.00	10.00
❑ 817 445-1	Bird on Verve, Vol. 4: Afro-Cuban Jazz	1985	2.50	5.00	10.00
❑ 817 446-1	Bird on Verve, Vol. 5: Charlie	1985	2.50	5.00	10.00
❑ 817 447-1	Bird on Verve, Vol. 6: South of the Border	1985	2.50	5.00	10.00
❑ 817 448-1	Bird on Verve, Vol. 7: Big Band	1985	2.50	5.00	10.00
❑ 817 449-1	Bird on Verve, Vol. 8: Charlie Parker in Hi-Fi	1985	2.50	5.00	10.00
❑ 823 250-1	The Cole Porter Songbook	1986	2.50	5.00	10.00
❑ 833 564-1	Charlie Parker Sides	198?	2.50	5.00	10.00
❑ 837 176-1	Bird: The Original Recordings of Charlie Parker	1987	2.50	5.00	10.00
VOGUE					
❑ LAE-12002 [M]	Memorial Album	1955	37.50	75.00	150.00
WARNER BROS.					
❑ 6BS 3159 [(6)]	The Complete Dial Recordings	1977	20.00	40.00	80.00
-- Limited edition of 4,000 box sets					
❑ 2WB 3198 [(2)]	The Very Best of Bird	1977	5.00	10.00	20.00
ZIM					
❑ 1001	Lullaby in Rhythm	197?	3.00	6.00	12.00
❑ 1003	At the Pershing Ballroom, Chicago, 1950	197?	3.00	6.00	12.00
❑ 1006	Apartment Jam	197?	3.00	6.00	12.00

PARKER, CHARLIE/STAN GETZ/WARDELL GRAY
Also see each artist's individual listings.
DESIGN

Number	Title	Yr	VG	VG+	NM
❑ DLP-183 [M]	Charlie Parker/Stan Getz/Wardell Gray	196?	3.75	7.50	15.00

PARKER, CHARLIE; DIZZY GILLESPIE; RED NORVO
Also see each artist's individual listings.
DIAL

Number	Title	Yr	VG	VG+	NM
❑ LP-903 [M]	Fabulous Jam Session	1951	150.00	300.00	600.00

PARKER, CHARLIE/DIZZY GILLESPIE/BUD POWELL/MAX ROACH
Also see each artist's individual listings.
SAVOY

Number	Title	Yr	VG	VG+	NM
❑ MG-9034 [10]	Bird, Diz, Bud, Max	1953	150.00	300.00	600.00

PARKER, CHARLIE/COLEMAN HAWKINS/GEORGIE AULD
Also see each artist's individual listings.
JAM

Number	Title	Yr	VG	VG+	NM
❑ 5006	Unearthed Masters, Vol. 1	198?	2.50	5.00	10.00

PARKER, JACY
Pianist and singer.
VERVE

Number	Title	Yr	VG	VG+	NM
❑ V-8424 [M]	Spotlight On Jacy Parker	1962	10.00	20.00	40.00
❑ V6-8424 [S]	Spotlight On Jacy Parker	1962	12.50	25.00	50.00

PARKER, JOHN
GOLDEN CREST

Number	Title	Yr	VG	VG+	NM
❑ GC-3051	Dixieland	196?	3.75	7.50	15.00

PARKER, KIM
Female singer; stepdaughter of Charlie.
SOUL NOTE

Number	Title	Yr	VG	VG+	NM
❑ SN-1033	Havin' Myself a Time	1981	3.00	6.00	12.00
❑ SN-1063	Good Girl	1982	3.00	6.00	12.00
❑ SN-1133	Sometimes I'm Blue	1986	3.00	6.00	12.00

PARKER, KNOCKY
Pianist.
AUDIOPHILE

Number	Title	Yr	VG	VG+	NM
❑ AP-28 [M]	Boogie Woogie Maxine	1956	10.00	20.00	40.00
❑ AP-102/5 [(4)]	The Complete Piano Works of Jelly Roll Morton	196?	12.50	25.00	50.00
-- In box with booklet; it's unknown whether the volumes also were issued individually					
EUPHONIC					
❑ 1215	Eight on Eighty-Eight	198?	2.50	5.00	10.00
❑ 1216	Classic Rags and Nostalgia	198?	2.50	5.00	10.00
GHB					
❑ GHB-19	Knocky Parker	1967	3.75	7.50	15.00
❑ 150	Knocky Parker and the Cake-Walkin' Jazz Band	1981	2.50	5.00	10.00
JAZZOLOGY					
❑ J-81	Cakewalk to Ragtime	197?	2.50	5.00	10.00
PROGRESSIVE					
❑ PLP-1 [10]	New Orleans Stomps	1954	12.50	25.00	50.00

PARKER, KNOCKY, AND SMOKEY MONTGOMERY
Montgomery is a banjo player. Also see KNOCKY PARKER.
CIRCLE

Number	Title	Yr	VG	VG+	NM
❑ CLP-10001	Texas Swing, Vol. 1: The Barrelhouse	1987	2.50	5.00	10.00
❑ CLP-10002	Texas Swing, Vol. 2: The Boogie-Woogie	1987	2.50	5.00	10.00
❑ CLP-10003	Texas Swing, Vol. 3: ... And the Blues	1987	2.50	5.00	10.00
❑ CLP-10004	Texas Swing, Vol. 4: Smokey and the Bearkats	1987	2.50	5.00	10.00

PARKER, LEO
Baritone saxophone player.
BLUE NOTE

Number	Title	Yr	VG	VG+	NM
❑ LT-1076	Rollin' with Leo	1980	2.50	5.00	10.00
❑ BLP-4087 [M]	Let Me Tell You 'Bout It	1961	15.00	30.00	60.00
-- With 61st St. address on label					
❑ BLP-4087 [M]	Let Me Tell You 'Bout It	1963	5.00	10.00	20.00
-- With "New York, USA" address on label					
❑ BLP-4095 [M]	Rollin' with Leo	1961	---	---	---
-- Canceled					
❑ BST-84087 [S]	Let Me Tell You 'Bout It	1961	20.00	40.00	80.00
-- With 61st St. address on label					
❑ BST-84087 [S]	Let Me Tell You 'Bout It	1963	6.25	12.50	25.00
-- With "New York, USA" address on label					
❑ BST-84087 [S]	Let Me Tell You 'Bout It	1967	3.75	7.50	15.00
-- With "A Division of Liberty Records" on label					
❑ BST-84095 [S]	Rollin' with Leo	1986	3.00	6.00	12.00
-- Originally scheduled for 1961 release, this was the first issue on its originally assigned number					
CHESS					
❑ LPV-413	The Late, Great King of Baritone Sax	1971	3.75	7.50	15.00
COLLECTABLES					
❑ COL-5329	Back to the Baritones	198?	2.50	5.00	10.00
SAVOY					
❑ MG-9009 [10]	Leo Parker	1952	62.50	125.00	250.00
❑ MG-9018 [10]	New Trends in Modern Music	1952	62.50	125.00	250.00

PARKER, MAYNARD
Guitarist.
PRESTIGE

Number	Title	Yr	VG	VG+	NM
❑ 10054	Midnight Rider	1973	5.00	10.00	20.00

PARKINS, LEROY
Woodwinds player.
BETHLEHEM

Number	Title	Yr	VG	VG+	NM
❑ BCP-6047 [M]	LeRoy Parkins and His Yazoo River Band	1960	7.50	15.00	30.00
❑ SBCP-6047 [S]	LeRoy Parkins and His Yazoo River Band	1960	10.00	20.00	40.00

Number	Title	Yr	VG	VG+	NM
PARLAN, HORACE					
Pianist.					
BLUE NOTE					
❏ BLP-4028 [M]	Movin' and Groovin'	1960	25.00	50.00	100.00
-- "Deep groove" version (deep indentation under label on both sides)					
❏ BLP-4028 [M]	Movin' and Groovin'	1960	20.00	40.00	80.00
-- Regular version, W. 63rd St. address on label					
❏ BLP-4028 [M]	Movin' and Groovin'	1963	5.00	10.00	20.00
-- With "New York, USA" address on label					
❏ BLP-4037 [M]	Us Three	1960	25.00	50.00	100.00
-- "Deep groove" version (deep indentation under label on both sides)					
❏ BLP-4037 [M]	Us Three	1960	20.00	40.00	80.00
-- Regular version, W. 63rd St. address on label					
❏ BLP-4037 [M]	Us Three	1963	5.00	10.00	20.00
-- With "New York, USA" address on label					
❏ BLP-4043 [M]	Speakin' My Piece	1960	25.00	50.00	100.00
-- "Deep groove" version (deep indentation under label on both sides)					
❏ BLP-4043 [M]	Speakin' My Piece	1960	20.00	40.00	80.00
-- Regular version, W. 63rd St. address on label					
❏ BLP-4043 [M]	Speakin' My Piece	1963	5.00	10.00	20.00
-- With "New York, USA" address on label					
❏ BLP-4062 [M]	Headin' South	1961	15.00	30.00	60.00
-- With W. 63rd St. address on label					
❏ BLP-4062 [M]	Headin' South	1963	5.00	10.00	20.00
-- With "New York, USA" address on label					
❏ BLP-4074 [M]	On the Spur of the Moment	1961	37.50	75.00	150.00
-- With W. 63rd St. address on label					
❏ BLP-4074 [M]	On the Spur of the Moment	1961	15.00	30.00	60.00
-- With 61st St. address on label					
❏ BLP-4074 [M]	On the Spur of the Moment	1963	5.00	10.00	20.00
-- With "New York, USA" address on label					
❏ BST-4074	On the Spur of the Moment	199?	6.25	12.50	25.00
-- Classic Records reissue on audiophile vinyl					
❏ BLP-4082 [M]	Up and Down	1961	15.00	30.00	60.00
-- With 61st St. address on label					
❏ BLP-4082 [M]	Up and Down	1963	5.00	10.00	20.00
-- With "New York, USA" address on label					
❏ BST-84028 [S]	Movin' and Groovin'	1960	20.00	40.00	80.00
-- With W. 63rd St. address on label					
❏ BST-84028 [S]	Movin' and Groovin'	1963	6.25	12.50	25.00
-- With "New York, USA" address on label					
❏ BST-84028 [S]	Movin' and Groovin'	1967	3.75	7.50	15.00
-- With "A Division of Liberty Records" on label					
❏ BST-84037 [S]	Us Three	1960	20.00	40.00	80.00
-- With W. 63rd St. address on label					
❏ BST-84037 [S]	Us Three	1963	3.75	7.50	15.00
-- With "A Division of Liberty Records" on label					
❏ BST-84037 [S]	Us Three	1967	6.25	12.50	25.00
-- With "New York, USA" address on label					
❏ BST-84043 [S]	Speakin' My Piece	1960	20.00	40.00	80.00
-- With W. 63rd St. address on label					
❏ BST-84043 [S]	Speakin' My Piece	1963	6.25	12.50	25.00
-- With "New York, USA" address on label					
❏ BST-84043 [S]	Speakin' My Piece	1967	3.75	7.50	15.00
-- With "A Division of Liberty Records" on label					
❏ BST-84062 [S]	Headin' South	1961	17.50	35.00	70.00
-- With W. 63rd St. address on label					
❏ BST-84062 [S]	Headin' South	1963	6.25	12.50	25.00
-- With "New York, USA" address on label					
❏ BST-84062 [S]	Headin' South	1967	3.75	7.50	15.00
-- With "A Division of Liberty Records" on label					
❏ BST-84074 [S]	On the Spur of the Moment	1961	50.00	100.00	200.00
-- With W. 63rd St. address on label					
❏ BST-84074 [S]	On the Spur of the Moment	1961	17.50	35.00	70.00
-- With 61st St. address on label					
❏ BST-84074 [S]	On the Spur of the Moment	1963	6.25	12.50	25.00
-- With "New York, USA" address on label					
❏ BST-84074 [S]	On the Spur of the Moment	1967	3.75	7.50	15.00
-- With "A Division of Liberty Records" on label					
❏ BST-84082 [S]	Up and Down	1961	17.50	35.00	70.00
-- With 61st St. address on label					
❏ BST-84082 [S]	Up and Down	1963	6.25	12.50	25.00
-- With "New York, USA" address on label					
❏ BST-84082 [S]	Up and Down	1967	3.75	7.50	15.00
-- With "A Division of Liberty Records" on label					
❏ BST-84134	Happy Frame of Mind	1986	3.00	6.00	12.00
-- "The Finest in Jazz Since 1939" issue					
INNER CITY					
❏ IC-2012	Arrival	197?	3.75	7.50	15.00
❏ IC-2056	No Blues	197?	3.75	7.50	15.00
STEEPLECHASE					
❏ SCS-1012	Arrival	198?	3.00	6.00	12.00
❏ SCS-1056	No Blues	198?	3.00	6.00	12.00
❏ SCS-1076	Frank-ly Speaking	198?	3.00	6.00	12.00
❏ SCS-1124	Blue Parlan	198?	3.00	6.00	12.00
❏ SCS-1141	Musically Yours	198?	3.00	6.00	12.00
❏ SCS-1167	The Maestro	198?	3.00	6.00	12.00
❏ SCS-1178	Like Someone in Love	1983	3.00	6.00	12.00
❏ SCS-1194	Glad I Met You	198?	3.00	6.00	12.00

Number	Title	Yr	VG	VG+	NM
PASS, JOE					
Guitarist.					
BASF					
❏ 20738	Intercontinental	197?	3.75	7.50	15.00
BLUE NOTE					
❏ LT-1053	The Complete "Catch Me" Sessions	1980	3.00	6.00	12.00
❏ LT-1103	Joy Spring	1981	2.50	5.00	10.00
DISCOVERY					
❏ DS-776	Guitar Interludes	197?	3.00	6.00	12.00
❏ DS-906	The Living Legends	1986	2.50	5.00	10.00
FANTASY					
❏ OJC-382	Montreux '77	1989	2.50	5.00	10.00
❏ OJC-602	I Remember Charlie Parker	1991	3.00	6.00	12.00
PABLO					
❏ 2310 593	The Best of Joe Pass	198?	3.00	6.00	12.00
❏ 2310 708	Virtuoso	1974	3.75	7.50	15.00
❏ 2310 716	Portrait of Duke Ellington	1975	3.00	6.00	12.00
❏ 2310 752	Montreux '75	1976	3.00	6.00	12.00
❏ 2310 788	Virtuoso #2	1976	3.00	6.00	12.00
❏ 2310 805	Virtuoso #3	1978	3.00	6.00	12.00
❏ 2310 877	Eximious	198?	3.00	6.00	12.00
❏ 2310 912	Whitestone	198?	2.50	5.00	10.00
❏ 2310 931	Blues for Fred	198?	2.50	5.00	10.00
❏ 2310 936	One for My Baby	1989	3.00	6.00	12.00
❏ 2310 939	Summer Nights	1990	3.75	7.50	15.00
❏ 2405 419	The Best of Joe Pass	198?	2.50	5.00	10.00
❏ 2640 102 [(2)]	Virtuoso #4	198?	3.75	7.50	15.00
PABLO LIVE					
❏ 2308 212	Montreux '77	1978	3.00	6.00	12.00
❏ 2308 239	Live at Long Beach City College	1987	2.50	5.00	10.00
❏ 2308 249	Joe Pass at Akron University	1987	2.50	5.00	10.00
❏ 2620 114 [(2)]	Joe Pass Trio Live at Donte's	198?	3.75	7.50	15.00
PABLO TODAY					
❏ 2312 109	I Remember Charlie Parker	1979	3.00	6.00	12.00
❏ 2312 133	Joe Pass Loves Gershwin	198?	3.00	6.00	12.00
PACIFIC JAZZ					
❏ PJ-73 [M]	Catch Me!	1963	6.25	12.50	25.00
❏ ST-73 [S]	Catch Me!	1963	7.50	15.00	30.00
❏ PJ-85 [M]	For Django	1964	6.25	12.50	25.00
❏ ST-85 [S]	For Django	1964	7.50	15.00	30.00
❏ LN-10086	Simplicity	198?	2.00	4.00	8.00
-- Budget-line reissue					
❏ LN-10132	For Django	198?	2.00	4.00	8.00
-- Budget-line reissue					
PAUSA					
❏ 7043	Intercontinental	198?	2.50	5.00	10.00
WORLD PACIFIC					
❏ WP-11844 [M]	A Sign of the Times	1966	3.75	7.50	15.00
❏ WP-11854 [M]	The Stones Jazz	1967	5.00	10.00	20.00
❏ WP-11865 [M]	Simplicity	1967	5.00	10.00	20.00
❏ ST-21844 [S]	A Sign of the Times	1966	5.00	10.00	20.00
❏ ST-21854 [S]	The Stones Jazz	1967	5.00	10.00	20.00
❏ ST-21865 [S]	Simplicity	1967	3.75	7.50	15.00

PASS, JOE, AND ROBERT CONTI

Also see each artist's individual listings.

Number	Title	Yr	VG	VG+	NM
DISCOVERY					
❏ 906	The Living Legends	1985	3.00	6.00	12.00

PASS, JOE, AND PAULINHO DA COSTA

Also see each artist's individual listings.

Number	Title	Yr	VG	VG+	NM
PABLO					
❏ 2310 824	Tudo Bem!	1978	3.00	6.00	12.00

PASS, JOE, AND NIELS-HENNING ORSTED PEDERSEN

Also see each artist's individual listings.

Number	Title	Yr	VG	VG+	NM
PABLO					
❏ 2310 830	Chops	1979	3.00	6.00	12.00
PABLO LIVE					
❏ 2308 811	North Sea Nights	1979	3.00	6.00	12.00

PASS, JOE, AND ARNOLD ROSS

Also see each artist's individual listings.

Number	Title	Yr	VG	VG+	NM
PACIFIC JAZZ					
❏ PJ-48 [M]	Sounds of Synanon	1962	6.25	12.50	25.00
❏ ST-48 [S]	Sounds of Synanon	1962	7.50	15.00	30.00

PASS, JOE, AND JIMMY ROWLES

Also see each artist's individual listings.

Number	Title	Yr	VG	VG+	NM
PABLO					
❏ 2310 865	Checkmate	1982	3.00	6.00	12.00

Number	Title	Yr	VG	VG+	NM

PASS, JOE; TOOTS THIELEMANS; NIELS-HENNING ORSTED PEDERSEN
Also see each artist's individual listings.
PABLO LIVE
| ❏ 2308 233 | Live in the Netherlands | 1981 | 3.00 | 6.00 | 12.00 |

PASSPORT
Fusion group led by KLAUS DOLDINGER.
ATCO
❏ SD 36-107	Cross-Collateral	1975	3.00	6.00	12.00
❏ SD 36-132	Infinity Machine	1976	3.00	6.00	12.00
❏ SD 36-149	Iguacu	1977	3.00	6.00	12.00
❏ SD 7042	Looking Through	1974	3.75	7.50	15.00
ATLANTIC
❏ SD 18162	Doldinger Jubilee '75	1976	3.00	6.00	12.00
❏ SD 19177	Sky Blue	1978	2.50	5.00	10.00
❏ SD 19233	Garden of Eden	1979	2.50	5.00	10.00
❏ SD 19265	Oceanliner	1980	2.50	5.00	10.00
❏ SD 19304	Blue Tattoo	1981	2.50	5.00	10.00
❏ 80034	Earthborn	1982	2.50	5.00	10.00
❏ 80144	Man in the Mirror	1983	2.50	5.00	10.00
❏ 81251	Running in Real Time	1985	2.50	5.00	10.00
❏ 81727	Heavy Nights	1986	2.50	5.00	10.00
❏ 81937	Talk Back	1989	2.50	5.00	10.00

PASTICHE
Vocal trio: Sandy Cressman; Jenny Meltzer; Becky West.
NOVA
| ❏ 8707 | That's R & B-Bop | 198? | 3.00 | 6.00 | 12.00 |

PASTOR, GUY
Male singer. Also see TONY PASTOR.
DISCOVERY
| ❏ DS-918 | This Is It | 1986 | 2.50 | 5.00 | 10.00 |

PASTOR, TONY
Tenor saxophone player and bandleader.
CIRCLE
| ❏ 31 | Tony Pastor and His Orchestra 1944-47 | 198? | 2.50 | 5.00 | 10.00 |
| ❏ CLP-121 | Tony Pastor and His Orchestra 1942-47 | 198? | 2.50 | 5.00 | 10.00 |
EVEREST
| ❏ SDBR-1031 [S] | P.S. – Plays and Sings Shaw | 1959 | 5.00 | 10.00 | 20.00 |
| ❏ LPBR-5031 [M] | P.S. – Plays and Sings Shaw | 1959 | 3.75 | 7.50 | 15.00 |
FORUM
| ❏ F-9009 [M] | Let's Dance with Tony Pastor | 196? | 3.00 | 6.00 | 12.00 |
| ❏ SF-9009 [S] | Let's Dance with Tony Pastor | 196? | 3.00 | 6.00 | 12.00 |
ROULETTE
| ❏ R-25024 [M] | Let's Dance | 1958 | 6.25 | 12.50 | 25.00 |
| ❏ R-25027 [M] | Guy Pastor and His Dad | 1958 | 6.25 | 12.50 | 25.00 |

PASTORIUS, JACO
Bass player. Also see WEATHER REPORT.
EPIC
| ❏ PE 33949 | Jaco Pastorius | 1976 | 2.50 | 5.00 | 10.00 |
IAI
| ❏ 37.38.46 | Jaco | 1975 | 5.00 | 10.00 | 20.00 |
WARNER BROS.
| ❏ BSK 3535 | Word of Mouth | 1981 | 2.50 | 5.00 | 10.00 |
| ❏ 23876 | Invitation | 1983 | 2.50 | 5.00 | 10.00 |

PATCHEN, KENNETH, WITH THE CHAMBER JAZZ SEXTET
Beat poet Patchen recites with a jazz band playing behind him.
CADENCE
| ❏ CLP-3004 [M] | Kenneth Patchen Reads His Poetry | 1957 | 75.00 | 150.00 | 300.00 |

PATE, JOHNNY
Bass player, composer and arranger.
GIG
| ❏ GLP-100 [M] | Subtle Sounds | 1956 | 25.00 | 50.00 | 100.00 |
KING
❏ 561 [M]	Jazz Goes Ivy League	1958	20.00	40.00	80.00
❏ 584 [M]	Swingin' Flute	1958	20.00	40.00	80.00
❏ 611 [M]	A Date with Johnny Pate	1959	20.00	40.00	80.00
STEPHENY
| ❏ 4002 [M] | Johnny Pate at the Blue Note | 1957 | 25.00 | 50.00 | 100.00 |
TALISMAN
| ❏ TLP-1 [10] | Johnny Pate Trio | 1956 | 30.00 | 60.00 | 120.00 |

PATITUCCI, JOHN
Bass player.
GRP
| ❏ GR-1049 | John Patitucci | 1988 | 2.50 | 5.00 | 10.00 |
| ❏ GR-9583 | On the Corner | 1989 | 3.00 | 6.00 | 12.00 |

PATTERSON, DON
Organist.
CADET
| ❏ LP-787 [M] | Goin' Down Home | 1967 | 7.50 | 15.00 | 30.00 |
| ❏ LPS-787 [S] | Goin' Down Home | 1967 | 5.00 | 10.00 | 20.00 |
MUSE
❏ MR-5005	The Return of Don Patterson	1974	3.75	7.50	15.00
❏ MR-5032	These Are Soulful Days	1975	3.75	7.50	15.00
❏ MR-5121	Movin' Up	1977	3.00	6.00	12.00
❏ MR-5148	Why Not	1979	3.00	6.00	12.00
PRESTIGE
❏ PRLP-7331 [M]	The Exiting New Organ of Don Patterson	1964	6.25	12.50	25.00
❏ PRST-7331 [S]	The Exciting New Organ of Don Patterson	1964	7.50	15.00	30.00
❏ PRLP-7349 [M]	Hip Cake Walk	1965	6.25	12.50	25.00
❏ PRST-7349 [S]	Hip Cake Walk	1965	7.50	15.00	30.00
❏ PRLP-7381 [M]	Patterson's People	1965	6.25	12.50	25.00
❏ PRST-7381 [S]	Patterson's People	1965	7.50	15.00	30.00
❏ PRLP-7415 [M]	Holiday Soul	1966	6.25	12.50	25.00
❏ PRST-7415 [S]	Holiday Soul	1965	7.50	15.00	30.00
❏ PRLP-7430 [M]	Satisfaction	1966	6.25	12.50	25.00
❏ PRST-7430 [S]	Satisfaction	1966	7.50	15.00	30.00
❏ PRLP-7466 [M]	The Boss Men	1967	7.50	15.00	30.00
❏ PRST-7466 [S]	The Boss Men	1967	6.25	12.50	25.00
❏ PRLP-7484 [M]	Soul Happening!	1967	6.25	12.50	25.00
❏ PRST-7484 [S]	Soul Happening!	1967	5.00	10.00	20.00
❏ PRLP-7510 [M]	Mellow Soul	1967	6.25	12.50	25.00
❏ PRST-7510 [S]	Mellow Soul	1967	5.00	10.00	20.00
❏ PRLP-7533 [M]	Four Dimensions	1967	6.25	12.50	25.00
❏ PRST-7533 [S]	Four Dimensions	1967	5.00	10.00	20.00
❏ PRST-7563	Boppin' and Burnin'	1968	5.00	10.00	20.00
❏ PRST-7577	Opus De Don	1968	5.00	10.00	20.00
❏ PRST-7613	Funk You	1969	5.00	10.00	20.00
❏ PRST-7640	Oh, Happy Days!	1969	5.00	10.00	20.00
❏ PRST-7704	The Best of Don Patterson	1969	3.75	7.50	15.00
❏ PRST-7738	Brothers-4	1970	3.75	7.50	15.00
❏ PRST-7772	Best of Jazz Giants	1971	3.75	7.50	15.00
❏ PRST-7816	Donnybrook	1971	3.75	7.50	15.00
❏ PRST-7852	Tune Up	1971	3.75	7.50	15.00

PATTERSON, KELLEE
Female singer.
BLACK JAZZ
| ❏ QD-12 | Maiden Voyage | 1974 | 5.00 | 10.00 | 20.00 |

PATTON, "BIG" JOHN
Organist.
BLUE NOTE
❏ BLP-4130 [M]	Along Came John	1963	7.50	15.00	30.00
❏ BLP-4143 [M]	Blue John	1963	---	---	---
-- Canceled						
❏ BLP-4174 [M]	The Way I Feel	1964	6.25	12.50	25.00
❏ BLP-4192 [M]	Oh Baby!	1964	6.25	12.50	25.00
❏ BLP-4229 [M]	Got a Good Thing Goin'	1966	6.25	12.50	25.00
❏ BLP-4239 [M]	Let 'Em Roll	1966	6.25	12.50	25.00
❏ BST-84130 [S]	Along Came John	1963	10.00	20.00	40.00
-- With "New York, USA" address on label						
❏ BST-84130 [S]	Along Came John	1967	3.75	7.50	15.00
-- With "A Division of Liberty Records" on label						
❏ BST-84143 [S]	Blue John	1986	3.00	6.00	12.00
-- "The Finest in Jazz Since 1939" issue; originally scheduled for 1963 release, but canceled						
❏ BST-84174 [S]	The Way I Feel	1964	7.50	15.00	30.00
-- With "New York, USA" address on label						
❏ BST-84174 [S]	The Way I Feel	1967	3.75	7.50	15.00
-- With "A Division of Liberty Records" on label						
❏ BST-84192 [S]	Oh Baby!	1964	7.50	15.00	30.00
-- With "New York, USA" address on label						
❏ BST-84192 [S]	Oh Baby!	1967	3.75	7.50	15.00
-- With "A Division of Liberty Records" on label						
❏ BST-84229 [S]	Got a Good Thing Goin'	1966	7.50	15.00	30.00
-- With "New York, USA" address on label						
❏ BST-84229 [S]	Got a Good Thing Goin'	1967	3.75	7.50	15.00
-- With "A Division of Liberty Records" on label						
❏ BST-84239 [S]	Let 'Em Roll	1966	7.50	15.00	30.00
-- With "New York, USA" address on label						
❏ BST-84239 [S]	Let 'Em Roll	1967	3.75	7.50	15.00
-- With "A Division of Liberty Records" on label						
❏ BST-84281 [S]	That Certain Feeling	1968	6.25	12.50	25.00
-- With "A Division of Liberty Records" on label						

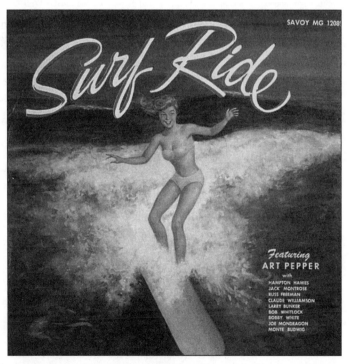

(Top left) Pianist Horace Parlan recorded half a dozen albums for Blue Note in the early 1960s, including this one, before becoming a sideman. He eventually moved to Denmark, where he resumed his recording career for Japan's SteepleChase label. (Top right) Joe Pass didn't become a guitar legend until the 1970s, when he was signed to Norman Granz' Pablo label. He had recorded for Pacific Jazz/World Pacific before that, though, and his *For Django* is considered a classic. (Bottom left) Passport, led by Klaus Doldinger, was one of the longest-lasting of the 1970s fusion groups. This album, *Earthborn*, was issued in 1982. (Bottom right) Alto sax man Art Pepper was the headliner on this Savoy collection from the 1950s.

Number	Title	Yr	VG	VG+	NM
❑ BST-84306 [S]	Understanding	1969	6.25	12.50	25.00
-- With "A Division of Liberty Records" on label					
❑ BST-84340 [S]	Accent on the Blues	1970	6.25	12.50	25.00
-- With "A Division of Liberty Records" on label					

PAULIN, DOC
Trumpeter and bandleader.
FOLKWAYS

Number	Title	Yr	VG	VG+	NM
❑ FA 2856	Doc Paulin's Marching Band	198?	2.50	5.00	10.00

PAULO, MICHAEL
Saxophone player.
MCA

Number	Title	Yr	VG	VG+	NM
❑ 42295	One Passion	1989	3.00	6.00	12.00

PAVAGEAU, ALCIDE "SLOW DRAG"
Bass player and bandleader.
GHB

Number	Title	Yr	VG	VG+	NM
❑ GHB-54	Half Fast Jazz Band	196?	3.75	7.50	15.00

PAXTON, GEORGE
Saxophone player, bandleader and arranger.
HINDSIGHT

Number	Title	Yr	VG	VG+	NM
❑ HSR-184	George Paxton and His Orchestra 1944-45	198?	2.50	5.00	10.00

PAYNE, BENNIE
Pianist and male singer.
KAPP

Number	Title	Yr	VG	VG+	NM
❑ KL-1004 [M]	Bennie Payne Plays and Sings	1955	20.00	40.00	80.00

PAYNE, CECIL
Baritone saxophone (and sometimes alto saxophone) player. Also see RANDY WESTON.
CHARLIE PARKER

Number	Title	Yr	VG	VG+	NM
❑ PLP-506 [M]	Shaw Nuff	1962	6.25	12.50	25.00
❑ PLP-506S [S]	Shaw Nuff	1962	7.50	15.00	30.00
❑ PLP-801 [M]	Cecil Payne Performing Charlie Parker's Music	1962	10.00	20.00	40.00
❑ PLP-801S [S]	Cecil Payne Performing Charlie Parker's Music	1962	12.50	25.00	50.00

MUSE

Number	Title	Yr	VG	VG+	NM
❑ MR-5061	Bird Gets the Worm	1976	3.00	6.00	12.00

SAVOY

Number	Title	Yr	VG	VG+	NM
❑ MG-12147 [M]	Patterns of Jazz	1959	20.00	40.00	80.00

SAVOY JAZZ

Number	Title	Yr	VG	VG+	NM
❑ SJL-1167	Patterns	1986	2.50	5.00	10.00

SIGNAL

Number	Title	Yr	VG	VG+	NM
❑ S-1203 [M]	Cecil Payne Quintet and Quartet	1955	50.00	100.00	200.00

STRATA-EAST

Number	Title	Yr	VG	VG+	NM
❑ SES-19734	The Zodiac	1973	6.25	12.50	25.00

PAYNE, CECIL, AND DUKE JORDAN
Also see each artist's individual listings.
MUSE

Number	Title	Yr	VG	VG+	NM
❑ MR-5015	Brooklyn Brothers	1974	3.75	7.50	15.00

PAYNE, FREDA
Female singer better known for her work in R&B and soul music.
ABC IMPULSE!

Number	Title	Yr	VG	VG+	NM
❑ AS-53 [S]	After the Lights Go Down Low... And Much More	1968	3.75	7.50	15.00

IMPULSE!

Number	Title	Yr	VG	VG+	NM
❑ A-53 [M]	After the Lights Go Down Low... And Much More	1964	7.50	15.00	30.00
❑ AS-53 [S]	After the Lights Go Down Low... And Much More	1964	10.00	20.00	40.00

PAYNE, JOHN, AND LOUIS LEVIN
Payne plays flute and saxophone; Levin is a keyboard player.
ARISTA/FREEDOM

Number	Title	Yr	VG	VG+	NM
❑ AF 1025	Bedtime	1976	3.00	6.00	12.00
❑ AF 1036	The Razor's Edge	1976	3.00	6.00	12.00

MERCURY

Number	Title	Yr	VG	VG+	NM
❑ SRM-1-1166	John Payne/Louis Levin Band	1977	3.75	7.50	15.00

PEACOCK, GARY
Bass player.
ECM

Number	Title	Yr	VG	VG+	NM
❑ 1101	Tale of Another	1977	3.00	6.00	12.00
❑ 1119	December Poems	1979	3.00	6.00	12.00

Number	Title	Yr	VG	VG+	NM
❑ 1165	Shift in the Wind	1981	2.50	5.00	10.00
❑ 1210	Voice from the Past	1982	2.50	5.00	10.00

PEAGLER, CURTIS
Alto and tenor saxophone player.
PABLO

Number	Title	Yr	VG	VG+	NM
❑ 2310 930	I'll Be Around	1988	2.50	5.00	10.00

PEARSON, DUKE
Pianist, composer and arranger.
ATLANTIC

Number	Title	Yr	VG	VG+	NM
❑ 3002 [M]	Honeybuns	196?	3.75	7.50	15.00
❑ SD 3002 [S]	Honeybuns	196?	3.75	7.50	15.00
❑ SD 3005 [S]	Prairie Dog	196?	3.75	7.50	15.00

BLUE NOTE

Number	Title	Yr	VG	VG+	NM
❑ BN-LA317-G	It Could Only Happen with You	1974	3.75	7.50	15.00
❑ BLP-4022 [M]	Profile -- Duke Pearson	1959	30.00	60.00	120.00
-- "Deep groove" version (deep indentation under label on both sides)					
❑ BLP-4022 [M]	Profile -- Duke Pearson	1959	20.00	40.00	80.00
-- Regular version with W. 63rd St. address on label					
❑ BLP-4022 [M]	Profile -- Duke Pearson	1963	6.25	12.50	25.00
-- With New York, USA address on label					
❑ BLP-4035 [M]	Tender Feelin's	1960	30.00	60.00	120.00
-- "Deep groove" version (deep indentation under label on both sides)					
❑ BLP-4035 [M]	Tender Feelin's	1960	20.00	40.00	80.00
-- Regular version with W. 63rd St. address on label					
❑ BLP-4035 [M]	Tender Feelin's	1963	6.25	12.50	25.00
-- With New York, USA address on label					
❑ BLP-4191 [M]	Wahoo!	1965	7.50	15.00	30.00
❑ BLP-4252 [M]	Sweet Honey Bee	1966	7.50	15.00	30.00
❑ B1-28269	The Right Touch	1994	3.00	6.00	12.00
-- Reissue of 84267					
❑ B1-35220	I Don't Care Who Knows It	1996	3.00	6.00	12.00
❑ BST-84022 [S]	Profile -- Duke Pearson	1959	15.00	30.00	60.00
-- With W. 63rd St. address on label					
❑ BST-84022 [S]	Profile -- Duke Pearson	1963	5.00	10.00	20.00
-- With New York, USA address on label					
❑ BST-84022 [S]	Profile -- Duke Pearson	1967	3.00	6.00	12.00
-- With "A Division of Liberty Records" on label					
❑ BST-84035 [S]	Tender Feelin's	1960	15.00	30.00	60.00
-- With W. 63rd St. address on label					
❑ BST-84035 [S]	Tender Feelin's	1963	5.00	10.00	20.00
-- With New York, USA address on label					
❑ BST-84035 [S]	Tender Feelin's	1967	3.00	6.00	12.00
-- With "A Division of Liberty Records" on label					
❑ B1-84191	Wahoo!	1986	3.00	6.00	12.00
-- "The Finest in Jazz Since 1939" reissue					
❑ BST-84191 [S]	Wahoo!	1965	7.50	15.00	30.00
-- With New York, USA address on label					
❑ BST-84191 [S]	Wahoo!	1967	3.00	6.00	12.00
-- With "A Division of Liberty Records" on label					
❑ BST-84252 [S]	Sweet Honey Bee	1966	7.50	15.00	30.00
-- With New York, USA address on label					
❑ BST-84252 [S]	Sweet Honey Bee	1967	3.00	6.00	12.00
-- With "A Division of Liberty Records" on label					
❑ BST-84267	The Right Touch	1968	6.25	12.50	25.00
❑ BST-84276	Introducing Duke Pearson's Big Band	1968	6.25	12.50	25.00
❑ BST-84293	The Phantom	1969	6.25	12.50	25.00
❑ BST-84308	Now Hear This	1969	6.25	12.50	25.00
❑ BST-84323	Merry Ole Soul	1970	5.00	10.00	20.00
❑ BST-84344	How Insensitive	1970	5.00	10.00	20.00
❑ B1-89792	Sweet Honey Bee	1993	3.00	6.00	12.00
-- Reissue of 84252					

JAZZTIME

Number	Title	Yr	VG	VG+	NM
❑ 33-02 [M]	Hush!	1962	10.00	20.00	40.00

PRESTIGE

Number	Title	Yr	VG	VG+	NM
❑ PRST-7729	Dedication	1970	3.75	7.50	15.00

PECK, BERT, AND THE KINGS OF DIXIELAND
PAULA

Number	Title	Yr	VG	VG+	NM
❑ 2225	New Orleans Beat	197?	2.50	5.00	10.00

PECORA, SANTO
Trombonist. Also see LU WATTERS.
CLEF

Number	Title	Yr	VG	VG+	NM
❑ MGC-123 [10]	Santo Pecora Collates	1953	25.00	50.00	100.00
-- With either Mercury or Clef cover; all labels are Clef					

MERCURY

Number	Title	Yr	VG	VG+	NM
❑ MGC-123 [10]	Dixieland Jazz Band	1953	---	---	---
-- Canceled; released on Clef 123					

SOUTHLAND

Number	Title	Yr	VG	VG+	NM
❑ SLP-213 [M]	Santo Pecora	1955	12.50	25.00	50.00

VIK

Number	Title	Yr	VG	VG+	NM
❑ XLA-1081 [M]	Dixieland Mardi Gras	1957	12.50	25.00	50.00

Number	Title	Yr	VG	VG+	NM

PEDICIN, MICHAEL, JR.
Saxophone player.
OPTIMISM

Number	Title	Yr	VG	VG+	NM
❑ OP-3106	City Song	198?	2.50	5.00	10.00
❑ OP-3211	Angles	1989	3.00	6.00	12.00

PEIFFER, BERNARD
Pianist and composer. Also see DON BYAS.
DECCA

❑ DL 8626 [M]	The Astounding Bernard Peiffer	1958	12.50	25.00	50.00
❑ DL 9203 [M]	Piano Ala Mood	1958	12.50	25.00	50.00
❑ DL 9218 [M]	The Pied Peiffer of the Piano	1959	12.50	25.00	50.00
❑ DL 79203 [S]	Piano Ala Mood	1958	10.00	20.00	40.00
❑ DL 79218 [S]	The Pied Peiffer of the Piano	1959	10.00	20.00	40.00

EMARCY

❑ MG-26036 [10]	Le Most	1954	20.00	40.00	80.00
❑ MG-36080 [M]	Bernie's Tunes	1956	12.50	25.00	50.00

LAURIE

❑ LLP-1006 [M]	Modern Jazz for People Who Like Original Music	1960	6.25	12.50	25.00
❑ SLP-1006 [S]	Modern Jazz for People Who Like Original Music	1960	7.50	15.00	30.00
❑ LLP-1008 [M]	Cole Porter's "Can Can"	1960	6.25	12.50	25.00
❑ SLP-1008 [S]	Cole Porter's "Can Can"	1960	7.50	15.00	30.00

NORGRAN

❑ MGN-11 [10]	Bernard Peiffer Et Son Trio	1954	20.00	40.00	80.00

PELL, DAVE
Saxophone player and clarinetist. Also see LUCY ANN POLK.
ATLANTIC

❑ 1216 [M]	Jazz and Romantic Places	1955	25.00	50.00	100.00
-- Black label					
❑ 1216 [M]	Jazz and Romantic Places	1961	7.50	15.00	30.00
-- Multicolor label, white "fan" logo at right					
❑ 1249 [M]	Love Story	1956	20.00	40.00	80.00
-- Black label					
❑ 1249 [M]	Love Story	1961	7.50	15.00	30.00
-- Multicolor label, white "fan" logo at right					

CAPITOL

❑ T 925 [M]	I Had The Craziest Dream	1958	7.50	15.00	30.00
-- Turquoise label					
❑ ST 1309 [S]	The Big Small Bands	1960	6.25	12.50	25.00
❑ T 1309 [M]	The Big Small Bands	1960	5.00	10.00	20.00
❑ ST 1512 [S]	Old South Wails	1961	6.25	12.50	25.00
❑ T 1512 [M]	Old South Wails	1961	5.00	10.00	20.00
❑ ST 1687 [S]	I Remember John Kirby	1962	6.25	12.50	25.00
❑ T 1687 [M]	I Remember John Kirby	1962	5.00	10.00	20.00

CORAL

❑ CRL 57248 [M]	Swingin' School Songs	1958	7.50	15.00	30.00
❑ CRL 757248 [S]	Swingin' School Songs	1958	6.25	12.50	25.00

GNP CRESCENDO

❑ GNPS-2122	Prez Conference	1978	2.50	5.00	10.00

HEADFIRST

❑ 715	Live at Alfonse's	198?	3.00	6.00	12.00

KAPP

❑ KL-1025 [M]	Dave Pell Plays Rodgers and Hart	1956	7.50	15.00	30.00
❑ KL-1034 [M]	Dave Pell Plays Burke and Van	1956	10.00	20.00	40.00

HEUSEN

❑ KL-1036 [M]	Dave Pell Plays Irving Berlin	1957	10.00	20.00	40.00

LIBERTY

❑ LRP-3298 [M]	Today's Hits in Jazz	1961	3.75	7.50	15.00
❑ LRP-3321 [M]	Jazz Voices in Video	1963	3.75	7.50	15.00
❑ LST-7298 [S]	Today;s Hits in Jazz	1961	5.00	10.00	20.00
❑ LST-7321 [S]	Jazz Voices in Video	1963	5.00	10.00	20.00
❑ LST-7631 [S]	Man-Ha-Man-Ha	1969	3.75	7.50	15.00

PRI

❑ 3002 [M]	Dave Pell Plays Harry James' Big Band Sounds	196?	5.00	10.00	20.00
❑ 3003 [M]	Dave Pell Plays Artie Shaw's Big Band Sounds	196?	5.00	10.00	20.00
❑ 3004 [M]	Dave Pell Plays Benny Goodman's Big Band Sounds	196?	5.00	10.00	20.00
❑ 3005 [M]	Dave Pell Plays Lawrence Welk's Big Band Sounds	196?	5.00	10.00	20.00
❑ 3006 [M]	Dave Pell Plays Perez Prado's Big Band Sounds	196?	5.00	10.00	20.00
❑ 3007 [M]	Dave Pell Plays Duke Ellington's Big Band Sounds	196?	5.00	10.00	20.00
❑ 3009 [M]	Dave Pell Plays Mantovani's Big Band Sounds	196?	5.00	10.00	20.00
❑ 3010 [M]	Dave Pell Plays the Dorsey Brothers' Big Band Sounds	196?	5.00	10.00	20.00

Number	Title	Yr	VG	VG+	NM
❑ 3011 [M]	Dave Pell Plays the Big Band Sounds	196?	5.00	10.00	20.00

RCA VICTOR

❑ LPM-1320 [M]	Jazz Goes Dancing	1956	12.50	25.00	50.00
❑ LPM-1394 [M]	Swingin' in the Ol' Corral	1957	12.50	25.00	50.00
❑ LPM-1524 [M]	Pell of a Time	1957	12.50	25.00	50.00
❑ LPM-1662 [M]	Campus Hop	1957	12.50	25.00	50.00

TREND

❑ TL-1003 [10]	Dave Pell Plays Irving Berlin	1953	30.00	60.00	120.00
❑ TL-1501 [M]	Dave Pell Plays Rodgers and Hart	1954	25.00	50.00	100.00

PELL, DAVE, AND JOE WILLIAMS
Also see each artist's individual listings.
GNP CRESCENDO

❑ GNPS-2124	Prez & Joe: In Celebration of Lester Young	1979	2.50	5.00	10.00

PEMBROKE, MIKE
JAZZOLOGY

❑ J-24	Mike Pembroke's Hot Seven	197?	2.50	5.00	10.00

PENAZZI, ANDRE
Percussionist.
DAUNTLESS

❑ 2020 [M]	Organ Jazz Samba Percussion	1963	3.75	7.50	15.00
❑ 7020 [S]	Organ Jazz Samba Percussion	1963	5.00	10.00	20.00

PENSYL, KIM
Pianist.
OPTIMISM

❑ OP-3210	Pensyl Sketches #1	1988	2.50	5.00	10.00

PENTAGON
Led by Cedar Walton.
EAST WIND

❑ 10002	Pentagon	1979	5.00	10.00	20.00

PEPLOWSKI, KEN
Clarinetist, also an alto and tenor saxophone player.
CONCORD JAZZ

❑ CJ-344	Double Exposure	1988	2.50	5.00	10.00
❑ CJ-376	Sonny Side	1989	3.00	6.00	12.00

PEPPER, ART
Alto saxophone player; also a tenor sax man and clarinetist. Also see CHET BAKER.
ANALOGUE PRODUCTIONS

❑ AP 010	Art Pepper Meets the Rhythm Section	199?	6.25	12.50	25.00
-- Reissue on audiophile vinyl					
❑ AP 012	Smack Up!	199?	6.25	12.50	25.00
-- Reissue on audiophile vinyl					
❑ AP 017	Art Pepper + Eleven: Modern Jazz Classics	199?	6.25	12.50	25.00
-- Reissue on audiophile vinyl					
❑ APR 3012	The New York Album	199?	3.75	7.50	15.00
❑ APR 3013	So in Love	199?	3.75	7.50	15.00
❑ APR 3014	The Intimate Art Pepper	199?	3.75	7.50	15.00

ARTISTS HOUSE

❑ 9412	So in Love	1979	3.00	6.00	12.00

BLUE NOTE

❑ BN-LA591-H2 [(2)]	Early Art	1976	3.75	7.50	15.00
❑ LT-1064	Omega Alpha	1980	2.50	5.00	10.00

CONTEMPORARY

❑ C-3532 [M]	Art Pepper Meets the Rhythm Section	1957	25.00	50.00	100.00
❑ M-3568 [M]	Art Pepper + Eleven: Modern Jazz Classics	1959	20.00	40.00	80.00
❑ M-3573 [M]	Gettin' Together!	1960	12.50	25.00	50.00
❑ M-3602 [M]	Smack Up!	1961	10.00	20.00	40.00
❑ M-3607 [M]	Intensity	1963	7.50	15.00	30.00
❑ M-3630 [M]	The Way It Was!	1966	6.25	12.50	25.00
❑ S-7532 [S]	Art Pepper Meets the Rhythm Section	1959	12.50	25.00	50.00
❑ S-7568 [S]	Art Pepper + Eleven: Modern Jazz Classics	1959	15.00	30.00	60.00
❑ S-7573 [S]	Gettin' Together!	1960	15.00	30.00	60.00
❑ S-7602 [S]	Smack Up!	1961	12.50	25.00	50.00
❑ S-7607 [S]	Intensity	1963	10.00	20.00	40.00
❑ S-7630 [S]	The Way It Was!	1966	7.50	15.00	30.00
❑ C-7633	Living Legend	197?	3.00	6.00	12.00
❑ C-7638	The Trip	197?	3.00	6.00	12.00

Number	Title	Yr	VG	VG+	NM
❏ C-7639	No Limit	1978	3.00	6.00	12.00
❏ C-7642	Thursday Night at the Village Vanguard	1979	3.00	6.00	12.00
❏ C-7643	Friday Night at the Village Vanguard	198?	2.50	5.00	10.00
❏ C-7644	Saturday Night at the Village Vanguard	198?	2.50	5.00	10.00
❏ C-7650	Art Pepper at the Village Vanguard, Vol. 4: More for Les	1986	2.50	5.00	10.00
DISCOVERY					
❏ 837	Among Friends	198?	2.50	5.00	10.00
❏ 3019 [10]	Art Pepper Quartet	1952	75.00	150.00	300.00
❏ 3023 [10]	Art Pepper Quintet	1954	62.50	125.00	250.00
FANTASY					
❏ OJC-169	Gettin' Together	198?	2.50	5.00	10.00
❏ OJC-176	Smack Up!	198?	2.50	5.00	10.00
❏ OJC-338	Art Pepper Meets the Rhythm Section	198?	2.50	5.00	10.00
❏ OJC-341	Modern Jazz Classics	198?	2.50	5.00	10.00
❏ OJC-387	Intensity	1989	2.50	5.00	10.00
❏ OJC-389	The Way It Was	1989	2.50	5.00	10.00
❏ OJC-408	Living Legend	1990	3.00	6.00	12.00
❏ OJC-410	The Trip	1990	3.00	6.00	12.00
❏ OJC-411	No Limit	1990	3.00	6.00	12.00
❏ OJC-474	Art Pepper Today	1990	3.00	6.00	12.00
❏ OJC-475	Straight Life	1990	3.00	6.00	12.00
GALAXY					
❏ 5119	Art Pepper Today	197?	2.50	5.00	10.00
❏ 5127	Straight Life	1979	2.50	5.00	10.00
❏ 5128	Landscape	197?	2.50	5.00	10.00
❏ 5140	Winter Moon	1980	2.50	5.00	10.00
❏ 5141	One September Afternoon	1981	2.50	5.00	10.00
❏ 5142	Roadgame	1982	2.50	5.00	10.00
❏ 5143	Goin' Home	1982	2.50	5.00	10.00
❏ 5145	Art Lives	1982	2.50	5.00	10.00
❏ 5147	Tete-a-Tete	198?	2.50	5.00	10.00
❏ 5148	Art Works	198?	2.50	5.00	10.00
❏ 5151	Art Pepper Quartet	198?	2.50	5.00	10.00
❏ 5154	The New York Album	1985	2.50	5.00	10.00
INTERLUDE					
❏ MO-512 [M]	Art Pepper Quartet	1959	12.50	25.00	50.00
❏ ST-1012 [S]	Art Pepper Quartet	1959	10.00	20.00	40.00
INTERPLAY					
❏ 7718	Among Friends	1979	2.50	5.00	10.00
INTRO					
❏ 606 [M]	Modern Art	1957	125.00	250.00	500.00
JAZZ WEST					
❏ JLP-10 [M]	The Return of Art Pepper	1956	125.00	250.00	500.00
MOSAIC					
❏ M3-105 [(3)]	The Complete Pacific Jazz Small Group Recordings of Art Pepper	198?	12.50	25.00	50.00
ONYX					
❏ 219	Omega Man	197?	2.50	5.00	10.00
PACIFIC JAZZ					
❏ PJ-60 [M]	The Artistry of Pepper	1962	10.00	20.00	40.00
SAVOY					
❏ MG-12089 [M]	Surf Ride	1956	25.00	50.00	100.00
SAVOY JAZZ					
❏ SJL-2217 [(2)]	Discoveries	197?	3.75	7.50	15.00
SCORE					
❏ SLP-4030 [M]	Modern Art	1958	25.00	50.00	100.00
❏ SLP-4031 [M]	The Art Pepper-Red Norvo Sextet	1958	25.00	50.00	100.00
❏ SLP-4032 [M]	The Return of Art Pepper	1958	25.00	50.00	100.00
STEREO RECORDS					
❏ S-7018 [S]	Art Pepper Meets the Rhythm Section	1958	20.00	40.00	80.00
TAMPA					
❏ TP-20 [M]	Art Pepper Quartet	1957	50.00	100.00	200.00
-- Colored vinyl					
❏ TP-20 [M]	Art Pepper Quartet	1958	25.00	50.00	100.00
-- Black vinyl					
❏ TS-1001 [S]	Art Pepper Quartet	1959	20.00	40.00	80.00
XANADU					
❏ 108	The Early Show	197?	2.50	5.00	10.00
❏ 117	The Late Show	198?	2.50	5.00	10.00

PEPPER, ART/SHELLY MANNE
Also see each artist's individual listings.

Number	Title	Yr	VG	VG+	NM
CHARLIE PARKER					
❏ PLP-836 [M]	Pepper/Manne	1963	6.25	12.50	25.00
❏ PLP-836S [S]	Pepper/Manne	1963	7.50	15.00	30.00

PEPPER, ART/SONNY REDD
Also see each artist's individual listings.

Number	Title	Yr	VG	VG+	NM
REGENT					
❏ MG-6069 [M]	Two Altos	1959	12.50	25.00	50.00
SAVOY					
❏ MG-12215 [M]	Art Pepper-Sonny Redd	1969	5.00	10.00	20.00

PEPPER, JIM
Tenor saxophone player, composer and male singer.

Number	Title	Yr	VG	VG+	NM
EMBRYO					
❏ 731	Powwow	1970	5.00	10.00	20.00

PERAZA, ARMANDO
Percussionist and occasional male singer.

Number	Title	Yr	VG	VG+	NM
SKYE					
❏ S-5D	Wild Thing	1970	3.75	7.50	15.00

PERIGEO
Fusion band from Italy: Franco D'Andrea (piano); Claudio Fassoli (tenor and soprano saxophones); Giovanni Tommaso (bass); others.

Number	Title	Yr	VG	VG+	NM
RCA VICTOR					
❏ TPL1-1080	Genealogia	197?	3.75	7.50	15.00
❏ APL1-1175	The Valley of the Temples	197?	3.00	6.00	12.00
-- Reissue with new prefix					
❏ TPL1-1175	The Valley of the Temples	197?	3.75	7.50	15.00
❏ TPL1-1228	Fata Morgana	197?	3.75	7.50	15.00

PERKINS, BILL
Mostly a tenor saxophone player, but has played both soprano and baritone saxes on record. Also see AL COHN; THE FIVE.

Number	Title	Yr	VG	VG+	NM
CONTEMPORARY					
❏ C-14011	Journey to the East	1985	2.50	5.00	10.00
INTERPLAY					
❏ 7721	Confluence	1979	2.50	5.00	10.00
❏ 8606	Remembrance of Dino's	1990	3.00	6.00	12.00
LIBERTY					
❏ LRP-3293 [M]	Bossa Nova	1963	5.00	10.00	20.00
❏ LST-7293 [S]	Bossa Nova	1963	6.25	12.50	25.00
PACIFIC JAZZ					
❏ PJ-1221 [M]	The Bill Perkins Octet On Stage	1956	25.00	50.00	100.00
RIVERSIDE					
❏ RS-3052	Quietly There	1969	6.25	12.50	25.00
SEA BREEZE					
❏ SB-2006	Many Ways to Go	1980	2.50	5.00	10.00
WORLD PACIFIC					
❏ WP-1221 [M]	The Bill Perkins Octet On Stage	1958	20.00	40.00	80.00

PERKINS, BILL, AND RICHIE KAMUCA
Also see each artist's individual listings.

Number	Title	Yr	VG	VG+	NM
LIBERTY					
❏ LRP-3051 [M]	Tenors Head On	1957	15.00	30.00	60.00

PERKINS, BILL; ART PEPPER; RICHIE KAMUCA
Also see each artist's individual listings.

Number	Title	Yr	VG	VG+	NM
PACIFIC JAZZ					
❏ PJM-401 [M]	Just Friends	1956	30.00	60.00	120.00
WORLD PACIFIC					
❏ PJM-401 [M]	Just Friends	1958	20.00	40.00	80.00

PERKINS, BILL, AND THE SAN FRANCISCANS

Number	Title	Yr	VG	VG+	NM
FAMOUS DOOR					
❏ 128	The Other Bill	197?	2.50	5.00	10.00

PERKINS, CARL
Pianist. Not to be confused with the rock 'n' roll singer of the same name.

Number	Title	Yr	VG	VG+	NM
DOOTO					
❏ DL-211 [M]	Introducing Carl Perkins	196?	3.75	7.50	15.00
DOOTONE					
❏ DL-211 [M]	Introducing Carl Perkins	1956	30.00	60.00	120.00
-- Black vinyl					
❏ DL-211 [M]	Introducing Carl Perkins	1956	50.00	100.00	200.00
-- Red vinyl					

PERRI
Vocal quartet: Carolyn, Darlene, Lori and Sharon Perry.

Number	Title	Yr	VG	VG+	NM
ZEBRA					
❏ ZR-5007	Perri	198?	3.00	6.00	12.00
❏ ZEB-5684	Celebrate!	1986	2.50	5.00	10.00
❏ ZEB-42017	The Flight	1987	2.50	5.00	10.00

Number	Title	Yr	VG	VG+	NM

PERSIP, CHARLIE
Drummer. Also see THE MODERN JAZZ SEXTET.
BETHLEHEM

Number	Title	Yr	VG	VG+	NM
❏ BCP-6046 [M]	Charlie Persip and the Jazz Statesmen	1960	10.00	20.00	40.00
❏ BCP-6046	Right Down Front	197?	3.00	6.00	12.00

-- Reissue, distributed by RCA Victor

❏ SBCP-6046 [S]	Charlie Persip and the Jazz Statesmen	1960	10.00	20.00	40.00

SOUL NOTE

❏ SN-1079	In Case You Missed It	1985	3.00	6.00	12.00
❏ 121179	No Dummies Allowed	1990	3.75	7.50	15.00

STASH

❏ ST-209	The Charlie Persip & Gerry LaFum Superband	198?	2.50	5.00	10.00

PERSON, HOUSTON
Tenor saxophone player.
FANTASY

❏ OJC-332	Goodness!	1988	2.50	5.00	10.00

MERCURY

❏ SRM-1-1104	Pure Pleasure	1976	3.00	6.00	12.00
❏ SRM-1-1151	Harmony	1977	3.00	6.00	12.00

MUSE

❏ MR-5110	Stolen Sweets	1977	3.00	6.00	12.00
❏ MR-5136	The Big Horn	197?	3.00	6.00	12.00
❏ MR-5161	Wild Flower	1977	3.00	6.00	12.00
❏ MR-5178	The Nearness of You	197?	3.00	6.00	12.00
❏ MR-5199	Suspicions	1980	3.00	6.00	12.00
❏ MR-5231	Very Personal	1981	2.50	5.00	10.00
❏ MR-5260	Heavy Juice	1982	2.50	5.00	10.00
❏ MR-5289	Always on My Mind	1986	2.50	5.00	10.00
❏ MR-5331	The Talk of the Town	1987	2.50	5.00	10.00
❏ MR-5344	Basics	1989	3.00	6.00	12.00
❏ MR-5376	Something in Common	1989	3.00	6.00	12.00
❏ MR-5433	Why Not!	1991	3.75	7.50	15.00

PRESTIGE

❏ PRLP-7491 [M]	Underground Soul	1967	7.50	15.00	30.00
❏ PRST-7491 [S]	Underground Soul	1967	5.00	10.00	20.00
❏ PRST-7517	Chocomotive	1968	5.00	10.00	20.00
❏ PRST-7548	Trust in Me	1968	5.00	10.00	20.00
❏ PRST-7566	Blue Odyssey	1968	5.00	10.00	20.00
❏ PRST-7621	Soul Dance!	1969	5.00	10.00	20.00
❏ PRST-7678	Goodness!	1969	5.00	10.00	20.00
❏ PRST-7767	The Truth!	1970	5.00	10.00	20.00
❏ PRST-7779	The Best of Houston Person	1970	3.75	7.50	15.00
❏ 10003	Person to Person	1971	6.25	12.50	25.00
❏ 10017	Houston Express	1971	5.00	10.00	20.00
❏ 10044	Broken Windows, Empty Hallways	1972	5.00	10.00	20.00
❏ 10055	Sweet Buns and Barbeque	1973	5.00	10.00	20.00

SAVOY

❏ 14471	Gospel Soul	197?	3.00	6.00	12.00

20TH CENTURY

❏ W-205	Houston Person	196?	6.25	12.50	25.00

WESTBOUND

❏ 205	Houston Person '75	1975	3.75	7.50	15.00
❏ 213	Get Outa My Way	1975	3.75	7.50	15.00

PERSSON, AAKE
Trombonist.
EMARCY

❏ MG-26039 [10]	Swedish Modern	1954	50.00	100.00	200.00

PERSSON, AAKE/ARNE DOMNERUS
Also see each artist's individual listings.
PRESTIGE

❏ PRLP-173 [10]	Aake Persson Swedish All Stars	1953	62.50	125.00	250.00

PERSSON, BENT
Trumpeter and cornet player.
STOMP OFF

❏ SOS-1167	Livin' High in London	198?	2.50	5.00	10.00

PERUNA JAZZMEN, THE
Members: Mikael Zuschlag (first cornet); Peter Aller (second cornet); Claus Forchhammer (clarinet); Arne Hojberg (trombone, leader); Anette Strauss (piano, vocals); John Neess (banjo); Mik "Count" Schack (washboard); Leo Hechmann (sousaphone).
STOMP OFF

❏ SOS-1003	Come On and Stomp, Stomp, Stomp	1981	2.50	5.00	10.00
❏ SOS-1020	Mean Blues	198?	2.50	5.00	10.00
❏ SOS-1105	Smoke House Blues	1986	2.50	5.00	10.00

PETERSEN, EDWARD
Tenor saxophone player.
DELMARK

Number	Title	Yr	VG	VG+	NM
❏ DS-445	Upward Spiral	1990	3.00	6.00	12.00

PETERSON, HANNIBAL MARVIN
Trumpeter, percussionist and male singer.
ENJA

❏ 3085	Angels of Atlanta	1981	3.00	6.00	12.00

INNER CITY

❏ IC-3020	Antibes	197?	3.75	7.50	15.00

PETERSON, JEANNE ARLAND
Pianist and female singer.
CELEBRATION

❏ 5004	Jeanne Arland Peterson	197?	3.75	7.50	15.00

PETERSON, OSCAR
Pianist and bandleader. Also see LOUIS ARMSTRONG; BUDDY DeFRANCO; STAN GETZ; COLEMAN HAWKINS; BILL HENDERSON; SONNY STITT; BEN WEBSTER; LESTER YOUNG.
AMERICAN RECORDING SOCIETY

❏ G-415 [M]	An Oscar for Peterson	1957	10.00	20.00	40.00
❏ G-438 [M]	Oscar Peterson Trio at Newport	1957	10.00	20.00	40.00

BASF

❏ 20713	Motions and Emotions	1972	3.00	6.00	12.00
❏ 20723	Hello Herbie	1972	3.00	6.00	12.00
❏ 20734	Tristeza on Piano	1972	3.00	6.00	12.00
❏ 20868	Walking the Line	1973	3.00	6.00	12.00
❏ 20905	In Tune	1973	3.00	6.00	12.00
❏ 20908	Reunion Blues	1973	3.00	6.00	12.00
❏ 21281	Great Connection	1974	3.00	6.00	12.00
❏ 25101 [(2)]	Exclusively for My Friends	1972	3.75	7.50	15.00
❏ 25156 [(2)]	In a Mellow Mood	1973	3.75	7.50	15.00

CLEF

❏ MGC-106 [10]	Oscar Peterson Piano Solos	1951	25.00	50.00	100.00

-- Reissue of Mercury 25024

❏ MGC-107 [10]	Oscar Peterson at Carnegie Hall	1951	25.00	50.00	100.00
❏ MGC-110 [10]	Oscar Peterson Collates	1952	25.00	50.00	100.00
❏ MGC-116 [10]	The Oscar Peterson Quartet	1952	25.00	50.00	100.00
❏ MGC-119 [10]	Oscar Peterson Plays Pretty	1952	25.00	50.00	100.00
❏ MGC-127 [10]	Oscar Peterson Collates No. 2	1953	20.00	40.00	80.00
❏ MGC-145 [10]	Oscar Peterson Sings	1954	20.00	40.00	80.00
❏ MGC-155 [10]	Oscar Peterson Plays Pretty No. 2	1954	20.00	40.00	80.00
❏ MGC-168 [10]	The Oscar Peterson Quartet No. 2	1954	20.00	40.00	80.00
❏ MGC-603 [M]	Oscar Peterson Plays Cole Porter	1953	15.00	30.00	60.00
❏ MGC-604 [M]	Oscar Peterson Plays Irving Berlin	1953	15.00	30.00	60.00
❏ MGC-605 [M]	Oscar Peterson Plays George Gershwin	1953	15.00	30.00	60.00
❏ MGC-606 [M]	Oscar Peterson Plays Duke Ellington	1953	15.00	30.00	60.00
❏ MGC-623 [M]	Oscar Peterson Plays Jerome Kern	1954	12.50	25.00	50.00
❏ MGC-624 [M]	Oscar Peterson Plays Richard Rodgers	1954	12.50	25.00	50.00
❏ MGC-625 [M]	Oscar Peterson Plays Vincent Youmans	1954	12.50	25.00	50.00
❏ MGC-648 [M]	Oscar Peterson Plays Harry Warren	1955	12.50	25.00	50.00
❏ MGC-649 [M]	Oscar Peterson Plays Harold Arlen	1955	12.50	25.00	50.00
❏ MGC-650 [M]	Oscar Peterson Plays Jimmy McHugh	1955	12.50	25.00	50.00
❏ MGC-688 [M]	The Oscar Peterson Quartet	1956	12.50	25.00	50.00

-- Reissue of 116

❏ MGC-694 [M]	Recital by Oscar Peterson	1956	12.50	25.00	50.00
❏ MGC-695 [M]	Nostalgic Memories by Oscar Peterson	1956	12.50	25.00	50.00
❏ MGC-696 [M]	Tenderly -- Music by Oscar Peterson	1956	12.50	25.00	50.00
❏ MGC-697 [M]	Keyboard Music by Oscar Peterson	1956	12.50	25.00	50.00
❏ MGC-698 [M]	An Evening with the Oscar Peterson Duo/Quartet	1956	12.50	25.00	50.00
❏ MGC-708 [M]	Oscar Peterson Plays Count Basie	1956	12.50	25.00	50.00
❏ MGC-751 [M]	The Oscar Peterson Trio at the Stratford Shakesperean Festival, Volume 1	1955	---	---	---

-- Canceled

❏ MGC-752 [M]	The Oscar Peterson Trio at the Stratford Shakesperean Festival, Volume 2	1955	---	---	---

-- Canceled
DCC COMPACT CLASSICS

❏ LPZ-2021	West Side Story	1996	6.25	12.50	25.00

-- Audiophile vinyl

Number	Title	Yr	VG	VG+	NM
EMARCY					
❏ 405 [(2)]	Oscar Peterson Trio Transition	1976	3.75	7.50	15.00
FANTASY					
❏ OJC-378	Oscar Peterson Jam -- Montreux	1989	2.50	5.00	10.00
❏ OJC-383	Oscar Peterson and the Bassists -- Montreux '77	1989	2.50	5.00	10.00
❏ OJC-498	Skol	1991	2.50	5.00	10.00
❏ OJC-603	Trumpet Summit Meets the Oscar Peterson Big Four	1991	2.50	5.00	10.00
❏ OJC-627	The Good Life	1991	2.50	5.00	10.00
LIMELIGHT					
❏ LM-82010 [M]	Canadiana Suite	1965	3.75	7.50	15.00
❏ LM-82023 [M]	Eloquence	1965	3.75	7.50	15.00
❏ LM-82029 [M]	With Respect to Nat	1966	3.75	7.50	15.00
❏ LM-82039 [M]	Blues Etude	1966	3.75	7.50	15.00
❏ LM-82044 [M]	Soul Espanol	1967	5.00	10.00	20.00
❏ LS-86010 [S]	Canadiana Suite	1965	5.00	10.00	20.00
❏ LS-86023 [S]	Eloquence	1965	5.00	10.00	20.00
❏ LS-86029 [S]	With Respect to Nat	1966	5.00	10.00	20.00
❏ LS-86039 [S]	Blues Etude	1966	3.75	7.50	15.00
❏ LS-86044 [S]	Soul Espanol	1967	3.75	7.50	15.00
MERCURY					
❏ MGC-106 [10]	Oscar Peterson Piano Solos	1951	30.00	60.00	120.00
❏ MGC-107 [10]	Oscar Peterson at Carnegie Hall	1951	30.00	60.00	120.00
❏ MGC-110 [10]	Oscar Peterson Collates	1952	30.00	60.00	120.00
❏ MGC-116 [10]	The Oscar Peterson Quartet	1952	30.00	60.00	120.00
❏ MGC-119 [10]	Oscar Peterson Plays Pretty	1952	30.00	60.00	120.00
❏ MGC-603 [M]	Oscar Peterson Plays Cole Porter	1953	25.00	50.00	100.00
❏ MGC-604 [M]	Oscar Peterson Plays Irving Berlin	1953	25.00	50.00	100.00
❏ MGC-605 [M]	Oscar Peterson Plays George Gershwin	1953	25.00	50.00	100.00
❏ MGC-606 [M]	Oscar Peterson Plays Duke Ellington	1953	25.00	50.00	100.00
❏ MG-20975 [M]	Oscar Peterson Trio + One	1964	6.25	12.50	25.00
❏ MG-25024 [10]	Oscar Peterson Piano Solos	1950	37.50	75.00	150.00
❏ SR-60975 [S]	Oscar Peterson Trio + One	1964	7.50	15.00	30.00
MGM					
❏ GAS-133	Oscar Peterson (Golden Archive Series)	1970	3.00	6.00	12.00
MOBILE FIDELITY					
❏ 1-243	Very Tall	1995	5.00	10.00	20.00
-- Audiophile vinyl					
PABLO					
❏ 2310-701	The Trio	1975	3.00	6.00	12.00
❏ 2310-739	Oscar Peterson and Roy Eldridge	1976	3.00	6.00	12.00
❏ 2310-740	Oscar Peterson and Dizzy Gillespie	1976	3.00	6.00	12.00
❏ 2310-741	Oscar Peterson and Harry Edison	1976	3.00	6.00	12.00
❏ 2310-742	Oscar Peterson and Clark Terry	1976	3.00	6.00	12.00
❏ 2310-743	Oscar Peterson and Jon Faddis	1976	3.00	6.00	12.00
❏ 2310-747	Montreux '75	1976	3.00	6.00	12.00
❏ 2310-779	Porgy and Bess	1976	3.00	6.00	12.00
❏ 2310-796	Giants	1977	3.00	6.00	12.00
❏ 2310-817	Jousts	1979	3.00	6.00	12.00
❏ 2310-895	History of An Artist, Volume 2	1983	3.00	6.00	12.00
❏ 2310-918	If You Could See Me Now	1987	2.50	5.00	10.00
❏ 2310-927	Oscar Peterson + Harry Edison + Eddie "Cleanhead" Vinson	1988	2.50	5.00	10.00
❏ 2310-940	Live	1990	2.50	5.00	10.00
❏ 2625-702 [(2)]	History of An Artist	1975	3.75	7.50	15.00
❏ 2625-705 [(2)]	A Salle Pleyel	1975	3.75	7.50	15.00
❏ 2625-711 [(2)]	Oscar Peterson in Russia	1976	3.00	6.00	12.00
❏ 2640-101 [(2)]	Freedom Songbook	1983	3.75	7.50	15.00
PABLO LIVE					
❏ 2308-208	Oscar Peterson Jam -- Montreux	1977	3.00	6.00	12.00
❏ 2308-213	Oscar Peterson and the Bassists -- Montreux '77	1978	3.00	6.00	12.00
❏ 2308-224	Digital at Montreux	1980	3.00	6.00	12.00
❏ 2308-231	Nigerian Marketplace	1982	3.00	6.00	12.00
❏ 2308-232	Skol	1982	3.00	6.00	12.00
❏ 2308-241	The Good Life	1983	3.00	6.00	12.00
❏ 2620-111 [(2)]	The London Concert	1979	3.75	7.50	15.00
❏ 2620-112 [(2)]	The Paris Concert	1979	3.75	7.50	15.00
❏ 2620-115 [(2)]	Live at the Northsea Jazz Festival, 1980	1981	3.75	7.50	15.00
PABLO TODAY					
❏ 2312-108	Night Child	1979	3.00	6.00	12.00
❏ 2312-129	A Royal Wedding Suite	198?	3.00	6.00	12.00
❏ 2312-135	The Personal Touch	1982	3.00	6.00	12.00
❏ 2313-103	Silent Partner	1980	3.00	6.00	12.00
PAUSA					
❏ 7044	Mellow Wood	1979	2.50	5.00	10.00
❏ 7059	Action	1980	2.50	5.00	10.00
❏ 7064	Girl Talk	1980	2.50	5.00	10.00
❏ 7069	My Favorite Instrument	1980	2.50	5.00	10.00
❏ 7073	In Tune	1980	2.50	5.00	10.00
❏ 7080	The Way I Really Play	1981	2.50	5.00	10.00
❏ 7099	Reunion Blues	1981	2.50	5.00	10.00
❏ 7102	Motions and Emotions	1982	2.50	5.00	10.00
❏ 7113	Great Connection	1983	2.50	5.00	10.00
❏ 7124	Tristeza on Piano	1983	2.50	5.00	10.00
❏ 7135	Another Day	1983	2.50	5.00	10.00
PRESTIGE					
❏ PRST-7595	Soul-O!	1968	3.75	7.50	15.00
❏ PRST-7620	The Great Oscar Peterson on Prestige!	1969	3.75	7.50	15.00
❏ PRST-7649	Oscar Peterson Plays for Lovers	1969	3.75	7.50	15.00
❏ PRST-7690	Easy Walker	1969	3.75	7.50	15.00
RCA VICTOR					
❏ LPT-3006 [10]	This Is Oscar Peterson	1952	30.00	60.00	120.00
TRIP					
❏ 5560	Eloquence	197?	2.50	5.00	10.00
VERVE					
❏ VSP-11 [M]	Stage Right	1966	3.00	6.00	12.00
❏ VSPS-11 [S]	Stage Right	1966	3.75	7.50	15.00
❏ MGV-2002 [M]	In a Romantic Mood -- Oscar Peterson with Strings	1956	10.00	20.00	40.00
❏ V-2002 [M]	In a Romantic Mood -- Oscar Peterson with Strings	1961	5.00	10.00	20.00
❏ MGV-2004 [M]	Pastel Moods by Oscar Peterson	1956	10.00	20.00	40.00
❏ V-2004 [M]	Pastel Moods by Oscar Peterson	1961	5.00	10.00	20.00
❏ MGV-2012 [M]	Romance -- The Vocal Styling of Oscar Peterson	1956	10.00	20.00	40.00
-- Reissue of Clef 145					
❏ V-2012 [M]	Romance -- The Vocal Styling of Oscar Peterson	1961	5.00	10.00	20.00
❏ MGV-2044 [M]	Recital by Oscar Peterson	1957	10.00	20.00	40.00
-- Reissue of Clef 694					
❏ V-2044 [M]	Recital by Oscar Peterson	1961	5.00	10.00	20.00
❏ MGV-2045 [M]	Nostalgic Memories by Oscar Peterson	1957	10.00	20.00	40.00
-- Reissue of Clef 695					
❏ V-2045 [M]	Nostalgic Memories by Oscar Peterson	1961	5.00	10.00	20.00
❏ MGV-2046 [M]	Tenderly -- Music by Oscar Peterson	1957	10.00	20.00	40.00
-- Reissue of Clef 696					
❏ V-2046 [M]	Tenderly -- Music by Oscar Peterson	1961	5.00	10.00	20.00
❏ MGV-2047 [M]	Keyboard Music by Oscar Peterson	1957	10.00	20.00	40.00
-- Reissue of Clef 697					
❏ V-2047 [M]	Keyboard Music by Oscar Peterson	1961	5.00	10.00	20.00
❏ MGV-2048 [M]	An Evening with Oscar Peterson	1957	10.00	20.00	40.00
-- Reissue of Clef 698					
❏ V-2048 [M]	An Evening with Oscar Peterson	1961	5.00	10.00	20.00
❏ MGV-2052 [M]	Oscar Peterson Plays the Cole Porter Songbook	1957	10.00	20.00	40.00
-- Reissue of Clef 603					
❏ V-2052 [M]	Oscar Peterson Plays the Cole Porter Songbook	1961	5.00	10.00	20.00
❏ V6-2052 [S]	Oscar Peterson Plays the Cole Porter Songbook	1961	3.75	7.50	15.00
-- Reissue of 6083					
❏ MGV-2053 [M]	Oscar Peterson Plays the Irving Berlin Songbook	1957	10.00	20.00	40.00
-- Reissue of Clef 604					
❏ V-2053 [M]	Oscar Peterson Plays the Irving Berlin Songbook	1961	5.00	10.00	20.00
❏ V6-2053 [S]	Oscar Peterson Plays the Irving Berlin Songbook	1961	3.75	7.50	15.00
-- Reissue of 6084					
❏ MGV-2054 [M]	Oscar Peterson Plays the George Gershwin Songbook	1957	10.00	20.00	40.00
-- Reissue of Clef 605					
❏ V-2054 [M]	Oscar Peterson Plays the George Gershwin Songbook	1961	5.00	10.00	20.00
❏ V6-2054 [S]	Oscar Peterson Plays the George Gershwin Songbook	1961	3.75	7.50	15.00
-- Reissue of 6085					
❏ MGV-2055 [M]	Oscar Peterson Plays the Duke Ellington Songbook	1957	10.00	20.00	40.00
-- Reissue of Clef 606					
❏ V-2055 [M]	Oscar Peterson Plays the Duke Ellington Songbook	1961	5.00	10.00	20.00
❏ V6-2055 [S]	Oscar Peterson Plays the Duke Ellington Songbook	1961	3.75	7.50	15.00
-- Reissue of 6086					
❏ MGV-2056 [M]	Oscar Peterson Plays the Jerome Kern Songbook	1957	10.00	20.00	40.00
-- Reissue of Clef 623					

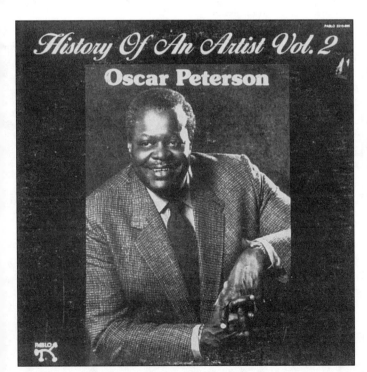

Pianist Oscar Peterson recorded early and often, and though sometimes criticized for repetitiveness in style, his work is also consistent and rarely disappoints. (Top left) Here's a stunning early 10-inch album cover from the Mercury/Clef period, complete with David Stone Martin artwork. (Top right) Peterson recorded for Verve for almost the entire decade of the 1960s, with a brief departure for Prestige late in the decade. This is one of his many LPs for Norman Granz' best-known label. (Bottom left) Pablo's *History of an Artist* series paired Peterson with former collaborators, with great success. This is the 1983 followup to the 1970s original. (Bottom right) Peterson worked with countless other artists through his career. *The Trio*, from the mid-1970s, finds him with frequent bandmate Joe Pass and less frequent partner Niels-Henning Orsted Pedersen (here with his name abbreviated).

Number	Title	Yr	VG	VG+	NM
❏ V-2056 [M]	Oscar Peterson Plays the Jerome Kern Songbook	1961	5.00	10.00	20.00
❏ V6-2056 [S]	Oscar Peterson Plays the Jerome Kern Songbook	1961	3.75	7.50	15.00
-- Reissue of 6087					
❏ MGV-2057 [M]	Oscar Peterson Plays the Richard Rodgers Songbook	1957	10.00	20.00	40.00
-- Reissue of Clef 624					
❏ V-2057 [M]	Oscar Peterson Plays the Richard Rodgers Songbook	1961	5.00	10.00	20.00
❏ V6-2057 [S]	Oscar Peterson Plays the Richard Rodgers Songbook	1961	3.75	7.50	15.00
-- Reissue of 6088					
❏ MGV-2058 [M]	Oscar Peterson Plays the Vincent Youmans Songbook	1957	---	---	---
-- Reissue planned but canceled					
❏ MGV-2059 [M]	Oscar Peterson Plays the Harry Warren Songbook	1957	10.00	20.00	40.00
-- Reissue of Clef 648					
❏ V-2059 [M]	Oscar Peterson Plays the Harry Warren Songbook	1961	5.00	10.00	20.00
❏ V6-2059 [S]	Oscar Peterson Plays the Harry Warren Songbook	1961	3.75	7.50	15.00
-- Reissue of 6090					
❏ MGV-2060 [M]	Oscar Peterson Plays the Harold Arlen Songbook	1957	10.00	20.00	40.00
-- Reissue of Clef 649					
❏ V-2060 [M]	Oscar Peterson Plays the Harold Arlen Songbook	1961	5.00	10.00	20.00
❏ V6-2060 [S]	Oscar Peterson Plays the Harold Arlen Songbook	1961	3.75	7.50	15.00
-- Reissue of 6091					
❏ MGV-2061 [M]	Oscar Peterson Plays the Jimmy McHugh Songbook	1957	10.00	20.00	40.00
-- Reissue of Clef 650					
❏ V-2061 [M]	Oscar Peterson Plays the Jimmy McHugh Songbook	1961	5.00	10.00	20.00
❏ V6-2061 [S]	Oscar Peterson Plays the Jimmy McHugh Songbook	1961	3.75	7.50	15.00
-- Reissue of 6092					
❏ MGV-2079 [M]	Soft Sands	1957	10.00	20.00	40.00
❏ V-2079 [M]	Soft Sands	1961	5.00	10.00	20.00
❏ MGV-2119 [M]	Oscar Peterson Plays "My Fair Lady"	1958	10.00	20.00	40.00
❏ V-2119 [M]	Oscar Peterson Plays "My Fair Lady"	1961	5.00	10.00	20.00
❏ V6-2119 [S]	Oscar Peterson Plays "My Fair Lady"	1961	3.75	7.50	15.00
-- Reissue of 6060					
❏ MGV-2156 [M]	The Oscar Peterson Trio with David Rose	1958	---	---	---
-- Canceled					
❏ UMV-2502	Oscar Peterson at the Stratford Shakespearean Festival	198?	2.50	5.00	10.00
❏ UMV-2626	Oscar Peterson at the Concertgebouw	198?	2.50	5.00	10.00
❏ MGVS-6036 [S]	A Night on the Town	1960	---	---	---
-- Canceled					
❏ MGVS-6060 [S]	Oscar Peterson Plays "My Fair Lady"	1960	7.50	15.00	30.00
❏ MGVS-6069 [S]	The Oscar Peterson Trio with the Modern Jazz Quartet at the Opera House	1960	7.50	15.00	30.00
❏ MGVS-6071 [S]	Songs for a Swingin' Affair -- A Jazz Portrait of Sinatra	1960	10.00	20.00	40.00
❏ MGVS-6083 [S]	Oscar Peterson Plays the Cole Porter Songbook	1960	7.50	15.00	30.00
❏ MGVS-6084 [S]	Oscar Peterson Plays the Irving Berlin Songbook	1960	7.50	15.00	30.00
❏ MGVS-6085 [S]	Oscar Peterson Plays the George Gershwin Songbook	1960	7.50	15.00	30.00
❏ MGVS-6086 [S]	Oscar Peterson Plays the Duke Ellington Songbook	1960	7.50	15.00	30.00
❏ MGVS-6087 [S]	Oscar Peterson Plays the Jerome Kern Songbook	1960	7.50	15.00	30.00
❏ MGVS-6088 [S]	Oscar Peterson Plays the Richard Rodgers Songbook	1960	7.50	15.00	30.00
❏ MGVS-6089 [S]	Oscar Peterson Plays the Vincent Youmans Songbook	1960	---	---	---
-- Canceled					
❏ MGVS-6090 [S]	Oscar Peterson Plays the Harry Warren Songbook	1960	7.50	15.00	30.00
❏ MGVS-6091 [S]	Oscar Peterson Plays the Harold Arlen Songbook	1960	7.50	15.00	30.00
❏ MGVS-6092 [S]	Oscar Peterson Plays the Jimmy McHugh Songbook	1960	7.50	15.00	30.00
❏ MGVS-6098 [S]	Porgy and Bess	1960	---	---	---
-- Canceled					
❏ MGVS-6116 [S]	The Jazz Soul of Oscar Peterson	1960	---	---	---
-- Canceled					
❏ MGVS-6119 [S]	Swinging Brass with the Oscar Peterson Trio	1960	7.50	15.00	30.00
❏ MGVS-6134 [S]	The Music from "Fiorello!"	1960	---	---	---
-- Canceled					
❏ MGV-8024 [M]	The Oscar Peterson Trio at the Stratford Shakespearean Festival	1957	10.00	20.00	40.00
❏ V-8024 [M]	The Oscar Peterson Trio at the Stratford Shakespearean Festival	1961	5.00	10.00	20.00
❏ MGV-8072 [M]	The Oscar Peterson Quartet No. 1	1957	10.00	20.00	40.00
❏ V-8072 [M]	The Oscar Peterson Quartet No. 1	1961	5.00	10.00	20.00
❏ MGV-8078 [M]	Recital by Oscar Peterson	1957	---	---	---
-- Canceled					
❏ MGV-8079 [M]	Nostalgic Memories by Oscar Peterson	1957	---	---	---
-- Canceled					
❏ MGV-8080 [M]	Tenderly -- Music by Oscar Peterson	1957	---	---	---
-- Canceled					
❏ MGV-8081 [M]	Keyboard Music by Oscar Peterson	1957	---	---	---
-- Canceled					
❏ MGV-8082 [M]	An Evening with Oscar Peterson	1957	---	---	---
-- Canceled					
❏ MGV-8092 [M]	Oscar Peterson Plays Count Basie	1957	10.00	20.00	40.00
-- Reissue of Clef 708					
❏ V-8092 [M]	Oscar Peterson Plays Count Basie	1961	5.00	10.00	20.00
❏ MGV-8239 [M]	The Oscar Peterson Trio with Sonny Stitt, Roy Eldredge and Jo Jones at Newport	1958	10.00	20.00	40.00
❏ V-8239 [M]	The Oscar Peterson Trio with Sonny Stitt, Roy Eldredge and Jo Jones at Newport	1961	5.00	10.00	20.00
❏ MGV-8268 [M]	The Oscar Peterson Trio at the Concertgebouw	1958	10.00	20.00	40.00
❏ V-8268 [M]	The Oscar Peterson Trio at the Concertgebouw	1961	5.00	10.00	20.00
❏ MGV-8269 [M]	The Oscar Peterson Trio with the Modern Jazz Quartet at the Opera House	1958	10.00	20.00	40.00
❏ V-8269 [M]	The Oscar Peterson Trio with the Modern Jazz Quartet at the Opera House	1961	5.00	10.00	20.00
❏ V6-8269 [S]	The Oscar Peterson Trio with the Modern Jazz Quartet at the Opera House	1961	3.75	7.50	15.00
-- Reissue of 6069					
❏ MGV-8287 [M]	A Night on the Town	1958	10.00	20.00	40.00
❏ V-8287 [M]	A Night on the Town	1961	5.00	10.00	20.00
❏ MGV-8334 [M]	Songs for a Swingin' Affair -- A Jazz Portrait of Sinatra	1959	12.50	25.00	50.00
❏ V-8334 [M]	Songs for a Swingin' Affair -- A Jazz Portrait of Sinatra	1961	5.00	10.00	20.00
❏ V6-8334 [S]	Songs for a Swingin' Affair -- A Jazz Portrait of Sinatra	1961	3.75	7.50	15.00
-- Reissue of 6071					
❏ MGV-8340 [M]	Porgy and Bess	1959	10.00	20.00	40.00
❏ V-8340 [M]	Porgy and Bess	1961	5.00	10.00	20.00
❏ V6-8340 [S]	Porgy and Bess	1961	3.75	7.50	15.00
❏ MGV-8351 [M]	The Jazz Soul of Oscar Peterson	1959	10.00	20.00	40.00
❏ V-8351 [M]	The Jazz Soul of Oscar Peterson	1961	5.00	10.00	20.00
❏ MGV-8364 [M]	Swinging Brass with the Oscar Peterson Trio	1959	10.00	20.00	40.00
❏ V-8364 [M]	Swinging Brass with the Oscar Peterson Trio	1961	5.00	10.00	20.00
❏ V6-8364 [S]	Swinging Brass with the Oscar Peterson Trio	1961	3.75	7.50	15.00
-- Reissue of 6119					
❏ MGV-8366 [M]	The Music from "Fiorello!"	1960	10.00	20.00	40.00
❏ V-8366 [M]	The Music from "Fiorello!"	1961	5.00	10.00	20.00
❏ MGV-8368 [M]	The Oscar Peterson Trio at J.A.T.P.	1960	10.00	20.00	40.00
❏ V-8368 [M]	The Oscar Peterson Trio at J.A.T.P.	1961	5.00	10.00	20.00
❏ MGV-8399 [M]	Carnival	1960	---	---	---
-- Canceled					
❏ V-8420 [M]	The Trio -- Live from Chicago	1961	6.25	12.50	25.00
❏ V6-8420 [S]	The Trio -- Live from Chicago	1961	7.50	15.00	30.00
❏ V-8429 [M]	Very Tall	1962	6.25	12.50	25.00
❏ V6-8429 [S]	Very Tall	1962	7.50	15.00	30.00
❏ V-8454 [M]	West Side Story	1962	6.25	12.50	25.00
❏ V6-8454 [S]	West Side Story	1962	7.50	15.00	30.00
❏ V-8476 [M]	Bursting Out with the All Star Big Band!	1962	6.25	12.50	25.00
❏ V6-8476 [S]	Bursting Out with the All Star Big Band!	1962	7.50	15.00	30.00
❏ V-8480 [M]	The Sound of the Trio	1962	6.25	12.50	25.00
❏ V6-8480 [S]	The Sound of the Trio	1962	7.50	15.00	30.00
❏ V-8482 [M]	The Modern Jazz Quartet and the Oscar Peterson Trio at the Opera House	1962	5.00	10.00	20.00
-- Reissue of 8269					

Number	Title	Yr	VG	VG+	NM
❑ V6-8482 [S]	The Modern Jazz Quartet and the Oscar Peterson Trio at the Opera House	1962	5.00	10.00	20.00
-- Reissue of 8269					
❑ V-8516 [M]	Affinity	1963	6.25	12.50	25.00
❑ V6-8516 [S]	Affinity	1963	7.50	15.00	30.00
❑ V-8538 [M]	Night Train	1963	6.25	12.50	25.00
❑ V6-8538 [S]	Night Train	1963	7.50	15.00	30.00
❑ V-8562 [M]	The Oscar Peterson Trio with Nelson Riddle	1963	6.25	12.50	25.00
❑ V6-8562 [S]	The Oscar Peterson Trio with Nelson Riddle	1963	7.50	15.00	30.00
❑ V-8581 [M]	Oscar Peterson Plays "My Fair Lady"	1964	3.75	7.50	15.00
❑ V6-8581 [S]	Oscar Peterson Plays "My Fair Lady"	1964	5.00	10.00	20.00
❑ V-8591 [M]	The Oscar Peterson Trio Plays	1964	3.75	7.50	15.00
❑ V6-8591 [S]	The Oscar Peterson Trio Plays	1964	5.00	10.00	20.00
❑ V-8606 [M]	We Get Requests	1965	3.75	7.50	15.00
❑ V6-8606 [S]	We Get Requests	1965	5.00	10.00	20.00
❑ V-8660 [M]	Put On a Happy Face	1966	3.75	7.50	15.00
❑ V6-8660 [S]	Put On a Happy Face	1966	5.00	10.00	20.00
❑ V-8681 [M]	Something Warm	1966	3.75	7.50	15.00
❑ V6-8681 [S]	Something Warm	1966	5.00	10.00	20.00
❑ V-8700 [M]	Thoroughly Modern '20s	1967	3.75	7.50	15.00
❑ V6-8700 [S]	Thoroughly Modern '20s	1967	3.75	7.50	15.00
❑ V-8740 [M]	Night Train, Volume 2	1967	5.00	10.00	20.00
❑ V6-8740 [S]	Night Train, Volume 2	1967	3.75	7.50	15.00
❑ V6-8775	Oscars -- Oscar Peterson Plays the Academy Awards	1969	3.75	7.50	15.00
❑ V6-8810 [(2)]	The Oscar Peterson Collection	1972	3.75	7.50	15.00
❑ V3G-8828	The Newport Years	1974	3.00	6.00	12.00
❑ V3HB-8842 [(2)]	Return Engagement	1975	3.75	7.50	15.00
❑ 810 047-1	We Get Requests	1986	2.50	5.00	10.00
❑ 821 289-1	Motions and Emotions	1984	2.50	5.00	10.00
-- Reissue					
❑ 821 663-1	Travelin' On	1985	2.50	5.00	10.00
❑ 821 849-1	Tracks	1985	2.50	5.00	10.00
❑ 821 987-1	Oscar Peterson Plays the Cole Porter Songbook	1986	2.50	5.00	10.00
-- Reissue of 2053					
❑ 823 249-1	Oscar Peterson Plays the George Gershwin Songbook	1985	2.50	5.00	10.00
-- Reissue of 2054					
❑ 825 099-1	The Oscar Peterson Trio Set	1985	2.50	5.00	10.00
❑ 825 769-1	Songs for a Swingin' Affair -- A Jazz Portrait of Sinatra	1985	2.50	5.00	10.00
-- Reissue of 8334					
❑ 825 865-1	Oscar Peterson Plays the Jerome Kern Songbook	1985	2.50	5.00	10.00
-- Reissue of 2056					
WING					
❑ SRW 16351	Canadiana Suite	1969	3.00	6.00	12.00

PETERSON, OSCAR, AND STEPHANE GRAPPELLI
Also see each artist's individual listings.

Number	Title	Yr	VG	VG+	NM
JAZZ MAN					
❑ 5054	Time After Time	1983	3.00	6.00	12.00
PABLO					
❑ 2310-907	Violins No End	198?	3.00	6.00	12.00
-- With Stuff Smith					
PRESTIGE					
❑ 24041 [(2)]	Oscar Peterson Featuring Stephane Grappelli	1974	3.75	7.50	15.00

PETERSON, OSCAR, AND MILT JACKSON
Also see each artist's individual listings.

Number	Title	Yr	VG	VG+	NM
PABLO					
❑ 2310-881	Two of the Few	1983	3.00	6.00	12.00

PETERSON, OSCAR/GERRY MULLIGAN
Also see each artist's individual listings.

Number	Title	Yr	VG	VG+	NM
VERVE					
❑ V-8559 [M]	The Oscar Peterson Trio and the Gerry Mulligan Four at Newport	1963	6.25	12.50	25.00
❑ V6-8559 [S]	The Oscar Peterson Trio and the Gerry Mulligan Four at Newport	1963	7.50	15.00	30.00

PETERSON, PAT
Male singer.

Number	Title	Yr	VG	VG+	NM
ENJA					
❑ 4020	Introducing Pat Peterson	1982	3.00	6.00	12.00

PETERSON, PETE
Bass player and bandleader.

Number	Title	Yr	VG	VG+	NM
PAUSA					
❑ 7143	Texas State of Mind	1982	2.50	5.00	10.00

Number	Title	Yr	VG	VG+	NM
❑ 7163	Jazz Journey	1984	2.50	5.00	10.00
❑ 7191	Playin' in the Park	1986	2.50	5.00	10.00

PETERSON, RALPH
Drummer.

Number	Title	Yr	VG	VG+	NM
BLUE NOTE					
❑ B1-91730	V	1989	3.00	6.00	12.00
❑ B1-92750	Tri-Angular	1989	3.00	6.00	12.00

PETERSTEIN, SHORTY

Number	Title	Yr	VG	VG+	NM
WORLD PACIFIC					
❑ WP-1274 [M]	The Wide Weird World of Shorty Petterstein	1959	10.00	20.00	40.00

PETRUCCIANI, MICHEL
Pianist and composer.

Number	Title	Yr	VG	VG+	NM
BLUE NOTE					
❑ B1-48679	Michel Plays Petrucciani	1988	2.50	5.00	10.00
❑ BT-85124	Pianism	1987	2.50	5.00	10.00
❑ BT-85133	Power of Three	1987	2.50	5.00	10.00
❑ B1-92563	Music	1989	3.00	6.00	12.00
GEORGE WEIN COLLECTION					
❑ GW-3001	100 Hearts	1984	3.00	6.00	12.00
❑ GW-3006	Live at the Village Vanguard	1985	3.00	6.00	12.00

PETTIFORD, OSCAR
Bass player and cellist. Also see SERGE CHALOFF; THE FOUR MOST; LES JAZZ MODES; THE MANHATTAN JAZZ SEPTETTE; LUCKY THOMPSON.

Number	Title	Yr	VG	VG+	NM
ABC-PARAMOUNT					
❑ ABC-135 [M]	Oscar Pettiford Orchestra in Hi-Fi	1956	25.00	50.00	100.00
❑ ABC-227 [M]	O.P.'s Jazz Men: Oscar Pettiford Orchestra in Hi-Fi, Vol. 2	1958	20.00	40.00	80.00
❑ ABCS-227 [S]	O.P.'s Jazz Men: Oscar Pettiford Orchestra in Hi-Fi, Vol. 2	1958	15.00	30.00	60.00
ATLANTIC					
❑ 8111 [M]	Live at Jilly's	1965	5.00	10.00	20.00
❑ SD 8111 [S]	Live at Jilly's	1965	6.25	12.50	25.00
BETHLEHEM					
❑ BCP-33 [M]	Oscar Pettiford Sextet	1955	25.00	50.00	100.00
❑ BCP-1003 [10]	Oscar Pettiford	1954	37.50	75.00	150.00
❑ BCP-1019 [10]	Basically Duke	1955	37.50	75.00	150.00
❑ BCP-6007	The Finest of Oscar Pettiford	197?	3.00	6.00	12.00
-- Reissue, distributed by RCA Victor					
DEBUT					
❑ DLP-8 [10]	Oscar Pettiford Sextet	1954	75.00	150.00	300.00
FANTASY					
❑ OJC-112	The New Sextet	198?	2.50	5.00	10.00
❑ 6010 [M]	My Little Cello	1964	7.50	15.00	30.00
❑ 6015 [M]	The Essen Jazz Festival	1964	7.50	15.00	30.00
❑ 86010 [R]	My Little Cello	1964	3.75	7.50	15.00
❑ 86015 [R]	The Essen Jazz Festival	1964	3.75	7.50	15.00
JAZZ MAN					
❑ 5036	Blue Brothers	198?	2.50	5.00	10.00
JAZZLAND					
❑ JLP-64 [M]	Last Recordings by the Late, Great Bassist	1962	12.50	25.00	50.00
❑ JLP-964 [R]	Last Recordings by the Late, Great Bassist	1962	7.50	15.00	30.00
PRESTIGE					
❑ PRST-7813	Memorial Album	1971	3.75	7.50	15.00
SAVOY JAZZ					
❑ SJL-1172	Discoveries	1986	2.50	5.00	10.00

PETTIFORD, OSCAR/VINNIE BURKE
Also see each artist's individual listings.

Number	Title	Yr	VG	VG+	NM
BETHLEHEM					
❑ BCP-6 [M]	Bass by Pettiford/Burke	1957	25.00	50.00	100.00

PETTIFORD, OSCAR/RED MITCHELL
Also see each artist's individual listings.

Number	Title	Yr	VG	VG+	NM
BETHLEHEM					
❑ BCP-2 [M]	Jazz Mainstream	1957	25.00	50.00	100.00

PHILLIPS, BARRE
Bass player.

Number	Title	Yr	VG	VG+	NM
ECM					
❑ 1011	Music for Two Basses	197?	3.75	7.50	15.00
❑ 1076	Mountainscapes	1976	3.00	6.00	12.00
❑ 1149	Journal Violone II	198?	3.00	6.00	12.00

Number	Title	Yr	VG	VG+	NM
❑ 1257	Call Me When You Get There	198?	3.00	6.00	12.00

OPUS ONE

Number	Title	Yr	VG	VG+	NM
❑ 2	Journal Violone	197?	3.75	7.50	15.00

PHILLIPS, ESTHER
Female singer. Best known for her work in R&B and soul, the below albums came out on jazz labels or numbering series.
ATLANTIC

Number	Title	Yr	VG	VG+	NM
❑ SD 1565	Burnin'	1970	6.25	12.50	25.00
❑ SD 1680	Confessin' the Blues	1975	3.75	7.50	15.00
❑ 90670	Confessin' the Blues	1987	2.50	5.00	10.00

-- Reissue of 1680
MUSE

Number	Title	Yr	VG	VG+	NM
❑ MR-5302	A Way to Say Goodbye	1986	3.00	6.00	12.00

SAVOY JAZZ

Number	Title	Yr	VG	VG+	NM
❑ SJL-2258	The Complete Savoy Recordings	1984	2.50	5.00	10.00

PHILLIPS, FLIP
Tenor saxophone player and clarinetist.
BRUNSWICK

Number	Title	Yr	VG	VG+	NM
❑ BL 58032 [10]	Tenor Sax Stylings	1953	37.50	75.00	150.00

CHOICE

Number	Title	Yr	VG	VG+	NM
❑ 1013	Phillips' Head	197?	3.00	6.00	12.00

CLEF

Number	Title	Yr	VG	VG+	NM
❑ MGC-105 [10]	Flip Phillips Quartet	1953	37.50	75.00	150.00
❑ MGC-109 [10]	Flip Phillips Collates	1953	37.50	75.00	150.00
❑ MGC-133 [10]	Flip Phillips Collates No. 2	1953	50.00	100.00	200.00
❑ MGC-158 [10]	Jumping Moods with Flip Phillips	1954	37.50	75.00	150.00
❑ MGC-634 [M]	The Flip Phillips-Buddy Rich Trio	1954	30.00	60.00	120.00
❑ MGC-637 [M]	The Flip Phillips Quintet	1954	30.00	60.00	120.00
❑ MGC-691 [M]	Flip Wails	1956	25.00	50.00	100.00
❑ MGC-692 [M]	Swinging with Flip Phillips and His Orchestra	1956	25.00	50.00	100.00
❑ MGC-693 [M]	Flip	1956	25.00	50.00	100.00
❑ MGC-740 [M]	Rock with Flip	1956	25.00	50.00	100.00

CONCORD JAZZ

Number	Title	Yr	VG	VG+	NM
❑ CJ-334	A Sound Investment	1988	2.50	5.00	10.00
❑ CJ-358	A Real Swinger	1988	2.50	5.00	10.00

DOCTOR JAZZ

Number	Title	Yr	VG	VG+	NM
❑ FW 39419	A Melody from the Sky	198?	2.50	5.00	10.00

MERCURY

Number	Title	Yr	VG	VG+	NM
❑ MGC-105 [10]	Flip Phillips Quartet	1951	62.50	125.00	250.00
❑ MGC-109 [10]	Flip Phillips Collates	1952	50.00	100.00	200.00
❑ MGC-133 [10]	Flip Phillips Collates No. 2	1953	---	---	---

-- Canceled; issued on Clef

Number	Title	Yr	VG	VG+	NM
❑ MG-25023 [10]	Flip Phillips Quartet	1950	75.00	150.00	300.00

ONYX

Number	Title	Yr	VG	VG+	NM
❑ 214	Flip Phillips in Florida	197?	3.00	6.00	12.00

PROGRESSIVE

Number	Title	Yr	VG	VG+	NM
❑ PRO-7063	Flipenstein	198?	2.50	5.00	10.00

SUE

Number	Title	Yr	VG	VG+	NM
❑ LP-1035 [M]	Flip Phillips Revisited	1965	7.50	15.00	30.00
❑ STLP-1035 [S]	Flip Phillips Revisited	1965	10.00	20.00	40.00

VERVE

Number	Title	Yr	VG	VG+	NM
❑ MGV-8075 [M]	Flip Wails	1957	20.00	40.00	80.00
❑ V-8075 [M]	Flip Wails	1961	6.25	12.50	25.00
❑ MGV-8076 [M]	Swingin' with Flip	1957	20.00	40.00	80.00
❑ V-8076 [M]	Swingin' with Flip	1961	6.25	12.50	25.00
❑ MGV-8077 [M]	Flip	1957	20.00	40.00	80.00
❑ V-8077 [M]	Flip	1961	6.25	12.50	25.00
❑ MGV-8116 [M]	Rock with Flip	1957	20.00	40.00	80.00
❑ V-8116 [M]	Rock with Flip	1961	6.25	12.50	25.00

PHILLIPS, FLIP, AND WOODY HERMAN
Also see each artist's individual listings.
CENTURY

Number	Title	Yr	VG	VG+	NM
❑ 1090	Together	1978	3.75	7.50	15.00

PHILLIPS, SONNY
Organist and pianist.
MUSE

Number	Title	Yr	VG	VG+	NM
❑ MR-5118	My Black Flower	1977	3.00	6.00	12.00
❑ MR-5157l	Concentrate on You	1979	3.00	6.00	12.00

PRESTIGE

Number	Title	Yr	VG	VG+	NM
❑ PRST-7737	Sure 'Nuff	1970	5.00	10.00	20.00
❑ PRST-7799	Black Magic	1970	5.00	10.00	20.00
❑ 10007	Black on Black	1971	5.00	10.00	20.00

PHILLIPS, WOOLF
British bandleader and arranger.
CORAL

Number	Title	Yr	VG	VG+	NM
❑ CRL 56036 [10]	Woolf Phillips Plays Duke Ellington Songs	1951	12.50	25.00	50.00

PHOENIX SYMPHONY RAGTIME ENSEMBLE
WORLD JAZZ

Number	Title	Yr	VG	VG+	NM
❑ 12	Phoenix Symphony Ragtime Ensemble	197?	2.50	5.00	10.00

PIANO CHOIR, THE
Created by STANLEY COWELL, it also featured HAROLD MABERN.
STRATA-EAST

Number	Title	Yr	VG	VG+	NM
❑ SES-19730 [(2)]	Handscapes	1973	6.25	12.50	25.00
❑ SES-19750	Handscapes 2	1975	5.00	10.00	20.00

PIANO RED
Real name: William Perryman. Pianist. Also recorded as "Dr. Feelgood."
ARHOOLIE

Number	Title	Yr	VG	VG+	NM
❑ 1064	William Perryman (Alone with Piano)	197?	3.00	6.00	12.00

EUPHONIC

Number	Title	Yr	VG	VG+	NM
❑ 1212	Percussive Piano	198?	2.50	5.00	10.00

GROOVE

Number	Title	Yr	VG	VG+	NM
❑ LG-1001 [M]	Jump Man, Jump	1956	---	---	---

-- The existence of this LP has not been confirmed

Number	Title	Yr	VG	VG+	NM
❑ LG-1002 [M]	Piano Red in Concert	1956	150.00	300.00	600.00

KING

Number	Title	Yr	VG	VG+	NM
❑ KS-1117	Happiness Is Piano Red	1970	5.00	10.00	20.00

RCA CAMDEN

Number	Title	Yr	VG	VG+	NM
❑ ACL1-0547	Rockin' with Red	1974	3.00	6.00	12.00

SOUTHLAND

Number	Title	Yr	VG	VG+	NM
❑ 8	Willie Perryman-Piano Red-Dr. Feelgood	1983	3.75	7.50	15.00

PIECES OF A DREAM
Members: James Lloyd (keyboards); Cedric Napoleon (bass, vocals); Curtis Harmon (drums).
ELEKTRA

Number	Title	Yr	VG	VG+	NM
❑ 6E-350	Pieces of a Dream	1981	2.50	5.00	10.00
❑ 60142	We Are One	1982	2.50	5.00	10.00
❑ 60270	Imagine This	1984	2.50	5.00	10.00

MANHATTAN

Number	Title	Yr	VG	VG+	NM
❑ ST-53023	Joyride	1986	2.50	5.00	10.00

PIERANUNZI, ENRICO
Pianist and occasional male singer.
SOUL NOTE

Number	Title	Yr	VG	VG+	NM
❑ 121221	No Man's Land	1990	3.75	7.50	15.00

PIERANUNZI, ENRICO, AND ART FARMER
Also see each artist's individual listings.
SOUL NOTE

Number	Title	Yr	VG	VG+	NM
❑ SN-1021	Isis	198?	3.00	6.00	12.00

PIERCE, BILLIE AND DEDE
Billie Pierce is a female singer and pianist. Also see DEDE PIERCE.
ARHOOLIE

Number	Title	Yr	VG	VG+	NM
❑ 2016	New Orleans Music	197?	2.50	5.00	10.00

BIOGRAPH

Number	Title	Yr	VG	VG+	NM
❑ CEN-15	Billie and Dede Pierce at Luthjen's	197?	2.50	5.00	10.00

JAZZOLOGY

Number	Title	Yr	VG	VG+	NM
❑ JCE-25	New Orleans Legends Live, Vol. 15	196?	3.75	7.50	15.00

RIVERSIDE

Number	Title	Yr	VG	VG+	NM
❑ RLP-370 [M]	Blues in the Classic Tradition	1961	7.50	15.00	30.00
❑ RLP-394 [M]	Blues and Tonks From the Delta	1961	7.50	15.00	30.00
❑ RS-9370 [R]	Blues in the Classic Tradition	1961	3.75	7.50	15.00
❑ RS-9394 [R]	Blues and Tonks From the Delta	1961	3.75	7.50	15.00

PIERCE, BILLY
Tenor and soprano saxophone player.
SUNNYSIDE

Number	Title	Yr	VG	VG+	NM
❑ SSC-1013	William the Conqueror	1986	2.50	5.00	10.00
❑ SSC-1026	Give and Take	1988	2.50	5.00	10.00

Number	Title	Yr	VG	VG+	NM

PIERCE, BOBBY
Keyboard player and male singer.
COBBLESTONE
| 9016 | Introducing Bobby Pierce | 197? | 3.75 | 7.50 | 15.00 |
MUSE
| MR-5030 | New York | 1974 | 3.00 | 6.00 | 12.00 |
| MR-5304 | Piercing | 198? | 2.50 | 5.00 | 10.00 |

PIERCE, DEDE
Trumpeter and male singer. Also see BILLIE AND DEDE PIERCE.
BIOGRAPH
| CEN-5 | Dede Pierce and the New Orleans Stompers | 197? | 2.50 | 5.00 | 10.00 |

PIERCE, NAT
Pianist and composer. Also see THE CAPP-PIERCE JUGGERNAUT.
CORAL
| CRL 57091 [M] | Kansas City Memories | 1957 | 12.50 | 25.00 | 50.00 |
| CRL 57128 [M] | Chamber Music for Moderns | 1957 | 10.00 | 20.00 | 40.00 |
FANTASY
| 3-14 [10] | Nat Pierce and the Herdsmen Featuring Dick Collins | 1954 | 20.00 | 40.00 | 80.00 |
KEYNOTE
| LP-1101 [M] | Nat Pierce Octet and Tentette | 1955 | 20.00 | 40.00 | 80.00 |
RCA VICTOR
| LPM-2543 [M] | Big Band at the Savoy Ballroom | 1962 | 6.25 | 12.50 | 25.00 |
| LSP-2543 [S] | Big Band at the Savoy Ballroom | 1962 | 7.50 | 15.00 | 30.00 |
VANGUARD
| VRS-8017 [10] | Nat Pierce Bandstand | 1955 | 20.00 | 40.00 | 80.00 |
ZIM
| 1005 | Nat Pierce and His Orchestra | 197? | 3.00 | 6.00 | 12.00 |
| 2003 | Ballad of Jazz Street | 198? | 2.50 | 5.00 | 10.00 |

PIERCE, NAT; DICK COLLINS; CHARLIE MARIANO
Also see each artist's individual listings.
FANTASY
| OJC-118 | Nat Pierce-Dick Collins Nonet/Charlie Mariano Sextet | 198? | 2.50 | 5.00 | 10.00 |
| 3224 [M] | Nat Pierce-Dick Collins Nonet/Charlie Mariano Sextet | 1956 | 30.00 | 60.00 | 120.00 |
-- Red vinyl
| 3224 [M] | Nat Pierce-Dick Collins Nonet/Charlie Mariano Sextet | 195? | 15.00 | 30.00 | 60.00 |
-- Black vinyl

PIERCE, NAT; MILT HINTON; BARRY GALBRAITH; OSIE JOHNSON
Also see each artist's individual listings.
MUSIC MINUS ONE
| Vol. 1 [M] | Nat Pierce and Milt Hinton and Barry Galbraith and Osie Johnson | 1956 | 7.50 | 15.00 | 30.00 |
-- With sheet music attached

PIKE, DAVE
Vibraphone player.
ATLANTIC
| 1457 [M] | Jazz for the Jet Set | 1966 | 3.75 | 7.50 | 15.00 |
| SD 1457 [S] | Jazz for the Jet Set | 1966 | 5.00 | 10.00 | 20.00 |
BASF
20739	Infra-Red	1972	3.75	7.50	15.00
21541	Salamao	1974	3.75	7.50	15.00
25112 [(2)]	Riff for Rent	1973	5.00	10.00	20.00
DECCA
| DL 4568 [M] | Manhattan Latin | 1965 | 3.75 | 7.50 | 15.00 |
| DL 74568 [S] | Manhattan Latin | 1965 | 5.00 | 10.00 | 20.00 |
EPIC
| LA 16025 [M] | Pike's Peak | 1962 | 7.50 | 15.00 | 30.00 |
| BA 17025 [S] | Pike's Peak | 1962 | 6.25 | 12.50 | 25.00 |
MOODSVILLE
| MVLP-36 [M] | Dave Pike Plays the Jazz Version of "Oliver" | 1963 | 12.50 | 25.00 | 50.00 |
-- Green label
| MVLP-36 [M] | Dave Pike Plays the Jazz Version of "Oliver" | 1965 | 6.25 | 12.50 | 25.00 |
-- Blue label, trident logo at right
MUSE
MR-5092	Times Out of Mind	197?	3.00	6.00	12.00
MR-5203	Let the Minstrels Play On	1980	2.50	5.00	10.00
MR-5261	Moon Bird	198?	2.50	5.00	10.00
NEW JAZZ
| NJLP-8281 [M] | Bossa Nova Carnival | 1962 | 12.50 | 25.00 | 50.00 |
-- Purple label
| NJLP-8281 [M] | Bossa Nova Carnival | 1965 | 6.25 | 12.50 | 25.00 |
-- Blue label, trident logo at right
| NJLP-8284 [M] | Limbo Carnival | 1962 | 12.50 | 25.00 | 50.00 |
-- Purple label
| NJLP-8284 [M] | Limbo Carnival | 1965 | 6.25 | 12.50 | 25.00 |
-- Blue label, trident logo at right
RIVERSIDE
| RLP-360 [M] | It's Time for David Pike | 1961 | 6.25 | 12.50 | 25.00 |
| RS-9360 [S] | It's Time for David Pike | 1961 | 7.50 | 15.00 | 30.00 |
TIMELESS
| LPSJP-302 | Bluebird | 1990 | 3.00 | 6.00 | 12.00 |
VORTEX
| 2007 | The Doors of Perception | 1970 | 5.00 | 10.00 | 20.00 |

PILHOFER, HERB
Pianist.
ARGO
| LP-657 [M] | Jazz | 1960 | 6.25 | 12.50 | 25.00 |
| LPS-657 [S] | Jazz | 1960 | 7.50 | 15.00 | 30.00 |
ZEPHYR
| ZP-12103-G [M] | Dick and Don Maw Present the Herb Pilhofer Octet—Jazz from the North Coast, Volume 2 | 1959 | 12.50 | 25.00 | 50.00 |

PILTZECKER, TED
Vibraphone player.
SEA BREEZE
| SB-2027 | Destinations | 1986 | 2.50 | 5.00 | 10.00 |

PINE, COURTNEY
Tenor and soprano saxophone player and flutist.
ANTILLES
(# unknown)	Journey to the Urge Within	1986	3.00	6.00	12.00
90697	Destiny's Song + The Image of Pursuance	1987	3.00	6.00	12.00
91334	The Vision's Tale	1989	3.00	6.00	12.00
510 769-1	Closer to Home	1992	5.00	10.00	20.00

PIRCHNER, WERNER; HARRY PEPL; JACK DeJOHNETTE
Pirchner plays accordion and vibes; Pepl is a guitarist. Also see JACK DeJOHNETTE.
ECM
| 1237 | Trio Recordings | 1985 | 3.00 | 6.00 | 12.00 |

PISANO, JOHNNY, AND BILLY BEAN
Pisano is a guitarist. Also see BILLY BEAN.
DECCA
DL 9206 [M]	Makin' It	1958	7.50	15.00	30.00
DL 9219 [M]	Take Your Pick	1958	7.50	15.00	30.00
DL 79206 [S]	Makin' It	1958	6.25	12.50	25.00
DL 79219 [S]	Take Your Pick	1958	6.25	12.50	25.00

PISTORIOUS, STEVE
Pianist.
JAZZOLOGY
| J-78 | Classic Piano Rags | 197? | 2.50 | 5.00 | 10.00 |

PIZZARELLI, BUCKY
Guitarist.
FLYING DUTCHMAN
| BDL1-1120 | Nightwings | 1975 | 3.00 | 6.00 | 12.00 |
MONMOUTH-EVERGREEN
7047	Green Guitar Blues	197?	3.75	7.50	15.00
7066	Bucky Pizzarelli Plays Beiderbecke, Challis, Kress	197?	3.75	7.50	15.00
7082	Bucky's Bunch	197?	3.00	6.00	12.00
7093	Bucky Pizzarelli with the Care Pierre Trio	197?	3.00	6.00	12.00
STASH
| ST-213 | Love Songs | 198? | 2.50 | 5.00 | 10.00 |
| ST-263 | Solo Flight | 1987 | 2.50 | 5.00 | 10.00 |

PIZZARELLI, BUCKY, AND VINNIE BURKE
Also see each artist's individual listings.
SAVOY
| MG-12158 [M] | Music Minus Many Men | 1960 | 7.50 | 15.00 | 30.00 |

PIZZARELLI, BUCKY, AND BUD FREEMAN
Also see each artist's individual listings.
FLYING DUTCHMAN
| BDL1-1378 | Buck & Bud | 1976 | 3.00 | 6.00 | 12.00 |

Number	Title	Yr	VG	VG+	NM
PIZZARELLI, BUCKY AND JOHN JR.					
Also see each artist's individual listings.					
STASH					
☐ ST-207	2 x 7 = Pizzarelli	1980	3.00	6.00	12.00
☐ ST-239	Swinging Sevens	198?	2.50	5.00	10.00
PIZZARELLI, JOHN JR.					
Guitarist and male singer. Also see BUCKY PIZZARELLI.					
STASH					
☐ ST-226	I'm Hip	1983	2.50	5.00	10.00
☐ ST-256	Hit That Jive, Jack!	1985	2.50	5.00	10.00
☐ ST-267	Sing! Sing! Sing!	1987	2.50	5.00	10.00
PIZZI, RAY					
Tenor and soprano saxophone player.					
DISCOVERY					
☐ 801	The Love Letter	1980	2.50	5.00	10.00
☐ 853	Espressivo	1982	2.50	5.00	10.00
PABLO					
☐ 2310 795	Conception	197?	3.00	6.00	12.00
PLANET, JANET					
Female singer.					
SEA BREEZE					
☐ SB-2026	Sweet Thunder	1986	3.00	6.00	12.00
PLAXICO, LONNIE					
Bass player.					
MUSE					
☐ MR-5389	Plaxico	1989	3.00	6.00	12.00
PLEASANT, BU					
Organist, female singer and composer.					
MUSE					
☐ MR-5033	Ms. Bu	1975	3.00	6.00	12.00
PLONSKY, JOHN					
GOLDEN CREST					
☐ GC-3014 [M]	Cool Man, Cool	1958	7.50	15.00	30.00
PLUMMER, BILL					
Bass player.					
ABC IMPULSE!					
☐ A-9164 [M]	Bill Plummer and the Cosmic Brotherhood	1968	10.00	20.00	40.00
☐ AS-9164 [S]	Bill Plummer and the Cosmic Brotherhood	1968	5.00	10.00	20.00
PODEWELL, POLLY					
Female singer.					
AUDIOPHILE					
☐ AP-136	All of Me	1980	2.50	5.00	10.00
POINDEXTER, PONY					
Alto and soprano saxophone player.					
EPIC					
☐ LA 16035 [M]	Pony's Express	1962	15.00	30.00	60.00
☐ BA 17035 [S]	Pony's Express	1962	20.00	40.00	80.00
INNER CITY					
☐ IC-1062	Poindexter	198?	3.00	6.00	12.00
NEW JAZZ					
☐ NJLP-8285 [M]	Pony Poindexter Plays the Big Ones	1962	20.00	40.00	80.00
-- Purple label					
☐ NJLP-8285 [M]	Pony Poindexter Plays the Big Ones	1965	6.25	12.50	25.00
-- Blue label, trident logo at right					
☐ NJLP-8297 [M]	Gumbo	1963	---	---	---
-- Canceled					
PRESTIGE					
☐ PRLP-16001 [M]	Gumbo	1964	10.00	20.00	40.00
POINTER, NOEL					
Violinist.					
BLUE NOTE					
☐ BN-LA736-H	Phantazia	1977	3.00	6.00	12.00
LIBERTY					
☐ LO-848	Hold On	1981	2.00	4.00	8.00
-- Reissue of United Artists 848					
☐ LT-1050	Calling	1981	2.00	4.00	8.00
-- Reissue of United Artists 1050					
☐ LT-1094	All My Reasons	1981	2.50	5.00	10.00
☐ LN-10235	Hold On	198?	2.00	4.00	8.00
-- Budget-line reissue					
☐ LN-10236	Phantazia	198?	2.00	4.00	8.00
-- Budget-line reissue					
☐ LN-10256	All My Reasons	198?	2.00	4.00	8.00
-- Budget-line reissue					
☐ LT-51123	Direct Hit	1982	2.50	5.00	10.00
UNITED ARTISTS					
☐ UA-LA848-H	Hold On	1978	2.50	5.00	10.00
☐ LT-1050	Calling	1980	2.50	5.00	10.00
POLAD, MIKE					
Mostly a pianist, he also has played banjo, guitar, clarinet and saxophone.					
JAZZOLOGY					
☐ J-77	The Cascades	197?	2.50	5.00	10.00
POLCER, ED					
Cornet player and bandleader.					
JAZZOLOGY					
☐ J-150	In the Condon Tradition	1987	2.50	5.00	10.00
POLK, LUCY ANN					
Female singer.					
INTERLUDE					
☐ MO-504 [M]	Easy Livin'	1959	12.50	25.00	50.00
☐ ST-1004 [S]	Easy Livin'	1959	10.00	20.00	40.00
MODE					
☐ LP-115 [M]	Lucky Lucy Ann	1957	37.50	75.00	150.00
TREND					
☐ TL-1008 [10]	Lucy Ann Polk with Dave Pell	1954	25.00	50.00	100.00
POLL WINNERS, THE					
Members: RAY BROWN; BARNEY KESSEL; SHELLY MANNE.					
CONTEMPORARY					
☐ C-3535 [M]	The Poll Winners	1957	12.50	25.00	50.00
☐ C-3556 [M]	The Poll Winners Ride Again	1958	12.50	25.00	50.00
☐ M-3576 [M]	Poll Winners Three	1960	10.00	20.00	40.00
☐ M-3581 [M]	Exploring the Scene	1960	10.00	20.00	40.00
☐ S-7535 [S]	The Poll Winners	1959	10.00	20.00	40.00
☐ S-7556 [S]	The Poll Winners Ride Again	1959	10.00	20.00	40.00
☐ S-7576 [S]	Poll Winners Three	1960	7.50	15.00	30.00
☐ S-7581 [S]	Exploring the Scene	1960	7.50	15.00	30.00
STEREO RECORDS					
☐ S-7010 [S]	The Poll Winners	1958	12.50	25.00	50.00
☐ S-7029 [S]	The Poll Winners Ride Again	1958	12.50	25.00	50.00
POLLACK, BEN					
Drummer and bandleader.					
BRUNSWICK					
☐ BL 58025 [10]	Ben Pollack	1951	15.00	30.00	60.00
SAVOY					
☐ MG-12090 [M]	Pick a Rib Boys	1956	12.50	25.00	50.00
☐ MG-12207 [M]	Dixieland Strut	196?	5.00	10.00	20.00
"X"					
☐ LX-3003 [10]	Ben Pollack and His Orchestra Featuring Benny Goodman	1954	15.00	30.00	60.00
POLLARD, TERRY					
Vibraphone player.					
BETHLEHEM					
☐ BCP-1015 [10]	Terry Pollard	1954	25.00	50.00	100.00
POLLARD, TERRY/BOBBY SCOTT					
Also see each artist's individual listings.					
BETHLEHEM					
☐ BCP-1 [M]	Young Moderns	1957	12.50	25.00	50.00
POMEROY, HERB					
Trumpeter, fluegel horn player and bandleader.					
ROULETTE					
☐ R-52001 [M]	Life Is A Many Splendored Gig	1958	20.00	40.00	80.00
☐ SR-52001 [S]	Life Is A Many Splendored Gig	1958	15.00	30.00	60.00
SHIAH					
☐ HP-1	Pramlatta's Hips	198?	3.75	7.50	15.00
TRANSITION					
☐ TRLP-1 [M]	Jazz in a Stable	1956	50.00	100.00	200.00
-- Deduct 25 percent if booklet is missing					

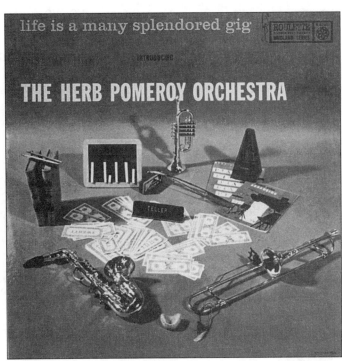

(Top left) Nat Pierce, a pianist firmly rooted in big-band styles, later would form the Capp-Pierce Juggernaut, a big band with drummer Frank Capp. Here's an earlier example of his small-group work. (Top right) Herb Pomeroy, a trumpeter and bandleader, had the first album issued on Roulette Records' "Birdland Series" jazz numbering system with R 52001, *Life Is a Many Splendored Gig*. (Bottom left) The most popular jazz violinist today, Jean-Luc Ponty, at different times worked with such disparate artists as Frank Zappa and Elton John. One of his many albums is this 1987 release on Columbia. (Bottom right) This Roulette album cover from 1965 is a bit misleading. The recordings within were his first new ones since 1958 – in the United States, anyway. As many other jazz musicians before and since, he spent some time in Europe in the interim.

Number	Title	Yr	VG	VG+	NM
UNITED ARTISTS					
❏ UAL-4015 [M]	Band in Boston	1959	20.00	40.00	80.00
❏ UAS-5015 [S]	Band in Boston	1959	15.00	30.00	60.00

PONDER, JIMMY
Guitarist.

Number	Title	Yr	VG	VG+	NM
ABC IMPULSE!					
❏ IA-9313	Illusions	197?	3.00	6.00	12.00
❏ IA-9327	White Room	197?	3.00	6.00	12.00
CADET					
❏ CA-50048	While My Guitar Gently Weeps	1974	3.00	6.00	12.00
MILESTONE					
❏ M-9121	Down Here on the Ground	1984	2.50	5.00	10.00
❏ M-9132	So Many Stars	1985	2.50	5.00	10.00
MUSE					
❏ MR-5324	Mean Streets, No Bridges	1987	2.50	5.00	10.00
❏ MR-5347	Jump	1988	2.50	5.00	10.00

PONTY, JEAN-LUC
Violinist and composer.

Number	Title	Yr	VG	VG+	NM
ATLANTIC					
❏ SD 16020	Civilized Evil	1980	2.50	5.00	10.00
❏ SD 18138	Upon the Wings of Music	1975	2.50	5.00	10.00
❏ SD 18163	Aurora	1976	2.50	5.00	10.00
❏ SD 18195	Imaginary Voyage	1976	2.50	5.00	10.00
❏ SD 19110	Enigmatic Ocean	1977	2.50	5.00	10.00
❏ SD 19136	Imaginary Voyage	1978	2.00	4.00	8.00
-- Reissue of 18195					
❏ SD 19158	Aurora	1978	2.00	4.00	8.00
-- Reissue of 18163					
❏ SD 19189	Cosmic Messenger	1978	2.50	5.00	10.00
❏ SD 19229	Jean-Luc Ponty: Live	1979	2.50	5.00	10.00
❏ SD 19253	A Taste for Passion	1979	2.50	5.00	10.00
❏ SD 19333	Mystical Adventures	1982	2.50	5.00	10.00
❏ 80098	Individual Choice	1983	2.00	4.00	8.00
❏ 80185	Open Mind	1984	2.00	4.00	8.00
❏ 81276	Fables	1985	2.00	4.00	8.00
BASF					
❏ 20645	Sunday Walk	1972	3.00	6.00	12.00
❏ 21288	Open Strings	1973	3.00	6.00	12.00
BLUE NOTE					
❏ BN-LA632-H2 [(2)]	Cantaloupe Island	1976	3.75	7.50	15.00
❏ LWB-632 [(2)]	Cantaloupe Island	1981	3.00	6.00	12.00
-- Reissue of BN-LA632-H2					
❏ LN-1102	Live at Donte's	1981	2.50	5.00	10.00
COLUMBIA					
❏ FC 40983	The Gift of Time	1987	2.00	4.00	8.00
❏ FC 45252	Storytelling	1989	3.00	6.00	12.00
DIRECT DISC					
❏ SD-16603	Cosmic Messenger	1980	7.50	15.00	30.00
-- Audiophile vinyl					
INNER CITY					
❏ 1003	Live at Montreux	197?	2.50	5.00	10.00
❏ 1005	Jean-Luc Ponty and Stephane Grappelli	197?	2.50	5.00	10.00
PACIFIC JAZZ					
❏ ST-20156	Electric Connection	1969	3.75	7.50	15.00
❏ ST-20168	The Jean-Luc Ponty Experience	1969	3.75	7.50	15.00
❏ ST-20172	King Kong -- Jean-Luc Ponty Plays the Music of Frank Zappa	1970	6.25	12.50	25.00
PAUSA					
❏ 7014	Jean-Luc Ponty Meets Giorgio Gaslini	1979	2.50	5.00	10.00
❏ 7033	Sunday Walk	1980	2.50	5.00	10.00
-- Reissue of BASF 20645					
❏ 7065	Open Strings	1980	2.50	5.00	10.00
-- Reissue of BASF 21288					
❏ 9001	The Jean-Luc Ponty Experience	1982	2.50	5.00	10.00
PRESTIGE					
❏ PRST-7676	Critic's Choice	1969	3.75	7.50	15.00
WORLD PACIFIC					
❏ ST-20134	More Than Meets the Ear	1969	3.75	7.50	15.00

POOLE, BILLIE
Female singer.

Number	Title	Yr	VG	VG+	NM
RIVERSIDE					
❏ RLP-425 [M]	Sermonette	1962	7.50	15.00	30.00
❏ RLP-458 [M]	Confessin' the Blues	1963	7.50	15.00	30.00
❏ RS-9425 [S]	Sermonette	1962	10.00	20.00	40.00
❏ RS-9458 [S]	Confessin' the Blues	1963	10.00	20.00	40.00

POPKIN, LENNY
Tenor saxophone player.

Number	Title	Yr	VG	VG+	NM
CHOICE					
❏ 1027	Falling Free	198?	2.50	5.00	10.00

PORT OF HARLEM JAZZMEN, THE
This all-star group recorded some of the first jazz on Blue Note Records.

Number	Title	Yr	VG	VG+	NM
MOSAIC					
❏ M-108	The Complete Recordings of the Port of Harlem Jazzmen	198?	5.00	10.00	20.00

PORTAL, MICHEL
Reeds player, often clarinet and bass clarinet.

Number	Title	Yr	VG	VG+	NM
HARMONIA MUNDI					
❏ HM-5186	Turbulence	1987	3.00	6.00	12.00

POTENZA, FRANK
Guitarist.

Number	Title	Yr	VG	VG+	NM
PALO ALTO/TBA					
❏ TB-206	Sand Dance	198?	2.50	5.00	10.00
❏ TB-222	Soft and Warm	1987	2.50	5.00	10.00

POTTER, TOMMY
Bass player.

Number	Title	Yr	VG	VG+	NM
EASTWEST					
❏ 4001 [M]	Tommy Potter's Hard Funk	1958	12.50	25.00	50.00

POTTS, BILL
Pianist, arranger and composer.

Number	Title	Yr	VG	VG+	NM
COLPIX					
❏ CP-451 [M]	Bye Bye Birdie	1963	7.50	15.00	30.00
❏ SCP-451 [S]	Bye Bye Birdie	1963	10.00	20.00	40.00
UNITED ARTISTS					
❏ UAL-403 [M]	The Jazz Soul of Porgy and Bess	1959	7.50	15.00	30.00
❏ UAS-5032 [S]	The Jazz Soul of Porgy and Bess	1959	10.00	20.00	40.00

POWELL, BADEN
Guitarist.

Number	Title	Yr	VG	VG+	NM
BASF					
❏ 25155 [(2)]	Canto on Guitar	197?	5.00	10.00	20.00
❏ 29057	Images on Guitar	197?	3.75	7.50	15.00
❏ 29194	Estudios	197?	3.75	7.50	15.00
❏ 29623	Tristeza on Guitar	197?	3.75	7.50	15.00
COLUMBIA					
❏ KC 32441	Solitude on Guitar	1974	3.00	6.00	12.00
PAUSA					
❏ 7078	Tristeza on Guitar	198?	2.50	5.00	10.00

POWELL, BUD
Pianist. Also see CHARLIE PARKER; THE QUINTET; SONNY STITT.

Number	Title	Yr	VG	VG+	NM
BLACK LION					
❏ 153	Invisible Cage	1974	3.00	6.00	12.00
BLUE NOTE					
❏ BLP-1503 [M]	The Amazing Bud Powell, Vol. 1	1955	50.00	100.00	200.00
-- "Deep groove" version (deep indentation under label on both sides)					
❏ BLP-1503 [M]	The Amazing Bud Powell, Vol. 1	1955	37.50	75.00	150.00
-- Regular version, Lexington Ave. address on label					
❏ BLP-1503 [M]	The Amazing Bud Powell, Vol. 1	1963	6.25	12.50	25.00
-- With "New York, USA" address on label					
❏ BLP-1504 [M]	The Amazing Bud Powell, Vol. 2	1955	50.00	100.00	200.00
-- "Deep groove" version (deep indentation under label on both sides)					
❏ BLP-1504 [M]	The Amazing Bud Powell, Vol. 2	1955	37.50	75.00	150.00
-- Regular version, Lexington Ave. address on label					
❏ BLP-1504 [M]	The Amazing Bud Powell, Vol. 2	1963	6.25	12.50	25.00
-- With "New York, USA" address on label					
❏ BLP-1571 [M]	Bud!	1957	37.50	75.00	150.00
-- "Deep groove" version (deep indentation under label on both sides)					
❏ BLP-1571 [M]	Bud!	1957	30.00	60.00	120.00
-- Regular version, W. 63rd St. address on label					
❏ BLP-1571 [M]	Bud!	1963	6.25	12.50	25.00
-- With "New York, USA" address on label					
❏ BST-1571 [S]	Bud!	1959	30.00	60.00	120.00
-- "Deep groove" version (deep indentation under label on both sides)					
❏ BST-1571 [S]	Bud!	1959	25.00	50.00	100.00
-- Regular version, W. 63rd St. address on label					
❏ BST-1571 [S]	Bud!	1963	5.00	120.00	20.00
-- With "New York, USA" address on label					
❏ BLP-1598 [M]	The Time Waits	1959	37.50	75.00	150.00
-- "Deep groove" version (deep indentation under label on both sides)					
❏ BLP-1598 [M]	The Time Waits	1959	30.00	60.00	120.00
-- Regular version, W. 63rd St. address on label					
❏ BLP-1598 [M]	The Time Waits	1963	6.25	12.50	25.00
-- With "New York, USA" address on label					

Number	Title	Yr	VG	VG+	NM
❏ BST-1598 [S]	The Time Waits	1959	30.00	60.00	120.00
-- "Deep groove" version (deep indentation under label on both sides)					
❏ BST-1598 [S]	The Time Waits	1959	25.00	50.00	100.00
-- Regular version, W. 63rd St. address on label					
❏ BST-1598 [S]	The Time Waits	1963	5.00	10.00	20.00
-- With "New York, USA" address on label					
❏ BLP-4009 [M]	The Scene Changes	1959	37.50	75.00	150.00
-- "Deep groove" version (deep indentation under label on both sides)					
❏ BLP-4009 [M]	The Scene Changes	1959	30.00	60.00	120.00
-- Regular version, W. 63rd St. address on label					
❏ BLP-4009 [M]	The Scene Changes	1963	6.25	12.50	25.00
-- With "New York, USA" address on label					
❏ BST-4009 [S]	The Scene Changes	1959	30.00	60.00	120.00
-- "Deep groove" version (deep indentation under label on both sides)					
❏ BST-4009 [S]	The Scene Changes	1959	25.00	50.00	100.00
-- Regular version, W. 63rd St. address on label					
❏ BST-4009 [S]	The Scene Changes	1963	5.00	10.00	20.00
-- With "New York, USA" address on label					
❏ BLP-5003 [10]	The Amazing Bud Powell, Vol. 1	1954	100.00	200.00	400.00
❏ BLP-5041 [10]	The Amazing Bud Powell, Vol. 2	1954	100.00	200.00	400.00
❏ B1-81503 [M]	The Amazing Bud Powell, Vol. 1	1989	3.75	7.50	15.00
-- "The Finest in Jazz Since 1939" reissue					
❏ BST-81503 [R]	The Amazing Bud Powell, Vol. 1	1967	3.00	6.00	12.00
-- With "A Division of Liberty Records" on label					
❏ B1-81504 [M]	The Amazing Bud Powell, Vol. 2	1989	3.75	7.50	15.00
-- "The Finest in Jazz Since 1939" reissue					
❏ BST-81504 [R]	The Amazing Bud Powell, Vol. 2	1967	3.00	6.00	12.00
-- With "A Division of Liberty Records" on label					
❏ BST-81571 [S]	Bud!	1967	3.75	7.50	15.00
-- With "A Division of Liberty Records" on label					
❏ BST-81571 [S]	Bud!	1986	2.50	5.00	10.00
-- "The Finest in Jazz Since 1939" reissue					
❏ BST-81598 [S]	The Time Waits	1967	3.75	7.50	15.00
-- With "A Division of Liberty Records" on label					
❏ BST-84009 [S]	The Scene Changes	1967	3.75	7.50	15.00
-- With "A Division of Liberty Records" on label					
❏ BST-84430	Alternate Takes	1985	3.00	6.00	12.00
❏ B1-93204	The Best of Bud Powell	1989	3.00	6.00	12.00
CLEF					
❏ MGC-102 [10]	Bud Powell Piano Solos	1953	---	---	---
-- Canceled					
❏ MGC-502 [10]	Bud Powell Piano Solos	1954	50.00	100.00	200.00
❏ MGC-507 [10]	Bud Powell Piano Solos, No. 2	1954	50.00	100.00	200.00
❏ MGC-610 [M]	Bud Powell's Moods	1954	37.50	75.00	150.00
❏ MGC-739 [M]	The Genius of Bud Powell	1956	30.00	60.00	120.00
COLUMBIA					
❏ CL 2292 [M]	A Portrait of Thelonious	1965	6.25	12.50	25.00
❏ CS 9092 [S]	A Portrait of Thelonious	1965	7.50	15.00	30.00
COLUMBIA JAZZ ODYSSEY					
❏ PC 36805	A Portrait of Thelonious	1980	2.50	5.00	10.00
COMMODORE					
❏ XFL-14943	The World Is Waiting	198?	2.50	5.00	10.00
DEBUT					
❏ DLP-3 [10]	Jazz at Massey Hall, Volume 2	1953	100.00	200.00	400.00
DELMARK					
❏ DL-406 [M]	Bouncing with Bud	1966	6.25	12.50	25.00
❏ DS-406	Bouncing with Bud	1987	2.50	5.00	10.00
❏ DS-9406 [S]	Bouncing with Bud	1966	7.50	15.00	30.00
DISCOVERY					
❏ 830	Bud Powell in Paris	198?	2.50	5.00	10.00
ELEKTRA/MUSICIAN					
❏ 60030	Inner Fires	1982	2.50	5.00	10.00
ESP-DISK'					
❏ BUD-1	Broadcasts, Volume 1	197?	3.75	7.50	15.00
❏ 1066 [S]	Bud Powell at the Blue Note Café, Paris	1968	6.25	12.50	25.00
FANTASY					
❏ OJC-111	Jazz at Massey Hall, Volume 2	198?	2.50	5.00	10.00
❏ 6006 [M]	Bud Powell Trio	1962	7.50	15.00	30.00
-- Black vinyl					
❏ 6006 [M]	Bud Powell Trio	1962	12.50	25.00	50.00
-- Red vinyl					
❏ 86006 [R]	Bud Powell Trio	1962	5.00	10.00	20.00
-- Blue vinyl					
❏ 86006 [R]	Bud Powell Trio	1962	7.50	15.00	30.00
-- Black vinyl					
MAINSTREAM					
❏ MRL-385	Ups 'n' Downs	1973	3.75	7.50	15.00
MERCURY					
❏ MGC-102 [10]	Bud Powell Piano	1950	62.50	125.00	250.00
❏ MGC-502 [10]	Bud Powell Piano Solos	1951	62.50	125.00	250.00
❏ MGC-507 [10]	Bud Powell Piano Solos, No. 2	1951	62.50	125.00	250.00
❏ MGC-610 [M]	Bud Powell's Moods	1953	50.00	100.00	200.00
❏ MG-35012 [10]	Bud Powell Piano	1950	75.00	150.00	300.00
MOSAIC					
❏ M5-116 [(5)]	The Complete Bud Powell Blue Note Recordings (1949-1958)	199?	20.00	40.00	80.00

Number	Title	Yr	VG	VG+	NM
MYTHIC SOUND					
❏ MS-6001	Early Years of a Genius, 1944-48	199?	3.00	6.00	12.00
❏ MS-6002	Burning in the USA, 1953-55	199?	3.00	6.00	12.00
❏ MS-6003	Cookin' at Saint-Germain, 1957-59	199?	3.00	6.00	12.00
❏ MS-6004	Relaxin' at Home, 1961-64	199?	3.00	6.00	12.00
❏ MS-6005	Groovin' at the Blue Note, 1959-61	199?	3.00	6.00	12.00
❏ MS-6006	Writin' for Duke, 1963	199?	3.00	6.00	12.00
❏ MS-6007	Tribute to Thelonious, 1964	199?	3.00	6.00	12.00
❏ MS-6008	Holiday in Edenville, 1964	199?	3.00	6.00	12.00
❏ MS-6009	Return to Birdland, 1964	199?	3.00	6.00	12.00
NORGRAN					
❏ MGN-23 [10]	Bud Powell Trio	1954	62.50	125.00	250.00
❏ MGN-1017 [M]	Jazz Original	1955	25.00	50.00	100.00
❏ MGN-1063 [M]	Jazz Giant	1956	25.00	50.00	100.00
❏ MGN-1064 [M]	Bud Powell's Moods	1956	25.00	50.00	100.00
❏ MGN-1077 [M]	Piano Interpretations by Bud Powell	1956	25.00	50.00	100.00
❏ MGN-1098 [M]	Bud Powell '57	1957	25.00	50.00	100.00
QUINTESSENCE					
❏ 25381	Bud Powell	1980	2.50	5.00	10.00
RCA VICTOR					
❏ LPM-1423 [M]	Strictly Powell	1957	25.00	50.00	100.00
❏ LPM-1507 [M]	Swingin' with Bud	1957	25.00	50.00	100.00
REPRISE					
❏ R-6098 [M]	Bud Powell in Paris	1964	7.50	15.00	30.00
❏ RS-6098 [S]	Bud Powell in Paris	1964	10.00	20.00	40.00
ROOST					
❏ LP-401 [10]	Bud Powell Trio	1950	100.00	200.00	400.00
❏ LP-412 [10]	Bud Powell Trio	1953	75.00	150.00	300.00
❏ LP-2224 [M]	Bud Powell Trio	1957	25.00	50.00	100.00
ROULETTE					
❏ R-52115 [M]	The Return of Bud Powell -- His First New Recordings Since 1958	1965	6.25	12.50	25.00
❏ SR-52115 [S]	The Return of Bud Powell -- His First New Recordings Since 1958	1965	7.50	15.00	30.00
STEEPLECHASE					
❏ SCC-6001	Bud Powell at the Golden Circle, Vol. 1	198?	3.00	6.00	12.00
❏ SCC-6002	Bud Powell at the Golden Circle, Vol. 2	198?	3.00	6.00	12.00
❏ SCC-6009	Bud Powell at the Golden Circle, Vol. 3	198?	3.00	6.00	12.00
❏ SCC-6014	Bud Powell at the Golden Circle, Vol. 4	198?	3.00	6.00	12.00
❏ SCC-6017	Bud Powell at the Golden Circle, Vol. 5	198?	3.00	6.00	12.00
VERVE					
❏ VSP-34 [M]	The Jazz Legacy of Bud Powell	1966	5.00	10.00	20.00
❏ VSPS-34 [R]	The Jazz Legacy of Bud Powell	1966	3.00	6.00	12.00
❏ VSP-37 [M]	This Was Bud Powell	1966	5.00	10.00	20.00
❏ VSPS-37 [R]	This Was Bud Powell	1966	3.00	6.00	12.00
❏ VE-2-2506 [(2)]	The Genius of Bud Powell, Vol. 1	197?	3.75	7.50	15.00
❏ VE-2-2526 [(2)]	The Genius of Bud Powell, Vol. 2	197?	3.75	7.50	15.00
❏ UMV-2571	Bud Powell '57	198?	2.50	5.00	10.00
❏ UMV-2573	Piano Interpretations	198?	2.50	5.00	10.00
❏ MGV-8115 [M]	The Genius of Bud Powell	1957	12.50	25.00	50.00
❏ V-8115 [M]	The Genius of Bud Powell	1961	6.25	12.50	25.00
❏ MGV-8153 [M]	Jazz Giant	1957	15.00	30.00	60.00
❏ V-8153 [M]	Jazz Giant	1961	6.25	12.50	25.00
❏ MGV-8154 [M]	Bud Powell's Moods	1957	15.00	30.00	60.00
❏ V-8154 [M]	Bud Powell's Moods	1961	6.25	12.50	25.00
❏ MGV-8167 [M]	Piano Interpretations by Bud Powell	1957	15.00	30.00	60.00
❏ V-8167 [M]	Piano Interpretations by Bud Powell	1961	6.25	12.50	25.00
❏ MGV-8185 [M]	Bud Powell '57	1957	12.50	25.00	50.00
❏ V-8185 [M]	Bud Powell '57	1961	6.25	12.50	25.00
❏ MGV-8218 [M]	Blues in the Closet	1958	12.50	25.00	50.00
❏ V-8218 [M]	Blues in the Closet	1961	6.25	12.50	25.00
❏ MGV-8301 [M]	The Lonely One...	1959	12.50	25.00	50.00
❏ V-8301 [M]	The Lonely One...	1961	6.25	12.50	25.00
XANADU					
❏ 102	Bud in Paris	197?	3.00	6.00	12.00

POWELL, LOVEY

Female singer.

Number	Title	Yr	VG	VG+	NM
TRANSITION					
❏ TRLP-1 [M]	Lovelady	1956	25.00	50.00	100.00
-- Deduct 25 percent if booklet is missing					

Number	Title	Yr	VG	VG+	NM
POWELL, MEL					
Pianist, arranger and composer.					
CAPITOL					
❏ T 615 [M]	Classics in Jazz	1955	10.00	20.00	40.00
COMMODORE					
❏ XFL-14943	The World Is Waiting	198?	2.50	5.00	10.00
PAUSA					
❏ 9023	The Unavailable Mel Powell	198?	2.50	5.00	10.00
VANGUARD					
❏ VRS-8004 [10]	Mel Powell Septet	1953	20.00	40.00	80.00
❏ VRS-8015 [10]	Bandstand	1954	20.00	40.00	80.00
❏ VRS-8501 [M]	Borderline	1954	12.50	25.00	50.00
❏ VRS-8503 [M]	Thingamagig	1954	12.50	25.00	50.00
❏ VRS-8506 [M]	Out on a Limb	1955	12.50	25.00	50.00
❏ VRS-8519 [M]	Easy Swing	1955	12.50	25.00	50.00
POWELL, ROGER					
Pianist and synthesizer player.					
ATLANTIC					
❏ SD 7251	Cosmic Furnace	1973	3.75	7.50	15.00
POWELL, SELDON					
Tenor saxophone player and flutist.					
ROOST					
❏ LP-2205 [M]	Seldon Powell Plays	1956	12.50	25.00	50.00
❏ LP-2220 [M]	Seldon Powell Sextet	1956	12.50	25.00	50.00
POWELL, SPECS					
Drummer and percussionist.					
ROULETTE					
❏ R-52004 [M]	Movin' In	1958	7.50	15.00	30.00
❏ SR-52004 [S]	Movin' In	1958	6.25	12.50	25.00
STRAND					
❏ SL-1027 [M]	Specs Powell Presents Big Band Jazz	1961	5.00	10.00	20.00
❏ SLS-1027 [S]	Specs Powell Presents Big Band Jazz	1961	6.25	12.50	25.00
POWER TOOLS					
Members: BILL FRISELL; Melvin Gibbs (bass); RONALD SHANNON JACKSON.					
ANTILLES					
❏ 90627	Strange Meeting	1987	2.50	5.00	10.00
POWERS, CHRIS					
CIRCLE					
❏ CLP-89	Chris Powers and His Orchestra 1985	1986	2.50	5.00	10.00
POWRIE, GLENNA					
Pianist.					
MUSE					
❏ MR-5392	Ashja	1990	3.00	6.00	12.00
POZAR, ROBERT					
SAVOY					
❏ MG-12189 [M]	Good Golly, Miss Nancy	1967	5.00	10.00	20.00
PREACHER ROLLO					
Drummer and bandleader.					
KING					
❏ 295-101 [10]	Dixieland	195?	30.00	60.00	120.00
MGM					
❏ E-95 [10]	Preacher Rollo and the Five Saints	1951	20.00	40.00	80.00
❏ E-217 [10]	Preacher Rollo at the Jazz Band Ball	1953	20.00	40.00	80.00
❏ E-3259 [M]	Dixieland Favorites	1955	12.50	25.00	50.00
❏ E-3403 [M]	Swanee River Jazz	1956	12.50	25.00	50.00
PRESERVATION HALL JAZZ BAND					
Among the most long-standing members: Percy Humphrey (trumpet); Willie Humphrey (clarinet); Frank Demond (trombone); Allan Jaffe (tuba).					
CBS MASTERWORKS					
❏ FM 37780	New Orleans, Volume 2	1982	2.50	5.00	10.00
❏ FM 38650	New Orleans, Volume 3	1983	2.50	5.00	10.00
❏ FM 44856	New Orleans, Volume 4	1989	3.00	6.00	12.00
❏ FM 44996	The Best of Preservation Hall Jazz Band	1989	3.00	6.00	12.00
COLUMBIA MASTERWORKS					
❏ M 34549	Preservation Hall Jazz Band	1977	3.00	6.00	12.00

Number	Title	Yr	VG	VG+	NM
PRESIDENT, THE					
Led by WAYNE HORVITZ.					
ELEKTRA/MUSICIAN					
❏ 60799	Bring Yr Camera	1989	3.00	6.00	12.00
PRESTER, ROB					
ANTILLES					
❏ 90967	Trillum	1988	2.50	5.00	10.00
PRESTIGE BLUES SWINGERS, THE					
Members: PEPPER ADAMS; RAY BRYANT; Buster Cooper (trombone); ART FARMER; JIMMY FORREST; TINY GRIMES; OSIE JOHNSON; WENDELL MARSHALL; JEROME RICHARDSON; IDRESS SULIEMAN; Jerry Valentine (trombone).					
PRESTIGE					
❏ PRLP-7145 [M]	Outskirts of Town	1958	20.00	40.00	80.00
❏ PRST-7787	Outskirts of Town	1970	3.75	7.50	15.00
SWINGVILLE					
❏ SVLP-2013 [M]	Stasch	1960	6.25	12.50	25.00
-- Blue label, trident logo at right					
❏ SVLP-2013 [M]	Stasch	1965	12.50	25.00	50.00
-- Purple label					
PRESTIGE JAZZ QUARTET, THE					
Members: TEDDY CHARLES; Addison Farmer (bass); Jerry Segal (drums); MAL WALDRON. Also see TEO MACERO.					
PRESTIGE					
❏ PRLP-7108 [M]	The Prestige Jazz Quartet	1957	12.50	25.00	50.00
PREVIN, ANDRE					
Pianist, composer and arranger. Also see SHORTY ROGERS.					
ANGEL					
❏ DS-37780	A Different Kind of Blues	1981	2.50	5.00	10.00
❏ DS-37799	It's a Breeze	1982	2.50	5.00	10.00
ARCHIVE OF FOLK AND JAZZ					
❏ 247	Early Years	1970	2.50	5.00	10.00
COLUMBIA					
❏ CL 1437 [M]	Like Love	1960	3.75	7.50	15.00
-- Red and black label with six "eye" logos					
❏ CL 1437 [M]	Like Love	1963	3.00	6.00	12.00
-- Red label with "Guaranteed High Fidelity" or "360 Sound Mono" at bottom					
❏ CL 1495 [M]	Rhapsody in Blue	1960	3.75	7.50	15.00
-- Red and black label with six "eye" logos					
❏ CL 1495 [M]	Rhapsody in Blue	1963	3.00	6.00	12.00
-- Red label with "Guaranteed High Fidelity" or "360 Sound Mono" at bottom					
❏ CL 1530 [M]	Give My Regards to Broadway	1960	5.00	10.00	20.00
-- Red and black label with six "eye" logos					
❏ CL 1530 [M]	Give My Regards to Broadway	1963	3.00	6.00	12.00
-- Red label with "Guaranteed High Fidelity" or "360 Sound Mono" at bottom					
❏ CL 1569 [M]	Camelot	1961	5.00	10.00	20.00
-- Red and black label with six "eye" logos					
❏ CL 1569 [M]	Camelot	1963	3.00	6.00	12.00
-- Red label with "Guaranteed High Fidelity" or "360 Sound Mono" at bottom					
❏ CL 1595 [M]	Thinking of You	1961	5.00	10.00	20.00
-- Red and black label with six "eye" logos					
❏ CL 1595 [M]	Thinking of You	1963	3.00	6.00	12.00
-- Red label with "Guaranteed High Fidelity" or "360 Sound Mono" at bottom					
❏ CL 1649 [M]	A Touch of Elegance	1961	5.00	10.00	20.00
-- Red and black label with six "eye" logos					
❏ CL 1741 [M]	Mack the Knife and Other Kurt Weill Music	1962	5.00	10.00	20.00
-- Red and black label with six "eye" logos					
❏ CL 1741 [M]	Mack the Knife and Other Kurt Weill Music	1963	3.00	6.00	12.00
-- Red label with "Guaranteed High Fidelity" or "360 Sound Mono" at bottom					
❏ CL 1786 [M]	Faraway Part of Town	1962	5.00	10.00	20.00
-- Red and black label with six "eye" logos					
❏ CL 1786 [M]	Faraway Part of Town	1963	3.00	6.00	12.00
-- Red label with "Guaranteed High Fidelity" or "360 Sound Mono" at bottom					
❏ CL 1888 [M]	The Light Fantastic	1962	5.00	10.00	20.00
-- Red and black label with six "eye" logos					
❏ CL 1888 [M]	The Light Fantastic	1963	3.00	6.00	12.00
-- Red label with "Guaranteed High Fidelity" or "360 Sound Mono" at bottom					
❏ CL 2034 [M]	Andre Previn in Hollywood	1963	3.75	7.50	15.00
-- Red label with "Guaranteed High Fidelity" at bottom					
❏ CL 2034 [M]	Andre Previn in Hollywood	1966	3.00	6.00	12.00
-- Red label with "360 Sound Mono" at bottom					
❏ CL 2114 [M]	The Soft and Swinging Music of Jimmy McHugh	1964	3.75	7.50	15.00
-- Red label with "Guaranteed High Fidelity" at bottom					
❏ CL 2114 [M]	The Soft and Swinging Music of Jimmy McHugh	1966	3.00	6.00	12.00
-- Red label with "360 Sound Mono" at bottom					
❏ CL 2195 [M]	My Fair Lady	1964	3.75	7.50	15.00
-- Red label with "Guaranteed High Fidelity" at bottom					
❏ CL 2195 [M]	My Fair Lady	1966	3.00	6.00	12.00
-- Red label with "360 Sound Mono" at bottom					

Number	Title	Yr	VG	VG+	NM
CL 2294 [M]	Popular Previn	1965	3.75	7.50	15.00
-- Red label with "Guaranteed High Fidelity" at bottom					
CL 2294 [M]	Popular Previn	1966	3.00	6.00	12.00
-- Red label with "360 Sound Mono" at bottom					
CS 8233 [S]	Like Love	1960	5.00	10.00	20.00
-- Red and black label with six "eye" logos					
CS 8233 [S]	Like Love	1963	3.75	7.50	15.00
-- Red label with "360 Sound Stereo" at bottom					
CS 8286 [S]	Rhapsody in Blue	1960	5.00	10.00	20.00
-- Red and black label with six "eye" logos					
CS 8286 [S]	Rhapsody in Blue	1963	3.75	7.50	15.00
-- Red label with "360 Sound Stereo" at bottom					
CS 8330 [S]	Give My Regards to Broadway	1960	6.25	12.50	25.00
-- Red and black label with six "eye" logos					
CS 8330 [S]	Give My Regards to Broadway	1960	3.75	7.50	15.00
-- Red label with "360 Sound Stereo" at bottom					
CS 8369 [S]	Camelot	1961	6.25	12.50	25.00
-- Red and black label with six "eye" logos					
CS 8369 [S]	Camelot	1963	3.75	7.50	15.00
-- Red label with "360 Sound Stereo" at bottom					
CS 8395 [S]	Thinking of You	1961	6.25	12.50	25.00
-- Red and black label with six "eye" logos					
CS 8395 [S]	Thinking of You	1963	3.75	7.50	15.00
-- Red label with "360 Sound Stereo" at bottom					
CS 8541 [S]	Mack the Knife and Other Kurt Weill Music	1962	6.25	12.50	25.00
-- Red and black label with six "eye" logos					
CS 8541 [S]	Mack the Knife and Other Kurt Weill Music	1962	3.75	7.50	15.00
-- Red label with "360 Sound Stereo" at bottom					
CS 8586 [S]	Faraway Part of Town	1962	6.25	12.50	25.00
-- Red and black label with six "eye" logos					
CS 8586 [S]	Faraway Part of Town	1963	3.75	7.50	15.00
-- Red label with "360 Sound Stereo" at bottom					
CS 8649 [S]	A Touch of Elegance	1961	6.25	12.50	25.00
-- Red and black label with six "eye" logos					
CS 8688 [S]	The Light Fantastic	1962	6.25	12.50	25.00
-- Red and black label with six "eye" logos					
CS 8688 [S]	The Light Fantastic	1963	3.75	7.50	15.00
-- Red label with "360 Sound Stereo" at bottom					
CS 8834 [S]	Andre Previn in Hollywood	1963	5.00	10.00	20.00
-- Red label with "360 Sound Stereo" in black at bottom					
CS 8834 [S]	Andre Previn in Hollywood	1966	3.75	7.50	15.00
-- Red label with "360 Sound Stereo" in white at bottom					
CS 8914 [S]	The Soft and Swinging Music of Jimmy McHugh	1964	5.00	10.00	20.00
-- Red label with "360 Sound Stereo" in black at bottom					
CS 8914 [S]	The Soft and Swinging Music of Jimmy McHugh	1966	3.75	7.50	15.00
-- Red label with "360 Sound Stereo" in white at bottom					
CS 8995 [S]	My Fair Lady	1964	5.00	10.00	20.00
-- Red label with "360 Sound Stereo" in black at bottom					
CS 8995 [S]	My Fair Lady	1966	3.75	7.50	15.00
-- Red label with "360 Sound Stereo" in white at bottom					
CS 9094 [S]	Popular Previn	1965	5.00	10.00	20.00
-- Red label with "360 Sound Stereo" in black at bottom					
CS 9094 [S]	Popular Previn	1966	3.75	7.50	15.00
-- Red label with "360 Sound Stereo" in white at bottom					

CONTEMPORARY

Number	Title	Yr	VG	VG+	NM
C-3543 [M]	Pal Joey	1957	12.50	25.00	50.00
C-3548 [M]	Gigi	1958	12.50	25.00	50.00
M-3558 [M]	Andre Previn Plays Vernon Duke	1959	12.50	25.00	50.00
M-3567 [M]	Andre Previn Plays Jerome Kern	1959	12.50	25.00	50.00
M-3570 [M]	Jazz Trio, King Size	1959	12.50	25.00	50.00
M-3572 [M]	West Side Story	1960	10.00	20.00	40.00
M-3575 [M]	Like Previn	1960	10.00	20.00	40.00
M-3586 [M]	Andre Previn Plays Harold Arlen	1960	10.00	20.00	40.00
S-7543 [S]	Pal Joey	1959	10.00	20.00	40.00
S-7548 [S]	Gigi	1959	10.00	20.00	40.00
S-7558 [S]	Andre Previn Plays Vernon Duke	1959	10.00	20.00	40.00
S-7567 [S]	Andre Previn Plays Jerome Kern	1959	10.00	20.00	40.00
S-7570 [S]	Jazz Trio, King Size	1959	10.00	20.00	40.00
S-7572 [S]	West Side Story	1960	7.50	15.00	30.00
S-7575 [S]	Like Previn	1960	7.50	15.00	30.00
S-7586 [S]	Andre Previn Plays Harold Arlen	1960	7.50	15.00	30.00

CORONET

Number	Title	Yr	VG	VG+	NM
170	Featuring Andre Previn	196?	3.00	6.00	12.00
181	The Magic Sounds of Andre Previn	196?	3.00	6.00	12.00

DECCA

Number	Title	Yr	VG	VG+	NM
DL 4115 [M]	Andre Previn Plays Pretty	1961	3.00	6.00	12.00
DL 4350 [M]	But Beautiful	1963	3.00	6.00	12.00
DL 8131 [M]	Let's Get Away From It All	1955	10.00	20.00	40.00
DL 8341 [M]	Hollywood at Midnight	1957	10.00	20.00	40.00
DL 74115 [S]	Andre Previn Plays Pretty	1961	3.75	7.50	15.00
DL 74350 [S]	But Beautiful	1963	3.75	7.50	15.00

FANTASY

Number	Title	Yr	VG	VG+	NM
OJC-157	Double Play!	198?	2.50	5.00	10.00
-- Reissue of Contemporary 7011					
OJC-170	Like Previn	198?	2.50	5.00	10.00
-- Reissue of Contemporary 7575					
OJC-422	West Side Story	1990	2.50	5.00	10.00
OJC-637	Pal Joey	1991	3.00	6.00	12.00

GUEST STAR

Number	Title	Yr	VG	VG+	NM
1436	Piano Greats	196?	3.00	6.00	12.00

HARMONY

Number	Title	Yr	VG	VG+	NM
HL 7348 [M]	Misty	1965	3.00	6.00	12.00
HL 7407 [M]	Starlight Piano	196?	3.00	6.00	12.00
HL 7429 [M]	Camelot	1967	3.00	6.00	12.00
HS 11148 [S]	Misty	1965	3.00	6.00	12.00
HS 11207 [S]	Starlight Piano	196?	3.00	6.00	12.00
HS 11229 [S]	Camelot	1967	3.00	6.00	12.00

JAZZ ODYSSEY

Number	Title	Yr	VG	VG+	NM
32-16-0260	Mack the Knife and Other Kurt Weill Music	196?	3.00	6.00	12.00
-- Reissue of Columbia 8541					

MGM

Number	Title	Yr	VG	VG+	NM
E-3716 [M]	Secret Songs for Young Lovers	1959	5.00	10.00	20.00
SE-3716 [S]	Secret Songs for Young Lovers	1959	6.25	12.50	25.00
E-3811 [M]	Like Blue	1960	5.00	10.00	20.00
SE-3811 [S]	Like Blue	1960	6.25	12.50	25.00
E-4186 [M]	Andre Previn -- Composer, Conductor, Arranger, Pianist	1964	3.75	7.50	15.00
SE-4186 [S]	Andre Previn -- Composer, Conductor, Arranger, Pianist	1964	5.00	10.00	20.00

MOBILE FIDELITY

Number	Title	Yr	VG	VG+	NM
1-095	West Side Story	1982	6.25	12.50	25.00
-- Audiophile vinyl					

MONARCH

Number	Title	Yr	VG	VG+	NM
203 [10]	All Star Jazz	1952	20.00	40.00	80.00
204 [10]	Andre Previn Plays Duke	1952	20.00	40.00	80.00

PRI

Number	Title	Yr	VG	VG+	NM
3026 [S]	The World's Most Honored Pianist	1962	6.25	12.50	25.00
-- Issued on yellow vinyl					

RCA CAMDEN

Number	Title	Yr	VG	VG+	NM
CAL-792 [M]	Love Walked In	1964	3.00	6.00	12.00
CAS-792 [R]	Love Walked In	1964	2.50	5.00	10.00

RCA VICTOR

Number	Title	Yr	VG	VG+	NM
LPM-1011 [M]	Gershwin	1955	10.00	20.00	40.00
LPM-1356 [M]	Three Little Words	1957	10.00	20.00	40.00
ANL1-2805	Pure Gold	1978	2.50	5.00	10.00
LPT-3002 [10]	Andre Previn Plays Harry Warren	1952	20.00	40.00	80.00
LPM-3491 [M]	Andre Previn Plays Music of the Young Hollywood Composers	1966	3.00	6.00	12.00
LSP-3491 [S]	Andre Previn Plays Music of the Young Hollywood Composers	1966	3.75	7.50	15.00
LPM-3551 [M]	Andre Previn with Voices	1966	3.00	6.00	12.00

SPRINGBOARD

Number	Title	Yr	VG	VG+	NM
SPB-4053	After Dark	197?	2.50	5.00	10.00

STEREO RECORDS

Number	Title	Yr	VG	VG+	NM
S-7004 [S]	Pal Joey	1958	12.50	25.00	50.00
S-7020 [S]	Gigi	1958	12.50	25.00	50.00

VERVE

Number	Title	Yr	VG	VG+	NM
V-8565 [M]	The Essential Andre Previn	1963	3.00	6.00	12.00
V6-8565 [S]	The Essential Andre Previn	1963	3.75	7.50	15.00

PREVIN, ANDRE; HERB ELLIS; SHELLY MANNE; RAY BROWN

Also see each artist's individual listings.

COLUMBIA

Number	Title	Yr	VG	VG+	NM
CL 2018 [M]	Four to Go	1963	3.75	7.50	15.00
CS 8818 [S]	Four to Go	1963	5.00	10.00	20.00

PREVIN, ANDRE, AND RUSS FREEMAN

Also see each artist's individual listings.

CONTEMPORARY

Number	Title	Yr	VG	VG+	NM
C-3537 [M]	Double Play!	1957	12.50	25.00	50.00
S-7011 [S]	Double Play!	1959	10.00	20.00	40.00

STEREO RECORDS

Number	Title	Yr	VG	VG+	NM
S-7011 [S]	Double Play!	1958	12.50	25.00	50.00

PREVITE, ROBERT

Drummer, percussionist, keyboard player, guitarist and bass player.

SOUND ASPECTS

Number	Title	Yr	VG	VG+	NM
SAS 008	Bump the Renaissance	1986	3.00	6.00	12.00

PRICE, RUTH

Female singer.

AVA

Number	Title	Yr	VG	VG+	NM
A-54 [M]	Live and Beautiful	1963	10.00	20.00	40.00
AS-54 [S]	Live and Beautiful	1963	12.50	25.00	50.00

Number	Title	Yr	VG	VG+	NM
CONTEMPORARY					
❏ M-3590 [M]	Ruth Price with Shelly Manne at the Manne-Hole	1961	12.50	25.00	50.00
❏ S-7590 [S]	Ruth Price with Shelly Manne at the Manne-Hole	1961	15.00	30.00	60.00
KAPP					
❏ KL-1006 [M]	My Name Is Ruth Price. I Sing.	1955	25.00	50.00	100.00
❏ KL-1054 [M]	The Party's Over	1957	25.00	50.00	100.00
ROOST					
❏ LP-2217 [M]	Ruth Price Sings!	1956	25.00	50.00	100.00

PRICE, SAMMY
Pianist and bandleader. Also see ROY ELDRIDGE.

Number	Title	Yr	VG	VG+	NM
CIRCLE					
❏ 73	Sammy Price and His Musicians, 1944	1985	2.50	5.00	10.00
CLASSIC JAZZ					
❏ 106	Fire	198?	2.50	5.00	10.00
CONCERT HALL JAZZ					
❏ 1008 [10]	Barrelhouse and Blues	1955	12.50	25.00	50.00
JAZZTONE					
❏ J-1207 [M]	Barrelhouse and Blues	1956	10.00	20.00	40.00
❏ J-1236 [M]	Les Jeunesses Musicales	1956	10.00	20.00	40.00
❏ J-1260 [M]	The Price Is Right	1957	10.00	20.00	40.00
SAVOY					
❏ MG-14004	Rock	196?	3.75	7.50	15.00
WORLD WIDE					
❏ 20016	Blues and Boogie	196?	3.75	7.50	15.00

PRICE, VITO
Tenor and alto saxophone player.

Number	Title	Yr	VG	VG+	NM
ARGO					
❏ LP-631 [M]	Swingin' the Loop	1958	10.00	20.00	40.00
❏ LPS-631 [S]	Swingin' the Loop	1958	7.50	15.00	30.00

PRIESTER, JULIAN
Trombonist.

Number	Title	Yr	VG	VG+	NM
ECM					
❏ 1044	Love, Love	197?	3.00	6.00	12.00
❏ 1098	Polarization	1977	3.00	6.00	12.00
JAZZLAND					
❏ JLP-25 [M]	Spiritsville	1960	7.50	15.00	30.00
❏ JLP-925 [S]	Spiritsville	1960	10.00	20.00	40.00
RIVERSIDE					
❏ RLP 12-316 [M]	Keep Swingin'	1960	7.50	15.00	30.00
❏ RLP 1163 [S]	Keep Swingin'	1960	10.00	20.00	40.00
❏ 6081	Keep Swingin'	197?	3.00	6.00	12.00

PRIMA, LOUIS
Trumpeter, male singer and bandleader.

Number	Title	Yr	VG	VG+	NM
CAPITOL					
❏ T 755 [M]	The Wildest	1956	12.50	25.00	50.00
❏ T 836 [M]	Call of the Wildest	1957	12.50	25.00	50.00
❏ T 908 [M]	The Wildest Show at Tahoe	1957	12.50	25.00	50.00
❏ T 1010 [M]	Las Vegas Prima Style	1958	12.50	25.00	50.00
❏ T 1132 [M]	Strictly Prima	1959	7.50	15.00	30.00
❏ T 1723 [M]	The Wildest Comes Home	1962	6.25	12.50	25.00
❏ ST 1723 [S]	The Wildest Comes Home	1962	7.50	15.00	30.00
❏ T 1797 [M]	Lake Tahoe Prima Style	1962	6.25	12.50	25.00
❏ ST 1797 [S]	Lake Tahoe Prima Style	1962	7.50	15.00	30.00
COLUMBIA					
❏ CL 1206 [M]	Breakin' It Up	1959	10.00	20.00	40.00
DOT					
❏ DLP-3262 [M]	His Greatest Hits	1960	6.25	12.50	25.00
❏ DLP-3264 [M]	Pretty Music Prima Style	1960	6.25	12.50	25.00
❏ DLP-3272 [M]	The Wildest Clan	1960	6.25	12.50	25.00
❏ DLP-3352 [M]	Wonderland by Night	1960	6.25	12.50	25.00
❏ DLP-3385 [M]	Blue Moon	1961	6.25	12.50	25.00
❏ DLP-3392 [M]	Return of the Wildest!	1961	6.25	12.50	25.00
❏ DLP-3410 [M]	Doin' the Twist	1961	6.25	12.50	25.00
❏ DLP-25262 [S]	His Greatest Hits	1960	7.50	15.00	30.00
❏ DLP-25264 [S]	Pretty Music Prima Style	1960	7.50	15.00	30.00
❏ DLP-25272 [S]	The Wildest Clan	1960	7.50	15.00	30.00
❏ DLP-25352 [S]	Wonderland by Night	1960	7.50	15.00	30.00
❏ DLP-25385 [S]	Blue Moon	1961	7.50	15.00	30.00
❏ DLP-25392 [S]	Return of the Wildest!	1961	7.50	15.00	30.00
❏ DLP-25410 [S]	Doin' the Twist	1961	7.50	15.00	30.00
MERCURY					
❏ MG-25142 [10]	Louis Prima Plays	1953	20.00	40.00	80.00
RONDO-LETTE					
❏ A-9 [M]	Louis Prima in All His Moods	1959	7.50	15.00	30.00

Number	Title	Yr	VG	VG+	NM
❏ A-25 [M]	Louis Prima Entertains	1959	7.50	15.00	30.00
SAVOY JAZZ					
❏ SJL-2264 [(2)]	Play Pretty for the People	198?	3.00	6.00	12.00
TOPS					
❏ 9759 [M]	Italian Favorites	195?	3.75	7.50	15.00

PRIMA, LOUIS, AND KEELY SMITH
Also see each artist's individual listings.

Number	Title	Yr	VG	VG+	NM
CAPITOL					
❏ T 1160 [M]	Hey Boy! Hey Girl!	1959	12.50	25.00	50.00
❏ SM-1531	The Hits of Louis and Keely	197?	2.50	5.00	10.00
-- Reissue with new prefix					
❏ ST 1531 [S]	The Hits of Louis and Keely	1961	7.50	15.00	30.00
❏ T 1531 [M]	The Hits of Louis and Keely	1961	6.25	12.50	25.00
CORONET					
❏ 121 [M]	Louis Prima Digs Keely Smith	196?	3.75	7.50	15.00
DOT					
❏ DLP-3210 [M]	Louis and Keely!	1959	7.50	15.00	30.00
❏ DLP-3263 [M]	Together	1960	6.25	12.50	25.00
❏ DLP-3266 [M]	Louis and Keely on Stage	1960	6.25	12.50	25.00
❏ DLP-25210 [S]	Louis and Keely!	1959	10.00	20.00	40.00
❏ DLP-25263 [S]	Together	1960	7.50	15.00	30.00
❏ DLP-25266 [S]	Louis and Keely on Stage	1960	7.50	15.00	30.00
RHINO					
❏ RNLP-70225	Zooma Zooma: The Best of Louis Prima Featuring Keely Smith	1986	2.50	5.00	10.00
SPIN-O-RAMA					
❏ 74 [M]	Box of Oldies	196?	3.75	7.50	15.00

PRINCE IGOR AND THE CZAR

Number	Title	Yr	VG	VG+	NM
DIFFERENT DRUMMER					
❏ 1002	From Russia	197?	3.75	7.50	15.00

PRINCE, BOB
Composer and bandleader.

Number	Title	Yr	VG	VG+	NM
RCA VICTOR					
❏ LPM-2435 [M]	Opus Jazz	1961	5.00	10.00	20.00
❏ LSP-2435 [S]	Opus Jazz	1961	6.25	12.50	25.00
WARNER BROS.					
❏ W 1240 [M]	N.Y. Export: Op. Jazz from Ballets U.S.A.; Ballet Music from Leonard Bernstein's West Side Story	1958	5.00	10.00	20.00
❏ WS 1240 [S]	N.Y. Export: Op. Jazz from Ballets U.S.A.; Ballet Music from Leonard Bernstein's West Side Story	1958	6.25	12.50	25.00
❏ W 1276 [M]	Charleston 1970	1959	5.00	10.00	20.00
❏ WS 1276 [S]	Charleston 1970	1959	6.25	12.50	25.00

PRINCE, ROLAND
Guitarist.

Number	Title	Yr	VG	VG+	NM
VANGUARD					
❏ VSD-79371	Color Visions	197?	2.50	5.00	10.00
❏ VSD-79388	Free Spirit	197?	2.50	5.00	10.00

PRINCETON TRIANGLE JAZZ BAND

Number	Title	Yr	VG	VG+	NM
BIOGRAPH					
❏ 12014	College Jazz in the '20s	1969	3.75	7.50	15.00

PRITCHARD, DAVID
Guitarist.

Number	Title	Yr	VG	VG+	NM
INNER CITY					
❏ IC-1047	Light-Year	1978	3.00	6.00	12.00
❏ IC-1070	City Dreams	1979	3.00	6.00	12.00

PRITCHETT, GEORGE
Guitarist.

Number	Title	Yr	VG	VG+	NM
KINNICKINNICK					
❏ 101	By Request	197?	5.00	10.00	20.00

PROBERT, GEORGE
Alto and soprano saxophone player.

Number	Title	Yr	VG	VG+	NM
GHB					
❏ GHB-70	The Incredible George Probert	197?	2.50	5.00	10.00

PROCOPE, RUSSELL
Alto saxophone player and clarinetist.

Number	Title	Yr	VG	VG+	NM
DOT					
❏ DLP 3010 [M]	The Persuasive Sax of Russell Procope	1956	10.00	20.00	40.00

Number	Title	Yr	VG	VG+	NM

PRYSOCK, ARTHUR
Male singer.

DECCA
❑ DL 4581 [M]	Strictly Sentimental	1965	3.75	7.50	15.00
❑ DL 4628 [M]	Showcase	1965	3.75	7.50	15.00
❑ DL 74581 [S]	Strictly Sentimental	1965	5.00	10.00	20.00
❑ DL 74628 [S]	Showcase	1965	5.00	10.00	20.00

KING
❑ KS-1064	The Country Side of Arthur Prysock	1969	3.00	6.00	12.00
❑ KS-1066	Where the Soul Trees Go	1970	3.00	6.00	12.00
❑ KS-1067	The Lord Is My Shepherd	1970	3.00	6.00	12.00
❑ KS-1088	Fly My Love	1970	3.00	6.00	12.00
❑ KS-1134	Unforgettable	1971	3.00	6.00	12.00

MCA
❑ 3061	Here's To Good Friends	1978	2.50	5.00	10.00

MGM
❑ GAS-134	Arthur Prysock (Golden Archive Series)	1970	3.00	6.00	12.00
❑ SE-4694	Arthur Prysock	1970	3.00	6.00	12.00

MILESTONE
❑ M-9139	A Rockin' Good Way	1986	2.50	5.00	10.00
❑ M-9146	This Guy's in Love with You	1987	2.50	5.00	10.00
❑ M-9157	Today's Love Songs, Tomorrow's Blues	1988	2.50	5.00	10.00

OLD TOWN
❑ LP-102 [M]	I Worry About You	1962	12.50	25.00	50.00
❑ LP-2004 [M]	Arthur Prysock Sings Only for You	1962	12.50	25.00	50.00
❑ LP-2005 [M]	Coast to Coast	1963	10.00	20.00	40.00
❑ LP-2006 [M]	A Portrait of Arthur Prysock	1963	10.00	20.00	40.00
❑ LP-2007 [M]	Everlasting Songs for Everlasting Lovers	1964	10.00	20.00	40.00
❑ LP-2008 [M]	Intimately Yours	1964	10.00	20.00	40.00
❑ LP-2009 [M]	A Double Header with Arthur Prysock	1965	10.00	20.00	40.00
❑ LP-2010 [M]	In a Mood	1965	10.00	20.00	40.00
❑ 12-001	Arthur Prysock '74	1973	3.00	6.00	12.00
❑ 12-002	Love Makes It Right	1974	3.00	6.00	12.00
❑ 12-004	All My Life	1976	3.00	6.00	12.00
❑ T-90604 [M]	A Portrait of Arthur Prysock	1965	10.00	20.00	40.00
-- Capitol Record Club edition					

POLYDOR
❑ PD-2-8901 [(2)]	Silk and Satin	1977	3.75	7.50	15.00

VERVE
❑ V6-650 [(2)]	24 Karat Hits	1969	3.75	7.50	15.00
❑ V-5009 [M]	Art and Soul	1966	3.00	6.00	12.00
❑ V6-5009 [S]	Art and Soul	1966	3.75	7.50	15.00
❑ V-5011 [M]	The Best of Arthur Prysock	1967	3.00	6.00	12.00
❑ V6-5011 [S]	The Best of Arthur Prysock	1967	3.75	7.50	15.00
❑ V-5012 [M]	A Portrait of Arthur Prysock	1967	3.75	7.50	15.00
❑ V6-5012 [S]	A Portrait of Arthur Prysock	1967	3.75	7.50	15.00
❑ V-5014 [M]	Mister Prysock	1967	3.75	7.50	15.00
❑ V6-5014 [S]	Mister Prysock	1967	3.75	7.50	15.00
❑ V-5029 [M]	Love Me	1968	3.75	7.50	15.00
❑ V6-5029 [S]	Love Me	1968	3.00	6.00	12.00
❑ V6-5038	The Best of Arthur Prysock, Volume 2	1968	3.00	6.00	12.00
❑ V6-5048	To Love or Not to Love	1968	3.00	6.00	12.00
❑ V6-5059	I Must Be Doing Something Right	1968	3.00	6.00	12.00
❑ V6-5070	This Is My Beloved	1969	3.00	6.00	12.00

PRYSOCK, ARTHUR/COUNT BASIE
Also see each artist's individual listings.

VERVE
❑ V-8646 [M]	Arthur Prysock/Count Basie	1966	3.75	7.50	15.00
❑ V6-8646 [S]	Arthur Prysock/Count Basie	1966	5.00	10.00	20.00
❑ 827 011-1	Arthur Prysock/Count Basie	1985	2.00	4.00	8.00
-- Reissue					

PUCHO AND THE LATIN SOUL BROTHERS
Pucho's real name is Henry Brown; he is a percussionist.

PRESTIGE
❑ PRLP-7471 [M]	Pucho and the Latin Soul Brothers	1967	10.00	20.00	40.00
❑ PRST-7471 [S]	Pucho and the Latin Soul Brothers	1967	7.50	15.00	30.00
❑ PRLP-7502 [M]	Saffron and Soul	1967	10.00	20.00	40.00
❑ PRST-7502 [S]	Saffron and Soul	1967	7.50	15.00	30.00
❑ PRLP-7528 [M]	Shuckin' and Jivin'	1967	12.50	25.00	50.00
❑ PRST-7528 [S]	Shuckin' and Jivin'	1967	7.50	15.00	30.00
❑ PRST-7555	Big Stick	1968	7.50	15.00	30.00
❑ PRST-7572	Heat!	1968	7.50	15.00	30.00
❑ PRST-7616	Dateline	1969	7.50	15.00	30.00
❑ PRST-7679	The Best of Pucho and the Latin Soul Brothers	1969	6.25	12.50	25.00

PUENTE, TITO
Timbales and vibraphone player, percussionist, composer and bandleader. A legend in Afro-Cuban music, he wrote "Oye Como Va," which was remade almost note-for-note by Santana in 1970. Also see WOODY HERMAN.

CONCORD PICANTE
❑ CJP-207	On Broadway	1983	2.50	5.00	10.00
❑ CJP-250	El Rey	1984	2.50	5.00	10.00
❑ CJP-283	Mambo Diablo	1985	2.50	5.00	10.00
❑ CJP-301	Sensacion	1987	2.50	5.00	10.00
❑ CJP-329	Un Poco Loco	1987	2.50	5.00	10.00
❑ CJP-354	Salsa Meets Jazz	1988	2.50	5.00	10.00

DECCA
❑ DL 4910 [M]	Brasilia Nueve	1967	6.25	12.50	25.00
❑ DL 74910 [S]	Brasilia Nueve	1967	5.00	10.00	20.00

GNP CRESCENDO
❑ GNP-70 [M]	The Exciting Tito Puente Band in Hollywood	196?	7.50	15.00	30.00
❑ GNPS-2048 [S]	Puente Now!	197?	2.50	5.00	10.00
-- Reissue of 70					

RCA VICTOR
❑ LPM-1251 [M]	Cuban Carnival	1955	12.50	25.00	50.00
❑ LPM-1312 [M]	Puente Goes Jazz	1956	15.00	30.00	60.00
❑ LPM-1354 [M]	Mambo on Broadway	1957	10.00	20.00	40.00
❑ LPM-1392 [M]	Let's Cha-Cha with Puente	1957	10.00	20.00	40.00
❑ LPM-1447 [M]	Night Beat	1957	10.00	20.00	40.00
❑ LPM-1479 [M]	Mucho Puente	1957	10.00	20.00	40.00
❑ LPM-1617 [M]	Top Percussion	1958	7.50	15.00	30.00
❑ LSP-1617 [S]	Top Percussion	1958	10.00	20.00	40.00
❑ LPM-1692 [M]	Dance Mania	1958	7.50	15.00	30.00
❑ LSP-1692 [S]	Dance Mania	1958	10.00	20.00	40.00
❑ LPM-1874 [M]	Dancing Under Latin Skies	1958	7.50	15.00	30.00
❑ LSP-1874 [S]	Dancing Under Latin Skies	1958	10.00	20.00	40.00
❑ LPM-2113 [M]	Mucho Cha Cha Cha	1959	7.50	15.00	30.00
❑ LSP-2113 [S]	Mucho Cha Cha Cha	1959	10.00	20.00	40.00
❑ LPM-2187 [M]	Cha Cha at Grossinger's	1959	7.50	15.00	30.00
❑ LSP-2187 [S]	Cha Cha at Grossinger's	1959	10.00	20.00	40.00
❑ LPM-2257 [M]	Tambo	1960	7.50	15.00	30.00
❑ LSP-2257 [S]	Tambo	1960	10.00	20.00	40.00
❑ LPM-2299 [M]	Revolving Bandstand	1960	7.50	15.00	30.00
❑ LSP-2299 [S]	Revolving Bandstand	1960	10.00	20.00	40.00
❑ LPM-2974 [M]	The Best of Tito Puente	1964	6.25	12.50	25.00
❑ LSP-2974(e) [P]	The Best of Tito Puente	1964	3.75	7.50	15.00

ROULETTE
❑ R-25193 [M]	Bossa Nova	1962	5.00	10.00	20.00
❑ SR-25193 [S]	Bossa Nova	1962	6.25	12.50	25.00
❑ R-25276 [M]	"My Fair Lady" Goes Latin	1964	5.00	10.00	20.00
❑ SR-25276 [S]	"My Fair Lady" Goes Latin	1964	6.25	12.50	25.00

TICO
❑ LP-101 [10]	Mambos, Volume 1	1951	25.00	50.00	100.00
❑ LP-103 [10]	Mambos, Volume 2	1952	20.00	40.00	80.00
❑ LP-107 [10]	Mambos, Volume 3	195?	20.00	40.00	80.00
❑ LP-114 [10]	Mambos, Volume 4	195?	20.00	40.00	80.00
❑ LP-120 [10]	The King of the Mambo and His Orchestra	195?	20.00	40.00	80.00
❑ LP-116 [10]	Mambos, Volume 5	195?	20.00	40.00	80.00
❑ LP-124 [10]	Tito Puente at the Vibes and His Rhythm Quartet	195?	20.00	40.00	80.00
❑ LP-128 [10]	Cha Cha Cha, Volume 1	195?	20.00	40.00	80.00
❑ LP-130 [10]	Cha Cha Cha, Volume 2	195?	20.00	40.00	80.00
❑ LP-131 [10]	Mambos, Volume 8	195?	20.00	40.00	80.00
❑ LP-133 [10]	Instrumental Mambos	195?	20.00	40.00	80.00
❑ LP-134 [10]	Cha Cha Cha, Volume 3	195?	20.00	40.00	80.00
❑ LP-1001 [M]	Mamborama	1955	15.00	30.00	60.00
❑ LP-1003 [M]	Mambo and Me	1955	15.00	30.00	60.00
❑ LP-1006 [M]	Mambos for Lovers	1955	15.00	30.00	60.00
❑ LP-1010 [M]	Dance the Cha Cha Cha	195?	15.00	30.00	60.00
❑ LP-1011 [M]	Puente in Percussion	1956	15.00	30.00	60.00
❑ LP-1025 [M]	Cha Cha Cha at the El Morocco	1956	15.00	30.00	60.00
❑ LP-1032 [M]	Basic Cha Cha Cha	1957	12.50	25.00	50.00
❑ LP-1049 [M]	Tito Puente Swings/Vicentico Valdes Sings	1958	12.50	25.00	50.00
❑ LP-1058 [M]	Puente in Love	1959	10.00	20.00	40.00
❑ LP-1083 [M]	Pachanga Con Puente	1961	7.50	15.00	30.00
❑ SLP-1083 [S]	Pachanga Con Puente	1961	10.00	20.00	40.00
❑ LP-1085 [M]	Vaya Puente	1962	7.50	15.00	30.00
❑ SLP-1085 [S]	Vaya Puente	1962	10.00	20.00	40.00
❑ LP-1086 [M]	El Rey Tito: Bravo Puente	1962	7.50	15.00	30.00
❑ SLP-1086 [S]	El Rey Tito: Bravo Puente	1962	10.00	20.00	40.00
-- This album contains the original version of "Oye Como Va"					
❑ LP-1088 [M]	Tito Puente in Puerto Rico	1963	6.25	12.50	25.00
❑ SLP-1088 [S]	Tito Puente in Puerto Rico	1963	7.50	15.00	30.00
❑ LP-1093 [M]	Tito Puente Bailables	1963	6.25	12.50	25.00
❑ SLP-1093 [S]	Tito Puente Bailables	1963	7.50	15.00	30.00

Number	Title	Yr	VG	VG+	NM
❑ LP-1106 [M]	Excitente Ritmo	196?	6.25	12.50	25.00
❑ SLP-1106 [S]	Excitente Ritmo	196?	7.50	15.00	30.00
❑ LP-1109 [M]	El Mundo Latino de Tito Puente	196?	6.25	12.50	25.00
❑ SLP-1109 [S]	El Mundo Latino de Tito Puente	196?	7.50	15.00	30.00
❑ LP-1115 [M]	Mucho Puente	196?	6.25	12.50	25.00
❑ SLP-1115 [S]	Mucho Puente	196?	7.50	15.00	30.00
❑ LP-1116 [M]	De Mi Para Ti	196?	6.25	12.50	25.00
❑ SLP-1116 [S]	De Mi Para Ti	196?	7.50	15.00	30.00
❑ LP-1121 [M]	Tito Puente Swings/The Exciting Lupe Sings	196?	5.00	10.00	20.00
❑ SLP-1121 [S]	Tito Puente Swings/The Exciting Lupe Sings	196?	6.25	12.50	25.00
❑ LP-1125 [M]	Tu Y Yo (You 'n' Me)	196?	5.00	10.00	20.00
❑ SLP-1125 [S]	Tu Y Yo (You 'n' Me)	196?	6.25	12.50	25.00
❑ LP-1127 [M]	Carnival in Harlem	196?	5.00	10.00	20.00
❑ SLP-1127 [S]	Carnival in Harlem	196?	6.25	12.50	25.00
❑ LP-1131 [M]	Homenaje a Rafael Hernandez	196?	5.00	10.00	20.00
❑ SLP-1131 [S]	Homenaje a Rafael Hernandez	196?	6.25	12.50	25.00
❑ LP-1136 [M]	Cuba Y Puerto Ricon Son	196?	5.00	10.00	20.00
❑ SLP-1136 [S]	Cuba Y Puerto Ricon Son	196?	6.25	12.50	25.00
❑ LP-1151 [M]	20th Anniversary	1967	6.25	12.50	25.00
❑ SLP-1151 [S]	20th Anniversary	1967	5.00	10.00	20.00
❑ LP-1154 [M]	El Rey Y Yo (The King and I)	1967	6.25	12.50	25.00
❑ SLP-1154 [S]	El Rey Y Yo (The King and I)	1967	5.00	10.00	20.00
❑ SLP-1172	El Rey (The King)	1968	5.00	10.00	20.00
❑ SLP-1191	Tito Puente En El Puente (On the Bridge)	1969	5.00	10.00	20.00
❑ SLP-1203	The Best of Tito Puente	1969	5.00	10.00	20.00
❑ SLP-1214	P'alante!	1970	5.00	10.00	20.00
❑ CLP-1301	Para Los Rumberos	1972	3.75	7.50	15.00
❑ CLP-1308	Tito Puente and His Concert Orchestra	1972	3.75	7.50	15.00
❑ CLP-1322	Unlimited Tito	1974	3.75	7.50	15.00
❑ JMTS-1413	The Legend	1976	3.75	7.50	15.00
❑ JMTS-1425	Homenaje a Beny More	1978	3.75	7.50	15.00
❑ JMTS-1430	La Pareja	1978	3.75	7.50	15.00
❑ JMTS-1439	Dance Mania 80's	198?	3.75	7.50	15.00
❑ JMTS-1440	Ce' Magnifique	198?	3.75	7.50	15.00

PUKWANA, DUDU
Alto and tenor saxophone player.
ARISTA/FREEDOM

Number	Title	Yr	VG	VG+	NM
❑ AF 1041	Diamond	1977	3.00	6.00	12.00

PULLEN, DON
Pianist.
ATLANTIC

Number	Title	Yr	VG	VG+	NM
❑ SD 1699	Tomorrow's Promises	1977	3.00	6.00	12.00
❑ SD 8802	Montreux '77	1978	3.00	6.00	12.00

BLACK SAINT

Number	Title	Yr	VG	VG+	NM
❑ BSR-0004	Capricorn Rising	198?	3.00	6.00	12.00
❑ BSR-0010	Healing Force	198?	3.00	6.00	12.00
❑ BSR-0019	Warriors	198?	3.00	6.00	12.00
❑ BSR-0028	Milano Strut	198?	3.00	6.00	12.00
❑ BSR-0038	The Magic Triangle	198?	3.00	6.00	12.00
❑ BSR-0080	Evidence of Things Unseen	198?	3.00	6.00	12.00
❑ BSR-0088	The Sixth Sense	1986	3.00	6.00	12.00

BLUE NOTE

Number	Title	Yr	VG	VG+	NM
❑ B1-91785	New Beginnings	1989	3.00	6.00	12.00

SACKVILLE

Number	Title	Yr	VG	VG+	NM
❑ 3008	Solo Piano Record	198?	2.50	5.00	10.00

PULLEN, DON, AND MILFORD GRAVES
Also see each artist's individual listings.
PULLEN-GRAVES MUSIC

Number	Title	Yr	VG	VG+	NM
❑ (# unknown)	Graves-Pullen Duo	1967	12.50	25.00	50.00

S.R.P.

Number	Title	Yr	VG	VG+	NM
❑ LP-290	Nommo	1968	10.00	20.00	40.00

PUMA, JOE
Guitarist.
BETHLEHEM

Number	Title	Yr	VG	VG+	NM
❑ BCP-1012 [10]	East Coast Jazz 3	1954	50.00	100.00	200.00

COLUMBIA

Number	Title	Yr	VG	VG+	NM
❑ CL 1618 [M]	Like Tweet	1961	7.50	15.00	30.00
❑ CS 8418 [S]	Like Tweet	1961	10.00	20.00	40.00

DAWN

Number	Title	Yr	VG	VG+	NM
❑ DLP-1118 [M]	Wild Kitten	1957	25.00	50.00	100.00

JUBILEE

Number	Title	Yr	VG	VG+	NM
❑ JLP-1070 [M]	Joe Puma Jazz	1958	20.00	40.00	80.00

PUNCH & HANDY'S CALIFORNIA CRUSADERS
Led by PUNCH MILLER and CAP'N JOHN HANDY.
GHB

Number	Title	Yr	VG	VG+	NM
❑ 191	Punch & Handy's California Crusaders, Vol. 1	1985	2.50	5.00	10.00
❑ 192	Punch & Handy's California Crusaders, Vol. 2	1985	2.50	5.00	10.00
❑ 193	Punch & Handy's California Crusaders, Vol. 3	1985	2.50	5.00	10.00

PURCELL, JOHN
Alto and baritone saxophone player and flutist.
MINOR MUSIC

Number	Title	Yr	VG	VG+	NM
❑ MM-006	Third Kind of Blue	1986	3.00	6.00	12.00

PURDIE, BERNARD
Drummer.
DATE

Number	Title	Yr	VG	VG+	NM
❑ TEM 3006 [M]	Soul Drums	1967	5.00	10.00	20.00
❑ TES 4006 [S]	Soul Drums	1967	5.00	10.00	20.00

PRESTIGE

Number	Title	Yr	VG	VG+	NM
❑ 10013	Purdie Good	1971	3.75	7.50	15.00
❑ 10038	Shaft	1972	5.00	10.00	20.00

PURIM, FLORA
Female singer. Also see RETURN TO FOREVER.
FANTASY

Number	Title	Yr	VG	VG+	NM
❑ OJC-315	Butterfly Dreams	1988	2.00	4.00	8.00
-- Reissue of Milestone 9052					
❑ OJC-619	Stories to Tell	1991	2.00	4.00	8.00
-- Reissue of Milestone 9058					

MILESTONE

Number	Title	Yr	VG	VG+	NM
❑ 9052	Butterfly Dreams	1974	2.50	5.00	10.00
❑ 9058	Stories to Tell	1975	2.50	5.00	10.00
❑ 9065	Open Your Eyes You Can Fly	1976	2.50	5.00	10.00
❑ 9070	500 Miles High	1976	2.50	5.00	10.00
❑ 9077	Encounter	1977	2.50	5.00	10.00
❑ 9081	That's What She Said	1978	2.50	5.00	10.00
❑ 9095	Love Reborn	1980	2.50	5.00	10.00

VENTURE

Number	Title	Yr	VG	VG+	NM
❑ 90995	The Midnight Sun	1988	2.50	5.00	10.00

WARNER BROS.

Number	Title	Yr	VG	VG+	NM
❑ BS 2985	Nothing Will Be As It Was...Tomorrow	1977	2.50	5.00	10.00
❑ BSK 3168	Everyday, Everynight	1978	2.50	5.00	10.00
❑ BSK 3344	Carry On	1979	2.50	5.00	10.00

PURIM, FLORA, AND AIRTO
Also see each artist's individual listings.
CROSSOVER

Number	Title	Yr	VG	VG+	NM
❑ CR-5001	The Magicians	1988	2.00	4.00	8.00
❑ CR-5003	The Sun Is Out	1989	2.50	5.00	10.00

GEORGE WEIN COLLECTION

Number	Title	Yr	VG	VG+	NM
❑ GW-3007	Humble People	1986	2.00	4.00	8.00

PURVIS, PAM, AND BOB ACKERMAN
Purvis is a female singer and keyboard player; Ackerman is a saxophone player, clarinetist and flutist.
BLACKHAWK

Number	Title	Yr	VG	VG+	NM
❑ BKH-51201	Heart Song	1986	2.50	5.00	10.00

Number	Title	Yr	VG	VG+	NM

Q

QUADRANT
Members: JOE PASS; MILT JACKSON; RAY BROWN; Mickey Roker (drums).
PABLO
| ❑ 2310 837 | Quadrant | 1978 | 3.00 | 6.00 | 12.00 |

PABLO TODAY
| ❑ 2312 117 | Quadrant Toasts Duke Ellington/ All Too Soon | 1980 | 3.00 | 6.00 | 12.00 |

QUARTET, THE
See THE MODERN JAZZ QUARTET.

QUARTETTE TRES BIEN
Members: Percy James; Albert St. James; Richard Simmons; Jeter Thompson (keyboards).
ATLANTIC
| ❑ 1461 [M] | Bully! | 1966 | 3.75 | 7.50 | 15.00 |
| ❑ SD 1461 [S] | Bully! | 1966 | 5.00 | 10.00 | 20.00 |

DECCA
❑ DL 4547 [M]	Boss Tres Bien	1964	3.75	7.50	15.00
❑ DL 4548 [M]	Kilimanjaro	1964	3.75	7.50	15.00
❑ DL 4617 [M]	Spring Into Spring	1965	3.75	7.50	15.00
❑ DL 4675 [M]	Stepping Out	1965	3.75	7.50	15.00
❑ DL 4715 [M]	Sky High	1966	3.75	7.50	15.00
❑ DL 4791 [M]	"In" Motion	1966	3.75	7.50	15.00
❑ DL 4822 [M]	Where It's At	1966	3.75	7.50	15.00
❑ DL 4893 [M]	Here It Is	1967	5.00	10.00	20.00
❑ DL 4958 [M]	Four of a Kind	1967	5.00	10.00	20.00
❑ DL 74547 [S]	Boss Tres Bien	1964	5.00	10.00	20.00
❑ DL 74548 [S]	Kilimanjaro	1964	5.00	10.00	20.00
❑ DL 74617 [S]	Spring Into Spring	1965	5.00	10.00	20.00
❑ DL 74675 [S]	Stepping Out	1965	5.00	10.00	20.00
❑ DL 74715 [S]	Sky High	1966	5.00	10.00	20.00
❑ DL 74791 [S]	"In" Motion	1966	5.00	10.00	20.00
❑ DL 74822 [S]	Where It's At	1966	5.00	10.00	20.00
❑ DL 74893 [S]	Here It Is	1967	3.75	7.50	15.00
❑ DL 74958 [S]	Four of a Kind	1967	3.75	7.50	15.00
❑ DL 75044	Our Thing	1969	3.75	7.50	15.00

GNP
❑ GNP-102 [M]	Quartette Tres Bien	1962	5.00	10.00	20.00
❑ GNPS-102 [S]	Quartette Tres Bien	1962	6.25	12.50	25.00
❑ GNP-107 [M]	Kilimanjaro	1963	5.00	10.00	20.00
❑ GNPS-107 [S]	Kilimanjaro	1963	6.25	12.50	25.00

QUEBEC, IKE
Tenor saxophone player and pianist.
BLUE NOTE
| ❑ LT-1052 | With a Song in My Heart | 1980 | 2.50 | 5.00 | 10.00 |
| ❑ BLP-4093 [M] | Heavy Soul | 1961 | 20.00 | 40.00 | 80.00 |
| -- With 61st St. address on label |
| ❑ BLP-4093 [M] | Heavy Soul | 1962 | 6.25 | 12.50 | 25.00 |
| -- With "New York, USA" address on label |
| ❑ BLP-4098 [M] | Blue and Sentimental | 1962 | 20.00 | 40.00 | 80.00 |
| -- With 61st St. address on label |
| ❑ BLP-4098 [M] | Blue and Sentimental | 1962 | 6.25 | 12.50 | 25.00 |
| -- With "New York, USA" address on label |
| ❑ BLP-4103 [M] | Easy Living | 1962 | --- | --- | --- |
| -- Canceled |
❑ BLP-4105 [M]	It Might As Well Be Spring	1962	7.50	15.00	30.00
❑ BLP-4114 [M]	Bossa Nova Soul Samba	1962	7.50	15.00	30.00
❑ B1-32090	Heavy Soul	1995	3.75	7.50	15.00
-- "The Finest in Jazz Since 1939" reissue
❑ BST-84093 [S]	Heavy Soul	1961	15.00	30.00	60.00
-- With 61st St. address on label
❑ BST-84093 [S]	Heavy Soul	1961	5.00	10.00	20.00
-- With "New York, USA" address on label
❑ BST-84093 [S]	Heavy Soul	1967	3.00	6.00	12.00
-- With "A Division of Liberty Records" on label
❑ BST-84098 [S]	Blue and Sentimental	1962	5.00	10.00	20.00
-- With "New York, USA" address on label
❑ BST-84098 [S]	Blue and Sentimental	1962	15.00	30.00	60.00
-- With 61st St. address on label
❑ BST-84098 [S]	Blue and Sentimental	1967	3.00	6.00	12.00
-- With "A Division of Liberty Records" on label
❑ BST-84098 [S]	Blue and Sentimental	1986	2.50	5.00	10.00
-- "The Finest in Jazz Since 1939" reissue
❑ BST-84103 [S]	Easy Living	1987	3.00	6.00	12.00
-- "The Finest in Jazz Since 1939" issue; originally scheduled for 1962 release
❑ BST-84105 [S]	It Might As Well Be Spring	1962	10.00	20.00	40.00
-- With "New York, USA" address on label
❑ BST-84105 [S]	It Might As Well Be Spring	1967	3.75	7.50	15.00
-- With "A Division of Liberty Records" on label
❑ BST-84114 [S]	Bossa Nova Soul Samba	1962	10.00	20.00	40.00
-- With "New York, USA" address on label
❑ BST-84114 [S]	Bossa Nova Soul Samba	1967	3.75	7.50	15.00
-- With "A Division of Liberty Records" on label
❑ BST-84114	Bossa Nova Soul Samba	199?	6.25	12.50	25.00
-- Classic Records reissue on audiophile vinyl

MOSAIC
| ❑ M4-107 [(4)] | The Complete Blue Note Forties Recordings of Ike Quebec and John Hardee | 199? | 17.50 | 35.00 | 70.00 |
| ❑ M3-121 [(3)] | The Complete Blue Note 45 Sessions of Ike Quebec | 199? | 15.00 | 30.00 | 60.00 |

QUEEN CITY RAGTIME ENSEMBLE
From Cincinnati, Ohio: Hank Troy (piano/leader); Marl Shanahan (drums); Maurie Walker (banjo); Bill Clark (tuba).
STOMP OFF
| ❑ SOS-1138 | Everybody's Rag | 1987 | 2.50 | 5.00 | 10.00 |

QUEST
Members: RICHIE BEIRACH; BILLY HART; DAVID LIEBMAN; RON McCLURE.
PATHFINDER
| ❑ PTF-8839 | Natural Selection | 1988 | 2.50 | 5.00 | 10.00 |

QUIGLEY, JACK
SAND
| ❑ C-28 [M] | Jack Quigley in Hollywood | 196? | 7.50 | 15.00 | 30.00 |
| -- Red vinyl; may or may not exist on black vinyl |
| ❑ CS-28 [S] | Jack Quigley in Hollywood | 196? | 5.00 | 10.00 | 20.00 |
| ❑ C-30 [M] | Class In Session | 196? | 7.50 | 15.00 | 30.00 |
| -- Red vinyl; may or may not exist on black vinyl |
| ❑ CS-30 [S] | Class In Session | 196? | 5.00 | 10.00 | 20.00 |
| ❑ C-32 [M] | Listen! Quigley | 196? | 7.50 | 15.00 | 30.00 |
| -- Red vinyl; may or may not exist on black vinyl |
❑ CS-32 [S]	Listen! Quigley	196?	5.00	10.00	20.00
❑ C-38 [M]	D'Jever	196?	5.00	10.00	20.00
❑ CS-38 [S]	D'Jever	196?	6.25	12.50	25.00

QUILL, GENE
Alto saxophone player and occasional clarinetist. Also see THE FOUR MOST; MUNDELL LOWE; PHIL WOODS.
ROOST
| ❑ LP-2229 [M] | Three Bones and a Quill | 1958 | 12.50 | 25.00 | 50.00 |

QUINICHETTE, PAUL
Tenor saxophone player. Also see JOHN COLTRANE; BENNIE GREEN; CHARLIE ROUSE; LESTER YOUNG.
BIOGRAPH
| ❑ BLP-12066 | The Kid from Denver | 199? | 3.00 | 6.00 | 12.00 |

DAWN
| ❑ DLP-1109 [M] | The Kid from Denver | 1956 | 25.00 | 50.00 | 100.00 |

EMARCY
❑ MG-26022 [10]	The Vice 'Pres'	1954	50.00	100.00	200.00
❑ MG-26035 [10]	Sequel	1954	50.00	100.00	200.00
❑ MG-36003 [M]	Moods	1955	25.00	50.00	100.00
❑ MG-36027 [M]	The Vice 'Pres'	1955	25.00	50.00	100.00

FANTASY
| ❑ OJC-076 | On the Sunny Side | 198? | 2.50 | 5.00 | 10.00 |

PRESTIGE
❑ PRLP-7103 [M]	On the Sunny Side	1957	20.00	40.00	80.00
❑ PRLP-7127 [M]	For Basie	1957	20.00	40.00	80.00
❑ PRLP-7147 [M]	Basie Reunion	1958	15.00	30.00	60.00

STATUS
| ❑ ST-2036 [M] | For Basie | 1966 | 5.00 | 10.00 | 20.00 |
| -- Reissue of Swingville 2036 |

SWINGVILLE
| ❑ SVLP-2036 [M] | For Basie | 1962 | 12.50 | 25.00 | 50.00 |
| -- Purple label |
| ❑ SVLP-2036 [M] | For Basie | 1965 | 6.25 | 12.50 | 25.00 |
| -- Blue label, trident logo at right |
| ❑ SVLP-2037 [M] | Basie Reunion | 1962 | 12.50 | 25.00 | 50.00 |
| -- Purple label |
| ❑ SVLP-2037 [M] | Basie Reunion | 1965 | 6.25 | 12.50 | 25.00 |
| -- Blue label, trident logo at right |

TRIP
| ❑ 5542 | The Vice 'Pres' | 197? | 2.50 | 5.00 | 10.00 |

UNITED ARTISTS
❑ UAL-4024 [M]	Like Basie	1959	12.50	25.00	50.00
❑ UAL-4054 [M]	Like Who?	1959	10.00	20.00	40.00
❑ UAL-4077 [M]	Paul Quinichette	1960	10.00	20.00	40.00
❑ UAS-5024 [S]	Like Basie	1959	10.00	20.00	40.00
❑ UAS-5054 [S]	Like Who?	1959	7.50	15.00	30.00
❑ UAS-5077 [S]	Paul Quinichette	1960	12.50	25.00	50.00

Number	Title	Yr	VG	VG+	NM	Number	Title	Yr	VG	VG+	NM

QUINICHETTE, PAUL, AND FRANK FOSTER
Also see each artist's individual listings.
DECCA
❑ DL 8058 [M]	Jazz Studio 1	1954	25.00	50.00	100.00

QUINICHETTE, PAUL/GENE ROLAND
Also see each artist's individual listings.
DAWN
❑ DLP-1122 [M]	Jazzville, Vol. 4	1957	25.00	50.00	100.00

QUINTET OF THE HOT CLUB OF FRANCE, THE
Members: Joseph Chaput (rhythm guitar); Roget Chaput (rhythm guitar); STEPHANE GRAPPELLI; DJANGO REINHARDT; Louis Vola (bass).
CAPITOL
❑ DT 2045 [R]	Hot Club of France	1964	5.00	10.00	20.00
❑ T 2045 [M]	Hot Club of France	1964	7.50	15.00	30.00

DIAL
❑ LP-214 [10]	Django Reinhardt and the Hot Club Quintet	1951	75.00	150.00	300.00
❑ LP-218 [10]	Django Reinhardt and the Quintet	1951	75.00	150.00	300.00

LONDON
❑ 810 [10]	Hot Club Quintet	1954	30.00	60.00	120.00
❑ LL 1344 [M]	Swing From Paris	1956	20.00	40.00	80.00

PRESTIGE
❑ PRST-7614 [R]	First Recordings	1969	3.75	7.50	15.00

QUINTET, THE
Members: DIZZY GILLESPIE; CHARLES MINGUS; CHARLIE PARKER; BUD POWELL; MAX ROACH.
DEBU
❑ DLP-2 [10]	Jazz at Massey Hall	1953	100.00	200.00	400.00
❑ DLP-4 [10]	Jazz at Massey Hall, Volume 3	1953	100.00	200.00	400.00
❑ DEB-124 [M]	Jazz at Massey Hall	1956	75.00	150.00	300.00

FANTASY
❑ 6006 [M]	Jazz at Massey Hall	1962	12.50	25.00	50.00
-- Red vinyl					
❑ 6006 [R]	Jazz at Massey Hall	1962	7.50	15.00	30.00
-- Black vinyl					
❑ 86006 [M]	Jazz at Massey Hall	1962	7.50	15.00	30.00
-- Blue vinyl					
❑ 86006 [R]	Jazz at Massey Hall	1962	5.00	10.00	20.00
-- Black vinyl					

QUIRE
RCA VICTOR
❑ BGL1-1700	Quire	1976	3.00	6.00	12.00

Number	Title	Yr	VG	VG+	NM

R

RA, SUN
See SUN RA in the "S" section.

RACHABANE, BARNEY
Alto saxophone player.
JIVE
| ❏ 1253-1-J | Barney's Way | 1989 | 3.00 | 6.00 | 12.00 |

RADER, DON
Trumpeter.
DISCOVERY
| ❏ 796 | Wallflower | 1979 | 3.00 | 6.00 | 12.00 |
PBR
| ❏ 10 | Now | 197? | 3.00 | 6.00 | 12.00 |

RADKE, FRED, AND MIKE VAX
Both Radke and Vax are trumpeters, arrangers and bandleaders.
MUSIC IS MEDICINE
| ❏ 9052 | The First Reunion | 198? | 3.00 | 6.00 | 12.00 |

RAE, JOHN
Vibraphone player.
SAVOY
| ❏ MG-12156 [M] | Opus De Jazz, Volume 2 | 1960 | 10.00 | 20.00 | 40.00 |

RAEBURN, BOYD
Soprano saxophone player, arranger and bandleader.
AIRCHECK
| ❏ 20 | Rhythms by Boyd Raeburn | 197? | 2.50 | 5.00 | 10.00 |
CIRCLE
| ❏ 22 | Boyd Raeburn and His Orchestra 1944-45 | 198? | 2.50 | 5.00 | 10.00 |
| ❏ CLP-113 | More Boyd Raeburn and His Orchestra 1944-45 | 1987 | 2.50 | 5.00 | 10.00 |
COLUMBIA
| ❏ CL 889 [M] | Dance Spectacular | 1956 | 7.50 | 15.00 | 30.00 |
| ❏ CL 957 [M] | Fraternity Rush | 1957 | 7.50 | 15.00 | 30.00 |
MUSICRAFT
| ❏ 505 | Experiments in Big Band Jazz 1945 | 198? | 2.50 | 5.00 | 10.00 |
SAVOY
❏ MG-12025 [M]	Man With the Horns	1955	10.00	20.00	40.00
❏ MG-12040 [M]	Boyd Meets Stravinsky	1955	10.00	20.00	40.00
❏ MG-15010 [10]	Innovations by Boyd Raeburn, Volume 1	1951	20.00	40.00	80.00
❏ MG-15011 [10]	Innovations by Boyd Raeburn, Volume 2	1951	20.00	40.00	80.00
❏ MG-15012 [10]	Innovations by Boyd Raeburn, Volume 3	1951	20.00	40.00	80.00
SAVOY JAZZ
| ❏ SJC-406 | Man with the Horns | 1985 | 2.50 | 5.00 | 10.00 |
| ❏ SJL-2250 [(2)] | Jewels Plus | 198? | 3.00 | 6.00 | 12.00 |

RAFF, RENEE
Female singer.
AUDIO FIDELITY
| ❏ AFLP-2142 [M] | Among the Stars | 1965 | 3.75 | 7.50 | 15.00 |
| ❏ AFSD-6142 [S] | Among the Stars | 1965 | 5.00 | 10.00 | 20.00 |

RAGTIME BANJO COMMISSION, THE
GHB
| ❏ GHB-154 | The Ragtime Banjo Commission | 1981 | 2.50 | 5.00 | 10.00 |

RAHIM, EMANUEL K.
Percussionist.
COBBLESTONE
| ❏ 9014 | Total Submission | 1972 | 6.25 | 12.50 | 25.00 |

RAHMLEE
Full name: Rahmlee Michael Davis. Trumpeter and fluegel horn player.
HEADFIRST
| ❏ 9703 | Rise of the Phoenix | 198? | 3.00 | 6.00 | 12.00 |

RAI, VASANT
From India. Sarod player.
VANGUARD
| ❏ VSD-79379 | Spring Flowers | 197? | 3.00 | 6.00 | 12.00 |

Number	Title	Yr	VG	VG+	NM
❏ VSD-79414	Autumn Song	1978	3.00	6.00	12.00

RAINBOW
Led by organist Will Boulware.
INNER CITY
| ❏ IC-6001 | Crystal Green | 197? | 3.75 | 7.50 | 15.00 |

RAINER, TOM
Pianist.
MUSIC IS MEDICINE
| ❏ 9042 | Night Music | 198? | 3.00 | 6.00 | 12.00 |

RAINEY, CHUCK
Bass player.
COBBLESTONE
| ❏ 9008 | Chuck Rainey Coalition | 1972 | 5.00 | 10.00 | 20.00 |

RAINEY, MA
Female singer, one of the pioneer blues singers.
BIOGRAPH
❏ LP-12001	Blues the World Forgot	1968	3.75	7.50	15.00
❏ LP-12011	Oh My Babe Blues	197?	3.00	6.00	12.00
❏ LP-12032	Queen of the Blues	197?	3.00	6.00	12.00
MILESTONE
❏ 2001	Immortal Ma Rainey	1967	3.75	7.50	15.00
❏ 2008	Blame It on the Blues	196?	3.75	7.50	15.00
❏ 2017	Down in the Basement	197?	3.00	6.00	12.00
❏ 47021 [(2)]	Ma Rainey	197?	3.75	7.50	15.00
RIVERSIDE
❏ RLP 12-108 [M]	Ma Rainey	1955	50.00	100.00	200.00
❏ RLP 12-137 [M]	Broken Hearted Blues	1956	25.00	50.00	100.00
❏ RLP-1003 [10]	Ma Rainey, Vol. 1	1953	62.50	125.00	250.00
❏ RLP-1016 [10]	Ma Rainey, Vol. 2	1953	62.50	125.00	250.00
❏ RLP-1045 [10]	Ma Rainey, Vol. 3	1954	62.50	125.00	250.00

RALKE, DON
Arranger and composer.
CROWN
| ❏ CLP-5019 [M] | Bongo Madness | 1957 | 6.25 | 12.50 | 25.00 |
WARNER BROS.
❏ W 1321 [M]	Bourbon Street Beat	1959	5.00	10.00	20.00
❏ WS 1321 [S]	Bourbon Street Beat	1959	6.25	12.50	25.00
❏ W 1360 [M]	But You've Never Heard Gershwin with Bongos	1960	5.00	10.00	20.00
❏ WS 1360 [S]	But You've Never Heard Gershwin with Bongos	1960	6.25	12.50	25.00
❏ W 1398 [M]	The Savage and Sensuous Bongos	1960	6.25	12.50	25.00
❏ WS 1398 [S]	The Savage and Sensuous Bongos	1960	7.50	15.00	30.00

RAMIREZ, RAM
Pianist and composer.
MASTER JAZZ
| ❏ 8122 | Rampant Ram | 1973 | 3.00 | 6.00 | 12.00 |

RAMPART STREET PARADERS, THE
Members: Clyde Hurley (trumpet); Abe Lincoln (trombone); MARTY MATLOCK (clarinet); EDDIE MILLER (saxophones); GEORGE VAN EPS (guitar).
COLUMBIA
❏ CL 648 [M]	Rampart and Vine	1955	10.00	20.00	40.00
-- Maroon label, gold print					
❏ CL 648 [M]	Rampart and Vine	1956	7.50	15.00	30.00
-- Red and black label with six "eye" logos					
❏ CL 785 [M]	Dixieland My Dixieland	1956	7.50	15.00	30.00
❏ CL 1061 [M]	Texas! U.S.A.	1957	7.50	15.00	30.00
HARMONY
| ❏ HL 7214 [M] | Real Dixieland | 196? | 3.75 | 7.50 | 15.00 |

RANDI, DON
Pianist, arranger and composer. Also see THE MUSIC COMPANY.
CAPITOL
| ❏ ST-287 | Love Theme from Romeo and Juliet | 1969 | 5.00 | 10.00 | 20.00 |
PALOMAR
| ❏ 24002 [M] | Don Randi! | 1965 | 3.75 | 7.50 | 15.00 |
| ❏ 34002 [S] | Don Randi! | 1965 | 5.00 | 10.00 | 20.00 |

Number	Title	Yr	VG	VG+	NM
POPPY					
❏ PY-5701	Don Randi Trio at the Baked Potato	1972	3.75	7.50	15.00
REPRISE					
❏ R-6229 [M]	Revolver Jazz	1966	5.00	10.00	20.00
❏ RS-6229 [S]	Revolver Jazz	1966	6.25	12.50	25.00
VERVE					
❏ V-8469 [M]	Where Do We Go From Here?	1962	3.00	6.00	12.00
❏ V6-8469 [S]	Where Do We Go From Here?	1962	3.75	7.50	15.00
❏ V-8524 [M]	Last Night With the Don Randi Trio	1963	3.00	6.00	12.00
❏ V6-8524 [S]	Last Night With the Don Randi Trio	1963	3.75	7.50	15.00
WORLD PACIFIC					
❏ ST-1297 [S]	Feelin' Like Blues	1960	6.25	12.50	25.00
❏ WP-1297 [M]	Feelin' Like Blues	1960	7.50	15.00	30.00

RANELIN, PHIL
Trombonist, composer and arranger.

Number	Title	Yr	VG	VG+	NM
TRIBE					
❏ PRSD-2226	Message from the Tribe	197?	25.00	50.00	100.00
❏ TRCD 4006	The Time Is Now!	1974	20.00	40.00	80.00

RANEY, DOUG
Guitarist. Also see JIMMY AND DOUG RANEY.

Number	Title	Yr	VG	VG+	NM
STEEPLECHASE					
❏ SCS-1082	Introducing Doug Raney	1978	3.00	6.00	12.00
❏ SCS-1105	Cuttin' Loose	198?	3.00	6.00	12.00
❏ SCS-1144	Listen	1981	3.00	6.00	12.00
❏ SCS-1166	I'll Close My Eyes	1982	3.00	6.00	12.00
❏ SCS-1191	Black and White	198?	3.00	6.00	12.00
❏ SCS-1200	Lazy Bird	198?	3.00	6.00	12.00
❏ SCS-1212	Guitar, Guitar, Guitar	198?	3.00	6.00	12.00

RANEY, JIMMY
Guitarist and composer. Also see BOB BROOKMEYER; KENNY BURRELL; THE MANHATTAN JAZZ ALL-STARS; ZOOT SIMS.

Number	Title	Yr	VG	VG+	NM
ABC-PARAMOUNT					
❏ ABC-129 [M]	Jimmy Raney Featuring Bob Brookmeyer	1956	12.50	25.00	50.00
❏ ABC-167 [M]	Jimmy Raney in Three Attitudes	1957	10.00	20.00	40.00
BIOGRAPH					
❏ LP-12060	Too Marvelous for Words	198?	2.50	5.00	10.00
DAWN					
❏ DLP-1120 [M]	Jimmy Raney Visits Paris	1958	10.00	20.00	40.00
FANTASY					
❏ OJC-1706	Jimmy Raney/A	1985	2.50	5.00	10.00
MUSE					
❏ MR-5004	Strings and Swings	1973	3.75	7.50	15.00
NEW JAZZ					
❏ NJLP-1101 [10]	Jimmy Raney Quartet Featuring Hall Overton	1953	75.00	150.00	300.00
❏ NJLP-1103 [10]	Jimmy Raney Ensemble Introducing Phil Woods	1953	75.00	150.00	300.00
PAUSA					
❏ 7021	Momentum	197?	2.50	5.00	10.00
PRESTIGE					
❏ PRLP-156 [10]	Jimmy Raney Plays	1953	37.50	75.00	150.00
❏ PRLP-179 [10]	Jimmy Raney in Sweden	1954	37.50	75.00	150.00
❏ PRLP-199 [10]	Jimmy Raney Quintet	1954	37.50	75.00	150.00
❏ PRLP-201 [10]	Jimmy Raney Quartet	1955	37.50	75.00	150.00
❏ PRLP-203 [10]	Jimmy Raney Ensemble	1955	37.50	75.00	150.00
❏ PRLP-7089 [M]	Jimmy Raney/A	1957	20.00	40.00	80.00
XANADU					
❏ 116	Influence	197?	3.00	6.00	12.00
❏ 132	Live in Tokyo	197?	3.00	6.00	12.00
❏ 140	Solo	1977	3.00	6.00	12.00

RANEY, JIMMY AND DOUG
Also see each artist's individual listings.

Number	Title	Yr	VG	VG+	NM
STEEPLECHASE					
❏ SCS-1118	Stolen Moments	198?	3.00	6.00	12.00
❏ SCS-1134	Duets	1980	3.00	6.00	12.00
❏ SCS-1184	Nardis	198?	3.00	6.00	12.00

RANEY, JIMMY/GEORGE WALLINGTON
Also see each artist's individual listings.

Number	Title	Yr	VG	VG+	NM
EMARCY					
❏ MG-36121 [M]	Swingin' in Sweden	1958	15.00	30.00	60.00

RANEY, SUE
Female singer.

Number	Title	Yr	VG	VG+	NM
CAPITOL					
❏ ST 1335 [S]	Songs for a Raney Day	1960	6.25	12.50	25.00
❏ T 1335 [M]	Songs for a Raney Day	1960	5.00	10.00	20.00
❏ ST 2032 [S]	All By Myself	1964	3.75	7.50	15.00
❏ T 2032 [M]	All By Myself	1964	5.00	10.00	20.00
DISCOVERY					
❏ DS-875	Sue Raney Sings the Music of Johnny Mandel	1982	2.50	5.00	10.00
❏ DS-913	Ridin' High	1984	2.50	5.00	10.00
IMPERIAL					
❏ LP-9323 [M]	Alive and In Love	1966	3.75	7.50	15.00
❏ LP-9355 [M]	New and Now	1967	6.25	12.50	25.00
❏ LP-9376 [M]	With a Little Help from My Friends	1968	7.50	15.00	30.00
❏ LP-12323 [S]	Alive and In Love	1966	5.00	10.00	20.00
❏ LP-12355 [S]	New and Now	1967	3.75	7.50	15.00
❏ LP-12376 [S]	With a Little Help from My Friends	1968	3.75	7.50	15.00

RANEY, SUE, AND BOB FLORENCE
Also see each artist's individual listings.

Number	Title	Yr	VG	VG+	NM
DISCOVERY					
❏ DS-931	Flight of Fancy: A Journey of Alan and Marilyn Bergman	1987	2.50	5.00	10.00
❏ DS-939	Quietly There	1988	2.50	5.00	10.00

RANGELL, NELSON
Soprano, alto and tenor saxophone player and flutist.

Number	Title	Yr	VG	VG+	NM
GRP					
❏ GR-9593	Playing for Keeps	1989	3.00	6.00	12.00

RATZER, KARL
Guitarist.

Number	Title	Yr	VG	VG+	NM
CMP					
❏ CMP-13-ST	Dancing on a String	198?	2.50	5.00	10.00
VANGUARD					
❏ VSD-79407	In Search of the Ghost	1978	3.00	6.00	12.00
❏ VSD-79423	Street Talk	1979	3.00	6.00	12.00

RAULSTON, FRED
Vibraphone player and percussionist.

Number	Title	Yr	VG	VG+	NM
INNER CITY					
❏ IC-1054	Open Stream	197?	3.00	6.00	12.00
❏ IC-1085	Uncharted Waters	198?	3.00	6.00	12.00
SEA BREEZE					
❏ SBD-104	Fred's Rescue	1987	2.50	5.00	10.00

RAVA, ENRICO
Trumpeter.

Number	Title	Yr	VG	VG+	NM
BLACK SAINT					
❏ BSR-0011	Il Giro Del Giorno	198?	3.00	6.00	12.00
ECM					
❏ 1063	Pilgrim	197?	3.00	6.00	12.00
❏ 1078	Plot	1976	3.00	6.00	12.00
❏ 1122	Enrico Rava Quartet	1978	3.00	6.00	12.00
❏ 1224	Opening Night	1981	2.50	5.00	10.00
SOUL NOTE					
❏ SN-1064	Andanada	198?	3.00	6.00	12.00
❏ SN-1114	String Band	1985	3.00	6.00	12.00

RAVAZZA, CARL
Male singer, violinist and bandleader.

Number	Title	Yr	VG	VG+	NM
HINDSIGHT					
❏ HSR-117	Carl Ravazza and His Orchestra 1940-44	198?	2.50	5.00	10.00

RAWLINS, STEVE
Pianist.

Number	Title	Yr	VG	VG+	NM
SEA BREEZE					
❏ SB-3003	Step Right Up	1985	2.50	5.00	10.00

RAWLS, LOU
Male singer. Has had hits in pop, R&B/soul and dance music as well as jazz.

Number	Title	Yr	VG	VG+	NM
ALLEGIANCE					
❏ AV-5016	Trying As Hard As I Can	198?	2.50	5.00	10.00
BELL					
❏ 1318	She's Gone	1974	3.00	6.00	12.00

(Top left) Blues singer Ma Rainey, who died in 1939, left behind approximately 100 recordings, many of which find her accompanied by jazz artists of the day. This is a sought-after collection, the first on 12-inch LP, of some of these performances. (Top right) Recorded by the Chick Corea/Al DiMeola/Stanley Clarke/Lenny White version of the group, Return to Forever's *Romantic Warrior* (1976) was the group's most popular among the general public, but at the time was widely panned by critics. It stands up much better today. (Bottom left) Even before Max Roach formed a classic quintet with doomed trumpeter Clifford Brown, he was in a quartet with Hank Mobley, and this rare 10-inch album resulted. Word has it that this LP has been very poorly mastered to CD, possibly from a far-less-than-mint copy of the original album. (Bottom right) Shorty Rogers spent many years writing film and television scores, but before that, he was respected as an arranger. His first album as a leader, after stints with, among others, Woody Herman and Stan Kenton, resulted in this 10-inch album, which is considered the precursor to what became known as "West Coast jazz."

Number	Title	Yr	VG	VG+	NM
BLUE NOTE					
❏ B1-91441	Stormy Monday	1990	3.00	6.00	12.00
-- Reissue of Capitol 1714					
❏ B1-91937	At Last	1989	3.00	6.00	12.00
❏ B1-93841	It's Supposed to Be Fun	1990	3.75	7.50	15.00
CAPITOL					
❏ ST-122	The Way It Was	1969	3.75	7.50	15.00
❏ ST-215	The Way It Was -- The Way It Is	1969	3.75	7.50	15.00
❏ SWBB-261 [(2)]	Close-Up	1969	5.00	10.00	20.00
-- Reissue of 1824 and 2042 in one package					
❏ ST-325	Your Good Thing	1969	3.75	7.50	15.00
❏ ST-427	You've Made Me So Very Happy	1970	3.75	7.50	15.00
❏ ST-479	Bring It On Home	1970	3.75	7.50	15.00
❏ STBB-720 [(2)]	Down Here on the Ground/I'd Rather Drink Muddy Water	1971	5.00	10.00	20.00
❏ SM-1714	Stormy Monday	197?	2.50	5.00	10.00
-- Reissue with new prefix					
❏ ST 1714 [S]	Stormy Monday	1962	6.25	12.50	25.00
❏ T 1714 [M]	Stormy Monday	1962	5.00	10.00	20.00
❏ ST 1824 [S]	Black and Blue	1963	6.25	12.50	25.00
❏ T 1824 [M]	Black and Blue	1963	5.00	10.00	20.00
❏ ST 2042 [S]	Tobacco Road	1964	6.25	12.50	25.00
❏ T 2042 [M]	Tobacco Road	1964	5.00	10.00	20.00
❏ ST 2273 [S]	Nobody But Lou	1965	6.25	12.50	25.00
❏ T 2273 [M]	Nobody But Lou	1965	5.00	10.00	20.00
❏ ST 2401 [S]	Lou Rawls and Strings	1965	6.25	12.50	25.00
❏ T 2401 [M]	Lou Rawls and Strings	1965	5.00	10.00	20.00
❏ SM-2459	Lou Rawls Live!	197?	2.50	5.00	10.00
-- Reissue with new prefix					
❏ ST 2459 [S]	Lou Rawls Live!	1966	5.00	10.00	20.00
❏ T 2459 [M]	Lou Rawls Live!	1966	3.75	7.50	15.00
❏ SM-2566	Lou Rawls Soulin'	197?	2.50	5.00	10.00
-- Reissue with new prefix					
❏ ST 2566 [S]	Lou Rawls Soulin'	1966	5.00	10.00	20.00
❏ T 2566 [M]	Lou Rawls Soulin'	1966	3.75	7.50	15.00
❏ ST 2632 [S]	Lou Rawls Carryin' On!	1966	5.00	10.00	20.00
❏ T 2632 [M]	Lou Rawls Carryin' On!	1966	3.75	7.50	15.00
❏ ST 2713 [S]	Too Much!	1967	3.75	7.50	15.00
❏ T 2713 [M]	Too Much!	1967	5.00	10.00	20.00
❏ ST 2756 [S]	That's Lou	1967	3.75	7.50	15.00
❏ T 2756 [M]	That's Lou	1967	5.00	10.00	20.00
❏ ST 2790 [S]	Merry Christmas, Ho, Ho, Ho	1967	3.00	6.00	12.00
❏ T 2790 [M]	Merry Christmas, Ho, Ho, Ho	1967	3.75	7.50	15.00
❏ ST 2864 [S]	Feelin' Good	1968	3.75	7.50	15.00
❏ T 2864 [M]	Feelin' Good	1968	7.50	15.00	30.00
❏ ST 2927	You're Good for Me	1968	3.75	7.50	15.00
❏ SKAO 2948	The Best of Lou Rawls	1968	3.75	7.50	15.00
❏ SM-2948	The Best of Lou Rawls	197?	2.50	5.00	10.00
-- Reissue with new prefix					
❏ SKBB-11585 [(2)]	The Best of Lou Rawls	1976	3.00	6.00	12.00
❏ SN-16096	The Best of Lou Rawls	1980	2.00	4.00	8.00
-- Budget-line reissue					
❏ SN-16097	Lou Rawls Live!	1980	2.00	4.00	8.00
-- Budget-line reissue					
EPIC					
❏ FE 37448	Now Is the Time	1982	2.50	5.00	10.00
❏ FE 38553	When the Night Comes	1983	2.50	5.00	10.00
❏ FE 39403	Close Company	1984	2.50	5.00	10.00
❏ FE 40210	Love All Your Blues Away	1986	2.50	5.00	10.00
MGM					
❏ SE-4771	Natural Man	1971	3.00	6.00	12.00
❏ SE-4809	Silk & Soul	1972	3.00	6.00	12.00
❏ SE-4861	A Man of Value	1973	3.00	6.00	12.00
❏ SE-4965	Live at the Century Plaza	1974	3.00	6.00	12.00
PHILADELPHIA INT'L.					
❏ PZ 33957	All Things in Time	1976	2.50	5.00	10.00
-- No bar code on cover					
❏ PZ 33957	All Things in Time	198?	2.00	4.00	8.00
-- With bar code on cover					
❏ PZ 34488	Unmistakably Lou	1977	2.50	5.00	10.00
-- No bar code on cover					
❏ PZ 34488	Unmistakably Lou	1986	2.00	4.00	8.00
-- Budget-line reissue					
❏ JZ 35036	When You Hear Lou, You've Heard It All	1977	2.50	5.00	10.00
❏ PZ2 35517 [(2)]	Lou Rawls Live	1978	3.00	6.00	12.00
❏ JZ 36006	Let Me Be Good to You	1979	2.50	5.00	10.00
❏ PZ 36006	Let Me Be Good to You	198?	2.00	4.00	8.00
-- Budget-line reissue					
❏ JZ 36304	Sit Down and Talk to Me	1979	2.50	5.00	10.00
❏ PZ 36304	Sit Down and Talk to Me	198?	2.00	4.00	8.00
-- Budget-line reissue					
❏ JZ 36774	Shades of Blue	1980	2.50	5.00	10.00
❏ FZ 39285	Classics	1984	2.50	5.00	10.00
PICKWICK					
❏ SPC-3156	Come On In, Mr. Blues	1971	2.50	5.00	10.00
❏ SPC-3228	Gee Baby	1972	2.50	5.00	10.00

Number	Title	Yr	VG	VG+	NM
POLYDOR					
❏ PD-1-6086	Naturally	1976	2.50	5.00	10.00

RAY, JOHNNIE
Male singer. Most of his output is pop, but the below features jazz-group backing.

Number	Title	Yr	VG	VG+	NM
COLUMBIA					
❏ CL 1225 [M]	'Til Morning	1958	10.00	20.00	40.00
-- Red and black label with six "eye" logos					
❏ CL 1225 [M]	'Til Morning	1963	5.00	10.00	20.00
-- Red label with either "Guraranteed High Fidelity" or "360 Sound Mono" at bottom					

REBILLOT, PAT
Pianist.

Number	Title	Yr	VG	VG+	NM
ATLANTIC					
❏ SD 1663	Free Fall	1974	3.00	6.00	12.00

REBIRTH BRASS BAND
Led by Keith Frazier (bass drum) and Philip Frazier (tuba).

Number	Title	Yr	VG	VG+	NM
ARHOOLIE					
❏ 1092	Here to Stay	1986	2.50	5.00	10.00
-- As "Rebirth Jazz Band of New Orleans"					
ROUNDER					
❏ 2093	Feel Like Funkin' It Up	1989	3.00	6.00	12.00

RECOIL
Led by PAT COIL.

Number	Title	Yr	VG	VG+	NM
PAUSA					
❏ 7117	Pardon My Fantasy	198?	2.50	5.00	10.00
❏ 7168	The Fantasy Continues	1985	2.50	5.00	10.00

RED ONION JAZZ BAND, THE

Number	Title	Yr	VG	VG+	NM
BIOGRAPH					
❏ LP-12012	There'll Be a Hot Time in the Old Town Tonight	1969	3.75	7.50	15.00
RIVERSIDE					
❏ RLP 12-260 [M]	Dance Off Both Your Shoes In Hi-Fi	1958	10.00	20.00	40.00

RED ONIONS AND OTTILIE
From Berlin, Germany.

Number	Title	Yr	VG	VG+	NM
STOMP OFF					
❏ SOS-1090	Mad Dog	1985	2.50	5.00	10.00

RED ROSE RAGTIME BAND
Led by Mike Schwimmer (washboard, vocals).

Number	Title	Yr	VG	VG+	NM
STOMP OFF					
❏ SOS-1128	A Rose Is a Rose Is a Rose	1987	2.50	5.00	10.00

RED ROSELAND CORNPICKERS, THE

Number	Title	Yr	VG	VG+	NM
STOMP OFF					
❏ SOS-1101	Double Talk	1985	2.50	5.00	10.00
❏ SOS-1102	That's No Bargain	1985	2.50	5.00	10.00
❏ SOS-1133	Handful of Keith	1987	2.50	5.00	10.00
❏ SOS-1153	Red Hot Band	1988	2.50	5.00	10.00

RED WING BLACKBIRDS RAGTIME BAND

Number	Title	Yr	VG	VG+	NM
STOMP OFF					
❏ SOS-1018	Two-Step Ball	198?	2.50	5.00	10.00

RED, SONNY
Alto saxophone player. Also see ART PEPPER.

Number	Title	Yr	VG	VG+	NM
BLUE NOTE					
❏ BLP-4032 [M]	Out of the Blue	1960	25.00	50.00	100.00
-- "Deep groove" version (deep indentation under label on both sides)					
❏ BLP-4032 [M]	Out of the Blue	1960	20.00	40.00	80.00
-- Regular version, W. 63rd St. address on label					
❏ BLP-4032 [M]	Out of the Blue	1963	6.25	12.50	25.00
-- With "New York, USA" address on label					
❏ ST-84032 [S]	Out of the Blue	1960	15.00	30.00	60.00
-- With W. 63rd St. address on label					
❏ ST-84032 [S]	Out of the Blue	1963	5.00	10.00	20.00
-- With "New York, USA" address on label					
❏ ST-84032 [S]	Out of the Blue	1967	3.75	7.50	15.00
-- With "A Division of Liberty Records" on label					
FANTASY					
❏ OJC-148	Images	198?	2.50	5.00	10.00
JAZZLAND					
❏ JLP-32 [M]	Breezin'	1960	7.50	15.00	30.00
❏ JLP-59 [M]	The Mode	1961	7.50	15.00	30.00
❏ JLP-74 [M]	Images	1962	7.50	15.00	30.00

Number	Title	Yr	VG	VG+	NM
❏ JLP-932 [S]	Breezin'	1960	10.00	20.00	40.00
❏ JLP-959 [S]	The Mode	1961	10.00	20.00	40.00
❏ JLP-974 [S]	Images	1962	10.00	20.00	40.00
MAINSTREAM					
❏ MRL-324	Sonny Red	1971	3.75	7.50	15.00

REDD, FREDDIE
Pianist and composer.

Number	Title	Yr	VG	VG+	NM
BLUE NOTE					
❏ BLP-4027 [M]	Music From "The Connection"	1960	30.00	60.00	120.00
-- "Deep groove" version (deep indentation under label on both sides)					
❏ BLP-4027 [M]	Music From "The Connection"	1960	25.00	50.00	100.00
-- Regular version, W. 63rd St. address on label					
❏ BLP-4027 [M]	Music From "The Connection"	1963	6.25	12.50	25.00
-- With "New York, USA" address on label					
❏ BLP-4045 [M]	Shades of Redd	1960	30.00	60.00	120.00
-- "Deep groove" version (deep indentation under label on both sides)					
❏ BLP-4045 [M]	Shades of Redd	1960	25.00	50.00	100.00
-- Regular version, W. 63rd St. address on label					
❏ BLP-4045 [M]	Shades of Redd	1963	6.25	12.50	25.00
-- With "New York, USA" address on label					
❏ BST-84027 [S]	Music From "The Connection"	1960	25.00	50.00	100.00
-- With W. 63rd St. address on label					
❏ BST-84027 [S]	Music From "The Connection"	1963	5.00	10.00	20.00
-- With "New York, USA" address on label					
❏ BST-84027 [S]	Music From "The Connection"	1967	3.75	7.50	15.00
-- With "A Division of Liberty Records" on label					
❏ BST-84045 [S]	Shades of Redd	1960	---	---	---
-- Canceled					
FANTASY					
❏ OJC-1748	San Francisco Suite For Jazz Trio	1990	3.00	6.00	12.00
INTERPLAY					
❏ 7715	Straight Ahead	1979	3.00	6.00	12.00
MOSAIC					
❏ M3-124 [(3)]	The Complete Blue Note Recordings of Freddie Redd	199?	10.00	20.00	30.00
PRESTIGE					
❏ PRLP-197 [10]	Introducing the Freddie Redd Trio	1954	37.50	75.00	150.00
RIVERSIDE					
❏ RLP 12-250 [M]	San Francisco Suite For Jazz Trio	1957	15.00	30.00	60.00
❏ 6184	San Francisco Suite For Jazz Trio	198?	3.00	6.00	12.00

REDD, FREDDIE, AND HAMPTON HAWES
Also see each artist's individual listings.

Number	Title	Yr	VG	VG+	NM
FANTASY					
❏ OJC-1705	Piano: East/West	1985	2.50	5.00	10.00
NEW JAZZ					
❏ NJLP-8307 [M]	Movin'	1963	---	---	---
-- Canceled; reassigned to Status					
PRESTIGE					
❏ PRLP-7067 [M]	Piano: East/West	1956	20.00	40.00	80.00
STATUS					
❏ ST-8307 [M]	Movin'	1965	10.00	20.00	40.00

REDD, VI
Female singer and alto saxophone player.

Number	Title	Yr	VG	VG+	NM
ATCO					
❏ 33-157 [M]	Lady Soul	1963	7.50	15.00	30.00
❏ SD 33-157 [S]	Lady Soul	1963	10.00	20.00	40.00
UNITED ARTISTS					
❏ UAJ-14016 [M]	Bird Call	1962	10.00	20.00	40.00
❏ UAJS-15016 [S]	Bird Call	1962	12.50	25.00	50.00

REDMAN, DEWEY
Tenor saxophone player, percussionist and male singer. Also see OLD AND NEW DREAMS.

Number	Title	Yr	VG	VG+	NM
ABC IMPULSE!					
❏ AS-9250	The Ear of the Behearer	1973	3.75	7.50	15.00
❏ AS-9300	Coincide	1974	3.75	7.50	15.00
ARISTA/FREEDOM					
❏ AF 1011	Look for the Black Star	1976	3.00	6.00	12.00
BLACK SAINT					
❏ 120123	Living on the Edge	1990	3.75	7.50	15.00
ECM					
❏ 1225	The Struggle Continues	1981	2.50	5.00	10.00
GALAXY					
❏ 5118	Musics	1980	3.00	6.00	12.00
❏ 5130	Soundsigns	198?	3.00	6.00	12.00

REDMAN, DEWEY, AND ED BLACKWELL
Blackwell played drums. Also see DEWEY REDMAN.

Number	Title	Yr	VG	VG+	NM
BLACK SAINT					
❏ BSR-0093	Red and Black in Willisau	1985	3.00	6.00	12.00

REDMAN, DON
Multi-instrumentalist, male singer, bandleader and arranger.

Number	Title	Yr	VG	VG+	NM
GOLDEN CREST					
❏ GC-3017 [M]	Park Avenue Patter	1958	10.00	20.00	40.00
RCA VICTOR					
❏ LPV-520 [M]	Master of the Big Band	1965	5.00	10.00	20.00
ROULETTE					
❏ R-25070 [M]	Dixieland in High Society	1960	5.00	10.00	20.00
❏ SR-25070 [S]	Dixieland in High Society	1960	6.25	12.50	25.00
STEEPLECHASE					
❏ SCC-6020	For Europeans Only	198?	3.00	6.00	12.00

REDMAN, GEORGE
Drummer.

Number	Title	Yr	VG	VG+	NM
SKYLARK					
❏ SKLP-20 [10]	The George Redman Group	1954	37.50	75.00	150.00

REDMOND, EDGAR

Number	Title	Yr	VG	VG+	NM
DISQUE-PHENOMENON					
❏ 2696 [10]	Edgar Redmond & the Modern String Ensemble	1965	7.50	15.00	30.00

REDOLFI, MICHEL
Composer, arranger and electronic instrumentalist. The below album was recorded entirely underwater!

Number	Title	Yr	VG	VG+	NM
HAT ART					
❏ 2002	Sonic Waters	1986	3.75	7.50	15.00

REECE, DIZZY
Trumpeter.

Number	Title	Yr	VG	VG+	NM
BEE HIVE					
❏ 7001	Manhattan Project	1976	3.00	6.00	12.00
BLUE NOTE					
❏ BLP-4006 [M]	Blues in Trinity	1958	37.50	75.00	150.00
-- "Deep groove" version (deep indentation under label on both sides)					
❏ BLP-4006 [M]	Blues in Trinity	1958	25.00	50.00	100.00
-- Regular version, W. 63rd St. address on label					
❏ BLP-4006 [M]	Blues in Trinity	1963	6.25	12.50	25.00
-- With "New York, USA" address on label					
❏ BST-4006 [S]	Blues in Trinity	1959	25.00	50.00	100.00
-- "Deep groove" version (deep indentation under label on both sides)					
❏ BST-4006 [S]	Blues in Trinity	1959	15.00	30.00	60.00
-- Regular version, W. 63rd St. address on label					
❏ BST-4006 [S]	Blues in Trinity	1963	5.00	10.00	20.00
-- With "New York, USA" address on label					
❏ BLP-4023 [M]	Star Bright	1959	30.00	60.00	120.00
-- "Deep groove" version (deep indentation under label on both sides)					
❏ BLP-4023 [M]	Star Bright	1959	20.00	40.00	80.00
-- Regular version, W. 63rd St. address on label					
❏ BLP-4023 [M]	Star Bright	1963	6.25	12.50	25.00
-- With "New York, USA" address on label					
❏ BLP-4033 [M]	Soundin' Off	1960	30.00	60.00	120.00
-- "Deep groove" version (deep indentation under label on both sides)					
❏ BLP-4033 [M]	Soundin' Off	1960	20.00	40.00	80.00
-- Regular version, W. 63rd St. address on label					
❏ BLP-4033 [M]	Soundin' Off	1963	6.25	12.50	25.00
-- With "New York, USA" address on label					
❏ B1-32093	Blues in Trinity	1995	3.75	7.50	15.00
❏ BST-84006 [S]	Blues in Trinity	1967	3.75	7.50	15.00
-- With "A Division of Liberty Records" on label					
❏ BST-84023 [S]	Star Bright	1959	15.00	30.00	60.00
-- With W. 63rd St. address on label					
❏ BST-84023 [S]	Star Bright	1963	5.00	10.00	20.00
-- With "New York, USA" address on label					
❏ BST-84023 [S]	Star Bright	1967	3.75	7.50	15.00
-- With "A Division of Liberty Records" on label					
❏ BST-84033 [S]	Soundin' Off	1960	15.00	30.00	60.00
-- With W. 63rd St. address on label					
❏ BST-84033 [S]	Soundin' Off	1963	5.00	10.00	20.00
-- With "New York, USA" address on label					
❏ BST-84033 [S]	Soundin' Off	1967	3.75	7.50	15.00
-- With "A Division of Liberty Records" on label					
DISCOVERY					
❏ 839	Moose the Mooche	198?	2.50	5.00	10.00
IMPERIAL					
❏ LP-9043 [M]	London Jazz	1957	20.00	40.00	80.00

Number	Title	Yr	VG	VG+	NM

NEW JAZZ

Number	Title	Yr	VG	VG+	NM
❑ NJLP-8274 [M]	Asia Minor	1962	12.50	25.00	50.00
-- Purple label					
❑ NJLP-8274 [M]	Asia Minor	1965	6.25	12.50	25.00
-- Blue label, trident logo at right					

REECE, DIZZY, AND TUBBY HAYES
Also see each artist's individual listings.
SAVOY

❑ MG-12111 [M]	Changing the Jazz at Buckingham Palace	1957	25.00	50.00	100.00

REED, LUCY
Female singer.
FANTASY

❑ 3212 [M]	The Singing Reed	195?	20.00	40.00	80.00
-- Black vinyl					
❑ 3212 [M]	The Singing Reed	1956	37.50	75.00	150.00
-- Red vinyl					
❑ 3243 [M]	This Is Lucy Reed	195?	20.00	40.00	80.00
-- Black vinyl					
❑ 3243 [M]	This Is Lucy Reed	1957	37.50	75.00	150.00
-- Red vinyl					

REED, WAYMON
Trumpeter.
ARTISTS HOUSE

❑ 10	46th and 8th	1980	3.00	6.00	12.00

REESE, DELLA
Female singer.
ABC

❑ 569 [M]	Della Reese Live	1966	3.75	7.50	15.00
❑ S-569 [S]	Della Reese Live	1966	5.00	10.00	20.00
❑ 589 [M]	One More Time	1967	5.00	10.00	20.00
❑ S-589 [S]	One More Time	1967	3.75	7.50	15.00
❑ 612 [M]	Della on Strings of Blue	1967	5.00	10.00	20.00
❑ S-612 [S]	Della on Strings of Blue	1967	3.75	7.50	15.00
❑ S-636	I Gotta Be Me...This Trip Out	1968	3.75	7.50	15.00
❑ AC-30002	The ABC Collection	1976	3.75	7.50	15.00

ABC-PARAMOUNT

❑ ABC-524 [M]	C'mon and Hear Della Reese	1965	3.75	7.50	15.00
❑ ABCS-524 [S]	C'mon and Hear Della Reese	1965	5.00	10.00	20.00
❑ ABC-540 [M]	I Like It Like Dat!	1966	3.75	7.50	15.00
❑ ABCS-540 [S]	I Like It Like Dat!	1966	5.00	10.00	20.00

AVCO EMBASSY

❑ 33004	Black Is Beautiful	1969	3.75	7.50	15.00
❑ 33017	Right Now	1970	3.75	7.50	15.00

JAZZ A LA CARTE

❑ 3	One of a Kind	1978	3.75	7.50	15.00

JUBILEE

❑ JLP-1026 [M]	Melancholy Baby	1957	7.50	15.00	30.00
❑ JLP-1071 [M]	A Date with Della Reese at Mr. Kelly's in Chicago	1959	6.25	12.50	25.00
❑ SDJLP-1071 [S]	A Date with Della Reese at Mr. Kelly's in Chicago	1959	7.50	15.00	30.00
❑ JLP-1083 [M]	Amen	1959	6.25	12.50	25.00
❑ SDJLP-1083 [S]	Amen	1959	7.50	15.00	30.00
❑ JLP-1095 [M]	The Story of the Blues	1960	6.25	12.50	25.00
❑ SDJLP-1095 [S]	The Story of the Blues	1960	7.50	15.00	30.00
❑ JLP-1109 [M]	What Do You Know About Love	1960	6.25	12.50	25.00
❑ JLP-1116 [M]	And That Reminds Me	1960	6.25	12.50	25.00
❑ JGM-5002 [M]	The Best of Della Reese	196?	3.75	7.50	15.00
❑ JGS-5002 [S]	The Best of Della Reese	196?	5.00	10.00	20.00

PICKWICK

❑ SPC-3058	And That Reminds Me	196?	3.00	6.00	12.00

RCA VICTOR

❑ LPM-2157 [M]	Della	1960	5.00	10.00	20.00
❑ LSP-2157 [S]	Della	1960	6.25	12.50	25.00
❑ LPM-2204 [M]	Della by Starlight	1960	5.00	10.00	20.00
❑ LSP-2204 [S]	Della by Starlight	1960	6.25	12.50	25.00
❑ LPM-2280 [M]	Della Della Cha-Cha-Cha	1961	5.00	10.00	20.00
❑ LSP-2280 [S]	Della Della Cha-Cha-Cha	1961	6.25	12.50	25.00
❑ LPM-2391 [M]	Special Delivery	1961	5.00	10.00	20.00
❑ LSP-2391 [S]	Special Delivery	1961	6.25	12.50	25.00
❑ LPM-2419 [M]	The Classic Della	1962	5.00	10.00	20.00
❑ LSP-2419 [S]	The Classic Della	1962	6.25	12.50	25.00
❑ LPM-2568 [M]	Della on Stage	1962	5.00	10.00	20.00
❑ LSP-2568 [S]	Della on Stage	1962	6.25	12.50	25.00
❑ LPM-2711 [M]	Waltz with Me	1963	5.00	10.00	20.00
❑ LSP-2711 [S]	Waltz with Me	1963	6.25	12.50	25.00
❑ LPM-2872 [M]	Della Reese at Basin Street East	1964	5.00	10.00	20.00
❑ LSP-2872 [S]	Della Reese at Basin Street East	1964	6.25	12.50	25.00

❑ LSP-4651	The Best of Della Reese	1972	3.00	6.00	12.00

REEVES, DIANNE
Female singer and composer.
BLUE NOTE

❑ BT-46906	Dianne Reeves	1987	2.50	5.00	10.00

EMI

❑ E1-92401	Never Too Far	1990	3.00	6.00	12.00

PALO ALTO

❑ PA-8026	Welcome to My Love	1983	3.75	7.50	15.00

PALO ALTO/TBA

❑ TB-203	For Every Heart	1984	3.00	6.00	12.00

REHAK, FRANK/ALEX SMITH
Rehak played trombone.
DAWN

❑ DLP-1107 [M]	Jazzville, Vol. 2	1956	25.00	50.00	100.00

REICHMAN, JOE
Pianist and bandleader.
CIRCLE

❑ CLP-84	The Pagliacci of the Piano	1986	2.50	5.00	10.00

HINDSIGHT

❑ HSR-166	Joe Reichman and His Orchestra 1944-49	198?	2.50	5.00	10.00

REID, IRENE
Female singer.
MGM

❑ E-4159 [M]	It's Only the Beginning for Irene Reid	1963	5.00	10.00	20.00
❑ SE-4159 [S]	It's Only the Beginning for Irene Reid	1963	6.25	12.50	25.00

POLYDOR

❑ 24-4040	The World Needs What I Need	1971	3.75	7.50	15.00

VERVE

❑ V-8621 [M]	Room for One More	1965	3.75	7.50	15.00
❑ V6-8621 [S]	Room for One More	1965	5.00	10.00	20.00

REID, RUFUS
Bass player.
SUNNYSIDE

❑ SSC-1010	Seven Minds	1985	2.50	5.00	10.00

THERESA

❑ 111	Perpetual Stroll	1980	3.00	6.00	12.00

REILLY, JACK
Keyboard player, arranger and composer.
CAROUSEL

❑ 1001	Blue-Sean-Green	197?	3.75	7.50	15.00
❑ 1002	Tributes	197?	3.75	7.50	15.00

REVELATION

❑ 35	Together (Again)... For the First Time	198?	2.50	5.00	10.00
❑ 36	Brinksman	198?	2.50	5.00	10.00

REINHARDT, DJANGO
Highly influential guitarist. Also see DIZZY GILLESPIE; THE QUINTET OF THE HOT CLUB OF FRANCE.
ANGEL

❑ ANG-36985	Django Reinhardt and the Quintet of the Hot Club of France	197?	2.50	5.00	10.00
❑ ANG.60003 [10]	Le Jazz Hot	1954	37.50	75.00	150.00
❑ ANG.60011 [10]	Django's Guitar	1955	37.50	75.00	150.00

ARCHIVE OF FOLK AND JAZZ

❑ 212 [R]	Django Reinhardt	1968	2.50	5.00	10.00
❑ 230 [R]	Django Reinhardt, Vol. 2	1969	2.50	5.00	10.00
❑ 255	Django Reinhardt, Vol. 3	197?	2.50	5.00	10.00
❑ 306	Django Reinhardt, Vol. 4	197?	2.50	5.00	10.00

BLUEBIRD

❑ 9988-1-RB	Djangology 49	1990	3.00	6.00	12.00

CAPITOL

❑ TBO 10226 [(2) M]	The Best Of Django Reinhardt	1960	12.50	25.00	50.00
-- Black colorband labels, Capitol logo at left					

CLEF

❑ MGC-516 [10]	The Great Artistry of Django Reinhardt	1954	37.50	75.00	150.00

Number	Title	Yr	VG	VG+	NM
COLUMBIA					
❏ C 31479	Swing It Lightly	1972	3.00	6.00	12.00
❏ PC 31479	Swing It Lightly	198?	2.00	4.00	8.00
-- Budget-line reissue					
EMARCY					
❏ 66004	Jazz Hot	1967	3.00	6.00	12.00
EPITAPH					
❏ E-4002	Django Reinhardt 1910-1953	1975	3.75	7.50	15.00
GNP CRESCENDO					
❏ GNP-9001	Django Reinhardt and the Quintet of the Hot Club of France	196?	2.50	5.00	10.00
❏ GNP-9002	Parisian Swing	197?	2.50	5.00	10.00
❏ GNP-9019	Django Reinhardt 1935-39	197?	2.50	5.00	10.00
❏ GNP-9023	Django Reinhardt 1935	197?	2.50	5.00	10.00
❏ GNP-9031	Django Reinhardt 1934	197?	2.50	5.00	10.00
❏ GNP-9038	The Immortal Django Reinhardt	198?	2.50	5.00	10.00
❏ GNP-9039	Legendary Django Reinhardt	198?	2.50	5.00	10.00
INNER CITY					
❏ IC-1104	Django Reinhardt and the Quintet of the Hot Club of France	198?	3.00	6.00	12.00
❏ IC-1105	Solos/Duos/Trios, Vol. 2	198?	3.00	6.00	12.00
❏ IC-1106	Compositions	198?	3.00	6.00	12.00
❏ IC-7004	The Versatile Giant	198?	3.00	6.00	12.00
JAY					
❏ 3008 [10]	Django Reinhardt	1954	45.00	90.00	180.00
LONDON					
❏ LB-810 [10]	Swing From Paris	1955	30.00	60.00	120.00
MERCURY					
❏ MGC-516 [10]	The Great Artistry of Django Reinhardt	1953	50.00	100.00	200.00
PERIOD					
❏ SPL-1100 [10]	Django Reinhardt Memorial, Volume 1	1954	30.00	60.00	120.00
❏ SPL-1101 [10]	Django Reinhardt Memorial, Volume 2	1954	30.00	60.00	120.00
❏ SPL-1102 [10]	Django Reinhardt Memorial, Volume 3	1954	30.00	60.00	120.00
❏ SPL-1201 [M]	Django Reinhardt Memorial Album, Volume 1	1956	12.50	25.00	50.00
❏ SPL-1202 [M]	Django Reinhardt Memorial Album, Volume 2	1956	12.50	25.00	50.00
❏ SPL-1203 [M]	Django Reinhardt Memorial Album, Volume 3	1956	12.50	25.00	50.00
❏ SPL-1204 [M]	The Best of Django Reinhardt	1956	12.50	25.00	50.00
❏ SPL-2204 [R]	The Best of Django Reinhardt	196?	6.25	12.50	25.00
PRESTIGE					
❏ PRST-7633 [R]	Django Reinhardt and American Jazz Giants	1969	3.75	7.50	15.00
RCA VICTOR					
❏ LPM-1100 [M]	Django Reinhardt	1955	25.00	50.00	100.00
❏ LPM-2319 [M]	Djangology	1961	10.00	20.00	40.00
❏ LSP-2319 [R]	Djangology	196?	6.25	12.50	25.00
REPRISE					
❏ R-6075 [M]	The Immortal Django Reinhardt	1963	6.25	12.50	25.00
❏ R9-6075 [R]	The Immortal Django Reinhardt	1963	3.75	7.50	15.00
SUTTON					
❏ SSU-274 [R]	Django Reinhardt and His Guitar	1966	3.00	6.00	12.00
❏ SU-274 [M]	Django Reinhardt and His Guitar	1966	5.00	10.00	20.00
SWING					
❏ SW-8420/7 [(7)]	Djanologie USA Volumes 1-7	1988	15.00	30.00	60.00
REMLER, EMILY					
Guitarist.					
CONCORD JAZZ					
❏ CJ-162	Firefly	1981	2.50	5.00	10.00
❏ CJ-195	Take Two	1982	2.50	5.00	10.00
❏ CJ-236	Transitions	1984	2.50	5.00	10.00
❏ CJ-265	Catwalk	1985	2.50	5.00	10.00
❏ CJ-356	East to Wes	1988	2.50	5.00	10.00
REMINGTON, DAVE					
JUBILEE					
❏ JLP-1017 [M]	Chicago Jazz Reborn	1956	10.00	20.00	40.00
TEMPUS					
❏ TL-101 [M]	Danceable Dixieland Jazz	1958	10.00	20.00	40.00
VEE JAY					
❏ LP-3009 [M]	Dixie on the Rocks	1960	6.25	12.50	25.00
❏ SR-3009 [S]	Dixie on the Rocks	1960	7.50	15.00	30.00
❏ LP-3030 [M]	Dixie Chicago Style	1962	5.00	10.00	20.00
❏ SR-3030 [S]	Dixie Chicago Style	1962	6.25	12.50	25.00

Number	Title	Yr	VG	VG+	NM
RENA, KID					
Trumpeter.					
CIRCLE					
❏ L-409 [10]	Kid Rena Delta Jazz Band	1951	20.00	40.00	80.00
RENAUD, HENRI					
Pianist, composer and bandleader.					
CONTEMPORARY					
❏ C-2502 [10]	The Henri Renaud All-Stars	1953	30.00	60.00	120.00
PERIOD					
❏ SPL-1211 [M]	The Birdlanders	1954	20.00	40.00	80.00
❏ SPL-1212 [M]	The Birdlanders	1954	20.00	40.00	80.00
RENDELL, DON					
Saxophone player (soprano, alto, tenor), clarinetist and flutist.					
JAZZLAND					
❏ JLP-51 [M]	Roarin'	1961	7.50	15.00	30.00
❏ JLP-951 [S]	Roarin'	1961	10.00	20.00	40.00
RENE, HENRI					
Accordion player, composer, arranger and bandleader.					
IMPERIAL					
❏ LP-9074 [M]	White Heat	1959	5.00	10.00	20.00
❏ LP-9096 [M]	Swingin' 59	1960	5.00	10.00	20.00
❏ LP-12021 [S]	White Heat	1959	7.50	15.00	30.00
❏ LP-12040 [S]	Swingin' 59	1960	7.50	15.00	30.00
RCA CAMDEN					
❏ CAL-130 [M]	Portfolio for Easy Listening	195?	3.75	7.50	15.00
❏ CAL-312 [M]	In Love Again	195?	3.75	7.50	15.00
❏ CAL-353 [M]	Melodic Magic	195?	3.75	7.50	15.00
RCA VICTOR					
❏ LPM-1033 [M]	Passion in Paint	1955	20.00	40.00	80.00
❏ LPM-1046 [M]	Music for Bachelors	1955	30.00	60.00	120.00
-- Cover model is Jayne Mansfield					
❏ LPM-1583 [M]	Music for the Weaker Sex	1957	6.25	12.50	25.00
❏ LPM-1947 [M]	Compulsion to Swing	1958	5.00	10.00	20.00
❏ LSP-1947 [S]	Compulsion to Swing	1958	7.50	15.00	30.00
❏ LPM-2002 [M]	Riot in Rhythm	1959	5.00	10.00	20.00
❏ LSP-2002 [S]	Riot in Rhythm	1959	7.50	15.00	30.00
❏ LSA-2396 [S]	Dynamic Dimensions	1961	7.50	15.00	30.00
❏ LPM-3049 [10]	Serenade to Love	1953	10.00	20.00	40.00
❏ LPM-3076 [10]	Listen to Rene	1953	10.00	20.00	40.00
RENTIE, DAMON					
PALO ALTO/TBA					
❏ TB-212	Designated Hitter	198?	2.50	5.00	10.00
❏ TB-219	Don't Look Back	1986	2.50	5.00	10.00
❏ TB-230	Skyline	1987	2.50	5.00	10.00
RENZI, MIKE					
Pianist and arranger.					
STASH					
❏ ST-273	A Beautiful Friendship	1988	2.50	5.00	10.00
REPERCUSSION UNIT					
Members: John Bergamo, Jim Hildebrandt, Gregg Johnson, Ed Mann, Lucky Mosko and Larry Stein. All play various percussion instruments and non-instruments.					
CMP					
❏ CMP-31-ST	In Need Again	1987	2.50	5.00	10.00
RESNICK, ART					
Pianist and composer.					
CAPRI					
❏ 74015	A Gift	198?	2.50	5.00	10.00
SYMPOSIUM					
❏ 2005	Jungleopolis	197?	3.75	7.50	15.00
RETURN TO FOREVER					
Landmark fusion group led by CHICK COREA. Among the other members at various times: AIRTO; STANLEY CLARKE; AL DiMEOLA; JOE FARRELL; EARL KLUGH; FLORA PURIM; LENNY WHITE.					
COLUMBIA					
❏ PC 34076	Romantic Warrior	1976	2.50	5.00	10.00
-- No bar code on cover					
❏ PC 34076	Romantic Warrior	198?	2.00	4.00	8.00
-- Reissue with bar code					
❏ PC 34682	Musicmagic	1977	2.50	5.00	10.00
-- No bar code on cover					
❏ PC 34682	Musicmagic	1985	2.00	4.00	8.00
-- Reissue with bar code					
❏ PCQ 34682 [Q]	Musicmagic	1977	5.00	10.00	20.00

Number	Title	Yr	VG	VG+	NM
❑ JC 35281	Return to Forever Live	1979	2.50	5.00	10.00
❑ JC 36359	The Best of Return to Forever	1980	2.50	5.00	10.00
❑ PC 36359	The Best of Return to Forever	198?	2.00	4.00	8.00
-- Budget-line reissue					
ECM					
❑ 1015	Return to Forever	1972	3.75	7.50	15.00
POLYDOR					
❑ PD-5525	Light As A Feather	1973	3.00	6.00	12.00
❑ PD-5536	Hymn of the Seventh Galaxy	1973	3.00	6.00	12.00
❑ PD-6509	Where Have I Known You Before	1974	3.00	6.00	12.00
❑ PD-6512	No Mystery	1975	3.00	6.00	12.00
❑ 825 336-1	Hymn of the Seventh Galaxy	198?	2.00	4.00	8.00
-- Reissue					

REVELERS, THE
Male vocal group with piano.
RONDO-LETTE

Number	Title	Yr	VG	VG+	NM
❑ A-50 [M]	Jazz at the Downstairs Club	1962	5.00	10.00	20.00
❑ SA-50 [S]	Jazz at the Downstairs Club	1962	6.25	12.50	25.00

REVERBERI
Italian group led by Gian Piero Reverberi.
PAUSA

Number	Title	Yr	VG	VG+	NM
❑ 7003	Reverberi and...	198?	2.50	5.00	10.00
❑ 7016	Timer	198?	2.50	5.00	10.00

REVOLUTIONARY ENSEMBLE, THE
Members: LEROY JENKINS; JEROME COOPER; Sirone (bass, trombone).
ESP-DISK'

Number	Title	Yr	VG	VG+	NM
❑ S-3007	The Revolutionary Ensemble at Peace Church	196?	3.75	7.50	15.00
HORIZON					
❑ SP-708	People's Republic	1975	3.00	6.00	12.00
INDIA NAVIGATION					
❑ IN-1023	Manhattan Cycles	197?	3.75	7.50	15.00
INNER CITY					
❑ IC-3016	The Revolutionary Ensemble	197?	3.00	6.00	12.00

REXROTH, KENNETH
Beat poet.
FANTASY

Number	Title	Yr	VG	VG+	NM
❑ 7008 [M]	Poetry and Jazz at the Blackhawk	1958	50.00	100.00	200.00
-- Red vinyl					
❑ 7008 [M]	Poetry and Jazz at the Blackhawk	1958	25.00	50.00	100.00
-- Black vinyl					

REXROTH, KENNETH, AND LAWRENCE FERLINGHETTI
Also see each artist's individual listings.
FANTASY

Number	Title	Yr	VG	VG+	NM
❑ 7002 [M]	Poetry Readings from the Cellar	1957	25.00	50.00	100.00
-- Black vinyl					
❑ 7002 [M]	Poetry Readings from the Cellar	1957	50.00	100.00	200.00
-- Red vinyl					

REY, ALVINO
Guitarist, bandleader and arranger.
CAPITOL

Number	Title	Yr	VG	VG+	NM
❑ ST 1085 [S]	Swingin' Fling	1959	6.25	12.50	25.00
❑ T 1085 [M]	Swingin' Fling	1959	5.00	10.00	20.00
❑ ST 1262 [S]	Ping Pong!	1959	6.25	12.50	25.00
❑ T 1262 [M]	Ping Pong!	1959	5.00	10.00	20.00
HINDSIGHT					
❑ HSR-121	Alvino Rey and His Orchestra 1946	198?	2.50	5.00	10.00
❑ HSR-167	Alvino Rey and His Orchestra 1946, Vol. 2	198?	2.50	5.00	10.00
❑ HSR-196	Alvino Rey and His Orchestra 1940-41	198?	2.50	5.00	10.00

REYNOLDS, TOMMY
Clarinet player and bandleader.
AUDIO LAB

Number	Title	Yr	VG	VG+	NM
❑ AL-1509 [M]	Dixieland All-Stars	1958	25.00	50.00	100.00
KING					
❑ 395-510 [M]	Jazz for Happy Feet	1956	20.00	40.00	80.00
ROYALE					
❑ 18117 [10]	Tommy Reynolds Orchestra with Bon Bon	195?	20.00	40.00	80.00

REYS, RITA
Female singer.
COLUMBIA

Number	Title	Yr	VG	VG+	NM
❑ CL 903 [M]	The Cool Voice of Rita Reys with Art Blakey and the Jazz Messengers	1956	25.00	50.00	100.00
EPIC					
❑ LN 3522 [M]	Her Name Is Rita Reys	1957	20.00	40.00	80.00
INNER CITY					
❑ IC-1157	Songs of Antonio Carlos Jobim	198?	3.00	6.00	12.00

RHODES, GEORGE
Pianist.
GROOVE

Number	Title	Yr	VG	VG+	NM
❑ LG-1005 [M]	Real George!	1956	15.00	30.00	60.00

RHYNE, MEL
Organist.
JAZZLAND

Number	Title	Yr	VG	VG+	NM
❑ JLP-16 [M]	Organizing	1960	7.50	15.00	30.00
❑ JLP-916 [S]	Organizing	1960	10.00	20.00	40.00

RHYTHM AND BLU
Violin trio: John Blake; DIDIER LOCKWOOD; MICHAL URBANIAK.
GRAMAVISION

Number	Title	Yr	VG	VG+	NM
❑ 18-8608	Rhythm and Blu	1986	3.00	6.00	12.00

RHYTHM COMBINATION, THE
German group led by Peter Herbolzheimer.
BASF

Number	Title	Yr	VG	VG+	NM
❑ 21751	Waitaminute	197?	3.75	7.50	15.00
❑ 25124	Power Play	197?	3.75	7.50	15.00

RHYTHMIC UNION, THE
Led by percussionist Robert Chappell.
INNER CITY

Number	Title	Yr	VG	VG+	NM
❑ IC-1100	Gentle Awakening	198?	3.00	6.00	12.00

RICE, DARYLE
Female singer and guitarist.
AUDIOPHILE

Number	Title	Yr	VG	VG+	NM
❑ AP-141	I Walk with Music	1980	2.50	5.00	10.00

RICH, BUDDY
Drummer, bandleader and male singer. Also see LIONEL HAMPTON; GENE KRUPA; FLIP PHILLIPS; LESTER YOUNG.
ARCHIVE OF FOLK AND JAZZ

Number	Title	Yr	VG	VG+	NM
❑ 260	Buddy Rich	197?	3.75	7.50	15.00
ARGO					
❑ LP-676 [M]	Playtime	1961	7.50	15.00	30.00
❑ LPS-676 [S]	Playtime	1961	10.00	20.00	40.00
EMARCY					
❑ EMS-2-402 [(2)]	Both Sides	1976	3.75	7.50	15.00
❑ 66006	Driver	1967	5.00	10.00	20.00
GREAT AMERICAN					
❑ 1030	Class of '78	1978	5.00	10.00	20.00
-- Direct-to-disc version of Gryphon 781					
GROOVE MERCHANT					
❑ 528	The Roar of '74	1974	3.00	6.00	12.00
❑ 3301	Very Live at Buddy's Place	1974	3.00	6.00	12.00
❑ 3303	The Last Blues Album, Vol. 1	1975	3.00	6.00	12.00
❑ 3307	The Big Band Machine	1976	3.00	6.00	12.00
❑ 4407 [(2)]	Tuff Dude!	197?	3.75	7.50	15.00
GRYPHON					
❑ 781	Class of '78	1978	3.00	6.00	12.00
LIBERTY					
❑ 11006	Keep the Customer Satisfied	1970	3.75	7.50	15.00
MCA					
❑ 5186	The Buddy Rich Band	1981	2.50	5.00	10.00
MERCURY					
❑ MG-20451 [M]	Richcraft	1959	15.00	30.00	60.00
❑ MG-20461 [M]	The Voice Is Rich	1959	12.50	25.00	50.00
❑ SR-60136 [S]	Richcraft	1959	17.50	35.00	70.00
❑ SR-60144 [S]	The Voice Is Rich	1959	15.00	30.00	60.00
NORGRAN					
❑ MGN-26 [10]	Buddy Rich Swingin'	1954	30.00	60.00	120.00
❑ MGN-1031 [M]	Sing and Swing with Buddy Rich	1955	20.00	40.00	80.00
❑ MGN-1052 [M]	The Swingin' Buddy Rich	1955	15.00	30.00	60.00
-- Reissue of 26					

Number	Title	Yr	VG	VG+	NM
❑ MGN-1078 [M]	The Wailing Buddy Rich	1956	15.00	30.00	60.00
❑ MGN-1088 [M]	This One's for Basie	1956	15.00	30.00	60.00
PACIFIC JAZZ					
❑ PJ-10113 [M]	Swingin' New Big Band	1966	6.25	12.50	25.00
❑ PJ-10117 [M]	Big Swing Face	1967	6.25	12.50	25.00
❑ LN-10089	Swingin' New Big Band	1981	2.00	4.00	8.00
-- Budget-line reissue					
❑ LN-10090	Big Swing Face	1981	2.00	4.00	8.00
-- Budget-line reissue					
❑ ST-20113 [S]	Swingin' New Big Band	1966	5.00	10.00	20.00
❑ ST-20117 [S]	Big Swing Face	1967	5.00	10.00	20.00
❑ ST-20126	A New One	1968	5.00	10.00	20.00
PAUSA					
❑ 9004	Buddy & Soul	1983	2.50	5.00	10.00
QUINTESSENCE					
❑ 25051	Mr. Drums	1978	3.00	6.00	12.00
RCA VICTOR					
❑ ANL1-1090	A Different Drummer	1975	2.50	5.00	10.00
-- Reissue of 4593					
❑ APL1-1503	Speak No Evil	1976	3.00	6.00	12.00
❑ CPL2-2273 [(2)]	Buddy Rich Plays & Plays & Plays	1977	3.75	7.50	15.00
❑ LSP-4593	A Different Drummer	1971	3.00	6.00	12.00
❑ AFL1-4666	Rich in London	1977	2.50	5.00	10.00
-- Reissue with new prefix					
❑ LSP-4666	Rich in London	1972	3.00	6.00	12.00
❑ AFL1-4802	Stick It	1977	2.50	5.00	10.00
-- Reissue with new prefix					
❑ LSP-4802	Stick It	1972	3.00	6.00	12.00
UNITED ARTISTS					
❑ UXS-86 [(2)]	Buddy Rich Superpak	1972	3.75	7.50	15.00
VERVE					
❑ VSP-40 [M]	Buddy Rich at J.A.T.P.	1966	3.75	7.50	15.00
❑ VSPS-40 [R]	Buddy Rich at J.A.T.P.	1966	3.00	6.00	12.00
❑ MGV-2009 [M]	Buddy Rich Sings Johnny Mercer	1956	15.00	30.00	60.00
❑ V-2009 [M]	Buddy Rich Sings Johnny Mercer	1961	5.00	10.00	20.00
❑ MGV-2075 [M]	Buddy Rich Just Sings	1957	15.00	30.00	60.00
❑ V-2075 [M]	Buddy Rich Just Sings	1961	5.00	10.00	20.00
❑ MGV-8142 [M]	The Swingin' Buddy Rich	1957	12.50	25.00	50.00
-- Reissue of Norgran 1052					
❑ V-8142 [M]	The Swingin' Buddy Rich	1961	5.00	10.00	20.00
❑ MGV-8168 [M]	The Wailing Buddy Rich	1957	12.50	25.00	50.00
-- Reissue of Norgran 1078					
❑ V-8168 [M]	The Wailing Buddy Rich	1961	5.00	10.00	20.00
❑ MGV-8176 [M]	This One's for Basie	1957	12.50	25.00	50.00
-- Reissue of Norgran 1086					
❑ V-8176 [M]	This One's for Basie	1961	5.00	10.00	20.00
❑ MGV-8285 [M]	Buddy Rich in Miami	1958	15.00	30.00	60.00
❑ V-8285 [M]	Buddy Rich in Miami	1961	5.00	10.00	20.00
❑ V-8425 [M]	Blues Caravan	1962	6.25	12.50	25.00
❑ V6-8425 [S]	Blues Caravan	1962	7.50	15.00	30.00
❑ V-8471 [M]	Burnin' Beat	1962	6.25	12.50	25.00
❑ V6-8471 [S]	Burnin' Beat	1962	7.50	15.00	30.00
❑ V-8484 [M]	Drum Battle: Gene Krupa vs. Buddy Rich	1962	6.25	12.50	25.00
❑ V6-8484 [S]	Drum Battle: Gene Krupa vs. Buddy Rich	1962	7.50	15.00	30.00
❑ V-8712 [M]	Big Band Shout	1967	5.00	10.00	20.00
❑ V6-8712 [S]	Big Band Shout	1967	3.75	7.50	15.00
❑ V6-8778	Super Rich	1969	3.75	7.50	15.00
❑ V6-8824 [(2)]	Monster	1973	3.75	7.50	15.00
WHO'S WHO IN JAZZ					
❑ 21006	Lionel Hampton Presents Buddy Rich	1978	3.00	6.00	12.00
WORLD PACIFIC					
❑ WPS-20113	The Buddy Rich Big Band	1968	3.75	7.50	15.00
❑ WPS-20133	Mercy, Mercy	1968	3.75	7.50	15.00
❑ WPS-20158	Buddy & Soul	1969	3.75	7.50	15.00
❑ WPS-20169	The Best of Buddy Rich	1970	3.75	7.50	15.00

RICH, BUDDY, AND SWEETS EDISON
Also see each artist's individual listings.

Number	Title	Yr	VG	VG+	NM
NORGRAN					
❑ MGN-1038 [M]	Buddy Rich and Sweets Edison	1955	20.00	40.00	80.00
VERVE					
❑ MGV-8129 [M]	Buddy and Sweets	1957	12.50	25.00	50.00
-- Reissue of Norgran 1038					
❑ V-8129 [M]	Buddy and Sweets	1961	5.00	10.00	20.00

RICH, BUDDY, AND MAX ROACH
Also see each artist's individual listings.

Number	Title	Yr	VG	VG+	NM
MERCURY					
❑ MG-20448 [M]	Rich Versus Roach	1959	15.00	30.00	60.00
❑ SR-60133 [S]	Rich Versus Roach	1959	17.50	35.00	70.00

RICH, LISA
Female singer.

Number	Title	Yr	VG	VG+	NM
DISCOVERY					
❑ 908	Listen Here	1986	2.50	5.00	10.00
TREND					
❑ 541	Touch of the Rare	1986	2.50	5.00	10.00

RICHARDS, ANN
Female singer.

Number	Title	Yr	VG	VG+	NM
ATCO					
❑ 33-136 [M]	Ann, Man!	1961	10.00	20.00	40.00
❑ SD 33-136 [S]	Ann, Man!	1961	15.00	30.00	60.00
CAPITOL					
❑ ST 1087 [S]	I'm Shooting High	1959	10.00	20.00	40.00
❑ T 1087 [M]	I'm Shooting High	1959	7.50	15.00	30.00
❑ ST 1406 [S]	The Many Moods of Ann Richards	1960	10.00	20.00	40.00
❑ T 1406 [M]	The Many Moods of Ann Richards	1960	7.50	15.00	30.00
❑ ST 1495 [S]	Two Much!	1961	10.00	20.00	40.00
❑ T 1495 [M]	Two Much!	1961	7.50	15.00	30.00
VEE JAY					
❑ LP-1070 [M]	Live...At the Losers	1963	10.00	20.00	40.00
❑ SR-1070 [S]	Live...At the Losers	1963	12.50	25.00	50.00

RICHARDS, EMIL
Percussionist.

Number	Title	Yr	VG	VG+	NM
ABC IMPULSE!					
❑ AS-9182 [S]	Spirit of '76	1968	5.00	10.00	20.00
❑ AS-9188 [S]	Journey to Bliss	1969	5.00	10.00	20.00
UNI					
❑ 3003 [M]	New Time Element	1967	6.25	12.50	25.00
❑ 3008 [M]	New Sound	1967	6.25	12.50	25.00
❑ 73003 [S]	New Time Element	1967	5.00	10.00	20.00
❑ 73008 [S]	New Sound	1967	5.00	10.00	20.00

RICHARDS, JOHNNY
Tenor saxophone player, composer, arranger and bandleader.

Number	Title	Yr	VG	VG+	NM
BETHLEHEM					
❑ BCP-6011 [M]	Something Else by Johnny Richards	1956	12.50	25.00	50.00
❑ BCP-6032	Something Else by Johnny Richards	197?	3.00	6.00	12.00
-- Reissue, distributed by RCA Victor					
CAPITOL					
❑ T 885 [M]	Wide Range	1957	10.00	20.00	40.00
❑ T 981 [M]	Experiments In Sound	1958	10.00	20.00	40.00
CORAL					
❑ CRL 57304 [M]	Walk Softly/Run Wild	1959	3.75	7.50	15.00
❑ CRL 757304 [S]	Walk Softly/Run Wild	1959	5.00	10.00	20.00
CREATIVE WORLD					
❑ ST-1052	Wide Range	198?	2.50	5.00	10.00
DISCOVERY					
❑ 915	Je Vous Adore	1986	2.50	5.00	10.00
ROULETTE					
❑ SR-25351	Aqui Se Habla Espanol	1967	5.00	10.00	20.00
❑ R-52008 [M]	The Rites of Diablo	1958	7.50	15.00	30.00
❑ SR-52008 [S]	The Rites of Diablo	1958	6.25	12.50	25.00
❑ R-52114 [M]	My Fair Lady	1964	3.75	7.50	15.00
❑ SR-52114 [S]	My Fair Lady	1964	5.00	10.00	20.00

RICHARDS, RED
Pianist.

Number	Title	Yr	VG	VG+	NM
SACKVILLE					
❑ 2017	I'm Shooting High	198?	3.00	6.00	12.00
WEST 54					
❑ 8000	Soft Buns	1979	3.00	6.00	12.00
❑ 8005	Mellow Tone	1980	3.00	6.00	12.00

RICHARDS, TREVOR
Drummer.

Number	Title	Yr	VG	VG+	NM
STOMP OFF					
❑ SOS-1222	The Trevor Richards New Orleans Trio	1991	3.00	6.00	12.00

Number	Title	Yr	VG	VG+	NM

RICHARDSON, JEROME
Saxophone player (soprano, alto, tenor, baritone), flutist and piccolo player. Also see THE PRESTIGE BLUES SWINGERS.
NEW JAZZ
| ❏ NJLP-8205 [M] | Jerome Richardson Sextet | 1958 | 20.00 | 40.00 | 80.00 |
| -- Purple label |
| ❏ NJLP-8205 [M] | Jerome Richardson Sextet | 1965 | 6.25 | 12.50 | 25.00 |
| -- Blue label, trident logo at right |
| ❏ NJLP-8226 [M] | Roamin' with Richardson | 1959 | 20.00 | 40.00 | 80.00 |
| -- Purple label |
| ❏ NJLP-8226 [M] | Roamin' with Richardson | 1965 | 6.25 | 12.50 | 25.00 |
| -- Blue label, trident logo at right |
UNITED ARTISTS
| ❏ UAJ-14006 [M] | Going to the Movies | 1962 | 7.50 | 15.00 | 30.00 |
| ❏ UAJS-15006 [S] | Going to the Movies | 1962 | 10.00 | 20.00 | 40.00 |
VERVE
| ❏ V-8729 [M] | Groove Merchant | 1967 | 5.00 | 10.00 | 20.00 |
| ❏ V6-8729 [S] | Groove Merchant | 1967 | 3.75 | 7.50 | 15.00 |

RICHARDSON, WALLY
Guitarist.
PRESTIGE
| ❏ PRST-7569 | Soul Guru | 1969 | 5.00 | 10.00 | 20.00 |

RICHMOND, DANNIE
Drummer.
ABC IMPULSE!
| ❏ AS-98 [S] | Dannie Richmond | 1968 | 3.75 | 7.50 | 15.00 |
GATEMOUTH
| ❏ 1004 | Dannie Richmond Quintet | 1980 | 3.00 | 6.00 | 12.00 |
IMPULSE!
| ❏ A-98 [M] | Dannie Richmond | 1966 | 5.00 | 10.00 | 20.00 |
| ❏ AS-98 [S] | Dannie Richmond | 1966 | 6.25 | 12.50 | 25.00 |
RED RECORD
| ❏ VPA-161 | Dionysius | 198? | 3.00 | 6.00 | 12.00 |
SOUL NOTE
| ❏ SN-1005 | Ode to Mingus | 198? | 3.00 | 6.00 | 12.00 |

RICHMOND, MIKE
Bass player.
INNER CITY
| ❏ IC-1065 | Dream Waves | 1978 | 3.00 | 6.00 | 12.00 |

RICHMOND, MIKE, AND ANDY LAVERNE
Also see each artist's individual listings.
STEEPLECHASE
| ❏ SCS-1101 | For Us | 198? | 3.00 | 6.00 | 12.00 |

RIDLEY, LARRY
Bass player.
STRATA-EAST
| ❏ SES-19759 | Sum of the Parts | 1975 | 6.25 | 12.50 | 25.00 |

RIEDEL, GEORGE
Bass player, composer and arranger.
PHILIPS
| ❏ PHM-200-140 [M] | Jazz Ballet | 1964 | 3.75 | 7.50 | 15.00 |
| ❏ PHS-600-140 [S] | Jazz Ballet | 1964 | 5.00 | 10.00 | 20.00 |

RIEMANN, KURT
Electronic instrumentalist and composer.
INNOVATIVE COMMUNICATION
| ❏ KS 80.047 | Electronic Nightworks | 1987 | 3.00 | 6.00 | 12.00 |

RIFKIN, JOSHUA
Classical pianist, arranger and composer. Most of his work is outside the scope of this book, but the below LPs helped to re-acquaint the United States with the long-neglected music of Scott Joplin.
NONESUCH
| ❏ H-71248 | Piano Rags by Scott Joplin | 1970 | 3.00 | 6.00 | 12.00 |
| ❏ H-71264 | Piano Rags by Scott Joplin, Vol. 2 | 1971 | 3.00 | 6.00 | 12.00 |

RILEY, DOUG
Pianist and organist.
PM
| ❏ 007 | Dreams | 1977 | 3.00 | 6.00 | 12.00 |

RIMINGTON, SAMMY
Clarinetist, alto saxophone player and bandleader.
GHB
❏ GHB-94	Sammy Rimington Plays George Lewis Classics	198?	2.50	5.00	10.00
❏ GHB-181	Sammy Rimington and the Mouldy Five, Vol. 1	1985	2.50	5.00	10.00
❏ GHB-182	Sammy Rimington and the Mouldy Five, Vol. 2	1985	2.50	5.00	10.00
JAZZ CRUSADE
| ❏ 1005 | Sammy Rimington Plays George Lewis Classics | 196? | 3.75 | 7.50 | 15.00 |
PROGRESSIVE
| ❏ PRO-7077 | The Exciting Sax of Sammy Rimington | 1987 | 2.50 | 5.00 | 10.00 |

RIPPINGTONS, THE
Members: Russ Freeman (leader, guitar, keyboards); Brandon Fields (alto, tenor and soprano sax, flute); Steve Reid (percussion); Tony Morales (drums). They appeared on all four of the below albums; others came and went.
GRP
| ❏ GR-9588 | Tourist in Paradise | 1989 | 3.00 | 6.00 | 12.00 |
| ❏ GR-9618 | Welcome to the St. James Club | 1990 | 3.75 | 7.50 | 15.00 |
PASSPORT JAZZ
| ❏ PJ 88019 | Moonlighting | 1987 | 3.00 | 6.00 | 12.00 |
| ❏ PJ 88042 | Kilimanjaro | 1988 | 3.00 | 6.00 | 12.00 |

RITENOUR, LEE
Guitarist. Also see DAVE GRUSIN.
ELEKTRA
❏ 6E-136	The Captain's Journey	1978	2.50	5.00	10.00
❏ 6E-192	Feel the Night	1979	2.50	5.00	10.00
❏ 6E-331	Rit	1981	2.50	5.00	10.00
❏ 60186	Rit/2	1982	2.50	5.00	10.00
❏ 60358	Banded Together	1984	2.50	5.00	10.00
ELEKTRA/MUSICIAN
| ❏ 60024 | Rio | 1982 | 2.50 | 5.00 | 10.00 |
| ❏ 60310 | On the Line | 1983 | 2.50 | 5.00 | 10.00 |
EPIC
| ❏ PE 33947 | First Course | 1976 | 2.50 | 5.00 | 10.00 |
| -- Orange label |
| ❏ PE 33947 | First Course | 1979 | 2.00 | 4.00 | 8.00 |
| -- Dark blue label |
| ❏ PE 34426 | Captain Fingers | 1977 | 2.50 | 5.00 | 10.00 |
| -- Orange label |
| ❏ PE 34426 | Captain Fingers | 1979 | 2.00 | 4.00 | 8.00 |
| -- Dark blue label |
| ❏ JE 36527 | The Best of Lee Ritenour | 1980 | 2.50 | 5.00 | 10.00 |
| ❏ PE 36527 | The Best of Lee Ritenour | 198? | 2.00 | 4.00 | 8.00 |
| -- Budget-line reissue |
GRP
❏ GR-1017	Rio	1986	2.00	4.00	8.00
❏ GR-1021	Earth Run	1986	2.50	5.00	10.00
❏ GR-1042	Portrait	1987	2.50	5.00	10.00
❏ GR-9570	Festival	1988	2.50	5.00	10.00
❏ GR-9594	Color Rit	1989	3.00	6.00	12.00
❏ GR-9615	Stolen Moments	1990	3.75	7.50	15.00
MOBILE FIDELITY
| ❏ 1-147 | Captain Fingers | 1985 | 6.25 | 12.50 | 25.00 |
| -- Audiophile vinyl |
NAUTILUS
| ❏ NR-41 | Rit | 198? | 10.00 | 20.00 | 40.00 |
| -- Audiophile vinyl |

RITZ, LYLE
Ukulele and bass player.
VERVE
❏ MGV-2087 [M]	How About Uke?	1957	10.00	20.00	40.00
❏ MGVS-6070 [S]	50th State Jazz	1960	10.00	20.00	40.00
❏ MGV-8333 [M]	50th State Jazz	1959	12.50	25.00	50.00
❏ V-8333 [M]	50th State Jazz	1961	6.25	12.50	25.00
❏ V6-8333 [S]	50th State Jazz	1961	5.00	10.00	20.00

RITZ, THE
Vocal group of Daryl Bosteels, Rebecca Hardiman, Sharon Harris and Bob Stoloff, with Jeff Auger (piano), Marty Ballou (bass) and Les Harris Jr. (drums).
PAUSA
| ❏ 7190 | Born to Bop | 1986 | 2.50 | 5.00 | 10.00 |

Number	Title	Yr	VG	VG+	NM

RIVERS, JAMES
Tenor saxophone player.
SPINDLETOP
| ❏ STP-101 | The Dallas Sessions | 1986 | 3.00 | 6.00 | 12.00 |

RIVERS, MAVIS
Female singer.
CAPITOL
| ❏ ST 1210 [S] | Take a Number | 1959 | 10.00 | 20.00 | 40.00 |
| ❏ T 1210 [M] | Take a Number | 1959 | 7.50 | 15.00 | 30.00 |
DELOS
| ❏ DMS-4002 | It's a Good Day | 1983 | 3.00 | 6.00 | 12.00 |
REPRISE
❏ R-2002 [M]	Mavis	1961	7.50	15.00	30.00
❏ R9-2002 [S]	Mavis	1961	10.00	20.00	40.00
❏ R-6074 [M]	Mavis Rivers Meets Shorty Rogers	1963	6.25	12.50	25.00
❏ RS-6074 [S]	Mavis Rivers Meets Shorty Rogers	1963	7.50	15.00	30.00
VEE JAY
| ❏ VJ-1132 [M] | We Remember Mildred Bailey | 1964 | 6.25 | 12.50 | 25.00 |
| ❏ VJS-1132 [S] | We Remember Mildred Bailey | 1964 | 10.00 | 20.00 | 40.00 |

RIVERS, RAY
Guitarist.
INSIGHT
| ❏ 202 | Let Me Hear Some Jazz | 198? | 2.50 | 5.00 | 10.00 |
PROJECT 3
| ❏ PR 5110 SD | Cool Cat on a Jazz Guitar | 1983 | 2.50 | 5.00 | 10.00 |

RIVERS, SAM
Saxophone player, flutist, pianist and composer.
ABC IMPULSE!
❏ AS-9251	Streams	1973	3.75	7.50	15.00
❏ AS-9286	Crystals	1974	3.75	7.50	15.00
❏ AS-9302	Hues	1974	3.75	7.50	15.00
❏ AS-9316	Sizzle	1975	3.75	7.50	15.00
❏ IA-9352 [(2)]	Sam Rivers Live	1978	3.75	7.50	15.00
BLACK SAINT
| ❏ BSR-0064 | Colours | 1982 | 3.00 | 6.00 | 12.00 |
BLUE NOTE
❏ BN-LA453-H2 [(2)]	Involution	1975	3.75	7.50	15.00
❏ BLP-4184 [M]	Fuchsia Swing Song	1964	6.25	12.50	25.00
❏ BLP-4206 [M]	Contours	1965	6.25	12.50	25.00
❏ BLP-4249 [M]	A New Conception	1966	6.25	12.50	25.00
❏ BLP-4261 [M]	Dimensions and Extensions	1966	---	---	---
-- Canceled					
❏ BST-84184 [S]	Fuchsia Swing Song	1964	7.50	15.00	30.00
-- With "New York, USA" address on label					
❏ BST-84184 [S]	Fuchsia Swing Song	1967	5.00	10.00	20.00
-- With "A Division of Liberty Records" on label					
❏ BST-84206 [S]	Contours	1965	7.50	15.00	30.00
-- With "New York, USA" address on label					
❏ BST-84206 [S]	Contours	1967	5.00	10.00	20.00
-- With "A Division of Liberty Records" on label					
❏ BST-84249 [S]	A New Conception	1966	7.50	15.00	30.00
-- With "New York, USA" address on label					
❏ BST-84249 [S]	A New Conception	1967	5.00	10.00	20.00
-- With "A Division of Liberty Records" on label					
❏ BST-84261 [S]	Dimensions and Extensions	1986	3.00	6.00	12.00
-- "The Finest in Jazz Since 1939" label; originally scheduled for 1966 release					
ECM
| ❏ 1162 | Contrasts | 1980 | 3.00 | 6.00 | 12.00 |
MCA
| ❏ 4149 [(2)] | Live Trio Session | 198? | 3.00 | 6.00 | 12.00 |
PAUSA
| ❏ 7015 | The Quest | 198? | 2.50 | 5.00 | 10.00 |
RED RECORD
| ❏ VPA-106 | The Quest | 198? | 3.00 | 6.00 | 12.00 |
TOMATO
| ❏ TOM-8002 | Waves | 1979 | 3.00 | 6.00 | 12.00 |

RIVERS, SAM, AND DAVE HOLLAND
Also see each artist's individual listings.
IAI
| ❏ 37.38.43 | Sam Rivers and Dave Holland | 197? | 3.75 | 7.50 | 15.00 |
| ❏ 37.38.48 | Sam Rivers and Dave Holland, Vol. 2 | 1976 | 3.75 | 7.50 | 15.00 |

RIVERSIDE JAZZ STARS, THE
Members include JIMMY HEATH; BLUE MITCHELL; CLARK TERRY; BOBBY TIMMONS; JULIUS WATKINS.
RIVERSIDE
| ❏ RLP-397 [M] | A Jazz Version of "Kean" | 1961 | 7.50 | 15.00 | 30.00 |
| ❏ RS-9397 [S] | A Jazz Version of "Kean" | 1961 | 10.00 | 20.00 | 40.00 |

RIZZI, TONY
Guitarist.
MILAGRO
| ❏ 1000 | Tony Rizzi Plays Charlie Christian | 197? | 3.00 | 6.00 | 12.00 |
STARLITE
| ❏ 6002 [10] | Tony Rizzi Guitar | 1954 | 12.50 | 25.00 | 50.00 |

ROACH, FREDDIE
Organist and composer.
BLUE NOTE
❏ BLP-4113 [M]	Down to Earth	1962	6.25	12.50	25.00
❏ BLP-4128 [M]	Mo' Greens, Please	1963	6.25	12.50	25.00
❏ BLP-4158 [M]	Good Move	1964	6.25	12.50	25.00
❏ BLP-4168 [M]	Brown Sugar	1964	6.25	12.50	25.00
❏ BLP-4190 [M]	All That's Good	1965	6.25	12.50	25.00
❏ BST-84113 [S]	Down to Earth	1962	7.50	15.00	30.00
-- With "New York, USA" address on label					
❏ BST-84113 [S]	Down to Earth	1967	3.75	7.50	15.00
-- With "A Division of Liberty Records" on label					
❏ BST-84128 [S]	Mo' Greens, Please	1963	7.50	15.00	30.00
-- With "New York, USA" address on label					
❏ BST-84128 [S]	Mo' Greens, Please	1967	3.75	7.50	15.00
-- With "A Division of Liberty Records" on label					
❏ BST-84158 [S]	Good Move	1964	7.50	15.00	30.00
-- With "New York, USA" address on label					
❏ BST-84158 [S]	Good Move	1967	3.75	7.50	15.00
-- With "A Division of Liberty Records" on label					
❏ BST-84168 [S]	Brown Sugar	1964	7.50	15.00	30.00
-- With "New York, USA" address on label					
❏ BST-84168 [S]	Brown Sugar	1967	3.75	7.50	15.00
-- With "A Division of Liberty Records" on label					
❏ BST-84190 [S]	All That's Good	1965	7.50	15.00	30.00
-- With "New York, USA" address on label					
❏ BST-84190 [S]	All That's Good	1967	3.75	7.50	15.00
-- With "A Division of Liberty Records" on label					
PRESTIGE
❏ PRLP-7490 [M]	The Soul Book	1967	7.50	15.00	30.00
❏ PRST-7490 [S]	The Soul Book	1967	5.00	10.00	20.00
❏ PRLP-7507 [M]	Mocha Motion	1967	7.50	15.00	30.00
❏ PRST-7507 [S]	Mocha Motion	1967	5.00	10.00	20.00
❏ PRLP-7521 [M]	My People -- Soul People	1967	7.50	15.00	30.00
❏ PRST-7521 [S]	My People -- Soul People	1967	5.00	10.00	20.00

ROACH, MAX
Drummer. Also see DUKE ELLINGTON; THE JAZZ ARTISTS GUILD; M'BOOM; CHARLES MINGUS; CHARLIE PARKER; THE QUINTET; BUDDY RICH; SONNY ROLLINS.
ABC IMPULSE!
| ❏ AS-8 [S] | Percussion Bitter Sweet | 1968 | 5.00 | 10.00 | 20.00 |
| ❏ AS-16 [S] | It's Time | 1968 | 10.00 | 20.00 | 40.00 |
ARGO
| ❏ LP-623 [M] | Max | 1958 | 12.50 | 25.00 | 50.00 |
| ❏ LPS-623 [S] | Max | 1958 | 10.00 | 20.00 | 40.00 |
ATLANTIC
❏ 1435 [M]	Max Roach Trio Featuring the Legendary Hasaan	1965	5.00	10.00	20.00
❏ SD 1435 [S]	Max Roach Trio Featuring the Legendary Hasaan	1965	6.25	12.50	25.00
❏ 1467 [M]	Drums Unlimited	1966	5.00	10.00	20.00
❏ SD 1467 [S]	Drums Unlimited	1966	6.25	12.50	25.00
❏ SD 1510 [S]	Members Don't Get Weary	1968	5.00	10.00	20.00
❏ SD 1587	Lift Every Voice and Sing	1972	3.00	6.00	12.00
BAINBRIDGE
| ❏ 1042 | Max Roach | 198? | 2.50 | 5.00 | 10.00 |
| ❏ 1044 | Max Roach/George Duvivier/ Sonny Clark | 198? | 2.50 | 5.00 | 10.00 |
CANDID
| ❏ CD-8002 [M] | We Insist -- Freedom Now Suite | 1960 | 15.00 | 30.00 | 60.00 |
| ❏ CS-9002 [S] | We Insist -- Freedom Now Suite | 1960 | 15.00 | 30.00 | 60.00 |
DEBUT
| ❏ DLP-13 [10] | Max Roach Quartet Featuring Hank Mobley | 1954 | 75.00 | 150.00 | 300.00 |
EMARCY
| ❏ MG-36098 [M] | Max Roach + 4 | 1957 | 25.00 | 50.00 | 100.00 |
| ❏ MG-36108 [M] | Jazz in 3/4 Time | 1957 | 20.00 | 40.00 | 80.00 |

Number	Title	Yr	VG	VG+	NM
❏ MG-36127 [M]	The Max Roach 4 Plays Charlie Parker	1958	20.00	40.00	80.00
❏ MG-36132 [M]	Max Roach + 4 on the Chicago Scene	1958	15.00	30.00	60.00
❏ MG-36140 [M]	Max Roach Plus Four At Newport	1958	15.00	30.00	60.00
❏ MG-36144 [M]	Max Roach with the Boston Percussion Ensemble	1958	15.00	30.00	60.00
❏ SR-80000 [S]	Max Roach + 4	1959	20.00	40.00	80.00
❏ SR-80002 [S]	Jazz in 3/4 Time	1959	15.00	30.00	60.00
❏ SR-80010 [S]	Max Roach Plus Four At Newport	1959	12.50	25.00	50.00
❏ SR-80015 [S]	Max Roach with the Boston Percussion Ensemble	1959	12.50	25.00	50.00
❏ SR-80019 [S]	The Max Roach 4 Plays Charlie Parker	1959	15.00	30.00	60.00
❏ SR-800?? [S]	Max Roach + 4 on the Chicago Scene	1959	12.50	25.00	50.00
❏ 814 190-1 [(2)]	Standard Time	198?	3.00	6.00	12.00
❏ 826 456-1	Jazz in 3/4 Time	1986	2.50	5.00	10.00
FANTASY					
❏ OJC-202	Max Roach Quartet Featuring Hank Mobley	1985	2.50	5.00	10.00
❏ OJC-304	Deeds, Not Words	1988	2.50	5.00	10.00
❏ 6007 [M]	Speak Brother, Speak	1963	6.25	12.50	25.00
❏ 86007 [S]	Speak Brother, Speak	1963	7.50	15.00	30.00
HAT ART					
❏ 4026 [(4)]	The Long March	1986	7.50	15.00	30.00
IMPULSE!					
❏ A-8 [M]	Percussion Bitter Sweet	1961	7.50	15.00	30.00
❏ AS-8 [S]	Percussion Bitter Sweet	1961	10.00	20.00	40.00
❏ A-16 [M]	It's Time	1962	5.00	10.00	20.00
❏ AS-16 [S]	It's Time	1962	7.50	15.00	30.00
JAZZLAND					
❏ JLP-79 [M]	Conversation	1962	7.50	15.00	30.00
❏ JLP-979 [S]	Conversation	1962	6.25	12.50	25.00
MCA					
❏ 29053	It's Time	1980	2.50	5.00	10.00
MERCURY					
❏ MG-20491 [M]	Quiet As It's Kept	1959	10.00	20.00	40.00
❏ MG-20539 [M]	Moon Faced and Starry-Eyed	1960	10.00	20.00	40.00
❏ MG-20760 [M]	Parisian Sketches	1962	7.50	15.00	30.00
❏ MG-20911 [M]	The Many Sides of Max	1964	6.25	12.50	25.00
❏ SR-60170 [S]	Quiet As It's Kept	1959	12.50	25.00	50.00
❏ SR-60215 [S]	Moon Faced and Starry-Eyed	1960	12.50	25.00	50.00
❏ SR-60760 [S]	Parisian Sketches	1962	10.00	20.00	40.00
❏ SR-60911 [S]	The Many Sides of Max	1964	7.50	15.00	30.00
MILESTONE					
❏ 47061 [(2)]	Conversations	198?	3.75	7.50	15.00
RIVERSIDE					
❏ RLP 12-280 [M]	Deeds, Not Words	1958	12.50	25.00	50.00
❏ RLP-1122 [S]	Deeds, Not Words	1959	10.00	20.00	40.00
❏ RS-3018 [S]	Deeds, Not Words	1968	3.75	7.50	15.00
SOUL NOTE					
❏ SN-1003	Pictures in a Frame	198?	3.00	6.00	12.00
❏ SN-1053	In the Light	1982	3.00	6.00	12.00
❏ SN-1093	Survivors	1985	3.00	6.00	12.00
❏ SN-1103	Scott Free	1985	3.00	6.00	12.00
❏ SN-1109	Easy Winners	1985	3.00	6.00	12.00
TIME					
❏ S-2087 [S]	Max Roach	1962	6.25	12.50	25.00
❏ 52087 [M]	Max Roach	1962	7.50	15.00	30.00
❏ ST-70003 [S]	Award Winning Drummer	1959	10.00	20.00	40.00
❏ T-70003 [M]	Award Winning Drummer	1959	12.50	25.00	50.00
TRIP					
❏ 5522	Max Roach + 4	197?	2.50	5.00	10.00
❏ 5559	Jazz in 3/4 Time	197?	2.50	5.00	10.00

ROACH, MAX/ART BLAKEY
Also see each artist's individual listings.
BLUE NOTE

Number	Title	Yr	VG	VG+	NM
❏ BLP-5010 [10]	Max Roach Quintet / Art Blakey and His Band	1952	150.00	300.00	600.00

ROACH, MAX, AND ANTHONY BRAXTON
Also see each artist's individual listings.
BLACK SAINT

Number	Title	Yr	VG	VG+	NM
❏ BSR-0024	Birth and Rebirth	198?	3.00	6.00	12.00
HAT HUT					
❏ 06 [(2)]	One in Two -- Two in One	1980	5.00	10.00	20.00

ROACH, MAX, AND CLIFFORD BROWN
See CLIFFORD BROWN.

ROACH, MAX; SONNY CLARK; GEORGE DUVIVIER
Duvivier is a bass player. Also see SONNY CLARK; MAX ROACH.
TIME

Number	Title	Yr	VG	VG+	NM
❏ S-2101 [S]	Max Roach, Sonny Clark, George Duvivier	1962	10.00	20.00	40.00
❏ 52101 [M]	Max Roach, Sonny Clark, George Duvivier	1962	7.50	15.00	30.00

ROACH, MAX, AND CONNIE CROTHERS
Also see each artist's individual listings.
NEW ARTISTS

Number	Title	Yr	VG	VG+	NM
❏ NA-1001	Swish	198?	3.00	6.00	12.00

ROACH, MAX, AND STAN LEVEY
Also see each artist's individual listings.
LIBERTY

Number	Title	Yr	VG	VG+	NM
❏ LRP-3064 [M]	Drummin' the Blues	1957	20.00	40.00	80.00

ROACH, MAX, AND ARCHIE SHEPP
Also see each artist's individual listings.
HAT HUT

Number	Title	Yr	VG	VG+	NM
❏ 13 [(2)]	The Long March	1980	5.00	10.00	20.00

ROACH, MAX, AND CECIL TAYLOR
Also see each artist's individual listings.
SOUL NOTE

Number	Title	Yr	VG	VG+	NM
❏ SN-1100/1 [(2)]	Historic Concerts	1985	3.75	7.50	15.00

ROANE, STEPHEN
Bass player.
LABOR

Number	Title	Yr	VG	VG+	NM
❏ 2	Siblings	1980	3.00	6.00	12.00

ROARING SEVEN JAZZBAND, THE
STOMP OFF

Number	Title	Yr	VG	VG+	NM
❏ SOS-1019	Hot Dance	198?	2.50	5.00	10.00

ROBBINS, ADELAIDE/MARIAN McPARTLAND/ BARBARA CARROLL
Robbins is a pianist. Also see BARBARA CARROLL; MARIAN McPARTLAND.
SAVOY

Number	Title	Yr	VG	VG+	NM
❏ MG-12097 [M]	Lookin' for a Boy	1957	12.50	25.00	50.00

ROBERT, GEORGE
Alto saxophone player.
CONTEMPORARY

Number	Title	Yr	VG	VG+	NM
❏ C-14037	Sun Dance	1988	2.50	5.00	10.00

ROBERTS, DAVID THOMAS
Pianist.
STOMP OFF

Number	Title	Yr	VG	VG+	NM
❏ SOS-1021	An Album of Early Folk Rags	198?	2.50	5.00	10.00
❏ SOS-1075	Through the Bottomlands	1985	2.50	5.00	10.00
❏ SOS-1132	The Amazon Rag	1986	2.50	5.00	10.00

ROBERTS, HANK
Cello player. Also a fiddler and male singer.
JMT

Number	Title	Yr	VG	VG+	NM
❏ 834 416-1	Black Pastels	1988	2.50	5.00	10.00

ROBERTS, HOWARD
Guitarist.
ABC IMPULSE!

Number	Title	Yr	VG	VG+	NM
❏ AS-9207	Antelope Freeway	1972	3.75	7.50	15.00
❏ AS-9299	Equinox Express Elevator	1974	3.75	7.50	15.00
CAPITOL					
❏ ST-336	Spinning Wheel	1970	3.75	7.50	15.00
❏ ST 1887 [S]	Color Him Funky	1963	7.50	15.00	30.00
❏ T 1887 [M]	Color Him Funky	1963	3.75	7.50	15.00
❏ SM-1961 [S]	H.R. Is A Dirty Guitar Player	1976	2.50	5.00	10.00
-- Reissue with new prefix					
❏ ST 1961 [S]	H.R. Is A Dirty Guitar Player	1963	5.00	10.00	20.00
❏ T 1961 [M]	H.R. Is A Dirty Guitar Player	1963	3.75	7.50	15.00
❏ ST 2214 [S]	Something's Cookin'	1965	5.00	10.00	20.00
❏ T 2214 [M]	Something's Cookin'	1965	3.75	7.50	15.00
❏ ST 2400 [S]	Goodies	1965	5.00	10.00	20.00

Number	Title	Yr	VG	VG+	NM
❏ T 2400 [M]	Goodies	1965	3.75	7.50	15.00
❏ ST 2478 [S]	Whatever's Fair	1966	5.00	10.00	20.00
❏ T 2478 [M]	Whatever's Fair	1966	3.75	7.50	15.00
❏ ST 2609 [S]	All-Time Great Instrumental Hits	1966	5.00	10.00	20.00
❏ T 2609 [M]	All-Time Great Instrumental Hits	1966	3.75	7.50	15.00
❏ ST 2716 [S]	Jaunty -- Jolly	1967	3.75	7.50	15.00
❏ T 2716 [M]	Jaunty -- Jolly	1967	6.25	12.50	25.00
❏ ST 2824 [S]	Guilty	1967	3.75	7.50	15.00
❏ T 2824 [M]	Guilty	1967	5.00	10.00	20.00
❏ ST 2901 [S]	Out Of Sight -- But In Mind	1968	3.75	7.50	15.00
❏ ST-11247	Sounds	1974	3.00	6.00	12.00

CONCORD JAZZ

Number	Title	Yr	VG	VG+	NM
❏ CJ-53	The Real Howard Roberts	1978	2.50	5.00	10.00

DISCOVERY

Number	Title	Yr	VG	VG+	NM
❏ 812	Turning to Spring	1980	3.00	6.00	12.00

NORGRAN

Number	Title	Yr	VG	VG+	NM
❏ MGN-1106 [M]	Mr. Roberts Plays Guitar	1955	---	---	---
-- Canceled

VERVE

Number	Title	Yr	VG	VG+	NM
❏ VSP-29 [M]	The Movin' Man	1966	5.00	10.00	20.00
❏ VSPS-29 [R]	The Movin' Man	1966	3.00	6.00	12.00
❏ UMV-2673	Mr. Roberts Plays Guitar	198?	3.00	6.00	12.00
❏ MGV-8192 [M]	Mr. Roberts Plays Guitar	1957	12.50	25.00	50.00
❏ V-8192 [M]	Mr. Roberts Plays Guitar	1961	6.25	12.50	25.00
❏ MGV-8305 [M]	Good Pickin's	1959	12.50	25.00	50.00
❏ V-8305 [M]	Good Pickin's	1961	6.25	12.50	25.00
❏ V-8662 [M]	Velvet Groove	1966	5.00	10.00	20.00
❏ V6-8662 [S]	Velvet Groove	1966	3.75	7.50	15.00

ROBERTS, JUDY
Pianist and female singer.
INNER CITY

Number	Title	Yr	VG	VG+	NM
❏ IC-1078	Judy Roberts Band	198?	3.00	6.00	12.00
❏ IC-1088	The Other World	198?	3.00	6.00	12.00
❏ IC-1138	Nights in Brazil	198?	3.00	6.00	12.00

PAUSA

Number	Title	Yr	VG	VG+	NM
❏ 7147	Judy Roberts Trio	198?	2.50	5.00	10.00
❏ 7176	You Are There	1985	2.50	5.00	10.00

ROBERTS, LUCKEY
Pianist and composer.
PERIOD

Number	Title	Yr	VG	VG+	NM
❏ RL-1929 [M]	Happy Go Luckey	1956	10.00	20.00	40.00

ROBERTS, LUCKEY, AND WILLIE "THE LION" SMITH
Also see each artist's individual listings.
GOOD TIME JAZZ

Number	Title	Yr	VG	VG+	NM
❏ L-12035 [M]	Harlem Piano Solos	1958	10.00	20.00	40.00
❏ S-10035 [S]	Harlem Piano Solos	1958	7.50	15.00	30.00

ROBERTS, MARCUS
Pianist.
NOVUS

Number	Title	Yr	VG	VG+	NM
❏ 3051-1-N	The Truth Is Spoken Here	1989	3.00	6.00	12.00
❏ 3078-1-N	Deep in the Shed	1990	3.75	7.50	15.00

ROBERTS, POLA
See GLORIA COLEMAN.

ROBERTS, WILLIAM NEIL
Harpsichordist.
KLAVIER

Number	Title	Yr	VG	VG+	NM
❏ 510	Great Scott!	197?	3.00	6.00	12.00
❏ 516	Scott Joplin Ragtime, Vol. 2	1974	3.00	6.00	12.00

ROBERTSON, HERB
Trumpeter, cornet and fluegel horn player.
JMT

Number	Title	Yr	VG	VG+	NM
❏ 834 420-1	Shades of Bud Powell	1988	2.50	5.00	10.00

ROBERTSON, PAUL
PALO ALTO

Number	Title	Yr	VG	VG+	NM
❏ PA-8002	The Song Is You	1981	2.50	5.00	10.00
❏ PA-8013	Old Friends, New Friends	1982	2.50	5.00	10.00

ROBICHAUX, JOE
Pianist and bandleader.
FOLKLYRIC

Number	Title	Yr	VG	VG+	NM
❏ 9032	Joe Robichaux and the Hot New Orleans Rhythm Boys	198?	2.50	5.00	10.00

ROBINS, CAROL JOY
Female singer.
OPTIMISM

Number	Title	Yr	VG	VG+	NM
❏ OP-3202	Joy Sings the Blues	1988	2.50	5.00	10.00

ROBINSON, FREDDY
Guitarist.
ENTERPRISE

Number	Title	Yr	VG	VG+	NM
❏ ENS-1025	Freddy Robinson at the Drive-In	1972	3.00	6.00	12.00

PACIFIC JAZZ

Number	Title	Yr	VG	VG+	NM
❏ ST-20162	The Coming Atlantis	1970	3.75	7.50	15.00
❏ ST-20176	Hot Fun in the Summertime	1971	3.75	7.50	15.00

ROBINSON, JIM
Trombonist and bandleader.
BIOGRAPH

Number	Title	Yr	VG	VG+	NM
❏ CEN-8	Jim Robinson and His New Orleans Band	197?	2.50	5.00	10.00
❏ CEN-16	Jim Robinson and His New Orleans Joymakers	197?	2.50	5.00	10.00

CENTER

Number	Title	Yr	VG	VG+	NM
❏ PLP-1 [M]	Jim Robinson and His New Orleans Band	196?	3.75	7.50	15.00

GHB

Number	Title	Yr	VG	VG+	NM
❏ GHB-28	Jim Robinson at the Jacinto Ballroom	197?	3.00	6.00	12.00
❏ GHB-185	Big Jim's Little Six	1986	2.50	5.00	10.00
❏ GHB-196	1944 Revisited	1986	2.50	5.00	10.00

JAZZ CRUSADE

Number	Title	Yr	VG	VG+	NM
❏ 2005	Jim Robinson	1965	3.75	7.50	15.00
❏ 2010	Jim Robinson's Little Six	196?	3.75	7.50	15.00
❏ 2015	1944 Revisited	196?	3.75	7.50	15.00

PEARL

Number	Title	Yr	VG	VG+	NM
❏ PS-5	Economy Hall Breakdown	197?	3.00	6.00	12.00

RIVERSIDE

Number	Title	Yr	VG	VG+	NM
❏ RLP-369 [M]	Jim Robinson's New Orleans Band	1961	7.50	15.00	30.00
❏ RLP-393 [M]	Jim Robinson Plays Spirituals and Blues	1961	7.50	15.00	30.00
❏ RS-9369 [R]	Jim Robinson's New Orleans Band	1961	3.75	7.50	15.00
❏ RS-9393 [R]	Jim Robinson Plays Spirituals and Blues	1961	3.75	7.50	15.00

ROBINSON, JIM, AND BILLIE AND DEDE PIERCE
Also see each artist's individual listings.
ATLANTIC

Number	Title	Yr	VG	VG+	NM
❏ 1409 [M]	Jim Robinson and Billie & DeDe Pierce	1963	5.00	10.00	20.00
❏ SD 1409 [S]	Jim Robinson and Billie & DeDe Pierce	1963	6.25	12.50	25.00

ROBINSON, PERRY
Clarinetist.
CHIAROSCURO

Number	Title	Yr	VG	VG+	NM
❏ 190	The Traveler	1977	3.75	7.50	15.00

IAI

Number	Title	Yr	VG	VG+	NM
❏ 37.38.56	Kundalini	1978	3.75	7.50	15.00

SAVOY

Number	Title	Yr	VG	VG+	NM
❏ MG-12177 [M]	Funk Dumpling	1962	6.25	12.50	25.00
❏ MG-12202 [M]	East Of Suez	196?	3.75	7.50	15.00

SAVOY JAZZ

Number	Title	Yr	VG	VG+	NM
❏ SJL-1180	Funk Dumpling	198?	2.50	5.00	10.00

ROBINSON, PETE
Keyboard player and composer.
TESTAMENT

Number	Title	Yr	VG	VG+	NM
❏ 4401	Dialogues for Piano and Reeds	197?	3.00	6.00	12.00

ROBINSON, PETER MANNING
Keyboard player and composer.
CMG

Number	Title	Yr	VG	VG+	NM
❏ CML-8018	Phoenix Rising	1989	3.00	6.00	12.00

Number	Title	Yr	VG	VG+	NM
ROBINSON, SPIKE					
Tenor saxophone player.					
CAPRI					
❑ 8984	London Reprise	1984	2.50	5.00	10.00
❑ 71785	Spring Can Really Hang You Up the Most	1985	2.50	5.00	10.00
❑ 72185	It's a Wonderful World	1985	2.50	5.00	10.00
DISCOVERY					
❑ 870	This Is Always: The Music of Harry Warren, Vol. 2	198?	2.50	5.00	10.00
ROBINSON, SPIKE, AND AL COHN					
Also see each artist's individual listings.					
CAPRI					
❑ 71787	Henry B. Meets Alvin G.	1987	2.50	5.00	10.00
ROBINSON, SUGAR CHILE					
CAPITOL					
❑ T 589 [M]	Boogie Woogie	1955	30.00	60.00	120.00
ROBINSON/LANGWORTHY/AXT JAZZ TRIO, THE					
Members: Charlie Robinson (guitar); Lew Langworthy (drums); Kevin Axt (bass).					
ASHLAND					
❑ 4963	The Robinson/Langworthy/Axt Jazz Trio	198?	3.00	6.00	12.00
ROCHE, BETTY					
Female singer.					
BETHLEHEM					
❑ BCP-64 [M]	Take the "A" Train	1956	20.00	40.00	80.00
❑ BCP-6026	Take the "A" Train	197?	3.00	6.00	12.00
-- Reissue, distributed by RCA Victor					
FANTASY					
❑ OJC-1718	Singin' and Swingin'	198?	2.50	5.00	10.00
PRESTIGE					
❑ PRLP-7187 [M]	Singin' and Swingin'	1961	12.50	25.00	50.00
❑ PRLP-7198 [M]	Lightly and Politely	1961	12.50	25.00	50.00
ROCHESTER-VEASLEY BAND, THE					
Led by Cornell Rochester (drums) and Gerald Veasley (bass, vocals).					
GRAMAVISION					
❑ 18-8505	One Minute of Love	1986	2.50	5.00	10.00
ROCKWELL, ROBERT					
ASI					
❑ 5002	Androids	1977	3.00	6.00	12.00
CELEBRATION					
❑ 5002	Androids	197?	3.75	7.50	15.00
RODGER, MART					
Clarinetist and bandleader.					
GHB					
❑ GHB-224	Jazz Tale of Two Cities	198?	2.50	5.00	10.00
RODGERS, GENE					
Pianist and arranger.					
EMARCY					
❑ MG-36145 [M]	Jazz Comes to the Astor	1958	10.00	20.00	40.00
RODGERS, IKE					
Trombonist.					
RIVERSIDE					
❑ RLP-1013 [10]	The Trombone of Ike Rodgers	1953	20.00	40.00	80.00
RODITI, CLAUDIO					
Trumpeter and fluegel horn player.					
MILESTONE					
❑ M-9158	Gemini Man	198?	2.50	5.00	10.00
❑ M-9175	Slow Fire	198?	2.50	5.00	10.00
RODNEY, RED					
Trumpeter. Also see GERRY MULLIGAN.					
ARGO					
❑ LP-643 [M]	Red Rodney Returns	1959	12.50	25.00	50.00
❑ LSP-643 [S]	Red Rodney Returns	1959	10.00	20.00	40.00
FANTASY					
❑ OJC-048	Modern Music from Chicago	198?	2.50	5.00	10.00
❑ 3208 [M]	Modern Music from Chicago	195?	20.00	40.00	80.00
-- Black vinyl					
❑ 3208 [M]	Modern Music from Chicago	1956	30.00	60.00	120.00
-- Red vinyl					
MUSE					
❑ MR-5034	Bird Lives!	1975	3.00	6.00	12.00
❑ MR-5046	Superbop	197?	3.00	6.00	12.00
❑ MR-5088	Red Tornado	1975	3.00	6.00	12.00
❑ MR-5111	Red White and Blues	1977	3.00	6.00	12.00
❑ MR-5135	Home Free	197?	3.00	6.00	12.00
❑ MR-5209	Live at the Village Vanguard	1980	3.00	6.00	12.00
❑ MR-5274	Night and Day	1981	2.50	5.00	10.00
❑ MR-5290	The 3 R's	198?	2.50	5.00	10.00
❑ MR-5307	Alive in New York	1986	2.50	5.00	10.00
❑ MR-5371	Bird Lives!	1989	2.50	5.00	10.00
ONYX					
❑ 204	Red Arrow	197?	3.00	6.00	12.00
PRESTIGE					
❑ PRLP-122 [10]	Red Rodney	1952	50.00	100.00	200.00
SAVOY					
❑ MG-12148 [M]	Fiery Red Rodney	1959	25.00	50.00	100.00
SIGNAL					
❑ S-1206 [M]	Red Rodney 1957	1957	150.00	300.00	600.00
❑ S-1206 [S]	Red Rodney 1957	199?	6.25	12.50	25.00
-- Classic Records reissue on audiophile vinyl (in stereo)					
RODNEY, RED, AND IRA SULLIVAN					
Also see each artist's individual listings.					
ELEKTRA/MUSICIAN					
❑ 60020	The Spirit Within	1982	2.50	5.00	10.00
❑ 60261	Sprint	198?	2.50	5.00	10.00
RODRIGUEZ, WILLIE					
Congas and bongos player.					
RIVERSIDE					
❑ RLP-469 [M]	Flatjacks	1963	6.25	12.50	25.00
❑ RS-9469 [S]	Flatjacks	1963	7.50	15.00	30.00
RODRIQUEZ, BOBBY					
Bass player.					
SEA BREEZE					
❑ SB-2030	Tell An Amigo	1986	2.50	5.00	10.00
ROESSLER, GEORGE					
Guitarist.					
EAGLE					
❑ SM-4195	Still Life and Old Dreams	1985	2.50	5.00	10.00
ROGERS, BOB					
Vibraphone player.					
INDIGO					
❑ 1501 [M]	All That and This, Too	1961	10.00	20.00	40.00
ROGERS, SHORTY					
Trumpeter, arranger and composer. Also see AL COHN; MAVIS RIVERS; BUD SHANK.					
ATLANTIC					
❑ 1212 [M]	The Swinging Mr. Rogers	1955	12.50	25.00	50.00
-- Black label					
❑ 1212 [M]	The Swinging Mr. Rogers	1961	6.25	12.50	25.00
-- Multicolor label, white "fan" logo at right					
❑ 1212 [M]	The Swinging Mr. Rogers	1963	5.00	10.00	20.00
-- Multicolor label, black "fan" logo at right					
❑ 1232 [M]	Martians, Come Back	1956	12.50	25.00	50.00
-- Black label					
❑ 1232 [M]	Martians, Come Back	1961	6.25	12.50	25.00
-- Multicolor label, white "fan" logo at right					
❑ 1232 [M]	Martians, Come Back	1963	5.00	10.00	20.00
-- Multicolor label, black "fan" logo at right					
❑ SD 1232 [S]	Martians, Come Back	1958	12.50	25.00	50.00
-- Green label					
❑ SD 1232 [S]	Martians, Come Back	1961	5.00	10.00	20.00
-- Multicolor label, white "fan" logo at right					
❑ SD 1232 [S]	Martians, Come Back	1963	3.75	7.50	15.00
-- Multicolor label, black "fan" logo at right					
❑ 1270 [M]	Way Up There	1957	12.50	25.00	50.00
-- Black label					
❑ 1270 [M]	Way Up There	1961	6.25	12.50	25.00
-- Multicolor label, white "fan" logo at right					
❑ 1270 [M]	Way Up There	1963	5.00	10.00	20.00
-- Multicolor label, black "fan" logo at right					
❑ 90042	The Swinging Mr. Rogers	1983	2.50	5.00	10.00

Number	Title	Yr	VG	VG+	NM
BLUEBIRD					
❑ 5917-1-RB [(2)]	Short Stops	1987	3.75	7.50	15.00
CAPITOL					
❑ H 294 [10]	Modern Sounds	1952	50.00	100.00	200.00
❑ ST 1960 [S]	Gospel Mission	1963	5.00	10.00	20.00
❑ T 1960 [M]	Gospel Mission	1963	6.25	12.50	25.00
DISCOVERY					
❑ 843	Jazz Waltz	1982	2.50	5.00	10.00
MGM					
❑ E-3798 [M]	Shorty Rogers Meets Tarzan	1960	7.50	15.00	30.00
❑ SE-3798 [S]	Shorty Rogers Meets Tarzan	1960	10.00	20.00	40.00
MOSAIC					
❑ M6-125 [(6)]	The Complete Atlantic and EMI Jazz Recordings of Shorty Rogers	199?	20.00	40.00	80.00
PAUSA					
❑ 9016	14 Historic Arrangements and Performances	198?	2.50	5.00	10.00
RCA VICTOR					
❑ LJM-1004 [M]	Shorty Rogers Courts the Count	1954	20.00	40.00	80.00
❑ LPM-1195 [M]	Shorty Rogers and His Giants	1956	17.50	35.00	70.00
❑ LPM-1326 [M]	Wherever the Five Winds Blow	1956	17.50	35.00	70.00
❑ LPM-1334 [M]	Collaboration	1956	15.00	30.00	60.00
❑ LPM-1350 [M]	The Big Shorty Rogers Express	1957	15.00	30.00	60.00
❑ LPM-1428 [M]	Shorty Rogers Plays Richard Rogers	1957	15.00	30.00	60.00
❑ LPM-1564 [M]	Portrait of Shorty	1957	15.00	30.00	60.00
❑ LPM-1696 [M]	Gigi Goes Jazz	1958	12.50	25.00	50.00
❑ LSP-1696 [S]	Gigi Goes Jazz	1958	15.00	30.00	60.00
❑ LPM-1763 [M]	Afro-Cuban Influence	1958	10.00	20.00	40.00
❑ LSP-1763 [S]	Afro-Cuban Influence	1958	12.50	25.00	50.00
❑ LPM-1975 [M]	Chances Are It Swings	1959	10.00	20.00	40.00
❑ LSP-1975 [S]	Chances Are It Swings	1959	12.50	25.00	50.00
❑ LPM-1997 [M]	The Wizard of Oz	1959	10.00	20.00	40.00
❑ LSP-1997 [S]	The Wizard of Oz	1959	12.50	25.00	50.00
❑ LPM-2110 [M]	The Swingin' Nutcracker	1960	10.00	20.00	40.00
❑ LSP-2110 [S]	The Swingin' Nutcracker	1960	12.50	25.00	50.00
❑ LPM-3137 [10]	Shorty Rogers' Giants	1953	50.00	100.00	200.00
❑ LPM-3138 [10]	Cool and Crazy	1953	50.00	100.00	200.00
REPRISE					
❑ R-6050 [M]	Bossa Nova	1962	5.00	10.00	20.00
❑ R9-6050 [S]	Bossa Nova	1962	6.25	12.50	25.00
❑ R-6060 [M]	Jazz Waltz	1962	5.00	10.00	20.00
❑ R9-6060 [S]	Jazz Waltz	1962	6.25	12.50	25.00
WARNER BROS.					
❑ W 1443 [M]	4th Dimension Jazz	1961	6.25	12.50	25.00
❑ WS 1443 [S]	4th Dimension Jazz	1961	7.50	15.00	30.00
XANADU					
❑ 148	Popi	198?	2.50	5.00	10.00

ROGERS, SHORTY/GERRY MULLIGAN
Also see each artist's individual listings.

Number	Title	Yr	VG	VG+	NM
CAPITOL					
❑ T 691 [M]	Modern Sounds	1956	20.00	40.00	80.00
❑ DT 2025 [R]	Modern Sounds	1963	3.00	6.00	12.00
❑ T 2025 [M]	Modern Sounds	1963	5.00	10.00	20.00

ROGERS, SHORTY, AND ANDRE PREVIN
Also see each artist's individual listings.

Number	Title	Yr	VG	VG+	NM
RCA VICTOR					
❑ LPM-1018 [M]	Collaboration	1954	15.00	30.00	60.00

ROGERS, SHORTY, AND BUDD SHANK
Also see each artist's individual listings.

Number	Title	Yr	VG	VG+	NM
CONCORD JAZZ					
❑ CJ-223	Yesterday, Today and Forever	1983	2.50	5.00	10.00

ROLAND, GENE
Trombonist, trumpeter, arranger and composer. Also see PAUL QUINICHETTE.

Number	Title	Yr	VG	VG+	NM
BRUNSWICK					
❑ BL 54114 [M]	Swingin' Friends	1963	10.00	20.00	40.00
❑ BL 754114 [S]	Swingin' Friends	1963	12.50	25.00	50.00
DAWN					
❑ DLP-1122 [M]	Jazzville, Volume 4	1958	20.00	40.00	80.00

ROLAND, JOE
Vibraphone player. Also see EDDIE SHU.

Number	Title	Yr	VG	VG+	NM
BETHLEHEM					
❑ BCP-17 [M]	Joe Roland Quintet	1955	12.50	25.00	50.00

Number	Title	Yr	VG	VG+	NM
SAVOY					
❑ MG-12039 [M]	Joltin' Joe Roland	1955	12.50	25.00	50.00
❑ MG-15034 [10]	Joe Roland Quartet	1954	30.00	60.00	120.00
❑ MG-15047 [10]	Joe Roland Quartet	1954	30.00	60.00	120.00

ROLDINGER, ADELHARD
Bass player.

Number	Title	Yr	VG	VG+	NM
ECM					
❑ 1221	Schattseite	1981	3.00	6.00	12.00

ROLLAND, BRIAN
Guitarist.

Number	Title	Yr	VG	VG+	NM
WUMAT					
❑ WM-1001	Guitar Bazaar	198?	3.00	6.00	12.00

ROLLINI, ADRIAN
Bass saxophone player, pianist, vibraphone player, "goofus" (keyed harmonica) and "hot fountain pen" (miniature clarinet) player and bandleader.

Number	Title	Yr	VG	VG+	NM
MERCURY					
❑ MG-20011 [M]	Chopsticks	1953	12.50	25.00	50.00
SUNBEAM					
❑ 134	Adrian Rollini and His Orchestra 1933-34	197?	2.50	5.00	10.00

ROLLINS, SONNY
Tenor saxophone player. Plays sax on the Rolling Stones' hit song "Waiting on a Friend" from 1981. Also see GARY BURTON; MILES DAVIS; ART FARMER; THELONIOUS MONK.

Number	Title	Yr	VG	VG+	NM
ABC IMPULSE!					
❑ AS-91 [S]	Sonny Rollins On Impulse!	1968	3.75	7.50	15.00
❑ AS-9121 [S]	East Broadway Run Down	1968	3.75	7.50	15.00
❑ AS-9236 [(2)]	Reevaluation: The Impulse Years	1973	3.75	7.50	15.00
❑ IA-9349	There Will Never Be Another You	1978	2.50	5.00	10.00
ANALOGUE PRODUCTIONS					
❑ AP 008	Way Out West	199?	6.25	12.50	25.00
-- Audiophile vinly					
ARCHIVE OF FOLK AND JAZZ					
❑ 220 [R]	Sonny Rollins with Guest Artist Thad Jones	1968	2.50	5.00	10.00
BLUE NOTE					
❑ BN-LA401-H2 [(2)]	Sonny Rollins	1975	3.75	7.50	15.00
❑ BN-LA475-H2 [(2)]	More from the Vanguard	1975	3.75	7.50	15.00
❑ BLP-1542 [M]	Sonny Rollins	1957	50.00	100.00	200.00
-- "Deep groove" version (deep indentation under label on both sides)					
❑ BLP-1542 [M]	Sonny Rollins	1957	37.50	75.00	150.00
-- Regular version, Lexington Ave. address on label					
❑ BLP-1542 [M]	Sonny Rollins	1963	6.25	12.50	25.00
-- With "New York, USA" address on label					
❑ BLP-1558 [M]	Sonny Rollins, Volume 2	1957	30.00	60.00	120.00
-- "Deep groove" version (deep indentation under label on both sides)					
❑ BLP-1558 [M]	Sonny Rollins, Volume 2	1957	20.00	40.00	80.00
-- Regular version, W. 63rd St. address on label					
❑ BLP-1558 [M]	Sonny Rollins, Volume 2	1963	6.25	12.50	25.00
-- With "New York, USA" address on label					
❑ BLP-1581 [M]	A Night at the Village Vanguard	1958	30.00	60.00	120.00
-- "Deep groove" version (deep indentation under label on both sides)					
❑ BLP-1581 [M]	A Night at the Village Vanguard	1958	20.00	40.00	80.00
-- Regular version, W. 63rd St. address on label					
❑ BLP-1581 [M]	A Night at the Village Vanguard	1963	6.25	12.50	25.00
-- With "New York, USA" address on label					
❑ BLP-4001 [M]	Newk's Time	1958	30.00	60.00	120.00
-- "Deep groove" version (deep indentation under label on both sides)					
❑ BLP-4001 [M]	Newk's Time	1958	20.00	40.00	80.00
-- Regular version, W. 63rd St. address on label					
❑ BLP-4001 [M]	Newk's Time	1963	6.25	12.50	25.00
-- With "New York, USA" address on label					
❑ BST-4001 [S]	Newk's Time	1959	20.00	40.00	80.00
-- "Deep groove" version (deep indentation under label on both sides)					
❑ BST-4001 [S]	Newk's Time	1959	15.00	30.00	60.00
-- Regular version, W. 63rd St. address on label					
❑ BST-4001 [S]	Newk's Time	1963	5.00	10.00	20.00
-- With "New York, USA" address on label					
❑ BST-81542 [R]	Sonny Rollins	1967	3.00	6.00	12.00
-- With "A Division of Liberty Records" on label					
❑ BST-81542 [M]	Sonny Rollins	1985	2.50	5.00	10.00
-- "The Finest in Jazz Since 1939" reissue					
❑ BST-81558 [R]	Sonny Rollins, Volume 2	1967	3.00	6.00	12.00
-- With "A Division of Liberty Records" on label					
❑ BST-81558 [M]	Sonny Rollins, Volume 2	1985	2.50	5.00	10.00
-- "The Finest in Jazz Since 1939" reissue					

Number	Title	Yr	VG	VG+	NM
❑ BST-81581 [R]	A Night at the Village Vanguard	1967	3.00	6.00	12.00
-- With "A Division of Liberty Records" on label					
❑ BST-81581 [M]	A Night at the Village Vanguard, Vol. 1	1987	2.50	5.00	10.00
-- "The Finest in Jazz Since 1939" reissue					
❑ BST-84001 [S]	Newk's Time	1967	3.75	7.50	15.00
-- With "A Division of Liberty Records" on label					
❑ BST-84001 [M]	Newk's Time	198?	2.50	5.00	10.00
-- "The Finest in Jazz Since 1939" reissue					
❑ B1-93203	The Best of Sonny Rollins	1989	3.00	6.00	12.00
BLUEBIRD					
❑ 5634-1-RB [(2)]	The Quartets Featuring Jim Hall	1986	3.75	7.50	15.00
CONTEMPORARY					
❑ C-3530 [M]	Way Out West	1957	25.00	50.00	100.00
❑ M-3564 [M]	Sonny Rollins and the Contemporary Leaders	1959	20.00	40.00	80.00
❑ S-7530 [S]	Way Out West	1959	12.50	25.00	50.00
❑ S-7564 [S]	Sonny Rollins and the Contemporary Leaders	1959	12.50	25.00	50.00
❑ C-7651	Alternate Takes	1986	2.50	5.00	10.00
DCC COMPACT CLASSICS					
❑ LPZ-2008	Saxophone Colossus	1995	6.25	12.50	25.00
-- Audiophile vinyl					
❑ LPZ-2022	Tenor Madness	1996	6.25	12.50	25.00
-- Audiophile vinyl					
FANTASY					
❑ OJC-007	Work Time	1982	2.50	5.00	10.00
❑ OJC-011	Sonny Rollins with the Modern Jazz Quartet	1982	2.50	5.00	10.00
❑ OJC-029	The Sound of Sonny	198?	2.50	5.00	10.00
❑ OJC-058	Moving Out	198?	2.50	5.00	10.00
❑ OJC-067	Freedom Suite	198?	2.50	5.00	10.00
❑ OJC-124	Tenor Madness	198?	2.50	5.00	10.00
❑ OJC-214	Sonny Rollins Plays for Bird	198?	2.50	5.00	10.00
❑ OJC-243	Sonny Rollins Plus 4	1987	2.50	5.00	10.00
❑ OJC-291	Saxophone Colossus	198?	2.50	5.00	10.00
❑ OJC-312	The Next Album	1988	2.50	5.00	10.00
❑ OJC-314	Horn Culture	198?	2.50	5.00	10.00
❑ OJC-337	Way Out West	198?	2.50	5.00	10.00
❑ OJC-340	Sonny Rollins and the Contemporary Leaders	198?	2.50	5.00	10.00
❑ OJC-348	Sonny Boy	198?	2.50	5.00	10.00
❑ OJC-468	The Cutting Edge: Montreux 1974	198?	2.50	5.00	10.00
❑ OJC-620	Nucleus	1991	2.50	5.00	10.00
GATEWAY					
❑ 7024	The Sound of Sonny	198?	2.50	5.00	10.00
IMPULSE!					
❑ A-91 [M]	Sonny Rollins On Impulse!	1966	6.25	12.50	25.00
❑ AS-91 [S]	Sonny Rollins On Impulse!	1966	7.50	15.00	30.00
❑ A-9121 [M]	East Broadway Run Down	1967	7.50	15.00	30.00
❑ AS-9121 [S]	East Broadway Run Down	1967	6.25	12.50	25.00
JAZZLAND					
❑ JLP-72 [M]	Sonny's Time	1962	10.00	20.00	40.00
❑ JLP-86 [M]	Shadow Waltz	1962	10.00	20.00	40.00
❑ JLP-972 [S]	Sonny's Time	1962	7.50	15.00	30.00
❑ JLP-986 [S]	Shadow Waltz	1962	7.50	15.00	30.00
MCA					
❑ 4127 [(2)]	Great Moments with Sonny Rollins	198?	3.00	6.00	12.00
❑ 29054	Sonny Rollins on Impulse!	1980	2.50	5.00	10.00
❑ 29055	There Will Never Be Another You	1980	2.50	5.00	10.00
MCA IMPULSE!					
❑ MCA-5655	Sonny Rollins on Impulse!	1986	2.50	5.00	10.00
METROJAZZ					
❑ E-1002 [M]	Sonny Rollins and the Big Brass	1958	15.00	30.00	60.00
❑ SE-1002 [S]	Sonny Rollins and the Big Brass	1958	12.50	25.00	50.00
❑ E-1011 [M]	Sonny Rollins at Music Inn	1958	15.00	30.00	60.00
❑ SE-1011 [S]	Sonny Rollins at Music Inn	1958	12.50	25.00	50.00
MILESTONE					
❑ M-9042	The Next Album	197?	3.00	6.00	12.00
❑ M-9051	Horn Culture	1974	3.00	6.00	12.00
❑ M-9059	The Cutting Edge: Montreux 1974	1975	3.00	6.00	12.00
❑ M-9064	Nucleus	1975	3.00	6.00	12.00
❑ M-9074	The Way I Feel	1976	3.00	6.00	12.00
❑ M-9080	Easy Living	1977	3.00	6.00	12.00
❑ M-9090	Don't Ask	1979	3.00	6.00	12.00
❑ M-9098	Love at First Sight	1980	3.00	6.00	12.00
❑ M-9104	No Problem	1981	2.50	5.00	10.00
❑ M-9108	Reel Life	1982	2.50	5.00	10.00
❑ M-9122	Sunny Days, Starry Nights	1984	2.50	5.00	10.00
❑ M-9150	G-Man	1987	3.00	6.00	12.00
❑ M-9155	Dancing in the Dark	1988	3.00	6.00	12.00
❑ M-9179	Falling in Love with Jazz	1990	3.75	7.50	15.00
❑ 47007 [(2)]	Freedom Suite Plus	197?	3.75	7.50	15.00
❑ 55005 [(2)]	Don't Stop the Carnival	1977	3.75	7.50	15.00
PRESTIGE					
❑ PRLP-137 [10]	Sonny Rollins Quartet	1952	75.00	150.00	300.00
❑ PRLP-186 [10]	Sonny Rollins Quartet	1954	62.50	125.00	250.00
❑ PRLP-190 [10]	Sonny Rollins	1954	62.50	125.00	250.00
❑ PRLP-7020 [M]	Work Time	1956	20.00	40.00	80.00
❑ PRLP-7029 [M]	Sonny Rollins with the Modern Jazz Quartet	1956	25.00	50.00	100.00
-- Green cover					
❑ PRLP-7029 [M]	Sonny Rollins with the Modern Jazz Quartet	1956	25.00	50.00	100.00
-- Blue cover					
❑ PRLP-7029 [M]	Sonny Rollins with the Modern Jazz Quartet	1956	20.00	40.00	80.00
-- Yellow cover					
❑ PRLP-7038 [M]	Sonny Rollins Plus 4	1956	20.00	40.00	80.00
❑ PRLP-7047 [M]	Tenor Madness	1956	20.00	40.00	80.00
❑ PRLP-7058 [M]	Moving Out	1956	20.00	40.00	80.00
❑ PRLP-7079 [M]	Saxophone Colossus	1957	20.00	40.00	80.00
❑ PRLP-7095 [M]	Rollins Plays for Bird	1957	20.00	40.00	80.00
❑ PRLP-7126 [M]	Tour De Force	1957	20.00	40.00	80.00
❑ PRLP-7207 [M]	Sonny Boy	1961	10.00	20.00	40.00
❑ PRLP-7246 [M]	Work Time	1962	10.00	20.00	40.00
❑ PRST-7246 [R]	Work Time	1962	6.25	12.50	25.00
❑ PRLP-7269 [M]	Sonny and the Stars	1963	10.00	20.00	40.00
❑ PRST-7269 [R]	Sonny and the Stars	1963	6.25	12.50	25.00
❑ PRLP-7326 [M]	Saxophone Colossus	1964	10.00	20.00	40.00
❑ PRST-7326 [R]	Saxophone Colossus	1964	6.25	12.50	25.00
❑ PRLP-7433 [M]	Sonny Rollins Plays Jazz Classics	1967	10.00	20.00	40.00
❑ PRST-7433 [R]	Sonny Rollins Plays Jazz Classics	1967	5.00	10.00	20.00
❑ PRST-7553 [R]	Sonny Rollins Plays for Bird	1968	3.75	7.50	15.00
❑ PRST-7657 [R]	Tenor Madness	1969	3.75	7.50	15.00
❑ PRST-7750	Worktime	1970	3.00	6.00	12.00
❑ PRST-7856	The First Recordings	1972	3.00	6.00	12.00
❑ 24004 [(2)]	Sonny Rollins	197?	3.75	7.50	15.00
❑ 24050 [(2)]	Saxophone Colossus and More	1974	3.75	7.50	15.00
❑ 24082 [(2)]	Taking Care of Business	198?	3.75	7.50	15.00
❑ 24096 [(2)]	Vintage Sessions	198?	3.75	7.50	15.00
QUINTESSENCE					
❑ 25181	Green Dolphin Street	197?	3.00	6.00	12.00
RCA VICTOR					
❑ AFL1-0859	The Bridge	1977	2.50	5.00	10.00
-- Reissue with new prefix					
❑ APL1-0859	The Bridge	1975	3.00	6.00	12.00
-- Reissue of LSP-2527					
❑ LPM-2527 [M]	The Bridge	1962	10.00	20.00	40.00
❑ LSP-2527 [S]	The Bridge	1962	17.50	35.00	70.00
❑ LSP-2527 [S]	The Bridge	199?	7.50	15.00	30.00
-- Classic Records reissue on audiophile vinyl					
❑ LSP-2527-45 [(4)]	The Bridge	1999	10.00	20.00	40.00
-- Classic Records reissue; 4 single-sided LPs that play at 45 rpm					
❑ LPM-2572 [M]	What's New?	1962	7.50	15.00	30.00
❑ LSP-2572 [S]	What's New?	1962	15.00	30.00	60.00
❑ LPM-2612 [M]	Our Man In Jazz	1962	7.50	15.00	30.00
❑ LSP-2612 [S]	Our Man In Jazz	1962	15.00	30.00	60.00
❑ LSP-2612 [S]	Our Man in Jazz	199?	6.25	12.50	25.00
-- Classic Records reissue on audiophile vinyl					
❑ LPM-2712 [M]	Sonny Meets Hawk!	1963	7.50	15.00	30.00
❑ LSP-2712 [S]	Sonny Meets Hawk!	1963	15.00	30.00	60.00
❑ LSP-2712 [S]	Sonny Meets Hawk!	199?	6.25	12.50	25.00
-- Classic Records reissue on audiophile vinyl					
❑ ANL1-2809	Pure Gold	1978	2.50	5.00	10.00
❑ LPM-2927 [M]	Now's the Time	1964	6.25	12.50	25.00
❑ LSP-2927 [S]	Now's the Time!	1964	7.50	15.00	30.00
❑ LSP-2927 [S]	Now's the Time!	199?	6.25	12.50	25.00
-- Classic Records reissue on audiophile vinyl					
❑ LPM-3355 [M]	The Standard Sonny Rollins	1965	6.25	12.50	25.00
❑ LSP-3355 [S]	The Standard Sonny Rollins	1965	7.50	15.00	30.00
RIVERSIDE					
❑ RLP 12-241 [M]	The Sound of Sonny	1957	25.00	50.00	100.00
-- White label, blue print					
❑ RLP 12-241 [M]	The Sound of Sonny	1959	12.50	25.00	50.00
-- Blue label, microphone logo at top					
❑ RLP-258 [M]	Freedom Suite	1958	20.00	40.00	80.00
❑ RLP-1124 [S]	The Sound of Sonny	1959	12.50	25.00	50.00
❑ RS-3010 [S]	Freedom Suite	1968	3.75	7.50	15.00
❑ 6044	Freedom Suite	197?	3.00	6.00	12.00
STEREO RECORDS					
❑ S-7017 [S]	Way Out West	1958	20.00	40.00	80.00
VERVE					
❑ VSP-32 [M]	Tenor Titan	1966	3.75	7.50	15.00

Number	Title	Yr	VG	VG+	NM
❏ VSPS-32 [S]	Tenor Titan	1966	3.00	6.00	12.00
❏ UMV-2555	Sonny Rollins/Brass, Sonny Rollins/Trio	198?	2.50	5.00	10.00
❏ V-8430 [M]	Sonny Rollins/Brass, Sonny Rollins/Trio	1962	7.50	15.00	30.00
❏ V6-8430 [S]	Sonny Rollins/Brass, Sonny Rollins/Trio	1962	6.25	12.50	25.00

ROLLINS, SONNY; CLIFFORD BROWN; MAX ROACH
Also see each artist's individual listings.
PRESTIGE

❏ PRLP-7291 [M]	Three Giants	1964	10.00	20.00	40.00
❏ PRST-7291 [R]	Three Giants	1964	6.25	12.50	25.00
❏ PRST-7821	Three Giants	1971	3.00	6.00	12.00

ROLLINS, SONNY/JIMMY CLEVELAND
Also see each artist's individual listings.
PERIOD

❏ SPL-1204 [M]	Sonny Rollins Plays/Jimmy Cleveland Plays	1956	25.00	50.00	100.00

ROMAN NEW ORLEANS JAZZ BAND, THE
RCA VICTOR

❏ LPT-3033 [10]	Around the World in Jazz -- Italy	1953	10.00	20.00	40.00

ROMAO, DOM UM
Drummer and percussionist.
MUSE

❏ MR-5013	Dom Um Romao	1974	3.75	7.50	15.00
❏ MR-5049	Spirit of the Times	197?	3.00	6.00	12.00
PABLO					
❏ 2310 777	Hotmosphere	197?	3.00	6.00	12.00

ROMERO, RAOUL
Guitarist.
SEA BREEZE

❏ SB-2031	The Music of Raoul Romero	1987	2.50	5.00	10.00

RONEY, WALLACE
Trumpeter.
MUSE

❏ MR-5335	Verses	1987	2.50	5.00	10.00
❏ MR-5346	Intuition	1989	3.00	6.00	12.00
❏ MR-5372	The Standard Bearer	1990	3.00	6.00	12.00

ROSE
French-American jazz-rock group.
MILLENNIUM

❏ BXL1-7749	Worlds Apart	1979	3.75	7.50	15.00

ROSE, DAVID
French violinist. Not to be confused with the American orchestra leader.
INNER CITY

❏ IC-1058	The Distance Between Dreams	197?	3.00	6.00	12.00

ROSE, WALLY
Pianist.
BLACKBIRD

❏ 12007	Wally Rose on Piano	196?	3.00	6.00	12.00
❏ 12010	Whippin' the Keys	197?	3.00	6.00	12.00
COLUMBIA					
❏ CL 782 [M]	Cake Walk to Lindy Hop	1956	10.00	20.00	40.00
❏ CL 6260 [10]	Wally Rose	1953	12.50	25.00	50.00
GOOD TIME JAZZ					
❏ S-10034 [S]	Ragtime Classics	1960	5.00	10.00	20.00
❏ L-12034 [M]	Ragtime Classics	1960	3.75	7.50	15.00
STOMP OFF					
❏ SOS-1057	Wally Rose Revisited	1982	2.50	5.00	10.00

ROSENGREN, BERNT
Tenor saxophone player.
STOMP OFF

❏ SOS-1177	Surprise Party	198?	2.50	5.00	10.00

ROSEWOMAN, MICHELE
Pianist and female singer.
ENJA

❏ R1-79607	Contrast High	1990	3.75	7.50	15.00

Number	Title	Yr	VG	VG+	NM
SOUL NOTE					
❏ SN-1072	The Source	1984	3.00	6.00	12.00

ROSIE O'GRADY'S GOOD TIME BAND
DIRECT DISK

❏ DD-103	Dixieland	1979	5.00	10.00	20.00
-- Audiophile recording

ROSNES, RENEE
Pianist.
BLUE NOTE

❏ B1-93561	Renee Rosnes	1990	3.75	7.50	15.00

ROSOLINO, FRANK
Trombonist. Also see VINCE GUARALDI.
BETHLEHEM

❏ BCP-26 [M]	I Play Trombone	1955	12.50	25.00	50.00
CAPITOL					
❏ H 6507 [10]	Frank Rosolino	1954	20.00	40.00	80.00
❏ T 6507 [M]	Frank Rosolino	1955	25.00	30.00	60.00
❏ T 6509 [M]	Frankly Speaking	1955	25.00	30.00	60.00
INTERLUDE					
❏ MO-500 [M]	The Legend of Frank Rosolino	1959	10.00	20.00	40.00
❏ ST-1000 [S]	The Legend of Frank Rosolino	1959	7.50	15.00	30.00
MODE					
❏ LP-107 [M]	Frank Rosolino Quintet	1957	25.00	50.00	100.00
REPRISE					
❏ R-6016 [M]	Turn Me Loose	1961	6.25	12.50	25.00
❏ R9-6016 [S]	Turn Me Loose	1961	7.50	15.00	30.00
SACKVILLE					
❏ 2014	Thinking About You	198?	2.50	5.00	10.00

ROSS, ANNIE
Female singer. Also see LAMBERT, HENDRICKS AND ROSS.
DECCA

❏ DL 4922 [M]	Fill My Heart with Song	1967	7.50	15.00	30.00
❏ DL 74922 [S]	Fill My Heart with Song	1967	5.00	10.00	20.00
KIMBERLY					
❏ 2018 [M]	Annie Ross Sings a Song with Mulligan!	1963	7.50	15.00	30.00
❏ 11018 [S]	Annie Ross Sings a Song with Mulligan!	1963	6.25	12.50	25.00
WORLD PACIFIC					
❏ ST-1020 [S]	Annie Ross Sings a Song with Mulligan!	1959	10.00	20.00	40.00
❏ ST-1028 [S]	Gypsy	1959	10.00	20.00	40.00
❏ WP-1253 [M]	Annie Ross Sings A Song With Mulligan!	1959	12.50	25.00	50.00
❏ ST-1285 [S]	A Gasser!	1960	10.00	20.00	40.00
❏ WP-1285 [M]	A Gasser!	1960	12.50	25.00	50.00
❏ WP-1808 [M]	Gypsy	1959	12.50	25.00	50.00

ROSS, ANNIE; DOROTHY DUNN; SHELBY DAVIS
All of the above are female singers. Also see ANNIE ROSS.
SAVOY

❏ MG-12060 [M]	Singin' 'N Swingin'	1956	10.00	20.00	40.00

ROSS, ARNOLD
Pianist, composer and bandleader. Also see JOE PASS; LENNIE TRISTANO.
CLEF

❏ MGC-134 [10]	Arnold Ross	1953	---	---	---
-- Evidently canceled

DISCOVERY					
❏ DL-2006 [M]	Arnold Ross	1954	12.50	25.00	50.00
MERCURY					
❏ MGC-134 [10]	Arnold Ross	1952	37.50	75.00	150.00

ROSS, RONNIE
Baritone saxophone player.
ATLANTIC

❏ 1333 [M]	The Jazz Makers	1960	7.50	15.00	30.00
❏ SD 1333 [S]	The Jazz Makers	1960	10.00	20.00	40.00

ROSS-LEVINE BAND, THE
Members: Billy Ross (flute, saxophone) and Machael Levine (keyboards) with Pete Harris (guitar); Cookie Lopez (percussion) and Steve Rucker (drums).
HEADFIRST

❏ 9701	That Summer Something	198?	3.00	6.00	12.00

Number	Title	Yr	VG	VG+	NM

ROUSE, CHARLIE
Tenor saxophone player. Also see LES JAZZ MODES.
BLUE NOTE
❏ BLP-4119 [M]	Bossa Nova Bacchanal	1962	7.50	15.00	30.00
❏ BST-84119 [S]	Bossa Nova Bacchanal	196?	5.00	10.00	20.00

-- With "A Division of Liberty Records" on label

❏ BST-84119 [S]	Bossa Nova Bacchanal	1962	10.00	20.00	40.00

-- With "New York, USA" address on label

DOUGLAS
❏ 7044	Cinnamon Flower	197?	3.75	7.50	15.00

EPIC
❏ LA 16012 [M]	Yeah!	1960	10.00	20.00	40.00
❏ LA 16018 [M]	We Paid Our Dues	1961	10.00	20.00	40.00
❏ BA 17012 [S]	Yeah!	1960	12.50	25.00	50.00
❏ BA 17012 [S]	Yeah!	199?	6.25	12.50	25.00

-- Classic Records reissue on audiophile vinyl

❏ BA 17018 [S]	We Paid Our Dues	1961	12.50	25.00	50.00

FANTASY
❏ OJC-491	Takin' Care of Business	1991	3.00	6.00	12.00

JAZZLAND
❏ JLP-19 [M]	Takin' Care of Business	1960	10.00	20.00	40.00
❏ JLP-919 [S]	Takin' Care of Business	1960	12.50	25.00	50.00

LANDMARK
❏ LLP-1521	Epistrophy	1989	3.00	6.00	12.00

STORYVILLE
❏ 4079	Moment's Notice	198?	2.50	5.00	10.00

STRATA-EAST
❏ SES-19746	Two Is One	1974	6.25	12.50	25.00

ROUSE, CHARLIE, AND PAUL QUINICHETTE
Also see each artist's individual listings.
BETHLEHEM
❏ BCP-6021 [M]	The Chase Is On	1958	12.50	25.00	50.00

ROVA
Saxophone quartet named after the first initials of their surnames: Jon Raskin (baritone, alto); Larry Ochs (tenor, sopranino); Andrew Voigt (alto, soprano, sopranino); Bruce Ackley (soprano, tenor).
BLACK SAINT
❏ BSR-0076	Rova Plays Lacy -- Favorite Street	1984	3.00	6.00	12.00
❏ 120126	Beat Kennel	1987	3.00	6.00	12.00

HAT ART
❏ 2013 [(2)]	Saxophone Diplomacy	1986	3.75	7.50	15.00
❏ 2032 [(2)]	The Crowd	1986	3.75	7.50	15.00

METALANGUAGE
❏ 101	Cinema Rovate	1978	5.00	10.00	20.00
❏ 106	The Removal of Secrecy	1979	5.00	10.00	20.00
❏ 10?	Daredevils	1979	5.00	10.00	20.00
❏ 118	As Was	1981	3.75	7.50	15.00

ROWLES, JIMMY
Pianist and male singer.
ANDEX
❏ A-3007 [M]	Weather in a Jazz Vane	1958	12.50	25.00	50.00
❏ AS-3007 [S]	Weather in a Jazz Vane	1958	10.00	20.00	40.00

CAPITOL
❏ ST 1831 [S]	Kinda Groovy!	1963	5.00	10.00	20.00
❏ T 1831 [M]	Kinda Groovy!	1963	3.75	7.50	15.00

CHOICE
❏ 1014	Grandpaws fresh	197?	3.00	6.00	12.00
❏ 1023	Paws That Refresh	197?	3.00	6.00	12.00

COLUMBIA
❏ FC 37639	Jimmy Rowles Plays Ellington and Strayhorn	1981	2.50	5.00	10.00

CONTEMPORARY
❏ C-14016	Jimmy Rowles	1986	2.50	5.00	10.00
❏ C-14032	I'm Glad There Is You	1988	2.50	5.00	10.00

HALCYON
❏ 110	Special Magic	197?	3.00	6.00	12.00

INTERLUDE
❏ MO-515 [M]	Upper Classmen	1959	10.00	20.00	40.00
❏ ST-1015 [S]	Upper Classmen	1959	7.50	15.00	30.00

JAZZZ
❏ 103	Fleeting Moment	197?	3.00	6.00	12.00

LIBERTY
❏ LRP-3003 [M]	Rare, But Well Done	1955	15.00	30.00	60.00

SIGNATURE
❏ SM-6011 [M]	Fiorello Uptown, Mary Sunshine Downtown	1960	15.00	30.00	60.00
❏ SS-6011 [S]	Fiorello Uptown, Mary Sunshine Downtown	1960	20.00	40.00	80.00

TAMPA
❏ TP-8 [M]	Let's Get Acquainted with Jazz... For People Who Hate Jazz	1957	37.50	75.00	150.00

-- Colored vinyl

❏ TP-8 [M]	Let's Get Acquainted with Jazz... For People Who Hate Jazz	1958	20.00	40.00	80.00

-- Black vinyl

❏ TPS-8 [S]	Let's Get Acquainted with Jazz... For People Who Hate Jazz	1958	12.50	25.00	50.00

XANADU
❏ 157	Make Such Beautiful Music Together	1980	3.00	6.00	12.00

ROWLES, JIMMY, AND GEORGE MRAZ
Mraz plays bass. Also see JIMMY ROWLES.
PROGRESSIVE
❏ PRO-7009	Music's the Only Thing on My Mind	198?	2.50	5.00	10.00

ROWLES, STACY AND JIMMY
Stacy is a trumpeter, fluegel horn player and female singer, and JIMMY ROWLES' daughter.
CONCORD JAZZ
❏ CJ-249	Tell It Like It Is	1984	2.50	5.00	10.00

ROY, WILLIAM
Pianist, composer and arranger.
AUDIOPHILE
❏ AP-213	When I Sing Alone	1986	2.50	5.00	10.00

ROYAL, ERNIE
Trumpeter.
URANIA
❏ UJLP-1203 [M]	Accent on Trumpet	1955	12.50	25.00	50.00

ROYAL, MARSHALL
Alto saxophone player.
CONCORD JAZZ
❏ CJ-88	First Chair	1979	2.50	5.00	10.00
❏ CJ-125	Royal Blue	1980	2.50	5.00	10.00

EVEREST
❏ SDBR-1087 [S]	Gordon Jenkins Presents Marshall Royal	1960	7.50	15.00	30.00
❏ LPBR-5087 [M]	Gordon Jenkins Presents Marshall Royal	1960	6.25	12.50	25.00

RUBIN, STAN
Bandleader, clarinetist and saxophone player.
CORAL
❏ CRL 57185 [M]	Dixieland Goes Broadway	1959	6.25	12.50	25.00
❏ CRL 757185 [S]	Dixieland Goes Broadway	1959	7.50	15.00	30.00

JUBLIEE
❏ JLP-4 [10]	The Tigertown Five, Vol. 1	1954	12.50	25.00	50.00
❏ JLP-5 [10]	The Tigertown Five, Vol. 2	1954	12.50	25.00	50.00
❏ JLP-6 [10]	The Tigertown Five, Vol. 3	1954	12.50	25.00	50.00
❏ JLP-1001 [M]	The College All Stars at Carnegie Hall	1955	10.00	20.00	40.00
❏ JLP-1003 [M]	College Jazz Comes to Carnegie Hall	1955	10.00	20.00	40.00
❏ JLP-1016 [M]	Tigertown Five	1956	10.00	20.00	40.00
❏ JLP-1024 [M]	Stan Rubin in Morocco	1956	10.00	20.00	40.00

PRINCETON
❏ LP-102 [10]	The Stan Rubin Tigertown Five	1954	15.00	30.00	60.00

RCA VICTOR
❏ LPM-1200 [M]	Dixieland Bash	1956	10.00	20.00	40.00
❏ LPM-3277 [10]	Stan Rubin's Dixieland Comes to Carnegie Hall	1955	12.50	25.00	50.00

RUCKER, ELLYN
Pianist and female singer.
CAPRI
❏ 10187	Ellyn	1987	3.00	6.00	12.00

Number	Title	Yr	VG	VG+	NM
RUDD, ROSWELL					

RUDD, ROSWELL
Trombonist and male singer.
ABC IMPULSE!

Number	Title	Yr	VG	VG+	NM
❑ AS-9126 [S]	Everywhere	1968	3.75	7.50	15.00

ARISTA/FREEDOM

| ❑ AF 1006 | Flexible Flyer | 1975 | 3.00 | 6.00 | 12.00 |
| ❑ AF 1029 | Inside Job | 1976 | 3.00 | 6.00 | 12.00 |

IMPULSE!

| ❑ A-9126 [M] | Everywhere | 1967 | 7.50 | 15.00 | 30.00 |
| ❑ AS-9126 [S] | Everywhere | 1967 | 6.25 | 12.50 | 25.00 |

JCOA

| ❑ 1007 | The Numatik String Band | 197? | 3.75 | 7.50 | 15.00 |

RUDD, ROSWELL, AND STEVE LACY
Also see each artist's individual listings.
SOUL NOTE

| ❑ SN-1054 | Regeneration | 1982 | 3.00 | 6.00 | 12.00 |

RUEDEBUSCH, DICK
Trumpeter.
ASCOT

| ❑ AM-13017 [M] | Dick Ruedebusch | 1964 | 3.00 | 6.00 | 12.00 |
| ❑ AS-16017 [S] | Dick Ruedebusch | 1964 | 3.75 | 7.50 | 15.00 |

JUBILEE

❑ JGM-5008 [M]	Meet Mr. Trumpet	1962	3.75	7.50	15.00
❑ JGS-5008 [S]	Meet Mr. Trumpet	1962	5.00	10.00	20.00
❑ JGM-5015 [M]	Dick Ruedebusch Remembers the Greats	1962	3.75	7.50	15.00
❑ JGS-5015 [S]	Dick Ruedebusch Remembers the Greats	1962	5.00	10.00	20.00
❑ JGM-5021 [M]	Mr. Trumpet, Volume 2	1963	3.75	7.50	15.00
❑ JGS-5021 [S]	Mr. Trumpet, Volume 2	1963	5.00	10.00	20.00

RUFF, WILLIE
Bass and French horn player. Also see THE MITCHELL-RUFF DUO.
COLUMBIA

| ❑ CS 9603 | The Smooth Side of Willie Ruff | 1968 | 5.00 | 10.00 | 20.00 |
-- Red "360 Sound" label

RUGOLO, PETE
Arranger, composer and bandleader.
COLUMBIA

| ❑ CL 604 [M] | Adventures in Rhythm | 1955 | 12.50 | 25.00 | 50.00 |
-- Maroon label, gold print
| ❑ CL 604 [M] | Adventures in Rhythm | 1956 | 10.00 | 20.00 | 40.00 |
-- Red and black label with six "eye" logos
| ❑ CL 635 [M] | Introducing Pete Rugolo | 1955 | 12.50 | 25.00 | 50.00 |
-- Maroon label, gold print
| ❑ CL 635 [M] | Introducing Pete Rugolo | 1956 | 10.00 | 20.00 | 40.00 |
-- Red and black label with six "eye" logos
| ❑ CL 689 [M] | Rugolomania | 1956 | 10.00 | 20.00 | 40.00 |
-- Red and black label with six "eye" logos
| ❑ CL 6289 [10] | Introducing Pete Rugolo | 1954 | 15.00 | 30.00 | 60.00 |

EMARCY

❑ MG-36082 [M]	Music for Hi-Fi Bugs	1956	10.00	20.00	40.00
❑ MG-36115 [M]	Out on a Limb	1957	10.00	20.00	40.00
❑ MG-36122 [M]	Percussion at Work	1958	10.00	20.00	40.00
❑ MG-36143 [M]	Rugolo Plays Kenton	1958	10.00	20.00	40.00

HARMONY

| ❑ HL 7003 [M] | New Sounds | 195? | 3.75 | 7.50 | 15.00 |

MERCURY

❑ PPS-2001 [M]	10 Trombones Like 2 Pianos	196?	5.00	10.00	20.00
❑ PPS-2016 [M]	10 Trombones and 2 Guitars	196?	5.00	10.00	20.00
❑ PPS-2023 [M]	10 Saxophones and 2 Basses	196?	5.00	10.00	20.00
❑ PPS-6001 [S]	10 Trombones Like 2 Pianos	196?	6.25	12.50	25.00
❑ PPS-6016 [S]	10 Trombones and 2 Guitars	196?	6.25	12.50	25.00
❑ PPS-6023 [S]	10 Saxophones and 2 Basses	196?	6.25	12.50	25.00
❑ MG-20118 [M]	Music from Outer Space	1957	12.50	25.00	50.00
❑ MG-202?? [M]	An Adventure in Sound: Reeds	1958	7.50	15.00	30.00
❑ MG-20260 [M]	Reeds in Hi-Fi	1958	7.50	15.00	30.00
❑ MG-20261 [M]	Brass in Hi-Fi	1958	7.50	15.00	30.00
❑ SR-60039 [S]	An Adventure in Sound: Reeds	1959	10.00	20.00	40.00
❑ SR-60043 [S]	Reeds in Hi-Fi	1959	10.00	20.00	40.00
❑ SR-60044 [S]	Brass in Hi-Fi	1959	10.00	20.00	40.00

RUIZ, HILTON
Pianist.
INNER CITY

| ❑ IC-2036 | Piano Man | 197? | 3.75 | 7.50 | 15.00 |

NOVUS

| ❑ 3011-1-N | Something Grand | 1987 | 2.50 | 5.00 | 10.00 |

| ❑ 3024-1-N | El Camino (The Road) | 1988 | 2.50 | 5.00 | 10.00 |
| ❑ 3053-1-N | Strut | 1989 | 3.00 | 6.00 | 12.00 |

STASH

| ❑ ST-248 | Cross Currents | 1985 | 2.50 | 5.00 | 10.00 |

STEEPLECHASE

❑ SCS-1036	Piano Man	198?	3.00	6.00	12.00
❑ SCS-1078	Excitation	198?	3.00	6.00	12.00
❑ SCS-1094	New York Hilton	198?	3.00	6.00	12.00
❑ SCS-1158	Steppin' Into Beauty	198?	3.00	6.00	12.00

RUIZ, JORGE LOPEZ
Bass player.
CATALYST

| ❑ 7908 | Amor Buenos Aires | 197? | 3.00 | 6.00 | 12.00 |

RUMMEL, JACK
Pianist and composer.
STOMP OFF

| ❑ SOS-1118 | Back to Ragtime | 1986 | 2.50 | 5.00 | 10.00 |

RUMSEY, HOWARD
Bass player and bandleader.
CONTEMPORARY

❑ C-2501 [10]	Sunday Jazz a la Lighthouse	1953	30.00	60.00	120.00
❑ C-2506 [10]	Howard Rumsey's Lighthouse All-Stars	1953	30.00	60.00	120.00
❑ C-2510 [10]	Howard Rumsey's Lighthouse All-Stars, Volume 4	1954	30.00	60.00	120.00
❑ C-2513 [10]	Howard Rumsey's Lighthouse All-Stars, Volume 1: The Quintet	1954	30.00	60.00	120.00
❑ C-2515 [10]	Howard Rumsey's Lighthouse All-Stars, Volume 2: The Octet	1954	30.00	60.00	120.00
❑ C-3501 [M]	Sunday Jazz a la Lighthouse	1955	20.00	40.00	80.00
❑ C-3504 [M]	Howard Rumsey's Lighthouse All-Stars, Vol. 6	1955	20.00	40.00	80.00
❑ C-3508 [M]	Howard Rumsey's Lighthouse All-Stars, Vol. 3	1955	20.00	40.00	80.00
❑ C-3509 [M]	Lighthouse at Laguna	1955	20.00	40.00	80.00
❑ C-3517 [M]	In the Solo Spotlight	1956	20.00	40.00	80.00
❑ C-3520 [M]	Howard Rumsey's Lighthouse All-Stars, Vol. 4: Oboe/Flute	1956	20.00	40.00	80.00
❑ C-3528 [M]	Music for Lighthousekeeping	1957	20.00	40.00	80.00
❑ S-7008 [S]	Music for Lighthousekeeping	1959	12.50	25.00	50.00
❑ C-14051	Jazz Invention	1989	3.00	6.00	12.00

FANTASY

❑ OJC-151	Sunday Jazz a la Lighthouse	198?	2.50	5.00	10.00
❑ OJC-154	Howard Rumsey's Lighthouse All-Stars, Vol. 4: Oboe/Flute	198?	2.50	5.00	10.00
❑ OJC-266	Howard Rumsey's Lighthouse All-Stars, Vol. 3	198?	2.50	5.00	10.00
❑ OJC-386	Howard Rumsey's Lighthouse All-Stars, Vol. 6	1989	2.50	5.00	10.00
❑ OJC-406	Lighthouse at Laguna	1989	2.50	5.00	10.00
❑ OJC-451	In the Solo Spotlight	1990	3.00	6.00	12.00

LIBERTY

| ❑ LRP-3045 [M] | Double or Nothin' | 1957 | 12.50 | 25.00 | 50.00 |
| ❑ LST-7014 [S] | Double or Nothin' | 1959 | 10.00 | 20.00 | 40.00 |

LIGHTHOUSE

| ❑ LP-300 [M] | Jazz Rolls-Royce | 1958 | 10.00 | 20.00 | 40.00 |
| ❑ LP-301 [M] | Sunday Jazz a la Lighthouse | 1958 | 10.00 | 20.00 | 40.00 |
-- Red vinyl

OMEGA

| ❑ OML-5 [M] | Jazz Rolls-Royce | 1960 | 7.50 | 15.00 | 30.00 |
| ❑ OSL-5 [S] | Jazz Rolls-Royce | 1960 | 7.50 | 15.00 | 30.00 |

PHILIPS

| ❑ PHM 200-012 [M] | Jazz Structures | 1961 | 5.00 | 10.00 | 20.00 |
| ❑ PHS 600-012 [S] | Jazz Structures | 1961 | 6.25 | 12.50 | 25.00 |

STEREO RECORDS

| ❑ S-7008 [S] | Music for Lighthousekeeping | 1958 | 17.50 | 35.00 | 70.00 |

RUSHEN, PATRICE
Female singer.
ARISTA

| ❑ AL-8401 | Watch Out! | 1987 | 2.50 | 5.00 | 10.00 |

ELEKTRA

❑ 6E-160	Patrice	1978	2.50	5.00	10.00
❑ 6E-243	Pizzazz	1979	2.50	5.00	10.00
❑ 6E-302	Posh	1980	2.50	5.00	10.00
❑ 60015	Straight from the Heart	1982	2.50	5.00	10.00
❑ 60360	Patrice Rushen Now	1984	2.50	5.00	10.00
❑ 60465	Anthology of Patrice Rushen	1986	2.50	5.00	10.00

Number	Title	Yr	VG	VG+	NM
PRESTIGE					
❏ 10089	Prelusion	1974	5.00	10.00	20.00
❏ 10098	Before the Dawn	1976	5.00	10.00	20.00
❏ 10101	Shout It Out	1977	3.75	7.50	15.00
❏ 10110	Let There Be Funk	1980	3.75	7.50	15.00
RUSHING, JIMMY					
Male singer and pianist.					
AUDIO LAB					
❏ AL-1512 [M]	Two Shades of Blue	1959	30.00	60.00	120.00
BLUESWAY					
❏ BL-6005 [M]	Everyday I Have the Blues	1967	5.00	10.00	20.00
❏ BLS-6005 [S]	Everyday I Have the Blues	1967	5.00	10.00	20.00
❏ BLS-6017	Livin' the Blues	1968	5.00	10.00	20.00
❏ BLS-6057	Sent for You Yesterday	1973	3.75	7.50	15.00
COLPIX					
❏ CP-446 [M]	Five Feet of Soul	1963	10.00	20.00	40.00
❏ SCP-446 [S]	Five Feet of Soul	1963	---	---	---
-- Not known to exist					
COLUMBIA					
❏ CL 963 [M]	The Jazz Odyssey of James Rushing, Esq.	1957	10.00	20.00	40.00
❏ CL 1152 [M]	Little Jimmy Rushing and the Big Brass	1958	10.00	20.00	40.00
❏ CL 1401 [M]	Rushing Lullabies	1959	10.00	20.00	40.00
❏ CL 1605 [M]	Jimmy Rushing and the Smith Girls	1961	7.50	15.00	30.00
❏ CS 8060 [S]	Little Jimmy Rushing and the Big Brass	1958	12.50	25.00	50.00
❏ CS 8196 [S]	Rushing Lullabies	1959	12.50	25.00	50.00
❏ CS 8405 [S]	Jimmy Rushing and the Smith Girls	1961	10.00	20.00	40.00
❏ C2 36419 [(2)]	Mister Five by Five	1979	3.00	6.00	12.00
JAZZTONE					
❏ J-1244 [M]	Listen to the Blues	195?	10.00	20.00	40.00
MASTER JAZZ					
❏ 8104	Gee, Baby	197?	3.75	7.50	15.00
❏ 8120	Who Was It Sang That Song?	1971	3.75	7.50	15.00
RCA VICTOR					
❏ LSP-4566	You and Me The Used to Be	1972	3.75	7.50	15.00
VANGUARD					
❏ VRS-65/66 [(2)]	Essential Jimmy Rushing	197?	3.75	7.50	15.00
❏ VSD-2008 [S]	If This Ain't the Blues	1958	15.00	30.00	60.00
❏ VRS-8011 [10]	Jimmy Rushing Sings the Blues	1955	25.00	50.00	100.00
❏ VRS-8505 [M]	Listen to the Blues	1955	12.50	25.00	50.00
❏ VRS-8513 [M]	If This Ain't the Blues	1957	12.50	25.00	50.00
❏ VRS-8518 [M]	Going to Chicago	1957	12.50	25.00	50.00
❏ VSD-73007	Listen to the Blues	1967	3.75	7.50	15.00
RUSHING, JIMMY; ADA MOORE; BUCK CLAYTON					
Also see each artist's individual listings.					
COLUMBIA					
❏ CL 778 [M]	Cat Meets Chick	1956	15.00	30.00	60.00
RUSSELL, GENE					
Pianist. Founder of the Black Jazz record label.					
BLACK JAZZ					
❏ 1	New Direction	1972	6.25	12.50	25.00
❏ QD-10	Talk to My Lady	1973	6.25	12.50	25.00
OVATION					
❏ OV-1803	Listen Here	197?	3.00	6.00	12.00
SEA BREEZE					
❏ SB-3001	Autumn Leaves	198?	2.50	5.00	10.00
RUSSELL, GEORGE					
Pianist, composer, arranger and bandleader.					
BASF					
❏ 25125 [(2)]	Live at Beethoven Hall	1973	3.75	7.50	15.00
BLUE NOTE					
❏ BT-85103	The African Game	198?	3.00	6.00	12.00
❏ BT-85132	So What	1987	3.75	7.50	15.00
CONCEPT					
❏ 002	Listen to the Silence	197?	3.00	6.00	12.00
DECCA					
❏ DL 4183 [M]	George Russell in Kansas City	1961	7.50	15.00	30.00
❏ DL 9216 [M]	New York, N.Y.	1958	12.50	25.00	50.00
❏ DL 9219 [M]	Jazz in the Space Age	1958	12.50	25.00	50.00
❏ DL 9220 [M]	George Russell at the Five Spot	1958	12.50	25.00	50.00
❏ DL 74183 [S]	George Russell in Kansas City	1961	10.00	20.00	40.00
❏ DL 79216 [S]	New York, N.Y.	1958	10.00	20.00	40.00
❏ DL 79219 [S]	Jazz in the Space Age	1958	10.00	20.00	40.00
❏ DL 79220 [S]	George Russell at the Five Spot	1958	10.00	20.00	40.00
FANTASY					
❏ OJC-070	Ezz-thetics	198?	2.50	5.00	10.00
❏ OJC-232	Stratusphunk	198?	2.50	5.00	10.00
❏ OJC-365	The Stratus Seekers	198?	2.50	5.00	10.00
❏ OJC-616	The Outer View	1991	3.00	6.00	12.00
FLYING DUTCHMAN					
❏ FD-122	Othello Ballet Suite/Electronic Organ Sonata No. 1	1970	5.00	10.00	20.0
❏ FD-124	Electronic Sonata for Souls Loved by Nature	1970	5.00	10.00	20.00
❏ FD-10122	Othello Ballet Suite/Electronic Organ Sonata No. 1	1971	3.75	7.50	15.00
❏ FD-10124	Electronic Sonata for Souls Loved by Nature	1971	3.75	7.50	15.00
MCA					
❏ 4017 [(2)]	New York, N.Y./Jazz in the Space Age	1974	3.75	7.50	15.00
MGM					
❏ E-3321 [M]	George Russell Octets	1955	20.00	40.00	80.00
MILESTONE					
❏ 47027 [(2)]	Outer Thoughts	197?	3.75	7.50	15.00
PETE					
❏ 1107	Easy Listening	1969	3.75	7.50	15.00
RCA VICTOR					
❏ LPM-1372 [M]	Jazz Workshop	1957	20.00	40.00	80.00
❏ LPM-2534 [M]	Jazz Workshop	1962	7.50	15.00	30.00
❏ LSP-2534 [R]	Jazz Workshop	1962	3.75	7.50	15.00
RIVERSIDE					
❏ RLP-341 [M]	Stratusphunk	1960	6.25	12.50	25.00
❏ RLP-375 [M]	Ezz-thetics	1961	6.25	12.50	25.00
❏ RLP-412 [M]	The Stratus Seekers	1962	6.25	12.50	25.00
❏ RLP-440 [M]	The Outer View	1963	6.25	12.50	25.00
❏ RS-3016	The Outer View	1968	5.00	10.00	20.00
❏ RS-3043	George Russell Sextet	1970	3.75	7.50	15.00
❏ 6112	Ezz-thetics	197?	3.00	6.00	12.00
❏ RS-9341 [S]	Stratusphunk	1960	7.50	15.00	30.00
❏ RS-9375 [S]	Ezz-thetics	1961	7.50	15.00	30.00
❏ RS-9412 [S]	The Stratus Seekers	1962	7.50	15.00	30.00
❏ RS-9440 [S]	The Outer View	1963	7.50	15.00	30.00
SOUL NOTE					
❏ SN-1009	Electronic Sonata for Souls Loved by Nature 1980	1980	3.00	6.00	12.00
❏ SN-1014	Othello Ballet Suite	198?	3.00	6.00	12.00
❏ SN-1019	Vertical Form VI	198?	3.00	6.00	12.00
❏ SN-1024	Listen to the Silence (A Mass for Our Time)	198?	3.00	6.00	12.00
❏ SN-1029	Trip to Pillar-Guri	198?	3.00	6.00	12.00
❏ SN-1034	Electronic Sonata for Souls Loved by Nature 1969	198?	3.00	6.00	12.00
❏ SN-1039	New York Big Band	198?	3.00	6.00	12.00
❏ SN-1044/5 [(2)]	The Essence of George Russell	198?	3.75	7.50	15.00
❏ SN-1049	Live in an American Time Spiral	1983	3.00	6.00	12.00
STRATA-EAST					
❏ SES-19761	Electronic Sonata for Souls Loved by Nature	1976	5.00	10.00	20.00
RUSSELL, HAL					
Saxophone player and bandleader.					
NESSA					
❏ N-21	NRG Ensemble	1981	5.00	10.00	20.00
❏ N-25	Generation	1982	5.00	10.00	20.00
RUSSELL, JIMMY					
CUCA					
❏ 4100 [M]	Jimmy Russell Trio	1965	6.25	12.50	25.00
DORIAN					
❏ 1020	The Swingin'est	1968	3.75	7.50	15.00
RUSSELL, LUIS					
Pianist and bandleader, a pioneer in swing music.					
COLUMBIA					
❏ CG 32338 [(2)]	Luis Russell and the Louisiana Swing Orchestra	1973	3.75	7.50	15.00
❏ PG 32338 [(2)]	Luis Russell and the Louisiana Swing Orchestra	197?	3.00	6.00	12.00
-- Reissue with new prefix					

Number	Title	Yr	VG	VG+	NM

RUSSELL, PEE WEE
Clarinetist and saxophone player. Also see RUBY BRAFF; COLEMAN HAWKINS; PEE WEE HUNT; JACK TEAGARDEN.

ABC IMPULSE!

Number	Title	Yr	VG	VG+	NM
❏ AS-96 [S]	Ask Me Now	1968	3.75	7.50	15.00
❏ AS-9137 [S]	College Concert of Pee Wee Russell with Henry "Red" Allen	1968	3.75	7.50	15.00
❏ IA-9359 [(2)]	Salute to Newport	1979	3.75	7.50	15.00

ARCHIVE OF FOLK AND JAZZ
| ❏ 233 [R] | Pee Wee Russell | 1969 | 2.50 | 5.00 | 10.00 |

ATLANTIC
| ❏ ALS-126 [10] | Pee Wee Russell All Stars | 1952 | 20.00 | 40.00 | 80.00 |

BARNABY
| ❏ BR-5018 | Jazz Reunion | 197? | 3.00 | 6.00 | 12.00 |

BELL
| ❏ LP-42 [M] | Pee Wee Russell Plays Pee Wee | 1961 | 6.25 | 12.50 | 25.00 |
| ❏ LPS-42 [S] | Pee Wee Russell Plays Pee Wee | 1961 | 7.50 | 15.00 | 30.00 |

COLUMBIA
| ❏ CL 1985 [M] | New Groove | 1963 | 3.75 | 7.50 | 15.00 |
| ❏ CS 8785 [S] | New Groove | 1963 | 5.00 | 10.00 | 20.00 |

COMMODORE
| ❏ XFL-16440 | Three Deuces and Hot Four: The Pied Piper of Jazz | 198? | 2.50 | 5.00 | 10.00 |

COUNTERPOINT
| ❏ 56? [M] | Portrait of Pee Wee | 1957 | 15.00 | 30.00 | 60.00 |

DCC COMPACT CLASSICS
| ❏ LPZ-2024 | Portrait of Pee Wee | 1996 | 6.25 | 12.50 | 25.00 |
| -- Audiophile vinyl | | | | | |

DISC
| ❏ DLP-??? [10] | Jazz Ensemble | 195? | 30.00 | 60.00 | 120.00 |

DOT
| ❏ DLP-3253 [M] | Pee Wee Russell Plays | 1960 | 6.25 | 12.50 | 25.00 |
| ❏ DLP-25253 [S] | Pee Wee Russell Plays | 1960 | 5.00 | 10.00 | 20.00 |

ESOTERIC
| ❏ 565 [M] | Pee Wee Russell All Stars | 1959 | 10.00 | 20.00 | 40.00 |
| ❏ 5565 [S] | Pee Wee Russell All Stars | 1959 | 7.50 | 15.00 | 30.00 |

FANTASY
| ❏ OJC-1708 | Rhythmakers and Teagarden | 1985 | 2.50 | 5.00 | 10.00 |

IMPULSE!
❏ A-96 [M]	Ask Me Now	1966	6.25	12.50	25.00
❏ AS-96 [S]	Ask Me Now	1966	7.50	15.00	30.00
❏ A-9137 [M]	College Concert of Pee Wee Russell with Henry "Red" Allen	1967	6.25	12.50	25.00
❏ AS-9137 [S]	College Concert of Pee Wee Russell with Henry "Red" Allen	1967	5.00	10.00	20.00

MAINSTREAM
| ❏ S-6026 [S] | A Legend | 1965 | 5.00 | 10.00 | 20.00 |
| ❏ 56026 [M] | A Legend | 1965 | 3.75 | 7.50 | 15.00 |

MCA
| ❏ 4150 [(2)] | Salute to Newport | 198? | 3.00 | 6.00 | 12.00 |

PRESTIGE
| ❏ PRST-7672 [R] | The Pee Wee Russell Memorial Album | 1969 | 3.75 | 7.50 | 15.00 |
| ❏ 24051 [(2)] | Jam Session in Swingville | 198? | 3.75 | 7.50 | 15.00 |

RIVERSIDE
| ❏ RLP 12-141 [M] | Rhythmakers and Teagarden | 1955 | 15.00 | 30.00 | 60.00 |

SAVOY JAZZ
| ❏ SJL-2228 [(2)] | The Individualism of Pee Wee Russell | 197? | 3.75 | 7.50 | 15.00 |

STEREO-CRAFT
| ❏ RTN-105 [M] | Pee Wee Plays Pee Wee | 196? | 5.00 | 10.00 | 20.00 |
| ❏ RTS-105 [S] | Pee Wee Plays Pee Wee | 196? | 6.25 | 12.50 | 25.00 |

STORYVILLE
| ❏ STLP-308 [10] | Pee Wee Russell | 1954 | 20.00 | 40.00 | 80.00 |
| ❏ STLP-909 [M] | We're In the Money | 1956 | 12.50 | 25.00 | 50.00 |

SWINGVILLE
❏ SVLP-2008 [M]	Swingin' with Pee Wee	1960	12.50	25.00	50.00
-- Purple label					
❏ SVLP-2008 [M]	Swingin' with Pee Wee	1965	6.25	12.50	25.00
-- Blue label, trident logo at right					

XANADU
| ❏ 192 | Over the Rainbow | 198? | 2.50 | 5.00 | 10.00 |

RUSSELL, PEE WEE/BILLY BANKS
Banks is a male singer. Also see PEE WEE RUSSELL.

JAZZ PANORAMA
| ❏ 1808 [10] | Pee Wee Russell / Billy Banks | 1951 | 20.00 | 40.00 | 80.00 |

RUSSELL, PEE WEE, AND RUBY BRAFF
Also see each artist's individual listings.

SAVOY
Number	Title	Yr	VG	VG+	NM
❏ MG-12034 [M]	Jazz At Storyville, Volume 1	1955	12.50	25.00	50.00
❏ MG-12041 [M]	Jazz At Storyville, Volume 2	1955	12.50	25.00	50.00

RUSSIAN JAZZ QUARTET, THE

ABC IMPULSE!
| ❏ AS-80 [S] | Happiness | 1968 | 3.75 | 7.50 | 15.00 |

IMPULSE!
| ❏ A-80 [M] | Happiness | 1965 | 5.00 | 10.00 | 20.00 |
| ❏ AS-80 [S] | Happiness | 1965 | 6.25 | 12.50 | 25.00 |

RUSSIN, BABE
Tenor saxophone player and clarinetist.

DOT
| ❏ DLP-3060 [M] | To Soothe the Savage | 1956 | 12.50 | 25.00 | 50.00 |

RUSSO, BILL
Trombonist, arranger, composer and bandleader. Also see STAN KENTON; SHELLY MANNE.

ATLANTIC
❏ 1241 [M]	The World of Alcina	1956	20.00	40.00	80.00
-- Black label					
❏ 1241 [M]	The World of Alcina	1961	7.50	15.00	30.00
-- Multicolor label, white "fan" logo at right					

DEE GEE
| ❏ 1001 [10] | A Recital in New American Music | 1952 | 50.00 | 100.00 | 200.00 |

FM
| ❏ 302 [M] | Stereophony | 1963 | 6.25 | 12.50 | 25.00 |
| ❏ S-302 [S] | Stereophony | 1963 | 7.50 | 15.00 | 30.00 |

ROULETTE
❏ R-52045 [M]	School of Rebellion	1960	6.25	12.50	25.00
❏ SR-52045 [S]	School of Rebellion	1960	7.50	15.00	30.00
❏ R-52063 [M]	Seven Deadly Sins	1960	6.25	12.50	25.00
❏ SR-52063 [S]	Seven Deadly Sins	1960	7.50	15.00	30.00

RUTHER, BULL
See MILT HINTON.

RUTHERFORD, PAUL
Trombonist and pianist.

EMANEM
| ❏ 3305 | Gentle Harm of the Bourgeoisie | 197? | 3.00 | 6.00 | 12.00 |

RYG, JORGEN
Trumpeter.

EMARCY
| ❏ MG-36099 [M] | Jorgen Ryg Jazz Quartet | 1956 | 12.50 | 25.00 | 50.00 |

RYPDAL, TERJE
Guitarist, flutist and keyboard player.

ECM
❏ 1031	What Comes After	1974	3.75	7.50	15.00
❏ 1045	Whenever I Seem to Be Far Away	1975	3.00	6.00	12.00
❏ 1067/8 [(2)]	Odyssey	1976	3.75	7.50	15.00
❏ 1083	After the Rain	1977	3.00	6.00	12.00
❏ 1110	Waves	1978	3.00	6.00	12.00
❏ 1125	Terje Rypdal/Miroslav Vitous/ Jack DeJohnette	1979	3.00	6.00	12.00
❏ 1144	Descendre	1979	3.00	6.00	12.00
❏ 1192	To Be Continued	198?	2.50	5.00	10.00
❏ 1303	Chaser	1986	2.50	5.00	10.00

RYPDAL, TERJE, AND DAVID DARLING
Also see each artist's individual listings.

ECM
| ❏ 23799 | EOS | 198? | 2.50 | 5.00 | 10.00 |

Number	Title	Yr	VG	VG+	NM

S

SABIEN, RANDY
Violinist and mandolin player.
FLYING FISH
Number	Title	Yr	VG	VG+	NM
❑ FF-297	In a Fog	198?	2.50	5.00	10.00

SABU
Full name: Sabu Martinez. Percussionist (bongos and conga drums) and male singer.
ALEGRE
| ❑ 802 [M] | Jazz Espagnole | 195? | 75.00 | 150.00 | 300.00 |
BLUE NOTE
❑ BLP-1561 [M]	Palo Congo	1957	37.50	75.00	150.00
-- "Deep groove" version (deep indentation under label on both sides)					
❑ BLP-1561 [M]	Palo Congo	1957	25.00	50.00	100.00
-- Regular version, W. 63rd St. address on label					
❑ BLP-1561 [M]	Palo Congo	1963	6.25	12.50	25.00
-- With "New York, USA" address on label					
❑ BST-81561 [R]	Palo Congo	1967	3.75	7.50	15.00
-- With "A Division of Liberty Records" on label					

SACBE
Mexican group: Eugenio Toussaint (piano, keyboards); Enrique Toussaint (bass); Fernando Toussaint (drums); Armando Montiel (percussion).
DISCOVERY
| ❑ 864 | Street Corner | 198? | 2.50 | 5.00 | 10.00 |
TREND
| ❑ TR-521 | Aztlan | 198? | 3.00 | 6.00 | 12.00 |
| ❑ TR-544 | The Sleeping Lady | 1986 | 2.50 | 5.00 | 10.00 |

SACHS, AARON
Clarinetist, tenor and alto saxophone player and flutist.
BETHLEHEM
| ❑ BCP-1008 [10] | Aaron Sachs Quintet | 1954 | 30.00 | 60.00 | 120.00 |
DAWN
| ❑ DLP-1114 [M] | Jazzville, Volume 3 | 1957 | 20.00 | 40.00 | 80.00 |
RAMA
| ❑ LP-1004 [M] | Clarinet and Co. | 1957 | 20.00 | 40.00 | 80.00 |

SACHS, AARON/HANK D'AMICO
Also see each artist's individual listings.
BETHLEHEM
| ❑ BCP-7 [M] | We Brought Our "Axes" | 1955 | 20.00 | 40.00 | 80.00 |

SACKVILLE ALL-STARS, THE
The below album features BUDDY TATE; JIM GALLOWAY; JAY McSHANN; Don Thompson (bass); and Terry Clarke (drums).
SACKVILLE
| ❑ 3028 | Saturday Night Function | 198? | 2.50 | 5.00 | 10.00 |

SADI, FATS
Vibraphone player.
BLUE NOTE
| ❑ BLP-5061 [10] | The Swinging Fats Sadi Combo | 1955 | 75.00 | 150.00 | 300.00 |

ST. CLAIRE, BETTY
Female singer.
JUBILEE
❑ JLP-15 [10]	Hal McKusick Plays -- Betty St. Clair Sings	1955	30.00	60.00	120.00
❑ JLP-23 [10]	Cool and Clearer	1955	25.00	50.00	100.00
❑ JLP-1011 [M]	What Is There to Say?	1956	12.50	25.00	50.00
SEECO
| ❑ SLP-456 [M] | Betty St. Claire at Basin Street | 1960 | 10.00 | 20.00 | 40.00 |
| ❑ SLP-4560 [S] | Betty St. Claire at Basin Street | 1960 | 10.00 | 20.00 | 40.00 |

ST. CYR, JOHNNY
Banjo player and guitarist. Also see PAUL BARBARIN.
SOUTHLAND
| ❑ 212 | Johnny St. Cyr and His Hot Five | 196? | 5.00 | 10.00 | 20.00 |

ST. LOUIS RAGTIMERS, THE
Members: Don Franz (tuba); Bill Mason (cornet, washboard); Al Stricker (banjo, vocals); Trebor Jay Tichenor (piano); Ed Freund (drums); Glenn Meyer (clarinet).
AUDIOPHILE
| ❑ AP-116 | The St. Louis Ragtimers | 1977 | 2.50 | 5.00 | 10.00 |
| ❑ AP-122 | Songs of the Showboat Era | 197? | 2.50 | 5.00 | 10.00 |

SALIM, A.K.
Arranger, composer and bandleader.
PRESTIGE
Number	Title	Yr	VG	VG+	NM
❑ PRLP-7379 [M]	Afro-Soul Drum Orgy	1966	6.25	12.50	25.00
❑ PRST-7379 [S]	Afro-Soul Drum Orgy	1966	7.50	15.00	30.00
SAVOY
❑ MG-12102 [M]	The Flute Suite	1957	20.00	40.00	80.00
❑ MG-12118 [M]	Pretty for the People	1957	20.00	40.00	80.00
❑ MG-12132 [M]	Blues Suite	1958	12.50	25.00	50.00
❑ SST-13001 [S]	Blues Suite	1959	10.00	20.00	40.00

SALIS, ANTONELLO
Pianist and accordion player.
HAT HUT
| ❑ 10 | Orange Juice/Nice Food | 1980 | 3.75 | 7.50 | 15.00 |

SALT CITY FIVE, THE
Among the members: Jack Maheu (clarinet); Bill Rubenstein (piano).
JUBILEE
❑ JLP-13 [10]	Salt City Five	1955	12.50	25.00	50.00
❑ JLP-24 [10]	Salt City Five, Volume 2	1955	12.50	25.00	50.00
❑ JLP-1012 [M]	Salt City Five	1956	10.00	20.00	40.00

SALUZZI, DINO
Bandoneon player, flutist and male singer.
ECM
| ❑ 1251 | Kultrum | 198? | 3.00 | 6.00 | 12.00 |
| ❑ 25042 | Once Upon a Time... Far Away in the South | 1986 | 2.50 | 5.00 | 10.00 |

SALVADOR, DOM
Pianist and arranger.
MUSE
| ❑ MR-5085 | My Family | 1976 | 3.00 | 6.00 | 12.00 |

SALVADOR, SAL
Guitarist and bandleader.
BEE HIVE
| ❑ BH-7002 | Starfingers | 1978 | 3.00 | 6.00 | 12.00 |
| ❑ BH-7009 | Juicy Lucy | 1979 | 3.00 | 6.00 | 12.00 |
BETHLEHEM
❑ BCP-39 [M]	Shades of Sal Salvador	1956	12.50	25.00	50.00
❑ BCP-59 [M]	Frivolous Sal	1956	12.50	25.00	50.00
❑ BCP-74 [M]	Tribute to the Greats	1957	12.50	25.00	50.00
BLUE NOTE
| ❑ BLP-5035 [10] | Sal Salvador Quintet | 1954 | 75.00 | 150.00 | 300.00 |
CAPITOL
| ❑ H 6505 [10] | Sal Salvador | 1954 | 30.00 | 60.00 | 120.00 |
| ❑ T 6505 [M] | Sal Salvador | 1955 | 20.00 | 40.00 | 80.00 |
DAUNTLESS
| ❑ DM-4307 [M] | You Ain't Heard Nothin' Yet | 1963 | 7.50 | 15.00 | 30.00 |
| ❑ DS-6307 [S] | You Ain't Heard Nothin' Yet | 1963 | 10.00 | 20.00 | 40.00 |
DECCA
❑ DL 4026 [M]	Beat for This Generation	1959	10.00	20.00	40.00
❑ DL 9210 [M]	Colors in Sound	1958	12.50	25.00	50.00
❑ DL 74026 [S]	Beat for This Generation	1959	12.50	25.00	50.00
❑ DL 79210 [S]	Colors in Sound	1958	10.00	20.00	40.00
GOLDEN CREST
| ❑ GC-1001 [M] | Sal Salvador Quartet | 1961 | 6.25 | 12.50 | 25.00 |
| ❑ GCS-1001 [S] | Sal Salvador Quartet | 1961 | 7.50 | 15.00 | 30.00 |
GP
| ❑ 5010 | Live at the University of Bridgeport | 197? | 3.00 | 6.00 | 12.00 |
ROULETTE
| ❑ R-25262 [M] | Music To Stop Smoking By | 1964 | 5.00 | 10.00 | 20.00 |
| ❑ RS-25262 [S] | Music To Stop Smoking By | 1964 | 6.25 | 12.50 | 25.00 |
STASH
❑ ST-224	In Our Own Sweet Way	198?	2.50	5.00	10.00
❑ ST-234	Sal Salvador Plays the World's Greatest Standards	198?	2.50	5.00	10.00
❑ ST-251	Sal Salvador Plays Gerry Mulligan	1985	2.50	5.00	10.00

SAMPLE, JOE
Keyboard player. Also see THE CRUSADERS.
ABC
| ❑ AA-1050 | Rainbow Seeker | 1978 | 2.50 | 5.00 | 10.00 |
| ❑ AA-1126 | Carmel | 1979 | 3.00 | 6.00 | 12.00 |
CRUSADERS
| ❑ 16001 | Carmel | 198? | 5.00 | 10.00 | 20.00 |
| -- Audiophile vinyl | | | | | |

Number	Title	Yr	VG	VG+	NM

MCA
- ❑ AA-1050 — Rainbow Seeker — 1979 — 2.00 — 4.00 — 8.00
  -- *Reissue of ABC 1050*
- ❑ AA-1126 — Carmel — 1979 — 2.50 — 5.00 — 10.00
  -- *Reissue of ABC 1126*
- ❑ 5172 — Voices in the Rain — 1981 — 2.50 — 5.00 — 10.00
- ❑ 5397 — The Hunter — 1983 — 2.50 — 5.00 — 10.00
- ❑ 5978 — Roles — 1987 — 2.50 — 5.00 — 10.00
- ❑ 27077 — Voices in the Rain — 198? — 2.00 — 4.00 — 8.00
  -- *Budget-line reissue*
- ❑ 37210 — Carmel — 198? — 2.00 — 4.00 — 8.00
  -- *Budget-line reissue*

MOBILE FIDELITY
- ❑ 1-016 — Rainbow Seeker — 1979 — 5.00 — 10.00 — 20.00
  -- *Audiophile vinyl*

STORYVILLE
- ❑ 4000 — Fancy Dance — 1980 — 3.00 — 6.00 — 12.00

WARNER BROS.
- ❑ 25781 — Spellbound — 1989 — 3.00 — 6.00 — 12.00
- ❑ 26318 — Ashes to Ashes — 1990 — 3.75 — 7.50 — 15.00

SAMPLE, JOE; RAY BROWN; SHELLY MANNE
Also see each artist's individual listings.

EAST WIND
- ❑ 10001 — The Three — 197? — 5.00 — 10.00 — 20.00

INNER CITY
- ❑ IC-6007 — The Three — 197? — 3.75 — 7.50 — 15.00

SAMPLE, JOE, AND DAVID T. WALKER
Also see each artist's individual listings.

CRUSADERS
- ❑ 16004 — Swing Street Café — 198? — 5.00 — 10.00 — 20.00
  -- *Audiophile vinyl*

MCA
- ❑ 5785 — Swing Street Café — 198? — 2.50 — 5.00 — 10.00

SAMPSON, EDGAR
Alto saxophone player, clarinetist and violinist.

CORAL
- ❑ CRL 57049 [M] — Swing Softly Sweet Sampson — 1957 — 10.00 — 20.00 — 40.00

MCA
- ❑ 1354 — Sampson Swings Again — 198? — 2.50 — 5.00 — 10.00

SAMS, GEORGE
Trumpeter.

HAT HUT
- ❑ 3506 — Nomadic Winds — 198? — 3.00 — 6.00 — 12.00

SAMUELS, DAVID
Vibraphone player and timpanist.

MCA
- ❑ 6328 — Ten Degrees North — 1988 — 2.50 — 5.00 — 10.00

SANBORN, DAVID
Saxophone player (mostly alto). Also see BOB JAMES.

REPRISE
- ❑ 25715 — Close-Up — 1988 — 2.50 — 5.00 — 10.00

WARNER BROS.
- ❑ BS 2873 — Taking Off — 1975 — 2.50 — 5.00 — 10.00
- ❑ BS 2957 — Sanborn — 1976 — 2.50 — 5.00 — 10.00
- ❑ BS 3051 — Promise Me the Moon — 1977 — 2.50 — 5.00 — 10.00
- ❑ BSK 3189 — Heart to Heart — 1978 — 2.50 — 5.00 — 10.00
- ❑ BSK 3379 — Hideaway — 1980 — 2.50 — 5.00 — 10.00
- ❑ BSK 3546 — Voyeur — 1981 — 2.50 — 5.00 — 10.00
- ❑ 23650 — As We Speak — 1982 — 2.50 — 5.00 — 10.00
- ❑ 23906 — Backstreet — 1983 — 2.50 — 5.00 — 10.00
- ❑ 25150 — Straight from the Heart — 1985 — 2.50 — 5.00 — 10.00
- ❑ 25479 — A Change of Heart — 1987 — 2.50 — 5.00 — 10.00

SANCHEZ, PONCHO
Percussionist.

CONCORD PICANTE
- ❑ CJP-201 — Sonando — 198? — 2.50 — 5.00 — 10.00
- ❑ CJP-239 — Bien Sabroso — 198? — 2.50 — 5.00 — 10.00
- ❑ CJP-286 — El Conguero — 1985 — 2.50 — 5.00 — 10.00
- ❑ CJP-310 — Papa Gato — 1987 — 2.50 — 5.00 — 10.00
- ❑ CJP-340 — Fuente — 1988 — 2.50 — 5.00 — 10.00
- ❑ CJP-369 — La Familia — 1989 — 2.50 — 5.00 — 10.00

DISCOVERY
- ❑ 799 — Poncho — 1979 — 3.00 — 6.00 — 12.00
- ❑ 813 — Straight Ahead — 1980 — 3.00 — 6.00 — 12.00

SANCIOUS, DAVID
Keyboard player. Formerly in Bruce Springsteen's band.

ELEKTRA/MUSICIAN
- ❑ 60130 — The Bridge — 1982 — 2.50 — 5.00 — 10.00

SANCTON, TOMMY
Clarinet player and bandleader.

GHB
- ❑ GHB-52 — Tommy Sancton's Galvanized Washboard Band — 1969 — 3.00 — 6.00 — 12.00

SANDERS, ANNETTE
Female singer.

SOVEREIGN
- ❑ SOV-502 — The Time Is Right — 198? — 3.00 — 6.00 — 12.00

SANDERS, PHAROAH
Tenor saxophone player. Also see THE JAZZ COMPOSERS ORCHESTRA; SUN RA.

ABC IMPULSE!
- ❑ A-9138 [M] — Tauhid — 1967 — 7.50 — 15.00 — 30.00
- ❑ AS-9138 [S] — Tauhid — 1967 — 5.00 — 10.00 — 20.00
- ❑ AS-9181 — Karma — 1969 — 5.00 — 10.00 — 20.00
- ❑ AS-9190 — Jewels of Thought — 1970 — 5.00 — 10.00 — 20.00
- ❑ AS-9199 — Summun Bukmun Umyum — 1970 — 5.00 — 10.00 — 20.00
- ❑ AS-9206 — Thembi — 1971 — 3.75 — 7.50 — 15.00
- ❑ AQ-9219 [Q] — Black Unity — 1974 — 4.50 — 9.00 — 18.00
- ❑ AS-9219 — Black Unity — 1972 — 3.75 — 7.50 — 15.00
- ❑ AQ-9227 [Q] — Live at the East — 1974 — 4.50 — 9.00 — 18.00
- ❑ AS-9227 — Live at the East — 1973 — 3.75 — 7.50 — 15.00
- ❑ AS-9229 [(2)] — The Best of Pharoah Sanders — 1973 — 5.00 — 10.00 — 20.00
- ❑ AS-9233 — Wisdom Through Music — 1973 — 3.75 — 7.50 — 15.00
- ❑ AQ-9254 [Q] — Village of the Pharoahs — 1974 — 4.50 — 9.00 — 18.00
- ❑ AS-9254 — Village of the Pharoahs — 1974 — 3.00 — 6.00 — 12.00
- ❑ AQ-9261 [Q] — Elevation — 1974 — 4.50 — 9.00 — 18.00
- ❑ AS-9261 — Elevation — 1974 — 3.00 — 6.00 — 12.00
- ❑ AQ-9280 [Q] — Love in Us All — 1975 — 4.50 — 9.00 — 18.00
- ❑ ASD-9280 — Love in Us All — 1975 — 3.00 — 6.00 — 12.00

ARISTA
- ❑ AL 4161 — Love Will Find a Way — 1978 — 3.00 — 6.00 — 12.00

ESP-DISK'
- ❑ 1003 [M] — Pharoah's First — 1965 — 6.25 — 12.50 — 25.00
- ❑ S-1003 [S] — Pharoah's First — 1965 — 7.50 — 15.00 — 30.00

GRP/IMPULSE!
- ❑ IMP-219 — Black Unity — 199? — 3.75 — 7.50 — 15.00
  -- *Reissue on audiophile vinyl*

INDIA NAVIGATION
- ❑ IN-1027 — Pharoah — 1977 — 3.00 — 6.00 — 12.00

MCA
- ❑ 4151 [(2)] — The Best of Pharoah Sanders — 1981 — 3.00 — 6.00 — 12.00
  -- *Reissue of Impulse 9229*
- ❑ 29056 — Tauhid — 1981 — 2.00 — 4.00 — 8.00
  -- *Reissue of Impulse 9138*
- ❑ 29057 — Karma — 1981 — 2.00 — 4.00 — 8.00
  -- *Reissue of Impulse 9181*
- ❑ 29058 — Jewels of Thought — 1981 — 2.00 — 4.00 — 8.00
  -- *Reissue of Impulse 9190*
- ❑ 29059 — Thembi — 1981 — 2.00 — 4.00 — 8.00
  -- *Reissue of Impulse 9206*

SIGNATURE
- ❑ FA 40952 — Oh Lord, Let Me Do No Wrong — 1989 — 3.00 — 6.00 — 12.00

STRATA-EAST
- ❑ 19733 — Izipho Sam (My Gifts) — 1973 — 3.75 — 7.50 — 15.00

THERESA
- ❑ 108/9 [(2)] — Journey to the One — 1980 — 3.75 — 7.50 — 15.00
- ❑ 112/13 [(2)] — Rejoice — 1981 — 3.75 — 7.50 — 15.00
- ❑ 116 — Pharoah Sanders Live — 1985 — 2.50 — 5.00 — 10.00
- ❑ 118 — Heart Is a Melody — 1986 — 2.50 — 5.00 — 10.00
- ❑ 121 — Shukuru — 1986 — 2.50 — 5.00 — 10.00

TIMELESS
- ❑ SJP-253 — Africa — 1990 — 3.00 — 6.00 — 12.00

UPFRONT
- ❑ 150 — Spotlight — 1973 — 3.00 — 6.00 — 12.00

SANDKE, JORDAN
Trumpeter. Brother of Randy.

STASH
- ❑ ST-259 — Rhythm Is Our Business — 1986 — 2.50 — 5.00 — 10.00

SANDKE, RANDY
Trumpeter and fluegel horn player. Brother of Jordan.

STASH
- ❑ ST-264 — New York Stories — 1987 — 2.50 — 5.00 — 10.00

Number	Title	Yr	VG	VG+	NM
SANDOLE BROTHERS, THE					

With DENNIS SANDOLE (guitar) and Adolphe Sandole (piano).

FANTASY

Number	Title	Yr	VG	VG+	NM
❏ 3209 [M]	Modern Music from Philadelphia	1956	12.50	25.00	50.00
-- Red vinyl					
❏ 3209 [M]	Modern Music from Philadelphia	1957	7.50	15.00	30.00
-- Black vinyl					

SANDOLE, DENNIS

Guitarist. Also see THE SANDOLE BROTHERS.

FANTASY

❏ 3251 [M]	Compositions and Arrangements for Guitar	1958	7.50	15.00	30.00

SANDOVAL, ARTURO

Trumpeter. Also see IRAKERE.

GRP

❏ GR-9634	Flight to Freedom	1991	3.75	7.50	15.00

SANGUMA

From Papua New Guinea.

ODE NEW ZEALAND

❏ SODE-194	Sanguma	1986	3.00	6.00	12.00

SANTAMARIA, MONGO

Conga player and bandleader. His version of the HERBIE HANCOCK composition "Watermelon Man" was a top-10 pop hit in 1963.

ATLANTIC

❏ SD 1567	Mongo '70	1970	3.00	6.00	12.00
❏ SD 1581	Mongo's Way	1971	3.00	6.00	12.00
❏ SD 1593	Mongo at Montreux	1972	3.00	6.00	12.00
❏ SD 1621	Up from the Roots	1974	3.00	6.00	12.00
❏ SD 8252	Feelin' Alright	1970	3.00	6.00	12.00

BATTLE

❏ B-6120 [M]	Watermelon Man!	1963	5.00	10.00	20.00
❏ B-6129 [M]	Mongo at the Village Gate	1964	5.00	10.00	20.00
❏ BS-96120 [S]	Watermelon Man!	1963	6.25	12.50	25.00
❏ BS-96129 [S]	Mongo at the Village Gate	1964	6.25	12.50	25.00

COLUMBIA

❏ CS 1060	Mongo's Greatest Hits	1970	3.00	6.00	12.00
❏ PC 1060	Mongo's Greatest Hits	198?	2.00	4.00	8.00
-- Reissue with new prefix					
❏ CL 2298 [M]	El Pussy Cat	1965	5.00	10.00	20.00
-- With "Guaranteed High Fidelity" in black at bottom of red label					
❏ CL 2298 [M]	El Pussy Cat	1965	3.00	6.00	12.00
-- With "360 Sound Mono" in white at bottom of red label					
❏ CL 2375 [M]	La Bamba	1965	3.75	7.50	15.00
❏ CL 2375 [M]	Mr. Watermelon Man	196?	3.00	6.00	12.00
-- Retitled reissue					
❏ CL 2411 [M]	El Bravo	1966	3.00	6.00	12.00
❏ CL 2473 [M]	Hey! Let's Party	1966	3.00	6.00	12.00
❏ CL 2612 [M]	Mongomania	1967	3.75	7.50	15.00
❏ CL 2770 [M]	Mongo Santamaria Explodes at the Village Gate	1967	3.75	7.50	15.00
❏ CS 9098 [S]	El Pussy Cat	1965	6.25	12.50	25.00
-- With "360 Sound Stereo" in black at bottom of red label					
❏ CS 9098 [S]	El Pussy Cat	1965	3.75	7.50	15.00
-- With "360 Sound Stereo" in white at bottom of red label					
❏ CS 9175 [S]	La Bamba	1965	5.00	10.00	20.00
❏ CS 9175 [S]	Mr. Watermelon Man	196?	3.75	7.50	15.00
-- Retitled reissue					
❏ CS 9211 [S]	El Bravo	1966	3.75	7.50	15.00
❏ CS 9273 [S]	Hey! Let's Party	1966	3.75	7.50	15.00
❏ CS 9412 [S]	Mongomania	1967	3.00	6.00	12.00
❏ CS 9570 [S]	Mongo Santamaria Explodes at the Village Gate	1967	3.00	6.00	12.00
❏ CS 9653	Soul Bag	1968	3.75	7.50	15.00
❏ CS 9780	Stone Soul	1969	3.75	7.50	15.00
❏ CS 9937	Workin' on a Groovy Thing	1969	3.75	7.50	15.00
❏ CS 9988	All Strung Out	1970	3.75	7.50	15.00

CONCORD JAZZ

❏ CJ-387	Ole Ola	1989	3.00	6.00	12.00

CONCORD PICANTE

❏ CJP-327	Soy Yo	1987	2.50	5.00	10.00
❏ CJP-362	Soca Me Nice	1988	2.50	5.00	10.00

FANTASY

❏ OJC-276	Yambu	1987	2.50	5.00	10.00
-- Reissue of 8012					
❏ OJC-281	Sabroso	1987	2.50	5.00	10.00
-- Reissue of 8058					
❏ OJC-490	Mongo at the Village Gate	1991	3.00	6.00	12.00
-- Reissue of Riverside 93529					

Number	Title	Yr	VG	VG+	NM
❏ OJC-626	Summertime	1991	3.00	6.00	12.00
-- Reissue of Pablo 2308 229					
❏ 3267 [M]	Yambu	1959	10.00	20.00	40.00
-- Red vinyl					
❏ 3267 [M]	Yambu	1959	7.50	15.00	30.00
-- Black vinyl					
❏ 3291 [M]	Mongo	1959	10.00	20.00	40.00
-- Red vinyl					
❏ 3291 [M]	Mongo	1959	7.50	15.00	30.00
-- Black vinyl					
❏ 3302 [M]	Our Man in Havana	1960	10.00	20.00	40.00
-- Red vinyl					
❏ 3302 [M]	Our Man in Havana	1960	7.50	15.00	30.00
-- Black vinyl					
❏ 3311 [M]	Mongo in Havana	1960	10.00	20.00	40.00
-- Red vinyl					
❏ 3311 [M]	Mongo in Havana	1960	7.50	15.00	30.00
-- Black vinyl					
❏ 3314 [M]	Sabroso	1960	10.00	20.00	40.00
-- Red vinyl					
❏ 3314 [M]	Sabroso	1960	7.50	15.00	30.00
-- Black vinyl					
❏ 3324 [M]	Arriba!	1961	10.00	20.00	40.00
-- Red vinyl					
❏ 3324 [M]	Arriba!	1961	7.50	15.00	30.00
-- Black vinyl					
❏ 3328 [M]	Mas Sabroso	1962	10.00	20.00	40.00
-- Red vinyl					
❏ 3328 [M]	Mas Sabroso	1962	7.50	15.00	30.00
-- Black vinyl					
❏ 3335 [M]	Viva Mongo!	1962	10.00	20.00	40.00
-- Red vinyl					
❏ 3335 [M]	Viva Mongo!	1962	7.50	15.00	30.00
-- Black vinyl					
❏ 3351 [M]	Mighty Mongo	1963	3.75	7.50	15.00
❏ MPF-4529	Mongo Santamaria's Greatest Hits	198?	2.00	4.00	8.00
-- Budget-line reissue					
❏ 8012 [S]	Yambu	1962	7.50	15.00	30.00
-- Blue vinyl					
❏ 8012 [S]	Yambu	1962	5.00	10.00	20.00
-- Black vinyl					
❏ 8032 [S]	Mongo	1962	7.50	15.00	30.00
-- Blue vinyl					
❏ 8032 [S]	Mongo	1962	5.00	10.00	20.00
-- Black vinyl					
❏ 8045 [S]	Our Man in Havana	1962	7.50	15.00	30.00
-- Blue vinyl					
❏ 8045 [S]	Our Man in Havana	1962	5.00	10.00	20.00
-- Black vinyl					
❏ 8055 [S]	Mongo in Havana	1962	7.50	15.00	30.00
-- Blue vinyl					
❏ 8055 [S]	Mongo in Havana	1962	5.00	10.00	20.00
-- Black vinyl					
❏ 8058 [S]	Sabroso	1962	7.50	15.00	30.00
-- Blue vinyl					
❏ 8058 [S]	Sabroso	1962	5.00	10.00	20.00
-- Black vinyl					
❏ 8067 [S]	Arriba!	1962	7.50	15.00	30.00
-- Blue vinyl					
❏ 8067 [S]	Arriba!	1962	5.00	10.00	20.00
-- Black vinyl					
❏ 8071 [S]	Mas Sabroso	1962	7.50	15.00	30.00
-- Blue vinyl					
❏ 8071 [S]	Mas Sabroso	1962	5.00	10.00	20.00
-- Black vinyl					
❏ 8087 [S]	Viva Mongo!	1962	7.50	15.00	30.00
-- Blue vinyl					
❏ 8087 [S]	Viva Mongo!	1962	5.00	10.00	20.00
-- Black vinyl					
❏ 8351 [S]	Mighty Mongo	1963	5.00	10.00	20.00
❏ 8373	Mongo Santamaria's Greatest Hits	1967	3.00	6.00	12.00
❏ 9431	Mongo Y La Lupe	1974	3.00	6.00	12.00

HARMONY

❏ H 30291	The Dock of the Bay	1971	2.50	5.00	10.00

MILESTONE

❏ 47012 [(2)]	Watermelon Man	1974	3.75	7.50	15.00
❏ 47038 [(2)]	Skins	1976	3.75	7.50	15.00

PABLO

❏ 2308 229	Summertime	1980	3.00	6.00	12.00

PRESTIGE

❏ 24018 [(2)]	Afro Roots	1973	3.75	7.50	15.00

RIVERSIDE

❏ RLP-423 [M]	Go, Mongo!	1962	6.25	12.50	25.00
❏ R-3008 [M]	Explosion	1967	6.25	12.50	25.00
❏ RS-3008 [S]	Explosion	1968	3.75	7.50	15.00
❏ RS-3045	Mongo Soul	1969	3.75	7.50	15.00
❏ RM-3523 [M]	Mongo Introduces La Lupe	1963	5.00	10.00	20.00

Number	Title	Yr	VG	VG+	NM
❏ RM-3529 [M]	Mongo at the Village Gate	1963	5.00	10.00	20.00
❏ RM-3530 [M]	Mongo Santamaria Explodes!	1964	5.00	10.00	20.00
❏ RS-9423 [S]	Go, Mongo!	1962	7.50	15.00	30.00
❏ RS-93523 [S]	Mongo Introduces La Lupe	1963	6.25	12.50	25.00
❏ RS-93529 [S]	Mongo at the Village Gate	1963	6.25	12.50	25.00
❏ RS-93530 [S]	Mongo Santamaria Explodes!	1964	6.25	12.50	25.00

TICO

Number	Title	Yr	VG	VG+	NM
❏ LP-137 [10]	Chango	1955	20.00	40.00	80.00
❏ LP-1037 [M]	Chango: Mongo Santamaria's Drums and Chants	1957	15.00	30.00	60.00
❏ LP-1149 [M]	Mongo Santamaria's Drums and Chants	1967	5.00	10.00	20.00

SANTANA, CARLOS, AND MAHAVISHNU JOHN McLAUGHLIN
Santana is a guitarist whose other work is outside the scope of this book. Also see JOHN McLAUGHLIN.
COLUMBIA

Number	Title	Yr	VG	VG+	NM
❏ KC 32034	Love Devotion Surrender	1973	2.50	5.00	10.00
❏ PC 32034	Love Devotion Surrender	197?	2.00	4.00	8.00

-- Reissue with new prefix

SANTIAGO, MIKE
Guitarist.
CHIAROSCURO

Number	Title	Yr	VG	VG+	NM
❏ 193	White Trees	1978	3.00	6.00	12.00

SANTOS BROTHERS, THE
METROJAZZ

Number	Title	Yr	VG	VG+	NM
❏ E-1015 [M]	Jazz For Two Trumpets	1958	12.50	25.00	50.00
❏ SE-1015 [S]	Jazz For Two Trumpets	1958	10.00	20.00	40.00

SANTOS, MOACIR
Saxophone player, clarinetist, composer and arranger.
BLUE NOTE

Number	Title	Yr	VG	VG+	NM
❏ BN-LA007-F	Maestro	1972	5.00	10.00	20.00
❏ BN-LA260-G	Saudade	1974	3.75	7.50	15.00
❏ BN-LA483-G	Carnival of the Spirits	1975	3.75	7.50	15.00

DISCOVERY

Number	Title	Yr	VG	VG+	NM
❏ 795	Opus 3, No. 1	1979	3.00	6.00	12.00

SARACHO
Full name: Gary Saracho. Keyboard player.
ABC IMPULSE!

Number	Title	Yr	VG	VG+	NM
❏ AS-9247	En Medio	1974	3.75	7.50	15.00

SARBIB, SAHEB
Bass player.
CADENCE JAZZ

Number	Title	Yr	VG	VG+	NM
❏ CJR-1001	Live at the Public Theatre	198?	2.50	5.00	10.00
❏ CJR-1008	U.F.O. -- Live on Tour	198?	2.50	5.00	10.00
❏ CJR-1010	Aisha	198?	2.50	5.00	10.00

SOUL NOTE

Number	Title	Yr	VG	VG+	NM
❏ SN-1048	Sessions	198?	3.00	6.00	12.00
❏ SN-1098	It Couldn't Happen Without You	198?	3.00	6.00	12.00

SASH, LEON
Accordion player, guitarist and vibraphone player.
DELMARK

Number	Title	Yr	VG	VG+	NM
❏ DS-9416	I Remember Newport	1968	3.75	7.50	15.00

STORYVILLE

Number	Title	Yr	VG	VG+	NM
❏ STLP-917 [M]	Leon Sash Quartet	1956	12.50	25.00	50.00

SATCHMO LEGACY BAND, THE
Members: Alvin Batiste (clarinet, vocals); RED CALLENDER (bass, tuba, vocals), AL CASEY (guitar, vocals); Alan Dawson (drums); CURTIS FULLER (trombone, vocals); FREDDIE HUBBARD (trumpet, fluegel horn, vocals); KIRK LIGHTSEY (piano, vocals).
SOUL NOTE

Number	Title	Yr	VG	VG+	NM
❏ 121116	Salute to Pops, Vol. 1	1990	3.75	7.50	15.00

SATOH, MASAHIKO
Pianist. Last name also spelled "Sato."
ENJA

Number	Title	Yr	VG	VG+	NM
❏ 2008	Trinity	197?	3.75	7.50	15.00

PORTRAIT

Number	Title	Yr	VG	VG+	NM
❏ OR 44194	Amorphism	1989	3.00	6.00	12.00

SATTERFIELD, ESTHER
Female singer.
A&M

Number	Title	Yr	VG	VG+	NM
❏ SP-3408	Once I Loved	1974	2.50	5.00	10.00
❏ SP-3411	The Need to Be	1975	2.50	5.00	10.00

SAUNDERS, HERM
Pianist.
VOGUE

Number	Title	Yr	VG	VG+	NM
❏ 101 [10]	Music at the Bantam Cock	1953	50.00	100.00	200.00

SAUNDERS, MERL
Keyboard player. Frequent collaborator with Jerry Garcia of the Grateful Dead.
CRYSTAL CLEAR

Number	Title	Yr	VG	VG+	NM
❏ 5006	Do I Move You	1980	5.00	10.00	20.00

-- Direct-to-disc recording
FANTASY

Number	Title	Yr	VG	VG+	NM
❏ MPF-4533	Keystone Encores, Vol. 1	1988	3.00	6.00	12.00
❏ MPF-4534	Keystone Encores, Vol. 2	1988	3.00	6.00	12.00
❏ MPF-4535	Live at the Keystone, Vol. 1	1988	3.00	6.00	12.00
❏ MPF-4536	Live at the Keystone, Vol. 2	1988	3.00	6.00	12.00
❏ 8421	Heavy Turbulence	1972	3.75	7.50	15.00
❏ 9421	Fire Up	1973	5.00	10.00	20.00
❏ 9460	Saunders	1974	3.75	7.50	15.00
❏ 9503	Leave Your Hat On	1976	3.00	6.00	12.00
❏ 79002 [(2)]	Live at the Keystone	198?	5.00	10.00	20.00

GALAXY

Number	Title	Yr	VG	VG+	NM
❏ 8209	Soul Grooving	197?	3.75	7.50	15.00

SAUNDERS, TEDDY
Pianist.
DISCOVERY

Number	Title	Yr	VG	VG+	NM
❏ 809	Sue Blue	1980	3.00	6.00	12.00

SAUNDERS, TOM
Cornet player and bandleader.
BOUNTIFUL

Number	Title	Yr	VG	VG+	NM
❏ 38002	Tom Saunders' Surf Side Six	197?	3.75	7.50	15.00

SAUSSY, TUPPER
Pianist. In the pop-rock world, his one-man band The Neon Philharmonic had one hit, "Morning Girl," in 1969.
MONUMENT

Number	Title	Yr	VG	VG+	NM
❏ MLP-8004 [M]	Discover Tupper Saussy	1964	5.00	10.00	20.00
❏ MLP-8027 [M]	Said I to Shostakovitch	1965	5.00	10.00	20.00
❏ MLP-8034 [M]	A Swinger's Guide to "Mary Poppins"	1965	5.00	10.00	20.00
❏ SLP-18004 [S]	Discover Tupper Saussy	1964	6.25	12.50	25.00
❏ SLP-18027 [S]	Said I to Shostakovitch	1965	6.25	12.50	25.00
❏ SLP-18034 [S]	A Swinger's Guide to "Mary Poppins"	1965	6.25	12.50	25.00

SAUTER-FINEGAN
Eddie Sauter (trumpet, arranger) and Bill Finegan (pianist, arranger). Also see RAY McKINLEY.
RCA VICTOR

Number	Title	Yr	VG	VG+	NM
❏ LJM-1003 [M]	Inside Sauter-Finegan	1954	20.00	40.00	80.00
❏ LPM-1009 [M]	The Sound of Sauter-Finegan	1954	20.00	40.00	80.00
❏ LPM-1051 [M]	Concert Jazz	1955	15.00	30.00	60.00
❏ LPM-1104 [M]	Sons of Sauter-Finegan	1955	15.00	30.00	60.00
❏ LPM-1227 [M]	New Directions in Music	1956	15.00	30.00	60.00
❏ LPM-1240 [M]	Adventure In Time	1956	15.00	30.00	60.00
❏ LPM-1341 [M]	Under Analysis	1957	12.50	25.00	50.00
❏ LPM-1497 [M]	Straight Down the Middle	1957	12.50	25.00	50.00
❏ LPM-2473 [M]	Inside Sauter-Finegan Revisited	1961	7.50	15.00	30.00
❏ LSP-2473 [S]	Inside Sauter-Finegan Revisited	1961	10.00	20.00	40.00
❏ LPM-3115 [10]	New Directions in Music	1953	30.00	60.00	120.00

UNITED ARTISTS

Number	Title	Yr	VG	VG+	NM
❏ WWR 3511 [M]	The Return of the Doodletown Fifers	1959	10.00	20.00	40.00
❏ WWS 7511 [S]	The Return of the Doodletown Fifers	1959	12.50	25.00	50.00

SAUTER-FINEGAN; CHICAGO SYMPHONY ORCHESTRA (FRITZ REINER, COND.)
RCA VICTOR RED SEAL

Number	Title	Yr	VG	VG+	NM
❏ LM-1888 [M]	Concerto for Jazz Band and Orchestra	1954	7.50	15.00	30.00

SAVITT, JAN
Violinist and bandleader.
HINDSIGHT

Number	Title	Yr	VG	VG+	NM
❏ HSR-213	Jan Savitt and His Top Hatters	198?	2.50	5.00	10.00

SAYE, JOE
Pianist.
EMARCY

Number	Title	Yr	VG	VG+	NM
❏ MG-36072 [M]	Scotch on the Rocks	1956	10.00	20.00	40.00

Number	Title	Yr	VG	VG+	NM
❏ MG-36112 [M]	A Wee Bit of Jazz	1957	10.00	20.00	40.00
❏ MG-36147 [M]	A Double Shot of Joe Saye	1958	10.00	20.00	40.00
❏ SR-80022 [S]	A Double Shot of Joe Saye	1958	7.50	15.00	30.00
MERCURY					
❏ SR-60052 [S]	A Wee Bit of Jazz	1959	7.50	15.00	30.00

SAYLES SILVER LEAF RAGTIME
GHB

Number	Title	Yr	VG	VG+	NM
❏ GHB-8	Sayles Sugar Leaf Ragtime	196?	3.75	7.50	15.00

SCALETTA, DON
Pianist.
CAPITOL

Number	Title	Yr	VG	VG+	NM
❏ ST 2204 [S]	Any Time, Any Groove	1965	5.00	10.00	20.00
❏ T 2204 [M]	Any Time, Any Groove	1965	3.75	7.50	15.00
❏ ST 2328 [S]	All in Good Time	1965	5.00	10.00	20.00
❏ T 2328 [M]	All in Good Time	1965	3.75	7.50	15.00
VERVE					
❏ V-5027 [M]	Sunday Afternoon at the Trident	1967	5.00	10.00	20.00
❏ V6-5027 [S]	Sunday Afternoon at the Trident	1967	3.75	7.50	15.00

SCANIAZZ
Swedish band.
STOMP OFF

Number	Title	Yr	VG	VG+	NM
❏ SOS-1004	Messin' Around	198?	2.50	5.00	10.00
❏ SOS-1038	Sunset Café Stomp	198?	2.50	5.00	10.00
❏ SOS-1056	It's Right Here for You	198?	2.50	5.00	10.00

SCHAEFER, HAL
Pianist.
DISCOVERY

Number	Title	Yr	VG	VG+	NM
❏ 781	Extraordinary Jazz Pianist	1979	2.50	5.00	10.00
RCA VICTOR					
❏ LPM-1106 [M]	Just Too Much	1955	12.50	25.00	50.00
❏ LPM-1199 [M]	The RCA Victor Jazz Workshop	1956	12.50	25.00	50.00
RENAISSANCE					
❏ 1000	Extraordinary Jazz Pianist	197?	3.00	6.00	12.00
UNITED ARTISTS					
❏ UAL-4021 [M]	Ten Shades of Blue	1959	10.00	20.00	40.00
❏ UAS-5021 [S]	Ten Shades of Blue	1959	10.00	20.00	40.00

SCHAERLI, PETER
Trumpeter.
HAT ART

Number	Title	Yr	VG	VG+	NM
❏ 2037 [(2)]	Schnipp Schnapp	1987	3.75	7.50	15.00

SCHECKTER, JANE
Female singer.
DRG

Number	Title	Yr	VG	VG+	NM
❏ MRS-711	I've Got My Standards	1989	3.00	6.00	12.00

SCHEER MUSIC
PALO ALTO

Number	Title	Yr	VG	VG+	NM
❏ TB-204	High Rise	198?	3.00	6.00	12.00
❏ PA-8025	Rappin' It Up	198?	3.00	6.00	12.00

SCHIFRIN, LALO
Pianist, composer and conductor. Much of his work for movies and TV is listed below.
AMERICAN INT'L.

Number	Title	Yr	VG	VG+	NM
❏ AILP 3003	The Amityville Horror	1979	2.50	5.00	10.00
AUDIO FIDELITY					
❏ AFLP-1981 [M]	Bossa Nova -- New Brazilian Jazz	1962	5.00	10.00	20.00
❏ AFLP-2117 [M]	Eso Es Latino Jazz	1963	5.00	10.00	20.00
❏ AFSD-5981 [S]	Bossa Nova -- New Brazilian Jazz	1962	6.25	12.50	25.00
❏ AFSD-6117 [S]	Eso Es Latino Jazz	1963	6.25	12.50	25.00
❏ AFSD-6195	The Other Side of Lalo Schifrin	1968	3.75	7.50	15.00
COLGEMS					
❏ COMO-5003 [M]	Murderer's Row	1967	12.50	25.00	50.00
❏ COSO-5003 [S]	Murderer's Row	1967	25.00	50.00	100.00
CTI					
❏ 5000	Black Widow	1976	3.00	6.00	12.00
❏ 5003	Towering Toccata	1977	3.00	6.00	12.00
DOT					
❏ DLP-3831 [M]	Music from Mission: Impossible	1967	7.50	15.00	30.00
❏ DLP-3833 [M]	Cool Hand Luke	1968	12.50	25.00	50.00
❏ DLP-25831 [S]	Music from Mission: Impossible	1967	10.00	20.00	40.00
❏ DLP-25833 [S]	Cool Hand Luke	1968	12.50	25.00	50.00

Number	Title	Yr	VG	VG+	NM
❏ DLP-25852	There's a Whole Lot of Schifrin Goin' On	1968	5.00	10.00	20.00
DRG					
❏ SBL-12591	The Fourth Protocol	1987	3.75	7.50	15.00
ENTR'ACTE					
❏ ERS-6508	Voyage of the Damned	1977	6.25	12.50	25.00
❏ ERS-6510	The Eagle Has Landed/The Four Musketeers	1980	3.00	6.00	12.00
MCA					
❏ 2284	Rollercoaster	1977	3.75	7.50	15.00
❏ 2374	Nunzio	1978	3.00	6.00	12.00
❏ 5185	The Competition	1980	2.50	5.00	10.00
❏ 25012	The Cincinnati Kid	1986	2.00	4.00	8.00
❏ 25137	Liquidator	1966	2.00	4.00	8.00
MGM					
❏ E-4110 [M]	Piano, Strings and Bossa Nova	1963	3.75	7.50	15.00
❏ SE-4110 [S]	Piano, Strings and Bossa Nova	1963	5.00	10.00	20.00
❏ E-4156 [M]	Between Broadway and Hollywood	1963	3.75	7.50	15.00
❏ SE-4156 [S]	Between Broadway and Hollywood	1963	5.00	10.00	20.00
❏ E-4313 [M]	The Cincinnati Kid	1965	5.00	10.00	20.00
❏ SE-4313 [S]	The Cincinnati Kid	1965	6.25	12.50	25.00
❏ E-4413 ST [M]	Liquidator	1966	5.00	10.00	20.00
❏ SE-4413 ST [S]	Liquidator	1966	6.25	12.50	25.00
❏ SE-4742	Medical Center and Other Great Themes	1971	5.00	10.00	20.00
NAUTILUS					
❏ NR-51	Ins and Outs	198?	10.00	20.00	40.00
-- Audiophile vinyl					
PALO ALTO					
❏ 8055	Ins and Outs	1983	3.00	6.00	12.00
PARAMOUNT					
❏ PAS-5002	More Music from Mission: Impossible	1969	10.00	20.00	40.00
❏ PAS-5004	Mannix	1969	7.50	15.00	30.00
ROULETTE					
❏ SR-42013	"Lalole" -- The Latin Sound	1968	3.75	7.50	15.00
❏ R 52088 [M]	Lalo Brilliance	1962	5.00	10.00	20.00
❏ SR 52088 [S]	Lalo Brilliance	1962	6.25	12.50	25.00
TABU					
❏ JZ 35436	Gypsies	1978	3.00	6.00	12.00
❏ JZ 36091	No One Home	1979	3.00	6.00	12.00
TETRAGRAMMATON					
❏ T-5006	Che!	1969	7.50	15.00	30.00
TICO					
❏ LP-1070 [M]	Piano Espanol	1960	6.25	12.50	25.00
❏ LPS-1070 [S]	Piano Espanol	1960	7.50	15.00	30.00
VARESE SARABANDE					
❏ STV-81198	The Osterman Weekend	1983	2.50	5.00	10.00
VERVE					
❏ V-8543 [M]	Samba Paros Dos	1963	3.75	7.50	15.00
❏ V6-8543 [S]	Samba Paros Dos	1963	5.00	10.00	20.00
-- With Bob Brookmeyer					
❏ V-8601 [M]	New Fantasy	1964	3.75	7.50	15.00
❏ V6-8601 [S]	New Fantasy	1964	5.00	10.00	20.00
❏ V-8624 [M]	Once a Thief and Other Themes	1965	3.75	7.50	15.00
❏ V6-8624 [S]	Once a Thief and Other Themes	1965	5.00	10.00	20.00
❏ V-8654 [M]	The Dissection and Reconstruction of Music from the Past	1966	3.75	7.50	15.00
❏ V6-8654 [S]	The Dissection and Reconstruction of Music from the Past	1966	5.00	10.00	20.00
❏ V6-8785	Insensatez	1968	3.75	7.50	15.00
❏ V6-8801	Rock Requiem	1971	3.00	6.00	12.00
WARNER BROS.					
❏ WS 1777	Bullitt	1968	12.50	25.00	50.00
❏ BS 2727	Enter the Dragon	1973	12.50	25.00	50.00
❏ BSK 3328	Boulevard Nights	1979	2.50	5.00	10.00

SCHNEIDER, ERIC
Alto, tenor and soprano saxophone player and clarinetist.
GATEMOUTH

Number	Title	Yr	VG	VG+	NM
❏ 1005	Eric's Alley	1981	3.00	6.00	12.00

SCHNEIDER, ERIC, AND EARL HINES
Also see each artist's individual listings.
GATEMOUTH

Number	Title	Yr	VG	VG+	NM
❏ 1003	Eric and Earl	1980	3.00	6.00	12.00

SCHNEIDER, KENT
DELMARK

Number	Title	Yr	VG	VG+	NM
❏ DS-418	Celebration for Modern Man	197?	3.00	6.00	12.00

(Top left) Sauter-Finegan (Eddie Sauter and Bill Finegan) tried to do innovative things with big band music in the 1950s, but the time had passed and the attempts proved to be a financial failure. They did produce some lasting music and one incredibly odd album cover in the process. (Top right) Another unusually interesting RCA Victor LP cover from almost the same time period as Sauter-Finegan was this one, for *Just Too Much* by Hal Schaefer on the piano. (Bottom left) Bob Scobey's Frisco Band was one of the wave of San Francisco-based Dixieland groups of the 1940s and 1950s, part of the last gasp of the already antiquated form. Of course, Dixieland never has gone away completely; it lives on in revival halls and jazz festivals around the world. (Bottom right) For most of jazz history, women have been relegated to the "girl singer" role. But Shirley Scott is a definite exception, as she is well-known and well-regarded for her jazz organ playing.

Number	Title	Yr	VG	VG+	NM
SCHNITTER, DAVID					
Tenor saxophone player.					
MUSE					
❏ MR-5108	Invitation	197?	3.00	6.00	12.00
❏ MR-5153	Goliath	1977	3.00	6.00	12.00
❏ MR-5197	Thundering	1979	3.00	6.00	12.00
❏ MR-5222	Glowing	1980	3.00	6.00	12.00
SCHOOF, MANFRED					
Trumpeter and fluegel horn player.					
ECM					
❏ 19004	Scales	1980	3.00	6.00	12.00
SCHULLER, GUNTHER					
Horn player, bandleader, composer and arranger.					
ANGEL					
❏ S-36060	Joplin	197?	3.00	6.00	12.00
ATLANTIC					
❏ 1368 [M]	Jazz Abstractions	1961	5.00	10.00	20.00
-- Multicolor label, white "fan" logo at right					
❏ 1368 [M]	Jazz Abstractions	1963	3.00	6.00	12.00
-- Multicolor label, black "fan" logo at right					
❏ SD 1368 [S]	Jazz Abstractions	1961	6.25	12.50	25.00
-- Multicolor label, white "fan" logo at right					
❏ SD 1368 [S]	Jazz Abstractions	1963	3.75	7.50	15.00
-- Multicolor label, black "fan" logo at right					
GM RECORDINGS					
❏ GM-3010	Jumpin' in the Future	1989	3.00	6.00	12.00
GOLDEN CREST					
❏ 31042 [(2)]	The Road from Rags to Jazz	197?	3.75	7.50	15.00
❏ 31043	Happy Feet: A Tribute to Paul Whiteman	197?	3.00	6.00	12.00
SCHUUR, DIANE					
Female singer and pianist.					
GRP					
❏ GR-1010	Deedles	1984	2.50	5.00	10.00
❏ GR-1022	Schuur Thing	1985	2.50	5.00	10.00
❏ GR-1030	Timeless	1986	2.50	5.00	10.00
❏ GR-1039	Diane Schuur and the Count Basie Orchestra	1987	2.50	5.00	10.00
❏ GR-9567	Talkin' 'Bout You	1988	2.50	5.00	10.00
❏ GR-9591	The Diane Schuur Collection	1989	3.00	6.00	12.00
❏ GR-9628	Pure Schuur	1991	3.75	7.50	15.00
MUSIC IS MEDICINE					
❏ 9057	Pilot of My Destiny	1982	5.00	10.00	20.00
SCHWARTZ, CHARLES					
Composer and conductor.					
INNER CITY					
❏ IC-1015	Professor Jive	197?	3.75	7.50	15.00
❏ IC-1164	Solo Brothers	198?	3.00	6.00	12.00
PABLO TODAY					
❏ 2312 115	Mother--! Mother--!	1980	3.75	7.50	15.00
SCHWARTZ, JONATHAN					
MUSE					
❏ MR-5325	Anyone Would Love You	1986	3.75	7.50	15.00
SCHWARTZ, THORNEL					
Guitarist.					
ARGO					
❏ LP-704 [M]	Soul Cookin'	1962	6.25	12.50	25.00
❏ LPS-704 [S]	Soul Cookin'	1962	7.50	15.00	30.00
SCHWEIZER, IRENE, AND RUDIGER CARL					
Scweizer is a pianist and drummer. Carl plays accordion, clarinet and saxophone and also is an arranger and composer.					
HAT HUT					
❏ X	The Very Centre of Middle Europe	1979	3.75	7.50	15.00
SCIANNI, JOSEPH					
Pianist.					
SAVOY					
❏ MG-12185 [M]	New Concepts	1965	7.50	15.00	30.00
SCOBEY, BOB					
Trumpeter.					
AMERICAN RECORDING SOCIETY					
❏ G-408 [M]	Bob Scobey's Frisco Band	1956	10.00	20.00	40.00

Number	Title	Yr	VG	VG+	NM
DOWN HOME					
❏ MGD-1 [M]	Bob Scobey's Frisco Band with Clancy Hayes	1954	12.50	25.00	50.00
GOOD TIME JAZZ					
❏ L-22 [10]	Bob Scobey's Frisco Band	1954	12.50	25.00	50.00
❏ L-12006 [M]	Bob Scobey's Frisco Band with Clancy Hayes	1955	10.00	20.00	40.00
❏ L-12009 [M]	Scobey and Clancy	1955	10.00	20.00	40.00
❏ L-12023 [M]	Direct from San Francisco	1955	10.00	20.00	40.00
❏ L-12032 [M]	Bob Scobey's Frisco Band, Volume 1	1957	10.00	20.00	40.00
❏ L-12033 [M]	Bob Scobey's Frisco Band, Volume 2	1957	10.00	20.00	40.00
JANSCO					
❏ 5231	The Great Bob Scobey, Volume 3	1967	3.75	7.50	15.00
❏ 6250	The Great Bob Scobey, Volume 1	1967	3.75	7.50	15.00
❏ 6252	The Great Bob Scobey, Volume 2	1967	3.75	7.50	15.00
RCA VICTOR					
❏ LPM-1344 [M]	Beauty and the Beat	1957	10.00	20.00	40.00
❏ LPM-1448 [M]	Swingin' on the Golden Gate	1957	10.00	20.00	40.00
❏ LPM-1567 [M]	Between 18th and 19th on Any Street	1957	10.00	20.00	40.00
❏ LPM-1700 [M]	College Classics	1958	10.00	20.00	40.00
❏ LPM-1889 [M]	Something Is Always Happening on the River	1958	10.00	20.00	40.00
❏ LPM-2086 [M]	Rompin' and Stompin'	1959	7.50	15.00	30.00
❏ LSP-2086 [S]	Rompin' and Stompin'	1959	10.00	20.00	40.00
VERVE					
❏ MGV-1001 [M]	Bob Scobey's Band	1956	10.00	20.00	40.00
❏ V-1001 [M]	Bob Scobey's Band	1961	5.00	10.00	20.00
❏ MGV-1009 [M]	Music from Bourbon Street	1956	10.00	20.00	40.00
❏ V-1009 [M]	Music from Bourbon Street	1961	5.00	10.00	20.00
❏ MGV-1011 [M]	The San Francisco Jazz of Bob Scobey	1957	10.00	20.00	40.00
❏ V-1011 [M]	The San Francisco Jazz of Bob Scobey	1961	5.00	10.00	20.00
SCOFIELD, JOHN					
Guitarist, bass player and bandleader.					
ARISTA/NOVUS					
❏ AN 3018	Who's Who?	1980	3.00	6.00	12.00
BLUE NOTE					
❏ B1-92894	Time on My Hands	1990	3.75	7.50	15.00
ENJA					
❏ 4004	Shinola	1981	3.00	6.00	12.00
❏ 4038	Out Like a Light	1982	3.00	6.00	12.00
GRAMAVISION					
❏ GR-8405	Electric Outlet	1984	2.50	5.00	10.00
❏ 18-8508-1	Still Warm	1985	2.50	5.00	10.00
❏ R1-79400	Flat Out	1989	3.00	6.00	12.00
INNER CITY					
❏ IC-3022	John Scofield Live	197?	3.75	7.50	15.00
❏ IC-3030	Rough House	1979	3.00	6.00	12.00
SCOOBY DOO					
ZEPHYR					
❏ ZMP-12002 [M]	Jerry Leiber Presents Scooby Doo	1959	12.50	25.00	50.00
SCOTT, BOBBY					
Pianist, male singer and composer. His best-known composition is "A Taste of Honey."					
ABC-PARAMOUNT					
❏ ABC-102 [M]	Scott Free	1956	12.50	25.00	50.00
❏ ABC-148 [M]	Bobby Scott and Two Horns	1957	12.50	25.00	50.00
ATLANTIC					
❏ 1341 [M]	The Compleat Musician	1960	5.00	10.00	20.00
-- Multicolor label, white "fan" logo at right					
❏ SD 1341 [S]	The Compleat Musician	1960	6.25	12.50	25.00
-- Multicolor label, white "fan" logo at right					
❏ 1355 [M]	A Taste of Honey	1960	5.00	10.00	20.00
-- Multicolor label, white "fan" logo at right					
❏ SD 1355 [S]	A Taste of Honey	1960	6.25	12.50	25.00
-- Multicolor label, white "fan" logo at right					
BETHLEHEM					
❏ BCP-8 [M]	The Compositions of Bobby Scott	1957	12.50	25.00	50.00
❏ BCP-1004 [10]	Great Scott	1954	30.00	60.00	120.00
❏ BCP-1009 [10]	The Compositions of Bobby Scott, Volume 1	1954	25.00	50.00	100.00
❏ BCP-1029 [10]	The Compositions of Bobby Scott, Volume 2	1955	25.00	50.00	100.00
MERCURY					
❏ MG-20701 [M]	Joyful Noises	1962	5.00	10.00	20.00

Number	Title	Yr	VG	VG+	NM
❏ MG-20767 [M]	When the Feeling Hits You	1963	5.00	10.00	20.00
❏ MG-20854 [M]	108 Pounds of Heartache	1963	5.00	10.00	20.00
❏ MG-20995 [M]	I Had a Ball	1964	5.00	10.00	20.00
❏ SR-60701 [S]	Joyful Noises	1962	6.25	12.50	25.00
❏ SR-60767 [S]	When the Feeling Hits You	1963	6.25	12.50	25.00
❏ SR-60854 [S]	108 Pounds of Heartache	1963	6.25	12.50	25.00
❏ SR-60995 [S]	I Had a Ball	1964	6.25	12.50	25.00

VERVE

Number	Title	Yr	VG	VG+	NM
❏ MGV-2106 [M]	Bobby Scott Sings the Best of Lerner and Loewe	1958	12.50	25.00	50.00
❏ V-2106 [M]	Bobby Scott Sings the Best of Lerner and Loewe	1961	6.25	12.50	25.00
❏ V6-2106 [S]	Bobby Scott Sings the Best of Lerner and Loewe	1961	5.00	10.00	20.00
❏ MGVS-6030 [S]	Bobby Scott Sings the Best of Lerner and Loewe	1960	10.00	20.00	40.00
❏ MGVS-6031 [S]	Serenate -- Bobby Scott, Pianist	1960	10.00	20.00	40.00
❏ MGVS-6065 [S]	Bobby Scott Plays the Music of Leonard Bernstein	1960	10.00	20.00	40.00
❏ MGV-8297 [M]	Serenate -- Bobby Scott, Pianist	1959	12.50	25.00	50.00
❏ V-8297 [M]	Serenate -- Bobby Scott, Pianist	1961	6.25	12.50	25.00
❏ V6-8297 [S]	Serenate -- Bobby Scott, Pianist	1961	5.00	10.00	20.00
❏ MGV-8326 [M]	Bobby Scott Plays the Music of Leonard Bernstein	1959	12.50	25.00	50.00
❏ V-8326 [M]	Bobby Scott Plays the Music of Leonard Bernstein	1961	6.25	12.50	25.00
❏ V6-8326 [S]	Bobby Scott Plays the Music of Leonard Bernstein	1961	5.00	10.00	20.00

SCOTT, CLIFFORD
Tenor saxophone player and flutist.
WORLD PACIFIC

Number	Title	Yr	VG	VG+	NM
❏ ST-1811 [S]	The Big Ones	1964	20.00	40.00	80.00
-- Green vinyl					
❏ ST-1811 [S]	The Big Ones	1964	7.50	15.00	30.00
-- Black vinyl					
❏ WP-1811 [M]	The Big Ones	1964	15.00	30.00	60.00
-- Green vinyl					
❏ WP-1811 [M]	The Big Ones	1964	5.00	10.00	20.00
-- Black vinyl					
❏ ST-1825 [S]	Lavender Sax	1964	10.00	20.00	40.00
❏ WP-1825 [M]	Lavender Sax	1964	7.50	15.00	30.00

SCOTT, CLIFFORD, AND LES McCANN
Also see each artist's individual listings.
PACIFIC JAZZ

Number	Title	Yr	VG	VG+	NM
❏ PJ-66 [M]	Out Front	1963	5.00	10.00	20.00
-- Black vinyl					
❏ PJ-66 [M]	Out Front	1963	10.00	20.00	40.00
-- Colored vinyl					
❏ ST-66 [S]	Out Front	1963	12.50	25.00	50.00
-- Colored vinyl					
❏ ST-66 [S]	Out Front	1963	6.25	12.50	25.00
-- Black vinyl					

SCOTT, HAZEL
Pianist and female singer.
CAPITOL

Number	Title	Yr	VG	VG+	NM
❏ H 364 [10]	Late Show	1953	20.00	40.00	80.00

COLUMBIA

Number	Title	Yr	VG	VG+	NM
❏ CL 6090 [10]	Great Scott	1950	20.00	40.00	80.00

CORAL

Number	Title	Yr	VG	VG+	NM
❏ CRL 56057 [10]	Hazel Scott	1952	20.00	40.00	80.00

DEBUT

Number	Title	Yr	VG	VG+	NM
❏ DLP-16 [10]	Relaxed Piano Moods	1955	50.00	100.00	200.00

DECCA

Number	Title	Yr	VG	VG+	NM
❏ DL 5130 [10]	Swinging the Classics	1950	20.00	40.00	80.00
❏ DL 8474 [M]	'Round Midnight	1957	10.00	20.00	40.00

FANTASY

Number	Title	Yr	VG	VG+	NM
❏ OJC-1702	Relaxed Piano Moods	1985	2.50	5.00	10.00

TIOCH

Number	Title	Yr	VG	VG+	NM
❏ TD-1013	Afterhours	198?	2.50	5.00	10.00

SCOTT, JIMMY
Male singer.
SAVOY

Number	Title	Yr	VG	VG+	NM
❏ MG-12027 [M]	Very Truly Yours	1955	15.00	30.00	60.00
❏ MG-12150 [M]	The Fabulous Little Jimmy Scott	1959	10.00	20.00	40.00
❏ MG-12181 [M]	If You Only Knew	1963	10.00	20.00	40.00
❏ MG-12300 [M]	Very Truly Yours	1969	3.75	7.50	15.00
❏ MG-12301 [M]	The Fabulous Songs of Jimmy	1969	3.75	7.50	15.00
❏ MG-12302 [M]	The Fabulous Voice of Jimmy	1969	3.75	7.50	15.00

TANGERINE

Number	Title	Yr	VG	VG+	NM
❏ TRC-1501 [M]	Falling in Love Is Wonderful	1963	3.75	7.50	15.00

Number	Title	Yr	VG	VG+	NM
❏ TRCS-1501 [S]	Falling in Love Is Wonderful	1963	5.00	10.00	20.00

SCOTT, ROBERT WILLIAM
WARNER BROS.

Number	Title	Yr	VG	VG+	NM
❏ WS 1886	In Memory of the Race	1970	3.75	7.50	15.00

SCOTT, SHIRLEY
Organist, pianist and female singer.
ABC IMPULSE!

Number	Title	Yr	VG	VG+	NM
❏ AS-51 [S]	For Members Only	1968	3.75	7.50	15.00
❏ AS-67 [S]	Great Scott!	1968	3.75	7.50	15.00
❏ AS-73 [S]	Everybody Loves a Lover	1968	3.75	7.50	15.00
❏ AS-81 [S]	Queen of the Organ	1968	3.75	7.50	15.00
❏ AS-93 [S]	Latin Shadows	1968	3.75	7.50	15.00
❏ AS-9109	On a Clear Day	1968	3.75	7.50	15.00
❏ AS-9119	Shirley Scott Plays the Big Bands	1968	3.75	7.50	15.00
❏ AS-9141	Girl Talk	1967	3.75	7.50	15.00
❏ IA-9341 [(2)]	The Great Live Sessions	1978	3.75	7.50	15.00

ATLANTIC

Number	Title	Yr	VG	VG+	NM
❏ SD 1515	Soul Song	1968	3.75	7.50	15.00
❏ SD 1532	Soul Saxes	1969	3.75	7.50	15.00
❏ SD 1561	Something	1970	3.75	7.50	15.00

CADET

Number	Title	Yr	VG	VG+	NM
❏ CA-50009	Mystical Lady	1972	3.00	6.00	12.00
❏ CA-50025	Lean On Me	1972	3.00	6.00	12.00
❏ CA-50036	Superstition	1973	3.00	6.00	12.00

FANTASY

Number	Title	Yr	VG	VG+	NM
❏ OJC-328	Blue Flames	1988	2.50	5.00	10.00

IMPULSE!

Number	Title	Yr	VG	VG+	NM
❏ A-51 [M]	For Members Only	1963	5.00	10.00	20.00
❏ AS-51 [S]	For Members Only	1963	6.25	12.50	25.00
❏ A-67 [M]	Great Scott!	1964	5.00	10.00	20.00
❏ AS-67 [S]	Great Scott!	1964	6.25	12.50	25.00
❏ A-73 [M]	Everybody Loves a Lover	1964	5.00	10.00	20.00
❏ AS-73 [S]	Everybody Loves a Lover	1964	6.25	12.50	25.00
❏ A-81 [M]	Queen of the Organ	1965	5.00	10.00	20.00
❏ AS-81 [S]	Queen of the Organ	1965	6.25	12.50	25.00
❏ A-93 [M]	Latin Shadows	1965	5.00	10.00	20.00
❏ AS-93 [S]	Latin Shadows	1965	6.25	12.50	25.00
❏ A-9109 [M]	On a Clear Day	1967	6.25	12.50	25.00
❏ AS-9109 [S]	On a Clear Day	1967	5.00	10.00	20.00
❏ A-9119 [M]	Shirley Scott Plays the Big Bands	1966	5.00	10.00	20.00
❏ AS-9119 [S]	Shirley Scott Plays the Big Bands	1966	6.25	12.50	25.00
❏ A-9141 [M]	Girl Talk	1967	7.50	15.00	30.00
❏ AS-9141 [S]	Girl Talk	1967	5.00	10.00	20.00

MCA

Number	Title	Yr	VG	VG+	NM
❏ 4152 [(2)]	The Great Live Sessions	1980	3.00	6.00	12.00

MOODSVILLE

Number	Title	Yr	VG	VG+	NM
❏ MVLP-5 [M]	Shirley Scott Trio	1960	12.50	25.00	50.00
-- Green label					
❏ MVLP-5 [M]	Shirley Scott Trio	1965	6.25	12.50	25.00
-- Blue label, trident logo at right					
❏ MVLP-19 [M]	Like Cozy	1961	12.50	25.00	50.00
-- Green label					
❏ MVLP-19 [M]	Like Cozy	1965	6.25	12.50	25.00
-- Blue label, trident logo at right					
❏ MVST-19 [S]	Like Cozy	1961	12.50	25.00	50.00
-- Green label					
❏ MVST-19 [S]	Like Cozy	1965	6.25	12.50	25.00
-- Blue label, trident logo at right					

MUSE

Number	Title	Yr	VG	VG+	NM
❏ MR-5388	Oasis	1990	3.00	6.00	12.00

PRESTIGE

Number	Title	Yr	VG	VG+	NM
❏ PRLP-7143 [M]	Great Scott!	1958	12.50	25.00	50.00
❏ PRLP-7155 [M]	Scottie	1959	12.50	25.00	50.00
❏ PRLP-7163 [M]	Scottie Plays Duke	1959	12.50	25.00	50.00
❏ PRLP-7173 [M]	Soul Searching	1960	12.50	25.00	50.00
❏ PRLP-7182 [M]	Mucho, Mucho	1960	12.50	25.00	50.00
❏ PRLP-7195 [M]	Shirley's Sounds	1961	10.00	20.00	40.00
❏ PRST-7195 [S]	Shirley's Sounds	1961	12.50	25.00	50.00
❏ PRLP-7205 [M]	Hip Soul	1961	10.00	20.00	40.00
-- Yellow label, Bergenfield, NJ address					
❏ PRLP-7205 [M]	Hip Soul	1965	5.00	10.00	20.00
-- Blue label, trident logo at right					
❏ PRLP-7226 [M]	Hip Twist	1962	10.00	20.00	40.00
-- Yellow label, Bergenfield, NJ address					
❏ PRLP-7226 [M]	Hip Twist	1965	5.00	10.00	20.00
-- Blue label, trident logo at right					
❏ PRST-7226 [S]	Hip Twist	1962	12.50	25.00	50.00
-- Silver label, Bergenfield, NJ address					
❏ PRST-7226 [S]	Hip Twist	1965	6.25	12.50	25.00
-- Blue label, trident logo at right					
❏ PRLP-7240 [M]	Shirley Scott Plays Horace Silver	1962	10.00	20.00	40.00

Number	Title	Yr	VG	VG+	NM
❑ PRST-7240 [S]	Shirley Scott Plays Horace Silver	1962	12.50	25.00	50.00
❑ PRLP-7262 [M]	Happy Talk	1963	10.00	20.00	40.00
❑ PRST-7262 [S]	Happy Talk	1963	12.50	25.00	50.00
❑ PRLP-7267 [M]	The Soul Is Willing	1963	10.00	20.00	40.00
-- Yellow label, Bergenfield, NJ address					
❑ PRLP-7267 [M]	The Soul Is Willing	1965	5.00	10.00	20.00
-- Blue label, trident logo at right					
❑ PRST-7267 [S]	The Soul Is Willing	1963	12.50	25.00	50.00
-- Silver label, Bergenfield, NJ address					
❑ PRST-7267 [S]	The Soul Is Willing	1965	6.25	12.50	25.00
-- Blue label, trident logo at right					
❑ PRLP-7283 [M]	Satin Doll	1963	10.00	20.00	40.00
❑ PRST-7283 [S]	Satin Doll	1963	12.50	25.00	50.00
❑ PRLP-7305 [M]	Drag 'Em Out	1964	10.00	20.00	40.00
❑ PRST-7305 [S]	Drag 'Em Out	1964	12.50	25.00	50.00
❑ PRLP-7312 [M]	Soul Shoutin'	1964	10.00	20.00	40.00
-- Yellow label, Bergenfield, NJ address					
❑ PRLP-7312 [M]	Soul Shoutin'	1965	5.00	10.00	20.00
-- Blue label, trident logo at right					
❑ PRST-7312 [S]	Soul Shoutin'	1964	12.50	25.00	50.00
-- Silver label, Bergenfield, NJ address					
❑ PRST-7312 [S]	Soul Shoutin'	1965	6.25	12.50	25.00
-- Blue label, trident logo at right					
❑ PRLP-7328 [M]	Travelin' Light	1964	6.25	12.50	25.00
❑ PRST-7328 [S]	Travelin' Light	1964	7.50	15.00	30.00
❑ PRLP-7338 [M]	Blue Flames	1965	6.25	12.50	25.00
❑ PRST-7338 [S]	Blue Flames	1965	7.50	15.00	30.00
❑ PRLP-7360 [M]	Sweet Soul	1965	6.25	12.50	25.00
❑ PRST-7360 [S]	Sweet Soul	1965	7.50	15.00	30.00
❑ PRLP-7376 [M]	Blue Seven	1965	6.25	12.50	25.00
❑ PRST-7376 [S]	Blue Seven	1965	7.50	15.00	30.00
❑ PRLP-7392 [M]	Soul Sisters	1965	6.25	12.50	25.00
❑ PRST-7392 [S]	Soul Sisters	1965	7.50	15.00	30.00
❑ PRLP-7424 [M]	Workin'	1966	6.25	12.50	25.00
❑ PRST-7424 [S]	Workin'	1966	7.50	15.00	30.00
❑ PRLP-7440 [M]	Now's the Time	1967	7.50	15.00	30.00
❑ PRST-7440 [S]	Now's the Time	1967	6.25	12.50	25.00
❑ PRST-7456 [S]	Stompin'	1968	6.25	12.50	25.00
❑ PRST-7707	The Best of Shirley Scott and Stanley Turrentine	1969	5.00	10.00	20.00
❑ PRST-7773	The Best for Beautiful People	1970	5.00	10.00	20.00
❑ PRST-7845	The Soul Is Willing	1971	3.75	7.50	15.00
STRATA-EAST					
❑ SES-7430	One for Me	197?	5.00	10.00	20.00

SCOTT, SHIRLEY, AND CLARK TERRY
Also see each artist's individual listings.
ABC IMPULSE!

Number	Title	Yr	VG	VG+	NM
❑ AS-9133 [S]	Soul Duo	1968	3.75	7.50	15.00
IMPULSE!					
❑ A-9133 [M]	Soul Duo	1967	6.25	12.50	25.00
❑ AS-9133 [S]	Soul Duo	1967	5.00	10.00	20.00

SCOTT, TOM
Saxophone player and flutist.
A&M

Number	Title	Yr	VG	VG+	NM
❑ SP-4330	Great Scott!	1972	3.75	7.50	15.00
ABC IMPULSE!					
❑ A-9163 [M]	Honeysuckle Breeze	1967	10.00	20.00	40.00
❑ AS-9163 [S]	Honeysuckle Breeze	1967	6.25	12.50	25.00
❑ AS-9171	Rural Still Life	1968	6.25	12.50	25.00
ATLANTIC					
❑ 80106	Target	1983	2.50	5.00	10.00
COLUMBIA					
❑ JC 35557	Intimate Strangers	1978	2.50	5.00	10.00
❑ PC 35557	Intimate Strangers	198?	2.00	4.00	8.00
-- Budget-line reissue					
❑ JC 36137	Street Beat	1979	2.50	5.00	10.00
❑ JC 36352	The Best of Tom Scott	1980	2.50	5.00	10.00
❑ FC 37419	Apple Juice	1981	2.50	5.00	10.00
ELEKTRA/MUSICIAN					
❑ 60162	Desire	1982	2.50	5.00	10.00
FLYING DUTCHMAN					
❑ 106	Hair	1969	5.00	10.00	20.00
❑ 114	Paint Your Wagon	1970	5.00	10.00	20.00
❑ BXL1-0833	Tom Scott in L.A.	1975	2.50	5.00	10.00
❑ AYL1-3875	Tom Scott in L.A.	1980	2.00	4.00	8.00
-- "Best Buy Series" reissue					
GRP					
❑ GR-1044	Streamlines	1987	2.50	5.00	10.00
❑ GR-9571	Flashpoint	1988	2.50	5.00	10.00
MCA					
❑ 29060	Rural Still Life	198?	2.00	4.00	8.00
-- Reissue of Impulse 9171					

Number	Title	Yr	VG	VG+	NM
ODE					
❑ PE 34952	Tom Scott and the L.A. Express	1977	2.00	4.00	8.00
-- Reissue of 77021					
❑ PE 34956	Tom Cat	1977	2.00	4.00	8.00
-- Reissue of 77029					
❑ PE 34959	New York Connection	1977	2.00	4.00	8.00
-- Reissue of 77033					
❑ PE 34966	Blow It Out	1977	2.50	5.00	10.00
❑ SP-77021	Tom Scott and the L.A. Express	1974	2.50	5.00	10.00
❑ SP-77029	Tom Cat	1975	2.50	5.00	10.00
❑ SP-77033	New York Connection	1976	2.50	5.00	10.00

SCOTT, TONY
Clarinetist, baritone saxophone player and pianist. Also see THE MODERN JAZZ SOCIETY; ZOOT SIMS.
ABC-PARAMOUNT

Number	Title	Yr	VG	VG+	NM
❑ ABC-235 [M]	South Pacific	1958	7.50	15.00	30.00
❑ ABCS-235 [S]	South Pacific	1958	6.25	12.50	25.00
BRUNSWICK					
❑ BL 54021 [M]	Tony Scott In Hi-Fi	1957	20.00	40.00	80.00
❑ BL 54056 [M]	Tony Scott Quartet	1957	30.00	60.00	120.00
❑ BL 58040 [10]	Music After Midnight	1953	30.00	60.00	120.00
❑ BL 58056 [10]	Tony Scott Quartet	1954	30.00	60.00	120.00
CORAL					
❑ CRL 57239 [M]	52nd Street Scene	1958	12.50	25.00	50.00
❑ CRL 757239 [S]	52nd Street Scene	1958	10.00	20.00	40.00
MUSE					
❑ MR-5230	Golden Moments	198?	2.50	5.00	10.00
❑ MR-5266	I'll Remember	198?	2.50	5.00	10.00
PERFECT					
❑ PL-12010 [M]	My Kind of Jazz	1960	10.00	20.00	40.00
❑ PL-14010 [S]	My Kind of Jazz	1960	12.50	25.00	50.00
RCA VICTOR					
❑ LJM-1022 [M]	Scott's Fling	1955	20.00	40.00	80.00
❑ LPM-1268 [M]	Both Sides of Tony Scott	1956	20.00	40.00	80.00
❑ LPM-1353 [M]	A Touch of Tony Scott	1956	20.00	40.00	80.00
❑ LPM-1452 [M]	The Complete Tony Scott	1957	20.00	40.00	80.00
SEECO					
❑ SLP-425 [M]	The Modern Art of Jazz	1959	7.50	15.00	30.00
❑ SLP-428 [M]	Hi-Fi Land of Jazz	1959	7.50	15.00	30.00
❑ SLP-4250 [S]	The Modern Art of Jazz	1959	10.00	20.00	40.00
❑ SLP-4280 [S]	Hi-Fi Land of Jazz	1959	10.00	20.00	40.00
SIGNATURE					
❑ SM-6001 [M]	Gypsy	1959	12.50	25.00	50.00
❑ SS-6001 [S]	Gypsy	1959	10.00	20.00	40.00
SOUL NOTE					
❑ SN-1083	African Bird: Come Back! Mother Africa	1984	3.00	6.00	12.00
SUNNYSIDE					
❑ SSC-1015	Sung Heroes	1987	2.50	5.00	10.00
VERVE					
❑ V-8634 [M]	Music for Zen Meditation	1965	3.75	7.50	15.00
❑ V6-8634 [S]	Music for Zen Meditation	1965	5.00	10.00	20.00
❑ V-8742 [M]	Music for Yoga Meditation and Other Joys	1967	5.00	10.00	20.00
❑ V6-8742 [S]	Music for Yoga Meditation and Other Joys	1967	3.75	7.50	15.00
❑ V6-8788 [S]	Homage to Lord Krishna	1969	3.75	7.50	15.00

SCOTT, TONY, AND TERRY GIBBS
Also see each artist's individual listings.
BRUNSWICK

Number	Title	Yr	VG	VG+	NM
❑ BL 58058 [10]	Hi-Fi Jazz	1955	30.00	60.00	120.00

SCOTT, TONY, AND JIMMY KNEPPER
Also see each artist's individual listings.
CARLTON

Number	Title	Yr	VG	VG+	NM
❑ LP-12-113 [M]	Free Blown Jazz	1959	12.50	25.00	50.00
❑ ST-12-113 [S]	Free Blown Jazz	1959	12.50	25.00	50.00

SCOTT, TONY, AND MAT MATTHEWS
Also see each artist's individual listings.
BRUNSWICK

Number	Title	Yr	VG	VG+	NM
❑ BL 58057 [10]	Jazz for GI's	1954	30.00	60.00	120.00

SCOTT-HERON, GIL
Male singer (proto-rapper), pianist and composer.
ARISTA

Number	Title	Yr	VG	VG+	NM
❑ AL 4030	The First Minute of a New Day	1975	2.50	5.00	10.00
❑ AL 4044	From South Africa to South	1975	2.50	5.00	10.00
❑ AL 4147	Bridges	1977	2.50	5.00	10.00
❑ AB 4189	Secrets	1978	2.50	5.00	10.00

Number	Title	Yr	VG	VG+	NM
A2L 5001 [(2)]	It's Your World	1976	3.00	6.00	12.00
AL 8248	The Best of Gil Scott-Heron	1984	2.50	5.00	10.00
AL 8301	The Mind of Gil Scott-Heron	1980	3.75	7.50	15.00
ALB6-8306	The Best of Gil Scott-Heron	1985	2.00	4.00	8.00

-- Reissue of 8248

Number	Title	Yr	VG	VG+	NM
AL 9514	1980	1980	2.50	5.00	10.00
AL 9540	Real Eyes	1980	2.50	5.00	10.00
AL 9566	Reflections	1981	2.50	5.00	10.00
AL 9606	Moving Target	1982	2.50	5.00	10.00

BLUEBIRD

| 6994-1-RB | The Revolution Will Not Be Televised | 1988 | 3.00 | 6.00 | 12.00 |

FLYING DUTCHMAN

| BLD1-0613 | The Revolution Will Not Be Televised | 1974 | 5.00 | 10.00 | 20.00 |
| BXL1-0613 | The Revolution Will Not Be Televised | 1978 | 3.00 | 6.00 | 12.00 |

-- Reissue with new prefix

| BXL1-2834 | Pieces of a Man | 1978 | 3.00 | 6.00 | 12.00 |

-- Reissue of 10143

| AYL1-3818 | The Revolution Will Not Be Televised | 1980 | 2.00 | 4.00 | 8.00 |

-- "Best Buy Series" reissue

| AYL1-3819 | Pieces of a Man | 1980 | 2.00 | 4.00 | 8.00 |

-- "Best Buy Series" reissue

| FD-10143 | Pieces of a Man | 1971 | 5.00 | 10.00 | 20.00 |
| FD-10153 | Free Will | 1972 | 5.00 | 10.00 | 20.00 |

STRATA-EAST

| SES-19742 | Winter in America | 1974 | 6.25 | 12.50 | 25.00 |

SEALY, JOE
Pianist and composer.
SACKVILLE

| 4007 | Clear Vision | 198? | 2.50 | 5.00 | 10.00 |

SEARS, AL
Tenor saxophone player.
AUDIO LAB

| AL-1540 [M] | Dance Music with a Swing Beat | 1959 | 30.00 | 60.00 | 120.00 |

SWINGVILLE

| SVLP-2018 [M] | Swing's the Thing | 1961 | 12.50 | 25.00 | 50.00 |

-- Purple label

| SVLP-2018 [M] | Swing's the Thing | 1965 | 6.25 | 12.50 | 25.00 |

-- Blue label, trident logo at right

SEBESKY, DON
Composer, arranger and trombonist.
CTI

| CTX-6031/2 [(2)] | Giant Box | 1974 | 3.75 | 7.50 | 15.00 |
| 6061 | The Rape of El Morro | 197? | 3.00 | 6.00 | 12.00 |

DOCTOR JAZZ

| FW 40155 | Moving Lines | 1986 | 2.50 | 5.00 | 10.00 |

GNP CRESCENDO

| GNPS-2164 | Full Circle | 198? | 2.50 | 5.00 | 10.00 |

GRYPHON

| 791 [(2)] | Three Works for Jazz Soloists and Symphony Orchestra | 1980 | 3.75 | 7.50 | 15.00 |

MOBILE FIDELITY

| 1-503 [(2)] | Three Works for Jazz Soloists and Symphony Orchestra | 198? | 15.00 | 30.00 | 60.00 |

-- Audiophile vinyl

VERVE

| V6-8756 | Don Sebesky and the Jazz-Rock Syndrome | 1968 | 5.00 | 10.00 | 20.00 |

SEEGER, BERT
Pianist.
ANTILLES

| AN-7086 | Time to Burn | 198? | 2.50 | 5.00 | 10.00 |
| AN-7088 | Because They Can | 198? | 2.50 | 5.00 | 10.00 |

SEGAL, GEORGE
Banjo player. Better known as an actor.
PHILIPS

| PHM 200-242 [M] | The Yama-Yama Man | 1967 | 5.00 | 10.00 | 20.00 |
| PHS 600-242 [S] | The Yama-Yama Man | 1967 | 5.00 | 10.00 | 20.00 |

SIGNATURE

| BSL1-0654 | A Touch of Ragtime | 1976 | 3.75 | 7.50 | 15.00 |

SEIFERT, ZBIGNIEW
Violinist.
CAPITOL

| ST-11618 | Zbigniew Seifert | 197? | 3.00 | 6.00 | 12.00 |

PAUSA

| 7077 | Man of the Light | 1979 | 2.50 | 5.00 | 10.00 |

SENENSKY, BERNIE
Pianist.
PM

| 006 | New Life | 197? | 3.00 | 6.00 | 12.00 |
| 021 | Free Spirit | 1986 | 2.50 | 5.00 | 10.00 |

SERRANO, PAUL
Trumpeter.
RIVERSIDE

| RLP-359 [M] | Blues Holiday | 1961 | 6.25 | 12.50 | 25.00 |
| RS-9359 [S] | Blues Holiday | 1961 | 7.50 | 15.00 | 30.00 |

SERRY, JOHN
Keyboard player.
CHRYSALIS

| CHS 1279 | Jazziz | 1979 | 2.50 | 5.00 | 10.00 |

SERTL, DOUG
Trombonist.
DISCOVERY

| 920 | Groovin' | 1986 | 2.50 | 5.00 | 10.00 |

SETE, BOLA
Guitarist. Also see VINCE GUARALDI.
ANALOGUE PRODUCTIONS

| APR 3003 | Tour de Force | 199? | 3.75 | 7.50 | 15.00 |

COLUMBIA

| KC 32375 | Goin' to Rio | 1973 | 3.00 | 6.00 | 12.00 |

DANCING CAT

| DC-3005 | Jungle Suite | 1985 | 3.00 | 6.00 | 12.00 |

FANTASY

OJC-286	Bossa Nova	1987	2.50	5.00	10.00
OJC-288	The Incomparable Bola Sete	1987	2.50	5.00	10.00
OJC-290	Autentico!	1987	2.50	5.00	10.00
3349 [M]	Bossa Nova	1963	3.75	7.50	15.00
3358 [M]	Tour de Force	1965	3.75	7.50	15.00
3364 [M]	The Incomparable Bola Sete	1965	3.75	7.50	15.00
3369 [M]	The Solo Guitar of Bola Sete	1966	3.75	7.50	15.00
3375 [M]	Autentico!	1966	3.75	7.50	15.00
8349 [S]	Bossa Nova	1963	5.00	10.00	20.00
8358 [S]	Tour de Force	1965	5.00	10.00	20.00
8364 [S]	The Incomparable Bola Sete	1965	5.00	10.00	20.00
8369 [S]	The Solo Guitar of Bola Sete	1966	5.00	10.00	20.00
8375 [S]	Autentico!	1966	5.00	10.00	20.00
8417	Shebaba	1971	3.00	6.00	12.00

LOST LAKE ARTS

| 82 | Ocean | 198? | 2.50 | 5.00 | 10.00 |

-- Reissue of Takoma LP

PARAMOUNT

| PAS-5011 | Workin' on a Groovy Thing | 1970 | 3.75 | 7.50 | 15.00 |

TAKOMA

| C-1049 | Ocean | 197? | 3.00 | 6.00 | 12.00 |

VERVE

| V-8689 [M] | Bola Sete At the Monterey Jazz Festival | 1967 | 5.00 | 10.00 | 20.00 |
| V6-8689 [S] | Bola Sete At the Monterey Jazz Festival | 1967 | 3.75 | 7.50 | 15.00 |

SETZER, BRIAN, ORCHESTRA
Guitarist formerly with rockabilly revival band Stray Cats, Setzer helped spur the late-1990s "swing" revival with the below LP.
INTERSCOPE

| 90183 | The Dirty Boogie | 1998 | 3.75 | 7.50 | 15.00 |

SEVENTH AVENUE
Members: Vincent Green (saxophones); Kenery Smith (bass); Ben Johnson (drums); Phillip Seed (guitar).
I.T.I.

| JL-022 | Heads Up | 1986 | 3.00 | 6.00 | 12.00 |

SEVENTH AVENUE STOMPERS
SAVOY JAZZ

| SJL-1139 | Fidgety Feet | 198? | 2.50 | 5.00 | 10.00 |

SEVERINSON, DOC
Trumpeter and bandleader.
ABC

| S-737 | 16 Great Performances | 1971 | 2.50 | 5.00 | 10.00 |

Number	Title	Yr	VG	VG+	NM
❑ X-771	Trumpets, Crumpets	1973	2.50	5.00	10.00

AMHERST

Number	Title	Yr	VG	VG+	NM
❑ AMH-3311	The Tonight Show Band with Doc Severinson	1986	2.50	5.00	10.00
❑ AMH-3312	The Tonight Show Band with Doc Severinson, Vol. II	1987	2.50	5.00	10.00
❑ AMH-3319	Facets	1988	2.50	5.00	10.00

ARCHIVE OF FOLK AND JAZZ

Number	Title	Yr	VG	VG+	NM
❑ 334	Doc Severinson and Friends	1978	2.50	5.00	10.00

COMMAND

Number	Title	Yr	VG	VG+	NM
❑ RS 33-819 [M]	Tempestuous Trumpet	1961	3.75	7.50	15.00
❑ RS 819 SD [S]	Tempestuous Trumpet	1961	5.00	10.00	20.00
❑ RS 33-837 [M]	The Big Band's Back in Town	1962	3.75	7.50	15.00
❑ RS 837 SD [S]	The Big Band's Back in Town	1962	5.00	10.00	20.00
❑ RS 33-859 [M]	Torch Songs for Trumpet	1963	3.75	7.50	15.00
❑ RS 859 SD [S]	Torch Songs for Trumpet	1963	5.00	10.00	20.00
❑ RS 33-883 [M]	High, Wide and Wonderful	1965	3.75	7.50	15.00
❑ RS 883 SD [S]	High, Wide and Wonderful	1965	5.00	10.00	20.00
❑ RS 33-893 [M]	Fever!	1966	3.00	6.00	12.00
❑ RS 893 SD [S]	Fever!	1966	3.75	7.50	15.00
❑ RS 33-901 [M]	Live!	1966	3.00	6.00	12.00
❑ RS 901 SD [S]	Live!	1966	3.75	7.50	15.00
❑ RS 33-904 [M]	Command Performances	1966	3.00	6.00	12.00
❑ RS 904 SD [S]	Command Performances	1966	3.75	7.50	15.00
❑ RS 33-909 [M]	Swinging and Singing	1967	3.75	7.50	15.00
❑ RS 909 SD [S]	Swinging and Singing	1967	3.00	6.00	12.00
❑ RS 33-917 [M]	The New Sound	1967	3.75	7.50	15.00
❑ RS 917 SD [S]	The New Sound	1967	3.00	6.00	12.00
❑ RS 927 SD	The Great Arrival	1968	3.00	6.00	12.00
❑ RS 937 SD	Doc Severinson with Strings	1969	3.00	6.00	12.00
❑ RS 950 SD	The Closet	1970	3.00	6.00	12.00
❑ RS 952 SD	The Best of Doc Severinson	1970	3.00	6.00	12.00
❑ QD-40003 [Q]	Fever!	1972	3.75	7.50	15.00

EPIC

Number	Title	Yr	VG	VG+	NM
❑ PE 34078	Night Journey	1976	2.50	5.00	10.00
❑ PE 34925	A Brand New Thing	1977	2.50	5.00	10.00

FIRSTLINE

Number	Title	Yr	VG	VG+	NM
❑ FDLP 5001	London Sessions	1980	3.00	6.00	12.00

JUNO

Number	Title	Yr	VG	VG+	NM
❑ 1001	I Feel Good	1970	3.00	6.00	12.00

MCA

Number	Title	Yr	VG	VG+	NM
❑ 4168 [(2)]	The Best of Doc Severinson	198?	2.50	5.00	10.00

PICKWICK

Number	Title	Yr	VG	VG+	NM
❑ SPC-3608	Torch Songs for Trumpet	1978	2.00	4.00	8.00

RCA VICTOR

Number	Title	Yr	VG	VG+	NM
❑ APL1-0273	Rhapsody for Now!	1973	3.00	6.00	12.00
❑ LSP-4522	Brass Roots	1971	3.00	6.00	12.00
❑ AFL1-4669	Doc	1977	2.50	5.00	10.00
-- Reissue with new prefix					
❑ LSP-4669	Doc	1972	3.00	6.00	12.00

SEVERSON, PAUL
Trombonist.
ACADEMY

Number	Title	Yr	VG	VG+	NM
❑ MWJ-1 [M]	Midwest Jazz	1956	12.50	25.00	50.00

SEVILLA, JORGE
Guitarist.
VERVE

Number	Title	Yr	VG	VG+	NM
❑ MGVS-6103 [S]	The Incredible Guitar of Jorge Sevilla	1960	10.00	20.00	40.00
❑ MGV-8342 [M]	The Incredible Guitar of Jorge Sevilla	1959	12.50	25.00	50.00
❑ V-8342 [M]	The Incredible Guitar of Jorge Sevilla	1961	6.25	12.50	25.00
❑ V6-8342 [S]	The Incredible Guitar of Jorge Sevilla	1961	5.00	10.00	20.00

SHAKATAK
Members: Bill Sharpe (keyboards); Keith Winter (guitar); Roger Odell (drums); Jill Saward (vocals); George Anderson (bass).
POLYDOR

Number	Title	Yr	VG	VG+	NM
❑ 823 017-1	Drivin' Hard	1987	2.50	5.00	10.00
❑ 839 578-1	Manic and Cool	1989	3.00	6.00	12.00

SHANK, BUD
Alto saxophone player and flutist. Also see LAURINDO ALMEIDA; CHET BAKER.
BAINBRIDGE

Number	Title	Yr	VG	VG+	NM
❑ CRS-6830	Live at the Haig	1985	2.50	5.00	10.00

CONCORD CONCERTO

Number	Title	Yr	VG	VG+	NM
❑ CC-2002	Explorations 1980: Suite for Flute and Piano	1981	2.50	5.00	10.00

CONCORD JAZZ

Number	Title	Yr	VG	VG+	NM
❑ CJ-20	Sunshine Express	1976	3.00	6.00	12.00
❑ CJ-58	Heritage	1979	3.00	6.00	12.00
❑ CJ-126	Crystal Comments	1980	2.50	5.00	10.00

CONTEMPORARY

Number	Title	Yr	VG	VG+	NM
❑ C-14012	California Concert	1985	2.50	5.00	10.00
❑ C-14019	That Old Feeling	1986	2.50	5.00	10.00
❑ C-14027	Bud Shank at Jazz Alley	1987	2.50	5.00	10.00
❑ C-14031	Serious Swingers	1988	2.50	5.00	10.00
-- With the Bill Perkins Quartet					
❑ C-14048	Tomorrow's Rainbow	1989	2.50	5.00	10.00

CROWN

Number	Title	Yr	VG	VG+	NM
❑ CST-311 [R]	Bud Shank	1963	3.00	6.00	12.00
❑ CLP-5311 [M]	Bud Shank	1963	3.75	7.50	15.00

KIMBERLY

Number	Title	Yr	VG	VG+	NM
❑ 2025 [M]	The Talents of Bud Shank	1963	5.00	10.00	20.00
❑ 11025 [S]	The Talents of Bud Shank	1963	6.25	12.50	25.00

MUSE

Number	Title	Yr	VG	VG+	NM
❑ MR-5309	This Bud's for You	198?	2.50	5.00	10.00

NOCTURNE

Number	Title	Yr	VG	VG+	NM
❑ NLP-2 [10]	Compositions of Shorty Rogers	1953	50.00	100.00	200.00

PACIFIC JAZZ

Number	Title	Yr	VG	VG+	NM
❑ PJ-4 [M]	Bud Shank Plays Tenor	1960	6.25	12.50	25.00
❑ ST-4 [S]	Bud Shank Plays Tenor	1960	7.50	15.00	30.00
❑ PJLP-14 [10]	Bud Shank with Three Trombones	1954	30.00	60.00	120.00
❑ PJLP-20 [10]	Bud Shank and Bob Brookmeyer	1954	30.00	60.00	120.00
❑ PJ-21 [M]	New Groove	1961	6.25	12.50	25.00
❑ ST-21 [S]	New Groove	1961	7.50	15.00	30.00
❑ PJ-58 [M]	Bossa Nova Jazz Samba	1962	6.25	12.50	25.00
❑ ST-58 [S]	Bossa Nova Jazz Samba	1962	7.50	15.00	30.00
❑ PJ-64 [M]	Brassamba Bossa Nova	1963	5.00	10.00	20.00
❑ ST-64 [S]	Brassamba Bossa Nova	1963	6.25	12.50	25.00
❑ PJ-89 [M]	Bud Shank and His Brazilian Friends	1965	5.00	10.00	20.00
❑ ST-89 [S]	Bud Shank and His Brazilian Friends	1965	6.25	12.50	25.00
❑ PJM-411 [M]	The Swing's to TV	1957	15.00	30.00	60.00
❑ PJ-1205 [M]	Bud Shank/Shorty Rogers	1955	20.00	40.00	80.00
❑ PJ-1213 [M]	Strings and Trombones	1956	20.00	40.00	80.00
❑ PJ-1215 [M]	The Bud Shank Quartet	1956	20.00	40.00	80.00
❑ PJ-1219 [M]	Jazz at Cal-Tech	1956	15.00	30.00	60.00
❑ PJ-1226 [M]	Flute 'n Oboe	1957	15.00	30.00	60.00
❑ PJ-1230 [M]	The Bud Shank Quartet	1957	15.00	30.00	60.00
❑ LN-10091	Bud Shank and the Sax Section	198?	2.50	5.00	10.00
❑ PJ-10110 [M]	Bud Shank and the Sax Section	1966	3.75	7.50	15.00
❑ ST-20110 [S]	Bud Shank and the Sax Section	1966	5.00	10.00	20.00

SUNSET

Number	Title	Yr	VG	VG+	NM
❑ SUM-1132 [M]	I Hear Music	1967	3.00	6.00	12.00
❑ SUS-5132 [S]	I Hear Music	1967	3.00	6.00	12.00

WORLD PACIFIC

Number	Title	Yr	VG	VG+	NM
❑ PJM-411 [M]	The Swing's to TV	1958	12.50	25.00	50.00
❑ WPM-411 [M]	The Swing's to TV	1958	10.00	20.00	40.00
❑ ST-1002 [S]	The Swing's to TV	1959	7.50	15.00	30.00
❑ ST-1018 [S]	Holiday in Brazil	1959	7.50	15.00	30.00
❑ WP-1205 [M]	Bud Shank/Shorty Rogers	1958	10.00	20.00	40.00
❑ WP-1215 [M]	The Bud Shank Quartet	1958	10.00	20.00	40.00
❑ WP-1219 [M]	Jazz at Cal-Tech	1958	10.00	20.00	40.00
❑ WP-1226 [M]	Flute 'n Oboe	1958	10.00	20.00	40.00
❑ WP-1230 [M]	The Bud Shank Quartet	1958	10.00	20.00	40.00
❑ WP-1251 [M]	I'll Take Romance	1958	10.00	20.00	40.00
❑ WP-1259 [M]	Holiday in Brazil	1959	10.00	20.00	40.00
❑ ST-1281 [S]	Latin Contrasts	1959	7.50	15.00	30.00
❑ WP-1281 [M]	Latin Contrasts	1959	10.00	20.00	40.00
❑ ST-1286 [S]	Flute 'n Alto	1960	10.00	20.00	40.00
❑ WP-1286 [M]	Flute 'n Alto	1960	7.50	15.00	30.00
❑ ST-1299 [S]	Koto 'n Flute	1960	10.00	20.00	40.00
❑ WP-1299 [M]	Koto 'n Flute	1960	7.50	15.00	30.00
❑ WP-1416 [M]	Improvisations	1961	6.25	12.50	25.00
❑ WP-1424 [M]	Koto 'n Flute	1962	6.25	12.50	25.00
❑ WP-1819 [M]	Folk 'n Flute	1965	3.75	7.50	15.00
❑ WP-1827 [M]	Flute, Oboe and Strings	1965	3.75	7.50	15.00
❑ WP-1840 [M]	Michelle	1966	3.75	7.50	15.00
❑ WP-1845 [M]	California Dreaming	1966	3.75	7.50	15.00
❑ WP-1853 [M]	Girl in Love	1967	5.00	10.00	20.00
❑ WP-1855 [M]	Brazil! Brazil! Brazil!	1967	5.00	10.00	20.00
❑ WP-1864 [M]	Bud Shank Plays Music from Today's Movies	1967	5.00	10.00	20.00
❑ ST-20170	Let It Be	1970	3.75	7.50	15.00
❑ ST-21819 [S]	Folk 'n Flute	1965	5.00	10.00	20.00
❑ ST-21827 [S]	Flute, Oboe and Strings	1965	5.00	10.00	20.00
❑ ST-21840 [S]	Michelle	1966	5.00	10.00	20.00
❑ ST-21845 [S]	California Dreaming	1966	5.00	10.00	20.00
❑ ST-21853 [S]	Girl in Love	1967	3.75	7.50	15.00
❑ ST-21855 [S]	Brazil! Brazil! Brazil!	1967	3.75	7.50	15.00

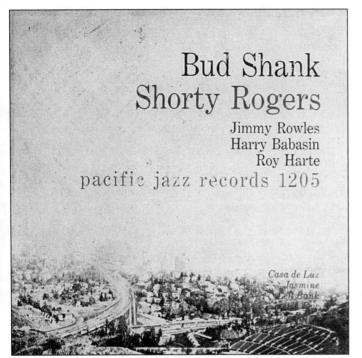

(Top left) This is one of the earliest albums from Bud Shank, a West Coast alto sax player known for his "cool" style, but who became more of a hard bopper in the 1980s. (Top right) Jack Sheldon, a trumpeter, made his recording debut as a leader on the obscure Jazz: West label. *Get Out of Town*, in fact, was the first 10-inch LP issue on the label. (Bottom left) Ben Sidran is a well-regarded jazz keyboardist who got his start as an unofficial member of the early Steve Miller Band (he co-wrote "Space Cowboy"). This is his 1988 album for the Windham Hill Jazz label. (Bottom right) Horace Silver was one of the most influential bop pianists and composers. Not only that, unlike most of his peers, he didn't move from label to label with alarming frequency; he recorded for Blue Note as a leader from the mid-1950s to 1980. Here is one of his classic 1950s releases.

Number	Title	Yr	VG	VG+	NM
❏ ST-21864 [S]	Bud Shank Plays Music from Today's Movies	1967	3.75	7.50	15.00
❏ ST-21868	A Spoonful of Jazz	1968	3.75	7.50	15.00
❏ ST-21873	Magical Mystery Tour	1968	3.75	7.50	15.00

SHANK, BUD/CHET BAKER
Also see each artist's individual listings.
KIMBERLY

Number	Title	Yr	VG	VG+	NM
❏ 2016 [M]	Swinging Soundtrack	1963	5.00	10.00	20.00
❏ 11016 [S]	Swinging Soundtrack	1963	6.25	12.50	25.00

SHANKAR
10-string double violin player, percussionist and male singer.
ECM

Number	Title	Yr	VG	VG+	NM
❏ 1195	Who's to Know	198?	3.00	6.00	12.00
❏ 25004	Vision	1985	2.50	5.00	10.00
❏ 25016	Song for Everyone	1985	2.50	5.00	10.00
❏ 25039	The Epidemics	1986	2.50	5.00	10.00

SHARON, RALPH
Pianist and composer.
ARGO

Number	Title	Yr	VG	VG+	NM
❏ LP-635 [M]	2:38 A.M.	1958	10.00	20.00	40.00

BETHLEHEM

Number	Title	Yr	VG	VG+	NM
❏ BCP-13 [M]	Mr. & Mrs. Jazz	1955	10.00	20.00	40.00
❏ BCP-41 [M]	Ralph Sharon Trio	1956	10.00	20.00	40.00

COLUMBIA

Number	Title	Yr	VG	VG+	NM
❏ CL 2321 [M]	Do I Hear A Waltz?	1965	6.25	12.50	25.00
❏ CS 9121 [S]	Do I Hear A Waltz?	1965	7.50	15.00	30.00

GORDY

Number	Title	Yr	VG	VG+	NM
❏ G-903 [M]	Modern Innovations on Country & Western Themes	1963	50.00	100.00	200.00

LONDON

Number	Title	Yr	VG	VG+	NM
❏ LB-733 [10]	Spring Fever	1953	12.50	25.00	50.00
❏ LB-842 [10]	Autumn Leaves	1954	12.50	25.00	50.00
❏ LL 1339 [M]	Spring Fever/Autumn Leaves	1955	10.00	20.00	40.00
❏ LL 1488 [M]	Easy Jazz	1956	10.00	20.00	40.00

RAMA

Number	Title	Yr	VG	VG+	NM
❏ RLP-1001 [M]	Jazz Around the World	1957	12.50	25.00	50.00

SHARROCK, SONNY
Guitarist.
VORTEX

Number	Title	Yr	VG	VG+	NM
❏ 2014	Black Woman	1970	5.00	10.00	20.00

SHAVERS, CHARLIE
Trumpeter, male singer, composer and arranger. Also see JONAH JONES; HAL SINGER.
AAMCO

Number	Title	Yr	VG	VG+	NM
❏ 310 [M]	The Most Intimate Charlie Shavers	1959	10.00	20.00	40.00

BETHLEHEM

Number	Title	Yr	VG	VG+	NM
❏ BCP-27 [M]	Gershwin, Shavers and Strings	1955	20.00	40.00	80.00
❏ BCP-67 [M]	The Complete Charlie Shavers with Maxine Sullivan	1957	20.00	40.00	80.00
❏ BCP-1007 [10]	Horn o' Plenty	1954	25.00	50.00	100.00
❏ BCP-1021 [10]	The Most Intimate Charlie Shavers	1955	25.00	50.00	100.00
❏ BCP-5002 [M]	The Most Intimate Charlie Shavers	1958	20.00	40.00	80.00
❏ BCP-6005 [M]	The Most Intimate Charlie Shavers	197?	3.00	6.00	12.00

-- Reissue, distributed by RCA Victor
CAPITOL

Number	Title	Yr	VG	VG+	NM
❏ ST 1883 [S]	Excitement Unlimited	1963	6.25	12.50	25.00
❏ T 1883 [M]	Excitement Unlimited	1963	5.00	10.00	20.00

EVEREST

Number	Title	Yr	VG	VG+	NM
❏ SDBR-1070 [S]	Girl of My Dreams	1960	6.25	12.50	25.00
❏ SDBR-1108 [S]	Here Comes Charlie	1960	6.25	12.50	25.00
❏ SDBR-1127 [S]	Like Charlie	1961	6.25	12.50	25.00
❏ LPBR-5070 [M]	Girl of My Dreams	1960	5.00	10.00	20.00
❏ LPBR-5108 [M]	Here Comes Charlie	1960	5.00	10.00	20.00
❏ LPBR-5127 [M]	Like Charlie	1961	5.00	10.00	20.00

JAZZTONE

Number	Title	Yr	VG	VG+	NM
❏ J-1229 [M]	Flow Gently, Sweet Rhythm	1956	10.00	20.00	40.00

MGM

Number	Title	Yr	VG	VG+	NM
❏ E-3765 [M]	Charlie Digs Paree	1959	6.25	12.50	25.00
❏ SE-3765 [S]	Charlie Digs Paree	1959	7.50	15.00	30.00
❏ E-3809 [M]	Charlie Digs Dixie	1960	6.25	12.50	25.00
❏ SE-3809 [S]	Charlie Digs Dixie	1960	7.50	15.00	30.00

PERIOD

Number	Title	Yr	VG	VG+	NM
❏ SPL-1113 [10]	Flow Gently, Sweet Rhythm	1955	30.00	60.00	120.00

PHOENIX

Number	Title	Yr	VG	VG+	NM
❏ 21	Trumpet Man	197?	2.50	5.00	10.00

SHAW, ARTIE
Clarinet player, composer and bandleader.
AIRCHECK

Number	Title	Yr	VG	VG+	NM
❏ 11	Artie Shaw and His Orchestra 1939-40	197?	2.50	5.00	10.00

ALLEGRO

Number	Title	Yr	VG	VG+	NM
❏ 1405 [M]	An Hour with Artie Shaw	1955	10.00	20.00	40.00
❏ 1466 [M]	Artie Shaw Hour	1955	10.00	20.00	40.00

ALLEGRO EILTE

Number	Title	Yr	VG	VG+	NM
❏ 4023 [10]	Artie Shaw Plays	195?	10.00	20.00	40.00
❏ 4107 [10]	Artie Shaw Plays Cole Porter	195?	10.00	20.00	40.00

ARCHIVE OF FOLK AND JAZZ

Number	Title	Yr	VG	VG+	NM
❏ 248	Artie Shaw	1970	2.50	5.00	10.00

BLUEBIRD

Number	Title	Yr	VG	VG+	NM
❏ AXM2-5517 [(2)]	The Complete Artie Shaw, Volume 1 (1938-39)	197?	3.75	7.50	15.00
❏ AXM2-5533 [(2)]	The Complete Artie Shaw, Volume 2 (1939)	197?	3.75	7.50	15.00
❏ AXM2-5556 [(2)]	The Complete Artie Shaw, Volume 3 (1939-40)	1979	3.75	7.50	15.00
❏ AXM2-5572 [(2)]	The Complete Artie Shaw, Volume 4 (1940-41)	1980	3.75	7.50	15.00
❏ AXM2-5576 [(2)]	The Complete Artie Shaw, Volume 5 (1941-42)	198?	3.75	7.50	15.00
❏ AXM2-5579 [(2)]	The Complete Artie Shaw, Volume 6 (1942-45)	198?	3.75	7.50	15.00
❏ AXM2-5580 [(2)]	The Complete Artie Shaw, Volume 7: Retrospective	198?	3.75	7.50	15.00
❏ 7637-1-RB	The Complete Gramercy Five Sessions	1989	3.00	6.00	12.00

CAPITOL

Number	Title	Yr	VG	VG+	NM
❏ ST 2992	Artie Shaw Re-Creates His Great '38 Band	1968	3.75	7.50	15.00

CLEF

Number	Title	Yr	VG	VG+	NM
❏ MGC-159 [10]	Artie Shaw and His Gramercy Five, Volume 1	1954	15.00	30.00	60.00
❏ MGC-160 [10]	Artie Shaw and His Gramercy Five, Volume 2	1954	15.00	30.00	60.00
❏ MGC-630 [M]	Artie Shaw and His Gramercy Five, Volume 3	1954	15.00	30.00	60.00
❏ MGC-645 [M]	Artie Shaw and His Gramercy Five, Volume 4	1955	15.00	30.00	60.00

COLUMBIA MASTERWORKS

Number	Title	Yr	VG	VG+	NM
❏ ML 4260 [M]	Modern Music for Clarinet	1950	12.50	25.00	50.00

DECCA

Number	Title	Yr	VG	VG+	NM
❏ DL 5286 [10]	Artie Shaw Dance Program	195?	12.50	25.00	50.00
❏ DL 5524 [10]	Speak to Me of Love	195?	12.50	25.00	50.00
❏ DL 8309 [M]	Did Someone Say Party?	1956	10.00	20.00	40.00

-- Black label, silver print
ENCORE

Number	Title	Yr	VG	VG+	NM
❏ EE 22023	Free for All	196?	3.75	7.50	15.00

EPIC

Number	Title	Yr	VG	VG+	NM
❏ LG 1006 [10]	Artie Shaw with Strings	1954	12.50	25.00	50.00
❏ LG 1017 [10]	Non-Stop Flight	1954	12.50	25.00	50.00
❏ LG 1102 [10]	Artie Shaw	1955	12.50	25.00	50.00
❏ LN 3112 [M]	Artie Shaw with Strings	1955	10.00	20.00	40.00
❏ LN 3150 [M]	Artie Shaw and His Orchestra	1955	10.00	20.00	40.00

HINDSIGHT

Number	Title	Yr	VG	VG+	NM
❏ HSR-139	Artie Shaw and His Orchestra, 1938	198?	2.50	5.00	10.00
❏ HSR-140	Artie Shaw and His Orchestra, 1938, Volume 2	198?	2.50	5.00	10.00
❏ HSR-148	Artie Shaw and His Orchestra, 1939	198?	2.50	5.00	10.00
❏ HSR-149	Artie Shaw and His Orchestra, 1939, Volume 2	198?	2.50	5.00	10.00
❏ HSR-176	Artie Shaw and His Orchestra, 1938-39	198?	2.50	5.00	10.00
❏ HSR-401 [(2)]	Artie Shaw and His Orchestra Play 22 Original Big Band Recordings	198?	3.00	6.00	12.00

INSIGHT

Number	Title	Yr	VG	VG+	NM
❏ 204	Artie Shaw and His Orchestra (1938-39)	198?	2.50	5.00	10.00

LION

Number	Title	Yr	VG	VG+	NM
❏ L-70058 [M]	Artie Shaw Plays Irving Berlin and Cole Porter	1958	6.25	12.50	25.00

MCA

Number	Title	Yr	VG	VG+	NM
❏ 4081 [(2)]	The Best of Artie Shaw	197?	3.00	6.00	12.00

MGM

Number	Title	Yr	VG	VG+	NM
❏ E-517 [10]	Artie Shaw Plays Cole Porter	1950	12.50	25.00	50.00

Number	Title	Yr	VG	VG+	NM

MUSICRAFT
| ❏ 503 | Artie Shaw and His Orchestra, Volume 1 | 198? | 2.50 | 5.00 | 10.00 |
| ❏ 507 | Artie Shaw and His Orchestra, Volume 2 | 198? | 2.50 | 5.00 | 10.00 |

PAIR
| ❏ PDL2-1012 [(2)] | Original Recordings | 1986 | 3.00 | 6.00 | 12.00 |

RCA CAMDEN
❏ CAL-465 [M]	The Great Artie Shaw	195?	5.00	10.00	20.00
❏ ACL1-0509	Greatest Hits	1974	2.50	5.00	10.00
❏ CAL-584 [M]	One Night Stand	1959	5.00	10.00	20.00
❏ CAL-908 [M]	September Song and Other Favorites	196?	5.00	10.00	20.00

RCA VICTOR
❏ LPT-28 [10]	Artie Shaw Favorites	195?	12.50	25.00	50.00
❏ LPM-30 [10]	Four Star Favorites	195?	12.50	25.00	50.00
❏ LPT-1020 [M]	My Concerto	195?	10.00	20.00	40.00
❏ ANL1-1089	The Best of Artie Shaw	1975	2.50	5.00	10.00
❏ LPM-1201 [M]	Both Feet in the Groove	1956	10.00	20.00	40.00
❏ LPM-1217 [M]	Back Bay Shuffle	1956	10.00	20.00	40.00
❏ LPM-1241 [M]	Artie Shaw and His Gramercy Five	1956	10.00	20.00	40.00
❏ LPM-1244 [M]	Moonglow	1956	10.00	20.00	40.00
❏ LPM-1570 [M]	Any Old Time	1957	10.00	20.00	40.00
❏ LPM-1648 [M]	A Man and His Dream	1957	10.00	20.00	40.00
❏ ANL1-2151	Backbay Shuffle	1977	2.50	5.00	10.00
❏ LPT-3013 [10]	This Is Artie Shaw	1952	12.50	25.00	50.00
❏ LPM-3675 [M]	The Best of Artie Shaw	1967	5.00	10.00	20.00
❏ LSP-3675 [R]	The Best of Artie Shaw	1967	3.00	6.00	12.00
❏ LPT-6000 [(2) M]	In the Blue Room/In the Café	195?	12.50	25.00	50.00
-- Originals are in a box; silver labels, red print					
❏ VPM-6039 [(2)]	This Is Artie Shaw	197?	3.75	7.50	15.00
❏ VPM-6062 [(2)]	This Is Artie Shaw, Volume 2	197?	3.75	7.50	15.00

SUNBEAM
| ❏ 207 | New Music 1936-37 | 197? | 2.50 | 5.00 | 10.00 |

VERVE
❏ MGV-2014 [M]	I Can't Get Started	1956	10.00	20.00	40.00
❏ V-2014 [M]	I Can't Get Started	1961	5.00	10.00	20.00
❏ MGV-2015 [M]	Sequence in Music	1956	10.00	20.00	40.00
❏ V-2015 [M]	Sequence in Music	1961	5.00	10.00	20.00

SHAW, BOBO
Drummer.
BLACK SAINT
| ❏ BSR-0021 | Junk Trap | 198? | 3.00 | 6.00 | 12.00 |
MUSE
| ❏ MR-5232 | P'NKJ'ZZ | 198? | 3.75 | 7.50 | 15.00 |
| ❏ MR-5268 | Bugle Boy Bop | 198? | 3.00 | 6.00 | 12.00 |

SHAW, GENE
Trumpeter.
ARGO
❏ LP-707 [M]	Breakthrough	1962	6.25	12.50	25.00
❏ LPS-707 [S]	Breakthrough	1962	7.50	15.00	30.00
❏ LP-726 [M]	Debut In Blues	1963	6.25	12.50	25.00
❏ LPS-726 [S]	Debut In Blues	1963	7.50	15.00	30.00
❏ LP-743 [M]	Carnival Sketches	1964	6.25	12.50	25.00
❏ LPS-743 [S]	Carnival Sketches	1964	7.50	15.00	30.00
CHESS
| ❏ CH-91564 | Debut In Blues | 198? | 2.50 | 5.00 | 10.00 |

SHAW, GEORGE
Trumpeter.
PALO ALTO/TBA
| ❏ TBA-218 | Encounters | 1986 | 2.50 | 5.00 | 10.00 |
| ❏ TBA-223 | Let Yourself Go | 1987 | 2.50 | 5.00 | 10.00 |

SHAW, LEE
Pianist.
CADENCE JAZZ
| ❏ CJR-1021 | OK! | 198? | 2.50 | 5.00 | 10.00 |

SHAW, MARLENA
Female singer.
BLUE NOTE
❏ BN-LA143-F	From the Depths of My Soul	1974	3.75	7.50	15.00
❏ BN-LA397-G	Who Is This Bitch, Anyway?	1975	3.75	7.50	15.00
❏ BN-LA606-G	Just a Matter	1976	3.75	7.50	15.00
❏ BST-84422	Marlena	1972	3.75	7.50	15.00
CADET
| ❏ LPS-803 | Different Bags | 1968 | 5.00 | 10.00 | 20.00 |
| ❏ LPS-833 | Spice of Life | 1969 | 5.00 | 10.00 | 20.00 |

COLUMBIA
❏ PC 34458	Sweet Beginnings	1977	3.00	6.00	12.00
❏ JC 35073	Acting Up	1978	3.00	6.00	12.00
❏ JC 35632	Take a Bite	1979	3.00	6.00	12.00
❏ JC 36367	The Best of Marlena Shaw	1980	2.50	5.00	10.00
VERVE
| ❏ 831 438-1 | It Is Love | 1987 | 2.50 | 5.00 | 10.00 |
| ❏ 837 312-1 | Love Is In Flight | 1988 | 2.50 | 5.00 | 10.00 |

SHAW, WOODY
Trumpeter.
COLUMBIA
❏ JC 35309	Rosewood	1977	3.00	6.00	12.00
❏ JC 35560	Stepping	1978	3.00	6.00	12.00
❏ JC 35977	Woody III	1979	3.00	6.00	12.00
❏ FC 36383	For Sure	1980	3.00	6.00	12.00
❏ FC 36519	The Best of Woody Shaw	1980	2.50	5.00	10.00
CONTEMPORARY
| ❏ C-7627/8 [(2)] | Blackstone Legacy | 1971 | 5.00 | 10.00 | 20.00 |
| ❏ C-7632 | Song of Songs | 197? | 3.75 | 7.50 | 15.00 |
ELEKTRA/MUSICIAN
| ❏ 60131 | Master of the Art | 1983 | 2.50 | 5.00 | 10.00 |
| ❏ 60299 | Night Music | 1984 | 2.50 | 5.00 | 10.00 |
ENJA
| ❏ 4018 | Lotus Flower | 1982 | 3.00 | 6.00 | 12.00 |
FANTASY
| ❏ OJC-180 | Song of Songs | 198? | 2.50 | 5.00 | 10.00 |
MOSAIC
| ❏ M4-142 [(4)] | The Complete CBS Studio Recordings of Woody Shaw | 199? | 20.00 | 40.00 | 80.00 |
MUSE
❏ MR-5058	Moontrane	1975	3.00	6.00	12.00
❏ MR-5074	Love Dance	1976	3.00	6.00	12.00
❏ MR-5103	Red's Fantasy	197?	3.00	6.00	12.00
❏ MR-5139	Concert Ensemble '76	1977	3.00	6.00	12.00
❏ MR-5160	The Iron Men	198?	3.00	6.00	12.00
❏ MR-5298	In the Beginning	198?	2.50	5.00	10.00
❏ MR-5318	Setting Standards	198?	2.50	5.00	10.00
❏ MR-5329	Solid	1987	2.50	5.00	10.00
❏ MR-5338	Imagination	1988	2.50	5.00	10.00
RED RECORD
| ❏ VPA-168 | The Time Is Right | 198? | 3.00 | 6.00 | 12.00 |

SHAY, SHERYL
LAUREL
| ❏ LR-506 | Sophisticated Lady | 1985 | 3.00 | 6.00 | 12.00 |

SHEA, TOM
Pianist.
STOMP OFF
| ❏ SOS-1022 | Little Wabash Special | 198? | 2.50 | 5.00 | 10.00 |

SHEARING, GEORGE
Pianist, arranger, composer and bandleader. Also see NAT KING COLE; MARIAN McPARTLAND.
ARCHIVE OF FOLK AND JAZZ
| ❏ 223 | Young George Shearing | 1968 | 2.50 | 5.00 | 10.00 |
| ❏ 236 | The Early Years, Vol. 2 | 1969 | 2.50 | 5.00 | 10.00 |
BASF
| ❏ 25340 | Light, Airy and Swinging | 1973 | 3.00 | 6.00 | 12.00 |
| ❏ 25351 | The Way We Are | 1974 | 3.00 | 6.00 | 12.00 |
CAPITOL
❏ SKAO-139	The Best of George Shearing, Vol. 2	1969	3.00	6.00	12.00
❏ ST-181	Fool on the Hill	1969	3.00	6.00	12.00
❏ T 648 [M]	The Shearing Spell	1956	7.50	15.00	30.00
-- Turquoise label					
❏ T 648 [M]	The Shearing Spell	1959	5.00	10.00	20.00
-- Black label with colorband, logo on left					
❏ DT 720 [R]	Velvet Carpet	196?	3.00	6.00	12.00
❏ T 720 [M]	Velvet Carpet	1956	7.50	15.00	30.00
-- Turquoise label					
❏ T 720 [M]	Velvet Carpet	1959	5.00	10.00	20.00
-- Black label with colorband, logo on left					
❏ T 720 [M]	Velvet Carpet	1962	3.75	7.50	15.00
-- Black label with colorband, logo on top					
❏ DT 737 [R]	Latin Escapade	196?	3.00	6.00	12.00
❏ T 737 [M]	Latin Escapade	1957	7.50	15.00	30.00
-- Turquoise label					
❏ T 737 [M]	Latin Escapade	1959	5.00	10.00	20.00
-- Black label with colorband, logo on left					
❏ T 737 [M]	Latin Escapade	1962	3.75	7.50	15.00
-- Black label with colorband, logo on top					

Number	Title	Yr	VG	VG+	NM
❏ ST 858 [S]	Black Satin	1959	5.00	10.00	20.00
-- Black label with colorband, logo on left
❏ ST 858 [S]	Black Satin	1962	3.75	7.50	15.00
-- Black label with colorband, logo on top
❏ T 858 [M]	Black Satin	1957	7.50	15.00	30.00
-- Turquoise label
❏ T 858 [M]	Black Satin	1959	5.00	10.00	20.00
-- Black label with colorband, logo on left
❏ T 858 [M]	Black Satin	1962	3.75	7.50	15.00
-- Black label with colorband, logo on top
❏ T 909 [M]	Shearing Piano	1957	7.50	15.00	30.00
-- Turquoise label
❏ T 909 [M]	Shearing Piano	1959	5.00	10.00	20.00
-- Black label with colorband, logo on left
❏ ST 1038 [S]	Burnished Brass	1959	6.25	12.50	25.00
-- Black label with colorband, logo on left
❏ ST 1038 [S]	Burnished Brass	1962	5.00	10.00	20.00
-- Black label with colorband, logo on top
❏ T 1038 [M]	Burnished Brass	1958	5.00	10.00	20.00
-- Black label with colorband, logo on left
❏ T 1038 [M]	Burnished Brass	1962	3.75	7.50	15.00
-- Black label with colorband, logo on top
❏ ST 1082 [S]	Latin Lace	1958	6.25	12.50	25.00
-- Black label with colorband, logo on left
❏ ST 1082 [S]	Latin Lace	1962	5.00	10.00	20.00
-- Black label with colorband, logo on left
❏ T 1082 [M]	Latin Lace	1958	5.00	10.00	20.00
-- Black label with colorband, logo on left
❏ T 1082 [M]	Latin Lace	1962	3.75	7.50	15.00
-- Black label with colorband, logo on top
❏ ST 1124 [S]	Blue Chiffon	1959	6.25	12.50	25.00
-- Black label with colorband, logo on left
❏ ST 1124 [S]	Blue Chiffon	1962	5.00	10.00	20.00
-- Black label with colorband, logo on top
❏ T 1124 [M]	Blue Chiffon	1959	5.00	10.00	20.00
-- Black label with colorband, logo on left
❏ T 1124 [M]	Blue Chiffon	1962	3.75	7.50	15.00
-- Black label with colorband, logo on top
❏ ST 1187 [S]	George Shearing On Stage	1959	6.25	12.50	25.00
-- Black label with colorband, logo on left
❏ ST 1187 [S]	George Shearing On Stage	1962	5.00	10.00	20.00
-- Black label with colorband, logo on left
❏ T 1187 [M]	George Shearing On Stage	1959	5.00	10.00	20.00
-- Black label with colorband, logo on left
❏ T 1187 [M]	George Shearing On Stage	1962	3.75	7.50	15.00
-- Black label with colorband, logo on top
❏ ST 1275 [S]	Latin Affair	1960	6.25	12.50	25.00
-- Black label with colorband, logo on left
❏ ST 1275 [S]	Latin Affair	1962	5.00	10.00	20.00
-- Black label with colorband, logo on left
❏ T 1275 [M]	Latin Affair	1960	5.00	10.00	20.00
-- Black label with colorband, logo on left
❏ T 1275 [M]	Latin Affair	1962	3.75	7.50	15.00
-- Black label with colorband, logo on top
❏ ST 1334 [S]	White Satin	1960	6.25	12.50	25.00
-- Black label with colorband, logo on left
❏ ST 1334 [S]	White Satin	1962	5.00	10.00	20.00
-- Black label with colorband, logo on top
❏ T 1334 [M]	White Satin	1960	5.00	10.00	20.00
-- Black label with colorband, logo on left
❏ T 1334 [M]	White Satin	1962	3.75	7.50	15.00
-- Black label with colorband, logo on top
❏ ST 1416 [S]	On the Sunny Side of the Strip	1960	6.25	12.50	25.00
-- Black label with colorband, logo on left
❏ ST 1416 [S]	On the Sunny Side of the Strip	1962	5.00	10.00	20.00
-- Black label with colorband, logo on top
❏ T 1416 [M]	On the Sunny Side of the Strip	1960	5.00	10.00	20.00
-- Black label with colorband, logo on left
❏ T 1416 [M]	On the Sunny Side of the Strip	1962	3.75	7.50	15.00
-- Black label with colorband, logo on top
❏ SM-1472	The Shearing Touch	1977	2.50	5.00	10.00
-- Reissue with new prefix
❏ ST 1472 [S]	The Shearing Touch	1961	6.25	12.50	25.00
-- Black label with colorband, logo on left
❏ ST 1472 [S]	The Shearing Touch	1962	5.00	10.00	20.00
-- Black label with colorband, logo on top
❏ T 1472 [M]	The Shearing Touch	1961	5.00	10.00	20.00
-- Black label with colorband, logo on left
❏ T 1472 [M]	The Shearing Touch	1962	3.75	7.50	15.00
-- Black label with colorband, logo on top
❏ ST 1567 [S]	Mood Latino	1961	6.25	12.50	25.00
-- Black label with colorband, logo on left
❏ ST 1567 [S]	Mood Latino	1962	5.00	10.00	20.00
-- Black label with colorband, logo on top
❏ T 1567 [M]	Mood Latino	1961	5.00	10.00	20.00
-- Black label with colorband, logo on left
❏ T 1567 [M]	Mood Latino	1962	3.75	7.50	15.00
-- Black label with colorband, logo on top
❏ ST 1628 [S]	Satin Affair	1961	6.25	12.50	25.00
-- Black label with colorband, logo on left
❏ ST 1628 [S]	Satin Affair	1962	5.00	10.00	20.00
-- Black label with colorband, logo on top
❏ T 1628 [M]	Satin Affair	1961	5.00	10.00	20.00
-- Black label with colorband, logo on left
❏ T 1628 [M]	Satin Affair	1962	3.75	7.50	15.00
-- Black label with colorband, logo on top
❏ ST 1715 [S]	San Francisco Scene	1962	5.00	10.00	20.00
❏ T 1715 [M]	San Francisco Scene	1962	3.75	7.50	15.00
❏ ST 1755 [S]	Concerto for My Love	1962	5.00	10.00	20.00
❏ T 1755 [M]	Concerto for My Love	1962	3.75	7.50	15.00
❏ ST 1827 [S]	Jazz Moments	1963	5.00	10.00	20.00
❏ T 1827 [M]	Jazz Moments	1963	3.75	7.50	15.00
❏ ST 1873 [S]	Bossa Nova	1963	5.00	10.00	20.00
❏ T 1873 [M]	Bossa Nova	1963	3.75	7.50	15.00
❏ ST 1874 [S]	Touch Me Softly	1963	5.00	10.00	20.00
❏ T 1874 [M]	Touch Me Softly	1963	3.75	7.50	15.00
❏ ST 1992 [S]	Jazz Concert	1963	5.00	10.00	20.00
❏ T 1992 [M]	Jazz Concert	1963	3.75	7.50	15.00
❏ ST 2048 [S]	Old Gold and Ivory	1964	3.75	7.50	15.00
❏ T 2048 [M]	Old Gold and Ivory	1964	3.00	6.00	12.00
❏ SM-2104	The Best of George Shearing	1977	2.50	5.00	10.00
-- Reissue with new prefix
❏ ST 2104 [S]	The Best of George Shearing	1964	3.75	7.50	15.00
❏ T 2104 [M]	The Best of George Shearing	1964	3.00	6.00	12.00
❏ ST 2143 [S]	Deep Velvet	1964	3.75	7.50	15.00
❏ T 2143 [M]	Deep Velvet	1964	3.00	6.00	12.00
❏ ST 2272 [S]	Out of the Woods	1965	3.75	7.50	15.00
❏ T 2272 [M]	Out of the Woods	1965	3.00	6.00	12.00
❏ ST 2326 [S]	Latin Rendezvous	1965	3.75	7.50	15.00
❏ T 2326 [M]	Latin Rendezvous	1965	3.00	6.00	12.00
❏ ST 2372 [S]	Here and Now	1965	3.75	7.50	15.00
❏ T 2372 [M]	Here and Now	1965	3.00	6.00	12.00
❏ ST 2447 [S]	Rare Form	1965	3.75	7.50	15.00
❏ T 2447 [M]	Rare Form	1965	3.00	6.00	12.00
❏ ST 2567 [S]	That Fresh Feeling	1966	3.75	7.50	15.00
❏ T 2567 [M]	That Fresh Feeling	1966	3.00	6.00	12.00
❏ ST 2699 [S]	George Shearing Today	1967	3.00	6.00	12.00
❏ T 2699 [M]	George Shearing Today	1967	3.75	7.50	15.00
❏ SM-11454	Latin Escapade	197?	2.50	5.00	10.00
❏ SM-11800	Black Satin	1978	2.50	5.00	10.00
CONCORD CONCERTO
❏ CC-2010	George Shearing and Barry Tuckwell Play the Music of Cole Porter	1986	2.50	5.00	10.00
CONCORD JAZZ
❏ CJ-110	Blues Alley Jazz	1980	2.50	5.00	10.00
❏ CJ-132	On a Clear Day	1981	2.50	5.00	10.00
-- With Brian Torff
❏ CJ-171	Alone Together	1981	2.50	5.00	10.00
❏ CJ-177	First Edition	1982	2.50	5.00	10.00
❏ CJ-246	Live at the Café Carlyle	1984	2.50	5.00	10.00
❏ CJ-281	Grand Piano	1985	2.50	5.00	10.00
❏ CJ-318	More Grand Piano	1987	2.50	5.00	10.00
❏ CJ-335	Breakin' Out	1988	2.50	5.00	10.00
❏ CJ-346	Dexterity	1988	2.50	5.00	10.00
❏ CJ-357	A Perfect Match	1988	2.50	5.00	10.00
-- With Ernestine Anderson
❏ CJ-371	The Spirit of 176	1989	3.00	6.00	12.00
-- With Hank Jones
❏ CJ-388	George Shearing in Dixieland	1989	3.00	6.00	12.00
❏ CJ-400	Piano	1989	3.00	6.00	12.00
DISCOVERY
❏ DL-3002 [10]	George Shearing Quintet	1950	15.00	30.00	60.00
LONDON
❏ LL 295 [10]	Souvenirs	1951	15.00	30.00	60.00
❏ LL 1343 [M]	By Request	1956	7.50	15.00	30.00
MGM
❏ E-90 [10]	A Touch of Genius	1951	12.50	25.00	50.00
❏ GAS-143	You're Hearing George Shearing	1970	3.00	6.00	12.00
❏ E-155 [10]	I Hear Music	1952	12.50	25.00	50.00
❏ E-226 [10]	When Lights Are Low	1953	12.50	25.00	50.00
❏ E-252 [10]	An Evening with George Shearing	1954	12.50	25.00	50.00
❏ E-518 [10]	You're Hearing the George Shearing Quartet	1950	15.00	30.00	60.00
❏ E-3122 [M]	An Evening with Shearing	1955	7.50	15.00	30.00
❏ E-3175 [M]	Shearing Caravan	1955	7.50	15.00	30.00
❏ E-3216 [M]	You're Hearing George Shearing	1955	7.50	15.00	30.00
❏ E-3264 [M]	When Lights Are Low	1955	7.50	15.00	30.00
❏ E-3265 [M]	Touch of Genius	1955	7.50	15.00	30.00
❏ E-3266 [M]	I Hear Music	1955	7.50	15.00	30.00
❏ E-3293 [M]	Shearing in Hi-Fi	1955	7.50	15.00	30.00
❏ E-4041 [M]	Satin Latin	1962	3.75	7.50	15.00
❏ SE-4041 [R]	Satin Latin	1962	3.00	6.00	12.00
❏ E-4042 [M]	Soft and Silky	1962	3.75	7.50	15.00
❏ SE-4042 [R]	Soft and Silky	1962	3.00	6.00	12.00
❏ E-4043 [M]	Smooth and Swinging	1962	3.75	7.50	15.00
❏ SE-4043 [R]	Smooth and Swinging	1962	3.00	6.00	12.00
❏ E-4169 [M]	The Very Best of George Shearing	1963	3.75	7.50	15.00
❏ SE-4169 [R]	The Very Best of George Shearing	1963	3.00	6.00	12.00

Number	Title	Yr	VG	VG+	NM
MOSAIC					
❏ MQ7-157 [(7)]	The Complete Capitol Live Recordings of George Shearing	199?	30.00	60.00	120.00
PAUSA					
❏ 7035	Light, Airy and Swinging	1977	2.50	5.00	10.00
❏ 7049	The Reunion	1979	2.50	5.00	10.00
-- With Stephane Grappelli					
❏ 7072	500 Miles High	1979	2.50	5.00	10.00
❏ 7088	Getting in the Swing of Things	1981	2.50	5.00	10.00
❏ 7116	On Target	198?	2.50	5.00	10.00
❏ 9030	The Shearing Touch	198?	2.50	5.00	10.00
❏ 9036	Jazz Moments	1985	2.50	5.00	10.00
PICKWICK					
❏ SPC-3039	Lullaby of Birdland	197?	2.50	5.00	10.00
❏ SPC-3100	You Stepped Out of a Dream	197?	2.50	5.00	10.00
SAVOY					
❏ MG-15003 [10]	Piano Solo	1951	15.00	30.00	60.00
SAVOY JAZZ					
❏ SJL-1117	So Rare	198?	2.50	5.00	10.00
SHEBA					
❏ 101	Out of This World	197?	3.00	6.00	12.00
❏ 103	George Shearing Trio	197?	3.00	6.00	12.00
❏ 104	George Shearing Quartet	197?	3.00	6.00	12.00
❏ 105	As Requested	197?	3.00	6.00	12.00
❏ 106	Music to Hear	197?	3.00	6.00	12.00
❏ 107	GAS	197?	3.00	6.00	12.00
VERVE					
❏ VSP-9 [M]	Classic Shearing	1966	3.75	7.50	15.00
❏ VSPS-9 [R]	Classic Shearing	1966	3.00	6.00	12.00
❏ 821 664-1	My Ship	198?	2.50	5.00	10.00
❏ 827 977-1 [(2)]	Lullaby of Birdland	1986	3.00	6.00	12.00

SHEARING, GEORGE, AND THE MONTGOMERY BROTHERS
Also see each artist's individual listings.

Number	Title	Yr	VG	VG+	NM
FANTASY					
❏ OJC-040	George Shearing and the Montgomery Brothers	198?	2.50	5.00	10.00
JAZZLAND					
❏ JLP-55 [M]	Love Walked In	1961	7.50	15.00	30.00
-- Cover has Shearing and the brothers					
❏ JLP-55 [M]	Love Walked In	1962	6.25	12.50	25.00
-- Cover has a woman					
❏ JLP-955 [S]	Love Walked In	1961	10.00	20.00	40.00
-- Cover has Shearing and the brothers					
❏ JLP-955 [S]	Love Walked In	1962	7.50	15.00	30.00
-- Cover has a woman					
RIVERSIDE					
❏ 6087	George Shearing and the Montgomery Brothers	197?	2.50	5.00	10.00
-- Reissue of Jazzland LP					

SHEARING, GEORGE, AND MEL TORME
Also see each artist's individual listings.

Number	Title	Yr	VG	VG+	NM
CONCORD JAZZ					
❏ CJ-190	An Evening with George Shearing and Mel Torme	1982	2.50	5.00	10.00
❏ CJ-219	Top Drawer	1983	2.50	5.00	10.00
❏ CJ-248	An Evening at Charlie's	1984	2.50	5.00	10.00
❏ CJ-294	An Elegant Evening	1985	2.50	5.00	10.00
❏ CJ-341	A Vintage Year	1988	2.50	5.00	10.00

SHEEN, MICKEY
Drummer.

Number	Title	Yr	VG	VG+	NM
HERALD					
❏ HLP-0105 [M]	Have Swing, Will Travel	1956	15.00	30.00	60.00

SHELDON, JACK
Trumpeter.

Number	Title	Yr	VG	VG+	NM
CAPITOL					
❏ ST 1851 [S]	Out!	1963	5.00	10.00	20.00
❏ T 1851 [M]	Out!	1963	3.75	7.50	15.00
❏ ST 2029 [S]	Play Buddy, Play!	1966	5.00	10.00	20.00
❏ T 2029 [M]	Play Buddy, Play!	1966	3.75	7.50	15.00
CONCORD JAZZ					
❏ CJ-229	Stand By for Jack Sheldon	1983	2.50	5.00	10.00
❏ CJ-339	Hollywood Heroes	1988	2.50	5.00	10.00
GENE NORMAN					
❏ GNP-60 [M]	Jack's Groove	1961	10.00	20.00	40.00
GNP CRESCENDO					
❏ GNPS-60	Jack's Groove	196?	3.00	6.00	12.00
❏ GNP-2029 [M]	Play, Buddy, Play!	1966	3.75	7.50	15.00
❏ GNPS-2029 [S]	Play, Buddy, Play!	1966	3.00	6.00	12.00

Number	Title	Yr	VG	VG+	NM
❏ GNPS-9036	Jack Sheldon and His All-Star Band	197?	2.50	5.00	10.00
JAZZ WEST					
❏ JWLP-1 [10]	Get Out of Town	1955	100.00	200.00	400.00
❏ JWLP-2 [10]	Jack Sheldon Quintet	1955	100.00	200.00	400.00
❏ JWLP-6 [M]	The Quartet and the Quintet	1956	75.00	150.00	30.00
REAL TIME					
❏ 303	Playin' It Straight	1981	3.75	7.50	15.00
REPRISE					
❏ R-2004 [M]	A Jazz Profile of Ray Charles	1961	6.25	12.50	25.00
❏ R9-2004 [S]	A Jazz Profile of Ray Charles	1961	7.50	15.00	30.00

SHELDON, NINA

Number	Title	Yr	VG	VG+	NM
PLUG					
❏ PLUG-2	Secret Places	1986	3.00	6.00	12.00

SHEPARD, TOMMY
Trombonist.

Number	Title	Yr	VG	VG+	NM
CORAL					
❏ CRL 57110 [M]	Shepard's Flock	1957	20.00	40.00	80.00

SHEPHERD, CYBILL
Female singer. Better known as an actress.

Number	Title	Yr	VG	VG+	NM
PARAMOUNT					
❏ PAS-1018	Cybill Does It...to Cole Porter	1974	5.00	10.00	20.00
-- With poster					

SHEPP, ARCHIE
Tenor saxophone player, pianist and male singer.

Number	Title	Yr	VG	VG+	NM
ABC IMPULSE!					
❏ AS-71 [S]	Four for Trane	1968	3.75	7.50	15.00
❏ AS-86 [S]	Fire Music	1968	3.75	7.50	15.00
❏ AS-97 [S]	On This Night	1968	3.75	7.50	15.00
❏ AS-9118 [S]	Live In San Francisco	1968	3.75	7.50	15.00
❏ AS-9134 [S]	Mama Too Tight	1968	3.75	7.50	15.00
❏ AS-9154 [S]	The Magic of Ju Ju	1968	5.00	10.00	20.00
❏ AS-9162 [S]	Three for a Quarter, One for a	1968	5.00	10.00	20.00
❏ AS-9170 [S]	The Way Ahead	1969	5.00	10.00	20.00
❏ AS-9188	For Losers	1970	5.00	10.00	20.00
❏ AS-9212	Things Have Got to Change	197?	3.75	7.50	15.00
❏ AS-9222	Africa Blues	197?	3.75	7.50	15.00
❏ AS-9231	Cry of My People	1973	3.75	7.50	15.00
❏ AS-9262	Kwanza	1974	3.75	7.50	15.00
ARISTA/FREEDOM					
❏ AF 1016	There's a Trumpet in My Soul	1975	3.00	6.00	12.00
❏ AF 1027	Montreux 1	197?	3.00	6.00	12.00
❏ AF 1034	Montreux 2	197?	3.00	6.00	12.00
BASF					
❏ 20651	Donaueschingen Festival	197?	3.75	7.50	15.00
BLACK SAINT					
❏ BSR-0002	A Sea of Faces	198?	3.00	6.00	12.00
DELMARK					
❏ DL-409 [M]	Archie Shepp in Europe	1968	7.50	15.00	30.00
❏ DS-9409 [S]	Archie Shepp in Europe	1968	5.00	10.00	20.00
DENON					
❏ 7538	Live in Tokyo	197?	3.75	7.50	15.00
❏ 7543	Lady Bird	197?	3.75	7.50	15.00
GRP/IMPULSE!					
❏ IMP-218	Four for Trane	199?	3.75	7.50	15.00
-- Reissue on audiophile vinyl					
IMPULSE!					
❏ A-71 [M]	Four for Trane	1964	6.25	12.50	25.00
❏ AS-71 [S]	Four for Trane	1964	7.50	15.00	30.00
❏ A-86 [M]	Fire Music	1965	6.25	12.50	25.00
❏ AS-86 [S]	Fire Music	1965	7.50	15.00	30.00
❏ A-97 [M]	On This Night	1966	7.50	15.00	30.00
❏ AS-97 [S]	On This Night	1966	6.25	12.50	25.00
❏ A-9118 [M]	Live In San Francisco	1967	7.50	15.00	30.00
❏ AS-9118 [S]	Live In San Francisco	1967	6.25	12.50	25.00
❏ A-9134 [M]	Mama Too Tight	1967	7.50	15.00	30.00
❏ AS-9134 [S]	Mama Too Tight	1967	6.25	12.50	25.00
INNER CITY					
❏ IC-1001	Doodlin'	197?	3.75	7.50	15.00
❏ IC-3002	Steam	1976	3.00	6.00	12.00
PRESTIGE					
❏ 10034	Black Gypsy	197?	3.75	7.50	15.00
❏ 10066	Coral Rock	197?	3.75	7.50	15.00
SACKVILLE					
❏ 3026	I Know About the Life	198?	2.50	5.00	10.00
SOUL NOTE					
❏ SN-1102	Down Home in New York	1985	3.00	6.00	12.00

Number	Title	Yr	VG	VG+	NM
STEEPLECHASE					
❑ SCS-1149	Looking at Bird	198?	3.00	6.00	12.00
❑ SCS-1169	Mama Rose	1982	3.00	6.00	12.00
❑ SCS-6013	The House I Live In	198?	3.00	6.00	12.00
TIMELESS					
❑ SJP-287	Lover Man	1990	3.00	6.00	12.00
VARRICK					
❑ VR-005	The Good Life	198?	2.50	5.00	10.00

SHEPP, ARCHIE, AND DOLLAR BRAND
Also see ARCHIE SHEPP; ABDULLAH IBRAHIM.

Number	Title	Yr	VG	VG+	NM
DENON					
❑ 7532	Duet	197?	3.75	7.50	15.00

SHEPP, ARCHIE, AND BILL DIXON
Also see each artist's individual listings.

Number	Title	Yr	VG	VG+	NM
SAVOY					
❑ MG-12178 [M]	The Archie Shepp-Bill Dixon Quartet	1962	7.50	15.00	30.00
❑ MG-12184 [M]	Archie Shepp and the New Contemporary 5/The Bill Dixon 7-Tette	1964	12.50	25.00	50.00
-- White bordered cover					
❑ MG-12184 [M]	Archie Shepp and the New Contemporary 5/The Bill Dixon 7-Tette	1965	6.25	12.50	25.00
-- Purple bordered cover					

SHEPP, ARCHIE, AND HORACE PARLAN
Also see each artist's individual listings.

Number	Title	Yr	VG	VG+	NM
STEEPLECHASE					
❑ SCS-1079	Goin' Home	197?	3.00	6.00	12.00
❑ SCS-1139	Trouble in Mind	1980	3.00	6.00	12.00

SHEPPARD, ANDY
Tenor and soprano saxophone player.

Number	Title	Yr	VG	VG+	NM
ANTILLES					
❑ 90692	Andy Sheppard	1988	2.50	5.00	10.00

SHERMAN, MARK
Vibraphone player, pianist and composer.

Number	Title	Yr	VG	VG+	NM
COLUMBIA					
❑ BFC 40360	A New Balance	1986	2.50	5.00	10.00

SHERRILL, JOYA
Female singer and composer.

Number	Title	Yr	VG	VG+	NM
COLUMBIA					
❑ CL 1378 [M]	Sugar and Spice	1959	6.25	12.50	25.00
❑ CS 8178 [S]	Sugar and Spice	1960	7.50	15.00	30.00
DESIGN					
❑ DLP-22 [M]	Joya Sherrill Jumps with Sammy Davis, Jr.	196?	3.00	6.00	12.00
20TH CENTURY FOX					
❑ TFL-3170 [M]	Joya Sherrill Sings Duke Ellington	196?	6.25	12.50	25.00
❑ TFS-4170 [S]	Joya Sherrill Sings Duke Ellington	196?	7.50	15.00	30.00

SHERWOOD, BOBBY
Guitarist, trumpeter, trombonist, pianist, composer, arranger and bandleader.

Number	Title	Yr	VG	VG+	NM
CAPITOL					
❑ H 320 [10]	Classics In Jazz	1952	15.00	30.00	60.00
❑ T 320 [M]	Classics In Jazz	1955	10.00	20.00	40.00
❑ H 463 [10]	Bobby Sherwood	1954	12.50	25.00	50.00
IAJRC					
❑ LP 35	Out of Sherwood's Forest	198?	2.50	5.00	10.00
JUBILEE					
❑ JLP-1040	I'm an Old Cowhand	1957	7.50	15.00	30.00
❑ JLP-1061	Pal Joey	1958	7.50	15.00	30.00
❑ SDJLP-1061	Pal Joey	1959	6.25	12.50	25.00

SHEW, BOBBY
Trumpeter.

Number	Title	Yr	VG	VG+	NM
INNER CITY					
❑ IC-1077	Outstanding in His Field	197?	3.00	6.00	12.00
JAZZ HOUNDS					
❑ 0002	Play Song	1980	2.50	5.00	10.00
PAUSA					
❑ 7171	Breakfast Wine	1985	2.50	5.00	10.00
❑ 7198	Shewhorn	1986	2.50	5.00	10.00

SHEW, BOBBY, AND CHUCK FINDLEY
Findley is a trumpeter. Also see BOBBY SHEW.

Number	Title	Yr	VG	VG+	NM
DELOS					
❑ DMS-4003	Trumpets No End	1984	2.50	5.00	10.00

SHEW, BOBBY, AND BILL MAYS
Also see each artist's individual listings.

Number	Title	Yr	VG	VG+	NM
JAZZ HOUNDS					
❑ 0003	Telepathy	198?	2.50	5.00	10.00

SHIELDS, BILL
Keyboard player.

Number	Title	Yr	VG	VG+	NM
OPTIMISM					
❑ OP-9001	Shieldstone	198?	2.50	5.00	10.00

SHIELDS, ROGER
Mostly a classical pianist, this is his one jazz-related LP.

Number	Title	Yr	VG	VG+	NM
TURNABOUT					
❑ 34579	The Age of Ragtime	197?	2.50	5.00	10.00

SHIHAB, SAHIB
Baritone and alto saxophone player and flutist.

Number	Title	Yr	VG	VG+	NM
ARGO					
❑ LP-742 [M]	Summer Dawn	1964	6.25	12.50	25.00
❑ LPS-742 [S]	Summer Dawn	1964	7.50	15.00	30.00
CHESS					
❑ CH-91563	Summer Dawn	198?	2.50	5.00	10.00
SAVOY					
❑ MG-12124 [M]	Jazz Sahib	1957	12.50	25.00	50.00
SAVOY JAZZ					
❑ SJL-2245 [(2)]	All-Star Sextets	197?	3.00	6.00	12.00

SHIHAB, SAHIB/HERBIE MANN
Also see each artist's individual listings.

Number	Title	Yr	VG	VG+	NM
SAVOY					
❑ MG-12112 [M]	The Jazz We Heard Last Summer	1957	12.50	25.00	50.00

SHOEMAKE, CHARLIE
Vibraphone player and bandleader.

Number	Title	Yr	VG	VG+	NM
DISCOVERY					
❑ 856	Away from the Crowd	198?	2.50	5.00	10.00
❑ 894	Charlie Shoemake Plays the Music of David Raksin	1986	2.50	5.00	10.00
❑ 924	I Think We're Almost There	1987	2.50	5.00	10.00
MUSE					
❑ MR-5193	Sunstroke	1978	3.00	6.00	12.00
❑ MR-5221	Blue Shoe	1979	3.00	6.00	12.00

SHOEMAKE, CHARLIE, AND BILL HOLMAN
Also see each artist's individual listings.

Number	Title	Yr	VG	VG+	NM
PAUSA					
❑ 7180	Collaboration	1985	2.50	5.00	10.00

SHOEMAKE, CHARLIE, AND HAROLD LAND
Also see each artist's individual listings.

Number	Title	Yr	VG	VG+	NM
CMG					
❑ CML-8016	Stand-Up Guys	1989	3.00	6.00	12.00

SHORE, DINAH
Female singer. Most of her output is pop, but the below was done with RED NORVO.

Number	Title	Yr	VG	VG+	NM
CAPITOL					
❑ ST 1354 [S]	Dinah Sings Some Blues with Red	1960	7.50	15.00	30.00
❑ T 1354 [M]	Dinah Sings Some Blues with Red	1960	6.25	12.50	25.00

SHORT, BOBBY
Male singer.

Number	Title	Yr	VG	VG+	NM
ATLANTIC					
❑ SD 2-606 [(2)]	Bobby Short Loves Cole Porter	1972	5.00	10.00	20.00
❑ SD 2-607 [(2)]	Mad About Noel Coward	1972	5.00	10.00	20.00
❑ SD 2-608 [(2)]	Bobby Short Is K-RA-Z-Y for Gershwin	1973	3.75	7.50	15.00
❑ SD 2-609 [(2)]	Live at Café Carlyle	1974	3.75	7.50	15.00
❑ SD 2-610 [(2)]	Bobby Short Celebrates Rodgers and Hart	197?	3.75	7.50	15.00
❑ 1214 [M]	Songs by Bobby Short	1955	7.50	15.00	30.00
-- Black label					
❑ 1214 [M]	Songs by Bobby Short	1961	5.00	10.00	20.00
-- White "fan" logo at right of label					
❑ 1214 [M]	Songs by Bobby Short	1963	3.75	7.50	15.00
-- Black "fan" logo at right of label					
❑ 1230 [M]	Bobby Short	1956	7.50	15.00	30.00
-- Black label					

Number	Title	Yr	VG	VG+	NM
❑ 1230 [M]	Bobby Short	1961	5.00	10.00	20.00
-- White "fan" logo at right of label					
❑ 1230 [M]	Bobby Short	1963	3.75	7.50	15.00
-- Black "fan" logo at right of label					
❑ 1262 [M]	Speaking of Love	1958	7.50	15.00	30.00
-- Black label					
❑ 1262 [M]	Speaking of Love	1961	5.00	10.00	20.00
-- White "fan" logo at right of label					
❑ SD 1262 [S]	Speaking of Love	1959	10.00	20.00	40.00
-- Green label					
❑ SD 1262 [S]	Speaking of Love	1961	6.25	12.50	25.00
-- White "fan" logo at right of label					
❑ 1285 [M]	Sing Me a Swing Song	1958	7.50	15.00	30.00
-- Black label					
❑ 1285 [M]	Sing Me a Swing Song	1961	5.00	10.00	20.00
-- White "fan" logo at right of label					
❑ 1285 [M]	Sing Me a Swing Song	1963	3.75	7.50	15.00
-- Black "fan" logo at right of label					
❑ 1302 [M]	The Mad Twenties	1959	7.50	15.00	30.00
-- Black label					
❑ 1302 [M]	The Mad Twenties	1961	5.00	10.00	20.00
-- White "fan" logo at right of label					
❑ 1302 [M]	The Mad Twenties	1963	3.75	7.50	15.00
-- Black "fan" logo at right of label					
❑ SD 1302 [S]	The Mad Twenties	1959	10.00	20.00	40.00
-- Green label					
❑ SD 1302 [S]	The Mad Twenties	1961	6.25	12.50	25.00
-- White "fan" logo at right of label					
❑ SD 1302 [S]	The Mad Twenties	1963	5.00	10.00	20.00
-- Black "fan" logo at right of label					
❑ 1321 [M]	On the East Side	1960	7.50	15.00	30.00
-- Black label					
❑ 1321 [M]	On the East Side	1961	5.00	10.00	20.00
-- White "fan" logo at right of label					
❑ 1321 [M]	On the East Side	1963	3.75	7.50	15.00
-- Black "fan" logo at right of label					
❑ SD 1321 [S]	On the East Side	1960	10.00	20.00	40.00
-- Green label					
❑ SD 1321 [S]	On the East Side	1961	6.25	12.50	25.00
-- White "fan" logo at right of label					
❑ SD 1321 [S]	On the East Side	1963	5.00	10.00	20.00
-- Black "fan" logo at right of label					
❑ SD 1535	Jump for Joy	1969	3.00	6.00	12.00
❑ SD 1574	Nobody Else But Me	1971	3.00	6.00	12.00
❑ SD 1620	The Very Best of Bobby Short	1973	3.00	6.00	12.00
❑ SD 1664	The Mad Twenties	1974	3.00	6.00	12.00
❑ SD 1689	Personal	1977	3.00	6.00	12.00
❑ 81715 [(4)]	50 from Bobby Short	1987	7.50	15.00	30.00
❑ 81778	Guess Who's in Town: The Lyrics of Andy Razaf	1988	2.50	5.00	10.00

ELEKTRA

Number	Title	Yr	VG	VG+	NM
❑ E1-60002	Moments Like This	1982	2.50	5.00	10.00

SHORTER, ALAN
Trumpeter and fluegel horn player.
VERVE

Number	Title	Yr	VG	VG+	NM
❑ V6-8769	Orgasm	1969	5.00	10.00	20.00

SHORTER, WAYNE
Tenor and soprano saxophone player, arranger and composer. Also see WEATHER REPORT; THE YOUNG LIONS.
BLUE NOTE

Number	Title	Yr	VG	VG+	NM
❑ BN-LA014-G	Moto Grosso Feio	1973	3.75	7.50	15.00
❑ LT-988	The Soothsayer	1979	3.00	6.00	12.00
❑ LT-1056	Etcetera	1980	3.00	6.00	12.00
❑ BLP-4173 [M]	Night Dreamer	1964	6.25	12.50	25.00
❑ BLP-4182 [M]	Juju	1965	6.25	12.50	25.00
❑ BLP-4194 [M]	Speak No Evil	1966	6.25	12.50	25.00
❑ BLP-4219 [M]	The All Seeing Eye	1966	6.25	12.50	25.00
❑ B1-29100	The All Seeing Eye	1994	3.75	7.50	15.00
❑ B1-32096	Schizophrenia	1995	3.75	7.50	15.00
❑ B1-33581	Etcetera	1995	3.75	7.50	15.00
❑ B1-46509	Speak No Evil	1997	3.75	7.50	15.00
-- Reissue on 180-gram vinyl					
❑ BST-84173 [S]	Night Dreamer	1964	7.50	15.00	30.00
-- With New York, USA address on label					
❑ BST-84173 [S]	Night Dreamer	1967	3.75	7.50	15.00
-- With "A Division of Liberty Records" on label					
❑ BST-84182 [S]	Juju	1965	7.50	15.00	30.00
-- With New York, USA address on label					
❑ BST-84182 [S]	Juju	1967	3.75	7.50	15.00
-- With "A Division of Liberty Records" on label					
❑ BST-84182	Juju	198?	2.50	5.00	10.00
-- "The Finest in Jazz Since 1939" reissue					
❑ BST-84194 [S]	Speak No Evil	1966	7.50	15.00	30.00
-- With New York, USA address on label					
❑ BST-84194 [S]	Speak No Evil	1967	3.75	7.50	15.00
-- With "A Division of Liberty Records" on label					
❑ BST-84219 [S]	The All Seeing Eye	1966	7.50	15.00	30.00
-- With New York, USA address on label					
❑ BST-84219 [S]	The All Seeing Eye	1967	3.75	7.50	15.00
-- With "A Division of Liberty Records" on label					
❑ BST-84232	Adam's Apple	1967	5.00	10.00	20.00
❑ BST-84232	Adam's Apple	1985	2.50	5.00	10.00
-- "The Finest in Jazz Since 1939" reissue					
❑ BST-84297	Schizophrenia	1969	5.00	10.00	20.00
❑ BST-84332	Super Nova	1970	5.00	10.00	20.00
❑ BST-84363	The Odyssey of Iska	1971	3.75	7.50	15.00
❑ B1-91141	The Best of Wayne Shorter	1988	2.50	5.00	10.00

COLUMBIA

Number	Title	Yr	VG	VG+	NM
❑ PC 33418	Native Dancer	1975	3.00	6.00	12.00
-- Originals have no bar code					
❑ PC 33418	Native Dancer	198?	2.00	4.00	8.00
-- Reissue with bar code					
❑ FC 40055	Atlantis	1985	2.50	5.00	10.00
❑ FC 40373	Phantom Navigator	1987	2.50	5.00	10.00
❑ FC 44110	Joy Ryder	1988	2.50	5.00	10.00

GNP CRESCENDO

Number	Title	Yr	VG	VG+	NM
❑ GNPS-2075 [(2)]	Wayne Shorter	1973	3.75	7.50	15.00

TRIP

Number	Title	Yr	VG	VG+	NM
❑ 5009 [(2)]	Shorter Moments	1974	3.00	6.00	12.00

VEE JAY

Number	Title	Yr	VG	VG+	NM
❑ LP-3006 [M]	Introducing Wayne Shorter	1960	10.00	20.00	40.00
❑ SR-3006 [S]	Introducing Wayne Shorter	1960	12.50	25.00	50.00
❑ VJS-3006	Introducing Wayne Shorter	1986	3.00	6.00	12.00
-- 1980s reissue on thinner vinyl					
❑ LP-3029 [M]	Wayning Moments	1962	7.50	15.00	30.00
❑ SR-3029 [S]	Wayning Moments	1962	10.00	20.00	40.00
❑ VJS-3029	Wayning Moments	198?	3.00	6.00	12.00
-- 1980s reissue on thinner vinyl					
❑ LP-3057 [M]	Second Genesis	1963	7.50	15.00	30.00
❑ SR-3057 [S]	Second Genesis	1963	10.00	20.00	40.00
❑ VJS-3057	Second Genesis	198?	3.00	6.00	12.00
-- 1980s reissue on thinner vinyl					

SHQ
Czech group led by Karel Velebny.
ESP-DISK'

Number	Title	Yr	VG	VG+	NM
❑ 1080 [S]	The Uhu Sleeps Only During the Day	1969	7.50	15.00	30.00

SHU, EDDIE
Tenor saxophone player, trumpeter and male singer.
BETHLEHEM

Number	Title	Yr	VG	VG+	NM
❑ BCP-1013 [10]	I Only Have Eyes For Shu	1954	25.00	50.00	100.00

SHU, EDDIE/BOB HARDAWAY
Also see each artist's individual listings.
BETHLEHEM

Number	Title	Yr	VG	VG+	NM
❑ BCP-3 [M]	Jazz Practitioners	1957	20.00	40.00	80.00

SHU, EDDIE/JOE ROLAND/"WILD" BILL DAVIS
Also see each artist's individual listings.
MERCER

Number	Title	Yr	VG	VG+	NM
❑ LP-1002 [10]	New Stars, New Sounds, Volume 1	1951	37.50	75.00	150.00

SHULMAN, JOEL
JAMAL

Number	Title	Yr	VG	VG+	NM
❑ 5162	Peninah	197?	5.00	10.00	20.00

SHUMATE, TED, AND IRA SULLIVAN
Shumate is a guitarist. Also see IRA SULLIVAN.
PAUSA

Number	Title	Yr	VG	VG+	NM
❑ 7188	Gulfstream	1986	2.50	5.00	10.00

SIDMAN, DAVID
Guitarist, composer and bandleader.
CADENCE JAZZ

Number	Title	Yr	VG	VG+	NM
❑ CJR-1033	Shades of Meaning	1988	2.50	5.00	10.00

SIDRAN, BEN
Keyboard player, pianist and male singer.
ANTILLES

Number	Title	Yr	VG	VG+	NM
❑ AN-1004	Old Songs for the New Depression	1981	2.50	5.00	10.00
❑ AN-1012	Bop City	1984	2.50	5.00	10.00

ARISTA

Number	Title	Yr	VG	VG+	NM
❑ AL 4081	Free in America	1976	3.00	6.00	12.00
❑ AL 4131	The Doctor Is In	1977	3.00	6.00	12.00
❑ AL 4178	A Little Kiss in the Night	1978	3.00	6.00	12.00

Number	Title	Yr	VG	VG+	NM
❑ AL 4218	Live at Montreux	1979	3.00	6.00	12.00
BLUE THUMB					
❑ BTS-40	I Lead a Life	1972	3.75	7.50	15.00
❑ BTS-55	Puttin' In Time on Planet Earth	1973	3.75	7.50	15.00
❑ BTS-6012	Don't Let Go	1974	3.00	6.00	12.00
BLUEBIRD					
❑ 6575-1-RB	That's Life I Guess	1988	2.50	5.00	10.00
CAPITOL					
❑ ST-825	Feel Your Groove	1971	5.00	10.00	20.00
HORIZON					
❑ SP-741	The Cat and the Hat	1980	3.00	6.00	12.00
MAGENTA					
❑ MA-0204	On the Cool Side	1985	2.50	5.00	10.00
❑ MA-0206	On the Live Side	1986	2.50	5.00	10.00
WINDHAM HILL JAZZ					
❑ WH-0108	Too Hot to Touch	1988	2.50	5.00	10.00

SIEGEL, DAN
Keyboards player.
CBS ASSOCIATED

Number	Title	Yr	VG	VG+	NM
❑ BZ 44026	Northern Nights	1987	2.50	5.00	10.00
❑ OZ 44490	Late One Night	1989	3.00	6.00	12.00
INNER CITY					
❑ IC-1046	Nite Ride	197?	3.00	6.00	12.00
❑ IC-1111	The Hot Shot	198?	3.00	6.00	12.00
❑ IC-1134	Oasis	198?	3.00	6.00	12.00
PAUSA					
❑ 7142	Reflections	198?	2.50	5.00	10.00
❑ 7164	Another Time, Another Place	1984	2.50	5.00	10.00
❑ 7179	On the Edge	1985	2.50	5.00	10.00

SIGNATURES, THE
Vocal and instrumental quintet: Bunny Phillips (lead voice); Ruth Alcivar (vocals, drums); Lee Humes (vocals, bass, trombone); Bob Alcivar (vocals, piano, arranger); Hal Curtis (vocals, trumpet).
WARNER BROS.

Number	Title	Yr	VG	VG+	NM
❑ W 1250 [M]	The Signatures Sing In	1958	7.50	15.00	30.00
❑ WS 1250 [S]	The Signatures Sing In	1958	10.00	20.00	40.00
❑ W 1353 [M]	Prepare to Flip!	1959	7.50	15.00	30.00
❑ WS 1353 [S]	Prepare to Flip!	1959	10.00	20.00	40.00
WHIPPET					
❑ WLP-702 [M]	The Signatures -- Their Voices and Instruments	1957	15.00	30.00	60.00

SIGNORELLI, FRANK
Pianist and composer.
DAVIS

Number	Title	Yr	VG	VG+	NM
❑ JD-103 [M]	Piano Moods	1951	12.50	25.00	50.00

SILVA, ALAN
Bass player.
CHIAROSCURO

Number	Title	Yr	VG	VG+	NM
❑ 2015	The Shout: Portrait for a Small Woman	197?	3.00	6.00	12.00
ESP-DISK'					
❑ 1091 [S]	Alan Silva	1969	5.00	10.00	20.00

SILVA, MARCOS
Keyboard player.
CROSSOVER

Number	Title	Yr	VG	VG+	NM
❑ CR-5004	Here We Go	1987	2.50	5.00	10.00
❑ CR-5006	White and Black	1989	3.00	6.00	12.00

SILVEIRA, RICARDO
Guitarist.
VERVE FORECAST

Number	Title	Yr	VG	VG+	NM
❑ 835 054-1	Long Distance	1988	2.50	5.00	10.00
❑ 837 696-1	Sky Light	1989	3.00	6.00	12.00

SILVER, HORACE
Pianist, bandleader and composer. Also see STAN GETZ.
BLUE NOTE

Number	Title	Yr	VG	VG+	NM
❑ BN-LA054-F	The Pursuit of the 27th Man	1973	3.75	7.50	15.00
❑ BN-LA402-H2 [(2)]	Horace Silver	1975	5.00	10.00	20.00
❑ BN-LA406-G	Silver 'n' Brass	1975	3.00	6.00	12.00
❑ BN-LA581-G	Silver 'n' Wood	1976	3.00	6.00	12.00
❑ BN-LA708-G	Silver 'n' Voices	1977	3.00	6.00	12.00
❑ BN-LA945-H	Sterling Silver	1979	3.00	6.00	12.00
❑ LWB-1033 [(2)]	Silver and Strings Play Music of the Spheres	1980	3.75	7.50	15.00

Number	Title	Yr	VG	VG+	NM
❑ BLP-1518 [M]	Horace Silver and the Jazz Messengers	1956	50.00	100.00	200.00
-- "Deep groove" version (deep indentation under label on both sides)					
❑ BLP-1518 [M]	Horace Silver and the Jazz Messengers	1956	37.50	75.00	150.00
-- Regular edition, Lexington Ave. address on label					
❑ BLP-1518 [M]	Horace Silver and the Jazz Messengers	1963	6.25	12.50	25.00
-- "New York, USA" address on label					
❑ BLP-1520 [M]	Spotlight on Drums	1956	50.00	100.00	200.00
-- "Deep groove" version (deep indentation under label on both sides)					
❑ BLP-1520 [M]	Spotlight on Drums	1956	37.50	75.00	150.00
-- Regular edition, Lexington Ave. address on label					
❑ BLP-1520 [M]	Spotlight on Drums	1963	6.25	12.50	25.00
-- "New York, USA" address on label					
❑ BLP-1539 [M]	Six Pieces of Silver	1957	50.00	100.00	200.00
-- "Deep groove" version (deep indentation under label on both sides)					
❑ BLP-1539 [M]	Six Pieces of Silver	1957	37.50	75.00	150.00
-- Regular edition, Lexington Ave. address on label					
❑ BLP-1539 [M]	Six Pieces of Silver	1963	6.25	12.50	25.00
-- "New York, USA" address on label					
❑ BLP-1562 [M]	The Stylings of Silver	1957	37.50	75.00	150.00
-- "Deep groove" version (deep indentation under label on both sides)					
❑ BLP-1562 [M]	The Stylings of Silver	1957	25.00	50.00	100.00
-- Regular edition, W. 63rd St. address on label					
❑ BLP-1562 [M]	The Stylings of Silver	1963	6.25	12.50	25.00
-- "New York, USA" address on label					
❑ BST-1562 [S]	The Stylings of Silver	1959	25.00	50.00	100.00
-- "Deep groove" version (deep indentation under label on both sides)					
❑ BST-1562 [S]	The Stylings of Silver	1959	20.00	40.00	80.00
-- Regular edition, W. 63rd St. address on label					
❑ BST-1562 [S]	The Stylings of Silver	1963	5.00	10.00	20.00
-- "New York, USA" address on label					
❑ BLP-1589 [M]	Further Explorations	1958	37.50	75.00	150.00
-- "Deep groove" version (deep indentation under label on both sides)					
❑ BLP-1589 [M]	Further Explorations	1958	25.00	50.00	100.00
-- Regular edition, W. 63rd St. address on label					
❑ BLP-1589 [M]	Further Explorations	1963	6.25	12.50	25.00
-- "New York, USA" address on label					
❑ BST-1589 [S]	Further Explorations	1959	25.00	50.00	100.00
-- "Deep groove" version (deep indentation under label on both sides)					
❑ BST-1589 [S]	Further Explorations	1959	20.00	40.00	80.00
-- Regular edition, W. 63rd St. address on label					
❑ BST-1589 [S]	Further Explorations	1963	5.00	10.00	20.00
-- "New York, USA" address on label					
❑ BLP-4008 [M]	Finger Poppin'	1959	37.50	75.00	150.00
-- "Deep groove" version (deep indentation under label on both sides)					
❑ BLP-4008 [M]	Finger Poppin'	1959	25.00	50.00	100.00
-- Regular edition, W. 63rd St. address on label					
❑ BLP-4008 [M]	Finger Poppin'	1963	6.25	12.50	25.00
-- "New York, USA" address on label					
❑ BST-4008 [S]	Finger Poppin'	1959	25.00	50.00	100.00
-- "Deep groove" version (deep indentation under label on both sides)					
❑ BST-4008 [S]	Finger Poppin'	1959	20.00	40.00	80.00
-- Regular edition, W. 63rd St. address on label					
❑ BST-4008 [S]	Finger Poppin'	1963	5.00	10.00	20.00
-- "New York, USA" address on label					
❑ BLP-4017 [M]	Blowin' the Blues Away	1959	30.00	60.00	120.00
-- "Deep groove" version (deep indentation under label on both sides)					
❑ BLP-4017 [M]	Blowin' the Blues Away	1959	20.00	40.00	80.00
-- Regular edition, W. 63rd St. address on label					
❑ BLP-4017 [M]	Blowin' the Blues Away	1963	6.25	12.50	25.00
-- "New York, USA" address on label					
❑ BLP-4042 [M]	Horace-Scope	1960	30.00	60.00	120.00
-- "Deep groove" version (deep indentation under label on both sides)					
❑ BLP-4042 [M]	Horace-Scope	1960	20.00	40.00	80.00
-- Regular edition, W. 63rd St. address on label					
❑ BLP-4042 [M]	Horace-Scope	1963	6.25	12.50	25.00
-- "New York, USA" address on label					
❑ BLP-4076 [M]	Doin' the Thing at the Village Gate	1961	15.00	30.00	60.00
-- 61st St. address on label					
❑ BLP-4076 [M]	Doin' the Thing at the Village Gate	1963	5.00	10.00	20.00
-- "New York, USA" address on label					
❑ BLP-4110 [M]	The Tokyo Blues	1962	7.50	15.00	30.00
❑ BLP-4131 [M]	Silver's Serenade	1963	7.50	15.00	30.00
❑ BLP-4185 [M]	Song for My Father (Cantiga Para Meu Pai)	1965	6.25	12.50	25.00
❑ BLP-4220 [M]	The Cape Verdean Blues	1965	6.25	12.50	25.00
❑ BLP-4250 [M]	The Jody Grind	1966	6.25	12.50	25.00
❑ BLP-5018 [10]	New Faces	1953	75.00	150.00	300.00
❑ BLP-5034 [10]	Horace Silver Trio, Vol. 2	1954	62.50	125.00	250.00
❑ BLP-5058 [10]	Horace Silver Quintet	1955	62.50	125.00	250.00
❑ BLP-5062 [10]	Horace Silver Quintet	1955	62.50	125.00	250.00
❑ B1-46548	Song for My Father	1997	3.75	7.50	15.00
-- Reissue on 180-gram vinyl					
❑ BST-81518 [R]	Horace Silver and the Jazz Messengers	1967	3.00	6.00	12.00

Number	Title	Yr	VG	VG+	NM
❏ BST-81518	Horace Silver and the Jazz Messengers	1985	2.50	5.00	10.00
-- "The Finest in Jazz Since 1939" reissue					
❏ B1-81520	The Horace Silver Trio	1989	2.50	5.00	10.00
-- "The Finest in Jazz Since 1939" reissue					
❏ BST-81520 [R]	Spotlight on Drums	1967	3.00	6.00	12.00
-- With "A Division of Liberty Records" on label					
❏ B1-81539	Six Pieces of Silver	1988	2.50	5.00	10.00
-- "The Finest in Jazz Since 1939" reissue					
❏ BST-81539 [R]	Six Pieces of Silver	1967	3.00	6.00	12.00
❏ BST-81562 [S]	The Stylings of Silver	1967	3.75	7.50	15.00
❏ BST-81589 [S]	Further Explorations	1967	3.75	7.50	15.00
❏ B1-84008	Finger Poppin'	198?	2.50	5.00	10.00
-- "The Finest in Jazz Since 1939" reissue					
❏ BST-84008 [S]	Finger Poppin'	1967	3.75	7.50	15.00
❏ BST-84017 [S]	Blowin' the Blues Away	1959	15.00	30.00	60.00
-- W. 63rd St. address on label					
❏ BST-84017 [S]	Blowin' the Blues Away	1963	5.00	10.00	20.00
-- "New York, USA" address on label					
❏ BST-84017 [S]	Blowin' the Blues Away	1967	3.75	7.50	15.00
-- "A Division of Liberty Records" on label					
❏ BST-84017	Blowin' the Blues Away	1985	2.50	5.00	10.00
-- "The Finest in Jazz Since 1939" reissue					
❏ BST-84042 [S]	Horace-Scope	1960	15.00	30.00	60.00
-- W. 63rd St. address on label					
❏ BST-84042 [S]	Horace-Scope	1963	5.00	10.00	20.00
-- "New York, USA" address on label					
❏ BST-84042 [S]	Horace-Scope	1967	3.75	7.50	15.00
-- "A Division of Liberty Records" on label					
❏ B1-84076	Doin' the Thing at the Village Gate	1989	2.50	5.00	10.00
-- "The Finest in Jazz Since 1939" reissue					
❏ BST-84076 [S]	Doin' the Thing at the Village Gate	1961	15.00	30.00	60.00
-- 61st St. address on label					
❏ BST-84076 [S]	Doin' the Thing at the Village Gate	1963	5.00	10.00	20.00
-- "New York, USA" address on label					
❏ BST-84076 [S]	Doin' the Thing at the Village Gate	1967	3.75	7.50	15.00
-- "A Division of Liberty Records" on label					
❏ BST-84110 [S]	The Tokyo Blues	1962	10.00	20.00	40.00
-- "New York, USA" address on label					
❏ BST-84110 [S]	The Tokyo Blues	1967	3.75	7.50	15.00
-- "A Division of Liberty Records" on label					
❏ BST-84131 [S]	Silver's Serenade	1963	10.00	20.00	40.00
-- "New York, USA" address on label					
❏ BST-84131 [S]	Silver's Serenade	1967	3.75	7.50	15.00
-- "A Division of Liberty Records" on label					
❏ BST-84185 [S]	Song for My Father (Cantiga Para Meu Pai)	1965	7.50	15.00	30.00
-- "New York, USA" address on label					
❏ BST-84185 [S]	Song for My Father (Cantiga Para Meu Pai)	1967	3.75	7.50	15.00
-- "A Division of Liberty Records" on label					
❏ BST-84185	Song for My Father (Cantiga Para Meu Pai)	1985	2.50	5.00	10.00
-- "The Finest in Jazz Since 1939" reissue					
❏ BST-84220 [S]	The Cape Verdean Blues	1965	7.50	15.00	30.00
-- "New York, USA" address on label					
❏ BST-84220 [S]	The Cape Verdean Blues	1967	3.75	7.50	15.00
-- "A Division of Liberty Records" on label					
❏ BST-84250 [S]	The Jody Grind	1966	7.50	15.00	30.00
-- "New York, USA" address on label					
❏ BST-84250 [S]	The Jody Grind	1967	3.75	7.50	15.00
-- "A Division of Liberty Records" on label					
❏ BST-84277	Serenade to a Soul Sister	1968	3.75	7.50	15.00
❏ BST-84309	You Gotta Take a Little Love	1969	3.75	7.50	15.00
❏ BST-84325	The Best of Horace Silver	1970	3.75	7.50	15.00
❏ BST-84352	That Healin' Feelin' (Phase 1)	1970	3.75	7.50	15.00
❏ BST-84368	Total Response (Phase 2)	1971	3.75	7.50	15.00
❏ BST-84420	Phase Three "All"	1972	3.75	7.50	15.00
❏ B1-91143	The Best of Horace Silver	1988	2.50	5.00	10.00
❏ B1-93206	The Best of Horace Silver, Vol. 2	1989	2.50	5.00	10.00
EPIC					
❏ LN 3326 [M]	Silver's Blue	1956	20.00	40.00	80.00
❏ LA 16006 [M]	Silver's Blue	1959	10.00	20.00	40.00
❏ BA 17006 [R]	Silver's Blue	196?	5.00	10.00	20.00

SIMEON, OMER
Clarinetist. Also see SIDNEY BECHET.

Number	Title	Yr	VG	VG+	NM
CONCERT HALL JAZZ					
❏ 1014 [10]	Clarinet A La Creole	195?	12.50	25.00	50.00
DISC					
❏ DLP-748 [10]	Omer Simeon Trio with James P. Johnson	195?	50.00	100.00	200.00

Number	Title	Yr	VG	VG+	NM
SIMMONS, NORMAN					
Pianist and composer.					
ARGO					
❏ LP-607 [M]	Norman Simmons Trio	1956	10.00	20.00	40.00
CREATIVE					
❏ LP-607 [M]	Interpolations	1956	20.00	40.00	80.00
MILLJAC					
❏ MLP-1001	Midnight Creeper	1979	3.75	7.50	15.00
❏ MLP-1002	I'm the Blues	1981	3.75	7.50	15.00

SIMMONS, SONNY
Alto saxophone player.

Number	Title	Yr	VG	VG+	NM
ARHOOLIE					
❏ 8003 [S]	Manhattan Egos	1969	3.75	7.50	15.00
CONTEMPORARY					
❏ M-3623 [M]	Rumasuma	1966	5.00	10.00	20.00
❏ S-7623 [S]	Rumasuma	1966	6.25	12.50	25.00
❏ S-7625/6 [(2)]	Burning Spirits	1970	5.00	10.00	20.00
ESP-DISK'					
❏ 1030 [M]	Sonny Simmons	1966	5.00	10.00	20.00
❏ S-1030 [S]	Sonny Simmons	1966	6.25	12.50	25.00
❏ 1043 [M]	Music from the Spheres	1967	6.25	12.50	25.00
❏ S-1043 [S]	Music from the Spheres	1967	5.00	10.00	20.00

SIMON AND BARD
FRED SIMON (keyboards, composer) and Michael Bard (saxophones).

Number	Title	Yr	VG	VG+	NM
FLYING FISH					
❏ FF-243	Musaic	1980	2.50	5.00	10.00
❏ FF-262	Tear It Up	1982	2.50	5.00	10.00
❏ FF-321	The Enormous Radio	198?	2.50	5.00	10.00

SIMON, ALAN
Pianist.

Number	Title	Yr	VG	VG+	NM
CADENCE JAZZ					
❏ CJR-1027	Rainsplash	198?	2.50	5.00	10.00

SIMON, FRED
Pianist and keyboard player. Also see SIMON AND BARD.

Number	Title	Yr	VG	VG+	NM
WINDHAM HILL					
❏ WH-1071	Usually/Always	1988	2.50	5.00	10.00

SIMON, RALPH
Tenor, soprano and alto saxophone player.

Number	Title	Yr	VG	VG+	NM
GRAMAVISION					
❏ 8002	Time Being	1981	2.50	5.00	10.00

SIMONE
Female singer from Brazil.

Number	Title	Yr	VG	VG+	NM
COLUMBIA					
❏ FC 44275	Vicio	1988	3.00	6.00	12.00

SIMONE, NINA
Female singer.

Number	Title	Yr	VG	VG+	NM
ACCORD					
❏ SN-7108	In Concert	1981	2.50	5.00	10.00
BETHLEHEM					
❏ BCP-6003	Nina Simone's Finest	197?	3.00	6.00	12.00
❏ BCP-6028 [M]	Jazz As Played in an Exclusive Side Street Club	1959	20.00	40.00	80.00
❏ BCP-6028 [M]	The Original Nina Simone	1961	7.50	15.00	30.00
-- Retitled reissue					
❏ SBCP-6028 [S]	Jazz As Played in an Exclusive Side Street Club	1959	25.00	50.00	100.00
❏ SBCP-6028 [S]	The Original Nina Simone	1961	10.00	20.00	40.00
-- Retitled reissue					
❏ BCP-6041 [M]	Nina Simone and Her Friends	1960	10.00	20.00	40.00
❏ SBCP-6041 [S]	Nina Simone and Her Friends	1960	12.50	25.00	50.00
-- With Carmen McRae and Chris Connor					
CANYON					
❏ 7705	Gifted and Black	1971	3.75	7.50	15.00
COLPIX					
❏ CP-407 [M]	The Amazing Nina Simone	1959	6.25	12.50	25.00
❏ SCP-407 [S]	The Amazing Nina Simone	1959	7.50	15.00	30.00
❏ CP-409 [M]	Nina at Town Hall	1960	6.25	12.50	25.00
❏ SCP-409 [S]	Nina at Town Hall	1960	7.50	15.00	30.00
❏ CP-412 [M]	Nina at Newport	1960	6.25	12.50	25.00
❏ SCP-412 [S]	Nina at Newport	1960	7.50	15.00	30.00
❏ CP-419 [M]	Forbidden Fruit	1961	6.25	12.50	25.00
❏ SCP-419 [S]	Forbidden Fruit	1961	7.50	15.00	30.00
❏ CP-421 [M]	Nina Simone at the Village Gate	1961	6.25	12.50	25.00
❏ SCP-421 [S]	Nina Simone at the Village Gate	1961	7.50	15.00	30.00
❏ CP-425 [M]	Nina Sings Ellington	1962	6.25	12.50	25.00

Number	Title	Yr	VG	VG+	NM
☐ SCP-425 [S]	Nina Sings Ellington	1962	7.50	15.00	30.00
☐ CP-443 [M]	Nina's Choice	1963	6.25	12.50	25.00
☐ SCP-443 [S]	Nina's Choice	1963	7.50	15.00	30.00
☐ CP-455 [M]	Nina Simone at Carnegie Hall	1963	6.25	12.50	25.00
☐ SCP-455 [S]	Nina Simone at Carnegie Hall	1963	7.50	15.00	30.00
☐ CP-465 [M]	Folksy Nina	1964	6.25	12.50	25.00
☐ SCP-465 [S]	Folksy Nina	1964	7.50	15.00	30.00
☐ CP-496 [M]	Nina with Strings	1966	6.25	12.50	25.00
☐ SCP-496 [S]	Nina with Strings	1966	7.50	15.00	30.00

CTI

☐ 7084	Baltimore	1978	3.00	6.00	12.00

PHILIPS

☐ PHM 200-135 [M]	Nina Simone In Concert	1964	3.75	7.50	15.00
☐ PHM 200-148 [M]	Broadway...Blues...Ballads	1964	3.75	7.50	15.00
☐ PHM 200-172 [M]	I Put a Spell on You	1965	3.75	7.50	15.00
☐ PHM 200-187 [M]	Pastel Blues	1965	3.75	7.50	15.00
☐ PHM 200-202 [M]	Let It All Out	1966	3.75	7.50	15.00
☐ PHM 200-207 [M]	Wild Is the Wind	1966	3.75	7.50	15.00
☐ PHM 200-219 [M]	The High Priestess of Soul	1967	3.75	7.50	15.00
☐ PHS 600-135 [S]	Nina Simone In Concert	1964	5.00	10.00	20.00
☐ PHS 600-148 [S]	Broadway...Blues...Ballads	1964	5.00	10.00	20.00
☐ PHS 600-172 [S]	I Put a Spell on You	1965	5.00	10.00	20.00
☐ PHS 600-187 [S]	Pastel Blues	1965	5.00	10.00	20.00
☐ PHS 600-202 [S]	Let It All Out	1966	5.00	10.00	20.00
☐ PHS 600-207 [S]	Wild Is the Wind	1966	5.00	10.00	20.00
☐ PHS 600-219 [S]	The High Priestess of Soul	1967	5.00	10.00	20.00
☐ PHS 600-298	The Best of Nina Simone	1969	5.00	10.00	20.00
☐ 822 846-1	The Best of Nina Simone	198?	2.50	5.00	10.00

PM

☐ 018	A Very Rare Evening	1979	3.00	6.00	12.00

QUINTESSENCE

☐ 25421	Silk and Soul	1979	2.50	5.00	10.00

RCA VICTOR

☐ AFL1-0241	It Is Finished -- Nina 1974	1977	2.50	5.00	10.00
-- Reissue with new prefix					
☐ APL1-0241	It Is Finished -- Nina 1974	1974	3.00	6.00	12.00
☐ AFL1-1788	Poets	1977	2.50	5.00	10.00
-- Reissue with new prefix					
☐ APL1-1788	Poets	1976	3.00	6.00	12.00
☐ LPM-3789 [M]	Nina Simone Sings the Blues	1967	6.25	12.50	25.00
☐ LSP-3789 [S]	Nina Simone Sings the Blues	1967	3.75	7.50	15.00
☐ LPM-3837 [M]	Silk and Soul	1967	6.25	12.50	25.00
☐ LSP-3837 [S]	Silk and Soul	1967	3.75	7.50	15.00
☐ LSP-4065	'Nuff Said	1968	3.75	7.50	15.00
☐ LSP-4102	Nina Simone and Piano	1968	3.75	7.50	15.00
☐ LSP-4152	To Love Somebody	1969	3.75	7.50	15.00
☐ LSP-4248	Black Gold	1970	3.75	7.50	15.00
☐ AFL1-4374	The Best of Nina Simone	1977	2.50	5.00	10.00
-- Reissue with new prefix					
☐ LSP-4374	The Best of Nina Simone	1970	3.75	7.50	15.00
☐ AFL1-4536	Here Comes the Sun	1977	2.50	5.00	10.00
-- Reissue with new prefix					
☐ LSP-4536	Here Comes the Sun	1971	3.75	7.50	15.00
☐ LSP-4757	Emergency Ward!	1972	3.75	7.50	15.00

SALSOUL

☐ SA-8546	Little Girl Blue	1982	2.50	5.00	10.00

TRIP

☐ 8020 [(2)]	Live in Europe	1973	3.00	6.00	12.00
☐ 8021 [(2)]	Black Is the Color	1973	3.00	6.00	12.00
☐ 9521	Portrait	197?	2.50	5.00	10.00

VERVE

☐ 831 437-1	Let It Be Me	1987	2.50	5.00	10.00

SIMPKINS, ANDY, AND DAVE MacKAY

Simpkins plays bass. Also see DAVID MacKAY.

STUDIO 7

☐ 403	Happying	197?	3.00	6.00	12.00

SIMPSON, CAROLE

Female singer.

CAPITOL

☐ T 878 [M]	All About Carole	1957	20.00	40.00	80.00

TOPS

☐ L-1732 [M]	Singin' and Swingin'	1960	6.25	12.50	25.00

SIMPSON, CASS

Pianist.

ABC-PARAMOUNT

☐ ABC-103 [M]	Cass Simpson	1956	10.00	20.00	40.00

SIMS, ZOOT

Tenor saxophone player. Also see PEPPER ADAMS; BOB BROOKMEYER; AL COHN; ROY ELDRIDGE; THE FOUR BROTHERS; STAN GETZ; JUTTA HIPP; THE MANHATTAN ALL-STARS; GERRY MULLIGAN; ORCHESTRA USA.

ABC IMPULSE!

☐ AS-9131 [S]	The Waiting Game	1968	5.00	10.00	20.00

ABC-PARAMOUNT

Number	Title	Yr	VG	VG+	NM
☐ ABC-155 [M]	Zoot Sims Plays Alto, Tenor and Baritone	1957	20.00	40.00	80.00
☐ ABC-198 [M]	Zoot Sims Plays Four Altos	1957	20.00	40.00	80.00

ARGO

☐ LP-608 [M]	Zoot	1956	20.00	40.00	80.00
-- Color cover					
☐ LP-608 [M]	Zoot	1957	12.50	25.00	50.00
-- Black and white cover					

BETHLEHEM

☐ BCP-6027	Down Home	197?	3.00	6.00	12.00
-- Reissue, distributed by RCA Victor					
☐ BCP-6051 [M]	Down Home	1960	10.00	20.00	40.00
☐ SBCP-6051 [S]	Down Home	1960	10.00	20.00	40.00

BIOGRAPH

☐ 12062	One to Blow On	198?	2.50	5.00	10.00

CADET

☐ LP-608 [M]	Zoot	1966	3.75	7.50	15.00

CHOICE

☐ 1006	Party	197?	3.75	7.50	15.00

CLASSIC JAZZ

☐ 21	Zoot Sims and Bucky Pizzarelli	197?	3.00	6.00	12.00

COLPIX

☐ CP-435 [M]	New Beat Bossa Nova	1962	10.00	20.00	40.00
☐ SCP-435 [S]	New Beat Bossa Nova	1962	12.50	25.00	50.00
☐ CP-437 [M]	New Beat Bossa Nova, Volume 2	1962	10.00	20.00	40.00
☐ SCP-437 [S]	New Beat Bossa Nova, Volume 2	1962	12.50	25.00	50.00

DAWN

☐ DLP-1102 [M]	The Modern Age of Jazz	1956	25.00	50.00	100.00
☐ DLP-1115 [M]	Zoot Sims Goes to Jazzville	1957	25.00	50.00	100.00

DISCOVERY

☐ DL-3015 [10]	The Zoot Sims Quartet In Paris	1951	62.50	125.00	250.00

FAMOUS DOOR

☐ HL-2000	At Ease	197?	3.75	7.50	15.00

FANTASY

☐ OJC-228	Zoot!	198?	2.50	5.00	10.00
☐ OJC-242	Zoot Sims Quartets	1987	2.50	5.00	10.00
☐ OJC-444	The Gershwin Brothers	1990	3.00	6.00	12.00

GROOVE MERCHANT

☐ 533	Nirvana	197?	3.75	7.50	15.00

IMPULSE!

☐ A-9131 [M]	The Waiting Game	1967	6.25	12.50	25.00
☐ AS-9131 [S]	The Waiting Game	1967	3.75	7.50	15.00

JAZZLAND

☐ JLP-2 [M]	Zoot Sims Quintet	1960	10.00	20.00	40.00
☐ JLP-92 [S]	Zoot Sims Quintet	1960	7.50	15.00	30.00

MCA

☐ 29069	Zoot Sims Plays Four Altos	1980	2.50	5.00	10.00

NEW JAZZ

☐ NJLP-1102 [10]	Zoot Sims in Hollywood	1954	50.00	100.00	200.00
☐ NJLP-8280 [M]	Good Old Zoot	1962	12.50	25.00	50.00
☐ NJLP-8302 [M]	Trotting	1963	---	---	---
-- Canceled; reassigned to Status					
☐ NJLP-8309 [M]	Koo Koo	1963	---	---	---
-- Canceled; reassigned to Status					

PABLO

☐ 2310 744	The Gershwin Brothers	197?	3.00	6.00	12.00
☐ 2310 770	Soprano Sax	197?	3.00	6.00	12.00
☐ 2310 783	Hawthorne Nights	197?	3.00	6.00	12.00
☐ 2310 831	Warm Tenor	1979	3.00	6.00	12.00
☐ 2310 861	Swinger	198?	2.50	5.00	10.00
☐ 2310 868	I Wish I Were Twins	198?	2.50	5.00	10.00
☐ 2310 872	The Innocent Years	198?	2.50	5.00	10.00
☐ 2310 898	Suddenly It's Spring	198?	2.50	5.00	10.00
☐ 2310 903	Quietly There	198?	2.50	5.00	10.00
☐ 2405 406	The Best of Zoot Sims	198?	2.50	5.00	10.00

PABLO TODAY

☐ 2312 120	Zoot Sims Plays Duke Ellington/Passion Flower	1980	3.00	6.00	12.00

PACIFIC JAZZ

☐ PJ-20 [M]	Choice	1961	10.00	20.00	40.00

PRESTIGE

☐ PRLP-117 [10]	Swingin' with Zoot Sims	1951	50.00	100.00	200.00
☐ PRLP-118 [10]	Tenor Sax Favorites	1951	50.00	100.00	200.00
☐ PRLP-138 [10]	Zoot Sims All Stars	1953	50.00	100.00	200.00
☐ PRLP-202 [10]	Zoot Sims Quintet	1955	37.50	75.00	150.00
☐ PRLP-7026 [M]	Zoot Sims Quartets	1956	30.00	60.00	120.00
☐ PRST-7817	First Recordings!	1970	3.75	7.50	15.00
☐ PRLP-16009 [M]	Trotting	1963	10.00	20.00	40.00
☐ 24061 [(2)]	Zootcase	197?	3.75	7.50	15.00

Number	Title	Yr	VG	VG+	NM
RIVERSIDE					
❏ RLP 12-228 [M]	Zoot!	1957	20.00	40.00	80.00
❏ 6103	Zoot	197?	3.00	6.00	12.00
SEECO					
❏ CELP-452 [M]	The Modern Art of Jazz	1960	10.00	20.00	40.00
❏ CELP-4520 [S]	The Modern Art of Jazz	1960	10.00	20.00	40.00
STATUS					
❏ ST-8280 [M]	Good Old Zoot	1965	10.00	20.00	40.00
❏ ST-8309 [M]	Koo Koo	1965	10.00	20.00	40.00
SWING					
❏ SW-8417	Zoot Sims in Paris	1987	2.50	5.00	10.00
TRIP					
❏ 5548	You 'n Me	197?	2.50	5.00	10.00
UNITED ARTISTS					
❏ UAL-4040 [M]	A Night at the Half Note	1959	10.00	20.00	40.00
❏ UAS-5040 [S]	A Night at the Half Note	1959	12.50	25.00	50.00
❏ UAJ-14013 [M]	Zoot Sims in Paris	1962	10.00	20.00	40.00
❏ UAJS-15013 [S]	Zoot Sims in Paris	1962	12.50	25.00	50.00
ZIM					
❏ 1008	Nash-ville	198?	2.50	5.00	10.00

SIMS, ZOOT, AND HARRY "SWEETS" EDISON
Also see each artist's individual listings.

Number	Title	Yr	VG	VG+	NM
FANTASY					
❏ OJC-499	Just Friends	1991	3.00	6.00	12.00
PABLO					
❏ 2310 841	Just Friends	198?	2.50	5.00	10.00

SIMS, ZOOT; JIMMY RANEY; JIM HALL
Also see each artist's individual listings.

Number	Title	Yr	VG	VG+	NM
MAINSTREAM					
❏ MRL-358	Otra Vez	1972	3.00	6.00	12.00
❏ S-6013 [S]	Two Jims and Zoot	1965	6.25	12.50	25.00
❏ 56013 [M]	Two Jims and Zoot	1965	5.00	10.00	20.00

SIMS, ZOOT, AND BUDDY RICH
Also see each artist's individual listings.

Number	Title	Yr	VG	VG+	NM
QUINTESSENCE					
❏ 25041	Air Mail Special	197?	3.00	6.00	12.00

SIMS, ZOOT, AND JIMMY ROWLES
Also see each artist's individual listings.

Number	Title	Yr	VG	VG+	NM
PABLO					
❏ 2310 803	Lucky	1977	3.00	6.00	12.00

SIMS, ZOOT; TONY SCOTT; AL COHN
Also see each artist's individual listings.

Number	Title	Yr	VG	VG+	NM
JAZZLAND					
❏ JLP-11 [M]	East Coast Sounds	1960	10.00	20.00	40.00
❏ JLP-911 [S]	East Coast Sounds	1960	10.00	20.00	40.00

SINATRA, FRANK
Male singer. Highly influenced by jazz, and highly influential on jazz as well, we have decided to include all his known American albums here rather than be selective. Also see TOMMY DORSEY; HARRY JAMES.

Number	Title	Yr	VG	VG+	NM
ARTANIS					
❏ ARZ 101 [(2)]	Sinatra '57 In Concert	1999	---	---	---
-- *Unissued; not officially canceled, though*					
BOOK-OF-THE-MONTH					
❏ (# unknown) [(6)]	Tommy Dorsey/Frank Sinatra: The Complete Sessions	1983	25.00	50.00	100.00
CAPITOL					
❏ DWBB-254 [(2) R]	Close-Up	1969	5.00	10.00	20.00
-- *Reissue in one package of "This Is Sinatra" and "This Is Sinatra, Volume Two"*					
❏ DKAO-374 [R]	Frank Sinatra's Greatest Hits	1969	3.00	6.00	12.00
❏ H 488 [10]	Songs for Young Lovers	1954	15.00	30.00	60.00
❏ H 528 [10]	Swing Easy	1954	15.00	30.00	60.00
❏ STBB-529 [(2)]	What Is This Thing Called Love?/The Night We Called It a Day	1970	3.75	7.50	15.00
❏ DW 581 [R]	In the Wee Small Hours	196?	3.00	6.00	12.00
❏ H1-581 [10]	In the Wee Small Hours, Part 1	1955	25.00	50.00	100.00
❏ H2-581 [10]	In the Wee Small Hours, Part 2	1955	25.00	50.00	100.00
❏ SM-581	In the Wee Small Hours	197?	2.00	4.00	8.00
❏ W 581 [M]	In the Wee Small Hours	1955	10.00	20.00	40.00
-- *Gray label original*					
❏ W 581 [M]	In the Wee Small Hours	1959	6.25	12.50	25.00
-- *Black label with colorband*					
❏ W 587 [M]	Swing Easy/Songs for Young Lovers	1955	10.00	20.00	40.00
-- *Gray label original; 12-inch version of two 10-inch LPs*					
❏ W 587 [M]	Swing Easy/Songs for Young Lovers	1959	6.25	12.50	25.00
-- *Black label with colorband*					
❏ DW 653 [R]	Songs for Swingin' Lovers!	196?	3.00	6.00	12.00
❏ SM-653	Songs for Swingin' Lovers!	197?	2.00	4.00	8.00
❏ W 653 [M]	Songs for Swingin' Lovers!	1956	10.00	20.00	40.00
-- *Gray label; cover has Sinatra facing toward the embracing couple*					
❏ W 653 [M]	Songs for Swingin' Lovers!	1956	12.50	25.00	50.00
-- *Gray label; cover has Sinatra facing away from the embracing couple*					
❏ W 653 [M]	Songs for Swingin' Lovers!	1959	6.25	12.50	25.00
-- *Black label with colorband*					
❏ STBB-724 [(2)]	My One and Only Love/Sentimental Journey	1971	3.75	7.50	15.00
❏ T 735 [M]	Frank Sinatra Conducts Tone Poems of Color	1956	15.00	30.00	60.00
-- *Turquoise label*					
❏ T 735 [M]	Frank Sinatra Conducts Tone Poems of Color	1959	10.00	20.00	40.00
-- *Black label with colorband*					
❏ DT 768 [R]	This Is Sinatra!	196?	3.00	6.00	12.00
❏ T 768 [M]	This Is Sinatra!	1956	7.50	15.00	30.00
-- *Turquoise label*					
❏ T 768 [M]	This Is Sinatra!	196?	3.75	7.50	15.00
-- *Gold "Starline" label*					
❏ T 768 [M]	This Is Sinatra!	196?	5.00	10.00	20.00
-- *Black "Starline" label*					
❏ DW 789 [R]	Close to You	196?	3.00	6.00	12.00
❏ W 789 [M]	Close to You	1957	7.50	15.00	30.00
-- *Gray label*					
❏ W 789 [M]	Close to You	1959	5.00	10.00	20.00
-- *Black label with colorband*					
❏ DW 803 [R]	A Swingin' Affair!	196?	3.00	6.00	12.00
❏ W 803 [M]	A Swingin' Affair!	1957	7.50	15.00	30.00
-- *Gray label*					
❏ W 803 [M]	A Swingin' Affair!	1957	5.00	10.00	20.00
-- *Black label with colorband*					
❏ SW 855 [S]	Where Are You?	1959	10.00	20.00	40.00
-- *Originals do not include "I Cover the Waterfront"*					
❏ SW 855 [S]	Where Are You?	196?	7.50	15.00	30.00
-- *Later releases restore "I Cover the Waterfront"*					
❏ W 855 [M]	Where Are You?	1957	7.50	15.00	30.00
-- *Gray label*					
❏ W 855 [M]	Where Are You?	1959	5.00	10.00	20.00
-- *Black label with colorband*					
❏ DT 894 [R]	The Sinatra Christmas Album	196?	2.50	5.00	10.00
-- *Rechanneled reissue of A Jolly Christmas with Frank Sinatra with same contents; some copies have this cover and "A Jolly Christmas" labels*					
❏ SM-894 [R]	The Sinatra Christmas Album	197?	2.00	4.00	8.00
-- *Reissue in rechanneled stereo; any color label*					
❏ T 894 [M]	The Sinatra Christmas Album	196?	5.00	10.00	20.00
-- *Reissue of A Jolly Christmas with Frank Sinatra with same contents; some copies have this cover and "A Jolly Christmas" labels*					
❏ W 894 [M]	A Jolly Christmas from Frank Sinatra	1957	10.00	20.00	40.00
-- *Gray label*					
❏ W 894 [M]	A Jolly Christmas from Frank Sinatra	1958	7.50	15.00	30.00
-- *Black colorband label*					
❏ SM-920	Come Fly with Me	197?	2.00	4.00	8.00
❏ SW 920 [S]	Come Fly with Me	1959	7.50	15.00	30.00
❏ W 920 [M]	Come Fly with Me	1958	10.00	20.00	40.00
-- *Gray label*					
❏ W 920 [M]	Come Fly with Me	1959	5.00	10.00	20.00
-- *Black label with colorband*					
❏ DW 982 [R]	This Is Sinatra, Volume Two	196?	3.00	6.00	12.00
❏ W 982 [M]	This Is Sinatra, Volume Two	1958	10.00	20.00	40.00
-- *Gray label*					
❏ W 982 [M]	This Is Sinatra, Volume Two	1959	5.00	10.00	20.00
-- *Black label with colorband*					
❏ SW 1053 [S]	Frank Sinatra Sings for Only the Lonely	1959	7.50	15.00	30.00
-- *Originals do not include "It's a Lonesome Old Town" and "Spring Is Here"*					
❏ SW 1053 [S]	Frank Sinatra Sings for Only the Lonely	196?	6.25	12.50	25.00
-- *Later releases restore "It's a Lonesome Old Town" and "Spring Is Here"*					
❏ W 1053 [M]	Frank Sinatra Sings for Only the Lonely	1958	10.00	20.00	40.00
-- *Gray label*					
❏ W 1053 [M]	Frank Sinatra Sings for Only the Lonely	1959	5.00	10.00	20.00
-- *Black label with colorband*					
❏ SW 1069 [S]	Come Dance with Me!	1959	7.50	15.00	30.00
❏ W 1069 [M]	Come Dance with Me!	1959	5.00	10.00	20.00
❏ DW 1164 [R]	Look to Your Heart	196?	3.00	6.00	12.00
❏ W 1164 [M]	Look to Your Heart	1959	7.50	15.00	30.00
❏ SM-1221	No One Cares	197?	2.00	4.00	8.00
❏ SW 1221 [S]	No One Cares	1959	7.50	15.00	30.00
❏ W 1221 [M]	No One Cares	1959	5.00	10.00	20.00
❏ SW 1417 [S]	Nice 'N' Easy	1960	6.25	12.50	25.00
❏ W 1417 [M]	Nice 'N' Easy	1960	5.00	10.00	20.00

Number	Title	Yr	VG	VG+	NM
❏ DW 1429 [R]	Swing Easy	1960	3.00	6.00	12.00
❏ W 1429 [M]	Swing Easy	1960	5.00	10.00	20.00
❏ DW 1432 [R]	Songs for Young Lovers	1960	3.00	6.00	12.00
❏ W 1432 [M]	Songs for Young Lovers	1960	5.00	10.00	20.00
❏ SM-1491	Sinatra's Swingin' Session!!!	197?	2.00	4.00	8.00
❏ SW 1491 [S]	Sinatra's Swingin' Session!!!	1961	6.25	12.50	25.00
❏ W 1491 [M]	Sinatra's Swingin' Session!!!	1961	5.00	10.00	20.00
❏ SW 1538 [S]	All the Way	1961	6.25	12.50	25.00
❏ W 1538 [M]	All the Way	1961	5.00	10.00	20.00
❏ SW 1594 [S]	Come Swing with Me!	1961	6.25	12.50	25.00
❏ W 1594 [M]	Come Swing with Me!	1961	5.00	10.00	20.00
❏ SM-1676	Point of No Return	197?	2.00	4.00	8.00
❏ SW 1676 [S]	Point of No Return	1962	6.25	12.50	25.00
❏ W 1676 [M]	Point of No Return	1962	5.00	10.00	20.00
❏ SWCO 1726 [(3) P]	Sinatra, The Great Years	1962	10.00	20.00	40.00
❏ WCO 1726 [(3) M]	Sinatra, The Great Years	1962	7.50	15.00	30.00
❏ SW 1729 [P]	Sinatra Sings...Of Love and Things	1962	5.00	10.00	20.00
❏ W 1729 [M]	Sinatra Sings...Of Love and Things	1962	5.00	10.00	20.00
❏ DW 1825 [R]	Sinatra Sings Rodgers and Hart	1963	3.00	6.00	12.00
❏ W 1825 [M]	Sinatra Sings Rodgers and Hart	1963	5.00	10.00	20.00
❏ DT 1919 [R]	Tell Her You Love Her	1963	3.00	6.00	12.00
❏ T 1919 [M]	Tell Her You Love Her	1963	5.00	10.00	20.00
❏ DW 1994 [R]	Sinatra Sings the Select Johnny Mercer	1963	3.00	6.00	12.00
❏ W 1994 [M]	Sinatra Sings the Select Johnny Mercer	1963	5.00	10.00	20.00
❏ DT 2036 [R]	The Greatest Hits of Frank Sinatra	1964	3.00	6.00	12.00
❏ T 2036 [M]	The Greatest Hits of Frank Sinatra	1964	5.00	10.00	20.00
❏ T 2123 [M]	Sinatra Sings the Select Harold Arlen	1964	25.00	50.00	100.00
-- Only released in Canada, Australia and the UK					
❏ PRO-2163/4/5/6 [(2) DJ]	Selections from Sinatra, The Great Years	1962	10.00	20.00	40.00
❏ DW 2301 [R]	Sinatra Sings the Select Cole Porter	1965	3.00	6.00	12.00
❏ W 2301 [M]	Sinatra Sings the Select Cole Porter	1965	5.00	10.00	20.00
❏ DT 2602 [R]	Forever Frank	1966	3.00	6.00	12.00
❏ T 2602 [M]	Forever Frank	1966	5.00	10.00	20.00
❏ DT 2700 [R]	The Movie Songs	1967	3.00	6.00	12.00
❏ T 2700 [M]	The Movie Songs	1967	5.00	10.00	20.00
❏ STFL 2814 [(6) P]	The Frank Sinatra Deluxe Set	1968	15.00	30.00	60.00
❏ TFL 2814 [(6) M]	The Frank Sinatra Deluxe Set	1968	25.00	50.00	100.00
❏ DKAO 2900 [R]	The Best of Frank Sinatra	1968	3.75	7.50	15.00
❏ PRO-2974/5 [DJ]	Frank Sinatra Minute Masters	1965	10.00	20.00	40.00
-- Edited version of 20 songs					
❏ DNFR 7630 [(6) P]	The Sinatra Touch	19??	15.00	30.00	60.00
❏ ST-11309	One More for the Road	1973	2.50	5.00	10.00
❏ SABB-11367 [(2) P]	Round #1	1974	3.75	7.50	15.00
❏ SM-11502	A Swingin' Affair!	1976	2.50	5.00	10.00
❏ SM-11801	Come Swing with Me	1978	2.50	5.00	10.00
❏ M-11883	This Is Sinatra!	1979	2.50	5.00	10.00
❏ SN-16109	The Best of Frank Sinatra	198?	2.00	4.00	8.00
-- Budget-line reissue					
❏ DN-16110	What Is This Thing Called Love	198?	2.00	4.00	8.00
-- Budget-line reissue					
❏ SN-16111	The Night We Called It a Day	198?	2.00	4.00	8.00
-- Budget-line reissue					
❏ N-16112	My One and Only Love	198?	2.00	4.00	8.00
-- Budget-line reissue					
❏ SN-16113	Sentimental Journey	198?	2.00	4.00	8.00
-- Budget-line reissue					
❏ N-16148	Look to Your Heart	198?	2.00	4.00	8.00
-- Budget-line reissue					
❏ SN-16149	Sinatra Sings...Of Love and Things	198?	2.00	4.00	8.00
-- Budget-line reissue					
❏ SN-16202	Frank Sinatra Sings for Only the Lonely	198?	2.00	4.00	8.00
-- Budget-line reissue					
❏ SN-16203	Come Dance with Me!	198?	2.00	4.00	8.00
-- Budget-line reissue					
❏ SN-16204	Nice 'N' Easy	198?	2.00	4.00	8.00
-- Budget-line reissue					
❏ SN-16205	All the Way	198?	2.00	4.00	8.00
-- Budget-line reissue					
❏ SN-16267	Where Are You	198?	2.00	4.00	8.00
-- Budget-line reissue					
❏ DN-16268	This Is Sinatra, Volume Two	198?	2.00	4.00	8.00
-- Budget-line reissue					

Number	Title	Yr	VG	VG+	NM
❏ C1-89611	Duets	1993	5.00	10.00	20.00
❏ DW 90986 [R]	Sentimental Journey	1966	3.75	7.50	15.00
-- Capitol Record Club issue					
❏ W 90986 [M]	Sentimental Journey	1966	6.25	12.50	25.00
-- Capitol Record Club issue					
❏ DQBO 91261 [(2) R]	Songs for the Young at Heart	196?	7.50	15.00	30.00
-- Capitol Record Club issue					
❏ C1-94777 [(5)]	The Capitol Years	1990	25.00	50.00	100.00
-- With book and wraparound banner. Only 5,000 were pressed					
❏ STBB-95191 [(2)]	Sinatra Sings the Great Ones	1973	5.00	10.00	20.00
-- Longines Symphonette (formerly Capitol) Record Club issue					

CAPITOL PICKWICK SERIES

Number	Title	Yr	VG	VG+	NM
❏ PC-3450 [M]	The Nearness of You	196?	3.00	6.00	12.00
❏ SPC-3450 [R]	The Nearness of You	196?	2.50	5.00	10.00
❏ PC-3452 [M]	Try a Little Tenderness	196?	3.00	6.00	12.00
❏ SPC-3452 [R]	Try a Little Tenderness	196?	2.50	5.00	10.00
❏ PC-3456 [M]	Nevertheless	196?	3.00	6.00	12.00
❏ SPC-3456 [R]	Nevertheless	196?	2.50	5.00	10.00
❏ PC-3457 [M]	Just One of Those Things	196?	3.00	6.00	12.00
❏ SPC-3457 [R]	Just One of Those Things	196?	2.50	5.00	10.00
❏ PC-3458 [M]	This Love of Mine	196?	3.00	6.00	12.00
❏ SPC-3458 [R]	This Love of Mine	196?	2.50	5.00	10.00
❏ PC-3463 [M]	My Cole Porter	196?	3.00	6.00	12.00
❏ SPC-3463 [R]	My Cole Porter	196?	2.50	5.00	10.00

COLUMBIA

Number	Title	Yr	VG	VG+	NM
❏ C2L 6 [(2) M]	The Frank Sinatra Story	1958	7.50	15.00	30.00
❏ C3L 42 [(3) M]	The Essential Frank Sinatra	1966	25.00	50.00	100.00
❏ C3S 42 [(3) R]	The Essential Frank Sinatra	1966	12.50	25.00	50.00
❏ CL 606 [M]	Frankie	1955	7.50	15.00	30.00
-- Cover has drawing of Frank Sinatra wearing a hat					
❏ CL 606 [M]	Frankie	1955	6.25	12.50	25.00
-- Cover has Frank with Debbie Reynolds					
❏ CL 743 [M]	The Voice	1956	6.25	12.50	25.00
❏ CL 743 [M]	The Voice	1999	6.25	12.50	25.00
-- Classic Records reissue on audiophile vinyl					
❏ CL 884 [M]	Frank Sinatra Conducts Music of Alec Wilder	1956	10.00	20.00	40.00
-- Reissue of Columbia Masterworks ML 4271					
❏ CL 902 [M]	That Old Feeling	1956	6.25	12.50	25.00
❏ CL 953 [M]	Adventures of the Heart	1957	6.25	12.50	25.00
❏ CL 1032 [M]	Christmas Dreaming	1957	20.00	40.00	80.00
❏ CL 1136 [M]	Put Your Dreams Away	1958	6.25	12.50	25.00
❏ CL 1241 [M]	Love Is a Kick	1958	6.25	12.50	25.00
❏ CL 1297 [M]	The Broadway Kick	1958	6.25	12.50	25.00
❏ CL 1359 [M]	Come Back to Sorrento	1959	6.25	12.50	25.00
❏ CL 1448 [M]	Reflections	1959	15.00	30.00	60.00
❏ CL 2474 [M]	Greatest Hits, The Early Years, Vol. 1	1966	3.75	7.50	15.00
❏ CAS 2475 [DJ]	The Voice: The Columbia Years Sampler	1986	10.00	20.00	40.00
❏ CL 2521 [10]	Get Happy	1955	15.00	30.00	60.00
-- "House Party Series" release					
❏ CL 2539 [10]	I've Got a Crush on You	1955	15.00	30.00	60.00
-- "House Party Series" release; different contents from CL 6290					
❏ CL 2542 [10]	Christmas with Sinatra	1955	15.00	30.00	60.00
-- "House Party Series" release					
❏ CL 2572 [M]	Greatest Hits, The Early Years, Vol. 2	1966	3.75	7.50	15.00
❏ CL 2739 [M]	The Essential Frank Sinatra, Volume 1	1967	6.25	12.50	25.00
❏ CL 2740 [M]	The Essential Frank Sinatra, Volume 2	1967	6.25	12.50	25.00
❏ CL 2741 [M]	The Essential Frank Sinatra, Volume 3	1967	6.25	12.50	25.00
❏ CL 2913 [M]	Frank Sinatra in Hollywood	1968	20.00	40.00	80.00
❏ CL 6001 [10]	The Voice of Frank Sinatra	1949	17.50	35.00	70.00
-- Original in pink paper cover					
❏ CL 6001 [10]	The Voice of Frank Sinatra	1950	15.00	30.00	60.00
-- Blue cardboard cover					
❏ CL 6019 [10]	Christmas Songs by Sinatra	1948	25.00	50.00	100.00
-- With "gingerbread man" cover					
❏ CL 6019 [10]	Christmas Songs by Sinatra	1949	20.00	40.00	80.00
-- With green vinylite cover					
❏ CL 6059 [10]	Frankly Sentimental	1951	15.00	30.00	60.00
❏ CL 6087 [10]	Songs by Sinatra, Volume 1	1952	15.00	30.00	60.00
❏ CL 6096 [10]	Dedicated to You	1952	25.00	50.00	100.00
-- Three of the tracks on this LP are alternate takes unavailable on vinyl anywhere else					
❏ CL 6143 [10]	Sing and Dance with Frank Sinatra	1953	15.00	30.00	60.00
❏ CL 6290 [10]	I've Got a Crush on You	1954	15.00	30.00	60.00
❏ CS 9274 [R]	Greatest Hits, The Early Years, Vol. 1	1966	2.50	5.00	10.00
❏ PC 9274	Greatest Hits, The Early Years, Vol. 1	197?	2.00	4.00	8.00
❏ CS 9372 [R]	Greatest Hits, The Early Years, Vol. 2	1966	2.50	5.00	10.00
❏ PC 9372	Greatest Hits, The Early Years, Vol. 2	197?	2.00	4.00	8.00

Number	Title	Yr	VG	VG+	NM
❏ CS 9539 [R]	The Essential Frank Sinatra, Volume 1	1967	3.00	6.00	12.00
❏ CS 9540 [R]	The Essential Frank Sinatra, Volume 2	1967	3.00	6.00	12.00
❏ CS 9541 [R]	The Essential Frank Sinatra, Volume 3	1967	3.00	6.00	12.00
❏ CS 9713 [R]	Frank Sinatra in Hollywood	1968	3.00	6.00	12.00
❏ KG 31358 [(2)]	In the Beginning	1971	10.00	20.00	40.00
❏ PG 31358 [(2)]	In the Beginning	197?	3.00	6.00	12.00
❏ C6X 40343 [(6)]	The Voice: The Columbia Years 1943-1952	1986	20.00	40.00	80.00
❏ C2X 40897 [(2)]	Hello Young Lovers	1988	7.50	15.00	30.00
❏ PC 40707	Christmas Dreaming	1987	7.50	15.00	30.00

-- Reissue of CL 1032 with an extra track

❏ PC 44238 [M]	Sinatra Rarities	1989	10.00	20.00	40.00

COLUMBIA MASTERWORKS

❏ ML 4271 [M]	Frank Sinatra Conducts Music of Alec Wilder	1955	25.00	50.00	100.00

HARMONY

❏ HL 7400 [M]	Have Yourself a Merry Little Christmas	1967	7.50	15.00	30.00
❏ HL 7405 [M]	Romantic Scenes from the Early Years	1967	7.50	15.00	30.00
❏ HS 11200 [R]	Have Yourself a Merry Little Christmas	1967	5.00	10.00	20.00
❏ HS 11205 [R]	Romantic Scenes from the Early Years	1967	3.00	6.00	12.00
❏ HS 11277 [R]	Someone to Watch Over Me	1968	3.75	7.50	15.00
❏ HS 11390 [R]	Frank Sinatra	1969	3.75	7.50	15.00
❏ KH 30318 [R]	Greatest Hits, Early Years	1971	3.75	7.50	15.00

LONGINES SYMPHONETTE

❏ LS-308A [(10)]	Sinatra: The Works	1972	18.75	37.50	75.00
❏ LS-309A [(6)]	Sinatra: The Works	1973	10.00	20.00	40.00

-- Abridged version of LS-308A

❏ SYS-5637	Sinatra Like Never Before	1972	6.25	12.50	25.00

-- Bonus LP with purchase of LS-308A

MOBILE FIDELITY

❏ SC-1 [(16)]	Sinatra	1983	150.00	300.00	600.00

-- Audiophile vinyl; only two of the 16 records in this box were released individually

❏ 1-086	Nice 'N' Easy	1981	10.00	20.00	40.00

-- Audiophile vinyl

❏ 1-135 [M]	A Jolly Christmas from Frank Sinatra	1984	10.00	20.00	40.00

-- Audiophile vinyl using the original title

PAIR

❏ PDL2-1027 [(2)]	All-Time Classics	1986	3.00	6.00	12.00
❏ PDL2-1028 [(2)]	Timeless	1986	3.00	6.00	12.00
❏ PDL2-1122 [(2)]	Classic Performances	1986	3.00	6.00	12.00

QWEST

❏ 25145	L.A. Is My Lady	1984	3.00	6.00	12.00

RCA VICTOR

❏ APL1-0497 [R]	What'll I Do	1974	3.00	6.00	12.00
❏ LPV-583 [M]	This Love of Mine	1971	10.00	20.00	40.00
❏ ANL1-1050 [R]	What'll I Do	1976	2.50	5.00	10.00
❏ LPM-1569 [M]	Frankie and Tommy	1957	15.00	30.00	60.00

-- First issue of this LP

❏ LPM-1569 [M]	Tommy Plays, Frankie Sings	1957	10.00	20.00	40.00

-- Second issue with new title

❏ LPM-1632 [M]	We Three	1958	15.00	30.00	60.00

-- First issue

❏ LPM-1632 [M]	We Three	1958	10.00	20.00	40.00

-- Second issue, "RE" on cover

❏ LPT-3063 [10]	Fabulous Frankie	1953	15.00	30.00	60.00
❏ CPL2-4334 [(2)]	The Sinatra/Dorsey Sessions, Vol. 1	1982	6.25	12.50	25.00
❏ CPL2-4335 [(2)]	The Sinatra/Dorsey Sessions, Vol. 2	1982	6.25	12.50	25.00
❏ CPL2-4336 [(2)]	The Sinatra/Dorsey Sessions, Vol. 3	1982	6.25	12.50	25.00
❏ AFL1-4741 [R]	Radio Years (Sinatra/Dorsey/Stordahl)	1983	3.75	7.50	15.00

REPRISE

❏ F 1001 [M]	Ring-a-Ding-Ding!	1961	5.00	10.00	20.00
❏ R9 1001 [S]	Ring-a-Ding-Ding!	1961	6.25	12.50	25.00
❏ F 1002 [M]	Swing Along with Me	1961	10.00	20.00	40.00

-- Original title

❏ F 1002 [M]	Sinatra Swings	1961	5.00	10.00	20.00

-- Retitled version of "Swing Along with Me"; Capitol threatened legal action because of its "Come Swing With Me!" collection

❏ R9 1002 [S]	Swing Along with Me	1961	12.50	25.00	50.00

-- Original title

❏ R9 1002 [S]	Sinatra Swings	1961	6.25	12.50	25.00

-- Retitled version of "Swing Along with Me"; Capitol threatened legal action because of its "Come Swing With Me!" collection

❏ F 1003 [M]	I Remember Tommy	1961	5.00	10.00	20.00
❏ R9 1003 [S]	I Remember Tommy	1961	6.25	12.50	25.00

Number	Title	Yr	VG	VG+	NM
❏ F 1004 [M]	Sinatra & Strings	1962	3.75	7.50	15.00
❏ R9 1004 [S]	Sinatra & Strings	1962	5.00	10.00	20.00
❏ F 1005 [M]	Sinatra and Swingin' Brass	1962	3.75	7.50	15.00
❏ R9 1005 [S]	Sinatra and Swingin' Brass	1962	5.00	10.00	20.00
❏ F 1006 [M]	Great Songs from Great Britain	1962	20.00	40.00	80.00

-- Only released in the UK

❏ R9 1006 [S]	Great Songs from Great Britain	1962	25.00	50.00	100.00

-- Only released in the UK

❏ F 1007 [M]	All Alone	1962	3.75	7.50	15.00
❏ R9 1007 [S]	All Alone	1962	5.00	10.00	20.00
❏ F 1008 [M]	Sinatra-Basie	1963	3.75	7.50	15.00
❏ R9 1008 [S]	Sinatra-Basie	1963	5.00	10.00	20.00
❏ F 1009 [M]	The Concert Sinatra	1963	3.75	7.50	15.00
❏ R9 1009 [S]	The Concert Sinatra	1963	6.25	12.50	25.00

-- Original pressings declare this was recorded in "35mm Stereo"

❏ R9 1009 [S]	The Concert Sinatra	196?	5.00	10.00	20.00

-- Without cover reference to "35mm Stereo"

❏ F 1010 [M]	Sinatra's Sinatra	1963	3.75	7.50	15.00
❏ R9 1010 [S]	Sinatra's Sinatra	1963	5.00	10.00	20.00
❏ F 1011 [M]	Days of Wine and Roses, Moon River, and Other Academy Award Winners	1964	3.75	7.50	15.00
❏ FS 1011 [S]	Days of Wine and Roses, Moon River, and Other Academy Award Winners	1964	5.00	10.00	20.00
❏ F 1012 [M]	It Might As Well Be Swing	1964	3.75	7.50	15.00
❏ FS 1012 [S]	It Might As Well Be Swing	1964	5.00	10.00	20.00
❏ F 1013 [M]	Softly, As I Leave You	1964	3.75	7.50	15.00
❏ FS 1013 [S]	Softly, As I Leave You	1964	5.00	10.00	20.00
❏ F 1014 [M]	September of My Years	1965	3.75	7.50	15.00
❏ FS 1014 [S]	September of My Years	1965	5.00	10.00	20.00
❏ F 1015 [M]	My Kind of Broadway	1965	3.75	7.50	15.00
❏ FS 1015 [S]	My Kind of Broadway	1965	5.00	10.00	20.00
❏ 2F 1016 [(2) M]	A Man and His Music	1965	5.00	10.00	20.00
❏ 2F/2FS 1016	A Man and His Music Special Box	1965	50.00	100.00	200.00

-- Blue slipcase with embossed silver front, raised letters, plus 4-page booklet and a signed card (deduct 50% if card missing). Add this to LP value.

❏ 2FS 1016 [(2) S]	A Man and His Music	1965	6.25	12.50	25.00
❏ F 1017 [M]	Strangers in the Night	1966	3.00	6.00	12.00
❏ FS 1017 [S]	Strangers in the Night	1966	3.75	7.50	15.00
❏ F 1018 [M]	Moonlight Sinatra	1966	3.75	7.50	15.00
❏ FS 1018 [S]	Moonlight Sinatra	1966	5.00	10.00	20.00
❏ 2F 1019 [(2) M]	Sinatra at the Sands	1966	5.00	10.00	20.00
❏ 2FS 1019 [(2) S]	Sinatra at the Sands	1966	6.25	12.50	25.00
❏ F 1020 [M]	That's Life	1966	3.00	6.00	12.00
❏ FS 1020 [S]	That's Life	1966	3.75	7.50	15.00
❏ F 1021 [M]	Francis Albert Sinatra & Antonio Carlos Jobim	1967	3.00	6.00	12.00
❏ FS 1021 [S]	Francis Albert Sinatra & Antonio Carlos Jobim	1967	3.75	7.50	15.00
❏ F 1022 [M]	Frank Sinatra (The World We Knew)	1967	3.75	7.50	15.00
❏ FS 1022 [S]	Frank Sinatra (The World We Knew)	1967	3.75	7.50	15.00
❏ FS 1023	The Sinatra Christmas Album	1967	25.00	50.00	100.00

-- Album never released; value is for cover slick

❏ FS 1024	Francis A. and Edward K.	1968	5.00	10.00	20.00
❏ FS 1025	Frank Sinatra's Greatest Hits	1968	3.75	7.50	15.00
❏ FS 1027	Cycles	1969	3.75	7.50	15.00
❏ FS 1028	SinatraJobim	1969	2,000.	3,000.	4,000.

-- Unreleased; test pressings exist (value is for one of these). 8-track tapes also exist and are 10% of this value

❏ FS 1029	My Way	1969	3.75	7.50	15.00
❏ FS4 1029 [Q]	My Way	1974	6.25	12.50	25.00
❏ FS 1030	A Man Alone & Other Songs of Rod McKuen	1969	3.75	7.50	15.00
❏ FS 1030	A Man Alone & Other Songs of Rod McKuen	1969	100.00	200.00	400.00

-- Signed copies with gatefold cover and hardbound book; 400 made

❏ FS 1031	Watertown	1970	6.25	12.50	25.00

-- With gatefold and poster

❏ FS 1032	Frank Sinatra's Greatest Hits, Vol. 2	1970	---	---	---

-- Canceled?

❏ FS 1033	Sinatra and Company	1971	3.75	7.50	15.00
❏ FS 1034	Frank Sinatra's Greatest Hits, Vol. 2	1972	3.75	7.50	15.00
❏ FS 2155	Ol' Blue Eyes Is Back	1973	3.00	6.00	12.00
❏ FS4 2155 [Q]	Ol' Blue Eyes Is Back	1974	6.25	12.50	25.00
❏ FS 2195	Some Nice Things I've Missed	1974	3.00	6.00	12.00
❏ FS4 2195 [Q]	Some Nice Things I've Missed	1974	6.25	12.50	25.00
❏ FS 2207	Sinatra -- The Main Event Live	1974	3.00	6.00	12.00
❏ 3FS 2300 [(3)]	Trilogy: Past, Present, Future	1980	5.00	10.00	20.00
❏ FS 2305	She Shot Me Down	1981	3.00	6.00	12.00
❏ 5004 [DJ]	A Man and His Music, Part II	1966	75.00	150.00	300.00

-- Promotional album for use by Budweiser

❏ 5230 [DJ]	Songbook, Vol. 1	1971	12.50	25.00	50.00
❏ 5267 [(2) DJ]	Songbook, Vol. 2	1972	25.00	50.00	100.00
❏ 5409 [DJ]	I Sing the Songs	1976	12.50	25.00	50.00

Number	Title	Yr	VG	VG+	NM
❑ F 6045 [M]	Sinatra Conducts Music from Pictures and Plays	1962	7.50	15.00	30.00
❑ R9 6045 [S]	Sinatra Conducts Music from Pictures and Plays	1962	10.00	2.00	40.00
❑ R 6167 [M]	Sinatra '65	1965	3.75	7.50	15.00
❑ RS 6167 [S]	Sinatra '65	1965	5.00	10.00	20.00
TIME-LIFE					
❑ SLGD-02 [(2)]	Legendary Singers	1982	6.25	12.50	25.00

SINGER, HAL, AND CHARLIE SHAVERS
Singer plays tenor saxophone. Also see CHARLIE SHAVERS.
PRESTIGE

Number	Title	Yr	VG	VG+	NM
❑ PRLP-7153 [M]	Blue Stompin'	1959	20.00	40.00	80.00
SWINGVILLE					
❑ SVLP-2023 [M]	Blue Stompin'	1961	12.50	25.00	50.00
-- Purple label					
❑ SVLP-2023 [M]	Blue Stompin'	1965	6.25	12.50	25.00
-- Blue label, trident logo at right					

SINGERS UNLIMITED, THE
Vocal quartet: Gene Puerling; Don Shelton (both formerly of THE HI-LO'S); Len Dresslar; and Bonnie Herman.
BASF

Number	Title	Yr	VG	VG+	NM
❑ 20903	Try to Remember	197?	3.00	6.00	12.00
❑ 21852	The Four of Us	197?	3.00	6.00	12.00
PAUSA					
❑ 7039	Friends	197?	2.50	5.00	10.00
❑ 7048	Just in Time	197?	2.50	5.00	10.00
❑ 7056	The Singers Unlimited with Rob McConnell and the Boss Brass	197?	2.50	5.00	10.00
❑ 7062	A Special Blend	197?	2.50	5.00	10.00
❑ 7068	Feeling Free	197?	2.50	5.00	10.00
❑ 7076	A Cappella III	1979	2.50	5.00	10.00
❑ 7100	A Cappella I	198?	2.50	5.00	10.00
❑ 7101	A Cappella II	198?	2.50	5.00	10.00
❑ 7109	Easy to Love	198?	2.50	5.00	10.00
❑ 7118	Eventide	198?	2.50	5.00	10.00
❑ 7121	Four of Us	198?	2.50	5.00	10.00
❑ 7136	Composer's Corner: The Singers Unlimited Sing Music of Lennon, McCartney and Ellington	198?	3.00	6.00	12.00
VERVE					
❑ 815 671-1	A Cappella	1985	2.50	5.00	10.00
❑ 817 486-1	The Singers Unlimited with Rob McConnell and the Boss Brass	198?	2.50	5.00	10.00
❑ 821 859-1	Christmas	198?	3.00	6.00	12.00

SINGLETON, ZUTTY/ART TATUM
Singleton played drums. Also see ART TATUM.
BRUNSWICK

Number	Title	Yr	VG	VG+	NM
❑ BL 58038 [10]	Battle of Jazz, Vol. 2	1953	12.50	25.00	50.00

SIRAVO, GEORGE
Reeds player, bandleader and arranger.
AD-LIB

Number	Title	Yr	VG	VG+	NM
❑ 226 [M]	Out on a Limb	196?	3.75	7.50	15.00
❑ S-226 [S]	Out on a Limb	196?	5.00	10.00	20.00
COLUMBIA					
❑ CL 6146 [10]	Your Dance Date with George Siravo	1951	10.00	20.00	40.00
DECCA					
❑ DL 8464 [M]	Portraits in Hi-Fi	1957	7.50	15.00	30.00
EPIC					
❑ BN 6?? [S]	Everything Goes	1961	5.00	10.00	20.00
❑ LN 3803 [M]	Everything Goes	1961	3.75	7.50	15.00
KAPP					
❑ KL-1016 [M]	Polite Jazz	1956	7.50	15.00	30.00
MERCURY					
❑ MG-20327 [M]	Darling, Please Forgive Me	1958	7.50	15.00	30.00
RCA CAMDEN					
❑ CAL-505 [M]	Siravo Swing Session	1959	3.75	7.50	15.00
❑ CAS-505 [S]	Siravo Swing Session	1959	5.00	10.00	20.00
RCA VICTOR					
❑ LPM-1970 [M]	Swingin' in Hi-Fi in Studio A	1959	6.25	12.50	25.00
❑ LSP-1970 [S]	Swingin' in Hi-Fi in Studio A	1959	7.50	15.00	30.00
TIME					
❑ S-2019 [S]	Seductive Strings	196?	5.00	10.00	20.00
❑ S-2115 [S]	And Then I Wrote Richard Rodgers	196?	5.00	10.00	20.00
❑ 52019 [M]	Seductive Strings	196?	3.75	7.50	15.00
❑ 52115 [M]	And Then I Wrote Richard Rodgers	196?	3.75	7.50	15.00

Number	Title	Yr	VG	VG+	NM
VIK					
❑ LX-1091 [M]	Old But New	1957	7.50	15.00	30.00
❑ LX-1125 [M]	Swing Hi, Swing Fi	1958	7.50	15.00	30.00

SIVUCA
Accordion player, guitarist, keyboard player and male singer.
VANGUARD

Number	Title	Yr	VG	VG+	NM
❑ VSD-79337	Sivuca	197?	3.75	7.50	15.00
❑ VSD-79352	Live at the Village Gate	197?	3.00	6.00	12.00

SIX AND SEVEN-EIGHTHS STRING BAND, THE
FOLKWAYS

Number	Title	Yr	VG	VG+	NM
❑ FP-671 [M]	The Six and Seven-Eighths String Band	1951	12.50	25.00	50.00
❑ FP-2671 [M]	The Six and Seven-Eighths String Band	195?	10.00	20.00	40.00

SIX, THE
Members: Bill Britto; JOHN GLASEL; BOB HAMMER; Eddie Phufe; Sonny Truitt; BOB WILBER.
BETHLEHEM

Number	Title	Yr	VG	VG+	NM
❑ BCP-28 [M]	The Six	1955	20.00	40.00	80.00
❑ BCP-57 [M]	The View From Jazzbo's Head	1956	25.00	50.00	100.00

SKJELBRED, RAY
Pianist.
EUPHONIC

Number	Title	Yr	VG	VG+	NM
❑ 1223	Chicago High Life	198?	2.50	5.00	10.00
STOMP OFF					
❑ SOS-1097	Gin Mill Blues	1985	2.50	5.00	10.00
❑ SOS-1124	Stompin' 'Em Down	1987	2.50	5.00	10.00

SKYWALK
Six-piece Canadian fusion band. Among the members: Kat Hendrikse (drums); Harris Van Berkel (guitar); Rene Worst (bass).
ZEBRA

Number	Title	Yr	VG	VG+	NM
❑ ZR 5004	Silent Witness	1984	3.00	6.00	12.00
❑ ZEB-5680	Silent Witness	1986	2.50	5.00	10.00
-- Reissue of 5004					
❑ ZEB-5715	The Bohemians	1986	2.50	5.00	10.00
❑ ZEB-42204	Paradiso	1988	2.50	5.00	10.00

SLACK, FREDDIE
Pianist and bandleader.
EMARCY

Number	Title	Yr	VG	VG+	NM
❑ MG-36094 [M]	Boogie-Woogie on the 88	1956	10.00	20.00	40.00
PAUSA					
❑ 9027	Behind the Eight-Beat	198?	2.50	5.00	10.00

SLAGLE, STEVE
Alto and soprano saxophone player, clarinetist, flutist and male singer.
ATLANTIC

Number	Title	Yr	VG	VG+	NM
❑ 81657	Rio Highlife	1986	2.50	5.00	10.00

SLEET, DON
Trumpeter.
JAZZLAND

Number	Title	Yr	VG	VG+	NM
❑ JLP-45 [M]	All Members	1961	6.25	12.50	25.00
❑ JLP-945 [S]	All Members	1961	7.50	15.00	30.00

SLICKAPHONICS
Members: Ray Anderson (trombone, vocals); Steve Elson (saxophones, vocals); AllanJaffe (guitar, vocals); Mark Helias (bass, vocals); Jim Payne (drums, vocals).
ENJA

Number	Title	Yr	VG	VG+	NM
❑ 4024	Wow Bag	1982	3.00	6.00	12.00

SLIDER-GLENN
I.T.I.

Number	Title	Yr	VG	VG+	NM
❑ JL-031	A Whispered Warning	1986	2.50	5.00	10.00
REEL DREAMS					
❑ 1007	A Whispered Warning	1983	3.75	7.50	15.00

SLINGER, CEES
Pianist and composer.
TIMELESS

Number	Title	Yr	VG	VG+	NM
❑ LPSJP-225	Sling Shot	1990	3.00	6.00	12.00

SLOANE, CAROL
Female singer.
AUDIOPHILE

Number	Title	Yr	VG	VG+	NM
❑ AP-195	Sophisticated Lady	1985	2.50	5.00	10.00

Number	Title	Yr	VG	VG+	NM
CHOICE					
❑ 1025	Cottontail	1979	3.00	6.00	12.00
COLUMBIA					
❑ CL 1766 [M]	Out of the Blue	1962	15.00	30.00	60.00
❑ CL 1923 [M]	Carol Sloane Live at 30th Street	1963	15.00	30.00	60.00
❑ CS 8566 [S]	Out of the Blue	1962	20.00	40.00	80.00
❑ CS 8723 [S]	Carol Sloane Live at 30th Street	1963	20.00	40.00	80.00
CONTEMPORARY					
❑ C-14049	Love You Madly	1989	3.00	6.00	12.00
❑ C-14060	The Real Thing	1990	3.75	7.50	15.00
PROGRESSIVE					
❑ PRO-7047	Carol Sings	1978	3.00	6.00	12.00

SMALL HERD, THE
See CHUBBY JACKSON.

SMALLEY, JUNE

Number	Title	Yr	VG	VG+	NM
CIRCLE					
❑ C-6	June Smalley Swings America	1979	2.50	5.00	10.00

SMALLS, CLIFF
Pianist.

Number	Title	Yr	VG	VG+	NM
MASTER JAZZ					
❑ 8131	Swing and Things	197?	3.00	6.00	12.00

SMART SET, THE
Vocal group.

Number	Title	Yr	VG	VG+	NM
WARNER BROS.					
❑ W-1203 [M]	A New Experience in Vocal Styles	1958	7.50	15.00	30.00
❑ WS-1203 [S]	A New Experience in Vocal Styles	1958	10.00	20.00	40.00

SMIAROWSKI, MIKE

Number	Title	Yr	VG	VG+	NM
SMEAR					
❑ SMR-891	Island Fantasy	1990	3.75	7.50	15.00

SMITH, BARTON

Number	Title	Yr	VG	VG+	NM
FOLKWAYS					
❑ FSP-33856	Realizations	198?	3.00	6.00	12.00

SMITH, BESSIE
Female singer and composer, one of the first recorded female blues singers.

Number	Title	Yr	VG	VG+	NM
COLUMBIA					
❑ GP 33 [(2)]	The World's Greatest Blues Singer	1970	5.00	10.00	20.00
❑ GL 503 [M]	The Bessie Smith Story, Volume 1	1951	12.50	25.00	50.00
-- *Maroon label, gold print*					
❑ GL 504 [M]	The Bessie Smith Story, Volume 2	1951	12.50	25.00	50.00
-- *Maroon label, gold print*					
❑ GL 505 [M]	The Bessie Smith Story, Volume 3	1951	12.50	25.00	50.00
-- *Maroon label, gold print*					
❑ GL 506 [M]	The Bessie Smith Story, Volume 4	1951	12.50	25.00	50.00
-- *Maroon label, gold print*					
❑ CL 855 [M]	The Bessie Smith Story, Volume 1	1956	6.25	12.50	25.00
-- *Red and black label with six "eye" logos*					
❑ CL 855 [M]	The Bessie Smith Story, Volume 1	1963	3.75	7.50	15.00
-- *Red label with "Guaranteed High Fidelity" or "360 Sound Mono"*					
❑ CL 856 [M]	The Bessie Smith Story, Volume 2	1956	6.25	12.50	25.00
-- *Red and black label with six "eye" logos*					
❑ CL 856 [M]	The Bessie Smith Story, Volume 2	1963	3.75	7.50	15.00
-- *Red label with "Guaranteed High Fidelity" or "360 Sound Mono"*					
❑ CL 857 [M]	The Bessie Smith Story, Volume 3	1956	6.25	12.50	25.00
-- *Red and black label with six "eye" logos*					
❑ CL 857 [M]	The Bessie Smith Story, Volume 3	1963	3.75	7.50	15.00
-- *Red label with "Guaranteed High Fidelity" or "360 Sound Mono"*					
❑ CL 858 [M]	The Bessie Smith Story, Volume 4	1956	6.25	12.50	25.00
-- *Red and black label with six "eye" logos*					
❑ CL 858 [M]	The Bessie Smith Story, Volume 4	1963	3.75	7.50	15.00
-- *Red label with "Guaranteed High Fidelity" or "360 Sound Mono"*					
❑ CG 30126 [(2)]	Any Woman's Blues	1971	3.75	7.50	15.00

Number	Title	Yr	VG	VG+	NM
❑ CG 30450 [(2)]	Empty Bed Blues	1971	3.75	7.50	15.00
❑ CG 30818 [(2)]	Empress	1972	3.75	7.50	15.00
❑ CG 31093 [(2)]	Nobody's Blues But Mine	1972	3.75	7.50	15.00
❑ C2 47091 [(2)]	The Complete Recordings Volume 1: Empress of the Blues	1991	5.00	10.00	20.00
-- *Box set; none of the subsequent volumes came out on vinyl*					
COLUMBIA MASTERWORKS					
❑ ML 4801 [M]	The Bessie Smith Story, Volume 1	1954	7.50	15.00	30.00
❑ ML 4802 [M]	The Bessie Smith Story, Volume 2	1954	7.50	15.00	30.00
❑ ML 4809 [M]	The Bessie Smith Story, Volume 3	1954	7.50	15.00	30.00
❑ ML 4810 [M]	The Bessie Smith Story, Volume 4	1954	7.50	15.00	30.00

SMITH, BILL
Clarinetist and composer.

Number	Title	Yr	VG	VG+	NM
CONTEMPORARY					
❑ M-3591 [M]	Folk Jazz	1961	5.00	10.00	20.00
❑ S-7591 [S]	Folk Jazz	1961	6.25	12.50	25.00
ONARI					
❑ 004	Pick a Number	198?	3.00	6.00	12.00

SMITH, BUSTER
Alto saxophone player. Also played clarinet and guitar.

Number	Title	Yr	VG	VG+	NM
ATLANTIC					
❑ 1323 [M]	The Legendary Buster Smith	1960	12.50	25.00	50.00
-- *Black label*					
❑ 1323 [M]	The Legendary Buster Smith	1961	5.00	10.00	20.00
-- *Multi-color label, white "fan" logo*					
❑ SD 1323 [S]	The Legendary Buster Smith	1960	12.50	25.00	50.00
-- *Green label*					
❑ SD 1323 [S]	The Legendary Buster Smith	1961	5.00	10.00	20.00
-- *Multi-color label, white "fan" logo*					

SMITH, CARRIE
Female singer.

Number	Title	Yr	VG	VG+	NM
AUDIOPHILE					
❑ AP-164	Fine and Mellow	198?	2.50	5.00	10.00
CLASSIC JAZZ					
❑ 139	Do Your Duty	197?	3.75	7.50	15.00
WEST 54					
❑ 8002	Carrie Smith	197?	3.75	7.50	15.00

SMITH, DAN

Number	Title	Yr	VG	VG+	NM
BIOGRAPH					
❑ LP-12036	God Is Not Dead	197?	2.50	5.00	10.00

SMITH, DEREK
Pianist. Also see DICK KATZ.

Number	Title	Yr	VG	VG+	NM
PROGRESSIVE					
❑ PRO-7002	Love for Sale	197?	3.00	6.00	12.00
❑ PRO-7035	The Man I Love	197?	3.00	6.00	12.00
❑ PRO-7055	Derek Smith Plays Jerome Kern	198?	2.50	5.00	10.00

SMITH, DWAYNE, AND ART JOHNSON
Smith is a pianist; Johnson plays guitar.

Number	Title	Yr	VG	VG+	NM
CAFÉ					
❑ L-729	Heartbound	1985	2.50	5.00	10.00

SMITH, GREG AND BEV
Both are baritone saxophone players. Greg also plays soprano sax and clarinet; Bev also plays bass clarinet and flute.

Number	Title	Yr	VG	VG+	NM
INTIMA					
❑ SJE-73291	Mr. and Mrs. Smith: No Baggage	1987	3.00	6.00	12.00

SMITH, HAL
Drummer and bandleader.

Number	Title	Yr	VG	VG+	NM
JAZZOLOGY					
❑ J-136	Hal Smith and His Rhythmakers with Butch Thompson	1985	2.50	5.00	10.00
STOMP OFF					
❑ SOS-1078	Do What Ory Say!	1985	2.50	5.00	10.00

SMITH, JABBO
Trumpeter.

Number	Title	Yr	VG	VG+	NM
MCA					
❑ 1347	Ace of Rhythm	198?	2.50	5.00	10.00
MELODEON					
❑ 7326	Trumpet Ace of the 20s, Vol. 1	197?	3.00	6.00	12.00
❑ 7327	Trumpet Ace of the 20s, Vol. 2	197?	3.00	6.00	12.00

SMITH, JIMMY

Organist. Also see BEVERLY KENNEY.

BLUE NOTE

Number	Title	Yr	VG	VG+	NM
❏ BN-LA400-H2 [(2)]	Jimmy Smith	1975	3.75	7.50	15.00
❏ LT-992	Confirmation	1979	2.50	5.00	10.00
❏ LT-1054	Cool Blues	1980	2.50	5.00	10.00
❏ LT-1092	On the Sunny Side	1981	2.50	5.00	10.00
❏ BLP-1512 [M]	Jimmy Smith at the Organ, Vol. 1	1956	37.50	75.00	150.00
-- "Deep groove" version (deep indentation under label on both sides)					
❏ BLP-1512 [M]	Jimmy Smith at the Organ, Vol. 1	1956	25.00	50.00	100.00
-- Regular edition, Lexington Ave. address on label					
❏ BLP-1512 [M]	Jimmy Smith at the Organ, Vol. 1	1963	6.25	12.50	25.00
-- With New York, USA address on label					
❏ BLP-1514 [M]	Jimmy Smith at the Organ, Vol. 2	1956	37.50	75.00	150.00
-- "Deep groove" version (deep indentation under label on both sides)					
❏ BLP-1514 [M]	Jimmy Smith at the Organ, Vol. 2	1956	25.00	50.00	100.00
-- Regular edition, Lexington Ave. address on label					
❏ BLP-1514 [M]	Jimmy Smith at the Organ, Vol. 2	1963	6.25	12.50	25.00
-- With New York, USA address on label					
❏ BLP-1525 [M]	The Incredible Jimmy Smith at the Organ, Vol. 3	1956	37.50	75.00	150.00
-- "Deep groove" version (deep indentation under label on both sides)					
❏ BLP-1525 [M]	The Incredible Jimmy Smith at the Organ, Vol. 3	1956	25.00	50.00	100.00
-- Regular edition, Lexington Ave. address on label					
❏ BLP-1525 [M]	The Incredible Jimmy Smith at the Organ, Vol. 3	1963	6.25	12.50	25.00
-- With New York, USA address on label					
❏ BLP-1528 [M]	The Incredible Jimmy Smith at Club Baby Grand, Wilmington, Delaware, Vol. 1	1956	37.50	75.00	150.00
-- "Deep groove" version (deep indentation under label on both sides)					
❏ BLP-1528 [M]	The Incredible Jimmy Smith at Club Baby Grand, Wilmington, Delaware, Vol. 1	1956	25.00	50.00	100.00
-- Regular edition, Lexington Ave. address on label					
❏ BLP-1528 [M]	The Incredible Jimmy Smith at Club Baby Grand, Wilmington, Delaware, Vol. 1	1963	6.25	12.50	25.00
-- With New York, USA address on label					
❏ BLP-1529 [M]	The Incredible Jimmy Smith at Club Baby Grand, Wilmington, Delaware, Vol. 2	1956	37.50	75.00	150.00
-- "Deep groove" version (deep indentation under label on both sides)					
❏ BLP-1529 [M]	The Incredible Jimmy Smith at Club Baby Grand, Wilmington, Delaware, Vol. 2	1956	25.00	50.00	100.00
-- Regular edition, Lexington Ave. address on label					
❏ BLP-1529 [M]	The Incredible Jimmy Smith at Club Baby Grand, Wilmington, Delaware, Vol. 2	1963	6.25	12.50	25.00
-- With New York, USA address on label					
❏ BLP-1547 [M]	A Date with Jimmy Smith, Vol. 1	1957	30.00	60.00	120.00
-- "Deep groove" version (deep indentation under label on both sides)					
❏ BLP-1547 [M]	A Date with Jimmy Smith, Vol. 1	1957	20.00	40.00	80.00
-- Regular edition, W. 63rd St. address on label					
❏ BLP-1547 [M]	A Date with Jimmy Smith, Vol. 1	1963	6.25	12.50	25.00
-- With New York, USA address on label					
❏ BLP-1548 [M]	A Date with Jimmy Smith, Vol. 2	1957	30.00	60.00	120.00
-- "Deep groove" version (deep indentation under label on both sides)					
❏ BLP-1548 [M]	A Date with Jimmy Smith, Vol. 2	1957	20.00	40.00	80.00
-- Regular edition, W. 63rd St. address on label					
❏ BLP-1548 [M]	A Date with Jimmy Smith, Vol. 2	1963	6.25	12.50	25.00
-- With New York, USA address on label					
❏ BLP-1551 [M]	Jimmy Smith at the Organ, Vol. 1	1957	30.00	60.00	120.00
-- "Deep groove" version (deep indentation under label on both sides)					
❏ BLP-1551 [M]	Jimmy Smith at the Organ, Vol. 1	1957	20.00	40.00	80.00
-- Regular edition, W. 63rd St. address on label					
❏ BLP-1551 [M]	Jimmy Smith at the Organ, Vol. 1	1963	6.25	12.50	25.00
-- With New York, USA address on label					
❏ BLP-1552 [M]	Jimmy Smith at the Organ, Vol. 2	1957	30.00	60.00	120.00
-- "Deep groove" version (deep indentation under label on both sides)					
❏ BLP-1552 [M]	Jimmy Smith at the Organ, Vol. 2	1957	20.00	40.00	80.00
-- Regular edition, W. 63rd St. address on label					
❏ BLP-1552 [M]	Jimmy Smith at the Organ, Vol. 2	1963	6.25	12.50	25.00
-- With New York, USA address on label					
❏ BLP-1556 [M]	The Sounds of Jimmy Smith	1957	30.00	60.00	120.00
-- "Deep groove" version (deep indentation under label on both sides)					
❏ BLP-1556 [M]	The Sounds of Jimmy Smith	1957	20.00	40.00	80.00
-- Regular edition, W. 63rd St. address on label					
❏ BLP-1556 [M]	The Sounds of Jimmy Smith	1963	6.25	12.50	25.00
-- With New York, USA address on label					
❏ BLP-1563 [M]	Jimmy Smith Plays Pretty Just for You	1957	30.00	60.00	120.00
-- "Deep groove" version (deep indentation under label on both sides)					
❏ BLP-1563 [M]	Jimmy Smith Plays Pretty Just for You	1957	20.00	40.00	80.00
-- Regular edition, W. 63rd St. address on label					
❏ BLP-1563 [M]	Jimmy Smith Plays Pretty Just for You	1963	6.25	12.50	25.00
-- With New York, USA address on label					
❏ BST-1563 [S]	Jimmy Smith Plays Pretty Just for You	1959	20.00	40.00	80.00
-- "Deep groove" version (deep indentation under label on both sides)					
❏ BST-1563 [S]	Jimmy Smith Plays Pretty Just for You	1959	12.50	25.00	50.00
-- Regular edition, W. 63rd St. address on label					
❏ BST-1563 [S]	Jimmy Smith Plays Pretty Just for You	1963	5.00	10.00	20.00
-- With New York, USA address on label					
❏ BLP-1585 [M]	Groovin' at Small's Paradise, Vol. 1	1958	30.00	60.00	120.00
-- "Deep groove" version (deep indentation under label on both sides)					
❏ BLP-1585 [M]	Groovin' at Small's Paradise, Vol. 1	1958	20.00	40.00	80.00
-- Regular edition, W. 63rd St. address on label					
❏ BLP-1585 [M]	Groovin' at Small's Paradise, Vol. 1	1963	6.25	12.50	25.00
-- With New York, USA address on label					
❏ BST-1585 [S]	Groovin' at Small's Paradise, Vol. 1	1959	20.00	40.00	80.00
-- "Deep groove" version (deep indentation under label on both sides)					
❏ BST-1585 [S]	Groovin' at Small's Paradise, Vol. 1	1959	12.50	25.00	50.00
-- Regular edition, W. 63rd St. address on label					
❏ BST-1585 [S]	Groovin' at Small's Paradise, Vol. 1	1963	5.00	10.00	20.00
-- With New York, USA address on label					
❏ BLP-1586 [M]	Groovin' at Small's Paradise, Vol. 2	1958	30.00	60.00	120.00
-- "Deep groove" version (deep indentation under label on both sides)					
❏ BLP-1586 [M]	Groovin' at Small's Paradise, Vol. 2	1958	20.00	40.00	80.00
-- Regular edition, W. 63rd St. address on label					
❏ BLP-1586 [M]	Groovin' at Small's Paradise, Vol. 2	1963	6.25	12.50	25.00
-- With New York, USA address on label					
❏ BST-1586 [S]	Groovin' at Small's Paradise, Vol. 2	1959	20.00	40.00	80.00
-- "Deep groove" version (deep indentation under label on both sides)					
❏ BST-1586 [S]	Groovin' at Small's Paradise, Vol. 2	1959	12.50	25.00	50.00
-- Regular edition, W. 63rd St. address on label					
❏ BST-1586 [S]	Groovin' at Small's Paradise, Vol. 2	1963	5.00	10.00	20.00
-- With New York, USA address on label					
❏ BLP-4002 [M]	House Party	1959	30.00	60.00	120.00
-- "Deep groove" version (deep indentation under label on both sides)					
❏ BLP-4002 [M]	House Party	1959	20.00	40.00	80.00
-- Regular edition, W. 63rd St. address on label					
❏ BLP-4002 [M]	House Party	1963	6.25	12.50	25.00
-- With New York, USA address on label					
❏ BST-4002 [S]	House Party	1959	20.00	40.00	80.00
-- "Deep groove" version (deep indentation under label on both sides)					
❏ BST-4002 [S]	House Party	1959	12.50	25.00	50.00
-- Regular edition, W. 63rd St. address on label					
❏ BST-4002 [S]	House Party	1963	5.00	10.00	20.00
-- With New York, USA address on label					
❏ BLP-4011 [M]	The Sermon	1959	30.00	60.00	120.00
-- "Deep groove" version (deep indentation under label on both sides)					
❏ BLP-4011 [M]	The Sermon	1959	20.00	40.00	80.00
-- Regular edition, W. 63rd St. address on label					
❏ BLP-4011 [M]	The Sermon	1963	6.25	12.50	25.00
-- With New York, USA address on label					
❏ BST-4011 [S]	The Sermon	1959	20.00	40.00	80.00
-- "Deep groove" version (deep indentation under label on both sides)					
❏ BST-4011 [S]	The Sermon	1959	12.50	25.00	50.00
-- Regular edition, W. 63rd St. address on label					
❏ BST-4011 [S]	The Sermon	1963	5.00	10.00	20.00
-- With New York, USA address on label					
❏ BLP-4030 [M]	Crazy Baby	1960	30.00	60.00	120.00
-- "Deep groove" version (deep indentation under label on both sides)					
❏ BLP-4030 [M]	Crazy Baby	1960	20.00	40.00	80.00
-- Regular edition, W. 63rd St. address on label					
❏ BLP-4030 [M]	Crazy Baby	1963	6.25	12.50	25.00
-- With New York, USA address on label					
❏ BLP-4050 [M]	Home Cookin'	1961	12.50	25.00	50.00
-- With W. 63rd St. address on label					
❏ BLP-4050 [M]	Home Cookin'	1963	5.00	10.00	20.00
-- With New York, USA address on label					
❏ BLP-4078 [M]	Midnight Special	1961	12.50	25.00	50.00
-- With 61st St. address on label					
❏ BLP-4078 [M]	Midnight Special	1963	5.00	10.00	20.00
-- With New York, USA address on label					
❏ BLP-4100 [M]	Jimmy Smith Plays Fats Waller	1962	12.50	25.00	50.00
-- With 61st St. address on label					
❏ BLP-4100 [M]	Jimmy Smith Plays Fats Waller	1963	5.00	10.00	20.00
-- With New York, USA address on label					

Number	Title	Yr	VG	VG+	NM
❏ BLP-4117 [M]	Back at the Chicken Shack	1963	6.25	12.50	25.00
❏ BLP-4141 [M]	Rockin' the Boat	1963	6.25	12.50	25.00
❏ BLP-4164 [M]	Prayer Meetin'	1964	6.25	12.50	25.00
❏ BLP-4200 [M]	Softly as a Summer Breeze	1965	6.25	12.50	25.00
❏ BLP-4235 [M]	Bucket!	1966	6.25	12.50	25.00
❏ BLP-4255 [M]	I'm Movin' On	1967	7.50	15.00	30.00
❏ BST-81512 [R]	Jimmy Smith at the Organ, Vol. 1	1967	3.00	6.00	12.00
❏ BST-81514 [R]	Jimmy Smith at the Organ, Vol. 2	1967	3.00	6.00	12.00
❏ BST-81525 [R]	The Incredible Jimmy Smith at the Organ, Vol. 3	1967	3.00	6.00	12.00
❏ BST-81528 [R]	The Incredible Jimmy Smith at Club Baby Grand, Wilmington, Delaware, Vol. 1	1967	3.00	6.00	12.00
❏ BST-81529 [R]	The Incredible Jimmy Smith at Club Baby Grand, Wilmington, Delaware, Vol. 2	1967	3.00	6.00	12.00
❏ BST-81547 [R]	A Date with Jimmy Smith, Vol. 1	1967	3.00	6.00	12.00
❏ BST-81548 [R]	A Date with Jimmy Smith, Vol. 2	1967	3.00	6.00	12.00
❏ BST-81551 [R]	Jimmy Smith at the Organ, Vol. 1	1967	3.00	6.00	12.00
❏ BST-81552 [R]	Jimmy Smith at the Organ, Vol. 2	1967	3.00	6.00	12.00
❏ BST-81556 [R]	The Sounds of Jimmy Smith	1967	3.00	6.00	12.00
❏ BST-81563 [S]	Jimmy Smith Plays Pretty Just for You	1967	3.75	7.50	15.00
❏ BST-81585 [S]	Groovin' at Small's Paradise, Vol. 1	1967	3.75	7.50	15.00
❏ BST-81586 [S]	Groovin' at Small's Paradise, Vol. 1	1967	3.75	7.50	15.00
❏ BST-84002 [S]	House Party	1967	3.75	7.50	15.00
❏ BST-84002	House Party	1985	2.50	5.00	10.00
-- "The Finest in Jazz Since 1939" reissue					
❏ BST-84011 [S]	The Sermon	1967	3.75	7.50	15.00
❏ B1-84030	Crazy Baby	1988	2.50	5.00	10.00
-- "The Finest in Jazz Since 1939" reissue					
❏ BST-84030 [S]	Crazy Baby	1960	12.50	25.00	50.00
-- With W. 63rd St. address on label					
❏ BST-84030 [S]	Crazy Baby	1963	5.00	10.00	20.00
-- With New York, USA address on label					
❏ BST-84030 [S]	Crazy Baby	1967	3.75	7.50	15.00
-- With "A Division of Liberty Records" on label					
❏ BST-84050 [S]	Home Cookin'	1961	12.50	25.00	50.00
-- With W. 63rd St. address on label					
❏ BST-84050 [S]	Home Cookin'	1963	5.00	10.00	20.00
-- With New York, USA address on label					
❏ BST-84050 [S]	Home Cookin'	1967	3.75	7.50	15.00
-- With "A Division of Liberty Records" on label					
❏ B1-84078	Midnight Special	1989	2.50	5.00	10.00
-- "The Finest in Jazz Since 1939" reissue					
❏ BST-84078 [S]	Midnight Special	1961	12.50	25.00	50.00
-- With 61st St. address on label					
❏ BST-84078 [S]	Midnight Special	1963	5.00	10.00	20.00
-- With New York, USA address on label					
❏ BST-84078 [S]	Midnight Special	1967	3.75	7.50	15.00
-- With "A Division of Liberty Records" on label					
❏ BST-84100 [S]	Jimmy Smith Plays Fats Waller	1962	12.50	25.00	50.00
-- With 61st St. address on label					
❏ BST-84100 [S]	Jimmy Smith Plays Fats Waller	1963	5.00	10.00	20.00
-- With New York, USA address on label					
❏ BST-84100 [S]	Jimmy Smith Plays Fats Waller	1967	3.75	7.50	15.00
-- With "A Division of Liberty Records" on label					
❏ BST-84117 [S]	Back at the Chicken Shack	1963	7.50	15.00	30.00
-- With New York, USA address on label					
❏ BST-84117 [S]	Back at the Chicken Shack	1967	3.75	7.50	15.00
-- With "A Division of Liberty Records" on label					
❏ BST-84117	Back at the Chicken Shack	1985	2.50	5.00	10.00
-- "The Finest in Jazz Since 1939" reissue					
❏ BST-84141 [S]	Rockin' the Boat	1963	7.50	15.00	30.00
-- With New York, USA address on label					
❏ BST-84141 [S]	Rockin' the Boat	1967	3.75	7.50	15.00
-- With "A Division of Liberty Records" on label					
❏ B1-84164	Prayer Meetin'	1988	2.50	5.00	10.00
-- "The Finest in Jazz Since 1939" reissue					
❏ BST-84164 [S]	Prayer Meetin'	1964	7.50	15.00	30.00
-- With New York, USA address on label					
❏ BST-84164 [S]	Prayer Meetin'	1967	3.75	7.50	15.00
-- With "A Division of Liberty Records" on label					
❏ BST-84200 [S]	Softly as a Summer Breeze	1965	7.50	15.00	30.00
-- With New York, USA address on label					
❏ BST-84200 [S]	Softly as a Summer Breeze	1967	3.75	7.50	15.00
-- With "A Division of Liberty Records" on label					
❏ BST-84225 [S]	Bucket!	1967	3.75	7.50	15.00
-- With "A Division of Liberty Records" on label					
❏ BST-84235 [S]	Bucket!	1966	7.50	15.00	30.00
-- With New York, USA address on label					
❏ BST-84255 [S]	I'm Movin' On	1967	5.00	10.00	20.00
❏ BST-84269	Open House	1968	5.00	10.00	20.00
❏ BST-84296	Plain Talk	1969	5.00	10.00	20.00
❏ B1-85125	Go For Whatcha Know	198?	2.50	5.00	10.00
❏ BST-89901 [(2)]	Jimmy Smith's Greatest Hits!	1969	6.25	12.50	25.00
❏ B1-91140	The Best of Jimmy Smith	1988	2.50	5.00	10.00

Number	Title	Yr	VG	VG+	NM
ELEKTRA/MUSICIAN					
❏ 60175	Off the Top	1983	2.50	5.00	10.00
❏ 60301	Keep On Comin'	1984	2.50	5.00	10.00
GUEST STAR					
❏ 1344 [M]	Jimmy Smith	196?	3.00	6.00	12.00
❏ G 1914 [M]	Jimmy Smith	196?	3.00	6.00	12.00
INNER CITY					
❏ 1121	The Cat Strikes Again	1981	2.50	5.00	10.00
MERCURY					
❏ SRM-1-1127	Sit On It!	1976	2.50	5.00	10.00
❏ SRM-1-1189	It's Necessary	1977	2.50	5.00	10.00
❏ SRM-1-3716	Unfinished Business	1978	2.50	5.00	10.00
METRO					
❏ M-521 [M]	Jimmy Smith at the Village Gate	1965	3.00	6.00	12.00
❏ MS-521 [S]	Jimmy Smith at the Village Gate	1965	3.00	6.00	12.00
MGM					
❏ GAS-107	Jimmy Smith (Golden Archive Series)	1970	3.75	7.50	15.00
❏ SE-4709	The Other Side	1970	3.00	6.00	12.00
❏ SE-4751	I'm Gon' Git Myself Together	1971	3.00	6.00	12.00
MILESTONE					
❏ M-9176	Prime Time	198?	2.50	5.00	10.00
MOSAIC					
❏ MQ5-154 [(5)]	The Complete February 1957 Jimmy Smith Blue Note Sessions	199?	20.00	40.00	80.00
PICKWICK					
❏ SPC-3023	Stranger in Paradise	196?	2.50	5.00	10.00
PRIDE					
❏ 6011	Black Smith	1974	3.00	6.00	12.00
SUNSET					
❏ SUM-1175 [M]	Jimmy Smith Plays the Standards	1967	3.75	7.50	15.00
❏ SUS-5175 [S]	Jimmy Smith Plays the Standards	1967	3.00	6.00	12.00
❏ SUS-5316	Just Friends	1971	3.00	6.00	12.00
VERVE					
❏ V6-652-2 [(2)]	24 Karat Hits	196?	3.75	7.50	15.00
❏ UMV-2073	Organ Grinder Swing	198?	2.50	5.00	10.00
-- Reissue of 8628					
❏ V-8474 [M]	Bashin'	1962	5.00	10.00	20.00
❏ V6-8474 [S]	Bashin'	1962	6.25	12.50	25.00
❏ V-8544 [M]	Hobo Flats	1963	5.00	10.00	20.00
❏ V6-8544 [S]	Hobo Flats	1963	6.25	12.50	25.00
❏ V-8552 [M]	Any Number Can Win	1963	5.00	10.00	20.00
❏ V6-8552 [S]	Any Number Can Win	1963	6.25	12.50	25.00
❏ V-8583 [M]	Who's Afraid of Virginia Woolf?	1964	5.00	10.00	20.00
❏ V6-8583 [S]	Who's Afraid of Virginia Woolf?	1964	6.25	12.50	25.00
❏ V-8587 [M]	The Cat	1964	5.00	10.00	20.00
❏ V6-8587 [S]	The Cat	1964	6.25	12.50	25.00
❏ V-8604 [M]	Christmas '64	1964	5.00	10.00	20.00
❏ V6-8604 [S]	Christmas '64	1964	6.25	12.50	25.00
❏ V-8618 [M]	The Monster	1965	3.75	7.50	15.00
❏ V6-8618 [S]	The Monster	1965	5.00	10.00	20.00
❏ V-8628 [M]	Organ Grinder Swing	1965	3.75	7.50	15.00
❏ V6-8628 [S]	Organ Grinder Swing	1965	5.00	10.00	20.00
❏ V-8641 [M]	Got My Mojo Workin'	1966	3.75	7.50	15.00
❏ V6-8641 [S]	Got My Mojo Workin'	1966	5.00	10.00	20.00
❏ V-8652 [M]	Peter and the Wolf	1966	5.00	10.00	20.00
❏ V6-8652 [S]	Peter and the Wolf	1966	6.25	12.50	25.00
❏ V-8666 [M]	Christmas Cookin'	1966	5.00	10.00	20.00
❏ V6-8666 [S]	Christmas Cookin'	1966	6.25	12.50	25.00
❏ V-8667 [M]	Hoochie Coochie Man	1966	3.75	7.50	15.00
❏ V6-8667 [S]	Hoochie Coochie Man	1966	5.00	10.00	20.00
❏ V-8705 [M]	Respect	1967	5.00	10.00	20.00
❏ V6-8705 [S]	Respect	1967	3.75	7.50	15.00
❏ V-8721 [M]	The Best of Jimmy Smith	1967	5.00	10.00	20.00
❏ V6-8721 [S]	The Best of Jimmy Smith	1967	3.75	7.50	15.00
❏ V6-8745 [S]	Stay Loose	1968	3.75	7.50	15.00
❏ V6-8750	Livin' It Up!	1968	3.75	7.50	15.00
❏ V6-8770	The Boss	1969	3.75	7.50	15.00
❏ V6-8794	Groove Drops	1970	3.75	7.50	15.00
❏ V6-8800	Plain Brown Wrapper	1971	3.00	6.00	12.00
❏ V6-8806	Root Down	1972	3.00	6.00	12.00
❏ V6-8809	Bluesmith	1973	3.00	6.00	12.00
❏ V6-8814 [(2)]	History of Jimmy Smith	1973	3.75	7.50	15.00
❏ V6-8832	Portuguese Soul	1974	3.00	6.00	12.00
❏ SMAS-90643 [S]	The Monster	1965	6.25	12.50	25.00
-- Capitol Record Club edition					
❏ 823 308-1	Bashin'	1986	2.50	5.00	10.00
-- Reissue of 8474					

Number	Title	Yr	VG	VG+	NM

SMITH, JIMMY, AND WES MONTGOMERY
Also see each artist's individual listings.
VERVE

Number	Title	Yr	VG	VG+	NM
❑ UMV-2069	Jimmy and Wes, The Dynamic	198?	2.50	5.00	10.00
-- Reissue of 8678					
❑ V-8678 [M]	Jimmy and Wes, The Dynamic	1967	5.00	10.00	20.00
❑ V6-8678 [S]	Jimmy and Wes, The Dynamic	1967	3.75	7.50	15.00
❑ V6-8766	The Further Adventures of Jimmy Smith and Wes Montgomery	1969	3.75	7.50	15.00

SMITH, JOHNNY
Guitarist and composer; he wrote "Moonlight in Vermont." Also see JERI SOUTHERN.
LEGENDE

Number	Title	Yr	VG	VG+	NM
❑ 1401 [10]	Annotations of the Muses	1955	25.00	50.00	100.00

ROOST

Number	Title	Yr	VG	VG+	NM
❑ R-410 [10]	A Three-Dimension Sound Recording of Jazz at NBC with the Johnny Smith Quintet	1953	37.50	75.00	150.00
❑ R-413 [10]	Johnny Smith Quintet	1953	30.00	60.00	120.00
❑ R-421 [10]	In a Mellow Mood	1954	25.00	50.00	100.00
❑ R-424 [10]	In a Sentimental Mood	1954	25.00	50.00	100.00
❑ LP-2201 [M]	Johnny Smith Plays Jimmy Van Heusen	1955	20.00	40.00	80.00
❑ LP-2203 [M]	Johnny Smith Quartet	1955	20.00	40.00	80.00
❑ LP-2211 [M]	Moonlight In Vermont	1956	20.00	40.00	80.00
❑ LP-2215 [M]	Moods	1956	15.00	30.00	60.00
❑ LP-2216 [M]	New Quartet	1956	15.00	30.00	60.00
❑ LP-2223 [M]	Johnny Smith Foursome, Volume 1	1956	12.50	25.00	50.00
❑ LP-2228 [M]	Johnny Smith Foursome, Volume 2	1957	12.50	25.00	50.00
❑ LP-2231 [M]	Flower Drum Song	1958	10.00	20.00	40.00
❑ SLP-2231 [S]	Flower Drum Song	1958	7.50	15.00	30.00
❑ LP-2233 [M]	Easy Listening	1959	10.00	20.00	40.00
❑ SLP-2233 [S]	Easy Listening	1959	7.50	15.00	30.00
❑ LP-2237 [M]	Favorites	1959	10.00	20.00	40.00
❑ SLP-2237 [S]	Favorites	1959	7.50	15.00	30.00
❑ LP-2238 [M]	Designed for You	1960	7.50	15.00	30.00
❑ SLP-2238 [S]	Designed for You	1960	10.00	20.00	40.00
❑ LP-2239 [M]	Dear Little Sweetheart	1960	7.50	15.00	30.00
❑ SLP-2239 [S]	Dear Little Sweetheart	1960	10.00	20.00	40.00
❑ LP-2242 [M]	Guitar and Strings	1960	7.50	15.00	30.00
❑ SLP-2242 [S]	Guitar and Strings	1960	10.00	20.00	40.00
❑ LP-2243 [M]	Johnny Smith Plus the Trio	1960	7.50	15.00	30.00
❑ SLP-2243 [S]	Johnny Smith Plus the Trio	1960	10.00	20.00	40.00
❑ LP-2246 [M]	The Sound of the Johnny Smith Guitar	1961	7.50	15.00	30.00
❑ SLP-2246 [S]	The Sound of the Johnny Smith Guitar	1961	10.00	20.00	40.00
❑ LP-2248 [M]	Man with the Blue Guitar	1962	7.50	15.00	30.00
❑ SLP-2248 [S]	Man with the Blue Guitar	1962	10.00	20.00	40.00
❑ LP-2250 [M]	Johnny Smith Plays Jimmy Van Heusen	1963	6.25	12.50	25.00
❑ SLP-2250 [S]	Johnny Smith Plays Jimmy Van Heusen	1963	7.50	15.00	30.00
❑ LP-2254 [M]	Guitar World	1963	6.25	12.50	25.00
❑ SLP-2254 [S]	Guitar World	1963	7.50	15.00	30.00
❑ LP-2259 [M]	Reminiscing	1965	6.25	12.50	25.00
❑ SLP-2259 [S]	Reminiscing	1965	7.50	15.00	30.00

VERVE

Number	Title	Yr	VG	VG+	NM
❑ V-8692 [M]	Johnny Smith	1967	7.50	15.00	30.00
❑ V6-8692 [S]	Johnny Smith	1967	5.00	10.00	20.00
❑ V-8737 [M]	Johnny Smith's Kaleidoscope	1968	7.50	15.00	30.00
❑ V6-8737 [S]	Johnny Smith's Kaleidoscope	1968	5.00	10.00	20.00
❑ V6-8767 [S]	Phase II	1969	5.00	10.00	20.00

SMITH, JOHNNY "HAMMOND"
See JOHNNY HAMMOND.

SMITH, KEELY
Female singer. Also see LOUIS PRIMA.
CAPITOL

Number	Title	Yr	VG	VG+	NM
❑ SW 914 [S]	I Wish You Love	1959	7.50	15.00	30.00
-- Black label with colorband, Capitol logo at left					
❑ SW 914 [S]	I Wish You Love	1962	3.75	7.50	15.00
-- Black label with colorband, Capitol logo at top					
❑ W 914 [M]	I Wish You Love	1957	12.50	25.00	50.00
-- Turquoise label					
❑ W 914 [M]	I Wish You Love	1959	7.50	15.00	30.00
-- Black label with colorband, Capitol logo at left					
❑ W 914 [M]	I Wish You Love	1962	3.75	7.50	15.00
-- Black label with colorband, Capitol logo at top					
❑ ST 1073 [S]	Politely!	1959	12.50	25.00	50.00
-- Black label with colorband, Capitol logo at left					
❑ ST 1073 [S]	Politely!	1962	5.00	10.00	20.00
-- Black label with colorband, Capitol logo at top					
❑ T 1073 [M]	Politely!	1958	10.00	20.00	40.00
-- Black label with colorband, Capitol logo at left					
❑ T 1073 [M]	Politely!	1962	3.75	7.50	15.00
-- Black label with colorband, Capitol logo at top					
❑ ST 1145 [S]	Swingin' Pretty	1959	12.50	25.00	50.00
-- Black label with colorband, Capitol logo at left					
❑ ST 1145 [S]	Swingin' Pretty	1962	5.00	10.00	20.00
-- Black label with colorband, Capitol logo at top					
❑ T 1145 [M]	Swingin' Pretty	1959	10.00	20.00	40.00
-- Black label with colorband, Capitol logo at left					
❑ T 1145 [M]	Swingin' Pretty	1962	3.75	7.50	15.00
-- Black label with colorband, Capitol logo at top					

DOT

Number	Title	Yr	VG	VG+	NM
❑ DLP-3241 [M]	Be My Love	1959	6.25	12.50	25.00
❑ DLP-3265 [M]	Swing, You Lovers	1960	6.25	12.50	25.00
❑ DLP-3287 [M]	Dearly Beloved	1961	6.25	12.50	25.00
❑ DLP-3345 [M]	A Keely Christmas	1961	6.25	12.50	25.00
❑ DLP-3415 [M]	Because You're Mine	1962	6.25	12.50	25.00
❑ DLP-3423 [M]	Twist with Keely Smith	1962	6.25	12.50	25.00
❑ DLP-3460 [M]	Cherokeely Swings	1962	6.25	12.50	25.00
❑ DLP-3461 [M]	What Kind of Fool Am I	1962	6.25	12.50	25.00
❑ DLP-25241 [S]	Be My Love	1959	7.50	15.00	30.00
❑ DLP-25265 [S]	Swing, You Lovers	1960	7.50	15.00	30.00
❑ DLP-25287 [S]	Dearly Beloved	1961	7.50	15.00	30.00
❑ DLP-25345 [S]	A Keely Christmas	1961	7.50	15.00	30.00
❑ DLP-25415 [S]	Because You're Mine	1962	7.50	15.00	30.00
❑ DLP-25423 [S]	Twist with Keely Smith	1962	7.50	15.00	30.00
❑ DLP-25460 [S]	Cherokeely Swings	1962	7.50	15.00	30.00
❑ DLP-25461 [S]	What Kind of Fool Am I	1962	7.50	15.00	30.00

HARMONY

Number	Title	Yr	VG	VG+	NM
❑ HS 11333	That Old Black Magic	1968	3.00	6.00	12.00

REPRISE

Number	Title	Yr	VG	VG+	NM
❑ R-6086 [M]	Little Girl Blue, Little Girl New	1963	5.00	10.00	20.00
❑ R9-6086 [S]	Little Girl Blue, Little Girl New	1963	6.25	12.50	25.00
❑ R-6132 [M]	The Intimate Keely Smith	1964	5.00	10.00	20.00
❑ RS-6132 [S]	The Intimate Keely Smith	1964	6.25	12.50	25.00
❑ R-6142 [M]	Keely Smith Sings the John Lennon/Paul McCartney Songbook	1964	6.25	12.50	25.00
❑ RS-6142 [S]	Keely Smith Sings the John Lennon/Paul McCartney Songbook	1964	7.50	15.00	30.00
❑ R-6175 [M]	That Old Black Magic	1965	5.00	10.00	20.00
❑ RS-6175 [S]	That Old Black Magic	1965	6.25	12.50	25.00

SMITH, KEITH
Trumpeter and bandleader.
GHB

Number	Title	Yr	VG	VG+	NM
❑ GHB-27	Keith Smith's Climax Jazz Band	196?	3.00	6.00	12.00

SMITH, LaVERGNE
Female singer.
COOK

Number	Title	Yr	VG	VG+	NM
❑ LP-1081 [10]	Angel in the Absinthe House	1955	37.50	75.00	150.00

SAVOY

Number	Title	Yr	VG	VG+	NM
❑ MG-12031 [M]	New Orleans Nightingale	1955	12.50	25.00	50.00

VIK

Number	Title	Yr	VG	VG+	NM
❑ LX-1056 [M]	La Vergne Smith	1956	12.50	25.00	50.00

SMITH, LEO
Trumpeter, fluegel horn player, flutist and percussionist.
BLACK SAINT

Number	Title	Yr	VG	VG+	NM
❑ BSR-0053	Go in Numbers	198?	3.00	6.00	12.00

ECM

Number	Title	Yr	VG	VG+	NM
❑ 1143	Divine Love	1979	3.00	6.00	12.00

KABELL

Number	Title	Yr	VG	VG+	NM
❑ CM-1	Creative Music-1	197?	3.75	7.50	15.00

NESSA

Number	Title	Yr	VG	VG+	NM
❑ N-19	Spirit Catcher	1980	3.75	7.50	15.00

SACKVILLE

Number	Title	Yr	VG	VG+	NM
❑ 3030	Rastafari	198?	2.50	5.00	10.00

SMITH, LONNIE
Organist.
BLUE NOTE

Number	Title	Yr	VG	VG+	NM
❑ B1-28266	Drives	1994	3.75	7.50	15.00
❑ B1-31249	Move Your Hand	1996	3.75	7.50	15.00
❑ B1-31880	Live at Club Mozambique	1995	3.75	7.50	15.00
❑ BST-84290	Think!	1968	5.00	10.00	20.00
❑ BST-84313	Turning Point	1969	5.00	10.00	20.00
❑ BST-84326	Move Your Hand	1970	3.75	7.50	15.00
❑ BST-84351	Drives	1971	3.75	7.50	15.00

CHIAROSCURO

Number	Title	Yr	VG	VG+	NM
❑ 2019	When the Night Is Right	1979	3.00	6.00	12.00

(Top left) La Vergne Smith is a little-known jazz singer who put out three collectible albums in the mid-1950s, including this one on Savoy. (Top right) Saxophone player Sonny Stitt was often at his best when he was "competing" with another name musician on an album. This Argo session, released in 1965, paired Stitt with trombonist Bennie Green. (Bottom left) If there is such a thing as an easy-to-find Sun Ra album, this would be among them. Chicago-based Delmark Records issued some 1950s sessions, in rechanneled stereo, on two different albums in the late 1960s. One of these is *Sound of Joy*. Most Sun Ra albums, especially on the Saturn label, are extremely difficult to locate. (Bottom right) Another highly collectible 10-inch album on the Blue Note label is this split LP, with half the tracks by The Swinging Swedes, the other half by The Cool Britons.

Number	Title	Yr	VG	VG+	NM
COLUMBIA					
❏ CL 2696 [M]	Finger-Lickin' Good Soul Organ	1967	6.25	12.50	25.00
❏ CS 9496 [S]	Finger-Lickin' Good Soul Organ	1967	5.00	10.00	20.00
GROOVE MERCHANT					
❏ 3308	Afro-Desia	1975	3.00	6.00	12.00
❏ 3312	Keep On Lovin'	1976	3.00	6.00	12.00
KUDU					
❏ 02	Mama Wailer	1972	3.00	6.00	12.00

SMITH, LONNIE LISTON
Pianist and keyboard player.

Number	Title	Yr	VG	VG+	NM
COLUMBIA					
❏ JC 35332	Loveland	1978	2.50	5.00	10.00
❏ JC 35654	Exotic Mysteries	1979	2.50	5.00	10.00
❏ JC 36141	Song for the Children	1979	2.50	5.00	10.00
❏ JC 36366	The Best of Lonnie Liston Smith	1980	2.50	5.00	10.00
❏ JC 36373	Love Is the Answer	1980	2.50	5.00	10.00
DOCTOR JAZZ					
❏ FW 38447	Dreams of Tomorrow	1983	2.50	5.00	10.00
❏ FW 39420	Silhouettes	1984	2.50	5.00	10.00
❏ FW 40063	Rejuvenation	1985	2.50	5.00	10.00
FLYING DUTCHMAN					
❏ BDL1-0591	Cosmic Funk	1974	3.00	6.00	12.00
❏ BXL1-0591	Cosmic Funk	1978	2.00	4.00	8.00
-- Reissue with new prefix					
❏ BDL1-0934	Expressions	1975	3.00	6.00	12.00
❏ BXL1-0934	Expressions	1978	2.00	4.00	8.00
-- Reissue with new prefix					
❏ BDL1-1196	Visions of a New World	1975	3.00	6.00	12.00
❏ BXL1-1196	Visions of a New World	1978	2.00	4.00	8.00
-- Reissue with new prefix					
❏ BDL1-1460	Reflections of a Golden Dream	1976	3.00	6.00	12.00
❏ BXL1-1460	Reflections of a Golden Dream	1978	2.00	4.00	8.00
-- Reissue with new prefix					
❏ 10163	Astral Travelling	1973	3.00	6.00	12.00
RCA VICTOR					
❏ AFL1-1822	Renaissance	1978	2.00	4.00	8.00
-- Reissue with new prefix					
❏ APL1-1822	Renaissance	1976	2.50	5.00	10.00
❏ AFL1-2433	Live!	1978	2.00	4.00	8.00
-- Reissue with new prefix					
❏ APL1-2433	Live!	1977	2.50	5.00	10.00
❏ AFL1-2897	The Best of Lonnie Liston Smith	1978	2.50	5.00	10.00
STARTRAK					
❏ STA-4021	Love Goddess	198?	2.50	5.00	10.00

SMITH, LOUIS
Trumpeter and fluegel horn player.

Number	Title	Yr	VG	VG+	NM
BLUE NOTE					
❏ BLP-1584 [M]	Here Comes Louis Smith	1958	37.50	75.00	150.00
-- "Deep groove" version (deep indentation under label on both sides)					
❏ BLP-1584 [M]	Here Comes Louis Smith	1958	30.00	60.00	120.00
-- Regular version, W. 63rd St. address on label					
❏ BST-1584 [S]	Here Comes Louis Smith	1959	25.00	50.00	100.00
-- "Deep groove" version (deep indentation under label on both sides)					
❏ BST-1584 [S]	Here Comes Louis Smith	1959	20.00	40.00	80.00
-- Regular version, W. 63rd St. address on label					
❏ BLP-1594 [M]	Smithville	1958	25.00	50.00	100.00
-- "Deep groove" version (deep indentation under label on both sides)					
❏ BLP-1594 [M]	Smithville	1958	20.00	40.00	80.00
-- Regular version, W. 63rd St. address on label					
❏ BST-1594 [S]	Smithville	1959	20.00	40.00	80.00
-- "Deep groove" version (deep indentation under label on both sides)					
❏ BST-1594 [S]	Smithville	1959	15.00	30.00	60.00
-- Regular version, W. 63rd St. address on label					
❏ BST-81584 [S]	Here Comes Louis Smith	1967	3.75	7.50	15.00
-- With "A Division of Liberty Records" on label					
❏ BST-81594 [S]	Smithville	1967	3.75	7.50	15.00
-- With "A Division of Liberty Records" on label					
STEEPLECHASE					
❏ SCS-1096	Just Friends	198?	3.00	6.00	12.00
❏ SCS-1121	Prancin'	1979	3.00	6.00	12.00

SMITH, MARVIN "SMITTY"
Drummer.

Number	Title	Yr	VG	VG+	NM
CONCORD JAZZ					
❏ CJ-325	Keeper of the Drums	1987	2.50	5.00	10.00
❏ CJ-379	The Road Less Traveled	1989	3.00	6.00	12.00

SMITH, MICHAEL

Number	Title	Yr	VG	VG+	NM
STORYVILLE					
❏ 4014	Reflection on Progress	1980	3.00	6.00	12.00

SMITH, MIKE
Alto saxophone player.

Number	Title	Yr	VG	VG+	NM
DELMARK					
❏ DS-444	Unit 7: A Tribute to Cannonball Adderley	1990	3.00	6.00	12.00

SMITH, OSBORNE
Male singer.

Number	Title	Yr	VG	VG+	NM
ARGO					
❏ LP-4000 [M]	Eyes of Love	1960	7.50	15.00	30.00
❏ LPS-4000 [S]	Eyes of Love	1960	10.00	20.00	40.00

SMITH, PAUL
Pianist and organist.

Number	Title	Yr	VG	VG+	NM
CAPITOL					
❏ H 493 [10]	Liquid Sounds	1954	20.00	40.00	80.00
❏ T 665 [M]	Cascades	1955	10.00	20.00	40.00
❏ T 757 [M]	Cool and Sparkling	1956	10.00	20.00	40.00
❏ T 829 [M]	Softly, Baby	1957	10.00	20.00	40.00
❏ ST 1017 [S]	Delicate Jazz	1958	6.25	12.50	25.00
❏ T 1017 [M]	Delicate Jazz	1958	7.50	15.00	30.00
DISCOVERY					
❏ DL-3009 [10]	Paul Smith	1950	25.00	50.00	100.00
❏ DL-3017 [10]	Paul Smith Trio	1952	20.00	40.00	80.00
MGM					
❏ E-4057 [M]	Memories of Paris	1962	5.00	10.00	20.00
❏ SE-4057 [S]	Memories of Paris	1962	6.25	12.50	25.00
OUTSTANDING					
❏ 002	The Master Touch	197?	3.00	6.00	12.00
❏ 004	The Art Tatum Touch	197?	3.00	6.00	12.00
❏ 005	The Ballad Touch	197?	3.00	6.00	12.00
❏ 007	The Art Tatum Touch, Vol. 2	197?	3.00	6.00	12.00
❏ 009	Heavy Jazz	197?	3.00	6.00	12.00
❏ 011	Heavy Jazz, Vol. 2	1978	3.00	6.00	12.00
❏ 012	This One Cooks!	197?	3.00	6.00	12.00
❏ 023	Jazz Spotlight on Porter and Gershwin	1980	3.75	7.50	15.00
❏ 024	Jazz Spotlight on Ellington and Rodgers	1980	3.75	7.50	15.00
PAUSA					
❏ 7172	Paul Smith Plays Steve Allen	1985	2.50	5.00	10.00
SAVOY					
❏ MG-12094 [M]	By the Fireside	1956	12.50	25.00	50.00
SKYLARK					
❏ SKLP-13 [10]	Paul Smith Quartet	1954	30.00	60.00	120.00
TAMPA					
❏ TP-9 [M]	Fine, Sweet and Tasty	1957	25.00	50.00	100.00
-- Colored vinyl					
❏ TP-9 [M]	Fine, Sweet and Tasty	1958	12.50	25.00	50.00
-- Black vinyl					
VERVE					
❏ MGV-2128 [M]	The Sound of Music	1960	10.00	20.00	40.00
❏ V-2128 [M]	The Sound of Music	1961	5.00	10.00	20.00
❏ V6-2128 [S]	The Sound of Music	1961	3.75	7.50	15.00
❏ MGV-2130 [M]	The Big Men	1960	10.00	20.00	40.00
❏ V-2130 [M]	The Big Men	1961	5.00	10.00	20.00
❏ V6-2130 [S]	The Big Men	1961	3.75	7.50	15.00
❏ MGV-2148 [M]	Latin Keyboards and Percussion	1960	10.00	20.00	40.00
❏ V-2148 [M]	Latin Keyboards and Percussion	1961	5.00	10.00	20.00
❏ V6-2148 [S]	Latin Keyboards and Percussion	1961	3.75	7.50	15.00
❏ MGV-4051 [M]	Carnival! In Percussion	1961	7.50	15.00	30.00
❏ V-4051 [M]	Carnival! In Percussion	1961	5.00	10.00	20.00
❏ V6-4051 [S]	Carnival! In Percussion	1961	6.25	12.50	25.00
❏ MGVS-6128 [S]	The Sound of Music	1960	7.50	15.00	30.00
❏ MGVS-6135 [S]	The Big Men	1960	7.50	15.00	30.00
VOSS					
❏ VLP1-42937	The Good Life	1988	2.50	5.00	10.00

SMITH, PAUL; RAY BROWN; LOUIS BELLSON
Also see each artist's individual listings.

Number	Title	Yr	VG	VG+	NM
DISCWASHER					
❏ 001	Intensive Care	1979	5.00	10.00	20.00

SMITH, PINE TOP
Pianist and male singer.

Number	Title	Yr	VG	VG+	NM
BRUNSWICK					
❏ BL 58003 [10]	Pine Top Smith	1950	30.00	60.00	120.00

SMITH, PLATO

Number	Title	Yr	VG	VG+	NM
LAND O' JAZZ					
❏ 1972	Dixieland Dance Date	1972	2.50	5.00	10.00

Number	Title	Yr	VG	VG+	NM
SMITH, RAY					
Pianist.					
STOMP OFF					
❑ SOS-1012	Jungle Blues	198?	3.00	6.00	12.00
SMITH, RICHARD					
Guitarist.					
CMG					
❑ CML-8011	Puma Creek	1988	2.50	5.00	10.00
SMITH, STEVE					
Drummer.					
COLUMBIA					
❑ FC 38955	Vital Information	1983	2.50	5.00	10.00
❑ FC 44334	Fiafiaga	1988	2.50	5.00	10.00
SMITH, STUFF					
Violinist and male singer.					
ARCHIVE OF FOLK AND JAZZ					
❑ 238	Stuff Smith/Guest Artist: Stephane Grappelly	1970	2.50	5.00	10.00
BASF					
❑ 20650	Black Violin	197?	3.75	7.50	15.00
PRESTIGE					
❑ PRST-7691 [R]	The Stuff Smith Memorial Album	1969	3.75	7.50	15.00
STORYVILLE					
❑ 4087	Swingin' Stuff	198?	2.50	5.00	10.00
20TH FOX					
❑ FTM-3008 [M]	Sweet Singin' Stuff	1959	7.50	15.00	30.00
❑ FTS-3008 [S]	Sweet Singin' Stuff	1959	6.25	12.50	25.00
VERVE					
❑ MGV-2041 [M]	Stuff Smith	1957	---	---	---
-- Canceled					
❑ MGVS-6097 [S]	Cat on a Hot Fiddle	1960	10.00	20.00	40.00
❑ MGV-8206 [M]	Soft Winds	1958	12.50	25.00	50.00
❑ V-8206 [M]	Soft Winds	1961	5.00	10.00	20.00
❑ MGV-8270 [M]	Stephane Grappelli With Stuff	1958	---	---	---
-- Canceled					
❑ MGV-8282 [M]	Have Violin, Will Swing	1958	12.50	25.00	50.00
❑ V-8282 [M]	Have Violin, Will Swing	1961	5.00	10.00	20.00
❑ MGV-8339 [M]	Cat on a Hot Fiddle	1959	12.50	25.00	50.00
❑ V-8339 [M]	Cat on a Hot Fiddle	1961	5.00	10.00	20.00
❑ V6-8339 [S]	Cat on a Hot Fiddle	1961	3.75	7.50	15.00
SMITH, TOMMY					
Alto and soprano saxophone player.					
BLUE NOTE					
❑ B1-91930	Step by Step	1989	3.00	6.00	12.00
STOMP OFF					
❑ SOS-1162	South Side Strut: A Tribute to Don Ewell	1989	2.50	5.00	10.00
SMITH, WILLIE					
Alto saxophone player. Also a baritone sax player, clarinetist and male singer.					
EMARCY					
❑ MG-26000 [10]	Relaxin' After Hours	1954	25.00	50.00	100.00
GNP CRESCENDO					
❑ GNPS-2055	The Best -- Alto Saxophone Supreme	196?	2.50	5.00	10.00
MERCURY					
❑ MG-25075 [10]	Alto Sax Artistry	1950	30.00	60.00	120.00
SMITH, WILLIE "THE LION"					
Pianist, composer and male singer. Also see LUCKEY ROBERTS.					
BLACK LION					
❑ 156	Pork and Beans	197?	3.75	7.50	15.00
BLUE CIRCLE					
❑ 1500-33 [10]	Willie "The Lion" Smith	1952	20.00	40.00	80.00
CHIAROSCURO					
❑ 104	Live at Blues Alley	197?	3.75	7.50	15.00
COMMODORE					
❑ XFL-15775	Willie "The Lion" Smith	198?	2.50	5.00	10.00
❑ DL-30004 [M]	The Lion of the Piano	1951	25.00	50.00	100.00
DIAL					
❑ LP-305 [10]	Harlem Memories	1953	62.50	125.00	250.00
DOT					
❑ DLP-3094 [M]	The Lion Roars	1958	12.50	25.00	50.00
GNP CRESCENDO					
❑ GNP-9011	Willie "The Lion" Smith	197?	2.50	5.00	10.00

Number	Title	Yr	VG	VG+	NM
GRAND AWARD					
❑ GA-33-368 [M]	The Legend of Willie Smith	1956	12.50	25.00	50.00
MAINSTREAM					
❑ S-6027 [R]	A Legend	1965	3.75	7.50	15.00
❑ 56027 [M]	A Legend	1965	6.25	12.50	25.00
RCA VICTOR					
❑ LSP-6016 [(2)]	Memoirs	1968	5.00	10.00	20.00
URANIA					
❑ UJLP-1207 [M]	Accent On Piano	1955	15.00	30.00	60.00
SMITH, WILLIE "THE LION", AND DON EWELL					
Also see each artist's individual listings.					
SACKVILLE					
❑ 2004	Grand Piano	198?	2.50	5.00	10.00
SMITH-GLAMANN QUINTET					
Members: Barry Galbraith (guitar); Betty Glamann (harp); Rufus Smith (bass); Nick Perito (accordion); Frank Garisto (drums).					
BETHLEHEM					
❑ BCP-22 [M]	Smith-Glamann Quintet	1955	12.50	25.00	50.00
SMITHSONIAN JAZZ REPERTORY ENSEMBLE, THE					
Members: PANAMA FRANCIS; Jack Gale (trombone); Major Holley (bass); DICK HYMAN; JIMMIE MAXWELL; DICK WELLSTOOD; BOB WILBER.					
SMITHSONIAN					
❑ N-021	The Music of Fats Waller and James P. Johnson	1988	3.75	7.50	15.00
SMOKER, PAUL					
Trumpeter.					
SOUND ASPECTS					
❑ SAS-006	Mississippi River Rat	1985	3.00	6.00	12.00
SNOW, VALAIDA					
Trumpeter and female singer.					
SWING					
❑ SW-8455/6 [(2)]	Swing Is the Thing	198?	3.00	6.00	12.00
SNOWDEN, ELMER					
Banjo player and bandleader.					
FANTASY					
❑ OJC-1756	Harlem Banjo	198?	2.50	5.00	10.00
IAJRC					
❑ LP 12	Elmer Snowden 1924-63	198?	2.50	5.00	10.00
RIVERSIDE					
❑ RLP-348 [M]	Harlem Banjo	1960	5.00	10.00	20.00
❑ RS-9348 [S]	Harlem Banjo	1960	6.25	12.50	25.00
SOCOLOW, FRANK					
Tenor and alto saxophone player.					
BETHLEHEM					
❑ BCP-70 [M]	Sounds By Socolow	1957	20.00	40.00	80.00
SOFTWARE					
Led by Peter Mergener and Michael Weissner.					
HEADFIRST					
❑ 9707	Marbles	198?	3.00	6.00	12.00
INNOVATIVE COMMUNICATION					
❑ D1-74766	Digital Dance	1988	3.00	6.00	12.00
❑ KS 80.050	Chip-Meditation	1987	3.75	7.50	15.00
❑ KS 80.055 [(2)]	Electronic Universe	1987	5.00	10.00	20.00
❑ IC 80.064	Syn-Code/Live in Concert	1988	3.75	7.50	15.00
SOLAL, MARTIAL					
Pianist; also a composer, clarinetist and saxophone player. Also see SIDNEY BECHET.					
CAPITOL					
❑ ST 10261 [S]	Martial Solal	1960	7.50	15.00	30.00
❑ T 10261 [M]	Martial Solal	1960	6.25	12.50	25.00
❑ ST 10354 [S]	Vive La France! Viva La Jazz! Vive Solal!	1961	6.25	12.50	25.00
❑ T 10354 [M]	Vive La France! Viva La Jazz! Vive Solal!	1961	5.00	10.00	20.00
CONTEMPORARY					
❑ C-2512 [10]	French Modern Sounds	1954	20.00	40.00	80.00
LIBERTY					
❑ LRP-3335 [M]	Martial Solal in Concert	1963	3.75	7.50	15.00
❑ LST-7335 [S]	Martial Solal in Concert	1963	5.00	10.00	20.00
MILESTONE					
❑ MLP-1001 [M]	Solal!	1967	6.25	12.50	25.00

Number	Title	Yr	VG	VG+	NM
❏ MSP-9001 [S]	Solal!	1967	3.75	7.50	15.00
❏ MSP-9014	On Home Ground	1969	3.75	7.50	15.00
PAUSA					
❏ 7061	Four Keys	197?	2.50	5.00	10.00
❏ 7103	Movability	198?	2.50	5.00	10.00
RCA VICTOR					
❏ LPM-2777 [M]	Martial Solal at Newport '63	1963	3.75	7.50	15.00
❏ LSP-2777 [S]	Martial Solal at Newport '63	1963	5.00	10.00	20.00
SOUL NOTE					
❏ SN-1060	Bluesine	1983	3.00	6.00	12.00

SOLAR PLEXUS
Swedish fusion group.
INNER CITY

Number	Title	Yr	VG	VG+	NM
❏ IC-1067	Solar Plexus	1979	3.00	6.00	12.00
❏ IC-1087	Earth Songs	1980	3.00	6.00	12.00

SOLOFF, LEW
Trumpeter.
PROJAZZ

Number	Title	Yr	VG	VG+	NM
❏ PAD-601	Hanalei Bay	1986	2.50	5.00	10.00

SOLUTION, THE
Members: Tom Barlage (sax and flute); Willem Ennes (keyboards); Ad Kooi (bass, replaced by Peter van der Sande, who was then replaced by Guus Willemse); Ap Alberts (sax); Frits Lagerwerff (trumpet); Frank de Graaf (vocals); Frits Schmidt (drums, replaced by Hans Waterman).
FIRST AMERICAN

Number	Title	Yr	VG	VG+	NM
❏ 7776	It's Only Just Begun	198?	2.50	5.00	10.00

SOMMERS, JOANIE
Female singer. Best known for her pop records (not included here).
WARNER BROS.

Number	Title	Yr	VG	VG+	NM
❏ W 1346 [M]	Positively the Most	1960	7.50	15.00	30.00
❏ WS 1346 [S]	Positively the Most	1960	10.00	20.00	40.00

SOMOA
PROJAZZ

Number	Title	Yr	VG	VG+	NM
❏ PAD-645	No Band Is an Island	1987	2.50	5.00	10.00

SONDHEIM, ALAN
ESP-DISK'

Number	Title	Yr	VG	VG+	NM
❏ 1048 [S]	Ritual-All-7-70	1969	5.00	10.00	20.00
❏ 1082 [S]	T'Other Little Tune	1969	5.00	10.00	20.00

SONN, LARRY
Trumpeter and pianist.
CORAL

Number	Title	Yr	VG	VG+	NM
❏ CRL 57057 [M]	The Sound of Sonn	1956	10.00	20.00	40.00
DOT					
❏ DLP-9005 [M]	Jazz Band Having a Ball	1958	6.25	12.50	25.00
❏ DLP-29005 [S]	Jazz Band Having a Ball	1958	7.50	15.00	30.00

SONS OF BIX, THE
Members: Tom Pletcher (cornet); Don Ingle (valve trombone); John Harker (clarinet); Russ Whitman (bass saxophone); Dave Miller (guitar, banjo); Don Gibson (piano); Wayne Jones (drums).
JAZZOLOGY

Number	Title	Yr	VG	VG+	NM
❏ J-59	Ostrich Walk	1979	2.50	5.00	10.00
❏ J-99	Copenhagen	1983	2.50	5.00	10.00

SOPRANO SUMMIT
Led by KENNY DAVERN and BOB WILBER on soprano sax.
CHIAROSCURO

Number	Title	Yr	VG	VG+	NM
❏ 149	Chalumeau Blue	197?	3.00	6.00	12.00
❏ 178	Crazy Rhythm	1977	3.00	6.00	12.00
CONCORD JAZZ					
❏ CJ-29	Soprano Summit in Concert	1976	3.00	6.00	12.00
❏ CJ-52	Live at Concord '77	1977	3.00	6.00	12.00
JAZZOLOGY					
❏ J-56	Live at Big Horn Jazzfest	197?	2.50	5.00	10.00
WORLD JAZZ					
❏ 5	Soprano Summit	197?	3.75	7.50	15.00

SOSKIN, MARK
Pianist.
PRESTIGE

Number	Title	Yr	VG	VG+	NM
❏ 10109	Rhythm Vision	1979	3.75	7.50	15.00

SOSSON, MARSHALL
Violinist.
TOWN HALL

Number	Title	Yr	VG	VG+	NM
❏ M26	Virtuoso Jazz Violin Classics	197?	3.00	6.00	12.00

SOUCHON, DR. EDMOND
Guitarist and bandleader.
GHB

Number	Title	Yr	VG	VG+	NM
❏ GHB-6	Dr. Edmond Souchon	1963	3.75	7.50	15.00
❏ GHB-131	Dr. Edmond Souchon and the Milneburg Boys	1969	3.00	6.00	12.00
GOLDEN CREST					
❏ GC-3021	Dixieland of New Orleans	196?	3.75	7.50	15.00
❏ GC-3065	Minstrel Days	196?	3.75	7.50	15.00
SOUTHLAND					
❏ 231	Dr. Edmond Souchon and the Milneburg Boys	1962	3.75	7.50	15.00

SOUL FLUTES
The "flutes" on this album were played by Joel Kaye, HERBIE MANN, George Marge, Romeo Penque and Stan Webb.
A&M

Number	Title	Yr	VG	VG+	NM
❏ SP-3009	Trust in Me	1969	5.00	10.00	20.00

SOULFUL STRINGS, THE
Arranged by RICHARD EVANS.
CADET

Number	Title	Yr	VG	VG+	NM
❏ LP-776 [M]	Paint It Black	1967	3.75	7.50	15.00
❏ LPS-776 [S]	Paint It Black	1967	3.00	6.00	12.00
❏ LPS-796	Groovin' with the Soulful Strings	1967	3.00	6.00	12.00
❏ LPS-805	Another Exposure	1968	3.00	6.00	12.00
❏ LPS-814	The Magic of Christmas	1968	3.00	6.00	12.00
❏ LPS-820	In Concert/Back by Demand	1969	3.00	6.00	12.00
❏ LPS-834	String Fever	1969	3.00	6.00	12.00
❏ LPS-846	Gamble-Huff	1971	2.50	5.00	10.00
❏ 50022 [(2)]	Best of the Soulful Strings	1973	3.00	6.00	12.00

SOUND OF FEELING
LIMELIGHT

Number	Title	Yr	VG	VG+	NM
❏ LS-86063	Spleen	1969	5.00	10.00	20.00

SOUNDS ORCHESTRAL
British studio group. The hit single "Cast Your Fate to the Wind," an almost note-for-note remake of VINCE GUARALDI's original, featured Johnny Pearson on piano.
JANUS

Number	Title	Yr	VG	VG+	NM
❏ JLS-3014	One More Time	197?	3.75	7.50	15.00
PARKWAY					
❏ P 7046 [M]	Cast Your Fate to the Wind	1965	3.75	7.50	15.00
❏ SP 7046 [S]	Cast Your Fate to the Wind	1965	5.00	10.00	20.00
❏ P 7050 [M]	Impressions of James Bond	1966	5.00	10.00	20.00
❏ SP 7050 [S]	Impressions of James Bond	1966	7.50	15.00	30.00

SOUNDSTAGE ALL-STARS, THE
DOT

Number	Title	Yr	VG	VG+	NM
❏ DLP-3204 [M]	More "Peter Gunn"	1959	6.25	12.50	25.00
❏ DLP-25204 [S]	More "Peter Gunn"	1959	7.50	15.00	30.00

SOUTER, EDDIE
See RAY McKINLEY.

SOUTH FRISCO JAZZ BAND, THE
Formed in 1956 by Vince Saunders (banjo).
SFJB

Number	Title	Yr	VG	VG+	NM
❏ 2-1978	Diggin' Clams	1978	3.75	7.50	15.00
STOMP OFF					
❏ SOS-1027	Live at Earthquake McGoon's	1981	2.50	5.00	10.00
❏ SOS-1035	These Cats Are Diggin' Us	198?	2.50	5.00	10.00
❏ SOS-1103	Jones Law Blues	1985	2.50	5.00	10.00
❏ SOS-1143	Sage Hen Strut	1987	2.50	5.00	10.00
❏ SOS-1180	Broken Promises	1988	2.50	5.00	10.00
VAULT					
❏ S-9008	Hot Tamale Man	196?	3.75	7.50	15.00

SOUTH, EDDIE
Violinist.
CHESS

Number	Title	Yr	VG	VG+	NM
❏ ACMJ-415	South Side Jazz	197?	3.00	6.00	12.00
MERCURY					
❏ MG-20401 [M]	The Distinguished Violin of Eddie South	1959	7.50	15.00	30.00

Number	Title	Yr	VG	VG+	NM
❏ SR-60070 [S]	The Distinguished Violin of Eddie South	1959	6.25	12.50	25.00
SWING					
❏ SW-8405	Eddie South	1985	2.50	5.00	10.00
TRIP					
❏ 5803	Dark Angel of the Fiddle	197?	2.50	5.00	10.00

SOUTHERN STOMPERS, THE
STOMP OFF

Number	Title	Yr	VG	VG+	NM
❏ SOS-1215	Echoes of King Oliver's Jazz Band	1991	2.50	5.00	10.00

SOUTHERN, JERI
Female singer and pianist.
CAPITOL

Number	Title	Yr	VG	VG+	NM
❏ ST 1173 [S]	Jeri Southern Meets Cole Porter	1959	10.00	20.00	40.00
-- Black colorband label, Capitol logo at left					
❏ ST 1173 [S]	Jeri Southern Meets Cole Porter	1963	5.00	10.00	20.00
-- Black colorband label, Capitol logo at top					
❏ T 1173 [M]	Jeri Southern Meets Cole Porter	1959	7.50	15.00	30.00
-- Black colorband label, Capitol logo at left					
❏ T 1173 [M]	Jeri Southern Meets Cole Porter	1963	3.75	7.50	15.00
-- Black colorband label, Capitol logo at top					
❏ ST 1278 [S]	Jeri Southern at the Crescendo	1960	10.00	20.00	40.00
-- Black colorband label, Capitol logo at left					
❏ ST 1278 [S]	Jeri Southern at the Crescendo	1963	5.00	10.00	20.00
-- Black colorband label, Capitol logo at top					
❏ T 1278 [M]	Jeri Southern at the Crescendo	1960	7.50	15.00	30.00
-- Black colorband label, Capitol logo at left					
❏ T 1278 [M]	Jeri Southern at the Crescendo	1963	3.75	7.50	15.00
-- Black colorband label, Capitol logo at top					

DECCA

Number	Title	Yr	VG	VG+	NM
❏ DL 5531 [10]	Intimate Songs	1954	20.00	40.00	80.00
❏ DL 8055 [M]	Southern Style	1955	12.50	25.00	50.00
❏ DL 8214 [M]	You Better Go Now	1956	12.50	25.00	50.00
❏ DL 8394 [M]	When Your Heart's on Fire	1956	12.50	25.00	50.00
❏ DL 8472 [M]	Jeri Southern Gently Jumps	1957	12.50	25.00	50.00
❏ DL 8745 [M]	Prelude to a Kiss	1958	12.50	25.00	50.00
❏ DL 8761 [M]	Southern Hospitality	1958	12.50	25.00	50.00

FORUM

Number	Title	Yr	VG	VG+	NM
❏ F-9030 [M]	Jeri Southern Meets Johnny Smith	196?	3.00	6.00	12.00
❏ SF-9030 [S]	Jeri Southern Meets Johnny Smith	196?	3.75	7.50	15.00

ROULETTE

Number	Title	Yr	VG	VG+	NM
❏ R-25039 [M]	Coffee, Cigarettes and Memories	1958	10.00	20.00	40.00
❏ R-52010 [M]	Southern Breeze	1958	10.00	20.00	40.00
❏ RS-52010 [S]	Southern Breeze	1958	12.50	25.00	50.00
❏ R-52016 [M]	Jeri Southern Meets Johnny Smith	1958	10.00	20.00	40.00
❏ RS-52016 [S]	Jeri Southern Meets Johnny Smith	1958	12.50	25.00	50.00

SPACE
Featuring ROSCOE MITCHELL and Gerald Oshita (saxophones).
1750 ARCH

Number	Title	Yr	VG	VG+	NM
❏ 1806	An Interesting Breakfast Conversation	198?	3.00	6.00	12.00

SPANIER, MUGGSY
Cornet player and bandleader.
ARCHIVE OF FOLK AND JAZZ

Number	Title	Yr	VG	VG+	NM
❏ 226	Muggsy Spanier	1968	2.50	5.00	10.00
❏ 326	Muggsy Spanier, Vol. 2	197?	2.50	5.00	10.00
AVA					
❏ A-12 [M]	Columbia, the Gem of the Ocean	1963	3.00	6.00	12.00
❏ AS-12 [S]	Columbia, the Gem of the Ocean	1963	3.75	7.50	15.00
COMMODORE					
❏ XFL-15777	Muggsy Spanier at Nick's New York, April 1944	198?	2.50	5.00	10.00
❏ FL-20009 [10]	Spanier's Ragtimers	1950	25.00	50.00	100.00
❏ FL-30016 [M]	Chicago Jazz	1957	12.50	25.00	50.00
DECCA					
❏ DL 5552 [10]	Hot Horn	1955	15.00	30.00	60.00
EMARCY					
❏ MG-26011 [10]	Muggsy Spanier and His Dixieland Band	1954	25.00	50.00	100.00
GLENDALE					
❏ GLS 6024	One of a Kind	198?	2.50	5.00	10.00
JAZZ ARCHIVES					
❏ JA-30	Little David Play Your Harp	198?	2.50	5.00	10.00
❏ JA-44	Jazz from California	198?	2.50	5.00	10.00

Number	Title	Yr	VG	VG+	NM
JAZZOLOGY					
❏ J-33	Muggsy Spanier	197?	2.50	5.00	10.00
❏ J-115	Relaxin' at Touro -- 1952	198?	2.50	5.00	10.00
LONDON					
❏ AL-3503 [S]	Muggsy, Tesch and the Chicagoans	195?	7.50	15.00	30.00
❏ LL 3528 [M]	Muggsy Spanier and the Bucktown Five	1959	10.00	20.00	40.00
MERCURY					
❏ MG-20171 [M]	Muggsy Spanier and His Dixieland Band	1956	12.50	25.00	50.00
❏ MG-25095 [10]	Muggsy Spanier and His Dixieland Band	1953	30.00	60.00	120.00
RCA VICTOR					
❏ LPM-1295 [M]	The Great 16	1956	12.50	25.00	50.00
❏ LPM-3043 [10]	Ragtime Favorites	195?	30.00	60.00	120.00
RIVERSIDE					
❏ RLP 12-107 [M]	Classic Early Recordings	1955	15.00	30.00	60.00
❏ RLP-1004 [10]	Muggsy Spanier and Frank Teschemacher	1953	30.00	60.00	120.00
❏ RLP-1035 [10]	Muggsy Spanier and His Bucktown Five	1954	30.00	60.00	120.00
STINSON					
❏ SLP 30 [M]	Muggsy Spanier's Ragtimers, Vol. 1	1962	12.50	25.00	50.00
-- Red vinyl					
❏ SLP 30 [M]	Muggsy Spanier's Ragtimers, Vol. 1	1962	6.25	12.50	25.00
-- Black vinyl					
❏ SLP 31 [M]	Muggsy Spanier's Ragtimers, Vol. 2	1962	12.50	25.00	50.00
-- Red vinyl					
❏ SLP 31 [M]	Muggsy Spanier's Ragtimers, Vol. 2	1962	6.25	12.50	25.00
-- Black vinyl					
STORYVILLE					
❏ 4020	Muggsy Spanier	198?	2.50	5.00	10.00
❏ 4053	Hot Horn	198?	2.50	5.00	10.00
❏ 4056	Muggsy Spanier at Club Hangover	198?	2.50	5.00	10.00
TRIP					
❏ 5532	Dixieland Session	197?	2.50	5.00	10.00
WEATHERS INDUSTRIES					
❏ W-5401 [M]	Dynamic Dixie	1954	15.00	30.00	60.00
ZEE GEE					
❏ 101 [10]	Muggsy Spanier's Ragtimers, Vol. 1	195?	30.00	60.00	120.00
❏ 102 [10]	Muggsy Spanier's Ragtimers, Vol. 2	195?	30.00	60.00	120.00

SPANN, LES
Guitarist and flutist.
JAZZLAND

Number	Title	Yr	VG	VG+	NM
❏ JLP-35 [M]	Gemini	1961	6.25	12.50	25.00
❏ JLP-935 [S]	Gemini	1961	7.50	15.00	30.00

SPARKS, MELVIN
Guitarist.
MUSE

Number	Title	Yr	VG	VG+	NM
❏ MR-5248	Sparkling	1981	3.75	7.50	15.00
PRESTIGE					
❏ 10001	Sparks!	1971	5.00	10.00	20.00
❏ 10016	Spark Plug	1972	5.00	10.00	20.00
❏ 10039	Akilah!	1973	5.00	10.00	20.00
WESTBOUND					
❏ 204	Melvin Sparks '75	1975	5.00	10.00	20.00

SPAULDING, JAMES
Alto saxophone player and flutist.
MUSE

Number	Title	Yr	VG	VG+	NM
❏ MR-5369	Brilliant Corners	1989	2.50	5.00	10.00
❏ MR-5413	Gotstabe a Better Way!	1990	3.00	6.00	12.00
STORYVILLE					
❏ 4034	Jame Spaulding Plays the Legacy of Duke	1980	3.00	6.00	12.00

SPECIAL EFX
Members: George Jinda (percussion); Chieli Minucci (guitar).
GRP

Number	Title	Yr	VG	VG+	NM
❏ GR-1007	Special EFX	1986	2.50	5.00	10.00
❏ GR-1014	Modern Manners	1986	2.50	5.00	10.00

Number	Title	Yr	VG	VG+	NM
❑ GR-1025	Slice of Life	1987	2.50	5.00	10.00
❑ GR-1033	Mystique	1987	2.50	5.00	10.00
❑ GR-1048	Double Feature	1988	2.50	5.00	10.00
❑ GR-9581	Confidential	1989	3.00	6.00	12.00

SPENCER, LEON, JR.
Organist.
PRESTIGE

Number	Title	Yr	VG	VG+	NM
❑ 10011	Sneak Preview!	1971	5.00	10.00	20.00
❑ 10033	Louisiana Slim	1972	5.00	10.00	20.00
❑ 10042	Bad Walking Woman	1973	5.00	10.00	20.00
❑ 10063	Where I'm Coming From	197?	3.75	7.50	15.00

SPHERE (1)
STRATA

Number	Title	Yr	VG	VG+	NM
❑ 103-74	Inside Ourselves	1974	3.75	7.50	15.00

SPHERE (2)
Tribute group to THELONIOUS MONK, including KENNY BARRON (piano); Ben Riley (drums); CHARLIE ROUSE (saxophones); Buster Williams (bass).
ELEKTRA/MUSICIAN

Number	Title	Yr	VG	VG+	NM
❑ 60166	Four in One	1982	2.50	5.00	10.00
❑ 60313	Flight Path	1984	2.50	5.00	10.00
RED RECORD					
❑ VPA-191	Sphere On Tour	1986	3.00	6.00	12.00
VERVE					
❑ 831 674-1	Four for All	1987	2.50	5.00	10.00
❑ 837 032-1	Bird Songs	198?	2.50	5.00	10.00

SPHEROE
French fusion group: Michel Perez (guitar); Gerard Maimone (keyboards); Rido Bayonne (bass, percussion); Patrick Cactus Garel (drums).
INNER CITY

Number	Title	Yr	VG	VG+	NM
❑ IC-1034	Spheroe	197?	3.75	7.50	15.00

SPIEGEL, VICTOR
Pianist.
EAGLE

Number	Title	Yr	VG	VG+	NM
❑ SM-4197	Wind on the Water	1985	3.00	6.00	12.00

SPINOZZA, DAVID
Guitarist and electric sitar player.
A&M

Number	Title	Yr	VG	VG+	NM
❑ SP-4677	Spinozza	1978	2.50	5.00	10.00

SPIRIT OF NEW ORLEANS JAZZ BAND, THE
Led by LOUIS COTTRELL.
GHB

Number	Title	Yr	VG	VG+	NM
❑ GHB-247	The Spirit of New Orleans Jazz Band	198?	2.50	5.00	10.00

SPITFIRE BAND, THE
Founded by Jackie Rae in 1981.
COLUMBIA

Number	Title	Yr	VG	VG+	NM
❑ FC 39891	Flight III	1985	2.50	5.00	10.00

SPIVAK, CHARLIE
Trumpeter and bandleader.
CIRCLE

Number	Title	Yr	VG	VG+	NM
❑ 16	Charlie Spivak and His Orchestra 1942	198?	2.50	5.00	10.00
❑ 17	Charlie Spivak and His Orchestra: Now!	1981	2.50	5.00	10.00
❑ CLP-80	Charlie Spivak and His Orchestra 1946	1985	2.50	5.00	10.00
HINDSIGHT					
❑ HSR-105	Charlie Spivak and His Orchestra 1943-46	198?	2.50	5.00	10.00
❑ HSR-188	Charlie Spivak and His Orchestra 1941	198?	2.50	5.00	10.00
INSIGHT					
❑ 215	Charlie Spivak and His Orchestra 1943-46	198?	2.50	5.00	10.00

SPIVAK, DUBBY
Male singer.
AUDIOPHILE

Number	Title	Yr	VG	VG+	NM
❑ AP-189	Dubby Swings Lightly	1986	2.50	5.00	10.00

SPONTANEOUS MUSIC ENSEMBLE, THE
Members on the below LP: John Stevens (drums, percussion, cornet, vocals); Trevor Watts (soprano saxophone).
EMANEM

Number	Title	Yr	VG	VG+	NM
❑ 303	Face to Face	1974	5.00	10.00	20.00

SPOTTS, ROGER HAMILTON
SEA BREEZE

Number	Title	Yr	VG	VG+	NM
❑ SB-5004	Roger Hamilton Spotts and His Big Band	1986	2.50	5.00	10.00

SPRAGUE, PETER
Guitarist.
CONCORD JAZZ

Number	Title	Yr	VG	VG+	NM
❑ CJ-237	Musica Del Mar	1984	2.50	5.00	10.00
❑ CJ-277	Na Pali Coast	1985	2.50	5.00	10.00
XANADU					
❑ 176	Dance of the Universe	1980	3.00	6.00	12.00
❑ 183	The Path	1981	2.50	5.00	10.00
❑ 184	Bird Raga	198?	2.50	5.00	10.00
❑ 193	Message Sent on the Wind	1982	2.50	5.00	10.00

SPRING STREET STOMPERS, THE
JUBILEE

Number	Title	Yr	VG	VG+	NM
❑ JLP-1002 [M]	The Spring Street Stompers at Carnegie Hall	1955	10.00	20.00	40.00
❑ JLP-1004 [M]	I Go, Hook, Line and Sinker	1955	10.00	20.00	40.00

SPYRO GYRA
Many personnel changes over the years, but the two constants have been Jay Beckenstein (saxophones) and Tom Schuman (keyboards).
AMHERST

Number	Title	Yr	VG	VG+	NM
❑ AMH-1014	Spyro Gyra	1978	3.75	7.50	15.00
GRP					
❑ GR-9608	Fast Forward	1990	3.75	7.50	15.00
INFINITY					
❑ INF-9004	Morning Dance	1979	3.00	6.00	12.00
MCA					
❑ 1445	City Kids	1986	2.00	4.00	8.00
-- Budget-line reissue					
❑ 5108	Catching the Sun	1980	2.50	5.00	10.00
❑ 5149	Carnaval	1981	2.50	5.00	10.00
❑ 5238	Freetime	1981	2.50	5.00	10.00
❑ 5368	Incognito	1982	2.50	5.00	10.00
❑ 5431	City Kids	1983	2.50	5.00	10.00
❑ 5606	Alternating Currents	1985	2.50	5.00	10.00
❑ 5753	Breakout	1986	2.50	5.00	10.00
❑ 6235	Rites of Summer	1988	2.50	5.00	10.00
❑ 6309	Point of View	1989	3.00	6.00	12.00
❑ 6893 [(2)]	Access All Areas	1984	3.00	6.00	12.00
❑ 16010	Catching the Sun	1982	10.00	20.00	40.00
-- Audiophile vinyl					
❑ 37148	Morning Dance	198?	2.00	4.00	8.00
-- Reissue of Infinity LP					
❑ 37149	Spyro Gyra	198?	2.00	4.00	8.00
-- Reissue of Amherst LP					
❑ 37176	Carnaval	198?	2.00	4.00	8.00
-- Budget-line reissue					
❑ 42046	Stories Without Words	1987	2.50	5.00	10.00
NAUTILUS					
❑ NR-9	Morning Dance	1979	10.00	20.00	40.00
-- Audiophile vinyl					

SQUIRREL NUT ZIPPERS
Neo-swing band founded by Jim Mathus (vocals, guitar, trombone) and Katharine Whalen (vocals, banjo) in 1993.
MAMMOTH

Number	Title	Yr	VG	VG+	NM
❑ MR 0105	The Inevitable	1995	2.00	4.00	8.00
❑ MR 0137	Hot	1996	2.00	4.00	8.00
❑ MR 0169	Perennial Favorites	1998	2.00	4.00	8.00

STACY, JESS
Pianist.
AIRCHECK

Number	Title	Yr	VG	VG+	NM
❑ 26	Jess Stacy On the Air	198?	2.50	5.00	10.00
ATLANTIC					
❑ 1225 [M]	A Tribute to Benny Goodman	1956	12.50	25.00	50.00
-- Black label					
❑ 90664	A Tribute to Benny Goodman	1988	2.50	5.00	10.00
BRUNSWICK					
❑ BL 54017 [M]	Piano Solos	1956	12.50	25.00	50.00
❑ BL 58029 [10]	Piano Solos	1951	20.00	40.00	80.00

Number	Title	Yr	VG	VG+	NM
CHIAROSCURO					
❏ 133	Stacy Still Swings	197?	3.00	6.00	12.00
❏ 177	Stacy's Still Swinging	1978	3.00	6.00	12.00
COLUMBIA					
❏ CL 6147 [10]	Piano Moods	1950	25.00	50.00	100.00
COMMODORE					
❏ XFL-15358	Jess Stacy and Friends	198?	2.50	5.00	10.00
HANOVER					
❏ HL-8010 [M]	The Return of Jess Stacy	1964	3.75	7.50	15.00
❏ HS-8010 [S]	The Return of Jess Stacy	1964	5.00	10.00	20.00
JAZZOLOGY					
❏ JCE-90	Blue Notion	198?	2.50	5.00	10.00

STADLER, HEINER
Composer.

Number	Title	Yr	VG	VG+	NM
LABOR					
❏ 7001	Brains on Fire	197?	3.75	7.50	15.00
❏ 7002	Brains on Fire, Vol. 2	1974	3.75	7.50	15.00
❏ 7003	Ecstasy	197?	3.75	7.50	15.00
❏ 7006	Jazz Alchemy	197?	3.75	7.50	15.00

STAETER, TED

Number	Title	Yr	VG	VG+	NM
ATLANTIC					
❏ 1218 [M]	Ted Staeter's New York	1955	12.50	25.00	50.00
-- Black label					
❏ 1218 [M]	Ted Staeter's New York	1961	6.25	12.50	25.00
-- Multicolor label, white "fan" logo at right					

STAFFORD, JO
Female singer.

Number	Title	Yr	VG	VG+	NM
BAINBRIDGE					
❏ 6234	Look at Me Now	1982	2.50	5.00	10.00
CAPITOL					
❏ H 75 [10]	American Folk Songs	1950	15.00	30.00	60.00
❏ H 197 [10]	Autumn in New York	195?	15.00	30.00	60.00
❏ T 197 [M]	Autumn in New York	1955	12.50	25.00	50.00
-- Turquoise or gray label					
❏ T 197 [M]	Autumn in New York	1959	7.50	15.00	30.00
-- Black colorband label, Capitol logo at left					
❏ H 247 [10]	Songs for Sunday Evening	195?	15.00	30.00	60.00
❏ T 423 [M]	Memory Songs	1955	12.50	25.00	50.00
-- Turquoise or gray label					
❏ T 423 [M]	Memory Songs	1959	7.50	15.00	30.00
-- Black colorband label, Capitol logo at left					
❏ H 435 [10]	Starring Jo Stafford	1953	15.00	30.00	60.00
❏ T 435 [M]	Starring Jo Stafford	1955	12.50	25.00	50.00
-- Turquoise or gray label					
❏ T 435 [M]	Starring Jo Stafford	1959	7.50	15.00	30.00
-- Black colorband label, Capitol logo at left					
❏ ST 1653 [S]	American Folk Songs	1962	6.25	12.50	25.00
❏ T 1653 [M]	American Folk Songs	1962	5.00	10.00	20.00
❏ ST 1921 [S]	The Hits of Jo Stafford	1963	6.25	12.50	25.00
❏ T 1921 [M]	The Hits of Jo Stafford	1963	5.00	10.00	20.00
❏ ST 2069 [S]	Sweet Hour of Prayer	1964	6.25	12.50	25.00
❏ T 2069 [M]	Sweet Hour of Prayer	1964	5.00	10.00	20.00
❏ ST 2166 [S]	The Joyful Season	1964	6.25	12.50	25.00
❏ T 2166 [M]	The Joyful Season	1964	5.00	10.00	20.00
❏ H 9014 [10]	Songs of Faith	1950	15.00	30.00	60.00
❏ SM-11889	The Hits of Jo Stafford	1979	2.50	5.00	10.00
COLUMBIA					
❏ CL 578 [M]	New Orleans	1954	10.00	20.00	40.00
-- Maroon label, gold print					
❏ CL 578 [M]	New Orleans	1955	7.50	15.00	30.00
-- Red and black label with six "eye" logos					
❏ CL 584 [M]	Jo Stafford Sings Broadway's Best	1954	10.00	20.00	40.00
-- Maroon label, gold print					
❏ CL 584 [M]	Jo Stafford Sings Broadway's Best	1955	7.50	15.00	30.00
-- Red and black label with six "eye" logos					
❏ CL 691 [M]	Happy Holiday	1955	15.00	30.00	60.00
❏ CL 910 [M]	Ski Trails	1956	10.00	20.00	40.00
❏ CL 968 [M]	Once Over Lightly	1957	10.00	20.00	40.00
❏ CL 1043 [M]	Songs of Scotland	1957	10.00	20.00	40.00
❏ CL 1124 [M]	Swingin' Down Broadway	1958	10.00	20.00	40.00
❏ CL 1228 [M]	Jo Stafford's Greatest Hits	1958	10.00	20.00	40.00
-- Red and black label with six "eye" logos					
❏ CL 1228 [M]	Jo Stafford's Greatest Hits	1963	5.00	10.00	20.00
-- Red label with "Guaranteed High Fidelity" in black					
❏ CL 1228 [M]	Jo Stafford's Greatest Hits	1965	3.75	7.50	15.00
-- Red label with "360 Sound Mono" in white					
❏ CL 1262 [M]	I'll Be Seeing You	1959	7.50	15.00	30.00
❏ CL 1339 [M]	Ballad of the Blues	1959	7.50	15.00	30.00
❏ CL 1561 [M]	Jo + Jazz	1960	10.00	20.00	40.00
❏ CL 2501 [10]	Soft and Sentimental	1955	10.00	20.00	40.00

Number	Title	Yr	VG	VG+	NM
❏ CL 2591 [10]	A Gal Named Jo	1955	10.00	20.00	40.00
❏ CL 6210 [10]	As You Desire Me	1952	12.50	25.00	50.00
❏ CL 6238 [10]	Jo Stafford Sings Broadway's Best	1953	12.50	25.00	50.00
❏ CL 6268 [10]	New Orleans	1954	12.50	25.00	50.00
❏ CL 6274 [10]	My Heart's in the Highland	1954	12.50	25.00	50.00
❏ CL 6286 [10]	Garden of Prayer	1954	12.50	25.00	50.00
❏ CS 8080 [S]	I'll Be Seeing You	1959	10.00	20.00	40.00
❏ CS 8139 [S]	Ballad of the Blues	1959	10.00	20.00	40.00
❏ CS 8361 [S]	Jo + Jazz	1960	15.00	30.00	60.00
CORINTHIAN					
❏ COR-105	G.I. Jo	1977	2.50	5.00	10.00
❏ COR-106	Greatest Hits	1977	2.50	5.00	10.00
❏ COR-108	Jo + Jazz	197?	2.50	5.00	10.00
❏ COR-110	Jo Stafford Sings American Folk Songs	197?	2.50	5.00	10.00
❏ COR-111	Songs of Faith, Hope and Love	197?	2.50	5.00	10.00
❏ COR-112	Jo + Broadway	197?	2.50	5.00	10.00
❏ COR-113	Ski Trails	197?	2.50	5.00	10.00
❏ COR-114	Jo + Blues	197?	2.50	5.00	10.00
❏ COR-115	International Hits	197?	2.50	5.00	10.00
❏ COR-118	Broadway Revisited	198?	2.50	5.00	10.00
❏ COR-119	By Request	198?	2.50	5.00	10.00
❏ COR-123	Music of My Life	1986	2.50	5.00	10.00
DECCA					
❏ DL 74973	Jo Stafford's Greatest Hits	1968	3.75	7.50	15.00
DOT					
❏ DLP-3673 [M]	Do I Hear a Waltz?	1966	3.75	7.50	15.00
❏ DLP-3745 [M]	This Is Jo Stafford	1967	3.75	7.50	15.00
❏ DLP-25673 [S]	Do I Hear a Waltz?	1966	5.00	10.00	20.00
❏ DLP-25745 [S]	This Is Jo Stafford	1967	5.00	10.00	20.00
REPRISE					
❏ R-6090 [M]	Getting Sentimental Over Tommy Dorsey	1963	5.00	10.00	20.00
❏ R9-6090 [S]	Getting Sentimental Over Tommy Dorsey	1963	6.25	12.50	25.00
STANYAN					
❏ 10073	Look at Me Now	197?	3.00	6.00	12.00
VOCALION					
❏ VL 73856 [R]	Happy Holidays	1968	3.00	6.00	12.00
❏ VL 73892	In the Mood for Love	1970	3.00	6.00	12.00

STAFFORD, JO, AND GORDON MacRAE
MacRae is a male singer not otherwise listed in this book. Also see JO STAFFORD.

Number	Title	Yr	VG	VG+	NM
CAPITOL					
❏ T 423 [M]	Memory Songs	1955	12.50	25.00	50.00
❏ SM-1696	Whispering Hope	1977	2.50	5.00	10.00
-- Reissue with new prefix					
❏ ST 1696 [S]	Whispering Hope	1962	6.25	12.50	25.00
❏ T 1696 [M]	Whispering Hope	1962	5.00	10.00	20.00
❏ ST 1916 [S]	Peace in the Valley	1963	6.25	12.50	25.00
❏ T 1916 [M]	Peace in the Valley	1963	5.00	10.00	20.00

STAFFORD, MARILYN, AND THE ERNIE CARSON BAND

Number	Title	Yr	VG	VG+	NM
CIRCLE					
❏ C-66	Jazz Goes Country	198?	2.50	5.00	10.00

STALLINGS, MARY, AND CAL TJADER
Stallings is a female singer. Also see CAL TJADER.

Number	Title	Yr	VG	VG+	NM
FANTASY					
❏ 3325 [M]	Cal Tjader Plays, Mary Stallings Sings	1962	12.50	25.00	50.00
-- Red vinyl					
❏ 3325 [M]	Cal Tjader Plays, Mary Stallings Sings	1962	7.50	15.00	30.00
-- Black vinyl					
❏ 8068 [S]	Cal Tjader Plays, Mary Stallings Sings	1962	5.00	10.00	20.00
-- Black vinyl					
❏ 8068 [S]	Cal Tjader Plays, Mary Stallings Sings	1962	10.00	20.00	40.00
-- Blue vinyl					

STAMM, MARVIN
Trumpeter.

Number	Title	Yr	VG	VG+	NM
PALO ALTO					
❏ PA-8022	Stampede	198?	2.50	5.00	10.00
VERVE					
❏ V6-8759	Machinations	1968	5.00	10.00	20.00

STANDBACK

Number	Title	Yr	VG	VG+	NM
SEA BREEZE					
❏ SB-3004	Norwegian Wood	198?	2.50	5.00	10.00

Number	Title	Yr	VG	VG+	NM

STANKO, TOMASZ
Trumpeter.
ECM
❏ 1071	Balladyna	1976	3.00	6.00	12.00

STARR, KAY
Female singer.
ABC
❏ S-631	When the Lights Go On Again	1968	3.00	6.00	12.00

CAPITOL
❏ H 211 [10]	Songs by Starr	1950	17.50	35.00	70.00
❏ T 211 [M]	Songs by Starr	1955	12.50	25.00	50.00
❏ H 363 [10]	Kay Starr Style	1953	17.50	35.00	70.00
❏ T 363 [M]	Kay Starr Style	1955	12.50	25.00	50.00
❏ DT 415 [R]	The Hits of Kay Starr	196?	3.00	6.00	12.00
❏ H 415 [10]	The Hits of Kay Starr	1953	17.50	35.00	70.00
❏ T 415 [M]	The Hits of Kay Starr	1955	12.50	25.00	50.00
-- Turquoise or gray label					
❏ T 415 [M]	The Hits of Kay Starr	1958	7.50	15.00	30.00
-- Black label with colorband, Capitol logo at left					
❏ T 415 [M]	The Hits of Kay Starr	1962	5.00	10.00	20.00
-- Black label with colorband, Capitol logo at top					
❏ T 580 [M]	In a Blue Mood	1955	12.50	25.00	50.00
❏ ST 1254 [S]	Movin'	1959	7.50	15.00	30.00
❏ T 1254 [M]	Movin'	1959	6.25	12.50	25.00
❏ ST 1303 [S]	Losers Weepers	1960	7.50	15.00	30.00
❏ T 1303 [M]	Losers Weepers	1960	6.25	12.50	25.00
❏ ST 1358 [S]	One More Time	1960	7.50	15.00	30.00
❏ T 1358 [M]	One More Time	1960	6.25	12.50	25.00
❏ ST 1374 [S]	Movin' on Broadway	1960	7.50	15.00	30.00
❏ T 1374 [M]	Movin' on Broadway	1960	6.25	12.50	25.00
❏ ST 1438 [S]	Kay Starr, Jazz Singer	1960	10.00	20.00	40.00
❏ T 1438 [M]	Kay Starr, Jazz Singer	1960	7.50	15.00	30.00
❏ ST 1468 [S]	All Starr Hits	1961	7.50	15.00	30.00
❏ T 1468 [M]	All Starr Hits	1961	6.25	12.50	25.00
❏ ST 1681 [S]	I Cry by Night	1962	6.25	12.50	25.00
❏ T 1681 [M]	I Cry by Night	1962	5.00	10.00	20.00
❏ ST 1795 [S]	Just Plain Country	1962	6.25	12.50	25.00
❏ ST-8-1795 [S]	Just Plain Country	196?	7.50	15.00	30.00
-- Capitol Record Club edition					
❏ T 1795 [M]	Just Plain Country	1962	5.00	10.00	20.00
❏ ST 2106 [S]	The Fabulous Favorites	1964	3.75	7.50	15.00
❏ T 2106 [M]	The Fabulous Favorites	1964	3.00	6.00	12.00
❏ ST 2550 [S]	Tears and Heartaches/Old Records	1966	3.75	7.50	15.00
❏ T 2550 [M]	Tears and Heartaches/Old Records	1966	3.00	6.00	12.00
❏ SM-11323	Kay Starrs Again	1977	2.00	4.00	8.00
-- Reissue with new prefix					
❏ ST-11323	Kay Starrs Again	1974	2.50	5.00	10.00
❏ SM-11880	Movin'	1979	2.50	5.00	10.00

CORONET
❏ CX-106 [M]	Kay Starr Sings	196?	3.00	6.00	12.00

GNP CRESCENDO
❏ GNPS-2083	Country	1974	2.50	5.00	10.00
❏ GNPS-2090	Back to the Roots	1975	2.50	5.00	10.00

HINDSIGHT
❏ HSR-214	Kay Starr 1947	1985	2.50	5.00	10.00

LIBERTY
❏ LRP-3280 [M]	Swingin' with the Starr	1963	6.25	12.50	25.00
-- Reissue of 9001					
❏ LRP-9001 [M]	Swingin' with the Starr	1956	12.50	25.00	50.00

PARAMOUNT
❏ PAS-5001	How About This	1969	3.00	6.00	12.00

RCA CAMDEN
❏ CAL-567 [M]	Kay Starr	196?	3.00	6.00	12.00

RCA VICTOR
❏ LPM-1149 [M]	The One and Only Kay Starr	1955	7.50	15.00	30.00
❏ ANL1-1311	Pure Gold	1976	2.00	4.00	8.00
❏ LPM-1549 [M]	Blue Starr	1957	7.50	15.00	30.00
❏ LPM-1720 [M]	Rockin' with Kay	1958	12.50	25.00	50.00
❏ LPM-2055 [M]	I Hear the Word	1959	6.25	12.50	25.00
❏ LSP-2055 [S]	I Hear the Word	1959	7.50	15.00	30.00

RONDO-LETTE
❏ A-3 [M]	Them There Eyes	1958	6.25	12.50	25.00

SUNSET
❏ SUM-1126 [M]	Portrait of a Starr	196?	3.75	7.50	15.00
❏ SUS-5126 [R]	Portrait of a Starr	196?	2.50	5.00	10.00

STARR, KAY/ERROLL GARNER
Also see each artist's individual listings.
CROWN
❏ CLP-5003 [M]	Singin' Kay Starr, Swingin' Erroll Garner	1957	7.50	15.00	30.00

Number	Title	Yr	VG	VG+	NM

MODERN
❏ LMP-1203 [M]	Singin' Kay Starr, Swingin' I Errol Garner	1956	20.00	40.00	80.00

STARSHIP ORCHESTRA
Led by NORMAN CONNORS.
COLUMBIA
❏ NJC 36456	Celestial Sky	1980	2.50	5.00	10.00

STATE STREET ACES, THE
STOMP OFF
❏ SOS-1011	Stuff	198?	2.50	5.00	10.00
❏ SOS-1041	Pass Out Lightly	198?	2.50	5.00	10.00
❏ SOS-1106	Old Folks Shuffle	198?	2.50	5.00	10.00

STATE STREET RAMBLERS, THE
Studio group of varying musicians led by JIMMY BLYTHE.
HERWIN
❏ 104	The State Street Ramblers, Vol. 1	197?	3.00	6.00	12.00
❏ 105	The State Street Ramblers, Vol. 2	197?	3.00	6.00	12.00

STATON, DAKOTA
Female singer.
CAPITOL
❏ DT 876 [R]	The Late, Late Show	196?	3.00	6.00	12.00
❏ SM-876	The Late, Late Show	1977	2.50	5.00	10.00
-- Reissue with new prefix					
❏ T 876 [M]	The Late, Late Show	1957	12.50	25.00	50.00
-- Turquoise or gray label					
❏ T 876 [M]	The Late, Late Show	1959	7.50	15.00	30.00
-- Black label with colorband, Capitol logo at left					
❏ T 876 [M]	The Late, Late Show	1962	3.75	7.50	15.00
-- Black label with colorband, Capitol logo at top					
❏ M-1003	In the Night	1976	2.50	5.00	10.00
-- Reissue with new prefix					
❏ T 1003 [M]	In the Night	1958	12.50	25.00	50.00
-- Turquoise or gray label					
❏ T 1003 [M]	In the Night	1959	7.50	15.00	30.00
-- Black label with colorband, Capitol logo at left					
❏ ST 1054 [S]	Dynamic!	1959	10.00	20.00	40.00
-- Black label with colorband, Capitol logo at left					
❏ ST 1054 [S]	Dynamic!	1962	5.00	10.00	20.00
-- Black label with colorband, Capitol logo at top					
❏ T 1054 [M]	Dynamic!	1958	7.50	15.00	30.00
-- Black label with colorband, Capitol logo at left					
❏ T 1054 [M]	Dynamic!	1962	3.75	7.50	15.00
-- Black label with colorband, Capitol logo at top					
❏ ST 1170 [S]	Crazy He Calls Me	1959	10.00	20.00	40.00
-- Black label with colorband, Capitol logo at left					
❏ ST 1170 [S]	Crazy He Calls Me	1962	5.00	10.00	20.00
-- Black label with colorband, Capitol logo at top					
❏ T 1170 [M]	Crazy He Calls Me	1959	7.50	15.00	30.00
-- Black label with colorband, Capitol logo at left					
❏ T 1170 [M]	Crazy He Calls Me	1962	3.75	7.50	15.00
-- Black label with colorband, Capitol logo at top					
❏ ST 1241 [S]	Time to Swing	1959	10.00	20.00	40.00
-- Black label with colorband, Capitol logo at left					
❏ ST 1241 [S]	Time to Swing	1962	5.00	10.00	20.00
-- Black label with colorband, Capitol logo at top					
❏ T 1241 [M]	Time to Swing	1959	7.50	15.00	30.00
-- Black label with colorband, Capitol logo at left					
❏ I 1241 [M]	Time to Swing	1962	3.75	7.50	15.00
-- Black label with colorband, Capitol logo at top					
❏ ST 1325 [S]	More Than the Most	1960	10.00	20.00	40.00
-- Black label with colorband, Capitol logo at left					
❏ ST 1325 [S]	More Than the Most	1962	5.00	10.00	20.00
-- Black label with colorband, Capitol logo at top					
❏ T 1325 [M]	More Than the Most	1960	7.50	15.00	30.00
-- Black label with colorband, Capitol logo at left					
❏ T 1325 [M]	More Than the Most	1962	3.75	7.50	15.00
-- Black label with colorband, Capitol logo at top					
❏ ST 1387 [S]	Ballads and the Blues	1960	10.00	20.00	40.00
-- Black label with colorband, Capitol logo at left					
❏ ST 1387 [S]	Ballads and the Blues	1962	5.00	10.00	20.00
-- Black label with colorband, Capitol logo at top					
❏ T 1387 [M]	Ballads and the Blues	1960	7.50	15.00	30.00
-- Black label with colorband, Capitol logo at left					
❏ T 1387 [M]	Ballads and the Blues	1962	3.75	7.50	15.00
-- Black label with colorband, Capitol logo at top					
❏ ST 1427 [S]	Softly	1961	10.00	20.00	40.00
-- Black label with colorband, Capitol logo at left					
❏ ST 1427 [S]	Softly	1962	5.00	10.00	20.00
-- Black label with colorband, Capitol logo at top					
❏ T 1427 [M]	Softly	1961	7.50	15.00	30.00
-- Black label with colorband, Capitol logo at left					

Number	Title	Yr	VG	VG+	NM
❑ T 1427 [M]	Softly	1962	3.75	7.50	15.00
-- Black label with colorband, Capitol logo at top					
❑ ST 1490 [S]	Dakota	1961	10.00	20.00	40.00
-- Black label with colorband, Capitol logo at left					
❑ ST 1490 [S]	Dakota	1962	5.00	10.00	20.00
-- Black label with colorband, Capitol logo at top					
❑ T 1490 [M]	Dakota	1961	7.50	15.00	30.00
-- Black label with colorband, Capitol logo at left					
❑ T 1490 [M]	Dakota	1962	3.75	7.50	15.00
-- Black label with colorband, Capitol logo at top					
❑ ST 1597 [S]	'Round Midnight	1961	10.00	20.00	40.00
-- Black label with colorband, Capitol logo at left					
❑ ST 1597 [S]	'Round Midnight	1962	5.00	10.00	20.00
-- Black label with colorband, Capitol logo at top					
❑ T 1597 [M]	'Round Midnight	1961	7.50	15.00	30.00
-- Black label with colorband, Capitol logo at left					
❑ T 1597 [M]	'Round Midnight	1962	3.75	7.50	15.00
-- Black label with colorband, Capitol logo at top					
❑ ST 1649 [S]	Dakota at Storyville	1962	6.25	12.50	25.00
❑ T 1649 [M]	Dakota at Storyville	1962	5.00	10.00	20.00

GROOVE MERCHANT

Number	Title	Yr	VG	VG+	NM
❑ 510	Madame Foo-Foo	1972	3.00	6.00	12.00
❑ 521	I Want a Country Man	1973	3.00	6.00	12.00
❑ 532	Ms. Soul	1974	3.00	6.00	12.00
❑ 4410 [(2)]	Confessin'	197?	3.75	7.50	15.00

LONDON

Number	Title	Yr	VG	VG+	NM
❑ PS 495 [S]	Dakota '67	1967	3.75	7.50	15.00
❑ LL 3495 [M]	Dakota '67	1967	5.00	10.00	20.00

MUSE

Number	Title	Yr	VG	VG+	NM
❑ MR-5401	Dakota Staton	1991	3.75	7.50	15.00

UNITED ARTISTS

Number	Title	Yr	VG	VG+	NM
❑ UAL-3292 [M]	From Dakota with Love	1963	5.00	10.00	20.00
❑ UAL-3312 [M]	Live and Swinging	1963	5.00	10.00	20.00
❑ UAL-3355 [M]	Dakota Staton with Strings	1964	5.00	10.00	20.00
❑ UAS-6292 [S]	From Dakota with Love	1963	6.25	12.50	25.00
❑ UAS-6316 [S]	Live and Swinging	1963	6.25	12.50	25.00
❑ UAS-6355 [S]	Dakota Staton with Strings	1964	6.25	12.50	25.00

VERVE

Number	Title	Yr	VG	VG+	NM
❑ V6-8799	I've Been There	1971	3.75	7.50	15.00

STEELE, JOAN

AUDIOPHILE

Number	Title	Yr	VG	VG+	NM
❑ AP-94	'Round Midnight	1975	3.00	6.00	12.00

STEELE, JOAN, AND JOHN MAGALDI

AUDIOPHILE

Number	Title	Yr	VG	VG+	NM
❑ AP-156	Lonesome No More	198?	2.50	5.00	10.00

STEIG, JEREMY
Flutist.

BLUE NOTE

Number	Title	Yr	VG	VG+	NM
❑ BST-84354	Wayfaring Stranger	1970	5.00	10.00	20.00

CAPITOL

Number	Title	Yr	VG	VG+	NM
❑ SM-662	Energy	1976	2.50	5.00	10.00
-- Reissue with new prefix					
❑ ST-662	Energy	1971	3.75	7.50	15.00

COLUMBIA

Number	Title	Yr	VG	VG+	NM
❑ CL 2136 [M]	Flute Fever	1964	3.00	6.00	12.00
❑ CS 8936 [S]	Flute Fever	1964	3.75	7.50	15.00
❑ KC 32579	Monium	1974	3.00	6.00	12.00
❑ KC 33297	Temple of Birth	1975	3.00	6.00	12.00

CTI

Number	Title	Yr	VG	VG+	NM
❑ 7075	Firefly	1977	3.00	6.00	12.00

GROOVE MERCHANT

Number	Title	Yr	VG	VG+	NM
❑ 2204	Fusion	197?	3.75	7.50	15.00

SOLID STATE

Number	Title	Yr	VG	VG+	NM
❑ SS-18059	This Is Jeremy Steig	1969	3.75	7.50	15.00
❑ SS-18068	Legwork	1970	3.75	7.50	15.00

STEIG, JEREMY, AND EDDIE GOMEZ
Also see each artist's individual listings.

CMP

Number	Title	Yr	VG	VG+	NM
❑ CMP-3-ST	Lend Me Your Ears	198?	2.50	5.00	10.00
❑ CMP-6-ST	Music for Flute and Double Bass	198?	2.50	5.00	10.00
❑ CMP-12-ST	Rain Forest	198?	2.50	5.00	10.00

ENJA

Number	Title	Yr	VG	VG+	NM
❑ 2098	Outlaws	198?	3.00	6.00	12.00

INNER CITY

Number	Title	Yr	VG	VG+	NM
❑ IC-3015	Outlaws	197?	3.00	6.00	12.00

STEIN, ANDY
Violinist.

STOMP OFF

Number	Title	Yr	VG	VG+	NM
❑ SOS-1146	Goin' Places	1987	2.50	5.00	10.00

STEIN, HAL, AND WARREN FITZGERALD
Stein plays alto and tenor saxophone; Fitzgerald plays trumpet.

PROGRESSIVE

Number	Title	Yr	VG	VG+	NM
❑ PLP-1002 [M]	Hal Stein-Warren Fitzgerald Quintet	1955	125.00	250.00	500.00

STEIN, LOU
Pianist.

AUDIOPHILE

Number	Title	Yr	VG	VG+	NM
❑ AP-198	Solo Piano	1984	2.50	5.00	10.00

BRUNSWICK

Number	Title	Yr	VG	VG+	NM
❑ BL 58053 [10]	Lou Stein	1953	12.50	25.00	50.00

CHIAROSCURO

Number	Title	Yr	VG	VG+	NM
❑ 140	Tribute to Tatum	197?	3.00	6.00	12.00
❑ 2027	Temple of the Gods	1979	3.00	6.00	12.00

DREAMSTREET

Number	Title	Yr	VG	VG+	NM
❑ DR-106	Lou Stein Trio Live at the Dome	1986	2.50	5.00	10.00

EPIC

Number	Title	Yr	VG	VG+	NM
❑ LG 3101 [M]	House Top	1955	10.00	20.00	40.00
❑ LN 3148 [M]	Three, Four and Five	1955	10.00	20.00	40.00
❑ LN 3186 [M]	From Broadway to Paris	1955	10.00	20.00	40.00

JUBILEE

Number	Title	Yr	VG	VG+	NM
❑ JLP-8 [10]	Six for Kicks	1954	12.50	25.00	50.00
❑ JLP-1019 [M]	Eight for Kicks, Four for Laughs	1956	10.00	20.00	40.00

STEPS AHEAD
Fusion supergroup: MICHAEL BRECKER (tenor sax); Steve Gadd (drums, replaced by PETER ERSKINE); EDDIE GOMEZ (bass); MIKE MAINIERI (vibes); DON GROLNICK (piano, replaced by ELIANE ELIAS, who was replaced by WARREN BERNHARDT).

ELEKTRA/MUSICIAN

Number	Title	Yr	VG	VG+	NM
❑ 60168	Steps	1983	2.50	5.00	10.00
❑ 60351	Modern Times	1985	2.50	5.00	10.00
❑ 60441	Magnetic	1986	2.50	5.00	10.00

STERLING, ARNOLD
Alto saxophone player.

JAM

Number	Title	Yr	VG	VG+	NM
❑ 010	Here's Brother Sterling	198?	3.00	6.00	12.00

STERN, LENI
Guitarist.

ENJA

Number	Title	Yr	VG	VG+	NM
❑ R1-79602	Secrets	1989	3.00	6.00	12.00

STERN, MIKE
Guitarist.

ATLANTIC

Number	Title	Yr	VG	VG+	NM
❑ 81656	Upside Downside	1986	2.50	5.00	10.00
❑ 81840	Time in Place	1988	2.50	5.00	10.00
❑ 82027	Jigsaw	1990	3.00	6.00	12.00

STEVENS, CLIVE
Tenor and soprano saxophone player and flutist.

CAPITOL

Number	Title	Yr	VG	VG+	NM
❑ ST-11263	Atmospheres	1973	3.75	7.50	15.00
❑ ST-11320	Voyage to Uranus	1974	3.75	7.50	15.00
❑ SM-11675	Atmospheres	1976	2.50	5.00	10.00
❑ SM-11676	Voyage to Uranus	1976	2.50	5.00	10.00

STEVENS, LEITH
Pianist, composer and conductor.

CORAL

Number	Title	Yr	VG	VG+	NM
❑ CRL 57283 [M]	Jazz Themes for Cops and Robbers	1958	12.50	25.00	50.00

DECCA

Number	Title	Yr	VG	VG+	NM
❑ DL 5515 [10]	Jazz Themes in "The Wild One"	1954	20.00	40.00	80.00

STEVENS, MIKE
Saxophone and keyboard player.

NOVUS

Number	Title	Yr	VG	VG+	NM
❑ 3042-1-N	Light Up the Night	1988	2.50	5.00	10.00
❑ 3080-1-N	Set the Spirit Free	1990	3.00	6.00	12.00

Number	Title	Yr	VG	VG+	NM

STEWARD, HERB
Tenor, alto and baritone saxophone player. Also see THE FOUR BROTHERS.

AVA

Number	Title	Yr	VG	VG+	NM
❏ A-9 [M]	So Pretty	1962	6.25	12.50	25.00
❏ AS-9 [S]	So Pretty	1962	7.50	15.00	30.00

FAMOUS DOOR

❏ 139	Three Horns of Herb Steward	1981	3.00	6.00	12.00

STEWART, BOB
Tuba player.

DAWN

❏ DLP-1103 [M]	Let's Talk About Love	1956	12.50	25.00	50.00

JMT

❏ 834 414-1	First Line	1988	2.50	5.00	10.00

STASH

❏ ST-266	In a Sentimental Mood	1987	2.50	5.00	10.00

STEWART, HELYNE
Female singer.

CONTEMPORARY

❏ M-3601 [M]	Love Moods	1962	7.50	15.00	30.00
❏ S-7601 [S]	Love Moods	1962	10.00	20.00	40.00

STEWART, JIMMY
Guitarist.

BLACKHAWK

❏ BKH-50301	The Touch	1986	2.50	5.00	10.00

CADENCE JAZZ

❏ CJR-1018	An Engineer of Sounds	198?	2.50	5.00	10.00

CATALYST

❏ 7621	Fire Flower	1977	3.00	6.00	12.00

STEWART, REX
Cornet and trumpet player.

AMERICAN RECORDING SOCIETY

❏ G-448 [M]	The Big Challenge	1958	10.00	20.00	40.00

ATLANTIC

❏ 1209 [M]	Big Jazz	1956	12.50	25.00	50.00

CONCERT HALL JAZZ

❏ 1202 [M]	Dixieland On Location	1954	20.00	40.00	80.00

DIAL

❏ LP-215 [10]	Ellingtonia	1951	62.50	125.00	250.00

FELSTED

❏ 2001 [S]	Rendezvous with Rex	1958	7.50	15.00	30.00
❏ 7001 [M]	Rendezvous with Rex	1958	10.00	20.00	40.00

GRAND AWARD

❏ GA 33-414 [M]	Just for Kicks	195?	10.00	20.00	40.00

HALL OF FAME

❏ 624	Reunion	197?	2.50	5.00	10.00

JAZZOLOGY

❏ J-36	The Irrepressible Rex Stewart	197?	3.00	6.00	12.00

JAZZTONE

❏ J-1202 [M]	Dixieland Free-for-All	1956	10.00	20.00	40.00
❏ J-1250 [M]	Rex Stewart Plays Duke Ellington	1957	10.00	20.00	40.00
❏ J-1268 [M]	The Big Challenge	1957	10.00	20.00	40.00
❏ J-1285 [M]	The Big Reunion	1957	10.00	20.00	40.00

MASTER JAZZ

❏ 8123	Rendezvous with Rex	197?	3.00	6.00	12.00

PRESTIGE

❏ PRST-7728	Memorial Album	1970	3.75	7.50	15.00
❏ PRST-7812	Trumpet Jive!	1971	3.75	7.50	15.00

SWING

❏ SW-8414	Porgy and Bess Revisited	1986	2.50	5.00	10.00

SWINGVILLE

❏ SVLP-2006 [M]	The Happy Jazz of Rex Stewart	1960	12.50	25.00	50.00

-- *Purple label*

❏ SVLP-2006 [M]	The Happy Jazz of Rex Stewart	1965	6.25	12.50	25.00

-- *Blue label, trident logo at right*

UNITED ARTISTS

❏ UAL-4009 [M]	Henderson Homecoming	1959	10.00	20.00	40.00
❏ UAS-5009 [S]	Henderson Homecoming	1959	7.50	15.00	30.00

URANIA

❏ UJLP-2012 [M]	Cool Fever	1955	15.00	30.00	60.00

WARNER BROS.

❏ W 1260 [M]	Porgy and Bess Revisited	1958	10.00	20.00	40.00
❏ WS 1260 [S]	Porgy and Bess Revisited	1958	7.50	15.00	30.00

"X"

❏ LX-3001 [10]	Rex Stewart and His Orchestra	1954	25.00	50.00	100.00

STEWART, REX/ILLINOIS JACQUET
Also see each artist's individual listings.

GRAND AWARD

Number	Title	Yr	VG	VG+	NM
❏ GA 33-315 [M]	Rex Stewart Plays Duke/Uptown Jazz	1955	10.00	20.00	40.00

STEWART, REX, AND DICKIE WELLS
Also see each artist's individual listings.

RCA VICTOR

❏ LPM-2024 [M]	Chatter Jazz	1959	6.25	12.50	25.00
❏ LSP-2024 [S]	Chatter Jazz	1959	7.50	15.00	30.00

STEWART, SANDY
Female singer. On the below LP, she is accompanied by DICK HYMAN on piano.

AUDIOPHILE

❏ AP-205	Sandy Stewart Sings Songs of Jerome Kern	1985	2.50	5.00	10.00

STEWART, SLAM
Bass player and male singer.

JAZZ MAN

❏ 5010	Slam Stewart with Milt Buckner and Jo Jones	198?	2.50	5.00	10.00

SAVOY

❏ MG-12067 [M]	Bowin' Singin' Slam	1956	10.00	20.00	40.00

STEWART, SLAM, AND BUCKY PIZZARELLI
Also see each artist's individual listings.

STASH

❏ ST-201	Dialogue	1978	3.00	6.00	12.00

STEWART, TOM
Tenor horn and bass trumpet player.

ABC-PARAMOUNT

❏ ABC-117 [M]	Tom Stewart Sextette/Quintet	1956	12.50	25.00	50.00

STEWART, TOMMY

PROGRESSIVE

❏ PRO-7009	Tommy Stewart and His Orchestra	198?	2.50	5.00	10.00

STILES, DANNY, AND BILL WATROUS
Stiles is a trumpeter. Also see BILL WATROUS.

FAMOUS DOOR

❏ 103	In Tandem	1974	3.75	7.50	15.00
❏ 112	One More Time	197?	3.00	6.00	12.00
❏ 126	In Tandem -- Into the 80s	1980	3.00	6.00	12.00

STITT, SONNY
Alto, tenor and baritone saxophone player. Also see STAN GETZ; THE MODERN JAZZ SEXTET; OSCAR PETERSON.

ABC IMPULSE!

❏ AS-43 [S]	Sonny Stitt Now!	1968	3.00	6.00	12.00
❏ AS-52 [S]	Salt and Pepper	1968	3.00	6.00	12.00

-- *With Paul Gonsalves*

ARGO

❏ LP-629 [M]	Sonny Stitt	1958	10.00	20.00	40.00
❏ LP-661 [M]	Burnin'	1960	6.25	12.50	25.00
❏ I PS-661 [S]	Burnin'	1960	7.50	15.00	30.00
❏ LP-683 [M]	Sonny Stitt at the D.J. Lounge	1961	6.25	12.50	25.00
❏ LPS-683 [S]	Sonny Stitt at the D.J. Lounge	1961	7.50	15.00	30.00
❏ LP-709 [M]	Rearin' Back	1962	6.25	12.50	25.00
❏ LPS-709 [S]	Rearin' Back	1962	7.50	15.00	30.00
❏ LP-730 [M]	Move On Over	1964	6.25	12.50	25.00
❏ LPS-730 [S]	Move On Over	1964	7.50	15.00	30.00
❏ LP-744 [M]	My Main Man	1965	6.25	12.50	25.00
❏ LPS-744 [S]	My Main Man	1965	7.50	15.00	30.00

ATLANTIC

❏ 1395 [M]	Sonny Stitt and the Top Brass	1962	6.25	12.50	25.00
❏ SD 1395 [S]	Sonny Stitt and the Top Brass	1962	7.50	15.00	30.00
❏ 1418 [M]	Stitt Plays Bird	1964	7.50	15.00	30.00
❏ SD 1418 [S]	Stitt Plays Bird	1964	10.00	20.00	40.00
❏ SD 3008	Deuces Wild	1970	3.75	7.50	15.00
❏ 90139	Sonny Stitt and Top Brass	198?	2.50	5.00	10.00

BLACK LION

❏ 307	Night Work	197?	2.50	5.00	10.00

CADET

❏ LP-629 [M]	Sonny Stitt	1966	3.75	7.50	15.00
❏ LP-661 [M]	Burnin'	1966	3.00	6.00	12.00
❏ LPS-661 [S]	Burnin'	1966	3.75	7.50	15.00
❏ LP-683 [M]	Sonny Stitt at the D.J. Lounge	1966	3.00	6.00	12.00

Number	Title	Yr	VG	VG+	NM
❑ LPS-683 [S]	Sonny Stitt at the D.J. Lounge	1966	3.75	7.50	15.00
❑ LP-709 [M]	Rearin' Back	1966	3.00	6.00	12.00
❑ LPS-709 [S]	Rearin' Back	1966	3.75	7.50	15.00
❑ LP-730 [M]	Move On Over	1966	3.00	6.00	12.00
❑ LPS-730 [S]	Move On Over	1966	3.75	7.50	15.00
❑ LP-744 [M]	My Main Man	1966	3.00	6.00	12.00
❑ LPS-744 [S]	My Main Man	1966	3.75	7.50	15.00
❑ LP-760 [M]	Inter-Action	1966	3.75	7.50	15.00
❑ LPS-760 [S]	Inter-Action	1966	5.00	10.00	20.00
❑ LP-770 [M]	Soul in the Night	1966	3.75	7.50	15.00
❑ LPS-770 [S]	Soul in the Night	1966	5.00	10.00	20.00
❑ 50026	Mr. Bojangles	1973	3.00	6.00	12.00
❑ 50039 [(2)]	I Cover the Waterfront	1974	3.75	7.50	15.00
❑ 50060	Satan	1974	3.00	6.00	12.00
❑ 60040	Never Can Say Goodbye	197?	3.00	6.00	12.00
CATALYST					
❑ 7608	Forecast	1976	3.00	6.00	12.00
-- With Red Holloway					
❑ 7616	I Remember Bird	1976	3.00	6.00	12.00
❑ 7620	Tribute to Duke Ellington	1977	3.00	6.00	12.00
CHESS					
❑ 405 [(2)]	Interaction	197?	3.75	7.50	15.00
-- With Zoot Sims					
❑ CH-9317	Sonny Stitt	1990	2.50	5.00	10.00
❑ CH-91523	Sonny Stitt at the D.J. Lounge	198?	2.50	5.00	10.00
COBBLESTONE					
❑ 9013	Tune-Up	1972	3.00	6.00	12.00
❑ 9021	Constellation	1973	3.00	6.00	12.00
COLPIX					
❑ CP-499 [M]	Broadway Soul	1964	7.50	15.00	30.00
❑ SCP-499 [S]	Broadway Soul	1964	7.50	15.00	30.00
DELMARK					
❑ 426	Made for Each Other	197?	3.00	6.00	12.00
FANTASY					
❑ OJC-009	Sonny Stitt/Bud Powell/ J.J. Johnson	198?	2.50	5.00	10.00
❑ OJC-060	Kaleidoscope	198?	2.50	5.00	10.00
FLYING DUTCHMAN					
❑ BDL1-1538	Stomp Off Let's Go	1976	2.50	5.00	10.00
GALAXY					
❑ 8204	In the Beginning	197?	3.00	6.00	12.00
GRP/IMPULSE!					
❑ IMP-210	Salt and Pepper	199?	3.75	7.50	15.00
-- Reissue on audiophile vinyl					
IMPULSE!					
❑ A-43 [M]	Sonny Stitt Now!	1963	6.25	12.50	25.00
❑ AS-43 [S]	Sonny Stitt Now!	1963	7.50	15.00	30.00
❑ A-52 [M]	Salt and Pepper	1964	6.25	12.50	25.00
❑ AS-52 [S]	Salt and Pepper	1964	7.50	15.00	30.00
-- With Paul Gonsalves					
JAZZ MAN					
❑ 5040	Night Work	198?	2.50	5.00	10.00
JAZZLAND					
❑ JLP-71 [M]	Low Flame	1962	6.25	12.50	25.00
❑ JLP-971 [S]	Low Flame	1962	7.50	15.00	30.00
JAZZTONE					
❑ J-1231 [M]	Early Modern	1956	12.50	25.00	50.00
❑ J-1263 [M]	Early Modern	1957	10.00	20.00	40.00
MUSE					
❑ MR-5006	12!	1973	3.00	6.00	12.00
❑ MR-5023	The Champ	1974	3.00	6.00	12.00
❑ MR-5067	Mellow	1975	3.00	6.00	12.00
❑ MR-5091	My Buddy: Plays for Ammons	1976	3.00	6.00	12.00
❑ MR-5129	Blues for Duke	197?	3.00	6.00	12.00
❑ MR-5204	Sonny's Back	1981	2.50	5.00	10.00
❑ MR-5228	In Style	1982	2.50	5.00	10.00
❑ MR-5269	The Last Stitt Sessions, Vol. 1	1983	2.50	5.00	10.00
❑ MR-5280	The Last Stitt Sessions, Vol. 2	1984	2.50	5.00	10.00
❑ MR-5323	Constellation	1986	2.50	5.00	10.00
❑ MR-5334	Tune-Up	1987	2.50	5.00	10.00
NEW JAZZ					
❑ NJLP-103 [10]	Sonny Stitt and Bud Powell	1950	75.00	150.00	300.00
PACIFIC JAZZ					
❑ PJ-71 [M]	My Mother's Eyes	1963	5.00	10.00	20.00
❑ ST-71 [S]	My Mother's Eyes	1963	6.25	12.50	25.00
PAULA					
❑ 4004	Soul Girl	1974	3.00	6.00	12.00
PHOENIX					
❑ 15	Superstitt	197?	2.50	5.00	10.00
❑ 19	Battles	197?	2.50	5.00	10.00
PRESTIGE					
❑ PRLP-103 [10]	Sonny Stitt Plays	1951	50.00	100.00	200.00

Number	Title	Yr	VG	VG+	NM
❑ PRLP-111 [10]	Mr. Saxophone	1951	50.00	100.00	200.00
❑ PRLP-126 [10]	Favorites, Volume 1	1952	50.00	100.00	200.00
❑ PRLP-148 [10]	Favorites, Volume 2	1953	50.00	100.00	200.00
❑ PRLP-7024 [M]	Sonny Stitt with Bud Powell and J.J. Johnson	1956	25.00	50.00	100.00
❑ PRLP-7077 [M]	Kaleidoscope	1957	25.00	50.00	100.00
❑ PRLP-7133 [M]	Stitt's Bits	1958	25.00	50.00	100.00
❑ PRLP-7244 [M]	Stitt Meets Brother Jack	1962	12.50	25.00	50.00
-- Yellow label					
❑ PRLP-7244 [M]	Stitt Meets Brother Jack	1964	6.25	12.50	25.00
-- Blue label with trident logo					
❑ PRST-7244 [S]	Stitt Meets Brother Jack	1962	12.50	25.00	50.00
❑ PRLP-7248 [M]	All God's Chillun Got Rhythm	1962	12.50	25.00	50.00
-- Yellow label					
❑ PRLP-7248 [M]	All God's Chillun Got Rhythm	1964	6.25	12.50	25.00
-- Blue label with trident logo					
❑ PRST-7248 [R]	All God's Chillun Got Rhythm	1962	7.50	15.00	30.00
❑ PRLP-7297 [M]	Soul Shack	1964	12.50	25.00	50.00
-- Yellow label					
❑ PRLP-7297 [M]	Soul Shack	1965	6.25	12.50	25.00
-- Blue label with trident logo					
❑ PRST-7297 [S]	Soul Shack	1964	12.50	25.00	50.00
-- Silver label					
❑ PRST-7297 [S]	Soul Shack	1965	6.25	12.50	25.00
-- Blue label with trident logo					
❑ PRLP-7302 [M]	Primitive Soul!	1964	10.00	20.00	40.00
-- Yellow label					
❑ PRLP-7302 [M]	Primitive Soul!	1965	6.25	12.50	25.00
-- Blue label with trident logo					
❑ PRST-7302 [S]	Primitive Soul!	1964	10.00	20.00	40.00
-- Silver label					
❑ PRST-7302 [S]	Primitive Soul!	1965	6.25	12.50	25.00
-- Blue label with trident logo					
❑ PRLP-7332 [M]	Shangri-La	1964	5.00	10.00	20.00
❑ PRST-7332 [S]	Shangri-La	1964	6.25	12.50	25.00
❑ PRLP-7372 [M]	Soul People	1965	5.00	10.00	20.00
❑ PRST-7372 [S]	Soul People	1965	6.25	12.50	25.00
❑ PRLP-7436 [M]	Night Crawler	1966	5.00	10.00	20.00
❑ PRST-7436 [S]	Night Crawler	1966	6.25	12.50	25.00
❑ PRLP-7452 [M]	'Nuther Fu'ther	1966	5.00	10.00	20.00
❑ PRST-7452 [S]	'Nuther Fu'ther	1966	6.25	12.50	25.00
❑ PRLP-7459 [M]	Pow!	1967	6.25	12.50	25.00
❑ PRST-7459 [S]	Pow!	1967	5.00	10.00	20.00
❑ PRST-7585	Stitt's Bits, Volume 1	1968	3.75	7.50	15.00
❑ PRST-7606	We'll Be Together Again	1969	3.75	7.50	15.00
❑ PRST-7612	Stitt's Bits, Volume 2	1969	3.75	7.50	15.00
❑ PRST-7635	Soul Electricity	1969	3.75	7.50	15.00
❑ PRST-7701	The Best of Sonny Stitt with Brother Jack McDuff	1969	3.75	7.50	15.00
❑ PRST-7759	Night Letter	1970	3.75	7.50	15.00
❑ PRST-7769	Best for Lovers	1970	3.75	7.50	15.00
❑ PRST-7839	Bud's Blues	1974	3.00	6.00	12.00
❑ 10012	Turn It On	1971	3.00	6.00	12.00
❑ 10032	Black Vibrations	1972	3.00	6.00	12.00
❑ 10048	Goin' Down Slow	1973	3.00	6.00	12.00
❑ 10074	So Doggone Good	1974	3.00	6.00	12.00
❑ 24044 [(2)]	Genesis	1974	3.75	7.50	15.00
PROGRESSIVE					
❑ 7034	Sonny Stitt Meets Sadik Hakim	1978	2.50	5.00	10.00
ROOST					
❑ LP-415 [10]	Sonny Stitt Plays Arrangements from the Pen of Johnny Richards	1952	75.00	150.00	300.00
❑ LP-418 [10]	Jazz at the Hi-Hat	1954	75.00	150.00	300.00
❑ LP-1203 [M]	Battle of Birdland	1955	20.00	40.00	80.00
❑ LP-1208 [M]	Sonny Stitt	1956	20.00	40.00	80.00
❑ LP-2204 [M]	Sonny Stitt Plays Arrangements of Quincy Jones	1957	12.50	25.00	50.00
❑ LP-2208 [M]	Sonny Stitt	1957	12.50	25.00	50.00
❑ LP-2219 [M]	37 Minutes and 48 Seconds of Sonny Stitt	1957	12.50	25.00	50.00
❑ LP-2226 [M]	Sonny Stitt with the New Yorkers	1958	12.50	25.00	50.00
❑ LP-2230 [M]	The Saxophone of Sonny Stitt	1959	10.00	20.00	40.00
❑ SLP-2230 [S]	The Saxophone of Sonny Stitt	1959	7.50	15.00	30.00
❑ LP-2235 [M]	A Little Bit of Stitt	1959	10.00	20.00	40.00
❑ SLP-2235 [S]	A Little Bit of Stitt	1959	7.50	15.00	30.00
❑ LP-2240 [M]	The Sonny Side of Stitt	1960	10.00	20.00	40.00
❑ SLP-2240 [S]	The Sonny Side of Stitt	1960	7.50	15.00	30.00
❑ LP-2244 [M]	Stittsville	1960	10.00	20.00	40.00
❑ SLP-2244 [S]	Stittsville	1960	7.50	15.00	30.00
❑ LP-2245 [M]	Sonny Side Up	196?	6.25	12.50	25.00
❑ SLP-2245 [S]	Sonny Side Up	196?	6.25	12.50	25.00
❑ LP-2247 [M]	Feelin's	1962	6.25	12.50	25.00
❑ SLP-2247 [S]	Feelin's	1962	6.25	12.50	25.00
❑ LP-2252 [M]	Sonny Stitt in Orbit	1963	6.25	12.50	25.00
❑ SLP-2252 [S]	Sonny Stitt in Orbit	1963	6.25	12.50	25.00
❑ LP-2253 [M]	Sonny Stitt Goes Latin	1963	6.25	12.50	25.00
❑ SLP-2253 [S]	Sonny Stitt Goes Latin	1963	6.25	12.50	25.00

Number	Title	Yr	VG	VG+	NM
ROULETTE					
❑ R-25339 [M]	The Matadors Meet the Bull	1965	5.00	10.00	20.00
❑ SR-25339 [S]	The Matadors Meet the Bull	1965	6.25	12.50	25.00
❑ R-25343 [M]	What's New?	1966	5.00	10.00	20.00
❑ SR-25343 [S]	What's New?	1966	6.25	12.50	25.00
❑ R-25348 [M]	I Keep Comin' Back	1967	6.25	12.50	25.00
❑ SR-25348 [S]	I Keep Comin' Back	1967	5.00	10.00	20.00
❑ SR-25354	Parallel-O-Stitt	1968	3.75	7.50	15.00
❑ SR-42035	Make Someone Happy	1969	3.00	6.00	12.00
❑ SR-42048	Stardust	1970	3.00	6.00	12.00
SAVOY					
❑ MG-9006 [10]	All Star Series: Sonny Stitt	1953	50.00	100.00	200.00
❑ MG-9012 [10]	New Sounds in Modern Music	1953	50.00	100.00	200.00
❑ MG-9014 [10]	New Trends of Jazz	1953	50.00	100.00	200.00
SAVOY JAZZ					
❑ SJL-1165	Symphony Hall Swing	1986	2.50	5.00	10.00
SOLID STATE					
❑ SS-18047	Little Green Apples	1968	3.75	7.50	15.00
❑ SS-18057	Come Hither	1969	3.75	7.50	15.00
TRIP					
❑ 5008 [(2)]	Two Sides of Sonny Stitt	1974	3.00	6.00	12.00
UPFRONT					
❑ UPF-196	Sonny's Blues	197?	2.50	5.00	10.00
VERVE					
❑ UMV-2558	New York Jazz	198?	2.50	5.00	10.00
❑ UMV-2634	Only the Blues	198?	2.50	5.00	10.00
❑ MGVS-6038 [S]	The Hard Swing	1960	10.00	20.00	40.00
❑ MGVS-6041 [S]	Sonny Stitt Plays Jimmy Giuffre Arrangements	1960	10.00	20.00	40.00
❑ MGVS-6108 [S]	Sonny Stitt Sits In with the Oscar Peterson Trio	1960	10.00	20.00	40.00
❑ MGVS-6149 [S]	Sonny Stitt Blows the Blues	1960	10.00	20.00	40.00
❑ MGVS-6149	Sonny Stitt Blows the Blues	1996	10.00	20.00	40.00
-- Audiophile reissue by Classic Records					
❑ MGVS-6149-45 [(4)]	Sonny Stitt Blows the Blues	1999	10.00	20.00	40.00
-- Audiophile reissue by Classic Records; plays at 45 rpm					
❑ MGVS-6154 [S]	Saxophone Supremacy	1960	---	---	---
-- Canceled					
❑ MGVS-6162 [S]	Sonny Stitt Swings the Most	1960	---	---	---
-- Canceled					
❑ MGV-8219 [M]	New York Jazz	1957	12.50	25.00	50.00
❑ V-8219 [M]	New York Jazz	1961	6.25	12.50	25.00
❑ MGV-8250 [M]	Only the Blues	1958	12.50	25.00	50.00
❑ V-8250 [M]	Only the Blues	1961	6.25	12.50	25.00
❑ MGV-8262 [M]	Sonny Side Up	1958	15.00	30.00	60.00
❑ V-8262 [M]	Sonny Side Up	1961	7.50	15.00	30.00
❑ MGV-8306 [M]	The Hard Swing	1959	12.50	25.00	50.00
❑ V-8306 [M]	The Hard Swing	1961	6.25	12.50	25.00
❑ V6-8306 [S]	The Hard Swing	1961	5.00	10.00	20.00
❑ MGV-8309 [M]	Sonny Stitt Plays Jimmy Giuffre Arrangements	1959	12.50	25.00	50.00
❑ V-8309 [M]	Sonny Stitt Plays Jimmy Giuffre Arrangements	1961	6.25	12.50	25.00
❑ V6-8309 [S]	Sonny Stitt Plays Jimmy Giuffre Arrangements	1961	5.00	10.00	20.00
❑ MGV-8324 [M]	Personal Appearance	1959	12.50	25.00	50.00
❑ V-8324 [M]	Personal Appearance	1961	6.25	12.50	25.00
❑ MGV-8344 [M]	Sonny Stitt Sits In with the Oscar Peterson Trio	1959	12.50	25.00	50.00
❑ V-8344 [M]	Sonny Stitt Sits In with the Oscar Peterson Trio	1961	6.25	12.50	25.00
❑ V6-8344 [S]	Sonny Stitt Sits In with the Oscar Peterson Trio	1961	5.00	10.00	20.00
❑ MGV-8374 [M]	Sonny Stitt Blows the Blues	1960	12.50	25.00	50.00
❑ V-8374 [M]	Sonny Stitt Blows the Blues	1961	6.25	12.50	25.00
❑ MGV-8377 [M]	Saxophone Supremacy	1960	12.50	25.00	50.00
❑ V6-8374 [S]	Sonny Stitt Blows the Blues	1961	5.00	10.00	20.00
❑ V-8377 [M]	Saxophone Supremacy	1961	6.25	12.50	25.00
❑ MGV-8380 [M]	Sonny Stitt Swings the Most	1960	12.50	25.00	50.00
❑ V-8380 [M]	Sommy Stitt Swings the Most	1961	6.25	12.50	25.00
❑ MGV-8403 [M]	Sonny Stitt	1960	---	---	---
-- Canceled					
❑ V-8451 [M]	The Sensual Sound of Sonny Stitt	1962	5.00	10.00	20.00
❑ V6-8451 [S]	The Sensual Sound of Sonny Stitt	1962	6.25	12.50	25.00
❑ V6-8837	Previously Unreleased Recordings	1974	3.00	6.00	12.00
WHO'S WHO IN JAZZ					
❑ 21022	Sonny, Sweets and Jaws	1981	2.50	5.00	10.00
❑ 21025	The Bubba's Sessions	1982	2.50	5.00	10.00

STITT, SONNY, AND GENE AMMONS
Also see each artist's individual listings.

Number	Title	Yr	VG	VG+	NM
CADET					
❑ LP-785 [M]	Jug and Sonny	1967	6.25	12.50	25.00

Number	Title	Yr	VG	VG+	NM
❑ LPS-785 [S]	Jug and Sonny	1967	3.75	7.50	15.00
CHESS					
❑ CH-91549	Jug and Sonny	198?	2.50	5.00	10.00
PRESTIGE					
❑ PRLP-107 [10]	Battle of the Saxes: Ammons vs. Stitt	1951	62.50	125.00	250.00
❑ PRLP-7234 [M]	Soul Summit	1962	10.00	20.00	40.00
-- Yellow label					
❑ PRST-7234 [S]	Soul Summit	1962	12.50	25.00	50.00
-- Yellow label					
❑ PRLP-7454 [M]	Soul Summit	1966	5.00	10.00	20.00
-- Blue label, trident logo at right					
❑ PRST-7454 [S]	Soul Summit	1966	6.25	12.50	25.00
-- Blue label, trident logo at right					
❑ PRST-7606	We'll Be Together Again	1969	5.00	10.00	20.00
VERVE					
❑ V-8426 [M]	Boss Tenors	1962	5.00	10.00	20.00
❑ V6-8426 [S]	Boss Tenors	1962	6.25	12.50	25.00
❑ V-8468 [M]	Boss Tenors in Orbit	1962	5.00	10.00	20.00
❑ V6-8468 [S]	Boss Tenors in Orbit	1962	6.25	12.50	25.00

STOLTZMAN, RICHARD
Clarinetist.

Number	Title	Yr	VG	VG+	NM
RCA					
❑ 5944-1-RC	New York Counterpoint	1987	2.50	5.00	10.00
RCA VICTOR					
❑ AML1-7124	Begin Sweet World	1986	2.50	5.00	10.00

STONE ALLIANCE
Primary members: Don Alias (drums, percussion); Steve Grossman (tenor saxophone); Gene Perla (bass). Also see MARCIO MONTARROYOS.

Number	Title	Yr	VG	VG+	NM
PM					
❑ 013	Stone Alliance	1976	3.00	6.00	12.00
❑ 015	Con Amigos	1977	3.00	6.00	12.00
❑ 020	Heads Up	1980	3.00	6.00	12.00

STOPAK, BERNIE

Number	Title	Yr	VG	VG+	NM
STASH					
❑ ST-274	Remember Me	1988	2.50	5.00	10.00

STORYVILLE STOMPERS, THE

Number	Title	Yr	VG	VG+	NM
TROPICANA					
❑ 1204 [M]	New Orleans Jazz	195?	10.00	20.00	40.00

STOVER, SMOKEY
Trumpeter and bandleader.

Number	Title	Yr	VG	VG+	NM
ARGO					
❑ LP-652 [DJ]	Smokey Stover's Original Firemen	1960	15.00	30.00	60.00
-- White label, multi-color vinyl					
❑ LP-652 [M]	Smokey Stover's Original Firemen	1960	6.25	12.50	25.00
❑ LPS-652 [S]	Smokey Stover's Original Firemen	1960	7.50	15.00	30.00
JAZZOLOGY					
❑ J-53	Smokey Stover and the Original Firemen	197?	2.50	5.00	10.00

STOWELL, JOHN
Guitarist.

Number	Title	Yr	VG	VG+	NM
INNER CITY					
❑ IC-1030	Golden Delicious	197?	3.00	6.00	12.00

STRAND, LES
Organist and pianist.

Number	Title	Yr	VG	VG+	NM
FANTASY					
❑ 3231 [M]	Les Strand on the Baldwin Organ	1956	12.50	25.00	50.00
-- Red vinyl					
❑ 3231 [M]	Les Strand on the Baldwin Organ	195?	5.00	10.00	20.00
-- Black vinyl					
❑ 3242 [M]	Jazz Classics on the Baldwin Organ	1956	12.50	25.00	50.00
-- Red vinyl					
❑ 3242 [M]	Jazz Classics on the Baldwin Organ	195?	5.00	10.00	20.00
-- Black vinyl					

STRATTON, DON
Trumpeter.

Number	Title	Yr	VG	VG+	NM
ABC-PARAMOUNT					
❑ ABC-118 [M]	Modern Jazz with Dixieland Roots	1956	10.00	20.00	40.00

STRAYHORN, BILLY
Pianist, arranger and composer most closely associated with the DUKE ELLINGTON Orchestra. Among the many songs he wrote were "Take the 'A' Train" and "Lush Life."

Number	Title	Yr	VG	VG+	NM
FELSTED					
❑ 2008 [S]	Billy Strayhorn Septet	1958	15.00	30.00	60.00
❑ 7008 [M]	Billy Strayhorn Septet	1958	20.00	40.00	80.00
MASTER JAZZ					
❑ 8116	Cue for Sax	197?	3.75	7.50	15.00
MERCER					
❑ LP-1001 [10]	Billy Strayhorn Trio	1951	50.00	100.00	200.00
❑ LP-1005 [10]	Billy Strayhorn and All-Stars	1951	50.00	100.00	200.00
ROULETTE					
❑ R-52119 [M]	Live!	1965	5.00	10.00	20.00
❑ SR-52119 [S]	Live!	1965	6.25	12.50	25.00
SOLID STATE					
❑ SS-18031	The Peaceful Side of Billy	1968	3.75	7.50	15.00
UNITED ARTISTS					
❑ UAJ-14010 [M]	The Peaceful Side of Billy	1962	10.00	20.00	40.00
❑ UAJS-15010 [S]	The Peaceful Side of Billy	1962	12.50	25.00	50.00

STRAZZERI, FRANK
Pianist.

Number	Title	Yr	VG	VG+	NM
CATALYST					
❑ 7607	After the Rain	1976	3.00	6.00	12.00
❑ 7623	Straz	1977	3.00	6.00	12.00
CREATIVE WORLD					
❑ ST-3003	View from Within	197?	3.00	6.00	12.00
DISCOVERY					
❑ DS-933	Kat Dancin'	1987	2.50	5.00	10.00
GLENDALE					
❑ 6002	Frames	197?	3.00	6.00	12.00
REVELATION					
❑ REV-10	That's Him and This Is New	1969	6.25	12.50	25.00
SEA BREEZE					
❑ SB-1007	Relaxin'	198?	3.00	6.00	12.00

STREETDANCER

Number	Title	Yr	VG	VG+	NM
DHARMA					
❑ 807	Rising	197?	3.75	7.50	15.00
FUTURE					
❑ 2001	Streetdancer	197?	3.75	7.50	15.00

STRING TRIO OF NEW YORK
Members: Diane Monroe (violin); James Emery (guitar); John Lindberg (bass).

Number	Title	Yr	VG	VG+	NM
BLACK SAINT					
❑ BSR-0031	First String	198?	3.00	6.00	12.00
❑ BSR-0048	Area Code 212	198?	3.00	6.00	12.00
❑ BSR-0058	Common Goal	198?	3.00	6.00	12.00
❑ BSR-0068	Rebirth of a Feeling	1984	3.00	6.00	12.00

STROZIER, FRANK
Alto saxophone player and composer. Also see THE YOUNG LIONS; YOUNG MEN FROM MEMPHIS.

Number	Title	Yr	VG	VG+	NM
INNER CITY					
❑ IC-2066	Remember Me	197?	3.75	7.50	15.00
JAZZLAND					
❑ JLP-56 [M]	Long Night	1961	6.25	12.50	25.00
❑ JLP-70 [M]	March of the Siamese Children	1962	6.25	12.50	25.00
❑ JLP-956 [S]	Long Night	1961	7.50	15.00	30.00
❑ JLP-970 [S]	March of the Siamese Children	1962	7.50	15.00	30.00
STEEPLECHASE					
❑ SCS-1066	Remember Me	198?	3.00	6.00	12.00
VEE JAY					
❑ LP-3005 [M]	Fantastic Frank Strozier	1960	7.50	15.00	30.00
❑ SR-3005 [S]	Fantastic Frank Strozier	1960	10.00	20.00	40.00

STRUNZ & FARAH
Guitarists Jorge Strunz and Ardeshir Farah.

Number	Title	Yr	VG	VG+	NM
MILESTONE					
❑ M-9123	Frontera	1984	2.50	5.00	10.00
❑ M-9136	Guitarras	1985	2.50	5.00	10.00

STUART, RORY
Guitarist.

Number	Title	Yr	VG	VG+	NM
CADENCE JAZZ					
❑ CJR-1016	Nightwork	1983	2.50	5.00	10.00
SUNNYSIDE					
❑ SSC-1021	Hurricane	1988	2.50	5.00	10.00

STUBBLEFIELD, JOHN
Tenor and soprano saxophone player.

Number	Title	Yr	VG	VG+	NM
SOUL NOTE					
❑ SN-1095	Confessin'	1985	3.00	6.00	12.00
STORYVILLE					
❑ 4011	Prelude	197?	3.00	6.00	12.00

STUBO, THORGEIR
Guitarist.

Number	Title	Yr	VG	VG+	NM
CADENCE JAZZ					
❑ CJR-1030	Rhythm-A-Ning	1987	2.50	5.00	10.00
❑ CJR-1036	End of a Tune	1988	2.50	5.00	10.00

STUERMER, DARYL
Guitarist.

Number	Title	Yr	VG	VG+	NM
GRP					
❑ GR-9573	Steppin' Out	1988	2.50	5.00	10.00

SUBRAMANIAM, DR. L.
Violinist.

Number	Title	Yr	VG	VG+	NM
CRUSADERS					
❑ 16003	Blossom	198?	5.00	10.00	20.00
-- Audiophile vinyl					
DISCOVERY					
❑ DS-202	Indian Classical Music	198?	3.00	6.00	12.00
MCA					
❑ 5784	Blossom	1986	2.50	5.00	10.00
MILESTONE					
❑ M-9114	Spanish Wave	198?	3.00	6.00	12.00
❑ M-9130	Conversations	1985	2.50	5.00	10.00
❑ M-9138	Mani & Co.	1986	2.50	5.00	10.00
STORYVILLE					
❑ 4075	Garland	198?	2.50	5.00	10.00
TREND					
❑ 524	Fantasy Without Limits	1980	3.00	6.00	12.00

SUDHALTER, DICK
Trumpeter and fluegel horn player.

Number	Title	Yr	VG	VG+	NM
AUDIOPHILE					
❑ AP-159	Friends with Pleasure	1981	2.50	5.00	10.00
STOMP OFF					
❑ SOS-1207	Get Out and Get Under the Moon	1991	3.00	6.00	12.00

SUDLER, MONETTE
Guitarist.

Number	Title	Yr	VG	VG+	NM
INNER CITY					
❑ IC-2062	Time for a Change	197?	3.75	7.50	15.00
STEEPLECHASE					
❑ SCS-1062	Time for a Change	198?	3.00	6.00	12.00
❑ SCS-1087	Brighter Days for You	198?	3.00	6.00	12.00
❑ SCS-1102	Live in Europe	198?	3.00	6.00	12.00

SULIEMAN, IDREES
Trumpeter and fluegel horn player. Also see THE PRESTIGE BLUES SWINGERS.

Number	Title	Yr	VG	VG+	NM
NEW JAZZ					
❑ NJLP-8202 [M]	Roots	1958	25.00	50.00	100.00
-- Yellow label					
❑ NJLP-8202 [M]	Roots	1958	15.00	30.00	60.00
-- Purple label					
❑ NJLP-8202 [M]	Roots	1965	6.25	12.50	25.00
-- Blue label, trident logo at right					
STEEPLECHASE					
❑ SCS-1052	Now Is the Time	198?	3.00	6.00	12.00
❑ SCS-1202	Bird's Grass	198?	3.00	6.00	12.00

SULLIVAN, CHARLES
Trumpeter.

Number	Title	Yr	VG	VG+	NM
INNER CITY					
❑ IC-1012	Genesis	1975	3.75	7.50	15.00

SULLIVAN, FRANK
Pianist.

Number	Title	Yr	VG	VG+	NM
REVELATION					
❑ 34	First Impressions	1981	2.50	5.00	10.00

SULLIVAN, IRA
Trumpeter, fluegel horn player, alto and tenor saxophone player, and flutist.

Number	Title	Yr	VG	VG+	NM
ATLANTIC					
❑ 1476 [M]	Horizons	1967	6.25	12.50	25.00

Number	Title	Yr	VG	VG+	NM
❏ SD-1476 [S]	Horizons	1967	3.75	7.50	15.00
DELMARK					
❏ DL-402 [M]	Blue Stroll	1961	7.50	15.00	30.00
❏ DS-402 [S]	Blue Stroll	1961	10.00	20.00	40.00
❏ DS-422	Nicky's Tune	197?	3.00	6.00	12.00
DISCOVERY					
❏ 873	Horizons	198?	2.50	5.00	10.00
FLYING FISH					
❏ FF-075	Ira Sullivan	1978	3.00	6.00	12.00
❏ FF-27075	Ira Sullivan	198?	2.50	5.00	10.00
-- Reissue					
GALAXY					
❏ 5114	Peace	1979	3.00	6.00	12.00
❏ 5137	Multimedia	198?	2.50	5.00	10.00
HORIZON					
❏ SP-706	Ira Sullivan	1976	3.00	6.00	12.00
MUSE					
❏ MR-5242	Doin' It All	1981	2.50	5.00	10.00
PAUSA					
❏ 7169	Strings Attached	1985	2.50	5.00	10.00
STASH					
❏ ST-208	The Incredible Ira Sullivan	1980	2.50	5.00	10.00
VEE JAY					
❏ LP-3003 [M]	Bird Lives!	1960	7.50	15.00	30.00
❏ SR-3003 [S]	Bird Lives!	1960	10.00	20.00	40.00
❏ VJS-3003 [S]	Bird Lives!	198?	3.00	6.00	12.00
-- Reissue with new prefix on thinner vinyl					

SULLIVAN, JOE
Pianist.

Number	Title	Yr	VG	VG+	NM
CAPITOL					
❏ T 636 [M]	Classics In Jazz	1955	10.00	20.00	40.00
DOWN HOME					
❏ MGD-2 [M]	Mr. Piano Man: The Music of Joe Sullivan	1956	12.50	25.00	50.00
EPIC					
❏ LG 1003 [10]	Joe Sullivan Plays Fats Waller Compositions	1954	20.00	40.00	80.00
FOLKWAYS					
❏ FJ-2851	Joe Sullivan Piano	197?	3.00	6.00	12.00
RIVERSIDE					
❏ RLP 12-202 [M]	New Solos by an Old Master	1955	15.00	30.00	60.00
VERVE					
❏ MGV-1002 [M]	Mr. Piano Man: The Music of Joe Sullivan	1957	10.00	20.00	40.00
❏ V-1002 [M]	Mr. Piano Man: The Music of Joe Sullivan	1961	5.00	10.00	20.00

SULLIVAN, MAXINE
Female singer.

Number	Title	Yr	VG	VG+	NM
ARCHIVE OF FOLK AND JAZZ					
❏ 307	Maxine Sullivan with Jack Teagarden	197?	2.50	5.00	10.00
ATLANTIC					
❏ 81783	Together	1987	2.50	5.00	10.00
AUDIOPHILE					
❏ AP-128	We Just Couldn't Say Goodbye	1979	2.50	5.00	10.00
❏ AP-154	Maxine Sullivan and the Ike Isaacs Trio	198?	2.50	5.00	10.00
❏ AP-167	Maxine	198?	2.50	5.00	10.00
❏ AP-185	It Was Great Fun	1984	2.50	5.00	10.00
❏ AP-193	Good Morning, Life!	1986	2.50	5.00	10.00
CIRCLE					
❏ 47	Maxine Sullivan and John Kirby 1940	198?	2.50	5.00	10.00
CONCORD JAZZ					
❏ CJ-288	Uptown	1986	2.50	5.00	10.00
MONMOUTH-EVERGREEN					
❏ 7038	Sullivan, Shakespeare and Hyman	197?	3.75	7.50	15.00
PERIOD					
❏ SPL-1207 [M]	Maxine Sullivan, Volume 2	1956	12.50	25.00	50.00
❏ RL-1909 [M]	Maxine Sullivan 1956	1956	12.50	25.00	50.00
STASH					
❏ ST-244	The Great Songs from the Cotton Club by Harold Arlen and Ted Koehler	1985	2.50	5.00	10.00
❏ ST-257	Maxine Sullivan Sings the Music of Burton Lane	1986	2.50	5.00	10.00

SULLIVAN, MAXINE, AND BOB WILBER
Also see each artist's individual listings.

Number	Title	Yr	VG	VG+	NM
MONMOUTH-EVERGREEN					
❏ 6917	Bob & Maxine	1969	3.75	7.50	15.00
❏ 6919	Maxine Sullivan and Bob Wilber	1969	3.00	6.00	12.00

SULLIVAN, PAT, JAZZ ORCHESTRA

Number	Title	Yr	VG	VG+	NM
PJS					
❏ WRC1-2536	Stairway Down to the Stars	1985	2.50	5.00	10.00

SUMMERLIN, ED
Composer, arranger and conductor. Also a tenor saxophone player.

Number	Title	Yr	VG	VG+	NM
ECCLESIA					
❏ ER-101 [M]	Liturgical Jazz	1959	15.00	30.00	60.00

SUMMERS, BILL
Percussionist.

Number	Title	Yr	VG	VG+	NM
PRESTIGE					
❏ 10102	Feel the Heat	1977	3.75	7.50	15.00
❏ 10103	Cayenne	1977	3.75	7.50	15.00
❏ 10105	Straight to the Bank	1978	3.75	7.50	15.00

SUN RA
Pianist, keyboard player, composer and bandleader (assorted Arkestras). The albums on the Saturn label are difficult to arrange into any sensible order – they are roughly numerical below, ignoring most punctuation, though some may not be. They also are much more difficult to find than the prices indicate. Rarely do any of them come up for sale, and when they do, the prices vary widely. We've opted to go on the side of caution, but be aware that a Sun Ra fanatic can pay a LOT more for some of these LPs. There are also many more variations than even listed below; if you have to know more, see Robert Campbell's *The Earthly Recordings Of Sun Ra* (Cadence Jazz Books; a new edition soon to be available on the website www.cadencebuilding.com).

Number	Title	Yr	VG	VG+	NM
A&M					
❏ SP-5260	Blue Delight	1989	3.75	7.50	15.00
ABC IMPULSE!					
❏ 1974	Welcome to Saturn	1974	6.25	12.50	25.00
❏ AS-9239	Atlantis	1973	5.00	10.00	20.00
❏ AS-9242	The Nubians of Plutonia	1974	5.00	10.00	20.00
❏ AS-9243	The Magic City	1973	5.00	10.00	20.00
❏ AS-9245	Angels and Demons at Play	1974	5.00	10.00	20.00
❏ AS-9255	Astro Black	1973	5.00	10.00	20.00
❏ ASD-9265	Jazz in Silhouette	1974	5.00	10.00	20.00
❏ AS-9270	Fate in a Pleasant Mood	1974	5.00	10.00	20.00
❏ AS-9271	Super Sonic Sounds	1974	5.00	10.00	20.00
❏ AS-9276	The Bad and the Beautiful	1974	5.00	10.00	20.00
❏ AS-9287	Night of the Purple Moon	1974	---	---	---
-- Canceled?					
❏ AS-9288	Planet Earth	1974	---	---	---
-- Canceled?					
❏ AS-9289	My Brother the Wind	1974	---	---	---
-- Canceled?					
❏ AS-9290	Sound Sound Pleasure	1974	---	---	---
-- Canceled?					
❏ AS-9291	Cosmic Tones for Mental Therapy	1974	---	---	---
-- Canceled?					
❏ AS-9292	We Travel the Spaceways	1974	---	---	---
-- Canceled?					
❏ AS-9293	Other Planes of There	1974	---	---	---
-- Canceled?					
❏ AS-9294	Art Forms from Dimensions Tomorrow	1974	---	---	---
-- Canceled?					
❏ AS-9295	Monorails and Satellites	1974	---	---	---
-- Canceled?					
❏ AS-9296	Cymbals	1974	---	---	---
-- Canceled?					
❏ AS-9297	Crystal Spears	1974	---	---	---
-- Canceled?					
❏ ASD-9298	Pathways to Unknown Worlds	1975	5.00	10.00	20.00
AFFINITY					
❏ AFF 10	The Solar-Myth Approach Volume I	1978	6.25	12.50	25.00
❏ AFF 76	The Solar-Myth Approach Volume II	1978	6.25	12.50	25.00
BASF					
❏ 20748	It's After the End of the World	1971	5.00	10.00	20.00
BLACK LION					
❏ 106	Pictures of Infinity	197?	5.00	10.00	20.00
BLACK SAINT					
❏ 120101	Reflections in Blue	1987	3.00	6.00	12.00
❏ 120111	Hours After	1990	3.75	7.50	15.00
BLUE THUMB					
❏ BTS-41	Space Is the Place	1973	5.00	10.00	20.00
DELMARK					
❏ DL-411 [M]	Sun Song	1967	7.50	15.00	30.00

Number	Title	Yr	VG	VG+	NM
❑ DS-411 [R]	Sun Song	1967	3.75	7.50	15.00
-- Reissue of Transition 10					
❑ DS-414 [R]	Sound of Joy	1968	3.00	6.00	12.00
DIW					
❑ DIWP-2 [PD]	Cosmo Omnibus Imaginable Illusion: Live at Pit-Inn	1988	12.50	25.00	50.00
-- Picture disc; limited to under 1,000 copies					
❑ 8024	Cosmo Omnibus Imaginable Illusion: Live at Pit-Inn	1988	3.75	7.50	15.00
ESP-DISK'					
❑ 1014 [M]	The Heliocentric Worlds of Sun Ra, Volume 1	1966	7.50	15.00	30.00
❑ S-1014 [S]	The Heliocentric Worlds of Sun Ra, Volume 1	1966	10.00	20.00	40.00
❑ 1017 [M]	The Heliocentric Worlds of Sun Ra, Volume 2	1966	3.75	7.50	15.00
-- With voices overdubbed on "The Sun Myth"					
❑ 1017 [M]	The Heliocentric Worlds of Sun Ra, Volume 2	1966	7.50	15.00	30.00
-- Without voices overdubbed on "The Sun Myth"					
❑ S-1017 [S]	The Heliocentric Worlds of Sun Ra, Volume 2	1966	5.00	10.00	20.00
-- With voices overdubbed on "The Sun Myth"					
❑ S-1017 [S]	The Heliocentric Worlds of Sun Ra, Volume 2	1966	10.00	20.00	40.00
-- Without voices overdubbed on "The Sun Myth"					
❑ S-1045 [S]	Nothing Is	1969	5.00	10.00	20.00
HAT ART					
❑ 2017 [(2)]	Sunrise in Different Directions	1986	3.75	7.50	15.00
HAT HUT					
❑ 17 [(2)]	Sunrise in Different Directions	1980	5.00	10.00	20.00
HORO					
❑ HDP-19/20 [(2)]	Unity	1978	6.25	12.50	25.00
❑ HDP-23/24 [(2)]	Other Voices, Other Blues	1978	6.25	12.50	25.00
❑ HDP-25/26 [(2)]	New Steps	1978	6.25	12.50	25.00
IAI					
❑ 37.38.50	Solo Piano Volume 1	197?	3.75	7.50	15.00
❑ 37.38.58	St. Louis Blues	197?	3.75	7.50	15.00
INNER CITY					
❑ IC-1020	Cosmos	1978	3.75	7.50	15.00
❑ IC-1039 [(2)]	Live at Montreux	1978	5.00	10.00	20.00
JIHAD					
❑ 1968 [S]	A Black Mass	1968	25.00	50.00	100.00
-- Color cover					
❑ 1968 [S]	A Black Mass	1968	37.50	75.00	150.00
-- Black and white cover					
LEO					
❑ LR-154	Love in Outer Space: Live in	1988	3.75	7.50	15.00
MELTDOWN					
❑ MPA-1	John Cage Meets Sun Ra	1987	5.00	10.00	20.00
PHILLY JAZZ					
❑ PJ-666	Lanquidity	1978	6.25	12.50	25.00
❑ PJ-1007	Of Mythic Worlds	1980	6.25	12.50	25.00
PRAXIS					
❑ CM 106	Sun Ra Arkestra Meets Salah Ragab in Egypt	1983	10.00	20.00	40.00
❑ CM 108	Live at Praxis Volume 1	1984	12.50	25.00	50.00
❑ CM 109	Live at Praxis Volume 2	1985	12.50	25.00	50.00
❑ CM 110	Live at Praxis 84 Volume 3	1985	12.50	25.00	50.00
RECOMMENDED					
❑ RR-11	Nuits de la Fondation Maeght Volume I	1981	7.50	15.00	30.00
-- Reissue of Shandar 10.001; plays at 45 rpm					
ROUNDER					
❑ 3035	Strange Celestial Road	1982	3.75	7.50	15.00
SATURN (INCLUDES EL SATURN)					
❑ CMIJ 78	Disco 3000	1978	5.00	10.00	20.00
❑ IHNY-165	Sun Ra and His Arkestra Featuring Pharoah Sanders and Black Harold	1976	10.00	20.00	40.00
❑ LP-200	Universe in Blue	197?	7.50	15.00	30.00
❑ LP-202 [M]	Fate in a Pleasant Mood	196?	7.50	15.00	30.00
-- Chicago address on label					
❑ LP-203 [M]	Interstellar Low Ways	1969	12.50	25.00	50.00
-- Chicago address on label					
❑ LP-204 [M]	Super-Sonic Jazz	1968	12.50	25.00	50.00
-- Blue or green cover; Chicago address on label					
❑ LP-205 [M]	Jazz in Silhouette	1967	12.50	25.00	50.00
-- Green label					
❑ LP-205 [M]	Jazz in Silhouette	1967	12.50	25.00	50.00
-- Red label					
❑ LP-206 [M]	Other Planes of There	1967	10.00	20.00	40.00
-- Chicago address on label					
❑ LP-207 [M]	Sun Ra Visits Planet Earth	196?	10.00	20.00	40.00
-- "El Saturn" label					

Number	Title	Yr	VG	VG+	NM
❑ LP-207 [M]	Sun Ra Visits Planet Earth	1968	12.50	25.00	50.00
-- Minneapolis address on label					
❑ LP-208 [M]	Secrets of the Sun	196?	12.50	25.00	50.00
-- Chicago address on label					
❑ SRLP-0216 [M]	Super-Sonic Jazz	1957	37.50	75.00	150.00
-- Blank cover					
❑ SRLP-0216 [M]	Super-Sonic Jazz	1957	75.00	150.00	300.00
-- Silk-screened cover					
❑ SRLP-0216 [M]	Super-Sonic Jazz	1958	37.50	75.00	150.00
-- Purple "keyboard" cover					
❑ SRLP-0216 [M]	Super-Sonic Jazz	1965	12.50	25.00	50.00
-- Blue or green cover					
❑ LP-402	When Sun Comes Out	196?	10.00	20.00	40.00
❑ LP-403 [M]	The Magic City	196?	7.50	15.00	30.00
-- Chicago address on label					
❑ LP-404 [M]	Art Forms of Dimensions Tomorrow	1969	7.50	15.00	30.00
-- Chicago address on label					
❑ LP-405	When Angels Speak of Love	196?	7.50	15.00	30.00
❑ LP-406 [M]	The Nubians of Plutonia	1969	12.50	25.00	50.00
-- Chicago address on label					
❑ LP-407 [M]	Angels and Demons at Play	196?	10.00	20.00	40.00
-- Chicago address on label					
❑ LP-408 [S]	Cosmic Tones for Mental Therapy	1967	50.00	100.00	200.00
-- Red label; Sun Ra art on cover					
❑ LP-409 [M]	We Travel the Spaceways	196?	6.25	12.50	25.00
-- "El Saturn" label					
❑ LP-485	Deep Purple	1973	10.00	20.00	40.00
❑ LP-487	Song of the Stargazers	1979	12.50	25.00	50.00
❑ LP-502 [S]	Strange Strings	1967	12.50	25.00	50.00
-- Red label					
❑ ESR-507 [S]	Atlantis	1969	7.50	15.00	30.00
-- "El Saturn" label					
❑ LP-509 [M]	Monorails and Satellites	1968	12.50	25.00	50.00
-- "El Saturn" label					
❑ LP-512	Sound Sun Pleasure!!	1970	10.00	20.00	40.00
❑ LP-519 [S]	Monorails and Satellites, Vol. II	1969	12.50	25.00	50.00
-- "El Saturn" label					
❑ ESR-520	Continuation	1969	6.25	12.50	25.00
❑ LP-520	Continuation	1970	12.50	25.00	50.00
❑ ESR-521	My Brother the Wind	1970	6.25	12.50	25.00
❑ LP-521	My Brother the Wind	197?	12.50	25.00	50.00
❑ LP-522	The Night of the Purple Moon	197?	12.50	25.00	50.00
❑ LP-523	My Brother the Wind, Volume II	1971	12.50	25.00	50.00
❑ LP-527	Space Probe	197?	12.50	25.00	50.00
❑ LP-529	The Invisible Shield	1974	20.00	40.00	80.00
-- Chicago address on label					
❑ LP-529	The Invisible Shield	1974	15.00	30.00	60.00
-- Philadelphia address on label					
❑ LP-530	Outer Spaceways Incorporated	1974	20.00	40.00	80.00
-- Chicago address on label					
❑ LP-530	Outer Spaceways Incorporated	1974	15.00	30.00	60.00
-- Philadelphia address on label					
❑ LP-538	Discipline 27-II	1973	12.50	25.00	50.00
❑ LP-539	What's New?	197?	12.50	25.00	50.00
❑ LP-564	Pathways to Unknown Worlds	1974	---	---	---
-- Canceled?					
❑ LPB-711 [M]	The Magic City	1966	20.00	40.00	80.00
-- Red label					
❑ LP-747	Some Blues But Not the Kind That's Blue	1977	10.00	20.00	40.00
❑ 752	What's New?	197?	5.00	10.00	20.00
❑ LP-771	The Soul Vibrations of Man	1977	10.00	20.00	40.00
❑ LP-772	Taking a Chance on Chances	1977	15.00	30.00	60.00
❑ LP-849	Horizon	1974	10.00	20.00	40.00
❑ 1272	Live in Egypt 1	1973	6.25	12.50	25.00
❑ LP-1966 [M]	When Angels Speak of Love	1966	75.00	150.00	300.00
-- Red cover with a "sideways" image of Sun Ra					
❑ ESR-1970	My Brother the Wind	1970	10.00	20.00	40.00
❑ 1978	Media Dream	1978	5.00	10.00	20.00
❑ 1981	Dance of Innocent Passion	1981	5.00	10.00	20.00
❑ 1984A/B	Just Friends	1984	5.00	10.00	20.00
❑ A/B1984SG-9	A Fireside Chat with Lucifer	1984	5.00	10.00	20.00
❑ C/D1984SG-9	Celestial Love	1984	5.00	10.00	20.00
❑ SRA-2000	My Brother the Wind, Volume II	1971	10.00	20.00	40.00
❑ LP-2066 [M]	When Sun Comes Out	1963	75.00	150.00	300.00
-- Green cover with yellow sun					
❑ LP-2066 [M]	When Sun Comes Out	1963	75.00	150.00	300.00
-- Black ameboid figure on cover					
❑ LP-2066 [M]	When Sun Comes Out	1963	50.00	100.00	200.00
-- Blank cover					
❑ LP-2066 [M]	When Sun Comes Out	1967	50.00	100.00	200.00
-- Spaceman at piano cover					
❑ KH-2772 [S]	Cosmic Tones for Mental Therapy	196?	7.50	15.00	30.00
-- Blue cover; Chicago address on label					
❑ ESR-5000	Universe in Blue	1972	7.50	15.00	30.00
❑ HK-5445 [M]	We Travel the Spaceways	1966	15.00	30.00	60.00
-- Red label					

Number	Title	Yr	VG	VG+	NM
❑ LP-5786 [M]	Jazz In Silhouette	1958	37.50	75.00	150.00
-- Yellow label					
❑ 6161	Song of the Stargazers	1979	12.50	25.00	50.00
❑ 6680	I, Pharaoh	1980	5.00	10.00	20.00
-- "El Saturn" label					
❑ 7771	Nidhamu	197?	5.00	10.00	20.00
❑ 7877	Somewhere Over the Rainbow	1977	5.00	10.00	20.00
❑ GH-9954-E/F [M]	Secrets of the Sun	1965	25.00	50.00	100.00
-- Red label					
❑ SR-9956 [M]	Art Forms of Dimensions Tomorrow	1965	12.50	25.00	50.00
-- Red label					
❑ SR-9956-2/A/B [M]	Fate In A Pleasant Mood	1965	20.00	40.00	80.00
-- Red label					
❑ SR-9956-2-M/N [M]	Rocket #9 Take Off For the Planet Venus	1966	75.00	150.00	300.00
-- Cover has "burning candle" logo					
❑ SR-9956-2/O/P [M]	Angels and Demons at Play	1965	20.00	40.00	80.00
-- Red label; metallic gold cover					
❑ SR-9956-11A/B [M]	Sun Ra Visits Planet Earth	1966	20.00	40.00	80.00
-- Red label					
❑ SR-9956-11E/F [M]	The Lady with the Golden Stockings	1966	75.00	150.00	300.00
-- Cover is generic and says "Tonal Views of Times Tomorrow"					
❑ 10480	Aurora Boralis	1980	5.00	10.00	20.00
❑ 11179	Sleeping Beauty	1979	20.00	40.00	80.00
❑ 13088A/12988B	Hidden Fire 2	1988	5.00	10.00	20.00
❑ 13188III/12988II	Hidden Fire 1	1988	5.00	10.00	20.00
❑ 14200 A/B	Space Probe	197?	7.50	15.00	30.00
❑ 19782	Sound Mirror	1978	5.00	10.00	20.00
❑ 19783	Media Dream	1978	5.00	10.00	20.00
❑ 19841	A Fireside Chat with Lucifer	1984	5.00	10.00	20.00
❑ 19842	Celestial Love	1984	5.00	10.00	20.00
❑ 52375	What's New?	1975	6.25	12.50	25.00
❑ 61674	Out Beyond the Kingdom Of	1974	10.00	20.00	40.00
❑ 72579	God Is More Than Love Can Ever Be	1979	5.00	10.00	20.00
❑ IX SR 72881	Oblique Parallax	1981	15.00	30.00	60.00
❑ 77771	Nidhamu	197?	6.25	12.50	25.00
❑ 81774	The Antique Blacks	1974	10.00	20.00	40.00
❑ MS 87976 [(2)]	Live at Montreux	1976	12.50	25.00	50.00
❑ 91379	Omniverse	1979	15.00	30.00	60.00
❑ 91780	Voice of the Eternal Tomorrow	1980	5.00	10.00	20.00
❑ 92074	Sub Underground	1974	10.00	20.00	40.00
❑ KH-98766 [M]	Other Planes of There	1966	20.00	40.00	80.00
-- Red label					
❑ 101477	Some Blues But Not the Kind That's Blue	1977	5.00	10.00	20.00
❑ 101185	Hiroshima	1985	5.00	10.00	20.00
❑ 101485	When Spaceships Appear	1985	5.00	10.00	20.00
❑ 101679	On Jupiter	1979	5.00	10.00	20.00
-- "El Saturn" label					
❑ 123180	Beyond the Purple Star Zone	1981	5.00	10.00	20.00
❑ 1014077	Some Blues But Not the Kind That's Blue	1977	6.25	12.50	25.00
❑ 1217718	Horizon	1974	5.00	10.00	20.00
❑ IX/1983220	Ra to the Rescue	1983	10.00	20.00	40.00
❑ 9121385	Outer Reach Intensity-Energy	1985	6.25	12.50	25.00
SATURN/RECOMMENDED					
❑ SRRD-1	Cosmo Sun Connection	1985	5.00	10.00	20.00
SAVOY					
❑ MG-12169 [M]	The Futuristic Sounds of Sun Ra	1961	20.00	40.00	80.00
SAVOY JAZZ					
❑ SJL-1141	We Are in the Future	198?	3.00	6.00	12.00
SHANDAR					
❑ SR 10.001	Nuits de la Fondation Maeght Volume I	1971	10.00	20.00	40.00
❑ SR 10.003	Nuits de la Fondation Maeght Volume II	1971	10.00	20.00	40.00
SWEET EARTH					
❑ SER 1003	The Other Side of the Sun	1979	5.00	10.00	20.00
THOTH INTERGALACTIC					
❑ LPB-711 [M]	The Magic City	1969	7.50	15.00	30.00
❑ IR-1972	The Night of the Purple Moon	1970	7.50	15.00	30.00
❑ KH-1272	Live in Egypt 1	1973	7.50	15.00	30.00
❑ KH-2772 [S]	Cosmic Tones for Mental Therapy	1969	7.50	15.00	30.00
❑ KH-5472 [M]	Strange Strings	196?	10.00	20.00	40.00
❑ 7771	Nidhamu	197?	7.50	15.00	30.00
❑ KH-98766 [M]	Other Planes of There	1969	10.00	20.00	40.00
TOTAL ENERGY					
❑ NER 3021	Outer Space Employment Agency	1999	3.00	6.00	12.00
❑ NER 3026	Life Is Beautiful	1999	2.50	5.00	10.00

Number	Title	Yr	VG	VG+	NM
TRANSITION					
❑ TLP-10 [M]	Jazz by Sun Ra	1957	62.50	125.00	250.00
-- With booklet (deduct 1/5 if missing)					

SUNDBOM, LARS "SUMPEN"
Trumpeter.
GHB
| ❑ GHB-148 | Hemma Hos Sumpen | 1979 | 2.50 | 5.00 | 10.00 |

SUNKEL, PHIL
Trumpeter, cornet player and composer.
ABC-PARAMOUNT
❑ ABC-136 [M]	Jazz Band	1956	20.00	40.00	80.00
❑ ABC-225 [M]	Gerry Mulligan and Bob Brookmeyer Play Phil Sunkel's Jazz Concerto Grosso	1958	12.50	25.00	50.00
❑ ABCS-225 [S]	Gerry Mulligan and Bob Brookmeyer Play Phil Sunkel's Jazz Concerto Grosso	1958	10.00	20.00	40.00

SUNSHINE, MONTY
Clarinet player best known for his playing on the CHRIS BARBER hit "Petite Fleur."
STOMP OFF
| ❑ SOS-1110 | New Orleans Hula | 1986 | 2.50 | 5.00 | 10.00 |

SUPERBLUE
Members at the time of the below LP: Don Sickler (trumpet); Roy Hargrove (trumpet); Frank Lacy (trombone); Bobby Watson (alto sax); Billy Pierce (tenor sax); Mulgrew Miller (piano); Bob Hurst (bass); Kenny Washington (drums).
BLUE NOTE
| ❑ B1-91731 | Superblue | 1989 | 3.75 | 7.50 | 15.00 |

SUPERSAX
Formed by Buddy Clark and MED FLORY. The band's premise was to arrange CHARLIE PARKER solos for a band.
CAPITOL
❑ ST-11177	Supersax Plays Bird	1973	2.50	5.00	10.00
❑ ST-11271	Supersax Plays Bird, Volume 2/ Salt Peanuts	1974	2.50	5.00	10.00
❑ ST-11371	Supersax Plays Bird with Strings	1975	2.50	5.00	10.00
COLUMBIA					
❑ FC 39140	Supersax and L.A. Voices	1984	2.50	5.00	10.00
❑ FC 39925	Supersax and L.A. Voices, Vol. 2	1985	2.50	5.00	10.00
❑ FC 44436	Stone Bird	1989	3.00	6.00	12.00
MOBILE FIDELITY					
❑ 1-511	Supersax Plays Bird	1981	10.00	20.00	40.00
-- Audiophile vinyl					
PAUSA					
❑ 7038	Chasin' the Bird	1977	2.50	5.00	10.00
❑ 7082	Dynamite!	1979	2.50	5.00	10.00
❑ 9028	Supersax Plays Bird, Volume 2/ Salt Peanuts	198?	2.00	4.00	8.00

SURMAN, JOHN
Saxophone player, clarinetist, keyboard player and percussionist.
ANTILLES
❑ AN-7004	Morning Glory	197?	3.00	6.00	12.00
ECM					
❑ 1148	Reflection	197?	3.00	6.00	12.00
❑ 1193	The Amazing Adventures of Simon Simon	1981	3.00	6.00	12.00
❑ 1295	Withholding Pattern	1986	3.00	6.00	12.00
❑ 23795	Such Winters of Memory	1983	2.50	5.00	10.00

SUSSMAN, RICHARD
Pianist and keyboard player.
INNER CITY
| ❑ IC-1045 | Free Fall | 1978 | 3.00 | 6.00 | 12.00 |
| ❑ IC-1068 | Tributaries | 1979 | 3.00 | 6.00 | 12.00 |

SUTTON, DICK
Trumpeter, composer and bandleader.
JAGUAR
| ❑ JP-802 [10] | Jazz Idiom | 1954 | 20.00 | 40.00 | 80.00 |
| ❑ JP-804 [10] | Progressive Dixieland | 1954 | 20.00 | 40.00 | 80.00 |

SUTTON, RALPH
Pianist.
ANALOGUE PRODUCTIONS
❑ AP 018	Partners in Crime	199?	6.25	12.50	25.00
-- Audiophile vinyl					
AUDIOPHILE					
❑ AP-163	Off the Cuff	198?	2.50	5.00	10.00

Number	Title	Yr	VG	VG+	NM
CIRCLE					
❏ L-413 [10]	Ralph Sutton	1951	20.00	40.00	80.00
COLUMBIA					
❏ CL 6140 [10]	Piano Moods	1950	20.00	40.00	80.00
COMMODORE					
❏ XFL-16570	Bix Beiderbecke Suite and Jazz Portraits	198?	2.50	5.00	10.00
❏ FL-30001 [M]	Ralph Sutton	1951	20.00	40.00	80.00
DECCA					
❏ DL 5498 [10]	I Got Rhythm	1953	20.00	40.00	80.00
DOWN HOME					
❏ MGD-4 [M]	Backroom Piano: The Ragtime Piano of Ralph Sutton	1955	15.00	30.00	60.00
❏ DH-1003 [10]	Ragtime Piano Solos	1953	20.00	40.00	80.00
HARMONY					
❏ HL 7109 [M]	Tribute to Fats	1958	5.00	10.00	20.00
JAZZ ARCHIVES					
❏ JA-45	Ralph Sutton and the All-Stars	198?	2.50	5.00	10.00
OMEGA					
❏ OML-51 [M]	Jazz At the Olympics	196?	3.75	7.50	15.00
❏ OSL-51 [S]	Jazz At the Olympics	196?	5.00	10.00	20.00
PROJECT 3					
❏ PR 5040 SD	Knocked Out Nocturne	1969	3.00	6.00	12.00
RIVERSIDE					
❏ RLP 12-212 [M]	Classic Jazz Piano	1956	15.00	30.00	60.00
ROULETTE					
❏ R-25232 [M]	Ragtime, U.S.A.	1963	3.75	7.50	15.00
❏ SR-25232 [S]	Ragtime, U.S.A.	1963	5.00	10.00	20.00
SACKVILLE					
❏ 2012	Piano Solos	198?	2.50	5.00	10.00
STORYVILLE					
❏ 4013	Ralph Sutton Quartet	198?	2.50	5.00	10.00
VERVE					
❏ MGV-1004 [M]	Backroom Piano: The Ragtime Piano of Ralph Sutton	1956	12.50	25.00	50.00

SVENSSON, REINHOLD
Pianist, organist and composer.

Number	Title	Yr	VG	VG+	NM
PRESTIGE					
❏ PRLP-106 [10]	Reinhold Svensson Piano	1951	50.00	100.00	200.00
❏ PRLP-129 [10]	Reinhold Svensson, Volume 2: Favorites	1952	50.00	100.00	200.00
❏ PRLP-155 [10]	New Sounds from Sweden, Volume 8	1953	50.00	100.00	200.00

SVENSSON, REINHOLD/BENGT HALLBERG
Also see each artist's individual listings.

Number	Title	Yr	VG	VG+	NM
PRESTIGE					
❏ PRLP-174 [10]	Piano Moderns	1953	50.00	100.00	200.00

SWALLOW, STEVE
Bass player.

Number	Title	Yr	VG	VG+	NM
ECM					
❏ 1160	Home	1979	3.00	6.00	12.00

SWANSON, RIC

Number	Title	Yr	VG	VG+	NM
AMERICAN GRAMAPHONE					
❏ AG-600	Urban Surrender	1985	2.50	5.00	10.00
OPTIMISM					
❏ OP-3220	Renewal	198?	3.00	6.00	12.00

SWARTZ, HARVIE
Bass player.

Number	Title	Yr	VG	VG+	NM
GRAMAVISION					
❏ 8202	Underneath It All	198?	2.50	5.00	10.00
❏ 18-8503-1	Urban Earth	1986	2.50	5.00	10.00

SWEDES FROM JAZZVILLE
Among the members: REINHOLD SVENSSON and ARNE DOMNERUS.

Number	Title	Yr	VG	VG+	NM
EPIC					
❏ LN 3309 [M]	Swedes from Jazzville	195?	12.50	25.00	50.00

SWEDISH JAZZ KINGS, THE
Formed by Tomas Ornberg (clarinet, soprano sax) in 1985.

Number	Title	Yr	VG	VG+	NM
STOMP OFF					
❏ SOS-1122	What Makes Me Love You So?	1986	2.50	5.00	10.00
❏ SOS-1188	After Midnight	1987	2.50	5.00	10.00

SWEET EMMA
See EMMA BARRETT.

SWIFT, DUNCAN
Pianist.

Number	Title	Yr	VG	VG+	NM
BLACK LION					
❏ 301	Piano Ragtime: Joplin and Morton	197?	3.00	6.00	12.00

SWINGING SWEDES, THE

Number	Title	Yr	VG	VG+	NM
TELEFUNKEN					
❏ LGX-66050 [M]	The Swinging Swedes	195?	12.50	25.00	50.00

SWINGING SWEDES, THE/THE COOL BRITONS

Number	Title	Yr	VG	VG+	NM
BLUE NOTE					
❏ BLP-5019 [10]	New Sounds from the Olde World	1951	75.00	150.00	300.00

SWINGLE SINGERS, THE
Formed by Ward Swingle of THE DOUBLE SIX OF PARIS. The basic premise was to take scat singing and apply it to classical works. Original members: Jean-Claude Briodin, Anne Germain, Jean Cussac, Claudine Meunier, Claude Germain, Christiane Legrand, Ward Swingle, Jeanette Baucomont. Many changes since.

Number	Title	Yr	VG	VG+	NM
COLUMBIA					
❏ PC 34194	Rags and All That Jazz	1976	2.50	5.00	10.00
COLUMBIA MASTERWORKS					
❏ M 33013	Love Songs for Madrigals and Madriguys	1976	2.50	5.00	10.00
MMG					
❏ 1115	Swingle Skyliner	198?	2.00	4.00	8.00
❏ 1125	Folio	198?	2.00	4.00	8.00
PHILIPS					
❏ PHS 2-5400 [(2)]	Bachanalia	1972	3.00	6.00	12.00
-- *Reissue of 600-197 and 600-126 in same package*					
❏ PHM 200-097 [M]	Bach's Greatest Hits	1963	2.50	5.00	10.00
❏ PHM 200-126 [M]	Going Baroque	1964	2.50	5.00	10.00
❏ PHM 200-149 [M]	Anyone for Mozart?	1965	2.50	5.00	10.00
❏ PHM 200-191 [M]	Getting Romantic	1965	2.50	5.00	10.00
❏ PHM 200-214 [M]	Rococo A-Go-Go	1966	2.50	5.00	10.00
❏ PHM 200-225 [M]	Encounter	1966	3.00	6.00	12.00
-- *With the Modern Jazz Quartet*					
❏ PHM 200-261 [M]	Spanish Masters	1967	2.50	5.00	10.00
❏ PHS 600-097 [S]	Bach's Greatest Hits	1963	3.00	6.00	12.00
❏ PHS 600-126 [S]	Going Baroque	1964	3.00	6.00	12.00
❏ PHS 600-149 [S]	Anyone for Mozart?	1965	3.00	6.00	12.00
❏ PHS 600-191 [S]	Getting Romantic	1965	3.00	6.00	12.00
❏ PHS 600-214 [S]	Rococo A-Go-Go	1966	3.00	6.00	12.00
❏ PHS 600-225 [S]	Encounter	1966	3.75	7.50	15.00
-- *With the Modern Jazz Quartet*					
❏ PHS 600-261 [S]	Spanish Masters	1967	3.00	6.00	12.00
❏ PHS 600-288	Back to Bach	1968	2.50	5.00	10.00
❏ PHS 700-004	The Joy of Singing	1973	2.50	5.00	10.00
❏ 824 544-1	Jazz Sebastian Bach	1985	2.00	4.00	8.00
❏ 824 545-1	Place Vendome	1985	2.00	4.00	8.00
-- *With the Modern Jazz Quartet; reissue of 600-225*					

SYMPHONY JAZZ ENSEMBLE

Number	Title	Yr	VG	VG+	NM
QCA					
❏ 364	Carmen	197?	3.75	7.50	15.00
❏ 378	Eastside Corridor	197?	3.75	7.50	15.00

SYMS, SYLVIA
Female singer.

Number	Title	Yr	VG	VG+	NM
ATLANTIC					
❏ ALS-137 [10]	Songs by Sylvia Syms	1952	25.00	50.00	100.00
❏ 1243 [M]	Songs by Sylvia Syms	1956	12.50	25.00	50.00
-- *Black label*					
❏ 1243 [M]	Songs by Sylvia Syms	1960	6.25	12.50	25.00
-- *Multicolor label, white "fan" logo at right*					
COLUMBIA					
❏ CL 1447 [M]	Torch Song	1960	7.50	15.00	30.00
-- *Red and black label with six "eye" logos*					
❏ CS 8243 [S]	Torch Song	1960	10.00	20.00	40.00
-- *Red and black label with six "eye" logos*					
DECCA					
❏ DL 8188 [M]	Sylvia Syms Sings	1955	12.50	25.00	50.00
-- *Black label, silver print*					
❏ DL 8639 [M]	Songs of Love	1958	10.00	20.00	40.00
-- *Black label, silver print*					
KAPP					
❏ KL-1236 [M]	That Man -- Love Songs to Frank Sinatra	1961	7.50	15.00	30.00
❏ KS-3236 [S]	That Man -- Love Songs to Frank Sinatra	1961	10.00	20.00	40.00
MOVIETONE					
❏ 2022 [M]	In a Sentimental Mood	1967	5.00	10.00	20.00

Number	Title	Yr	VG	VG+	NM		Number	Title	Yr	VG	VG+	NM
❏ 72022 [S]	In a Sentimental Mood	1967	3.75	7.50	15.00		**SZAKCSI**					
PRESTIGE							Pianist.					
❏ PRLP-7439 [M]	Sylvia Is!	1965	5.00	10.00	20.00		**GRP**					
❏ PRST-7439 [S]	Sylvia Is!	1965	6.25	12.50	25.00		❏ GR-1045	Sa-chi	1988	2.50	5.00	10.00
❏ PRLP-7489 [M]	For Once in My Life	1967	6.25	12.50	25.00		❏ GR-9577	Mystic Dreams	1989	3.00	6.00	12.00
❏ PRST-7489 [S]	For Once in My Life	1967	5.00	10.00	20.00							
20TH CENTURY FOX							**SZOBEL, HERMANN**					
❏ TFM-4123 [M]	The Fabulous Sylvia Syms	1963	6.25	12.50	25.00		**ARISTA**					
❏ TFS-4123 [S]	The Fabulous Sylvia Syms	1963	7.50	15.00	30.00		❏ AL 4058	Szobel	1976	3.00	6.00	12.00
VERSION												
❏ VLP-103 [10]	After Dark	1954	20.00	40.00	80.00							

SYNTHESIS
CHIAROSCURO

Number	Title	Yr	VG	VG+	NM
❏ 172	Six by Six	197?	3.00	6.00	12.00

SZABO, GABOR
Guitarist.
ABC IMPULSE!

Number	Title	Yr	VG	VG+	NM
❏ AS-9105	Gypsy 66	1968	3.00	6.00	12.00
❏ AS-9123	Spellbinder	1968	3.00	6.00	12.00
❏ AS-9128	Jazz Raga	1968	3.00	6.00	12.00
❏ AS-9146	The Sorcerer	1968	3.00	6.00	12.00
❏ AS-9151	Wind, Sky and Diamonds	1968	3.75	7.50	15.00
❏ AS-9159	Light My Fire	1968	3.75	7.50	15.00
❏ AS-9167	More Sorcery	1968	3.75	7.50	15.00
❏ AS-9173	The Best of Gabor Szabo	1968	3.75	7.50	15.00
❏ AS-9204 [(2)]	His Great Hits	1971	3.75	7.50	15.00

BLUE THUMB

Number	Title	Yr	VG	VG+	NM
❏ BTS-28	High Contrast	1972	3.00	6.00	12.00
-- With Bobby Womack					
❏ 6014	Live	1974	3.00	6.00	12.00
❏ BTS-8823	Magical Connection	1971	3.00	6.00	12.00

BUDDAH

Number	Title	Yr	VG	VG+	NM
❏ 18-SK	Watch What Happens	1970	3.00	6.00	12.00
❏ 20-SK	Blowin' Some Old Smoke	1971	3.00	6.00	12.00

CTI

Number	Title	Yr	VG	VG+	NM
❏ 6026	Mizrab	1973	3.00	6.00	12.00
❏ 6035	Rambler	1974	3.00	6.00	12.00

GRP/IMPULSE!

Number	Title	Yr	VG	VG+	NM
❏ IMP-211	The Sorcerer	199?	3.75	7.50	15.00
-- Reissue on audiophile vinyl					

IMPULSE!

Number	Title	Yr	VG	VG+	NM
❏ A-9105 [M]	Gypsy 66	1966	5.00	10.00	20.00
❏ AS-9105 [S]	Gypsy 66	1966	6.25	12.50	25.00
❏ A-9123 [M]	Spellbinder	1966	5.00	10.00	20.00
❏ AS-9123 [S]	Spellbinder	1966	6.25	12.50	25.00
❏ A-9128 [M]	Jazz Raga	1967	6.25	12.50	25.00
❏ AS-9128 [S]	Jazz Raga	1967	5.00	10.00	20.00
❏ A-9146 [M]	The Sorcerer	1967	6.25	12.50	25.00
❏ AS-9146 [S]	The Sorcerer	1967	5.00	10.00	20.00
❏ AS-9151	Wind, Sky and Diamonds	1968	6.25	12.50	25.00
-- This exists on the pre-ABC Impulse! label, though theoretically it shouldn't					

MCA

Number	Title	Yr	VG	VG+	NM
❏ 4155 [(2)]	His Great Hits	198?	3.00	6.00	12.00

MERCURY

Number	Title	Yr	VG	VG+	NM
❏ SRM-1-1091	Nightflight	1976	2.50	5.00	10.00
❏ SRM-1-1141	Faces	1976	2.50	5.00	10.00

PEPITA

Number	Title	Yr	VG	VG+	NM
❏ 707	Femme Fatale	198?	2.50	5.00	10.00

SALVATION

Number	Title	Yr	VG	VG+	NM
❏ 704	Macho	1975	3.00	6.00	12.00

SKYE

Number	Title	Yr	VG	VG+	NM
❏ SK-3	Bacchanal	1968	3.75	7.50	15.00
❏ SK-7	Dreams	1969	3.75	7.50	15.00
❏ SK-9	Gabor Szabo 1969	1969	3.75	7.50	15.00
❏ SK-15	Lena & Gabor	1970	3.75	7.50	15.00
-- With Lena Horne					

SZABO, RICH
Trumpeter.
BBW

Number	Title	Yr	VG	VG+	NM
❏ 2001	Best of Both Worlds	198?	3.00	6.00	12.00

SZAJNER, BOB
RMS

Number	Title	Yr	VG	VG+	NM
❏ 77003	Sound Ideas	198?	3.00	6.00	12.00
❏ 77004	Afterthoughts	198?	3.00	6.00	12.00

SEEDS & STEMS

Number	Title	Yr	VG	VG+	NM
❏ SSH-7802	Jazz Opus 20/40	1979	3.00	6.00	12.00

Number	Title	Yr	VG	VG+	NM

T

T-SQUARE
Japanese fusion group: Masahiro Andoh (guitars); Takeshi Itoh (saxophones); Hirotaka Izumi (piano, keyboards); Hiroyuke Noritake (drums); Mitsuru Sutoh (bass).
PORTRAIT
| ❏ FR 44193 | Truth | 1988 | 2.50 | 5.00 | 10.00 |

TABACKIN, LEW
Saxophone player and flutist.
INNER CITY
❏ IC-1028	Dual Nature	1976	3.00	6.00	12.00
❏ IC-1038	Tabackin	1977	3.00	6.00	12.00
❏ IC-6048	Tenor Gladness	197?	3.75	7.50	15.00
❏ IC-6052	Rites of Pan	197?	3.75	7.50	15.00
JAM
| ❏ 5005 | Black and Tan Fantasy | 198? | 3.00 | 6.00 | 12.00 |

TABOR, ERON
Male singer.
STUDIO ONE
| ❏ S-104 | Eron Tabor | 196? | 5.00 | 10.00 | 20.00 |

TACUMA, JAMAALADEEN
Bass player.
GRAMAVISION
❏ GR-8301	Showstopper	1983	3.00	6.00	12.00
❏ GR-8308	Renaissance Man	1984	2.50	5.00	10.00
❏ 18-860?	Music World	1986	2.50	5.00	10.00
❏ 18-8803	Jukebox	1988	2.50	5.00	10.00

TAILGATE RAMBLERS, THE
Members: Wild Bill Davison; Bruce Gerletti; John McDonald; Bob Butler; Eddie Collins; Jim Joseph; Frank Foguth.
JAZZOLOGY
| ❏ J-32 | Pause | 1968 | 3.00 | 6.00 | 12.00 |
| ❏ J-43 | Swing | 197? | 3.00 | 6.00 | 12.00 |

TALBERT, THOMAS (TOM)
Pianist, composer and arranger.
ATLANTIC
❏ 1250 [M]	Bix Fats Duke Interpreted by Thomas Talbert	1957	10.00	20.00	40.00
-- Black label					
❏ 1250 [M]	Bix Fats Duke Interpreted by Thomas Talbert	1961	5.00	10.00	20.00
-- Multicolor label, white "fan" logo at right					
❏ SD 1250 [S]	Bix Fats Duke Interpreted by Thomas Talbert	1958	10.00	20.00	40.00
-- Green label					
❏ SD 1250 [S]	Bix Fats Duke Interpreted by Thomas Talbert	1961	5.00	10.00	20.00
-- Multicolor label, white "fan" logo at right					
SEA BREEZE
| ❏ SB-2038 | Things As They Are | 198? | 2.50 | 5.00 | 10.00 |

TAMBA FOUR, THE
A&M
| ❏ SP-3004 | We and the Sea | 1968 | 5.00 | 10.00 | 20.00 |
| ❏ SP-3013 | Samba Blim | 1969 | 5.00 | 10.00 | 20.00 |

TAPSCOTT, HORACE
Pianist and composer.
FLYING DUTCHMAN
| ❏ FDS-107 | The Giant Is Awakened | 1969 | 5.00 | 10.00 | 20.00 |
| ❏ FD-10107 | The Giant Is Awakened | 197? | 3.75 | 7.50 | 15.00 |
INTERPLAY
| ❏ 7714 | Songs of the Unsung | 197? | 3.00 | 6.00 | 12.00 |
| ❏ 7724 | Horace Tapscott in New York | 197? | 3.00 | 6.00 | 12.00 |

TARIKA BLUE
CHIAROSCURO
| ❏ 141 | Blue Path | 197? | 3.75 | 7.50 | 15.00 |

TATE, BUDDY
Tenor saxophone and clarinet player. Also see BUCK CLAYTON.
BASF
| ❏ 20740 | Unbroken | 197? | 3.75 | 7.50 | 15.00 |

BLACK LION
| ❏ 312 | Kansas City Woman | 197? | 3.75 | 7.50 | 15.00 |
CHIAROSCURO
| ❏ 123 | Buddy Tate and His Buddies | 1973 | 3.75 | 7.50 | 15.00 |
CONCORD JAZZ
| ❏ CJ-163 | The Great Buddy Tate | 1981 | 2.50 | 5.00 | 10.00 |
FANTASY
| ❏ OJC-184 | Tate-a-Tate | 1985 | 2.50 | 5.00 | 10.00 |
FELSTED
| ❏ 2004 [S] | Swinging Like Tate | 1958 | 20.00 | 40.00 | 80.00 |
| ❏ 7004 [M] | Swinging Like Tate | 1958 | 20.00 | 40.00 | 80.00 |
MASTER JAZZ
| ❏ 8127 | Swinging Like Tate | 197? | 3.00 | 6.00 | 12.00 |
| ❏ 8128 | Texas Twister | 197? | 3.00 | 6.00 | 12.00 |
MUSE
| ❏ MR-5198 | Buddy Tate and the Muse All-Stars Live at Sandy's | 1979 | 2.50 | 5.00 | 10.00 |
| ❏ MR-5249 | Hard Blowin': Live at Sandy's | 198? | 2.50 | 5.00 | 10.00 |
PAUSA
| ❏ 7030 | Unbroken | 198? | 2.50 | 5.00 | 10.00 |
SACKVILLE
❏ 3017	Sherman Shuffle	198?	2.50	5.00	10.00
❏ 3027	Buddy Tate Quartet	198?	2.50	5.00	10.00
❏ 3034	The Ballad of Artistry	198?	2.50	5.00	10.00
SWINGVILLE
❏ SVLP-2003 [M]	Tate's Date	1960	12.50	25.00	50.00
-- Purple label					
❏ SVLP-2003 [M]	Tate's Date	1965	6.25	12.50	25.00
-- Blue label, trident logo at right					
❏ SVLP-2014 [M]	Tate-A-Tate	1960	12.50	25.00	50.00
-- Purple label					
❏ SVLP-2014 [M]	Tate-A-Tate	1965	6.25	12.50	25.00
-- Blue label, trident logo at right					
❏ SVLP-2029 [M]	Groovin' with Buddy Tate	1961	12.50	25.00	50.00
-- Purple label					
❏ SVLP-2029 [M]	Groovin' with Buddy Tate	1965	6.25	12.50	25.00
-- Blue label, trident logo at right					

TATE, BUDDY, AND DOLLAR BRAND
Also see ABDULLAH IBRAHIM; BUDDY TATE.
CHIAROSCURO
| ❏ 165 | Buddy Tate and Dollar Brand | 1977 | 3.00 | 6.00 | 12.00 |

TATE, GRADY
Drummer and percussionist.
ABC IMPULSE!
| ❏ ASD-9330 | The Master | 197? | 3.00 | 6.00 | 12.00 |
BUDDAH
| ❏ BDS-5623 | By Special Request | 1973 | 3.00 | 6.00 | 12.00 |
JANUS
| ❏ 3050 | She Is My Lady | 197? | 3.00 | 6.00 | 12.00 |
| ❏ 7010 | Movin' Day | 197? | 3.00 | 6.00 | 12.00 |
SKYE
❏ SK-4	Windmills of My Mind	1969	5.00	10.00	20.00
❏ SK-17	After the Long Ride Home	197?	3.75	7.50	15.00
❏ SK-1007	Feeling Life	197?	3.75	7.50	15.00

TATRO, DUANE
Saxophone player, arranger and composer.
CONTEMPORARY
| ❏ C-3514 [M] | Jazz for Moderns | 1956 | 20.00 | 40.00 | 80.00 |

TATUM, ART
Pianist. Also see LIONEL HAMPTON; ZUTTY SINGLETON.
AIRCHECK
| ❏ 21 | Radio Broadcasts | 197? | 2.50 | 5.00 | 10.00 |
ASCH
| ❏ ALP-356 [10] | Art Tatum | 1950 | 37.50 | 75.00 | 150.00 |
AUDIOPHILE
| ❏ AP-88 | The Remarkable Art Tatum | 198? | 2.50 | 5.00 | 10.00 |
BRUNSWICK
❏ BL 54004 [M]	Here's Art Tatum	1955	30.00	60.00	120.00
❏ BL 58013 [10]	Art Tatum Trio	1950	25.00	50.00	100.00
❏ BL 58023 [10]	Art Tatum Piano Solos	1950	25.00	50.00	100.00
CAPITOL
❏ H 216 [10]	Art Tatum	1950	25.00	50.00	100.00
❏ T 216 [M]	Art Tatum	1955	20.00	40.00	80.00
❏ H 269 [10]	Art Tatum Encores	1951	25.00	50.00	100.00
❏ H 408 [10]	Art Tatum Trio	1953	25.00	50.00	100.00
❏ M-11028	Art Tatum	1972	3.00	6.00	12.00

Number	Title	Yr	VG	VG+	NM
CLEF					
❏ (no #) [(4) M]	Art Tatum	1954	75.00	150.00	300.00
-- Boxed set with volumes 2, 3, 4 and 5 of The Genius of Art Tatum					
❏ MGC-612 [M]	The Genius of Art Tatum #1	1954	20.00	40.00	80.00
❏ MGC-613 [M]	The Genius of Art Tatum #2	1954	20.00	40.00	80.00
❏ MGC-614 [M]	The Genius of Art Tatum #3	1954	20.00	40.00	80.00
❏ MGC-615 [M]	The Genius of Art Tatum #4	1954	20.00	40.00	80.00
❏ MGC-616 [M]	The Genius of Art Tatum	1954	---	---	---
-- Canceled					
❏ MGC-617 [M]	The Genius of Art Tatum	1954	---	---	---
❏ MGC-618 [M]	The Genius of Art Tatum #5	1954	20.00	40.00	80.00
❏ MGC-619 [M]	The Genius of Art Tatum	1954	---	---	---
-- Canceled					
❏ MGC-620 [M]	The Genius of Art Tatum	1954	---	---	---
-- Canceled					
❏ MGC-621 [M]	The Genius of Art Tatum	1954	---	---	---
-- Canceled					
❏ MGC-657 [M]	The Genius of Art Tatum #6	1955	20.00	40.00	80.00
❏ MGC-658 [M]	The Genius of Art Tatum #7	1955	20.00	40.00	80.00
❏ MGC-659 [M]	The Genius of Art Tatum #8	1955	20.00	40.00	80.00
❏ MGC-660 [M]	The Genius of Art Tatum #9	1955	20.00	40.00	80.00
❏ MGC-661 [M]	The Genius of Art Tatum #10	1955	20.00	40.00	80.00
❏ MGC-712 [M]	The Genius of Art Tatum #11	1956	20.00	40.00	80.00
❏ MGC-741 [M]	The Art Tatum Trio	1955	---	---	---
-- Canceled					
❏ MGC-746 [M]	Presenting the Art Tatum Trio	1955	---		---
-- Canceled					
CMS/SAGA					
❏ 6915	The Rarest Solos	197?	2.50	5.00	10.00
COLUMBIA					
❏ GL 101 [10]	Gene Norman Concert at Shrine Auditorium, May 1949	1952	37.50	75.00	150.00
❏ CL 2565 [10]	The Tatum Touch	1956	12.50	25.00	50.00
❏ CL 6301 [10]	An Art Tatum Concert	1954	20.00	40.00	80.00
❏ CS 9655	Piano Starts Here	1968	5.00	10.00	20.00
-- Red "360 Sound" label					
❏ CS 9655	Piano Starts Here	1971	2.50	5.00	10.00
-- Orange label					
❏ PC 9655	Piano Starts Here	198?	2.00	4.00	8.00
-- Reissue with new prefix					
DECCA					
❏ DL 5086 [10]	Art Tatum Piano Solos	1950	30.00	60.00	120.00
❏ DL 8715 [M]	The Art of Tatum	1958	12.50	25.00	50.00
DIAL					
❏ LP-206 [10]	Art Tatum Trio	1950	62.50	125.00	250.00
EMARCY					
❏ 826 129-1 [(2)]	20th Century Piano Genius	1986	3.00	6.00	12.00
FOLKWAYS					
❏ FL-33 [10]	Art Tatum Trio	1951	20.00	40.00	80.00
❏ F-12293	Footnotes to Jazz	197?	3.00	6.00	12.00
GNP CRESCENDO					
❏ GNP-9025	Art Tatum at the Crescendo, Vol. 1	197?	2.50	5.00	10.00
❏ GNP-9026	Art Tatum at the Crescendo, Vol. 2	197?	2.50	5.00	10.00
HARMONY					
❏ HL 7006 [M]	An Art Tatum Concert	1957	6.25	12.50	25.00
JAZZ MAN					
❏ 5024	The Genius	198?	2.50	5.00	10.00
❏ 5030	Get Happy	198?	2.50	5.00	10.00
JAZZZ					
❏ 101	Works of Art	197?	3.00	6.00	12.00
MCA					
❏ 4019 [(2)]	Tatum Masterpieces	197?	3.00	6.00	12.00
❏ 42327	Solos	1990	3.00	6.00	12.00
MOVIETONE					
❏ 2021 [M]	The Legendary Art Tatum	1967	3.75	7.50	15.00
❏ 72021 [R]	The Legendary Art Tatum	1967	3.00	6.00	12.00
ONYX					
❏ 205	God Is in the House	197?	3.00	6.00	12.00
PABLO					
❏ 2310 720	The Tatum Group Masterpieces with Lionel Hampton, Buddy Rich	197?	2.50	5.00	10.00
❏ 2310 723	The Tatum Solo Masterpieces, Vol. 1	197?	2.50	5.00	10.00
❏ 2310 729	The Tatum Solo Masterpieces, Vol. 2	197?	2.50	5.00	10.00
❏ 2310 730	The Tatum Solo Masterpieces, Vol. 3	197?	2.50	5.00	10.00
❏ 2310 731	The Tatum Group Masterpieces with Lionel Hampton, Sweets Edison, Barney Kessel	197?	2.50	5.00	10.00

Number	Title	Yr	VG	VG+	NM
❏ 2310 732	The Tatum Group Masterpieces with Benny Carter, Vol. 1	197?	2.50	5.00	10.00
❏ 2310 733	The Tatum Group Masterpieces with Benny Carter, Vol. 2	197?	2.50	5.00	10.00
❏ 2310 734	The Tatum Group Masterpieces with Roy Eldridge	197?	2.50	5.00	10.00
❏ 2310 735	The Tatum Group Masterpieces with Jo Jones	197?	2.50	5.00	10.00
❏ 2310 736	The Tatum Group Masterpieces with Buddy DeFranco	197?	2.50	5.00	10.00
❏ 2310 737	The Tatum Group Masterpieces with Ben Webster	197?	2.50	5.00	10.00
❏ 2310 775	The Tatum Group Masterpieces with Lionel Hampton, Buddy Rich, Vol. 2	198?	2.50	5.00	10.00
❏ 2310 789	The Tatum Solo Masterpieces, Vol. 4	197?	2.50	5.00	10.00
❏ 2310 790	The Tatum Solo Masterpieces, Vol. 5	197?	2.50	5.00	10.00
❏ 2310 791	The Tatum Solo Masterpieces, Vol. 6	197?	2.50	5.00	10.00
❏ 2310 792	The Tatum Solo Masterpieces, Vol. 7	197?	2.50	5.00	10.00
❏ 2310 793	The Tatum Solo Masterpieces, Vol. 8	198?	2.50	5.00	10.00
❏ 2310 835	The Tatum Solo Masterpieces, Vol. 9	198?	2.50	5.00	10.00
❏ 2310 862	The Tatum Solo Masterpieces, Vol. 10	198?	2.50	5.00	10.00
❏ 2310 864	The Tatum Solo Masterpieces, Vol. 11	198?	2.50	5.00	10.00
❏ 2310 870	The Tatum Solo Masterpieces, Vol. 12	198?	2.50	5.00	10.00
❏ 2310 875	The Tatum Solo Masterpieces, Vol. 13	198?	2.50	5.00	10.00
❏ 2310 887	The Best of Art Tatum	198?	2.50	5.00	10.00
❏ 2405 418	The Best of Art Tatum	198?	2.50	5.00	10.00
❏ 2625 703 [(13)]	The Tatum Solo Masterpieces	197?	25.00	50.00	100.00
-- Box set with all 13 volumes included					
❏ 2625 706 [(8)]	The Tatum Group Masterpieces	197?	15.00	30.00	60.00
-- Boxed set with eight volumes (except 2310 775) included					
PAUSA					
❏ 9017	The Legend	198?	2.50	5.00	10.00
REMINGTON					
❏ 2 [10]	Tatum Piano	1950	25.00	50.00	100.00
STINSON					
❏ SLP-40 [10]	Art Tatum Trio	1950	37.50	75.00	150.00
❏ SLP-40 [M]	Art Tatum Solos and Trio	195?	10.00	20.00	40.00
STORYVILLE					
❏ 4108	Masters of Jazz, Vol. 8	199?	3.00	6.00	12.00
20TH CENTURY FOX					
❏ 3162 [M]	This Is Art Tatum, Volume 1	196?	3.75	7.50	15.00
❏ 3163 [M]	This Is Art Tatum, Volume 2	196?	3.75	7.50	15.00
❏ S-4162 [R]	This Is Art Tatum, Volume 1	196?	3.00	6.00	12.00
❏ S-4163 [R]	This Is Art Tatum, Volume 2	196?	3.00	6.00	12.00
20TH FOX					
❏ FTM-102-2 [(2) M]	Piano Discoveries	1961	7.50	15.00	30.00
❏ FTS-102-2 [(2) R]	Piano Discoveries	1961	5.00	10.00	20.00
❏ FTM-3029 [M]	Piano Discoveries Vol. I	1960	5.00	10.00	20.00
❏ FTS-3029 [R]	Piano Discoveries Vol. I	1960	3.75	7.50	15.00
❏ FTM-3033 [M]	Piano Discoveries Vol. II	1960	5.00	10.00	20.00
❏ FTS-3033 [R]	Piano Discoveries Vol. II	1960	3.75	7.50	15.00
VARESE SARABANDE					
❏ VC 81021	The Keystone Sessions	197?	3.75	7.50	15.00
VERVE					
❏ VSP-33 [M]	The Art of Art	1966	3.75	7.50	15.00
❏ VSPS-33 [R]	The Art of Art	1966	3.00	6.00	12.00
❏ MGV-8036 [M]	The Genius of Art Tatum #1	1957	12.50	25.00	50.00
❏ V-8036 [M]	The Genius of Art Tatum #1	1961	5.00	10.00	20.00
❏ MGV-8037 [M]	The Genius of Art Tatum #2	1957	12.50	25.00	50.00
❏ V-8037 [M]	The Genius of Art Tatum #2	1961	5.00	10.00	20.00
❏ MGV-8038 [M]	The Genius of Art Tatum #3	1957	12.50	25.00	50.00
❏ V-8038 [M]	The Genius of Art Tatum #3	1961	5.00	10.00	20.00
❏ MGV-8039 [M]	The Genius of Art Tatum #4	1957	12.50	25.00	50.00
❏ V-8039 [M]	The Genius of Art Tatum #4	1961	5.00	10.00	20.00
❏ MGV-8040 [M]	The Genius of Art Tatum #5	1957	12.50	25.00	50.00
❏ V-8040 [M]	The Genius of Art Tatum #5	1961	5.00	10.00	20.00
❏ MGV-8055 [M]	The Genius of Art Tatum #6	1957	12.50	25.00	50.00
❏ V-8055 [M]	The Genius of Art Tatum #6	1961	5.00	10.00	20.00
❏ MGV-8056 [M]	The Genius of Art Tatum #7	1957	12.50	25.00	50.00
❏ V-8056 [M]	The Genius of Art Tatum #7	1961	5.00	10.00	20.00
❏ MGV-8057 [M]	The Genius of Art Tatum #8	1957	12.50	25.00	50.00
❏ V-8057 [M]	The Genius of Art Tatum #8	1961	5.00	10.00	20.00
❏ MGV-8058 [M]	The Genius of Art Tatum #9	1957	12.50	25.00	50.00
❏ V-8058 [M]	The Genius of Art Tatum #9	1961	5.00	10.00	20.00
❏ MGV-8059 [M]	The Genius of Art Tatum #10	1957	12.50	25.00	50.00
❏ V-8059 [M]	The Genius of Art Tatum #10	1961	5.00	10.00	20.00

Number	Title	Yr	VG	VG+	NM
❏ MGV-8095 [M]	The Genius of Art Tatum #11	1957	12.50	25.00	50.00
❏ V-8095 [M]	The Genius of Art Tatum #11	1961	5.00	10.00	20.00
❏ MGV-8101-5 [(5) M]	Art Tatum, Volume 1	1957	50.00	100.00	200.00
-- Boxed set with volumes 1-5 of The Genius of Art Tatum					
❏ MGV-8102-5 [(5) M]	Art Tatum, Volume 2	1957	50.00	100.00	200.00
-- Boxed set with volumes 6-10 of The Genius of Art Tatum					
❏ MGV-8118 [M]	Presenting the Art Tatum Trio	1957	12.50	25.00	50.00
❏ V-8118 [M]	Presenting the Art Tatum Trio	1961	5.00	10.00	20.00
❏ MGV-8220 [M]	The Art Tatum-Ben Webster Quartet	1958	12.50	25.00	50.00
❏ V-8220 [M]	The Art Tatum-Ben Webster Quartet	1961	5.00	10.00	20.00
❏ MGV-8323 [M]	The Greatest Piano of Them All	1959	12.50	25.00	50.00
❏ V-8323 [M]	The Greatest Piano of Them All	1961	5.00	10.00	20.00
❏ MGV-8332 [M]	The Incomparable Music of Art Tatum	1959	12.50	25.00	50.00
❏ V-8332 [M]	The Incomparable Music of Art Tatum	1961	5.00	10.00	20.00
❏ MGV-8347 [M]	More of the Greatest Piano of Them All	1959	12.50	25.00	50.00
❏ V-8347 [M]	More of the Greatest Piano of Them All	1961	5.00	10.00	20.00
❏ MGV-8360 [M]	Still More of the Greatest Piano of Them All	1960	12.50	25.00	50.00
❏ V-8360 [M]	Still More of the Greatest Piano of Them All	1961	5.00	10.00	20.00
❏ V-8433 [M]	The Essential Art Tatum	1962	5.00	10.00	20.00

TATUM, ART; BENNY CARTER; LOUIS BELLSON
Also see each artist's individual listings.
CLEF

Number	Title	Yr	VG	VG+	NM
❏ MGC-643 [M]	Tatum-Carter-Bellson	1955	20.00	40.00	80.00
VERVE					
❏ MGV-8013 [M]	The Three Giants	1957	12.50	25.00	50.00
❏ V-8013 [M]	The Three Giants	1961	5.00	10.00	20.00
❏ MGV-8227 [M]	Makin' Whoopee	1958	12.50	25.00	50.00
❏ V-8227 [M]	Makin' Whoopee	1961	5.00	10.00	20.00

TATUM, ART, AND BUDDY DeFRANCO
Also see each artist's individual listings.
AMERICAN RECORDING SOCIETY

Number	Title	Yr	VG	VG+	NM
❏ G-412 [M]	The Art Tatum-Buddy DeFranco Quartet	1956	10.00	20.00	40.00
CLEF					
❏ MGC-715 [M]	The Art Tatum-Buddy DeFranco Quartet	1955	---	---	---
-- Canceled					
VERVE					
❏ MGV-8229 [M]	The Art Tatum-Buddy DeFranco Quartet	1958	12.50	25.00	50.00
❏ V-8229 [M]	The Art Tatum-Buddy DeFranco Quartet	1961	5.00	10.00	20.00

TATUM, ART; ROY ELDRIDGE; ALVIN STOLLER; JOHN SIMMONS
CLEF

Number	Title	Yr	VG	VG+	NM
❏ MGC-679 [M]	The Art Tatum-Roy Eldridge-Alvin Stoller-John Simmons Quartet	1955	30.00	60.00	120.00
VERVE					
❏ MGV-8064 [M]	The Art Tatum-Roy Eldridge-Alvin Stoller-John Simmons Quartet	1957	20.00	40.00	80.00
❏ V-8064 [M]	The Art Tatum-Roy Eldridge-Alvin Stoller-John Simmons Quartet	1961	6.25	12.50	25.00

TATUM, ART/ERROLL GARNER
Also see each artist's individual listings.
JAZZTONE

Number	Title	Yr	VG	VG+	NM
❏ J-1203 [M]	Kings of the Keyboard	1956	10.00	20.00	40.00
ROOST					
❏ LP-2213 [M]	Giants of the Piano	1956	12.50	25.00	50.00

TATUM, ART/JAMES P. JOHNSON
Also see each artist's individual listings.
MCA

Number	Title	Yr	VG	VG+	NM
❏ 4112 [(2)]	Tatum Masterpieces Vol. 2/ Johnson Plays Fats Waller	197?	3.00	6.00	12.00

TATUM, ART/MARY LOU WILLIAMS
Also see each artist's individual listings.
HALL OF FAME

Number	Title	Yr	VG	VG+	NM
❏ 607	King and Queen	197?	2.50	5.00	10.00

Number	Title	Yr	VG	VG+	NM
JAZZTONE					
❏ J-1280 [M]	The King and Queen	1958	10.00	20.00	40.00

TAYLOR, ART
Drummer. Also see LES JAZZ MODES.
BLUE NOTE

Number	Title	Yr	VG	VG+	NM
❏ BLP-4047 [M]	A.T.'s Delight	1960	20.00	40.00	80.00
-- Regular version, W. 63rd St. address on label					
❏ BLP-4047 [M]	A.T.'s Delight	1960	30.00	60.00	120.00
-- "Deep groove" version (deep indentation under label on both sides)					
❏ BST-84047 [S]	A.T.'s Delight	1960	15.00	30.00	60.00
-- W. 63rd St. address on label					
❏ BST-84047 [S]	A.T.'s Delight	1985	2.50	5.00	10.00
-- "The Finest in Jazz Since 1939" reissue					
FANTASY					
❏ OJC-094	Taylor's Wailers	198?	2.50	5.00	10.00
NEW JAZZ					
❏ NJLP-8219 [M]	Taylor's Tenors	1959	12.50	25.00	50.00
-- Purple label					
❏ NJLP-8219 [M]	Taylor's Tenors	1965	6.25	12.50	25.00
-- Blue label, trident logo at right					
PRESTIGE					
❏ PRLP-7117 [M]	Taylor's Wailers	1957	25.00	50.00	100.00

TAYLOR, BILLY
Pianist. Also see ERROLL GARNER; JOE HOLIDAY; MUNDELL LOWE.
ABC IMPULSE!

Number	Title	Yr	VG	VG+	NM
❏ AS-71 [S]	My Fair Lady Loves Jazz	1968	3.75	7.50	15.00
ABC-PARAMOUNT					
❏ ABC-112 [M]	Evergreens	1956	12.50	25.00	50.00
❏ ABC-134 [M]	Billy Taylor At the London House	1956	12.50	25.00	50.00
❏ ABC-162 [M]	Billy Taylor Introduces Ira Sullivan	1957	12.50	25.00	50.00
❏ ABC-177 [M]	My Fair Lady Loves Jazz	1957	12.50	25.00	50.00
❏ ABC-226 [M]	The New Trio	1958	12.50	25.00	50.00
❏ ABCS-226 [S]	The New Trio	1958	10.00	20.00	40.00
ARGO					
❏ LP-650 [M]	Taylor Made Flute	1959	12.50	25.00	50.00
❏ LPS-650 [S]	Taylor Made Flute	1959	10.00	20.00	40.00
ATLANTIC					
❏ ALR-113 [10]	Piano Panorama	1951	37.50	75.00	150.00
❏ 1277 [M]	The Billy Taylor Touch	1958	12.50	25.00	50.00
-- Black label					
❏ 1277 [M]	The Billy Taylor Touch	1961	6.25	12.50	25.00
-- Multicolor label, white "fan" logo at right					
❏ 1329 [M]	One for Fun	1960	12.50	25.00	50.00
-- Black label					
❏ SD 1329 [S]	One for Fun	1960	12.50	25.00	50.00
-- Green label					
BELL					
❏ S-6049	OK Billy!	1970	3.75	7.50	15.00
CAPITOL					
❏ ST 2039 [S]	Right Here, Right Now	1963	6.25	12.50	25.00
❏ T 2039 [M]	Right Here, Right Now	1963	5.00	10.00	20.00
❏ ST 2302 [S]	Midnight Piano	1965	6.25	12.50	25.00
❏ T 2302 [M]	Midnight Piano	1965	5.00	10.00	20.00
CONCORD JAZZ					
❏ CJ-145	Where've You Been	1981	2.50	5.00	10.00
FANTASY					
❏ OJC-015	The Billy Taylor Trio with Candido	1982	2.50	5.00	10.00
❏ OJC-1730	Cross Section	198?	2.50	5.00	10.00
IMPULSE!					
❏ A-71 [M]	My Fair Lady Loves Jazz	1965	5.00	10.00	20.00
❏ AS-71 [S]	My Fair Lady Loves Jazz	1965	6.25	12.50	25.00
MERCURY					
❏ MG-20722 [M]	Impromptu	1962	5.00	10.00	20.00
❏ SR-60722 [S]	Impromptu	1962	6.25	12.50	25.00
MONMOUTH-EVERGREEN					
❏ 7089	Jazz Alive	1978	3.00	6.00	12.00
MOODSVILLE					
❏ MVLP-16 [M]	Interlude	1961	12.50	25.00	50.00
-- Green label					
❏ MVLP-16 [M]	Interlude	1965	6.25	12.50	25.00
-- Blue label, trident logo at right					
NEW JAZZ					
❏ NJLP-8313 [M]	Live! At Town Hall	1963	---	---	---
-- Canceled; reassigned to Status					
PAUSA					
❏ 7096	Sleeping Bee	198?	2.50	5.00	10.00

Number	Title	Yr	VG	VG+	NM
PRESTIGE					
❏ PRLP-139 [10]	Billy Taylor Trio, Volume 1	1953	55.00	110.00	220.00
❏ PRLP-165 [10]	Billy Taylor Trio, Volume 2	1953	55.00	110.00	220.00
❏ PRLP-168 [10]	Billy Taylor Trio, Volume 3	1953	55.00	110.00	220.00
❏ PRLP-184 [10]	Billy Taylor Trio	1954	50.00	100.00	200.00
❏ PRLP-188 [10]	Billy Taylor Trio	1954	50.00	100.00	200.00
❏ PRLP-194 [10]	Billy Taylor Trio In Concert at Town Hall, December 17, 1954	1955	50.00	100.00	200.00
❏ PRLP-7001 [M]	A Touch of Taylor	1955	20.00	40.00	80.00
❏ PRLP-7015 [M]	Billy Taylor Trio, Volume 1	1956	20.00	40.00	80.00
❏ PRLP-7016 [M]	Billy Taylor Trio, Volume 2	1956	20.00	40.00	80.00
❏ PRLP-7051 [M]	The Billy Taylor Trio with Candido	1956	20.00	40.00	80.00
❏ PRLP-7071 [M]	Cross Section	1956	20.00	40.00	80.00
❏ PRLP-7093 [M]	Billy Taylor Trio at Town Hall	1957	20.00	40.00	80.00
❏ PRST-7664 [R]	A Touch of Taylor	1969	3.75	7.50	15.00
❏ PRST-7762	Today!	1970	3.75	7.50	15.00
RIVERSIDE					
❏ RLP 12-306 [M]	Billy Taylor with Four Flutes	1959	12.50	25.00	50.00
❏ RLP 12-319 [M]	Billy Taylor Trio Uptown	1960	12.50	25.00	50.00
❏ RLP 12-339 [M]	Warming Up	1960	12.50	25.00	50.00
❏ RLP-1151 [S]	Billy Taylor with Four Flutes	1959	10.00	20.00	40.00
❏ RLP-1168 [S]	Billy Taylor Trio Uptown	1960	10.00	20.00	40.00
❏ RLP-1195 [S]	Warming Up	1960	10.00	20.00	40.00
ROOST					
❏ R-406 [10]	Jazz at Storyville	1952	30.00	60.00	120.00
❏ R-409 [10]	Taylor Made Jazz	1952	30.00	60.00	120.00
SAVOY					
❏ MG-9035 [10]	Billy Taylor Piano	1953	30.00	60.00	120.00
SESAC					
❏ N-3001 [M]	Custom Taylored	1959	15.00	30.00	60.00
❏ SN-3001 [S]	Custom Taylored	1959	12.50	25.00	50.00
STATUS					
❏ ST-8313 [M]	Live! At Town Hall	1965	10.00	20.00	40.00
SURREY					
❏ S-1033 [M]	Easy Life	1966	6.25	12.50	25.00
❏ SS-1033 [S]	Easy Life	1966	7.50	15.00	30.00
TOWER					
❏ ST-5111 [S]	I Wish I Knew	1968	6.25	12.50	25.00
WEST 54					
❏ 8008	Live at Storyville	198?	3.00	6.00	12.00

TAYLOR, CECIL

Pianist and composer. Also see DONALD BYRD; JAZZ COMPOSERS ORCHESTRA.

Number	Title	Yr	VG	VG+	NM
A&M					
❏ 75021 5286 1	In Florescence	1990	3.00	6.00	12.00
AMERICAN RECORDING SOCIETY					
❏ G-437 [M]	Modern Jazz	195?	10.00	20.00	40.00
ARISTA/FREEDOM					
❏ AF 1005	Silent Tongues	1975	3.00	6.00	12.00
❏ AF 1038	Indent	197?	3.00	6.00	12.00
❏ AF 1905 [(2)]	Nefertiti	197?	3.75	7.50	15.00
BARNABY					
❏ Z 30562	Cecil Taylor Quartet	1971	3.75	7.50	15.00
❏ KZ 31035	New York City R&B	1972	3.75	7.50	15.00
BLUE NOTE					
❏ BN-LA458-H2 [(2)]	In Transition	197?	3.75	7.50	15.00
❏ BLP-4237 [M]	Unit Structures	1966	6.25	12.50	25.00
❏ BLP-4260 [M]	Conquistador	1967	7.50	15.00	30.00
❏ RST-84237 [S]	Unit Structures	1966	7.50	15.00	30.00
-- With "New York, USA" on label					
❏ BST-84237 [S]	Unit Structures	1967	3.75	7.50	15.00
-- With "A Division of Liberty Records" on label					
❏ B1-84260 [S]	Conquistador	1989	3.00	6.00	12.00
-- "The Finest in Jazz Since 1939" reissue					
❏ BST-84260 [S]	Conquistador	1967	6.25	12.50	25.00
-- With "A Division of Liberty Records" on label					
CANDID					
❏ CD-8006 [M]	The World of Cecil Taylor	1960	12.50	25.00	50.00
❏ CS-9006 [S]	The World of Cecil Taylor	1960	10.00	20.00	40.00
CONTEMPORARY					
❏ C-3562 [M]	Looking Ahead!	1959	12.50	25.00	50.00
❏ S-7562 [S]	Looking Ahead!	1959	10.00	20.00	40.00
FANTASY					
❏ OJC-452	Looking Ahead	1990	3.00	6.00	12.00
❏ 6014 [M]	Live At the Café Montmarte	1964	5.00	10.00	20.00
❏ 86014 [S]	Live At the Café Montmarte	1964	6.25	12.50	25.00
HAT ART					
❏ 1993/4 [(2)]	Garden	1986	3.75	7.50	15.00
-- Reissue of Hat Hut 1993/4					
❏ 2036 [(2)]	The Eight	1987	3.75	7.50	15.00

Number	Title	Yr	VG	VG+	NM
❏ 3011 [(3)]	One Too Many Salty Swift & Not Goodbye	1986	5.00	10.00	20.00
-- Reissue of Hat Hut 02					
HAT HUT					
❏ 02 [(3)]	One Too Many Salty Swift & Not Goodbye	197?	6.25	12.50	25.00
❏ 16 [(2)]	It Is In the Brewing Luminous	198?	3.75	7.50	15.00
❏ 1993/4 [(2)]	Garden	198?	5.00	10.00	20.00
❏ 3508	Calling It the 8th	1981	3.00	6.00	12.00
INNER CITY					
❏ IC-3001	The Dark to Themselves	197?	3.75	7.50	15.00
❏ IC-3021	Air Above	1977	3.75	7.50	15.00
JAZZ MAN					
❏ 5026	The World of Cecil Taylor	198?	2.50	5.00	10.00
❏ 5031	New York R & B	198?	2.50	5.00	10.00
JCOA					
❏ 1002	Cecil Taylor with the Jazz Composers Orchestra	197?	3.75	7.50	15.00
MOSAIC					
❏ M6-127 [(6)]	The Complete Candid Recordings of Cecil Taylor and Buell Neidlinger	199?	25.00	50.00	100.00
NEW WORLD					
❏ 201	Cecil Taylor	1978	3.00	6.00	12.00
❏ 303	Three Phasis	197?	3.00	6.00	12.00
PAUSA					
❏ 7053	Live in the Black Forest	198?	2.50	5.00	10.00
❏ 7108	Fly! Fly! Fly!	198?	2.50	5.00	10.00
PRESTIGE					
❏ 34003 [(3)]	Great Concert	197?	5.00	10.00	20.00
SOUL NOTE					
❏ SN-1089	Winged Serpent (Sliding Quadrants)	1986	3.00	6.00	12.00
❏ 121150	For Olim	199?	3.00	6.00	12.00
TRANSITION					
❏ TRLP-19 [M]	Jazz Advance	1956	50.00	100.00	200.00
-- With booklet (deduct 1/4 if missing)					
UNIT CORE					
❏ 30551	Spring of Two Blue-J's	197?	5.00	10.00	20.00
UNITED ARTISTS					
❏ UAL-4014 [M]	Hard Driving Jazz	1959	12.50	25.00	50.00
❏ UAL-4046 [M]	Love for Sale	1959	12.50	25.00	50.00
❏ UAS-5014 [S]	Stereo Drive	1959	10.00	20.00	40.00
❏ UAS-5046 [S]	Love for Sale	1959	10.00	20.00	40.00

TAYLOR, CREED

Arranger and producer, best known for his hand in other people's recordings. The below albums are generally conceded to have been recorded by a group led by Kenyon Hopkins.

Number	Title	Yr	VG	VG+	NM
ABC-PARAMOUNT					
❏ ABC-259 [M]	Shock Music in Hi-Fi	1958	10.00	20.00	40.00
❏ ABCS-259 [S]	Shock Music in Hi-Fi	1958	15.00	30.00	60.00
❏ ABC-308 [M]	Lonelyville "The Nervous Beat"	1960	6.25	12.50	25.00
❏ ABCS-308 [S]	Lonelyville "The Nervous Beat"	1960	7.50	15.00	30.00
❏ ABC-317 [M]	The Best of the Barracks Ballads	1960	6.25	12.50	25.00
❏ ABCS-317 [S]	The Best of the Barracks Ballads	1960	7.50	15.00	30.00

TAYLOR, DICK

Trombonist.

Number	Title	Yr	VG	VG+	NM
SKYLARK					
❏ SKLP-18 [10]	Blue Moon	1954	20.00	40.00	80.00

TAYLOR, JOE

Drummer.

Number	Title	Yr	VG	VG+	NM
PROJAZZ					
❏ PAD-635	Mystery Walk	1988	2.50	5.00	10.00

TAYLOR, LYNN

Number	Title	Yr	VG	VG+	NM
GRAND AWARD					
❏ GA-33-3?? [M]	Lynn Taylor Sings	195?	75.00	150.00	300.00

TAYLOR, MARTIN

Guitarist.

Number	Title	Yr	VG	VG+	NM
CONCORD JAZZ					
❏ CJ-184	Skye Boat	198?	2.50	5.00	10.00

TAYLOR, RUSTY

Number	Title	Yr	VG	VG+	NM
STOMP OFF					
❏ SOS-1028	Good Old Bad Old Days	198?	2.50	5.00	10.00
❏ SOS-1082	Give Me a Call	1985	2.50	5.00	10.00
❏ SOS-1186	Let's Misbehave	1988	2.50	5.00	10.00

Number	Title	Yr	VG	VG+	NM

TAYLOR, SAM "THE MAN"
Tenor and baritone saxophone player and clarinetist.

DECCA
❑ DL 4302 [M]	Misty Mood	1962	3.75	7.50	15.00
❑ DL 4417 [M]	It's A Blue World	1963	3.75	7.50	15.00
❑ DL 4573 [M]	Somewhere in the Night	1964	3.75	7.50	15.00
❑ DL 74302 [S]	Misty Mood	1962	5.00	10.00	20.00
❑ DL 74417 [S]	It's A Blue World	1963	5.00	10.00	20.00
❑ DL 74573 [S]	Somewhere in the Night	1964	5.00	10.00	20.00

LION
❑ L-70054 [M]	Sam "The Man" Taylor	1958	6.25	12.50	25.00

METROJAZZ
❑ E-1008 [M]	Jazz for Commuters	1958	12.50	25.00	50.00
❑ SE-1008 [S]	Jazz for Commuters	1958	10.00	20.00	40.00

MGM
❑ GAS-146	Sam "The Man" Taylor (Golden Archive Series)	1970	3.75	7.50	15.00
❑ E-293 [10]	Music with the Big Beat	195?	25.00	50.00	100.00
❑ E-3292 [M]	Blue Mist	1955	15.00	30.00	60.00
-- Yellow label					
❑ E-3380 [M]	Out of This World	1956	15.00	30.00	60.00
-- Yellow label					
❑ E-3473 [M]	Music with the Big Beat	1956	20.00	40.00	80.00
-- Yellow label					
❑ E-3482 [M]	Music for Melancholy Babies	1957	15.00	30.00	60.00
-- Yellow label					
❑ E-3553 [M]	Rockin' Sax and Rollin' Organ	1957	15.00	30.00	60.00
-- Yellow label					
❑ E-3573 [M]	Prelude to Blues	1957	15.00	30.00	60.00
-- Yellow label					
❑ E-3607 [M]	Lush Life	1957	---	---	---
-- Canceled					
❑ E-3783 [M]	More Blue Mist	1959	7.50	15.00	30.00
❑ SE-3783 [S]	More Blue Mist	1959	10.00	20.00	40.00
❑ E-3967 [M]	Sam "The Man" Taylor Plays Hollywood	1960	7.50	15.00	30.00
❑ SE-3967 [S]	Sam "The Man" Taylor Plays Hollywood	1960	10.00	20.00	40.00
❑ E-3973 [M]	Blue Mist	1961	7.50	15.00	30.00
❑ SE-3973 [S]	Blue Mist	1961	6.25	12.50	25.00
-- Possibly a re-recording of 3292					

MOODSVILLE
❑ MVLP-24 [M]	The Bad and the Beautiful	1962	12.50	25.00	50.00
-- Green label					
❑ MVLP-24 [M]	The Bad and the Beautiful	1965	6.25	12.50	25.00
-- Blue label, trident logo at right					

TCHICAI, JOHN
Saxophone player and composer. Many guest appearances, including, bizarrely, on the John Lennon/Yoko Ono album *Unfinished Music No. 2: Life with the Lions*. Also see THE NEW YORK ART QUINTET.

BLACK SAINT
❑ 120094	Timo's Message	1990	3.00	6.00	12.00

STEEPLECHASE
❑ SCS-1075	The Real Tchicai	198?	3.00	6.00	12.00

TCHICAI, JOHN, AND PIERRE DORGE
Also see each artist's individual listings.

STEEPLECHASE
❑ SCS-1174	Ball at Louisiana	1982	3.00	6.00	12.00

TEAGARDEN, JACK
Trombonist and occasional male singer. Also see RED ALLEN; BENNY GOODMAN; LIONEL HAMPTON.

AIRCHECK
❑ 9	Jack Teagarden and Frankie Trumbauer	197?	2.50	5.00	10.00
❑ 24	Jack Teagarden on the Air	198?	2.50	5.00	10.00

ARCHIVE OF FOLK AND JAZZ
❑ 335	Original Dixieland	198?	2.50	5.00	10.00
❑ 352	Big Band Jazz	198?	2.50	5.00	10.00

BETHLEHEM
❑ BCP-32 [M]	Jazz Great	1955	12.50	25.00	50.00

BIOGRAPH
❑ C-2	Great Soloist	197?	2.50	5.00	10.00

BLUEBIRD
❑ 9986-1-RB	That's a Serious Thing	1990	3.00	6.00	12.00

CAPITOL
❑ T 721 [M]	This Is Teagarden	1956	10.00	20.00	40.00
❑ T 820 [M]	Swing Low Sweet Spiritual	1957	10.00	20.00	40.00
❑ ST 1095 [S]	Big T's Dixieland Band	1959	6.25	12.50	25.00
❑ T 1095 [M]	Big T's Dixieland Band	1959	5.00	10.00	20.00
❑ ST 1143 [S]	Shades of Night	1959	6.25	12.50	25.00

❑ T 1143 [M]	Shades of Night	1959	5.00	10.00	20.00

COLUMBIA SPECIAL PRODUCTS
❑ JSN 6044 [(3) M]	King of the Blues Trombone	197?	6.25	12.50	25.00

COMMODORE
❑ 20015 [10]	Big T	195?	20.00	40.00	80.00

DECCA
❑ DL 4540 [M]	The Golden Horn of Jack	1964	3.75	7.50	15.00
❑ DL 8304 [M]	Big T's Jazz	1956	10.00	20.00	40.00
❑ DL 74540 [R]	The Golden Horn of Jack	1964	3.00	6.00	12.00

EPIC
❑ SN 6044 [(3) M]	King of the Blues Trombone	1963	20.00	40.00	80.00
❑ LN 24045 [M]	King of the Blues Trombone, Vol. 1	1963	6.25	12.50	25.00
❑ LN 24046 [M]	King of the Blues Trombone, Vol. 2	1963	6.25	12.50	25.00
❑ LN 24047 [M]	King of the Blues Trombone, Vol. 3	1963	6.25	12.50	25.00

FOLKWAYS
❑ FJ-2819	The Big Band Sound of Jack Teagarden and Bunny Berigan	198?	3.00	6.00	12.00

JAZZTONE
❑ J-1222 [M]	Big T	195?	7.50	15.00	30.00
-- Reissue of Period material					

JOLLY ROGER
❑ 5026 [10]	Jack Teagarden	1955	12.50	25.00	50.00

MCA
❑ 227	The Golden Horn of Jack	1973	2.50	5.00	10.00
-- Black rainbow label					

MOSAIC
❑ MQ6-168 [(6)]	The Complete Capitol Fifties Jack Teagarden Sessions	199?	25.00	50.00	100.00

PERIOD
❑ SLP-1106 [10]	Meet Me Where They Play the	1955	20.00	40.00	80.00
❑ SLP-1110 [10]	Original Dixieland	1955	20.00	40.00	80.00

RCA VICTOR
❑ LPV-528 [M]	Jack Teagarden	1965	5.00	10.00	20.00

RONDO-LETTE
❑ A-18 [M]	The Blues and Dixie	1958	6.25	12.50	25.00

ROULETTE
❑ R-25091 [M]	Jack Teagarden at the Round Table	1960	3.75	7.50	15.00
❑ SR-25091 [S]	Jack Teagarden at the Round Table	1960	5.00	10.00	20.00
❑ R-25119 [M]	Jazz Maverick	1961	3.75	7.50	15.00
❑ SR-25119 [S]	Jazz Maverick	1961	5.00	10.00	20.00
❑ R-25177 [M]	Dixie Sound	1962	3.75	7.50	15.00
❑ SR-25177 [S]	Dixie Sound	1962	5.00	10.00	20.00
❑ R-25243 [M]	Portrait of Mr. T	1963	3.75	7.50	15.00
❑ SR-25243 [S]	Portrait of Mr. T	1963	5.00	10.00	20.00

ROYALE
❑ 18156 [10]	The Blues	195?	20.00	40.00	80.00

SAVOY JAZZ
❑ SJL-1162	Varsity Sides	1986	2.50	5.00	10.00

SOUNDS
❑ S-1203	Jack Teagarden in Concert	197?	3.75	7.50	15.00

TRIP
❑ 6	Jack Teagarden	197?	2.50	5.00	10.00

URANIA
❑ UJLP-1001 [10]	Meet the New Jack Teagarden	1954	25.00	50.00	100.00
❑ UJLP-1002 [10]	Jack Teagarden Sings and Plays	1954	25.00	50.00	100.00

VERVE
❑ V-8416 [M]	Mis'ry and the Blues	1961	3.75	7.50	15.00
❑ V6-8416 [S]	Mis'ry and the Blues	1961	5.00	10.00	20.00
❑ V-8465 [M]	Think Well of Me	1962	3.75	7.50	15.00
❑ V6-8465 [S]	Think Well of Me	1962	5.00	10.00	20.00
❑ V-8495 [M]	Jack Teagarden!!	1962	3.75	7.50	15.00
❑ V6-8495 [S]	Jack Teagarden!!	1962	5.00	10.00	20.00

TEAGARDEN, JACK/BOBBY HACKETT
Also see each artist's individual listings.

COMMODORE
❑ FL-30012 [M]	Jack Teagarden and Bobby Hackett	1959	7.50	15.00	30.00

TEAGARDEN, JACK/JONAH JONES
Also see each artist's individual listings.

AAMCO
❑ ALP-309 [M]	Two Boys from Dixieland	196?	6.25	12.50	25.00
-- Reissue of Bethlehem material					

BETHLEHEM
❑ BCP-6042 [M]	Dixieland	1959	10.00	20.00	40.00

Number	Title	Yr	VG	VG+	NM
TEAGARDEN, JACK/MAX KAMINSKY					
Also see each artist's individual listings.					
COMMODORE					
❑ XFL-14940	Big T and Mighty Max	198?	2.50	5.00	10.00
HALL OF FAME					
❑ 616	Jack and Max	197?	2.50	5.00	10.00
TEAGARDEN, JACK/PEE WEE RUSSELL					
Also see each artist's individual listings.					
FANTASY					
❑ OJC-1708	Jack Teagarden's Big Eight / Pee Wee Russell's Rhythmakers	1985	2.50	5.00	10.00
RIVERSIDE					
❑ RLP 12-141	Jack Teagarden's Big Eight / Pee Wee Russell's Rhythmakers	1956	15.00	30.00	60.00
TEDESCO, TOMMY					
Six- and 12-string guitarist. Best known for his session work on Phil Spector-produced records, among others.					
DISCOVERY					
❑ 789	When Do We Start	1978	3.00	6.00	12.00
❑ 851	My Desiree	1982	2.50	5.00	10.00
❑ 928	Hollywood Gypsy	1986	2.50	5.00	10.00
IMPERIAL					
❑ LP-9263 [M]	The Electric 12 String Guitar of Tommy Tedesco	1964	3.75	7.50	15.00
❑ LP-9295 [M]	Guitars	1965	3.75	7.50	15.00
❑ LP-9321 [M]	Calypso Soul	1966	3.75	7.50	15.00
❑ LP-12263 [S]	The Electric 12 String Guitar of Tommy Tedesco	1964	5.00	10.00	20.00
❑ LP-12295 [S]	Guitars	1965	5.00	10.00	20.00
❑ LP-12321 [S]	Calypso Soul	1966	5.00	10.00	20.00
TREND					
❑ TR-514	Autumn	1978	5.00	10.00	20.00
-- Direct-to-disc recording					
❑ TR-517	Alone at Last	1979	5.00	10.00	20.00
-- Direct-to-disc recording					
❑ TR-534	Carnival Time	1983	3.00	6.00	12.00
TEITELBAUM, RICHARD					
Synthesizer player and composer.					
ARISTA/FREEDOM					
❑ AF 1037	Time Zones	197?	3.00	6.00	12.00
TEMIZ, OKAY					
Drummer and percussionist.					
FINNADAR					
❑ 9032	Drummer of Two Worlds	198?	3.75	7.50	15.00
TEMPERLEY, JOE, AND JIMMY KNEPPER					
Temperley is a baritone, tenor and alto saxophone player and clarinetist. Also see JIMMY KNEPPER.					
HEP					
❑ 2003	Just Friends	198?	2.50	5.00	10.00
TEMPLETON, ALEC					
Pianist and composer.					
ATLANTIC					
❑ 1222 [M]	The Magic Piano	1956	10.00	20.00	40.00
-- Black label					
❑ 1222 [M]	The Magic Piano	1961	5.00	10.00	20.00
-- Multicolor label, white "fan" logo at right					
TEMPLIN, RAY					
EUPHONIC					
❑ 1219	A Flash at the Piano	198?	2.50	5.00	10.00
TERRACE, PETE					
Percussionist and bandleader.					
FANTASY					
❑ 3203 [M]	Going Loco	1956	15.00	30.00	60.00
-- Red vinyl					
❑ 3203 [M]	Going Loco	195?	6.25	12.50	25.00
-- Black vinyl					
❑ 3215 [M]	Invitation to the Mambo	1956	15.00	30.00	60.00
-- Red vinyl					
❑ 3215 [M]	Invitation to the Mambo	195?	6.25	12.50	25.00
-- Black vinyl					
❑ 3234 [M]	The Pete Terrace Quintet	1957	15.00	30.00	60.00
-- Red vinyl					
❑ 3234 [M]	The Pete Terrace Quintet	195?	6.25	12.50	25.00
-- Black vinyl					

Number	Title	Yr	VG	VG+	NM
FORUM					
❑ F-9041[M]	Cole Porter in Latin America	196?	3.75	7.50	15.00
❑ SF-9041 [S]	Cole Porter in Latin America	196?	3.00	6.00	12.00
TICO					
❑ LP-1023 [M]	A Night in Mambo Jazzland	1956	10.00	20.00	40.00
❑ LP-1028 [M]	The Nearness of You	1956	10.00	20.00	40.00
❑ LP-1036 [M]	Cha Cha Cha in New York	1957	10.00	20.00	40.00
❑ LP-1050 [M]	Pete with a Latin Beat	1958	7.50	15.00	30.00
❑ LP-1057 [M]	My One and Only Love	1959	7.50	15.00	30.00
❑ LP-1063 [M]	Cole Porter in Latin America	1959	7.50	15.00	30.00
❑ LP-1082 [M]	Bella Pachanga	1961	6.25	12.50	25.00
❑ SLP-1082 [S]	Bella Pachanga	1961	7.50	15.00	30.00
TERRY, BUDDY					
Tenor and soprano saxophone player and flutist.					
MAINSTREAM					
❑ MRL-336	Awareness	1972	3.75	7.50	15.00
❑ MRL-356	Pure Dynamite	1973	3.75	7.50	15.00
❑ MRL-391	Lean On Him	1974	3.00	6.00	12.00
PRESTIGE					
❑ PRLP-7525 [M]	Electric Soul	1967	7.50	15.00	30.00
❑ PRST-7525 [S]	Electric Soul	1967	6.25	12.50	25.00
❑ PRLP-7541 [M]	Natural Soul	1967	7.50	15.00	30.00
❑ PRST-7541 [S]	Natural Soul	1967	6.25	12.50	25.00
TERRY, CLARK					
Trumpeter and fluegel horn player. Also see GARY BURTON; KENNY DORHAM; COLEMAN HAWKINS; THE RIVERSIDE JAZZ STARS; SHIRLEY SCOTT.					
ABC IMPULSE!					
❑ AS-64 [S]	The Happy Horn of Clark Terry	1968	3.75	7.50	15.00
❑ AS-9127 [S]	Spanish Rice	1968	3.75	7.50	15.00
❑ AS-9157 [S]	It's What's Happenin'	1968	5.00	10.00	20.00
ARGO					
❑ LP-620 [M]	Out on a Limb	1957	12.50	25.00	50.00
CAMEO					
❑ C-1064 [M]	More	1964	7.50	15.00	30.00
❑ CS-1064 [S]	More	1964	10.00	20.00	40.00
❑ C-1071 [M]	Tread Ye Lightly	1964	7.50	15.00	30.00
❑ CS-1071 [S]	Tread Ye Lightly	1964	10.00	20.00	40.00
CANDID					
❑ CD-8009 [M]	Color Changes	1960	12.50	25.00	50.00
❑ CS-9009 [S]	Color Changes	1960	10.00	20.00	40.00
EMARCY					
❑ MG-36007 [M]	Clark Terry	1955	20.00	40.00	80.00
❑ MG-36093 [M]	The Jazz School	1956	15.00	30.00	60.00
ETOILE					
❑ CPR-1	Clark Terry's Big Bad Band	197?	5.00	10.00	20.00
FANTASY					
❑ OJC-066	Serenade to a Bus Seat	198?	2.50	5.00	10.00
❑ OJC-229	Duke with a Difference	1990	2.50	5.00	10.00
❑ OJC-302	In Orbit	1988	2.50	5.00	10.00
❑ OJC-604	Memories of Duke	1991	2.50	5.00	10.00
IMPULSE!					
❑ A-64 [M]	The Happy Horn of Clark Terry	1964	6.25	12.50	25.00
❑ AS-64 [S]	The Happy Horn of Clark Terry	1964	7.50	15.00	30.00
❑ A-9127 [M]	Spanish Rice	1966	6.25	12.50	25.00
❑ AS-9127 [S]	Spanish Rice	1966	7.50	15.00	30.00
JAZZ MAN					
❑ 5046	Color Changes	198?	2.50	5.00	10.00
MAINSTREAM					
❑ MRL-320	Straight No Chaser	1971	3.75	7.50	15.00
❑ MRL-347	Angyumaluma	1972	3.75	7.50	15.00
❑ MRL-373	Clark Terry and the W.B. Brookmeyer Quintet	1973	3.75	7.50	15.00
❑ MRL-803 [(2)]	What'd He Say	197?	5.00	10.00	20.00
❑ S-6043 [S]	Clark Terry Tonight	1965	6.25	12.50	25.00
❑ S-6054 [S]	The Power of Positive Swinging	1965	6.25	12.50	25.00
❑ S-6066 [S]	Mumbles	1966	6.25	12.50	25.00
❑ S-6086	Clark Terry with Bob Brookmeyer	196?	5.00	10.00	20.00
❑ 56043 [M]	Clark Terry Tonight	1965	5.00	10.00	20.00
❑ 56054 [M]	The Power of Positive Swinging	1965	5.00	10.00	20.00
❑ 56066 [M]	Mumbles	1966	5.00	10.00	20.00
MILESTONE					
❑ 47032 [(2)]	Cruising	197?	3.75	7.50	15.00
MOODSVILLE					
❑ MVLP-20 [M]	Everything's Mellow	1961	12.50	25.00	50.00
-- Green label					
❑ MVLP-20 [M]	Everything's Mellow	1965	6.25	12.50	25.00
-- Blue label, trident logo at right					

Number	Title	Yr	VG	VG+	NM
❑ MVLP-26 [M]	The Jazz Version of "All American"	1962	12.50	25.00	50.00
-- Green label					
❑ MVLP-26 [M]	The Jazz Version of "All American"	1965	6.25	12.50	25.00
-- Blue label, trident logo at right					
PABLO TODAY					
❑ 2312 105	Ain't Misbehavin'	1980	3.00	6.00	12.00
❑ 2312 118	Memories of Duke	1980	3.00	6.00	12.00
❑ 2313 127	Yes, the Blues	1981	3.00	6.00	12.00
PAUSA					
❑ 7131	Wham!	198?	2.50	5.00	10.00
POLYDOR					
❑ 24-5002	Clark Terry at Montreux Jazz Festival	1970	3.75	7.50	15.00
RIVERSIDE					
❑ RLP 12-237 [M]	Serenade to a Bus Seat	1957	37.50	75.00	150.00
❑ -- White label, blue print					
❑ RLP 12-237 [M]	Serenade to a Bus Seat	1957	12.50	25.00	50.00
❑ -- Blue label, microphone logo at top					
❑ RLP 12-246 [M]	Duke with a Difference	1957	25.00	50.00	100.00
❑ RLP 12-271 [M]	In Orbit	1958	25.00	50.00	100.00
❑ RLP 12-295 [M]	Top and Bottom Brass	1959	25.00	50.00	100.00
❑ RLP-1108 [S]	Duke with a Difference	1959	20.00	40.00	80.00
❑ RLP-1137 [S]	Top and Bottom Brass	1959	20.00	40.00	80.00
❑ RM-3009 [M]	C.T. Meets Monk	1967	6.25	12.50	25.00
❑ RS-3009 [S]	C.T. Meets Monk	1967	5.00	10.00	20.00
❑ 6167	In Orbit	198?	3.00	6.00	12.00
❑ 6209	Serenade to a Bus Seat	198?	3.00	6.00	12.00
SWING					
❑ 8406	Paris 1960	1985	2.50	5.00	10.00
TRIP					
❑ 5528	Swahili	197?	2.50	5.00	10.00
20TH CENTURY FOX					
❑ TFM-3137 [M]	What Makes Sammy Swing	1963	5.00	10.00	20.00
❑ TFS-4137 [S]	What Makes Sammy Swing	1963	6.25	12.50	25.00
VANGUARD					
❑ VSD-79355	Clark Terry Big Band Live at Wichita Fest '74	1975	3.00	6.00	12.00
❑ VSD-79365	Clark Terry and His Jolly Giants	197?	3.00	6.00	12.00
❑ VSD-79373	Clark Terry Big Band Live at Buddy's Place	1976	3.00	6.00	12.00
❑ VSD-79393	Globetrotter	1977	3.00	6.00	12.00
VERVE					
❑ V6-8836	Previously Unreleased Recordings	197?	3.75	7.50	15.00
WING					
❑ MGW-60002 [M]	The Jazz School	1955	20.00	40.00	80.00

TERRY, CLARK/COLEMAN HAWKINS
Also see each artist's individual listings.

Number	Title	Yr	VG	VG+	NM
COLPIX					
❑ CP-450 [M]	Eddie Costa Memorial Concert	1963	10.00	20.00	40.00
❑ SCP-450 [S]	Eddie Costa Memorial Concert	1963	12.50	25.00	50.00

TERRY, LILLIAN

Number	Title	Yr	VG	VG+	NM
SOUL NOTE					
❑ SN-1047	A Dream Comes True	198?	3.00	6.00	12.00
❑ SN-1147	Oo-Shoo-Be-Doo-Be...Oo...Oo... Oo ...Oo	1986	3.00	6.00	12.00

TERRY, PAT, JR.
Banjo player.

Number	Title	Yr	VG	VG+	NM
CIRCLE					
❑ C-54	All Jazzed Up	1981	2.50	5.00	10.00

TESCHEMACHER, FRANK
Clarinetist, alto saxophone player, violinist and banjo player.

Number	Title	Yr	VG	VG+	NM
BRUNSWICK					
❑ BL 58017 [10]	Tesch Plays Jazz Classics	1950	20.00	40.00	80.00

THESAURUS RHYTHM MAKERS

Number	Title	Yr	VG	VG+	NM
SUNBEAM					
❑ 101	The Thesaurus Rhythm Makers, Vol. 1	197?	2.50	5.00	10.00
❑ 102	The Thesaurus Rhythm Makers, Vol. 2	197?	2.50	5.00	10.00

Number	Title	Yr	VG	VG+	NM
❑ 103	The Thesaurus Rhythm Makers, Vol. 3	197?	2.50	5.00	10.00

THESELIUS, GOSTA
Tenor saxophone player and pianist.

Number	Title	Yr	VG	VG+	NM
BALLY					
❑ BAL-12002 [M]	Swedish Jazz	1956	12.50	25.00	50.00

THEUS, FATS
Tenor saxophone player.

Number	Title	Yr	VG	VG+	NM
CTI					
❑ 1005	Black Out	1972	3.75	7.50	15.00

THIELEMANS, TOOTS
Harmonica player.

Number	Title	Yr	VG	VG+	NM
A&M					
❑ SP-3613	Yesterday and Today	1974	3.00	6.00	12.00
ABC-PARAMOUNT					
❑ ABC-482 [M]	The Whistler and His Guitar	1965	6.25	12.50	25.00
❑ ABCS-482 [S]	The Whistler and His Guitar	1965	7.50	15.00	30.00
CHOICE					
❑ 1007	Captured Alive	197?	3.75	7.50	15.00
COLUMBIA					
❑ CL 658 [M]	The Sound	1955	12.50	25.00	50.00
COMMAND					
❑ RS 33-906 [M]	Contrasts	1967	5.00	10.00	20.00
❑ RS 906 SD [S]	Contrasts	1967	3.75	7.50	15.00
❑ RS 33-918 [M]	Guitars and Strings... And Things	1967	5.00	10.00	20.00
❑ RS 918 SD [S]	Guitars and Strings... And Things	1967	3.75	7.50	15.00
❑ RS 930 SD	Toots!	1968	3.75	7.50	15.00
❑ RSSD 978-2 [(2)]	The Salient One	1973	3.75	7.50	15.00
CONCORD JAZZ					
❑ CJ-355	Only Trust Your Heart	1988	2.50	5.00	10.00
DECCA					
❑ DL 9204 [M]	Time Out for Toots	1958	12.50	25.00	50.00
❑ DL 79204 [S]	Time Out for Toots	1958	10.00	20.00	40.00
FANTASY					
❑ OJC-1738	Man Bites Harmonica	198?	2.50	5.00	10.00
INNER CITY					
❑ IC-1145	Live	198?	3.00	6.00	12.00
❑ IC-1146	Live 2	198?	3.00	6.00	12.00
❑ IC-1147	Live 3	198?	3.00	6.00	12.00
❑ IC-1148	Spotlight	198?	3.00	6.00	12.00
JAZZ MAN					
❑ 5016	Slow Motion	198?	2.50	5.00	10.00
RIVERSIDE					
❑ RLP 12-257 [M]	Man Bites Harmonica	1958	25.00	50.00	100.00
SIGNATURE					
❑ SM-6006 [M]	The Soul of Toots Thielmans	1960	20.00	40.00	80.00
❑ SS-6006 [S]	The Soul of Toots Thielmans	1960	15.00	30.00	60.00

THIGPEN, ED
Drummer and percussionist.

Number	Title	Yr	VG	VG+	NM
GNP CRESCENDO					
❑ GNPS-2098	Action Re-Action	197?	2.50	5.00	10.00
VERVE					
❑ V-8663 [M]	Out of the Storm	1966	5.00	10.00	20.00
❑ V6-8663 [S]	Out of the Storm	1966	6.25	12.50	25.00

THILO, JESPER
Danish tenor saxophone player.

Number	Title	Yr	VG	VG+	NM
STORYVILLE					
❑ 4065	Swingin' Friends	198?	2.50	5.00	10.00
❑ 4072	Tribute to Frog	198?	2.50	5.00	10.00

THOMAS, DAVID
Pianist.

Number	Title	Yr	VG	VG+	NM
STOMP OFF					
❑ SOS-1072	Through the Bottomlands	1984	2.50	5.00	10.00

THOMAS, GARY
Tenor and soprano saxophone player and flutist.

Number	Title	Yr	VG	VG+	NM
ENJA					
❑ R1-79604	Code Violations	1989	3.00	6.00	12.00
JMT					
❑ 834 432-1	By Any Means Necessary	198?	2.50	5.00	10.00

Number	Title	Yr	VG	VG+	NM

THOMAS, JEANNIE
Female singer.
STRAND
| ❑ SL-1030 [M] | Jeannie Thomas Sings for the Boys | 1961 | 10.00 | 20.00 | 40.00 |
| ❑ SLS-1030 [S] | Jeannie Thomas Sings for the Boys | 1961 | 12.50 | 25.00 | 50.00 |

THOMAS, JOE (1)
Trumpeter; among others, he played in FLETCHER HENDERSON's early orchestras. See VIC DICKENSON.

THOMAS, JOE (2)
Tenor saxophone player.
UPTOWN
| ❑ 27.01 | Raw Meat | 198? | 3.00 | 6.00 | 12.00 |

THOMAS, JOE (2), AND JAY McSHANN
Also see each artist's individual listings.
UPTOWN
| ❑ 27.12 | Blowin' In from Kansas City | 198? | 3.00 | 6.00 | 12.00 |

THOMAS, JOE (3)
Tenor saxophone player and flutist. Not to be confused with Joe Thomas (2), who was a tenor saxophone player with the JIMMIE LUNCEFORD orchestra.
CHIAROSCURO
| ❑ 2018 | Flash | 1979 | 3.00 | 6.00 | 12.00 |
GROOVE MERCHANT
| ❑ 504 | Joy of Cookin' | 197? | 5.00 | 10.00 | 20.00 |
| ❑ 3310 | Masada | 197? | 3.75 | 7.50 | 15.00 |

THOMAS, JOE (?), AND BILL ELLIOTT
Which Joe Thomas is this? We're not sure.
SUE
| ❑ LP-1025 [M] | Speak Your Piece | 1964 | 12.50 | 25.00 | 50.00 |

THOMAS, KID
See KID THOMAS in the letter K.

THOMAS, LEON
Male singer.
FLYING DUTCHMAN
❑ FD-10115	Spirits Known and Unknown	197?	5.00	10.00	20.00
❑ FD-10132	The Leon Thomas Album	197?	5.00	10.00	20.00
❑ FD-10155	Blues and the Soulful Truth	197?	3.75	7.50	15.00
❑ FD-10164	Facets	197?	3.75	7.50	15.00
❑ FD-10167	Full Circle	197?	3.75	7.50	15.00
MEGA
| ❑ M51-5003 | Gold Sunrise on Magic Mountain | 197? | 5.00 | 10.00 | 20.00 |
PORTRAIT
| ❑ FR 44161 | The Leon Thomas Blues Band | 1988 | 2.50 | 5.00 | 10.00 |

THOMAS, PAT
Male singer.
MGM
❑ E-4103 [M]	Desafinado	1962	3.75	7.50	15.00
❑ SE-4103 [S]	Desafinado	1962	5.00	10.00	20.00
❑ E-4206 [M]	Moody's Mood	1964	3.75	7.50	15.00
❑ SE-4206 [S]	Moody's Mood	1964	5.00	10.00	20.00
STRAND
| ❑ SL-1015 [M] | Jazz Patterns | 1961 | 10.00 | 20.00 | 40.00 |
| ❑ SLS-1015 [S] | Jazz Patterns | 1961 | 12.50 | 25.00 | 50.00 |

THOMAS, RENE
Guitarist.
FANTASY
| ❑ OJC-1725 | Guitar Groove | 198? | 2.50 | 5.00 | 10.00 |
JAZZLAND
| ❑ JLP-27 [M] | Guitar Groove | 1960 | 7.50 | 15.00 | 30.00 |
| ❑ JLP-927 [S] | Guitar Groove | 1960 | 10.00 | 20.00 | 40.00 |

THOMAS, WALTER "FOOTS"
Alto, tenor and baritone saxophone player, clarinetist and bandleader.
PRESTIGE
| ❑ PRST-7584 | Walter "Foots" Thomas All-Stars | 196? | 3.75 | 7.50 | 15.00 |

THOMPSON, BOB
Pianist and keyboard player.
INTIMA
❑ SJ-73238	Brother's Keeper	1987	2.50	5.00	10.00
❑ SJ-73284	7 In, 7 Out	1987	2.50	5.00	10.00
-- Reissue of Rainbow 2010					
❑ D1-73331	Say What You Want	1988	2.50	5.00	10.00
❑ D1-73519	Wilderness	1989	3.00	6.00	12.00
RAINBOW
| ❑ 2010 | 7 In, 7 Out | 1986 | 5.00 | 10.00 | 20.00 |

THOMPSON, BUTCH
Pianist and bandleader.
JAZZOLOGY
| ❑ J-146 | Butch Thompson and His Boys in Chicago | 1986 | 2.50 | 5.00 | 10.00 |
STOMP OFF
| ❑ SOS-1037 | A' Solas | 198? | 2.50 | 5.00 | 10.00 |

THOMPSON, BUTCH, AND CHET ELY
Also see each artist's individual listings.
JAZZOLOGY
| ❑ J-79 | Jelly Rolls On | 197? | 2.50 | 5.00 | 10.00 |

THOMPSON, BUTCH, AND HAL SMITH
Also see each artist's individual listings.
STOMP OFF
| ❑ SOS-1075 | Echoes from Storyville, Vol. 1: If You Don't Shake | 1985 | 2.50 | 5.00 | 10.00 |
| ❑ SOS-1116 | Echoes from Storyville, Vol. 2: Milenberg Joys | 1986 | 2.50 | 5.00 | 10.00 |

THOMPSON, CHESTER
Organist.
BLACK JAZZ
| ❑ 6 | Powerhouse | 197? | 6.25 | 12.50 | 25.00 |

THOMPSON, DON
Pianist, bass player, vibraphone player, arranger and composer.
CONCORD JAZZ
| ❑ CJ-243 | Beautiful Friendship | 198? | 2.50 | 5.00 | 10.00 |
PM
| ❑ 008 | Country Place | 1976 | 3.00 | 6.00 | 12.00 |

THOMPSON, LES
RCA VICTOR
| ❑ LPT-3102 [10] | Gene Norman Presents "Just Jazz" | 1952 | 37.50 | 75.00 | 150.00 |

THOMPSON, LUCKY
Tenor and soprano saxophone player. Also see THE MODERN JAZZ SOCIETY.
ABC-PARAMOUNT
| ❑ ABC-111 [M] | Lucky Thompson Featuring Oscar Pettiford, Volume 1 | 1956 | 20.00 | 40.00 | 80.00 |
| ❑ ABC-171 [M] | Lucky Thompson Featuring Oscar Pettiford, Volume 2 | 1957 | 20.00 | 40.00 | 80.00 |
DAWN
| ❑ DLP-1113 [M] | Lucky Thompson | 1957 | 20.00 | 40.00 | 80.00 |
FANTASY
| ❑ OJC-194 | Lucky Strikes | 1985 | 2.50 | 5.00 | 10.00 |
GROOVE MERCHANT
❑ 508	Goodbye Yesterday	197?	3.75	7.50	15.00
❑ 517	I Offer You	197?	3.75	7.50	15.00
❑ 4411 [(2)]	Illuminations	197?	5.00	10.00	20.00
LONDON
| ❑ D-93098 [10] | Recorded in Paris '56 | 1956 | 20.00 | 40.00 | 80.00 |
MOODSVILLE
❑ MVLP-39 [M]	Lucky Thompson Plays Jerome Kern and No More	1963	10.00	20.00	40.00
-- Green label					
❑ MVLP-39 [M]	Lucky Thompson Plays Jerome Kern and No More	1965	5.00	10.00	20.00
-- Blue label, trident logo at right					
❑ MVST-39 [S]	Lucky Thompson Plays Jerome Kern and No More	1963	12.50	25.00	50.00
-- Green label					
❑ MVST-39 [S]	Lucky Thompson Plays Jerome Kern and No More	1965	6.25	12.50	25.00
-- Blue label, trident logo at right					

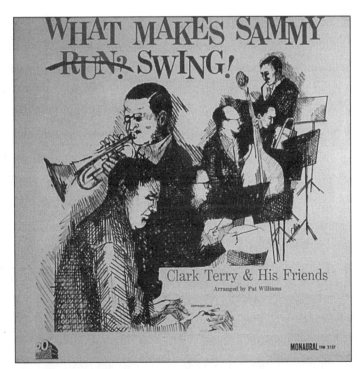

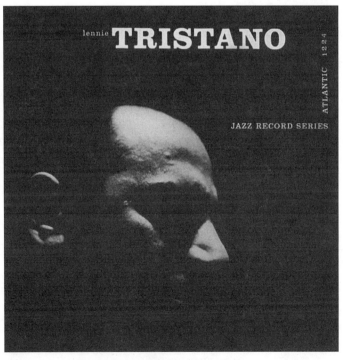

(Top left) Art Tatum was one of the great jazz piano soloists in addition to doing some fine trio work. The collection of albums he recorded for Norman Granz in the 1950s remain classics of the genre. Here is the first in the series of "The Genius Of" albums that came out originally on the Clef label. (Top right) Another pianist of long standing was Billy Taylor. In the early days of the label, ABC-Paramount released a lot of jazz albums, and this, *Evergreens*, was one of them. (Bottom left) Trumpeter Clark Terry spent time with both Duke Ellington's and Count Basie's orchestras before forming his own group. This 1963 release was his only one on the 20th Century Fox label. (Bottom right) Pianist Lennie Tristano was best known for his work with Lee Konitz. He recorded rarely as a leader; one of those was the 1955 album *Lenny Tristano* on the Atlantic label.

Number	Title	Yr	VG	VG+	NM
NESSA					
❑ N-13	Body and Soul	198?	3.00	6.00	12.00
PRESTIGE					
❑ PRLP-7365 [M]	Lucky Strikes	1965	6.25	12.50	25.00
❑ PRST-7365 [S]	Lucky Strikes	1965	7.50	15.00	30.00
❑ PRLP-7394 [M]	Happy Days Are Here Again	1965	6.25	12.50	25.00
❑ PRST-7394 [S]	Happy Days Are Here Again	1965	7.50	15.00	30.00
RIVOLI					
❑ 40 [M]	Lucky Is Back!	1965	6.25	12.50	25.00
❑ S-40 [S]	Lucky Is Back!	1965	7.50	15.00	30.00
❑ 44 [M]	Kinfolk's Corner	1965	6.25	12.50	25.00
❑ S-44 [S]	Kinfolk's Corner	1965	7.50	15.00	30.00
SWING					
❑ 8404	Paris 1956, Vol. 1	1985	2.50	5.00	10.00
TOPS					
❑ L-928 [10]	Jazz at the Auditorium	1954	30.00	60.00	120.00
TRANSITION					
❑ TRLP-21 [M]	Lucky Strikes	1956	62.50	125.00	250.00
-- With booklet (deduct 1/5 if missing)					
URANIA					
❑ UJLP-1206 [M]	Accent on Tenor	1955	25.00	50.00	100.00
XANADU					
❑ 204	Brown Rose	1985	2.50	5.00	10.00

THOMPSON, MALACHI
Trumpeter.

Number	Title	Yr	VG	VG+	NM
DELMARK					
❑ DS-442	Spirit	1989	3.00	6.00	12.00

THOMPSON, SIR CHARLES
Pianist, organist, bandleader and arranger. Also see THE MANHATTAN JAZZ ALL-STARS.

Number	Title	Yr	VG	VG+	NM
AMERICAN RECORDING SOCIETY					
❑ G-447 [M]	Basically Swing	1957	7.50	15.00	30.00
APOLLO					
❑ 103 [10]	Sir Charles Thompson and His All-Stars	1951	100.00	200.00	400.00
COLUMBIA					
❑ CL 1364 [M]	Sir Charles Thompson and the Swing Organ	1959	6.25	12.50	25.00
❑ CL 1663 [M]	Rockin' Rhythm	1961	6.25	12.50	25.00
❑ CS 8205 [S]	Sir Charles Thompson and the Swing Organ	1959	7.50	15.00	30.00
❑ CS 8463 [S]	Rockin' Rhythm	1961	7.50	15.00	30.00
EUPHONIC					
❑ 1221	The Neglected Professor	198?	2.50	5.00	10.00
SACKVILLE					
❑ 3037	Portrait of a Piano	199?	3.00	6.00	12.00
VANGUARD					
❑ VRS-8003 [10]	Sir Charles Thompson Sextet	1953	25.00	50.00	100.00
❑ VRS-8006 [10]	Sir Charles Thompson Quartet	1954	25.00	50.00	100.00
❑ VRS-8009 [10]	Sir Charles Thompson and His Band	1954	37.50	75.00	150.00
❑ VRS-8018 [10]	Sir Charles Thompson Trio	1955	25.00	50.00	100.00

THORNE, FRAN
Pianist.

Number	Title	Yr	VG	VG+	NM
TRANSITION					
❑ TRLP-27 [M]	Piano Reflections	1956	50.00	100.00	200.00
-- With booklet (deduct 1/4 if missing)					

THORNHILL, CLAUDE
Pianist, bandleader, composer and arranger.

Number	Title	Yr	VG	VG+	NM
CIRCLE					
❑ C-19	Claude Thornhill and His Orchestra 1941 & 1947	198?	2.50	5.00	10.00
COLUMBIA					
❑ CL 709 [M]	Dancing After Midnight	1955	10.00	20.00	40.00
❑ CL 6035 [10]	Piano Reflections	1949	20.00	40.00	80.00
❑ CL 6050 [10]	Dance Parade	1949	20.00	40.00	80.00
❑ CL 6164 [10]	Claude Thornhill Encores	1951	20.00	40.00	80.00
❑ KG 32906 [(2)]	The Memorable Claude Thornhill	1973	3.00	6.00	12.00
DECCA					
❑ DL 8722 [M]	Claude on a Cloud	1958	6.25	12.50	25.00
❑ DL 8878 [M]	Dance to the Sound of Claude Thornhill	1958	6.25	12.50	25.00
❑ DL 78722 [S]	Claude on a Cloud	1958	7.50	15.00	30.00
❑ DL 78878 [S]	Dance to the Sound of Claude Thornhill	1958	7.50	15.00	30.00

Number	Title	Yr	VG	VG+	NM
DESIGN					
❑ DLP-50 [M]	Sleepy Serenade	1957	3.75	7.50	15.00
HARMONY					
❑ HL 7088 [M]	The Thornhill Sound	1957	6.25	12.50	25.00
HINDSIGHT					
❑ HSR-108	Claude Thornhill and His Orchestra 1947	198?	2.50	5.00	10.00
INSIGHT					
❑ 207	Claude Thornhill and His Orchestra	198?	2.50	5.00	10.00
KAPP					
❑ KL-1058 [M]	Two Sides of Claude Thornhill	1958	7.50	15.00	30.00
❑ KS-3058 [S]	Two Sides of Claude Thornhill	1958	6.25	12.50	25.00
RCA CAMDEN					
❑ CAL-307 [M]	Dinner for Two	1958	6.25	12.50	25.00
TREND					
❑ TL-1001 [10]	Dream Stuff	1953	20.00	40.00	80.00
❑ TL-1002 [10]	Claude Thornhill Plays the Great Jazz Arrangements of Gerry Mulligan and Ralph Aldrich	1953	20.00	40.00	80.00

THORNTON, ARGONNE
See SADIK HAKIM.

THORNTON, CLIFFORD
Trumpeter.

Number	Title	Yr	VG	VG+	NM
JCOA					
❑ 1008	Gardens of Harlem	197?	3.75	7.50	15.00
THIRD WORLD					
❑ 9636 [S]	Freedom and Unity	1969	6.25	12.50	25.00
❑ 12372	Communications Network	197?	3.75	7.50	15.00

THORNTON, TERI
Female singer.

Number	Title	Yr	VG	VG+	NM
COLUMBIA					
❑ CL 2094 [M]	Open Highway	1963	7.50	15.00	30.00
❑ CS 8894 [S]	Open Highway	1963	10.00	20.00	40.00
DAUNTLESS					
❑ DM-4306 [M]	Somewhere in the Night	1963	6.25	12.50	25.00
❑ DS-6306 [S]	Somewhere in the Night	1963	7.50	15.00	30.00
RIVERSIDE					
❑ RLP-352 [M]	Devil May Care	1961	10.00	20.00	40.00
❑ RM-3525 [M]	Lullabye of the Leaves	1964	6.25	12.50	25.00
❑ 6142	Devil May Care	198?	3.00	6.00	12.00
❑ RS-9352 [S]	Devil May Care	1961	7.50	15.00	30.00
❑ RS-93525 [S]	Lullabye of the Leaves	1964	7.50	15.00	30.00

THREADGILL, HENRY
Alto and tenor saxophone player, clarinetist and bass flutist. Also see AIR.

Number	Title	Yr	VG	VG+	NM
ABOUT TIME					
❑ 1004	When Was That?	198?	3.00	6.00	12.00
❑ 1005	Just the Facts and Pass the Bucket	198?	3.00	6.00	12.00
NOVUS					
❑ 3013-1-N	You Know the Number	1987	2.50	5.00	10.00
❑ 3025-1-N	Easily Slip Into Another World	1988	2.50	5.00	10.00
❑ 3052-1-N	Rag, Bush and All	1989	2.50	5.00	10.00

THREE
Members: KHAN JAMAL; JOHNNY DYANI; PIERRE DORGE.

Number	Title	Yr	VG	VG+	NM
STEEPLECHASE					
❑ SCS-1201	Three	198?	3.00	6.00	12.00

THREE CATS AND A FIDDLE

Number	Title	Yr	VG	VG+	NM
REPEAT					
❑ S-150 [M]	Three Cats and a Fiddle	1964	3.75	7.50	15.00

THREE DEUCES, THE

Number	Title	Yr	VG	VG+	NM
STOMP OFF					
❑ SOS-1185	Stompin' 'n' Slidin'	1988	2.50	5.00	10.00

THREE JOLLY MINERS, THE

Number	Title	Yr	VG	VG+	NM
HISTORICAL					
❑ 23 [M]	The Three Jolly Miners 1925-28	1968	3.75	7.50	15.00

Number	Title	Yr	VG	VG+	NM

THREE SOULS, THE
Members: Henry Cain; Albert Coleman; Will Scott.
ARGO
❑ LP-4005 [M]	Almost Like Being In Love	1960	---	---	---
-- Canceled					
❑ LPS-4005 [S]	Almost Like Being In Love	1960	---	---	---
-- Canceled					
❑ LP-4036 [M]	Dangerous Dan Express	1964	5.00	10.00	20.00
❑ LPS-4036 [S]	Dangerous Dan Express	1964	6.25	12.50	25.00
❑ LP-4044 [M]	Soul Sounds	1965	5.00	10.00	20.00
❑ LPS-4044 [S]	Soul Sounds	1965	6.25	12.50	25.00

THREE SOUNDS, THE
Members: GENE HARRIS (piano); Bill Dowdy (drums); Andrew Simpkins (bass). Harris later recorded as "Gene Harris and the Three Sounds" with studio musicians; those albums are listed under Harris' name.
BLUE NOTE
❑ BLP-1600 [M]	Introducing the Three Sounds	1958	30.00	60.00	120.00
-- "Deep groove" version (deep indentation under label on both sides)					
❑ BLP-1600 [M]	Introducing the Three Sounds	1958	20.00	40.00	80.00
-- Regular version, W. 63rd St. address on label					
❑ BLP-1600 [M]	Introducing the Three Sounds	1963	6.25	12.50	25.00
-- With "New York, USA" address on label					
❑ BST-1600 [S]	Introducing the Three Sounds	1959	20.00	40.00	80.00
-- "Deep groove" version (deep indentation under label on both sides)					
❑ BST-1600 [S]	Introducing the Three Sounds	1959	15.00	30.00	60.00
-- Regular version, W. 63rd St. address on label					
❑ BST-1600 [S]	Introducing the Three Sounds	1963	5.00	10.00	20.00
-- With "New York, USA" address on label					
❑ BLP-4014 [M]	Bottoms Up	1959	30.00	60.00	120.00
-- "Deep groove" version (deep indentation under label on both sides)					
❑ BLP-4014 [M]	Bottoms Up	1959	20.00	40.00	80.00
-- Regular version, W. 63rd St. address on label					
❑ BLP-4014 [M]	Bottoms Up	1963	6.25	12.50	25.00
-- With "New York, USA" address on label					
❑ BST-4014 [S]	Bottoms Up	1959	20.00	40.00	80.00
-- "Deep groove" version (deep indentation under label on both sides)					
❑ BST-4014 [S]	Bottoms Up	1959	15.00	30.00	60.00
-- Regular version, W. 63rd St. address on label					
❑ BST-4014 [S]	Bottoms Up	1963	5.00	10.00	20.00
-- With "New York, USA" address on label					
❑ BLP-4020 [M]	Good Deal	1959	30.00	60.00	120.00
-- "Deep groove" version (deep indentation under label on both sides)					
❑ BLP-4020 [M]	Good Deal	1959	20.00	40.00	80.00
-- Regular version, W. 63rd St. address on label					
❑ BLP-4020 [M]	Good Deal	1963	6.25	12.50	25.00
-- With "New York, USA" address on label					
❑ BLP-4044 [M]	Moods	1960	30.00	60.00	120.00
-- "Deep groove" version (deep indentation under label on both sides)					
❑ BLP-4044 [M]	Moods	1960	20.00	40.00	80.00
-- Regular version, W. 63rd St. address on label					
❑ BLP-4044 [M]	Moods	1963	6.25	12.50	25.00
-- With "New York, USA" address on label					
❑ BLP-4072 [M]	Feelin' Good	1961	20.00	40.00	80.00
-- With W. 63rd St. address on label					
❑ BLP-4072 [M]	Feelin' Good	1963	6.25	12.50	25.00
-- With "New York, USA" address on label					
❑ BLP-4088 [M]	Here We Come	1961	20.00	40.00	80.00
-- With 61st St. address on label					
❑ BLP-4088 [M]	Here We Come	1963	6.25	12.50	25.00
-- With "New York, USA" address on label					
❑ BLP-4102 [M]	Hey! There	1962	7.50	15.00	30.00
❑ BLP-4120 [M]	It Just Got to Be	1963	7.50	15.00	30.00
❑ BLP-4155 [M]	Black Orchid	1963	7.50	15.00	30.00
❑ BLP-4197 [M]	Out of This World	1965	7.50	15.00	30.00
❑ BLP-4248 [M]	Vibrations	1966	7.50	15.00	30.00
❑ BLP-4265 [M]	Live at the Lighthouse	1967	7.50	15.00	30.00
❑ BST-81600 [S]	Introducing the Three Sounds	1967	3.75	7.50	15.00
-- With "A Division of Liberty Records" on label					
❑ BST-84014 [S]	Bottoms Up	1967	3.75	7.50	15.00
-- With "A Division of Liberty Records" on label					
❑ BST-84020 [S]	Good Deal	1959	12.50	25.00	50.00
-- With W. 63rd St. address on label					
❑ BST-84020 [S]	Good Deal	1963	5.00	10.00	20.00
-- With "New York, USA" address on label					
❑ BST-84020 [S]	Good Deal	1967	3.75	7.50	15.00
-- With "A Division of Liberty Records" on label					
❑ BST-84044 [S]	Moods	1960	12.50	25.00	50.00
-- With W. 63rd St. address on label					
❑ BST-84044 [S]	Moods	1963	3.75	7.50	15.00
-- With "A Division of Liberty Records" on label					
❑ BST-84044 [S]	Moods	1967	5.00	10.00	20.00
-- With "New York, USA" address on label					
❑ BST-84072 [S]	Feelin' Good	1961	12.50	25.00	50.00
-- With W. 63rd St. address on label					
❑ BST-84072 [S]	Feelin' Good	1963	5.00	10.00	20.00
-- With "New York, USA" address on label					
❑ BST-84072 [S]	Feelin' Good	1967	3.75	7.50	15.00
-- With "A Division of Liberty Records" on label					
❑ BST-84088 [S]	Here We Come	1961	12.50	25.00	50.00
-- With 61st St. address on label					
❑ BST-84088 [S]	Here We Come	1963	5.00	10.00	20.00
-- With "New York, USA" address on label					
❑ BST-84088 [S]	Here We Come	1967	3.75	7.50	15.00
-- With "A Division of Liberty Records" on label					
❑ BST-84102 [S]	Hey! There	1962	7.50	15.00	30.00
-- With "New York, USA" address on label					
❑ BST-84102 [S]	Hey! There	1967	3.75	7.50	15.00
-- With "A Division of Liberty Records" on label					
❑ BST-84120 [S]	It Just Got to Be	1963	7.50	15.00	30.00
-- With "New York, USA" address on label					
❑ BST-84120 [S]	It Just Got to Be	1967	3.75	7.50	15.00
-- With "A Division of Liberty Records" on label					
❑ BST-84155 [S]	Black Orchid	1963	7.50	15.00	30.00
-- With "New York, USA" address on label					
❑ BST-84155 [S]	Black Orchid	1967	3.75	7.50	15.00
-- With "A Division of Liberty Records" on label					
❑ BST-84197 [S]	Out of This World	1965	7.50	15.00	30.00
-- With "New York, USA" address on label					
❑ BST-84197 [S]	Out of This World	1967	3.75	7.50	15.00
-- With "A Division of Liberty Records" on label					
❑ BST-84248 [S]	Vibrations	1966	7.50	15.00	30.00
-- With "New York, USA" address on label					
❑ BST-84248 [S]	Vibrations	1967	3.75	7.50	15.00
-- With "A Division of Liberty Records" on label					
❑ BST-84265 [S]	Live at the Lighthouse	1967	5.00	10.00	20.00
-- With "A Division of Liberty Records" on label					
❑ BST-84285 [S]	Coldwater Flat	1968	5.00	10.00	20.00
-- With "A Division of Liberty Records" on label					
❑ BST-84301 [S]	Elegant Soul	1968	5.00	10.00	20.00
-- With "A Division of Liberty Records" on label					
❑ BST-84341 [S]	Soul Symphony	1969	5.00	10.00	20.00
-- With "A Division of Liberty Records" on label					

LIMELIGHT
❑ LM-82014 [M]	Three Moods	1965	5.00	10.00	20.00
❑ LM-82026 [M]	Beautiful Friendship	1965	5.00	10.00	20.00
❑ LS-86014 [S]	Three Moods	1965	6.25	12.50	25.00
❑ LS-86026 [S]	Beautiful Friendship	1965	6.25	12.50	25.00

MERCURY
❑ MG-20776 [M]	Jazz On Broadway	1963	6.25	12.50	25.00
❑ MG-20839 [M]	Some Like It Modern	1963	6.25	12.50	25.00
❑ MG-20921 [M]	Live at the Living Room	1963	6.25	12.50	25.00
❑ SR-60776 [S]	Jazz On Broadway	1963	7.50	15.00	30.00
❑ SR-60839 [S]	Some Like It Modern	1963	7.50	15.00	30.00
❑ SR-60921 [S]	Live at the Living Room	1963	7.50	15.00	30.00

VERVE
❑ V-8513 [M]	Blue Genes	1963	6.25	12.50	25.00
❑ V6-8513 [S]	Blue Genes	1963	7.50	15.00	30.00

THURSDAY GROUP, THE
Members: Douglas Lichterman (guitar); Clayton Englar (tenor, soprano and bass sax, flute); Jim Kerwin (bass); Vinnie Johnson (drums, replaced by Tony Manno).
PATHFINDER
❑ PTF-8307	The Thursday Group	1983	3.00	6.00	12.00
❑ PTF-8807	Uncle Mean	1988	3.00	6.00	12.00

TIBBETTS, STEVE
Guitarist, kalimba player and synthesizer player.
ECM
❑ 1218	Northern Song	198?	2.50	5.00	10.00
❑ 25002	Safe Journey	1984	2.50	5.00	10.00

TICHENOR, TREBOR
Pianist. Also see THE ST. LOUIS RAGTIMERS.
DIRTY SHAME
❑ 2001	King of Folk Ragtime	197?	3.00	6.00	12.00

TILLES, NURIT
Pianist.
JAZZOLOGY
❑ JCE-87	Ragtime, Here and Now!	1982	2.50	5.00	10.00

TIMELESS ALL-STARS, THE
Members: CURTIS FULLER; BILLY HIGGINS; BOBBY HUTCHERSON; HAROLD LAND; CEDAR WALTON; BUSTER WILLIAMS.
TIMELESS
❑ LPSJP-178	It's Timeless	1988	2.50	5.00	10.00

Number	Title	Yr	VG	VG+	NM

TIMMENS, JIM, AND HIS JAZZ ALL-STARS
Arranger and conductor. Some of the musicians on this album were KENNY BURRELL; DONALD BYRD; and JOE VENUTO.
WARNER BROS.
| ❏ W 1278 [M] | Gilbert and Sullivan Revisited | 1958 | 5.00 | 10.00 | 20.00 |
| ❏ WS 1278 [S] | Gilbert and Sullivan Revisited | 1958 | 6.25 | 12.50 | 25.00 |

TIMMONS, BOBBY
Pianist. Also see JOE ALEXANDER; JOHN JENKINS; THE RIVERSIDE JAZZ STARS; THE YOUNG LIONS.
FANTASY
| ❏ OJC-104 | This Here Is Bobby Timmons | 198? | 2.50 | 5.00 | 10.00 |
| ❏ OJC-364 | Bobby Timmons In Person | 198? | 2.50 | 5.00 | 10.00 |
MILESTONE
❏ MSP-9011	Got to Get It	1969	5.00	10.00	20.00
❏ MSP-9020	Do You Know the Way	1969	5.00	10.00	20.00
❏ 47031 [(2)]	Moanin'	197?	3.75	7.50	15.00
PRESTIGE
❏ PRLP-7335 [M]	Little Barefoot Soul	1964	6.25	12.50	25.00
❏ PRST-7335 [S]	Little Barefoot Soul	1964	7.50	15.00	30.00
❏ PRLP-7351 [M]	Chun-King	1965	6.25	12.50	25.00
❏ PRST-7351 [S]	Chun-King	1965	7.50	15.00	30.00
❏ PRLP-7387 [M]	Workin' Out	1966	6.25	12.50	25.00
❏ PRST-7387 [S]	Workin' Out	1966	7.50	15.00	30.00
❏ PRLP-7414 [M]	Holiday Soul	1966	6.25	12.50	25.00
❏ PRST-7414 [S]	Holiday Soul	1966	7.50	15.00	30.00
❏ PRLP-7429 [M]	Chicken and Dumplin's	1966	6.25	12.50	25.00
❏ PRST-7429 [S]	Chicken and Dumplin's	1966	7.50	15.00	30.00
❏ PRLP-7465 [M]	Soul Man	1967	6.25	12.50	25.00
❏ PRST-7465 [S]	Soul Man	1967	5.00	10.00	20.00
❏ PRLP-7483 [M]	Soul Food	1967	6.25	12.50	25.00
❏ PRST-7483 [S]	Soul Food	1967	5.00	10.00	20.00
❏ PRST-7780	The Best of Soul Piano	1970	3.75	7.50	15.00
RIVERSIDE
❏ RLP 12-317 [M]	This Here Is Bobby Timmons	1960	10.00	20.00	40.00
❏ RLP-334 [M]	Soul Time	1960	7.50	15.00	30.00
❏ RLP-363 [M]	Easy Does It	1961	6.25	12.50	25.00
❏ RLP-391 [M]	The Bobby Timmons Trio In Person	1961	6.25	12.50	25.00
-- Recorded "Live" at the Village Vanguard					
❏ RLP-422 [M]	Sweet and Soulful Sounds	1962	6.25	12.50	25.00
❏ RLP-468 [M]	Born to Be Blue!	1963	6.25	12.50	25.00
❏ RLP-1164 [S]	This Here Is Bobby Timmons	1960	7.50	15.00	30.00
❏ RS-3053	From the Bottom	196?	3.75	7.50	15.00
❏ R-6050	This Here Is Bobby Timmons	197?	3.00	6.00	12.00
❏ R-6110	Bobby Timmons In Person	197?	3.00	6.00	12.00
❏ RS-9334 [S]	Soul Time	1960	10.00	20.00	40.00
❏ RS-9363 [S]	Easy Does It	1961	7.50	15.00	30.00
❏ RS-9391 [S]	The Bobby Timmons Trio In Person	1961	7.50	15.00	30.00
-- Recorded 'Live' At the Village Vanguard					
❏ RS-9422 [S]	Sweet and Soulful Sounds	1962	7.50	15.00	30.00
❏ RS-9468 [S]	Born to Be Blue!	1963	7.50	15.00	30.00

TIRABASSO, JOHN
Drummer.
DISCOVERY
| ❏ DS-884 | Live at Dino's | 198? | 2.50 | 5.00 | 10.00 |
DOBRE
| ❏ 1022 | Diamond Cuff Links and Mink | 197? | 3.75 | 7.50 | 15.00 |

TISO, WAGNER
Pianist, keyboard player, arranger and composer.
PHILIPS
| ❏ 834 632-1 | Manu Carue | 1989 | 3.00 | 6.00 | 12.00 |
VERVE
| ❏ 831 819-1 | Giselle | 1987 | 2.50 | 5.00 | 10.00 |

TJADER, CAL
Vibraphone player. The most prominent non-Latino in the Latin jazz realm. Also see DAVE BRUBECK; DON ELLIOTT; MARY STALLINGS.
CONCORD JAZZ
| ❏ CJ-159 | Shining Sea | 1981 | 2.50 | 5.00 | 10.00 |
CONCORD PICANTE
❏ CJP-113	La Onda Va Bien	1979	3.00	6.00	12.00
❏ CJP-133	Gozame! Pero Ya...	1980	3.00	6.00	12.00
❏ CJP-176	A Fuego Vivo	1981	2.50	5.00	10.00
❏ CJP-247	Good Vibes	1983	2.50	5.00	10.00
CRYSTAL CLEAR
| ❏ 8003 | Huracan | 1978 | 6.25 | 12.50 | 25.00 |
| -- Direct-to-disc recording | | | | | |
FANTASY
| ❏ 3-9 [10] | The Cal Tjader Trio | 1953 | 37.50 | 75.00 | 150.00 |
| -- Any of various non-black vinyl pressings | | | | | |

Number	Title	Yr	VG	VG+	NM
❏ 3-9 [10]	The Cal Tjader Trio	1953	25.00	50.00	100.00
-- Black vinyl					
❏ 3-17 [10]	Ritmo Caliente	1954	37.50	75.00	150.00
-- Any of various non-black vinyl pressings					
❏ 3-17 [10]	Ritmo Caliente	1954	25.00	50.00	100.00
-- Black vinyl					
❏ OJC-271	Mambo with Tjader	1987	2.50	5.00	10.00
-- Reissue of 3202					
❏ OJC-274	Tjader Plays Mambo	1987	2.50	5.00	10.00
-- Reissue of 3221					
❏ OJC-277	San Francisco Moods	1987	2.50	5.00	10.00
-- Reissue of 8017					
❏ OJC-278	A Night at the Blackhawk	1987	2.50	5.00	10.00
-- Reissue of 8026					
❏ OJC-279	Concert on the Campus	1987	2.50	5.00	10.00
-- Reissue of 8044					
❏ OJC-285	Cal Tjader Plays the Harold Arlen Songbook	1987	2.50	5.00	10.00
-- Reissue of 8072					
❏ OJC-436	Jazz at the Blackhawk	1990	2.50	5.00	10.00
-- Reissue of 8096					
❏ OJC-642	Latin Kick	1991	3.00	6.00	12.00
-- Reissue of 8033					
❏ OJC-643	Cal Tjader's Latin Concert	1991	3.00	6.00	12.00
-- Reissue of 8014					
❏ 3202 [M]	Mambo with Tjader	1955	25.00	50.00	100.00
-- Red vinyl					
❏ 3202 [M]	Mambo with Tjader	1956	12.50	25.00	50.00
-- Black vinyl, red label, non-flexible vinyl					
❏ 3202 [M]	Mambo with Tjader	196?	6.25	12.50	25.00
-- Black vinyl, red label, flexible vinyl					
❏ 3211 [M]	Tjader Plays Tjazz	1956	25.00	50.00	100.00
-- Red vinyl					
❏ 3211 [M]	Tjader Plays Tjazz	1956	12.50	25.00	50.00
-- Black vinyl, red label, non-flexible vinyl					
❏ 3216 [M]	Ritmo Caliente	1956	25.00	50.00	100.00
-- Red vinyl					
❏ 3216 [M]	Ritmo Caliente	1956	12.50	25.00	50.00
-- Black vinyl, red label, non-flexible vinyl					
❏ 3216 [M]	Ritmo Caliente	196?	6.25	12.50	25.00
-- Black vinyl, red label, flexible vinyl					
❏ 3221 [M]	Tjader Plays Mambo	1956	25.00	50.00	100.00
-- Red vinyl					
❏ 3221 [M]	Tjader Plays Mambo	1956	12.50	25.00	50.00
-- Black vinyl, red label, non-flexible vinyl					
❏ 3221 [M]	Tjader Plays Mambo	196?	6.25	12.50	25.00
-- Black vinyl, red label, flexible vinyl					
❏ 3227 [M]	Cal Tjader Quartet	1956	25.00	50.00	100.00
-- Red vinyl					
❏ 3232 [M]	The Cal Tjader Quintet	1956	25.00	50.00	100.00
-- Red vinyl					
❏ 3232 [M]	The Cal Tjader Quintet	1956	12.50	25.00	50.00
-- Black vinyl, red label, non-flexible vinyl					
❏ 3232 [M]	The Cal Tjader Quintet	196?	6.25	12.50	25.00
-- Black vinyl, red label, flexible vinyl					
❏ 3241 [M]	Jazz at the Blackhawk	1957	12.50	25.00	50.00
-- Red vinyl					
❏ 3241 [M]	Jazz at the Blackhawk	1957	7.50	15.00	30.00
-- Black vinyl, red label, non-flexible vinyl					
❏ 3241 [M]	Jazz at the Blackhawk	196?	3.75	7.50	15.00
-- Black vinyl, red label, flexible vinyl					
❏ 3250 [M]	Latin Kick	1957	12.50	25.00	50.00
-- Red vinyl					
❏ 3250 [M]	Latin Kick	1957	7.50	15.00	30.00
-- Black vinyl, red label, non-flexible vinyl					
❏ 3250 [M]	Latin Kick	196?	3.75	7.50	15.00
-- Black vinyl, red label, flexible vinyl					
❏ 3253 [M]	Cal Tjader	1958	15.00	30.00	60.00
-- Red vinyl					
❏ 3253 [M]	Cal Tjader	1958	10.00	20.00	40.00
-- Black vinyl, non-flexible vinyl					
❏ 3262 [M]	Mas Ritmo Caliente	1958	12.50	25.00	50.00
-- Red vinyl					
❏ 3262 [M]	Mas Ritmo Caliente	1958	7.50	15.00	30.00
-- Black vinyl, red label, non-flexible vinyl					
❏ 3262 [M]	Mas Ritmo Caliente	196?	3.75	7.50	15.00
-- Black vinyl, red label, flexible vinyl					
❏ 3271 [M]	San Francisco Moods	1958	12.50	25.00	50.00
-- Red vinyl					
❏ 3271 [M]	San Francisco Moods	1958	7.50	15.00	30.00
-- Black vinyl, red label, non-flexible vinyl					
❏ 3271 [M]	San Francisco Moods	196?	3.75	7.50	15.00
-- Black vinyl, red label, flexible vinyl					
❏ 3275 [M]	Cal Tjader's Latin Concert	1958	12.50	25.00	50.00
-- Red vinyl					
❏ 3275 [M]	Cal Tjader's Latin Concert	1958	7.50	15.00	30.00
-- Black vinyl, red label, non-flexible vinyl					
❏ 3275 [M]	Cal Tjader's Latin Concert	196?	3.75	7.50	15.00
-- Black vinyl, red label, flexible vinyl					
❏ 3278 [M]	Tjader Plays Tjazz	1958	12.50	25.00	50.00
-- Red vinyl; reissue of 3211					

Number	Title	Yr	VG	VG+	NM
❏ 3278 [M]	Tjader Plays Tjazz	1958	7.50	15.00	30.00
-- Black vinyl, red label, non-flexible vinyl					
❏ 3278 [M]	Tjader Plays Tjazz	196?	3.75	7.50	15.00
-- Black vinyl, red label, flexible vinyl					
❏ 3279 [M]	Latin for Lovers	1958	12.50	25.00	50.00
-- Red vinyl					
❏ 3279 [M]	Latin for Lovers	1958	7.50	15.00	30.00
-- Black vinyl, red label, non-flexible vinyl					
❏ 3279 [M]	Latin for Lovers	196?	3.75	7.50	15.00
-- Black vinyl, red label, flexible vinyl					
❏ 3283 [M]	A Night at the Blackhawk	1959	12.50	25.00	50.00
-- Red vinyl					
❏ 3283 [M]	A Night at the Blackhawk	1959	7.50	15.00	30.00
-- Black vinyl, red label, non-flexible vinyl					
❏ 3283 [M]	A Night at the Blackhawk	196?	3.75	7.50	15.00
-- Black vinyl, red label, flexible vinyl					
❏ 3289 [M]	Tjader Goes Latin	1959	12.50	25.00	50.00
-- Red vinyl					
❏ 3289 [M]	Tjader Goes Latin	1959	7.50	15.00	30.00
-- Black vinyl, red label, non-flexible vinyl					
❏ 3289 [M]	Tjader Goes Latin	196?	3.75	7.50	15.00
-- Black vinyl, red label, flexible vinyl					
❏ 3295 [M]	Concert by the Sea	1959	12.50	25.00	50.00
-- Red vinyl					
❏ 3295 [M]	Concert by the Sea	1959	7.50	15.00	30.00
-- Black vinyl, red label, non-flexible vinyl					
❏ 3295 [M]	Concert by the Sea	196?	3.75	7.50	15.00
-- Black vinyl, red label, flexible vinyl					
❏ 3299 [M]	Concert on the Campus	1960	10.00	20.00	40.00
-- Red vinyl					
❏ 3299 [M]	Concert on the Campus	1960	6.25	12.50	25.00
-- Black vinyl, red label, non-flexible vinyl					
❏ 3299 [M]	Concert on the Campus	196?	3.75	7.50	15.00
-- Black vinyl, red label, flexible vinyl					
❏ 3307 [M]	Cal Tjader Quartet	1960	10.00	20.00	40.00
-- Red vinyl					
❏ 3307 [M]	Cal Tjader Quartet	1960	6.25	12.50	25.00
-- Black vinyl, red label, non-flexible vinyl					
❏ 3307 [M]	Cal Tjader Quartet	196?	3.75	7.50	15.00
-- Black vinyl, red label, flexible vinyl					
❏ 3309 [M]	Demasiado Caliente	1960	10.00	20.00	40.00
-- Red vinyl					
❏ 3309 [M]	Demasiado Caliente	1960	6.25	12.50	25.00
-- Black vinyl, red label, non-flexible vinyl					
❏ 3309 [M]	Demasiado Caliente	196?	3.75	7.50	15.00
-- Black vinyl, red label, flexible vinyl					
❏ 3310 [M]	West Side Story	1960	10.00	20.00	40.00
-- Red vinyl					
❏ 3310 [M]	West Side Story	1960	6.25	12.50	25.00
-- Black vinyl, red label, non-flexible vinyl					
❏ 3310 [M]	West Side Story	196?	3.75	7.50	15.00
-- Black vinyl, red label, flexible vinyl					
❏ 3313 [M]	Cal Tjader Quintet	196?	3.75	7.50	15.00
-- Black vinyl, red label, flexible vinyl					
❏ 3313 [M]	Cal Tjader Quintet	1961	6.25	12.50	25.00
-- Black vinyl, red label, non-flexible vinyl					
❏ 3313 [M]	Cal Tjader Quintet	1961	10.00	20.00	40.00
-- Red vinyl; evidently a different album than 3232					
❏ 3315 [M]	Cal Tjader Live and Direct	1961	10.00	20.00	40.00
-- Red vinyl					
❏ 3315 [M]	Cal Tjader Live and Direct	1961	6.25	12.50	25.00
-- Black vinyl, red label, non-flexible vinyl					
❏ 3315 [M]	Cal Tjader Live and Direct	196?	3.75	7.50	15.00
-- Black vinyl, red label, flexible vinyl					
❏ 3326 [M]	Mambo	1961	10.00	20.00	40.00
-- Red vinyl					
❏ 3326 [M]	Mambo	1961	6.25	12.50	25.00
-- Black vinyl, red label, non-flexible vinyl					
❏ 3326 [M]	Mambo	196?	3.75	7.50	15.00
-- Black vinyl, red label, flexible vinyl					
❏ 3330 [M]	Cal Tjader Plays the Harold Arlen Songbook	1961	10.00	20.00	40.00
-- Red vinyl					
❏ 3330 [M]	Cal Tjader Plays the Harold Arlen Songbook	1961	6.25	12.50	25.00
-- Black vinyl, red label, non-flexible vinyl					
❏ 3330 [M]	Cal Tjader Plays the Harold Arlen Songbook	196?	3.75	7.50	15.00
-- Black vinyl, red label, flexible vinyl					
❏ 3339 [M]	Latino	1962	10.00	20.00	40.00
-- Red vinyl					
❏ 3339 [M]	Latino	1962	6.25	12.50	25.00
-- Black vinyl, red label, non-flexible vinyl					
❏ 3339 [M]	Latino	196?	3.75	7.50	15.00
-- Black vinyl, red label, flexible vinyl					
❏ 3341 [M]	Concert by the Sea, Volume 2	1962	10.00	20.00	40.00
-- Red vinyl					
❏ 3341 [M]	Concert by the Sea, Volume 2	1962	6.25	12.50	25.00
-- Black vinyl, red label, non-flexible vinyl					
❏ 3341 [M]	Concert by the Sea, Volume 2	196?	3.75	7.50	15.00
-- Black vinyl, red label, flexible vinyl					

Number	Title	Yr	VG	VG+	NM
❏ 3366 [M]	Cal Tjader's Greatest Hits	1965	3.75	7.50	15.00
❏ 3374 [M]	Cal Tjader's Greatest Hits, Volume 2	1966	3.75	7.50	15.00
❏ MPF-4527	Cal Tjader's Greatest Hits	1987	2.50	5.00	10.00
-- Reissue of 8366					
❏ MPF-4530	Cal Tjader's Greatest Hits, Volume 2	1987	2.50	5.00	10.00
-- Reissue of 8374					
❏ 8003 [S]	Mas Ritmo Caliente	196?	7.50	15.00	30.00
-- Blue vinyl					
❏ 8003 [S]	Mas Ritmo Caliente	196?	5.00	10.00	20.00
-- Black vinyl, blue label, non-flexible vinyl					
❏ 8003 [S]	Mas Ritmo Caliente	196?	3.00	6.00	12.00
-- Black vinyl, blue label, flexible vinyl					
❏ 8014 [S]	Cal Tjader's Latin Concert	196?	7.50	15.00	30.00
-- Blue vinyl					
❏ 8014 [S]	Cal Tjader's Latin Concert	196?	5.00	10.00	20.00
-- Black vinyl, blue label, non-flexible vinyl					
❏ 8014 [S]	Cal Tjader's Latin Concert	196?	3.00	6.00	12.00
-- Black vinyl, blue label, flexible vinyl					
❏ 8016 [S]	Latin for Lovers	196?	7.50	15.00	30.00
-- Blue vinyl					
❏ 8016 [S]	Latin for Lovers	196?	5.00	10.00	20.00
-- Black vinyl, blue label, non-flexible vinyl					
❏ 8016 [S]	Latin for Lovers	196?	3.00	6.00	12.00
-- Black vinyl, blue label, flexible vinyl					
❏ 8017 [S]	San Francisco Moods	196?	7.50	15.00	30.00
-- Blue vinyl					
❏ 8017 [S]	San Francisco Moods	196?	5.00	10.00	20.00
-- Black vinyl, blue label, non-flexible vinyl					
❏ 8017 [S]	San Francisco Moods	196?	3.00	6.00	12.00
-- Black vinyl, blue label, flexible vinyl					
❏ 8019 [S]	Latin for Dancers	196?	25.00	50.00	100.00
-- Blue vinyl; the existence of this has been confirmed. Black vinyl copies of 8019 are unknown.					
❏ 8026 [S]	A Night at the Blackhawk	196?	7.50	15.00	30.00
-- Blue vinyl					
❏ 8026 [S]	A Night at the Blackhawk	196?	5.00	10.00	20.00
-- Black vinyl, blue label, non-flexible vinyl					
❏ 8026 [S]	A Night at the Blackhawk	196?	3.00	6.00	12.00
-- Black vinyl, blue label, flexible vinyl					
❏ 8030 [S]	Tjader Goes Latin	196?	7.50	15.00	30.00
-- Blue vinyl					
❏ 8030 [S]	Tjader Goes Latin	196?	5.00	10.00	20.00
-- Black vinyl, blue label, non-flexible vinyl					
❏ 8030 [S]	Tjader Goes Latin	196?	3.00	6.00	12.00
-- Black vinyl, blue label, flexible vinyl					
❏ 8033 [S]	Latin Kick	196?	7.50	15.00	30.00
-- Blue vinyl					
❏ 8033 [S]	Latin Kick	196?	5.00	10.00	20.00
-- Black vinyl, blue label, non-flexible vinyl					
❏ 8033 [S]	Latin Kick	196?	3.00	6.00	12.00
-- Black vinyl, blue label, flexible vinyl					
❏ 8038 [S]	Concert by the Sea	196?	7.50	15.00	30.00
-- Blue vinyl					
❏ 8038 [S]	Concert by the Sea	196?	5.00	10.00	20.00
-- Black vinyl, blue label, non-flexible vinyl					
❏ 8038 [S]	Concert by the Sea	196?	3.00	6.00	12.00
-- Black vinyl, blue label, flexible vinyl					
❏ 8044 [S]	Concert on the Campus	196?	7.50	15.00	30.00
-- Blue vinyl					
❏ 8044 [S]	Concert on the Campus	196?	5.00	10.00	20.00
-- Black vinyl, blue label, non-flexible vinyl					
❏ 8044 [S]	Concert on the Campus	196?	3.00	6.00	12.00
-- Black vinyl, blue label, flexible vinyl					
❏ 8053 [S]	Demasiado Caliente	196?	7.50	15.00	30.00
-- Blue vinyl					
❏ 8053 [S]	Demasiado Caliente	196?	5.00	10.00	20.00
-- Black vinyl, blue label, non-flexible vinyl					
❏ 8053 [S]	Demasiado Caliente	196?	3.00	6.00	12.00
-- Black vinyl, blue label, flexible vinyl					
❏ 8054 [S]	West Side Story	196?	7.50	15.00	30.00
-- Blue vinyl					
❏ 8054 [S]	West Side Story	196?	5.00	10.00	20.00
-- Black vinyl, blue label, non-flexible vinyl					
❏ 8054 [S]	West Side Story	196?	3.00	6.00	12.00
-- Black vinyl, blue label, flexible vinyl					
❏ 8057 [S]	Mambo	1962	7.50	15.00	30.00
-- Blue vinyl					
❏ 8057 [S]	Mambo	1962	5.00	10.00	20.00
-- Black vinyl, blue label, non-flexible vinyl					
❏ 8057 [S]	Mambo	196?	3.00	6.00	12.00
-- Black vinyl, blue label, flexible vinyl					
❏ 8059 [S]	Cal Tjader Live and Direct	1962	7.50	15.00	30.00
-- Blue vinyl					
❏ 8059 [S]	Cal Tjader Live and Direct	1962	5.00	10.00	20.00
-- Black vinyl, blue label, non-flexible vinyl					
❏ 8059 [S]	Cal Tjader Live and Direct	196?	3.00	6.00	12.00
-- Black vinyl, blue label, flexible vinyl					
❏ 8072 [S]	Cal Tjader Plays the Harold Arlen Songbook	1962	7.50	15.00	30.00
-- Blue vinyl					

Number	Title	Yr	VG	VG+	NM
❏ 8072 [S]	Cal Tjader Plays the Harold Arlen Songbook	1962	5.00	10.00	20.00
-- Black vinyl, blue label, non-flexible vinyl					
❏ 8072 [S]	Cal Tjader Plays the Harold Arlen Songbook	196?	3.00	6.00	12.00
-- Black vinyl, blue label, flexible vinyl					
❏ 8077 [R]	Ritmo Caliente	1962	7.50	15.00	30.00
-- Blue vinyl					
❏ 8077 [R]	Ritmo Caliente	1962	5.00	10.00	20.00
-- Black vinyl, blue label, non-flexible vinyl					
❏ 8077 [R]	Ritmo Caliente	196?	3.00	6.00	12.00
-- Black vinyl, blue label, flexible vinyl					
❏ 8079 [S]	Latino	1962	7.50	15.00	30.00
-- Blue vinyl					
❏ 8079 [S]	Latino	1962	5.00	10.00	20.00
-- Black vinyl, blue label, non-flexible vinyl					
❏ 8079 [S]	Latino	196?	3.00	6.00	12.00
-- Black vinyl, blue label, flexible vinyl					
❏ 8083 [R]	Cal Tjader Quartet	1962	7.50	15.00	30.00
-- Blue vinyl					
❏ 8083 [R]	Cal Tjader Quartet	1962	5.00	10.00	20.00
-- Black vinyl, blue label, non-flexible vinyl					
❏ 8083 [R]	Cal Tjader Quartet	1962	3.00	6.00	12.00
-- Black vinyl, blue label, flexible vinyl					
❏ 8084 [S]	Cal Tjader Quintet	1962	7.50	15.00	30.00
-- Blue vinyl; stereo version of 3313					
❏ 8084 [S]	Cal Tjader Quintet	1962	5.00	10.00	20.00
-- Black vinyl, blue label, non-flexible vinyl					
❏ 8084 [S]	Cal Tjader Quintet	1962	3.00	6.00	12.00
-- Black vinyl, blue label, flexible vinyl					
❏ 8085 [R]	The Cal Tjader Quintet	196?	7.50	15.00	30.00
-- Blue vinyl; stereo version of 3232					
❏ 8085 [R]	The Cal Tjader Quintet	196?	5.00	10.00	20.00
-- Black vinyl, blue label, non-flexible vinyl					
❏ 8085 [R]	The Cal Tjader Quintet	196?	3.00	6.00	12.00
-- Black vinyl, blue label, flexible vinyl					
❏ 8096 [R]	Jazz at the Blackhawk	1962	7.50	15.00	30.00
-- Blue vinyl					
❏ 8096 [R]	Jazz at the Blackhawk	1962	5.00	10.00	20.00
-- Black vinyl, blue label, non-flexible vinyl					
❏ 8096 [R]	Jazz at the Blackhawk	196?	3.00	6.00	12.00
-- Black vinyl, blue label, flexible vinyl					
❏ 8097 [R]	Tjader Plays Tjazz	1962	7.50	15.00	30.00
-- Blue vinyl					
❏ 8097 [R]	Tjader Plays Tjazz	1962	5.00	10.00	20.00
-- Black vinyl, blue label, non-flexible vinyl					
❏ 8097 [R]	Tjader Plays Tjazz	196?	3.00	6.00	12.00
-- Black vinyl, blue label, flexible vinyl					
❏ 8098 [S]	Concert by the Sea, Volume 2	1962	7.50	15.00	30.00
-- Blue vinyl					
❏ 8098 [S]	Concert by the Sea, Volume 2	1962	5.00	10.00	20.00
-- Black vinyl, blue label, non-flexible vinyl					
❏ 8098 [S]	Concert by the Sea, Volume 2	196?	3.00	6.00	12.00
-- Black vinyl, blue label, flexible vinyl					
❏ 8366 [S]	Cal Tjader's Greatest Hits	1965	3.00	6.00	12.00
❏ 8374 [S]	Cal Tjader's Greatest Hits, Volume 2	1966	3.00	6.00	12.00
❏ 8379	West Side Story	1967	3.00	6.00	12.00
-- Reissue of 8054					
❏ 8406	Tjader	1970	3.00	6.00	12.00
❏ 8416	Agua Dulce	1971	3.00	6.00	12.00
❏ 9409	Live at the Funky Quarters	1970	3.00	6.00	12.00
❏ 9422	Primo	1972	3.00	6.00	12.00
❏ 9424	Mambo with Tjader	1973	3.00	6.00	12.00
❏ 9446	Last Bolero in Berkeley	1974	3.00	6.00	12.00
❏ 9463	Puttin' It Together	1974	3.00	6.00	12.00
❏ 9482	Last Night When We Were Young	1975	3.00	6.00	12.00
❏ 9502	Amazonas	1975	3.00	6.00	12.00
❏ 9521	At Grace Cathedral	1977	3.00	6.00	12.00
❏ 9533	Guarabe	1977	3.00	6.00	12.00
❏ 24712 [(2)]	Los Ritmos Caliente	197?	3.75	7.50	15.00
GALAXY					
❏ 5107	Breathe Easy	1977	3.00	6.00	12.00
❏ 5121	Here	1978	3.00	6.00	12.00
MGM					
❏ 10008	Sonido Nuevo	197?	3.75	7.50	15.00
PRESTIGE					
❏ 24026 [(2)]	The Monterey Concerts	1973	3.75	7.50	15.00
SAVOY					
❏ MG-9036 [10]	Cal Tjader -- Vibist	1954	25.00	50.00	100.00
SKYE					
❏ SK-1	Solar Heat	1968	5.00	10.00	20.00
❏ SK-10	Cal Tjader Plugs In	1969	5.00	10.00	20.00
❏ SK-19	Tjader-Ade	1970	3.75	7.50	15.00
VERVE					
❏ V-8419 [M]	In a Latin Bag	1961	5.00	10.00	20.00

Number	Title	Yr	VG	VG+	NM
❏ V6-8419 [S]	In a Latin Bag	1961	6.25	12.50	25.00
❏ V-8459 [M]	Saturday Night...Sunday Night at the Blackhawk	1962	5.00	10.00	20.00
❏ V6-8459 [S]	Saturday Night...Sunday Night at the Blackhawk	1962	6.25	12.50	25.00
❏ V-8470 [M]	The Contemporary Music of Mexico and Brazil	1962	5.00	10.00	20.00
❏ V6-8470 [S]	The Contemporary Music of Mexico and Brazil	1962	6.25	12.50	25.00
❏ V-8507 [M]	Several Shades of Jade	1963	5.00	10.00	20.00
❏ V6-8507 [S]	Several Shades of Jade	1963	6.25	12.50	25.00
❏ V-8531 [M]	Sona Libre	1963	5.00	10.00	20.00
❏ V6-8531 [S]	Sona Libre	1963	6.25	12.50	25.00
❏ V-8575 [M]	Breeze from the East	1964	5.00	10.00	20.00
❏ V6-8575 [S]	Breeze from the East	1964	6.25	12.50	25.00
❏ V-8585 [M]	Warm Wave	1964	5.00	10.00	20.00
❏ V6-8585 [S]	Warm Wave	1964	6.25	12.50	25.00
❏ V-8614 [M]	Soul Sauce	1965	5.00	10.00	20.00
❏ V6-8614 [S]	Soul Sauce	1965	6.25	12.50	25.00
❏ V-8626 [M]	Soul Bird: Whippenpoof	1965	5.00	10.00	20.00
❏ V6-8626 [S]	Soul Bird: Whippenpoof	1965	6.25	12.50	25.00
❏ V-8637 [M]	Soul Burst	1965	5.00	10.00	20.00
❏ V6-8637 [S]	Soul Burst	1965	6.25	12.50	25.00
❏ V-8651 [M]	El Soni Do Nuevo -- The New Soul Sound	1966	3.75	7.50	15.00
❏ V6-8651 [S]	El Soni Do Nuevo -- The New Soul Sound	1966	5.00	10.00	20.00
❏ V-8671 [M]	Along Comes Cal	1966	3.75	7.50	15.00
❏ V6-8671 [S]	Along Comes Cal	1966	5.00	10.00	20.00
❏ V-8725 [M]	The Best of Cal Tjader	1967	3.75	7.50	15.00
❏ V6-8725 [S]	The Best of Cal Tjader	1967	5.00	10.00	20.00
❏ V-8730 [M]	Hip Vibrations	1967	5.00	10.00	20.00
❏ V6-8730 [S]	Hip Vibrations	1967	3.75	7.50	15.00
❏ V6-8769	The Prophet	1969	3.75	7.50	15.00
❏ 827 756-1	Soul Sauce	1986	2.50	5.00	10.00
-- Reissue of 8614					

TJADER, CAL, AND CHARLIE BYRD
Also see each artist's individual listings.
FANTASY

❏ 9453	Tambu	1974	3.00	6.00	12.00

TJADER, CAL/DON ELLIOTT
Also see each artist's individual listings.
SAVOY

❏ MG-12054 [M]	Vib-Rations	1956	10.00	20.00	40.00
-- Reissue of 9036 and 9033					

TJADER, CAL, AND STAN GETZ
Also see each artist's individual listings.
FANTASY

❏ 3266 [M]	Cal Tjader-Stan Getz Sextet	1958	12.50	25.00	50.00
-- Red vinyl					
❏ 3266 [M]	Cal Tjader-Stan Getz Sextet	1958	7.50	15.00	30.00
-- Black vinyl, red label, non-flexible vinyl					
❏ 3266 [M]	Cal Tjader-Stan Getz Sextet	196?	3.75	7.50	15.00
-- Black vinyl, red label, flexible vinyl					
❏ 3348 [M]	Cal Tjader-Stan Getz Sextet	1963	3.75	7.50	15.00
-- Reissue of 3266					
❏ 8005 [S]	Cal Tjader-Stan Getz Sextet	196?	7.50	15.00	30.00
-- Blue vinyl					
❏ 8005 [S]	Cal Tjader-Stan Getz Sextet	196?	5.00	10.00	20.00
-- Black vinyl, blue label, non-flexible vinyl					
❏ 8005 [S]	Cal Tjader-Stan Getz Sextet	196?	3.00	6.00	12.00
-- Black vinyl, blue label, flexible vinyl					
❏ 8348 [S]	Cal Tjader-Stan Getz Quartet	1963	3.00	6.00	12.00
-- Reissue of 8005					

TJADER, CAL, AND CARMEN McRAE
Also see each artist's individual listings.
CONCORD JAZZ

❏ CJ-189	Heat Wave	1982	2.50	5.00	10.00

TODD, RICHARD
French horn player.
GM RECORDINGS

❏ 2010	New Ideas	1986	3.00	6.00	12.00

TOGASHI, MASAHIKO
Drummer and bandleader.
INNER CITY

❏ IC-6011	Spiritual Nature	197?	3.75	7.50	15.00

Number	Title	Yr	VG	VG+	NM

TOGAWA, PAUL
Drummer and bandleader.
MODE
| ❑ LP-104 [M] | Paul Togawa Quartet | 1957 | 20.00 | 40.00 | 80.00 |

TOLLIVER, CHARLES
Trumpeter and composer.
ARISTA/FREEDOM
| ❑ AF 1002 | Paper Man | 1975 | 3.00 | 6.00 | 12.00 |
| ❑ AF 1017 | The Ringer | 1975 | 3.00 | 6.00 | 12.00 |
STRATA-EAST
❑ SES-1971	Music Inc.	1971	5.00	10.00	20.00
❑ SES-1972	Live at Slugs'	1972	5.00	10.00	20.00
❑ SES-8001	Compassion	1980	3.00	6.00	12.00
❑ SES-19720	Live at Slugs', Vol. 2	1972	5.00	10.00	20.00
❑ SES-19740/1 [(2)]	Live at the Loosdrecht Jazz	1974	6.25	12.50	25.00
❑ SES-19745	Live in Tokyo	1974	5.00	10.00	20.00
❑ SES-19757	Impact	1975	3.75	7.50	15.00

TOLONEN, JUKKA
Guitarist.
TERRA
| ❑ T-6 | Touch Wood | 1985 | 3.00 | 6.00 | 12.00 |

TOMPKINS, FRED
Composer and conductor.
F.K.T.
❑ 101	Compositions	1980	2.50	5.00	10.00
❑ 102	Somesville	1980	2.50	5.00	10.00
❑ 103	Cecile	1980	3.00	6.00	12.00
FESTIVAL
| ❑ 9001 | Compositions | 197? | 3.00 | 6.00 | 12.00 |
| ❑ 9002 | Somesville | 1975 | 3.00 | 6.00 | 12.00 |

TOMPKINS, ROSS
Pianist.
CONCORD JAZZ
❑ CJ-28	Scrimshaw	1976	3.00	6.00	12.00
❑ CJ-46	Lost in the Stars	1977	3.00	6.00	12.00
❑ CJ-65	Ross Tompkins and His Good Friends	1978	3.00	6.00	12.00
❑ CJ-117	Festival Time	198?	2.50	5.00	10.00
FAMOUS DOOR
❑ HL-143	Street of Dreams	198?	2.50	5.00	10.00
❑ HL-146	Symphony	198?	2.50	5.00	10.00
❑ HL-151	L.A. After Dark	1986	2.50	5.00	10.00
❑ HL-153	In the Swing of Things	1987	2.50	5.00	10.00

TOMPKINS, ROSS, AND JOE VENUTI
Also see each artist's individual listings.
CONCORD JAZZ
| ❑ CJ-51 | Live '77 | 1978 | 3.00 | 6.00 | 12.00 |

TONIGHT SHOW BAND, THE
See DOC SEVERINSON.

TORFF, BRIAN
Bass player and composer.
AUDIOPHILE
| ❑ AP-182 | Manhattan Hoe-Down | 1983 | 2.50 | 5.00 | 10.00 |
OPTIMISM
| ❑ OP-2601 | Hitchhiker of Karoo | 198? | 2.50 | 5.00 | 10.00 |

TORKANOWSKY, DAVID
Organist and pianist.
ROUNDER
| ❑ 2090 | Steppin' Out | 198? | 2.50 | 5.00 | 10.00 |

TORME, MEL
Male singer, pianist, drummer and composer, best known probably for his "The Christmas Song," made popular by NAT KING COLE.
ALLEGRO ELITE
| ❑ 4117 [10] | Mel Torme Sings | 195? | 7.50 | 15.00 | 30.00 |
ARCHIVE OF FOLK AND JAZZ
| ❑ 324 | The Velvet Fog | 198? | 2.50 | 5.00 | 10.00 |
ATLANTIC
❑ 8066 [M]	Mel Torme at the Red Hill Inn	1962	7.50	15.00	30.00
❑ SD 8066 [S]	Mel Torme at the Red Hill Inn	1962	10.00	20.00	40.00
❑ 8069 [M]	Comin' Home Baby	1962	7.50	15.00	30.00
❑ SD 8069 [S]	Comin' Home Baby	1962	10.00	20.00	40.00
❑ 8091 [M]	Sunday in New York	1963	7.50	15.00	30.00
❑ SD 8091 [S]	Sunday in New York	1963	10.00	20.00	40.00
❑ SD 18129	Live at the Maisonette	1975	3.00	6.00	12.00
❑ 80078	Songs of New York	1982	2.50	5.00	10.00
AUDIOPHILE
| ❑ 67 | Mel Torme Sings About Love | 198? | 5.00 | 10.00 | 20.00 |
BETHLEHEM
❑ BCP-34 [M]	It's a Blue World	1956	12.50	25.00	50.00
❑ BCP-52 [M]	Mel Torme and the Marty Paich Dektette	1956	12.50	25.00	50.00
❑ BCP 6013 [M]	Mel Torme Sings Fred Astaire	1957	12.50	25.00	50.00
❑ BCP 6016 [M]	California Suite	1957	12.50	25.00	50.00
❑ BCP 6020 [M]	Mel Torme Live at the Crescendo	1958	12.50	25.00	50.00
❑ BCP 6031 [M]	Songs for Any Taste	1959	12.50	25.00	50.00
CAPITOL
| ❑ P 200 [10] | California Suite | 1950 | 25.00 | 50.00 | 100.00 |
| ❑ ST-313 | A Time for Us | 1969 | 3.00 | 6.00 | 12.00 |
COLUMBIA
❑ CL 2318 [M]	That's All -- A Lush Romantic	1965	3.75	7.50	15.00
❑ CL 2535 [M]	Mel Torme Right Now	1966	3.00	6.00	12.00
❑ CS 9118 [S]	That's All -- A Lush Romantic	1965	5.00	10.00	20.00
❑ CS 9335 [S]	Mel Torme Right Now	1966	3.75	7.50	15.00
COLUMBIA SPECIAL PRODUCTS
| ❑ P 13090 | That's All | 1976 | 3.00 | 6.00 | 12.00 |
CONCORD JAZZ
❑ CJ-306	Mel Torme with Rob McConnell and the Boss Brass	1986	2.50	5.00	10.00
❑ CJ-360	Reunion	1988	2.50	5.00	10.00
❑ CJ-382	In Concert Tokyo	1989	2.50	5.00	10.00
-- Above two with the Marty Paich Dek-Tette					
CORAL
| ❑ CRL 57012 [M] | Gene Norman Presents Mel Torme "Live" at the Crescendo | 1955 | 12.50 | 25.00 | 50.00 |
| ❑ CRL 57044 [M] | Musical Sounds Are the Best Songs | 1956 | 12.50 | 25.00 | 50.00 |
DISCOVERY
| ❑ 910 | Sings His California Suite | 1986 | 2.50 | 5.00 | 10.00 |
| -- Reissue of Capitol 200 | | | | | |
FINESSE
| ❑ W2X 37484 [(2)] | Mel Torme & Friends Recorded at Marty's, New York City | 1981 | 3.00 | 6.00 | 12.00 |
GLENDALE
| ❑ 6007 | Mel Torme | 1978 | 2.50 | 5.00 | 10.00 |
| ❑ 6018 | Easy to Remember | 1979 | 2.50 | 5.00 | 10.00 |
GRYPHON
| ❑ 796 | A New Album | 1979 | 2.50 | 5.00 | 10.00 |
LIBERTY
| ❑ LST-7560 | A Day in the Life of Bonnie and Clyde | 1968 | 5.00 | 10.00 | 20.00 |
METRO
| ❑ M-523 [M] | I Wished on the Moon | 1965 | 3.00 | 6.00 | 12.00 |
| ❑ MS-523 [S] | I Wished on the Moon | 1965 | 3.75 | 7.50 | 15.00 |
MGM
| ❑ E 552 [10] | Songs by Mel Torme | 1952 | 25.00 | 50.00 | 100.00 |
MUSICRAFT
❑ 508	Mel Torme, Volume 1	1983	2.50	5.00	10.00
❑ 510	It Happened in Monterey	1983	2.50	5.00	10.00
❑ 2005	Gone with the Wind	1986	2.50	5.00	10.00
STASH
| ❑ ST-252 | 'Round Midnight | 1985 | 2.50 | 5.00 | 10.00 |
STRAND
| ❑ SL-1076 [M] | Mel Torme Sings | 1960 | 5.00 | 10.00 | 20.00 |
| ❑ SLS-1076 [S] | Mel Torme Sings | 1960 | 6.25 | 12.50 | 25.00 |
TOPS
| ❑ L-1615 [M] | Prelude to a Kiss | 1958 | 6.25 | 12.50 | 25.00 |
VERVE
❑ MGV 2105 [M]	Torme	1958	12.50	25.00	50.00
❑ V-2105 [M]	Torme	1961	5.00	10.00	20.00
-- Reissue					
❑ V6-2105 [S]	Torme	1961	6.25	12.50	25.00
-- Reissue					
❑ MGV 2117 [M]	Ole Torme! Mel Torme Goes South of the Border with Billy May	1959	12.50	25.00	50.00
❑ V-2117 [M]	Ole Torme! Mel Torme Goes South of the Border with Billy May	1961	5.00	10.00	20.00
-- Reissue					
❑ V6-2117 [S]	Ole Torme! Mel Torme Goes South of the Border with Billy May	1961	6.25	12.50	25.00
-- Reissue					
❑ MGV 2120 [M]	Back in Town	1959	12.50	25.00	50.00
❑ V-2120 [M]	Back in Town	1961	5.00	10.00	20.00
-- Reissue					

Number	Title	Yr	VG	VG+	NM
❑ V6-2120 [S]	Back in Town	1961	6.25	12.50	25.00
-- Reissue					
❑ MGV 2132 [M]	Mel Torme Swings Schubert Alley	1960	12.50	25.00	50.00
❑ V-2132 [M]	Mel Torme Swings Schubert Alley	1961	5.00	10.00	20.00
-- Reissue					
❑ V6-2132 [S]	Mel Torme Swings Schubert Alley	1961	6.25	12.50	25.00
-- Reissue					
❑ MGV 2144 [M]	Swingin' on the Moon	1960	12.50	25.00	50.00
❑ V-2144 [M]	Swingin' on the Moon	1961	5.00	10.00	20.00
-- Reissue					
❑ V6-2144 [S]	Swingin' on the Moon	1961	6.25	12.50	25.00
❑ MGV 2146 [M]	Broadway, Right Now	1961	12.50	25.00	50.00
❑ V-2146 [M]	Broadway, Right Now	1961	5.00	10.00	20.00
-- Reissue					
❑ V6-2146 [S]	Broadway, Right Now	1961	6.25	12.50	25.00
❑ MGV 2153 [M]	I Dig the Duke! I Dig the Count!	1961	---	---	---
-- Canceled; moved to 8491					
❑ UMV-2521	Mel Torme Swings Shubert Alley	1981	2.50	5.00	10.00
❑ UMV-2675	Back in Town	1982	2.50	5.00	10.00
❑ MGVS 6015 [S]	Torme	1960	12.50	25.00	50.00
❑ MGVS 6058 [S]	Ole Torme! Mel Torme Goes South of the Border with Billy May	1960	12.50	25.00	50.00
❑ MGVS 6063 [S]	Back in Town	1960	12.50	25.00	50.00
❑ MGVS 6146 [S]	Mel Torme Swings Schubert Alley	1960	12.50	25.00	50.00
❑ V-8440 [M]	My Kind of Music	1962	6.25	12.50	25.00
❑ V6-8440 [S]	My Kind of Music	1962	7.50	15.00	30.00
❑ V-8491 [M]	I Dig the Duke! I Dig the Count!	1962	6.25	12.50	25.00
❑ V6-8491 [S]	I Dig the Duke! I Dig the Count!	1962	7.50	15.00	30.00
❑ V-8593 [M]	Verve's Choice -- The Best of Mel Torme	1964	3.00	6.00	12.00
❑ V6-8593 [S]	Verve's Choice -- The Best of Mel Torme	1964	3.75	7.50	15.00
❑ 823 248-1	The Duke Ellington and Count Basie Songbooks	1984	2.50	5.00	10.00
-- Reissue of Verve 8491					
VOCALION					
❑ VL 73905	The Velvet Fog	197?	2.50	5.00	10.00

TORME, MEL, AND BUDDY RICH
Also see each artist's individual listings.
CENTURY

Number	Title	Yr	VG	VG+	NM
❑ 1100	Together Again -- For the First Time	1978	6.25	12.50	25.00
-- Direct-to-disc recording					
GRYPHON					
❑ 784	Together Again -- For the First Time	1978	2.50	5.00	10.00

TORN, DAVID, AND GEOFFREY GORDON
Torn is a guitarist; Gordon a percussionist.
ECM

Number	Title	Yr	VG	VG+	NM
❑ 1284	Best Laid Plans	1985	3.00	6.00	12.00

TORRES, NESTOR
Flutist.
VERVE FORECAST

Number	Title	Yr	VG	VG+	NM
❑ 839 387-1	Morning Ride	1989	3.00	6.00	12.00

TOSHIKO
See TOSHIKO AKIYOSHI.

TOUFF, CY
Bass trumpet player.
ARGO

Number	Title	Yr	VG	VG+	NM
❑ LP-606 [M]	Doorway to Dixie	1956	10.00	20.00	40.00
❑ LP-641 [M]	Touff Assignment	1959	7.50	15.00	30.00
❑ LPS-641 [S]	Touff Assignment	1959	6.25	12.50	25.00
PACIFIC JAZZ					
❑ PJ-42 [M]	Keester Parade	1962	10.00	20.00	40.00
❑ PJ-1211 [M]	Cy Touff, His Octet and Quintet	1956	25.00	50.00	100.00
WORLD PACIFIC					
❑ PJM-410 [M]	Havin' a Ball	1958	15.00	30.00	60.00

TOWNER, RALPH
Guitarist, pianist, synthesizer player, French horn player, cornet player and percussionist.
ECM

Number	Title	Yr	VG	VG+	NM
❑ 1032	Diary	1973	3.75	7.50	15.00
❑ 1060	Solstice	197?	3.00	6.00	12.00
❑ 1095	Sound and Shadows	197?	3.00	6.00	12.00
❑ 1121	Batik	1978	3.00	6.00	12.00
❑ 1153	Old Friends, New Friends	197?	2.50	5.00	10.00
❑ 1173	Solo Concert	1979	2.50	5.00	10.00
❑ 23788	Blue Sun	1983	2.50	5.00	10.00

TOWNER, RALPH, AND JOHN ABERCROMBIE
Also see each artist's individual listings.
ECM

Number	Title	Yr	VG	VG+	NM
❑ 1207	Five Years Later	198?	2.50	5.00	10.00

TOWNER, RALPH, AND GARY BURTON
Also see each artist's individual listings.
ECM

Number	Title	Yr	VG	VG+	NM
❑ 1056	Matchbook	197?	3.00	6.00	12.00
❑ 25038	Slide Show	1986	2.50	5.00	10.00

TOWNER, RALPH, AND GLEN MOORE
Also see each artist's individual listings.
ECM

Number	Title	Yr	VG	VG+	NM
❑ 1025	Trios/Solos	197?	3.00	6.00	12.00

TRACEY, STAN
Pianist and composer.
LONDON

Number	Title	Yr	VG	VG+	NM
❑ LL 3107 [M]	Showcase	195?	10.00	20.00	40.00

TRACEY, STAN, AND KEITH TIPPETT
Tippett also plays piano. Also see STAN TRACEY.
EMANEM

Number	Title	Yr	VG	VG+	NM
❑ 3307	TNT	1975	3.75	7.50	15.00

TRAUT, ROSS
Guitarist. Also see TRAUT/RODBY DUO.
HEADFIRST

Number	Title	Yr	VG	VG+	NM
❑ 9709	Ross Traut	198?	3.75	7.50	15.00

TRAUT/RODBY DUO
ROSS TRAUT (guitar) and Steve Rodby (bass).
COLUMBIA

Number	Title	Yr	VG	VG+	NM
❑ FC 44472	The Great Lawn	1989	3.00	6.00	12.00

TRAVIS, NICK
Trumpeter. Also see THE MANHATTAN JAZZ ALL-STARS.
RCA VICTOR

Number	Title	Yr	VG	VG+	NM
❑ LPM-1010 [M]	The Panic Is On	1954	20.00	40.00	80.00

TREVOR, JEANNIE
Female singer.
MAINSTREAM

Number	Title	Yr	VG	VG+	NM
❑ S-6075 [S]	Jeannie Trevor Sings!!	1965	7.50	15.00	30.00
❑ 56075 [M]	Jeannie Trevor Sings!!	1965	6.25	12.50	25.00

TRIO, THE
Members: KENNY CLARKE; HANK JONES; WENDELL MARSHALL.
SAVOY

Number	Title	Yr	VG	VG+	NM
❑ MG-12023 [M]	The Trio	1955	25.00	50.00	100.00

TRISTANO, LENNIE
Pianist and composer. Also see LEE WILEY.
ATLANTIC

Number	Title	Yr	VG	VG+	NM
❑ 1224 [M]	Lennie Tristano with Lee Konitz	1955	20.00	40.00	80.00
-- Black label					
❑ 1224 [M]	Lennie Tristano with Lee Konitz	1960	6.25	12.50	25.00
-- Multicolor label, white "fan" logo at right					
❑ 1224 [M]	Lennie Tristano with Lee Konitz	1964	3.75	7.50	15.00
-- Multicolor label, black "fan" logo at right					
❑ 1357 [M]	The New Tristano	196?	12.50	25.00	50.00
-- Multicolor label, white "fan" logo at right					
❑ 1357 [M]	The New Tristano	1960	3.75	7.50	15.00
-- Multicolor label, black "fan" logo at right					
❑ SD 2-7003 [(2)]	Requiem	198?	3.75	7.50	15.00
❑ SD 2-7006 [(2)]	Lennie Tristano Quartet	198?	3.75	7.50	15.00
ELEKTRA/MUSICIAN					
❑ 60264	Manhattan	1984	2.50	5.00	10.00
EMARCY					
❑ MG-26029 [10]	Holiday in Piano	1954	37.50	75.00	150.00
INNER CITY					
❑ IC-6002	Descent Into the Maelstrom	197?	3.75	7.50	15.00
JAZZ					
❑ JR-1	Live at Birdland 1949	198?	2.50	5.00	10.00
❑ JR-5	Live in Toronto 1952	198?	2.50	5.00	10.00

Number	Title	Yr	VG	VG+	NM
❏ JR-6	Continuity	198?	2.50	5.00	10.00

MOSAIC

Number	Title	Yr	VG	VG+	NM
❏ MQ10-174 [(10)]	The Complete Atlantic Recordings of Lennie Tristano, Lee Konitz and Warne Marsh	199?	45.00	90.00	180.00

NEW JAZZ

Number	Title	Yr	VG	VG+	NM
❏ NJLP-101 [10]	Lennie Tristano with Lee Konitz	1950	62.50	125.00	250.00

PRESTIGE

Number	Title	Yr	VG	VG+	NM
❏ PRLP-101 [10]	Lennie Tristano with Lee Konitz	1951	50.00	100.00	200.00

TRISTANO, LENNIE; JOE BUSHKIN; BOBBY SCOTT; MARIAN McPARTLAND
Also see each artist's individual listings.

SAVOY

Number	Title	Yr	VG	VG+	NM
❏ MG-12043 [M]	The Jazz Keyboards of Lennie Tristano, Joe Bushkin, Bobby Scott & Marian McPartland	1955	12.50	25.00	50.00

TRISTANO, LENNIE/ARNOLD ROSS
Also see each artist's individual listings.

EMARCY

Number	Title	Yr	VG	VG+	NM
❏ MG-26029 [10]	Holiday Piano	1953	30.00	60.00	120.00

TROMBONES UNLIMITED
LIBERTY

Number	Title	Yr	VG	VG+	NM
❏ LRP-3449 [M]	These Bones are Made for Walking	1966	3.75	7.50	15.00
❏ LRP-3472 [M]	You're Gonna Hear from Me	1966	3.75	7.50	15.00
❏ LRP-3494 [M]	Big Boss Bones	1967	5.00	10.00	20.00
❏ LRP-3527 [M]	Holiday for Trombones	1967	5.00	10.00	20.00
❏ LRP-3549 [M]	One of Those Songs	1968	6.25	12.50	25.00
❏ LST-7449 [S]	These Bones are Made for Walking	1966	5.00	10.00	20.00
❏ LST-7472 [S]	You're Gonna Hear from Me	1966	5.00	10.00	20.00
❏ LST-7494 [S]	Big Boss Bones	1967	3.75	7.50	15.00
❏ LST-7527 [S]	Holiday for Trombones	1967	3.75	7.50	15.00
❏ LST-7549 [S]	One of Those Songs	1968	3.75	7.50	15.00
❏ LST-7592	Grazing in the Grass	1968	3.75	7.50	15.00

TROUP, BOBBY
Pianist, male singer and composer. His best-known song was "Route 66."

AUDIOPHILE

Number	Title	Yr	VG	VG+	NM
❏ AP-98	In a Class Beyond Compare	198?	2.50	5.00	10.00

BETHLEHEM

Number	Title	Yr	VG	VG+	NM
❏ BCP-19 [M]	Bobby Troup Sings Johnny Mercer	1955	12.50	25.00	50.00
❏ BCP-35 [M]	The Distinctive Style of Bobby	1955	12.50	25.00	50.00
❏ BCP-1030 [10]	Bobby Troup	1955	15.00	30.00	60.00

CAPITOL

Number	Title	Yr	VG	VG+	NM
❏ H 484 [10]	Bobby	1953	20.00	40.00	80.00
❏ T 484 [M]	Bobby	1955	12.50	25.00	50.00

INTERLUDE

Number	Title	Yr	VG	VG+	NM
❏ MO-501 [M]	Cool	1959	10.00	20.00	40.00
❏ ST-1001 [S]	Cool	1959	10.00	20.00	40.00

LIBERTY

Number	Title	Yr	VG	VG+	NM
❏ LRP-3002 [M]	Bobby Troup and His Trio	1955	12.50	25.00	50.00
❏ LRP-3026 [M]	Do Re Mi	1957	12.50	25.00	50.00
❏ LRP-3078 [M]	Here's to My Lady	1958	12.50	25.00	50.00

MODE

Number	Title	Yr	VG	VG+	NM
❏ LP-111 [M]	Bobby Swings Tenderly	1957	25.00	50.00	100.00

PAUSA

Number	Title	Yr	VG	VG+	NM
❏ 9032	Bobby Troup	198?	2.50	5.00	10.00

RCA VICTOR

Number	Title	Yr	VG	VG+	NM
❏ LPM-1959 [M]	Bobby Troup and His Jazz All-Stars	1959	10.00	20.00	40.00
❏ LSP-1959 [S]	Bobby Troup and His Jazz All-Stars	1959	12.50	25.00	50.00

TRUMPET KINGS, THE
Members: ROY ELDRIDGE; DIZZY GILLESPIE; CLARK TERRY.

ANALOGUE PRODUCTIONS

Number	Title	Yr	VG	VG+	NM
❏ APR-3010	Alternate Blues	199?	3.75	7.50	15.00

PABLO

Number	Title	Yr	VG	VG+	NM
❏ 2310 754	Montreux '75	1975	3.00	6.00	12.00

TRUMPET SUMMIT
Members: DIZZY GILLESPIE; FREDDIE HUBBARD; CLARK TERRY.

PABLO TODAY

Number	Title	Yr	VG	VG+	NM
❏ 2312 114	Trumpet Summit Meets the Oscar Peterson Big 4	198?	3.00	6.00	12.00

TRYFOROS, BOB
Guitarist.

PURITAN

Number	Title	Yr	VG	VG+	NM
❏ 5002	Joplin on Guitar	197?	3.00	6.00	12.00

TRYNIN, JENNIFER
Female singer, guitarist and composer. After a recording hiatus, she returned as a more pop-oriented singer for the Warner Bros. label.

PATHFINDER

Number	Title	Yr	VG	VG+	NM
❏ PTF-8827 [EP]	Trespassing	1988	3.75	7.50	15.00

TUCK & PATTI
Tuck Andress (guitar) and Patti Cathcart (vocals).

WINDHAM HILL

Number	Title	Yr	VG	VG+	NM
❏ WH-0111	Tears of Joy	1988	2.50	5.00	10.00
❏ WH-0116	Love Warriors	1989	3.00	6.00	12.00

TUCKER, MICKEY
Pianist.

MUSE

Number	Title	Yr	VG	VG+	NM
❏ MR-5174	Mister Mysterious	1978	3.00	6.00	12.00
❏ MR-5223	The Crawl	1979	3.00	6.00	12.00

XANADU

Number	Title	Yr	VG	VG+	NM
❏ 128	Triplicity	1976	3.00	6.00	12.00
❏ 143	Sojourn	1977	3.00	6.00	12.00

TUCKER, TOMMY
Male singer and bandleader.

CIRCLE

Number	Title	Yr	VG	VG+	NM
❏ C-15	Tommy Tucker and His Orchestra 1942-1947	198?	2.50	5.00	10.00
❏ CLP-124	Tommy Tucker and His Californians 1933	1991	3.00	6.00	12.00

TURNER, JIM
Pianist.

EUPHONIC

Number	Title	Yr	VG	VG+	NM
❏ 1222	Old Fashioned Love: A Tribute to James P. Johnson	198?	2.50	5.00	10.00

TURNER, JOE
Male singer. Also popular in rhythm & blues.

ARHOOLIE

Number	Title	Yr	VG	VG+	NM
❏ 2004 [M]	Jumpin' the Blues	1962	5.00	10.00	20.00

ATCO

Number	Title	Yr	VG	VG+	NM
❏ SD 33-376	Joe Turner -- His Greatest Recordings	1971	3.75	7.50	15.00

ATLANTIC

Number	Title	Yr	VG	VG+	NM
❏ 1234 [M]	The Boss of the Blues	1956	30.00	60.00	120.00
-- Black label					
❏ 1234 [M]	The Boss of the Blues	1960	25.00	50.00	100.00
-- White "bullseye" label					
❏ 1234 [M]	The Boss of the Blues	1961	10.00	20.00	40.00
-- White "fan" logo on label					
❏ 1234 [M]	The Boss of the Blues	1963	3.75	7.50	15.00
-- Black "fan" logo on label					
❏ SD 1234 [S]	The Boss of the Blues	1959	45.00	90.00	180.00
-- Green label					
❏ SD 1234 [S]	The Boss of the Blues	1960	37.50	75.00	150.00
-- White "bullseye" label					
❏ SD 1234 [S]	The Boss of the Blues	1961	12.50	25.00	50.00
-- White "fan" logo on label					
❏ SD 1234 [S]	The Boss of the Blues	1963	5.00	10.00	20.00
-- Black "fan" logo on label					
❏ 1332 [M]	Big Joe Rides Again	1959	37.50	75.00	150.00
-- Black label					
❏ 1332 [M]	Big Joe Rides Again	1960	10.00	20.00	40.00
-- White "fan" logo on label					
❏ 1332 [M]	Big Joe Rides Again	1963	3.75	7.50	15.00
-- Black "fan" logo on label					
❏ SD 1332 [S]	Big Joe Rides Again	1959	50.00	100.00	200.00
-- Green label					
❏ SD 1332 [S]	Big Joe Rides Again	1960	12.50	25.00	50.00
-- White "fan" logo on label					
❏ SD 1332 [S]	Big Joe Rides Again	1963	5.00	10.00	20.00
-- Black "fan" logo on label					
❏ 8005 [M]	Joe Turner	1957	37.50	75.00	150.00
-- Black label					
❏ 8005 [M]	Joe Turner	1961	10.00	20.00	40.00
-- White "fan" logo on label					
❏ 8005 [M]	Joe Turner	1963	3.75	7.50	15.00
-- Black "fan" logo on label					

Number	Title	Yr	VG	VG+	NM
❑ 8023 [M]	Rockin' the Blues	1958	30.00	60.00	120.00
-- Black label					
❑ 8023 [M]	Rockin' the Blues	1960	10.00	20.00	40.00
-- White "fan" logo on label					
❑ 8023 [M]	Rockin' the Blues	1963	3.75	7.50	15.00
-- Black "fan" logo on label					
❑ 8033 [M]	Big Joe Is Here	1959	30.00	60.00	120.00
-- Black label					
❑ 8033 [M]	Big Joe Is Here	1960	25.00	50.00	100.00
-- White "bullseye" label					
❑ 8033 [M]	Big Joe Is Here	1960	10.00	20.00	40.00
-- White "fan" logo on label					
❑ 8033 [M]	Big Joe Is Here	1963	3.75	7.50	15.00
-- Black "fan" logo on label					
❑ 8081 [M]	The Best of Joe Turner	1963	12.50	25.00	50.00
❑ SD 8812	Boss of the Blues	1981	2.50	5.00	10.00
-- Reissue of 1234					
❑ 81752	Greatest Hits	1987	2.50	5.00	10.00
BLUES SPECTRUM					
❑ BS-104	Great Rhythm and Blues Oldies Vol. 4	197?	3.75	7.50	15.00
BLUESTIME					
❑ 9002 [M]	The Real Boss of the Blues	196?	10.00	20.00	40.00
❑ 29002 [S]	The Real Boss of the Blues	196?	7.50	15.00	30.00
BLUESWAY					
❑ BL 6006 [M]	Singing the Blues	1967	5.00	10.00	20.00
❑ BLS-6006 [S]	Singing the Blues	1967	6.25	12.50	25.00
❑ S-6060	Roll 'Em	1973	3.75	7.50	15.00
CHIAROSCURO					
❑ 147	King of Stride	1976	3.75	7.50	15.00
CLASSIC JAZZ					
❑ 138	Effervescent	1976	3.75	7.50	15.00
DECCA					
❑ DL 8044 [M]	Joe Turner Sings Kansas City Jazz	1953	62.50	125.00	250.00
FANTASY					
❑ OJC-497	Trumpet Kings Meet Joe Turner	1991	3.00	6.00	12.00
INTERMEDIA					
❑ QS-5008	Rock This Joint	198?	2.50	5.00	10.00
❑ QS-5026	The Very Best of Joe Turner -- Live	198?	2.50	5.00	10.00
❑ QS-5030	The Blues Boss -- Live	198?	2.50	5.00	10.00
❑ QS-5036	Everyday I Have the Blues	198?	2.50	5.00	10.00
❑ QS-5043	Roll Me Baby	198?	2.50	5.00	10.00
KENT					
❑ KST-542	Joe Turner Turns On the Blues	1973	3.75	7.50	15.00
MCA					
❑ 1325	Early Big Joe	198?	2.50	5.00	10.00
MUSE					
❑ MR-5293	Blues Train	198?	2.50	5.00	10.00
-- With Roomful of Blues and Dr. John					
PABLO					
❑ 2310 717	Trumpet Kings Meet Joe Turner	197?	3.00	6.00	12.00
❑ 2310 760	Nobody in Mind	197?	3.00	6.00	12.00
❑ 2310 763	Another Epoch Stride Piano	197?	3.00	6.00	12.00
❑ 2310 776	In the Evening	197?	3.00	6.00	12.00
❑ 2310 800	Things That I Used to Do	197?	3.00	6.00	12.00
❑ 2310 818	Every Day I Have the Blues	198?	3.00	6.00	12.00
❑ 2310 848	The Best of Joe Turner	1980	3.00	6.00	12.00
❑ 2310 863	Have No Fear, Joe Turner Is Here	1983	3.00	6.00	12.00
❑ 2310 883	Singing the Same, Sad, Happy, Forever Blues	1983	3.00	6.00	12.00
❑ 2310 913	Patcha, Patcha, All Night Long	198?	3.00	6.00	12.00
❑ 2310 937	Flip, Flop and Fly	1989	3.00	6.00	12.00
❑ 2405 404	The Best of "Big" Joe Turner	198?	3.00	6.00	12.00
SAVOY					
❑ MG-14012 [M]	Blues'll Make You Happy	1958	37.50	75.00	150.00
❑ MG-14106 [M]	Careless Love	1963	20.00	40.00	80.00
SAVOY JAZZ					
❑ SJC-406	Blues'll Make You Happy	1985	2.50	5.00	10.00
-- Reissue of Savoy 14012					
❑ SJL-2223 [(2)]	Have No Fear	197?	3.75	7.50	15.00

TURNER, JOE, AND PETE JOHNSON

Johnson was the pianist for vocalist Joe Turner in his early days.

EMARCY

Number	Title	Yr	VG	VG+	NM
❑ MG-36014 [M]	Joe Turner and Pete Johnson	1955	50.00	100.00	200.00

Number	Title	Yr	VG	VG+	NM
TURNER, RAY					
Pianist.					
CAPITOL					
❑ H 306 [10]	Kitten on the Keys	1952	12.50	25.00	50.00
TURRE, STEVE					
Trombonist.					
STASH					
❑ ST-270	Viewpoint	1987	2.50	5.00	10.00
❑ ST-275	Fire and Ice	1988	2.50	5.00	10.00
TURRENTINE, STANLEY					
Tenor saxophone player. Also see SHIRLEY SCOTT.					
BAINBRIDGE					
❑ 1038	Stan the Man	1981	2.50	5.00	10.00
BLUE NOTE					
❑ BN-LA883-J2 [(2)]	Jubilee Shout!!	1977	3.75	7.50	15.00
❑ LT-933	New Time Shuffle	1978	2.50	5.00	10.00
❑ LT-1037	In Memory Of…	1980	2.50	5.00	10.00
❑ LT-1075	Mr. Natural	1980	2.50	5.00	10.00
❑ LT-1095	Ain't No Way	1981	2.50	5.00	10.00
❑ BLP-4039 [M]	Look Out!	1960	30.00	60.00	120.00
-- "Deep groove" version (deep indentation under label on both sides)					
❑ BLP-4039 [M]	Look Out!	1960	20.00	40.00	80.00
-- Regular version with W. 63rd St. address on label					
❑ BLP-4039 [M]	Look Out!	1963	6.25	12.50	25.00
-- With "New York, USA" address on label					
❑ BLP-4057 [M]	Blue Hour	1961	20.00	40.00	80.00
-- With W. 63rd St. address on label					
❑ BLP-4057 [M]	Blue Hour	1963	6.25	12.50	25.00
-- With "New York, USA" address on label					
❑ BLP-4065 [M]	Comin' Your Way	1961	---	---	---
-- Canceled					
❑ BLP-4069 [M]	Up at Minton's, Volume 1	1961	20.00	40.00	80.00
-- With W. 63rd St. address on label					
❑ BLP-4069 [M]	Up at Minton's, Volume 1	1963	6.25	12.50	25.00
-- With "New York, USA" address on label					
❑ BLP-4070 [M]	Up at Minton's, Volume 2	1961	20.00	40.00	80.00
-- With W. 63rd St. address on label					
❑ BLP-4070 [M]	Up at Minton's, Volume 2	1963	6.25	12.50	25.00
-- With "New York, USA" address on label					
❑ BLP-4081 [M]	Dearly Beloved	1961	18.75	37.50	75.00
-- With 61st St. address on label					
❑ BLP-4081 [M]	Dearly Beloved	1963	6.25	12.50	25.00
-- With "New York, USA" address on label					
❑ BLP-4096 [M]	That's Where It's At	1962	15.00	30.00	60.00
-- With 61st St. address on label					
❑ BLP-4096 [M]	That's Where It's At	1963	6.25	12.50	25.00
-- With "New York, USA" address on label					
❑ BLP-4122 [M]	Jubilee Shout!!!	1963	---	---	---
-- Canceled					
❑ BLP-4129 [M]	Never Let Me Go	1963	7.50	15.00	30.00
❑ BLP-4150 [M]	A Chip Off the Old Block	1963	7.50	15.00	30.00
❑ BLP-4162 [M]	Hustlin'	1964	7.50	15.00	30.00
❑ BLP-4201 [M]	Joyride	1965	6.25	12.50	25.00
❑ BLP-4234 [M]	Stanley Turrentine	1965	---	---	---
-- Canceled					
❑ BLP-4240 [M]	Rough 'n Tumble	1966	6.25	12.50	25.00
❑ BLP-4256 [M]	The Spoiler	1967	6.25	12.50	25.00
❑ BLP-4268 [M]	Easy Walker	1967	6.25	12.50	25.00
❑ BST-84039 [S]	Look Out!	1960	15.00	30.00	60.00
-- With W. 63rd St. addresss on label					
❑ BST-84039 [S]	Look Out!	1963	5.00	10.00	20.00
-- With "New York, USA" address on label					
❑ BST-84039 [S]	Look Out!	1967	3.75	7.50	15.00
-- With "A Division of Liberty Records" on label					
❑ BST-84057 [S]	Blue Hour	1961	15.00	30.00	60.00
-- With W. 63rd St. address on label					
❑ BST-84057 [S]	Blue Hour	1963	5.00	10.00	20.00
-- With "New York, USA" address on label					
❑ BST-84057 [S]	Blue Hour	1967	3.75	7.50	15.00
-- With "A Division of Liberty Records" on label					
❑ BST-84057 [S]	Blue Hour	1970	2.50	5.00	10.00
-- With United Artists distribution					
❑ BST-84057	Blue Hour	1986	2.50	5.00	10.00
-- "The Finest in Jazz Since 1939" label reissue					
❑ B1-84065	Comin' Your Way	1988	2.50	5.00	10.00
-- "The Finest in Jazz Since 1939" label; first issue of LP					
❑ BST-84065 [S]	Comin' Your Way	1961	---	---	---
-- Canceled					
❑ BST-84069 [S]	Up at Minton's, Volume 1	1961	15.00	30.00	60.00
-- With W. 63rd St. addresss on label					
❑ BST-84069 [S]	Up at Minton's, Volume 1	1963	5.00	10.00	20.00
-- With "New York, USA" address on label					
❑ BST-84069 [S]	Up at Minton's, Volume 1	1967	3.75	7.50	15.00
-- With "A Division of Liberty Records" on label					

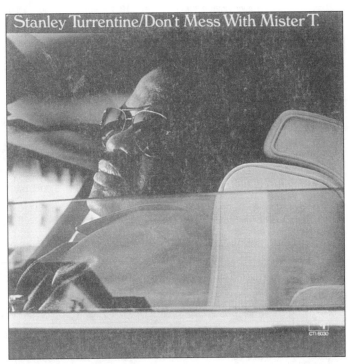

Tenor saxophone player Stanley Turrentine began as an R&B musician, which helps explain why most of his music is so funky and is sought-after by "soul jazz" collectors. (Top left) *That's Where It's At* is among his 1960s classics on the Blue Note label. (Top right) Turrentine's greatest commercial success came on the CTI label. *Salt Song*, from 1971, was the follow-up to the critically acclaimed *Sugar* LP. (Bottom left) Long before there was a TV star in gold chains who went by that name, Turrentine was known as "Mister T," as this 1973 CTI release shows. (Bottom right) After CTI, Turrentine went to the Fantasy label, where both his music and his album covers, as illustrated by the 1977 *Nightwings*, got increasingly cheesy.

Number	Title	Yr	VG	VG+	NM
❏ BST-84070 [S]	Up at Minton's, Volume 2	1961	15.00	30.00	60.00
-- With W. 63rd St. adress on label					
❏ BST-84070 [S]	Up at Minton's, Volume 2	1963	5.00	10.00	20.00
-- With "New York, USA" address on label					
❏ BST-84070 [S]	Up at Minton's, Volume 2	1967	3.75	7.50	15.00
-- With "A Division of Liberty Records" on label					
❏ BST-84081 [S]	Dearly Beloved	1961	15.00	30.00	60.00
-- With 61st St. address on label					
❏ BST-84081 [S]	Dearly Beloved	1963	5.00	10.00	20.00
-- With "New York, USA" address on label					
❏ BST-84081 [S]	Dearly Beloved	1967	3.75	7.50	15.00
-- With "A Division of Liberty Records" on label					
❏ BST-84096 [S]	That's Where It's At	1962	15.00	30.00	60.00
-- With 61st St. address on label					
❏ BST-84096 [S]	That's Where It's At	1963	5.00	10.00	20.00
-- With "New York, USA" address on label					
❏ BST-84096 [S]	That's Where It's At	1967	3.75	7.50	15.00
-- With "A Division of Liberty Records" on label					
❏ BST-84096	That's Where It's At	1986	2.50	5.00	10.00
-- "The Finest in Jazz Since 1939" reissue					
❏ BST-84122	Jubilee Shout!!	1986	3.00	6.00	12.00
-- "The Finest in Jazz Since 1939" label; first issue of LP					
❏ BST-84129 [S]	Never Let Me Go	1963	7.50	15.00	30.00
-- With "New York, USA" address on label					
❏ BST-84129 [S]	Never Let Me Go	1967	3.75	7.50	15.00
-- With "A Division of Liberty Records" on label					
❏ BST-84150 [S]	A Chip Off the Old Block	1963	7.50	15.00	30.00
-- With "New York, USA" address on label					
❏ BST-84150 [S]	A Chip Off the Old Block	1967	3.75	7.50	15.00
-- With "A Division of Liberty Records" on label					
❏ BST-84162 [S]	Hustlin'	1964	7.50	15.00	30.00
-- With "New York, USA" address on label					
❏ BST-84162 [S]	Hustlin'	1967	3.75	7.50	15.00
-- With "A Division of Liberty Records" on label					
❏ BST-84162 [S]	Hustlin'	1970	2.50	5.00	10.00
-- With United Artists distribution					
❏ BST-84201 [S]	Joyride	1964	6.25	12.50	25.00
-- With "New York, USA" address on label					
❏ BST-84201 [S]	Joyride	1967	3.75	7.50	15.00
-- With "A Division of Liberty Records" on label					
❏ BST-84201	Joyride	1984	2.50	5.00	10.00
-- "The Finest in Jazz Since 1939" label reissue					
❏ BST-84234 [S]	Stanley Turrentine	1965	---	---	---
-- Canceled					
❏ BST-84240 [S]	Rough 'n Tumble	1966	5.00	10.00	20.00
-- With "New York, USA" address on label					
❏ BST-84240 [S]	Rough 'n Tumble	1967	3.75	7.50	15.00
-- With "A Division of Liberty Records" on label					
❏ BST-84256 [S]	The Spoiler	1967	5.00	10.00	20.00
❏ BST-84268 [S]	Easy Walker	1967	5.00	10.00	20.00
❏ BST-84286	The Look of Love	1968	5.00	10.00	20.00
-- With "A Division of Liberty Records" on label					
❏ BST-84286	The Look of Love	1970	3.75	7.50	15.00
-- With United Artists distribution					
❏ BST-84298	Always Something There	1968	5.00	10.00	20.00
❏ BST-84315	Common Touch!	1969	5.00	10.00	20.00
❏ BST-84336	Another Story	1969	5.00	10.00	20.00
❏ BST-84424	Z.T.'s Blues	1985	2.50	5.00	10.00
❏ BST-85105	Straight Ahead	1984	2.50	5.00	10.00
❏ BST-85140	Wonderland	1987	2.50	5.00	10.00
❏ B1-90261	La Place	1987	2.50	5.00	10.00
❏ B1-93201	The Best of Stanley Turrentine	1989	3.00	6.00	12.00
CTI					
❏ 6005	Sugar	1971	3.00	6.00	12.00
❏ 6010	Salt Song	1971	3.00	6.00	12.00
❏ 6017	Cherry	1972	3.00	6.00	12.00
❏ 6030	Don't Mess with Mister T.	1973	3.00	6.00	12.00
❏ 6048	The Baddest Turrentine	1974	3.00	6.00	12.00
❏ 6052	The Sugar Man	1975	3.00	6.00	12.00
❏ 8006	Sugar	1981	2.50	5.00	10.00
-- Reissue					
❏ 8008	Salt Song	1981	2.50	5.00	10.00
-- Reissue					
❏ 8010	Cherry	1981	2.50	5.00	10.00
-- Reissue					
❏ 8011	Don't Mess with Mister T.	1981	2.50	5.00	10.00
-- Reissue					
ELEKTRA					
❏ 6E-217	Betcha	1979	2.50	5.00	10.00
❏ 6E-269	Inflation	1980	2.50	5.00	10.00
❏ 5E-534	Tender Togetherness	1981	2.50	5.00	10.00
❏ 60201	Home Again	1982	2.50	5.00	10.00
FANTASY					
❏ FPM-4002 [Q]	Pieces of Dreams	1974	5.00	10.00	20.00
❏ 9465	Pieces of Dreams	1974	2.50	5.00	10.00
❏ 9478	In the Pocket	1975	2.50	5.00	10.00
❏ 9493	Have You Ever Seen the Rain	1975	2.50	5.00	10.00
❏ 9508	Everybody Come On Out	1976	2.50	5.00	10.00
❏ 9519	The Man with the Sad Face	1976	2.50	5.00	10.00

Number	Title	Yr	VG	VG+	NM
❏ 9534	Nightwings	1977	2.50	5.00	10.00
❏ 9548	West Side Highway	1978	2.50	5.00	10.00
❏ 9563	What About You!	1978	2.50	5.00	10.00
❏ 9604	Use the Stairs	1980	2.50	5.00	10.00
IMPULSE!					
❏ AS-9115	Let It Go	1967	6.25	12.50	25.00
MAINSTREAM					
❏ S-6041 [S]	Tiger Tail	1965	6.25	12.50	25.00
❏ 56041 [M]	Tiger Tail	1965	5.00	10.00	20.00
SUNSET					
❏ SUS-5255	The Soul of Stanley Turrentine	196?	3.00	6.00	12.00
TIME					
❏ S-2086 [S]	Stan the Man	1962	10.00	20.00	40.00
❏ 52086 [M]	Stan the Man	1962	10.00	20.00	40.00

TURRENTINE, TOMMY
Trumpeter.

Number	Title	Yr	VG	VG+	NM
BAINBRIDGE					
❏ 1047	Tommy Turrentine	198?	2.50	5.00	10.00
TIME					
❏ ST-70008 [S]	Tommy Turrentine	1960	12.50	25.00	50.00
❏ T-70008 [M]	Tommy Turrentine	1960	10.00	20.00	40.00

TURTLE ISLAND STRING QUARTET
Members: Darol Anger (violin, fiddle); David Balakrishnan (violin, baritone violin); Irene Sazer (viola); Mark Summer (cello).

Number	Title	Yr	VG	VG+	NM
WINDHAM HILL					
❏ WH-0110	Turtle Island String Quartet	1988	2.50	5.00	10.00
❏ WH-0114	Metropolis	1989	3.00	6.00	12.00

TUSA, FRANK
Bass player.

Number	Title	Yr	VG	VG+	NM
ENJA					
❏ 2056	Father Time	197?	3.75	7.50	15.00

TWARDZIK, RICHARD
Pianist. Also see RUSS FREEMAN.

Number	Title	Yr	VG	VG+	NM
PACIFIC JAZZ					
❏ PJ-37 [M]	The Last Set	1962	15.00	30.00	60.00

TYLE, TEDDY
Tenor saxophone player.

Number	Title	Yr	VG	VG+	NM
GOLDEN CREST					
❏ GC-3060 [M]	Moon Shot	1959	10.00	20.00	40.00

TYLER, ALVIN "RED"
Tenor saxophone player and composer.

Number	Title	Yr	VG	VG+	NM
ROUNDER					
❏ 2047	Heritage	1986	3.00	6.00	12.00
❏ 2061	Graciously	1987	2.50	5.00	10.00

TYLER, CHARLES
Alto and baritone saxophone player and clarinetist.

Number	Title	Yr	VG	VG+	NM
ADELPHI					
❏ 5011	Sixty Minute Man	1980	3.00	6.00	12.00
ESP-DISK'					
❏ 1029 [M]	The Charles Tyler Ensemble	1966	5.00	10.00	20.00
❏ S-1029 [S]	The Charles Tyler Ensemble	1966	6.25	12.50	25.00
❏ S-1059 [S]	Eastern Man Alone	1968	5.00	10.00	20.00
NESSA					
❏ N-16	Saga of the Outlaws	197?	3.75	7.50	15.00
SILKHEART					
❏ SH-118	Autumn in Paris	199?	3.00	6.00	12.00
STORYVILLE					
❏ 4098	Definite, Vol. 1	198?	2.50	5.00	10.00

TYNER, McCOY
Pianist.

Number	Title	Yr	VG	VG+	NM
ABC IMPULSE!					
❏ AS-18	Inception	1968	3.00	6.00	12.00
❏ AS-33	Reaching Fourth	1968	3.00	6.00	12.00
❏ AS-39	Nights of Ballads and Blues	1968	3.00	6.00	12.00
❏ AS-48	McCoy Tyner Live at Newport	1968	3.00	6.00	12.00
❏ AS-63	Today and Tomorrow	1968	3.00	6.00	12.00
❏ AS-79	McCoy Tyner Plays Duke Ellington	1968	3.00	6.00	12.00
❏ IA-9235 [(2)]	Reevaluation: The Impulse! Years	197?	3.75	7.50	15.00
❏ IA-9338 [(2)]	Early Trios	1978	3.75	7.50	15.00
BLUE NOTE					
❏ BN-LA022-F	Extensions	1973	3.75	7.50	15.00

Number	Title	Yr	VG	VG+	NM
❑ BN-LA223-G	Asante	1974	3.75	7.50	15.00
❑ BLP-4264 [M]	The Real McCoy	1967	6.25	12.50	25.00
❑ BST-84264 [S]	The Real McCoy	1967	5.00	10.00	20.00
-- With "A Division of Liberty Records" on label					
❑ BST-84264	The Real McCoy	1970	3.00	6.00	12.00
-- With United Artists distribution					
❑ BST-84264	The Real McCoy	1987	2.50	5.00	10.00
-- "The Finest in Jazz Since 1939" label					
❑ BST-84275	Tender Moments	1968	5.00	10.00	20.00
-- With "A Division of Liberty Records" on label					
❑ BST-84275	Tender Moments	1970	3.00	6.00	12.00
-- With United Artists distribution					
❑ BST-84275	Tender Moments	1985	2.50	5.00	10.00
-- "The Finest in Jazz Since 1939" label					
❑ BST-84307	Time for Tyner	1969	5.00	10.00	20.00
-- With "A Division of Liberty Records" on label					
❑ BST-84307	Time for Tyner	1987	2.50	5.00	10.00
-- "The Finest in Jazz Since 1939" label					
❑ BST-84338	Expansions	1969	5.00	10.00	20.00
-- With "A Division of Liberty Records" on label					
❑ BST-84338	Expansions	1970	3.00	6.00	12.00
-- With United Artists distribution					
❑ BST-84338	Expansions	1984	2.50	5.00	10.00
-- "The Finest in Jazz Since 1939" label					
❑ B1-91651	Revelations	1989	3.00	6.00	12.00

COLUMBIA

Number	Title	Yr	VG	VG+	NM
❑ FC 37375	La Leyenda de la Hora (The Legend of the Hour)	1981	2.50	5.00	10.00
❑ FC 38053	Looking Out	1982	2.50	5.00	10.00

ELEKTRA/MUSICIAN

Number	Title	Yr	VG	VG+	NM
❑ 60350	Dimensions	1984	2.50	5.00	10.00

FANTASY

Number	Title	Yr	VG	VG+	NM
❑ OJC-311	Sahara	1988	2.50	5.00	10.00
-- Reissue of Milestone 9039					
❑ OJC-313	Song for My Lady	1988	2.50	5.00	10.00
-- Reissue of Milestone 9044					
❑ OJC-618	Song of the New World	1991	2.50	5.00	10.00
-- Reissue of Milestone 9049					
❑ OJC-650	Echoes of a Friend	1991	2.50	5.00	10.00
-- Reissue of Milestone 9055					

GRP/IMPULSE!

Number	Title	Yr	VG	VG+	NM
❑ 216	McCoy Tyner Plays Duke Ellington	1997	5.00	10.00	20.00
-- Reissue on audiophile vinyl					
❑ 220	Inception	1997	5.00	10.00	20.00
-- Reissue on audiophile vinyl					
❑ 221	Nights of Ballads and Blues	1997	5.00	10.00	20.00
-- Reissue on audiophile vinyl					

IMPULSE!

Number	Title	Yr	VG	VG+	NM
❑ A-18 [M]	Inception	1962	6.25	12.50	25.00
❑ AS-18 [S]	Inception	1962	6.25	12.50	25.00
❑ A-33 [M]	Reaching Fourth	1963	6.25	12.50	25.00
❑ AS-33 [S]	Reaching Fourth	1963	6.25	12.50	25.00
❑ A-39 [M]	Nights of Ballads and Blues	1963	6.25	12.50	25.00
❑ AS-39 [S]	Nights of Ballads and Blues	1963	6.25	12.50	25.00
❑ A-48 [M]	McCoy Tyner Live at Newport	1963	6.25	12.50	25.00
❑ AS-48 [S]	McCoy Tyner Live at Newport	1963	6.25	12.50	25.00
❑ A-63 [M]	Today and Tomorrow	1964	6.25	12.50	25.00
❑ AS-63 [S]	Today and Tomorrow	1964	6.25	12.50	25.00
❑ A-79 [M]	McCoy Tyner Plays Duke Ellington	1965	6.25	12.50	25.00
❑ AS-79 [S]	McCoy Tyner Plays Duke Ellington	1965	6.25	12.50	25.00

MCA

Number	Title	Yr	VG	VG+	NM
❑ 4126 [(2)]	Great Moments with McCoy Tyner	1981	3.00	6.00	12.0
❑ 4156 [(2)]	Reevaluation: The Impulse Years	1981	3.00	6.00	12.00
-- Reissue of Impulse! 9235					
❑ 4157 [(2)]	Early Trios	1981	3.00	6.00	12.00
-- Reissue of Impulse! 9338					

MILESTONE

Number	Title	Yr	VG	VG+	NM
❑ FPM-4006 [Q]	Song of the New World	197?	5.00	10.00	20.00
❑ 9039	Sahara	197?	2.50	5.00	10.00
❑ 9044	Song for My Lady	197?	2.50	5.00	10.00
❑ 9049	Song of the New World	197?	2.50	5.00	10.00
❑ 9055	Echoes of a Friend	1974	2.50	5.00	10.00
❑ 9056	Sama Layuca	1974	2.50	5.00	10.00
❑ 9063	Trident	1975	2.50	5.00	10.00
❑ 9067	Fly with the Wind	1976	2.50	5.00	10.00
❑ 9072	Focal Point	1977	2.50	5.00	10.00
❑ 9079	Inner Voices	1978	2.50	5.00	10.00
❑ 9085	The Greeting	1978	2.50	5.00	10.00
❑ 9087	Together	1979	2.50	5.00	10.00
❑ 9091	Passion Dance	1979	2.50	5.00	10.00
❑ 9094	Horizon	1980	2.50	5.00	10.00
❑ 9102	13th House	1981	2.50	5.00	10.00
❑ 9167	Uptown/Downtown	1988	2.50	5.00	10.00

Number	Title	Yr	VG	VG+	NM
❑ 47062	Reflections	198?	2.50	5.00	10.00
❑ 55001 [(2)]	Enlightenment	197?	3.00	6.00	12.00
❑ 55002 [(2)]	Atlantis	1975	3.00	6.00	12.00
❑ 55003 [(2)]	Supertrios	1977	3.00	6.00	12.00
❑ 55007 [(2)]	4 x 4	1980	3.00	6.00	12.00

PALO ALTO

Number	Title	Yr	VG	VG+	NM
❑ PA-8083	Just Feelin'	1985	2.50	5.00	10.00

PAUSA

Number	Title	Yr	VG	VG+	NM
❑ 9007	Time for Tyner	198?	2.00	4.00	8.00
-- Reissue of Blue Note 84307					

QUICKSILVER

Number	Title	Yr	VG	VG+	NM
❑ QS-4010	Just Feelin'	1990	2.50	5.00	10.00
-- Reissue of Palo Alto LP					

TIMELESS

Number	Title	Yr	VG	VG+	NM
❑ SJP-260	Bon Voyage	1990	2.50	5.00	10.00

Number	Title	Yr	VG	VG+	NM

U

UEMATSU, YOSHITAKA
See JEFF HITTMAN.

ULANO, SAM
Drummer.
LANE
Number	Title	Yr	VG	VG+	NM
❏ LP-140 [M]	Sam Ulano	195?	12.50	25.00	50.00
❏ LP-151 [M]	Sam Ulano Is Mr. Rhythm	195?	12.50	25.00	50.00

ULMER, JAMES "BLOOD"
Guitarist and male singer.
ARTISTS HOUSE
| ❏ 13 | Are You Glad to Be in America? | 1980 | 5.00 | 10.00 | 20.00 |
| ❏ AH 9407 | Tales of Captain Black | 1979 | 5.00 | 10.00 | 20.00 |
BLUE NOTE
| ❏ BT-85136 | America -- Do You Remember the Love? | 1987 | 3.00 | 6.00 | 12.00 |
CARAVAN OF DREAMS
| ❏ CDP 85004 | Live at the Caravan of Dreams | 1986 | 3.75 | 7.50 | 15.00 |
COLUMBIA
❏ ARC 37493	Free Lancing	1981	5.00	10.00	20.00
❏ ARC 38285	Black Rock	1982	5.00	10.00	20.00
❏ BFC 38900	Odyssey	1983	3.00	6.00	12.00
IN+OUT
| ❏ 7007 | Revealing | 1990 | 3.00 | 6.00 | 12.00 |

UNCLE FESTIVE
Members: John Pondel (guitar); Ron Pedley (keyboards); Bud Harner (drums); Marc Levine (bass).
NOVA
| ❏ 8703-1 | Money's No Object | 198? | 2.50 | 5.00 | 10.00 |
OPTIMISM
| ❏ OP-3107 | Say Uncle | 1988 | 2.50 | 5.00 | 10.00 |

UPCHURCH, PHIL
Guitarist and bandleader. His "You Can't Sit Down" was a hit single in the early 1960s.
BLUE THUMB
| ❏ BTS-59 | Lovin' Feelin' | 1973 | 3.00 | 6.00 | 12.00 |
| ❏ BTS-6005 [(2)] | Darkness, Darkness | 1971 | 5.00 | 10.00 | 20.00 |
BOYD
| ❏ B-398 [M] | You Can't Sit Down | 1961 | 20.00 | 40.00 | 80.00 |
| ❏ BS-398 [S] | You Can't Sit Down | 1961 | 25.00 | 50.00 | 100.00 |
CADET
| ❏ LPS-826 | Upchurch | 1969 | 3.75 | 7.50 | 15.00 |
| ❏ LPS-840 | The Way I Feel | 1970 | 3.75 | 7.50 | 15.00 |
JAM
| ❏ 007 | Free and Easy | 198? | 3.00 | 6.00 | 12.00 |
KUDU
| ❏ 22 | Phil Upchurch and Tennyson Stevens | 1975 | 3.00 | 6.00 | 12.00 |
MILESTONE
| ❏ MSP-9010 | Feeling Blue | 1968 | 3.75 | 7.50 | 15.00 |
UNITED ARTISTS
❏ UAL-3162 [M]	You Can't Sit Down, Part 2	1961	7.50	15.00	30.00
❏ UAL-3175 [M]	Big Hit Dances	1962	6.25	12.50	25.00
❏ UAS-6162 [S]	You Can't Sit Down, Part 2	1961	10.00	20.00	40.00
❏ UAS-6175 [S]	Big Hit Dances	1962	7.50	15.00	30.00

UPTOWN LOWDOWN JAZZ BAND
Founded and led by Bert Barr (cornet) in 1971.
GHB
| ❏ GHB-149 | Uptown Lowdown Jazz Band | 1979 | 2.50 | 5.00 | 10.00 |
| ❏ GHB-159 | Hauling Ash | 1981 | 2.50 | 5.00 | 10.00 |
STOMP OFF
| ❏ SOS-1030 | Uptown Lowdown Jazz Band in Colonial York, Pa. | 198? | 2.50 | 5.00 | 10.00 |
ULJB
❏ UL-101	Uptown Lowdown Jazz Band	197?	2.50	5.00	10.00
❏ UL-1??	Seattle Style	1985	2.50	5.00	10.00
❏ UL-1??	Jingle Jazz	1989	2.50	5.00	10.00

UPTOWN STRING QUARTET, THE
Members: Eileen Folson (cello); Diane Monroe (violin); Maxine Roach (viola); Lesa Terry (violin).
PHILIPS
| ❏ 838 358-1 | Max Roach Presents the Uptown String Quartet | 1989 | 3.00 | 6.00 | 12.00 |

URBAN EARTH FEATURING HARVIE SWARTZ
Also see HARVIE SWARTZ.
BLUEMOON
Number	Title	Yr	VG	VG+	NM
❏ R1-79150	Full Moon Dancer	1989	3.00	6.00	12.00

URBANIAK, MICHAL
Violinist.
ARISTA
| ❏ AL 4086 | Body English | 1976 | 3.00 | 6.00 | 12.00 |
CATALYST
| ❏ 7909 [(2)] | Beginning | 197? | 3.75 | 7.50 | 15.00 |
COLUMBIA
❏ KC 32852	Fusion	1974	3.00	6.00	12.00
❏ KC 33184	Atma	1975	3.00	6.00	12.00
❏ PC 33542	Fusion III	1975	3.00	6.00	12.00
EASTWEST
| ❏ 90992 | Urban Express | 1989 | 3.00 | 6.00 | 12.00 |
INNER CITY
| ❏ IC-1036 | Urbaniak | 1977 | 3.00 | 6.00 | 12.00 |
JAM
| ❏ 5004 | Jam at Sandy's | 198? | 3.00 | 6.00 | 12.00 |
OPTIMISM
| ❏ OP-5012 | Milky Way | 198? | 2.50 | 5.00 | 10.00 |
PAUSA
| ❏ 7047 | Heritage | 197? | 2.50 | 5.00 | 10.00 |
| ❏ 7114 | Daybreak | 198? | 2.50 | 5.00 | 10.00 |
STEEPLECHASE
| ❏ SCS-1159 | My One and Only Love | 1981 | 3.00 | 6.00 | 12.00 |
| ❏ SCS-1195 | Take Good Care of My Heart | 198? | 3.00 | 6.00 | 12.00 |

URSO, PHIL
Tenor saxophone player.
REGENT
| ❏ MG-6003 [M] | Sentimental Journey | 1956 | 12.50 | 25.00 | 50.00 |
SAVOY
| ❏ MG-12056 [M] | The Philosophy of Urso | 1956 | 12.50 | 25.00 | 50.00 |
| ❏ MG-15041 [10] | Bob Brookmeyer with Phil Urso | 1954 | 37.50 | 75.00 | 150.00 |

URTREGER, RENE
See DICK KATZ.

US3
Created by Geoff Wilkinson (producer) and Mel Simpson (producer, keyboards), this jazz-rap melange spawned a hit single, "Cantaloop (Flip Fantasia)." Its extensive samples from the Blue Note back catalog, much of which still had not been reissued on CD in 1993, helped revive interest in the legendary label.
BLUE NOTE
| ❏ B1-30027 | Broadway & 52nd | 1997 | 3.75 | 7.50 | 15.00 |
| ❏ B1-80883 | Hand on the Torch | 1993 | 3.75 | 7.50 | 15.00 |

USSELTON, BILLY
Tenor saxophone player.
KAPP
| ❏ KL-1051 [M] | Bill Usselton -- His First Album | 1957 | 12.50 | 25.00 | 50.00 |

Number	Title	Yr	VG	VG+	NM

V

V.S.O.P. QUINTET
See HERBIE HANCOCK.

VACHE, ALLAN
Clarinetist and saxophone player.
AUDIOPHILE
❏ AP-176	Vache's Jazz Moods	1983	2.50	5.00	10.00
❏ AP-192	High Speed Swing	1986	2.50	5.00	10.00

VACHE, ALLAN, AND CHUCK HUGHES
Hughes also plays clarinet. Also see ALLAN VACHE.
JAZZOLOGY
❏ J-131	Clarinet Climax	198?	2.50	5.00	10.00

VACHE, WARREN
Cornet and fluegel horn player.
AUDIOPHILE
❏ AP-196	First Time Out	1986	2.50	5.00	10.00
CONCORD JAZZ
❏ CJ-87	Jillian	1979	2.50	5.00	10.00
❏ CJ-98	Polished Brass	1980	2.50	5.00	10.00
❏ CJ-153	Iridescence	1981	2.50	5.00	10.00
❏ CJ-203	Midtown Jazz	1982	2.50	5.00	10.00
❏ CJ-323	Easy Going	1987	2.50	5.00	10.00
❏ CJ-392	Warm Evenings	1989	3.00	6.00	12.00
DREAMSTREET
❏ 101	Blues Walk	197?	3.75	7.50	15.00
MONMOUTH-EVERGREEN
❏ 7081	First Time Out	197?	3.75	7.50	15.00

VALENTIN, DAVE
Flutist.
GRP
❏ GR-1004	Flute Juice	198?	2.50	5.00	10.00
❏ GR-1009	Kalahari	198?	2.50	5.00	10.00
❏ GR-1016	Jungle Garden	198?	2.50	5.00	10.00
❏ GR-1028	Light Struck	198?	2.50	5.00	10.00
❏ GR-1043	Mind Time	1988	2.50	5.00	10.00
❏ GR-9568	Live at the Blue Note	1988	2.50	5.00	10.00
GRP/ARISTA
❏ GL 5001	Legends	1978	3.00	6.00	12.00
❏ GL 5006	Hawk	1979	2.50	5.00	10.00
❏ GL 5505	Pied Piper	198?	2.50	5.00	10.00
❏ GL 5511	In Love's Time	198?	2.50	5.00	10.00

VAN DAMME, ART
Accordion player.
BASF
❏ 21755	Squeezing Art and Tender Flutes	197?	3.75	7.50	15.00
❏ 22016	Invitation	197?	3.75	7.50	15.00
❏ 25113 [(2)]	The Many Moods of Art Van Damme	197?	5.00	10.00	20.00
❏ 25257 [(2)]	Star Spangled Rhythm	197?	5.00	10.00	20.00
CAPITOL
❏ H 178 [10]	Cocktail Capers	1950	12.50	25.00	50.00
❏ T 178 [M]	Cocktail Capers	1954	10.00	20.00	40.00
❏ L 300 [10]	More Cocktail Capers	1952	12.50	25.00	50.00
❏ T 300 [M]	More Cocktail Capers	1954	10.00	20.00	40.00
COLUMBIA
❏ C2L 7 [(2) M]	They're Playing Our Song	1958	10.00	20.00	40.00
❏ CL 544 [M]	The Van Damme Sound	1955	7.50	15.00	30.00
❏ CL 630 [M]	Martini Time	1955	7.50	15.00	30.00
❏ CL 801 [M]	Manhattan Time	1956	7.50	15.00	30.00
❏ CL 876 [M]	The Art of Van Damme	1956	7.50	15.00	30.00
❏ CL 1382 [M]	Everything's Coming Up Music	1959	6.25	12.50	25.00
❏ CL 1563 [M]	Accordion A La Mode	1960	6.25	12.50	25.00
❏ CL 1794 [M]	Art Van Damme Swings Sweetly	1962	3.75	7.50	15.00
❏ CL 2013 [M]	A Perfect Match	1963	3.75	7.50	15.00
❏ CL 2192 [M]	The New Sound Of the Art Van Damme Septet	1964	3.00	6.00	12.00
❏ CL 2585 [10]	The Art Van Damme Quintet	1956	10.00	20.00	40.00
❏ CL 6265 [10]	Martini Time	1953	10.00	20.00	40.00
❏ CS 8177 [S]	Everything's Coming Up Music	1959	7.50	15.00	30.00
❏ CS 8363 [S]	Accordion A La Mode	1960	7.50	15.00	30.00
❏ CS 8594 [M]	Art Van Damme Swings Sweetly	1962	5.00	10.00	20.00
❏ CS 8813 [S]	A Perfect Match	1963	5.00	10.00	20.00
❏ CS 8992 [S]	The New Sound Of the Art Van Damme Septet	1964	3.75	7.50	15.00

DESIGN
❏ DLP-905 [M]	3 of a Kind	196?	3.00	6.00	12.00
❏ SDLP-905 [R]	3 of a Kind	196?	2.00	4.00	8.00
HARMONY
❏ HL-7439 [M]	Music for Lovers	196?	3.00	6.00	12.00
❏ HS-11439 [S]	Music for Lovers	196?	2.50	5.00	10.00
PAUSA
❏ 7027	Blue World	197?	2.50	5.00	10.00
❏ 7066	Invitation	197?	2.50	5.00	10.00
❏ 7104	Keep Going	198?	2.50	5.00	10.00
❏ 7126	Squeezing Art and Tender Flutes	198?	2.50	5.00	10.00
❏ 7151	Art Van Damme and Friends	198?	2.50	5.00	10.00
PICKWICK
❏ PC-3009 [M]	Best Of Art Van Damme	196?	3.00	6.00	12.00
❏ PCS-3009 [R]	Best Of Art Van Damme	196?	2.00	4.00	8.00
SONIC ARTS
❏ 12	By Request	1980	3.00	6.00	12.00

VAN DER GELD, TOM
Vibraphone player.
ECM
❏ 1113	Patience	1977	3.00	6.00	12.00
❏ 1134	Path	1979	3.00	6.00	12.00

VAN DYKE, LOUIS
Pianist.
COLUMBIA MASTERWORKS
❏ M 34511	'Round Midnight	1977	2.50	5.00	10.00

VAN EPS, GEORGE
Seven-string guitarist. Also see EDDIE MILLER; THE RAMPART STREET PARADERS.
CAPITOL
❏ ST-267	Soliloquy	1969	3.75	7.50	15.00
❏ ST 2533 [S]	My Guitar	1966	5.00	10.00	20.00
❏ T 2533 [M]	My Guitar	1966	3.75	7.50	15.00
❏ ST 2783	Seven String Guitar	1968	3.75	7.50	15.00
COLUMBIA
❏ CL 929 [M]	Mellow Guitar	1956	10.00	20.00	40.00
CORINTHIAN
❏ 121	Mellow Guitar	198?	2.50	5.00	10.00

VAN'T HOF, JASPER
Pianist.
PAUSA
❏ 7084	Live in Montreux	1979	2.50	5.00	10.00

VARNER, TOM
French horn player.
SOUL NOTE
❏ SN-1017	TV	198?	3.00	6.00	12.00
❏ SN-1067	Motion/Stillness	198?	3.00	6.00	12.00

VASCONCELOS, NANA
Percussionist and male singer.
ANTILLES
❏ 90698	Bush Dance	1987	2.50	5.00	10.00
ECM
❏ 1147	Saudades	1979	3.00	6.00	12.00

VAUGHAN, SARAH
Female singer, one of the great interpreters of popular song.
ACCORD
❏ SN-7195	Simply Divine	1981	2.50	5.00	10.00
ALLEGRO
❏ 1592 [M]	Sarah Vaughan	1955	12.50	25.00	50.00
❏ 1608 [M]	Sarah Vaughan	1955	12.50	25.00	50.00
❏ 3080 [10]	Early Sarah	195?	20.00	40.00	80.00
ALLEGRO ELITE
❏ 4106 [10]	Sarah Vaughan Sings	195?	7.50	15.00	30.00
ARCHIVE OF FOLK AND JAZZ
❏ 250	Sarah Vaughan	197?	2.50	5.00	10.00
❏ 271	Sarah Vaughan, Volume 2	197?	2.50	5.00	10.00
❏ 325	Sarah Vaughan, Volume 3	197?	2.50	5.00	10.00
ATLANTIC
❏ SD 16037	Songs of the Beatles	1981	3.00	6.00	12.00
CBS MASTERWORKS
❏ FM 37277	Gershwin Live!	1982	2.50	5.00	10.00
-- With the Los Angeles Philharmonic Orchestra					
❏ FM 42519	Brazilian Romance	1987	2.50	5.00	10.00

Number	Title	Yr	VG	VG+	NM
COLUMBIA					
❏ CL 660 [M]	After Hours with Sarah Vaughan	1955	12.50	25.00	50.00
❏ CL 745 [M]	Sarah Vaughan in Hi-Fi	1956	12.50	25.00	50.00
❏ CL 914 [M]	Linger Awhile	1956	12.50	25.00	50.00
❏ CL 6133 [10]	Sarah Vaughan	1950	30.00	60.00	120.00
COLUMBIA SPECIAL PRODUCTS					
❏ P 13084	Sarah Vaughan in Hi-Fi	1976	2.50	5.00	10.00
-- Reissue of Columbia 745					
❏ P 14364	Linger Awhile	1978	2.50	5.00	10.00
-- Reissue of Columbia 914					
CONCORD					
❏ 3018 [M]	Sarah Vaughan Concert	1957	7.50	15.00	30.00
CORONET					
❏ 277	Sarah Vaughan Belts the Hits	196?	3.75	7.50	15.00
EMARCY					
❏ EMS-2-412 [(2)]	Sarah Vaughan Live	197?	3.00	6.00	12.00
❏ MG-26005 [10]	Images	1954	20.00	40.00	80.00
❏ MG-36004 [M]	Sarah Vaughan	1955	20.00	40.00	80.00
❏ MG-36058 [M]	In the Land of Hi-Fi	1956	20.00	40.00	80.00
❏ MG-36089 [M]	Sassy	1956	12.50	25.00	50.00
❏ MG-36109 [M]	Swingin' Easy	1957	12.50	25.00	50.00
❏ 814 187-1 [(2)]	The George Gershwin Songbook	1983	3.00	6.00	12.00
❏ 824 864-1	The Rodgers & Hart Songbook	1985	2.50	5.00	10.00
❏ 826 454-1	In the Land of Hi-Fi	1986	2.50	5.00	10.00
-- Reissue of 36058					
FORUM					
❏ F-9034 [M]	Dreamy	196?	3.00	6.00	12.00
❏ SF-9034 [S]	Dreamy	196?	3.75	7.50	15.00
HARMONY					
❏ HL 7158 [M]	The Great Sarah Vaughan	196?	3.00	6.00	12.00
LION					
❏ L 70052 [M]	Tenderly	1958	6.25	12.50	25.00
MAINSTREAM					
❏ MRL 340	Time in My Life	1972	3.75	7.50	15.00
❏ MRL 361	Sarah Vaughan/Michel Legrand	1972	3.75	7.50	15.00
❏ MRL 379	Feelin' Good	1973	3.75	7.50	15.00
❏ MRL 404	Sarah Vaughan and the Jimmy Rowles Quintet	1974	3.75	7.50	15.00
❏ MRL 419	More Sarah Vaughan from Japan	1974	3.75	7.50	15.00
MASTERSEAL					
❏ MS-55 [M]	Sarah Vaughan Sings	195?	6.25	12.50	25.00
MERCURY					
❏ MGP-2-100 [(2) M]	Great Songs from Hit Shows	1957	15.00	30.00	60.00
❏ MGP-2-101 [(2) M]	Sarah Vaughan Sings George Gershwin	1957	15.00	30.00	60.00
❏ MG-20094 [M]	Sarah Vaughan at the Blue Note	1956	10.00	20.00	40.00
❏ MG-20219 [M]	Wonderful Sarah	1957	10.00	20.00	40.00
❏ MG-20223 [M]	In a Romantic Mood	1957	10.00	20.00	40.00
❏ MG-20244 [M]	Great Songs from Hit Shows, Vol. 1	1958	7.50	15.00	30.00
❏ MG-20245 [M]	Great Songs from Hit Shows, Vol. 2	1958	7.50	15.00	30.00
❏ MG-20310 [M]	Sarah Vaughan Sings George Gershwin, Vol. 1	1958	7.50	15.00	30.00
❏ MG-20311 [M]	Sarah Vaughan Sings George Gershwin, Vol. 2	1958	7.50	15.00	30.00
❏ MG-20326 [M]	Sarah Vaughan and Her Trio at Mr. Kelly's	1958	10.00	20.00	40.00
❏ MG-20370 [M]	Vaughan and Violins	1958	10.00	20.00	40.00
❏ MG-20383 [M]	After Hours at the London House	1958	10.00	20.00	40.00
❏ MG-20438 [M]	The Magic of Sarah Vaughan	1959	7.50	15.00	30.00
❏ MG-20441 [M]	No 'Count Sarah	1959	7.50	15.00	30.00
❏ MG-20540 [M]	The Divine Sarah Vaughan	1960	6.25	12.50	25.00
❏ MG-20580 [M]	Close to You	1960	6.25	12.50	25.00
❏ MG-20617 [M]	My Heart Sings	1961	6.25	12.50	25.00
❏ MG-20645 [M]	Sarah Vaughan's Golden Hits	1961	5.00	10.00	20.00
❏ MG-20831 [M]	Sassy Swings the Tivoli	1962	5.00	10.00	20.00
❏ MG-20882 [M]	Vaughan with Voices	1963	5.00	10.00	20.00
❏ MG-20941 [M]	Viva Vaughan	1964	3.75	7.50	15.00
❏ MG-21009 [M]	Sarah Vaughan Sings the Mancini Songbook	1965	3.75	7.50	15.00
❏ MG-21069 [M]	The Pop Artistry of Sarah Vaughan	1966	3.75	7.50	15.00
❏ MG-21079 [M]	The New Scene	1966	3.75	7.50	15.00
❏ MG-21116 [M]	Sassy Swings Again	1967	3.75	7.50	15.00
❏ MG-21122 [M]	It's a Man's World	1967	3.75	7.50	15.00
❏ MG-25188 [10]	Divine Sarah	1955	25.00	50.00	100.00
❏ SR-60020 [S]	After Hours at the London House	1959	10.00	20.00	40.00
❏ SR-60038 [S]	Vaughan and Violins	1959	10.00	20.00	40.00
❏ SR-60041 [S]	Great Songs from Hit Shows, Vol. 1	1959	10.00	20.00	40.00
❏ SR-60045 [S]	Sarah Vaughan Sings George Gershwin, Vol. 1	1959	10.00	20.00	40.00
❏ SR-60046 [S]	Sarah Vaughan Sings George Gershwin, Vol. 2	1959	10.00	20.00	40.00

Number	Title	Yr	VG	VG+	NM
❏ SR-60078 [S]	Great Songs from Hit Shows, Vol. 2	1959	10.00	20.00	40.00
❏ SR-60110 [S]	The Magic of Sarah Vaughan	1959	10.00	20.00	40.00
❏ SR-60116 [S]	No 'Count Sarah	1959	10.00	20.00	40.00
❏ SR-60240 [S]	Close to You	1960	7.50	15.00	30.00
❏ SR-60255 [S]	The Divine Sarah Vaughan	1960	7.50	15.00	30.00
❏ SR-60617 [S]	My Heart Sings	1961	7.50	15.00	30.00
❏ SR-60645 [S]	Sarah Vaughan's Golden Hits	1961	6.25	12.50	25.00
-- Original black label version					
❏ SR-60831 [S]	Sassy Swings the Tivoli	1962	6.25	12.50	25.00
❏ SR-60882 [S]	Vaughan with Voices	1963	6.25	12.50	25.00
❏ SR-60941 [S]	Viva Vaughan	1964	5.00	10.00	20.00
❏ SR-61009 [S]	Sarah Vaughan Sings the Mancini Songbook	1965	5.00	10.00	20.00
❏ SR-61069 [S]	The Pop Artistry of Sarah Vaughan	1966	5.00	10.00	20.00
❏ SR-61079 [S]	The New Scene	1966	5.00	10.00	20.00
❏ SR-61116 [S]	Sassy Swings Again	1967	5.00	10.00	20.00
❏ SR-61122 [S]	It's a Man's World	1967	5.00	10.00	20.00
❏ 826 320-1 [(6)]	The Complete Sarah Vaughan on Mercury Vol. 1: Great Jazz Years (1954-56)	1986	10.00	20.00	40.00
❏ 826 327-1 [(5)]	The Complete Sarah Vaughan on Mercury Vol. 2: Great American Songs (1956-57)	1986	10.00	20.00	40.00
❏ 826 333-1 [(6)]	The Complete Sarah Vaughan on Mercury Vol. 3: Great Show on Stage (1954-56)	1986	10.00	20.00	40.00
❏ 830 721-1 [(4)]	The Complete Sarah Vaughan on Mercury Vol. 4 Part 1: Live in Europe (1963-64)	1987	10.00	20.00	40.00
❏ 830 726-1 [(5)]	The Complete Sarah Vaughan on Mercury Vol. 4 Part 2: Sassy Swings Again	1987	10.00	20.00	40.00
METRO					
❏ M-539 [M]	Tenderly	1965	3.00	6.00	12.00
❏ MS-539 [S]	Tenderly	1965	3.75	7.50	15.00
MGM					
❏ E-165 [10]	Tenderly	1950	30.00	60.00	120.00
❏ E-544 [10]	Sarah Vaughan Sings	1951	30.00	60.00	120.00
❏ E-3274 [M]	My Kinda Love	1955	12.50	25.00	50.00
-- Combination of two 10-inch LPs on one 12-inch LP					
MUSICRAFT					
❏ 504	Divine Sarah	197?	2.50	5.00	10.00
❏ MVS-2002	The Man I Love	1986	2.50	5.00	10.00
❏ MVS-2006	Lover Man	1986	2.50	5.00	10.00
PABLO					
❏ 2310 821	How Long	1978	2.50	5.00	10.00
❏ 2310 885	The Best of Sarah Vaughan	1983	2.50	5.00	10.00
❏ 2312 101	I Love Brazil	1978	2.50	5.00	10.00
❏ 2312 111	The Duke Ellington Songbook One	1979	2.50	5.00	10.00
❏ 2312 116	The Duke Ellington Songbook Two	1980	2.50	5.00	10.00
❏ 2312 125	Copacabana	1981	2.50	5.00	10.00
❏ 2312 137	Crazy and Mixed Up	1981	2.50	5.00	10.00
❏ 2405 416	The Best of Sarah Vaughan	1990	2.50	5.00	10.00
PALACE					
❏ 5191 [M]	Sarah Vaughan Sings	195?	6.25	12.50	25.00
PICKWICK					
❏ PCS-3035	Fabulous Sarah Vaughan	197?	2.50	5.00	10.00
REMINGTON					
❏ RLP-1024 [10]	Hot Jazz	1953	50.00	100.00	200.00
RIVERSIDE					
❏ RLP 2511 [10]	Sarah Vaughan Sings with John Kirby	1955	25.00	50.00	100.00
RONDO-LETTE					
❏ A-35 [M]	Songs of Broadway	1958	6.25	12.50	25.00
❏ A-53 [M]	Sarah Vaughan Sings	1959	6.25	12.50	25.00
ROULETTE					
❏ 103 [(2)]	Echoes of An Era	197?	3.00	6.00	12.00
❏ R 52046 [M]	Dreamy	1960	7.50	15.00	30.00
❏ SR 52046 [S]	Dreamy	1960	10.00	20.00	40.00
❏ R 52060 [M]	Divine One	1960	6.25	12.50	25.00
❏ SR 52060 [S]	Divine One	1960	7.50	15.00	30.00
❏ R 52070 [M]	After Hours	1961	6.25	12.50	25.00
❏ SR 52070 [S]	After Hours	1961	7.50	15.00	30.00
❏ R 52082 [M]	You're Mine	1962	6.25	12.50	25.00
❏ SR 52082 [S]	You're Mine	1962	15.00	30.00	60.00
-- Red vinyl					
❏ SR 52082 [S]	You're Mine	1962	7.50	15.00	30.00
-- Black vinyl					
❏ R 52091 [M]	Snowbound	1962	5.00	10.00	20.00
❏ SR 52091 [S]	Snowbound	1962	6.25	12.50	25.00
❏ R 52092 [M]	The Explosive Side of Sarah	1962	5.00	10.00	20.00
❏ SR 52092 [S]	The Explosive Side of Sarah	1962	6.25	12.50	25.00
❏ R 52100 [M]	Star Eyes	1963	3.75	7.50	15.00
❏ SR 52100 [S]	Star Eyes	1963	5.00	10.00	20.00
❏ R 52104 [M]	Lonely Hours	1963	3.75	7.50	15.00
❏ SR 52104 [S]	Lonely Hours	1963	5.00	10.00	20.00
❏ R 52109 [M]	The World of Sarah Vaughan	1964	3.75	7.50	15.00

Sarah Vaughan was one of the great jazz singers, though sometimes overlooked because she did have some straight pop hits in the 1950s as well. (Top left) One of the earliest compilations of her music into LP form was on this 10-incher from the mid-1950s on Mercury, *The Divine Sarah*. (Top right) *In the Land of Hi-Fi*, a 1955 issue on Mercury's EmArcy jazz label, includes some nice solos from Cannonball Adderley on alto sax with Vaughan's golden voice. (Bottom left) *After Hours at the London House* was the first Sarah Vaughan album to be released in true stereo (the mono version is pictured above). (Bottom right) In the early 1970s, Vaughan recorded a series of LPs for the Mainstream label. Among these was this album of highlights from some concerts in Japan.

Number	Title	Yr	VG	VG+	NM
❑ SR 52109 [S]	The World of Sarah Vaughan	1964	5.00	10.00	20.00
❑ R 52112 [M]	Sweet 'N Sassy	1964	3.75	7.50	15.00
❑ SR 52112 [S]	Sweet 'N Sassy	1964	5.00	10.00	20.00
❑ R 52116 [M]	Sarah Sings Soulfully	1965	3.75	7.50	15.00
❑ SR 52116 [S]	Sarah Sings Soulfully	1965	5.00	10.00	20.00
❑ R 52118 [M]	Sarah Plus Two	1965	3.75	7.50	15.00
❑ SR 52118 [S]	Sarah Plus Two	1965	5.00	10.00	20.00

SCEPTER

Number	Title	Yr	VG	VG+	NM
❑ CTN-18029	The Best of Sarah Vaughan	1972	3.00	6.00	12.00

SPIN-O-RAMA

Number	Title	Yr	VG	VG+	NM
❑ 73 [M]	Sweet, Sultry and Swinging	196?	10.00	20.00	40.00
❑ S-73 [S]	Sweet, Sultry and Swinging	196?	12.50	25.00	50.00
❑ 114 [M]	The Divine Sarah Vaughan	196?	10.00	20.00	40.00
❑ S-114 [S]	The Divine Sarah Vaughan	196?	12.50	25.00	50.00

TRIP

Number	Title	Yr	VG	VG+	NM
❑ 5501	Sarah Vaughan	197?	2.50	5.00	10.00
❑ 5517	Sassy	197?	2.50	5.00	10.00
❑ 5523	In the Land of Hi-Fi	197?	2.50	5.00	10.00
❑ 5551	Swingin' Easy	197?	2.50	5.00	10.00

WING

Number	Title	Yr	VG	VG+	NM
❑ MGW-12123 [M]	All Time Favorites	1963	3.00	6.00	12.00
❑ MGW-12280 [M]	The Magic of Sarah Vaughan	1964	3.00	6.00	12.00
❑ SRW-16123 [S]	All Time Favorites	1963	3.75	7.50	15.00
❑ SRW-16123 [S]	The Magic of Sarah Vaughan	1964	3.75	7.50	15.00

VAUGHAN, SARAH, AND COUNT BASIE
Also see each artist's individual listings.
PABLO

Number	Title	Yr	VG	VG+	NM
❑ 2312 130	Send In the Clowns	1980	2.50	5.00	10.00

ROULETTE

Number	Title	Yr	VG	VG+	NM
❑ R 52061 [M]	Count Basie and Sarah Vaughan	1960	6.25	12.50	25.00
❑ SR 42018	Count Basie and Sarah Vaughan	1968	3.75	7.50	15.00
❑ SR 52061 [S]	Count Basie and Sarah Vaughan	1960	7.50	15.00	30.00

VAUGHAN, SARAH, AND BILLY ECKSTINE
Also see each artist's individual listings.
EMARCY

Number	Title	Yr	VG	VG+	NM
❑ 822 526-1	The Irving Berlin Songbook	1984	2.50	5.00	10.00

LION

Number	Title	Yr	VG	VG+	NM
❑ L-70088 [M]	Billy and Sarah	195?	6.25	12.50	25.00

MERCURY

Number	Title	Yr	VG	VG+	NM
❑ MG-20316 [M]	Sarah Vaughan and Billy e Eckstin Sing the Best of Irving Berlin	1959	7.50	15.00	30.00
❑ SR-60002 [S]	Sarah Vaughan and Billy Eckstine Sing the Best of Irving Berlin	1959	10.00	20.00	40.00

VAUGHAN, SARAH; DINAH WASHINGTON; JOE WILLIAMS
Also see each artist's individual listings.
ROULETTE

Number	Title	Yr	VG	VG+	NM
❑ R 52108 [M]	We Three	1964	3.75	7.50	15.00
❑ SR 52108 [S]	We Three	1964	5.00	10.00	20.00

VAUGHN, FATHER TOM
Pianist.
CONCORD JAZZ

Number	Title	Yr	VG	VG+	NM
❑ CJ-16	Joyful Jazz	1976	3.00	6.00	12.00

RCA VICTOR

Number	Title	Yr	VG	VG+	NM
❑ LPM-3577 [M]	Jazz In Concert at the Village Gate	1966	3.75	7.50	15.00
❑ LSP-3577 [S]	Jazz In Concert at the Village Gate	1966	5.00	10.00	20.00
❑ LPM-3708 [M]	Cornbread (Meat Loaf, Greens and Deviled Eggs)	1967	5.00	10.00	20.00
❑ LSP-3708 [S]	Cornbread (Meat Loaf, Greens and Deviled Eggs)	1967	3.75	7.50	15.00
❑ LPM-3845 [M]	Motor City Soul	1967	5.00	10.00	20.00
❑ LSP-3845 [S]	Motor City Soul	1967	3.75	7.50	15.00

VAZQUEZ, ROLAND
Drummer, percussionist and composer.
GRP/ARISTA

Number	Title	Yr	VG	VG+	NM
❑ GL 5002	Roland Vazquez and the Urban Ensemble	1978	3.75	7.50	15.00

HEADFIRST

Number	Title	Yr	VG	VG+	NM
❑ 9710	Feel Your Dream	198?	3.00	6.00	12.00

SOUNDWINGS

Number	Title	Yr	VG	VG+	NM
❑ SW-2106	The Tides of Time	1988	2.50	5.00	10.00

VEGA, AL
Pianist.
PRESTIGE

Number	Title	Yr	VG	VG+	NM
❑ PRLP-152 [10]	Al Vega Piano Solos With Bongos	1953	37.50	75.00	150.00

VELEBNY, KAREL
See SHQ.

VELEZ, GLEN
Drummer and percussionist.
CMP

Number	Title	Yr	VG	VG+	NM
❑ CMP-23-ST	Internal Combustion	1987	2.50	5.00	10.00
❑ CMP-30-ST	Seven Heaven	1988	2.50	5.00	10.00
❑ CMP-42-ST	Assyrian Rose	1989	2.50	5.00	10.00

VENTURA, CAROL
Female singer.
PRESTIGE

Number	Title	Yr	VG	VG+	NM
❑ PRLP-7358 [M]	Carol!	1965	6.25	12.50	25.00
❑ PRST-7358 [S]	Carol!	1965	7.50	15.00	30.00
❑ PRLP-7405 [M]	I Love to Sing!	1965	6.25	12.50	25.00
❑ PRST-7405 [S]	I Love to Sing!	1965	7.50	15.00	30.00

VENTURA, CHARLIE
Saxophone player (tenor, alto, baritone, bass). Also see GENE KRUPA.
BATON

Number	Title	Yr	VG	VG+	NM
❑ 1202 [M]	New Charlie Ventura in Hi-Fi	1957	12.50	25.00	50.00

BRUNSWICK

Number	Title	Yr	VG	VG+	NM
❑ BL 54025 [M]	Here's Charlie	1957	20.00	40.00	80.00

CLEF

Number	Title	Yr	VG	VG+	NM
❑ MGC-117 [10]	Charlie Ventura Collates	1953	50.00	100.00	200.00

CORAL

Number	Title	Yr	VG	VG+	NM
❑ CRL 56067 [10]	Open House	1952	30.00	60.00	120.00

CRAFTSMAN

Number	Title	Yr	VG	VG+	NM
❑ 8039 [M]	Charlie Ventura Plays for the People	1960	6.25	12.50	25.00

CRYSTALETTE

Number	Title	Yr	VG	VG+	NM
❑ 5000 [10]	Stomping With the Sax	1950	37.50	75.00	150.00

DECCA

Number	Title	Yr	VG	VG+	NM
❑ DL 8046 [M]	Charlie Ventura Concert	1954	25.00	50.00	100.00

EMARCY

Number	Title	Yr	VG	VG+	NM
❑ MG-26028 [10]	F.Y.I. Ventura	1954	30.00	60.00	120.00
❑ MG-36015 [M]	Jumping with Ventura	1955	20.00	40.00	80.00

FAMOUS DOOR

Number	Title	Yr	VG	VG+	NM
❑ 115	Chazz '77	1977	2.50	5.00	10.00

GENE NORMAN

Number	Title	Yr	VG	VG+	NM
❑ GNP-1 [M]	Charlie Ventura In Concert	1954	25.00	50.00	100.00

GNP CRESCENDO

Number	Title	Yr	VG	VG+	NM
❑ GNP-1 [M]	Charlie Ventura In Concert	196?	3.00	6.00	12.00
❑ GNPS-1 [R]	Charlie Ventura In Concert	196?	2.50	5.00	10.00

HALL OF FAME

Number	Title	Yr	VG	VG+	NM
❑ 605	Charlie Ventura Quintet	197?	2.50	5.00	10.00

IMPERIAL

Number	Title	Yr	VG	VG+	NM
❑ IM-3002 [10]	Charlie Ventura and His Sextet	1953	50.00	100.00	200.00

KING

Number	Title	Yr	VG	VG+	NM
❑ 543 [M]	Adventure with Charlie Ventura	1958	20.00	40.00	80.00

MCA

Number	Title	Yr	VG	VG+	NM
❑ 42330	Gene Norman Presents a Charlie Ventura Concert	1990	3.00	6.00	12.00

MERCURY

Number	Title	Yr	VG	VG+	NM
❑ MGC-117 [10]	Charlie Ventura Collates	1952	55.00	110.00	220.00

MOSAIC

Number	Title	Yr	VG	VG+	NM
❑ MQ9-182 [(9)]	The Complete Verve/Clef Charlie Ventura/Flip Phillips Studio Sessions	199?	37.50	75.00	150.00

NORGRAN

Number	Title	Yr	VG	VG+	NM
❑ MGN-8 [10]	Charlie Ventura Quartet	1953	50.00	100.00	200.00
❑ MGN-1041 [M]	Charlie Ventura's Carnegie Hall Concert	1955	30.00	60.00	120.00
❑ MGN-1073 [M]	Charlie Ventura in a Jazz Mood	1956	25.00	50.00	100.00
❑ MGN-1075 [M]	Blue Saxophone	1956	25.00	50.00	100.00
❑ MGN-1103 [M]	Charley's Parley	1956	25.00	50.00	100.00

PHOENIX

Number	Title	Yr	VG	VG+	NM
❑ 6	Charlie Boy	197?	2.50	5.00	10.00

RCA VICTOR

Number	Title	Yr	VG	VG+	NM
❑ LPM-1135 [M]	It's All Bop to Me	1955	30.00	60.00	120.00

REGENT

Number	Title	Yr	VG	VG+	NM
❑ MG-6064 [M]	East of Suez	1958	12.50	25.00	50.00

SAVOY JAZZ

Number	Title	Yr	VG	VG+	NM
❑ SJL-2243 [(2)]	Euphoria	198?	3.00	6.00	12.00

TOPS

Number	Title	Yr	VG	VG+	NM
❑ L-1528 [M]	Charlie Ventura Plays Hi-Fi Jazz	1958	6.25	12.50	25.00

TRIP

Number	Title	Yr	VG	VG+	NM
❑ 5536	Jumping with Ventura	197?	2.50	5.00	10.00

(Top left) Art Van Damme played many keyboard instruments, but was best known for his work on the accordion, one of the most unlikely of jazz instruments. This is one of his earliest albums as a leader, on the Capitol label. (Top right) Singer Carol Ventura made a splash with two albums on Prestige in the mid-1960s. This was her second, and last, release. (Bottom left) As you might be able to deduce from the album cover, Leroy Vinnegar was renowned for his "walking bass" playing and became known as "The Walker." He continued to perform right up until his death in August 1999. (Bottom right) Mal Waldron is sometimes overlooked in the list of great jazz pianists. But he shouldn't be, not with albums like *The Quest,* which he recorded with Eric Dolphy and Booker Ervin and was issued in 1962. And he also has the distinction of the first LP release on ECM Records, *Free at Last* (ECM 1001).

Number	Title	Yr	VG	VG+	NM
VERVE					
❏ MGV-8132 [M]	Charlie Ventura's Carnegie Hall Concert	1957	20.00	40.00	80.00
❏ V-8132 [M]	Charlie Ventura'a Carnegie Hall Concert	1961	6.25	12.50	25.00
❏ MGV-8163 [M]	Charlie Ventura in a Jazz Mood	1957	15.00	30.00	60.00
❏ V-8163 [M]	Charlie Ventura in a Jazz Mood	1961	6.25	12.50	25.00
❏ MGV-8165 [M]	Blue Saxophone	1957	15.00	30.00	60.00
❏ V-8165 [M]	Blue Saxophone	1961	6.25	12.50	25.00
ZIM					
❏ 1004	Charlie Ventura in Chicago	197?	2.50	5.00	10.00

VENTURA, CHARLIE/CHARLIE KENNEDY
Charlie Kennedy played alto saxophone. Also see CHARLIE VENTURA.

Number	Title	Yr	VG	VG+	NM
REGENT					
❏ MG-6047 [M]	Crazy Rhythms	1957	15.00	30.00	60.00
SAVOY					
❏ MG-12200	Crazy Rhythms	197?	3.00	6.00	12.00

VENTURA, CHARLIE, AND MARY ANN McCALL
Also see each artist's individual listings.

Number	Title	Yr	VG	VG+	NM
NORGRAN					
❏ MGN-20 [10]	An Evening with Mary Ann McCall and Charlie Ventura	1954	37.50	75.00	150.00
❏ MGN-1013 [M]	Another Evening with Charlie Ventura and Mary Ann McCall	1954	30.00	60.00	120.00
❏ MGN-1053 [M]	An Evening with Mary Ann McCall and Charlie Ventura	1955	25.00	50.00	100.00
VERVE					
❏ MGV-8143 [M]	An Evening with Mary Ann McCall and Charlie Ventura	1957	20.00	40.00	80.00
❏ V-8143 [M]	An Evening with Mary Ann McCall and Charlie Ventura	1961	6.25	12.50	25.00

VENUTI, JOE
Violinist, basically the first to use the instrument in jazz.

Number	Title	Yr	VG	VG+	NM
ARCHIVE OF FOLK AND JAZZ					
❏ 349	Joe Venuti and the Dutch Swing College Band	197?	2.50	5.00	10.00
AUDIOPHILE					
❏ AP-118	Incredible	197?	2.50	5.00	10.00
CHIAROSCURO					
❏ 134	Blue Four	1975	3.00	6.00	12.00
❏ 203	The Best of Joe Venuti	1979	2.50	5.00	10.00
FLYING FISH					
❏ FF-077	Joe in Chicago, 1978	1979	3.00	6.00	12.00
GOLDEN CREST					
❏ GC-3100 [M]	Joe Venuti Plays Gershwin	1959	7.50	15.00	30.00
❏ GC-3101 [M]	Joe Venuti Plays Jerome Kern	1959	7.50	15.00	30.00
GRAND AWARD					
❏ GA-33-351 [M]	Fiddle on Fire	1956	10.00	20.00	40.00
PAUSA					
❏ 7034	Doin' Things	197?	2.50	5.00	10.00
TOPS					
❏ L 923 [10]	Twilight on the Trail	195?	7.50	15.00	30.00
VANGUARD					
❏ VSD-79396	Joe Venuti in Milan	197?	2.50	5.00	10.00
❏ VSD-79405	Jazz Violin	197?	2.50	5.00	10.00
YAZOO					
❏ 1062	Violin Jazz	198?	2.50	5.00	10.00

VENUTI, JOE, AND GEORGE BARNES
Also see each artist's individual listings.

Number	Title	Yr	VG	VG+	NM
CONCORD JAZZ					
❏ CJ-14	Gems	197?	3.00	6.00	12.00
❏ CJ-30	Live at the Concord Summer Festival	197?	3.00	6.00	12.00

VENUTI, JOE, AND EARL HINES
Also see each artist's individual listings.

Number	Title	Yr	VG	VG+	NM
CHIAROSCURO					
❏ 145	Hot Sonatas	1975	3.00	6.00	12.00

VENUTI, JOE/EDDIE LANG
Also see each artist's individual listings.

Number	Title	Yr	VG	VG+	NM
COLUMBIA					
❏ C2L 24 [(2) M]	Swinging the Blues	1963	6.25	12.50	25.00
-- "Guaranteed High Fidelity" on labels					
❏ C2L 24 [(2) M]	Swinging the Blues	1965	5.00	10.00	20.00
-- "360 Sound Mono" on labels					

Number	Title	Yr	VG	VG+	NM
"X"					
❏ LVA-3036 [M]	Joe Venuti and Eddie Lang	1955	10.00	20.00	40.00

VENUTI, JOE, AND DAVE McKENNA
Also see each artist's individual listings.

Number	Title	Yr	VG	VG+	NM
CHIAROSCURO					
❏ 160	Alone at the Palace	1977	3.00	6.00	12.00

VENUTI, JOE, AND MARIAN McPARTLAND
Also see each artist's individual listings.

Number	Title	Yr	VG	VG+	NM
HALCYON					
❏ 112	Maestro and Friend	197?	3.00	6.00	12.00

VENUTI, JOE, AND LOUIS PRIMA
Also see each artist's individual listings.

Number	Title	Yr	VG	VG+	NM
DESIGN					
❏ DLP-54 [M]	Hi-Fi Lootin'	195?	5.00	10.00	20.00

VENUTI, JOE, AND ZOOT SIMS
Also see each artist's individual listings.

Number	Title	Yr	VG	VG+	NM
CHIAROSCURO					
❏ 128	Joe and Zoot	197?	3.75	7.50	15.00
❏ 142	Joe Venuti and Zoot Sims	1975	3.00	6.00	12.00

VER PLANCK, BILLY
Trombonist and composer.

Number	Title	Yr	VG	VG+	NM
SAVOY					
❏ MG-12101 [M]	Dancing Jazz	1957	10.00	20.00	40.00
❏ MG-12121 [M]	Jazz for Playgirls	1957	10.00	20.00	40.00

VER PLANCK, MARLENE
Female singer.

Number	Title	Yr	VG	VG+	NM
AUDIOPHILE					
❏ AP-121	You'd Better Love	197?	2.50	5.00	10.00
❏ AP-138	Marlene Ver Planck Loves Johnny Mercer	197?	2.50	5.00	10.00
❏ AP-160	A New York Singer	1980	2.50	5.00	10.00
❏ AP-169	A Warmer Place	1981	2.50	5.00	10.00
❏ AP-186	I Like to Sing	1984	2.50	5.00	10.00
❏ AP-218	Marlene Ver Planck Sings Alec Wilder	1986	2.50	5.00	10.00
❏ AP-235	Pure and Natural	1988	2.50	5.00	10.00
SAVOY					
❏ MG-12058 [M]	I Think of You with Every Breath I Take	1956	12.50	25.00	50.00
-- As "Marlene"					

VERGARI, MADELINE
Female singer.

Number	Title	Yr	VG	VG+	NM
SEA BREEZE					
❏ SB-108	This Is My Lucky Day	198?	2.50	5.00	10.00

VERHEYEN, CARL
Guitarist.

Number	Title	Yr	VG	VG+	NM
CMG					
❏ CML-8012	No Borders	198?	2.50	5.00	10.00

VERNON, MILLI(E)
Female singer.

Number	Title	Yr	VG	VG+	NM
AUDIOPHILE					
❏ AP-178	Old Shoes	1989	2.50	5.00	10.00
STORYVILLE					
❏ STLP-910 [M]	Introducing Milli Vernon	1956	75.00	150.00	300.00

VERY SPECIAL ENVOY

Number	Title	Yr	VG	VG+	NM
ROULETTE					
❏ SR-42003	Very Special Envoy	1968	5.00	10.00	20.00

VESALA, EDWARD
Drummer, composer and arranger.

Number	Title	Yr	VG	VG+	NM
ECM					
❏ 1088	Satu	197?	3.00	6.00	12.00

VIBRATION SOCIETY, THE
Among the members: Steve Turre (trombone); Hilton Ruiz (piano).

Number	Title	Yr	VG	VG+	NM
STASH					
❏ ST-261	The Music of Rahsaan Roland Kirk	1986	2.50	5.00	10.00

Number	Title	Yr	VG	VG+	NM
VICK, HAROLD					
Tenor saxophone player.					
BLUE NOTE					
❑ BLP-4138 [M]	Steppin' Out	1963	10.00	20.00	40.00
❑ BST-84138 [S]	Steppin' Out	1963	12.50	25.00	50.00
-- With "New York, USA" address on label					
❑ BST-84138 [S]	Steppin' Out	1967	3.75	7.50	15.00
-- With "A Division of Liberty Records" on label					
MUSE					
❑ MR-5054	Commitment	197?	3.00	6.00	12.00
RCA VICTOR					
❑ LPM-3677 [M]	The Caribbean Suite	1966	3.75	7.50	15.00
❑ LSP-3677 [S]	The Caribbean Suite	1966	5.00	10.00	20.00
❑ LPM-3761 [M]	Straight Up	1967	5.00	10.00	20.00
❑ LSP-3761 [S]	Straight Up	1967	3.75	7.50	15.00
STRATA-EAST					
❑ SES-7431	Don't Look Back	197?	5.00	10.00	20.00
VIDEO ALL STARS, THE					
Organized and led by Skip Martin. Some of the musicians were BOB COOPER; SHELLY MANNE; RED MITCHELL; and FRANK ROSOLINO.					
SOMERSET					
❑ SF-8800 [M]	The Video All Stars Play TV Jazz Themes	1956	30.00	60.00	120.00
VIENNA ART ORCHESTRA					
Led and conducted by Mathias Ruegg.					
HAT HUT					
❑ 1980/1 [(2)]	Concerto Piccolo	1980	5.00	10.00	20.00
❑ 1991/2 [(2)]	Suite for the Green Eighties	1981	5.00	10.00	20.00
❑ 1999/2000 [(2)]	From No Time to Rag Time	1982	5.00	10.00	20.00
❑ 2005 [(2)]	The Minimalism of Erik Satie	1984	3.75	7.50	15.00
❑ 2024 [(2)]	Perpetuum Mobile	1985	3.75	7.50	15.00
VIG, TOMMY					
Percussionist.					
DISCOVERY					
❑ 780	Encounter with Time	197?	2.50	5.00	10.00
DOBRE					
❑ 1015	1978	1978	3.00	6.00	12.00
MILESTONE					
❑ MSP-9007	Sounds of the Seventies	1968	5.00	10.00	20.00
VILLAGE STOMPERS, THE					
Dixieland-style band from New York. Their hit was "Washington Square."					
EPIC					
❑ LN 24078 [M]	Washington Square	1963	3.75	7.50	15.00
❑ LN 24090 [M]	More Sounds of Washington Square	1964	3.75	7.50	15.00
❑ LN 24109 [M]	Around the World with the Village Stompers	1964	3.00	6.00	12.00
❑ LN 24161 [M]	Some Folk, a Bit of Country and a Whole Lot of Dixie	1965	3.00	6.00	12.00
❑ LN 24180 [M]	A Taste of Honey	1965	3.00	6.00	12.00
❑ LN 24235 [M]	One More Time	1966	3.00	6.00	12.00
❑ LN 24318 [M]	The Village Stompers' Greatest Hits	1967	3.00	6.00	12.00
❑ BN 26078 [S]	Washington Square	1963	5.00	10.00	20.00
❑ BN 26090 [S]	More Sounds of Washington Square	1964	5.00	10.00	20.00
❑ BN 26109 [S]	Around the World with the Village Stompers	1964	3.75	7.50	15.00
❑ BN 26161 [S]	Some Folk, a Bit of Country and a Whole Lot of Dixie	1965	3.75	7.50	15.00
❑ BN 26180 [S]	A Taste of Honey	1965	3.75	7.50	15.00
❑ BN 26235 [S]	One More Time	1966	3.75	7.50	15.00
❑ BN 26318 [S]	The Village Stompers' Greatest Hits	1967	3.75	7.50	15.00
VILLEGAS					
Full name: Enrique Mono Villegas. Pianist.					
COLUMBIA					
❑ CL 787 [M]	Introducing Villegas	1956	7.50	15.00	30.00
❑ CL 877 [M]	Very, Very Villegas	1956	7.50	15.00	30.00
VINNEGAR, LEROY					
Bass player.					
CONTEMPORARY					
❑ C-3542 [M]	Leroy Walks!	1957	20.00	40.00	80.00
❑ M-3608 [M]	Leroy Walks Again!	1962	7.50	15.00	30.00
❑ S-7003 [S]	Leroy Walks!	1959	12.50	25.00	50.00
❑ S-7542 [S]	Leroy Walks!	197?	3.00	6.00	12.00

Number	Title	Yr	VG	VG+	NM
❑ S-7608 [S]	Leroy Walks Again!	1962	10.00	20.00	40.00
FANTASY					
❑ OJC-160	Leroy Walks!	198?	2.50	5.00	10.00
❑ OJC-454	Leroy Walks Again!	1990	2.50	5.00	10.00
LEGEND					
❑ 1001	Glass of Water	197?	3.75	7.50	15.00
PBR					
❑ 6	The Kid	197?	3.00	6.00	12.00
STEREO RECORDS					
❑ S-7003 [S]	Leroy Walks!	1958	15.00	30.00	60.00
VEE JAY					
❑ LP-2502 [M]	Jazz's Great Walker	1964	7.50	15.00	30.00
❑ LPS-2502 [S]	Jazz's Great Walker	1964	7.50	15.00	30.00
VINSON, EDDIE "CLEANHEAD"					
Alto saxophone player and male singer.					
AAMCO					
❑ 312 [M]	Cleanhead's Back in Town	196?	10.00	20.00	40.00
BETHLEHEM					
❑ BCP-5005 [M]	Eddie "Cleanhead" Vinson Sings	1957	25.00	50.00	100.00
❑ BCP-6036	Back in Town	1978	3.75	7.50	15.00
BLUESWAY					
❑ BL-6007 [M]	Cherry Red	1967	6.25	12.50	25.00
❑ BLS-6007 [S]	Cherry Red	1967	6.25	12.50	25.00
CIRCLE					
❑ CLP-57	Kidney Stew	1983	3.00	6.00	12.00
DELMARK					
❑ 631	Old Kidney Stew Is Fine	1980	3.00	6.00	12.00
FLYING DUTCHMAN					
❑ 31-1012	You Can't Make Love Alone	197?	3.75	7.50	15.00
KING					
❑ KS-1087	Cherry Red	1969	6.25	12.50	25.00
MUSE					
❑ MR-5116	The Clean Machine	1978	3.75	7.50	15.00
❑ MR-5208	Eddie "Cleanhead" Vinson and the Muse All-Stars: Live at Sandy's	1979	3.00	6.00	12.00
❑ MR-5243	Eddie "Cleanhead" Vinson and the Muse All-Stars: Hold It Right There	198?	3.00	6.00	12.00
❑ MR-5282	Cleanhead and Roomful of Blues	1982	3.00	6.00	12.00
❑ MR-5310	Eddie "Cleanhead" Vinson Sings the Blues	198?	3.00	6.00	12.00
PABLO					
❑ 2310 866	I Want a Little Girl	198?	3.00	6.00	12.00
REGGIES					
❑ 1000	Rollin' Over the Devil	1981	3.00	6.00	12.00
RIVERSIDE					
❑ RLP-502 [M]	Back Door Blues	1965	10.00	20.00	40.00
❑ RLS-9502 [S]	Back Door Blues	1965	10.00	20.00	40.00
VINSON, EDDIE "CLEANHEAD"/JIMMY WITHERSPOON					
Also see each artist's individual listings.					
KING					
❑ 634 [M]	Battle of the Blues, Volume 3	1960	375.00	750.00	1,500.
VIOLA, AL					
Guitarist.					
LEGEND					
❑ 1002	Alone Again	197?	3.75	7.50	15.00
MODE					
❑ LP-121 [M]	Solo Guitar	1957	20.00	40.00	80.00
PBR					
❑ 7	Salutations F.S.	197?	3.00	6.00	12.00
❑ 11	Prelude to a Kiss	197?	3.00	6.00	12.00
VISION					
MUSIC IS MEDICINE					
❑ 9027	Vision	198?	3.00	6.00	12.00
VISITORS, THE					
Members: Earl Grubbs (soprano saxophone); Carl Grubbs (alto sax).					
COBBLESTONE					
❑ 9010	Neptune	197?	5.00	10.00	20.00
MUSE					
❑ MR-5024	In My Youth	197?	3.00	6.00	12.00
❑ MR-5047	Rebirth	197?	3.00	6.00	12.00
❑ MR-5094	Motherland	1976	3.00	6.00	12.00
❑ MR-5195	Neptune	197?	2.50	5.00	10.00

Number	Title	Yr	VG	VG+	NM

VITOUS, MIROSLAV
Bass player. Also see WEATHER REPORT.
ARISTA
| ❏ AL 4099 | Majesty Music | 197? | 2.50 | 5.00 | 10.00 |
ARISTA/FREEDOM
| ❏ AF 1040 | Vitous | 1976 | 3.00 | 6.00 | 12.00 |
ATLANTIC
| ❏ SD 1622 | Mountain in the Clouds | 1972 | 3.00 | 6.00 | 12.00 |
ECM
| ❏ 1145 | First Meeting | 1979 | 3.00 | 6.00 | 12.00 |
| ❏ 1185 | Miroslav Vitous Group | 198? | 3.00 | 6.00 | 12.00 |
EMBRYO
| ❏ SD 524 | Infinite Search | 1970 | 3.75 | 7.50 | 15.00 |
WARNER BROS.
| ❏ BS 2925 | Magical Shepherd | 1976 | 2.50 | 5.00 | 10.00 |

VITRO, ROSEANNA
Female singer.
SKYLINE
| ❏ SKYP-1001 | A Quiet Place | 1987 | 2.50 | 5.00 | 10.00 |
TEXAS ROSE
| ❏ TRM-1001 | Listen Here | 1984 | 2.50 | 5.00 | 10.00 |

VIZZUTTI, ALLEN
Trumpeter.
BAINBRIDGE
| ❏ 6246 | Red Metal | 198? | 2.50 | 5.00 | 10.00 |
HEADFIRST
| ❏ 9700 | Vizzutti | 198? | 3.00 | 6.00 | 12.00 |

VOCAL JAZZ INCORPORATED
GRAPEVINE
| ❏ 3310 | Vocal Jazz Incorporated | 197? | 3.00 | 6.00 | 12.00 |

VOLLENWEIDER, ANDREAS
Harpist.
CBS MASTERWORKS
| ❏ FM 37793 | ...Behind the Gardens...Behind the Wall...Under the Tree... | 1984 | 2.50 | 5.00 | 10.00 |
| ❏ FM 37827 | Caverna Magica (...Under the Tree-In the Cave...) | 1984 | 2.50 | 5.00 | 10.00 |
CBS/FM
| ❏ FM 39963 | White Winds | 1985 | 2.50 | 5.00 | 10.00 |
| ❏ FM 42255 | Down to the Moon | 1986 | 2.50 | 5.00 | 10.00 |
COLUMBIA
| ❏ OC 45154 | Dancing with the Lion | 1989 | 3.00 | 6.00 | 12.00 |

VON OHLEN, JOHN "THE BARON"
Drummer.
CREATIVE WORLD
| ❏ ST-3001 | The Baron | 197? | 2.50 | 5.00 | 10.00 |

VON SCHLIPPENBACH, ALEXANDER
Pianist.
ENJA
| ❏ 2012 | Payan | 197? | 3.75 | 7.50 | 15.00 |

VUCKOVICH, LARRY
Pianist, arranger and composer.
INNER CITY
| ❏ IC-1096 | Blue Balkan | 198? | 3.00 | 6.00 | 12.00 |
PALO ALTO
| ❏ PA-8012 | City Sounds | 1981 | 2.50 | 5.00 | 10.00 |

Number	Title	Yr	VG	VG+	NM	Number	Title	Yr	VG	VG+	NM

W

WACKER, FRED
CADET
| ☐ LP-4050 [M] | Fred Wacker Swings Cool | 1966 | 3.00 | 6.00 | 12.00 |
| ☐ LPS-4050 [S] | Fred Wacker Swings Cool | 1966 | 3.75 | 7.50 | 15.00 |

DOLPHIN
| ☐ 9 [M] | Freddy Wacker and His Windy City Seven | 195? | 12.50 | 25.00 | 50.00 |

WADDELL, STEVE
Waddell (trombone, vocals) leads a trad jazz band called Creole Bells.
STOMP OFF
| ☐ SOS-1172 | Frisco Comes to Melbourne | 1987 | 2.50 | 5.00 | 10.00 |

WADUD, ABDUL
Cellist.
RED RECORD
| ☐ VPA-147 | Straight Ahead/Free at Last | 198? | 3.00 | 6.00 | 12.00 |

WAGNER, LARRY
A44
| ☐ AP-501 [10] | Larry Wagner | 1954 | 15.00 | 30.00 | 60.00 |

WALCOTT, COLLIN
Sitar and tabla player, violinist, percussionist and male singer. Also see CODONA.
ECM
| ☐ 1062 | Cloud | 1976 | 3.00 | 6.00 | 12.00 |
| ☐ 1096 | Grazing | 1977 | 3.00 | 6.00 | 12.00 |

WALD, JERRY
Clarinetist and bandleader.
KAPP
| ☐ KL-1043 [M] | Listen to the Music of Jerry Wald | 1956 | 10.00 | 20.00 | 40.00 |

LION
| ☐ L-70014 [M] | Tops in Pops -- Designed for Dancing | 1958 | 6.25 | 12.50 | 25.00 |

WALDEN, NARADA MICHAEL
Drummer, male singer and producer.
ATLANTIC
☐ SD 19141	I Cry, I Smile	1978	2.50	5.00	10.00
☐ SD 19222	Awakening	1979	2.50	5.00	10.00
☐ SD 19259	The Dance of Life	1979	2.50	5.00	10.00
☐ SD 19279	Victory	1980	2.50	5.00	10.00
☐ SD 19351	Confidence	1981	2.50	5.00	10.00
☐ 80058	You, Looking at Me	1982	2.50	5.00	10.00

REPRISE
| ☐ 25694 | Divine Emotion | 1988 | 2.50 | 5.00 | 10.00 |

WARNER BROS.
| ☐ 25176 | The Nature of Things | 1984 | 2.50 | 5.00 | 10.00 |

WALDO'S GUTBUCKET SYNCOPATORS
Also see TERRY WALDO.
BLACKBIRD
| ☐ 6002 | Ohio Theatre Concert | 197? | 2.50 | 5.00 | 10.00 |
| ☐ 12009 | Jazz in the Afternoon | 197? | 3.00 | 6.00 | 12.00 |

STOMP OFF
| ☐ SOS-1001 | Feelin' Devilish | 198? | 2.50 | 5.00 | 10.00 |
| ☐ SOS-1036 | Presents | 198? | 2.50 | 5.00 | 10.00 |

WALDO'S RAGTIME ORCHESTRA
Also see TERRY WALDO.
STOMP OFF
| ☐ SOS-1007 | Smiles and Chuckles | 198? | 2.50 | 5.00 | 10.00 |
| ☐ SOS-1069 | Spectacular Ragtime | 198? | 2.50 | 5.00 | 10.00 |

WALDO, TERRY
Pianist and male singer. Also see WALDO'S GUTBUCKET SYNCOPATORS; WALDO'S RAGTIME ORCHESTRA.
DIRTY SHAME
| ☐ 1237 | Snookums Rag | 197? | 3.00 | 6.00 | 12.00 |

STOMP OFF
| ☐ SOS-1002 | Wizard of the Keyboard | 198? | 2.50 | 5.00 | 10.00 |
| ☐ SOS-1120 | Terry Waldo and the Gotham City Band | 1987 | 2.50 | 5.00 | 10.00 |

WALDRON, MAL
Pianist and composer. Also see THE PRESTIGE JAZZ QUARTET.
ARISTA/FREEDOM
| ☐ AF 1013 | Blues for Lady Day | 1975 | 3.00 | 6.00 | 12.00 |
| ☐ AF 1042 | Signals | 1977 | 3.00 | 6.00 | 12.00 |

BETHLEHEM
| ☐ BCP-6045 [M] | Left Alone | 1960 | 10.00 | 20.00 | 40.00 |
| ☐ SBCP-6045 [S] | Left Alone | 1960 | 10.00 | 20.00 | 40.00 |

ENJA
☐ 2004	Black Glory	197?	3.75	7.50	15.00
☐ 2034	Up Popped the Devil	197?	3.75	7.50	15.00
☐ 2050	Hard Talk	197?	3.75	7.50	15.00
☐ 3075	Mingus Lives	198?	3.00	6.00	12.00
☐ 4010	What It Is	198?	3.00	6.00	12.00

FANTASY
☐ OJC-082	The Quest	198?	2.50	5.00	10.00
☐ OJC-132	Impressions	198?	2.50	5.00	10.00
☐ OJC-611	Mal/1	1991	3.00	6.00	12.00

INNER CITY
| ☐ IC-3018 [(2)] | Moods | 1979 | 3.75 | 7.50 | 15.00 |

MUSE
| ☐ MR-5305 | Encounters | 198? | 2.50 | 5.00 | 10.00 |

MUSIC MINUS ONE
☐ 175 [M]	Fun With Brushes	1960	5.00	10.00	20.00
☐ 1012 [M]	Moonglow and Stardust	1960	5.00	10.00	20.00
☐ 1015 [M]	Music of Duke Ellington	1960	5.00	10.00	20.00
☐ 1016 [M]	Music of McHugh	1960	5.00	10.00	20.00
☐ 1017 [M]	Mal Waldron	1960	5.00	10.00	20.00
☐ 1018 [M]	For Singers 'N Singer	1960	5.00	10.00	20.00
☐ 4005 [M]	Blue Drums	1961	5.00	10.00	20.00
☐ 4007 [M]	For Pianists Only	1961	5.00	10.00	20.00
☐ 4008 [M]	They Laughed When I Sat Down to Play	1961	5.00	10.00	20.00

NEW JAZZ
☐ NJLP-8201 [M]	Mal/3: Sounds	1958	25.00	50.00	100.00
-- Yellow label					
☐ NJLP-8201 [M]	Mal/3: Sounds	1958	12.50	25.00	50.00
-- Purple label					
☐ NJLP-8201 [M]	Mal/3: Sounds	1965	6.25	12.50	25.00
-- Blue label, trident logo at right					
☐ NJLP-8208 [M]	Mal/4: Trio	1958	12.50	25.00	50.00
-- Purple label					
☐ NJLP-8208 [M]	Mal/4: Trio	1965	6.25	12.50	25.00
-- Blue label, trident logo at right					
☐ NJLP-8242 [M]	Impressions	1960	12.50	25.00	50.00
-- Purple label					
☐ NJLP-8242 [M]	Impressions	1965	6.25	12.50	25.00
-- Blue label, trident logo at right					
☐ NJLP-8269 [M]	The Quest	1962	12.50	25.00	50.00
-- Purple label					
☐ NJLP-8269 [M]	The Quest	1965	6.25	12.50	25.00
-- Blue label, trident logo at right					
☐ NJLP-8316 [M]	The Dealers	1963	---	---	---
-- Canceled; reassigned to Status					

PALO ALTO
| ☐ PA-8014 | One Entrance, Many Exits | 1982 | 2.50 | 5.00 | 10.00 |

PAULA
| ☐ LPS-4000 | Mal Waldron on the Steinway | 197? | 3.00 | 6.00 | 12.00 |

PRESTIGE
☐ PRLP-7090 [M]	Mal/1	1957	20.00	40.00	80.00
☐ PRLP-7111 [M]	Mal/2	1957	20.00	40.00	80.00
☐ PRST-7579 [S]	The Quest	1969	5.00	10.00	20.00
☐ 24068 [(2)]	Mal Waldron/1 and 2	197?	3.75	7.50	15.00
☐ 24107 [(2)]	After Hours	197?	3.75	7.50	15.00

SOUL NOTE
☐ 121118	The Go-Go -- Live at the Village Gate	1989	3.00	6.00	12.00
☐ 121130	Update	1989	3.00	6.00	12.00
☐ 121148	The Seagulls of Kristiansund	1990	3.75	7.50	15.00

STATUS
| ☐ ST-8316 [M] | The Dealers | 1965 | 10.00 | 20.00 | 40.00 |

WEST 54
| ☐ 8010 | Live/Left Alone | 1980 | 3.00 | 6.00 | 12.00 |

WALDRON, MAL, AND STEVE LACY
Also see each artist's individual listings.
HAT ART
| ☐ 2038 [(2)] | Let's Call This | 1987 | 3.75 | 7.50 | 15.00 |

INNER CITY
| ☐ IC-3010 | One-upsmanship | 197? | 3.00 | 6.00 | 12.00 |

SOUL NOTE
| ☐ 121170 | Sempre Amore | 1990 | 3.75 | 7.50 | 15.00 |

Number	Title	Yr	VG	VG+	NM

WALDRON, MAL, AND GARY PEACOCK
Also see each artist's individual listings.
CATALYST
| ❑ 7906 | First Encounter | 197? | 3.00 | 6.00 | 12.00 |

WALI AND THE AFRO-CARAVAN
SOLID STATE
| ❑ SS-18065 | Home Lost and Found | 1969 | 5.00 | 10.00 | 20.00 |

WALKER, KIT
Keyboard player, composer and producer.
WINDHAM HILL
| ❑ WH-0109 | Dancing on the Edge of the World | 1987 | 2.50 | 5.00 | 10.00 |
| ❑ WH-0117 | Fire in the Lake | 1989 | 3.00 | 6.00 | 12.00 |

WALKER, T-BONE
Guitarist and male singer.
ATLANTIC
❑ 8020 [M]	T-Bone Blues	1959	55.00	110.00	220.00
-- Black label					
❑ 8020 [M]	T-Bone Blues	1960	17.50	35.00	70.00
-- Red and purple label					
❑ SD 8256	T-Bone Blues	1970	5.00	10.00	20.00
BLUE NOTE
| ❑ BN-LA533-H2 [(2)] | Classics | 1975 | 5.00 | 10.00 | 20.00 |
BLUESTIME
| ❑ 29004 | Everyday I Have the Blues | 1968 | 7.50 | 15.00 | 30.00 |
| ❑ 29010 | Blue Rocks | 1969 | 7.50 | 15.00 | 30.00 |
BLUESWAY
❑ BLS-6008	Stormy Monday Blues	1968	7.50	15.00	30.00
-- Reissue of Wet Soul LP?					
❑ BLS-6014	Funky Town	1968	7.50	15.00	30.00
❑ BLS-6058	Dirty Mistreater	1973	3.75	7.50	15.00
BRUNSWICK
| ❑ BL 754126 | The Truth | 1968 | 7.50 | 15.00 | 30.00 |
CAPITOL
❑ H 370 [10]	Classics in Jazz	1953	250.00	500.00	1,000.
❑ T 370 [M]	Classics in Jazz	1953	75.00	150.00	300.00
❑ T 1958 [M]	Great Blues Vocal and Guitar	1963	37.50	75.00	150.00
-- Black "The Star Line" label (existence of black colorband label not confirmed)					
DELMARK
| ❑ D-633 [M] | I Want a Little Girl | 1967 | 10.00 | 20.00 | 40.00 |
| ❑ DS-633 [S] | I Want a Little Girl | 1967 | 12.50 | 25.00 | 50.00 |
IMPERIAL
❑ LP-9098 [M]	T-Bone Walker Sings the Blues	1959	75.00	150.00	300.00
❑ LP-9116 [M]	Singing the Blues	1960	62.50	125.00	250.00
❑ LP-9146 [M]	I Get So Weary	1961	75.00	150.00	300.00
MOSAIC
| ❑ M9-130 [(9)] | The Complete Recordings of T-Bone Walker 1940-1954 | 199? | 50.00 | 100.00 | 200.00 |
POLYDOR
| ❑ 24-4502 | Good Feelin' | 1972 | 3.75 | 7.50 | 15.00 |
| ❑ PD-5521 | Fly Walker Airlines | 1973 | 3.75 | 7.50 | 15.00 |
REPRISE
| ❑ 2RS 6483 [(2)] | Very Rare | 1973 | 5.00 | 10.00 | 20.00 |
WET SOUL
| ❑ 1002 | Stormy Monday Blues | 1967 | 12.50 | 25.00 | 50.00 |

WALL, DAN
Organist.
AUDIOPHILE
| ❑ AP-143 | Dan Wall Trio | 198? | 2.50 | 5.00 | 10.00 |
PROGRESSIVE
| ❑ PRO-7016 | The Trio | 198? | 3.00 | 6.00 | 12.00 |

WALLACE, BENNIE
Tenor saxophone player.
AUDIOQUEST
| ❑ AQLP-1017 | The Old Songs | 1993 | 3.75 | 7.50 | 15.00 |
BLUE NOTE
| ❑ BT-48014 | Border Town | 1988 | 3.00 | 6.00 | 12.00 |
| ❑ BT-85107 | Twilight Time | 198? | 3.00 | 6.00 | 12.00 |
ENJA
❑ 3091	Wallace Plays Monk	198?	3.00	6.00	12.00
❑ 4028	Bennie Wallace and Chick Corea	1982	3.00	6.00	12.00
❑ 4046	Big Jim's Tango	1982	3.00	6.00	12.00

INNER CITY
| ❑ IC-3025 | Fourteen Bar Blues | 1979 | 3.00 | 6.00 | 12.00 |
| ❑ IC-3034 | Live at the Public Theater | 1979 | 3.00 | 6.00 | 12.00 |

WALLER, FATS
Pianist, organist, male singer and composer.
ARCHIVE OF FOLK AND JAZZ
| ❑ 319 | Fats Waller Plays Fats Waller | 197? | 2.50 | 5.00 | 10.00 |
| ❑ 337 | Ain't Misbehavin' | 197? | 2.50 | 5.00 | 10.00 |
BIOGRAPH
❑ 1002	Rare Piano Rolls	197?	2.50	5.00	10.00
❑ 1005	Rare Piano Rolls, Volume 2	197?	2.50	5.00	10.00
❑ 1015	Rare Piano Rolls, Volume 3	197?	2.50	5.00	10.00
BLUEBIRD
❑ AXM2-5511 [(2)]	The Complete Fats Waller, Volume 1	197?	3.75	7.50	15.00
❑ AXM2-5518 [(2)]	Piano Solos	197?	3.75	7.50	15.00
❑ AXM2-5575 [(2)]	The Complete Fats Waller, Volume 2	198?	3.75	7.50	15.00
❑ AXM2-5583 [(2)]	The Complete Fats Waller, Volume 3	198?	3.75	7.50	15.00
❑ 5905-1-RB [(2)]	The Complete Fats Waller, Volume 4	1987	3.75	7.50	15.00
❑ 6288-1-RB	The Joint Is Jumpin'	1987	2.50	5.00	10.00
❑ 9983-1-RB [(4)]	The Last Years: Fats Waller and His Rhythm, 1940-1943	198?	7.50	15.00	30.00
BULLDOG
| ❑ BDL-2004 | 20 Golden Pieces of Fats Waller | 198? | 2.50 | 5.00 | 10.00 |
GIANTS OF JAZZ
| ❑ GOJ-1029 | Live at the Yacht Club | 198? | 2.50 | 5.00 | 10.00 |
| ❑ GOJ-1035 | Live, Volume 2 | 198? | 2.50 | 5.00 | 10.00 |
RCA VICTOR
❑ LPT-8 [10]	Fats Waller 1934-42	1951	37.50	75.00	150.00
❑ LPT-14 [10]	Fats Waller Favoites	1951	37.50	75.00	150.00
❑ LPV-473 [M]	The Real Fats Waller	1965	6.25	12.50	25.00
❑ LPV-516 [M]	Fats Waller '34/35	1965	5.00	10.00	20.00
❑ LPV-525 [M]	Valentine Stomp	1966	5.00	10.00	20.00
❑ LPV-550 [M]	Smashing Thirds	1968	5.00	10.00	20.00
❑ LPV-562 [M]	African Ripples	1969	5.00	10.00	20.00
❑ LPT-1001 [M]	Fats Waller Plays and Sings	1954	20.00	40.00	80.00
❑ LPM-1246 [M]	Ain't Misbehavin'	1956	12.50	25.00	50.00
❑ LPM-1502 [M]	Handful of Keys	1957	12.50	25.00	50.00
❑ LPM-1503 [M]	One Never Knows, Do One?	1959	12.50	25.00	50.00
❑ CPL1-2904	A Legendary Performer	1979	2.50	5.00	10.00
❑ LPT-3040 [10]	Swingin' the Organ	1953	30.00	60.00	120.00
❑ LPM-6000 [(2) M]	Fats	1960	20.00	40.00	80.00
❑ LPT-6001 [(2) M]	Fats Waller Radio Transcriptions	1954	30.00	60.00	120.00
-- Boxed set with booklet					
RIVERSIDE
❑ RLP 12-103 [M]	The Young Fats Waller	1955	15.00	30.00	60.00
❑ RLP 12-109 [M]	The Amazing Mr. Waller	1955	15.00	30.00	60.00
❑ RLP-1010 [10]	Rediscovered Fats Waller Piano Solos	1953	37.50	75.00	150.00
❑ RLP-1021 [10]	Fats Waller at the Organ	1953	37.50	75.00	150.00
❑ RLP-1022 [10]	Jiving with Fats Waller	1953	37.50	75.00	150.00
STANYAN
| ❑ 10057 | The Undiscovered Fats Waller | 197? | 2.50 | 5.00 | 10.00 |
SWING
| ❑ SW-8442/3 [(2)] | Fats Waller in London | 198? | 3.00 | 6.00 | 12.00 |
TRIP
| ❑ J-4 | Fats Waller on the Air | 197? | 2.50 | 5.00 | 10.00 |
| ❑ 5042 [(2)] | A Legend in His Lifetime | 197? | 3.00 | 6.00 | 12.00 |
"X"
| ❑ LVA-3035 [10] | The Young Fats Waller | 1955 | 37.50 | 75.00 | 150.00 |

WALLINGTON, GEORGE
Pianist and composer. Also see JAMES MOODY; JIMMY RANEY.
ATLANTIC
❑ 1275 [M]	Knight Music	1958	20.00	40.00	80.00
-- Black label					
❑ 1275 [M]	Knight Music	1961	6.25	12.50	25.00
-- Multicolor label, white "fan" logo at right					
❑ SD 1275 [S]	Knight Music	1958	20.00	40.00	80.00
-- Green label					
❑ SD 1275 [M]	Knight Music	1961	5.00	10.00	20.00
-- Multicolor label, white "fan" logo at right					
BLUE NOTE
| ❑ BLP-5045 [10] | George Wallington and His All-Star Band | 1954 | 100.00 | 200.00 | 400.00 |
EAST-WEST
| ❑ 4004 [M] | The Prestidigitator | 1958 | 37.50 | 75.00 | 150.00 |

Number	Title	Yr	VG	VG+	NM
FANTASY					
❑ OJC-1704	Jazz for the Carriage Trade	1985	2.50	5.00	10.00
❑ OJC-1754	The George Wallington Trios	198?	2.50	5.00	10.00
NEW JAZZ					
❑ NJLP-8207 [M]	The New York Scene	1958	37.50	75.00	150.00
-- Purple label					
❑ NJLP-8207 [M]	The New York Scene	1965	10.00	20.00	40.00
-- Blue label, trident logo at right					
NORGRAN					
❑ MGN-24 [10]	The Workshop of the George Wallington Trio	1954	37.50	75.00	150.00
❑ MGN-1010 [M]	George Wallington with Strings	1954	25.00	50.00	100.00
PRESTIGE					
❑ PRLP-136 [10]	The George Wallington Trio	1952	62.50	125.00	250.00
❑ PRLP-158 [10]	The George Wallington Trio, Volume 2	1953	62.50	125.00	250.00
❑ PRLP-7032 [M]	Jazz for the Carriage Trade	1956	125.00	250.00	500.00
❑ PRST-7587 [R]	The George Wallington Trios	1968	5.00	10.00	20.00
❑ PRST-7820	At Café Bohemia '55	1971	3.75	7.50	15.00
❑ 24093 [(2)]	Our Delight	197?	3.75	7.50	15.00
PROGRESSIVE					
❑ PLP-1001 [M]	George Wallington Quintet at the Bohemia	1955	250.00	500.00	1,000
❑ 3001 [10]	The George Wallington Trio	1952	62.50	125.00	250.00
❑ PRO-7001	The George Wallington Quintet at the Café Bohemia, 1955	198?	2.50	5.00	10.00
SAVOY					
❑ MG-12081 [M]	The George Wallington Trio	1956	20.00	40.00	80.00
❑ MG-12122 [M]	Jazz at Hotchkiss	1957	20.00	40.00	80.00
❑ MG-15037 [10]	The George Wallington Trio	1954	25.00	50.00	100.00
SAVOY JAZZ					
❑ SJL-1122	Dance of the Infidels	198?	2.50	5.00	10.00
VERVE					
❑ MGV-2017 [M]	Variations	1956	20.00	40.00	80.00

WALRATH, JACK
Trumpeter and composer.

Number	Title	Yr	VG	VG+	NM
BLUE NOTE					
❑ BT-46905	Master of Suspense	1987	3.00	6.00	12.00
❑ B1-91101	Neohippus	1989	3.00	6.00	12.00
GATEMOUTH					
❑ 1002	Demons in Pursuit	1979	3.00	6.00	12.00
MUSE					
❑ MR-5362	Wholly Trinity	198?	2.50	5.00	10.00
RED RECORD					
❑ VPA-182	Live at Umbria Jazz Festival, Vol. 1	1986	3.00	6.00	12.00
❑ VPA-186	Live at Umbria Jazz Festival, Vol. 2	1986	3.00	6.00	12.00
STASH					
❑ ST-221	Revenge of the Fat People	198?	2.50	5.00	10.00
❑ ST-223	A Plea for Sanity	198?	2.50	5.00	10.00
STEEPLECHASE					
❑ SCS-1172	Jack Walrath in Europe	1982	3.00	6.00	12.00

WALTER, CY
Pianist and composer.

Number	Title	Yr	VG	VG+	NM
ATLANTIC					
❑ 1236 [M]	Rodgers Revisited	1956	10.00	20.00	40.00
-- Black label					
❑ 1236 [M]	Rodgers Revisited	1961	5.00	10.00	20.00
-- Multicolor label, white "fan" logo at right					
MGM					
❑ E-4393 [M]	Cy Walter at the Drake	1966	3.00	6.00	12.00
❑ SE-4393 [S]	Cy Walter at the Drake	1966	3.75	7.50	15.00
WESTMINSTER					
❑ WP-6120 [M]	Dry Martini, Please	195?	6.25	12.50	25.00
❑ WPS-15054 [S]	Dry Martini, Please	195?	7.50	15.00	30.00

WALTON, CEDAR
Pianist and composer.

Number	Title	Yr	VG	VG+	NM
CLEAN CUTS					
❑ 704	Solos	1980	3.75	7.50	15.00
COBBLESTONE					
❑ 9011	Breakthrough	197?	3.75	7.50	15.00
COLUMBIA					
❑ JC 36285	Soundscapes	1980	2.50	5.00	10.00
FANTASY					
❑ OJC-462	Cedar!	1990	2.50	5.00	10.00
❑ OJC-6002	Cedar Walton Plays Cedar Walton	1988	2.50	5.00	10.00

Number	Title	Yr	VG	VG+	NM
INNER CITY					
❑ IC-6009	The Pentagon	197?	3.00	6.00	12.00
❑ IC-6019	Pit Inn	198?	3.00	6.00	12.00
MUSE					
❑ MR-5010	A Night at Boomer's, Vol. 1	1973	3.00	6.00	12.00
❑ MR-5022	A Night at Boomer's, Vol. 2	1973	3.00	6.00	12.00
❑ MR-5059	Firm Roots	197?	3.75	7.50	15.00
❑ MR-5244	The Maestro	1981	2.50	5.00	10.00
PRESTIGE					
❑ PRLP-7519 [M]	Cedar!	1967	6.25	12.50	25.00
❑ PRST-7519 [S]	Cedar!	1967	5.00	10.00	20.00
❑ PRST-7591	Spectrum	1968	5.00	10.00	20.00
❑ PRST-7618	The Electric Boogaloo Song	1969	5.00	10.00	20.00
❑ PRST-7693	Soul Cycle	1970	5.00	10.00	20.00
RCA VICTOR					
❑ APL1-1009	Mobius	1975	5.00	10.00	20.00
❑ APL1-1435	Beyond Mobius	1976	5.00	10.00	20.00
RED RECORD					
❑ VPA-179	Cedar's Blues	1986	3.00	6.00	12.00
STEEPLECHASE					
❑ SCS-1085	First Set	198?	3.00	6.00	12.00
❑ SCS-1179	Third Set	198?	3.00	6.00	12.00

WALTON, CEDAR, AND HANK MOBLEY
Also see each artist's individual listings.

Number	Title	Yr	VG	VG+	NM
MUSE					
❑ MR-5132	Breakthrough	197?	3.00	6.00	12.00

WALTON, FRANK

Number	Title	Yr	VG	VG+	NM
DELMARK					
❑ DS-436	Reality	197?	2.50	5.00	10.00

WALTON, JON

Number	Title	Yr	VG	VG+	NM
GATEWAY					
❑ 7006	Jon Walton Swings Again	1964	3.75	7.50	15.00

WANDERLEY, WALTER
Organist. His "Summer Samba" was a top-40 hit in 1966.

Number	Title	Yr	VG	VG+	NM
A&M					
❑ SP-3018	When It Was Done	1969	3.00	6.00	12.00
❑ SP-3022	Moondreams	1969	3.00	6.00	12.00
CANYON					
❑ 7711	Return of the Original Sound	196?	3.00	6.00	12.00
GNP CRESCENDO					
❑ GNPS-2137	Brazil's Greatest Hits	197?	2.50	5.00	10.00
❑ GNPS-2142	Perpetual Motion Love	197?	2.50	5.00	10.00
PHILIPS					
❑ PHM 200-227 [M]	Brazilian Blend	1967	3.00	6.00	12.00
❑ PHM 200-233 [M]	Organ-ized	1967	3.00	6.00	12.00
❑ PHS 600-227 [S]	Brazilian Blend	1967	3.75	7.50	15.00
❑ PHS 600-233 [S]	Organ-ized	1967	3.75	7.50	15.00
TOWER					
❑ ST 5047 [S]	From Rio with Love	1966	3.75	7.50	15.00
❑ ST 5058 [S]	Murmurio	1967	3.75	7.50	15.00
❑ T 5047 [M]	From Rio with Love	1966	3.75	7.50	15.00
❑ T 5058 [M]	Murmurio	1967	3.75	7.50	15.00
VERVE					
❑ V-8658 [M]	Rain Forest	1966	3.75	7.50	15.00
❑ V-8676 [M]	Cheganca	1966	3.75	7.50	15.00
❑ V-8706 [M]	Batucada	1967	5.00	10.00	20.00
❑ V-8739 [M]	Kee-Ka-Roo	1967	5.00	10.00	20.00
❑ V6-8658 [S]	Rain Forest	1966	5.00	10.00	20.00
❑ V6-8676 [S]	Cheganca	1966	5.00	10.00	20.00
❑ V6-8706 [S]	Batucada	1967	3.75	7.50	15.00
❑ V6-8739 [S]	Kee-Ka-Roo	1967	3.75	7.50	15.00
WORLD PACIFIC					
❑ WP-1856 [M]	Samba So!	1967	5.00	10.00	20.00
❑ WP-1866 [M]	Quarteto Bossamba	1967	6.25	12.50	25.00
❑ ST-21856 [S]	Samba So!	1967	3.75	7.50	15.00
❑ ST-21866 [S]	Quarteto Bossamba	1967	3.75	7.50	15.00

WAR
R&B group; the below album, which is not much different than their usual material, was, until the mid-1990s, the only gold record in the history of the Blue Note label.

Number	Title	Yr	VG	VG+	NM
BLUE NOTE					
❑ BN-LA690-G [(2)]	Platinum Jazz	1977	3.00	6.00	12.00

WARBURTON, PAUL, AND DALE BRUNING
Warburton is a bass player, Bruning is a guitarist.

Number	Title	Yr	VG	VG+	NM
CAPRI					
❑ 7986	Our Delight	198?	2.50	5.00	10.00

Number	Title	Yr	VG	VG+	NM

WARD, HELEN
Female singer.
COLUMBIA
| ❏ CL-6271 [10] | It's Been So Long | 1954 | 12.50 | 25.00 | 50.00 |
PAX
| ❏ 6004 [10] | Wild Bill Davison with Helen Ward | 1954 | 15.00 | 30.00 | 60.00 |

WARDELL, ROOSEVELT
Pianist.
RIVERSIDE
| ❏ RLP-350 [M] | The Revelation | 1960 | 6.25 | 12.50 | 25.00 |
| ❏ RS-9350 [S] | The Revelation | 1960 | 7.50 | 15.00 | 30.00 |

WARE, DAVID S.
Tenor saxophone player and composer.
HAT HUT
| ❏ W | Birth of a Being | 1978 | 3.75 | 7.50 | 15.00 |

WARE, WILBUR
Bass player.
FANTASY
| ❏ OJC-1737 | The Chicago Sound | 198? | 2.50 | 5.00 | 10.00 |
RIVERSIDE
| ❏ RLP 12-252 [M] | The Chicago Sound | 1957 | 20.00 | 40.00 | 80.00 |
| ❏ 6048 | The Chicago Sound | 197? | 3.00 | 6.00 | 12.00 |

WARE, WILBUR; JOHNNY GRIFFIN; JUNIOR MANCE
Also see each artist's individual listings.
JAZZLAND
| ❏ JLP-12 [M] | The Chicago Cookers | 1960 | 10.00 | 20.00 | 40.00 |

WARREN, EARLE
Alto saxophone player and clarinetist.
MUSE
| ❏ MR-5312 | Earle Warren and the Count's Men | 198? | 2.50 | 5.00 | 10.00 |

WARREN, PETER
Bass player.
ENJA
| ❏ 2018 | Bass Is | 197? | 3.75 | 7.50 | 15.00 |

WASHINGTON, DINAH
Female singer and occasional vibraphone player. Also see SARAH VAUGHAN.
ACCORD
| ❏ SN-7207 | Retrospective | 1982 | 2.50 | 5.00 | 10.00 |
ARCHIVE OF FOLK AND JAZZ
| ❏ 297 | Dinah Washington | 197? | 3.00 | 6.00 | 12.00 |
COLLECTABLES
| ❏ COL-5200 | Golden Classics | 1989 | 2.50 | 5.00 | 10.00 |
DELMARK
| ❏ DL-451 | Mellow Mama | 1992 | 5.00 | 10.00 | 20.00 |
EMARCY
❏ EMS-2-401 [(2)]	Jazz Sides	197?	3.75	7.50	15.00
❏ MG-26032 [10]	After Hours with Miss D	1954	30.00	60.00	120.00
❏ MG-36000 [M]	Dinah Jams	1955	12.50	25.00	50.00
❏ MG-36011 [M]	For Those in Love	1955	12.50	25.00	50.00
❏ MG-36028 [M]	After Hours with Miss D	1955	12.50	25.00	50.00
-- Reissue of 26032
❏ MG-36065 [M]	Dinah	1956	12.50	25.00	50.00
❏ MG-36073 [M]	In the Land of Hi-Fi	1956	12.50	25.00	50.00
❏ MG-36104 [M]	The Swingin' Miss "D"	1956	12.50	25.00	50.00
❏ MG-36119 [M]	Dinah Washington Sings Fats Waller	1957	12.50	25.00	50.00
❏ MG-36130 [M]	Dinah Washington Sings Bessie Smith	1957	12.50	25.00	50.00
❏ MG-36141 [M]	Newport '58	1958	10.00	20.00	40.00
❏ 814 184-1 [(2)]	Slick Chick (On the Mellow Side)	1983	3.00	6.00	12.00
❏ 824 883-1 [(2)]	Jazz Sides	198?	3.00	6.00	12.00
-- Reissue of 401
| ❏ 826 453-1 | In the Land of Hi-Fi | 1986 | 2.50 | 5.00 | 10.00 |
GRAND AWARD
| ❏ GA-33-318 [M] | Dinah Washington Sings the Blues | 1955 | 12.50 | 25.00 | 50.00 |
-- Add 50% if removable wrap-around cover is still there
HARLEM HIT PARADE
| ❏ 8002 | Finer Dinah | 197? | 2.50 | 5.00 | 10.00 |
MERCURY
| ❏ MGP-2-103 [(2) M] | This Is My Story | 1963 | 6.25 | 12.50 | 25.00 |
-- Combines 20788 and 20789 in one package

| ❏ MGP-2-603 [(2) S] | This Is My Story | 1963 | 7.50 | 15.00 | 30.00 |
-- Combines 60788 and 60789 in one package
❏ MG-20119 [M]	Music for a First Love	1957	12.50	25.00	50.00
❏ MG-20120 [M]	Music for Late Hours	1957	12.50	25.00	50.00
❏ MG-20247 [M]	The Best in Blues	1958	12.50	25.00	50.00
❏ MG-20439 [M]	The Queen	1959	7.50	15.00	30.00
❏ MG-20479 [M]	What a Diff'rence a Day Makes!	1960	7.50	15.00	30.00
❏ MG-20523 [M]	Newport '58	1960	7.50	15.00	30.00
-- Reissue of EmArcy 36141
| ❏ MG-20525 [M] | Dinah Washington Sings Fats Waller | 1960 | 7.50 | 15.00 | 30.00 |
-- Reissue of EmArcy 36119
❏ MG-20572 [M]	Unforgettable	1961	6.25	12.50	25.00
❏ MG-20604 [M]	I Concentrate on You	1961	6.25	12.50	25.00
❏ MG-20614 [M]	For Lonely Lovers	1961	6.25	12.50	25.00
❏ MG-20638 [M]	September in the Rain	1961	6.25	12.50	25.00
❏ MG-20661 [M]	Tears and Laughter	1962	6.25	12.50	25.00
❏ MG-20729 [M]	I Wanna Be Loved	1962	6.25	12.50	25.00
❏ MG-20788 [M]	This Is My Story -- Dinah Washington's Golden Hits, Volume 1	1963	3.75	7.50	15.00
❏ MG-20789 [M]	This Is My Story -- Dinah Washington's Golden Hits, Volume 2	1963	3.75	7.50	15.00
❏ MG-20829 [M]	The Good Old Days	1963	3.75	7.50	15.00
❏ MG-20928 [M]	The Queen and Quincy	1965	3.75	7.50	15.00
❏ MG-21119 [M]	Dinah Discovered	1967	5.00	10.00	20.00
❏ MG-25060 [10]	Dinah Washington	1950	30.00	60.00	120.00
❏ MG-25138 [10]	Dynamic Dinah	1952	30.00	60.00	120.00
❏ MG-25140 [10]	Blazing Ballads	1952	30.00	60.00	120.00
❏ SR-60111 [S]	The Queen	1959	10.00	20.00	40.00
❏ SR-60158 [S]	What a Diff'rence a Day Makes!	1960	10.00	20.00	40.00
❏ SR-60200 [S]	Newport '58	1960	10.00	20.00	40.00
❏ SR-60202 [S]	Dinah Washington Sings Fats Waller	1960	10.00	20.00	40.00
❏ SR-60232 [S]	Unforgettable	1961	7.50	15.00	30.00
❏ SR-60604 [S]	I Concentrate on You	1961	7.50	15.00	30.00
❏ SR-60614 [S]	For Lonely Lovers	1961	7.50	15.00	30.00
❏ SR-60638 [S]	September in the Rain	1961	7.50	15.00	30.00
❏ SR-60661 [S]	Tears and Laughter	1962	7.50	15.00	30.00
❏ SR-60729 [S]	I Wanna Be Loved	1962	7.50	15.00	30.00
❏ SR-60788 [S]	This Is My Story -- Dinah Washington's Golden Hits, Volume 1	1963	5.00	10.00	20.00
❏ SR-60789 [S]	This Is My Story -- Dinah Washington's Golden Hits, Volume 2	1963	5.00	10.00	20.00
❏ SR-60829 [S]	The Good Old Days	1963	5.00	10.00	20.00
❏ SR-60928 [S]	The Queen and Quincy	1965	5.00	10.00	20.00
❏ SR-61119 [S]	Dinah Discovered	1967	3.75	7.50	15.00
❏ 818 815-1	What a Diff'rence a Day Makes!	198?	2.00	4.00	8.00
-- Reissue
| ❏ 822 867-1 | This Is My Story -- Dinah Washington's Golden Hits, Volume 1 | 1985 | 2.00 | 4.00 | 8.00 |
-- Reissue
PICKWICK
❏ SPC-3043	Dinah Washington	196?	2.50	5.00	10.00
❏ SPC-3230	I Don't Hurt Anymore	197?	2.50	5.00	10.00
❏ SPC-3536	Greatest Hits	197?	2.50	5.00	10.00
ROULETTE
❏ RE 104 [(2)]	Echoes of An Era	196?	3.75	7.50	15.00
❏ RE 117 [(2)]	Queen of the Blues	1971	3.75	7.50	15.00
❏ RE 125 [(2)]	The Immortal Dinah Washington	1973	3.75	7.50	15.00
❏ R 25170 [M]	Dinah '62	1962	3.75	7.50	15.00
❏ SR 25170 [S]	Dinah '62	1962	5.00	10.00	20.00
❏ R 25180 [M]	In Love	1962	3.75	7.50	15.00
❏ SR 25180 [S]	In Love	1962	5.00	10.00	20.00
❏ R 25183 [M]	Drinking Again	1962	3.75	7.50	15.00
❏ SR 25183 [S]	Drinking Again	1962	5.00	10.00	20.00
❏ R 25189 [M]	Back to the Blues	1963	3.75	7.50	15.00
❏ SR 25189 [S]	Back to the Blues	1963	5.00	10.00	20.00
❏ R 25220 [M]	Dinah '63	1963	3.75	7.50	15.00
❏ SR 25220 [S]	Dinah '63	1963	5.00	10.00	20.00
❏ R 25244 [M]	In Tribute	1963	3.75	7.50	15.00
❏ SR 25244 [S]	In Tribute	1963	5.00	10.00	20.00
❏ R 25253 [M]	A Stranger on Earth	1964	3.75	7.50	15.00
❏ SR 25253 [S]	A Stranger on Earth	1964	5.00	10.00	20.00
❏ R 25269 [M]	Dinah Washington	1964	3.75	7.50	15.00
❏ SR 25269 [S]	Dinah Washington	1964	5.00	10.00	20.00
❏ R 25289 [M]	The Best of Dinah Washington	1965	3.75	7.50	15.00
❏ SR 25289 [S]	The Best of Dinah Washington	1965	5.00	10.00	20.00
❏ SR-42014	The Best of Dinah Washington	1968	3.00	6.00	12.00
-- Reissue of 25289
TRIP
❏ 5500	Dinah Jams	1973	2.50	5.00	10.00
❏ 5516	After Hours	1973	2.50	5.00	10.00
❏ 5524	Tears and Laughter	1974	2.50	5.00	10.00
❏ 5556	Dinah Washington Sings Bessie Smith	197?	2.50	5.00	10.00

Number	Title	Yr	VG	VG+	NM
❏ 5565	The Swingin' Miss D	197?	2.50	5.00	10.00
❏ TLX 9505 [(2)]	Sad Songs -- Blue Songs	197?	3.00	6.00	12.00
VERVE					
❏ 818 930-1	The Fats Waller Songbook	1984	2.50	5.00	10.00
WING					
❏ PKW-2-121 [(2)]	The Original Queen of Soul	1969	5.00	10.00	20.00
❏ MGW-12140 [M]	The Late Late Show	1963	3.00	6.00	12.00
❏ MGW-12271 [M]	Dinah Washington Sings Fats Waller	1964	3.00	6.00	12.00
❏ SRW-16140 [S]	The Late Late Show	1963	3.00	6.00	12.00
❏ SRW-16271 [S]	Dinah Washington Sings Fats Waller	1964	3.00	6.00	12.00
❏ SRW-16386	The Original Soul Sister	196?	3.00	6.00	12.00

WASHINGTON, DINAH, AND BROOK BENTON
Benton is a male singer not otherwise listed in this book. Also see DINAH WASHINGTON.

Number	Title	Yr	VG	VG+	NM
MERCURY					
❏ MG-20588 [M]	The Two of Us	1960	6.25	12.50	25.00
❏ SR-60588 [S]	The Two of Us	1960	7.50	15.00	30.00
❏ 824 823-1	The Two of Us	1985	2.00	4.00	8.00
-- Reissue					

WASHINGTON, EARL
Pianist and composer.

Number	Title	Yr	VG	VG+	NM
JAZZ WORKSHOP					
❏ JWS-202 [M]	All Star Jazz	1963	15.00	30.00	60.00
❏ JWS-213 [M]	Reflections	1963	15.00	30.00	60.00

WASHINGTON, ERNESTINE
Female singer best known in the gospel realm.

Number	Title	Yr	VG	VG+	NM
DISC					
❏ DLP-712 [10]	Ernestine Washington with Bunk Johnson	195?	50.00	100.00	200.00

WASHINGTON, GROVER, JR.
Saxophone player. Very popular in the 1970s into the early 1980s, his biggest hit (with a vocal assist from R&B singer Bill Withers) was "Just the Two of Us."

Number	Title	Yr	VG	VG+	NM
COLUMBIA					
❏ FC 40510	Strawberry Moon	1987	2.50	5.00	10.00
❏ OC 44256	Then and Now	1988	2.50	5.00	10.00
❏ OC 45253	Time Out of Mind	1989	2.50	5.00	10.00
❏ C 48530	Next Exit	1992	5.00	10.00	20.00
ELEKTRA					
❏ 6E-182	Paradise	1979	2.50	5.00	10.00
❏ 6E-305	Winelight	1980	2.50	5.00	10.00
❏ 5E-562	Come Morning	1981	2.50	5.00	10.00
❏ 60215	The Best Is Yet to Come	1982	2.50	5.00	10.00
❏ 60318	Inside Moves	1984	2.50	5.00	10.00
❏ 60415	Anthology of Grover Washington,	1985	2.50	5.00	10.00
KUDU					
❏ KS-03	Inner City Blues	1971	3.00	6.00	12.00
❏ KS-07	All the King's Horses	1972	3.00	6.00	12.00
❏ KS-20	Mister Magic	1975	3.00	6.00	12.00
❏ KS-24	Feels So Good	1975	3.00	6.00	12.00
❏ KS-32	A Secret Place	1976	3.00	6.00	12.00
❏ KSQX-1213 [(2) Q]	Soul Box	1973	6.25	12.50	25.00
❏ KSX-1213 [(2)]	Soul Box	1973	3.75	7.50	15.00
❏ KSX-3637 [(2)]	Live at the Bijou	1977	3.75	7.50	15.00
MOTOWN					
❏ M5-165V1	A Secret Place	1981	2.00	4.00	8.00
-- Reissue of Kudu 32					
❏ M5-175V1	Mister Magic	1981	2.00	4.00	8.00
-- Reissue of Kudu 20					
❏ M5-177V1	Feels So Good	1981	2.00	4.00	8.00
-- Reissue of Kudu 24					
❏ M5-184V1	Soul Box Vol. 1	1981	2.00	4.00	8.00
-- Reissue of half of Kudu 1213					
❏ M5-186V1	All the King's Horses	1981	2.00	4.00	8.00
-- Reissue of Kudu 07					
❏ M5-187V1	Soul Box Vol. 2	1981	2.00	4.00	8.00
-- Reissue of half of Kudu 1213					
❏ M5-189V1	Inner City Blues	1981	2.00	4.00	8.00
-- Reissue of Kudu 03					
❏ M7-910	Reed Seed	1978	2.50	5.00	10.00
❏ M7-933	Skylarkin'	1980	2.50	5.00	10.00
❏ M9-940 [(2)]	Baddest	1980	3.00	6.00	12.00
❏ M9-961 [(2)]	Anthology	1981	3.00	6.00	12.00
❏ 5232 ML	Skylarkin'	1982	2.00	4.00	8.00
-- Reissue of 933					
❏ 5236 ML	Reed Seed	1982	2.00	4.00	8.00
-- Reissue of 910					
❏ 5307 ML	Greatest Performances	198?	2.50	5.00	10.00
❏ 6126 ML	Grover Washington Jr. at His Best	198?	2.50	5.00	10.00

Number	Title	Yr	VG	VG+	NM
❏ 8239 ML2 [(2)]	Live at the Bijou	198?	3.00	6.00	12.00
NAUTILUS					
❏ NR-39	Winelight	1981	12.50	25.00	50.00
-- Audiophile vinyl					

WASHINGTON, TUTS
Pianist.

Number	Title	Yr	VG	VG+	NM
ROUNDER					
❏ 2041	New Orleans Piano Professor	198?	2.50	5.00	10.00

WASHINGTON, TYRONE
Tenor saxophone player.

Number	Title	Yr	VG	VG+	NM
BLUE LABOR					
❏ 102	Do Right	197?	5.00	10.00	20.00
BLUE NOTE					
❏ BST-84274	Natural Essence	1968	6.25	12.50	25.00

WASSERMAN, ROB
Bass player.

Number	Title	Yr	VG	VG+	NM
MCA					
❏ 42131	Duets	1988	2.50	5.00	10.00
ROUNDER					
❏ 0179	Solo	198?	3.00	6.00	12.00

WATANABE, KAZUMI
Guitarist.

Number	Title	Yr	VG	VG+	NM
GRAMAVISION					
❏ GR-8404	Mobo I	1984	3.00	6.00	12.00
❏ GR-8406	Mobo II	1984	3.00	6.00	12.00
❏ 18-8506	Mobo Club	1985	2.50	5.00	10.00
❏ 18-8602	Mobo Splash	1986	2.50	5.00	10.00
❏ 18-8706	Spice of Life	1987	2.50	5.00	10.00
❏ 18-8810	Spice of Life Too	1988	2.50	5.00	10.00
❏ R1-79415	Kilowatt	1989	3.00	6.00	12.00
INNER CITY					
❏ IC-6071	Mermaid Boulevard	198?	3.00	6.00	12.00

WATANABE, SADAO
Saxophone player (alto, soprano, sopranino) and flutist.

Number	Title	Yr	VG	VG+	NM
CATALYST					
❏ 7911	Sadao Watanabe and Charlie Mariano	197?	3.00	6.00	12.00
COLUMBIA					
❏ C2X 36818 [(2)]	How's Everything	1980	3.00	6.00	12.00
❏ FC 37433	Orange Express	1981	2.50	5.00	10.00
ELEKTRA					
❏ 60431	Maisha	1986	2.50	5.00	10.00
❏ 60475	Parker's Mood	1986	2.50	5.00	10.00
❏ 60748	Birds of Passage	1987	2.50	5.00	10.00
❏ 60803 [(2)]	Selected Sadao Watanabe	1989	3.75	7.50	15.00
❏ 60816	Elis	1988	2.50	5.00	10.00
❏ 60906	Front Seat	1989	3.00	6.00	12.00
ELEKTRA/MUSICIAN					
❏ 60297	Fill Up the Night	1984	2.50	5.00	10.00
❏ 60371	Rendezvous	1985	2.50	5.00	10.00
INNER CITY					
❏ IC-6015	I'm Old Fashioned	197?	3.00	6.00	12.00
❏ IC-6060	Morning Island	198?	3.00	6.00	12.00
❏ IC-6061	Bird of Paradise	198?	3.00	6.00	12.00
❏ IC-6062	California Shower	197?	3.00	6.00	12.00
❏ IC-6063	My Dear Life	198?	3.00	6.00	12.00
❏ IC-6064	Autumn Blow	198?	3.00	6.00	12.00
VANGUARD					
❏ VSD-79344	Round Trip	1974	3.00	6.00	12.00

WATERGATE SEVEN PLUS ONE, THE

Number	Title	Yr	VG	VG+	NM
STOMP OFF					
❏ SOS-1165	Ostrich Walk and Alligator Crawl	1989	2.50	5.00	10.00

WATERS, BENNY
Saxophone player, clarinetist and male singer.

Number	Title	Yr	VG	VG+	NM
MUSE					
❏ MR-5340	From Paradise (Small's) to Shangri-La	1987	2.50	5.00	10.00
STOMP OFF					
❏ SOS-1210	Memories of the Twenties	1991	2.50	5.00	10.00

WATERS, ETHEL
Female singer, a pioneer of the blues.

Number	Title	Yr	VG	VG+	NM
BIOGRAPH					
❏ 12022	Ethel Waters 1921/24	197?	2.50	5.00	10.00

Number	Title	Yr	VG	VG+	NM
❏ 12025	Jazzin' Babies Blues	197?	2.50	5.00	10.00
COLUMBIA					
❏ CL 2792 [M]	On Stage and Screen 1925-1940	1968	3.75	7.50	15.00
❏ KG 31571 [(2)]	Her Greatest Years	1972	3.75	7.50	15.00
❏ PG 31571 [(2)]	Her Greatest Years	197?	3.00	6.00	12.00
-- Reissue with new prefix					
GLENDALE					
❏ GL-9011	Ethel Waters	198?	2.50	5.00	10.00
MERCURY					
❏ MG-20051 [M]	Ethel Waters	1954	12.50	25.00	50.00
MONMOUTH-EVERGREEN					
❏ 6812	Miss Ethel Waters	1968	3.00	6.00	12.00
REMINGTON					
❏ RLP-1025 [10]	Ethel Waters	1950	12.50	25.00	50.00
WORD					
❏ WST-8044	His Eye Is On the Sparrow	197?	3.00	6.00	12.00
"X"					
❏ LVA-1009 [M]	Ethel Waters	1955	12.50	25.00	50.00

WATERS, KIM
Soprano and alto saxophone player.

Number	Title	Yr	VG	VG+	NM
WARLOCK					
❏ WAR-2713	Sweet and Saxy	1989	3.00	6.00	12.00
❏ WAR-2720	All Because of You	1990	3.00	6.00	12.00

WATERS, PATTY
Female singer.

Number	Title	Yr	VG	VG+	NM
ESP-DISK'					
❏ 1025 [M]	Patty Waters Sings	1966	6.25	12.50	25.00
❏ S-1025 [S]	Patty Waters Sings	1966	7.50	15.00	30.00
❏ 1055 [S]	Patty Waters College Tour	1968	15.00	30.00	60.00

WATKINS, DOUG
Bass player. Also see THE MANHATTAN JAZZ ALL-STARS.

Number	Title	Yr	VG	VG+	NM
NEW JAZZ					
❏ NJLP-8238 [M]	Soulnik	1960	12.50	25.00	50.00
-- Purple label					
❏ NJLP-8238 [M]	Soulnik	1965	6.25	12.50	25.00
-- Blue label, trident logo at right					
PHILIPS					
❏ PHM 200-001 [M]	French Horns for My Lady	1962	5.00	10.00	20.00
❏ PHS 600-001 [S]	French Horns for My Lady	1962	6.25	12.50	25.00
TRANSITION					
❏ TRLP-20 [M]	Watkins at Large	1956	250.00	500.00	1,000.
-- Deduct 1/10 if booklet is missing					

WATKINS, JOE
Drummer and occasional male singer.

Number	Title	Yr	VG	VG+	NM
GHB					
❏ GHB-74	Last Will and Testament	197?	2.50	5.00	10.00

WATKINS, JULIUS
French horn player and composer. Also see LES JAZZ MODES.

Number	Title	Yr	VG	VG+	NM
BLUE NOTE					
❏ BLP-5053 [10]	Julius Watkins Sextet	1954	100.00	200.00	400.00
❏ BLP-5064 [10]	Julius Watkins Sextet, Volume 2	1955	100.00	200.00	400.00

WATKINS, MARY
Female singer?

Number	Title	Yr	VG	VG+	NM
OLIVIA					
❏ LF-919	Something Moving	198?	2.50	5.00	10.00
PALO ALTO					
❏ PA-8030	Wind of Change	198?	2.50	5.00	10.00
REDWOOD					
❏ R-8506	Spiritsong	1985	2.50	5.00	10.00

WATKINS, MITCH
Guitarist.

Number	Title	Yr	VG	VG+	NM
ENJA					
❏ R1-79603	Underneath It All	1989	3.00	6.00	12.00

WATROUS, BILL
Trombonist.

Number	Title	Yr	VG	VG+	NM
COLUMBIA					
❏ KC 33090	Manhattan Wild Life Refuge	1974	2.50	5.00	10.00
❏ PC 33701	Tiger of San Pedro	1975	2.50	5.00	10.00

Number	Title	Yr	VG	VG+	NM
FAMOUS DOOR					
❏ HL-101	'Bone Straight Ahead	197?	3.00	6.00	12.00
❏ HL-127	Watrous in Hollywood	1979	3.00	6.00	12.00
❏ HL-134	I'll Play for You	1980	3.00	6.00	12.00
❏ HL-136	Coronary Trombossa	1981	2.50	5.00	10.00
❏ HL-137	La Zorra	1981	2.50	5.00	10.00
❏ HL-144	Roarin' Back Into New York	1982	2.50	5.00	10.00
❏ HL-147	The Best of Bill Watrous	198?	2.50	5.00	10.00
SOUNDWINGS					
❏ SW-2100	Someplace Else	1986	2.50	5.00	10.00
❏ SW-2104	Reflections	1987	2.50	5.00	10.00

WATSON, BOBBY
Alto saxophone player.

Number	Title	Yr	VG	VG+	NM
BLUE NOTE					
❏ B1-90262	No Question About It	1988	3.00	6.00	12.00
❏ B1-91915	The Inventor	1990	3.00	6.00	12.00
RED RECORD					
❏ VPA-173	Perpetual Groove (Live in Europe)	198?	3.00	6.00	12.00
❏ VPA-184	Appointment in Milano	1986	3.00	6.00	12.00
ROULETTE					
❏ SR-5009	Estimated Time of Arrival	1977	3.00	6.00	12.00
-- As "Robert Watson"					

WATT, TOMMY
British bandleader.

Number	Title	Yr	VG	VG+	NM
BETHLEHEM					
❏ BCP-6052 [M]	Watt's Cooking	1961	7.50	15.00	30.00

WATTERS, LU
Trumpeter and bandleader. Also see BOB HELM; BUNK JOHNSON.

Number	Title	Yr	VG	VG+	NM
CLEF					
❏ MGC-103 [10]	Lu Watters Jazz	1954	---	---	---
-- Canceled					
❏ MGC-503 [10]	Lu Watters Jazz	1954	20.00	40.00	80.00
DOWN HOME					
❏ MGD-5 [10]	Lu Watters and His Yerba Buena Jazz Band	1955	15.00	30.00	60.00
GOOD TIME JAZZ					
❏ L-A [(3) M]	San Francisco Style	195?	15.00	30.00	60.00
❏ L-8 [10]	Lu Watters and His Yerba Buena Jazz Band	1952	12.50	25.00	50.00
❏ L-12001 [M]	Dawn Club Favorites	1954	10.00	20.00	40.00
❏ L-12002 [M]	Originals and Ragtime	1954	10.00	20.00	40.00
❏ L-12003 [M]	Stomps, Etc. and the Blues	1954	10.00	20.00	40.00
❏ L-12007 [M]	1942 Series	1955	10.00	20.00	40.00
HOMESPUN					
❏ 101	Lu Watters and the Yerba Buena Jazz Band, Vol. 1	197?	2.50	5.00	10.00
❏ 102	Lu Watters and the Yerba Buena Jazz Band, Vol. 2	197?	2.50	5.00	10.00
❏ 103	Live Recordings from Hambone Kelly's	197?	2.50	5.00	10.00
❏ 104	Lu Watters and the Yerba Buena Jazz Band, Vol. 4	197?	3.00	6.00	12.00
❏ 105	Memories of the Bodega Battle	197?	3.00	6.00	12.00
❏ 106	Lu Watters and the Yerba Buena Jazz Band, Vol. 6	197?	2.50	5.00	10.00
❏ 107	Lu Watters and the Yerba Buena Jazz Band, 1941	197?	2.50	5.00	10.00
MERCURY					
❏ MGC-103 [10]	Lu Watters and the Yerba Buena Jazz Band	1950	25.00	50.00	100.00
❏ MGC-503 [10]	Lu Watters Jazz	1951	25.00	50.00	100.00
❏ MGC-510 [10]	Lu Watters and His Yerba Buena Jazz Band	1952	25.00	50.00	100.00
❏ MG-35013 [10]	Lu Watters and the Yerba Buena Jazz Band	1950	30.00	60.00	120.00
RIVERSIDE					
❏ RLP 12-213 [M]	San Francisco Style	1956	15.00	30.00	60.00
❏ RLP-2513 [10]	Lu Watters 1947	1955	20.00	40.00	80.00
VERVE					
❏ MGV-1005 [M]	Lu Watters and His Yerba Buena Jazz Band	1956	12.50	25.00	50.00
❏ V-1005 [M]	Lu Watters and His Yerba Buena Jazz Band	1961	5.00	10.00	20.00

WATTERS, LU/SANTO PECORA
Also see each artist's individual listings.

Number	Title	Yr	VG	VG+	NM
VERVE					
❏ MGV-1008 [M]	Dixieland Jamboree	1956	12.50	25.00	50.00
❏ V-1008 [M]	Dixieland Jamboree	1961	6.25	12.50	25.00

Number	Title	Yr	VG	VG+	NM

WATTS, CHARLIE
Drummer, best known as a member of The Rolling Stones.
COLUMBIA
| FC 40570 | The Charlie Watts Orchestra Live Fulham Town Hall | 1986 | 3.75 | 7.50 | 15.00 |

CONTINUUM
| 19308 | From One Charlie | 1990 | 6.25 | 12.50 | 25.00 |

-- Box set with LP, book ("Ode to a High Flying Bird") and photo of Charlie Parker

WATTS, ERNIE
Tenor saxophone player.
ELEKTRA
| 6E-285 | Look in Your Heart | 1980 | 2.50 | 5.00 | 10.00 |
PACIFIC JAZZ
| PJ-20155 | Planet Love | 1969 | 7.50 | 15.00 | 30.00 |
QWEST
| 25283 | Musician | 1985 | 2.50 | 5.00 | 10.00 |
VAULT
| LP-9011 | Wonderbag | 1968 | 5.00 | 10.00 | 20.00 |

WATTS, MARZETTE
Bass clarinetist and soprano and alto saxophone player.
ESP-DISK'
| 1044 [S] | Marzette Watts and Company | 1971 | 5.00 | 10.00 | 20.00 |
SAVOY
| MG-12193 [M] | The Marzette Watts Ensemble | 1968 | 5.00 | 10.00 | 20.00 |

WAVE, THE
ATLANTIC
| 81883 | Second Wave | 1988 | 2.50 | 5.00 | 10.00 |

WAYLAND QUARTET, THE
4 CORNERS OF THE WORLD
| FCS-4249 | Jazz Bach | 1968 | 3.75 | 7.50 | 15.00 |

WAYNE, CHUCK
Guitarist.
FOCUS
| FL-333 [M] | Tapestry | 1964 | 6.25 | 12.50 | 25.00 |
| FS-333 [M] | Tapestry | 1964 | 7.50 | 15.00 | 30.00 |
PRESTIGE
| PRLP-7367 [M] | Morning Mist | 1965 | 5.00 | 10.00 | 20.00 |
| PRST-7367 [S] | Morning Mist | 1965 | 6.25 | 12.50 | 25.00 |
PROGRESSIVE
| 3003 [10] | The Chuck Wayne Quintet | 1953 | 50.00 | 100.00 | 200.00 |
| PRO-7008 | Traveling | 1976 | 3.00 | 6.00 | 12.00 |
SAVOY
| MG-12077 [M] | The Jazz Guitarist | 1956 | 12.50 | 25.00 | 50.00 |
SAVOY JAZZ
| SJL-1144 | Tasty Pudding | 198? | 2.50 | 5.00 | 10.00 |
VIK
| LX-1098 [M] | String Fever | 1957 | 12.50 | 25.00 | 50.00 |

WAYNE, CHUCK, AND JOE PUMA
Also see each artist's individual listings.
CHOICE
| 1004 | Interactions | 197? | 3.00 | 6.00 | 12.00 |

WAYNE, FRANCES
Female singer.
ATLANTIC
| 1263 [M] | The Warm Sound of Frances Wayne | 1957 | 12.50 | 25.00 | 50.00 |
-- Black label
| 1263 [M] | The Warm Sound of Frances Wayne | 1961 | 5.00 | 10.00 | 20.00 |
-- White "fan" logo at right of label
BRUNSWICK
| BL 54022 [M] | Frances Wayne | 1958 | 10.00 | 20.00 | 40.00 |
CORAL
| CRL 56019 [10] | Salute to Ethel Waters | 195? | 15.00 | 30.00 | 60.00 |
EPIC
| LN 3222 [M] | Songs for My Man | 1956 | 12.50 | 25.00 | 50.00 |

WEATHER REPORT
Important fusion band whose "Birdland," from the Heavy Weather album, has become a jazz standard. The constants were JOE ZAWINUL (keyboards) and WAYNE SHORTER (saxophones). Among those who came and went were AIRTO; VICTOR BAILEY; ALPHONSE MOUZON; JACO PASTORIUS; and MIROSLAV VITOUS.
ARC
| JC 35358 | Mr. Gone | 1978 | 2.50 | 5.00 | 10.00 |

| PC 36358 | Mr. Gone | 1980 | 2.00 | 4.00 | 8.00 |
-- Budget-line reissue
PC2 36030 [(2)]	8:30	1979	3.00	6.00	12.00
JC 36793	Night Passage	1980	2.50	5.00	10.00
PC 36793	Night Passage	198?	2.00	4.00	8.00
-- Budget-line reissue
| FC 37616 | Weather Report | 1982 | 2.50 | 5.00 | 10.00 |
| PC 37616 | Weather Report | 198? | 2.00 | 4.00 | 8.00 |
-- Budget-line reissue
| HC 47616 | Weather Report | 1982 | 10.00 | 20.00 | 40.00 |
-- Half-speed mastered edition
COLUMBIA
| C 30661 | Weather Report | 1971 | 3.00 | 6.00 | 12.00 |
| KC 30661 | Weather Report | 1974 | 2.50 | 5.00 | 10.00 |
-- Reissue of C 30661
| PC 30661 | Weather Report | 1977 | 2.00 | 4.00 | 8.00 |
-- Reissue
| KC 31352 | I Sing the Body Electric | 1972 | 3.00 | 6.00 | 12.00 |
| PC 31352 | I Sing the Body Electric | 1977 | 2.00 | 4.00 | 8.00 |
-- Reissue
KC 32210	Sweetnighter	1973	3.00	6.00	12.00
CQ 32494 [Q]	Mysterious Traveller	1974	5.00	10.00	20.00
KC 32494	Mysterious Traveller	1974	3.00	6.00	12.00
PC 32494	Mysterious Traveller	1977	2.00	4.00	8.00
-- Reissue
| PC 33417 | Tale Spinnin' | 1975 | 3.00 | 6.00 | 12.00 |
-- No bar code on cover
| PC 33417 | Tale Spinnin' | 1977 | 2.00 | 4.00 | 8.00 |
-- Budget-line reissue with bar code
| PCQ 33417 [Q] | Tale Spinnin' | 1975 | 5.00 | 10.00 | 20.00 |
| PC 34099 | Black Market | 1976 | 3.00 | 6.00 | 12.00 |
-- No bar code on cover
| PC 34418 | Heavy Weather | 1977 | 3.00 | 6.00 | 12.00 |
-- No bar code on cover
| PC 34418 | Heavy Weather | 198? | 2.00 | 4.00 | 8.00 |
-- Budget-line reissue with bar code
FC 38427	Procession	1983	2.50	5.00	10.00
FC 39147	Domino Theory	1984	2.50	5.00	10.00
FC 39908	Sportin' Life	1985	2.50	5.00	10.00
FC 40280	This Is This	1986	2.50	5.00	10.00
HC 44418	Heavy Weather	198?	10.00	20.00	40.00
-- Half-speed mastered edition

WEATHERBIRD JAZZ BAND, THE
STOMP OFF
| SOS-1034 | Fireworks | 198? | 2.50 | 5.00 | 10.00 |

WEATHERBURN, RONN
Pianist.
STOMP OFF
| SOS-1107 | After the Ball | 198? | 2.50 | 5.00 | 10.00 |

WEBB, ART
Flutist.
ATLANTIC
| SD 18212 | Mr. Flute | 197? | 2.50 | 5.00 | 10.00 |
| SD 18226 | Love Eyes | 197? | 2.50 | 5.00 | 10.00 |

WEBB, CHICK
Drummer and bandleader.
CIRCLE
| CLP-81 | Stompin' at the Savoy, 1936 | 198? | 2.50 | 5.00 | 10.00 |
COLUMBIA
| CL 2639 [M] | The Immortal Chick Webb | 1967 | 6.25 | 12.50 | 25.00 |
| CS 9439 [R] | The Immortal Chick Webb | 1967 | 3.00 | 6.00 | 12.00 |
DECCA
| DL 79223 [R] | Chick Webb 1937-39 | 1958 | 6.25 | 12.50 | 25.00 |
| DL 9223 [M] | Chick Webb 1937-39 | 1958 | 10.00 | 20.00 | 40.00 |
FOLKWAYS
| FJ-2818 | Chick Webb Featuring Ella Fitzgerald | 197? | 2.50 | 5.00 | 10.00 |
MCA
1303	Legend	198?	2.50	5.00	10.00
1327	Ella Swings the Band	198?	2.50	5.00	10.00
1348	Princess of the Savoy	198?	2.50	5.00	10.00
4107 [(2)]	The Best of Chick Webb	197?	3.00	6.00	12.00
TRIP
| J-5 | On the Air | 197? | 2.50 | 5.00 | 10.00 |

WEBB, GEORGE
One of the leaders of the British "trad jazz" movement.
JAZZOLOGY
| J-122 | George Webb's Dixielanders | 1985 | 2.50 | 5.00 | 10.00 |

Number	Title	Yr	VG	VG+	NM

WEBB, ROGER
SWAN
| ❏ SLP-516 [M] | John, Paul and All That Jazz | 1964 | 7.50 | 15.00 | 30.00 |

WEBER, EBERHARD
Bass player.
ECM
❏ 1042	Colours of Chloe	197?	3.75	7.50	15.00
❏ 1066	Yellow Fields	197?	3.00	6.00	12.00
❏ 1086	Following Morning	197?	3.00	6.00	12.00
❏ 1107	Silent Feet	1978	2.50	5.00	10.00
❏ 1137	Fluid Rustle	1979	2.50	5.00	10.00
❏ 1188	Little Movements	1980	2.50	5.00	10.00
❏ 1231	Later That Evening	198?	2.50	5.00	10.00
❏ 1288	Chorus	1985	3.00	6.00	12.00

WEBER, HAJO, AND ULRICH INGENBOLD
ECM
| ❏ 1235 | Winterreise | 198? | 3.00 | 6.00 | 12.00 |

WEBSTER, BEN
Tenor saxophone player, pianist and arranger. Also see DON BYAS; BENNY CARTER; COLEMAN HAWKINS; ILLINOIS JACQUET; GERRY MULLIGAN; ART TATUM.
ABC IMPULSE!
| ❏ AS-65 [S] | See You at the Fair | 1968 | 3.75 | 7.50 | 15.00 |
ANALOGUE PRODUCTIONS
| ❏ AP 011 | Ben Webster at the Renaissance | 199? | 6.25 | 12.50 | 25.00 |
BASF
| ❏ 20658 | Ben Webster Meets Don Byas | 197? | 3.75 | 7.50 | 15.00 |
BLACK LION
❏ 111	Atmosphere for Lovers and	197?	3.75	7.50	15.00
❏ 190	Duke's in Bed!	197?	3.00	6.00	12.00
❏ 302	Saturday Montmartre	197?	3.00	6.00	12.00
BRUNSWICK
| ❏ BL 58031 [10] | Tenor Sax Stylings | 1952 | 75.00 | 150.00 | 300.00 |
CIRCLE
| ❏ 41 | The Horn | 198? | 2.50 | 5.00 | 10.00 |
| ❏ 42 | The Horn -- Alternate Takes | 198? | 2.50 | 5.00 | 10.00 |
DISCOVERY
| ❏ 818 | The Warm Moods of Ben Webster | 198? | 2.50 | 5.00 | 10.00 |
EMARCY
| ❏ MG-26006 [10] | The Big Tenor | 1954 | 62.50 | 125.00 | 250.00 |
| ❏ 824 836-1 [(2)] | The Complete Ben Webster on EmArcy | 1986 | 3.75 | 7.50 | 15.00 |
ENJA
| ❏ 2038 | Live at Pio's | 197? | 3.00 | 6.00 | 12.00 |
FIDELIO
| ❏ FL-4475 | Gentle Ben | 198? | 2.50 | 5.00 | 10.00 |
IMPULSE!
| ❏ A-65 [M] | See You at the Fair | 1964 | 6.25 | 12.50 | 25.00 |
| ❏ AS-65 [S] | See You at the Fair | 1964 | 7.50 | 15.00 | 30.00 |
INNER CITY
| ❏ IC-2008 | My Man | 197? | 3.75 | 7.50 | 15.00 |
JAZZ ARCHIVES
| ❏ JA-15 | Ben: A Tribute to a Great Jazzman | 198? | 2.50 | 5.00 | 10.00 |
| ❏ JA-35 | Ben and the Boys | 198? | 2.50 | 5.00 | 10.00 |
JAZZ MAN
| ❏ 5007 | Atmosphere for Lovers | 198? | 2.50 | 5.00 | 10.00 |
NESSA
| ❏ N-8 | Did You Call? | 197? | 5.00 | 10.00 | 20.00 |
NORGRAN
❏ MGN-1001 [M]	The Consummate Artistry of Ben Webster	1954	37.50	75.00	150.00
❏ MGN-1018 [M]	Music for Loving	1955	50.00	100.00	200.00
❏ MGN-1039 [M]	Ben Webster Plays Music with Feeling	1955	50.00	100.00	200.00
❏ MGN-1089 [M]	King of the Tenors	1956	30.00	60.00	120.00
PRESTIGE
| ❏ 24031 [(2)] | At Work in Europe | 197? | 3.75 | 7.50 | 15.00 |
REPRISE
| ❏ R-2001 [M] | The Warm Moods of Ben Webster | 1961 | 6.25 | 12.50 | 25.00 |
| ❏ R9-2001 [S] | The Warm Moods of Ben Webster | 1961 | 7.50 | 15.00 | 30.00 |
STEEPLECHASE
| ❏ SCS-1008 | My Man | 198? | 3.00 | 6.00 | 12.00 |

VERVE
❏ MGV-2026 [M]	Sophisticated Lady -- Ben Webster with Strings	1956	12.50	25.00	50.00
❏ V-2026 [M]	Sophisticated Lady -- Ben Webster with Strings	1961	6.25	12.50	25.00
❏ UMV-2081	King of the Tenors	198?	2.50	5.00	10.00
❏ UMV-2515	Ben Webster and Associates	198?	3.00	6.00	12.00
❏ VE-2-2530 [(2)]	Ballads	197?	3.75	7.50	15.00
❏ VE-2-2536 [(2)]	Soulville	197?	3.75	7.50	15.00
❏ MGVS-6056 [S]	Ben Webster and Associates	1959	10.00	20.00	40.00
❏ MGVS-6114 [S]	Ben Webster Meets Oscar Peterson	1960	10.00	20.00	40.00
❏ MGVS-6124 [S]	The Soul of Ben Webster	1960	---	---	---
-- Canceled					
❏ MGV-8020 [M]	King of the Tenors	1957	12.50	25.00	50.00
❏ V-8020 [M]	King of the Tenors	1961	6.25	12.50	25.00
❏ MGV-8130 [M]	Music with Feeling -- Ben Webster with Strings	1957	12.50	25.00	50.00
❏ V-8130 [M]	Music with Feeling -- Ben Webster with Strings	1961	6.25	12.50	25.00
❏ MGV-8274 [M]	Soulville	1958	12.50	25.00	50.00
❏ V-8274 [M]	Soulville	1961	6.25	12.50	25.00
❏ MGV-8318 [M]	Ben Webster and Associates	1959	12.50	25.00	50.00
❏ V-8318 [M]	Ben Webster and Associates	1961	6.25	12.50	25.00
❏ V6-8318 [S]	Ben Webster and Associates	1961	5.00	10.00	20.00
❏ MGV-8349 [M]	Ben Webster Meets Oscar Peterson	1959	12.50	25.00	50.00
❏ V-8349 [M]	Ben Webster Meets Oscar Peterson	1961	6.25	12.50	25.00
❏ V6-8349 [S]	Ben Webster Meets Oscar Peterson	1961	5.00	10.00	20.00
❏ MGV-8359 [M]	The Soul of Ben Webster	1960	12.50	25.00	50.00
❏ V-8359 [M]	The Soul of Ben Webster	1961	6.25	12.50	25.00
❏ 833 550-1 [(2)]	Ballads	198?	3.00	6.00	12.00
❏ 833 551-1 [(2)]	Soulville	198?	3.00	6.00	12.00

WEBSTER, BEN, AND DON BYAS
Also see each artist's individual listings.
COMMODORE
| ❏ XFL-14938 | Kings of Tenor Sax | 198? | 2.50 | 5.00 | 10.00 |

WEBSTER, BEN, AND HARRY "SWEETS" EDISON
Also see each artist's individual listings.
COLUMBIA
| ❏ CL 1891 [M] | Ben Webster-Sweets Edison | 1962 | 6.25 | 12.50 | 25.00 |
| ❏ CS 8691 [S] | Ben Webster-Sweets Edison | 1962 | 7.50 | 15.00 | 30.00 |
COLUMBIA JAZZ MASTERPIECES
| ❏ CJ 40853 | Ben and "Sweets" | 1987 | 2.50 | 5.00 | 10.00 |
COLUMBIA JAZZ ODYSSEY
| ❏ PC 37036 | Ben and "Sweets" | 1981 | 2.50 | 5.00 | 10.00 |

WEBSTER, BEN, AND COLEMAN HAWKINS
Also see each artist's individual listings.
COLUMBIA
| ❏ KG 32774 [(2)] | Giants of the Tenor Saxophone | 1973 | 3.75 | 7.50 | 15.00 |
VERVE
| ❏ VE-2-2520 [(2)] | Tenor Giants | 197? | 3.75 | 7.50 | 15.00 |

WEBSTER, BEN, AND JOE ZAWINUL
Also see each artist's individual listings.
FANTASY
| ❏ OJC-109 | Soulmates | 198? | 2.50 | 5.00 | 10.00 |
MILESTONE
| ❏ 47056 [(2)] | Trav'lin' Light | 198? | 3.00 | 6.00 | 12.00 |
RIVERSIDE
| ❏ RLP-476 [M] | Soulmates | 1964 | 6.25 | 12.50 | 25.00 |
| ❏ RS-9476 [S] | Soulmates | 1964 | 7.50 | 15.00 | 30.00 |

WECHTER, JULIUS
Vibraphone player and percussionist. Best known for creating the Baja Marimba Band, which is outside the scope of this book.
JAZZ: WEST
| ❏ LP-9 [M] | Linear Sketches | 1956 | 50.00 | 100.00 | 200.00 |

WEED, BUDDY
Pianist and bandleader.
COLUMBIA
| ❏ CL 6160 [10] | Piano Moods | 1951 | 12.50 | 25.00 | 50.00 |
CORAL
| ❏ CRL 57087 [M] | Piano Solos with Rhythm Accompaniment | 1957 | 10.00 | 20.00 | 40.00 |

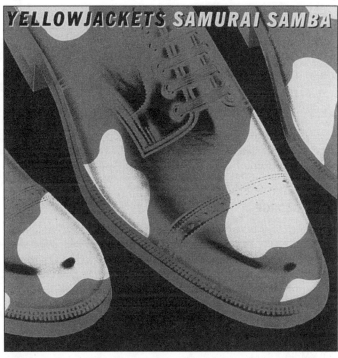

(Top left) First issued on EmArcy in mono only in 1958, *Dinah Washington Sings Fats Waller* was re-assigned to parent label Mercury in 1960 when it was mixed into stereo. It proved that even as she was going pop, she could still sing the jazz greats. (Top right) Weather Report ranks as among the foremost of the jazz-rock fusion bands, and even spawned a standard, "Birdland." The 1985 LP *Sportin' Life* was the last one released while they were still together; they were no more by the time 1987's *This Is This* came out. (Bottom left) Tenor saxophone player Steve White made one album as a leader, but it was this 1950s Liberty release with a truly wild cover, befitting the title *Jazz Mad*. (Bottom right) The group Yellowjackets often transcends the connotations of the term "fusion," incorporating R&B and older jazz into the electrified mix. *Samurai Samba* was their third album before switching for a few years to MCA and GRP, then returning to Warner Bros. in the 1990s.

Number	Title	Yr	VG	VG+	NM

WEEKS, ANSON

Bandleader and composer. Popular in the 1920s and early 1930s, he came out of retirement in the 1950s to make the series of albums for Fantasy.

FANTASY

Number	Title	Yr	VG	VG+	NM
❏ 3258 [M]	Dancin' with Anson	1958	7.50	15.00	30.00
-- Red vinyl					
❏ 3258 [M]	Dancin' with Anson	1958	3.75	7.50	15.00
-- Black vinyl					
❏ 3269 [M]	Memories	1958	7.50	15.00	30.00
-- Red vinyl					
❏ 3269 [M]	Memories	1958	3.75	7.50	15.00
-- Black vinyl					
❏ 3297 [M]	More Dancin' with Anson	1959	7.50	15.00	30.00
-- Red vinyl					
❏ 3297 [M]	More Dancin' with Anson	1959	3.75	7.50	15.00
-- Black vinyl					
❏ 3306 [M]	Cruisin' with Anson	1960	7.50	15.00	30.00
-- Red vinyl					
❏ 3306 [M]	Cruisin' with Anson	1960	3.75	7.50	15.00
-- Black vinyl					
❏ 3333 [M]	Dancin' at Anson's	1961	6.25	12.50	25.00
-- Red vinyl					
❏ 3333 [M]	Dancin' at Anson's	1961	3.00	6.00	12.00
-- Black vinyl					
❏ 3338 [M]	Old Favorites and New	1962	6.25	12.50	25.00
-- Red vinyl					
❏ 3338 [M]	Old Favorites and New	1962	3.00	6.00	12.00
-- Black vinyl					
❏ 3355 [M]	Reminiscing at the Mark	1964	3.00	6.00	12.00
❏ 8001 [S]	Dancin' with Anson	1960	6.25	12.50	25.00
-- Blue vinyl					
❏ 8001 [S]	Dancin' with Anson	1960	3.00	6.00	12.00
-- Black vinyl					
❏ 8006 [S]	Memories	1960	6.25	12.50	25.00
-- Blue vinyl					
❏ 8006 [S]	Memories	1960	3.00	6.00	12.00
-- Black vinyl					
❏ 8043 [S]	More Dancin' with Anson	1960	6.25	12.50	25.00
-- Blue vinyl					
❏ 8043 [S]	More Dancin' with Anson	1960	3.00	6.00	12.00
-- Black vinyl					
❏ 8051 [S]	Cruisin' with Anson	1960	6.25	12.50	25.00
-- Blue vinyl					
❏ 8051 [S]	Cruisin' with Anson	1960	3.00	6.00	12.00
-- Black vinyl					
❏ 8076 [S]	Dancin' at Anson's	1961	7.50	15.00	30.00
-- Blue vinyl					
❏ 8076 [S]	Dancin' at Anson's	1961	3.75	7.50	15.00
-- Black vinyl					
❏ 8090 [S]	Old Favorites and New	1962	7.50	15.00	30.00
-- Blue vinyl					
❏ 8090 [S]	Old Favorites and New	1962	3.75	7.50	15.00
-- Black vinyl					
❏ 8355 [S]	Reminiscing at the Mark	1964	3.75	7.50	15.00

HINDSIGHT

Number	Title	Yr	VG	VG+	NM
❏ HSR-146	Anson Weeks and the Hotel Mark Hopkins Orchestra 1932	198?	2.50	5.00	10.00

WEIN, GEORGE

Pianist, male singer and bandleader.

ATLANTIC

Number	Title	Yr	VG	VG+	NM
❏ 1221 [M]	Wein, Women and Song	1955	12.50	25.00	50.00
-- Black label					
❏ 1221 [M]	Wein, Women and Song	1961	6.25	12.50	25.00
-- Multicolor label, white "fan" logo at right					
❏ SD 1533 [S]	George Wein and the Newport All-Stars	1969	3.75	7.50	15.00

BETHLEHEM

Number	Title	Yr	VG	VG+	NM
❏ BCP-6050 [M]	George Wein and the Storyville Sextet -- Jazz at the Modern	1960	10.00	20.00	40.00
❏ SBCP-6050 [S]	George Wein and the Storyville Sextet -- Jazz at the Modern	1960	10.00	20.00	40.00

COLUMBIA

Number	Title	Yr	VG	VG+	NM
❏ CS 9631 [S]	Alive and Well in Mexico	1968	3.75	7.50	15.00

IMPULSE!

Number	Title	Yr	VG	VG+	NM
❏ A-31 [M]	George Wein and the Newport All-Stars	1963	5.00	10.00	20.00
❏ AS-31 [S]	George Wein and the Newport All-Stars	1963	6.25	12.50	25.00

RCA VICTOR

Number	Title	Yr	VG	VG+	NM
❏ LPM-1332 [M]	The Magic Horn of George Wein	1956	10.00	20.00	40.00

WEISBERG, TIM

Flutist.

A&M

Number	Title	Yr	VG	VG+	NM
❏ SP-3039	Tim Weisberg	1971	3.00	6.00	12.00
❏ SP-3045	Dreamspeaker	1973	2.50	5.00	10.00
❏ SP-3121	Tim Weisberg 4	198?	2.00	4.00	8.00
-- Budget-line reissue					
❏ SP-3261	Smile/The Best of Tim Weisberg	198?	2.00	4.00	8.00
-- Budget-line reissue					
❏ SP-3658	Tim Weisberg 4	1974	2.50	5.00	10.00
❏ SP-4352	Hurtwood Edge	1972	3.00	6.00	12.00
❏ SP-4545	Listen to the City	1975	2.50	5.00	10.00
❏ SP-4600	Live at Last!	1976	2.50	5.00	10.00
❏ SP-4749	Smile/The Best of Tim Weisberg	1979	2.50	5.00	10.00

CYPRESS

Number	Title	Yr	VG	VG+	NM
❏ YL-0123	Outrageous Temptations	1989	3.00	6.00	12.00
❏ 661 112-1	High Risk	1986	2.50	5.00	10.00

DESERT ROCK

Number	Title	Yr	VG	VG+	NM
❏ DR-001	High Risk	1985	3.75	7.50	15.00

LIBERTY

Number	Title	Yr	VG	VG+	NM
❏ LN-10029	Rotations	198?	2.00	4.00	8.00
-- Budget-line reissue					
❏ LN-10031	The Tim Weisberg Band	198?	2.00	4.00	8.00
-- Budget-line reissue					

MCA

Number	Title	Yr	VG	VG+	NM
❏ 3084	Night-Rider!	1979	2.50	5.00	10.00
❏ 5125	Party of One	1980	2.50	5.00	10.00
❏ 5245	Travelin' Light	1981	2.50	5.00	10.00

NAUTILUS

Number	Title	Yr	VG	VG+	NM
❏ NR-7	Tip of the Weisberg	1980	7.50	15.00	30.00
-- Audiophile vinyl					

UNITED ARTISTS

Number	Title	Yr	VG	VG+	NM
❏ UA-LA773-G	The Tim Weisberg Band	1977	2.50	5.00	10.00
❏ UA-LA857-H	Rotations	1978	2.50	5.00	10.00

WELCH, ELISABETH

Female singer.

DRG

Number	Title	Yr	VG	VG+	NM
❏ SL-5202	Where Have You Been?	1987	2.50	5.00	10.00

WELDON, MAXINE

Female singer.

MAINSTREAM

Number	Title	Yr	VG	VG+	NM
❏ MRL-319	Right On	1971	3.00	6.00	12.00
❏ MRL-339	Chilly Wind	1972	3.00	6.00	12.00

WELLS, DICKY

Trombonist. Also see REX STEWART.

FELSTED

Number	Title	Yr	VG	VG+	NM
❏ SJA-2006 [S]	Bones for the King	1958	10.00	20.00	40.00
❏ SJA-2009 [S]	Trombone Four in Hand	1958	10.00	20.00	40.00
❏ FAJ-7006 [M]	Bones for the King	1958	10.00	20.00	40.00
❏ FAJ-7009 [M]	Trombone Four in Hand	1958	10.00	20.00	40.00

MASTER JAZZ

Number	Title	Yr	VG	VG+	NM
❏ 8118	Trombone Four-in-Hand	197?	3.00	6.00	12.00

PRESTIGE

Number	Title	Yr	VG	VG+	NM
❏ PRST-7593 [R]	Dicky Wells in Pais 1937	1968	6.25	12.50	25.00

UPTOWN

Number	Title	Yr	VG	VG+	NM
❏ 27.07	Lonesome Road	198?	2.50	5.00	10.00

WELLSTOOD, DICK

Pianist.

CHIAROSCURO

Number	Title	Yr	VG	VG+	NM
❏ 109	From Ragtime On	197?	3.00	6.00	12.00
❏ 129	Dick Wellstood Featuring Kenny Davern	197?	3.00	6.00	12.00
❏ 139	One-Man Jazz Machine	1975	3.00	6.00	12.00

CLASSIC JAZZ

Number	Title	Yr	VG	VG+	NM
❏ 10	From Dixie to Swing	197?	2.50	5.00	10.00

JAZZOLOGY

Number	Title	Yr	VG	VG+	NM
❏ JCE-73	Alone	197?	2.50	5.00	10.00

PICKWICK

Number	Title	Yr	VG	VG+	NM
❏ SPC-3376	Music from "The Sting"	197?	2.50	5.00	10.00
❏ SPC-3575	Ragtime Music of Scott Joplin	197?	2.50	5.00	10.00

RIVERSIDE

Number	Title	Yr	VG	VG+	NM
❏ RLP-2506 [10]	Dick Wellstood	1955	25.00	50.00	100.00

WELLSTOOD, DICK, AND CLIFF JACKSON

Jackson is a pianist. Also see DICK WELLSTOOD.

SWINGVILLE

Number	Title	Yr	VG	VG+	NM
❏ SVLP-2026 [M]	Uptown and Downtown	1961	12.50	25.00	50.00
-- Purple label					
❏ SVLP-2026 [M]	Uptown and Downtown	1965	6.25	12.50	25.00
-- Blue label, trident logo at right					

Number	Title	Yr	VG	VG+	NM

WERNER, KEN
Pianist.
INNER CITY
| ❑ IC-3036 | Beyond the Forest of Mirkwood | 198? | 3.00 | 6.00 | 12.00 |

WESS, FRANK
Tenor saxophone player and flutist.
COMMODORE
| ❑ FL-20031 [10] | Frank Wess Quintet | 1952 | 30.00 | 60.00 | 120.00 |
| ❑ FL-20032 [10] | Frank Wess | 1952 | 30.00 | 60.00 | 120.00 |
ENTERPRISE
| ❑ 5001 | To Memphis | 197? | 3.75 | 7.50 | 15.00 |
MAINSTREAM
| ❑ S-6033 [R] | Award Winner | 1965 | 3.00 | 6.00 | 12.00 |
| ❑ 56033 [M] | Award Winner | 1965 | 6.25 | 12.50 | 25.00 |
MOODSVILLE
❑ MVLP-8 [M]	Frank Wess Quartet	1960	12.50	25.00	50.00
-- Green label					
❑ MVLP-8 [M]	Frank Wess Quartet	1965	6.25	12.50	25.00
-- Blue label, trident logo at right					
PRESTIGE
❑ PRLP-7231 [M]	Southern Comfort	1962	10.00	20.00	40.00
❑ PRST-7231 [S]	Southern Comfort	1962	12.50	25.00	50.00
❑ PRLP-7266 [M]	Yo Ho! Poor You, Little Me	1963	10.00	20.00	40.00
❑ PRST-7266 [S]	Yo Ho! Poor You, Little Me	1963	12.50	25.00	50.00
PROGRESSIVE
| ❑ PRO-7057 | Flute Juice | 198? | 2.50 | 5.00 | 10.00 |
SAVOY
❑ MG-12022 [M]	Flutes and Reeds	1955	20.00	40.00	80.00
❑ MG-12072 [M]	North, South, East, Wess	1956	20.00	40.00	80.00
❑ MG-12095 [M]	Jazz for Playboys	1956	20.00	40.00	80.00
SAVOY JAZZ
| ❑ SJL-1136 | I Hear Ya Talkin' | 198? | 2.50 | 5.00 | 10.00 |
STATUS
| ❑ ST-7266 [S] | Yo Ho! Poor You, Little Me | 1965 | 5.00 | 10.00 | 20.00 |

WESS, FRANK, AND KENNY BURRELL
Also see each artist's individual listings.
PRESTIGE
| ❑ PRLP-7278 [M] | Steamin' | 1963 | 10.00 | 20.00 | 40.00 |
| ❑ PRST-7278 [R] | Steamin' | 1963 | 6.25 | 12.50 | 25.00 |

WESS, FRANK, AND JOHNNY COLES
Also see each artist's individual listings.
UPTOWN
| ❑ 27.14 | Two at the Top | 198? | 2.50 | 5.00 | 10.00 |

WESS, FRANK, AND THAD JONES
Also see each artist's individual listings.
NEW JAZZ
| ❑ NJLP-8310 [M] | Touche | 1963 | --- | --- | --- |
| -- Canceled; reassigned to Status | | | | | |
STATUS
| ❑ ST-8310 [M] | Touche | 1965 | 10.00 | 20.00 | 40.00 |

WEST END JAZZ BAND
STOMP OFF
| ❑ SOS-1042 | Red Hot Chicago | 1982 | 2.50 | 5.00 | 10.00 |
| ❑ SOS-1085 | Chicago Breakdown | 1985 | 2.50 | 5.00 | 10.00 |

WEST, ALVY
Alto saxophone player and bandleader.
COLUMBIA
| ❑ CL 6062 [10] | Alvy West and His Little Band | 1949 | 15.00 | 30.00 | 60.00 |

WESTBROOK, FORREST
Keyboard player.
REVELATION
| ❑ REV-11 | This Is Their Time, Oh Yes | 197? | 3.75 | 7.50 | 15.00 |

WESTBROOK, MIKE
Pianist, composer and bandleader.
HAT ART
❑ 2012 [(2)]	On Duke's Birthday	1986	3.75	7.50	15.00
❑ 2031 [(2)]	Love for Sale	198?	3.75	7.50	15.00
❑ 2040 [(2)]	Westbrook-Rossini	1987	3.75	7.50	15.00

WESTCHESTER WORKSHOP, THE
Among the members was trombonist EDDIE BERT.
UNIQUE
| ❑ LP-103 [M] | Unique Jazz | 1957 | 12.50 | 25.00 | 50.00 |

WESTON, PAUL
Pianist, bandleader and arranger whose Music for Dreaming, first issued on 78s in 1944, is considered the first "mood music" or "lounge" album.
CAPITOL
❑ H 222 [10]	Music for Dreaming	195?	10.00	20.00	40.00
❑ ST 1154 [S]	Music for Dreaming	1959	3.75	7.50	15.00
❑ T 1154 [M]	Music for Dreaming	1959	3.00	6.00	12.00
❑ ST 1192 [S]	Music for the Fireside	1959	3.75	7.50	15.00
❑ T 1192 [M]	Music for the Fireside	1959	3.00	6.00	12.00
❑ ST 1222 [S]	Music for Memories	1959	3.75	7.50	15.00
❑ T 1222 [M]	Music for Memories	1959	3.00	6.00	12.00
❑ ST 1563 [S]	Music for My Love	1961	3.75	7.50	15.00
❑ T 1563 [M]	Music for My Love	1961	3.00	6.00	12.00
❑ ST-91212	Romantic Reflections	196?	3.75	7.50	15.00
-- Capitol Record Club exclusive					
COLUMBIA
❑ CL 572 [M]	Caribbean Cruise	1955	3.75	7.50	15.00
❑ CL 693 [M]	Mood for 12	1955	3.75	7.50	15.00
❑ CL 794 [M]	Love Music	1956	3.75	7.50	15.00
❑ CL 879 [M]	Solo Mood	1956	3.75	7.50	15.00
❑ CL 909 [M]	Moonlight Becomes You	1956	3.75	7.50	15.00
❑ CL 977 [M]	Crescent City	1956	3.75	7.50	15.00
❑ CL 1112 [M]	Hollywood	1958	3.75	7.50	15.00
❑ CL 6232 [10]	Whispers in the Dark	195?	10.00	20.00	40.00
CORINTHIAN
❑ 107	Cinema Cameos	198?	2.00	4.00	8.00
❑ 109	Easy Jazz	198?	2.00	4.00	8.00
❑ 116	Crescent City	198?	2.00	4.00	8.00
HARMONY
| ❑ KH 31578 | Paul Weston Plays Jerome Kern | 1972 | 2.50 | 5.00 | 10.00 |
| ❑ KH 31603 | Paul Weston Plays Jerome Kern, Vol. 2 | 1972 | 2.50 | 5.00 | 10.00 |

WESTON, RANDY
Pianist and composer.
ARISTA/FREEDOM
❑ AF 1004	Carnival	1975	3.00	6.00	12.00
❑ AF 1014	Blues Africa	197?	3.00	6.00	12.00
❑ AF 1026	Berkshire Blues	197?	3.00	6.00	12.00
ATLANTIC
| ❑ SD 1609 | African Cookbook | 197? | 3.75 | 7.50 | 15.00 |
COLPIX
| ❑ CP-456 [M] | Highlight | 1963 | 7.50 | 15.00 | 30.00 |
| ❑ SCP-456 [S] | Highlight | 1963 | 15.00 | 30.00 | 60.00 |
CTI
| ❑ 6016 | Blue Moses | 197? | 3.00 | 6.00 | 12.00 |
DAWN
| ❑ DLP-1116 [M] | The Modern Art of Jazz | 1957 | 20.00 | 40.00 | 80.00 |
FANTASY
| ❑ OJC-1747 | Jazz A La Bohemia | 1990 | 2.50 | 5.00 | 10.00 |
INNER CITY
| ❑ IC-1013 | African Nite | 1975 | 3.00 | 6.00 | 12.00 |
JAZZLAND
| ❑ JLP-4 [M] | Zulu! | 1960 | 10.00 | 20.00 | 40.00 |
JUBILEE
| ❑ JLP-1060 [M] | Piano A La Mode | 1957 | 10.00 | 20.00 | 40.00 |
MILESTONE
| ❑ 7206 [(2)] | Zulu | 197? | 3.75 | 7.50 | 15.00 |
PAUSA
| ❑ 7017 | Randy Weston | 198? | 2.50 | 5.00 | 10.00 |
POLYDOR
| ❑ PD-5055 | Tanjah | 197? | 3.00 | 6.00 | 12.00 |
RIVERSIDE
❑ RLP 12-203 [M]	Get Happy	1956	15.00	30.00	60.00
❑ RLP 12-214 [M]	With These Hands...	1956	15.00	30.00	60.00
❑ RLP 12-227 [M]	Randy Weston Trio and Solo	1957	15.00	30.00	60.00
❑ RLP 12-232 [M]	Jazz A La Bohemia	1957	15.00	30.00	60.00
❑ RLP-2508 [10]	Cole Porter in a Modern Mood	1954	30.00	60.00	120.00
❑ RLP-2515 [10]	Randy Weston Trio	1955	30.00	60.00	120.00
❑ 6063	Get Happy	197?	3.00	6.00	12.00
❑ 6208	Trio and Solo	198?	2.50	5.00	10.00
ROULETTE
| ❑ R-65001 [M] | Uhuru Afrika | 1960 | 7.50 | 15.00 | 30.00 |
| ❑ RS-65001 [S] | Uhuru Afrika | 1960 | 10.00 | 20.00 | 40.00 |
1750 ARCH
| ❑ 1802 | Blue | 198? | 3.00 | 6.00 | 12.00 |
TRIP
| ❑ 5033 | Blues | 197? | 2.50 | 5.00 | 10.00 |
UNITED ARTISTS
| ❑ UAL-4011 [M] | Little Niles | 1959 | 10.00 | 20.00 | 40.00 |

Number	Title	Yr	VG	VG+	NM
❑ UAL-4045 [M]	Destry Rides Again	1959	10.00	20.00	40.00
❑ UAL-4066 [M]	Live at the Five Spot	1959	10.00	20.00	40.00
❑ UAS-5011 [S]	Little Niles	1959	12.50	25.00	50.00
❑ UAS-5045 [S]	Destry Rides Again	1959	12.50	25.00	50.00
❑ UAS-5066 [S]	Live at the Five Spot	1959	12.50	25.00	50.00

WESTON, RANDY, AND CECIL PAYNE
Also see each artist's individual listings.
JAZZLAND

Number	Title	Yr	VG	VG+	NM
❑ JLP-13 [M]	Greenwich Village Jazz	1960	10.00	20.00	40.00

WESTON, RANDY/LEM WINCHESTER
Also see each artist's individual listings.
METROJAZZ

Number	Title	Yr	VG	VG+	NM
❑ E-1005 [M]	New Faces at Newport	1958	12.50	25.00	50.00
❑ SE-1005 [S]	New Faces at Newport	1958	10.00	20.00	40.00

WETMORE, DICK
Violinist.
BETHLEHEM

Number	Title	Yr	VG	VG+	NM
❑ BCP-1035 [10]	Dick Wetmore	1955	25.00	50.00	100.00

WETTLING, GEORGE
Drummer.
COLUMBIA

Number	Title	Yr	VG	VG+	NM
❑ CL 2559 [10]	George Wettling's Jazz Band	1956	12.50	25.00	50.00

HARMONY

Number	Title	Yr	VG	VG+	NM
❑ HL 7080 [M]	Dixieland in Hi-Fi	1957	5.00	10.00	20.00

KAPP

Number	Title	Yr	VG	VG+	NM
❑ KL-1005 [M]	Ragtime Duo	1955	10.00	20.00	40.00
❑ KL-1028 [M]	Jazz Trios	1956	10.00	20.00	40.00

WEATHERS INDUSTRIES

Number	Title	Yr	VG	VG+	NM
❑ 5501 [M]	High Fidelity Rhythms	1955	10.00	20.00	40.00

WGJB
See YANK LAWSON AND BOB HAGGART; THE WORLD'S GREATEST JAZZ BAND.

WHALUM, KIRK
Player of various saxophones and keyboards.
COLUMBIA

Number	Title	Yr	VG	VG+	NM
❑ FC 40221	Floppy Disk	1985	2.50	5.00	10.00
❑ FC 40812	And You Know That!	1988	2.50	5.00	10.00
❑ FC 45215	The Promise	1989	3.00	6.00	12.00

WHEELER, CLARENCE
Saxophone player.
ATLANTIC

Number	Title	Yr	VG	VG+	NM
❑ SD 1551	Doin' What We Wanna	197?	10.00	20.00	40.00
❑ SD 1585	The Love I've Been Looking For	197?	5.00	10.00	20.00
❑ SD 1636	New Chicago Blues	197?	3.75	7.50	15.00

WHEELER, KENNY
Trumpeter, fluegel horn player and cornet player.
ECM

Number	Title	Yr	VG	VG+	NM
❑ 1069	Gnu High	197?	3.00	6.00	12.00
❑ 1102	Deer Wan	1977	2.50	5.00	10.00
❑ 1156	Around 6	1979	2.50	5.00	10.00
❑ 25000	Double, Double You	1984	2.50	5.00	10.00

WHIGHAM, JIGGS
Trombonist.
PAUSA

Number	Title	Yr	VG	VG+	NM
❑ 7134	Hope	198?	2.50	5.00	10.00

WHITCOMB, IAN
Male singer and accordion and ukulele player. Best known as a rock star during the British Invasion of the mid-1960s (his big hit was "You Turn Me On"), from the 1970s on he has been an aficionado of more traditional forms of music.
AUDIOPHILE

Number	Title	Yr	VG	VG+	NM
❑ AP-115	Treasures of Tin Pan Alley	197?	3.00	6.00	12.00
❑ AP-147	At the Ragtime Ball	1983	3.00	6.00	12.00

FIRST AMERICAN

Number	Title	Yr	VG	VG+	NM
❑ 7704	Crooner Tunes	1979	2.50	5.00	10.00
❑ 7725	Red Hot "Blue Heaven"	1980	2.50	5.00	10.00
❑ 7729	The Rock and Roll Years	1981	2.50	5.00	10.00
❑ 7751	Instrumentals	1981	2.50	5.00	10.00
❑ 7789	In Hollywood	1982	2.50	5.00	10.00

RHINO

Number	Title	Yr	VG	VG+	NM
❑ RNLP-127	The Best of Ian Whitcomb (1964-1968)	1986	2.00	4.00	8.00

SIERRA

Number	Title	Yr	VG	VG+	NM
❑ 8708	Pianomelt	1980	2.50	5.00	10.00

TOWER

Number	Title	Yr	VG	VG+	NM
❑ DT 5004 [R]	You Turn Me On	1965	5.00	10.00	20.00
❑ T 5004 [M]	You Turn Me On	1965	6.25	12.50	25.00
❑ ST 5042 [S]	Mod, Mod Music Hall	1966	5.00	10.00	20.00
❑ T 5042 [M]	Mod, Mod Music Hall	1966	3.75	7.50	15.00
❑ ST 5071 [S]	Yellow Underground	1967	5.00	10.00	20.00
❑ T 5071 [M]	Yellow Underground	1967	3.75	7.50	15.00
❑ ST 5100	Sock Me Some Rock	1968	5.00	10.00	20.00

UNITED ARTISTS

Number	Title	Yr	VG	VG+	NM
❑ UA-LA021-F	Under the Ragtime Moon	1972	2.50	5.00	10.00

WHITCOMB, IAN, AND DICK ZIMMERMAN
Zimmerman is a pianist. Also see IAN WHITCOMB.
AUDIOPHILE

Number	Title	Yr	VG	VG+	NM
❑ AP-225	Steppin' Out	1987	2.50	5.00	10.00

STOMP OFF

Number	Title	Yr	VG	VG+	NM
❑ SOS-1017	Don't Say Goodbye Miss Ragtime	198?	3.00	6.00	12.00
❑ SOS-1049	My Wife Is Dancing Mad	198?	3.00	6.00	12.00

WHITE EAGLE JAZZ BAND, THE
GHB

Number	Title	Yr	VG	VG+	NM
❑ GHB-204	The White Eagle Jazz Band	1988	2.50	5.00	10.00

WHITE, ANDREW
Tenor saxophone player who, in addition to his vast catalog on his own label, has transcribed and published the solos of JOHN COLTRANE and ERIC DOLPHY in book form. Also see THE J.F.K. QUINTET.
ANDREW'S MUSIC

Number	Title	Yr	VG	VG+	NM
❑ AM-1	Andrew Nathaniel White III	197?	5.00	10.00	20.00
❑ AM-2 [(2)]	Live at the "New Thing"	197?	6.25	12.50	25.00
❑ AM-3	Live in Bucharest	197?	5.00	10.00	20.00
❑ AM-4	Who Got Da Funk?	197?	5.00	10.00	20.00
❑ AM-5	Passion Flower	197?	5.00	10.00	20.00
❑ AM-6	Songs for a French Lady	197?	5.00	10.00	20.00
❑ AM-7	Theme	1975	5.00	10.00	20.00
❑ AM-8	Live at the Foolery, Vol. 1	1975	3.75	7.50	15.00
❑ AM-9	Live at the Foolery, Vol. 2	1975	3.75	7.50	15.00
❑ AM-10	Live at the Foolery, Vol. 3	1975	3.75	7.50	15.00
❑ AM-11	Live at the Foolery, Vol. 4	1975	3.75	7.50	15.00
❑ AM-12	Live at the Foolery, Vol. 5	1975	3.75	7.50	15.00
❑ AM-13	Live at the Foolery, Vol. 6	1975	3.75	7.50	15.00
❑ AM-14	Collage	1975	3.75	7.50	15.00
❑ AM-15	Marathon '75, Vol. 1	1976	3.75	7.50	15.00
❑ AM-16	Marathon '75, Vol. 2	1976	3.75	7.50	15.00
❑ AM-17	Marathon '75, Vol. 3	1976	3.75	7.50	15.00
❑ AM-18	Marathon '75, Vol. 4	1976	3.75	7.50	15.00
❑ AM-19	Marathon '75, Vol. 5	1976	3.75	7.50	15.00
❑ AM-20	Marathon '75, Vol. 6	1976	3.75	7.50	15.00
❑ AM-21	Marathon '75, Vol. 7	1976	3.75	7.50	15.00
❑ AM-22	Marathon '75, Vol. 8	1976	3.75	7.50	15.00
❑ AM-23	Marathon '75, Vol. 9	1976	3.75	7.50	15.00
❑ AM-24	Spotts, Maxine and Brown	1976	3.75	7.50	15.00
❑ AM-25	Countdown	1976	3.75	7.50	15.00
❑ AM-26	Red Top	1977	3.00	6.00	12.00
❑ AM-27	Trinkle, Trinkle	1977	3.00	6.00	12.00
❑ AM-28	Ebony Glaze	1977	3.00	6.00	12.00
❑ AM-29	Miss Ann	1977	3.00	6.00	12.00
❑ AM-30	Seven Giant Steps for Coltrane	1977	3.75	7.50	15.00
❑ AM-31	Live in New York Vol. 1	1977	3.00	6.00	12.00
❑ AM-32	Live in New York Vol. 2	1977	3.00	6.00	12.00
❑ AM-33	Bionic Saxophone	1978	3.00	6.00	12.00
❑ AM-36	Saxophonitis	1979	3.00	6.00	12.00
❑ AM-37	Weekend at One Step, Vol. 1: Fonk Update	1980	3.00	6.00	12.00
❑ AM-38	Weekend at One Step, Vol. 2: I Love Japan	1980	3.00	6.00	12.00
❑ AM-39	Weekend at One Step, Vol. 3: Have Band Will Travel	1980	3.00	6.00	12.00
❑ AM-42	Profile: White	1983	3.00	6.00	12.00

WHITE, BRIAN, AND ALAN GRESTY
White is a clarinetist and male singer; Gresty is a trumpeter.
JAZZOLOGY

Number	Title	Yr	VG	VG+	NM
❑ J-116	Muggsy Remembered	1988	2.50	5.00	10.00

WHITE, CARLA
Female singer.
STASH

Number	Title	Yr	VG	VG+	NM
❑ ST-237	Andruline	1983	2.50	5.00	10.00

WHITE, JOHN
Percussionist and male singer.
MAINSTREAM

Number	Title	Yr	VG	VG+	NM
❑ MRL-330	John White	1972	3.00	6.00	12.00

Number	Title	Yr	VG	VG+	NM
WHITE, KITTY					
Female singer.					
EMARCY					
❏ MG-36020 [M]	A New Voice in Jazz	1955	12.50	25.00	50.00
❏ MG-36068 [M]	Kitty White	1955	12.50	25.00	50.00
PACIFICA					
❏ PL-802 [10]	Kitty White	1955	25.00	50.00	100.00
WHITE, LENNY					
Drummer. His group Twennynine was popular in R&B circles in the early 1980s. Also see RETURN TO FOREVER.					
ELEKTRA					
❏ 6E-121	Adventures of Astral Pirates	1978	2.50	5.00	10.00
❏ 6E-164	Streamline	1978	2.50	5.00	10.00
❏ 6E-223	Best of Friends	1979	2.50	5.00	10.00
❏ 6E-304	Twennynine with Lenny White	1980	2.50	5.00	10.00
❏ 5E-551	Just Like Dreamin'	1981	2.50	5.00	10.00
NEMPEROR					
❏ SD 435	Venusian Summer	1975	3.00	6.00	12.00
❏ SD 441	Big City	1977	3.00	6.00	12.00
WHITE, MICHAEL					
Violinist.					
ABC IMPULSE!					
❏ AS-9215	Spirit Dance	197?	3.75	7.50	15.00
❏ AS-9221	Pneuma	197?	3.75	7.50	15.00
❏ AS-9241	Land of Spirit and Light	1973	3.75	7.50	15.00
❏ AS-9268	Father Music, Mother Dance	1974	3.75	7.50	15.00
❏ ASD-9281	Go with the Flow	1974	3.75	7.50	15.00
ELEKTRA					
❏ 6E-138	X Factor	1978	2.50	5.00	10.00
WHITE, MIKE					
SEECO					
❏ SLP-442 [M]	Dixieland Jazz	1960	5.00	10.00	20.00
❏ SLP-4420 [S]	Dixieland Jazz	1960	6.25	12.50	25.00
WHITE, STEVE					
Tenor saxophone player.					
LIBERTY					
❏ LJH-6006 [M]	Jazz Mad -- The Unpredictable Steve White	1955	12.50	25.00	50.00
WHITEMAN, PAUL					
Violinist and bandleader. The self-proclaimed "King of Jazz," his band's highly polished and arranged music was a forerunner to the big bands. Many of his musicians were jazz greats (TOMMY DORSEY, BIX BEIDERBECKE and JOE VENUTI just to name several), and he helped make BING CROSBY a star.					
CAPITOL					
❏ T 622 [M]	Classics in Jazz	1955	12.50	25.00	50.00
❏ DT 1678 [R]	Paul Whiteman Conducts George Gershwin	1962	3.00	6.00	12.00
❏ T 1678 [M]	Paul Whiteman Conducts George Gershwin	1962	3.75	7.50	15.00
COLUMBIA					
❏ CL 2830 [M]	Paul Whiteman Featuring Bing Crosby	1968	3.75	7.50	15.00
CORAL					
❏ CRL 57021 [M]	The Great Gershwin	1955	5.00	10.00	20.00
GRAND AWARD					
❏ GA-208 SD [S]	Hawaiian Magic	1958	7.50	15.00	30.00
❏ GA-241 SD [S]	The Night I Played at 666 Fifth	1960	7.50	15.00	30.00
❏ GA-244 SD [S]	Cavalcade of Music	1960	7.50	15.00	30.00
❏ GA-33-351 [M]	Fiddle on Fire	195?	7.50	15.00	30.00
❏ GA-33-356 [M]	Hawaiian Magic	1958	5.00	10.00	20.00
❏ GA-33-409 [M]	The Night I Played at 666 Fifth	1960	5.00	10.00	20.00
❏ GA-33-412 [M]	Cavalcade of Music	1960	5.00	10.00	20.00
❏ GA-33-502 [M]	Great Whiteman Hits	195?	7.50	15.00	30.00
❏ GA-33-503 [M]	The Greatest Stars of My Life	195?	12.50	25.00	50.00
-- In red velvet jacket					
❏ GA-33-901 [(2) M]	Paul Whiteman/50th Anniversary	1956	12.50	25.00	50.00
MARK 56					
❏ 761 [M]	Tribute to Gershwin 1936	197?	3.00	6.00	12.00
RCA VICTOR					
❏ LPV-555 [M]	Paul Whiteman, Volume 1	195?	3.75	7.50	15.00
SUNBEAM					
❏ 18 [M]	In Concert 1927-32	197?	3.00	6.00	12.00
"X"					
❏ LVA-3040 [10]	Paul Whiteman's Orchestra Featuring Bix Beiderbecke	1955	20.00	40.00	80.00
WHITEMAN, PAUL, ORCHESTRA					
New recordings of arrangements used by the original PAUL WHITEMAN Orchestra. Conceived by trumpeter Dick Sudhalter and conducted by Alan Cohen.					
MONMOUTH-EVERGREEN					
❏ 7074	The Classic Arrangements of Challis, Satterfield, Hayton	197?	3.00	6.00	12.00
❏ 7078	Live in '75	1975	3.00	6.00	12.00
WHITING, MARGARET					
Female singer.					
AUDIOPHILE					
❏ AP-152	Too Marvelous for Words	198?	2.50	5.00	10.00
❏ AP-173	Come a Little Closer	198?	2.50	5.00	10.00
❏ AP-207	This Lady's in Love with You	1986	2.50	5.00	10.00
CAPITOL					
❏ H 163 [10]	South Pacific	1950	12.50	25.00	50.00
❏ H 209 [10]	Margaret Whiting Sings Rodgers and Hart	1950	12.50	25.00	50.00
❏ H 234 [10]	Songs	1950	12.50	25.00	50.00
❏ T 410 [M]	Love Songs	1954	10.00	20.00	40.00
❏ T 685 [M]	For the Starry-Eyed	1955	10.00	20.00	40.00
DOT					
❏ DLP 3072 [M]	Goin' Places	1957	6.25	12.50	25.00
❏ DLP 3113 [M]	Margaret	1958	3.75	7.50	15.00
❏ DLP 3176 [M]	Margaret Whiting's Great Hits	1959	3.75	7.50	15.00
❏ DLP 3235 [M]	Ten Top Hits	1960	3.75	7.50	15.00
❏ DLP 3337 [M]	Just a Dream	1960	3.75	7.50	15.00
❏ DLP 25113 [S]	Margaret	1958	5.00	10.00	20.00
❏ DLP 25176 [S]	Margaret Whiting's Great Hits	1959	5.00	10.00	20.00
❏ DLP 25235 [S]	Ten Top Hits	1960	5.00	10.00	20.00
❏ DLP 25337 [S]	Just a Dream	1960	5.00	10.00	20.00
HAMILTON					
❏ HLP 143 [M]	My Ideal	196?	3.00	6.00	12.00
❏ HLP 12143 [S]	My Ideal	196?	3.75	7.50	15.00
LONDON					
❏ PS 497 [S]	The Wheel of Hurt	1967	3.75	7.50	15.00
❏ PS 510 [S]	Maggie Isn't Margaret Anymore	1967	3.75	7.50	15.00
❏ PS 527	Pop Country	1968	3.75	7.50	15.00
❏ LL 3497 [M]	The Wheel of Hurt	1967	5.00	10.00	20.00
❏ LL 3510 [M]	Maggie Isn't Margaret Anymore	1967	5.00	10.00	20.00
MGM					
❏ E-4006 [M]	Past Midnight	1961	3.75	7.50	15.00
❏ SE-4006 [S]	Past Midnight	1961	5.00	10.00	20.00
VERVE					
❏ V-4038 [M]	The Jerome Kern Song Book	1960	3.75	7.50	15.00
❏ V6-4038 [S]	The Jerome Kern Song Book	1960	5.00	10.00	20.00
WHITNEY, DAVE					
Trumpeter and bandleader.					
JAZZOLOGY					
❏ J-68	Dave Whitney and His Jazz Band	198?	2.50	5.00	10.00
WHYTE, RONNIE					
Male singer and pianist.					
AUDIOPHILE					
❏ AP-127	I Love a Piano	198?	2.50	5.00	10.00
❏ AP-151	Ronnie Whyte at the Conservatory	198?	2.50	5.00	10.00
❏ AP-204	Soft Whyte	1986	2.50	5.00	10.00
MONMOUTH-EVERGREEN					
❏ 7088	New York State of Mind	197?	3.00	6.00	12.00
PROGRESSIVE					
❏ PRO-7075	Something Wonderful	1986	2.50	5.00	10.00
WIDESPREAD DEPRESSION ORCHESTRA, THE					
Swing revival band about 20 years ahead of its time. Members: Dean Nicyper (tenor sax); Michael Hashim (alto sax); David Lillie (baritone sax); Jordan Sandke (trumpet); Tim Atherton (trombone); Phil Flanagan (bass); John Ellis (drums); Michael LeDonne (piano); Jonny Holtzman (vocals).					
STASH					
❏ ST-203	Downtown Uproar	1979	2.50	5.00	10.00
❏ ST-206	Boogie in the Barnyard	1980	2.50	5.00	10.00
❏ ST-212	Time to Jump and Shout	198?	2.50	5.00	10.00
WIDESPREAD JAZZ ORCHESTRA					
Among the members were Dan Barrett (trombone).					
ADELPHI					
❏ 5015	Swing Is the Thing	1983	2.50	5.00	10.00

Number	Title	Yr	VG	VG+	NM
COLUMBIA					
❏ FC 40034	Paris Blues	1985	2.50	5.00	10.00
WIGGINS, GERALD					
Pianist.					
CHALLENGE					
❏ CHP-604 [M]	The King and I	1957	15.00	30.00	60.00
CLASSIC JAZZ					
❏ 117	Wig Is Here	198?	2.50	5.00	10.00
CONTEMPORARY					
❏ M-3595 [M]	Relax and Enjoy It	1961	7.50	15.00	30.00
❏ S-7595 [S]	Relax and Enjoy It	1961	10.00	20.00	40.00
DIG					
❏ LP-102 [M]	Gerald Wiggins Trio	1956	15.00	30.00	60.00
DISCOVERY					
❏ DL-2003 [10]	Gerald Wiggins Trio	1953	30.00	60.00	120.00
FANTASY					
❏ OJC-173	Relax and Enjoy It	198?	2.50	5.00	10.00
HIFI					
❏ J-618 [M]	Wiggin' Out	1961	7.50	15.00	30.00
❏ JS-618 [S]	Wiggin' Out	1961	10.00	20.00	40.00
MOTIF					
❏ 504 [M]	Reminiscin' with Wig	1956	15.00	30.00	60.00
SPECIALTY					
❏ SP-2101 [S]	Around the World	1969	5.00	10.00	20.00
TAMPA					
❏ TP-1 [M]	The Loveliness of You	1957	25.00	50.00	100.00
-- Colored vinyl					
❏ TP-1 [M]	The Loveliness of You	1958	12.50	25.00	50.00
-- Black vinyl					
❏ TP-33 [M]	Gerald Wiggins Trio	1957	25.00	50.00	100.00
-- Colored vinyl					
❏ TP-33 [M]	Gerald Wiggins Trio	1958	12.50	25.00	50.00
-- Black vinyl					
WIGGS, JOHNNY					
Cornet player.					
GHB					
❏ GHB-100	Johnny Wiggs and the New Orleans Kids	197?	2.50	5.00	10.00
NEW ORLEANS					
❏ 7206	Congo Square	197?	2.50	5.00	10.00
❏ 47045	Congo Square	197?	2.50	5.00	10.00
PARAMOUNT					
❏ CJS 107 [10]	Johnny Wiggs' New Orleanians Playing Jazz Favorites and Featuring Ray Burke	195?	15.00	30.00	60.00
SOUTHLAND					
❏ LP-200 [10]	Johnny Wiggs	1954	12.50	25.00	50.00
❏ LP-200 [M]	Johnny Wiggs	195?	7.50	15.00	30.00
WIGGS, JOHNNY, AND RAY BURKE					
Also see each artist's individual listings.					
S/D					
❏ LP-1001 [10]	Chamber Jazz	1955	12.50	25.00	50.00
WILBER, BOB					
Clarinetist and soprano saxophone player. Also see SOPRANO SUMMIT.					
CIRCLE					
❏ CLP-98	Reflections	1986	2.50	5.00	10.00
❏ L-406 [10]	Bob Wilbur Jazz Band	1951	12.50	25.00	50.00
CLASSIC JAZZ					
❏ 5	Spreadin' Joy	197?	2.50	5.00	10.00
❏ 8	New Clarinet in Town	197?	2.50	5.00	10.00
❏ 9	Blowin' the Blues Away	197?	2.50	5.00	10.00
JAZZOLOGY					
❏ J-44	Bob Wilber and His Famous Jazz Band	198?	2.50	5.00	10.00
❏ J-141	Live at Bechet's	1986	2.50	5.00	10.00
❏ J-142	Ode to Bechet	1986	2.50	5.00	10.00
MONMOUTH-EVERGREEN					
❏ 6917	The Music of Hoagy Carmichael	197?	3.00	6.00	12.00
RIVERSIDE					
❏ RLP-2501 [10]	Young Men With Horns	1952	20.00	40.00	80.00
WILBER, BOB, AND SCOTT HAMILTON					
Also see each artist's individual listings.					
CHIAROSCURO					
❏ 171	Bob Wilber and Scott Hamilton	1977	3.00	6.00	12.00

Number	Title	Yr	VG	VG+	NM
WILCOX, LARRY					
Arranger.					
COLUMBIA					
❏ CL 2147 [M]	Hot Rod Jazz	1964	7.50	15.00	30.00
❏ CS 8947 [S]	Hot Rod Jazz	1964	10.00	20.00	40.00
COLUMBIA SPECIAL PRODUCTS					
❏ CSRP 8947 [M]	Hot Rod Jazz	196?	5.00	10.00	20.00
WILDER, ALEC					
Composer. Also see FRANK SINATRA.					
COLUMBIA					
❏ CL 6181 [10]	Alec Wilder Octet	1951	15.00	30.00	60.00
MERCURY					
❏ MG 25008 [10]	Alec Wilder and His Octet	1949	15.00	30.00	60.00
WILDER, JOE					
Trumpeter.					
COLUMBIA					
❏ CL 1319 [M]	Jazz from "Peter Gunn"	1959	7.50	15.00	30.00
❏ CL 1372 [M]	The Pretty Sound of Joe Wilder	1959	7.50	15.00	30.00
❏ CS 8121 [S]	Jazz from "Peter Gunn"	1959	10.00	20.00	40.00
❏ CS 8173 [S]	The Pretty Sound of Joe Wilder	1959	10.00	20.00	40.00
SAVOY					
❏ MG-12063 [M]	'N' Wilder....	1956	10.00	20.00	40.00
SAVOY JAZZ					
❏ SJL-1191	Softly with Feeling	1989	2.50	5.00	10.00
WILEY, LEE					
Female singer. Also see ELLIS LARKINS.					
ALLEGRO ELITE					
❏ 4019 [10]	Lee Wiley Sings -- Lennie Tristano Plays	195?	25.00	50.00	100.00
AUDIOPHILE					
❏ AP-1	Lee Wiley Sings Ira and George Gershwin and Cole Porter	1986	2.50	5.00	10.00
❏ AP-10	Lee Wiley Sings the Songs of Richard Rodgers and Lorenz Hart and Harold Arlen	1990	3.00	6.00	12.00
COLUMBIA					
❏ CL 656 [M]	Night in Manhattan	1955	20.00	40.00	80.00
❏ CL 6169 [10]	Night in Manhattan	1951	25.00	50.00	100.00
❏ CL 6215 [10]	Lee Wiley Sings Vincent Youmans	1952	25.00	50.00	100.00
❏ CL 6216 [10]	Lee Wiley Sings Irving Berlin	1952	25.00	50.00	100.00
JAZZTONE					
❏ J-1248 [M]	The Songs of Rodgers and Hart -- Intimate Jazz	1956	12.50	25.00	50.00
JJC					
❏ M-2002 [M]	The One and Only Lee Wiley	195?	12.50	25.00	50.00
❏ M-2003 [M]	The Classic Interpretations of the Immortal Cole Porter	195?	12.50	25.00	50.00
LIBERTY MUSIC SHOP					
❏ 1003 [10]	Cole Porter Songs by Lee Wiley	195?	75.00	150.00	300.00
❏ 1004 [10]	George Gershwin Songs by Lee Wiley	195?	75.00	150.00	300.00
MONMOUTH-EVERGREEN					
❏ 6807	Lee Wiley Plays Rodgers & Hart/Harold Arlen	1968	3.75	7.50	15.00
❏ 7034	Lee Wiley Sings Gershwin & Porter	1970	3.00	6.00	12.00
❏ 7041	Back Home Again	1971	3.00	6.00	12.00
RCA VICTOR					
❏ LPM-1408 [M]	West of the Moon	1957	20.00	40.00	80.00
❏ LPM-1566 [M]	Touch of the Blues	1957	15.00	30.00	60.00
RIC					
❏ M-2002 [M]	The One and Only Lee Wiley	1964	5.00	10.00	20.00
❏ S-2002 [S]	The One and Only Lee Wiley	1964	6.25	12.50	25.00
STORYVILLE					
❏ STLP-312 [10]	Lee Wiley Sings Rodgers and Hart	1954	50.00	100.00	200.00
TOTEM					
❏ 1021	Lee Wiley on the Air	197?	2.50	5.00	10.00
❏ 1033	Lee Wiley on the Air, Vol. 2	198?	2.50	5.00	10.00
WILKERSON, DON					
Tenor saxophone player.					
BLUE NOTE					
❏ BLP-4107 [M]	Preach, Brother!	1962	7.50	15.00	30.00
❏ BLP-4121 [M]	Elder Don	1963	7.50	15.00	30.00
❏ BLP-4145 [M]	Shoutin'	1963	7.50	15.00	30.00
❏ BST-84107 [S]	Preach, Brother!	1962	10.00	20.00	40.00
-- With "New York, USA" address on label					

Number	Title	Yr	VG	VG+	NM
❏ BST-84107 [S]	Preach, Brother!	1967	5.00	10.00	20.00
-- With "A Division of Liberty Records" on label					
❏ BST-84121 [S]	Elder Don	1963	10.00	20.00	40.00
-- With "New York, USA" address on label					
❏ BST-84121 [S]	Elder Don	1967	5.00	10.00	20.00
-- With "A Division of Liberty Records" on label					
❏ BST-84145 [S]	Shoutin'	1963	10.00	20.00	40.00
-- With "New York, USA" address on label					
❏ BST-84145 [S]	Shoutin'	1967	5.00	10.00	20.00
-- With "A Division of Liberty Records" on label					
RIVERSIDE					
❏ RLP-332 [M]	Texas Twister	1960	10.00	20.00	40.00
❏ RLP-1186 [S]	Texas Twister	1960	10.00	20.00	40.00

WILKES, RAY
Guitarist.
INNER CITY

Number	Title	Yr	VG	VG+	NM
❏ IC-1051	Dark Blue Man	197?	3.00	6.00	12.00

WILKINS, ERNIE
Tenor and alto saxophone player, arranger and composer. Also see KENNY CLARKE.
EVEREST

Number	Title	Yr	VG	VG+	NM
❏ SDBR-1077 [S]	Here Comes the Swingin' Mr. Wilkins	1959	7.50	15.00	30.00
❏ SDBR-1104 [S]	The Big New Band of the '60s	1960	7.50	15.00	30.00
❏ LPBR-5077 [M]	Here Comes the Swingin' Mr. Wilkins	1959	6.25	12.50	25.00
❏ LPBR-5104 [M]	The Big New Band of the '60s	1960	6.25	12.50	25.00
MAINSTREAM					
❏ MRL-305	Hard Mother Blues	1971	3.75	7.50	15.00
❏ MRL-806 [(2)]	Screaming Mothers	197?	3.75	7.50	15.00
RCA CAMDEN					
❏ CAL-543 [M]	The Greatest Songs Ever Swung	195?	3.75	7.50	15.00
SAVOY					
❏ MG-12044 [M]	Top Brass Featuring 5 Trumpets	1955	15.00	30.00	60.00
STEEPLECHASE					
❏ SCS-1190	Montreux	198?	3.00	6.00	12.00
STORYVILLE					
❏ 4051	Ernie Wilkins and the Almost Big Band	198?	2.50	5.00	10.00

WILKINS, JACK
Guitarist.
CHIAROSCURO

Number	Title	Yr	VG	VG+	NM
❏ 156	Merge	1977	3.00	6.00	12.00
❏ 185	You Can't Live Without It	1978	3.00	6.00	12.00
MAINSTREAM					
❏ MRL-396	Windows	197?	3.00	6.00	12.00

WILLETTE, BABY FACE
Organist.
ARGO

Number	Title	Yr	VG	VG+	NM
❏ LP-739 [M]	No Rock	1964	6.25	12.50	25.00
❏ LPS-739 [S]	No Rock	1964	7.50	15.00	30.00
❏ LP-749 [M]	Behind the 8-Ball	1965	6.25	12.50	25.00
❏ LPS-749 [S]	Behind the 8-Ball	1965	7.50	15.00	30.00
BLUE NOTE					
❏ BLP-4068 [M]	Face to Face	1961	37.50	75.00	150.00
-- With W. 63rd St. address on label					
❏ BLP-4068 [M]	Face to Face	1963	6.25	12.50	25.00
-- With "New York, USA" address on label					
❏ BLP-4084 [M]	Stop and Listen	1962	30.00	60.00	120.00
-- With 61st St. address on label					
❏ BLP-4084 [M]	Stop and Listen	1963	6.25	12.50	25.00
-- With "New York, USA" address on label					
❏ BST-84068 [S]	Face to Face	1961	30.00	60.00	120.00
-- With W. 63rd St. address on label					
❏ BST-84068 [S]	Face to Face	1963	5.00	10.00	20.00
-- With "New York, USA" address on label					
❏ BST-84068 [S]	Face to Face	1967	3.75	7.50	15.00
-- With "A Division of Liberty Records" on label					
❏ BST-84084 [S]	Stop and Listen	1962	25.00	50.00	100.00
-- With 61st St. address on label					
❏ BST-84084 [S]	Stop and Listen	1963	5.00	10.00	20.00
-- With "New York, USA" address on label					
❏ BST-84084 [S]	Stop and Listen	1967	3.75	7.50	15.00
-- With "A Division of Liberty Records" on label					
CADET					
❏ LP-739 [M]	No Rock	1966	3.00	6.00	12.00
❏ LPS-739 [S]	No Rock	1966	3.75	7.50	15.00
❏ LP-749 [M]	Behind the 8-Ball	1966	3.00	6.00	12.00
❏ LPS-749 [S]	Behind the 8-Ball	1966	3.75	7.50	15.00

WILLIAMS, AL
RENAISSANCE

Number	Title	Yr	VG	VG+	NM
❏ 9565	Sandance	1976	3.00	6.00	12.00

WILLIAMS, ANN
Female singer.
CHARLIE PARKER

Number	Title	Yr	VG	VG+	NM
❏ PLP-807 [M]	First Time Out	1963	10.00	20.00	40.00
❏ PLP-807S [S]	First Time Out	1963	10.00	20.00	40.00

WILLIAMS, ANTHONY
See TONY WILLIAMS.

WILLIAMS, BILLY
Male singer.
CORAL

Number	Title	Yr	VG	VG+	NM
❏ CRL 57184 [M]	Billy Williams	1957	15.00	30.00	60.00
❏ CRL 57251 [M]	Half Sweet, Half Beat	1959	12.50	25.00	50.00
❏ CRL 57343 [M]	The Billy Williams Revue	1960	12.50	25.00	50.00
❏ CRL 757251 [S]	Half Sweet, Half Beat	1959	20.00	40.00	80.00
❏ CRL 757343 [S]	The Billy Williams Revue	1960	15.00	30.00	60.00
MERCURY					
❏ MG 20317 [M]	Oh Yeah!	1958	15.00	30.00	60.00
MGM					
❏ E-3400 [M]	The Billy Williams Quartet	1957	15.00	30.00	60.00
WING					
❏ MGW-12131 [M]	Vote for Billy Williams	1959	10.00	20.00	40.00

WILLIAMS, BUSTER
Bass player.
BUDDAH

Number	Title	Yr	VG	VG+	NM
❏ BDS-5728	Dreams Come True	1980	3.00	6.00	12.00
MUSE					
❏ MR-5080	Pinnacle	1975	3.00	6.00	12.00
❏ MR-5101	Reflections	1976	3.00	6.00	12.00
❏ MR-5171	Heartbeat	1979	3.00	6.00	12.00

WILLIAMS, CHARLES
Alto saxophone player.
MAINSTREAM

Number	Title	Yr	VG	VG+	NM
❏ MRL-312	Charles Williams	1971	3.00	6.00	12.00
❏ MRL-345	Trees and Grass and Things	1972	3.00	6.00	12.00
❏ MRL-381	Stickball	1973	3.00	6.00	12.00

WILLIAMS, CLARENCE
Pianist, male singer, bandleader, composer and arranger.
BIOGRAPH

Number	Title	Yr	VG	VG+	NM
❏ 12006	Clarence Williams Volume 1, 1927-29	197?	2.50	5.00	10.00
❏ 12038	Clarence Williams Volume 2, 1927-28	197?	2.50	5.00	10.00
MCA					
❏ 1349	Music Mann	198?	2.50	5.00	10.00
RIVERSIDE					
❏ RLP-1033 [10]	Clarence Williams and Orchestra	1954	15.00	30.00	60.00

WILLIAMS, CLAUDE
Violinist and male singer.
CLASSIC JAZZ

Number	Title	Yr	VG	VG+	NM
❏ 135	Fiddler's Dream	198?	2.50	5.00	10.00

WILLIAMS, COOTIE
Trumpeter.
HALL OF FAME

Number	Title	Yr	VG	VG+	NM
❏ 602	The Big Challenge	197?	2.50	5.00	10.00
JARO					
❏ JAM-5001 [M]	Around Midnight	1959	25.00	50.00	100.00
❏ JAS-8001 [S]	Around Midnight	1959	20.00	40.00	80.00
MOODSVILLE					
❏ MVLP-27 [M]	The Solid Trumpet of Cootie Williams	1962	12.50	25.00	50.00
-- Green label					
❏ MVLP-27 [M]	The Solid Trumpet of Cootie Williams	1965	6.25	12.50	25.00
-- Blue label, trident logo at right					
PHOENIX					
❏ 1	Cootie Williams Sextet and Orchestra	197?	2.50	5.00	10.00

Number	Title	Yr	VG	VG+	NM
RCA VICTOR					
❏ LPM-1718 [M]	Cootie Williams in Hi-Fi	1958	20.00	40.00	80.00
WARWICK					
❏ W-2027 [M]	Do Nothing Till You Hear From Me	1960	10.00	20.00	40.00
❏ W-2027ST [S]	Do Nothing Till You Hear From Me	1960	15.00	30.00	60.00

WILLIAMS, COOTIE/JIMMY PRESTON
Preston was a male singer and alto saxophone player. Also see COOTIE WILLIAMS.

Number	Title	Yr	VG	VG+	NM
ALLEGRO ELITE					
❏ 4109 [10]	Rock 'N' Roll	195?	12.50	25.00	50.00

WILLIAMS, DAVID "FAT MAN"
Pianist and male singer.

Number	Title	Yr	VG	VG+	NM
NEW ORLEANS					
❏ 7204	Apple Tree	197?	2.50	5.00	10.00

WILLIAMS, GEORGE
Composer, arranger and bandleader.

Number	Title	Yr	VG	VG+	NM
BRUNSWICK					
❏ BL 54020 [M]	The Fox	1957	12.50	25.00	50.00
RCA VICTOR					
❏ LPM-1205 [M]	We Could Make Such Beautiful Music	1956	10.00	20.00	40.00
❏ LPM-1301 [M]	Rhythm Was His Business	1956	10.00	20.00	40.00

WILLIAMS, GRIFF
Pianist and bandleader.

Number	Title	Yr	VG	VG+	NM
HINDSIGHT					
❏ HSR-175	Griff Williams and His Orchestra 1946-1951	198?	2.50	5.00	10.00

WILLIAMS, HERBIE
Trumpeter.

Number	Title	Yr	VG	VG+	NM
WORKSHOP JAZZ					
❏ WSJ-216 [M]	The Soul and Sound of Herbie Williams	1963	15.00	30.00	60.00

WILLIAMS, JAMES
Pianist.

Number	Title	Yr	VG	VG+	NM
CONCORD JAZZ					
❏ CJ-104	Everything I Love	1980	2.50	5.00	10.00
❏ CJ-140	Images (Of the Things to Come)	1981	2.50	5.00	10.00
❏ CJ-192	The Arioso Touch	1982	2.50	5.00	10.00
EMARCY					
❏ 832 859-1	The Magical Trio	1988	2.50	5.00	10.00
❏ 834 368-1	Magical Trio 2	1989	3.00	6.00	12.00
SUNNYSIDE					
❏ SSC-1007	Alter Ego	1985	2.50	5.00	10.00
❏ SSC-1012	Progress Report	1986	2.50	5.00	10.00
ZIM					
❏ 2005	Flying Colors	1977	3.00	6.00	12.00

WILLIAMS, JESSICA
Pianist.

Number	Title	Yr	VG	VG+	NM
ADELPHI					
❏ 5003	The Portal of Antrim	1976	3.75	7.50	15.00
❏ 5005 [(2)]	Portraits	197?	3.75	7.50	15.00
BLACKHAWK					
❏ BKH-51301	Nothin' But the Truth	1986	2.50	5.00	10.00
CLEAN CUTS					
❏ 701	Rivers of Memory	1979	3.00	6.00	12.00
❏ 703	Orgonomic Music	198?	3.00	6.00	12.00
❏ 706	Update	1982	3.00	6.00	12.00

WILLIAMS, JOE
Male singer. Also see COUNT BASIE; SARAH VAUGHAN.

Number	Title	Yr	VG	VG+	NM
BLUE NOTE					
❏ BST-84355	Worth Waiting For	1970	3.75	7.50	15.00
BLUEBIRD					
❏ 6464-1-RB	The Overwhelming Joe Williams	1988	2.50	5.00	10.00
DELOS					
❏ DMS-4001	Nothin' But the Blues	1984	3.00	6.00	12.00
FANTASY					
❏ OJC-438	Joe Williams Live	1990	2.50	5.00	10.00
❏ F-9441	Joe Williams Live	1974	3.00	6.00	12.00
FORUM					
❏ F-9033 [M]	That Kind of Woman	196?	3.00	6.00	12.00
❏ SF-9033 [S]	That Kind of Woman	196?	3.75	7.50	15.00
JASS					
❏ J-6	Chains of Love	198?	2.50	5.00	10.00
PAUSA					
❏ 9008	Worth Waiting For	198?	2.50	5.00	10.00
RCA VICTOR					
❏ LPM-2713 [M]	Jump for Joy	1963	6.25	12.50	25.00
❏ LSP-2713 [S]	Jump for Joy	1963	7.50	15.00	30.00
❏ LPM-2762 [M]	Joe Williams at Newport '63	1963	6.25	12.50	25.00
❏ LSP-2762 [S]	Joe Williams at Newport '63	1963	7.50	15.00	30.00
❏ LPM-2879 [M]	Me and the Blues	1964	6.25	12.50	25.00
❏ LSP-2879 [S]	Me and the Blues	1964	7.50	15.00	30.00
❏ LPM-3433 [M]	The Song Is You	1965	5.00	10.00	20.00
❏ LSP-3433 [S]	The Song Is You	1965	6.25	12.50	25.00
❏ LPM-3461 [M]	The Exciting Joe Williams	1965	5.00	10.00	20.00
❏ LSP-3461 [S]	The Exciting Joe Williams	1965	6.25	12.50	25.00
REGENT					
❏ MG-6002 [M]	Everyday	1956	12.50	25.00	50.00
ROULETTE					
❏ SR-42016	A Man Ain't Supposed to Cry	1968	3.75	7.50	15.00
❏ R-52005 [M]	A Man Ain't Supposed to Cry	1958	7.50	15.00	30.00
❏ SR-52005 [S]	A Man Ain't Supposed to Cry	1958	10.00	20.00	40.00
❏ R-52030 [M]	Joe Williams Sings About You!	1959	7.50	15.00	30.00
❏ SR-52030 [S]	Joe Williams Sings About You!	1959	10.00	20.00	40.00
❏ R-52039 [M]	That Kind of Woman	1960	7.50	15.00	30.00
❏ SR-52039 [S]	That Kind of Woman	1960	10.00	20.00	40.00
❏ R-52066 [M]	Sentimental and Melancholy	1961	7.50	15.00	30.00
❏ SR-52066 [S]	Sentimental and Melancholy	1961	10.00	20.00	40.00
❏ R-52069 [M]	Together	1961	7.50	15.00	30.00
❏ SR-52069 [S]	Together	1961	10.00	20.00	40.00
-- With Harry "Sweets" Edison					
❏ R-52071 [M]	Have a Good Time with Joe Williams	1961	7.50	15.00	30.00
❏ SR-52071 [S]	Have a Good Time with Joe Williams	1961	10.00	20.00	40.00
❏ R-52085 [M]	Swingin' Night at Birdland	1962	6.25	12.50	25.00
❏ SR-52085 [S]	Swingin' Night at Birdland	1962	7.50	15.00	30.00
❏ R-52102 [M]	One Is a Lonesome Number	1963	6.25	12.50	25.00
❏ SR-52102 [S]	One Is a Lonesome Number	1963	7.50	15.00	30.00
❏ R-52105 [M]	New Kind of Love	1964	6.25	12.50	25.00
❏ SR-52105 [S]	New Kind of Love	1964	7.50	15.00	30.00
SAVOY					
❏ MG-12216 [M]	Joe Williams Sings	196?	3.75	7.50	15.00
-- Reissue of Regent LP					
SAVOY JAZZ					
❏ SJL-1140	Everyday I Have the Blues	198?	2.50	5.00	10.00
SHEBA					
❏ 102	Heart and Soul	197?	3.00	6.00	12.00
SOLID STATE					
❏ SM-17008 [M]	Presenting Joe Williams and the Jazz Orchestra	1967	6.25	12.50	25.00
❏ SS-18008 [S]	Presenting Joe Williams and the Jazz Orchestra	1967	5.00	10.00	20.00
❏ SS-18015 [S]	Something Old, New and Blue	1968	5.00	10.00	20.00
TEMPONIC					
❏ 29561	With Love	197?	3.75	7.50	15.00
VERVE					
❏ 833 236-1	Every Night	1987	2.50	5.00	10.00
❏ 837 932-1	In Good Company	1989	3.00	6.00	12.00

WILLIAMS, JOHN
Bass player.

Number	Title	Yr	VG	VG+	NM
EMARCY					
❏ MG-26047 [10]	John Williams	1955	25.00	50.00	100.00
❏ MG-36061 [M]	John Williams Trio	1956	12.50	25.00	50.00

WILLIAMS, JOHN TOWNER
Pianist, composer and arranger. This is the John Williams who became famous for his film scores and as conductor of the Boston Pops Orchestra.

Number	Title	Yr	VG	VG+	NM
BETHLEHEM					
❏ BCP-6025 [M]	World on a String	1958	12.50	25.00	50.00

WILLIAMS, KEITH
Trumpeter, arranger and bandleader.

Number	Title	Yr	VG	VG+	NM
EDISON INERNATIONAL					
❏ 501 [M]	Big Band Jazz Themes	1960	5.00	10.00	20.00
❏ SDP-501 [S]	Big Band Jazz Themes	1960	6.25	12.50	25.00
LIBERTY					
❏ LRP-3040 [M]	The Dazzling Sound	1957	5.00	10.00	20.00

Number	Title	Yr	VG	VG+	NM

WILLIAMS, MARY LOU
Pianist and composer. Also see BARBARA CARROLL; AL HAIG; ART TATUM.
ASCH
| ❏ ALP-345 [10] | Mary Lou Williams Trio | 1950 | 50.00 | 100.00 | 200.00 |

ATLANTIC
| ❏ ALR-114 [10] | Piano Panorama, Volume 2 | 1951 | 30.00 | 60.00 | 120.00 |

AUDIOPHILE
| ❏ AP-8 | Roll 'Em | 1988 | 2.50 | 5.00 | 10.00 |

CHIAROSCURO
| ❏ 103 | From the Heart | 197? | 3.00 | 6.00 | 12.00 |
| ❏ 146 | Live at the Cookery | 197? | 3.00 | 6.00 | 12.00 |

CIRCLE
| ❏ 412 [10] | Piano Contempo | 1951 | 30.00 | 60.00 | 120.00 |

CONCERT HALL JAZZ
| ❏ 1007 [10] | A Keyboard History | 1955 | 12.50 | 25.00 | 50.00 |

CONTEMPORARY
| ❏ C-2507 [10] | Piano '53 | 1953 | 25.00 | 50.00 | 100.00 |

EMARCY
| ❏ MG-26033 [10] | Mary Lou | 1954 | 25.00 | 50.00 | 100.00 |

FOLKWAYS
❏ FP-32 [10]	Rehearsal -- Jazz Session/Footnotes to Jazz, Vol. 3	1951	25.00	50.00	100.00
❏ FS-2843 [M]	Mary Lou Williams	196?	3.75	7.50	15.00
❏ FS-2860 [M]	History of Jazz	197?	3.00	6.00	12.00
❏ FJ-2966 [(2)]	The Asch Recordings 1944-1947	197?	3.75	7.50	15.00
❏ FS-32843 [R]	Mary Lou Williams	196?	3.00	6.00	12.00
❏ FJ-32844	Zodiac Suite	196?	3.00	6.00	12.00

GNP CRESCENDO
| ❏ GNPS-9029 | Mary Lou Williams in London | 198? | 2.50 | 5.00 | 10.00 |

INNER CITY
| ❏ IC-2043 | Free Spirits | 197? | 3.75 | 7.50 | 15.00 |

JAZZTONE
| ❏ J-1206 [M] | A Keyboard History | 1955 | 10.00 | 20.00 | 40.00 |

KING
| ❏ 295-85 [10] | Progressive Piano Stylings | 1953 | 37.50 | 75.00 | 150.00 |

MARY
| ❏ 101 | Black Christ of the Andes | 197? | 3.75 | 7.50 | 15.00 |
-- Reissue with new number
❏ 102	Mary Lou's Mass	197?	3.75	7.50	15.00
❏ 103	Zoning	1974	3.75	7.50	15.00
❏ 32843 [M]	Black Christ of the Andes	1964	6.25	12.50	25.00
❏ 32843 [S]	Black Christ of the Andes	1964	7.50	15.00	30.00
❏ 282489 [M]	Music for Peace	1964	6.25	12.50	25.00
❏ 282489 [S]	Music for Peace	1964	7.50	15.00	30.00

PABLO
| ❏ 2310 819 | My Mama Pinned a Rose | 1978 | 3.00 | 6.00 | 12.00 |
| ❏ 2405 412 | The Best of Mary Lou Williams | 198? | 2.50 | 5.00 | 10.00 |

PABLO LIVE
| ❏ 2308 218 | Solo Recital/Montreux Jazz Festival 1978 | 1979 | 3.00 | 6.00 | 12.00 |

STEEPLECHASE
| ❏ SCS-1043 | Free Spirits | 198? | 3.00 | 6.00 | 12.00 |

STINSON
❏ SLP-24 [10]	Mary Lou Williams	1950	37.50	75.00	150.00
❏ SLP-24 [M]	Mary Lou Williams	195?	7.50	15.00	30.00
❏ SLP-29 [10]	Jazz Variation	1950	37.50	75.00	150.00

WILLIAMS, MARY LOU/RALPH BURNS
Also see each artist's individual listings.
JAZZTONE
| ❏ J-1255 [M] | Composers -- Pianists | 1956 | 10.00 | 20.00 | 40.00 |

WILLIAMS, MARY LOU, AND DON BYAS
Also see each artist's individual listings.
GNP CRESCENDO
| ❏ GNP-9030 | Mary Lou Williams and Don Byas | 197? | 2.50 | 5.00 | 10.00 |

WILLIAMS, MARY LOU, AND DON BYAS/BUCK CLAYTON AND ALIX COMBELLE
Combelle played tenor saxophone. Also see DON BYAS; BUCK CLAYTON; MARY LOU WILLIAMS.
STORYVILLE
| ❏ STLP-906 [M] | Messin' 'Round in Montmarte | 1956 | 12.50 | 25.00 | 50.00 |

WILLIAMS, MARY LOU/JUTTA HIPP
Also see each artist's individual listings.
SAVOY JAZZ
| ❏ SJL-1202 | First Ladies of Jazz | 1990 | 3.00 | 6.00 | 12.00 |

WILLIAMS, MARY LOU, AND CECIL TAYLOR
Also see each artist's individual listings.
PABLO LIVE
| ❏ 2620 108 [(2)] | Embraced | 1978 | 3.75 | 7.50 | 15.00 |

WILLIAMS, NORMAN
Alto saxophone player. Known as "Bishop."
THERESA
❏ 101	The Bishop	1979	3.00	6.00	12.00
❏ 102	The Bishop's Bag	1979	3.00	6.00	12.00
❏ 105	One for Bird	1980	3.00	6.00	12.00

WILLIAMS, PATRICK
Composer, arranger and conductor.
ALLEGIANCE
| ❏ AV-443 | Dreams and Themes | 1985 | 2.50 | 5.00 | 10.00 |
-- Reissue of PCM album
CAPITOL
| ❏ ST-11242 | Threshold | 1974 | 2.50 | 5.00 | 10.00 |

COLUMBIA
| ❏ JC 36318 | An American Concerto | 1979 | 2.50 | 5.00 | 10.00 |

PAUSA
| ❏ 7060 | Theme | 1980 | 2.50 | 5.00 | 10.00 |

PCM
| ❏ PAA 1001 | Dreams and Themes | 1984 | 3.00 | 6.00 | 12.00 |

SOUNDWINGS
| ❏ SW-2103 | 10th Avenue | 1987 | 2.50 | 5.00 | 10.00 |
| ❏ SW-2107 | Threshold | 1988 | 2.50 | 5.00 | 10.00 |

WILLIAMS, RICHARD
Trumpeter, fluegel horn player and composer.
BARNABY
| ❏ BR-5014 | New Horn in Town | 197? | 2.50 | 5.00 | 10.00 |

CANDID
| ❏ CD-8003 [M] | New Horn in Town | 1960 | 10.00 | 20.00 | 40.00 |
| ❏ CS-9003 [S] | New Horn in Town | 1960 | 12.50 | 25.00 | 50.00 |

WILLIAMS, ROD
Pianist.
MUSE
| ❏ MR-5380 | Hanging in the Balance | 198? | 2.50 | 5.00 | 10.00 |

WILLIAMS, TONY
Drummer.
BLUE NOTE
❏ BLP-4180 [M]	Life Time	1964	6.25	12.50	25.00
❏ BLP-4216 [M]	Spring	1965	6.25	12.50	25.00
❏ BT-48494	Angel Street	1988	3.00	6.00	12.00
❏ BST-84180 [S]	Life Time	1964	7.50	15.00	30.00
-- With "New York, USA" address on label
| ❏ BST-84180 [S] | Life Time | 1967 | 3.75 | 7.50 | 15.00 |
-- With "A Division of Liberty Records" on label
| ❏ BST-84216 [S] | Spring | 1965 | 7.50 | 15.00 | 30.00 |
-- With "New York, USA" address on label
| ❏ BST-84216 [S] | Spring | 1967 | 3.75 | 7.50 | 15.00 |
-- With "A Division of Liberty Records" on label
| ❏ BST-84216 [S] | Spring | 1985 | 2.50 | 5.00 | 10.00 |
-- "The Finest in Jazz Since 1939" reissue
❏ BT-85119	Foreign Intrigue	198?	3.00	6.00	12.00
❏ BT-85138	Civilization	1987	3.00	6.00	12.00
❏ B1-93170	Native Heart	1990	3.00	6.00	12.00

COLUMBIA
❏ PC 33836	Believe It	1975	2.50	5.00	10.00
❏ PC 34263	Million Dollar Legs	1976	2.50	5.00	10.00
❏ JC 35705	Joy of Flying	1979	2.50	5.00	10.00
❏ JC 36397	The Best of Tony Williams	1980	2.50	5.00	10.00
❏ HC 45705	Joy of Flying	198?	12.50	25.00	50.00
-- Half-speed mastered edition
POLYDOR
❏ 25-3001 [(2)]	Emergency	1969	5.00	10.00	20.00
❏ PD-4017	Emergency, Vol. 1	197?	3.00	6.00	12.00
❏ PD-4021	Turn It Over	197?	3.00	6.00	12.00
❏ PD-4065	Ego	197?	3.00	6.00	12.00
❏ PD-5040	The Old Bums Rush	197?	3.00	6.00	12.00

VERVE
| ❏ VE-2-2541 [(2)] | Once in a Lifetime | 198? | 3.00 | 6.00 | 12.00 |

WILLIAMS, VALDO
Pianist.
SAVOY
| ❏ MG-12188 [M] | New Advanced Jazz | 1967 | 7.50 | 15.00 | 30.00 |

Number	Title	Yr	VG	VG+	NM
WILLIAMSON, CLAUDE					
Pianist.					
BETHLEHEM					
❑ BCP-54 [M]	Claude Williamson	1956	10.00	20.00	40.00
❑ BCP-69 [M]	'Round Midnight	1957	10.00	20.00	40.00
CAPITOL					
❑ H 6502 [10]	Claude Williamson	1954	12.50	25.00	50.00
❑ H 6511 [10]	Keys West	1955	12.50	25.00	50.00
❑ T 6511 [10]	Keys West	1956	10.00	20.00	40.00
CONTRACT					
❑ 15001 [M]	The Fabulous Claude Williamson Trio	196?	7.50	15.00	30.00
❑ 15003 [M]	Theatre Party	196?	7.50	15.00	30.00
CRITERION					
❑ 601 [M]	Claude Williamson Mulls the Mulligan Scene	1958	10.00	20.00	40.00
DISCOVERY					
❑ 862	La Fiesta	198?	2.50	5.00	10.00
INTERPLAY					
❑ 7708	Holography	1977	3.00	6.00	12.00
❑ 7717	New Departure	1978	3.00	6.00	12.00
❑ 7727	La Fiesta	1979	3.00	6.00	12.00
WILLIAMSON, STU					
Trumpeter and valve trombonist.					
BETHLEHEM					
❑ BCP-31 [M]	Stu Williamson Plays	1955	20.00	40.00	80.00
❑ BCP-55 [M]	Stu Williamson	1956	20.00	40.00	80.00
❑ BCP-1024 [10]	Stu Williamson Plays	1955	30.00	60.00	120.00
WILLIS, LARRY					
Pianist.					
GROOVE MERCHANT					
❑ 514	Inner Crisis	197?	3.75	7.50	15.00
WILLIS, PETE					
CIRCLE					
❑ C-45	The One and Only Pete Willis	1982	2.50	5.00	10.00
PROGRESSIVE					
❑ PRO-7013	The One and Only Pete Willis	198?	2.50	5.00	10.00
WILSON, CASSANDRA					
Female singer and composer.					
JMT					
❑ 834 404-1	Point of View	1987	2.50	5.00	10.00
❑ 834 412-1	Days Aweigh	1987	2.50	5.00	10.00
❑ 834 419-1	Blue Skies	1988	2.50	5.00	10.00
❑ 860 004-1	Point of View	1986	3.75	7.50	15.00
-- Original edition					
WILSON, CLIVE					
Trumpeter.					
NEW ORLEANS					
❑ NOR-7210	Clive Wilson Plays New Orleans Jazz	1986	2.50	5.00	10.00
WILSON, GERALD					
Trumpeter, composer and arranger.					
AUDIO LAB					
❑ AL-1538 [M]	Big Band Modern	1959	37.50	75.00	150.00
DISCOVERY					
❑ 833	Lomelin	1981	2.50	5.00	10.00
❑ 872	Corcovado	1983	2.50	5.00	10.00
FEDERAL					
❑ 295-93 [10]	Gerald Wilson	1953	75.00	150.00	300.00
PACIFIC JAZZ					
❑ PJ-34 [M]	You Better Believe It	1961	6.25	12.50	25.00
❑ ST-34 [S]	You Better Believe It	1961	7.50	15.00	30.00
❑ PJ-61 [M]	Moment of Truth	1962	6.25	12.50	25.00
❑ ST-61 [S]	Moment of Truth	1962	7.50	15.00	30.00
❑ PJ-80 [M]	Portraits	1964	6.25	12.50	25.00
❑ ST-80 [S]	Portraits	1964	7.50	15.00	30.00
❑ PJ-88 [M]	Gerald Wilson on Stage	1964	6.25	12.50	25.00
❑ ST-88 [S]	Gerald Wilson on Stage	1964	7.50	15.00	30.00
❑ PJ-LA889-H	The Best of the Gerald Wilson Orchestra	1978	2.50	5.00	10.00
❑ LN-10097	You Better Believe It	1981	2.00	4.00	8.00
-- Budget-line reissue					
❑ LN-10098	Moment of Truth	1981	2.00	4.00	8.00
-- Budget-line reissue					
❑ PJ-10099 [M]	Feelin' Kinda Blue	1964	3.75	7.50	15.00
❑ LN-10100	Gerald Wilson on Stage	1981	2.00	4.00	8.00
-- Budget-line reissue					
❑ LN-10101	Feelin' Kinda Blue	1981	2.00	4.00	8.00
-- Budget-line reissue					
❑ PJ-10111 [M]	Golden Sword	1966	3.75	7.50	15.00
❑ PJ-10118 [M]	Live and Swinging	1967	5.00	10.00	20.00
❑ ST-20099 [S]	Feelin' Kinda Blue	1966	5.00	10.00	20.00
❑ ST-20111 [S]	Golden Sword	1966	5.00	10.00	20.00
❑ ST-20118 [S]	Live and Swinging	1967	3.75	7.50	15.00
❑ ST-20132 [S]	Everywhere	1968	3.75	7.50	15.00
❑ ST-20135 [S]	California Soul	1969	3.75	7.50	15.00
❑ ST-20160 [S]	Eternal Equinox	1969	3.75	7.50	15.00
❑ ST-20174	The Best of Gerald Wilson	1970	3.75	7.50	15.00
TREND					
❑ TR-537	Calafia	1985	3.00	6.00	12.00
WILSON, GLENN					
Baritone saxophone player.					
CADENCE JAZZ					
❑ CJR-1023	Impasse	198?	2.50	5.00	10.00
SUNNYSIDE					
❑ SSC-1030	Elusive	1988	2.50	5.00	10.00
WILSON, JACK					
Pianist.					
ATLANTIC					
❑ 1406 [M]	Jack Wilson Quartet	1963	7.50	15.00	30.00
❑ SD 1406 [S]	Jack Wilson Quartet	1963	10.00	20.00	40.00
❑ 1427 [M]	The Two Sides of Jack Wilson	1964	7.50	15.00	30.00
❑ SD 1427 [S]	The Two Sides of Jack Wilson	1964	10.00	20.00	40.00
BLUE NOTE					
❑ BLP-4251 [M]	Something Personal	1967	10.00	20.00	40.00
❑ BST-84251 [S]	Something Personal	1967	5.00	10.00	20.00
-- With "A Division of Liberty Records" on label					
❑ BST-84251 [S]	Something Personal	1967	7.50	15.00	30.00
-- With "New York, USA" address on label					
❑ BST-84270 [S]	Easterly Winds	1968	5.00	10.00	20.00
-- With "A Division of Liberty Records" on label					
❑ BST-84328 [S]	Song for My Daughter	1969	5.00	10.00	20.00
-- With "A Division of Liberty Records" on label					
DISCOVERY					
❑ 777	Innovations	1977	3.00	6.00	12.00
❑ 805	Margo's Theme	1979	3.00	6.00	12.00
❑ 872	Corcovado	198?	2.50	5.00	10.00
VAULT					
❑ LP-9001 [M]	Brazilian Mancini	1964	6.25	12.50	25.00
❑ LPS-9001 [S]	Brazilian Mancini	1964	7.50	15.00	30.00
❑ LP-9002 [M]	Ramblin'	1964	6.25	12.50	25.00
❑ LPS-9002 [S]	Ramblin'	1964	7.50	15.00	30.00
❑ LP-9008 [M]	Jazz Organs	1965	6.25	12.50	25.00
❑ LPS-9008 [S]	Jazz Organs	1965	7.50	15.00	30.00
WILSON, JOE LEE					
Male singer.					
INNER CITY					
❑ IC-1042	Secrets from the Sun	197?	3.00	6.00	12.00
❑ IC-1064	Without a Song	197?	3.00	6.00	12.00
OBLIVION					
❑ 5	Livin' High Off Nickels and Dimes	197?	3.75	7.50	15.00
SURVIVAL					
❑ 110	What Would It Be	1975	3.00	6.00	12.00
WILSON, LESETTE					
HEADFIRST					
❑ 9708	Now That I've Got Your Attention	198?	3.00	6.00	12.00
WILSON, MARIE					
STASH					
❑ ST-250	I Thought About You	1985	2.50	5.00	10.00
WILSON, NANCY					
Female singer.					
CAPITOL					
❑ ST-148	Nancy	1969	3.75	7.50	15.00
❑ ST-234	Son of a Preacher Man	1969	3.75	7.50	15.00
❑ SWBB-256 [(2)]	Close-Up	1969	5.00	10.00	20.00
-- Combines 1828 and 1934 into one package					
❑ ST-353	Hurt So Bad	1969	3.75	7.50	15.00
❑ ST-429	Can't Take My Eyes Off You	1970	3.75	7.50	15.00
❑ ST-541	Now I'm a Woman	1970	3.75	7.50	15.00
❑ STBB-727 [(2)]	For Once in My Life/Who Can I Turn To	1971	5.00	10.00	20.00

Number	Title	Yr	VG	VG+	NM
❏ ST-763	The Right to Love	1971	3.75	7.50	15.00
-- Retitled reissue of 2757					
❏ SM-798	But Beautiful	197?	2.50	5.00	10.00
-- Reissue					
❏ ST-798	But Beautiful	1971	3.75	7.50	15.00
❏ ST-842	Kaleidoscope	1971	3.75	7.50	15.00
❏ ST 1319 [S]	Like in Love	1960	7.50	15.00	30.00
-- Black label with colorband, Capitol logo on left					
❏ ST 1319 [S]	Like in Love	1960	5.00	10.00	20.00
-- Black label with colorband, Capitol logo on top					
❏ T 1319 [M]	Like in Love	1960	6.25	12.50	25.00
-- Black label with colorband, Capitol logo on left					
❏ T 1319 [M]	Like in Love	1960	3.75	7.50	15.00
-- Black label with colorband, Capitol logo on top					
❏ ST 1440 [S]	Something Wonderful	1960	7.50	15.00	30.00
-- Black label with colorband, Capitol logo on left					
❏ ST 1440 [S]	Something Wonderful	1960	5.00	10.00	20.00
-- Black label with colorband, Capitol logo on top					
❏ T 1440 [M]	Something Wonderful	1960	6.25	12.50	25.00
-- Black label with colorband, Capitol logo on left					
❏ T 1440 [M]	Something Wonderful	1960	3.75	7.50	15.00
-- Black label with colorband, Capitol logo on top					
❏ ST 1524 [S]	The Swingin's Mutual	1961	7.50	15.00	30.00
-- Black label with colorband, Capitol logo on left					
❏ ST 1524 [S]	The Swingin's Mutual	1961	5.00	10.00	20.00
-- Black label with colorband, Capitol logo on top					
❏ T 1524 [M]	The Swingin's Mutual	1961	3.75	7.50	15.00
-- Black label with colorband, Capitol logo on top					
❏ T 1524 [M]	The Swingin's Mutual	1961	6.25	12.50	25.00
-- Black label with colorband, Capitol logo on left					
❏ ST 1767 [S]	Hello Young Lovers	1962	6.25	12.50	25.00
❏ T 1767 [M]	Hello Young Lovers	1962	5.00	10.00	20.00
❏ SM-1828	Broadway My Way	197?	2.50	5.00	10.00
-- Reissue					
❏ ST 1828 [S]	Broadway My Way	1963	5.00	10.00	20.00
❏ T 1828 [M]	Broadway My Way	1963	3.75	7.50	15.00
❏ SM-1934	Hollywood My Way	197?	2.50	5.00	10.00
-- Reissue					
❏ ST 1934 [S]	Hollywood My Way	1963	5.00	10.00	20.00
❏ T 1934 [M]	Hollywood My Way	1963	3.75	7.50	15.00
❏ ST 2012 [S]	Yesterday's Love Songs/Today's Blues	1964	5.00	10.00	20.00
❏ T 2012 [M]	Yesterday's Love Songs/Today's Blues	1964	3.75	7.50	15.00
❏ ST 2082 [S]	Today, Tomorrow, Forever	1964	5.00	10.00	20.00
❏ T 2082 [M]	Today, Tomorrow, Forever	1964	3.75	7.50	15.00
❏ KAO 2136 [M]	The Nancy Wilson Show!	1965	3.75	7.50	15.00
❏ SKAO 2136 [S]	The Nancy Wilson Show!	1965	5.00	10.00	20.00
❏ ST 2155 [S]	How Glad I Am	1964	5.00	10.00	20.00
❏ T 2155 [M]	How Glad I Am	1964	3.75	7.50	15.00
❏ ST 2321 [S]	Today -- My Way	1965	5.00	10.00	20.00
❏ T 2321 [M]	Today -- My Way	1965	3.75	7.50	15.00
❏ ST 2351 [S]	Gentle Is My Love	1965	5.00	10.00	20.00
❏ T 2351 [M]	Gentle Is My Love	1965	3.75	7.50	15.00
❏ ST 2433 [S]	From Broadway with Love	1966	5.00	10.00	20.00
❏ T 2433 [M]	From Broadway with Love	1966	3.75	7.50	15.00
❏ SM-2495	A Touch of Today	197?	2.50	5.00	10.00
-- Reissue					
❏ ST 2495 [S]	A Touch of Today	1966	5.00	10.00	20.00
❏ T 2495 [M]	A Touch of Today	1966	3.75	7.50	15.00
❏ ST 2555 [S]	Tender Loving Care	1966	5.00	10.00	20.00
❏ T 2555 [M]	Tender Loving Care	1966	3.75	7.50	15.00
❏ ST 2634 [S]	Nancy -- Naturally	1967	5.00	10.00	20.00
❏ T 2634 [M]	Nancy -- Naturally	1967	3.75	7.50	15.00
❏ ST 2712 [S]	Just for Now	1967	5.00	10.00	20.00
❏ T 2712 [M]	Just for Now	1967	3.75	7.50	15.00
❏ ST 2757 [S]	Lush Life	1967	3.75	7.50	15.00
❏ T 2757 [M]	Lush Life	1967	5.00	10.00	20.00
❏ ST 2844 [S]	Welcome to My Love	1968	3.75	7.50	15.00
❏ T 2844 [M]	Welcome to My Love	1968	6.25	12.50	25.00
❏ ST 2909	Easy	1968	3.75	7.50	15.00
❏ SKAO 2947	The Best of Nancy Wilson	1968	3.75	7.50	15.00
❏ ST 2970	The Sound of Nancy Wilson	1968	3.75	7.50	15.00
❏ SY-4575	Broadway My Way	197?	2.50	5.00	10.00
-- Odd reissue					
❏ ST-11131	I Know I Love Him	1972	3.00	6.00	12.00
❏ ST-11317	All in Love Is Fair	1974	3.00	6.00	12.00
❏ ST-11386	Come Get to This	1975	3.00	6.00	12.00
❏ ST-11518	This Mother's Daughter	1976	3.00	6.00	12.00
❏ ST-11659	I've Never Been to Me	1977	3.00	6.00	12.00
❏ SM-11767	How Glad I Am	1978	2.50	5.00	10.00
-- Reissue of 2155					
❏ SMAS-11786	Music on My Mind	1978	3.00	6.00	12.00
❏ SM-11802	Easy	1978	2.50	5.00	10.00
-- Reissue of 2909					
❏ SM-11819	Come Get to This	1978	2.50	5.00	10.00
-- Reissue of 11386					
❏ SM-11884	Nancy -- Naturally	1979	2.50	5.00	10.00
-- Reissue of 2634					
❏ ST-11943	Life, Love and Happiness	1979	3.00	6.00	12.00

Number	Title	Yr	VG	VG+	NM
❏ SM-12031	Can't Take My Eyes Off You	1980	2.50	5.00	10.00
-- Reissue of 429					
❏ ST-12055	Take My Love	1980	3.00	6.00	12.00
❏ SN-16198	The Best of Nancy Wilson	198?	2.00	4.00	8.00
-- Budget-line reissue					
COLUMBIA					
❏ FC 40330	Keep You Satisfied	1986	2.50	5.00	10.00
❏ FC 40787	Forbidden Lover	1987	2.50	5.00	10.00
❏ FC 44464	Nancy Now!	1989	2.50	5.00	10.00
PAUSA					
❏ PR-9041	Nancy -- Naturally	1985	2.50	5.00	10.00
PICKWICK					
❏ SPC-3273	Goin' Out of My Head	197?	2.50	5.00	10.00
❏ SPC-3348	The Good Life	197?	2.50	5.00	10.00

WILSON, NANCY, AND CANNONBALL ADDERLEY

Also see each artist's individual listings.

Number	Title	Yr	VG	VG+	NM
CAPITOL					
❏ SM-1657	Nancy Wilson/Cannonball Adderley	197?	2.50	5.00	10.00
-- Reissue					
❏ ST 1657 [S]	Nancy Wilson/Cannonball Adderley	1962	7.50	15.00	30.00
-- Black label with colorband, Capitol logo on left					
❏ ST 1657 [S]	Nancy Wilson/Cannonball Adderley	1962	5.00	10.00	20.00
-- Black label with colorband, Capitol logo on top					
❏ T 1657 [M]	Nancy Wilson/Cannonball Adderley	1962	3.75	7.50	15.00
-- Black label with colorband, Capitol logo on top					
❏ T 1657 [M]	Nancy Wilson/Cannonball Adderley	1962	6.25	12.50	25.00
-- Black label with colorband, Capitol logo on left					

WILSON, PHIL

Trombonist.

Number	Title	Yr	VG	VG+	NM
FAMOUS DOOR					
❏ HL-109	That's All	197?	3.00	6.00	12.00
❏ HL-133	Boston-New York Axis	1980	3.00	6.00	12.00
OUTRAGEOUS					
❏ 1	Getting It All Together	197?	3.75	7.50	15.00

WILSON, PHIL, AND RICH MATTESON

Matteson plays valve trombone. Also see PHIL WILSON.

Number	Title	Yr	VG	VG+	NM
ASI					
❏ 203	Sound of Wasp	197?	3.00	6.00	12.00
❏ 5000	Sound of Wasp	197?	2.50	5.00	10.00
-- Reissue of 203					

WILSON, PHILLIP

Drummer and percussionist.

Number	Title	Yr	VG	VG+	NM
HAT HUT					
❏ Q	Esoteric	197?	3.75	7.50	15.00

WILSON, REG

Number	Title	Yr	VG	VG+	NM
HERALD					
❏ HLP-0104 [M]	All By Himself	1956	12.50	25.00	50.00

WILSON, REUBEN

Organist and composer.

Number	Title	Yr	VG	VG+	NM
BLUE NOTE					
❏ BST-84295	On Broadway	1968	6.25	12.50	25.00
-- With "A Division of Liberty Records" on label					
❏ BST-84317	Love Bug	1969	6.25	12.50	25.00
-- With "A Division of Liberty Records" on label					
❏ BST-84343	Blue Mode	1970	6.25	12.50	25.00
❏ BST-84365	Groovy Situation	1971	6.25	12.50	25.00
❏ BST-84377	Set Us Free	1972	6.25	12.50	25.00
CADET					
❏ CA-60033	Got to Get Your Own	1975	3.75	7.50	15.00
GROOVE MERCHANT					
❏ 511	Sweet Life	1973	5.00	10.00	20.00
❏ 523	The Cisco Kid	1974	3.75	7.50	15.00
❏ 4404 [(2)]	Bad Stuff	197?	5.00	10.00	20.00

WILSON, TEDDY

Pianist.

Number	Title	Yr	VG	VG+	NM
ALLEGRO					
❏ 4024 [10]	All Star Sextet	1954	25.00	50.00	100.00
❏ 4031 [10]	All Star Sextet	1954	25.00	50.00	100.00
BLACK LION					
❏ 177	Moonglow	197?	3.00	6.00	12.00
❏ 209	Runnin' Wild Montreux	197?	3.00	6.00	12.00

Number	Title	Yr	VG	VG+	NM
❏ 308	Striding After Fats	197?	3.00	6.00	12.00
CAMEO					
❏ C-1059 [M]	Teddy Wilson 1964	1964	7.50	15.00	30.00
❏ CS-1059 [S]	Teddy Wilson 1964	1964	7.50	15.00	30.00
CHIAROSCURO					
❏ 111	With Billie in Mind	1973	3.00	6.00	12.00
❏ 150	Teddy Wilson and the All-Stars	197?	3.00	6.00	12.00
❏ 168	Teddy Martin Revamps Rodgers and Hart	197?	3.00	6.00	12.00
CLASSIC JAZZ					
❏ 32	Live at Santa Tecia	1976	2.50	5.00	10.00
❏ 101	Three Little Words	197?	2.50	5.00	10.00
CLEF					
❏ MGC-140 [10]	The Didactic Mr. Wilson	1953	30.00	60.00	120.00
❏ MGC-156 [10]	Soft Moods with Teddy Wilson	1954	30.00	60.00	120.00
COLUMBIA					
❏ CL 748 [M]	Mr. Wilson	1956	15.00	30.00	60.00
❏ CL 1318 [M]	Mr. Wilson and Mr. Gershwin	1959	10.00	20.00	40.00
❏ CL 1352 [M]	Gypsy	1959	7.50	15.00	30.00
❏ CL 1442 [M]	And Then They Wrote	1960	7.50	15.00	30.00
❏ CL 6040 [10]	Teddy Wilson Featuring Billie Holiday	1949	100.00	200.00	400.00
❏ CL 6098 [10]	Teddy Wilson and His Piano	1950	62.50	125.00	250.00
❏ CL 6153 [10]	Piano Moods	1950	30.00	60.00	120.00
❏ CS 8160 [S]	Gypsy	1959	10.00	20.00	40.00
❏ CS 8242 [S]	And Then They Wrote	1960	10.00	20.00	40.00
❏ CG 31617 [(2)]	Teddy Wilson and His All-Stars	1972	3.75	7.50	15.00
COMMODORE					
❏ FL-20029 [10]	Town Hall Concert	1952	50.00	100.00	200.00
DIAL					
❏ LP-213 [10]	Teddy Wilson All Stars	1950	75.00	150.00	300.00
GNP CRESCENDO					
❏ GNP-9014	Teddy Wilson	197?	2.50	5.00	10.00
JAZZ ARCHIVES					
❏ JA-28	Teddy Wilson Sextet 1944, Vol. 1	198?	2.50	5.00	10.00
❏ JA-36	Teddy Wilson Sextet 1944, Vol. 2	198?	2.50	5.00	10.00
JAZZOLOGY					
❏ J-86	Teddy's Choice	198?	2.50	5.00	10.00
MERCURY					
❏ MG-25172 [10]	Piano Pastries	1953	30.00	60.00	120.00
MGM					
❏ E-129 [10]	Runnin' Wild	1951	50.00	100.00	200.00
MOSAIC					
❏ MQ8-173 [(8)]	The Complete Verve Recordings of the Teddy Wilson Trio	199?	37.50	75.00	150.00
MUSICRAFT					
❏ 502	Teddy Wilson and His All Stars, Vol. 1	198?	2.50	5.00	10.00
❏ 2007	As Time Goes By	1986	2.50	5.00	10.00
❏ 2008	Sunny Morning	1986	2.50	5.00	10.00
NORGRAN					
❏ MGN-1019 [M]	The Creative Teddy Wilson	1955	25.00	50.00	100.00
PRESTIGE					
❏ PRST-7696 [S]	The Teddy Wilson Trio in Europe	1969	3.75	7.50	15.00
QUICKSILVER					
❏ QS-9002	Into the Sky	198?	2.50	5.00	10.00
ROYALE					
❏ 18169 [10]	Teddy Wilson and His All Stars	195?	25.00	50.00	100.00
SACKVILLE					
❏ 2005	Teddy Wilson in Tokyo	198?	2.50	5.00	10.00
STORYVILLE					
❏ 4046	Teddy Wilson Revisits the Goodman Years	198?	2.50	5.00	10.00
VERVE					
❏ MGV-2011 [M]	Intimate Listening	1956	12.50	25.00	50.00
❏ V-2011 [M]	Intimate Listening	1961	5.00	10.00	20.00
❏ MGV-2029 [M]	For Quiet Lovers	1956	15.00	30.00	60.00
❏ V-2029 [M]	For Quiet Lovers	1961	6.25	12.50	25.00
❏ MGV-2073 [M]	I Got Rhythm	1957	12.50	25.00	50.00
❏ V-2073 [M]	I Got Rhythm	1961	5.00	10.00	20.00
❏ MGV-8272 [M]	The Impeccable Mr. Teddy Wilson	1958	12.50	25.00	50.00
❏ V-8272 [M]	The Impeccable Mr. Teddy Wilson	1961	5.00	10.00	20.00
❏ MGV-8299 [M]	These Tunes Remind Me of You	1959	12.50	25.00	50.00
❏ V-8299 [M]	These Tunes Remind Me of You	1961	5.00	10.00	20.00
❏ MGV-8330 [M]	The Touch of Teddy Wilson	1959	12.50	25.00	50.00
❏ V-8330 [M]	The Touch of Teddy Wilson	1961	5.00	10.00	20.00

Number	Title	Yr	VG	VG+	NM
WHO'S WHO IN JAZZ					
❏ 21009	Lionel Hampton Presents Teddy Wilson	1979	2.50	5.00	10.00

WILSON, TEDDY, AND MARIAN McPARTLAND
Also see each artist's individual listings.

Number	Title	Yr	VG	VG+	NM
HALCYON					
❏ 106	Elegant Piano	197?	3.00	6.00	12.00

WILSON, TEDDY/GERRY MULLIGAN
Also see each artist's individual listings.

Number	Title	Yr	VG	VG+	NM
VERVE					
❏ UMV-2622 [M]	The Teddy Wilson Trio and the Gerry Mulligan Quartet at Newport	198?	3.00	6.00	12.00
❏ MGV-8235 [M]	The Teddy Wilson Trio and the Gerry Mulligan Quartet at Newport	1958	12.50	25.00	50.00
❏ V-8235 [M]	The Teddy Wilson Trio and the Gerry Mulligan Quartet at Newport	1961	5.00	10.00	20.00
❏ V6-8827	Newport Years	197?	3.00	6.00	12.00

WINCHESTER, LEM
Vibraphone player. Also see RANDY WESTON.

Number	Title	Yr	VG	VG+	NM
ARGO					
❏ LP-642 [M]	Lem Winchester with the Ramsey Lewis Trio	1959	12.50	25.00	50.00
❏ LPS-642 [S]	Lem Winchester with the Ramsey Lewis Trio	1959	10.00	20.00	40.00
FANTASY					
❏ OJC-1719	Winchester Special	198?	2.50	5.00	10.00
MGM					
❏ E-1005 [M]	New Faces at Newport	1960	10.00	20.00	40.00
MOODSVILLE					
❏ MVLP-11 [M]	Lem Winchester with Feeling	1960	12.50	25.00	50.00
-- Green label					
❏ MVLP-11 [M]	Lem Winchester with Feeling	1965	6.25	12.50	25.00
-- Blue label, trident logo at right					
NEW JAZZ					
❏ NJLP-8223 [M]	Winchester Special	1959	20.00	40.00	80.00
-- Purple label					
❏ NJLP-8223 [M]	Winchester Special	1965	6.25	12.50	25.00
-- Blue label, trident logo at right					
❏ NJLP-8239 [M]	Lem's Beat	1960	12.50	25.00	50.00
-- Purple label					
❏ NJLP-8239 [M]	Lem's Beat	1965	6.25	12.50	25.00
-- Blue label, trident logo at right					
❏ NJLP-8244 [M]	Another Opus	1960	12.50	25.00	50.00
-- Purple label					
❏ NJLP-8244 [M]	Another Opus	1965	6.25	12.50	25.00
-- Blue label, trident logo at right					

WIND CHILL FACTOR

Number	Title	Yr	VG	VG+	NM
QCA					
❏ 372	City Streets	1978	3.00	6.00	12.00

WINDHURST, JOHNNY
Trumpeter.

Number	Title	Yr	VG	VG+	NM
JAZZOLOGY					
❏ J-3	The Imaginative Johnny Windhurst	1963	3.75	7.50	15.00
TRANSITION					
❏ TRLP-2 [M]	Jazz at Columbus Ave.	1956	50.00	100.00	200.00
-- Deduct 1/4 if booklet is missing					

WINDING, KAI
Trombonist and composer. Best known for his hit instrumental recording of "More (Theme from Mondo Cane)." Also see STAN GETZ; J.J. JOHNSON; GERRY MULLIGAN; FATS NAVARRO.

Number	Title	Yr	VG	VG+	NM
A&M					
❏ SP-3008	Israel	1969	3.00	6.00	12.00
ABC IMPULSE!					
❏ AS 3 [S]	The Incredible Kai Winding Trombones	1968	3.00	6.00	12.00
-- Black and red label					
COLUMBIA					
❏ CL 936 [M]	Trombone Sound	1956	12.50	25.00	50.00
❏ CL 999 [M]	Trombone Panorama	1957	12.50	25.00	50.00
❏ CL 1264 [M]	Swingin' State	1958	12.50	25.00	50.00
❏ CL 1329 [M]	Dance to the City Beat	1959	10.00	20.00	40.00
❏ CS 8062 [S]	Swingin' State	1958	10.00	20.00	40.00
❏ CS 8136 [S]	Dance to the City Beat	1959	7.50	15.00	30.00
GATEWAY					
❏ 7022	Jazz Showcase	1979	2.50	5.00	10.00

Number	Title	Yr	VG	VG+	NM
GLENDALE					
❏ 6003	Danish Blue	1976	2.50	5.00	10.00
❏ 6004	Caravan	1977	2.50	5.00	10.00
HARMONY					
❏ HL 7341 [M]	The Great Kai Winding Sound	1962	3.75	7.50	15.00
IMPULSE!					
❏ A 3 [M]	The Incredible Kai Winding Trombones	1960	7.50	15.00	30.00
❏ AS 3 [S]	The Incredible Kai Winding Trombones	1960	6.25	12.50	25.00
-- Orange and black label					
MCA					
❏ 29062	Incredible Kai Winding Trombones	198?	2.50	5.00	10.00
-- Reissue of Impulse! 3					
PICKWICK					
❏ SPC-3004	Trombones	196?	3.00	6.00	12.00
RED RECORD					
❏ VPA-143	Duo Bones	198?	3.00	6.00	12.00
ROOST					
❏ LP 408 [10]	Kai Winding All Stars	1952	30.00	60.00	120.00
SAVOY					
❏ MG-9017 [10]	New Trends of Jazz	1952	30.00	60.00	120.00
❏ MG-12119 [M]	In the Beginning	196?	3.75	7.50	15.00
VERVE					
❏ V-8427 [M]	Kai Ole	1962	6.25	12.50	25.00
❏ V6-8427 [S]	Kai Ole	1962	6.25	12.50	25.00
❏ V-8493 [M]	Suspense Themes in Jazz	1962	6.25	12.50	25.00
❏ V6-8493 [S]	Suspense Themes in Jazz	1962	6.25	12.50	25.00
❏ V-8525 [M]	Kai Winding Solo	1963	6.25	12.50	25.00
❏ V6-8525 [S]	Kai Winding Solo	1963	6.25	12.50	25.00
❏ V-8551 [M]	More!!!	1963	6.25	12.50	25.00
❏ V6-8551 [S]	More!!!	1963	6.25	12.50	25.00
❏ V-8556 [M]	The Lonely One	1963	6.25	12.50	25.00
❏ V6-8556 [S]	The Lonely One	1963	6.25	12.50	25.00
❏ V-8573 [M]	Mondo Cane #2	1964	6.25	12.50	25.00
❏ V6-8573 [S]	Mondo Cane #2	1964	7.50	15.00	30.00
❏ V-8602 [M]	Modern Country	1964	3.75	7.50	15.00
❏ V6-8602 [S]	Modern Country	1964	5.00	10.00	20.00
❏ V-8620 [M]	Rainy Day	1965	3.75	7.50	15.00
❏ V6-8620 [S]	Rainy Day	1965	5.00	10.00	20.00
❏ V-8639 [M]	The "In" Instrumentals	1965	3.75	7.50	15.00
❏ V6-8639 [S]	The "In" Instrumentals	1965	5.00	10.00	20.00
❏ V-8657 [M]	More Brass	1966	3.00	6.00	12.00
❏ V6-8657 [S]	More Brass	1966	3.75	7.50	15.00
❏ V-8661 [M]	Dirty Dog	1966	3.00	6.00	12.00
❏ V6-8661 [S]	Dirty Dog	1966	3.75	7.50	15.00
❏ V-8691 [M]	Penny Lane and Time	1967	3.75	7.50	15.00
❏ V6-8691 [S]	Penny Lane and Time	1967	3.00	6.00	12.00
WHO'S WHO IN JAZZ					
❏ 21001	Lionel Hampton Presents Kai Winding	1978	2.50	5.00	10.00

WINDING, KAI, AND SONNY STITT
Also see each artist's individual listings.

Number	Title	Yr	VG	VG+	NM
HALL OF FAME					
❏ 612	Early Modern	197?	2.50	5.00	10.00

WINDMILL SAXOPHONE QUARTET
Formed by Clayton Englar (saxophonist, flutist, composer, arranger) in 1984. Other members: Jesse Meman, Ken Plant, and Tom Monroe, all of whom play various saxophones plus flutes and clarinets.

Number	Title	Yr	VG	VG+	NM
PATHFINDER					
❏ PTF-8801	Very Scary	1988	2.50	5.00	10.00

WINDOWS
Members: Skipper Wise (bass, guitar); Tim Timmermans (drums, percussion, keyboards); Ed Cohen (acoustic and electric keyboards, percussion); Michael Acosta (tenor and soprano saxes).

Number	Title	Yr	VG	VG+	NM
(LABEL UNKNOWN)					
❏ (# unknown)	Windows	1985	5.00	10.00	20.00
CYPRESS					
❏ YL-0214	The French Laundry	1989	3.00	6.00	12.00
INTIMA					
❏ SJ-73218	Is It Safe	1987	2.50	5.00	10.00
❏ SJ-73219	Windows	1987	2.50	5.00	10.00
-- Reissue of self-titled debut album					
❏ D1-73298	Mr. Bongo	1988	2.50	5.00	10.00

WINDY CITY BANJO BAND, THE

Number	Title	Yr	VG	VG+	NM
PINNACLE					
❏ 107	The Windy City Banjo Band	1963	3.75	7.50	15.00

WINDY CITY SEVEN, THE
See FRED WACKER.

WINKLER, MARK
Male singer and composer.

Number	Title	Yr	VG	VG+	NM
CMG					
❏ CML-7207	Ebony Rain	1988	2.50	5.00	10.00
❏ CML-8021	Hottest Night of the Year	1989	3.00	6.00	12.00

WINSTON, MURIEL
Female singer.

Number	Title	Yr	VG	VG+	NM
STRATA-EAST					
❏ SES-7411	A Fresh Viewpoint	197?	3.75	7.50	15.00

WINSTON, SHERRY
Flutist.

Number	Title	Yr	VG	VG+	NM
HEADFIRST					
❏ 634	Do It for Love	198?	2.50	5.00	10.00
WARLOCK					
❏ WAR-2724	Love Is	1991	3.00	6.00	12.00

WINTER, PAUL
Saxophone player, clarinetist, composer and bandleader – first a sextet, then the Paul Winter Consort. He was an early advocate of "world music," which has since been lumped in with the "new age" movement. Members of the Consort since 1980 are EUGENE FRIESEN (cello); Paul Halley (piano, organ); and Glen Velez (percussion).

Number	Title	Yr	VG	VG+	NM
A&M					
❏ SP-4170	The Winter Consort	1968	3.75	7.50	15.00
❏ SP-4207	Something in the Wind	1969	3.75	7.50	15.00
❏ SP-4279	The Road	1970	3.75	7.50	15.00
❏ SP-4653	Earthdance	1977	3.00	6.00	12.00
❏ SP-4698	Common Ground	1978	3.00	6.00	12.00
COLUMBIA					
❏ CL 1925 [M]	Jazz Meets the Bossa Nova	1962	3.75	7.50	15.00
❏ CL 1997 [M]	Jazz Premiere: Washington	1963	3.75	7.50	15.00
❏ CL 2064 [M]	New Jazz on Campus	1963	3.75	7.50	15.00
❏ CL 2155 [M]	Jazz Meets the Folk Song	1964	3.75	7.50	15.00
❏ CL 2272 [M]	The Sound of Ipanema	1965	3.75	7.50	15.00
❏ CL 2315 [M]	Rio	1965	3.75	7.50	15.00
❏ CS 8725 [S]	Jazz Meets the Bossa Nova	1962	5.00	10.00	20.00
❏ CS 8797 [S]	Jazz Premiere: Washington	1963	5.00	10.00	20.00
❏ CS 8864 [S]	New Jazz on Campus	1963	5.00	10.00	20.00
❏ CS 8955 [S]	Jazz Meets the Folk Song	1964	5.00	10.00	20.00
❏ CS 9072 [S]	The Sound of Ipanema	1965	5.00	10.00	20.00
❏ CS 9115 [S]	Rio	1965	5.00	10.00	20.00
EPIC					
❏ KE 31643	Icarus	1972	3.00	6.00	12.00
❏ PE 31643	Icarus	197?	2.50	5.00	10.00
-- Reissue					
LIVING MUSIC					
❏ LMR-1 [(2)]	Callings	1981	5.00	10.00	20.00
-- With 20-page booklet					
❏ LM-0001 [(2)]	Callings	198?	3.75	7.50	15.00
-- Reissue of LMR-1					
❏ LMR-2 [(2)]	Missa Gaia/Earth Mass	1983	5.00	10.00	20.00
❏ LMR-3	Sun Singer	1984	3.00	6.00	12.00
❏ LM-0003	Sun Singer	198?	2.50	5.00	10.00
-- Reissue of LMR-3					
❏ LMR-4	Icarus	1985	3.00	6.00	12.00
-- Reissue of Epic LP					
❏ LM-0004	Icarus	198?	2.50	5.00	10.00
-- Reissue of LMR-4					
❏ LMR-5	Concert for the Earth Live at the United Nations	1985	3.00	6.00	12.00
❏ LMR-6	Canyon	1986	3.00	6.00	12.00
❏ LM-0012	Wintersong	1986	2.50	5.00	10.00
❏ LM-0015	Earthbeat	1987	2.50	5.00	10.00

WINTER, PAUL, AND PAUL HALLEY
Halley is a pianist and organist. Also see PAUL WINTER.

Number	Title	Yr	VG	VG+	NM
LIVING MUSIC					
❏ LM-0013	Whales Alive!	1987	2.50	5.00	10.00

WINTER, RAYMOND

Number	Title	Yr	VG	VG+	NM
INNER CITY					
❏ IC-1135	Tropic Woods	198?	3.00	6.00	12.00

WINTERS, JERRI
Female singer.

Number	Title	Yr	VG	VG+	NM
BETHLEHEM					
❏ BCP-76 [M]	Somebody Loves Me	1957	12.50	25.00	50.00
FRATERNITY					
❏ F-1001 [M]	Winter's Here	1955	15.00	30.00	60.00

Number	Title	Yr	VG	VG+	NM

WINTERS, PINKY
ARGO
Number	Title	Yr	VG	VG+	NM
❑ LP-604 [M]	Lonely One	1956	10.00	20.00	40.00

CREATIVE
| ❑ LP-604 [M] | Lonely One | 1956 | 15.00 | 30.00 | 60.00 |

WINTERS, SMILEY
Drummer.
ARHOOLIE
| ❑ 8004/5 [(2)] | Smiley Etc. | 1969 | 5.00 | 10.00 | 20.00 |

WISHFUL THINKING
Members: Tim Weston (guitar); David Garibaldi (drums); Chris Boardman (keyboards); Jerry Watts Jr. (bass); Dave Shank (vibes, percussion).
PAUSA
| ❑ 7187 | Wishful Thinking | 1986 | 2.50 | 5.00 | 10.00 |
| ❑ 7205 | Think Again | 1987 | 3.00 | 6.00 | 12.00 |

SOUNDWINGS
| ❑ SW-2109 | Way Down West | 1988 | 2.50 | 5.00 | 10.00 |

WISNER, JIMMY
Pianist.
CHANCELLOR
| ❑ CHJ-5014 [M] | Aper-Sepshun | 1960 | 6.25 | 12.50 | 25.00 |
| ❑ CHJS-5014 [S] | Aper-Sepshun | 1960 | 7.50 | 15.00 | 30.00 |

FELSTED
| ❑ FL-2509 [S] | Blues for Harvey | 1962 | 6.25 | 12.50 | 25.00 |
| ❑ FL-7509 [M] | Blues for Harvey | 1962 | 7.50 | 15.00 | 30.00 |

WITHERSPOON, JIMMY
Male singer. Also see EDDIE "CLEANHEAD" VINSON.
ABC
| ❑ 717 | Handbags and Gladrags | 1970 | 6.25 | 12.50 | 25.00 |

ANALOGUE PRODUCTIONS
| ❑ APR 3008 | Evenin' Blues | 199? | 3.75 | 7.50 | 15.00 |

BLUE NOTE
| ❑ BN-LA534-G | Spoonful | 1976 | 3.00 | 6.00 | 12.00 |

BLUESWAY
❑ BLS-6026	Blues Singer	1969	6.25	12.50	25.00
❑ BLS-6040	Hunh	1970	6.25	12.50	25.00
❑ BLS-6051	The Best of Jimmy Witherspoon	1970	6.25	12.50	25.00

CAPITOL
| ❑ ST-11360 | Love Is a Five Letter Word | 1975 | 3.00 | 6.00 | 12.00 |

CHESS
| ❑ CH-93003 | Spoon So Easy: The Chess Years | 1990 | 3.00 | 6.00 | 12.00 |

CONSTELLATION
| ❑ CM 1422 [M] | Take This Hammer | 1964 | 12.50 | 25.00 | 50.00 |
| ❑ CMS 1422 [R] | Take This Hammer | 1964 | 7.50 | 15.00 | 30.00 |

CROWN
| ❑ CST-215 [R] | Jimmy Witherspoon Sings the Blues | 1961 | 20.00 | 40.00 | 80.00 |
-- Red vinyl
| ❑ CST-215 [R] | Jimmy Witherspoon Sings the Blues | 1961 | 5.00 | 10.00 | 20.00 |
-- Black vinyl
| ❑ CLP-5156 [M] | Jimmy Witherspoon | 1959 | 20.00 | 40.00 | 80.00 |
-- Black label, silver print
| ❑ CLP-5156 [M] | Jimmy Witherspoon | 1961 | 6.25 | 12.50 | 25.00 |
-- Gray label, black print
| ❑ CLP-5192 [M] | Jimmy Witherspoon Sings the Blues | 1959 | 20.00 | 40.00 | 80.00 |
-- Black label, silver print
| ❑ CLP-5192 [M] | Jimmy Witherspoon Sings the Blues | 1961 | 6.25 | 12.50 | 25.00 |
-- Gray label, black print

FANTASY
| ❑ OBC-511 | Evenin' Blues | 1988 | 3.00 | 6.00 | 12.00 |
-- Reissue of Prestige 7300
| ❑ OBC-527 | Baby, Baby, Baby | 1990 | 3.00 | 6.00 | 12.00 |
-- Reissue of Prestige 7290
| ❑ 9660 | Rockin' L.A. | 1989 | 3.00 | 6.00 | 12.00 |
| ❑ 24701 [(2)] | The 'Spoon Concerts | 1972 | 5.00 | 10.00 | 20.00 |

HIFI
❑ R-421 [M]	At the Monterey Jazz Festival	1959	25.00	50.00	100.00
❑ SR-421 [S]	At the Monterey Jazz Festival	1959	15.00	30.00	60.00
❑ R-422 [M]	Feelin' the Spirit	1959	25.00	50.00	100.00
❑ SR-422 [S]	Feelin' the Spirit	1959	15.00	30.00	60.00
❑ R-426 [M]	Jimmy Witherspoon at the Renaissance	1959	25.00	50.00	100.00
❑ SR-426 [S]	Jimmy Witherspoon at the Renaissance	1959	15.00	30.00	60.00

JAZZ MAN
Number	Title	Yr	VG	VG+	NM
❑ 5013	Jimmy Witherspoon Sings the	1980	3.00	6.00	12.00

LAX
| ❑ PW 37115 | Love Is a Five Letter Word | 1981 | 2.50 | 5.00 | 10.00 |
-- Reissue of Capitol LP

MUSE
| ❑ MR-5288 | Jimmy Witherspoon Sings the | 1983 | 2.50 | 5.00 | 10.00 |
| ❑ MR-5327 | Midnight Lady Called the Blues | 1986 | 2.50 | 5.00 | 10.00 |

PRESTIGE
❑ PRLP-7290 [M]	Baby, Baby, Baby	1963	10.00	20.00	40.00
❑ PRST-7290 [S]	Baby, Baby, Baby	1963	10.00	20.00	40.00
❑ PRLP-7300 [M]	Evenin' Blues	1964	10.00	20.00	40.00
❑ PRST-7300 [S]	Evenin' Blues	1964	10.00	20.00	40.00
❑ PRLP-7314 [M]	Blues Around the Clock	1964	10.00	20.00	40.00
❑ PRST-7314 [S]	Blues Around the Clock	1964	10.00	20.00	40.00
❑ PRLP-7327 [M]	Blue Spoon	1964	10.00	20.00	40.00
❑ PRST-7327 [S]	Blue Spoon	1964	10.00	20.00	40.00
❑ PRLP-7356 [M]	Some of My Best Friends Are the Blues	1965	6.25	12.50	25.00
❑ PRST-7356 [S]	Some of My Best Friends Are the Blues	1965	6.25	12.50	25.00
❑ PRLP-7418 [M]	Spoon in London	1966	6.25	12.50	25.00
❑ PRST-7418 [S]	Spoon in London	1966	6.25	12.50	25.00
❑ PRLP-7475 [M]	Blues for Easy Livers	1967	6.25	12.50	25.00
❑ PRST-7475 [S]	Blues for Easy Livers	1967	5.00	10.00	20.00
❑ PRST-7713	The Best of Jimmy Witherspoon	1969	5.00	10.00	20.00
❑ PRST-7855	Mean Old Frisco	1974	3.75	7.50	15.00

RCA VICTOR
| ❑ ANL1-1048 | Goin' to Kansas City Blues | 1976 | 2.50 | 5.00 | 10.00 |
-- Reissue
| ❑ LPM-1639 [M] | Goin' to Kansas City Blues | 1957 | 25.00 | 50.00 | 100.00 |

REPRISE
❑ R-2008 [M]	Spoon	1961	10.00	20.00	40.00
❑ R9-2008 [S]	Spoon	1961	15.00	30.00	60.00
❑ R-6012 [M]	Hey, Mrs. Jones	1961	10.00	20.00	40.00
❑ R9-6012 [S]	Hey, Mrs. Jones	1961	15.00	30.00	60.00
❑ R-6059 [M]	Roots	1962	10.00	20.00	40.00
❑ R9-6059 [S]	Roots	1962	15.00	30.00	60.00

UNITED
| ❑ 7715 | A Spoonful of Blues | 197? | 3.00 | 6.00 | 12.00 |

VERVE
❑ V-5007 [M]	Blue Point of View	1966	5.00	10.00	20.00
❑ V6-5007 [S]	Blue Point of View	1966	6.25	12.50	25.00
❑ V-5030 [M]	Blues Is Now	1967	6.25	12.50	25.00
❑ V6-5030 [S]	Blues Is Now	1967	5.00	10.00	20.00
❑ V-5050 [M]	A Spoonful of Soul	1968	7.50	15.00	30.00
❑ V6-5050 [S]	A Spoonful of Soul	1968	5.00	10.00	20.00

WORLD PACIFIC
| ❑ WP-1267 [M] | Singin' the Blues | 1959 | 25.00 | 50.00 | 100.00 |
| ❑ WP-1402 [M] | There's Good Rockin' Tonight | 1961 | 15.00 | 30.00 | 60.00 |
-- Reissue of 1267

WITHERSPOON, JIMMY, AND RICHARD "GROOVE" HOLMES
Also see each artist's individual listings.
OLYMPIC GOLD MEDAL
| ❑ 7107 | Groovin' and Spoonin' | 1974 | 3.00 | 6.00 | 12.00 |

SURREY
| ❑ S-1106 [M] | Blues for Spoon and Groove | 1965 | 6.25 | 12.50 | 25.00 |
| ❑ SS-1106 [S] | Blues for Spoon and Groove | 1965 | 7.50 | 15.00 | 30.00 |

WITHERSPOON, JIMMY, AND GERRY MULLIGAN
Also see each artist's individual listings.
ARCHIVE OF FOLK AND JAZZ
| ❑ 264 | Jimmy Witherspoon and Gerry Mulligan | 197? | 3.00 | 6.00 | 12.00 |

WITHERSPOON, JIMMY, AND BEN WEBSTER
Also see each artist's individual listings.
VERVE
| ❑ V6-8835 | Previously Unreleased Recordings | 197? | 3.75 | 7.50 | 15.00 |

WITTWER, JOHNNY
Pianist. Also see KID ORY.
STINSON
| ❑ SLP-58 | Piano Rags | 195? | 5.00 | 10.00 | 20.00 |

WOFFORD, MIKE
Pianist.
DISCOVERY
| ❑ 778 | Bird of Paradise | 1977 | 3.00 | 6.00 | 12.00 |

Number	Title	Yr	VG	VG+	NM
❏ 784	Afterthoughts	1978	3.00	6.00	12.00
❏ 808	Mike Wofford Plays Jerome Kern	1979	2.50	5.00	10.00
❏ 816	Mike Wofford Plays Jerome Kern, Volume 2	1980	2.50	5.00	10.00
❏ 827	Mike Wofford Plays Jerome Kern, Volume 3	198?	2.50	5.00	10.00

EPIC

❏ LN 24225 [M]	Strawberry Wine	1967	5.00	10.00	20.00
❏ BN 26225 [S]	Strawberry Wine	1967	3.75	7.50	15.00

FLYING DUTCHMAN

❏ BDL1-1372	Joplin: Interpretations '76	1976	3.00	6.00	12.00

MILESTONE

❏ MPS-9012	Summer Night	1968	5.00	10.00	20.00

TREND

❏ TR-552	Funkalero	1988	2.50	5.00	10.00

WOFSEY, GARY
Trumpet and flugel horn player, sometimes playing both simultaneously! Also a bandleader (The Contemporary Jazz Orchestra).

AMBI

❏ 1519	My Grandfather's Clock	198?	3.00	6.00	12.00
❏ 1520	Mel	198?	3.00	6.00	12.00
❏ 1521	Kef's Pool	198?	3.00	6.00	12.00

WOLFE, NEIL
Pianist.

COLUMBIA

❏ CL 2239	Piano – My Way	1964	3.00	6.00	12.00
❏ CL 2378	Out of This World	1965	3.00	6.00	12.00
❏ CS 9039	Piano – My Way	1964	3.75	7.50	15.00
❏ CS 9178	Out of This World	1965	3.75	7.50	15.00
❏ CS 9600	Piano for Barbra	1968	3.00	6.00	12.00

IMPERIAL

❏ LP-9169	Neil Swings Nicely	1962	3.75	7.50	15.00
❏ LP-9192	One Order of Blues	1962	3.75	7.50	15.00
❏ LP-12084	Neil Swings Nicely	1962	5.00	10.00	20.00
❏ LP-12192	One Order of Blues	1962	5.00	10.00	20.00

WOLFE, NEIL, AND NOAH YOUNG
Also see each artist's individual listings.

WK

❏ 101	I Am Music/I Am Song	197?	3.75	7.50	15.00

WOLFE, STEVE, AND NANCY KING
Wolfe is a tenor saxophone player, pianist, flutist and oboist. King is a female singer.

INNER CITY

❏ IC-1049	First Date	197?	3.00	6.00	12.00

WOLLMAN, TERRY
Guitarist.

NOVA

❏ 8706	Bimini	1987	2.50	5.00	10.00

WOOD, BOOTY
Trombonist.

MASTER JAZZ

❏ 8102	Hang In There	197?	3.75	7.50	15.00

WOOD, JOHN

LOS ANGELES

❏ 1001	Freeway of Love	197?	3.75	7.50	15.00
❏ 1002	Until Goodbye	1976	3.75	7.50	15.00

RANWOOD

❏ RLP-8036	Introducing the John Wood Trio	1969	3.75	7.50	15.00

WOODARD, LYMAN
Keyboard player.

STRATA

❏ 105-75	Saturday Night Special	197?	3.75	7.50	15.00

WOODEN JOE
See WOODEN JOE NICHOLAS.

WOODING, SAM
Pianist and bandleader.

BIOGRAPH

❏ 12026	Chocolate Dandies	197?	2.50	5.00	10.00

WOODS, CHRIS
Alto saxophone player and flutist.

DELMARK

❏ DS-434	Somebody Stole My Blues	197?	3.00	6.00	12.00
❏ DS-437	Modus Operandi	1979	2.50	5.00	10.00

WOODS, JIMMY
Alto and tenor saxophone player.

CAPITOL

❏ ST-654	Essence	1971	3.75	7.50	15.00

CONTEMPORARY

❏ M-3605 [M]	Awakening	1962	6.25	12.50	25.00
❏ M-3612 [M]	Conflict	1963	6.25	12.50	25.00
❏ S-7605 [S]	Awakening	1962	7.50	15.00	30.00
❏ S-7612 [S]	Conflict	1963	7.50	15.00	30.00

WOODS, PHIL
Alto and soprano saxophone player, clarinetist and male singer. Also see THE MANHATTAN JAZZ ALL-STARS; ORCHESTRA USA; JIMMY RANEY.

ABC IMPULSE!

❏ AS-9143 [S]	Greek Cooking	1968	3.75	7.50	15.00

ADELPHI

❏ 5010	More Live	198?	2.50	5.00	10.00

ANTILLES

❏ AN-1006	Birds of a Feather	1982	2.50	5.00	10.00
❏ AN-1013	At the Vanguard	198?	2.50	5.00	10.00

BARNABY

❏ BR-5016	Rights of Swing	197?	2.50	5.00	10.00
-- Reissue					
❏ KZ 31036	Rights of Swing	1972	3.00	6.00	12.00

BLACKHAWK

❏ BKH-50401	Heaven	1986	2.50	5.00	10.00

CANDID

❏ CD-8016 [M]	Rights of Swing	1960	10.00	20.00	40.00
❏ CS-9016 [S]	Rights of Swing	1960	12.50	25.00	50.00

CENTURY

❏ 1050	Songs for Sisyphus	197?	5.00	10.00	20.00

CLEAN CUTS

❏ 702	Phil Woods Quartet, Vol. 1	1979	3.00	6.00	12.00

CONCORD JAZZ

❏ CJ-345	Bop Stew	1988	2.50	5.00	10.00
❏ CJ-361	Evolution	1988	2.50	5.00	10.00
❏ CJ-377	Bouquet	1989	3.00	6.00	12.00

EMBRYO

❏ SD 530	Phil Woods at the Frankfurt Jazz Festival	197?	3.75	7.50	15.00

ENJA

❏ 3081	Three for All	1981	3.00	6.00	12.00

EPIC

❏ LN 3436 [M]	Warm Woods	1958	12.50	25.00	50.00

FANTASY

❏ OJC-052	Woodlore	1982	2.50	5.00	10.00
❏ OJC-092	Paring Off	198?	2.50	5.00	10.00
❏ OJC-1732	The Young Bloods	198?	2.50	5.00	10.00
❏ OJC-1735	Bird Feathers	198?	2.50	5.00	10.00

GRYPHON

❏ 782	Sisyphus	1978	3.00	6.00	12.00
❏ 788	I Remember	1979	3.00	6.00	12.00

IMPULSE!

❏ A-9143 [M]	Greek Cooking	1967	7.50	15.00	30.00
❏ AS-9143 [S]	Greek Cooking	1967	6.25	12.50	25.00

INNER CITY

❏ IC-1002	European Rhythm Machine	197?	3.75	7.50	15.00

JAZZ MAN

❏ 5001	Rights of Swing	1982	2.50	5.00	10.00

MGM

❏ SE-4695	Phil Woods at the Montreux Jazz Festival	197?	3.75	7.50	15.00

MOSAIC

❏ MQ7-159 [(7)]	The Phil Woods Quartet/Quintet 20th Anniversary Set	199?	30.00	60.00	120.00

MUSE

❏ MR-5037	Musique de Bois	1974	3.00	6.00	12.00

NEW JAZZ

❏ NJLP-1104 [10]	Phil Woods New Jazz Quintet	1954	75.00	150.00	300.00
❏ NJLP-8291 [M]	Pot Pie	1962	20.00	40.00	80.00
-- Purple label					
❏ NJLP-8291 [M]	Pot Pie	1965	6.25	12.50	25.00
-- Blue label, trident logo at right					

Number	Title	Yr	VG	VG+	NM
❏ NJLP-8304 [M]	Sugan	1963	---	---	---
-- Canceled, reassigned to Status					
PALO ALTO/TBA					
❏ PA-8084	Live from New York	1985	2.50	5.00	10.00
PRESTIGE					
❏ PRLP-191 [10]	Phil Woods New Jazz Quartet	1954	62.50	125.00	250.00
❏ PRLP-204 [10]	Phil Woods New Jazz Quintet	1955	62.50	125.00	250.00
❏ PRLP-7018 [M]	Woodlore	1956	25.00	50.00	100.00
❏ PRLP-7046 [M]	Paring Off	1956	25.00	50.00	100.00
❏ PRLP-7080 [M]	The Young Bloods	1957	25.00	50.00	100.00
❏ PRST-7673 [R]	Early Quintets	1969	3.75	7.50	15.00
❏ 24065 [(2)]	Altology	197?	3.75	7.50	15.00
QUICKSILVER					
❏ QS-4011	Live from New York	1991	3.00	6.00	12.00
RCA VICTOR					
❏ BGL1-1027	Images	1975	3.00	6.00	12.00
❏ BXL1-1027	Images	1978	2.50	5.00	10.00
-- Reissue with new prefix					
❏ BGL1-1391	The New Album	1976	3.00	6.00	12.00
❏ BXL1-1391	The New Album	1978	2.50	5.00	10.00
-- Reissue with new prefix					
❏ BGL1-1800	Floresta	1976	3.00	6.00	12.00
❏ BXL1-1800	Floresta	1978	2.50	5.00	10.00
-- Reissue with new prefix					
❏ BGL2-2202 [(2)]	Live from the Showboat	1977	3.75	7.50	15.00
RED RECORD					
❏ VPA-163	European Tour Live	198?	3.00	6.00	12.00
❏ VPA-177 [(2)]	Integrity	1985	3.75	7.50	15.00
SAVOY JAZZ					
❏ SJL-1179	Bird Calls: Vol. 1	1987	2.50	5.00	10.00
STATUS					
❏ ST-8304 [M]	Sugan	1965	10.00	20.00	40.00
TESTAMENT					
❏ 4402	New Music	197?	3.75	7.50	15.00
VERVE					
❏ V6-8791	Round Trip	1969	3.75	7.50	15.00

WOODS, PHIL, AND GENE QUILL
Also see each artist's individual listings.

Number	Title	Yr	VG	VG+	NM
COLUMBIA JAZZ ODYSSEY					
❏ PC 36806	Phil Talks with Quill	1980	2.50	5.00	10.00
EPIC					
❏ BN 554 [S]	Phil Talks with Quill	1959	10.00	20.00	40.00
❏ BN 554 [S]	Phil Talks with Quill	199?	6.25	12.50	25.00
-- Classic Records reissue on audiophile vinyl					
❏ LN 3521 [M]	Phil Talks with Quill	1959	12.50	25.00	50.00
FANTASY					
❏ OJC-215	Phil and Quill with Prestige	198?	2.50	5.00	10.00
PRESTIGE					
❏ 2508	Four Altos	198?	3.00	6.00	12.00
❏ PRLP-7115 [M]	Phil and Quill with Prestige	1957	20.00	40.00	80.00
RCA VICTOR					
❏ LPM-1284 [M]	The Woods-Quill Sextet	1956	20.00	40.00	80.00

WOODS, PHIL; GENE QUILL; JACKIE McLEAN; JOHN JENKINS; HAL McKUSICK
Also see each artist's individual listings.

Number	Title	Yr	VG	VG+	NM
NEW JAZZ					
❏ NJLP-8204 [M]	Bird Feathers	1958	25.00	50.00	100.00
-- Yellow label					
❏ NJLP-8204 [M]	Bird Feathers	1959	12.50	25.00	50.00
-- Purple label					
❏ NJLP-8204 [M]	Bird Feathers	1965	6.25	12.50	25.00
-- Blue label, trident logo at right					

WOODS, PHIL, AND CHRIS SWANSON
Swanson is a trombonist. Also see PHIL WOODS.

Number	Title	Yr	VG	VG+	NM
SEA BREEZE					
❏ SB-2008	Crazy Horse	198?	2.50	5.00	10.00
❏ SB-2019	Piper at the Gates of Dawn	1984	2.50	5.00	10.00

WOODS, PHIL, AND LEW TABACKIN
Also see each artist's individual listings.

Number	Title	Yr	VG	VG+	NM
OMNISOUND					
❏ 1033	Phil Woods and Lew Tabackin	198?	2.50	5.00	10.00

WORLD BASS VIOLIN ENSEMBLE
Members: Phil Bowler; Greg Maker; Rufus Reid; Bob Cunningham; Brian Smith; Fred Hopkins.

Number	Title	Yr	VG	VG+	NM
BLACK SAINT					
❏ BSR-0063	Bassically Yours	198?	3.00	6.00	12.00

WORLD RHYTHM BAND

Number	Title	Yr	VG	VG+	NM
DISCOVERY					
❏ 865	Ibex	198?	2.50	5.00	10.00

WORLD SAXOPHONE QUARTET
Members: JULIUS HEMPHILL (soprano, alto, tenor saxes, flute); OLIVER LAKE (soprano, alto, tenor saxes, flute); DAVID MURRAY (tenor sax, bass clarinet); HAMIET BLUIETT (baritone sax, alto clarinet, alto flute).

Number	Title	Yr	VG	VG+	NM
BLACK SAINT					
❏ BSR-0027	Steppin'	198?	3.00	6.00	12.00
❏ BSR-0046	W.S.Q.	198?	3.00	6.00	12.00
❏ BSR-0056	Revue	198?	3.00	6.00	12.00
❏ BSR-0077	Live in Zurich	198?	3.00	6.00	12.00
ELEKTRA/MUSICIAN					
❏ 60864	Rhythm and Blues	1989	3.00	6.00	12.00
ELEKTRA/NONESUCH					
❏ 79137	World Saxophone Quartet Plays Duke Ellington	1987	2.50	5.00	10.00
❏ 79164	Dances and Ballads	1988	2.50	5.00	10.00

WORLD'S GREATEST JAZZ BAND, THE
Continuation of the listings of YANK LAWSON AND BOB HAGGART.

Number	Title	Yr	VG	VG+	NM
ARCHIVE OF FOLK AND JAZZ					
❏ 314	The World's Greatest Jazz Band	197?	2.50	5.00	10.00
FLYING DUTCHMAN					
❏ BDL1-1371	The World's Greatest Jazz Band In Concert	1976	3.00	6.00	12.00
WORLD JAZZ					
❏ 1	Century Plaza	197?	3.00	6.00	12.00
❏ 2	Hark the Herald Angels Swing	197?	3.00	6.00	12.00
❏ 3	The World's Greatest Jazz Band in Concert, Vol. 1	197?	3.00	6.00	12.00
❏ 4	The World's Greatest Jazz Band in Concert, Vol. 2	197?	3.00	6.00	12.00
❏ 6	The World's Greatest Jazz Band Plays Cole Porter	197?	3.00	6.00	12.00
❏ 7	The World's Greatest Jazz Band Plays Rodgers and Hart	197?	3.00	6.00	12.00
❏ 8	The World's Greatest Jazz Band On Tour	197?	3.00	6.00	12.00
❏ 9	The World's Greatest Jazz Band Plays Duke Ellington	197?	3.00	6.00	12.00
❏ 10	The World's Greatest Jazz Band On Tour II	197?	3.00	6.00	12.00
❏ 11	The World's Greatest Jazz Band Plays George Gershwin	1978	3.00	6.00	12.00

WRICE, LARRY "WILD"

Number	Title	Yr	VG	VG+	NM
PACIFIC JAZZ					
❏ PJ-24 [M]	Wild!	1961	6.25	12.50	25.00
❏ ST-24 [S]	Wild!	1961	7.50	15.00	30.00

WRIGHT, BERNARD
Keyboard player and male singer.

Number	Title	Yr	VG	VG+	NM
ARISTA					
❏ ALB8-8103	Funky Beat	198?	2.50	5.00	10.00
GRP/ARISTA					
❏ GL 5011	'Nard	1980	3.00	6.00	12.00
MANHATTAN					
❏ ST-53014	Mr. Wright	1985	2.50	5.00	10.00

WRIGHT, DEMPSEY
Guitarist.

Number	Title	Yr	VG	VG+	NM
ANDEX					
❏ A-3006 [M]	The Wright Approach	1958	15.00	30.00	60.00
❏ AS-3006 [S]	The Wright Approach	1958	12.50	25.00	50.00

WRIGHT, FRANK
Tenor saxophone player.

Number	Title	Yr	VG	VG+	NM
CHIAROSCURO					
❏ 2014	Kevin, My Dear Son	1979	3.00	6.00	12.00
ESP-DISK'					
❏ 1023 [M]	Frank Wright Trio	1966	6.25	12.50	25.00
❏ S-1023 [S]	Frank Wright Trio	1966	5.00	10.00	20.00
❏ 1053 [S]	Your Prayer	1968	5.00	10.00	20.00

WRIGHT, JOHN
Pianist.

Number	Title	Yr	VG	VG+	NM
FANTASY					
❏ OJC-1743	South Side Soul	1990	2.50	5.00	10.00

Number	Title	Yr	VG	VG+	NM
NEW JAZZ					
❑ NJLP-8322 [M]	The Last Amen	196?	---	---	---
-- *Canceled; reassigned to Status*					
PRESTIGE					
❑ PRLP-7190 [M]	South Side Soul	1960	10.00	20.00	40.00
❑ PRLP-7197 [M]	Nice 'N' Nasty	1961	10.00	20.00	40.00
❑ PRLP-7212 [M]	Makin' Out	1961	10.00	20.00	40.00
❑ PRLP-7233 [M]	Mr. Soul	1962	7.50	15.00	30.00
❑ PRST-7233 [S]	Mr. Soul	1962	10.00	20.00	40.00
STATUS					
❑ ST-8322 [M]	The Last Amen	1965	10.00	20.00	40.00

WRIGHT, LEO
Alto saxophone player, flutist and clarinetist.

Number	Title	Yr	VG	VG+	NM
ATLANTIC					
❑ 1358 [M]	Blues Shout	196?	3.75	7.50	15.00
-- *Multicolor label, black "fan" logo at right*					
❑ 1358 [M]	Blues Shout	1960	6.25	12.50	25.00
-- *Multicolor label, white "fan" logo at right*					
❑ 1393 [M]	Suddenly the Blues	1962	6.25	12.50	25.00
-- *Multicolor label, black "fan" logo at right*					
❑ SD 1358 [S]	Blues Shout	196?	5.00	10.00	20.00
-- *Multicolor label, black "fan" logo at right*					
❑ SD 1358 [S]	Blues Shout	1960	7.50	15.00	30.00
-- *Multicolor label, white "fan" logo at right*					
❑ SD 1358 [S]	Suddenly the Blues	1962	7.50	15.00	30.00
-- *Multicolor label, black "fan" logo at right*					
ROULETTE					
❑ SR-5007	Evening Breeze	1977	2.50	5.00	10.00
VORTEX					
❑ 2011	Soul Talk	197?	5.00	10.00	20.00

WRIGHT, LEFTY
Pianist.

Number	Title	Yr	VG	VG+	NM
"X"					
❑ LXA-3028 [10]	Boogie Woogie Piano	1954	15.00	30.00	60.00

WRIGHT, NAT
Male singer.

Number	Title	Yr	VG	VG+	NM
WARWICK					
❑ W-2040 [M]	The Biggest Voice in Jazz	1961	12.50	25.00	50.00
❑ W-2040ST [S]	The Biggest Voice in Jazz	1961	20.00	40.00	80.00

WYNN, ALBERT
Trombonist and bandleader.

Number	Title	Yr	VG	VG+	NM
RIVERSIDE					
❑ RLP-426 [M]	Albert Wynn and His Gutbucket Seven	1962	7.50	15.00	30.00
❑ RS-9426 [R]	Albert Wynn and His Gutbucket Seven	1962	5.00	10.00	20.00

Number	Title	Yr	VG	VG+	NM

Y

YAGED, SOL
Clarinetist.
HERALD
❑ HLP-0103 [M]	It Might As Well Be Swing	1956	12.50	25.00	50.00

LANE
❑ LP-149 [M]	Live at the Gaslight Club	195?	12.50	25.00	50.00
❑ LP-154 [M]	One More Time	195?	12.50	25.00	50.00
❑ LPS-154 [S]	One More Time	195?	12.50	25.00	50.00
❑ LP-155 [M]	Sol Yaged at the Gaslight Club	195?	12.50	25.00	50.00
❑ LPS-155 [S]	Sol Yaged at the Gaslight Club	195?	12.50	25.00	50.00

PHILIPS
❑ PHM 200-002 [M]	Jazz at the Metropole	1961	3.75	7.50	15.00
❑ PHS 600-002 [S]	Jazz at the Metropole	1961	5.00	10.00	20.00

YALE DIXIELAND BAND, THE
COLUMBIA
❑ CL 736 [M]	Eli's Chosen Six	1955	10.00	20.00	40.00

YAMA YAMA JAZZ BAND, THE
JAZZOLOGY
❑ J-78	New Orleans Jazz -- Australian Style, Vol. 1	198?	2.50	5.00	10.00
❑ J-79	New Orleans Jazz -- Australian Style, Vol. 2	198?	2.50	5.00	10.00

YAMAMOTO, TSUYOSHI
Pianist and composer.
CONCORD JAZZ
❑ CJ-218	Zephyr	1981	2.50	5.00	10.00

THREE BLIND MICE
❑ TBM-23	Midnight Sugar	1995	7.50	15.00	30.00
-- Audiophile vinyl					
❑ TBM-30	Misty	199?	7.50	15.00	30.00
-- Audiophile vinyl					

YAMASHITA, STOMU
Percussionist.
KUCKUCK
❑ KU-072	Sea and Sky	198?	3.00	6.00	12.00

YANCEY, JIMMY
Pianist.
ATLANTIC
❑ ALS-103 [10]	Yancey Special	1950	25.00	50.00	100.00
❑ ALS-130 [10]	Yancey Special	1952	20.00	40.00	80.00
❑ ALS-134 [10]	Piano Solos	1952	20.00	40.00	80.00
❑ 1283 [M]	Pure Blues	1958	12.50	25.00	50.00
-- Black label					
❑ 1283 [M]	Pure Blues	1961	5.00	10.00	20.00
-- Multicolor label, white "fan" logo at right					
❑ 1283 [M]	Pure Blues	1964	3.75	7.50	15.00
-- Multicolor label, black "fan" logo at right					

JAZZOLOGY
❑ J-51	In the Beginning	197?	2.50	5.00	10.00

PARAMOUNT
❑ CJS-101 [10]	Yancey Special	1951	25.00	50.00	100.00

PAX
❑ LP-6011 [10]	1943 Mixture	1954	20.00	40.00	80.00
❑ LP-6012 [10]	Evening With the Yanceys	1954	20.00	40.00	80.00

RIVERSIDE
❑ RLP 12-124 [M]	Yancey's Getaway	1956	15.00	30.00	60.00
❑ RLP-1028 [10]	Lost Recording Date	1954	25.00	50.00	100.00

"X"
❑ LX-3000 [10]	Blues and Boogie	1954	25.00	50.00	100.00

YANCEY, MAMA, AND ART HODES
Yancey is a female singer. Also see ART HODES.
VERVE FOLKWAYS
❑ FV-9015 [M]	Blues	1965	5.00	10.00	20.00
❑ FVS-9015 [S]	Blues	1965	6.25	12.50	25.00

YANKEE RHYTHM KINGS
Formed in 1974 in Boston. Among the members: Bob Connors (trombone); Jeff Hughes (cornet, trumpet, fluegel horn); Jim Mazzy (banjo, vocals).
GHB
❑ GHB-83	Yankee Rhythm Kings, Vol. 1	197?	2.50	5.00	10.00
❑ GHB-97	Classic Jazz of the 20s	1978	2.50	5.00	10.00
❑ GHB-151	Classic Jazz of the 20s	1980	2.50	5.00	10.00

Number	Title	Yr	VG	VG+	NM

YARBROUGH, CAMILLE
Female singer and composer.
VANGUARD
❑ VSD-79356	The Iron Pot Cooker	197?	3.00	6.00	12.00

YAZ-KAZ
GRAMAVISION
❑ 18-7013	Jonon-Sho	198?	3.00	6.00	12.00

YELL CHASERS, THE
REALTIME
❑ 822	I've Got My Fingers	197?	5.00	10.00	20.00
-- Direct-to-disc recording; plays at 45 rpm					

YELLIN, PETE
Alto saxophone player and flutist.
MAINSTREAM
❑ MRL-363	Dance of Allegra	197?	3.75	7.50	15.00
❑ MRL-397	It's the Right Thing	1974	3.75	7.50	15.00

YELLOWJACKETS
Members: Russell Ferrante (keyboards); Jimmy Haslip (bass); Mark Russo (alto sax through 1990); Ricky Lawson (drums, replaced by William Kennedy in 1986); Robben Ford (guitar through 1983).
MCA
❑ 5752	Shades	1986	2.50	5.00	10.00
❑ 5994	Four Corners	1987	2.50	5.00	10.00
❑ 6236	Politics	1988	2.50	5.00	10.00
❑ 6304	The Spin	1989	3.00	6.00	12.00

WARNER BROS.
❑ BSK 3573	The Yellowjackets	1982	2.50	5.00	10.00
❑ 23813	Mirage A Trois	1983	2.50	5.00	10.00
❑ 25204	Samurai Samba	1985	2.50	5.00	10.00

YERBA BUENA JAZZ BAND, THE
See LU WATTERS.

YORK, BETH
Pianist.
LADYSLIPPER
❑ LR-104	Transformations	1986	3.00	6.00	12.00

YOST, PHIL
Bass player, soprano saxophone player, flutist, guitarist and banjo player. On the below albums, he played all the instruments.
TAKOMA
❑ C-1016	Bent City	196?	5.00	10.00	20.00
❑ C-1021	Fog-Hat Ramble	196?	5.00	10.00	20.00

YOSUKE, YAMASHITA
Pianist and keyboard player.
WEST 54
❑ 8009	Breathtake	1980	3.00	6.00	12.00

YOUNG LIONS, THE (1)
Members: Bob Cranshaw; LOUIS HAYES; ALBERT HEATH; LEE MORGAN; WAYNE SHORTER; BOBBY TIMMONS.
TRIP
❑ 5011 [(2)]	Lions of Jazz	197?	3.00	6.00	12.00

VEE JAY
❑ LP-3013 [M]	The Young Lions	1960	10.00	20.00	40.00
❑ SR-3013 [S]	The Young Lions	1960	12.50	25.00	50.00
❑ VJS-3013 [S]	The Young Lions	197?	2.50	5.00	10.00
-- Reissue on thinner, more flexible vinyl					

YOUNG LIONS, THE (2)
Approximately 17 young musicians in a gig recorded live at Carnegie Hall.
ELEKTRA MUSICIAN
❑ 60196 [(2)]	The Young Lions	1983	3.00	6.00	12.00

YOUNG MEN FROM MEMPHIS
Members: BOOKER LITTLE, Louis Smith (trumpet); FRANK STROZIER (alto sax); GEORGE COLEMAN (tenor sax); PHINEAS NEWBORN (piano); Calvin Newborn (guitar); George Joyner, aka Jamil Nasser (bass); Charles Crosby (drums).
UNITED ARTISTS
❑ UAL-4029 [M]	Down Home Reunion	1959	12.50	25.00	50.00
❑ UAS-5029 [S]	Down Home Reunion	1959	10.00	20.00	40.00

Number	Title	Yr	VG	VG+	NM

YOUNG TUXEDO BRASS BAND, THE
Members at the time of recording: John Casimir (E-flat clarinet, leader); Andrew Anderson (trumpet), John "Pickey" Brunious (trumpet); Albert "Fernandez" Walters (trumpet); Clement Tervalon (trombone), Jim Robinson (trombone), Herman Sherman (alto sax), Andrew Morgan (tenor sax), Wilbert Tillman (sousaphone), Emile Knox (bass drum), Paul Barbarin (snare drum).

ATLANTIC

Number	Title	Yr	VG	VG+	NM
❏ 1297 [M]	Jazz Begins	1958	10.00	20.00	40.00
-- Black label					
❏ 1297 [M]	Jazz Begins	1961	5.00	10.00	20.00
-- Multicolor label, white "fan" logo at right					
❏ 1297 [M]	Jazz Begins	1964	3.75	7.50	15.00
-- Multicolor label, black "fan" logo at right					
❏ SD 1297 [M]	Jazz Begins	1958	12.50	25.00	50.00
-- Green label					
❏ SD 1297 [M]	Jazz Begins	1961	3.75	7.50	15.00
-- Multicolor label, white "fan" logo at right					
❏ SD 1297 [M]	Jazz Begins	1964	3.00	6.00	12.00
-- Multicolor label, black "fan" logo at right					

YOUNG, CECIL
Trumpeter.

AUDIO LAB

Number	Title	Yr	VG	VG+	NM
❏ AL-1516 [M]	Jazz on the Rocks	1959	20.00	40.00	80.00

KING

Number	Title	Yr	VG	VG+	NM
❏ 295-1 [10]	A Concert of Cool Jazz	1952	25.00	50.00	100.00

YOUNG, DAVID
Tenor saxophone player.

MAINSTREAM

Number	Title	Yr	VG	VG+	NM
❏ MRL-323	David Young	1972	3.75	7.50	15.00

YOUNG, ELDEE
Bass player; was a member of the classic RAMSEY LEWIS Trio of the 1960s. Also see YOUNG-HOLT UNLIMITED.

ARGO

Number	Title	Yr	VG	VG+	NM
❏ LP-699 [M]	Just for Kicks	1962	3.75	7.50	15.00
❏ LPS-699 [S]	Just for Kicks	1962	5.00	10.00	20.00
❏ LP-1003 [M]	Eldee Young and Company	1962	5.00	10.00	20.00
❏ LPS-1003 [S]	Eldee Young and Company	1962	6.25	12.50	25.00

YOUNG, JOHN
Pianist.

ARGO

Number	Title	Yr	VG	VG+	NM
❏ LP-612 [M]	Young John Young	1957	10.00	20.00	40.00
❏ LP-692 [M]	Themes and Things	1962	6.25	12.50	25.00
❏ LPS-692 [S]	Themes and Things	1962	7.50	15.00	30.00
❏ LP-713 [M]	A Touch of Pepper	1962	6.25	12.50	25.00
❏ LPS-713 [S]	A Touch of Pepper	1962	7.50	15.00	30.00

CADET

Number	Title	Yr	VG	VG+	NM
❏ LP-692 [M]	Themes and Things	1966	3.00	6.00	12.00
❏ LPS-692 [S]	Themes and Things	1966	3.75	7.50	15.00

DELMARK

Number	Title	Yr	VG	VG+	NM
❏ DL-403 [M]	The John Young Trio	1961	7.50	15.00	30.00
❏ DS-403 [S]	The John Young Trio	1961	10.00	20.00	40.00

VEE JAY

Number	Title	Yr	VG	VG+	NM
❏ VJS-3060	Opus de Funk	1974	5.00	10.00	20.00

YOUNG, LARRY
Organist and composer.

ARISTA

Number	Title	Yr	VG	VG+	NM
❏ AL 4072	Spaceball	1976	3.00	6.00	12.00

BLUE NOTE

Number	Title	Yr	VG	VG+	NM
❏ LT-1038	Mother Ship	1980	3.00	6.00	12.00
❏ BLP-4187 [M]	Into Somethin'	1964	7.50	15.00	30.00
❏ BLP-4221 [M]	Unity	1966	7.50	15.00	30.00
❏ BLP-4242 [M]	Of Love and Peace	1966	7.50	15.00	30.00
❏ BLP-4266 [M]	Contrasts	1967	10.00	20.00	40.00
❏ BST-84187 [S]	Into Somethin'	1964	10.00	20.00	40.00
-- With "New York, USA" address on label					
❏ BST-84187 [S]	Into Somethin'	1967	5.00	10.00	20.00
-- With "A Division of Liberty Records" on label					
❏ BST-84221 [S]	Unity	1966	10.00	20.00	40.00
-- With "New York, USA" address on label					
❏ BST-84221 [S]	Unity	1967	5.00	10.00	20.00
-- With "A Division of Liberty Records" on label					
❏ BST-84221	Unity	198?	2.50	5.00	10.00
-- "The Finest in Jazz Since 1939" reissue					
❏ BST-84242 [S]	Of Love and Peace	1966	10.00	20.00	40.00
-- With "New York, USA" address on label					
❏ BST-84242 [S]	Of Love and Peace	1967	5.00	10.00	20.00
-- With "A Division of Liberty Records" on label					
❏ BST-84266 [S]	Contrasts	1967	7.50	15.00	30.00
-- With "A Division of Liberty Records" on label					
❏ BST-84304 [S]	Heaven on Earth	1968	7.50	15.00	30.00
-- With "A Division of Liberty Records" on label					

MOSAIC

Number	Title	Yr	VG	VG+	NM
❏ M9-137 [(9)]	The Complete Blue Note Recordings of Larry Young	199?	30.00	60.00	120.00

NEW JAZZ

Number	Title	Yr	VG	VG+	NM
❏ NJLP-8249 [M]	Testifying	1960	12.50	25.00	50.00
-- Purple label					
❏ NJLP-8249 [M]	Testifying	1965	6.25	12.50	25.00
-- Blue label, trident logo at right					
❏ NJLP-8264 [M]	Young Blues	1961	12.50	25.00	50.00
-- Purple label					
❏ NJLP-8264 [M]	Young Blues	1965	6.25	12.50	25.00
-- Blue label, trident logo at right					

PRESTIGE

Number	Title	Yr	VG	VG+	NM
❏ PRLP-7237 [M]	Groove Street	1962	10.00	20.00	40.00
❏ PRST-7237 [S]	Groove Street	1962	10.00	20.00	40.00

YOUNG, LESTER
Tenor saxophone player, clarinetist and male singer. His nickname "Pres" was coined by BILLIE HOLIDAY. Also see COLEMAN HAWKINS.

ALADDIN

Number	Title	Yr	VG	VG+	NM
❏ LP-705 [10]	Lester Young Trio	1953	75.00	150.00	300.00
❏ LP-706 [10]	Easy Does It	1954	75.00	150.00	300.00
❏ LP-801 [M]	Lester Young and His Tenor Sax, Volume 1	1956	30.00	60.00	120.00
❏ LP-802 [M]	Lester Young and His Tenor Sax, Volume 2	1956	30.00	60.00	120.00

AMERICAN RECORDING SOCIETY

Number	Title	Yr	VG	VG+	NM
❏ G-417 [M]	Pres and Teddy	1957	12.50	25.00	50.00

ARCHIVE OF FOLK AND JAZZ

Number	Title	Yr	VG	VG+	NM
❏ 287	Pres	197?	2.50	5.00	10.00

BLUE NOTE

Number	Title	Yr	VG	VG+	NM
❏ BN-LA456-H2 [(2)]	Pres: The Aladdin Sessions	1975	3.75	7.50	15.00

CHARLIE PARKER

Number	Title	Yr	VG	VG+	NM
❏ CLP-402 [M]	Pres	1961	12.50	25.00	50.00
❏ CLP-405 [M]	Pres Is Blue	1961	12.50	25.00	50.00

CLEF

Number	Title	Yr	VG	VG+	NM
❏ MGC-104 [10]	The Lester Young Trio	1953	62.50	125.00	250.00
❏ MGC-108 [10]	Lester Young Collates	1953	62.50	125.00	250.00
❏ MGC-124 [10]	Lester Young Collates No. 2	1953	62.50	125.00	250.00
-- Some copies of this have Mercury covers; no difference in value					
❏ MGC-135 [10]	The Lester Young Trio No. 2	1953	62.50	125.00	250.00

COLUMBIA

Number	Title	Yr	VG	VG+	NM
❏ JG 33502 [(2)]	The Lester Young Story, Vol. 1	1975	3.75	7.50	15.00
❏ JG 34837 [(2)]	The Lester Young Story, Vol. 2: Romance	1976	3.75	7.50	15.00
❏ JG 34840 [(2)]	The Lester Young Story, Vol. 3: Enter Count	1976	3.75	7.50	15.00

COMMODORE

Number	Title	Yr	VG	VG+	NM
❏ XFL-14937	The Kansas City Six and Five	198?	2.50	5.00	10.00
❏ XFL-15352	A Complete Session	198?	2.50	5.00	10.00
❏ FL-20021 [10]	Kansas City Style	1952	75.00	150.00	300.00
❏ FL-30014 [M]	Kansas City Style	1959	25.00	50.00	100.00

CROWN

Number	Title	Yr	VG	VG+	NM
❏ CST-305 [R]	Nat "King" Cole Meets Lester Young	196?	3.00	6.00	12.00
❏ CLP-5305 [M]	Nat "King" Cole Meets Lester Young	196?	6.25	12.50	25.00

EMARCY

Number	Title	Yr	VG	VG+	NM
❏ SRE-66010	Lester Young At His Very Best	1967	3.75	7.50	15.00

EPIC

Number	Title	Yr	VG	VG+	NM
❏ LN 3107 [M]	Lester Leaps In	1956	25.00	50.00	100.00
❏ LN 3168 [M]	Let's Go to Pres	1956	25.00	50.00	100.00
❏ LN 3576 [M]	Lester Young Memorial Album, Volume 1	1959	12.50	25.00	50.00
❏ LN 3577 [M]	Lester Young Memorial Album, Volume 2	1959	12.50	25.00	50.00
❏ SN 6031 [(2) M]	Lester Young Memorial Album	1959	37.50	75.00	150.00

IMPERIAL

Number	Title	Yr	VG	VG+	NM
❏ LP-9181-A [M]	The Immortal Lester Young	1962	12.50	25.00	50.00
❏ LP-9187-A [M]	The Great Lester Young, Volume 2	1962	12.50	25.00	50.00
❏ LP-12181-A [R]	The Immortal Lester Young	196?	5.00	10.00	20.00
❏ LP-12187-A [R]	The Great Lester Young, Volume 2	196?	5.00	10.00	20.00

INTRO

Number	Title	Yr	VG	VG+	NM
❏ LP-602 [M]	Swinging Lester Young	1957	25.00	50.00	100.00
❏ LP-603 [M]	The Greatest	1957	25.00	50.00	100.00

JAZZ ARCHIVES

Number	Title	Yr	VG	VG+	NM
❏ JA-18	Jammin' with Lester, Vol. 1	198?	2.50	5.00	10.00
❏ JA-34	Jammin' with Lester, Vol. 2	198?	2.50	5.00	10.00

Number	Title	Yr	VG	VG+	NM
❑ JA-42	Lester Young and Charlie Christian 1939-40	198?	2.50	5.00	10.00
MAINSTREAM					
❑ S-6002 [R]	The Influence of Five	1965	3.00	6.00	12.00
❑ S-6004 [R]	Town Hall Concert	1965	3.00	6.00	12.00
❑ S-6008 [R]	Chairman of the Board	1965	3.00	6.00	12.00
❑ S-6009 [R]	52nd Street	1965	3.00	6.00	12.00
❑ S-6012 [R]	Prez	1965	3.00	6.00	12.00
❑ 56002 [M]	The Influence of Five	1965	6.25	12.50	25.00
❑ 56004 [M]	Town Hall Concert	1965	6.25	12.50	25.00
❑ 56008 [M]	Chairman of the Board	1965	6.25	12.50	25.00
❑ 56009 [M]	52nd Street	1965	6.25	12.50	25.00
❑ 56012 [M]	Prez	1965	6.25	12.50	25.00
MERCURY					
❑ MGC-104 [10]	The Lester Young Trio	1951	75.00	150.00	300.00
❑ MGC-108 [10]	Lester Young Collates	1951	75.00	150.00	300.00
❑ MGC-124 [10]	Lester Young Collates No. 2	1953	---	---	---
-- Canceled; issued on Clef					
NORGRAN					
❑ MGN-5 [10]	Lester Young with the Oscar Peterson Trio No. 1	1954	50.00	100.00	200.00
❑ MGN-6 [10]	Lester Young with the Oscar Peterson Trio No. 2	1954	50.00	100.00	200.00
❑ MGN-1005 [M]	The President	1954	50.00	100.00	200.00
❑ MGN-1022 [M]	Lester Young	1955	50.00	100.00	200.00
❑ MGN-1043 [M]	Pres and Sweets	1955	50.00	100.00	200.00
❑ MGN-1054 [M]	The President Plays with the Oscar Peterson Trio	1955	25.00	50.00	100.00
❑ MGN-1071 [M]	Lester's Here	1956	25.00	50.00	100.00
❑ MGN-1072 [M]	Pres	1956	25.00	50.00	100.00
❑ MGN-1074 [M]	Lester Young and the Buddy Rich Trio	1956	25.00	50.00	100.00
❑ MGN-1093 [M]	Lester Swings Again	1956	25.00	50.00	100.00
❑ MGN-1100 [M]	Lester Young	1956	25.00	50.00	100.00
ONYX					
❑ 218	Prez in Europe	197?	3.00	6.00	12.00
PABLO					
❑ 2405 420	The Best of Lester Young	198?	2.50	5.00	10.00
PABLO LIVE					
❑ 2308 219	Lester Young in Washington, D.C., at Olivia Davis', Vol. 1	1979	3.00	6.00	12.00
❑ 2308 225	Lester Young in Washington, D.C., at Olivia Davis', Vol. 2	1980	3.00	6.00	12.00
❑ 2308 228	Lester Young in Washington, D.C., at Olivia Davis', Vol. 3	198?	2.50	5.00	10.00
❑ 2308 230	Lester Young in Washington, D.C., at Olivia Davis', Vol. 4	198?	2.50	5.00	10.00
PICKWICK					
❑ SPC-5015	Prez Leaps Again	197?	2.50	5.00	10.00
SAVOY					
❑ MG-9002 [10]	Lester Young (All Star Be Bop)	1951	75.00	150.00	300.00
❑ MG-12068 [M]	Blue Lester	1956	20.00	40.00	80.00
❑ MG-12071 [M]	The Master's Touch	1956	20.00	40.00	80.00
❑ MG-12155 [M]	The Immortal Lester Young	1959	15.00	30.00	60.00
SAVOY JAZZ					
❑ SJL-1109	Pres Lives	197?	2.50	5.00	10.00
❑ SJL-1133	Master Takes	198?	2.50	5.00	10.00
❑ SJL-2202 [(2)]	The Complete Lester Young (1944-49)	197?	3.75	7.50	15.00
SCORE					
❑ SLP-4019 [M]	Lester Young / The King Cole Trio	1958	20.00	40.00	80.00
❑ SLP-4028 [M]	Swinging Lester Young	1958	20.00	40.00	80.00
❑ SLP-4029 [M]	The Great Lester Young	1958	20.00	40.00	80.00
SUNSET					
❑ SUS-5181	Giant of Jazz	1967	3.00	6.00	12.00
TRIP					
❑ 5519	Pres at His Best	197?	2.50	5.00	10.00
VERVE					
❑ VSP-27 [M]	Pres and His Cabinet	1966	6.25	12.50	25.00
❑ VSPS-27 [R]	Pres and His Cabinet	1966	3.00	6.00	12.00
❑ VSP-30 [M]	Giants 3	1966	6.25	12.50	25.00
❑ VSPS-30 [R]	Giants 3	1966	3.00	6.00	12.00
-- With Buddy Rich and Nat King Cole					
❑ VSP-41 [M]	Lester Young at J.A.T.P.	196?	3.75	7.50	15.00
❑ VSPS-41 [R]	Lester Young at J.A.T.P.	196?	3.00	6.00	12.00
❑ VE-2-2502 [(2)]	Pres & Teddy & Oscar	197?	3.75	7.50	15.00
❑ VE-2-2516 [(2)]	Lester Swings	197?	3.75	7.50	15.00
❑ VE-2-2527 [(2)]	Jazz Giants '56	197?	3.75	7.50	15.00
❑ UMV-2528	Pres and Sweets	198?	2.50	5.00	10.00
❑ VE-2-2538 [(2)]	Mean to Me	197?	3.75	7.50	15.00
❑ UMV-2672	Pres	198?	2.50	5.00	10.00
❑ MGV-8134 [M]	Pres and Sweets	1957	15.00	30.00	60.00
❑ V-8134 [M]	Pres and Sweets	1961	6.25	12.50	25.00
❑ MGV-8144 [M]	The President Plays with the Oscar Peterson Trio	1957	15.00	30.00	60.00
❑ V-8144 [M]	The President Plays with the Oscar Peterson Trio	1961	6.25	12.50	25.00
❑ MGV-8161 [M]	Lester's Here	1957	15.00	30.00	60.00
❑ V-8161 [M]	Lester's Here	1961	6.25	12.50	25.00
❑ MGV-8162 [M]	Pres	1957	15.00	30.00	60.00
❑ V-8162 [M]	Pres	1961	6.25	12.50	25.00
❑ MGV-8164 [M]	Lester Young and the Buddy Rich Trio	1957	15.00	30.00	60.00
❑ V-8164 [M]	Lester Young and the Buddy Rich Trio	1961	6.25	12.50	25.00
❑ MGV-8181 [M]	Lester Swings Again	1957	15.00	30.00	60.00
❑ V-8181 [M]	Lester Swings Again	1961	6.25	12.50	25.00
❑ MGV-8187 [M]	It Don't Mean a Thing (If It Ain't Got That Swing)	1957	15.00	30.00	60.00
❑ V-8187 [M]	It Don't Mean a Thing (If It Ain't Got That Swing)	1961	6.25	12.50	25.00
❑ MGV-8205 [M]	Pres and Teddy	1957	15.00	30.00	60.00
❑ V-8205 [M]	Pres and Teddy	1961	6.25	12.50	25.00
❑ MGV-8308 [M]	The Lester Young Story	1959	15.00	30.00	60.00
❑ V-8308 [M]	The Lester Young Story	1961	6.25	12.50	25.00
❑ MGV-8378 [M]	Lester Young in Paris	1960	15.00	30.00	60.00
❑ V-8378 [M]	Lester Young in Paris	1961	6.25	12.50	25.00
❑ MGV-8398 [M]	The Essential Lester Young	1961	15.00	30.00	60.00
❑ V-8398 [M]	The Essential Lester Young	1961	6.25	12.50	25.00
❑ 833 554-1 [(2)]	Lester Swings	198?	3.00	6.00	12.00

YOUNG, LESTER/COUNT BASIE
Also see each artist's individual listings.

Number	Title	Yr	VG	VG+	NM
MERCURY					
❑ MG-25015 [10]	Lester Young Quartet/Count Basie Seven	1950	62.50	125.00	250.00

YOUNG, LESTER/CHU BERRY
Also see each artist's individual listings.

Number	Title	Yr	VG	VG+	NM
JAZZTONE					
❑ J-1218 [M]	Tops on Tenor: Pres and Chu	1956	17.50	35.00	70.00

YOUNG, LESTER; ROY ELDRIDGE; HARRY "SWEETS" EDISON
Also see each artist's individual listings.

Number	Title	Yr	VG	VG+	NM
VERVE					
❑ UMV-2694	Laughin' to Keep From Cryin'	198?	2.50	5.00	10.00
❑ MGVS-6054 [S]	Laughin' to Keep from Cryin'	1960	17.50	35.00	70.00
❑ MGVS-6054 [S]	Laughin' to Keep from Cryin'	199?	6.25	12.50	25.00
-- Classic Records reissue on audiophile vinyl					
❑ MGV-8298 [M]	Going for Myself	1959	15.00	30.00	60.00
❑ V-8298 [M]	Going for Myself	1961	6.25	12.50	25.00
❑ MGV-8316 [M]	Laughin' to Keep from Cryin'	1960	15.00	30.00	60.00
❑ V-8316 [M]	Laughin' to Keep from Cryin'	1961	6.25	12.50	25.00
❑ V6-8316 [S]	Laughin' to Keep from Cryin'	1961	7.50	15.00	30.00

YOUNG, LESTER, AND ILLINOIS JACQUET
Also see each artist's individual listings.

Number	Title	Yr	VG	VG+	NM
ALADDIN					
❑ LP-701 [10]	Battle of the Saxes	1953	100.00	200.00	400.00

YOUNG, LESTER, AND PAUL QUINICHETTE
Also see each artist's individual listings.

Number	Title	Yr	VG	VG+	NM
EMARCY					
❑ MG-26021 [10]	Pres Meets Vice-Pres	1954	62.50	125.00	250.00

YOUNG, NOAH
Bass player.

Number	Title	Yr	VG	VG+	NM
LAUGHING ANGEL					
❑ LAR 33	Unicorn Dream	1981	3.75	7.50	15.00

YOUNG, SNOOKY
Trumpeter and fluegel horn player.

Number	Title	Yr	VG	VG+	NM
CONCORD JAZZ					
❑ CJ-55	The Snooky Young/Marshal Royal Album	1977	3.00	6.00	12.00
❑ CJ-91	Horn of Plenty	1979	3.00	6.00	12.00
MASTER JAZZ					
❑ 8130	Dayton	197?	3.00	6.00	12.00

YOUNG, STERLING
Violinist and bandleader.

Number	Title	Yr	VG	VG+	NM
HINDSIGHT					
❑ HSR-113	Sterling Young and His Orchestra 1939-1940	198?	2.50	5.00	10.00

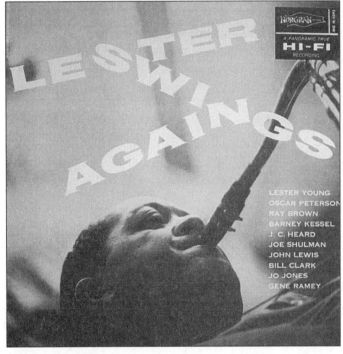

Lester Young was the not-so-missing saxophone link between swing and bebop and a fixture on Billie Holiday recordings. Ironically, "Pres" and Lady Day died about four months apart in 1959. (Top left) Early in his career, Young was in a trio with Nat King Cole on piano and Red Callender on bass. This 10-inch album released by Aladdin in 1953 is a document of that all-star group. (Top right) A different Lester Young Trio recorded for Norman Granz' Clef label in the early 1950s; among the results is this 10-inch LP. (Bottom left) This rather striking cover adorned Lester Young, a 12-inch collection issued on Norgran in 1955. (Bottom right) *Lester Swings Again* was first issued on the Norgran label in 1956, then quickly reissued on the unified Verve label (MGV-8181).

Number	Title	Yr	VG	VG+	NM

YOUNG, WEBSTER
Trumpeter.
FANTASY

Number	Title	Yr	VG	VG+	NM
❑ OJC-1716	For Lady	198?	2.50	5.00	10.00

PRESTIGE

Number	Title	Yr	VG	VG+	NM
❑ PRLP-7106 [M]	For Lady	1957	25.00	50.00	100.00

YOUNG-HOLT UNLIMITED
Group formed by RED HOLT and ELDEE YOUNG after they left the RAMSEY LEWIS Trio. In late 1968-early 1969, they had a Top 10 hit single with the instrumental "Soulful Strut."
ATLANTIC

Number	Title	Yr	VG	VG+	NM
❑ SD 1634	Oh Girl	1973	3.00	6.00	12.00

BRUNSWICK

Number	Title	Yr	VG	VG+	NM
❑ BL 54121 [M]	Wack-Wack	1966	5.00	10.00	20.00
-- As "Young-Holt Trio"					
❑ BL 54125 [M]	On Stage	1967	5.00	10.00	20.00
-- As "Young-Holt Trio"					
❑ BL 54128 [M]	The Beat Goes On	1967	7.50	15.00	30.00
❑ BL 754121 [S]	Wack-Wack	1966	5.00	10.00	20.00
-- As "Young-Holt Trio"					
❑ BL 754125 [S]	On Stage	1967	5.00	10.00	20.00
-- As "Young-Holt Trio"					
❑ BL 754128 [S]	The Beat Goes On	1967	5.00	10.00	20.00
❑ BL 754141	Funky But!	1968	5.00	10.00	20.00
❑ BL 754144	Soulful Strut	1968	3.75	7.50	15.00
❑ BL 754150	Just a Melody	1969	3.75	7.50	15.00

CADET

Number	Title	Yr	VG	VG+	NM
❑ LP-791 [M]	Feature Spot	1967	7.50	15.00	30.00
❑ LPS-791 [S]	Feature Spot	1967	5.00	10.00	20.00
-- As "Eldee Young and Red Holt (of the Ramsey Lewis Trio)"					

COTILLION

Number	Title	Yr	VG	VG+	NM
❑ SD 18001	Mellow Dreamin'	1971	3.00	6.00	12.00
❑ SD 18004	Born Again	1972	3.00	6.00	12.00

PAULA

Number	Title	Yr	VG	VG+	NM
❑ LPS-4002	Super Fly	1973	5.00	10.00	20.00

YOUR FRIENDLY NEIGHBORHOOD BIG BAND
See MATT CATINGUB.

YUTAKA
Keyboard player.
GRP

Number	Title	Yr	VG	VG+	NM
❑ GR-1046	Yutaka	1988	2.50	5.00	10.00

Number	Title	Yr	VG	VG+	NM

Z

ZACK, GEORGE
Pianist and male singer.
COMMODORE
❑ FL-20001 [10]	Party Piano of the Roaring '20s	1950	12.50	25.00	50.00

ZAHARA
ANTILLES
❑ AN-1011	Flight of the Spirit	198?	3.00	6.00	12.00

ZAPPA, FRANK
Guitarist, keyboard player, composer, bandleader and male vocalist, Zappa is prominent as a rock musician, but he's impossible to pigeonhole. Many of his albums, especially on the Barking Pumpkin and Bizarre labels, are jazzy. Zappa was chosen by jazz critics to the Down Beat Magazine Jazz Hall of Fame in 1994.

ANGEL
❑ DS-38170	Boulez Conducts Zappa: The Perfect Stranger	1983	3.00	6.00	12.00

BARKING PUMPKIN
❑ 7X4-1	The Old Masters Sampler	1984	6.25	12.50	25.00
❑ AS 995 [DJ]	Tinsel Town Rebellion	1981	5.00	10.00	20.00
-- Promo-only sampler					
❑ BPR-1111	Shut Up 'N' Play Yer Guitar	1981	5.00	10.00	20.00
-- Mail-order item only					
❑ BPR-1112	Shut Up 'N' Play Yer Guitar Some More	1981	5.00	10.00	20.00
-- Mail-order item only					
❑ BPR-1113	Return of the Son of Shut Up 'N' Play Yer Guitar	1981	5.00	10.00	20.00
-- Mail-order item only					
❑ BPRP-1114 [PD]	Zappa	1982	3.75	7.50	15.00
-- Picture disc with two songs					
❑ BPRP-1115 [PD]	Baby Snakes	1983	3.75	7.50	15.00
-- Picture disc					
❑ AS 1294 [DJ]	You Are What You Is Special Clean Cuts Edition	1981	5.00	10.00	20.00
❑ 7777 [(8)]	The Old Masters, Box 1	1984	15.00	30.00	60.00
-- Boxed set					
❑ 8888 [(8)]	The Old Masters, Box 2	1986	15.00	30.00	60.00
-- Another boxed set					
❑ 8888X	The Old Masters Sampler 2	1986	6.25	12.50	25.00
❑ 9999 [(8)]	The Old Masters, Box 3	1987	15.00	30.00	60.00
-- Still another boxed set					
❑ PW2 37336 [(2)]	Tinsel Town Rebellion	1981	5.00	10.00	20.00
❑ PW2 37537 [(2)]	You Are What You Is	1981	5.00	10.00	20.00
❑ FW 38066	Ship Arriving Too Late to Save a Drowning Witch	1982	3.00	6.00	12.00
❑ W3X-38290 [(3)]	Shut Up 'N' Play Yer Guitar	1982	6.25	12.50	25.00
-- Box set containing all three "Shut Up 'N' Play Yer Guitar" albums					
❑ FW 38403	Man from Utopia	1983	3.00	6.00	12.00
❑ FW 38820	London Symphony Orchestra	1983	3.00	6.00	12.00
❑ SVBO-74200 [(2)]	Them Or Us	1984	3.75	7.50	15.00
❑ SWCO-74201 [(3)]	Thing-Fish	1984	5.00	10.00	20.00
❑ ST-74202	Francesco Zappa	1985	2.50	5.00	10.00
❑ ST-74203	Frank Zappa Meets the Mothers of Prevention	1985	2.50	5.00	10.00
❑ ST-74205	Jazz from Hell	1986	2.50	5.00	10.00
❑ 74206 [(3)]	Joe's Garage, Acts 1, 2 and 3	1986	12.50	25.00	50.00
-- Box set, two gatefolds, with insert					
❑ SJ-74207	London Symphony Orchestra, Volume 2	1987	2.50	5.00	10.00
❑ D1-74212 [(2)]	Guitar	1988	2.50	5.00	10.00
❑ D1-74213 [(3)]	You Can't Do That on Stage Anymore Sampler	1988	2.50	5.00	10.00
❑ R1 74213	You Can't Do That on Stage Anymore Sampler	1988	3.00	6.00	12.00
❑ D1-74217 [(3)]	You Can't Do That on Stage Anymore Vol. 2	1988	2.50	5.00	10.00
❑ D1-74218	Broadway the Hard Way	1988	2.50	5.00	10.00

BIZARRE
❑ MS-2024 [(2)]	Uncle Meat	1969	8.75	17.50	35.00
-- Originals come with a booklet; blue label					
❑ MS-2024 [(2)]	Uncle Meat	1973	5.00	10.00	20.00
-- Reissue with brown Reprise label					
❑ MS-2028	Weasels Ripped My Flesh	1970	6.25	12.50	25.00
-- Blue label original					
❑ MS-2028	Weasels Ripped My Flesh	1973	3.75	7.50	15.00
-- Reissue with brown Reprise label					
❑ MS-2030	Chunga's Revenge	1970	6.25	12.50	25.00
-- Blue label original					
❑ MS-2030	Chunga's Revenge	1973	3.75	7.50	15.00
-- Reissue with brown Reprise label					
❑ MS 2030 [DJ]	Chunga's Revenge	1970	12.50	25.00	50.00
-- White label promo					

Number	Title	Yr	VG	VG+	NM
❑ MS-2042	Fillmore East, June 1971	1971	6.25	12.50	25.00
-- Blue label original					
❑ MS-2042	Fillmore East, June 1971	1973	2.75	7.50	15.00
-- Reissue with brown Reprise label					
❑ MS 2075	Just Another Band from L.A.	1972	6.25	12.50	25.00
-- Blue label original					
❑ MS 2075	Just Another Band from L.A.	1973	3.75	7.50	15.00
-- Reissue with brown Reprise label					
❑ MS 2093	The Grand Wazoo	1972	6.25	12.50	25.00
-- Blue label original					
❑ MS 2093	The Grand Wazoo	1973	3.75	7.50	15.00
-- Reissue with brown Reprise label					
❑ MS 2094	Waka/Jawaka	1972	6.25	12.50	25.00
-- Blue label original					
❑ MS 2094	Waka/Jawaka	1973	3.75	7.50	15.00
-- Reissue with brown Reprise label					
❑ RS-6356	Hot Rats	1969	12.50	25.00	50.00
-- Blue label original					
❑ RS-6356	Hot Rats	1973	3.75	7.50	15.00
-- Reissue with brown Reprise label					
❑ RS-6370	Burnt Weenie Sandwich	1970	6.25	12.50	25.00
-- Blue label original; with booklet					
❑ RS-6370	Burnt Weenie Sandwich	1973	3.75	7.50	15.00
-- Reissue with brown Reprise label					

COLUMBIA
❑ (no #) [(4) DJ]	Lather	1977	187.50	375.00	750.00
-- Test pressing only; parts of this LP are on DSK 2291, 2292 and 2294; released as a whole only after Zappa's death, with vinyl only coming out in Japan					

DISCREET
❑ MS 2149	Over-Nite Sensation	1973	5.00	10.00	20.00
❑ MS4 2149 [Q]	Over-Nite Sensation	1973	10.00	20.00	40.00
❑ DS 2175	Apostrophe (')	1974	3.75	7.50	15.00
❑ DS 2175	Apostrophe (')	1974	12.50	25.00	50.00
-- White label promo					
❑ DS4 2175 [Q]	Apostrophe (')	1974	8.75	17.50	35.00
❑ 2DS 2202 [(2)]	Roxy and Elsewhere	1974	6.25	12.50	25.00
❑ DS 2216	One Size Fits All	1975	3.75	7.50	15.00
❑ DS 2234	Bongo Fury	1975	3.75	7.50	15.00
❑ DSK 2288	Over-Nite Sensation	1977	3.00	6.00	12.00
-- Reissue of DiscReet 2149 with new number					
❑ DSK 2289	Apostrophe (')	1977	3.00	6.00	12.00
-- Reissue with new number					
❑ 2D 2290 [(2)]	Zappa in New York	1978	62.50	125.00	250.00
-- Stock copy with "Punky's Whips" erroneously listed on jacket					
❑ 2D 2290 [(2)]	Zappa in New York	1978	5.00	10.00	20.00
❑ 2D 2290 [(2) DJ]	Zappa in New York	1978	100.00	200.00	400.00
-- Test pressing with "Punky's Whips"					
❑ DSK 2291	Studio Tan	1978	3.75	7.50	15.00
❑ DSK 2292	Sleep Dirt	1978	3.75	7.50	15.00
❑ DSK 2294	Orchestral Favorites	1978	3.75	7.50	15.00

FOO-EEE
❑ R1-70372 [(11)]	Beat the Boots #2	1992	25.00	50.00	100.00
-- Legitimate box-set release by Rhino of 11 bootlegged concerts					
❑ R1-70907 [(10)]	Beat the Boots	1991	25.00	50.00	100.00
-- Legitimate box-set release by Rhino of eight bootlegged concerts					

MCA
❑ 4183 [(2)]	200 Motels (movie soundtrack)	1986	3.75	7.50	15.00
-- Reissue					

MGM
❑ GAS-112	The Mothers of Invention	1970	12.50	25.00	50.00
❑ GAS-112 [DJ]	The Mothers of Invention	1970	25.00	50.00	100.00
-- Yellow label promo					
❑ SE-4754	The Worst of the Mothers	1971	12.50	25.00	50.00
❑ SE-4754 [DJ]	The Worst of the Mothers	1971	37.50	75.00	150.00
-- Yellow label promo					

RHINO/DEL-FI
❑ RNEP-604	Rare Meat: The Early Productions of Frank Zappa	1984	10.00	20.00	40.00
-- With original cover					

RYKO ANALOGUE
❑ RALP 10503	We're Only in It for the Money	1995	3.00	6.00	12.00
-- Vinyl reissue; Frank Zappa/The Mothers of Invention					
❑ RALP 40500 [(2)]	Strictly Commercial: The Best of Frank Zappa	1995	5.00	10.00	20.00
-- Issued with obi					

UNITED ARTISTS
❑ UAS-9956 [(2)]	200 Motels (movie soundtrack)	1971	12.50	25.00	50.00

VERVE
❑ V-5005-2 [(2) M]	Freak Out!	1966	100.00	200.00	400.00
-- White label promo					
❑ V-5005-2 [(2) M]	Freak Out!	1966	50.00	100.00	200.00
-- Cover version 1: Has blurb inside gatefold on how to get a map of "freak-out hot spots" in L.A.					
❑ V-5005-2 [(2) M]	Freak Out!	1966	37.50	75.00	150.00
-- Cover version 2: Has no blurb inside on getting a map of "freak-out hot spots"					
❑ V6-5005-2 [(2) S]	Freak Out!	1966	75.00	150.00	300.00
-- Yellow label promo					
❑ V6-5005-2 [(2) S]	Freak Out!	1966	20.00	40.00	80.00
-- Cover version 1: Has blurb inside gatefold on how to get a map of "freak-out hot spots" in L.A.					
❑ V6-5005-2 [(2) S]	Freak Out!	1966	15.00	30.00	60.00
-- Cover version 2: Has no blurb inside on getting a map of "freak-out hot spots"					

Number	Title	Yr	VG	VG+	NM
❑ V-5013 [M]	Absolutely Free	1967	30.00	60.00	120.00
❑ V-5013 [M]	Absolutely Free	1967	50.00	100.00	200.00
-- White label promo					
❑ V6-5013 [S]	Absolutely Free	1967	15.00	30.00	60.00
❑ V-5045 [M]	We're Only in It for the Money	1968	75.00	150.00	300.00
-- White label promo					
❑ V-5045 [M]	We're Only in It for the Money	1968	37.50	75.00	150.00
-- With sheet of cut-outs a la "Sgt. Pepper's Lonely Hearts Club Band"					
❑ V6-5045 [S]	We're Only in It for the Money	1968	15.00	30.00	60.00
-- Un-censored version, with cut-outs					
❑ V6-5045 [S]	We're Only in It for the Money	1968	37.50	75.00	150.00
-- Censored version: the songs "Who Needs the Peace Corps?" and "Let's Make the Water Turn Black" have lines deleted					
❑ V6-5055	Cruising with Ruben and the Jets	1968	15.00	30.00	60.00
❑ V6-5055 [DJ]	Cruising with Ruben and the Jets	1968	37.50	75.00	150.00
-- Yellow label promo					
❑ V6-5068	Mothermania -- The Best of the Mothers	1969	18.75	37.50	75.00
❑ V6-5068 [DJ]	Mothermania -- The Best of the Mothers	1969	37.50	75.00	150.00
-- Yellow label promo					
❑ V6-5074	The XXXX of the Mothers	1969	12.50	25.00	50.00
❑ V6-5074 [DJ]	The XXXX of the Mothers	1969	37.50	75.00	150.00
-- Yellow label promo					
❑ V6-8741	Lumpy Gravy	1968	12.50	25.00	50.00
❑ V6-8741 [DJ]	Lumpy Gravy	1968	50.00	100.00	200.00
-- Yellow label promo					
WARNER BROS.					
❑ BS-2970	Zoot Allures	1976	3.75	7.50	15.00
ZAPPA					
❑ MK-78 [DJ]	Sheik Yerbouti Clean Cuts	1979	8.75	17.50	35.00
❑ MK-129 [DJ]	Joe's Garage Acts I, II and III Sampler	1980	8.75	17.50	35.00
❑ SRZ-2-1501 [(2)]	Sheik Yerbouti	1979	5.00	10.00	20.00
❑ SRZ-2-1502 [(2)]	Joe's Garage, Acts II and III	1980	5.00	10.00	20.00
❑ SRZ-1-1603	Joe's Garage, Act I	1979	3.75	7.50	15.00

ZAWINUL, JOE

Keyboard player and composer (wrote "Mercy, Mercy, Mercy" and "Birdland"). Two of the albums on Columbia were released as "Zawinul Syndicate." Also see WEATHER REPORT; BEN WEBSTER.

Number	Title	Yr	VG	VG+	NM
ATLANTIC					
❑ SD 1579	Zawinul	1970	5.00	10.00	20.00
❑ SD 1694	Concerto	1976	3.75	7.50	15.00
❑ 3004 [M]	Money in the Pocket	1966	5.00	10.00	20.00
❑ SD 3004 [S]	Money in the Pocket	1966	6.25	12.50	25.00
COLUMBIA					
❑ FC 40081	Dialects	1986	2.50	5.00	10.00
❑ FC 40969	Immigrants	1988	2.50	5.00	10.00
❑ FC 44316	Black Water	1989	3.00	6.00	12.00
VORTEX					
❑ 2002	The Rise and Fall of the 3rd Stream	1968	5.00	10.00	20.00

ZEITLIN, DENNY

Pianist.

Number	Title	Yr	VG	VG+	NM
COLUMBIA					
❑ CL 2182 [M]	Cathexis	1964	5.00	10.00	20.00
❑ CL 2340 [M]	Carnival	1965	5.00	10.00	20.00
❑ CL 2463 [M]	My Shining Hour	1966	3.75	7.50	15.00
❑ CL 2748 [M]	Zeitgeist	1966	3.75	7.50	15.00
❑ CS 8982 [S]	Cathexis	1964	6.25	12.50	25.00
❑ CS 9140 [S]	Carnival	1965	6.25	12.50	25.00
❑ CS 9263 [S]	My Shining Hour	1966	5.00	10.00	20.00
❑ CS 9548 [S]	Zeitgeist	1966	5.00	10.00	20.00
LIVING MUSIC					
❑ LM-0011	Homecoming	1986	2.50	5.00	10.00
1750 ARCH					
❑ 1758	Expansions	197?	3.75	7.50	15.00
❑ 1759	Syzygy	197?	3.75	7.50	15.00
❑ 1770	Soundings	1979	3.75	7.50	15.00
WINDHAM HILL					
❑ WH-0112	Denny Zeitlin Trio	1988	2.50	5.00	10.00
❑ WH-0121	In the Moment	1989	3.00	6.00	12.00

ZEITLIN, DENNY, AND CHARLIE HADEN

Also see each artist's individual listings.

Number	Title	Yr	VG	VG+	NM
ECM					
❑ 1239	Time Remembers One Time Once	1981	3.00	6.00	12.00

ZENITH HOT STOMPERS, THE

British group.

Number	Title	Yr	VG	VG+	NM
STOMP OFF					
❑ SOS-1191	20th Anniversary Album	1991	3.00	6.00	12.00

ZENITH SIX, THE

British group, it once shared a bill with The Beatles at the Cavern Club in Liverpool (October 13, 1962, to be exact).

Number	Title	Yr	VG	VG+	NM
GHB					
❑ GHB-12	The Zenith Six, Vol. 1	196?	3.00	6.00	12.00
❑ GHB-13	The Zenith Six, Vol. 2	196?	3.00	6.00	12.00

ZETTERLUND, MONICA

Female singer.

Number	Title	Yr	VG	VG+	NM
INNER CITY					
❑ IC-1082	It Only Happens Every Time	197?	3.75	7.50	15.00

ZIMMERMAN, DICK

See IAN WHITCOMB.

ZINN'S RAGTIME STRING QUARTET

Number	Title	Yr	VG	VG+	NM
CLASSIC JAZZ					
❑ 13	Zinn's Ragtime String Quartet	197?	2.50	5.00	10.00

ZITO, PHIL

Drummer and bandleader.

Number	Title	Yr	VG	VG+	NM
COLUMBIA					
❑ CL 6110 [10]	International City Dixielanders	1950	12.50	25.00	50.00

ZITRO, JAMES

Drummer and composer. Also see ZYTRON.

Number	Title	Yr	VG	VG+	NM
ESP-DISK'					
❑ 1052 [S]	Zitro	1968	6.25	12.50	25.00

ZOLLER, ATTILA

Guitarist.

Number	Title	Yr	VG	VG+	NM
EMARCY					
❑ SPE-66013	The Horizon Beyond	1968	6.25	12.50	25.00
EMBRYO					
❑ SD 523	Gypsy Cry	1970	5.00	10.00	20.00
INNER CITY					
❑ IC-3008	Dream Bells	1976	3.75	7.50	15.00

ZONJIC, ALEXANDER

Flutist.

Number	Title	Yr	VG	VG+	NM
OPTIMISM					
❑ OP-3102	When Is It Real	198?	2.50	5.00	10.00
❑ OP-3206	Elegant Evening	198?	2.50	5.00	10.00
❑ OP-3207	Romance with You	198?	2.50	5.00	10.00

ZORN, JOHN

Horn player, composer and bandleader.

Number	Title	Yr	VG	VG+	NM
ELEKTRA					
❑ 60844	Spy vs. Spy	1989	3.00	6.00	12.00
ELEKTRA/NONESUCH					
❑ 79139	The Big Gundown	1987	2.50	5.00	10.00
❑ 79172	Spillane/Two-Lane Highway/Forbidden Fruit	1987	2.50	5.00	10.00
❑ 79238	Naked City	1990	3.00	6.00	12.00
HAT ART					
❑ 2034 [(2)]	Cobra	1987	3.75	7.50	15.00

ZOTTOLA, GLENN

Trumpeter.

Number	Title	Yr	VG	VG+	NM
DREAMSTREET					
❑ 105	Live at Eddie Condon's	1980	3.00	6.00	12.00
❑ 107	Steamin' Mainstream	1986	2.50	5.00	10.00
FAMOUS DOOR					
❑ HL-141	Secret Love	1981	3.00	6.00	12.00
❑ HL-149	Stardust	1983	3.00	6.00	12.00

ZUNIGER, RICK

Guitarist.

Number	Title	Yr	VG	VG+	NM
HEADFIRST					
❑ 675	New Frontier	198?	3.00	6.00	12.00

ZURKE, BOB

Pianist.

Number	Title	Yr	VG	VG+	NM
RCA VICTOR					
❑ LPM-1013 [M]	The Tom Cat on the Keys	1955	20.00	40.00	80.00

ZYTRON

Led by JAMES ZITRO and DAVE LIEBMAN.

Number	Title	Yr	VG	VG+	NM
PACIFIC ARTS					
❑ PACB7-120	New Moon in Zytron	197?	3.75	7.50	15.00

Number	Title	Yr	VG	VG+	NM

ORIGINAL CAST RECORDINGS

Almost by definition, there are few jazz albums that fit in this category. The below albums contain no dialogue or songs, as most original cast LPs do; these contain instrumental music that was used in the background of the play. For albums of music used in television programs, see the "Television Albums" section.

CLARA (BEG, BORROW OR STEAL)
❑ Commentary CYN-02 [M] — 1960 — 15.00 — 30.00 — 60.00

MY PEOPLE
❑ Contact C-1 [M] — 1966 — 5.00 — 10.00 — 20.00
❑ Contact CS-1 [S] — 1966 — 6.25 — 12.50 — 25.00

SOUNDTRACKS

The below albums contain music written for films that was contained in the films. It does not include "Jazz Impressions Of" albums or other interpretive works. Also, many albums are listed under the composer or artist's name, so if you don't see it below, be sure to look it up there. Some soundtrack music can be found under DUKE ELLINGTON; ELLA FITZGERALD; QUINCY JONES; HENRY MANCINI; and LALO SCHIFRIN, just to name a few.

If an album has movie music of a "jazzy" nature, and is listed neither below nor in the artist section, then we'd like to know about it so it can be included in future editions of the Goldmine Jazz Album Price Guide.

Title	Yr	VG	VG+	NM
ALFIE				
❑ Impulse! A-9111 [M]	1966	7.50	15.00	30.00
❑ Impulse! AS-9111 [S]	1966	7.50	15.00	30.00
❑ ABC Impulse! AS-9111 [S]	1968	3.75	7.50	15.00
ALL NIGHT LONG				
❑ Epic LA 16032 [M]	1962	10.00	20.00	40.00
❑ Epic BA 17032 [S]	1962	12.50	25.00	50.00
ANATOMY OF A MURDER				
❑ Columbia CL 1360 [M]	1959	10.00	20.00	40.00
❑ Columbia CS 8166 [S]	1959	12.50	25.00	50.00
BABY DOLL				
❑ Columbia CL 958 [M]	195?	12.50	25.00	50.00
-- No ads for LPs on back cover				
❑ Columbia CL 958 [M]	1956	15.00	30.00	60.00
-- Ads for other Columbia LPs on back cover				
BAREFOOT ADVENTURE				
❑ Pacific Jazz PJ-35 [M]	1961	10.00	20.00	40.00
❑ Pacific Jazz ST-35 [S]	1961	15.00	30.00	60.00
BLACK ORPHEUS				
❑ Epic LN 3672 [M]	1959	10.00	20.00	40.00
❑ Fontana MGF-27520 [M]	1963	5.00	10.00	20.00
❑ Fontana SRF-67520 [R]	1963	3.75	7.50	15.00
BLACKBIRDS OF 1928				
❑ Columbia Masterworks OL 6770 [M]	1968	3.75	7.50	15.00
❑ Revue 1 [M]	196?	7.50	15.00	30.00
❑ Sutton SSU-270 [R]	196?	3.00	6.00	12.00
❑ Sutton SU-270 [M]	196?	5.00	10.00	20.00
BLOW-UP				
❑ MGM E-4447 [M]	1967	10.00	20.00	40.00
❑ MGM SE-4447 [S]	1967	12.50	25.00	50.00
COLLEGE CONFIDENTIAL				
❑ Chancellor CHL-5016 [M]	1960	10.00	20.00	40.00
❑ Chancellor CHLS-5016 [S]	1960	12.50	25.00	50.00
THE CONNECTION				
❑ Charlie Parker PLP-806 [M]	1962	7.50	15.00	30.00
❑ Charlie Parker PLP-806S [S]	1962	10.00	20.00	40.00
❑ Felsted 2512 [S]	1960	75.00	150.00	300.00
❑ Felsted 7512 [M]	1960	50.00	100.00	200.00
COOL WORLD				
❑ Philips PHM 200-138 [M]	1964	12.50	25.00	50.00
❑ Philips PHS 600-138 [S]	1964	20.00	40.00	80.00
DAKTARI				
❑ Leo the Lion CH-1043 [M]	1967	5.00	10.00	20.00
❑ MGM CH-1043 [M]	1967	5.00	10.00	20.00
THE DEADLY AFFAIR				
❑ Verve V-8679 [M]	1966	6.25	12.50	25.00
❑ Verve V6-8679 [S]	1966	7.50	15.00	30.00
DESTINATION MOON				
❑ Columbia CL 6151 [10]	1950	30.00	60.00	120.00
❑ Omega OL-3 [M]	1959	10.00	20.00	40.00
❑ Omega OSL-3 [S]	196?	20.00	40.00	80.00
EAST SIDE, WEST SIDE				
❑ Columbia CL 2123 [M]	1963	6.25	12.50	25.00
❑ Columbia CS 8923 [S]	1963	10.00	20.00	40.00
THE FALCON AND THE SNOWMAN				
❑ EMI America SV-17150	1985	2.50	5.00	10.00
THE FIVE PENNIES				
❑ Dot DLP-9500 [M]	1959	6.25	12.50	25.00
❑ Dot DLP-29500 [S]	1959	12.50	25.00	50.00

Number	Title	Yr	VG	VG+	NM
THE FUGITIVE KIND					
❑ United Artists UAL-4065 [M]		1959	12.50	25.00	50.00
❑ United Artists UAS-5065 [S]		1959	17.50	35.00	70.00
THE GENE KRUPA STORY					
❑ Verve MGVS-6105 [S]		1959	25.00	50.00	100.00
-- *Original stereo issue*					
❑ Verve MGV-15010 [M]		1959	12.50	25.00	50.00
❑ Verve V-15010 [M]		1961	5.00	10.00	20.00
❑ Verve V6-15010 [S]		1963	20.00	40.00	80.00
-- *Early reissue*					
THE GENTLE RAIN					
❑ Mercury MG-21016 [M]		1966	5.00	10.00	20.00
❑ Mercury SR-61016 [S]		1966	6.25	12.50	25.00
THE GLENN MILLER STORY					
❑ Decca DL 5519 [10]		1954	10.00	20.00	40.00
❑ Decca DL 8226 [M]		1956	7.50	15.00	30.00
❑ Decca DL 9123 [M]		196?	5.00	10.00	20.00
-- *Reissue of 8226*					
❑ Decca DL 79123 [R]		196?	3.75	7.50	15.00
GOLDEN BOY					
❑ Colpix CP-478 [M]		1964	5.00	10.00	20.00
❑ Colpix SCP-478 [S]		1964	6.25	12.50	25.00
GONE WITH THE WAVE					
❑ Colpix CP-492 [M]		1965	10.00	20.00	40.00
❑ Colpix SCP-492 [S]		1965	15.00	30.00	60.00
HEAVY TRAFFIC					
❑ Fantasy F-9436		1973	6.25	12.50	25.00
HELL TO ETERNITY					
❑ Warwick W 2030 [M]		1960	30.00	60.00	120.00
❑ Warwick WST 2030 [S]		1960	50.00	100.00	200.00
I WANT TO LIVE					
❑ United Artists UAL-4006 [M]		1958	7.50	15.00	30.00
❑ United Artists UAS-4006 [S]		1958	10.00	20.00	40.00
-- *Jazz music by Gerry Mulligan, Shelly Mann and Art Farmer*					
❑ United Artists UXL 1 [(2) M]		1958	15.00	30.00	60.00
-- *Combines 4005 and 4006 into one package*					
❑ United Artists UXS 51 [(2) S]		1958	20.00	40.00	80.00
-- *Combines 5005 and 5006 into one package*					
THE INTERNS					
❑ Colpix CP 427 [M]		1962	7.50	15.00	30.00
❑ Colpix SCP 427 [S]		1962	10.00	20.00	40.00
THE JAMES DEAN STORY					
❑ Capitol W 881 [M]		1957	15.00	30.00	60.00
❑ Kimberly 2016 [M]		1960	10.00	20.00	40.00
❑ Kimberly 11016 [S]		1960	12.50	25.00	50.00
-- *Reissue of World Pacific 2005*					
❑ World Pacific P-2005 [M]		1958	25.00	50.00	100.00
KWAMINA					
❑ Mercury MG-20654 [M]		1961	6.25	12.50	25.00
❑ Mercury SR-60654 [S]		1961	7.50	15.00	30.00
LES LIAISONS DANGEREUSES					
❑ Charlie Parker PLP-813 [M]		1962	6.25	12.50	25.00
❑ Charlie Parker PLP-813S [S]		1962	7.50	15.00	30.00
❑ Epic LA 16022 [M]		1961	10.00	20.00	40.00
❑ Epic BA 17022 [S]		1961	7.50	15.00	30.00
❑ Fontana MGF-27539 [M]		1965	5.00	10.00	20.00
❑ Fontana SRF-67539 [R]		1965	3.75	7.50	15.00
LOVE LIFE					
❑ Heritage 600 [M]		195?	15.00	30.00	60.00
A MAN CALLED ADAM					
❑ Reprise R 6180 [M]		1966	3.75	7.50	15.00
❑ Reprise RS 6180 [S]		1966	5.00	10.00	20.00
THE MAN WITH THE GOLDEN ARM					
❑ Decca DL 8257 [M]		1956	10.00	20.00	40.00
MICKEY ONE					
❑ MGM E-4312 [M]		1965	5.00	10.00	20.00
❑ MGM SE-4312 [S]		1965	6.25	12.50	25.00
A MILANESE STORY					
❑ Atlantic 1388 [M]		1962	5.00	10.00	20.00
❑ Atlantic SD 1388 [S]		1962	6.25	12.50	25.00
-- *Composed by JOHN LEWIS*					
MR. BUDDWING					
❑ Verve V-8638 [M]		1965	3.75	7.50	15.00
❑ Verve V6-8638 [S]		1965	6.25	12.50	25.00

Number	Title	Yr	VG	VG+	NM
A NEW KIND OF LOVE					
❑ Mercury MG-20859 [M]		1963	3.75	7.50	15.00
❑ Mercury SR-60859 [S]		1963	5.00	10.00	20.00
ODDS AGAINST TOMORROW					
❑ United Artists UAL-4061 [M]		1959	7.50	15.00	30.00
❑ United Artists UAS-5061 [S]		1959	12.50	25.00	50.00
ORCHESTRA WIVES					
❑ RCA Victor LPT-3065 [10]		1954	15.00	30.00	60.00
PAPER MOON					
❑ Paramount PAS-1012		1973	5.00	10.00	20.00
PARIS BLUES					
❑ United Artists UAL-4092 [M]		1961	6.25	12.50	25.00
❑ United Artists UAS-5092 [S]		1961	7.50	15.00	30.00
PETE KELLY'S BLUES					
❑ Columbia CL 690 [M]		1955	10.00	20.00	40.00
❑ Decca DL 8166 [M]		1955	12.50	25.00	50.00
-- *Black label, silver print*					
PRIVATE HELL 36					
❑ Coral CRL 56122 [10]		1954	25.00	50.00	100.00
THE PROPER TIME					
❑ Contemporary M-3587 [M]		1960	7.50	15.00	30.00
❑ Contemporary S-7587 [S]		1960	10.00	20.00	40.00
THE RAT RACE					
❑ Dot DLP-3306 [M]		1960	10.00	20.00	40.00
❑ Dot DLP-25306 [S]		1960	12.50	25.00	50.00
THE REPORTER					
❑ Columbia CL 2269 [M]		1963	7.50	15.00	30.00
❑ Columbia CS 9069 [S]		1963	10.00	20.00	40.00
❑ Coral CRL 56122 [10]		1954	25.00	50.00	100.00
SATAN IN HIGH HEELS					
❑ Charlie Parker PLP-406 [M]		1962	12.50	25.00	50.00
-- *Gatefold cover*					
❑ Charlie Parker PLP-406 [M]		1962	7.50	15.00	30.00
-- *Standard cover*					
❑ Charlie Parker PLP-406S [S]		1962	15.00	30.00	60.00
-- *Gatefold cover*					
❑ Charlie Parker PLP-406S [S]		1962	10.00	20.00	40.00
-- *Standard cover*					
SLIPPERY WHEN WET					
❑ World Pacific WP-1265 [M]		1959	12.50	25.00	50.00
ST. LOUIS BLUES					
❑ Capitol W 993 [M]		1958	12.50	25.00	50.00
-- *Turquoise or gray label*					
❑ Capitol W 993 [M]		1959	6.25	12.50	25.00
-- *Black colorband label, logo at left*					
❑ Capitol W 993 [M]		196?	5.00	10.00	20.00
-- *Black colorband label, logo at top*					
ST. LOUIS WOMAN					
❑ Capitol L 355 [10]		1955	20.00	40.00	80.00
THE STING					
❑ MCA 390		1973	3.00	6.00	12.00
-- *Original edition*					
❑ MCA 2040		197?	2.50	5.00	10.00
❑ MCA 37091		1981	2.00	4.00	8.00
THE STRANGE ONE					
❑ Coral CRL 57132 [M]		1957	17.50	35.00	70.00
SUN VALLEY SERENADE					
❑ RCA Victor LPT-3064 [10]		1954	15.00	30.00	60.00
SWEET LOVE, BITTER					
❑ Impulse! A-9141 [M]		1967	10.00	20.00	40.00
❑ Impulse! AS-9141 [S]		1967	7.50	15.00	30.00
❑ ABC Impulse! AS-9141 [S]		1968	3.75	7.50	15.00
THE SWEET SMELL OF SUCCESS					
❑ Decca DL 8610 [M]		1957	15.00	30.00	60.00
THIS PROPERTY IS CONDEMNED					
❑ Verve V-8664 [M]		1966	5.00	10.00	20.00
❑ Verve V6-8664 [S]		1966	7.50	15.00	30.00
THE V.I.P.S THEME					
❑ MGM E-4184 [M]		1963	5.00	10.00	20.00
❑ MGM SE-4184 [S]		1963	6.25	12.50	25.00
-- *Music by Bill Evans*					
THE WILD ONE					
❑ Decca DL 5515 [10]		1954	20.00	40.00	80.00

Number	Title	Yr	VG	VG+	NM
❑ Decca DL 8349 [M]		1956	10.00	20.00	40.00
THE YELLOW CANARY					
❑ Verve V-8548 [M]		1963	5.00	10.00	20.00
❑ Verve V6-8548 [S]		1963	6.25	12.50	25.00
YOUNG BILLY YOUNG					
❑ United Artists UAS-5199		1969	6.25	12.50	25.00
YOUNG MAN WITH A HORN					
❑ Columbia CL 582 [M]		1950	7.50	15.00	30.00
❑ Columbia CL 6106 [10]		1950	12.50	25.00	50.00

TELEVISION ALBUMS

The following section includes albums with content related to television programs, whether a series, miniseries or special. As with the soundtrack albums, there are some records listed under the artist's name; some of these can be found under VINCE GUARALDI; HENRY MANCINI; and LALO SCHIFRIN, among others.

If an album has music of a "jazzy" nature, is from a television show of any kind, and is listed neither below nor in the artist section, then we'd like to know about it so it can be included in future editions of the Goldmine Jazz Album Price Guide.

Number	Title	Yr	VG	VG+	NM
A CHARLIE BROWN CHRISTMAS					
❑ Charlie Brown 3701		1977	5.00	10.00	20.00

-- Complete soundtrack with dialogue, plus music by Vince Guaraldi; includes 12-page bound-in booklet with script and illustrations

Number	Title	Yr	VG	VG+	NM
ELEVEN AGAINST THE ICE					
❑ RCA Victor LPM-1618 [M]		1958	15.00	30.00	60.00
THE MUSIC FROM M SQUAD					
❑ RCA Victor LPM-2062 [M]		1959	7.50	15.00	30.00
❑ RCA Victor LSP-2062 [S]		1959	10.00	20.00	40.00
RICHARD DIAMOND					
❑ EmArcy MG-36162 [M]		1959	12.50	25.00	50.00
❑ EmArcy SR-80045 [S]		1959	20.00	40.00	80.00
77 SUNSET STRIP					
❑ Warner Bros. W 1289 [M]		1959	7.50	15.00	30.00
❑ Warner Bros. WS 1289 [S]		1959	10.00	20.00	40.00
THRILLER					
❑ Time S-2034 [S]		1960	10.00	20.00	40.00
❑ Time 52034 [M]		1960	7.50	15.00	30.00

Number	Title	Yr	VG	VG+	NM

VARIOUS ARTISTS COLLECTIONS

For the most part, the below listing covers jazz-related albums with three or more different artists featured. There are some exceptions, though. The listings do contain some with only one or two artists if they were part of a various-artists series (for example, Jazz at the Philharmonic). Also, some multi-artist albums are contained in the main listings.

In addition, some of the below are what can be called "blowing sessions," leaderless jams of artists who were all part of one record label's signings. These generally fetch more than the average various-artists album.

Albums with the same name are grouped together, even when they do not have the same contents! If we know they are different albums, we indicate this in the listings.

Over 1,600 various-artists LPs appear below. Our research here is truly just beginning. If you have a multi-artist set that is neither below nor under any of the individual artists in the main listings, please let us know.

AC-DC BLUES
❑ Stash ST-106   197?   2.50   5.00   10.00

ACCENT ON PIANO
❑ Urania UJLP-1207 [M]   1955   7.50   15.00   30.00

ACCENT ON TROMBONE
❑ Urania UJLP-1205 [M]   1955   7.50   15.00   30.00

ADD-A-PART JAZZ
❑ Columbia CL 908 [M]   1956   6.25   12.50   25.00

THE ADVANCE GUARD OF THE '40S
❑ EmArcy MG-36016 [M]   1955   12.50   25.00   50.00

AFRO SUMMIT
❑ BASF 20675   197?   5.00   10.00   20.00
❑ Pausa 7026   198?   2.50   5.00   10.00

AFRO-COOL
❑ GNP Crescendo GNP-48 [M]   1959   5.00   10.00   20.00

AFRO-CUBAN JAZZ
❑ Verve VE-2-2522 [(2)]   197?   3.75   7.50   15.00
❑ Verve 833 561-1 [(2)]   198?   3.00   6.00   12.00

AFTER HOUR JAZZ
❑ Epic LN 320? [M]   1955   7.50   15.00   30.00

AFTER HOURS BLUES, 1949
❑ Biograph 12010   1969   3.00   6.00   12.00

ALIVEMUTHERFORYA
❑ Columbia JC 35349   197?   3.00   6.00   12.00

ALL DAY LONG
❑ Prestige PRLP-7081 [M]   1957   25.00   50.00 100.00
-- Reissued as Prestige 7277; see KENNY BURRELL.

ALL NIGHT LONG
❑ Prestige PRLP-7073 [M]   1957   25.00   50.00 100.00
-- Reissued as Prestige 7289; see KENNY BURRELL.

ALL STAR JAZZ
❑ Halo 50223 [M]   195?   7.50   15.00   30.00

ALL STAR SESSIONS
❑ Capitol M-11031   1973   3.00   6.00   12.00

ALL STAR SWING GROUPS
❑ Savoy Jazz SJL-2218 [(2)]   198?   3.00   6.00   12.00

ALL STAR TRIBUTE TO TATUM
❑ American Recording Society G-424 [M]   1957   7.50   15.00   30.00

ALL-STAR DATES
❑ RCA Victor LPT-21 [10]   1951   12.50   25.00   50.00

ALL-STAR STOMPERS
❑ Circle L-402 [M]   1951   10.00   20.00   40.00

ALTO ALTITUDE
❑ EmArcy MG-36018 [M]   1955   12.50   25.00   50.00

ALTO ARTISTRY
❑ Trip 5543   197?   2.50   5.00   10.00

ALTO SAXES
❑ Norgran MGN-1035 [M]   1955   20.00   40.00   80.00
❑ Verve MGV-8126 [M]   1957   7.50   15.00   30.00
❑ Verve V-8126 [M]   1961   5.00   10.00   20.00

ALTO SUMMIT
❑ Prestige PRLP-7684   1969   3.75   7.50   15.00

AMERICA'S GREATEST JAZZMEN PLAY COLE PORTER
❑ Moodsville MVLP-34 [M]   1963   10.00   20.00   40.00
-- Green label
❑ Moodsville MVLP-34 [M]   1965   5.00   10.00   20.00
-- Blue label, trident logo at right
❑ Moodsville MVST-34 [S]   1963   10.00   20.00   40.00
-- Green label
❑ Moodsville MVST-34 [S]   1965   5.00   10.00   20.00
-- Blue label, trident logo at right

AMERICA'S GREATEST JAZZMEN PLAY GEORGE GERSHWIN
❑ Moodsville MVLP-33 [M]   1963   10.00   20.00   40.00
-- Green label
❑ Moodsville MVLP-33 [M]   1965   5.00   10.00   20.00
-- Blue label, trident logo at right
❑ Moodsville MVST-33 [S]   1963   10.00   20.00   40.00
-- Green label
❑ Moodsville MVST-33 [S]   1965   5.00   10.00   20.00
-- Blue label, trident logo at right

AMERICA'S GREATEST JAZZMEN PLAY RICHARD RODGERS
❑ Moodsville MVLP-35 [M]   1963   10.00   20.00   40.00
-- Green label
❑ Moodsville MVLP-35 [M]   1965   5.00   10.00   20.00
-- Blue label, trident logo at right
❑ Moodsville MVST-35 [S]   1963   10.00   20.00   40.00
-- Green label
❑ Moodsville MVST-35 [S]   1965   5.00   10.00   20.00
-- Blue label, trident logo at right

AMERICA'S GREATEST JAZZMEN PLAY THE BROADWAY SCENE
❑ Moodsville MVLP-38 [M]   1963   10.00   20.00   40.00
-- Green label
❑ Moodsville MVLP-38 [M]   1965   5.00   10.00   20.00
-- Blue label, trident logo at right
❑ Moodsville MVST-38 [S]   1963   10.00   20.00   40.00
-- Green label
❑ Moodsville MVST-38 [S]   1965   5.00   10.00   20.00
-- Blue label, trident logo at right

AMERICAN JAZZ FESTIVAL AT NEWPORT '56, NO. 1
-- See LOUIS ARMSTRONG.

AMERICAN JAZZ FESTIVAL AT NEWPORT '56, NO. 2
-- See DAVE BRUBECK.

AMERICAN JAZZ FESTIVAL AT NEWPORT '56, NO. 3
-- See DUKE ELLINGTON.

AMERICAN JAZZ FESTIVAL AT NEWPORT '56, NO. 4
-- See DUKE ELLINGTON.

AMERICANS ABROAD, VOL. 1
❑ Pax LP-6009 [10]   1955   10.00   20.00   40.00

AMERICANS ABROAD, VOL. 2
❑ Pax LP-6015 [10]   1955   10.00   20.00   40.00

AMERICANS IN EUROPE, VOL. 1
❑ ABC Impulse! AS-36 [S]   1968   3.00   6.00   12.00
❑ Impulse! A-36 [M]   1963   5.00   10.00   20.00
❑ Impulse! AS-36 [S]   1963   6.25   12.50   25.00

AMERICANS IN EUROPE, VOL. 2
❑ ABC Impulse! AS-37 [S]   1968   3.00   6.00   12.00
❑ Impulse! A-37 [M]   1963   5.00   10.00   20.00
❑ Impulse! AS-37 [S]   1963   6.25   12.50   25.00

THE ANATOMY OF IMPROVISATION
❑ Verve MGV-8230 [M]   1958   7.50   15.00   30.00
❑ Verve V-8230 [M]   1961   5.00   10.00   20.00

ANNIVERSARY
❑ Xanadu 201   1986   2.50   5.00   10.00

ANOTHER MONDAY NIGHT AT BIRDLAND
❑ Roulette R 52022 [M]   1959   7.50   15.00   30.00
❑ Roulette SR 52022 [S]   1959   7.50   15.00   30.00

AN ANTHOLOGY OF CALIFORNIA MUSIC
❑ Jazz: West Coast JWC-500 [M]   1955   37.50   75.00 150.00

AN ANTHOLOGY OF CALIFORNIA MUSIC, VOL. 2
❑ Jazz: West Coast JWC-501 [M]   1956   37.50   75.00 150.00

ANTHROPOLOGY
❑ Zim 1002   197?   3.00   6.00   12.00

THE ART OF JAZZ PIANO
❑ Epic LN 3295 [M]   1956   7.50   15.00   30.00

Number	Title	Yr	VG	VG+	NM
THE ART OF THE BALLAD					
❏ Verve VSP-17 [M]		1966	3.75	7.50	15.00
❏ Verve VSPS-17 [R]		1966	2.50	5.00	10.00
THE ART OF THE BALLAD 2					
❏ Verve VSP-38 [M]		1966	3.75	7.50	15.00
❏ Verve VSPS-38 [R]		1966	2.50	5.00	10.00
THE ART OF THE JAM SESSION: MONTREUX '77					
❏ Pablo Live 2620 106 [(8)]		1978	17.50	35.00	70.00
ASIAN JOURNAL					
❏ Music of the World H-303		198?	2.50	5.00	10.00
ASSORTED FLAVORS OF PACIFIC JAZZ					
❏ Pacific Jazz HFS-1 [M]		1956	12.50	25.00	50.00
THE ATLANTIC FAMILY LIVE AT MONTREUX					
❏ Atlantic SD-2-3000 [(2)]		1977	3.75	7.50	15.00
ATLANTIC JAZZ					
❏ Atlantic 81712 [(15)]		1987	62.50	125.00	250.00
-- Boxed set with all 12 volumes in 15 records, liner notes and credits					
ATLANTIC JAZZ: BEBOP					
❏ Atlantic 81702		1987	2.50	5.00	10.00
ATLANTIC JAZZ: FUSION					
❏ Atlantic 81711		1987	2.50	5.00	10.00
ATLANTIC JAZZ: INTROSPECTION					
❏ Atlantic 81710		1987	2.50	5.00	10.00
ATLANTIC JAZZ: KANSAS CITY					
❏ Atlantic 81701		1987	2.50	5.00	10.00
ATLANTIC JAZZ: MAINSTREAM					
❏ Atlantic 81704		1987	2.50	5.00	10.00
ATLANTIC JAZZ: NEW ORLEANS					
❏ Atlantic 81700		1987	2.50	5.00	10.00
ATLANTIC JAZZ: PIANO					
❏ Atlantic 81707 [(2)]		1987	3.00	6.00	12.00
ATLANTIC JAZZ: POST BOP					
❏ Atlantic 81705		1987	2.50	5.00	10.00
ATLANTIC JAZZ: SINGERS					
❏ Atlantic 81706 [(2)]		1987	3.00	6.00	12.00
ATLANTIC JAZZ: SOUL					
❏ Atlantic 81708 [(2)]		1987	3.00	6.00	12.00
ATLANTIC JAZZ: THE AVANT-GARDE					
❏ Atlantic 81709		1987	2.50	5.00	10.00
ATLANTIC JAZZ: WEST COAST					
❏ Atlantic 81703		1987	2.50	5.00	10.00
THE ATLANTIC NEW ORLEANS JAZZ SESSIONS					
❏ Mosaic MQ6-179 [(6)]		199?	30.00	60.00	120.00
ATLANTIC RECORDS: GREAT MOMENTS IN JAZZ					
❏ Atlantic 81907 [(3)]		1989	6.25	12.50	25.00
AUDIO MASTER PLUS SAMPLER					
❏ A&M SP6-3003		198?	3.00	6.00	12.00
AUDIO MASTER PLUS SAMPLER II					
❏ A&M SP6-3021		198?	3.00	6.00	12.00
AUTOBIOGRAPHY IN JAZZ					
❏ Debut DEB-198 [M]		1955	37.50	75.00	150.00
❏ Fantasy OJC-115		198?	2.50	5.00	10.00
AWARD ALBUM JAZZ VOCALS					
❏ Bethlehem BCP-6060 [M]		1961	6.25	12.50	25.00
BACKGROUNDS OF JAZZ, VOL. 1: COUNTRY & URBAN BLUES					
❏ "X" LVA-3016 [10]		1954	20.00	40.00	80.00
BACKGROUNDS OF JAZZ, VOL. 1: THE JUG BANDS					
❏ "X" LX-3009 [10]		1954	20.00	40.00	80.00
BACKGROUNDS OF JAZZ, VOL. 3: KINGS OF THE BLUES					
❏ "X" LVA-3032 [10]		1955	20.00	40.00	80.00
BACKWOOD BLUES					
❏ Riverside RLP-1039 [10]		1954	20.00	40.00	80.00
BALLROOM BANDSTAND					
❏ Columbia CL 611 [M]		1955	6.25	12.50	25.00
BARGAIN DAY					
❏ EmArcy MG-36087 [M]		1956	10.00	20.00	40.00

Number	Title	Yr	VG	VG+	NM
BARREL HOUSE PIANO					
❏ Brunswick BL 58022 [10]		1951	15.00	30.00	60.00
BARRELHOUSE BOOGIE					
❏ Bluebird 8334-1-RB		198?	2.50	5.00	10.00
BARRELHOUSE PIANO 1927-36					
❏ Yazoo 1028		197?	2.50	5.00	10.00
THE BASS					
❏ ABC Impulse! AS-9284 [(3)]		197?	5.00	10.00	20.00
BATTLE OF BANDS					
❏ Capitol H 235 [10]		1950	12.50	25.00	50.00
BATTLE OF JAZZ, VOL. 1					
-- See BUD FREEMAN.					
BATTLE OF JAZZ, VOL. 2					
-- See ART TATUM.					
BATTLE OF JAZZ, VOL. 3					
❏ Brunswick BL 58039 [10]		1953	12.50	25.00	50.00
BATTLE OF JAZZ, VOL. 4					
-- See EDMOND HALL.					
BATTLE OF JAZZ, VOL. 5					
-- See BOBBY HACKETT.					
BATTLE OF JAZZ, VOL. 6					
-- See RED ALLEN.					
BATTLE OF JAZZ, VOL. 7					
-- See ROY ELDRIDGE.					
BATTLE OF JAZZ, VOL. 8					
-- See JOHNNY DODDS.					
BATTLE OF THE BIG BANDS					
❏ Capitol T 667 [M]		1956	7.50	15.00	30.00
BATTLE OF THE SAXES					
❏ Aladdin LP-701 [10]		1950	125.00	250.00	500.00
BATTLE OF THE SAXES-TENOR ALL STARS					
❏ EmArcy MG-36023 [M]		1955	12.50	25.00	50.00
❏ Trip 5527		197?	2.50	5.00	10.00
BE OUR GUEST					
❏ Gene Norman GNP-20 [M]		1955	6.25	12.50	25.00
THE BE-BOP ERA					
❏ RCA Victor LPV-519		1965	5.00	10.00	20.00
BE-BOP SINGERS					
❏ Prestige PRST-7828		1971	3.00	6.00	12.00
BEBOP AND BEYOND					
❏ Concord Jazz CJ-244		1984	2.50	5.00	10.00
BEBOP BOYS					
❏ Savoy Jazz SJL-2225 [(2)]		198?	3.00	6.00	12.00
THE BEBOP ERA					
❏ Columbia Jazz Masterpieces CJ 40972		1988	2.50	5.00	10.00
BEBOP REVISITED, VOL. 1					
❏ Xanadu 120		197?	2.50	5.00	10.00
BEBOP REVISITED, VOL. 2					
❏ Xanadu 124		197?	2.50	5.00	10.00
BEBOP REVISITED, VOL. 3					
❏ Xanadu 172		197?	2.50	5.00	10.00
BEBOP REVISITED, VOL. 4					
❏ Xanadu 197		197?	2.50	5.00	10.00
BEBOP REVISITED, VOL. 5					
❏ Xanadu 205		1986	2.50	5.00	10.00
BEBOP REVISITED, VOL. 6					
❏ Xanadu 208		1987	2.50	5.00	10.00
BEST COAST JAZZ					
❏ EmArcy MG-36039 [M]		1955	20.00	40.00	80.00
BEST FROM THE WEST: MODERN SOUNDS FROM CALIFORNIA, VOL. 1					
❏ Blue Note BLP-5059 [10]		1955	50.00	100.00	200.00
BEST FROM THE WEST: MODERN SOUNDS FROM CALIFORNIA, VOL. 2					
❏ Blue Note BLP-5060 [10]		1955	50.00	100.00	200.00
THE BEST OF ARGO JAZZ					
❏ Argo ALPS-1 [M]		1961	7.50	15.00	30.00

Number / Title	Yr	VG	VG+	NM
THE BEST OF BLUE NOTE, VOL. 1				
❏ Blue Note BST-84429 [(2)]	197?	5.00	10.00	20.00
THE BEST OF BLUE NOTE, VOL. 2				
❏ Blue Note BST-84433 [(2)]	197?	5.00	10.00	20.00
BEST OF DIXIELAND				
❏ RCA Victor ANL1-1431	1976	2.50	5.00	10.00
❏ RCA Victor LPM-2982 [M]	1965	5.00	10.00	20.00
❏ RCA Victor LSP-2982 [R]	1965	3.00	6.00	12.00
BEST OF THE BIG NAME BANDS				
❏ RCA Camden CAL-368 [M]	1958	6.25	12.50	25.00
BETHLEHEM'S BEST				
❏ Bethlehem EXLP-6 [(3) M]	1958	17.50	35.00	70.00
-- Box set of 82, 83, and 84				
BETHLEHEM'S BEST, VOLUME 1				
❏ Bethlehem BCP-82 [M]	1958	7.50	15.00	30.00
BETHLEHEM'S BEST, VOLUME 2				
❏ Bethlehem BCP-83 [M]	1958	7.50	15.00	30.00
BETHLEHEM'S BEST, VOLUME 3				
❏ Bethlehem BCP-84 [M]	1958	7.50	15.00	30.00
BETHLEHEM'S GRAB BAG				
❏ Bethlehem EXLP-2 [M]	1958	10.00	20.00	40.00
THE BIG 18 -- LIVE ECHOES OF THE SWINGING BANDS				
❏ RCA Victor LPM-1921 [M]	1959	10.00	20.00	40.00
❏ RCA Victor LSP-1921 [S]	1959	12.50	25.00	50.00
BIG BAND CONTRAST				
❏ Bethlehem BCP-6037 [M]	1960	7.50	15.00	30.00
BIG BAND JAZZ				
❏ Brunswick BL 58050 [10]	1953	12.50	25.00	50.00
BIG BAND JAZZ: TULSA TO HARLEM				
❏ Delmark DL-439	1989	2.50	5.00	10.00
BIG BAND STEREO				
❏ Capitol SW 1055 [S]	1959	6.25	12.50	25.00
BIG BANDS				
❏ Capitol STFL-293 [(6)]	1969	7.50	15.00	30.00
-- One album each by Les Brown, Glen Gray, Duke Ellington, Benny Goodman, Harry James and Woody Herman				
THE BIG BANDS 1933				
❏ Prestige PRLP-7645	1969	3.75	7.50	15.00
BIG BANDS ARE BACK				
❏ Commodore J2-15596 [(2)]	198?	3.00	6.00	12.00
BIG BANDS OF THE SINGING YEARS, VOLUME 1				
❏ Collectables COL-5096	198?	2.50	5.00	10.00
BIG BANDS OF THE SINGING YEARS, VOLUME 2				
❏ Collectables COL-5097	198?	2.50	5.00	10.00
BIG BANDS OF THE SWING YEARS				
❏ Archive of Folk and Jazz 359	198?	2.50	5.00	10.00
BIG BANDS UPTOWN				
❏ MCA 1323	198?	2.50	5.00	10.00
BIG BANDS UPTOWN, VOL. 1				
❏ Decca DL 79242	1969	3.00	6.00	12.00
BIG BANDS!				
❏ Onyx 202	197?	3.00	6.00	12.00
BIG BANDS' GREATEST HITS				
❏ Columbia CG 30009 [(2)]	197?	3.00	6.00	12.00
-- "CG" prefix is a reissue of "G"				
❏ Columbia G 30009 [(2)]	1970	5.00	10.00	20.00
-- Red "360 Sound" labels				
❏ Columbia G 30009 [(2)]	1970	3.75	7.50	15.00
-- Orange labels				
BIG BANDS' GREATEST HITS, VOL. 2				
❏ Columbia CG 31213 [(2)]	197?	3.00	6.00	12.00
-- "CG" prefix is a reissue of "G"				
❏ Columbia G 31213 [(2)]	1972	3.75	7.50	15.00
THE BIG BEAT				
❏ Milestone 47016 [(2)]	1990	3.75	7.50	15.00
BIG LITTLE BANDS				
❏ Onyx 220	197?	3.00	6.00	12.00
BIG NAME DIXIE				
❏ Score SLP-4024 [M]	1958	12.50	25.00	50.00
BILL EVANS: A TRIBUTE				
❏ Palo Alto PA-8028 [(2)]	1982	3.75	7.50	15.00
BILLIE HOLIDAY REVISITED				
❏ Mainstream MRL-409	197?	3.00	6.00	12.00
BILLIE, ELLA, LENA, SARAH!				
❏ Columbia Jazz Odyssey PC 36811	198?	2.50	5.00	10.00
BING CROSBY AND ROSEMARY CLOONEY: WHITE CHRISTMAS				
❏ Holiday/Collector's Gold 598	1980	2.50	5.00	10.00
-- Crosby recordings are from a radio broadcast				
BIRD FEATHERS				
-- See PHIL WOODS.				
BIRD'S NIGHT -- THE MUSIC OF CHARLIE PARKER				
❏ Savoy MG-12138 [M]	1958	12.50	25.00	50.00
BIRD'S NIGHT: A CELEBRATION OF THE MUSIC OF CHARLIE PARKER, LIVE AT THE FIVE SPOT				
❏ Savoy Jazz SJL-2257 [(2)]	198?	3.00	6.00	12.00
BIRDLAND ALL STARS AT CARNEGIE HALL				
❏ Roulette RE-127 [(2)]	197?	3.00	6.00	12.00
BIRDLAND DREAM BAND, VOL. 1				
❏ Vik LX-1070 [M]	1957	7.50	15.00	30.00
BIRDLAND DREAM BAND, VOL. 2				
❏ Vik LX-1077 [M]	1957	7.50	15.00	30.00
THE BIRDLAND STARS ON TOUR, VOL. 1				
❏ RCA Victor LPM-1327 [M]	1956	10.00	20.00	40.00
THE BIRDLAND STARS ON TOUR, VOL. 2				
❏ RCA Victor LPM-1328 [M]	1956	10.00	20.00	40.00
THE BIRDLAND STORY				
❏ Roulette RB-2 [(2) M]	1961	10.00	20.00	40.00
❏ Roulette SRB-2 [(2) S]	1961	10.00	20.00	40.00
BIRDLANDERS				
❏ Archive of Folk and Jazz 275	197?	2.50	5.00	10.00
THE BIRTH OF BOP, VOL. 1				
❏ Savoy MG-9022 [10]	1953	37.50	75.00	150.00
THE BIRTH OF BOP, VOL. 2				
❏ Savoy MG-9023 [10]	1953	37.50	75.00	150.00
THE BIRTH OF BOP, VOL. 3				
❏ Savoy MG-9024 [10]	1953	37.50	75.00	150.00
THE BIRTH OF BOP, VOL. 4				
❏ Savoy MG-9025 [10]	1953	37.50	75.00	150.00
THE BIRTH OF BOP, VOL. 5				
❏ Savoy MG-9026 [10]	1953	37.50	75.00	150.00
BIRTH OF SOUL				
❏ Decca DL 79245	1969	3.00	6.00	12.00
BLACK AND WHITE RAGTIME, 1921-39				
❏ Biograph 12047	197?	3.00	6.00	12.00
BLACK CALIFORNIA, VOL. 1				
❏ Savoy Jazz SJL-2215 [(2)]	198?	3.00	6.00	12.00
BLACK CALIFORNIA, VOL. 2				
❏ Savoy Jazz SJL-2242 [(2)]	198?	3.00	6.00	12.00
BLACK GIANTS				
❏ Columbia CG 33402 [(2)]	197?	3.75	7.50	15.00
BLACK LION AT MONTREUX				
❏ Black Lion 213	197?	3.75	7.50	15.00
THE BLACK SWING TRADITION				
❏ Savoy Jazz SJL-2246 [(2)]	198?	3.00	6.00	12.00
BLACKBERRY JAM 1943-45				
❏ Sunbeam 214	197?	2.50	5.00	10.00
BLOWIN' SESSIONS				
❏ Blue Note BN-LA521-H2 [(2)]	1975	5.00	10.00	20.00
BLOWOUT AT MARDI GRAS				
❏ Cook LP-1084 [M]	1955	10.00	20.00	40.00
BLUE NOTE '86: A GENERATION OF JAZZ				
❏ Blue Note BQ-85127	1986	3.00	6.00	12.00
THE BLUE NOTE 50TH ANNIVERSARY COLLECTION VOL. 1: FROM BOOGIE TO BOP, 1939-1956				
❏ Blue Note B1-92465 [(2)]	1989	3.75	7.50	15.00

Number	Title	Yr	VG	VG+	NM
THE BLUE NOTE 50TH ANNIVERSARY COLLECTION VOL. 2: THE JAZZ MESSAGE, 1956-1965					
❑ Blue Note B1-92468 [(2)]		1989	3.75	7.50	15.00
THE BLUE NOTE 50TH ANNIVERSARY COLLECTION VOL. 3: FUNK AND BLUES, 1956-1967					
❑ Blue Note B1-92471 [(2)]		1989	3.75	7.50	15.00
THE BLUE NOTE 50TH ANNIVERSARY COLLECTION VOL. 4: OUTSIDE IN, 1964-1989					
❑ Blue Note B1-92474 [(2)]		1989	3.75	7.50	15.00
THE BLUE NOTE 50TH ANNIVERSARY COLLECTION VOL. 5: LIGHTING THE FUSE, 1970-1989					
❑ Blue Note B1-92477 [(2)]		1989	3.75	7.50	15.00
BLUE NOTE CLASSICS					
❑ Blue Note B-6509 [M]		1969	3.75	7.50	15.00
BLUE NOTE LIVE AT THE ROXY					
❑ Blue Note BN-LA663-J2 [(2)]		1976	3.75	7.50	15.00
BLUE NOTE MEETS THE L.A. PHILHARMONIC					
❑ Blue Note BN-LA870-H		1977	3.75	7.50	15.00
BLUES 'N' FOLK					
❑ Bethlehem BCP-6071 [M]		1963	15.00	30.00	60.00
THE BLUES AND ALL THAT JAZZ					
❑ MCA 1353		198?	2.50	5.00	10.00
BLUES FOR TOMORROW					
❑ Fantasy OJC-030		198?	2.50	5.00	10.00
❑ Riverside RLP 12-243 [M]		1957	10.00	20.00	40.00
BLUES IN CONCERT					
❑ Groove Merchant 4405 [(2)]		197?	5.00	10.00	20.00
THE BLUES IN MODERN JAZZ					
❑ Atlantic 1337 [M]		1961	5.00	10.00	20.00
-- Multicolor label, white "fan" logo at right					
❑ Atlantic 1337 [M]		1963	3.75	7.50	15.00
-- Multicolor label, black "fan" logo at right					
❑ Atlantic SD 1337 [R]		1969	3.00	6.00	12.00
THE BLUES IN STEREO					
❑ World Pacific ST-1021 [S]		1959	7.50	15.00	30.00
THE BLUES, VOL. 2					
❑ Pacific Jazz JWC-502 [M]		1956	12.50	25.00	50.00
❑ World Pacific JWC-502 [M]		1958	10.00	20.00	40.00
THE BLUES, VOL. 2: HAVE BLUES, WILL TRAVEL					
❑ World Pacific JWC-509 [M]		1958	10.00	20.00	40.00
THE BLUES, VOL. 3: BLOWIN' THE BLUES					
❑ World Pacific JWC-512 [M]		1958	10.00	20.00	40.00
❑ World Pacific ST-1029 [S]		1959	7.50	15.00	30.00
BODY AND SOUL					
❑ RCA Victor LPV-501		1964	5.00	10.00	20.00
BONING UP ON 'BONES					
❑ EmArcy MG-36038 [M]		1955	12.50	25.00	50.00
BOOGIE WOOGIE					
❑ Decca DL 5248 [10]		1950	12.50	25.00	50.00
BOOGIE WOOGIE KINGS AND QUEENS					
❑ Decca DL 5249 [10]		1950	12.50	25.00	50.00
BOOGIE WOOGIE PIANO					
❑ Brunswick BL 58018 [10]		1950	15.00	30.00	60.00
BOOGIE WOOGIE PIANOS					
❑ Columbia KC 32708		197?	2.50	5.00	10.00
BOOGIE WOOGIE RARITIES (1927-43)					
❑ Milestone M-2009		197?	3.00	6.00	12.00
BOOGIE WOOGIE TRIO					
❑ Storyville 4006		198?	2.50	5.00	10.00
BOOTY					
❑ Mainstream MRL-413		197?	3.00	6.00	12.00
BOP CITY: EVIDENCE					
❑ Boplicity BOPM-12		198?	2.50	5.00	10.00
BOP CITY: MIDNIGHT					
❑ Boplicity BOPM-9		198?	2.50	5.00	10.00
BOP CITY: STRAIGHT AHEAD					
❑ Boplicity BOPM-10		198?	2.50	5.00	10.00

Number	Title	Yr	VG	VG+	NM
BOP CITY: THINGS ARE GETTING BETTER					
❑ Boplicity BOPM-11		198?	2.50	5.00	10.00
BOP LIVES					
❑ Pickwick SPC-5011		197?	2.50	5.00	10.00
BRASS FEVER					
❑ ABC Impulse! AS-9308		197?	3.00	6.00	12.00
BRASS FEVER: TIME IS RUNNING OUT					
❑ ABC Impulse! AS-9319		197?	3.00	6.00	12.00
BRITISH FESTIVAL OF JAZZ CONCERT					
❑ Decca DL 5422 [10]		1952	12.50	25.00	50.00
BRITISH JAZZ FESTIVAL					
❑ Decca DL 5424 [10]		1952	12.50	25.00	50.00
BROTHERS AND OTHER MOTHERS					
❑ Savoy Jazz SJL-2210 [(2)]		198?	3.00	6.00	12.00
BROTHERS AND OTHER MOTHERS, VOL. 2					
❑ Savoy Jazz SJL-2236 [(2)]		198?	3.00	6.00	12.00
BUSHKIN-SAFRANSKI-WILSON GROUPS					
❑ Allegro 1590 [10]		1955	12.50	25.00	50.00
CAFÉ SOCIETY					
❑ Onyx 210		197?	3.00	6.00	12.00
CALIFORNIA CONCERT					
❑ CTI CTX 2 + 2 [(2)]		197?	3.75	7.50	15.00
THE CATS					
❑ Fantasy OJC-079		198?	2.50	5.00	10.00
❑ New Jazz NJLP-8217 [M]		1959	20.00	40.00	80.00
-- Purple label					
❑ New Jazz NJLP-8217 [M]		1965	7.50	15.00	30.00
-- Blue label, trident logo at right					
CATS AND JAMMER KIDS					
❑ Angel ANG-60007 [10]		1955	12.50	25.00	50.00
CATS VS. CHICKS					
❑ MGM E-255 [10]		1954	12.50	25.00	50.00
A CELEBRATION OF DUKE					
❑ Fantasy OJC-605		1991	3.00	6.00	12.00
❑ Pablo Today 2312 119		197?	3.75	7.50	15.00
CENTRAL AVENUE BREAKDOWN, VOL. 1					
❑ Onyx 212		197?	3.00	6.00	12.00
CENTRAL AVENUE BREAKDOWN, VOL. 2					
❑ Onyx 215		197?	3.00	6.00	12.00
THE CHANGING FACE OF HARLEM					
❑ Savoy Jazz SJL-2208 [(2)]		198?	3.00	6.00	12.00
THE CHANGING FACE OF HARLEM, VOL. 2					
❑ Savoy Jazz SJL-2224 [(2)]		198?	3.00	6.00	12.00
CHARLIE PARKER 10TH MEMORIAL CONCERT					
❑ Limelight LM-82017 [M]		1965	3.75	7.50	15.00
❑ Limelight LS-86017 [S]		1965	5.00	10.00	20.00
❑ Trip 5510		197?	2.50	5.00	10.00
CHARLIE PARKER MEMORIAL CONCERT					
❑ Cadet 2CA-60002 [(2)]		1971	5.00	10.00	20.00
❑ Chess CH-92510		198?	3.00	6.00	12.00
CHICAGO / AUSTIN HIGH SCHOOL					
❑ RCA Victor LPM-1508 [M]		1957	7.50	15.00	30.00
CHICAGO AND ALL THAT JAZZ!					
❑ Verve V-8441 [M]		1961	6.25	12.50	25.00
❑ Verve V6-8441 [S]		1962	7.50	15.00	30.00
CHICAGO JAZZ ALBUM					
❑ Decca DL 8029 [M]		1954	10.00	20.00	40.00
CHICAGO JAZZ, 1923-29					
❑ Biograph 12005		1968	3.00	6.00	12.00
CHICAGO JAZZ, VOLUME 2, 1925-29					
❑ Biograph 12043		197?	3.00	6.00	12.00
CHICAGO SOUTH SIDE					
❑ Historical 10		1968	2.50	5.00	10.00
CHICAGO SOUTH SIDE, VOL. 2					
❑ Historical 30		1969	2.50	5.00	10.00
CHICAGO STYLE JAZZ					
❑ Columbia CL 632 [M]		1955	6.25	12.50	25.00

Number Title	Yr	VG	VG+	NM
CHICAGO'S BOSS TENORS				
❏ Chess CHV-414	1970	3.75	7.50	15.00
CHICAGO: THE LIVING LEGENDS, VOL. 1				
❏ Riverside RLP-389 [M]	196?	5.00	10.00	20.00
❏ Riverside RS-9389 [R]	196?	3.00	6.00	12.00
CHICAGO: THE LIVING LEGENDS, VOL. 2				
❏ Riverside RLP-390 [M]	196?	5.00	10.00	20.00
❏ Riverside RS-9390 [R]	196?	3.00	6.00	12.00
THE CHICAGOANS				
❏ Decca DL 79231	1968	3.00	6.00	12.00
CHOCOLATE DANDIES, 1928-1933				
❏ Swing SW-8448	198?	2.50	5.00	10.00
CLAMBAKE ON BOURBON STREET				
❏ Cook LP-1085 [10]	1955	12.50	25.00	50.00
CLASSIC BLUES ACCOMPANISTS				
❏ Riverside RLP-1052 [10]	1955	20.00	40.00	80.00
CLASSIC CAPITOL JAZZ SESSIONS				
❏ Mosaic MQ19-170 [(19)]	199?	100.00	200.00	400.00
CLASSIC JAZZ PIANO STYLES				
❏ RCA Victor LPV-544 [M]	1967	5.00	10.00	20.00
CLASSIC PIANOS				
❏ Doctor Jazz FW 38851	198?	2.50	5.00	10.00
CLASSIC TENORS, VOL. 2				
❏ Doctor Jazz FW 39519	198?	2.50	5.00	10.00
CLASSICS IN JAZZ				
❏ Capitol T 320 [M]	1954	7.50	15.00	30.00
CLASSICS IN JAZZ: COOL AND QUIET				
❏ Capitol H 371 [10]	1953	12.50	25.00	50.00
CLASSICS IN JAZZ: DIXIELAND STYLISTS				
❏ Capitol H 321 [10]	1952	12.50	25.00	50.00
CLASSICS IN JAZZ: SMALL COMBOS				
❏ Capitol H 322 [10]	1952	12.50	25.00	50.00
COLLECTOR'S JACKPOT, VOL. 1				
❏ Jazz Archives JA-21	198?	2.50	5.00	10.00
COLLECTOR'S JACKPOT, VOL. 2				
❏ Jazz Archives JA-40	198?	2.50	5.00	10.00
COLLECTORS ITEMS, VOL. 2				
❏ Riverside RLP-1040 [10]	1954	20.00	40.00	80.00
COLLECTORS' CHOICE				
❏ Verve V-8408 [M]	1961	---	---	---
-- Canceled				
COLLECTORS' ITEMS, 1922-30				
❏ Historical 11	1967	2.50	5.00	10.00
COLLECTORS' ITEMS, 1925-29				
❏ Historical 20	1968	2.50	5.00	10.00
COLLEGE ALBUM				
❏ Verve MGV-8341 [M]	1959	---	---	---
-- Canceled				
COLLEGE JAZZ: DIXIELAND				
❏ Columbia CL 736 [M]	1956	5.00	10.00	20.00
COLORADO JAZZ PARTY				
❏ BASF 25099 [(2)]	197?	5.00	10.00	20.00
COLUMBIA JAZZ FESTIVAL				
❏ Columbia JJ-1 [M]	1959	6.25	12.50	25.00
COLUMBIA'S ALL NEW TIME-RELEASE CAPSULE				
❏ Columbia AS 247 [DJ]	1977	3.75	7.50	15.00
-- Promo-only sampler				
COMBO JAZZ				
❏ Jazztone J-1221 [M]	1956	7.50	15.00	30.00
COMPARATIVE BLUES				
❏ Hall of Fame 603	197?	2.50	5.00	10.00
❏ Jazztone J-1258 [M]	1957	7.50	15.00	30.00
THE COMPLETE COMMODORE JAZZ RECORDINGS, VOLUME I				
❏ Mosaic M23-123 [(23)]	199?	100.00	200.00	400.00
THE COMPLETE COMMODORE JAZZ RECORDINGS, VOLUME II				
❏ Mosaic M23-128 [(23)]	199?	100.00	200.00	400.00
THE COMPLETE COMMODORE JAZZ RECORDINGS, VOLUME III				
❏ Mosaic M20-134 [(20)]	199?	75.00	150.00	300.00
THE COMPLETE KEYNOTE COLLECTION				
❏ Keynote 830 121-1 [(21)]	1986	62.50	125.00	250.00
THE COMPLETE MASTER JAZZ PIANO SERIES				
❏ Mosaic M6-140 [(6)]	199?	25.00	50.00	100.00
COMPOSERS AT PLAY: HAROLD ARLEN AND COLE PORTER				
❏ "X" LVA-1003 [M]	1955	10.00	20.00	40.00
THE COMPOSITIONS OF BENNY GOLSON				
❏ Riverside RLP-3505 [M]	1962	3.75	7.50	15.00
❏ Riverside RS-93505 [S]	1962	5.00	10.00	20.00
THE COMPOSITIONS OF BOBBY TIMMONS				
❏ Riverside RLP-3512 [M]	1962	3.75	7.50	15.00
❏ Riverside RS-93512 [S]	1962	5.00	10.00	20.00
THE COMPOSITIONS OF CHARLIE PARKER				
❏ Riverside RLP-3506 [M]	1962	3.75	7.50	15.00
❏ Riverside RS-93506 [S]	1962	5.00	10.00	20.00
THE COMPOSITIONS OF COLE PORTER				
❏ Riverside RM-3515 [M]	1963	3.75	7.50	15.00
❏ Riverside RS-93515 [S]	1963	5.00	10.00	20.00
THE COMPOSITIONS OF DIZZY GILLESPIE				
❏ Riverside RLP-3508 [M]	1962	3.75	7.50	15.00
❏ Riverside RS-93508 [S]	1962	5.00	10.00	20.00
THE COMPOSITIONS OF DUKE ELLINGTON				
❏ Riverside RLP-3507 [M]	1962	3.75	7.50	15.00
❏ Riverside RS-93507 [S]	1962	5.00	10.00	20.00
THE COMPOSITIONS OF DUKE ELLINGTON, VOL. 2				
❏ Riverside RLP-3510 [M]	1962	3.75	7.50	15.00
❏ Riverside RS-93510 [S]	1962	5.00	10.00	20.00
THE COMPOSITIONS OF GEORGE GERSHWIN				
❏ Riverside RM-3517 [M]	1963	3.75	7.50	15.00
❏ Riverside RS-93517 [S]	1963	5.00	10.00	20.00
THE COMPOSITIONS OF HAROLD ARLEN				
❏ Riverside RM-3518 [M]	1963	3.75	7.50	15.00
❏ Riverside RS-93518 [S]	1963	5.00	10.00	20.00
THE COMPOSITIONS OF HORACE SILVER				
❏ Riverside RLP-3509 [M]	1962	3.75	7.50	15.00
❏ Riverside RS-93509 [S]	1962	5.00	10.00	20.00
THE COMPOSITIONS OF IRVING BERLIN				
❏ Riverside RM-3519 [M]	1963	3.75	7.50	15.00
❏ Riverside RS-93519 [S]	1963	5.00	10.00	20.00
THE COMPOSITIONS OF JEROME KERN				
❏ Riverside RM-3516 [M]	1963	3.75	7.50	15.00
❏ Riverside RS-93516 [S]	1963	5.00	10.00	20.00
COMPOSITIONS OF LIONEL HAMPTON				
❏ Crown CLP-5107 [M]	195?	6.25	12.50	25.00
THE COMPOSITIONS OF MILES DAVIS				
❏ Riverside RLP-3504 [M]	1962	3.75	7.50	15.00
❏ Riverside RS-93504 [S]	1962	5.00	10.00	20.00
THE COMPOSITIONS OF RICHARD RODGERS				
❏ Riverside RM-3514 [M]	1963	3.75	7.50	15.00
❏ Riverside RS-93514 [S]	1963	5.00	10.00	20.00
THE COMPOSITIONS OF TADD DAMERON				
❏ Riverside RLP-3511 [M]	1962	3.75	7.50	15.00
❏ Riverside RS-93511 [S]	1962	5.00	10.00	20.00
THE COMPOSITIONS OF THELONIOUS MONK				
❏ Riverside RLP-3503 [M]	1962	3.75	7.50	15.00
❏ Riverside RS-93503 [S]	1962	5.00	10.00	20.00
CONCEPTION				
❏ Prestige PRLP-7013 [M]	1956	25.00	50.00	100.00
CONCERT IN ARGENTINA				
❏ Halcyon 113 [(2)]	197?	3.75	7.50	15.00
CONCERT IN JAZZ				
❏ Tops L-1532 [M]	1958	5.00	10.00	20.00
CONCERT JAZZ				
❏ Brunswick BL 54027 [M]	1956	7.50	15.00	30.00
A CONCORD JAM				
❏ Concord Jazz CJ-142	1981	2.50	5.00	10.00
A CONCORD JAM, VOL. 2				
❏ Concord Jazz CJ-180	1982	2.50	5.00	10.00

Number	Title	Yr	VG	VG+	NM
A CONCORD JAM, VOL. 3: A GREAT AMERICAN EVENING					
❏ Concord Jazz CJ-220		1984	2.50	5.00	10.00
CONCORD JAZZ GUITAR COLLECTION, VOL. 1 AND 2					
❏ Concord Jazz CJ-160 [(2)]		198?	3.00	6.00	12.00
THE CONCORD SOUND, VOL. 1					
❏ Concord Jazz CJ-278		1985	2.50	5.00	10.00
COOL AND CAREFREE					
❏ Columbia Special Products CSP 119 [M]		1963	3.00	6.00	12.00
-- Sold only by Carrier air conditioner dealers					
COOL CALIFORNIA					
❏ Savoy Jazz SJL-2254 [(2)]		198?	3.00	6.00	12.00
COOL EUROPE					
❏ MGM E-3157 [M]		1955	7.50	15.00	30.00
COOL GABRIELS					
❏ Groove LG-1003 [M]		1956	15.00	30.00	60.00
COOL JAZZ					
❏ Seeco CELP-465 [M]		1960	5.00	10.00	20.00
COOL JAZZ FROM HOLLAND					
❏ Epic LN 1126 [10]		1955	10.00	20.00	40.00
COOLIN'					
❏ New Jazz NJLP-8216 [M]		1959	15.00	30.00	60.00
-- Purple label					
❏ New Jazz NJLP-8216 [M]		1965	7.50	15.00	30.00
-- Blue label, trident logo at right					
COPULATIN' BLUES					
❏ Stash ST-101		197?	3.75	7.50	15.00
COPULATIN' BLUES, VOL. 2					
❏ Stash ST-122		198?	3.75	7.50	15.00
COPULATIN' RHYTHM					
❏ Jass J-3		198?	3.75	7.50	15.00
COPULATIN' RHYTHM, VOL. 2					
❏ Jass J-5		198?	3.75	7.50	15.00
THE CORE OF JAZZ					
❏ MGM SE-4737		1970	3.00	6.00	12.00
COTTON CLUB STARS					
❏ Stash ST-124 [(2)]		198?	3.00	6.00	12.00
CRITICS' CHOICE					
❏ Dawn DLP-1123 [M]		1958	20.00	40.00	80.00
CRUISIN'					
❏ Jazzland JLP-7 [M]		1960	6.25	12.50	25.00
❏ Jazzland JLP-97 [S]		1960	7.50	15.00	30.00
CTI SUMMER JAZZ AT THE HOLLYWOOD BOWL: LIVE ONE					
❏ CTI 7076		197?	3.00	6.00	12.00
CTI SUMMER JAZZ AT THE HOLLYWOOD BOWL: LIVE THREE					
❏ CTI 7078		197?	3.00	6.00	12.00
CTI SUMMER JAZZ AT THE HOLLYWOOD BOWL: LIVE TWO					
❏ CTI 7077		197?	3.00	6.00	12.00
CYLINDER JAZZ					
❏ Saydisc SDL-334		198?	2.50	5.00	10.00
DANCE BAND HITS					
❏ RCA Victor LPT-2 [10]		1951	10.00	20.00	40.00
DANCE TO THE BANDS					
❏ Capitol TBO 727 [(2) M]		1956	10.00	20.00	40.00
❏ Capitol T 977 [M]		1958	5.00	10.00	20.00
DANCE, BE HAPPY!					
❏ Columbia CL 967 [M]		1957	5.00	10.00	20.00
DANCING WITH THE STARS					
❏ Epic LN 3136 [M]		1955	7.50	15.00	30.00
DAS IS JAZZ!					
❏ Decca DL 8229 [M]		1956	7.50	15.00	30.00
A DATE WITH GREATNESS					
❏ Imperial LP-9188A [M]		1962	12.50	25.00	50.00
❏ Imperial LP-12188A [R]		1962	6.25	12.50	25.00
-- Features Aladdin tracks by Coleman Hawkins, Howard McGhee and Lester Young					
A DATE WITH RIVERSIDE					
❏ Riverside S-4 [M]		195?	10.00	20.00	40.00
DECADE OF JAZZ, VOLUME 1, 1939-49					
❏ Blue Note BN-LA158-G2 [(2)]		1974	3.75	7.50	15.00
DECADE OF JAZZ, VOLUME 2, 1949-59					
❏ Blue Note BN-LA159-G2 [(2)]		1974	3.75	7.50	15.00
DECADE OF JAZZ, VOLUME 3, 1959-69					
❏ Blue Note BN-LA160-G2 [(2)]		1974	3.75	7.50	15.00
DEEP PURPLE					
-- See SHELLY MANNE.					
THE DEFINITIVE JAZZ SCENE, VOL. 1					
❏ ABC Impulse! AS-99 [S]		1968	3.00	6.00	12.00
❏ Impulse! A-99 [M]		1966	3.75	7.50	15.00
❏ Impulse! AS-99 [S]		1966	5.00	10.00	20.00
THE DEFINITIVE JAZZ SCENE, VOL. 2					
❏ ABC Impulse! AS-100 [S]		1968	3.00	6.00	12.00
❏ Impulse! A-100 [M]		1966	3.75	7.50	15.00
❏ Impulse! AS-100 [S]		1966	5.00	10.00	20.00
THE DEFINITIVE JAZZ SCENE, VOL. 3					
❏ ABC Impulse! AS-9101 [S]		1968	3.00	6.00	12.00
❏ Impulse! A-9101 [M]		1966	3.75	7.50	15.00
❏ Impulse! AS-9101 [S]		1966	5.00	10.00	20.00
DIGITAL III AT MONTREUX					
❏ Pablo Live 2308 223		1980	3.00	6.00	12.00
DIXIE LAND U.S.A.					
❏ Promenade 2134 [M]		195?	3.75	7.50	15.00
DIXIE, LONDON STYLE					
❏ London LL 1337 [M]		1956	5.00	10.00	20.00
DIXIELAND -- NEW ORLEANS					
❏ Mainstream 56003 [M]		1965	6.25	2.50	25.00
❏ Mainstream S-6003 [R]		1965	3.00	6.00	12.00
DIXIELAND AT CARNEGIE HALL					
❏ Forum F-9011 [M]		196?	5.00	10.00	20.00
❏ Forum SF-9011 [S]		196?	6.25	12.50	25.00
DIXIELAND AT ITS BEST					
❏ RCA Camden CAL-838 [M]		1964	3.00	6.00	12.00
❏ RCA Camden CAS-838 [R]		1964	2.50	5.00	10.00
DIXIELAND AT JAZZ, LTD.					
❏ Atlantic 1261 [M]		1957	10.00	20.00	40.00
-- Black label					
❏ Atlantic 1261 [M]		1961	6.25	12.50	25.00
-- Multicolor label, white "fan" logo at right					
DIXIELAND AT JAZZ, LTD., VOL. 1					
❏ Atlantic ALS-139 [10]		1952	15.00	30.00	60.00
DIXIELAND AT JAZZ, LTD., VOL. 2					
❏ Atlantic ALS-140 [10]		1952	15.00	30.00	60.00
DIXIELAND CLASSICS					
❏ Jazztone J-1216 [M]		1956	7.50	15.00	30.00
DIXIELAND CONTRASTS					
❏ Jazzman LJ-334 [M]		1954	7.50	15.00	30.00
DIXIELAND DETOUR					
❏ Capitol H 312 [10]		1952	12.50	25.00	50.00
DIXIELAND FESTIVAL, VOL. 1					
❏ Vik LX-1057 [M]		1956	7.50	15.00	30.00
DIXIELAND HITS					
❏ Swingville SVLP-2040 [M]		1962	10.00	20.00	40.00
-- Purple label					
❏ Swingville SVLP-2040 [M]		1965	5.00	10.00	20.00
-- Blue label, trident logo at right					
DIXIELAND IN OLD NEW ORLEANS					
❏ Golden Crest GC-3021 [M]		1958	5.00	10.00	20.00
DIXIELAND JAZZ					
❏ Audiophile XL-325 [M]		1954	7.50	15.00	30.00
❏ Audiophile XL-330 [M]		1954	7.50	15.00	30.00
❏ Grand Award GA 33-310 [M]		1955	6.25	12.50	25.00
-- Without wrap-around outer cover					
❏ Grand Award GA 33-310 [M]		1955	15.00	30.00	60.00
-- With wrap-around outer cover					
DIXIELAND JAZZ GEMS					
❏ Commodore FL-20010 [10]		1950	12.50	25.00	50.00
DIXIELAND MAIN STREAM					
❏ Savoy MG-12213 [M]		196?	5.00	10.00	20.00
DIXIELAND RHYTHM KINGS					
❏ Paradox LP-6002 [10]		1951	12.50	25.00	50.00
DIXIELAND SERIES, VOL. 1					
❏ Savoy MG-15005 [10]		1952	20.00	40.00	80.00

Number / Title	Yr	VG	VG+	NM
DIXIELAND SERIES, VOL. 2				
❑ Savoy MG-15009 [10]	1952	20.00	40.00	80.00
DIXIELAND VS. BIRDLAND				
❑ MGM E-231 [10]	1954	12.50	25.00	50.00
DIZZY ATMOSPHERE				
❑ Specialty LP-2110 [M]	1957	10.00	20.00	40.00
DOUBLE BARREL JAZZ				
❑ Bethlehem BCP-87 [M]	1958	7.50	15.00	30.00
DOWN BEAT CRITICS POLL WINNERS				
❑ Clef MGC-742 [M]	1955	---	---	---
-- Canceled				
DOWN BEAT JAZZ CONCERT				
❑ Dot DLP-9003 [M]	1958	7.50	15.00	30.00
❑ Dot DLP-29003 [S]	1958	6.25	12.50	25.00
DOWN BEAT JAZZ CONCERT, VOL. 2				
❑ Dot DLP-3188 [M]	1959	7.50	15.00	30.00
❑ Dot DLP-25188 [S]	1959	6.25	12.50	25.00
DOWN BEAT'S HALL OF FAME, VOL. 1				
❑ Verve MGV-8320 [M]	1959	12.50	25.00	50.00
❑ Verve V-8320 [M]	1961	5.00	10.00	20.00
DREAMING ON THE RIVER TO NEW ORLEANS				
❑ Southland SLP-238	1963	3.75	7.50	15.00
THE DRUMS				
❑ ABC Impulse! AS-9272 [(3)]	197?	5.00	10.00	20.00
DRUMS ON FIRE				
❑ World Pacific WP-1247 [M]	1958	10.00	20.00	40.00
THE EARL BAKER CYLINDERS				
❑ Jazz Archives JA-43	198?	2.50	5.00	10.00
EARLY AND RARE: CLASSIC JAZZ "COLLECTORS ITEMS"				
❑ Riverside RLP 12-134 [M]	1957	10.00	20.00	40.00
EARLY BONES				
❑ Prestige 24067 [(2)]	197?	3.75	7.50	15.00
EARLY JAZZ GREATS, VOL. 1				
❑ Jazztone J-1249 [M]	1957	7.50	15.00	30.00
EARLY JAZZ GREATS, VOL. 2				
❑ Jazztone J-1252 [M]	1957	7.50	15.00	30.00
EARLY MODERN				
❑ Milestone M-9035	197?	3.00	6.00	12.00
EARLY VIPER JIVE				
❑ Stash ST-105	197?	2.50	5.00	10.00
EARTHY!				
❑ Prestige PRLP-7102 [M]	1957	25.00	50.00	100.00
THE EAST COAST JAZZ SCENE, VOL. 1				
❑ Coral CRL 57035 [M]	1956	12.50	25.00	50.00
EASY LISTENING				
❑ Audiophile AP-27 [M]	1953	7.50	15.00	30.00
❑ Audiophile AP-38 [M]	1953	7.50	15.00	30.00
❑ Audiophile XL-327 [M]	1954	7.50	15.00	30.00
ECHOES OF AN ERA				
❑ Elektra 60021	1982	2.50	5.00	10.00
-- With Stanley Clarke, Chick Corea, Chaka Khan and Joe Henderson				
ECHOES OF AN ERA VOLUME 2: THE CONCERT				
❑ Elektra/Musician 60165	1983	2.50	5.00	10.00
ECHOES OF ENJA				
❑ Enja 4000	197?	3.00	6.00	12.00
ECHOES OF NEW ORLEANS				
❑ Southland SLP-239	1963	3.75	7.50	15.00
EIGHT WAYS TO JAZZ				
❑ Riverside RLP 12-272 [M]	1958	7.50	15.00	30.00
ENCYCLOPEDIA OF JAZZ IN THE '60'S, VOL. 1				
❑ Verve V-8677 [M]	1966	3.75	7.50	15.00
❑ Verve V6-8677 [S]	1966	5.00	10.00	20.00
THE ENCYCLOPEDIA OF JAZZ IN THE 70S				
❑ RCA Victor APL2-1984 [(2)]	1977	3.75	7.50	15.00
THE ENCYCLOPEDIA OF JAZZ ON RECORDS				
❑ Decca DXF 140 [(4) M]	1957	25.00	50.00	100.00
-- Box set; individually issued as Decca 8398, 8399, 8400 and 8401				
THE ENCYCLOPEDIA OF JAZZ ON RECORDS, VOL. 1: JAZZ OF THE TWENTIES				
❑ Decca DL 8398 [M]	1957	5.00	10.00	20.00
THE ENCYCLOPEDIA OF JAZZ ON RECORDS, VOL. 2: JAZZ OF THE THIRTIES				
❑ Decca DL 8399 [M]	1957	5.00	10.00	20.00
THE ENCYCLOPEDIA OF JAZZ ON RECORDS, VOL. 1 AND 2: JAZZ OF THE TWENTIES/JAZZ OF THE THIRTIES				
❑ MCA 4061 [(2)]	197?	3.75	7.50	15.00
THE ENCYCLOPEDIA OF JAZZ ON RECORDS, VOL. 3: JAZZ OF THE FORTIES				
❑ Decca DL 8400 [M]	1957	5.00	10.00	20.00
THE ENCYCLOPEDIA OF JAZZ ON RECORDS, VOL. 4: JAZZ OF THE FIFTIES				
❑ Decca DL 8401 [M]	1957	5.00	10.00	20.00
THE ENCYCLOPEDIA OF JAZZ ON RECORDS, VOL. 3 AND 4: JAZZ OF THE FORTIES/JAZZ OF THE FIFTIES				
❑ MCA 4062 [(2)]	197?	3.75	7.50	15.00
THE ENCYCLOPEDIA OF JAZZ ON RECORDS, VOL. 5: JAZZ OF THE SIXTIES				
❑ MCA 4063 [(2)]	197?	3.75	7.50	15.00
ENERGY ESSENTIALS				
❑ ABC Impulse! ASD-9228 [(3)]	197?	5.00	10.00	20.00
ERA OF THE CLARINET				
❑ Mainstream S-6011 [R]	1965	3.00	6.00	12.00
❑ Mainstream 56011 [M]	1965	6.25	12.50	25.00
ESCAPADE REVIEWS THE JAZZ SCENE				
❑ Liberty SL-9005 [M]	1957	7.50	15.00	30.00
ESCAPE				
❑ Gene Norman GNP-27 [M]	1958	6.25	12.50	25.00
ESQUIRE'S 2ND ANNUAL ALL-AMERICAN JAZZ CONCERT				
❑ Sunbeam 219 [(2)]	197?	3.00	6.00	12.00
ESQUIRE'S ALL-AMERICAN HOT JAZZ				
❑ RCA Victor LPV-544 [M]	1967	5.00	10.00	20.00
ESQUIRE'S WORLD OF JAZZ				
❑ Capitol STBO 1970 [(2) S]	1963	5.00	10.00	20.00
❑ Capitol TBO 1970 [(2) M]	1963	5.00	10.00	20.00
THE ESSENTIAL JAZZ VOCALS				
❑ Verve V-8505 [M]	1963	5.00	10.00	20.00
❑ Verve V6-8505 [S]	1963	6.25	12.50	25.00
AN EVENING OF JAZZ				
❑ Norgran MGN-1065 [M]	1956	20.00	40.00	80.00
❑ Verve MGV-8155 [M]	1957	7.50	15.00	30.00
❑ Verve V-8155 [M]	1961	5.00	10.00	20.00
EZZ-THETIC				
-- See LEE KONITZ.				
FANTASY SAMPLER				
❑ Fantasy FS-654 [M]	195?	5.00	10.00	20.00
-- Red vinyl				
THE FEMININE TOUCH				
❑ Decca DL 5486 [10]	1953	12.50	25.00	50.00
❑ Decca DL 8316 [M]	1956	7.50	15.00	30.00
FESTIVAL JAZZ, VOL. 1				
❑ Jim Taylor Presents 106	197?	3.00	6.00	12.00
FESTIVAL JAZZ, VOL. 2				
❑ Jim Taylor Presents 107	197?	3.00	6.00	12.00
FIFTEEN STAR SAXOPHONES				
❑ Bethlehem BCP-6035 [M]	1959	7.50	15.00	30.00
50 YEARS OF JAZZ GREATS				
❑ Columbia Musical Treasury P3S 5932 [(3)]	197?	5.00	10.00	20.00
50 YEARS OF JAZZ GUITAR				
❑ Columbia CG 33566 [(2)]	1973	3.75	7.50	15.00
52ND STREET JAZZ				
❑ Waldorf Music Hall MH 33-148 [10]	195?	25.00	50.00	100.00
52ND STREET, VOL. 1				
❑ Onyx 203	197?	3.00	6.00	12.00
52ND STREET, VOL. 2				
❑ Onyx 217	197?	3.00	6.00	12.00

Number / Title	Yr	VG	VG+	NM
FILL YOUR HEAD WITH JAZZ				
❑ Columbia G 30217 [(2)]	1971	3.75	7.50	15.00
FIRE INTO MUSIC				
❑ CTI CTS-2	197?	3.75	7.50	15.00
FIRST ALBUM OF JAZZ				
❑ Folkways FP-712 [10]	1951	12.50	25.00	50.00
FIRST SESSIONS 1949-50				
❑ Prestige 24081 [(2)]	197?	3.75	7.50	15.00
FIVE BIRDS AND A MONK				
❑ Galaxy 5134	1979	3.00	6.00	12.00
FIVE FEET OF SWING				
❑ Decca DL 8045 [M]	1954	10.00	20.00	40.00
FOOTNOTES TO JAZZ, VOL. 1				
-- See JOHNNY DODDS.				
FOOTNOTES TO JAZZ, VOL. 2: ANATOMY OF A JAZZ COMPOSITION				
❑ Folkways FP-31 [10]	1951	12.50	25.00	50.00
FOOTNOTES TO JAZZ, VOL. 3				
-- See MARY LOU WILLIAMS.				
FOR DANCERS ONLY				
❑ Epic LN 3120 [M]	1955	7.50	15.00	30.00
FOR JAZZ LOVERS				
❑ EmArcy MG-36086 [M]	1956	10.00	20.00	40.00
FOREMOST!				
❑ Onyx 201	197?	3.00	6.00	12.00
FOUNDATIONS				
❑ MCA 4153 [(2)]	198?	3.00	6.00	12.00
FOUNDATIONS OF MODERN JAZZ				
❑ Archive of Folk and Jazz 229	196?	2.50	5.00	10.00
FOUR ALTOS				
❑ Prestige PRLP-7116 [M]	1957	25.00	50.00	100.00
FOUR DECADES OF JAZZ				
❑ Xanadu 5001 [(2)]	197?	3.75	7.50	15.00
FOUR FRENCH HORNS				
❑ Savoy MG-12173 [M]	1961	12.50	25.00	50.00
THE FOUR MOST GUITARS				
❑ ABC-Paramount ABC-109 [M]	1956	7.50	15.00	30.00
❑ Paramount LP-109 [10]	1954	15.00	30.00	60.00
THE FOUR ROSES DANCE PARTY				
❑ Columbia Special Products XTV 68933/4 [M]	1961	3.75	7.50	15.00
FOUR TO GO				
❑ Columbia CL 2018 [M]	1963	5.00	10.00	20.00
❑ Columbia CS 8818 [S]	1963	3.75	7.50	15.00
FOUR TROMBONES... THE DEBUT RECORDINGS				
❑ Prestige 24097 [(2)]	197?	3.75	7.50	15.00
FRANK BULL AND GENE NORMAN PRESENT DIXIELAND JUBILEE				
❑ Decca DL 7022 [10]	1952	12.50	25.00	50.00
FRENCH FESTIVAL				
❑ Classic Jazz 133	197?	3.00	6.00	12.00
FRENCH TOAST				
❑ Angel ANG-60009 [10]	1956	12.50	25.00	50.00
FRIDAY THE 13TH, COOK COUNTY JAIL				
❑ Groove Merchant 515	197?	3.75	7.50	15.00
FROM CANADA WITH LOVE				
❑ PM 011	198?	2.50	5.00	10.00
FROM SPIRITUALS TO SWING				
❑ Vanguard VSD-47/48 [(2)]	197?	3.75	7.50	15.00
❑ Vanguard VMS-73131	197?	2.50	5.00	10.00
FUN ON THE FRETS: EARLY JAZZ GUITAR				
❑ Yazoo 1061	197?	2.50	5.00	10.00
FUNKY BLUES NO. 2				
❑ American Recording Society G-404 [M]	1956	7.50	15.00	30.00
GARY MOORE PRESENTS "MY KIND OF MUSIC"				
❑ Columbia CL 717 [M]	1956	6.25	12.50	25.00
GEMS OF JAZZ, VOL. 1				
❑ Decca DL 5133 [10]	1950	12.50	25.00	50.00
❑ Decca DL 8039 [M]	1954	10.00	20.00	40.00
GEMS OF JAZZ, VOL. 2				
❑ Decca DL 5134 [10]	1950	12.50	25.00	50.00
❑ Decca DL 8040 [M]	1954	10.00	20.00	40.00
GEMS OF JAZZ, VOL. 3				
❑ Decca DL 5383 [10]	1952	12.50	25.00	50.00
❑ Decca DL 8041 [M]	1954	10.00	20.00	40.00
GEMS OF JAZZ, VOL. 4				
❑ Decca DL 5384 [10]	1952	12.50	25.00	50.00
❑ Decca DL 8042 [M]	1954	10.00	20.00	40.00
GEMS OF JAZZ, VOL. 5				
❑ Decca DL 8043 [M]	1954	10.00	20.00	40.00
GENE NORMAN PRESENTS JUST JAZZ				
❑ RCA Victor LPM-3102 [10]	1953	12.50	25.00	50.00
GET IT TOGETHER				
❑ Mainstream MRL-350	197?	3.00	6.00	12.00
GIANTS OF BOOGIE WOOGIE				
❑ Riverside RLP 12-106 [M]	1956	10.00	20.00	40.00
GIANTS OF JAZZ (Three different albums)				
❑ American Recording Society G-401 [M]	1956	7.50	15.00	30.00
❑ Columbia CL 1970 [M]	1963	7.50	15.00	30.00
❑ George Wein Collection GW-3004	198?	2.50	5.00	10.00
GIANTS OF JAZZ ORGAN				
❑ King 837 [M]	1963	30.00	60.00	120.00
GIANTS OF JAZZ, VOL. 1				
❑ Who's Who in Jazz 21012	197?	2.50	5.00	10.00
GIANTS OF JAZZ VOL. 2				
❑ American Recording Society G-444 [M]	1957	7.50	15.00	30.00
GIANTS OF JAZZ, VOL. 2				
❑ Who's Who in Jazz 21014	197?	2.50	5.00	10.00
GIANTS OF SMALL BAND SWING, VOL. 1				
❑ Fantasy OJC-1723	1990	2.50	5.00	10.00
❑ Riverside RLP 12-143 [M]	1957	10.00	20.00	40.00
GIANTS OF SMALL BAND SWING, VOL. 2				
❑ Fantasy OJC-1724	1990	2.50	5.00	10.00
❑ Riverside RLP 12-145 [M]	1957	10.00	20.00	40.00
GIANTS OF THE BLUES TENOR SAX				
❑ Prestige 24101 [(2)]	197?	3.75	7.50	15.00
GIANTS OF THE FUNK TENOR SAX				
❑ Prestige 24102 [(2)]	197?	3.75	7.50	15.00
GIANTS OF TRADITIONAL JAZZ				
❑ Savoy Jazz SJL-2251 [(2)]	198?	3.00	6.00	12.00
THE GIRLS SING				
❑ Savoy MG-12220 [M]	196?	5.00	10.00	20.00
GOD REST YE MERRY, JAZZMEN				
❑ Columbia FC 37551	1981	3.00	6.00	12.00
❑ Columbia PC 37551	198?	2.00	4.00	8.00
-- Budget-line reissue				
THE GOLDEN ERA OF JAZZ, VOL. 1				
❑ Savoy MG-15015 [10]	1952	20.00	40.00	80.00
THE GOLDEN ERA OF JAZZ, VOL. 2				
❑ Savoy MG-15018 [10]	1952	20.00	40.00	80.00
GOLDEN JAZZ INTRSUMENTALS				
❑ Bethlehem BCP-6065 [M]	1962	6.25	12.50	25.00
THE GREAT BANDS				
❑ Columbia Musical Treasury P2M 5267 [(2)]	1968	5.00	10.00	20.00
GREAT BLUES				
❑ Riverside RLP-1074 [10]	1955	20.00	40.00	80.00
GREAT BLUES SINGERS				
❑ Riverside RLP 12-121 [M]	1957	10.00	20.00	40.00
❑ Riverside RLP-1032 [10]	1954	20.00	40.00	80.00
GREAT GUITARS AT THE WINERY				
❑ Concord Jazz CJ-131	1980	3.00	6.00	12.00
GREAT GUITARS OF JAZZ				
❑ MGM SE-4691	1970	3.00	6.00	12.00
GREAT JAZZ				
❑ Rondo-lette A-31 [M]	195?	6.25	12.50	25.00

Number	Title	Yr	VG	VG+	NM
THE GREAT JAZZ ALBUM					
❏ Project 3 PR 6009/10 [(2)]		197?	3.75	7.50	15.00
THE GREAT JAZZ ALBUM, VOLUME 2					
❏ Project 3 PR 6023/24 [(2)]		197?	3.75	7.50	15.00
GREAT JAZZ BRASS					
❏ RCA Camden CAL-383 [M]		1958	6.25	12.50	25.00
GREAT JAZZ PIANISTS					
❏ RCA Camden CAL-328 [M]		1958	6.25	12.50	25.00
GREAT JAZZ PIANISTS OF OUR TIME					
❏ RCA Camden CAL-882 [M]		1965	3.75	7.50	15.00
❏ RCA Camden CAS-882 [R]		1965	2.50	5.00	10.00
GREAT JAZZ REEDS					
❏ RCA Camden CAL-339 [M]		1958	6.25	12.50	25.00
THE GREAT JAZZ SINGERS					
❏ Halo 50269 [M]		1957	3.75	7.50	15.00
THE GREAT SWING BANDS					
❏ Jazztone J-1245 [M]		1957	7.50	15.00	30.00
THE GREAT TENOR JAZZMEN					
❏ Allegro 1634 [M]		195?	10.00	20.00	40.00
GREAT TRUMPET ARTISTS					
❏ RCA Victor LPT-26 [10]		1951	12.50	25.00	50.00
❏ RCA Victor LPT-35 [10]		1952	12.50	25.00	50.00
GREATEST HITS					
❏ Harmony HL 7255 [M]		1960	3.75	7.50	15.00
THE GREATEST JAZZ CONCERT EVER					
❏ Prestige 24024 [(2)]		197?	3.75	7.50	15.00
THE GREATEST JAZZ CONCERT IN THE WORLD					
❏ Pablo 2625 704 [(4)]		197?	7.50	15.00	30.00
GRETSCH DRUM NIGHT AT BIRDLAND					
❏ Roulette R 52049 [M]		1960	7.50	15.00	30.00
❏ Roulette SR 52049 [S]		1960	7.50	15.00	30.00
GRETSCH DRUM NIGHT, VOLUME 2					
❏ Roulette R 52067 [M]		1961	7.50	15.00	30.00
❏ Roulette SR 52067 [S]		1961	7.50	15.00	30.00
THE GRIFFITH PARK COLLECTION					
❏ Elektra/Musician 60025		1982	2.50	5.00	10.00
-- All-star session with STANLEY CLARKE; CHICK COREA; JOE HENDERSON; FREDDIE HUBBARD; LENNY WHITE.					
THE GRIFFITH PARK COLLECTION VOL. 2: THE CONCERT					
❏ Elektra/Musician 60262 [(2)]		198?	3.00	6.00	12.00
A GRP CHRISTMAS COLLECTION					
❏ GRP GR-9574		1988	3.00	6.00	12.00
GRP LIVE IN SESSION					
❏ GRP GR-1023		1985	2.50	5.00	10.00
GRP SAMPLER, VOL. 1					
❏ GRP F-7701		198?	2.50	5.00	10.00
GRP SUPER LIVE IN CONCERT					
❏ GRP GR-2-1650 [(2)]		1988	3.00	6.00	12.00
GUIDE TO JAZZ					
❏ RCA Victor LPM-1393 [M]		1956	7.50	15.00	30.00
GUITAR PLAYER					
❏ MCA 6002 [(2)]		197?	3.75	7.50	15.00
❏ MCA 8012 [(2)]		1976	3.75	7.50	15.00
-- Original issue					
GUITAR PLAYER PRESENTS JAZZ GUITAR CLASSICS					
❏ Fantasy OJC-6012		1990	3.75	7.50	15.00
GUITAR PLAYERS					
❏ Mainstream MRL-410		197?	3.00	6.00	12.00
GUITAR SESSION					
❏ Inner City IC-6050		198?	3.00	6.00	12.00
GUITAR SOUL					
-- See KENNY BURRELL.					
GUITAR WORKSHOP					
❏ Pausa 7089		198?	2.50	5.00	10.00
GUT BUCKET BLUES AND STOMPS					
❏ Herwin 112		197?	3.00	6.00	12.00
GUTIAR STARS					
❏ MCA 42126		1988	2.50	5.00	10.00

Number	Title	Yr	VG	VG+	NM
HANDFUL OF COOL JAZZ					
❏ Bethlehem BCP-90 [M]		1959	7.50	15.00	30.00
HAPPY JAZZ					
❏ Jazztone J-1215 [M]		1956	7.50	15.00	30.00
HARD COOKIN'					
-- See ART FARMER.					
THE HARD SWING					
❏ Pacific Jazz JWC-508 [M]		1957	12.50	25.00	50.00
❏ World Pacific JWC-508 [M]		1958	10.00	20.00	40.00
HARLEM COMES TO LONDON					
❏ Swing SW-8444		198?	2.50	5.00	10.00
HARLEM JAZZ 1930					
❏ Brunswick BL 58024 [10]		1951	12.50	25.00	50.00
HARLEN ODYSSEY					
❏ Xanadu 112		197?	2.50	5.00	10.00
HEAD START -- BOB THIELE EMERGENCY					
❏ Flying Dutchman FDS-104 [(2)]		1969	6.25	12.50	25.00
HERE AND NOW					
❏ Catalyst 7613		197?	2.50	5.00	10.00
HERE COME THE GIRLS					
❏ Verve MGV-2036 [M]		1956	10.00	20.00	40.00
❏ Verve V-2036 [M]		1961	5.00	10.00	20.00
HERE COME THE SWINGING BANDS					
❏ Verve MGV-8207 [M]		1957	7.50	15.00	30.00
❏ Verve V-8207 [M]		1961	5.00	10.00	20.00
HI-FI JAZZ					
❏ Brunswick BL 58058 [10]		1954	12.50	25.00	50.00
HI-FI JAZZ SESSION					
❏ Masterseal MSLP 5013 [M]		1957	6.25	12.50	25.00
A HI-FI SALUTE TO THE GREAT ONES					
❏ MGM E-3325 [M]		1956	7.50	15.00	30.00
A HI-FI SALUTE TO THE GREAT ONES, VOL. 2					
❏ MGM E-3354 [M]		1956	7.50	15.00	30.00
HIGHLIGHTS IN JAZZ: TWELFTH ANNIVERSARY CONCERT					
❏ Stash ST-254		1985	2.50	5.00	10.00
THE HISTORIC DONAUESCHINGEN JAZZ CONCERT 1957					
❏ Pausa 7081		198?	2.50	5.00	10.00
HISTORIC JAZZ CONCERT AT MUSIC INN					
❏ Atlantic 1298 [M]		1958	10.00	20.00	40.00
-- Black label					
❏ Atlantic 1298 [M]		1961	6.25	12.50	25.00
-- Multicolor label, white "fan" logo at right					
❏ Atlantic 1298 [M]		1963	5.00	10.00	20.00
-- Multicolor label, black "fan" logo at right					
HISTORY OF CLASSIC JAZZ					
❏ Riverside SDP-11 [(5) M]		1956	75.00	150.00	300.00
-- Five-record set in leatherette album with booklet; records were available separately as Riverside 112, 113, 114, 115 and 116.					
HISTORY OF CLASSIC JAZZ, VOL. 1					
❏ Riverside RLP 12-112 [M]		1957	10.00	20.00	40.00
HISTORY OF CLASSIC JAZZ, VOL. 2					
❏ Riverside RLP 12-113 [M]		1957	10.00	20.00	40.00
HISTORY OF CLASSIC JAZZ, VOL. 3					
❏ Riverside RLP 12-114 [M]		1957	10.00	20.00	40.00
HISTORY OF CLASSIC JAZZ, VOL. 4					
❏ Riverside RLP 12-115 [M]		1957	10.00	20.00	40.00
HISTORY OF CLASSIC JAZZ, VOL. 5					
❏ Riverside RLP 12-116 [M]		1957	10.00	20.00	40.00
HISTORY OF JAZZ, VOL. 1: NEW ORLEANS ORIGINS					
❏ Capitol T 793 [M]		1956	6.25	12.50	25.00
HISTORY OF JAZZ, VOL. 1: THE SOLID SOUTH					
❏ Capitol H 239 [10]		1950	12.50	25.00	50.00
HISTORY OF JAZZ, VOL. 2: THE GOLDEN ERA					
❏ Capitol H 240 [10]		1950	12.50	25.00	50.00
HISTORY OF JAZZ, VOL. 2: THE TURBULENT '20S					
❏ Capitol T 794 [M]		1956	6.25	12.50	25.00
HISTORY OF JAZZ, VOL. 3: EVERYBODY SWINGS					
❏ Capitol T 795 [M]		1956	6.25	12.50	25.00

Number Title	Yr	VG	VG+	NM
HISTORY OF JAZZ, VOL. 3: THEN CAME SWING				
❏ Capitol H 241 [10]	1950	12.50	25.00	50.00
HISTORY OF JAZZ, VOL. 4: ENTER THE COOL				
❏ Capitol H 242 [10]	1950	12.50	25.00	50.00
❏ Capitol T 796 [M]	1956	6.25	12.50	25.00
THE HITS ARE ON VERVE				
❏ Verve V-201 [M]	1964	3.75	7.50	15.00
❏ Verve V6-201 [S]	1964	5.00	10.00	20.00
HODGE PODGE OF OFF-BEAT JAZZ				
❏ Sunbeam 1	197?	2.50	5.00	10.00
HODGE PODGE OF OFF-BEAT JAZZ, VOL. 2				
❏ Sunbeam 5	197?	2.50	5.00	10.00
HOLIDAY IN SAX				
❏ EmArcy MG-26019 [10]	1954	20.00	40.00	80.00
HOLIDAY IN TRUMPET				
❏ EmArcy MG-26015 [10]	1954	20.00	40.00	80.00
HONKERS AND BAR WALKERS				
❏ Delmark DL-438	198?	2.50	5.00	10.00
HOT CANARIES				
❏ Columbia CL 2534 [10]	1954	7.50	15.00	30.00
HOT CLARINETS				
❏ Historical 25	1969	2.50	5.00	10.00
THE HOT ONES				
❏ Columbia Special Products CSP-107 [M]	1963	5.00	10.00	20.00
-- Available only from Johnson Sea Horse boat dealers				
HOT PIANOS				
❏ Historical 29	1969	2.50	5.00	10.00
HOT TRUMPETS				
❏ Historical 28	1969	2.50	5.00	10.00
HOT VS. COOL: A BATTLE OF JAZZ				
❏ MGM E-211 [10]	1953	12.50	25.00	50.00
HOUSE RENT PARTY				
❏ Savoy MG-12199 [M]	1961	12.50	25.00	50.00
HOW BLUE CAN YOU GET? GREAT BLUES VOCALS IN THE JAZZ TRADITION				
❏ Bluebird 6758-1-RB	1989	3.00	6.00	12.00
HOW HIGH THE MOON				
❏ Clef MGC-608 [M]	1955	10.00	20.00	40.00
-- Reissue of Mercury 608				
❏ Clef MGC-Vol. 1 [M]	1955	12.50	25.00	50.00
-- Reissue of 608				
❏ Mercury MGC-Vol. 1 [10]	1951	15.00	30.00	60.00
-- Reissue of 35001				
❏ Mercury MGC-608 [M]	1953	20.00	40.00	80.00
-- Reissue of Vol. 1				
❏ Mercury MG-35001 [10]	1950	20.00	40.00	80.00
❏ Verve MGV-Vol. 1 [M]	1957	7.50	15.00	30.00
-- Reissue of 12-inch Clef Vol. 1				
(I GOT NO KICK AGAINST) MODERN JAZZ				
❏ GRP GR-9827 [(2)]	1995	3.75	7.50	15.00
-- Jazz artists do songs made famous by the Beatles				
I JUST LOVE JAZZ PIANO!				
-- See HAMPTON HAWES.				
I LIKE JAZZ!				
❏ Columbia JZ 1 [M]	1955	7.50	15.00	30.00
I REMEMBER BEBOP				
❏ Columbia C2 35381 [(2)]	197?	3.75	7.50	15.00
I'M WILD ABOUT MY LOVIN'				
❏ Historical 32	1969	2.50	5.00	10.00
IMPULSE ARTISTS ON TOUR				
❏ ABC Impulse! AS-9264	197?	3.00	6.00	12.00
IMPULSIVELY!				
❏ ABC Impulse! AS-9266 [(2)]	197?	3.75	7.50	15.00
IN CONCERT, VOL. 2				
❏ CTI 6049	197?	3.00	6.00	12.00
IN FROM THE STORM: THE MUSIC OF JIMI HENDRIX				
❏ RCA Victor 68233-1 [PD]	1995	3.00	6.00	12.00
-- Limited edition picture disc (no regular U.S. vinyl exists)				
IN THE BEGINNING…BEBOP				
-- See FATS NAVARRO.				

Number Title	Yr	VG	VG+	NM
INDIVIDUALS				
❏ Columbia CG 36213 [(2)]	197?	3.00	6.00	12.00
INFORMAL SESSION AT SQUIRREL'S BY THE SONS OF BIX				
❏ Paramount LP-104 [(2) 10]	1954	20.00	40.00	80.00
INTERCOLLEGIATE MUSIC FESTIVAL, VOL. 1				
❏ Impulse! A-9145 [M]	1967	5.00	10.00	20.00
❏ Impulse! AS-9145 [S]	1967	3.75	7.50	15.00
❏ ABC Impulse! AS-9145 [S]	1968	3.00	6.00	12.00
INTERNATIONAL JAM SESSIONS				
❏ Xanadu 122	197?	2.50	5.00	10.00
INTERNATIONAL JAZZ WORKSHOP				
❏ EmArcy MGE-26002 [M]	1964	6.25	12.50	25.00
❏ EmArcy SRE-66002 [S]	1964	7.50	15.00	30.00
INTERPLAY FOR TWO TRUMPETS AND TWO TENORS				
❏ Prestige PRLP-7112 [M]	1957	25.00	50.00	100.00
INTRODUCTION TO JAZZ				
❏ Decca DL 8244 [M]	1956	7.50	15.00	30.00
ISLES OF JAZZ				
❏ Discovery DL-2010 [10]	1954	12.50	25.00	50.00
ITALIAN JAZZ STARS				
❏ Angel ANG-60001 [10]	1955	12.50	25.00	50.00
IVY LEAGUE JAZZ				
❏ Decca DL 8282 [M]	1956	7.50	15.00	30.00
❏ Golden Crest GC-3039 [M]	1958	5.00	10.00	20.00
JAM SESSION				
❏ Clef MGC-4001/7 [(7) M]	1953	75.00	150.00	300.00
-- Boxed set containing 4001-4007				
❏ EmArcy MG-36002 [M]	1954	12.50	25.00	50.00
JAM SESSION #1				
❏ Clef MGC-601 [M]	1954	10.00	20.00	40.00
❏ Clef MGC-651 [M]	1955	10.00	20.00	40.00
-- Reissue of 4001				
❏ Clef MGC-4001 [M]	1953	12.50	25.00	50.00
❏ Mercury MGC-601 [M]	1953	20.00	40.00	80.00
❏ Verve MGV-8049 [M]	1956	7.50	15.00	30.00
-- Reissue of Clef 651				
JAM SESSION #2				
❏ Clef MGC-602 [M]	1954	10.00	20.00	40.00
❏ Clef MGC-652 [M]	1955	10.00	20.00	40.00
-- Reissue of 4002				
❏ Clef MGC-4002 [M]	1953	12.50	25.00	50.00
❏ Mercury MGC-602 [M]	1953	20.00	40.00	80.00
❏ Verve MGV-8050 [M]	1956	7.50	15.00	30.00
-- Reissue of Clef 652				
JAM SESSION #3				
❏ Clef MGC-653 [M]	1955	10.00	20.00	40.00
-- Reissue of 4003				
❏ Clef MGC-4003 [M]	1953	12.50	25.00	50.00
❏ Verve MGV-8051 [M]	1956	7.50	15.00	30.00
-- Reissue of Clef 653				
JAM SESSION #4				
❏ Clef MGC-654 [M]	1955	10.00	20.00	40.00
-- Reissue of 4004				
❏ Clef MGC-4004 [M]	1953	12.50	25.00	50.00
❏ Verve MGV-8052 [M]	1956	7.50	15.00	30.00
-- Reissue of Clef 654				
JAM SESSION #5				
❏ Clef MGC-655 [M]	1955	10.00	20.00	40.00
-- Reissue of 4005				
❏ Clef MGC-4005 [M]	1953	12.50	25.00	50.00
❏ Verve MGV-8053 [M]	1956	7.50	15.00	30.00
-- Reissue of Clef 655				
JAM SESSION #6				
❏ Clef MGC-656 [M]	1955	10.00	20.00	40.00
-- Reissue of 4006				
❏ Clef MGC-4006 [M]	1953	12.50	25.00	50.00
❏ Verve MGV-8054 [M]	1956	7.50	15.00	30.00
-- Reissue of Clef 656				
JAM SESSION #7				
❏ Clef MGC-677 [M]	1955	10.00	20.00	40.00
❏ Verve MGV-8062 [M]	1957	7.50	15.00	30.00
-- Reissue of Clef 677				
JAM SESSION #8				
❏ Clef MGC-711 [M]	1955	10.00	20.00	40.00
❏ Verve MGV-8094 [M]	1957	7.50	15.00	30.00
-- Reissue of Clef 711				

Number	Title	Yr	VG	VG+	NM
JAM SESSION #9					
❑ Verve MGV-8196 [M]		1957	7.50	15.00	30.00
JAM SESSION AT CARNEGIE HALL					
❑ Columbia CL 557 [M]		1954	7.50	15.00	30.00
JAM SESSION AT COMMODORE					
❑ Commodore FL-30006 [M]		1951	10.00	20.00	40.00
JAM SESSION COAST TO COAST					
❑ Columbia CL 547 [M]		1954	7.50	1.00	30.00
JAM SESSION, VOL. 2					
❑ Skylark SKLP-12 [10]		1954	62.50	125.00	250.00
THE JAM SESSIONS: MONTREUX '77					
❑ Pablo Live 2620 105 [(2)]		1978	3.75	7.50	15.00
❑ Fantasy OJC-385		1989	2.50	5.00	10.00
JAMMIN' IN SWINGVILLE					
❑ Prestige 24051 [(2)]		197?	3.75	7.50	15.00
JAMMING AT RUDI'S, VOL. 1					
❑ Circle L-407 [M]		1951	10.00	20.00	40.00
JAMMING AT RUDI'S, VOL. 2					
❑ Circle L-410 [M]		1951	10.00	20.00	40.00
THE JATP ALL STARS: HOW HIGH THE MOON					
❑ Verve VSP-15 [M]		1966	3.75	7.50	15.00
❑ Verve VSPS-15 [R]		1966	2.50	5.00	10.00
THE JATP ALL STARS: PERDIDO					
❑ Verve VSP-16 [M]		1966	3.75	7.50	15.00
❑ Verve VSPS-16 [R]		1966	2.50	5.00	10.00
THE JATP ALL-STARS AT THE OPERA HOUSE					
❑ Verve MGVS-6029 [S]		1960	7.50	15.00	30.00
❑ Verve MGV-8267 [M]		1958	10.00	20.00	40.00
❑ Verve V-8267 [M]		1961	5.00	10.00	20.00
❑ Verve V6-8267 [S]		1961	3.75	7.50	15.00
❑ Verve MGV-8284 [M]		1959	---	---	---
-- Canceled					
❑ Verve V-8489 [M]		1962	6.25	12.50	25.00
❑ Verve V6-8489 [S]		1962	7.50	15.00	30.00
THE JATP ALL-STARS: FUNKY BLUES					
❑ Verve V-8486 [M]		1962	6.25	12.50	25.00
❑ Verve V6-8486 [S]		1962	7.50	15.00	30.00
JAZZ					
(At least two different albums)					
❑ Royale 1883 [10]		195?	7.50	15.00	30.00
❑ Halo 50242 [M]		1957	3.75	7.50	15.00
❑ Mainstream MRL-408		197?	3.00	6.00	12.00
JAZZ A LA MIDNIGHT					
❑ Hall of Fame 608		197?	2.50	5.00	10.00
❑ Jazztone J-1282 [M]		1957	7.50	15.00	30.00
JAZZ A LA MOOD					
❑ Jazztone J-1254 [M]		1957	7.50	15.00	30.00
JAZZ ALL STARS, VOL. 1					
❑ Who's Who in Jazz 21010		197?	3.00	6.00	12.00
JAZZ AMERICANA					
❑ Tampa TP-11 [M]		1957	25.00	50.00	100.00
-- Colored vinyl					
❑ Tampa TP-11 [M]		1958	10.00	20.00	40.00
-- Black vinyl					
JAZZ AND POPS FROM THE SOVIET UNION					
❑ Colosseum CRLP-171 [M]		1955	7.50	15.00	30.00
JAZZ ANTHOLOGY OF WEST COAST JAZZ					
❑ Jazztone J-1243 [M]		1957	7.50	15.00	30.00
JAZZ AT CARNEGIE HALL					
❑ Arco AL-4 [10]		1950	20.00	40.00	80.00
❑ Mercury MG-35002 [10]		1950	20.00	40.00	80.00
-- Reissue of Arco 4					
JAZZ AT CARNEGIE HALL, VOLUME 2					
❑ Arco AL-8 [10]		195?	20.00	40.00	80.00
JAZZ AT COLUMBIA -- COLLECTORS ITEMS					
❑ Columbia CB-16 [M]		195?	5.00	10.00	20.00
-- Columbia Record Club "bonus record" in generic sleeve with die-cut circle in middle					
JAZZ AT COLUMBIA -- DIXIELAND					
❑ Columbia CB-8 [M]		195?	5.00	10.00	20.00
-- Columbia Record Club "bonus record" in generic sleeve with die-cut circle in middle					
JAZZ AT JAZZ LTD.					
❑ Atlantic 1338 [M]		1961	6.25	12.50	25.00
-- Multicolor label, white "fan" logo at right					

Number	Title	Yr	VG	VG+	NM
JAZZ AT MASSEY HALL					
-- See THE QUINTET.					
JAZZ AT PRESERVATION HALL					
❑ Atlantic 1408 [M]		1964	3.00	6.00	12.00
❑ Atlantic SD 1408 [S]		1964	3.75	7.50	15.00
JAZZ AT PRESERVATION HALL, VOL. 2					
❑ Atlantic 1409 [M]		1964	3.00	6.00	12.00
❑ Atlantic SD 1409 [S]		1964	3.75	7.50	15.00
JAZZ AT PRESERVATION HALL, VOL. 3					
❑ Atlantic 1410 [M]		1964	3.00	6.00	12.00
❑ Atlantic SD 1410 [S]		1964	3.75	7.50	15.00
JAZZ AT STORYVILLE					
❑ Paradox LP-6003 [10]		1951	12.50	25.00	50.00
❑ Savoy MG-15001 [10]		1952	20.00	40.00	80.00
❑ Savoy MG-15014 [10]		1952	20.00	40.00	80.00
❑ Storyville STLP-319 [10]		1955	20.00	40.00	80.00
JAZZ AT STORYVILLE, VOL. 2					
❑ Savoy MG-15016 [10]		1952	20.00	40.00	80.00
JAZZ AT STORYVILLE, VOL. 3					
❑ Savoy MG-15019 [10]		1953	20.00	40.00	80.00
JAZZ AT STORYVILLE, VOL. 4					
❑ Savoy MG-15020 [10]		1953	20.00	40.00	80.00
JAZZ AT THE BOSTON ARTS FESTIVAL					
❑ Storyville STLP-311 [10]		1954	20.00	40.00	80.00
JAZZ AT THE HOLLYWOOD BOWL					
❑ Verve MGV-8231-2 [(2) M]		1958	12.50	25.00	50.00
❑ Verve V-8231-2 [(2) M]		1961	6.25	12.50	25.00
JAZZ AT THE NEW SCHOOL					
❑ Chiaroscuro 110		197?	3.75	7.50	15.00
JAZZ AT THE PHILHARMONIC					
❑ Stinson SLP-23 [10]		1950	30.00	60.00	120.00
-- See-through red vinyl; the first pressing of the first volume to be issued					
❑ Stinson SLP-23 [10]		195?	20.00	40.00	80.00
-- Black vinyl					
❑ Stinson SLP-23 [10]		195?	20.00	40.00	80.00
-- Opaque red vinyl					
❑ Stinson SLP-23 [M]		195?	5.00	10.00	20.00
JAZZ AT THE PHILHARMONIC, NEW VOLUME 2					
❑ Clef MGC-Vol. 2 [M]		1955	12.50	25.00	50.00
-- Side 1 is the 10-inch Vol. 2; Side 2 is the 10-inch Vol. 3					
JAZZ AT THE PHILHARMONIC, NEW VOLUME 3					
❑ Clef MGC-Vol. 3 [M]		1955	12.50	25.00	50.00
-- Side 1 is the 10-inch Vol. 4; Side 2 is the 10-inch Vol. 5					
JAZZ AT THE PHILHARMONIC, NEW VOLUME 4					
❑ Clef MGC-Vol. 4 [M]		1955	12.50	25.00	50.00
-- Combines the 10-inch Vol. 6 and Vol. 14 on one record					
JAZZ AT THE PHILHARMONIC, NEW VOLUME 5					
❑ Clef MGC-Vol. 5 [M]		1955	12.50	25.00	50.00
-- Combines the 10-inch Vol. 7, 10 and 11 on one record					
JAZZ AT THE PHILHARMONIC, NEW VOLUME 6					
❑ Clef MGC-Vol. 6 [M]		1955	12.50	25.00	50.00
-- Combines the 10-inch Vol. 8 and Vol. 9 on one record					
JAZZ AT THE PHILHARMONIC, NEW VOLUME 7					
❑ Clef MGC-Vol. 7 [M]		1955	12.50	25.00	50.00
-- Combines the 10-inch Vol. 12 and 13 on one record					
JAZZ AT THE PHILHARMONIC, VOLUME 2					
❑ Arco AL-1 [10]		1950	20.00	40.00	80.00
❑ Clef MGC-Vol. 2 [10]		1953	15.00	30.00	60.00
-- Reissue of Mercury Vol. 2					
❑ Mercury MG-35003 [10]		1950	20.00	40.00	80.00
-- Reissue of Arco 1					
❑ Mercury MGC-Vol. 2 [10]		1951	15.00	30.00	60.00
-- Reissue of 35003					
❑ Verve MGV-Vol. 2 [M]		1957	7.50	15.00	30.00
-- Reissue of 12-inch Clef Vol. 2					
JAZZ AT THE PHILHARMONIC, VOLUME 3					
❑ Arco AL-2 [10]		1950	20.00	40.00	80.00
❑ Clef MGC-Vol. 3 [10]		1953	15.00	30.00	60.00
-- Reissue of Mercury Vol. 3					
❑ Mercury MG-35004 [10]		1950	20.00	40.00	80.00
-- Reissue of Arco 2					
❑ Mercury MGC-Vol. 3 [10]		1951	15.00	30.00	60.00
-- Reissue of 35004					
❑ Verve MGV-Vol. 3 [M]		1957	7.50	15.00	30.00
-- Reissue of 12-inch Clef Vol. 3					

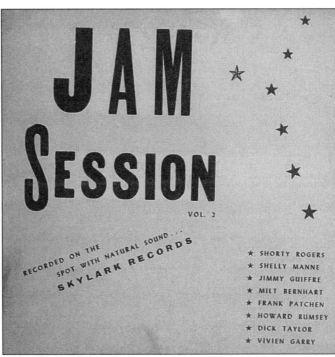

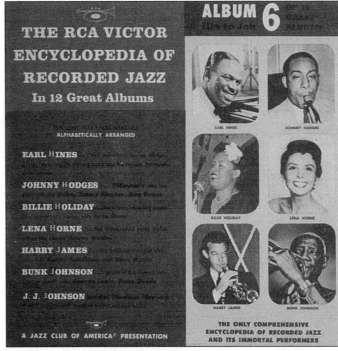

(Top left) *The History of Jazz, Volume Four* was part of a four-volume set originally issued on 10-inch LP in the early 1950s. When Capitol re-issued them on 12-inch, the volume subtitled *Enter the Cool* was the only one to keep the same subtitle. (Top right) *Jam Session,* on the small Skylark label, was a 10-inch LP "blowing session" that looks only slightly more dignified than a bootleg. It's one of the rarest and most sought-after of all albums of this type. (Bottom left) *Jazz Is Busting Out All Over* was a compilation on the Savoy label, which put out many such albums in the 1950s and 1960s. (Bottom right) One of the most well-known early LP collections of jazz was *The RCA Victor Encyclopedia of Recorded Jazz,* a 12-album set issued by the Jazz Club of America in 1956. Even though they are 10-inch albums, which usually command a premium, they haven't increased in value as much as other 10-inch LPs.

Number　　Title	Yr	VG	VG+	NM
JAZZ AT THE PHILHARMONIC, VOLUME 4				
❑ Clef MGC-Vol. 4 [10]	1953	15.00	30.00	60.00
-- Reissue of Mercury Vol. 4				
❑ Mercury MG-35005 [10]	1950	20.00	40.00	80.00
❑ Mercury MGC-Vol. 4 [10]	1951	15.00	30.00	60.00
-- Reissue of 35005				
❑ Verve MGV-Vol. 4 [M]	1957	7.50	15.00	30.00
-- Reissue of 12-inch Clef Vol. 4				
JAZZ AT THE PHILHARMONIC, VOLUME 5				
❑ Clef MGC-Vol. 5 [10]	1953	15.00	30.00	60.00
-- Reissue of Mercury Vol. 5				
❑ Mercury MG-35006 [10]	1950	20.00	40.00	80.00
❑ Mercury MGC-Vol. 5 [10]	1951	15.00	30.00	60.00
-- Reissue of 35006				
❑ Verve MGV-Vol. 5 [M]	1957	7.50	15.00	30.00
-- Reissue of 12-inch Clef Vol. 5				
JAZZ AT THE PHILHARMONIC, VOLUME 6				
❑ Clef MGC-Vol. 6 [10]	1953	15.00	30.00	60.00
-- Reissue of Mercury Vol. 6				
❑ Mercury MG-35007 [10]	1950	20.00	40.00	80.00
❑ Mercury MGC-Vol. 6 [10]	1951	15.00	30.00	60.00
-- Reissue of 35007				
❑ Verve MGV-Vol. 6 [M]	1957	7.50	15.00	30.00
-- Reissue of 12-inch Clef Vol. 6				
JAZZ AT THE PHILHARMONIC, VOLUME 7				
❑ Clef MGC-Vol. 7 [10]	1953	15.00	30.00	60.00
-- Reissue of Mercury Vol. 7				
❑ Mercury MG-35008 [10]	1950	20.00	40.00	80.00
❑ Mercury MGC-Vol. 7 [10]	1951	15.00	30.00	60.00
-- Reissue of 35008				
❑ Verve MGV-Vol. 7 [M]	1957	7.50	15.00	30.00
-- Reissue of 12-inch Clef Vol. 7				
JAZZ AT THE PHILHARMONIC, VOLUME 8				
❑ Clef MGC-Vol. 8 [10]	1953	15.00	30.00	60.00
-- Reissue of Mercury Vol. 8				
❑ Mercury MG-35000 [10]	1950	20.00	40.00	80.00
❑ Mercury MGC-Vol. 8 [10]	1951	15.00	30.00	60.00
-- Reissue of 35000				
❑ Verve MGV-Vol. 8 [(3) M]	1957	15.00	30.00	60.00
-- Reissue of Clef Vol. 15				
JAZZ AT THE PHILHARMONIC, VOLUME 9				
❑ Clef MGC-Vol. 9 [10]	1953	15.00	30.00	60.00
-- Reissue of Mercury Vol. 9				
❑ Mercury MG-35009 [10]	1950	20.00	40.00	80.00
❑ Mercury MGC-Vol. 9 [10]	1951	15.00	30.00	60.00
-- Reissue of 35009				
❑ Verve MGV-Vol. 9 [(3) M]	1957	15.00	30.00	60.00
-- Reissue of Clef Vol. 16				
JAZZ AT THE PHILHARMONIC, VOLUME 10				
❑ Clef MGC-Vol. 10 [10]	1953	15.00	30.00	60.00
-- Reissue of Mercury Vol. 10				
❑ Mercury MG-35010 [10]	1950	25.00	50.00	100.00
❑ Mercury MGC-Vol. 10 [10]	1951	15.00	30.00	60.00
-- Reissue of 35010				
❑ Verve MGV-Vol. 10 [(3) M]	1957	15.00	30.00	60.00
-- Reissue of Clef Vol. 17				
JAZZ AT THE PHILHARMONIC, VOLUME 11				
❑ Clef MGC-Vol. 11 [10]	1953	15.00	30.00	60.00
-- Reissue of Mercury Vol. 11				
❑ Mercury MG-35011 [10]	1950	20.00	40.00	80.00
❑ Mercury MGC-Vol. 11 [10]	1951	15.00	30.00	60.00
-- Reissue of 35011				
❑ Verve MGV-Vol. 11 [(3) M]	1957	15.00	30.00	60.00
-- Reissue of Clef Vol. 18				
JAZZ AT THE PHILHARMONIC, VOLUME 12				
❑ Clef MGC-Vol. 12 [10]	1953	15.00	30.00	60.00
-- Reissue of Mercury Vol. 12				
❑ Mercury MGC-Vol. 12 [10]	1951	15.00	30.00	60.00
❑ Verve MGV-Vol. 12 [(2) M]	195?	---	---	---
-- Advertised, but unreleased?				
JAZZ AT THE PHILHARMONIC, VOLUME 13				
❑ Clef MGC-Vol. 13 [10]	1953	15.00	30.00	60.00
-- Reissue of Mercury Vol. 13				
❑ Mercury MGC-Vol. 13 [10]	1951	15.00	30.00	60.00
JAZZ AT THE PHILHARMONIC, VOLUME 14				
❑ Clef MGC-Vol. 14 [10]	1953	15.00	30.00	60.00
-- Reissue of Mercury Vol. 14				
❑ Mercury MGC-Vol. 14 [10]	1951	15.00	30.00	60.00
JAZZ AT THE PHILHARMONIC, VOLUME 15				
❑ Clef MGC-Vol. 15 [10]	1953	15.00	30.00	60.00
-- Reissue of Mercury Vol. 15				
❑ Clef MGC-Vol. 15 [(3) M]	1954	20.00	40.00	80.00
-- Boxed set of new material with program				

Number　　Title	Yr	VG	VG+	NM
❑ Mercury MGC-Vol. 15 [10]	1951	15.00	30.00	60.00
JAZZ AT THE PHILHARMONIC, VOLUME 16				
❑ Clef MGC-Vol. 16 [(3) M]	1954	20.00	40.00	80.00
-- Boxed set of new material with program				
JAZZ AT THE PHILHARMONIC, VOLUME 17				
❑ Clef MGC-Vol. 17 [(3) M]	1955	20.00	40.00	80.00
-- Boxed set of new material with photo booklet				
JAZZ AT THE PHILHARMONIC, VOLUME 18				
❑ Clef MGC-Vol. 18 [(3) M]	1955	20.00	40.00	80.00
-- Boxed set of new material with booklet				
JAZZ AT THE PHILHARMONIC: BIRD & PRES, CARNEGIE HALL 1949				
❑ Verve 815 150-1	1984	2.50	5.00	10.00
JAZZ AT THE PHILHARMONIC: BIRD & PRES, THE '46 CONCERTS				
❑ Verve VE-2-2518 [(2)]	197?	3.75	7.50	15.00
❑ Verve 833 565-1 [(2)]	198?	3.00	6.00	12.00
JAZZ AT THE PHILHARMONIC: BLUES IN CHICAGO, 1955				
❑ Verve 815 155-1	1984	2.50	5.00	10.00
JAZZ AT THE PHILHARMONIC: CARNEGIE BLUES				
❑ Verve 825 101-1	1985	2.50	5.00	10.00
JAZZ AT THE PHILHARMONIC: HARTFORD 1953				
❑ Pablo Live 2308 240	198?	2.50	5.00	10.00
JAZZ AT THE PHILHARMONIC: HISTORIC RECORDINGS				
❑ Verve VE-2-2504 [(2)]	197?	3.75	7.50	15.00
JAZZ AT THE PHILHARMONIC: IN TOKYO 1983				
❑ Pablo Live 2620 117 [(3)]	1984	5.00	10.00	20.00
JAZZ AT THE PHILHARMONIC: LONDON 1969				
❑ Pablo Live 2620 119 [(2)]	198?	3.00	6.00	12.00
JAZZ AT THE PHILHARMONIC: MONTREUX '75				
❑ Pablo 2310 748	197?	3.75	7.50	15.00
JAZZ AT THE PHILHARMONIC: NORGRAN BLUES 1950				
❑ Verve 815 151-1	1984	2.50	5.00	10.00
JAZZ AT THE PHILHARMONIC: ONE O'CLOCK JUMP 1953				
❑ Verve 815 153-1	1984	2.50	5.00	10.00
JAZZ AT THE PHILHARMONIC: THE 1940S				
❑ Verve UMV-9070/2 [(3)]	197?	6.25	12.50	25.00
JAZZ AT THE PHILHARMONIC: THE CHALLENGES, 1954				
❑ Verve 815 154-1	1984	2.50	5.00	10.00
JAZZ AT THE PHILHARMONIC: THE COLEMAN HAWKINS SET				
❑ Verve 815 148-1	1984	2.50	5.00	10.00
JAZZ AT THE PHILHARMONIC: THE DRUM BATTLE				
❑ Verve 815 146-1	1984	2.50	5.00	10.00
JAZZ AT THE PHILHARMONIC: THE ELLA FITZGERALD SET				
❑ Verve 815 147-1	1984	2.50	5.00	10.00
JAZZ AT THE PHILHARMONIC: THE EXCITING BATTLE -- STOCKHOLM '55				
❑ Pablo 2310 713	197?	3.00	6.00	12.00
JAZZ AT THE PHILHARMONIC: THE GETZ & J.J. SET				
❑ Verve 825 100-1	1985	2.50	5.00	10.00
JAZZ AT THE PHILHARMONIC: THE OSCAR PETERSON SET				
❑ Verve 825 099-1	1985	2.50	5.00	10.00
JAZZ AT THE PHILHARMONIC: THE RAREST CONCERTS				
❑ Verve 815 149-1	1984	2.50	5.00	10.00
JAZZ AT THE PHILHARMONIC: TRUMPET BATTLE, 1952				
❑ Verve 815 152-1	1984	2.50	5.00	10.00
JAZZ AT THE PHILHARMONIC ALL STARS				
❑ American Recording Society G-416 [M]	1957	7.50	15.00	30.00
JAZZ AT THE PHILHARMONIC IN EUROPE				
❑ Verve V6-8823 [(2)]	197?	5.00	10.00	20.00
JAZZ AT THE PHILHARMONIC IN EUROPE, VOL. 1				
❑ Verve V-8539 [M]	1963	5.00	10.00	20.00
❑ Verve V6-8539 [S]	1963	6.25	12.50	25.00
JAZZ AT THE PHILHARMONIC IN EUROPE, VOL. 2				
❑ Verve V-8540 [M]	1963	5.00	10.00	20.00
❑ Verve V6-8540 [S]	1963	6.25	12.50	25.00
JAZZ AT THE PHILHARMONIC IN EUROPE, VOL. 3				
❑ Verve V-8541 [M]	1963	5.00	10.00	20.00
❑ Verve V6-8541 [S]	1963	6.25	12.50	25.00

If any series of various-artists collections has collector's cachet, it's the Norman Granz *Jazz at the Philharmonic* series. The different volumes have been issued and reissued countless times in many forms on a bunch of different labels, with the last vinyl reissues coming in the 1980s on the reactivated Verve label. (Top left) The very first *JATP* album was issued on the Stinson label; it's the only one Granz did not retain the rights to, and Stinson kept it in print for decades, first as a 10-inch album, then on 12-inch. (Top right) When Granz started issuing his own *JATP* albums, this one, usually called *How High the Moon*, became the de facto Volume 1. (Bottom left) The first *JATP* set that Granz leased rather than sold was dubbed *Volume Two* and originally appeared on the tiny Arco label. (Bottom right) One of the later 10-inch volumes in the series, *Vol. 9* would later be consolidated into the 12-inch *New Volume 6*, which later became simply *Volume 6*. Confused yet?

Number / Title	Yr	VG	VG+	NM
JAZZ AT THE PHILHARMONIC IN EUROPE, VOL. 4				
❏ Verve V-8542 [M]	1963	5.00	10.00	20.00
❏ Verve V6-8542 [S]	1963	6.25	12.50	25.00
JAZZ AT THE PHILHARMONIC IN TOKYO				
❏ Pablo Live 2620 104 [(3)]	198?	6.25	12.50	25.00
JAZZ AT THE SANTA MONICA CIVIC '72				
❏ Pablo 2625 701 [(3)]	197?	6.25	12.50	25.00
JAZZ BAND BALL				
❏ Good Time Jazz L-12005 [M]	1954	5.00	10.00	20.00
JAZZ BANDS 1926-30				
❏ Historical 16	1967	2.50	5.00	10.00
JAZZ CITY PRESENTS				
❏ Bethlehem BCP-80 [M]	1957	7.50	15.00	30.00
JAZZ COMMITTEE FOR LATIN AMERICAN AFFAIRS				
❏ FM LP-303 [M]	1963	12.50	25.00	50.00
JAZZ CONCERT				
(Two different albums)				
❏ Jazztone J-1219 [M]	1956	7.50	15.00	30.00
❏ Mercury MGJC-1 [(2) M]	1953	30.00	60.00	120.00
-- Combines 601 and 602 in a box				
❏ Norgran MGN-3501-2 [(2) M]	1956	30.00	60.00	120.00
-- Reissue of Mercury MGJC-1				
JAZZ CONCERT WEST COAST				
❏ Savoy MG-12012 [M]	1955	20.00	40.00	80.00
❏ Savoy MG-12196 [M]	1961	12.50	25.00	50.00
JAZZ CONFIDENTIAL				
❏ Crown CLP-5056 [M]	1959	5.00	10.00	20.00
JAZZ CORNUCOPIA				
❏ Coral CRL 57149 [M]	1958	7.50	15.00	30.00
JAZZ CRITICS' CHOICE				
❏ Columbia Jazz Odyssey PC 36807	198?	2.50	5.00	10.00
JAZZ CRYSTALLIZATIONS				
❏ Pausa 7020	198?	2.50	5.00	10.00
JAZZ DANCE				
❏ Jaguar JP-801 [10]	1954	12.50	25.00	50.00
JAZZ DUPLEX				
❏ Pax LP-6006 [10]	1954	7.50	15.00	30.00
JAZZ FESTIVAL				
(Two different albums)				
❏ Imperial LP-9233 [M]	1963	5.00	10.00	20.00
❏ Imperial LP-12233 [S]	1963	6.25	12.50	25.00
❏ Kapp KS-1 [M]	1956	5.00	10.00	20.00
JAZZ FESTIVAL IN HI-FI: NEAR IN AND FAR OUT				
❏ Warner Bros. W 1281 [M]	1959	6.25	12.50	25.00
JAZZ FESTIVAL IN STEREO: NEAR IN AND FAR OUT				
❏ Warner Bros. WS 1281 [S]	1959	7.50	15.00	30.00
JAZZ FESTIVAL, VOLUME 2				
❏ Imperial LP-9238 [M]	1963	5.00	10.00	20.00
❏ Imperial LP-12238 [S]	1963	6.25	12.50	25.00
JAZZ FOR A SUNDAY AFTERNOON				
❏ Solid State SS-18027	1968	3.75	7.50	15.00
JAZZ FOR A SUNDAY AFTERNOON, VOL. 2				
❏ Solid State SS-18028	1968	3.75	7.50	15.00
JAZZ FOR A SUNDAY AFTERNOON, VOL. 3				
❏ Solid State SS-18037	1968	3.75	7.50	15.00
JAZZ FOR A SUNDAY AFTERNOON, VOL. 4				
❏ Solid State SS-18052	1969	3.75	7.50	15.00
JAZZ FOR ART'S SAKE				
❏ Dotted Eighth 101 [M]	195?	10.00	20.00	40.00
JAZZ FOR HI-FI LOVERS				
❏ Dawn DLP-1124 [M]	1958	20.00	40.00	80.00
JAZZ FOR LOVERS				
❏ Riverside RLP 12-244 [M]	1957	10.00	20.00	40.00
JAZZ FOR PEOPLE WHO HATE JAZZ				
❏ RCA Victor LJM-1008 [M]	1954	12.50	25.00	50.00
JAZZ FOR PLAYBOYS				
❏ Savoy Jazz SJC-412	1985	2.50	5.00	10.00
JAZZ FOR PLAYGIRLS				
❏ Savoy Jazz SJC-413	1985	2.50	5.00	10.00
JAZZ FOR SURF-NIKS				
❏ Bethlehem BCP-6073 [M]	1961	7.50	15.00	30.00
JAZZ FROM DOWN UNDER				
❏ Jaguar JP-803 [10]	1954	12.50	25.00	50.00
JAZZ FROM NEW YORK, 1928-32				
❏ Historical 33	1969	2.50	5.00	10.00
JAZZ FROM SWEDEN				
❏ Discovery DL-2002 [10]	1953	12.50	25.00	50.00
JAZZ FROM THE FAMOUS DOOR				
❏ GHB GHB-116	197?	2.50	5.00	10.00
JAZZ GALA CONCERT				
❏ Atlantic SD 1693	197?	3.00	6.00	12.00
JAZZ GIANTS				
❏ Biograph 3002	196?	3.00	6.00	12.00
JAZZ GIANTS '56				
❏ Verve UMV-2511	197?	3.00	6.00	12.00
❏ Verve MGV-8146 [M]	1957	7.50	15.00	30.00
❏ Verve V-8146 [M]	1961	5.00	10.00	20.00
JAZZ GIANTS '58				
❏ Verve UMV-2540	197?	3.00	6.00	12.00
❏ Verve MGV-8248 [M]	1958	12.50	25.00	50.00
❏ Verve V-8248 [M]	1961	6.25	12.50	25.00
THE JAZZ GIANTS				
❏ Norgran MGN-1056 [M]	1956	20.00	40.00	80.00
JAZZ GIANTS, VOL. 1				
❏ EmArcy MG-36048 [M]	1955	10.00	20.00	40.00
❏ Trip 5504	197?	2.50	5.00	10.00
JAZZ GIANTS, VOL. 2: THE PIANO PLAYERS				
❏ EmArcy MG-36049 [M]	1955	10.00	20.00	40.00
❏ Trip 5518	197?	2.50	5.00	10.00
JAZZ GIANTS, VOL. 3: REEDS, PART 1				
❏ EmArcy MG-36050 [M]	1955	10.00	20.00	40.00
❏ Trip 5538	197?	2.50	5.00	10.00
JAZZ GIANTS, VOL. 3: REEDS, PART 2				
❏ EmArcy MG-36051 [M]	1955	10.00	20.00	40.00
❏ Trip 5555	197?	2.50	5.00	10.00
JAZZ GIANTS, VOL. 4: FOLK BLUES				
❏ EmArcy MG-36052 [M]	1955	10.00	20.00	40.00
JAZZ GIANTS, VOL. 5: BRASS				
❏ EmArcy MG-36053 [M]	1955	10.00	20.00	40.00
JAZZ GIANTS, VOL. 6: MODERN SWEDES				
❏ EmArcy MG-36054 [M]	1955	10.00	20.00	40.00
JAZZ GIANTS, VOL. 7: DIXIELAND				
❏ EmArcy MG-36055 [M]	1955	10.00	20.00	40.00
JAZZ GIANTS, VOL. 8: DRUM ROLE				
❏ EmArcy MG-36071 [M]	1956	10.00	20.00	40.00
JAZZ GOES TO BROADWAY				
❏ Kapp KL-1007 [M]	1956	5.00	10.00	20.00
JAZZ GREATS				
(Two different albums)				
❏ Gateway 10111	197?	3.00	6.00	12.00
❏ Tops L-1508 [M]	1958	5.00	10.00	20.00
JAZZ GREATS!				
❏ Allegro 737 [M]	1958	7.50	15.00	30.00
JAZZ GREATS 2				
❏ Gateway 10112	197?	3.00	6.00	12.00
JAZZ GREATS 3				
❏ Gateway 10113	197?	3.00	6.00	12.00
JAZZ GREATS, VOL. 2				
❏ Columbia Special Products P 13230	1976	2.50	5.00	10.00
-- Custom manufactured for Radio Shack				
JAZZ HALL OF FAME, VOL. 2				
❏ Design DLP-113	196?	5.00	10.00	20.00
THE JAZZ HOUR				
❏ Savoy MG-12126 [M]	1957	12.50	25.00	50.00
JAZZ IN A VERTICAL GROOVE, 1925-28				
❏ Biograph 12057	197?	2.50	5.00	10.00
JAZZ IN HOLLYWOOD				
❏ Liberty LJH-6001 [M]	1955	7.50	15.00	30.00

Number Title	Yr	VG	VG+	NM
JAZZ IN THE THIRTIES				
❑ Swing SW-8457/8 [(2)]	198?	3.00	6.00	12.00
JAZZ IN TRANSITION				
❑ Transition TRLP-30 [M]	1956	50.00	100.00	200.00
-- With booklet (deduct 1/4 if missing)				
JAZZ INTERPLAY				
❑ Prestige PRLP-7341 [(2) M]	1964	10.00	20.00	40.00
❑ Prestige PRLP-7341 [(2) R]	1964	6.25	12.50	25.00
JAZZ IS BUSTING OUT ALL OVER				
❑ Savoy MG-12123 [M]	1957	12.50	25.00	50.00
❑ Savoy Jazz SJC-408	198?	2.50	5.00	10.00
JAZZ JAMBOREE				
❑ Halo 50229 [M]	1957	5.00	10.00	20.00
JAZZ LAB				
❑ Starlite ST-7003 [M]	1955	12.50	25.00	50.00
THE JAZZ LIFE				
❑ Candid CD-8019 [M]	1960	10.00	20.00	40.00
❑ Candid CS-9019 [S]	1960	7.50	15.00	30.00
JAZZ LIFE!				
❑ Barnaby BR-5021	197?	3.00	6.00	12.00
JAZZ LTD.				
❑ Regal LP-11 [10]	1951	12.50	25.00	50.00
THE JAZZ MAKERS				
❑ Columbia CL 1036 [M]	1957	5.00	10.00	20.00
JAZZ MONTAGE				
❑ Liberty LRP-3292 [M]	1963	3.75	7.50	15.00
❑ Liberty LST-7292 [S]	1963	5.00	10.00	20.00
JAZZ MUSIC FOR BIRDS				
❑ Bethlehem BCP-6039 [M]	1959	7.50	15.00	30.00
JAZZ MUSIC FOR PEOPLE WHO DON'T CARE ABOUT MONEY				
❑ Bethlehem BCP-88 [M]	1958	7.50	15.00	30.00
JAZZ ODYSSEY: THE SOUND OF CHICAGO				
❑ Columbia C3L 32 [(3) M]	1964	10.00	20.00	40.00
JAZZ ODYSSEY: THE SOUND OF HARLEM				
❑ Columbia C2L 33 [(3)]	1964	10.00	20.00	40.00
JAZZ ODYSSEY: THE SOUND OF NEW ORLEANS				
❑ Columbia C3L 30 [(3) M]	1964	10.00	20.00	40.00
JAZZ OF THE FORTIES, VOL. 1				
❑ Folkways FJ-2841	197?	3.00	6.00	12.00
JAZZ OF THE ROARING 20'S				
❑ Riverside RLP 12-801 [M]	195?	12.50	25.00	50.00
JAZZ OF THE ROARING TWENTIES: DANCE MUSIC OF THE CHARLESTON ERA				
❑ Riverside RLP 12-108 [M]	1956	10.00	20.00	40.00
JAZZ OF THE SIXTIES				
❑ Vee Jay VJS-2-1008 [(2)]	1974	5.00	10.00	20.00
JAZZ OF TWO DECADES				
❑ EmArcy DEM-2 [M]	1956	10.00	20.00	40.00
JAZZ OFF THE AIR, VOL. 1				
❑ Esoteric ESJ-2 [10]	1952	20.00	40.00	80.00
JAZZ OFF THE AIR, VOL. 2				
❑ Esoteric ESJ-3 [10]	1952	20.00	40.00	80.00
JAZZ OMNIBUS				
❑ Columbia CL 1020 [M]	1957	5.00	10.00	20.00
JAZZ ON THE AIR				
❑ Brunswick BL 58048 [10]	1953	12.50	25.00	50.00
JAZZ ON THE SCREEN				
❑ Fontana MGF-27532 [M]	1965	7.50	15.00	30.00
❑ Fontana SRF-67532 [S]	1965	10.00	20.00	40.00
JAZZ PIANISTS GALORE				
❑ Jazz: West Coast JWC-506 [M]	1956	37.50	75.00	150.00
THE JAZZ PIANO				
❑ RCA Victor LPM-3499 [M]	1966	5.00	10.00	20.00
❑ RCA Victor LSP-3499 [S]	1966	6.25	12.50	25.00
A JAZZ PIANO ANTHOLOGY				
❑ Columbia PG 32355 [(2)]	197?	3.75	7.50	15.00
JAZZ PIANO GREATS				
❑ Folkways FJ-2852	197?	3.00	6.00	12.00
JAZZ PIONEERS 1933-36				
❑ Prestige PRLP-7647	1969	3.75	7.50	15.00
JAZZ POLL WINNERS				
❑ Columbia CL 1610 [M]	1960	5.00	10.00	20.00
JAZZ POTPOURRI				
❑ Audiophile AP-24 [M]	1953	7.50	15.00	30.00
THE JAZZ RECORD STORY				
❑ Jazzology J-82	197?	2.50	5.00	10.00
THE JAZZ ROUND				
❑ Verve VSP-24 [M]	1966	3.75	7.50	15.00
❑ Verve VSPS-24 [R]	1966	2.50	5.00	10.00
JAZZ SAHIB				
❑ Savoy Jazz SJC-409	1985	2.50	5.00	10.00
A JAZZ SALUTE TO FREEDOM				
❑ Core 100 [(2) M]	196?	6.25	12.50	25.00
THE JAZZ SCENE				
❑ American Recording Society G-419 [M]	1957	7.50	15.00	30.00
❑ Clef MGC-674 [M]	1955	10.00	20.00	40.00
-- Reissue of 4007				
❑ Clef MGC-4007 [M]	1953	12.50	25.00	50.00
❑ Clef Special Edition (no #) [(2) 10]	1953	25.00	50.00	100.00
-- Two 10-inch LPs in box. Buyers had the option of purchasing a collection of photos that had been used in the original 78 rpm album; add another 50 percent if these photos are included				
❑ Verve MGV-8060 [M]	1957	7.50	15.00	30.00
-- Reissue of Clef 674				
❑ Verve V-8060 [M]	1961	5.00	10.00	20.00
THE JAZZ SINGERS				
❑ Prestige 24113 [(2)]	197?	3.75	7.50	15.00
JAZZ SOUL OF "CLEOPATRA"				
❑ New Jazz NJLP-8292 [M]	1962	10.00	20.00	40.00
-- Purple label				
❑ New Jazz NJLP-8292 [M]	1965	5.00	10.00	20.00
-- Blue label, trident logo at right				
THE JAZZ SOUND				
❑ Columbia Special Products CSP 298 [M]	1966	2.50	5.00	10.00
JAZZ SOUTH PACIFIC				
❑ Regent MG-6001 [M]	1956	12.50	25.00	50.00
❑ Savoy MG-12205 [M]	196?	5.00	10.00	20.00
THE JAZZ STORY				
❑ Coral CJE-100 [(3) M]	195?	25.00	50.00	100.00
-- Box set; narrated by Steve Allen				
JAZZ STUDIO 1				
-- See PAUL QUINICHETTE.				
JAZZ STUDIO 2				
-- See JOHN GRAAS.				
JAZZ STUDIO 3				
-- See JOHN GRAAS.				
JAZZ STUDIO 4				
-- See JACK MILLMAN.				
JAZZ STUDIO 5				
-- See RALPH BURNS.				
JAZZ SUPER HITS				
❑ Atlantic SD 1528	1969	6.25	12.50	25.00
JAZZ SUPER HITS, VOL. 2				
❑ Atlantic SD 1559	1970	5.00	10.00	20.00
JAZZ SURPRISE				
❑ Crown CLP-5008 [M]	1957	5.00	10.00	20.00
JAZZ SWINGS BROADWAY				
❑ Pacific Jazz PJM-404 [M]	1956	12.50	25.00	50.00
❑ World Pacific PJM-404 [M]	1958	10.00	20.00	40.00
JAZZ TIME U.S.A. -- VOLUME 1				
❑ Brunswick BL 54000 [M]	1952	7.50	15.00	30.00
JAZZ TIME U.S.A. -- VOLUME 2				
❑ Brunswick BL 54001 [M]	1953	7.50	15.00	30.00
JAZZ TIME U.S.A. -- VOLUME 3				
❑ Brunswick BL 54002 [M]	1954	7.50	15.00	30.00
JAZZ TRUMPET, VOL. 1				
❑ Prestige 24111 [(2)]	198?	3.75	7.50	15.00
THE JAZZ TRUMPET, VOL. 2				
❑ Prestige 24112 [(2)]	198?	3.75	7.50	15.00

Number Title	Yr	VG	VG+	NM
JAZZ VARIATIONS, VOL. 1				
❏ Stinson SLP-20 [10]	195?	15.00	30.00	60.00
❏ Stinson SLP-20 [M]	196?	6.25	12.50	25.00
JAZZ VARIATIONS, VOL. 2				
❏ Stinson SLP-29 [M]	196?	6.25	12.50	25.00
JAZZ VIOLINS OF THE 40S				
❏ Folkways FJ-2854	197?	3.00	6.00	12.00
JAZZ VOCALS AWARD ALBUM				
❏ Bethlehem BCP-6068 [M]	1963	6.25	12.50	25.00
JAZZ WEST COAST, VOL. 1				
❏ Pacific Jazz JWC-500 [M]	1956	12.50	25.00	50.00
❏ World Pacific JWC-500 [M]	1958	10.00	20.00	40.00
JAZZ WEST COAST, VOL. 2				
❏ Pacific Jazz JWC-501 [M]	1956	12.50	25.00	50.00
❏ World Pacific JWC-501 [M]	1958	10.00	20.00	40.00
JAZZ -- WEST COAST VOL. III				
❏ Jazztone J-1274 [M]	195?	7.50	15.00	30.00
JAZZ WEST COAST, VOL. 3				
❏ Pacific Jazz JWC-507 [M]	1957	12.50	25.00	50.00
❏ World Pacific JWC-507 [M]	1958	10.00	20.00	40.00
JAZZ WEST COAST, VOL. 4				
❏ World Pacific JWC-510 [M]	1958	10.00	20.00	40.00
❏ World Pacific ST-1009 [S]	1959	7.50	15.00	30.00
JAZZ WEST COAST, VOL. 5				
❏ World Pacific JWC-511 [M]	1958	10.00	20.00	40.00
JAZZ WIZARDS, VOL. 1				
❏ Herwin 106	197?	3.00	6.00	12.00
JAZZ WIZARDS, VOL. 2				
❏ Herwin 107	197?	3.00	6.00	12.00
JAZZ WOMEN: A FEMINIST RETROSPECTIVE				
❏ Stash ST-109 [(2)]	197?	3.75	7.50	15.00
THE JAZZ WORLD				
❏ Columbia Special Products CSS 524 [S]	1967	2.50	5.00	10.00
JAZZ YEARS: 25TH ANNIVERSARY				
❏ Atlantic SD-2-316 [(2)]	197?	3.75	7.50	15.00
JAZZ, SKIFFLE AND JUG STYLE				
❏ Herwin 113	197?	3.00	6.00	12.00
JAZZ, VOL. 1: THE SOUTH				
❏ Folkways FP-53/4 [M]	1951	6.25	12.50	25.00
❏ Folkways FJ-2801 [M]	197?	3.00	6.00	12.00
JAZZ, VOL. 2: THE BLUES				
❏ Folkways FP-55/6 [M]	1951	6.25	12.50	25.00
❏ Folkways FJ-2802 [M]	197?	3.00	6.00	12.00
JAZZ, VOL. 3: NEW ORLEANS				
❏ Folkways FP-57/8 [M]	1951	6.25	12.50	25.00
❏ Folkways FJ-2803 [M]	197?	3.00	6.00	12.00
JAZZ, VOL. 4: JAZZ SINGERS				
❏ Folkways FP-59/60 [M]	1951	6.25	12.50	25.00
❏ Folkways FJ-2804 [M]	197?	3.00	6.00	12.00
JAZZ, VOL. 5: CHICAGO				
❏ Folkways FP-63/4 [M]	1951	6.25	12.50	25.00
❏ Folkways FJ-2805 [M]	197?	3.00	6.00	12.00
JAZZ, VOL. 6: CHICAGO #2				
❏ Folkways FP-65/6 [M]	1951	6.25	12.50	25.00
❏ Folkways FJ-2806 [M]	197?	3.00	6.00	12.00
JAZZ, VOL. 7: NEW YORK 1922-1934				
❏ Folkways FP-67/8 [M]	1951	6.25	12.50	25.00
❏ Folkways FJ-2807 [M]	197?	3.00	6.00	12.00
JAZZ, VOL. 8: BIG BANDS BEFORE 1938				
❏ Folkways FP-69/70 [M]	1951	6.25	12.50	25.00
❏ Folkways FJ-2808 [M]	197?	3.00	6.00	12.00
JAZZ, VOL. 9: PIANO				
❏ Folkways FP-71/2 [M]	1951	6.25	12.50	25.00
❏ Folkways FJ-2809 [M]	197?	3.00	6.00	12.00
JAZZ, VOL. 10: BOOGIE WOOGIE, JUMP, KANSAS CITY				
❏ Folkways FP-73/4 [M]	1951	6.25	12.50	25.00
❏ Folkways FJ-2810 [M]	197?	3.00	6.00	12.00
JAZZ, VOL. 11: ADDENDA				
❏ Folkways FP-75/6 [M]	1951	6.25	12.50	25.00
❏ Folkways FJ-2811 [M]	197?	3.00	6.00	12.00

Number Title	Yr	VG	VG+	NM
THE JAZZ-ROCK-SOUL PROJECT				
❏ Riverside 3048	197?	5.00	10.00	20.00
JAZZ: THE 60S, VOLUME 1				
❏ Pacific Jazz PJ-LA893-H	1977	2.50	5.00	10.00
JAZZ: THE 60S, VOLUME 2				
❏ Pacific Jazz PJ-LA895-H	1977	2.50	5.00	10.00
JAZZMEN -- DETROIT				
❏ Savoy MG-12083 [M]	1956	20.00	40.00	80.00
THE JAZZOLOGY POLL WINNERS 1964				
❏ GHB GHB-200	1986	2.50	5.00	10.00
JAZZTIME, U.S.A.				
❏ MCA 4113 [(2)]	197?	3.00	6.00	12.00
JAZZTONE SAMPLER				
❏ Jazztone J-SPEC-100 [10]	1955	12.50	25.00	50.00
-- With booklet				
JAZZVILLE, VOL. 1				
❏ Dawn DLP-1101 [M]	1956	20.00	40.00	80.00
JAZZVILLE, VOL. 2				
-- See FRANK REHAK.				
JAZZVILLE, VOL. 3				
-- See AARON SACHS.				
JAZZVILLE, VOL. 4				
-- See PAUL QUINICHETTE.				
JAZZVISIONS: ALL STRINGS ATTACHED				
❏ Verve 841 291-1	1989	3.00	6.00	12.00
JAZZVISIONS: BRIZILIAN KNIGHTS AND A LADY				
❏ Verve 841 292-1	1989	3.00	6.00	12.00
JAZZVISIONS: ECHOES OF ELLINGTON, VOL. 1				
❏ Verve 841 288-1	1989	3.00	6.00	12.00
JAZZVISIONS: ECHOES OF ELLINGTON, VOL. 2				
❏ Verve 841 289-1	1989	3.00	6.00	12.00
JAZZVISIONS: JUMP THE BLUES AWAY				
❏ Verve 841 287-1	1989	3.00	6.00	12.00
JAZZVISIONS: LATIN FAMILIA				
❏ Verve 841 290-1	1989	3.00	6.00	12.00
JAZZVISIONS: RIO REVISITED				
❏ Verve 841 286-1	1989	3.00	6.00	12.00
JAZZVISIONS: THE MANY FACES OF BIRD				
❏ Verve 841 285-1	1989	3.00	6.00	12.00
A JAZZY WONDERLAND				
❏ Columbia 1P 8120	1990	3.75	7.50	15.00
-- Available on vinyl through Columbia House only				
JINGLE BELL JAZZ				
❏ Columbia CL 1893 [M]	1962	5.00	10.00	20.00
❏ Columbia CS 8693 [S]	1962	3.75	7.50	15.00
❏ Columbia PC 36803	1980	2.50	5.00	10.00
-- Reissue of Harmony KH 32529 on the "Jazz Odyssey" series				
❏ Harmony KH 32529	1973	3.00	6.00	12.00
-- Reissue of CS 8693 with one track changed				
JOHN COLTRANE IN THE WINNER'S CIRCLE				
❏ Bethlehem BCP-6066 [M]	1961	6.25	12.50	25.00
-- Reissue of 6024 with new title				
JOHN HAMMOND PRESENTS "FROM SPIRITUALS TO SWING" AT CARNEGIE HALL 1938				
❏ Vanguard VRS-8523 [M]	1959	10.00	20.00	40.00
JOHN HAMMOND PRESENTS "FROM SPIRITUALS TO SWING" AT CARNEGIE HALL 1939				
❏ Vanguard VRS-8524 [M]	1959	10.00	20.00	40.00
JOURNEYS INTO JAZZ, VOL. 1				
❏ GHB GHB-65	197?	2.50	5.00	10.00
JOURNEYS INTO JAZZ, VOL. 2				
❏ GHB GHB-66	197?	2.50	5.00	10.00
JUST JAZZ				
❏ Imperial LP-9246 [M]	1963	5.00	10.00	20.00
❏ Imperial LP-12246 [S]	1963	6.25	12.50	25.00
KANSAS CITY IN THE '30S				
❏ Capitol T 1057 [M]	1958	6.25	12.50	25.00
KANSAS CITY JAZZ				
❏ Decca DL 8044 [M]	1954	10.00	20.00	40.00

Number / Title	Yr	VG	VG+	NM
KANSAS CITY PIANO				
☐ Decca DL 9226 [M]	1967	7.50	15.00	30.00
☐ Decca DL 79226 [R]	1967	3.00	6.00	12.00
KBIG CHOICES				
☐ World Pacific KBIG-1 [S]	1964	6.25	12.50	25.00
KELLOGG'S PRESENTS…BIG BAND CLASSICS				
☐ RCA Special Products DPL1-0438(e)	1980	2.50	5.00	10.00
KEYBOARD KINGS				
☐ MGM E-100 [10]	1951	12.50	25.00	50.00
KEYBOARD KINGS OF JAZZ				
☐ RCA Victor LPT-4 [10]	1951	10.00	20.00	40.00
KINGS AND QUEENS OF IVORY				
☐ MCA 1329	198?	2.50	5.00	10.00
KINGS OF CLASSIC JAZZ				
☐ Riverside RLP 12-131 [M]	1957	10.00	20.00	40.00
KINGS OF SWING				
☐ Pickwick PTP-2072 [(2)]	197?	3.00	6.00	12.00
KINGS OF THE KEYBOARD				
☐ American Recording Society G-406 [M]	1956	7.50	15.00	30.00
KNOW YOUR JAZZ				
☐ ABC-Paramount ABC-115 [M]	1956	7.50	15.00	30.00
LEGENDARY BLACK JAZZ STARS IN THEIR FIRST FILMS				
☐ Biograph M-3	198?	2.50	5.00	10.00
LENNY TRISTANO MEMORIAL CONCERT				
☐ Jazz Records JR-3 [(5)]	198?	10.00	20.00	40.00
LEONARD FEATHER'S ENCYCLOPEDIA OF JAZZ				
☐ Vee Jay VJSP-400 [(2)]	1977	6.25	12.50	25.00
LEONARD FEATHER'S ENCYCLOPEDIA OF JAZZ, VOLUME ONE: GIANTS OF THE SAXOPHONE				
☐ Vee Jay LP-2501 [M]	1964	5.00	10.00	20.00
☐ Vee Jay VJS-2501 [S]	1964	6.25	12.50	25.00
LEONARD FEATHER'S ENCYCLOPEDIA OF JAZZ OF THE '60S: BLUES BAG				
☐ Vee Jay LP-2506 [M]	1964	5.00	10.00	20.00
LESTORIAN MODE				
-- See STAN GETZ.				
LIGHTS OUT SAN FRANCISCO				
☐ Blue Thumb BT 6004	1970	6.25	12.50	25.00
LISTEN TO OUR VISION				
☐ Gramavision 18-8509	1986	2.50	5.00	10.00
LIVE AT THE FESTIVAL				
☐ Enja 2030	197?	3.75	7.50	15.00
THE LIVELY SOUND OF UNIVERSITY				
☐ Capitol Custom (no #) [M]	1966	5.00	10.00	20.00
-- "Mustang Sweepstakes Prize Winner" on front cover				
LIVING MUSIC COLLECTION '86				
☐ Living Music LM-0006	1986	2.50	5.00	10.00
LOADED				
☐ Savoy MG-12074 [M]	1956	12.50	25.00	50.00
LONDON BROIL				
☐ Angel ANG-60004 [10]	1955	12.50	25.00	50.00
A LOOK AT YESTERDAY				
☐ Mainstream S-6025 [R]	1965	3.00	6.00	12.00
☐ Mainstream 56025 [M]	1965	6.25	12.50	25.00
LOOKIN' FOR A BOY				
-- See ADELAIDE ROBBINS.				
A LOT OF YARN BUT A WELL-KNITTED JAZZ ALBUM				
☐ Bethlehem BCP-91 [M]	1958	7.50	15.00	30.00
LULLABY OF BIRDLAND				
☐ RCA Victor LPM-1146 [M]	1955	12.50	25.00	50.00
LUSTY MOODS				
☐ Moodsville MVLP-37 [M]	1963	10.00	20.00	40.00
-- Green label				
☐ Moodsville MVLP-37 [M]	1965	5.00	10.00	20.00
-- Blue label, trident logo at right				
☐ Moodsville MVST-37 [S]	1963	10.00	20.00	40.00
-- Green label				
☐ Moodsville MVST-37 [S]	1965	5.00	10.00	20.00
-- Blue label, trident logo at right				

Number / Title	Yr	VG	VG+	NM
☐ New Jazz NJLP-8319 [M]	1963	---	---	---
-- Canceled				
☐ Status ST-8319 [M]	1965	7.50	15.00	30.00
THE MAGIC HORN				
☐ RCA Victor LPM-1332 [M]	1956	10.00	20.00	40.00
MAGNAVOX PRESENTS A REPRISE OF GREAT HITS				
☐ Reprise PRO 578	1973	2.50	5.00	10.00
MAMBO JAZZ				
☐ Prestige PRLP-135 [10]	1952	37.50	75.00	150.00
THE MAN WITH A HORN				
☐ Decca DL 5191 [10]	1950	12.50	25.00	50.00
MANASSAS JAZZ FESTIVAL				
☐ Jazzology J-17	196?	2.50	5.00	10.00
THE MANY FACES OF THE BLUES				
☐ Savoy MG-12125 [M]	1957	12.50	25.00	50.00
MASTER JAZZ PIANO				
☐ Master Jazz 8105	197?	3.00	6.00	12.00
MASTER JAZZ PIANO, VOL. 2				
☐ Master Jazz 8108	197?	3.00	6.00	12.00
MASTER JAZZ PIANO, VOL. 3				
☐ Master Jazz 8117	197?	3.00	6.00	12.00
MASTER JAZZ PIANO, VOL. 4				
☐ Master Jazz 8129	197?	3.00	6.00	12.00
MASTERS OF THE MODERN PIANO				
☐ Verve VE-2-2514 [(2)]	197?	3.75	7.50	15.00
THE MELLOW MOODS OF JAZZ				
☐ RCA Victor LPM-1365 [M]	1956	10.00	20.00	40.00
MELLOW THE MOOD/JAZZ IN A MELLOW MOOD				
☐ Blue Note BLP-5001 [10]	1951	50.00	100.00	200.00
MEMORABLE SESSIONS IN JAZZ				
☐ Blue Note BLP-5026 [10]	1953	50.00	100.00	200.00
MEMPHIS JAZZ FESTIVAL				
☐ Jazzology J-134	198?	2.50	5.00	10.00
THE MERCURY 40TH ANNIVERSARY V.S.O.P. ALBUM				
☐ Mercury 824 116-1 [(4)]	1985	10.00	20.00	40.00
METRONOME ALL STARS 1956				
☐ Clef MGC-743 [M]	1956	10.00	20.00	40.00
☐ Verve MGV-8030 [M]	1957	10.00	20.00	40.00
☐ Verve V-8030 [M]	1961	5.00	10.00	20.00
METRONOME ALL-STARS (AT LEAST TWO DIFFERENT ALBUMS)				
☐ Columbia CL 2528 [10]	1954	7.50	15.00	30.00
☐ Harmony HL 7044 [M]	1957	6.25	12.50	25.00
☐ RCA Camden CAL-426 [M]	1958	6.25	12.50	25.00
MIDNIGHT JAZZ AT CARNEGIE HALL				
☐ Verve MGV-8189-2 [(2) M]	1957	12.50	25.00	50.00
☐ Verve V-8189-2 [(2) M]	1961	6.25	12.50	25.00
MILESTONE JAZZSTARS IN CONCERT				
☐ Milestone M-55006 [(2)]	198?	3.75	7.50	15.00
MILESTONE TWOFER GIANTS				
☐ Milestone MSP-1 [(2)]	197?	3.75	7.50	15.00
MISSING LINKS				
☐ MCA 42206	1988	2.50	5.00	10.00
THE MODERN IDIOM				
☐ Capitol H 325 [10]	1952	12.50	25.00	50.00
MODERN JAZZ				
(Two different albums)				
☐ Tops L-1521 [M]	1958	5.00	10.00	20.00
☐ London LL 1185 [M]	1955	5.00	10.00	20.00
MODERN JAZZ CONCERT				
☐ Adventures in Sound WL-127 [M]	1958	10.00	20.00	40.00
MODERN JAZZ FESTIVAL				
☐ Harmony HL 7196 [M]	1958	5.00	10.00	20.00
MODERN JAZZ GALLERY				
☐ Kapp KXL-5001 [M]	195?	5.00	10.00	20.00
MODERN JAZZ GREATS				
☐ Crown CLP-5212 [M]	196?	3.75	7.50	15.00
MODERN JAZZ GREATS, VOL. 2				
☐ Crown CLP-5220 [M]	196?	3.75	7.50	15.00

Number / Title	Yr	VG	VG+	NM
MODERN JAZZ HALL OF FAME				
❏ Design DLP-29 [M]	196?	3.00	6.00	12.00
❏ Design DLPS-29 [R]	196?	2.00	4.00	8.00
MODERN JAZZ PIANO				
❏ RCA Camden CAL-384 [M]	1958	6.25	12.50	25.00
MODERN JAZZ PIANO ALBUM				
❏ Savoy Jazz SJL-2247 [(2)]	198?	3.00	6.00	12.00
MODERN JAZZ SPECTACULAR				
❏ Jazztone J-1231 [M]	1956	7.50	15.00	30.00
MODERN JAZZ TRUMPETS				
❏ Prestige PRLP-113 [10]	1951	50.00	100.00	200.00
MODERN MOODS				
❏ Moodsville MVLP-2 [M]	1961	10.00	20.00	40.00
-- Green label				
❏ Moodsville MVLP-2 [M]	1965	5.00	10.00	20.00
-- Blue label, trident logo at right				
MONARCH ALL STAR JAZZ, VOL. 1				
❏ Monarch LP-201 [10]	1952	12.50	25.00	50.00
MONARCH ALL STAR JAZZ, VOL. 2				
❏ Monarch LP-202 [10]	1952	12.50	25.00	50.00
MONARCH ALL STAR JAZZ, VOL. 3				
❏ Monarch LP-203 [10]	1952	12.50	25.00	50.00
MONARCH ALL STAR JAZZ, VOL. 4				
❏ Monarch LP-204 [10]	1952	12.50	25.00	50.00
MONARCH ALL STAR JAZZ, VOL. 5				
❏ Monarch LP-205 [10]	1952	12.50	25.00	50.00
MONDAY NIGHT AT BIRDLAND				
❏ Roulette R 52015 [M]	1958	7.50	15.00	30.00
❏ Roulette SR 52015 [S]	1959	7.50	15.00	30.00
MONTAGE				
❏ Savoy MG-12029 [M]	1955	20.00	40.00	80.00
THE MONTREUX '77 COLLECTION				
❏ Pablo Live 2620 107 [(8)]	1978	17.50	35.00	70.00
THE MONTREUX COLLECTION				
❏ Pablo 2625 707 [(2)]	197?	3.75	7.50	15.00
MONTREUX SUMMIT				
❏ Columbia JG 35005 [(2)]	1978	3.75	7.50	15.00
MONTREUX SUMMIT, VOLUME 2				
❏ Columbia JG 35090 [(2)]	1978	3.75	7.50	15.00
MOOD IN BLUE				
❏ Urania UJLP-1209 [M]	1955	7.50	15.00	30.00
MOOD TO BE WOOED				
❏ Cadet LP-784 [M]	1967	5.00	10.00	20.00
❏ Cadet LPS-784 [S]	1967	3.75	7.50	15.00
MORE DRUMS ON FIRE				
❏ World Pacific ST-1022 [S]	1960	7.50	15.00	30.00
❏ World Pacific WP-1261 [M]	1960	10.00	20.00	40.00
MORE LIVE ECHOES OF THE SWINGING BANDS				
❏ RCA Victor LPM-1983 [M]	1959	10.00	20.00	40.00
❏ RCA Victor LSP-1983 [S]	1959	12.50	25.00	50.00
THE MOST				
❏ Forum Circle FC-9079 [M]	1963	3.00	6.00	12.00
❏ Forum Circle FCS-9079 [S]	1963	3.00	6.00	12.00
THE MOST, VOLUME 1				
❏ Roulette R 52050 [M]	1960	5.00	10.00	20.00
❏ Roulette SR 52050 [S]	1960	6.25	12.50	25.00
THE MOST, VOLUME 2				
❏ Roulette R 52053 [M]	1960	5.00	10.00	20.00
❏ Roulette SR 52053 [S]	1960	6.25	12.50	25.00
THE MOST, VOLUME 3				
❏ Roulette R 52057 [M]	1961	5.00	10.00	20.00
❏ Roulette SR 52057 [S]	1961	6.25	12.50	25.00
THE MOST, VOLUME 4				
❏ Roulette R 52062 [M]	1961	5.00	10.00	20.00
❏ Roulette SR 52062 [S]	1961	6.25	12.50	25.00
THE MOST, VOLUME 5				
❏ Roulette R 52075 [M]	1961	5.00	10.00	20.00
❏ Roulette SR 52075 [S]	1961	6.25	12.50	25.00
MOTOR CITY SCENE				
❏ Bethlehem BCP-6056 [M]	1961	12.50	25.00	50.00
MUSIC FOR THE BOY FRIEND…HE REALLY DIGS JAZZ				
❏ Decca DL 8314 [M]	1956	7.50	15.00	30.00
MUSIC FROM THE DANCING YEARS				
❏ RCA Victor PR-112 [M]	1961	3.75	7.50	15.00
-- Created for Dole Pineapple				
MUSIC FROM THE SOUTH, VOL. 1: COUNTRY BRASS BANDS				
❏ Folkways FA-2650 [M]	195?	5.00	10.00	20.00
THE MUSIC OF NEW ORLEANS, VOL. 1				
❏ Folkways FA-2461 [M]	1959	5.00	10.00	20.00
THE MUSIC OF NEW ORLEANS, VOL. 2				
❏ Folkways FA-2462 [M]	1959	5.00	10.00	20.00
THE MUSIC OF NEW ORLEANS, VOL. 3: DANCE HALLS				
❏ Folkways FA-2463 [M]	1959	5.00	10.00	20.00
THE MUSIC OF NEW ORLEANS, VOL. 4: THE BIRTH OF JAZZ				
❏ Folkways FA-2464 [M]	1959	5.00	10.00	20.00
THE MUSIC OF NEW ORLEANS, VOL. 5: NEW ORLEANS JAZZ				
❏ Folkways FA-2465 [M]	1959	5.00	10.00	20.00
A MUSICAL HISTORY OF JAZZ				
❏ Grand Award GA 33-322 [M]	1955	5.00	10.00	20.00
MY FAIR LADY				
❏ New Jazz NJLP-8315 [M]	1963	---	---	---
-- Canceled				
❏ Status ST-8315 [M]	1965	7.50	15.00	30.00
THE NAMES OF DIXIELAND				
❏ Baronet B-108 [M]	195?	5.00	10.00	20.00
NATIVE NEW ORLEANS JAZZ				
❏ Dot DLP-3009 [M]	1956	7.50	15.00	30.00
NEW AMERICAN MUSIC VOL. 1: JAZZ				
❏ Folkways FA-33901	197?	3.00	6.00	12.00
NEW BLUE HORNS				
❏ Fantasy OJC-256	198?	2.50	5.00	10.00
❏ Riverside RLP 12-294 [M]	1958	7.50	15.00	30.00
THE NEW BREED				
❏ ABC Impulse! IA-9339 [(2)]	197?	3.75	7.50	15.00
NEW CHAMBER JAZZ				
❏ Epic LN 1124 [10]	1955	7.50	15.00	30.00
NEW FACES AT NEWPORT				
❏ Metrojazz E-1005 [M]	1959	10.00	20.00	40.00
❏ Metrojazz SE-1005 [S]	1959	7.50	15.00	30.00
NEW MUSIC: SECOND WAVES				
❏ Savoy Jazz SJL-2235 [(2)]	198?	3.00	6.00	12.00
NEW ORLEANS ALL-STARS				
❏ GHB GHB-35	196?	3.00	6.00	12.00
NEW ORLEANS BRASS BANDS: DOWN YONDER				
❏ Rounder 2062	198?	2.50	5.00	10.00
NEW ORLEANS DIXIELAND				
❏ Southland SLP-216 [M]	1955	6.25	12.50	25.00
NEW ORLEANS ENCORE				
❏ Riverside RLP-2503 [10]	1954	20.00	40.00	80.00
NEW ORLEANS EXPRESS				
❏ EmArcy MG-36022 [M]	1955	12.50	25.00	50.00
NEW ORLEANS HORNS				
❏ Riverside RLP-1005 [10]	1953	20.00	40.00	80.00
NEW ORLEANS JAZZ				
❏ Decca DL 5483 [10]	1953	12.50	25.00	50.00
❏ Decca DL 8283 [M]	1956	7.50	15.00	30.00
NEW ORLEANS JAZZ AND HERITAGE FESTIVAL, 10TH ANNIVERSARY				
❏ Flying Fish FF-089	198?	2.50	5.00	10.00
NEW ORLEANS JAZZ AND HERITAGE FESTIVAL, 1976				
❏ Rhino R1-71111 [(2)]	1989	3.75	7.50	15.00
NEW ORLEANS JAZZ AT THE KITTY HALLS				
❏ Arhoolie 1013	198?	2.50	5.00	10.00
NEW ORLEANS JAZZ BABIES				
❏ Southland SLP-214 [M]	1955	6.25	12.50	25.00
NEW ORLEANS JAZZ KINGS				
❏ Southland SLP-217 [M]	1955	6.25	12.50	25.00
NEW ORLEANS JAZZ STARS				
❏ Southland SLP-211 [M]	1955	6.25	12.50	25.00

Number / Title	Yr	VG	VG+	NM
NEW ORLEANS LEGENDS				
❏ Riverside RLP 12-119 [M]	1957	10.00	20.00	40.00
NEW ORLEANS REVIVAL				
❏ Riverside RLP-1047 [10]	1954	20.00	40.00	80.00
NEW ORLEANS RHYTHM KINGS				
❏ Riverside RLP 12-102 [M]	195?	15.00	30.00	60.00
-- Also see NEW ORLEANS RHYTHM KINGS in the main A-Z listings.				
NEW ORLEANS STYLE				
❏ "X" LVA-3029 [10]	1954	20.00	40.00	80.00
NEW ORLEANS TO LOS ANGELES				
❏ Southland SLP-215 [M]	1955	6.25	12.50	25.00
NEW ORLEANS: THE LIVING LEGENDS, VOL. 1				
❏ Riverside RLP-356 [M]	196?	5.00	10.00	20.00
❏ Riverside RS-9356 [R]	196?	3.00	6.00	12.00
NEW ORLEANS: THE LIVING LEGENDS, VOL. 2				
❏ Riverside RLP-357 [M]	196?	5.00	10.00	20.00
❏ Riverside RS-9357 [R]	196?	3.00	6.00	12.00
NEW SOUNDS FROM SWEDEN, VOL. 1: THE DARING YOUNG SWEDES				
❏ Prestige PRLP-119 [10]	1951	50.00	100.00	200.00
NEW SOUNDS FROM SWEDEN, VOL. 2				
-- See BENGT HALLBERG.				
NEW SOUNDS FROM SWEDEN, VOL. 3				
-- See ARNE DOMNERUS.				
NEW SOUNDS FROM SWEDEN, VOL. 4				
-- See ARNE DOMNERUS.				
NEW SOUNDS FROM SWEDEN, VOL. 5				
-- See LARS GULLIN.				
NEW SOUNDS FROM SWEDEN, VOL. 6				
-- See BENGT HALLBERG.				
NEW SOUNDS FROM SWEDEN, VOL. 7				
-- See LARS GULLIN.				
NEW SOUNDS FROM SWEDEN, VOL. 8				
-- See REINHOLD SVENSSON.				
A NEW VISION FROM GRAMAVISION				
❏ Gramavision 18-8510	1986	2.50	5.00	10.00
NEW VOICES				
❏ Dawn DLP-1125 [M]	1956	20.00	40.00	80.00
THE NEW WAVE IN JAZZ				
❏ ABC Impulse! AS-90 [S]	1968	3.00	6.00	12.00
❏ Impulse! A-90 [M]	1966	3.75	7.50	15.00
❏ Impulse! AS-90 [S]	1966	5.00	10.00	20.00
NEW YORK JAZZ OF THE TWENTIES				
❏ Riverside RLP-1048 [10]	1954	20.00	40.00	80.00
NEWPORT JAZZ FESTIVAL				
❏ RCA Victor LPM-3369 [M]	1965	3.75	7.50	15.00
❏ RCA Victor LSP-3369 [S]	1965	5.00	10.00	20.00
NEWPORT JAZZ FESTIVAL ALL STARS				
❏ Atlantic 1331 [M]	1961	6.25	12.50	25.00
-- Multicolor label, white "fan" logo at right				
❏ Atlantic SD 1331 [S]	1961	7.50	15.00	30.00
-- Multicolor label, white "fan" logo at right				
NEWPORT JAZZ FESTIVAL: LIVE				
❏ Columbia C2 38262 [(2)]	198?	3.00	6.00	12.00
A NIGHT AT EDDIE CONDON'S				
❏ Decca DL 8281 [M]	1956	7.50	15.00	30.00
A NIGHT AT THE FIVE SPOT: A MEMORIAL CONCERT DEDICATED TO THE 1930S, VOL. 1				
❏ Aircheck 1	197?	2.50	5.00	10.00
1944 ESQUIRE JAZZ ALL-STARS				
❏ Aircheck 27	197?	2.50	5.00	10.00
1947 WNEW SATURDAY NIGHT SWING SESSION				
❏ Archive of Folk and Jazz 231	196?	2.50	5.00	10.00
1959 MONTEREY JAZZ FESTIVAL				
❏ Archive of Folk and Jazz 239	196?	2.50	5.00	10.00
THE MUSIC OF CHARLIE PARKER				
❏ Signal S-1204 [M]	1957	30.00	60.00	120.00
NO 'COUNT				
❏ Savoy MG-12078 [M]	1956	15.00	30.00	60.00
NO ENERGY CRISIS				
❏ ABC Impulse! AS-9267 [(2)]	1974	5.00	10.00	20.00
NO SOUR GRAPES, JUST PURE JAZZ				
❏ Bethlehem BCP-92 [M]	1958	7.50	15.00	30.00
NORMAN GRANZ JAM SESSION				
❏ Verve VE-2-2508 [(2)]	197?	3.75	7.50	15.00
NORMAN GRANZ JAZZ CONCERT				
❏ Norgran MGN-2501 [M]	1954	20.00	40.00	80.00
❏ Norgran MGN-2502 [M]	1954	20.00	40.00	80.00
NOTHING CHEESY ABOUT THIS JAZZ				
❏ Bethlehem BCP-85 [M]	1958	7.50	15.00	30.00
OLEO				
❏ Pausa 7025	198?	2.50	5.00	10.00
OLIO				
❏ Prestige PRLP-7084 [M]	1957	25.00	50.00	100.00
-- Reissued as Status 8310; see FRANK WESS.				
ON THE TRAIL				
❏ Pausa 7024	198?	2.50	5.00	10.00
ON-THE-ROAD JAZZ				
❏ Riverside RLP 12-127 [M]	1957	10.00	20.00	40.00
ONE NIGHT STAND: A KEYBOARD EVENT				
❏ Columbia KC2 37100 [(2)]	198?	3.00	6.00	12.00
❏ Columbia HC2 47100 [(2)]	198?	12.50	25.00	50.00
-- "Half-Speed Mastered" edition				
ONE NIGHT WITH BLUE NOTE PRESERVED				
❏ Blue Note BTDK-85117 [(4)]	1985	15.00	30.00	60.00
-- Box set containing all 4 volumes				
ONE NIGHT WITH BLUE NOTE PRESERVED, VOL. 1				
❏ Blue Note BT-85113	1985	3.00	6.00	12.00
ONE NIGHT WITH BLUE NOTE PRESERVED, VOL. 2				
❏ Blue Note BT-85114	1985	3.00	6.00	12.00
ONE NIGHT WITH BLUE NOTE PRESERVED, VOL. 3				
❏ Blue Note BT-85115	1985	3.00	6.00	12.00
ONE NIGHT WITH BLUE NOTE PRESERVED, VOL. 4				
❏ Blue Note BT-85116	1985	3.00	6.00	12.00
ONE WORLD JAZZ				
❏ Adventures in Sound WL-162 [M]	1959	12.50	25.00	50.00
❏ Adventures in Sound WS-314 [S]	1959	10.00	20.00	40.00
OPUS DE BLUES				
❏ Savoy MG-12142 [M]	1959	15.00	30.00	60.00
OPUS DE BOP				
-- See STAN GETZ.				
OPUS DE JAZZ				
❏ Savoy MG-12036 [M]	1955	20.00	40.00	80.00
OPUS IN SWING				
❏ Savoy MG-12085 [M]	1956	15.00	30.00	60.00
THE ORCHESTRA "HOUSE OF SOUND"				
❏ Brunswick BL 54003 [M]	1954	7.50	15.00	30.00
ORIGINAL BLUE NOTE JAZZ, VOL. 1				
❏ Blue Note B-6504	1969	5.00	10.00	20.00
ORIGINAL BLUE NOTE JAZZ, VOL. 2				
❏ Blue Note B-6506	1970	5.00	10.00	20.00
THE ORIGINAL SOUND OF THE 20'S				
❏ Columbia C3L 35 [(3)]	1965	10.00	20.00	40.00
OUR BEST				
❏ Clef MGC-639 [M]	1955	12.50	25.00	50.00
❏ Norgran MGN-1021 [M]	1955	20.00	40.00	80.00
OUT CAME THE BLUES				
❏ MCA 1352	198?	2.50	5.00	10.00
PABLO ALL-STARS JAM: MONTREUX '77				
❏ Fantasy OJC-380	1989	2.50	5.00	10.00
❏ Pablo Live 2308 210	197?	3.75	7.50	15.00
PANORAMA OF BRITISH JAZZ				
❏ Discovery DL-2001 [10]	1953	12.50	25.00	50.00
PARAMOUNT CORNET BLUES RARITIES CHICAGO 1924-27				
❏ Herwin 111	197?	3.00	6.00	12.00
PARAMOUNT HOT JAZZ RARITIES 1926-28				
❏ Herwin 110	197?	3.00	6.00	12.00

Number	Title	Yr	VG	VG+	NM
PARLOR PIANO: BLUES AND STOMPS					
❑ Biograph 1001		197?	2.50	5.00	10.00
PARTY AFTER HOURS					
❑ Aladdin LP-703 [10]		1950	2,000.	4,000.	8,000.
-- Red vinyl					
❑ Aladdin LP-703 [10]		1950	1,000.	2,000.	4,000.
-- Black vinyl					
PERCUSSION PROFILES					
❑ ECM 19002		1977	3.00	6.00	12.00
PERCUSSION UNABRIDGED					
❑ Kimberly 2022 [M]		1963	5.00	10.00	20.00
❑ Kimberly 11022 [S]		1963	6.25	12.50	25.00
PERFECT FOR DANCING: ALL TEMPOS					
❑ RCA Victor LPM-1072 [M]		1954	7.50	15.00	30.00
PERFECT FOR DANCING: FOX TROTS					
❑ RCA Victor LPM-1070 [M]		1954	7.50	15.00	30.00
PERFECT FOR DANCING: JITTERBUG OR LINDY					
❑ RCA Victor LPM-1071 [M]		1954	7.50	15.00	30.00
PERIOD'S JAZZ DIGEST					
❑ Period SPL-302 [M]		1956	12.50	25.00	50.00
PERIOD'S JAZZ DIGEST VOL. 2					
❑ Period SPL-304 [M]		1955	12.50	25.00	50.00
PIANISTS GALORE					
❑ Pacific Jazz JWC-506 [M]		1957	12.50	25.00	50.00
❑ World Pacific JWC-506 [M]		1958	10.00	20.00	40.00
PIANO ARTISTRY					
❑ Audiophile AP-28 [M]		1953	7.50	15.00	30.00
PIANO GIANTS					
❑ Prestige 24052 [(2)]		197?	3.75	7.50	15.00
PIANO IN STYLE					
❑ MCA 1332		198?	2.50	5.00	10.00
PIANO INTERPRETATIONS					
❑ Norgran MGN-1036 [M]		1955	20.00	40.00	80.00
❑ Verve MGV-8125 [M]		1957	7.50	15.00	30.00
❑ Verve V-8125 [M]		1961	5.00	10.00	20.00
PIANO JAZZ, VOLUME 1					
❑ Brunswick BL 54014 [M]		1955	7.50	15.00	30.00
PIANO JAZZ, VOLUME 2					
❑ Brunswick BL 54015 [M]		1955	7.50	15.00	30.00
PIANO MODERN					
❑ Verve VSP-13 [M]		1966	3.75	7.50	15.00
❑ Verve VSPS-13 [R]		1966	2.50	5.00	10.00
PIANO MUSIC FOR PARTIES					
❑ Columbia CL 603 [M]		1955	6.25	12.50	25.00
PIANO MUSIC FOR TWO					
❑ Columbia CL 602 [M]		1955	6.25	12.50	25.00
PIANO ONE					
❑ Private Music 2004-1-P		1986	2.50	5.00	10.00
THE PIANO PLAYERS					
❑ Xanadu 171		197?	3.00	6.00	12.00
PIANO RAGTIME OF THE FORTIES					
❑ Herwin 403		197?	3.00	6.00	12.00
PIANO RAGTIME OF THE TEENS, TWENTIES AND THIRTIES					
❑ Herwin 402		197?	3.00	6.00	12.00
PIANO RAGTIME OF THE TEENS, TWENTIES AND THIRTIES, VOL. 2					
❑ Herwin 405		197?	3.00	6.00	12.00
PIANO RAGTIME OF THE TEENS, TWENTIES AND THIRTIES, VOL. 3					
❑ Herwin 406		197?	3.00	6.00	12.00
PIANO ROLL HALL OF FAME					
❑ Sounds 1202		196?	3.00	6.00	12.00
PIANO ROLL TRANSCRIPTIONS					
❑ Riverside RLP 12-110 [M]		1956	10.00	20.00	40.00
❑ Riverside RLP 12-126 [M]		1957	10.00	20.00	40.00
PIANO STYLISTS					
❑ Capitol H 323 [10]		1952	12.50	25.00	50.00
PIANO TWO					
❑ Private Music 2027-1-P		1988	2.50	5.00	10.00
PICK UP THE BEAT					
❑ Epic LN 3127 [M]		1955	7.50	15.00	30.00
PIONEERS OF BOOGIE WOOGIE					
❑ Riverside RLP-1009 [10]		1953	20.00	40.00	80.00
PIONEERS OF BOOGIE WOOGIE, VOL. 2					
❑ Riverside RLP-1034 [10]		1954	20.00	40.00	80.00
PIONEERS OF THE JAZZ GUITAR					
❑ Yazoo 1057		197?	2.50	5.00	10.00
PLAYBOY ALL STARS VOLUME 1					
❑ Playboy PB-1957 [(2) M]		1957	10.00	20.00	40.00
PLAYBOY ALL STARS VOLUME 2					
❑ Playboy PB-1958 [(2) M]		1958	10.00	20.00	40.00
PLAYBOY ALL STARS VOLUME 3					
❑ Playboy PB-1959 [(3) M]		1959	15.00	30.00	60.00
THE PLAYERS' ASSOCIATION					
❑ Vanguard VSD-79384		197?	3.00	6.00	12.00
POP PARADE					
❑ MGM E-194 [10]		1953	12.50	25.00	50.00
POPULAR FAVORITES					
❑ Columbia CL 6057 [10]		1949	10.00	20.00	40.00
PORGY AND BESS					
❑ Bethlehem EXLP-1 [(3) M]		1956	17.50	35.00	70.00
❑ Bethlehem BCP-6040 [M]		1959	7.50	15.00	30.00
PORTRAITS IN JAZZ					
❑ Reprise R-6084 [M]		1963	3.00	6.00	12.00
❑ Reprise R9-6084 [S]		1963	3.75	7.50	15.00
POT, SPOON, PIPE AND JUG					
❑ Stash ST-102		197?	2.50	5.00	10.00
A POTPOURRI OF JAZZ					
❑ Verve MGV-2032 [M]		1956	10.00	20.00	40.00
❑ Verve V-2032 [M]		1961	5.00	10.00	20.00
POWER, GLORY AND MUSIC					
❑ Salvation 1000		197?	3.75	7.50	15.00
PRESTIGE CLASSIC JAM SESSIONS, VOL. 1					
❑ Prestige 24107 [(2)]		198?	3.75	7.50	15.00
PRESTIGE GROOVY GOODIES, VOL. 1					
❑ Prestige PRLP-7298 [M]		1964	7.50	15.00	30.00
❑ Prestige PRST-7298 [R]		1964	5.00	10.00	20.00
PRESTIGE SOUL MASTERPIECES					
❑ Fantasy OJC-1201		1988	3.00	6.00	12.00
PRESTIGE TWOFER GIANTS, VOL. 1					
❑ Prestige PRP-1 [(2)]		197?	3.75	7.50	15.00
PRESTIGE TWOFER GIANTS, VOL. 2					
❑ Prestige PRP-2 [(2)]		197?	3.75	7.50	15.00
PRIMITIVE PIANO					
❑ Tone 1 [M]		195?	7.50	15.00	30.00
PROGRESSIVE PIANO					
❑ RCA Victor LJM-3001 [10]		1952	12.50	25.00	50.00
THE PROGRESSIVE RECORDS ALL STAR TENOR SAX SPECTACULAR					
❑ Progressive PRO-7019		1978	3.00	6.00	12.00
THE PROGRESSIVE RECORDS ALL STAR TROMBONE SPECTACULAR					
❑ Progressive PRO-7018		1978	3.00	6.00	12.00
THE PROGRESSIVE RECORDS ALL STAR TRUMPET SPECTACULAR					
❑ Progressive PRO-7015		1978	3.00	6.00	12.00
THE PROGRESSIVE RECORDS ALL STAR TRUMPET SPECTACULAR, VOL. 2					
❑ Progressive PRO-7017		1978	3.00	6.00	12.00
THE PROGRESSIVES					
❑ Columbia CG 31574 [(2)]		197?	3.00	6.00	12.00
-- "CG" prefix is a reissue of "KG"					
❑ Columbia KG 31574 [(2)]		1972	3.75	7.50	15.00
RAGTIME PIANO ROLL, VOL. 1					
❑ Riverside RLP-1006 [10]		1953	25.00	50.00	100.00
RAGTIME PIANO ROLL, VOL. 2					
❑ Riverside RLP-1025 [10]		1954	20.00	40.00	80.00
RAGTIME PIANO ROLL, VOL. 3					
❑ Riverside RLP-1049 [10]		1954	20.00	40.00	80.00
RAGTIMERS' IMMORTAL PERFORMANCES					
❑ RCA Victor LPT-1000 [M]		1954	7.50	15.00	30.00

Number Title	Yr	VG	VG+	NM
RARE BANDS OF THE 20S, VOL. 1				
❑ Historical ASC-3	1966	3.00	6.00	12.00
RARE BANDS OF THE 20S, VOL. 2				
❑ Historical ASC-6	1966	3.00	6.00	12.00
RARE BANDS OF THE 20S, VOL. 3				
❑ Historical ASC-7	1966	3.00	6.00	12.00
RARE HOT CHICAGO JAZZ				
❑ Herwin 109	197?	3.00	6.00	12.00
RARE VERTICAL JAZZ				
❑ Historical ASC-8	1966	3.00	6.00	12.00
THE RCA VICTOR ENCYCLOPEDIA OF RECORDED JAZZ, ALBUM 1				
❑ RCA Victor LEJ-1 [10]	1956	10.00	20.00	40.00
THE RCA VICTOR ENCYCLOPEDIA OF RECORDED JAZZ, ALBUM 2				
❑ RCA Victor LEJ-2 [10]	1956	10.00	20.00	40.00
THE RCA VICTOR ENCYCLOPEDIA OF RECORDED JAZZ, ALBUM 3				
❑ RCA Victor LEJ-3 [10]	1956	10.00	20.00	40.00
THE RCA VICTOR ENCYCLOPEDIA OF RECORDED JAZZ, ALBUM 4				
❑ RCA Victor LEJ-4 [10]	1956	10.00	20.00	40.00
THE RCA VICTOR ENCYCLOPEDIA OF RECORDED JAZZ, ALBUM 5				
❑ RCA Victor LEJ-5 [10]	1956	10.00	20.00	40.00
THE RCA VICTOR ENCYCLOPEDIA OF RECORDED JAZZ, ALBUM 6				
❑ RCA Victor LEJ-6 [10]	1956	10.00	20.00	40.00
THE RCA VICTOR ENCYCLOPEDIA OF RECORDED JAZZ, ALBUM 7				
❑ RCA Victor LEJ-7 [10]	1956	10.00	20.00	40.00
THE RCA VICTOR ENCYCLOPEDIA OF RECORDED JAZZ, ALBUM 8				
❑ RCA Victor LEJ-8 [10]	1956	10.00	20.00	40.00
THE RCA VICTOR ENCYCLOPEDIA OF RECORDED JAZZ, ALBUM 9				
❑ RCA Victor LEJ-9 [10]	1956	10.00	20.00	40.00
THE RCA VICTOR ENCYCLOPEDIA OF RECORDED JAZZ, ALBUM 10				
❑ RCA Victor LEJ-10 [10]	1956	10.00	20.00	40.00
THE RCA VICTOR ENCYCLOPEDIA OF RECORDED JAZZ, ALBUM 11				
❑ RCA Victor LEJ-11 [10]	1956	10.00	20.00	40.00
THE RCA VICTOR ENCYCLOPEDIA OF RECORDED JAZZ, ALBUM 12				
❑ RCA Victor LEJ-12 [10]	1956	10.00	20.00	40.00
THE REAL AMBASSADORS				
❑ Columbia CL 5850 [M]	1962	5.00	10.00	20.00
❑ Columbia OS 2250 [S]	1962	6.25	12.50	25.00
REBIRTH OF BEALE STREET				
❑ Beale Street BS-1	1983	50.00	100.00	200.00
-- Limited edition of 1,000 made for the city of Memphis				
RECORD HOP				
❑ Decca DL 8067 [M]	1955	7.50	15.00	30.00
RECORDED IN NEW ORLEANS, VOL. 1				
❑ Good Time Jazz L-12019 [M]	1955	5.00	10.00	20.00
RECORDED IN NEW ORLEANS, VOL. 2				
❑ Good Time Jazz L-12020 [M]	1955	5.00	10.00	20.00
RED HOT AND BLUE JAZZ				
❑ Waldorf Music Hall MH 33-141 [10]	195?	50.00	100.00	200.00
REEFER SONGS				
❑ Stash ST-100	197?	3.75	7.50	15.00
RELAXED SAXOPHONE MOODS				
❑ Prestige PRLP-141 [10]	1953	25.00	50.00	100.00
REMEMBERING CHRISTMAS WITH THE BIG BANDS				
❑ RCA Special Products DPM1-0506 [M]	1981	3.00	6.00	12.00
REQUESTED BY YOU				
❑ Columbia CL 607 [M]	1955	6.25	12.50	25.00
RHYTHM & BLUES				
❑ RCA Camden CAL-371 [M]	1958	6.25	12.50	25.00
RHYTHM AND BLUES				
❑ Savoy MG-15008 [10]	1952	20.00	40.00	80.00
RHYTHM PLUS ONE				
❑ Epic LN 3297 [M]	1956	7.50	15.00	30.00
THE RHYTHM SECTION				
❑ Epic LN 3271 [M]	1956	7.50	15.00	30.00
RHYTHM, BLUES AND BOOGIE-WOOGIE				
❑ Decca DL 4011 [M]	1960	7.50	15.00	30.00

Number Title	Yr	VG	VG+	NM
RIDIN' IN RHYTHM				
❑ Swing SW-8453/4 [(2)]	198?	3.00	6.00	12.00
RINGSIDE AT CONDON'S				
❑ Savoy MG-15029 [10]	1954	20.00	40.00	80.00
RINGSIDE AT CONDON'S VOL. 2				
❑ Savoy MG-15030 [10]	1954	20.00	40.00	80.00
RIVERBOAT JAZZ				
❑ Brunswick BL 58026 [10]	1951	12.50	25.00	50.00
RIVERSIDE DRIVE				
❑ Riverside RLP 12-267 [M]	1958	7.50	15.00	30.00
RIVERSIDE MODERN JAZZ SAMPLER				
❑ Riverside S-3 [M]	1956	10.00	20.00	40.00
THE ROARING 20'S				
❑ Saydisc SDL-344	198?	2.50	5.00	10.00
RODGERS AND HART GEMS				
❑ World Pacific JWC-504 [M]	1958	10.00	20.00	40.00
ROGERS & HART GEMS				
❑ Pacific Jazz JWC-504 [M]	1956	12.50	25.00	50.00
ROOST 5TH ANNIVERSARY ALBUM				
❑ Roost RST-1201 [M]	1955	12.50	25.00	50.00
ROOTS				
-- See IDREES SULIEMAN.				
THE ROOTS OF DIXIELAND JAZZ				
❑ Archive of Folk and Jazz 274	197?	2.50	5.00	10.00
THE ROOTS OF DIXIELAND JAZZ, VOL. 2				
❑ Archive of Folk and Jazz 320	198?	2.50	5.00	10.00
'ROUND MIDNIGHT				
❑ Milestone M-9144	1986	3.00	6.00	12.00
-- Compilation of seven versions of the title song, released not long after the movie of the same name				
ST. LOUIS JAZZ, 1925-27				
❑ Herwin 114	197?	3.00	6.00	12.00
SAX GREATS				
❑ Archive of Folk and Jazz 331	198?	2.50	5.00	10.00
THE SAX SECTION				
❑ Epic LN 3278 [M]	1956	10.00	20.00	40.00
SAX STYLISTS				
❑ Capitol H 328 [10]	1952	12.50	25.00	50.00
THE SAXOPHONE				
❑ ABC Impulse! AS-9253 [(3)]	197?	5.00	10.00	20.00
SAXOPHONE REVOLT				
❑ Riverside RLP 12-284 [M]	1958	7.50	15.00	30.00
A SCRAPBOOK OF BRITISH JAZZ, 1926-1956				
❑ London LL 1444 [M]	1956	5.00	10.00	20.00
SECOND SESSION AT SQUIRREL'S				
❑ Paramount LP-108 [10]	1954	15.00	30.00	60.00
SESSION AT MIDNIGHT				
❑ Capitol T 707 [M]	1956	7.50	15.00	30.00
SESSION AT RIVERSIDE				
❑ Capitol T 761 [M]	1956	7.50	15.00	30.00
THE SEVEN AGES OF JAZZ				
❑ Metrojazz 2-E-1009 [(2) M]	1959	15.00	30.00	60.00
❑ Metrojazz 2-SE-1009 [(2) S]	1959	12.50	25.00	50.00
THE 77 SESSIONS				
❑ GHB GHB-250	198?	2.50	5.00	10.00
SHADES OF NEW ORLEANS				
❑ GHB GHB-140	198?	2.50	5.00	10.00
❑ Southland SLP-240	1963	3.75	7.50	15.00
SHOUTIN', SWINGIN' AND MAKIN' LOVE				
❑ Chess CHV-412	1970	3.75	7.50	15.00
SIGNALS				
❑ Savoy Jazz SJL-2231 [(2)]	198?	3.00	6.00	12.00
SILVER BLUE				
❑ Xanadu 137	197?	3.00	6.00	12.00
SINGIN' AND SWINGIN'				
❑ Savoy MG-12060 [M]	---	---	---	---
-- See ANNIE ROSS.				
❑ Savoy MG-12217 [M]	196?	5.00	10.00	20.00

Number / Title	Yr	VG	VG+	NM
SINGIN' THE BLUES				
❏ MCA 4064 [(2)]	197?	3.00	6.00	12.00
SITTIN' IN				
❏ Verve MGV-8225 [M]	1958	12.50	25.00	50.00
❏ Verve V-8225 [M]	1961	6.25	12.50	25.00
$64,000 JAZZ				
❏ Columbia CL 777 [M]	1955	12.50	25.00	50.00
SMALL COMBO HITS				
❏ RCA Victor LPT-3 [10]	1951	10.00	20.00	40.00
SMART, LUSCIOUS, BEAUTIFUL				
❏ Bethlehem BCP-6034 [M]	1960	7.50	15.00	30.00
THE SMITHSONIAN COLLECTION OF CLASSIC JAZZ				
❏ Smithsonian/CSP P6 11891 [(6)]	1973	12.50	25.00	50.00
❏ Smithsonian/CSP P7 19477 [(7)]	1987	10.00	20.00	40.00
-- Revised version of 1973 original				
SMOKE RINGS				
❏ RCA Victor LPT-13 [10]	1951	10.00	20.00	40.00
SOFT PEDAL				
❏ Columbia CL 2511 [10]	1954	7.50	15.00	30.00
SOLO FLIGHT				
❏ Pacific Jazz JWC-505 [M]	1956	12.50	25.00	50.00
❏ World Pacific JWC-505 [M]	1958	10.00	20.00	40.00
SOME LIKE IT COOL				
❏ United Artists SX-71 [S]	1959	10.00	20.00	40.00
❏ United Artists X-71 [M]	1959	10.00	20.00	40.00
SOMETHING FOR BOTH EARS				
❏ World Pacific HFS-2 [S]	1958	10.00	20.00	40.00
-- Stereo sampler				
SOMETHING NEW, SOMETHING BLUE				
❏ Columbia CL 1388 [M]	1959	5.00	10.00	20.00
SONGS BY RODGERS AND HART AND JOHNNY GREEN				
❏ Discovery DL-3014 [10]	1951	12.50	25.00	50.00
SOUL JAZZ, VOL. 1				
❏ Bluesville BVLP-1009 [M]	1960	12.50	25.00	50.00
-- Blue label, silver print				
❏ Bluesville BVLP-1009 [M]	1965	6.25	12.50	25.00
-- Blue label, trident logo at right				
SOUL JAZZ, VOL. 2				
❏ Bluesville BVLP-1010 [M]	1960	12.50	25.00	50.00
-- Blue label, silver print				
❏ Bluesville BVLP-1010 [M]	1965	6.25	12.50	25.00
-- Blue label, trident logo at right				
SOUL JAZZ GIANTS				
❏ Prestige PRST-7791	1970	3.75	7.50	15.00
THE SOUL OF JAZZ				
❏ Riverside S-5 [M]	1957	10.00	20.00	40.00
❏ World Wide MGS-20002 [S]	1958	20.00	40.00	80.00
THE SOUL OF JAZZ PERCUSSION				
❏ Warwick W 5003 [M]	1961	7.50	15.00	30.00
❏ Warwick W 5003ST [S]	1961	10.00	20.00	40.00
THE SOUL OF JAZZ PIANO				
❏ Riverside 9S-7 [S]	196?	7.50	15.00	30.00
THE SOUND OF BIG BAND JAZZ IN HI-FI				
❏ World Pacific WP-1257 [M]	1960	10.00	20.00	40.00
THE SOUND OF BIG BAND JAZZ IN STEREO				
❏ World Pacific ST-1015 [S]	1960	7.50	15.00	30.00
THE SOUND OF JAZZ				
❏ Columbia CL 1098 [M]	1957	5.00	10.00	20.00
THE SOUND OF PICANTE				
❏ Concord Picante CJP-295	1986	2.50	5.00	10.00
SOUTH SIDE JAZZ				
❏ Chess CHV-415	1971	3.00	6.00	12.00
SOUTHERN MEETIN'				
❏ Kimberly 2017 [M]	1963	5.00	10.00	20.00
❏ Kimberly 11017 [S]	1963	6.25	12.50	25.00
THE SPANISH SIDE OF JAZZ				
❏ Roulette SR-42001	1968	5.00	10.00	20.00
SPIRITUALS TO SWING: JOHN HAMMOND'S 30TH ANNIVERSARY CONCERT 1967				
❏ Columbia CG 30776 [(2)]	197?	3.00	6.00	12.00
-- "CG" prefix is a reissue of "G"				
❏ Columbia G 30776 [(2)]	1971	3.75	7.50	15.00

Number / Title	Yr	VG	VG+	NM
STABLE MATES				
❏ Savoy MG-12115 [M]	1957	12.50	25.00	50.00
STARS OF JAZZ '61				
❏ Jazzland JLP-1001 [M]	1961	6.25	12.50	25.00
STARS OF THE APOLLO				
❏ Columbia CG 30788 [(2)]	197?	3.00	6.00	12.00
-- "CG" prefix is a reissue of "G"				
❏ Columbia G 30788 [(2)]	1971	3.75	7.50	15.00
STRAIGHT NO CHASER				
❏ Blue Note B1-28263 [(2)]	1994	5.00	10.00	20.00
-- Compilation of original recordings that were sampled by US3, plus others				
STRETCHING OUT				
❏ United Artists UAL-4023 [M]	1959	30.00	60.00	120.00
❏ United Artists UAS-5023 [S]	1959	25.00	50.00	100.00
STRICTLY BEBOP				
❏ Capitol M-11059	1973	3.00	6.00	12.00
STRICTLY FROM DIXIE				
❏ MGM E-3262 [M]	1956	7.50	15.00	30.00
A STRING OF SWINGIN' PEARLS				
❏ RCA Victor LPM-1373 [M]	1956	7.50	15.00	30.00
SUMMIT MEETING				
(Two different albums)				
❏ Vanguard VSD-79390	1977	3.00	6.00	12.00
❏ Vee Jay SR-3026 [S]	1961	6.25	12.50	25.00
SWEDES FROM JAZZVILLE				
❏ Epic LN 3309 [M]	1957	12.50	25.00	50.00
SWEDISH PASTRY				
❏ Discovery DL-2008 [10]	1954	12.50	25.00	50.00
SWING 1946				
❏ Prestige PRLP-7604	1969	3.75	7.50	15.00
SWING AGAIN!				
❏ Capitol DT 1386 [R]	196?	3.00	6.00	12.00
❏ Capitol T 1386 [M]	1960	5.00	10.00	20.00
SWING CLASSICS 1935				
❏ Prestige PRLP-7646	1969	3.75	7.50	15.00
THE SWING ERA, VOL. 1				
❏ "X" LVA-3030 [10]	1955	20.00	40.00	80.00
SWING GOES DIXIE				
❏ American Recording Society G-420 [M]	1957	7.50	15.00	30.00
SWING GUITARS				
❏ Norgran MGN-1033 [M]	1955	20.00	40.00	80.00
❏ Verve MGV-8124 [M]	1957	7.50	15.00	30.00
❏ Verve V-8124 [M]	1961	5.00	10.00	20.00
SWING HI, SWING LO				
❏ Blue Note BLP-5027 [10]	1953	50.00	100.00	200.00
❏ Blue Note B-6507 [M]	1969	3.75	7.50	15.00
SWING LIGHTLY				
❏ Jazztone J-1265 [M]	1957	7.50	15.00	30.00
SWING... NOT SPRING!				
❏ Savoy MG-12062 [M]	1956	12.50	25.00	50.00
SWING POTPOURRI				
❏ Audiophile AP-23 [M]	1953	7.50	15.00	30.00
SWINGIN': BIG BAND SWING AND JAZZ FROM THE 1930S AND 1940S				
❏ Folkways FJ-2861	1986	3.00	6.00	12.00
A SWINGIN' GIG				
❏ Tampa TP-2 [M]	1957	25.00	50.00	100.00
-- Colored vinyl				
❏ Tampa TP-2 [M]	1958	10.00	20.00	40.00
-- Black vinyl				
SWINGIN' LIKE SIXTY, VOL. 1				
❏ World Pacific ST-1289 [S]	1960	7.50	15.00	30.00
SWINGIN' LIKE SIXTY, VOL. 2				
❏ World Pacific ST-1290 [S]	1960	7.50	15.00	30.00
SWINGIN' LIKE SIXTY, VOL. 3				
❏ World Pacific ST-1291 [S]	1960	7.50	15.00	30.00
SWINGIN' SOUNDS				
❏ Columbia Special Products XTV 82030 [M]	1962	6.25	12.50	25.00
-- Issued for the W.A. Sheaffer Pen Co.				

(Top left) *Session at Riverside* is a Capitol album that was issued in 1956. It's not clear from the cover whether this is a compilation or jam session – the former seems more likely. Among the more prominent people on the LP are Coleman Hawkins, Billy Butterfield, Urbie Green and Charlie Shavers. (Top right) One of the most acclaimed collections of jazz music ever produced was *The Smithsonian Collection of Classic Jazz*, first issued as a 6-LP set in 1973 (the version pictured above). It was one of the most wide-ranging collections of its kind, as it cross-licensed from just about every jazz label in existence at the time. The collection was updated in 1987 and re-issued on LP and (for the first time) compact disc. (Bottom left) Another collection from an obscure label is this World Wide stereo release, *The Soul of Jazz*. (Bottom right) In the wake of the gold-record success of US3's *Hand on the Torch*, which sampled from the Blue Note catalog, the label issued this 2-LP sampler of the full-length versions of songs that the US3 album had sampled. The liner notes revealed just what kind of shape the Blue Note catalog was in at the time: Almost half of the albums from which the songs were taken had not been reissued on CD as of 1994.

Number / Title	Yr	VG	VG+	NM
SWINGING BROADWAY				
❑ Kimberly 11024 [S]	1963	6.25	12.50	25.00
❑ Kimberly 2024 [M]	1963	5.00	10.00	20.00
SWINGING FOR THE KING				
❑ Mercury MG-20133 [M]	1956	12.50	25.00	50.00
SWINGING SMALL BANDS				
❑ MCA 1324	198?	2.50	5.00	10.00
SWINGING SOUNDTRACK				
❑ Kimberly 2016 [M]	1963	5.00	10.00	20.00
❑ Kimberly 11016 [S]	1963	6.25	12.50	25.00
SWINGTIME JIVE				
❑ Stash ST-108	197?	2.50	5.00	10.00
THE SWINGVILLE ALL-STARS				
❑ Swingville SVLP-2010 [M]	1960	10.00	20.00	40.00
-- Purple label				
❑ Swingville SVLP-2010 [M]	1965	5.00	10.00	20.00
-- Blue label, trident logo at right				
A TASTE OF JAZZ				
❑ Concord Jazz CJ-93	197?	2.50	5.00	10.00
TEA PAD SONGS, VOL. 1				
❑ Stash ST-103	197?	2.50	5.00	10.00
TEA PAD SONGS, VOL. 2				
❑ Stash ST-104	197?	2.50	5.00	10.00
TENOR CONCLAVE				
❑ Prestige PRLP-7074 [M]	1957	25.00	50.00	100.00
-- Reissued as Prestige 7249; see JOHN COLTRANE.				
TENOR JAZZ				
❑ Mercury MG-20016 [10]	1950	25.00	50.00	100.00
-- Issued in a paper sleeve				
TENOR SAX				
❑ Concord 3012 [M]	195?	10.00	20.00	40.00
TENOR SAX SOLOS, VOL. 1				
❑ Savoy MG-9008 [10]	1952	37.50	75.00	150.00
TENOR SAX SOLOS, VOL. 2				
❑ Savoy MG-9013 [10]	1952	37.50	75.00	150.00
TENOR SAX SOLOS, VOL. 3				
❑ Savoy MG-9021 [10]	1953	37.50	75.00	150.00
TENOR SAXES				
❑ Norgran MGN-1034 [M]	1955	20.00	40.00	80.00
❑ Verve MGV-8127 [M]	1957	7.50	15.00	30.00
❑ Verve V-8127 [M]	1961	5.00	10.00	20.00
TENORS ANYONE?				
❑ Dawn DLP-1126 [M]	1958	20.00	40.00	80.00
TERRITORY BANDS 1926-31				
❑ Historical 26	1969	2.50	5.00	10.00
TERRITORY BANDS 1929-33				
❑ Historical 24	1968	2.50	5.00	10.00
THAT'S THE WAY I FEEL NOW (A TRIBUTE TO THELONIOUS MONK)				
❑ A&M SP-6006 [(2)]	198?	3.75	7.50	15.00
THEME SONGS				
(Two different albums)				
❑ Columbia CL 6016 [10]	1949	10.00	20.00	40.00
❑ RCA Victor LPT-1 [10]	1951	10.00	20.00	40.00
THESAURUS OF CLASSIC JAZZ				
❑ Columbia C4L 18 [(4)]	1961	12.50	25.00	50.00
THEY ALL PLAYED RAGTIME				
❑ Jazzology JCE-52	197?	2.50	5.00	10.00
THEY ALL PLAYED THE MAPLE LEAF RAG				
❑ Herwin 401	197?	3.00	6.00	12.00
A THIRD SESSION AT SQUIRREL'S				
❑ Paramount LP-110 [10]	1954	15.00	30.00	60.00
THIS COULD LEAD TO LOVE				
❑ Riverside RLP 12-808 [M]	195?	12.50	25.00	50.00
THIS IS THE BIG BAND ERA				
❑ RCA Victor VPM-6043 [(2)]	197?	3.75	7.50	15.00
THIS IS THE BLUES				
❑ Kimberly 2020 [M]	1963	5.00	10.00	20.00
❑ Kimberly 11020 [S]	1963	6.25	12.50	25.00
THIS IS THE BLUES, VOL. 1				
❑ Pacific Jazz PJ-13 [M]	1961	7.50	15.00	30.00
THIS IS THE BLUES, VOL. 2				
❑ Pacific Jazz PJ-30 [M]	1962	6.25	12.50	25.00
❑ Pacific Jazz ST-30 [M]	1962	7.50	15.00	30.00
THIS IS THEIR TIME, OH YEAH				
❑ Revelation REV-11	1970	3.75	7.50	15.00
THREE DECADES OF MUSIC, 1939-49, VOL. 1				
❑ Blue Note BST-89902 [(2)]	1969	6.25	12.50	25.00
THREE DECADES OF MUSIC, 1949-59, VOL. 1				
❑ Blue Note BST-89903 [(2)]	1969	6.25	12.50	25.00
THREE DECADES OF MUSIC, 1959-69, VOL. 1				
❑ Blue Note BST-89904 [(2)]	1969	6.25	12.50	25.00
THREE ROADS TO JAZZ				
❑ American Recording Society LP-100 [M]	1956	7.50	15.00	30.00
TIME SPEAKS: DEDICATED TO THE MEMORY OF CLIFFORD BROWN				
❑ Timeless LPSJP-187	1990	3.00	6.00	12.00
-- With Benny Golson, Freddie Hubbard, Woody Shaw, Kenny Barron, Cecil McBee, Ben Riley				
TOOTIN' THROUGH THE ROOF, VOL. 1				
❑ Onyx 209	197?	3.00	6.00	12.00
TOOTIN' THROUGH THE ROOF, VOL. 2				
❑ Onyx 213	197?	3.00	6.00	12.00
TOWN HALL CONCERT				
❑ Mainstream S-6004 [R]	1965	3.00	6.00	12.00
❑ Mainstream 56004 [M]	1965	6.25	12.50	25.00
TRADITIONAL JAZZ				
❑ London LL 1242 [M]	1955	5.00	10.00	20.00
TRADITIONAL JAZZ AT THE ROYAL FESTIVAL HALL				
❑ London LL 1184 [M]	1955	5.00	10.00	20.00
TRIBUTE TO CHARLIE PARKER FROM THE NEWPORT JAZZ FESTIVAL				
❑ RCA Victor LPM-3738 [M]	1967	7.50	15.00	30.00
❑ RCA Victor LSP-3738 [S]	1967	5.00	10.00	20.00
A TRIBUTE TO DUKE				
❑ Concord Jazz CJ-50	197?	3.00	6.00	12.00
TRIBUTE TO MONK AND BIRD				
❑ Tomato TOM-9002 [(2)]	1979	3.75	7.50	15.00
TROMBONE BAND STAND				
❑ Bethlehem BCP-6036 [M]	1960	7.50	15.00	30.00
TROMBONE SCENE				
❑ Vik LX-1087 [M]	1957	7.50	15.00	30.00
TROMBONES				
❑ Savoy MG-12086 [M]	1956	15.00	30.00	60.00
THE TROMBONES, INC.				
❑ Warner Bros. W 1272 [M]	1959	6.25	12.50	25.00
❑ Warner Bros. WS 1272 [S]	1959	7.50	15.00	30.00
TRUE BLUE				
❑ Xanadu 136	197?	2.50	5.00	10.00
THE TRUMPET ALBUM				
❑ Savoy Jazz SJL-2237 [(2)]	198?	3.00	6.00	12.00
TRUMPET BLUES 1925-29				
❑ Historical 27	1969	2.50	5.00	10.00
TRUMPET INTERLUDE				
❑ EmArcy MG-36017 [M]	1955	12.50	25.00	50.00
TRUMPET STYLISTS				
❑ Capitol H 326 [10]	1952	12.50	25.00	50.00
TRUMPET TRIBUTE TO FATS NAVARRO, CLIFFORD BROWN, BOOKER LITTLE				
❑ Trip 5036 [(2)]	197?	3.00	6.00	12.00
TRUMPETER'S HOLIDAY				
❑ Epic LN 3252 [M]	1956	7.50	15.00	30.00
TRUMPETS ALL OUT				
❑ Savoy MG-12096 [M]	1957	15.00	30.00	60.00
❑ Prestige PRLP-7344 [M]	---	---	---	---
-- See ART FARMER.				
24 KARAT GOLD FOR GROOVIN'				
❑ Verve V6-6654 [(2)]	1968	5.00	10.00	20.00
25 YEARS OF PRESTIGE				
❑ Prestige 24046 [(2)]	197?	3.75	7.50	15.00

Number Title	Yr	VG	VG+	NM
UNDER ONE ROOF				
❏ EmArcy MG-36088 [M]	1956	10.00	20.00	40.00
UNEXPURGATED JAZZ				
❏ Audiophile AP-43 [M]	1953	7.50	15.00	30.00
UNFORGETTABLE PERFORMANCES BY THE JAZZ IMMORTALS				
❏ Dot DLP-3444 [M]	196?	3.00	6.00	12.00
UP SWING				
❏ RCA Victor LPT-12 [10]	1951	10.00	20.00	40.00
UPRIGHT AND LOWDOWN				
❏ Columbia CL 685 [M]	1955	5.00	10.00	20.00
THE VERVE COMPENDIUM OF JAZZ, NO. 1				
❏ Verve MGV-8194 [M]	1957	7.50	15.00	30.00
❏ Verve V-8194 [M]	1961	5.00	10.00	20.00
THE VERVE COMPENDIUM OF JAZZ, NO. 2				
❏ Verve MGV-8195 [M]	1957	7.50	15.00	30.00
❏ Verve V-8195 [M]	1961	5.00	10.00	20.00
VERY SAXY				
❏ Fantasy OJC-458	1990	3.00	6.00	12.00
❏ Prestige PRLP-7167 [M]	1959	15.00	30.00	60.00
❏ Prestige PRST-7790	1971	5.00	10.00	20.00
-- *Reissue of 7167*				
VICEROY CIGARETTES CAMPUS JAZZ FESTIVAL				
❏ RCA Custom KO7P-1544 [M]	1959	7.50	15.00	30.00
-- *Available thoruigh Viceroy cigarettes*				
THE VIOLIN SUMMIT				
❏ Prestige PRLP-7631	1969	3.75	7.50	15.00
VOODOO DRUMS IN HI-FI				
❏ Atlantic 1296 [M]	1958	10.00	20.00	40.00
-- *Black label*				
❏ Atlantic 1296 [M]	1961	6.25	12.50	25.00
-- *Multicolor label, white "fan" logo at right*				
❏ Atlantic 1296 [M]	1963	5.00	10.00	20.00
-- *Multicolor label, black "fan" logo at right*				
WASHBOARD RHYTHM KINGS, VOL. 1				
❏ "X" LVA-3021 [10]	1954	20.00	40.00	80.00
WE CUT THIS ALBUM FOR BREAD				
❏ Bethlehem BCP-86 [M]	1958	7.50	15.00	30.00
WE LIKE BANDS				
❏ Coral CRL 57229 [M]	195?	3.00	6.00	12.00
WE'VE BUILT A JAZZ ALBUM FOR YOU				
❏ Bethlehem BCP-89 [M]	1958	7.50	15.00	30.00
WEED: A RARE BATCH				
❏ Stash ST-107	197?	3.00	6.00	12.00
WEST COAST JAZZ, VOL. 2				
❏ Jazztone J-12?? [M]	1957	7.50	15.00	30.00
WEST COAST VS. EAST COAST				
❏ MGM E-3390 [M]	1956	7.50	15.00	30.00
WHEELIN' AND DEALIN'				
❏ Prestige PRLP-7131 [M]	1957	25.00	50.00	100.00
-- *Reissued as Status 8327; see JOHN COLTRANE.*				
THE WIDE, WIDE WORLD OF JAZZ				
❏ RCA Victor LPM-1325 [M]	1956	7.50	15.00	30.00
WILDFLOWERS: NEW YORK LOFT JAZZ 1				
❏ Douglas 7045	1976	3.00	6.00	12.00
WILDFLOWERS: NEW YORK LOFT JAZZ 2				
❏ Douglas 7046	1976	3.00	6.00	12.00
WILDFLOWERS: NEW YORK LOFT JAZZ 3				
❏ Douglas 7047	1976	3.00	6.00	12.00
WILDFLOWERS: NEW YORK LOFT JAZZ 4				
❏ Douglas 7048	1976	3.00	6.00	12.00
WILDFLOWERS: NEW YORK LOFT JAZZ 5				
❏ Douglas 7049	1976	3.00	6.00	12.00
WINNER'S CIRCLE				
❏ Bethlehem BCP-6024 [M]	1958	10.00	20.00	40.00
WINNERS ALL! THE DOWN BEAT JAZZ POLL '64				
❏ Verve V-8579 [M]	1964	5.00	10.00	20.00
❏ Verve V6-8579 [S]	1964	6.25	12.50	25.00
WINNERS CIRCLE LIMITED EDITION				
❏ Columbia GB-4 [M]	1959	6.25	12.50	25.00

Number Title	Yr	VG	VG+	NM
A WINNING SEASON OF JAZZ FROM CBS RECORDS				
❏ Columbia AS 374 [DJ]	1977	3.75	7.50	15.00
-- *Promo-only sampler*				
THE WOMEN IN JAZZ				
❏ Storyville STLP-916 [M]	1956	12.50	25.00	50.00
WOMEN IN JAZZ, VOL. 1: ALL-WOMAN GROUPS				
❏ Stash ST-111	198?	2.50	5.00	10.00
WOMEN IN JAZZ, VOL. 2: PIANISTS				
❏ Stash ST-112	198?	2.50	5.00	10.00
WOMEN IN JAZZ, VOL. 3: SWINGTIME TO MODERN				
❏ Stash ST-113	198?	2.50	5.00	10.00
WORLD'S GREATEST MUSIC SERIES POP/JAZZ				
❏ Artia-Parliament WGM 2-A [(5)]	196?	10.00	20.00	40.00
-- *First of two five-record sets*				
❏ Artia-Parliament WGM 2-AB [(10)]	196?	25.00	50.00	100.00
-- *Box set of material from the Roulette label. Also issued as two five-record boxes.*				
❏ Artia-Parliament WGM 2-B [(5)]	196?	10.00	20.00	40.00
-- *Second of two five-record sets*				
XANADU AT MONTREUX, VOL. 1				
❏ Xanadu 162	198?	2.50	5.00	10.00
XANADU AT MONTREUX, VOL. 2				
❏ Xanadu 163	198?	2.50	5.00	10.00
XANADU AT MONTREUX, VOL. 3				
❏ Xanadu 164	198?	2.50	5.00	10.00
XANADU AT MONTREUX, VOL. 4				
❏ Xanadu 165	198?	2.50	5.00	10.00
XANADU IN AFRICA				
❏ Xanadu 180	1981	3.00	6.00	12.00
YAZOO'S HISTORY OF JAZZ				
❏ Yazoo 1070	197?	2.50	5.00	10.00
YESTERDAY				
❏ Mainstream MRL-364	197?	3.00	6.00	12.00
YOU'VE GOT TO HEAR IT TO BELIEVE IT				
❏ Solid State SS-94	1966	5.00	10.00	20.00
THE YOUNG AT BOP				
❏ EmArcy MG-26001 [10]	1954	20.00	40.00	80.00
THE YOUNG ONES OF JAZZ				
❏ EmArcy MG-36085 [M]	1956	10.00	20.00	40.00
YOURS				
❏ Harmony HL 7042 [M]	1957	5.00	10.00	20.00
YULE STRUTTIN' -- A BLUE NOTE CHRISTMAS				
❏ Blue Note 1P 8119	1990	3.00	6.00	12.00
-- *Available on vinyl through Columbia House only*				
ZENITH SALUTES THE SWINGIN' BANDS				
❏ Columbia Special Products CSS 525 [M]	1966	3.75	7.50	15.00
-- *Available from Zenith dealers*				

GET INTO THE GROOVE

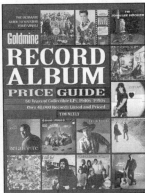

Goldmine Record Album Price Guide
by Tim Neely
Now you can value record albums with confidence and celebrate 50 years of the LP, the 1940s through the 1990s. More than 40,000 albums, valued at $20.00 or more, are listed and priced in up to three grades of condition.
Softcover • 8-1/2 x 11 • 552 pages
100 b&w photos
REA1 • $24.95

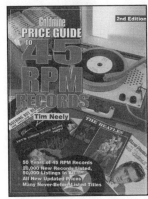

Goldmine Price Guide to 45 RPM Records
2nd Edition
by Tim Neely
A new, larger format makes room for many new artists and 20,000 new listings - 50,000 records in all. All prices have been reviewed, providing the most accurate values in three grades of condition. Learn more about your favorite artists with the updated discographies from the '50s through the '90s. The handy checklist format helps you inventory your favorite records.
Softcover • 8-1/2 x 11 • 544 pages
100 b&w photos
R452 • $22.95

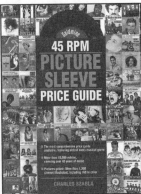

Goldmine 45 RPM Picture Sleeve Price Guide
by Charles Szabla
Record collectors have discovered that it's not just their vinyl that has value - 45 RPM picture sleeves are also in high demand. Now you can quickly identify, date and value your collection-in two grades of condition with the first and only comprehensive price guide available. Alphabetical listings for more than 10,000 sleeves, covering more than 40 years of U.S. releases.
Softcover • 8-1/2 x 11 • 320 pages
1,200 b&w photos
RPS01 • $19.95

The Complete Book of Doo-Wop
by Dr. Anthony J. Gribin & Dr. Andrew M. Schiff
This book transports you back to nostalgic times of hanging out with friends at the malt shop, dances at the hop, and first romances and makes you want to scan the radio in the hopes of hearing a song by Dion & the Belmonts, the Chiffons or Little Anthony & the Imperials. An extensive history of doo-wop from 1950 through the early 1970s is given, along with 150 photos, 64 sheet-music covers and prices for 1,000 top doo-wop records.
Softcover • 8-1/2 x 11 • 500 pages
150 b&w photos
DWRB • $24.95

Goldmine KISS Collectibles Price Guide
by Tom Shannon
KISS is still one of the hottest bands in the world today and the most collectible musical group, next to Elvis and the Beatles. This book, featuring 2,000 listings and 500 color photos of the band's merchandise, offers detailed listings for every U.S. recording, as well as a large number of foreign releases. There are also detailed listings of more than 250 licensed products produced from 1974-1998, from action figures, Beanies and die-cast cars, to Halloween costumes, posters and videos.
Softcover • 8-1/4 x 10-7/8 • 176 pages
500 color photos
KISS • $24.95

Goldmine Promo Record & CD Price Guide
2nd Edition
by Fred Heggeness, Edited by Tim Neely
More than 10,000 total individual promotional 45s, 78s, LPs, LLPs, EPs, 12-inch singles and sleeves and covers from 1950 to 1997 are listed. Easily identify your records with 1,100 photographic replications of labels, sleeves and covers.
Softcover • 8-1/2 x 11 • 464 pages
1,100 b&w photos
PRC02 • $24.95

Goldmine

Krause Publications • 700 E. State Street • Iola, WI 54990-0001 • www.krausebooks.com

Monday-Friday, 7 a.m. - 8 p.m. • Saturday, 8 a.m. - 2 p.m., CST

For a FREE catalog or to place a credit card order, call

800-258-0929

Dept. REBR

SATISFACTION GUARANTEE:
If for any reason you are not completely satisfied with your purchase, simply return it within 14 days and receive a full refund, less shipping.

Shipping and Handling: $3.25 1st book; $2 ea. add'l. Call for UPS delivery rates. Foreign orders $15 per shipment plus $5.95 per book.
Sales tax: CA 7.25%, IA 6%, IL 6.25%, PA 6%, TN 8.25%, VA 4.5%, WA 8.2%, WI 5.5%.